THE EIGHTH MENTAL MEASUREMENTS YEARBOOK

Edited by

OSCAR KRISEN BUROS

Director, The Buros Institute of Mental Measurements

Volume II

THE GRYPHON PRESS

HIGHLAND PARK · NEW JERSEY

1978

DESIGNED BY LUELLA BUROS

LC 39–3422, ISBN 910674–24–8

MANUFACTURED BY PORT CITY PRESS, BALTIMORE, MARYLAND
PRINTED IN THE UNITED STATES OF AMERICA

3/14/79

Table of Contents

VOLUME II

VOLUME I

THE EIGHTH MENTAL MEASUREMENTS YEARBOOK

Volume II
714—INDEXES

Tests and Reviews
(CONTINUED)

READING

REVIEWS BY *Ira E. Aaron, John Charles Alderson, Nicholas J. Anastasiow, J. Douglas Ayers, Rebecca C. Barr, Allen Berger, N. Dale Bryant, Kathryn Hoover Calfee, Robert C. Calfee, Thorsten R. Carlson, David J. Carroll, Richard C. Cox, A. Garr Cranney, Dennis J. Deloria, Randy Demaline, Thomas F. Donlon, John Downing, Priscilla A. Drum, Ralph D. Dutch, Carol Anne Dwyer, Robert Dykstra, Warwick B. Elley, Roger Farr, Shirley C. Feldmann, Nikola N. Filby, Robert A. Forsyth, Edward B. Fry, John J. Geyer, Gene V Glass, Patrick Groff, John T. Guthrie, A. Ralph Hakstian, Larry A. Harris, Ruth N. Hartley, Joyce E. Hood, Dale D. Johnson, Marjorie S. Johnson, Richard T. Johnson, Lawrence M. Kasdon, Thomas Kellaghan, Barbara K. Keogh, Albert J. Kingston, Martin Kling, Roy A. Kress, Eleanor M. Ladd, John W. Lombard, John McLeod, Carolyn E. Massad, William R. Merz, Jason Millman, Charles T. Myers, Doris E. Nason, Anthony J. Nitko, P. David Pearson, Douglas A. Pidgeon, Gus P. Plessas, Barton B. Proger, Fred Pyrczak, Earl F. Rankin, Alton L. Raygor, H. Alan Robinson, Richard D. Robinson, Nancy L. Roser, Roger A. Ruth, Richard Rystrom, Darrell L. Sabers, Gilbert Sax, Robert L. Schreiner, Carleton B. Shay, Sidney W. Shnayer, Harry Singer, Edward R. Sipay, Kenneth J. Smith, William L. Smith, Richard A. Thompson, J. Jaap Tuinman, William J. Valmont, Byron H. Van Roekel, James L. Wardrop, Blaine R. Worthen and William Yule.*

---

[714]

*ACER Primary Reading Survey Tests. Grades 1, 2, 3, 4, 5, 6; 1971–73; no data on reliability for Levels A–C and parts 1 and 2 of Level D; 1–2 forms; 6 levels; interim manuals: Levels AA–BB ('73, 34 pages), Levels A–D ('72, 31 pages), Level D, parts 1A–1C ('73, 26 pages); separate answer sheets must be used for grades 3–6; Aus $2 per interim manual; 60¢ per 10 answer sheets; 30¢ per key; specimen sets: $3.20 per Levels AA–BB, $5.50 per Levels A–D (Form R), $3.80 per levels A–D (Form S), $3 per level D (parts 1A–1C); postpaid within Australia; interim manuals prepared by G. P. Withers in collaboration with M. L. Clark, W. T. Renehan (manual A–D), and

B. Rechter (manual A–D); Australian Council for Educational Research [Australia]. *

a) LEVEL AA. Grade 1; 1972–73; word recognition; Forms R, S, ('72, 4 pages); Aus $1.25 per 10 tests; 16(27) minutes.

b) LEVEL BB. Grade 2; 1972–73; 2 forms; 2 parts.
 1) *Part 1: Word Knowledge.* Forms R, S, ('72, 3 pages); Aus $1.25 per 10 tests; 16(27) minutes.
 2) *Part 2: Comprehension.* Forms R, S, ('72, 6 pages); Aus 25¢ per test; 20(30) minutes.

c) LEVEL A. Grade 3; 1971–72; 1–2 forms; 2 parts.
 1) *Part 1: Word Knowledge.* Form R ('71, 3 pages); Aus 80¢ per 10 tests; 20(28) minutes.

2) *Part 2: Comprehension.* Forms R, S, ('71, 7 pages) ; Aus $1.50 per 10 tests ; 30(40) minutes.

d) LEVEL B. Grade 4 ; 1971–72 ; 1–2 forms ; 2 parts ; prices same as for c.

　1) *Part 1: Word Knowledge.* Form R ('71, 3 pages) ; 20(28) minutes.

　2) *Part 2: Comprehension.* Forms R, S, ('71, 8 pages) ; 30(40) minutes.

e) LEVEL C. Grade 5 ; 1971–72 ; 1–2 forms ; 2 parts ; prices same as for c.

　1) *Part 1: Word Knowledge.* Form R ('71, 3 pages) ; 20(28) minutes.

　2) *Part 2: Comprehension.* Forms R, S, ('71, 8 pages) ; 30(40) minutes.

f) LEVEL D. Grade 6 ; 1971–73 ; 1–2 forms ; 5 parts ; Aus 60¢ per 10 special answer sheets for Dictionary Skills.

　1) *Part 1: Word Knowledge.* Form R ('71, 3 pages) ; Aus $1.25 per 10 tests ; 20(28) minutes.

　2) *Part 2: Comprehension.* Forms R, S, ('71, 7 pages) ; Aus 25¢ per test ; 30(40) minutes.

　3) *Part 1A: Word Discrimination.* Form R ('72, 4 pages) ; Aus $1.25 per 10 tests ; 15(23) minutes.

　4) *Part 1B: Word Formation.* Form R ('72, 4 pages) ; Aus $1.25 per 10 tests ; 30(38) minutes.

　5) *Part 1C: Dictionary Skills.* Form R ('72, 4 pages) ; Aus $1.25 per 10 tests ; 30(38) minutes.

[715]

★**ACT Proficiency Examination in Corrective and Remedial Instruction in Reading.** College and adults ; 1975–76 ; for college accreditation of nontraditional study, advanced placement, or assessment of educational achievement ; test administered 4 times annually (February, May, August, November) at centers established by the publisher ; developed and administered in New York State as a part of their College Proficiency Examinations Program ; 9 graduate credits recommended ; no data on reliability ; Form ZZ ('75, 24 pages, reprinted with 1976 copyright) ; study guide ('76, 3 pages) ; for further information and program accessories, see 470 ; examination fee, $35 per candidate (includes reporting of score to the candidate and one college) ; 180(210) minutes ; developed by the New York State Education Department ; American College Testing Program. *

[716]

★**ACT Proficiency Examinaion in Reading Instruction in the Elementary School.** College and adults ; 1973–76 ; for college accreditation of nontraditional study, advanced placement, or assessment of educational achievement ; test administered 4 times annually (February, May, August, November) at centers established by the publisher ; developed and administered in New York State as a part of their College Proficiency Examinations Program ; 6 semester credits recommended ; no data on reliability ; Form ZZ ('73, 11 pages, reprinted with 1976 copyright) ; study guide ('76, 4 pages) ; for further information and program accessories, see 470 ; examination fee, $30 per candidate (includes reporting of score to the candidate and one college) ; 180(210) minutes ; developed by the New York State Education Department ; American College Testing Program. *

[717]

*****American School Achievement Tests: Part 1, Reading, Revised Edition.** Grades 2–3, 4–6, 7–9 ; 1941 75 ; previous edition ('55–58) still available ; 3 scores : sentence and word meaning, paragraph meaning, average ; no data on reliability of average score ; no norms for average score ; Forms X, Y, ('75, 4 pages, self-marking) ; 3 levels ; no specific manual ;

ACER Primary Reading Survey Tests

$4.90 per 35 tests ; 80¢ per specimen set of any one level ; postage extra ; Willis E. Pratt, George A. W. Stouffer, Jr., and Joan R. Yanuzzi ; Bobbs-Merrill Co., Inc. *

a) PRIMARY BATTERY 2. Grades 2–3 ; battery manual ('75, 19 pages) ; 25(35) minutes.

b) INTERMEDIATE BATTERY. Grades 4–6 ; battery manual ('75, 29 pages) ; 25(35) minutes.

c) ADVANCED BATTERY. Grades 7–9 ; battery manual ('75, 30 pages) ; 30(40) minutes.

For reviews by Russell G. Stauffer and Agatha Townsend of an earlier edition, see 5 :620. For reviews of the complete battery, see 4 (2 reviews, 1 excerpt), 6 :2 (2 reviews), 5 :1 (2 reviews), 4 :1 (1 review), and 3 :1 (2 reviews).

REFERENCES

1. LANE, HELEN S., AND BAKER, DOROTHEA. "Reading Achievement of the Deaf: Another Look." *Volta R* 76(8): 489–99 N '74. * (PA 53:5725)

EDWARD B. FRY, *Professor of Education, Rutgers, The State University of New Jersey, New Brunswick, New Jersey.*

The *American School Achievement Tests: Reading* are solid, well-developed group testing instruments. The authors have selected the two most widely used and most academically defensible kind of subtests : sentence and word meaning, and paragraph meaning. Separate scores and norms are given for each, and the two may be averaged together, if desired.

The sentence completion type of items used in the sentence and word meaning subtest seem particularly appropriate for the lower elementary pupils though they are appropriate for upper levels as well. This type of subtest is often called vocabulary on other tests, but it is more flexible than some formats such as the use of antonyms. It should also make the tests more usable with remedial or disadvantaged groups.

The authors state that the goals of the battery, of which this test is a part, are to measure pupil progress, to assist in individualization of instruction (classification of pupils), and to furnish data for diagnostic programs in the language arts. These goals are a bit ambitious for the reading test. The tests will certainly permit comparison of the student or class with national norms or with other pupils or classes in a locality, but they are "diagnostic" only in a very limited sense. If the whole battery is given, one could diagnose whether the pupil had relative strengths in spelling or arithmetic computation as opposed to reading paragraph meaning. But these tests are certainly not diagnostic in the sense of criterion referenced tests or diagnostic-prescriptive batteries. In other words, these tests will help the teacher or supervisor in measuring a pupil's general progress ; it will help the teacher in grouping pupils, but it will not tell her what to teach. It will not point out strengths or weaknesses in any more detail than the titles of the subtests indicate. This is not really a fault; it is what most group reading achievement reading tests really do.

The content validity is good. The contents of this test are based on a survey of elementary textbooks, courses of study, literature on children's vocabulary, and the judgment of teachers, supervisors, and curriculum specialists. The concurrent validity is excellent; this test correlates from .88 to .93 with reading tests of the *California Achievement Test,* the *Metropolitan Achievement Test,* and the *Stanford Achievement Test.*

The reliability is also good (.89 to .94). The standard errors of measurement are given for both subtests at all levels. For teachers wise enough to use them, the standard error of measurement indicates a band about five months wide at the primary level, and about 1.8 years at the advanced level. That we only know, or rather can estimate, that a student's true score is in a band 1.8 years wide two-thirds of the time, is not a fault of this test; all tests are similar, but it needs to be continually pointed out to teachers who tend to place more faith in the obtained score than the test maker says is warranted. Reporting reading scores in band scores (which this test does not) is one way to remind the teacher of this validity.

The standardization is also adequate in regional representation, but the manual regrettably lacks data on size. It is interesting and praiseworthy that the standardization group included "Public schools at all stages of integration, private nonsectarian, and private sectarian schools."

The testing time is relatively brief; 35 to 40 minutes for both reading tests including time for preliminaries. Test booklets have a self-scoring feature by using a carbon type sheet. The publisher states that hand and machine scoring services are available. The manual is both informative and clear.

The manual states in several places that the tests attempt to provide for students at the lower end of the scale, but caution should be used as it is possible to obtain scores below the chance guessing level. Perhaps future editions can cure this by adding a correction for guessing, or simply telling the teacher to use a lower level

test and refusing to give a grade score below the chance level. On the average, the score that could be obtained by a student who just randomly filled in the blanks would be grade equivalency scores of 2.0 on the primary, 3.0 on the intermediate, and 2.7 on the advanced level of the sentence and word meaning subtest.

In summary, the *American School Achievement Tests: Reading* is a first class group achievement test, convenient to administer and easy to understand. The reliability and validity are good, and they should appeal to many educators because they are short and they test children in a sensible manner.

[718]

★Basic Educational Skills Inventory: Reading. Grades kgn–6; 1972–73; criterion referenced; for battery entry, see 5; no data on reliability; no description of procedures and normative groups used in obtaining grade level equivalencies; individual; 1 form; 2 levels; battery user's guide ('73, 15 pages); directions for administering ('72, 21 pages); stimulus booklet ('72, 94 pages); response booklet ('72, 11 pages) for Level A; scoring booklet ['72, 6 pages] for each level; $40 per set of testing materials for both levels including 35 response booklets and 35 sets of scoring booklets; $7.75 per 35 scoring booklets; postage extra; (40–90) minutes; Gary Adamson, Morris Shrago, and Glen Van Etten; B. L. Winch & Associates. *

a) LEVEL A. 12 scores: memory for sentences, direction in space, same or different, naming the alphabet from memory, printing capital letters from memory, manuscript printing of dictated small letters, naming printed letters, matching letters, writing and naming capital cursive letters, naming cursive written letters, sight words, total.

b) LEVEL B. 23 scores: rhyming sounds, initial consonants and vowels, final consonants, initial consonant blends and digraphs (2 scores), final consonant blends and digraphs, auditory blending of words, initial consonants, final consonants, initial vowels, medial vowels, printed vowels and consonants, printed letter blends and digraphs, beginning and ending word patterns, blending printed words, blending phonetic elements, double vowels and diphthongs, hard and soft sounds, prefixes, suffixes, prefixes—suffixes, syllabification, total.

For reviews of the complete battery, see 5 (2 reviews).

PRISCILLA A. DRUM, *Assistant Professor of Education, University of California, Santa Barbara, California.*

This test purports to assess the word recognition skills of elementary pupils. In fact, only 10 of the 33 tasks ask a pupil to respond to a printed word, though the test is intended to diagnose word recognition problems. If the purpose is instead to diagnose pre-word recognition problems, subskills that may be needed to decode words, then at least such primary skills as differences between long and short vowels, single letters with multiple sound correspondences, and silent letters should have been included. Instead, the same questions are asked over and over again. Seven of the 11 tasks in Level A ask the pupil to name, to write, or to recognize the letters of the alphabet. Twelve of the 22 tasks in Level B require the segmentation or sounding out of letter, blends, and digraph sounds from pictures or oral stimuli.

This test does not provide as much information as either of the authors' recommended screening devices, the *Wide Range Achievement Test* or the *Metropolitan Achievement Tests*. It is quite expensive and would be time-consuming to administer. Further, there are no reliability data nor any description of the normative groups used in obtaining the ranges for the grade level equivalencies provided in the user's guide. Instead, the expectancies—the authors' synonymous term for the grade level ranges—are based on an unknown procedure for "careful analysis of a broad range of scope and sequence charts" from an unspecified number of unnamed basal reader series.

The procedures for administration have numerous problems. In the first place, the teacher will be very busy while administering this test. The directions for administering, which include the verbal directions the teacher is to give, are in one book, the scoring sheets are separate, and the stimulus booklet is used intermittently for different tasks. Notwithstanding all of these materials, the teacher is required to say what is to be done, to point to the correct stimulus, and to score the separate responses in very quick succession. Certain instructions that the teacher is to provide the child are inaccurate. In the nonsense or infrequent word pronunciation task, the teacher says, "These next words will be ones you have never heard of," but the list includes *fade, gat, trek, whiff,* and *gloat* among the 12 words—words that undoubtedly some of the children have heard.

The pupil may have difficulty in interpreting other instructions. In one task, the child is asked to "draw a straight diagonal line from one top corner of the page to the bottom corner opposite that." In another instance, both the directions and the format of the test appear unnecessarily complicated.

The scoring sheets do not provide for correct responses that diverge from the test writers'

expectations. The last task examines the rules of hyphenation rather than syllabification, the task name.

Whether grade level equivalencies should be provided when diagnosis of specific skills is being assessed is another question. The grade at which cursive (versus manuscript) writing is introduced seems dependent upon the particular curriculum to which the child has been exposed. The context differences for hard and soft *c* and *g* are sometimes taught in first grade, sometimes in second. The authors do warn that the grade level designation should be cross-referenced with the particular curriculm used. Given the peculiar method of obtaining grade level scores (scope and sequence charts) these equivalencies should have been omitted. Also, these scores have limited value as given. The maximum correct score (the ceiling) is expected to be reached on 10 tasks or subtasks by first grade and on 13 more by second grade. On every task, the teacher may place at least one score in at least two grade levels. The only score which would have meaning for assessing progress would be a numerical gain score. If the test were given twice, it would be a fairly simple matter to determine progress on any of the 33 tasks that the teacher wished to measure.

This test could be used to find out if the pupil knows the alphabet and can segment and produce sounds of letters and letter clusters, but there are many simpler, less expensive ways to obtain this information. In summary, this reviewer does not believe that this test serves a purpose.

[719]
*California Achievement Tests: Reading, 1970 Edition. Grades 1.5–2, 2–4, 4–6, 6–9, 9–12; 1933–74; 1957 edition with 1963 norms still available; 3 scores: vocabulary, comprehension, total; 2 forms; 5 levels; no specific manual; for battery manuals and accessories, see 10; separate answer sheets (CompuScan, Digitek, IBM 1230, Scoreze) must be used in grades 4–12; postage extra; Ernest W. Tiegs and Willis W. Clark; CTB/McGraw-Hill. *

a) LEVEL 1. Grades 1.5–2; Forms A ('70, 12 pages), B ('71, 12 pages); 2 editions; $5 per specimen set of both editions; 46(65) minutes.
1) *Hand Scorable Booklet.* $10.15 per 35 tests.
2) *CompuScan Machine Scorable Booklet.* $14.70 per 35 tests; scoring service, 55¢ and over per test ($50 minimum).

b) LEVEL 2. Grades 2–4; Forms A ('70, 12 pages), B ('71, 12 pages); 2 editions; hand scorable, CompuScan machine scorable; prices same as for level 1; 40(68) minutes.

c) LEVEL 3. Grades 4–6; Forms A ('70, 14 pages), B ('71, 14 pages); $12.25 per 35 tests; $4 per 50 CompuScan answer sheets; $5 per 50 Digitek or IBM answer sheets; $4.25 per 25 Scoreze answer sheets; $2.50 per IBM hand scoring stencil; Digitek scoring stencil not available; $5 per specimen set; CompuScan scoring service, 35¢ and over per test ($50 minimum); 45(70) minutes.

d) LEVEL 4. Grades 6–9; Forms A ('70, 15 pages), B ('71, 15 pages); prices same as for level 3; 50(75) minutes.

e) LEVEL 5. Grades 9–12; Forms A ('70, 16 pages), B ('71, 16 pages); prices same as for level 3; 50(75) minutes.

See T2:1536 (27 references), 7:683 (29 references), 6:784 (13 references), and 5:622 (5 references); for reviews by John C. Flanagan and James R. Hobson and an excerpted review by Laurance F. Shaffer of the 1950 edition, see 4:530; for a review by Frederick B. Davis of an earlier edition, see 2:1563; for reviews by Ivan A. Booker and Joseph C. Dewey, see 1:1110. For reviews of the complete battery, see 10 (2 reviews), 6:3 (2 reviews), 5:2 (1 review), 4:2 (3 reviews), 3:15 (1 review), 2:1193 (2 reviews), and 1:876 (1 review, 1 excerpt).

REFERENCES

1–5. See 5:622.
6–18. See 6:784.
19–47. See 7:683.
48–74. See T2:1536; also includes a cumulative name index to the first 74 references, 5 reviews, and 1 excerpt for this test.
75. CHADWICK, CAROLE C.; MICHAEL, WILLIAM B.; AND HANSHUMAKER, JAMES. "Correlates of Success in Practice Teaching in Music at the University of Southern California." *Ed & Psychol Meas* 32(4):1073–8 w '72. *
76. HICKS, RETA DANIELS. *A Comparative Analysis Among the Variables, Father's Occupational Level, Sex, Intelligence, and Reading Achievement With Fourth Grade Children's Ability to Read Technical and Basic Vocabularies.* Doctor's thesis, University of Southern Mississippi (Hattiesburg, Miss.), 1972. (DAI 33:1320A)
77. JONGSMA, EUGENE. "California Reading Test: A Review," pp. 9–11. In *Reading Tests for the Secondary Grades.* Edited by William Blanton and others. Newark, Del.: International Reading Association, Inc., 1972. Pp. iv, 55. *
78. MILLER, WALLACE D. "Usefulness of the Peabody Picture Vocabulary Test and the Slosson Intelligence Test in a Teacher Training Program." *South J Ed Res* 6(2):71–8 Ap '72. * (PA 50:7800)
79. FREDERICK, NANCY ANN. *A Study of the Relationship Among General Ability, Reading Achievement, Sex and Knowledge of Selected Phoneme-Grapheme Correspondences in Grades Four, Five and Six.* Doctor's thesis, Florida State University (Tallahassee, Fla.), 1973. (DAI 34:508A)
80. GALL, STEFANIE SWINDLE. *An Investigation of Growth in Critical Reading Ability in Grades Four, Five and Six.* Doctor's thesis, Florida State University (Tallahassee, Fla.), 1973. (DAI 34:510A)
81. HOCKMAN, CAROL H. "Black Dialect Reading Tests in the Urban Elementary School." *Read Teach* 26(6):581–3 Mr '73. *
82. McCARTHY, KAREN A., AND STECKLER, JANE F. "Temporal Stability and Concurrent Validity of the PPVT With Typical First Grade Students." *Ed & Psychol Meas* 33(2):469–72 su '73. * (PA 51:5990)
83. RANCOURT, KAREN LOGOZZO. *The Moderation of Comprehension in Reading by Three Perception Formats and Three Fatigue Levels.* Doctor's thesis, University of Maryland (College Park, Md.), 1973. (DAI 35:1881A)
84. CALLAWAY, BYRON; JERROLDS, BOB W.; AND GWALTNEY, WAYNE. "The Relationship Between Reading and Language Achievement and Certain Sociological and Adjustment Factors." *Read Improv* 11(1):19–26 sp '74. *
85. COLEMAN, BETSY E. *The Relationship Between Auditory and Visual Perceptual Skills and First Grade Reading Achievement Under an Initial Phonemics-Reading Approach and Under an Initial Structural Linguistics Reading Approach.* Doctor's thesis, University of Pittsburgh (Pittsburgh, Pa.), 1974. (DAI 35:2118A)
86. LORD, FREDERIC M. "Quick Estimates of the Relative Efficiency of Two Tests as a Function of Ability Level." *J Ed Meas* 11(4):247–54 w '74. *
87. LORET, PETER G.; SEDER, ALAN; BIANCHINI, JOHN C.; AND VALE, CAROL A. *Anchor Test Study: Equivalence and Norms Tables for Selected Reading Achievement Tests (Grades 4, 5, and 6).* DHEW Publication S/N 1780–01312. Washington, D.C.: Government Printing Office, 1974. Pp. ix, 92. *
88. MARWIT, SAMUEL J., AND NEUMANN, GAIL. "Black and White Children's Comprehension of Standard and Nonstandard English Passages." *J Ed Psychol* 66(3):329–32 Je '74. * (PA 52:10124)
89. MATHENY, ADAM P., JR., AND DOLAN, ANNE BROWN. "A Twin Study of Genetic Influences in Reading Achievement." *J Learn Dis* 7(2):99–102 F '74. * (PA 52:6326)
90. SEITHER, FRANCES G. "A Predictive Validity Study of Screening Measures Used to Select Practical Nursing Students." *Nursing Res* 23(1):60–3 Ja–F '74. * (PA 52:5486)
91. TUINMAN, J. JAAP. "Determining the Passage Dependency of Comprehension Questions in 5 Major Tests." *Read Res Q* 9(2):206–23 '73–74 ['74]. * (PA 53:2010)
92. LINN, ROBERT L. "Anchor Test Study: The Long and the Short of It." *J Ed Meas* 12(3):201–13 f '75. *
93. MACHOWSKY, HERBERT, AND MEYERS, JOEL. "Auditory Discrimination, Intelligence, and Reading Achievement at Grade 1." *Percept & Motor Skills* 40(2):363–8 Ap '75. * (PA 54:10586)
94. PEARSON, LINDA BOWEN. *The Relationship of Eye-Hand Drawing Coordination to Reading Achievement in a Group of Selected First- and Second-Grade Children.* Doctor's thesis, University of Alabama (University, Ala.), 1975. (DAI 36:7854A)
95. ROBINSON, WILLIAM BYRON. *A Study to Determine the Relationships Among Reading Achievement, Self-Concept and Selected Motor Performance Tests for Sixth Grade Male Students.* Doctor's thesis, University of Mississippi (University, Miss.), 1975. (DAI 36:4128A)
96. WILLIAMS, CAROLYN CHANDLER. *The Relationship Between Selected Reading Skills and Other Personal Variables of Sixth and Seventh Grade Students and Achievement in Science and Social Studies.* Doctor's thesis, Mississippi State University (State College, Miss.), 1975. (DAI 36:4132A)
97. HANEY, RUSSELL; MICHAEL, WILLIAM B.; AND MARTOIS, JOHN. "The Prediction of Success of Three Ethnic Groups in the Academic Components of a Nursing-Training Program at a Large Metropolitan Hospital." *Ed & Psychol Meas* 36(2):421–31 su '76. *
98. KAUFMAN, MAURICE. "Measuring Oral Reading Accuracy." *Read World* 15(4):216–25 My '76. *
99. KILIAN, GLORIA LAVERNE. *The Relationship Between Readability of Assigned Textbooks and Reading Level of Students in a School of Nursing.* Doctor's thesis, Kansas State University (Manhattan, Kan.), 1976. (DAI 37:1290A)
100. SHEN, SHINE MING SUN. *Factors of Language Development and Reading Achievement at Grade Levels Two Through Six.* Doctor's thesis, University of Southern Mississippi (Hattiesburg, Miss.), 1976. (DAI 37:2160A)

JOHN W. LOMBARD, *President, Educational Materials Corporation, Chicago, Illinois.*

The *California Achievement Tests* are a nationally standardized battery of tests in reading, math, and language arts for grades 1 to 12. The reading test can be used independently from the rest of the battery and might be considered if one is seeking a short, well-constructed group survey test of general reading achievement. This edition of the test was developed for standardization in spring 1970, and is thus fairly old for a major test.

The 1970 CAT Reading was developed in the fashion usual for such broad-based tests. Since content validity is the only type of validity described in the technical manual, it is crucial that anyone considering the use of CAT Reading understand its development rationale. The objectives to be measured were selected after a study of the recommended curricula objectives and courses of studies from many states, and a review of texts recommended or adopted at the state levels. Items were then written, pretested, and selected to reflect the major objectives. It is to the publisher's credit that the manuals supporting the test show the guidelines used for selecting items after pretesting and list the specific matching of items and objectives in the final forms. This information should help a test

California Achievement Tests: Reading

selection committee decide whether the test scores would reflect achievement of most of the important reading objectives of their school system.

The test items are well written and edited, although they would not pass the scrutiny of a committee reviewing the test for sex bias. For example, the first five items involving people in Level 1, Form A depict three male and two female stereotypic situations (active boys; passive, domestic females). Whether this has any proven effect on measurement seems irrelevant, and items in the new edition will undoubtedly have been tested to show lack of bias against sex and ethnic groups. Reviewers of the test content should note specifically the inclusion of at least six items in each of Levels 2–5 directed toward reference skills but categorized as reading comprehension. Also, some of the items in Levels 3–5 related to comprehension of mathematically oriented reading passages may test math and/or logic as much as reading skills. In general, however, item quality is high and content validity should follow.

Judging from raw score data, Levels 1 and 2 are too easy for above average students in the upper grades of their intended use, and this point is noted in a promotional brochure and test coordinator's handbook. How one decides if students are above average is not clear, however.

The technical manual provides a great deal of data about the test, but nowhere does it report how many usable records, by grade and level, went into formation of the norms. Many studies of reliability (internal consistency, interform, interlevel articulation) are reported, and all are quite acceptable. No statistical studies of validity are given; the publisher rests the case for validity with the arguments that only content validity is relevant to such national achievement tests. Various scores are available, including grade equivalents; percentile ranks and stanines for beginning, middle, and end of each grade; and the special achievement development scale scores, which are given major emphasis in the interpretive material. The achievement development scale is an equal interval scale, continuous from grade 1.5 to 12, independent of level, form, and time of year tested, and possessing other features that make it useful in research. Such scales, now common in most publishers' achievement batteries, are indeed superior to GEs, but

despite lengthy explanations of the problems associated with them, GEs continue to be made routinely available. The slow, lingering deaths of the IQ and GE scores reflect the publishers' problem of improving measurement, yet marketing successfully.

Another score is available if one uses CAT Reading with CTB's *Short Form Test of Academic Aptitude*. It is alleged that SFTAA scores, used with the scale scores on any CAT test, provide a measure of anticipated achievement, but since the SFTAA correlates in the low .80s with CAT Reading above grade 2, the use of such scores, especially in individual diagnosis, is not recommended until far more research data are made available.

CAT Reading is an acceptable test of achievement of nationally emphasized reading objectives. Its major use should be to survey group achievement, report results to the public, evaluate curriculum strategies, and chart trends over time or across grades. Individual scores might be a starting point in working with a student, but the scores are too general to be considered diagnostic. Anyone considering the use of this test can make a decision only by studying the objectives and items and determining whether this test, more than its many equally valid competitors, is a "match" with local educational objectives. Other considerations—such as the numerous scoring features, special norms, ease of administration, and even price—are quite secondary.

KENNETH J. SMITH, *Professor of Reading and Head of the Department, The University of Arizona, Tucson, Arizona.*

Two procedures were used in the selection of items for this and other tests in the battery of *California Achievement Tests:* (a) selection of content based on a study of textbooks, recommended objectives, and courses of study; and (b) selection of only those items which "discriminate between the high and low scoring students in a group."

It is questionable whether a single test item can meet both of these criteria. For instance, if an item is designed to determine performance on a very important objective, a conscientious teacher will want *all* of the children to meet that objective. If the children are successful, they presumably will answer the item acceptably and everyone will be pleased. Of course, if this were

California Achievement Tests: Reading

to happen, the item would be thrown out of the test! The point is that an item can be designed to measure a child's performance in meeting an objective, or it can be designed to compare a child's performance with that of other children, *but not both*. The *California Achievement Tests* claim both, but actually are designed to accomplish the latter.

The weighting of isolated, out-of-context vocabulary is notable. For instance, Level 3 has a total of 82 items, 40 of which are vocabulary (the others are "comprehension"). Such a test will, of course, discriminate among children, but it won't tell much about their reading skills. Furthermore, the selection of 40 words to represent a child's vocabulary is necessarily arbitrary and therefore dangerous.

The examiner's manual is quite clear and easy to follow. An examiner who is familiar with the manual should have little difficulty. The students, however, may have more of a problem. For instance, on Level 2, they must understand such terms as booklet, questionnaire, scratch paper, left, complete your birthdate, oral, and basic skills. Also on Level 2, the children are instructed to find the word that follows "in an a-b-c order." Children may, of course, know instead "alphabetical order," but if the examiner interprets or explains such directions, the norms will be thrown off.

The choices of scoring procedures, along with the clear presentation of scores on profile sheets, continues to be an advantage of the California tests. The directions are clear and complete. Scores are reported in terms of percentiles, grade equivalents, and stanines, all of which are well explained. A standard score is also available for charting student growth.

Since the standardization was completed in February and March, schools should consider administration at that time if they want norms to be accurate. Extrapolation into other months is guesswork. The standardization sample seems reasonable to the degree that it is possible to represent such a diverse population. However, the definition of a "city" as "population 25,000 or more" is interesting; it places Jonesboro, Arkansas, and New York City in the same urban category! Catholic schools were sampled separately. Very small districts and non-Catholic private schools were not included in the sample.

The norming procedure seems appropriate within its limitations. However, users are warned that the norms are based on administration of each level only to the appropriate grades. For instance, Level 5 was administered to high school students, but norms are available down to kindergarten. But Level 5 was not administered to kindergarten children, so such norms are only extrapolations and should be used with great caution. It also is interesting to note that a student taking Level 5 could ignore the test, mark the answer sheet by guess, and get a grade equivalent score of 4.1 in reading (with average luck). Not bad for a non-reader!

An additional problem is that one or two items often can make a substantial difference in the score yielded, a particularly dangerous matter when the high guessing factor on this test is considered. This problem is addressed in the technical report, but not convincingly so.

SUMMARY. The *California Achievement Test: Reading* is a standardized test emphasizing vocabulary and comprehension. It is barely adequate for comparing a child's performance in these two areas with the performance of the norm group. It is not useful for learning much about a child's reading skills and abilities.

In short, the *California Achievement Test: Reading* has the problems of any standardized test which claims more than it can produce. Finally, it is seriously flawed and should be used with caution, even if the examiner's purposes are limited to broad comparisons.

[720]

★Cloze Procedure [Ebbinghaus Completion Method] as Applied to Reading. Invented in 1897 by Ebbinghaus (*1*), this historical testing procedure has been used to measure reading comprehension as well as intelligence, achievement in college courses, association, imagination, language ability, and "numerous other 'faculties'"; many different names were used to refer to the procedure and its modifications, e.g., Ebbinghaus completion test, mutilated sentence (or text) test, combination/method, sentence (or story) completion, missing word test, conjectural test, incomplete sentences test, completion exercise, controlled completion test, and multiple-choice Ebbinghaus; in 1953, Taylor (*28*) applied the technique (designating it the cloze procedure) to measuring the readability or difficulty of textual materials—the designation quickly caught on to include all missing-word techniques used to measure both reading comprehension and readability of textual material (the cloze procedure is unique in that in addition to measuring examinee responses as other tests do, it is sometimes used solely to measure the readability of the test material itself); a variety of names have since been used for cloze procedures, e.g., precloze, postcloze, multiple choice cloze, random cloze, and rational cloze; since few users of the procedure are aware of the early use of the Ebbinghaus completion method, brief annotations have been presented for the references listed below published in 1930 or earlier.

REFERENCES

1. EBBINGHAUS, H. "Ueber eine neue Methode zur Prüfung geistiger Fähigkeiten und ihre Anwendung bei Schulkindern." *Zeitsch. fur Psych. und Phys. der Sinnesorgane* 13:401–57 '97. (*Reference not seen.*)

2. TERMAN, LEWIS M. "Genius and Stupidity: A Study of Some of the Intellectual Processes of Seven 'Bright' and Seven 'Stupid' Boys." Part 7, "Test of the Mastery of Language": Sect. 2, "The Mutilated Text," pp. 342–7. *Pedagog Sem* 13:307–73 S '06. * (Presents two Ebbinghaus completion tests—possibly the first published in English. One test consists of a 197-word story with 91 percent of the words omitted and 3 percent of the words reduced to the first 2 to 4 letters. In the second test the complete story is read aloud before the test is taken.)

3. BROWN, WILLIAM. "Some Experimental Results in the Correlation of Mental Abilities." *Brit J Psychol* 3:296–322 O '10. * (Used "the well-known *Combinations Methode* of Ebbinghaus in which the subject is shown a passage of continuous prose with from one-third to one-quarter of the words replaced by blanks, and is asked to supply the missing words or words of similar significance.")

4. SIMPSON, BENJAMIN R. "Correlations of Mental Abilities." *Teach Col Contrib Ed* 53:1–122 '12. * (Presents reliability data on the "Ebbinghaus Mutilated Text" and correlations with 14 other tests of "general intelligence.")

5. TERMAN, LEWIS M., AND CHILDS, H. G. "A Tentative Revision and Extension of the Binet-Simon Measuring Scale of Intelligence: Part 2, Supplementary Tests." Section 2, "The Completion Test," pp. 198–202. *J Ed Psychol* 3:198–208 Ap '12. * (Presents a story completion test with four degrees of mutilation—33⅓, 45, 54, and 66⅔ percent of words omitted—for grades 4–8.)

6. WEISS, A. P. "The Ebbinghaus Conjectural Method for Examination Purposes." *J Exp Pedagogy & Train Col Rec* (England) 1(4):320–34 Je '12. * (Recommends the use of the "conjectural test" for measuring student knowledge in college courses.)

7. WYATT, STANLEY. "The Quantitative Investigation of Higher Mental Processes." *Brit J Psychol* 6:109–33 Je '13. * (Among 15 tests, analogies and completion tests gave the highest correlations with subjective estimates of intelligence. The author used the Terman-Child completion tests.)

8. BOYD, WILLIAM. "The Value of the Combination Method for Examination Purposes." *J Exp Pedagogy & Train Col Rec* (England) 2(6):449–57 D '14. * (Concludes "that the Combination Method test can never completely take the place of the ordinary examination. But the ease with which it can be done and corrected, the advantage which it gives to certain students who usually fail to do themselves justice in examinations, the steadiness of the examiner's marking, the superiority of the results got when the marks of the two kinds of examinations are combined, all go to indicate that it has considerable value when used occasionally to supplement the ordinary examination.")

9. TRABUE, M. R. "Some Results of a Graded Series of Completion Tests." *Sch & Soc* 1:537–40 Ap 10 '15. * (A reduction of his 1914 graded series of completion tests to 24 sentences, each with 1 to 7 words omitted, for grades 2–13. Norms and scoring directions are presented.)

10. WHIPPLE, GUY MONTROSE. "Ebbinghaus' Completion-Method," pp. 283–300. In his *Manual of Mental and Physical Tests: Part 2, Complex Processes, Second Edition*. Baltimore, Md.: Warwick & York, Inc., 1915. Pp. v, 336. *

11. TRABUE, MARION REX. "Completion-Test Language Scales." *Teach Col Contrib Ed* 77:1–118 '16. * (Presents detailed scoring directions and normative data on eight additional sentence completion tests for grades 2–13. "Professor H. Ebbinghaus, who invented the completion-test method, characterized it as 'a real test of intelligence.' It has been variously classified by psychologists, as a test of 'imagination,' as an 'association test,' as a test of 'memory,' and as a test of numerous other 'faculties.' *As a matter of fact, the completion of incomplete sentences correlates remarkably well with almost any other measure of desirable qualities* [italics added]. * the obvious dependence of the ability to complete sentences upon the ability to read and think about printed words, and the magnitude of the correlations obtained between the completion test and other tests of language ability seemed to justify the classification of the completion-test scales for educational purposes as 'language scales.' ")

12. KELLEY, TRUMAN L. "Individual Testing With Completion Test Exercises." *Teach Col Rec* 18:371–82 S '17. * (Presents two parallel forms, *Completion Exercise Alpha* and *Completion Exercise Beta*, of 40 scaled sentences, each with 1 to 7 words omitted. "In view of the high reliability of this completion test and of its high correlation with so important a function as scholastic standing the writer would highly recommend it.")

13. OTIS, ARTHUR S. *Otis Group Intelligence Test.* Yonkers, N.Y.: World Book Co., 1918. * (Subtest 9, Narrative Com-

pletion, is probably the first published multiple choice cloze test. The unmutilated text of one test, for example, consists of a continuous story of 203 words; 57 of the words were omitted but only 25 of the omissions were used for testing.)

14. BALLARD, PHILIP BOSWOOD. *Mental Tests*, pp. 147–54. London: University of London Press, Ltd., 1920. Pp. xv, 235. * (An early example of a post-cloze test, a test in which the complete text is read before taking the cloze test.)

15. HAGGERTY, M. E.; TERMAN, L .M.; THORNDIKE, E. L.; WHIPPLE, G. M.; AND YERKES, R. M. *National Intelligence Tests*. Yonkers, N.Y.: World Book Co., 1920. * (Subtest 2 of this test for grades 2–8 consists of 20 mutilated sentences, each of which has one or two words missing.

16. TRABUE, M. R., AND STOCKBRIDGE, FRANK PARKER. *Measure Your Mind: The Mentimeter and How to Use It*, pp. 225–9, 346. Garden City, N.Y.: Doubleday, Page & Co., 1920. Pp. vii, 349. * [Subtest 23, Completion of Sentences, consists of 20 sentences, graduated in difficulty for grades 2 through college, with 1 to 7 words omitted per sentence. The authors state: "Although it has been used by many teachers and supervisors as a test of reading ability, it should probably be classified rather as an intelligence test than as an educational measuring instrument."]

17. BURT, CYRIL. *Mental and Scholastic Tests*, pp. 233–5, 281–2. London: P. S. King & Son, Ltd., 1921. Pp. xv, 432. *

18. BALLARD, PHILIP BOSWOOD. *Group Tests of Intelligence*, pp. 27–8, 70–3. London: University of London Press, Ltd., 1922. Pp. x, 252. * (Describes an intelligence test—used by the British Civil Service for selecting women clerks—with two "completion and missing-word" subtests and two similar subtests in "fool-proof form"—"fool-proof" meaning "multiple-choice.")

19. BALLARD, PHILIP BOSWOOD. Chap. 15, "Silent Reading," pp. 160–6. In his *The New Examiner*. London: University of London Press, Ltd., 1923. Pp. 269. * (Because of its heavy emphasis on memory, the author replaced his 1920 post-cloze test with a cloze test, for ages 9–14, in which the pupil sees only the mutilated text in order to place the emphasis on reading comprehension.)

20. MALMUD, ROSE S. "The Controlled *vs.* the Free Completion." *Am J Psychol* 36:401–11 Jl '25. * (PA 1:498) (Comparison of Trabue's *Completion-Test Language Scales* with the same mutilated texts but with groups of words from which correct answers are to be selected. The author concluded: "The controlled completion . . . . is an improved instrument in what it measures and in the accuracy with which it measures it. It is a better measure of language ability and a finer index of general intelligence.")

21. WOOLLEY, HELEN THOMPSON. "Mutilated Text," pp. 105–10, 281–6, 368–9, 486–8. In her *An Experimental Study of Children at Work and in School Between the Ages of Fourteen and Eighteen Years*. New York: Macmillan Co., 1926. Pp. xv, 762. *

22. BRONNER, AUGUSTA F.; HEALY, WILLIAM; LOWE, GLADYS M.; AND SHIMBERG, MYRA E. "Language Completion," pp. 40–2, 181–2. In their *A Manual of Individual Mental Tests and Testing*. Boston, Mass.: Little, Brown & Co., 1927. Pp. x, 287. * (Presents three modifications of the "Ebbinghaus Mutilated Text Test" with norms.)

23. HAMILTON, E. R. *The Art of Interrogation: Studies in the Principles of Mental Tests and Examinations*, pp. 33–5, 104. London: Kegan Paul, Trench, Trubner & Co., Ltd., 1929. Pp. xii, 174. * (Presents examples of Ebbinghaus' completion test—missing words in sentences and in paragraphs—and the "multiple-choice Ebbinghaus.")

24. KENT, GRACE H., AND WELLS, E. FRANCES. "Story Completion Tests." *J Ed Psychol* 21:703–11 D '30. * (PA 5:2063) (Presents two story completion tests, with norms for grades 3–9, based on "two simple and well-known fables.")

25. BURT, CYRIL. *Mental and Scholastic Tests, Second Edition.* pp. 245–7, 309–10. London: Staples Press Ltd., 1947. Pp. xxi, 467. *

26. SHANNON, C. E. "A Mathematical Theory of Communication." *Bell System Tech J* 27:379–423, 623–56 Jl, O '48. *

27. SHANNON, C. E. "Prediction and Entropy of Printed English." *Bell System Tech J* 30:50–64 Ja '51. *

28. TAYLOR, WILSON L. "'Cloze Procedure': A New Tool for Measuring Readability." *Journalism Q* 30:415–33 f '53. * (PA 29:850)

29. CHAPANIS, ALPHONSE. "The Reconstruction of Abbreviated Printed Messages." *J Exp Psychol* 48:496–510 D '54. * (PA 29:7205)

30. TAYLOR, WILSON LEWIS. *Application of "Cloze" and Entropy Measures to the Study of Contextual Constraint in Samples of Continuous Prose.* Doctor's thesis, University of Illinois (Urbana, Ill.), 1954. (DA 15:464)

31. WILSON, KELLOGG, AND CARROLL, JOHN B. "Applications of Entropy Measures to Problems of Sequential Structure." *J Abn & Soc Psychol Sup* 49:103–12 '54. *

32. TAYLOR, WILSON L. "Recent Developments in the Use of 'Cloze Procedure.'" *Journalism Q* 33:42–8 w '56. * (PA 31:2936)

Cloze Procedure [*Ebbinghaus Completion Method*] *as Applied to Reading*

33. HVISTENDAHL, J. K. "Use of 'Cloze' Procedure to Obtain 'Live' Statistics." *Journalism Q* 34:255 sp '57. *

34. JENKINSON, MARION DIXON. *Selected Processes and Difficulties of Reading Comprehension.* Doctor's thesis, University of Chicago (Chicago, Ill.), 1957.

35. MILLER, GEORGE A., AND FRIEDMAN, ELIZABETH A. "The Reconstruction of Mutilated English Texts." *Inf & Control* 1:38–55 S '57. *

36. TAYLOR, WILSON L. " 'Cloze' Readability Scores as Indices of Individual Differences in Comprehension and Aptitude." *J Appl Psychol* 41:19–26 F '57. * (*PA* 32:960)

37. HVISTENDAHL, J. K. "Language Ability as a Factor in 'Cloze' Scores." *Journalism Q* 35:353–4 su '58. *

38. RANKIN, EARL FREDERICK, JR. *An Evaluation of the Cloze Procedure as a Technique for Measuring Reading Comprehension.* Doctor's thesis, University of Michigan (Ann Arbor, Mich.), 1958. (*DA* 19:733)

39. RUBENSTEIN, HERBERT, AND ABORN, MURRAY. "Learning, Prediction, and Readability." *J Appl Psychol* 42:28–32 F '58. * (*PA* 33:5652)

40. ABORN, MURRAY; RUBENSTEIN, HERBERT; AND STERLING, THEODOR D. "Sources of Contextual Constraint Upon Words in Sentences." *J Exp Psychol* 57:171–80 Mr '59. * (*PA* 34:1280)

41. FLETCHER, JUNIOR EUGENE. *A Study of the Relationships Between Ability to Use Context as an Aid in Reading and Other Verbal Abilities.* Doctor's thesis, University of Washington (Seattle, Wash.), 1959. (*DA* 20:2675)

42. NICOL, MARGARET A., AND MILLER, KENNETH M. "Word Redundancy in Written English." *Austral J Psychol* 11:81–91 Je '59. * (*PA* 34:4294)

43. RANKIN, EARL F. "Uses of the Cloze Procedure in the Reading Clinic." *Int Read Assn Conf Proc* 4:228–31 '59. *

44. RANKIN, EARL F., JR. "The Cloze Procedure—Its Validity and Utility." *Nat Read Conf Yearb* 8:131–44 '59. *

45. KING, DAVID J., AND COFER, CHARLES N. "Exploratory Studies of Stories Varying in the Adjective-Verb Quotient." *J General Psychol* 62:199–221 Ap '60. * (*PA* 34:7705)

46. MACGINITIE, WALTER HAROLD. *Contextual Constraint in English Prose.* Doctor's thesis, Columbia University (New York, N.Y.), 1960. (*DA* 21:126)

47. HARMS, L. S. "Listener Comprehension of Speakers of Three Status Groups." *Lang & Speech* (England) 4:109–12 '61. * (*PA* 37:4903)

48. MACGINITIE, WALTER H. "Contextual Constraint in English Prose Paragraphs." *J Psychol* 51:121–30 Ja '61. * (*PA* 35:5706)

49. WEAVER, WENDELL WILLIAM. *An Examination of Some Differences in Oral and Written Language Using the Cloze Procedure.* Doctor's thesis, University of Georgia (Athens, Ga.), 1961. (*DA* 22:2702)

50. BLOOMER, RICHARD H. "The Cloze Procedure as a Remedial Reading Exercise." *J Develop Read* 5:173–81 sp '62. *

51. BORMUTH, JOHN ROBERT. *Cloze Tests as Measures of Readability and Comprehension Ability.* Doctor's thesis, Indiana University (Bloomington, Ind.), 1962. (*DA* 23:4218)

52. BROOKS, SADYE TUNE. *Effects of Locus of Control and Anxiety on the Ability of Mentally Retarded Children to Use Context Clues in Reading.* Doctor's thesis, George Peabody College for Teachers (Nashville, Tenn.), 1962. (*DA* 23:2003)

53. FILLENBAUM, SAMUEL, AND JONES, LYLE V. "An Application of 'Cloze' Technique to the Study of Aphasic Speech." *J Abn & Social Psychol* 65:183–9 Ag '62. * (*PA* 38:10327, title only)

54. SALZINGER, KURT; PORTNOY, STEPHANIE; AND FELDMAN, RICHARD S. "The Effect of Order of Approximation to the Statistical Structure of English on the Emission of Verbal Responses." *J Exp Psychol* 64:52–7 Jl '62. * (*PA* 37:4382)

55. BORMUTH, JOHN. "Cloze as a Measure of Readability." *Int Read Assn Conf Proc* 8:131–4 '63. *

56. COLEMAN, E. B., AND BLUMENFELD, J. P. "Cloze Scores of Nominalizations and Their Grammatical Transformations Using Active Verbs." *Psychol Rep* 13:651–4 D '63. * (*PA* 38:8328)

57. FELDSTEIN, STANLEY, AND JAFFE, JOSEPH. "Language Predictability as a Function of Psychotherapeutic Interaction." *J Consult Psychol* 27:123–6 Ap '63. * (*PA* 37:8059)

58. FILLENBAUM, SAMUEL; JONES, LYLE V.; AND RAPOPORT, AMNON. "The Predictability of Words and Their Grammatical Classes as a Function of Rate of Deletion From a Speech Transcript." *J Verbal Learning & Verbal Behav* 2:186–94 Ag '63. *

59. HONIGFELD, GILBERT. "The Ability of Schizophrenics to Understand Normal, Psychotic, and Pseudo-Psychotic Speech." *Dis Nerv System* 24:692–4 N '63. *

60. HONIGFELD, GILBERT. "Effects of an Hallucinogenic Agent on Verbal Behavior." *Psychol Rep* 13:383–5 O '63. * (*PA* 38:7565)

61. ROTHKOPF, ERNST Z. "Learning From Written Sentences: Within-Sentence Order in the Acquisition of Name-Clause Equivalences." *J Verbal Learning & Verbal Behav* 2:470–5 D '63. * (*PA* 38:7347)

62. RUDDELL, ROBERT BYRON. *An Investigation of the Effect of the Similarity of Oral and Written Patterns of Language Structure on Reading Comprehension.* Doctor's thesis, Indiana University (Bloomington, Ind.), 1963. (*DA* 24:5207)

63. WEAVER, WENDELL W., AND KINGSTON, ALBERT J. "A Factor Analysis of the Cloze Procedure and Other Measures of Reading and Language Ability." *J Commun* 13:252–61 D '63. *

64. BORMUTH, JOHN R. "Experimental Applications of Cloze Tests." *Int Read Assn Conf Proc* 9:303–6 '64. *

65. CLARK, RUTH ANNE. *The Influence of Syntactic and Referential Information on Word Predictability.* Doctor's thesis, University of Wisconsin (Madison, Wis.), 1964. (*DA* 25:3738)

66. COHEN, SANDRA RUTH. *Redundancy in the Written Language of the Deaf: Predictability of Deaf and Hearing Story Paraphrases.* Doctor's thesis, Columbia University (New York, N.Y.), 1964. (*DA* 26:4792)

67. DICKENS, MILTON, AND WILLIAMS, FREDERICK. "An Experimental Application of Cloze Procedure and Attitude Measures to Listening Comprehension." *Speech Monogr* 31:103–8 Je '64. *

68. FRIEDMAN, MILDRED McELHINNEY. *The Use of the Cloze Procedure for Improving the Reading Comprehension of Foreign Students at the University of Florida.* Doctor's thesis, University of Florida (Gainesville, Fla.), 1964. (*DA* 25:3420)

69. GALLANT, RUTH MARGARET FRANCES. *An Investigation of the Use of Cloze Tests as a Measure of Readability of Materials for the Primary Grades.* Doctor's thesis, Indiana University (Bloomington, Ind.), 1964. (*DA* 25:6431)

70. GREENE, FRANK PIERREPONT. *A Modified Cloze Procedure for Assessing Adult Reading Comprehension.* Doctor's thesis, University of Michigan (Ann Arbor, Mich.), 1964. (*DA* 25:5734)

71. HAFNER, LAWRENCE E. "Relationships of Various Measures to the 'Cloze.' " *Yearb Nat Read Conf* 13:135–45 '64. *

72. HONIGFELD, GILBERT; PLATZ, ARTHUR; AND GILLIS, RODERIC D. "Verbal Style and Personality: Authoritarianism." *J Commun* 14:215–8 D '64. * (*PA* 39:10197)

73. JENTZ, DOROTHY R. *An Evaluation of the Cloze Procedure for Improving Reading Comprehension.* Master's thesis, Northern Illinois University (DeKalb, Ill.), 1964.

74. MANIS, MELVIN, AND DAWES, ROBYN M. "Cloze Score as a Function of Attitude." *Psychol Rep* 9:79–84 Ag '64. *

75. RUDDELL, ROBERT B. "A Study of Cloze Comprehension Technique in Relation to Structurally Controlled Reading Material." *Int Read Assn Conf Proc* 9:298–303 '64. *

76. SALZINGER, KURT; PORTNOY, STEPHANIE; AND FELDMAN, RICHARD S. "Verbal Behavior of Schizophrenic and Normal Subjects." *Ann N Y Acad Sci* 105:845–60 S 8 '64. * (*PA* 40:1826)

77. ANDERSON, JONATHAN. "Research in Readability for the Classroom Teacher." *J Read* 8:402–3+ My '65. *

78. BLOOMER, RICHARD H., AND HEITZMAN, ANDREW J. "Pre-Testing and the Efficiency of Paragraph Reading." *J Read* 8:219–23 Mr '65. * (*PA* 40:8063)

79. BORMUTH, J. R., AND MACDONALD, O. L. "Cloze Tests as a Measure of Ability to Detect Literary Style." *Int Read Assn Conf Proc* 10:287–90 '65. *

80. BORMUTH, JOHN R. "Optimum Sample Size and Cloze Test Length in Readability Measurement." *J Ed Meas* 2:111–6 Je '65. *

81. BORMUTH, JOHN R. "Validities of Grammatical and Semantic Classifications of Cloze Test Scores." *Int Read Assn Conf Proc* 10:283–6 '65. *

82. CLARK, RUTH ANNE; WILLIAMS, FREDERICK; AND TANNENBAUM, PERCY H. "Effects of Shared Referential Experience Upon Encoder-Decoder Agreement." *Lang & Speech* (England) 8:252–9 O–D '65. *

83. COLEMAN, E. B. "Learning of Prose Written in Four Grammatical Transformations." *J Appl Psychol* 49:332–41 O '65. * (*PA* 40:154)

84. CRONENBERGER, PATRICIA LOUISE. *Cloze Tests: A Comparison of Two Approaches to Construction.* Master's thesis, Indiana University (Bloomington, Ind.), 1965.

85. DeVITO, JOSEPH A. "Comprehension Factors in Oral and Written Discourse of Skilled Communicators." *Speech Monogr* 32:124–8 Je '65. *

86. GALLANT, RUTH. "Use of Cloze Tests as a Measure of Readability in the Primary Grades." *Int Read Assn Conf Proc* 10:286–7 '65. *

87. GREENE, FRANK B. "Modification of the Cloze Procedure and Changes in Reading Test Performance." *J Ed Meas* 2:213–7 D '65. *

88. HAFNER, LAWRENCE E. "A One-Month Experiment in Teaching Context Aids in Fifth Grade." *J Ed Res* 58:472–4 Jl–Ag '65. * (*PA* 40:764)

89. HAFNER, LAWRENCE E. "Implications of Cloze." *Yearb Nat Read Conf* 14:151–8 '65. *

90. HONIGFELD, GILBERT. "Temporal Effects of LSD-25 and Epinephrine on Verbal Behavior." *J Abn Psychol* 70:303–6 Ag '65. * (*PA* 39:14275)

91. LOUTHAN, VINCENT. "Some Systematic Grammatical Deletions and Their Effects on Reading Comprehension." *Engl J* 54:295–9 Ap '65. *

Cloze Procedure [*Ebbinghaus Completion Method*] *as Applied to Reading*

92. PEISACH, ESTELLE CHERRY. "Children's Comprehension of Teacher and Peer Speech." *Child Develop* 36:467–80 Je '65. * *(PA* 39:11973)

93. PLATZ, ARTHUR, AND HONIGFELD, GILBERT. "Some Effects of Anxiety on the Intelligibility of Verbal Communication in Psychotherapy." *J Pers & Social Psychol* 2:122–5 Jl '65. * *(PA* 39:12425)

94. RANKIN, EARL F., JR. "Closure and Cloze Procedure." *Yearb North Central Read Assn* 3–4:54–84 '65. *

95. RANKIN, EARL F., JR. "The Cloze Procedure—A Survey of Research." *Yearb Nat Read Conf* 14:133–50 '65. *

96. RANSOM, PEGGY ELAINE HITCHCOCK. *A Study to Determine Reading Levels of Elementary School Children by Cloze Testing.* Doctor's thesis, Ball State University (Muncie, Ind.), 1965. *(DA* 26:3705)

97. RUDDELL, ROBERT B. "The Effect of Oral and Written Patterns of Language Structure on Reading Comprehension." Comments by Theodore Clymer. *Read Teach* 18:270–5 Ja '65. *

98. RUDDELL, ROBERT B. "Effect of the Similarity of Oral and Written Patterns of Language Structure on Reading Comprehension." *El Engl* 42:403–10 Ap '65. *

99. RUDDELL, ROBERT B. "Reading Comprehension and Structural Redundancy in Written Material." *Int Read Assn Conf Proc* 10:308–11 '65. *

100. SCHNEYER, J. WESLEY. "Use of the Cloze Procedure for Improving Reading Comprehension." *Read Teach* 19:174–9 D '65. * *(PA* 40:8077)

101. STREET, ROY F. Chap. 3, "Completion Tests and the Nature of Intellect," pp. 12–20. In his *A Gestalt Completion Test: A Study of a Cross Section of Intellect.* Teachers College, Columbia University Contributions to Education No. 481. New York: Bureau of Publications, the College, 1931. Pp. vii, 65. *

102. SZALAY, T. G. "Validation of the Coleman Readability Formulas." *Psychol Rep* 17:965–6 D '65. * *(PA* 40:3546)

103. WEAVER, WENDELL W. "Theoretical Aspects of the Cloze Procedure." *Yearb Nat Read Conf* 14:115–32 '65. *

104. BLOOMER, RICHARD H. "The Effects of Non-overt Reinforced Cloze Procedure Upon Reading Comprehension." *Yearb Nat Read Conf* 15:31–40 '66. *

105. BLUMENFELD, JACOB P., AND MILLER, GERALD R. "Improving Reading Through Teaching Grammatical Constraints." *El Engl* 43:752–5 N '66. *

106. BORMUTH, JOHN R. "Readability: A New Approach." *Read Res Q* 1:79–132 sp '66. * *(PA* 40:11114)

107. DONOHEW, LEWIS. "Decoder Behavior on Incongruent Political Material: A Pilot Study." *J Commun* 16:133–42 Je '66. * *(PA* 40:11122)

108. GREGORY-PANOPOULOS, JOHN FRED. *An Experimental Application of "Cloze" Procedure as a Diagnostic Test of Listening Comprehension Among Foreign Students.* Doctor's thesis, University of Southern California (Los Angeles, Calif.), 1966. *(DA* 27:2213A)

109. HAFNER, LAWRENCE E. "Cloze Procedure." *J Read* 9:415–21 My '66. *

110. KLARE, GEORGE R. "Comments on Bormuth's Readability: A New Approach." *Read Res Q* 1:119–25 su '66. *

111. KNIGHT, DAVID W. *The Reading Performance of Students With Ninth Grade Reading Achievement on Occupational Information Materials Written With Various Levels of Readability.* Doctor's thesis, Florida State University (Tallahassee, Fla.), 1966. *(DA* 27:2425A)

112. KOHLER, EMMETT THEODORE. *An Investigation of Cloze Scores in Terms of Selected Cognitive Variables.* Doctor's thesis, Florida State University (Tallahassee, Fla.), 1966. *(DA* 27:114A)

113. McLEOD, J., AND ANDERSON, J. "Readability Assessment and Word Redundancy of Printed English." *Psychol Rep* 18:35–8 F '66. * *(PA* 40:7051)

114. MOROZ, MYRON, AND FOSMIRE, FREDERICK R. "Application of Cloze Procedures to Schizophrenic Language." *Dis Nerv System* 27:408–10 Je '66. *

115. BEARD, JACOB G. "Comprehensibility of High School Textbooks: Association with Content Area." *J Read* 11:229–34 D '67. *

116. BORMUTH, JOHN R. "Comparable Cloze and Multiple-choice Comprehension Test Scores." *J Read* 10:291–9 F '67. * *(PA* 41:6248)

117. BRISTOR, JANET E. *The Cloze Test as a Measure of Reading Comprehension—Grade Three.* Master's thesis, California State College (California, Pa.), 1967.

118. HEITZMAN, ANDREW J., AND BLOOMER, RICHARD H. "The Effect of Non-overt Reinforced Cloze Procedure Upon Reading Comprehension." *J Read* 11:213–23 D '67. *

119. JUROVCIK, PAUL. *Comprehension and the Cloze Procedure.* Master's thesis, California State College (California, Pa.), 1967.

120. KINGSTON, ALBERT J., AND WEAVER, WENDELL W. "Recent Developments in Readability Appraisal." *J Read* 11:44–7 O '67. *

121. KIRBY, CLARA LOU LAUGHLIN. *A Comparison of Scores Obtained on Standardized Oral and Silent Reading Tests and a Cloze Test.* Doctor's thesis, Ball State University (Muncie, Ind.), 1967. *(DA* 28:4512A)

122. MILLER, G. R., AND COLEMAN, E. B. "A Set of Thirty-Six Prose Passages Calibrated for Complexity." *J Verbal Learning & Verbal Behav* 6:851–4 D '67. * *(PA* 42:8908)

123. MOORES, DONALD FREDERICK. *Applications of "Cloze" Procedures to the Assessment of Psycholinguistic Abilities of the Deaf.* Doctor's thesis, University of Illinois (Urbana, Ill.), 1967. *(DA* 28:3032A)

124. RANKIN, EARL F., JR. "Research Design and the Cloze Procedure." *Int Read Assn Conf Proc* 11(1):489–91 '67. *

125. STEWART, ELNEITA WALLACE. *A Comparative Study of the Effectiveness of Cloze and Textbook Procedures in a College Reading Program.* Doctor's thesis, University of Houston (Houston, Tex.), 1967. *(DA* 28:4835A)

126. WEAVER, WENDELL W., AND BICKLEY, A. C. "Some Differences in Encoding and Decoding Messages." *J Read Specialist* 7:18–9+ O '67. * *(PA* 42:2528)

127. ALEXANDER, HENRY WILLIAM. *An Investigation of the Cloze Procedure as a Measuring Device Designed to Identify the Independent, Instruction, and Frustration Reading Levels of Pupils in the Intermediate Grades.* Doctor's thesis, University of Illinois (Urbana, Ill.), 1968. *(DA* 29:4314A)

128. BORMUTH, JOHN R. "Cloze Test Readability: Criterion Reference Scores." *J Ed Meas* 5:189–96 f '68. * *(PA* 44:11209)

129. BORMUTH, JOHN R. "The Cloze Readability Procedure." *El Engl* 45:429–36 Ap '68. *

130. COLEMAN, E. B., AND MILLER, G. R. "A Measure of Information Gained During Prose Learning." *Read Res Q* 3:369–86 sp '68. * *(PA* 42:13694)

131. CRANNEY, ADELBERT GARR, JR. *A Comparison of a Free-Response and Multiple-Choice Cloze Reading Test.* Doctor's thesis, University of Minnesota (Minneapolis, Minn.), 1968. *(DA* 29:811A)

132. GREENE, FRANK P.; CRANNEY, A. GARR; BLOOMER, RICHARD; RANKIN, EARL; WEAVER, WENDELL; AND BROWN, ERIC. "Cloze Symposium." Discussion by Wilson Taylor and others. *Yearb Nat Read Conf* 17:110–31 '68. *

133. KIRCHHOFF, LEO HENRY. *A Study Utilizing the Cloze Test Procedure to Determine Reading Levels of First Grade Children Who Have Been Taught Beginning Reading by Four Different Approaches.* Doctor's thesis, University of Kansas (Lawrence, Kan.), 1968. *(DA* 29:3329A)

134. LISKE, WILFRED WALLACE. *The Cloze Procedure for Determining Readability of Encyclopedia Material for Elementary School Pupils.* Doctor's thesis, University of Maryland (College Park, Md.), 1968. *(DA* 29:4189A)

135. MARTIN, RUBY WHEELER. *Transformational Grammar, Cloze, and Performance in College Freshmen.* Doctor's thesis, Syracuse University (Syracuse, N.Y.), 1968. *(DAI* 30:70A)

136. PORTNOY, STEPHANIE. *A Comparison of Oral and Written Verbal Behavior.* Doctor's thesis, Columbia University (New York, N.Y.), 1968. *(DA* 29:1191B)

137. POTTER, THOMAS CLIFFORD. *Reading Skills in Young Children: Closure and Comprehension.* Doctor's thesis, University of California (Los Angeles, Calif.), 1968. *(DA* 29:1051A)

138. RANSOM, PEGGY. "Determining Reading Levels of Elementary School Children by Cloze Testing." *Int Read Assn Conf Proc* 12(1):477–82 '68. *

139. RANSOM, PEGGY E. "Determining Reading Levels of Elementary School Children by Cloze Testing." *Proc Int Read Assn* 12(1):477–82 '68. *

140. ROTHKOPF, ERNST Z. "Textual Constraint as Function of Repeated Inspection." *J Ed Psychol* 59:20–5 F '68. * *(PA* 42:6609)

141. WEAVER, WENDELL W.; WHITE, WILLIAM F.; AND KINGSTON, ALBERT J., JR. "Affective Correlates of Reading Comprehension." *J Psychol* 68:87–95 Ja '68. * *(PA* 42:7878)

142. WEINTRAUB, SAMUEL. "The Cloze Procedure." *Read Teach* 21:567–71+ Mr '68. *

143. ANDERSON, JONATHAN. *Application of Cloze Procedure to English Learned as a Foreign Language.* Doctor's thesis, University of New England (Armidale, N.S.W., Australia), 1969.

144. AQUINO, MILAGROS R. "The Validity of the Miller-Coleman Readability Scale." *Read Res Q* 4(3):342–57 sp '69. *

145. AQUINO, MILAGROS; MOSBERG, LUDWIG; AND SHARRON, MARGE. "Reading Comprehension Difficulty as a Function of Content Area and Linguistic Complexity." *J Exp Ed* 37(4):1–4 su '69. *

146. BAILEY, LARRY J. "Cloze Procedure—A Technique for Evaluating Instructional Materials." *J Indus Teach Ed* 6(4):57–60 su '69. *

147. BORMUTH, JOHN R. "Empirical Determination of the Instructional Reading Level." *Int Read Assn Conf Proc* 13(1):716–21 '69. *

148. BORMUTH, JOHN R. "Factor Validity of Cloze Tests as Measures of Reading Comprehension." *Read Res Q* 4(3):358–65 sp '69. *

149. DELCAMP, RITA M. *Reading and Listening Comprehension of Fifth Grade Pupils as Measured by the Cloze Procedure.* Master's thesis, Rutgers—The State University (New Brunswick, N.J.), 1969.

150. ESTRADA, FRANK XAVIER. *The Effect of Increasing Syntactic Complexity on Reading Comprehension.* Master's thesis, University of California (Los Angeles, Calif.), 1969.

Cloze Procedure [*Ebbinghaus Completion Method*] *as Applied to Reading*

151. GOODSTEIN, HENRY ARTHUR. *The Performance of Educable Mentally Handicapped and Average-IQ Children on Two Modified Cloze Tasks for Oral Language.* Doctor's thesis, University of Connecticut (Storrs, Conn.), 1969. (*DAI* 30:3320A)

152. GUICE, BILLY M. "The Use of the Cloze Procedure for Improving Reading Comprehension of College Students." *J Read Behav* 1(3):81–92 su '69. * (*PA* 45:3035)

153. HATER, MARY ANN. *The Cloze Procedure as a Measure of the Reading Comprehensibility and Difficulty of Mathematical English.* Doctor's thesis, Purdue University (Lafayette, Ind.), 1969. (*DAI* 30:4829A)

154. HENRY, PEGGY ELAINE. *The Effect of Interest on Reading Comprehension as Measured by Cloze and Multiple Choice Tests.* Doctor's thesis, University of Iowa (Iowa City, Iowa), 1969. (*DAI* 30:3857A)

155. JEFFERSON, GEORGE LEE, JR. *Lexical and Structural Items as Predictors of Readability for High and Low Ability Readers.* Doctor's thesis, University of Georgia (Athens, Ga.), 1969. (*DAI* 30:5287A)

156. MILLER, DAVID L. *The Utility of "Cloze" for the Measurement of the Ability to Use Linguistic Context in the Aural Perception of Language.* Master's thesis, Utah State University (Logan, Utah), 1969.

157. RANKIN, EARL F., AND CULHANE, JOSEPH W. "Comparable Cloze and Multiple-Choice Comprehension Test Scores." *J Read* 13(3):193–8 D '69. * (*PA* 44:9267)

158. RANKIN, EARL F., AND DALE, LOTHAR H. "Cloze Residual Gain—A Technique for Measuring Learning Through Reading." *Yearb Nat Read Conf* 18:17–26 '69. *

159. RANKIN, EARL F., AND OVERHOLSER, BETSY M. "Reaction of Intermediate Grade Children to Contextual Clues." *J Read Behav* 1(3):50–73 su '69. * (*PA* 45:2168)

160. RENTEL, VICTOR MICHAEL. *Form Class and Word Length as Indices of the Difficulty of Predicting Cloze Entries in a Sample of Continuous Prose.* Doctor's thesis, University of South Carolina (Columbia, S.C.), 1969. (*DAI* 30:4284A)

161. SAUER, FREDA MAE. *The Determination of Reading Instructional Level of Disabled Fourth Grade Readers Utilizing Cloze Testing Procedure.* Doctor's thesis, Oklahoma State University (Stillwater, Okla.), 1969. (*DAI* 31:4046A)

162. SKYER, GIL. "A Comparison of the Cloze Procedure and the Short Answer Achievement Test in Determining Subject Matter Comprehension." *Grad Res Ed & Related Discip* 5(1):29–45 f '69. *

163. SMITH, WILLIAM LEWIS. *The Effect of Snytax on Reading.* Doctor's thesis, Florida State University (Tallahassee, Fla.), 1969. (*DAI* 30:4970A)

164. TANNENBAUM, PERCY H.; WILLIAMS, FREDERICK; AND CLARK, RUTH ANNE. "Effects of Grammatical Information on Word Predictability." *J Commun* 19(1):41–8 Mr '69. * (*PA* 43:12951)

165. WEAVER, WENDELL W.; KINGSTON, ALBERT J.; BICKLEY, A. C.; AND WHITE, WILLIAM F. "Information-Flow Difficulty in Relation to Reading Comprehension." *J Read Behav* 1(3):41–9 su '69. * (*PA* 45:2355)

166. WEIL, A. T., AND ZINBERG, N. E. "Acute Effects of Marihuana on Speech." *Nature* 222(5192):434–7 My 3, '69. *

167. WHITE, WILLIAM F., AND AARON, ROBERT. "Non-Verbal Cues as Determinants of Reading Comprehension." *J Read Behav* 1(4):53–65 f '69. *

168. BICKLEY, A. C.; ELLINGTON, BILLIE J.; AND BICKLEY, RACHEL T. "The Cloze Procedure: A Conspectus." *J Read Behav* 2:232–49 su '70. * (*PA* 46:2986)

169. BLAKE, JAMES HERBERT. *Cloze Scores, Agreement Scores, and Approximated Equivalence Scores as Indices of Contextual Constraint.* Doctor's thesis, Syracuse University (Syracuse, N.Y.), 1970. (*DAI* 31:5923A)

170. CHARLES, EDWARD. *An Investigation of the Use of Cloze Tests to Compare Gain Scores of Students in Science Who Have Used Individualized Science Materials and Those Who Have Used Traditional Textbook Materials.* Doctor's thesis, Lehigh University (Bethlehem, Pa.), 1970. (*DAI* 31:5026A)

171. CRAWFORD, ALAN NEAL. *The Cloze Procedure as a Measure of the Reading Comprehension of Elementary Level Mexican-American and Anglo-American Children.* Doctor's thesis, University of California (Los Angeles, Calif.), 1970. (*DAI* 31:3162A)

172. CULHANE, JOSEPH W. "CLOZE Procedures and Comprehension." *Read Teach* 23(5):410–3 F '70. *

173. DARNELL, DONALD K. "Clozentropy: A Procedure for Testing English Language Proficiency of Foreign Students." *Speech Monogr* 37(1):36–46 Mr '70. *

174. FROELICH, DONALD MAX. *A Comparison of Two Methods of Assessing Textbook Readability of Selected College Level Electronics Textbooks.* Doctor's thesis, University of Missouri (Columbia, Mo.), 1970. (*DAI* 31:3917A)

175. FROESE, VICTOR. *A Cross-Validation of the Dale-Chall Readability Formula Using the Cloze Procedure and Sixth Grade Science Textbook Materials.* Master's thesis, Western Washington State College (Bellingham, Wash.), 1970.

176. GEYER, JAMES RUSH. *The Cloze Procedure as a Predictor of Comprehension in Secondary Social Studies Material.* Doctor's thesis, University of Maryland (College Park, Md.), 1970. (*DAI* 31:2002A)

177. GOODSTEIN, HENRY A. "Performance of Mentally Handicapped and Average-IQ Children on Two Modified Cloze Tasks for Oral Language." *Am J Mental Def* 75(3):290–7 N '70. * (*PA* 46:3605)

178. KINGSTON, ALBERT J., AND WEAVER, WENDELL W. "Feasibility of Cloze Techniques for Teaching and Evaluating Culturally Disadvantaged Beginning Readers." *J Social Psychol* 82(2):205–14 D '70. * (*PA* 45:6050)

179. KIRBY, CLARA L. "Using the Cloze Procedure as a Testing Technique." *Int Read Assn Conf Proc* 13(4):68–77 '70. *

180. MCLEOD, JOHN, AND ANDERSON, JONATHAN. "An Approach to Assessment of Reading Ability Through Information Transmission." *J Read Behav* 2(2):116–43 sp '70. * (*PA* 45:503)

181. MARSHALL, WILLIAM A. "Contextual Constraint on Deaf and Hearing Children: Investigating the Effect at Fourth Grade Reading Level Using the Cloze Procedure." *Am Ann Deaf* 115(7):682–9 N '70. * (*PA* 45:10471)

182. MARSHALL, WILLIAM JAMES ALOYSIUS. *Investigating the Effect of Contextual Constraint on Deaf and Hearing Children at the Fourth Grade Reading Level, Using the Cloze Procedure.* Doctor's thesis, University of Illinois (Urbana, Ill.), 1970. (*DAI* 31:2218A)

183. MOORES, DONALD F. "An Investigation of the Psycholinguistic Functioning of Deaf Adolescents." *Excep Children* 36(9):645–52 My '70. * (*PA* 46:5509)

184. OHNMACHT, FRED W.; WEAVER, WENDELL W.; AND KOHLER, EMMETT T. "Cloze and Closure: A Factorial Study." *J Psychol* 74(2):205–17 Mr '70. * (*PA* 44:12542)

185. SEMMEL, MELVYN I.; BARRITT, LOREN S.; AND BENNETT, STANLEY W. "Performance of EMR and Nonretarded Children on a Modified Cloze Task." *Am J Mental Def* 74(5):681–8 Mr '70. * (*PA* 44:15171)

186. SMITH, ELMER L. "Use of the Cloze Procedure in Improving Comprehension of Junior College Readers." *Yearb Nat Read Conf* 19(2):171–6 '70. *

187. SWANSON, PAULA R. *A Pilot Study to Investigate the Use of Teacher Made Cloze Tests to Determine Reading Grade Level.* Master's thesis, California State College (Los Angeles, Calif.), 1970.

188. TAYLOR, WILSON L., AND WALDMAN, IVAN N. "Latency and Focus Methods of Cloze Quantification." *Yearb Nat Read Conf* 19(2):241–62 '70. *

189. THOMPSON, GAIL PARKS. *An Evaluation of the Use of the Cloze Procedure as a Measure of Readability.* Master's thesis, Washington State University (Pullman, Wash.), 1970.

190. WEAVER, WENDELL W.; HOLMES, C. CURTIS; AND REYNOLDS, RICHARD J. "The Effect of Reading Variation and Punctuation Conditions Upon Reading Comprehension." *J Read Behav* 2(1):75–84 w '70. * (*PA* 45:664)

191. ANDERSON, J. "A Technique for Measuring Reading Comprehension and Readability." *Engl Lang Teach* (England) 25(2):178–82 F '71. *

192. BASSETT, CAROL M. *The Cloze Technique as a Tool for Improving and Testing Comprehension in Reading: A Survey of the Literature.* Master's thesis, University of Wisconsin (Eau Claire, Wis.), 1971.

193. BLACKWELL, JANET M.; THOMPSON, RICHARD A.; AND DZIUBAN, CHARLES D. "An Investigation Into the Effectiveness of the Cloze Procedure as a Vocabulary Teaching Toll." *J Read Behav* 4(4):53–4 f '71–72 ['71]. *

194. BLANTON, B. ELGIT, AND TUINMAN, J. JAAP. "Objective and Subjective Information Value of Words." *Psychol Rep* 29(3):972 D '71. * (*PA* 47:8849)

195. BOWERS, FREDERICK, AND NACKE, PHIL L. "Cloze, Transformational Theory and Redundancy." *J Read Behav* 4(1):20–33 w '71–72 ['71]. *

196. BYRNE, MARY ANN; FELDHUSEN, JOHN F.; AND KANE, ROBERT B. "The Relationships Among Two Cloze Measurement Procedures and Divergent Thinking Abilities." *Read Res Q* 6(3):378–93 sp '71. * (*PA* 47:3624)

197. CARVER, RONALD P.; JOHNSON, RAYMOND L.; AND FRIEDMAN, HERBERT L. "Factor Analysis of the Ability to Comprehend Time-Compressed Speech." *J Read Behav* 4(1):40–9 w '71–72 ['71]. *

198. COLEMAN, EDMUND B. "Developing a Technology of Written Instruction: Some Determiners of the Complexity of Prose," pp. 155–204. "Discussion of Professor Coleman's Paper" by Walter H. MacGinitie, pp. 205–15. In *Verbal Learning Research and the Technology of Written Instruction.* Edited by Ernst Z. Rothkopf and Paul E. Johnson. New York: Teachers College Press, 1971. Pp. xi, 367. *

199. CRAKER, HAZEL VIOLA. *Clozentropy Procedure as an Instrument for Measuring Oral English Competencies of First Grade Children.* Doctor's thesis, University of New Mexico (Albuquerque, N.M.), 1971. (*DAI* 32:6286A)

200. DAUGHERTY, JOAN. *The Effect of the Cloze Procedure and Interspersed Questions as an Aid to Reading Comprehension.* Doctor's thesis, University of Akron (Akron, Ohio), 1971. (*DAI* 32:664A)

201. DULIN, KENNETH L. "Measuring the Difficulty of Reading Materials." *Read Improv* 8(1):3–6 sp '71. *

202. FAUBION, NORMA NELL. *The Effect of Training in the Use of Cloze on the Ability of Fourth Grade Pupils to Gain Information From Written Discourse.* Doctor's thesis, Texas

Cloze Procedure [Ebbinghaus Completion Method] as Applied to Reading

A & M University (College Station, Tex.), 1971. (*DAI* 32: 4486A)

203. GUSCOTT, CHARLES EDGAR. *The Effect of Cloze Procedure Exercises on the Improvement of Reading Achievement and of Reading Comprehension of Selected Sixth-Grade Students.* Doctor's thesis, University of Akron (Akron, Ohio), 1971. (*DAI* 32:3861A)

204. HAFNER, LAWRENCE E.; GWALTNEY, WAYNE; AND ROBINSON, RICHARD. "Reading in Bookkeeping: Predictions and Performance." *J Read* 14(8):537–46 My '71. *

205. HARTSOUGH, WALTER ROSS. *An Analysis of Performance as a Function of Locus of Control on Tasks Utilizing "Cloze" Technique Under Skill, Chance, and Ambiguous Set Conditions.* Doctor's thesis, University of Connecticut (Storrs, Conn.), 1971. (*DAI* 33:2811B)

206. HOUSKA, JOSEPH THOMAS. *The Efficacy of the Cloze Procedure as a Readability Tool on Technical Content Material as Used in Industrial Education at the High School Level.* Doctor's thesis, University of Illinois (Urbana, Ill.), 1971. (*DAI* 32: 4500A)

207. JONGSMA, EUGENE. *The Cloze Procedure as a Teaching Technique.* Newark, Del.: International Reading Association, 1971. Pp. 42. *

208. KELLY, NANCY L. *A Comparison of Readability Formula Ratings With Written Cloze Scores on Primary Level Reading Material.* Master's thesis, Rutgers—The State University (New Brunswick, N.J.), 1971.

209. KENNEDY, DELORES KESSLER. *Training With the Cloze Procedure, Visually and Auditorially, to Improve the Reading and Listening Comprehension of Third Grade Underachieving Readers.* Doctor's thesis, Pennsylvania State University (University Park, Pa.), 1971. (*DAI* 32:6206A)

210. LEVINE, HELEN FAITH. "Linguistic and Paralinguistic Changes in Spanish-Speakers Learning English." *Engl Lang Teach* (England) 25(3):288–96 Je '71. * [Errata: 26(3):198–200 F '72. *]

211. LISMAN, LINDA C. *Vowel Deletion and Cloze Tests Compared With a Reading Ability Test.* Master's thesis, Rutgers—The State University (New Brunswick, N.J.), 1971.

212. MORK, THEODORE A. "Clozing the Placement Gap: A New Tool for Administrators and Teachers." *Ed Leadership* 28(7):763–7 Ap '71. *

213. OLLER, JOHN W., JR., AND CONRAD, CHRISTINE A. "The Cloze Technique and ESL Proficiency." *Lang Learning* 21(2): 183–95 D '71. *

214. OLLER, JOHN W., JR., AND INAL, NEVIN. "A Cloze Test of English Prepositions." *TESOL Q* 5(4):315–26 D '71. *

215. RANKIN, EARL F. "Grade Level Interpretation of Cloze Readability Scores." *Yearb Nat Read Conf* 20:30–7 '71. *

216. REILLY, RICHARD R. "A Note on 'Clozentropy: A Procedure for Testing English Language Proficiency of Foreign Students.'" *Speech Monogr* 38(4):350–3 N '71. *

217. ROBINSON, RICHARD DAVID. *An Investigation Into the Use of the Cloze Procedure With a Group of Functionally Illiterate Adults.* Doctor's thesis, University of Georgia (Athens, Ga.), 1971. (*DAI* 32:3572A)

218. RYNDERS, PETER. *Use of the Cloze Procedure to Develop Comprehension Skill in the Intermediate Grades.* Doctor's thesis, Syracuse University (Syracuse, N.Y.), 1971. (*DAI* 32: 5676A)

219. SIKES, HELEN CRUSE. *A Comparative Study of Cloze Procedure Scores on Original and Published Materials.* Doctor's thesis, University of Southern Mississippi (Hattiesburg, Miss.), 1971. (*DAI* 32:2320A)

220. STEPHENS, ROBERT GERALD. *Use of the Cloze Procedure as a Criterion for Evaluating the Applicability of Selected Readability Formulas to Science Reading Materials.* Doctor's thesis, Indiana University (Bloomington, Ind.), 1971. (*DAI* 32:6020A)

221. SWALM, JAMES E. *Comparison of Oral Reading, Silent Reading, and Listening Comprehension Assessed by Cloze.* Doctor's thesis, Rutgers—The State University (New Brunswick, N.J.), 1971. (*DAI* 32:3578A)

222. TUINMAN, J. JAAP. "The Removal of Information Procedure (RIP): A First Analysis." *J Read Behav* 3(2):44–50 sp '70–71 ['71]. *

223. TUINMAN, JAAP, AND HAFNER, LAWRENCE E. "Information Value of Adjectives in Relation to Their Position in Sentences." *Psychol Rep* 28(3):987–90 Je '71. * (*PA* 46:10135)

224. WEAVER, WENDELL W., AND KINGSTON, ALBERT J. "Oral and Written Language Measures With First Grade Pupils." *Yearb Nat Read Conf* 20:219–26 '71. *

225. WEAVER, WENDELL W.; KINGSTON, ALBERT J.; AND DINNAN, JAMES A. "Vertical and Horizontal Constraints in the Context Reading of Sentences." *J Read Behav* 3(2):39–43 sp '70–71 ['71]. *

226. WIECHELMAN, DUANE SYLVESTER. *A Comparison of Cloze Procedure Scores and Informal Reading Inventory Results for Estimating Functional Reading Levels for Students at Eighth Grade Level.* Doctor's thesis, University of Northern Colorado (Greeley, Colo.), 1971. (*DAI* 32:3583A)

227. ANDERSON, JONATHAN. "The Application of Cloze Procedure to English Learned as a Foreign Language in Papua and New Guinea." *Engl Lang Teach* (England) 27(1):66–72 O '72. *

228. CARROLL, JOHN B. "Defining Language Comprehension: Some Speculations," pp. 1–30. "Supplying Missing Elements in Messages," pp. 18–9. In *Language Comprehension and the Acquisition of Knowledge.* Edited by John B. Carroll and Roy O. Freedle. Washington, D.C.: V. H. Winston & Sons, 1972. Pp. xv, 380. *

229. CRANNEY, A. GARR. "The Construction of Two Types of Cloze Reading Tests for College Students." *J Read Behav* 5(1): 60–4 w '72–73 ['72?]. *

230. CULHANE, JOSEPH WILLIAM. *The Use of an Iterative Research Process to Study the Adaptation of Cloze for Improving the Reading Comprehension of Expository Materials.* Doctor's thesis, Syracuse University (Syracuse, N.Y.), 1972. (*DAI* 34:997A)

231. ELLINGTON, BILLIE JEAN. *Evaluation of the Cloze Procedure as a Teaching Device for Improving Reading Comprehension.* Doctor's thesis, University of Georgia (Athens, Ga.), 1972. (*DAI* 33:5031A)

232. ELZENGA, ROBERT D. *The Cloze Procedure and Informal Reading Inventory: A Correlative Study.* Master's thesis, Central Washington State College (Ellensburg, Wash.), 1972.

233. FRAM, RALPH D. *A Review of the Literature Related to the Cloze Procedure.* Master's thesis, Boston University (Boston, Mass.), 1972.

234. GEYER, JAMES R., AND CAREY, ALBERT R. "Predicting and Improving Comprehensibility of Social Studies Materials: The Roles of Cloze Procedure and Readability Adjustment." *Read World* 12(2):85–93 D '72. * (*PA* 50:1772)

235. GINTHER, DEAN WEBSTER. *Cloze Estimation of the Instructional Reading Level.* Master's thesis, University of Illinois (Urbana, Ill.), 1972.

236. GUTHRIE, JOHN T. "Learnability Versus Readability of Texts." *J Ed Res* 65(6):273–80 F '72. * (*PA* 48:5786)

237. HARGIS, CHARLES H. "A Comparison of Retarded and Nonretarded Children on the Ability to Use Context in Reading." *Am J Mental Def* 76(6):726–8 My '72. * (*PA* 48:12067)

238. HODGES, ELAINE JOY. *A Comparison of the Functional Reading Levels of Selected Third Grade Students of Varying Reading Abilities.* Doctor's thesis, University of Northern Colorado (Greeley, Colo.), 1972. (*DAI* 33:896A)

239. HOLMES, CHARLES CURTIS. *Specific Effects of Test Anxiety on Reading Comprehension as Measured by the Cloze Procedure.* Doctor's thesis, University of Georgia (Athens, Ga.), 1972. (*DAI* 33:4939A)

240. KLARE, G. R.; SINAIKO, H. W.; AND STOLUROW, L. M. "The Cloze Procedure: A Convenient Readability Test for Training Materials and Translations." *Int R Appl Psychol* (England) 21(2):77–106 O '72. * (*PA* 49:10259)

241. MARTIN, CLESSEN J., AND HERNDON, MARY ANNE. "Development of Telegraphic Prose Based on a Random Word Deletion Scheme." *Yearb Nat Read Conf* 21:30–4 '72. *

242. MOLLACH, FRANCIS L. "The Use of Cloze Procedure to Study the Reading Capabilities of Community College Freshmen." *Res Teach Engl* 6(1):20–35 sp '72. *

243. NEIE, VAN E. "Verbal Predictive Ability and Performance on Selected Science Process Tasks." *J Res Sci Teach* 9(3):213–21 '72. *

244. NESTVOLD, KARL J. "Cloze Procedure Correlation With Perceived Readability." *Journalism Q* 49(3):592–4 au '72. *

245. OHNMACHT, FRED W., AND FLEMING, JAMES T. "Cloze and Closure: A Second Analysis." *Yearb Nat Read Conf* 21: 35–44 '72. *

246. OHNMACHT, FRED W., AND FLEMING, JAMES T. "Perceptual Closure and Cloze Performance: A Replication With Older Subjects." *J General Psychol* 87(2):225–9 O '72. * (*PA* 49:6035)

247. OLLER, JOHN W., JR. "Assessing Competence in ESL: Reading." *TESOL Q* 6(4):313–23 D '72. *

248. OLLER, JOHN W., JR. "Scoring Methods and Difficulty Levels for Cloze Tests of Proficiency in English as a Second Language." *Mod Lang J* 56(3):151–8 Mr '72. *

249. OLLER, JOHN W., JR.; BOWEN, J. DONALD; DIEN, TON THAT; AND MASON, VICTOR W. "Cloze Tests in English, Thai, and Vietnamese: Native and Non-native Performance." *Lang Learning* 22(1):1–15 Je '72. *

250. PETERSON, JOE; PETERS, NAT; AND PARADIS, ED. "Validation of the Cloze Procedure as a Measure of Readability With High School Trade School and College Populations." *Yearb Nat Read Conf* 21:45–50 '72. *

251. POOLE, MILLICENT E. "Social Class Differences in Language Predictability." *Brit J Ed Psychol* 42(2):127–36 Je '72. * (*PA* 49:832)

252. RAMANAUSKAS, SIGITA. "Contextual Constraints Beyond a Sentence on Cloze Responses of Mentally Retarded Children." *Am J Mental Def* 77(3):338–45 N '72. * (*PA* 50:3297)

253. RAMANAUSKAS, SIGITA. "The Responsiveness of Cloze Readability Measures to Linguistic Variables Operating Over Segments of Text Longer Than a Sentence." *Read Res Q* 8(1): 72–91 f '72. * (*PA* 50:5826)

254. RATEKIN, NED H. "The Adequacy of the Cloze in Measuring Comprehension of Different Logical Patterns." *Yearb Nat Read Conf* 21:59–65 '72. *

255. ROACH, DANIEL J. *Determining What Predictive Validity the Cloze Procedure Has in Establishing Instructional Reading Levels in a Commercially Prepared Basal Reading Sys-*

Cloze Procedure [Ebbinghaus Completion Method] as Applied to Reading

tem. Master's thesis, Eastern Connecticut State College (Willimantic, Conn.), 1972.

256. ROBINSON, RICHARD D. *An Introduction to the Cloze Procedure: An Annotated Bibliography.* Newark, Del.: International Reading Association, 1972. Pp. 12. *

257. ROUSCH, PETER DESMOND. *A Psycholinguistic Investigation Into the Relationship Between Prior Conceptual Knowledge, Oral Reading Miscues, Silent Reading, and Post-Reading Performance.* Doctor's thesis, Wayne State University (Detroit, Mich.), 1972. (*DAI* 33:6074A)

258. RUFENER, JANTORN BURANABANPOTE. *Use of the Cloze Procedure With Thai School Children: An Exploratory Study of Readability and Individual Differences in Reading.* Doctor's thesis, University of Illinois (Urbana, Ill.), 1972. (*DAI* 33:2774A)

259. SCHELL, LEO M. "Promising Possibilities for Improving Comprehension." *J Read* 15(6):415–24 Mr '72. *

260. SILVERMAN, GERALD. "Psycholinguistics of Schizophrenic Language." *Psychol Med* (England) 2(3):254–9 Ag '72. * (*PA* 49:11493)

261. SINAIKO, H. WALLACE, AND KLARE, GEORGE R. "Further Experiments in Language Translation: Readability of Computer Translation." *ITL* 15:1–29 '72. *

262. SWALM, JAMES E. "Comparison of Oral Reading, Silent Reading and Listening Comprehension Assessed by Cloze." *Ed* 92(4):11–5 Ap–My '72. *

263. TAYLOR, WILSON L. "Relative Influences of Preceding, Following and Surrounding Contexts on Cloze Performance." *Yearb Nat Read Conf* 21:66–73 '72. *

264. TUINMAN, J. JAAP. "The Relationships Among Cloze, Associational Fluency, and the Removal of Information Procedure—A Validity Study." *Ed & Psychol Meas* 32(2):469–72 su '72. *

265. TUINMAN, J. JAAP. "Speculations on Cloze as a Research Procedure." *Yearb Nat Read Conf* 21:74–84 '72. *

266. TURNER, BARBARA, AND GILLILAND, JOHN. "The Use of Cloze Procedure in the Measurement of Schools Council Humanities Project Materials." *Reading* (England) 6(2):4–13 Je '72. *

267. VAN HAUWERMEIREN, P. "A Method for Measuring the Effects of Translation on Readability." *ITL* 18:47–53 '72. *

268. WILLIAMSON, JAMES EARL. *Context Clues Used by Sixth Grade Readers of Expository and Narrative Discourse.* Doctor's thesis, University of Arizona (Tucson, Ariz.), 1972. (*DAI* 33:2827A)

269. AARONSON, SHIRLEY. "The Use of a Student-Designed Cloze Procedure as a Vocabulary Tool." *Yearb Nat Read Conf* 22(2):1–6 '73. *

270. BARNES, JUDY ANNE. *A Comparative Study of the Dale-Chall Formula and the Cloze Test Procedure for Determining the Readability of Six Selections From Different Genre.* Master's thesis, University of Kansas (Lawrence, Kan.), 1973.

271. BENNING, BARBARA MARSHALL. *An Investigation Concerning the Differential Effect of Five Selected Cloze Procedure Deletion Patterns on Narrative Science Material.* Doctor's thesis, University of Maryland (College Park, Md.), 1973. (*DAI* 34:3681A)

272. BONOMO, JACQUELYN. *An Investigation of the Relationship Between Specific and Broad Inference.* Master's thesis, Rutgers—The State University (New Brunswick, N.J.), 1973.

273. BORTNICK, ROBERT, AND LOPARDO, GENEVIEVE S. "An Instructional Application of the Cloze Procedure." *J Read* 16(4):296–300 Ja '73. *

274. BURNHAM, BLAINE WINDSOR. *Use of the Cloze Procedure to Increase Mathematical Facility.* Doctor's thesis, Arizona State University (Tempe, Ariz.), 1973. (*DAI* 33:3187B)

275. CARPENTER, TERYLE, AND GRAY, GORDON. "Cloze Assessment of Cultural Response Variation." *Yearb Nat Read Conf* 22(1):258–62 '73. *

276. CARVER, RONALD P. "Understanding, Information Processing, and Learning From Prose Materials." *J Ed Psychol* 64(1):76–84 F '73. * (*PA* 50:187)

277. CONNOLLY, PATRICK R., AND KNABE, WILLIAM E. "Assessing Inter-Group Differences in the Use of Language." *Central States Speech J* 24(1):43–7 sp '73. *

278. CULHANE, JOSEPH W. "On Understanding Instructional Materials." *Clearing House* 48(3):191–2 N '73. *

279. DOYLE, JAMES THOMAS, JR. *A Lexical-Structural Cloze Procedure Approach to Reading Comprehension.* Doctor's thesis, University of Southern California (Los Angeles, Calif.), 1973. (*DAI* 34:3828A)

280. EDWARDS, ROBERT DURGIN. *The Cloze Procedure as a Measure of the Reading Comprehension of Poetry.* Doctor's thesis, University of Arizona (Tucson, Ariz.), 1973. (*DAI* 34:4982A)

281. ELLINGTON, ALLEN RALPH. *The Cloze Procedure and Selected Measures as a Means of Predicting Success in First Year Shorthand.* Doctor's thesis, University of Georgia (Athens, Ga.), 1973. (*DAI* 34:4954A)

282. FLEMING, JAMES T.; OHNMACHT, FRED W.; AND NILES, JEROME A. "Effects of Selected Strategies and Contextual Constraint on Cloze Performance." *Yearb Nat Read Conf* 22(1):92–100 '73. *

283. FROESE, VICTOR. "Cloze Readability Versus the Dale-Chall Formula," pp. 23–30. In *Teachers, Tangibles, Techniques: Comprehension of Content in Reading.* Edited by Bonnie Smith Schulwitz. Newark, Del.: International Reading Association, 1973. Pp. 167. *

284. GALLOWAY, PRISCILLA. "How Secondary Students and Teachers Read Textbooks." *J Read* 17(3):216–9 D '73. *

285. GROUWS, DOUGLAS A., AND ROBINSON, RICHARD D. "Some Ideas Concerning the Readability of Classroom Mathematics Materials." *Sch Sci & Math* 73(9):711–6 D '73. *

286. HASKELL, JOHN FARLEY. *Refining the Cloze Testing and Scoring Procedures for Use With ESL Students.* Doctor's thesis, Columbia University (New York, N.Y.), 1973. (*DAI* 34:3206A)

287. HELM, ESTELLE BAILEY. "Use of the Cloze Procedure in Elementary Schools." *Yearb Nat Read Conf* 22(2):44–8 '73. *

288. HORTON, RAYMOND JOSEPH. *The Construct Validity of Cloze Procedure: An Exploratory Factor Analysis of Cloze, Paragraph Reading, and Structure-of-Intellect.* Doctor's thesis, Hofstra University (Hempstead, N.Y.), 1973. (*DAI* 34:3140A)

289. KAZMIERSKI, PAUL REGIS. *The Effects of the Cloze Procedure Upon the Literal Understanding of Text Materials by Post Secondary Deaf Students.* Doctor's thesis, Syracuse University (Syracuse, N.Y.), 1973. (*DAI* 34:7047A)

290. KEEN, ROBERT H. "The '20-Questions' Technique: Prediction of Visual Threshold and Measurement of Redundancy." *J Exp Psychol* 100(1):158–61 S '73. * (*PA* 51:10376)

291. KENNEDY, DELORES KESSLER, AND WEENER, PAUL. "Vexing Criticisms of Research on Reading: A Response to Wardrop and Essex." *Read Res Q* 8(4):558–65 su '73. * (*PA* 51:11911)

292. KENNEDY, DELORES KESSLER, AND WEENER, PAUL. "Visual and Auditory Training With the Cloze Procedure to Improve Reading and Listening Comprehension." *Read Res Q* 8(4):524–41 su '73. * (*PA* 51:11912)

293. KLINE, JOHN A., AND HULLINGER, JAMES L. "Redundancy, Self Orientation, and Group Consensus." *Speech Monogr* 40(1):72–4 Mr '73. * (*PA* 52:833)

294. LEFKOW, SYLVIA E. *A Comparison Between the Efficacy of the Cloze Procedure and the Question-and-Answer Procedure in Improving Reading Comprehension.* Master's thesis, California State University (Sacramento, Calif.), 1973.

295. OLLER, JOHN W., JR. "Cloze Tests of English Language Proficiency and What They Are." *Lang Learning* 23(1):106–18 Je '73. *

296. OLLER, JOHN W., JR. "Cloze Tests of Second Language Proficiency and What They Measure." *Lang Learning* 23(1):105–18 Je '73. *

297. PAPALLO, PATRICIA M. *Cloze Procedure: A Method of Diagnosing, Evaluating, and Correcting Reading Difficulties.* Master's thesis, Central Connecticut State College (New Britain, Conn.), 1973.

298. PENNOCK, CLIFFORD D. "Selecting Instructional Materials to Meet Students' Reading Performance Level." *Alberta J Ed Res* (Canada) 19(1):30–6 Mr '73. *

299. PENNOCK, CLIFFORD D. "Using Cloze to Select Appropriate Level Instructional Materials." *El Engl* 50(6):940–1 S '73. *

300. PETERSON, JOE; PARADIS, ED; AND PETERS, NAT. "Revalidation of the Cloze Procedure as a Measure of the Instructional Level for High School Students." *Yearb Nat Read Conf* 22(1):144–9 '73. *

301. PHILLIPS, BONNIE DARLENE. *The Effect of the Cloze Procedure on Content Achievement and Reading Skills in a Junior College Introduction to Business Course.* Doctor's thesis, University of Northern Colorado (Greeley, Colo.), 1973. (*DAI* 34:212A)

302. PRANGE, JANET L. *An Investigation of the Relationships Obtaining Between Cloze Test Measures of Reading Performance and Measures of Critical Reading, General Reading, Intelligence and Sex.* Doctor's thesis, State University of New York (Buffalo, N.Y.), 1973. (*DAI* 34:6459A)

303. RILEY, PAMELA M. *The Cloze Procedure—A Selected Annotated Bibliography.* Lae, Papua New Guinea: Papua New Guinea University of Technology, 1973. Pp. vi, 33. *

304. ROBINSON, RICHARD D. "The Cloze Procedure: A New Tool for Adult Education." *Adult Ed* (U.S.) 23(2):87–98 w '73. * (*PA* 50:3885)

305. RUPLEY, WILLIAM H. "The Cloze Procedure." *J Read* 16(6):496–502 Mr '73. *

306. SEDLAK, ROBERT ALAN. *A Comparison of Good and Poor EMH Arithmetic Problem Solvers on Modified Cloze Problems.* Doctor's thesis, Pennsylvania State University (University Park, Pa.), 1973. (*DAI* 35:3557A)

307. SPRAY, GARY DELMAR. *The Relationships Between Eleventh Graders' Cloze Scores and Comprehension of a U.S. History Textbook.* Doctor's thesis, University of Arizona (Tucson, Ariz.), 1973. (*DAI* 34:1182A)

308. THOMPSON, KELLY GORDON. *The Concurrent Validity of a Non-Reinforced Cloze Test in Determining Three Levels of Readability of Selected Fourth Grade Students.* Doctor's thesis, University of Alabama (University, Ala.), 1973. (*DAI* 34:6372A)

309. TUINMAN, J. JAAP; FLANIGAN, MICHAEL C.; AND BLANTON, B. ELGIT. "Subjects' Awareness of Response Alternatives

Cloze Procedure [Ebbinghaus Completion Method] as Applied to Reading

in Cloze Tasks." *J General Psychol* 88(1):13–21 Ja '73. * (*PA* 49:10514)

310. WALTER, RICHARD BARRY. *An Investigation Into the Relationships Between Cloze Test Scores and Informal Reading Inventory Scores of Fifth Grade Pupils.* Doctor's thesis, Ball State University (Muncie, Ind.), 1973. (*DAI* 34:2941A)

311. WARDROP, JAMES L., AND ESSEX, DIANE L. " 'Vexing Problems' Revisited: Pitfalls for the Unwary Researcher (A Reaction to Kennedy and Weener)." *Read Res Q* 8(4):542–57 su '73. * (*PA* 51:11938)

312. ANDERSON, THOMAS H. "Cloze Measures as Indices of Achievement Comprehension When Learning From Extended Prose." *J Ed Meas* 11(2):83–92 su '74. * (*PA* 53:1983)

313. BACKUS, MARY GIAFAGLEONE. *Conservation and Reading Comprehension.* Master's thesis, Rutgers—The State University (New Brunswick, N.J.), 1974.

314. BEAGLE, BARBARA A. *A Comparison of Oral and Written Responses on Cloze Tests.* Master's thesis, Rutgers—The State University (New Brunswick, N.J.), 1974.

315. BINKLEY, JANET RAMAGE. *Cloze Procedure in German for Teaching and Testing Reading at the Intermediate Level.* Doctor's thesis, University of Kansas (Lawrence, Kan.), 1974. (*DAI* 36:677A)

316. CARVER, RONALD P. "Measuring the Primary Effect of Reading: Reading-Storage Technique, Understanding Judgments, and Cloze." *J Read Behav* 6(3):249–74 S '74. * (*PA* 54:6363)

317. CORLETT, DONNA. "Evaluation of Reading in the Classroom." *Read Improv* 11(3):20–2 w '74. *

318. COX, JO ANN KUX. *A Comparison of Two Instructional Methods Utilizing the Cloze Procedure and a More Traditional Method for Improving Reading Comprehension and Vocabulary in Context in a Disadvantaged Fourth-Grade Elementary School Sample.* Doctor's thesis, University of Sotuhern Mississippi (Hattiesburg, Miss.), 1974. (*DAI* 35:6569A)

319. DAUGS, DONALD R., AND DAUGS, FRED. "Readability of High School Biology Materials." *Sci Ed* 58(4):471–82 O '74. *

320. ECHOLS, STANLEY LAVURLE. *An Investigation of Fourth-, Fifth-, and Sixth-Grade Children's Comprehension of Selected Syntactic Structures Based on Pupil Responses to Systematically Deleted Cloze Tests.* Doctor's thesis, Mississippi State University (State College, Miss.), 1974. (*DAI* 35:7720A)

321. ERICKSON, LAWRENCE, AND HANSEN, LEE H. "Performance on Cloze Passages In and Out of Context." *Yearb Nat Read Conf* 23:158–62 '74. *

322. FLEMING, JOSEPH BRUCE. *Analysis of the Readability of Fifth Grade Social Studies Textbooks Using the Cloze Procedure.* Doctor's thesis, Utah State University (Logan, Utah), 1974. (*DAI* 36:104A)

323. GREENEWALD, MARY JANE. *The Effects of Specific Training in Cloze and Contextual Clue Exercises Upon Third-Year French Students' Ability to Utilize Context.* Doctor's thesis, University of Wisconsin (Madison, Wis.), 1974. (*DAI* 35:4128A)

324. HERRON, MARGIE J. *Relationship of Scores Obtained on Two Modified Cloze Tests to Functional Reading Scores as Obtained From a Silent IRI With Second Grade Pupils.* Doctor's thesis, University of Northern Colorado (Greeley, Colo.), 1974. (*DAI* 35:2531A)

325. HICKS, DONNA WHEELER. *Validation Study of the Hicks Cloze-Reading Test for Grades Two–Six.* Doctor's thesis, Oklahoma State University (Stillwater, Okla.), 1974. (*DAI* 35:6437A)

326. HUTSON, BARBARA A., AND NILES, JEROME A. "Parallel Analysis of Oral Language and Reading Miscues." *Yearb Nat Read Conf* 23:232 '74. *

327. IRVINE, PATRICIA; ATAI, PARVIN; AND OLLER, JOHN W., JR. "Cloze, Dictation, and the Test of English as a Foreign Language." *Lang Learning* 24(2):245–52 D '74. *

328. JOHNSON, DAVID CHARLES. *The Evaluation of Comprehension When English Is a Second Language by Use of the Cloze Procedure.* Doctor's thesis, University of Georgia (Athens, Ga.), 1974. (*DAI* 35:5121A)

329. JONES, MARGARET B., AND PIKULSKI, EDNA C. "Cloze for the Classroom." *J Read* 17(6):432–8 Mr '74. *

330. KEIL, ALYCE. *Validation of a Readability Formula With Written Cloze Test Scores.* Master's thesis, Rutgers—The State University (New Brunswick, N.J.), 1974.

331. KENNEDY, DOLORES. "The Cloze Procedure: Use It to Develop Comprehension Skills." *Instructor* 84:82+ N '74. *

332. KING, DOROTHY VIRGINIA. *A Study of the Use of the Cloze Procedure in Teaching Plane Geometry.* Doctor's thesis, University of Missouri (Columbia, Mo.), 1974. (*DAI* 36:108A)

333. LINDQUIST, ALBERT ALLEN. *Set Induction Effects on Reading Comprehension in Content Fields as Measured by Cloze Exercises for Selected Seventh and Eighth Grade Students.* Doctor's thesis, University of Southern California (Los Angeles, Calif.), 1974. (*DAI* 35:802A)

334. LYNCH, F. DENNIS. "Clozentropy: A New Technique for Analyzing Audience Response to Film." *Speech Monogr* 41(3):245–52 Ag '74. * (*PA* 54:3076)

335. McNINCH, GEORGE; KAZELSKIS, RICHARD; AND COX, JO ANN. "Appropriate Cloze Deletion Schemes for Determin-

ing Suitability of College Textbooks." *Yearb Nat Read Conf* 23:249–53 '74. *

336. MARANDOS, SAM A. *Analysis of the Cloze Procedure as a Measure of Reading Comprehension.* Master's thesis, California State University (Sacramento, Calif.), 1974.

337. MILLER, WALLACE D., AND FRENCH, SUSAN. "Using the Cloze Procedure to Determine the Suitability of Social Science and Science Textbooks." *Yearb Nat Read Conf* 23:254–8 '74. *

338. NEVILLE, MARY H., AND PUGH, A. K. "Context in Reading and Listening: A Comparison of Children's Errors in Cloze Tests." *Brit J Ed Psychol* 44(3):224–32 N '74. * (*PA* 53:10561)

339. OHNMACHT, FRED W., AND FLEMING, JAMES T. "Further Effects of Selected Deletion Strategies and Varying Contextual Constraints on Cloze Performance." *Yearb Nat Read Conf* 23:163–71 '74. *

340. OLLER, JOHN W., JR., AND NAGATO, NAOKO. "The Long-term Effect of FLES: An Experiment." *Mod Lang J* 58(1–2):15–9 Ja–F '74. * (*PA* 53:3999)

341. PETERSON, JOE, AND CARROLL, MARTHA. "The Cloze Procedure as an Indicator of the Instructional Level for Disabled Readers." *Yearb Nat Read Conf* 23:153–7 '74. *

342. RANKIN, EARL F. "The Cloze Procedure Revisited." *Yearb Nat Read Conf* 23:1–8 '74. *

343. REID, MARION S. *The Effects of Sentence Order on the Cloze Responses of Fourth Grade Students.* Master's thesis, University of New Orleans (New Orleans, La.), 1974.

344. RICHMOND, MARK G., AND SMITH, CARL B. "The Use of Cloze as a Readability-Comprehensibility Measure for First, Second and Third Grade Students." *South J Ed Res* 8(4):352–66 f '74. *

345. SALUP, BERNICE J. *An Investigation of the Cloze Technique for Measuring the Reading Comprehension of College Freshmen.* Doctor's thesis, Temple University (Philadelphia, Pa.), 1974. (*DAI* 36:3525A)

346. SAUNDERS, BARBARA J. *The Application of the Cloze Procedure to Determine the Ability of Eleventh Grade Students at Luther Burbank High School to Read Selected Literature and History Books.* Master's thesis, California State University (Sacramento, Calif.), 1974.

347. SCHLIEF, MABEL, AND WOOD, ROBERT W. "A Comparison of Procedures to Determine Readability Level of Non-text Materials." *Read Improv* 11(2):57–64 f '74. *

348. SCHULTZ, KATHRYN WRIGHT. *The Relationship Among Cloze Scores, Reading Comprehension, and Intelligence of Fourth Grade Students.* Master's thesis, Texas Woman's University (Denton, Tex.), 1974.

349. SEDLAK, ROBERT A. "Performance of Good and Poor Problem Solvers on Arithmetic Word Problems Presented in a Modified Cloze Format." *J Ed Res* 67(10):467–71 Jl–Ag '74. * (*PA* 53:3448)

350. SMITH, PAULA JEAN. *Kindergarten Children's Abilities to Use Context on Aural Cloze Passages.* Doctor's thesis, University of Arizona (Tucson, Ariz.), 1974. (*DAI* 35:3500A)

351. STUBBS, JOSEPH B., AND TUCKER, G. RICHARD. "The Cloze Test as a Measure of English Proficiency." *Mod Lang J* 58(5–6):239–41 S–O '74. * (*PA* 53:10568)

352. THELEN, JUDITH N. "Using the Cloze Test With Science Textbooks." *Sci & Child* 12(3):26–7 N '74. *

353. ALMEIDA, PAMELA MASON. *Practical Implications of the Cloze Test for Placement in Instructional Materials.* Doctor's thesis, Harvard University (Cambridge, Mass.), 1975. (*DAI* 36:7367A)

354. BALYEAT, RALPH, AND NORMAN, DOUGLAS. "LEA-Cloze Comprehension Test." *Read Teach* 28(6):555–60 Mr '75. *

355. BARTOO, ROY KENNETH. *The Effect of Cumulative Context Upon Cloze Task Performance of Tenth Graders.* Doctor's thesis, State University of New York (Buffalo, N.Y.), 1975. (*DAI* 36:842A)

356. BERRENT, HOWARD IRA. *The Effects of Anxiety on Cloze Measures of Reading Comprehension for Third and Fifth Grade Average Readers.* Doctor's thesis, Hofstra University (Hempstead, N.Y.), 1975. (*DAI* 37:187A)

357. BLACKWELL, JANET MOORE. *An Investigation of Language Behavior of Pupils Measured by Phrase-Marked and Nonphrase-Marked Cloze Scores.* Doctor's thesis, Boston University (Boston, Mass.), 1975. (*DAI* 36:1429A)

358. BORMUTH, JOHN R. Chap. 4, "Literacy in the Classroom," pp. 60–90. In *Help for the Reading Teacher: New Directions in Research.* Edited by William D. Page. Urbana, Ill.: National Conference on Research in English, 1975. Pp. ii, 110. *

359. CARSTENS, PAUL W., AND McKEAG, ROBERT A. "Cloze Test Scores for Assessing Reading Comprehension: Some Considerations for Interpreting Data." *Read Improv* 12(1):8–10 sp '75. *

360. CARVER, RONALD P. "Revised Procedures for Developing Reading-Input Materials and Reading-Storage Tests." *J Read Behav* 7(2):155–72 su '75. *

361. COHEN, JUDITH H. "Effect of Content Area Material on Cloze Test Performance." *J Read* 19(3):247–50 D '75. *

362. COHEN, JUDITH HELENE. *An Examination of the Effect of Content Area Reading in Literature, Social Studies and Science Textbooks Upon Cloze Test Performance of Seventh*

Cloze Procedure [Ebbinghaus Completion Method] as Applied to Reading

Grade Students. Doctor's thesis, Hofstra University (Hempstead, N.Y.), 1975. (*DAI* 35:7782A)

363. DECK, DENNIS DORIAN. *Validation of a Word Deletion Procedure as a Measure of Reading Comprehension.* Doctor's thesis, Pennsylvania State University (University Park, Pa.), 1975. (*DAI* 37:927A)

364. EBERWEIN, LOWELL. "Does Pronouncing Unknown Words Really Help?" *Acad Ther* 11(1):23–9 f '75. *

365. FARRIS, LINDA SCHOENBECK. *A Comparison of Cloze and Multiple Choice Procedures for Measuring Reading Comprehension.* Doctor's thesis, University of North Carolina (Chapel Hill, N.C.), 1975. (*DAI* 36:6627A)

366. FEELY, THEODORE M., JR. "How to Match Reading Materials to Student Reading Levels: 2, The Cloze and the Maze." *Social Studies* 66(6):252–8 N–D '75. *

367. FINN, PATRICK J. "The Use of the Relative Frequency Coefficient to Identify High Information Words and to Measure Readability." *Yearb Nat Read Conf* 24:286–90 '75. *

368. FLORIANI, BERNARD PAUL. *A Psycholinguistic Analysis of Structure Word Performance and Cloze Errors in Sentences of Varied Syntactic Complexity.* Doctor's thesis, Memphis State University (Memphis, Tenn.), 1975. (*DAI* 36:6631A)

369. GOVE, MARY K. "Using the Cloze Procedure in a First Grade Classroom." *Read Teach* 29(1):36–8 O '75. *

370. HENNING, GRANT H. "Measuring Foreign Language Reading Comprehension." *Lang Learning* 25(1):109–14 Je '75. *

371. HORTON, RAYMOND JOSEPH. "The Construct Validity of Cloze Procedure: An Exploratory Factor Analysis of Cloze, Paragraph Reading, and Structure-of-Intellect Tests (Abstract)." *Read Res Q* 10(2):248–51 '74–75 ['75]. *

372. JOHNSON, DAVID C. "The Evaluation of Comprehension When English Is a Second Language by Use of the Cloze Procedure." Abstract. *Yearb Nat Read Conf* 24:207 '75. *

373. LOPARDO, GENEVIEVE S. "LEA—Cloze Reading Material for the Disabled Reader." *Read Teach* 29(1):42–4 O '75. *

374. LOWRY, DENNIS T., AND MARR, THEODORE J. "Clozentropy as a Measure of International Communication Comprehension." *Pub Opin Q* 39(3):301–12 f '75. * (*PA* 56:7572)

375. MCLEOD, JOHN. "Uncertainty Reduction Language Through Reading Comprehension." *J Psycholinguistic Res* 4(4):343–55 O '75. * (*PA* 55:1588)

376. MILLER, LAWRENCE R. "A Direct Comparison of the Predictive Capabilities of Two Cloze-Derived Readability Formulas." *Psychol Rep* 37(3, pt 2):1207–11 D '75. * (*PA* 56:3250)

377. MILLER, LAWRENCE R. "Predictive Powers of Multiple-Choice and Cloze-Derived Readability Formulas." *Read Improv* 12(1):52–8 sp '75. *

378. PAGE, WILLIAM D. "The Post Oral Reading Cloze Test: New Link Between Oral Reading and Comprehension." *J Read Behav* 7(4):383–9 w '75. *

379. PARADIS, EDWARD; TIERNEY, ROBERT; AND PETERSON, JOE. "A Systematic Examination of the Reliability of the Cloze Procedure." Abstract. *Yearb Nat Read Conf* 24:273 '75. *

380. RODRIGUEZ T., NELSON, AND HANSEN, LEE H. "Performance of Readability Formulas Under Conditions of Restricted Ability Level and Restricted Difficulty of Materials." *J Exp Ed* 44(1):8–14 f '75. *

381. ROSENKRANZ, CATHERINE ISABELLA ROGERS. *The Efficacy of Cloze Procedure for Estimating Reading Ability of Students and Readability of Materials in Adult Fundamental Education Programs.* Doctor's thesis, University of Wisconsin (Madison, Wis.), 1975. (*DAI* 36:4964A)

382. SPRING, KAREN STROM. "How Much Do Community College Students Learn From Their Textbooks?" *J Read* 19(2):131–6 N '75. *

383. SUHORSKY, JOSEPH. *An Investigation of the Relationship Between Undeleted Text Preceding a Cloze Test and Cloze Test Results.* Doctor's thesis, University of Maryland (College Park, Md.), 1975. (*DAI* 36:3393A)

384. TUINMAN, J. JAAP; BLANTON, WILLIAM E.; AND GRAY, GORDON. "A Note on Cloze as a Measure of Comprehension." *J Psychol* 90(2):159–62 Jl '75. * (*PA* 54:10672)

385–6. WHITMER, ROBERT LEE. *An Investigation Into the Effectiveness of Cloze and Inferential Techniques Upon French Reading Comprehension at the Intermediate College Level.* Doctor's thesis, University of Pittsburgh (Pittsburgh, Pa.), 1975. (*DAI* 36:3465A)

387. ANDERSON, JONATHAN. *Psycholinguistic Experiments in Foreign Language Testing.* St. Lucia, Queensland, Australia: University of Queensland Press, 1976. Pp. x, 159. *

388. ELLEY, WARWICK B. "The 'Cloze' Procedure: A Method of Testing, Teaching, and Assessing Readability," pp. 55–71. In *New Directions for Teaching: Selected Proceedings of the Fifth New Zealand Conference on Reading and the Fifth World Congress on Reading.* Edited by David B. Doake and Brian T. O'Rourke. Wellington, New Zealand: New Zealand Educational Institute, 1976. Pp. 279. *

389. GOMBERG, ADELINE WISHENGRAD. "Freeing Children to Take a Chance." *Read Teach* 29(5):455–7 F '76. *

390. GREATHOUSE, LARRY J., AND NEAL, BARBARA J. "Letter Cloze Will Conquer Contractions." *Read Teach* 30(2):173–6 N '76. *

391. HOUSTON, ARNEIDA. *An Analysis of the Effectiveness of the Cloze Procedure as a Teaching Technique With Disadvantaged Children.* Doctor's thesis, University of Connecticut (Storrs, Conn.), 1976. (*DAI* 36:6459A)

392. MCKENNA, MICHAEL. "Synonymic Versus Verbatim Scoring of the Cloze Procedure." *J Read* 20(2):141–3 N '76. *

393. NEVILLE, MARY H., AND PUGH, A. K. "Context in Reading and Listening: Variations in Approach to Cloze Tasks." *Read Res Q* 12(1):13–31 '76–77 ['76]. *

394. PAGE, WILLIAM D. "Pseudocues, Supercues, and Comprehension." *Read World* 15(4):232–8 My '76. *

395. PIKULSKI, JOHN J. "Using the Cloze Technique." *Lang Arts* 53(3):317–8+ Mr '76. *

396. PORTER, D. "Modified Cloze Procedure: A More Valid Reading Comprehension Test." *Engl Lang Teach J* (England) 30(2):151–5 Ja '76. *

397. STREIB, RACHEL. "Context Utilization in Reading by Educable Mentally Retarded Children." *Read Res Q* 12(1):32–54 '76–77 ['76]. *

398. SZABO, ROBERT J. "The Effect of Adverbial Subordinate Clause Position on Reading Comprehension." *J Ed Res* 69(9):331–2 My–Je '76. *

399. PIKULSKI, JOHN J., AND PIKULSKI, EDNA C. "Cloze, Maze, and Teacher Judgment." *Read Teach* 30(7):766–70 Ap '77. *

400. WHITE, WILLIAM F., AND ELAM, KAY. "Affective Predictors of Reading Comprehension." *Percept & Motor Skills* 44(3, pt 2):1059–64 Je '77. *

JOHN CHARLES ALDERSON, *Department of Linguistics, University of Edinburgh, Edinburgh, Scotland.*

Any discussion of the cloze procedure must first define what it means since different procedures are subsumed under the same heading in the literature. (*a*) In its most general use, cloze procedure means the principled deletion of words from a text, without further specification of the principle governing the selection of words deleted. (*b*) At the next most general level, cloze procedure means the deletion of words selected either rationally or randomly. The rational cloze involves the selection of words for deletion according to some linguistic principle— only nouns are deleted, or only verbs, or only markers of cohesion. The random cloze—more appropriately, the pseudo-random cloze—deletes every nth word, regardless of its linguistic characteristics; n can be any number, but is usually between 5 and 10. (*c*) A more specific use of the term cloze procedure defines it as the deletion of every fifth word, regardless of its linguistic nature.

In most uses of cloze, the subject has to replace the deleted words with words which he thinks most likely to have been deleted. (Although multiple choice versions of cloze have been used, they will be ignored in this review.) Usually the subject is given credit only for a restoration which exactly matches the deleted word. This is known as the exact word scoring procedure. However, the term cloze procedure can validly be applied to a procedure which scores restorations correct if they are from the same form class as the deleted item. It can be

Cloze Procedure [Ebbinghaus Completion Method] as Applied to Reading

seen that definitions of terms are important in order to compare like with like. Indeed, one of the greatest problems in evaluating the cloze procedure is how to compare different procedures applied to the same text, or even the same procedure applied to different texts. For the purpose of this review, the rational cloze is ignored—since it almost certainly tests something quite different from the random cloze—and the cloze procedure is defined as the deletion of every nth word from a text, for subsequent restoration, in some form, by subjects.

Since the 1950s, many investigations have been made into the cloze procedure, and many studies have used cloze as a criterion measure. Although initially it was validated as a measure of readability against readability formulas, it was quickly assumed to be superior to those formulas. From an initial use in readability studies, it was soon used to measure the reading comprehension abilities of subjects, and many studies showed that cloze correlated, to varying degrees, but always positively, with respected and widely used measures of reading ability. However, not only has cloze been used as a presumed measure of reading ability, and as a measure of the readability of text (including algebra textbooks, headlines, telegrams, captions, and the like), it has been put to many other uses—in one study (166), to show that smoking marihuana may affect retrieval from the short-term memory store. Nevertheless, the main use of cloze remains the measurement of reading abilities. It has recently also been used with nonnative speakers of English as a measure not only of reading ability, but of general proficiency in English. Initially validated against more traditional tests of proficiency in English as a foreign language, its increased use is being justified by the claim that it is superior to these traditional measures. The general conclusion from most of the cloze studies has been that cloze is a reliable and valid measure of reading comprehension and, for nonnative speakers, of proficiency in English as a foreign language.

Most studies using the cloze procedure make certain assumptions about the procedure and its methodology, assumptions which are not necessarily justified. These are: (a) That one cloze test on a text is sufficient to characterise either the readability of that text or the subject's ability to comprehend the text. (b) That the fre-quency of word deletion beyond every fifth word has no effect on the measurement of the text's readability or the subject's comprehension of it. Not all studies have deleted every fifth word, but the tacit assumption seems to have been that whatever deletion rate was used is equivalent to any other deletion rate that might have been used. (c) That the exact word scoring procedure is the most valid way of scoring restorations.

It is necessary, however, to show that these assumptions are justified before one can recommend use of the cloze procedure. Bormuth's study (64) throws light on the first assumption, and suggests that it is unjustified since, in over half of the cases, he found significant differences between different cloze versions on the same text. In other words, deleting every fifth word starting at the second or third word of the text does not usually produce the same results as are achieved by deleting every fifth word starting with the first word of the text. Clearly the differences must be due in part at least to the fact that different versions delete different words.

This is also the case when using different deletion frequencies on the same passage, and evidence is accumulating in this reviewer's research that different deletion rates on the same text *do* result in differences. It has been assumed in the past that if at least 50 items are deleted, the effect of using a different deletion frequency will be neutralised, but the recent evidence suggests that this might not be the case.

The third assumption has received more consideration than the first two. In general, it has been found that other scoring procedures—particularly those which give credit for synonyms of the deletions as well as the exact word deleted—correlate highly with the exact word scoring procedure, and so add little information to that already supplied by the exact word. However, reservations must be made about these studies, since most of them compare the exact word method to procedures where extra weight is given to the exact word rather than a synonym of it. This has the effect of biasing the results in favour of the exact word procedure. Furthermore, while it is clearly *easier* to accept only restorations exactly matching the word deleted, the validity of this procedure is rarely questioned.

It is conceivable that a scoring procedure giv-

Cloze Procedure [Ebbinghaus Completion Method] as Applied to Reading

ing equal weight to exact word answers and to acceptable response answers (various definitions of acceptability are, of course, possible—semantic or syntactic acceptability, pragmatic or communicative equivalence) might well measure something different from whatever is measured by the exact word scoring procedure. At present, the question of whether other scoring procedures might test different abilities is underinvestigated.

Thus, unsolved problems in the use of the cloze procedure include the fact that, for any given text, a cloze test might give different results if the deletions either started at a different point in the text or were less or more frequent. Moreover, the validity of the exact word scoring procedure has not yet been sufficiently established for one to be able wholeheartedly to recommend its use over another scoring procedure.

A somewhat more fundamental problem than these, which has received recent attention, is: what is it that a cloze test tests? In the past, correlational studies claim to have shown that cloze is a valid measure of reading comprehension, but recent studies cast some doubt on the adequacy of cloze as such a measure. The factorial study by Weaver and Kingston (63), which appeared to show that cloze was unrelated to measures of reading comprehension and to be more a measure of redundancy, has received recent support from Tuinman, Blanton, and Gray (384) who suggest that cloze measures the redundancy of a text rather than the comprehension of its message content. Evidence from Miller and Coleman (122) that the constraint operating on a cloze item is from within the sentence in which the item is to be found rather than from outside that sentence is supported by the findings of both Bartoo (355) and Suhorsky (383) that adding unmutilated context to a cloze test does not improve the reader's performance. If cloze were a measure of overall comprehension of a passage, however, one would expect the addition of relevant information to result in a greater cloze score, where the original score is less than perfect.

It has also been suggested in the past that decreasing the deletion frequency might increase a cloze score, but MacGinitie (48) showed, to a limited extent, that this was not so. Recent research of this reviewer has confirmed this and

has shown that a cloze item's score is not affected by varying the amount of context around a gap beyond five words. This is further confirmation of the suggestion (228) that cloze measures local redundancy, and that it is sentence-bound. If it were true that cloze scores are largely unaffected by the nature (or indeed absence or presence) of the nonimmediate environment, then it would appear that the same cloze scores could be gained from the procedure applied to individual, unconnected sentences rather than to passages. This suggests that the cloze procedure only correlates with other measures of reading comprehension to the extent that they measure aspects of sentence comprehension rather than text comprehension. It also suggests that cloze is incapable of measuring the abilities to make inferences from a text, to relate the text to the outside world, and to evaluate the text—in short, the higher order reading skills.

Indeed, in retrospect, it seems surprising that the cloze procedure should have been thought capable of measuring such abilities, since the procedure itself samples words, not ideas or semantic features. Precisely because the procedure is word-based, a large part of the sample is redundant information or, more precisely, grammatical information, and thus related to lower order linguistic abilities rather than higher order inferential reading processes. It is possible that a statistical sample of words is an adequate means of characterising part of the readability of a text, but it does not seem to be adequate for measuring overall reading comprehension abilities, since these presumably involve more than word comprehension, recognition of syntax, or even sentence comprehension. It is possible that a nonrandom cloze procedure, the rational cloze, might provide a better measure of these skills—while still suffering from the handicap of being word-based—but the area of rational cloze is underresearched. For example, no guidelines can be offered the test user and constructor at present as to which linguistic selection of words might provide such a measure.

The problem of the noncomparability of different cloze tests—based on different texts, deleting different words, at different frequencies, and scoring responses differently—bedevils an evaluation of the cloze procedure, since what may well be true for one application of the procedure to one text may be invalid for another application. It is an apparently simple tool for the test user since all one has to do is select a text, remove some words, and see how close to the original text the subjects come, with no further knowledge of test construction or interpretation needed. But it is in this very simplicity that the danger lies since there can be no guarantee that one has produced a good *test* as a result of the application of the *procedure*. What evidence there is suggests that current assumptions in the methodology of cloze testing (random selection) are unjustified and that different results might indeed have been gained if different words had been deleted, a different deletion frequency had been used, or a different scoring procedure had been employed. This is probably enough to make any test user very wary in his use of such a procedure without further investigation. Unless he has special reasons for using the procedure—because he is interested in proficiency in English as a foreign language, for example—he might feel disinclined to use the procedure at all if, as recent research suggests, it should prove to be merely a measure of the redundancy of a text, rather than comprehension of the content of a text and overall reading ability.

WARWICK B. ELLEY, *Reader in Educational Psychology, University of the South Pacific, Suva, Fiji.*

Taylor's designation of the "cloze procedure" as a measure of readability represented a significant breakthrough. By omitting words from the text according to some preordained rule, rather than at the whim of the test constructor, Taylor provided the required degree of objectivity which made possible the assessment of the readability of prose and the amount of information the reader had gained in reading it, in addition to its traditional function as a test of language comprehension.

RATIONALE. Taylor used the word "cloze" to describe the procedure because the reader is presumed to go through a Gestalt process of "closure" when guessing the deleted words, on the basis of the surrounding context. If the reader can reproduce the exact word he is more "in tune" with the writer and his message than if he chooses an inappropriate word. As Wilson and Carroll (*31*) put it: "If the encoder produc-

ing a message and the decoder receiving it happen to have highly similar semantic and grammatical habit systems the decoder ought to be able to predict or anticipate what the encoder will produce at each moment with considerable accuracy." By this rationale, the cloze procedure provides an estimate of the degree of similarity in language habits between writer and reader. A reader who cannot respond correctly has missed some part of the writer's message. Even if he chooses a word of similar meaning, the connotations associated with the word are presumed to be different. Thus, credit is not normally given for synonyms. How relevant is the approach of communication theory to the needs of the teacher trying to discover whether Johnny has understood the main point of a story?

In an unpublished paper, MacGinitie argues that a student taking the cloze test can often replace the words correctly because he is familiar with the recurrent regularities of English prose; yet he may understand nothing about the substance. Admittedly, such structural words as articles, conjunctions, auxiliaries, and prepositions are easily replaceable by those familiar with English, and such words crop up approximately 50 percent of the time. In fact, some students can gain high scores on meaningless material provided it contains some grammatical cues. Nevertheless, children and poor readers do make mistakes in these structural items, thereby reflecting a weaker grasp of these conventions and regularities which in themselves represent important props and cues for the proficient reader. If there is validity in current analyses of reading as a "psycho-linguistic guessing game" in which competent readers set up and confirm expectations on the basis of minimal cues, then readers who are familiar with the structural markers and how they relate to context will have real advantages over those less familiar. They will demonstrate their advantage in their response to both the reading task and to the cloze test.

Studies have shown that cloze tests which examine only function words are measuring different processes from tests of content words (*38*) and this finding should warn us against preparing tests of reading which confine themselves to one or the other. However, the popular procedure of omitting every fifth word normally does ensure a reasonable balance of the two, provided the test is long enough.

Carroll (*228*) also claims that cloze scores are dependent mainly on "local redundancy," usually from cues in the same sentence. He cites the factor analysis of Weaver and Kingston (*63*) which appeared to identify a special aptitude for using redundancy in prose. Carroll finds no evidence that cloze tests measure the main ideas that run through a discourse and believes that they depend too much on inferential processes. On the last point, one's position will depend on one's concept of reading comprehension. There is no doubt that correct replacements are sometimes made by means of painstaking reasoning processes, but the reasoning in question surely draws on (*a*) the reader's previous knowledge of the topic, (*b*) other relevant information contained in the passage, (*c*) the reader's familiarity with language conventions, and (*d*) his reasoning skills. In this reviewer's opinion, all these components determine whether meaningful reading comprehension takes place.

While there may be some artificiality in the cloze testing process, as Carroll claims, it must be remembered that the multiple choice test is not immune from such criticism. In neither case, however, does this artificiality account for much of the variance. Indeed, Weaver and Kingston's redundancy factor was shown only with college students, and is not consistent with studies on a full cross section of schoolchildren. Until we know more about the nature of the construct "reading comprehension," we can scarcely deny a place for the cloze procedure on logical grounds. It is too useful for that.

EMPIRICAL FINDINGS. Research findings on the reliability and validity of the cloze procedure as an index of reading comprehension are numerous and quite impressive.

There is little doubt that it is a reliable measure of reading competence per unit of testing time. Using the Australian GAP test of 42 items, the writer has obtained parallel-forms reliability coefficients close to .90 after only 15 minutes testing of 9-year-olds.

The GAPADOL test for older students also reports internal-consistency coefficients above .90 for a (generous) 30-minute time limit. Bormuth, who has made intensive studies of the procedure, typically finds reliability coefficients between .85 and .90 for 50-item cloze tests used

with schoolchildren. For children below age 8, the reliability data are less impressive.

Concurrent validity coefficients, using multiple choice tests as a criterion, cluster for the most part between .65 and .90. Coefficients over .80 are typically shown, however, when the same passages have been used for both cloze test and multiple choice tests (*34*). Lower correlations obtained in some studies can usually be explained in terms of dissimilarities in the content of the passages used, an important source of variance in comprehension, or in terms of low reliability and restriction of range.

MEASUREMENT OF READABILITY. In developing the cloze procedure, Taylor was primarily concerned with its potential for assessing readability. He pointed out, with justification, that in comparison with the cloze, traditional readability formulas are insensitive to the previous knowledge of the topic which is shown by the particular set of readers sampled. Moreover, such formulas are less effective with nonidiomatic or unconventional prose, as he demonstrated in his early experiments. The cloze makes fewer assumptions about the abilities of the readers. Rather than systematically counting the elements presumed to be difficult, it manages to measure all their effects at once.

For the uninitiated, however, there are traps in using the method for assessing readability. There is now much evidence that cloze difficulty indices vary predictably according to the word class of the deletions—the most difficult being nouns, verbs, and adjectives. In a study of the readability of textbooks, this reviewer (*388*) showed disconcerting variations in difficulty on the same 200-word passages when five different sets of words were deleted according to rotating cloze principles. These variations were largely attributable to differences in the proportions of content words tested. As it is unrealistic to expect many teachers to prepare five parallel forms on each passage, it seems that in the test preparation phase, the user should always check, at least, that the ratio of nouns and verbs deleted is similar to that found in the passage as a whole.

One of the advantages of the cloze method of assessing readability is that it provides an objective criterion for deciding whether a given reader can profit from reading the material in question. Bormuth (*128*) has recommended that a criterion level of 44 percent be used to decide whether a passage is of suitable difficulty for instructional purposes, and 57 percent for independent reading. These figures are roughly equivalent to 75 and 90 percent, respectively, on multiple choice tests. Later investigators (*157, 300*) have found similar figures, using different materials and techniques. However, the range of materials and grade levels used in these studies needs to be extended to inspire greater confidence. There is an inevitable arbitrariness inherent in difficulty levels obtained from multiple choice questions, which must leave uncertainty about the meaning of a 75 percent criterion. Easy questions can be asked about hard passages, and vice versa. Despite these caveats, this advantagē of the cloze procedure must be seen as a distinct breakthrough, deserving of further study.

CONCLUSION. The cloze procedure warrants regular use by teachers, both in assessing comprehension and in measuring readability. It is relatively easy for classroom teachers to prepare, and provides flexibility in choice of materials. It produces high reliability per unit of time, and is generally popular with pupils. While scoring must be done by hand, it often provides the teacher with insights for follow-up work. Where norm data are required, the teacher may wish to resort to conventional standardized tests, but a few normed cloze tests are now available.

For measuring readability, the cloze procedure is recommended when accurate assessments are needed, or when large investments are to be made in new textbooks. The cloze has the advantage of making no assumptions about the ability levels of the target pupils, or the relative importance of the factors which make for difficulty in reading. Teachers would need guidance in selecting sample passages and in preparing and scoring the tests, but the results are of such practical value that the effort required for such professional training is readily justifiable.

Research workers will also find ample scope for experimenting with the procedure in measuring information gain, for assessing attitudes or the quality of translations, or for evaluating achievement in cross-national studies, but technical complexities put such exercises out of the range of all but a few. There is, however, untapped potential in the cloze for teacher diagnosis of children's misconceptions in language usage.

While more will doubtless be learned of the value and limitations of the procedure, this reviewer is sufficiently impressed to agree with Oller (*296*) that the cloze represents "a stroke of raw genius." Taylor's hypothesis now has strong support. When random deletions from a passage are replaced by the reader, the results do signify something important about the quality of the communication between writer and reader.

WILLIAM L. SMITH, *Associate Professor of Education, Boston University, Boston, Massachusetts.*

The cloze procedure is a technique by which words are systematically deleted from a prose passage. Three key concepts in this description make the cloze procedure valuable in testing: "technique," "systematically," and "passage." (*a*) Technique. The cloze procedure is not a test, but rather a means by which one can devise a test. This is an important point because, while many tests exist, there are very few elegant means of testing which can readily be understood and utilized by people with little or no training in research technology. (*b*) Systematically. Although there are other common techniques by which one can test (multiple choice, free recall, sentence completion, essay, etc.), all of these involve an experimenter variable; that is, the test maker selects and frames the items to be tested and determines the correct answers. When using the cloze procedure, however, the test maker selects only the text; the procedure dictates the test items, and thus the experimenter variable is more fully controlled. (*c*) Passage. While the passage chosen affects the results, and an ill-advised selection can produce confounded conclusions, the cloze procedure provides a measure of control, for it should only be used with a passage which is sufficient and complete (i.e., free standing). Thus, it is quite unlike the single sentence completion because the subject is allowed to utilize a full range of contextual clues. He can read around the missing word and, when a word is inserted, can use that word in the determination of other missing words. The subject can even reread the passage to produce more appropriate insertions. Conse-

Cloze Procedure [Ebbinghaus Completion Method] as Applied to Reading

quently, the cloze procedure provides for the use of sentential and supersentential clues.

While the cloze procedure came into prominence in the 1950s, the concept of deleting words from a running text to determine a subject's knowledge of the material is probably as old as writing itself. Evidence of the technique dates back to Ebbinghaus' experiments in the late nineteenth century. The technique was also used, particularly with regard to intelligence testing, in the early twentieth century.

Taylor, Bormuth, and other experimenters formalized the procedure. They determined that for most testing (disregarding specialized knowledge retrieval) every fifth word should be deleted, except in the first and last sentences which should remain intact, and that only exact-word replacements should be considered correct. There are two alternative strategies: one counting synonyms as correct and the other counting words from the same form class as correct. Both of these strategies present difficulties which limit their usefulness. If synonyms are counted, the experimenter must have some technique for determining appropriate synonyms. This imposes an experimenter variable, for the experimenter is dictating from his own semantic system. Current knowledge of semantics makes the assumption that all speakers have the same system questionable if not untenable, particularly when subjects are not of the same age or culture as the experimenter. However, it should be noted that allowances for dialectally different but semantically congruent words probably should be allowed (e.g., polecat/skunk, brook/creek, mongrel/cur, soda/tonic/pop).

The admission of words from the same class (e.g., noun, verb) is even more questionable. Again, the experimenter would become a variable, for he would have to make an a priori decision on the potential members of each form class. This task is particularly formidable for two reasons. First, there is no single linguistic theory which is sufficiently developed to allow the experimenter to predict exactly the words for each class. Second, the range of possible choices would depend upon the subject's linguistic maturity. Present knowledge of the acquisition of such features, while too incomplete to allow viable predictions, certainly indicates that one's concept of inclusiveness within each class changes with maturity.

The cloze procedure is typically used to determine the readability of a passage or to determine a subject's reading ability. Indeed, it has been found to be a reliable and valid measure of both. The validity is particularly evident when placed in a context of current linguistic theory and research.

Linguistic research has been primarily concerned with the variables in oral language, but this information can also be applied to reading. There are two particularly potent variables: (*a*) the reader's ability to use the language (a combination of language development and reading ability) and (*b*) the reader's familiarity with the subject matter being presented.

As one's ability to use the language increases (i.e., as one linguistically matures), he is able to make more precise predictions about the material being read. He is able to use more and more complex syntactic and semantic clues in order to guess what will appear next. In essence, the reader is limiting the probabilities of what words will appear. Therefore, the reader is able to understand more while actually *reading* less. The cloze procedure provides an indication of this ability level, particularly in the responses to deleted function words.

Function words are those which do not provide principal meaning, but rather provide the linkages between the content-bearing words. Roughly, function words are all those not being used as nouns, verbs, adjectives, or adverbs. A child's early use of language is particularly devoid of function words. They begin to appear as more complex thoughts are expressed. The same is true in writing. Young writers tend to use very simple sentences, each expressing a single concept. More mature writers put many of these concepts into a single sentence; consequently, that sentence will be more complex, and this complexity necessitates the increased use of function words. As one increases in ability to read and understand more complex material, one must increase in ability to understand function words. An examination of material written for young children and that written for adults will evidence this increase.

Of course, as one linguistically matures, one increases vocabulary size both in number of words and in the complexity of meaning for each word. Therefore, the ability to insert nouns, verbs, adjectives, and adverbs (usually called

---

Cloze Procedure [Ebbinghaus Completion Method] as Applied to Reading

open class words) will increase also. However, the ability to predict open class words is also dependent upon the reader's familiarity with the subject matter being presented. The more one knows about the subject matter the higher the probability of inserting a correct response. This, of course, is not surprising; one reads familiar material with greater efficiency because one is able to guess more words, thus actually reading fewer. This process can be demonstrated by the poem, "Jabberwocky." The poem is not hard to recite because the function words are real English words and the syntactic relationships are preserved. However, deriving meaningfulness is difficult because the content-bearing words are nonsense words. Consequently, the poem is apparently read with low comprehension. If the cloze procedure were applied to a passage like "Jabberwocky," the results would indicate only the language development of the reader, for no one could predict the made-up words; only the function words would be predictable.

While the "Jabberwocky" example is extreme, it does provide an insight into a necessary precaution if cloze is to be used to determine reading ability or readability. When determining the reading ability of a student, it is important to analyze the passage to be used in order to preclude particularly unique words or concepts. It is quite possible for two students of quite different ability to have identical scores. If student 1 is lower on the language development scale, yet happens to know more about the content of the particular passage, that knowledge will inflate his score. Student 2, on the other hand, may do well on function words, but his lack of knowledge of the specific content will depress his score. It is also possible for a passage written at a syntactic level quite different from the student's maturity level to provide false or misleading information.

In determining reading ability, the cloze procedure can effectively be used in two ways. One can determine the readability of a book for a student by selecting a sample passage for testing. It is crucial here that the passage reflect the complexity and content of the entire book. Using the same procedure, one can also predict the readability of a book for a group. The necessary constraint is that the students being tested represent the entire group.

While the cloze procedure cannot provide either the detailed diagnostic information or grade level placements one receives from the standardized reading tests, it can be used to supplement the information typically gleaned from informal reading inventories and will provide necessary information about the suitability of reading materials. Consequently, all teachers can and should profit from its use. Compared with other testing techniques, it is simpler to construct, can effectively control the experimenter variable, can be applied to any prose passage, and, if used with proper precautions, will yield valid, reliable information about reading ability, language maturity, and the readability of written materials.

[721]

*Comprehensive Tests of Basic Skills: Reading, Expanded Edition. Grades kgn.6–1.9, 1.6–2.9, 2.5–4.9, 4.5–6.9, 6.5–8.9, 8.5–12.9; 1968–76; previous edition (Forms Q and R) still available; 1 form; 6 levels; 1 or 2 editions; no specific manual; battery coordinator's handbook ('76, 59 pages); battery technical bulletin no. 1 ('74, 75 pages); $2.50 per coordinator's handbook; $2.50 per technical bulletin; postage extra; specimen set not available; CTB/McGraw-Hill. *
a) READING. Grades kgn.6–1.9, 1.6–2.9; 1 form; 2 levels; 2 editions: hand scored, CompuScan machine scored; battery manual ('74, 69–87 pages) for each level; $10.15 per 35 hand scored tests; $14.70 per 35 CompuScan tests; CompuScan scoring service, 55¢ per test.
    1) Level B. Grades kgn.6–1.9; 5 scores: letter sounds, word recognition (2 scores), reading comprehension, total; Form S ('73, 12 pages); (90) minutes in 2 sessions.
    2) Level C. Grades 1.6–2.9; 4 scores: vocabulary, sentences, passages, total; Form S ('73, 9–10 pages); (101) minutes in 2 sessions.
b) READING AND REFERENCE SKILLS. Grades 2.5–4.9, 4.5–6.9, 6.5–8.9, 8.5–12.9; 4 scores: reading (vocabulary, comprehension, total), reference skills; 1 form; 4 levels; battery manual ('74, 70–95 pages) for each level; separate answer sheets (Digitek, IBM 1230, Scoreze) must be used except for level 1 CompuScan booklet; Digitek scoring stencil not available.
    1) Level 1. Grades 2.5–4.9; Form S ('73, 12–13 pages); 2 editions: consumable, reusable; $14.70 per 35 CompuScan machine scored tests; $10.15 per 35 reusable tests; answer sheets: $5 per 50 Digitek or IBM, $4.25 per 25 Scoreze; $2.50 per IBM hand scoring stencil; CompuScan scoring service, 55¢ per test; (105) minutes in 2 sessions.
    2) Level 2. Grades 4.5–6.9; Form S ('73, 18 pages); $10.15 per 35 tests; answer sheets: $5 per 50 Digitek or IBM, $4.25 per 25 Scoreze; $2.50 per IBM hand scoring stencil; (99) minutes in 2 sessions.
    3) Level 3. Grades 6.5–8.9; Form S ('73, 18 pages); prices same as for level 2; (92) minutes in 2 sessions.
    4) Level 4. Grades 8.5–12.9; Form S ('73, 20 pages); prices same as for level 2; (91) minutes in 2 sessions.
    See T2:1542 (3 references); for a review by Earl F. Rankin of Forms Q and R, see 7:685. For reviews of the complete battery, see 12 (2 reviews) and 7:9 (2 reviews, 3 excerpts).

Cloze Procedure [Ebbinghaus Completion Method] as Applied to Reading

REFERENCES

1–3. See T2:1542.
4. CAMPBELL, BILLY RANDOLPH. *A Study of the Relationship of Reading Ability of Students in Grades 4, 5, and 6, and Comprehension of Social Studies and Science Textbook Selections.* Doctor's thesis, Florida State University (Tallahassee, Fla.), 1972. (*DAI* 33:3146A)
5. DEXTER, HALE GENE. *A Study of the Relationship Between Selected Grading Criteria and the Use of Standardized Test Scores as Predictors of Grades.* Doctor's thesis, University of Missouri (Kansas City, Mo.), 1973. (*DAI* 34:3864A)
6. INGERSOLL, G. M., AND JOHNSON, P. "Attitudes and Reading Comprehension: A Preliminary Investigation." *Read Improv* 11(2):52–6 f '74. *
7. LORD, FREDERIC M. "Quick Estimates of the Relative Efficiency of Two Tests as a Function of Ability Level." *J Ed Meas* 11(4):247–54 w '74. *
8. LORET, PETER G.; SEDER, ALAN; BIANCHINI, JOHN C.; AND VALE, CAROL A. *Anchor Test Study: Equivalence and Norms Tables for Selected Reading Achievement Tests (Grades 4, 5, and 6).* DHEW Publication S/N 1780–01312. Washington, D.C.: Government Printing Office, 1974. Pp. ix, 92. *
9. BUTTERWORTH, THOMAS W., AND MICHAEL, WILLIAM B. "The Relationship of Reading Achievement, School Attitude, and Self-Responsibility Behaviors of Sixth-Grade Pupils to Comparative and Individualized Reporting Systems: Implications for Improvement of Validity of the Evaluation of Pupil Progress." *Ed & Psychol Meas* 35(4):987–91 w '75. * (*PA* 55:13535)
10. LINN, ROBERT L. "Anchor Test Study: The Long and the Short of It." *J Ed Meas* 12(3):201–13 f '75. *
11. MALONE, ABRIAN MCCOY. *The Correlation Between Children's Reading Ability and Their Cognitive Development, as Measured by Their Performance on Piagetian-Based Test.* Doctor's thesis, St. Louis University (St. Louis, Mo.), 1975. (*DAI* 37:2133A)
12. ADOLINA, MICHELE. *A Comparison of Traditional and Automated Testing and an Analysis of the Effect of Testing on Attitude Between High and Low Achieving Students.* Doctor's thesis, Boston University (Boston, Mass.), 1976. (*DAI* 37:1503A)

RANDY DEMALINE, *Research Associate, The Evaluation Center, Western Michigan University, Kalamazoo, Michigan.*

In developing these reading tests, the publisher involved experienced primary and nursery school teachers and curriculum specialists in the identification of appropriate content areas and their measures. This concern for test content and its validity was a major emphasis throughout the development of the tests.

The selection process of items to be included on Form S consisted of choosing the best items from the previous two forms by applying four item selection criteria concerning discrimination in difficulty, test consistency, and reliability. The proportion of identical or revised items on each level remaining from the previous forms ranges from .15 to .83 for reading vocabulary, from .00 to .40 for reading comprehension, and from .45 to 1.00 for the reference skills subtest.

The battery technical bulletin and manuals are very comprehensive for both the reading test and other tests in the battery. A wide variety of score types is available, including raw scores, national and/or local percentiles or stanines, grade equivalent scores, and the publisher's scale scores. Some people will probably cringe at the sight of grade equivalent scores, but the manual does caution the user about grade equivalent scores and suggests they *not* be used for reporting to "persons not trained in testing." This is probably as close to a condemnation as the publisher can get.

The expanded standard score is presented as "a single, equal interval scale of scores across all grades for use with all levels." These scores could be useful in observing growth in achievement through the school years. However, some inservice training of teachers would be required for interpretation.

The publisher has done an excellent job of providing information in the technical bulletin about the sampling procedure involved in setting the norms for the test. Community type, school type, school enrollment, geographic region, and other demographic data were considered in selecting the 130,000 students in the norming sample.

Within-grade K-R reliabilities for reading subtests for Levels 1–4 range from .89 to .94. The reliabilities for total reading scores range from .94 to .97. The reference skills sections do not fare as well, with reliabilities from .76 to .86, but still are generally acceptable. For levels B and C these coefficients are generally in the .80s and .90s.

The technical bulletin includes the item difficulties for three to five grades within each level. An idiosyncrasy occurs in the reading comprehension subtest in Level 4, and the cause is not clear. Item difficulty indices tend to increase as desired, but, for a third of the items, these indices level off at the end of grade 10 and then actually decrease. The leveling off is mentioned but not the decrease, and no explanation is presented. One wonders whether this decrease violates the assumptions of the expanded standard score model and thereby affects its use in later grades.

Some of the information in the technical bulletin is in response to previous criticism. For example, an empirical study to validate the reliability of hand-scored versus machine-scored testbooks for primary students is reported. Other new information is a result of current concerns about test bias with black or Spanish-speaking minority groups. The results of an item point-biserial comparison used to identify biased items are presented for Level 2; these show that there is some bias, but it is considered too small to be of concern. Also in response to

Comprehensive Tests of Basic Skills: Reading

the anticipated question of whether comparable results are obtained at grade levels in the overlap regions of the six test levels, tables giving correlation coefficients as measures of interlevel articulation are presented for Levels 1–4. These range from .69 to .89; they are not high, but are sufficient.

It is difficult, in the face of all this, to say that any data are missing. The CTBS is weak in the area of validity. The publisher's primary concern has properly been with content validity, but other types of validity are scoffed at: "Since it is not the aim of an achievement test to predict or substitute for some criterion, its correlation with a criterion or other achievement test is not useful in the evaluation of the test." Somewhat begrudgingly, the publisher does present intercorrelation coefficients for the subtests of Levels 1–4 and the language and nonlanguage IQ sections of the *Short Form Test of Academic Aptitude*. It is doubtful that this meets the criticisms of the lack of predictive or concurrent validity statistics.

In summary, these reading and reference skills tests are examples of well-constructed and well-researched tests. The publisher is to be applauded on the amount of relevant and responsive data presented in the technical bulletin and on the quality of the manuals. The potential tester should find the test both usable and useful. I agree with the publisher's statement: "The final evaluation of a test's validity for a particular school district must be based on that district's own objectives and curriculum." If the potential user is satisfied with the content covered, the CTBS/S reading can certainly be recommended.

[722]

Cooperative Primary Tests: Reading. Grades 1.5–2.5, 2.5–3; 1965–67; 2 forms; 2 levels; no specific manual; battery manual ('67, 104 pages); $3.75 per 20 tests; $3 per battery manual; cash orders postpaid; specimen set not available; (35) minutes; Educational Testing Service; Addison-Wesley Publishing Co., Inc. *
a) GRADES 1.5–2.5. Forms 12A, 12B, ('65, 10 pages).
b) GRADES 2.5–3. Forms 23A, 23B, ('65, 10 pages).
For reviews of the complete battery, see 13 (1 review) and 7:10 (2 excerpts).

REFERENCES

1. MacKay, Robert. Chap. 5, "Standardized Tests: Objective/Objectified Measures of 'Competence,'" pp. 218–47. In *Language Use and School Performance.* By Aaron V. Cicourel and others. New York: Academic Press, Inc., 1974. Pp. ix, 368. *

Shirley C. Feldmann, *Professor of Education and Head, Reading Program, The City*

Comprehensive Tests of Basic Skills: Reading

College and The Graduate School, The City University of New York, New York, New York.

This test, part of a larger achievement battery, measures "understanding of phonetic and structural properties of words," that is, knowledge about language. It deals with the child's general abilities to attack words rather than with each sound and rule.

In part 1 the tester reads the items while the child marks the responses in the testbook. The tasks are associating sounds with letters, sounds with written words, and letters with sounds, as well as recognizing probable letter sequences. In part 2 the child works independently to match letter configuration, discriminate letter configurations, match beginning letters to picturable words, recognize words in compound words, and deal with contractions, derivatives of root words, and roots of derived words. There are 60 items and two samples, with a three-choice format.

The format of the test is attractive, and simple directions are maintained throughout the test. The items to be marked are pictures, words, or word parts. The pictures seem relatively unambiguous and easy to interpret.

The tests were normed on a sample balanced by geographical areas and size of school district. Ethnic groups were not identified in the sample. Fall and spring samples were used and about 1,800 children per grade were tested. The standardization procedures seem well-conceived and thorough.

Reliability was determined by internal consistency measures and by correlation of alternate forms, with both measures in the range of .82 to .93. Mean item difficulties range from .58 to .86. Since the items are easy for the second and third grade samples, there may be ceiling effects for all the upper-ability children.

Validity is described as content validity, with the judgment of practitioners and authorities having been used to create the domain for the test. This domain is not well described in the handbook, nor are reasons given for the selection of particular word analysis skills over others. In an area as well specified as word analysis skills, in contrast to more elusive reading comprehension skills, a large group of skills could be considered for inclusion. While the test does not err by presenting examples of every skill, it still does not have a clear rationale for those that are included. In addition, since only a few items are used in a skill area, reliability of diagnostic information obtained from the scores is doubtful. For these reasons, the test is probably better used primarily for general ranking in the overall word analysis area.

Another problem with the test is its high correlation with the reading test of the series. Correlations of .73 to .78 indicate considerable overlap of content areas, and therefore use of both tests might not be indicated, as their information yield is so similar.

In summary, the test is attractive, well-standardized, easy to take, and relatively free of distracting features, but it appears to have limited value for classroom planning. The tests are easy for many primary level children; their lack of adequate rationale and low level of diagnostic yield may lessen their effectiveness for the teacher. Finally, the high correlation with the reading test may make the word analysis test superfluous if the battery is used. The test seems to have value for determining the relative position of children on general word analysis skills.

NANCY L. ROSER, *Associate Professor of Curriculum and Instruction, The University of Texas, Austin, Texas.*

This test represents an effort to "survey understandings and skills considered basic to future development in reading." Each form is composed of 50 three-choice items and is easily handscored with the accompanying scoring sheets. Both levels of the test employ words, sentences, and paragraphs as stimuli, and pictures, words, and sentences as responses. On the lower level forms, pictures comprise about 40 percent of the responses, whereas on the upper level forms they comprise only about 15 percent. A 10-item pilot test, to be administered before the lower level forms, gives a "practice" experience with test format and question types. The tests have attractive formats, maintain consistent directions, and set no formal time limits.

Items were designed to measure: (*a*) comprehension; (*b*) extraction; and (*c*) interpretation, evaluation, and inference. It is unusual to find a primary level reading test with as much emphasis on inference. Distractors are included that vary only slightly from the correct choice, i.e., in only one phoneme or one picture detail, in

order to provide the teacher with diagnostic information. In isolated instances, items appear to be more a reflection of experience than of reading ability. In addition, the testing of words in isolation presents a somewhat unrealistic set for reading. Both a boy child and a letter are distractors for the stimulus word "mail." The variable upon which that item isolates may be spelling unless context is offered. A strength of the handbook is that it directs attention to the item response, recognizing that "while a short achievement test cannot be considered precisely diagnostic, a study of errors for individual pupils may also suggest appropriate procedures."

One preliminary form for each final test form was tried out experimentally in Cincinnati schools, chosen to represent a cross-section of ability levels. It was determined that the testing procedure was adequate, and that very few item replacements or revisions were necessary. It must be noted that the replacement items, therefore, have not been tested.

Two nationwide samples were tested to provide a fall set and a spring set of normative data. In both samplings there were three stages. School districts were chosen "with a probability proportional to the total enrollments in the districts, so that districts enrolling many pupils were more likely to be chosen than districts enrolling relatively few." Next, there was a random sampling of schools within districts. Finally, although all the children of the appropriate grades were tested at each chosen school, only data from 10 per grade level, chosen randomly, were analyzed by ETS. Three problems suggest themselves here: First, as noted in the handbook, since the probability weighting by size of sampling unit was not carried out beyond the choice of school districts, a child in a small school, in an already-chosen district, had a better chance of selection than a child in a larger school in the same district. Second, as Hanna (7:10) points out, there were no stratification procedures employed to assure representation proportional to the population on such features as SES of community, geographical region, or size of school district. Hanna realizes this type of stratification to be most desirable in light of the low (38 percent) participation of invited school districts. Even though ETS found that the districts actually used matched the population fairly closely in geographical region and size of school districts, the potential exists for some variable to systematically influence the norms when such a low percentage of the invited districts respond. Third, there were certain districts which, because they did not offer grades 1–3, were not included. If one of these was chosen, the replacement was the one immediately following it in an alphabetized list. This method of substituting unduly raises the following district's chances of inclusion.

These problems aside, the normative data provided for the CPT reading tests are quite complete. Each raw score is transformed into a scaled score and mid-percentile ranks are computed. In addition, some schools provided data from both forms of one level, and other schools provided data from both levels. Therefore, even though there was some relatively unexplained discarding of data, raw scores on alternate forms and raw scores on corresponding tests at the two levels can be related. Indeed, raw score to scaled score conversions are possible for all tests, making direct comparisons possible.

The handbook offers a thorough description of the statistical characteristics of the final forms. The internal-consistency coefficients for the lower level forms range from .86 to .90, and for the upper level forms from .89 to .91. The correlation coefficients between alternate forms were .82 and .85 (two orders of presentation) for the lower level, and .85 and .91 for the upper level. The reading tests were relatively difficult at the lower level, ranging from 49 to 56 percent correct; the upper level tests ranged from 55 to 72 percent. The difficulty of the lower level tests is also reflected in the percentile rank of 25 for a chance score.

No independent measure of validity was attempted. The handbook states that "content validity is best ensured by entrusting test construction to persons well qualified to judge the relationship of the test content to teaching objectives" and recommends that "each test user make an individual judgment of content validity with respect to his own instructional practices and educational aims."

In spite of the criticisms discussed above, the CPT: Reading appears to be a well-designed, carefully standardized, and easily administered measure of children's reading/thinking abilities.

Cooperative Primary Tests: Reading

[723]

★**Criterion Reading: Individualized Learning Management System.** Grades kgn, 1, 2–3, 4–6, 7–adult basic education; 1970–71; criterion referenced; 2 series: diagnostic (2 forms), instructional (called process skills); the 5 levels together cover 451 overlapping specific-objective subtests; level 1—90 nonreading subtests (86 percent consist of 1 to 4 items) in 3 areas: motor skills (28 subtests), visual matching (21), auditory matching (41); levels 2–5—361 subtests (68 percent consisting of 2 to 8 items) in 5 areas: phenology (68 subtests), structural analysis (70), verbal information (100), syntax (56), comprehension (67); no data on reliability; no norms; mastery is 100% for tests of fewer than 20 items, 95% for all others; no supporting data or information for grade placement of specific objectives and mastery standards; tests: level 1 ('71, 104 pages), levels 2–5 ('71, 43–169 pages in 2 booklets per level); directions for administration: level 1 ('71, 133 pages), levels 2–5 ('71, 48–184 pages in 2 booklets per level); teacher's guide ('71, 75 pages); individual record form ('71, 15 pages) for levels 1–5; group record form ('71, 23 pages) for levels 1–5; set of test booklets for 5 students: $13.80 for level 1, $24.48 for 2, $24.93 for 3, $25.74 for 4 or 5; directions for administration: $2.97 for level 1, $5.37 for 2, $8.37 for 3, $9.09 for 4, $9.07 for 5; $2.07 per teacher's guide; 36¢ per record form; postpaid; specimen set not available; administration time not reported; Marie G. Hackett; Random House, Inc. *

REFERENCES

1. FREMER, JOHN. "Review of Criterion Reading." *Read Teach* 26(5):521–7 F '73. *
2. THOMPSON, RICHARD A., AND DZIUBAN, CHARLES D. "Criterion Referenced Reading Tests in Perspective." *Read Teach* 27(3):292–4 D '73. *

Read Teach 26(5):521–7 F '73. John Fremer. * the developers of *Criterion Reading* sought a comprehensive system that would help teachers carry out a continuing and integrated evaluation of a pupil's development of reading skills. This goal merits approval, but the resultant system has serious flaws that make it difficult to applaud more than the developer's purpose and effort. If the materials were presented with well-justified modesty, as drafts requiring a great deal of further work, perhaps a gentler treatment would be appropriate. Unfortunately, the publisher has chosen to resort to overblown and unsupported statements * In several instances, a form of definitional magic has been employed that promises what cannot be delivered. A noteworthy example is the following: "CRITERION READING is performance-based. This means that each pupil will acquire the skill as it is set forth in the performance objective, and he will perform the skill under the conditions which the objective states. Since the skills are ranked in a hierarchy based on current psychological and educational theory, a child gains measurable competence in reading as he masters skill upon skill. When he has mastered all the skills, he has become an effective and able reader." Are we really to believe that *"each pupil"* will acquire all those skills merely because Criterion Reading is *"performance-based"?* Wariness is called for here. * *Criterion Reading*....purports to provide information about a student's mastery of some 450 "skills" that are represented to be necessary for reading and language competence. * One of the pillars on which *Criterion Reading* rests is a Hierarchy of Skills that serves as an overall structuring and sequencing device for the system. It seems reasonable to suppose, therefore, that the *Criterion Reading* hierarchy has an experimental as well as a logical base. If this is so, no evidence is presented for it in the teacher's manual or supporting materials accompanying a specimen set. The manual indicates that the hierarchy of skills "taken together, define the full range of competencies a child must exhibit in order to be able to read." Yet, this reviewer found it difficult to accept the assertion that the following skills from the motor skills area were essential to effective reading: "(*a*) Pupil is able to balance on one foot while the teacher slowly counts to five. (*b*) The pupil is able to tie his shoelaces in a bow with ease. (*c*) The pupil is able to throw a beanbag into a wastepaper basket from a distance of eight feet. (*d*) The pupil is able to catch a beanbag from a distance of eight feet." Although there is undoubtedly some relationship between these "critical" skills and such motor activities as page turning, one is inclined to wonder whether balancing, tying, catching, and throwing, are not listed and emphasized primarily because they are traditional classroom activities for the kindergarten? It would be possible to design and execute studies to assess the extent to which these motor skills are prerequisites to other skills listed in the hierarchy. Some outcomes that can be hypothesized are that many students learn skills that are placed higher in the Criterion Reading hierarchy long before, or even without ever, mastering these motor skills. For some students with physical handicaps, these supposedly prerequisite reading skills are clearly unattainable. Another problem with the Hierarchy of Skills and its role in the *Criterion Reading* system, is the apparent assumption that the sequence of development of reading skills needs to be highly similar for all children. This assumption can be detected in the analysis of the development of

reading skills that is offered in the teacher's manual. After noting gross sequential dependencies, that is, one must be able to read words before one can read paragraphs, the manual goes on to describe a process by which all reading skills can be analyzed on logical grounds into sequentially dependent subskills. It is unassailably true that it is possible to carry out such logical analyses; the *Criterion Reading* Hierarchy of Skills represents only one of the available efforts. What remains to be demonstrated, however, is that all, or even the majority of children, actually do acquire competencies in the logical sequence that is described. Even if the *majority* of students did follow the indicated pattern, it is hard to justify the inflexible use of *Criterion Reading* for *all* students as an *"individualized* learning management system." If a child can function effectively at higher level skills, why continue to focus energy on unmastered lower level skills? Perhaps for this child, some skills can be bypassed. *Criterion Reading* fails to address itself to this possibility. To this measurement trained reviewer, the aspect of the *Criterion Reading* assessment system that is most faulty is reflected in the following statement from the teacher's manual: "When a pupil has mastered the given skill." The statement makes no allusion to the possibility of measurement error and the system simply ignores this possibility. * a student's mastery of an objective is based on performance on some small number of questions * About 10 percent of the time only three questions are used, but six or seven are more common and only rarely are more than twelve questions used. * Isn't it possible that one or more of the items associated with a particular objective might not be very good measures of that objective? And what about the myriad factors influencing a student's response? Given unambiguous and otherwise technically adequate questions, carefully developed directions, standardized testing conditions, and skilled administrators, the influence of irrelevant factors can be minimized, but not eliminated. Failure to achieve the "mastery level" will often be attributable to such factors rather than to a student's failure to develop a competency. The measurement situation is further confounded by the fact that a common criterion level (95 percent accuracy) is specified for all objectives. * The idea that raising standards raises performance has a long history, but it is a principle that is widely misapplied. When the number of questions varies from three to twenty-six and when the degree of complexity of objective, and thus the homogeneity of items, is also quite variable, the 95 percent rule actually has the effect of applying quite different standards to different objectives. The establishment of a criterion level should involve both logical and empirical procedures. A common sense approach to setting such tentative levels as four out of five or three out of six, depending upon the objective, would clearly be preferable to the inflexible application of arbitrary standards. * The breadth of the questions is certainly impressive. The developers have produced questions that employ a much more diverse array of multiple choice item types than is typically the case for survey tests of reading achievement. * An examination of the questions associated with each skill does not reveal any consistent connection between the complexity of the skill and the level of difficulty or the number of questions. The main determinants of the number of questions per skill may have been the ease of construction and time to administer, as brief questions occur in much longer sets than lengthy questions. The technical adequacy of the individual questions varies considerably across skill areas and even within sets, but in general they appear to be appropriate measures of the stated skills. Only a small proportion of the entire pool of questions have multiple keys or ambiguous wording. The vocabulary load of the items seems very high, though, throughout the materials. It is likely that many students would have difficulty with the questions associated with a skill because of difficulty with the vocabulary—for example, the third grade consonant sound items using the words *leech* and *stag,* and the junior high analogy item *"foreigner* is to *alien."* There is also a forced and awkward quality to much of the language used in the test questions. Many sentences have a written-for-a-test flavor to them. This reviewer would advise classroom teachers not to use *Criterion Reading,* at least not in the way suggested by the test publisher. It would clearly be helpful, though, as a source for ideas regarding testing and reporting techniques so it might be worthwhile to obtain a specimen set. If *Criterion Reading* is revised in the future to be a more flexible system without arbitrary and inappropriate standards, it may be worthy of serious consideration. It might even be possible to use *Criterion Reading* in its present form if teachers are willing and have the necessary time to develop revised procedures for using the tests.

[724]

Edinburgh Reading Tests. Ages 8.5–10.5, 10.0–12.5; 1972–73; ERT; 1 form; 2 levels; postpaid within U.K.; (30–35) minutes for practice test, (75–95) minutes in 2 sessions for test; Hodder & Stoughton Educational [England]. *
a) STAGE 2. Ages 8.5–10.5; 1972; 7 scores: vocabulary, comprehension of sequences, retention of significant details, use of context, reading rate, comprehension of essential ideas, total; no data on reliability for reading rate; Parts 1 (9 pages), 2 (8 pages); manual (39 pages); profile (1 page); practice test (8 pages); £2.40 per 20 copies of Part 1; £2 per 20 copies of Part 2; 90p per 20 profiles; £1.40 per 20 practice tests; 80p per manual; 95p per specimen set; test by Godfrey Thomson Unit, University of Edinburgh, in association with Scottish Education Department and Educational Institute of Scotland; manual by M. J. Hutchings and E. M. J. Hutchings.
b) STAGE 3. Ages 10.0–12.5; 1972–73; 6 scores: reading for facts, comprehension of sequences, retention of main ideas, comprehension of points of view, vocabulary, total; Parts 1 ('72, 15 pages), 2 ('72, 8 pages); manual ('73, 39 pages); profile ('73, 1 page); practice test ('72, 8 pages); £2.50 per 20 copies of Part 1; £1.60 per 20 copies of Part 2; 50p per 20 profiles; £1.40 per 20 practice tests; 80p per manual; 95p per specimen set; test by Moray House College of Education in association with Scottish Education Department and Educational Institute of Scotland; manual by J. F. McBride and P. C. McNaught.

DOUGLAS A. PIDGEON, *Head, Reading Research Unit, Child Development and Educational Psychology, University of London Institute of Education, London, England.*

These tests form part of a very ambitious project to provide a series of tests in five levels or stages for children from age 7 upwards. So far only Stages 2 and 3 are available.

The standardisation was carried out separately in Scotland and in England and Wales; and while the final achieved samples used can by no means be described as probability ones, local authorities, schools, and classes within schools appear to have been chosen with some considerable care so that reasonable confidence can be placed on their representativeness. As is the usual practice in the U.K., conversion tables, incorporating age allowances, are provided yielding deviation quotients having a mean of 100 and a standard deviation of 15, although tables of reading ages are also supplied. The total test reliability for both stages, calculated by

K-R 20 from random samples of scripts, is .97. The reliabilities of the subtests are surprisingly high, ranging from .81 to .91 for Stage 2 and from .81 to .95 for Stage 3.

So far so good. On the question of validity, however, the manuals, while pointing out that it is hoped to provide estimates of concurrent and predictive validity after further work has been carried out, rest their case on content validity having been incorporated by the test constructors working in association with steering committees of teachers and reading experts on whose judgements they could rely. It is clearly important to examine the tests' content very carefully.

The working of the all-important committees is not described. For example, it is not clear whether the subtest areas were defined and described first and then items constructed to measure them, or whether, from a collection of items of all kinds, groups with similar characteristics were selected and given a collective name. Certainly, some item types are quite ingenious, but many appear to have been chosen because they displayed good item characteristics. One might question, for example, the relevance of items requiring the testee to identify the correct order of four or five short sentences set down in a mixed-up order. But justification is provided "because of the consistently high discriminatory qualities of these items and the high correlations of this test with the overall score." Similarly, it is not easy to see in what way, within the context provided by a given sentence, "allowed" as a synonym for "permitted" differs from "distinct" as a synonym for "clear." Yet the former is included in a vocabulary subtest and the latter occurs in a subtest entitled "Use of Context."

No justification or explanation is given as to why particular subtests are included, and no reference is made to people such as Gray, Robinson, Barrett, Clymer, or Bormuth, to name but a few, who have examined in some depth the question of what reading comprises or have attempted to produce taxonomies of reading behaviours and skills. The fault is not that other people's expertise has been ignored, but that the tests are based on no coherent plan at all. Not only is there a complete lack of structure within each stage but, judging from the two stages produced so far, there is no overall plan

for the series either. If "reading for facts" is deemed necessary at Stage 3, surely it should also be included for younger children at Stage 2. Part of the trouble is that not only do subtests vary across the two stages but so too do the nomenclature and descriptive words used. What is "comprehension of essential ideas" at Stage 2 appears as "comprehension of points of view" at Stage 3.

Going by the work of the authors mentioned above, many aspects of reading are omitted altogether, yet both stages include some subtests of doubtful significance. There is one, for example, called "retention of significant details" at Stage 2 and "retention of main ideas" at Stage 3, which simply measures short-term memory through the recall (unseen) of facts given in short paragraphs. This is frankly described in one manual as seemingly "to stand somewhat aside from the main business of reading"; and although a verbal justification for it is given, no empirical evidence is provided in support.

The intercorrelations of the subtests are generally high—in the low .70s for Stage 2 and the high .70s for Stage 3—and the manual authors stress the fact that the separate results are "in most cases small and educationally insignificant." Their conclusion is that "reading can be thought of as a unified ability," which in terms of the actual content of these tests is a fully justified statement. Despite this, elaborate descriptions are given for providing profiles of standardised subtest scores, and although strong warnings are given about possible misinterpretations, the implication is that the tests have a useful diagnostic value. It should be added that there is one subtest which breaks the general rule, and that is the one measuring "reading rate" at Stage 2. It has an average correlation with the other subtests of only .46, demonstrating that there is one aspect of reading at least which might have some relatively independent existence.

It must be said that in all aspects but one both the tests and manuals reach the high standard of excellence to be expected from the institutions that constructed them. The exception is the most important, however—validity. Unfortunately, a collection of well-constructed but homogeneous item types alone does not necessarily make a good test. With the official backing given to the production of this series of tests, it seems a pity that the opportunity was missed to build them on a more solid foundation. Perhaps it is not too late for a rescue operation to be made on the stages still to come.

As for the present tests, they will obviously show high concurrent validities with other "comprehension" tests and therefore they could be useful for survey purposes, but not for anything else.

EARL F. RANKIN, *Professor of Education, University of Kentucky, Lexington, Kentucky.*

These tests are intended for use throughout the English-speaking world. However, norms are available only for Scotland and England/Wales and are presently being developed for Australia. In the reviewer's opinion, portions of the content, vocabulary, and style of the reading passages are distinctly British in character. These linguistic and stylistic characteristics, together with the cultural limitations of the test norms, raise questions about the usefulness of the test for children in the United States.

According to the manuals, the test was constructed, through the combined efforts of teachers, researchers, and government officials, to measure a wide range of cognitive skills involved in reading. Claims for validity rest primarily on the content of the test as a whole; yet we are not told precisely how the test content was produced to reflect either the reading curriculum or the nature of the reading process. There is no doubt that the subtests measure several high-level cognitive processes involved in reading; but why these specific skills were measured to the exclusion of others is left open to question. One wonders, for example, why reading rate is measured at Stage 2 but not at Stage 3. No information is provided regarding either criterion-related or construct validity.

A K-R 20 reliability of .97 is reported for total scores at both levels. Subtest reliabilities range from .81 to .95, with median .89. Apparently, these reliabilities were computed for wide-range samples representing all ages for which each level is used. Unfortunately, no standard errors of measurement are provided.

Norms for each level were developed on the basis of random samples of approximately 2,800 children in Scotland and the same number in England/Wales. Since these children were enrolled in state schools, they are not representative of the total population even within these countries.

Test results are expressed in the form of "reading quotients," "reading ages," and "standardized scores." All subtest scores are portrayed on a rather elaborate "subtest profile." Reading quotients relate a child's performance to his or her age group. Only the total score is expressed as a reading quotient, with a mean of 100 and a standard deviation of 15. The reading age expresses a child's performance in relation to the average scores of other age groups. Thus, a child's score can be compared with both his or her own age group and with other age groups. The profile of subtest scores is well designed for diagnostic purposes.

While British teachers might not have difficulty in following the statistics involved in recording and interpreting these test results, most American teachers would probably not understand many of these concepts. Despite careful instructions not to interpret the reading quotient as an indication of aptitude, perhaps the analogy between the reading quotient and the intelligence quotient is strong enough to produce precisely this effect. Since the teacher is asked to interpret reading quotients in terms of the percentages of students falling below a given quotient, it would seem more desirable to provide normalized percentiles for this purpose. One questions the use of the reading age norms, not only because the norms are limited to values between the precise age groups for whom the two tests were intended, but also because unequal measurement units are found between various points on the age-norm distribution. If used, reading ages are generally more meaningful for lower-age levels, where achievement is more closely related to maturation than it is for students in secondary school.

From a practical point of view, strengths as well as weaknesses arise from the fact that for both stages there are a practice test and two other tests, requiring three periods for administration. If we wish to measure reading diagnostically, we must be ready to spend an amount of time commensurate with this important purpose; yet many teachers would be reluctant to invest this amount of class time for testing. On the more positive side, administration of the practice test should be helpful in reducing test anxiety.

Edinburgh Reading Tests

Teachers are given good advice regarding interpretation of test results. Excellent descriptions of the precise characteristics of subtests and even individual items are provided. An interesting procedure for evaluating relatively high or low group performance in relation to the average performance of that group constitutes a desirable feature of this test. An undesirable feature is the fact that only one test form has been constructed thus far for each level.

The chief weakness of this test as a diagnostic instrument lies in the high correlations among most of the subtests. The sole exception to this is the reading rate test in Stage 2. It is well known that different measures of comprehension skills and vocabulary are highly interrelated. Virtually all factor analysis studies of reading comprehension point to two factors accounting for most of the variance in such measurements. It is also well known that when we have high correlations between tests, the difference between one test score and another (such as might be found in a diagnostic profile) must be exceedingly high in order for the difference in the two test scores to surpass the standard error of the difference between those scores. This is due to the effect of the correlation between two tests upon the reliability of the difference between two test scores. For example, if we take two scores on subtests D and E for Stage 3 for a child in Scotland, the reliability coefficients for these two subtests are .94 and .88, respectively. The correlation between these two tests is .84. It can be shown, therefore, that the reliability of the difference between two scores on these two subtests is approximately .44, despite the substantial reliability coefficients for each. The diagnostic value of this test is questionable, even though the profile sheet indicates "significantly" extreme scores for each individual only in relation to the median score in his particular pattern of five subtest scores.

Although constructed as a diagnostic test, the chief value of the *Edinburgh Reading Tests* lies in the total score as an excellent measure of general reading achievement. The comparison of subtests for diagnostic purposes is of little value except for infrequently occurring extreme differences among reading skills.

[725]

★Fountain Valley Teacher Support System in Reading. Grades 1, 2, 3, 4, 5, 6; 1971–75; FVTSS-R;

criterion referenced; the 6 levels together cover 367 specific-objective subtests (77% consist of 2 or 3 items) in 5 areas: comprehension (12–20 subtests), phonetic analysis (16–71, grades 1–3), structural analysis (13–15, grades 1–3), study skills (10–18), vocabulary development (3–10); no data on reliability; no norms; mastery defined as 100% for 2- and 3-item subtests and 67–88% for subtests of other lengths; no supporting data or information for grade placement of specific objectives and mastery standards; tape cassette available for administration; 2 editions: self-scoring, hand scoring; 77 tests ('71, 1 page each); manuals ('74, 39–67 pages) for each grade level; administration manual, experimental edition ('75, 183 pages); individual record forms ('71, 4 pages); looseleaf prescription guide for each grade level; 50 sets of tests for any one grade level: $25.75–$43.25 for hand scoring, $49.50–$104.50 for self-scoring; $9–$19 per set of scoring stencils for any one grade level; $6.50 per 50 record forms; $51.25–$99.50 per set of cassettes and manual for any one grade level; $15 per administration manual; postage extra; specimen set not available; (5–21) minutes per test; Richard L. Zweig Associates, Inc. *

REFERENCES
1. THOMPSON, RICHARD A., AND DZIUBAN, CHARLES D. "Criterion Referenced Reading Tests in Perspective." *Read Teach* 27(3):292–4 D '73. *

ANTHONY J. NITKO, *Associate Professor of Education, University of Pittsburgh, Pittsburgh, Pennsylvania.*

The *Fountain Valley Teacher Support System in Reading* consists of sets of test items organized into five curricular areas, a collection of 367 specific behavioral objectives keyed to each of the items, and an extensive list of teaching materials from a variety of commercial publishers each element of which is keyed to a specific objective. The sets of test items within each curricular area are organized into series of tests in presumably ascending order of difficulty. This allows one to begin testing at a different level within each area, if one so chooses.

The tests are to be used in the following way. Each student is administered a set of items in each of the curricular areas. The item scores are used to make judgments about whether a student needs further instruction on each objective or is to be declared a "master" and, hence, not in need of further study on specific objectives. If it is decided that a student needs additional study on particular objectives, "prescriptions" can be developed by consulting the list of teaching materials that have been keyed to each objective. Materials are provided for recording test results and for monitoring pupil progress through the objectives. Tests are usually administered via cassette tapes, and answers are recorded on self-scoring or teacher-scored answer sheets.

Fountain Valley Teacher Support System in Reading

The unfortunate thing about the FVTSSR is that no data are supplied to support the use of the tests for any of these purposes. The user is cautioned to examine these materials carefully and keep several points in mind.

One should examine the objectives covered by the system. The series claims to cover the first six years of reading instruction. However, over half of the objectives are linked to the lowest two levels of the program (roughly the first two years). This is because of the specificity of the objectives (e.g., each tiny grapheme-phoneme correspondence constitutes an objective). Taken as a whole over all levels, the objectives seem not to form a complete reading program and seem to focus on the more easily measured objectives. For example, the important beginning reading skill of blending phonemes to produce words is ignored and the user is left with no measure (nor diagnosis) of this process. Another example is in the area of reading comprehension. These skills when tested by such norm-referenced tests as the *Iowa Tests of Basic Skills* or the *Comprehensive Tests of Basic Skills* appear broader, richer, and more nearly like the terminal behaviors to which one would hope that six years of reading instruction would lead. Perhaps, for certain remedial programs more specific and narrow objectives may be appropriate.

Another claim is made that the objectives are arranged in a learning sequence. No evidence supports this use of the tests. In fact, many of the objectives seem to represent an arbitrary, rather than optimal, arrangement.

Thirdly, there is a claim that one can diagnose, prescribe, and judge mastery on the basis of the scores. No mention is made of the (highly) likely occurrence of erroneous classifications and decisions. No evidence is presented to support this use. Of the 367 objectives, 57 percent are tested with only two items; 20 percent with three items. Thus, the great majority of decisions will be based on very few test items. These items are usually multiple choice with three alternatives each. Clearly there are not enough items per objective to make the kinds of mastery decisions and diagnoses intended. In the past, norm-referenced tests have been criticized because they have only one or two items measuring specific skills. Should objective-based tests be exempt from this criticism?

A fourth point to keep in mind is the quality of the items. A commercial product that is professionally developed should be expected to contain quality items. The items of the Fountain Valley system lack this characteristic on the whole. For example, many items function like matching exercises and there is perfect matching; often items are written with incomplete stems where direct questions would be more appropriate; and some completion items have blanks in awkward places. Also, forcing each item into a format so that it can be administered by a cassette, leads to difficulties. This is especially evident where directions change in the middle of a test and no sample item is presented. Such directions presented aurally would seem to be difficult to comprehend for average students working independently and encountering these item-types for the first time.

To place a child into the appropriate level to begin testing, the publisher recommends the use of grade equivalent scores from norm-referenced reading tests and/or some combination of judgment, past performance, or less formal testing. The manual gives two hypothetical examples: one using the grade equivalent score from a standardized test and the other illustrating an instance where the student did "not have a standardized reading test score." Thus, the implication is that using the grade equivalent score from a standardized test is to be preferred. No mention is made of the fact that one's grade equivalent may be different for different tests and bear little relation to the local curriculum within which the student must learn.

Finally, there are claims that the tests will identify students with auditory perception problems, visual perception problems, and those who learn best by "auditory mode." No explanation is given as to what is meant by any of these constructs, nor is there evidence that in fact the test can do any of this.

In short, this test lacks evidence (*a*) for content, construct, and criterion-oriented validity and (*b*) for reliability (however this might be defined in the context of criterion-referenced testing). Users should insist that criterion-referenced tests meet minimum standards of technical quality and that invocation of the term "criterion-referenced" should not result in a dispensation from providing evidence that supports claims of quality.

Fountain Valley Teacher Support System in Reading

GUS P. PLESSAS, *Professor of Education, California State University, Sacramento, California.*

The FVTSSR consists of 77 one-page tests and a reference guide to a variety of commercially produced instructional materials for use in grades 1–6. The system is diagnostic and prescriptive in design. It is intended to provide classroom teachers with a means of diagnosis, a guide to remedial prescription, and a method of pupil placement in reading, including "pretest for fast learners" as well as "posttest for the average and slow learners."

Related to the FVTSSR are objectives stated in behavioral terms for the individual learner and limited to a specific skill in reading. For each grade, behavioral objectives are number coded by reading skill areas; each behavioral objective numeral corresponds with a criterion test numeral. Similarly coded is the cross-referenced manual called Teaching Alternatives Supplement. Such a numbering system facilitates easy identification of tests and of reteaching prescriptions, making this feature one of the strong practical elements of the program.

However, central to the use of FVTSSR in general and the reading tests in particular must be the acceptance of the stated behavioral objectives. It is essential that users of the tests ascertain first the values of the specific objectives to judge the worth of many of the criterion-referenced test items. No data are given to support the validity or construction of the 367 behavioral objectives that form the FVTSSR.

Consider, for example, the behavioral objective relating to the initial consonant *b*, "The student will demonstrate his ability to recognize the sound-symbol relationship of the initial consonant *b* by selecting from a set of printed choices, the word that begins with the initial consonant *b* when: the stimulus word with the sound of initial consonant *b* and the set of printed choices are read aloud, and [when] the stimulus word alone is read aloud." The question is how important is such an objective in the actual process of word identification in reading? Does successful performance on such a criterion task insure the application of initial consonant *b* knowledge to an unfamiliar word that starts with the letter *b*? Conversely, does an unsuccessful performance on the task indicate an inability to analyze an unknown word that starts with the letter *b*? It would be very difficult to estimate the relationship between results on the criterion-referenced tests and the actual reading performance of a student, due in large part to the undetermined values of the given behavioral objectives as they are formulated and to the uncertain accuracy of the test performance.

Although all the tests are classified by purpose according to coded objectives and by levels of difficulty, again no supporting evidence is given to explain the delineation of grade placement levels of specific objectives. How were these levels determined? What criteria were employed to distinguish the hierarchy of difficulty? Are the levels valid for purposes of testing in each of the areas designated? How were the test words selected? Unfortunately, the stated behavioral objectives do not identify what words should be included in the operation to be performed. Thus what is measured when, for example, a student is to demonstrate ability to distinguish compound words or rhyming words or to recognize an antonym? What is the significance of word analysis or vocabulary objectives when target words are not included as part of the performance objective?

One final note on the Fountain Valley behavioral objectives concerns the construction of the comprehension objectives and their criterion-referenced test items. Even though a variety of comprehension subskills are described in performance terms, the given conditions for the application of these comprehension operations are not described. What does it mean in a statement of objectives that the learner be able "to compare and contrast ideas," or "to read creatively and react personally," when the type of material to be read is not disclosed in the objective? The problem is further complicated by lack of evidence from validity studies to support the assessment of comprehension in terms of distinct subskill areas as discrete and unrelated elements of comprehension.

The FVTSSR tests do have some commendable qualities. They include ease of test administration, readable teacher's guide, uncomplicated scoring procedures, and practical color and number codes for test identification and for remedial prescriptions. The program would have been further enhanced if data on test reliability were provided. It would be helpful to know the chance factor in student performance.

Fountain Valley Teacher Support System in Reading

There are tape directions provided for each of the tests. However, it seems unnecessary to use the cassettes for administration because the tests are not standardized. Rather, the FVTSSR tests should be given by the teacher personally. In this way, the testing conditions would be similar to the conditions under which teaching-learning occurs.

In sum, the FVTSSR is a carefully organized and packaged program. But its use would depend mainly on the acceptance of the stated objectives, and test effectiveness appears uneven at best.

[726]

GAPADOL. Ages 10–16; 1972; upward extension for "adolescent children" of *GAP Reading Comprehension Test;* cloze technique; Forms G, Y, (16 pages); manual (12 pages); Aus $8.95 per 25 sets of both forms, postage extra; specimen set not available; 60(65) minutes; J. McLeod and J. Anderson; Heinemann Educational Australia Pty Ltd. [Australia]. *

IRA E. AARON, *Professor of Education, The University of Georgia, Athens, Georgia.*

GAPADOL is designed to assess reading achievement by means of the cloze technique. Each form contains six paragraphs of approximately 100 to 150 words each, with approximately 80 words omitted in each form. Words omitted are those "of high redundancy but not.... completely redundant." Deletions range from adjacent words (in one instance) to 16 words, with all parts of speech except interjections being included among the deletions. On the average, approximately every eighth word has been deleted.

Though a time limit of 30 minutes has been set, the test is a power test; this time appears to be quite adequate. The test booklet is 4¼x11 inches in size. The deleted words must be printed in blocks to the right of the paragraph, and children are not penalized for misspellings. Two brief practice exercises precede the test itself.

The manual presents clear directions to the examiner. Norms consist of reading age scores along with the 10th and 90th raw score percentiles for each month of chronological age from 7–5 to 16–11. The manual gives no information about how these norms were established. However, a communication from the publisher indicates that the test norms are based on the testing of more than 5,000 students in grades 2 through 12 in Saskatoon, Canada—the entire population for these grades.

Hoyt reliability coefficients for five different year groups range from .84 to .93, with a median of .90.

No validity data are presented in the manual. However, according to the publisher, a correlation of .78 was found "between the GAP and GAPADOL tests, for children with reading ages up to about 10½ years." The publisher also said that "the validity of the cloze-type tests has been well established over the years." Not all persons in the areas of reading and measurement have such confidence in the technique itself. Further, it would seem that the question of validity would be specific to the test itself and not to the technique used in the test. The assumption is also made that the original GAP test is valid for measuring comprehension—this assumption may or may not be true.

Despite limitations, GAPADOL can be used to determine quickly the relative reading achievement standings of adolescents. However, almost any of the widely used reading achievement tests would better serve the needs of test users in the United States.

[726A]

Gates-MacGinitie Reading Tests. Grades 1, 2, 3, 2.5–3, 4–6, 7–9; 1926–72; GMRT; 6 levels; 2 editions; technical manual ('72, 12 pages); postage extra; Arthur I. Gates and Walter H. MacGinitie; Houghton Mifflin Co. *
a) PRIMARY A. Grade 1; 1926–72; 2 scores: vocabulary, comprehension; 40(50) minutes in 2 sessions.
  1) *Hand Scored Edition.* Forms 1, 2, ('64, 8 pages); manual ('65, 8 pages); $6.24 per 35 tests; $1.50 per specimen set.
  2) *Machine Scored Edition.* Forms 1M, 2M, ('70, 8 pages); manual ('71, 12 pages); $11.25 per 35 tests; $3 per specimen set; scoring service, 35¢ and over per test.
b) PRIMARY B. Grade 2; 1926–72; remaining details same as for Primary A.
c) PRIMARY C. Grade 3; 1939–72; 2 scores: vocabulary, comprehension; forms and prices same as for Primary A; 50(60) minutes in 2 sessions.
d) PRIMARY CS. Grades 2.5–3; 1926–65; speed and accuracy; 7(15) minutes.
  1) *Hand Scored Edition.* Forms 1, 2, 3, ('64, 3 pages); manual ('65, 8 pages); $3.75 per 35 tests; $1 per specimen set.
  2) *Machine Scored Edition.* Forms 1M, 2M, 3M, ('70, 4 pages); manual ('71, 11 pages); $8.55 per 35 tests; $1.50 per specimen set; scoring service, 35¢ and over per test.
e) SURVEY D. Grades 4–6; 1939–72; 3 scores: speed and accuracy, vocabulary, comprehension; $6.24 per 35 tests of either edition; $1.50 per specimen set.
  1) *Consumable Booklet Edition.* Forms 1, 2, 3, ('64, 8 pages); manual ('65, 12 pages); 45(60) minutes in 2 sessions.
  2) *Separate Answer Sheet Edition.* Forms 1M, 2M, 3M, ('64, 8 pages); manual ('65, 16 pages); separate answer sheets (Digitek, IBM 805, IBM 1230, MRC,

Fountain Valley Teacher Support System in Reading

NCS) must be used; answer sheets: $2.40 per 35 Digitek, $2.25 per 35 IBM 805, $2.40 per 35 IBM 1230, $5.10 per 35 MRC, $10 per 100 NCS; $2 per set of IBM 805 scoring stencils; $1.20 per NCS scoring stencil; MRC scoring service, 30¢ and over per test; NCS scoring service, 25¢ and over per test; 46(60) minutes in 2 sessions.

f) SURVEY E. Grades 7–9; 1939–72; $6.24 per 35 tests of either edition; $1.50 per specimen set; 44(60) minutes in 2 sessions.

1) *Consumable Booklet Edition.* Forms 1, 2, 3, ('64, 8 pages); manual ('65, 12 pages).

2) *Separate Answer Sheet Edition.* Forms 1M, 2M, 3M, ('64, 8 pages); manual ('65, 16 pages); answer sheets and prices same as for *e2.*

See T2:1552 (18 references); for reviews by Carolyn L. Burke and Byron H. Van Roekel and an excerpted review by William R. Powell, see 7:689.

REFERENCES

1–18. See T2:1552.
19. ALLBAUGH, RONALD J. *A Comparison of the Functional Reading Levels of Fifth Grade Students of Varying Reading Abilities.* Doctor's thesis, University of Northern Colorado (Greeley, Colo.), 1972. (*DAI* 33:3142A)
20. ANDERSON, WILLIAM F., AND STERN, DAVID. "The Relative Effects of the Frostig Program, Corrective Reading Instruction, and Attention Upon the Reading Skills of Corrective Readers With Visual Perceptual Deficiencies." *J Sch Psychol* 10(4):387–95 D '72. * (*PA* 50:3665)
21. ASHLEY, HELEN CATHERINE. *A Study of the Relationships of Several Measures of Interpretive Skills in Literature and Achievement in Reading.* Doctor's thesis, State University of New York (Buffalo, N.Y.), 1972. (*DAI* 33:1580A)
22. BLANTON, WILLIAM E. "Gates-MacGinitie Reading Tests: A Review," pp. 23–6. In *Reading Tests for the Secondary Grades.* Edited by William Blanton and others. Newark, Del.: International Reading Association, Inc., 1972. Pp. iv, 55. *
23. CONDREN, RAYMOND J. *Characteristics of the Chronically Unemployed in Relation to Reading Retardation.* Doctor's thesis, Texas Tech University (Lubbock, Tex.), 1972. (*DAI* 33:2788B)
24. DEIGNAN, MARGARET CORCORAN. *Reading Achievement of High Risk Children: Variables Influencing Performance.* Doctor's thesis, Yeshiva University (New York, N.Y.), 1972. (*DAI* 33:3433A)
25. GOULD, KATHRYN LEWIS. *Relationships of Creativity, Reading Comprehension, Intelligence, and Response to a Literature Selection for Fourth Grade Inner-City Children.* Doctor's thesis, Ohio State University (Columbus, Ohio), 1972. (*DAI* 33:893A)
26. KING, ETHEL M., AND FRIESEN, DORIS T. "Children Who Read in Kindergarten." *Alberta J Ed Res* (Canada) 18 (3):147–61 S '72. *
27. KIRBY, EDWARD A.; LYLE, WILLIAM; AND AMBLE, BRUCE R. "Reading and Psycholinguistic Processes of Inmate Problem Readers." *J Learn Dis* 5(5):295–8 My '72. * (*PA* 48:7457)
28. LEE, JACKSON FREDERICK, JR. *Prediction of Student Success at the North Carolina Advancement School.* Doctor's thesis, Duke University (Durham, N.C.), 1972. (*DAI* 33:4947A)
29. LEVINE, DANIEL U.; LACHOWICZ, HOLLY; OXMAN, KAREN; AND TANGEMAN, AHDEN. "The Home Environment of Students in a High-Achieving Inner-City Parochial School and a Nearby Public School." *Sociol Ed* 45(4):435–45 f '72. * (*PA* 49:7882)
30. McALLISTER, ROBERT J. *A Correlational Study of the Raven Test of Colored Progressive Matrices, the Ottawa School Behavior Checklist, and the Gates MacGinitie Primary Reading Tests, A and B.* Master's thesis, Niagara University (Niagara University, N.Y.), 1972.
31. PRZYWANSKY, WALTER B. "Effects of Perceptual-Motor Training and Manuscript Writing on Reading Readiness Skills in Kindergarten." *J Ed Psychol* 63(2):110–5 Ap '72. * (*PA* 48:7862)
32. REILLY, DAVID H. "Auditory-Visual Integration, School Demographic Features and Reading Achievement." *Percept & Motor Skills* 35(3):995–1001 D '72. * (*PA* 49:12054)
33. THOMPSON, MERITA LEE. *Relationships Between Perceptual-Motor Development and Reading Achievement of Third Grade Students.* Doctor's thesis, University of Alabama (University, Ala.), 1972. (*DAI* 33:5541A)
34. APPLEBEE, ARTHUR N. "Toward Independent Measures of Speed of Reading." *J Learn Dis* 6(1):16–20 Ja '73. * (*PA* 50:3667)
35. BREKKE, BEVERLY, AND WILLIAMS, JOHN D. "Teachers' Prediction of Reading Readiness." *Percept & Motor Skills* 37(2):521–2 O '73. * (*PA* 51:9910)
36. BREKKE, BEVERLY W.; WILLIAMS, JOHN D.; AND HARLOW, STEVEN D. "Conservation and Reading Readiness." *J Genetic Psychol* 123(1):133–8 S '73. * (*PA* 51:7944)
37. BURGETT, R. E., AND GLASER, N. A. "Appraising the Revised Standardized Reading Test." *El Engl* 50(1):71–4 Ja '73. *
38. DeRUITER, JAMES ALLEN. *A Bayesian Approach to the Use of Test Data for the Identification of Learning Disability in School-Age Children.* Doctor's thesis, University of Arizona (Tucson, Ariz.), 1973. (*DAI* 34:4919A)
39. DuBOIS, NELSON F., AND BROWN, FOSTER LLOYD. "Selected Relationships Between Frostig Scores and Reading Achievement in a First Grade Population." *Percept & Motor Skills* 37(2):515–9 O '73. * (*PA* 51:9914)
40. JOHNSON, DALE D. "Sex Differences in Reading Across Cultures." *Read Res Q* 9(1):67–86 '73–74 ['73]. * (*PA* 51:11949)
41. KENT, ANITA HUTT. *The Relationships of Reading Comprehension, Conservation Ability, Auditory Discrimination, and Visual-Motor Development of Third-Grade Pupils.* Doctor's thesis, University of Oklahoma (Norman, Okla.), 1973. (*DAI* 34:2924A)
42. RICCI, JOYCE. *The Relationship Between the Scores on the Gates-MacGinitie Reading Test of the Open Court Correlated Language Arts Program and the Basal Series in the Killingly School System.* Master's thesis, Eastern Connecticut State College (Willimantic, Conn.), 1973.
43. SAVILLE, PETER, AND BLINKHORN, STEPHEN. *The Gates-MacGinitie Reading Tests: Primary A, Form 1, British Supplement of Norms.* Windsor, Berks, England: NFER Publishing Co. Ltd., 1973. Pp. 10. *
44. HOLMES, GARY DONALD. *A Comparison of the Comprehensive Tests of Basic Skills and the Metropolitan Readiness Tests in Predicting Reading Success of First Grade Children as Measured by the Gates-MacGinitie Reading Tests in Floyd County, Georgia Schools.* Doctor's thesis, Mississippi State University (State College, Miss.), 1974. (*DAI* 35:4912A)
45. LORET, PETER G.; SEDER, ALAN; BIANCHINI, JOHN C.; AND VALE, CAROL A. *Anchor Test Study: Equivalence and Norms Tables for Selected Reading Achievement Tests (Grades 4, 5, and 6).* DHEW Publication S/N 1780–01312. Washington, D.C.: Government Printing Office, 1974. Pp. ix, 92. *
46. STITT, JACQUELIN ANN. *Extrinsic Motivation and Test Taking in the Elementary School Child.* Doctor's thesis, Indiana University (Bloomington, Ind.), 1974. (*DAI* 35:5940A)
47. JACKSON, SHEILA M. *An Evaluation of Oral Reading Miscues in Second Grade Subjects.* Doctor's thesis, University of South Carolina (Columbia, S.C.), 1975. (*DAI* 37:250A)
48. LINN, ROBERT L. "Anchor Test Study: The Long and the Short of It." *J Ed Meas* 12(3):201–13 f '75. *
49. YEARBY, MARY ELIZABETH. *The Effect of Instruction in Test-Taking Skills on the Standardized Reading Test Scores of White and Black Third-Grade Children of High and Low Socioeconomic Status.* Doctor's thesis, Indiana University (Bloomington, Ind.), 1975. (*DAI* 36:4426A)
50. KENNAN, DONNA METZ. *A Study of the Relationship Between Tenth Grade Students' Reading Ability and Their Comprehension of Certain Assigned Textbooks.* Doctor's thesis, Florida State University (Tallahassee, Fla.), 1976. (*DAI* 37:6391A)
51. PREISS, LORRAINE CECILIA. *An Investigation to Determine the Adequacy of the Gates-MacGinitie Reading Tests as a Predictor of Success in the First Semester Anatomy and Physiology Course in an Open Admissions Community College.* Doctor's thesis, University of Michigan (Ann Arbor, Mich.), 1976. (*DAI* 37:6198A)
52. GLAZZARD, MARGARET. "The Effectiveness of Three Kindergarten Predictors for First-Grade Achievement." *J Learn Dis* 10(2):95–9 F '77. * (*PA* 58:4423)

[727]

Gates-MacGinitie Reading Tests: Survey F. Grades 10–12; 1969–72; lower levels of the Gates-MacGinitie Reading Tests listed separately in this volume; 4 scores: speed and accuracy (number attempted, number correct), vocabulary, comprehension; 2 forms; 2 editions; technical supplement ('70, 6 pages); grade score norms ('72, 4 pages, derived from data reported in 1970 technical supplement); $6.24 per 35 tests; $1.50 per specimen set of either edition; postage extra; 49(60) minutes; Arthur I. Gates and Walter H. MacGinitie; Houghton Mifflin Co. *

a) CONSUMABLE BOOKLET EDITION. Forms 1, 2, ('69, 8 pages); manual ('69, 12 pages).

b) SEPARATE ANSWER SHEET EDITION. Forms 1M, 2M, ('69, 8 pages); manual ('69, 16 pages); separate answer sheets (Digitek, IBM 805, IBM 1230, MRC, NCS) must be used; answer sheets: $5.10 per 35

Digitek or IBM 1230, $2.70 per 35 IBM 805, $2.85 per 35 MRC, $10 per 100 NCS; hand scoring stencils: $2 per set of IBM 805, $1 per NCS; MRC scoring service, 35¢ and over per test; NCS scoring service, 20¢ and over per test; NCS materials and scoring service available from NCS Interpretive Scoring Systems.

For a review by Jason Millman, see 7:690.

REFERENCES

1. BLANTON, WILLIAM E. "Gates-MacGinitie Reading Tests: A Review," pp. 23-6. In *Reading Tests for the Secondary Grades*. Edited by William Blanton and others. Newark, Del.: International Reading Association, Inc., 1972. Pp. iv, 55. *
2. JOHNS, JERRY L. "Can Teachers Use Standardized Reading Tests to Determine Students' Instructional Levels?" *Ill Sch Res* 11(3):29-35 sp '75. *

ALBERT J. KINGSTON, *Professor of Educational Psychology, The University of Georgia, Athens, Georgia.*

Survey F presumes to assess three aspects of reading: speed and accuracy, vocabulary, and comprehension.

Speed and accuracy are measured in four minutes by 36 items, each consisting of one to three sentences with the last word deleted. The examinee completes the sentence by selecting one of four words. The selections are highly varied in content but are comparatively easy. Pupils who have made normal progress in reading should have little difficulty in answering the items, which are assumed to provide a measure of a student's ability to read rapidly with comprehension.

The vocabulary test is traditional. A stimulus word is presented, followed by five other words. The student selects the word most closely resembling the initial word. Fifteen minutes is allowed for 50 items. There is no penalty for guessing and students are urged to guess. These instructions differ from those in the speed and accuracy section, where students are advised to proceed to the next item if they don't know an answer and to "work as fast as [they] can without making errors." No reasons for this difference are provided. An examination of the selected words suggests that care was taken to avoid choosing those which might be learned in formal academic study. Generally the five alternate words seem to be well chosen and likely to attract the unwary.

The comprehension subtest consists of 21 narrative passages with two or three words deleted in each. The student must select from the five words presented the correct one for each deletion. Thus the test resembles the popular "cloze procedure" often employed in reading

and language research. The passages range in length from 30 words to slightly more than 100 and represent varying content. The time limit is 25 minutes and 80 percent of students can be expected to complete the items. Again there is no penalty for guessing and students are encouraged to answer even if uncertain about the answer. Neither the manual nor the technical supplement provides information designed to help the teacher interpret the scores of those who fail to finish the test as compared to the scores of those who finish the test but are inaccurate.

The excellent technical supplement describes in considerable detail the methods employed in trying out items and norming the test. Pertinent information concerning reliability and validity, as well as procedures for utilizing and transforming scores, also is provided. Scores can be interpreted in the form of raw scores, percentile ranks, or standardized scores. The tables provided in the manual are clear and readily used. The alternate form reliabilities by grade average .88 for comprehension, .90 for vocabulary, .72 for speed (number attempted), and .80 for speed (number correct). The reliabilities of the speed section are somewhat lower than desirable. Another weakness in Survey F is the high correlation between the comprehension and vocabulary scores. Coefficients range from .82 for twelfth graders to .86 for eleventh graders. These high positive correlations suggest a commonality that may not justify the use of two subtests. The problem is further compounded by the high reported correlations between these sections and the Lorge-Thorndike verbal IQ, at or just under .80 at all three grade levels. Reading, of course, is a thought process involving language. At the high school level it is expected that some overlap between various measures will occur. The high degree of relationship found between some of these subtests, however, tends to cast doubt upon the uniqueness of whatever is supposedly being measured. Perhaps one major shortcoming lies in the type of reading behavior being measured. Reading specialists emphasize that reading is a complex skill which consists of many subskills. High school students presumably need to have mastered not only literal comprehension but such interpretative comprehension abilities as making inferences, separating fact and opinion, and determining the writer's fairness and objectivity. These important comprehension skills are not assessed in this instrument.

Finally, the manual and technical supplement are well done. The manual is well written and the average classroom teacher should be able to administer, score, and interpret the test results without difficulty. The technical supplement provides excellent tables and explanations for those interested in further statistical interpretation.

[728]

Group Reading Assessment. End of first year junior school; 1962–64; 1 form ('62, 4 pages); manual ('64, 16 pages, 1975 reprinting has minor revisions); 75p per 20 tests; 40p per manual; 45p per specimen set; postpaid within U.K.; (20–30) minutes; Frank A. Spooncer; Hodder & Stoughton Educational [England]. *

DAVID J. CARROLL, *Research Associate, The Godfrey Thomson Unit for Academic Assessment, The University of Edinburgh, Edinburgh, Scotland.*

The author emphasises that he sets out to test the mechanics of reading, rather than reading comprehension; the underlying concept of "mechanical reading" must therefore be evaluated.

The first part of the test covers aural discrimination, or spelling, since the words are put in the context of a sentence. The distractors appear to have been well chosen, and there is ample scope for reversals, hard-soft confusions, and the like. The second part, consisting of sentence completion items, is bedevilled by the testers' problem of making a sentence adequate context for an item. It is possible that we make too much of this need for each item to be complete in itself. Sentences in prose very rarely are, but this does not mean that cloze items load very much on more than local redundancy. The result for a sentence completion test is a strange kind of journalese, in which each sentence supplies its own context, to the detriment of naturalism. Even sentences which are complete units—e.g., newspaper headlines, notice boards—depend very much for their meaning on context. There are, in addition, one or two departures from contemporary usage which might confuse the reader, e.g., "the flowers are a pretty picture in our garden," "tumble" as a verb, "quarrelsome," "full of mischief." Part 3 requires the subjects to locate the word or words having the same sound as the first one on the line. Again, this is obvi-

ously the work of a seasoned test constructor, although he has missed the fact that, in Scotland, "wh" is aspirated ("which" and "witch" are not the same sound).

The important assumptions behind such a test, which a teacher should examine before using, are as follows: (a) that there is such a thing as mechanical reading, (b) that reading is related significantly to spoken language, (c) that it is possible to construct, in vacuo, a syntactic and semantic context in a single sentence, which will be naturalistic, and (d) that the sound of a word is useful to reader.

It is undoubtedly true that "barking at print," the mechanical translation of graphemes into spoken sounds, does exist. Whether it is healthy that this should be so or whether it would exist if we did not teach it, this test measures it effectively. It is also true that we teach reading via the spoken language. But in fluent readers, especially when they are reading rapidly, the subvocalisation tends to be vestigial, or absent, suggesting that it is not an integral part of reading. The sounding of words, however, is a useful strategy, used by fluent readers to come to terms with new or unfamiliar words. Is there any reason, however, why the "mechanics" of reading should be lexis, rather than syntax, or concepts of print, or graphic signals? This reviewer believes that all of these merit a place in such a test; moreover, such a test as this, it should be remembered, is, by its nature, profoundly artificial for any reader until he fails— then it becomes naturalistic, and functions successfully.

The instructions for administration are clear and well thought out. The examples used illuminate the principles involved and should present no difficulty to any child in a U.K. junior school class. However, the suggested sentences for Part 1 should be modified if it is felt that they are out of touch with contemporary usage: "weigh out," for example, is now a rare verb. The author acknowledges that less able children may have difficulty with Part 3.

Construction, item writing, and item analysis are dealt with fully and explicitly. The author provides two standardisations: a conversion to mean 100 and SD 15 and a scale of reading ages. None of these scores are divided by sex. The only reference to sex differences is a footnote which shows the sex difference to be 4.7 at the median. Surely, in view of the accepted preponderance of boys amongst those with reading problems and of the magnitude of this difference, sex differences should be acknowledged.

Reliability is attested by a K-R 20 and two test-retest coefficients, all fully described. Validity evidence consists of correlation coefficients among a variety of tests.

To summarise, this is a well-made, but conservative, test. It is practical, and has a well-written manual. These virtues should commend it to the conservatives in U.K. schools. It is possible to have reservations about the author's model of reading, but, in fairness, it should be pointed out that it almost certainly reflects school practice, which, in turn, feeds on such tests as this.

THOMAS KELLAGHAN, *Director, Educational Research Centre, St. Patrick's College, Dublin, Ireland.*

The purpose of this test is to assess the reading level of children at the end of their first year in junior school (at about age 8). The test is simple in format and relatively short, being made up of four pages containing 57 items. One section of the test (16 items) is made up of items with four stimulus words, one of which has to be identified by the child when the teacher reads it in a sentence. "Suggested sentences" are provided in the manual, with the odd corollary that the sentences may be varied by the teacher. The first part of the test appears on the cover page, which makes one wonder about an instruction not to open the booklets as they are distributed. The second section is made up of 25 incomplete sentences, the child's task being to select an appropriate word from four stimulus words to complete a sentence. Strangely, the teacher is again free to vary instructions "according to the ability of the class." One wonders to what extent administrative procedures were varied in the standardization of the test or what effect such variation might have on pupils' scores. In the final section of the test (16 items), the child has to select from five words, one or more that sound the same as an underlined stimulus word. The reviewer had difficulty with two items, as in the English to which he is accustomed, "which" is not pronounced "witch," and "wail" does not sound the same as "whale."

No information is provided in the manual on the specifications followed in the writing of the 132 items which were tried out in constructing the test. In selecting the final 57 items for the test, difficulty level, according to which items were sequenced in the test, and discrimination indices were taken into account. However, while there are general statements about the relative difficulty of items in one section as compared to another, no item statistics for difficulty or discrimination are provided.

Two sets of norms are provided. Raw scores may be converted to reading ages or to standardized scores with a mean of 100 and a standard deviation of 15. The reading age norms were arrived at by administering Vernon's *Graded Word Reading Test* to a sample of children who had taken the *Group Reading Assessment*, and using a method of equivalent percentiles. The median reading age of children with a chronological age of 8 years 2 months was found to be 8 years 5 months, "suggesting either that the sample was a little above average, or that the norms of the individual test were slightly lenient." Rather than disturb teachers' notions concerning the lapidary quality of norms, it was decided to adjust the new norms to the old. This procedure ignores the possibility that observed differences might have been due to differences in the standardization samples, differences in the methods of measurement, or changes in standards of reading over time. Given the method of calculating reading ages and the temptation to reify such scores, it seems preferable that teachers should use standardized scores rather than reading ages.

A measure of the internal consistency of the test (K-R 20) for "one age-group" was found to be .97. The manual does not make clear what is meant by an "age-group," and no internal-consistency data are provided for other than this one group. A test-retest correlation of .96 over a three-month interval and another of .91 over an eight-month interval were found. These measures of reliability are all satisfactory. Means and variances for the reliability sample, however, are not reported.

Various uses are suggested for the test—to survey the reading levels of complete age groups, to group children for instruction according to reading ability, to discover children backward in reading, and to relate a child's performance in reading to that of "a large group of children of his own age." Unfortunately, no evidence of validity for the recommended uses is provided. Nor is any adequate information provided about the "large group of children" with whom comparisons may be made; neither the normative population nor the method of sampling for standardization is described.

In summary, the manual for this test is flimsy and fails to meet many of the requirements expected of contemporary test manuals, such as those laid down in *Standards for Educational and Psychological Tests*. Given the lack of information on the selection of items, on test validity, and on the normative population, together with the rather strange procedure used in determining reading age norms, it is difficult to know precisely how a teacher should interpret scores. Teachers with an accumulated experience of using word recognition tests may find the test of some value. It certainly is easier and less time-consuming to administer than an individual test. Some information, however, such as clues to the nature of children's difficulties, that can be obtained by having children respond orally to word stimuli will be lost in the group administration. Since the test manual does not provide the relevant information, teachers who use the test will have to decide, on the basis of their own experience, how well the test serves the functions set out in the manual.

[729]

Group Reading Test. Ages 6–10; 1968–69; GRT; Forms A, B, ('69, 2 pages); manual ('68, 35 pages); 45p per 20 tests; 30p per scoring stencil; 50p per manual; 55p per specimen set; postpaid within U.K.; 13(20) minutes; D. Young; Hodder & Stoughton Educational [England]. *

RALPH D. DUTCH, *Principal Lecturer in Educational Psychology, Aberdeen College of Education, Aberdeen, Scotland.*

Each form of this easily administered reading test consists of two parts, one on either side of a single sheet of paper. In Part 1 the child has to select, from among three to five words, the one word that matches a picture. In Part 2 the child has to select a synonym for a given word in a multiple choice, sentence completion format. The total score can be converted to either a reading age or a reading quotient. The test is easily and quickly scored.

The manual is clearly and helpfully written.

The standardisation has obviously been very carefully carried out so that even small points such as advice on how to mark the tests or how to allow for practice effects are based on investigation rather than on hunch. More important, the manual contains sensible warnings against investing the results of short tests like this with more precision and significance than they justify. Reliability coefficients, presented mainly in terms of standard errors of measurement, are provided. The validity measures, nearly all of concurrent validity, are based on the high correlations with other reading tests and on the rather higher than usual correlations with teachers' estimates. The author has provided equivalent reading scores on five other reading tests; some test users may find this useful. The test is highly practicable in the sense of being easy to give, quick to score, easy to interpret, cheap, and readily available.

On the other hand, although the norms are based on a sample of over 7,000 children, beyond the age of 10 "50 percent were above the ceiling of the test." This obviously led to great difficulties in producing acceptable standard scores, and means that the test is really useless for measuring the attainment of good readers in the top half of the age scale. Finally, although this test is as good as most of its kind, and although the author stresses that it should be seen as complementary to other types of test, it is still not clear to this reviewer how a knowledge of the simple results it provides would be of much use to a teacher looking for help to improve the reading competencies of children in her class.

[730]

Iowa Silent Reading Tests. Grades 6–9, 9–14, 11–16; 1927–73; ISRT; previous edition still available; 2 forms; 3 levels; manual ('73, 30–37 pages) for each level; guide for interpretation and use ('73, 67–71 pages) for each level; profile ('73, 2 pages, self-marking); separate answer sheets or folders (Digitek, IBM 1230, MRC, hand scored) must be used; supplementary directions ('73, 3–6 pages) for Digitek, IBM; $11.60 per 35 tests; answer sheets: $9 per 35 sets of Digitek or IBM for Level 1 or 2, $6 for Level 3, $14 per 100 MRC for Level 1 or 2, $9.50 for Level 3, $3.50 per 35 hand scored; hand scoring stencils: $5 per set of Digitek or IBM for Level 1 or 2, $3 for Level 3, $4.25 per set of hand scored for Level 1 or 2, $2.70 for Level 3; $4 per 35 profiles; $5 per guide for interpretation and use; $2.75 per specimen set of any one level; postage extra; Digitek or IBM scoring service: $1.05 and over per test for Level 1 or 2, 95¢ and over per test for Level 3; MRC scoring service: 50¢ and over per test for Level 1 or 2, 45¢ and over per test for Level 3; coordinating editor: Roger Farr; Psychological Corporation. *

Iowa Silent Reading Tests

a) LEVEL 1. Grades 6–9; 5 scores: vocabulary, reading comprehension, total, directed reading, reading efficiency; Forms E, F, ('72, 15 pages); 91(140) minutes in 3 sessions.

b) LEVEL 2. Grades 9–14; 5 scores: same as for Level 1; Forms E, F, ('72, 15 pages); 86(136) minutes in 3 sessions.

c) LEVEL 3. Grades 11–16; 4 scores: vocabulary, reading comprehension, total, reading efficiency; Forms E, F, ('72, 10 pages); 56(96) minutes in 2 sessions.

See T2:1560 (42 references); for a review by Worth R. Jones of an earlier edition, see 6:794 (40 references); for reviews by Frederick B. Davis and William W. Turnbull and excerpted reviews by Earl R. Gabler and Margaret Pankaskie, see 3:489 (21 references); for reviews by Ivan A. Booker and Holland D. Roberts, see 2:1547 (6 references).

REFERENCES

1–6. See 2:1547.
7–27. See 3:489.
28–67. See 6:794.
68–109. See T2:1560; also includes a cumulative name index to the first 109 references, 5 reviews, and 2 excerpts for this test.
110. JOHNSON, RONALD. "Iowa Silent Reading Tests: A Review," pp. 26–8. In *Reading Tests for the Secondary Grades.* Edited by William Blanton and others. Newark, Del.: International Reading Association, Inc., 1972. Pp. iv, 55. *
111. LIVINGSTON, HOWARD F. "What the Reading Test Doesn't Test—Reading." *J Read* 15(6):402–10 Mr '72. *
112. REED, MARY MAHONEY. *Some Effects of Oral Presentation on Reading Achievement in Grades Seven and Eight in an Inner City School.* Doctor's thesis, University of Pittsburgh (Pittsburgh, Pa.), 1972. (*DAI* 33:6737A)
113. DURHAM, LINDA LARUE. *An Investigation of the Remedial Reading Program and Its Alternatives for Seventh Graders in Laramie Public Schools.* Doctor's thesis, University of Wyoming (Laramie, Wyo.), 1973. (*DAI* 34:2290A)
114. FENNEMAN, GLENN CARL. *The Validity of Previous Experience, Aptitude, and Attitude Toward Mathematics as Predictors of Achievement in Freshman Mathematics at Wartburg College.* Doctor's thesis, University of Northern Colorado (Greeley, Colo.), 1973. (*DAI* 34:7100A)
115. THOMPSON, HUBERT WENDELL. *The Analysis of the Reading Performance of College Freshmen Students at Four Undergraduate Institutions of Higher Education as Evidenced by Selected Standardized Test Results.* Doctor's thesis, Kansas State University (Manhattan, Kan.), 1974. (*DAI* 35:2734A)
116. DAVIS, FREDERICK B. "Review of the Iowa Silent Reading Tests." *J Ed Meas* 12(1):57–60 sp '75. *
117. HUNTER, RUSSELL, AND HOEFFNER, RALPH. "Review of the Iowa Silent Reading Tests." *Meas & Eval Guid* 8(2):123–6 Jl '75. *
118. LIVINGSTON, CATHERINE LUCILLE. *A Study of the Effects of Different Levels of Initial Diagnosis on Gains in Reading Achievement for Adults in a Community College.* Doctor's thesis, University of Illinois (Urbana, Ill.), 1975. (*DAI* 36:2574A)

NIKOLA N. FILBY, *Research Associate, Far West Laboratory for Educational Research and Development, San Francisco, California.*

The 1973 edition of the *Iowa Silent Reading Tests* replaces earlier editions (as reviewed in the 6th MMY) with a newly conceptualized and organized set of reading measures. This review discusses each of the component tests in this new edition, and briefly discusses the norms and manuals provided with the tests.

VOCABULARY. The vocabulary test is a 50-item multiple choice test of synonyms. In each item, options form a cluster related by association, requiring the pupil to make a precise identification of the stimulus word's meaning. For example, the options for the word "talent" are "effort," "performance," "ability," and "fame." This careful selection of response options is a desirable feature, justifying the authors' claim of measuring depth and precision in knowledge of word meaning.

READING COMPREHENSION. The reading comprehension section is composed of two parts. Part A involves answering questions based on short passages available to the student as he responds. Part B, at Levels 1 and 2, is a short-term retention test.

The test developers have selected interesting reading passages that represent varied styles and content. They have taken care to ensure that questions are "based solely on the information specifically set forth in the passage," rather than testing general knowledge independent of the passage. On these points the tests measure up quite well.

Far too many of the questions are, unfortunately, detail questions. The use of detail questions is not wholly unreasonable in Part A, where the student has the passage available to him. Emphasis on detail is inappropriate in the short-term retention test. The interpretive manual claims that the retention test measures "key points, major facts, and general ideas and points of view expressed by the writer." The reader's ability to grasp key points and general ideas is an important skill, and a comprehensive battery of reading skills should measure this ability. The ISRT fails to do so very convincingly.

DIRECTED READING. This section deals with work-study skills. Part A covers reference material, including dictionary usage and knowledge of reference sources. Part B requires the reader to "skim and scan" a complex encyclopedia article in order to answer specific questions.

This section of the test seems well designed. The dictionary usage questions are based on a set of invented dictionary entries. This reduces the effect of prior familiarity with specific word meanings. The skim-and-scan section has the questions printed directly on the response sheet to facilitate efficient performance.

Unfortunately, Directed Reading is not included in the Level 3 battery. Ostensibly this is done because Level 3 students "have already mastered dictionary use and library research skills." Research skills become even more important in advanced work. Certainly the ability to skim and scan is an important skill at this level. Elimination of this section illustrates to me the difficulty of measuring complex and/or applied skills in a standardized paper-and-pencil test. This is a general limitation of the field, which users should keep in mind when evaluating all reading tests.

READING EFFICIENCY. This test measures reading speed and error rate using a modified cloze procedure. A passage is written with a content word deleted at the *end* of each sentence or pair of sentences. Responses are intended to be highly predictable from the immediately preceding context.

Of the set of scores in the ISRT, the reading efficiency score is the most independent statistically. The reading efficiency score can potentially give the user useful information about individual differences on a dimension other than basic ability to comprehend.

In a test of this type, an important consideration is the extent to which responses are in fact readily predictable from context. To ensure valid items, "items were chosen so that most students who reach an item in the time allotted can answer it correctly." In practice, "most students" ranges from 75% to 93% correct responses. Some items are definitely more straightforward than others, but the range is at an acceptable level.

NORMS. Each manual of directions provides norms for each grade level of the target range for that test level. The manual states that the standardization samples were "defined on the basis of geographic location, size of school district, and socioeconomic index based on median family income and median years of schooling of adults in the community." Unfortunately, descriptive data on the standardization sample are given only for geographic location. There is no way to evaluate fully the nature of the standardization population. This severely limits the interpretability of the norms.

MANUALS. One strength of the ISRT is the complete and well-written set of manuals. Each level has a Manual of Directions and, in addition, a Guide for Interpretation and Use. This guide covers test interpretation, use of the ISRT for instructional purposes and for administrative purposes, and development and structure of the tests. Considering all these different sections, this guide is a somewhat formidable document; but users should be encouraged to go through it.

Different sections are addressed to different audiences, and the writers do a good job of covering major points and giving interesting suggestions.

SUMMARY. The 1973 edition of the *Iowa Silent Reading Tests* brings the ISRT out of the realm of old, outmoded tests and into the front ranks of contemporary reading comprehension batteries. This new edition is the product of a careful, long-term developmental effort. It contains interesting subtests, with a variety of scoring options. It is well packaged and presented. The Guide for Interpretation and Use is a model of thoroughness and clarity. One could wish for different emphasis or more inventiveness `in some of the tests themselves. For instance, the comprehension test is heavily loaded with detail questions. This problem exists, however, in most standardized reading tests. Given the range of tests available, the ISRT is an outstanding candidate and can be recommended for use.

A. RALPH HAKSTIAN, *Associate Professor of Psychology, The University of British Columbia, Vancouver, British Columbia, Canada.*

The 1973 edition of the *ISRT* represents the second revision of a reading assessment battery first published in 1927 and revised in 1943. Many of the earlier features of the battery—its organization and multifaceted view of reading— are present in the new revision, but the latter is sufficiently different in major respects to be considered a new test series.

Whereas the earlier ISRT editions comprised two levels extending from grade 4 through college, the 1973 edition includes three: Level 1, for grades 6 through 9; Level 2, for grades 9 through 14; and Level 3, for academically accelerated students in grades 11 and 12, and college students. It could be argued that the grade levels spanned by the ISRT are not the critical ones for the assessment of reading and diagnosis of reading deficiencies, and the series would perhaps have been more useful with additional test levels for the primary and intermediate elementary school grades.

At each level, there are separate tests of vocabulary, reading comprehension, and reading efficiency, and at Levels 1 and 2 there is also a test of directed reading. The reading efficiency test assesses speed and accuracy and yields a "reading efficiency index." The reading comprehension test contains two parts: Part A, in which the examinee reads several short passages and, with the opportunity to look back to the passages, answers questions about the literal meaning, relationship of ideas, implications, mood, etc., of the passages; and Part B, in which, in Levels 1 and 2, the examinee reads one longer passage and, without looking back, answers similar questions. In Part B of the Level 3 test, this "reading for retention" section is replaced by "parallel passages," in which the examinee, after reading two passages on the same subject, compares and contrasts the viewpoints expressed in the passages.

In the vocabulary test, at all three levels, careful use has been made of well-documented educational sources for word choice. In the reading comprehension tests, similar care is evident in the selection of reading passages of appropriate readability and carefully varied content. Perhaps more important, the questions on these passages call for far more than simply the word knowledge and determining-meaning-from-context skills that seem, unfortunately, to be stressed in other reading comprehension tests.

ADMINISTRATION AND SCORING. The various tests of the ISRT are easily administered. The excellent manual provides detailed instructions for the examiner. Scoring is similarly straightforward, with either machine or hand scoring possibilities. The manual also gives planning, scheduling, and pretest orientation suggestions, as well as guidance concerning the meaning and use of the various derived scores, and construction of student profiles.

INTERPRETATION AND NORMS. The user is also provided with a clear and informative guide for interpretation and use. Included is an excellent discussion of the characteristics, applications, and interpretation of raw and derived scores. In addition, much backup information is provided concerning planning a reading assessment program and using the results for both instructional and administrative purposes. One noteworthy feature of the ISRT is that, through a large equating study and the use of Thurstonian scaling procedures, a system of continuous interlevel standard scores has been developed that permits the user to relate scores obtained for a given test at one level to performance on the test at the other two levels.

The norms for the ISRT appear more than satisfactory, being based on representative public school standardization samples, in terms of geographical location, size of school district, and social class factors. These samples are also sufficiently large to render their performance levels stable, typically ranging from about 2,000 to 3,000 students in each grade, at each level, on each of Forms E and F. Such large, carefully specified, and representative norms give the ISRT an interpretive appeal enjoyed by few other reading tests.

Although the Level 2 and, particularly, Level 3 tests are of sufficient difficulty and discriminating power to be used with college students—and, in fact, are described as covering this range—no norms beyond grade 12 are provided. The user *could* use the norms for grade 12 students "planning to attend a 4-year college or university" with students actually attending college or university, but normative interpretation would be difficult. Thus, at this time, the ISRT really has somewhat restricted usefulness at the college level or beyond. Colleges and universities could, of course, develop local norms, but a welcome further addition to the ISRT interpretive materials would be college and university norms.

RELIABILITY AND VALIDITY. Reliability was assessed at each level by an alternate-forms study, with a two to three week interval and counterbalanced order, and by calculation of K-R 21 coefficients (except for the speeded reading efficiency test). All students in one grade in an entire school district were used in the assessment of alternate-forms reliability. The median reliabilities for the subtests follow: vocabulary, .86; comprehension, .83; directed reading, .81; efficiency, .77; power (vocabulary and comprehension), .90. It should be noted that an undesirably high degree of student heterogeneity for reliability assessment (1,052 grade 7 students in a school district, for example) may have inflated these coefficients somewhat. The internal-consistency coefficients are similarly inflated, but to an even greater extent, since they are based on entire norm groups, with resulting tremendous heterogeneity. This inflation is offset to an unknown extent, however, by the inexplicable use of the K-R 21 formula to obtain "estimates of Kuder-Richardson Formula #20 reliability coefficients." Surely it is unnecessary, with modern-

Iowa Silent Reading Tests

day computing capabilities, to "estimate," rather than calculate, K-R 20! The use of entire norm samples, or random subsamples of them, in reliability estimation is not uncommon; it is, nonetheless, poor psychometric practice, giving a higher reliability estimate than that which would be realized by a particular user, with a relatively homogeneous sample. It seems true that the individual ISRT tests are adequately reliable. The reliability assessment procedures, however, are not the best, and more defensible estimates could be provided.

Validity data are scanty. Regarding content validity, the user is invited to consult the rationale for, and content of, each test, as discussed in the supporting documents. Concurrent validation results are given, for Levels 1 and 2, in the form of correlations between scores on the ISRT vocabulary and reading comprehension tests (and their sum), and those on the corresponding tests of the *Metropolitan Reading Tests*. These correlations, presented separately by grade, tend to be in the .70s and .80s, but again considerable heterogeneity of range is a factor to be considered. No predictive validity data are presented. However, it may well be that, particularly at the grade levels covered by the ISRT, it makes more sense to consider reading ability as a *criterion,* rather than predictor, variable. Some correlational results between the ISRT tests and various academic achievement criteria would, nonetheless, have been informative.

SUMMARY. The ISRT is likely the best test series currently available for the assessment of reading skills at the grade 6 level and up. The tests are carefully constructed and based on sound principles, and appear to have adequate reliability and excellent interpretive qualities through their careful and thorough standardization. Although it seems conceptually sensible to regard reading ability as *multifaceted,* there is no evidence that the ISRT vocabulary, reading comprehension, directed reading, and reading efficiency tests are *multifactorial.* The intercorrelations given, for example, for 2,707 grade 7 students taking the Level 1 Form E tests, between the vocabulary test and the other three tests are .84, .80, and .67. The remaining three correlations (excluding vocabulary) are .83, .70, and .68. After disattenuation, it is clear that the individual ISRT tests tap, to a major extent,

the differential psychologist's "verbal ability" trait, and this is undoubtedly true of other reading tests. Quite clearly, one and only one common factor accounts for the above correlations. For this reason, it is difficult to envision the ISRT—or its competitors—as having much *diagnostic* utility. For *assessment* purposes, however, the 1973 ISRT series is, all things considered, an impressive addition to the current inventory of reading tests.

J Ed Meas 12(1):57–60 sp '75. Frederick B. Davis. * Because most of the subtests appear to be somewhat speeded and one of the subtests at each level is moderately speeded, the administrator must be well informed about the procedures, alert, conscientious, and equipped with an accurate timing device that has a second hand. Consequently, the reviewer suggests that trained examiners be used to administer these tests with classroom teachers acting only as proctors. Although the scores on each subtest are based on the number of items marked correctly (without correction for guessing), the examinees are not explicitly told this and the examiner is enjoined not to emphasize the importance of speed or guessing beyond the instructions provided in the manual. Since questions are invited in the oral directions for some subtests, there may be some awkward moments when examinees ask whether their scores are to be corrected for guessing or include a subtraction for wrong answers. The examiner must apparently evade the question because he has not been instructed to state the facts and professional ethics forbid him to lie. The directions for the most highly speeded subtest (Reading Efficiency) tell the examiner that "pupils are not to be informed of the time limits; to do so places too great an emphasis on very rapid reading instead of efficient reading." What rate of work each examinee sets for himself depends on what he thinks is best when he is told that the purpose of the test is "to find out how ACCURATE you are when you read FAST." Without knowledge of how much time he is to be allowed, he has to decide what "fast" means in practice. Would it be better to tell him the time limit and ask him to "read as fast as you can without making careless mistakes?" The directions for Test 1 include the statement, "If you are not sure of the answer to a question, make the best choice you can, but do not make any wild guesses." A variant of this appears in the directions for some, but not all, other parts. A test-wise examinee knows that he is most likely not to lower his score by marking an answer to every item even if he makes "wild guesses" on some of them (especially those he doesn't have time to reach in the time limit), and may raise it by so doing. So he ignores the directions. However, the conscientious or naive examinee tends to follow them and thus place himself at a disadvantage relative to his more sophisticated or less conscientious fellow examinees. To the extent that this occurs, the validity of the scores as measures of reading skills suffers. To prevent this, the edition of the *Standards for Educational and Psychological Tests and Manuals* that was current when the tests were published recommends (on page 33) that correction for guessing be used unless there is "a generous time limit *and* a warning is given by the proctor near the end concerning the amount of time remaining *and* instructions are unequivocal to mark every item, including pure guesses. ESSENTIAL." Inspection of the items in the subtests indicates that they are generally of good quality. The passages on which the reading-comprehension items are based seem varied in subject matter, appropriate, and intrinsically interesting in many instances. An effort has been made to measure the major operational skills of comprehension in a balanced way in each of Forms E and F. The reviewer judges that success in marking items correctly without reading or referring to the passages on which they are based (a skill that, in any event, greatly overlaps that of marking items correctly after reading or referring to the passages) is of trivial consequence in determining scores on these tests. Furthermore, random marking of all items yields percentile ranks that tend to be low. Whether dictionary skills or knowledge of how to use library resources (like a card catalogue) should be included in a reading test the reviewer does not know. Since the Directed-Reading scores (which these work-study skills help to determine) are reported separately, they do not influence the reading-comprehension scores. The intercorrelations of the subtest scores suggest that the Reading-Efficiency scores are determined to a considerable degree by the way examinees react to directions to read "fast"

when "fast" has not been defined for them in terms of a time limit for a specified number of items. * Stanines are recommended for intersubtest comparisons in profile charts even though, strictly speaking, their comparability in new groups rests on the assumption that all of the subtest scores are equally reliable. In general, it would appear that the reliability coefficients of most of the subtests in the *Iowa Silent Reading Tests* are high enough to warrant reporting scores in more than the nine stanine categories * Standard errors of measurement for subtest raw scores based on a counter-balanced administration of both Forms E and F.... are reported * Since standard scores, stanines, or percentile ranks are actually reported for examinees, the over-all standard errors of measurement are of no value to most test users. In short, only a small amount of conveniently useful reliability data are provided for interpretive purposes. To be sure, standard errors of measurement for standard scores are included in the tables that report data based on the use of Kuder-Richardson equation no. 21. But, to the extent that the tests are speeded, these standard errors of measurement may be too small to a degree that varies from subtest to subtest. Strictly speaking, the correlation coefficient between two parallel forms of a test is not a reliability coefficient unless the variances of the two forms are identical, or at least insignificantly different at some preselected level. Since this requirement is not met by scores for some of the subtests, some of the coefficients reported represent slightly inflated alternate-forms reliability coefficients. Perhaps the best estimates, given the subtest data provided in the manuals, would be obtained by using the equation: $r_{EE'} = r_{FF'} = 2S_E S_F r_{EF}/(V_E + V_F)$. Reliability coefficients are chiefly useful for research purposes, so they should be reported as accurately as possible. The *Guide for Interpretation and Use* for each of Levels 1–3 includes excellent suggestions for reporting and interpreting scores. The material is outstandingly helpful. In addition, some technical data are provided. Fortunately, no space is wasted on studies of the predictive, concurrent, or congruent validity of the tests.

Meas & Eval Guid 8(2):123–6 Jl '75. Russell Hunter and Ralph Hoepfner. * The manuals are comprehensive, well organized, and provide useful information. * Despite the fact that the

Iowa Silent Reading Tests

manual states that level 3 is for use with college students, no norms are provided for this population. * Considerable space is devoted to suggestions as to how the results might be employed, but prescriptive suggestions are not made for the individual teacher. Nor is genuine diagnostic information provided, except that of the most general nature. National standardization was performed in 1972 for levels 1, 2, and 3 on the populations of 20, 23, and 15 school districts, respectively. The manuals do not explain the discrepancy of numbers nor do they state the extent of mutual inclusivity of the districts. The norm sample was described as being chosen on the basis of geographic location, size of school district, and a socioeconomic index based on income and education of adults in the community, but no specifics are provided. The schools were selected to represent students "most likely to be taking the ISRT"; however, this would imply that the norm sample is biased to the higher end of the socioeconomic scale. * The ISRT is a comprehensive, norm-referenced test of various aspects of reading that may be used from the sixth through the twelfth grades. The tests were competently developed; the manuals provide a wealth of information for the user; and the test has been exhaustively analyzed statistically. In terms of technical competence, the publishers have maintained the highest measurement standards in its preparation. Due to their highly academic nature and their time requirements, however, the subtests of the ISRT should be considered as special and intensive reading tests and not as components of a comprehensive testing program.

[731]

*Maintaining Reading Efficiency Tests. Grades 7–16 and adults; 1966–74; MRET; 3 scores: rate, comprehension accuracy, reading efficiency; no norms for grades 8–10 and 12; 5 forms; reading booklet ('70, 13 pages) for each form; test booklet ('70, 4 pages) for each form; no manual; interpretive data and answer keys ['74, 4 pages]; $7.50 per 20 reading booklets; $2.50 per test booklet; $2.50 per specimen set; cash orders postpaid; [30–40] minutes; Lyle L. Miller; Developmental Reading Distributors. *
a) TEST 1, HISTORY OF BRAZIL, 1970 REVISION. 1966–70.
b) TEST 2, HISTORY OF JAPAN, 1970 REVISION. 1966–70.
c) TEST 3, HISTORY OF INDIA. 1970.
d) TEST 4, HISTORY OF NEW ZEALAND. 1970.
e) TEST 5, HISTORY OF SWITZERLAND. 1970.

ALTON L. RAYGOR, *Professor of Educational Psychology and Coordinator, Reading and* *Study Skills Center, University of Minnesota, Minneapolis, Minnesota.*

These tests consist of five selections, each describing the history of a country, followed by 50 comprehension items. Rate of reading is determined by timing for 10 minutes. Scores on the comprehension measure are influenced by the rate score, since the student answers only questions covered in the portion completed for the rate measure.

Timing varies from student to student. All receive 10 minutes to read, but some who read more than 500 words per minute can start answering comprehension questions immediately. No time limit is imposed on the comprehension part.

The usual procedures for item development and selection were apparently not followed in this test. The five selections "were designed at the same level of readability as measured by the Flesch Formula" and the passages "were standardized at the same length and with the same number of questions." All test exercises were balanced with the same proportion of completion, multiple choice, and true-false questions. All five tests were reviewed by four or more staff members and "were used experimentally with 25 or more students."

No information is given on item development, scope and sequence considerations, item-analysis, item difficulty, or any of the usual expected topics.

It is difficult to address the questions usually considered in a test review because of the lack of information provided. No reliability or validity information is given, and the normative information consists of distributions of four groups.

The tests are unusual in several respects: (a) The items are a mixture of completion, multiple choice, and true-false. (b) The rate scores are calibrated from 0 to 60,000 words per minute. (c) The rate in words per minute is multiplied by the percent of items correct out of a variable number tried to get a "rate of comprehension" score which is then reported in the norm tables. (d) No directions are given for administering the tests other than what can be found on the student's answer sheet.

In summary, these tests appear to be put together without the usual attention to test development procedures. As a result, it is even hard to discuss them in the same way. They are more like tests that are teacher-constructed for use in a classroom than they are like standardized tests. This reviewer would not recommend them for anything other than informal use, possibly as practice exercises in a class.

[732]

*Metropolitan Achievement Tests: Reading Tests. Grades 2.5–3.4, 3.5–4.9, 5.0–6.9, 7.0–9.5; 1931–73; 3 scores: word knowledge, reading, total; 3 forms; 4 levels; battery manual for interpreting ('73, 120 pages); battery teacher's handbook ('71, 16–17 pages) for each level; $8.50 per 35 tests; $1.50 per set of hand scoring stencils; $7 per battery manual for interpreting; postage extra; specimen set not available; Walter N. Durost, Harold H. Bixler, J. Wayne Wrightstone, George A. Prescott, and Irving H. Balow; Psychological Corporation. *
a) PRIMARY 2. Grades 2.5–3.4; Forms F ('70), G ('71), H ('71), (8 pages); directions ('70, 8 pages); scoring service, $1.30 and over per test; 48(60) minutes.
b) ELEMENTARY. Grades 3.5–4.9; Forms F ('70), G ('71), H ('71), (8 pages); battery directions ('70, 13 pages); separate answer sheets (MRC) may be used; $8.50 per 100 answer sheets; $1 per MRC hand scoring stencil; scoring service: 40¢ and over per answer sheet, $1.30 and over per test booklet; 40(50) minutes.
c) INTERMEDIATE. Grades 5.0–6.9; Forms F ('70), G ('71), H ('71), (7 pages); battery directions ('70, 19 pages); separate answer sheets (Digitek, IBM 805, IBM 1230, MRC) may be used; answer sheets: $3 per 35 Digitek or IBM 1230, $2.50 per 35 IBM 805, $2.85 per 35 MRC; $1 per Digitek or IBM scoring stencil; $1 per MRC hand scoring stencil; Digitek or IBM scoring service, 60¢ and over per test; MRC scoring service, 40¢ and over per test; 40(50) minutes.
d) ADVANCED. Grades 7.0–9.5; Forms F ('70), G ('71), H ('71), (8 pages); battery directions ('70, 19 pages); answer sheets, prices, and time same as for intermediate level.

See T2:1567 (12 references) and 7:696 (16 references); for a review by H. Alan Robinson of an earlier edition, see 6:797 (4 references); for reviews by James R. Hobson and Margaret G. McKim, see 4:543; for a review by D. A. Worcester, see 2:1551; for reviews by Ivan A. Booker and Joseph C. Dewey, see 1:1105. For reviews of the complete battery, see 22 (2 reviews, 1 excerpt), 6:15 (2 reviews), 4:18 (1 review), 2:1189 (2 reviews), and 1:874 (3 reviews).

REFERENCES

1–4. See 6:797.
5–20. See 7:696.
21–32. See T2:1567; also includes a cumulative name index to the first 32 references and 6 reviews for this test.
33. DAVIS, FREDERICK B. "Reporting Test Data in the Media: Two Case Studies." Read Teach 26(3):305–10 D '72. *
34. FOLLMAN, JOHN, AND LOWE, A. J. "Empirical Examination of Critical Reading and Critical Thinking—An Overview." J Read Behav 5(3):159–68 su '72–73. * (PA 51:12009)
35. GUTHRIE, JOHN T.; GOLDBERG, HERMAN K.; AND FINUCCI, JOAN. "Independence of Abilities in Disabled Readers." J Read Behav 4(2):129–38 sp '72. *
36. HUTCHINSON, JUNE O'SHIELDS. "Reading Tests and Nonstandard Language." Read Teach 25(5):430–7 F '72. * (PA 49:3202) (For reply, see 37.)
37. KARLSEN, BJORN. "Test Prejudice: A Reply." Letter. Read Teach 26(1):73+ O '72. *
38. KELLY, JANET SHEARER. Variables Related to Academic Achievement in Lower Socioeconomic Status Intermediate School Children. Doctor's thesis, New York University (New York, N.Y.), 1972. (DAI 33:2908B)
39. LIVINGSTON, HOWARD F. "What the Reading Test Doesn't Test—Reading." J Read 15(6):402–10 Mr '72. *
40. PETERSON, JOE. "Metropolitan Achievement Tests: Reading, Advanced Level: A Review," pp. 28–31. In Reading Tests for the Secondary Grades. Edited by William Blanton and others. Newark, Del.: International Reading Association, Inc., 1972. Pp. iv, 55. *
41. COHEN, SHELDON; GLASS, DAVID C.; AND SINGER, JEROME E. "Apartment Noise, Auditory Discrimination, and Reading Ability in Children." J Exp Social Psychol 9(5):407–22 S '73. * (PA 51:8197)
42. DURHAM, LINDA LARUE. An Investigation of the Remedial Reading Program and Its Alternatives for Seventh Graders in Laramie Public Schools. Doctor's thesis, University of Wyoming (Laramie, Wyo.), 1973. (DAI 34:2290A)
43. FOWLER, ELAINE D. "Predicting Reading Achievement of Spanish-Speaking First Grade Children." Read Improv 10(3):7–11 w '73. *
44. FRY, MAURINE A., AND JOHNSON, CAROLE SCHULTE. "Oral Language Production and Reading Achievement Among Selected Students." J Am Indian Ed 13(1):22–7 O '73. *
45. OAKLAND, THOMAS D.; WILLIAMS, FERN C.; AND HARMER, WILLIAM R. "A Longitudinal Study of Auditory Perception and Reading Instruction With First-Grade Negro Children." J Spec Ed 7(2):141–54 su '73. * (PA 52:4081)
46. SCOTT, DIANA. The Effectiveness of Teaching Strategies Related to Modality Preferences of Pupils With Reading Difficulties at the End of Grade One. Doctor's thesis, Ball State University (Muncie, Ind.), 1973. (DAI 34:2446A)
47. JONES, SUE ANN. Concept Attainment and Reading Achievement. Doctor's thesis, University of Missouri (Columbia, Mo.), 1974. (DAI 36:1178A)
48. LOMBARDI, VINCENT A. The Effect of Test Anxiety on the Relationship Between Intelligence and Reading Achievement in a Group of Seventh Grade Suburban Children. Doctor's thesis, Temple University (Philadelphia, Pa.), 1974. (DAI 35:3528A)
49. LORD, FREDERIC M. "Quick Estimates of the Relative Efficiency of Two Tests as a Function of Ability Level." J Ed Meas 11(4):247–54 w '74. *
50. LORET, PETER G.; SEDER, ALAN; BIANCHINI, JOHN C.; AND VALE, CAROL A. Anchor Test Study: Equivalence and Norms Tables for Selected Reading Achievement Tests (Grades 4, 5, and 6). DHEW Publication S/N 1780–01312. Washington, D.C.: Government Printing Office, 1974. Pp. ix, 92. *
51. MARCO, GARY L. "A Comparison of Selected School Effectiveness Measures Based on Longitudinal Data." J Ed Meas 11(4):225–34 w '74. *
52. MARSH, LINDA KESSLER. Self-Esteem, Achievement Responsibility, and Reading Achievement of Lower-Class Black, White, and Hispanic Seventh-Grade Boys. Doctor's thesis, New York University (New York, N.Y.), 1974. (DAI 35:6514A)
53. PAULUS, NANCY JANE. Analysis of Socioeconomic Group and Racial Group Score Differences on a Comparison of Two Measures of Reading Comprehension Achievement Earned by Fifth Grade Students. Doctor's thesis, Duke University (Durham, N.C.), 1974. (DAI 35:4872A)
54. PUSSER, H. ELLISON, AND McCANDLESS, BOYD R. "Socialization Dimensions Among Inner-City Five-Year-Olds and Later School Success: A Follow-Up." J Ed Psychol 66(3):285–90 Je '74. * (PA 52:11024)
55. TAPSCOTT, BARBARA McCAULEY. An Investigation of the Impact of Instructional Objectives on the Reading Achievement of Students in the Primary Grades. Doctor's thesis, University of North Carolina (Chapel Hill, N.C.), 1974. (DAI 35:4952A)
56. TUINMAN, J. JAAP. "Determining the Passage Dependency of Comprehension Questions in 5 Major Tests." Read Res Q 9(2):206–23 '73–74 ['74]. * (PA 53:2010)
57. COPPEDGE, JOYCE LUVERNE. The Academic Achievement, Self Concept, Social Behavior, and Attendance of Ethnically Different, but Racially Similar Children Attending an Urban Public School. Doctor's thesis, Fordham University (New York, N.Y.), 1975. (DAI 36:5899A)
58. DIVINE, JAMES HAROLD. An Investigation Into the Relationship Between Self-Esteem and Reading Achievement. Doctor's thesis, Northern Illinois University (DeKalb, Ill.), 1975. (DAI 36:2095A)
59. LINN, ROBERT L. "Anchor Test Study: The Long and the Short of It." J Ed Meas 12(3):201–13 f '75. *
60. McCORMICK, CHARLES HAROLD. The Prediction of Arithmetic and Reading Achievement From Selected Affective Measures. Doctor's thesis, Northern Illinois University (DeKalb, Ill.), 1975. (DAI 36:2107A)
61. POLIRSTOK, SUSAN ROVET. "The Relationship Between Birth Order and Reading Ability in Urban Ninth Grade Junior High School Students." Grad Res Ed & Related Discip 8(1):68–97 sp '75. *
62. DRISKILL, ROBERT EUGENE. Selected Factors Relating to Reading Achievement. Doctor's thesis, University of Arizona (Tucson, Ariz.), 1976. (DAI 37:1384A)
63. NYSTROM, ROBERTA KAY. Standardized Achievement Measurement With the Educationally Handicapped—Normalization or Further Segregation? Doctor's thesis, University of

Southern California (Los Angeles, Calif.), 1976. (*DAI* 37: 2082A)
    64. OLSON, PATRICIA HAGEY. *The Relationship of Selected Oral Language Components to Reading Achievement of Third Grade Students.* Doctor's thesis, University of Arizona (Tucson, Ariz.), 1976. (*DAI* 37:1390A)

FRED PYRCZAK, *Associate Professor of Education, California State University, Los Angeles, California.*

This test, a major norm-referenced reading test, is accompanied by a large amount of technical data. This review highlights some of its special strengths and weaknesses.

ITEMS. Although most of the items in this test are skillfully written, some are clearly flawed. For example, many of the word knowledge items have keyed answers that are not, strictly speaking, correct. Combining stems with the keyed choices, we often obtain such incorrect statements as these: "A *loud noise* is a bang" and "To *notice* is to observe." Although this type of flaw may not adversely affect the students' performance on the test, it is distasteful to both students and teachers who strive for scholarly precision in the use of words. The *Cooperative English Tests: Reading Comprehension* is an example of a test with word knowledge items that are relatively free from this type of flaw.

Some of the comprehension items, based on associated passages, are actually passage-independent. That is, it is possible for the examinee to determine the correct answers to the items without actually reading the associated passages. Tuinman (56) reported data on the passage-independence of items based on passages in five major reading tests, including the Metropolitan. He found that all five were deficient to some extent in terms of this characteristic.

At the lower levels, many of the items on associated passages lack attractive distractors. For example, in Primary 2, Form F, the distractors for an item are "Saturday" and "Tuesday"; neither of these days is mentioned in the associated passage. "Sunday," the correct answer, is mentioned in the passage. It is not necessary to comprehend the passage, the item, or even the word "Sunday," to recognize that "Sunday" is probably the correct answer. This type of flaw is common in reading tests written for the primary grades.

Those who plan to use the test with culturally diverse groups will find Report No. 23 of special interest. In it, the authors describe selected items that were revised or eliminated from the Metropolitan on the basis of reviews by members of minority groups. The authors are to be commended for taking this step. In future reports, it would be desirable to list the minority groups that were represented by reviewers and to indicate what criteria were used in reviewing the items.

INTERPRETATION. The material on interpreting scores in both the battery Teacher's Handbook and the battery Manual for Interpreting is clearly written and, for the most part, sound. A strong point is the stress placed on the inherent defects of grade equivalents.

Some of the interpretations suggested in the handbook would be better made with the aid of criterion-referenced reading tests. Metropolitan reading scores will reliably indicate only broad areas of strength and weakness in reading and will be of little use in the selection of instructional materials. Criterion-referenced tests such as those that accompany the *Fountain Valley Teacher Support System in Reading* will perform these functions much more adequately.

The section in the handbook on the comparison of achievement scores with aptitude scores probably will encourage teachers to make such comparisons for individual students. Unfortunately, the material does not adequately warn against the pitfalls in comparing aptitude scores with achievement scores; it fails to point out the need for an aptitude test that measures those specific skills that underlie the achievement domain in question.

TECHNICAL CONSIDERATIONS. The procedures followed to insure content validity are appropriate for a norm-referenced reading test designed for national use. The handbook correctly warns, however, that "Since each school has its own curriculum, the content validity of *Metropolitan Achievement Tests* must be evaluated by each school."

The K-R 20 and corrected split-half reliability coefficients for subtests are acceptably high. Unfortunately, reliability estimates based upon more than one administration of the test are not given. The authors argue that such estimates are irrelevant since they may be influenced by sources of error that are not inherent characteristics of the test. It seems to this writer, however, that it is important for test users to have estimates of all sources of error variance.

Metropolitan Achievement Tests: Reading Tests

The standardization program seems more than adequate, considering the complexities of such programs.

SUMMARY. Even though this reviewer has pointed out some weaknesses in individual items, in the interpretative material for teachers, and in the estimation of reliability, the *Metropolitan Achievement Tests: Reading Tests* is good for obtaining a rough indication of broad areas of strength and weakness in reading.

DARRELL L. SABERS, *Professor of Educational Psychology, The University of Arizona, Tucson, Arizona.*

These tests, often referred to as the *Metropolitan Reading Tests,* are part of the larger achievement battery and are offered as separate tests for the primary 2 through advanced levels.

The total reading score is a combination of the word knowledge and reading subtests. The word knowledge subtest measures vocabulary and word recognition. The reading subtest is a measure of sentence meaning and paragraph meaning at the primary level, paragraph meaning at the elementary level, and paragraph plus larger selection comprehension at the intermediate and advanced levels. The items are multiple choice. Perhaps as many as one-half of the items can be answered correctly, especially by the well-informed student, without reading the passage.

Although the 1970 edition differs very little from the previous edition, it should continue to be a popular survey instrument. In addition to a separate teacher's handbook for each level, the excellent battery technical manual, called Manual for Interpreting, and many special reports are available from the publishers. These materials present suggestions for using the scores that appear to be understandable and should result in proper and justified score interpretation if more educators using the tests would utilize them.

From a technical viewpoint, the tests are excellent. The standardization was based on a very large sample representative of the national population of school children. Tables are available for obtaining grade equivalents, percentiles, and stanines. To use these tables, raw scores are first converted to "standard scores," which in this case are actually scaled scores. There is one obvious omission with respect to the norm data; there are no provisions for interpreting school system averages or classroom standing.

The reliabilities of the tests are adequate for survey instruments providing a general measure of reading achievement. Reliability coefficients for the subtests are above .90 and for the total reading score are near .95. The standard errors of measurement are well below one-half a grade unit. Both the standard errors and the split-half reliabilities are based on an odd-even split of items, a procedure which is inappropriate for reading tests that have several items based on one passage. The effect of this incorrect procedure will be slight but will make the test appear more reliable.

Report No. 2 provides a complete table of specifications to help one in assessing the content validity of the tests. The authors suggest that each staff considering the tests should decide for themselves whether the tests have content validity for their school, because no test can be universally valid.

There is one aspect of the reading tests that differs from the other subtests of the *Metropolitan Achievement Tests.* The reading tests do not have the ridiculous Don't Know (DK) and the often misunderstood Not Given (NG) distractors found in the other Metropolitan subtests. These aspects of the other tests in the battery make the norms invalid (e.g., see the battery review by Findley in the Sixth MMY). This reviewer has visited two schools where the students refer to NG as No Good and say that they mark DK when the answer is not given. The reading tests avoid these problems.

One problem facing any teacher using standardized tests is to determine how much test practice to give students. This problem may be especially prominent when the teacher reads in the handbook: "If pupils are coached or practiced on the test, the teacher may not get an accurate picture of the pupils." Obviously, the students should not practice on the actual test items, but the statement tends to discourage the necessary practice with standardized test formats. Because standardized tests are very different from the tasks faced daily by most students, there is a real need to allow the students to become familiar with timed, multiple choice tests. Practice in taking standardized tests is especially important for students in classrooms using an "open education" or a language-experi-

ence approach to reading. The former often produces children who have difficulty attending to a
multiple choice test for a sustained period of
time unless there has been provision for such
practice, and the latter often produces children
who relate better to their own experiences than
to the printed page in isolation.

In one aspect it is evident the MAT authors
are aware of children's test behavior. The directions for these tests do not include telling the
time limits to young children. This omission is
very good, because young children may either
feel panic because the time is too short or give
up because the tasks take too long.

The directions for administering and scoring
are clear and uncomplicated with one exception.
In scoring, the teacher is told that items are
either right, wrong, or omitted. The score is the
number right. The teacher might well wonder
how omits differ from wrongs when all are considered wrong in computing the score. The
items are, in fact, either right or wrong.

In summary, these tests are as good as any
and better than most standardized reading tests.
The decision as to whether to use the Metropolitan or other reading tests should be based
on how the content of the competing tests agrees
with the user's definition of reading. The authors of the *Metropolitan Reading Tests* consider reading to be approximately equal parts
of word knowledge and sentence or paragraph
meaning, but what is actually measured is best
assessed by the potential user examining each
item on the test.

[733]

★National Teacher Examinations: Introduction
to the Teaching of Reading. College seniors and
teachers; 1972–76; test administered 3 times annually
(February, July, November) at centers established by
the publisher; Forms VNT1, S-VNT1, VNT2, ('73,
21 pages); descriptive booklet ('72, 8 pages); for program accessories, see 381; examination fee, $11 per
candidate; 120(165) minutes; Educational Testing
Service. *
For reviews of the testing program, see 381 (2 reviews).

[734]

*National Teacher Examinations: Reading Spe-
cialist. College seniors and teachers; 1969–76; test
administered 3 times annually (February, July, November) at centers established by the publisher; formerly entitled *National Teacher Examinations: Reading Specialist—Elementary School;* Forms WNT1
('74, 23 pages), WNT2 ('74, 20 pages); descriptive
booklet ('73, 9 pages); for program accessories, see
381; examination fee, $13 per candidate; 120(165)
minutes; Educational Testing Service. *

For reviews of the testing program, see 381 (2 reviews) and 7:582 (2 reviews).

H. ALAN ROBINSON, *Professor of Reading,
Hofstra University, Hempstead, New York.*
[Review of Forms WNT1 and WNT2.]

The Reading Specialist examination is a
paper-and-pencil test containing 150 five-choice
items focused on the teaching and supervising of
reading, kindergarten through grade twelve.
The examination must be completed within 120
minutes. According to the nine-page booklet
made available to candidates who want to prepare for the examination, the test is designed to
assess knowledge and understanding of methods
and materials. The examination is suggested as
most appropriate for those with advanced preparation who expect to become reading specialists.

Test items were constructed and/or reviewed
by a committee of highly qualified reading specialists. The test runs a gamut from broad questions related to principles of instruction, to specifics about content and techniques, to questions
about the roles of a reading specialist. The overall impression is of an eclectic approach to reading, although the test taker whose training and
conceptual framework are largely psycholinguistic may be somewhat penalized. Of ten sample
questions in the booklet about the examination,
this reviewer, who views reading as a psycholinguistic process, earned a score of 80 percent
—one item correct through logical guessing.
One "error" was the result of not knowing two
tests for "checking the child's blending skills."
The other "error" occurred because the question couldn't be answered by someone operating
out of this reviewer's conceptual framework.

The Educational Testing Service has not published normative data about this test. The reviewer had to depend on a 1974 in-house test
analysis report concerned with a description of
test characteristics and only suggestive of
norms.

Although in an oral discussion with the NTE
Program Administrator and in the description
of the test, it is said to have been designed "for
candidates with advanced preparation who expect to have special responsibilities related to
teaching reading at any grade level from kindergarten through twelve," the "norming" data
were based on results from 128 seniors in teachers' colleges and candidates for teaching positions. Although only 120 tests were analyzed,

the "norm" group appeared to consist of 98 " 'best prepared' candidates" and 30 "other candidates"; the meanings of "best prepared" and "others" were not clarified. In addition, though the Program Director assured this reviewer that only an error was made in using the wrong title, the test analysis report consistently used the title "Reading Specialist in the Elementary School" in discussing the analytical findings.

The K-R 20 estimate of the reliability coefficient is .86. Only 77.5 percent of the candidates were able to complete the test.

Aside from the problems related to making decisions about "knowledge and understanding" on a limited 150-item test of this nature and the problems seemingly involved in "norming," one must raise questions about purposes and uses of such an examination. In a booklet for candidates, four purposes and uses are cited: "[1] to measure the candidate's competence in the area of reading instruction; [2] to provide information useful in identifying strengths and weaknesses in the candidate's preparation; [3] to serve educational institutions in their efforts to improve the preparation of reading teachers and specialists; [4] to provide one type of quantitative information useful in the selection or certification of reading teachers and specialists."

Purpose 1. Can "competence in the area of reading instruction" be evaluated with such an examination? The answer is obviously dependent upon one's concept of "competence" and what is meant by "the area of reading instruction." To this reviewer "competence" means the ability and skill to execute a task. Certainly this paper-and-pencil test cannot measure teaching ability, application of procedures, and interaction with students. Even if "competence" is equated with "knowledge and understanding," a problem exists. One may have *knowledge* without understanding. One may have *understanding* without the ability to implement.

Purpose 2. There was no evidence of any effort to cluster items together for diagnostic purposes. And if there were, it is doubtful that reliability could be established for the few items that would cluster together around a specific strength or weakness. At best the instrument would serve as an extremely rough and preliminary measurement of strengths and weaknesses related to the conceptual frameworks of the designers.

Purpose 3. Perhaps the examination would have some use in helping an institution look at its program, since all students would be coping with the same experience—IF the tests could then be analyzed and discussed by the group. There is some confusion in this purpose and the next one in regard to the use of the term "reading teachers and specialists." The examination is supposed to be for reading specialists; yet the descriptive material distinguishes between those who teach and those who supervise. Does the one examination adequately cope with both?

Purpose 4. The admirable part of this purpose is that the term "one type of quantitative information" is used. Indeed, that is what this examination represents—one small piece of quantitative information. The second part of this statement of purpose, "useful in the selection or certification of reading teachers and specialists," can be a dangerous and erroneous concept unless many other valuable means of evaluation are included. One hopes that students and classroom teachers will be serviced by reading specialists who possess knowledge, understanding, competence, and humanitarianism.

The *National Teacher Examination: Reading Specialist* needs better and clearer "norming" procedures. Its construction also needs to be evaluated: Should the committee of examiners be broadened to include a larger representation from a number of conceptual frameworks? Is multiple choice the best means of measuring whatever is to be measured—knowledge? understanding? competence? Should more attention be paid to larger reliable clusters of questions that might be used to ascertain candidates' strengths and weaknesses? Certainly the suggested purposes and uses ought to be reconsidered and spelled out in nonambiguous terms.

Unless the "norming" procedures can be clarified in relation to the target population, and the purposes and uses carefully delineated, this reviewer does not recommend this examination even as one type of quantitative information on which to base decisions about the prospective reading specialist.

[735]

Nelson-Denny Reading Test, Forms C and D. Grades 9-16 and adults; 1929-76; NDRT; previous edition (Forms A and B, '60) still available; 4 scores: vocabulary, comprehension, total, rate; Forms C, D, ('73, 12 pages); manual ('73, 45 pages); student report folder ('73, 4 pages); profile-norms ('76, 2 pages) for adults; separate answer sheets (Digitek, IBM 1230, self-marking) or cards (MRC) must be used; $9 per 35 tests; $55.50 per 500 Digitek answer sheets; $42 per 500 IBM answer sheets; $9 per set of 35 self-marking answer sheets, 35 report folders, and manual; $5.40 per 100 MRC answer cards; $1.05 per Digitek or IBM scoring stencil; $2.40 per 35 report folders; $2.40 per 35 profiles; $1.65 per manual; $2.40 per specimen set; postage extra; MRC scoring service, 24¢ and over per test ($12 minimum); 30(35) minutes for regular administration, 22.5(28) minutes for administration to superior students and adults; James I. Brown, M. J. Nelson, and E. C. Denny; Houghton Mifflin Co. *

See T2:1572 (46 references); for reviews by David B. Orr and Agatha Townsend and an excerpted review by John O. Crites of Forms A and B, see 6:800 (13 references); for a review by Ivan A. Booker, see 4:544 (17 references); for a review by Hans C. Gordon, see 2:1557 (6 references).

REFERENCES

1–6. See 2:1557.
7–23. See 4:544.
24–36. See 6:800.
37–82. See T2:1572; also includes a cumulative name index to the first 82 references, 4 reviews, and 1 excerpt for this test.
83. MANN, HORACE, JR. A Study of Selected Academic and Interest Variables in Relation to Achievement in a College of Engineering. Doctor's thesis, Oklahoma State University (Stillwater, Okla.), 1971. (DAI 33:591A)
84. STUART, EUDENE MAY. The Relationship Between Selected Language Arts and Proofreading Performance. Doctor's thesis, University of North Dakota (Grand Forks, N.D.), 1971. (DAI 33:232A)
85. FARR, ROGER. "Nelson-Denny Reading Test: A Review," pp. 31–4. In Reading Tests for the Secondary Grades. Edited by William Blanton and others. Newark, Del.: International Reading Association, Inc., 1972. Pp. iv, 55. *
86. KOZIEY, P. W., AND BRAUER, J. H. "Using Mental Practice to Improve Reading Performance." Alberta J Ed Res (Canada) 18(3):190–5 S '72. * (PA 49:9972)
87. PYRCZAK, FRED. "Objective Evaluation of the Quality of Multiple-Choice Test Items Designed to Measure Comprehension of Reading Passages." Read Res Q 8(1):62–71 f '72. * (PA 50:5825)
88. SLOTHOWER, MAMIE. A Descriptive Analysis of Personality and Academic Characteristics of Freshman Students at Langston University. Doctor's thesis, Oklahoma State University (Stillwater, Okla.), 1972. (DAI 34:2399A)
89. CARVER, RONALD P. "The Chunked Reading Test as a Measure of Thoughts Understood." Yearb Nat Read Conf 22(1):150–3 '73. *
90. CARVER, RONALD P., AND DARBY, CHARLES A., JR. "Analysis of the Chunked Reading Test and Reading Comprehension." J Read Behav 5(4):282–96 f '73. * (PA 52:1822)
91. GNEWUCH, MINNIE M. The Effect of Vocabulary Training Upon the Development of Vocabulary, Comprehension, Total Reading, and Rate of Reading of College Students. Doctor's thesis, Oklahoma State University (Stillwater, Okla.), 1973. (DAI 34:6254A)
92. GOOLSBY, THOMAS M., JR. "Levels of Performance and Concurrent Validity of Two Measures of Vocabulary and Reading for Certain Graduate Students." Ed & Psychol Meas 33(4):947–9 w '73. * (PA 52:4021)
93. TASCHOW, HORST G. "Raw Score Method of the Residual Gain Procedure Versus the Crude Gain Method in Measuring Reading Improvement." Yearb Nat Read Conf 22(1):169–77 '73. *
94. AMBROSINO, ROBERT J.; BRADING, PAUL L.; AND NOVAL, LORRAINE K. "Reading: A Potential Source of Academic Difficulty in Medical School." J Read Behav 6(4):367–73 D '74. * (PA 54:8389)
95. COCHRAN, JUDITH ANN. A Descriptive Study Examining Grades, Reading Ability and Attrition of Certain Low Income Freshmen at Arizona State University. Doctor's thesis, Arizona State University (Tempe, Ariz.), 1974. (DAI 35:4042A)
96. COLLIGAN, JOHN TERRENCE. Achievement and Personality Characteristics as Predictors of Observed Tutor Behavior. Doctor's thesis, Arizona State University (Tempe, Ariz.), 1974. (DAI 35:4293A)
97. NENNICH, FLORENCE. A Predictor Index for Use in Elementary Shorthand. Doctor's thesis, Temple University (Philadelphia, Pa.), 1974. (DAI 35:4325A)
98. SOUTH, J. J. "Early Career Performance of Engineers—Its Composition and Measurement." Personnel Psychol 27(2):225–43 su '74. *
99. STARKS, DAVID D., AND FELDHUSEN, JOHN F. "Prediction of Unit Test Grades Within a College Course." Improving Col & Univ Teach 22(4):218–9 au '74. *
100. SULLIVAN, EMILIE PAUL. Internal Reading Flexibility Patterns Among Texas A & M University Undergraduates. Doctor's thesis, Texas A & M University (College Station, Tex.), 1974. (DAI 35:5068A)
101. CHERNEY, ELAINE ETHEL. Relationship of Reading Ability of Remedial Track University Freshmen to Text Readability and Instructional Methodology. Doctor's thesis, Michigan State University (East Lansing, Mich.), 1975. (DAI 36:3432A)
102. CHESTER, ROBERT D.; DULIN, KENNETH L.; AND CARVELL, ROBERT. "Mature Readers' Nelson-Denny Comprehension Scores With and Without Syntactically- and Semantically-Simplified Item-Stems and/or Item-Foils." Yearb Nat Read Conf 24:227–34 '75. *
103. CRADDOCK, MARTHA CLEVELAND. An Examination of a Heuristic Approach to Developmental Reading in Freshman English Classes at Lynchburg College. Doctor's thesis, University of Virginia (Charlottesville, Va.), 1975. (DAI 36:3438A)
104. HANKINS, DONALD RAY. A Comparative Study of Communication Skills in Technical-Vocational and College Parallel Students. Doctor's thesis, North Texas State University (Denton, Tex.), 1975. (DAI 36:2766A)
105. HENARD, KAY FIELDS. Life Change and Reading Achievement as Predictors of Academic Performance for Selected Community College Freshmen. Doctor's thesis, Texas A & M University (College Station, Tex.), 1975. (DAI 36:5082A)
106. McCORD, MICHAEL T. "A Semantic Analysis of Reading Comprehension Tests." Yearb Nat Read Conf 24:211–9 '75. *
107. PEDRINI, D. T., AND PEDRINI, B. S. "College Grades and Reading Abilities." Read Improv 12(2):75–80 su '75. *
108. PEDRINI, D. T., AND PEDRINI, BONNIE C. "Reading Abilities and College Grades." Col Stud J 9(1):37–42 F–Mr '75. * (PA 54:12591)
109. SCHACHNER, STEPHEN P. An Examination of the Interaction Effects of Anxiety, Task Difficulty, and Instructions on a Reading Comprehension Task. Doctor's thesis, University of Pittsburgh (Pittsburgh, Pa.), 1975. (DAI 36:2111A)
110. SLOVAK, PAULINE ANDERSON. The Reading Achievement Levels of Community College Freshmen Enrolled in a Modular English Course Compared With the Readability Levels of Books Assigned in the Course. Doctor's thesis, East Texas State University (Commerce, Tex.), 1975. (DAI 36:5096A)
111. THURMOND, VERA BELINDA. Relationship Between Students' Perceptions of Their Reading Ability and Scores on a Standardized Test. Doctor's thesis, University of Georgia (Athens, Ga.), 1975. (DAI 36:5658A)
112. BALSER, ELIZABETH ANN. The Relationship Between Text Readability and Student Reading Level and its Effect on College Achievement. Doctor's thesis, West Virginia University (Morgantown, W.Va.), 1976. (DAI 37:2098A)
113. ZÁRATE, NARCISA. Predictive Factors of Academic Success for Freshmen of a Multicultural University. Doctor's thesis, New Mexico State University (University Park, N.M.), 1976. (DAI 37:1381A)

ROBERT A. FORSYTH, Professor of Education, The University of Iowa, Iowa City, Iowa.

Forms C and D of the Nelson-Denny Reading Test were developed to supplement, but not replace, Forms A and B. The authors state: "The four forms now available reflect slightly different subject matter emphases and slightly different levels of difficulty; they should provide greater latitude for users in selecting the particular form most appropriate for a specific purpose and for individual needs." However, guidelines for selecting the best form for a particular purpose and need are not provided.

The test is intended to "serve predictive, screening, and broadly diagnostic purposes" with students in grades 9 through 16. The publishers have made a praiseworthy effort to supply representative norms for high school students. The manual contains a very detailed discussion of the development of these norms. Beginning-of-year, middle-of-year, and end-of-year percentile norms are supplied for grades 9 through 12. The beginning-of-year norms are empirical norms obtained from the test standardization in October and November of 1972. The other two sets of norms are extrapolated (or interpolated) norms.

On the other hand, the normative data supplied for grades 13 through 16 do not permit any very descriptive norm-referenced interpretations of the test scores. The college level norms cannot be considered as representing any well defined population.

Despite the lack of representativeness of the college norms, the test seems more suitable for college students than for high school students. The content of the test certainly appears to be directed at college students. In the comprehension subtest, for example, only one reading passage was selected because of its relevance for high school students. The other seven selections were apparently chosen from college level sources.

In addition, this test would be very difficult for most high school students. For example, consider the vocabulary subtest, which has 100 items. The median raw scores (beginning-of-year) for Form C are 15, 17, 20, and 23 for grades 9, 10, 11, and 12, respectively. Form D medians are very similar. [Note that chance score for a 100-item test with 5 alternatives is 20.]

One of the major factors contributing to the difficulty of the vocabulary subtest is the time limit set for it. The examinee has only 10 minutes to answer the 100 items. No data related to the effects of the time limit are supplied. However, as noted above, the median scores for the vocabulary subtest are very low, indicating the possibility of a speed factor.

For grades 9, 10, 11, and 12, split-half and alternate forms reliability estimates are provided for the vocabulary, comprehension, and total scores. Only split-half estimates are furnished for these three scores at grades 13–16. For grades 9–12, only alternate forms reliabilities are given for the reading rate score; no reliability estimates are provided for grades 13 through 16. Since speed does seem to be an important factor, the alternate forms estimates of reliability seem more appropriate. For the vocabulary test these reliabilities are .82, .87, .91, and .91 for grades 9, 10, 11, and 12, respectively. The comprehension estimates are .68, .66, .78, and .74 and the reading rate estimates are .54, .62, .69, and .66.

As can be seen above, the vocabulary scores are the most reliable. However, it should be noted that the directions to the examinees specifically state that "it is to your advantage to attempt to answer all questions." Given these directions and the nature of the vocabulary test, one wonders how much of the true score variance is really accounted for by differences among students in test-taking strategy. Perhaps, under such conditions, it would have been better to employ some type of scoring procedure that attempts to minimize the effects of differences in test-taking strategy.

The test manual emphasizes screening, predictive, and broadly diagnostic uses for the test results. Given the relatively low reliabilities of the reading rate and comprehension scores and the difficulty level of the vocabulary subtest, this test probably would be judged as having a low degree of validity for most purposes when it is used with high school students. For example, it is difficult to believe that it could be of much help in identifying "students who need special help with reading problems." Perhaps the test may have some validity as a screening device for identifying highly gifted readers at the high school level; or, perhaps, at the college level it may have some validity for identifying people who need remedial work. However, very little empirical evidence is given to support the use of the test as a screening device in any setting. Likewise, relatively little evidence is given to support its use as a predictive instrument. The evidence that is provided pertains primarily to University of Minnesota students and relates the Nelson-Denny to grades in several college courses and overall grade point average. Actually, the given data represent rather weak evidence of predictive validity. In general, on the basis of this evidence it seems reasonable to conclude that the Nelson-Denny adds little to our ability to predict grades beyond what we can do with high school rank alone.

Probably the major use emphasized by the authors and publishers is the diagnostic use

Nelson-Denny Reading Test

(broadly conceived) of these tests. The form used to convey the test results to the student emphasizes the use of the score profiles to identify areas of strength and weakness and discusses the implications of these strengths and weaknesses. For example, a student whose reading rate percentile rank is the lowest is told the following: "If rate is your lowest score, you should be pleased to know that your vocabulary, comprehension, and total scores are probably underestimates of your real ability. Since you read at a rate below that expected of one with your word power you need to increase your reading rate." This type of interpretation must be undertaken with extreme caution for several reasons: (a) The relationship between rate, comprehension, and vocabulary seems to be much more complex than that implied by these simple interpretive statements. (b) The reliabilities of the rate and comprehension scores are relatively low and the intercorrelations of the various subtests are relatively high. Therefore, the reliability of the differences between scores will definitely be low. (c) Many of the interpretations of the profiles assume that the vocabulary score is the most important score. Given the difficulty of the vocabulary subtest for high school students, it seems unreasonable to place too much emphasis on this score for these students.

In summary, the *Nelson-Denny Reading Test* appears to be most useful at the college level. At this level, if local norms are developed, the test may validly serve the predictive, screening, and diagnostic purposes for which it was developed. However, at the high school level, other reading tests designed more specifically for the high school population would probably be more useful than the *Nelson-Denny Reading Test*.

ALTON L. RAYGOR, *Professor of Educational Psychology and Coordinator, Reading and Study Skills Center, University of Minnesota, Minneapolis, Minnesota.*

Forms C and D are recently published (1973) forms of the test. Forms A and B are still in use. The manual states that it was "desirable to develop additional forms of the *Nelson-Denny Reading Test* to provide users with an even more accurate and useful measure of this important ability." The new forms are different in subject matter and difficulty and "should pro-

vide greater latitude for users in selecting the particular form most appropriate for a specific purpose and for individual needs." Unfortunately, nothing more is said to help the user to select forms. The format is identical to Forms A and B, but the user is left completely without any information as to the equivalence of Forms C and D to the older forms.

Administration procedures are well described. The section on advanced preparation is especially helpful and may prevent some of the frequent errors of the inexperienced test administrator.

Criticisms of the previous forms of the test have apparently had some impact on the preparation of the manual for these new forms. Some predictive validity data now reported suggest that scores are somewhat predictive of college grades, even though some of the generalizations made are questionable. For example, the manual indicates that in one sample the NDRT was "slightly better" than the *Minnesota Scholastic Aptitude Test* in prediction, when the two zero-order correlations involved were .397 and .384, respectively, and both were lower than high school rank at .585. Unfortunately, the data given on predictive validity seems to be related to the previously published forms. Since the new forms are presumably different in content and difficulty, we are left with little usable information on which to base judgments about the predictive validity of the forms.

DIAGNOSTIC USES. In a section of the manual labeled "Diagnostic Uses" some suggestions which relate to differences in test profiles are given. This part would be of value to teachers who might be inexperienced in using such "diagnostic" information if it were not so filled with oversimplified and questionable explanations of student difficulties. For example, in one discussed profile a student has percentile ranks as follows: vocabulary, 65; comprehension, 45; and reading rate, 20. The pattern is explained in terms of "word power" not being used with the "expected skill." It is suggested that in addition to the possibility of motivation, interest, or concentration problems, the student might "suffer from background deficiency, regressing, vocalizing, and word-by-word reading." Ignoring the fact that no information has been given to indicate that such score variations might have been the result of the testing situations or might have occurred by chance alone, the "explanation" is still questionable. One is forced to wonder if the manual was prepared by a "reading expert" who didn't know (a) that all readers necessarily show some regressions while reading; (b) that vocalizing or sub-vocalizing is probably universally present in normal reading and improves comprehension on the kind of difficult material used in this test; and (c) that according to good studies of the mechanics of the reading process, the average college student sees 1.1 words per eye-fixation and is essentially a "word-by-word" reader.

In another example of this diagnostic "helpfulness," the manual refers to a study by Holmes and Singer which has been severely criticized because of its misuse of multiple regression analysis and inappropriate interpretation of the reading process. The manual suggests that since Holmes and Singer reported three factors influencing vocabulary (vocabulary in context, vocabulary in isolation, and prefixes) and since one of the three (prefixes) could be related to items, this information should be used for diagnosis. Items that have prefixes are listed and some suggestions are given for instruction. No mention is made of any data relevant to the reliability or validity of the sub-subscales thus created, and no cautions are given to the user concerning interpretation of them.

A similar process is then recommended for use on the items of the comprehension test. Again, no reference is made to the dangers of this procedure.

TECHNICAL INFORMATION. Generally acceptable procedures were followed in item production, informal tryout, and item selection. The major criticism this reviewer has to make is that the test was developed on a very high-level population in which 87 percent of the sample were above the status of college freshmen and 64 percent were upperclass college students, graduates, and faculty. This seems to be a strange population on which to develop items for use down through grade 9 (with grade level norms reported down to grade 6!)

The procedures for standardization seem reasonable, given the difficulty of achieving a real "census sample." The grade-level norms are probably better than the college norms, since the college norms are a mixture of two-year and four-year schools. No effort is made to differentiate between the two types of colleges in spite of widespread evidence of rather large differences in measured reading ability.

The section on validity suggests an examination of the test by the user "to see if it meets your local objectives." An item-by-item examination by this reviewer produced an overwhelming impression of *very* difficult, bookish passages followed by highly artificial questions of the sort that one would not ask in real life.

Alternate form reliabilities, reported over a three-week interval, range from .54 to .91 with median .80.

DIFFICULTY. The one area of most concern to this reviewer is the general level of difficulty of the passages, the vocabulary, and the comprehension items.

A look at the norm tables makes the point quickly. Take, for example, the widely accepted criterion that a test will discriminate best in a population in which half of the items are answered correctly. On the vocabulary section of this test one must go up to the grade 16 level before this is true. The obvious conclusion is that the test will do best at that level. Since the items were developed and selected initially on a very high level population, it is not surprising.

One way of examining the difficulty of a test is to make totally random responses (the "blind monkey with a pencil" technique) and to see how the results compare with real people. This reviewer did it by taking Form C and making the center ("C") response to each item. This "blind monkey" obtained a grade level of 12.0 on vocabulary, 7.0 on comprehension, and 9.3 on the total test!

Further examination shows that 70 percent of beginning ninth graders get below chance scores on the vocabulary test. Fifty-nine percent of tenth graders, 49 percent of eleventh graders, and 40 percent of twelfth graders also get below chance scores. College freshmen only average 33 out of the 100 items correct.

A FINAL COMMENT. The various difficulties discussed in this review, important as they are, pale into insignificance in relation to the problems posed by the extreme difficulty level. To use this test on anyone other than highly selected college students or adults will produce very questionable measurement results. Worse than that, it will provide a difficult, defeating, and frustrating experience to many of the students—especially those who have already had enough of such experiences.

OISE Achievement Tests in Silent Reading: Advanced Primary Battery. Grade 2; 1969–71; 5 scores: words in use, multiple word meanings, Part A comprehension, Part B comprehension, total; Forms A, B, ('69, 21 pages); manual ('70, 16 pages); technical handbook ('71, 34 pages); Can $5.35 per 25 tests; $1.35 per set of scoring stencils; $1.35 per handbook; $1.35 per specimen set; postage extra; 90(110) minutes in 3 sessions; Ontario Institute for Studies in Education and Patricia Tracy (handbook); distributed by Guidance Centre [Canada]. *

JOHN MCLEOD, *Director, Institute of Child Guidance and Development, University of Saskatchewan, Saskatoon, Canada.*

The manual and technical handbook which accompany this test provide the information that the tests were designed to supersede the *Dominion Achievement Tests in Silent Reading,* that the revision got underway in 1964, and that the tests are related to the needs of teachers, counsellors and administrators.

What do each of these professional persons require for a test of reading comprehension in the early grades? The administrator presumably would like an indication of the general level of reading achievement in the schools within his or her jurisdiction and will probably be particularly interested in the number of children likely to require corrective reading or remedial education. Likewise, the class teacher will be interested in checking his or her own assessments of children's reading achievement against an externally standardized criterion and will be looking for the additional bonus of diagnostic clues to help those children whose reading achievement is not up to par. If an elementary school is so fortunate as to have a counsellor in the early grades, then this person will be looking particularly for in-depth information about children whose reading achievement deviates significantly from the average.

If a test is designed merely to measure the level of reading achievement, it should be brief, straightforward to administer and have sufficient reliability and validity to identify those children whose reading disability warrants further investigation. The OISE tests certainly have impressive reliability (.97) and acceptable validity (correlation of about .75 with teachers' estimates) but they require three test sessions, taking up a total of 90 minutes actual testing

time exclusive of preliminary instructions, etc. As reliabilities of the order of .80 have been obtained from cloze tests with approximately 50 deletions, one suspects that a reliability coefficient of .97 is no greater than could be achieved through a cloze test made up of random deletions, but of sufficient length to occupy 90 minutes of actual testing time.

But, it might be argued, a test such as the OISE test which is made up of subtests of "words in use," "multiple word meanings," and "comprehension" yields diagnostic information over and above level of achievement, which is all that could be expected of the home-made cloze test, and the standardized test provides an index of achievement level which is itself more informative, as individual achievements may be interpreted against the background of the scores of a representative sample of young elementary students.

But is this so? Examination of individual children's responses to any reading test can provide diagnostic information to the perceptive teacher but simply because a test has subtests purporting to measure particular skills is no guarantee that they do in fact measure those skills. For instance, subtest 2, entitled Multiple Word Meanings, takes the form of a series of sentences in which one word is underlined and the child is required to pick out, from a multiple choice format, one of four words which is closest in meaning to the underlined word. The test items are arranged in pairs, adjacent items using the same word in different contexts which give the word a different meaning. The pairs of items are said to have been arranged in order of difficulty, the most difficult of the pair being the criterion. But what undoubtedly contributes to the difficulty of several items in this subtest is the difficulty of the context in which the word is placed and/or the difficulty of the multiple choice answers. For example, item 25 (out of 30) tests the child's knowledge of the meaning of the word "pet." This simple consonant-vowel-consonant word, which can probably be read by the majority of grade 1 children and its meaning understood by them, is contained in the sentence "Judy had a raccoon as a *pet,*" and in order to figure out the correct answer, the child is required to decode "tame," and discount detractor answers which contain the words "funny," "quiet," and "small." Again, in order to assess whether a child understands the meaning of the relatively easy "ring," a child has to read the words "sound," "horn," "whistle," and "harp." The preliminary sample item reveals the vintage of the test, requiring the child to pick out a synonym for the word "top" in the sentence "Sue had a new blue top." At least one literate, intelligent girl of 8 years had difficulty finding the correct answer from "wall," "table," "roof," and "toy" as she interpreted it to be the upper garment that goes with a skirt or pair of jeans.

The other subtests are a sentence completion test which taps the child's semantic comprehension (but not comprehension related to syntax), and a traditional comprehension test consisting of four short paragraphs (two of which are describing animals) followed by questions on content. There is a further section to the comprehension subtest which requires a child to place four sentences in correct order to make up a continuous text.

Standardization seems to have been comprehensive and well carried out, but limited to the province of Ontario in Canada. Unfortunately, tables are provided to translate raw scores into stanines and percentile ranks only. And, despite the authors' assurance that "educators find percentile ranks easy to understand and to interpret to parents," it has been the perplexing experience of this reviewer over a period of many years that many teachers have great difficulty in comprehending percentile ranks and have never heard of stanines. In view of the limited range of this test (stanines and percentile ranks are provided for children aged 7 years 5 months through 8 years 4 months), the more familiar reading ages or grade equivalents would have provided a rather limited table, but this is no reason for not providing the information. It would have been helpful and informative to many teachers if cutoff scores had been extracted from the standardization tables, indicating the score below which a child of a particular age, tested at a particular time of the year, should be considered for further diagnosis.

In summary, a good deal of psychometric blood and sweat went into the preparation of these tests but as they take so much longer to administer than most other reading tests, without producing a commensurate amount of information, the teachers, counsellors, and adminis-

trators for whom they are allegedly designed would be better served by administering a relatively short group test of achievement to the whole class, and using the additional time in carrying out in-depth diagnostic testing of children who need it with one of the several excellent tests available for the purpose.

[737]

★Primary Reading Assessment Units. Grades 1–3; 1973; PRAU; no data on reliability; norms consist of means only; 10 tests; 1–3 levels; the grade designations below indicate tests made up of items in the 40–60% difficulty range; 1 form; manual (19 pages); technical report (no date, 52 pages) for this and 1 other test; separate answer sheets must be used; Can $46.80 per 15 sets of tests and answer sheets and 1 manual; $2 per technical report; $4.25 per specimen set; postage extra; [10–15] minutes per test; Ellen Campbell, Patricia Tracy, and Eileen McErlaine (except technical report); Ontario Institute for Studies in Education [Canada]. *
a) RECOGNIZING FEELINGS. Grade 1; test A (8 pages).
b) FINDING REASONS, PREDICTING RESULTS. Grades 1, 2; 2 levels: tests A (8 pages), B (4 pages).
c) CHOOSING IDEAS AND DETAILS. Grades 1, 2, 3; 3 levels: tests A (8 pages), B (4 pages), C (7 pages).
d) DISCOVERING IDEAS AND DETAILS. Grades 1, 2, 3; 3 levels: tests A (8 pages), B, C, (6 pages).
e) FINDING THE RIGHT ORDER. Grade 2; test B (4 pages).
f) FOLLOWING DIRECTIONS. Grade 2; test B (6 pages).
g) READING GRAPHS. Grade 2; test B (7 pages).
h) FINDING OUT WHAT THE WRITER MEANS. Grades 2, 3; 2 levels: tests B, C, (4 pages).
i) READING CHARTS. Grade 3; test C (7 pages).
j) READING MAPS. Grade 3; test C (8 pages).

[738]

Progressive Achievement Tests of Reading. Standards 2–4 and Forms I–IV; 1969–70; PATR; raw scores are converted into "levels of achievement" regardless of age or class and into percentile ranks within half-year age groups; 2 forms; 2 tests; 7 overlapping levels called Parts 2 (Standard 2), 3 (3), 4 (4), 5 (Form I), 6 (II), 7 (III), 8 (IV) in a single booklet; manual ('69, 32 pages); separate answer sheets must be used; NZ 40¢ per 20 answer sheets for any one level; 15¢ per scoring stencil; $1.25 per manual; $4 per specimen set; postage extra; Warwick B. Elley and Neil A. Reid; New Zealand Council for Educational Research [New Zealand]. *
    Australian edition: Grades 3–9; 1970–73; manual ('73, 119 pages) by M. L. Clark; Australian Council for Educational Research [Australia]. *
a) READING COMPREHENSION. Forms A ('69, 23 pages), B ('70, 23 pages); $5 per 20 tests; 40(50) minutes.
b) READING VOCABULARY. Forms A ('69, 12 pages), B ('70, 12 pages); $4 per 20 tests; 30(40) minutes.
    See T2:1579 (1 reference); for excerpted reviews by Milton L. Clark and J. Elkins, see 7:699.

REFERENCES

1. See T2:1579.
2. REID, N. A., AND HUGHES, D. C. "A Factorial Analysis of the PAT: Reading Comprehension, Reading Vocabulary, and Listening Comprehension Tests." N Zeal J Ed Studies 9(1):18–30 My '74. * (PA 53:12568)

OISE Achievement Tests in Silent Reading

DOUGLAS A. PIDGEON, *Head, Reading Research Unit, Child Development and Educational Psychology, University of London Institute of Education, London, England.*

The design and presentation of these tests is to be commended. They consist of two reusable booklets, each covering the age range 8 to 14 (grades 3 to 9), providing separate measures of reading comprehension and vocabulary. The items are arranged in an overlapping format, with seven different starting and finishing points, and the number of items and range of difficulty increase with age and grade.

The items in the vocabulary test require a choice from five plausible alternatives of the best synonym to replace a word underlined in a given sentence. The comprehension items aim to measure both factual and inferential comprehension of prose material. After reading a narrative or descriptive or expository passage, the testee is presented with from four to six multiple choice factual or inferential items; the proportion of expository passages and inferential items are gradually increased for older pupils.

Both criterion- and norm-referenced interpretations from the raw data are possible. In the New Zealand manual, in a simple but seemingly effective procedure, raw scores are related to 10 reading comprehension or reading vocabulary levels. For any pupil, his level score indicates what he knows or can do, thus providing the teacher with a guide for selecting further suitable reading materials and exercises. Level scores can also be converted into percentile ranks, derived from a very thorough national standardisation, thus permitting a comparison of an individual's standing with others of his own class or grade group.

Notably, the Australian manual gives greater emphasis to the norm-referenced aspect; and, from a separate and rather less satisfactory standardisation, separate tables of percentile ranks and stanines for each Australian state and the Capital Territory are provided. Tentative level scores are also given. In the United Kingdom, the criterion-referenced aspect only is emphasized, since no local norming has as yet been carried out—it being supposed that the New Zealand norms are equally applicable in UK schools, although no evidence for this is supplied.

All praise should be given to the authors of the original NZ manual. It is a model of clarity in its description of the construction and use of the tests, its explanation of the more technical details of scaling and norming, and its warnings about the possible misuse of the results. Unfortunately, this very clarity has led to a separation of the section dealing with the uses to which the tests can be put from that concerned with the test's validity. As a result, a number of uses are suggested for which no validatory evidence is supplied. For example, the tests are recommended for providing advice on pupils' educational and vocational plans, but no predictive evidence of any kind is given in support. Also, it is suggested that a teacher may be alerted to possible signs of underachievement by comparing scores on PATR with other tests having minimal emphasis on reading, such as listening comprehension, oral vocabulary, or nonverbal intelligence. However, no empirical evidence is supplied to support this suggestion, nor, incidentally, is any suggestion made as to how a teacher should react to signs of overachievement which, if the statistical evidence had been provided, would have been shown to occur with approximately equal frequency.

The section on validity is more concerned with the tests per se than with their intended uses and there is a concentration on content and concurrent validity. Concerning the latter, some 21 correlations with other reading and intelligence tests are given in the NZ manual and a further 54 in the Australian one. Most vary between .65 and .85, but it is difficult to interpret their meaning. Since they are relatively easy to obtain, one suspects they are given just to impress.

The evidence on content validity is, on the face of it, more impressive. A great deal of time and effort went into the planning and construction of the tests so that they "will assess those reading skills which are commonly accepted as important by the majority of informed teachers of reading in New Zealand." It reflects sadly on those concerned with teaching reading that, from ages 8 to 14, reading should be thought of only in terms of vocabulary and comprehension. Are there not other reading behaviours and skills which should also be taught and tested? What about verifying and evaluating the author's intentions, or developing appropriate study skills, to mention but two? Were these

Progressive Achievement Tests of Reading

considered and rejected by the committees of reading specialists who framed the policy for the tests, or were they not even considered? Apparently reading speed tests were specifically not recommended. So the tests measure only vocabulary and comprehension and the correlations between these are not far short of the reliability coefficients of the tests, as is the case with the items measuring the factual and inferential reading skills. Yet, in the latter case, it was considered too unreliable to produce separate scores.

It is hoped that a wrong impression of these tests is not being conveyed. To sum up, they are well-planned, well-constructed, and well-standardised tests that are equal to, if not better than, many other tests of a similar kind already on the market. The idea of using them as criterion-referenced tests is certainly to be commended. As they now stand, however, and with the evidence presented in the manual, they are probably more suited for survey and screening purposes than for diagnostic purposes for which their value is somewhat limited. It would be good to see some equally well-made tests of other aspects of reading coming from the same stable.

[739]

★Reading Placement Test. Students entering postsecondary institutions with open-door policies; 1976, c1962–76; subtest of *CGP Self-Scoring Placement Tests in English and Mathematics;* self-scoring edition of the reading test (Form UPG) in the *Comparative Guidance and Placement Program;* publisher recommends use of local norms; 1 form ('72, 8 pages, identical with test copyrighted 1969 except for format); for battery accessories, see 7; separate answer sheets (self-marking) must be used; $3.50 per 10 tests; $10 per 25 answer sheets; $1 per specimen set; cash orders postpaid; 25(30) minutes; published for the College Entrance Examination Board by Educational Testing Service. *

For reviews of the complete battery, see 7 (2 reviews). For reference to reviews of the CGP Program, see 475.

[740]

*The Reading Progress Scale. Grades 3–12, 13–14; 1970–75; RPS; test consists of 4 paragraphs estimated to be at difficulty levels grades 1–3, 4–6, 7–9, and 10–12, each paragraph scored 0 or 1; reliability data based on grades 3–12; no norms; 2 forms; 2 levels; manual ('71, 13 pages); $4 per manual; cash orders postpaid; 7(15) minutes; Ronald P. Carver; Revrac Publications. *

a) [ORIGINAL TEST.] Grades 3–12; 1970–71; Forms 2, 5, ('70, 2 pages); directions for students ('70, 1 page); directions for administering ('71, 2 pages); student report/information sheet (no date, 2 pages); $15 per 100 tests; $1 per set of scoring stencils; $7.50 per 100

directions for students; $7.50 per 100 student report/information sheets; $5 per specimen set.
b) [COLLEGE VERSION.] Grades 13–14; 1970–75; "an adaptation" for use as a screening test at the college level; Forms 2C, 5C, ('75, c1970, 3 pages, self-marking, identical to the 1970 test for grades 3–12 except for format, one change in punctuation, and omission of one article); manual supplement (no date, 2 pages); directions for administering (no date, 1 page); $20 per 100 tests; $6 per specimen set.

REFERENCES

1. FELDMANN, SHIRLEY C. "Review of the Reading Progress Scale." *J Read* 15(6):451+ Mr '72. *
2. INGERSOLL, G. M., AND JOHNSON, P. "Attitudes and Reading Comprehension: A Preliminary Investigation." *Read Improv* 11(2):52–6 f '74. *

BLAINE R. WORTHEN, *Director of Evaluation and Research, Northwest Regional Educational Laboratory, Portland, Oregon.*[1]

The *Reading Progress Scale* is intended to measure "reading-input performance," described by the author as the ability to decode or translate graphic symbols "into a form which can be subsequently stored or understood." Comprehension skills are not measured, and the term "read" is used by the author "to mean the ability to input the information not necessarily understand it."

The test has two forms, each of which consists of four paragraphs, printed on a single sheet. For each form, the first paragraph is proposed as comparable in reading difficulty to material used in grades 1–3; the second paragraph supposedly corresponds in difficulty to material used in grades 4–6; the third paragraph, grades 9–10; and the fourth paragraph, grades 10–12.

Each paragraph contains 20 two-choice cloze format items, formed by providing an alternative incorrect choice for every fifth word in the paragraph. The distractor is generally a word which would not be used because of its grammatical or syntactical form. Students are allowed seven minutes to complete the test. In the scoring of the test, one point is given for each paragraph on which 18 of the items (90 percent) are answered correctly. The total score for a student is, therefore, the number of paragraphs passed and can range only from 0 to 4.

Administration is uncomplicated, and explicit directions for test administrators and practice items for students are included. Punched scoring templates are also provided for each form.

_____
[1] The reviewer is indebted to his colleague, Randy Demaline, for observations about the *Reading Progress Scale* which have influenced this review. Full responsibility for the content of this review rests, however, with the reviewer.

There are perplexing questions about the rationale for several key features of the *Reading Progress Scale*. Unfortunately, these questions are not answered by the accompanying manual, which describes how test procedures were devised but not why. In the absence of such justification, many features of the test must be viewed as questionable or unacceptable.

For example, no rationale is given for using civics for the content of one form and geography for content of the other. Parallelism is claimed on the basis of Bormuth's "cloze level scores," but the possible impact of subject matter knowledge is apparently discounted. Correct responses to items such as "oxidation is (heavy, rapid)" and "cold (every, deserts) lie near the poles (and, continent) on high plateaus," clearly require content knowledge in addition to reading input ability.

No information is given about the rationale and underlying assumptions of the cloze deletion procedures used for generating test items. The decision to delete every fifth word was based on "fragmentary information collected in pilot studies." The assumption that this pattern is ideal across all grade levels is questionable. More serious, strict adherence to this deletion pattern pays no attention to the number of items which deal with various parts of speech. The questionable result of these procedures is seen in one paragraph where "the" is the correct response to 5 of the 20 items.

It is unclear how item distractors were chosen or their relative plausibility determined. Many of the distractors are patently implausible. Others are so plausible that it is difficult to defend the designated correct responses as preferable. For example, "the dairy (has, is) to stop selling its (milk, sold)" and "circulation of (the, a) petition." Although seven alternatives were "vetoed" as impossible or too difficult and therefore replaced, the criteria used in these decisions are questionable.

The manual refers to non-subjective "alternative selection procedures" but fails to describe them. It appears one common method was to choose words which were correct responses to other items in the same paragraph. For example, in one paragraph, the correct response "soluble" appears three times and is also used twice as a distractor, resulting in a single word comprising over 12 percent of the response options in the paragraph.

The test and manual appear to have been casually put together. Statements are imprecise. For example, the statement that "the ability to read the easiest paragraph on the test is a milestone that all readers must reach and most students reach by the second grade" is inconsistent with the facts that "in grade 2, no data were available" and 21 percent of the third-grade students in the sample failed that paragraph. References in the text to research are not always supplied in the reference list. Form 2 contains a non-sentence. One of the scoring keys is not punched. Although these inadequacies are nontrivial in and of themselves, they also serve as unsettling indicators that the missing rationale for the test and item development procedures may be as casual.

There are several factors which limit the utility of this test. Chief among them is the very narrow range of scores possible. With a purported reading progress scale for grades 1–12 yielding only five possible scores, only three-year leaps in reading progress can be discerned. This seems little more useful to the educator than a thermometer which registered only low, medium, and high would be to the physician. It is suggested in the manual that examiners may elect to record the exact number attempted and correct for each paragraph, but there are no aids provided for how to interpret such scores, judge their reliability, or use the information diagnostically. This lack is especially critical in the absence of a rationale for distractors which might help teachers use incorrect responses diagnostically.

Although this test is relatively quick and simple to administer and score, these advantages are offset by its low information yield and difficulty in interpreting the scores. For example, classroom teachers who accept the definition of reading-input performance as a helpful measure of reading progress are likely to have difficulty explaining it to parents without reverting to oversimplified and questionable interpretations such as those included on the individual report sheet for the test. It will also prove baffling to many parents just how the test can fail to measure understanding and yet report desired scores for students at various grade levels.

Reading Progress Scale

Although the *Reading Progress Scale* is presented as a criterion-referenced test, the author includes norms for the interpretation of its results. Unfortunately, these norms are grossly inadequate. The norm group is "471, 3rd to 12th graders in a school in a small town, population 1,000" in Missouri. This is hardly a sufficiently representative group to support the assertion that this school is "average." The inadequacy of the norms is further highlighted by the facts that an average of fewer than 50 students per grade were tested, and first and second grades were omitted entirely. Yet the individual report sheet for use in reporting results to students and parents bases its interpretations and progress reports on these norms. There also appears to be inconsistency in the use of these norms. For example, it is stated in the individual report sheet "all third grade graduates....should score 1," but it is then noted that only "79% of the third graders....scored 1 or higher and about 87% of the fourth graders.... scored 1 or higher."

Validity data on the scale are limited and exist only for grades 3 through 6. Teachers' predictions of their students' scores on the test are reported in relation to the students' actual scores. With 191 students, fewer than 12 percent failed a paragraph which their teachers had estimated they "could read and understand given an unlimited amount of reading time." It is also reported that the RPS level for 81 percent of the actual scores on Form 5 and 73 percent of scores on Form 2 "coincided with or was one level higher" than the teacher ratings. Scores of 93 percent of the students on Form 5 and 84 percent of the students on Form 2 were within one level of teacher ratings. Unfortunately, no information is provided on how many students' scores coincided precisely with teacher estimates.

These validity data are unconvincing. First, given the three-grade range for each single score on this instrument, the apparent high degree of correspondence is still below what would be anticipated with such undiscriminating indices. Second, it seems at best misleading to use teacher estimates of students' ability to read *and understand,* given unlimited time, as a basis for establishing validity of a speeded test which purports to measure only reading input

ability and claims to explicitly avoid measurement of understanding.

Another consideration relevant to validity is the selection of 90 percent as the criterion level for passing each paragraph. "Obviously, there is little difference between one individual who answers 17 correct and another who answers 18 correct." Yet the scoring system can result in such persons being rated as much as three grades apart in their reading progress. Such a procedure seems a flagrant disregard for the real meaning underlying the final test results.

A "traditional alternate-form reliability estimate" of .84 is reported for 471 students. Of these students, 64 percent made exactly the same score, while 33 differed by one paragraph and 3 percent by two or more paragraphs. Such differences become problematic because of the three-grade band width of a score. It seems indefensible to use a procedure where measurement error alone can easily result in a student being judged on one day as reading at the ninth-grade level and, on the next, at the sixth-grade level.

The appropriateness of the seven-minute time limit is questionable, since it was not actually tested in the pilot study. Error rates for five and six minutes were found to be 31 and 23 percent, respectively, but with different forms of the test. The selection of seven minutes seems an arbitrary projection from the data. An analysis of the scalar qualities of the test suggests, however, that the scores may not be overly influenced by the time factor.

SUMMARY. The *Reading Progress Scale* represents an effort to develop a convenient, simple measure of reading progress for teachers, researchers, and national policymakers. The test has little to offer for these uses, however. Its narrow focus on one aspect of reading performance makes the proposed interpretations of scores as indicators of grade-level reading progress misleading. The rationale for the test and development procedures are unclear and in some cases contradictory. The decision to reduce reading progress across the entire spectrum of grades 1–12 to only five possible descriptors seems ill-advised and leads to several serious problems in interpretation and use of test results.

Considerable work would be required before the *Reading Progress Scale* could be considered a serious competitor in this area of testing. The basic rationale of the test must be clarified and justified. Test development procedures should be justified, especially those which give rise to problems noted in this review. Errors and contradictions must be removed and more care and attention given to accuracy and documentation of assertions about the test. Until these steps are taken, this reviewer would advise against the use of this test.

J Read 15(6):451+ Mr '72. Shirley C. Feldmann. * a group-administered speed test containing four paragraphs to be read silently. Each paragraph represents a level of difficulty, the first representing grades 1–3 and the last, grades 10–12. A forced-choice cloze procedure is used for the twenty test points in each paragraph; the reader is required to check one of two words which makes the most sense in the sentence. If 90 percent of his selections are correct the paragraph is assumed to have been read capably. The resultant score places the reader on a scale from zero to four. While the test rationale and procedures for measuring it seem ingenious and well thought through, other features of the test are not, with the result that the test looks more like an experimental rather than final edition. The test format seems cluttered, and directions for administration and scoring are difficult to follow. The scoring key included was not operational. More importantly, the test is complex in format so that the test procedures might present considerable difficulty to younger children. Rather than the second grade to adult range claimed for the test a fourth grade level might be more appropriate as a floor. Although the test was constructed as a criterion-referenced rather than norm-referenced test, some norms are included. These are based on a surprisingly small and atypical sample, so that interpretation using the normative data is questionable. One hopes that continued development of the test might bring much needed changes in its practical aspects so that its potential as a measure of reading input could be evaluated. * may eventually prove interesting and useful in measuring components of reading achievement, but....[it does not seem] to meet that promise in its present form.

[741]
Reading Test (Comprehension and Speed): Municipal Tests: National Achievement Tests.

Grades 3–6, 6–8; 1938–57; subtest of *Municipal Battery;* 5 scores: following directions, sentence meaning, paragraph meaning, reading speed, total; no data on reliability; no norms for part scores; 2 forms (A and B, identical with tests copyrighted 1938 and 1939, respectively); 2 levels; $2 per specimen set of either level; postage extra; Robert K. Speer and Samuel Smith; Psychometric Affiliates. *
a) GRADES 3–6. 1938–57; Forms A ('54, 8 pages), B ('55, 8 pages); directions-norms-key for Forms A ('57, 4 pages), B ('39, 4 pages); $5 per 25 tests; 33 (38) minutes.
b) GRADES 6–8. 1938–54; Forms A ('50, 6 pages), B ('54, 6 pages); directions-norms-key for Forms A ('38, 4 pages), B ('39, 4 pages); $4.50 per 25 tests; 32(37) minutes.
For reviews of the complete battery, see 5:18 (1 review), 4:20 (1 review), and 2:1191 (2 reviews).

LARRY A. HARRIS, *Professor of Education, Virginia Polytechnic Institute and State University, Blacksburg, Virginia.*

Only an extraordinarily good reading test written nearly 40 years ago could still have value for test users today. This test first appeared in 1938 and has not been revised since that time. It is not a good test and is not recommended for use.

The four-page manual includes no discussion of the purposes of the test, nor is there any explanation of the content or how the test was developed. No test objectives are reported and no information is given on how to interpret or use the results.

Total scores are converted into grade equivalents; there are no norms for subtests. No description is given of how the norms were established, nor is any norming sample discussed. A table titled "Efficiency Norms" enables the test user to determine the number of months the child's "achievement is above or below the achievement to be expected for his I.Q. and grade." IQ scores are divided into categories as follows: below 90, 90–109, and above 109. No explanation is given as to how this table was developed or is to be used for instructional purposes.

No validity information is reported for the tests and no skills classification is provided for determining validity locally. Reliability coefficients are reported, in a catalog available from the publisher, as .92 for the grades 3–6 edition and .91 for the grades 6–8 edition. There is no explanation of how the above coefficients were obtained.

In Part 1, Following Directions, the tasks begin at a relatively easy level and grow progressively more complex. The more complex items require the child to perform mathematical calculations, alphabetize, understand points of the compass, and solve problems of logic. Obviously, more than following directions is measured here.

The sentences presented in Part 2, Sentence Meaning, are on the order of slogans or homilies. For example, one item presents the statement, "It is possible to be pennywise and pound foolish." There are two possible difficulties with the use of such moralistic admonitions in a reading test. First, the language employed is not natural. The sentence structure is stilted and ponderous; the vocabulary is uncommon and, from a child's standpoint, used in an almost esoteric way. Second, there is a good chance that some children may be familiar with some of the homilies used in the test and will consequently have an advantage over those who are not familiar with these sayings.

Part 3, Paragraph Meaning, presents 10 paragraphs dealing with topics quite remote from the experiences of children in grades 3–8 (i.e., astrology, commerce, laws of nature). The questions deal with literal understanding only. A check of the vocabulary used suggests that the difficulty level is quite advanced for the grades intended.

The final subtest, Reading Speed, is clearly not long enough (2 or 3 minutes depending on level) to gain a reliable measure of reading speed. Only one story is presented at each level. This means that third graders and sixth graders must read the same material on a subtest as dependent on the difficulty of material as on reading speed. Comprehension is checked by having the child underline in the story "every sentence which tells that Henry was sad or unhappy" (grades 6–8) or "that John went home" (grades 3–6). This seems to be a terribly gross measure of understanding.

This reviewer has been unable to find anything about the test which merits a positive recommendation. It is a very old instrument, but age alone is not relevant here. What is more basic is that the test makers fail completely in their obligation to provide clear test objectives, reliability and validity information, a description of the norming sample and procedures, and a description of how the test results can be used to improve instruction.

[742]

★SPAR Reading Test. Ages 7–0 to 15–11; 1976; based upon *Group Reading Test* and uses the same scoring stencils; may be administered with *SPAR Spelling Test* or independently; Forms A, B, (2 pages); combined manual (35 pages) for this and the spelling test; 50p per 20 tests; 30p per scoring stencil for either form; 75p per manual; 85p per specimen set; postpaid within U.K.; 13(20) minutes; D. Young; Hodder & Stoughton Educational [England]. *

J. DOUGLAS AYERS, *Professor of Education, University of Victoria, Victoria, British Columbia, Canada.*

The test is composed of 15 items requiring the matching of four or five words with a picture, and 20 incomplete sentences, each with six alternatives. The stems of the sentences are composed usually of not more than two or three words and require a general information response or a synonym to be chosen. Frequently, the alternatives appear more difficult than the words in the stem. The manual does not report the basis on which the test was constructed. The manual presents no reasons for including reading quotients, and the reviewer can find no defensible reasons for providing two sets of reading quotients or for providing norms above age 10.

The intended purpose of the SRT is to provide a complementary approach to the testing of literacy and to alert the teacher to the need for remedial measures; but the extremely high intercorrelations with several tests, including the companion *SPAR Spelling Test,* show that it is unnecessary to administer both SPAR tests. It would be more profitable to administer a test that supplied diagnostic information to replace one or both of them.

[743]

★St. Lucia Reading Comprehension Test. Grades 2–4; 1974; Forms A, B, (4 pages); manual (10 pages); Aus $7.50 per 25 tests of each form; postage extra; (15–30) minutes; J. Elkins and R. J. Andrews; Teaching and Testing Resources [Australia]. *

[744]

Sequential Tests of Educational Progress: Reading, Series II. Grades 4–6, 7–9, 10–12, 13–14; 1956–72; original 70 minute series (Series I) still available; 2 forms ('69, 11–18 pages); Forms 4A and 4B (grades 4–6), 3A and 3B (grades 7–9), 2A and 2B (grades 10–12), 1A and 1B (grades 13–14); for battery manuals and accessories, see 28; separate answer sheets (Digitek, IBM 805, IBM 1230) must be used; $7 per 20 tests; $5.50 per 100 answer sheets; $1.50 per 10 IBM (805, 1230 hand) scoring stencils (answer pattern must be punched out locally); Digitek scoring stencils not available; cash orders postpaid; specimen

Reading Test (Comprehension and Speed): Municipal Tests: National Achievement Tests

set not available; 45(55) minutes; Educational Testing Service; Addison-Wesley Publishing Co., Inc. *

See T2:1599 (25 references); for reviews by Emmett Albert Betts and Paul R. Lohnes of the original edition (Series I), see 6:810 (6 references); for reviews by Eric F. Gardner, James R. Hobson, and Stephen Wiseman, see 5:653. For reviews of the complete battery, see 28 (2 reviews), 6:25 (2 reviews), and 5:24 (2 reviews, 1 excerpt).

REFERENCES

1–6. See 6:810.
7–31. See T2:1599; also includes a cumulative name index to the first 31 references and 5 reviews for this test.
32. ESTES, THOMAS. "Sequential Tests of Educational Progress, Series 2: Reading: A Review," pp. 38–40. In *Reading Tests for the Secondary Grades.* Edited by William Blanton and others. Newark, Del.: International Reading Association, Inc., 1972. Pp. iv, 55. *
33. ESSER, MARIE WALSH. *A Study of the Development of Critical Reading Abilities in Seventh and Eighth Grade Students.* Master's thesis, St. Cloud State College (St. Cloud, Minn.), 1973.
34. SULLIVAN, JOANNA. "The Relationship of Creative and Convergent Thinking to Literal and Critical Reading Ability of Children in the Upper Grades." *J Ed Res* 66(8):374–7 Ap '73. * (*PA* 50:12116)
35. LORD, FREDERIC M. "Quick Estimates of the Relative Efficiency of Two Tests as a Function of Ability Level." *J Ed Meas* 11(4):247–54 w '74. *
36. LORET, PETER G.; SEDER, ALAN; BIANCHINI, JOHN C.; AND VALE, CAROL A. *Anchor Test Study: Equivalence and Norms Tables for Selected Reading Achievement Tests (Grades 4, 5, and 6).* DHEW Publication S/N 1780–01312. Washington, D.C.: Government Printing Office, 1974. Pp. ix, 92. *
37. LAWSON, ANTON E.; NORDLAND, FLOYD H.; AND KAHLE, JANE B. "Levels of Intellectual Development and Reading Ability in Disadvantaged Students and the Teaching of Science." *Sci Ed* 59(1):113–25 Ja–Mr '75. *
38. LINN, ROBERT L. "Anchor Test Study: The Long and the Short of It." *J Ed Meas* 12(3):201–13 f '75. *

RICHARD T. JOHNSON, *Associate Professor of Education, Virginia Polytechnic Institute and State University, Reston, Virginia.*

Previous reviewers of the earlier STEP reading test have termed it well-written, interesting to pupils, an outstanding professional achievement. Series II has continued in that tradition, making many improvements in response to earlier criticisms by MMY reviewers. But some problems persist.

One of the most serious criticisms was that the reading test had limited diagnostic use, that it gave little information useful in adapting materials or instructional procedures to individual pupils. The criticism still applies. In the present version, the 60 items are split into a 30-item, 15-minute vocabulary test and a 30-item, 30-minute paragraph comprehension test which are combined to yield a single score. The test apparently was divided for ease in administration; separate scores are not calculated. Thus, this test might be useful as a broad screening device for overall reading skills, or to provide gross information for making administrative decisions in grouping or programming. But those users who have more diagnostic purposes in mind should look elsewhere.

Administrators who are willing to use a single-score general reading test for such purposes as assessing the effects of experimentation and innovation should consider the ETS norming process if they plan to compare their students' scores with national norms. Norming data for all but the college students were collected the last two weeks of April and first week of May 1970. The norms tables are based on the assumption that students will achieve the same score in the spring and the following fall, an assumption that seems too tenuous to permit fall-to-spring norm-referenced evaluations of growth in reading. ETS points out that it is "virtually impossible to establish different sets of norms for fall and spring that accurately reflect the sometimes antithetical effects of forgetting and maturation during the three or four months of summer." Rather than testing twice a year, users would be wise to test once a year in the spring.

Criticisms concerning the lack of validity data apparently have been disregarded. No information is presented on the factorial composition of the tests, no demonstration of differential predictive validities between the STEP reading and SCAT verbal is made, no concurrent or predictive studies are reported, and no longitudinal data are shown. The only evidence for validity is "content validity," which turns out to be the weakest possible substitute for substantial data. Questions have been classified by the type of skill they require of students (comprehension, translation and inference, and analysis). Although this is a technically accurate classification, there appears to be confusion in its application.

In Part 1 of all the reading tests, for example, comprehension is simply inferring meanings from context—finding synonyms—and comprehension questions are indistinguishable from translation and inference questions except in form.

In addition, labeling an item "comprehension" or "translation and inference" in Part 2 seems arbitrary. For example, an item such as item 9 in Form 1A—"The author suggests that to the casual viewer the paintings of Paul Klee may appear to be all of the following EXCEPT"—is classed as translation and inference, whereas item 12—"The author would probably describe the work of Paul Klee as all of the following EXCEPT"—is classed as comprehension. On Form 4A, item 2—"How did Luke feel about finding the cave?"—is labeled translation and inference whereas item 16—"How does the child in the poem feel about washing?"—is labeled analysis. None of the answers is directly given; all must be inferred in essentially the same way.

However, the further ordering of these skills into the four content areas of narrative, humanities, science, and social studies (perhaps in response to an earlier criticism that the tests were too limited in content) is a spurious classification since one of the classes—narrative—overlaps all others and is not of the same kind; it is not a subject matter area but a style of prose in which any subject matter might be written. Because this classification is so profoundly flawed, it is impossible for an individual classifying the items independently to arrange them as ETS has done in the item classification tables in the handbook, even after discovering the "key word" system largely used. In Part 1 of all tests, if an item contains a word such as "librarian," "actor," "painting," or "book," it is assigned to humanities regardless of the intent of the question. That is, it is assigned to humanities even though it does not tap knowledge about actors, paintings, librarians, or books, and though other words could have been substituted for these without changing the answer. In the same way, if words denoting natural objects or animals are present, the item is designated as scientific. Any item with no such definite key word falls under narrative, which as a category most often deals with people's attitudes and how they affect their behavior and so probably should be listed under social studies; e.g., "Despite his air of politeness, his early departure betrayed his real displeasure at the way the meeting was going." Even if a user painstakingly determined that a student missed most of the science or social studies or humanities-content questions, what conclusions could be drawn? Because of the incorrect and highly contrived classification scheme, the item tables serve no useful purpose for Part 1 of the tests and very little for Part 2.

The test includes generally interesting straightforward comprehension, inference from context, and reading passage items. In contrast to the earlier series, the current test presents varying numbers of questions for each passage rather than a consistent five. Because all levels of the test have 60 items plus the same timing and examples, different levels can be administered simultaneously in a classroom, a distinct advantage in reading where considerable heterogeneity exists.

The user's manual covers the entire battery of STEP tests, providing only a scanty section on the reading test, and little or no help in using the results constructively.

However, for the sophisticated psychometrician, the technical section of the handbook contains detailed descriptions of the data collection and analysis, including a good discussion of statistical error, the reliability of difference scores, and the construction of local norms. Most of the cases of lack of information pointed out in previous reviews have been corrected: there is new alternate form reading test reliability data (coefficients range from .76 to .93), correlations between SCAT verbal and STEP reading are presented (.75 to .83), and sex differences in reading are not as large now although girls consistently outperform boys approximately one converted score point.

The STEP reading test is technically one of the best gross measures of reading available, and Form A appears to be the better of the two forms. Series II represents a definite improvement over the earlier one, with generally credible answers to criticisms of MMY reviewers. However, any user who hopes to find a reading test that can be used for diagnostic purposes and which also makes some attempt at providing validity data should choose another test.

JAMES L. WARDROP, *Associate Professor of Educational Psychology and Chairperson of the Department, University of Illinois at Urbana-Champaign, Urbana, Illinois.*

The STEP reading tests are a part of a battery that is technically very sound. The description of the test development process, reliability data—including both internal consistency and alternate-forms estimates and a lucid discussion of the reliability of difference scores—and information about interrelationships of reading with other STEP subtests are commendably complete. Norm groups are carefully and clearly described, although one might wish for subgroup norms of several sorts besides the traditional girl-boy breakdown presented in the series handbook: by type of community, separating urban from suburban from rural communities; by socioeconomic level of schools, districts, or communities; by geographic region. Admittedly, to provide such information would have required a much more costly sampling plan than was used in norming the STEP battery. The norm groups appear to constitute representative national samples at all except the college level. The separate reporting of "school means" norms in addition to norms for individual scores is laudatory.

Evidence for the validity of STEP-R, as for most standardized achievement tests, is primarily in terms of content validity. Unlike many of its competitors, however, the test is not geared to a set of specific instructional objectives. This difference is consistent with the philosophy underlying both STEP and the closely related *Cooperative Primary Tests* (designed for use in grades 1.5–3, while STEP covers grades 4–14). As noted in the series handbook, these instruments were conceived to probe basic understandings, rather than "simple memorization of arbitrary rules and so-called 'facts.' " Accordingly, items requiring interpretation, evaluation, or inference are more prevalent in STEP-R than in many other reading tests. Correlations of STEP-R scores with those from the verbal subtest of the *School and College Ability Tests* are also provided. These correlations range from .75 to .83, with median .78, and are only slightly lower than correlations between alternate forms for STEP-R itself.

Norms tables allow conversion from raw scores to "converted scores," percentile ranks, and stanines. That the publishers have avoided using the much misunderstood grade-equivalent scores, but have instead created a "continuous" scale across all levels of the STEP, is commendable. That percentile ranks are downplayed and percentile bands emphasized for score interpretation is also worthy of positive comment.

All levels and forms of the tests have two parts: Part 1, containing 30 "sentence comprehension" (i.e., vocabulary) items; and Part 2, consisting of 30 "passage comprehension" items distributed over six brief reading selections. Items for both parts are categorized into "skill" areas (comprehension, translation and inference, and analysis), although no theoretical

basis is provided for presuming that these areas represent unique and important components of the reading process. Items are additionally categorized according to content (narrative, humanities, science, and social studies). (In STEP-R, none of the sentence comprehension items is classified as reflecting analysis skills; in fact, the distribution of "analysis" items—according to the publisher's own classification—ranges from a low of four items on Form 2B to a high of only eight items on Form 3B. The lack of a systematic progression from few to many analysis items and from many to fewer comprehension items as one moves from lower to higher grade levels is puzzling.) The skills-by-content classification matrix is presented in the early pages of the handbook, definitely preferable to the practice of those publishers who provide such information in what often seem to be the most unlikely places. The classification of items contains some strange anomalies; e.g., in the category "Translation and Inference—Narrative" are found both an item that requires the examinee to equate a "frosted pane" with a window and an item that asks (about a poem), "What was the child's main objection to washing?" Elsewhere, to select the best meaning for "examination" and to select "the best title" for a story are both categorized under "Comprehension—Narrative." It would require an unusual model of the reading process to justify a claim that the two items in each pair assess the same skill. It is reasonable to view the classification matrix as a heuristic means for obtaining appropriately broad coverage of the area of reading, but the user who wishes to carry out more detailed analyses of "groups of related questions" should examine the individual items carefully rather than relying on the publisher's classification.

Only a single "reading" score is reported. No separate part scores for vocabulary ("sentence comprehension") or comprehension ("passage comprehension") are given, although the correlation between these two parts is frequently lower than the correlation of reading scores with other STEP subtests (English expression, science, and especially social studies) for which separate scores *are* reported.

The STEP is a superb example of a standardized test of reading achievement. The handbook, consisting of a manual and the technical report, is thorough, complete, and clear. The test content assesses the so-called "higher-level" skills more adequately than the typical achievement test. Uses and limitations of scores are clearly described. If users are aware of the limitations of the published item-classification matrix and comfortable with the lack of systematic progression towards more analysis and fewer comprehension items as one moves from lower to higher levels of the test, they should find STEP-R a highly satisfactory standardized test of reading achievement.

[745]

*Stanford Achievement Test: Reading Tests, 1973 Edition. Grades 1.5–2.4, 2.5–3.4, 3.5–4.4, 4.5–5.4, 5.5–6.9, 7.0–9.5; 1923–75; 1964 edition still available; catalog uses the title *1973 Stanford Reading Tests;* 2 forms; 6 levels; 2 editions for primary levels 1–3; for battery accessories, see 29; separate answer sheets (Digitek, IBM 805, IBM 1230, MRC) may be used in grades 4.5–9.5; postage extra; specimen set not available; Richard Madden, Eric F. Gardner, Herbert C. Rudman, Bjorn Karlsen, and Jack C. Merwin; Psychological Corporation. *

a) PRIMARY LEVEL 1. Grades 1.5–2.4; 6 scores: reading (word, comprehension, word plus comprehension), word study skills, total, vocabulary; Forms A, B, ('73, c1972, 12 pages); 2 editions: hand scored, MRC scored; Form A manual ('73, 10 pages), Form B manual ('74, 10 pages); $8.95 per 35 hand scored tests; $2.25 per set of scoring stencils; $14.25 per 35 MRC scored tests; hand scoring service, $1.80 and over per test; MRC scoring service, 55¢ and over per test; (120) minutes in 2 sessions.

b) PRIMARY LEVEL 2. Grades 2.5–3.4; 6 scores: same as for primary level 1; Forms A, B, ('73, c1972, 12 pages); 2 editions: hand scored, MRC scored; Form A manual ('73, 11 pages), Form B manual ('74, 11 pages); $10.25 per 35 hand scored tests; $2.25 per set of scoring stencils; $15.25 per 35 MRC scored tests; scoring services and time same as for primary level 1.

c) PRIMARY LEVEL 3. Grades 3.5–4.4; 4 scores: comprehension, word study skills, total, vocabulary; Forms A, B, ('73, c1972, 12 pages); 2 editions: hand scored, MRC scored; Form A manual ('73, 10 pages), Form B manual ('74, 10 pages); $10.25 per 35 hand scored tests; $2.25 per set of scoring stencils; $15.25 per 35 MRC scored tests; scoring services same as for primary level 1; (110) minutes in 2 sessions.

d) INTERMEDIATE LEVEL 1. Grades 4.5–5.4; 4 scores: same as for primary level 3; Forms A, B, ('73, c1972, 10 pages); Form A manual ('73, 12 pages), Form B manual ('74, 12 pages); $10.25 per 35 tests; $2.25 per set of scoring stencils; answer sheets: $3 per 35 Digitek or IBM 1230, $2.50 per 35 IBM 805, $2.85 per 35 MRC; $2 per set of Digitek or IBM scoring stencils; $1 per MRC hand scoring stencil; Digitek or IBM scoring service, 80¢ and over per test; MRC scoring service, 40¢ and over per test; (115) minutes in 2 sessions.

e) INTERMEDIATE LEVEL 2. Grades 5.5–6.9; 4 scores: same as for primary level 3; Forms A, B, ('73, c1972, 10 pages); Form A manual ('73, 12 pages), Form B manual ('74, 12 pages); prices same as for intermediate level 1; (110) minutes in 2 sessions.

f) ADVANCED. Grades 7.0–9.5; 3 scores: vocabulary, comprehension, total; Forms A, B, ('73, c1972, 10 pages); manual ('73, 10 pages); $10.25 per 35 tests; $2.25 per set of scoring stencils; answer sheets: $3 per 35 Digitek or IBM 1230, $2.50 per 35 IBM 805, $2.85 per 35 MRC; $1 per Digitek or IBM scoring stencil; $1 per MRC hand scoring stencil; Digitek or IBM scoring service, 70¢ and over per test; MRC scoring service, 40¢ and over per test; (75) minutes in 2 sessions.

See T2:1603 (32 references); for a review by Arthur E. Traxler of the 1964 edition, see 7:708 (16 references); see also 6:813 (1 reference); for reviews by Helen M. Robinson and Agatha Townsend of an earlier edition, see 5:656; for a review by James R. Hobson, see 4:555 (4 references); for a review by Margaret G. McKim, see 3:503. For reviews of the complete battery, see 29 (2 reviews, 2 excerpts), 7:25 (1 excerpt), 6:26 (1 review, 1 excerpt), 5:25 (1 review), 4:25 (2 reviews), and 3:18 (2 reviews).

REFERENCES

1–4. See 4:555.
5. See 6:813.
6–21. See 7:708.
22–53. See T2:1603; also includes a cumulative name index to the first 53 references and 5 reviews for this test.
54. COLLINGWOOD, MADELINE DUCKWORTH. *A Descriptive Analysis of Reading Achievement Levels in Grade Four—A Follow-Up of a Three Year Experimental Study of Factors Affecting Learning to Read.* Doctor's thesis, University of Pittsburgh (Pittsburgh, Pa.), 1972. (*DAI* 34:1475A)
55. FILLMER, H. T.; BUSBY, WALTER A.; AND SMITTLE, PATRICIA. "Visual Perception and Self Concept: New Directions in Reading." *J Read Behav* 4(3):17–20 su '72. *
56. LOHNES, PAUL R. "Statistical Descriptors of School Classes." *Am Ed Res J* 9(4):547–56 f '72. *
57. NEWMAN, ANABEL P. "Later Achievement Study of Pupils Underachieving in Reading in First Grade." *Read Res Q* 7(3):477–508 sp '72. * (*PA* 49:10005)
58. SABATINO, DAVID A.; HAYDEN, DAVID L.; AND KELLING, KENT. "Perceptual, Language, and Academic Achievement of English, Spanish, and Navajo Speaking Children Referred for Special Classes." *J Sch Psychol* 10(1):39–46 Mr '72. * (*PA* 48:12198)
59. SANDERS, PAULINE M. *The Relationship of Culturally-Related Variables to the Reading Achievement of Nonreservation Cherokee Indian Pupils.* Doctor's thesis, University of Arkansas (Fayetteville, Ark.), 1972. (*DAI* 33:1989A)
60. CALLENBACH, CARL. "The Effects of Instruction and Practice in Content-Independent Test-Taking Techniques Upon the Standardized Reading Test Scores of Selected Second-Grade Students." *J Ed Meas* 10(1):25–30 sp '73. *
61. GALLISTEL, ELIZABETH. "Achievement on a Test of Specific Coding Skills Contrasted With Achievement on Global Tests of Reading Skills." *J Learn Dis* 6(1):1–5+ Ja '73. * (*PA* 50:3762)
62. GAVIN, JAMES F., AND TOOLE, DAVID L. "Validity of Aptitude Tests for the 'Hardcore Unemployed.'" *Personnel Psychol* 26(1):139–46 sp '73. * (*PA* 51:1988)
63. O'BRIEN, DONALD. *An Investigation of Relationships Existing Between Cloze Form Measures of Reading Comprehension and Reading Behaviors Determined by the Reading Inventory Technique and Standardized Reading Tests.* Doctor's thesis, State University of New York (Buffalo, N.Y.), 1973. (*DAI* 35:324A)
64. PRANGE, JANET L. *An Investigation of the Relationships Obtaining Between Cloze Test Measures of Reading Performance and Measures of Critical Reading, General Reading, Intelligence and Sex.* Doctor's thesis, State University of New York (Buffalo, N.Y.), 1973. (*DAI* 34:6459A)
65. RYAN, ROBERT ARCHER. *An Investigation of Psycholinguistic Factors as They Relate to Reading Ability of Mentally Retarded Students.* Doctor's thesis, University of South Carolina (Columbia, S.C.), 1973. (*DAI* 34:1710A)
66. SANDERS, COLUMBUS NELSON. *Correlations of Reading Achievement With Various Phonic Word-Recognition Skills for Inner-City Black Children.* Doctor's thesis, University of Oregon (Eugene, Ore.), 1973. (*DAI* 34:3041A)
67. BURNHAM, CAROLYN JOAN STIGMAN. *Reading Achievement Survey in Granite School District—A Diagnostic Study of Skills and Deficiencies of Seventh Grade Students.* Doctor's thesis, University of Utah (Salt Lake City, Utah), 1974. (*DAI* 35:4119A)
68. CHARROW, V. R., AND FLETCHER, J. D. "English as the Second Language of Deaf Children." *Develop Psychol* 10(4):463–70 Jl '74. * (*PA* 52:12761)
69. EMANUEL, JANE M., AND SAGAN, EDGAR L. "The Intelligence, Reading Achievement, and Arithmetic Achievement Scores of Head Start Attendees Compared to Head Start

Non-Attendees in the First, Second and Third Grades."
Training Sch B 71(2):119–32 Ag '74. *

70. LORD, FREDERIC M. "Quick Estimates of the Relative Efficiency of Two Tests as a Function of Ability Level." *J Ed Meas* 11(4):247–54 W '74. *

71. LORET, PETER G.; SEDER, ALAN; BIANCHINI, JOHN C.; AND VALE, CAROL A. *Anchor Test Study: Equivalence and Norms Tables for Selected Reading Achievement Tests (Grades 4, 5, and 6).* DHEW Publication S/N 1780-01312. Washington, D.C.: Government Printing Office, 1974. Pp. ix, 92. *

72. MEISEL, STEPHEN M. *A Comparison of the Oral Language of Average Achieving Male Readers and Low Achieving Male Readers in Fourth Grade.* Doctor's thesis, Hofstra University (Hempstead, N.Y.), 1974. (*DAI* 35:7788A)

73. GRAY, JERRY L., AND KNIEF, LOTUS M. "The Relationship Between Cognitive Style and School Achievement." *J Exp Ed* 43(4):67–71 su '75. *

74. LINN, ROBERT L. "Anchor Test Study: The Long and the Short of It." *J Ed Meas* 12(3):201–13 f '75. *

75. RUBIN, ROSALYN A. "Reading Ability and Assigned Materials: Accommodation for the Slow but Not the Accelerated." *El Sch J* 75(6):373–7 Mr '75. * (*PA* 54:6274)

GENE V GLASS, *Professor of Education, University of Colorado, Boulder, Colorado.*

The coverage of reading skills in this test adequately represents reading which is taught in the schools and which is currently validly measurable by written tests. An innovation with this sixth edition is an auditory vocabulary test at all levels below advanced.

In addition to the test booklets, directions, keys, and norms, the user may purchase a wealth of auxiliary battery materials: guides to interpretation, indices of instructional objectives with item difficulties, a technical report, and a series of research reports. The test has been thoroughly studied and its properties carefully documented.

The test norms provide percentile ranks, stanine scores, grade equivalent scores, and "scaled" scores. A slight comparative advantage of this test over its competition is that the norms at the lowest two primary levels are based on testings in October, February, and May instead of only one or two testings during the year. The norms are based on data from over 275,000 pupils in 109 school districts in 43 states. The matching of the norm group characteristics with data on the entire nation is quite close.

The content validity of the test appears to be adequate. It purports to test reading, and any reasonable observer would agree that it does. Curriculum analyses, expert reviews, and field tryouts preceded item selection. In the indices of instructional objectives, items are grouped under objectives, and "p values" (percent of norm group answering correctly) are reported for each item. It is unclear what use one would make of these; they are too molecular to guide instruction. Considering that the test would be given only once in a school year, of what instruc-

tional value is it to a teacher to learn in May, for example, that the class cannot spell words involving the "schwa" sound? Insufficient norm data are given at the level of the global objectives (of which there are about a dozen at each level of the test). The best use one could make of these data at the objectives level is to plot trends across years for a school or district.

Reliability data abound, but they are all based on split-half or K-R 20 coefficients. The former could be omitted without loss, since they are nearly identical to the latter and would have been expected to be so. Information about the stability reliability of the test—say over a period of 12 and 24 months, which might represent the typical intervals between obtaining a score and making a decision with it—is lacking and would be welcomed.

In technical quality, content validity, and completeness, this test is the equal of the other major achievement tests, viz., Metropolitan, Iowa, and California. There is no real choice among these four tests on technical grounds. The user can select the test which most conveniently fits his particular needs with the confidence that he is purchasing a competent piece of psychometric workmanship.

EARL F. RANKIN, *Professor of Education, University of Kentucky, Lexington, Kentucky.*

The reading component of the 1973 edition of the Stanford test battery yields three to six scores (depending upon test level) for major dimensions of reading achievement. Therefore, this component should be viewed as a survey test of general reading achievement. Although these tests may serve some diagnostic purposes, they were not designed primarily as diagnostic instruments.

Stanford Reading Tests have been widely used for many years and enjoy a deservedly prestigious reputation. In keeping with a tradition of excellence, these tests have undergone five revisions since the first edition appeared in 1923.

In contrast with the 1964 edition, the present revision has been changed in several respects: (*a*) Whereas the last edition produced scores mainly for reading vocabulary and paragraph meaning, the present edition yields, at various levels, scores for vocabulary (dictated), vocabulary (reading), reading (comprehension), word study skills, and total reading. (*b*) The item format for measuring reading comprehension has been changed from sentence completion to multiple choice. (*c*) The dictated vocabulary subtest and another test in the battery, listening comprehension, can be combined to produce a total auditory score for diagnostic purposes. (*d*) This test is designed not only for norm-referenced interpretation but also for instructional-objective interpretation, with extensive advice to teachers for classroom use. (*e*) In keeping with the current emphasis on decoding, word study skills are measured beyond the primary grades through grade 6.9. (*f*) A common scale of measurement relates this battery to the *Stanford Early School Achievement Test,* the *Stanford Test of Academic Skills* (secondary-college level), and the *Otis-Lennon Mental Ability Test.* (*g*) Provisions have been made for extended normative grade coverage at each test level to accommodate use by schools having widely different levels of achievement. (*h*) The number of test levels has been increased from five to six by adding an additional primary level test and modifying the span of grades covered by each level. (*i*) Many features involving new types of norms and extensive scoring and reporting services have been added. Besides the usual individual pupil norms, special group norms such as "p values" and "school group stanines" should prove most helpful in evaluating the effectiveness of the curriculum and in making administrative decisions. It is clear that the present edition represents a major attempt to update the tests to meet contemporary educational and social needs.

In the writer's judgment, most of the new features of this edition are highly commendable. The new pattern of subtests provides more specific and useful information than the last edition. However, the exclusion of a reading vocabulary subtest for both the primary 3 and intermediate level tests is puzzling. The dictated vocabulary score and the total auditory score should be helpful in separating listening vocabulary from reading vocabulary problems for both prognostic and diagnostic purposes. Although it is doubtful that multiple choice items will measure reading comprehension more validly than sentence completion items, this change probably increases "item acceptability" and certainly facilitates interpretation in relation to instructional

objectives. The focus of all test items upon the attainment of specific objectives should be of value to teachers. However, the interpretation of skill grouping scores must be made cautiously due to probable large measurement error stemming from the small number of items within some skill groupings. Given current variations in achievement at the same grade levels in different schools, the extended grade coverage norms may be useful. The manual states: "It is always possible to use any battery level with children in any grade and translate scores into grade equivalents or scaled scores since both are continuous scales across all grades." However, this usage may lead to some bizarre interpretations of reading achievement. For example, a third grade level test could be administered to a sixth grade class from a low socioeconomic environment; grade equivalent scores of six or better might be erroneously interpreted as "reading up to grade level." Obviously, such a grade equivalent score of six would only apply to facility in reading third grade materials, not sixth.

New features that are particularly outstanding are the publisher's scoring services which, together with the use of scaled scores and special group norms, offer unique assistance in evaluating the effectiveness of instruction. Advice in the manual regarding the complex problem of measuring reading improvement is comprehensive, but the writer doubts that the simple use of scaled scores is an adequate solution to this problem.

From a technical standpoint, the test is well constructed, with some minor exceptions. Test development was carried out in a careful and thorough manner involving a very large representative standardization sample. Reported reliability coefficients are impressive, generally in the high .80s to mid-.90s. It should be noted that the probable effect of speed upon split-half and K-R reliability coefficients is extrapolated from research on the 1953 edition. In view of the otherwise extensive statistical and measurement data provided for these tests, it is odd that no reliability coefficients are provided for the total reading score. Although evidence for content and construct validity is convincing, no studies are reported for "criterion related" validity. Even though we are told that the test forms were equated upon the basis of "inter-

Stanford Achievement Test: Reading Tests

preted scores," no evidence is presented concerning the equivalence of means and variances or the magnitude of correlations among these presumably equivalent forms.

Mention should be made of the attractive test format, very complete and informative manuals, and excellent research bulletins. Instructions for test administration and interpretation are well written. Despite some lapses, technical data are very complete. In general, this recent edition of a well-known test represents a marked improvement over the previous edition, incorporates several desirable new features, and deserves a high rating.

[746]
*Sucher-Allred Reading Placement Inventory. Reading level grades 1–9; 1968–73; SARPI; 3 major scores: independent, instructional, and frustrational grade reading levels; no data on reliability and validity; individual; 1 form ('73, 16 pages in manual); manual ('73, 33 pages plus test and record forms); record booklet ('73, 8 pages); $2.97 per 35 record booklets; $2.49 per manual; postpaid; (20) minutes; Floyd Sucher and Ruel A. Allred; Economy Co. *
See T2:1604 (1 reference).

REFERENCES
1. See T2:1604.
2. DAINES, DELVA, AND MASON, LYNNE G. "A Comparison of Placement Tests and Readability Graphs." J Read 15(8): 597–603 My '72. *
3. JOHNS, JERRY. "Review of the Sucher-Allred Reading Placement Inventory." Read World 12(1):72–4 O '72. *
4. STAFFORD, JERRY. "Review of the Sucher-Allred Reading Placement Inventory." Read World 14(4):269–71 My '75. *

MARJORIE S. JOHNSON, *Professor of Reading and Chairman, Psychology of Reading Department, Temple University, Philadelphia, Pennsylvania.*

The objectives of this test are important ones for any teacher to accomplish—to identify the child's reading levels and common word-recognition and comprehension errors in order to place him in appropriate materials for instruction. The tests and the directions provided in the manual, however, would seem to lead to superficiality in the accomplishment of these objectives.

The statement, for example, that this can be done in 20 minutes per child is one which would encourage superficiality. In actuality, this testing is designed to follow a "gross screening" conducted to "identify each student's general reading ability." Six steps are prescribed for this screening. The only recommendations given are that the child's reading of materials he chooses (one selection for oral rereading and one for oral reading at sight) be rated "read very well,

or fair, or poorly" and the level recorded as a guide to a starting place for the inventory. If done thoroughly, this gross screening could provide the same information as the inventory itself and would certainly involve a considerable amount of time.

Another factor in the superficiality of results is the recommended procedure for recording responses. In the word recognition test, there is no instruction to record the child's actual responses. A check is recorded to indicate either an incorrect response or no response. Therefore, no diagnostic information is made available. Likewise, except for a suggestion that "in some cases it is helpful to record the student's response," reading comprehension questions are simply marked for amount of credit. A minimum amount of data would be accumulated, therefore, for analysis of specific strengths and weaknesses which were revealed in the course of the testing.

A second major problem is that the inventory would tend to overestimate the reading levels of students for a number of reasons. First, no criteria are given for correct responses to comprehension questions. In fact, one or sometimes two possible answers are given and the directions state that "credit should be given for these or other reasonable responses." Each of the selections has five questions, each of which purports to measure one of the following: main idea (always choosing a title), facts, sequence (always telling what event followed a stated one), inference, and critical thinking. For the last type, the questions can, in most cases, be answered yes or no, which must be followed by a reason. In only one case do the authors indicate a stand on whether the selection leads to a particular judgment. Where the suggested answer is "yes or no, depending on a reasonable explanation," it is difficult to see, on the basis of many selections, how diametrically opposed judgments could be reasonably explained. The lack of stated criteria for correct responses opens up the possibility that the level of comprehension might be grossly inflated through the acceptance of less-than-good responses. Second, the starting point for the inventory seems too high, especially when one considers that the identification of an independent reading level is one of the objectives. It is suggested that the oral reading be begun one level below that at which the child "made five or more errors on the Word-Recognition Test" unless there are indications that he has "extreme reading difficulties" or is "apprehensive about the test." No instructions are given about what the examiner should do if the child performs poorly on the starting level. There is inconsistency about this starting level in that it is suggested that it is an "approximate instructional level" and yet testing is begun only one level lower, leaving little room for an independent level. Third, in the area of word recognition, the scores may be inflated by the treatment of proper nouns. Instructions are that errors on these are to be counted only once, regardless of how often they occur. Each repetition of the name, however, is tallied in the word count. Thus, Selection A has 51 words, four of which are Tom and five of which are Jim. If errors on these are to be counted only once, it would seem that the repetitions should be eliminated from the word count. The two allowable errors for the independent level would therefore be two errors out of 44 words rather than 51 and would place the child below the criterion level set for the independent reading level. Further, ambiguity exists about the significance of "uncounted errors" such as corrections, hesitations, and repetitions of less than three words. These do not seem to be used in determining levels unless there is a choice of instructional levels indicated by the scores.

Several other questions arise about the inventory. The criteria used for the independent, instructional, and frustrational levels differ from those usually given in other materials on informal reading inventories. No source for these criteria or justification of them is given. Information on the word selection is vague; and, although treatment of certain words in the readability study is indicated, no rationale for that treatment is stated. Finally, the fact that only one form is provided limits the use of the inventory.

Modifications of standard procedures for informal reading inventories include only an untimed word recognition test rather than a flashed and an untimed measure, elimination of silent reading as a measure, and reduction of the number of comprehension questions. This pattern follows that of the *Classroom Reading Inventory,* but in the Sucher-Allred no attention

is paid to these modifications and no provision is made for flexibility of administration such as that offered in the CRI.

The effort to provide an inventory and a self-teaching manual is a worthy one. Teachers do need to be able to place children correctly for instruction and to know their assets and liabilities as readers in order to plan an effective program for them. The *Sucher-Allred Reading Placement Inventory* appears to oversimplify this whole process.

JAMES L. WARDROP, *Associate Professor of Educational Psychology, and Chairperson of the Department, University of Illinois at Urbana-Champaign, Urbana, Illinois.*

This test consists of two parts: a word-recognition task and an oral-reading task. Each part contains 12 "graded" sections covering the range from primer through grade 9. The test materials are embedded in a manual that is a self-instructional presentation of information about how to use the inventory.

Unfortunately, the manual is entirely prescriptive, with essentially no justification presented for any of the assertions the authors make. In this respect, the Sucher-Allred is like those dozens of other "diagnostic" reading tests or informal reading inventories that depend primarily on the authors' conception of what is important to look at in assessing a child's reading proficiency or problems. If the test has any redeeming feature, it is the modesty of the claims made for its utility.

The single form, lack of reliability and validity data, simplistic conception of the skills involved in reading, and inadequate scoring instructions are flaws which place the Sucher-Allred outside any reasonable boundaries for what can properly be considered a "test." It is unfortunate that it is marketed as a "test" and that, in spite of the suggestion that it can be used "for placing each student at the appropriate reading levels," no guidance is provided for identifying appropriate instructional materials or strategies once an "instructional level" has been identified.

The single form consists of 12 vocabulary lists (little information is given about the guidelines used to determine what words would be included in these lists) and 12 passages "ranging in degree of difficulty from primer through ninth-grade reading level." For the "word-recognition" subtest, the pupil simply pronounces each of the words in a list; while for the "oral reading" test, the pupil reads a passage aloud while the teacher records errors, and then answers five "comprehension questions" about the passage. The only hint of reliability or validity data is the cryptic statement that "a study was conducted to determine which words were the best predictors for each grade level."

For comprehension questions, "the teacher judges the adequacy of each answer and records full, partial, or no errors (1, 3/4, 1/2, 1/4, 0)." However, the only guidance given for scoring are lists that give one or two possible answers for each question. No guidelines are given for determining how much credit is to be given for an answer or what features of an answer are to be considered in scoring.

Some teachers may find the Sucher-Allred useful as a preliminary gross screening instrument, but there is no justification for using it as anything more.

*Read World 12(1):72–4 O '72. Jerry Johns. *
There are....several comments of a somewhat critical nature which this reviewer would like to raise. First, the criteria for determining the independent, instructional, and frustration levels are not based on the traditional criteria developed by Emmett A. Betts. Consequently, teachers who use the *Sucher-Allred Reading Placement Inventory* should remember that the three reading levels may be slightly different from those determined with the Betts criteria. Although there is recent evidence to suggest that the Betts criteria are too high, there is insufficient evidence to indicate with assurance what criteria are most suitable. Second, the placement inventory relies heavily on oral reading selections to estimate the pupil's reading levels. While this procedure is probably adequate for the primary grades, silent reading becomes more important at the upper grade levels. For this reason, it would have been desirable to include silent reading passages, in addition to the oral reading selections, at levels four through nine. Third, for each of the graded selections there are five questions which deal with main ideas, facts, sequence, inference, and critical thinking. The inference and critical thinking questions for many of the graded selections are, in this reviewer's opinion, mislabeled. Many of the

so-called "inference" questions might be more accurately labeled opinion questions. Practically all of the "critical thinking" questions would be better identified as experience and/or evaluation questions since the student is given credit if the pupil gives a reasonable answer. Because the authors provide no definitions of what they mean by an inference question or a critical thinking question, prospective users of the placement inventory should evaluate the questions before assuming that the questions tap the skills of inference and/or critical thinking. Misclassifying questions is a very common error in both published and informal reading inventories. Finally, as the pupil reads the graded selections the teacher records omissions, substitutions, insertions, and the like. These miscues in word recognition are merely counted as errors in determining the pupil's reading levels. Recent research in miscue analysis would suggest a need for a qualitative analysis of "errors" instead of a mere quantitative analysis. Interested teachers could, nevertheless, conduct such an analysis. It is unfortunate that the authors did not include a few basic questions (Does the miscue make sense?, Is the miscue acceptable grammatically?, Is there graphic similarity?, Is there sound similarity?) to assist teachers in conducting a qualitative analysis of the pupil's miscues. Although the *Sucher-Allred Reading Placement Inventory* has a number of limitations (something which plagues all currently published reading inventories), it is well organized, has an attractive format, and should be an asset to any classroom teacher interested in identifying each pupil's reading levels. After all, the single greatest step teachers could take to improve reading instruction would be to place pupils in reading materials which are at their instructional levels.

*Read World 14(4):269–71 My '75. Jerry Stafford. * designed for use by classroom teachers to identify students' independent, instructional and frustrational reading levels; identify common word recognition and comprehension errors; and to place students in appropriate materials for instruction * The test purports to identify common comprehension errors on the part of the reader. It seems likely that many students would read so few passages that a truly reliable pattern of comprehension errors would be impossible to arrive at. Furthermore, presenting questions to be answered after the student has read seems to be inconsistent with the current instructional practice of establishing purposes for reading prior to reading. * Accuracy in reading using the S-ARPI is determined by simply counting the number of errors the student makes while reading the word lists and the reading passages. This procedure is questionable for several reasons. First, recent investigation suggests that the errors (miscues) children make while reading are not of equal importance. * Second, there are data which suggest that the errors made at the instructional level differ from the errors made at the frustrational level. * Third, the S-ARPI is designed for use by classroom teachers. The literature suggests that examiners have considerable difficulty in accurately coding children's oral reading errors. * The S-ARPI identifies students' independent, instructional and frustrational reading levels using the following performance criteria: at least 97% accuracy in word recognition and at least 80% accuracy in comprehension for independent level; 92% to 96% accuracy in word recognition and from 60% to 79% in comprehension accuracy for instructional level; and less than 92% in word accuracy and less than 60% in comprehension accuracy for frustrational level. An examination of the literature on the topic suggests that there is considerable disagreement among authorities as to the performance criteria that should be used for determining independent, instructional and frustrational levels. The authors provide no data to suggest why these performance criteria were chosen for their test. Moreover, there are data which suggest that students in the primary and intermediate levels may need different performance criteria. Furthermore, the manual offers no suggestion as to what should happen if a student reads at the instructional level for word recognition and the frustrational level in comprehension or vice versa. The original philosophy of the informal reading inventory suggested that the materials used for testing be the same materials that are going to be used for teaching. S-ARPI is an obvious violation of this philosophy. In discussing the use of commercially produced inventories as opposed to teacher made inventories using instructional materials, Beldin raises the following question: "Can this be done safely, or do we get more

valid results by developing test materials from the classroom instructional materials?" The authors of the S-ARPI have provided no data which suggest that their test is valid for its intended purpose.

[747]

Wide-span Reading Test. Ages 7–15; 1972; Forms A, B, (8 pages); manual (30 pages); separate answer sheets must be used; £2.50 per 25 tests; 65p per 25 answer sheets; 65p per manual; specimen set not available; postage extra; 30(35) minutes; Alan Brimer (incorporating material by Herbert Gross); Thomas Nelson & Sons Ltd. [England]. *

DAVID J. CARROLL, *Research Associate, The Godfrey Thomson Unit for Academic Assessment, The University of Edinburgh, Edinburgh, Scotland.*

This test aims to assess reading comprehension at all levels from the beginning of silent reading to "the full development of reading comprehension effectiveness." Reading comprehension is defined as decoding print into sounds, fitting meaning to groups of sounds, and construing the structure (syntactic and semantic) of a text. Continuous passages are not used. Output takes the form of standard scores, a nominal scale, and three categories of "diagnostic" information. There are two parallel forms, and information about both first and second occasions of testing.

This test is certainly both original and ambitious. It sets out to provide a great deal of information, and to do it in a novel way. The "stem" of each item is a sentence with one chosen word omitted. In this way it could be said to resemble modified cloze procedure, the more so, as there is now evidence that cloze procedure is substantially sentence, or even clause, bound—i.e., that ambiguity is resolved within the boundaries of the clause, before any connections are made. The novelty consists in the way in which the possible range of answers is constrained, not by a multiple choice group, but by the provision of a sentence, from which the correct word is extracted.

The manual contains no indication of rationale, beyond that item difficulty will depend upon "the complexity of the incomplete sentence, the embeddedness of the missing word in the second sentence, and the counter-suggestion of inappropriate alternatives." This is not self-evident. Discussion with fluent readers suggests that, when taking the test they were not, after the first few items, misled by the structure of the second sentence. None of them could remember anything of any of these sentences beyond the first five, having used them simply as a source of words to check against the syntactic and semantic constraints of the incomplete sentences. It is possible, however, that less fluent readers would not grasp that this could be done, and would be confronted with such difficulties as transforming a word which, in the second sentence, is object (noun) into object (verb), before it will fit. This will increase discrimination, and is undoubtedly relevant to reading, but will penalise those who can read the second sentences more than those who can only extract individual words.

No rationale is given, again, for the three diagnostic subscores; (*a*) decoding (should perhaps be called encoding) loads entirely on difficulty in translating words into graphemes; (*b*) vocabulary includes any word which is semantically inappropriate; and (*c*) linguistic includes anything that is not syntactically appropriate. There is no indication of the relative frequency with which these three diagnostic categories occur, or of their stability on test-retest—which is the more unfortunate, since it appears that all the children in the standardisation sample were tested twice over. They are unlikely, however, to be rare since the indicators are divided into six classes and each category contains three classes, a category being signaled if half or more of the total number of indicators occur in it.

The "interpretation" section of the manual describes these diagnostic categories in general terms, but makes no suggestion for interpretation, beyond that a specific diagnosis should be made. Of decoding skills, it says: "since such inadequacy occurs in relation to incorrect responses, there is some reason to suppose that it inhibits effective reading comprehension." However, since the diagnosis loads *only* on wrong responses, this claim is perhaps overstated.

Administration instructions are clear. Younger children may find difficulty in manipulating both test booklet and answer sheet, and in grasping that they have to find in one sentence a word to fill in a gap in another sentence, then write this word down in the correct place on an altogether separate piece of paper. Diagnostic marking would be easier if examples were given, and if

there were somewhere to sum the various diagnostic totals for the two pages of answer sheet.

Parallel-form reliabilities range from .89 to .94, with median .92, for eight year groups.

The method of standardisation chosen is inadequately described. The method of sampling is not described at all, beyond assurances as to its adequacy. However, the numbers involved, and the sample parameters, are included. Tables are provided for year of schooling, occasion of administration, form, and age, but not sex. The age allowance is calculated from the regression of raw score on age but there is no evidence whether it was simply calculated at the 50th percentile, or at others, or what form the averaging took.

This method of standardisation has several advantages, where a test is intended to be administered to widely-differing groups. It is capable of reflecting the differing levels of the subsections of the population, and their differing rates of progress. These variations are not lost in the spurious smoothness of a single conversion table. It is, however, vulnerable, especially at the extremes, to error. Because the various tables are constructed independently, it is not wise to rely on them either for a reading age (none are calculated) or for a measure of progress from year to year. In extreme cases, a child may make no progress whatever in a year of schooling, or even slip back, while retaining his percentile position in the year group. Alternatively, a child with four years of schooling can score lower than one of the same age with three years of schooling. This is counter-intuitive, and would be removed by other methods of standardisation. The tables themselves are difficult to follow. They consist of 17 columns of small type, with few lines to guide the eye.

There is no information given in the manual about test construction, validity, and correlation with other tests. One can, however, draw some conclusions about validity.

The length of the test is between 23 and 45 items, depending upon the age range of the subjects. It should be used with caution for Junior 1 children, where it is unlikely to be informative about below-average children, and with Secondary 3 and 4 children, to whom it seems to be losing its relevance. There is some practice effect, which is not due to difficulty in understanding gap-filling, but probably to the need to

Wide-span Reading Test

"unlearn" normal reading, when dealing with the selection of words. No provision is made for guessing in completing the diagnostic categories. Inspection suggests that the range of words tested is heavily biased away from structure words, and the syntax savours of constructors' standbys, such as the opposite analogy and the masked definition, seldom seen in ordinary prose.

In summary, the test is competently constructed, but evidence is needed to justify its rationale. The constructors should have studied the *Standards for Educational and Psychological Tests* before writing their manual. The potential purchaser should assure himself that he is able to interpret the results before choosing this test in preference to the many simpler group reading tests now on the market.

WILLIAM YULE, *Senior Lecturer in Psychology, Institute of Psychiatry, University of London, London, England.*

This is an interesting test of reading comprehension, intended for use in groups. The test consists of 80 items. For each item, the child has to read two short sentences. In the second sentence, a word has been omitted, and the child has to complete the blank with the appropriate word from the first sentence. In arriving at the total score, spelling errors are ignored, although they are examined in the diagnostic scales. Children start the test at different points according to their age, but all are allowed 30 minutes for completion.

When the test is used for diagnostic purposes, children who do poorly are asked to complete earlier items. If at least 10 errors can be coded, the diagnostic scales can be employed. Errors are classified as decoding, linguistic, or vocabulary errors. The author claims that the predominant error indicates the nature of the child's reading disability. No evidence is cited to substantiate this claim.

Although the instructions for administering the test as a group test seem clear, the administrator has to decide at the end of the time limit whether to ask the child to continue in order to obtain diagnostic data.

The test has been standardized on over 900 children in each of eight age groups. The children were drawn from many schools over England and Wales. The manual provides no descriptive data on the social class, rural-urban, immigrant-nonimmigrant nature of the sample. Parallel-form reliabilities range from .89 to .94. Surprisingly, no validity data at all are provided.

This test has face validity as a test of reading comprehension. In view of its interesting, novel format, it would have been more valuable had the author provided data on how it relates to other, better established, reading tests. The diagnostic scales seem arbitrary, and not related to any particular theory of reading disability. The suggestion that they can help teachers identify appropriate remedial activities owes more to hope and commercial sales talk than to empirical findings.

DIAGNOSTIC

[748]
★**Analysis of Skills: Reading.** Grades 1–2, 3–4, 5–6, 7–8; 1974–76; also called *ASK-Reading* and *STS-ASK: Reading;* "objective-referenced and norm-referenced"; 4 area scores (word analysis, comprehension, study skills, total) plus 43 to 48 skill scores [3 items per skill: mastery (3 items correct or 2 items including the most difficult), partial mastery (2 easiest items correct), non-mastery (0 or 1 item correct)]: discrimination (1 to 5 skills, grades 1–4 only), phonetic analysis—consonants (2 to 7 skills), phonetic analysis—vowels (2 to 6), structural analysis (3 to 6) word recognition (5, grades 1–2 only), vocabulary in context (5), literal comprehension (4 to 6), inferential comprehension (3 to 9), critical comprehension (1 to 7), library and reference skills (3 to 6), organization skills (1 to 3), pictorial and graphic material (1 to 2), following directions (2, grades 3–8 only); no data on reliability; no norms for skill scores; 4 levels; general manual ('74, 22 pages); directions manual ('74, 20 pages) for levels 34–78; interpretive manual ('74, 12 pages); master skills outline ('74, 2 pages); interpretive folder for students ('74, 3 pages) for each level; content outline ('74, 4 pages) for each level; separate answer sheets (NCS) must be used for levels 34–78; $12 per 20 tests; $8.50 per 50 answer sheets; $1.50 per general manual; postage extra; $2 per specimen set, cash orders only; scoring service, 52¢ per test; rental and scoring service, $1.30 and over per student for level 12, $1 and over for levels 34–78; O. F. Anderhalter (series director) and Frances Shands (reading coordinator); Scholastic Testing Service, Inc. *
a) LEVEL 12. Grades 1–2; 1974–76; 47 skills; 1 form ('74, 28 pages, NCS scorable); directions manual ('76, 26 pages); (165–185) minutes in 3 sessions.
b) LEVEL 34. Grades 3–4; 1974; 43 skills; 1 form (19 pages); (125–145) minutes in 3 sessions.
c) LEVEL 56. Grades 5–6; 1974; 48 skills; 1 form (19 pages); (145–165) minutes in 3 sessions.
d) LEVEL 78. Grades 7–8; 1974; 45 skills; 1 form (18 pages); (145–165) minutes in 3 sessions.

Wide-span Reading Test

JOHN T. GUTHRIE, *Director of Research, International Reading Association, Newark, Delaware.*

The authors claim to have developed a criterion-referenced test based on reading skills that are commonly taught. The objectives for this test were developed by examining textbooks used in grades 1 through 8 and by using taxonomies from national, state, and local sources. From this search came a list of 60 objectives for reading instruction. These are spread over the eight grade levels; not all grades include all of the objectives. The objectives are reading skills that the authors believe children should learn. The skills are clearly stated and the items are representative of the defined skills. Over the four levels (12, 34, 56, 78) from first to eighth grade, the emphasis on word analysis skills decreases, which makes good sense. The emphasis on vocabulary and literal comprehension is equally high at all levels. Study skills are also included at all levels. The number of items that are claimed to measure inferential comprehension and critical (evaluative) comprehension increases from grades 1 through 8. Administration of the test is generally quite straightforward. The interpretive booklet for the administrator and the general manual are clear, as are the instructions to the examinees in the manuals for the separate forms.

Content validity, which is important for a criterion-referenced test, depends firstly on whether the content is well defined. The authors define the content as the components of reading that should be taught in instructional programs. However, a rationale for these components is not provided and the number of subskills or components in reading is highly controversial. For instructional purposes, we need to have measurements on the minimum number of distinguishable skills that affect the most complex outcome of reading, comprehension, and memory, of a passage of text. For example, we would not refer to uttering the sound /k/ for the letter "k" as a component of reading, since that particular behavior would be unlikely to affect paragraph comprehension except under unusual circumstances. However, producing the sounds often associated with all single consonants would certainly influence paragraph comprehension and might be called a component. Understanding homonyms (pair, pare) is not

regarded as a component, since in itself it could hardly make a difference in comprehension of most paragraphs. But the size of a child's oral vocabulary, a more general skill, may legitimately be considered a component.

Although we wish to identify as many important components of reading as possible, there is reason to believe that this test has isolated too many. For example, consonant digraphs are tested as a component. It is unlikely that inability to recognize and pronounce consonant digraphs will impair reading comprehension significantly. This task is too microscopic to be called a component. However, a class of consonant rules, including consonant digraphs, consonant blends, and consonant variants, might be formed that would be powerful enough to qualify. In addition, there are two subtests, inferential comprehension-figurative language, and word meanings from context, that are very similar. In both cases, the child is presented a sentence with an underlined word or phrase. The child's task is to select the printed word or phrase that contains the same meaning from a set of alternatives. For example, to test understanding of figurative language, examinees are given the sentence, "George *saw the light* when the coach explained the play the second time." The alternatives are: (a) looked at a neon sign, (b) saw the sun, (c) blinked his eyes, (d) flipped, (e) understood. In a different subtest, word meanings from context, one sentence is: "I did not *witness* the robbery because I was blindfolded." The alternatives are: (a) see or observe, (b) sit during, (c) wait for, (d) stand up, (e) listen to. Both subtests require examinees to predict the meaning of a few underlined words from the rest of the information in the sentence and from the reader's knowledge. In the figurative language subtest, some metaphoric information is contained in the underlined words. In the other subtest, almost no information is available in the underlined word since it is unknown to most readers in the age group for whom the level is intended. The minor distinction between the cognitive operations needed to perform these tasks does not justify separate subtests, since the distinction will not be likely to make a difference in paragraph comprehension. This test errs on the side of splitting reading into too many subskills. The consequence is that measurement and teaching are

Analysis of Skills: Reading

directed to immaterial tasks, rather than substantial components of reading.

No other indications of validity are provided. There are no data correlating a total score on this measure with total scores on other measures; there is no evidence of intercorrelation between subtests of this measure and subtests in other measures. Finally, the face validity of this test is doubtful, since the topography of reading is not mapped to scale by the subskills. Trivial objectives, such as recognizing homographs, and important ones, such as understanding synonyms for words, are both measured by three-item subtests which give them equal weight in scoring and interpretation.

A basic purpose of this test is to measure how well subskills have been mastered. The scoring guide is intended to facilitate this usage by illustrating nonmastery, partial mastery, or mastery for each skill. However, the concept of mastery for reading subskills is tenuous. Consider, for example, synonyms, a subtest in all levels. Items contain presentation of a sentence such as "The *loud* engine hurt my ears." The child's task is to identify a word with the same meaning as loud from the following set: soft, noisy, low, red. It does not seem sensible to say that a child in second grade can master synonyms in a generic sense, since not even Shakespeare managed that feat. A child cannot be said to master even a limited set of words, say "second-grade words," since meanings for the simplest word, e.g., "man," can grow through a lifetime. Relative proficiency is another matter; a child might be superior to his peer group, without the implication of mastery. A scale of performance on synonyms might be constructed in which children at different ages could be placed at different points, although it has not been provided for this test. The concept of mastery is not well conceived here and the scoring procedures for mastery are likely to be misleading.

Reliability is not treated in any of the manuals or other materials. The authors suggest that the results should be interpreted in terms of the subtest scores rather than the total score. However, the subscores are based on three items each. With this small number of items, reliability of the subskill measurements is likely to be extremely low. Decisions about mastery and

nonmastery based on only three items are not likely to be consistent.

The authors claim that the test is norm-referenced as well as criterion-referenced. They offer to provide classroom, local, and national norms for the three major content categories and the total score. However, no other normative information is provided in the manuals. Since a description of the population on which the national norms are based is not provided, we should be skeptical about the value of the measure for norm-referenced purposes.

Finally, there are a few specific shortcomings that should be pointed out. In comprehension items that contain questions and passages, the two elements should be interdependent; that is, there should be passage dependency. Two sources of low passage dependency are knowledge about the world and interquestion cueing. Regarding the former, if a child can answer a comprehension question on the basis of what he knows from experience rather than on the basis of what he reads in the selected paragraph, the item measures his knowledge rather than reading comprehension. The other contributor to low passage dependency, interitem cueing, is exemplified by item 105, Level 12, clearly providing the answer to item 103. There are examples of low passage dependency in all four levels. In Level 78, items 48–52 have low dependency, whereas 53–57 have high passage dependency. We need evidence from the authors that answering paragraph comprehension questions actually requires reading the paragraph.

Another shortcoming is that some items contain words that exceed the difficulty of the sentences or paragraphs they are intended to test. For instance, in Level 12, "coiled" occurs as a key word testing a simple first grade sentence. Control for this disruptive difficulty is important and should be maintained. A technical flaw is that in the vocabulary and paragraph comprehension sections, there is often more than one plausible alternative. In Level 12, items 91 and 108 each have three plausible answers out of the four alternatives provided.

The need for criterion-referenced tests in reading is urgent. Most objective-based teaching programs or diagnostic/prescriptive approaches require them. However, this test is not likely to meet the need. The measure does not have an adequate rationale, since it does not provide the

Analysis of Skills: Reading

criteria for deciding the number and nature of skills to be included. The authors do not produce any empirical evidence of the validity and reliability of the test. Flaws in item construction are abundant. One's initial flush of enthusiasm for a criterion-referenced test of reading fades on close inspection of this measure.

P. DAVID PEARSON, *Associate Professor of Education, University of Minnesota, Minneapolis, Minnesota.*

This group administered, objectives-referenced testing package consists of four levels, each spanning two grades. There are 60 objectives overall in the three domains of word analysis (23 objectives), comprehension (27 objectives), and study skills (10 objectives). Each level uses three items per objective to measure some 43–48 objectives. Proceeding from the first level to the fourth, emphasis shifts from word analysis to comprehension and study skills.

The tests are also criterion-referenced in that mastery criteria are applied to the three-item test for each objective: 0 items or 1 item correct represents nonmastery; 2 (provided that one of the correct items is the most difficult of the three items) or 3 items correct represents mastery; partial mastery is represented by correct responses to the two easiest items for an objective. National or local normative data (stanines and grade equivalents) are provided upon request, although the normative data appear to be based upon a higher level of aggregation than the objective (i.e., the three domains of word analysis, comprehension, and study skills).

There is a general manual describing test development, data reduction procedures, interpretation, and normative reporting options. In addition, there is a manual of directions for administering Level 12 and a second manual of directions for Levels 34, 56, and 78.

An implicit claim for the content validity of the items stems from the test development procedures. The objectives were derived by consulting a large number of developmental reading systems to locate commonly taught objectives. These objectives were checked for completeness by comparing them to lists used by several school districts. Finally, a range of educators was consulted to develop the final master list of objectives.

The hierarchy of difficulty within each objective was accomplished either logically or empirically. At times there was a natural hierarchy of difficulty within an objective (i.e., one item was obviously harder than the others). When all items appeared comparable, the set was administered to a sample of students to derive an empirical sequence of difficulty.

Within the burgeoning field of criterion-referenced testing and skills management systems, this test appears to have adopted a middle ground. The developers have not—as with some systems—gone to the extreme of listing 200 or so objectives with but one item per objective; nor have they adopted the more conservative approach of those systems that choose fewer objectives, say 20–30, and use 15 to 20 items per objective. The developers have also taken a middle position on the norm-referenced versus criterion-referenced issue; they have recognized the fact that by aggregating scores across objectives they can provide schools with potentially reliable normative data as well as the more explicit criterion-referenced data for individuals and classrooms. A third indication of their middle ground is related to their approach to test interpretation and subsequent instructional activities. While they do suggest subskill grouping for remedial work, they do not provide a list of workbook pages or ditto sheets from various reading systems that could be used to teach those skills.

With respect to technical information, the general manual is deficient. It appears that no attempts were made to determine construct validity or concurrent validity. Because of the fact that the publisher has a normative reporting capability, one suspects that item analysis data and reliability data are available. However, no such data are provided in the manual; nor is there any indication that it is available to the potential test user.

If one accepts the assumptions and practices of criterion-referenced and objectives-referenced testing systems, this test compares well in relation to competing systems. Its developers have recognized the difficulty of establishing mastery criteria and have tried to develop criteria which would take into account factors such as guessing and item difficulty. They have recognized that criterion-referenced goals and norm-referenced goals need not be mutually exclusive. By adopt-

Analysis of Skills: Reading

ing a middle ground in terms of the number of objectives, they have developed a system which is not so complex that it defies implementation by a teacher or a school. Finally, its objectives are representative of reading instruction in today's schools.

However, some of the assumptions and practices of criterion-referenced and objectives-referenced testing systems are questionable: (a) Few, if any, of these systems have demonstrated any construct validity; that is, few have demonstrated that mastery of a given skill contributes to something we might want to call overall reading ability. In fact, the hierarchical assumptions of such systems (i.e., that some skills are logically prerequisite to others) have yet to be empirically validated. (b) Paper-and-pencil tests test phonics skills in a recognition rather than a production mode. Research has shown that such recognition measures often do not correlate very well with children's ability to perform comparable production tasks in an actual reading situation. Some concurrent validity information would boost confidence in these recognition measures. (c) The very notion of mastery has not yet been validated. Presumably, a student who has demonstrated mastery can *use* the skill in transfer situations; a student who has not, cannot. The reading and testing professions have not, to this reviewer's knowledge, carried out such validation studies. These are but some of the knotty issues that must be dealt with in the next few years if we are to develop a technical data base to support the intuitive level of confidence presently attributed to criterion-referenced and objectives-referenced testing programs available for the evaluation of reading skills.

As far as the *Analysis of Skills: Reading* is concerned, it is assuredly a viable alternative among the numerous systems available for fine-grained analysis of reading skills in group testing situations. The larger question that faces the test user is whether or not such systems ought to be used at all. Granted, these systems facilitate the process of making instructional decisions about individuals and groups of students, but are the decisions any better than those made using more traditional measures?

[749]
*Classroom Reading Inventory, Third Edition. Grades 2–10; 1965–76; CRI; 6 scores: word recogni-

Analysis of Skills: Reading

tion, independent reading level, instructional reading level, frustration level, hearing capacity level, spelling; no data on reliability; no norms; individual in part; Forms A, B, C, ('76, 15 pages, identical with test copyrighted 1973 except for 1 new passage in Form A); manual ('76, 28 pages plus test materials—perforated pages permit removal of test materials); record sheets and teacher's worksheets ('69, 10–12 pages) must be reproduced locally; $3.95 per manual, postage extra; (12) minutes for individual parts, administration time for spelling not reported; Nicholas J. Silvaroli; Wm. C. Brown Co. Publisher. *

See T2:1618 (1 reference); for an excerpted review by Donald L. Cleland of an earlier edition, see 7:715.

REFERENCES

1. See T2:1618.
2. DAINES, DELVA, AND MASON, LYNNE G. "A Comparison of Placement Tests and Readability Graphs." *J Read* 15(8): 597–603 My '72. *
3. SWARTZ, DARLENE J. UNRUH. *The Relationship of Self-Esteem to Reading Performance.* Doctor's thesis, University of Northern Colorado (Greeley, Colo.), 1972. (*DAI* 33: 508A)
4. AVINGER, JUANITA HUNT. *An Analysis of the Oral Language Development of Selected Fourth-Grade Black Readers in Relation to Reading Difficulties.* Doctor's thesis, Baylor University (Waco, Tex.), 1974. (*DAI* 35:7023A)
5. BREKKE, BEVERLY, AND WILLIAMS, JOHN D. "Conservation and Reading Achievement of Second Grade Bilingual American Indian Children." *J Psychol* 86(1):65–9 Ja '74. * (*PA* 52:6310)
6. JOHNS, JERRY L. "Can Teachers Use Standarized Reading Tests to Determine Students' Instructional Levels?" *Ill Sch Res* 11(3):29–35 sp '75. *
7. KUTZMAN, SONDRA LOU KLEMENTIS. *The Technique of Testing and Instructional Levels of Informal Reading Inventories.* Doctor's thesis, University of Southern Mississippi (Hattiesburg, Miss.), 1975. (*DAI* 36:1921A)

MARJORIE S. JOHNSON, *Professor of Reading and Chairman, Psychology of Reading Department, Temple University, Philadelphia, Pennsylvania.*

The most recent editions of the CRI have increased its flexibility for teacher use in that there is now a third form of each of the subtests. The author has, from the start, recognized that, to gain a time advantage for the teacher, he has sacrificed some of the thoroughness of conventional informal reading inventories. Provision of three forms of the inventory, with B and C designated as optional, does make it more likely that his suggestions for their use as silent reading materials or a means of appraising hearing comprehension might be followed and that materials would still remain available for posttesting. The author makes no claim that use of Form A, as directed for the basic testing, will provide adequate diagnostic information on all children. He presents the CRI almost as a compromise between group achievement tests, which he characterizes as "able to classify children of comparable ages or grade groups according to above average, average and below average reading ability," and a full and thorough individual informal reading inventory, which he considers capable of yielding the kinds of information on specific needs essential as the basis for formulation of an instructional program.

Of the modifications made to save time in administration, one of the disadvantages cannot really be overcome even through the suggested uses of Forms B and C; this is the limitation of comprehension questions to five for each selection. Although this may be adequate coverage for some of the very short lower-level selections, it does not seem thorough enough to appraise complete understanding of some of the longer selections. Therefore, deficiencies in comprehension may go undetected.

The author's instructions for recording of the child's reading performance are designed to provide a maximum amount of information to the teacher. He recommends, for example, that all word errors in Part 1, the graded word lists, be recorded so that the teacher can determine exactly how the child responded to the words. Similar detailed recording of word-recognition performance is recommended during the oral reading in Part 2. From his record, the teacher should be able to reconstruct the exact way in which the child responded to the particular paragraph. For the comprehension questions, possible answers are provided with the caution that these are merely guides. The final responsibility for judging a response which is not provided rests with the teacher. The author suggests that it may be helpful, in some cases, to record the actual response. For full diagnostic information and for really considered judgment of the response, recording of all responses would be desirable. If the child gives one of the expected responses, it could be checked off. If he gives another, it should be recorded.

One other weakness of the comprehension appraisal, in addition to the limited number of questions, is the overbalance of factual recall questions. The distribution of factual, inferential, and vocabulary-type questions varies considerably from selection to selection. Further, some of the inferential questions seem to tap rather low-level inferences, and leave most of the higher-level thinking abilities untapped.

Matters of type, style, etc., leave something to be desired. The print is the same for all levels, thus working a possible hardship on children who, in their instructional material, have been reading only books with larger type. There are some inconsistencies between the illustrations and the text, as in the placement of the name of the car in Form B, "Salt Flat Speed." Some inaccuracies in content occur, as in Form C, "Birds." In some cases, lack of punctuation makes reading more difficult, as in Form B, "The Conestoga Wagon," where a comma after "when this old wagon reached a river," would facilitate phrasing and understanding. In general, however, the selections seem interesting although not of high literary quality.

One problem arises in relation to the treatment of the titles of the selections. They are not counted in the numbers of words recorded for each selection. However, the child is apparently expected to include them in his reading as no mention is made of them as something used in the motivation for reading. Handling of the reading of the title could affect the word recognition scores obtained and, therefore, the setting of the levels.

The addition in the manual of a section on interpretation makes more explicit the handling of scoring, the setting of levels, etc. It should allow the neophyte clinician to proceed with more confidence.

Overall, the CRI seems to be an adequate instrument to achieve its stated purposes—to provide the teacher with information on the child's reading levels and on his word recognition and comprehension abilities so that he can develop appropriate reading instruction and independent activities for the child. Appropriate cautions are provided so that one could not easily be mislead to believe that the inventory must be given to every child or that it is a diagnostic panacea. As a quick inventory, it should be a valuable asset to the classroom program.

[750]

The Cooper-McGuire Diagnostic Word-Analysis Test. Grades 1–5 and over; 1970–72; criterion referenced; 3 readiness-for-word-analysis goals (letter names and shapes, auditory discrimination of letter sounds and blending ability, visual discrimination of word forms), 2 phonic analysis goals (consonant sounds, vowel sounds), 4 structural analysis goals (root words and endings, compound words and contractions, prefixes and suffixes, syllables); 32 overlapping tests with 1 to 13 tests administered at a given reader level; no norms; minimum acceptable achievement level is either 80% (9 tests) or 100% (23 tests); individual in part; Forms A, B, ('70, 43 pages for all 32 tests, spirit masters for local duplicating); manual ('72, 32 pages); revised directions for administration ('72, 140 pages); class record chart ('70, 8 pages) for each form; additional instructional material available;

$13 per spirit master set of 32 tests; $1 per set of class record charts for both forms; $1.40 per manual; $4 per directions; postage extra; administration time not reported; J. Louis Cooper and Marion L. McGuire; Croft Educational Services, Inc. *

JOHN McLEOD, *Director, Institute of Child Guidance and Development, University of Saskatchewan, Saskatoon, Canada.*

This test consists of 32 separate tests which comprehensively and rationally analyze word-attack skills into five readiness goals, 17 phonics goals and 10 goals related to structural analysis.

The authors reject the feasibility or desirability of establishing test norms, arguing correctly that it is preferable in a diagnostic test to construct items that indicate the extent to which a pupil has or has not developed certain skills. This argument follows from the authors' distinction between norm-referenced tests, which are useful as predictive screening devices, whereas "the main value of criterion-referenced tests lies in their ability to diagnose specific strengths and weaknesses."

So far, so good. And, in developing the analysis of word-attack skills, the authors go on to point out that long-term goals "may be broken down into a number of instructional tasks, each of which represents a step toward the realization of the goal." Instructional objectives, which must be very specifically defined, are derived "by analyzing the component skills and concepts of each major goal. These skills and concepts are presented with the simple ones followed by those that are more complex. When a learner achieves all of the objectives, he has achieved the goal."

While the authors are perfectly justified in claiming that the trappings of standardized scores are unnecessary in a diagnostic (i.e., analytic) reading test, they cannot lightly dismiss demands for some evidence of reliability and validity, especially when the subtests are presumably considered to be in a hierarchical order. There is no doubt that the user is encouraged to believe that the tests *are* in hierarchical order; the manual states that *"readiness for any skill is achieved when the learner knows the lower-level skills necessary to the development or use of the new skill to be taught"* (test authors' stress). Nowhere in the test manual is there indication of empirical evidence that the tests are in hierarchical sequential order or that the validity or reliability of individual tests or

test items has been examined. The reliability and validity of responses to individual items are particularly important when, as in several of the tests, knowledge of a particular digraph, etc., is checked by only a single item.

At the outset of this review, the word "rationally" was used to describe the analysis of the reading process that forms the basis of these tests, and the word was used advisedly. It is *rational,* and reasonable, to contend that a reader must be able to "tell which of the vowel's variable sounds it will have in unfamiliar words." But, in order to test the child's mastery of vowel principles, Test P-15 presents five sentences, the longest of which contains 27 words, describing 5 "vowel principles," and the child is requested to indicate which of the 5 principles is involved in 10 presented stimulus words. In a snap check, this reviewer found that a reading level somewhere between 5th and 6th grade seems to be necessary to comprehend the "vowel principles" as set down in this test, yet children with a reading level of grade 3.5 could read all the words in the test, thus illustrating that they had mastered the vowel principles which they could probably not verbalize. (Incidentally, it is difficult to understand the authors' insistence in the manual that nonsense words be used in this test, when none of the words used in Form B is a nonsense word.)

Likewise, in Test P-16, there are about 200 words of oral instruction followed by quite a complex task, when it would have been much more straightforward to assess the child's ability to apply vowel principles by having him or her read the 10 words of the test.

This brings us to a basic issue which applies not only to the Cooper-McGuire tests but also to several established diagnostic reading tests. In the context of the test under review, we might begin by asking why the test forms have been produced on spirit masters, and the obvious answer is that this will facilitate the administration of the test on a group basis. And, if the test is to be presented on a group basis, then clearly the teacher or examiner has to read out instructions and the children have to write down responses on a piece of paper; it would be unthinkable that all children should respond verbally. Hence, the test situation is one in which an auditory stimulus is received by the child who, in turn, has to respond by making a visual

Cooper-McGuire Diagnostic Word-Analysis Test

match in a multiple choice format. In the actual reading process, however, a child is presented with a visual stimulus and has to respond verbally in an open-ended (i.e., not multiple choice) situation.

In the majority of cases, correlation between linguistic tasks of the two types indicated above is very high, but in the case of a child with a significant learning disability in reading, it cannot be taken for granted that an assessment of auditory reception and visual/motor response faithfully reflects the child's functioning in the reading situation which calls for visual reception followed by verbal expression. Test P-9 presents a good example of a rational, logical approach which is at variance with the clinically observed difficulty of final blends and digraphs. In P-9, the child is given a couple of stimulus words which end with the same consonant blends. He or she is then presented with four printed words and has to circle the consonant blend (at the end of one of these four words) which is the same as those just spoken by the examiner. In responding to this test, if the child is able to isolate the final heard consonant blend, response is simply a matter of scrutinizing the end of each of the four words and marking the appropriate digraph. In other words, the rest of the printed words can be ignored as irrelevant. In the actual clinical reading situation, however, final consonant blends and digraphs are far more difficult to read than the initial blends and digraphs, a fact which, one speculates, is largely due to the fact that in responding, the child has not only to decode the final digraph but also to hold in immediate memory the preceding letter sounds and then synthesize the whole. In other words, "Final Blends and Digraphs" is an ambiguous title, and what is tested is not necessarily a valid criterion against which to assess whether the child is progressing along that sequential hierarchy to the ultimate goal.

These tests represent useful reference material to be used as a check to conform, or infirm, diagnostic hunches arrived at through more general tests. Their value would be enhanced if empirical evidence were available to support their effectiveness; and if the tasks could be modified (making the test individual rather than group) so that more of the subtests called for a direct simulation of some aspect of the reading process.

[751]

Cooperative Primary Tests: Word Analysis. Grades 1.5–3; 1965–67; Forms 13A, 13B, ('65, 7 pages); no specific manual; battery manual ('67, 104 pages); $3.75 per 20 tests; $3 per battery manual; cash orders postpaid; specimen set not available; (40) minutes; Educational Testing Service; Addison-Wesley Publishing Co., Inc. *

For reviews of the complete battery, see 13 (1 review) and 7:10 (2 excerpts).

SHIRLEY C. FELDMANN, *Professor of Education and Head, Reading Program, The City College and The Graduate School, The City University of New York, New York, New York.*

This test, one part of a larger achievement battery, is a group-administered reading test for primary grade children. Its stated purpose is to test the understandings and skills basic to future development in reading. Rather than test minutiae, it aims to tap the child's understanding and thinking, with an emphasis on improvable skills. There are two levels of reading tests, with an alternate form of each, one for upper first and second grade and the other for grades two and three. Each has 50 items, with two samples, and a three-choice response format. There are no time limits on the tests, but 35 minutes is suggested. The items progress through presentation of words and sentences to paragraphs. The handbook states, however, that easy and difficult items are interspersed throughout the test so as not to discourage the child. The child is required to mark pictures or words in response to words or sentences. Responses require both recall and interpretation of items, with the latter involving inference, categorization, a title, or a rhyme to fit a category. The upper level test has fewer word and sentence items and more paragraph items.

The format is uncluttered and provides visual cues to move the child from the test item to the answer choices. Pictures are simplified line drawings which seem unambiguous, in most cases. It seems unlikely that many children would be confused by the directions or be distracted by the format. The format is clearly superior to that found on many other achievement tests.

Scores may be converted to percentile ranks for each grade. Such percentile ranks may be useful generally but may give little diagnostic information about knowledge of reading skills. Scoring keys are provided.

The tests were normed with samples balanced

by geographical area and by size of the school district, but no ethnic groups were identified. A fall and a spring sample were used with about 1,800 children in each grade sample. The standardization procedures seem carefully planned and executed.

Reliability was determined by internal consistency measures and correlation of alternate forms, with measures in both cases in the range of .86–.91. Item difficulties for grade 1 range from .18 to .90, with median .43.

Validity is described in the handbook as content validity. While this is common practice for reading achievement tests, very little information is given about the performance domain used. Criterion-related validity measures, such as the relationship to other standardized reading tests, might give the user more information about the nature of the test.

There are several areas of concern. First, seven different combinations of skills and response modes are used in the test. The directions are the same for all, thus reducing some possible confusion for the child but little is known of other confusions that may result. In some cases very few items are presented in one mode so that the reliability of such may be questioned. Whether this particular combination of modes, or any other combination that could be made, is optimal for obtaining a better estimate of reading skills is open to question and should be explored. On the whole, interpretation of test results is very limited in the handbook, in terms of both class and individual use.

Another concern is the high correlations reported between the reading and word analysis tests, from .73 to .78, indicating a major overlap of skills. While this might be expected in two areas within the reading-language domain, it does seem inefficient to have two tests when one might do.

Lastly, it is not clear whether the 10-item pilot test, which is given for practice at the beginning of the entire battery, should be given when only one part of it is to be administered.

In summary, the test seems well constructed and normed, except for validity data. Its format is uncluttered and provides easy access to the tasks at hand. It should be as effective as other published reading tests for classroom use.

Cooperative Primary Tests: Word Analysis

★**Diagnosis: An Instructional Aid: Reading.** Grades 1–4, 3–6; 1973–74; criterion-referenced tests consisting of a series of diagnostic tests (called probes) and an optional "survey test"; no data on reliability; no norms; 2 levels; $7.20 per specimen set of either level; postage extra; administration time not reported; Science Research Associates, Inc. *

a) DIAGNOSTIC TESTS (PROBES). The two levels together cover 518 specific-objective subtests (73% of which consist of 1 or 2 items) in 5 areas: comprehension (48 subtests), phonetic analysis (242), structural analysis (55), study skills (32), vocabulary (141); tests within a given level may be administered in any order; no scores obtained for the tests or subtests; teacher must decide from missed items which specific objectives need further study.

1) *Reading Level A.* Grades 1–4; 1973; 34 tests (294 specific objectives) in 5 areas: comprehension (9 tests, 25 subtests), phonetic analysis (12, 160), structural analysis (5, 34), study skills (3, 11), vocabulary (5, 64); phonetic analysis administered by tape cassette; tests (2 pages each plus record page); manual (32 pages); prescription guide (32 pages); $119.50 per set of test materials (including survey test) for 25 pupils; $53.96 per 25 sets of tests.

2) *Reading Level B.* Grades 3–6; 1974; 30 tests (224 specific objectives) in 5 areas: comprehension (9 tests, 23 subtests), phonetic analysis (4, 82), structural analysis (4, 21), study skills (7, 21), vocabulary (6, 77); the first four tests are used to determine whether the corresponding Level A tests should be administered; tests (2 pages each plus record page); manual (32 pages); prescription guide (114 pages); $87.50 per set of test materials (including survey test) for 25 pupils; $53.95 per 25 sets of tests.

b) SURVEY TEST. Grades 1–4, 3–6; 1973–74; an optional test to determine which diagnostic tests should be administered; test consists of 2-item subtests (except for 4 3-item subtests in Level B) paralleling the diagnostic tests; if both items of a subtest are missed, the corresponding diagnostic test "probably should be administered"; pupils missing only one of the two items should be checked informally to determine whether the corresponding diagnostic test should be administered; Level A: Forms X, Y, ('73, 8 pages); Level B: Forms X, Y, ('74, 8 pages); $10.80 per 25 tests.

RICHARD C. COX, *Director, Office of Measurement and Evaluation, University of Pittsburgh, Pittsburgh, Pennsylvania.*

Diagnosis: An Instructional Aid: Reading is, according to the teacher's handbook, an educational tool designed to diagnose the reading skills of a pupil in terms of specific learning objectives and to suggest prescriptions for the remediation of identified weaknesses. While there are several components in the *Diagnosis* kit, this review is concerned with only the criterion-referenced diagnostic and survey tests.

The teacher's handbook indicates that the criterion-referenced diagnostic probes are the heart of *Diagnosis*. Each diagnostic test is a single four-page booklet on which pupils work directly on the front and back. A carbon inter-leaf reproduces the answers on the key which is printed on the inside of the front page. It would be helpful if there were printed directions to the pupils to turn the booklet over and complete the back.

The carbon interleaf does not allow the test-taker to erase. Instead, the pupil must circle the first response and record another answer nearby. This can be quite inconvenient and difficult for pupils in the early grades.

Directions for scoring the diagnostic tests are clearly specified in the handbook. Directions for *using* the scores are lacking in detail. The only suggestion provided is that a pupil may be weak in a skill in which one or more items are missed. It is certainly appropriate to utilize and encourage teacher judgment; however, some further guidelines seem to be warranted.

As expected with criterion-referenced tests, there are no norms available for either the diagnostic or survey tests. Nor is there any information concerning reliability or validity of these tests. Also, there is no description of item development or tryout. In short, the teacher's handbook is completely devoid of data. Technical data concerning *Diagnosis* are not available from the publisher. These omissions raise an issue that must be addressed now that criterion-referenced tests are being published in greater numbers. Just what information should be provided to the prospective test user? Surely the information will be different from that typically provided for a norm-referenced measure, but what exactly should it be? To help the consumer select a test, there should be some guidelines to ensure consistent information from test to test. Certainly enough has been written concerning the evaluative aspects of criterion-referenced tests to fill this information gap.

In most instances the issue of validity must be addressed by the consumer. In general, the items on the diagnostic tests appear to be measuring the specified objectives. The consumer must evaluate whether or not the objectives being tested are consistent with those to be learned. Do the items on the tests measure the objectives in a way the teacher finds useful? Any manual for a criterion-referenced test should clearly specify the objectives for each instructional unit and should indicate which items test which objectives.

Reliability data should be provided as well. The reliability issue is the same as for norm-referenced tests; i.e., is there consistent measurement? This is especially important when decisions are made on the basis of only one or two test items.

Administration of the survey test is one starting point suggested by the handbook. It is possible also for a teacher to use the results of the *SRA Achievement Series,* particularly the individual skills profile, if it is available. The suggestion to do so is probably more lucrative to SRA than it is convenient for a teacher. Another suggested way to assess *Diagnosis* is simply to use other information about individual pupil achievement as a guide to selecting the appropriate diagnostic tests. This latter suggestion may be appealing, since it utilizes teacher judgment. However, further directions on using this other information systematically would be desirable.

If a teacher chooses to use a survey test, there is a choice between the Level A, grades 1–4, test and the Level B, grades 3–6, test. There is no explanation of the overlap nor are there any instructions concerning which test to administer to third and fourth grade pupils. The teacher's handbook indicates that both Level A and B tests have another form available if pre and post measures are desired. It is not made clear whether or not these are parallel tests; thus, it is difficult to judge if using them as pre and post measures is appropriate.

The teacher's handbook contains specific directions for administering the survey tests. The phonetic analysis section on both the Level A and B survey tests is administered orally. Unfortunately, there are no cautions about correct pronunciation, loudness of voice, and other potential problems in using oral directions with young children.

In the Level A survey test several nonsense words are used both as distractors and as correct options. No explanation or rationale is provided for this practice.

In general, the directions for the survey tests are fairly clear and easy to follow, although there could be more specificity concerning the directions the user should give to the pupil following the oral sections. As the test now stands, there is a void and one can only assume

Diagnosis: An Instructional Aid: Reading

that the pupils are told to proceed by reading the directions and completing the test.

Another feature suggested by the handbook is that survey test items deemed inappropriate for the pupils being tested can be omitted. *Diagnosis* is not a standardized set of tests because it is not intended to be; yet if a teacher uses the test results for instructional decisions, there ought to be some standardization in the process.

In most instances there are only two items on the survey test to indicate mastery or non-mastery of a skill. The directions indicate that a student getting one of the two items correct should be checked "informally" to see if a diagnostic test should be administered. There are no clues as to how the informal check should proceed. If both items are missed, the directions indicate that the diagnostic test should "probably" be administered. This looseness in procedure may be more confusing than helpful. The lack of discussion or information about the reliability of decisions based upon two test items is a serious weakness if the survey tests are used as indicators of mastery/non-mastery.

Diagnosis presents a difficult situation for a test reviewer. There are certainly test materials involved in the kit, yet many of the typical checkpoints are not addressed by the manual. There is, in fact, not a manual with information that is usually associated with tests. The user will have to assess validity by examining the learning objectives being measured by the diagnostic tests. Reliability information is not available in the kit. A technical report could shed further light on these issues and on item development and selection.

The survey and diagnostic tests from *Diagnosis* have several attractive features. They are constructed so as to be visually and psychologically pleasing to the test-taker. There is some novelty in the scoring system. Once the system is thoroughly understood by the teacher and pupils, it can be used quite efficiently in an individualized classroom setting. There is also room for improvement on both types of tests. Test administration procedures need to be tightened. Directions for both test-giver and test-taker need to be more specific. And then there is the larger specter of lack of information concerning reliability, validity, and item development. Until such information is available,

Diagnosis should be used with a great deal of caution.

[753]

*Diagnostic Reading Scales, Revised Edition. Grades 1–6 and poor readers in grades 7–12; 1963–75; DRS; previous edition ('63) still available; 12 or 13 scores: word recognition, instructional level (oral reading), independent level (silent reading), rate of silent reading (optional), potential level (auditory comprehension), and 8 phonics scores (consonant sounds, vowel sounds, consonant blends, common syllables, blends, letter sounds, initial consonants, auditory discrimination); individual; 1 form ('72, 29 pages); 2 manuals ('72, 38 pages, identical—including norms—except for different directions for administering and scoring Oral Reading); record booklet ('72, 34 pages); technical bulletin ('75, 23 pages); $3 per test; $19.95 per 35 record booklets; $1.50 per manual; $2.50 per technical bulletin; $7.50 per specimen set; postage extra; (40–50) minutes; George D. Spache; CTB/McGraw-Hill. *

See T2:1624 (4 references); for a review by Rebecca C. Barr of the earlier edition, see 7:717 (7 references); for a review by N. Dale Bryant, see 6:821.

REFERENCES

1–7. See 7:717.
8–11. See T2:1624.
12. ELLER, WILLIAM, AND ATTEA, MARY. "Three Diagnostic Reading Tests: Some Comparisons." *Int Read Assn Conf Proc* 11(1):562–6 '67. *
13. WINKLEY, CAROL K. "What Do Diagnostic Reading Tests Really Diagnose?" pp. 64–80. In *Diagnostic Viewpoints in Reading.* Edited by Robert E. Leibert. Newark, Del.: International Reading Association, Inc., 1971. Pp. viii, 133. *
14. DAINES, DELVA, AND MASON, LYNNE G. "A Comparison of Placement Tests and Readability Graphs." *J Read* 15(8):597–603 My '72. *
15. BROGAN, WESLEY GAMBLE. *A Comparative Analysis of the Reading Errors of Retarded and Non-Retarded Females.* Doctor's thesis, University of North Carolina (Chapel Hill, N.C.), 1973. (*DAI* 34:5749A)
16. GICKLING, EDWARD ERIC. *The Interaction Effects of Sensory-Motor and Aspiration Variables on the Prediction of Reading Subtest Scores for Institutionalized Mentally Retarded Students.* Doctor's thesis, Southern Illinois University (Carbondale, Ill.), 1973. (*DAI* 34:1734A)
17. CALLAWAY, BYRON; JERROLDS, BOB W.; AND TISDALE, LOUISE. "A Study of the Relationship of Subtest Scores on the California Test of Personality to Selected Parts of the Diagnostic Reading Scales." *South J Ed Res* 8(1):192–6 w '74. * (*PA* 52:10999)
18. GICKLING, EDWARD E., AND JOINER, LEE M. "Complex Interactions of an Auditory Ability and Aspiration in Predicting Specific Reading Deficits." *Am J Mental Def* 79(2):162–8 S '74. * (*PA* 53:3435)
19. STAFFORD, JERRY. "Reading Test Review: Reflections on the Diagnostic Reading Scales." *Read World* 14(1):5–8 O '74. * (*PA* 53:8411)
20. DAVIS, EVERETT E. "Reading Frustration Level as Indicated by the Polygraph." *J Ed Res* 68(8):286–8 Ap '75. * (*PA* 54:8398)
21. McCORD, MICHAEL T. "A Semantic Analysis of Reading Comprehension Tests." *Yearb Nat Read Conf* 24:211–9 '75. *
22. NUMMEDAL, ALICIA MAY CIESLAR. *A Comparison of Silent and Oral Reading Comprehension of Deaf Children.* Doctor's thesis, University of Illinois (Urbana, Ill.), 1975. (*DAI* 36:220A)
23. ROWELL, ELIZABETH HANSEN. *The Relationship Between Silent and Oral Reading Comprehension in Grades Three and Five.* Doctor's thesis, University of Connecticut (Storrs, Conn.), 1975. (*DAI* 35:6946A)
24. MUZYCZKA, MARJORIE J., AND ERICKSON, MARILYN T. "WISC Characteristics of Reading Disabled Children Identified by Three Objective Methods." *Percept & Motor Skills* 43(2):595–602 O '76. *
25. ALLINGTON, RICHARD L.; CHODOS, LAURA; DOMARACKI, JANE; AND TRUEX, SHARON. "Passage Dependency: Four Diagnostic Oral Reading Tests." *Read Teach* 30(4):369–75 Ja '77. *
26. JORGENSON, GERALD W. "Relationship of Classroom Behavior to the Accuracy of the Match Between Material Difficulty and Student Ability." *J Ed Psychol* 69(1):24–32 F '77. * (*PA* 58:6135)

Diagnosis: An Instructional Aid: Reading

NANCY L. ROSER, *Associate Professor of Curriculum and Instruction, The University of Texas, Austin, Texas.*

The *Diagnostic Reading Scales* are individually administered tests that provide an estimate of the instructional, independent, and potential reading levels, an estimate of the student's independent reading and evidence as to how the student attacks or analyzes words. While the definitions of instructional and potential levels are commonly accepted ones, the term "independent level" deviates markedly from its standard usage, and test users should carefully note the difference. The revised edition offers an expanded manual, well-organized and highly readable, a less confusing format for the student's test book, and the addition of a technical bulletin. Other alterations since the 1963 edition of the DRS include revision of certain comprehension questions, some rearrangement of items within the phonics test, and inclusion of two additional phonics subtests. The complete battery now consists of three word recognition lists, 22 reading passages (two each representing 11 difficulty levels from primer through eighth grade), and eight supplementary phonics tests.

Within-grade, test-retest reliability coefficients ("retest after 2–8 weeks") are reported for small samples of 19 to 62 students as follows: word recognition, .91 to .96, with median .935; instructional level, .70 to .92, with median .85; independent level, .66 to .83, with median .685; potential level (grades 1–3 only), .58 to .75, with median .59; rate, .42 to .89, with median .62; and phonics, .30 to .98, with median .77.

WORD RECOGNITION LISTS. The three lists (40–50 words each) are graduated in difficulty and designed primarily "to estimate the student's instructional level" to serve as an indicator of the level at which the student should enter the passages, and secondarily "to reveal the student's method of word attack and analysis" and "to evaluate the student's sight-word vocabulary." Words were selected from Durrell's 1940 word list and were included for their discriminating power and ordered by difficulty on the basis of the original tryouts. Changes in cultural and school-related experiences might mandate revision of the vocabulary list, but the list placed 72 percent of the students in the tryout sample one level above their instructional level score,

considered to be the optimal prediction. Difficulties that may be encountered in using the lists include the lack of specific directions for interpreting responses when they deviate from the printed word, and the problem of recognizing dialect-distinct pronunciations without benefit of context. The lists appear most useful as a test for entry point, and less useful in fulfilling another stated purpose—to reveal the student's method of word attack and analysis. The latter will depend upon the expertise of the examiner.

READING PASSAGES. Difficulty levels of the 22 reading passages were determined by using the Spache or Dale-Chall formulas. Passages represent narrative, expository, and descriptive selections, each followed by 7 or 8 comprehension questions. Nearly all questions tap recall of information rather than higher level comprehension skills. The testing situation requires the examiner to monitor oral reading in order to record omissions, additions, substitutions or mispronunciations, repetitions, reversals, and words added. When either reading errors or inappropriate responses to questions exceed a critical cutoff point, the oral reading is stopped. Instructional level is defined as the level preceding the point of failure. The description as to how the cutoff points for oral reading errors were determined is incomplete. They appear especially generous at the lowest levels, where words are frequently repeated, since a repeated error counts only once. The comprehension cutoff score is more fully described as a minimum of 60 percent correct response for instructional level (reading orally), independent level (reading silently), and potential level (listening).

There is limited description of test construction procedure. No mention is made of other tests against which selected passages had to demonstrate validity; how validity was demonstrated in these comparisons is not discernible. While it is stated that instructional levels were constantly compared with teacher judgments, there is no indication of the frequency of agreement. The manual states that the "procedures followed in constructing the instrument constitute the basic evidence for the validity of the Scales," yet there is insufficient evidence to support the claim.

PHONICS TESTS. The placement of two addi-

Diagnostic Reading Scales

tional phonics subtests after the original six produces a somewhat arbitrary sequence. The manual dictates that the tests be administered in the order given, yet the last test, auditory discrimination of word pairs, appears to be prerequisite to successful performance on earlier tests of blending and substitution. Initial consonant substitution requires the student to pronounce a new word that would be obtained if the initial consonant of a given word were changed to one presented parenthetically. The skill becomes one of mentally "moving" the substituted consonant, seemingly more remote and abstract than attacking known parts. In addition, the tests present some potential problems if the student's reading program has not emphasized synthetic phonics. Students are asked to pronounce the "sounds" of consonants and blends in isolation, and to pronounce syllables (e.g., di, ent, ed) divorced from any word. This isolation of word parts may provide the examiner with little useful information. The five nonsense words offered to test vowel sounds contain three real words (nit, ret, and tot) which may be confusing since the student must pronounce the word with both long and short vowel sounds.

SUMMARY. The DRS appears to have greatest use for examiners seeking comparative data for a student's instructional progress. Because of the difficulty in translating the obtained Instructional Level into an instructional placement in widely divergent reading materials, it is suggested that those seeking instructional information might better use an informal inventory built from classroom materials. More realistic information as to the student's ability to apply phoneme-grapheme relationships could be gleaned from careful scrutiny of errors on the oral reading passages. Finally, the accompanying diagnostic checklists lack specificity and thus provide little instructional payoff for the time spent completing them.

ROBERT L. SCHREINER, *Professor of Education, University of Minnesota, Minneapolis, Minnesota.*

This standardized battery of individually administered reading tests is designed to assess strengths and weaknesses in various components of the reading process. It is normed for students in grades 1–8, except for the phonics subtests

which are normed for grades 2–4. The scales contain materials measuring the following skills or abilities: word recognition, oral reading, silent reading, reading potential (listening ability), reading comprehension, and phonics.

The testing materials consist of a reusable test book with three separate lists of words to assess word recognition, 22 graded passages for measuring oral, silent, and potential reading levels, and eight supplemental phonics tests. An examiners record booklet is provided for recording student responses and norms for the various subtests. Comprehension questions following the graded reading passages are found in the record booklet; the booklet also includes a word analysis checklist, a checklist of reading difficulties, and a summary record blank. The manual provides description and rationale for the subtests; information pertaining to administration, scoring, and interpretation of results; and a technical section describing reliability and validity studies that have been conducted using the scales.

WORD RECOGNITION LISTS. Three separate word lists are available for assessing the student's level of sight vocabulary and to determine the beginning passage for oral reading diagnosis. The student begins the test by pronouncing words from the appropriate list, one at a time. This test is discontinued after five consecutive pronunciation errors. The raw score is then translated into a grade-equivalent score. Reliability and validity data provided confirm that the results are useful to estimate the appropriate passage to begin oral reading diagnosis. The score might be a more useful estimate of the student's level of sight vocabulary if the sample included a full range of words. The ceiling (6.5) is reached upon correct pronunciation of 29 of 40 words on the most difficult list. One questions the usefulness of such a score if instructional levels achieved later on the test are higher than the 6.5 ceiling.

READING PASSAGES. After an estimate of the student's instructional level is obtained from the word recognition test, the student then begins reading aloud at one reading grade level lower than that level. The reading passages, ranging in difficulty from low-first- to mid-eighth-grade levels, provide for the assessment of instructional, independent, and potential levels. Two separate passages at each of 11

Diagnostic Reading Scales

levels represent the type and range found in school reading materials. Data are provided substantiating the readability levels of the passages. The passages at the primary grade levels are mostly of a narrative style; the upper-grade passages are more expository in nature. The accompanying comprehension questions frequently require the student to recall information immediately read. Depending upon the student's background, some of the questions could be answered without reading the accompanying passages. Norms for oral reading errors and correct responses to reading comprehension questions are provided. The acceptable criterion level of 60 percent accuracy for each passage read is inordinately low; most users would demand greater reading accuracy from their students.

The interpretation of instructional and independent reading levels and the determination of student performance are unduly complicated and confusing. It is not clear from reading the manual whether a student's silent reading score is always the independent level and/or the oral reading score is the instructional level. Interpretation of these scores is further complicated by the fact that the definitions used by the author are different from the generally accepted definitions of instructional and independent reading levels.

Despite the rationale presented in the manual, this reviewer cannot accept the notion that a score received on a listening test is a valid estimate of reading potential. Listening and reading are not the same types of tasks. To estimate and predict that students, with appropriate instruction in listening, will achieve at a higher level in reading is dangerous and potentially harmful. In any event, it is incumbent upon the test author and the publisher to justify the concept of potential reading level. Sufficient data and research justifying this concept are not presented.

PHONICS TESTS. Eight separate subtests, listed in the entry above, are available to provide an estimate of the student's ability in phonics. The user will need to review the subtests to determine which of them are most useful for primary or intermediate level students. A criterion-referenced approach has been used to assign grade scores to student scores with these tests. This approach is used because phonic tests do not have sufficient ceiling to discriminate among students. However, the results of these tests appear to have a great deal of content validity and would prove useful for designating instructional strategies.

SUMMARY. Test results must provide instructionally useful information to users. It has been this reviewer's experience that the grade-level scores obtained from all three reading portions of the scales tend to overestimate student performance. Thus, the scores do not directly translate to appropriate instructional materials. Discrepancies may be the result of passage length or the relatively low criterion set for comprehension of passages. They may also be related to the fact that most instructional materials were not constructed with the same degree of precision as were the passages in the scales. Nevertheless, the user must consider these shortcomings.

Finally, the manual is extremely difficult to follow. Sentences and directions are too complex. It would be more helpful if a step-by-step format were used in order to apprise users of standardized procedures.

Read World 14(1):5–8 O '74. Jerry Stafford. * The *Diagnostic Reading Scales* is also used as a means to determine the student's Independent Level, where Independent Level is defined as "that grade level to supplementary instructional and recreational reading materials which the pupil can read to himself with adequate comprehension...." This level is identified through having the student read *silently* at levels just above the obtained Instructional Level. Silent reading is continued on progressively more difficult passages until the student fails to answer at least 60% of the questions for the passage read. Provisions in any test for finding both the Instructional Level and the Independent Level are laudable even though the criteria for determining such levels are often arbitrary. However, Independent Level as presented in this test appears to differ considerably from the meaning usually associated with the term. Independent Level, as discussed in the literature, is customarily lower than the Instructional Level. In the *Diagnostic Reading Scales* the Independent Level in many cases will be higher than the Instructional Level as obtained through the oral reading portion of the test. It follows that using the Independent Level of the test will place students in materials that are more difficult for recreational reading than for instruction. This is precisely opposite of what should happen if customary procedures are used. Moreover, using oral reading to identify Instructional Level and silent reading to identify Independent Level appears to be based on the assumption that instruction in reading will be oral. Current teaching practices, especially at intermediate levels, do not appear to support this assumption. Furthermore, one must question whether a comprehension which may go as low as 60% is adequate for recreational reading. It appears likely that using the Independent Level of the *Diagnostic Reading Scales* with its possible low of 60% comprehension will place students in materials that are too difficult for the intended purpose. One of the most desirable features of the *Diagnostic Reading Scales* is its provision for finding the student's reading potential. The procedure is simple and straightforward requiring the examiner to read aloud to the student passages above the Independent Level and ask the questions that accompany the passages. The highest level at which the student answers 60% or more of the questions is identified as his potential level. * The *Diagnostic Reading Scales* appears to offer considerable potential in diagnosing a wide variety of reading skills and needs. A more in-depth *Examiner's Manual* describing the procedures used in determining validity and reliability and presenting suggestions for recording oral reading behavior would assist in realizing this potential. In addition, a review of the procedures used for determining Instructional and Independent Levels would be beneficial as the procedures used in this test appear to contradict the current understanding of those levels.

[754]

*Diagnostic Reading Tests. Various grades kgn–13; 1947–74; DRT; 3 levels; interpretation booklet, second edition ('68, 92 pages); revised norms ('74, 52 pages, with 1948–73 norms); separate answer sheets (IBM 805-Digitek, IBM 1230, hand scored) may be used (except for section 4, part 1) for grades 2–13; 25¢ per key for any one booklet; 7¢ per machine scored answer sheet; 4¢ per hand scored answer sheet; 25¢ per scoring stencil; 25¢ per directions for any one booklet; $2.50 per interpretation booklet; $1.50 per norms booklet; postage extra; Committee on Diagnostic Reading Tests, Inc. *
a) DIAGNOSTIC READING TESTS : KINDERGARTEN THROUGH

Diagnostic Reading Scales

FOURTH GRADES. Various grades kgn–4 (except for section 4, part 1); 1957–68; 2 sections, 5 booklets; 25¢ per copy of booklet 2 or 3; 20¢ per copy of other booklets; $2.50 per specimen set of all 5 booklets and directions for each.
  1) *Survey Section*. Grades kgn–1, 1, 2, 3–4; 1957–68; 4 levels.
    (*a*) Reading Readiness Booklet. Grades kgn–1; 5 scores: relationships, eye-hand coordination, visual discrimination, auditory discrimination, vocabulary; Form B ('57, 16 pages); revised directions for administering ('66, 12 pages, essentially the same as mimeographed 1957 directions except for format and a few minor changes); administration time not reported.
    (*b*) Booklet 1. Grade 1; 12 scores: visual discrimination, auditory discrimination (3 subscores plus total), vocabulary (3 subscores plus total), story reading (2 subscores plus total); reliability data for total subscores only; Form A ('57, 23 pages); revised directions ('66, 16 pages, essentially the same as mimeographed 1957 directions except for format and a few minor changes); administration time not reported.
    (*c*) Booklet 2. Grade 2; 3 scores: word recognition, comprehension, total; Forms A, B, ('57, 15 pages); combined revised directions ('66, 10 pages) for this test and (*d*) below; [30] minutes.
    (*d*) Booklet 3. Grades 3–4; details same as for (*c*) above.
  2) *Section 4: Word Attack, Part 1: Oral*. Grades 1–8; 1958–68; no data on reliability; individual; Forms A, B, ('58, 8 pages); revised directions for administering ('58, 8 pages) for grades 1–13; [20] minutes.
b) DIAGNOSTIC READING TESTS : LOWER LEVEL. Grades 4–8; 1947–72; 2 sections, 4 booklets; $1.75 per specimen set of all 4 booklets and directions for each.
  1) *Survey Section*. Grades 4–8; 1952–72; 3 parts in 2 booklets; revised directions for administering ('72, 16 pages); supplementary directions with IBM 1230 answer sheets ('67, 4 pages); 25¢ per copy of either booklet; (30) minutes per booklet; Braille edition available from American Printing House for the Blind, Inc.
    (*a*) Booklet 1: Part 1, Word Recognition and Comprehension. 2 scores: word recognition, comprehension; Forms A, B, C, D, ('57, 12 pages, Form B identical with test copyrighted 1952 except for format and cover page).
    (*b*) Booklet 2: Parts 2 and 3, Vocabulary-Story Reading. 3 scores: vocabulary, rate of reading, story comprehension; Forms A ('52), B ('57, identical with test copyrighted 1952 except for cover page and, in vocabulary section, revised option order in most items and minor revision in 1 item), C ('57), D ('57), (12 pages).
  2) *Section 4: Word Attack*. Various grades 1–13; 1947–69; 2 parts.
    (*a*) Part 1, Oral. Grades 1–8; see *a*2 above.
    (*b*) Part 2, Silent. Grades 4–13; 1947–69; 3 scores: identification of sounds, syllabication, total; Forms A, B, ('47, 6 pages), C, D, ('58, 4 pages); revised directions for administering ('69, 4 pages, essentially the same as 1958 directions except for deletions and minor changes); 15¢ per test; (30) minutes.
c) DIAGNOSTIC READING TESTS : UPPER LEVEL. Grades 7–13; 1947–73; 5 sections, 6 booklets; $4.50 per specimen set of all 6 booklets and directions for each.
  1) *Survey Section*. 1947–73; 5 scores: rate of reading, comprehension check, vocabulary, total compre-

hension, total; no reliability data or norms for comprehension check subtest; Forms A, B, ('66, essentially the same as 1947 tests except for substitution of a new reading selection in Part 3), C ('70), D ('67, essentially the same as 1947 test except for minor revisions in 8 items in Parts 1 and 2 and a revised reading selection in Part 3); E, F, ('71), G ('50), H ('71), (22–23 pages); revised directions for administering ('70, 8 pages, essentially the same as 1947 and 1956 directions except for format, revision of 1 table, and minor changes in directions); 30¢ per test; 40(50) minutes; Braille edition available from American Printing House for the Blind, Inc.

2) *Section 1: Vocabulary (Revised).* 1947–68; 5 scores: English, mathematics, science, social studies, total; no data on reliability of total score; Forms A, B, ('52, 9 pages); revised directions for administering ('66, 4 pages); 15¢ per test; 35(40) minutes.

3) *Section 2: Comprehension: Silent and Auditory.* 1947–68; no norms for grade 13; revised Forms A, B, C, D, ('57, c1948, 28–34 pages); revised directions for administering ('66, 12 pages, identical—including norms—with mimeographed 1958 directions except for deletion of norms date, format, and addition of 2 paragraphs of instructions for administering as a silent comprehension test when using answer sheets); may be administered as a listening comprehension test; 25¢ per test; [30] minutes as a silent reading test.

4) *Section 3: Rates of Reading: Part 1, General.* 1947–68; 4 scores: normal rate of reading, comprehension at normal rate, maximum rate of reading, comprehension at maximum rate; Forms A, B, ('47, 14 pages); revised directions for administering ('50, 12 pages, identical with directions published 1948 except for cover page); 15¢ per test; 30(35) minutes.

5) *Section 4: Word Attack.* 1947–68; 2 parts.
(*a*) Part 1, Oral. 1948–68; no data on reliability; no norms for grades 9–13; individual; Forms A, B, ('48, 15 pages); revised directions for administering ('58, 8 pages) for grades 1–13; 20¢ per test; (20) minutes.
(*b*) Part 2, Silent. Grades 4–13; see *b*2(*b*) above.
See T2:1626 (21 references); for reviews by Albert J. Kingston and B. H. Van Roekel, see 6:823 (21 references); for reviews by Frederick B. Davis, William W. Turnbull, and Henry Weitz, see 4:531 (19 references).

REFERENCES

1–19. See 4:531.
20–40. See 6:823.
41–61. See T2:1626; also includes a cumulative name index to the first 61 references and 5 reviews for this test.
62. GUTHRIE, HARRIET MAY. *A Factor Analytic Study of Reading Comprehension as the Extrapolated Function of a Three Dimensional Model of the Reading Process.* Doctor's thesis, University of Missouri (Kansas City, Mo.), 1972. (*DAI* 34:1585A)
63. JONGSMA, EUGENE. "Diagnostic Reading Tests: A Review," pp. 19–23. In *Reading Tests for the Secondary Grades.* Edited by William Blanton and others. Newark, Del.: International Reading Association, Inc., 1972. Pp. iv, 55. *
64. DEMBO, MYRON H., AND WILSON, DONALD A. "A Performance Contract in Speed Reading." *J Read* 16(8):627–33 My '73. *
65. MOORE, KENNETH THOMPSON. *Reading Subskills and Success in the College Freshman Year.* Doctor's thesis, University of Florida (Gainesville, Fla.), 1975. (*DAI* 37:4100A)

[755]

★**Diagnostic Screening Test: Reading.** Grades 1–12; 1976; DSTR; 15 scores: comfort level, instructional level, frustration level, comprehension level, phonics/sight ratio, consolidation index, and 9 word attack scores; no data on reliability; individual; 1 form (6 pages); manual (11 pages plus comprehension subtest); $7.50 per 20 tests, postage extra; specimen set not available; [5–10] minutes; Thomas D. Gnagey; Facilitation House. *

P. DAVID PEARSON, *Associate Professor of Education, University of Minnesota, Minneapolis, Minnesota.*

The *Diagnostic Screening Test: Reading,* a set of short tests to be individually administered to students in grades 2–12, is designed to give educators a quick (5–10 minutes) diagnostic picture of a student's word attack skills and instructional reading level, "which can be immediately translated into practical, helpful classroom learning activities."

More specifically, test data can allegedly be translated into the following indices: (1) Word Reading Comfort Level (that grade level of materials at which a student should know almost all the words), (2) Word Reading Instructional Level (that grade level at which the student knows 85–90% of the words), (3) Word Reading Frustration Level (that grade level at which a student misses so many words that the task is unpleasant or incomprehensible), (4) Comprehension of Passages Level (essentially a grade level score for comprehension of material read silently), (5) Consolidation Index (a measure of how efficiently a student can apply the skills he or she has apparently learned), and (6) Phonics to Sight Ratio (an index of the relative strength of a student's ability to read words which exemplify rule-predictable versus rule-unpredictable patterns). There are, in addition, several other minor indices which can be derived.

All indices except the Comprehension of Passages Level are derived from a word list test consisting of 63 basic and 21 advanced words. The procedures for converting word reading performance into the various indices are spelled out; however, some examples of computation would help the test administrator. Furthermore, the directions are ambiguous regarding how one should administer the word reading test; it isn't clear whether the basic and advanced words are to be administered separately or interspersed.

The Comprehension of Passages Level is derived by counting the number of correct answers a student gives to questions after he or she has silently read two short paragraphs. The questions are read orally by the test administrator;

the student may not refer to the text while answering. The raw scores for passages are converted to grade equivalent scores which are averaged to derive the index.

The manual includes some technical data, an interpretation section, and some guidelines for making instructional recommendations. While the test construction and norming procedures do not meet the rigorous standards of most standardized tests, they are superior to the procedures typical of many informal or individual diagnostic reading tests on the market. The test words were selected from among a pool of 3,221 words suggested as "typical" of grade level by 71 teachers in grades 1–12. The words were then placed into 8 categories (corresponding to 7 phonics rules plus sight words). The pool was reduced to 84 by finding "grade appropriate words," i.e., words that were known by 35% to 100% of students at one grade level but known by 30% or fewer of students at the next lower grade level. These 84 words were administered to 240 grade 1–12 students and the scores were compared with three other criteria for grade placement of students: teacher judgment and the SRA and WRAT reading tests. The manual reports the proportion of students at each grade level for which the grade equivalent score of the DSTR and each of the three criteria differed by fewer than two months. The proportions range from .72 to .97. It would have been useful to test users if the manual also reported correlations with the criterion measures.

The manual reports the average raw score obtained on each passage for students who had grade equivalent scores of 2–13 on the SRA reading test. The number of correct answers increases across grade levels fairly well through grade 7, after which the ceiling is reached on two of the passages. No reliability data are reported for either the word test or the passage test.

DSTR has three basic practical problems: (1) The directions for administration are not at all clear. Exactly where one starts, what materials have to be used, and how one proceeds from one step to the next often have to be inferred. (2) With no reliability data and with such serious ceiling problems on the comprehension test, users will have to question the reliability of judgments at upper grade levels. (3)

There is no supporting normative data for the subtests measuring various phonics skills; any judgments made on the basis of so few items (a maximum of 7 words per skill) for which there is no supporting data can be only speculative at best.

There are also some conceptual concerns: (1) The notion of finding a set of words that corresponds to a grade level such that a student might know some predictable percentage of them is a worthy goal but a pragmatic impossibility. There is not enough consistency between schools, books, programs, or students to make such a construct meaningful. (2) The DSTR starts out with a fairly modest goal typical of *screening* tests: to give the administrator some idea of a place to start with a particular student. But then it goes on to claim that it can provide much more specific data regarding subskill strengths and weaknesses, the amount of instructional effort that should be directed to phonic or sight word analysis, and whether a student's skills profile is or is not on a par with his or her general reading level. In short, the suggestions for data analysis exceed the capacity of the data base. (3) There are so many questions for the comprehension passages that comprehension is (and can only be) tested at a very atomistic level. For example, there are 12 questions for passage 1, which has a total of 26 words. One wonders whether anything but memory of the order of specific words in the passage is being tested. At the least, the directions ought to inform the students, beforehand, of the detailed nature of the questions.

The strength of the test is that one can get some important information about where to place a child instructionally with a minimum expenditure of time and effort. Furthermore, compared to alternative informal placement tests, the DSTR is as sound as many and utilizes better norming procedures than most. As long as one recognizes the limitations of the instrument, it can serve as a preliminary component in a larger testing program. "DST" stands for "diagnostic screening test"; the test can be useful if the emphasis is placed on *screening*. If the emphasis is placed on diagnosis, the test falls far short of its goal.

[756]

★Domain Phonic Tests. Ages 5–9; 1972; no scores (except for auditory discrimination subtest), 6 areas: initial single consonants, final single consonants, con-

Diagnostic Screening Test: Reading

sonant blends, single vowels, vowel blends, auditory discrimination; no data on reliability; no norms; individual; 1 form (4 cards plus 1 page in record booklet); manual (38 pages); record booklet (7 pages); corrective exercises (63 pages) for use after testing; £4.40 per examiner's kit including 2 sets of tests, 5 record booklets, and 5 sets of corrective exercises; 65p per 5 record booklets; £2.65 per 5 sets of corrective exercises; postage extra; administration time not reported; J. McLeod and J. Atkinson; Oliver & Boyd [Scotland]. *

[757]

Doren Diagnostic Reading Test of Word Recognition Skills, 1973 Edition. Grades 1–4; 1956–73; DDRT; 13 scores: letter recognition, beginning sounds, whole word recognition, words within words, speech consonants, ending sounds, blending, rhyming, vowels, discriminate guessing, spelling, sight words, total; no norms; 1 form ('73, 24 pages); manual ('73, 38 pages); $6.80 per 25 tests; $5.90 per overlay key booklet; $2.35 per manual; postage extra; $3 per specimen set, postpaid; (60–180) minutes; Margaret Doren; American Guidance Service, Inc. *

See T2:1627 (2 references); for reviews by B. H. Van Roekel and Verna L. Vickery of an earlier edition, see 5:659.

REFERENCES

1–2. See T2:1627.
3. BANNATYNE, ALEX. "Review of the Doren Diagnostic Reading Test of Word Recognition Skills." *J Learn Dis* 7(9): 535–8 N '74. *
4. FELDMANN, SHIRLEY. "Review of the Doren Diagnostic Reading Test of Word Recognition Skills." *Read Teach* 28(1): 93 O '74. *
5. OTTO, WAYNE. "Review of the Doren Diagnostic Reading Test of Word Recognition Skills." *J Sch Psychol* 13(3): 276–7 f '75. *

ROBERT L. SCHREINER, *Professor of Education, University of Minnesota, Minneapolis, Minnesota.*

The DDRT is a group administered test with diagnostic implications for individual students in grades 1–4. The test consists of 395 items in 12 subtests, each with separate components that assess the following skills: (*a*) Letter Recognition (identity, case, and forms); (*b*) Beginning Sounds (sound identity and context selection); (*c*) Whole Word Recognition (word identity and similarity); (*d*) Words Within Words (compound and hidden words, and discrimination); (*e*) Speech Consonants (auditory and visual); (*f*) Ending Sounds (consonant, variant, and plurals); (*g*) Blending; (*h*) Rhyming (auditory, visual, and dissimilar rhyming and similar nonrhyming); (*i*) Vowels (word choice, vowel identity, vowel rules and sounds, rule exceptions, double vowels: choice and sound, diphthongs, and sound exceptions); (*j*) Discriminate Guessing; (*k*) Spelling (phonetic and nonphonetic); and (*l*) Sight Words.

The testing materials consist of consumable test booklets, an overlay key to assist the user in scoring, and a manual. The manual contains information regarding the rationale for the test, item selection, general directions for administration, an extensive section devoted to activities for remedial teaching, and a brief technical section. Correlational data, by grade level, are provided between the Doren and the *Coordinated Scales of Attainment,* the coefficients ranging from .77 at grade 1 to .92 at grade 4, with an overall coefficient of .90. Descriptive data about sampling procedures or subjects are not provided. Correlations between subtest scores and total score range from .53, letter recognition, to .88, blending. No evidence of independence of skills is presented to justify profile reporting of student scores. Difficulty indices are not reported. Normative data or procedures for translating student scores into standard scores are not utilized. The number of errors by subskill, reported in raw score form, are used to calculate student scores.

This test is an ambitious attempt to assess many beginning reading skills. It fails on many counts. While the test, because of the emphasis on the commonly accepted content of basal reading systems, may have satisfactory content validity, its lack of predictive and construct validity is readily apparent. It is claimed that the results obtained from the test can be directly translated into immediate and effective classroom practices. These claims are unwarranted and unsubstantiated. The names assigned to the skills do not accurately describe the reading processes or skills being assessed. For example, several of the subtests require the student to choose a correct word to complete a sentence. In one part of Beginning Sounds, the student chooses between two words with different sounds to complete the *meaning* of the sentence. The correct response depends on the context of the sentence; the initial sounds of the words are irrelevant to making the correct choice. Similar context strategies are used to measure speech consonants, ending sounds, and blending. The parts of these subtests utilizing context do not assess the skills their names imply.

Two additional subtests, Letter Recognition and Discriminate Guessing do not serve as useful indicators of the degree of reading disability of individual students. Thus, they have limited predictive usefulness. In one part of the letter recognition subtest, students are asked to encircle various forms of uppercase letters. These forms include both lower and upper case and manuscript and cursive formation of the letters. Since discrimination among cursive letters has little to do with beginning reading tasks, it seems a highly questionable type of item. In the discriminate guessing subtest, students read a riddle and then complete the context by filling in a blank. Correct responses are strictly a function of the student's general knowledge and do not assist the user in the diagnostic process.

While each of the subtests of the Doren may be a useful criterion-referenced instrument for the assessment of highly specific phonic skills, a potentially dangerous situation occurs when the user computes a profile of student performance by subtest. In addition to the previously mentioned shortcomings of this instrument regarding profile scores, the visual interpretation and display of student performance is seriously questioned. A gray or danger area is printed on the lower portion of the profile on the front cover of the student test booklet. A score is placed in the gray area when the student makes seven or more errors on any of the subtests. The authors states, "All skill totals that fall below the level of proficiency, in the shaded area on the Profile, indicate the skills which need remedial teaching." This scoring procedure allows student errors to range from 47% for Discriminate Guessing to 16% for Whole Word Recognition and Vowels before remediation is necessary. No justification is provided for this scoring procedure. Normative data are sorely needed for such practices.

In summary, the amount of time required to administer and score this test and the lack of normative and item analysis data make it of questionable usefulness.

J Learn Dis 7(9):535–8 N '74. Alex Bannatyne. * definitely fills a gap in our diagnostic testing procedures. A careful study of the test, even without using it with children, is an education in itself. Many of us do not realize just how complex reading is, even on an academic level, let alone when considering sensory-motor processing, motivation and psychoneurological factors. Although one may feel it is not necessary to teach each of the twelve skills assessed by this test as a deliberate procedure in the classroom, the competent teacher of reading and spelling should be aware of their separate existence and of their interrelationships within the learning-to-read process. The Doren Diagnostic Test will need to be supplemented with other reading tests. Comprehension, paragraph reading, fluency, reading rate and basic sensory motor functions such as auditory closure and recall memory for designs are not included. The Doren Test is a probe of word recognition in details, not depth, but that is sufficient to qualify it for a place in your battery of available tests. *

J Sch Psychol 13(3):276–7 f '75. Wayne Otto. * the reviewer grew up with the 1956 edition of the *Doren;* it was used extensively in his training and in his early experience as a reading specialist. Consequently, it has the comfortable feel of an old shoe. So it evokes all the warm, positive, even affectionate, feelings of comfortable old shoes and dependable old friends. Furthermore, the reviewer has a profound respect for the common sense approach to reading instruction and to the solution of reading problems. The *Doren* embodies much common sense in its approach to the diagnosis of reading difficulties. * The 1973 Revision of the *Doren* retains its high face validity with people who bear responsibility for the on-line, day-to-day teaching of reading. In general, the skills that are covered are the ones teachers worry about and the ones that good readers have mastered. The format of the test lends well to ease of administration and scoring. The directions are—for the most part—explicit and clear. The test will, in the judgment of this reviewer, deservedly continue to be used widely and with enthusiasm. It has the splendid appeal of common sense, and people *with* common sense will use it to improve their teaching of word recognition skills. But let's face it. Like everything else the *Doren* has limitations, and some of them are virtually unpardonable. A minor kind of limitation is the labeling of certain of the subtests. The subtest called Letter Identity, for example, is very simply a letter *matching* test; the Word Identity subtest of the Whole Word Recognition skill area amounts to a simple matching test, too. The Plural Endings subtest of the Ending Sounds skill area has very little to do with ending *sounds.* But these are relatively minor concerns. No need to quibble about titles if we can agree that the behaviors are important to success in reading. A more serious limitation is the fact that a few of the subtests are preceded by very complex directions that would seem to boggle the minds of many primary school children. The directions for the Blending test are an example of this complexity. The most serious limitation is that there are no item statistics at all to demonstrate reliability of the tests and subtests. The *Manual* says only that "the items in this test have been selected from a larger number of tested items." This is the unpardonable limitation; but it is one that presumably could easily be remedied by publication of available data. On the positive side, some validity data are given in the last section of the *Manual*. And, again, there is a good demonstration of common sense: "Failure to discriminate letter forms is rarely a cause of reading difficulty. In a diagnostic test, however, it is necessary to include items basic to reading success." So Letter Recognition continues as a subtest *because* it is basic and *despite* the fact that it does not correlate highly with total test scores. This review seems to boil down to two paradoxical points. As an empiricist with some appreciation for the niceties of test construction, I hate the *Doren*. But as a pragmatist with some appreciation for the realities of teaching kids to read, I love it!

Read Teach 28(1):93 O '74. *Shirley Feldmann.* * The test measures, according to its author, discrimination in word recognition based on "a whole to its parts" approach, rather than on analysis of word construction. However promising such an approach, the test does not live up to its rationale. Inspection of the subtests shows that many measure more than one reading skill. Other tests seem to be misnamed, thus casting doubt on the validity of the information obtained. Confounding these problems are the inordinately confusing directions and tasks required, often too complex for primary level children. For the thirty odd subtests there are at least ten different test tasks. Many different item formats are used, some with vertical columns, others with horizontal rows, and still others with unnumbered items and ambiguous formats. Thus, errors made may not be clear indicators of a child's actual skill. In addition, the technical data furnished are inadequate, slighting reliability and validity questions as well as a description of the tryout sample. The subtests are not normed, a defensible position

for a diagnostic test, but no explanation is given of the scoring procedure used. Why one score is acceptable but another indicates need of remedial work seems to be an arbitrary decision. Despite the pressing need for reading diagnostic instruments, this test has flaws in construction and in administration procedures which seem to limit its usefulness for the classroom teacher.

[758]

★**Fountain Valley Teacher Support System in Secondary Reading.** Grades 7–12; 1976; FVTSS-SR; upward extension of the *Fountain Valley Teacher Support System in Reading*; criterion referenced; 61 specific-objective subtests (69% consist of 4 or 6 items) in 3 areas: comprehension (20 subtests), study skills (24), vocabulary development (17); no data on reliability; no norms; mastery passing mark is 67 to 83%; 38 test sheets, each covering 1 to 3 subtests; manual and resource guide (32–50 pages) for each area; individual record forms (2 pages); optional survey test (10 pages) available for identifying students for whom these tests are too difficult; $331.50 per 50 sets of testing materials; $15 per 50 survey tests; $3.75 per 50 survey test answer sheets; $6.50 per 50 record forms; (5–15) minutes per test; [30] minutes per survey test; Richard L. Zweig Associates, Inc. *

GILBERT SAX, *Professor of Education and Psychology, University of Washington, Seattle, Washington.*

This test consists of three "strands," each of which is divided into three "domains": vocabulary development (word meaning, structural analysis, and vocabulary in content areas), comprehension (interpretive comprehension and descriptive language), and study skills (using reference sources, using the library, and organizing information). Each domain, in turn, is measured by a number of criterion-referenced tests that are tied to behaviorally-stated objectives. The 61 tests include 17 for vocabulary, 20 for comprehension, and 24 for study skills. In addition, a survey test consisting of 25 multiple choice items, 23 of which contain three alternatives, is provided. The stated purpose of the survey test is to identify students who will find the secondary reading materials too difficult for them.

The system contains a number of useful ideas. A "continuous pupil progress profile" allows teachers to identify students for whom reteaching is necessary; if students have learned a skill to proficiency (the criteria are listed on each test sheet), that fact is indicated on the profile. A class record sheet is also available to help group students who have not reached proficiency levels for each test. Another useful adjunct to the system is a box of Action/Mark crayons. Whenever a correct answer is marked, a latent image of a plus sign is made apparent; incorrect answers are indicated either by the number of the objective being measured by that test or, on the survey test, by three small boxes. Students are warned to use the crayons only to mark their final answers.

A "teacher's manual and resource guide" accompanies each strand. Each describes the system in general terms, specifies the behavioral objectives for that strand, and includes a rather exhaustive bibliography of textbooks, audiovisual aids, laboratory materials and kits, workbooks, and spirit masters that can be used to help teach each objective.

The survey test presents a number of problems. First, no evidence regarding reliability, validity, or the effectiveness of the cutoff score for placement purposes is presented. Teachers are told only that a score of 20 or more items correct (out of 25) is necessary before students should be permitted to work on the objectives for the secondary level. Teachers are not told that the system might be too easy for some students although that is certainly a possibility. The survey test items are a conglomeration of the types of items found in the criterion-referenced tests; but since there are only 25 items and 61 objectives, one would expect to find some rationale for selecting these particular items. Unfortunately, no rationale appears in any of the materials supplied to purchasers. Most of the items contain only three alternatives (and thus capitalize on guessing), and clues to the correct answer are present in numerous items. Students are told, for example, that "a less common [dictionary] meaning" for a term is the second, third, or fourth entry. A dictionary entry is given, and the student is asked to pick the one with "a less common meaning." Students are also told what homonyms, synonyms, and antonyms are, and then they are asked if two words are homonyms, synonyms, or antonyms. In another set of items, students are told that they will be asked to select a word in social studies or science that best completes a definition, but in the question on science only one option is related to science; thus, to respond correctly does not require any understanding of the definition. Another item uses an analogy that can be an-

swered solely by the length of the words. One item contains a potentially confusing choice of words, and items on topic sentences and the main idea of a paragraph can be answered by reading only the first line of a paragraph. In a few items, more than one response might be justified as the correct answer. Except for providing a cutoff score, teachers are not told how results on the survey test are to be interpreted. None of the items is linked to any of the criterion-referenced tests, thus making it difficult to determine which prerequisite skills need to be taught or retaught.

The criterion-referenced tests appear to be tied closely to their behaviorally-stated objectives, but they, too, present some problems. The most serious difficulty is that only one form of each test is available, even though teachers are told that these tests can serve both as pretests and posttests. The effect of using the same test for both purposes is to increase greatly the probability that students will appear to have mastered a given objective when, in fact, they may have learned only how to avoid previously made errors.

No evidence regarding reliability, validity, or the effectiveness of cutoff scores is presented for any of the criterion-referenced tests. No evidence tells users if items were selected randomly from each domain or what the criteria for item selection were.

The teacher's manual and resource guide contains hundreds of references that can be used to teach the behavioral objectives for each strand. Even here, however, there is some question regarding the usefulness of this information. Most teachers will have access to only a few of the materials that are referenced; some are quite old and some (such as alphabetizing to the fifth and sixth letter) hardly require an external source.

The FVTSS-SR will be of greatest value to junior high school teachers who are unacquainted with the objectives of secondary-school reading instruction and who want a conveniently packaged set of workbook-like materials. This convenience will, however, be costly. Because the system provides no teaching materials per se, most teachers will find it just as easy and much less expensive to use a good basal text along with a workbook or two for each student who needs special help.

Fountain Valley Teacher Support System in Secondary Reading

CARLETON B. SHAY, *Professor of Education, California State University, Los Angeles, California.*

The FVTSS-SR differs from its parent test at the elementary level by utilizing printed directions instead of cassettes and nonconsumable test booklets in two of three content areas, and by providing the optional survey test as a screening device. Based on research in secondary curriculum guides and text series and on consultation with teachers and reading experts, the FVTSS-SR tests the 61 skills most often emphasized in secondary reading programs. These skills are grouped in three "strands" (comprehension, study skills, and vocabulary development), each of which is, in turn, subdivided into three "domains," whose behavioral objectives vary in number from 2 to 18. All test items are multiple choice with 3 or 4 choices. The behavioral objectives for each skill are clearly defined in the separate manual and resource guide provided for each strand, and are coded for ease of cross-referencing. A useful section in each manual is a glossary of terms which range from those of general use to those helpful in understanding the FVTSS-SR.

For those desiring a criterion-referenced test, the FVTSS-SR has several attractive features. First, a small number of objectives may be tested at one time, and they may be given in almost any order; the answer sheets include test items for only one to three objectives. In fact, the authors recommend that no more than two tests be given to a student in any one testing period. Second, the results are immediately available through the Action/Mark scoring system which uses invisible ink on the answer sheet and a special scoring crayon which reveals a plus for a correct response and the objective code number for an incorrect response. The test is, in this way, diagnostic of an unmastered objective. Third, one of two performance levels may be selected for each objective on the answer sheet: mastery (100 percent) or proficiency (75–83 percent), which instructs the student to proceed to the next objective. Teachers are instructed to "reteach" objectives not satisfied at mastery or proficiency level, whichever criterion is selected. Fourth, each manual contains a list, by coded objective, of references in a large number of commonly used texts, workbooks, laboratory, and AV materials. In this way, presumably, a

teacher could test attainment of a specific objective following its study in the text; however, it would be more helpful for this purpose to provide a sequence of objectives by text, even though this would probably reveal text objectives not tested by the FVTSS-SR. Since the manual states that the resource guide is updated regularly, this reverse-classification could be included in such revisions. Finally, the FVTSS-SR is easy to administer, since it may be self-administered and scored, and is untimed. This advantage may be outweighed by the logistics involved in individualization of testing by objective, or the lack of availability of machine scoring, but is clearly superior from the standpoint of criterion-referenced, individualized testing.

The greatest deficiency of the FVTSS-SR is the complete absence of reliability and validity data. Reliability is never even referred to, and the only mention of validity is the unsubstantiated claim "it has been validated through the use of vocabulary and readability guides, and through trial and field test evaluations." Information supplied to the reviewer by the publisher tends to support these claims, but there is no excuse for not including some of the data in the manuals.

The first trial administration was given in the Fountain Valley School District, California. Among the findings pertinent to validity are these: "eighth grade students performed better than seventh grade students," "few skills were found inappropriate for the seventh grade level," and "the use of an 80% proficiency level produced the best correlation between student performance and teacher ranking of students." These statements are at least probably reflective of data, though the data are not supplied. Following revision, the field test was given in 1975 to 1,585 students in 61 classes (31 seventh grade, 29 eighth grade, one ninth grade) in Fountain Valley; Tucson, Arizona; and Linden, New Jersey. Item analyses were performed.

First, items were considered suspect when their item difficulty levels (percentage of correct responses) were outside the interval 60 to 80 and/or the responses to the distractors were not more or less evenly distributed. Item difficulty levels were used only as a guide to faulty items and not to delete them automatically as might be the case with norm-referenced tests, where the desire is to maximize score variance. Second, measures of item discrimination were calculated. All students were given the reading comprehension and vocabulary subtests of the *Stanford Achievement Test,* and divided into three groups according to their grade equivalent scores. The percentages of correct responses of the upper and lower groups were compared as a measure of item discrimination. In addition, correlation coefficients were calculated between the behavioral objective score on the main test and each test item on the survey test, and with the total survey test score. Extensive revision followed. These data should be interpreted with caution since they are norm-referenced criteria applied to criterion-referenced tests (in the absence of generally accepted indices for such tests), and in any case, the criteria were not necessarily applied rigorously to eliminate "faulty" items.

Further validity data were given to the reviewer in terms of a study of passage-dependency to determine the degree to which the test items are dependent upon their related passages and not on prior information. This study found 54 percent (89 of 166 items) nondependent for various reasons, resulting in further revision of the FVTSS-SR. No additional data were supplied to validate any of the revisions.

No data were furnished to support directly the contention that "a vocabulary and reading level appropriate to the junior high school was established," although the item analysis data, along with further information about the vocabulary list employed, could have been used. One further criticism may be made of the FVTSS-SR. There is only one form of the test available, even though the manual suggests that the FVTSS-SR "may be used to pretest as well as posttest." In addition, the same test must be used following less-than-mastery scores and reteaching on any objective. It is hoped that a second form will be made available, and that equivalent-forms reliabilty data will be supplied.

In summary, at a comparatively early stage of development, the FVTSS-SR seems to be a promising test, whose potential virtues are not yet fully realized. The lack of reliability and validity data cannot be justified; more studies need to be performed and data reported in the manuals. Its best potential seems to be in the direction of measures of teacher-selected objectives keyed to the text rather than as a general survey (more appropriate to a norm-referenced test, unless there is a correspondence between the teacher's objectives and the totality of those tested by the FVTSS-SR). Because of its attention to passage-dependency and similar concerns, it may have more potential than other tests of its type.

[759]

Gates-McKillop Reading Diagnostic Tests. Grades 2-0 to 6-0; 1926–62; revision of *Gates Reading Diagnostic Tests;* 28 scores: omissions, additions, repetitions, mispronunciation (reversals, partial reversals, total reversals, wrong beginnings, wrong middle, wrong ending, wrong in several parts, total), oral reading total, words-flash presentation, words-untimed presentation, phrases-flash presentation, recognizing and blending common word parts, giving letter sounds, naming capital letters, naming lower-case letters, recognizing the visual form of sounds (nonsense words, initial letters, final letters, vowels), auditory blending, spelling, oral vocabulary, syllabication, auditory discrimination; no data on reliability; no norms for auditory discrimination score; individual; Forms 1, 2, ('62, 9 pages); manual ('62, 20 pages); pupil record-response booklet ('62, 16 pages) for each form; separate record-response booklets must be used; $1.50 per test; $6.50 per 25 record-response booklets; 10¢ per tachistoscope for flash presentation of subtests; 50¢ per manual; $4 per specimen set; postage extra; (60) minutes; Arthur I. Gates and Anne S. McKillop; Teachers College Press. *

See T2:1629 (11 references); for reviews by N. Dale Bryant and Gabriel M. Della-Piana, see 6:824 (2 references); for a review by George D. Spache of the earlier edition, see 5:662; for a review by Worth J. Osburn, see 4:563 (2 references); for a review by T. L. Torgerson, see 3:510 (3 references).

REFERENCES

1–3. See 3:510.
4–5. See 4:563.
6–7. See 6:824.
8–18. See T2:1629; also includes a cumulative name index to the first 18 references and 5 reviews for this test.
19. Eller, William, and Attea, Mary. "Three Diagnostic Reading Tests: Some Comparisons." *Int Read Assn Conf Proc* 11(1):562–6 '67. *
20. Berends, Margery Lois. *An Analysis of Error Patterns, Rates and Grade Equivalent Scores on Selected Reading Measures at Three Levels of Performance.* Doctor's thesis, Oklahoma State University (Stillwater, Okla.), 1971. (*DAI* 33:582A)
21. Winkley, Carol K. "What Do Diagnostic Reading Tests Really Diagnose?" pp. 64–80. In *Diagnostic Viewpoints in Reading.* Edited by Robert E. Leibert. Newark, Del.: International Reading Association, Inc., 1971. Pp. viii, 133. *
22. Daines, Delva, and Mason, Lynne G. "A Comparison of Placement Tests and Readability Graphs." *J Read* 15(8): 597–603 My '72. *
23. Kiniry, Martha Sue Murphy. *Differentiating Elementary Children With Learning Disabilities Using the Illinois Test of Psycholinguistic Abilities.* Doctor's thesis, East Texas State University (Commerce, Tex.), 1972. (*DAI* 33:1046A)
24. Denney, Douglas R. "Relationship of Three Cognitive Style Dimensions to Elementary Reading Abilities." *J Ed Psychol* 66(5):702–9 O '74. * (*PA* 53:8332)
25. Eberwein, Lowell. "Does Pronouncing Unknown Words Really Help?" *Acad Ther* 11(1):23–9 f '75. *
26. Lucas, Marilyn S., and Singer, Harry. "Dialect in Relation to Oral Reading Achievement: Recoding, Encoding, or Merely a Code?" *J Read Behav* 7(2):137–48 su '75. * (*PA* 57:6843)

Harry Singer, *Professor of Education and Chairman, Reading and Language Development*

Program, University of California, Riverside, California.

The earliest edition of this test was one of the first standardized diagnostic tests in reading.

The manual suffers from lack of data on reliability and validity, and from other psychometric problems. The publication seven years earlier of the AERA-NCMUE *Technical Recommendations for Achievement Tests* urging test authors and publishers to prepare more informative manuals apparently had no influence on the authors of this test. The manual presents no information whatsoever on the reliability and validity of the 28 subtests.

A major shortcoming lies in the gradation and standardization of the oral reading paragraphs. Paragraphs 1 to 4 are about equally spaced in difficulty, but a large increment in difficulty occurs between paragraphs 4 and 5 and again between paragraphs 6 and 7. Also, the content and language of the last three paragraphs, which include such words as "vassal," "kinsmen," and "mayhap," are quaint and outmoded. Furthermore, standardization of and directions for administering the test require that all testees complete the first four paragraphs regardless of errors made, thus making the test unduly difficult for beginning readers and limiting its appropriateness for primary graders. This limitation is serious since early detection of reading difficulties is necessary for ease of correction and for prevention of further difficulties.

The test uses four expectancy criteria (mental age, oral reading status, grade level, and oral vocabulary level), but the manual does not discuss the significance of discrepancies between any of these expectancy criteria and oral reading performance.

Content validity of a test can be determined from a table of specifications or a list of behavioral objectives, but no explicit information of this type is provided in the manual.

Although extensive tables of norms are provided, no data are given on the characteristics, sample procedure, or size of the standardization population. Neither percentiles nor standard scores are provided, only grade equivalent norms. Grade equivalent norms are notoriously unreliable because a difference in relatively few items results in large grade-equivalent differences, especially at extreme ends of the scales which are usually based on extrapolated data.

Scoring is time-consuming. But more important, oral reading "errors" are weighted equally and not differentiated according to any theory of reading development. For example, repetition of two or more words is counted as an error even if the student is rereading a sentence to self-correct, and self-correction of errors is what good readers do earlier than poor readers in learning to read. Moreover, oral errors, which are simply departures from the text, are not differentiated according to whether an error could result in a change in meaning. Finally, no validity data are provided on changes in performance on any of the subtests as a result of specific instruction or even of general reading improvement, nor are suggestions even made for teaching students how to overcome errors in reading.

What, then, is the value of the test? The well-organized manual provides detailed instructions for administering, scoring, and interpreting test results. The test assesses a variety of functions taught in a skills sequence approach to reading instruction; particularly desirable for assessing this skills sequence are the subtests of sight word recognition, blending, syllabication, and oral vocabulary. But a comprehensive assessment of a skills sequence instruction is precluded because missing from the diagnostic battery are subtests on use of syntax, semantics, and grapheme-phoneme correspondences in identifying words in context. However, the test user may infer, albeit somewhat unsystematically, from performance on the paragraph reading subtest, particularly on paragraphs with relatively difficult word recognition tasks, whether the examinee is using contextual constraints and phonemic responses to graphemes.

The test has not been revised since 1962, despite subsequent critical reviews of it. As theories and concepts of test construction, standardization, and norming continue to improve, the discrepancy between the Gates-McKillop and criteria for an excellent test increases. Unless modified soon, the test is headed towards obsolescence. Until such time as the test is revised to meet the criteria currently required for excellence in diagnostic testing of oral reading, test users might be able to capitalize on some of its desirable features, yet must be aware of its many limitations. Or, better still, use another test which has more advantages and fewer limitations, for example, Spache's *Diagnostic Reading Scales*.

[760]
Gillingham-Childs Phonics Proficiency Scales. Grades 2–8; 1966–73; GCPPS; criterion referenced; no data on reliability and validity; no norms; no suggested standards of mastery; 2 levels; cash orders postpaid; (10–15) minutes per scale; Educators Publishing Service, Inc. *
a) SERIES 1: BASIC READING AND SPELLING. 1966–70; 17 subtest scores in each of 2 areas: reading, spelling; individual in part; 1 form ('70, 47 pages, essentially the same as test copyrighted 1967 except for minor changes); directions ('70, 8 pages); reading record ('69, 22 pages); spelling record ('70, 47 pages); $2.50 per test; 70¢ per reading record; $1.50 per spelling record; Sally B. Childs, Anna Gillingham (test), and Bessie W. Stillman (test).
b) SERIES 2: ADVANCED READING. 1970–73; 20 subtest scores; individual; 1 form ('71, 56 pages); directions ('73, 11 pages); advanced reading record ('71, 23 pages); $2.50 per test; 70¢ per reading record; Sally B. Childs and Ralph de S. Childs.

SHIRLEY C. FELDMANN, *Professor of Education and Head, Reading Program, The City College and The Graduate School, The City University of New York, New York, New York.*

These scales are mastery tests in reading and spelling, designed to check knowledge of the sequential steps of reading of Gillingham's reading program, which espouses a coding or phonic approach for teaching initial skills. The program starts with sounds, and proceeds in systematic and sequential steps through multisyllabic words, covering elementary grade skills. Reading and spelling are considered almost completely interchangeable in this program; that is, as defined, they are complementary processes used in changing back and forth between the code, or written symbols, and spoken words.

The tests are individually given. Each series has a spiral-bound booklet for the child to read, disposable individual record booklets for reading and for spelling, and a booklet giving directions for use. The subtests are to be given after instruction in a particular skill area in order to judge learning proficiency, so it is unlikely that more than a few subtests in either scale series would be given at any one time.

Series 1, Basic Reading and Spelling, includes skills for the introductory period of teaching. The items contain letter-sound connections, three-letter regular and nonce (nonsense) words, consonant digraphs and blends in regular

and nonce words, monosyllables ending in *f, l, s,* vowel-consonant-*e* regular and nonce words, syllable division between two consonants with regular and nonce words, and doubling final consonants in monosyllables. Extra skills presented include knowing the alphabet, irregular words, basic plural rule, and adding suffixes to vowel-consonant *e* words.

The tester is instructed that the sounds must be clearly and correctly made by the child, so that unless there is a perfect performance need for further practice is indicated. The sounding out of words by the child while pronouncing them is considered incorrect.

Series 2, Advanced Reading, has no spelling component. It tests elaborations of the basic steps of Series 1, given in a systematic and developmental sequence. Phonograms, digraphs, variations of consonant and vowel sounds, suffixes, irregular words, reading pronunciations, and syllable divisions are included. The tester is instructed to record any deviation from standard pronunciation of the items, using a system of marks given in the directions.

The skills presented in the scales are comprehensive and appear to be presented in ascending order of difficulty. A teacher using the reading program to which they are tied can obtain minute knowledge of any child's reading and spelling skills. As mastery tests go, these have a typical format and, therefore, should present no problems for administration in the classroom.

These seem slim advantages, however, in relation to the weaknesses apparent in the scales. Although the scales are based on a definition of reading that is viewed today as narrow and confining, even a teacher who structures her program around such a definition may find the scales of limited value. They are so linked to the Gillingham method in definition of item correctness that most other "phonic method" users may find them arbitrary and limited in the possible diagnostic information to be derived. Such users might feel that less arduous assessments of the same reading and spelling skills might yield sufficient information for curriculum planning.

More serious lacks are the unstated assumptions made about the scales. There is no information given about the procedures used in constructing the items. There is little mention of any kind of scoring procedures or interpretation of results. Reliability data are absent and, although a case could be made for it, content validity is not mentioned. No discussion is included concerning the use of test information in curriculum planning. The scales are similar to many teacher-made mastery scales; they have achieved the status of tests only through virtue of publication. The burden of proof of their usefulness in the classroom rests entirely on the user.

In summary, the scales would seem to have limited value for teachers not using the reading program upon which they were based. Shorter and less formal measures could give the same information about the reading skills of a child in a more efficient way. Lack of any information on construction procedures casts extreme doubt on their value as reading and spelling measures.

LAWRENCE M. KASDON, *Professor of Education, Yeshiva University, New York, New York.*

These scales of phonics skills are designed to be used with the Gillingham approach to teaching reading. The directions for administering are so specifically attuned to Gillingham's methodology that one not familiar with this approach would be at a disadvantage in using these scales.

The manuals do not give any information about the construction, reliability, or validity of the scales. Content validity can be assumed since they were authored by the originator of the Gillingham approach and a close associate.

Most of the scales possess three parts and the directions are not clear as to whether or not all three need to be administered. At the Series 1 level there are three additional scales of nonce words (nonsense syllables) for each of four subtests. In Series 2, the additional nonce words occur only in the summary subtests.

According to the directions, "Every sound must be clearly and correctly made, and any ambiguity, addition, omission, substitution, reversal or self-correction is an error. The goal is perfect performance so that any error indicates the need for further practice." Such standards are overly stringent; a slip of the tongue or a pronunciation different from Gillingham's, but correct according to current dictionaries or the pupil's dialect, can be counted as an error. The scales contain numerous examples of discrepancies with current scholarship. For example, consider the Series 2 scale which requires pupils to pronounce words which have been spelled phonetically: (*a*) the majority of the pronunciations contain inaccuracies according to current dictionaries; (*b*) the phonetic symbols are peculiar to the Gillingham program and do not correspond to the diacritics used in current dictionaries; (*c*) they indicate that words are syllabified in speech; and (*d*) *average* difficulty of the words is approximately eighth grade, which means that many of these scales will not be in the speaking or listening vocabulary of many pupils. In summary, the scales represent thinking about phonics of a generation ago.

These scales are limited in use to the Gillingham approach and are in serious need of revision in terms of current scholarship. A reading teacher looking for a criterion-referenced, word attack test for the primary grades might wish to consider the *Wisconsin Tests of Reading Skill Development: Word Attack.*

[761]

Group Phonics Analysis. Reading level grades 1–3; 1971; GPA; criterion referenced; no scores, 11 areas: number reading, letter reading, hearing consonants, alphabetization, recognition (vowels, short sounds, long vowel sounds in words), vowel digraph rule, final e rule, open and closed syllables, syllabification; no data on reliability; no norms; no suggested standards of mastery; 1 form (1 page, self-marking); manual (4 pages); $4.95 per 30 tests; $2 per specimen set of this and 4 other tests; cash orders postpaid; [10–15] minutes; Edward Fry; Dreier Educational Systems, Inc. *

REFERENCES

1. FULD, PAULA ALTMAN. "Review of the Group Phonics Analysis Test." *J Read* 16(1):85+ O '72. *

PATRICK GROFF, *Professor of Education, San Diego State University, San Diego, California.*

The *Group Phonics Analysis* claims to be a "diagnostic group test" helpful "in determining which of several basic phonics skills pupils have mastered," and "in discovering which pupils need help in this important method of word attack." An inspection of this test reveals, however, that the attainment of these goals is not possible through the use of the GPA.

One reason the GPA fails to fulfill its acclaimed goals is that it involves its teacher-administrator in certain activities that have been demonstrated not to be related to the accomplishment of phonics skills by children. In this respect, the GPA tests children's abilities to read numbers, their knowledge of the names of letters, their ability to alphabetize, and their understanding of the term "vowel." It is highly doubtful whether the teacher of phonics needs this information.

It is also noticeable that the manual and the content of the GPA both violate certain established bits of information about linguistics and orthography. The GPA in this regard wrongly subscribes to the notion that phonemes can be spoken and heard as such in isolation. There is no support from phoneticians for this belief. Yet, almost all the subtests of the GPA ask the beginning reader to listen to phonemes supposedly articulated in isolation, and then to mark letters or words that represent these sounds—which actually are heard as facsimile speech sounds. As well, linguists would reject GPA's advocacy of dictionary syllabication. Wrong, then, is GPA's notion that "when there are two consonants between two separated vowel sounds, the consonants are divided to form the syllable division" or that "when only one consonant is found between two separated vowel sounds, the consonant goes with the last consonant." Not only are these rules confusing since it is not always apparent what is meant here by consonant, phoneme, or grapheme; it is also clear that none of the linguistic theories of the highly debatable phenomenon called the syllable endorse these practices of syllabication by dictionaries. The GPA also appears to ignore the fact that educational research reveals it is highly unlikely that teaching children dictionary syllabication helps them to any exceptional extent to learn to read or spell. An equally dubious statement from GPA is that in reading vowel digraphs "the first vowel [letter] is pronounced long and the second is silent." Actually, this cannot be a rule of phonics since to read correctly a majority of the vowel digraphs in words this "rule" must be violated.

It is also regrettable that the GPA gives no specific information as to its reliability or validity. Its author explains that the skills tested are "presented in the same order that they are frequently introduced in reading textbooks and teachers' manuals." This is an unfortunate guide for establishing its validity, however, since it is known that the phonics content of basal readers (and their manuals) of the past has been notoriously inaccurate. The validity of the GPA is also said to be based on the content of phonics as offered by "reading authorities." The errors of the GPA, as described so far, however, cast

doubt on the credentials of the experts Fry chose for this purpose.

A further weakness of the GPA lies in the wording of some of the directions given to children who take the test. For example, in subtest 9 the child hears, "I want you to mark the three *vowels.*" In subtest 16 he is told, "Mark the vowel sound you hear in the word READ." It is apparent that the GPA refers in subtest 9 to letters, but does not specifically say so. In subtest 16 the child is asked to perform the impossible; of course, it is obvious that *sounds* cannot be marked.

Finally, the claim by the GPA, that it "is designed to assist the teacher and curriculum specialist in determining strengths and weaknesses" of pupils learning phonics, is not met by the test. This is because the GPA provides no standards of attainment or pupil performance criteria for the teacher's use. This reference information is necessary, however, if the teacher of any given grade level is to be able to use the scores gained from the GPA to decide how much and what kinds of phonics knowledge a particular child still needs to learn. The GPA does not tell the teacher how any score less than a perfect score on its subtests should be interpreted. What score must a child make here, one must ask, if he is considered by the GPA to have "weaknesses" in phonics skills? Neither this question, nor that of whether a certain subset test score (or total GPA test score) means that a child is a low, average, or high achiever in phonics for his age, intelligence, reading or grade level, is answered by the GPA. There is no evidence offered by the GPA, therefore, that its scores are either predictive or reflective about instruction in phonics, or to what extent they relate to children's overall reading abilities. The most pressing need of phonics teachers has long been for information as to when children's accomplishments in phonics indicate that instruction in a certain item of phonics can be discontinued so that the teacher can move on to the next more difficult item in the phonics hierarchy of skills. It is obvious that the GPA in no way helps the teacher solve this urgent problem unless the pupil scores 100 percent on a given subtest.

In summary, the GPA is not to be recommended for the measurement of phonics because it tests irrelevant matters, contains several linguistic and orthographic errors, presents no con-

Group Phonics Analysis

vincing argument that it is reliable or valid, offers directions that are sometimes confusing, and presents no achievement norms. Accordingly, tests of phonics with fewer of these flaws should be used for this purpose. These would include the *Cooperative Primary Tests: Word Analysis,* the phonics section of the *Diagnostic Reading Scales,* the word attack section of the *Diagnostic Reading Tests,* and the *Silent Reading Diagnostic Tests.*

J Read 16(1):85+ O '72. Paula Altman Fuld. * The phonics tests may be particularly helpful in giving the new teacher a convenient summary of the grapheme-phoneme correspondences commonly taught, but the user should bear in mind the fact that the form of response on the group test—that is, recognition of nonsense words that contain a specific sound—is not the same as with reading either silently or aloud. The difference may be critical for readers who would be diagnosed as dyslexic; for such readers, both the group and the individual tests might give misleading results. These problems are common to all phonics tests of which this reviewer is aware; but teachers should be cautioned about them in the manuals. Since tests like these have been available for years, their claim to being criterion referenced needs to be evaluated. * criterion referenced skill tests should yield scores that are related somehow to the level of mastery needed for the skill to be adequate for use * True criterion referenced reading skill tests do not yet seem to be feasible; they will not become so until a more precise understanding of the processes involved in reading is attained.

[762]
Individual Phonics Criterion Test. Grades 1–8; 1971; IPCT; formerly called *Phonics Criterion Test;* criterion referenced; no scores, 14 areas: easy consonants, short vowels, long and silent vowels, difficult consonants, consonant digraphs, consonant second sounds, schwa sounds, long vowel digraphs, vowel plus r, broad o, diphthongs, difficult vowels, consonant blends, consonant exceptions; no data on reliability; no norms; no suggested standards of mastery; individual; 1 form (4 pages, reprinted with minor changes in 2 items and 1976 copyright date); no manual; $3.95 per 40 tests; $2 per specimen set of this and 4 other tests; cash orders postpaid; [30–45] minutes; Edward Fry; Dreier Educational Systems, Inc. *

JOYCE E. HOOD, *Director, Children's Reading Clinic, The University of Iowa, Iowa City, Iowa.*

The value of this test depends partly on the point of view of the person considering it. Some people believe that grapheme-phoneme correspondences are learned indirectly, through actual reading experience, and applied only in combination with other cue sources. Others consider it worthwhile to evaluate a reader's ability to apply grapheme-phoneme correspondences overtly and in isolation from other cue sources. These are the people who may want to examine this test which is the sort of informal evaluation instrument that many reading clinicians have prepared for their own use. The test's value would then be one of convenience. The test may also be welcomed as an inexpensive, simple procedure for assessing an individual reader's ability to apply grapheme-phoneme knowledge in identifying unfamiliar words.

In the IPCT, nonsense words are used to test phonic knowledge in word attack. If it had tested each grapheme-phoneme correspondence in isolation, then an examinee might have been able to demonstrate mastery of these correspondences as paired-associate items and yet not have been able to apply them. If real words had been employed, some of a subject's correct answers might have been based on previous identifications of the words by means of context clues rather than on mastery of particular grapheme-phoneme correspondences. In a phonics test which employs nonsense words one can at least be sure the examinee is attempting to apply his phonic knowledge to a word unfamiliar in print. The test situation is artificial, however, because the examinee cannot check his attempted pronunciation against his memory bank of spoken words to judge its correctness. The ideal test would be made up of words familiar to a given examinee in spoken form and meaning but not hitherto encountered in print. One who has detailed knowledge of an examinee's prior reading experience might prepare such a test for that particular person but the test probably would not be appropriate for another reader. In a test intended for general use it seems justifiable that nonsense words be employed, even though there are problems connected with their use.

One potential problem with nonsense words concerns the manner in which a reader not trained in synthetic phonics might approach them. Children are likely to expect an unfamiliar printed word to represent a familiar spoken one whenever their previous instruction involved a sight-word approach with word-frequency control. They may be dissatisfied with a synthetic phonic pronunciation of a nonsense word and, in a search for a meaningful response, may guess a real word that contains some, but not all, of the same phonemes. Their erroneous pronunciation would not necessarily indicate lack of knowledge of the grapheme-phoneme correspondences involved. A child trained in synthetic phonics may have had previous experiences with words which to him are nonsense words if his instructional material did not employ word-frequency control, or if nonsense words have been included in his phonic drill. The test is probably more appropriate for children taught by a phonics rather than a meaning-emphasis approach.

The 99 grapheme-phoneme correspondences in the *Individual Phonics Criterion Test* were selected by the author as the most frequently used phonic elements in several high-frequency word lists. Grapheme-phoneme correspondences vary with orthographic context, however, and it would have been better in several cases if the nonsense words used in this test had been constructed with orthographic patterns also taken into account. For example, final /f/ is tested with the word *vof* even though the letter *f* represents the phoneme /v/ in the word *of,* and the final phoneme /f/ is usually spelled with the letters *ff*. Final /ch/ is tested in the word *rach* even though the letters *ch* represent the /k/ phoneme in the word *stomach* and the /ch/ phoneme in final position is most often spelled *-tch*. The phoneme /u̇/ is tested in the word *fush* even though *u* followed by *sh* more often represents the short vowel *u* and the /u̇/ phoneme is more often represented by the letter *u* when it follows *b* or *p* or precedes *ll*. The final silent *gh* is tested in the word *begh* even though the letters *egh* are not found at the end of any familiar English word.

Each item tests one grapheme-phoneme correspondence twice, once as the initial phoneme and once as the final phoneme in a word whenever appropriate The examiner is to score only the grapheme-phoneme correspondence being tested, ignoring any errors on any other parts of the word. The examinee is not told the focus of each section, and this may affect the way he responds. For example, he may commit vowel errors in the second section either because he developed a set to respond with short *a* or *o* in the first section or because he was not previously corrected for any mispronunciations of vowels. These errors would not necessarily indicate an inability to apply the short-vowel rule. It might be preferable to introduce each section by instructing the pupil to pay special attention to the particular class of phonic elements involved.

No information is provided as to the average ages or grade levels at which children may be expected to know various proportions of the items on this test. It is a criterion test in the sense that a teacher is to inventory phonic knowledge with the test and then to teach the grapheme-phoneme correspondences represented by any items missed. It is not a criterion test in the sense that mastery of these 99 grapheme-phoneme correspondences has been found a necessary prerequisite for successful reading. Although phonics knowledge in general is associated with good reading, there is no evidence that knowing these 99 items is essential to the development of reading ability.

In summary, the test is simple, inexpensive, and convenient to use. It will probably appeal to teachers who prefer a phonics approach to teaching reading and be more appropriate for children taught by that approach. The use of nonsense words makes it possible to test the application of phonic knowledge in words known to be unfamiliar, but may cause some children to make errors because they are searching for a meaningful response. Children might demonstrate their knowledge more accurately if they knew the class of phonic elements which is the focus of each section of the test. Some items do not represent English orthographic patterns as faithfully as they might. Teachers should consider these problems when scoring the test. The author chose to test these 99 grapheme-phoneme correspondences because they occur often in familiar words, but he presents no evidence that knowledge of these particular items is prerequisite to successful reading. The test is recommended as a clinical tool for teachers who are aware of the pitfalls of this type of testing and who can help a child integrate phonic knowledge with other cues to meaning.

Individual Phonics Criterion Test

[763]

★Individual Pupil Monitoring System—Reading.
Grades 1, 2, 3, 4, 5, 6; 1974; IPMS—Reading; criterion referenced; the general skills structure is the
same for all grades although some specific skills are
not tested in all grades; each test booklet contains
from 11 to 29 5-item tests, "each test measuring mastery of one behavioral objective"; 2 types of scores:
individual scores for each objective (a 5-item subtest),
class mean score for each objective; no data on reliability; no norms; no suggested standards of mastery
—"Based on your expectations, you might decide that
three correct answers (out of a possible five) is satisfactory for one student but unsatisfactory for another";
2 forms; 3 tests; 6 levels; teacher's guide (38–44
pages) for each level; behavioral objectives (49 pages)
for this and customized service which is available;
pupil progress record (4–5 pages) for each test and
each level; teacher's management record (13 pages)
for each level; 8 cross-reference booklets (24–53
pages) to 8 reading textbook series; separate answer
sheets (hand scored, self-scoring) may be used for
levels 3–6; self-scoring answer sheets ("insta-mark")
require the use of special crayons; $18.15–$19.50 per
35 tests and pupil progress records; $21 per 500 hand
scored answer sheets; $11.70 per 100 insta-mark an-
swer sheets; $3.90 per box of 12 insta-mark crayons;
$3.90 per teacher's kit of guide, management record,
and behavioral objectives for level 1 or 2 ($3.75 for
any level 3–6); $1.80–$2.70 per cross-reference booklet; $3.90 per specimen set; postage extra; Houghton
Mifflin Co. *

a) WORD-ATTACK. Overlapping behavioral objectives in
3 areas: phonics, structure, context.
1) *Level 1.* Grade 1; 19 objectives; Forms A, B,
(22 pages); [105–135] minutes.
2) *Level 2.* Grade 2; 28 objectives; Forms A, B,
(31 pages); [135–165] minutes.
3) *Level 3.* Grade 3; 29 objectives; Forms A, B,
(33 pages); [135–165] minutes.
4) *Level 4.* Grade 4; 23 objectives; Forms A, B,
(28 pages); [105–135] minutes.
5) *Level 5.* Grade 5; 21 objectives; Forms A, B,
(26 pages); [90–120] minutes.
6) *Level 6.* Grade 6; 18 objectives; Forms A, B,
(22 pages); [75–105] minutes.

b) VOCABULARY AND COMPREHENSION. Overlapping behavioral objectives in 2 areas: vocabulary, comprehension.
1) *Level 1.* Grade 1; 12 objectives; Forms A, B,
(21 pages); [90–120] minutes.
2) *Level 2.* Grade 2; 19 objectives; Forms A, B,
(25 pages); [60–90] minutes.
3) *Level 3.* Grade 3; 19 objectives; Forms A, B,
(33 pages); [150–180] minutes.
4) *Level 4.* Grade 4; 19 objectives; Forms A, B,
(27 pages); [150–180] minutes.
5) *Level 5.* Grade 5; 23 objectives; Forms A, B,
(37 pages); [150–180] minutes.
6) *Level 6.* Grade 6; 22 objectives; Forms A, B,
(32 pages); [150–180] minutes.

c) DISCRIMINATION/STUDY SKILLS. Overlapping behavioral objectives in 2 areas: discrimination, study skills.
1) *Level 1.* Grade 1; 12 objectives; Forms A, B,
(14 pages); [60–90] minutes.
2) *Level 2.* Grade 2; 13 objectives; Forms A, B,
(16 pages); [60–90] minutes.
3) *Level 3.* Grade 3; 11 objectives; Forms A, B,
(19 pages); [60–90] minutes.
4) *Level 4.* Grade 4; 16 objectives; Forms A, B,
(24 pages); [105–135] minutes.

5) *Level 5.* Grade 5; 19 objectives; Forms A, B,
(31 pages); [120–150] minutes.
6) *Level 6.* Grade 6; 20 objectives; Forms A, B,
(31 pages); [120–150] minutes.

DALE D. JOHNSON, *Professor of Education,
University of Wisconsin-Madison, Madison,
Wisconsin.*

The *Individual Pupil Monitoring System—
Reading* is a criterion-referenced testing program intended for pupils in grades 1–6. Three
areas of reading are tested—word-attack, vocabulary and comprehension, and discrimina-
tion/study skills. A separate test booklet (available in two forms) is provided for each area at
each of the six grade levels.

The IPMS has divided "reading" into 343
overlapping subskills (behavioral objectives),
each of which is tested with a five-item test.
These 343 subskills include 138 in word-attack,
114 in vocabulary and comprehension, and 91 in
discrimination/study skills. The word-attack
booklets measure three categories of skills:
phonics, structure, and context. Four categories
of skills—vocabulary, literal comprehension,
interpretive comprehension, and evaluative comprehension—are tested in the vocabulary and
comprehension booklets. Subskills tested in the
discrimination/study skills booklets are categorized as follows: auditory discrimination, visual discrimination, reference skills, pictorial
and graphic, organizing information, and following directions.

Before critically analyzing the IPMS it is
necessary to distinguish between program *dependent* and program *independent* skills monitoring systems—the IPMS falls into the latter
category. Program *dependent* management systems are designed to facilitate the use of a published basal reader program, and they are
interlocked with that instructional program.
Program *independent* management systems, on
the other hand, are not related to nor are they
integral to any one published reading program.

A major philosophical problem with skills
monitoring systems in general and with the
IPMS in particular is that they generally evoke
a "reading-as-skill" perspective. Reading ability
is equated with the development of skills which
can be used for instructional grouping. Learning
to read is equated with mastering those isolated
skills. Skills monitoring systems, by their nature, fractionate the reading act into tiny, atom-

Individual Pupil Monitoring System—Reading

istic parts despite our knowledge that the phonological, morphological, and syntactic components of language are interdependent. Closely related is the implicit emphasis on sequence of skills. Certainly sequences are pedagogically necessary; everything cannot be taught or learned at once. However, publishers of skills monitoring systems such as the IPMS are obligated to state clearly that their sequences are not hierarchical but are purely arbitrary. This may be viewed as a "straw person" concern, but the fact is that when sequences are committed to paper and published, many teachers get the message that there is some logical, sensible rationale for such sequences.

Skills monitoring systems are first and foremost testing programs. The basic question is whether or not the IPMS tests are appropriate for educational decision making, for if a test is not going to be used for decision making why bother giving it in the first place? Purchasers of the IPMS testing program are given no data on test reliability, and being criterion-referenced tests, no norms are provided.

With regard to validity, users are informed that: (a) prevalent behavioral objectives in use in reading were selected and arranged in six levels of difficulty; (b) qualified persons were selected to write test items to measure performance on each objective; (c) experimental editions were assembled and test tryouts were conducted on a national sample of students (which was neither identified nor described); and (d) revisions were made for the final IPMS.

No mastery levels are offered. The publishers state, "In order to ensure the adaptability of the IPMS, no achievement standards have been set ....Your own knowledge of your students' capabilities will dictate your definition of a 'satisfactory' test score. Based on your expectations, you might decide that three correct answers (out of a possible five) is satisfactory for one student but unsatisfactory for another. A close analysis of individual test scores is a necessary part of a flexible testing program."

A major concern is the validity of the testing instruments. Are the tests provided for measuring the attainment of objectives (competencies) valid indices of the skills at issue? Do the tests measure what they say they do? The answer to both of these questions when applied to a number of the IPMS tests is a clear NO.

Most of the phonics tests are tests of encoding not decoding. They are, in essence, multiple choice spelling tests. The purpose of instruction in phonics is to help children pronounce unfamiliar printed words, with the hopeful expectation that, once pronounced, the word will be recognized from the child's speaking/listening vocabulary. Thus phonics involves attaching sounds to letters and letter clusters. Spelling, on the other hand, involves attaching letters to sounds. If the English language were similar to some languages (e.g., Spanish, Finnish) which have a nearly perfect one-to-one relationship between letters and sounds, a spelling test of phonic relationships might possibly be appropriate. English, though, with its 26 letters and 45 phonemes has many hundreds of letter-sound relationships.

Many of the phonic tests in IPMS, especially at the lower levels, require the child to look at a picture and find the letter that makes the beginning (or middle or ending) sound of the word represented by the picture from a choice of three or four letters That task requires spelling, not decoding.

Other word-attack tests with questionable validity employ these formats: (a) A picture is shown alongside an incomplete word; from among three or four distractors, the child selects the missing letters which will correctly spell the word. (b) The child is shown an incomplete word; the task is to select, from among three or four choices, a letter or letters which will form a real, not a nonsense word. (c) Plurals are tested by looking at a picture and choosing, for example, the word jack or jacks to correctly label the picture.

In the above examples, the first is another spelling test and the second and third are variations of vocabulary tests. Since they do not measure what they purport to (i.e., phonics for the first two, structure for the third), they are invalid.

Similar validity problems occur on the vocabulary and comprehension tests, and on the discrimination/study skills tests; for example, one vocabulary test asks that a meaning be selected (from a choice of four) for a nonsense word embedded in a sentence. That format tests one's ability to use context; it does not test vocabulary. A first grade interpretive comprehension test (main idea, pictures) requires the

Individual Pupil Monitoring System—Reading

child to look at a picture and choose the most appropriate title. As with any group test of interpretive comprehension, many of the "right" answers are doubtful; a case could be made for each of the distractors.

With regard to the discrimination/study skills tests, one must wonder why such a wedding occurred in the first place. What do auditory and visual discrimination have to do with reference skills, pictorials and graphics, or organizing information? It would have seemed more logical to have separate tests of discrimination (appropriate for the primary grades) and other tests which would incorporate the four categories of study skills included. Perhaps publishing costs and packaging contributed to a greater degree to the decision to wed these two diverse areas than did instructional practice or common sense. Though combining these two areas seems illogical, the various subtests under this umbrella possess high face validity. In virtually all cases they very accurately measured what they say they measure.

In summary, a number of the word-attack tests and a smaller number of the vocabulary and comprehension tests lack validity because of improper format choice or improper test labeling.

In the reviewer's opinion, the major validity assumption is that mastering all these separate skills has something to do with what most of us would call "reading." The question is, in principle, empirically solvable. Practically speaking, one probably could not determine the contribution of each individual skill but one could determine whether or not mastery of a set of subskills contributed to increased oral reading fluency or comprehension of written discourse. Publishers of skills monitoring systems like the IPMS seem obligated to conduct such needed research with their products.

Most criterion-referenced tests have adopted a criterion level of 80 or 90 percent to indicate mastery of their competencies and objectives. The IPMS has chosen not to recommend a criterion level and instead has suggested that teachers use their best judgment for each individual. Nonetheless, the question exists, mastery of what? Are three items sufficient or do we need five or ten or more? The IPMS states that it has provided a five-item test for each of its 343 objectives. Perhaps the problem has more to do with the nature of the objectives than with the notion of mastery, though in practical terms for potential users, it relates to both.

For example, the first grade long-vowel test has two items measuring *a,* and one each measuring *o, e,* and *i*—no items measure *u.* It seems improper to include this array of long vowels on one test and relegate mastery decisions to the teacher. If the teacher chose three out of five to indicate mastery of long vowels, pupils could demonstrate their mastery of long vowels in an amazing variety of ways. One could show mastery and not know *a,* or *i,* or *e,* or *o.* And *u* is not tested at all.

This is but one of a number of observations of specific subtests which have problems related to mastery. In one sense the publishers of IPMS have gotten themselves "off the hook" by not recommending the usual 80 percent criterion level that most other skills monitoring systems employ. But whether mastery is to be 80 percent, or "three of five," or determined by teacher judgment, a sufficient number of *related* items need to be provided (and validly constructed) so one can determine what it is that has been mastered.

A more critical problem is the issue of what it means to master a skill. As stated earlier, the whole notion of test validity is critical here. Are the test items really representative of the skill as it is to be used? Also, while the concept of mastering a word-attack skill makes sense intuitively, the corollary concept of mastering a comprehension skill makes no sense whatever. One can visualize a situation in which a teacher might decide to cut a pupil off from final-consonants-skill activities (although one must be careful about an *allegedly* mastered skill), but it is hard to imagine why a teacher would stop all main idea or multiple meanings activities simply because a child answers three of five such items correctly. One would hope that no child could test out of cause and effect, or sequence, for example, because one could demonstrate his or her lack of mastery simply by increasing the conceptual difficulty of the words or contextual relationships. Comprehension is, by its nature, an ongoing, never-ending process with no precise starting or stopping point. It is pervasive to all reading—to all verbal discourse.

CONCLUSION. The IPMS—Reading is a program independent (external) skills monitoring

Individual Pupil Monitoring System—Reading

system which tests three broad categories of reading subskills across six grade levels. The publishers have provided no reliability or norming data for their tests of 343 overlapping objectives. Some of the tests of word-attack and vocabulary and comprehension appear to lack validity, and the system's treatment of mastery is troublesome. In comparison with other external skills monitoring systems, however, such as the *Fountain Valley Teacher Support System in Reading* and the *Wisconsin Tests of Reading Skill Development,* the IPMS would probably hold its own.

BYRON H. VAN ROEKEL, *Professor of Education and Director, Reading Center, Michigan State University, East Lansing, Michigan.*

Even at first glance one senses that the publisher of the IPMS—Reading is using a currently popular movement in education to appeal to potential users of this testing program—for prominently displayed on the cover of each of the booklets that comprise the IPMS—Reading is the slogan "Criterion-Referenced Assessment."

Unfortunately, it reflects a considerable distortion of meaning to classify the tests which make up the IPMS—Reading as criterion-referenced measures. This is true simply because the producers of these tests have failed to provide criteria against which to judge performance. Criteria are nonexistent because the designers of these tests have seemingly not taken cognizance of the characteristics which distinguish criterion-referenced and norm-referenced measures; and, as a result, have, in the development of these tests, apparently viewed the terms "criterion" and "behavioral objective" as being synonymous.

The essential difference between norm-referenced measurement and criterion-referenced measurement rests in the quantitative scales used to express how much the individual can do. In norm-referenced measurement, an individual's test performance (score) is compared to a scale derived from the test performance of a particular group of individuals. In criterion-referenced measurement, an individual's test performance is judged against a scale, a score at the top of the scale indicating complete acquisition of some specifically defined abilities or behaviors and a score at the bottom indicating

total absence of attainment in those abilities. Inherent, then, in the concept of criterion-referenced measurement are specifically defined abilities (usually stated as behavioral objectives) and quantitative scales (criteria) to express how much of those abilities have been mastered.

Individuals examining the printed matter which comprises the IPMS—Reading will have no difficulty ascertaining the behavioral objectives the tests purport to measure, for each of several hundred objectives are listed in a behavioral objectives booklet, inside the front cover of the test booklets and at the top of the corresponding test page. But, search as one may, what turns out to be missing are the quantitative scales for judging how much an individual can do. If the tests from the IPMS—Reading were truly "criterion-referenced," such quantitative scales would have been included.

The primary function of criterion-referenced measurement is to tell us in meaningful terms what an individual knows or can do. It is used to determine if a person has acquired certain competencies or mastered a specific set of objectives. In the school setting, criterion-referenced measures are used to determine whether a pupil has acquired sufficient knowledge and skill to meet the demands of new instruction. Pupils whose scores equal or exceed the criterion score are judged to be ready to advance to the next level of instruction. At first glance, this form of measurement appears most attractive until one reflects on the difficulties which face the test designer who must produce criterion-referenced tests that are practically useful. Good criterion-referenced measures are difficult to obtain because of limitations inherent in the concept of criterion-referenced measurement itself. Because only highly specified behavioral objectives will suffice, the test designer must have a means for determining specific behaviors which are essential to the acquisition of some generalized ability, such as reading. Because the school curriculum proceeds on the assumption that a hierarchical arrangement of subject matter is desirable, he must have a means for ordering subject matter so that mastery of one ability provides positive transfer to the learning of another, next in sequence. And, because criterion-referenced measurement is concerned with entry level, he must have a means of determining the level of proficiency required in one ability to advance successfully to the next. Unfortunately, given the content and process of much of school subject matter, there are few techniques available for identifying and sequencing behaviors which are critical and establishing criteria which are meaningful.

The purpose of the IPMS—Reading is rather obscure. The first sentence in the introduction to the teacher's guide reads, "An understanding of the purpose and scope of the *Individual Pupil Monitoring System—Reading* is necessary for effective use of the program." But, search as one may, nary a word can be found describing the purposes of the tests unless one is willing to accept as a statement of purpose the sentence that it "can be used both as a diagnostic tool and as a means of final assessment."

Equally obscure is other information useful in judging the quality of the tests. It would have added a professional touch had the authors made a reasonable effort to follow the recommendations presented in *Standards for Educational and Psychological Tests*. Notably absent, except for cursory comment here and there, is information describing the test's rationale, development, technical characteristics, and interpretation. At best, all one can glean is that "the initial step in preparing the criterion-referenced reading tests was to analyze the reading behavioral objectives most prevalent in the United States"; that "the behavioral objectives for the program were then written and placed in ascending difficulty in the six levels that closely correspond to the six elementary grades"; that "qualified persons [reading educators and administrators] were selected to write items that would measure the performance of students on each behavioral objective"; that "the items corresponding to behavioral objectives were assembled into experimental editions for validation tryouts"; that "the purpose of the tryouts was twofold: 1) to validate the placement of behavioral objectives in specific grade levels, and 2) to validate the items corresponding to each behavioral objective"; that "tryouts of the items corresponding to behavioral objectives were then conducted on a national sample of students"; and that "all this information [thus gathered] was used in the development of the final IPMS—Reading behavioral objectives list and in the item revision and format planning of the final tests."

Had the manual met professional standards,

it would have stated explicitly the purposes and applications for which the test is recommended; described clearly the psychological and educational reasoning underlying the test and the nature of the characteristics it is intended to measure; described fully the development of the test, including the rationale, specifications followed in writing items, and results of item analysis or other research; described the professional qualifications of the item writers; and clearly described the population from which was drawn the national sample of students used in the tryout of the tests.

A perusal of the behavioral objectives should lead the potential user to ask from whence the formulators of these objectives determined the relevance of the objectives to the acquisition of reading. That this is a particularly crucial question is reinforced by the interdisciplinary surge of interest, during the last decade or so, in the nature of those mental operations, the acquisition of which are necessary for learning to read. It would probably have added significantly to the stature of the IPMS—Reading had its developers examined the component structures of the models of reading acquisition resulting from these interdisciplinary efforts—at least it might have contributed to the face validity of their objectives.

That the validity of the objectives and the items designed to measure them should be examined carefully is illustrated by objective 205: "Consonants, Ending-Blends and Digraphs: Identify the 2-letter blend (*br, tr,* etc.) or digraph (*ch,* etc.) that makes the ending sound of a word that is shown as a picture." Not only is the wording awkward but the choice of examples in the forepart of the objective is unfortunate simply because English writing does not have words which end with either of the letter combinations *br* or *tr*. The question of validity is compounded when one examines the items which purportedly measure level of performance in this objective. Item 3, Form A, consists of a picture of a shirt followed by the letter combinations *rd, rt, rk,* and *rl.* The pupil is to choose the letter combination that represents the ending sound heard in shirt. The directions are ambiguous for two reasons: (*a*) the phonemic features of the letter combinations from among which the child must choose extend beyond the boundaries of a single phoneme, and (*b*) the phoneme represented by the letter *r* is very close in relationship to the vowel which precedes it in *shirt* and, in the pronunciation of many of us, is phonetically a vocalic *er* which functions as a single vowel heavily influenced by the retroflex pronunciation of *r*. Item 4 consists of a picture of a witch followed by the letter combinations *tch, ch, th,* and *rth*. A casual inspection of this item suggests that any of several conditions may influence the selection of a response. For the alert child, the presence of two foils which are neither 2-letter blends nor digraphs, in effect, reduces it to a two-option item. For the less vigilant child who has mastered the spelling of *witch,* the odds are likely to favor the selection of *tch*. For the child who relies strictly on the regularity of phoneme-grapheme correspondences in English orthography, the choice is likely to be an arbitrary one between *tch* and *ch* since both are frequently occurring graphemic representations of the voiceless affricate one hears at the end of *witch*.

An examination of the section of the teacher's guide dealing with the use of the IPMS—Reading gives one the impression that the program is intended to be a sort of jack-of-all trades. Preferring to characterize it as a "flexible program that can be used both as a diagnostic tool and as a means of final assessment," the publisher claims that because two forms are available, "the IPMS may be used to test students' skill mastery before instruction (pre-testing) and their mastery after instruction (post-testing). Another option is to administer one form of a test after instruction and then to administer the alternate form after students have practiced the skill." The IPMS—Reading might have been viewed with much more favor had the publisher felt an obligation to provide evidence to support the usefulness of the tests as diagnostic and achievement measures and to report data by which to judge the comparability of Forms A and B. As it stands, the IPMS—Reading features the major limitations of criterion-referenced measures and realistically should be characterized as an informal reading inventory.

[764]

★**Individualized Criterion Referenced Testing: Reading.** Grades kgn, 1, 2, 3, 4, 5, 6, 7, 8; 1973–76; ICRTR; 9 levels consisting of 46 tests covering 345 overlapping specific-objective subtests (2 items each in grades 1–8) not classified other than by grade (kgn: 8 tests, 41 objectives; grade 1: 9 tests, 72 objectives;

grade 2: 6 tests, 48 objectives; grade 3: 5 tests, 40 objectives; grades 4–6: 4 tests, 32 objectives for each grade; grade 7: 2 tests, 16 objectives; grade 8: 4 tests, 32 objectives); mastery defined as a perfect score on a 2-item test except for kgn; no data on reliability; kgn: 1 form ('73, 8 booklets, 4–5 pages); grades 1–8: Forms A, B, ('73, 2–9 booklets, 2–7 pages each); manual ('76, 104 pages); individual record folder ['73, 4 pages); orientation cassette available; separate 2-item tests, called *Benchmarks: Reading,* are available for each of the 288 objectives for grades 1–8; separate answer sheets (NCS, hand scored) may be used in grades 1–2, must be used in grades 3–8; all answer sheets accomodate 5 tests; NCS scorable tests available for grades 1–2; $15 per 10 sets of all tests for any one level (levels 7 and 8 are combined); $1.75 per 50 hand scored answer sheets; $1.95 per scoring stencil; $3.95 per 10 individual record folders; $4.95 per manual; NCS scoring service (including answer sheet but not tests), $1.35 per student (5 tests); postage extra; administration time not reported; Educational Development Corporation. *

Ruth N. Hartley, *Associate Professor of Education, California State University, Sacramento, California.*

An operational skills survey (Worksheet S) is to be used prior to Level A to determine the child's readiness to enter the test program. No information is given on how the items were selected nor on their validity and reliability for determining such readiness. Level A is a prereading level and again no information is provided on the items in relation to their validity. Levels 1–8 contain a varied number of test booklets per level with Forms A and B for each booklet. These are referred to as alternate forms; however, no information is given on how it was determined that Forms A and B are equivalent. Each booklet contains 16 questions and covers eight objectives. Information is not given on how the objectives were selected for each booklet nor on how they were sequenced, nor on how or why the decision was made to use two items to test each objective. The ICRT Benchmarks are divided into eight levels and contain two questions to test each objective to be used to monitor student progress objective by objective. This is the only information provided on the benchmarks.

The manual suggests that the tests may be used for diagnosis and prescription; however, no specific information is given on how to use the tests for these purposes except through the test reports. Another suggested use is as a pretest and a posttest. The use of these tests in pretest and posttest situations appears to be questionable because criterion-referenced tests were not designed to provide comparative data but to provide information on student achievement or mastery of specific tasks. Further, criterion-referenced tests were designed to test student achievement or mastery on tasks as the student progresses through the curriculum.

The general directions for administering the tests are clear. However, the determination of which test booklets to use with individual students is not clear. The tests may be hand scored or machine scored. The manual describes in detail how to have the student fill out the answer sheets. It also describes in detail the types of score reports that can be provided to the teacher. These reports do provide good information to the teacher on each student's performance.

The manual discusses several definitions of validity but it does not give any information on the validity of this test program. The items appear to have face validity in that they appear to test the content of the objectives.

Definitions of reliability are also discussed but, again, no information is reported on the reliability of this test series. The manual does provide a formula for an individual district to determine the reliability of the two test items for any objective. This is a questionnaire technique and, moreover, does not provide reliability information to the test user in test selection. The reliability and validity of the scoring procedures are discussed on the basis of accumulative probability values with the statement that "all are above the 5% confidence level." This discussion is not clear and is meaningless to the general test user.

Items for the program were field tested on approximately 80,000 students in grades 1–8 in six districts in Orange County, California. Originally the objectives were arranged on a continuum by a committee of teachers at each grade level in each district. Therefore, each district had a different continuum. According to the manual, "the test results indicated some question about content validity of the testing continuum. For this reason, it was recommended that the districts use a professionally developed continuum as opposed to a democratically developed one. The Audio Reading Progress Laboratory was identified as the best materials-free professional sequence available." No information is given on how or by whom this sequence was selected. These objectives were

then matched to revised field-tested items which were common to four or more of the six districts. The test items were revised based on the results of the field test.

There is no information provided on field testing of the revised items matched to the Audio Reading Progress Laboratory objectives continuum. Therefore, there appears to be no field-test information on the final test forms.

SUMMARY. ICRT: Reading is an attractive set of materials with extensive score report information and a management system. However, the manual does not provide adequate information on the placement of students in the test program, validity and reliability of the tests, field-test information on the final test forms, assignment of objectives to a level, development of the continuum, item difficulty, and the relationship of the objectives and the test items to the reading process.

MARTIN KLING, *Professor of Education, Rutgers, The State University of New Jersey, New Brunswick, New Jersey.*

ICRT: Reading consists of "a set of specified instructional objectives which describe the developmental instructional program." Reading objectives are purported to be arranged from very elementary to most difficult in order to reflect an instructional continuum.

The central question that the potential consumer of these criterion tests of reading should ask is to what extent is this instructional continuum achieved? The answer to this question is vaguely given in a section of the teacher's manual entitled "Field Test." The field test (1972–1973) began when teachers in grades 1 through 8 in six different elementary school districts selected their own reading objectives from a bank of 1,200 such objectives. The objectives were arranged on a continuum by the teachers, and an average of 64 items were administered to each of approximately 80,000 students. Six hundred objectives were selected from the 1,200, based on the criterion of being included in at least four out of six districts. After this testing, it was noted that there was "some question about the content validity of the testing continuum." The manual states that therefore "it was recommended that the districts use a professionally developed continuum as opposed to a democratically developed one."

Individualized Criterion Referenced Testing: Reading

Notwithstanding the fact that approximately 400,000 additional students participated in a 1973–1974 final version of the ICRT : Reading, little additional information is provided about the content validity of the reading objectives. It is not known how the original 1,200 items were identified or what specific substantive criteria were used to reduce the number to 600 reading objectives, and finally to 329, the total number of objectives in the present testing program. When experts were utilized, details have not been provided about the relevant experiences of, qualifications of, or directions given to the experts. Likewise, no information is given about the method of selecting the sample of students, the type of school system, and characterization of the learners or the learning context. A criterion-referenced instrument cannot be separated from the learner, the teacher, or the instructional materials. There is no rationale for the selection of the skills. Instead, face validity and cross-referencing of test objectives to commercially available instructional materials seem to be the prevailing approach.

Problems of judgment arise in determining at what level to begin testing a student. For example, standardized test scores are suggested as one of the criteria, and the manual states that "standardized test scores generally reflect the *highest* point at which the student is able to achieve. Therefore, it is usually necessary to subtract one-half to one full year from a current standardized score to find an appropriate placement in ICRT." No data or logic is provided for making this decision. It is known that there are some reading tests in which students typically score high and others in which students typically score low. The developers of the ICRT should have provided information about how students score on various standardized reading tests.

The discussion of reliability is inadequate and misleading. The authors fail to make clear the unreliability of mastery ratings based on two-item multiple choice tests. Such short tests are always better measures of ignorance than of knowledge. Whereas strong inferences can be drawn when one or both items are answered incorrectly, only weak inferences can be made when both items are answered correctly. For example, most test users realize that if a pupil knows neither question on a four-response test,

the probability is .06 that, on an average, a mastery score may be obtained by guessing. However, it is less well known that if a pupil does know the answer to one of the items, the probability of obtaining a mastery score is .25. Furthermore, these probabilities are underestimates since they do not include errors of sampling from a population of items. For example, assume that a pupil knows 50 percent of the domain of items which measure a particular objective—the probability of the student obtaining a mastery score would be .39 when both sampling and guessing errors are considered. It is obvious that mastery of a specific objective cannot be determined by two-item subtests.

The manual presents a confusing and irrelevant discussion of the reliability of obtaining at least five (or six?) mastery scores for the eight specific-objective subtests in a given test booklet. This reviewer would advise test users to give no attention to the analysis presented in the manual. In a criterion-referenced test, one should consider only the reliabilities for specific items.

The results of a student's performance are printed out in a student summary, which lists the objective number and paraphrases the name of the reading objective. Objectives are further classified as to "you were able to" if the student answered both items correctly, "you need to review" if only one of the items was correct, and "you need to learn how to" if both were missed. Associated curriculum materials are also listed next to each objective, with up to five instructional resources. Other printouts which the consumer can use are a class instructional grouping report, a building summary, and a district summary.

Three methods for assessing each student's progress in mastering objectives are : administering the ICRT tests from time to time in order to analyze each student's skill ; ICRT Benchmarks, which are an alternate set of test items to evaluate each skill ; and a cumulative student profile folder. The benchmarks are a novel approach to continuous monitoring of pupil progress as well as an aid for review and a supplement to basal readers.

In summary, the promise of fulfilling an instructional reading continuum has to be taken at face value. Any decisions about the use of ICRT : Reading should be tempered by a knowl-

Individualized Criterion Referenced Testing: Reading

edge of the learner, the teacher, resources available, the context of the learning situation, and, of most importance, the unreliability of two-item tests for measuring mastery of a specific objective.

In the final analysis, the critical problems with validity and reliability are so serious as to question the usefulness of ICRT: Reading in the classroom.

[765]

★McGrath Diagnostic Reading Test. Grades 1–13; 1974–76; the *McGrath Test of Reading Skills* must also be administered, since its 3 subtests are subtests of this test; 19 scores: letter recognition (2 scores), oral spelling, MTRS subtests (oral word recognition, oral paragraph reading, word meanings), comprehension (2 scores), consonant sounds, blends, short vowels, auditory fusion, auditory memory (2 scores), laterality (3 scores), visual perception and memory, visual discrimination; no data on reliability; no norms; individual; 1 form ('76, 11 pages, identical with test copyrighted 1974 except for directions); manual ('76, 17 pages, replaces 1974 cassette tape); $30 per 30 tests; $2 per single copy; postage extra; (30) minutes; Joseph E. McGrath; McGrath Publishing Co. *

[766]

★Mastery: An Evaluation Tool: Reading. Grades kgn, 1, 2, 3, 4, 5, 6, 7, 8, 9; 1974–76; SOBAR (System for Objective-Based Assessment—Reading); criterion referenced; 23–35 subtest scores in 6 areas: comprehension (grades kgn–9), letter recognition (kgn), phonic analysis (kgn–4), structural analysis (1–9), study skills (1–9), vocabulary (kgn–9); each test consists of 23–35 3-item single-objective subtests; no data on reliability; no norms; mastery defined as a perfect score on a 3-item subtest; Forms L ('75), M ('76); test booklets 12–27 pages each; 10 levels; user's guide ('75, 18 pages) for this test and one other; grades kgn–2 form-level manuals, (dates same as for tests, 14 pages); grades 3–9 manual ('75, 9 pages); grades 3–9 form-level manual supplements (dates same as for tests, 3–7 pages); separate answer sheets must be used for grades 3–9; $17.69 per 25 NCS scorable tests for grades kgn–2; $12.29 per 25 tests for grades 3–9; $10.71 per 100 answer sheets; 70¢ per user's guide; $8.20 per specimen set; postage extra; scoring service: $1.40 or less per test for grades kgn–2, 98¢ or less per test for grades 3–9; (3) minutes per subtest; customized tests covering locally chosen objectives are available in both English and Spanish; Center for the Study of Evaluation, University of California at Los Angeles; Science Research Associates, Inc. *

REFERENCES

1. GREENE, FRANK. "Review of the Mastery: An Evaluation Tool: Reading Test." *Read Teach* 30(7):822–3 Ap '77. *

THORSTEN R. CARLSON, *Professor of Education, Sonoma State College, Rohnert Park, California.*

SOBAR (System for Objective-Based Assessment—Reading) is an impressive and overwhelming set of assessment materials. The potential user has the option of using the "catalog" tests or of selecting from two catalogs of objectives those objectives that one would desire to have measured by a "customized" test. Each objective is measured by three test items. Mastery of an objective is ostensibly attained if the learner responds correctly to all three of the items for an objective. The two catalogs list a total of 302 objectives (there is some overlapping of objectives). Since all the objectives for Levels K-B (K–grade 2) or for Levels C-I (grades 3–9) cannot be measured in any one test, sampling must be used. This issue and the criteria for mastery will be discussed later.

Two forms are provided in the catalog tests, Forms L and M. These two forms are presumably equivalent, though no data are provided for evaluation of equivalence. Neither is any information furnished as to reliability or validity. No evidence is provided on the relationship of the objectives to reading performance. In the meantime, for sampling purposes, it appears that the authors assume that the objectives are equally related to performance. If not, how was the sampling accomplished?

No norms are provided, except the arbitrary and questionable criterion for mastery. No difficulty or discrimination data are provided for any of the items. The lack of such data makes diagnostic and achievement evaluation difficult, since different items covering the same objectives oftentimes yield different item data. The guide, on page 4, does promise that statistical studies of the *mastery* items will be forthcoming, including information on "the sensitivity of the items to instruction."

Though technical information is lacking, the guide, manuals, and manual supplements provide adequate information for administering the tests. Scoring services available include, for each pupil, for the class, or for a system, information on performance on each objective tested, as well as on the total test. No diagnostic information is furnished on the major sections in the catalogs of objectives, i.e., Letter Recognition, Phonic Analysis, Structural Analysis, Vocabulary, Comprehension, and Study Skills.

The use of the manuals is in some instances somewhat awkward in that the teacher needs to use for Levels C and D the manual for the directions for completing identifying information and for the sample test practice. Then the teacher must transfer to the manual supplement for the "Special Oral Instructions."

Also, the manuals for Levels K, A, and B identify the directions for each item using the number for each objective. One must refer to the test sheets for this number in order to find the directions for a given item. This is an unnecessarily awkward arrangement. The problem has been corrected in the directions for Levels C-I, in which the items are numbered serially.

The objectives identified in Form M, Level A as 1A, 1C, 1G, and 1B and in Form M, Level B as 2A, 2D, 2G, and 2F appear in the Catalog of Objectives for Level A as PE8, 10, 18, and 11 and for Level B as PE7, 10, 19, and 11, respectively. This discrepancy in designating objectives needs to be reconciled.

Since many of the objectives are assessed at more than one grade level, there is considerable overlapping of items. For example, Levels C and D have 24 identical items; Levels E and F have 27; and Levels F and G have 39 identical items. In the levels that were checked, the duplication ranged from approximately 24 to 41 percent. The need of assessing some of the same objectives at different levels seems obvious and necessary, but the use of so many identical items seems questionable. The full extent of the use of identical items in measuring overlapping objectives should be studied at all levels.

For further diagnosis, the manual recommends another set of tests, *Diagnosis: An Instructional Aid.* This is another program of criterion-referenced tests, or probes. The probes were apparently developed independently of SOBAR. There are no instructional suggestions with SOBAR except a recommendation to use the probes, which include instructional prescriptions comprised of suggested pages from basal textbooks and supplementary materials. As a diagnostic instrument SOBAR would be more helpful if it provided suggestions for materials and procedures to deal with deficiencies in specific areas of reading skills.

Criterion-referenced tests are predicated on the importance of assessing specific learning objectives. Criteria for mastery are arbitrarily determined. In the catalog tests of this series, mastery is assumed if all three items covering a given objective are correctly answered.

Objective-based test theory holds that for assessment to be sufficiently specific, a test should sample objectives extensively, or even completely if possible. The theory does not usually allow any assumption of mastery of objectives that are not specifically tested. In spite of the theory, the authors of this test have had to cope with reality by sampling the objectives rather than assessing the mastery of each. The materials provided do not explain how the objectives were sampled. There is no statement of the authors' conceptualization of the reading process nor consideration of any reading model serving as a framework for the two catalogs of objectives. The catalogs are apparently just that; they do not represent a framework derived from philosophical, linguistic, and psychological considerations of the reading process.

Though no account is given of how the sampling was accomplished for the catalog tests, the following observations from an examination of the two catalogs are revealing. Of the 162 objectives in the K–2 catalog, 90 objectives are not sampled at any level, 64 objectives are sampled at one level, 7 at two grade levels, and only one objective is measured at each of the three grade levels. Note the following data for the subsections: of 24 objectives in Letter Recognition, 13 are not tested at any level. A total of 34, or one-half, of the 68 objectives for Phonic Analysis are not measured. In Structural Analysis, 22 of the 27 objectives are not sampled at all. Five of the 11 objectives in Vocabulary are not measured. Six of the 19 objectives in Comprehension are not sampled at all. In Study Skills, 10 of the 13 objectives are not sampled.

Of the 140 objectives in the 3–9 catalog, 44 objectives are not tested at any grade level, 34 objectives are sampled or tested at one level, 32 at two grade levels, 14 at three grade levels, 3 at four levels, 3 at five levels, 2 objectives at each of six levels, and 8 objectives are assessed at each of the seven grade levels. The sampling within sections might be questioned for Phonic Analysis, for which 13 of the 32 objectives are not sampled, and for Structural Analysis, for which 21 of the 43 objectives are not sampled.

Explanation of the authors' conceptualization of the reading process and their rationale for the sampling of objectives or components of the process would have been helpful in the evaluation of the test instruments. To sample, as has been done for the catalog tests, without explanation of the rationale for the prospective user is a

Mastery: An Evaluation Tool: Reading

dubious practice. This is particularly true since the test is avowedly a criterion-based mastery test.

In ordering customized tests, 10 to 30 objectives for K–2 and 10 to 40 for grades 3–9 may be selected for each test. SRA then selects items. Two forms, L and M, are available for customized and catalog tests. Since no norms or other item difficulty data are available, it is difficult for this reviewer to understand why SOBAR is to be preferred over the mastery-type tests that accompany many current reading programs. Such tests may be more "customized" than a test compiled from an arbitrarily limited and undoubtedly often fortuitous selection from two overlapping catalogs of objectives.

Judging from the sampling, it is apparent that the authors have found that not all the objectives can be measured in one test or even in 10 tests, one at each level K–9. If it is discovered that children's learning is more general than 302 objectives (less the overlap in the two catalogs) would imply, the SOBAR tests may evolve into patterns not greatly different from conventional achievement tests that have recognized and always used sampling procedures. Standard test construction procedures further provide the user the advantage of a defined and rational conceptualization of what the authors presume to be the reading process, identification of the objectives that are measured, and an explanation of the sampling of the objectives in test construction.

The data presented on sampling raise questions as to the diagnostic value of the catalog tests. Can a test with such sampling be considered "objective-based," a label which carries the presumption of extensive sampling or even complete coverage? Also in question is the assertion that three items can determine the mastery of an objective. The probability table in the guide on attaining mastery by chance alone seems to be convincing, but it should be noted that the table is based on the assumption of random behavior. Item successes do not come about in random fashion.

The instructions apparently assume that third grade pupils will be given test Level C; fourth grade pupils, Level D; fifth grade, Level E; etc. No provision, suggestion, or procedures are offered for what is often called "out-of-level testing." If, for example, the sampling and general difficulty of Level C is not appropriate for below-level achieving third grade pupils, what can be done? For whom and under what circumstances are the various levels appropriate? How can the level of entry for certain pupils be determined? The problem is equally crucial for the poor achiever and the gifted pupil.

Most achievement tests provide item difficulty information. Where such information is not available, as in the case of SOBAR, it is difficult to judge whether failure on an item is due to lack of mastery of an objective or to the difficulty of the item. The value of the three-item criterion for mastery may be, in spite of the reservations expressed, adequate for analyzing a class but inadequate for individual diagnosis.

The two catalogs of objectives are impressive lists of item descriptions rather than descriptions of expected pupil behavior or response. The two lists overlap to some degree. The K–2 catalog includes objectives in such areas as guide words, definitions, encyclopedia, index, and maps. The inclusion of such categories raises some question as to what is taught and what can be expected in grades K–2. Similar concerns developed from an examination of the practice sheet, which is identical for grades 3–9. The reading level of its content is too difficult for many third graders. Also, the concept of prefix may not be known at this point. Practice tests should be provided for at least two levels of difficulty, including one at easy third grade level. The practice of having pupils read the directions independently is not a good practice—particularly if the directions are too difficult for many pupils.

Many of the items are excellent, as in Form L, Level I, items 1–6; some are quite clever as in Form L, Level K, items 67–69. The paragraphs for comprehension are interesting and well written. There are items that would benefit from further editing. The tests should be carefully checked for technical errors in item writing.

The items in Phonic Analysis are predominantly spelling oriented. The pupil is presented with an oral stimulus and then selects from four options, the correct orthographic, or visual, response. In many, if not most, instances, the decoys are so different from the correct response that it is difficult to understand how they would draw meaningful response from pupils except on a chance basis. Some of the items seem to involve mastery of unusual spellings.

Mastery: An Evaluation Tool: Reading

As contrasted with the spelling orientation, a reading approach would require a visual, or written, situation with an oral-aural response or the selection of a written option from among three or four that would be reasonable possibilities in reading material. In reading, the word *each,* for example, is in the orthographic form *each.* The learner needs to determine whether *ea* represents /ā/, /ē/, or /ĕ/. In spelling, on the other hand, the learner responds to the oral-aural /ēch/. In that situation he must decide whether /ē/ is spelled by *ea, ee,* or *e.* The options in reading, or decoding, are different from those in spelling, or encoding, a sound. It seems reasonable that authors of tests of reading phonics should, whenever possible, construct items in the reading mode, with reading options. The SOBAR items in phonic analysis are constructed entirely in the spelling mode, that is, the pupils select the *spellings* rather than *"sound the spellings."*

In items dealing with initial, medial, and final consonant sounds, the assumption is apparent that they should be measured as discrete learnings. What evidence is there that consonant sounds need to be taught in all three positions? In spelling, the position of the consonant sound is of some concern, as medial and final consonant sounds are characterized by greater variability in the letters that represent them.

Examination of the phonics objectives raises a number of perhaps minor concerns. Objective PB20 refers to the "sound /*x*/." The letter *x* represents the *sounds* of either /gz/ or /ks/, as in *exact* and *box.* The term "consonant digraph sound" is used, as in PB37, and "vowel digraph sound," as in PB58. Digraphs are graphemic forms and should probably not be discussed as sounds except for some special cases such as /ch/ and /th/. The practice is particularly confusing in the case of vowels where, for example, the digraph form *ea* may spell /ē/, /ā/, or /ĕ/; both *oa* and *o* spell /ō/; *ew, oo,* and *u* may spell /yü/. Obviously, digraph spellings cannot be generally designated as distinctive digraph sounds.

The sounds spelled by *wh* and erroneously designated in PB38 as "the sound /wh/" are subject to dialectal considerations. The sound cluster, /hw/, has practically disappeared from speech in American schools. The term "consonant blend sound" is used throughout rather than the more descriptive term "consonant cluster." Moreover, consonant clusters are combinations, not single sound units.

The use of the term "silent letters" is inadvisable and inaccurate. If letters do not make sounds, how can we designate only some letters as silent? And, more importantly, many letters, as in the digraph spellings, do have linguistic functions and are not really "silent," like the *g* in *sign* and *signal.* These concerns are not the result of intense and comprehensive analysis by this reviewer. However, any set of objectives that serves as a basis for a program of instruction or assessment needs a thorough analysis for scholarship by whatever disciplines are involved.

In summary, before considering use of either the "customized" or "catalog" versions of this assessment system, one should wait for forthcoming technical data assuring acceptable quality of the objectives and test items. Minimally, data are needed on the sampling of objectives as well as on item reliability, validity, discrimination, relevance, and difficulty. Information on the readability of the materials would also be helpful.

Another deficiency is the absence of instructional suggestions except that the user purchase from the publisher another system of objective-referenced tests which include prescriptive references to basal textbooks and supplementary materials. When technical data are available for proper evaluation of items, the "customized" tests may be useful for the users who have conceptualized clearly what they wish to measure in reading and who find that selected SOBAR objectives coincide with their conceptualization.

So until technical data are available and until other problems discussed in this review have been dealt with, those seeking a criterion-referenced assessment system need to consider other instruments.

Read Teach 30(7):822–3 *Ap '77. Frank Greene.* This is a set of materials offering a wide variety of ways to put together reading tests. * For local tests, someone selects ten to forty objectives that seem relevant to the local curriculum. SRA then prints a test with three multiple choice questions for each objective. For already constructed tests, SRA has put together tests for each grade K through nine by selecting objectives which seem to be common end-of-grade mastery objectives. * The development is logical. The objectives are clear. The items are content valid in that they are direct samples of the specific objectives. The printing is neat. The answer sheets are clear and as uncluttered as such sheets can be. The whole package is elegant. The whole package is also unnecessary. Specific items are new, but the whole test (any combination of items or the off-the-shelf ones) looks and feels just like the rest of the standardized reading tests already on the market. The same multiple choice format. The same types of choices, where most of the distractors could be argued for and test wiseness sure helps mark the "best" answers. The topics covered and the manner in which they are covered are all the same old ones. Reading samples are still limited to short passages with short questions. I won't bother with extended item analysis since the problem is not statistics as much as meaningfulness. Just one example. After reading a short passage on two sibs building a raft which they were not allowed to use because it might be unsafe, which then saved the whole family when the nearby river flooded, the reader is asked a question on how the children probably felt. Three of the four choices were negative (disappointed, angry, upset) and one positive (pleased). Not much of an item, even if it has a low error rate. Oh well. Not everybody likes brand X and therefore it may not be a bad idea to have many brands for people to choose from. This is not a bad choice, not really needed, but not bad.

[767]

★Objectives-Referenced Bank of Items and Tests: Reading and Communication Skills. Grades kgn–12 and adults; 1975; ORBIT:RCS; customized, criterion-referenced tests (consisting of 4-item, single-objective subtests) covering up to 50 objectives locally chosen from a list of 335 objectives (233 specific objectives and 102 category objectives) in 10 areas: visual discrimination, phonic analysis, structural analysis, word meaning, literal comprehension, interpretive comprehension, critical comprehension, reference skills, language mechanics, language expression; subtests are categorized according to grade level of the most difficult word in the subtest (primer, 13 subtests; grade 1, 16; grade 2, 36; grade 3, 50; grade 4, 52; grade 5, 46; grade 6, 39; grade 7, 30; grade 8, 31; grade 9, 5; grade 10, 19); no data on reliability; no norms; mastery defined as at least 3 out of 4 items correct; 335 subtests (1–4 pages each); 2 formats; combined examiner's manual (22 pages) for this test and one other; objectives booklet (43 pages); $3 per objectives booklet; postage extra; specimen set not available; (5) minutes per objective; CTB/McGraw-Hill. *

a) MULTI-OBJECTIVE TESTS. Separate answer sheets (CompuScan) may be used; 68¢ per test of 27–30 objectives for 1–500 tests ($500 minimum); $4.50 per 50 answer sheets; scoring service, 40¢ and over per test ($175 minimum).
b) SINGLE-OBJECTIVE SUBTESTS. 335 subtests (1–4 pages each); 7–10¢ per subtest ($250 minimum); $1 per examiner's manual.

[768]

★Power Reading Survey Test. Grades 1–3, 4–6, 7–12; 1973–75; criterion-referenced tests covering 195 overlapping objectives (105 different objectives) in 3 areas: word recognition (90 overlapping objectives, 47 different), comprehension (53, 25), study skills (52, 33); part of the Power Reading System, a program for diagnosis and remedial instruction in reading, which includes lesson plans and additional tests which must be reproduced locally; 83% of the objectives are measured by 3-item tests with mastery defined as at least 2 of the 3 items correct; 3 levels (students reaching the mastery criteria for 80% of the tests at any one level should proceed to the next higher level); no data on reliability; no norms; a few tests are individual; 1 form; teacher's guide ('75, 42 pages); $10.98 per set of 10 tests, 10 individual checklists, manual, and 1 group record for any one level; $2 per teacher's guide; $5.95 per specimen set of any one level; postage extra; administration time not reported; William E. Blanton, James L. Laffey, Edward L. Robbins, and Carl B. Smith; BFA Educational Media. *
a) POWER 1. Grades 1–3; 1973–75; 46 specific-objective tests in 1 booklet: word recognition (27 tests), comprehension (10), study skills (9); 1 form ('73, 12 pages); manual ('73, 15 pages); individual checklist ('73, 4 pages); group record ('73, 1 page).
b) POWER 2. Grades 4–6; 1974–75; 68 specific-objective tests in 1 booklet: word recognition (34 tests), comprehension (18), study skills (16); 1 form ('74, 23 pages); manual ('74, 15 pages); individual checklist ('74, 5 pages); group record ('74, 1 page).
c) POWER 3. Grades 7–12; 1975; 81 specific-objective tests in 1 booklet: word recognition (29 tests), comprehension (25), study skills (27); 1 form (35 pages); manual (11 pages); individual checklist (6 pages); group record (1 page).

REFERENCES
1. DuBois, Jessie J. "Review of the Power Reading Survey Tests." Read Teach 28(2):214–5 N '74. *

IRA E. AARON, *Professor of Education, The University of Georgia, Athens, Georgia.*

The *Reading Survey Test* is the diagnostic part of the Power Reading System. According to the teacher's guide, the Power Reading System offers "tools and techniques to diagnose individual reading deficiencies and prescribe remedies for those deficiencies."

Each item is keyed to a program behavioral objective, and a criterion level has been set for satisfactory performance of each subskill. Over items, with the criterion for success usually 80 percent of the subskills are measured by three being at least two of the three correct; almost all the other subskills are measured by two or four items each. In all, there are 195 objectives in the three tests, with overlapping cutting the total number of different skills down to 105.

Test 1 contains 108 group-administered and 4 individually-administered items that assess 44 subskills. Test 2, with 192 group and 3 individual items, assesses 68 subskills. Test 3 has 237 group and 4 individual items to assess 81 subskills.

No specific discussions of reliability and validity are offered. The authors evidently considered the Power Reading System as instructional materials and thus did not supply reliability and validity data for the tests.

The reading skills tested are typical of those found in published series of traditional basal readers and other reading instructional materials. How they were selected and ordered, though, is not discussed in the teacher's guide or in the manuals. Choices had to be made from among the many possible subskills, and the test authors' selections seem satisfactory.

Administration time is not reported. For group testing, this reviewer estimates one hour for the primary test, two hours for the intermediate, and five hours for the secondary test. Although five hours is excessive, a test that long is needed for adequate coverage. Individual testing requires an estimated 15 minutes for the primary, 15–20 minutes for the intermediate, and 25 minutes for the secondary test. It would be impractical for a classroom teacher to administer the individual test to all of his/her students. From 6 to 10 hours would be needed.

Overall, the tests and manuals are adequately prepared. Directions, for the most part, are easy to follow by both student and teacher. However, the instructions state over and over: "Repeat the procedure used for Number ——." Instructions for Test 2 include 98 instances of this statement. Each time the teacher must look back to the item referred to and remember to make whatever modification the item needs. The format could have been changed to make it easier for the teacher to administer.

Teachers considering use of these materials should study the skills lists carefully to determine how good a fit there is with the skills in their major instructional materials. These materials are for use in supplementing an ongoing program and thus should be compatible with that program. They do *not* constitute a total program.

Schools using programs that teach the skills assessed in these tests would likely find them helpful, but using them in a program that has many differences in skills could be wasteful. This latter statement would apply to *all* materials, not just to the test. There is no need to assess skills that are not a part of the planned instructional program.

A similar "system" which includes similar tests is the Wisconsin Design for Reading Skill Development. The WDRSD materials were prepared with greater care and are more extensive. Schools wanting a more elaborate "skills management system" would likely prefer the WDRSD.

WILLIAM R. MERZ, *Associate Professor of Behavioral Sciences in Education, California State University, Sacramento, California.*

The *Power Reading System* is designed for three uses: as a general organizer, as a supplemental basal program, and as a remedial program. The kit for each of the three levels contains *Power Reading Survey Tests,* lesson plans, student worksheets, "student assessments," skills checklists, and group ledgers. The program is attractively packaged and organized. Objectives are clearly stated in the teacher's guide, and items for the two types of tests in the program—survey tests and student assessments—are referenced to each objective.

It is difficult to evaluate the tests without examining both the instructional material and the record system. As an instructional tool, the system has many desirable features. It is clear what is being taught. In addition, the material is well organized, attractively formatted, clearly printed, and straightforward. However, the tests present many technical problems.

The first problem is content validity. The 195 overlapping objectives define the whole of what is measured and what is taught. But why these particular objectives? While they appear similar to those included in the specifications tables of many other reading tests, no rationale for their selection is given. This leaves the question of content validity open. No evidence on construct or criterion validity is presented either. Certainly evidence for both must be presented in order to show that the materials function as they were intended.

The larger problem is that no effort was made

Power Reading Survey Test

to follow the recommendations in the *Standards for Educational and Psychological Tests* in the material included in the kit, and no supplemental technical reports are referenced. Even though no elaborate claims are made for the tests and for the diagnostic-prescriptive materials, there is no evidence that they have even been tried and that they help the pupils attain the objectives on which the system is based. There is no description of how the tests were developed or of how test items were selected. No item analysis data, difficulty levels, or discrimination indices are presented. While the *Power Reading Survey Tests,* designed for diagnosis, are of reasonable length, the student assessments designed for post instructional assessment are very short; often mastery of an objective is assessed with only three items. The criterion for passing most of the objectives is two or three items correct out of three. Without information on item characteristics, setting a passing score becomes an arbitrary effort which may be subverted by chance. If an item has three options, there is one chance in nine that a pupil can attain two items of three correct by guessing alone. If a pupil knows the answer to one question, there is one chance in three that a student could get a second item correct by guessing alone.

There is no information on reliability either. In the absence of reliability data, the criterion problem is compounded because the aids to interpretation simply suggest that if the pupil answers questions correctly then the skill has been mastered. There are no warnings about the reliability of a mastery level, no warnings about the reliability of the three item tests measuring an objective, and no warnings about the reliability of whole tests. Without some estimate of reliability, no standard error can be used to adjust for chance.

No norming or scaling information is presented, so it is impossible to tell whether or not a teacher's pupils perform like other pupils of the same age or at the same grade level. Some pupil assessments are individually administered which means that pupils must self administer tests or teachers must arrange for individual testing. Data obtained from all of the assessment instruments must be recorded and kept track of to use this system. This alone requires a good deal of time and effort, no matter how convenient the record keeping procedure is.

All in all, the lack of technical information and of guidance on score interpretation yielded by the system is devastating. As the materials are now presented, questions about content validity must be answered by the user's going over the objectives and the material with no help from the authors or the editors. Judgments on construct and criterion-related validity cannot be made, and evidence on reliability of the test scores and the prescriptions is nonexistent. While the materials initially appear appropriate and well done, none of the technical information is present so that they can be used with a reasonable degree of confidence. It is incumbent on materials developers to provide such information.

Read Teach 28(2):214–5 N '74. Jessie J. DuBois. Power Reading 1 is a management system for gathering information and for making instructional decisions. The system is a diagnostic prescriptive approach to reading. It includes behavioral objectives, criterion-referenced assessment elements, a file drawer organizational arrangement, lesson plans and student worksheets for each skill, and an individual and group record keeping system. * The price of the system is not unreasonable. In fact, it is an excellent investment when the quality and quantity of the contents are considered. * The *Power Reading System* incorporates the implications of research findings and is representative of current trends in reading instruction. It is a systematic diagnostic prescriptive monitoring system which allows teachers to keep a continuous record of each child's progress. There are four basic steps involved in the system: 1) determining reading abilities and deficiencies, 2) student grouping and teaching of reading skills, 3) assessing results of reading instruction, and 4) recording assessment performance and regrouping. *

[769]

*Prescriptive Reading Inventory. Grades kgn.0–1.0, kgn.5–2.0, 1.5–2.5, 2.0–3.5, 3.0–4.5, 4.0–6.5; 1972–77; PRI; 2 criterion-referenced tests; 30 to 42 scores (mastery, needs review, nonmastery) covering 90 reading objectives for Levels A–D and 30 objectives (10 specific, 20 category) for Levels 1 and 2; 6 levels; additional instructional and staff development materials available; postage extra; CTB/McGraw-Hill. *
a) PRESCRIPTIVE READING INVENTORY. 1972–76; 84 percent of the scores based on 3 and 4 item tests; no norms; mastery defined as 66⅔% and 75% correct on 3 and 4 item tests, respectively; Levels 1 and 2 may be

administered by tape cassette; interpretive handbook ('76, 18 pages) for Levels 1 and 2; interpretive handbook ('72, 53 pages) for Levels A–D; technical report ('76, 127 pages) for Levels A–D; checklist of observable behaviors ('76, 3 pages) for Levels 1 and 2; list of objectives ('76, 1 page) for Levels 1 and 2; program reference guides available for Levels A–D for each textbook series keyed to PRI; $8.95 per tape cassette for Level 1 or 2; $2.50 per technical report; $2.50 per program reference guide; $10 per multilevel specimen set, $5 per specimen set of any one level, (without technical report); CompuScan scoring service, 90¢ per test booklet, 60¢ per answer sheet, ($50 minimum).

1) *Level 1.* Grades kgn.0–1.0; 1976; 30 scores: 2 scores (each based on 3 items) plus total in each of 10 categories (sound discrimination, sound matching, form matching, visual reasoning, sound-symbol correspondence, letter names, oral language, literal comprehension, interpretive comprehension, attention skills); no data on reliability; 1 form (24 pages); 2 formats: CompuScan scored, hand scored; manual (34 pages); pretest (4 pages); key/diagnostic map (4 pages); $20.65 per 35 CompuScan tests, $16.45 per 35 hand scorable tests; (10) minutes for pretest, (75–85) minutes in 3 or more sessions for test.

2) *Level 2.* Grades kgn.5–2.0; 1976; 30 scores: 2 scores (each based on 3 items) plus total in each of 10 categories (sound discrimination, sound matching, sound-symbol correspondence, visual reasoning, oral language, sight vocabulary, initial reading, attention skills, literal comprehension, interpretive comprehension); no data on reliability; 1 form (24 pages); 2 formats: CompuScan scored, hand scored; manual (35 pages); pretest (4 pages); key/diagnostic map (4 pages); prices and time same as for Level 1.

3) *Level A.* Grades 1.5–2.5; 1972–76; 34 scores (each based on 3–5 items): recognition of sounds and symbols (2 scores), phonic analysis (4 scores), structural analysis (9 scores), translation (7 scores), literal comprehension (3 scores), interpretive comprehension (7 scores), critical comprehension (2 scores); no data on reliability for 27 scores; 1 form ('72, 28 pages); 2 formats: CompuScan scored, hand scored; manual ('72, 22 pages); key/diagnostic map ('74, 6 pages); optional practice exercises ('69, 4 pages); $20.65 per 35 CompuScan tests, $16.45 per 35 hand scorable tests; (190–200) minutes in 4 sessions.

4) *Level B.* Grades 2.0–3.5; 1972–76; 41 scores (each based on 3–6 items): recognition of sounds and symbols (2 scores), phonic analysis (8 scores), structural analysis (8 scores), translation (7 scores), literal comprehension (3 scores), interpretive comprehension (12 scores), critical comprehension (1 score); no data on reliability for 33 scores; 1 form ('72, 36 pages); 2 formats: CompuScan scored, hand scored; manual ('72, 22 pages); key/diagnostic map ('74, 6 pages); $20.65 per 35 CompuScan tests, $16.45 per 35 hand scorable tests; (175–185) minutes in 4 sessions.

5) *Level C.* Grades 3.0–4.5; 1972–76; 42 scores (each based on 3–8 items): phonic analysis (4 scores), structural analysis (8 scores), translation (8 scores), literal comprehension (5 scores), interpretive comprehension (13 scores), critical comprehension (4 scores); no data on reliability for 33 scores; 1 form ('72, 31 32 pages); 3 formats: CompuScan scored, hand scored, reusable; manual ('72, 13 pages); key/diagnostic map ('74, 7 pages); separate answer sheets (CompuScan) may be used

with hand scorable booklet; $20.65 per 35 CompuScan tests, $16.10 per 35 hand scorable tests, $14.85 per 35 reusable tests and 50 answer sheets; $4 per 50 answer sheets; (175–185) minutes in 4 sessions.

6) *Level D.* Grades 4.0–6.5; 1972–76; 38 scores (each based on 3–6 items): phonic analysis (3 scores), structural analysis (5 scores), translation (6 scores), literal comprehension (3 scores), interpretive comprehension (12 scores), critical comprehension (9 scores); no data on reliability for 28 scores; 1 form ('72, 31 pages); manual ('72, 10 pages); key/diagnostic map ('74, 6 pages); separate answer sheets (CompuScan) must be used; $16.60 per 35 tests and 50 answer sheets when machine scoring ($21.85 when hand scoring); $4 per 50 answer sheets; (160–170) minutes in 4 sessions.

b) PRI INTERIM TESTS. 1972–77; "short, teacher-scored tests for each of PRI's objectives"; 20–42 tests (14–25 single-sheet skills tests and 9–24 comprehension tests in 3–7 booklets) each based on 3 (Levels 1 and 2) or 5 (Levels A–D) items; no data on reliability; no norms; mastery defined as 100% correct for 3 item tests (and for 6 item category scores) and 80% for 5 item tests; manual ('76, 50 pages) for Levels 1 and 2; $75 per 32 sets of tests for Level 1, 2, A, or B; $80 per 32 sets of tests for Level C or D; (5–10) minutes per skills test, (20–25) minutes per comprehension booklet.

1) *Level 1.* Grades kgn.0–1.0; 1976; 20 skills tests (1 page).

2) *Level 2.* Grades kgn.5–2.0; 1976; 20 skills tests (1 page).

3) *Level A.* Grades 1.5–2.5; 1972–77; 25 skills tests ('77, 1–2 pages), 9 comprehension tests in 3 booklets ('77, 8–9 pages); manual ('77, 45 pages).

4) *Level B.* Grades 2.0–3.5; 1972–77; 25 skills tests ('77, 1–2 pages), 16 comprehension tests in 5 booklets ('77, 8–10 pages); manual ('77, 47 pages).

5) *Level C.* Grades 3.0–4.5; 1972–77; 20 skills tests ('77, 1–2 pages), 22 comprehension tests in 7 booklets ('77, 8–11 pages); manual ('77, 21 pages).

6) *Level D.* Grades 4.0–6.5; 1972–77; 14 skills tests ('77, 1–2 pages), 24 comprehension tests in 7 booklets ('77, 8–10 pages); manual ('77, 20 pages).

REFERENCES

1. THOMPSON, RICHARD A., AND DZIUBAN, CHARLES D. "Criterion Referenced Reading Tests in Perspective." *Read Teach* 27(3):292–4 D '73. *
2. MALLEY, JOHN DAVID. *An Investigation of the Use of the Prescriptive Reading Inventory, California Achievement Test, and Wide Range Achievement Test for the Measurement of Reading Skills.* Doctor's thesis, Baylor University (Waco, Tex.), 1974. (*DAI* 35:2993B)
3. ROUDABUSH, GLENN E. "An Empirical Structure for Reading Objectives." *J Read Behav* 6(4):403–19 D '74. * (*PA* 54:8511)
4. MALLEY, T. DAVID. "The Measurement of Reading Skills." *J Learn Dis* 8(6):377–81 Jl '75. *
5. WAKEFIELD, JAMES A., JR.; VESELKA, RONALD E.; AND MILLER, LESLIE. "A Comparison of the Iowa Tests of Basic Skills and the Prescriptive Reading Inventory." *J Ed Res* 68(9):347–9 My–Je '75. * (*PA* 54:8519)

ROGER FARR, *Associate Dean, School of Education, Indiana University, Bloomington, Indiana.* [Review of Levels A–D and the experimental edition of the PRI Interim Tests.]

The *Prescriptive Reading Inventory* has as its major purpose the assessment of individual students' achievement on a set of specific reading objectives. The *Prescriptive Reading Inventory Interim Tests* are designed for use as a monitoring system to follow instruction which would presumably have been based on the PRI tests. These two sets of tests are based on the same set of objectives and generally use the same item formats.

The PRI tests were developed prior to the PRI Interim Tests and provide the structure for the PRI Interim Tests. The PRI tests are accompanied by considerable technical data while the PRI Interim Tests are labelled "experimental editions." For these reasons this review will first focus on the PRI tests. The PRI Interim Tests will be reviewed as an extension of the PRI tests.

The *Prescriptive Reading Inventory* is designed to "provide evaluation relevant to classroom instruction." The test seems to have its base in the behavioral objectives movement and criterion-referenced test movement which gained the attention of educators in the late 60s and seems to be continuing into the 70s. The review of this test will focus on how well it accomplishes its stated purpose of providing guidance for classroom instruction. Three basic questions will be discussed. First, does the test measure important aspects of reading instruction? Second, how well does the test measure those things it purports to measure? Third, is the test practical for use by those who teach reading?

Does the test measure what is important? The test developers decided that what was important to measure were those reading objectives that were included in the "five most widely used basal reading programs." On the surface this seems like a logical decision. It means that if a teacher uses one of these basal readers, the objectives of that basal will be included on the test. But there are problems with this approach.

The major problem is that compiling a list of objectives from five basal reading programs will lead to a "smorgasbord" of objectives if there is no theory of reading to guide the objectives selection. For the PRI, no theory of reading was stated as a guide for the selection of objectives. The result is a list of objectives which are only loosely related because they did not evolve from a stated definition of reading. The PRI test developers do organize the objectives into major categories but in doing so admit that the categorization does not constitute a definition of reading. The following statement in the technical report emphasizes the point: "This classi-

fication scheme is not meant to be definitive, but it provides a way to organize and work with a large number of specific reading objectives." The result of this "atheoretical" position is that the test user would need to impose a definition of reading on the test and use only the test items that assess those objectives which matched his definition.

Because of the lack of a clear definition of reading, the test developers have compiled a long list of redundant and overlapping objectives. This list of 90 objectives breaks reading into a fractionated set of test items that could lead to fractionated reading instruction. For example, one objective is that "the student will be able to identify synonyms for given words." Another is that "the student will be able to identify antonyms for given words." These two objectives can be used to write two different item types, but the reading teacher is not interested in the children's recognition of antonyms or synonyms but in increasing vocabulary strength. While the teacher may use antonym or synonym type exercises to improve vocabulary, she does not see these as different objectives; and if she does, such reading instruction becomes a nonsensical "mastery" of narrow objectives or test item types rather than a mastery of important reading skills.

Related to the first question, does the test measure what is important, is the concern with the publication dates of the basal readers on which the test is based. At the time of the writing of this review, all of the five basal readers on which the PRI is based have been replaced by newer editions. Such is the fate of tying a test to specific instructional materials. While the changing of materials is one problem with the selection of the objectives, another problem is how the objectives were actually determined. The test developers "reviewed the reading materials page by page to identify the reading behaviors implicit in the program's instruction." This means test users are dependent on what the test developers "thought" the authors of the reading materials were trying to accomplish. This may answer the question as to why recognition of antonyms is a separate objective. The author of the instructional materials may have merely been using an "antonym type exercise" to accomplish some objective such as the student's use of reading context to identify the meaning of words.

How well does the test measure what it purports to measure? In general the test format is clear and the items seem to be well written. However, there are some serious problems. First, the format changes after every three or four items. For example on the Red Level (grades 1.5 to 2.5), for the first three items the task is to match the vowel sound in a stimulus word with one of three choices; for the next three items the task is to find a particular vowel sound such as long i in one of four choices; for the next three items the task is to select, from three choices, the best word to complete a statement. This constant changing of item format continues throughout the test. After 123 items of constantly changing formats, primary grade students may be quite confused.

Some of the item types also seem to be questionable approaches to measuring the objectives they purport to measure. For example, for the assessment of matching like vowel sounds, the teacher gives the following instruction: "Find the word that has *the same vowel sound* as the underlined word." This item seems to be measuring more than the matching of vowel sounds. The first or second grader must also know what is meant by the term "vowel sound." This item type seems to be an assessment of terminology as well as the assessment of a reading skill. There are other item types on the test that also seem to be relatively poor measures of the objectives. The potential user should carefully review the test to determine if this is a serious problem for him. There are enough of these problems to cause this reviewer to rate the PRI relatively low on this criterion.

Another aspect of how well the test measures the objectives is reliability. There are only three to five test items for each objective. For three-item objectives, two or three items correct indicate mastery, one correct is needs review, and none correct is nonmastery. Such criterion levels are common on criterion-referenced tests and they seem to this reviewer to be nonsense. The reviewer tested the reliability of the first 15 objectives of the Red Level by marking the items at random and scoring according to the above criteria. Two of the objectives were mastered, four needed review, and nine were failed. That result was achieved by random marking

with no knowledge of the questions; one wonders how many objectives would be mastered if there were just a little knowledge. In order to demonstrate the reliability that could be added by increasing the number of items per objective, the same 15 objectives were scored as five objectives each including nine or more items. The criteria levels were increased proportionately in the scoring. This time all five objectives were failed. Why didn't the test developers include more items per objective? If they did, the test would be far too lengthy—if the long list of objectives were retained—but then the test would be strengthened if a shorter, more realistic list of objectives were developed.

Is the test practical for use by those who teach reading? The answer in this reviewer's opinion is no. Reading is fractioned into a long, overlapping list of objectives. Such long lists of objectives get in the way of reading instruction. While skills are important in learning to read, this long list does not provide a well-thought-out list of skills that relate to one another. It is just what it was designed to be, a potpourri of objectives that the test developers thought that the authors of reading materials were attempting to teach.

Perhaps the major question facing the classroom reading teacher is the placement of students in the appropriate level of the reading program. For this important question, this test provides no information. The classroom teacher of reading would be much better off planning informal assessment as a part of the ongoing instructional program than trying to adapt, select from, and interpret this test as the central focus for planning reading instruction. If a teacher knew enough to adapt this test to her needs, she would also know that she would not need to use this test.

Most of the concerns with the PRI tests also apply to the PRI Interim Tests, such as the construct validity of the objectives included on the test, the lack of a specific guiding definition of reading for the development of the test, the manner in which the objectives were discerned from the instructional materials, the copyright dates of the instructional materials on which the tests are based, the congruency between some item types and the objectives they are supposed to be measuring, and the lengthy list of redundant objectives which the test attempts to assess.

Prescriptive Reading Inventory

The major types of information that are missing include any type of reliability information, validity evidence for the criterion scoring levels, and any review of item tryouts which could lead to an explanation as to how well the test items discriminate. Without this information, the test user is left with merely an attractively packaged set of test pages that include exercises that look like those found in many reading workbooks.

The lack of reliability information is especially important. Without such information, the test user has no basis on which to determine whether the results a student achieves will be consistent from one testing time to another. Since the test developers propose that important individual instructional decisions be made on the basis of these test results, it is absolutely essential that the developers indicate how reliable these results can be expected to be.

In summary, these tests seem to have too many major flaws to provide the kind of information a teacher needs to "get on with" instruction. As with most criterion-referenced tests that include long lists of objectives and complicated management systems, there is concern that these systems may be relied on in place of thoughtful, ongoing diagnosis by a competent teacher.

CAROLYN E. MASSAD, *Examiner, Elementary and Secondary School Programs, Educational Testing Service, Princeton, New Jersey.* [Review of Levels A–D and the experimental edition of the PTR Interim Tests.]

Although the publisher does not state explicitly a theory of reading on which the PRI and the PRI Interim Tests are based, material in the interpretive handbook appears to indicate the assumption that reading is a somewhat hierarchical order of skills that follows "a continuum from early decoding skills to aspects of critical thinking in reading comprehension." However, it is not exactly clear how the publisher thinks all these skills are related except that "the reading behaviors [expressed as objectives] are not necessarily acquired in separate, sequential steps, but may overlap as they develop." Because of this, some of the objectives are measured at more than one level. Nevertheless, several objectives could have been tested at more levels than they are, in varying degrees of difficulty.

As indicated, the unifying characteristics among the skills tested are not made evident. Since the PRI and the PRI Interim Tests are criterion-referenced tests, this is not unusual. Such an approach seems to treat learning as if it were acquired by adding separate, discrete units to the collection of things learned rather than as if it were the building of a structure of numerous, interrelated concepts and skills. Yet this approach can be quite helpful in identifying students' strengths and weaknesses and those of programs when the tests adequately reflect the objectives of the programs.

Ideally, for diagnosis in the strictest sense of the word, a test should be extremely reliable. For the PRI, the publisher admits that an "unorthodox" form of reliability information is presented, but feels that the "effectiveness of the whole test in guiding students through an appropriate instructional sequence was more important." This same attitude appears to have prevailed for the PRI Interim Tests. To be reliable, a measure must have a sufficient number of items measuring what it is intended to measure. Both the PRI and the PRI Interim Tests have too few items per objective for reliable measurement of any single objective.

For the PRI, the publisher appears to be satisfied with only three or four items to measure "mastery" of most of the objectives; and "mastery" is defined as, for example, a score of two out of three items correct on one objective. In comparison, the PRI Interim Tests use five items to measure "mastery"; mastery is defined as having at least four out of five items correct. No data are currently available to support the validity of the cutoff scores that indicate "mastery" of an objective. This is understandable for the PRI Interim Tests since they are only in experimental form; but, the PRI has been in use for several years and there certainly should be some evidence as to whether students are properly classified by the PRI as "masters" of the objectives. Also, inconsistency across the PRI and the PRI Interim Tests regarding the number of correct responses needed for "mastery" of an objective adds to the questionableness of the cutoff scores.

A definite weakness is that insufficient information is currently available for the test consumer to judge the concurrent and diagnostic validity of these tests. This is a most serious omission since the lack of such data sheds some doubt on the ability of the tests to provide the information needed to group students and/or to pinpoint a student's weaknesses. Unfortunately, having so few items per objective can lead to errors in judgment about individual students, although judgments about groups of students are less susceptible to error. As with all test results, before a definitive judgment is made regarding the achievement of an individual student on a given objective other information should also be considered. Therefore, the cost in time and money for both testing and gathering of other necessary information for decision making must be considered in the test selection process.

With regard to content validity, there may be an insufficient number of items to provide for the representativeness needed in measuring some of the objectives. Indeed, the term "mastery" as the publisher uses it may be quite misleading since complete mastery of any but the simplest ideas and skills is generally unattainable. Clearly, an inspection of the items and format is necessary before the PRI is used and decisions made on the basis of the test results.

The publisher explains that "terminal objectives," defined as "the behavior the student will be able to display after instruction," are being measured rather than "process objectives," defined as that "activity through which a student acquires a behavior." Yet the behavioral objectives generally specify an activity in which the behavior is to take place. In fact, a given behavior is sometimes present in more than one objective, the activity being the varying factor among some objectives. Consequently, it would seem that the objectives are not the "terminal objectives" that the publisher claims to measure. Nevertheless, stating the activity in which the behavior is to be observed should not necessarily be a handicap. If the activity happens to be a part of a student's program of instruction, then the evaluation is clearly one of the program and the student's achievement in that program. And for those unfamiliar with the activity, perhaps transfer of learning is being measured. Moreover, the publisher provides suggested classroom activities, all of which are keyed to the objectives measured and can be used to teach toward them. Hopefully, however, these activities will not become the sole basis of a reading

Prescriptive Reading Inventory

program, one that does not necessarily provide for building an interrelated structure of skills.

A decided advantage of the PRI Interim Tests is that they can be used much like teacher-made tests that follow a specific unit of study, thus saving valuable teacher-preparation time. In addition, they can be reused later to determine retention of learning. Because each objective has its own test, greater flexibility is provided in using the PRI Interim Tests as compared to the PRI. Not all students need to take every test at the same time or in the same order, nor does every student need to take all of the tests. The PRI, on the other hand, is a rather long test and should be divided into reasonably short sessions, not exceeding 45 minutes each, so that students are not fatigued.

In summary, the adequacy of the PRI and the PRI Interim Tests depends upon the kinds of decisions to be made based on the test results. Decisions about grouping students according to needs in skill areas could be made with the understanding that regrouping will be needed when errors in assignments to groups are detected. In making definitive decisions about individual students, it is necessary also to consider information other than the test results. Where samples of students' work, teacher observations, results of informal reading inventories, etc., are also considered with test results, these tests are highly recommended. However, a review of the contents and objectives of the tests to determine their appropriateness for the students' program is, of course, necessary before a decision is made to use the tests.

[770]

★Ransom Program Reading Tests. Grades kgn, 1, 2, 3, 4, 5, 6; 1974–75; 278 criterion-referenced tests covering 202 overlapping specific objectives in 5 areas: cognitive and affective comprehension (36 objectives), conceptual vocabulary (39), linguistic comprehension (27), location and study skills (29), perceptual vocabulary (71); tests are provided for only 37.3% of the 541 objectives presented in the Ransom Program; minimum mastery levels range from 67 to 100%; 19 levels (students passing 75 to 80% of tests at any one level should proceed to next higher level); 18 tests cover 2–4 objectives although only one score is obtained; no data on reliability; no norms; no supporting data or information for grade placement of specific objectives and mastery standards; instructional guide available for each of 8 basic reading series; teacher's handbook ('75, 146 pages); individual record form ('75, 2 pages); $22.68 per 35 record forms; $42.87 per handbook; cash orders postpaid; specimen set not available; administration time not reported; Grayce A. Ransom; Addison-Wesley Publishing Co., Inc. *
a) LEVELS 1–13. Grades kgn, 1, 2, 3; 1974–75; levels

and number of specific objective tests: kgn (levels 1–3, 32 tests), grade 1 (4–7, 48), grade 2 (8–10, 56), grade 3 (11–13, 56); only one test can be administered at a time since the directions for each item are given orally; tests ('74, 1–3 pages each, spirit masters for local duplicating); teacher instructions ('74, 39–75 pages) for each grade; $42.12 ($35.64 for kgn) per set of spirit masters and instructions for any one grade. b) LEVELS 14–19. Grades 4, 5, 6; 1975; levels and number of specific objective tests: grade 4 (levels 14–15, 30 tests), grade 5 (16–17, 28), grade 6 (18–19, 28); test booklets (29–30 pages each) contain tests for 2 levels; teacher instructions (12 pages) for each grade; separate answer sheets must be used for each level (also serves for listing books read relevant to 8 additional objectives); $27.27 per 35 tests and instructions for any one grade; $9.72 per 35 answer sheets for any one level.

RICHARD A. THOMPSON, *Professor of Education and Director, Educational Development Program, Florida Technological University, Orlando, Florida.*

The Ransom Reading Management Program is an instructional system developed to facilitate individualization of reading instruction. Familiarity with other commercial or homemade reading management systems should tune in the reader to the structure and functional value of these programs. Although there are differences among all programs, the basic concept is the same. In essence it is: cull the basal manuals for reading skills; state them in behavioral terms; create test items for measuring each behavioral objective; and correlate or key the basal textbook, workbook pages and other instructional reading materials to the listed objectives.

Because the Ransom system is a well-thought-out reading management program, it is usable with any basal program or within any reading curriculum. Its flexible design is of functional value to teachers and specialists to organize, assess, and utilize existing reading resources for effective management at the elementary school level. At the center of this program is a taxonomy of reading objectives which can be coded to the various reading materials available within a school.

Ransom's criterion-referenced tests are an integral part of the program used for continually assessing each student's strengths and weaknesses in terms of specific reading skill needs. The results are consolidated on individual and group profile forms which are used to plan individualized instructional needs of each student. Arrayed to cover the extensive range of reading skills found in widely used K–6 basal readers, the 500 plus behavioral and subordinate objectives are spread over 19 test levels. The purpose of constructing this number of levels was to allow students to be tested throughout school terms and continuously through grade six.

It does not appear that the 19 test levels are an unreasonable number. With each test covering from 9 to 21 skills, the median number being 14, there is considerable variability in the number of objectives assessed by each test. As a minor suggestion, it would probably be advantageous to have some reassignment of objectives to reduce the size of the objectives covered on the tests with the larger number of skills listed. The utility value for the students would be that a smaller number of learning outcomes in these instances would expedite movement from one level to the next without the necessity of spending unusually long periods of time at any one particular level. In any case, regardless of the number of skills tested at any one level, with this organization students can master skills at one level of complexity before working on related skills or the same skill at a greater level of complexity.

Subsequent to pilot testing of the criterion-referenced tests, 76 schools field tested the experimental program providing "input to the author and publisher as the final version was developed." The author purports that "the extensive field testing....has shown the validity of its major features."

Content validity for a criterion-referenced test such as Ransom's is best determined by considering whether the test items are valid measures of the objectives they are intended to measure and whether the objectives are a valid representation of the K–6 reading curriculum. By this reviewer's inspection, the test items seem to validly measure the prescribed objectives, but this inspection and judgment should not be thought of as having equal validity with a formal item analysis using a sensitivity index such as was done by CTB/McGraw Hill in the development of their *Prescriptive Reading Inventory.*

While most of the objectives appear to be valid, this reviewer questions the relationship of a few objectives to reading ability, or the relationship might be so minimal that time spent learning the objective may be better applied to skills with stronger relationships to reading ability. For example, the grammar skills listed are not likely to have a relationship to reading skill inasmuch as there is no empirical evidence that knowledge of grammar skills, kernel sentence patterns, sentence transformations and the like is related to reading ability.

There should be a demonstrated relationship that knowledge of objectives affects reading skill before students are asked to learn these skills. Time wasted trying to learn nonexistent or unrelated skills could be avoided if test publishers were exacting in test development.

A large "plus" factor is that the Ransom system is unquestionably comprehensive in covering reading skills, even the higher level skills such as cause and effect relationships, detecting propaganda, drawing conclusions, recognizing implied assumptions, irony, and hyperboles. This comprehensiveness should make the program attractive to teachers regardless of reading materials available.

On balance, the objectives covered, with the exception of the few mentioned, appear to have content validity; that is, in this reviewer's judgment, the skills are likely to have a direct relationship to reading ability. Knowledgeable teachers using these tests can use discretion and have students skip dubious objectives.

Another unsubstantiated assumption in criterion-referenced tests in general and in the Ransom tests in particular is that there exists an empirically derived hierarchy of reading skills. Certainly this hierarchical arrangement is implicit when students must pass one skill before proceeding to the next, but as yet this assumption is unsubstantiated. No evidence is available supporting this contention. Knowing this, teachers using these tests need to use judgment and not permit students to lose too much time learning a particular skill before discontinuing the pursuit in favor of another skill on the continuum.

Legibility, clarity, and attractiveness merit attention. It must be said that the Ransom materials from the teacher's handbook through teacher instructions including the test duplicating masters are expertly written, printed, and packaged.

CONCLUSION. In perspective, the Ransom system has great potential for use by reading teachers. Although the criterion-referenced tests are

useful, they could be further refined to demonstrate that all of the skill objectives show a relationship to reading ability and the test items are sensitive to instruction. Knowledgeable teachers having a solid acumen of reading skill development would find this system useful in pinpointing students' reading skill needs. With knowledge gained from criterion-referenced assessment, teachers can prescribe appropriate instructional strategies for direct assault on precise students needs, the surest way of increasing students' reading power.

Flexibility is the key to criterion-referenced testing, and the nature of the Ransom tests makes them of especial interest to classroom teachers. That reading is a complex skill composed of many subskills makes a valid criterion-referenced test a valuable teaching tool, and the Ransom program makes appropriate use of this capability for individualizing reading instruction. It is a well-thought-out, useful management system with particular applicability in helping teachers individualize their instructional programs. For teachers who view themselves as diagnostic/prescriptive reading instructors rather than reading technicians who follow recipe programs, the Ransom program is worth investigating.

[771]

★**Reading: IOX Objectives-Based Tests.** Grades kgn–6; 1973–76; criteron referenced; 78 tests (spirit masters for local duplicating) in 2 areas; no data on reliability; 2 forms; series description ('73, 4 pages); folder of support forms ('74, 14 pages); 4% extra for postage and handling; specimen booklet (sample pages only) for these and other tests is available free on request; (5–10) minutes per test; series description by W. James Popham; tests developed under the direction of John McNeil, Nola Paxton, and Linda Paulson; Instructional Objectives Exchange. *
a) WORD ATTACK SKILLS. 38 tests; "skills represent those which should be mastered at the end of primary school"; Forms A, B, ('73, 1–2 pages); manual ('73, 22 pages); comparative data ('76, 10 pages); $25 per set of testing materials for either form, $45 for both forms.
b) COMPREHENSION SKILLS. 40 tests; Forms A, B, ('73, 1–2 pages); manual ('73, 30 pages); comparative data ('76, 13 pages); $25 per set of testing materials for either form, $45 for both forms.

REBECCA C. BARR, *Research Associate, The University of Chicago, Chicago, Illinois.*

The IOX tests differ from most standardized achievement tests in two respects. First, items are selected not on the basis of their sensitivity to individual differences, but rather in accord with specified instructional objectives. Second, tests are homogeneous in content and separable, allowing school personnel to select those tests which accord with the instructional objectives in specific classes. The authors specify that the test may be used for individualized instruction, pretest-posttest evaluation of instructional sequences in the classroom, and supplementation of school-wide or district-wide educational evaluations.

The comprehension tests are designed to measure literal interpretation of material (syntactical structures, sequence, punctuation, and affixes) and inferential reasoning from material (main idea, conclusions, and context clues). The 2 to 10 tests within each of the seven areas are ordered on the basis of test item complexity. For example, under Conclusions, the material in the second test (simple logical reasoning) consists of one or two simple factual sentences in active voice to be read orally by the test administrator; by contrast, the material in the fifth test (identifying situations from information) consists of a short descriptive paragraph of no more than six simple, compound, or complex sentences, to be read by the child. Each comprehension test consists typically of 5, but sometimes 10, items.

The 38 word attack tests are patterned after the objectives and the test items of the *Wisconsin Tests of Reading Skill Development: Word Attack*. Except for six tests administered individually by the teacher (with five items each), the word attack tests contain 10 items each. The tests are purportedly arranged in a sequence of difficulty, though the criteria used in judging difficulty are not explicit and the particular position in the sequence of some tests appears to have been arbitrarily determined.

The authors emphasize that though the tests are numbered sequentially, the sequence is not rigid and teachers may select those objectives and tests which are appropriate for their purposes. In order to facilitate selective use, tests are distributed as boxed collections of preprinted spirit masters of one or two pages each.

Directions and an example (uncompleted on elementary tests, but completed on more advanced tests) are included on all tests. Test administrators are encouraged to insure that students understand the directions and to respond to student questions pertaining to the example. However, there are no procedures specified through which the teacher can determine whether or not pupils understand the directions and the example.

Tests may be hand scored using the scoring key accompanying each collection of tests. For each student taking a test, the number of correct responses (uncorrected for guessing) and percentage of correct responses may be derived, and the latter score may be compared to a locally determined criterion level to judge mastery.

Two important questions must be considered: do the tests consistently yield the same scores for individuals, and are the forms comparable in difficulty? No evidence is reported concerning the first question. Because the tests contain few items and typically two or three response alternatives, scores from the tests might be expected to yield inconsistent test-retest scores. Because the tests are recommended for use in instructional planning for individuals, it is hoped that evidence concerning this aspect of reliability will be forthcoming.

No data are provided pertaining to the comparability of forms, but there is some indirect evidence. Over 2,000 Los Angeles pupils were assigned tests and forms through a matrix sampling procedure; discrepancies between results on the two forms of some of the tests suggest that caution should be exercised in making pretest-posttest comparisons for individuals, and that a form balancing procedure (as described in the series description booklet) should be used in the assessment of class, school, and district learning.

The content validity is supported by the detailed specification of item content and form in the "amplified" objectives. Nevertheless, an examination of item content suggests some problems that may interfere with the assessment of the intended objective. Concerning the word attack tests, four tests involving the matching of sounds may be completed on the basis of visual letter matching since the stimulus words, to be spoken by the teacher, are printed on the tests along with response alternatives. Nine of the 38 tests depend on correct picture identification by pupils, whereas nine other tests include as response alternatives words with which children are assumed to be familiar. For these 18 tests, failure to correctly identify the pictures or words may interfere with children being able

Reading: IOX Objectives-Based Tests

to demonstrate the knowledge that the tests were designed to elicit.

Similarly, on the comprehension tests, the success with which students perform comprehension operations may be more a reflection of familiarity with passage words than the comprehension process the test purports to measure. For example, students who are unfamiliar with the vocabulary of a passage would not be able to demonstrate whether or not they are able to predict outcomes or order events as they occur in a passage.

Pictorial or textual characteristics may not interfere with valid assessment of the stated objectives; nevertheless, concurrent validation of each of the tests is needed to insure that the process or knowledge that the test was designed to measure is actually being elicited.

The authors make no claim that the mastery of tested concepts will result in general reading competence; nevertheless, the question of what instruction in specific skills contributes to general reading competence is an extremely important one. The question is not simply one of concurrent or predictive validity estimates based on correlations between the IOX reading tests and indices of general reading proficiency, but rather the assessment of what a change in the status of particular skills contributes to general reading proficiency.

SUMMARY. There is a clear need in educational practice and research for tests designed in the manner of the IOX tests. Nevertheless, content validity is not a sufficient basis for judging their validity. For such criterion-referenced tests to become useful educational tools, reliability of single tests, comparability of forms, and the specific and general concurrent validity of the tests must be established.

BARTON B. PROGER, *Coordinator, Program Evaluation Services, Montgomery County Intermediate Unit, Norristown, Pennsylvania.*

The IOX reading tests represent a logical outgrowth of IOX's earlier, extensive work in objectives, which in itself has made a substantial contribution to the instructional process. This review is written from the perspective of one who has wrestled over several years with the problems of criterion-referenced measurement, program evaluation, curricular task analysis by objectives, and construction of curriculum management systems in several areas. The reviewer has focused on the structural framework rather than getting caught up in the nuances of the specific item contents themselves.

The purposes of IOX tests are twofold: classroom management and program evaluation. The reviewer concludes that the former area possesses several problems but that a major advance has been made in the latter area. The reading tests are well suited to local program evaluation purposes. Clearly, the authors devoted much effort to designing a system that is flexible for meeting local demands of specific curricula. One has a certain degree of programmatic freedom (albeit still limited, as will be emphasized later) in choosing separate tests, each of which has been built to reflect a single major objective, rather than a cluster of several objectives. For example, the 40 specific-objective tests in Comprehension Skills are grouped into the major areas: main idea (5 tests), conclusions (10 tests), sequence (7 tests), context clues (9 tests), punctuation (3 tests), syntactical structure (4 tests), and affixes (2 tests).

A folder of support forms gives procedures to assist in the local design of a specific program evaluation system. The local school program evaluator would distribute the "Rating Form" to members of the staff or other concerned groups to obtain ratings (on a five-point scale) of importance for each objective. The program evaluator would then use the "Priority Rating Summary Sheet" to assign numerical weights to the various rater groups and compute weighted average ratings on each objective across groups. These ratings are then used in the selection of the specific tests to be used.

The other major purpose, classroom management, has not been achieved satisfactorily. A basic issue involves whether a criterion-referenced measurement system should be curriculum-embedded or curriculum-free. There appear to be at least six major criteria by which to evaluate any mastery-oriented, classroom management system: (*a*) specificity of objectives, (*b*) appropriateness of CRM-oriented test items, (*c*) simplicity of usage, (*d*) guidelines for usage and interpretation of results for instructional decision-making, (*e*) frequency of CRM feedback, and (*f*) flexibility of meshing CRM tests and objectives to existing curricular offerings so as to make rational decision-making possible (the issue of hierarchical sequencing). Of the above criteria, IOX tests are relatively strong in (*a*), (*b*), and (*c*); the system leaves much to be desired in (*d*), (*e*), and (*f*). With regard to (*d*), very minimal details are given. The support form folder discusses usage very briefly, and the test manuals are quite nebulous in this regard. If one speaks about either individualization or group instruction, some directionality should be offered. The reviewer does not see how (*e*) and (*f*) can be achieved because of the large *range* of very specific skills that each test sheet embodies. For instance, in Word Attack Skills, test 10 (Matching Final Consonant Sounds to Written Single Letters) covers letters b, d, g, f, k, l, m, n, p, and r. In most curricular series, this range of skills is taught over an extended period of time (there is often also spiral presentation over time of related specific skills, which complicates the picture). Another problem is that each test was devised for grades K to 6; this is particularly a problem in the Comprehension Skills collection, if one is trying to customize the selection of tests to the grade level and to a specific sequence-area within that grade. Curriculum-free management systems continue to proliferate, but the pre-set versions will always suffer from the above flaws.

The test manuals, while not offering much of a specific, directional nature, nonetheless serve a valuable function in providing an explanation of each objective. The reviewer is somewhat puzzled regarding the development of the tests. The criteria for initially selecting objectives are clearly stated and appear to pose no problem. The objectives are given for review to "one or more" external consultants, to "a practicing teacher," and to IOX staff for "three separate internal....reviews." What is not clear is just how tightly controlled and how extensive the total review process was, and how many individuals were actually involved. Nor is it clear, even more importantly, whether the tests were produced mainly by field-oriented efforts or by think-tank efforts.

A brochure, by Popham, on the series of IOX tests puts forth an explanation (viz., lack of funds) as to why no technical development data are provided (e.g., reliability, item homogeneity), and the reviewer can accept this. However, for those who wish to pursue these topics lo-

cally, the publisher should have pointed out the large body of literature available on the continuing debates about validity and reliability considerations specifically geared to CRM.

It appears to be a psychometric schizophrenia to have to address the topic of normative data in a CRM review, but for each of the two reading collections a document on "comparative data" is provided. The purpose is to help teachers and others to set "realistic performance expectations." Frankly, however, the reviewer cannot accept this approach to setting expectancies. While the issue is admittedly a difficult one, there are a number of commonsense, practical ways other than "tests being normed" that can be used. Further, the manner in which the data were obtained leaves much to be desired. Fall testing was conducted in 1975 on about 2,300 students as a measure of what mastery should have existed at the end of the previous grade in spring! What about the summer lag phenomenon? (The document admits this problem, but the danger of invalidity remains.) There is, however, a considerably worse problem in the possible misinterpretation by the lay user. The expectancy data are relevant only to what levels should be exhibited in spring of a given grade at the *end* of the school year; in other words, the only appropriate use would be for summative program evaluation purposes, and even here the reviewer himself would not rely on such normative data for CRM-based materials. The real danger, however, arises if the teacher begins to use the data for making instructional decisions for test/objectives given *during* the year. Total invalidity would be the consequence.

SUMMARY. The authors have made a valuable contribution in program evaluation work but their work suffers to some extent for curriculum management purposes. In the latter regard, the reviewer would look at the materials far more favorably if they had been put forth for global, instructional placement purposes at the start of the year or at major points within the year, rather than as an in-process management system for use throughout the year.

[772]

★**Reading Skills Diagnostic Test.** Grades 2–8; 1967–71; 6 scores: letter identification, simple phonics, consistent words, inconsistent words, letters in context, words in context; no norms for 4 subtests; 1 form (no date, 8 pages); manual ('71, 48 pages); $2.50

Reading Skills Diagnostic Test

per 25 tests; $3.50 per manual; specimen set not available; postage extra; administration time not reported; Richard H. Bloomer; Brador Publications, Inc. *

See T2:1644 (1 reference).

IRA E. AARON, *Professor of Education, The University of Georgia, Athens, Georgia.*

This test aims to provide the teacher with an uncomplicated "system of diagnosis of basic skill problems such that the teacher will know specifically what she has to teach each child." The test contains 350 items. Only one form is available.

The 50-item Letter Identification subtest assesses knowledge of letters of the alphabet. The teacher says a letter and the child circles one of three letters to indicate the one read (items 1–26) or one of three words to indicate the word containing the letter (items 27–50). All letters are tested in the 26 items containing letters. All letters except q and x are checked in the 24 items dealing with words. The correct letter in the last 24 items is an initial consonant 14 times, a final consonant twice, a medial consonant three times, and medial vowels five times.

Simple Phonics contains 50 items and requires the child to relate sounds to letter shapes. The examiner says a sound and children identify the letter (items 1–25) or two letters (items 26–50) from among three possibilities. Of the first 25, 18 sounds to be identified are initial consonants, one a final consonant, one a medial consonant (*axe*, on the basis of spelling but not of sound), four medial vowels, and one an initial vowel. Items 26–50 are all initial consonants plus a short vowel sound (as *da* in *dad*).

The 50-item Phonetically Consistent Words subtest checks the subject's ability to recognize words that are spelled as they sound. The child indicates which of three phonetically regular words the examiner said. Directions in the manual are inadequate for this subtest. Words given are the same 50 groups of three that are on the test itself, with no indication of which word of each group the examiner is to read. Through use of a diagnostic chart, the examiner in some cases may determine laboriously the words the author intended to be read. As the manual now is, this subtest is useless because of this important omission.

Phonetically Inconsistent Words is similar to the previous subtest except that it contains 87

items and deals with the subject's ability to identify words spelled differently from the way they sound. Again, it is impossible from the manual to administer this subtest. The author again failed to give the list of words to be read.

Letters in Context consists of 23 sentences in which one letter has been omitted from 40 words, one or two from each sentence. The task of the subject is to write in the missing letter. All letters missing are closely tied to context. However, a few words could be given any one of several different letters. For instance, one sentence refers to throwing a *rope* over a branch. *Rose* (letter s) or *robe* (letter b) also could fit.

The final subtest is Words in Context. Seven sections have from 11 to 21 words deleted. The total number of words deleted is 102. The subject's task is to determine the deleted word from the context. Approximately every tenth word has been omitted. Instructions to the examiner suggest stopping if the child takes more than 15 minutes on a single paragraph. To wait for 15 minutes seems much too long. To spend as much as 5 minutes on one paragraph would seem excessive. Grade norms, from 4.0 to 8.0, are reported for this subtest. No explanation for the basis of these norms is given.

Using 212 pupils from grades 1–6, tested 14 weeks apart, test-retest reliability coefficients for the subtests range from .48 (Letters in Context) to .92 (Phonetically Inconsistent Words), with mean .73. Total test reliability is .94.

The only data on validity consist of eight correlations between total scores on the RSDT and scores on the *Metropolitan Achievement Tests*, "Gates Reading Tests" [sic], and *Stanford Achievement Tests*. The correlations range from .66 to .75, with median .70. Since these correlations were computed "from situations involving pupils in total range grades 1–6," they are greatly inflated.

Since the RSDT is a diagnostic test where, hopefully, pupils' strengths and weaknesses may be pinpointed, correlating the total score with norm-referenced tests seems inappropriate. In a diagnostic test each of the subtest scores must be validated.

Thirty pages of the manual are devoted to "General Remediation Techniques." The author suggests somewhat mechanical procedures to follow in remediation. Most suggestions offered are *not* in line with those given in widely used

Reading Skills Diagnostic Test

texts on remedial reading instruction and in current instructional materials in reading. The quality of the suggestions ranges from inferior (on most specific instructional suggestions) to good (on a few general guides for working with children).

The test presupposes a hierarchical arrangement of skills in line with the order in which subtests are presented. Further, a subskill mastery concept is used, as indicated by the suggestion of mastery of one subarea then moving to the next. This reviewer questions these statements. Research evidence does *not* tell us *the* hierarchical arrangement of skills. On the basis of logic, the order in which subtests are given seems appropriate for most subtests. However, why wait for mastery of one before beginning instruction on another? Meaning comes in the last subtest. This reviewer prefers seeing it from the beginning.

The several typographical errors in the manual caused this reviewer to question the care with which the manual was constructed.

Finally, the early subtests reflect a synthetic approach to phonics instruction. No reference is made to the existence of an analytic approach, and the majority of the core reading instructional programs in the United States are predominantly analytic in nature.

In its present form, this test appears of limited use to classroom teachers or clinicians. A teacher would fare better by using an inventory that matches his or her core instructional program in reading.

EDWARD R. SIPAY, *Professor of Education and Director of Reading Clinics, State University of New York at Albany, Albany, New York.*

Although the manual also contains a remedial program and other teaching suggestions, this review focuses on the test, alluding to the other sections of the manual only as they relate directly to the test. Potential test users, however, should carefully read the remedial methodology and procedures sections to determine if the tasks required of the test are in keeping with the suggested remediation, and to help them better understand and interpret the test.

The six subtests sample letter-name knowledge, decoding, word recognition, and comprehension skills. The directions for administering the test, though perhaps too brief for young children, are adequate except in a few instances. In all but the last subtest, the first item is used as the sample, with the answer being given if necessary. Time limits are suggested for a few subtests, but specific guidelines for terminating subtests are lacking—perhaps because this is a group test. Information regarding interpretation and use of some subtest results are less than adequate. Scoring keys for four subtests are found in the manual; none are indicated for the two word recognition subtests. Since the test is usually group administered, some type of scoring mask or overlay would expedite scoring. Even if the test is administered individually, as suggested for young children, the tasks remain the same as in a group test.

According to the manual, the subtests are hierarchically arranged, with attainment of each successive skill level dependent upon mastery of the preceding level. No rationale or evidence is presented to justify or verify this claim. Presumably, testing is always begun with the first subtest, with the next one in the sequence being given only after the skills at the preceding level have been mastered. But what constitutes mastery? Surely children can learn to read before they know the names of all 26 letters, and most can learn some sight words before all or even any phonic skills are known. Thus the claims for a hierarchical order of subtests and the need for mastery at each level seem unwarranted.

LETTER IDENTIFICATION. Despite what the manual implies, prior associational learning and not visual discrimination is the primary factor sampled by this subtest. On the first 26 items (one for each letter of the alphabet), the task is to select from three lowercase letters, the one named by the examiner. In most items, the distractors are very similar visually to the correct response.

Items 27–50 (*q* and *x* are omitted) require the child to select from three words, the one containing the letter named by the examiner. In a few printed stimuli, the letter is part of a consonant blend or vowel combination. No rationale is presented for measuring letter-name knowledge both in isolation and word context. Although the manual calls for mastery of all the letter names prior to going on to simple phonics, it is not clear whether they must be learned in isolation, in word context, or both. Furthermore, the importance placed on letter-name

Reading Skills Diagnostic Test

knowledge prior to learning phonics is confusing in light of the statement that "letter names have no meaning in a phonics lesson."

SIMPLE PHONICS. This test samples the ability to make sound-symbol associations. That is, the child must select from three choices the letter or letter combination that represents the sound pronounced in isolation. Such a task differs from the ability to make symbol-sound associations, going from the printed symbol to its sound. A child may be able to perform the task required by this subtest, but be unable to make or to utilize the symbol-sound associations required in decoding unknown printed words.

The first 25 items sample all the letters except q, with only the short vowel sounds and the hard sounds of c and g being included. Stimuli for items 26–50 involve a variety of consonant-short vowel combinations. The printed choices vary among the items. For some items, the same letter is not repeated in the other two choices. For others, the same letter appears in two choices; and in still others, only the initial consonant or final vowel differs in all three choices. What effect this has upon test results and the diagnostic implications are not clear, but use of such various stimuli makes it more difficult to determine the possible reasons for incorrect choices.

PHONETICALLY CONSISTENT WORDS. Because the manual does not indicate which words the examiner is to pronounce, most of the following comments are based on the sample item and inferences made by working "backwards" from the diagnostic chart.

In all 50 items, the task is to select from three printed words, the one pronounced by the examiner. In almost every set of choices the distractors are similar to the correct response in one or more visual elements (e.g., for mop, the distractors are mom and top).

The manual implies that children who make errors on this test should be taught "to put words together" (blending). Yet it is not clear how many errors constitute such a need. It would seem that if a child obtains a majority of correct responses, blending ability is intact. Or perhaps it merely means that the words are in his sight vocabulary. In any regard, there are more reasons than blending ability for correct and incorrect responses on this subtest. Nothing in the manual tells how to determine these possi-

ble reasons. Thus, in this reviewer's opinion, the subtest is not diagnostic.

Extreme care should be exercised in using the diagnostic chart. For example, item 1 is listed as sampling the "short o" associations. But since all three choices contain an o, an incorrect response on this element is impossible. In the other short o item (the number of samples per phonic element range from one to four), only two of the printed choices contain an o, both of which represent /ŭ/! On items such as 29 (rope, cloak, smoke), the child could choose the correct response (cloak) by cuing on the initial blend, alone, and thereby be credited with knowing the association for oa.

PHONETICALLY INCONSISTENT WORDS. Again, except for the sample item, there is no indication in the manual as to which words the examiner is to pronounce for the other 86 items. The sample item is go, but this reviewer does not understand why go is classified as phonetically inconsistent. Similarly in item 64, all three choices contain ight, a phonogram which consistently represents the same "sound."

LETTERS IN CONTEXT. In each of the 40 items contained in the 23 unrelated sentences contained in this subtest, the skill is to fill in one letter to complete the word (the blanks are in various positions in the words). This "comprehension" subtest, which has the lowest reliability (.48), has a suggested maximum time of 15 minutes. While the use of context clues is involved in the task, experiential background might play an important role in some items (e.g., He _urried his horse in the s_all). On other items, more than the indicated acceptable responses seem reasonable. For instance, h or even p or s may be just as logical as j in the sentence, "He ate toast with _am."

Five grade-equivalent scores (2.0 to 6.0) are presented for five raw scores, but there is no description of the norming sample.

The references to "Section VII" are obviously typographical errors since there are only six sections. Other typographical errors also appear in the test.

WORDS IN CONTEXT. This comprehension subtest is a modified cloze test, primarily using an every tenth word deletion. There are seven unrelated sections each containing from 11 to 21 deletions, for a total of 102 items. Synonyms are accepted in scoring. A time limit of 15 minutes

Reading Skills Diagnostic Test

per paragraph is suggested. So if the child were given all seven sections, the subtest might take 1 hour and 45 minutes to administer.

The manual states that the paragraphs are of increasing difficulty, but no data are furnished. Although it may occur by chance, the words that are deleted probably have some influence on the difficulty of the task and paragraph. For example in section 7, which has 14 deletions, 5 of the possible responses are *the* and 2 are *it.*

Grade-equivalent scores (4.0 to 8.0) are given for five raw scores, but again no data regarding the sample are provided. It would seem that this subtest is inappropriate for most primary-grade children.

RELIABILITY AND VALIDITY. Test-retest reliability data are reported for each subtest (.48–.92) and the total test (.94). Only the reliability of the phonetically consistent and inconsistent words subtests reach the .90 often used as a guideline for use of tests with individuals. Therefore, the use of the other four subtests in planning remedial programs for individuals is questionable. Furthermore, the lack of sufficient reliability for four subtests seriously opens to question the stated need of achieving mastery before going on to the next level. If test scores fluctuate greatly, how can one be sure that mastery has been attained? It also jeopardizes the claim that noting errors on one-sample items offers useful diagnostic information.

It is difficult to interpret the reported coefficients because other than the ambiguous statement that "Data presented here is [sic] only from situations involving pupils in total range grades 1–6," no descriptive information regarding the sample is provided. Among the questions raised by the lack of such information are: Did all 212 children take all six subtests? If so, does this not violate the test procedures and philosophy? If not, how was a total test reliability determined?

Also reported are eight validity coefficients, ranging from .66 to .75, between the total test score and three standardized tests. Again interpretation is difficult. For example, it is not clear whether the total achievement battery or just the reading tests (or which reading subtests) were used for the Metropolitan and Stanford tests.

SUMMARY. *The Reading Skills Diagnostic Test* suffers from the limitations of any group test that attempts to assess specific reading skills, particularly in the area of decoding. In this reviewer's opinion, despite its label, the test is really not diagnostic because it does not reveal or help the examiner to determine why certain errors were made. For these reasons, plus the questions and points raised above, it would be difficult to recommend this test for diagnostic purposes. If the reliability of the four subtests were improved, the test might provide some useful information for classroom teachers who ascribe to the philosophy of teaching reading expounded in the manual.

[773]

SPIRE Individual Reading Evaluation. Reading levels grades primer–6, 4–10; 1970–73; SPIRE (Student Problem Individual Reading Evaluation); 2 tests: diagnostic reading evaluation, quick placement test; 8 scores: 3 diagnostic scores (individual word recognition, oral and silent retention, oral and silent comprehension), 2 quick placement scores (individual word recognition, reading), and 3 derived scores (instructional level, frustration level, independent level); no data on how standards for levels were determined; individual; 2 levels; $45 per set of testing materials for either level; 5% extra for postage and handling; [20–30] minutes for diagnostic test, [5] minutes for quick placement test; Harvey Alpert and Alvin Kravitz; New Dimensions in Education, Inc. *
a) SPIRE 1. Reading level grades primer–6; 1970–73; 1 form; reading selections ('73, 21 cards); digit-scope ('73, 7 cards); duplicating masters ('73, 50 pages including summary sheet); guide ('73, 34 pages).
b) SPIRE 2. Reading level grades 4–10; 1971; 1 form; reading selections (21 pages); digit-scope (8 cards); duplicating masters (50 pages including summary sheet); guide (34 pages).

REFERENCES

1. KRAVITZ, ALVIN. *The Evaluation of a Summer Reading Program and Validation of the SPIRE Individual Reading Quick Placement Test.* Doctor's thesis, Hofstra University (Hempstead, N.Y.), 1972. (*DAI* 32:6714A)

N. DALE BRYANT, *Professor of Psychology and Education, Teachers College, Columbia University, New York, New York.*

SPIRE 1 and 2 are well-designed, attractive, easy-to-use, unnormed tests that are, in effect, informal reading inventories. They do not identify the actual reading level of a child in relation to how children at a given grade level usually read. However, this is not a problem for the major purpose of the test: identifying level of material to be used for instruction. Knowing a child's reading level does not automatically indicate the optimum level that should be used for instructional material. (Assumptions must be made about whether below or at level is best for instructional material.) The SPIRE tests do identify levels of materials appropriate for instructing a child in reading within the substantial limitations of: (a) the assumptions underlying informal reading inventories, e.g., that children learn best with reading materials on which they make a specific number of oral reading errors (usually 5 or fewer per 100 words) and on which they can answer a particular number of questions (usually 75 percent) about the material; and (b) the adequacy of the unanalyzed questions and the representativeness of the selection in terms of the number and kind of reading errors it is likely to generate. (Two selections with the same readability level according to formulas can still give substantially different numbers of errors when both are read by the same children. Also, questions asked about two selections of the same readability level may vary tremendously in difficulty due either to differences in content and style or to chance variation in the work of the test constructor.) In the present tests, the subjective cutting scores used to determine reading levels are based upon the authors' assumptions as applied to varying materials and levels of performance. In spite of these limitations, SPIRE 1 and 2 are probably better than the majority of informal reading inventories.

Three major types of scores are used: comprehension questions, oral passage reading, and words read from word lists. Test materials are graded so that children either pass or fail each type of score at a specific grade level. Comprehension tests are judged to be passed if at least 6 out of 10 questions are answered correctly. Scores for a representative sample of children from the grade for which each selection was designed would have provided a basis for more equivalent "passing" scores and would certainly vary from selection to selection.

The criteria for passing oral reading is about 7 or fewer errors per 100 words. While passages have been selected using a readability formula, the number of errors made by a norming group would certainly vary from grade to grade and selection to selection.

Word lists for each grade level were checked on a "representative, random sample of children in the grades for which the test was intended." The number and source of the sample is not specified. A word was selected for a list if 70-80 percent of the children in that grade pronounced it correctly and if fewer than 70 percent of the

children in the next lower grade and more than 80 percent of the children in the next higher grade pronounced it correctly.

There are two major parts to the tests: the Quick Placement Tests, intended to identify a child's instructional level based upon word recognition and silent reading comprehension; and the Diagnostic Reading Evaluation, which provides more data for clinical judgments but is primarily aimed at identifying a "hard" and "easy" as well as "medium" instructional level. These levels are based upon number of errors in oral reading and the number of questions answered correctly on oral and silent reading selections.

There are useful procedures for identifying which levels should be tested. Useful summary sheets are provided for describing oral errors and for describing the child's reading. While much clinical information can be obtained from the performance on the selections, the detail in the summary sheets can be misleading except in relatively extreme cases. The measurement is not adequate for making some of the judgments on categories such as making inferences, finding ideas, and finding details. Besides problems with categorizing comprehension questions, a child may be asked only three to five main idea questions in all the various selections administered. This is an insufficient number to either check or not check the summary statement, "Problems with Finding Main Ideas." The test is designed for classroom teacher use, and the judgments using much of the data, other than reading level, are more appropriate to a cautious clinician who possesses other confirming evidence.

The tests are beautifully prepared with ditto masters of all the expendable sheets. The selections are interesting and appropriate for their level. The adequacy of the questions is hard to evaluate and is what would be expected in trying to make up 10 questions for 75 to 200 words. Only a few can be answered by children without reading the selection.

Concurrent validities indicate that whatever the test is measuring, it is very much the same as is measured by other reading tests, and that simple word recognition can account for most of the variance. The split-half reliability coefficients are very high: .97 and .98 (N = 60, range of sample not given). Alternate-form reliabilities could have been computed for grade levels

4, 5, and 6, where SPIRE 1 and SPIRE 2 overlap. Also, none of these statistics indicate whether or not the reading level identified by the tests is an accurate measure of the child's reading level. (A test that gives each child's score as one year below that of the normed tests could correlate perfectly with the normed test.)

In summary, the SPIRE tests are predominantly excellent "informal reading inventories," with all of the advantages, unvalidated assumptions, and potentially variable test results that such tests are likely to produce. They provide a useful, though limited, guide for selecting instructional levels. The classroom teacher might find the five minutes required by the Quick Placement Test a worthwhile investment of time, since she would get a better "feeling" of the child's reading than is provided by group achievement test scores. However, due to the fact that the diagnostic section requires about 30 minutes and provides additional data requiring some caution and expertise in interpretation, it might be better used by a reading specialist, although classroom teachers may find it useful for a few selected children.

Few instruments cover as wide a range as do these two tests together, and few provide the variations of word recognition, oral reading errors, and oral/silent reading comprehension (with and without rereading). While the tests provide a guide to selecting the level of reading material to be used in instruction, the value of that guidance is limited by the many unvalidated assumptions that are made. Research on the validity of the assumptions and provision of normative data could make these tests outstanding instruments.

EDWARD R. SIPAY, *Professor of Education and Director of Reading Clinics, State University of New York at Albany, Albany, New York.*

Because SPIRE 1 and 2 have primarily the same overall format and procedures (the word lists and reading selections are different), the following comments apply to both kits, except as noted. Basically, SPIRE consists of two discrete individually administered tests. The Quick Placement Test (QPT) yields an instructional level, operationally defined as the highest grade (reader) level at which the arbitrarily determined criteria for both the word recognition (70 percent) and silent reading (60 percent)

subtests are met. Since QPT testing is terminated if the criterion for silent reading is met on the first selection given, the child's QPT instructional level cannot exceed his score on the word recognition subtest. The administration sample is misleading in this regard because it indicates that since the criterion is met, the next higher level should be administered.

Four types of questions (main idea, detail, inference, and vocabulary) are asked on this and the other SPIRE oral and silent reading selections. However, most of the questions involve details. Not every selection has the same number of each type question or even at least one question of every type. Nor is there an equal total number of each type. Such an unequal distribution is very likely to influence test interpretation as suggested in the manual. How many of each type a child is asked, and therefore the number answered correctly and incorrectly, will depend upon which selections are read. Some main ideas are factual, others inferential, but this distinction is not indicated. Many users probably will disagree with some of the classifications (e.g., some detail questions appear to call for inferences).

The questions and suggested answers should be studied carefully by potential test users. For example, one question asks, "What evidence did the author have that the Indians were not to blame for the dead saguaros?" "None" is the suggested answer; however, the last sentence in the selection reads, "All the evidence indicated the Indians were at fault until, one day, I heard a man remark that many saguaros far south of our land were dying." In another case the answer to a silent reading question is given in the oral selection which is read prior to the silent selection.

The QPT score is less likely to be accurate for children at the initial stages of learning to read. At these levels of ability, silent reading (one of the criteria) usually receives little emphasis or practice.

The other SPIRE test, the Diagnostic Individual Reading Evaluation (DIRE), uses the same word lists as the QPT. But the DIRE word recognition subtest allows an additional 7 seconds for each word not responded to correctly in 3 seconds. Correct responses on these second attempts are added to the number originally correct to determine if the 70 percent criterion has been met. Therefore, it is possible for one child to meet the criterion for successful word recognition using a 3-second criterion, another to do so using a combination of criteria, and yet another to be successful only when a 10-second criterion is employed.

Although one's initial impression, perhaps due to the manual format, is that there are separate oral and silent subtests, both the oral and silent selection at a given level are administered before going on to the next higher level. Separate oral and silent reading scores are not yielded by the DIRE, although they could be derived by deviating from the suggested administration and scoring procedures.

When judging the learner's instructional level, examiners should take into consideration the number of words for which the student just meets the 7-second criterion in oral reading and the 10-second criterion in word recognition. Although both sight vocabulary and decoding skills may be employed in reading, any child who needs the maximum time to decode many words at a given level very probably will find that material difficult, even though he may pass the comprehension criterion (the test is untimed and the child is allowed to consult the selection). Placing a child in daily instruction using such reading material may put him in a continual stressful situation.

Oral reading errors are scored as either one point or a half-point, but clearcut guidelines are not offered for making some decisions. Nor is the rationale for the distinction between one-point and half-point errors always apparent. For instance, why should omissions of all pronouns count only a half-point, when pronouns often are important to obtaining meaning? Allowances for dialect variations in scoring are not mentioned; thus, many black dialect renditions would be counted as at least half-point errors.

The oral word accuracy, combined retention, and the combined comprehension scores (simply whether the criterion for each was passed or failed) are used, singularly and in combination, in deciding what action to take after the oral and silent reading selections at a given level have been administered. A key to aid in making such decisions is provided, but a few directions are confusing or unclear. For example, in three situations the examiner is instructed to go up one level and down one level if this is the first

selection given. No rationale for the procedure is offered. Is the lower selection administered first, then the higher selection? Is the higher selection still given if the student fails the criterion on the lower level? The final direction on page 18 is very confusing. It states that testing is completed when the actions prescribed in the key have been taken. If the criteria for all three scores are met, the examiner is instructed to go up one level. Certainly testing is not terminated if all three criteria are also met at the next higher level; or is it?

The key for determining the student's independent, instructional, and frustration levels indicates that the same single and combined scores are used as in determining the range of testing. These levels also are based on arbitrarily set standards (e.g., 60 percent for retention and for comprehension). Four instructional levels are so defined (1 hard, 2 medium, and 1 easy), but how does one use this information? If the student's instructional levels are 6, 7, and 8, as in the SPIRE 2 example, what level of reading material is used for which instructional purposes?

The Student Problem Individual Reading Evaluation form is used for recording the student's instructional, frustration, and independent levels. It also contains a 24-item problem checklist which is filled out after analyzing the student's performance on the DIRE. Only the reading levels are directly derived from the test scores; the other information is based on an analysis of the student's performance, primarily in oral reading. A few checklist items present some problems. For example, on what basis does one decide whether a child "does not understand meaning of words usually found at grade level"? Such decisions could not be based on the student's performance on the vocabulary items on the comprehension check because some levels do not contain such items. Even where three vocabulary items occur at a level, does two correct out of three indicate a strength or weakness? For the reasons cited in the second paragraph of this review, it would be very difficult to make decisions regarding weaknesses in the various types of comprehension.

RELIABILITY AND VALIDITY. Reliability coefficients ranging from .95 to .98 are reported for scores on word accuracy (diagnostic only), oral and silent comprehension, and quick placement.

SPIRE Individual Reading Evaluation

No explanation is given for omitting such data for oral and silent reading retention scores, which are used in making administration and interpretation decisions. Reliability data are not reported for the DIRE instructional levels, which appear to be the main scores derived from the test; nor are any relationships between QPT and DIRE instructional levels indicated. Such information would be of value in test interpretation.

Surprisingly, exactly the same reliability coefficients are reported for both SPIRE 1 and 2. Was the same inadequately described sample of 60 subjects used for both forms? Even if not, the small number of subjects spread across 7 or 10 grade levels may have contributed to these extremely high reliability coefficients.

Exactly the same validity coefficients comparing the DIRE (.91) medium instructional level (which one?) and the QPT instructional level (.88) with the sample's scores on a standardized reading achievement paragraph meaning subtest are again reported for both SPIRE 1 and 2. Validity coefficients, ranging from .73 to .88, also are indicated for SPIRE 1 QPT scores and subtests of two other tests. Overall, these coefficients indicate the test has satisfactory concurrent validity.

SUMMARY. If the questions raised in this review were answered satisfactorily, if the noted weaknesses were overcome, and if the reliability and validity data were verified with a larger, well-defined sample, SPIRE could prove to be a useful test in determining a student's instructional reading levels. A great deal more would be required to make it a diagnostic test.

[774]

★Sand: Concepts About Print Test. Ages 5-0 to 7-0; 1972; early detection of reading difficulties; individual; 1 form (20 pages); no specific manual; combined manual (31 pages) for this and other diagnostic measures; NZ $1.50 per test; $1.50 per manual; postage extra; (5–10) minutes; Marie M. Clay; Heinemann Educational Books Ltd. [New Zealand]. *

[775]

Sipay Word Analysis Tests. Grades 1–adult; 1974; SWAT; criterion referenced; item, part, trial, and total test scores are reported as fractions (number correct over number presented); fraction scores are converted into qualitative ratings of specific skill strengths and weaknesses based on "arbitrarily chosen criteria"—can or probably can perform the skill (68–100% correct), may be able to perform the skill (51–67%), cannot or probably cannot perform the skill (0–50%)—and "performance objective scores" (95%

correct); no data on reliability; no norms; individual; 1 form; 17 tests; battery manual (34 pages); $73 per set of testing materials including 12 sets of answer sheets and report forms; 12 answer sheets and report forms: $1.80 (Tests 1–3, 8–10, 13, 16), $2.70 (Tests 11, 12, 15), $3.60 (Tests 4, 6, 7), $4.50 (Test 5), $7.20 (Test 14); $2.50 per specimen set (complete set of test cards not included); cash orders postpaid; (10–20) minutes per test; Edward R. Sipay; Educators Publishing Service, Inc. *

a) SURVEY TEST. For determining which specific tests and parts of other tests should be administered; each referral is based upon the first failed item in 3 trials; 58 cards; manual (2 pages); answer sheet (1 page); 90¢ per 12 answer sheets.

b) TEST 1, LETTER NAMES. 2 parts: lower case, upper case; items administered 3 times in different order; 30 scores; 56 cards; manual (3 pages); answer sheet (1 page); report form (2 pages).

c) TEST 2, SYMBOL-SOUND ASSOCIATION: SINGLE LETTERS. 2 parts (sounds, words) for consonants, vowels; items administered 3 times in different order; 28 scores; 29 cards (same as for Test 1); manual (4 pages); answer sheet (2 pages); report form (2 pages).

d) TEST 3, SUBSTITUTION: SINGLE LETTERS. 3 parts: initial consonants, final consonants, medial vowels; 7 scores; 61 cards; manual (6 pages); answer sheet (1 page); report form (2 pages).

e) TEST 4, CONSONANT-VOWEL-CONSONANT TRIGRAMS. 3 parts: initial consonants, final consonants, vowels; 4 scores; 69 cards; manual (7 pages); answer sheet (3 pages); report form (3 pages).

f) TEST 5, INITIAL CONSONANT BLENDS AND DIGRAPHS. 3 parts: blends, digraphs, triple clusters; 12 scores; 109 cards; manual (7 pages); answer sheet (7 pages); report form (2 pages).

g) TEST 6, FINAL CONSONANT BLENDS AND DIGRAPHS. 2 parts: blends, digraphs; 8 scores; 62 cards; manual (7 pages); answer sheet (5 pages); report form (2 pages).

h) TEST 7, VOWEL COMBINATIONS. 4 parts: vowel digraphs, diphthongs, vowel combinations (more common, less common); 16 scores; 76 cards; manual (8 pages); answer sheet (5 pages); report form (2 pages).

i) TEST 8, OPEN-SYLLABLE GENERALIZATION. 6 scores; 16 cards; manual (4 pages); answer sheet (1 page); report form (2 pages).

j) TEST 9, FINAL SILENT E GENERALIZATION. 6 scores; 16 cards; manual (4 pages); answer sheet (1 page); report form (2 pages).

k) TEST 10, VOWEL VERSATILITY. 6 scores; 25 cards; manual (5 pages); answer sheet (1 page); report form (1 page).

l) TEST 11, VOWELS + R. 3 parts: single vowel + r, 2 vowels + r, single vowel + r + silent e; 12 scores; 49 cards; manual (5 pages); answer sheet (2 pages); report form (2 pages).

m) TEST 12, SILENT CONSONANTS. 4 scores; 22 cards; manual (5 pages); answer sheet (2 pages); report form (2 pages).

n) TEST 13, VOWEL SOUNDS OF Y. 4 scores; 10 cards; manual (4 pages); answer sheet (1 page); report form (2 pages).

o) TEST 14, VISUAL ANALYSIS. 3 parts: monosyllabic words, root words and affixes, syllabication; 53 scores; 104 cards; manual (13 pages); answer sheet (6 pages in 2 parts); report form (8 pages in 3 parts).

p) TEST 15, VISUAL BLENDING. 2 parts: component elements into syllables, syllables into words; 9 scores;

32 cards; manual (5 pages); answer sheet (2 pages); report form (2 pages).

q) TEST 16, CONTRACTIONS. 17 scores; 22 cards; manual (3 pages); answer sheet (2 pages); report form (2 pages).

REFERENCES

1. ROVELLI, VIRGINIA ANNE. *A Comparison of Three Instructional Sequences for Learning the Grapheme-Phoneme Vowel Correspondences.* Doctor's thesis, State University of New York (Albany, N.Y.), 1972. (*DAI* 33:2623A)
2. BROWN, VIRGINIA L. "Review of the Sipay Word Analysis Tests." *J Learn Dis* 9(4):201–5 Ap '76. *
3. FELDMANN, SHIRLEY C. "Review of the Sipay Word Analysis Tests." *Read Teach* 29(4):411–2 Ja '76. *
4. *Read Teach* 30(5):546–7 F '77. [See letters by Else S. Carter, Edward R. Sipay, and Shirley C. Feldmann.]

ROY A. KRESS, *Professor of Psychology of Reading, Temple University, Philadelphia, Pennsylvania.*

The *Sipay Word Analysis Tests* are designed to measure a reader's ability to apply decoding skills in the recognition of unknown words in three basic areas: visual analysis, phonic analysis, and visual blending. There are 17 tests in all: a survey test which provides basic information about the reader's word analysis skills and serves as an entry battery, and 16 additional tests which are to be used selectively as indicated by the results of the survey test. The total battery represents a very comprehensive coverage of the sequence of phonic and structural analysis skills usually taught in the basic word recognition program developed in the primary grades.

Each test has four components: (*a*) a minimanual containing instructions for the administration, recording, scoring, and suggested follow-up testing; (*b*) a set of test cards; (*c*) an answer sheet; and (*d*) an individual report form. There also is a separate manual which contains general information regarding the construction and use of the entire series of tests. The author claims content validity because the tests "measure the skills needed to decode words not recognized at sight" and, since each skill is tested three times, reliability is also "assured." However, no data regarding either reliability or validity are presented.

The SWAT is designed primarily as individual diagnostic tools for use with learners of any age who are experiencing difficulty with decoding. Since the tests are basically diagnostic in nature, the label of "criterion-referenced test" is ill-conceived although, by definition, correct.

Since SWAT is to be used selectively, administration time will vary according to the learner and the number of tests employed. Since each test item is exposed for a maximum of five seconds and the number of items on the separate tests vary, no set time for administration can be estimated. However, maximum time for the longest test (156 items) would be about 15 minutes. The author estimates that 10 to 20 minutes would be "reasonable" for administration to any one child. The time required for analysis and interpretation of test results will depend upon the examiner's skill and ability to use the detailed suggestions provided in the manual(s).

Skills are measured in isolation (without context) using letters, letter combinations, nonsense syllables, and whole words, depending upon the specific skill involved. In some instances, combinations of skill application must be utilized by the examinee. In constructing the test stimuli, the author employed two basic criteria: no stimulus word could appear on Dale's list of 3000 familiar words and no word could appear in print more than once in approximately 100,000 words according to the *Word Frequency Book.* Test items were sequenced on the basis of frequency in American English based upon a cited study by Hanna et al.

SWAT may be used as an effective diagnostic tool in a variety of situations. (*a*) In a clinic setting where little is known about the child's ability, use of the survey test and the subsequent administration of the appropriate follow-up tests would provide valuable diagnostic information. In a similar manner it could be employed by the classroom teacher at the beginning of the school year. (*b*) Selectively, a particular test(s) may be used to confirm learning or lack thereof following a period of instruction with respect to the specific skill(s) included in the test. (*c*) Since the skills are sequenced, a higher level test might be used to assess a child's knowledge of certain skills *prior* to a planned period of instruction in those skills and thus reduce redundant learning activity for the child. (*d*) Conceivably, SWAT could also be used as one measure of the effectiveness of a particular skill development program.

SWAT is a well prepared diagnostic test of word analysis ability. Based upon sound research data, the content is effectively sequenced and will provide a valuable diagnostic tool for clinicians, classroom teachers, and researchers who wish to measure rather precisely a child's ability to attack unknown words *out of context and without meaningful semantic feedback.* Two major limitations are inherent in the tests. (*a*) The use of words (real or nonsense) in isolation prevents the examinee from employing two of the most important clues to word recognition— context and an oral known counterpart against which to monitor the correctness of his/her response. Because of this, the tests, at the various criterion levels established in the manual, no doubt require a higher level of decoding ability than is actually needed for reading in context. (*b*) Validity and reliability have not been statistically established although the author has indicated that these data are forthcoming.

WILLIAM J. VALMONT, *Associate Professor of Reading, University of Arizona, Tucson, Arizona.*

Each of the 16 tests in SWAT may be used individually or in combination to evaluate a subject's performance over those phonic and structural analysis skills typically taught in first through third or fourth grades. Rather than considering this battery appropriate for a given school grade, users should determine whether or not the tests are appropriate for analyzing skills to which their subjects have been exposed. Length of time for administering tests is variable, depending upon which are used.

A serious limitation of the SWAT is the lack of statistically determined "precision" of the test items. The author indicates that because elements are presented in isolation, the SWAT probably requires a higher level of decoding ability than actually needed for reading, since semantic and syntactic variables are not operable. This being the case, the test may needlessly refer students for teaching or remedial activities. Content validity may be debatable for two reasons: (*a*) the isolation of elements, and (*b*) the use of real words which some subjects may recognize as sight words, even though some precautions have been taken against this event.

The recommended practice of "detailed analysis" (e.g., administering the Vowel Digraph test and then analyzing beginning and final consonants in addition to the element being tested) is cumbersome and redundant. There are specific tests for such elements in other sections of the battery which could be administered and evaluated more easily. If the precision of each item in each test were determined, there would

be no value in continuing to reevaluate similar items in other tests.

Potential users of the instrument should consider the following points: (*a*) Test 2 (Symbol-Sound Associations) requires subjects to produce "letter sounds" in isolation. This test would be pertinent only for those subjects learning to read through synthetic phonics programs. (*b*) The stimulus cards in Test 8 (Open-Syllable Generalizations) contain artificially divided words to which subjects respond by pronouncing the first syllable. It is questionable that this contrived circumstance permits examiners to determine accurately the way subjects would process words in reading situations. (*c*) Test 15 (Visual Blending) also contains artificially divided stimulus cards, and the same concern applies. (*d*) All "report forms" contain arbitrarily chosen "performance objectives" stated in terms that might appear to be more appropriate to norm-referenced tests. These statements are of no value in reporting to others the exact phonic or other skill difficulties of any subject.

While most tests and items in the SWAT battery appear to be technically accurate, it would behoove potential users to examine the instrument carefully. The author has presented many suggestions for further testing (trial teaching) when difficulties arise and has presented ample suggestions for overcoming diagnosed difficulties. Test cards and the 16 minimanuals permit great flexibility in selecting appropriate tests tailored to an individual, but instructions and procedures are tremendously redundant. The SWAT should be useful to clinicians and reading specialists but of limited use to classroom teachers because of time and analysis factors.

J Learn Dis 9(4):201–5 Ap '76. Virginia L. Brown. Probably a great portion of remedial and developmental programs in learning disabilities involves word analysis skills, especially symbol-sound correspondence, or phonics. Whether or not the time and effort spent on these skills can be justified, it is nevertheless probable that the practice will endure. Consequently, continuing attention should be paid to the status of tests and techniques in word analysis. * Sipay assumes that a learner eventually should acquire word analysis or decoding skills

Sipay Word Analysis Tests

and, further, that these skills are usually taught in isolation, "although they probably do not function in isolation" (*Manual,* p. 1). This test, or series of 17 tests, is designed to provide detailed symbol-sound correspondence information for planning individualized programs of isolated decoding skills. * (User note: The kit that holds copies of answer sheets and report forms is not durable. The lack of lid arrangement makes storage a problem, and the kit is not easily portable. In addition, cards are lost unless handled carefully—a rubber band will help hold them in place.) * In order to prevent learner confusion and thus mislead the analysis of responses, real words or syllables from real words are used rather than nonsense words and syllables. * The deliberate use of words likely to be outside the learner's speaking/meaning vocabulary removes a powerful cue to word analysis that is usually available to the reader. The intent here is to isolate the word analysis skill as much as possible from other acquired language techniques. This intent is also reflected in the decision to use words and syllables rather than words in context. The removal of words from their context or linguistic environment is intended to focus on the skill in isolation. * Sipay's criteria for stimulus selection are usually well considered. Especially commendable is the notion of moving from visual stimuli to pronunciation. This procedure is in contrast to the practice of having the student write a graphic or letter response to stimuli presented vocally, or to select from several alternatives. This reviewer's primary question relates to the validity of employing any such isolated procedures to test a skill that is rarely, if ever, used in isolation from the usual cues. Commendably, Sipay tempers his discussion regarding the nature of word analysis skills with words such as *likely, probably,* and *may.* His approach is a refreshing contrast to those who treat their constructs as reality. Three skill areas are discussed at great length by the author. These are visual analysis, phonic analysis, and visual blending. It is assumed that these skills are applied rapidly and sequentially by the reader who is trying to decode an unfamiliar word. The author also considers that many other skills contribute to success in word analysis, but his discussion is limited to these three areas. Sipay relies heavily upon Burmeister's (1971) reading related

analysis of the sound-to-symbol spelling data developed by Hanna et al. (1966). The choice of Hanna as a base, rather than the more relevant work of Weir (1964) or the earlier work of Venezky (1967), is puzzling. Hanna is concerned with sound-to-symbol relationships (spelling), while Weir and Venezky deal with spelling-to-sound relationships (reading). The discussion of this section is laden with the esoteric terminology of word analysis. In fact, it is so burdensome in its hypotheses about how learners analyze words that I wonder if the processes described are grounded in child-based data about the reading process or in adult logic. This question is critical because the latter opens the door to calling a student learning disabled because he or she does not understand and use a laborious process superimposed by adults. Evident throughout the Sipay manual is the assumption that because a student is able to make the appropriate symbol-sound associations, he or she knows the generalizations they represent. Conversely, if a student does not make the associations, it is because he does not know the generalizations. Further, most remedial programs actually teach the generalization as a means of getting the student to make the association. This practice is analogous to that of the language clinician who notes a problem with production of appropriate verb tenses. It is unlikely that the clinician would teach the child the rules of syntax in order to change his behavior. Rule-memorizing and deductive approaches to learning appear to be unnecessary and undesirable in much of general language training, with the notable exception of reading behavior. (Somehow, only teachers seem determined to teach both grammar and reading by making children memorize rules.) We must ask the hard question of why this appears to be so, especially since we have little data about the efficacy of rule-learning approaches to the learning-to-read process. * the assumption that word recognition errors made during oral reading are due to faulty symbol-sound correspondence is certainly incomplete. This heavy implication is especially unfortunate because Sipay otherwise notes the problems of trying to isolate these elements, especially in the reality of connected discourse. Sipay says that his tests possess content validity because they require the decoding of words not recognized by sight. This comment is

Sipay Word Analysis Tests

somewhat circuitous in that any word unknown to the student should meet that criterion. The value of these tests seems to be in the preselection of target stimuli and in the systematic arrangement of stimuli. What the test purports to measure is, "the decoding aspect of the reading act" (*Manual*, p. 1). Careful selection of stimuli was made to increase the probability that most of the useful generalizations and associations needed to decode unfamiliar words were tapped. The stimuli themselves cannot be separated (for test purposes) from how the responses are coded and interpreted. The question is whether or not the symbol-sound correspondence skills noted are indeed adequate representations of the universe of skills needed to decode unfamiliar words. This is not likely the case. Sipay himself notes throughout the manual that other skills are necessary for word recognition. Yet, he never says where these skills fit into the total program of word analysis. * it is improbable that the tests offer adequate representations of the constructs, visual analysis, phonic analysis, and visual blending, even as they are defined in the SWAT manual * Reliability is said to be accounted for by providing at least three different items for each symbol-sound association sampled. This statement does not deal with how often students make correct responses to one, two or three of these item sets. Neither does it consider inter- and intra-examiner reliability, or test-retest reliability. By calling SWAT a criterion-referenced test, one can assume that Sipay felt no need to deal further with reliability, or to present normative data. The user is cautioned, then, against making any normative comparisons or statements about a learner's performance on the SWAT. In order to make any such comments, the examiner would have to know a great deal about what the student and his or her peers have been taught, i.e., the instructional history of the student(s). He or she also would have to know about other aspects of the learner's reading behavior that are normatively based. This reviewer believes that the author's neglect of the preceding questions is unfortunate, yet helpful in that it forces individual consideration of the student's responses rather than a normative statement. The Sipay Word Analysis Tests have received analytical attention because they are a relatively good representation of tests of this genre. Many features

of the SWAT could well be used as a basis for comparing similar word analysis tests. Focus upon individual vocal response to written symbols, careful selection and arrangement of stimuli, and certainly the improved recording and reporting formats are well worth careful consideration by the learning disabilities clinician involved in word analysis. At least as many questions are raised as are answered here. It may well be that it is impossible to design a reading test that adequately will assess in isolation a skill that in practice is used in a complex combination of many other abilities. In spite of reservations, this reviewer believes that Sipay's procedures are a cut above those generally available to learning disabilities.

Read Teach 29(4):411–2 Ja '76. *Shirley C. Feldmann.* * The tests seem clearly structured and designed to obtain a thorough analysis of the learner's word analysis skills. The answer sheets require a careful listing of each response. The individual report form details specific strengths and weaknesses, performance objectives, analysis of performance, trial teaching, and suggested follow-up testing for each skill. Yet the thoroughness with which each skill is analyzed prompts some questions about the tests as a whole. First, at a suggested time of ten to twenty minutes per test, *SWAT* has an administration time of three to five-and-a-half hours per child. Although the mini-manuals suggest selective administration, the criteria given are complex and do not lead to easy selection or ordering of priorities. There is also a question whether the tests measure the skills needed to read unknown words. The manual warns that children may be able to apply the skills in the separate tests but still be unable to decode unknown words. It further suggests that an oral reading sample be used as a pretest for determining which tests to give. Perhaps oral reading alone might be more efficient for determining the child's ability to integrate and apply known skills than assessment of separate skills. The rationale and interpretation of the tests also have some weaknesses. The claim that *SWAT* is criterion-referenced is weak, since the definitions of behavioral objectives and criteria for mastery are vague. The tables for classification of specific skill strengths and weaknesses are not only difficult to interpret but seem to have no rationale. The most serious fault is the complete absence of evidence that the test does what it is said to do. Reliability and validity are slighted in the manual and no mention is made of test tryouts with children. These are unthinkable omissions for a test published in a time when the value of all reading assessment is being questioned. Therefore, despite *SWAT*'s efficient packaging, the tests seem to have some serious limitations. Before buying *SWAT* one should ask whether the same information could be obtained from a shorter battery, and more importantly, do the tests yield the information needed to help a child with his reading.

[776]

★**Skills Monitoring System: Reading.** Grades 3, 4, 5; 1974-75; SMSR; 3 levels; 2 areas: word identification (grade 3 only), comprehension; criterion-referenced tests for a given level and area consist of a diagnostic survey test (Skill Locator) and a series of specific-objective tests (Skill Minis); the Skill Locator tests for a given level and area consist of test booklets containing 27–36 2-item specific-objective subtests (items are selected from the corresponding Skill Mini tests) with mastery defined as both items correct; the Skill Mini tests for a given level and area consist of 27–36 specific-objective tests (98% of which have 8–12 items) with mastery defined as 80% correct; the Skill Locator tests identify objectives not mastered, the Skill Mini tests are used for checking results which seem questionable to the teacher and for determining mastery following further instruction; reliability based on 1974 field test version; no norms; 1 form; teacher handbook ('75, 48–49 pages) for each level and area; individual record ('75, 1 page) for each level and area; special markers must be used with self-scoring latent-image Skill Mini tests; $2 per 35 individual records; $6 per 12 markers; $3 per teacher handbook; $2.50 per specimen set of any one level and area; postage extra; scoring service for Skill Locator tests, 75¢ and over per test; (45–60) minutes per Skill Locator, (6–10) minutes per Skill Mini; Psychological Corporation. *

a) WORD IDENTIFICATION. Grade 3; 27 objectives: visual perception (3), phonic analysis (14), morphemic elements (10).

1) *Skill Locator.* Test booklet ('75, 7 pages, MRC scorable); $17.50 per 35 tests; $1.25 per key.
2) *Skill Mini.* 27 tests ('75, 2 pages each); $67.50 per 16 sets of tests.

b) COMPREHENSION. Grades 3, 4, 5; 25–28 objectives (29–36 subtests) at any one level: word meaning in context (5–7 objectives), literal meaning (6–8 objectives), interpretation (8–12 objectives), critical reading (2–5 objectives).

1) *Skill Locator.* Test booklets ('75, 11–12 pages, MRC scorable); $22 per 35 tests; $1.25 per key.
2) *Skill Mini.* 29 tests (grade 3), 35 tests (grade 4), 36 tests (grade 5); tests ('75, 2 pages each); 16 sets of tests: $72.50 for grade 3, $87.50 for grade 4, $90 for grade 5.

JASON MILLMAN, *Professor of Educational Research Methodology, Cornell University, Ithaca, New York.*

The *Skills Monitoring System: Reading* includes two types of tests, Skill Minis and Skill Locators. The Skill Minis are one-sheet tests consisting of eight or more items measuring a single reading skill. The Skill Locators are multi-skill survey tests containing items similar to those appearing on the Minis. (Typically, two items on the Locator reference each skill.) Also available are class and individual record sheets, suggestions for classroom instructional management patterns, and a teacher resource book that suggests additional instructional resource material.

The SMS is not tied to a particular reading curriculum. The 27 word identification skills measured at the third grade level and the 100 overlapping reading comprehension skills assessed over grades 3–5 have been selected on the basis of their recognized importance. The SMS is intended to provide a means by which the educator can monitor proficiency on these skills. Advocacy of the use of the assessment materials presupposes that specific skill instruction is an effective means toward the goal of improved reading.

The tests are designed to permit criterion-referenced interpretations; that is, to identify specific skills that the student has or has not mastered. The tests are not timed and relative comparisons among students are discouraged. (No norms are provided, for example.)

It is recommended that the Locator test be given first to allow an initial determination, based on the 2-item subtests, of the student's mastery/nonmastery status on each skill. After instruction on the skills referenced by the subtests not passed, the proficiency status of the student is then assessed with the longer, corresponding Skill Mini instrument. Only one form of each Skill Mini test is available, thus preventing retesting with a fresh set of items.

Scoring of the Skill Mini tests can be facilitated by using the latent image feature of these tests. The students "erase" the answer boxes with the "magic crayon" to expose whether or not the choice is correct ("Y" for yes or "N" for no appears). This feature permits students to correct their own Skill Mini tests. Obtaining the roughly 30 subtest results from each student's Locator answer sheet is a more formidable task. These test results are placed on class and individual student record sheets by hand, or

Sipay Word Analysis Tests

by computer if the user elects to use the publisher's test scoring service.

The user is provided with brief statements describing each skill, e.g., "Identify the sentence that has the same meaning as a given sentence." Such statements provide some information about the skill area but are not sufficient descriptors of the behaviors to be shown by the learners and of the stimuli to be used to elicit the behaviors. Missing is information about the test items' possible content, how the wrong options were created, how the items were sampled, and so on. Admittedly, few publishers of criterion-referenced tests provide this information, but without it the user does not know what the student can or can't do after taking a Skill Mini test. By changing the item content, the attractiveness of the incorrect choices, or other features of the item, the test writer can control whether only a few or most students will be labeled "masters" while still producing a test that measures the stated skill or objective. What then does it mean to say the student has or has not passed? Since the test items were not sampled from a defined population, the user cannot make generalized, criterion-referenced interpretations from the Skill Mini test scores.

Except for the problem of lack of domain specification mentioned above, the test construction effort has followed reasonable and responsible procedures for item tryout and for detecting needed revisions. Field test sample sizes and reliability indicators are quite acceptable.

Having eight or more items in each Skill Mini test is a strong feature of the SMS. Many other criterion-referenced tests attempt to determine mastery on the basis of only one or two items. As the SMS instructions imply, the results of the two-item subtests on the survey Locator test should not be taken as the final word.

The consumer does have to pay the costs associated with development and packaging. Less expensive criterion-referenced reading tests are available (e.g., reusable spirit masters distributed by the Instructional Objectives Exchange or locally constructed devices), but in these instances, the user perhaps sacrifices quality and convenience for economy of price.

SUMMARY. The educator who wishes a system to assess specific reading skills of students in grades 3–5 that is independent of any particular reading curriculum should seriously consider the SMS. Strong points include its responsible test development effort, test reliability, the latent image feature, the availability of the survey Locator test, and teacher resource and management suggestions.

The fact that the test items are not sampled from a well-defined population of tasks, the lack of an alternative form of the tests, the record keeping associated with individual student/specific objective monitoring assessment systems, and the price may be considered negative features.

[777]

*Stanford Diagnostic Reading Test. Grades 1.5–3.5, 2.5–5.5, 4.5–9.5, 9–13; 1966–76; SDRT; previous edition (Levels 1 and 2) still available; 2 forms; 4 levels; 2 editions (hand scored, MRC scored) for grades 1.5–5.5; $3 per specimen set; postage extra; Bjorn Karlsen, Richard Madden, and Eric F. Gardner; Psychological Corporation. *

a) RED LEVEL. Grades 1.5–3.5; 1966–76; 6 scores: word reading, comprehension, total, auditory vocabulary, auditory discrimination, phonetic analysis; Forms A, B, ('76, 14 pages); manual ('76, 95 pages); $12.50 per 35 hand scored tests; $14.95 per 35 MRC scored tests; $3.50 per set of hand scoring stencils; MRC scoring service, 90¢ and over per test; (150) minutes in 3–5 sessions.

b) GREEN LEVEL. Grades 2.5–5.5; 1966–76; 7 scores: auditory vocabulary, auditory discrimination, phonetic analysis, structural analysis, comprehension (literal, inferential, total); Forms A, B, ('76, 15 pages); manual ('76, 96 pages); prices same as for a; (165) minutes in 3–5 sessions.

c) BROWN LEVEL. Grades 4.5–9.5; 1966–76; 7 scores: auditory vocabulary, comprehension (literal, inferential, total), phonetic analysis, structural analysis, reading rate; Forms A, B, ('76, 11 pages); manual ('76, 106 pages); separate answer folders (MRC, hand scored) must be used; $12.50 per 35 tests; $7.70 per 35 MRC answer folders; $3.50 per 35 hand scored answer folders; $2.75 per set of hand scoring stencils; MRC scoring service, 85¢ and over per test; (113) minutes in 1–5 sessions.

d) LEVEL 3 [BLUE LEVEL]. Grades 9–13; 1974; 12 scores: comprehension (literal, inferential, total), vocabulary (word meaning, word parts, total), decoding (phonetic analysis, structural analysis, total), rate (scanning and skimming, fast reading, total); Forms A and B consist of 2 parts: reusable test booklet (14 pages), MRC test-answer booklet (4 pages); manual (48 pages); $14.50 per 35 tests; $8 per 35 answer booklets; $3.25 per set of scoring stencils; $3 per specimen set; scoring service, 60¢ and over per test.

See T2:1651 (2 references); for a review by Lawrence M. Kasdon of Levels 1–2 of the earlier edition, see 7:725 (3 references).

REFERENCES

1–3. See 7:725.
4–5. See T2:1651.
6. WINKLEY, CAROL K. "What Do Diagnostic Reading Tests Really Diagnose?" pp. 64–80. In Diagnostic Viewpoints in Reading. Edited by Robert E. Leibert. Newark, Del.: International Reading Association, Inc., 1971. Pp. viii, 133. *
7. BURG, LESLIE ANNE. An Analysis of Factors Related to Reading Disability as Evidenced in Three Specifically Identified

Groups. Doctor's thesis, Boston University (Boston, Mass.), 1972. (*DAI* 33:1311A)

8. NAYLOR, MARILYN JO. *Reading Skill Variability Within and Among Fourth, Fifth and Sixth Grade Students Attaining the Same Reading Achievement Score.* Doctor's thesis, University of Minnesota (Minneapolis, Minn.), 1972. (*DAI* 33:6239A)

9. RAISCH, VIRGINIA. *An Evaluation of the Effectiveness of Group Reading Instruction on Skills as Defined in the Stanford Diagnostic Reading Test.* Master's thesis, California State University (Hayward, Calif.), 1972.

10. RHODES, LEE ROY, JR. *The Effect of a Cloze Procedure Methodology on Reading Comprehension of Sixth Grade Students of Varying Reading Ability.* Doctor's thesis, University of Maine (Orono, Me.), 1972. (*DAI* 33:6598A)

11. STOLL, PATRICIA DONATH. "A Study of the Construct and Criterion-Related Validity of the Stanford Diagnostic Reading Test." *J Ed Res* 66(4):184–9 D '72. *

12. BELL, ANNE WOODS. *A Study of the Shift in Error Patterns Between Instructional and Frustration Levels Among Grade Developmental Readers.* Doctor's thesis, Oklahoma State University (Stillwater, Okla.), 1973. (*DAI* 34:5466A)

13. KARNES, FRANCES NESSLER. *A Comparative Analysis of Individual and Group Auditory Discrimination Tests for Disabled Third Grade Readers in a Lower Socio-Economic Group.* Doctor's thesis, University of Illinois (Urbana, Ill.), 1973. (*DAI* 34:7468A)

14. SANDERS, COLUMBUS NELSON. *Correlations of Reading Achievement With Various Phonic Word-Recognition Skills for Inner-City Black Children.* Doctor's thesis, University of Oregon (Eugene, Ore.), 1973. (*DAI* 34:3041A)

15. BURNHAM, CAROLYN JOAN STIGMAN. *Reading Achievement Survey in Granite School District—A Diagnostic Study of Skills and Deficiencies of Seventh Grade Students.* Doctor's thesis, University of Utah (Salt Lake City, Utah), 1974. (*DAI* 35:4119A)

16. HOFF, JEAN ESTELLE. *The Effect of IOX Objectives-Based Reading Test Collections Upon Fifth-Grade Comprehension and Word-Attack Skills.* Doctor's thesis, North Texas State University (Denton, Tex.), 1974. (*DAI* 35:6940A)

17. LETON, DONALD A. "The Structure of the Stanford Diagnostic Reading Test in Relation to the Assessment of Learning-Disabled Pupils." *Psychol Sch* 11(1):40–7 Ja '74. * (*PA* 52:6384)

18. THURMOND, VERA BELINDA. "The Effect of Black English on the Reading Test Performance of High School Students." *J Ed Res* 70(3):160–3 Ja–F '77. *

BYRON H. VAN ROEKEL, *Professor of Education and Director, Reading Center, Michigan State University, East Lansing, Michigan.*

Users of the first edition of the SDRT may have difficulty recognizing the 1976 revision. Even a cursory examination of the new edition reveals significant alterations in format, subtest content, manuals, methods of expressing test scores, and the interpretation and use of test results. Acknowledging the merits of the first edition, the changes incorporated in the revision have contributed materially to the quality and usefulness of the test.

The primary purpose of the 1976 edition is consistent with the basic philosophy which influenced the development of the tests 10 years earlier; namely, that the purpose of diagnostic reading assessment is to lead to the improvement of the reading ability of all pupils. Accordingly, the primary purpose of the test is "to diagnose pupils' strengths and weaknesses in reading." Because the SDRT was designed to provide particularly accurate assessment of low-achieving pupils, the authors caution that "the test will have limited usefulness in classes of gifted pupils or in situations where many pupils

are superior readers." This should not be perceived as a serious limitation, simply because gifted pupils and children who are superior readers are not likely to exhibit serious deficits in the first place.

Previous users of the SDRT will recall that the 1966 edition was published in two levels, designed for use with pupils in grades 2.5 to 4.5 and in grades 4.5 to 8.5. In the new edition, the coverage of these tests has been expanded to provide for the assessment of pupils from the end of grade 1 to the end of grade 8 and the test content has been assigned to a hierarchy of three levels: Red Level—for end of grade 1 and grade 2 (and low achievers in grades 3 and over); Green Level—for grades 3 and 4 (and low achievers in grades 5 and over); and Brown Level—for grades 5 through 8 (and low achievers in grades 9 and over). Because no explanation is given, one can only speculate that the authors, in the interests of greater precision, resorted to a three-level hierarchy to reduce the grade range coverage of the lower level tests. A fourth level, now known as the Blue Level, was published in 1974 for use with high school and community college students.

Because the serious diagnostician will want more from these tests than a cursory listing of attributes, shortcomings, and technical data, it may be propitious to examine the assumptions and rationale which guided the authors in the development of the SDRT. From the manuals, one learns that "the SDRT authors view reading as a developmental process with four major components: decoding, vocabulary, comprehension, and rate." Other statements in the manual and a careful study of the content and structure of the tests reveal that the authors assume a hierarchical set of component skills which lead to the acquisition of reading—hierarchical in the sense that the learning of lower level skills is prerequisite to the learning of skills later in the sequence. Accordingly, each of the levels is said to provide for the measurement of various components of the reading-decoding and reading-comprehension acts, sequenced according to order of complexity. The desired performances on the various subtests at each level are described in terms of behavioral objectives which have been classified in a sort of three-tiered structure proceeding from "Skill Domain" objectives to "Item Cluster" objectives to "Item"

Stanford Diagnostic Reading Test

objectives—the distinction among which, despite the intriguing labels, is mainly a matter of increasing specificity.

The previous comment should alert the potential user to examine two crucial matters which shaped the content and structure of the tests: (a) From whence came the objectives? (b) What influences determined the sequencing and placement of the objectives along the hierarchy of skills measured by these tests? For the former, the authors are said to have identified the "instructional objectives" common to most reading programs by reviewing state and city curriculum materials and major reading series, a process which leads one, at once, to question the sufficiency of common practice as a measure of validity. In the case of the latter, "Each objective was assigned to the level at which the target population should have developed the skill," although neither the identity of the target population nor the means for determining the expected achievement level is revealed. This reviewer would have viewed with much more favor a set of objectives derived from an empirically based theoretical model of reading acquisition and a hierarchical sequencing based on some form of component task analysis.

The authors have been painstaking in the construction and refinement of the testing materials. The manual is well done and meets professional standards for describing the rationale, development, and technical characteristics of the test. Procedures for administering and scoring the tests and interpreting and using the test results are clear, concise, and complete. Technical characteristics seem to be highly satisfactory—K-R 20 reliabilities range from .79 to .98 for the various subtests across levels, with a vast majority of the coefficients exceeding .90. Inter-subtest correlations, for the most part, fall substantially below reliabilities, suggesting at least some degree of independence among the skills measured by the subtests.

The authors feature two types of scores, content-referenced scores and norm-referenced scores. The norm-referenced scores include the usual fare of percentile ranks, stanines, grade equivalents, and scaled scores. Content-referenced scores include raw scores and progress indicators—the latter apparently a coinage for criterion raw scores which supposedly distinguish among pupils who are competent in the

measured skill and those who have not acquired the skill in sufficient degree to advance to the next level of instruction.

The use of content-referenced scores should appeal to diagnosticians who are obliged to determine where in the hierarchy of reading skills measured by this test the pupil should begin his study in order to maximally adapt instruction to his needs It should also appeal to teachers who must manage and adapt instruction for groups composed of pupils referred from different levels of grade placement. However, the user of these tests will want to evaluate "the goodness of fit" of the test objectives and progress indicators (criterion scores) with the objectives and expected level of competency of the local curriculum by asking these questions: (a) Are the skills needed for successful performance on this test those we believe to be essential to the acquisition of reading? (b) Do the test items adequately define our objectives of reading instruction? (c) Do the criterion scores provide a sound basis for generalizing a pupil's performance on similar collections of skill domains? Such inquiry is desirable simply because techniques for validating learning hierarchies and content-referenced scores are not readily available. In recognition of this, the authors have provided suggestions for selecting the test performance information most useful in the local school.

Considerable attention is given to the use of the test results. In one 10-page section of the manual, the authors describe three patterns of organizing groups of pupils for "prescriptive teaching," which is claimed to be more individual than traditional grouping because it groups together pupils who need help with the same skills. Included are a variety of instructional alternatives which the authors describe as specific suggestions for helping pupils in each group. A casual inspection of the more than 80 itemized suggestions will reveal that most of them are not sufficiently explicit and precise to insure that independent teachers would teach the same skills to the same pupils, and an experienced teacher will note a striking similarity to the "kitchen hints" found in textbooks designed for use in method courses in reading.

The SDRT has few peers among group diagnostic reading tests. It provides test information that should prove useful to teachers without spe-

Stanford Diagnostic Reading Test

cial training in diagnosis and remediation. Teachers will need to give careful attention to the interpretation and use of the test data simply because the directions for using the results assume considerable sophistication in test theory. Users of this test should recognize the limitations of group diagnostic testing and refer the more severely deficient pupils to a skilled and experienced diagnostician.

[778]

Wisconsin Tests of Reading Skill Development: Word Attack. Grades kgn–2, 1, 1–3, 2–4, 3–6; 1970–72; WTRSD:WA; part of the Wisconsin Design for Reading Skill Development; criterion referenced; 6–16 "single-skill" scores at each of 5 levels; no norms; 80% mastery criterion suggested for each subtest with retesting at next higher level if a child fails not more than one subtest, and retesting at next lower level if a child passes not more than one subtest; 2 forms ('72); 2 formats: consumable booklet, ditto masters; administrator's manual ('72, 12–28 pages) for each level; teacher's planning guide ('72, 41 pages); Design overview ('72, 173 pages); profile card ('72, 2 pages); additional instructional materials available; $12 per 100 profile cards; $1.50 per administrator's manual; $4 per planning guide; $5 per Design overview; cash orders postpaid; sampler free (sample pages only); overview and planning guide by Wayne Otto (principal investigator) and Eunice Askov; tests and manuals by Karlyn Kamm, Pamela J. Miles, Deborah M. Stewart, Virginia L. Van Blaricom (tests), and Margaret L. Harris (tests); NCS Interpretive Scoring Systems. *
a) LEVEL A. Grades kgn–2; "early readiness" level; 6 scores: rhyming words, rhyming phrases, shapes, letters and numbers, words and phrases, initial consonants; Forms P (16-page booklet or 16 ditto masters), Q (16 ditto masters); $17 per 35 consumable booklets and manual; $16 per set of ditto masters; (105) minutes in 4 sessions.
b) TRANSITION LEVEL A–B. Grade 1; "advanced readiness or preprimer" level; selected items from Levels A and B; 7 scores: rhyming words, rhyming phrases, words and phrases, initial consonants, beginning consonants, ending consonants, consonant blends; Forms P (16-page booklet or 14 ditto masters), Q (14 ditto masters); $17 per 35 consumable booklets and manual; ditto masters must be assembled from Levels A and B; (110) minutes in 4 sessions.
c) LEVEL B. Grades 1–3; "primer or first reader" level; 11 scores: beginning consonants, ending consonants, consonant blends, rhyming elements, short vowels, consonant digraphs, compound words, contractions, base words and endings, plurals, possessives; Forms P (12-page booklet or 11 ditto masters), Q (11 ditto masters); $13.50 per 35 consumable booklets and manual; $11 per set of ditto masters; (120) minutes in 4 sessions.
d) LEVEL C. Grades 2–4; "second reader" level; 16 scores: consonant variants, consonant blends, long vowels, vowel plus r/a plus l/a plus w, diphthongs, long and short oo, middle vowel, 2 vowels separated, 2 vowels together, final vowel, consonant digraphs, base words, plurals, homonyms, synonyms and antonyms, multiple meanings; Forms P (20-page booklet or 17 ditto masters), Q (17 ditto masters); $20.50 per 35 consumable booklets and manual; $17 per set of ditto masters; (175) minutes in 5 sessions.
e) LEVEL D. Grades 3–6; "third reader" level; 6 scores: 3-letter consonant blends, silent letters, syllabication, accent, unaccented schwa, possessives; Forms P (8-page booklet or 7 ditto masters), Q (7 ditto masters); $10 per 35 consumable booklets and manual; $7 per set of ditto masters; (65) minutes in 2 sessions.
See T2:1655 (1 reference).

REFERENCES

1. See T2:1655.
2. Askov, Eunice N. "The Word Attack Element of the Design." Yearb Nat Read Conf 21:249–52 '72. *
3. Otto, Wayne. "Rational and Overview of the Wisconsin Design." Yearb Nat Read Conf 21:245–8 '72. *
4. Rude, Robert T. "Implementation and Field Testing of the Design." Yearb Nat Read Conf 21:265–72 '72. *
5. Cox, Janet Elizabeth. A Comparative Study of Two Approaches for Teaching Reading: Basal Reader Plus Management System Versus Basal Reader. Doctor's thesis, University of Georgia (Athens, Ga.), 1975. (DAI 36:4986A)
6. Rude, Robert T.; Niquette, Sheldon; and Foxgrover, Phyllis. "The Retention of Visual and Auditory Discrimination Reading Skills." J Ed Res 68(5):192–6 Ja '75. * (PA 53:12503)
7. Rude, Robert T.; Otto, Wayne; and Klumb, Roger W. "Retention of Specific Reading Skills by Primary Grade Pupils Under Varied Teacher Incentive Conditions." J Ed Res 69(9):323–30 My–Je '76. *

Rebecca C. Barr, *Research Associate, The University of Chicago, Chicago, Illinois.*

The Wisconsin Word Attack tests are designed to aid elementary teachers in instructional planning and evaluation. Each skill area tested is keyed to appropriate instructional activities within selected published materials and within the Wisconsin Design Teacher's Resource File. Pupil performance on the skill tests in relation to mastery criterion provides the basis for determining the level and emphasis of instruction.

ORGANIZATION. For each of the five levels described above there is a booklet edition which contains all group-administered skill tests, and an edition of separate tests for each of the skills included in the booklet edition. There are two parallel forms, P and Q, for the separate tests edition, but only Form P for the booklet edition. In addition, six skill tests (Distinguishes Colors at Level A; Sight Vocabulary at Levels B, C, and D; Left-to-Right Sequence at Level B; and Independent and Varied Word Attack Skills at Level C) must be administered individually and are therefore not included with the booklet and separate edition tests. The booklet edition is recommended for initial group testing, and the separate tests edition for retesting prior to instruction and evaluation following instruction.

ADMINISTRATION AND SCORING. Directions for test administration, to be read "word for word," appear to be adequate for the higher level tests. For Levels A and A–B, however, the provision

Stanford Diagnostic Reading Test

of only one example may be insufficient for some children.

The authors make recommendations concerning appropriate group sizes at each of the five levels and for pacing particular tests, all of which are untimed. A disadvantage of the tests is the total time required for their administration: four class periods for the first three levels, five for Level C, and two for Level D. Tests yield the following information for each skill: raw score, uncorrected for guessing; percentage of items correct; and mastery determined in accord with the local criterion.

RELIABILITY. In the test administrator's manuals accompanying each level, evidence is summarized in one sentence: "Reliabilities of individual tests are in the .70's and .80's with a few in the .90's." These 1972 administrator's manuals then state that "further specific information appears in the *Technical Manual: Word Attack.*" Unfortunately, no such technical manual has been published to date!

VALIDITY. The tests are criterion referenced; test items were constructed to measure the word attack skills that were identified by the test authors and defined in behavioral terms. On this basis the authors claim the content validity of the tests.

Certain problems that frequently attend content interpretation have been avoided. For example, pictures included in the tests are named by the teacher so as to eliminate a potential source of confusion. Most of the skill tests are homogeneous in item content, and typically the test label indicates test content. However, the tests of beginning consonant sounds and ending consonant sounds (Level B) contain two item types: tests of sound-symbol associations and of auditory discrimination. Only one test is grossly mislabeled, Base Words (Level C). Since base words are constant within items and affixes vary, the test appears to measure children's ability to select a contextually appropriately affixed word. Several tests (A-2, B-10, C-13, C-18) seem to measure how children use contextual information rather than or in addition to their knowledge of rhyming, contractions, multiple meanings, and base words.

The extensive use of nonsense words—in more than a third of the tests—may be problematic. No evidence is presented indicating that the brief training provided to familiarize students with nonsense words is sufficient to eliminate the difficulties that some children experience with them. About a third of the tests require spelling, as opposed to reading, processes. Most of these, pertaining to consonant and vowel letter-sound associations (Levels B and C), involve the processes of listening to a nonsense word and selecting a spelling that corresponds to a portion of the nonsense word. Though reading and spelling processes are related, they are clearly not isomorphic in English.

The use of nonsense words and spelling processes may not invalidate the tests, but concurrent validation is necessary to substantiate the claim that reading skills are being assessed.

Because this collection of tests is used for instructional planning, it is important to know the degree to which tested skills are necessary and sufficient for word attack and contextual reading. The test authors state, "Like other components of the *Design,* the Word Attack tests are based on an outline of skills essential for reading skill development in the elementary school years." Yet they provide no evidence to support this assertion. Further, assumptions concerning the interdependence and difficulty of skill tests determine the order of tests within and between levels. This order, in turn, influences the sequence of instruction; but no evidence to support the hierarchical arrangement of word attack skills is provided. A distinction needs to be made between skill sequences for which there is some logical or empirical basis and those which are, in fact, arbitrary and therefore may be treated flexibly.

SUMMARY. The tests have the advantage of requiring little expertise on the part of the teacher for test administration and instructional planning. Potential problems of content validity, failure to provide evidence concerning the reliability and concurrent validity of specific tests, and failure to demonstrate the contribution of specific skills to word attack proficiency and contextual reading competence should lead to caution in the use of the tests.

RICHARD RYSTROM, *Associate Professor of Reading and Linguistics, The University of Georgia, Athens, Georgia.*

The purpose of the Wisconsin Word Attack tests is to determine how well students have mastered the word attack skills identified within

Wisconsin Tests of Reading Skill Development: Word Attack

the Wisconsin Design. In general, satisfactory performance is set at 80 percent. In determining what the word attack skills are, the authors state that they "have taken a rather traditional and eclectic approach to Word Attack in reflecting the broadest possible base in terms of school practice in the teaching of word attack skills." As the authors point out, "the levels are arranged in sequence, but the skills within a given level are not necessarily arranged in a hierarchical sequence."

Most of the skills tests are untimed group tests in which the teacher leads the students through the items one by one or through individual sections. When all have finished, they move together to the next item or section. The entire test is also available in sections, so teachers can select any particular section to administer to individual students (for example, to evaluate a new student in the classroom). To assist in grouping for after-test instruction, there are McBee-type cards teachers can use to place children into skill groups.

There are three substantial advantages to the Wisconsin Word Attack tests. First, the tests are exceptionally comprehensive. Virtually every reading behavior a teacher could want (or need) to measure is included in the tests. Second, the tests can be used to make an objective diagnostic evaluation of each child's strengths and weaknesses. The authors state, in a discussion of postassessment and regrouping, that "experience in our pilot schools indicated that children who were dismissed from skill groups on the basis of teacher judgment only did not retain at a later date as many skills as children dismissed on the basis of satisfactory performance on the parallel form of the WTRSD subtest. Therefore, formal assessment after instruction is recommended." Third, there are activity materials which teachers can use prior to testing, designed to increase the probability that children will know the skills on which they will be tested. In the event children do not meet the criterion, there are also supplementary materials available, as well as an exceptionally complete index to where, in all of the materials available at the end of 1974, teachers could find instructional material in printed and audiovisual sources.

It was noted earlier that the Wisconsin Word Attack tests were derived from the practices of classroom teachers. This approach to test construction produces mixed feelings. On the one hand, it enhances the usefulness of the tests for classroom teachers, it frees them from being tied to any particular reading series, and it increases the probability that they will use the tests. On the other, it means that the tests are a somewhat miscellaneous collection of skills, without a comprehensive theory of reading behind the selection or omission of any particular skill. As the authors point out, "Differences from certain other approaches, particularly those with a linguistic orientation, may appear to be irreconcilable, and we admit that we have not discovered a way to resolve the conflict to everyone's satisfaction." This "conflict" has led to some peculiar, and unnecessary, anomalies within the tests. In Level B, Test 6, for instance, children are asked to find which word rhymes with *log: lag, bag, bog, leg.* The *-og* words are notorious for their variability across dialects. In some regions, all *-og* words are pronounced identically; in others, there are as many as four different pronunciations. Another item from the same test presents *book: read, crook, booked, boot.* While *crook* is clearly the intended answer, one reason why children might logically select *booked* as the answer is that many younger children do not consistently and accurately use this morphological feature, and that fact in no way interferes with their reading comprehension.

In Level C, Test 7, children are asked to decide whether *-oo-* words contain long or short vowels, where *book* is considered short and *moose* long. The problem is that the long vowel sound in *moose* is the long-*u* vowel sound, cf. *dun, dune.* In English orthography, the vowel sound in *book* is usually spelled *-oo-*, but the vowel sound in *boot* is usually *-u-*. These sounds are long and short (if "long" means a vowel is rounded or glided), but they are not related to each other in the same ways the vowel pairs *back-bake, them-theme,* and *long-lone* are. In Level D, Test 5, where children's ability to pick out accented syllables is being measured, one of the items is the word *July,* given first syllable stress in some regions of the United States, second syllable stress in others; the answer key allows only the latter choice.

Some of the test anomalies are, of course, the inevitable result of writing any test: unfortunate but unavoidable. Much more serious are those which have resulted from a willing dismissal of forty-plus years' examination of the nature of language and its relationships to our orthographic system. When the members of the Wisconsin Design, who are an exceptionally able group of scholars, chose to make the best possible tests they could, assuming they would restrict themselves to normal schoolroom practices, they chose to be followers rather than leaders.

In sum, the *Wisconsin Tests of Reading Skill Development: Word Attack* is a thorough and well-developed set of tests measuring the skills identified within the Wisconsin Design as those practices commonly employed in most classrooms. They provide an accurate estimate of children's reading skills and diagnostic information about which skills need additional work, with some indications of where teachers might begin instruction. In all ways, the tests do an excellent job of attaining the goals the test makers set for themselves. The only criticism is that the authors could have set their goals higher by choosing to lead our collective wisdom rather than to follow it.

[779]

Woodcock Reading Mastery Tests. Grades kgn-12; 1972-73; WRMT; 6 scores (letter identification, word identification, word attack, word comprehension, passage comprehension, total) plus derived scores in these same 6 areas at each of 4 levels (easy reading level [96% mastery], reading grade score [90% mastery], failure reading level [75% mastery], relative mastery of grade level); individual; Forms A, B, ('73, 155 pages); manual ('73, 129 pages); response forms ('73, 6 pages) for each form; $22 per kit of either form, 25 response forms, and manual; $3.85 per 25 response forms; $3.50 per manual; postage extra; (20–30) minutes; Richard W. Woodcock; American Guidance Service, Inc. *

REFERENCES

1. BANNATYNE, ALEX. "Review of the Woodcock Reading Mastery Tests." *J Learn Dis* 7(7):398–9 Ag–S '74. *
2. PROGER, BARTON B. "Review of the Woodcock Reading Mastery Tests." *J Spec Ed* 9(4):439–44 W '75. *
3. ALLINGTON, RICHARD L. "Review of the Woodcock Reading Mastery Tests." *J Read* 20(2):162–3 N '76. *
4. DeGRAFFENRIED, HELEN LEE. *Use of the WISC-R to Determine Intellectual Differences Between Average and Retarded Readers and to Predict Reading Achievement as Measured by the Woodcock Reading Mastery Test.* Doctor's thesis, Brigham Young University (Provo, Utah), 1976. (*DAI* 37:877A)
5. FOUSE, ANNA BETH FORRESTER. *A Study of Auditory Perception, Visual Perception, and Phonics Abilities of Fourth and Sixth Graders.* Doctor's thesis, Texas Woman's University (Denton, Texas), 1976. (*DAI* 37:4278A)
6. HOUCK, CHERRY, AND HARRIS, LARRY A. "Review of the Woodcock Reading Mastery Tests." *J Sch Psychol* 14(1):77–9 sp '76. *
7. WILLIAMSON, ANN POLLARD. *An Analysis of Error Patterns of Disabled Readers at the Secondary Level.* Doctor's thesis, Texas Woman's University (Denton, Texas), 1976. (*DAI* 37:4292A)

CAROL ANNE DWYER, *Program Director, Elementary and Secondary School Programs, Educational Testing Service, Princeton, New Jersey.*

The *Woodcock Reading Mastery Tests* are an ambitious, carefully constructed series of individual reading tasks which promise solutions to many of the problems of teachers, clinicians, and researchers through application of the latest psychometric techniques to reading assessment. Unhappily, this promise remains largely unfulfilled.

H. L. Mencken described hope as the pathological belief in the occurrence of the impossible. The keen sense of disappointment inspired by these tests may well be due in part to the very high, perhaps impossible, expectations they generated among reading and psychometric professionals. The Woodcock tests have as their fundamental objective to provide very precise meaures of reading ability which are easy to administer and interpret. This objective has been only partially achieved.

The tests are available in two parallel forms, each of which is intended for use with students from kindergarten through grade 12. The coverage of this wide age span with a single instrument, coupled with the availability of parallel forms, is an especially useful feature for the reading researcher, who is often faced with the problem of noncomparable test content between elementary and secondary school reading measures. The five subtests are letter identification (45 questions), word identification (150 questions), word attack (50 questions), word comprehension (70 questions), and passage comprehension (85 questions). An index of total reading is also generated.

The test booklet is a sturdy easel-type ring binder which is placed between the test taker and the administrator so that the stimuli are provided to the taker at the same time the stimuli, notes, and directions are visible to the administrator. The tests, graphics, and overall design are attractive but the artwork is somewhat old-fashioned. The type used in the stimuli is almost primer size and quite clear. A very comprehensive manual is provided which incorporates background information, administration instructions, and technical data.

The titles of the subtests seem similar to those found in many familiar survey reading tests, but there are important differences which preclude making comparisons among them without reference to the actual test content and response format.

The letter identification subtest requires the student to name 45 letters. The importance of including such a subtest in a general reading test is questionable, particularly in a test which aspires to administrative efficiency. Letter identification is more useful as a readiness measure than as a measure of reading per se. In addition, the performance ceiling has been artificially raised through the inclusion of unusual typefaces and letter shapes, including cursive, gothic, roman, and italic variations. The generalization of a child's visual discrimination skills to these typefaces would appear to be of little interest to most reading practitioners.

The word identification subtest consists of single words in isolation. Great care was taken in the choice of these words and their sources are well documented in the manual. The range of difficulty covered is very wide ("go" to "facetious"), and items include irregularly pronounced words as well as those which may be correctly pronounced through application of pronunciation generalizations. This subtest will certainly offend those who stress word recognition through use of context clues, but it stands as a well-done example of a traditional reading task. The same may be said of the word attack subtest, which utilizes single "nonsense" words. This task is not universally accepted as salient to fluent adult level reading, but the subtest itself is well constructed and could be useful in individual diagnosis of reading errors for planning classroom instruction.

The word comprehension subtest is much more than simple single-word comprehension. The task for the student is to complete a series of single-word analogies. While vocabulary is certainly a large part of this task, it is also confounded with distinct reasoning and classification skills at the lower as well as at the upper ranges of difficulty, since the rationales for the analogies are varied and occasionally complex (e.g., building is to body as girders is to—; and two is to four as three is to—).

The passage comprehension subtest also presents difficulty in its interpretation and use. The manual describes this subtest as a "modified cloze procedure," and modified it is. Words are deleted from the passage comprehension materials not by mechanical and prespecified rules, but by purposeful deletion of key words and concepts. In many instances, the deletion quite transparently implies a direct question based on the preceding material and might more usefully have been cast in that format. In addition, pictures have been included as comprehension aids in the earlier items.

There is no evidence of attempts to measure higher level reading skills such as inference, evaluation of logic, or analysis; instead, the use of abstruse materials seems to be relied on for difficulty.

Overall, the test content gives the impression of trying to serve too many masters. Some of the material is clearly useful primarily in a diagnostic context; other sections seem to be useful only as predictors of complex skills and to have no discernable diagnostic or instructional utility. Yet these distinctions are not alluded to anywhere in the manual. The test content as a whole seems best suited for use as a global screening measure for reading disability and not for any more precise decision.

The test content is noticeably sex-role stereotyped. Although the Woodcock materials were prepared several years ago, there has certainly been time enough available to edit them for sexism. Girls and women appear less frequently in the stimulus materials, and usually in the roles of mother, wife, nurse, and pupil, in contrast to the portrayal of boys and men in a wide range of roles and activities. It is especially disturbing to see a new test introduced with this sort of material included, when there will probably be no major revision of it for ten years or so.

The manual combines administration instructions and technical data. To the reading or assessment professional, the manual is clear, complete, and accurate. However, the mass of data presented could overwhelm the test administrator who is simply seeking "how-to" guidance. The manual suggests that the tests can be administered by paraprofessionals, but the manual itself was certainly not written with them in mind.

The appendices describe a wide variety of administrative and interpretive procedures. The interpretive options, however, dwell on the procedures to follow, rather than on establishing a rationale for selecting them. Information is provided on use of separate percentile ranks for boys and girls and on use of SES-adjusted per-

Woodcock Reading Mastery Tests

centile ranks, but no mention is made of why one would wish to do this. These "alternate interpretive procedures" simply describe other sets of norm tables that are available, and how to determine a testee's SES.

Once the directions for administering the test have been located, actual administration is relatively simple. The easel format is convenient and much useful information is provided on the examiner's side of the page. The easel and its contents are of exceptionally sturdy materials, which will be especially appreciated by those who work with young children. The administration time is relatively short for an individual test, but this advantage is offset by the difficulty of scoring and interpretation, to the point where a group test might actually prove more efficient.

The tests present an ambitious combination of innovative and traditional approaches to measurement. The test items were analyzed and calibrated using Rasch-Wright procedures. The manual does not present enough information on the procedures to determine if the Rasch-Wright model's assumptions were met. Since this was such an important part of the test's development, it is disappointing not to have a full technical description in this area. However, the test development procedures described indicate such an outstanding attention to high quality procedures that one feels confident of the quality of other test content and assembly procedure standards.

The Woodcock tests seem stronger in the area of technical procedures than in interpretation of these procedures and their results. For example, the manual defines criterion-referenced testing at length, citing Cronbach's rather inclusive definition of CRT as testing in which "provision is made for translating the test score into a statement about the behavior to be expected of a person with that score." Even with such a definition in hand, the Woodcock tests are very clearly designed as norm-referenced tests. In addition, the test content is such that meaningful CR interpretations would be difficult even to derive, and are certainly not provided by the test makers.

The norms provided are clearly presented, thoroughly researched, and well constructed. The separate-sex and SES-adjusted norms provided seem technically sound, but their rationale is weak. The manual suggests that the separate-sex norms will probably not be of significance for most users—but then, the user asks, why supply them? To whom are they of interest, and why? The user is left without guidelines for when and how they should be used. Absence of guidelines can only aggravate the problems reading specialists now encounter in dealing with the knotty question of sex differences in reading. The SES-adjusted norms present a similar problem, but in addition, the score adjustments required are done on an individual basis, require a great deal of detailed background information, and are time-consuming for the practitioner to calculate.

Split-half and alternative-form reliabilities for the current form are reported only for grades 2 and 7. The inclusion of pretest reliability data is not useful and probably misleading, since the pretests are not identical with the final forms. The publisher's catalog claims that "split-half reliabilities for the five tests generally were in the .90 to .99 range." In fact, the subscore reliabilities range from .02 to .99 by the split-half method. Of the 20 final-form subscore reliabilities given, 7 are below .9 and 13 at or above .9. The test-retest reliabilties range from .16 to .94, with median .84. These are not disgraceful reliability estimates, but neither are they exceptional for an individual measure. Some of the subtests have quite low reliabilities for decision-making at the individual level; the test-retest reliability of .83 reported for the total score in grade 7 is quite low for individual use. In the matter of validity, again the claims far exceed the data, although the data are probably no worse than those of other major reading tests. Shortcomings of content validity have been discussed above. What is called "predictive validity" in the manual is a clear example of parallel form reliability, and claims for multimethod, multitrait analyses are totally without foundation.

CONCLUSION. The *Woodcock Reading Mastery Tests* are an interesting and ambitious effort but seriously flawed. They make claims to innovation and technical quality that are, upon close examination, not supported by data, and will thus be disappointing to many measurement and reading specialists.

Woodcock Reading Mastery Tests

J. JAAP TUINMAN, *Professor of Education, Simon Fraser University, Burnaby, British Columbia, Canada.*

Psychometrically, the *Woodcock Reading Mastery Tests* is the most unusual battery of diagnostic reading tests published in this decade because of the variety of derived scores. Raw scores are first converted into "mastery scores" which are then used to obtain the normed scores. It would have been less misleading had the author used the term "standard scores," since the "mastery scores" do *not* indicate the degree of mastery of learning. For example, a "mastery" score of 120 on the five subtests represents a range of grade scores from 1.9 to 12.9; and a range of percentages which raw scores are of the possible scores from 38 to 85 percent. Yet the author claims that the "mastery" scale consists of *"equal"* units; that is, "the units on the scale are the same size at any level, therefore they have the same meaning at every level." Woodcock goes on to say, "Any given difference between two points on the Mastery Scale has the same meaning at any level and in any of the five skill areas measured by the test." Woodcock's definition of "same meaning" is difficult to accept. For example, a pupil with a "mastery" score of 90 on all five tests would obtain grade scores of 1.3, 1.7, 2.5, 4.6, and 3.4; and percentages of possible scores of 43, 20, 30, 46, and 39. If the pupil were to increase his "mastery" score to 120, however, he would receive grade scores of 1.9 (up .6), 2.1 (up .4), 7.5 (up 5.0), 12.9 (up 8.3), and 7.8 (up 4.4); and percentages of possible scores of 67 (up 24), 38 (up 18), 85 (up 55), 76 (up 30), and 73 (up 34). Thus a gain of 30 mastery points is equivalent to a range of grade score gains from .4 to 8.3; and a range in percentage of possible score gains ranging from 18 to 55.

Although the test claims to be a criterion-referenced test as well as a norm-referenced test, no interpretative use is made of item or total raw scores. Even the grade scores are ambiguous and difficult to interpret. Traditional grade scores are not used. Instead, three estimated grade score equivalents are provided representing the grade levels at which pupils' mastery of "reading tasks" averages 75 percent ("failure reading level"), 90 percent ("reading grade score"), and 96 percent ("easy reading level"). The "reading tasks" are obviously not all the

test items since 90 percent mastery of the tests items is equivalent to grade scores of 3.3, 8.8, 12.3, and 12.9 on the five tests.

In addition, the test provides an "achievement index" score which indicates the number of points a student's raw score is above or below the median raw score obtained in the norm group for his grade level. The "relative mastery at G" score is a prediction of percentage mastery a student would obtain if presented with reading "tasks similar to those that the average pupil at the subject's grade level could perform with 90 percent mastery." Percentile ranks within grades are also provided.

THE SUBTESTS. The selection of subtests is traditional and apparently not based on a specific theory of the reading process. The inclusion of the Letter Identification (LI) test is unusual, and the most useless, containing 45 letters printed in upper and lower case roman, sans serif cursive, and specialty typefaces. By the end of fourth grade most pupils are expected to achieve a perfect score. Since the LI score is added with the average, a fourth grader scoring at 4.9 on all other tests, with the expected perfect LI score, would have an inflated overall score by about .3 grade months. Moreover, missing one item drops the grade score from 12.9 to 6.2, thus illustrating the artificiality of the LI score scale.

In the Word Identification Test "there is no assumption that the subject knows the meaning of the word nor that he has ever seen the word before." However, some children manage to get a number of easy items right because they know them as sight words but fail to decode those words outside their sight vocabulary, while others rely on word attack skills. The test tends to measure different functions for different children.

The Word Attack Test measures "the subject's ability to identify nonsense words through the application of phonic and structural analysis skills." Despite the objection of many reading experts to this use of nonsense words, the test may potentially provide practical diagnostic information for those who operate in the context of phonics-based reading programs. However, as with the preceding test, error analysis rather than overall score is of most utility. The student is explicitly told that the test is made up of nonsense words yet several words, including a sam-

Woodcock Reading Mastery Tests

ple item, are real words. Contrary to the author's expectation, some children do recognize this fact. Again it appears that statistical criteria in item selection supersede considerations of content validity.

The Word Comprehension Test presents special problems with content validity. The author uses an analogy format. If a third grader misses the item: "book–read radio–_____" (for which the answer is listen), is one to conclude that the student does not know the meaning of "listen"? This test appears to be more one of reasoning than knowledge of words per se. Furthermore, while the examiner reads the sample items to the subject, during the actual test the subject must decode the word silently and then give the answer. Consequently, many children who are given the test *because* they are poor readers are penalized.

The Passage Comprehension Test is "of a modified cloze procedure type." Scores on this test again reflect decoding and comprehension problems. The poorer a decoder a student is, relative to the norming group, the more the test becomes a measure of word attack rather than of comprehension skills. Both this and the preceding test could have been made far more useful had additional norms been established for responses of students to whom the stimulus materials had been read.

There are two additional problems of content validity with this test. Twenty-nine percent of the items in both forms use pictures. Many poorly decoding students do well on these items, responding exclusively to the picture, and then fail to do any further items correctly. It is difficult to see in what sense these items measure "passage" or even "sentence" comprehension. Again, some of the research literature on the cloze technique shows that it is largely a measure of local redundancy and that it fails to measure understanding of large idea units. Moreover, correlations between cloze and conventional comprehension tests can vary as a function of grade; thus it may be assumed that the Passage Comprehension Test measures different functions for the lower grades than it does for the higher grades.

TECHNICAL DATA. The information on reliability is clear and sufficient. Corrected split-half reliabilities for four of the subtests are quite high, ranging from .83 to .99. Above the 2.9

grade level the reliability of the Letter Identification Test drops sharply and becomes negligible at the 7.9 grade level. In general, the tests are more reliable for the lower grades. The standard errors of measurement generally do not exceed two or three grade months, values quite acceptable for most school-based diagnosis.

Evidence for the validity of the test is far less satisfactory. Issues of content validity are discussed in part above. The publisher presents data from a multimethod-multitrait matrix, but correctly acknowledges that perhaps using alternate forms as different methods is conceptually inadequate. It is. A study to test the prediction of scores on one form from performance on the other is presented but, while of interest, the data add relatively little to the case for validity. No validity studies involving external criteria are reported. This is a decided weakness.

The major criticism regarding validity, however, involves the claim, central to the development of the test, of providing the user with a criterion-referenced set of scores. A recurrent theme in the manual is that the tests allow, with great precision, a prediction of "the subject's level of performance on content like that in the test." The basic problem is that "content like that in the test" has no operational meaning. Except, perhaps, in the case of the Letter Identification Test, the domain of behaviors underlying the items in the test has been left undefined. The test user must somehow extrapolate from the items the range and kinds of tasks on which the students will be successful/unsuccessful. To this end, the author provides "Reference Scales" which list the grade levels at which a person with a given mastery score has demonstrated 50 or 90 percent mastery on a "sample task." A child attaining a mastery scale score of 146 has a grade scale score of 2.9 indicating 50 percent mastery of identifying words like the sample task "certain." It takes a grade score of 3.6 to do the same at a 90 percent mastery level. The issue is that no criterion is provided the teacher to construct a domain of words of which "certain" is a representative! The "sample tasks" are provided, but what do they mean?

GENERAL EVALUATION. The strong points of this test are quickly evident. A wide variety of interpretive scores, highly reliable even for subtests, are available; a clear and concise manual is provided; test directions are easy and

Woodcock Reading Mastery Tests

largely void of ambiguity; and the multiple choice format has been avoided—all answers are open-ended. Three of the five subtests are of a type often used in reading diagnosis; the added precision provided by this test is welcome. The parallel of the relative mastery scores with the three reading levels yielded by conventional informal reading inventories is noted by the author.

Among the weaknesses of the tests are some minor ones, which can be easily corrected in subsequent editions. The administration time, "20–30 minutes," is unrealistic for most of the poor readers the test is likely to be used with. An administration time of 30–50 minutes would be more realistic, even if one urges on the non-responding subject after a few seconds, as the author recommends.

The derived scores assume a 90 percent success rate as proper mastery. Many measurement experts and reading education practitioners settle for 80 percent. The choice of the arbitrary 90 percent may by questioned by some users.

Finally, the two important and overriding criticisms are that the utility of two of the tests for the assessment of reading skills is very low and that claims for criterion-referenced interpretation are, when viewed from the perspective of instructional decision making, largely ungrounded.

The *Woodcock Reading Mastery Tests*, due to the precision of the measurements performed, can be a valuable tool in the hands of an experienced reading diagnostician. They are not recommended for a more general usage.

J Learn Dis 7(7):398–9 Ag–S '74. Alex Bannatyne. * An innovative feature is the provision of SES (socioeconomic status) adjusted norms; these are based on communities having similar SES characteristics to the local area. * The mastery tests will be particularly useful for clinical or research purposes and in many other situations for which precise measures of reading achievement are useful. * The tests are suspended on an easel which helps facilitate administration. Altogether it is a sturdy package unlikely to show wear even with years of use. * Unfortunately, the Woodcock Reading Mastery Tests do not assess speed or rate of reading (fluency), nor do they cover a knowledge of syntax (or grammatic closure). Even so, as

they stand, these tests are a remarkable achievement and a valuable addition to the diagnosticians' assessment battery. They are simple to administer and score, and are recommended to L.D. teachers and psychologists.

J Read 20(2):162–3 N '76. Richard L. Allington. * only rarely is a test developed that offers a variety of unique features while at the same time maintaining or improving both the assessment effectiveness and efficiency of its predecessors. Such is the case with the Woodcock Reading Mastery Tests * designed particularly for clinical use or research purposes and other situations where precise determinations of individual achievement are deemed desirable * The validity and reliability data provided are quite impressive and detailed * A somewhat unique feature that underlies both the selection of items and the norming of the test was the author's use of the Rasch analysis procedures. * another unique feature of the WRMT is the development of a criterion-referenced Mastery Scale which can be used for a variety of purposes * After nearly a year of use of the WRMT, this reviewer has found the combination of Word Identification, Word Comprehension, and Passage Comprehension Tests the most useful for assessing reading achievement in both clinical and research applications. The Word Attack Test is used at times for subjects referred from districts having reading programs with heavy emphasis on word attack skills. The Word Attack Test does tell one whether a subject can decode nonsense words, but experience demonstrates that unless previous instruction has focused on this behavior, subjects often score quite poorly in relation to the other tests. Several other features of the WRMT deserve mention. While the scoring of the various tests and the calculation of grade equivalents, mastery scores, and so forth seem a bit confusing at times to the novice who is more accustomed to simply recording a raw score or grade equivalent, the manual quite clearly presents complete and precise directions for completing these tasks. In addition, the manual presents substantial information on the interpretation of test results. The testing materials are well designed and present a nearly ideal administration package. All tests are contained in a single loose-leaf-style notebook which opens into an easy to use easel format. Stimuli for the subjects are easily

Woodcock Reading Mastery Tests

changed by flipping pages, with no awkward materials changes necessary. The availability of an alternate equivalent form makes retesting after a short period of time possible while eliminating the hazard of familiarity with particular items. In summary, experience using the WRMT supports the promotional and technical data provided by the publisher. It is an excellent individual reading achievement test which can be used to gather reading achievement data for a variety of purposes.

J Sch Psychol 14(1):77–9 sp '76. Cherry Houck and Larry A. Harris. * a battery of five tests (Letter Identification, Word Identification, Word Attack, Word Comprehension, and Passage Comprehension) that are designed to achieve the following objectives: (1) measure reading achievement with greater precision, (2) provide for ease of administration, and (3) allow more useful interpretation of test results by incorporating new reporting procedures. Some difficulty is encountered in evaluating the degree to which the first objective has been reached. This difficulty results primarily from the lack.... of any quantitative data to support the instrument's external validity. * In terms of content validity....the method for assessment of Word Comprehension and Passage Comprehension is open to question. An analogy format is used to measure a subject's knowledge of word meanings. It appears that responses to these items could be somewhat confounded by a subject's reasoning and classification abilities. Additionally, the "modified cloze procedure type" employed to measure Passage Comprehension is just that; it is modified. A reference to Bormuth (1969) for procedural documentation is not convincing inasmuch as the test items do not appear to meet Bormuth's criterion of "using a set of mechanically objective and prespecified rules" for determining the location of the deletions. In fact, the items resemble more closely a completion test where deletions are made "using subjective concepts such as key words." The modifications include the addition of picture clues for some items and, based on inspection, a nonspecified word deletion procedure. A means of assessing a subject's ability to remember details of what he has read or to make inference is not included. We question the importance of including a Letter Identification Test in a general measure of reading achievement. While research evidence links knowledge of letter names to early success in reading, results on such tests are primarily useful as a readiness measure. The Letter Identification Test artificially creates a range of item difficulty that extends into grade 4 by presenting the examinee with eight different type faces (including cursive and Roman). Whether children can generalize their visual discrimination skills to recognize unusual type faces seems to be an especially narrow question for a test of this kind to address. Given the stated objective for this test regarding precision of measurement, it seems reasonable to expect that a new instrument would reflect current psycholinguistic thought and research which indicates that recognizing words in isolation is a difficult and even artificial task. As with many word identification tests, words are presented in isolation without benefit of contextual clues in this test. Ample evidence is available to predict that children will fail to correctly identify words on this subtest that they can recognize and understand in context. More useful information would be yielded if the words were presented in a short phrase. The use of multitrait-multimethod matrix analysis to evidence convergent and discriminant validation is somewhat misleading as Woodcock admits. While there is reference to Campbell and Fiske (1959) for justification of the analysis procedure, inspection of the original article suggests that the assumptions which are associated with the analysis are not satisfied. Specifically, the multitrait-multimethod validation process assumes that multitraits are being assessed and that they are being assessed by at least two independent methods (Campbell & Fiske, 1959). It is difficult to interpret the use of Forms A and B of the WRMT (two different forms of the same test) as being two independent methods of measurement. The final procedure, a study "designed to evaluate and demonstrate the predictive capabilities of the WRMT" again is somewhat misleading. Predictions are made not to an independent measure, but to a subject's score when he is tested using an alternate form of the WRMT one week later. The author claims that the data resulting from this predictive study support the hypothesis of no difference, i.e., the hypothesis could not be rejected for each of the five subtests as well as the total reading score. The concluding statement "The results of this

Woodcock Reading Mastery Tests

study provide some evidence for the validity of making differential predictions of reading success at various grade levels from a subject's score on the Woodcock Reading Mastery Tests" seems to lack the necessary qualifiers. There appear to be no present data to support any prediction other than subject's scores when administered an alternate form of WRMT following a one-week interval. It seems that these data better support alternate form reliability than validity. Aside from the above considerations which may, following other studies to assess the instrument's external validity, prove of lesser importance, the second objective was met more closely. The WRMT manual presents precise directions for administration and scoring and, because of the packaging format, it is relatively easy to administer. Assessment over only a critical range permits more rapid completion, which should enable the subject to sustain his best effort. The additional feature of exposure to only one or a few items per page should decrease the amount of frustration encountered by subjects who have perceived their failure on previous item-cluttered tests. Test objective three is certainly approached. The user is provided with traditional as well as innovative reporting methods. * three concepts each represent newer interpretation procedures: (1) Relative Mastery, which suggests an instructional range; (2) the Achievement Index, which suggests the degree of reading retardation; and (3) the Relative Mastery at Grade, which predicts the degree of success a subject would have when given a test similar to those that an average pupil at the subject's grade could perform with 90% mastery. Unfortunately, a procedure for interpreting a subject's scores in terms of his socioeconomic status is involved and requires the collection of data for 11 factors. Although these data are readily available from census reports, users may find the adjustment procedure more time consuming than desirable inasmuch as a given school district may encompass several different communities with varying socioeconomic characteristics. This is unfortunate because normative data often do not permit sufficient consideration of a divergent population. One seemingly over-rated component is the joint norm-referenced criterion-referenced scale. The degree to which the developed reference scales represent a "developmental summary of reading

task mastery" is open to question. The assumptions made regarding the grade level at which certain skills will be mastered are questionable. First, the instructional program used with a child will obviously have a marked effect on the sequence of skills he has been exposed to. The sequence assumed by the author of this test will not apply equally well to children in various instructional programs. Second, despite the use of "mastery" in the label given to the test, it is plainly norm-based. Furthermore, without performance objectives for each item, the requirements for a criterion-referenced test are not met, thus making it difficult to make specific prescriptive statements from the Reference Scales. In summary, the WRMT comes to a market which longs for a precise method of assessing reading skills. The possibility that such an instrument could lead to diagnostic prescriptions using criterion-referenced procedures brings the practitioner to complete attention. Unfortunately, such a product is not here yet. The practitioner will need to collect additional data before specific diagnostic prescriptions may be developed. With further evidence of the WRMT's external validity, it may well be that it can serve effectively as a screening device for identifying children who are experiencing reading difficulties.

J Spec Ed 9(4):439–44 w '75. *Barton B. Proger.* * the only formal instrument....that has legitimately built into it several soundly constructed options for both CRM [criterion referenced measurement] and NRM [norm referenced measurement] * One of the more interesting features of the WRMT is that a test publisher has embodied a highly complicated but psychometrically pleasing model of test development based upon the work of George Rasch. * This provides a mechanism that not only gives a child's degree of mastery but also his predicted degrees of mastery on easier and harder material. * Despite the superb technical quality of the WRMT test development, it is questionable whether many test consumers can appreciate and take advantage of all the nuances of that development process. The manual presents a tremendous amount of detail on how the test was developed, which becomes confusing to one not immersed in the same processes as the author. The potential test consumer might be overwhelmed by the dialogue in certain parts of the manual (fortunately, large portions of this technical exposition, mainly in Part IV, are not crucial to successful use of the WRMT). Apart from this theoretical complexity, there is the practical problem of learning how to use the many NRM and (especially) CRM and CRM/NRM reporting options. As a consequence of the tremendous flexibility of the WRMT, problems in interpretation have increased. This means that it will therefore take the consumer longer than usual to become familiar with the reporting and interpretation procedures. Further, there is a puzzling policy of giving or not giving examples in the various subtests. In particular, Paragraph Comprehension has no examples (there are, however, pictorial cues). How much danger is there of this subtest being invalidated by a child's inability to understand directions? * Generally, the instructions to the child seem to be clear, and there should not be problems of note in this area. Apart from its length and variegated complexity, the WRMT manual is excellent. One cannot fault its 124 pages for poor documentation! Procedures of deriving NRM and CRM test scores are explained in full with examples. An extensive set of tables is provided for almost every interpretive option one can think of. Indeed, the manual goes so far as to give tightly structured procedures for shortening (or lengthening!) the test battery, as well as other adaptations of test administration (e.g., lessening the basal-ceiling restrictions) and interpretation (e.g., qualifying results by socioeconomic status). However, case studies are missing of what the two blank panels under each test on the score sheet might look like: "Diagnostic Interpretation of Errors" and "Implications for Instructions." It would have been desirable to have a few well-chosen examples to indicate how far one can go with test results, assuming that the consumer has adequate experience to make such recommendations. The validity data are somewhat sparse. It appears that while far, far more effort went into careful development and standardization of the test than one might reasonably expect, validity studies were given short shift. The predictive validity study is valuable in verifying the mastery scoring NRM/CRM procedures. However, the multimethod-multitrait study is somewhat misleading in that no *external* criteria were used; thus, there is really much less here than meets the eye. In this regard, there is the logistical problem of giving more than one lengthy individualized test to many children; however, some small-sample study could have been completed with truly independent criteria. Finally, some comments are in order on the format of the WRMT. The Easel-Kit is a sophisticated and suitable package for such an individually given test, although one must be careful that the loose-leaf ring mechanism does not become undone through careless closing of the booklet. One could question why Forms A and B are in separate Easel-Kits; both would fit in one binder, thus reducing the cost. *Conclusions.* The WRMT stands as a tribute to the current cutting edge of test-development theory. Its careful deployment of the Rasch model is noteworthy. The legitimate embodiment of both CRM and NRM should make the WRMT a useful addition to almost anyone's battery of clinical reading instruments. Not to be forgotten are the possibilities of research, program evaluation, and teacher training in sophisticated measurement procedures.

MISCELLANEOUS

[780]

The Instant Word Recognition Test. Reading level grades 1–4; 1971; IWRT; criterion referenced; no data on reliability; no norms except mean score for grade 1; Forms 1, 2, in a single test sheet (1 page, self-marking); manual (4 pages); $4.95 per 30 tests; $2 per specimen set of this and 4 other tests; cash orders postpaid; [15–25] minutes; Edward Fry; Dreier Educational Systems, Inc. *

REFERENCES

1. FULD, PAULA ALTMAN. "Review of the Instant Word Recognition Test." *J Read* 16(1):85+ O '72. *

PRISCILLA A. DRUM, *Assistant Professor of Education, University of California, Santa Barbara, California.*

This test is described as a "criterion referenced test." The content tested is recognition knowledge of words selected from the author's "Instant Words," a frequency count of the 600 most common words used in reading material for children. The frequency counts were obtained by cross-referencing other frequency counts, such as those by Thorndike-Lorge, Dolch, and Rinsland. The final frequency list was then edited, adding some items and deleting others in order to provide a basic vocabulary consistent with the materials used in teaching beginning reading. According to the author, the first 300 words represent from 58 to 77 percent of the words used in a number of basal series.

The purpose given for the test is to assess what words the pupils know in order to decide where to begin in teaching the "Instant Words." The words are divided by grade; the first 100 words are to be mastered by the end of first grade, the second 100 by the end of second grade, and so forth. The words progress from easy to hard, with successive pairs of items representing samples from subgroup lists of 25 instant words each. The principle used in establishing easy to hard seems to be based on frequency; group 1a begins with *the*. The criterion for scoring, though not given, is mastery of all words sampled from the appropriate grade level. Since the test can be given twice, both initial placement and improvement after instruction can be assessed.

One problem within the test itself is that alternate lines of the test supposedly can be used to determine different reading problems. The first line of every pair presents a random selection of words from the set of 25 words; the second line has items from the same set but also with two or three words with the same beginning sound. If errors are confined to the second line of each pair, then one might suspect that the pupils are just examining the beginning letter in their selections. Unfortunately, the child has only four chances at each grade list to exhibit this pattern, and his choices are limited to one out of two or one out of three words for each item. It would be difficult to obtain a consistent error pattern from such a limited sample.

The test is easy to administer. The teacher says a word, then a sentence in which the word is used, and then repeats the word. The pupils mark an X above the appropriate word, which is one of five choices for each item. The second form of each level uses the same student test sheet. The teacher follows the same procedure, using a different word, but the pupils now select from only four choices. The tests can be torn apart and self-scored by noting whether the X appears in the shaded box.

Little information about the scores is provided. The test was "administered to 153 first graders in December and their mean score was 11.1" items. The entire lower level of 24 items must have been used rather than just the first eight items which correspond to the 100 words appropriate for first grade. The average score indicates that these first graders were capable of recognizing almost half of the words sampled from the second grade list. Thus, the original designation of word groups as appropriate for certain grades is questioned by these results.

This test presents a sound to sight procedure, which, as the author states, "is a little easier than the skill of reading them aloud." However, the purpose behind sight vocabularies is for the reader to see and, without further analysis, immediately say the word. Since only a few words are sampled at each grade level, it would be more consistent just to ask each pupil individually to read the words aloud.

The major consideration for use of this test is based on its content domain. Successive mastery of sight word lists over four grades of reading instruction is questionable. Basic sight vocabularies are often taught to both beginning and remedial readers as paired associate tasks, i.e., see the word and say it without further analysis of the letters into sounds. Given a small number of such associations, this is not a difficult task, and the child can learn to respond appropriately to certain printed words in a very short period of time. If the words are both frequent in the material used and irregular in their sight to sound correspondence, then this would be an efficient strategy for a limited number of words at an initial stage of reading acquisition. To continue such instruction through four grades with a corpus of 600 words, many of which are regular in their sight to sound correspondence, appears to encourage the teaching of reading as a rote memorization task, an inefficient procedure for an alphabetic language.

In summary, beyond grade one, *The Instant Word Recognition Test* has dubious value. Even for initial placement, the child should be asked to read the words not just recognize them.

J Read 16(1):85+ O '72. Paula Altman Fuld. * a discussion of validity and reliability for various purposes is missed. The scoring of these tests is easily done through keyed second sheets onto which the student's answers are automatically transferred. * Since tests like these have been available for years, their claim to being criterion referenced needs to be evaluated. * criterion referenced skill tests should

Instant Word Recognition Test

yield scores that are related somehow to the level of mastery needed for the skill to be adequate for use * True criterion referenced reading skill tests do not yet seem to be feasible; they will not become so until a more precise understanding of the processes involved in reading is attained.

[781]

*Inventory of Teacher Knowledge of Reading, Revised Edition. Elementary school teachers and college students in methods courses; 1971–75; no norms; 1 form ('75, 27 pages); no manual; information and answer key (no date, 4 pages); directions are for separate answer sheets but that must be provided locally if use desired; $35 per 35 tests; postage extra; specimen copy available to qualified users on request; "most respondents" require (60–75) minutes; A. Sterl Artley and Veralee B. Hardin; Lucas Brothers Publishers. *

REFERENCES

1. ALDRIDGE, THURMAN EUGENE. *The Elementary Principal as an Instructional Leader for Reading Instruction.* Doctor's thesis, University of Missouri (Columbia, Mo.), 1973. (*DAI* 35:1888A)
2. CLARY, LINDA MIXON. *Teacher Personality, Teacher Knowledge of Reading and Selected Teacher Characteristics as Predictors of Successful Student Achievement in Reading.* Doctor's thesis, University of Georgia (Athens, Ga.), 1974. (*DAI* 35:5184A)
3. KINGSTON, ALBERT J.; BROSIER, GLENN F.; AND HSU, YI-MING. "The Inventory of Teacher Knowledge of Reading: A Validation." *Read Teach* 29(2):133–6 N '75. * (*PA* 55:10679)
4. RORIE, IVA LaVERNE. *Analysis and Validation of the Inventory of Teacher Knowledge of Reading.* Doctor's thesis, University of Missouri (Columbia, Mo.), 1975. (*DAI* 36:4423A)
5. JOHNSON, DARWIN B. *Teacher Knowledge of Reading and the Reading Development of Students in Grades Two Through Four.* Doctor's thesis, Northern Illinois University (DeKalb, Ill.), 1976. (*DAI* 37:1387A)
6. VANROOSENDAAL, MARY LINDA. *Selected Factors Involved in Elementary Teachers' Knowledge of the Teaching of Reading.* Doctor's thesis, Northern Illinois University (DeKalb, Ill.), 1976. (*DAI* 36:7193A)

Read World 12(4):296–8 My '73. Daniel T. Fishco. [Review of original edition.] What should one make of a multiple-choice "inventory of teacher knowledge of reading" to which a teacher's responses are said to be *wrong* (that is, he is said to not have a proper knowledge of reading) if he answers "yes" to these statements:

1, Oral language development should be of major concern to kindergarten and first grade teachers because: children will not learn to read unless their speech patterns are like those used in books. 2, A reader who is able to pronounce the unfamiliar word, *returnable,* by noting the prefix, *re;* the root, *turn;* and the suffix, *able* is making use of a: semantic clue. 4, Attitudes toward reading and interest in reading: are not actually areas which should be part of routine evaluation. 5, One of the most important instructional goals in reading in grades IV, V, and VI is to: develop the abilities involved in the reading of literature. 10, As an instructional goal the ability to read critically is especially important because it stresses the importance of: careful attention to sentence meaning. 15, It has been said that comprehension should be a thinking, reasoning process. Comprehension becomes this type of process as: physical and mental maturity take place. 16, Reading instruction with severely disabled readers seems most effective: when it is conducted within the regular classroom by a special reading teacher. 18, If a pupil is experiencing difficulties of a mild or less severe nature his needs: require tutorial instruction and specialized materials. 22, Background of experience is an important prerequisite for comprehension because it: provides the foundation for any assumption that the reader might make about the selection. 24, Although individual differences of various types exist among a group of readers, these differences typically: are not so prevalent among first graders.

These examples, taken from the first one fourth of the items of the Artley-Hardin *Inventory of Teacher Knowledge of Reading* (the remaining three-fourths of the test exhibit a like proportion of such items) lead to the critical question to be asked of this purported test of teacher knowledge. This is: How many instructors in "basic reading methods and in-service programs" for whom this test was written teach that statements as the above are false? What if this number is small? If so, as I suspect it is, then the acceptability of the Artley-Hardin *Inventory* as a guide, as they put it, in "determining the extent of growth taking place over a period of time as the result of instruction given" will of necessity be limited. And even if one accepts the beliefs of the *Inventory* as to what is authentic knowledge of reading one would be hard pressed to explain away other significant aspects of the test which adversely affect its testworthiness. For example, one wonders at the vague approach in items like: "3, If *plast* were a real word the *a* would likely stand for the '*a* of at. *a* of ate. *a* of far. *a* of about.'" Obviously, these *a*'s are all the same grapheme, so any of the preferred answers could be argued to be correct. * the dubious nature of some stems of questions makes a search for a "correct" response to them almost impossible, e.g., "48, Probably the most effective way to cope with heterogeneity in reading achievement is through:" * Since when has the creation of such heterogeneity by the teacher been considered the wrong thing to do? * Of doubtful validity, as well, are items that require the test taker to select purported purposes of specific standardized tests of reading, intelligence, and visual perception. The last requirement seems particularly irrelevant, of course, since correlations found between perception scores and reading in the primary grades are too low to be used for predictive purposes. * In summary, it is obvious

Inventory of Teacher Knowledge of Reading

that in Artley and Hardin's reading classes in Missouri, teachers are taught to reject reading information whose authenticity other teacher educators would not question. These different opinions as to what constitutes the respectable knowledge of reading illustrates the major difficulty in accepting this test, especially for competency-based teacher education courses. When one can argue disparately with Artley and Hardin via their test, as to what reading truly is, surely their *Inventory* fails in its pose as the ideal or uniform test of teacher learnings in criterion-based teacher education, or in the traditional forms, for that matter.

[782]
★Speed Scale for Determining Independent Reading Level. Grades 1–12; 1975; 3 grade level scores: word recognition [pronunciation], comprehension [vocabulary], independent reading [average of pronunciation and vocabulary levels]; no data on reliability of independent reading level scores; no data on validity; no description of normative populations; individual in part; 1 form (4 pages); word card (1 page); manual (8 pages); $2.50 per set of word card and 25 tests; $1.50 per manual; postage extra; specimen set not available; Ward Cramer and Roger Trent; Academic Therapy Publications. *

J. JAAP TUINMAN, *Professor of Education, Simon Fraser University, Burnaby, British Columbia, Canada.*

The word recognition part of this test consists of 20 words for each grade from 1 to 9 and 20 words for grades 10–12 combined. The student is asked to pronounce these words. Grade level is defined as the highest level in which no more than three words are missed. No justification for this criterion is provided. The words reputedly are randomly drawn from the Kucera-Francis word list and cross-referenced with the *American Heritage Word Frequency Book,* referred to casually by the authors as "the Heritage computerized word list." Since the Kucera-Francis list was compiled without reference to grade and the American Heritage list contains only words which occurred in the curriculum texts for grades 3–9, questions exist regarding the source of grade 1 and 2 words and how the grade 10–12 words were "cross-referenced."

The comprehension test contains 50 vocabulary items, consisting of an underlined stimulus word (in isolation) followed by four alternatives. The student's task is to find the word "that goes best" with the underlined word. The relationship between the correct alternative (as

determined by the answer key) and the stimulus word varies: sometimes synonymy is involved (victory-triumph), at other times the relationships are less clear (whisper-voice, but "spoke" is listed as a wrong alternative). Functional, superordinate, and subordinate relationships are all included. In at least 10 of the 50 items there is no clear-cut "best" answer. Green: yellow or grass? Blue: red or color? Performance: theater, musical or tragedy? "Holiday" is listed as the correct answer for "ornament." Since "glitter" is also an option, one assumes this to be a typographical error. Again without any justification presented, grade levels are assigned to number of correct answers: through grade 6, every four correct answers means one added grade level, grades 7–9 require five more answers correct each, and any student achieving more than 39 correct answers attains a grade 10–12 level.

The comprehension words were selected in the same manner as those in the word recognition test. Their assignment to a particular grade level is based on a tryout with 876 students (the "standardization sample") from grades 1 through 12. Criteria for selection of these particular words from a larger pool or for their exact grade assignment are not elaborated upon. The authors are satisfied to state that "only those items which met the predetermined statistical characteristics for a given grade were used (e.g., the difficulty of an item must decrease as the grade placement increased)."

This rather cavalier attitude toward the technical side of test development permeates the test manual (six pages of print in all). Reliability data are sparse: test-retest correlations (one-week interval) of .98 and .97 for the two subtests, respectively, are quoted. However, these coefficients are based upon a sample of 120 students across 12 grades. (No breakdown of subjects per grade is provided.) It is reasonable to assume that reliabilities will vary greatly from grade to grade, yet the relevant information is not available. Moreover, additional reliability data, notably coefficients of internal consistency, are desirable.

In addition to the sparse information on content validity, the authors mention that they asked 12 reading specialists "to judge whether or not the items were representative of the total word recognition and comprehension domain at a particular grade level." Inexplicably, they do not report any data on the responses. Finally, a study is reported on the agreement between independent reading levels of 100 students attained with the Speed Scale and as determined by four "expert reading specialists." Unfortunately, insufficient details regarding procedures are provided to meaningfully evaluate the degree to which this study establishes concurrent validity.

The Speed Scale was developed to establish a student's independent reading level. This level is defined in terms of 80 percent accuracy in word recognition and comprehension. More conventional definitions, parenthetically, define the independent reading level in terms of more than 99 percent accuracy in word recognition, and a minimum of 90 percent comprehension, a far more stringent, and probably more realistic, criterion.

No evidence is presented by the test authors that the levels established by their scale are valid, i.e., correspond directly to levels of material difficulty (such as estimated by readability formulae) which the students can read with 80 percent accuracy in word recognition and 80 percent comprehension. Using established older instruments such as the Gray or the Spache oral reading test, or some of the subtests on the newly developed *Woodcock Reading Mastery Tests,* or even a carefully developed informal reading inventory, most experienced test users can obtain more relevant and more valid information on the reading level of students than that obtained from the Speed Scale.

The authors of the Speed Scale provide an illustration of how their test can be used by a classroom teacher in need of "placing" a student recently transferred from a school outside the district. Rather than relying on a single observation with an instrument whose reliability and validity have not been established, a teacher is well advised to rely on her own observations of the work done by a new student in his first few weeks in the class. The uncertainty of one's informal judgment is much to be preferred over the false security of an invalid test score.

ORAL

[783]

*The Burt Word Reading Test, 1974 Revision.
Ages 5 and over; 1921–76; BWRT; revision of *The*

Burt (Rearranged) Word Reading Test; pronunciation; individual; 1 form ('76, 1 card, words identical with 1938 test except for order); manual ('76, 22 pages); £1 per 20 tests; 75p per manual; postpaid within U.K.; [5–10] minutes; original test by Cyril Burt; earlier revision by P. E. Vernon; current revision by Scottish Council for Research in Education; Hodder & Stoughton Educational [England]. *

See T2:1680 (7 references) and 7:738 (3 references).

REFERENCES

1–3. See 7:738.
4–10. See T2:1680; also includes a cumulative name index to the first 10 references for this test.
11. WILSON, J. A. "Personality and Attainment in the Primary School: 2, Personality Structure and Attainment for Ten-Year-Olds." *Res Ed* (England) 7:1–10 My '72. * (*PA* 49:5584)
12. COCKBURN, JUNE M. "Annual Surveys of Reading Disability in a Scottish County." *Brit J Ed Psychol* 43(2):188–91 Je '73. * (*PA* 51:7949)
13. VERNON, PHILIP E. "A Restandardization of the Burt-Vernon Graded Word Reading Test." *Western Psychologist* (Canada) 4(3):72–8 '73. * (*PA* 53:12577)
14. BROADLEY, G., AND BROADLEY, KATHLEEN M. "Rural Standardisation of the Burt-Vernon Graded Word Reading Test." *Alberta J Ed Res* (Canada) 21(4):289–94 D '75. * (*PA* 56:1492)
15. SHEARER, ERIC, AND APPS, RYCHARD. "A Restandardization of the Burt-Vernon and Schonell Graded Word Reading Tests." *Ed Res* (England) 18(1):67–73 N '75. * (*PA* 55:8658)

[784]

★Cutrona Reading Inventory. Grades kgn–6, 7–12 and adult; 1975; word pronunciation; criterion referenced; 3 grade scores: independent reading, instructional reading, frustration reading; no data on reliability; no norms; 94–100% indicates "independent reading grade level," 75–93% indicates "instructional reading grade level," 74% and lower represents "frustration reading grade level"; individual; 1 form ('75, 4 pages, test consists of 16 words for each grade); 2 levels; no manual; $3 per 20 tests; $1 per specimen copy; cash orders postpaid; [10] minutes; M. P. Cutrona; Cutronics Educational Institute. *
a) A BASIC SCREENING. Grades kgn–6; information sheet ['75, 1 page].
b) ADVANCED LEVEL. Grades 7–12 and adult.

[785]

Gilmore Oral Reading Test. Grades 1–8; 1951–68; GORT; 3 scores: accuracy, comprehension, rate; individual; Forms C, D; record blanks ('68, 12 pages); reading paragraphs ('68, 25 pages) for both forms; manual ('68, 31 pages); $7.75 per 35 record blanks; $5 per reading paragraphs; $1.65 per manual; $2.50 per specimen set; postage extra; (15–20) minutes; John V. Gilmore and Eunice C. Gilmore; Psychological Corporation. *

See T2:1679 (5 references); for reviews by Albert J. Harris and Kenneth J. Smith, see 7:737 (17 references); for reviews by Lydia A. Duggins and Maynard C. Reynolds of the original edition, see 5:671.

REFERENCES

1–17. See 7:737.
18–22. See T2:1679; also includes a cumulative name index to the first 22 references and 4 reviews for this test.
23. RODENBORN, LEO V., JR. "The Importance of Memory and Integration Factors to Oral Reading Ability." *J Read Behav* 3(1):51–9 w '70–71 ['71]. *
24. ANDERSON, WILLIAM F., AND STERN, DAVID. "The Relative Effects of the Frostig Program, Corrective Reading Instruction, and Attention Upon the Reading Skills of Corrective Readers With Visual Perceptual Deficiencies." *J Sch Psychol* 10(4):387–95 D '72. * (*PA* 50:3665)
25. CHEEK, MARTHA DIANE COLLINS. *Relationship of Oral Reading, Spelling and Knowledge of Graphemic Options.* Doctor's thesis, Florida State University (Tallahassee, Fla.), 1972. (*DAI* 33:2608A)

Gilmore Oral Reading Test

26. DAINES, DELVA, AND MASON, LYNNE G. "A Comparison of Placement Tests and Readability Graphs." *J Read* 15(8): 597–603 My '72. *

27. STOLL, PATRICIA DONATH. "A Study of the Construct and Criterion-Related Validity of the Stanford Diagnostic Reading Test." *J Ed Res* 66(4):184–9 D '72. *

28. WAYNANT, LOUISE FISHER. *An Investigation of the Relationship Between Technique of Testing and Oral Reading Performance.* Doctor's thesis, University of Maryland (College Park, Md.), 1972. (*DAI* 33:669A)

29. MORRIS, OUIDA FAE. *Reading Performance of Normally Sighted and Partially Sighted Third and Fourth Grade Students Using Regular Print and Large Print.* Doctor's thesis, University of Minnesota (Minneapolis, Minn.), 1973. (*DAI* 34:7076A)

30. STAFFORD, JERRY. "Oral Reading Diagnosis and Purposes for Reading." *Read World* 13(1):5–12 O '73. *

31. WATSON, CLIFFORD DEAN. *An Analysis of Cognitive and Affective Skills in Judging the Effectiveness of a Contingency Management System for Low Socio-Economic Minority Students Who Have Academic and Social Adjustment Problems.* Doctor's thesis, Wayne State University (Detroit, Mich.), 1973. (*DAI* 35:1537A)

32. DENNY, DOUGLAS R. "Relationship of Three Cognitive Style Dimensions to Elementary Reading Abilities." *J Ed Psychol* 66(5):702–9 O '74. * (*PA* 53:8332)

33. CHAMBLESS, MARTHA S. *A Study to Determine the Relationship Between Selected Oral Reading Errors and Self-Concept.* Doctor's thesis, University of Arkansas (Fayetteville, Ark.), 1975. (*DAI* 36:3220A)

34. STAFFORD, JERRY. "Review of the Gilmore Oral Reading Test." *Read World* 14(3):216–8 Mr '75. * (*PA* 54:6424)

35. STRADER, SUSAN GENTRY. *The Relationship Between Rate and Comprehension in Beginning Reading.* Doctor's thesis, University of Georgia (Athens, Ga.), 1975. (*DAI* 36:7753A)

36. BRADLEY, JOHN M. "Evaluating Reading Achievement for Placement in Special Education." *J Spec Ed* 10(3):237–45 f '76. * (*PA* 57:6918)

37. KAUFMAN, MAURICE. "Measuring Oral Reading Accuracy." *Read World* 15(4):216–25 My '76. *

38. ALLINGTON, RICHARD L.; CHODOS, LAURA; DOMARACKI, JANE; AND TRUEX, SHARON. "Passage Dependency: Four Diagnostic Oral Reading Tests." *Read Teach* 30(4):369–75 Ja '77. *

39. SILBERBERG, NORMAN E., AND SILBERBERG, MARGARET C. "A Note on Reading Tests and Their Role in Defining Reading Difficulties." *J Learn Dis* 10(2):100–3 F '77. * (*PA* 58:3604)

Read World 14(3):216–8 Mr '75. Jerry Stafford. * A student's performance in oral reading accuracy is determined by simply counting the number of substitutions, mispronunciations, insertions, hesitations, repetitions, omissions, etc., made while reading. In light of recent psycholinguistic research, it is difficult to conceive that each of these error categories could be of equal weight. The error coding procedure of the GORT could benefit considerably from a weighing procedure which recognizes the relative importance of errors in terms of their contribution to the understanding of the passage. The authors of the test have pointed out that practice is needed to develop facility in recording reading errors. Investigation on the topic suggests that even after considerable training and practice teachers tend to record inaccurately a large percentage of the errors. More recent study indicates that even with the benefit of audio tapes, trained personnel often have difficulty in analyzing students' oral reading performance. The *Manual of Directions* is remiss in its failure to include data describing the reliability with which the various errors can be

Gilmore Oral Reading Test

coded. The reading passages in the GORT represent a continuous story in a middle class suburban setting. The passages in each form show rather regular increases in difficulty as determined by the number of polysyllabic words, the percentage of complex sentences, word difficulty and paragraph length. Each passage is accompanied by five comprehension questions that are concerned mainly with the recall of facts directly stated in the passage. Little concern is given to assessing higher order comprehension skills. The reasons behind the method used for computing comprehension in the GORT need to be explained. A student who performs poorly in accuracy but who has done well in comprehension up to the ceiling level is assumed to have greater skills in comprehension and consequently is credited for answering questions beyond the level at which testing is concluded. Thus, it is assumed that if the student could read subsequent passages with greater accuracy he could also demonstrate better comprehension. In-depth investigation into the relationships between oral reading accuracy and oral reading comprehension cast serious doubt on this assumption. * The GORT is commonly used for diagnosing the reading needs of students identified as having reading problems. The discussion of the test's standardization was not sufficiently detailed to determine what portion of the students used were identified as having reading problems.

[786]

★McGrath's Preliminary Screening Test in Reading. Grades 1–13; 1973–76; earlier forms entitled *Oral Word-Recognition Test;* items are from the word recognition subtest of the *McGrath Test of Reading Skills;* word pronunciation; no data on reliability; no norms; individual; 1 form ('76, 2 pages, test consists of 10 words for each grade); no manual; directions ('76, 1 page); $2 per 10 tests, postage extra; (1–3) minutes; Joseph E. McGrath; McGrath Publishing Co. *

[787]

Oral Reading Criterion Test. Reading level grades 1–7; 1971; ORCT; criterion referenced; 3 reading level scores: independent, instructional, frustration; no data on reliability; no norms; individual; 1 form (4 pages); no manual; $3.95 per 40 tests; $2 per specimen set of this and 4 other tests; cash orders postpaid; [10–15] minutes; Edward Fry; Dreier Educational Systems, Inc. *

REFERENCES

1. FULD, PAULA ALTMAN. "Review of the Oral Reading Criterion Test." *J Read* 16(1):85+ O '72. *

J Read 16(1):85+ O '72. Paula Altman Fuld. * includes a graph that can help the teacher estimate the readability level of available materials. This innovation is more convenient than the use of a formula for estimating readability * Fry's procedure is greatly simplified and it could probably be handled easily by a competent ninth grade student assistant or by a para-professional * Fry's new procedure may be an important contribution, especially where teacher turnover is high. As with other such procedures, of course, the teacher must also consider the pupil's familiarity with, and interest in, the subject matter of the book before assigning it. * A teacher-made inventory, however, contains actual passages from the reader to be used; it is therefore automatically valid for placing children in that series. For a separately constructed test, on the other hand, validity for various purposes must be established experimentally and discussed in the teacher's manual. The manual for the *Oral Reading Test* completely lacks such a discussion. Since this test seems to be flawed in a number of ways, its validity seems open to question. The first problem with this test is that the paragraphs are poorly written and edited. Desirable punctuation is lacking in several places (paragraphs 1-A, 2-A, 3-A, and 5), there is more than one lengthy sentence in which the clauses are not as closely related as they should be (paragraphs 3-B and 5), and the word "it" is used with unclear reference in a few places (paragraphs 2-B and 3-B). An additional problem is that the directions do not include clear criteria for defining the three reading levels that the test is supposed to reveal. The statement under *Scoring* merely says, ". . . . one mistake gives the Independent Level on the first paragraph." Would one mistake also define the Independent Level for the longer and harder paragraphs? One error is about six percent of Paragraph 1-A but less than two percent of Paragraphs 5 through 7. A single error is therefore more disruptive in earlier passages than in later passages on this test, and the manual should include some discussion of this problem. Furthermore, questions like the following are certain to arise: What is it best for the teacher to do when a pupil makes several errors on the first passage but does better on the next few passages? At what point should testing be discontinued? Such questions should be anticipated and answered in the manual, according to the *Standards for Educational and Psychological Tests and Manuals*. In the absence of this information, and without any discussion of problems of validity and reliability for various purposes, the teacher is better off constructing her own informal test. * Since tests like these have been available for years, their claim to being criterion referenced needs to be evaluated. * criterion referenced skill tests should yield scores that are related somehow to the level of mastery needed for the skill to be adequate for use * True criterion referenced reading skill tests do not yet seem to be feasible; they will not become so until a more precise understanding of the processes involved in reading is attained.

[788]

★**Oral Word-Recognition Test.** Grades 1-13; 1973; catalog uses the title *A Preliminary Screening Test in Reading;* items are from the word recognition subtest of the *McGrath Test of Reading Skills;* no data on reliability; no norms; no directions for administration and scoring; individual; Forms A, B, C, (1 page, test consists of 5 words for each grade); $2 per 75 tests, postage extra; (1-2) minutes; Joseph E. McGrath; McGrath Publishing Co. *

[789]

★**Reading Classification Test.** Ages 7.5-11.5; 1972-76; adaptation of oral word reading subtest of *Individual Reading Test;* word pronunciation; reliability data based on prepublication form; individual; 1 form ['72, 5 cards in manual]; revised manual ('76, 20 pages plus test cards, essentially the same as manual copyrighted 1962 except for revision of section on readability levels and addition of diagnostic information); record sheet ('72, 1 page); Aus 30¢ per 10 record sheets; $1.80 per manual; postpaid within Australia; [5-25] minutes; H. J. Williamson and I. L. Ball; Educational Resources [Australia]. *

REFERENCES

1. WILLIAMSON, H. J., AND BALL, I. L. "An Investigation of the Discriminant Validity, Reliability Estimates and Some Correlates of a Word Recognition Test for Children—Ages 7 to 11." B Victorian Inst Ed Res 22:1–21 Je '70.

[790]

Reading Miscue Inventory. Grades 1-8; 1972; RMI; catalog title is *The Goodman-Burke Reading Miscue Inventory;* "deviations" (errors) are called *"miscues* to suggest that they are not random errors but, in fact, are cued by the thought and language of the reader"; tape recorder must be used to record the examinee's reading of a 15 to 20 minute selection (difficult enough to produce at least 25 errors) and the immediate retelling of what was read; 6 scores: retelling score, percentage breakdown of oral reading errors with comprehension loss (none, partial, total), percentage breakdown of oral reading errors (excluding omissions) with sound similarity (high, some, none) to text, percentage breakdown of oral reading errors (excluding omissions) with graphic similarity (high, some, none) to text, percentage breakdown of oral reading errors (excluding omissions) with grammatical function similarity (identical, indeterminate, different) to text, percentage breakdown of 18 possible oral reading error patterns—corrected, grammatically acceptable, semantically acceptable—characterizing the examinee's ability (strength, partial strength, weakness, overcorrection) in "using the grammatical and meaning cueing systems"; no data on reliability and validity; no norms; individual; 1 form; reading selections (62 pages); manual (132 pages); worksheets (103 pages, spirit masters for local duplicating); coding sheet (1 page); profile (1 page); practice manual (130 pages); practice tapes; $84.75 per set of testing materials including 100 coding and profile sheets; $5.13 per 100 coding or profile sheets; $6.60 per manual; postage extra; [45] minutes; Yetta M. Goodman and Carolyn L. Burke; Macmillan Publishing Co., Inc. *

See T2:1686 (1 reference).

REFERENCES

1. See T2:1686.
2. Burke, Carolyn. "Preparing Elementary Teachers to Teach Reading," pp. 15–29. In *Miscue Analysis.* Edited by Kenneth S. Goodman. Urbana, Ill.: ERIC Clearinghouse on Reading and Communications, 1973. Pp. iv, 120. *
3. Goodman, Yetta M. "Miscue Analysis for In-Service Reading Teachers," pp. 49–64. In *Miscue Analysis.* Edited by Kenneth S. Goodman. Urbana, Ill.: ERIC Clearinghouse on Reading and Communications, 1973. Pp. iv, 120. *
4. Hollander, Sheila K. *Strategies of Selected Sixth Graders Reading and Working Verbal Arithmetic Problems.* Doctor's thesis, Hofstra University (Hempstead, N.Y.), 1973. (*DAI* 34:6258A)
5. Kaplan, Elaine M. *An Analysis of the Oral Reading Miscues of Selected Fourth Grade Boys Identified as Having High or Low Manifest Anxiety.* Doctor's thesis, Hofstra University (Hempstead, N.Y.), 1973. (*DAI* 35:4253A)
6. Kolczynski, Richard Gerald. *A Psycholinguistic Analysis of Oral Reading Miscues in Selected Passages From Science, Social Studies, Mathematics, and Literature.* Doctor's thesis, Ohio State University (Columbus, Ohio), 1973. (*DAI* 34:7108A)
7. Miller, Joan W. "An Interdisciplinary View of Reading as a Qualitative Process." *Read Improv* 10(2):40–5 f '73. *
8. Nieratka, Suzanne. "Miscue Analysis in a Special Education Resource Room," pp. 100–2. In *Miscue Analysis.* Edited by Kenneth S. Goodman. Urbana, Ill.: ERIC Clearinghouse on Reading and Communications, 1973. Pp. iv, 120. *
9. Tatum, Barbara Jean. *A Quantitative and Qualitative Analysis of Oral Reading Miscues as Related to the Comprehension of Selected Passages From Literature, Mathematics, Science, and Social Studies Texts.* Master's thesis, Ohio State University (Columbus, Ohio), 1973.
10. Watson, Dorothy J. "Helping the Reader: From Miscue Analysis to Strategy Lessons," pp. 103–15. In *Miscue Analysis.* Edited by Kenneth S. Goodman. Urbana, Ill.: ERIC Clearinghouse on Reading and Communications, 1973. Pp. iv, 120. *
11. Watson, Dorothy J. Harper. *A Psycholinguistic Description of the Oral Reading Miscues Generated by Selected Readers Prior to and Following Exposure to a Saturated Book Program.* Doctor's thesis, Wayne State University (Detroit, Mich.), 1973. (*DAI* 34:4094A)
12. Anderson, Dorothy Jean. *A Psycholinguistic Description of the Oral Reading Miscues of Selected First Grade Students Participating in a Supplemental Language Based Program.* Doctor's thesis, Virginia Polytechnic Institute (Blacksburg, Va.), 1974. (*DAI* 35:2755A)
13. Carder, Mary Elizabeth. *A Comparison of Oral Reading Miscues of Poor Readers Assigned to Learning Disability Classes With Those Assigned to Remedial Reading Classes.* Doctor's thesis, University of Northern Colorado (Greeley, Colo.), 1974. (*DAI* 35:6933A)
14. Goodman, Yetta. "I Never Read Such a Long Story Before." *Engl J* 63(8):65–71 N '74. *
15. Hayden, John Blair. *Psycholinguistic Analysis of Oral Reading of Three Selected Groups of Seventh Grade Students.* Doctor's thesis, University of Southern California (Los Angeles, Calif.), 1974. (*DAI* 34:7101A)
16. Little, Larry J. *A Study of the Relationship Between Syntactic Development and Oral Reading Substitution Miscues of Average and Disabled Third Grade Readers.* Doctor's thesis, University of Kansas (Lawrence, Kan.), 1974. (*DAI* 35:5971A)
17. Tortelli, James Peter. *A Psycholinguistic Description of the Effects of Strategy Lessons Upon the Oral Reading Behavior of Twelve Below-Average Readers of Differing Linguistic Backgrounds, Grades Four, Five, and Six.* Doctor's thesis, Wayne State University (Detroit, Mich.), 1974. (*DAI* 35:4142A)
18. Williamson, Leon E., and Young, Freda. "The IRI and RMI Diagnostic Concepts Should be Synthesized." *J Read Behav* 6(2):183–94 Jl '74. * (*PA* 53:12509)
19. Brown, Virginia. "Reading Miscue Analysis." *J Learn Dis* 8(10):605–11 D '75. *
20. Jackson, Sheila M. *An Evaluation of Oral Reading Miscues in Second Grade Subjects.* Doctor's thesis, University of South Carolina (Columbia, S.C.), 1975. (*DAI* 37:250A)
21. Readence, John Edward. *A Psycholinguistic Analysis of the Oral Reading Miscues of Impulsive and Reflective Third Grade Children.* Doctor's thesis, Arizona State University (Tempe, Ariz.), 1975. (*DAI* 37:3366A)
22. Stenroos, Carol J. *A Psycholinguistic Description of Selected Gifted Readers Relating Prior Conceptual Knowledge to the Concept Density of Varied Contextual Materials.* Doctor's thesis, Wayne State University (Detroit, Mich.), 1975. (*DAI* 36:7173A)
23. Wofford, Barbara Ann. *Using Reading Miscue Analysis to Investigate Publishers' Suggested Readability Levels for Elementary Science Textbooks: A Comparative Study.* Doctor's thesis, Virginia Polytechnic Institute and State University (Blacksburg, Va.), 1975. (*DAI* 36:2514A)
24. Brazee, Phyllis Ellen. *A Qualitative and Quantitative Description of Eighth Grade Students' Oral Reading in Both Narrative and Expository Materials.* Doctor's thesis, University of Northern Colorado (Greeley, Colo.), 1976. (*DAI* 37:2032A)
25. Hodes, Phyllis. *A Psycholinguistic Study of Reading Miscues of Yiddish-English Bilingual Children.* Doctor's thesis, Wayne State University (Detroit, Mich.), 1976. (*DAI* 37:2694A)
26. Norton, Donna Elithe. *A Comparison of the Oral Reading Errors of High and Low Ability First and Third Graders Taught by Two Approaches—Synthetic Phonic and Analytic-Eclectic.* Doctor's thesis, University of Wisconsin (Madison, Wis.), 1976. (*DAI* 37:3399A)
27. Strong, Betty Jay VanSandt. *Expressive Styles in Art and Strategies in Reading.* Doctor's thesis, Memphis State University (Memphis, Tenn.), 1976. (*DAI* 37:6907A)
28. Vorhaus, Renée Pool. *Analysis and Comparison of Oral Miscues Generated by First Grade Students on Four Different Reading Tasks.* Doctor's thesis, University of Pennsylvania (Philadelphia, Pa.), 1976. (*DAI* 37:163A)

Nicholas J. Anastasiow, *Director, Institute for Child Study, Indiana University, Bloomington, Indiana.*

The *Reading Miscue Inventory* may more properly be labeled a system for the diagnosis and evaluation of children's oral reading and recall of a story than a test. While the RMI may be a development towards remediating some of the limitations of more traditionally normed tests, it does not have some of the advantages of the latter. The RMI approach is unique in that it is derived directly from a theory of reading which is supported by a substantial amount of research evidence by Kenneth Goodman, the authors of the inventory, and their students. The theory is the psycholinguistic interpretation of speech, reading, and writing, which perceives the reader as the active interpreter of the written page.

Basically, the RMI authors posit that the errors a child makes in reading are not random but are direct products of the reader's stage of language and cognitive development, dialect, and previous experience. To the authors, not all miscues are of equal significance. For example, some errors, such as reading "mus" for "must," are dialectical, whereas "dipided" (for "depended") is a nonword substitute which completely changes the meaning of the sentence read. However, no evidence is provided to jus-

Reading Miscue Inventory

tify the conclusion that analysis of a reader's miscues is therefore the appropriate means to assess his reading level for instruction. In the absence of such support, the user should be cognizant that no matter how intuitively appealing the theory may be, the bridge from miscue analysis to daily instruction is barely built on research data.

In this respect, the absence of reliability data is troubling and the lack of validation data more so. The latter becomes an even greater issue when one notes that the administration, scoring, and analysis of the child's oral reading is a complex and time-consuming process that depends upon the user's skill in applying comprehensive but complex diagnoses of samples of a child's oral reading. The manual, however, is quite comprehensive in explaining how to measure, score, and analyze the nine areas of oral miscues presented: dialect, intonation, graphic similarity, sound similarity, grammatical function, correction, grammatical acceptability, semantic acceptability, and meaning change. In addition, a scheme for analyzing comprehension is presented by having the child recall the story after he finishes reading it. The manual's comprehensiveness will require the administrator of the inventory to be well versed in the reading process. The effectiveness of the diagnosis will depend upon the teacher's ability to use the complex set of marking schemes, to understand the psycholinguistic approach, and to find the time to administer the inventory, score it, and analyze each child's protocol. A skilled RMI user may spend as much as two hours with each child, a novice much longer.

Many of the scoring judgments about the miscues are subjective and the teacher is not provided with evidence to explain whether the frequency of types of miscues is typical among children of a given age. Developing frequencies or norms may be a contradiction to the authors' theory of diagnosis; however, case studies which provide types of error patterns for children of different ages would greatly assist the teacher in determining the seriousness of a problem encountered among the class. In addition, the RMI's comprehension score is dependent upon the teacher's subjective judgment as to the adequacy of the child's recall. Extensive teacher pre- or in-service training obviously will be needed before most teachers will be able to utilize the manual effectively.

The manual provides a limited number of instructional suggestions for remediating each of the listed miscue types. No data are presented to indicate that remediating a miscue will improve a student's reading ability or that such remediation can be effective. Teachers who have individualized their instruction or who utilize non-graded techniques may find the RMI suitable for part of their needs. However, while the manual provides examples of children's miscues and the actual script of a child as an example of both errors and scoring procedures, it does not provide guidance for the beginning teacher on where a beginning reader or mature reader of any given age might score. Again, to provide this information would be in contradiction to the philosophy of the authors. The user is instructed to select unfamiliar reading material and have the child read at a level on which he or she will make 25 miscues. Reading series vary widely from company to company and are not controlled across series for vocabulary level. Thus, the teacher must be cautioned that the RMI is designed to determine not the level of performance but the type and quality of performance. A well-designed achievement test provides information to enable a teacher to gauge roughly at what level to begin instruction. The RMI, in most cases, will not. The RMI used with other measures should aid the skilled teacher in a comprehensive diagnosis of a child's oral reading and ability to recall detail of a story after it has been read orally.

HARRY SINGER, *Professor of Education, University of California, Riverside, California.*

The RMI requires the audio-taping of a student reading orally, without help on any word identification problems, a selection which is one grade level above his or her "usual" class assigned material, generates a minimum of 25 miscues, and takes 15 to 20 minutes to read. Comprehension is immediately assessed by having the student retell the selection under guided questioning, as he had been informed he would be required to do. Up to a total of 100 points can be received for correctly retelling the characterization, plot, events, and theme of literary selections or the specifics, concepts, and generalizations of informational material.

Reading Miscue Inventory

Miscues, defined as discrepancies between oral responses and printed materials, are assumed to be not "random errors" but responses "cued by the language and thought the reader brings to the written material in his attempt to extract meaning from his reading." In a novel contribution to diagnosis of oral reading, each miscue is then evaluated by a series of nine questions which determine whether the reader's miscues are similar to the graphemes or their sounds, are dialect-determined, contain an intonation shift, maintain grammatical functions and relationships, are self-corrected, or involve meaning changes that result in comprehension losses. The answers to these questions are entered on coding sheets, summarized, computed into percentages, and transferred to reader profile sheets.

Reading strategies are identified according to similarity of miscues to graphic, sound, and grammatical relationships. Reading strategy lessons are then provided for reducing each pattern of miscues.

Four types of readers are defined by a combination of comprehension pattern (comprehension loss, partial loss, and no loss) and retelling score. They are labelled as "ineffective," "some effective," "moderately effective," and "highly effective" use of reading strategies. Suggestions are given for improving the comprehension of each type of reader.

The strength of RMI is that the inventory procedures, evaluation and interpretation of miscues, and reading strategy lessons are based upon and are consistent with a psycholinguistic theory of reading. Briefly stated, the theory is that orally reconstructed responses to printed material are cued and determined by an interaction among graphophonemic, semantic, and syntactic systems. Meaning may then be associated with the orally reconstructed responses and tested for consistency with the expected meaning. If the associated meaning is inconsistent with the anticipated meaning, a correction may be made through a regressive eye movement to a previous point in the text; but if it is consistent, then the meaning may be stored or encoded into an oral response. Consequently, RMI's rationale for evaluation of miscues is based not only on their departures from expected responses but also on whether they result in changes from textual meaning and whether

the reader tests for meaning consistency and attempts to self-correct miscues. The inventory thus provides insight into a reader's strategies for obtaining meaning from relatively difficult materials. Since this insight complements information gleaned from any survey test and from any other diagnostic test, RMI should be a necessary part of a clinician's diagnostic procedures and should be used in teaching graduate courses on diagnosis and improvement of reading.

However, RMI would be a more valuable diagnostic tool if its weaknesses could be reduced. The limitations and shortcomings of RMI stem from the fact that it is only an "inventory," which is a set of *procedures* for obtaining and evaluating miscues and for assessing comprehension. RMI is not a standardized test nor a scale for measuring and diagnosing reading ability. But, since RMI does quantify its results and has the appearance of being more than an informal reading inventory, it should be evaluated on the same criteria used for appraising any scientific instrument that purports to diagnose reading and any procedure that prescribes strategies for improving reading processes and comprehension. According to these criteria, RMI lacks standardized directions and selections, explicit rationale and stipulated criteria for determining cutting points for its diagnostic patterns, norms for interpreting scores, reliability and validity data for diagnoses and for prescribed reading strategies. Furthermore, judged only as an inventory, RMI's procedures are vague, arbitrary, and subjective.

Vagueness begins with the reading selections. Although the RMI kit provides selections graded from 1 to 7, neither the grading information nor the readability formula on which the selections were graded are given in the manual. These omissions can be readily corrected by clinicians who know how to apply a readability formula, but RMI apparently does not consider such information to be necessary. In fact, teachers are advised to select *any* material that is "novel" to the reader, one grade level above material "usually" assigned in class to the reader, and comprised of concepts and situations which the reader can "comprehend." These vague directions and odd comprehensibility requirements signify that reading selections will vary from one tester to another in degree of

Reading Miscue Inventory

novelty, level of difficulty, and comprehensibility. Consequently, these variations will tend to adversely affect the reliability and validity of diagnosis and restrict the generalizability of the diagnosis to the kind of material used in the reading selection.

The directions for selecting reading materials also assume that teachers know the reading levels of their students and can judge reading material accurately. What the manual does not explicitly require, but what testers would have to do anyway to objectify selection of reading material, is use a survey test to determine a student's level of reading ability and then apply a readability formula to select and confirm that a reading selection is one level above the student's reading level. Testers would presumably still have to employ subjective procedures to satisfy the novelty and comprehensibility criteria.

However, limitations in selection could be offset by directions standardized on representative selections, perhaps those contained in the kit. If they were, then other measurement standards could also be realized. For example, normative data resulting from repeated administration of the same selections could be provided. Apparently Goodman and Burke are not averse to provision and use of such normative data because they state that repeated use of the same selections would make it "possible to compare the readings of the same child or of different children on the same material."

Standardization would also tend to offset another problem: difficulties in making judgments, particularly borderline decisions, on the categorization and evaluation of miscues. Although the manual seems to have clear examples for categorizing miscues, testers nevertheless have difficulty because miscues obtained do not always fit the examples given in the manual. For instance, how much can a word depart in meaning from an expected word before it cannot be considered as a synonym? Testers also encounter decision difficulties in guiding retelling of the selection, in constructing an outline for assessing comprehension, and in determining the "fewer" number of points to give when some part of the retelling is incomplete. A comprehensive coding manual, content outline, and explicit assessment procedures would tend to objectify categorization of miscues and measurement of comprehension. Then Goodman and

Burke would have a basis on which to provide reliability and validity data on categorization and evaluation of miscues and on diagnosis of reading strategies and comprehension patterns. Perhaps they would also be able to validate their reading lessons for reducing miscues and for improving comprehension.

The division of comprehension patterns and retelling scores into four general categories based on "effectiveness" of reading strategies is obviously arbitrary. The categories are not determined by any specific reading strategies nor by any specific comprehension difficulties, but only by comprehension loss pattern and range of retelling score. Using these summary scores diminishes the diagnostic value of RMI. Consequently, the comprehension strategy lessons for improving comprehension are at best only grossly relatable to either of the variables—comprehension loss pattern or retelling score—that define each type of reader. Although the reading strategy lessons may be appropriate, particularly those related to specific processes, no evidence of their validity is reported in the manual. For all these reasons, RMI's procedures for assessment and improvement of comprehension are the weakest and least defensible part of RMI.

The best parts of RMI are its evaluative procedure for diagnosing miscues, its interpretations of a reader's strategies for reading relatively difficult material, and its strategies for reducing particular miscues. This information centers on the coding sheet. However, in the summarizing and transferring to the reader profile, significant diagnostic information on corrections and semantic acceptability on miscues, which are retained in grammatical relationships and in comprehension loss computations, are omitted in computing "graphic and sound relationships." For parallel organization, the reader profile should have summarized graphic and sound *functions* along with grammatical *functions,* and graphic and sound *relationships* along with grammatical *relationships.* The manual offers no explanation for this differentiation and lack of parallel summaries. Nor does the manual explain why information on grammatical functions is summarized and listed on the reader profile but not interpreted.

More diagnostic information could have been obtained had miscues been grouped for types of miscues within graphic, sound, and grammatical categories. For example, developmental levels could have been obtained had graphic and sound miscues been grouped for beginning, middle, and ends of words.

While reading strategy lessons are provided for repeated miscues in graphic, sound, and grammatical associations, none were formulated for "conceptual habitual associations." While Goodman and Burke may be correct in their judgment that these associations lie outside the reading process and within the purview of content area instruction, conceptual miscues are nevertheless highly related to meaning and to students' ability to gain information from text. Furthermore, content area teachers want help from reading specialists on how to teach students to use and develop conceptual responses to printed materials. Consequently, it is disappointing that strategy lessons for conceptual responses to reading were not included in the manual, especially since RMI does stress meaning as a criterion for evaluating reading processes.

SUMMARY. RMI is a desirable pedagogical tool and heuristic procedure for evaluating miscues, but its procedures are not objective enough for obtaining reliable and valid diagnoses and are too time consuming for informal use in the classroom. However, RMI can be made into a more objective instrument and its time factor can possibly be reduced, perhaps by combining the scoring sheet with the reader profile. If so, then the hope expressed in the conclusion to the manual would more likely be realized: "The *Reading Miscue Inventory*, hopefully, is a tool that will first help the teacher to become increasingly knowledgeable about reading, and will then help to facilitate the task of learning to read."

[791]

★Salford Sentence Reading Test. Ages 6-10 to 10-6; 1976; SSRT; individual; Forms A, B, C, (test-directions card); manual (11 pages); 95p per set of cards; 60p per manual; postpaid within U.K.; [2–3] minutes; G. E. Bookbinder; Hodder & Stoughton Educational [England]. *

J. DOUGLAS AYERS, *Professor of Education, University of Victoria, Victoria, British Columbia, Canada.*

The author's arguments for developing a new reading test are the following: first, many available tests are out of date; second, most reading

tests have only one form; third, most other tests employ word recognition only, a limitation that deprives students of an opportunity to derive meaning from context. In Britain, where a great deal of stress is placed on individualized approaches to reading and the lack of alternative equivalent forms means the child is tested "year after year, and sometimes on a number of occasions within a year," practice effect can lead to "exaggerated reading ages." For the very reasons that this test will appeal to primary teachers in Great Britain, it is unlikely to be used in North America. In any case, new norms would have to be established on a sample of children in North America, because the current norms are based on children who are taught to read after age 5 at the discretion of the teacher.

The SSRT is an individual oral reading test that has three forms, each consisting of 13 sentences of increasing length and vocabulary difficulty corresponding to four sizes of print. While nearly all statements are simple sentences, selection of words was not based on any word list but rather on "increase in word length and, to a lesser extent, the estimated unfamiliarity of the words in successive sentences." Numerous tryouts and revisions were made until norms were equated and correlations were .95 with Schonell's *Graded Word Reading Test* in "the relevant age range" (6 to 10). Because of the limited number of sentences for such a wide range of ages, the reviewer is concerned with the content validity of the test.

Directions for administering and scoring are simple and straightforward.

Two types of standardization were done. First, 250 children aged 5-9 to 9-9 from five Salford schools were administered the Schonell GWRT and the SSRT to establish age norms. Whether the children were administered one or all three forms is not indicated, and nowhere is there any evidence that the tests are parallel, although it is reported that "at each age level, the median reading age was equated with or came very close to the median chronological age"; that the results were similar for the Schonell and the SSRT; and that the intercorrelations with the Schonell varied from .95 to .99 for "each yearly age group." In the second stage Form C was administered to 20,000 children in the age range 6-9 to 11-9 and from these a representative sample of one quarter of the entire population was used for establishing percentile norms. The percentile distributions reported for each three-month age range are based on 250 to 300 children. Separate norms are not provided for boys and girls, despite the fact that the data show sizable differences in favor of girls for three age groups.

There is no evidence presented with regard to retest or between forms reliability as such, although in one table labelled "predictive reliability," the correlations between Forms A and C over a retest period of one-year and a two-year age range for small samples of boys and girls were, respectively, .95 and .91.

SUMMARY. Given the apparent high reliability and concurrent validity of the SSRT, this individually administered test provides a quick and accurate assessment of reading achievement up to age 10. Data on equivalence of test characteristics and between forms reliability for single age groups must be reported. Also, separate norms should probably be developed for boys and girls. Despite the high recommendation for use in Britain, it is unlikely that this type of test would be acceptable in North America at the present time for the reasons presented earlier.

[792]

Standardized Oral Reading Check Tests. Grades 1–2, 2–4, 4–6, 6–8; 1923 (no date on test materials); 2 scores: rate, accuracy; no data on reliability; no information on basis for obtaining grade equivalents; individual; 5 forms (2 pages); 4 levels; directions (2 pages); record sheet (2 pages); norms (1 page); $4.95 per 20 copies of all forms of any one level; $2.20 per specimen set; postage extra; (1–3) minutes; William S. Gray; Bobbs-Merrill Co., Inc. *
a) SET 1. Grades 1–2.
b) SET 2. Grades 2–4.
c) SET 3. Grades 4–6.
d) SET 4. Grades 6–8.
See T2:1689 (7 references); for reviews by David H. Russell and Clarence R. Stone, see 2:1570 (1 reference).

KENNETH J. SMITH, *Professor of Reading and Head of the Department, The University of Arizona, Tucson, Arizona.*

Gray's *Standardized Oral Reading Check Tests,* published in 1923, were a pretty clever idea for their day. They consist of five presumably matched tests for each level. Each test, individually administered, yields a rate score and an accuracy score, with standard scores for each grade level provided.

More important, however, and more interesting, is the very real effort at detailed diagnosis

of oral reading behaviors. An individual record sheet provides a checklist of oral reading errors which could stand simplification and improvements, but which is as good as many more modern efforts. Furthermore, the examiner is directed to note "tendencies to change the meaning by substitutions or omissions of words or changes in their order." That sounds a lot like being told to look for good and bad miscues, doesn't it? The examiner is further instructed to prepare daily "tests" of 50 or more words, each for similar analysis; to administer additional forms of the test at intervals of two, three, or four weeks; and to use the accumulated data to adjust the "character of the instruction."

The concentration on rate of oral reading probably is irrelevant. Even the inclusion of "standard" scores for accuracy adds nothing useful for diagnostic purposes, and the scores almost certainly are inaccurate. The whole effort to "standardize" a diagnostic test probably is unfortunate, but, then, who had heard of criterion-referenced tests in 1923? Finally, there are no statistical data provided, and the "stories" in the tests aren't too good.

No doubt the Gray tests are limited in purpose and somewhat technically out of date. They cannot be recommended as part of a test battery. However, they are impressive as an early effort at an essentially criterion-referenced diagnostic test for the purpose of improving instructional efficiency. They do not confuse oral reading with comprehension, as is done in some recent tests. Furthermore, they recognize the contribution of context without dismissing the essential graphic identification necessary to accurate reading. They are deserving of respect for what they can do, particularly in view of their publication date. There probably are no better published oral reading tests available to date. A well-designed informal reading inventory is probably our best bet until the state of the art improves.

[793]

Standardized Oral Reading Paragraphs. Grades 1–8; 1915; SORP; no data on reliability; no information on bases for obtaining grade equivalents; individual; 1 form (4 pages); directions-class record, 1955 edition (2 pages, essentially the same as directions-record sheet issued 1915 except for revision of scoring directions based on 1915 "standard" scores); $3.50 per 35 tests; 80¢ per specimen set; postage extra; (3–8) minutes; William S. Gray; Bobbs-Merrill Co., Inc. *

See T2:1690 (19 references) ; for reviews by David Kopel and Clarence R. Stone, see 2:1571 (7 references).

KENNETH J. SMITH, *Professor of Reading and Head of the Department, The University of Arizona, Tucson, Arizona.*

First published in 1915, Gray's *Standardized Oral Reading Paragraphs* is unquestionably of historical interest and value. It is an individually administered, standardized (somehow) test which combines oral reading *rate* and oral reading *accuracy* in order to arrive at a "B" score. This "B" score, similar to a grade equivalent, is intended to be used to determine whether a child should be "promoted." The content of the test is a group of successively more difficult paragraphs to be read by the child while the examiner marks errors in a manner remarkably similar to that used in modern informal reading inventories. This careful scoring procedure, however, is not used in analysis of the student's performance, as errors are merely counted in order to arrive at a final score.

One could quickly conclude, and quite properly so, that this test has *only* historical value. Certainly one would not wish to "promote" a child on the basis of the combined oral reading accuracy and rate score yielded. However, one can but marvel at the lack of progress made in oral reading testing in more than 60 years. Without pausing to review more recent tests, it is interesting to note that the primary additions which recent tests have made to Gray's efforts are: (*a*) the addition of "comprehension" questions, usually of the factual recall, *memory* type, to material read orally, a practice having doubtful validity; (*b*) the addition of context clues to the scoring analysis, sometimes at the expense of other analyses; and (*c*) the inclusion of statistical data, a generally desirable practice, but one which commonly obscures failure to establish validity.

Given such factors as inadequate standardization and scoring procedures, as well as unfortunate recommendations for test use, the *Standardized Oral Reading Paragraphs* has no place in a modern testing program, but students of reading testing will find it interesting, and practitioners are cautioned that a more recent copyright date does not necessarily imply improvement.

Standardized Oral Reading Paragraphs

READINESS

[794]

The APELL Test: Assessment Program of Early Learning Levels. Ages 4.5–7; 1969; program for identifying educational deficiencies, suggesting remedial instruction, and retesting; 16 scores: 4 pre-reading (visual discrimination, auditory discrimination, letter names, total), 4 pre-math (attributes, number concepts, number facts, total), 7 language (nouns, pronouns, verbs, adjectives, plurals, prepositions, total), total; norms for total score only; no description of normative population; 1 form (58 pages); manual (110 pages); separate answer cards must be used; $9.35 per test; $7.90 per manual; $330 per school set (35 tests plus manual); $17.35 per 35 sets of answer cards (includes scoring service); postpaid; (40) minutes in 2 sessions; Eleanor V. Cochran and James L. Shannon; Edcodyne Corporation. *

See T2:1692 (1 reference).

J Spec Ed 5(2):195–8 su '71. Barton B. Proger. * truly unique among extensively developed achievement tests in that it is criterion-referenced * The....manual....does not present sufficient details on the criterion-referenced nature of the test. The only clue to this method of interpretation is the absence of norms and the examples provided (although insufficient and inadequate in depth) for interpreting different types of performance profiles. * The response instructions seem to be easy to follow for any child of the age recommended for the test; the enlarged sample item that is used on the blackboard should eliminate any confusion. APELL is pictorial in content and will probably present no major problems to either disadvantaged or less verbally oriented pupils. * Different types of items are not mixed, except in one instance: an item from the "verbs" section is embedded within the "pronouns" section. * The single exception....appears to be an error in production, although one that probably will not have disastrous results. The teacher's manual is well documented and practical. * In summary, APELL should be a useful screening instrument at the early-childhood level. In the teacher's manual Cochran describes the test as "a validated system of instructional diagnosis and design [p. iii]." Only with number concepts and nouns are more than four items ever used; it can be debated whether approximately four items are an adequate sampling of behavior to be used for diagnosis in the classical educational sense. Nonetheless, APELL yields much detailed preliminary information that can be useful for preliminary screenings. Where doubt does exist about weaknesses in any specific areas, more intensive analysis may be carried out using teacher-made exercises.

[795]

Academic Readiness Scale. First grade entrants; 1968; ARS; a similar rating scale, *End of First Grade Progress Scale,* "suitable for older children," is available without a manual; ratings by teachers in 14 areas: motor, perceptual-motor (2 scores), persistence, memory, attention, number recognition, counting, word recognition, vocabulary, interest in curriculum, social, humor, emotional; also includes form for recording opinions of teachers and parents regarding children being considered for retention or special class placement; no information is given on how to obtain item and total scores; no norms; 1 form; 2 levels; $4.60 per 25 scales; $4.35 per specimen set; 10% extra for postage and handling; [5–10] minutes; Harold F. Burks; Arden Press. *

See T2:1693 (1 reference).

REFERENCES

1. See T2:1693.
2. MAULDIN, WILLIAM TIMOTHY. *Prediction of First Grade Reading Scores Utilizing Burks' Academic Readiness Scale and the Metropolitan Readiness Tests.* Master's thesis, California State University (Long Beach, Calif.), 1973.

DENNIS J. DELORIA, *Chief of Evaluation, Office of Child Development, Department of Health, Education, and Welfare, Washington, D.C.*

The author states that this test is primarily intended "to identify slow maturing or otherwise handicapped children who may need to be retained or to be placed in a special class or be given a modified curriculum in the first grade." Although the manual also suggests the ARS can be used "to single out more able pupils," the score form and manual are almost exclusively oriented toward the first stated purpose, identifying children with potential learning handicaps. It is a preliminary screening device that is not intended to replace professional diagnosis.

The 14 items are in a rating scale format, each consisting of a page-wide line divided into six segments, with reference statements of child behavior to guide the teachers in placing their checkmarks. The manual gives no instructions about how to complete the score form, but teachers should have little difficulty because the reference statements are largely self-explanatory.

There is no provision for obtaining either total or subtotal scores from the scale, and no numeric computations are involved in the use of the test for making decisions about a particular child. Rather, the recommended scoring is visual, wherein "children who are rated well to the left of center on the ARS may be considered for retention or special class placement." Although troublesome at first glance, this peculiar

scoring procedure has much to recommend it for the intended purpose of the scale: it is simple and easy, only extreme overall ratings will come to the scorer's attention; it discourages careless labeling of children with scores that have a false appearance of precision; it encourages the rater to place more weight on other circumstances in the child's life before deciding to retain the child or place the child in special education; and it allows parents more freedom for questions and opinions since the appearance of finality inspired by fixed scores is absent.

The general effect, then, should be to discourage misuse of results, and to throw responsibility for decisions back to the people who must, in reality, make the decisions anyway. In the process of doing this, the scale could easily provoke deeper and more enlightened discussions between the teacher and parents, counselors, and school officials. Indeed, the author commendably downplays the importance of the ARS results throughout the manual by encouraging a commonsense approach to decisions. He presents the ARS results as just one indicator among many that need to be considered in deciding about a particular child. If a child is a candidate for retention, the teacher is urged to answer 11 additional questions printed on the back of the ARS, and to confer with parents about 9 more questions. The teacher questions bring age, physical size, health, regularity of school attendance, and other child characteristics into consideration. The parent questions overlap items on the ARS considerably, but explicitly bring in the viewpoint of parents.

The chief problem with the additional teacher and parent questions is that no empirical evidence is presented in their support. For example, how much does it matter whether a child has established hand dominance? Is it really an argument for retention if parents have shown continuing interest in the progress of their child? For the most part, though, the additional questions appear to be relevant and useful.

Correlations between ratings and re-ratings 10 days apart ranged from .64 to .83 for the various categories. While these figures are not high, they seem adequate given the low-key application of results recommended by the author. Inter-rater reliability estimates are not presented.

As evidence of validity, the author presents

correlations between the ARS ratings of kindergartners with reading achievement scores one year later in two school systems. The correlations for item ratings range from .17 to .47, with median .32; the correlations for total score range from .41 to .48, with median .43. These statistics give little evidence for the probability of correctly screening a particular child. No needed contingency tables or frequency data are presented. Although systematic sex and socioeconomic class differences were found in the standardization data, possible differences due to age were unexplainably omitted from investigation.

In spite of weaknesses in standardization and norming, the ARS should prove useful to kindergarten teachers who are considering retention or special placement for certain children. The ARS seems to be worthwhile simply as a device to facilitate discussions between the teacher and parents. Risk of misuse of the results is minimized by the scoring system and judicious instructions. The author deserves credit for conscientiously avoiding the false promises so commonly found in other readiness scales and their manuals.

ELEANOR M. LADD, *Associate Professor of Psychology of Reading, Temple University, Philadelphia, Pennsylvania.*

The ARS attempts to structure and harness the expertise and observational skills of kindergarten and first grade teachers in order to identify children who need special placement or who are being considered for retention.

No norms are provided. Guidelines for evaluation indicate that the child "whose profile falls sharply to the left is likely to be a first grade risk."

The manual includes a discussion of abilities related to school readiness, factors to be considered in the early identification of "at risk" children and a rationale for the categories chosen. The 42 correlations range from .17 to .42.

No inter-rater reliabilities are reported. Intra-rater reliabilities, with the same teachers rating 110 kindergarten children 10 days apart, range from .64 to .83.

It is difficult to judge the accuracy of the claims made for the scale because of the lack of data in the manual. In the 10 years since the development of the ARS, critical new findings which impinge on all evaluation have been provided by developmental, behavioral, and cognitive psychologists. Particularly, one misses items involving the new understandings of the psycholinguistic nature and structure of language. In addition, suggestions for planning curricula for "unready" children do not reflect current educational philosophy and procedures.

The ARS reflects the philosophic position that the burden of proof for success lies wholly upon the child. Nowhere is teacher input considered. The teacher is not asked to consider quality of instruction, the degree of trust the child has, the quality of communication between teacher and child, or the learning styles of the child. In the parent interview, no questions are posed to determine the child's perceptions of the school milieu as viewed in the home.

The majority of the categories included in the ARS will, in all probability, remain important as signals of academic success and, used in conjunction with formal and informal tests, the scale can add a measure of protection for the child. However, the general nature of the categories and the absence of language-related categories limit its usefulness.

[796]
Analysis of Readiness Skills: Reading and Mathematics. Grades kgn–1; 1972, c1969–72; 5 scores: visual perception of letters, letter identification, mathematics (identification, counting), total; orally administered in English or Spanish; 1 form (8 pages); manual (22 pages); $6 per 25 tests; $1.95 per specimen set; postage extra; (30–40) minutes; Mary C. Rodrigues, William H. Vogler, and James F. Wilson; Houghton Mifflin Co. *

JOHN T. GUTHRIE, *Director of Research, International Reading Association, Newark, Delaware.*

The concept of readiness for reading and arithmetic implies that there is a time when a child has come of age for formal teaching. A child is ready for instruction when his physical maturity, experiential background, emotional adjustment, cognitive abilities, and motivation have developed to the point where focused instruction is beneficial. In making the decision about whether "children are ready for the more challenging experiences of reading and mathematics," the authors state that "the *Analysis of Readiness Skills,* supported by teacher judgment, offers a most effective basis for selecting children for such programs."

Administration of this readiness test is very straightforward. The directions are clear and are read verbatim by the teacher. One potential value of this test is that the directions are presented in English and Spanish. To determine whether the tests in the two languages were equivalent, I asked a native-speaking Spanish professor of literature to look at the Spanish translation. He said that it was not only substantively correct but surprisingly precise.

The reliability of the total score is based on a national sample stratified on income, region, and size of community. For the English population, K-R 21 is .90; for the Spanish group, .81. The subtests for the English group range from .59 to .87; for the Spanish group, .54 to .71. These scores indicate that the subtests do not have adequate reliability to be used in isolation. Based on reliability information, all we can assess from this measure is school readiness; the test cannot be used to obtain diagnostic information. A low score on the measure cannot be broken down to suggest which types of readiness training might be given to children.

Predictive validity is the single most important aspect of a readiness test. A high score on the test should imply that the child will benefit from reading instruction and show high reading achievement at a later point in time. Unfortunately, the test manual provides no data on validity and we could not locate any studies that used this test. In the absence of data, we may ask whether the subtests include skills that are likely to have predictive validity. Certainly, the letter-naming and number-naming subtests qualify. However, most readiness tests seem to contain two factors: a familiarity factor including the alphabet, numbers, and matching tasks found here and elsewhere; and an oral language factor, including word meaning, listening, and following directions. This test does not contain the language factor which lends stability and relevance to readiness measures. Consequently, its promise for predictive validity is doubtful.

Scores that result from the administration of the test are recorded in raw scores and percentiles. The manual suggests that "children with total raw scores of 31 or better may be started immediately in appropriate programs." As there is no rationale for this score, this recommendation seems doctrinaire and should be tempered with judgments about the other char-

acteristics of the children and the program they will enter. It should be noted that the test is more sensitive for English-speaking than Spanish-speaking groups. A range of 11 raw score points separates the 20th and 60th percentiles for the English-speaking group, whereas a range of only 5 raw score points separates these percentiles for the Spanish-speaking group. In other words, the Spanish-speaking child is most likely to score very high or very low on this test; this does not give optimal information to teachers and administrators.

The option of giving this test in Spanish to Spanish-speaking children raises some dilemmas for decision-making. When children are learning to read English and the language of instruction is English, the test of readiness should usually be given in English. In learning to read Spanish taught in Spanish, a readiness test in Spanish should be used, if possible. It would be unwise to give this test to monolingual children in Spanish and use the results for placement in a program for reading English, for many children might perform well on the test but poorly in the program.

There are likely to be some Spanish-speaking children who also speak English reasonably well and who are ready to learn to read English. If these children perform well on this test when it is given in Spanish and poorly when it is given in English, they should probably be taught in a bilingual program. They may be ready for reading instruction in English, but they also need a substantial amount of English language teaching. Children can be taught to speak English and to read it at the same time, provided they have at least moderate oral language proficiency in English prior to instruction.

For most purposes, I would prefer one of the better developed readiness tests, such as the *Murphy-Durrell Reading Readiness Analysis* or the *Metropolitan Readiness Test,* to this one. I would rather select a measure with a broader range of subtests, the combination of which has substantial, well-documented predictive validity. Under the rare circumstances in which there is a bilingual teacher or school program in which language, reading, and mathematics may be taught in English by a Spanish-speaking teacher who can bridge the language gap, this test may possibly be used as a supplement to teacher

Analysis of Readiness Skills: Reading and Mathematics

judgment for decisions about entering children into formal instruction programs.

CHARLES T. MYERS, *Administrative Associate, Educational Testing Service, Princeton, New Jersey.*

This is certainly not the only test whose title is somewhat too grandiose. A much more appropriate title would have been "Letter and Numeral Identification Skills Test." But sales and promotional departments of test publishers do seem to have a way of interfering with the good intentions of test writers and, in this reviewer's judgment, it is not likely that the test authors had an entirely free hand in the development of the supplementary test materials.

The test itself appears to be simple and straightforward and probably effective for a limited purpose, that of finding out which children can properly identify letters and numerals. But the test manual does not identify that as the test's purpose and it gives only a vague indication of how the test should be used. For example, the manual states that this test was compared with the *Metropolitan Readiness Test* and that "it was found that the two tests correlated highly with each other, but only moderately with teacher judgments." If such correlation coefficients had been computed, it is inexcusable that complete numerical data (the means, the standard deviations, and certainly the correlation coefficients) were not reported. On the other hand, if the coefficients had not been computed, it is unfortunate that such a statement was made. Furthermore, the "moderate" correlation with teacher judgments really should be explained. When a test does not have a good correlation with a reasonable criterion, it is quite possible that there is a good reason; but the test user ought to be told something about it.

The test manual indicates that this test should be used to help decide "the most appropriate time for each child to enter reading and mathematics programs." The manual also provides percentile norms for the total test score for children beginning kindergarten. What the authors fail to do is to give any suggestion of what percent of the norms group children were judged to be ready for such programs. Further, they fail to give any definition of what kind of "reading and mathematics programs" they have in mind. Such programs differ widely in the extent of readiness assumed. Thus an inexperienced teacher would need a year's experience with the test, including a trial use of the test, before the test scores became at all meaningful. The publisher should know better than to provide such vague guidance.

Perhaps a more serious criticism is that the ability measured by this test, the ability to identify letters and numerals, is only a small part of the complex development that gets a child ready for beginning formal school work in reading and mathematics. The advertising blurb for this test says: "Three tests comprising the *Analysis of Readiness Skills* tell whether or not your kindergarten or beginning first-grade children are ready for introductory reading and mathematics programs." That statement just is not true. There is more to readiness than just being able to identify letters and numbers in a test situation. Fortunately the manual does make some effort to correct this unfortunate claim.

The test itself probably does a good job of doing the limited task it sets out to do, although there are a number of minor flaws. All tests have flaws, however, so the reader should consider whether these flaws are serious or not. For one thing, this test is designed for right-handed children only. The child is instructed to keep his place in the test by putting his finger on a picture at the left end of each line and then told to mark his answer choice in the test booklet somewhere to the right of that. Doing that task left-handed would be extremely difficult, whereas it would have been easy to have put the identifying pictures at both ends of each line. It may also be a flaw that the test takes about 40 minutes to administer and the manual does not give any suggestion as to whether beginning kindergarten children have to do the whole test in one sitting or whether the teacher may break up the administration for children who may not be ready to sit still and concentrate for so long a time. Also, it would probably have been better if the children were instructed to draw a line around their answer choice, or to underline it, rather than crossing out the right answer. This answer format makes it difficult for a child who may answer impulsively and then change his mind. Another complaint is that the teacher is told to say "number or numeral" 10 times over in the course of administration. It would be better for the teacher to use the one word his

Analysis of Readiness Skills: Reading and Mathematics

pupils were familiar with and to omit the other. "Numeral" is probably the fashionable word these days, but how many kindergarten children know that or care?

This test is attractively printed and should be easy to administer and to score. For teachers in some parts of this country, it will be useful to know that it can be administered in Spanish and that there are norms for Spanish-speaking children. Thus, for both English-speaking children and Spanish-speaking children it should be easy to get test scores. The serious problem is that once you have obtained the scores, there is inadequate information given in the manual as to how the scores may reasonably be used. Information about the validity of the test and about the interpretation of the norms is practically nonexistent. The possibility that this is a common problem is not an adequate excuse. Teachers may very well know better than to take the test title at face value, but how many parents and school board members would not put undue pressure on the teachers to misuse the scores?

This test looks like a nice little test. It may be useful under certain conditions, but the user is warned that the test and manual together make an inadequate package and the usefulness of the test will depend on the wisdom and experience of the teacher. As is generally true for educational questions, additional evidence beyond the test score must certainly be considered in deciding about a child's readiness. But more than that, the meaning of any particular test score level in terms of the implied degree of readiness will have to be determined on the basis of the teacher's own experience. The manual is insufficient for that purpose.

[797]

★Cognitive Skills Assessment Battery. Prekgn-kgn; 1974; CSAB; criterion referenced; "designed to provide a profile of the child's strengths and weaknesses" and to "explore curriculum needs of the entire class"; 84 item scores (40 consist of plus or minus) in 20 areas: basic information (4 scores), identification of body parts (4 scores), color identification (3 scores), shape identification (4 scores), number knowledge (9 scores), information from pictures (4 scores), picture comprehension (3 scores), story comprehension (5 scores), multiple directions (3 scores), large muscle coordination (3 scores), auditory memory, visual-motor coordination (6 scores), sentence recall, vocabulary (6 scores), visual memory, symbol discrimination (8 scores), letter naming (2 scores), visual-auditory discrimination (4 scores), auditory discrimination (5 scores), response during assessment (8 scores); no data on reliability; individual; 1 form; card manual (91 pages); response

sheet (4 pages); preliminary manual (19 pages); $17.50 per kit of testing materials including 50 response sheets; $6 per 32 response sheets; 50¢ per preliminary manual; $1.50 per specimen set (without card manual); postage extra; (20–25) minutes; Ann E. Boehm and Barbara R. Slater; Teachers College Press. *

KATHRYN HOOVER CALFEE, *Palo Alto Unified School District, Palo Alto, California.*

This battery is intended to provide the preschool or kindergarten teacher with information about the perceptual and mental competencies of each child. The authors have attempted to sample those competencies "deemed relevant to success at the kindergarten and grade one levels by teachers in the field." The profile of individual strengths and weaknesses is intended to be useful for instructional purposes.

The authors list several areas of competency that are presumably covered by the battery: orientation toward and familiarity with one's environment (jargon for "what the child knows about his world"), coordination, discrimination, memory, and comprehension and concept formation. They claim that the battery provides information about the child's ability in each of these areas, information that will allow the teacher to make independent and instructionally valid decisions. This is a worthy goal; unfortunately, there is no evidence that the authors have achieved the goal through this test.

At several points in the manual, the authors stress the criterion-referenced character of the test and emphasize that its most appropriate application is in planning and guiding instruction. It is, therefore, surprising to read the suggestion that administration follow the fall-spring pattern typical of standardized achievement tests. Presumably the class profile in September is to guide instruction for the next nine months, and then the student's gains are to be measured by readministration. Also surprising, given the clinical nature of the test, are the instructions that "no directions be *repeated* or *changed* and that no cues be given unless the *Card Manual* specifically gives such instruction." This mandate seems at variance with the effort to design the test to yield levels of response for each item, with the advice to conduct further exploration of the child's competence when failure occurs, and with the allowance for multiple sessions when required by a child.

The battery has a nice appearance. The items

Cognitive Skills Assessment Battery

are printed in a large, clear format on heavy card stock. The test booklet folds out into a stand-alone triangle, with the stimulus facing the child and the instructions facing the tester. A minor irritation is that the triangle forms such a sharp angle upward that the tester cannot easily look at the student's responses. Instead, it is necessary to lay the booklet flat on the table during testing. A more serious problem is that since the instructions are sometimes unclear, the tester will encounter surprises if he is not thoroughly prepared. For instance, item 5 requires eight blocks that are not included in the kit. Item 15 requires that the tester have a watch or clock that measures seconds.

Scoring criteria in the appendices provide some help in defining which level the child has attained. However, it is surprising to find that some tests have separate criteria for prekindergartners and kindergartners. The items that require copying of geometric shapes and letters put the left-handed child at a disadvantage: the placement of the item to be copied turns the task into a visual memory task as well; the child's hand and arm cover the object to be copied. Determining the "level of response" for many of the items entails a fairly complex decision strategy on the part of the tester. Better design of the instructions accompanying each item could make the tester's job easier and more reliable.

More consistent use of the "levels" concept might also be reasonable. Some items are scored + and −, while others are scored 2 (highest level), 1, and N. However, many of the +/− items could be scored as totally correct, partially correct, and altogether wrong or no response. The child who points to "u" in response to "n" knows more than the student who points to "w" or attempts no answer at all. Similarly, the student who chooses the tall *or* red flowers when asked "Point to all the flowers that are tall and red" shows that he understands the question to some degree.

Although the battery is still in a preliminary edition, there is some effort to present data on its properties. Field testing was carried out with about 900 prekindergartners and kindergartners balanced on socioeconomic status and geographical area. Technical information from this study is limited to the percent responding at the different levels for each item, broken down according to age and socioeconomic status. There are no data on reliability or validity. The authors state that only items considered by teachers as "illustrative of competency" were considered for inclusion. "Items were also examined to determine if they were sensitive to instruction" and whether they differentiated children "who had achieved competency in an area as opposed to those who had not." The authors state that "these procedures provide the *content validity* for the battery." No evidence is provided in support of these statements, unfortunately.

Examination of the item data shows an apparent ceiling effect for many of the items. For instance, body parts were correctly identified by more than three-quarters of the poorest group for whom data are reported, and the average over all groups for this portion of the battery is approximately 90 percent correct. Such high performance levels suggest that this portion of the battery is nondiscriminating and may be a waste of time. Similar remarks hold for other sections of the battery. Incidentally, the reviewer assumes that the data for item 11, "2 + 5 = ?," are in error; it seems unlikely that 99 percent of the low socioeconomic prekindergartners answered the item correctly.

The test resembles a number of other tests now on the market. Some of the apparent flaws in this version will undoubtedly be remedied in the final version. The materials for the student are well presented in this test; the tester is not so well treated. The selection of items is comprehensive, though possibly redundant and too simple in some instances. This test is no better nor worse than many others now on the market. Its use with children who present special educational problems may be defensible. A better use of testing dollars may be the acquisition of a variety of specimen tests, so the classroom teacher of beginners becomes aware of the areas considered important to measure. The best assessment for young children continues to be an informed and knowledgeable teacher.

BARBARA K. KEOGH, *Professor of Education and Chairman, Department of Special Education, University of California, Los Angeles, California.*

Current enthusiasm for early identification of educationally high risk and high potential children has led to a proliferation of screening

Cognitive Skills Assessment Battery

techniques designed for use at the preschool and kindergarten levels. The CSAB appears to be one of the better efforts in this regard. The test is nicely packaged, has reasonably well defined administrative and scoring guides (including an appendix containing scoring criteria and examples), and for the most part includes items which have at least consensual validation as appropriate for kindergarten pupils. The CSAB has not been age normed in the traditional sense. By the authors' statement the test is "a criterion-referenced measure," aimed at assessing competencies of young children which are presumed to be relevant to success in school. Specific items were selected by examination of curriculum guides, analysis of teacher-defined goals, and observations of children in classrooms. Items were evaluated additionally in terms of their presumed relevance to school tasks and to expectations for children's abilities at kindergarten. The CSAB was field tested on samples of 391 prekindergarten and 507 kindergarten children in four geographic areas of the United States, the samples including children from families of middle and low socioeconomic status. The authors claim that content validity for the battery is provided by the procedures used in the selection of the areas and the items. No further validity or reliability analyses are reported. Tables summarizing percent of field samples responding to each item suggest that socioeconomic status (SES) influences some but not all items. Comparison of success percentages for prekindergarten and kindergarten samples also reveals clear variation among items; a number of items were passed at such high rates as to be nondiscriminatory, while others had high proportions of less successful responses according to both age and SES groups. There appears to be real variability as to the power of individual items, and the lack of reported statistical data as to item analysis, reliability, and validity detracts from the use of the test for systematic program evaluation or for research purposes.

No total score is obtained; rather, the authors recommend that the test be used to structure a profile of abilities and educational needs for a given child or for a whole class. Pertinent to an evaluation of that recommendation is the question of whether curricular or educational programs should be tied to the content domains represented in the CSAB. As with other cri-

terion-referenced tests, there is a possible circularity of assessment, teaching, and curricular goals. The CSAB, weakened by lack of external validity referents, is especially in need of firm data demonstrating the predictive validity of the items for subsequent achievement in school. While many items have intuitive appeal and are consistent with other kindergarten screening measures, it is likely that some lack reliability and have questionable relevance to school readiness. Particular caution must be exercised in interpreting performance of children from non-English or other cultural minority backgrounds. It is likely that the very items with the highest relevance for school performance are the ones which are most influenced by cultural and language differences, thus possibly penalizing the able child from a nonmajority background.

A particularly interesting and potentially valuable aspect of the CSAB is a section assessing subjective aspects of children's performance during testing. Included are four-point ratings of task persistence, attention span, rapport, confidence, and the like. Affective and motivational influences on test performance are always of importance; they may be particularly important when assessing prekindergarten and kindergarten children. Formal recognition of this aspect of assessment adds an important dimension to the interpretation of performance on the other items and strengthens the utility of the CSAB.

In sum, although a number of items appear more noncognitive than cognitive, taken as a whole the test provides a way of developing a profile, or picture, of a child relative to behavioral expectancies at kindergarten. The breadth of the repertoire of items and the concern with affective, social, and motivational characteristics adds strength to the test. Major weaknesses have to do with inadequate item analysis and limited validity data. From a practical point of view, the time and expense involved in assessing large numbers of children with this test must be weighed against the usefulness of the information gained. While likely gratuitous, the point should be emphasized that screening approaches may be defended only if they lead to appropriately differentiated educational programs. Demonstration of instructional implications of the CSAB profiles is a necessary and important step.

Cognitive Skills Assessment Battery

[798]

★**Hess School Readiness Scale.** Ages 3.5–7.0; 1975; HSRS; prediction of school success based upon mental ability; individual; 1 form (22 pages); manual (36 pages); record form (2 pages); $24.95 per set of testing materials including 25 record forms, cash orders postpaid; specimen set not available; (8) minutes; Richard J. Hess; Mafex Associates, Inc. *

REFERENCES

1. KATHERMAN, RUTH P. *A Reliability Study of the Hess School Readiness Scales.* Master's thesis, Millersville State College (Millersville, Pa.), 1969.
2. SCRANTON, GARY B. *A Comparison Study of the Hess School Readiness Scale With the ABC Inventory.* Master's thesis, Millersville State College (Millersville, Pa.), 1971.
3. HESS, RICHARD J., AND HAHN, ROLAND T., II. "Prediction of School Failure and the Hess School Readiness Scale." *Psychol Sch* 11(2):134–6 Ap '74. * (PA 52:13188)

RICHARD C. COX, *Director, Office of Measurement and Evaluation, University of Pittsburgh, Pittsburgh, Pennsylvania.*

The *Hess School Readiness Scale* is an ambitious attempt to evaluate the general intelligence of preschool children in order to judge their readiness for school. According to the manual, the HSRS is designed as an individual test which can be administered and scored in eight minutes. It was developed to provide a more convenient measure than the major individual intelligence tests suitable for young children. The author feels that it is important to measure intelligence as part of a preschool evaluation because of his assumption that intelligence is the single most important variable affecting success in school. Even if a potential user is willing to accept that assumption, there are other serious problems which may limit the usefulness of the scale.

The test consists of 45 items divided into 12 subtests. While the manual covers most of the appropriate areas of concern for both the layman and the measurement specialist, it does not present enough information on most topics. For example, there is only a short paragraph concerning the qualifications of the examiner, a vital concern for any individually administered intelligence scale. There appears to be no information about how the items were constructed. Directions for administering individual items are not specific enough so that standardization will be maintained. Typographical errors and obvious corrections appear throughout the manual.

The standardization sample of 3,000 was selected from rural, urban, and suburban areas of Eastern Pennsylvania. Only 8 percent of the sample was nonwhite. The representativeness

of the sample must be questioned, and a more specific description of the norming procedures should have been included.

Reliability and validity data are interesting but sparse. Only test-retest reliability is reported, using 323 children with a three-week interval between testings. The resultant coefficient of .91 is quite surprising considering the test length and the lack of consistency in performance by young children. Content validity is claimed on the basis of the fact that HSRS subtests include content similar to other general intelligence tests. Evidence of criterion-related validity consists mainly of correlations of the HSRS and Stanford-Binet for males, females, prekindergarten, prefirst grade, and rural, urban, and suburban groups. These coefficients range from .81 to .97, with a median of .88. Predictive validity data are presented, with school performance the following year as the criterion. Both teacher ratings and standardized achievement tests were used to measure school performance. Again, these coefficients are quite high. Further studies of reliability and validity would add considerably to these promising initial findings.

The test booklet is by far the poorest part of the HSRS. It is difficult to turn the pages and the durability of the binding is questionable. Organization of the booklet is poor, the art work is lacking in quality, and the pictures are badly reproduced. The counting frame used to measure number concepts is poorly constructed and easily bent, making it very difficult to slide the blocks. Reproduction of the record form is of such poor quality that it is difficult to read. It seems wasteful to spend considerable time on test conceptualization and on reliability and validity studies, and yet produce a shoddy looking instrument.

There is some similarity between HSRS and Stanford-Binet items. There is also an attempt made to emulate the Binet mental age equivalents, the end result being the HSRS intelligence quotient. At first glance the HSRS appears to be a mini-Binet but the similarities are only superficial; the HSRS is technically and psychometrically not comparable to the Binet.

It is possible to list many reasons why the HSRS should not be considered a useful instrument. Surely the basic assumption that intelligence is a crucial variable that should be measured to screen preschoolers will find argument. The traditionalist will most certainly scoff at the idea of being able to administer and score an individual intelligence test for preschool children in eight minutes or less and have it mean anything. Yet there are the initial reliability and validity studies which suggest a promising instrument. Perhaps further studies are warranted; certainly further refinement of the instrument is necessary before it should be considered seriously. Even these suggestions may be irrelevant since other instruments, which are quite acceptable for assessing school readiness, already exist.

[799]

Initial Survey Test. First grade entrants; 1970–72; IST; skills for "success in beginning primary learning"; 8 scores: reading (language meanings, auditory ability, visual ability, letter recognition, sound-letter relationships, total), mathematics, total; the five reading subtests originally published under the title *Initial Reading Survey Test;* no data on reliability of part scores; no data on validity; Forms A, B, ('72, 16 pages); manual ('72, 45 pages) for each form; flash cards (no date, 11 cards); score sheet (no date, 1 page); $5.34 per 35 tests, postage extra; [120–150] minutes in 4 sessions; Marion Monroe, John C. Manning, Joseph M. Wepman, and E. Glenadine Gibb; Scott, Foresman & Co. *

REFERENCES
1. SHERMAN, JUDY SAIFF. *A Comparative Study of Achievement on the Scott, Foresman Initial Survey Test of First Grade Children With and Without Siblings and the Social Adjustment of the First and Second Grade Children.* Master's thesis, State University of New York (Oswego, N.Y.), 1973.

ROBERT C. CALFEE, *Professor of Education and Psychology and Director, Stanford Center for Research and Development in Teaching, Stanford University, Stanford, California.*

The *Initial Survey Test* consists of the *Initial Reading Survey Test,* published in 1970, plus a short mathematics subtest. The reading battery provides information in five reading-related skills. This group-administered test is designed to assess "how extensively [*sic*] children have acquired the abilities and understandings that contribute to success in primary learning." The manual suggests that the subtest scores may be used as a "guide for planning and pacing appropriate instruction for each child."

The authors assume that the first grader can work as part of a group during the testing, can understand instructions on how to make a correct answer, and knows the associations between cues spoken by the tester and the pictures or letters on the test page. The manual states that the directions may be given in the children's

native language, but test items must be presented only in English. This advice could lead to some rather absurd situations.

The 16-page test booklet contains many small, detailed pictures printed in full color, which seem likely to cause difficulty for the child not used to such materials. The manual includes model pages identical to the test booklet along with the dialogue and procedure, a format which is most helpful.

The directions for administering the test assume a conventional first grade setting, with separate desks for each child, all facing in the same direction. The manual states that "a test of this kind can be given to an entire class," but the teacher is also advised that "you may divide the class into groups if you wish to do so." While this is probably good advice, differences in grouping procedures seem likely to lead to differences in performance that could invalidate the normative scores.

Some of the suggestions for administration are useful, and others are less valuable. For instance, the teacher is told to terminate testing of "any child who becomes upset by inability to respond meaningfully." The sound-letter subtest is to be cancelled for the child who becomes upset during the letter-recognition subtest. These suggestions make sense only if the test is individually administered—otherwise, what happens to the group when the teacher says that one child can stop taking the test and what happens to that child? And what is the basis for the recommendations? The last item on the letter-recognition subtest requires the child to choose from "b d q p," a difficult and possibly frustrating task. The sound-letter test uses only capital letters as stimuli, and it is entirely possible that the child who gives up on letter recognition because of the difficulty of handling lowercase letters might do reasonably well on the letter-recognition subtest that follows.

Test administration is divided into four sessions. Teacher judgment is the basis for deciding whether more than one session per day is to be attempted. No time limit is given; the teacher is advised to "administer the items at a pace that allows just enough time for *most* of the children to mark an item." The student of moderate ability is thus likely to score poorly if he is in a high-ability class, while he will be the star in a low-ability class. This seems an undesirable property of a test.

The section on scoring the test will discourage, mystify, and perhaps offend the user, depending on his knowledge and experience. The advice to score correct responses by *not* marking will bother the tester who believes in the value of positive scoring. And why go through the task of finding percentile and standard scores, when the chief purpose of the test is to fit instruction to the needs of children within the individual class? The instructions in this section ask the tester to do a lot of work to no apparent purpose, a recommendation which will strengthen the impression that tests are largely busywork. The user would be better advised to spend time looking for patterns for individual students, isolating the items that are hard for the class, making notes about possible instruction plans—all excellent words of advice given in the manual just before the instructions to look up percentiles, standard scores, and so on.

The section by Manning and Gibb on "Implications for Instruction" contains thoughtful and useful comments about the relation between assessment and instruction, more than is found in many other reading readiness tests. Manning cautions about misinterpreting total test scores. His subtest interpretations are specific; a close look at the skills necessary to answer the questions in any of the subtests shows that different underlying processes are being tapped within subtests. For example, the auditory ability subtest contains items measuring auditory discrimination, rhyming skills, auditory memory, and matching of beginning sounds. The teacher can use these item differences to direct instructional time to clearly focused objectives, rather than trying to improve the global "skill" of auditory ability.

Unfortunately, some of Manning's suggestions are also off the mark, in my opinion. After cautioning the user about reliance on total test scores, he suggests that the total scores will help the teacher "in ranking pupils in terms of *present* levels of understanding and skill and in grouping pupils of similar levels for effective beginning instruction." However, the teacher should ask how this score provides a basis for instruction, and "effective beginning reading instruction" in what? The total score is strongly weighted toward letter knowledge (65 out of

135 items), whereas vocabulary is sparsely represented (20 items).

As another instance, the statement that language differences (second language and dialect variations) "cause instructional problems for the classroom teacher" is a questionable generalization not supported without qualification by research. Finally, the relation between alphabet knowledge and reading is well established, but so is the fact that learning the alphabet, "the visual symbols which represent sounds," is not per se "fundamental to reading success."

The section entitled "Standardization of the Test" must be read with care to be fully appreciated. An initial standardization appears to have been reasonably well designed and based on an adequate sample size. However, the final standardization is based on a sample of fewer than 1,000 students of unspecified origin. This suggests that percentiles and standard scores should be taken with a grain of salt. Reliability of the total test score is estimated at .96 for Form A and .95 for Form B. Subtest reliabilities are unreported, and there is no information on subtest intercorrelations. Neither are there any data on validity. A detailed item analysis is reported, with information about the distractibility of each alternative. This could be of considerable usefulness to the teacher in evaluating the students' error patterns.

Overall, this is not a bad test for the purpose intended, compared with others on the market. The teacher could probably obtain the same (or better) information more cheaply and quickly, without the paraphernalia of percentiles and standard scores, by adapting materials available in the classroom and following the tasks laid out in the test manual as simply and directly as possible. The teacher might worry that such an approach would be suspect because of the lack of established standardization data. However, many data are not necessary for instructional assessment, and may actually lead to misuse.

SIDNEY W. SHNAYER, *Professor of Education, California State University, Chico, California.*

One purpose of this test is to measure the degree to which "children have acquired the abilities and understandings that contribute to success in beginning primary learning." As a second purpose, the authors suggest that there is diagnostic value to the subtests, which "are designed to serve as an initial guide for planning and pacing appropriate instruction for each child."

Normative data are based on "children who had just begun the first year of school." The norms, which include standard scores, stanines and percentiles, were derived from children two-thirds of whom "had at least three to five months of kindergarten, and 81 children who had either no kindergarten or no more than eight weeks in a summer kindergarten."

As an aside, the publishers and the authors produce a reading series with a well developed prereading program. This instrument seems designed to measure the effects of that specific instructional program rather than for use by a school providing other kinds of prereading experiences.

The basic information concerning norming procedures is difficult to describe because it must be ferreted out from several different places. The manual is less informative than usually expected.

The reported odd-even reliabilities (.96 for Form A, .95 for Form B) for the total are certainly acceptable. However, if the subtests are to be used in the diagnostic manner suggested, the subtests also must have a high degree of reliability. No information is available on their reliability. The diagnostic utility of each of the subtests might be viewed by examining the item analysis data. Comparison of an item analysis for a class with the item analysis data in the manual, in a test of this kind, would be a valuable contribution to the teacher willing to take the time to make the analysis. It is recommended for the items which are relevant to the curriculum of the school. There are no data with respect to predictive or concurrent validity, even though a major purpose of the test is to predict success in beginning primary learning.

Directions for administration are clear and provide opportunity for additional examples for portions of the test, such as the rhyming section, where children may need added practice in understanding the task and the terminology (such as "pairs of words" and "last sound" in a word).

The printing of the colored pictures is somewhat blurry, dark, and uneven. While row markers (small sketches) are effectively placed *outside* of the item boxes on the first subtest,

row markers placed *inside* the item boxes on three other subtests may prove confusing to children who associate the picture markers with the word letter or sound test stimulus in the same box.

In summary, the IST would seem to be an appropriate and useful test if the content is specifically related to the curricular expectations of a school district. Furthermore, the specificity of the subtests and the length of total test would be advantageous if a teacher or school wished to measure the relationship of what has been taught to what has been learned. In that sense, then, use of the test as a criterion-referenced instrument might yield its greatest value. As an instrument which meets its stated purposes, it has too many shortcomings. At the present time this test is not recommended as an instrument to measure "the abilities and understandings that contribute to success in primary learning." On the other hand, it is one of the better developed tests tied to a specific prereading program.

[800]

★Jansky Screening Index. Kgn; 1972; JSI; no reliability data or norms for total score; authors recommend use of local cutoff points to identify high-risk groups; individual; 1 form; no separate manual (manual contained in 9 below); score sheet (no date, 1 page); $16.50 per kit of testing materials (except manual) including 35 score sheets and 35 word matching tests; $1.25 per 35 score sheets or word matching tests; postage extra; (15–20) minutes; Jeannette Jansky and Katrina de Hirsch (manual); Matt-Jansky. *

REFERENCES
1. DE HIRSCH, KATRINA; JANSKY, JEANETTE J.; AND LANG-FORD, WILLIAM S. "Early Prediction of Reading Failure." *B Orton Soc* 16:1–13+ '66. *
2. DE HIRSCH, KATRINA; JANSKY, JEANNETTE JEFFERSON; AND LANGFORD, WILLIAM S. *Predicting Reading Failure.* New York: Harper & Row, Publishers, Inc., 1966. Pp. xv, 144. *
3. DE HIRSCH, KATRINA, AND JANSKY, JEANETTE. "Kindergarten Protocols of Failing Readers," pp. 30–42. In *Reading Diagnosis and Evaluation.* Edited by Dorothy L. De Boer. Newark, Del.: International Reading Association, 1970. Pp. vi, 138. *
4. TRIMBLE, AUBREY C. "Can Remedial Reading Be Eliminated?" *Acad Ther* 5(3):207–13 sp '70. * (*PA* 44:19420)
5. ZAESKE, ARNOLD. "The Validity of Predictive Index Tests in Predicting Reading Failure at the End of Grade One," pp. 28–33. In *Reading Difficulties: Diagnosis, Correction, and Remediation.* Edited by William K. Durr. Newark, Del.: International Reading Association, 1970. Pp. vii, 276. *
6. ADKINS, PATRICIA L.; HOLMES, GEORGE R.; AND SCHNACKENBERG, ROBERT C. "Factor Analyses of the de Hirsch Predictive Index." *Percept & Motor Skills* 33(3):1319–25 D '71. * (*PA* 48:3655)
7. WEIMER, WAYNE ROBERT. *A Perceptuomotor and Oral Language Program for Children Identified as Potential Failures.* Doctor's thesis, University of New Mexico (Albuquerque, N.M.), 1971. (*DAI* 32:3877A)
8. EAVES, L. C.; KENDALL, D. C.; AND CRICHTON, J. U. "The Early Detection of Minimal Brain Dysfunction." *J Learn Dis* 5(8):454–62 O '72. * (*PA* 49:7436)
9. JANSKY, JEANNETTE, AND DE HIRSCH, KATRINA. *Preventing Reading Failure: Prediction, Diagnosis, Intervention,* pp. 39–66, 146–59. New York: Harper & Row, Publishers, 1972. Pp. xi, 207. *

10. MILLER, WILMA H. "Predicting Achievement in First-Grade Reading and Writing." *Ill Sch Res* 8(3):17–23 sp '72. *

11. WALLBROWN, JANE D.; WALLBROWN, FRED H.; AND ENGIN, ANN W. "The Relative Importance of Mental Age and Selected Assessors of Auditory and Visual Perception in the Metropolitan Readiness Test." *Psychol Sch* 11(2):136–43 Ap '74. * (*PA* 52:13209)

12. CAMP, BONNIE W. "Review of Jansky Screening Index," pp. 495–7. In *Pediatric Screening Tests.* Edited by William K. Frankenburg and Bonnie W. Camp. Springfield, Ill.: Charles C Thomas, Publisher, 1975. Pp. xii, 549. *

13. GOLDSTEIN, ARNOLD. "Review of Jansky Screening Index," pp. 494–5. In *Pediatric Screening Tests.* Edited by William K. Frankenburg and Bonnie W. Camp. Springfield, Ill.: Charles C Thomas, Publisher, 1975. Pp. xii, 549. *

14. WALLBROWN, JANE D.; ENGIN, ANN W.; WALLBROWN, FRED H.; AND BLAHA, JOHN. "The Prediction of First Grade Reading Achievement With Selected Perceptual-Cognitive Tests." *Psychol Sch* 12(2):140–9 Ap '75. * (*PA* 55:1605)

[801]

The Macmillan Reading Readiness Test, Revised Edition. First grade entrants; 1965–70; 6 or 8 scores: rating scale, visual discrimination, auditory discrimination, vocabulary and concepts, letter names, total for tests 1–5, visual-motor (optional), total for tests 1–6; 1 form ('70, 12 pages); manual ('70, 15 pages); $6.60 per 10 tests; $3.16 per specimen set; postage extra; [75–90] minutes in 3 to 5 sessions; Albert J. Harris and Edward R. Sipay; Macmillan Co. *

REFERENCES

1. STALLINGS, JANE AINEL. *Reading Methods and Sequencing Abilities: An Interaction Study in Beginning Reading.* Doctor's thesis, Stanford University (Stanford, Calif.), 1970. (*DAI* 31:6415A)

2. WHITE, GENEVIEVE. *Procedures for Predicting Children's Success in First Grade Achievement.* Master's thesis, Arkansas State University (State University, Ark.), 1970.

3. MAHAFFEY, JAMES PERRY. *An Investigation of the Relationship of Selected Oral Language and Readiness Factors to First-Grade Reading Achievement.* Doctor's thesis, University of South Carolina (Columbia, S.C.), 1974. (*DAI* 36:695A)

KATHRYN HOOVER CALFEE, *Palo Alto Unified School District, Palo Alto, California.*

The *Macmillan Reading Readiness Test* is designed primarily to aid in "determining which children are ready for beginning reading instruction," and secondarily for "evaluating the success of a reading readiness program." The concept of readiness has been challenged by a number of educators in recent years. It is true that some children come to school with experiences and knowledge that leave them better prepared than others to benefit from the reading instruction that is typically offered. In fact, some children enter first grade already reading with considerable skill and fluency; such children will do quite well on this test. Suppose, on the other hand, that a child cannot read and is poorly prepared to benefit from typical instruction (whatever that may be). Is the teacher to wait while the child becomes ready? Of course not. Reading builds on continuous development of a complex of skills that begins with the early growth of language, reaches a peak in the elementary grades, and continues to be refined through college. For the kindergarten and first

grade teacher, it is not a question of knowing who is ready—every child is ready to be taught something. The usefulness of a test like the Macmillan lies in helping the teacher decide what the child knows and what he does not know, as a basis for planning an instructional program for the child.

The manual recommends giving the test in three to five sessions at the end of kindergarten or a few weeks after the child begins first grade. Each session takes about 20 minutes. It is suggested that "the class should be divided for testing into groups of between ten and fifteen children," and that "it is desirable for each teacher to test her [*sic*] own children and to be assisted by a helper (preferably another teacher)." With a class of 30 children, administration of the testing may require as much as five hours of the teacher's time, plus an equal amount of another teacher's time. A careful job of scoring is likely to take another 10 hours.

The pictures presented to the student for the auditory discrimination and the vocabulary and concepts subtests are small and contain irrelevant detail and shading that are likely to make the test more difficult. The vocabulary test is biased toward knowledge within the experience of the middle class child—monkeys play tricks while fish, ducks, and pigs do not; magicians make things disappear, but policemen don't; dolphins and anacondas are rare in inner-city ghettos. The format of the copying subtest requires answers to be drawn in a box to the right of the form, so that left-handed children are penalized.

The manual also has certain flaws. The print is small and the dialogue is not set apart from the rest of the material. The format of the auditory subtest is different from the other subtests, in that the child must mark *both* of two correct answers for each item, and receives no partial credit. The instructions are ambiguous on how the student is to be told to mark *two* answers for each item. On the positive side, scoring the test is simplified by stencils provided in the test kit. However, the copying (visual-motor) test poses quite a challenge. A plastic template and nearly two full pages of guidelines and scoring details must be mastered.

No weight at all is given to the optional word-recognition subtest. No data are provided about this subtest and, although the other subtests are numbered, it is not even assigned a number. This is surprising, since this subtest comes closer to measuring reading than do any of the others. The authors do suggest that if the child performs above the chance level on this test, "his reading ability should be checked out individually." Indeed, the teacher might even want to check out the child's reading ability *before* administering the Macmillan test, if there is any likelihood that the student knows how to read.

The instructional applications section of the manual is rather terse, less than half a page in length. The teacher is told to assign each student's performance to one of five levels that range from "very high" (top 10%) to "very low" (bottom 10%). The student in the top level is supposed to be ready for an immediate start in reading instruction, and should make rapid progress. The student in the lowest level is likely to be seriously handicapped and the teacher should not expect the child to make reasonable progress in the early stages of reading instruction. The authors suggest further diagnostic evaluation by a specialist for children in the bottom category. They state that some of these children "may be mentally retarded, others may show the effects of severe cultural deprivation, and still others may have physical defects or emotional disturbances that are likely to interfere with learning to read. One child may need eyeglasses; a second, intensive psychotherapy; a third, activities to compensate for cultural handicaps; a fourth, placement in a special class for mentally retarded children." Nowhere is there a suggestion that these children may not have had an opportunity to learn what the test measures, that they may be normal children who will respond to instruction. To the contrary, the stated opinion is that simply delaying the start of reading instruction and providing a uniform readiness program will be ineffective.

All in all, it is not clear why the teacher would want to spend the time and energy required to administer, score, and interpret the *Macmillan Reading Readiness Test*. The test might be useful for program evaluation, but this is not the teacher's concern. Since the test depends largely on teacher observation and rating, why not build on this principle, adding objective information as required for the individual stu-

dent? For instance, in place of the complex copying test, the teacher can ask the child to copy letters, words, or sentences, depending on his level of skill. The test of letter names is easy to administer by showing the student letter cards and asking him to name each one. This eliminates guessing. Knowledge of word meanings and auditory-phonetic principles can be gained through direct interaction with the student. Such information is not standardized nor is it norm-referenced, to be sure. But these characteristics of the Macmillan seem likely to lead to misuse more often than not.

ROGER A. RUTH, *Associate Professor of Education, University of Victoria, Victoria, British Columbia, Canada.*

The directions to the teacher recommend that children be taught the specific vocabulary of test administration and the manner of marking responses, before testing. Many teachers would have recognized the desirability of this pretest instruction, but its explication in the test manual lends assurance that the standardization group also enjoyed this advantage.

The sections on visual discrimination (of letter similarity and word similarity), vocabulary and concepts, and letter names are objective in scoring, and the marking task is eased by provision of scoring templates.

The rating scale will pose some difficulty for the teacher in deciding which of five ratings (from very low to very high) to assign to a child's status in such characteristics as muscular coordination, maturity of pronunciation, and richness and variety of experience. Since the test is standardized for administration "early in the school year," it would be of particular interest to know the resources teachers would be expected to draw upon in rating "parental interest in schooling." Given Harris' long interest in handedness and cerebral dominance, it is surprising that the teacher is given no specific instruction on how to determine "hand preference."

A principal potential problem in administration is lack of a device for directing the attention of the child to the particular item under consideration. While items are numbered, the teacher is advised not to identify the item by its number, but to have the subjects locate it by moving a marker "under the next row." This

Macmillan Reading Readiness Test

procedure presents obvious opportunity for the child to lose his place, invalidating responses on succeeding items.

Although the test is represented as being usable either late in the kindergarten year or early in the first grade, there is nothing in the standardization procedure that would legitimate its use with the kindergarten group. Given the very considerable differences in academic emphasis from one kindergarten program to another, use of the rating scale would seem to be especially suspect.

The manual invites potential users of the MRRT to "judge its content validity for themselves." This seems to be a less-than-sufficient concern for the adequacy of task selection, on two accounts: the teacher-user is unlikely to be as familiar with research on predictive efficiency of various readiness measures as are the test authors, and could be expected to benefit from a more thorough discussion of the basis for selection; and the accumulated evidence that group intelligence tests predict beginning reading success as effectively as do reading readiness tests should alert the authors of the latter to a greater concern for content validity.

Another sort of content validity that needs consideration is the selection of particular items within tasks that, in principle, appear to have logical relationship to the reading task. On this basis, one may question the seemingly high proportion of stimulus words and response pictures in the vocabulary and concept subtest that would be alien to the experiences of disadvantaged urban children, and the age-appropriateness and culture-fairness of such vocabulary items as picnic, inside, twins, pedals, cliff, disappear, dolphin, dough, and anaconda.

With the exception of the rating scale, reliability coefficients are satisfactorily high (.80 to .95), and the MRRT total score would appear to predict first grade reading success about as well (r = .66) as other well-constructed readiness tests. As noted earlier, this is not significantly better than the predictions of group intelligence tests, but present-day politics of education may make it preferable to base instructional strategies on readiness scores rather than on intelligence indices, even if the two are equally efficient predictors.

Lastly, it must be observed that the empirical validity of the MRRT depends on the statistic

Macmillan Reading Readiness Test

the teacher elects as a basis for instructional planning. The raw scores and their percentile equivalents have been tested for their predictive validity. However, the manual offers an interpretation of these statistics as reflecting one of five "expectancy levels." It can be expected that most teacher-users ultimately will make instructional decisions respecting these expectancy levels, and no rationale—statistical or otherwise —is offered by the test authors for their assignments.

SUMMARY. In view of the considerable number of specific criticisms offered above, my summary reaction to the *Macmillan Reading Readiness Test* may seem incongruous, even perverse: I think that it is as good as most of its kind; better than many. Whether it would be the best choice for a particular teacher depends on the characteristics of that teacher's instructional program and students. I would think it more appropriate for a phonetic approach to reading than other approaches; and for predicting success of middle class children, than that of disadvantaged children. Even within these constraints, my preference would be the *Clymer-Barrett Prereading Battery,* if only because of the latter's provision for specific test-item identification.

[802]
*Metropolitan Readiness Tests, 1976 Edition. First half kgn, second half kgn and first grade entrants; 1933–76; MRT; 2 forms; 2 levels; 2 editions (hand scored, MRC scored); practice test ('74, 4 pages); parent-teacher conference report ('76, 4 pages) for each level; $11.75 per 35 hand scored tests; $26 per 35 MRC scored tests; $3.95 per specimen set; postage extra; MRC scoring service, $1 and over per test; Joanne R. Nurss and Mary E. McGauvran; Psychological Corporation. *

a) LEVEL 1. First half kgn; 1974–76; 9 or 10 scores: auditory memory, rhyming, visual skills (letter recognition, visual matching, total), language skills (school language listening, quantitative language, total), total, copying (optional); no reliability data or norms for copying score; Forms P, Q, ('74, 25 pages); interpretation manual ('76, 31 pages); directions for administering ('76, 29 pages) for each form; (105) minutes in 7 sessions.

b) LEVEL 2. Second half kgn and first grade entrants; 1933–76; previous edition still available; 4–6 scores: auditory skills, visual skills, language skills, total, quantitative skills (optional), copying (optional); no data on reliability for part scores; norms consist of means and standard deviations for part scores, no norms for copying score; Forms P, Q, ('74, 23 pages); interpretation manual ('76, 30 pages); directions for administering ('76, 29 pages) for each form; (110) minutes in 5 sessions.

See T2:1716 (55 references); for reviews by Robert Dykstra and Harry Singer of an earlier edition, see

7:757 (124 references); for a review by Eric F. Gardner and an excerpted review by Fay Griffith, see 4:570 (3 references); for a review by Irving H. Anderson, see 3:518 (5 references); for a review by W. J. Osburn, see 2:1552 (10 references).

REFERENCES

1–10. See 2:1552.
11–15. See 3:518.
16–18. See 4:570.
19–142. See 7:757.
143–197. See T2:1716; also includes a cumulative name index to the first 197 references, 5 reviews, and 1 excerpt for this test.
198. McCartin, Rose Amata, and Meyers, C. E. "An Exploration of six Semantic Factors at First Grade." *Multiv Behav Res* 1(1):74–94 Ja '66. * (*PA* 41:1415)
199. Long, Barbara H., and Henderson, Edmund H. "Teacher Judgments of Black and White School Beginners." *Sociol Ed* 44(3):358–68 su '71. *
200. Abrahamson, Roy E. "The Development of an Instrument for Measuring the Degrees of Divergent Responses Revealed in Clay Images Formed by First Grade School Children." *Studies Art Ed* 14(1):47–58 f '72. *
201. Alalouf, Albert Emanuel. *The Placement of First Grade Children With Special Attention Toward Teacher and Pupil Characteristics.* Doctor's thesis, University of Southern California (Los Angeles, Calif.), 1972. (*DAI* 33:3173A)
202. Armbruster, Rudolph A. *Perceptual Motor, Gross Motor, and Sensory Motor Skills Training: The Effect Upon School Readiness and Self Concept Development of Kindergarten Children.* Doctor's thesis, Wayne State University (Detroit, Mich.), 1972. (*DAI* 33:6644A)
203. Ayllon, Teodoro, and Kelly, Kathy. "Effects of Reinforcement on Standardized Test Performance." *J Appl Behav Analysis* 5(4):477–84 w '72. * (*PA* 49:11329)
204. Benenson, Thea Fuchs. *The Relationship Between Visual Memory for Designs and Early Reading Achievement.* Doctor's thesis, Columbia University (New York, N.Y.), 1972. (*DAI* 33:186A)
205. Byrnes, Elizabeth G. *A Validity Study of the Kirk Teachers Estimate of Kindergarten Pupils Abilities When Compared With the Results of Teacher Prediction and the Metropolitan Readiness Tests.* Master's thesis, University of Kansas (Lawrence, Kan.), 1972.
206. Cicirelli, Victor G. "A Note on the Factor Analysis of Disadvantaged Children's Illinois Test of Psycholinguistic Abilities and Achievement Test Scores." *J Exp Ed* 41(1):5–8 f '72. * (*PA* 49:9877)
207. Drummond, Robert J. "Concurrent and Predictive Validity of the Cooperative Preschool Inventory." *El Sch Guid & Counsel* 7(1):60–1 O '72. *
208. Fisher, Maurice D., and Turner, Robert V. "The Effects of a Perceptual-Motor Training Program Upon the Academic Readiness of Culturally Disadvantaged Kindergarten Children." *J Negro Ed* 41(2):142–50 sp '72. * (*PA* 49:5390)
209. Geuder, Ralph W. *Sex as a Factor in the Prediction of Academic Performance.* Doctor's thesis, University of Maryland (College Park, Md.), 1972. (*DAI* 34:663A)
210. Haberman, Irene. *Comparative Validity of the Metropolitan Reading Readiness Test and Teacher Prediction of Pupil Success in Reading.* Master's thesis, Fairleigh Dickinson University (Rutherford, N.J.), 1972.
211. Hammond, Ruth Kartchner. *A Predictive Study of Mathematical Readiness and Achievement: A Longitudinal Study From First Grade Entrance Through Third Grade.* Doctor's thesis, Purdue University (Lafayette, Ind.), 1972. (*DAI* 33:637A)
212. Hauptman, Eileen B. *Predictability of the Metropolitan Readiness Test for First Grade Reading Achievement in Bellmawr.* Master's thesis, Glassboro State College (Glassboro, N.J.), 1972.
213. Lohnes, Paul R., and Gray, Marian M. "Intelligence and the Cooperative Reading Studies." *Read Res Q* 7(3):466–76 sp '72. * (*PA* 49:9987)
214. Minton, Judith Haber. *The Impact of Sesame Street on Reading Readiness of Kindergarten Children.* Doctor's thesis, Fordham University (New York, N.Y.), 1972. (*DAI* 33:3396A)
215. Morgan, Edwin W. *The Identification and Treatment of Children With Potential Learning Difficulties Related to Reading Based on Extensive Background Factors Provided by a Professional Team.* Doctor's thesis, University of Montana (Missoula, Mont.), 1972. (*DAI* 33:84A)
216. Morrison, James B., Jr. *The Prediction of Reading Achievement in Grade One.* Doctor's thesis, Boston University (Boston, Mass.), 1972. (*DAI* 33:1325A)
217. Newman, Anabel P. "Later Achievement Study of Pupils Underachieving in Reading in First Grade." *Read Res Q* 7(3):477–508 sp '72. * (*PA* 49:10005)
218. Oakland, Thomas. "The Effects of Test-Wiseness Materials on Standardized Test Performance of Preschool Disadvantaged Children." *J Sch Psychol* 10(4):355–60 D '72. * (*PA* 50:3860)
219. Plant, Walter T., and Southern, Mara L. "The Intellectual and Achievement Effects of Preschool Cognitive Stimulation of Poverty Mexican-American Children." *Genetic Psychol Monogr* 86(1):141–73 Ag '72. * (*PA* 49:1349)
220. Price, Eleanor, and Rosemier, Robert. "Some Cognitive and Affective Outcomes of Same-Sex Versus Coeducational Grouping in First Grade." *J Exp Ed* 40(4):70–7 su '72. * (*PA* 49:3289)
221. Rubin, Rosalyn. "Sex Differences in Effects of Kindergarten Attendance on Development of School Readiness and Language Skills." *El Sch J* 72(5):265–74 F '72. *
222. Rupp, Jane Downs. *The Prediction of Reading Readiness With Auditory and Visual Assessors and Intelligence Test in Three Sub-Samples.* Doctor's thesis, Ohio State University (Columbus, Ohio), 1972. (*DAI* 33:575A)
223. Serwer, Blanche, J.; Shapiro, Bernard J.; and Shapiro, Phyllis P. "Achievement Prediction of 'High-Risk' Children." *Percept & Motor Skills* 35(2):347–54 O '72. * (*PA* 49:7970)
224. Severson, Roger A. "Early Detection of Children With Potential Learning Disabilities: A Seven-Year Effort." Abstract. *Proc 80th Ann Conv Am Psychol Assn* 7(2):561–2 '72. * (*PA* 48:5679)
225. Wallner, Nancy Kubin. "The Development of a Test of Listening Comprehension for Kindergarten and Beginning First Grade—A Preliminary Report." *South J Ed Res* 6(1): 39–48 Ja '72. *
226. Aliotti, Nicholas C., and Blanton, William E. "Creative Thinking Ability, School Readiness, and Intelligence in First Grade Children." *J Psychol* 84(1):137–43 My '73. * (*PA* 50:7620)
227. Asbury, Charles A. "Cognitive Correlates of Discrepant Achievement in Reading." *J Negro Ed* 42(2):123–33 sp '73. * (*PA* 51:3884)
228. Bennett, Dale Eugene. *The Differential Predictive Effectiveness of Selected Pre-Reading Measures on Success in Reading at the End of Grade One Under Each of Six Major Approaches to First-Grade Reading Instruction.* Doctor's thesis, University of Minnesota (Minneapolis, Minn.), 1973. (*DAI* 34:3680A)
229. Bolig, John R., and Fletcher, Gerald O. "The MRT vs. Ratings of Kindergarten Teachers as Predictors of Success in First Grade." *Ed Leadership* 30(7):637–40 Ap '73. *
230. Brecht, Richard David. *The Effects of Visual Tracking Training on Kindergarten Reading Readiness Scores.* Doctor's thesis, University of Missouri (Columbia, Mo.), 1973. (*DAI* 35:907A)
231. Buckland, Pearl, and Balow, Bruce. "Effect of Visual Perceptual Training on Reading Achievement." *Excep Children* 39(4):299–304 Ja '73. * (*PA* 50:5643)
232. Caspers, Earl Marcus. *A Study of the Relationship Between Teacher Judgment of Kindergarten Pupils and Their Performance on Three Major Reading Readiness Tests.* Doctor's thesis, Southern Illinois University (Carbondale, Ill.), 1973. (*DAI* 34:6492A)
233. Coury, Janine Peschard. *Screening for Learning Disabilities Among Inner-City First Graders.* Doctor's thesis, University of Tennessee (Knoxville, Tenn.), 1973. (*DAI* 34:2382A)
234. Crum, Lauren Ellen. *The Effect of Perceptual-Motor Training on the Reading Readiness of Kindergarten Children as Measured by the Metropolitan Readiness Test.* Master's thesis, Ohio State University (Columbus, Ohio), 1973.
235. Denson, Teresa Ann. *An Experimental Study of the Effect of a Listening Skills Training Program in Kindergarten on the Development of Pre-Reading Skills.* Doctor's thesis, University of Southern California (Los Angeles, Calif.), 1973. (*DAI* 34:3986A)
236. Goodman, Libby, and Wiederholt, J. Lee. "Predicting Reading Achievement in Disadvantaged Children." *Psychol Sch* 10(2):181–5 Ap '73. * (*PA* 50:9860)
237. Hartlage, Lawrence C., and Lucas, David G. "Early Predictors of Optimum Educational Approaches to Preventing Reading Failure in First-Grade Children." Abstract. *Proc 81st Ann Conv Am Psychol Assn* 8(2):717–8 '73. * (*PA* 50:7731)
238. Johnson, Bonnie Lee. *The Effect of Three Visual Perceptual Programs on the Readiness of Kindergarten Children.* Doctor's thesis, Texas A & M University (College Station, Tex.), 1973. (*DAI* 34:3836A)
239. Kreamer, Thomas Lawrence. *Listening Comprehension as a Predictor of First Grade Reading Achievement.* Doctor's thesis, McNeese State University (Lake Charles, La.), 1973. (*DAI* 34:1487A)
240. Kulberg, Janet M., and Gershman, Elaine S. "School Readiness: Studies of Assessment Procedures and Comparison of Three Types of Programming for Immature 5-Year-Olds." *Psychol Sch* 10(4):410–20 O '73. * (*PA* 51:9975)
241. Lessler, Ken, and Bridges, Judith S. "The Prediction of Learning Problems in a Rural Setting: Can We Improve on Readiness Tests?" *J Learn Dis* 6(2):90–4 F '73. * (*PA* 50:3820)
242. McCleskey, Joyce Anne. *Specific Language Training as a Method of Facilitating Reading Readiness for a Select*

Group of First Grade Children. Doctor's thesis, University of Southern Mississippi (Hattiesburg, Miss.), 1973. (*DAI* 34: 4572A)

243. MAULDIN, WILLIAM TIMOTHY. *Prediction of First Grade Reading Scores Utilizing Burks' Academic Readiness Scale and the Metropolitan Readiness Tests.* Master's thesis, California State University (Long Beach, Calif.), 1973.

244. MILLS, JAMES CHARLES. "The Effect of Art Instruction Upon a Reading Development Test: An Experimental Study With Rural Appalachian Children." *Studies Art Ed* 14(3):4–8 sp '73. *

245. MOORE, RUTH C., AND OGLETREE, EARL J. "A Comparison of the Readiness and Intelligence of First Grade Children With and Without a Full Year of Head Start Training." *Ed* 93(3):266–70 F–Mr '73. *

246. MUNDY, MICHAEL JEROME. *An Analysis of an Academically Structured Head Start Program for: (1) Geographic, (2) Academic Treatment, and (3) High-Low Subject Ability Variables.* Doctor's thesis, Auburn University (Auburn, Ala.), 1973. (*DAI* 34:2395A)

247. OGSTON, D. G. "The Technical Standards of Intellective Tests Used in Alberta Elementary Schools: A Review." *Alberta J Ed Res* (Canada) 19(4):270–83 D '73. *

248. PIKULSKI, JOHN. "Predicting Sixth Grade Achievement by First Grade Scores." *Read Teach* 27(3):284–7 D '73. * (*PA* 51:11961)

249. RUBIN, ROSALYN A.; ROSENBLATT, CYNTHIA; AND BALOW, BRUCE. "Psychological and Educational Sequelae of Prematurity." *Pediatrics* 52(3):352–63 S '73. *

250. RUDE, ROBERT T. "Readiness Tests: Implications for Early Childhood Education." *Read Teach* 26(6):572–80 Mr '73. * (*PA* 51:5998)

251. RUDOLPH, CHARLES ERNEST. *A Comparison of the Dimensions of the Cooperative Preschool Inventory With Selected Measures of Intelligence and Readiness.* Doctor's thesis, Mississippi State University (State College, Miss.), 1973. (*DAI* 34:4888A)

252. SHEPHERD, RICHARD CHARLES. *An Investigation of Selected Factors in Oral Language Performance Related to Readiness for Beginning Reading Instruction.* Doctor's thesis, Temple University (Philadelphia, Pa.), 1973. (*DAI* 34:1713A)

253. WILBURN, DAVID JOSEPH. *First Grade Entrance Age as a Factor in Sixth Grade Achievement Across Readiness Levels.* Doctor's thesis, University of Maryland (College Park, Md.), 1973. (*DAI* 34:3481B)

254. WILLIS, EVA HARRELL. *"Sesame Street" Viewing in Early Childhood in Relation to Readiness Skills and Achievement as Measured by Standardized Tests.* Doctor's thesis, University of Northern Colorado (Greeley, Colo.), 1973. (*DAI* 34:2293B)

255. YORE, LARRY DEAN. *A Comparison Study of Reading Readiness Skills Acquisition by Two Methods: A Traditional Reading Readiness Program and a Kindergarten Science Curriculum.* Doctor's thesis, University of Minnesota (Minneapolis, Minn.), 1973. (*DAI* 34:7071A)

256. ATWATER, BETTIE CHAMBERLAIN. *Relationships of Parent and Teacher Ratings of Specific Learning, Motivation, Creativity, and Leadership Behaviors to Readiness Scores of First Grade Early Entrance Selectees.* Doctor's thesis, Florida State University (Tallahassee, Fla.), 1974. (*DAI* 35:6001A)

257. AYERS, JERRY B.; ROHR, MICHAEL E.; AND AYERS, MARY N. "Perceptual-Motor Skills, Ability to Conserve, and School Readiness." *Percept & Motor Skills* 38(2):491–4 Ap '74. * (*PA* 53:842)

258. BOOK, ROBERT M. "Predicting Reading Failure: A Screening Battery for Kindergarten Children." *J Learn Dis* 7(1):43–7 Ja '74. * (*PA* 52:1802)

259. BUSCH, ROBERT F. *Predicting First-Grade Reading Achievement.* Doctor's thesis, University of Missouri (Columbia, Mo.), 1974. (*DAI* 36:216A)

260. DENSON, TERI A., AND MICHAEL, WILLIAM B. "The Rutgers Drawing Test as a Midyear Kindergarten Predictor of End-of-Kindergarten Readiness for First Grade." *Ed & Psychol Meas* 34(4):999–1002 w '74. * (*PA* 54:6378)

261. DEVRIES, RHETA. "Relationships Among Piagetian, IQ, and Achievement Assessments." *Child Develop* 45(3):746–56 S '73. *

262. DOKES, MARION A. *The Effect of Oral Language on the Performance of Kindergarten Children on the Metropolitan Reading Readiness Test.* Master's thesis, Texas Woman's University (Denton, Tex.), 1974.

263. ELIJAH, DAVID VICTOR, JR. *Teacher Expectations: Determinants of Pupils' Reading Achievement.* Doctor's thesis, Oklahoma State University (Stillwater, Okla.), 1974. (*DAI* 35:6570A)

264. ENGIN, ANN W. "The Relative Importance of the Subtests of the Metropolitan Readiness Test in the Prediction of First Grade Reading and Arithmetic Achievement Criteria." *J Psychol* 88(2):289–98 N '74. * (*PA* 54:1971)

265. HOLMES, GARY DONALD. *A Comparison of the Comprehensive Tests of Basic Skills and the Metropolitan Readiness Tests in Predicting Reading Success of First Grade Children as Measured by the Gates-MacGinitie Reading Tests in Floyd County, Georgia Schools.* Doctor's thesis, Mississippi State University (State College, Miss.), 1974. (*DAI* 35:4912A)

266. HUBERTY, CARL J., AND SWAN, WILLIAM W. "Preschool Classroom Experience and First-Grade Achievement." *J Ed Res* 67(7):311–6 My '74. * (*PA* 52:11012)

267. HUESING, RALPH ADOLF. *Developmental Predictor Variables for Subsequent Academic Achievement.* Doctor's thesis, St. Louis University (St. Louis, Mo.), 1974. (*DAI* 35:4284A)

268. LEWIS, JOHN. "A Study of the Validity of the Metropolitan Readiness Tests." *Ed & Psychol Meas* 34(2):415–6 su '74. * (*PA* 53:4098)

269. McCLESKEY, JOYCE. "Specific Language Training as a Method of Facilitating Reading Readiness for a Select Group of First Grade Children." *South J Ed Res* 8(2):236–54 sp '74. * (*PA* 53:3993)

270. McNINCH, GEORGE. "Awareness of Aural and Visual Word Boundary Within a Sample of First Graders." *Percept & Motor Skills* 38(3, pt 2):1127–34 Je '74. * (*PA* 53:1949)

271. MAITLAND, SUZANNE; NADEAU, J. B. E.; AND NADEAU, GRETCHEN. "Early School Screening Practices." *J Learn Dis* 7(10):645–9 D '74. * (*PA* 53:10558)

272. MARGOLIS, HOWARD. *The Effects of an Impulsive or Reflective Conceptual Tempo Upon the Auditory Perceptual, Reading Readiness, and Intelligence Test Performances of Kindergarten Children.* Doctor's thesis, Hofstra University (Hempstead, N.Y.), 1974. (*DAI* 35:1503A)

273. MASELLI, DOMINIC. *A Correlational Study of the Metropolitan Readiness Tests and Sixth Grade Reading Achievement.* Master's project, California State University (San Jose, Calif.), 1974.

274. MURPHY, MAUREEN CARTWRIGHT. "Academic Implications of a High School Entrance Examination for Economically Disadvantaged and Other Students." *J Ed Res* 67(7):303–6 Mr '74. * (*PA* 52:11022)

275. PASEWARK, RICHARD A.; SCHERR, STEPHEN S.; AND SAWYER, ROBERT N. "Correlations of Scores on the Vane Kindergarten, Wechsler Preschool and Primary Scale of Intelligence and Metropolitan Reading Readiness Tests." *Percept & Motor Skills* 38(2):518 Ap '74. * (*PA* 53:884)

276. PETERSON, VERNA LEE M. *The Kindergarten: The Interrelationships of Self-Concept, Language Age, Readiness, Socio-Economic Status, Sex, Family Size and Achievement.* Doctor's thesis, Texas Woman's University (Denton, Tex.), 1974. (*DAI* 36:5808A)

277. POWERS, SANDRA M. "The Validity of the Vane Kindergarten Test in Predicting Achievement in Kindergarten and First Grade." *Ed & Psychol Meas* 34(4):1003–7 w '74. * (*PA* 54:6416)

278. PUSSER, H. ELLISON, AND McCANDLESS, BOYD R. "Socialization Dimensions Among Inner-City Five-Year-Olds and Later School Success: A Follow-Up." *J Ed Psychol* 66(3): 285–90 Je '74. * (*PA* 52:11024)

279. RUBIN, ROSALYN A. "Preschool Application of the Metropolitan Readiness Tests: Validity, Reliability, and Preschool Norms." *Ed & Psychol Meas* 34(2):417–22 su '74. * (*PA* 53:4116)

280. TELEGDY, GABRIEL A. "A Factor Analysis of Four School Readiness Tests." *Psychol Sch* 11(2):127–33 Ap '74. * (*PA* 52:13283)

281. TELEGDY, GABRIEL A. "The Relationship Between Socioeconomic Status and School Readiness." *Psychol Sch* 11(3): 351–6 Jl '74. * (*PA* 53:10497)

282. THOMAS, JERRY R., AND CHISSOM, BRAD S. "Prediction of First Grade Academic Performance From Kindergarten Perceptual-Motor Data." *Res Q* 45(2):148–53 My '74. *

283. THOMAS, JERRY R.; CHISSOM, BRAD S.; AND BOOKER, LYNN. "Perceptual-Motor and Academic Relationships for Disadvantaged Children Classified as Learning Disabled and Normal." *Am Correct Ther J* 28(3):95–9 My–Je '74. * (*PA* 53:8380)

284. VAN HORN, K. ROGER, AND HOLLAND, JEAN M. "Relationships Between the ABC Inventory and the Metropolitan Readiness Test." *Psychol Sch* 11(4):396–9 O '74. * (*PA* 54:2002)

285. VEGA, MANUEL, AND POWELL, ARNOLD. "Visual Defects and Performance on Psychological Tests." *J Negro Ed* 43(1): 127–30 w '74. * (*PA* 54:3514)

286. WALLBROWN, JANE D.; WALLBROWN, FRED H.; AND ENGIN, ANN W. "The Relative Importance of Mental Age and Selected Assessors of Auditory and Visual Perception in the Metropolitan Readiness Test." *Psychol Sch* 11(2):136–43 Ap '74. * (*PA* 52:13209)

287. WALLNER, NANCY KUBIN. "The Development of a Listening Comprehension Test for Kindergarten and Beginning First Grade." *Ed & Psychol Meas* 34(2):391–6 su '74. * (*PA* 53:4123)

288. WEBB, SARAH LEVESCY. *A Comparison of Three-Dimensional Mock-Up and Paper-Pencil Presentations of Readiness Test Material to First-Grade Students From Different Socioeconomic Levels.* Doctor's thesis, University of Oklahoma (Norman, Okla.), 1974. (*DAI* 35:1886A)

289. WHITE, WILLIAM F., AND SIMMONS, MARGARET. "First-Grade Readiness Predicted by Teachers' Perception of Students' Maturity and Students' Perception of Self." *Percept & Motor Skills* 30(1, pt 2):395–9 Ag '74. *

290. BEWLEY, WESLEY LEON. *The Effects of Family Structure Socioeconomic Status, and Pupil Gender Upon Children's*

Reading Readiness Scores. Doctor's thesis, University of Oklahoma (Norman, Okla.), 1975. (*DAI* 36:4982A)

291. CABALLERO, JANE ALEXIS. *A Comparison of Piagetian Conservation Concepts With Reading Achievement.* Doctor's thesis, University of South Carolina (Columbia, S.C.), 1975. (*DAI* 36:7182A)

292. CRUZ, SYLVIA; HEINRIHAR, INES; QUEZADA, ROSE; AND ZIRKEL, PERRY. "Spanish-Speaking Students and the Language Factor in the MRT." *Integrated Ed* 13(6):43–4 N–D '75. *

293. ELLER, WILLIAM, AND FARR, ROGER. "Consumer Awareness in Testing Reading," pp. 30–5. In *Issues in Evaluating Reading.* Edited by Stanley Wanat. Arlington, Va.: Center for Applied Linguistics, 1977. Pp. xiii, 63. *

294. DRAKE, SUZANNE V. "How Is Language Competence Related to Reading Readiness?" *Ill Sch Res* 11(3):15–8 sp '75. *

295. DRAKE, SUZANNE VIRGINIA. *Factors of Reading Readiness.* Doctor's thesis, University of Connecticut (Storrs, Conn.), 1975. (*DAI* 35:7524A)

296. EASLEY, DOROTHY JOHNSON. *A Comparative Study of the Kindergarten Child's Comprehensive Vocabulary Development and Readiness-to-Read Vocabulary Development.* Doctor's thesis, East Texas State University (Commerce, Tex.), 1975. (*DAI* 36:4988A)

297. MINTON, JUDITH HABER. "The Impact of Sesame Street on Readiness." *Sociol Ed* 48(2):141–51 sp '75. * (*PA* 54:8357)

298. TELEGDY, GABRIEL A. "The Effectiveness of Four Readiness Tests as Predictors of First Grade Academic Achievement." *Psychol Sch* 12(1):4–11 Ja '75. * (*PA* 54:10670)

299. TREADWAY, KATHRYN ANN. *The Relationship Between Pre-Reading Patterns of Behavior and Success With Specific Reading Methods of Kindergarten Children.* Doctor's thesis, Oklahoma State University (Stillwater, Okla.), 1975. (*DAI* 36:7193A)

300. BROWN, NINA W. "Non-Cognitive Characteristics in the Prediction of Reading Readiness." *Ed & Psychol Meas* 36(2):537–42 su '76. *

301. BUTTRAM, JOAN; COVERT, ROBERT W.; AND HAYES, MARJORIE. "Prediction of School Readiness and Early Grade Achievement by Classroom Teachers." *Ed & Psychol Meas* 36(2):543–6 su '76. *

302. COLLIGAN, ROBERT C. "Prediction of Kindergarten Reading Success From Preschool Report of Parents." *Psychol Sch* 13(3):304–8 Jl '76. * (*PA* 57:2001)

303. LORTON, ELLEN F. *Prediction of Academic Achievement With the First Grade Screening Test and the McCarthy Scales of Children's Abilities.* Doctor's thesis, Texas Woman's University (Denton, Tex.), 1976. (*DAI* 37:4285A)

304. MARGOLIS, HOWARD. "Relationship Between Auditory-Visual Integration, Reading Readiness, and Conceptual Tempo." *J Psychol* 93(2):181–9 Jl '76. * (*PA* 56:9645)

305. SALEZ, CAROLE JOAN. *A Study of the Relationships Among the Visual Discrimination and Auditory Discrimination Measures Found in Five Reading Readiness Batteries.* Doctor's thesis, University of Wisconsin (Madison, Wis.), 1976. (*DAI* 37:5065A)

306. BECHER, RHODA McSHANE, AND WOLFGANG, CHARLES H. "An Exploration of the Relationship Between Symbolic Representation in Dramatic Play and Art and the Cognitive and Reading Readiness Levels of Kindergarten Children." *Psychol Sch* 14(3):377–81 Jl '77. *

307. LAIDLAW, JOHN RUXTON. *A Study of Pre-Kindergarten Screening at Selected Elementary Schools.* Doctor's thesis, Arizona State University (Tempe, Ariz.), 1977. (*DAI* 37:6875A)

308. RANDEL, MILDRED A.; FRY, MAURINE A.; AND RALLS, ELIZABETH M. "Two Readiness Measures as Predictors of First and Third-Grade Reading Achievement." *Psychol Sch* 14(1):37–40 Ja '77. * (*PA* 58:6427)

[803]
Murphy-Durrell Reading Readiness Analysis.
First grade entrants; 1949–65, c1947–65; MDRRA; revision of *Murphy-Durrell Diagnostic Reading Readiness Test;* 6 scores: sound recognition, letter names (capitals, lower case, total), learning rate, total; 1 form ('64, 8 pages); flash cards ('65, 1 sheet); manual ('65, 20 pages); $8.50 per 35 tests; $2.25 per specimen set; postage extra; (60) minutes in 2 sessions; Helen A. Murphy and Donald D. Durrell; Psychological Corporation. *

See T2:1717 (7 references); for reviews by Rebecca C. Barr and Harry Singer, see 7:758 (10 references); for reviews by Joan Bollenbacher and S. S. Dunn of the earlier edition, see 5:679 (2 references); see also 4:571 (2 references).

REFERENCES

1–2. See 4:571.
3–4. See 5:679.

5–14. See 7:758.
15–21. See T2:1717; also includes a cumulative name index to the first 21 references and 4 reviews for this test.

22. COWEN, SHEILA RING. *The Use of a Moderated Stepwise Regression Technique in Determining Differential Predictability for Readers in First Grade.* Doctor's thesis, University of Pennsylvania (Philadelphia, Pa.), 1972. (*DAI* 33:1313A)

23. GRUEN, RONALD S. "Prediction of End-of-Year Reading Achievement for First- and Third-Grade Pupils." Abstract. *Proc 80th Ann Conv Am Psychol Assn* 7(2):563–4 '72. * (*PA* 48:5813)

24. KING, ETHEL M., AND FRIESEN, DORIS T. "Children Who Read in Kindergarten." *Alberta J Ed Res* (Canada) 18(3):147–61 S '72. *

25. LOHNES, PAUL R. "Statistical Descriptors of School Classes." *Am Ed Res J* 9(4):547–56 f '72. *

26. LOHNES, PAUL R., AND GRAY, MARIAN M. "Intelligence and the Cooperative Reading Studies." *Read Res Q* 7(3):466–76 sp '72. * (*PA* 49:9987)

27. NEWMAN, ANABEL P. "Later Achievement Study of Pupils Underachieving in Reading in First Grade." *Read Res Q* 7(3):477–508 sp '72. * (*PA* 49:10005)

28. BENNETT, DALE EUGENE. *The Differential Predictive Effectiveness of Selected Pre-Reading Measures on Success in Reading at the End of Grade One Under Each of Six Major Approaches to First-Grade Reading Instruction.* Doctor's thesis, University of Minnesota (Minneapolis, Minn.), 1973. (*DAI* 34:3680A)

29. PIKULSKI, JOHN. "Predicting Sixth Grade Achievement by First Grade Scores." *Read Teach* 27(3):284–7 D '73. * (*PA* 51:11961)

30. RUDE, ROBERT T. "Readiness Tests: Implications for Early Childhood Education." *Read Teach* 26(6):572–80 Mr '73. * (*PA* 51:5998)

31. RUDE, ROBERT T.; NIQUETTE, SHELDON; AND FOXGROVER, PHYLLIS. "The Retention of Visual and Auditory Discrimination Reading Skills." *J Ed Res* 68(5):192–6 Ja '75. * (*PA* 53:12503)

32. STAFFORD, JERRY. "Review of the Murphy-Durrell Reading Readiness Analysis." *Read World* 15(2):114–5 D '75. *

33. YOUNG, DOROTHY JUNE. *The Relationship Between Pre-Reading Behavior Patterns and Success of Specific Reading Methods With Kindergarten Children.* Doctor's thesis, Oklahoma State University (Stillwater, Okla.), 1975. (*DAI* 36:7195A)

34. SALEZ, CAROLE JOAN. *A Study of the Relationships Among the Visual Discrimination and Auditory Discrimination Measures Found in Five Reading Readiness Batteries.* Doctor's thesis, University of Wisconsin (Madison, Wis.), 1976. (*DAI* 37:5065A)

Read World 15(2):114–5 D '75. Jerry Stafford. * made up of three group measures designed to test abilities described as essential to success in beginning reading. The three tests are a *Phonemes Test,* a *Letter Names Test* and a *Learning Rate Test.* * *The Learning Rate Test* assesses students' ability to "learn" and recognize nine sight words. The words are taught in a systematic way by presenting them on a chalkboard, on flash cards, and in the test booklet. Words used in the test were chosen because of their meaningfulness to children. In all three situations in which the words are presented to the child, meaning is also emphasized. One hour after teaching, the students are tested to determine how many words they can recognize. Precisely why a one hour time period was used was not discussed by the authors. Nor were there any research data presented to support the use of such a time period. In addition, the *Learning Rate Test* did not include the use of a pretest. It is quite possible that for many children the test assesses what children knew prior to testing and not how well they learn. *

The *Manual of Directions* contains simple and easy to follow directions for administering and scoring the test. Also found in the *Manual of Directions* are suggestions for grouping and teaching students based on the results of the tests. The process of translating diagnostic data into productive learning is threatened from many sources. One possible source of difficulty is the inherent weakness found within the diagnostic instrument. Another potential source of difficulty is the misuse of data that the diagnostic instrument provides. Even a good testing instrument can be rendered useless if the test data are not used wisely. The instructional suggestions found in the *Manual*....if followed may actually preclude good instruction. As indicated in the *Manual*....the instructional suggestions are provided to assist teachers in providing instruction using three groups within a class. While it is true that many children will have their needs met using three groups, it is also true that many children's needs will not be met using such a grouping strategy. The failure....to include suggestions for the use of a variety of grouping strategies (especially flexible/skill grouping) is a serious omission. This apparent weakness is complicated by yet another factor. The *Manual*....recommends that instruction be based on the findings from this test. The fact that some children may need assistance in areas other than those measured by the M-DRRA is only incidently mentioned or totally ignored.

[804]

*PMA Readiness Level. Grades kgn–1; 1946–74; revision of still-in-print 1962 edition of *SRA Primary Mental Abilities* for grades kgn–1; 5 tests; examiner's manual ('74, 23 pages); user's manual ('74, 23 pages); profile ('74, 3 pages plus auditory discrimination test); $12 per 30 sets of tests and 1 set of manuals; $1.42 per specimen set; postage extra; (60) minutes for the battery; Thelma Gwinn Thurstone; Science Research Associates, Inc. *
a) AUDITORY DISCRIMINATION. 1974; 1 form (1 page in profile); [10] minutes.
b) VERBAL MEANING. 1946–74; 1 form ('74, 4 pages); [15] minutes.
c) PERCEPTUAL SPEED. 1946–74; 1 form ('74, 4 pages, abbreviated version of test copyrighted 1962); 3[10] minutes.
d) NUMBER FACILITY. 1946–74; 1 form ('74, 4 pages); [15] minutes.
e) SPATIAL RELATIONS. 1946–74; 1 form ('74, 4 pages, abbreviated adaptation of test copyrighted 1962); [15] minutes.

ROBERT DYKSTRA, *Professor of Education and Chairman, Department of Curriculum and In-*struction, University of Minnesota, Minneapolis, Minnesota.

The *PMA Readiness Level* is a revision of the 1962 edition of the *SRA Primary Mental Abilities* tests for kindergarten and first grade. The four tests used in the K–1 level of the 1962 PMA tests (verbal meaning, perceptual speed, number facility, and spatial relations) remain in the current battery, although they have been modified somewhat. Auditory discrimination has been added.

The manual states that the battery "is designed to provide both a measure of certain critical behaviors children bring into the classroom and information about each individual's level of development compared with that of other children." The manual suggests further that scores on the test battery are designed to suggest areas for instructional focus to help the child become "ready" for school learning.

A number of uses for information gathered are suggested in the manual. Teachers are encouraged, for example, to use the test results to check their own impressions about how individual children function in a learning situation. They are also advised to use the test data to assist them in selecting appropriate instructional materials. The manual does not suggest the nature of materials that might be appropriate in light of how a pupil or group of pupils perform on the various subtests. It suggests instead that test results can help in determining the *level* of instructional materials best suited to a given pupil or class. This suggestion appears to have extremely limited utility. A child who scores very well on the battery, for example, if placed in the middle of a primary reading program might still encounter considerable frustration because of unfamiliarity with specific prerequisite reading skills that would have been introduced in earlier levels of the program.

A third proposed use of the test instrument is to determine the rate of instruction for children. This suggestion undoubtedly reflects the IQ orientation of earlier editions of the PMA battery. In this regard, it is interesting to note that the current battery does not provide a total score but rather only separate scores for each of the tests. The battery does not provide, therefore, a single estimate of scholastic aptitude that might be used as a predictor of learning rate. Moreover, the manual fails to suggest how

Murphy-Durrell Reading Readiness Analysis

one should plan the rate of instruction for children whose five test scores reveal them to be above average in some mental abilities, below average in others.

Another suggested use of test data is to identify special needs of individual pupils or groups. This implies that the battery can be used diagnostically, a questionable implication in light of less than optimal test reliabilities and rather substantial test intercorrelations. Moreover, no evidence is provided that instruction in the abilities measured by the various tests improves performance in the respective primary mental abilities let alone the more general types of school learning.

The manual also suggests using test data to facilitate grouping for instruction. It would seem more appropriate, however, to group children on the basis of specific instructional needs in kindergarten and first grade rather than on more general measures of mental ability. One could also question the battery's proposed use as a device for communicating with parents. The tests by and large are not closely enough related to the curriculum in kindergarten and first grade to provide useful information about academic progress. At the same time, the battery is probably less than an adequate measure of scholastic aptitude if the school chose to provide parents with such information. Therefore, its value as a device for communicating with parents is far from clear.

Questions should also be raised about certain aspects of the battery from the standpoint of test construction, validity, and standardization. Some of the items on the auditory discrimination test, for example, appear to have questionable validity. In one item pupils are asked to discriminate between the pronunciations of petal and pedal. For many pupils and their teachers (who will be required to administer the item) these words are pronounced identically. In another item the examiner asks the pupil to mark a pitcher rather than a picture when illustrations of the two are presented side by side. It is likely that many children fail this item not because of faulty auditory discrimination but because their dialect fails to differentiate between the pronunciation of pitcher and picture.

The matter of test validity is discussed in the manual in terms of predictive validity, concurrent validity, and construct validity. Since the PMA is a readiness battery, one would expect a fairly comprehensive discussion of predictive validity. Such is not supplied, however. Predictive validity is discussed solely in terms of a single investigation in which correlations were obtained between the performance of 64 first grade pupils on an experimental edition of the battery and end-of-year achievement as indicated by academic grades (presumably awarded by teachers). It is certainly difficult to justify the use of teacher grades as the sole criterion measure of pupil achievement. This is especially true in light of the legitimate concern expressed by many that pupil performance on batteries such as this influences teacher expectations of what a pupil can achieve, which, in turn, may have an indirect influence on pupil achievement itself.

Norms for the test are provided separately for kindergarten and first grade pupils and are differentiated according to whether the child was tested in the beginning, middle, or end of the year. Tests were administered to the standardization sample, however, only in May, so only end-of-year norms represent actual performance. Scores for beginning and intermediate kindergarten and first grade pupils are extrapolated. It is interesting to note that the battery was not standardized on beginning first grade pupils even though that is the most likely point at which the tests would be administered in the actual school situation.

In fairness to the author and publisher, it should be said that the user's manual and examiner's manual exhibit a good deal of cautious and tentative language in their discussion of the use of test data. Much of their advice to teachers about the implication of types of test performance is clearly conjectural and is presented as such. All of this tentativeness tends to confirm, however, the doubts a potential user should have about the usefulness of the *PMA Readiness Level* as an instructional tool. It appears to try to be too many things to too many potential users and as a result makes a limited contribution to the assessment of specific readiness skills such as those related to reading. In the typical situation, moreover, it is these more specific reading-related readiness skills that are of interest to kindergarten and first grade teachers.

PMA Readiness Level

[805]

PreReading Expectancy Screening Scales. First grade entrants; 1973; PRESS; predicting reading problems in beginning readers; 4 scores: visual sequencing, visual/auditory spatial, auditory sequencing, letter identification; 1 form (5 pages); manual (18 pages); profiles for boys, girls, (1 page); $12.50 per 25 tests; $4.50 per 25 profiles; $4.50 per manual; $5.75 per specimen set; postage extra; (25–35) minutes; Lawrence C. Hartlage and David G. Lucas; Psychologists and Educators, Inc. *

REFERENCES

1. HARTLAGE, LAWRENCE C., AND LUCAS, DAVID G. "Group Screening for Reading Disability in First Grade Children." *J Learn Dis* 6(5):317–21 My '73. * (PA 51:1920)

ROBERT DYKSTRA, *Professor of Education and Chairman, Department of Curriculum and Instruction, University of Minnesota, Minneapolis, Minnesota.*

The authors describe this instrument as a group diagnostic battery for predicting reading problems in beginning readers. It includes tests of visual sequencing, visual/auditory space, auditory sequencing, and letter identification.

PRESS has little to recommend it and much to raise questions about. The materials, for example, include no clear statement concerning what the scales are designed to do or not to do. The manual subtitle indicates that the scales constitute a group *diagnostic* test. The directions for scoring, however, suggest that converting a given raw score to a percentile equivalent will help *predict* readiness to profit from initial reading instruction. Nothing more explicit in the way of a statement of purpose is given anywhere.

There is no evidence that the battery has diagnostic value in the usual sense of the word, despite the inclusion of a profile sheet which the manual suggests is designed to provide a graphic picture of a given child's strengths and weaknesses in readiness for reading. Virtually no rationale is given for the particular subtests included in the battery so it is difficult to determine how the authors relate performance on each measure to the process of learning to read. No data concerning intercorrelations among the various subtests are provided so it is impossible to estimate the degree to which the measures assess similar or different aspects of readiness; such information is essential if one is considering using a battery for differential diagnosis. Moreover, no evidence is provided that instruction aimed at improving performance on any of the subtests is related in any way to improving

a child's chances of success in beginning reading.

The battery's value as a predictive instrument is also subject to question. Among the four subtests, for example, only the visual sequencing test was significantly related to first grade reading achievement in each of three separate investigations. Multiple correlations between pupil performance on the total battery and a criterion measure of end-of-first-grade reading achievement ranged from .23 to .45 for six separate samples. The correlation of .23, moreover, failed to reach statistical significance at the .01 level of probability. In terms of this limited usefulness in prediction, it would be extremely difficult to justify the time and expense involved in administering the battery as a predictive instrument.

Another major weakness of the test is its failure to suggest even minimal instructional implications for a child who performs poorly on the various scales. The manual suggests that a child whose scores fall above the 40th percentile on all four subtests is an excellent candidate for success in initial reading instruction, whereas a child whose scores on all four subtests fall at or below the 30th percentile is likely not ready to profit from initial reading instruction. If the child scores well on the battery, a move ahead into formal reading instruction is clearly implied because there is little chance of failure. On the other hand, the sum total of the advice given to teachers about what to do with children who are classified as "not ready" is to suggest that they probably require either "fairly extensive enrichment or diferrment [*sic*] of reading instruction." It is interesting that the authors suggest enrichment (whatever that means) rather than remediation even though the battery is described as a diagnostic test. Furthermore, the teacher who opts to defer beginning reading instruction, in accordance with the test authors' suggestion, is given no advice about what to do with the "not-ready" child. It is implied that the teacher merely wait until the child attains readiness as measured by the subtests of this battery. Such implied advice is not very useful.

A number of other problems and unanswered questions remain. For example, the labeling of subtests is inconsistent. The manual provides directions for a memory test; the profile sheet lists no such test, but an auditory sequencing test instead. Separate profile sheets and percentile norms are provided for boys and girls with no explanation of why this is done. In fact, if the tests are to be used either diagnostically or predictively, why would a teacher wish to know how a given child's performance compared with only that of his same-sex peers rather than with that of the total population of first grade pupils? What would be the instructional implications of providing such information?

The norming of the test also raises questions. Children from a single school system were used, thereby casting doubts on the generalizability of the normative data provided. The only information provided about the standardization sample, moreover, is that the pupils scored slightly above the 50th percentile on the *Metropolitan Readiness Tests*. One could also question the choice of the word recognition subtest from the *Wide Range Achievement Test* as the sole standardized criterion measure of reading achievement against which to calculate the predictive validity of PRESS. A comprehensive reading test developed specifically for the primary grades might provide a more appropriate assessment of first grade reading ability for the purpose of validating a readiness battery.

There are also some practical problems with the test from a user's standpoint, only a few of which will be mentioned. The instructions for the visual/auditory space test appear to be unnecessarily complex. Only one practice item is provided for the visual sequencing test after which children are expected to understand the testing task. Certain tables in the manual are numbered differently from what the narrative suggests. The sample profile sheet in the manual indicates that a raw score of 15 on the letter identification test corresponds with a percentile rank of 80 despite the fact that the maximum score on the test is 13.

The *Prereading Expectancy Screening Scales* are not in the same league with reading readiness tests such as the Murphy-Durrell, the Clymer-Barrett, or the Metropolitan. Too little information is provided to enable the test user to know what a given test score means, let alone to suggest what instructional implications might be associated with the performance of any child or group of children on either a single subtest or the entire battery. When I think about the serious questions raised about the data provided by the better readiness tests, I am hard-pressed to suggest appropriate uses for this test.

JOYCE E. HOOD, *Director, Children's Reading Clinic, The University of Iowa, Iowa City, Iowa.*

The authors consider the four subtests in this instrument to represent variables which accumulated research evidence suggests are related to acquisition of reading skills. Three of the subtests were selected because they yielded significant correlations (ranging from .31 to .78) with the reading scores from the *Wide Range Achievement Test* and with teacher rankings of reading ability for 44 first graders. The letter identification subtest was added to replace the two subtests from the tryout test that did not yield significant correlations.

The authors cite low correlations with scores on *Progressive Matrices, Bender Gestalt Test,* and a draw-a-person test, based on the 44 first graders, as evidence that the subtests are not simply general ability measures. Stronger evidence would be afforded by significant partial correlations of these subtests with reading ability when intelligence is controlled. Although data were available for computing these partial correlations, they were not computed, or at least are not reported in the manual.

The authors do not offer a rationale relating the subtest tasks to aspects of the reading process. Nor do they present evidence that these are the best choices out of the many possible tasks which have at one time or another accurately predicted reading success. The test items, except those in Test 4, are similar to those typically found in intelligence or other capacity tests.

In physical appearance, neither the manual nor the answer forms seems to have been carefully prepared. The instructions read to the examinees do not seem detailed enough to explain the test's relatively difficult tasks to first graders. Since the operations required in the subtests do not seem related to the reading process, it is difficult to understand how a teacher would plan remediation for children screened out as not ready to read.

The reliability and validity data for this test

are based on a fall administration to 1,384 first graders in a single school system. Odd-even reliability coefficients for the subtests were computed on 200 randomly selected subjects. They range from .78 to .91. Subtest intercorrelations are not reported.

The criterion measures used in attempting to establish predictive validity were the reading scores from the WRAT and teacher rankings of reading ability at the end of first grade. Correlation coefficients are reported for each subtest for boys and girls separately and for the total group, within the three different instructional programs used in the school district. These coefficients range from .00 to .44. The authors suggest that children whose scores on all four subtests fall at or below the 30th percentile are probably not ready to read, although they reported that 19 percent of the children in the standardization group who scored thus attained a WRAT reading grade equivalent at or above 2.0 by the end of first grade. Among children reading at or above 2.0 level there were none with any subtest scores below the 40th percentile.

There would seem to be better choices of criterion measures than the WRAT reading score and teacher rankings of reading ability. To achieve a grade-equivalent of 2.0 on the WRAT, a child needs only to label 13 capital letters and identify 13 words correctly. And, if one is willing to use a first grade teacher's rankings of reading ability to establish the predictive validity of a screening test, one might consider using a kindergarten teacher's rankings as measures of reading readiness and dispensing with the screening test altogether.

SUMMARY. A number of weaknesses of the *Prereading Expectancy Screening Scales* have been discussed. The validity coefficients of under .45 are far too low for accurate prediction. They are based on data representing only one school district and related to criterion measures of doubtful merit. The choice of these particular subtests as suitable for first grade screening is not substantiated either logically or empirically. The subtests do not provide clues to possible remediation for children who do not score well. For these reasons the use of this test cannot be recommended.

PreReading Expectancy Screening Scales

[806]

Riley Preschool Developmental Screening Inventory. Ages 3–5; 1969; RPDSI; school readiness; 2 scores: design, make-a-boy (girl); no data on reliability; individual; 1 form (4 pages); manual (12 pages plus test); $8.50 per 25 tests and manual; $6.50 per 25 tests; $2.50 per manual; 8% extra for postage and handling; [3–10] minutes; Clara M. D. Riley; Western Psychological Services. *

DORIS E. NASON, *Professor Emeritus of Education, The University of Connecticut, Storrs, Connecticut.*

This inventory "is designed to help determine quickly, and fairly accurately, which children may have the most serious problems and need professional guidance."

Very explicit directions are given for the prospective examiner regarding the attitude toward subject(s) and choice of words. The specific wording for each task is given both in Spanish and in English. Acceptable facial and verbal responses by the examiner to a pupil's performance are rigidly prescribed.

The test booklet cover presents directions for scoring, a grid for recording pupil responses to copying the test designs (circle, cross, square, triangle, and diamond) and a checklist for body parts the pupil includes in the drawing of a boy or girl. Both quantitative and qualitative analyses are made, using a somewhat inadequate scoring key. Very arbitrary decisions must be made on data which are highly subjective in nature.

No information is given in the manual regarding reliability, validity, and the derivation of the "developmental ages."

This reviewer compared the developmental ages with those assigned by the researchers who produced the 1960 Stanford-Binet. All the items to be copied, except the cross, are used both in the Riley inventory and in the Stanford-Binet. While the developmental age levels for the four items which appear on both tests are the same, the scoring standards differ. Directions for scoring are much more explicit in the Stanford-Binet manual.

The scoring of the Make-a-Boy (Girl) test is based upon a quantitative analysis of the performance of 600 low-income children in Los Angeles County. In the Stanford-Binet, the credits for adding items to a partially formed figure are for the most basic parts of a body: arms, legs, eyes, nose, and mouth. In the Riley inventory, the pupil's score is the total number

of items included. Hence, a score could be artificially high because embellishments would
count as much as major body items.

The author makes categorical claims for
which she offers no evidence. For example, (*a*)
a child's refusal to make a drawing probably
means that the child does not trust the examiner enough to try. (*b*) "Perseveration has
been found by the author to correspond to behavior that is hyperactive." (*c*) "Children who
fail to draw the circle correctly are likely to
have neurological or organicity problems."

Administering and scoring the inventory can
be easily done. However, to use the interpretations of test scores as given by the author would
lead to faulty diagnoses. Types of conclusions
which could be reached only after much observation and testing by teams of such specialists
as clinical psychologists, pediatricians, speech
clinicians, reading clinicians, and child psychiatrists are claimed possible using this inventory.

From summaries of research and from many
years experience in clinical diagnosis and remedial treatment for young children, this reviewer
believes that preschool screening is crucial in
the planning of appropriate school experiences
for each child. The screening required to gain
relevant, accurate information in the many
areas of development which affect learning cannot be done by a single instrument. An inventory which is valid and quite comprehensive
would be one source of data. The Riley inventory is neither valid nor comprehensive. All the
items included have been borrowed from other
sources. Such vital areas as oral language, hearing capacity, visual and auditory acuity, visual
and auditory discrimination, general health,
home background, perseverance, attentiveness,
rate of learning, and emotional maturity are not
touched upon in the Riley inventory.

[807]

*School Readiness Survey, Second Edition. Ages
4–6; 1967–75; to be administered and scored by parents
with school supervision; 8 scores: number concepts,
discrimination of form, color naming, symbol matching,
speaking vocabulary, listening vocabulary, general information, total, plus unscored general readiness checklist; reliability data based on 1967 edition; 1 form
('69, 30 pages); "restandardized" manual ('75, 15
pages); $12.50 per 25 tests; 75¢ per manual; $1 per
specimen set; postage extra; [15–30] minutes; F. L.
Jordan and James Massey; Consulting Psychologists
Press, Inc. *

For excerpted reviews by Dale E. Bennett and
Byron Egeland, see 7:763.

REFERENCES
1. SASSENRATH, J. M., AND MADDUX, ROBERT E. "The Factor
Structure of Three School Readiness or Diagnostic Tests for
Disadvantaged Kindergarten Children." *Psychol Sch* 10(3):
287–93 Jl '73. * (*PA* 51:6000)
2. SASSENRATH, JULIUS M., AND MADDUX, ROBERT E. "Language Instruction, Background, and Development of Disadvantaged Kindergarten Children." *Calif J Ed Res* 25(2):61–8 Mr
'74. * (*PA* 53:1954)
3. THORPE, HELENE S., AND WERNER, EMMY E. "Developmental Screening of Preschool Children: A Critical Review of
Inventories Used in Health and Educational Programs." *Pediatrics* 53(3):362–70 Mr '74. *

JOHN DOWNING, *Professor of Psychological
Foundations in Education, University of Victoria, Victoria, British Columbia, Canada.*

According to the manual, "the *School Readiness Survey* is designed to help professional
personnel, in the elementary schools and elsewhere, to involve the parents of preschool children in evaluating their youngsters' developmental level and in preparing the youngsters
for kindergarten." Only items that could be
administered and scored by parents were included in the test. In addition, an unscored
checklist of observable general behavior characteristics was developed for those qualities that
did not lend themselves to test responses.

Reliability is indicated by a correlation of .79
in a study in which 32 children were tested by
teachers in June and again in October. In
another study of 20 children tested by parents
in June and by teachers in October, the correlation was .64. Parents tended to score their
children between two and five points higher
than the teachers did. No information is provided on the reliability of the part scores.

A validity study involved 383 pre-school
children from 20 schools in two California
counties. A first testing was done by parents in
May prior to kindergarten entrance in September; a year later the kindergarten teachers
rated each child's progress on a five-point scale.
The correlation between the SRS scores obtained by parent and teacher ratings was .62.
Unfortunately, no data are reported on any
relationship between scores on the survey and
other objective criteria such as other readiness
tests or measures of academic achievement.

With regard to the norms, the authors admit
that the sample was not representative of the
United States. They state that the "interpretation of the scores given in the test booklet has
been adjusted somewhat to compensate for this
bias in the norms"; they do not, however, specify how this adjustment was made. Cumulative
percentage norms are given by sex but not by

age, but the chief purpose of the test is to discriminate at the lower end of the scales. A child scoring "substantially below" 70 percent "is very likely to need special assistance or additional time for growth before entering school." No explanation is given as to what scores are "substantially below" 70 percent. Included in the test booklet are some suggestions to parents headed "How you can help your child to be ready for school." These suggestions have some face validity but no data are offered to show that the activities proposed enhance children's readiness for school.

The chief problem with this survey is that it is associated with rather limited and somewhat outmoded concepts of school readiness. Apart from four or five items in the checklist, responses to which do not count in the score, the survey is limited to the cognitive domain, whereas an important part of the child guidance concept of school readiness is concerned with such affective characteristics as control of the emotions, self-discipline, and social adjustment. Furthermore, the opening sentences of the authors' foreword in the manual reveal the outdated assumption underlying the construction of the survey. They say: "In 1965 the authors....met to discuss a problem that has been plaguing educators for years: how do you answer a parent who asks, 'should I keep Johnny out of school for another year?'" This concept of school readiness was common prior to the mid-sixties, but since then it has been replaced in many schools by a more dynamic view of readiness. School readiness is now seen as much a matter of fitting the school to the child as it is a matter of fitting the child to the school.

In summary, this *School Readiness Survey* has very little to recommend its use. Its validity has been inadequately demonstrated both by testing and by logic.

[808–9]

★**School Readiness Test.** Grades kgn–1; 1974–77; 8 scores: word recognition, identifying letters, visual discrimination, auditory discrimination, comprehension and interpretation, handwriting readiness, number readiness, total; no data on validity; norms for total score only; subtest scores convert to "OK," "probably needs help," or "definitely needs help" (no basis given for these categorizations); 1 form ('74, 16 pages); manual ('75, 23 pages); technical supplement ('77, 4 pages); $11.20 per 35 tests; $1 per specimen set; postage extra; Spanish manual ('77) available; (60) minutes in 2 sessions; O. F. Anderhalter; Scholastic Testing Service, Inc. *

School Readiness Survey

THORSTEN R. CARLSON, *Professor of Education, Sonoma State College, Rohnert Park, California.*

The primary purpose of this test is "to divide pupils into groups that are *ready* for formal learning, and groups that could use varying amounts of further *readiness experience*." Neither the subtests nor the manual provide any meaningful information on the nature of the readiness experiences that each group would need. The authors also claim that the test can be used "to diagnose the strengths and weaknesses of the individual pupils as related to readiness for formal learning in the different skill areas—reading, writing, numbers, and so on."

The test is provided in only one form. A 4-page technical supplement reports K–R 20 reliabilities of .91 for samples of approximately 400 each at the kindergarten and first grade levels. The estimates for subtest scores range from .54 to .88 (median .75). The reliabilities of the eight subtests are not adequate for diagnosing individual strengths and weaknesses. The supplement also reports subtest intercorrelations ranging from .26 to .63. This is interpreted to mean that "the several subtests do contribute relatively independent measures which can be useful for broad diagnostic purposes." However, the intercorrelations may be low because of unacceptably low reliability coefficients, which have the effect of lowering the intercorrelations. The authors do not elaborate on what they mean by the usefulness of the instrument for "broad diagnostic purposes." Even under the presumption of the independence of the subtest measures, the individual subtests do not appear to be useful for individual diagnosis because of the low reliability coefficients.

The test does not provide specific information on pupil deficits nor does the manual supply or even imply what should be done instructionally. To be of diagnostic value, the instrument should sample adequately the important aspects of school readiness; provide normative criteria of performance for individual pupils; and describe, as specifically as possible, at least the nature of the experiences needed to correct the deficits.

No data are provided on validity. Neither is any information provided on item discrimination, relevance, or difficulty. Nor, for any sub-test, is information supplied on sampling or the ordering of the items. The author has not provided any conceptualization of what constitutes school readiness or any listing of the objectives assessed by the test instrument. The absence of such data precludes the effective use of the test for either prognostic or diagnostic purposes, or, for that matter, for any prospective use at either the kindergarten or first grade levels.

Test 1, word recognition, actually attempts to measure vocabulary. No explanation is given for the choice of words. The sampling is limited to nouns that can be pictured. It is difficult to believe that some of the options used would draw the responses of any pupils, except by chance. Some of the pictures rely on stereotypes or exaggerations. Note for example, that the doctor is a man with a stethoscope attached to his ears and that the Earth is represented by a globe.

Test 2, identifying letters, is a sampling of pupils' recognition of upper and lowercase printed letters. The sans serif type, though used in workbooks, is not common to early reading materials. The pupil is asked to identify 10 uppercase letters and 10 lowercase letters. No explanation is made for the choices. How is the diagnostic function of the test carried out when the sampling for each of the two kinds of letters is limited to less than 40 percent of the alphabet?

Test 3, visual discrimination, requires the pupils to select from among four choices the response that matches a given geometric form, or number or letter sequence. Although a strict time limit is imposed, the pupil is not informed of this. Within the items are a number of decoys that involve reversals of individual letters within words. No word is presented in reversed form among the decoys and only one set of numbers is a full reversal. In reading, a reversal is the pronunciation of a word in reverse, as *no* for *on* or *part* for *trap*. In the sampling of reversal tendencies, it would seem advisable to include among the decoys reversible words such as *not* for *ton,* or *was* for *saw*.

Test 4, auditory discrimination, has a 10-second time limit for each item; the pupils are advised to work quickly. Only beginning consonants are used. The test is one of auditory recognition rather than discrimination. Since the name of each object accompanies its picture, the task may be for many pupils one of identifying the letter visually.

Test 5, comprehension and interpretation, requires the pupil to identify pictures that are each described by a sentence. Four choices are provided and the correct choice is usually distinguished by some detail provided in the descriptive sentence. Some decoys are quite unrelated, and some responses require rather stereotyped and limited conceptions of the object or activity involved while others require quite a bit of imagination in picture interpretation. For example, to interpret the apple in item 8 as rolling from the tree takes some imagination. Item 10 requires a stereotyped concept of what constitutes "a table in a classroom." Three of the four could be such tables and the fourth is totally unrelated to the descriptive sentence.

Test 6, handwriting readiness, involves some subjectivity in scoring. No guidelines for scoring are provided. Apparently the person who scores the test will need to judge what constitutes a reasonable rendition of each example. In the absence of any explanation, even an examination of the face validity fails to provide any clear picture or conception of what constitutes handwriting readiness.

Test 7, number readiness, goes far beyond readiness for number activities. Items that require the recognition of fractional parts, that involve dealing with measures of time and money, and that require knowledge of order among numbers are hardly skills and understandings associated with beginning number readiness. The use of "number" and "numeral" has been confused in the directions, as in items 3, 8, and many others.

The directions for some of the tests could be simplified by standardizing them. In Test 1 the pupils are directed to "put a mark" (X) on the correct answer. To put X on the "right" answer may be confusing since such a mark is usually reserved for a mistake or a wrong answer. In Test 2, the pupil is asked to "put a ring" around the right answer. In the same test, he is subsequently asked to "draw a ring" and then later to "mark" the correct answer, ostensibly with a circle and not with an X. In Test 5, the pupils "mark" each answer, but there are no instructions as to whether a circle or an X should be

School Readiness Test

used. In Test 7, a "big mark," which again could be an X or a circle is used.

The objects used to identify the test pages and items should be carefully chosen and illustrated. Such a choice as the animal *bat* for item 2 of Test 1 is probably unwise as it is not as familiar to children as is the correct response to the item, *ant*. Other choices and illustrations need further scrutiny and analysis.

Percentile norms are provided for the total test for the end of kindergarten and beginning of grade 1. There is no adequate description of the norming population. No norms are provided for the subtests. Five arbitrary classifications of degrees of readiness are suggested based on "experience." Just what "experience" gave rise to the classifications is not developed in the guide. Neither are suggestions given to the teacher as to what might be done for each of the five groups, except that particular attention should be given to those who fall in the three lowest groups.

Ratings are given for the part scores. Pupils on each subtest can be rated as "OK," "probably needs help," or "definitely needs help." No explanation is given as to how these ratings were arrived at. The guide recommends that these ratings be studied for the three lowest groups and the readiness experiences be "centered upon the areas which are rated" as probably in need of help or definitely in need of help.

In summary, this test is lacking in several respects. Only one form is available. The reliability coefficients for the total test are not impressive and the coefficients for the subtests are not adequate for either diagnostic or prognostic purposes, whether with individuals or groups, large or small. There are no data on the validity of the instrument. No technical information is provided for individual items. Norms are not available for the subtests. There is no conceptualization provided of the nature of school readiness on which the test is predicated. No objectives are provided and there are no data and no rationale for the nature of the sampling represented by the items. For either diagnosis or prognosis, there are more adequate instruments available for evaluation.

[810]

★Thackray Reading Readiness Profiles. Ages 4-8 to 5-8; 1974; TRRP; 3 scores: vocabulary, auditory discrimination, visual discrimination, plus unscored general ability (draw-a-man); 1 form (16 pages);

manual (35 pages); £2.20 per 10 tests; 55p per manual; 75p per specimen set; postpaid within U.K.; (70) minutes; Derek Thackray and Lucy Thackray; Hodder & Stoughton Educational [England]. *

REFERENCES

1. FRANCIS-WILLIAMS, J. M. "Review of the Thackray Reading Readiness Profiles." *Develop Med & Child Neurol* (England) 17(2):260-1 Ap '75. *
2. PATTISON, DOUGLAS. "Review of the Thackray Reading Readiness Profiles." *Remedial Ed* (England) 10(1):45-6 '75. *
3. PREEN, BRIAN. "Review of the Thackray Reading Readiness Profiles." *Read Teach* 29(2):199-200 N '75. *
4. LANSDOWN, RICHARD. "Review of the Thackray Reading Readiness Profiles." *J Child Psychol & Psychiatry* (England) 17(2):167-8 Ap '76. *

Develop Med & Child Neurol (England) 17(2):260-1 Ap '75. J. M. Francis-Williams. * this is the first original British reading readiness test, based on research with British children, to be published in this country * The test is planned to assess reading readiness in four different areas: Profile 1—vocabulary; Profile 2—auditory discrimination; Profile 3—visual discrimination; Profile 4—general ability. The first three profiles aim to measure directly three abilities and, in order to complete these satisfactorily, the child must be able to follow the directions and examine the pictures and words in a left-to-right sequence. General ability Profile 4 is assessed on the child's skill in drawing his mother. This, the authors claim, "indicates the stage the child has reached in perception and motor control and provides a good estimate of intellectual maturity." So many factors contribute to the quality of a child's achievement in drawing a person that it would seem to be making a very doubtful estimate of his intellectual maturity on the basis of this "Profile" alone. It is difficult to judge the value of this test without experimenting with it. I tried it with a group of children who had started school two months previously. They were selected by their teacher on the basis of her judgement of their problems and abilities. The results of the readiness test confirmed the teacher's judgements. She is a particularly experienced and perceptive teacher, but the test may be helpful to a teacher of less experience, particularly in assessing visual and auditory discrimination separately.

J Child Psychol & Psychiatry (England) 17(2):167-8 Ap '76. Richard Lansdown. * The Thackray profiles start with a test of vocabulary and concept formation consisting of a Peabody-type approach to vocabulary. This is followed by an assessment of auditory discrimination in which children have to match initial sounds in words. Surprisingly only consonants are tested; the teacher who is accustomed to a/u discrimination difficulties will find the omission of vowels odd. Visual discrimination is assessed by a matching-to-sample technique using letters only. There is some attempt at tapping reversals and sequencing skills in this scale but no assessment is made of the child's use of word shape. The final scale is called "general ability" and is no more than a simplified scoring for the Draw-a-Man test. Apart from the vagueness of the concept of intellectual maturity the use of this part of the battery is questionable because of the alarming page of interpretations of errors given. Despite words of caution some teachers will fasten on an absence of legs as suggestive of insecurity and one wonders if this will be in the child's best interest. The profiles were standardised on 5,500 children aged 4/8 to 5/8. This rather narrow age limit, plus the use of a stringent item analysis, means that the scales have a high floor: the visual discrimination profile, e.g. omits single letters. Split half reliability is between 0.8 and 0.9 and early versions of the whole scale have a predictive validity of between 0.4 and 0.6. No factor analysis is quoted but a correlation matrix gives a range of inter scale coefficients of 0.31 to 0.52. It would cost a three-form-entry primary school £24 to give this test to its new entrants. The value of such a blanket use is not yet proven. An experimental evaluation of the use of this test is necessary before conclusions can be drawn but initial thoughts about it are lukewarm.

Read Teach 29(2):199–200 N '75. Brian Preen. * The manual....is clear, to the point, and easily followed * The readiness assessment is quickly and easily administered * While the information in the section Interpretation of Scores (Profiles 1–3) is clear and meaningful to any teacher with a background in basic statistics, problems of interpretation could arise for those teachers who lack such an understanding, and therefore, may cause confusion over questions such as: Which children need remediation? What specific remediation is required in any one profile? These questions were raised regularly by teachers who experimented with this assessment. This readiness assessment should be of considerable value to both classroom teachers and children. It should assist in promoting early reading programs for children

who are ready, as well as isolating for remedial assistance those children who are at risk so far as early reading development is concerned.

SPECIAL FIELDS

[811]

The Adult Basic Reading Inventory. Functionally illiterate adolescents and adults; 1966; ABRI; test booklets with the title *Basic Reading Inventory* (BRI) are available for school use; scores in 5 areas: sight words, sound and letter discrimination, word meaning (reading), word meaning (listening), context reading; no data on reliability for scores on Parts 1, 2, 4, and 5; no norms; Form A (16 pages); manual (23 pages); technical report (4 pages); $10.50 per 20 tests; 55¢ per technical report; postage extra; $1 per specimen set, cash orders only; (60) minutes; Richard W. Burnett; Scholastic Testing Service, Inc. *
For a review by Albert J. Kingston, see 7:769.

THOMAS F. DONLON, *Senior Research Psychologist, Educational Testing Service, Princeton, New Jersey.*

The ABRI offers its users a seemingly sensible way to spend about an hour trying to gauge the reading ability of those who are reading at or below the fourth or fifth grade level. During this hour, the user asks the subject to select the one among four printed words which names a picture; to select the one printed word among four which begins with a sound like the beginning sound of a word read aloud; to find the printed word among three that most closely resembles in general meaning a printed stimulus word. (For example, is *dog* more like *pet, sky,* or *go?* Is *look* more like *see, cow,* or *train?*) A fourth task is the third task read aloud but with the printed words in front of the subject again. Finally, the fifth task presents three brief reading comprehension passages with five questions about each.

It seems self-evident that readers do better on such tasks than nonreaders or poor readers. The vocabulary is appropriate. The explanation of tasks is given orally; the examples are read aloud. All in all, one could feel confident that rough differences in reading level could be appraised by considering score differences on the ABRI.

The basic questions would seem to be: Why spend an hour? Why not spend about 10 minutes giving the 40 vocabulary ("synonym") multiple choice questions of Part 3? This procedure alone yields reliabilities approximating those of the full-length test. It is so designed that the first 10 words are more relevant to grade 2, the second 10 to grade 3, etc., so that some grade-placements can be attempted. Given this high reliability, this quasi-grade-reference or scaling, why give the whole test? What decisions about readers will be helped by the additional information one receives?

The meagre psychometric information provided with the test does not help with these questions. Such information as is given tends to suggest that the largely verbal appeals for the "diagnostic" value of Parts 1, 2, 4, and 5 are just window dressing. Unless users can substantiate diagnostic applications on their own evidence, testing with more than the single, 40-item, 10-minute Part 3 is of little value. If they *do* decide to use this 40-item section, the test information offers very little guidance to assist them.

What is wrong with this test is mostly the implicit claims that it offers reliable measurement of important and analyzable aspects of reading. Its component subtests focus on picture-recognition, initial-sound recognition, coping with oral presentation, and coping with passages. Each of these may plausibly be a separate, worrisome aspect of reading deficiency. But there is no evidence that this separateness is, in fact, the case; no evidence that teachers of reading learn something of value from an initial-consonant-detection score such as derived from Part 2 of this test. If, in fact, the logic of Part 2 is sound, why is no initial-consonant score derived from Part 1? Each of the 20 questions in Part 1 offers a wrong answer which has the same initial sound as the correct response. Why go to such pains to build this property in and then never use it, if, in fact, it is of sufficient importance to warrant an entire section devoted to it?

The word "adult" is a variable component of the title. The publisher's catalog calls this the *Adult Basic Reading Inventory* and says, "It is not for school use except when illiteracy is suspected." It then says, in the pricing section, "For school use, booklets entitled 'Basic Reading Inventory'—omitting 'Adult' from the title—may be ordered." It seemed to this reviewer that this kind of verbal variability is unfortunate. "Adult illiterates" are quite different from many "school illiterates," who, by the definition

of these materials, are those reading at grade levels one through four. One can imagine the same materials used for each group, with psychometric success, but one can be concerned about psychological inappropriateness if people in their middle years confront stories of Dick and Jane and the puppy, or second graders read about "want ads." The present test seems clearly aimed at adults. The vocabulary is limited, but the approach is not to a child. This probably could be a selling point. In point of fact, congruence of test content and reader age and interest is not mentioned in the materials.

Overall, this test is a weak offering because of the limited developmental work. It probably can differentiate poor readers, but it is doubtful that it can diagnose them. As a 40-item vocabulary test, it seems overpriced.

[812]

Reading/Everyday Activities in Life. Ages 10 and over; 1972; R/EAL; functional literacy; criterion referenced; no norms, standards of mastery set at 80–100% correct for functional literacy, 50–79% marginal, below 50% illiterate; individually administered by tape cassette; 1 form (20 pages); manual (51 pages); $1 per test; $6 per cassette; $6.50 per manual; postage extra; Spanish edition (tape cassette only) available; [50–90] minutes; Marilyn Lichtman; CAL Press, Inc. *

REFERENCES

1. LICHTMAN, MARILYN. "The Development and Validation of R/EAL, an Instrument to Assess Functional Literacy." *J Read Behav* 6(2):167–82 Jl '74. *

ALBERT J. KINGSTON, *Professor of Educational Psychology, The University of Georgia, Athens, Georgia.*

R/EAL, designed to assess the functional literacy of teenagers and adults who have limited schooling, was deliberately constructed to be different in design and content from the typical reading survey test.

R/EAL attempts to appraise those reading skills which the author regards as essential for adults living in the modern or "real" world. Nine categories of reading activities are included: signs and labels; schedules and tables; maps; categorized listings and indices; high-interest, factual narrative passages; illustrated advertisements; technical documents; sets of directions; and fill-in-the-blank forms. The author claims to have analysed each of these activities and to have prepared subtests which measure each type of skill needed by the different reading activities.

The test is individually administered and

self-pacing; hence it is recommended that each examinee have a tape recorder and cassette. The author recognizes that this testing procedure is slow and expensive but apparently feels that more life-like and realistic measures are obtained. Cassettes are available in both English and Spanish. This reviewer did not secure a Spanish version but the English version seems well done. Instructions are given by a male with excellent intonation and a pleasant voice. The instructions themselves require that the examinee turn off the recorder while he answers questions. Considering the type of examinee the test is designed for, this procedure may lead to some confusion. Examinees also are requested to write their answers in the test booklet; machine scoring and special answer sheets are not available. The examinee is provided with only limited practice before the test is administered. He is asked to read a facsimile of a newspaper movie advertisement and to answer merely two practice questions. The cassette instructs the examinee to turn off the tape, raise his hand and ask for help if unable to answer the questions. The manual, however, fails to specify just what help may be given under these circumstances. For each of the nine subtests the testee answers five questions by writing in the space provided in the test booklet. Thus, each reading activity has equal weight.

The first subtest presumes to measure the ability to read signs and labels and requires that the examinee identify various road signs. The next subtest, designed to appraise the ability to read schedules and tables, presents a facsimile of a typical newspaper television schedule. The third test concerns the making of a cheese pizza and the examinee answers questions pertaining to instructions printed on the facsimile of a package. The fourth test is more traditional in that it consists of a narrative passage dealing with the subject of narcotics; the selection was selected because it presumably is of high interest. The fifth test is a newspaper grocery store advertisement and the sixth represents an apartment lease. The seventh subtest consists of reading a road map similar to those given by various gasoline stations. The eighth test is a newspaper help-wanted advertisement and the ninth subtest consists of a job application form which the examinee completes as

directed. Generally, the instructions to the examinee are clear, realistic, and precise.

The nine reading tasks at first glance appear to assess validly the reading abilities of adults in nonacademic situations. They seem to represent a variety of different reading tasks and situations. One may question, however, whether each of the nine types of reading should have equal weight. Is reading a road map of equal importance to reading a lease, reading a grocery advertisement, or completing a job application? Presumably the format which consists of five items per subtest indicates that the author may believe the affirmative to be the case. It may be, however, that the common format was utilized because it was felt that each reading task could be adequately appraised only if at least five items were included on each subtest. The manual stresses the fact that each category was selected on the basis of its interest, importance, and frequency of use. Task analyses were employed in establishing terminal and enabling objectives for each set of materials.

In view of the nonacademic background and consequent lack of familiarity with testing procedures which one might expect to find with adults for whom this test was developed, one can only wonder how much time and effort are needed to teach examinees the proper use of the tape recorder. Moreover, the lack of separate answer sheets increases the costs of using R/EAL.

There are other drawbacks to the measure. Although the test is merely a few years old, inflation has caught up with at least one section. The facsimile grocery advertisement lists prices that are considerably less than most of us now pay for meat and produce. Finally, it is likely that some questions may be answered on the basis of personal experience rather than from the reading tasks themselves, e.g., knowledge of road sign messages by virtue of the shapes of the signs.

R/EAL is said to be of value for both diagnostic and evaluative purposes. The manual suggests that the nine subtests should be examined and profiled to obtain evidence concerning the reading needs of examinees. However, some general reading ability seems to be involved in performance on all of the subtests. A correlation of .74 between R/EAL scores and the *Stanford Achievement Test: Reading*

Reading/Everyday Activities in Life

is reported in the manual, and point biserial correlations for individual test items and total test score range from a low of .25 to a high of .66. In addition, the diagnostic value of the test is questionable as most reading specialists would desire more specific diagnostic information than this test yields, e.g., word attack skills, vocabulary, literal and interpretive comprehension, flexibility of rate, etc.

Finally, because R/EAL is a criterion-referenced measure, the entire problem of what exactly is meant by "functional literacy" becomes important. The author appears to have been aware of this problem and attempted to use the best information available. She deserves a great deal of credit for attempting to develop a test which assesses this concept. The task analysis approach is a good one. However, whether the subtests developed actually represent the categories claimed is open to argument. For example, the category of reading signs and labels includes such diverse reading acts as reading clothing tags, medicine labels, billboards, and road signs. One wonders why labels on food packages and cans also are not included. Again, reading a recipe is included in the same category as sewing with a pattern or using tools, machinery, and equipment. Probably most specialists will disagree with some aspects of the author's categories of common printed materials or the degree to which the sample subtest measures the assumed reading ability. Moreover, it seems likely that vocabulary and general reading ability may underlie success in these and similar reading tasks.

RICHARD D. ROBINSON, *Associate Professor of Education, University of Missouri—Columbia, Columbia, Missouri.*

This test was developed to assess mastery of basic or functional literacy skills in a manner which would enable the results to be used for diagnostic and/or evaluative purposes. It is intended primarily to be used with students from the age of 10 through adulthood who for various reasons have had unsuccessful experiences in reading, especially those related to traditional forms of evaluation. As defined by the author, "the functional literate is the person who can extract necessary and essential information from a variety of printed stimuli and demonstrate his ability to use such informa-

tion." In determining a student's literacy level, material for this test was selected from what the author considered, "reading experiences encountered in daily living."

The test is divided into nine reading selections which are taken from a wide variety of sources: a set of road signs, a TV schedule, a food recipe, a reading selection on drugs, a food market ad, an apartment lease, a road map, a want ad, and a job application. Comprehension of these passages is measured through the use of a student-administered tape cassette which asks five questions on each passage.

Despite the intent of this test as a measure of the functional literacy level of an individual, it can best be described as basically an indication of factual recall with little emphasis on the degree of understanding. Subtest format and content are reflective of this narrow definition of functional literacy.

A major weakness of R/EAL is the subject matter of the individual subtests, which, in the reviewer's opinion, do not reflect reading material and reading level most often encountered by those for whom this test was designed. The author indicates in the manual that the selected activities were done on the basis of "a logical and common-sense approach." This rather questionable procedure for the selection of appropriate test material is evident in several of the sections. The passages on narcotic drugs, the lease agreement, and the want ad present problems because of the advanced concepts and vocabulary encountered by the reader. Readability level of each of these passages, as measured by the Dale-Chall Readability Formula, indicates that they are all written at a reading level above grade 7. Each contains terminology which is seldom encountered, even by good readers. Terms such as paregoric, demerol, covenants, lessee, and tenancy are examples of vocabulary in these particular subtests.

The content of two other sections, road signs and the television schedule, are also open to question as to what is actually being measured. In these examples the emphasis is placed on the use of shapes and numbers rather than words. Conceivably, a correct response might be given to the question "What sign tells you to give the right of way to another car?" not because the student recognized the word "yield," but because he knew the shape of the sign. Likewise, a correct answer to the question "What program is on channel 7 at 9:00 p.m.?" might indicate only that the student could identify numbers successfully as presented orally from the tape presentation, rather than actually comprehending the printed television schedule.

The test booklet seems particularly inappropriate for those who have had previous unsuccessful experiences in assessing their functional literacy skills. The size of the type used in several of the subtests, most notably the lease agreement and the want ad, may cause readability problems for some students. In addition, the illustrations accompanying both the road map and the want ad contain an exorbitant amount of detail. While it may be argued that these tasks represent reality in terms of what a reader must contend with in a real-life situation, they still seem to this reviewer an unnecessarily complicated situation for those who have had previous problems with testing procedures.

Score interpretation of R/EAL is a major shortcoming of this test. Despite the inclusion of a brief task analysis description for each of the nine subtest areas, there is still insufficient information provided for any but the most experienced clinician to plan a meaningful literacy program. The two short case studies which are included for illustrative purposes have very limited application.

In summary, R/EAL does not furnish the basic diagnostic information which is essential in the development of a literacy skills program for the individual student. In fact, more useful knowledge could probably be obtained from the administration of a teacher-constructed informal or subjective inventory.

[813]

*SRA Reading Index. Job applicants ages 14 and over with poor educational backgrounds; 1968–74; total score and a proficiency level (picture-word association, word decoding, phrase comprehension, sentence comprehension, or paragraph comprehension); no norms for proficiency levels, minimum proficiency levels for particular jobs to be set locally; 1 form ('68, 8 pages, self-marking); combined manual ('74, 23 pages) for this and *SRA Arithmetic Index;* tape cassette available for administration; $8.75 per 25 tests; $15 per tape cassette; $1 per manual; $2 per specimen set; postage extra; (25–30) minutes; manual by Bruce A. Campbell with the assistance of LaVonne Macaitis; Science Research Associates, Inc. *

For a review by Dorothy C. Adkins of this test and the *SRA Arithmetic Index,* see 7:20.

REFERENCES

1. SCIENCE RESEARCH ASSOCIATES. *Validation: Procedures and Results: Part 2, Results From SRA Test Validation Stud-

ies. Chicago, Ill.: Science Research Associates, Inc., 1972. Pp. ii, 62. *
2. TOOLE, DAVID L.; GAVIN, JAMES F.; MURDY, LEE B.; AND SELLS, SAUL B. "The Differential Validity of Personality, Personal History, and Aptitude Data for Minority and Nonminority Employees." *Personnel Psychol* 25(4):661–72 w '72. *
3. SCIENCE RESEARCH ASSOCIATES. *Validation: Procedures and Results: Part 3, Supplementary Results, Third Edition.* Chicago, Ill.: Science Research Associates, 1974. Pp. ii, 90. *

SPEED

[814]

Basic Reading Rate Scale. Grades 3–16; 1970–71, c1947–71; BRRS; the two forms consist of the first 97 or 98 items in the corresponding 450-item forms of *Tinker Speed of Reading Test* ('55); no college norms; Forms A, B, ('70, 6 pages); manual ('71, 10 pages); individual report sheet (no date, 2 pages); $15 per 50 tests; $1 per set of scoring stencils; $7.50 per set of 100 individual report sheets; $4 per manual; $6 per specimen set; cash orders postpaid; 5(15) minutes; original test by Miles A. Tinker, shortened by Ronald P. Carver; Revrac Publications. *

For a review by Leonard S. Feldt of the full length test, see 5:687.

REFERENCES

1. FELDMANN, SHIRLEY C. "Review of the Basic Reading Rate Scale." *J Read* 15(6):451+ Mr '72. *

A. GARR CRANNEY, *Associate Professor of Education and Director, Reading and Study Skills Center, University of Florida, Gainesville, Florida.*

The test uses the first 98 or 97 items from the *Tinker Speed of Reading Test* for Forms A and B, respectively. A words-per-minute score is calculated, and readers are categorized into "beginning," "good," "better," and "best" groupings at arbitrarily-determined 100-word increments. Some minimal basis for the categories is provided in a table of test results as a function of grade level and age. The total group for ten grades, 3 to 12, was 471 students, a small but adequately described sample. The test was also given to an unreported number of college students who placed mostly in the "better" reader category (201–300 wpm).

Each 30-word item consists of one or two sentences described as easy reading with vocabulary based on the first 1,000 words in *The Teacher's Word Book of 30,000 Words.* The comprehension check consists of marking the one wrong word near the end of each item which spoils the meaning or is inappropriate to it.

The manual reports a correlation of .75 with the speed of comprehension score of the *Davis Reading Test.* An alternate forms reliability of .96 is reported for "471 third to twelfth graders in a school in a small town." The author's statement that this is "a very high reliability estimate for a five minute test" is unacceptable because of the wide range of grades used to estimate the reliability. A test which is extremely unreliable for differentiating within a single grade group may be highly reliable for differentiating among students in grades 3–12. The *Standards for Educational and Psychological Tests* state that "when a test is recommended or ordinarily employed in homogeneous subsamples, the reliability and standard error of measurement should be independently investigated within each subsample and reported in the test manual." Had the author followed this recommendation, he would have reported reliability data separately for each of the 10 grades.

Strengths of the test include the short administration time, relative freedom from problems associated with traditional multiple choice comprehension testing, comparability of forms, and appropriateness for research and evaluation of rate improvement.

Weaknesses of the test include a manual that is difficult to read, minimal validity information, inadequate and misleading reliability data, and the arbitrary nature of the four reading-rate categories. Test booklets are not reusable. The comprehension check is very different from the more integrated thought processes required in paragraph or story comprehension tasks of most conventional reading tests. Since a different topic is introduced in each item, there is constant interruption in thought process. Additionally, as each item is considered, the scanning process probably used in reading the first sentence may not represent the kind of reading task desired by most test users. This kind of comprehension check also does not adequately measure knowledge gained or amount comprehended from typical reading test passages where a main idea is developed at some length.

In summary, the BRRS is recommended for research or estimating improvement in some instructional situations where rate is emphasized. It may be less than satisfying, however, to test users who want a more representative comprehension check measuring the kind of reading most people do.

J Read 15(6):451+ Mr '72. Shirley C. Feldmann. * a revised version of Tinker's

Basic Reading Rate Scale

Speed of Reading Test, 1955. It is a group-administered test providing a measure of the rate at which very easy material can be read. Forms A and B are provided. The reader is given five minutes to read the items, which are uniform in difficulty level, and is required to cross out a word in each item which does not fit in with the meaning of the material. The number of correct items is converted into an average word-per-minute score, with speeds of from zero to 300 or more words-per-minute used to determine designations of Beginning, Good, Better or Best reader. The content of this test....seems difficult for the below fourth grade reader since the format used is an adult one. The manuals and procedures are not easily usable, and the norm tables are again based on the same small and atypical sample as is the other test. These features detract considerably from the potential usefulness of the test. * may eventually prove interesting and useful in measuring components of reading achievement, but....[it does not seem] to meet that promise in its present form.

STUDY SKILLS

[815]

The Cornell Learning and Study Skills Inventory. Grades 7–13, 13–16; 1970; CLASSI; 9 scores: goal orientation, activity structure, scholarly skills, lecture mastery, textbook mastery, examination mastery, self mastery, total, reading validity index; no data on reliability of part scores; 1 form; 2 levels; manual (31 pages); separate answer sheets must be used; $17.25 per 25 tests; $4.25 per 25 answer sheets; $4.25 per set of scoring stencils; $4.25 per 25 profiles; $4.25 per manual; $5.75 per specimen set of either level; postage extra; (30–50) minutes; Walter Pauk and Russell Cassel; Psychologists & Educators, Inc. *
a) SECONDARY SCHOOL FORM. Grades 7–13; 1 form (7 pages); profiles: junior high, high school, junior college, (1 page).
b) COLLEGE FORM. Grades 13–16; 1 form (10 pages); profile (1 page).
See T2:1756 (2 references).

REFERENCES

1–2. See T2:1756.
3. CULLOTY, MARGARET B. "Review of the Cornell Learning and Study Skills Inventory." *Read World* 12(1):71–2 O '72. *

ALLEN BERGER, *Professor of Language Communications, University of Pittsburgh, Pittsburgh, Pennsylvania.*

Each level contains 120 items in the following categories: goal orientation, 13 items; activity structure, 16; scholarly skills, 20; lecture mastery, 17; textbook mastery, 23; examination mastery, 15; and self-mastery, 16. Except for minor changes in wording, each of the secondary school level items is comparable to the corresponding college level item.

The most noticeable difference between the two levels is in the way students are to respond: true or false on the secondary school form; seldom-sometimes-frequently-usually-always on the college form. It is not clear why "never" is not used to balance "always."

On the basis of student responses, a profile can be drawn by connecting the scores for the seven categories. A reading validity index and a total score are also part of the scoring procedure. The reading validity index "is comprised of 11 pairs of items," spread through each form, "intended primarily for use in determining whether or not subjects....have read and deliberated on each item, or whether they merely placed random marks."

There is very little information about the manner in which this instrument was standardized. The authors state the test "was developed and standardized over a six year period of time, and with populations coming largely from New York and Wisconsin. Scores for persons contained in the various norms, however, came from more than 30 different states in the United States, and from Liberia in West Africa."

The profile sheets for the high school level show only the number of students at various grade levels on whom the norms are based. The college profile sheet provides even less information.

From the sparse information in the manual, it is difficult to understand the rationale underlying the norming procedure. How can one norm be used for "college freshmen, seniors, and indeed university graduates"? Who were the people on whom the test was normed? Are the students in the norm groups typical? Were they selected for superior learning and study skills?

Reliability data are contained in a single paragraph and a table showing correlations for internal consistency and test-retest reliabilities ranging from .82 to .92 for total scores; no information is given on the reliability of part scores.

The authors make claims for face, status, and training validity. Their claim for what they call status validity is supported by a table containing low correlations between the inventory and grade point averages of junior high school students and four tables containing low intercorrelations of part to total scores on the secondary school and college levels. Their paragraph on face validity has the ring of authors writing an advertisement for themselves; and their claim for training validity includes a plug for two training films which they have developed. In short, their claims for validity are less impressive than their claims for reliability.

In summary, this reviewer is left with serious reservations about this instrument. It contains typographical errors, and some of the items (such as wanting to finish high school) are clearly inappropriate for college students who, the authors say, can be given the secondary level. The normative, reliability, and validity data are neither convincing nor sufficient to explain the rationale behind claims made by the authors and the publisher. Until they produce better data, it would be advisable to use another study skills inventory.

RICHARD D. ROBINSON, *Associate Professor of Education, University of Missouri-Columbia, Columbia, Missouri.*

This inventory was designed as a measure of the "specific competencies that are requisite for effective learning at the secondary school and college levels of instruction."

The inventory is based primarily on testing conducted at several university reading-study centers. The college form of the test was normed on a sample population consisting of approximately 1,600 students obtained at one eastern university, two midwestern universities, and an African university. The secondary level was standardized using students drawn primarily from eastern and midwestern junior and senior high schools. No descriptive information is provided on either sample as to selection criteria, previous scholastic performance, or socioeconomic background. In view of the fact that the test user is provided with so limited a description of these norm populations and with such a relatively small and unrepresentative sample at the college level, there is a question regarding the appropriateness of the standardization process.

No specific information is given in the manual

on the procedures followed in the selection of the content to be tested. Despite the authors' statement that the "items contained in the inventory are easily recognized as dealing with pertinent factors in relation to the learning effectiveness of individuals," the evidence to support this claim is not provided. The test user must simply rely on face validity as related to the content selection in light of the paucity of supporting data.

As is true with most study skills inventories, there are items appearing on this test which are certainly open to differences of opinion, especially when considering the scoring value assigned to a particular question by the authors. For example: (31) "While studying, I like to listen to background music"; (39) "When I worry, I stop studying and try to solve the problem right then and there"; and (61) "I take my lecture notes in pencil; so that I can make changes easily." For maximum credit on each of these items, the student must mark "seldom" which appears to this reviewer a very arbitrary decision. These and other similar questions would seem to necessitate a rather flexible evaluation procedure on the part of the teacher or counselor when using this inventory.

The most important aspect of any test such as this should be its usefulness as a means whereby a teacher or counselor could take the results and develop a meaningful program of study skills for an individual. While the manual does include a rather extended discussion of what the authors believe are the important dimensions of the study skills area, very little information is provided which would aid in the interpretation of a student's performance on this inventory. The assumption is that the user of this test will have the necessary background in study skills to suggest to students viable learning approaches which will fit individual strengths and weaknesses.

In summary, CLASSI is a rather superficial assessment of a student's study skills. To be effective, this inventory should be used by those who have had a great deal of experience in this area since the manual provides little, if any, help in the establishment of a study skills program. When compared to inventories such as the *Survey of Study Habits and Attitudes*, CLASSI is of limited value.

Cornell Learning and Study Skills Inventory

Read World 12(1):71–2 O '72. Margaret B. Culloty. * For the most part individual items are clear. The secondary school form is answered by a yes or no response. The college form, however, is scored on the basis of a scale from 1 to 5 (1 equals seldom, 5 equals always). Though this second format may be more accurate, it presents numerous problems if one attempts to hand score the items. Continued readjustment of the scored value of an answer must be made in moving from item to item. This is the most serious drawback to the use of the inventory on a large scale without an available computer. Though this learning and study skills inventory is not without problems, it should be of use to some teachers. It is a valuable addition to the materials needed for skill development programs at both the high school and college levels.

[816]

★**Effective Study Test.** Grades 8–12, 11–13; 1964–72; EST; 6 scores: reality orientation, study organization, writing behavior, reading behavior, examination behavior, total; no data on reliability; no norms for grade 8; 1 form; 2 levels: grades 8–12 ('64, 4 pages), grades 11–13 ('72, 4 pages); manual ('64, 11 pages); separate answer sheets must be used; 25¢ per test; 12¢ per answer sheet; 60¢ per scoring stencil; 60¢ per manual; $1.35 per specimen set; postage extra; Spanish edition ('72) available; (35–45) minutes; William F. Brown; Effective Study Materials. *

REFERENCES

1. GALLESSICH, JUNE. "An Investigation of Correlates of Academic Success of Freshmen Engineering Students." *J Counsel Psychol* 17(2):173–6 Mr '70. * (PA 44:9340)
2. GADZELLA, BERNADETTE M., AND GOLDSTON, JOHN. "Effect of Study Guides and Classroom Discussions on Students' Perceptions of Study Habits." *Percept & Motor Skills* 44(3, pt 1):901–2 Je '77. *

A. GARR CRANNEY, *Associate Professor of Education and Director, Reading and Study Skills Center, University of Florida, Gainesville, Florida.*

This 125-item, true-false test is designed to measure knowledge about effective study practices. It differs from most study skills inventories in not requiring students to make judgments about their own practices.

Both high school and college forms have clear instructions and an uncomplicated hand-scoring procedure. Horizontal, row-by-row answer sheet numbering may be confusing to some students.

The manual appropriately indicates counseling, instructional, research, and screening uses for the test. Instructionally, it may be used with the Brown-Holtzman *Effective Study Guide.*

Commendably, diagnostic use of individual items as well as the five subscale scores are recommended in the counseling section.

Development of items and subscales involved several revisions and followed conventional measurement practices. Coverage of the study skills field is adequate. On both forms, note-taking practices are included in the writing behavior scale. Items are generally well constructed and have face validity. Keyed responses reflect research-based and accepted practices in the field, except for item 70 on the high school form, which is incorrectly keyed. Laudably, some items on this form were modified or replaced to suit younger students. Since, however, according to the Dale-Chall estimate, readability is at the 11th and 12th grade level, students in the 8th or 9th grade or those with severe reading problems may have difficulty reading the test.

Norm tables are limited to Texas schools and were tabulated in 1962–63. Norm groups are named, but not described. Between-grade levels differences in raw scores at the higher percentile ranks tend to be small. No norms for the 8th grade are included although the test is recommended for use with that grade.

Validity information for both forms is well described. Correlations with grade-point averages are higher than the .30 to .40 level usually reported for study skills inventories. Acceptable correlations are also reported for both forms, including information on subscale independence and correlations with other tests. More recent validation information using students from other geographical areas would improve the validity section of the manual.

No reliability information is presented. In light of an otherwise well-written manual, this raises questions about the consistency of the test as a measuring instrument. Similarly, no information is given about the Spanish form of the test. On occasion, tests translated from English into another language undergo subtle changes affecting measurement characteristics.

With the exception of the lack of reliability information, the impression of the test and its manual is favorable. Test users, however, should not infer that knowledge about study practices indicates that the practices are actually in use. For the purpose of obtaining a self-report of practices in use, the *Survey of Study Habits and Attitudes* is recommended. In addition, the *MHBSS Study Skills Test* combines knowledge of study practices with a self-report of student practice. Though not without their own imperfections, both tests are recommended, depending on the purpose of the test user.

[817]

★**Goyer Organization of Ideas Test.** College; 1966–68; GOIT; Form S ('68, 8 pages); no manual; mimeographed report ('66, 18 pages); separate answer sheets (IBM 805) must be used; $25 per 25 tests; $10 per scoring stencil; postpaid; specimen set free; (20–40) minutes; Robert S. Goyer; the Author. *

REFERENCES

1. GOYER, ROBERT S. "A Test to Measure the Ability to Organize Ideas." *J Ed Meas* 4(2):63–4 su '67. * (*PA* 42:4483)

[818]

*Study Attitudes and Methods Survey. High school and college; 1972–76; SAMS; 6 scores: academic interest, academic drive, study methods, study anxiety, manipulation, alienation toward authority; only reliability and validity data are for college population; no description of high school normative population; 1 form ('72, 6 pages); preliminary manual ('72, 10 pages); profile ('76, 2 pages) for high school; profile ('72, 1 page) for college; separate answer sheets (IBM 1230) must be used; $9.50 per 25 tests; $4.50 per 50 answer sheets; $4 per set of hand scoring stencils; $4 per 50 profiles; $1.25 per manual; $2.25 per specimen set; postage extra; (55) minutes; William B. Michael, Joan J. Michael, and Wayne S. Zimmerman; EdITS/Educational and Industrial Testing Service. *

See T2:1766 (4 references).

REFERENCES

1–4. See T2:1766.
5. KNAPP, LISA J. "The Validity of the Study Attitudes and Methods Survey for Predicting Grades in High School Biology." *Ed & Psychol Meas* 33(4):959–61 w '73. * (*PA* 52:4039)
6. MICHAEL, JOAN J.; CROOK, ROBERT; MICHAEL, WILLIAM B.; AND HOLLY, KEITH. "The Relationship of Each of the Six Scales of the Study Attitudes and Methods Survey (SAMS) to Each of Three Different Criteria of Academic Achievement for a Sample of High School Seniors." *Ed & Psychol Meas* 33(4):955–7 w '73. * (*PA* 52:13197)
7. THAMES, JOHN A.; ZIMMERMAN, WAYNE S.; AND MICHAEL, WILLIAM B. "The Concurrent Validity of Each of the Six Scales of the Study Attitudes and Methods Survey (SAMS) With Achievement and Aptitude Measures for a Sample of Female High School Seniors." *Ed & Psychol Meas* 33(2):473–6 su '73. * (*PA* 51:6010)
8. HALL, PERRY L. *A Comparison of Nondisabled and Physically Disabled Freshman College Students on Seven Study and Attitudinal Variables.* Doctor's thesis, University of Cincinnati (Cincinnati, Ohio), 1975. (*DAI* 36:4399A)
9. HOOK, ORA MACDONALD. *The Relationship of Cognitive, Affective, Demographic, and School-Related Variables to Membership of Community College Students in Four Ethnic Groups and to Their Academic Achievement.* Doctor's thesis, University of Southern California (Los Angeles, Calif.), 1976. (*DAI* 36:7294A)
10. PAULSON, DORIS ELEANOR. *The Prediction of Academic Performance in a Community College From Intellective Variables and From Nonintellective Variables Emphasizing Study Attitudes and Methods.* Doctor's thesis, University of Southern California (Los Angeles, Calif.), 1976. (*DAI* 37:2083A)

ALLEN BERGER, *Professor of Language Communications, University of Pittsburgh, Pittsburgh, Pennsylvania.*

The authors state that "the purpose of this test is twofold, (1) to identify those students who might experience difficulty in their school work due to poor study methods or to specific attitudinal factors, and (2) to diagnose for purposes of counseling or guidance those areas which might contribute to such difficulty."

The test consists of 150 items such as "I find studying to be one of the most pleasurable and satisfying experiences in my life," "I size up people I meet to determine whether they can be useful to me," and "I nod my head up and down to impress the teacher that I understand and agree with what he is saying." To each item students choose one of four responses: N (not at all like me, or different from me), 1 (seldom, or somewhat like me), 2 (frequently, or much like me), or 3 (almost always, or very much like me).

The test was normed on 947 community college students "in a large suburban two-year college within a few miles of the Civic Center of Los Angeles. Of those who participated, approximately 500 were males and 450 were females, of whom 90 percent fell in the age range from 17 to 26. The breakdown of the sample by ethnic groups closely approximates the population breakdown by ethnic identification in the county of Los Angeles."

Questions should be asked in regard to the norms for this instrument. What sampling basis was used to determine whether these students are representative of community college students elsewhere? The profile sheet for high school students gives no information about their number, grade placement, or how they were selected—information deemed essential in the *Standards for Educational and Psychological Tests.*

The authors refer to a study reporting "evidence concerning the relationship of SAMS scores to grade point average in a sample of community college students." They acknowledge that the correlations are low (.13 to .37, median .19) but statistically significant. The evidence that they present is not persuasive.

Reliability data range from .83 to .90 for internal consistency and .68 to .79 for test-retest. The authors suggest that the reliability is "adequate for counseling purposes." Counselors, however, might feel more confident and find this survey more helpful if it were backed up with studies showing greater reliability, a wider range of normative data, and convincing evidence to support different kinds of validity. Until such time, this instrument should be used with caution.

John W. Lombard, *President, Educational Materials Corporation, Chicago, Illinois.*

This test is the outcome of various studies of noncognitive factors associated with school success begun in the early 1950s by the senior author. The 150 items, describing school-related situations, are evenly distributed over six subtests, which emerged from several factor analytic studies. Students scoring high on the first three subtests and low on the last three are believed to possess "desirable habit and motivational characteristics," and likely to be high achievers.

As with all such self-descriptive surveys, the honesty, frankness, and self-awareness of the respondent is crucial, and this point is stressed in both the survey directions and interpretive manual. Thus, it seems inappropriate for the promotional materials for SAMS to suggest it might be used as a college entrance examination, since widespread faking would likely occur.

The items are relevant and well edited, although there appears to be considerable redundancy and a few items require self-insights that would perplex trained practitioners. As an example of the redundancy problem, items 4, 34, 82, 106, 130, and 142 all probe anxiety about examinations in thinly disguised variations as shown by item 34, "I dread taking examinations even when I am reasonably well prepared," and item 142, "I am anxious before an examination even when I have studied for it." Perplexing items, at least to this reviewer, include those that ask whether one most frequently derives his motivation from a desire to succeed rather than from a fear of failure, or whether he "gets along better" out of school than in school.

The four alternatives for each item form a continuum from "Not at all like me, or different from me—applies to me less than 5 percent of the time, or is less than 5 percent like me" to "Almost always, or very much like me—applies to me more than 85 percent of the time, or is more than 85 percent like me." No rationale is given for the very narrow range assigned to the first category nor why its range is so much less than that assigned to the last category. In

Study Attitudes and Methods Survey

addition, no data are given on the distribution of responses to the items, individually or collectively.

Actually, the interpretive manual and norms are so sketchy that I cannot recommend use of SAMS. Four years after publication, the manual is still called "preliminary," and its 10 pages provide meager assistance to the user.

After one takes the survey and hand scores it (a process made easy by purposeful item layout and separate stencils for each of the six subtests), little help is provided in interpreting the results or using them in counseling. Two profile sheets (with college norms and high school norms) are available that enable one to plot the six raw scores and convert them instantly to T scores and percentiles. Unfortunately, the college "normative" data are based on only 947 students from a single community college near Los Angeles, tested at some unreported date.

Although unisex norms are given for college students, separate sex norms are given for high school students. No information is given on the size or composition of the high school norms group. The high school norms differ greatly from the college norms on two scales, manipulation and alienation toward authority.

The present "preliminary" manual presents some data from two studies: the "normative" study, and another involving 280 community college students. Subtest reliabilities are adequate; intercorrelations range from .51 to .77 among the first three scales and .40 to .66 among the last three. Correlations between the first three tests and the last three tests are low, − .02 to − .21. SAMS scores for the 280 students were also correlated with grade point average (GPA) for at least one semester of junior college work. The subtest correlating highest with GPA was academic drive (.25 and .37 in administrations four months apart). Multiple correlations of the six SAMS subtests with GPA are .31 and .42, but note that the academic drive scale alone show correlations of .25 and .37. Thus SAMS shows some evidence of validity, but it is inadequate in scope to draw any final conclusion.

Another major fault is the scant attention paid in the manual to interpretation and recommendations for subsequent action based on SAMS scores. Far more work should be done

to help counselors make use of the scores. Until this is done, and more comprehensive norms are developed, SAMS is not recommended for general use.

[819]

★Study Skills Surveys. Grades 9–16; 1965–70; SSS; 4 scores: study organization, study techniques, study motivation, total; no data on reliability; norms for grades 9 and 13 only; 1 form ('65, 4 pages); manual ('65, 4 pages); workbook ('70, 4 pages); separate answer sheets must be used; 25¢ per test; 12¢ per answer-profile sheet; 15¢ per workbook; 35¢ per manual; 75¢ per specimen set; postage extra; Spanish edition ('65) available; (15–20) minutes; William F. Brown; Effective Study Materials. *

[820]

Survey of Study Habits and Attitudes. Grades 7–12, 12–14; 1953–67; SSHA; original edition called Brown-Holtzman Survey of Study Habits and Attitudes; 7 scores: study habits (delay avoidance, work methods, total), study attitudes (teacher approval, education acceptance, total), total; 1 form; 2 levels; manual ('67, 30 pages); separate answer sheets (IBM 805, IBM 1230) must be used; $4.25 per 25 tests; $2.90 per 50 IBM 805 answer sheets; $3.40 per 50 IBM 1230 answer sheets; $1.25 per manual and IBM 805 scoring keys; $1.60 per manual and IBM 1230 scoring keys; $1.75 per specimen set; postage extra; scoring service, 55¢ and over per test; Spanish edition ('71) available; (20–25) minutes; William F. Brown and Wayne H. Holtzman; Psychological Corporation. *
a) FORM H. Grades 7–12; 1967; 1 form (6 pages).
b) FORM C. Grades 12–14; 1965–67; 1 form ('65, 6 pages).
See T2:1772 (33 references); for a review by Carleton B. Shay and excerpts by Martin J. Higgins and Albert E. Roark (with Scott A. Harrington), see 7:782 (69 references); see also 6:856 (12 references); for reviews by James Deese and C. Gilbert Wrenn (with Roy D. Lewis) of the original edition, see 5:688 (14 references).

REFERENCES

1–14. See 5:688.
15–26. See 6:856.
27–95. See 7:782.
96–128. See T2:1772; also includes a cumulative name index to the first 128 references, 3 reviews, and 2 excerpts for this test.
129. ORPEN, CHRISTOPHER. "Factors in University Success: An Empirical Investigation at the University of Cape Town." Onderwys-Education Bulletin (South Africa) 15(4):162–7 D '70. *
130. FEENSTRA, HENRY J., AND SANTOS-CASTILLO, EMMA H. "Aptitude, Attitude and Motivation in Second Language Acquisition: A Look at Two Cultures." Philippine J Psychol 4(1):62–9 Je '71. * (PA 49:1286)
131. BODDEN, JACK L.; OSTERHOUSE, ROBERT; AND GELSO, CHARLES J. "The Value of a Study Skills Inventory for Feedback and Criterion Purposes in an Educational Skills Course." J Ed Res 65(7):309–11 Mr '72. * (PA 48:7726)
132. DRAAYER, DONALD R., AND McLURE, JOHN W. "A Comparison of Student Study Habits and Attitudes on Traditional and Modular Scheduling." North Central Assn Q 46(3):348–59 W '72. *
133. DuCETTE, JOSEPH, AND WOLK, STEPHEN. "Ability and Achievement as Moderating Variables of Student Satisfaction and Teacher Perception." J Exp Ed 41(1):12–7 f '72. * (PA 49:7779)
134. GOLDBERG, LEWIS R. "Student Personality Characteristics and Optimal College Learning Conditions: An Extensive Search for Trait-By-Treatment Interaction Effects." Instructional Sci (Netherlands) 1(2):153–210 Jl '72. *
135. LIDDICOAT, JAMES PATTERSON. Differences Between Under- and Overachievers at a Small Liberal Arts Women's College. Doctor's thesis, Lehigh University (Bethlehem, Pa.), 1972. (DAI 32:6133A)

Survey of Study Habits and Attitudes

136. MITCHELL, KENNETH R., AND NG, KIM T. "Effects of Group Counseling and Behavior Therapy on the Academic Achievement of Test-Anxious Students." *J Counsel Psychol* 19(6):491–7 N '72. * (*PA* 49:7902)

137. PEARCE, RICHARD MOTT. *An Evaluation of Expressed Level of Aspiration as a Determinant of Performance in an Under-Graduate Biology Course.* Doctor's thesis, Oregon State University (Corvallis, Ore.), 1972. (*DAI* 32:5635A)

138. TUSCHER, MELVIN FELIX. *A Proposed Model for Predicting Success in a First Course of College Calculus in the Community Junior College.* Doctor's thesis, University of Southern California (Los Angeles, Calif.), 1972. (*DAI* 33:1468A)

139. WITTMAIER, BRUCE C. "Test Anxiety and Study Habits." *J Ed Res* 65(8):352–4 Ap '72. * (*PA* 48:9669)

140. ADAMS, CLARENCE LANCELOT, JR. *A Study of Factors Which May Affect Academic Success Among "SEEK" Students.* Doctor's thesis, Yeshiva University (New York, N.Y.), 1973. (*DAI* 34:2275B)

141. COSTARIS, MICHAEL J. *Nonintellective Characteristics of Open Door Admittees to a Community College.* Doctor's thesis, Rutgers—The State University (New Brunswick, N.J.), 1973. (*DAI* 34:6378A)

142. DRAHEIM, CHARLES KENNETH. *A Comparative Study of Grade Point Averages, Study Habits, and Scores on the Personal Orientation Inventory Between Groups of College Students in Relation to Educational Attitudes as Determined by the Teacher Approval and Educational Acceptance Scales of the Survey of Study Habits and Attitudes.* Doctor's thesis, University of South Dakota (Vermillion, S.D.), 1973. (*DAI* 35:817A)

143. GOLDFRIED, MARVIN R., AND D'ZURILLA, THOMAS J. "Prediction of Academic Competence by Means of the Survey of Study Habits and Attitudes." *J Ed Psychol* 64(1):116–22 F '73. * (*PA* 50:1777)

144. LIN, Y., AND MCKEACHIE, W. J. "Student Characteristics Related to Achievement in Introductory Psychology Courses." *Brit J Ed Psychol* 43(1):70–6 F '73. * (*PA* 50:0934)

145. MACKIE, JOAN BARCY. "Comparison of Student Satisfaction With Educational Experiences in Two Teaching Process Models." *Nursing Res* 22(3):262–6 My–Je '73. * (*PA* 52:7750)

146. SHAFFER, PHYLLIS E. "Academic Progress of Disadvantaged Minority Students: A Two-Year Study." *J Col Stud Personnel* 14(1):41–6 Ja '73. * (*PA* 50:7859)

147. WORK, WALTER PAXTON. *A Study of Selected Intellectual and Nonintellectual Variables for the Purpose of Developing an Academic Advising Model.* Doctor's thesis, Kent State University (Kent, Ohio), 1973. (*DAI* 34:5647A)

148. AYERS, JERRY B., AND ROHR, MICHAEL E. "Relationship of Selected Variables to Success in a Teacher Preparation Program." *Ed & Psychol Meas* 34(4):933–7 w '74. * (*PA* 54:6355)

149. BURKETT, SANDRA PRICE. *An Investigation of Selected Intellective and Non-Intellective Factors as Predictors of Academic Success for Educationally-Economically Disadvantaged College Freshmen.* Doctor's thesis, Mississippi State University (State College, Miss.), 1974. (*DAI* 35:5050A)

150. GALE, ANDREW. *Underachievement Among Black and White Male Junior College Students.* Doctor's thesis, Illinois Institute of Technology (Chicago, Ill.), 1974. (*DAI* 35:6070A)

151. KILPATRICK, RETHA HOOVER. *Predicting Achievement in Business Communications.* Doctor's thesis, University of Georgia (Athens, Ga.), 1974. (*DAI* 35:5056A)

152. MCCAUSLAND, DONALD F., AND STEWART, NANCY E. "Academic Aptitude, Study Skills, and Attitudes and College GPA." *J Ed Res* 67(8):354–7 Ap '74. * (*PA* 52:11020)

153. MEEHAN, WILLIAM JOSEPH. *A Correlation of Selected Personal Characteristics of Students Identified as High- or Low-Variable on Academic Performance.* Doctor's thesis, Oklahoma State University (Stillwater, Okla.), 1974. (*DAI* 35:636oA)

154. MITTANCK, ROBERT GENE. *The Relationship of Selected Non-Cognitive Variables to Academic Performance in Black College Students.* Doctor's thesis, University of Texas (Austin, Tex.), 1974. (*DAI* 35:265A)

155. PROCIUK, TERRY J., AND BREEN, LAWRENCE J. "Locus of Control, Study Habits and Attitudes, and College Academic Performance." *J Psychol* 88(1):91–5 S '74. * (*PA* 53:6190)

156. SCHRUPP, HAROLD ALLAN. *An Evaluation of a Community College Instructional Program for the Educationally Disadvantaged.* Doctor's thesis, University of California (Los Angeles, Calif.), 1974. (*DAI* 35:2016A)

157. WAKEFIELD, JAMES A., JR.; ALSTON, HERBERT L.; YOM, B. LEE; AND DOUGHTIE, EUGENE B. "Related Factors of the Survey of Study Habits and Attitudes and the Vocational Preference Inventory." *J Voc Behav* 5(2):215–9 O '74. * (*PA* 53:6261)

158. BRUCE, CHARLES WILLIAM, III. *A Study of the Effects of Tutoring Upon Academic Achievement, Self-Concept, and Study Habits and Attitudes of Freshman Male Athletes.* Doctor's thesis, George Peabody College for Teachers (Nashville, Tenn.), 1975. (*DAI* 36:5076A)

159. CURRIE, SARA RUTH. *An Investigation of the Impact of Selected Readings From College Study and Orientation Man-uals on the Attitudes of Junior College Freshmen.* Doctor's thesis, Boston University (Boston, Mass.), 1975. (*DAI* 36:4979A)

160. FRANKLIN, THOMAS EDWIN. *The Prediction of Achievement and Time Spent in Instruction in a Self-Paced Individualized Course.* Doctor's thesis, West Virginia University (Morgantown, W.Va.), 1975. (*DAI* 36:4347A)

161. KHAN, S. B., AND ROBERTS, DENNIS M. "Structure of Academic Attitudes and Study Habits." *Ed & Psychol Meas* 35(4):835–42 w '75. * (*PA* 55:11022)

162. MITCHELL, KENNETH R.; HALL, RALPH F.; AND PIATKOWSKA, OLGA E. "A Group Program for Bright Failing Underachievers." *J Col Stud Personnel* 16(4):306–12 Jl '75. *

163. RAMANAIAH, NERELLA V.; RIBICH, FRED D.; AND SCHMECK, RONALD R. "Internal External Control of Reinforcement as a Determinant of Study Habits and Academic Attitudes." *J Res Personality* 9(4):375–84 D '75. * (*PA* 55:13427)

164. RUTKOWSKI, KATHLEEN, AND DOMINO, GEORGE. "Interrelationship of Study Skills and Personality Variables in College Students." *J Ed Psychol* 67(6):784–9 D '75. * (*PA* 55:8265)

165. SCIMONELLI, FRANK JOSEPH. *A Study of Selected Variables Related to the Achievement of Music Majors in Two-Year Community Colleges.* Doctor's thesis, Catholic University of America (Washington, D.C.), 1975. (*DAI* 36:1366A)

166. CALDWELL, JAMES FRANKLIN. *A Descriptive Study of Academically Unsuccessful Arts and Sciences Freshmen.* Doctor's thesis, Oklahoma State University (Stillwater, Okla.), 1976. (*DAI* 37:5597A)

167. JEARAKUL, PRAPHON. *A Study of Some Factors Associated With Academic Performance of Tenth-Graders in Provincial High Schools of Northeastern Thailand.* Doctor's thesis, University of Colorado (Boulder, Colo.), 1976. (*DAI* 37:1961A)

168. LEVINE, FREDERIC J. "Influence of Field-Independence and Study Habits on Academic Performance of Black Students in a Predominantly White University." *Percept & Motor Skills* 42(3, pt 2):1101–2 Je '76. *

169. ROBYAK, JAMES EDWARD. *Relationships Among Personality Type, Classroom Structure and Performance in a Study Skills Course.* Doctor's thesis, University of Utah (Salt Lake City, Utah), 1976. (*DAI* 37:203A)

170. WEN, SHIH-SUNG, AND LIU, AN-YEN. "The Validity of Each of the Four Scales of the Survey of Study Habits and Attitudes (SSHA) for Each of two Samples of College Students and Under Each of two Treatment Conditions Involving use of Released Class Time." *Ed & Psychol Meas* 36(2):565–8 su '76. *

171. GIBSON, H. B.; CORCORAN, M. E.; AND CURRAN, J. D. "Hypnotic Susceptibility and Personality: The Consequences of Diazepam and the Sex of Objects." *Brit J Psychol* 68(1):51–9 F '77. *

172. GOLDSTON, JOHN; ZIMMERMANN, MARC; SENI, CHRISTINE; AND GADZELLA, BERNADETTE M. "Study Habits and Attitudes Characteristic of Sex and Locus-of-control Groups." *Psychol Rep* 40(1):271–4 F '77. * (*PA* 58:6305)

173. SHEEHAN, DANIEL S., AND HAMBLETON, RONALD K. "A Predictive Study of Success in an Individualized Science Program." *Sch Sci & Math* 77(1):13–20 Ja '77. *

[821]

★**Test of Library/Study Skills.** Grades 2–5, 4–9, 8–12; 1975; no data on reliability; no norms; 3 levels; no manual; separate answer cards must be used; $6 per 100 answer cards; $1 per scoring stencil; postpaid; sample copy of test free; (50) minutes; Irene Gullette and Frances Hatfield; Larlin Corporation. *

a) LEVEL 1. Grades 2–5; 1 form (7 pages); $11 per 50 tests.

b) LEVEL 2. Grades 4–9; 1 form (11 pages); $13 per 50 tests.

c) LEVEL 3. Grades 8–12; 1 form (10 pages); $13 per 50 tests.

[822]

Watson-Glaser Critical Thinking Appraisal. Grades 9–16 and adults; 1942–64; WGCTA; Forms YM, ZM, ('61, 8 pages); manual ('64, 16 pages); separate answer sheets (IBM 805, IBM 1230) must be used; $14.25 per 35 tests; $2.50 per 35 IBM 805 answer sheets; $3 per 35 IBM 1230 answer sheets; $1 per IBM scoring stencil; $2.75 per specimen set; postage extra; scoring service, 60¢ per test ($15 minimum); (50–60) minutes; Goodwin Watson and Edward M. Glaser; Psychological Corporation. *

See T2:1775 (35 references); for excerpted reviews

Survey of Study Habits and Attitudes

by John O. Crites and G. C. Helmstadter, see 7:783 (74 references) ; see also 6:867 (24 references) ; for reviews by Walker H. Hill and Carl I. Hovland of an earlier edition, see 5:700 (8 references) ; for a review by Robert H. Thouless and an excerpted review by Harold P. Fawcett, see 3:544 (3 references).

REFERENCES

1–3. See 3:544.
4–11. See 5:700.
12–35. See 6:867.
36–109. See 7:783.
110–144. See T2:1775; also includes a cumulative name index to the first 144 references, 3 reviews, and 3 excerpts for this test.
145. NYFIELD, GILLIAN; SAVILLE, PETER; FIELD, JANICE; AND HODGKISS, JOHN. British Supplement to the Watson-Glaser Thinking Appraisal (Form YM). Windsor, Berks, England: NFER Publishing Co. Ltd., 1964. Pp. ii, 24. *
146. BISHOP, TERRY. "Predicting Potential: Selection for Science-Based Industries." Personnel Management (England) 3(7):31–3 Jl '71. *
147. MARRS, LAWRENCE WAYNE. The Relationship of Critical Thinking Ability and Dogmatism to Changing Regular Class Teachers' Attitudes Toward Exceptional Children. Doctor's thesis, University of Texas (Austin, Tex.), 1971. (DAI 33:638A)
148. ALSTON, DORIS N. "An Investigation of the Critical Reading Ability of Classroom Teachers in Relation to Selected Background Factors." Ed Leadership 29(4):341–3 Ja '72. *
149. BRUBAKER, HERBERT LEE. Selection of College Major by the Variables of Intelligence, Creativity and Critical Thinking. Doctor's thesis, Temple University (Philadelphia, Pa.), 1972. (DAI 33:1507A)
150. BYBEE, JOHN RALEIGH. Prediction in the College of Education Doctoral Program at the Ohio State University. Doctor's thesis, Ohio State University (Columbus, Ohio), 1972. (DAI 33:4111A)
151. COBLE, CHARLES R., AND HOUNSHELL, PAUL B. "Teacher Self-Actualization and Student Progress." Sci Ed 56(3):311–6 Jl–S '72. *
152. HIMAYA, MAKRAM I. Identification of Possible Variables for Predicting Student Changes in Physical Science Courses Designed for Nonscience Majors. Doctor's thesis, University of Iowa (Iowa City, Iowa), 1972. (DAI 34:67A)
153. HUDSON, VERNON C., JR. A Study of the Relationship Between the Social Studies Student Teacher's Divergent Thinking Ability and His Success in Promoting Divergent Thinking in Class Discussion. Doctor's thesis, University of Arkansas (Fayetteville, Ark.), 1972. (DAI 33:2219A)
154. JAMES, REUBEN J. "Traits Associated With the Initial and Persistent Interest in the Study of College Science." J Res Sci Teach 9(3):231–4 '72. *
155. LITTLE, THOMAS LEE. The Relationship of Critical Thinking Ability to Intelligence, Personality Factors, and Academic Achievement. Doctor's thesis, Memphis State University (Memphis, Tenn.), 1972. (DAI 33:5554A)
156. LUCAS, A. M. "Inflated Posttest Scores Seven Months After Pretest." Sci Ed 56(3):381–7 Jl–S '72. *
157. LUCAS, A. M., AND BROADHURST, N. A. "Changes in Some Content-Free Skills, Knowledge, and Attitudes During Two Terms of Grade 12 Biology Instruction in Ten South Australian Schools." Austral Sci Teach J 18(1):66–74 My '72. *
158. SCHAFER, PAUL JOSEPH. An Inquiry Into the Relationship Between the Critical Thinking Ability of Teachers and Selected Variables. Doctor's thesis, University of Pittsburgh (Pittsburgh, Pa.), 1972. (DAI 33:1066A)
159. SKINNER, S. BALLOU, AND HOUNSHELL, PAUL B. "The Effect of the St. Andrews College Natural Science Course Upon Critical Thinking Ability." Sch Sci & Math 72(6):555–62 Je '72. *
160. STEVENS, JOHN TRUMAN. A Study of the Relationships Between Selected Teacher Affective Characteristics and Student Learning Outcomes in a Junior High School Science Program. Doctor's thesis, University of Virginia (Charlottesville, Va.), 1972. (DAI 33:3430A)
161. TAYLOR, LOREN ELDON. Predicted Role of Prospective Activity-Centered vs Textbook-Centered Elementary Science Teachers Correlated With 16 Personality Factors and Critical Thinking Abilities. Doctor's thesis, University of Idaho (Moscow, Idaho), 1972. (DAI 34:2415A)
162. VANCE, JIMMY STIRMAN. The Influence of a Teacher Questioning Strategy on Attitude and Critical Thinking. Doctor's thesis, Arizona State University (Tempe, Ariz.), 1972. (DAI 33:669A)
163. AWOMOLO, AMOS ADEMOLA. Teacher Discussion Leadership Behaviour in a Public Issues Curriculum and Some Cognitive and Personality Correlates. Doctor's thesis, University of Toronto (Toronto, Ont., Canada), 1973. (DAI 35:316A)
164. HUNT, DENNIS, AND RANDHAWA, BIKKAR S. "Relationship Between and Among Cognitive Variables and Achievement in Computational Science." Ed & Psychol Meas 33(4):921–8 w '73. * (PA 52:4026)

165. MATHIAS, ROBERT OWEN. Assessment of the Development of Critical Thinking Skills and Instruction in Grade Eight Social Studies in Mt. Lebanon School District. Doctor's thesis, University of Pittsburgh (Pittsburgh, Pa.), 1973. (DAI 34:1064A)
166. MOORE, MICHAEL RICHARD. An Investigation of the Relationships Among Teacher Behavior, Creativity and Critical Thinking Ability. Doctor's thesis, University of Missouri (Columbia, Mo.), 1973. (DAI 35:1270A)
167. MURPHY, ANTHONY J. The Relationship of Leadership Potential to Selected Admission Criteria for the Advanced Programs in Educational Administration. Doctor's thesis, State University of New York (Albany, N.Y.), 1973. (DAI 34:1545A)
168. NIXON, JOHN TIMOTHY. The Relationship of Openness to Academic Performance, Critical Thinking, and School Morale in Two School Settings. Doctor's thesis, George Peabody College for Teachers (Nashville, Tenn.), 1973. (DAI 34:3999A)
169. O'NEILL, MARGARET ROSE. A Study of Critical Thinking, Open-Mindedness, and Emergent Values Among High School Seniors and Their Teachers. Doctor's thesis, Fordham University (New York, N.Y.), 1973. (DAI 34:2278A)
170. SEYMOUR, LOWELL A., AND SUTMAN, FRANK X. "Critical Thinking Ability, Open-Mindedness, and Knowledge of the Processes of Science of Chemistry and Non-Chemistry Students." J Res Sci Teach 10(2):159–63 '73. *
171. BUNT, DON DUANE. Prediction of Academic Achievement and Critical Thinking of Eighth Graders in Suburban, Urban, and Private Schools Through Specific Personality, Ability, and School Variables. Doctor's thesis, Northern Illinois University (DeKalb, Ill.), 1974. (DAI 35:2042A)
172. BURNS, ROBERT LLOYD. The Testing of a Model of Critical Thinking Ontogeny Among Central Connecticut State College Undergraduates. Doctor's thesis, University of Connecticut (Storrs, Conn.), 1974. (DAI 34:5467A)
173. CANNON, ALLAN GORDON. The Development and Testing of a Policy-Capturing Model for the Selection of School Administrators in a Large Urban School District. Doctor's thesis, University of Texas (Austin, Tex.), 1974. (DAI 35:2565A)
174. CORLETT, DONNA. "Library Skills, Study Habits and Attitudes, and Sex as Related to Academic Achievement." Ed & Psychol Meas 34(4):967–9 w '74. * (PA 54:6370)
175. GARRIS, CHARLES W. A Study Comparing the Improvement of Students' Critical Thinking Ability Achieved Through the Teacher's Increased Use of Classroom Questions Resulting From Individualized or Group Training Programs. Doctor's thesis, Pennsylvania State University (University Park, Pa.), 1974. (DAI 35:7123A)
176. HINOJOSA, THOMAS RODOLFO, JR. The Influence of Idiographic Variables on Leadership Style: A Study of Special Education Administrators (Plan A) in Texas. Doctor's thesis, University of Texas (Austin, Tex.), 1974. (DAI 35:2082A)
177. McCLOUDY, CARL WINDELL. An Experimental Study of Critical Thinking Skills as Affected by Intensity and Types of Sound. Doctor's thesis, East Texas State University (Commerce, Tex.), 1974. (DAI 35:4086A)
178. SCHAFER, PAUL J. "Critical Thinking Ability of Teachers." J Instruct Psychol 1(4):39–40 f '74. * (PA 53:12388)
179. SIMON, A., AND WARD, L. O. "The Performance on the Watson-Glaser Critical Thinking Appraisal of University Students Classified According to Sex, Type of Course Pursued, and Personality Score Category." Ed & Psychol Meas 34(4):957–60 w '74. * (PA 64:21)
180. STORY, LLOYD EDWARD, JR. The Effect of the BSCS Inquiry Slides on the Critical Thinking Ability and Process Skills of First-Year Biology Students. Doctor's thesis, University of Southern Mississippi (Hattiesburg, Miss.), 1974. (DAI 35:2796A)
181. CARLSON, DONN ARVID. Training in Formal Reasoning Abilities Provided by the Inquiry Role Approach and Achievement on the Piagetian Formal Operational Level. Doctor's thesis, University of Northern Colorado (Greeley, Colo.), 1975. (DAI 36:7308A)
182. CRUCE-MAST, ADA LOU. The Interrelationship of Critical Thinking, Empathy and Social Interest With Moral Judgment. Doctor's thesis, Southern Illinois University (Carbondale, Ill.), 1975. (DAI 36:7945A)
183. HILLIS, SHELBY ROSS. The Relationship of Inquiry Orientation in Secondary Physical Science Classrooms and Student's Critical Thinking Skills, Attitudes and Views of Science. Doctor's thesis, University of Texas (Austin, Tex.), 1975. (DAI 36:805A)
184. HOOGSTRATEN, JOH., AND CHRISTIAANS, H. H. C. M. "The Relationship of the Watson-Glaser Critical Thinking Appraisal to Sex and Four Selected Personality Measures for a Sample of Dutch First-Year Psychology Students." Ed & Psychol Meas 35(4):969–73 w '75. * (PA 55:11302)
185. RAWLS, JAMES R., AND NELSON, OSCAR TIVIS, JR. "Characteristics Associated With Preferences for Certain Managerial Positions." Psychol Rep 36(3):911–8 Je '75 * (PA 54:10730)
186. ROSS, GEORGE ROBERT, JR. A Factor Analytic Study of Inductive Reasoning Tests. Doctor's thesis, Florida State University (Tallahassee, Fla.), 1975. (DAI 36:2111A)
187. CAMPBELL, ISABEL CORDLE. The Effect of Selected Facets

Watson-Glaser Critical Thinking Appraisal

of Critical Reading Instruction Upon Active Duty Servicemen and Civilian Evening College Adults. Doctor's thesis, University of Georgia (Athens, Ga.), 1976. (*DAI* 37:2591A)

188. COOK, MARLENE MARY. *A Study of the Interaction of Student and Program Variables for the Purpose of Developing a Model for Predicting Graduation From Graduate Programs in Educational Administration at the State University of New York at Buffalo.* Doctor's thesis, State University of New York (Buffalo, N.Y.), 1976. (*DAI* 37:827A)

189. DE LOACH, STANLEY STEVE. *Level of Ego Development, Degree of Psychopathology, and Continuation or Termination of Outpatient Psychotherapy Involvement.* Doctor's thesis, Georgia State University (Atlanta, Ga.), 1976. (*DAI* 37:5348B)

190. LANDIS, RICHARD ELLIOT. *The Psychological Dimensions of Three Measures of Critical Thinking and Twenty-Four Structure-of-Intellect Tests for a Sample of Ninth-Grade Students.* Doctor's thesis, University of Southern California (Los Angeles, Calif.), 1976. (*DAI* 37:5705A)

191. MOORE, MARY LOU. *Effects of Value Clarification on Dogmatism, Critical Thinking, and Self-Actualization.* Doctor's thesis, Arizona State University (Tempe, Ariz.), 1976. (*DAI* 37:907A)

192. GRASZ, CAROL SCAVNICKY. *A Study to Determine the Validity of Test Scores and Other Selected Factors as Predictors of Success in a Basic Course in Educational Administration.* Doctor's thesis, Rutgers—The State University of New Jersey (New Brunswick, N.J.), 1977. (*DAI* 37:7436A)

193. SMITH, DARYL G. "College Classroom Interactions and Critical Thinking." *J Ed Psychol* 69(2):180–90 Ap '77. *

[823]

Wisconsin Tests of Reading Skill Development: Study Skills. Grades kgn–1, 1–2, 2–3, 3–4, 4–5, 5–6, 6–7; 1970–73; WTRSD:SS; part of the Wisconsin Design for Reading Skill Development; criterion referenced; 2–14 "single-skill" scores at each of 7 levels; no norms; 80% mastery criterion suggested for each subtest, with retesting at next higher level if a child fails not more than one subtest and retesting at next lower level if a child passes not more than one subtest; 1–2 forms ('73); administrator's manual ('73, 12–22 pages) for each level; teacher's planning guide ('73, 43 pages); Design overview ('72, 173 pages); profile card ('73, 2 pages); additional instructional materials available; $16 per 100 profile cards; $1.50 per administrator's manual; $4 per planning guide; $5 per Design overview; cash orders postpaid; sampler free (sample pages only); overview and planning guide by Wayne Otto (principal investigator), Eunice Askov, and Robert D. Chester (planning guide); manuals by Deborah M. Stewart, Karlyn Kamm, James Allen, and Diane K. Sals (*c–e*); NCS Interpretive Scoring Systems. *

a) LEVEL A. Grades kgn–1; 2 scores: position of objects, measurement (size); Form P (8-page booklet or 6 ditto masters); $10 per 35 consumable booklets and 1 manual; $6 per set of ditto masters; (25) minutes; test by Karlyn Kamm, Deborah M. Stewart, and Virginia L. Van Blaricom.

b) LEVEL B. Grades 1–2; 4 scores: picture symbols, picture grids, measurement (distance), graphs (relative amounts); Form P (16-page booklet or 15 ditto masters); $17 per 35 consumable booklets and 1 manual; $15 per set of ditto masters; (65) minutes in 2 sessions; test by Karlyn Kamm, Deborah M. Stewart, and Virginia L. Van Blaricom.

c) LEVEL C. Grades 2–3; 10 scores: nonpictorial symbols, color keys, number-letter grids, measurement (size, distance), graphs (exact amounts, differences), tables (relative amounts, one cell), alphabetizing; Form P (24-page booklet or 25 ditto masters plus 4-page color maps booklet); Form Q ditto master available for the alphabetizing test; $24.50 per 35 consumable booklets and 1 manual; $25 per set of Form P ditto masters; $1 per Form Q ditto master; $15 per 35 reusable color maps booklets; (130) minutes in 3 sessions; test by Karlyn Kamm, Deborah M. Stewart, Virginia L. Van Blaricom, James Allen, and Mary L. Ramberg.

d) LEVEL D. Grades 3–4; 12 scores: point and line symbols, scale (whole units), graphs (differences, approximate amounts), tables (differences), reference (indexes, tables of contents, alphabetizing, guide words, headings and subheadings, selecting sources, facts or opinions); Form P (28-page booklet or 28 ditto masters); Form Q ditto masters available for the 7 reference tests; $28 per 35 consumable booklets and 1 manual; $28 per set of Form P ditto masters; $12 per set of Form Q ditto masters; (160) minutes in 4 sessions; test by Karlyn Kamm, Deborah M. Stewart, Virginia L. Van Blaricom, Evelyn Weible, James Allen, J. Laird Marshall, Mary L. Ramberg, and Diane K. Sals.

e) LEVEL E. Grades 4–5; 14 scores: point-line-area symbols, intermediate directions, scale (multiple whole units), graphs (differences, purpose and summary), tables (multiplicative differences, purpose and summary), reference (indexes, dictionary meanings, cross references, guide words, guide cards, specialized references, fact checking); Forms P, Q, in a single booklet (61 pages, Form Q is for the 7 reference tests only); separate answer sheets (ditto masters) must be used; $60 per 35 tests; $3 per set of ditto masters for answer sheets; (190) minutes in 5 sessions.

f) LEVEL F. Grades 5–6; 12 scores: maps (analysis), map projections, inset maps, different scales, graphs (differences), schedules (relationship), reference (*Subject Index*, dictionary pronunciation, card filing rules, Dewey Decimal System, outlining, catalog cards); Forms P, Q, in a single booklet (49 pages, Form Q is for the 6 reference tests only); answer sheet and price information same as for Level E; (195) minutes in 5 sessions.

g) LEVEL G. Grades 6–7; 10 scores: maps (synthesis), latitude and longitude, meridians and parallels, scale (fractional units), graphs (multiplicative differences, projecting and relating), schedules (problem solving), references (*Reader's Guide*, card catalogs, outlining); Forms P, Q, in a single booklet (52 pages, Form Q is for the 3 reference tests only); answer sheet and price information same as for Level E; (180) minutes in 4 sessions.

REFERENCES

1. KAMM, KARLYN. "The Study Skills Component of the Design." *Yearb Nat Read Conf* 21:253–7 '72. *

2. OTTO, WAYNE. "Rational and Overview of the Wisconsin Design." *Yearb Nat Read Conf* 21:245–8 '72. *

3. ZIMMERMAN, WAYNE S.; PARKS, HENRY; AND GRAY, KENNETH. "The Validity of Traditional Cognitive Measures and of Scales of the Study Attitudes and Methods Survey in the Prediction of the Academic Success of Educational Opportunity Program Students." *Ed & Psychol Meas* 37(2):465–70 su '77. *

JOHN J. GEYER, *Associate Professor of Education and Psychology, Rutgers, The State University of New Jersey, New Brunswick, New Jersey.*

The Wisconsin Tests of Reading Skills Development: Study Skills are formal, criterion-referenced tests designed specifically for use with the massive Wisconsin Design for Reading Skill Development. In conjunction with informal procedures, they comprise the diagnostic and evaluative component of the study skills element one of six such elements making up the total program. Their purpose is to determine a student's skill proficiencies and deficien-

Watson-Glaser Critical Thinking Appraisal

cies prior to specific skill instruction and to monitor his progress after instruction.

The emphasis of the tests (and the program) is heavily upon skills. The tests do not cover such familiar topics as attitudes toward school, management of time, preparing for and taking examinations, preparing projects and papers, or similar broad procedures and attitudes often found under a study skills heading. The tests focus tightly on eight "strands" concerned with the skills necessary for locating, interpreting, and using maps, graphs, tables, and reference materials. They are available at seven levels of difficulty.

The tests give every evidence of careful professionalism in their construction and appearance. Considerable effort has gone into making the tasks required of the child as realistic as possible through a lavish use of illustrations and simulations of actual materials. Directions seem clear and appropriate to the ages being tested. The tests are untimed and examiners are encouraged to help individual children with further explanations as required.

Since the tests are criterion-referenced, no norm data are supplied. Rather, the tests are referenced to specific performance objectives (and through them to the instructional record-keeping components). Scoring is simple percentage correct with a score of 80 percent recommended as signifying "mastery." It is intended that "mastery" of a strand at a certain level also certifies mastery at lower levels.

Reliability and validity information provided in the administrator's manuals is sparse and, to some extent, misleading. Each manual contains a statement such as, "Reliabilities of individual tests are in the .70's and .80's with a few in the .90's" and another statement that "further specific information appears in the *Technical Manual: Study Skills.*" The teacher's planning guide states: "Each of the tests has demonstrated reliability at a reasonably high level. In general, the reliability coefficients are .80 or better." Unfortunately, the technical manuals are not available and the technical data provided to this reviewer did not entirely support the statements quoted. Of the 64 reliabilities reported, 17 were below .70, ranging downward to a low of .32. The sample sizes these correlations were based on were quite small for a project of this magnitude.

To some extent the weakness in test statistics is a problem endemic to criterion-referenced measurement. The small number of items on each of the many tests and the relative homogeneity of the students tested virtually preclude the magnitude of correlations familiar in norm-referenced measurement. The problem is lessened by the function of the tests in guiding instruction over the short term. These scores do not rest in files forever stigmatizing children. However, reliabilities on a few of the tests appear weak enough to raise serious questions concerning their validity even for the use intended.

The weaknesses discussed apply to only a few of the tests and should not prevent the use of the program by those who are otherwise pleased with it. They do point up the need for additional test development, a need which is continuous in the testing field.

SCIENCE

REVIEWS BY *J. Arthur Campbell, Peter A. Dahl, Edward F. deVillafranca, Frank J. Fornoff, Arlen R. Gullickson, Mario Iona, George G. Mallinson, Jacqueline V. Mallinson, Clarence H. Nelson, John P. Penna, Gerald R. Van Hecke, Wayne W. Welch,* and *Victor L. Willson.*

[824]
*CLEP General Examinations: Natural Sciences. 1–2 years or equivalent; 1964–76; for college accreditation of nontraditional study, advanced placement, or assessment of educational attainment; 3 scores: biological, physical, total; normative, reliability, and validity data based on 1963 testing; Forms PCT1, PCT2, ('67, 14 pages); manual ('74, 17 pages) for CLEP General Examinations; for CLEP program accessories, see 473; separate answer sheets (IBM 850-Digitek, IBM 1230) must be used; rental fee, $4 per test; postpaid; 75(85) minutes; program administered for the

College Entrance Examination Board by Educational Testing Service. *

REFERENCES

1. COHEN, ALLAN STUART. *Comparison of Decision-Making Strategies for Awarding College Credit Based on College Level Examination Program Examinations.* Doctor's thesis, University of Iowa (Iowa City, Iowa), 1972. (*DAI* 33:6723A)
2. GRANDY, JERILEE, AND SHEA, WALTER M. *The CLEP General Examinations in American Colleges and Universities.* Princeton, N.J.: Educational Testing Service, 1976. Pp. 23. *

GEORGE G. MALLINSON, *Distinguished Professor of Science Education, Western Michigan University, Kalamazoo, Michigan.* [Review of the 1972 natural sciences examination in the *CLEP General Examinations,* Form UCT1.]

As stated in the series manual, "more and more colleges and universities have accepted the principle that college-level learning, however acquired, should be credited toward a degree." Certainly this attitude has spread in recent decades. University personnel now acknowledge that there are many ways to acquire college-level knowledge, other than by sitting in a college classroom. However, one of the most difficult tasks of implementing such a philosophy is equating out-of-school experience with college-level earned credit. The College-Level Examination Program has been one such attempt. According to the manual, "a program of the College Entrance Examination Board, CLEP is a national system of credit-by-examination offering people of all ages and all backgrounds an opportunity to obtain recognition for college-level achievement. This chance is offered regardless of when, where, or how one's knowledge has been acquired."

The CLEP battery consists of two types of tests, General Examinations and Subject Examinations. The test reviewed here is one of the five basic tests of liberal arts included in the General Examinations, other areas being English composition, humanities, mathematics, and social sciences and history. The tests purport to evaluate material ordinarily covered in the first two years of college within the general studies, or liberal arts, areas. The booklet states, "The General Examinations, which were not developed from the viewpoint of any particular approach or curriculum, sample these common areas."

Each of the five General Examinations is a 60-minute, five-option multiple choice test. The examination in natural sciences contains 85 items. A booklet distributed by the publisher, indicates that:

The content of the test covers three major areas: (1) Information about science as a field in which people work and its relationship to other areas of knowledge is the basis for about 15 percent of the questions * (2) Questions about biology and related sciences make up about 42 or 43 percent of the test. Most of these questions are based on concepts and principles that apply to both animals and plants, and the rest are about equally divided between material about these two aspects of biology. (3) The physical sciences are the basis for the other 42 or 43 percent of the test. About a third of such questions deal with physics, a third with chemistry, and the final third are related to astronomy, geology and meteorology.

In the opinion of this reviewer, the rationale for such a distribution is consistent with the goals of the typical general-education science requirement. In addition, a careful perusal of the test items and a tally of item type by content show that the test adheres to these specifications.

The items are interesting, many dealing with the analysis of graphs or diagrams. Others consist of a paragraph of information to be studied and analyzed. One minor point that puzzles this reviewer is the division of the test into two parts, labelled Part A and Part B. Part A presents seven "clusters" of data interpretation items, varying from three to six items per group. Part B starts out with single items—33 to be precise. However, these 33 items are followed by several more "clusters" of three, four or five items each. If, as one may first assume, Part A is made up of groups, or clusters, of items, then those at the end of the test should also have been placed in Part A.

Another minor criticism of the examination is the format of the printed material. The type is relatively small and closely spaced. For a student taking the entire battery of General Examinations in one day, this factor could add greatly to fatigue. Also, with several items the options are listed in paragraph style, whereas in other cases they are listed vertically, one under the other. This inconsistency could prove to be confusing, particularly to a student who is not accustomed to responding on a separate answer sheet.

Other than these two minor criticisms, the items are more than adequate. There appears to be an appropriate "mix" of factual recall items and thinking, reasoning items. The content balance, as outlined above, is adhered to well. An analysis of the items failed to reveal scientific inaccuracies.

CLEP General Examinations: Natural Sciences

There does appear to be a wide range of difficulty among the items. For example, one item deals with the distinction between a "vertebrate" and an "invertebrate." This item could easily be included in an upper-elementary-school science examination. At the other end of the spectrum of difficulty, the testee is required to analyze and apply Kepler's harmonic law. However, since the test is designed to be general, covering many aspects of natural sciences, the range of difficulty can be defended. Further, descriptive information provided to students assures them that no one is expected to know the correct responses to all, or even a majority of, the items.

Since extensive normative data are provided in the series manual, a detailed discussion is not included here. Suffice to say, however, the test appears to have more than adequate face validity, and the reliabilities of both the biological science and physical science parts are .86.

If a college or university is willing to grant credit by examination, the use of the CLEP tests would be most useful. A student who could pass this test would certainly possess a "general studies," or "liberal arts," level of science knowledge. The reviewer recommends this test for the purpose for which it is claimed to be designed.

[825]

★Comprehensive Tests of Basic Skills: Science, Expanded Edition. Grades 4.5–6.9, 6.5–8.9; 1973–76; Form S ('73, 14 pages) for Levels 2 (grades 4.5–6.9), 3 (grades 6.5–8.9); no specific manual; battery manual ('74, 70–72 pages) for each level; battery coordinator's handbook ('76, 59 pages); battery technical bulletin No. 1 ('74, 75 pages); separate answer sheets (Digitek, IBM 1230, Scoreze for science and social studies combined) must be used; $10.50 per 35 tests; answer sheets: $5 per 50 Digitek or IBM, $4.25 per 25 Scoreze; $2.50 per IBM hand scoring stencil; Digitek scoring stencil not available; $2.50 per coordinator's handbook; $2.50 per technical bulletin; postage extra; specimen set not available; (66) minutes; CTB/McGraw-Hill. *

For reviews of the complete battery, see 12 (2 reviews).

ARLEN R. GULLICKSON, *Associate Professor of Education, The University of South Dakota, Vermillion, South Dakota.*

Test content is divided into seven major categories: recognition, classification, quantification, identification of trend, prediction from data, hypothesis evaluation, and design analysis. Those classifications represent an ordering of cognitive skills with recognition at the lower

end and design analysis at the upper end. Level 2 emphasizes the lower order skills with only four of 36 total items in the upper two levels, three in hypothesis evaluation, and one in design analysis. Level 3 gives much more emphasis to those two latter classifications with eight of 41 total items on hypothesis evaluation and three on design analysis.

A multiple choice test with four response alternatives per item, it uses A, B, C, and D for response options on all odd-numbered items and E, F, G, and H on the even items. Such a format reduces the chance for a recording error on a test answer sheet when a test item is skipped. Both a battery technical bulletin and a battery examiner's manual are provided. The technical bulletin enhances interpretation by providing reliability, validity, and demographic information relative to the norm sample. Such information allows a user to see how closely the characteristics of his community fit those of the community from which norm data were obtained.

Several scoring options are available. Each has its own advantages and disadvantages. For example, an acetate stencil key enables rapid hand scoring of tests. However, in using this method no record of correct and incorrect responses is retained, and no content analysis may be made on the basis of the stencil scoring. Consequently, by using such a scoring technique, one loses some of the interpretative richness. Other more expensive scoring options provide greater flexibility in interpretation and use of test results.

With the many interpretative options available, users should carefully consider the limitations of the test. As an achievement test it is designed for comparison on a national level; i.e., its norms are based upon a national sample and the items reflect many curricula, not any one curriculum. It should not be used as the determiner of student achievement in a course nor as a determiner of the quality of any particular science course.

Perhaps the most significant concern relative to use of the test is its difficulty. For example, for Level 2, percentile rank tables indicate that at the end of grade four approximately one-third scored within a range obtainable by chance (random guessing). Only when the Level 2 test was administered to sixth grade students did more than 80 percent of the students score outside the range of chance. To a slightly lesser extent the same problem exists for Level 3. The high difficulty level of the test is of particular concern here because the manual encourages overinterpretation by providing grade-equivalent scores for persons scoring within the chance range. In cases where class achievement is well below average, class interpretation, as well as individual interpretation, may have little meaning. That is especially true if the cognitive categories are being evaluated. It would never be appropriate to interpret the category results on an individual basis. The manuals do not suggest such use, and reliability and validity information are not provided for such interpretative purposes.

The rather high percentage of scores falling within the chance range undoubtedly is a contributing factor to the rather low reliability of the test, which ranges from a low of .79 at grade 4.7 to a high of .90 at grade 8.7.

The test developer has exercised care to ensure content validity, and has gone to considerable effort to remove racial bias from the test. The technical bulletin also attests to the significant efforts made in the use of item analysis in improving individual items and therefore the whole test. One aspect of validation that is not included in the technical bulletin is the test's relationship with other tests designed to measure the same levels of science achievement. Data on such relationships would greatly facilitate comparison of this test with other comparable but established tests.

SUMMARY. The test manuals show the attendance to the necessary developmental activities that a standardized test should have. The norms are recently developed, 1972–73, and care has been taken to ensure that the test operates appropriately across grade levels. In light of these considerations, the test is a welcome addition to the CTBS battery. The rather high difficulty level of the test, particularly at the lower grades for which each level is designed makes it more appropriate for better-than-average students and correspondingly less appropriate for use among low achieving students. Finally, potential users should be aware that CTBS has a national focus. Therefore, selection of the test should be based upon the fit between CTBS and the school curricula, which requires a careful content analysis of the test at the school level.

[826]

Cooperative Science Tests: Advanced General Science. Grades 8–9; 1962–65; Forms A ('62, 23 pages), B ('62, 20 pages); no specific manual; series handbook ('64, 76 pages); student bulletin ('65, 2 pages); separate answer sheets (Digitek, IBM 805, IBM 1230, NCS) must be used; $6 per 20 tests; $5.50 per 100 answer sheets; $1.50 per 10 IBM scoring stencils (answer pattern must be punched out locally); Digitek scoring stencils not available; $2 per series handbook; $3 per 100 student bulletins; $3.50 per specimen set of this and 4 other science tests; cash orders postpaid; NCS scoring and statistical analysis service, 45¢ and over per test; 80(92) minutes; Educational Testing Service; Addison-Wesley Publishing Co., Inc. *

For a review by Carl J. Olson, see 7:788 (1 reference). For excerpted reviews by Irvin J. Lehmann (with Clarence H. Nelson) and William Mehrens of the series, see 7:787.

GEORGE G. MALLINSON, *Distinguished Professor of Science Education, Western Michigan University, Kalamazoo, Michigan.*

This test is designed for use primarily in grade 9 general science classes, or "superior grade 8" science classes. It "covers the same content area as" does the *Cooperative General Science Test,* but, according to the catalog, "more comprehensively and at a higher level of difficulty." There are two forms of the test, both consisting of two 40-minute parts. Part 1 of each form consists of 30 biology items and a total of 30 in the areas of astronomy, geology, and meteorology. Part 2 consists of 30 physics items and 30 chemistry items.

Both forms of the test are comprised of five-option multiple choice items. In both forms, the options for odd-numbered items are designated "A, B, C, D, and E," while those for even-numbered items are designated "F, G, H, J, and K." While it may seem trivial to mention such a detail, such option designations are extremely valuable in helping students avoid responding in the wrong place on the separate answer sheet. It would be desirable if more standardized test publishers followed this procedure.

If one peruses the handbook carefully, he cannot help but be impressed by the vast amount of information provided. The handbook gives detailed information on administration, test scoring, and score interpretation. Much information is also provided concerning the preparation, equating, and norming of the tests, as well as the usual statistical information concerning validity, reliability, item discrimination, speededness, difficulty, and equivalence of the alternate forms. From the statistical standpoint, one can only give the tests a high rating.

The balance between the traditional subject matter areas of general science seems adequate, that is, one-fourth each in the biological, earth science, physics, and chemistry fields. This certainly "stacks up" with the content taught in a traditional ninth grade general science class. Although the test is recommended for "superior grade 8" students, it would be suitable only if such students had experienced "traditional" general science courses in grades 7 and 8. It probably would not be an adequate measure of achievement if students had experienced "compartmentalized" science courses in grades 7 and 8 (typically, biological science in grade 7 and earth or physical science in grade 8).

The authors have classified the items according to the skills they purport to measure. These skills are knowledge; comprehension; and application, analysis, and evaluation. This reviewer "took" both forms of the test to see if his answers matched the keyed responses. In all cases they did. Further, he "classified" the items according to the three categories above before he checked the classifications in the handbook. In most cases, the classifications agreed. The numbers of items on Form A in the categories knowledge; comprehension; and application, analysis, and evaluation are well balanced, with 35, 37, and 48 items, respectively. On Form B there is less evidence of balance, with 26, 35, and 59 items, respectively.

In general, the items are interesting—a "plus" value for any test. However, in some cases, students must do a great deal of reading in order to answer an item. This is especially true for some of the data interpretation groups in which a number of items relate to a given paragraph or diagram. For students who have reading problems, this may be a severe handicap.

In the opinion of this reviewer, one of the most serious shortcomings of the test is its speededness. According to the information given in the handbook, in no case did 100 percent of the norm group reach the three-quarter point of the tests and no more than 74.2 percent answered the last item. If, indeed, this is a test of achievement and comprehension, it would appear that either the test should be shortened or the time for administration should be lengthened. Making a test so long (or so difficult) that no students complete it seems to serve little purpose.

In spite of these shortcomings, the test appears to be a better-than-average standardized test for grade 9 general science. It is certainly better than most teacher-made tests. If a school system has a science curriculum that "matches" the areas covered by this test, the *Cooperative Science Test: Advanced General Science* should be most useful in evaluating student achievement. This reviewer would not hesitate to recommend it.

[827]

Cooperative Science Tests: General Science. Grades 7–9; 1962–65; Forms A, B, ('62, 10–11 pages); no specific manual; series handbook ('64, 76 pages); student bulletin ('65, 2 pages); separate answer sheets (Digitek, IBM 805, IBM 1230, NCS) must be used; $6 per 20 tests; $5.50 per 100 answer sheets; $1.50 per 10 IBM scoring stencils (answer pattern must be punched out locally); Digitek scoring stencils not available; $2 per series handbook; $3 per 100 student bulletins; $3.50 per specimen set of this and 4 other science tests; cash orders postpaid; NCS scoring and statistical analysis service, 45¢ and over per test; 40(45) minutes; Educational Testing Service; Addison-Wesley Publishing Co., Inc. *

For a review by Clarence H. Nelson, see 7:789 (1 reference). For excerpted reviews by Irvin J. Lehmann (with Clarence H. Nelson) and William Mehrens of the series, see 7:787.

[828]

*National Teacher Examinations: Biology and General Science. College seniors and teachers; 1940–77; test administered 3 times annually (February, July, November) at centers established by the publisher; Forms YNT ('76, 24 pages), ZNT ('77, 22 pages); descriptive booklet ('76, 10 pages); for program accessories, see 381; examination fee, $13 per candidate; 120(165) minutes; Educational Testing Service. *

For reviews of the testing program, see 381 (2 reviews), 7:582 (2 reviews), 6:700 (1 review), and 5:538 (3 reviews).

[829]

*National Teacher Examinations: Chemistry, Physics, and General Science. College seniors and teachers; 1940–77; test administered 3 times annually (February, July, November) at centers established by the publisher; Forms YNT ('76, 27 pages), ZNT ('77, 31 pages); descriptive booklet ('70, 11 pages); for program accessories, see 381; examination fee, $13 per candidate; 120(165) minutes; Educational Testing Service. *

For reviews of the testing program, see 381 (2 reviews), 7:582 (2 reviews), 6:700 (1 review), and 5:538 (3 reviews).

JACQUELINE V. MALLINSON, *Adjunct Associate Professor of Science Education, Western*

Michigan University, Kalamazoo, Michigan.
[Review of Forms UNT and YNT.]

This examination is designed to measure a candidate's preparation for teaching biology and general science at the secondary school level. Both forms consist of 160 five-choice items, requiring a 120-minute administration time.

The descriptive booklet for candidates indicates that the questions are categorized according to content (biological sciences and general sciences—namely chemistry, physics, and earth sciences) and also according to various abilities and understandings.

The reviewer "took" both forms of the examination and, while so doing, tabulated the items according to abilities and subject matter. The reviewer can say without hesitation that the two forms of the examination are consistent with the specifications outlined by the publisher.

The subject-matter items cover areas of understanding in which anyone prepared to teach secondary school biology and/or general science should be competent. The items represent a good coverage of content, ranging from understanding concepts and applying principles to knowledge of names and terms.

The "ability" items are realistic in that they present typical classroom situations, such as real test-question responses that the candidate must "score" and analyze for students' understandings (or misunderstandings). Some items also require an analysis of a laboratory situation or the determination of the best way to carry out a classroom demonstration.

The examination has good reliability, .95. The mean item difficulty is satisfactory. Speededness is not a problem; 99.7 percent of the norm group completed 75 percent of the examination, and at least 80 percent completed the entire examination.

In summary, this examination is a more than adequate measuring device for the purposes for which it is designed. It should be a useful instrument for assessing the subject-matter background and teaching "know-how" of education majors, teaching candidates, and teachers applying for state certification. As with all such measures, the results of the test cannot, and should not, be used in an absolute fashion. But the results could be combined with a number of pieces of information for evaluating a candidate's potential worth as a secondary teacher of biology and general science.

[830]

Sequential Tests of Educational Progress: Science, Series II. Grades 4–6, 7–9, 10–12, 13–14; 1956–72; original 70 minute series (Series I) still available; 2 forms ('69, 11–19 pages): Forms 4A and 4B (grades 4–6), 3A and 3B (grades 7–9), 2A and 2B (grades 10–12), 1A and 1B (grades 13–14); for battery manuals and accessories, see 28; separate answer sheets (Digitek, IBM 805, IBM 1230) must be used; $7 per 20 tests; $5.50 per 100 answer sheets; $1.50 per 10 IBM (805, 1230 hand) scoring stencils (answer pattern must be punched out locally); Digitek scoring stencils not available; cash orders postpaid; specimen set not available; 40(50) minutes for grades 4–9, 60(70) minutes for grades 10–14; Educational Testing Service; Addison-Wesley Publishing Co., Inc. *

See T2:1794 (18 references); for reviews by John C. Flanagan and George G. Mallinson of the original edition (Series I), see 6:882 (2 references); for reviews by Palmer O. Johnson, Julian C. Stanley (with M. Jacinta Mann), and Robert M. W. Travers, see 5:716. For reviews of the complete battery, see 28 (2 reviews), 6:25 (2 reviews), and 5:24 (2 reviews, 1 excerpt).

REFERENCES

1–2. See 6:882.
3–20. See T2:1794; also includes a cumulative name index to the first 20 references and 5 reviews for this test.
21. Leake, John B., and Hinerman, Charles O. "Scientific Literacy and School Characteristics." *Sch Sci & Math* 73(9):772–82 D '73. *
22. Keating, Daniel P. "The Study of Mathematically Precocious Youth." *J Spec Ed* 9(1):45–62 sp '75. * (PA 56:4069)
23. Lawson, Anton E.; Nordland, Floyd H.; and DeVito, Alfred. "Relationship of Formal Reasoning to Achievement, Aptitudes, and Attitudes in Preservice Teachers." *J Res Sci Teach* 12(4):423–31 O '75. *
24. Williams, Carolyn Chandler. *The Relationship Between Selected Reading Skills and Other Personal Variables of Sixth and Seventh Grade Students and Achievement in Science and Social Studies.* Doctor's thesis, Mississippi State University (State College, Miss.), 1975. (DAI 36:4132A)

Wayne W. Welch, *Professor of Educational Psychology, University of Minnesota, Minneapolis, Minnesota.*

Reviewing tests, like writing them, is a difficult task. Specific criteria are not well established, there is heavy reliance on the printed word, presumed impact on students is examined rather than actual performance, and potential for reviewer bias is great.

The reader is probably in a better position to judge this review if he knows how each of the above problems was addressed. First, criteria were established prior to examining the test battery. Approximately two dozen characteristics were examined within five major categories: development, item characteristics, instructions, validity and reliability, and interpretation. Second, like most tests, this review is almost entirely words. Third, I have not given these tests to anyone except my fourteen-year-old daughter and myself. I tried to use my experience with a variety of other tests to judge what reactions students might have. Finally, I did have an opinion about these tests before I began. It was positive, and based on a 1966 examination of Series I.

In spite of some concerns, I found STEP Science, Series II, to be of sufficient quality to recommend it to those facing decisions in science education. Information generated by the series would be helpful in both individual and group evaluations.

Particular strengths of the series are noted in the areas of format, item characteristics, development, reliability, and interpretation.

The tests are pleasant in appearance. The items are well laid out with enough sketches and graphs to make them appear interesting to examinees. The matrix of content and level of items appears well represented. I picked two forms at random (Form 2A, 4B) and noted the following item distribution: biology, 31 and 25 items, respectively; chemistry, 13 and 5; physics, 19 and 12; earth science, 12 and 8; total, 75 and 50. In addition, the item distribution on the same two forms for various cognitive abilities is as follows: knowledge, 12 and 15 items, respectively; comprehension, 15 and 10; application, 40 and 23; higher levels, 8 and 2. Of course, one person's comprehension item could be another's knowledge item depending on the individual's prior information. But the publishers are to be commended for their attempt to broaden the domain being tested.

The manual is not clear on the rationale for selecting relative content emphases (e.g., 50 percent biological science in some tests), but if a user finds the content consistent with his educational goals there should be few problems here.

Test reliability is reported both for parallel forms (range is .71 to .88) and for K-R 20 internal consistency (.81 to .91). These coefficients are about average for tests of this type.

The manuals provide considerable information for administering, scoring, and interpreting results. The publishers are to be lauded for providing extensive information for test users, although some time is required to become familiar with the materials.

Limitations of the science tests appear to occur in the categories of instructions, domain

definition, and validity. In addition, there are problems associated with mass-producing batteries of tests in several disciplines. Of course, there are always questions to be raised about individual items and format.

The three-column "General Directions" on the cover of each test are difficult to read. Perhaps more space between the columns would help. The example item refers only to a Digitek format when, in fact, there are answer sheets with quite different markings. This could confuse students. In my opinion, the multi-purpose optical scanning sheets used with these tests have high error potential. They are covered with a maze of spaces to darken, overlapped with directions, and easily voided by stray pencil marks. I would urge simplicity to reduce errors. I have found an error rate as high as 10 percent in marking and optically scoring these forms. Users are cautioned to check answer sheets carefully and hand score a sample of tests as a quality check.

Although the content domain sampled is broader than that of most tests, it ignores such things as the relationships of science and society, student attitude toward science, and laboratory skills; and little attention is given to the processes of science. These are important outcomes. Users of this set of tests may want to augment their science testing program with some of the more recent attempts to test these important concepts, for example, the *Test on Understanding Science.*

I have some concerns about the lack of validity information provided with the tests. Some mention is made of content validity because experts were used in the development. However, no information is presented on other types of validity, e.g., concurrent or predictive validity. Do students who we are quite sure know more science score higher on these tests? For example, do third year science students outperform those in their first year of science? How closely do these tests correlate with other measures of science? Information of this kind is not presented in the handbook.

The extremely high correlations between the science tests and other tests in the series—reading, social science, mathematics—are bothersome. The median correlation between the eight different science tests and the social science tests is .81. Yet the correlations between Forms

Sequential Tests of Educational Progress: Science

A and B in science are only slightly higher, with a median of about .83. Similarly, the correlation between the science tests and the SCAT total is nearly .80. It would appear that all of these tests are measuring about the same thing. It may be unfair to label one test as science and another as social science. Interesting, clever, probing, multiple choice items in the higher cognitive levels may be largely content free. Perhaps what is being measured is ability to answer these kinds of questions (intelligence?) and not achievement in a particular subject. Further study or reporting of available information on validity seems warranted.

I would question the classification of a few of the items, and I think the foil layout might be confusing to some students. However, I don't think these are major problems.

In summary, I believe these tests measure something quite well and present a plethora of interpretative information for the user. Just what it is that they are measuring and whether or not they are measuring all the things they should be are yet to be determined.

VICTOR L. WILLSON, *Assistant Professor of Educational Evaluation and Research, The University of South Dakota, Vermillion, South Dakota.*

The STEP II science tests have been developed to measure student progress in general scientific literacy. The authors' emphasis on utilizing results is for individual prescription rather than for class, school, or district use. The continued insistence by test publishers on such usage flies in the face of actual district usage, lack of specific validity, low reliability, and small item samples for making decisions about individual students. Tests such as this ought to be promoted for uses to which they may more properly be put: class, school, or district assessment of achievement, evaluation of curriculum, and research at the local level.

Forms 4 and 3 are one-part, timed tests with 50 items each. Reasonable care has been taken to select items across content areas of biology, chemistry, physics, and earth science. Items were also developed to reflect hierarchical cognitive processes. This reviewer asked science education professors and doctoral candidates to classify random samples of items by subject and cognitive level. For Form 4 (A and B),

agreement between test developers and the judges was 80 percent on subject matter and 33 percent on cognitive level. For Form 3 (A and B), the agreement was 92 percent for subject matter and 46 percent for cognitive level. A similar analysis for Forms 1 and 2 resulted in 89 percent agreement between test authors and judges on content area and 46 percent on cognitive level. While neither the test publishers nor the judges selected for this little study may necessarily be correct, these results suggest that a school district should review the items and classify them in a way most meaningful to the district or school using the tests. The judges reviewing the tests agreed that the reading levels for Forms 4 and 3 were of appropriate difficulty for the grade levels intended.

K-R 20 reliabilities range from .81 to .91, with median .88. More important are the parallel-form reliabilities, which range from .71 to .88, with median .84.

Forms 1 and 2 are two-part tests, with the first part designed to assess cognitive achievement based on the student's background and the second part designed to assess the student's ability to utilize information presented to him. Correlations between part scores range from .60 to .78, with median .75.

Validity data are scanty, with only correlations among the STEP tests and between them and SCAT tests presented. The correlations between science and SCAT verbal scores range from .69 to .78, with median .73; the correlations with the SCAT quantitative scores are lower, .60 to .78, with median .715. It is interesting that the median correlation between the science tests and other STEP tests are quite high: social studies, .815; reading, .765; English expression, .745; mathematics basic concepts, .735; mathematics computation, .71; and mechanics of writing, .63. These correlations are difficult to rationalize.

Norming procedures are excellent. The inclusion of a list of school districts participating in norming is useful. A criticism of the norm sample at the college level is that no large land-grant universities are represented. Thus, norms may not be useful for large state universities, but this limitation is not serious.

Test administration instructions are clear and concise. Instructions for hand scoring are so abbreviated as to be useless for a naive teacher. The use of the punchout scoring stencil should be made clearer in the manual for each level.

Norm tables are clear and easy to read. The use of percentile bands for given observed scores is excellent, even though the confidence interval is at .68 probability. Of course, .95 confidence intervals, which probably should have been included, would have been so broad that they would clearly highlight the difficulty of making decisions concerning individual placement or remediation.

The STEP II science tests appear to have sufficient reliability and content validity to be considered by schools for program evaluation, local science assessment, or research. The use of items in specific subjects of science or at specific cognitive levels given in the manual does not have validity information to support it and such use should be for research purposes only.

Users are cautioned that use of the science tests in making decisions about individual students is not recommended.

BIOLOGY

[831]

*Advanced Placement Examination in Biology. High school students desiring credit for college level courses and admission to advanced courses; 1956–77; available to secondary schools for annual administration on specified days in May; Form ZBP ('77, 24 pages) in 2 booklets (objective, essay); course description ('76, 44 pages); sample syllabi ('76, 32 pages); grading guidelines ('76, 22 pages); previous essay questions available; for program accessories, see 471; examination fee, $32 per student; 180(200) minutes; an inactive form [Form YBP ('76, 22 pages)] is available to colleges for local administration and scoring (rental fee, $2 per test); program administered for the College Entrance Examination Board by Educational Testing Service. *

See 7:807 (1 reference); for a review by Clarence H. Nelson of earlier forms, see 6:893 (1 reference); for a review by Clark W. Horton, see 5:724. For reviews of the APE program, see 471 (2 reviews) and 7:662 (2 reviews).

REFERENCES

1. See 6:893.
2. See 7:807.
3. KASTRINOS, WILLIAM, AND ERK, FRANK C. "Advanced Placement Exam in Biology." *Am Biol Teach* 36(5):282–91 My '74. *

[832]

*CLEP Subject Examination in Biology. 1 year or equivalent; 1970–76; for college accreditation of nontraditional study, advanced placement, or assessment of educational achievement; tests administered monthly at centers throughout the United States; 3 scores: knowledge, analysis, total; Forms SCT1 ('70, 19 pages), UCT1 ('70, 21 pages); optional essay supplement scored by college: Forms SCT1A, SCT1B, SCT2A, SCT2B, ('70, 2 pages); for program accessories, see 473; rental and scoring fee, $20 per student (includes reporting of scores to the candidate and one college); postpaid; 90(95) minutes, same for essay supplement; program administered for the College Entrance Examination Board by Educational Testing Service. *

For reviews of the CLEP program, see 473 (3 reviews) and 7:664 (3 reviews).

CLARENCE H. NELSON, *Professor Emeritus, Office of Evaluation Services, Michigan State University, East Lansing, Michigan.* [Review of Form SCT1.]

The *CLEP Subject Examination in Biology* has been designed to measure attainment of the content and objectives of a typical two-semester course in college biology, mainly for the purpose of determining whether or not college credit should be granted to individuals who have prepared themselves by independent study without being enrolled in the equivalent college course. This instrument appears to be very well suited to that purpose. It derives its validity from its construction procedures. Questions were contributed by individuals teaching introductory college biology courses and by test specialists who, with the assistance of a review committee of biology professors, made revisions, refinements, and adjustments necessary to produce a final product that conforms as closely as possible to the content and ability specifications previously established. And to the student who has diligently prepared himself/ herself, the examination content should look familiar. The very commendable reliability of .91, obtained from initial administration to nearly 4,000 students, also reflects the generally high level of workmanship that has gone into the production of this examination.

The content covered is categorized under three headings: cell biology (25 percent), organism biology (40 percent), and population biology (35 percent). Abilities measured are designated as knowledge of facts, principles, and processes of biology (60 percent); understanding of means by which information is collected, interpreted, and used in formulating hypotheses, drawing conclusions, and making predictions (30 percent); and understanding that science is a human endeavor with social consequences (10 percent). Section 1, consisting of independent multiple choice items, is designated as the "Knowledge Test," and Section 2, containing 40 multiple choice items associated with reading selections, is regarded as the "Analysis Test." It would be helpful if the individual items had been classified on a two-axis grid to show the content and ability each item purports to measure. This reviewer, curious as to which 10 items (10 percent) may have been allotted to the third abilities category, was unable to find that many items in the examination which *unequivocally* and *forthrightly* measure "understanding that science is a human endeavor with social consequences." However, this criticism should be tempered somewhat by the acknowledgment that most textbooks don't address themselves to this objective in a very meaningful way either. In view of the overall general excellence of the examination, this is no serious flaw.

A few minor infelicities of item construction were encountered. In principle, the stem of a computational type multiple-choice item should be capable of standing alone as an open-ended, free-response question and yield one, but *only one,* right answer. To satisfy this criterion, the stem of item 2 should provide one more bit of information—namely, CD 4. In item 15, the elaborate phraseology in response C, in contrast to the relatively simpler phraseology used in the other responses, tends to attract attention to it as the possible right answer. A very perceptive student who was not quite sure of the correct answer might reason, "Nobody would be likely to go to all the trouble of wasting abstruse words like exponential and semilogarithmic in a mere wrong answer."

In item 50, the verbal association between "oxygen" in the stem and "oxidative" in response C may tend to provide an irrelevant clue to the answer. In items 58–60, the response list is slightly nonhomogeneous in that four of the responses are names of physical entities, while response B is the name of a process. In item 92, the stem does not set the task (contains no verb) but depends upon the responses to do this. The foregoing are examples of very minor lapses that would not impair the essential overall effectiveness of the examination.

One of the most noteworthy and commendable aspects is the grading procedure recommended by the CLEP Council. It appears to be the epitome of fairness. Standard score norms were obtained by administering the CLEP biol-

ogy examination to a sample of 3,656 undergraduate students near the end of a year's course in biology. Course instructors were asked to indicate the final grade (A=highest, E=failing) for each student. The CLEP Council recommends that course credit be awarded to any individual who attains the mean standard score (49) earned by C students who had actually taken the year's course. This appears to be very equitable. Mean scores could be used for awarding other grades (53 for B, 61 for A), though each institution may wish to adjust these slightly to reflect its own prevailing standards.

The *CLEP Subject Examination in Biology* represents a high level of careful and imaginative workmanship. The content and objectives coverage parallels very closely most first-year college biology courses. The student should feel that he/she has been rigorously tested but upon receiving the grade report should have no basis for feeling that the grade is unfair. This examination can be highly recommended as a basis for granting credit and a grade for two semesters of introductory college biology learned by independent study.

An optional essay section is also provided for the examinee to take if the credit-granting institution requires it. The essay answers are mailed directly to the institution to which the examinee's objective examination score report is sent. The essays are then graded by the faculty of that institution rather than by the testing agency.

The optional essay section consists of four global questions of which the examinee is directed to answer any three, budgeting approximately 30 minutes per question. An exceedingly well-prepared student could hardly do justice to three of these questions in 90 minutes, but a poorly prepared student might find 90 minutes superfluous. The nature of the optional essay section is such that, varying only the degree of comprehensiveness of the answers expected, the same questions could serve equally well for college freshmen, for senior biology majors, and for master's degree candidates. The problem in grading the CLEP papers would seem to be how not to confuse these various levels of expectation. Perhaps the fairest way to grade the CLEP essays would be to compare them with essay examination papers written by students nearing completion of their first-year biology course in the same institution, assigning corresponding grades for comparable levels of work.

In summary, the objective examination alone would be adequate to measure the student's competency in first-year college biology. If, however, an assessment of writing ability is also desired, the student's answers to the optional essay section should provide a basis for obtaining this additional data for his credential. The major concern would be to assign a grade to the written work that corresponds to grades given for comparable levels of writing by regularly enrolled first-year biology students.

[833]

*College Board Achievement Test in Biology. Candidates for college entrance; 1915–76; test administered 6 times annually (January, March, May, June, November, December) at centers established by the publisher; Forms YCB4, YCB5, ZCB1, ZCB2, ZCB3, ZCB4, ('75–76, 13–18 pages); for more complete information, see 472; examination fee, $12.50 per candidate; 60(80) minutes; an inactive form, entitled *College Placement Test in Biology,* is available for local administration and scoring; program administered for the College Entrance Examination Board by Educational Testing Service. *

See 7:813 (2 references) and 6:892 (3 references); for a review by Elizabeth Hagen of an earlier form, see 5:723; for a review by Clark W. Horton, see 4:600. For reviews of the testing program, see 6:760 (2 reviews).

REFERENCES

1–3. See 6:892.
4–5. See 7:813.
6. GROBE, CARY H. "A Regression Approach to Evaluating Instructional Programs in Science." *J Res Sci Teach* 10(1): 55–62 '73. *

[834]

*College Placement Test in Biology. Entering college freshmen; 1962–75, c1961–75; inactive form of *College Board Achievement Test in Biology* available for local administration and scoring; Form PPL1 ['67, 14 pages, reprint of 1963 test]; separate answer sheets (Digitek, IBM 805, IBM 1230) must be used; for program accessories, see 474; rental fee, $2 per student; 60(70) minutes; program administered for the College Entrance Examination Board by Educational Testing Service. *

For a review by Elizabeth Hagen of an earlier form, see 5:723; for a review by Clark W. Horton, see 4:600. For a review of the CPT program, see 7:665.

REFERENCES

1. WHITE, GORDON W.; MILLER, DONALD M.; MATTEN, LAWRENCE C.; ENGLERT, DuWAYNE C.; AND SCOTT, M. DOUGLAS. "National and Local Proficiency Tests: Their Validity for an Introductory Biology Course." *Ed & Psychol Meas* 36(4): 993–6 w '76. * (*PA* 58:2280)

[835]

*The Graduate Record Examinations Advanced Biology Test. Graduate school candidates; 1939–76; test administered 5 times annually (January, April, June, October, December) at centers established by the publisher; 4 scores: cellular and subcellular, organismal, population, total; 5 current forms ('73–76, 29–33 pages); descriptive booklet ('75, 12 pages); for program accessories, see 476; examination fee, $10.50 per candidate; 170(190) minutes; an inactive form is available for local administration (rental fee, $5.50 per test); Educational Testing Service. *

For a review by Clark W. Horton of an earlier form, see 5:727. For reviews of the GRE program, see 7:667 (1 review) and 5:601 (1 review).

[836]

*UP Field Test in Biology. College; 1969–77; formerly called *The Undergraduate Record Examinations: Biology;* Form SUR ('70, 24 pages); descriptive booklet ('71, 15 pages); for program accessories, see 480; rental fee, $4 per test, postage extra; 120(140) minutes; Educational Testing Service. *

CLARENCE H. NELSON, *Professor Emeritus, Office of Evaluation Services, Michigan State University, East Lansing, Michigan.* [Review of Form SUR.]

This biology test consists of 150 items to be answered in a two-hour period, which appears to be a reasonable time allotment. It was developed by a committee of college and university biology faculty members whose knowledge of current trends in college biology curricula is reflected in, and gives content validity to, the test. Some of the technical details of item refinement and editing were ably handled by two Educational Testing Service staff members. On the whole, the instrument produced by this group should serve very well the stated purpose of measuring the academic abilities and achievements of undergraduates nearing completion of their majors in biological science, enabling each student to find out how his/her performance compares with others within the same institution and also "on a national scale, with a wide variety of students from many kinds of colleges in many geographic areas."

The 150 items in this test are distributed percentage-wise among five major categories as follows: structure and function (50), interaction with environment (30), biosociology (10), biology as a science (5), and practical biology (5). While these categories give a general overview of the content, the organizational scheme implicit in the list seems to lack the finely-tuned integration that a carefully conceived undergraduate biology program for majors should possess. Actually the test itself is much better structured than the above outline would indicate. Would not items 116–120, 125–128, 129–134, 135–138, 139–143 and 147–150, which exemplify the kind of thinking, reasoning, and methodology a scientist employs in problem solving, be stellar candidates for inclusion under the category, "biology as a science"?

On the whole the items are very well constructed, with a few minor exceptions. In item 61, no unit is specified. Shall we assume the same unit of surface area is intended in each response? Item 65 seems to be inordinately difficult for the students. Why include it? With items 90–94 and 95–99, there is an even match. If the student knows four of the five answers, the fifth one drops into place automatically. For item 142, the conclusion keyed as the correct answer seems difficult to arrive at without a bit more information or data being supplied.

The sets of items associated with descriptive or experimental situations (112–150), involving an interpretation and analysis of data, are highly desirable for this kind of test, for they challenge the students to draw upon the knowledge, understandings, and skills they have acquired to *deduce* answers rather than merely to regurgitate what has been memorized.

A very useful item summary worksheet is provided listing the index of difficulty for each item in one column for the reference group sample consisting of juniors and in the next column for seniors. A third column provides space for recording similar data for "your institution" and a fourth column for recording a comparison (+ or −). To the right is checked the suggested content category for each item. This affords an opportunity to compare student performance with the national norm on each item. The accompanying materials suggest that items involving content not covered in the local curriculum may be deleted from scoring, but to do so would render the local total scores noncomparable to the national total score norms, unless some correction factor were devised and applied.

Nowhere in the accompanying materials does a reliability estimate for this particular form appear. A booklet on the AP series reports a K-R 20 reliability of .93 for an unidentified form. Furthermore, no relevant information needed to interpret this reliability estimate is provided—no description of the group tested, its size, the time of testing, and the mean and standard deviation. The publisher should supply this information to prospective users.

UP Field Test in Biology

In summary, the *UP Field Test in Biology* is, on the whole, well constructed and should serve adequately as a means of obtaining comparative data on the performance of undergraduates nearing completion of their biology major requirements. Such data can be useful not only to the students, but also to the institution as one basis for self-study of its biology program.

CHEMISTRY

[837]
*ACS Cooperative Examination in General Chemistry. 1 year college; 1934–76; current Forms 1973 ('73, 8 pages), 1975 ['75, 12 pages], 1975S ('76, 12 pages); retired Forms 1965 ('65, 12 pages), 1967 ('67, 12 pages), 1970S ('72, 11 pages) available to secondary schools; no specific manual; general directions ['70, 4 pages]; norms (2–6 pages) for each form; separate answer sheets (IBM 805 for 1965 and 1967 forms, IBM 1230 for later forms) must be used; $12 per 25 tests; $1.50 per 25 answer sheets; $1 per scoring stencil; $3 per specimen set; postage extra; 105(110) minutes; Examinations Committee, American Chemical Society. *

See T2:1819 (1 reference) and 7:826 (5 references); for reviews by J. A. Campbell and William Hered and an excerpted review by S. L. Burson, Jr. of earlier forms, see 6:902 (3 references); for reviews by Frank P. Cassaretto and Palmer O. Johnson, see 5:732 (2 references); for a review by Kenneth E. Anderson, see 4:610 (1 reference); for reviews by Sidney J. French and Florence E. Hooper, see 3:557 (3 references); see also 2:1593 (5 references).

REFERENCES

1–5. See 2:1593.
6–8. See 3:557.
9. See 4:610.
10–11. See 5:732.
12–14. See 6:902.
15–19. See 7:826.
20. See T2:1819; also includes a cumulative name index to the first 20 references, 7 reviews, and 1 excerpt for this test.
21. AMERICAN CHEMICAL SOCIETY, DIVISION OF CHEMICAL EDUCATION. "Condensed Norms: ACS Cooperative Examinations." *J Chem Ed* 49(3):216+ Mr '72. *
22. AMERICAN CHEMICAL SOCIETY, DIVISION OF CHEMICAL EDUCATION. "Examinations Committee—ACS Spring Testing Program." *J Chem Ed* 51(3): 214–5 Mr '74. *
23. AMERICAN CHEMICAL SOCIETY, DIVISION OF CHEMICAL EDUCATION. "Condensed Norms: ACS Cooperative Examinations." *J Chem Ed* 53(4):264–5 Ap '76. *

FRANK J. FORNOFF, *Senior Examiner in Science, Higher Education and Careers Programs, Educational Testing Service, Princeton, New Jersey.*

Probably the most widely used of all chemistry tests, the *ACS Cooperative Examination in General Chemistry* in its 1975 edition follows the pattern of other recent forms. There are 70 four-choice questions and one matching set of 10 questions. Questions are arranged in parts by content areas, and patterns for offering the examination in more than one session by requiring candidates to answer the questions in different parts at different times are described. The printing of the test, however, is not such as to prevent a student during the first session from reading questions to be answered during subsequent testing sessions.

The content areas are the ones covered in the large majority of chemistry courses, and the distribution of numbers of questions among the areas is probably about what most chemistry professors would choose. There might be less agreement as to the selection of questions within some of the content areas. Free energy is not mentioned in the questions on thermochemistry, thermodynamics, and kinetics, for example. I probably would not include four questions that are essentially nomenclature questions in the twelve reserved for descriptive chemistry.

The wording of most of the questions seems clear and unambiguous. The distinguished panel of chemical educators has done its work well. I spotted one question with a significant figure problem. On one point, the committee and I disagree about the wording of questions. The opening directions urge the candidate: "Whenever possible, arrive at your own answer to a question before looking at the responses." Yet questions are regularly worded to give the candidate no clue as to whether the desired answer is the global one or is the one from those that are offered. I acknowledge that "of the following" adds words to a stem, but I believe the phrase also clarifies the question being asked when the global response is not offered.

For more than 4,000 students from about 60 institutions, the mean score on the first 70 questions was about 37.5, indicating that the test is not improperly difficult.

I suspect that the test is not speeded. Therefore, the inclusion of a few questions that take some time to answer is not inappropriate. However, I have observed that many students omit such questions and get their scores on questions that can be answered more quickly. I believe that somewhat better measurement results when complexities unrelated to the chemistry being tested are minimized.

I am not as favorably impressed by the laboratory matching questions as by the rest of the examination. The laboratory is more than selecting equipment, but the format used limits all of the laboratory questions to this topic. Incidentally, I am not sure that "to best accomplish or most simply carry out" the distinguishing of an electrolyte from a nonelectrolyte one selects a conductivity cell and a source of alternating current, at least not with the conductivity cells shown in my texts.

Norms based on the performances of more than 2,100 students in 1975 and 700 students in 1976 are provided for the first 70 questions and of somewhat fewer students in 1975 and for almost 1,900 in 1976 for the full 80 questions. The norms populations are fully described. The Kuder-Richardson reliability is reported as varying from .84 to .90 for the 70 questions and the 80 questions on the basis of the 1975 norms data.

The examination seems to me to provide a good measure of performance in what is at present the conventional general chemistry course and to permit a comparison of the achievement of one's students with a sizable sample of other students across the country.

[838]

*ACS Cooperative Examination in Inorganic Chemistry. College juniors and seniors (Form 1976 for graduate level also); 1961–76; 3 scores (except for Form 1976 which has total score only): part 1, part 2, total; no reliability data or norms for 1970 and 1971 versions of Form 1969 part 2; Forms 1969 (12 pages), 1972 (8 pages), 1976 (10 pages); part 2 of Forms 1969 and 1972 consists of essay-type questions and for Form 1969 it includes alternate 1970 and 1971 versions; Forms 1969 and 1972 are available to secondary schools; no specific manual; general directions ['61, 4 pages]; norms (2–3 pages) for each form; separate answer sheets (IBM 1230) must be used; $12 per 25 tests; $1.50 per 25 answer sheets; $1 per scoring stencil; $3 per specimen set; postage extra; 110(120) minutes for Form 1976, 115(120) minutes for Forms 1969 and 1972; Examinations Committee, American Chemical Society. *

See T2:1820 (1 reference) and 7:827 (2 references); for a review by Frank J. Fornoff and an excerpted review by George B. Kauffman of an earlier form, see 6:903 (1 reference).

REFERENCES

1. See 6:903.
2–3. See 7:827.
4. See T2:1820.
5. GOWENLOCK, B. G.; MCINTOSH, D. M.; AND MACKAILL, A. W. "ACS Standardized Exams Versus Conventional Papers at a British University." *J Chem Ed* 50(2):139–40 F '73. *
6. AMERICAN CHEMICAL SOCIETY, DIVISION OF CHEMICAL EDUCATION. "Examinations Committee—ACS Spring Testing Program." *J Chem Ed* 51(3):214–5 Mr '74. *

[839]

*ACS Cooperative Examination in Inorganic-Organic-Biological Chemistry (for Allied Health Science Programs). 1–4 quarters of chemistry for paramedical students; 1970–74; title on 1971 test is *ACS Cooperative Examination in Inorganic-Organic-*

Biological Chemistry (for Paramedical Programs);
4 scores: inorganic, organic, biological, total; each
subtest has 2 parts and various combinations of subtests and parts may be administered to fit a particular
course; Forms 1971 ('70, 20 pages), 1974 ('74, 16
pages); no specific manual; general directions ['70, 4
pages]; norms (4 pages) for each form; separate
answer sheets (IBM 1230) must be used; $12 per 25
tests; $1.50 per 25 answer sheets; $1 per set of scoring
stencils; $3 per specimen set; postage extra; 35(40)
minutes for Part A of each subtest, 20(25) minutes for
Part B of each subtest; Examinations Committee,
American Chemical Society. *

REFERENCES

1. AMERICAN CHEMICAL SOCIETY, DIVISION OF CHEMICAL
EDUCATION. "Condensed Norms: ACS Cooperative Examinations." *J Chem Ed* 49(3):216+ Mr '72. *
2. AMERICAN CHEMICAL SOCIETY, DIVISION OF CHEMICAL
EDUCATION. "Condensed Norms: ACS Cooperative Examinations." *J Chem Ed* 53(4):264-5 Ap '76. *

[840]

***ACS Cooperative Examination in Organic
Chemistry.** 1 year college; 1942-74; an earlier edition
called *A.C.S. Cooperative Organic Chemistry Test;*
current Forms 1971, 1974, (16 pages); retired Form
1968 (19 pages) available to secondary schools; no
specific manual; general directions ['70, 4 pages];
norms (2 pages) for each form; separate answer sheets
(IBM 1230) must be used; $12 per 25 tests; $1.50 per
25 answer sheets; $1 per scoring stencil; $3 per specimen set; postage extra; 100(110) minutes; Examinations Committee, American Chemical Society. *

See 7:831 (3 references) and 6:905 (4 references);
for a review by Shailer Peterson of an earlier form,
see 3:558.

REFERENCES

1-4. See 6:905.
5-7. See 7:831.
8. AMERICAN CHEMICAL SOCIETY, DIVISION OF CHEMICAL
EDUCATION. "Condensed Norms: ACS Cooperative Examinations." *J Chem Ed* 49(3):216+ Mr '72. *
9. GOWENLOCK, B. G.; MCINTOSH, D. M.; AND MACKAILL,
A. W. "ACS Standardized Exams Versus Conventional Papers
at a British University." *J Chem Ed* 50(2):139-40 F '73. *
10. HOLMES, ROY A.; MICHAEL, JOAN J.; AND MICHAEL,
WILLIAM B. "The Comparative Validities of Three Scoring
Systems Applied to an Objective Achievement Examination in
Chemistry." *Ed & Psychol Meas* 34(2):387-9 su '74. *

[841]

***ACS Cooperative Examination in Organic
Chemistry, Graduate Level.** Entering graduate
students; 1961-74; an earlier edition called *A.C.S. Cooperative Examination for Graduate Placement in
Organic Chemistry;* Forms 1971-O (16 pages), 1974-O
(14 pages); no specific manual; general directions
['70, 4 pages]; norms (2-3 pages) for each form;
distribution restricted to graduate schools; separate
answer sheets (IBM 1230) must be used; $12 per 25
tests; $1.50 per 25 answer sheets; $1 per scoring
stencil; $3 per specimen set; postage extra; 90(100)
or 120(130) minutes; Examinations Committee,
American Chemical Society. *

See 7:832 (1 reference) and 6:900 (1 reference).

REFERENCES

1. See 6:900.
2. See 7:832.
3. AMERICAN CHEMICAL SOCIETY, DIVISION OF CHEMICAL
EDUCATION. "Condensed Norms: ACS Cooperative Examinations." *J Chem Ed* 49(3):216+ Mr '72. *
4. AMERICAN CHEMICAL SOCIETY, DIVISION OF CHEMICAL
EDUCATION. "Condensed Norms: ACS Cooperative Examinations." *J Chem Ed* 53(4):264-5 Ap '76. *

[842]

***ACS Cooperative Examination in Physical
Chemistry.** 1 year college; 1946-76; reliability data

and norms for Form 1976 expected to be available
after the 1977 testing; current forms: Form 1973 (consists of three 7-8 page tests: thermodynamics, chemical
dynamics, and quantum chemistry, which may be administered separately or together), Form 1975 (8
pages, for a full year course), Form 1976 (7 pages,
thermodynamics only); retired Form 1969 (8 pages)
available to secondary schools; no specific manual;
general directions ['61, 4 pages]; norms (2-4 pages)
for each form except Form 1976; separate answer
sheets (IBM 1230) must be used; $12 per 25 tests;
$1.50 per 25 answer sheets; $1 per scoring stencil; $3
per specimen set; postage extra; 90(100) minutes for
Form 1973 (per test) and Form 1976, 110(120) minutes for Form 1975; Examinations Committee, American Chemical Society. *

See T2:1826 (2 references), 7:833 (2 references),
and 6:904 (1 reference); for a review by Alfred S.
Brown of an earlier form, see 3:559.

REFERENCES

1. See 6:904.
2-3. See 7:833.
4-5. See T2:1826.
6. GOWENLOCK, B. G.; MCINTOSH, D. M.; AND MACKAILL,
A. W. "ACS Standardized Exams Versus Conventional Papers
at a British University." *J Chem Ed* 50(2):139-40 F '73. *
7. MAYBURY, P. CALVIN; HOPKINS, HARRY P., JR.; HALL,
LOWELL H.; AND WARRICK, PERCY. "A Report From the Physical Chemistry Examination Subcommittee on the 1972-1973
Tests." *J Chem Ed* 51(7):493-4 Jl '74. *

GERALD R. VAN HECKE, *Associate Professor
of Chemistry, Harvey Mudd College, Claremont, California.*

Form 1975 is comprehensive, covering thermodynamics, dynamics, and quantum chemistry; Form 1976 covers only thermodynamics.

Form 1976 Thermodynamics consists of 45
questions with a total working time of 90 minutes. The examination is in two parts, Part A
consisting of 30 questions to be answered in 50
minutes, and Part B consisting of 15 questions
to be answered in the remaining 40 minutes.
Since students who finish Part A early are
not prevented from working on B and those who
finish B early are allowed to return to work on
A, the examination could just as well be given
in its entirety for one set period of time, for
which the 90 minutes seems quite adequate.
Scoring is done by counting correct answers,
with no penalty for guessing. Many questions
are such that immediately the choice of correct
answer is narrowed to only two of the four
options. Thus intelligent guessing can well be
an important factor in overall performance.

Form 1975 consists of 49 questions to be answered in 110 minutes. The overall weighting
and division of areas included is good and the
coverage is reasonably thorough. Moreover, the
questions are designed to require a minimum
of numerical calculations and this design has
been accomplished. Again, the score is the num-

ber of correct answers. The correct answer can, in most instances, immediately be narrowed to two of the four choices, and then, recognition that the sign of one or more of the quantities sought must be plus or minus decides between the last two choices. This is a strength of the examination but also a weakness, since it allows "intelligent guessing" often to obtain the correct answer without adequate understanding. To discuss Form 1975 in some detail, the questions in the thermodynamic section are straightforward and, if anything, often too simple for use by instructors after a typical one-year physical chemistry course usually taken by junior and senior chemistry majors. Specifically, the items in the thermodynamic section can be roughly divided into questions covering the first law (4 questions), second law (3), third law (3), chemical equilibrium (3), phase equilibrium (3), ideal gas properties and thermodynamic relationships (5), and electrochemical cells (2). Weaknesses in coverage occur mainly in the areas of chemical and phase equilibria. The chemical equilibrium questions are essentially of the type: given three of the four terms in the equation $\Delta G = \Delta H - T\Delta S$ calculate the remaining one. The phase equilibrium questions deal only with vapor-liquid systems, there being no questions on solid-liquid equilibria for either one or two component systems. Further, no questions appear that would test understanding of any of the Clausius-Clapeyron relationships. The weaknesses in these areas come from too many questions on first law thermodynamic cycles. Given the general simplicity of the questions in this section, the sophistication required to answer one of the electrochemistry questions is surprising.

The questions (total of 11) in the dynamics section are the best overall in terms of being penetrating and requiring considerable understanding of the area. Two questions appear on the kinetic theory of gases, one question on transport properties, one on ionic conductance, and the remainder on chemical kinetics. On first reading the examination, the single question on transport properties came as a surprise and seemed out of place. Either additional questions in this area should have been included or none at all.

The quantum chemistry section, consisting of 13 questions, is considerably too simple.

Some questions require good understanding of principles and their application but too many simply require recognition of a correct name or formula (for example: "DeBroglie's hypothesis leads to the relationship"—followed by four formula choices). Also many questions deal with just the hydrogen atom or its atomic spectra. The questions have been designed to cover the area comprehensively and that they do reasonably well, the only weakness being in molecular quantum chemistry; but the level of the questions is too low and they could well be answered by a freshman student after a good first year course.

Form 1976 Thermodynamics covers the following areas on thermodynamics: the first law (9 questions), the second law (6), the third law (3), relationships between thermodynamic variables (8), chemical equilibrium (10), phase equilibrium (7), and electrochemical cells (2). The overall division into traditional thermodynamic areas is good and in keeping with general areas of emphasis in current physical chemistry courses, except perhaps for electrochemistry which seems to have been slightly neglected. Most of the questions in the first part are as the test authors intended, simple, testing a very basic comprehension of thermodynamic principles. There are, however, a significant number of good questions requiring more than just simple recognition of a name or formula. The questions on phase and chemical equilibria are the most demanding in Part A. Curiously the questions on various types of thermodynamic cycles are the most demanding in Part B. As stated in the instructions, numerical calculations are minimal in Part A. The more involved questions of Part B require thinking through some calculations but here the answers are all, except for two, choices between numerical values set up for final computation. What is, perhaps, misleading is that while the questions in B have longer answers, they are really not more rigorous than the good questions in A, and, in fact, some are simpler than in A.

Overall, Form 1975 is comprehensive and short, but aimed at a level that seems too low for juniors and seniors who have completed a full-year physical chemistry course. Form 1975 could serve well to provide a ground-level measure of comprehension in a final examination supplemented with more rigorous questions of

ACS Cooperative Examination in Physical Chemistry

the instructor's choosing. Form 1976, on the other hand, is a good test of basic thermodynamics, aimed at a level of comprehension higher than that of Form 1975, comparing, of course, only the thermodynamics portion of the two examinations. The level, however, of Form 1976 Thermodynamics still seems a bit low for use with juniors and seniors after a typical full-year course in physical chemistry. The instructor using this examination—which to repeat, does provide a good test of basic concepts— would more than likely wish to supplement it with problems of his own choosing. One attractive option might be to use only Part A, taking 50 minutes, to give a good overall test which could then be nicely supplemented with more rigorous problems to complete the typical three-hour final examination period.

For both examinations the instruction booklets and examination sheets are clear and pose no difficulties for the instructor. The norms published for Form 1975 seem to be reasonable but so few colleges and universities have reported results that the question of how representative the norms are is left unanswered. This question is of some concern since most of the reporting institutions tend to be small and less well known than the large state universities. Norms for Form 1976 were not available when this review was written.

[843]

ACS Cooperative Examination in Physical Chemistry, Graduate Level. Entering graduate students; 1961-72; an earlier edition called *A.C.S. Cooperative Examination for Graduate Placement in Physical Chemistry;* Forms 1967-P (7 pages), 1972-P (8 pages); no specific manual; general directions ['70, 4 pages]; norms (2-3 pages) for each form; distribution restricted to graduate schools; separate answer sheets (IBM 805 for Form 1967-P, IBM 1230 for Form 1972-P) must be used; $12 per 25 tests; $1.50 per 25 answer sheets; $1 per scoring stencil; $3 per specimen set; postage extra; 120(130) minutes; Examinations Committee, American Chemical Society. *

See 7:834 (2 references) and 6:901 (1 reference).

REFERENCES

1. See 6:901.
2-3. See 7:834.
4. AMERICAN CHEMICAL SOCIETY, DIVISION OF CHEMICAL EDUCATION. "Examinations Committee—ACS Spring Testing Program." *J Chem Ed* 51(3):214-5 Mr '74. *

GERALD R. VAN HECKE, *Associate Professor of Chemistry, Harvey Mudd College, Claremont, California.*

Two physical chemistry graduate level examinations, Forms 1967-P and 1972-P, are available to assist in the placement of beginning graduate students. The cover of each examination states that the "anticipated time allowance is two hours" and that supplementary items may be added if necessary.

The Form 1967-P examination consists of 33 items. There is a penalty for incorrect responses which helps reduce unrepresentative high scores obtained by "intelligent guessing." Three major areas are covered: thermodynamics (19 questions), dynamics (6), and quantum chemistry (8).

Form 1972-P consists of 50 items. There is no penalty for guessing. The two-hour time limit may be insufficient, as this examination is considerably more rigorous and thought-provoking than Form 1967-P. The time allotments between these two examinations are not consistent in view of the difference in number and difficulty of the questions. The major coverage areas in Form 1972-P are: thermodynamics (21 questions), statistical thermodynamics (5), dynamics (7), and quantum chemistry and spectroscopy (17). The inclusion of statistical thermodynamics is new compared to 1967-P and its inclusion is welcome, especially in light of the increasing time spent discussing this topic in current physical chemistry courses.

Overall, the questions on Form 1967-P seem to be either too simple—recognize the correct formula or name of principle—or one-significant-figure numerical estimations requiring a reasonable amount of computation but not testing any great understanding. In contrast, Form 1972-P questions range from good to difficult. Many questions, requiring the recognition of which of a number of given statements is true (or false in some cases), are quite subtle and require considerable understanding of the principles being tested.

To mention some details of Form 1967-P, several questions appear out of place in the examination. One of these deals with the temperature dependence of the dielectric constant of a dilute gas, an area which is not given much time in current physical chemistry courses. Another question that seems better suited to a freshman physics examination deals with the determination of an object's density from its weight in two solvents. One of the numerical type questions deals with the estimation of Avogadro's number from information about a crystal's unit cell dimensions and density. The answers are given in the form of numbers ready to be evaluated to obtain a final answer. Indeed, it is possible with understanding of the principles involved to choose which combination of numbers gives the correct (and best) estimate. (By the way, two options can immediately be eliminated by simple unit analysis.) However, the student with a calculator would simply numerically evaluate each answer and choose the one giving the closest estimate without understanding any principle involved.

From the distribution of questions already mentioned, it might be surmised that Form 1967-P is mainly thermodynamics, which is true. Unfortunately, many questions are too trivial for a graduate level examination. Further, only one question pertains to the second law and no questions to the third law. Five questions cover chemical equilibrium but they are all of the type merely requiring use of $\Delta G° = -RT \ln K$ or $\Delta G° = \Delta H° - T\Delta S°$. Moreover, questions on phase equilibria are almost non-existent. It is almost inconceivable that an examination aimed at placing graduate students would have no questions covering any aspect of phase equilibria in binary systems. The most subtle question on the examination deals with the enthalpy of vaporization of a fluid near its critical point—again, a question not really in the mainstream of current physical chemistry courses. Electrochemical cells are, on the other hand, nicely covered by two good questions testing understanding of basic principles.

The coverage of reaction kinetics in Form 1967-P is very poor, amounting to only three questions of the type: if the temperature is changed by X, what happens to the rate? Among the dynamics items are three questions on kinetic theory which require recall of the proportionality of the mean free path on variables such as temperature and pressure.

Finally, the quantum chemistry questions of Form 1967-P are of such a trivial nature that they could easily be answered by a freshman after a good first year chemistry course.

The questions on Form 1972-P are much more balanced. The numerical options have been chosen to make guessing difficult; unit analysis alone cannot be used to eliminate possibilities. Within the thermodynamics area there is good coverage of phase and chemical equilibria, seven and five questions respectively.

Also, electrochemical cells is well covered, perhaps too esoterically, with a question included on transference numbers. The seven questions on dynamics, kinetic theory, and reaction kinetics reasonably cover the subject area with, perhaps, some slighting of kinetic theory. The greatest improvement in Form 1972-P over 1967-P comes in the area of quantum chemistry and spectroscopy where the questions now require good understanding of the principles, and not simply name or formula recognition.

The norms for Form 1967-P represent results reported by only 13 institutions, mostly in the East, and cannot be taken as very representative. The norms for Form 1972-P are based on students in 43 institutions representing a good geographical distribution.

Instructors planning to use Form 1972-P should note an error in the examination booklet. The instructions on the first page of the booklet indicate that there are five choices for each of the items but, in fact, there are only four. Since the answer sheets which accompany the examination are marked for five responses, the instructor should clearly point out the difficulty to the students.

Overall, Form 1972-P is an excellent, comprehensive examination, well suited to its purpose of graduate student placement. It could be used as a challenging examination for junior and senior students who have completed a strong full-year physical chemistry course. In this latter case, it is unlikely that an instructor would find it necessary to supplement the examination. Form 1967-P pales by comparison to the 1972-P version and is in the main too trivial for use without employing extensive supplemental questions.

[844]

*ACS-NSTA Cooperative Examination in High School Chemistry, [Advanced Level]. Advanced high school classes; 1963–74; Forms 1968 Adv (15 pages), 1970 Adv (12 pages), 1972 Adv (12 pages), 1974 Adv (11 pages); no specific manual; general directions ['70, 4 pages]; norms (4 pages) for each form; separate answer sheets (IBM 1230) must be used; $10 per 25 tests; $1.50 per 25 answer sheets; $1 per scoring stencil; $3 per specimen set; postage extra; 80(90) minutes; sponsored jointly with the National Science Teachers Association; Examinations Committee, American Chemical Society. *

For a review by Irvin J. Lehmann of the 1970 and earlier forms, see 7:838 (3 references); for reviews by Frank J. Fornoff and William Hered, see 6:909.

REFERENCES

1–3. See 7:838.
4. FAST, KENNETH VERNON. *An Analysis and Classification*

of the Twelve ACS-NSTA High School Chemistry Achievement Tests, 1957–1971, Using Bloom's Taxonomy of Educational Objectives Handbook I: Cognitive Domain. Doctor's thesis, University of Maryland (College Park, Md.), 1972. (*DAI* 33:2194A)

PETER A. DAHL, *Head of Science Department, Lowell High School, San Francisco, California.* [Review of Form 1974 Adv.]

The 1974 form of this advanced level test in high school chemistry consists of 40 nonmathematical items and 20 items involving some mathematics. Although some previous forms of this test were scored with a correction for guessing, the 1974 form is scored number of right answers; this simplifies hand scoring.

This test is the best final examination available for advanced placement chemistry classes, since it covers all the important chemical topics of first year college chemistry and places about the same emphasis on these chemical topics as the multiple choice part of the *Advanced Placement Examination in Chemistry,* i.e., structure of matter, 10 percent; states of matter, 20; reactions and equations, 24; equilibrium-kinetics-thermodynamics, 36; and descriptive, 10. The only noticeable difference between the two tests is that the APEC has more questions directly related to laboratory work.

The 1974 form is quite difficult. The median score is 38 percent of the possible score; this is much more difficult than the corresponding part of the APEC in recent years. This level of difficulty is too high. A median of about 50 percent would give the necessary spreading without discouraging students unnecessarily.

Each form is pretested in many high schools; inappropriate questions are discarded, and the wording of questions is improved before public distribution. These well-written tests are appropriate for any high school chemistry course which covers first-year, college-level chemistry. I strongly recommend it for use in advanced placement chemistry courses in high schools.

JOHN P. PENNA, *Science Teacher, Governor Livingston High School, Berkeley Heights, New Jersey.* [Review of Form 1974 Adv.]

This 1974 edition follows very much the pattern of its even-year predecessors. The test is constructed for advanced or honor classes and is suggested as suitable for an advanced placement course. Likewise, it is recommended to colleges as a tool in solving placement problems. These suggestions and recommendations have

no represented statistical support. However, the success of the program seems to indicate that the test satisfies a need.

The test consists of Part 1, containing 40 general information items, and Part 2, containing 20 quantitative items. Only the right answers are scored and the parts can be given separately or together. The total test is suggested for complete coverage.

The test booklet contains a reference table of relevant information and a periodic table. Students are allowed to use a table of logarithms and slide rule. No mention is made of hand calculators. For school systems or classes where their use is allowed, some statement of definite approval or disapproval should be made. This issue looms important, since the norms on this timed test are based on voluntary submission of the data by the users. A calculator generation forced to use a slide rule would be at a disadvantage compared to those tacitly allowed to use calculators.

The testmakers are to be complimented for their clarity of question construction, as well as for the sophisticated array of topics. It is easy to see how such a test will differentiate a group of elitist students, and any high school teacher should be proud of a class that could field such a formidable battery of questions.

The teacher is provided with a manual which aids in the administration and scoring of the test. However, it is a general manual and not specific to this test. Percentile ranks, standard deviations, and reliability coefficients for part and total scores are presented for the total norms group and for three subgroups derived from the entire group according to number of semesters of chemistry, physics, and mathematics. The population of the entire group is characterized according to grade, sex, type of school, professional goals, and amount of lecture, laboratory, and class time. This sparsity of statistical data is hardly commendable. A mean, along with the percentage of students answering each item correctly, could be added. The attempt to classify items according to Bloom's Taxonomy is good. Perhaps a general listing of subject matter could accompany that listing. The low number of items in the category of analysis is glaring, but when one realizes the dubious nature of this type of classification, it is not so startling. Many items defy single classification. More laboratory analysis questions would please this reviewer and perhaps fill the gap.

The small number of students used to establish the norms is undoubtedly due to the number of reporting institutions, the elitist nature of the test, and the desire for rapid publication. This deficiency may be understandable but hardly commendable.

While appreciating the range of topics used in the test, this reviewer wonders about the content validity. In no way is this meant to challenge the makers, since, having used the previous tests, I was indeed pleased, but some rationale as to the distribution and choice of topics would be appreciated. Perhaps a listing of the range of topics used in the testing would provide a basis of unifying the content of advanced high school chemistry.

In summary, the 1974 edition is a clearly well constructed, challenging test for high-ability high school chemistry students. Statistical data are sparse and need improvement, while the small size of the sample may be an insurmountable barrier given the goals of the program. Content validity and distribution of items within the test need to be justified. The test booklet should clarify the problem of calculator use. These criticisms notwithstanding, this test is a good instrument for differentiating among high-ability high school chemistry students and is one I would gladly use on my advanced placement chemistry students.

[845]

*ACS-NSTA Cooperative Examination in High School Chemistry, [Lower Level]. 1 year high school; 1957–75; Forms 1971 ('71), 1971S ('71, Form 1971 with item sequence changed), 1973 ('73), 1973S ('74), 1975 ('75), (12 pages), 1975S ('75, 8 pages); no specific manual; general directions ['70, 4 pages]; norms (4–6 pages) for each form; separate answer sheets (IBM 1230) must be used; $10 per 25 tests; $1.50 per 25 answer sheets; $1 per scoring stencil; $3 per specimen set; postage extra; 80(90) minutes; sponsored jointly with the National Science Teachers Association; Examinations Committee, American Chemical Society. *

See T2:1830 (3 references); for reviews by William R. Crawford and Irvin J. Lehmann of Form 1971 and earlier forms, see 7:837 (9 references); for reviews by Frank J. Fornoff and William Hered and excerpted reviews by Christine Jansing and Joseph Schmuckler, see 6:908 (5 references); for reviews by Edward G. Rietz and Willard G. Warrington, see 5:729.

REFERENCES

1–5. See 6:908.
6–14. See 7:837.
15–17. See T2:1830; also includes a cumulative name index to the first 17 references, 6 reviews, and 2 excerpts for this test.
18. AMERICAN CHEMICAL SOCIETY, DIVISION OF CHEMICAL EDUCATION. "Condensed Norms: ACS Cooperative Examinations." *J Chem Ed* 49(3):216+ Mr '72. *
19. CANGEMI, MARY CLARE. *A Study of Relationships Among Verbal Interaction, Student Achievement, and Attitude in Selected Two and Four Year College General Chemistry Classes.* Doctor's thesis, New York University (New York, N.Y.), 1972. (*DAI* 33:628A)
20. FAST, KENNETH VERNON. *An Analysis and Classification of the Twelve ACS-NSTA High School Chemistry Achievement Tests, 1957–1971, Using Bloom's Taxonomy of Educational Objectives Handbook I: Cognitive Domain.* Doctor's thesis, University of Maryland (College Park, Md.), 1972. (*DAI* 33: 2194A)
21. DENNY, RITA T. "Questions About Inner City High School Chemistry." *Sch Sci & Math* 73(5):355–8 My '73. *
22. AMERICAN CHEMICAL SOCIETY, DIVISION OF CHEMICAL EDUCATION. "Examinations Committee—ACS Spring Testing Program." *J Chem Ed* 51(3):214–5 Mr '74. *
23. FAST, KENNETH V. "An Analysis and Classification of the ACS-NSTA High School Chemistry Achievement Tests Using Bloom's Taxonomy-Cognitive Domain." *Sci Ed* 58(1): 17–21 Ja–Mr '74. *
24. SEDDON, G. M. "A Comparison of Three Different Measures for Predicting Achievement in Chemistry in the Age Range 15 to 18-Plus." *Res Ed* (England) 12:63–70 N '74. * (*PA* 54:1997)
25. COVERDELL, ANNA-MARIA. "The New Look of the ACS-NSTA High School Chemistry Examination." *Sci Teach* 42(3): 47–8 Mr '75. *
26. GRAYSON, THOMAS DAVID. *An Analysis of the Relationships Between Certain Pupil Characteristics and the Grading System Used in a Science Course.* Doctor's thesis, University of Texas (Austin, Tex.), 1975. (*DAI* 36:2729A)
27. YEKESON, STEPHEN MARKA. *A Study of Selected Variables for Prediction of Success and Placement in General Chemistry at Western Michigan University.* Doctor's thesis, Western Michigan University (Kalamazoo, Mich.), 1975. (*DAI* 36:7320A)
28. AMERICAN CHEMICAL SOCIETY, DIVISION OF CHEMICAL EDUCATION. "Condensed Norms: ACS Cooperative Examinations." *J Chem Ed* 53(4):264–5 Ap '76. *

EDWARD F. deVILLAFRANCA, *Teacher of Chemistry, Kent School, Kent, Connecticut.*

While this test covers a commendably wide range of topics, too many of the questions are aimed at a level of achievement which would not constitute any challenge for a student with any depth of understanding of chemistry fundamentals. In order to prepare students for this test, a teacher would be advised to cover many topics somewhat superficially. Even with this rather broad coverage, there are several topics, considered important by most chemistry teachers, that are covered inadequately or not at all. For example, descriptive chemistry of any consequence is not included nor are gases considered at any conditions other than STP—rather impractical laboratory conditions.

There are a few, unfortunately too few, questions designed to enable a teacher to draw some conclusions about a student who answers them correctly. Far more questions leave much doubt as to whether or not a student really has any significant understanding, even when the questions have been answered correctly. One question, for example, is set up in such a way that it could have tested the concept of a substance in excess in a stoichiometrical relationship. The question is destroyed, however, by the choice of answers offered, three of the four being obviously impossible. This reduces the item to one which intelligent and test-wise students can get right without knowing any chemistry. Many more questions have good beginnings and potential, but often end by asking the obvious or the trivial. There is a difference between easy questions that really test a concept and questions that prove nothing, and many of the items in this test fail to negotiate that fine distinction.

While there have been some tests of higher quality in this series, the 1975 edition seems most suitable for students of very modest ability. After a full-year course, would not one expect more of a student than to know that evaporation means going from the liquid to the gaseous state or to be able to compute the molecular weight of a compound when given its formula and the necessary atomic weights? Able students will find many items almost patronizing in their objectives.

In conclusion, the 1975 edition of this test is commendable for its topical coverage, and it is modern in its emphasis. Yet a lack of professionalism in construction of many items mars its overall impact. There are few technical errors and the key is without fault, but many questions give no real insight into a student's achievement and could just as well be left unasked. Compared, for example, to the *College Board Achievement Test in Chemistry,* the 1975 ACS-NSTA test does not challenge the able student and does not probe for any sophistication in the understanding of basic principles and concepts.

[846]

*Advanced Placement Examination in Chemistry.** High school students desiring credit for college level courses and admission to advanced courses; 1954–77; available to secondary schools for annual administration on specified days in May; Form ZBP ('77, 20 pages) in 2 booklets (objective, essay); course description ('76, 42 pages); sample syllabi ('76, 18 pages); grading guidelines ('76, 23 pages); previous essay questions available; for program accessories, see 471; examination fee, $32 per student; 180(200) minutes; an inactive form [Form YBP ('76, 20 pages)] is available to colleges for local administration and scoring (rental fee, $2 per test); program administered for the College Entrance Examination Board by Educational Testing Service. *

See T2:1832 (1 reference) and 6:915 (1 reference); for a review by Theo. A. Ashford of an earlier form, see 5:743. For reviews of the APE program, see 471 (2 reviews) and 7:662 (2 reviews).

J. ARTHUR CAMPBELL, *Professor of Chemistry and Chairman of the Department, Harvey Mudd College, Claremont, California.* [Review of Forms XBP and YBP.]

I was sent copies of Forms XBP and YBP, both copyrighted in 1975 by Educational Testing Service. They were accompanied by the usual voluminous and detailed analysis one has come to expect from ETS. Some 4,000 students took these examinations and the results are available for examination by potential users. There is a booklet describing the examination, another one describing its grading, and a third analyzing the tests in terms of reliability (objective section .89, composite about .9, with the correlation between objective and essay .82), some evidence of speededness in the objective scores, score distributions, subscore data, means, and standard deviations. The only analyses that I would like to have seen but which are missing, are those concerning the reliability of individual items, and a correlation chart between test items and subject matter normally covered in such a course. It is hard to imagine that a potential user would have any difficulty in understanding the materials I have just mentioned and in finding them useful in reaching conclusions in the absence of the test.

But that raises the more important point as to what the conclusion might be were the test itself to be examined. As I point out in my discussion of the CLEP Examination (see 847), the AP and CLEP exams are remarkably similar. If they are really designed to do two different jobs, it is difficult to see how their construction processes promote this similarity. But the AP exam is well established and is clearly used, and has been for many years, to allow colleges to evaluate the attainment of the student in a high school course for which advanced placement in the college might be given. Most colleges (and many have used the examination) have found these results useful and continue to assume their validity. I see no reason why they should change from this program.

I must point out that these exams, like all objective tests I have examined, have an unfortunate number of ambiguous questions. In one form, I raised questions with respect to 11 of the 73 objective items; in the other, 15 of the 80 objective items. On the essays, the corresponding figures are 2 out of 18 and 4 out of 9 ques-

ACS-NSTA Cooperative Examination in High School Chemistry

tions. Most of these are at the nit-picking level, but I believe they could cause problems to the students, especially good students. However, in each exam there are some problems that it seems to me are truly serious. For example, a catalyst may increase the order of a reaction as well as providing an alternate path; snow could disappear from the ground by diffusion, by dispersion, or by sublimation; either the statement that the conductivity of metallic copper decreases with increase in temperature or the statement that copper is the best of the metallic conductors could be true, depending on what one means by "best"; knowledge either of the order of the reaction or of the activation energy could be most useful for developing a reaction mechanism, depending on the system; for a chemical reaction that is neither exothermic nor endothermic the activation energy could either be zero or not affected by a catalyst; there is evidence that Cl_2 rather that OCl^- is the active ingredient in some household bleaches; the effect of a catalyst on a reaction can be on both the enthalpy or entropy of a reaction or either if by reaction one refers to the formation of the activated complex; for the formation of two moles of gas from three moles of gas the formation of product may be favored by either an increase in pressure or the addition of a catalyst; the statement that the change in free energy for a reaction increases can be interpreted with equal validity as becoming either more positive or more negative. In spite of the number of objections I raise here, there are only two or three questions on each exam that I think really must be reworked. This is not bad in terms of my own experience with a large number of objective tests. Thus I would not fault the test too seriously on this basis.

I have more serious reservations about the almost total lack of questions involving laboratory work, as well as an almost complete lack of questions which would involve situations novel to the student. The great majority of items, in fact almost all of them, will be straight memory questions for most students. This is not to say the student cannot apply reasoning if he has forgotten the answer, but he will have seen the answer most of the time. It is quite possible to pose questions on objective and essay tests which do indeed deal directly with laboratory work. It is also possible to pose ques-

tions involving novel situations. In fact, it is possible to pose questions which involve novel situations in a laboratory set-up, combining both features of what it seems to me would make a desirable examination in chemistry. It also seems to me that ETS should begin to consider that SI units are no longer novel. In almost all the world except the United States, science courses have gone to SI units almost completely. We are moving in that direction also. National tests should contain, as a minimum, mention of SI units and allow students with background in them at least an equal chance to students who are still learning in the older sets of units.

The main purpose of a placement test is to provide a means of identifying those students who have learned enough so that they need not repeat the college course. For that purpose, the AP tests have done a good job. If ETS continues to produce this kind of test, the results should continue favorable. I do feel the tests can be improved. In the marginal cases, a different emphasis in the questions would allow students of a slightly different background to show that they too have learned quite enough to opt out of the college-level program and get advanced standing. We should be concerned not only with the fact that students who have succeeded on our tests go on to show that they have learned something, but also with whether or not the students who failed the present test really didn't learn enough to get their advanced placements.

[847]

*CLEP Subject Examination in General Chemistry. 1 year or equivalent; 1964-76; for college accreditation of nontraditional study, advanced placement, or assessment of educational achievement; tests administered monthly at centers throughout the United States; Forms VCT1, VCT2, ('73, 14 pages); optional essay supplement scored by college: Forms MCT-A ('64, 5 pages), VCT-A, VCT-B, ('73, 5 pages); for program accessories, see 473; rental and scoring fee, $20 per student (includes reporting of scores to the candidate and one college); postpaid; 90(95) minutes, same for essay supplement; program administered for the College Entrance Examination Board by Educational Testing Service. *
For reviews of the CLEP program, see 473 (3 reviews) and 7:664 (3 reviews).

J. ARTHUR CAMPBELL, *Professor of Chemistry and Chairman of the Department, Harvey Mudd College, Claremont, California.* [Review of Form VCT1.]

I received a copy of Form VCT1, one of two

forms initially issued in 1973. It is "designed to measure knowledge and understanding of the material usually covered in a one-year introductory course in general chemistry at the college level." A primary purpose is to allow evaluation of work done outside a given college in order to judge eligibility for credit. There is a booklet, published in 1977, which devotes more than a page to discussing the general chemistry exam. There is also an in-house test analysis form which discusses the appropriateness of the test to group (very difficult), the reliability (.865), the speededness (not speeded), the mean item difficulty (mean observed Δ of 14.6, middle difficulty reference value of 12.0) and mean biserial correlation (mean of .35 based on the 100-item total scores). Few tests are used more widely (several thousand students annually). Complete group statistics are available, and the raw scores are converted into percentile ranks so that the evaluator can compare individual students with a national sample.

Documentation such as that listed above is impressive, full, and probably reliable in itself. One cannot argue with the thoroughness with which the results of the test are studied and reported. What one needs to explore, more importantly, is the nature of the test items.

I reviewed the CLEP exam and the *Advanced Placement Examination in Chemistry* (see 846). I find the two indistinguishable except for the number of questions asked. I found no questions on CLEP which could not be on the AP Examination and vice versa. They are prepared by different committees, but the end results are not differentiable as far as I can see. One wonders if there is any reason to have the separate examinations, at least as long as they are so similar.

Then one comes to the question of the items themselves. The CLEP Examination consists of 100 objective items plus six essay questions. Each section of the test is to be done in 90 minutes. What dismays me is the number of items with which I took issue. Devoting my full nit-picking skills, I found changes that I would make in 32 of the 100 objective items and in two of the six essay questions.

I differed seriously with about 10 of the objective items and one of the essay questions. For example, question 4 in the essay tests asked one to define the terms associated with the symbols ΔG, ΔH, and ΔS. What is really meant is, presumably, $\Delta G°$, $\Delta H°$, and $\Delta S°$. These are not the same and should not be used interchangeably.

In the same question it is essential that "the standard state" be specified, but this is not done either. At least I presume this was the intent of the questioners, for the student is asked to predict the sign of the three quantities. This is not possible, in general, except in the standard state. Or is it possible that the questioners are willing to accept the general answer that ΔG is less than zero and ΔS is greater than zero for every reaction occurring when mixtures of pure substances are put together? If this is the intent of the questioners, I can support them. But I doubt very much, on the basis of what is usually taught in freshman chemistry, that this is their intent.

I have similar questions on those items in the objective test which suggest that a hydronium ion can never be a base; that the average atomic weight of carbon is used as a standard; that only oxidation-reduction (and not hydrolysis or neutralization) can serve as a source of energy in a voltaic cell; that complete miscibility cannot be shown by both solid-solid and liquid-liquid systems; that H_3O^+, HCl, NH_3, and OH^- cannot all act either as an acid or a base in the Bronsted approach; that significant figures should be mentioned as important and yet violated in several items; that C_7H_{14} cannot be a saturated organic compound; that it is not possible to consider both phosphate ions and nitrate ions as stabilized by resonance; that merely asking if ΔS is negative allows a definitive answer when it could be the entropy change of the system, the surroundings, or the total change; that the word electron always refers to a negatively charged particle (rather than sometimes to positrons); or that calling a solution acidic or basic gives sufficient identification of the concentration to be considered. There are other wordings to which I also object, as I have indicated above.

Now I am willing to consider that most chemistry courses do not make major issues of these points, but some do. In fact, any careful treatment of the subject would make the above distinctions clear. Furthermore, it would be possible to make the tests no harder and yet

CLEP Subject Examination in General Chemistry

avoid these ambiguities merely by slightly rephrasing the questions.

I must say that I have never picked up an objective test to which I did not have objections. This statement even applies to those I have given when I looked at them later. But when the objections are so numerous, and, at least to me, of such gravity, I believe that the test is seriously flawed, regardless of its statistical validity. It must be noted that I was reading a 1973 test submitted to me and that more recent forms may have a much higher accuracy in their questions. This I cannot judge. But I would strongly suggest that this particular form, at least, be retired from service if that has not already been done.

This takes me back to the more central question of whether a CLEP-type exam is needed. Such an exam may well have a place, but I do not feel it should be interchangeable with the *Advanced Placement Test in Chemistry,* as is the case if this form is indicative. It seems to me a higher level of performance might be expected for a person who is to get college credit than for one who is to be given advanced standing. The AP exams are normally used either to discharge a college requirement or to give placement into a second-semester course. The CLEP exam, as I understand it, is more commonly used to see whether a student is qualified for an advanced course. The only real difference I can see now is that the college itself grades the essay part of the CLEP exam but not of the AP exam. If these tests are to be used for additional purposes, I would strongly recommend that the examinations be made more different than they currently are.

It is hard to argue with the continued success of this testing program sponsored by the College Entrance Examination Board. Unfortunately, the VCT1 CLEP exam is so seriously flawed that it cannot, in my opinion, serve as an adequate test. It is quite possible, indeed probable, that more recent versions have been greatly improved.

[848]

*College Board Achievement Test in Chemistry. Candidates for college entrance; 1901–76; test administered 6 times annually (January, March, May, June, November, December) at centers established by the publisher; Forms YCB4, YCB5, ZCB1, ZCB2, ZCB3, ZCB4, ('75–76, 11–12 pages); for more complete information, see 472; examination fee, $12.50 per candidate; 60(80) minutes; inactive forms, entitled

College Placement Test in Chemistry, are available for local administration and scoring; program administered for the College Entrance Examination Board by Educational Testing Service. *

See 7:844 (3 references); for a review by William Hered of earlier forms, see 6:914 (4 references); for a review by Max D. Engelhart, see 5:742 (2 references); for a review by Evelyn Raskin, see 4:617 (4 references). For reviews of the testing program, see 6:760 (2 reviews).

[849]

*College Placement Test in Chemistry. Entering college freshmen; 1962–75, c1956–75; inactive forms of *College Board Achievement Test in Chemistry* available for local administration and scoring; Forms PPL1 ('67, reprint of 1964 test), PPL2, ('67, reprint of 1965 test) in a single booklet (27 pages); separate answer sheets (Digitek, IBM 805, IBM 1230) must be used; for program accessories, see 474; rental fee, $2 per student; 60(70) minutes; program administered for the College Entrance Examination Board by Educational Testing Service. *

For a review by William Hered of earlier forms, see 6:914; for a review by Max D. Engelhart, see 5:742; for a review by Evelyn Raskin, see 4:617. For a review of the CPT program, see 7:665.

[850]

Cooperative Science Tests: Chemistry. Grades 9–12; 1963–65; 3 scores: general concepts and principles, laboratory, total; Forms A, B, ('63, 20 pages); no specific manual; series handbook ('64, 76 pages); student bulletin ('65, 2 pages); separate answer sheets (Digitek, IBM 805, IBM 1230, NCS) must be used; $6 per 20 tests; $5.50 per 100 answer sheets; $1.50 per 10 IBM scoring stencils (answer pattern must be punched out locally); $2 per series handbook; Digitek scoring stencils not available; $3.50 per specimen set of this and 4 other science tests; cash orders postpaid; NCS scoring and statistical analysis service, 45¢ and over per test; 80(92) minutes; Educational Testing Service; Addison-Wesley Publishing Co., Inc. *

For excerpted reviews by Irvin J. Lehmann (with Clarence H. Nelson) and William Mehrens of the series, see 7:787.

EDWARD F. deVILLAFRANCA, *Teacher of Chemistry, Kent School, Kent, Connecticut.*

This test has been very competently and professionally put together in almost every way. A good balance is obtained in the choice of topics tested as well as in the wide range of degree of difficulty of different items. The impression is that most of the items are originally conceived and interestingly presented and, further, that they measure much more than pure factual recall. Many questions require the student to use care, give some thought, and to have had some experience—all this without making too difficult or sophisticated the concepts and principles needed.

Each form consists of two parts; the first part tests general concepts and principles while the second part is strongly oriented towards laboratory procedures and operations, including some items on factual descriptive chemistry.

A serious reservation concerning these tests is that a significant number of items test aspects of chemistry no longer emphasized in high school courses of the late 1970s. This reviewer's impression that the tests would have been excellent for a course taught 15 years ago was confirmed by a glance at the copyright date—1963! Undoubtedly, there is a wide variation between courses in different schools and even between individual teachers as to what is emphasized in the way of course content. Probably no consensus is possible, but items on industrial chemistry seemed too many and too specialized. For example, does a modern course emphasize the Frasch Process, the Bessemer Converter, the commercial preparation of HCl, or even the fractionation of crude oil? In addition to the industrial chemistry items, there are also questions involving equivalent weights and normality—not bad except that the modern trend is to stick with moles.

A comparison of the two forms indicates that Form A is the better test for several reasons. First, it is less oriented towards the non-modern aspects mentioned above. Second, it has practically no technical errors. Eight items in Form B have various problems: more than one reasonable choice of answer presented, no good answer, ambiguity in the answer, or the wrong key. Also, Part 2 of Form B belabors certain aspects of lab work almost as if the authors were running out of ideas and needed to come up with 55 items in any way possible!

Two features of these tests that appeal are: (a) the format of each item consists of a stem and five possible responses; (b) in alternate questions the five responses are labeled ABCDE and then FGHJK—this helps the student avoid mis-numbering his answers on the answer sheet.

The tests are of high professional quality but so badly outdated, compared, for example, to the *College Board Achievement Test in Chemistry,* that they would not be particularly valid for any high school chemistry students except those in the most traditional of courses of 15 years ago.

Cooperative Science Tests: Chemistry

JOHN P. PENNA, *Science Teacher, Governor Livingston High School, Berkeley Heights, New Jersey.*

This chemistry test purports to assess "knowledge and understanding of basic concepts and principles, ability to apply knowledge in problem situations, and ability to analyze and evaluate scientific ideas and procedures" as presented in most conventional high school chemistry courses. Part 1 is concerned with material presented in the text and classroom, while Part 2 assesses important laboratory abilities.

Form A and Form B, each consisting of 115 items, are divided into 40-minute segments for ease of administering, and the multiple-choice structure provides for rapid scoring. A detailed and comprehensive series handbook contains a welter of statistical information. For example, each item is catalogued for its place in a taxonomy of skills (knowledge, comprehension, application, and analysis and evaluation), as well as according to subject matter. Each item is logged with the percentage of students answering the item correctly. Percentile norms based on national and urban testing are presented for both part and total scores. Norms based on "two or three selected suburban school systems" are also reported. Part 2 of the test provides a refreshing set of items which call for analytical reasoning about laboratory activities, as well as some challenging questions for the astute student.

The validity of a nationally standardized test for high school chemistry courses is a much debated question. Is there sufficient uniformity of content to allow for a nationwide standardized test? The question was never answered to this reviewer's satisfaction. Be that as it may, the validity of any test depends upon whether it measures what one wants it to measure. Ultimately, the users of this test must judge whether there is content validity with respect to their own course content and educational aims. Regardless of such judgments, this test can be criticized assuredly for its age. Since 1963, when it was copyrighted, many changes have occured in the educational scene and most certainly in chemistry. Students enrolled in experimental curricula were deliberately excluded from the norming population. Even as a measure of traditional, or conventional, chemistry courses, a cursory view of conventional text-books over the last 14 years shows a marked change. "Conventional" texts and courses have been altered to reflect the influences of the newer curricula developed during the late '50s and early '60s. The trend has been supposedly away from descriptive chemistry toward theoretical chemistry, with more theory and less memory, and movement from observation to principle to application. This test reflects a decided lack of that changed emphasis. Electron configuration notation, orbital notation, electron dot diagrams, and electron and molecular structure are points that are definitely not a part of this test but are a part of high school chemistry in 1977. It should be mentioned, however, that the overlap of content with modern courses far exceeds the lack of coverage. Commercial preparation of elements, commercial processes (Bessemer, Haber, Frasch), diffusion rates of gases—no matter how noteworthy—have received definite de-emphasis in a contemporary course. "Inert gases" (item 27, Part 1, Form A) would now be called "noble gases." One wonders if students should be required to memorize the activity series of metals (item 51, Part 2, Form A), although these metals may be familiar enough. The availability of a reference table would in no way detract from the question. It may even help a student who hasn't memorized the products of the electrolysis of sodium chloride solution reason to the correct answer for item 9, Part 1, Form A. Items 56 and 57 (Part 1, Form A) are a good application of the principle of freezing point depression to non-aqueous solution. A parallel question should have been included in Form B. Part 2 questions in general are well constructed and show good application of theory, reasoning, and technique to laboratory work. However, some of the items would be difficult, if not impossible, for students who had never seen the experiments performed (items 52 and 53, Form B).

The classification of items according to skill shows a marked emphasis on the skills of application and analysis and evaluation over knowledge and comprehension for the total test. However, the classification of certain items is indeed dubious. While one item may employ application or analysis, knowledge is a necessary prerequisite for the question, the result being that

it does not simply involve application. The cataloguing is somewhat misleading. Likewise, many items lack uniqueness of skill and therefore defy clear classification in one category or another.

The classification of each item according to percentage right is useful, but perhaps a division of the percentage right among students in grades 10, 11, and 12 would indicate the mathematical sophistication needed for some questions or the caliber of student at each level. The reviewer would find the percentile norms for each of grades 10, 11, and 12 more revealing than norms for national and suburban populations. This would certainly be more useful to the individual or class.

In summary, these tests are an excellent measure of traditional chemistry, and the handbook is a model for all such standardized tests. However, given the evolution that has occurred over the last 14 years, its standard in terms of a national norm is doubtful. Some vocabulary has changed, new concepts have been introduced and other concepts have been de-emphasized. In general, there has been a shift from descriptive to more theoretical chemistry. Classification of items is helpful in showing the emphasis of the test but dubious in some cases. Although this reviewer sees parts of the test as dated, the usefulness of the majority of items is beyond question, especially since the organizers had the wisdom to include percentage of students who got each item correct, as well as to suggest ways of using items or groups of items.

[851]

Emporia Chemistry Test. 1, 2 semesters high school; 1962–64; first published 1962–63 in the Every Pupil Scholarship Test series; Forms A, B, (64, 4 pages); 2 levels labeled Tests 1, 2; manual ('64, 3 pages); $3.50 per 25 tests; $1.50 per specimen set; postage extra; 40(45) minutes; A. T. Ericson and M. W. Sanders; Bureau of Educational Measurements. *

PETER A. DAHL, *Head of Science Department, Lowell High School, San Francisco, California.*

The *Emporia Chemistry Test* comes in two forms for each of two levels: Forms A and B of Test 1 are designed to be used at the end of one semester of high school chemistry; Forms A and B of Test 2, at the end of a year of high school chemistry. Each form consists of 100 multiple choice questions.

The "test is based on the common content of leading textbooks and courses of study" as of pre-1962 and covers "definitions, formulas, equations, principles, theories, and problems." Test 2 differs from Test 1 by including reaction kinetics, equilibrium, solubility, oxidation and reduction, normality, Lewis Acid-Base concepts, and organic chemistry. All of the tests contain questions which are appropriate only for the older, descriptive-type course in fashion before CHEM Study or CBA. There are no mathematical problems dealing with reaction kinetics or equilibria (like solubility products or ionization constants of acids or bases). Instead, definitions, formulas, and equations are accented.

Unfortunately, the tests are not well written. There are a few typographical errors ("One oxygen atom weights") and many poorly worded or ambiguous questions; for example, "The most abundant element is 1. iron 2. aluminum 3. sodium 4. nitrogen 5. oxygen" is terribly ambiguous. The given key is oxygen, so the Earth's crust is meant; but considering the Earth as a whole makes iron the answer. Considering the atmosphere, nitrogen is correct. The way the question is actually worded, the correct key (hydrogen) is not even given as an option! Another example of a poor item is: "In the electrolysis of a concentrated sodium chloride solution the substance produced at the positive electrode is 1. sodium 2. sodium hydroxide 3. chlorine 4. hydrogen 5. sodium chloride." The anode should not be identified as the positive electrode, since sign conventions for electrodes are not the same everywhere. In order to complete a calculation in another item, the student has to have memorized the heat of fusion for water. Most high school teachers do not require this kind of memorization on a final test.

If an unenlightened teacher is using a pre-1960 high school chemistry textbook and teaching a descriptive course, then these tests might be useful. However, for the vast majority of teachers, who are using modern chemistry textbooks (like CHEM Study revisions, CBA, and others), these tests would not be adequate. Instead, the *ACS-NSTA Cooperative Examination in High School Chemistry* is most appropriate. These examinations are constantly being updated to reflect changes in textbooks and in the material taught in high school chemistry, and new forms are published about every other year.

[852]

*The Graduate Record Examinations Advanced Chemistry Test.** Graduate school candidates; 1939–76; test administered 5 times annually (January, April, June, October, December) at centers established by the publisher; 5 current forms ('73–76, 24–32 pages); descriptive booklet ('75, 11 pages); for program accessories, see 476; examination fee, $10.50 per candidate; 170(190) minutes; an inactive form is available for local administration (rental fee, $5.50 per test); Educational Testing Service. *

See 7:848 (1 reference); for a review by Max D. Engelhart of an earlier form, see 6:919. For reviews of the GRE program, see 7:667 (1 review) and 5:601 (1 review).

REFERENCES

1. See 7:848.
2. EDUCATIONAL TESTING SERVICE. *The Prediction of Doctorate Attainment in Psychology, Mathematics and Chemistry.* GRE Board Research Report, No. 69-6aR. Princeton, N.J.: Educational Testing Service, 1974. Pp. 19. *

[853]

*Toledo Chemistry Placement Examination.** College entrants; 1959–74; TCPE; 7 scores: arithmetic and algebra, general knowledge, formulas and nomenclature, equations, algebraic formulations, chemical problems, total; no data on reliability; no norms for part scores for Form 1967; Forms 1967, 1974, (8 pages); no specific manual; general directions ['70, 4 pages]; norms (1–2 pages) for each form; separate answer sheets (IBM 805 for Form 1967, IBM 1230 for Form 1974) must be used; $12 per 25 tests; $1.50 per 25 answer sheets; $1 per scoring stencil; $3 per specimen set; postage extra; 55(60) minutes: Albertine Krohn; Examinations Committee, American Chemical Society. *

See T2:1847 (2 references); for reviews by Kenneth E. Anderson and William R. Crawford of earlier forms, see 6:920 (1 reference).

REFERENCES

1. See 6:920.
2–3. See T2:1847.
4. COLEY, NEIL ROY. *An Investigation of Prediction of Academic Success in a Community Junior College.* Doctor's thesis, University of Southern California (Los Angeles, Calif.), 1972. (*DAI* 33:3317A)
5. COLEY, NEIL R. "Prediction of Success in General Chemistry in Community Colleges." *J Chem Ed* 50(9):613–5 S '73 .*
6. AMERICAN CHEMICAL SOCIETY, DIVISION OF CHEMICAL EDUCATION. "Condensed Norms: ACS Cooperative Examinations." *J Chem Ed* 53(4):264–5 Ap '76. *

FRANK J. FORNOFF, *Senior Examiner in Science, Higher Education and Careers Programs, Educational Testing Service, Princeton, New Jersey.*

This test is designed for students entering college general chemistry. On the basis of the scores, students may be placed in remedial or regular sections.

Organization of the test is as follows: arithmetic and algebra, 15 questions; general knowledge (largely of chemistry), 25 questions; formulas and nomenclature, 6 questions;

equations, 6 questions; algebraic formulations, 6 questions; and chemical problems, 5 questions.

Weighted scoring is recommended, with the questions in the first three parts weighted less heavily than those in the last three parts.

In general, the questions are worded clearly and concisely. About half of the Part 2 questions are probably application questions for most students, and this is a good percentage for such a test. One problem involving gas volumes does not specify conditions, and another does so only incompletely. In general, I found no troublesome ambiguities, though one question was miskeyed.

Norms based on 1,224 students are presented, but the nature of the population is not described. For the norming population, the test is of appropriate difficulty: a mean of 52 percent. Norms for the first three parts combined and for each of the last three parts, as well as for total score, are provided.

I would not consider comparing the grades on the test for students with and those without high school chemistry to be appropriate since the latter must be at a very serious disadvantage on Parts 2, 3, 4, and 6.

Though the description of the development of the several forms mentions validity, no information on either reliability or validity is presented with the test.

Though I do not believe the test should be used for granting college credit in chemistry, I feel sure that it can satisfactorily serve to identify superior students and those at risk of failure.

[854]

*UP Field Test in Chemistry. College; 1969–77; formerly called *The Undergraduate Record Examinations: Chemistry Test;* Form TUR ('71, 17 pages); descriptive booklet ('72, 16 pages); for UAP accessories, see 480; rental fee, $4 per test, postage extra; 120(140) minutes; Educational Testing Service. *

GEOLOGY

[855]

*The Graduate Record Examinations Advanced Geology Test. Graduate school candidates; 1939–76; test administered 5 times annually (January, April, June, October, December) at centers established by the publisher; 4 scores: stratigraphy-paleontology-geomorphology, structural geology and geophysics, mineralogy-petrology-geochemistry, total; 3 current forms ('73–76, 31–36 pages); descriptive booklet ('75, 12 pages); for program accessories, see 476; exami-

nation fee, $10.50 per candidate; 170(190) minutes; an inactive form is available for local administration (rental fee, $5.50 per test); Educational Testing Service. *

See 7:852 (1 reference). For reviews of the GRE program, see 7:667 (1 review) and 5:601 (1 review).

[856]

*UP Field Test in Geology. College; 1969–77; formerly called *The Undergraduate Record Examinations: Geology Test,* Form RUR ('69, 15 pages); descriptive booklet ('70, 7 pages); for UAP accessories, see 480; rental fee, $4 per test, postage extra; 120(140) minutes; Educational Testing Service. *

MISCELLANEOUS

[857]

★ACT Proficiency Examination in Anatomy and Physiology. College and adults; 1975–76; for college accreditation of nontraditional study, advanced placement, or assessment of educational achievement; test administered 4 times annually (February, May, August, November) at centers established by the publisher; developed and administered in New York State as a part of their College Proficiency Examinations Program; 6 semester credits recommended; no data on reliability; Form ZZ ('76, 30 pages); study guide ('76, 4 pages); for further information and program accessories, see 470; examination fee, $30 per candidate (includes reporting of score to the candidate and one college); 180(210) minutes; developed by the New York State Education Department; American College Testing Program. *

[858]

★ACT Proficiency Examination in Earth Science. College and adults; 1966–76; for college accreditation of nontraditional study, advanced placement, or assessment of educational achievement; test administered 4 times annually (February, May, August, November) at centers established by the publisher; developed and administered in New York State as a part of their College Proficiency Examinations Program; 6 semester credits recommended; no data on reliability; 2 parts: objective, essay; single letter grade; 2 parts: Form ZZ ('75, 10 pages, reprinted with 1976 copyright; objective part), Form ZZ ('76, 4 pages; essay part); study guide ('76, 3 pages); for further information and program accessories, see 470; examination fee, $30 per candidate (includes reporting of score to the candidate and one college); 180(210) minutes; developed by the University of the State of New York; American College Testing Program. *

[859]

NM Concepts of Ecology Test. Grades 6–8, 9–12; 1973; NMCET; criterion referenced; no suggested standards of mastery for item and total scores; 2 levels; separate answer sheets must be used; $8.50 per 35 tests; $2 per 35 answer sheets; $1 per scoring stencil; $1.50 per manual; $3 per specimen set of either level; postpaid; 20(25) minutes; Educational Evaluation Associates for and in cooperation with the New Mexico State Department of Education; Monitor. *

a) LEVEL I. Grades 6–8; no reliability data or norms for grades 7 and 8; 1 form (3 pages); manual (3 pages).

NM Concepts of Ecology Test

b) LEVEL 2. Grades 9–12; no reliability data or norms for grades 10 and 11; 1 form (3 pages); manual (4 pages).

JACQUELINE V. MALLINSON, *Adjunct Associate Professor of Science Education, Western Michigan University, Kalamazoo, Michigan.*

The manuals describe the *NM Concepts of Ecology Test* as "a criterion-referenced test that was designed to assess specific learner objectives in the area of ecology" in grades 6–12. Each level consists of 20 multiple choice items. Both levels have two to six items in each of the following areas: geographic evolution and conservation, plant and animal dependencies, natural adaptation, and life processes. The lower level, for grades 6–8, also has 2 or 3 items in each of three additional areas: natural balance, natural resources, and pollution. No explanation is presented for the broader scope of the lower level test.

The classifications of some items are contradictory. For example, item 15, in Level 1, is classified as a "pollution" item; but in Level 2, an almost identical item is classified as a "life processes" item. There are several other such discrepancies.

Many of the items used on both levels of this test "skirt around" the edges of meaningful topics of ecology. It would be helpful if there was more emphasis on the relationships between living things and the non-living resources of the environment, and on the interrelationships among living things. The tests would be greatly improved by the inclusion of some energy-related items; some "food-and-people" items; and some dealing with the impact of human activity on the environment, both living and non-living.

There is a considerable amount of overlap in the items used in the two levels of the test. Of the 20 items on each form, 7 are essentially the same in both forms, differing only slightly in wording. Yet, the slight differences in wording can make the difference between "night and day" as indicated by this example: "Which of the following is a producer in the food web?" The Level 1 options are skunk, cow, corn, and lizard; the Level 2 options are the same except for the substitution of "cloud" for "cow." Although the keyed answer is "corn" in each case, 46 percent of the sixth graders in the norm group selected "cow" and 34 percent selected

the keyed answer. One can imagine that in the minds of these youngsters, cows, from which we get milk, butter, ice cream, and cheese, certainly *are* "producers." By substituting the "cloud" for "cow," the item became one of the easiest ones in the Level 2 test, whereas it was one of the most difficult in the Level 1 test. This certainly illustrates the great importance of carefully selecting and wording all options.

No validity data are provided for the two levels of this test. The internal-consistency reliability coefficients reported are low, .67 to .74.

Although the test is called a criterion-referenced test, there are no suggestions for setting standards of mastery, possibly because the test proved very difficult. Percentages of the norm groups having an item correct ranged from .17 to .85, median .45 in grade 6; .32 to .78, median .47 in grade 9; and .36 to .84, median .68 in grade 12. Had corrections for guessing been made, the median percentage of correct answers would have been .27, .29, and .57, respectively.

The lack of norms for grades 7, 8, 10, and 11 does not allow for meaningful comparisons of students of these grade levels who might be administered the tests.

The title of this test sounded exciting, and certainly reflects an area of the curriculum in great need of evaluation. In its present form, however, this reviewer cannot recommend use of the test. A thoughtful classroom teacher, willing to spend one evening, could probably construct a test as good or better.

[860]

Tests of Basic Experiences: Science. Prekgn–kgn, kgn–grade 1; 1970–72; 1 form; Levels K ('70, 34 pages), L ('70, 18 pages); no specific manual; for battery manuals and accessories, see 34; $12 per 30 tests, postage extra; (25) minutes; Margaret H. Moss; CTB/McGraw-Hill. *

For reviews of the complete battery, see 34 (1 review, 2 excerpts) and 7:33 (1 review).

ARLEN R. GULLICKSON, *Associate Professor of Education, The University of South Dakota, Vermillion, South Dakota.*

This test is designed to provide an indication of how well a child's experiences have prepared him for his introduction to science. The author also indicates the test may provide a means for placing students in homogeneous learning groups. The test does not require reading ability on the part of the student.

For Level K each child is provided with a

booklet, each page of which has four picture drawings, representing the options for one test item. For each item the test administrator tells the students to mark one drawing, for example, "Mark the one that flies." The total test includes four example items and 28 test items. Level L has the same format with one exception. In it two items are placed on each page. This reduces the number of pages necessary to complete the test but results in a test that is somewhat awkward to administer, especially when compared to Level K.

Procedurally the test is well prepared. Instructions for administration are clear and complete, scoring is straightforward, and record forms are provided to compile both individual and class scores. In addition, the manual is careful to advocate the use of proctors in administering the test to the young children.

Norms are provided for users which can serve to provide a general "feel" for interpreting test results. In obtaining the norm data, four geographical region types and four community types were tested. Although the developer has made an effort to test students from a substantial number of schools in a variety of locations, the reference group is not a probability sample and the norms are unlikely to be truly representative of any region or community type. For most teachers who choose to use the test, the development of local norms would be more satisfactory.

Neither of the two levels has a high reliability. The highest reliability coefficient cited for Level L is .79 for first graders. The reliability for Level K is slightly higher, .84 for kindergarten students. Such reliability presents a problem that is most striking for persons who score about average on the test. For example, if on Level K a kindergarten child scored 18 (above average), by using the standard error of measurement one would predict that his true score lies somewhere between 13.7 and 22.3 (95 percent confidence interval). In terms of percentile ranks, that is an interval which spans from approximately the 23rd percentile to the 74th percentile—approximately 50 percentage points.

Aside from a content validation, the manual does not provide validity information pertinent to the test's use in assessment for science purposes. The manual itself recommends that the test *not* be used as a principal determiner of "readiness." Although the author advocates use of the test for prescribing instruction, available evidence does not support such use. In particular, the author has provided 28 3 x 5 cards, one card per test item, "to help the teacher apply test results in the classroom." The obvious purpose of the cards is to teach a desired concept to those students who missed an item, or to teach the concept to the whole class if a large percent of the class missed the item. The individual items are simply not strong enough to be used as determiners of whether either individuals or a group as a whole understands a concept which the author believes the item measures. If the test is to be advocated for predictive or diagnostic situations, research evidence should be provided which validates such use.

The test is interesting and imaginative, and is administratively well prepared. However, much work remains to be done before it can be said that the test is valid for the expressed purposes of grouping students or prescribing the teaching of specific concepts.

[861]

★Understanding in Science Test. Grades 7–9; 1975; experimental form; categorization into one of 4 Piagetian stages: early concrete (0–29 percent of possible score), late concrete (32–56 percent), early formal (56–76 percent), late formal (79–100 percent); no data presented on the basis of the categorization; no data on reliability; no norms; 1 form (12 pages); manual (12 pages); some testing materials must be assembled locally; separate answer sheets must be used; Aus 30¢ per test; 50¢ per 10 answer sheets; $1.25 per manual; postpaid within Australia; (40) minutes; R. P. Tisher and L. G. Dale; Australian Council for Educational Research [Australia]. *

PHYSICS

[862]

*Advanced Placement Examinations in Physics. High school students desiring credit for college level courses and admission to advanced courses; 1954–77; available to secondary schools for annual administration on specified days in May; Form ZBP ('77, 29 pages) in 2 booklets (objective, essay); 2 levels (candidate elects only one); course description ('76, 56 pages); sample syllabi ('76, 31 pages); grading guidelines ('76, 48 pages); previous essay questions available; for program accessories, see 471; examination fee, $32 per student; an inactive form [Form YBP ('76, 26–28 pages)] is available to colleges for local administration and scoring (rental fee, $2 per test); program administered for the College Entrance Examination Board by Educational Testing Service. *
a) PHYSICS B. Equivalent of 1 year terminal course in college physics; 180(200) minutes.
b) PHYSICS C. Equivalent of 1 year nonterminal course

in college physics; 1 or 2 scores: mechanics (part 1), electricity and magnetism (part 2); 2 parts in each test booklet (candidate elects either one or both parts); 90(100) minutes for each part.

See 6:927 (2 references); for a review by Leo Nedelsky of an earlier form, see 5:750. For reviews of the APE program, see 471 (2 reviews) and 7:662 (2 reviews).

REFERENCES

1–2. See 6:927.
3. THOMPSON, RAYMOND E.; FINN, EDWARD J.; AND PASQUESI, ROBERT J. "The Advanced Placement Program in Physics." *Physics Teach* 10(7):391–7 O '72. *
4. PFEIFFENBERGER, WILL. "1974 Advanced Placement Examinations in Physics." *Physics Teach* 14(7):423–30 O '76. *
5. PFEIFFENBERGER, G. WILL, AND MODU, CHRISTOPHER C. "A Validity Study of the Multinle-Choice Component of the Advanced Placement Physics C Examination." *Am J Physics* 45(11):1066–9 N '77. *

MARIO IONA, *Professor of Physics, University of Denver, Denver, Colorado.* [Review of Forms XBP and YBP.]

These examinations serve the very specific purpose of evaluating high school students' standing after taking a year's college level physics course or independent preparation for placement into the physics program when entering college. There are two separate examinations. Physics B, based on a college level physics course without calculus, covers all areas of physics often described as terminal. Physics C consists of two parts, each of which can be taken separately. These two parts are based on the mechanics and the electricity and magnetism segments of a beginning college physics course using calculus. All examinations consist of a multiple choice section of qualitative and problem questions and a free response (essay) section of problems, sometimes requiring comments, for which work has to be shown. The objective and essay sections each take half the available time and the maximum scores in each section receive equal weight in establishing the final grade. The free response questions of previous examinations are available and the new questions that have been used are published annually with details on their grading. The examinations are revised annually with some multiple choice questions used from previous examinations for standardization of the scores. The format and content of the examinations change little from year to year, and the major changes are outlined in the announcements, which also present sample questions.

The level of difficulty seems to be fairly well chosen for the intended purpose. This is demonstrated by the approximately bell-shaped curves of the raw scores. However, the questions seem somewhat hard even for this selected group of students since the distribution of raw scores have a mean which is usually a little below the middle of the range. When the distributions are skewed, an attempt is made to take this into consideration in setting the cutoff raw scores in assigning the reported grades of 1 (low) to 5 (high). Although the examinations are described as usually providing sufficient time, the fact that on the average 8 to 11 percent of the answers are omitted seems to indicate that the examinations are either too long for some students, or that the coverage does not match the topics of the courses taken, or that they are too difficult. The students may also have been discouraged from guessing by possible misunderstanding of the instructions, which point out the grading procedure of subtracting a percentage of wrong choices. Especially on Physics B, which covers a wide range of subject matter, the score may be affected more by lack of coverage than by lack of comprehension of the covered topics.

The examinations are intended to be based on course descriptions given in annually revised announcements. The course description emphasizes the advantage and need of laboratory work in an advanced placement physics program; however, the examinations do not seem to require any specific laboratory experience. The detailed list of topics to be covered in such a course is mirrored by the questions asked, although occasionally questions seem to be more difficult than one would expect in most beginning college courses. This seems especially true of some quantitative questions in atomic physics and of some questions dealing with mechanical systems which will rarely have been discussed quantitatively, but which can be analyzed in a qualitative way. Most questions are directly concerned with applying the basic principles, as taught in traditional introductory courses, to straightforward problems. Not all wrong options for the multiple choice questions are specifically chosen to distract the student from the correct one so that occasionally some can be eliminated without positive knowledge of the correct answer. Most of the questions are carefully and simply stated, but a few questions do not have a clearly correct answer so that the choice has to be based on whichever option one considers as the "best" answer. A very critical reader will find room for improvement in the formulation of some questions. However, the effect on students will be minimal.

Many colleges seem reluctant to commit themselves to allowing definite benefits on the basis of the examination grades reported, probably because they have little information about the equivalency to college accomplishments. Some studies have shown that grades of 3 and above are often equivalent to B and A grades at many demanding colleges, although there is a wide range of overlap of grades. Colleges have to make their decision on the basis of a single reported grade, based on both the objective and essay sections or, in addition, on their own evaluation of the answers to the free response sections, since those are available upon request. Colleges which choose this latter way of evaluation may wish that separate grades for the two sections had been reported, since they do not know how the part they are evaluating in detail entered into the overall grade. Although in such a limited examination not all abilities can be demonstrated, it would appear that placement on the basis of the upper grades would be as valid as placement on the basis of most transfer grades, as far as ability to handle physics problems is concerned.

There is some evidence that the two sections of the examinations deal with different aspects of the ability to solve problems in physics. Because of the time limitation, the multiple choice section emphasizes the memorization and simple application of many detailed relations, while in the free response section there is some emphasis on deriving the specific relations from fundamental principles. Nevertheless, the correlation between the two sections is usually above .70.

Although there are only few comparison data available, some colleges may find the examinations instructive in comparing their own students with the AP students.

The examinations are intended for a very limited purpose which they seem to serve adequately for those who obtain the higher grades.

Each institution has to make its own judgment which grade to accept for the various purposes of placement, exemption, or credit; the decision may vary considerably on the basis of the image the institution has in its own estimation or wishes to project. Since the conse-

quences of overly cautious evaluation are relatively minor, i.e., requiring the taking of a course for which the student might qualify already, I prefer erring on the "safe" side and therefore feel that the classification of the grade 3 as "qualified" is perhaps somewhat optimistic for many institutions if it means qualified for college credit.

[863]

*College Board Achievement Test in Physics. Candidates for college entrance; 1901–76; test administered 6 times annually (January, March, May, June, November, December) at centers established by the publisher; Forms YCB4, YCB5, ZCB1, ZCB2, ZCB3, ZCB4, ('75–76, 11–14 pages); for more complete information, see 472; examination fee, $12.50 per candidate; 60(80) minutes; inactive forms, entitled *College Placement Test in Physics,* are available for local administration and scoring; program administered for the College Entrance Examination Board by Educational Testing Service. *

See 7:855 (2 references) and 6:926 (4 references); for a review by Theodore G. Phillips of an earlier form, see 5:749 (2 references); for a review by Palmer O. Johnson, see 4:633 (3 references). For reviews of the testing program, see 6:760 (2 reviews).

REFERENCES

1–3. See 4:633.
4–5. See 5:749.
6–9. See 6:926.
10–11. See 7:855; see also T2:1859 for a cumulative name index to the first 11 references and 2 reviews for this test.
12. PFEIFFENBERGER, G. W. "National Testing in Physics: Recent Trends and Future Implications." *Physics Teach* 12(7): 391–5 O '74. *

[864]

*College Placement Test in Physics. Entering college freshmen; 1962–75, c1954–75; inactive forms of *College Board Achievement Test in Physics* available for local administration and scoring; Forms PPL ['67, reprint of 1964 test], SPL ['70, reprint of 1964 test] in a single booklet (30 pages); separate answer sheets (Digitek, IBM 805, IBM 1230) must be used; for program accessories, see 474; rental fee, $2 per student; 60(70) minutes; program administered for the College Entrance Examination Board by Educational Testing Service. *

For a review by Theodore G. Phillips of an earlier form, see 5:749; for a review by Palmer O. Johnson, see 4:633. For a review of the CPT program, see 7:665.

[865]

Cooperative Science Tests: Physics. Grades 10–12; 1963–65; 3 scores: general concepts and principles, laboratory, total; Forms A, B, ('63, 20–22 pages); no specific manual; series handbook ('64, 76 pages); student bulletin ('65, 2 pages); separate answer sheets (Digitek, IBM 805, IBM 1230, NCS) must be used; $6 per 20 tests; $5.50 per 100 answer sheets; $1.50 per 10 IBM scoring stencils (answer pattern must be punched out locally); Digitek scoring stencils not available; $2 per series handbook; $3 per 100 student bulletins; $3.50 per specimen set of this and 4 other science tests; cash orders postpaid; NCS scoring and statistical analysis service, 45¢ and over per test; 80(92) minutes; Educational Testing Service; Addison-Wesley Publishing Co., Inc. *

Cooperative Science Tests: Physics

For a review by Alexander Even, see 7:857. For excerpted reviews by Irvin J. Lehmann (with Clarence H. Nelson) and William Mehrens of the series, see 7:787.

WAYNE W. WELCH, *Professor of Educational Psychology, University of Minnesota, Minneapolis, Minnesota.*

Perhaps more than any other subject, high school physics has been the target of curriculum reform supported by the federal government. In the late 50s and early 60s, the PSSC physics development effort was the model for dozens of curriculum revision efforts that followed. Some claim more than 40 percent of high school physics students were using the course in the late 60s.

A second major curriculum effort, Harvard Project Physics (HPP), appeared about 1970. Markedly different from PSSC in philosophy and style, the HPP course represented a second generation of curriculum renewal efforts in science. Course developers now claim that HPP is used by 25 percent of the physics students in the USA. There has been a decline in PSSC enrollment since the advent of the HPP course, but recent estimates place about one-half of the physics students taking either one or the other of these two courses. In addition, the impact of this curriculum development effort is apparent from examining the content, problems, laboratory equipment, and teacher manuals of the more conventional texts. Revised editions of these books have incorporated much of the philosophy and content of the newer courses.

Unfortunately, the Cooperative physics test has not kept pace with the above developments. With few exceptions, the tests look like they were written with very little knowledge of the recent curriculum revision efforts. This may have occurred because the current version of the test was started about 1958. However, item writing was not completed until 1962, several years after PSSC was initiated. And certainly, the historical and humanistic flavor of the HPP course is not found in any of the items in the 1963 version of the Cooperative physics tests.

The tests (two forms with two parts to each form) are fairly adequate, albeit difficult, tests of content which apeared in physics books in the 30s and 40s. The domain of items includes mechanics, heat, sound, light, electricity and magnetism, and atomic physics. Compare this with the six units of the Project Physics course; motion, astronomy, mechanics, light and electromagnetism, models of the atom, and the nucleus. Clearly a difference exists. The content of PSSC Physics is different as well. In my opinion, the Cooperative physics test is not testing the physics taught to a large share of our students. As such, this reviewer cannot recommend its use, unless a user is interested in student performance on very conventional measures.

If such is the case, a few comments on the tests seem in order. The item classification indicates a heavy emphasis on application items. Half or more of the items on both forms are judged to be at this level. In addition, about 20 percent of the items are classified analysis or evaluation, and about 15 percent comprehension. The remainder are knowledge items. The heavy emphasis on application is somewhat of a puzzle, but at least there is a scattering across the various levels of the cognitive domain.

Part 2 of the tests is purported to measure laboratory applications including several questions about laboratory experiments and equipment. However, asking a question about equipment doesn't necessarily mean the item is measuring understanding of scientific methods and procedures. In fact, I don't believe any of the 12 items (3 in Form A, 9 in Form B) claimed to be measuring scientific methods are, in fact, measuring those skills normally considered part of scientific method. For example, an item which refers to a Boyle's Law apparatus asks, "If the product of the two variables (pressure P and volume V) proves to be a constant, one can conclude that....(B) the variables are inversely proportional to one another." This seems to test little more than the meaning of "inversely proportional," certainly not application of scientific method as is claimed in the handbook.

There are other criticisms of the test. The items are quite difficult; the mean number of items correct is 47 percent. Since the tests are speeded rather than power tests, it is not possible to determine how much of this difficulty is due to speededness. No concurrent validity information is presented. Student instructions for the example problem do not make sense for some of the available answer sheets. This is certain to cause some confusion.

Cooperative Science Tests: Physics

In addition, the copy of the handbook I received had six duplicate pages in it, and was missing pages 7–14 and 63–70. An inserted errata sheet identified two incorrectly keyed items in the handbook, but failed to note the duplicate classification of item 1, Part 2, Form A. Mistakes such as these will create problems for test users.

In spite of the above concerns, there are some strengths in these physics tests. Test appearance and item layout are good. K-R 20 reliabilities are high (.90 and .91), although no doubt inflated by the test's speededness. The items are well written and adequately test the limited content of traditional physics. The items are interesting and challenging but, given their rather high difficulty levels, may be more appropriate for college students.

However, a revision of this test is badly needed to represent more adequately current physics content and the increasing attention being given to the intangible outcomes of science instruction; e.g., attitudes, impact of science on society, scientific processes, and decision making.

[866]

*The Graduate Record Examinations Advanced Physics Test. Graduate school candidates; 1939–76; test administered 5 times annually (January, April, June, October, December) at centers established by the publisher; 5 current forms ('73–75, 18–20 pages); descriptive booklet ('75, 12 pages); for program accessories, see 476; examination fee, $10.50 per candidate; 170(190) minutes; an inactive form is available for local administration (rental fee, $5.50 per test); Educational Testing Service. *

For a review by Theodore G. Phillips, see 6:931; for a review by Leo Nedelsky, see 5:754. For reviews of the GRE program, see 7:667 (1 review) and 5:601 (1 review).

REFERENCES

1. PFEIFFENBERGER, G. W. "National Testing in Physics: Recent Trends and Future Implications." *Physics Teach* 12(7): 391–5 O '74. *

[867]

*UP Field Test in Physics. College; 1969–77; formerly called *The Undergraduate Record Examinations: Physics Tests;* Form TUR ('71, 16 pages); descriptive booklet ('72, 16 pages); for UAP accessories, see 480; rental fee, $4 per test, postage extra; 120(140) minutes; Educational Testing Service. *

SENSORY-MOTOR

REVIEWS BY *Brad S. Chissom, Richard E. Darnell, John J. Geyer, Donald A. Leton, Thomas Oakland, Jerome D. Pauker, Homer B. C. Reed, Jr., James C. Reed, James A. Rice, Carl L. Rosen, and Alida S. Westman.*

[868]

★The Bender-Purdue Reflex Test: For Signs of Symmetric Tonic Neck Reflex Immaturity. Ages 6–12; 1976; child's posture as "he creeps on hands and knees, first forward, then backward, against manual resistance," as related to current or latent learning disabilities; no data on reliability; no norms; individual; 1 form (6 pages); manual (72 pages plus sample forms); $5 per 25 tests; $7.50 per manual; postage extra; [30–40] minutes; Miriam L. Bender; Academic Therapy Publications. *

RICHARD E. DARNELL, *Director, Curriculum in Physical Therapy, Department of Physical Medicine and Rehabilitation, Medical School, University of Michigan, Ann Arbor, Michigan.*

This test and training manual is derived from an experimental study to determine the relationship existing between the presence of learning disorders and persisting symmetric tonic neck reflex activity among children of elementary school age and to determine the relationship of intelligence and/or increasing chronological age on such reflex activity. The test examines six different behavioral signs of symmetrical tonic neck activity in both forward and backward creeping: (*a*) characteristic creeping posture, (*b*) head control, (*c*) arm and hand position, (*d*) trunk, hip, and knee position, (*e*) ankle and foot position, (*f*) creeping patterns and rhythm. Judgments are made with regard to each sign in which the absence or presence of reflex activity can be noted utilizing an eight-point scale indicating absence to strong presence.

Test validity is supported by an impressive description of the significance of that reflex in the development of gross motor patterns, and minor reference to its use in current therapeutic approaches. A conceptual model is also presented for its implications in perceptual and conceptual development. Test items are well constructed and relatively free from ambiguity. No statistical evidence for concurrent or predictive validity is presented. Intercorrelations between test items are not reported.

Coefficients of reliability are not present although the presence of interrater reliability is reported as part of the experimental procedure. Reliabilities for individual subject groups, individual test items, and reliabilities of difference scores are not available.

Norms are limited to experimental groupings: older and younger children, children of higher and lower intelligence, and total experimental group; and control groupings: older and younger children, and total control group. Norms for individual test items are not available. The lack of adequate presentation of normative data represents a major deficiency of the test and seriously detracts from its usefulness in pediatric or educational settings.

The manual appears adequate to allow appropriate scoring although some subjective judgments and qualitative interpretations are necessary. Instructions for observing and evaluating are given in detail, and the test blank is both attractive and convenient to use. An outstanding component of the manual is a developmental training program designed to stimulate maturation of the reflex, which emphasizes resisted creeping and walking activities. It is well presented and excellently illustrated, and is appropriate for use by professionals, paraprofessionals, parents, and parent surrogates of children with learning disabilities.

Within the limitations described above, the test and associated training manual constitute a unique and valuable asset in evaluation and therapeutic intervention in children whose level of activity can incorporate quadruped activity. For individual children, it allows the determination of an objective data base, provides treatment suggestions in an orderly and efficient manner, and allows determination of progress. Although it is by design exceedingly narrow in scope, dealing with only one of a large number of primitive reflexes which may impede motor development, it is highly recommended for its clinical usefulness with children with learning disabilities and/or associated developmental delay in the achievement of major motor milestones.

Bender-Purdue Reflex Test

[869]

★**Cleary-Now Test of Perceptual-Motor Readiness.** Grades kgn–1; 1973–74; "visual-perceptual readiness for reading"; no information on basis for obtaining norms, which consist of cutoff scores only; individual; 1 form ('73, 17 cards plus 2 practice cards); manual ('74, 14 pages); scoring sheet ('73, 1 page); $20 per set of testing materials including 50 scoring sheets; $1 per 50 scoring sheets; postpaid; (15–20) minutes; Brian Cleary and Joseph Now; Curtis Blake Child Development Center, American International College. *

[870]

Developmental Test of Visual-Motor Integration. Ages 2–8, 2–15; 1967; VMI; 2 levels; manual (76 pages); technical report (46 pages); $6.81 per technical report and set of cards for *b*; $5.55 per manual; $2.40 per specimen set (complete test and manual not included); postage extra; [15–20] minutes; Keith E. Beery and Norman A. Buktenica (test); Follett Publishing Co. *
a) [SHORT FORM.] Ages 2–8; 1 form (10 pages, identical with Long Form except for omission of 9 items); $7.11 per 15 tests.
b) [LONG FORM.] Ages 2–15; 1 form (14 pages); set of 24 stimulus cards available for remedial work; assessment and remediation worksheets (40 pages); $10.20 per 15 tests; $24.90 per 10 sets of worksheets.
See T2:1875 (6 references); for a review by Brad S. Chissom, see 7:867 (5 references).

REFERENCES

1–5. See 7:867.
6–11. See T2:1875; also includes a cumulative name index to the first 11 references and 1 review for this test.
12. ARMBRUSTER, RUDOLPH A. *Perceptual Motor, Gross Motor, and Sensory Motor Skills Training: The Effect Upon School Readiness and Self Concept Development of Kindergarten Children.* Doctor's thesis, Wayne State University (Detroit, Mich.), 1972. (*DAI* 33:6644A)
13. BURG, LESLIE ANNE. *An Analysis of Factors Related to Reading Disability as Evidenced in Three Specifically Identified Groups.* Doctor's thesis, Boston University (Boston, Mass.), 1972. (*DAI* 33:1311A)
14. KRAUFT, VIRGINIA R., AND KRAUFT, CONRAD C. "Structured vs Unstructured Visual-Motor Tests for Educable Retarded Children." *Percept & Motor Skills* 34(3):691–4 Je '72. * (*PA* 48:12193)
15. KRAUSEN, R. "The Relationship of Certain 'Pre-Reading Skills to General Ability and Social Class in Nursery Children.'" *Ed Res* (England) 15(1):72–9 N '72. *
16. PAPAGNO, NANCY ISABELLA. *A Study of the Reliability of the Short Form of the Developmental Test of Visual-Motor Integration.* Master's thesis, Pennsylvania State University (University Park, Pa.), 1972.
17. RYCKMAN, DAVID B.; RENTFROW, ROBERT; FARGO, GEORGE; AND MCCARTIN, ROSEMARIE. "Reliabilities of Three Tests of Form-Copying." *Percept & Motor Skills* 34(3):917–8 Je '72. * (*PA* 48:11277)
18. KELLAGHAN, THOMAS, AND GREANEY, BETTY JANE. "A Factorial Study of the Characteristics of Preschool Disadvantaged Children." *Irish J Ed* 7(2):53–65 w '73. *
19. CARLSON, ROLF STANELY. *The Performance of Problem Readers on the Wechsler Intelligence Scale for Children, the Developmental Test of Visual-Motor Integration and Piagetian Variables.* Doctor's thesis, University of North Carolina (Chapel Hill, N.C.), 1973. (*DAI* 35:497B)
20. PACKARD, SANDRA. "Creative Tempo in Children's Art Production." *Studies Art Ed* 14(3):18–25 sp '73. *
21. SERAPIGLIA, THERESA. *Self-Selected and Teacher Matched Word Recognition Tasks Presented to Measured Perceptual Modalities of Primary Children.* Doctor's thesis, Pennsylvania State University (University Park, Pa.), 1973. (*DAI* 35:1536A)
22. BUSCH, ROBERT F. *Predicting First-Grade Reading Achievement.* Doctor's thesis, University of Missouri (Columbia, Mo.), 1974. (*DAI* 36:216A)
23. CARR, JAMES VINCENT. *The Use of the Gesell Developmental Examination to Identify Children Prone to Emotional Maladjustment and Visual Motor Problems.* Doctor's thesis, Boston College (Chestnut Hill, Mass.), 1974. (*DAI* 35:1524A)
24. NELSON, DONALD GORDEN. *A Comparison of the Performance of the Trainable Mentally Retarded on Tests Measuring*

Mental Age, Achievement, and Cognitive and Visual-Motor Development. Doctor's thesis, University of Nebraska (Lincoln, Neb.), 1974. (*DAI* 35:5176A)
25. RATLIFF, WILLIAM RANDALL, JR. *A Comparison of Two Methods of Evaluation of Selected Psychological Variables in Learning Between Learning Disabled and Normal 7, 8, 9, and 10 Year-Old Children.* Doctor's thesis, East Texas State University (Commerce, Tex.), 1974. (*DAI* 35:4258A)
26. COSTELLO, CHRISTINE THERESE. *A Factor Analytic Comparison of Three Tests of Visual Perception for Children.* Doctor's thesis, St. Louis University (St. Louis, Mo.), 1975. (*DAI* 37:1892B)
27. EATON, IRA E. *The Relationship Between Perceptual-Motor Ability and Reading Success.* Doctor's thesis, St. Louis University (St. Louis, Mo.), 1975. (*DAI* 36:3562A)
28. HILL, NANCY CAROLYN. *A Factor Analytic Study of Selected Tests of Specific Components of Academic Learning.* Doctor's thesis, University of Missouri (Columbia, Mo.), 1975. (*DAI* 36:6600A)
29. LIEMOHN, WENDELL, AND WAGNER, PATRICK. "Motor and Perceptual Determinants of Performance on the Bender-Gestalt and the Beery Developmental Scale by Retarded Males." *Percept & Motor Skills* 40(2):524-6 Ap '75. * (*PA* 54:9967)
30. DUFFEY, JAMES B.; RITTER, DAVID R.; AND FEDNER, MARK. "Developmental Test of Visual-Motor Integration and the Goodenough Draw-A-Man Test as Predictors of Academic Success." *Percept & Motor Skills* 43(2):543-6 O '76. *
31. HARTLAGE, LAWRENCE C., AND LUCAS, TOMMIE L. "Differential Correlates of Bender-Gestalt and Beery Visual Motor Integration Test for Black and for White Children." *Percept & Motor Skills* 43(3, pt 2):1039-42 D '76. * (*PA* 58:2505)
32. KRAETSCH-HELLER, GAYLA. "Use of the Beery Visual-Motor Integration Test With Partially Sighted Students." *Percept & Motor Skills* 43(1):11-4 Ag '76. * (*PA* 57:4759)
33. KING, CHARLES HENRY. *Predictive Variables in Two Learning Disabilities Programs.* Doctor's thesis, Hofstra University (Hempstead, N.Y.), 1976. (*DAI* 37:5359B)
34. PARK, ROSEMARIE JANET. *Performance on Geometric Figure-Copying Tests as Predictors of Types of Error in Decoding.* Doctor's thesis, Harvard University (Cambridge, Mass.), 1976. (*DAI* 37:3399A)
35. TUCKER, RUTH ELAINE. *The Relationship Between Perceptual-Motor Development and Academic Achievement.* Doctor's thesis, University of Alabama (University, Ala.), 1976. (*DAI* 37:7536A)

DONALD A. LETON, *Professor of Educational Psychology, University of Hawaii at Manoa, Honolulu, Hawaii.*

Geometric designs were first constructed by Wertheimer as laboratory instruments for establishing principles of perception. They were developed to validate Gestalt theory rather than to test individual differences in perception. Ever since Bender adopted these as a clinical procedure in neuropsychiatry they have been misused and overused in clinical psychology. There is now a proliferation of tests using geometric form reproduction, including the *Memory-for-Designs Test, Benton Visual Retention, Minnesota Percepto-Diagnostic Test, Rutgers Drawing Test, Perceptual Forms Test, Purdue Perceptual Motor Survey,* and this test. There is some communality among their purposes: to assess brain damage, visual memory, perceptual disturbance, motor maturation and, for the VMI, to identify the learning disabled. Their general validity is that heterogeneous groups of brain-damaged, neurally-handicapped subjects tend to perform poorly in reproducing geometric designs.

In the development of the VMI, an item pool of 72 geometric designs was sequentially reduced to an age scale of 30 items, and then to a scale of 24 items. Several of the Wertheimer designs survived the age-differentiation criterion. The majority of the VMI designs, 17 of 24, are straight-line, angular configurations. Five have circular elements. Only two of the 24 designs, numbers 14 and 18, have discontinuous details involving visual closure. There are no designs requiring directional changes in continuous curved lines. The last four designs, numbers 21 through 24, are three-dimensional.

The response requirement for the VMI is essentially a drawing skill with a perceptual subability. The perceptual analysis of the designs is relatively simple compared to spatial perceptual tests using figure analogies, matrix relationships, block designs, and embedded figures. Interpretations about a child's perceptual abilities on the basis of VMI drawings are therefore tenuous.

There are a number of graphomotor skills which are not assessed in the reproduction of the VMI designs. There are various criterion-referenced scripting skills such as: "Print your name"; "Write the letters of the alphabet"; "Write the numbers from 1 to 20"; copying lazy eights, continuous lower-case c's, cursive upper-case L's; and other drawing tasks, such as "Draw a clock," which are generally useful for assessing graphomotor skills of children. It would be very shortsighted for teachers and psychologists to rely solely on the limited sample of VMI drawings to judge visual-motor integration.

The manual describes the VMI as a tool for educational assessment and for identification and remediation of learning disorders. The relationships of performance on the VMI with specific academic achievements are not identified. The need for studies of predictive validity was recognized in the previous MMY review of the test (see 7:867). There have been subsequent doctoral theses and journal reports pertaining to the reliability and factorial validity of the VMI, but there are only a few studies evaluating its predictive validity.

The age-norms provided in the VMI manual are not sufficient bases for the identification of learning disorders. There is no indication that children with visual-motor handicaps were systematically excluded from the norm group, nor intentionally included to represent the range of "normal" differences. To the extent that drawing skills are bound to the maturation of neuro-muscular structures, then negatively-skewed leptokurtic distributions of scores on drawing tests may be expected. The shapes of the score distributions at consecutive age levels are not described. Separate male and female age-equivalent tables are provided; however, the necessity for different sex norms is not discussed. There may have been a greater frequency of boys with exogenous graphomotor problems in the tails of the age-distributions; there may have been a developmental superiority for females across the score ranges; or both. This disregard for the shapes of the raw score distributions is a technical oversight.

The single age-equivalent score implies a unidimensional trait; however, in the technical report, Beery states that "certain discontinuities in development were suggested in the nine- to ten-year-old range." Beery also observed developmental changes in drawing vertical, horizontal, and oblique dimensions; open and closed forms; symmetrical forms; component parts of composite forms; relative sizes; relative spacing; and proportionality. The age progression for these skill changes may be implicit in the sequence of the 24 designs, but specific error features are not systematically considered in the scoring. The types of errors included in various scoring strategies for other geometric form tests include rotation, distortion, diminution, constriction, angulation, work-over, tremor, rounding, confabulation, fragmentation, simplification, closure, and perseveration. In the VMI booklet, however, the restriction of copying space and the boundaries for the reproductions preclude the occurrence of a number of these errors.

Much debate has arisen about the degrees of departure from accurate design reproductions and the types of errors which hold clinical significance. Inasmuch as Beery and Buktenica did not obtain drawing responses from a criterion group of children with graphomotor problems, the diagnostic validity of the VMI to identify learning disabled has not been demonstrated.

JAMES A. RICE, Associate Professor of Psychology, University of Houston, Houston, Texas.

Developmental Test of Visual-Motor Integration

The VMI purports to measure the integration of visual perception and motor behavior in young children. The author postulates five developmental levels on the road to such integration: motor proficiency, tactual-kinesthetic tracing, visual perception, and visual motor integration. The integration of relevant functions is considered a prerequisite to academic success; the VMI is specifically concerned with the visual motor aspect. There is reasonable concern for whether or not the construct, visual motor integration, is adequately defined for evaluation by a relatively simplistic copying task. The development of functional integration, and thus a capacity for higher order processing, is as fundamental to more sophisticated learning as it is complex. The issue of validity requires serious attention before the VMI can be presumed to measure an important, relevant attribute. The author reports a study (*1*) in which Buktenica correlated a variety of tests with language arts achievement for 342 low and middle class first grade children, obtaining coefficients of .33 to .50 for the VMI and the criterion variables, but differential performance for the diagnostic groups with which Beery is presumably concerned—learning disabled, minimal brain dysfunction, perceptual dysfunctioned—is not demonstrated. Another study is described in which Bateman obtained correlations of .70 and .73, respectively, between the VMI and the ITPA subtests, Visual-Motor Association and Visual Sequencing. Such correlations are interesting, but largely circular, for the ITPA is, simply, another instrument, not a get-at-able, relevant validity criterion.

Directions for both individual and group administration are explicit; scoring is either pass or fail, samples of actual reproductions by children are given in the manual for each of the 24 designs, after the manner of Terman in the Stanford-Binet. With the scoring criteria for each design are age norms, developmental comments, and either expectations based on earlier research, or developmental trends with a series of sample reproductions illustrating the range of expectation for each of the several relevant age levels. Age equivalent scores (2-10 to 15-11), guidelines for children 3 and under, and procedures for assessment and remediation of visual-motor difficulties complete the manual. A standardization sample of 1,039 appears adequate and the procedures appear sound. The interjudge reliability for one judge is reported as .96; test-retest coefficients range from .80 to .90, depending upon sex and length of interval; the age ranges on which these correlations were obtained are not reported. Correlations between VMI scores and age in groups having an age range of 3 through 14 are .88 for girls and .89 for boys.

Conceding worthy forerunners, e.g., *Bender-Gestalt Test Memory for Designs Test,* and *Benton Visual Retention Test,* Beery justifies the VMI, noting the shortcomings in similar instruments: restricted age ranges, poor standardization, lack of developmental information, and absence of a group testing format. These shortcomings are valid issues, even with some of the more widely heralded and utilized instruments.

Recent, vociferous disenchantment with the exhaustively researched construct, intelligence, has led to an intense concern with other, presumably more educationally relevant, constructs, not the least of which is visual perceptual-motor functioning. The function has been defined in various manners; an absence or deficiency has been described by numerous terms, frequently related to a variety of human conditions, e.g., brain damage. There yet remains much research before the construct is effectively harnessed for purposes of validity. Deficits in visual perceptual-motor functioning are clearly identifiable to the sophisticated professional, and frequently to others, but it has steadfastly defied those who would generate *meaningful,* psycho-educationally relevant validity criteria.

The VMI, while relatively new and lacking established validity, is more carefully researched and precisely standardized than the more prominently utilized instruments with a generally similar purpose. Inter item steps are much smaller than for either the *Bender-Gestalt Test* or the *Benton Visual Retention Test,* thus, a potential researcher may expect higher correlations with other variables simply on a statistical basis. Users may expect to benefit for the very reasons that Beery has given as shortcomings with other instruments, for these are indeed valid. However, although visual motor integration as a construct is promising, it is not a new concept, and it still remains to be defined in terms of meaningful and useful criteria. Correlating the VMI with other tests, especially those Beery regards as lacking, will not add meaningfully to validity; correlation with such tests as the ITPA is circular, the constructs presumably measured in both yet to be operationally (educationally) defined.

[871]

Frostig Movement Skills Test Battery, Experimental Edition. Ages 6–12; 1972; FMSTB; 6 summary scores: hand-eye coordination, strength, balance, visually guided movement, flexibility, total; no data on reliability of summary scores; no norms for summary scores; individual; 1 form; manual (35 pages); record sheet (1 page); testing materials may be assembled locally or purchased for $50 per kit (a stopwatch and two 12-foot 2 × 4's must be obtained locally); $2.50 per 50 record sheets; $3 per manual and sample record sheet; postage extra; (20–25) minutes; R. E. Orpet; Consulting Psychologists Press, Inc. *

REFERENCES

1. GRUEN, RONALD S. "Prediction of End-of-Year Reading Achievement for First- and Third-Grade Pupils." Abstract. *Proc 8th Ann Conv Am Psychol Assn* 7(2):563–4 '72. * (PA 48:5813)
2. SEVERSON, ROGER A. "Early Detection of Children With Potential Learning Disabilities: A Seven-Year Effort." Abstract. *Proc 8th Ann Conv Am Psychol Assn* 7(2):561–2 '72. * (PA 48:5679)
3. THOMPSON, MERITA LEE. *Relationships Between Perceptual-Motor Development and Reading Achievement of Third Grade Students.* Doctor's thesis, University of Alabama (University, Ala.), 1972. (DAI 33:5541A)
4. ARNHEIM, DANIEL D., AND SINCLAIR, WILLIAM A. "The Effect of a Motor Development Program on Selected Factors in Motor Ability, Personality, Self-Awareness and Vision." *Am Correct Ther J* 28(6):167–71 N–D '74. * (PA 56:6696)

THOMAS OAKLAND, *Professor of Educational Psychology, The University of Texas, Austin, Texas.*

The manual identifies six areas of psychological development which are important to children's learning and behavior: language, perception, higher cognitive processes, social adjustment, emotional adjustment, and sensory-motor and movement skills. Recognizing the need for an evaluation instrument in this last area, FMSTB was developed as an age scale to assess strengths and weaknesses in the sensory-motor development of children between the chronological ages (CA) of 6 through 12. In addition to being one of the six important developmental areas, sensory-motor abilities are described as influencing the development of the other five areas.

Theoretical support for the test battery comes from research with adults and adolescents which established separate factors for sensory-motor competence: hand-eye coordination, balance, strength, flexibility, endurance, and agility. The 12 subtests within the FMSTB are utilized to arrive at an assessment of the first four factors; endurance and agility are not assessed. One factor, visually guided movement, was not hypothesized but was obtained and included within the test.

Hand-eye coordination is assessed by three subtests: bead stringing, fist-edge-palm coordinated hand movements, and block transfer. Balance or equilibrium is assessed by two subtests: walking board (balance beam) and one-foot balance with eyes open or closed. Strength is assessed by five subtests: broad jumping, shuttle run, changing body positions from lying and standing positions, sit-ups, and push-ups. Flexibility is assessed by measuring how far a child can bend forward from a sitting position. Visually guided movement is assessed by throwing 15 bean bags overhand at a target 10 feet away.

The administration time for the FMSTB is 20 to 25 minutes for each child. The author suggests that this time can be shortened by having the examiner explain and demonstrate each task to a group of 3 to 4 children and request each child to perform the task immediately. The subtests are administered quite easily, requiring a minimum level of professional sophistication by the examiner. The administration of the test requires the following items in addition to the materials obtained in the test kit: furniture (e.g., a table and two chairs), a stopwatch, lumber required for the walking board, and a 5-foot square piece of carpet with a nonskid backing or a gymnastic mat.

Raw scores for each subtest are converted to standard scores; separate tables are provided for males and females within each of the seven CA groups. The scale score for each of the three factors (i.e., hand-eye coordination, strength, and balance) comprising two or more subtests is determined by calculating the mean scale score of its subtests. A composite mean scale score is derived by determining the mean scale score of all subtests administered.

The standardization sample consists of 744 Caucasian elementary school children (grades K–6) from only one school district in southern California. Approximately 106 children are included within each of the seven CA groups. While the absolute number of children included within the standardization sample is adequate,

the sample clearly was not drawn so as to represent children nationally.

Reliability estimates derived from a factor analysis for each of the seven CA groups and described in terms of common factor variance range from .44 to .88, with the median coefficients within the mid-.60s. Many if not most of these coefficients are too low to enable one accurately to determine placement, programmatic, and evaluation decisions for individual children. Test-retest reliability estimates and standard errors of measurement are not reported.

Evidence pertaining to the battery's validity also is provided by the factor analysis of the intercorrelations for each age group within the standardization sample. The five factors obtained were used as the basis for grouping the 12 subtests into the five major subtests. In general, the factors are quite consistent across the seven CA groups. The manual does identify subtests that do not maintain consistent associations with their factor across all CA groups. Inconsistencies in the factor loadings are most prominent within the older ages. The manual, however, does not suggest ways to alter the interpretations of data which are inconsistent with the test's factorial structure. The limited number of subtests included within the battery precludes the possibility of finding many separate factors. This limitation, recognized in the manual, probably could have been averted by including within the battery more subtests measuring fine motor coordination—skills which are particularly important for school-related behaviors during the elementary grades. Unfortunately, no criterion-related validity data are reported.

The manual emphasizes the importance of acquiring adequate information in order to develop a comprehensive remedial program geared to each child's individual pattern of abilities and disabilities; it does not provide evidence for using the FMSTB in this way. The reliability estimates generally are too low, the validity data are meager, and relationships between test results and developmental or remedial programs are unspecified. While the scale may be of limited use in making norm-referenced evaluations of children's gross sensory-motor skills, using the scale to initiate

Frostig Movement Skills Test Battery

diagnostic-intervention activities is not warranted.

Labeling the test "Experimental Edition" suggests the need for more complete research on the battery, with the author and publisher assuming responsibility for initiating research and for revising the manual. This apparently has not been done. Thus, the FMSTB should be limited to research purposes until more evidence is available to warrant its use in applied activities with children. Also, the publisher should be encouraged to remove statements from its catalog which state that the test "enables a teacher to pin-point any area of sensory-motor development requiring special attention," and "is useful for test-retest research." Inaccurate statements such as these unfortunately serve to provide support to those persons demanding "truth in testing" legislation.

CARL L. ROSEN, *Professor of Education and Director, Educational Child Study Center, Kent State University, Kent, Ohio.*[1]

This test is an "experimental" edition initiated in 1967. Although it was published in 1972, the reviewer, on his request for more information, was told that "the manual you have is still the latest edition." An experimental denotation does not exempt a published test from rigorous examination; such a denotation assumes continued experimentation, scrutiny, and refinement, which in this case seems required.

The manual provides a sparse section on the rationale, importance, and background of the test. Selective use of mostly nonempirical secondary sources as supportive references is misleading to potential users. Comments are made regarding the importance of "motor functions," "movement skills," and "movement education" to global constructs of behavior ("total development and learning, social and emotional development, estimation of self-worth" and "development of social skills"). No attention, however, is provided to the research literature regarding the contribution of motor abilities to the prediction of specific variables within these domains, and there is a latent form of circular reasoning implying that what is important to assess for the handicapped is also important for children in general.

[1] The technical assistance of Sonya Blixt, Associate Professor of Education and Director of the Bureau of Research and Services, College of Education, Kent State University is gratefully acknowledged.

While the movement skills of this test are adequately described, inadequate explicit attention is given to specific recommended uses, and there are no specifications of cautions for misuse nor suggestions as to qualifications for test users. The subtests themselves involve a range of motor tasks whose content and value to school "learning," for example, seem uncertain (bean-bag throwing at a target; flexing the spine, back muscles, and hamstring ligaments; leg strength in a standing broad jump, speed and agility in moving from standing to lying positions). "Factorial Validity" has been explored, yet real concern about what this test is valid for is not demonstrated by any studies of predictive or concurrent validity. Given no clear criteria for use of the test, validity is a relative matter.

The manual ends after a section on administration procedures with no comment whatsoever on interpretation and use of various individual and summary scaled scores derived from raw scores; no illustrations are provided of sample profiles; no suggestions are given for follow-up "situational" observations of pupils whose test performance is suspect; and no recommendations are available suggesting signs and indicators for special referrals or programs of remediation. An undated supplementary bulletin accompanying test equipment makes reference to the "Frostig Move-Grow-Learn" program for "use in conjunction with the materials in this kit," with no explicit tie-in to this test. Such assistance seems important to proper use of a published test such as this.

Given the special nature of the attributes being measured, the demanding nature of some of the tasks, the age range of subjects involved, and the limited samples of motor behaviors elicited (several tests involve 20 or 30 seconds for first tries; some provide no, or inadequate, attention to practice; a few measure performance based on best of several tries), the absence of special recommendations for scheduling, establishing rapport, managing, differentially observing, recording, and interpreting test performance is unfortunate.

While there are comments for the tester's reference to test procedures and photos for visualizing a subject's performance in various tasks, there are no standard directions for administering approximately 9 of the 13 subtests

Frostig Movement Skills Test Battery

(subtests 2, 3, 5, 7–12). One purpose of a standardized test is to obtain measurements that are comparable with measurements made with the norm groups. It is imperative to standardized test construction that directions be fixed in manuals of such tests, or variations in directions to subjects will result in wide inconsistency in administration and, hence, measurement. Collecting normative data is not profitable and scoring a test such as this is a useless task unless testing directions are standard.

The normative description is also inadequate. N's within age groups are suggestive of a restricted sample, and the representativeness of a norms group representing one community is questionable. The descriptive statistics show some inconsistencies in developmental changes by age (subtests 5, 10, 11b for males; 5, 10, 11a and b, 12 for females) and constricted dispersion of scores in some categories. Given questionable norming, the use of scaled scores seems to be of little value if not potentially misleading.

The information on reliability reflects these problems. In place of test-retest or interexaminer reliabilities, only subtest reliabilities, based upon communalities from the factor analysis, are available. The manual notes the "range" (.44 to .88) of communalities, commenting that "only 14" of the 91 are "less than .60." While reliability data based upon communalities are referred to in the manual as "minimum estimates," the particular analysis technique used is often inaccurate and may produce communalities considerably higher than the reliability estimates. Given that traditional standards for interpreting reliability consider coefficients of .80 or above as adequate, and communalities which probably represent inflated coefficients are presented, this interpretation of test reliability is questionable. Tabulations based on criteria of less than .70, for example, resulted in a count of approximately 56 of the 91 communalities to be unsatisfactory. Given this tabulation, the reliability of this test could be questioned for five of the seven age groups (6, 7, 9, 10 and 11). More than half of the communalities presented were below .70.

In brief, inadequacies make this test unacceptable in its present state. While there is danger of grave misuse of this test, there is need for acceptable standardized tests in this area.

Frostig Movement Skills Test Battery

The denotation of experimental edition calls for further experimentation.

[872]

Minnesota Percepto-Diagnostic Test (Revised). Ages 5–16; 1962–69; MPDT; brain damage and emotional disturbances; individual; Forms A ('62, 6 cards and protractor), B (same stimulus cards presented in reverse order, '69); revised manual ('69, 83 pages); profile ('69, 1 page) for children; profile ('62, 1 page) for adults; $4.50 per set of test cards; $3.50 per 50 profiles; $5 per manual; cash orders postpaid; (5–20) minutes; G. B. Fuller and J. T. Laird (test); Clinical Psychology Publishing Co., Inc. *

See T2:1485 (17 references) and P:457 (19 references); for reviews by Richard W. Coan and Eugene E. Levitt of the original edition, see 6:231 (2 references).

REFERENCES

1–2. See 6:231.
3–21. See P:457.
22–38. See T2:1485; also includes a cumulative name index to the first 38 references and 2 reviews for this test.
39. FISCHER, R., AND SCHEIB, J. "Creative Performance and the Hallucinogenic Drug-Induced Creative Experience or One Man's Brain-Damage Is Another's Creativity." *Confinia Psychiatrica* (Switzerland) 14(3–4):174–202 '71. * (PA 51:2599)
40. DUDLEY, HAROLD K., JR.; MASON, MARK; AND HUGHES, RONALD C. "The Extent of Drug Abuse Among Young State Hospital Patients." *Adolescence* 7(27):371–91 f '72. * (PA 50:1236)
41. FISCHER, ROLAND; FOX, RONALD; AND RALSTIN, MARY. "Creative Performance and the Hallucinogenic Drug-Induced Creative Experience." *J Psychedelic Drugs* 5(1):29–36 f '72. * (PA 51:8697)
42. GRAY, JOHN E., AND TREHERNE, A. DAVID. "Retest Reliability Performance of Children on the Minnesota Percepto-Diagnostic Test After 7 Years." *J Clin Psychol* 28(3):359–60 Jl '72. * (PA 51:2105)
43. LEVINE, MAUREEN, AND FULLER, GERALD. "Psychological, Neuropsychological, and Educational Correlates of Reading Deficit." *J Learn Dis* 5(9):563–71 N '72. * (PA 49:9983)
44. LEVINE, MAUREEN, AND FULLER, GERALD. "Sex Differences on Psychoeducational Tests With Three Classified Deficit Reading Groups." *Slow Learning Child* (Australia) 19(3):165–74 N '72. *
45. RYCKMAN, DAVID B.; RENTFROW, ROBERT; FARGO, GEORGE; AND McCARTIN, ROSEMARIE. "Reliabilities of Three Tests of Form-Copying." *Percept & Motor Skills* 34(3):917–8 Je '72. * (PA 48:11277)
46. CROOKES, T. G., AND COLEMAN, JEAN A. "The Minnesota Percepto-Diagnostic Test (MPD) in Adult Psychiatric Practice." *J Clin Psychol* 29(2):204–6 Ap '73. * (PA 51:9252)
47. FRIEDRICH, DOUGLAS, AND FULLER, GERALD B. "Visual-Motor Performance: Delineation of the 'Perceptual Deficit' Hypothesis." *J Clin Psychol* 29(2):207–9 Ap '73. * (PA 51:9445)
48. FULLER, GERALD B. "Three Categories of Visual-Motor Performance of Children With a Reading Disability and Their Theoretical Implications." *Psychol Sch* 10(1):19–23 Ja '73. * (PA 50:3758)
49. FULLER, GERALD, AND FRIEDRICH, DOUGLAS. "Predicting Potential School Problems." *Percept & Motor Skills* 37(2):453–4 O '73. * (PA 51:9917)
50. GEORGE, JANE. "Differentiating Clinical Groups by Means of the Minnesota Percepto-Diagnostic Test." *J Clin Psychol* 29(2):210–2 Ap '73. * (PA 51:9213)
51. LIN, YI-GUANG, AND RENNICK, PHILLIP M. "WAIS Correlates of the Minnesota Percepto-Diagnostic Test in a Sample of Epileptic Patients: Differential Patterns for Men and Women." *Percept & Motor Skills* 37(2):643–6 O '73. * (PA 51:9508)
52. FRIEDRICH, DOUGLAS, AND FULLER, GERALD B. "Visual-Motor Performance: Additional Delineation of the 'Perceptual Deficit' Hypothesis." *J Clin Psychol* 30(1):30–3 Ja '74. * (PA 52:3360)
53. FULLER, GERALD, AND FRIEDRICH, DOUGLAS. "A Diagnostic Approach to Differentiate Brain-Damaged From Non-Brain-Damaged Adolescents." *J Clin Psychol* 30(3):361–3 Jl '74. * (PA 56:4321)
54. FULLER, GERALD B., AND FRIEDRICH, DOUGLAS. "Three Diagnostic Patterns of Reading Disabilities." *Acad Ther* 10(2):219–31 w '74–75 ['74]. * (PA 54:8439)
55. HOLLAND, TERRILL R., AND WADSWORTH, HELEN M. "Incidence Versus Degrees of Rotation on the Minnesota Percepto-

Diagnostic Test in Brain-Damaged and Schizophrenic Patients."
Percept & Motor Skills 38(1):131–4 F '74. * (PA 52:7799)
56. LASCH, LYNN D.; HOLLAND, JEAN; AND LASCH, RONALD
W. "A New Group Administration Procedure for the Minnesota
Percepto-Diagnostic Test." Psychol Sch 11(4):403–7 O '74. *
(PA 54:1985)
57. PODIETZ, LENORE. Perceptual Behavior as Reflected in the
Minnesota Percepto-Diagnostic Test and a Shift in Body Pos-
ture. Doctor's thesis, Temple University (Philadelphia, Pa.),
1974. (DAI 35:3032B)
58. HOLLAND, TERRILL R.; WADSWORTH, HELEN M.; AND
ROYER, FRED L. "The Performance of Brain-Damaged and
Schizophrenic Patients on the Minnesota Percepto-Diagnostic
Test Under Standard and BIP Conditions of Administration."
J Clin Psychol 31(1):21–5 Ja '75. * (PA 56:4151)
59. KILPATRICK, DEAN G.; MILLER, WILLIAM C.; ALLAIN,
ALBERT N.; HUGGINS, MARY B.; AND LEE, WILLIAM H. "The
Use of Psychological Test Data to Predict Open-Heart Surgery
Outcome: A Prospective Study." Psychosom Med 37(1):62–73
Ja–F '75. * (PA 54:3853)
60. WALLBROWN, JANE D.; WALLBROWN, FRED H.; AND EN-
GIN, ANN W. "The Validity of Two Clinical Tests of Visual-
Motor Perception." J Clin Psychol 33(2):491–5 Ap '77. *

[873]

The Primary Visual Motor Test. Ages 4–8; 1964–
70; PVMT; individual; 1 form ('70, 16 geometric
designs to be copied by examinee); manual ('70, 184
pages); scoring form ('70, 4 pages); $4 per set of
test cards; $8.50 per 50 scoring forms; $4.75 per 100
test sheets; $16 per manual; cash orders postpaid;
(10–20) minutes; Mary R. Haworth; Grune &
Stratton, Inc. *

For a review by Dale B. Harris, and an excerpted
review by A. Barclay, see 7:873 (1 reference).

REFERENCES

1. See 7:873.
2. SHERIDAN, MARY D. "Review of the Primary Visual Motor Test." Develop Med & Child Neurol (England) 13(6):
820–1 D '71. *
3. ALLEMAN, SARAH A. "Review of the Primary Visual Motor Test." J Pers Assess 36(1):80–1 F '72. *
4. GREENBERG, JANEY BERSON. Differential Prediction of Reading Ability at the First Grade Level. Doctor's thesis, University
of Pennsylvania (Philadelphia, Pa.), 1972. (DAI 33:3304B)
5. HAWORTH, MARY R. "Relationships Between the Primary
Visual Motor Test, S-B Vocabulary Subtest and Mental Age."
J Clin Psychol 30(3):326–30 Jl '74. * (PA 56:4965)
6. RANCK, SHIRLEY ANN. A Factor Analysis of Five Perceptual Motor Tests of First Grade Children. Doctor's thesis,
Fordham University (New York, N.Y.), 1976. (DAI 37:983B)

Develop Med & Child Neurol (England)
13(6):820–1 D '71. Mary D. Sheridan. * The
author firmly states that the test is a clinical
instrument and should only be administered by
properly trained persons. The warning is wise
and necessary. Like many other clinical tools
which at first sight appear deceptively simple,
it undoubtedly requires considerable experience in application and, even more important, in
correct interpretation. In the hands of amateur
examiners, however well-intentioned, the test
results would probably be invalid and possibly
dangerous if decisions regarding educational or
institutional placement were involved. On the
evidence presented, the P.V.M. test, properly
administered and interpreted, appears to offer a
valuable addition to the test-batteries at present
in use for the detection of visual-motor disorders
in young children between 4 and 7 years,
especially as it also seems to provide signposts
for therapy. The book is well produced and

excellently illustrated. There is a useful reference list and index. It should be carefully
studied by professional workers in child psychology, child psychiatry and developmental
paediatrics. *

J Pers Assess 36(1):80–1 F '72. Sarah A.
Alleman. The PVM is a drawing task, similar
to the Bender-Gestalt, whose purpose is the
evaluation of visual motor development in
children 4–8 years of age. Sixteen drawings
are presented to the subject to be copied. Several of these are geometric designs, and some
are simple representations of familiar objects
such as a tree, house, arrow, and face. A recording blank and scoring sheet are provided, and
each drawing is scored on as many as 14
criteria. Normative tables are given for normal
children by chronological age, and retarded
children by mental age. Separate tables are
given for trainable (I.Q. 30–49) and educable
(I.Q. 50–79) retarded children. It is not intended as a test of intelligence, but rather as a
test of visual motor development. The PVM has
been shown to be a reliable test, and the manual
presents the scoring criteria clearly enough to
ensure a high degree of interjudge agreement.
Scoring reliabilities as high as .98 are reported,
and no lower than .82. Test-re-test reliability is
also high, when the test sessions were 2 months
apart. Since some "gain" in skill is to be expected, the obtained correlation is more than
adequate. The mean PVM scores "show a
definite and consistent improvement with increasing age," and thus seem to possess satisfactory validity. Other validity studies with this
and similar tests are reported in the manual.
The greatest deficiency as the PVM now stands
—and one which is freely acknowledged by the
author—is the lack of experimental data on
various clinical groups. The manual contains
brief descriptions of the kinds of test performance shown by children suffering from diseases
of the central nervous system, traumatic head
injuries, PKU, deafness, language disorders,
learning disabilities, and childhood psychosis.
Many of the findings are tentative, anecdotal, or
based on a small number of Ss. In view of the
available data, however incomplete, the test
shows considerable promise. There can be question of the need for means of identifying children with visual motor problems in a preschool
setting.

Primary Visual Motor Test

[874]

The Purdue Perceptual-Motor Survey. Ages 6–10; 1966; PPMS; to identify those children lacking perceptual-motor abilities necessary for acquiring academic success; 22 scores: balance and posture (walking board [3 scores], jumping), body image and differentiation (identification of body parts, imitation of movements, obstacle course, Krauss-Weber, angels in the snow), perceptual-motor match (chalkboard [4 scores], rhythmic writing [3 scores]), ocular control (4 scores), form perception (2 scores); individual; 1 form; manual (87 pages); record form (11 pages); $7.95 per manual and set of cards; $4.95 per 25 record forms; postage extra; some testing materials must be assembled locally; administration time not reported; Eugene G. Roach and Newell C. Kephart; Charles E. Merrill Publishing Co. *

See T2:1883 (9 references); for reviews by Colleen B. Jamison and Daniel Landis, see 7:874 (25 references).

REFERENCES

1–25. See 7:874.
26–34. See T2:1883; also includes a cumulative name index to the first 34 references and 2 reviews for this test.
35. EASON, JULIA ELLEN. *The Comparison of the Effects of Two Programs of Physical Activity on Perceptual-Motor Development and Primary Mental Abilities of Pre-School Aged Children.* Doctor's thesis, George Peabody College for Teachers (Nashville, Tenn.), 1972. (*DAI* 33:2147A)
36. ELROD, JOE MARLAN. *The Effects of Perceptual-Motor Training and Music on Perceptual-Motor Development and Behavior of Educable Mentally Retarded Children.* Doctor's thesis, Louisiana State University (Baton Rouge, La.), 1972. (*DAI* 33:2148A)
37. FISHER, MAURICE D., AND TURNER, ROBERT V. "The Effects of a Perceptual-Motor Training Program Upon the Academic Readiness of Culturally Disadvantaged Kindergarten Children." *J Negro Ed* 41(2):142–50 sp '72. * (*PA* 49:5390)
38. GEDDES, DOLORES. "Factor Analytic Study of Perceptual-Motor Attributes as Measured by Two Test Batteries." *Percept & Motor Skills* 34(1):227–30 F '72. * (*PA* 48:6892)
39. HAMMOND, RUTH KARTCHNER. *A Predictive Study of Mathematical Readiness and Achievement: A Longitudinal Study From First Grade Entrance Through Third Grade.* Doctor's thesis, Purdue University (Lafayette, Ind.), 1972. (*DAI* 33:637A)
40. HANNUM, MICHAEL CLAYTON. *Validation Study: Perceptual-Motor Behavior Screening Checklist (Experimental Model).* Doctor's thesis, University of Northern Colorado (Greeley, Colo.), 1972. (*DAI* 33:3437A)
41. KESKINER, A.; MULLGARDT, M.; AND FRANZEL, G. A. "Perceptual-Motor Dysfunction and Schizophrenic Behavior." *World J Psychosynthesis* 4(6):34–8 Je '72. *
42. LIETZ, ENNO S. "Perceptual-Motor Abilities of Disadvantaged and Advantaged Kindergarten Children." *Percept & Motor Skills* 35(3):887–90 D '72. * (*PA* 49:10334)
43. NEEMAN, RENATE L. "Perceptual-Motor Attributes of Normal School Children: A Factor Analytic Study." *Percept & Motor Skills* 34(2):471–4 Ap '72. * (*PA* 49:10348)
44. NEEMAN, RENATE L. "'A Review of an Occupational Therapist's Research on Perceptual-Motor Attributes of Mental Retardates': Can Perceptual-Motor Theory be Experimentally Proved." *Austral Occup Ther J* 19(1):35–40 Ja–F '72. * (*PA* 49:4804)
45. THOMPSON, MERITA LEE. *Relationships Between Perceptual-Motor Development and Reading Achievement of Third Grade Students.* Doctor's thesis, University of Alabama (University, Ala.), 1972. (*DAI* 33:5541A)
46. BARKER, MARIE ESMAN. *The Purdue Perceptual-Motor Survey: The Spanish Edition, Development and Standardization.* Doctor's thesis, New Mexico State University (University Park, N.M.), 1973. (*DAI* 34:5614A)
47. RIDER, BARBARA A. "Perceptual-Motor Dysfunction in Emotionally Disturbed Children." *Am J Occup Ther* 27(6):316–20 S '73. * (*PA* 51:7314)
48. SCHOENFELDT, BARBARA BARLIANT. *The Perceptual-Motor Survey as a Reading Clinic Diagnostic Tool.* Doctor's thesis, University of Georgia (Athens, Ga.), 1973. (*DAI* 34:7112A)
49. AYERS, JERRY B.; ROHR, MICHAEL E.; AND AYERS, MARY N. "Perceptual-Motor Skills, Ability to Conserve, and School Readiness." *Percept & Motor Skills* 38(2):491–4 Ap '74. * (*PA* 53:842)
50. EATON, IRA E. *The Relationship Between Perceptual-Motor Ability and Reading Success.* Doctor's thesis, St. Louis University (St. Louis, Mo.), 1975. (*DAI* 36:3562A)
51. LEVENSPIEL, MARY JOSEPHINE. *A Study of the Relationships Between Selected Perceptual-Motor Behaviors and:*

Achievement in Reading; Achievement in Mathematics; Classroom Behavior; Academic Self-Concept; and Academic Motivation for First and Third Grade Boys and Girls. Doctor's thesis, Oregon State University (Corvallis, Ore.), 1975. (*DAI* 36:818A)
52. PUETZ, WILLIAM J., JR. *A Comparison of Perceptual-Motor Ability Programs on Reading Ability of Second Grade Students.* Master's thesis, Kansas State College (Pittsburg, Kan.), 1975.
53. CROSBIE, RONALD LEWIS. *The Effect of an Individualized Developmental Motor Activity Program on the Perceptual-Motor Performance and IQ Scores of Selected Trainable Mentally Retarded Children.* Doctor's thesis, West Virginia University (Morgantown, W.Va.), 1976. (*DAI* 37:2054A)
54. SHICK, JACQUELINE, AND PLACK, JERALYN J. "Kephart's Perceptual Motor Training Program." *J Phys Ed & Rec* 47(6):58–9 Je '76. *
55. TUCKER, RUTH ELAINE. *The Relationship Between Perceptual-Motor Development and Academic Achievement.* Doctor's thesis, University of Alabama (University, Ala.), 1976. (*DAI* 37:7536A)

[875]

Southern California Sensory Integration Tests. Ages 4–10 with learning problems; 1962–72; SCSIT; a battery of tests consisting of *The Ayres Space Test* (SV), *Southern California Figure-Ground Visual Perception Test* (FG), *Southern California Kinesthesia and Tactile Perception Tests* (KIN, MFP, FI, GRA, LTS, DTS), *Southern California Perceptual-Motor Tests* (MAC, IP, CML, BMC, RLD, SBO, SBC), and two new tests: design copying (DC), position in space (PS); 17 scores: space visualization (SV), figure-ground perception (FG), kinesthesia (KIN), manual form perception (MFP), finger identification (FI), graphesthesia (GRA), localization of tactile stimuli (LTS), double tactile stimuli perception (DTS), motor accuracy (MAC), imitation of postures (IP), crossing midline of body (CML), bilateral motor coordination (BMC), right-left discrimination (RLD), standing balance with eyes open (SBO), standing balance with eyes closed (SBC), design copying (DC), position in space (PS); no data on validity in battery manual; no norms for ages 9–10 except for space visualization, figure-ground perception, position in space, and design copying; individual; 1 form; manual ('72, 75 pages plus record booklet); record booklet ('72, 6 pages); design copying test ('72, 2 pages); motor accuracy test ('72, 4 pages); profile ('72, 1 page); $98.50 per kit of testing materials including 25 sets of record booklets, design copying tests, motor accuracy tests, and profiles, and manual; $7.50 per 25 record booklets; $9.50 per 100 design copying tests or profiles; $6.50 per 25 motor accuracy tests; $8.50 per manual; 8% extra for postage and handling; (75–90) minutes; A. Jean Ayres; Western Psychological Services. *

See T2:1887 (18 references). For reviews of *The Ayres Space Test,* see 6:63 (2 reviews); *Southern California Figure-Ground Visual Perception Tests,* see 7:876 (1 review); *Southern California Kinesthesia and Tactile Perception Tests,* see 7:877 (1 review); *Southern California Motor Accuracy Test,* see 7:878 (1 review, 1 excerpt); *Southern California Perceptual-Motor Tests,* see 7:879 (1 review, 1 excerpt).

REFERENCES

1–18. See T2:1887.
19. RIDER, BARBARA A. "Perceptual-Motor Dysfunction in Emotionally Disturbed Children." *Am J Occup Ther* 27(6):316–20 S '73. * (*PA* 51:7314)
20. JOHNSON, DANESSA WISE. *Neural Basis for Reading: The Relationship of Sensorimotor Integration to Reading Achievement in Third Grade Youngsters.* Doctor's thesis, Temple University (Philadelphia, Pa.), 1974. (*DAI* 35:1531A)
21. McCRACKEN, ALICE. "Tactile Function of Educable Mentally Retarded Children." *Am J Occup Ther* 29(7):397–402 Ag '75. * (*PA* 54:12089)
22. SILBERZAHN, MARY. "Sensory Integrative Function in a Child Guidance Clinic Population." *Am J Occup Ther* 29(1):28–34 Ja '75. * (*PA* 53:11932)

23. SEARS, CAROL JOYCE. *A Study to Determine Relationships Existing Between Sensory Integration Syndromes and Psycholinguistic Abilities in Children With Learning Disabilities.* Doctor's thesis, American University (Washington, D.C.), 1976. (*DAI* 37:7079A)

HOMER B. C. REED, JR., *Associate Professor of Pediatrics (Psychology), Tufts University School of Medicine, Boston, Massachusetts.*

This battery of 17 tests has been designed to elucidate the dysfunction in underlying neural systems that is thought to accompany the perceptual and learning problems presented by children of late preschool and school age.

It is useful, in attempting to evaluate SCSIT, to consider the frame of reference within which the measures have been developed. The author's professional identification is with occupational therapy, and her tests reflect the clinical observations and activities of years of work with handicapped children. The descriptive phrases that come most readily to mind when one views the test materials are "sensory-perceptual" and "perceptual-motor." There is an immediate "goodness of fit" between such phrases and the names of the individual subtests (design copying, figure-ground perception, kinesthesia, imitation of postures, right-left discrimination, etc.). The names of the subtests reflect their content and simultaneously describe a litany of diagnostic and therapeutic activities in which occupational therapists traditionally interact with children who present neurological and musculoskeletal handicaps. The orientation of the diagnostic and therapeutic activities is explicitly biological in character. The children to whom the activities are applied typically have biologically based disorders of growth and development, and the charge given to the occupational therapist is that of exploring and ameliorating the sensory-perceptual-motor deficits that the patient presents. The diagnostic and therapeutic activities of occupational therapy have been adopted and applied, albeit frequently in an uncritical manner, by personnel in special education. The author herself has been active in this movement, writing and publishing research designed to interest both audiences and designed also to further the development of a common conceptual framework.

It is difficult, then, in reviewing SCSIT, to know whether to evaluate the battery of tests as a possible contribution to occupational therapy or whether instead to adopt a special education frame of reference and to examine its possible usefulness in that field. The author's intent for her test should presumably be the key to this question and should be apparent from examining the criterion information supplied by the test manual. This line of reasoning results quickly in the major evaluative conclusion that the reviewer has formed regarding SCSIT. It is not possible, on the basis of presently available information, to assess the validity of the test battery. This conclusion applies whether one looks for neurological confirmation of test performances or whether one looks instead for relationships between SCSIT performances and measures of educational aptitudes or achievement. It is possible to answer questions regarding reliability of test scores, and it is certainly possible to speculate on how one might use the information generated by the test battery; but traditional indices of relationships between the battery and either neurological or educational criteria are virtually impossible to locate.

It is reasonable to ask if an entire battery of tests can indeed be published with everyone overlooking the niggling question of whether or not the battery is good for anything. The answer is, "Probably not," but some knowledge of how this particular battery of tests evolved is helpful. The test manual states, "SCSIT and their theoretical foundations have been in the process of evolving through clinical application and research over several decades." The reader is referred to a series of seven factor analytic studies that has formed the basis for the theoretical model for SCSIT, and the reviewer located the four (*3–5, 11*) of these seven studies that have appeared in standard professional journals. These four studies are of questionable merit, having in common the fault of applying too many tests to too few subjects. Certainly, it is true that such studies can provide only the most vulnerable kind of theoretical foundation for a battery of tests. In fact, the explanation for this battery of tests is probably to be found more in unpublished clinical work than in published research. Even if one has only very limited interaction with occupational therapists throughout the country, one encounters the author's tests and this phenomenon has been true for the past decade. There is a priesthood of believers toiling in the bowels of nearly all large hospitals, publishing little or nothing but working mightily. Individually and collectively, the members of this group share a frame of reference in child development and developmental neurology that makes these tests attractive and useful. For such a group, the absence of experimentally and statistically sound validational studies may well be of little importance. However, potential users of SCSIT (e.g., special education personnel) who do not have the sophistication bestowed both by medical training and relevant clinical experience would be well advised to save their money.

ALIDA S. WESTMAN, *Associate Professor of Psychology, Eastern Michigan University, Ypsilanti, Michigan.*

This battery is designed to help diagnose children's dysfunctions in very basic areas: form and space perception, postural and bilateral integration, tactile perception, and motor skills. At this point, however, the diagnostic procedure provided is sufficiently incomplete that administration and interpretation should be done only by persons experienced with dysfunctions in children and this battery used only to help structure the interview(s) and evaluation. Weaknesses show in the normative, validity, and reliability data, and in the tests themselves. These will be discussed in turn.

The norm groups were variable in size but all were very small, e.g., 30 children per age group. Backgrounds are unspecified, but it is unlikely that any group adequately represented the "geographic and socioeconomic levels of metropolitan Los Angeles and surrounding areas." Since the norm groups together are said to do so, different norms probably represent different populations, possibly calculated as individual tests were constructed. Hence, the norms are of questionable value.

In addition, standard scores are presented, but how these were calculated is not always clear. An unknown number were obtained by an unspecified method of extrapolation from data. In addition, to "correct sampling error," interpolated "adjusted" means and standard deviations are reported in addition to the values obtained from the data; these "adjusted" values differ at times substantially from the data values. Hence, the tester should exercise extreme caution when using standard scores.

Furthermore, absence of norms by sex and of data on groups with recognized dysfunctions

places heavy reliance upon looking at all data about the child and upon personal intuition. For each age group by test, sex differences were evaluated by using the t test; hence it is unclear without crossvalidation which of the differences are reliable.

Validity data are virtually nonexistent. Most helpful are four sample profiles of children who have particular problems. Factor analyses yielded clusters which are listed in the manual, but these clusters have not been well tested against independent measurements.

Reliability, except for one test, was measured by test-retest with an unknown period between tests and is reported for all 4-year-olds, 5-year-olds, etc. The results are extremely variable; correlations range from .01 to .89. Therefore, any test user should check the reliabilities of each test used for age related vs. random variability and check the standard error of measurement before crediting a score with significance. Many scores are too unreliable to use. Motor Accuracy's reliability was not by test-retest but by internal consistency and was good; r values range from .67 to .94.

The testing procedure is generally but not always clear. In particular, the testee usually is not told when performance is timed and is then penalized for time taken. Behavior of impulsive children is sometimes mentioned but other types of behaviors are not.

All tests are reasonably brief. When there is a difference in difficulty of items, difficulty generally increases gradually. However, not all tests are equally good for children 4 to 8 years of age; some are too hard for the younger ones and some too easy for the older children.

The first three tests are visual tests and do not require motor skills. SV, Ayres Space, consists of indicating which form fits a form board. The criterion of final choice has been clarified. This test is fun, but there is a ceiling effect for older children. On the other hand, FG, Figure-ground, and PS, Position in Space, are very problematic for younger children. FG consists of pointing out superimposed or imbedded figures, whereas PS requires the child to point out the same form(s) in a different orientation.

The latter test and Design Copying are new additions to the battery. PS seems valid, since the drawings represent objects, rather than letters whose orientation would be critical, e.g.,

Southern California Sensory Integration Tests

p≠b. For PS instructions, possible vocabulary problems are pointed out. Feedback and learning take place during the test. However, Part 2 poses two problems. Scoring depends primarily on time taken, yet use of a shield to expose one choice at a time is recommended. Second, it is unclear which response is scored if the child changes an answer.

Design Copying demands motor skill; it consists of connecting increasingly more dots. Since only straight lines are used, this test has little applicability to writing or reading. Measurement is of the least accurate line drawn and scoring by ruler is difficult. The tester may wish to make plastic overlays for the different deviations from straightness permitted for children of different ages. This test does not discriminate among 4-year-olds and is reported to be invalidated through experience.

The other tests are concerned with motor, kinesthetic, or postural factors, and tactile defense. These tests have been reviewed before—as have SV and FG. Let me add briefly that the child taking Manual Form Perception, Finger Identification, and Graphesthesia always is presented the stimulus without being able to see, but tested with vision. In Localization of Tactile Stimuli the child is tested with vision still impossible. Adding this condition to the other three tests would help determine the effect of sensory integration compared to the child's sensitivity to touch by itself. In addition, the reason for testing manual form perception with flat, smooth, geometrical shapes is unclear. Three-dimensional objects of approximately equal size and with surface texture controlled would seem more useful.

In summary, these tests are a helpful clinical tool. Basic areas rarely included elsewhere, e.g., kinesthesia and tactile perception, are included. A disadvantage is that the tester must become an expert on all behaviors measured and on the battery itself in order to use it safely. Specifically, testing procedures are not always completely outlined and the normative, validity, and reliability data are weak. As a result, heavy reliance must be placed upon looking at all of the data about a child and upon personal intuition.

[876]

*Spatial Orientation Memory Test. Ages 5-9; 1971-75; SOMT; individual; Forms 1, 2, ('71, 45 pages); manual ('75, 8 pages); score sheet ('71, 2 pages, reprinted with 1975 copyright); $20 per set of testing materials including 50 score sheets; $5 per 50 score sheets; postpaid; specimen set not available; [5-7] minutes; Joseph M. Wepman and Dainis Turaids; Language Research Associates, Inc. *

JOHN J. GEYER, *Associate Professor of Education and Psychology, Rutgers, The State University of New Jersey, New Brunswick, New Jersey.*

This test is one of a large and growing number of tests competing for the attention of those employing the specific learning disability approach to the teaching of reading. The test is designed to "assess the development of a child's ability to retain and recall the orientation (direction) of visually presented forms." This skill is asserted to be important to "individual letter discrimination recall; the sequential ordering of letters in words; the ease of learning that print in English always proceeds from left to right," and the establishment of right-left dominance.

The test consists of 20 designs and an equal number of arrays of four or five of the same designs in different orientations. The test is administered individually by presenting each design for five seconds and then asking the child to point to the same design (on a separate card) which is "turned exactly in the same direction." Scores, the number correct, may be converted to five ratings ranging from −2 (below level of threshold adequacy) to +2 (indicates very good development). The five grades represent a percentage distribution of 15–20–30–20–15 in an unspecified sample. The reason for the choice of the 15th percentile as the minimum "adequately threshold" is not explained. Scores are not corrected for chance, and minimum "adequate" levels at the lower ages are at chance levels and below.

Standardization data reported consist of a few hundred "unselected" cases distributed across ages 5 through 10. Reliabilities are reported for ages 5 through 8 only, and validity rests on two reported correlations with a reading readiness test (.42, age 6 only) and the reading test of an achievement battery (.51, age 7 only). These data seem irrelevant to support the validity of a spatial orientation memory test. K-R 20 reliabilities (mysteriously labeled "Form I vs. Form II") within age groups range from .60 to .74, with median .62. These reliabilities are very low, and far too low for the individual diagnosis recommended.

The major problem with this test is the issue of validity. The correlations with the two reading measures are of unimpressive magnitude; furthermore, even substantial correlations with reading measures would not validate this test. The authors suggests that certain reading problems are caused by an impairment of an "important perceptual factor" called spatial orientation memory. This suggestion is neither documented nor intuitively obvious. Until the authors can make a better case that the *Spatial Orientation Memory Test* measures something worth measuring, there seems to be little purpose in using it.

[877]

A Standardized Road-Map Test of Direction Sense. Ages 7–18; 1965; right-left directional orientation; no data on reliability; individual; 1 form (2 pages, reprinted with 1976 copyright); manual (32 pages, reprinted with 1976 copyright); $3 per 50 tests; $1 per scoring stencil; $5 per manual; postage extra; [10–15] minutes; John Money; Academic Therapy Publications. *

For a review by James C. Reed and excerpted reviews by C. H. Ammons and Joseph L. French, see 7:880 (6 references).

REFERENCES

1–6. See 7:880.
7. SABATINO, DAVID A., AND BECKER, JOHN T. "Relationship Between Lateral Preference and Selected Behavioral Variables for Children Failing Academically." *Child Develop* 42(6): 2055–60 D '71. * (PA 48:9861)
8. KRICHEV, ALAN. "Review of the Standardized Road-Map Test of Direction Sense." *Psychol Sch* 14(2):247–8 Ap '77. *

Psychol Sch 14(2):247–8 Ap '77. Alan Krichev. * There is no indication of reliability or validity. The author anticipates that reliability would be quite high for individuals who have developed directional-sense skills; however, this might not be true for those individuals who had not yet fully developed this sense. From an examination of the material presented in the manual, I would have to question the value of using this test with anyone under the age of 10. I suspect you would find out just as much by asking the child to show right and left on himself and on others. Money feels that it would certainly be of value in a neuropsychological assessment. That may be so for children older than age 10; however, I am not yet prepared to categorically agree with him. In the absence of validity studies, the question certainly must be raised as to whether there is a need for standardized tests of this sort. What might have been helpful in a test of a patient

Spatial Orientation Memory Test

with Turner's Syndrome may not necessarily be of value to the average school psychologist.

[878]

Symbol Digit Modalities Test. Ages 8 and over; 1973; SDMT; "early screening of apparently normal children and adults for possible covert manual motor, visual, learning and/or other cerebral defects"; no data on reliability; 1 form (2 pages); manual (10 pages plus test); $12.50 per kit of 100 tests, scoring stencil, and manual; $8.50 per 100 tests; $2.50 per manual; 8% extra for postage and handling; 1.5(10) minutes; Aaron Smith; Western Psychological Services. *

See T2:1889 (4 references).

BRAD S. CHISSOM, *Associate Professor of Educational Psychology, Texas A&M University, College Station, Texas.*

This test of brain damage in children is more of a screening device than a diagnostic instrument, as the manual implies. The test is a coding task. After responding to 10 practice items, the subject is given 90 seconds in which to respond to a full page of similar items. The SDMT contains 110 items, a number sufficient to preclude the completion of all items within the time limit.

A unique feature is the oral version in which the subject responds orally and the examiner records the responses. No experience is required to administer or score the test.

According to the manual, "If both written and oral retest scores are more than one standard deviation below the age-sex norms, *the child should be referred for more detailed neuropsychologic studies, and especially examinations of visual acuity.*" No information is presented in support of this cutoff score.

The author presents no data on reliability, although he does refer to a comparison of mean scores on tests administered 20 to 37 months apart as "reliability data"!

Validity information is somewhat more acceptable, even though the information presented is based on personal communications with the author, thus making them inaccessible to the test user. Several tables are presented that show low mean scores for groups of subjects ranging from mental retardates to diagnosed schizophrenics. Construct validity of the SMDT has been successfully documented with a body of theoretical and empirical evidence. However, there is not sufficient specific validity information to indicate how successful the SMDT is as a screening instrument for brain-damaged subjects. The percentage of correct and incorrect identifications through the use of the test is vital evidence necessary to establish its validity. No evidence of this sort is presented.

In summary, it appears that the SDMT may possess the potentials of a good screening instrument. It is short, easy to administer, inexpensive, and easy to score. Norms currently offered are not adequate for widespread usage geographically. Additional normative information is, for example, necessary for minority group subjects; this weakness is mentioned in the manual. More reliability and validity information must be provided before the SDMT can be considered an adequate screening device. At present, the SDMT should probably not be considered for use either as a screening instrument or for research purposes.

JAMES C. REED, *Associate Professor of Pediatrics, Tufts University School of Medicine, Boston, Massachusetts.*

The *Symbol Digit Modalities Test* is similar to the Wechsler digit symbol tests except that numbers are substituted for symbols rather than symbols being substituted for numbers. Consequently, the test can be administered in either written or oral form. The directions for the test are clear, precise, and easy to follow. The test is easy to score.

The purpose of the SDMT is to provide a screening instrument for detecting patients, children as well as adults, who have disease, damage, or dysfunction implicating the cerebral hemispheres. The author also suggests that the test can be used to detect learning disabilities, to predict reading disabilities, as a diagnostic aid in an individual with a suspected brain lesion, or to measure the speed and accuracy with which bilingual subjects can think in different languages.

The rationale of the SDMT is based on the literature of clinical neuropsychology. The perception of numbers, verbal symbols, and nonverbal visual designs involves different cerebral hemispheric mechanisms. In general, the left cerebral hemisphere (at least in adults) is dominant for language functions, and lesions of the right cerebral hemispheres result in disturbances of visuoperceptual and spatial constructional functions. Digit substitution tests, of which the SDMT is one version, are believed to tap many different cerebral mechanisms involving both cerebral hemispheres. Consequently, it is "not surprising that 'brain damaged' (sic) children and adults will show reduced efficiency in one or more of the chains of cerebral mechanisms resulting in impaired SDMT written and oral performance."

I do not question the rationale for this test. The author is forthright in stating that poor oral or written scores *alone* should not be considered diagnostically definitive; he is appropriately cautious about how the test should be interpreted. I do have reservations about the technical merits of the SDMT.

The standardization and normative data were obtained from 3,680 children in 15 different schools, grades 3–12, ages 8–17, in the Omaha public schools. The sample is restricted geographically, and restriction in geographic representativeness, while a realistic fact of life because of the economic problems of data collection, is, nevertheless, still a limitation. Means and standard deviations are presented by sex for each group for both written and oral presentations. Gains for test-retest practice effects are also given. Means and standard deviations (written form) are also provided for small samples (8 to 21) of New York City public school children and for University of Michigan graduate and undergraduate students. However, no reliability coefficients are given.

The value of the validity data is questionable. Mean scores are presented for various diagnostic groups—mentally retarded, brain-damaged, stroke patients, traumatic aphasics, split-brain patients, and patients with various language disorders. These mean scores are compared with similar values from normals equated for age and sex, or with digit symbol scores. From these data, one can infer that organic groups may, indeed, score lower than comparable normals, or that cerebral disease will result in a lowered SDMT score. However, on the basis of these data, it is not possible to evaluate the number of false positives or false negatives. The hit rates are not given. What is the significance of a low score on the SDMT even in the absence of motor impairment and in the presence of an IQ value within the normal range or higher? Possibilities are suggested, but the data are not presented.

As a practicing neuropsychologist, I have a

Symbol Digit Modalities Test

bias against screening tests for cerebral dysfunction. I do not see the value of administering tests to a large number of persons to detect possible cerebral dysfunction, especially if such dysfunction is static in course. If an individual has a clinical complaint, screening tests do not give the etiology. Much more comprehensive tests have to be employed, regardless of the findings on a screening test. If there are no clinical complaints, why bother? For those who have a different bias, the SDMT is probably as useful as, if not more useful than, most screening tests for cerebral dysfunction on the market.

MOTOR

[879]

Motor Problems Inventory. Preschool through grade 5; 1972; MPI; individual; 1 form (2 pages); manual (7 pages plus test); $9.50 per kit of 100 tests and manual; $8.50 per 100 tests; $2.50 per manual; 8% extra for postage and handling; (5–10) minutes; Glyndon D. Riley; Western Psychological Services. *

BRAD S. CHISSOM, *Associate Professor of Educational Psychology, Texas A&M University, College Station, Texas.*

This inventory consists of 15 motor items divided into four categories listed as small muscle coordination, laterality, gross motor coordination, and general observations. The items are scored, with a marked degree of subjectivity, on a three-point scale ranging from 0, indicating no problem, to 2, indicating that the subject exhibited much of a problem in the performance of the task required by the item. The MPI is administered to subjects on an individual basis by an examiner who needs at least some experience or training in the use of the MPI.

The items were selected on a rational basis according to three criteria: simple enough for general use, abnormal responses need to be readily observable, and part of a traditional examining procedure. Traditional procedures used in speech and language pathology, psychological examinations, and neurological examinations provided the background for the selection.

No special equipment is necessary to administer the MPI, but a room designated as a testing area is desirable. Administration time is approximately 10 minutes per child depending upon the age of the child and other pertinent

factors. A response sheet for the examiner lists the items and provides a blank to record observations. All item scores are summed for a total score and this total score is compared to a norm based on the results obtained from the administration of the inventory to groups of normal children.

Norms—consisting of the categories "normal range," "significant problem," and "severe problem"—are presented for each of grades P, K, 1, 3, and 5, based on 30 to 60 children per grade. No descriptive information is provided for the norm sample making it of indeterminant origin. In addition to the inadequate norm sample size and lack of descriptive information, norms are not provided directly for grades 2 and 4; for these grades, the norms are interpolated.

A test-retest reliability of .77 is reported for a clinic population of 24 children from 5–11 years of age. Comparison of the responses of 15 trained clinicians to the videotaped responses of five children yielded an interscorer reliability of .91. No age levels or descriptive data are indicated about the children rated and no information is given about the clinicians. These reliability data are inadequate, and more information should be reported.

Face validity is a positive feature of this inventory since the items are based on traditional examining procedures from the three areas listed earlier in this review. The items were selected by a rational process, but all of the items have theoretical and empirical bases. There is no rationale or empirical evidence indicating the reasons the four areas were selected or the reasons for weighting the areas in which three items represent the areas of laterality and gross motor coordination and five items determine the area labeled general observations.

Two research studies relating to validity are described in the manual. Neither of these studies is referenced to enable the test user to make a more complete examination of the data. A factor analysis study provides some justification for the inclusion of the items in the inventory, while the second study compares the MPI to a human figure drawing test yielding a contingency coefficient of .74. The manual provides no additional empirical evidence concerning the validity of the MPI and there are no bibliographical references to any of the studies that are described in the manual. Information is included in the manual about shortened versions of the inventory using only a portion of the 15 items. Due to the lack of data about the reliability and validity of the total inventory, it would seem the use of shortened versions of the MPI is questionable.

Although the MPI may have some possibility as a clinical instrument for screening purposes, there is a lack of any solid empirical evidence that would support the ability of this instrument to detect motor problems any better than other similar instruments. It has a well-founded theoretical basis, and some of the attributes of a good screening device; that is, it is short, relatively easy to administer, and inexpensive; but the lack of adequate norms, sufficient reliability data, and of any substantial validity information and the complete absence of documentation indicates that any test user should be cautious about decisions that are based on the MPI scores.

[880]

★Perceptual Motor Test. Grades 1–3; 1972–73; "developed initially to predict potential learning problems of children entering the first grade and to diagnose deficiencies in children manifesting learning difficulties in the primary grades"; 2 scores (reading potential, writing potential) based on 9 subtest scores: posture, flexibility, balance, awareness, bilaterality, unilaterality, crosslaterality, hand-eye-foot preference, eye control; no data on reliability and validity; no data on relevance of scores to current or future performance in reading and writing; no norms; 1 form; manual ('73, 21 pages plus 6 copies of 2-page score sheet); $1.95 per manual; additional score sheets must be reproduced locally; postage extra; (15–30) minutes; Paul Smith; Educational Activities, Inc. *

RICHARD E. DARNELL, *Director, Curriculum in Physical Therapy, Department of Physical Medicine and Rehabilitation, Medical School, University of Michigan, Ann Arbor, Michigan.*

This test purports to measure posture, balance, flexibility, laterality, eye-hand-foot preference and eye control. It is a refinement of earlier tests in which 1,000 children were tested in grades 1 to 3.

Evidence for concurrent and predictive validity is presented in an extremely brief and highly global manner, suggesting the relationship of the functions listed with learning achievement. Statistical measures of validity are not offered. However, the test manual indicates efforts to insure validity of test items,

although intercorrelations are not reported. No data on reliability are offered. The author does not present age or grade norms or size of subgroups tested.

The standardization of test items is extremely poor, with background information and suggestions for interpretation often confounded with instructions. Scoring of the items is highly suggestive in nature, although pictures indicating the difference between correct and incorrect responses are employed for some items.

The scoring sheet allows an entry of a score for each item in either or both of two separate columns to allow judgment in reading and writing proficiency. Ranges of test scores for very poor, poor, fair, good, and very good reading and writing abilities are presented. The scoring sheet is extremely confusing, with samples of student scores offered rather than directions for scoring. This confusion is heightened by the presentation of a 14-item descriptive code, supposedly to annotate numerically scored items, with no explanation of appropriate use, as well as by the use in items related to laterality, unilaterality, and crosslaterality of letter codes to which no apparent reference is made.

The test manual contains, in addition to the presentation of the Kraus-Weber test (without appropriate citation) in an appendix, a description of the development of the test, explanations of space and equipment necessary to administer the test, test items description and interpretation, as well as suggestions for corrective skills. In general, suggestions for interpretation and correction are extremely simplistic and may actually be contraindicated in children with learning disabilities associated with developmental orthopedics or neurological disability. For example, suggestions for modification of postural abnormalities by stretching or strengthening can be extremely damaging if not carried out both with appropriate medical consultation and by properly trained persons.

It is unfortunate that this test has few if any merits to support its use, in terms of either the qualities desired in adequate measurement or appropriate therapeutic practice.

JAMES A. RICE, *Associate Professor of Psychology, University of Houston, Houston, Texas.*

The *Perceptual Motor Test* was "developed initially to predict potential learning problems of children entering the first grade and to diagnose deficiencies in children manifesting learning difficulties in the primary grades." Nine types of tasks produce the nine subtest scores listed above.

There is no evidence of reliability. After an inference that the test is neurophysiological, validity is presumed for predicting success in reading and writing on the basis of a relationship with teacher checklists of behaviors traditionally regarded as reading- and writing-related. Scores on the *Metropolitan Achievement Test* and the PMT are said to be related, but no correlations are given, nor is there evidence of a systematic validity study. The tasks required in this test are described as developmental, and, by an allusion to "recent research" relating developmental and academic learnings, the case for validity is closed.

After presentation of the tasks required of the child, comments are made urging belief that the behavior sampled is predictive of reading and/or writing skills. For example, in reference to posture, the author writes: "posture may result in either reading or writing problems because of the skewed signals the eyes send to the brain." The author is reaching far and wide for validity in this utterly absurd remark. Scoring is purely subjective; again, for posture: "Estimate on a continuum of 0–20 (with 0 being terrible and 20 being perfect) a score based on the child's head and shoulder posture." Suggestions for remediation follow.

One is reminded of the organismic age concept and many false impressions following thereon, when reviewing this naive commentary by the author of the PMT. Many characteristics are correlated, especially in the primary-grade age range, where development is very rapid for perceptual-motor and many other skills. The extraordinary degree of subjectivity in administration, scoring, and interpretation, even if the PMT had an a priori basis for prediction, renders it psychometrically unsound.

[881]

Test of Motor Impairment. Ages 5–14; 1972; TMI; motor deficiency resulting from neural dysfunction; cutoff score arbitrarily set to obtain 10–15 percent impaired at each age level; 1 form; manual (93 pages); record form (4 pages); 4 response sheets (1 page); $120 per set of test materials for 35–50 subjects; $6 per 50 record forms; $5 per manual; postage extra; (20–60) minutes; D. H. Stott, F. A. Moyes, and

S. E. Henderson; Brook Educational Publishing Ltd. [Canada]. *
See T2:1904 (4 references).

REFERENCES

1–4. See T2:1904.
5. NAIDOO, SANDHYA. *Specific Dyslexia: The Research Report of the ICAA Word Blind Centre for Dyslexic Children.* London: Sir Isaac Pitman & Sons Ltd., 1972. Pp. xv, 165. *
6. STOTT, D. H.; MARSTON, N. C.; AND NEILL, SARA J. Chap. 11, "Maladjustment and Motor Impairment," pp. 125–36. In their *Taxonomy of Behaviour Disturbance.* London: University of London Press Ltd., 1975. Pp. viii, 184. *

JEROME D. PAUKER, *Research Director and Chief Psychologist, Family Court Clinic, Clarke Institute of Psychiatry; and Associate Professor of Life Sciences (Psychology—Scarborough College) and of Behavioural Sciences, University of Toronto, Toronto, Ontario, Canada.*

This is a carefully and well-constructed test. Starting with the items of the *Oseretzky Tests of Motor Proficiency,* the authors pruned and grafted through four revisions of the TMI to arrive at the present battery of 45 items, with norms based on 854 children between their 6th and 15th birthdays attending 31 schools in an industrial city of Ontario. It is not clear how many of the children were of each sex or at each age.

There are five items at each of nine age-levels: ages 4 and lower, ages 5 through 10 at yearly intervals, a combined 11–12 year-level, and age 13 and over. At each age-level, there is an item devoted to each of the following categories of motor function: (a) "control and balance of the body while immobile," (b) "control and coordination of the upper limbs," (c) "control and coordination of the whole body while in motion," (d) "manual dexterity with the emphasis on speed," and (e) "simultaneous movement and precision." The criteria for item selection emphasize the minimizing of perceptual, cognitive, motivational, temperamental, experiential, muscular, physical stature, sex, and cultural factors; and valiant attempts were made during the successive revisions to detect and adjust for these variables. Rather than have a few items, each with successive difficulty levels for successive years, the task within each category of motor function changes from age-level to age-level so that a culturally-determined difficulty or other experientially-related problem with one specific activity will not unduly penalize a child across several year-levels. Demonstrations of a task can be repeated several times; instructions can be repeated, varied, and simplified; and testing may be done in more than one session.

Three general testing procedures are outlined. In the standard procedure, recommended for surveys and research, each child is tested at his/her own age-level, and testing either stops if all five items are passed or is continued at lower age-levels until all five items at an age-level are passed. The shortened procedure is used when a sample population is large enough to compensate for some loss in accuracy; after being tested at age-level, further testing at lower age-levels is restricted to those categories of motor function which were failed. The clinical procedure is used where the most thorough exploration of a child's motor ability is required; here, testing is done both at the child's own age-level and at the one below, regardless of success at his/her own age-level. Scoring is for failure rather than success, so that a well coordinated child scores zero and any score above that is a measure of impairment.

The manual is clear, for the most part, in its description of each test item and its presentation of instructions and scoring criteria. For each age-level, there is a list of the equipment provided with the test and of the additional equipment to be supplied by the tester, e.g., stop watch, tennis ball, masking tape. Each item description is accompanied by a picture of a child performing the task.

Retest reliability (test-retest and interscorer) is mostly high; reliability studies revealed a few items on which recorder accuracy was not up to standard, and revisions in response-recording were made to counteract these lapses.

Validity studies reported in the manual show a close correspondence between TMI scores and teachers' ratings of motor ability, and significant correlations between motor impairment scores and several categories of maladjustment as checklisted on the *Bristol Social Adjustment Guides*. The latter finding is important for Stott's argument that at least some aspects of maladjustment are related to subtle neurological impairment, and that the TMI serves as an independent means of measuring such impairment. A finding of higher motor-impairment scores for children with behaviors in a "neurological" grouping (e.g., has unwilled twitches and jerks; too restless and overactive to heed

even for a moment) "strengthens the supposition that the common factor in the relationship between motor impairment and maladjustment ....is one of neural dysfunction."

This test is straightforward, with considerable face and content validity in addition to the other validity indicators noted above. There are occasional lapses in clarity in the manual, but for the most part it serves its purpose well. The test equipment supplied with the kit is sturdy and nicely packaged in a carrying case. Materials which must be supplied by the tester are easily obtainable. One possible drawback could be the test room requirements (it must be at least 18 by 12 feet, it must have one blank wall suitable for ball throwing, and at least part of the floor must be uncarpeted), but a school gymnasium would serve the purpose.

One can argue about the contention that the motor impairment measured by this test likely results from neural dysfunction, but the motor performance itself does appear to be measured objectively, reliably, and validly.

VISION

[882]

Marianne Frostig Developmental Test of Visual Perception, Third Edition. Ages 3–8; 1961–66; DTVP; 7 scores: eye-motor coordination, figure-ground discrimination, form constancy, position in space, spatial relations, total, perceptual quotient; 1 form ('63, c1961, 19 pages); demonstration cards ['63, 11 cards]; revised administration and scoring manual ('66, 38 pages); monograph on 1963 standardization ('64, 37 pages); $10 per kit of 10 tests, scoring keys, demonstration cards, monograph, and manual; $10 per 25 tests; $5 per specimen set; postage extra; (30–45) minutes for individual administration, (40–60) minutes for group administration; Marianne Frostig in collaboration with D. Welty Lefever, John R. B. Whittlesey, and Phyllis Maslow (monograph); Consulting Psychologists Press, Inc. *

See T2:1921 (43 references); for reviews by Brad S. Chissom, Newell C. Kephart, and Lester Mann, see 7:871 (117 references); for reviews by James M. Anderson and Mary C. Austin, see 6:553 (7 references).

REFERENCES

1–7. See 6:553.
8–124. See 7:871.
125–167. See T2:1921; also includes a cumulative name index to the first 167 references and 5 reviews for this test.
168. MYERS, PATRICIA I., AND HAMMILL, DONALD D. Chap. 9, "The Test-Related Systems," pp. 239–66. In their *Methods for Learning Disorders.* New York: John Wiley & Sons., Inc., 1969. Pp. xiii, 313. *
169. ANDERSON, WILLIAM F., AND STERN, DAVID. "The Relative Effects of the Frostig Program, Corrective Reading Instruction, and Attention Upon the Reading Skills of Corrective Readers With Visual Perceptual Deficiencies." *J Sch Psychol* 10(4): 387–95 D '72. * (*PA* 50:3665)
170. BRAITHWAITE, R. J. "The Frostig Test and Training Programme—How Valuable?" *Slow Learning Child* (Australia) 19(2):86–91 Jl '72. * (*PA* 49:9857)

171. CHAPMAN, L. J., AND WEDELL, K. "Perceptual-Motor Abilities and Reversal Errors in Children's Handwriting." *J Learn Dis* 5(6):321–5 Je–Jl '72. * *(PA* 49:1275)

172. CHISSOM, BRAD S.; THOMAS, JERRY R.; AND BIASIOTTO, JUDSON. "Canonical Validity of Perceptual-Motor Skills for Predicting an Academic Criterion." *Ed & Psychol Meas* 32(4): 1095–8 w '72. *

173. DRISCOLL, MARY COOK, AND ABELSON, CAROL. "Programmed Instruction Versus Therapist Instruction." *Am J Occup Ther* 26(2):78–80 Mr '72. * *(PA* 48:5662)

174. FISHER, MAURICE D., AND TURNER, ROBERT V. "The Effects of a Perceptual-Motor Training Program Upon the Academic Readiness of Culturally Disadvantaged Kindergarten Children." *J Negro Ed* 41(2):142–50 sp '72. * *(PA* 49:5390)

175. GAYTON, WILLIAM F.; NEIFERT, JAMES T.; WARNER, WILLIAM R.; AND WILSON, WINSTON T. "Abbreviation of the Frostig Test of Developmental Visual Perception." *Percept & Motor Skills* 35(1):221–4 Ag '72. * *(PA* 49:3512)

176. HASKELL, SIMON H. "Visuoperceptual, Visuomotor, and Scholastic Skills of Alternating and Uniocular Squinting Children." *J Spec Ed* 6(1):3–8 sp '72. * *(PA* 49:5420)

177. KRAUSEN, R. "The Relationship of Certain 'Pre-Reading Skills to General Ability and Social Class in Nursery Children.'" *Ed Res* (England) 15(1):72–9 N '72. *

178. LAWHON, DELBERT ALLEN. *A Study of the Use of Concrete and Abstract Stimuli in the Development of Perceptual Abilities of Disadvantaged Five Year Old Children.* Doctor's thesis, West Virginia University (Morgantown, W.Va.), 1972. *(DAI* 33:2695A)

179. MAXWELL, DONNA M. LUCAS. *An Evaluation of the Effectiveness of the Wepman Auditory Discrimination Test, Sub-Test II and V, of the Frostig Test of Visual Discrimination, and Peabody Picture Vocabulary Test as a Predictor of First Grade Reading.* Master's thesis, California State University (Hayward, Calif.), 1972.

180. MLODNOSKY, LUCILLE BLAIN. "The Bender Gestalt and the Frostig as Predictors of First-Grade Reading Achievement Among Economically Deprived Children." *Psychol Sch* 9(1): 25–30 Ja '72. * *(PA* 48:7883)

181. NEEL, RICHARD SCOTT. *A Psychometric Investigation of Identification of Learning Disabled Children.* Doctor's thesis, University of Southern California (Los Angeles, Calif.), 1972. *(DAI* 33:1554A)

182. PEREBOOM, MARGARET JANE GAMBLE. *The Relationship Among Perceptual Functioning, Socioeconomic Status and Race in Young Children.* Doctor's thesis, University of Texas (Austin, Tex.), 1972. *(DAI* 34:862B)

183. RAUTENSTRAUCH, CAROL ANN. *A Reliability Study of the Frostig Developmental Test of Visual Perception Over Different Time Intervals Using Kindergarten and First Grade Children.* Master's thesis, Pennsylvania State University (University Park, Pa.), 1972.

184. RUBIN, ELI Z.; BRAUN, JEAN S.; BECK, GAYLE R.; AND LLORENS, LELA A. *Cognitive Perceptual Motor Dysfunction.* Detroit, Mich.: Wayne State University Press, 1972. Pp. 173. *

185. SERWER, BLANCHE J.; SHAPIRO, BERNARD J.; AND SHAPIRO, PHYLLIS P. "Achievement Prediction of 'High-Risk' Children." *Percept & Motor Skills* 35(2):347–54 O '72. * *(PA* 49:7970)

186. SILVERSTEIN, A. B. "Another Look at Sources of Variance in the Developmental Test of Visual Perception." *Psychol Rep* 31(2):557–8 O '72. * *(PA* 49:5796)

187. SMITH, PHILIP A., AND MARX, RONALD W. "Some Cautions on the Use of the Frostig Test: A Factor Analytic Study." *J Learn Dis* 5(6):357–62 Je–Jl '72. * *(PA* 49:56)

188. THOMAS, JERRY R.; CHISSOM, BRAD S.; AND BIASIOTTO, JUDSON. "Investigation of the Shane-O Ball Test as a Perceptual-Motor Task for Pre-Schoolers." *Percept & Motor Skills* 35(2): 447–50 O '72. * *(PA* 49:5799)

189. WIEDERHOLT, J. LEE. *The Predictive Validity of Frostig's Constructs as Measured by the Developmental Test of Visual Perception.* Doctor's thesis, Temple University (Philadelphia, Pa.), 1972. *(DAI* 33:1556A)

190. WRIGHT, LOGAN. "Intellectual Sequelae of Rocky Mountain Spotted Fever." *J Abn Psychol* 80(3):315–6 D '72. * *(PA* 49:9500)

191. BECKER, JOHN T., AND SABATINO, DAVID A. "Frostig Revisited." *J Learn Dis* 6(3):180–4 Mr '73. * *(PA* 50:6439)

192. BLACK, F. WILLIAM. "Neurogenic Findings in Reading-Retarded Children as a Function of Visual Perceptual Ability." *Percept & Motor Skills* 36(2):359–62 Ap '73. * *(PA* 51:3467)

193. BUCCELLATO, LEONARD ANDREW. *The Role of Visual Perception in the Oral Language Production of Educable Mentally Retarded Children.* Doctor's thesis, Georgia State University (Atlanta, Ga.), 1973. *(DAI* 34:5617A)

194. BUCKLAND, PEARL, AND BALOW, BRUCE. "Effect of Visual Perceptual Training on Reading Achievement." *Excep Children* 39(4):299–304 Ja '73. * *(PA* 50:5643)

195. CARDOZO, CAROL WILCOX. *Visual Perceptual Maturity and Cognitive Development in Normal and Educable Retarded Children.* Doctor's thesis, University of Miami (Coral Gables, Fla.), 1973. *(DAI* 34:387B)

196. COURY, JANINE PESCHARD. *Screening for Learning Dis-*

abilities Among Inner-City First Graders. Doctor's thesis, University of Tennessee (Knoxville, Tenn.), 1973. *(DAI* 34:2382A)

197. DUBOIS, NELSON F. "Selected Correlations Between Reading Achievement and Various Visual Abilities of Children in Grades 2 and 4." *Percept & Motor Skills* 37(1):45–6 Ag '73. * *(PA* 51:9915)

198. DUBOIS, NELSON F., AND BROWN, FOSTER LLOYD. "Selected Relationships Between Frostig Scores and Reading Achievement in a First Grade Population." *Percept & Motor Skills* 37(2):515–9 O '73. * *(PA* 51:9914)

199. GOODMAN, LIBBY, AND WIEDERHOLT, J. LEE. "Predicting Reading Achievement in Disadvantaged Children." *Psychol Sch* 10(2):181–5 Ap '73. * *(PA* 50:9860)

200. GREENSPAN, STEVEN BARRY. *Children's Perceptual-Motor Reversal Confusions: Correlates and Therapy.* Doctor's thesis, Illinois Institute of Technology (Chicago, Ill.), 1973. *(DAI* 35:1077B)

201. HENSLEY, BONNIE LEE. *The Relationship of Selected Oral Language, Perceptual, Demographic, and Intellectual Factors to the Reading Achievement of Good, Average, and Poor First Grade Reading Groups.* Doctor's thesis, University of Southern Mississippi (Hattiesburg, Miss.), 1973. *(DAI* 34:4562A)

202. ISAAC, BLANCHE K. "Perceptual-Motor Development of First Graders as Related to Class, Race, Intelligence, Visual Discrimination, and Motivation." *J Sch Psychol* 11(1):47–56 Mr '73. * *(PA* 51:1923)

203. MARTIN, NORA MAE WHITE. *The Effects of Training in Visual Constancy and Role-Playing on Reading Ability.* Doctor's thesis, University of Michigan (Ann Arbor, Mich.), 1973. *(DAI* 34:4931A)

204. MEAD, MICHAEL DEAN. *The Construction and Testing of a Scale for Measuring Visual Perception: A Pilot Study.* Doctor's thesis, University of Northern Colorado (Greeley, Colo.), 1973. *(DAI* 34:3469B)

205. REJTO, ALICE. "Music as an Aid in the Remediation of Learning Disabilities." *J Learn Dis* 6(5):286–95 My '73. *

206. SAND, PATRICIA L.; TAYLOR, NEAL; RAWLINGS, MARY; AND CHITNIS, SUNEETI. "Performance of Children With Spina Bifida Manifesta on the Frostig Developmental Test of Visual Perception." *Percept & Motor Skills* 37(2):539–46 O '73. * *(PA* 52:1344)

207. SILVERSTEIN, A. B. "Reliability and Abnormality of Differences Between DTVP Subtest Scores." *Psychol Sch* 10(2): 204–6 Ap '73. * *(PA* 50:8131)

208. STAPLETON, LEROY EARL. *A Long-Range, Diagnostic-Prescriptive Reading Intervention Program Employing the Frostig Test of Visual Perceptual Development and the Illinois Test of Psycholinguistic Abilities With Low Socioeconomic, Semi-Urban, Elementary Students of the Okaloosa County Florida Public Schools.* Doctor's thesis, Florida State University (Tallahassee, Fla.), 1973. *(DAI* 34:3161A)

209. THOMAS, JERRY R., AND CHISSOM, BRAD S. "Note on Factor Structure of the Frostig Developmental Test of Visual Perception." *Percept & Motor Skills* 36(2):510 Ap '73. * *(PA* 51:2776)

210. WOOD, PATRICIA ANN. *The Role of Age and School Experience in Performance on Certain Visual Perception Tests.* Doctor's thesis, University of Illinois (Urbana, Ill.), 1973. *(DAI* 34:5737A)

211. ALLEN, JERRY C. "Relationships Between Visual Perception and Oral Language Production of Young Children." *Percept & Motor Skills* 38(3, pt 2):1319–27 Je '74. * *(PA* 53:200)

212. CHISSOM, BRAD S.; THOMAS, JERRY R.; AND COLLINS, DELORES G. "Relationships Among Perceptual-Motor Measures and Their Correlations With Academic Readiness for Preschool Children." *Percept & Motor Skills* 39(1, pt 2):467–73 Ag '74. * *(PA* 56:10765)

213. FEE, F. "An Analysis of Two Diagnostic Tests: The Frostig and the I.T.P.A." *Irish J Psychol* 2(3):176–82 w '74. * *(PA* 53:10708)

214. HENSLEY, BONNIE. "The Relationship of Selected Oral Language, Perceptual, Demographic, and Intellectual Factors to the Reading Achievement of Good, Average, and Poor First Grade Reading Groups." *South J Ed Res* 8(2):256–71 sp '74. * *(PA* 53:4024)

215. LIEMOHN, WENDELL P., AND KNAPCZYK, DENNIS R. "Factor Analysis of Gross and Fine Motor Ability in Developmentally Disabled Children." *Res Q* 45(4):424–32 D '74. * *(PA* 56:4153)

216. SABATINO, DAVID A.; ABBOTT, JOHN C.; AND BECKER, JOHN T. "What Does the Frostig DTVP Measure?" *Excep Children* 40(6):453–4 Mr '74. * *(PA* 52:11080)

217. THOMAS, JERRY R.; CHISSOM, BRAD S.; AND BOOKER, LYNN. "Perceptual-Motor and Academic Relationships for Disadvantaged Children Classified as Learning Disabled and Normal." *Am Correct Ther J* 28(3):95–9 My–Je '74. * *(PA* 53:8380)

218. THOMAS, JERRY R., AND CHISSOM, BRAD S. "Prediction of First Grade Academic Performance From Kindergarten Perceptual-Motor Data." *Res Q* 45(2):148–53 My '74. *

219. CASSEL, RUSSELL N., AND KLAS, JOHN O. "Using Factor Analysis to Compare Test Data." *Calif J Ed Res* 26(3):137–44 My '75. * *(PA* 54:10631)

Marianne Frostig Developmental Test of Visual Preception

220. COLARUSSO, RONALD P.; MARTIN, HANNAH; AND HARTUNG, JOSEPH. "Specific Visual Perceptual Skills as Long-Term Predictors of Academic Success." *J Learn Dis* 8(10):651–5 D '75. * (*PA* 56:1496)

221. COSTELLO, CHRISTINE THERESE. *A Factor Analytic Comparison of Three Tests of Visual Perception for Children.* Doctor's thesis, St. Louis University (St. Loius, Mo.), 1975. (*DAI* 37:1892B)

222. DIBACCO, JOHN PHILIP. *The Efficacy of Group and Individually Administered Perceptual Tests in Predicting Multi-Criteria First Grade Achievement.* Doctor's thesis, George Peabody College for Teachers (Nashville, Tenn.), 1975. (*DAI* 36:1901B)

223. FERREE, ROBERT GRAY, III. *Effects of Positive Reinforcement on an Assessment Measure of Visual Perception Behavior.* Doctor's thesis, University of North Carolina (Greensboro, N.C.), 1975. (*DAI* 37:1403A)

224. KRACKE, ILSE. "Assessment of the Suitability of Frostig's Test and Training Programme for a School for Children With Language and Learning Problems." *Teach Deaf* (England) 73(430):86–92 Mr '75. *

225. PITCHER-BAKER, GEORGIA. "Clinical and Psychometric Merits of the Frostig Developmental Test of Visual Perception." *Psychol Sch* 12(3):315–8 Jl '75. * (*PA* 54:12658)

226. PLACK, JERALYN J., AND SHICK, JACQUELINE. "Physical Education: Is There Evidence to Support the Use of the Frostig Developmental Training Program in Physical Education?" *J Phys Ed & Rec* 46(5):58–9 My '75. *

227. THOMPSON, LONDON JEAN JOHNSON. *The Relationship of Visual Perception to Reading Achievement and the Effects of Two Types of Visual Perceptual Training on Reading Achievement in the First-Grade Year.* Doctor's thesis, University of Southern Mississippi (Hattiesburg, Miss.), 1975. (*DAI* 36:5027A)

228. BISAGA, JEFFREY STEVEN. *Sources of Variance in the Scores of Learning Disabled Children on the Marianne Frostig Developmental Test of Visual Perception.* Doctor's thesis, Fuller Theological Seminary (Pasadena, Calif.), 1976. (*DAI* 37:6297B)

229. BLACK, F. WILLIAM. "Cognitive, Academic, and Behavioral Findings in Children With Suspected and Documented Neurological Dysfunction." *J Learn Dis* 9(3):182–7 Mr '76. * (*PA* 56:4310)

230. FORGONE, CHARLES. "Effects of Visual Perception and Language Training Upon Certain Abilities of Retarded Children." *Ed & Train Mental Retard* 11(3):212–7 O '76. *

231. GONYO, MARILYN E. *The Relationship Between Visual Perception and Arithmetical Computation Skills Among Learning Disabled Second and Third Grade Children.* Doctor's thesis, Rutgers, The State University of New Jersey (New Brunswick, N.J.), 1976. (*DAI* 37:7591A)

232. JUSTEN, JOSEPH E., III, AND HARTH, ROBERT. "The Relationship Between Figure-Ground Discrimination and Color Blindness in Learning Disabled Children." *J Learn Dis* 9(2):96–9 F '76. *

233. PENDER, ROBERT HUGH. *A Comparison of Visual Perception and Selected Motor Fitness Test Items Between Congenital Deaf and Hearing Children.* Doctor's thesis, University of Southern Mississippi (Hattiesburg, Miss.), 1976. (*DAI* 37:2060A)

234. RANCK, SHIRLEY ANN. *A Factor Analysis of Five Perceptual Motor Tests of First Grade Children.* Doctor's thesis, Fordham University (New York, N.Y.), 1976. (*DAI* 37:983B)

235. SCHECKEL, LEE WALSHE. *An Inquiry Into the Relationship of Visual Perception and Territoriality Among Residents in a Home for the Aged.* Doctor's thesis, American University (Washington, D.C.), 1976. (*DAI* 37:6219A)

236. SILVERSTEIN, A. B. "Redundancy in Five Psychological Tests." *Psychol Rep* 39(3, pt 2):1072–4 D '76. *

237. TEW, BRIAN. "Some Doubts About the Frostig Test of Visual Perception." *Remedial Ed* (England) 11(1):32–5 '76. *

238. TOWER, DARRYL Q. "Relationships Between Perceptual Responses and Accident Patterns in Children: A Pilot Study." *Am J Occup Ther* 30(8):498–501 S '76. * (*PA* 57:3738)

239. WOOD, NANCY E. "Directed Art, Visual Perception, and Learning Disabilities." *Acad Ther* 12(4):455–62 su '77. *

[883]

Motor-Free Visual Perception Test. Ages 4–8; 1972; MVPT; individual; 1 form (51 plates); manual (27 pages); scoring sheet (2 pages); $12.50 per plates booklet; $1.50 per 25 scoring sheets; $3.50 per manual; postage extra; (10) minutes; Ronald P. Colarusso and Donald D. Hammill; Academic Therapy Publications. *

REFERENCES

1. NEWCOMER, PHYLLIS, AND HAMMILL, DONALD. "Visual Perception of Motor Impaired Children: Implications for Assessment." *Excep Children* 39(4):335–7 Ja '73. * (*PA* 50:5471)

2. HUDGINS, ANNE LOCKE. *Assessment of Visual-Motor Disabilities in Young Children.* Doctor's thesis, University of Georgia (Athens, Ga.), 1975. (*DAI* 36:7950A)

3. GONYO, MARILYN E. *The Relationship Between Visual Perception and Arithmetical Computation Skills Among Learning Disabled Second and Third Grade Children.* Doctor's thesis, Rutgers, The State University of New Jersey (New Brunswick, N.J.), 1976. (*DAI* 37:7591A)

4. HILL, DAVID STEWART. *The Definition of Learning Disabilities: An Application of Cattell's Constructs of Gf and Gc.* Doctor's thesis, Temple University (Philadelphia, Pa.), 1976. (*DAI* 37:2110A)

5. JOHNSON, D. LA MONT; BREKKE, BEVERLY; AND FOLLMAN, DENNIS E. "Appropriateness of the Motor-Free Visual Perception Test When Used With the Trainable Mentally Retarded." *Percept & Motor Skills* 43(3, pt 2):1346 D '76. * (*PA* 58:2558)

6. KRICHEV, ALAN. "Review of the Motor-Free Visual Perception Test." *Psychol Sch* 13(3):365–6 Jl '76. *

7. SEXTON, LARRY CHARLES. *Auditory and Visual Perception, Sex, and Academic Aptitude as Predictors of Achievement for First Grade Children.* Doctor's thesis, Ball State University (Muncie, Ind.), 1976. (*DAI* 37:6162A)

8. WRIGHT, JULIA ANN. *Relation of Visual and Motor Perception to Reading Achievement Among Children With One Year of Study in School.* Doctor's thesis, Ohio State University (Columbus, Ohio), 1976. (*DAI* 37:2758A)

9. HUDGINS, ANNE LOCKE. "Assessment of Visual-Motor Disabilities in Young Children: Toward Differential Diagnosis." *Psychol Sch* 14(3):252–60 Jl '77. *

CARL L. ROSEN, *Professor of Education and Director, Educational Child Study Center, Kent State University, Kent, Ohio.*[1]

The MVPT is described as a "quick, highly reliable and valid measure of overall visual perceptual processing ability in children." The 36-item test is individually administered, and multiple choice responses reduce what the authors refer to as a "confounding variable" in the measurement of visual perception; namely, the influence of motor ability on test performance.

They indicate that this test "can be used by teachers, psychologists, educational specialists and others." The impression is obtained that the authors believe any personnel needing some quick measure of a child's (or children's) ability in this area, could administer the MVPT. They state that the test is for screening, diagnostic, and research purposes.

No clear rationale nor evidence is provided, as to precisely why a "motor-free" test of visual perception might be any more desirable for the screening and diagnosis of these abilities than the typical tests. Why specifically should such a separation be a consideration of importance in testing typical children is not dealt with. Their claim that "while motor and visual perception skills are often clearly associated, they can also be very separate abilities," is neither fully explained, documented, nor delimited. The types of children or the kinds of conditions when the two abilities are important to test separately are not defined.

[1] Thanks for technical assistance to Sonya L. Blixt, Associate Professor of Education and Director of the Bureau of Educational Research and Services, Kent State University.

Motor-Free Visual Perception Test

There is present (as is not infrequently the case in test manuals on visual perception) the potential for the unsophisticated user to draw from assumptions on what just might be necessary for the testing of some exceptional children, the mistaken inference that the same assumptions hold in the measurement of typical children.

The behavior of most human beings, however, is a unity, with sensory, motor, perceptual, cognitive, and affective dimensions operating in a highly complex interactive and interfacilitative manner. The activation of these interconnected dimensions is probably hierarchical and their engagement fully holistic. To single out some hypothetically finite subsystem such as visual perceptual processing from such a dynamic flux and to specify some "motor-free" construct of it for "screening" and "diagnosis," requires not only a far more adequate rationale than is made available in this manual, but also more satisfactory evidence substantiating the relevance of this type of test for something and the importance of this particular test as a measure of these hypothetical abilities.

No information is presented regarding the relevance of visual perception for some desirable, if not necessary, outcome; hence, the need for such measurement is uncertain. The authors acknowledge that the low correlations (between MVPT and school achievement and aptitude measures) in their validity data is not unique to the MVPT. They indicate that their test, as well as other tests of visual perception, tend to account for little of the variability in school achievement and academic aptitude measures. While they are to be credited for clearly indicating that they are not making claims about high relationships between perception, reading and other school abilities, this is not a satisfactory basis for validating a test of visual perception. What is this test relevant for? The statement of their own belief that visual perception is not "unimportant to a child's development," is rather general and should be more sufficiently supported by data. If the MVPT is a measure of "motor-free" visual perception, we need to know how important it is to measure such an ability and what useful or critical outcomes do motor-free visual perception abilities contribute to.

In regard to the question, does the MVPT

measure the abilities purported, the authors' contention that: "moderately high correlations between the MVPT and visual-motor tests with lower correlations between the MVPT and achievement and intelligence tests would be supportive evidence that the MVPT measures visual perception" is not upheld in their data. The median correlation of .49 between MVPT and the other tests indicates that the various perception tests are not measuring the same thing. Given, among other things, the lack of comparability between samples of subjects in their data who received the perception tests, and those samples who received the achievement and intelligence tests, the comparison of correlations leads to tenuous if not unsubstantiated conclusions.

There are also definitive problems with the interpretation of the normative data. While the authors wisely caution that both the perceptual ages and perceptual quotients derived from raw scores should not be interpreted without considering the standard error of measurement, it is uncertain why the authors used the split-half reliabilities in calculating the standard error of measurement when the Kuder-Richardson coefficients were available (and were, in all cases lower than the split-half data). Also, in reporting an overall standard error of measurement, they used data for the combined group, but have wisely used individual age group data for calculating perceptual quotients. It would seem that the use of a single standard error of measurement for tables built around different age groups could potentially lead to misclassification problems in screening and in subsequent remediation of pupils. The authors' recommendation that a "PQ 85 or less (minus 1 standard deviation) be the criteria for inadequacy on the test," appears not to be defended by either the validity or the reliability data available.

Finally, there is an absence of any of the kinds of assistance and refinements that test users would benefit from in the skilled day-to-day screening uses of tests such as these. If a child does perform "inadequately" on this test, how is the teacher to (as is suggested) "verify this conclusion by evaluating the child's performance in the classroom?" Will she, without adequate assistance, know what to look for, or will she make sure that she finds "problems"?

Motor-Free Visual Perception Test

What kinds of behavior should she look for? What sorts of behaviors would inadequacy on this test be congruent with in everyday behavior that the user can be guided to look for? No assistance is given. Towards the final part of the manual, the authors indicate that remediation should begin "immediately," if the teacher "is convinced a problem exists," but little on "what" and "how" specifically to remediate is offered except for a mixed collection of references. They curiously urge that perceptual training not be at the expense of regular classroom academic activities—but if it is "not important," why test?

In summary, while this test claims to be a quick practical screening and diagnostic instrument, inadequate evidence is presented to substantiate its validity for either screening or diagnosis. Consequently, the MVPT cannot be recommended in its present state.

Psychol Sch 13(3):365–6 Jl '76. *Alan Krichev.* * The Manual includes an excellent, concise description of the selection procedure for included items, each item's validity factor and pass-fail percentage, the results of several validity and reliability studies, and the normative population of 883 subjects. The last description could have been detailed more fully, but this did not seem to be a serious failing. The authors obviously have attempted to follow the guidelines of the APA's 1966 *Standards for Educational and Psychological Tests and Manuals.* The authors claim that the MVPT is "practical for screening, diagnostic, and research purposes." They see it as a "quick, highly reliable, and valid measure of overall visual perceptual processing ability in children." Frankly, so do I.

[884]

***Stycar Vision Tests.** Normal and handicapped children 6 months and over; 1958–76; SVT; individual; 5 levels; revised manual ('76, 53 pages); £28.60 per set of testing materials; £1.60 per manual; postpaid within U.K.; Mary D. Sheridan; distributed by NFER Publishing Co. Ltd. [England]. *

a) MINIATURE TOYS TEST. Nonspeaking handicapped children mental ages 21 months and over who are unable to recognize letters; 1958–76; 1 form ['58]; record form for miniature toys and graded balls ['70, 2 pages]; £5.70 per set of toys (items priced individually); £1.10 per 25 record forms; [5–10] minutes.

b) GRADED BALLS TEST. Ages 6–30 months (also handicapped children with mental ages within this range); 1968–76; 1 form ['68]; record form same as for *a*;

£4.40 per set of testing materials (10 balls and record form); [5] minutes.

c) AGES 3, 4–5. 1958–76; 1 form ['58]; 2 levels: 5-letter booklet for 3 year olds, 7-letter booklet for 4–5 year olds; key card ['70, 1 card]; record form ['70, 2 pages]; £4.30 per set of testing materials (without manual); £1.10 per 25 record forms; [5–10] minutes.

d) AGES 5–7. 1958–76; 9-letter charts, Forms A ['58, 1 page], B ['68, 1 page]; key card ['70, 1 card]; record form same as for *c*; £1.20 per chart; set *c* must be purchased to obtain 9-letter key card; (4) minutes.

e) PANDA TEST. Severely visually handicapped children ages 6–30 months (also handicapped children with mental ages within this range); 1973–76; 1 form (27 letter cards, 9 plastic letters for use with multi-handicapped children); £5.10 per set of cards; £7 per set of plastic letters; [10] minutes.

See T2:1931 (5 references).

REFERENCES

1–5. See T2:1931.
6. KEITH, C. G.; DIAMOND, Z.; AND STANSFIELD, A. "Visual Acuity Testing in Young Children." *Brit J Ophthal* 56(11): 827–32 N '72. *
7. WOODRUFF, M. EMERSON. "Observations on the Visual Acuity of Children During the First Five Years of Life." *Am J Optom* 49(3):205–15 Mr '72. * (PA 48:8836)
8. SHERIDAN, MARY D. "The STYCAR Graded-Balls Vision Test." *Develop Med & Child Neurol* (England) 15(4):423–32 Ag '73. * (PA 51:8274)
9. SHERIDAN, MARY D. "The STYCAR Panda Test for Children With Severe Visual Handicaps." *Develop Med & Child Neurol* (England) 15(6):728–35 D '73. * (PA 52:3471)
10. BROWDER, J. A., AND LEVY, W. J. "Vision Testing of Young and Retarded Children." *Clin Pediatrics* 13(11):983–6 N '74. *
11. SHERIDAN, MARY D. "What Is Normal Distance Vision at Five to Seven Years?" *Develop Med & Child Neurol* (England) 16(2):189–95 Ap '74. * (PA 52:12000)
12. DAVENS, EDWARD. "Review of Stycar Vision Tests," pp. 306–9. In *Pediatric Screening Tests*. Edited by William K. Frankenburg and Bonnie W. Camp. Springfield, Ill.: Charles C Thomas, Publisher, 1975. Pp. xii, 549. *
13. SAVITZ, ROBERTA. "Review of Stycar Vision Tests," pp. 309–12. In *Pediatric Screening Tests*. Edited by William K. Frankenburg and Bonnie W. Camp. Springfield, Ill.: Charles C Thomas, Publisher, 1975. Pp. xii, 549. *

[885]

The 3-D Test of Visualization Skill. Ages 3–8; 1972; no data on reliability and validity; individual, although manual states "may be given either as an individual or a group test"; 1 form (6 geometric forms); manual (90 pages); checklist (6 pages); individual scoring sheet (1 page); $18.50 per set of geometric forms; $3.50 per 25 checklists; $1 per 25 scoring sheets; $4.50 per manual; postage extra; (20–25) minutes; Grace Petitclerc; Academic Therapy Publications. *

DONALD A. LETON, *Professor of Educational Psychology, University of Hawaii at Manoa, Honolulu, Hawaii.*

The construction of this test evolved "quite by chance" from the use of three-dimensional forms—a sphere, a cube, and a pyramid—in teaching drawing skills to several nonreaders. Although the test was designed for use by classroom teachers, the author states that this "does not forbid its use by or lessen its value to school psychologists, practicing psychiatrists, pediatricians, reading specialists, or specialists in other fields of therapy." Nevertheless, she also acknowledges that "for the test to ask and hold the respect of such specialists, however, the scoring results will need to be correlated with prevailing intelligence and achievement tests." It may be an insult to the teaching profession to imply that correlational studies are unnecessary for a test to be used by teachers, but necessary for a test to be used by other specialists.

In discussing the need for correlational studies, the author is inconsistent. On the one hand the manual promises, "In the near future, the [correlation] results will be published"; on the other hand the manual states, "this evaluation scale makes no correlation between prevailing I.Q. scores and the Three-Dimensional Test scores; nor is such a correlation possible. The factors evaluated in the Three-Dimensional Test are not examined in tests slanted toward academic knowledge, even though the Three-Dimensional Test factors are the necessary undergirding for accumulating and operating higher skills."

The test claims to measure three levels of visualization skills in seven subtests, as follows, Level 1: shape identification, size perception, and visual equilibrium; Level 2: visual memory and operational imagery; and Level 3: image transformation. The visualization levels are referenced to Piaget's theory of the development of mental imagery as figurative, operational, and transformational skills.

The test stimuli consist of six wooden forms, i.e., two spheres, two cubes, and two pyramids, of unequal size. Response materials are a box of colored chalk and four 9" × 15" sheets of paper. The instructions are fairly explicit and administration procedures are easy. Subjective judgments are required to assign ratings of 0 to 3 to the qualities of the drawings and to the verbal responses. Single illustrations are provided for each rating at each age level, years 3 through 8. Three-dimensional drawing renditions of the sphere, cube, and pyramid by 7- and 8-year-old children receive ratings of 3. Below 7 years of age, however, the outline renditions of a circle, square, and triangle are adequate for ratings of 3. Six-year-old children producing three-dimensional renditions receive the same ratings as those producing circle, square, and triangle outlines.

A score table presents the ranges of ratings and median placements for the three visualiza-

tion test levels at six age-levels. The table is based on a sample of 127 randomly selected children; however, the population source of the sample is not identified. The author does not explain why unequal subsamples of 12, 17, 21, 28, 27, and 22 were selected for the 3- to 8-year-age levels, respectively. The samples are not adequate for age norms, nor to verify three growth levels in visualization skills. Furthermore, the median is not an appropriate statistic to summarize a small sample of ratings. On the Level 3 subtest, the median of the distribution of ratings for 8-year-olds is not as high as the medians for 6- and 7-year-olds. This is contrary to the expected developmental growth, and may have been due to variabilities in the age samples or to unreliabilities in the ratings. The manual does not report interrater reliabilities. Because of the fluctuations in the age-level performances occurring on the Level 1 and Level 2 subtests, the score table does not provide any useful indication of visual maturity.

The individual scoring sheet indicates a total possible score of 81, and the rating instructions for each of the subtests are consistent with this total. A maximum of 54 points is indicated for the three Level 1 subtests; of 6 points, for the two Level 2 subtests; and of 21 points, for the Level 3 subtest. Discrepant with this, however, maximum obtained scores of 22 to 36 are reported for the Level 2 subtest in the score table.

The child is instructed to "Take any color of chalk" to draw the form. Relative to the first choice of color, the manual states, "Research indicates that a choice of cool colors—blue, green, purple—is indicative of a retiring, reflective, probably creative character; while a choice of warm colors—red, orange, yellow—implies a gregarious, active, high-spirited character." The research validating this personality interpretation is not referenced in the manual. It is doubtful that children 3 to 8 years of age would be consistent enough in their color choices to provide reliable response data, and the validity of this interpretation is even more dubious.

The author makes the following clinical interpretations for difficulties in visualizing and drawing the forms. A mark or scribble implies an "embryo" image, or one of three physical sensory imbalances: "right-left conflict; undeveloped eye-hand coordinations; or dormancy or blockage in nerve channels that affect the image in transit from touch to brain or brain to hand." The concepts of an *embryo* stage of imagery, of *conflicts* in laterality, and of *dormancy* or *blockage* in nerve channels are semantic, without neurologic reality. There are no corresponding nerve states or nerve conditions to define these concepts.

In view of the lack of validity and reliability studies and the lack of adequate norms, *the presentation of this rating procedure as a test is inappropriate.* Longitudinal research will be necessary to confirm the hypothesized growth changes in visualization skills, and to validate them as subabilities of academic achievement. It will also be necessary to contrast the performances of criterion groups of children with known visual-motor impairments to the performances of normal children, in order to justify the clinical interpretations and proposed use with learning disabled children. In its present state, the 3-D test is just about as useless as any "test" could possibly be.

SOCIAL STUDIES

REVIEWS BY *Mary Friend Adams, Harry D. Berg, Lee H. Ehman, Hulda Grobman, Richard E. Gross, James O. Hodges, Dana G. Kurfman, Howard D. Mehlinger, Irving Morrissett, Ina V. S. Mullis, Jack L. Nelson, and Anna S. Ochoa.*

[886]
CLEP General Examinations: Social Sciences and History. 1–2 years or equivalent; 1964–76; for college accreditation of nontraditional study, advanced placement, or assessment of educational attainment; 3 scores: social sciences, history, total; normative, reliability, and validity data based on 1963 testing; Forms PCT1 ('67, 14 pages), PCT2 ('67, 17 pages); manual ('74, 17 pages) for CLEP General Examinations; for CLEP program accessories, see 473; separate answer sheets (IBM 805-Digitek, IBM 1230) must be used; rental fee, $4 per test; postpaid; 75(85) minutes; program administered for the College Entrance Examination Board by Educational Testing Service. *

REFERENCES
1. GRANDY, JERILEE, AND SHEA, WALTER M. *The CLEP General Examinations in American Colleges and Universities.* Princeton, N.J.: Educational Testing Service, 1976. Pp. 23. *

RICHARD E. GROSS, *Professor of Education, Stanford University, Stanford, California.* [Review of the 1976 social science and history examination in the *CLEP General Examinations,* Form YCT1.]

The descriptive booklets available on these tests explain the development of the program over the years and the use of committees of specialists to produce and keep the tests up to date. Unfortunately the examiners are only identified by their collegial affiliation and there is no way of ascertaining the balance between the different academic disciplines, by subject field, that exists or has existed on the part of the committees of examiners.

The norms for this test and hence the cutting scores are based on 1963's college sophomores. Reliability and standard error data, based on the foregoing sample, are .92 and .28, respectively. Validity claims are based on concurring claims: scores are higher for subjects with greater course background and for subjects intending to major in social science or history. About 60 percent of the scores on this test which were submitted to colleges by the subjects resulted in the student's receiving credit for college work. The median amount of credit was six semester hours; the range, depending upon the institution, was 2–10 semester hours. The median cutting score for college was 488 on a scale of 200–800. Most of the students who receive credit on this test take no further course work in social science or history; those students who do take further course work tend to receive average or better grades.

This test appears to be used primarily to provide an option for students who need to meet a social science/history requirement. It is apparently not too difficult for them to do so. Given this use of the test, it seems fair to ask whether a 60-minute, 90-question exam is a satisfactory measure of what the student knows about basic subject matter in history, economics, geography, anthropology, sociology, and social psychology. (It should be noted the CLEP also offers more complete and specialized tests in the foregoing fields except in anthropology, geography, and social psychology.) This CLEP examination in social sciences and history apportions about one-third of the queries to history and about two-thirds of these are on American history. The remaining questions are widely scattered among the social science disciplines. Economics and sociology have a slightly greater emphasis, with social psychology and social science methods receiving the least treatment. Questions about relatively contemporary events comprise about as much of the test as those devoted to political science.

The test format is entirely multiple choice with five options provided in each case. This reviewer believes the bulk of the items are well designed with a few being quite ingenious, such as, for example, item 68; several excellent skill-oriented charts and tables are included, such as items 27, 28, and 54. Unfortunately, this form included no analyses of maps, cartoons, or pictures. Most questions are factual or definitional. This reviewer found several items (26 and 55) somewhat confusing because of their negative wording; others somewhat picayune (29 and 62) in the details sought; and a few others seemingly very simple (12, 34, 42, and 65) in terms of college level comprehension. A few of the items are also limited by poor foils; see, for example, items 2, 53, and 60. The testers in this case provide rather impossible or silly foils because of the maintenance of five choices in each instance. Many of the items would provide adequate assessment with merely four options.

As is usual in objective tests, a few questions would actually penalize the more sophisticated or knowledgeable respondent; see, for example, items 27, 44, 68, and 79. Other questions seem to be somewhat arbitrary in that plausible arguments for different answers could be made; see, for example, items 1 and 4. The reviewer's major criticism of the test items relates to the fairness of considering all questions equal. A mere recall of fact response cannot be compared with the competencies measured in the analysis

of a complex graph. A number of the items are much more time-consuming than others. Item 44 is probably the most involved question, calling for an evaluation of alternate inferences, as well as tabular interpretation, and the correct answer would seem to be deserving of much more "credit" than is true when one has to identify the individual who wrote an important basic work in the social science (62).

In conclusion, to return to an earlier reservation, after reviewing the total test, one is led to question its ability to truly assess history and social science attainment in this single instrument. As suggested, the questions are exceedingly disparate. For this reviewer, the ability to achieve a passing score does not guarantee an appreciation of social reality, let alone a depth of knowledge of history and the various social sciences. (On the other hand, often course work sufficient to meet requirements may not result in these qualities either.) It is the reviewer's opinion that a number of social scientists from the different disciplines included in the test might well challenge the adequacy of the instrument in sampling their particular subject. This would probably be especially true in relation to the investigative processes followed in the research phases of their disciplines. The test would be greatly strengthened with the inclusion of more items devoted to such competencies.

[887]
*College Board Achievement Test in American History and Social Studies. Candidates for college entrance; 1901–76; test administered 6 times annually (January, March, May, June, November, December) at centers established by the publisher; Forms YCB4, YCB5, ZCB1, ZCB2, ZCB3, ZCB4, ('75–76, 13–18 pages) ; for more complete information, see 472; examination fee, $12.50 per candidate; 60(80) minutes; an inactive form, entitled *College Placement Test in American History and Social Studies,* is available for local administration and scoring; program administered for the College Entrance Examination Board by Educational Testing Service. *

See T2:1939 (1 reference) ; for a review by Howard R. Anderson of earlier forms, see 6:966; for a review by Ralph W. Tyler, see 5:786 (3 references) ; for a review by Robert L. Thorndike, see 4:662 (6 references). For reviews of the testing program, see 6:760 (2 reviews).

[888]
*College Board Achievement Test in European History and World Cultures. Candidates for college entrance; 1901–76; test administered 2 times annually (May, December) at centers established by the publisher; Forms YCB5, ZCB3, ('75–76, 18–19 pages) ; for more complete information, see 472;

examination fee, $12.50 per candidate; 60(80) minutes; an inactive form, entitled *College Placement Test in European History and World Cultures,* is available for local administration and scoring; program administered for the College Entrance Examination Board by Educational Testing Service. *

For a review by David K. Heenan of earlier forms, see 6:967. For reviews of the testing program, see 6:760 (2 reviews).

[889]

*College Placement Test in American History and Social Studies.** Entering college freshmen; 1962–75; inactive form of *College Board Achievement Test in American History and Social Studies* available for local administration and scoring; Form K-PPL ['67, 14 pages, reprint of 1964 test]; separate answer sheets (Digitek, IBM 805, IBM 1230) must be used; for program accessories, see 474; rental fee, $2 per student; 60(70) minutes; program administered for the College Entrance Examination Board by Educational Testing Service. *

For a review by Howard R. Anderson of an earlier form, see 6:966; for a review by Ralph W. Tyler, see 5:786; for a review by Robert L. Thorndike, see 4:662. For a review of the CPT program, see 7:665.

[890]

*College Placement Test in European History and World Cultures.** Entering college freshmen; 1963–75; inactive form of *College Board Achievement Test in European History and World Cultures* available for local administration and scoring; Form OPL ('66, 16 pages, reprint of 1963 test); separate answer sheets (Digitek, IBM 805, IBM 1230) must be used; for program accessories, see 474; rental fee, $2 per student; 60(70) minutes; program administered for the College Entrance Examination Board by Educational Testing Service. *

For a review by David K. Heenan of Form OPL (formerly LAC1), see 6:967. For a review of the CPT program, see 7:665.

[891]

*National Teacher Examinations: Social Studies.** College seniors and teachers; 1940–76; test administered 3 times annually (February, July, November) at centers established by the publisher; Forms XNT1 ('75, 23 pages), YNT ('76, 25 pages); descriptive booklet ('75, 8 pages); for program accessories, see 381; examination fee, $13 per candidate; 120(165) minutes; Educational Testing Service. *

For a review by Harry D. Berg of an earlier form, see 6:974. For reviews of the testing program, see 381 (2 reviews), 7:582 (2 reviews), 6:700 (1 review), 5:538 (3 reviews), and 4:802 (1 review).

JACK L. NELSON, *Professor of Education, Rutgers, The State University of New Jersey, New Brunswick, New Jersey.* [Review of Forms XNT1 and YNT.]

Purposes described by ETS for this test in social studies include the measurement of "academic competence in the content and methodology of the social studies," assistance for teacher education institutions to "improve the preparation of social studies teachers," and provision of "quantitative information useful in the selection of teachers." The descriptive booklet for this test states that the test measures understanding of history and the social sciences, inquiry skills characteristic of those disciplines and professional aspects of social studies education. While there is a professed emphasis on the application of social science concepts and generalizations, the booklet notes that the items test a knowledge of basic terms and facts. Major categories of questions are identified as professional education, political science, economics, history, geography, and sociology/anthropology.

This review covers Forms XNT1 and YNT. The most recent test analysis data available from ETS at the time this review was prepared are for Forms XNT and XNT1. Thus, general statistical analyses included here are for Form XNT1. Data used in the analysis were generated from an April 1975 administration to graduating seniors and candidates for teaching positions. The examination was administered to 2,096 persons at that time, from which a sample of 1,030 was drawn for analysis.

The test contains 150 items, though the current ETS analysis deleted one item. Reliability estimates were found to be .92, with a standard error of measurement of 6.4. The mean raw score in the sample was 48.2 and the standard deviation, 23.0. These statistics show the test to be satisfactory in reliability and somewhat difficult for the sample. No claims of validity are made and no statistical data on validity are provided.

Data on speededness show that over 76 percent of the sample completed the test and over 99 percent finished 75 percent of the items.

Statistical data supporting use of the test for teacher candidates are good, but an examination of individual items in the test raises questions about the claims for judging teacher candidates' knowledge in the broad range of the social sciences and the application of social science inquiry skills. For example, on Form XNT1 items covering factual information in history comprised almost one-third of the test, with sociology/anthropology next most frequent at about 20 percent. Professional education items were approximately 10 percent of the test, and geography items accounted for only about 3 percent. This imbalance is understandable in terms of teacher production when the vast majority are majors in history and where many of the professional education items are presumably in the Common Examination of the NTE. However, the accompanying literature by ETS should properly describe the contents and show the relative weight each subject has. Also, the test is limited to a narrow range of identified social sciences and, with few exceptions, excludes law, religion, and philosophy, in addition to multi-field social issues, which are an increasingly large area in social studies instruction.

A second concern revolves around the ETS brochure statement that the test emphasizes application of concepts, generalizations, and inquiry skills. There are a number of such items but they are not in the majority. Some of the inquiry application items are excellent, but there should be more of that type and quality to justify claiming emphasis. The majority of items are traditional recall or vocabulary items. A number of professional items are ambiguously phrased.

SUMMARY. This test is suitable for making limited judgments about achievement in history and selected social sciences. Reliability and difficulty data are favorable. Test items are heavily loaded in the area of facts and term definition, with some application of social science generalizations. Applications of newer teacher methodology and social science inquiry skills are included but minimal. Subject knowledge covered does not comprehensively treat social studies taught in the schools but concentrates on history, sociology, economics, and political science.

[892]

Sequential Tests of Educational Progress: Social Studies, Series II. Grades 4-6, 7-9, 10-12, 13-14; 1956-72; original 70 minute series (Series I) still available; 2 forms ('69, 15-23 pages): Forms 4A and 4B (grades 4-6), 3A and 3B (grades 7-9), 2A and 2B (grades 10-12), 1A and 1B (grades 13-14); for battery manuals and accessories, see 28; separate answer sheets (Digitek, IBM 805, IBM 1230) must be used; $7 per 20 tests; $5.50 per 100 answer sheets; $1.50 per 10 IBM (805, 1230 hand) scoring stencils (answer pattern must be punched out locally); Digitek scoring stencils not available; cash orders postpaid; specimen set not available; 45(55) minutes for grades 4-9, 60(70) minutes for grades 10-14; Educational Testing Service; Addison-Wesley Publishing Co., Inc. *

See T2:1948 (13 references); for reviews by Jonathon C. McLendon and Donald W. Oliver of the original edition (Series I), see 6:971 (1 reference); for reviews by Richard E. Gross, S. A. Rayner, and Ralph W. Tyler, see 5:792. For reviews of the complete battery, see 28 (2 reviews), 6:25 (2 reviews), and 5:24 (2 reviews, 1 excerpt).

National Teacher Examinations: Social Studies

REFERENCES

1. See 6:971.
2-14. See T2:1948; also includes a cumulative name index to the first 14 references and 5 reviews for this test.
15. WILLIAMS, CAROLYN CHANDLER. *The Relationship Between Selected Reading Skills and Other Personal Variables of Sixth and Seventh Grade Students and Achievement in Science and Social Studies.* Doctor's thesis, Mississippi State University (State College, Miss.), 1975. (*DAI* 36:4132A)

HOWARD D. MEHLINGER, *Professor of Education and History and Director, Social Studies Development Center, Indiana University, Bloomington, Indiana.*

According to the handbook, "The social studies tests are designed to measure student development in the broad skills and understandings that every citizen should possess to be effective. The skills include the ability to read, organize, interpret, and evaluate information presented in tabular, pictorial, or prose form. The understandings include the nature of social change; the interdependence of individuals, communities, and societies; the way in which society directs and regulates the behavior of its members; the nature of a democratic society; the effects of the geographical environment on man's way of life and man's increasing control over the forces of nature; the ways in which man tries to understand and adjust to his environment; and man's economic needs and how they are satisfied." These are worthy, ambitious goals. That the tests sometimes fall short of their stated aspirations does not detract from the fact that the tests are superior to most other social studies tests on the market at any grade level and continue to provide models for good item construction.

While the overall quality of the tests is high, they present some problems for social studies educators. Test developers fully appreciate the impact achievement tests can have on the development of a subject field. If standardized tests continue to represent traditional ways of thinking about a field, they may impede needed reforms. If they appear to be far in advance of current practice in a field, they may be written off as "faddist" and thus ignored.

The tests were developed between 1966 and 1970, a period marking the end of the first phase of the "new social studies." During this phase, emphasis was placed on teaching inquiry skills, on imparting the "structure" of the academic disciplines, and in general on strengthening the intellectual side of social studies. It is not by accident that the description for the tests notes that the content for the test items was drawn from such fields as political science, sociology, anthropology, economics, history, and geography.

But the field of social studies has changed in several ways since these tests were published. The National Council for the Social Studies has published a set of curriculum guidelines that identify four broad concerns: knowledge, skills, values, and social participation. The tests treat the first two but largely ignore the latter two. Since 1970 social studies teachers have devoted greater attention to such topics as value/moral education, law-related education, global education, and environmental education. The items on economics, political science, and geography especially seem out of phase with much current social studies practice. Moreover, sociology items do not reflect current concerns about the position of racial and ethnic minorities, and women in society. In short, social studies educators who might have been pleased that their students performed well on these tests in 1969 and 1970 would be less certain today that the tests fully tap what students should gain from good social studies instruction.

In summary, the STEP II social studies tests are good and can still be recommended. Nevertheless, they are becoming less satisfactory with each passing year. It is time for ETS to plan a revision, one that will maintain the same high standards of the current series while reflecting the changes that have occurred in social studies instruction since 1970.

INA V. S. MULLIS, *Senior Research Analyst, National Assessment of Educational Progress, Denver, Colorado.*

The "tests are designed to measure student development in the broad skills and understandings that every citizen should possess to be effective." In the skills area, the test measures a variety of critical thinking skills involving logical relationships—including symbol recognition, interpretation, comparison and contrast, and interpolation.

The format and the critical skills required are essentially the same for each of the four levels of the test. Each question or group of questions begins with a picture, cartoon, map, graph, chart, or reading passage, and the emphasis is on cognitive process rather than knowledge con-

tent. Respondents are asked to read, organize, and analyze the information presented. The items in different levels differ in complexity of situation, context, difficulty of vocabulary, and level of abstraction. At the high school and post-secondary levels, the graphics involve more variables and the content is more esoteric. The properties and processes involved become progressively more complex throughout the series, since the situations become farther away in time and space and the visual materials become more abstract; nevertheless the critical thinking skills required are the same at all grade levels.

A well-organized and easy-to-use item classification system is provided in the manual for each series. Items are classified by skill level—organizing, interpreting, or evaluating information; by discipline topic; and by type of stimulus material. Percentages of the normative sample passing each item are given, so that even though the test is not divided into subtests, users can reference specific skills, even one as unique as the ability to interpret cartoons.

The manual's claims to measure such broad understandings as "the nature of social change," the "nature of a democratic society," and "man's economic needs and how they are satisfied" are not justified by the items. Although the items often pertain to information or concepts related to these understandings, they rarely require demonstration of concept acquisition beyond the information provided. For example, the ability to interpret a political cartoon or a shaded representation of the overlapping powers of nation and states does not necessarily imply an understanding of the nature of a democratic government. There are a few scattered knowledge questions, but they are insufficient to determine broad understandings. The authors' failure to classify items according to understandings is perhaps due to this weakness.

The STEP II social studies test score is closely related to total score on SCAT II. The within-grade correlations range from .75 to .83, with median .81. These correlations are higher than the corresponding correlations for any of the other six tests in the STEP II series. These correlations are not far below the alternate-form reliabilities of the social studies tests: .60 to .93, with median .85. These correlations raise serious questions as to whether or not the social studies test is too heavily weighted with items placing an emphasis on intelligence rather than social studies outcomes.

The manuals for each age level include clear and complete administration and scoring instructions. They also present norms for individuals and school means, explain how to use standard errors, and include percentile bands. However, the appropriateness of using any of the norms for comparison purposes is quite questionable. Because achievement tests (SAT, ACT, ITBS, CTBS, NAEP) have been declining since the late 1960s, the norms for these 1969 tests are probably seriously outdated.

Still, this test is generally an excellent measure of critical thinking skills. Because of its emphasis on cognitive process, the content does not appear particularly outmoded. The test is specifically recommended for use within a district, school, or class to provide information about particularized instructional strategies, such as reading for specific purposes in the content area, interpretation of information, or logical reasoning. The test would also be useful as a diagnostic tool either to help individual teachers select appropriate reading materials and instructional strategies or to aid districts shifting their instructional emphasis from knowledge of content to cognitive process.

In summary, if this 1969 test is used to provide information for instructional purposes and not to make national comparisons, it is recommended as a measure of cognitive process. It is not suggested for use if course instruction is organized primarily around the more traditional approach of fact concept learning, since it would not be an adequate measure of pupil achievement in terms of instruction.

[893]

Zimmerman-Sanders Social Studies Test. 1, 2 semesters in grades 7–8; 1962–64; first published 1962–63 in the Every Pupil Scholarship Test series; Forms A, B, (164, 2 pages); 2 levels labeled Tests 1, 2; manual ('64, 3 pages); $3.50 per 25 tests; $1.50 per specimen set; postage extra; 30(35) minutes; John J. Zimmerman and M. W. Sanders; Bureau of Educational Measurements. *

MARY FRIEND ADAMS, *Assistant Professor of Education, Indiana University, Bloomington, Indiana.*

This test purports to measure seventh and eighth grade students' knowledge of important social studies content based on textbooks and

courses of study being used in several different states. Four so-called "equivalent" forms of the test are available, of which three include 85 and one includes 75 multiple choice, factual recall items. The catalog, however, states that Forms 1A and 1B are for the first semester and Forms 2A and 2B for the second semester.

The authors suggest that the results of the test may be used to: (a) measure student achievement, (b) evaluate teaching effectiveness, (c) determine student grades, (d) motivate desirable habits of learning, and (e) detect weaknesses in the learning process.

As a measure of student achievement in social studies, this test is inadequate. An analysis of the content of one form (2A) revealed that all of the items fell into one of four broad recall categories: (a) location, where X occurred or where X is; (b) identification of famous people and the jobs they held; (c) recognition of the contribution a famous person made; and (d) capitals of various countries. In no case did an item require the students to go beyond the recall of miscellaneous facts.

These items reflect poor objectives for social studies instruction and have little relevance to social understanding. Social understanding requires that students be able to use historical data to form and test hypotheses, make predictions, and develop explanations; to provide good reasons for a position; and to define social phenomena operationally. Students who are proficient at these functional skills may perform poorly on this particular test. The relevance of these items to social science knowledge or processes is questionable.

As a measure of teaching effectiveness, this test is also poor. The validity and reliability of the test were established in 1963. The items were based on the content of textbooks being used in schools in various states at that time. The objectives and materials of social studies textbooks have changed considerably since then. Social studies instruction which stresses process skills, critical thinking, and social issues cannot effectively be evaluated with a test based on questions from textbooks used in 1963.

The manual provides a table for translating raw scores into percentile scores. The percentile scores are then translated into letter grades. To use any commercially prepared test as a means of awarding grades is questionable. One should examine one's instructional objectives carefully to determine whether the objectives of the test are consistent with one's own objectives before using this test as a measuring device.

As a means of motivating desirable habits of learning, this test should be ignored. As stated earlier, this test does not measure learning. It merely measures a student's ability to recall a random assortment of facts. This learning does not reflect any habits that seem necessary for coping or surviving in the world today. The test does not aid a teacher in detecting "weaknesses in the learning pattern." Learning is not synonymous with remembering.

In summary, this test is one of the poorest available for measuring a student's learning patterns or knowledge of social studies content. A teacher interested in evaluating either of the above would do better to develop his own test than to use this one. This test is useful only for those teachers whose goals are to teach miscellaneous facts—and questionable ones at that!

ECONOMICS

[894]

★CLEP Subject Examination in Introductory Macroeconomics. 1 semester or equivalent; 1974–76; for college accreditation of nontraditional study, advanced placement, or assessment of educational achievement; tests administered monthly at centers throughout the United States; Form WCT1 ('74, 15 pages); optional essay supplement Form WCT-B ('74, 2 pages) scored by college; for program accessories, see 473; rental and scoring fee, $20 per student (includes reporting of scores to the candidate and one college); postpaid; 90(95) minutes, same for essay supplement; program administered for the College Entrance Examination Board by Educational Testing Service. *
For reviews of the CLEP program, see 473 (3 reviews).

[895]

★CLEP Subject Examination in Introductory Micro- and Macroeconomics. 1–2 semesters or equivalent; 1974–76; for college accreditation of nontraditional study, advanced placement, or assessment of educational achievement; tests administered monthly at centers throughout the United States; Form WCT1 ('74, 17 pages); optional essay supplement Form WCT-C ('74, 2 pages) scored by college; for program accessories, see 473; rental and scoring fee, $20 per student (includes reporting of scores to the candidate and one college); postpaid; 90(95) minutes, same for essay supplement; program administered for the College Entrance Examination Board by Educational Testing Service. *
For reviews of the CLEP program, see 474 (3 reviews).

[896]

★CLEP Subject Examination in Introductory Microeconomics. 1 semester or equivalent; 1974–76; for college accreditation of nontraditional study, advanced placement, or assessment of educational achievement; tests administered monthly at centers throughout the United States; Form WCT1 ('74, 17 pages); optional essay supplement Form WCT-A ('74, 2 pages) scored by college; for program accessories, see 473; rental and scoring fee, $20 per student (includes reporting of scores to the candidate and one college); postpaid; 90(95) minutes, same for essay supplement; program administered for the College Entrance Examination Board by Educational Testing Service. *
For reviews of the CLEP program, see 473 (3 reviews).

[897]

*The Graduate Record Examinations Advanced Economics Test. Graduate school candidates; 1939–76; test administered 5 times annually (January, April, June, October, December) at centers established by the publisher; 5 current forms ('72–76, 29–31 pages); descriptive booklet ('75, 11 pages); for program accessories, see 476; examination fee, $10.50 per candidate; 170(190) minutes; an inactive form is available for local administration (rental fee, $5.50 per test); Educational Testing Service. *
See 6:987 (1 reference). For reviews of the GRE program, see 7:667 (1 review) and 5:601 (1 review).

IRVING MORRISSETT, *Professor of Economics, University of Colorado, Boulder, Colorado.* [Review of Form K-WGR.]

This is a 170-item multiple choice test, having five options for each item, to be completed in two hours and 50 minutes. It is used as an important criterion for admittance to graduate programs in economics in the vast majority of colleges and universities. It is administered five times a year in hundreds of colleges and universities throughout the United States and in many foreign countries, along with the general examinations in verbal and quantitative ability and 19 other advanced examinations. From October 1971 through September 1974, more than 12,000 persons took the economics examination.

The content and scope of the test were determined by a committee of five economists appointed by Educational Testing Service (ETS) with the assistance of the American Economic Association. Assisted by testing specialists from ETS and by other subject-matter specialists, the committee then developed the test. There is no report of the test having been field tested.

The test has clearly been constructed with the best of test-construction and content expertise. With a very few exceptions, items are clearly written, cover significant economic content, and present good sets of optional responses. A few questions turn on exceptionally fine points of theory, and many are particularly difficult to answer without the use of scratch paper, which is prohibited under the testing rules. While test results depend heavily on knowledge of modern economic theory, they depend equally on an agile mind.

The test description states that approximately 60 percent of the test is evenly divided between macroeconomic and microeconomic analysis, with the remainder devoted to questions from topics such as money and banking, international economics, public finance, labor economics, and economic development. Questions from the latter areas, however, are for the most part highly theoretical and closely linked to macro- and, especially microeconomics, to the virtual exclusion of historical and institutional content.

Test results are reported only for the entire test, not for subparts. Of the 20 advanced tests now given in all areas, 9 are reported in two or three subparts; for example, separate scores are reported for human geography and physical geography, as well as a total score. Reporting by subparts probably would be advantageous for economics. The obvious division would be into macro and micro, although some economists might also wish to add a historical-institutional section, which would require a substantial change in content from the current test. Such a change would of course entail greater difficulties in test construction than in the current test, since theory is largely axiomatic and deductive and therefore highly amenable to multiple choice responses; whereas historical and institutional content, unless purely factual, is harder to put into multiple choice items on which experts agree.

Analysis of the test has been made with the substantial expertise and thoroughness that can be afforded by such a strong institution as ETS. The latest analysis is based on 715 of the 741 tests administered to candidates for admission to graduate schools and fellowship candidates in December 1974. The analysis yielded a highly satisfactory reliability estimate of .94. The test was also judged, not so convincingly, to be "less speeded than it might at first appear to be," particularly on the basis of completion of 75 percent of the test by 96 percent of the examinees.

The analysis also yielded the well substantiated judgment that the test is very "difficult."

With 170 items, the mean raw score was 59.4, the standard deviation 27.7, the range −6 to 142, and the skewness moderately positive. (Negative scores are possible because of error penalties; the expected value of the score of a completely uninformed person with or without guessing is zero.) Thus, with the mean and median almost a standard deviation below the middle possible (positive) score and the standard deviation less than one-third of the middle possible score, it seems that the test is pointed more toward the discovery of determination and genius than to maximum discrimination.

Raw scores are converted to scaled scores, with a possible range of 200 to 990, rounded to the nearest 10 points, so that all scores end in zero. The reason for using a three-digit score is to get away from any implied connection with the 0 to 100 grading scale common to education; the reason for setting the third digit at zero is to avoid the appearance of spurious accuracy. The method of converting to the scaled score is one which preserves the comparability of any revised test with previous tests. This is done by using a subset of questions common to a new test and the preceding test—34 items in the present case.

While the level of difficulty of successive revised tests, as indicated by the scaled scores, is held constant, so that a given scaled score in 1977 is comparable to the same scaled score in any of the preceding tests, the percentile rankings are not comparable. These are normed on recent groups of examinees. Two recent sets of norms are supplied, for all 12,134 examinees who took the advanced economics test from October 1971 through September 1974 and for a subset of 1,916 examinees who took the test from October 1974 through June 1975, the subset consisting only of college seniors and non-enrolled college graduates. This subset, by excluding the graduate students and college sophomores and juniors who took the test, may provide a more useful basis for judging incoming graduate students.

Content validity of the test, given the types of knowledge covered by the test, is well assured by the expertise of the examining committee. Some information on the general predictive ability is given. A brief review of a number of studies, using various criteria of success, concludes that "A weighted composite including under-

Graduate Record Examinations Advanced Economics Test

graduate GPA and one or more GRE scores typically provided a validity coefficient in the .40–.45 range for various criteria of success and for different academic fields. This is somewhat higher than the coefficient obtained with GRE scores alone and substantially higher than that obtained from use of undergraduate GPA alone."

All in all, this is a highly professional and very demanding test. It is the best in the field, not only because it is the only test in the field but also because of the expert and plentiful resources, both substantive and technical, that have gone into its construction, revision, analysis, and norming. As indicated above, the test is more difficult than it should be, both from the standpoint of getting maximum discrimination and maintaining the morale of examinees. It is heavily weighted on the theoretical side, which is in line with the emphases of most graduate schools today, but not calculated to please those economists who would like to see somewhat more attention given to the historical and institutional aspects of their subject.

[898]

★Junior High School Test of Economics. Grades 7–9; 1973–74; 1 form ('73, 7 pages); manual ('74, 39 pages); separate answer sheets must be used; $6 per 25 tests; $2 per manual; postage extra; answer sheets must be reproduced locally; specimen set not available; (40) minutes; Leon M. Schur, Robert Donegan, Marlin L. Tanck, David Zitlow, and Gerald A. Weston; Joint Council on Economic Education. *

LEE H. EHMAN, *Associate Professor of Education, Indiana University, Bloomington, Indiana.*

This test is based on an item-sampling matrix including eleven content categories (both macro- and micro-economics) and three cognitive categories—knowledge, comprehension, and application. The content categories lead to a reasonable coverage, although a few items do seem misplaced in the matrix. For example, this item is supposed to measure comprehension of GNP: "If we wanted to find out whether an increase in wages over a period of time represented an actual increase in living standards, we should look at what has happened to:" (answer: "Consumer prices"). This next item is supposed to measure application of GNP knowledge: "Which one of the following is likely to cause more people to be out of work?" (answer: "A decrease in business spending"). Neither item appears to measure the GNP con-

tent category. The content category "International Trade" has items which measure only effects of tariffs and not the content explained at length in the manual. Similar problems are encountered in the categorization by cognitive dimensions. Nevertheless, there is a good range of items across the three cognitive levels.

An important flaw is the lack of validity evidence. The test was constructed by "five teachers and economists" who declared it to have "content validity." An independent group of content specialists should have judged the content validity of the test according to specified procedures and criteria. Also, no experimental data comparing groups with instruction to those without are available to establish construct validity. No concurrent validity data are developed. The mean scores for seventh, eighth, and ninth grades increase, suggesting that some maturational factors influence the test scores. More substantial validity evidence is needed before credence can be placed in the use of this test.

The test manual does give extensive rationale statements for each item, and these could be of considerable value to the user. Other specific item data are missing, however. Item-to-total score correlation coefficients are mentioned but not given. Response distributions for each answer and the distractors are omitted. What is given is the proportion correct by item for the entire sample used to construct norms. Six of the 40 proportions are at or near the chance, or guessing, level. The relatively modest reliabilities are undoubtedly affected. These items probably also contributed to what appears to be a floor effect for the test—the raw means for seventh, eighth, and ninth grade are 14.25, 17.68, and 19.12 out of a possible 40, respectively.

The norms for the test are based on what is described as a national sample. The user should understand, however, that the schools which cooperated were all associated with programs of the Joint Council on Economic Education, and there is a pronounced Midwestern/Southern bias—only Pittsburgh and Utah schools are exceptions and they are only two out of 22 school systems used.

A few items have very questionable "answers." For example: "The long lines of consumers waiting outside many stores in Russia tell us that many consumer goods there are probably:" (answer: "priced too low"). This "answer" seems to miss the point, which is that supply is too low (and/or demand is too high) for the price placed on the items. Similarly: "In a capitalistic economic system, such as the United States, who has the most influence in deciding what will be produced?" (answer: "Consumers"; other foils are "labor unions"; "the federal government"; "businessmen"). This item may or may not be correctly answered, in the quantitative sense, by "consumers." The term "most influence" is a tricky notion in the U.S. economy!

As stated in the test manual, this instrument does fill a gap for the junior high level, and that is an important point. But the lack of clearly established validity, the questionable content coverage (despite the manual's claims), the relatively high number of chance-level items, and the weaknesses in several other items, all suggest that this test needs a thorough item-by-item revision and complete validity studies before it can be used confidently as a pedagogical and/or research tool.

[899]

Modern Economics Test: Content Evaluation Series. Grades 10–12; 1971; 1 form (9 pages); manual (16 pages); separate answer sheets (MRC) must be used; $12 per 35 tests; $6.30 per 35 answer sheets and 1 manual; 75¢ per scoring stencil; $1.35 per specimen set; postage extra; scoring service, 30¢ per test ($15 minimum); 45(50) minutes; Morris G. Sica, Sylvia Lane, and John D. Lafky; Houghton Mifflin Co. *

LEE H. EHMAN, *Associate Professor of Education, Indiana University, Bloomington, Indiana.*

This test is accompanied by a clear and complete set of directions for administration, scoring, and interpretation of results. But the lack of completeness in describing the development and validation of the test weakens confidence in its use.

The 45 items cover four content areas deemed important by three major reports by the Joint Council on Economic Education published in the 1960s. The authors, with the aid of ten high school economics teachers, developed a pool of items which covered the four content areas and varying levels of Bloom's taxonomy. Unfortunately, no classification of items by taxonomic levels is reported; the eight "behaviors" outlined in the manual, which are supposed to be represented by the items, are not described in

terms of Bloom's work. Nevertheless, there seems to be an adequate range of items at various cognitive levels for each content area. One significant omission in content is in the area of public economic policy. No item reflects the recent problem of high inflation which is accompanied by high unemployment.

There are some weak items. For example, the stem of item 19 tends to give the answer for item 21. Items 29 through 32 depend on a supply/demand schedule diagram for a leather shoe market. The diagram is perfectly clear. But the items, apparently through a typographical error, all refer to changes in price, demand, and supply of leather—not leather shoes. This difference is important in the four items and could lead to incorrect answers or, at least, to confusion and doubt for a knowledgeable student. Items 33 and 34 (on wage fluctuations and employment opportunity) seem based on erroneous assumptions about reality, in that they ignore the function of unions and wage stability on wage levels. Item 41 seems oversimplified, and item 25 is not correct—its keyed answer is "that the income tax has proven to be the largest source of revenue for the government." This is *presently* correct, but has not always been so—corporate taxes were not too long ago a larger source, for example—and this certainly has not always been "the major argument in favor of the progressive Federal Income Tax," as the item asserts.

Although fault can be found with the content of the test items, a more damaging criticism is that there is no evidence whatever for the test's validity. The authors claim "content" validity—actually they refer to face validity. Only one "curriculum expert" judged the table of specifications and items sampled within this matrix. No independent group of content experts—economists—judged the items for their accuracy, coverage, and congruence with the table of specifications. Thus, content validity has not been established.

Construct validity evidence is wholly lacking. Studies showing differences on this test between students instructed in economics and those not instructed are not reported. Nor has any concurrent validity study to show a relationship between this test and others in the content field been made. The split-halves reli-

Junior High School Test of Economics

ability of the test is fairly high (.87), although no test-retest reliability study is reported.

A sophisticated school sampling plan for field testing is described in the manual, but the schools involved in the standardization study are heavily from the Midwest and South. Twenty-five schools are from the former region, and ten from the latter. Only four are from the Northeast, and the remaining four from the West. The discrepancy of proportional sampling by region is not explained by the authors and calls into question the regional representativeness of the norming data.

In short, the test is well-supported by a complete manual for administration, scoring, and interpretation. It is not supported by complete evidence for validity. The reliability is quite high, but some individual items need reworking. The main need is for validity evidence, which will either increase our confidence in the scientific use of this test or lead to its rejection or revision. At present, confidence is not warranted.

IRVING MORRISSETT, *Professor of Economics, University of Colorado, Boulder, Colorado.*

The purpose of this 45-item multiple-choice test is "to discern whether the individual comprehends the essential concepts and principles of economics and can apply them to evaluate the functioning of the American economy, analyze its persistent problems, and rationally judge the viability and validity of economic decisions implemented by decision makers. In addition, the test can discern whether the individual possesses the appropriate background for making rational economic decisions." At this high level of abstraction, the stated purpose is exemplary, and one to which any economics testmaker might aspire. More concretely, it is a test of the content of a standard high school economics text. The 45 items are classified as national income, 22 percent; monetary and fiscal policy, 31 percent; price system, 27 percent; and international economics and economic development, 20 percent.

Procedures for development of the test were eminently sound. Construction of test items by a group of high school economics teachers, followed by appropriate rounds of testing with students and reviews by content and test experts, resulted in a test with "suitable ranges of difficulty and discrimination." The use of Bloom's *Taxonomy of Educational Objectives,* claimed by the publisher as a part of the developmental process, is less in evidence than the other developmental features. Most responses would qualify as application and comprehension questions. There are few factual questions (although comprehension and application responses may be memorized) and little or nothing that can be called analysis or synthesis. The one question described as concerned with value judgments is on comparative advantage and unrelated to value judgments. The lack of higher-order questions is, of course, common to most testing procedures.

The test items are well constructed. As with any multiple-choice test, there may be some disputes about how right some of the right answers are—a matter that is most likely to trouble brighter students. For a good score on the test, a student should accept the textbook presentations of orthodox price theory and a simple Keynesian macro-model, saving the "yes-buts" for class discussion. An example is item 11: "If the flow of income in country x is not large enough to absorb all the goods and services produced, the price level will tend to (A) fall, (B) fluctuate within narrow limits, (C) rise, (D) remain stationary." Some students, after answering (A), would feel impelled to say, "It depends on what country you are talking about and how prices are determined in that country."

Students' scores will obviously be affected by the particular economics content to which they have been exposed. Many high school courses cover the subject matter of this test as it is described above, but students in a course that gives major emphasis to microeconomics, which comprises only 27 percent of the test, may score low, as would students who took a course which limits coverage of international economics (20 percent on the test). In short, the test is closely geared to a particular type of economics course. There is little or no coverage of some types of content that many economists would consider useful, including factual knowledge, such as orders of magnitude; and knowledge of institutions, such as economic pressure groups. But then, a 45-item test can't do everything.

The manual gives useful information about background, administration, and interpretation of the test. Blow-by-blow suggestions are given

Modern Economics Test: Content Evaluation Series

for test administration. The manual provides a table for converting raw scores into standard scores, stanines, percentile ranks, and percentile bands. The comments on the use and interpretation of the scores are only moderately useful. Caution is advised about interpreting the scores in the light of local circumstances, an admonition which may take the sting out of low scores that are compared to national norms but otherwise doesn't help much. The test is said to be "essentially diagnostic in nature," but suggestions for diagnostic procedures are not given. However, since all items are classified into general content areas, as indicated above, a simple diagnosis can take the form of examining high and low scores on these content areas.

The test was standardized in 1970 with a sample of 2,481 students from 43 high schools in 32 school systems in 17 states. The sampling procedure, with stratification by community size and socioeconomic rating, was quite sound. An important lack in the description of the norming procedure is information about what economics courses had been experienced by the sample students. Since the norming was done in May and June, perhaps it can be assumed that the sample students had recently completed a typical one-semester high school economics course. A still more important omission in the norming data is the lack of pre- and post-test results. The usefulness of the norming procedure would have been greatly enhanced if the sample had been divided into students who had and those who had not taken an economics course.

This is a sound and usable test for measuring economic knowledge as typically covered in a high school text. In this respect, it is comparable with the *Test of Economic Understanding*. However, the latter test has two advantages—it comes in two approximately equivalent forms (of 50 items each), which can be used for pre- and post-testing, and it provides pre- and post-test norms.

[900]

Primary Test of Economic Understanding. Grades 2–3; 1971; PTEU; norms based on grade 3 only; 1 form (11 pages); manual (26 pages plus test); $6 per 25 tests; $2 per manual; specimen set not available; postage extra; (40) minutes; Donald G. Davison and John H. Kilgore; Bureau of Business and Economic Research, University of Iowa; distributed by Joint Council on Economic Education. *

See T2:1967 (1 reference).

REFERENCES

1. See T2:1967.
2. BRANDENBURG, DALE C., AND WHITNEY, DOUGLAS R. "Matched Pair True-False Scoring: Effect on Reliability and Validity." *J Ed Meas* 9(4):297–302 w '72. * (*PA* 50:39)

JAMES O. HODGES, *Assistant Professor of Education, Virginia Commonwealth University, Richmond, Virginia.*

This test was designed to measure mastery of certain economics concepts, understandings, and generalizations that might be taught as a part of the content of primary level social studies. In a broader sense, it may be used to measure student achievement resulting from the introduction of new materials, teaching strategies, and the increased knowledge of teachers participating in in-service and pre-service programs which include an emphasis on economics education. Hence, it may be used to test the teacher's ability to teach, as well as the student's level of understanding of basic economics concepts.

The manual identifies from the discipline of economics five major generalizations which provided the conceptual framework for the development of the test. Included with each generalization are related major understandings, major concepts, and subconcepts developed by the authors. The scope and nature of the economic content is appropriate for primary level, and the test appears to be an excellent instrument for evaluating knowledge of economics content. While the authors consider the test "highly valid for a spiral and developmental economic education program," it is suggested that each school system or test evaluator assess content validity by determining whether the test measures the economic content of a particular program or programs in the system.

The 64 statements, 32 matched pairs, to which the student responds by circling "yes" or "no," have survived a thorough testing and analysis procedure. The test was administered during the development process to approximately 100 second grade students and has been evaluated in its present form as a research experiment with 504 second grade students in 24 classrooms of Des Moines, Iowa. While the norming process was based on a wide sample of third grade students in 135 schools in 18 states, the samples were selected partly for "convenience and accessibility." Consequently, the authors of the test make no claim that the data obtained represent a well defined repre-

Modern Economics Test: Content Evaluation Series

sentative population, although they state that the frequency distribution of scores resembles a normal distribution.

The "limited reading ability of primary grade students" was a major factor in influencing the form of the test. The manual suggests that the teacher read each item twice and direct the students to circle the "yes" or "no." The matched-pair format "involved writing reversed items for each concept or bit of information tested." To receive credit for a correct answer, the student must answer correctly each of the items making up a matched pair. While a multiple choice test would have permitted the development of higher-level questions, the authors indicate that efforts to use multiple choice items consisting of pictures was too costly and time-consuming. It was decided that the 32 matched-pair items were sufficient to obtain a justifiable reliability level and yet not be so lengthy as to tire or bore the students. Directions for administering and scoring the test are very clear and understandable.

An obtained K-R 20 reliability of .78 is deemed adequate for making decisions about groups. The authors state, however, that the test should not be used as the only source of information for making decisions about individual students.

Two charts provided in the manual will enable the examiner to evaluate results achieved by individual students in comparison with the norming group. The first table provides the corresponding percentile rank for each raw score. The second table enables the examiner to compare individual students with the norming group on each question by identifying the percent of students who answered each item correctly.

The *Primary Test of Economic Understanding* is a useful and appropriate evaluation instrument. It has been carefully developed and tested. It appears adequate for the primary grades in terms of the type of test items and the relative ease in administering the test. It is based on worthwhile economics content.

ANNA S. OCHOA, *Associate Professor of Social Studies Education, Indiana University, Bloomington, Indiana.*

This 64-item test is designed to measure selected economic generalizations and concepts in grades 2 and 3. These concepts are derived from economic content guidelines developed by Project DEEP (Developmental Economic Education Program), which, during the 1960s, was a pioneer effort to identify appropriate economic content for school curricula.

The test developers used a yes-no matched-pair format; e.g., item 1 is paired with item 33, item 2 with item 34, and so on through item 32 which is paired with item 64. To receive credit for a correct answer, the learner must get both paired items correct. The format is a thoughtful one that minimizes the acquiescent set of young children. There is no penalty for guessing. In fact, the directions to the user encourage guessing, as well as erasing wrong answers.

Is this test reflective of current trends in elementary social studies? The perspective of this review is that the primary social studies curriculum should include the following components: knowledge, thinking and inquiry, valuing, and social participation. While knowledge should include powerful theories and related concepts and generalizations, these theories should be applied to social issues. At the primary level the relationship of this knowledge to the lives of children should be made clear.

The test focuses exclusively on the knowledge base derived from economists, teachers, and curriculum developers. The economic generalizations and understandings that are listed in the manual are descriptive rather than explanatory. However, the testmakers were confined to the curriculum trends of the late 1960s. It is only recently that some attention has been given to curriculum based on theories rather than selected generalizations.

The test items do not reflect systematic application of concepts and generalizations to economic issues that children face. Although a few items deal with personal savings, allowances, and earnings, such items are few. No items deal with poverty, housing problems, or environmental issues. Rather, this test supports a curriculum that seeks to teach economic generalizations without explicit application to the social or economic issues that impinge upon children's immediate lives.

Use of sexist language is evident in several test items. A few items reveal sex stereotypes. For example, item 8 applies the division-of-labor concept to mother and sister doing the dishes. Item 27 asks if a business*man* "needs a

Primary Test of Economic Understanding

wife, a car, materials and workers" before *he* can go into business. Although the answer to this item is "no," the item still supports a bias about the role of women.

No explicit attention is given to cultural diversity. The names of children used in a few test items are common Anglo-Saxon names. None of the items are cast in terms that represent ethnic or racial groups. It should be noted that sensitivity to sexism and pluralism were only emerging when this test was under development. Revision of the test should reflect these social concerns.

The conceptual framework does not reflect attention to higher level thinking or inquiry skills. This omission violates recent trends in elementary social studies. In this decade, textbooks and new social studies curricula have emphasized intellectual development. The work of learning theorists such as Bruner, Piaget, and Gagne is ignored by the test developers. The test items are largely confined to the knowledge and comprehension levels of Bloom's taxonomy. There are no items that involve children in hypothesizing (making plausible guesses), identifying data sources, evaluating evidence, or drawing conclusions. If the testmakers would present problem situations, they could design items that would address these important intellectual skills.

In the 1970s, social studies educators have done substantial work in values education. The work of Taba, Fraenkel, Kohlberg, and others has provided insight as well as instructional models and materials appropriate for primary youngsters. Children can and do make decisions in their daily lives. Test items can ask them to identify plausible alternatives and to predict consequences. Such items could be developed in the yes-no matched-pair format. A revision of this test should consider this important component of social studies.

Like other tests for young children, this one also ignores this component of social participation. It does not provide students with items that would ask them what they would do if they had spent their allowance and needed more money. It does not ask them what they would do if they didn't have playground equipment because the school could not afford it. Other items might have them identify the adults who might be useful in helping them solve a problem.

Appropriately, the test developers clearly identify some of the limitations of the instrument in the manual. They point out that the validity of the test depends upon the objectives of the local social studies program. They point out that the test norms were derived only from a third grade population. In addition, the manual cautions that decisions about an individual student should not be based solely on the student's score on this test and that no effort was made to compare this test with controlled, normative samples for other standardized tests. These are important limitations that should guide the user.

More importantly, the test taps a limited knowledge base that has limited power in helping children explain their economic world. Intellectual operations are ignored, as are valuing skills and social participation. Although the test seems to measure some of the understandings identified, it ignores important components of the social studies. Without substantial revision, this test (one of the few economic tests designed for young children) should be confined to diagnostic use.

[901]

Test of Elementary Economics, Revised Experimental Edition. Grades 4–6; 1971; TEE; no data on reliability; norms based on grade 6 only; 1 form (8 pages); manual (27 pages); separate answer sheets must be used; $6 per 25 tests; $2 per manual; postage extra; answer sheets must be reproduced locally; specimen set not available; 30(35) minutes; developed by Economic Education Enrichment Program, West Springfield (Mass.) Public Schools; Joint Council on Economic Education. *

REFERENCES
1. NAPPI, ANDREW T. "An Evaluation of Award-Winning Elementary Teaching Materials From the Kazanjian Program." *J Econ Ed* 5(2):82–8 sp '74. *

MARY FRIEND ADAMS, *Assistant Professor of Education, Indiana University, Bloomington, Indiana.*

This test was designed to evaluate student understanding of seven basic economic concepts: household, business, government, exchange, technology, market, and the national economy. These concepts are a fair representation of the major concepts around which economic instruction in the elementary school is most frequently developed. The test was developed to evaluate the impact of the intermediate elementary section of a K–12 curriculum in which economic concepts were integrated into the existing social studies curriculum. The

Primary Test of Economic Understanding

test is an excellent measure of the concepts and skills emphasized in the curriculum project.

As a measure of economic understanding for classes not using the prepared curriculum materials, one may find that the complexity and sophistication of economic understanding required in the test is beyond that normally achieved in elementary social studies classes where sociological, historical, and political concepts are emphasized. The manual is well-prepared, especially the section providing a rationale for each item on the test. Teachers not using the prepared curriculum materials can read the rationale for each item to determine whether the test equitably measures their teaching objectives and instruction. The rationale could serve as a guideline for teachers interested in designing their own instructional materials.

The test items have been designed to measure three levels of cognition: knowledge, comprehension, and application. Knowledge items are subdivided into factual and defining items. Items have not been developed for all three cognitive levels for each of the seven concepts; however, a reasonable distribution among cognitive levels exists (knowledge, 13; comprehension, 18; application, 9). Of the 40 items on the test, the concepts of household and exchange are heavily stressed, while the concepts of technology and national economy are included in only four and two items, respectively.

The manual includes an explanation of the types of questions on the test, an item rationale, a report of preliminary technical data, directions for using and scoring the test, and a feedback form for reporting results of the test. Norms are available for grade 6 only; no data on reliability or validity are available. The developers are soliciting information on the student population and test results from teachers using the test. The manual is written in clear, precise language and is easily understood by teachers unfamiliar with the language of statistics and test construction. The developers of the test have done an outstanding job of explaining the philosophy, goals, and uses of the test results. Teachers are encouraged to use the test as a diagnostic, as well as an achievement measure. In either capacity, this test measures many of the important social studies concepts and processes necessary to economic understanding today.

While the test was developed in 1971, the items are free of dated information. The knowledge items do not emphasize specific factual information which is related to a specific time period, but rather emphasize knowledge of basic concepts and their attributes. The conceptual emphasis of the items keeps them from being restricted to instruction based on one specific curriculum. Any person with an understanding of the seven basic concepts included on the test should be able to perform successfully.

Although this test is still in an experimental stage, it is probably one of the best measures of economic understanding available today. This test is one of the few available elementary social studies tests which measure higher level cognition and conceptually organized knowledge. Evaluation utilizing this instrument can encourage good teaching of economics in the elementary school.

JAMES O. HODGES, *Assistant Professor of Education, Virginia Commonwealth University, Richmond, Virginia.*

This test, referred to in the manual as "an experimental evaluation instrument" for intermediate level, was designed for use and tested in sixth grade. Although identified as a test for grades 4–6, there is no evidence that the test was given to either 4th or 5th grade students in the piloting and revision stages. Nor is there any information on its use in these grades since its development. For the most part, the test was given to pupils from middle-class homes, and there is no available evidence that the test is appropriate for pupils of varying academic abilities from a broad spectrum of socioeconomic backgrounds. As the manual indicates, the test results are not sufficient to establish norms.

The instrument is designed to test understanding of seven specific economic concepts: household, business, government, exchange, technology, market, and national economy. Since it focuses on major concepts of the discipline of economics, it is consistent with the goals and objectives of social studies education. While the use of multiple choice items is generally recognized as appropriate for testing almost any understanding or ability, this test is limited to questions of actual knowledge and definitions, comprehension, and application. There are no questions designed to test interpretation or analysis of charts, graphs, documents, etc. Nor are there questions to test critical thinking or problem-solving skills. In a matrix including the seven major concepts, the manual identifies 13 knowledge questions, 18 comprehension questions, and 9 application questions.

The quality of the 40 multiple choice items is excellent. They are well-stated and contain appropriate distractors. It appears that the test is most appropriate to use in evaluating achievement following an extended period of instruction in economics. The questions are heavily loaded with economic concepts, which would make them difficult for students with limited reading ability and those who lack the conceptual basis for understanding the questions. Because of its specialized language, not many students can be expected to do well on this instrument if it is used as a pre-assessment tool.

There are a number of reasons to believe that this test would be very difficult for large numbers of students in the target group. First, even for the select testing group, 29 correct answers out of 40 questions was sufficient to rank students at the 99th percentile. The students who correctly answered one-half the questions ranked at the 74th percentile. It is likely that as the test is administered at lower grade levels and to students in different socioeconomic and ability levels, the number of correct answers would be so few that the test's value would be limited.

A second factor which might contribute to the difficulty of this test is reading level. Although there is no information on reading level, a large number of questions contain highly abstract and specialized terminology. An example is the question which asks the students to identify the requirement for "the development of an industrial economy" from such choices as "an increase in investment in capital equipment," "a stable population," and "a decrease in amount of saving." Saving, investment, capital equipment, and industrial economy are abstract and highly specialized concepts and it is questionable whether many students in grades 4–6 are likely to acquire an image of these concepts that is indicative of functional economic literacy.

A few questions concern specific periods in American history and probably would be difficult for students who lack the historical background. They might also necessitate a perspective of historical time that is lacking in many

intermediate children. One question asks the student to select the answer which "*best* describes the economy of the United States during the period 1750–1799." Another asks the student what happened to "a large proportion of the profits in the United States during 1800–1899." The correct answer is that they were "reinvested in capital equipment" rather than "reinvested in consumer goods," "exported," or "saved but not reinvested." Again, such knowledge is very specialized and not likely to be acquired by students in grades 4–6 unless they have gone through a very effective program in economics education.

The manual provides two sections that may be particularly useful to the teacher who wishes to analyze the test results. The first of these is the section titled "item rationale." This label is misleading, since the section does not provide an explanation of why the substance of each of these questions is important to the needs of the learner or the needs of society, but instead identifies the correct answer to each question and elaborates on the content in a way that explains the answer. An example is the question which asks the student to recognize the factors of production. The "rationale" statement simply explains what the factors of production are. These explanations, apparently intended for the teacher, do not seem sufficient to help those teachers who lack a conceptual understanding of the disciplines of economics.

The section of the manual which may be of more value to the teacher provides an analysis of each test item based on experience with 1,755 students primarily from New England. One table provides the results of analysis of each item in terms of the percentage of students answering correctly and incorrectly, the percentage of students in the top 27 percent and bottom 27 percent who answered correctly, and the extent to which the item discriminates between the upper and lower groups. Another table shows the percentages of students responding to each alternative answer. The analysis would be more valuable if norms had been established with a more representative cross section of students in grades 4–6. Such an analysis could help to show where misconceptions exist by pinpointing those distractors selected by a substantial number of students.

In summary, this is a conceptually sound test

Test of Elementary Economics

of economic understanding and the questions are well written. Norms should be established for grades 4–6, and across a variety of socio-economic backgrounds. There are enough difficult questions to provide ample discrimination among students. The test is perhaps too difficult for grades 4 and 5. It could probably be used effectively in the middle schools, following instruction in economics.

[902]

Test of Understanding in Personal Economics.
High school; 1971; TUPE; norms for grades 9 and 12 only; 1 form (7 pages); manual (28 pages); separate answer sheets must be used; $6 per 25 tests; $2 per manual; postage extra; answer sheets must be reproduced or obtained locally; specimen set not available; (45) minutes; Joint Council on Economic Education. *

REFERENCES

1. KIM, PAUL YUNG TAIK. *An Analysis of Personal Economic Understanding Developed in Selected General College Business and Economics Courses.* Doctor's thesis, University of Minnesota (Minneapolis, Minn.), 1973. (*DAI* 34:3817A)
2. MILLER, HELEN MINER. *A Study of Personal Economic Concepts and Personal Finance Attitudes of Wisconsin Winnebago Indian Youth Compared With White Youth in Selected Wisconsin Public Schools.* Doctor's thesis, Northern Illinois University (DeKalb, Ill.), 1975. (*DAI* 36:6432A)
3. POOLER, ANNE ELIZABETH. *An Analysis of General and Personal Economic Understanding Among Selected Maine Eleventh Grade U.S. History Students.* Doctor's thesis, University of Maine (Orono, Me.), 1975. (*DAI* 36:6452A)
4. DUFF, THOMAS BERT. *Measurement of Personal Economic Understanding Developed in Basic Business.* Doctor's thesis, University of Minnesota (Minneapolis, Minn.), 1976. (*DAI* 37:7487A)
5. FEESE, SHARRON SUZANNE MICHAELS. *Incidental Learning of Consumer Economic Concepts in Second-Semester Typewriting.* Doctor's thesis, Kansas State University (Manhattan, Kan.), 1976. (*DAI* 37:5544A)

HULDA GROBMAN, *Professor of Health Education, Saint Louis University Medical Center, Saint Louis, Missouri.*

This test is intended to measure information and skills included in the Joint Council on Economic Education guidelines for teaching personal economics through social studies, business and home economics curricula, "to teach the application of economic analysis to personal decisions and to emphasize the interrelatedness of economic matters, both personal and social. The goal is the improvement of various competencies in students' roles as workers, consumers and citizens." The student is told that "these questions will measure how well you understand the principles of economics and the way our economy operates."

The test is appropriate for any high school economics, general social studies, or contemporary affairs course. However, the basic assumptions about learning underlying the test rationale are questionable. Since the statement of purpose appears to define "understanding" as a

higher cognitive process, the proportion of items devoted to knowledge and direct application might be questioned. Further, there is an implicit assumption that knowledge of a fact is a sufficient condition for use of that fact to promote understanding. Thus, the "rationale" provided for each test item includes such statements as: "This is a factual matter which provides an understanding of...." Or, the student who recognizes that "the American economic system functions primarily through.... markets" is presumed to have "an appreciation for the role of markets in our economic system" and this appreciation "will enable students to judge and act for their best interest in market situations they are involved in."

The norms (spring 1970) are percentile ranks for 9th and 12th grade students in home economics, business education, and social studies classes, who have not studied the Council's guide materials. The data are admittedly not on a representative sample, but the data and their presentation are reasonably successful in the stated purpose of providing useful information to teachers. Thus, for example, each item is discussed in terms of why it is included, and why the keyed answer is correct and the distractors are not. Percentages of the norm group passing each item are given, though frequency of selection of distractors is not. Reliability and validity data are reported in an easy-to-understand fashion and, within the limitations of the sample, are acceptable.

Although the test layout is professional looking, there are several serious flaws in presentation: answering item 29 depends on information in the stem of item 28, rather than having common information provided in an introductory statement to both items and separating the pair of items from the preceding and following items; the reference back to item 28 is implicit rather than explicit in the item wording. For some items, the writers clearly had difficulty developing three plausible distractors. The distribution of keyed responses among the four alternatives is relatively even, although in three instances the keyed answer appears in the same position on the answer sheet for three successive items.

A minor difficulty shared with many other test developers in the social sciences is the problem of avoiding wording of items in a way that may make them obsolete or change their meaning during the life of the test. Item 40 refers to the GNP forecasts "between now and 1980." While the answer does not depend on a specific time frame, since it is a hypothetical if/then question (If GNP increases, what must also have happened?), such temporal references can reduce the life of a test. Currency and pertinence of other items appear highly acceptable despite the age of the instrument.

[903]

*UP Field Test in Economics. College; 1969–73; formerly called *The Undergraduate Record Examinations: Economics Test;* Form SUR ('70, 19 pages); descriptive booklet ('72, 14 pages); for UAP accessories, see 480; rental fee, $4 per test, postage extra; 120(140) minutes; Educational Testing Service. *

GEOGRAPHY

[904]

*The Graduate Record Examinations Advanced Geography Test. Graduate school candidates; 1966–76; test administered 5 times annually (January, April, June, October, December) at centers established by the publisher; 3 scores: human geography, physical geography, total; 3 current forms ('73–76, 31–32 pages); descriptive booklet ('75, 11 pages); for program accessories, see 476; examination fee, $10.50 per candidate; 170(190) minutes; an inactive form is available for local administration (rental fee, $5.50 per test); Educational Testing Service. *

For a review of the GRE program, see 7:667 (1 review).

[905]

*UP Field Test in Geography. College; 1969–77; formerly called *The Undergraduate Record Examinations: Geography Test;* Form K-RUR ('71, 33 pages); descriptive booklet ('70, 7 pages); for UAP accessories, see 480; rental fee, $4 per test, postage extra; 120(140) minutes; Educational Testing Service. *

HISTORY

[906]

★ACT Proficiency Examination in African and Afro-American History. College and adults; 1972–76; for college accreditation of nontraditional study, advanced placement, or assessment of educational achievement; test administered 4 times annually (February, May, August, November) at centers established by the publisher; developed and administered in New York State as a part of their College Proficiency Examinations Program; 6 semester credits recommended; no data on reliability; Form ZZ ('72, 13 pages, reprinted with 1976 copyright); study guide ('76, 4 pages); for further information and program accessories, see 470; examination fee, $30 per candidate (includes reporting of score to the candidate and one college); 180(210) minutes; developed by the New York State Education Department; American College Testing Program. *

Test of Understanding in Personal Economics

[907]

*Advanced Placement Examination in American History. High school students desiring credit for college level courses and admission to advanced courses; 1956–77; available to secondary schools for annual administration on specified days in May; Form ZBP ('77, 28 pages) in 2 booklets (objective, essay); course description ('76, 50 pages); sample syllabi ('75, 33 pages); grading guidelines ('76, 42 pages); previous essay questions available; for program accessories, see 471; examination fee, $32 per student; 180 (200) minutes; an inactive form [Form YBP ('76, 35 pages)] is available to colleges for local administration and scoring (rental fee, $2 per test); program administered for the College Entrance Examination Board by Educational Testing Service. *

See T2:1980 (1 reference); for a review by Harry D. Berg of an earlier form, see 6:1000 (1 reference); for reviews by James A. Field, Jr. and Christine McGuire, see 5:812. For reviews of the APE program, see 471 (2 reviews) and 7:662 (2 reviews).

[908]

*Advanced Placement Examination in European History. High school students desiring credit for college level courses and admission to advanced courses; 1956–77; available to secondary schools for annual administration on specified days in May; Form ZBP ('77, 30 pages) in 2 booklets (objective, essay); course description ('76, 35 pages); sample syllabus ('76, 31 pages); grading guidelines ('76, 30 pages); previous essay questions available; for program accessories, see 471; examination fee, $32 per student; 180(200) minutes; an inactive form [Form YBP ('76, 22 pages)] is available to colleges for local administration and scoring (rental fee, $2 per test); program administered for the College Entrance Examination Board by Educational Testing Service. *

See 6:1001 (2 references). For reviews of the APE program, see 471 (2 reviews) and 7:662 (2 reviews).

REFERENCES

1–2. See 6:1001.
3. ALPERN, MILDRED. "Advanced Placement European History." *Col Board R* 93:2–6+ f '74. *

[909]

★Black History: A Test to Create Awareness and Arouse Interest. Teachers; 1974; no data on reliability; no norms; 1 form (20 pages); no manual or directions for administration and scoring; bibliography and suggested uses (18 pages); separate answer sheets may be used; $50 per 30 tests, postpaid; specimen set not available; machine scoring service available; [40] minutes; Gregory C. Coffin, Elsie F. Harley, and Bessie M. L. Rhodes; Coffin Associates. *

REFERENCES

1. COFFIN, GREGORY C.; HARLEY, ELSIE F.; AND RHODES, BESSIE M. L. "A Test in Black History." *J Negro Ed* 43(3): 353–79 su '74. *

[910]

*CLEP Subject Examination in Afro-American History. 1 semester or equivalent; 1973–76; for college accreditation of nontraditional study, advanced placement, or assessment of educational achievement; tests administered monthly at centers throughout the United States; Forms VCT1, VCT2, ('73, 14 pages); optional essay supplement scored by college: Forms UCT-A, UCT-B, ('72, 2 pages); for program accessories, see 473; rental and scoring fee, $20 per student (includes reporting of scores to the candidate and one college); postpaid; 90(95) minutes, same for essay supplement; program administered for the College Entrance Examination Board by Educational Testing Service. *

For reviews of the CLEP program, see 473 (3 reviews).

[911]

*CLEP Subject Examination in American History. 1 year or equivalent; 1970–76; for college accreditation of nontraditional study, advanced placement, or assessment of educational achievement; tests administered monthly at centers throughout the United States; 3 scores: before 1865, since 1865, total; Form UCT1 ('70, 15 pages); optional essay supplement scored by college: Forms SCT1A, SCT1-B, SCT2-A, SCT2-B, ('70 2 pages); for program accessories, see 473; rental and scoring fee, $20 per student (includes reporting of scores to the candidate and one college); postpaid; 90(95) minutes, same for essay supplement; program administered for the College Entrance Examination Board by Educational Testing Service. *

For reviews of the CLEP program, see 473 (3 reviews) and 7:664 (3 reviews).

HARRY D. BERG, *Professor, Office of Evaluation Services, Michigan State University, East Lansing, Michigan.* [Review of Form SCT1.]

As stated above, the CLEP tests in American history are offered by the College Entrance Examination Board as a basis for granting college credit to those who believe they have gained competence in the subject through non-classroom means. If this purpose is to be properly served, useful norms should be provided, and the tests should have content validity for the courses to which they are intended to apply. As the developers indicate in the accompanying manuals, there are inherent problems in achieving these ends.

A test analysis, based on testing 1,173 students finishing a one-year introductory course in eight colleges, shows that the tests are very difficult. The mean scores of the sixty item subtests (before 1865 and after 1865) ranged from 19 to 26 percent of the possible score. These low scores can be partially explained by the fact that correction for guessing led to many omissions. This reviewer feels that the test items are of appropriate difficulty for a college level course.

Norms are presented both in terms of scaled scores and percentile ranks. Different editions have been equated so that their scaled scores are comparable. The correlation with the course grades in the norming population is surprisingly low, only .54. This suggests that course grades are given on some basis other than the kind of achievement measured by the tests. The relia-

bilities reported for two forms are .88 and .90, about as high as can be expected.

The College Board wisely suggests that users develop norms based on their own students as a basis for granting credit. To assist in this, the CEEB offers a local standard-setting administration for 50 to 200 students. If local norms are not used, the Board suggests that the scaled scores for C students be taken as the minimum score for awarding college credit.

The evaluation of the content validity of the tests is, of course, a subjective matter and will vary from user to user. This reviewer feels that, from a technical and subject coverage point of view, the tests are probably as good as can be made. They are well balanced as to broad areas (economic, political, social and cultural, foreign affairs, and geographical). A few items deal with rather obscure details, but, on the whole, items are concerned with applications, relationships, and comparisons involving concepts which should be derived from an introductory course wherever taken. The items meet the requirements of good item writing. There are few ambiguities, and the items are free from clues and nonfunctioning content.

[912]

*CLEP Subject Examination in Western Civilization. 1 year or equivalent; 1964–76; for college accreditation of nontraditional study, advanced placement, or assessment of educational achievement; tests administered monthly at centers throughout the United States; Forms VCT1 ('73, 16 pages), VCT2 ('73, 15 pages); optional essay supplement scored by college: Forms MCT-A, MCT-B, ('64, 2 pages), UCT-A, UCT-B, ('72, 2 pages); for program accessories, see 473; rental and scoring fee, $20 per student (includes reporting of scores to the candidate and one college); postpaid; 90(95) minutes, same for essay supplement; program administered for the College Entrance Examination Board by Educational Testing Service. *

For reviews of the CLEP program, see 473 (3 reviews) and 7:664 (3 reviews).

[913]

*The Graduate Record Examinations Advanced History Test. Graduate school candidates; 1939–76; test administered 5 times annually (January, April, June, October, December) at centers established by the publisher; 3 scores: European history, American history, total; 4 current forms ('74–76, 29–35 pages); descriptive booklet ('75, 12 pages); for program accessories, see 476; examination fee, $10.50 per candidate; 170(190) minutes; an inactive form is available for local administration (rental fee, $5.50 per test); Educational Testing Service. *

See 7:919 (1 reference); for a review by Robert H. Ferrell of an earlier form, see 5:818. For reviews of the GRE program, see 7:667 (1 review) and 5:601 (1 review).

[914]

Hollingsworth-Sanders Intermediate History Test. 1, 2 semesters in grades 5–6; 1962–64; first published 1962–63 in the Every Pupil Scholarship Test series; Forms A, B, ('64, 4 pages); 2 levels labeled Tests 1, 2; manual ('64, 3 pages); $3.50 per 25 tests; 20¢ per key; 20¢ per manual; $1.50 per specimen set; postage extra; 30(35) minutes; Leon Hollingsworth and M. W. Sanders; Bureau of Educational Measurements. *

DANA G. KURFMAN, *Supervisor of Social Studies, Prince George's County Public Schools, Upper Marlboro, Maryland.*

This instrument is questionable as a measure of contemporary objectives for intermediate level social studies programs. Developed in the early sixties, it is primarily a test of American history information. Although the test claims to consider the application of information and reasoning, as well as knowledge of facts, virtually all items deal with specific pieces of information. In fact, almost half of the test items in both forms of both tests ask for information about specific people. There is no evidence of any effort to measure the concepts which have been the major emphasis of social studies in the last 15 years.

The *Hollingsworth-Sanders Intermediate History Test* may have some use in determining student knowledge of basic information about American history. Even when the test is used for this limited purpose, care needs to be taken. First, it should be noted that the test is really two tests, one dealing with the first semester, and a second test, ostensibly covering two semesters of work. This is not the case. Test 1 deals with information about American history through the American Revolution. Test 2 deals with information about American history from the time of the American Revolution to the present. Thus, Test 2 should not be used on the assumption that it provides some measure of a full year's study of American history.

The major reservation about each of the two tests is the lack of balance between Form A and Form B. Apparently there was no planned division of items into topics or periods of American history; nor was there even a random distribution of items from an item pool. Three topical comparisons will illustrate this point for Test 1. Form A has just 1 item, while Form B has 8 items dealing wtih conditions in Europe prior to exploration. Form A has just 17 items dealing with the colonial period, whereas Form

B has 30 items. When Form A and Form B of Test 1 are compared with respect to the period of the American Revolution, Form A has 19 items and Form B just 2. The same sort of imbalance prevails with respect to Test 2. For some inexplicable reason, the American revolutionary period is treated again. In this test there is only 1 item in Form A, while there are 9 in Form B. Form A has 10 items on sectional development and politics, whereas Form B has only 2. Form A has 11 items on the War of 1812 and the Mexican War, whereas Form B has only 2. Form B makes up for this by having 13 items on foreign relations since the Civil War, whereas Form A has only 1. These differences in the two forms of each test suggest that users should not consider them interchangeable forms.

Given the marked changes in performance by students today compared to students in the early sixties, it will be inadvisable to rely too much on the norms that are provided with the tests. The norms suggest that the tests were of appropriate difficulty for the norming sample, but given the conceptual emphasis of contemporary social studies, these tests are likely to be much more difficult for today's students.

[915]

Meares-Sanders Junior High School History Test. 1, 2 semesters in grades 7–8; 1962–64; first published 1962–63 in the Every Pupil Scholarship Test series; Forms A, B, ('64, 4 pages); 2 levels labeled Tests 1, 2; manual ('64, 3 pages); $3.50 per 25 tests; $1.50 per specimen set; postage extra; 40(50) minutes; Shirley Meares and M. W. Sanders; Bureau of Educational Measurements. *

INA V. S. MULLIS, *Senior Research Analyst, National Assessment of Educational Progress, Denver, Colorado.*

This test is, for the most part, chronologically organized, with Forms 1A and 1B representing a survey of American history from exploration through reconstruction and Forms 2A and 2B surveying latter 19th century economic development through the 1950s. Since the tests were developed in the early 1960s, the Form 2 tests are outdated. They also suffer from an overemphasis on economic and political history and a notable lack of items devoted to black history and the social issues of the 1960s. In addition, the chronological organization makes this test unsuitable for courses that are presented topically.

Unfortunately, a test can be no better than its component items. Despite the assertion in the manual that "items include knowledge of facts, as well as the application of information and reasoning," all the items are knowledge reproduction items. There are no items based on stimulus materials such as graphs, pictures, or reading selections, which would require interpretation, hypothesizing, or evaluating. Admittedly, this may be a weakness of many objective history tests. A more critical failing is that most of the items probe knowledge of isolated facts rather than understanding of concepts or generalizations. Furthermore, in the opinion of this reviewer, about half the items deal with historically insignificant facts. About one-third of the items are "who" questions that would be more effective as "why" questions. For example, one item reads: "The Proclamation of 1763 and the Stamp Act of 1765 were part of the colonial program of British Prime Minister: (1) William Pitt, (2) George Grenville, (3) Charles Townsend, (4) Edmund Andros." It would be more significant to ask what immediate effect these acts had on the American colonists. Other items that are not "who" questions also hint at important concepts in the stem, but ask for a less significant fact. One such item is "The most important of the early canals was the: (1) Pennsylvania Canal, (2) Cumberland Canal, (3) Erie Canal, (4) Illinois-Michigan Canal." Finally, several items like "Before he became President, Dwight D. Eisenhower served as president of: (1) Yale, (2) Stanford, (3) the University of Minnesota, (4) Columbia," are merely trivial.

The brief manual of directions reports percentile norms and raw scores for 7th and 8th grades for all four forms of the test. However, the norming procedures are not specifically described beyond the use of "12,619 pupils who were located in many representative schools in a large number of states." Essential information about the number of schools, the number of states, and why the schools were considered representative is missing. Percentile norms must be used to make comparisons across forms, since Form A is more difficult than Form B for both tests. The manual also directs users to base their results on previous year norms, midyear norms, or end of year norms that either are not provided or are insufficiently labeled.

The split-half reliabilities of the four forms of the test range from .89 to .92.

The manual states, "The test results may be profitably used....(1) for determining pupil achievement; (2) for checking the efficiency of instruction; (3) for assigning school marks; (4) for analyzing pupil and class weaknesses; and (5) for motivating pupil effort." However, this test is undesirable as a measure of pupil achievement in American history, except in those courses which may emphasize memorization of historical facts in their instruction. Even in this case, close scrutiny is recommended to insure that the facts asked by the test are truly considered important by the potential user and that each item not only pertains to an important concept, but asks a significant question.

[916]

*UP Field Test in History. College; 1969–77; formerly called *The Undergraduate Record Examinations: History Test;* Form SUR ('70, 22 pages); descriptive booklet ('72, 13 pages); for UAP accessories, see 480; rental fee, $4 per test, postage extra; 120(140) minutes; Educational Testing Service. *

POLITICAL SCIENCE

[917]

★American Government: IOX Objectives-Based Tests. Grades 10–12; 1973–74; criterion referenced; 32 tests (spirit masters for local duplicating); no data on reliability; no norms; no suggested standards of mastery; Forms A, B, ('73, 1–2 pages); manual ('73, 23 pages); series description ('73, 4 pages); folder of support forms ('74, 14 pages); $25 per set of testing materials for either form, $45 for both forms; 4% extra for postage and handling; specimen booklet (sample pages only) for this and 3 other tests is available free on request; (5–10) minutes per test; series description by W. James Popham; tests developed under the direction of Barbara S. Cummings; Instructional Objectives Exchange. *

DANA G. KURFMAN, *Supervisor of Social Studies, Prince George's County Public Schools, Upper Marlboro, Maryland.*

These tests deserve discussion both as innovations in testing and as measures of typical American government course objectives. They bring to classroom teachers and school administrators a meaningful example of criterion-referenced testing. They bring to American government teachers a number of useful examples of how to test student attainment of specific American government objectives.

Each test consists of five to ten items designed to measure a single objective. There are

32 such tests in each of the two forms. Thus, teachers and school systems can choose those tests which measure the objectives to which they subscribe. No data are provided on the tests either in the form of reliability estimates or in the form of average test or item difficulties. The publisher states that such data are not provided because of the expense involved; therefore, school systems and teachers will have to develop their own data.

The availability of these tests extends considerably a teacher's capability for both individualizing instruction and determining the effectiveness of his/her teaching strategies. Having concise measures of single objectives should encourage teachers to develop learning stations to teach the capability described by the objective. Moreover, the two forms of the test permit pretesting and posttesting to evaluate instructional performance.

For administrators, these tests illustrate how a great variety of educational objectives can be measured without overburdening student patience through extended time periods of testing. Suggestions for using these tests (or testlets) in a program of matrix sampling should offer a valuable insight for many administrators who would like to determine the effectiveness of their programs in helping their students attain a wide variety of educational objectives.

Teachers will find these tests to be particularly useful because they can select the ones that measure what they want their students to know. Some teachers may question the lack of objectives, and accompanying tests, dealing with political processes. For example, there is little attention to the ways decisions are made within our political institutions. But for most teachers it will be useful to have as wide an array of objective measures as are provided by these 32 tests.

Each objective is stated behaviorally and then carefully amplified. Most important, each objective has with it a sample item which is really a model for all the items that appear in both forms of the test. By far the most common type of sample item calls for the classification of hypothetical situations. The number of hypothetical situations that can be formulated is extensive. The stage is set by directions such as the following: "Read each paragraph below. Decide which branch of the federal government

would be responsible for dealing with the situation described, and write the letter of your choice in the blank preceding each situation description. A) legislative branch B) executive branch C) judicial branch."

The hypothetical situation given in the test manual is: "In December, 1941, following the Japanese attack on Pearl Harbor, the United States declared war against the Axis Powers—Japan, Germany, and Italy. This step marked United States entry into the Second World War. Which branch of the federal government made the declaration?"

This item and several like it measure the objective: "Given a description of an actual or hypothetical situation in which the jurisdiction of one of the three branches of the federal government is involved, the student will indicate which branch would be responsible for dealing with the situation in question."

Some tests are based on many more options than usual in multiple choice testing. For example, one dealing with the individual's civil rights has 17 such rights, from "freedom of speech" to "no excessive fines or bails." As noted before, most of the items in the tests are of this matching sort, using hypothetical examples. From the way items are generated, teachers will find many suggestions for generating their own questions dealing with each objective.

The major problem with this particular set of tests is the apparent difficulty of the items. There is no way of checking this impression objectively because no data about item difficulty are provided. But to this reviewer, at any rate, most of the items seem far more appropriate for a college government class than for any senior high school American government class, let alone a ninth grade civics class. Part of the problem is in the reading level of the items and part is in the inherent difficulty of the tasks imposed by the items. The use of hypothetical examples requires students to read far more than they probably are accustomed to. It may be true that teaching to such clearly defined objectives will result in a level of student performance suggesting mastery of the objectives, but it appears more likely that many high school students will simply become discouraged by the apparent difficulty of the tasks posed by most of the questions. There is no way to tell this for

American Government: IOX Objectives-Based Tests

sure without some empirical data. Teachers are advised to look over the tests and determine for themselves whether they are at an appropriate level of difficulty.

In short, then, the IOX objectives-based tests in American government suggest new modes of evaluation which teachers and administrators will find challenging. They put into effect in a meaningful way what the supporters of behavioral objectives have been advocating for many years. As such, they are a valuable contribution to improved social studies teaching.

JACK L. NELSON, *Professor of Education, Rutgers, The State University of New Jersey, New Brunswick, New Jersey.*

The two forms of this set of tests, designed for use in classroom management and program evaluation, differ from most measurement instruments in their rationale, structure, and use.

The rationale is consistent with the movement toward specific instructional objectives, criterion-referenced testing, and mastery learning. Basically this movement stresses behavioral or competency objectives which can differ according to classroom, school, or community situation and which require measurement devices to diagnose weaknesses and judge change after instruction. The primary interest in these tests is learner outcomes. Thus, the intention is to develop items that directly measure specific learning objectives. Criterion-referencing occurs by use of a rating form for teacher judgments of the relative importance of the various skills tested.

The physical format of the tests consists of a box which contains a statement of description and use of the tests, several forms for marking the teacher's judgment on importance for each objective and related information on test results, a scoring guide, test manual, and 32 spiritmaster short tests on American government.

No statistical data on reliability or validity are provided, presumably because of the opportunity for local criterion-referencing. The manual notes that the items were developed and reviewed by classroom teachers and were field tested in one high school. No data on the field tests are provided. The manual states that the tests cover concepts dealt with in most American government textbooks and that the content should be mastered in a one-semester course.

Administrative directions are included, but not in detail. Most tests require 5 to 10 minutes to complete. Pre- and posttest arrangements can be made by using both forms.

The test manual includes sample items with specific objectives and amplified objectives. The stated objectives are of a general format which goes something like: Given information on this subject, the student will select an appropriate response. The amplified objective usually includes some teaching techniques, more information on the topic, and proposed student responses. The tests themselves do not contain objectives; they are one and two page tests with a brief set of directions and a few items. The items are of a quick-scoring response type.

Some of the items included on the short tests are innovative and thoughtful. These call for application of knowledge about government. Most of the items, however, are variations of factual recall or definitional questions. Much of the content of the tests is drawn from standard texts in the field and incorporates information on the formal structure and operation of government rather than the more contemporary curricular interests in political behavior and applied politics. This heavy stress on descriptions and formal operations seems typical of behavioral objectives viewpoints which concern themselves with physically observable and mechanistic concepts of knowledge. In that sense, the specific objectives listed in the teacher's manual and the test item emphasis on "book" answers are consistent. Unfortunately, for teachers who want to stress interrelationships, political reality, and social issues of government, these tests offer no more than do end-of-chapter check-ups in textbooks or teacher-made tests.

SUMMARY. Although the idea of criterion-referenced tests has substance in providing a local classroom teacher or department with options, this set of tests does not adequately cover the possible needs of a variety of situations. The convenience of spiritmasters is of practical assistance for the harried teacher, but the narrow framework of the majority of test items limits their use to fact-oriented teaching.

Statistically sound standardized tests lack sensitivity to reflective thinking. Reflective thinking tests lack solid comparative validity and reliability data. The objectives-based tests reviewed here lack both statistical bases and reflective thinking. They might be useful for classroom management, but are unsuitable for program evaluation.

[918]

★American Political Behavior Achievement Test. High school; 1974; also called *APB Achievement Test;* 2 scores: political knowledge, political science skills; no norms; 1 form (14 pages); manual (8 pages); $8.25 per 35 tests; $2.05 per specimen set; postage extra; (40) minutes for knowledge subtest, (50–60) minutes for skills subtest; John J. Patrick and Allen D. Glenn; Personnel Press. *

RICHARD E. GROSS, *Professor of Education, Stanford University, Stanford, California.*

This test is designed for use particularly by instructors offering the American Political Behavior program. The authors claim that it can also be used in other government and civics courses; but this reviewer believes that many of the items are directly related to the particular program for which the test was developed and, therefore, that since offerings in other high school political science courses have somewhat different aims and often quite different emphases, such teachers would have to use this test with great caution as an achievement test for their programs. Even certain of the terminology in the test, such as "political efficacy" and "political alienation," are concepts that would demand special emphasis by teachers offering more traditional civics courses.

The test consists of two sections, political knowledge and political science skills. The original pool of items was validated by "several political scientists and social studies educators." In addition to this unclarified procedure for content validity, some high school social studies teachers and their students were asked to judge the items from the standpoint of readability and clarity.

Split-half reliability coefficients, obtained from three small samples (17, 20, and 49 students), ranged from .88 to .92 for the political knowledge scores and .77 to .90 for political science skills scores.

The political knowledge subtest consists of 70 true-false items that primarily measure recall of facts about American government and politics. The knowledge demanded is not trivial. It calls for understanding of party differences, separation of powers, voting requirements, political structure, socio-economic influences on political

behavior, and fundamental concepts of American democracy. Several sets of questions require students to apply their knowledge to hypothetical individuals or situations. Only a few items that are treated as facts are somewhat subject to interpretation; the right answer to item 3, for example, depends on whether the testee decides upon the actual answer or the legal answer. There are also several questions that are practical "give-aways" such as item 4. In these and a number of other questions the thorough thinker is likely to be penalized, e.g., item 37. While this is a better-than-average true/false test, there is really no excuse for testmakers to use this type of question when all of its weaknesses are so well known. Using such tests, instead of, for example, multiple choice items, is detrimental to the entire movement to improve evaluation as it tends to perpetuate this bad practice among teachers.

The political science skills subtest consists of 40 multiple choice items calling on students to employ a number of intellectual skills and to use information in a variety of ways. Included are the skills of interpreting charts and graphs, distinguishing facts from values, using criteria for evaluating items, categorizing concepts, defining, employing polling methods, and analyzing evidence from raw data in order to evaluate conclusions. The reviewer finds this portion of the APB test to be quite impressive. It examines a number of very important competencies which should characterize the young citizen. One of the great challenges in the social studies is to move teachers from the old emphasis upon imparting and demanding regurgitation of facts to one which features the able employment of the skills of learning. Assessment items of the type featured here can do much to help bring about this much needed change.

One of the major faults of the first section of this test is that so few of the true and false items ask questions of a "why" nature; the second section could also do more with such elements instead of so frequently focusing upon "what." However, the political science skills section seems to be a far superior instrument for "new" social studies purposes than the political knowledge section. Unfortunately, here too, students who have taken the American Political Behavior course will probably far outperform most other civics students because once again terminology reflects the specific APB course, and the kinds of skills assessed are those featured in such classes. This reviewer found very few items on which to demur and generally they are well constructed, sometimes seeking the best answer rather than the right one. Additionally, a frequent choice is to declare that evidence provided is insufficient for drawing any of the suggested conclusions. While the reviewer would differ on the correct answer given for item 22, it is the only one about which he has reservations.

This achievement test is a step in the right direction. A thorough revision of the political knowledge subtest, eliminating the true-false approach and with fewer purely factual recall items, would make this test the best instrument available for civics courses in the area of American government.

[919]

*CLEP Subject Examination in American Government. 1 semester or equivalent; 1965–76; for college accreditation of nontraditional study, advanced placement, or assessment of educational achievement; tests administered monthly at centers throughout the United States; Form K-UCT2 ('72, 15 pages); optional essay supplement scored by college: Forms NCT-A, NCT-B, ('65, 2 pages), UCT-A, UCT-B, ('72, 2 pages); for program accessories, see 473; rental and scoring fee, $20 per student (includes reporting of scores to the candidate and one college); postpaid; 90(95) minutes, same for essay supplement; program administered for the College Entrance Examination Board by Educational Testing Service. *

For reviews of the CLEP program, see 473 (3 reviews) and 7:664 (3 reviews).

HOWARD D. MEHLINGER, *Professor of Education and History and Director, Social Studies Development Center, Indiana University, Bloomington, Indiana.* [Review of Form K-UCT2.]

This examination covers concepts and generalizations commonly featured in a freshman or sophomore introductory college course in American government. The test was designed with two main uses in mind. Some high school juniors and seniors might wish to take this test following the completion of an advanced course in American government taught in their high schools. Such a course, limited to able students and patterned after introductory college courses in American government, would likely prepare them to perform successfully on this examination. If the college or university these students attend accepts CLEP, the students may receive college credit for American government without having to enroll in the course; success on the exam might also qualify them for admission to more advanced courses in political science than entering freshmen are ordinarily permitted to take. A second test client is the person who cannot attend classes on a college campus and who wishes to study independently, taking examinations over courses to earn college credit. A few institutions enable students to complete college degrees without ever attending classes on campus.

This test is not appropriate as a general achievement test for high school students because the level of knowledge expected exceeds that normally called for in typical high school American government courses. However, an especially able and motivated high school senior who is interested in politics and government and who has read widely in the field might do well on the examination and should be encouraged to attempt it.

The test consists of two parts: a 98-item multiple choice examination requiring 90 minutes to complete and an optional essay examination, also of 90 minutes, containing four questions from which students must select three for response.

The main focus of the multiple choice examination is on the structure and process of the national government. The questions are divided roughly among the following topics: presidency, bureaucracy, and congress (30 percent); courts and civil liberties (15 percent); political participation (25 percent); political parties and pressure groups (25 percent); and federalism and constitutional background (5 percent). Although the test has a 1972 copyright, it has remained quite current and up-to-date by focusing primarily upon enduring structural and procedural aspects of government and politics and thus largely avoiding items that test for knowledge of current political issues and personalities.

The essay examination is a less accurate guide to what students know about American government and politics. The items seemed designed primarily to promote student speculation and to offer an opportunity to display skill in linking ideas in an appealing narrative form.

CLEP provides a general guide to the program and a booklet on how to interpret test scores. Both are written in a simple style that should be understandable even to a beginner.

The care invested in the development and testing of this examination was plain to the reviewer. The test is difficult, but the items are unambiguous and treat significant topics. A person may question whether satisfactory performance on a 90-minute multiple choice examination and a 90-minute essay examination provides sufficient evidence to determine whether a student who has not attended college classes in American government knows as much as one who has and thus deserves credit. But if a college or university has elected to provide this option to students and if students prefer or are able to secure college credit only in this manner, then this examination may be used confidently. It employs principles of good examination construction and provides a reasonably valid measure of the content of introductory courses in American government.

[920]

Cooperative Social Studies Tests: Civics. Grades 8–9; 1964–65; Forms A, B, ('64, 11 pages); no specific manual; series manual ('65, 46 pages); student bulletin ('65, 2 pages); separate answer sheets (Digitek, IBM 805, IBM 1230, NCS) must be used; $6 per 20 tests; $5.50 per 100 answer sheets; $1.50 per 10 IBM scoring stencils (answer pattern must be punched out locally); Digitek scoring stencils not available; $2 per series manual; $3 per 100 student bulletins; $3.50 per specimen set of this and 5 other social studies tests; cash orders postpaid; NCS scoring and statistical analysis service, 45¢ and over per test; 40(50) minutes; Educational Testing Service; Addison-Wesley Publishing Co., Inc. *
For a review by Vincent N. Campbell, see 7:928.

Anna S. Ochoa, *Associate Professor of Social Studies Education, Indiana University, Bloomington, Indiana.*

The publisher classifies the 70 items in this civics test as measuring three skills: remembering (21 items), understanding (23 items), and analyzing (26 items). The items are also classified across five subject matter areas: constitution and national government (Form A, 19 items; Form B, 22 items); state and local government (5, 7 items); citizenship and political participation (20, 13 items); government services, controls, and finances (16, 17 items); and national defense and international relations (10, 11 items).

This review is based on the Social Studies Curriculum Guidelines, a position statement of the National Council for the Social Studies.

The guidelines identify four essential components of a social studies curriculum: knowledge, higher level thinking skills and inquiry processes, values, and social participation.

The authors of this test give systematic attention to higher level intellectual operations, as evidenced in their table of specifications and in the items themselves. This aspect of the test was probably ahead of its time. However, the test does not incorporate elements of the inquiry process. Through the use of short vignettes, graphs, or cartoons, new items could present data for students to manipulate. Such data could be followed by items that ask students to identify the most appropriate hypothesis. Other items could present a hypothesis and ask students to identify the most useful sources of data needed to test that hypothesis. Although the test in its present form asks students to interpret graphs, cartoons, and maps, the items that accompany them do not test the ability to hypothesize, identify evidence, and draw conclusions.

Examining values represents another important component of social studies education. In spite of their attention to some thinking operations, the authors did not include decision making or value analysis among their skill areas. It should be noted that social studies trends in 1964 were not as concerned with values education as they are now. However, the current literature presents a wide range of instructional approaches. Further, textbook materials are incorporating value related exercises in their teacher and student materials. The questioning strategies embedded in these approaches can be converted into test items without much difficulty. Such items would ask students to identify alternatives and predict consequences in response to a problem situation. Other items could ask students to select the best reasons that support political decisions of their choice. In this way, the authors would support the values education thrust that is found in current social studies materials.

Providing young people with opportunities for community participation is another important component of social studies education. While 24 percent of the items are on citizenship and political participation, these items specify actions taken in the public arena—they do not focus on the political lives of youth.

The test could present political action situations that reflect the immediate political contexts of school and community—items which ask students to identify strategies which would be most effective or most consistent with their values. Other items might ask students to evaluate alternative ways of influencing political decisions in their classroom, school, and community.

The knowledge base of this test gives emphasis to the structure of government. Constitutional provisions, agencies of government, and political processes are basic themes of the test. The following concepts are illustrative of many test items: filibustering, political machine, logrolling, electoral college, checks and balances, and the federal system. While understanding of these concepts deserves some attention, it would also be desirable to include concepts that represent political behavior; e.g., mobilizing, influencing, bargaining, and compromising. Testmakers and curriculum developers must recognize that adolescents are sociocentric. At this age they are increasingly influenced by a peer culture whose values are not always supportive of academic achievement. Since testing is one significant factor that influences the nature of teaching and learning, test developers should pay more attention to those learnings that correspond to social development of youth.

The content of civics instruction should reflect persistent social issues. Such issues receive only superficial treatment in this civics test. Knowledge of the Bill of Rights is included, but the test items speak mainly to the provisions of the Bill of Rights. The items do not apply these rights to issues such as racism, equal opportunity, poverty, and crime.

Sexism and cultural diversity are two issues that deserve special attention. Given its 1965 publication date, the test has remarkably few instances of sexist language or sex stereotyping. Vestiges of a sexist orientation are found in cartoons that present only male characters. These cartoon characters are also all white. Further, none of the items focus on racism, ethnic diversity, or sexism as compelling social concerns of this society. A revision of the test could easily accommodate these concerns.

The conventional canons of testing were carefully followed as these tests were developed. In both forms of the test, however, responses to a few items depend on the correct response to previous items. This practice should be avoided.

In its present form the test has a number of deficiencies. Its knowledge base does not give sufficient attention to social issues, and the concepts tested are not directly related to the political action and behavior of youth. Although treatment of intellectual skills compares favorably with other tests, the test could be strengthened in this area. More attention to decision making and value analysis would be welcome as well. Although this test was thoughtfully constructed in terms of the instructional materials of the early sixties, it needs considerable revision to represent current trends in social studies. Until such a revision is completed, use of the test is not recommended.

[921]

*The Graduate Record Examinations Advanced Political Science Test. Graduate school candidates, 1939–76; test administered 5 times annually (January, April, June, October, December) at centers established by the publisher; 4 current forms ('73–76, 27–32 pages); descriptive booklet ('75, 12 pages); for program accessories, see 476; examination fee, $10.50 per candidate; 170(190) minutes; an inactive form is available for local administration (rental fee, $5.50 per test); Educational Testing Service. *

For a review by Christine McGuire of an earlier form, see 5:835. For reviews of the GRE program, see 7:667 (1 review) and 5:601 (1 review).

[922]

★Informeter: An International Technique for the Measurement of Political Information. Older adolescents and adults; 1972; no data on reliability and validity; no norms; 1 form (2 pages); no manual; copy of test free (may be locally duplicated); postpaid; [15] minutes; Panos D. Bardis; the Author. *

[923]

*National Teacher Examinations: Texas Government. College seniors and teachers; 1972–76; test administered 3 times annually (February, July, November) at centers established by the publisher; Form VNT ('73, 16 pages); descriptive booklet ('72, 8 pages); for program accessories, see 381; examination fee, $13 per candidate; 120(165) minutes; Educational Testing Service. *

For reviews of the testing program, see 381 (2 reviews).

[924]

*UP Field Test in Political Science. College; 1969–77; formerly called The Undergraduate Record Examinations: Political Science Test; Form UUR ('72, 24 pages); descriptive booklet ('72, 14 pages); for UAP accessories, see 480; rental fee, $4 per test, postage extra; 120(140) minutes; Educational Testing Service. *

SOCIOLOGY

[925]

*CLEP Subject Examination in Introductory Sociology. 1 year or equivalent; 1965–76; for college accreditation of nontraditional study, advanced placement, or assessment of educational achievement; tests administered monthly at centers throughout the United States; Forms WCT1 ('74, 15 pages), WCT2 ('74, 17 pages); optional essay supplement scored by college: Forms NCT-A ('65, 2 pages), WCT-A, WCT-B, ('74, 2 pages); for program accessories, see 473; rental and scoring fee, $20 per student (includes reporting of scores to the candidate and one college); postpaid; 90(95) minutes, same for essay supplement; program administered for the College Entrance Examination Board by Educational Testing Service. *

For reviews of the CLEP program, see 473 (3 reviews) and 7:664 (3 reviews).

[926]

*The Graduate Record Examinations Advanced Sociology Test. Graduate school candidates; 1939–76; test administered 5 times annually (January, April, June, October, December) at centers established by the publisher; 4 current forms ('73–76, 28–33 pages); descriptive booklet ('75, 10 pages); for program accessories, see 476; examination fee, $10.50 per candidate; 170(190) minutes; an inactive form is available for local administration (rental fee, $5.50 per test); Educational Testing Service. *

For a review by J. Richard Wilmeth, see 6:1021. For reviews of the GRE program see 7:667 (1 review) and 5:601 (1 review).

[927]

*UP Field Test in Sociology. College; 1969–77; formerly called *The Undergraduate Record Examinations: Sociology Test;* Form SUR ('70, 20 pages); descriptive booklet ('72, 13 pages); for UAP accessories, see 480; rental fee, $4 per test, postage extra; 120(140) minutes; Educational Testing Service. *

SPEECH & HEARING

REVIEWS BY *Charles V. Anderson, Lear Ashmore, Nicholas W. Bankson, Daniel R. Boone, Katharine G. Butler, Margaret C. Byrne, Courtney B. Cazden, Lon L. Emerick, Marie C. Fontana, J. Joseph Freilinger, Ronald Goldman, Raphael M. Haller, Harvey Halpern, Stephen B. Hood, James B. Lingwall, R. Duane Logue, Leija V. McReynolds, Manfred J. Meier, Thomas Oakland, Harold A. Peterson, Robert L. Rosenbaum, Eugene C. Sheeley, Ralph L. Shelton, Lawrence D. Shriberg, Ronald K. Sommers, Joel Stark, James A. Till, Lawrence J. Turton, and Harris Winitz.*

---

[928]

The Ohio Tests of Articulation and Perception of Sounds. Ages 5–8; 1973; OTAPS; 8 scores: articulation (sounds in words, sounds in phrases, nonsense words in context, stimulability of nonsense words), listening (identification of sounds by self, by examiner, comparator perception of sounds by self, by examiner); norms consist of means and standard deviations; individual; 1 form (131-page test card booklet); manual (77 pages); scoring folder-profile (6 pages); score sheet (1 page); $11.50 per set of card booklet, 25 scoring folder-profiles, and manual; $2 per 25 scoring folder-profiles; 75¢ per 50 score sheets; $2.50 per manual; postage extra; [80] minutes; Ruth Beckey Irwin and Marcia Stevenson Abbate (test); Stanwix House, Inc. * (Canadian publisher: J. M. Dent & Sons (Canada) Ltd. [Canada].)

See T2:2023 (4 references).

REFERENCES

1–4. See T2:2023.
5. BRADLEY, BETTY H. "Responses of Retardates to Three Auditory Discrimination Tests." *Slow Learning Child* (Australia) 19(1):22–7 Mr '72. * (*PA* 49:9298)
6. IRWIN, RUTH BECKEY. "Evaluating the Perception and Articulation of Phonemes of Children, Ages 5 to 8." *J Commun Disorders* 7(1):45–63 Mr '74. * (*PA* 52:9046)
7. CRITE, ANTJE E. "Review of Ohio Tests of Articulation and Perception of Sounds," pp. 457–9. In *Pediatric Screening Tests.* Edited by William K. Frankenburg and Bonnie W. Camp. Springfield, Ill.: Charles C Thomas, Publisher, 1975. Pp. xii, 549. *

8. O'KEEFE, JUDITH STUCHEL. *A Comparative Study of the Auditory Perceptual Abilities of Legally Blind and Sighted Children, With Varying Learning and Speech Abilities.* Doctor's thesis, Ohio State University (Athens, Ohio), 1976. (*DAI* 37:4705A)

HARRIS WINITZ, *Professor of Psychology and Speech Science, University of Missouri, Kansas City, Missouri.*

Articulation assessment is a primary responsibility of speech clinicians. Testing of auditory discrimination of phonetic units is often made as an additional assessment of articulatory functioning.

This test, designed to "identify articulatory and perceptual inadequacies" of children ages 5–8, consists of four articulation (speech) subtests and four auditory perception (listening) tests. A score is obtained for each of the subtests, but there are no total scores for the four speech tests, the four listening tests, or for the eight subtests (see the test description above).

Norms are presented for each of the eight subtests at each of five age levels (5, 5½, 6, 7, and 8). Unfortunately, these norms consist of means and standard deviations only. Furthermore, the norms at each level are based on a small, but carefully selected, sample of 40 children. In speaking about the articulation tests, the manual states that "the scores improved progressively as the ages increased." This statement is only partly true—there are five instances where an older age group does less well than a younger group. In the listening tests, there are two such retrogressions. These retrogressions are probably caused by sampling variations resulting from using only 40 cases for obtaining norms.

Test materials include an attractive spiral-bound booklet of test cards, forms for scoring responses, and a manual. Although the manual presents considerable statistical information, it fails to present adequate directions for administering and scoring the test. The profiling of the subscores is not at all clear and it is extremely time consuming since the profile forms do not list the scores to be profiled. One must enter the norms table of mean scores for the five age levels to obtain by interpolation the age scores, which can then be entered on the profile. Unfortunately, poorer scores sometimes have higher age equivalencies than better scores—e.g., a score of 73 errors on subtest 4 is equivalent to an age level of 5½, while a score of 74 errors is equivalent to an age level of 6.

The intercorrelations among the four articulation tests are fairly high for the lowest three age levels; the median correlations being .65, .77, and .64. The median intercorrelations for age levels 7 and 8 are much lower, .30 and .44. The high correlations (.60 to .97, median .91) between sounds in words and sounds in phrases suggests that the same articulation skills are measured by both subtests. The intercorrelations for the listening tests display a similar pattern.

Test-retest reliabilities, based on only 20 children tested a week apart, are reported. The obtained correlations are .73 to .89 for the articulation tests and .24 to .88 for the listening tests. Because of the small sample size, these correlations are not very trustworthy. Furthermore, the coefficients are inflated because they are based on a wide-range group consisting of both first and second graders. The one-week interval between testing also contributed to

inflating these reliabilities since too little time elapsed to minimize memory effects. The manual does not say whether the retesting was done by a different examiner. If both testings were done by the same examiner, the reliabilities are practically meaningless.

No data are presented on the validity of the listening tests. The four articulation tests were correlated with the screening test of the *Templin-Darley Tests of Articulation,* "since its reliability and validity had been established for identification of misarticulations." These correlations equal or exceed .87; however, little confidence can be placed on these measures of concurrent validity. The correlations are based on only 32 subjects about whom no information is presented—the sample may have been drawn from two or three grades, resulting in inflated correlations. Furthermore, the Templin-Darley test defined validity in the narrow sense of severity ratings.

This test was developed to include additional assessments of auditory functioning and to correlate these findings with articulatory development. Unfortunately the results suggest that the auditory tests are highly related and, therefore, individual assessment of each auditory test is not recommended or needed. There is no evidence to suggest that a developmental lag will predict the persistence of an articulation error. Neither is there evidence that this test, or any other developmental articulation tests, can be used successfully for diagnostic purposes.

[929]

Preschool Language Scale. Ages 2–6; 1969; PLS; 3 scores: auditory comprehension, verbal ability, total, plus an articulation section; no data on reliability and validity; individual; 1 form; picture book (36 pages); record booklet (18 pages); manual (88 pages); $9.50 per set of picture book, record booklet, and manual; $7.50 per 10 record booklets; postage extra; (30) minutes; Irla Lee Zimmerman, Violette G. Steiner, and Roberta L. Evatt; Charles E. Merrill Publishing Co. *

See T2:2024 (1 reference); for a review by Joel Stark and an excerpted review by C. H. Ammons, see 7:965.

REFERENCES

1. See T2:2024.
2. MAURER, EUGENIA F. *An Investigation of the Validity and Reliability of the Pre-School Language Scale.* Master's thesis, Illinois State University (Normal, Ill.), 1973.
3. ZIMMERMAN, IRLA LEE; STEINER, VIOLETTE G.; AND POND, ROBERTA L. "Language Status of Preschool Mexican-American Children—Is There a Case Against Early Bilingual Education?" *Percept & Motor Skills* 38(1):227–30 F '74. * (PA 52:8632)
4. LASS, NORMAN J., AND GOLDEN, SHEILA S. "A Comparative Study of Children's Performance on Three Tests for Receptive Language Abilities." *J Auditory Res* 15(3):177–82 Jl '75. * (PA 57:6127)

J Spec Ed 5(1):86–8 w–sp '71. *Barton B. Proger.* * The inventory is divided into two main parts: Auditory Comprehension Scale.... and Verbal Ability Scale * A supplementary "Articulation Section"....appears to have been included as something of an afterthought. For the latter part of the inventory, no explanation is given as to how it relates to the two main portions of the scale. * A highly desirable feature of the Auditory Comprehension Scale is its attempt to divorce itself from verbal responses. * The only information on validity contained in the manual is the subjective assertion of utility for each of the two main scales by workers in the field * Each developmental task on both main tests is accompanied by a well-written description of Material, Procedure, Score, Rationale, and Reference. * Developmental ages are assigned to various groups of item-tasks. For the stated purposes of preliminary screening or evaluation, such age interpretations are probably sufficient for most accepted uses of the *PLS*. One must not, however, interpret such developmental ages in the sense of genuine norms derived statistically. Since it is quite obvious that not all normal children of a given chronological age are at the same developmental stage as that outlined by the manual, and since the reader is not told what percentage of a given age group would fall at slightly different developmental stages, one cannot consider the manual's age placements in the usual normative sense. * the *PLS* looks appealing to would-be examiners because clearly described items are neatly pigeon-holed under various developmental ages. However, when one uses the informal inventory for preliminary screening purposes, one must not forget that the items have come from several different contexts and have been used with different child populations. Placing the same developmental weight of one and one-half months on each of any two items deriving from different sources can be questioned. Nonetheless, the *PLS* appears to be among the more sophisticated of the informal inventories.

[930]

★**Symbolic Play Test, Experimental Edition.** Ages 1–3; 1976; SPT; language potential; individual; 1 form; manual (36 pages); record form (2 pages); £30 per set of testing materials including 25 record forms; £1 per 25 record forms; £3 per manual; postpaid within U.K.; (10–15) minutes; Marianne Lowe

Preschool Language Scale

and Anthony J. Costello; NFER Publishing Co. Ltd. [England]. *

[931]

***UP Field Test in Speech Pathology and Audiology.** College; 1969–77; formerly called *The Undergraduate Record Examinations: Speech and Hearing Test;* Form TUR ('69, 15 pages); descriptive booklet ('71, 15 pages); for UAP accessories, see 480; rental fee, $4 per test; rental and scoring fee, $5.50 per test; postage extra; 120(140) minutes; Educational Testing Service. *

KATHERINE G. BUTLER, *Acting Dean of Graduate Studies and Research and Director, Speech and Hearing Center, San Jose State University, San Jose, California.*

This test is designed to demonstrate student competency in speech pathology *and* audiology at the undergraduate, preprofessional level. The descriptive booklet states that the test is broad enough and comprehensive enough to serve "students and faculty with an objective and standard measure of academic performance. Viewed as a supplementary examination, the test provides information on how the student compares not only with other students within a class or department but also, on a national scale, with a wide variety of students from many kinds of colleges in many geographical areas." ETS states specifically that this test is not for admissions purposes, and transcripts of the test scores are not sent to "any agency, graduate institution or fellowship program."

No standardization information is provided. Date of test construction is not provided. An item summary worksheet provides the percentage of senior students who passed each item correctly. Size of the reference group sample is not provided to the user.

Of the 120 items on this two-hour, multiple choice test, "50 questions deal with descriptive phonetics, voice production, articulation, acoustics of voice and speech, the anatomy and physiology of the speech mechanism, experimental phonetics, semantics, and language development." Unfortunately, the test does not reflect the current research on acquisition of language and linguistic development to the extent that would be helpful for the measurement of skills of the students in present-day speech pathology/audiology training programs. Those utilizing this test would need to construct additional items "in house" in order to measure the prerequisite skills currently demanded of speech and language pathology students upon completion of their undergraduate program.

"Forty questions deal with speech pathology: functional voice and articulation disorders, organic disorders of speech, stuttering, and psychological problems related to speech pathology." Here again, the emphasis reflects the training patterns of institutions of a decade or more ago. Such matters as distinctive feature analysis and language sampling are not addressed.

"Thirty questions are concerned directly with audiology: hearing theory, hearing testing, and hearing rehabilitation." Again, the most recent information in such areas as impedance audiometry, dichotic listening, and ear advantage is not included.

About 20 percent of the questions deal directly with therapy. However, as programs at the undergraduate level stress preprofessional training, and provide fewer hours of clinical practicum experience, this portion of the test may become less relevant.

In conclusion, while this examination may have considerable benefit if the measurement of academic knowledge of undergraduates is desired, based on an external, nationally-prepared test, it is important to note that internal questions should be generated and supplementary testing devised which would lead to the measurement of competency. This test, in its present form, does not provide sufficient information regarding student competency in such areas as language acquisition, phonology, syntax, language sampling, pragmatics, distinctive feature analysis, and more recent trends in audiological evaluation and instrumentation.

HEARING

[932]

Auditory Discrimination Test. Ages 5–8; 1958–73; ADT; "ability to recognize the fine differences that exist between the phonemes used in English speech"; individual; orally administered; 2 forms; 2 editions; $8 per 50 tests; $2 per manual for either edition; $3 per specimen set; postpaid; (5–10) minutes; Joseph M. Wepman; Language Research Associates, Inc. *
a) ORIGINAL EDITION. 1958; forms 1, 2, (2 pages); manual (4 pages).
b) 1973 REVISION. 1958–73; forms 1A, 2A, ('73, 1 page, identical with test copyrighted 1958 except for use of correct score rather than an error score); manual ('73, 8 pages).
See T2:2028 (82 references); for a review by Louis

M. DiCarlo of the original edition, see 6:940 (2 references).

REFERENCES
1–2. See 6:940.
3–84. See T2:2028; also includes a cumulative name index to the first 84 references and 1 review for this test.
85. BUKTENICA, NORMAN A. *Relative Contributions of Auditory and Visual Perception to First-Grade Language Learning.* Doctor's thesis, University of Chicago (Chicago, Ill.), 1966.
86. WEPMAN, JOSEPH M. "Auditory Discrimination: Its Role in Language Comprehension, Formulation and Use." *Pediat Clin North Am* 15(3):721–7 Ag '68. *
87. DAVIS, JOAN CAROLYN. *Auditory Discrimination in Culturally Disadvantaged Children.* Master's thesis, Vanderbilt University (Nashville, Tenn.), 1970.
88. HUTSON, KATHY. *Non-Verbal Auditory Discrimination in Culturally Disadvantaged Children.* Master's thesis, Vanderbilt University (Nashville, Tenn.), 1970.
89. BOZMAN, MAURICE WILSON. *The Contribution of Selected Variables to the Diagnoses of Problem Readers by a Reading Specialist in the Areas of Phonics and Comprehension.* Doctor's thesis, University of Maryland (College Park, Md.), 1972. (*DAI* 33:5403A)
90. BRADLEY, BETTY H. "Responses of Retardates to Three Auditory Discrimination Tests." *Slow Learning Child* (Australia) 19(1):22–7 Mr '72. * (*PA* 49:9298)
91. DAHLE, ARTHUR J., AND DALY, DAVID A. "Influence of Verbal Feedback on Auditory Discrimination Test Performance of Mentally Retarded Children." *Am J Mental Def* 76(5):586–90 Mr '72. * (*PA* 48:12063)
92. EAVES, L. C.; KENDALL, D. C.; AND CRICHTON, J. U. "The Early Detection of Minimal Brain Dysfunction." *J Learn Dis* 5(8):454–62 O '72. * (*PA* 49:7436)
93. ELENBOGEN, ELAINE MANHEIM, AND THOMPSON, GLEN ROBBINS. "A Comparison of Social Class Effects in Two Tests of Auditory Discrimination." *J Learn Dis* 5(4):209–12 Ap '72. * (*PA* 48:6950)
94. GRAHAM, DOROTHY MARGUERITE. *A Comparison Between the Indian and Non-Indian Children in Southern Saskatchewan Based on Listening Comprehension, Reading Comprehension, Auditory Discrimination, and I.Q.* Doctor's thesis, University of Northern Colorado (Greeley, Colo.), 1972. (*DAI* 33:894A)
95. GUTHRIE, JOHN T.; GOLDBERG, HERMAN K.; AND FINUCCI, JOAN. "Independence of Abilities in Disabled Readers." *J Read Behav* 4(2):129–38 sp '72. *
96. MARQUARDT, THOMAS P., AND SAXMAN, JOHN H. "Language Comprehension and Auditory Discrimination in Articulation Deficient Kindergarten Children." *J Speech & Hearing Res* 15(2):382–9 Je '72. *
97. MAXWELL, DONNA M. LUCAS. *An Evaluation of the Effectiveness of the Wepman Auditory Discrimination Test, Sub-Test II and V, of the Frostig Test of Visual Discrimination, and Peabody Picture Vocabulary Test as a Predictor of First Grade Reading.* Master's thesis, California State University (Hayward, Calif.), 1972.
98. NAIDOO, SANDHYA. *Specific Dyslexia: The Research Report of the ICAA Word Blind Centre for Dyslexic Children.* London: Sir Isaac Pitman & Sons Ltd., 1972. Pp. xv, 165. *
99. NEEL, RICHARD SCOTT. *A Psychometric Investigation of Identification of Learning Disabled Children.* Doctor's thesis, University of Southern California (Los Angeles, Calif.), 1972. (*DAI* 33:1554A)
100. NEWMAN, ANABEL P. "Later Achievement Study of Pupils Underachieving in Reading in First Grade." *Read Res Q* 7(3):477–508 sp '72. * (*PA* 49:10005)
101. O'LEARY, EMMETT LAURENCE. *An Investigation of Receptive Language Deficiency in a Male Prison Population.* Doctor's thesis, University of Nebraska (Lincoln, Neb.), 1972. (*DAI* 34:453B)
102. RAGOSIN, EDRIA MIRIAM, AND WEIDNER, WILLIAM E. "Speech Sound Discrimination: Comparing Articulatory Defective and Proficient Children." *Acta Symbolica* 3(2):106–7 f '72. * (*PA* 49:2719)
103. ROBINSON, HELEN M. "Visual and Auditory Modalities Related to Methods for Beginning Reading." *Read Res Q* 8(1):7–39 f '72. * (*PA* 50:5833)
104. RUPP, JANE DOWNS. *The Prediction of Reading Readiness With Auditory and Visual Assessors and Intelligence Test in Three Sub-Samples.* Doctor's thesis, Ohio State University (Columbus, Ohio), 1972. (*DAI* 33:575A)
105. SAPIR, SELMA G. "Auditory Discrimination With Words and Nonsense Syllables." *Acad Ther* 7(3):307–13 sp '72. * (*PA* 48:8761)
106. SERWER, BLANCHE J.; SHAPIRO, BERNARD J.; AND SHAPIRO, PHYLLIS P. "Achievement Prediction of 'High-Risk' Children." *Percept & Motor Skills* 35(2):347–54 O '72. * (*PA* 49:7970)
107. SEVERSON, ROGER A. "Early Detection of Children With Potential Learning Disabilities: A Seven-Year Effort." Abstract. *Proc 80th Ann Conv Am Psychol Assn* 7(2):561–2 '72. * (*PA* 48:5679)
108. SNYDER, ROBERT, AND POPE, PEGGY. "Auditory and

Visual Inadequacies in Maturation at the First Grade Level." *J Learn Dis* 5(10):620–5 D '72. * (*PA* 50:749)

109. VELLUTINO, FRANK R.; DESETTO, LOUIS; AND STEGER, JOSEPH A. "Categorical Judgment and the Wepman Test of Auditory Discrimination." *J Speech & Hearing Disorders* 37(2):252–7 My '72. *

110. WEBBER, MARGARET SHARP. *Prediction of Word Recognition Deficits From Articulation and Auditory Discrimination Ability at Time of First-Grade Entrance.* Doctor's thesis, Temple University (Philadelphia, Pa.), 1972. (*DAI* 33:1532A)

111. WEINER, PAUL S. "The Perceptual Level Functioning of Dysphasic Children: A Follow-Up Study." *J Speech & Hearing Res* 15(2):423–38 Je '72. * (*PA* 49:11508)

112. BRYEN, DIANE NELSON. *The Construction and Validation of Language-Related Tests of Speech-Sound Discrimination for Specific Language Populations in First and Second Grades.* Doctor's thesis, Temple University (Philadelphia, Pa.), 1973. (*DAI* 35:4723A)

113. COHEN, SHELDON; GLASS, DAVID C.; AND SINGER, JEROME E. "Apartment Noise, Auditory Discrimination, and Reading Ability in Children." *J Exp Social Psychol* 9(5):407–22 S '73. * (*PA* 51:8197)

114. COURY, JANINE PESCHARD. *Screening for Learning Disabilities Among Inner-City First Graders.* Doctor's thesis, University of Tennessee (Knoxville, Tenn.), 1973. (*DAI* 34:2382A)

115. DAWKINS, ARTHUR C. *The Effects of Music and Instruction on Auditory Discrimination Test Scores of Disadvantaged Preschool Students.* Doctor's thesis, Catholic University of America (Washington, D.C.), 1973. (*DAI* 34:4862A)

116. DYSON, JANIE FAYE. *The Relationship Between Auditory Discrimination and Beginning Reading of Selected First Grade Children.* Doctor's thesis, University of Alabama (University, Ala.), 1973. (*DAI* 34:6251A)

117. HENSLEY, BONNIE LEE. *The Relationship of Selected Oral Language, Perceptual, Demographic, and Intellectual Factors to the Reading Achievement of Good, Average, and Poor First Grade Reading Groups.* Doctor's thesis, University of Southern Mississippi (Hattiesburg, Miss.), 1973. (*DAI* 34:4562A)

118. JARVIS, ELIZABETH ORYSIA. *Auditory Abilities of Primary School Children: A Study of the Relationship of Auditory Abilities to Each Other and to Reading Achievement, and an Investigation of the Relationships Among Selected Auditory Test Profiles.* Doctor's thesis, University of Toronto (Toronto, Ont., Canada), 1973. (*DAI* 35:890A)

119. KARNES, FRANCES NESSLER. *A Comparative Analysis of Individual and Group Auditory Discrimination Tests for Disabled Third Grade Readers in a Lower Socio-Economic Group.* Doctor's thesis, University of Illinois (Urbana, Ill.), 1973. (*DAI* 34:7468A)

120. KENT, ANITA HUTT. *The Relationships of Reading Comprehension, Conservation Ability, Auditory Discrimination, and Visual-Motor Development of Third-Grade Pupils.* Doctor's thesis, University of Oklahoma (Norman, Okla.), 1973. (*DAI* 34:2924A)

121. MCNELLY, CHARLES HOUSTON. *Auditory Speech Discrimination Under Various Background Noise Conditions of Learning Disabled, Brain Damaged Boys and Normal Boys.* Doctor's thesis, University of Michigan (Ann Arbor, Mich.), 1973. (*DAI* 35:517B)

122. MORENCY, ANNE, AND WEPMAN, JOSEPH M. "Early Perceptual Ability and Later School Achievement." *El Sch J* 73(6):323–7 Mr '73. * (*PA* 50:0962)

123. NOBER, LINDA W. "Auditory Discrimination and Classroom Noise." *Read Teach* 27(3):288–91 D '73. * (*PA* 51:12026)

124. NOBER, LINDA WEISSBRODT. *A Study of Classroom Noise as a Factor Which Effects the Auditory Discrimination Performance of Primary Grade Children.* Doctor's thesis, University of Massachusetts (Amherst, Mass.), 1973. (*DAI* 33:6756A)

125. OAKLAND, THOMAS D.; WILLIAMS, FERN C.; AND HARMER, WILLIAM R. "A Longitudinal Study of Auditory Perception and Reading Instruction With First-Grade Negro Children." *J Spec Ed* 7(2):141–54 su '73. * (*PA* 52:4081)

126. SANDERS, COLUMBUS NELSON. *Correlations of Reading Achievement With Various Phonic Word-Recognition Skills for Inner-City Black Children.* Doctor's thesis, University of Oregon (Eugene, Ore.), 1973. (*DAI* 34:3041A)

127. SASSENRATH, J. M., AND MADDUX, ROBERT E. "The Factor Structure of Three School Readiness or Diagnostic Tests for Disadvantaged Kindergarten Children." *Psychol Sch* 10(3):287–93 Jl '73. * (*PA* 51:6000)

128. STRAG, GERALD A., AND RICHMOND, BERT O. "Auditory Discrimination Techniques for Young Children." *El Sch J* 73(8):447–54 My '73. * (*PA* 50:10033)

129. DAHLE, ARTHUR J., AND DALY, DAVID A. "Tangible Rewards in Assessing Auditory Discrimination Performance of Mentally Retarded Children." *Am J Mental Def* 78(5):625–30 Mr '74. * (*PA* 52:8003)

130. FESHBACH, SEYMOUR, AND ADELMAN, HOWARD. "Remediation of Learning Problems Among the Disadvantaged." *J Ed Psychol* 66(1):16–28 F '74. * (*PA* 52:4070)

131. HENSLEY, BONNIE. "The Relationship of Selected Oral Language, Perceptual, Demographic, and Intellectual Factors to the Reading Achievement of Good, Average, and Poor First Grade Reading Groups." *South J Ed Res* 8(2):256–71 sp '74. * (*PA* 53:4024)

132. KALEITA, ANNETTE MARIE. *A Study of the Impact of Instruction on the Auditory Discrimination Abilities of Kindergarten Children.* Doctor's thesis, University of Maryland (College Park, Md.), 1974. (*DAI* 36:3237A)

133. LEACH, MOZELLE PHILLIPS. *Selected Environmental Factors Influencing Auditory Discrimination Skills of First Grade Students.* Doctor's thesis, University of Oklahoma (Norman, Okla.), 1974. (*DAI* 35:4999A)

134. MARGOLIS, HOWARD. *The Effects of an Impulsive or Reflective Conceptual Tempo Upon the Auditory Perceptual, Reading Readiness, and Intelligence Test Performances of Kindergarten Children.* Doctor's thesis, Hofstra University (Hempstead, N.Y.), 1974. (*DAI* 35:1503A)

135. NICHOLS, DONALD ARTHUR. *Auditory Discrimination by Virgin Islands Children of Different Dialects of English.* Doctor's thesis, Boston University (Boston, Mass.), 1974. (*DAI* 35:1535A)

136. ROSS, HELEN WARREN. *Auditory Discrimination in Six-Year-Old Children as a Function of Ethnic Group Membership.* Doctor's thesis, Catholic University of America (Washington, D.C.), 1974. (*DAI* 35:269A)

137. SASSENRATH, JULIUS M., AND MADDUX, ROBERT E. "Language Instruction, Background, and Development of Disadvantaged Kindergarten Children." *Calif J Ed Res* 25(2):61–8 Mr '74. * (*PA* 53:1954)

138. WALLBROWN, JANE D.; WALLBROWN, FRED H.; AND ENGIN, ANN W. "The Relative Importance of Mental Age and Selected Assessors of Auditory and Visual Perception in the Metropolitan Readiness Test." *Psychol Sch* 11(2):136–43 Ap '74. * (*PA* 52:13209)

139. WRIGHT, LOYD S. "Conduct Problem or Learning Disability?" *J Spec Ed* 8(4):331–6 w '74. * (*PA* 56:4935)

140. WRIGHT, LLOYD S. "Perceptual Characteristics of Third Grade Conduct Problem Boys." *Slow Learning Child* (Australia) 21(1):53–61 Mr '74. * (*PA* 53:4069)

141. CARTER, JOHN L. "Auditory Discrimination and Training Effects for Educable Retarded Children." *Ed & Train Mental Retard* 10(2):94–5 Ap '75. * (*PA* 54:7884)

142. FERENCE, TERRY LYNN. *The Performance of Kindergarten Children on the Wepman Auditory Discrimination Test With and Without Visual Cues.* Master's thesis, California State University (Sacramento, Calif.), 1975.

143. GROFF, PATRICK. "Reading Ability and Auditory Discrimination: Are They Related?" *Read Teach* 28(8):742–7 My '75. * (*PA* 55:3250)

144. HILL, NANCY CAROLYN. *A Factor Analytic Study of Selected Tests of Specific Components of Academic Learning.* Doctor's thesis, University of Missouri (Columbia, Mo.), 1975. (*DAI* 36:6600A)

145. HOCHSTETLER, MIRIAM ELAINE. *A Study of Factors Related to the Reading Ability of Beginning Kindergarten Children.* Doctor's thesis, Ball State University (Muncie, Ind.), 1975. (*DAI* 37:183A)

146. MCGOVERN, JILL ELIZABETH. *A Comparison of Auditory Perception Between Learning Disabled and Nonlearning Disabled Culturally Different Pupils.* Doctor's thesis, University of New Orleans (New Orleans, La.), 1975. (*DAI* 37:223A)

147. MACHOWSKY, HERBERT, AND MEYERS, JOEL. "Auditory Discrimination, Intelligence, and Reading Achievement at Grade 1." *Percept & Motor Skills* 40(2):363–8 Ap '75. * (*PA* 54:10586)

148. MANZELLA, ROBERT ANTHONY. *An Examination of Auditory Discrimination Skills and Articulatory Behavior Among Children With Lateral /s/ Misarticulations.* Doctor's thesis, State University of New York (Buffalo, N.Y.), 1975. (*DAI* 36:4967B)

149. RIEDL, PAMELA SEARS. *Performance of Articulatory-Impaired Children on Several Psycholinguistic Measures.* Doctor's thesis, Michigan State University (East Lansing, Mich.), 1975. (*DAI* 36:6095B)

150. SCHULTZ, JEROME JOSEPH. *Four Measures of Auditory Discrimination: A Factor-Analytic Determination of Their Relative Equivalence.* Doctor's thesis, Boston College (Chestnut Hill, Mass.), 1975. (*DAI* 36:224A)

151. WALLBROWN, JANE D.; ENGIN, ANN W.; WALLBROWN, FRED H.; AND BLAHA, JOHN. "The Prediction of First Grade Reading Achievement With Selected Perceptual-Cognitive Tests." *Psychol Sch* 12(2):140–9 Ap '75. * (*PA* 55:1605)

152. WILLIAMS, PEGGY E. Chap. 5, "Auditory Discrimination: Differences Versus Deficits," pp. 91–100. In *Help for the Reading Teacher: New Directions in Research.* Edited by William D. Page. Urbana, Ill.: National Conference on Research in English, 1975. Pp. ii, 110. *

153. FOUSE, ANNA BETH FORRESTER. *A Study of Auditory Perception, Visual Perception, and Phonics Abilities of Fourth and Sixth Graders.* Doctor's thesis, Texas Woman's University (Denton, Tex.), 1976. (*DAI* 37:4278A)

154. LARSEN, STEPHEN C.; ROGERS, DOROTHY; AND SOWELL, VIRGINIA. "The Use of Selected Perceptual Tests in Differentiating Between Normal and Learning Disabled Children." *J Learn Dis* 9(2):85–90 F '76. * (*PA* 56:4972)

Auditory Discrimination Test

155. NEEL, RICHARD S. "A Psychometric Investigation of Identification of Children With Academic Difficulties." *J Spec Ed* 10(1):91–5 sp '76. *

156. STEVENSON, HAROLD W.; PARKER, TIMOTHY; WILKINSON, ALEXANDER; HEGION, ADA; AND FISH, ENRICA. "Longitudinal Study of Individual Differences in Cognitive Development and Scholastic Achievement." *J Ed Psychol* 68(4):377–400 Ag '76. *

157. HARE, BETTY A. "Perceptual Deficits Are Not a Cue to Reading Problems in Second Grade." *Read Teach* 30(6):624–8 Mr '77. *

158. MARGOLIS, HOWARD. "Auditory Perceptual Test Performance and the Reflection-Impulsivity Dimension." *J Learn Dis* 10(3):164–72 Mr '77. *

[933]

Auditory Memory Span Test. Ages 5–8; 1973; "ability to recall single syllable spoken words in progressively increasing series"; individual; Forms 1 (1 page), 2 (1 page, consists of rearranged items from Form 1 except for 2 revised items); manual (8 pages); $8 per 50 tests; $2 per manual; $3 per specimen set; postpaid; [5–7] minutes; Joseph M. Wepman and Anne Morency; Language Research Associates, Inc. *

REFERENCES

1. MORENCY, ANNE S.; WEPMAN, JOSEPH M.; AND HAAS, SARAH K. "Developmental Speech Inaccuracy and Speech Therapy in the Early School Years." *El Sch J* 70(4):219–44 Ja '70. *

2. MORENCY, ANNE, AND WEPMAN, JOSEPH M. "Early Perceptual Ability and Later School Achievement." *El Sch J* 73(6):323–7 Mr '73. * (*PA* 50:9962)

J. JOSEPH FREILINGER, *Consultant, Clinical Speech Services, Department of Public Instruction, Des Moines, Iowa.*

The *Auditory Memory Span Test* purports to test the "ability to recall single syllable spoken words in progressively increasing series" for children ages 5 through 8. Each form of the test contains fifteen items: three items in each of five series. The first series consists of two words in each item; the second series, three words; and progressing to the fifth series consisting of six words in each item.

The authors claim that there is "a strong positive relationship....between auditory memory ability and child's development of speech, language, and learning-to-learn to read." If a child obtains a score in the lowest 15 percent of his age group, his performance is considered to be "below level of threshold of adequacy." Adequacy for what is not explained. At any rate, if a 5- or 6-year-old child scores at the 15th percentile or lower, the authors consider a score "below level of threshold of adequacy" of great importance since they recommend that "the classroom teacher, school psychologist, and others in the child's school environment be alerted to the child's developmental status." Furthermore, "the parents' role during this developmental stage should be explained to them in terms of avoiding unrealistic expectations and making unreasonable demands on the child in areas of performance that are effected by auditory memory ability." The classroom teacher is then expected "to adjust her instructional procedures accordingly." The school psychologist is expected to adjust "oral instruction of intelligence and achievement tests....to shortened sentences."

There is no evidence whatsoever that scoring in the lowest 15 percent on this test indicates learning difficulties which will be eliminated or diminished by "proper intervention" by teachers, psychologists, and parents. The correlations with scores on achievement tests (.18 to .32, median .26) are inconsequential and, more importantly, irrelevant to learning difficulties which the test is presumably measuring.

Because of the complete absence of information on validity, this test cannot be recommended.

[934]

Auditory Sequential Memory Test. Ages 5–8; 1973; digit recall; reliability data consists of one coefficient; individual; no reading by examinees; Forms 1, 2, (1 page); manual (6 pages); $8 per 50 tests; $2 per manual; $3 per specimen set; postpaid; [5–7] minutes; Joseph M. Wepman and Anne Morency; Language Research Associates, Inc. *

J. JOSEPH FREILINGER, *Consultant, Clinical Speech Services, Department of Public Instruction, Des Moines, Iowa.*

This memory-for-digits test purports to test sequential order recall in children ages 5–8. Each form contains 7 pairs of items ranging from two digits to eight digits.

To receive credit, the child must repeat the digits in the exact order presented. If the child is successful on either item of a pair, the examiner proceeds with the test until the child fails both sequences of a level. Credit is given for each correct sequence with a value equal to the number of digits; the maximum score is 70. The raw score is converted into a score of -2 ("below the level of the threshold of adequacy," lowest 15 percent), -1 ("a moderately low ability indicative of a continuing problem," next 20 percent), 0 ("an average ability," middle 30 percent), 1 ("a positive but not yet fully developed ability," next 20 percent), and 2 ("indicates very good development," highest 15 percent). The specimen test provided to this reviewer did not have a horizontal line to separate the "0" from "-1" on the rating scale. One assumes that the line would intersect between the credits "20" and "19" in the age eight column. Thus, in order to obtain an average ability as indicated by the rating scale, a child, age five, must obtain a score of 10; age six, a score of 10; age seven, a score of 20; and, age eight, a score of 20.

It is important to note the author's caveat that any child showing a deficit in auditory sequencing, discrimination, or memory should be evaluated to rule out a loss of hearing acuity. The other paragraphs in the interpretation section of the manual are helpful in understanding test findings.

The test-retest coefficient of reliability is reported as .82 but the number of subjects is not reported. Seven validity and standardization studies are cited; however, three are not listed in the reference list and bibliography.

SUMMARY. The test, easy and quick to administer and score, provides an assessment of sequential order recall for children 5 through 8 years of age. For the pupil showing a deficit, one cannot conclude whether the deficit is one of auditory sequential memory or auditory memory (a common failing of memory-for-digits tests). The manual is adequate.

The information the authors present under validity suggests relationships between auditory sequential memory and learning disabilities and reading in the second grade, but it does not necessarily support the validity of the test. Auditory sequential memory may be only one aspect of reading or contributing to a learning disability.

For one interested in a memory-for-digits test for pupils five through eight years of age, the test can be recommended as one which is inexpensive and both easy and quick to administer and score.

[935–6]
★F.A.T.S.A. Test (Flowers Auditory Test of Selective Attention), Experimental Edition. Grades 1–6; 1972; FATSA; no data on reliability for grades 4–6; no data on validity; test administered by tape recording (5 inch reel) or tape cassette; 1 form (13 pages); manual (14 pages); $39.50 per set of 12 test booklets, tape recording, cassette, and manual; $7.50 per 12 tests; postage extra; (30) minutes; Arthur Flowers; Perceptual Learning Systems. *

STEPHEN B. HOOD, *Professor of Communication Disorders, Bowling Green State University, Bowling Green, Ohio.*

This test was designed to assess "auditory vigilance and/or auditory watch-keeping" skills

within the more general construct of auditory attention span. The author states the "auditory skills assessed are more specifically selective attention skills rather than general attention skills." The test was conceived of as an indicator of central auditory abilities and is inappropriate for children with peripheral hearing loss. The author considers "the test to be most useful with young children who are experiencing auditory attention problems in a learning situation." The nature of these learning difficulties is not explained.

The FATSA is strictly experimental. Since the test was developed as a group test, the normative data are not appropriate for children who are individually tested. Limited normative data are available for regular class children ages 6–12, and for two groups of mentally handicapped. Since, in all cases, the number of children comprising the normative groups is inadequate, the experimental edition does not meet the requirements of a properly standardized test.

The test consists of 3 practice items and 32 test items. The instructions, practice/demonstration items, and test items are presented from either a reel-to-reel or cassette tape to an optimum group of 12 children. Although a calibration tone is present on the tape, the fact that in actual practice the test will most likely be presented at a most comfortable loudness level, is a potential test weakness because it is difficult to insure that all children will receive the test stimuli at an optimum loudness level.

The test booklet has three rows of seven stimuli on each page. The rows correspond to the test questions. The child's task is to mark the picture(s) that are preceded by the key word "George." That is, if the auditory stimulus is "Put a mark on George Cow," the child should put a mark on the cow. If the auditory stimulus is "put a mark on cow," the child should not put a mark on the cow. After completing 3 practice items, the child then completes the next 32 test items.

The rate at which the auditory stimuli are presented is variable, but without an explanation of the underlying rationale. Beginning with stimulus 22, most of the auditory stimuli are superimposed upon background noise and/or speech. The noise and/or speech is both constant and variable and the loudness and pitch of the examiner's voice changes. Information relative to the signal/noise ratios is not presented, but it should be. The rationale and experimental details of procedure are not presented and it is not at all clear what is being tested.

Each item is scored as correct or incorrect. An item is correct only if the child identifies the exact number of stimulus pictures preceded by the word "George." The total possible score is 32. A raw score can be compared to the mean, standard deviation, and one to three selected percentiles which serve as norms. The author states that "when very small numbers of children are to be given a CAA test, an audiometric screening test should precede" testing. But when "large numbers" are tested, the audiometric testing should be "used as a follow-up for those individuals who score below the norm [mean] for the grade level being tested." Incidentally, the only grade norms presented are for mentally retarded children (11 to 25 children per grade) and for 60 first grade children having learning problems.

K-R 20 reliabilities are reported only for wide-range groups of elementary school children, and consequently are inflated—.69 for grades 1 and 2 and .82 for grades 3 and 4. The test is sufficiently reliable for measuring groups but not for individuals.

The FATSA is at best a gross screening device for identification of children with deficits in selective auditory attention. As pointed out by the author, no validity data are available.

While the test may have the ability to discriminate some children who lack "auditory vigilance," the concepts of "auditory vigilance" and "auditory watch-keeping skills" are not operationally defined. Furthermore, other constructs—such as auditory memory span, distractibility, perseveration, and fatigue—will probably enter as confounding variables.

Without further standardization and more adequate data on the construction, reliability, validity, and usefulness of the test, it should be viewed with caution. Furthermore, since the construct of central auditory abilities and selective attention are so complex, it is hoped that normative data will be made available for children who are tested individually. Until more normative research is available, and until the underlying constructs, principles, methodology, and rationale supporting FATSA are clearly

stated in the manual, the test's place in an assessment battery cannot be recommended.

EUGENE C. SHEELEY, *Professor of Communicative Disorders and Director, Audiological Services, The University of Alabama, University, Alabama.*

This 32-item test is intended for use either by a professional or by a supervised paraprofessional. Its purpose is to identify basic auditory perceptual deficits in young children, namely deficits in selective auditory attention, auditory attention span, auditory vigilance, auditory watchkeeping, and specific verbal signal monitoring. The preceding terms are not defined, but overlap is implied. Once a deficit is identified, remediation can be employed, specifically the author's programs in vigilance training.

The test requires the listener to mark the pictures named by a male talker with a general American dialect. The procedure is something like "Simon Says": the key word "George" must precede the name of each picture to be marked. For each item, a row of line drawings —representing bike, cow, cup, fish, ball, dog, and clock—appears on the answer sheet. Each answer sheet includes three rows of pictures. Color coded pages enable the test administrator to see that all children are on the correct page. The recording includes instructions and three practice items. The item number and carrier phrase are spoken before each series of names. A competing signal, which accompanies the last 11 items, begins as a soft "hum" and ends as a second male talker a few decibels below the first talker.

Each child must be given a hearing screening test before the FATSA, or else those who score "below the norm" must be screened afterward. When necessary, children must be given preliminary work on concepts such as "put a mark on the picture" and "top row."

The manual describes seating when the test is given through a loudspeaker to a group of 12 children. The sound pressure level is to be 80 decibels at the front row; if a sound level meter is not available, the volume is adjusted to a comfortable loudness for a listener in the last row. An "electronic intensity calibration system" and "special speaker system" are reported as "optional," but these are not described. Pro-

F.A.T.S.A. Test (Flowers Auditory Test of Selective Attention)

grams of instruction, one primary and one advanced, are recommended for use with children who score low on the test, but details are not given.

The test is considered experimental for use only as a screening tool. There are no data on validity. K-R 20 reliabilities, based on unspecified numbers of children, are reported for grades 1 and 2 combined (.69), and for grades 2 and 3 combined (.82); had single grade groups been used, the reliabilities would have been appreciably less. Norms were obtained by group administration of the test to 231 children aged 6.1 to 12.0 years who were in regular classes. Fiftieth, 25th, and 10th percentiles, as well as means and standard deviations, are given. Data are also supplied for 143 educable mentally handicapped children, 218 mildly retarded children, and 120 learning disabled children. Comparison of data from group to group is sometimes impossible because the same percentiles are not always given, the range is given for only one group, and the age-grade classification system is different for each group.

The test has face validity for certain auditory skills. Auditory attention span is clearly involved since 30 minutes of listening are required with only a one-minute break. Auditory memory is utilized in remembering the key word, and auditory vigilance is demanded by the use of a competing signal. Since the test is recommended for screening, pass-fail criteria are implied. None are specifically given, although the author suggests that any score below the 25th percentile of "regular class children" in his age group "be considered a poor score." It is suggested that each school district will wish to develop its own "norms." It might have been more helpful to have given tentative pass-fail criteria with suggestions for modifying them for different school populations.

The test vocabulary should be familiar to first graders and the pictures are well drawn. The answer booklet is well designed but the 13 oversize sheets may present storage problems. The author's precautions to rule out the contribution of hearing loss are appropriate. Instructions for scoring the test are precise and clear. Procedures for administering the test, however, are sometimes equivocal: the reel-to-reel recording is strongly recommended but not required; three different ways are given to determine the

volume setting. Perhaps equivocations are necessary at this point in the development of the test. The manual itself could benefit from editorial work, e.g., "distances between rows of desks or tables should be no greater than what is allowed for chairs to be used by the children" and "entire intact classes." The tape recording is not described in the manual as far as the monitoring of the signal, the signal-to-noise ratios, a rationale for signal levels, and choice of signals, etc., are concerned. The tape recording was carelessly produced: the instructions sound ad-libbed, switching is clearly audible, and a spoken error is followed by a spoken correction.

At present, the test has limited use even as a screening tool because of the lack of data on validity, the minimal data on reliability, and the absence of pass-fail criteria for various ages, grades, or special populations. Perhaps further study using the experimental version will supply the lacks as well as develop alternate forms and an analysis of errors with implications for remediation. The author might consider adopting a rationale for the use of competing signals similar to that used in the Auditory Selective Attention Test of the Goldman-Fristoe-Woodcock battery, which uses three distinct types of competing signals and a systematic increase in level until the competing signal exceeds the primary signal.

[937]

★Goldman-Fristoe-Woodcock Auditory Skills Test Battery. Ages 3 and over; 1974–76; also called *G-F-W Battery;* 12 tests in 5 easel-kits; individual; tests administered by tape (cassette or 5 inch reel, 3¾ ips), earphones recommended; technical manual ('76, 40 pages); profile ('75, 4 pages); $98 per set of 5 easel-kits (each kit includes test items and manual, 25 response forms and profiles, tape cassette or reel, and technical manual); $3.90 per 25 response forms for any one easel-kit; $4 per 25 profiles; $6.50 per cassette or reel for *a, b, d,* or *e* ($7 for *c*); $2.50 per technical manual; postage extra; specimen set not available; (10–15) minutes per test; Ronald Goldman, Macalyne Fristoe, and Richard W. Woodcock; American Guidance Service, Inc. *
a) GFW AUDITORY SELECTIVE ATTENTION TEST. 5 scores: quiet, fan-like noise, cafeteria noise, voice, total; no norms for quiet score; 1 form ('74, 254 pages); manual ('74, 19 pages); response form ('74, 4 pages); $20.50 per kit.
b) GFW DIAGNOSTIC AUDITORY DISCRIMINATION TEST. 3 parts in 2 easel-kits; manual ('74, 14 pages in part 1 kit).
    1) *Part 1.* 1 form ('74, 236 pages); response form ('74, 5 pages, including Sound Confusion Inventory, a diagnostic scoring process to be completed if all 3 parts are administered); $20 per kit.

F.A.T.S.A. Test (Flowers Auditory Test of Selective Attention)

2) *Parts 2 and 3.* Administered to those below 25th percentile on part 1; 2 scores: total of parts 1 and 2, total of parts 1, 2, and 3; 1 form ('74, 277 pages); response form ('74, 3 pages); $26 per kit.

c) GFW AUDITORY MEMORY TESTS. 3 tests: recognition memory, memory for content, memory for sequence; 1 form ('74, 167 pages); manual ('74, 24 pages); response form ('74, 5 pages); $25.50 per kit.

d) GFW SOUND-SYMBOL TESTS. 7 tests: sound mimicry, sound recognition, sound analysis, sound blending, sound-symbol association, reading of symbols, spelling of sounds; 1 form ('74, 182 pages); manual ('74, 33 pages); response form ('74, 8 pages); $20.75 per kit.

KATHERINE G. BUTLER, *Acting Dean of Graduate Studies and Research and Director, Speech and Hearing Center, San Jose State University, San Jose, California.*

This very extensive test battery provides diagnostic instruments for both clinical and research use, primarily by speech pathologists and audiologists, school psychologists, reading specialists and special educators. Its usefulness is increased by the considerable amount of development and collection of normative data which preceded its issuance.

The authors point to the importance of auditory perception as it relates to auditory comprehension and mental functioning. The G-F-W battery specifically measures selective attention, auditory discrimination, recognition memory, memory for content, memory for sequence, and, in addition, provides for a series of seven subtests under the rubric "sound-symbol" tests. The technical manual notes that the tests were "designed primarily for clinical use, to provide fine discriminations among subjects at lower developmental levels and among subjects whose performance is deficient for their ages." The manual also states that the battery "should provide detailed diagnostic information in at least two areas of auditory skill: speech-sound discrimination and knowledge of grapheme-to-phoneme correspondence."

The norming data were gathered on a representative sample of subjects, ages 3 to 80. A limited number of school sites were involved in California, Florida, and Maine, with the majority of testing sites being located in Minnesota. The manual provides age and race data by age groups of 3 to 8 years, 9 to 18 years, and 19 years and over, rather than by chronological ages per se. For example, the selective attention test was administered to 228 children ages 3 to 8, 256 children ages 9 to 18, and 101 subjects 19 years or older, for a total of 585 subjects, of whom 90.2 percent were white, 6.7 percent were black, and 3.1 percent were "other." Similar information is provided for all tests. The norming samples range in number from 405 to 4,790, with a mean of approximately 500 across the three age groupings for most tests. A clinical sample was also utilized, distributed across two groups, one with mild speech and learning difficulties and the other with severe learning difficulties. The split-half reliabilities for the 12 tests in the three age groups vary considerably, ranging from .46 to .97, with median .85. The battery tests are least reliable (median .81) for ages 9 to 18; the median reliability in the other two groups is .90. No test-retest reliabilities are reported. These reliabilties are inflated since they are based on wide-range age groups, rather than on within-age or within-grade groups.

Test intercorrelations, with the effect of age range removed, indicate that the various tests in the battery do, for the most part, measure distinctly different auditory traits or skills. The age-relatedness of auditory skills is determined through cross-sectional rather than longitudinal data and relates positively to other research data.

Five of the 12 tests utilize pictures and require only a pointing response. There is a training section for every test that makes use of pictures to be used in the later administration of the test, thus reducing vocabulary differences among subjects and teaching the picture-word associations to be used. Another five of the tests use nonsense words, while the final two tests utilize a list of familiar words as stimuli.

Well-constructed easel-kits are used, with the examiner reading certain instructions and the auditory test stimuli presented by prerecorded audiotape, available either in reel-to-reel or cassette tapes. Earphones are recommended, and the authors note that "the use of low-quality equipment or the absence of earphones may result in reduced performance to an unknown degree; however, such equipment may still be preferable to live voice administration." Difficulty may be encountered by an examiner who provides earphones for the subject, but does not have access to a stereo playback to monitor the subject's responses.

The manuals provided with the easel-kits are clear, particularly when reviewed in the context of the technical manual. Users may find the

Goldman-Fristoe-Woodcock Auditory Skills Test Battery

norm-referenced information more helpful than the criterion-referenced information. A battery profile may be constructed for those subjects given the complete battery, or it is possible to utilize only portions of the battery in conjunction with other test instruments. Considerable information can be determined from even a partial administration of specific tests or subtests within the battery. The profiles can be utilized for both diagnostic and remediation purposes.

SUMMARY. The G-F-W battery may be utilized for in-depth diagnosis and therapeutic planning for subjects with suspected language or learning handicaps. While the tests are relatively easy to administer, the administration of the entire battery is time-consuming. However, the data obtained may be of real value in identifying the existence of specific auditory processing difficulties. Subject fatigue may limit the usefulness of the entire battery with preschool and kindergarten subjects. It should be particularly helpful to teachers of learning disabled children ages 8–18. In an area where many instruments are experimental in nature only, this battery has been produced only after considerable attention had been paid to its development, standardization, and statistical analysis, and to the provision of normative data and profiles for interpretative purposes. As such, it deserves serious consideration by those interested in the measurement of auditory processing skills.

THOMAS OAKLAND, *Professor of Educational Psychology, The University of Texas, Austin, Texas.*

The G-F-W battery was designed to identify and describe deficient auditory perception skills in persons aged 3 through 80. Emphasis is placed on differentiating more finely among persons with defective auditory perception than among those with normal perception. The conceptual basis for the battery describes auditory perception as the ability to extract and process auditory information and to relate this information to other experiences; auditory perception is viewed as a cluster of abilities between those of auditory acuity and auditory comprehension.

Six criteria guided the development of the battery: (*a*) to assess " a broad spectrum" of auditory perception skills; (*b*) "to provide fine discriminations among subjects at lower devel-

opmental levels and among subjects whose performance is deficient for their ages"; (*c*) to "provide detailed diagnostic information in at least two areas of auditory skills: speech-sound discrimination and knowledge of grapheme-to-phoneme correspondence"; (*d*) "to minimize the effects of irrelevant subjective characteristics"; (*e*) to have easy-to-acquire administration procedures; and (*f*) "to maximize the likelihood of correct, standardized administration."

The battery presents the most comprehensive assessment of auditory skills presently available. Twelve individually administered tests comprise four major clusters which progressively require greater cognitive complexity. An examiner may administer a single test, a combination of tests, or the full battery.

Auditory selective attention refers to a person's ability to attend to an important auditory signal while ignoring distracting background noises which become increasingly intense. Auditory discrimination refers to a person's ability to distinguish between sounds which are highly similar. Three auditory memory tests measure short-term retention of information; recognition memory is defined as the ability to recognize an auditory event which has occurred in the immediate past; recognition for content refers to the ability to recognize the elements in an auditory event without regard for the sequence of those elements; memory for sequences is described as the ability to remember the order of a set of elements in an auditory event.

The seven sound-symbol cluster tests measure several basic abilities prerequisite to advanced language skills, including reading and spelling; sound mimicry refers to the ability to translate from the aural to the oral modality; the sound recognition test measures the ability to identify a familiar word when presented with an isolated sequence of phonemes of that word; sound analysis refers to the ability to distinguish specific phonemes contained in nonsense syllables; the sound blending test measures the ability to synthesize isolated sounds into meaningful words; sound-symbol association is a paired-associate learning task which measures a person's ability to learn new associations between novel auditory and visual symbols; reading of symbols refers to the ability to make grapheme-to-phoneme translations of 70 non-

Goldman-Fristoe-Woodcock Auditory Skills Test Battery

sense words; the spelling of sounds test measures the ability to make phoneme-to-grapheme translations of nonsense words.

Normative data gathered for this battery were based on the testing of 5,773 subjects aged 3 to 80 in four states (California, Florida, Maine, and Minnesota); in each of the first three states the sample was drawn from only one city. The percentages of the norming sample for three broad age groups are as follows: 35 percent, ages 3–8; 48 percent, ages 9–18; and 17 percent, ages 19–80. The norms for the reading of symbols test are based on "data gathered for norming the Word Attack Test of the *Woodcock Reading Mastery Tests.*"

The technical manual does not report the actual number of persons included in the standardization sample at each chronological age. The mean number of persons included for the various tests within the three broad age ranges was 186 for ages 3–8, 250 for ages 9–18, and 89 for ages 19–80. This means that the average number tested at each age was only 32 for each of the ages 3–8; 25 for each of the ages 9–18; and less than 2 persons at each of the higher ages.

Despite the small numbers at each age level, percentile rank norms are presented for 40 age intervals! Each set of percentile ranks is based on an average of only 11 persons in the age 3–8 group; 25 in the age 9–18 group; and less than 2 in the age 19–80 group. The percentile ranks cannot possibly have been computed from so few cases. The authors do not explain how it is possible to obtain as many as 73 percentiles when testing approximately 25 persons. Until more convincing data are made available, these percentile rank norms probably should not be used.

It is impossible to judge the significance of the split-half reliabilities reported because they are based on such wide ranges of ages. These reliabilities are certainly greatly inflated because of the correlations between GFW scores and age—.34 to .80 (median .56) in the group 3 to 8 years; −.04 to .58 (median .30), 9 to 18 years; and −.19 to −.72 (median −.60), 19 to 80 years. The authors should have reported either within-age or within-grade reliabilities, including test-retest as well as split-half procedures. Considering only the 11 reliabilities based upon the entire norms sample, the reli-

abilities reported for the three wide-range groups are: 3 to 8 years, .78 to .97 with median .87; 9 to 18 years, .46 to .96 with median .77; and 19 to 80, .73 to .97 with median .90. Fifty-eight percent of these wide-range-based reliabilities are .89 or lower and 30 percent are .79 or lower. The within-grades, within-schools reliabilities must be appreciably lower. One must conclude that the tests are not as reliable as tests should be for the profile analysis of individuals.

The technical manual summarizes the major similarities and differences between tests in a succinct and helpful manner as a means of examining the battery's content validity. The construct validity is examined in three ways. First, intercorrelations among the tests, with age effects removed through partial correlation procedures, generally are sufficiently low to infer that the tests measure different abilities rather than a general auditory perception ability. Second, correlations between age and test scores tend to be high and positive for ages 3–8, lower and positive for ages 9–18, and high and negative for ages 19–80. The third method of demonstrating validity compares the performance of normals to the mild and the moderate-to-severe dysfunctional groups. In contrast to the scores from normals, the mildly dysfunctional persons scored lower on 9 of the 12 tests and the moderately-to-severely dysfunctional persons scored lower on every test. These data suggest that the battery does differentiate between persons with dysfunctional abilities and those who are normal. However, there is little evidence that the battery effectively discriminates among persons within the lower developmental levels. While the analyses reported in the technical manual provide for age effects, they do not control for other factors (e.g., intelligence, years of education, socioeconomic status) which contribute significantly to differential performance on these tests.

The battery has a number of commendable features which help insure an equitable and proper administration. One is the use of earphones and prerecorded tapes for tests using auditory stimuli. On those tests which utilize pictures, a training procedure is incorporated into the administration which teaches picture-word associations used and which minimizes the effects of vocabulary differences among persons

Goldman-Fristoe-Woodcock Auditory Skills Test Battery

taking the test. Procedures for administering and scoring are clearly presented and conveniently bound in self-contained booklets which allow the client and examiner to view the test materials simultaneously and the examiner to see the directions for administering and scoring each item.

The test materials are both heavy (13¾ lbs.) and somewhat bulky. The addition of a tape recorder and two sets of earphones decreases its transportability.

Clinicians and researchers interested in language and learning disorders should find the G-F-W battery interesting and useful. The battery may be most useful in evaluating various auditory perception skills of children below age 9 and persons with severe defects. Older children tend to receive nearly perfect scores on some of the tests and few adults are included in the standardization sample—factors which limit the battery's usefulness with these persons. The reading error inventory and sound confusion inventory also may be a useful diagnostic device to uncover some perceptual abilities depressing the development of speech, language, and reading skills.

In addition to identifying persons with auditory problems, the authors suggest that the auditory discrimination and auditory selective attention tests are useful in assessing certain hearing problems and in evaluating the effectiveness of hearing aids. While this may be true, no guidelines are provided for their use in these ways.

SUMMARY. The G-F-W battery does assess a broad spectrum of auditory perception skills, minimizes many irrelevant factors, and provides clear administration and scoring procedures. Its effectiveness in differentiating among persons with poorly developed auditory skills is somewhat questionable. As always in using norm-referenced measures, the development and initiation of intervention programs for individual persons based on results from one battery is risky. The battery may provide helpful diagnostic information, but is insufficient in its detail to justify an intervention program with demonstrated effectiveness. Additional research and development is needed to ascertain the battery's reliability, to further explicate its construct validity, and to clarify its standardization sample.

Goldman-Fristoe-Woodcock Auditory Skills Test Battery

[938]

Goldman-Fristoe-Woodcock Test of Auditory Discrimination. Ages 4 and over; 1970; GFW; speech-sound discrimination scores under 2 conditions: quiet, background noise; individual; 1 form; 3 parts; examiner's test kit (50 pages); manual (31 pages); record sheet (1 page); stimulus test words tape (7½ ips, 5 inch reel or cassette); use of earphones recommended; pretraining picture cards also available; $23 per kit of test materials and 50 response sheets; $3.50 per 50 response sheets; $1.75 per manual; postage extra; (10–15) minutes; Ronald Goldman, Macalyne Fristoe, and Richard W. Woodcock; American Guidance Service, Inc. *

See T2:2037 (4 references); for reviews by Eugene C. Sheeley and Ralph L. Shelton and an excerpted review by Barton B. Proger, see 7:938.

REFERENCES

1–4. See T2:2037.
5. HORD, CHARLCIE LEE. *Effects of Preschool Language Instruction on Auditory Discrimination Skills.* Master's thesis, Vanderbilt University (Nashville, Tenn.), 1970.
6. BURG, LESLIE ANNE. *An Analysis of Factors Related to Reading Disability as Evidenced in Three Specifically Identified Groups.* Doctor's thesis, Boston University (Boston, Mass.), 1972. (DAI 33:1311A)
7. SCHMIDT, JEAN WALSH. *The Effect of Kindergarten Auditory Perceptual Training Program on Selected Auditory Abilities.* Doctor's thesis, New York University (New York, N.Y.), 1972. (DAI 33:482B)
8. SWEM, THOMAS WILLIAM. *A Comparative Investigation of the Auditory Discrimination Abilities of Children in Special Education and Regular Education Classrooms in the San Luis Valley of Colorado.* Doctor's thesis, University of New Mexico (Albuquerque, N.M.), 1972. (DAI 33:3369B)
9. BROWER, CARTER G. *The Relationship Between Children and Performance on the Goldman-Fristoe-Woodcock Test of Auditory Discrimination and Teacher Ratings of Attention on the Devereaux Elementary School Rating Scale.* Master's thesis, University of New Mexico (Albuquerque, N.M.), 1973.
10. FINKENBINDER, RONALD L. "A Descriptive Study of the Goldman-Fristoe-Woodcock Test of Auditory Discrimination and Selected Reading Variables With Primary School Children." *J Spec Ed* 7(2):125–31 su '73. * (PA 52:4071)
11. KARNES, FRANCES NESSLER. *A Comparative Analysis of Individual and Group Auditory Discrimination Tests for Disabled Third Grade Readers in a Lower Socio-Economic Group.* Doctor's thesis, University of Illinois (Urbana, Ill.), 1973. (DAI 34:7468A)
12. SCHUBERT, GEORGE W.; MEYER, ROBERT C.; and SCHMIDT, JACQUE I. "Evaluation of the Noise Subtest of the Goldman-Fristoe-Woodcock Test of Auditory Discrimination." *J Auditory Res* 13(1):42–4 Ja '73. * (PA 54:8778)
13. WATSON, MICHAEL ALLEN. *Development and Validation of a Group Test of Developmental Learning Skills and Its Relation to Similar Individual Tests in the Field.* Doctor's thesis, Northern Illinois University (DeKalb, Ill.), 1973. (DAI 34:1143A)
14. WEINER, PAUL S., AND HOOCK, WILLIAM C. "The Standardization of Tests: Criteria and Criticisms." *J Speech & Hearing Res* 16(4):616–26 D '73. * (PA 52:8073)
15. WRUCK, DONALD KURT. *The Relationship Between Speech Sound Discrimination and Oral Stereognosis to Articulation.* Doctor's thesis, Bowling Green State University (Bowling Green, Ohio), 1973. (DAI 34:4115B)
16. NERBONNE, MICHAEL A.; McMULLIN, BRENT R.; HIPSKIND, NICHOLAS M.; and OLSON, ARDELL. "Presentation Level in Auditory Discrimination Tests for Children." *J Auditory Res* 14(4):258–62 O '74. * (PA 56:3366)
17. BANNATYNE, ALEX. "Review of the Goldman-Fristoe-Woodcock Test of Auditory Discrimination." *J Learn Dis* 8(3):130–2 Mr '75. *
18. BLUE, C. MILTON, AND VERGASON, GLENN A. "Auditory Discrimination in Conditions of Noise and Quiet by Black and White Disadvantaged Children." *Percept & Motor Skills* 41(1):35–40 Ag '75. * (PA 55:4224)
19. NEUFELD, GORDON ARTHUR. *The Relationship of Speech-Sound Discrimination to the Development of Ear Asymmetries in Grade-School Children.* Doctor's thesis, University of British Columbia (Vancouver, B.C., Canada), 1975. (DAI 36:3653B)
20. SCHULTZ, JEROME JOSEPH. *Four Measures of Auditory Discrimination: A Factor-Analytic Determination of Their Relative Equivalence.* Doctor's thesis, Boston College (Chestnut Hill, Mass.), 1975. (DAI 36:224A)
21. OWENS, EDNA KELL. *An Investigation of Auditory Memory and Its Relationship to Reading Achievement of Elementary Pupils.* Doctor's thesis, Memphis State University (Memphis, Tenn.), 1976. (DAI 37:3474A)

22. SEXTON, LARRY CHARLES. *Auditory and Visual Perception, Sex, and Academic Aptitude as Predictors of Achievement for First Grade Children.* Doctor's thesis, Ball State University (Muncie, Ind.), 1976. (*DAI* 37:6162A)

J Learn Dis 8(3):130–2 Mr '75. Alex Bannatyne. The one major problem I have with this test is that it is a test of auditory closure.... and not, as the authors believe, a test of auditory discrimination. A case in point is the presentation of the memory process required by the G-F-W discrimination task, diagrammed on page 8 of the test manual. On that page the authors also diagram the memory process required by the traditional same-different discrimination test. This, too, is termed a discrimination task. It is scientifically confusing to have the single term "discrimination" applied to both types of memory process since auditory closure requires a matching against past experience, requiring long-term memory, while auditory discrimination is an immediate comparison between two stimuli presented almost simultaneously to the subject. * The first part of the test is administered without any background noise and is called the Quiet Subtest. This is followed by the Noise Subtest which presents 30 stimulus words against a "cafeteria" background noise. For me, this Noise Subtest is a clear-cut auditory closure test. * The validity of the G-F-W Test of Auditory Discrimination was not established against any traditional word-pair discrimination test. This is a pity because I suspect the correlations would have been quite low. * The test discriminated quite well between normal subjects and learning disability children, disadvantaged children, mentally retarded children, the hard of hearing children with school learning problems, and children with speech and language problems. Of course all these groups could equally well have problems of auditory closure. Note that poor auditory discrimination almost always means poor auditory closure, but the reverse is not necessarily true. In my experience, most learning disability children tested check out diagnostically as normal on a paired-word auditory discrimination test, but prove to have auditory closure problems on the ITPA Auditory Closure Subtest. Certainly the validity question on all these auditory tests cries out for much more extensive research into the various categories of auditory processing and how they are interrelated in both theory and practice. The G-F-W Test of Auditory Discrimination does break down the phonemes tested in the stimulus words into their distinctive features. These are voiced and unvoiced sounds on one dimension against plosive continuant and nasals on the second dimension. The place of articulation is also considered. Unfortunately, the frequency of occurrence of these distinctive features is too small to make an analysis of them reliable when examining individual children. However, they should prove very useful for group comparisons in research projects. The test is easy to administer, but requires a high fidelity tape recorder and earphones. * Finally I would like to raise the unpopular topic (these days) of sex differences on tests. * the authors of this test of so-called auditory discrimination found a significant difference due to sex which is discounted in the norms, the two groups being combined. On the Noise Subtest especially, the females made slightly fewer errors than the males up to $10\frac{1}{2}$ years of age. It is all very well to ignore cognitive and perceptual sex differences in the "normal" populations used for standardizing tests, but we in learning disabilities are working with children who have significant deficits in one or more of these cognitive and perceptual processes. Boys with learning disabilities outnumber girls with learning disabilities *at least* three to one. * Perhaps it is time we stopped quietly brushing sex differences under the rug. Exploratory research into the topic might lead to new methods of preventing learning disabilities, of screening out high risk children, and of developing curricula which would be a help rather than a hindrance to LD children.

[939]

★**K.S.U. Speech Discrimination Test.** Persons with hearing loss grades 3 and over; 1967–69; norms consist of means and standard deviations; individual; forms A, B, C, D, E, F, G, H, ('67, 1 page); no manual; reprint of *2* below provided; tape cassette available for administration; $7.50 per set of tape, reprint, and 9 sets of answer sheets for all forms; $1 per 9 sets of answer sheets; cash orders postpaid; (4) minutes; Kenneth W. Berger; Audiotone. *

REFERENCES

1. NACKES, MARY. *An Examination of the Relationship Between Speech Discrimination Performance and Hearing Handicap.* Master's thesis, Kent State University (Kent, Ohio), 1967.
2. BERGER, KENNETH W. "A Speech Discrimination Task Using Multiple-Choice Key Words in Sentences." *J Auditory Res* 9(3):247–62 Jl '69. * (*PA* 45:9247)
3. BERGER, KENNETH W.; KEATING, LAWRENCE W.; AND ROSE, DARRELL E. "An Evaluation of the Kent State University (KSU) Speech Discrimination Test on Subjects With Sensory-Neural Loss." *J Auditory Res* 11(2):140–3 Ap '71. *

HARRIS WINITZ, *Professor of Psychology and Speech Science, University of Missouri, Kansas City, Missouri.*

This test is designed to measure auditory perception of word units within the context of short sentences. Each of the eight forms of this hearing test has 13 items, consisting of "five phonetically similar key words within each sentence, any one of which will complete the sentence. The tester however, reads only one of the key words and the subject is to cross out on the printed answer sheet the key word which he believes he heard." The sentences may either be read by the examiner or be tape administered. Key words are one or two syllables in length, and frequent in appearance in conversational speech. Only preliminary experimentation was conducted to establish that the multiple-word choices were logically appropriate and of equal probability.

The author claims that the test measures "how efficiently one can utilize his hearing for daily communication." He also states that he "found the present test particularly useful with persons having a foreign accent" and suggests "that the test might be useful in auditory training." No information is presented on specific ways that the test results may be useful.

Only preliminary normative scales are provided. Statistically stable scores remain to be determined. No information is given as to the range of phonetic elements sampled within and across alternate forms. The format of the presentation can be easily followed from the instructions. This test is potentially an important contribution to auditory testing, because it examines test words within the context of sentences. In effect, this test examines a person's ability to extract phonetic information from an acoustically variable signal, a fundamental process when listening to conversational speech. Large-scale revision of this test is, therefore, recommended; populations reflective of normal and abnormal hearing should be selected. Reduction to two test forms, sentence difficulty, and the probabilities of foil items need to be considered. Validity should be determined independently of other hearing tests using clinically defined populations.

[940]

Kindergarten Auditory Screening Test. Grades kgn–1; 1971; KAST; 3 scores: speech in environmental noise, phonemic synthesis, same/different; no

K.S.U. Speech Discrimination Test

data on reliability; 1 form (33⅓ rpm record); teacher's guide (21 pages); student response booklet (20 pages); $7.65 per set of record and guide; $4.14 per 15 response booklets; $2.40 per specimen set (complete record and guide not included); postage extra; (20) minutes; Jack Katz; Follett Publishing Co. *

REFERENCES

1. MARGOLIS, HOWARD. *The Effects of an Impulsive or Reflective Conceptual Tempo Upon the Auditory Perceptual, Reading Readiness, and Intelligence Test Performances of Kindergarten Children.* Doctor's thesis, Hofstra University (Hempstead, N.Y.), 1974. (*DAI* 35:1503A)
2. MARGOLIS, HOWARD. "The Kindergarten Auditory Screening Test as a Predictor of Reading Disability." *Psychol Sch* 399–403 O '76. *
3. MARGOLIS, HOWARD. "Auditory Perceptual Test Performance and the Reflection-Impulsivity Dimension." *J Learn Dis* 10(3):164–72 Mr '77. *

NICHOLAS W. BANKSON, *Associate Professor of Speech Pathology and Audiology, Boston University, Boston, Massachusetts.*

The KAST is a 29-item screening test of auditory perceptual skills designed for kindergarten and first grade children. Test stimuli are presented via a phonograph recording and require the child to record his responses in a picture-response booklet. The test is designed for individual and group administration, with a pretraining period recommended prior to administration. The three subtests comprising the instrument are speech in noise (identification of spoken words with increasing levels of environmental noise in the background), phonemic synthesis (identification of spoken words wherein the separate sounds of the word are produced at 1½ second intervals), and same/different discrimination (indicating whether paired spoken nonsense and real words, one of which is spoken by a man and the other by a boy, are the same or different).

The author states that the subtests of this instrument were selected on the basis of deficits evidenced on these tasks by 200 children referred for suspected learning disabilities to the Menorah Medical Center, Kansas City, Missouri.

An attempt to indicate predictive validity is based upon the finding that 40 normal children who were tested with the three subtests passed each of them; however, specific numbers of accurate predictions of learning disabilities made from such testing, as well as false positives and false negatives, are not reported. In addition, the criteria by which these children were categorized as normal are not presented. The author reports that his experience indicates that classroom teachers can identify more than 90 percent of children who have auditory perceptual deficiencies with this test, though supporting data for this statement is lacking. While cutoff scores for pass, borderline, and fail performances are indicated for both kindergarten and first grade children on each of the subtests, the criteria upon which these were determined is not reported. No reliability information is presented for the measure.

The response booklet is comprised of black and white line drawings of objects which are easily identifiable. In some pictures, the abundance of lines used to provide detail and shadings could prove a source of distraction for children with visual perceptual problems.

For the speech in noise subtest, the child must look at a picture and mark two or three stimulus items after each is named. In the sound blending subtest, the child must select from among four pictures the one depicting the word the narrator pronounces. The same/different discrimination subtest requires the child to mark either a rectangle in which two circles are drawn for auditory stimuli that are the same, or a rectangle containing a circle and a square for stimuli that are different. On this task the child must not only decide whether two spoken words or nonsense words are the same, but he must make this evaluation despite differences in the voices of the two speakers, and then determine the appropriate rectangle to mark. The manual states that this subtest can pick up a discrimination problem, some memory disorders, and other auditory perceptual abnormalities. Information is not presented to explain or further support this statement.

Since this test is a screening instrument, the author suggests that children who fail one or more subtests be referred to medical and/or speech and hearing specialists for further evaluation. A question one must face in using this test concerns the nature of auditory perception, its relationship to learning disabilities, and the types of diagnostic tests which should be used in follow-up. If the practitioner does not have answers to these questions, he may fall into the trap of defining auditory perception as that which is measured on this screening test, with subsequent remediation based thereupon. If the relationship of such specific skills to learning performance is not well established, the possibility exists that one may be teaching isolated and non-meaningful skills.

In summary, the KAST is a viable instrument for a quick screening of selected auditory perceptual skills. While the phonograph recording is of high fidelity, repeated usage will decrease that fidelity. The potential examiner will need to give careful consideration to the utilization he can make of the information derived from the test.

[941]

★Language-Structured Auditory Retention Span Test. Mental ages 3.7 to adult; 1973-75; LARS; immediate recall of words and sentences presented orally; 2 scores: mental age, "quotient" (MA/CA); no data on reliability and validity; no information presented on the derivation of mental age equivalents; no description of standardization procedures; individual; Forms A, B, ('73, 4 pages); manual ('75, 27 pages); $3.50 per 25 tests; $4.50 per manual; postage extra; specimen set not available; [20] minutes; Luis Carlson; Academic Therapy Publications. *

REFERENCES

1. KRICHEV, ALAN. "Review of the Language-Structured Auditory Retention Span Test." *Psychol Sch* 13(3):366 Jl '76. *

JAMES B. LINGWALL, *Professor of Speech Pathology and Audiology and Head of the Department, The University of Kansas, Lawrence, Kansas.*

This sentence recall test consists of 58 items ("sentences") ranging in complexity from single words (e.g., Mama) to sentences "long enough to challenge the....average adult" (e.g., "When they came to the crossroads they were baffled about their choices."). The author describes the test as "a new tool designed for those who have a need to define and remediate or circumvent disabilities in language functioning for children of mental age three years and seven months old through adult, individually tested."

It is virtually impossible to learn from the manual just what specific purposes the test is intended to serve. The author describes it as a sentence recall test but the particular applications to be made are extremely vague. As a test of "immediate recall of auditory stimuli," it is of questionable value. The basis for selecting 58 different sentences apears to be strictly arbitrary. Increasing length of each "sentence" in terms of additional letters does not correspond with a systematic increase in the number of spoken phonemes in each sentence. Further, there is no systematic control for syntactical differences in the difficulty of sentence items.

Instructions for administration and scoring are vaguely described. The test is extremely difficult to administer and score; in fact, this reviewer cannot ascertain just how the test could be scored.

There is a complete absence of information on the construction, standardization, reliability, and validity of the test. Oddly enough, although the author never refers to the test as an intelligence test, the raw scores are converted to mental ages and "verbal IQs." The author speaks of using the test "to remediate any problems detected by the test," but gives no clues as to the problems which may be detected.

In summary, the use of this test cannot be recommended. It is astonishing that the author and publisher were willing to market a test without any data as to its validity, reliability, and usefulness.

Psychol Sch 13(3):366 Jl '76. Alan Krichev. * LARS' main drawback is that....its manual obviously was written for teachers with no training in psychometrics. The Manual includes no information as to the test's reliability and validity, the equivalence of the two forms, or the normative sample. No references are given as to where this information might be obtained. Unsophisticated testers might wish to accept the existence of pertinent data on faith. To them, I would undoubtedly recommend the use of LARS as a handy instrument to assess language-based short-term memory. School psychologists are, I hope, too sophisticated to use and interpret an instrument which does not offer *any* data to allow the user the opportunity to evaluate its reliability and validity, and which does not give the applicability of the included norms. I'm afraid this is an instrument which might gain widespread acceptance among teacher-testers but which school psychologists will more comfortably leave unused except for specific experimental purposes.

[942]

Lindamood Auditory Conceptualization Test. Grades kgn–12; 1971; LACT; 3 scores: isolated sounds in sequence, sounds within syllable pattern, total; no data on reliability of part scores; no norms for sounds within syllables score; individual; no reading by examinees; Forms A, B, (2 pages); preliminary manual (35 pages); set of colored blocks; tape cassette of directions for administering; examiner's cue sheet (2 pages); $13.95 per set of testing materials including 50 sets of both forms; $4.75 per 50 sets of both forms; postage extra; (10–35) minutes; Charles H. Lindamood and Patricia C. Lindamood; Teaching Resources Corporation. *

REFERENCES

1. BUTCHEE, JEAN ANNELLE. *The Usefulness of the Lindamood Auditory Conceptualization Test as a Screening Tool for Identification of Children With Auditory Perceptual Difficulties and as a Predictor of Reading Achievement.* Master's thesis, University of Tulsa (Tulsa, Okla.), 1973.
2. CALFEE, ROBERT C.; LINDAMOOD, PATRICIA; AND LINDAMOOD, CHARLES. "Acoustic-Phonetic Skills and Reading—Kindergarten Through Twelfth Grade." *J Ed Psychol* 64(3):293–8 Je '73. * (PA 50:11947)
3. KARNES, FRANCES NESSLER. *A Comparative Analysis of Individual and Group Auditory Discrimination Tests for Disabled Third Grade Readers in a Lower Socio-Economic Group.* Doctor's thesis, University of Illinois (Urbana, Ill.), 1973. (DAI 34:7468A)
4. KRACKOWIZER, DAGA, AND JAMISON, JENNIFER. "Possibilities for Use of the LAC and ADD by Teachers and Speech Specialists." *Lang Speech & Hearing Services Sch* 5(2):98–102 Ap '74. * (PA 52:11041)
5. MATHEWSON, GROVER C., AND PEREYRA-SUAREZ, DENISE M. "Spanish Language Interference With Acoustic-Phonetic Skills and Reading." *J Read Behav* 7(2):187–96 su '75. * (PA 57:6844)

KATHARINE G. BUTLER, *Acting Dean of Graduate Studies and Research and Director, Speech and Hearing Center, San Jose State University, San Jose, California.*

LACT is a relatively brief instrument which identifies "conceptualization" of "isolated phonemic units" and "contrasts within and between syllables, in respect to phonemic identity and sequence." This individually administered instrument purports to measure two auditory perceptual encoding abilities, i.e., discrimination between speech sounds and the perception of the number and order of sounds within spoken patterns (syllables). The authors indicate that it has relevance to the diagnosis of, and educational planning for, individuals with speech, language, reading, or spelling problems.

The test was normed on 660 students, K–12, in Monterey, California, public schools. While ethnic and socioeconomic data are not provided, the authors state that a full range of socio-economic-ethnic groups were represented. Teachers selected the subjects based on "upper" and "lower" classroom performance. Sixty students, equally divided between boys and girls, were utilized at each grade level, K–6; and 240 in grades 7–12.

Reliability data were determined by test-retest, with alternate forms utilizing 4 children at each grade level (total N, 52 students). The resultant reliability is reported to be .96. Thus, reliability data are rather limited, particularly in view of the authors' statement that there is "no average facility by grade level" after the second grade, and that "individuals tend to evidence extremes of adequate or inadequate performance."

This 28-item test provides for a five-item "precheck" to establish the subject's ability to demonstrate the receptive understanding of sameness and difference, number concepts to four, left to right order, and the first and last concepts. The examiner's verbal directions at the close of the precheck include: "Show me three blocks and make only the first one and the last one the same." These rather complex directions provide difficulty for children with receptive language difficulties, and reduce the test's effectiveness with young or handicapped children.

While the manual indicates that the test may be administered in approximately 10 minutes, test time is usually considerably longer, due to precheck and demonstration items. When the test is administered to young children, the administration time is more likely to be 20 to 35 minutes. However, there are no prescribed time limits.

The two equivalent forms assist in test-retest evaluation. The test items themselves are well constructed. The materials provided in the kit include 18 colored blocks, an audiotape which provides for examiner training (but not for test administration) in the verbal delivery of isolated phonemes, and a simple, well-designed, but incomplete record sheet. The authors indicate that the test may be administered by educators, testing and guidance personnel, physicians, and parents who have familiarized themselves with the procedure and the stimuli presentation. This reviewer would hope, however, that the test be administered primarily by trained personnel with a background in the International Phonetic Alphabet and/or with training and validation of phonetic skills. The examiner must deliver the isolated phonemic stimuli at a rate of two per second, which requires at least a moderate amount of experience.

SUMMARY. This test goes well beyond the traditional auditory discrimination tasks represented by so many tests on the market. It provides a rather unique method of evaluating the subject's ability to manipulate aurally-perceived stimuli, both cognitively and motorically. It is likely to be more useful with older subjects, since a considerable number of children below age 7 have difficulty in mastering the skills required on the precheck items. Examiner variability provides some difficulty and results by untrained or informally trained examiners are questionable. Since the test utilizes isolated

phonemes and syllables, linguistic interpretations are not required. Even with the exclusion of semantically meaningful material, a number of auditory processing skills are involved, including short-term memory storage, sequencing, and analysis of both auditory and visual stimuli, etc. It is suggested that this test would be most useful to examiners with broad backgrounds in speech and language pathology, reading, and auditory processing disorders.

JAMES A. TILL, *Assistant Professor of Speech and Hearing Sciences, University of Washington, Seattle, Washington.*

The LACT was designed to identify individuals who have difficulty with what is labeled by the authors as "auditory conceptualization." Curiously, this term was omitted from the list of terms defined in the manual. It is apparent from the manual, however, that the authors include both the ability to discriminate among speech sounds and the ability to specify where a difference occurs in a speech sound pattern as the basic components of auditory conceptualization.

The test requires live-voice presentation of speech sounds either in a sequence of isolated speech sounds or in coarticulated syllables containing two to four speech sounds. The subject is required to demonstrate knowledge of the number of speech sounds produced and their similarity or dissimilarity by placing colored blocks in a row with the first sound represented on the left and the last sound in the sequence represented on the right. Association of a specific color to a specific sound is avoided in the test by allowing the child the initial choice of colors from a central pile of blocks. A precheck procedure is administered prior to the test to determine if the necessary concepts of same/different, number concepts to four, and left to right progression are present. The authors advise that if several errors are made during the five precheck items, the precheck may be given again; and, if the "concepts are present," the remainder of the test should be given. They do not, however, give a specific criterion of success necessary before the remainder of the test may be given.

The test kit contains an audiotape which is included to control some of the variability associated with live-voice presentation. It provides

Lindamood Auditory Conceptualization Test

prototypical pronunciation of the speech sounds used in the test and an example of test administration. The tape is of fair quality although some editing is noticeable upon listening to it. The instructions provided on the tape are, for the most part, redundant with the instructions in the manual, but the recording is useful in providing examples of pronunciation and the rate of stimulus presentation. Despite the examples provided by the audiotape, the disadvantages associated with live-voice presentation remain present in this test. Variations in pronunciation and rate can be expected to occur among different examiners and even among different presentations from the same examiner. The authors argue that this mode of presentation allows the use of visual cues as well as auditory cues and also makes the testing situation more natural. Nevertheless, live-voice presentation and the variability it introduces may impair the reliability and validity of the test.

The manual claims that the LACT is valuable in identifying children who will later have difficulty in spelling and reading. No data are presented in support of this claim. It is also noted that the test should be "a valuable diagnostic instrument in the area of speech pathology," although no further mention of the specific relation of LACT results to oral speech and language occurs in the manual.

Although the administration procedure is complex, the directions and examples given in the manual are clear and concise. The scoring form, likewise, is well organized and easy to use.

The test items are composed of 17 English consonants and five English vowels. The authors identify the sounds used as a representative sample of the English phonemes and state that they were selected after "years of experimentation and research," but do not report any data or rationale for the specific sound combinations used. They do acknowledge that less visible and less different sounds may be more difficult in the isolated sounds subtest, at least for younger subjects. It is hard to determine whether they are referring to acoustic properties of the sounds or some other intuitive basis of difference either in the above statement or when they later write of "wide and narrow contrasts." They indicate that performance on the coarticulated syllable task is unaffected by

the specific sounds used, but again, present no data.

The students on whom the LACT was standardized were selected randomly after a larger sample was stratified on the basis of sex and upper and lower academic performance. The entire sample, however, was selected from a very limited geographical area. The authors state that all testing was done by trained school personnel, but do not specify the degree of training. This would be of particular importance in a test which utilizes live-voice presentation as noted above.

The normative data consist of frequency distributions (using percentages rather than frequencies) of the scores of 60 students at each of the grade levels K–6 and of the scores of 240 students in grades 7–12 combined. No further statistics (such as percentile ranks, means, and standard deviations) are reported. The means, calculated by the reviewer, follow for the eight groups: K, 29.2; 1, 41.0; 2, 56.5; 3, 57.8; 4, 64.8; 5, 68.2; 6, 69.7; 7–12, 67.7. The mean for grades 7–12 is actually lower than the means for grades 5 and 6. These statistics suggest a need for larger samples.

The authors report an alternate forms reliability of .96 based on a sample of 52 students, 4 students from each grade K–12. This reliability is practically meaningless because of the extremely heterogenous sample—kindergartners to high school seniors. Within-grade reliabilities should have been reported.

Minimum scores are reported for each grade level which, if not exceeded, should result in educational intervention according to the authors. The manner in which these scores were determined is not described. The educational strategies offered in the manual strongly advocate the teaching of the skills tested by the LACT as a preventative measure for children who initially score poorly on the test. Numerous procedures are described, but additional research regarding the value of these procedures in preventing future reading and spelling difficulties is necessary.

In summary, the LACT provides some unique information regarding one aspect of auditory perception in children. The ability to discriminate among speech sounds as well as the ability to segment the acoustic signal into phoneme classes is assessed. The relation of

LACT results to oral speech and language is, at present, unclear. There is a need for additional research in this area as well as additional normative information, before the LACT can be recommended to speech clinicians or remedial teachers.

[943]

*National Teacher Examinations: Audiology.
College seniors and teachers; 1970–77; test administered 3 times annually (February, July, November) at centers established by the publisher; Forms YNT ('76, 24 pages), ZNT ('77, 22 pages); descriptive booklet ('70, 6 pages); for program accessories, see 381; examination fee, $13 per candidate; 120(165) minutes; Educational Testing Service. *

For reviews of the testing program, see 381 (2 reviews) and 7:582 (2 reviews).

[944]

Oliphant Auditory Discrimination Memory Test.
Grades 1–8; 1971; OADMT; no data on reliability and validity; no description of population used to derive "average error scores" and the "significant weakness" cutoff scores; 1 form; directions (2 pages including test); separate answer sheets must be used; $1.50 per set of 12 answer sheets and 2 directions; 75¢ per specimen set of this and test 945; cash orders postpaid; [10–15] minutes; Genevieve G. Oliphant; Educators Publishing Service, Inc. *

See T2:2049 (1 reference).

LEAR ASHMORE, *Professor of Speech Communication and Education, The University of Texas at Austin, Austin, Texas.*

This test is designed as an auditory discrimination screening test for use in grades 2–6. The response required of the children is somewhat involved. Two words are presented which are either alike or minimally different and then a third word is said, and the child must decide whether the third word is the same as word 1 or word 2 or that all three words are the same. On the response sheet the child circles for each set of words either 1 (which means that the third word was like the first) or 2 (which means the third word was like the second) or S (which means all three words were alike). On the test, words are all single-syllable words in a consonant-vowel-consonant (CVC) format and the variations may be in initial or final consonant position or internal vowel position. There are 20 response sets.

The mode of response on this test seems rather involved and it is possible that the child could recognize the differences or similarities in the words but be confused in what symbol to circle on the response sheet. The response mode has been a problem since the beginning of

auditory discrimination testing; most available tests require a relatively sophisticated listener to accomplish the task accurately. Unfortunately, most of the children with whom one wishes to explore discrimination ability (those who are having problems in speech, reading, language skills) may be the very ones who have difficulty understanding the instructions and how they are to respond rather than difficulty recognizing similarities and differences between stimuli. The Oliphant test does nothing to simplify or compensate for these difficulties; in fact, the response mode is more complicated than on some of the established tests of auditory discrimination. Additionally, the author relates the response form to the memory function, in that the child has to retain the first stimulus and second stimulus and then compare them to the third stimulus. All auditory discrimination tests require short-term memory function because the child has to retain the stimulus item or stimuli long enough to make some decision and then respond in terms of that decision. Therefore, the response form on the Oliphant test brings nothing unique to the memory task which is inherent in auditory discrimination testing and is no more a test of memory than the traditional "same or different" minimal pair form.

The author does present average error scores and scores indicating significant weaknesses for the grade levels tested. There is no evidence as to where these scores came from or the number of children tested to derive these scores. The author indicates a strong correlation between scores on this test and scores of other tests of language related skills, but presents no definitive data which would allow a user of the test to compare results with those from another test population.

There is little about the Oliphant test to evaluate critically and this in itself is a negative evaluation. There is no indication of the system for selecting the words used, and prior research indicates that item selection is a very important variable in discrimination testing. There is no explanation of the choice of the particular phoneme contrasts used in the test. Again, for most users of discrimination tests, phonemic content is an important consideration. Was selection based on some confusion matrix, most frequently appearing sounds, or sounds which are close in articulatory or acoustic properties?

The greatest lack in the test is in rationale for the particular test format. There is no indication of reasons for organizing the tasks in the way presented. What advantages does this form have over more traditional "same-different," "right-wrong" designs? What does it discover about a child's discrimination abilities that other tests do not explore?

The art of auditory discrimination testing reached a plateau many years ago and the science of auditory discrimination has yet to appear. This test contributes little or nothing toward meeting the need for more scientifically based information concerning the nature of auditory discrimination and its relationship to the learning of language-related abilities.

[945]

Oliphant Auditory Synthesizing Test. Grades 1–8; 1971; OAST; no data on reliability; norms consist of a mean and standard deviation; individual; no reading by examinees; 1 form (2 pages); directions sheet (2 pages); $1.50 per 12 tests; 75¢ per specimen set of this and test 944; cash orders postpaid; [10–15] minutes; Genevieve Oliphant; Educators Publishing Service, Inc. *

See T2:2050 (1 reference).

Lon L. Emerick, *Professor of Speech Pathology, Northern Michigan University, Marquette, Michigan.*

This test is designed to "assess the ability of a child to listen to a word spoken in separate phonemes, to hold these phonemes in his memory in the correct sequence, and to blend these phonemes mentally and assign them a linguistic meaning." The author points out that "these abilities are critical to successful performance in the areas of speech, reading, or spelling." Additionally, the test is useful, according to the author, in differential diagnosis of perceptual functioning and in assessing children with developmental learning disabilities.

We have for many years employed an informal evaluation of auditory synthesis—Van Riper termed it "vocal phonics"—in examining children presenting disorders of articulation. Our clinical impressions suggest that the ability to receive and hold phonemes in memory, blend them into a sequence, and assign semantic value to the sequence is, indeed, related to speech acquisition as well as to other areas of linguistic functioning. So, it was with some enthusiasm

that we greeted the present diagnostic instrument by Oliphant.

The OAST consists of a practice unit (three words) and three testing units. The test units are each comprised of 10 stimulus words: Unit 1 employs words having two phonemes (for example, "her," "go"); Unit 2, words of three phonemes ("sun," "mad"); and the final unit, words of four phonemes ("sleep," "cold"). The entire test is administered individually. The worker utters the words carefully, one sound at a time, and the child is asked to respond by saying the word. If the child's first response is not correct, the words are repeated and the respondent is then asked to indicate which of three choices (for example, if the stimulus word is "out," the child is asked to choose from "town," "out," and "our") is correct.

The author suggests that any first grade child achieving a score of 47 (about 1 SD above the mean) or better possesses excellent auditory synthesizing ability and that a child scoring below 20 shows serious deficiencies. It is suggested that the clinician can interpolate scores for older children, but the instructions are vague and it is doubtful if the test in its present form is useful beyond the first grade.

The OAST represents an initial attempt at formulation of a measure of vocal phonics but has serious limitations. Since auditory synthesis is an age-related ability, the usefulness of the test would be enhanced with longitudinal norms—the interpolation suggested in the manual seems totally inadequate. The author gives no information as to how the stimulus words were selected—on the basis of frequency of occurrence, phonemic balance? I would recommend an ordinal scale for evaluating responses.

In summary, the OAST is a provocative initial attempt at formulating an instrument to assess auditory synthesis ability. In the hands of a skillful and informed worker, it would be of value, even in its present heuristic form, in evaluating speech and language impaired youngsters. Although it cannot be recommended unequivocally—because of the limitations delineated herein—speech clinicians, special education teachers, and teachers of the learning disabled will find some clinical utility in the OAST. To the best of my knowledge, there is

Oliphant Auditory Discrimination Memory Test

at the present time no other instrument that assesses auditory synthesis abilities in children.

[946]

★**STARS Test (Short Term Auditory Retrieval and Storage), Experimental Edition.** Grades 1–6; 1972; STARS; recognition of pairs and triads of words presented simultaneously; no data on reliability for grades 3–6; no data on validity; test administered by tape recording (5 inch reel) or tape cassette; 1 form (13 pages); manual (14 pages); $39.50 per set of 12 tests, tape recording, cassette, and manual; $7.50 per 12 tests; postage extra; (20–30) minutes; Arthur Flowers; Perceptual Learning Systems. *

[947]

*****Stycar Hearing Tests.** Ages 6 months to 7 years (normal and mentally retarded); 1958–76; SHT; no data on reliability; no norms; individual; 1 form; revised manual ('76, 60 pages); record blank ('59, 2 pages); £11.25 per set of testing materials, 25 record blanks, and manual; £1.05 per 25 record blanks; £1.55 per manual; postpaid within U.K.; administration time not reported; Mary D. Sheridan; NFER Publishing Co. Ltd. [England]. *

RONALD GOLDMAN, *Professor of Biocommunication, Center for Developmental and Learning Disorders, The University of Alabama in Birmingham, Birmingham, Alabama.*

The *Stycar Hearing Tests* were designed, according to the author, as a response to the urgent need for a series of procedures that could be routinely administered by physicians and educational psychologists specifically interested in assessing the hearing of young handicapped children. This screening technique was designed primarily as a means of obtaining "reliable information concerning the child's capacity to hear with comprehension in everyday situations."

The test items were developed to provide an opportunity for observing young children's responses to speech and nonspeech auditory stimulation. The auditory stimuli include environmental noisemakers (rattle, bell, etc.), nonsense syllables, and meaningful words and sentences. The young children taking this test are expected to respond by localizing sound, manipulating simple objects, pointing to objects or pictures, and repeating words and sentences. The specific speech and nonspeech stimuli were selected, according to the author, to provide a sampling of various acoustic sound frequencies that occur in the speech range.

For children 6 to 14 months, the response requirements are relatively simple in that the subject needs only to localize a set of speech and environmental sounds produced by the examiner. This method lacks sophistication in controlling either the frequency or intensity characteristics of the sounds generated. In reviewing the noisemakers provided in the Stycar test, it was observed that the Nuffield rattle produced both intermittent and uncontrollable sounds. It seemed as though the particles within the rattle bulb would adhere to the inner surface, thereby creating no sound or sound with minimal intensity. If greater precision is sought, it would be best obtained by utilizing a speech audiometer.

For older subjects taking this test, the demands are more complex. The children are required to either manipulate objects, point to pictures, or repeat words and sentences when presented with auditory commands. Although the author attempts to control for such variables as vocabulary and picture-word association ability, the technique for accomplishing this goal is not presented as a formal procedure. For this age group, it would be difficult to determine whether an incorrect response is a function of decreased hearing sensitivity or an inability to recognize the vocabulary incorporated in the test procedure. For example, in the six-toy test, there is an item designated "brick," which evidently describes the North American term "block." If the youngster does not have this word in his lexicon, he is likely to respond inappropriately because he lacks the lexical entry rather than the ability to perceive the auditory signal. Since this test was developed in England, the North American examiner must be cognizant of potential language differences, such as the above example, that may occur within the procedure.

At the higher-age test levels, the procedure requires the subjects to repeat a series of word lists and sentences. As indicated in the manual, the procedure offers the examiner some useful information regarding auditory responses as well as articulatory proficiency. Unfortunately, there is no method of ferreting out the confounding effects that auditory memory and language proficiency may have on the test results. The sentence repetition procedures labeled by some language clinicians as "elicited imitation" are frequently considered as a method for assessing linguistic competence.

Although the tests provide screening techniques to ascertain some aspects of hearing competence in children 6 months to 11 years of age, the test title may be confusing since other listening skills in addition to signal detection are evaluated. The procedures also assess such related skill areas as auditory discrimination, auditory memory, and articulatory proficiency, as well as language competence. It is difficult, however, for this reviewer to determine how to separate the specific skills being assessed at any given level.

The Stycar tests were designed to be administered individually. The administration could be relatively uncomplicated and should not require a great deal of time. However, general instructions for administration are frequently unclear and at points rather ambiguous. The author's style of interspersing theory and clinical notations with specific instructions on test administration is somewhat distracting. Her recommendation that the test be given to a large number of children prior to carrying out a valid test administration might be eliminated if a highly-structured test administration format were employed. A more structured style would be particularly advantageous for professionals with minimal experience.

The test manual fails to provide adequate information regarding interpretation of test results. For example, if a child responds appropriately at her/his age level, this may not necessarily mean that a hearing loss is absent. It is possible that the youngster with a mild hearing loss or with certain audiometric configurations might pass this screening procedure. On the other hand, it would be extremely difficult to interpret poor performance on this test since failure could be the result of cognitive and/or language delay, articulatory inaccuracies, examiner variability in sound production, and/or a hearing problem. The less sophisticated examiner may not elicit sufficient information from this test to make appropriate recommendations for the types of diagnostic procedures that should follow.

The response form is somewhat helpful for summarizing results. Unfortunately, the form does not always coincide with the test procedures described within the manual. For example, the reviewer was unable to locate a section on the form to describe the assessment of repetition of sentences. It is difficult to determine the correctness or incorrectness of a re-peated word or sentence if the examiner does not have a detailed description of a child's articulatory pattern.

The manual does not provide statistical information regarding reliability and validity. The author states, "The screening procedures here described are intended to provide information regarding the presence of everyday auditory competence. They are basically clinical procedures, evoking highly individualistic response and therefore not susceptible to sophisticated statistical evaluation." This reviewer must disagree with this statement since lack of such important information leaves many unanswered questions regarding both the reliability and validity of this screening assessment technique.

SUMMARY. In general, the *Stycar Hearing Tests* may more appropriately be labeled as an inventory for obtaining gross estimates of auditory performance. The general information obtained through the use of this procedure can usually be secured by an astute clinician during the course of a routine examination. For the less experienced examiner, the somewhat structured procedures, along with the necessary materials, could have some value for screening auditory responses to nonspeech and speech stimulation. The usefulness of this procedure could be enhanced if more details for interpretation of test results were provided and if test norms were available. Currently there is a lack in the availability of instruments to assess the hearing skills of young handicapped children which these tests attempt to screen. There is a decided need for structured instruments with demonstrated reliability and validity to meet this objective. It is unfortunate that the *Stycar Hearing Tests* do not meet this need.

[948]
★Test of Auditory Discrimination. Grades kgn-6; 1975; TAD; manual title is *The Testing-Teaching Module of Auditory Discrimination;* 6 scores: initial consonants, initial consonant blends and digraphs, final consonants, final consonant blends and digraphs, vowels, auditory blending; no data on reliability and validity; no norms; individual; 1 form (8 pages); manual (137 pages); item analysis sheet (2 pages); $3.50 per 25 tests; $4 per manual; postage extra; specimen set not available; [20–30] minutes; Victoria Risko; Academic Therapy Publications. *

LEAR ASHMORE, *Professor of Speech Communication and Education, The University of Texas at Austin, Austin, Texas.*

This test was developed for use by the classroom or reading teacher to assist in evaluating specific auditory discrimination skills. There is also an accompanying teaching program. According to the author, this test goes beyond the usual auditory discrimination task of recognizing similarities and differences between minimal pairs of words and evaluates the child's ability to recognize whether parts within words are similar, which is a more discriminating task and one that more closely relates to the skills required for reading.

Some attention was paid to phonetic categories in the construction of the test items and manner of articulation (plosives, nasals, etc.); consonant blends, long and short vowels, and diphthongs were included. The one-syllable words were selected from an auditory discrimination manual written by Charles L. Shedd (apparently well-known to reading teachers). The words were equated in length and then paired by a number of criteria such as phonetic category of initial and final sounds. Blends and digraphs and medial vowel sounds were matched for length and medial diphthongs were matched.

The subtests involving auditory discrimination require the child to indicate whether two words begin (or end) with the same sound. The vowels are tested in the same ways. In the auditory blending subtest, the child is required to synthesize a set of sounds into the correct word. The number of responses in each subtest varies from five to ten. There is also an optional subset in each subtest.

TAD was administered individually to 81 children enrolled in the first three grades (no information as to school, etc.) during the first semester of the school year. Reading performance was measured at the completion of the school year, using the *Metropolitan Achievement Tests*. Data analysis revealed that the TAD was highly related to reading achievement in each grade and that in each grade a set of variables was predictive of reading achievement. An example of this predictive statement is that for first grade children, when three words were presented in serial order, the combination of discrimination of single final consonant sounds and auditory blending predicted reading achievement accounting for 61 percent of the variance at the .01 level. Similar types of data are presented for the other two grade levels

tested. Data analysis is not helpful in measuring the meaningfulness of the children's performances.

Data are not presented which allow one to compare scores of one child with scores of another child. The test is designed to explore strengths and weaknesses in auditory discrimination abilities in a child, not between children. Supposedly, then, from a child's performance on the TAD, the teacher would have information about a starting place in the teaching module which accompanies the test. Theoretically, the availability of a teaching program in association with a test rates a favorable reaction from the test users. The word "theoretically" is used advisedly because the evidence of improvement in the language related abilities with improvement in auditory discrimination abilities is equivocal.

It is interesting that new auditory discrimination tests continue to appear year after year, and few of them present anything unique or more definitive to the art of discrimination testing. From the early design of determining whether or not the child could distinguish two speech stimuli differing by one sound (pa-ma or pan-man), there have developed a number of variations in the way the stimuli are presented (live voice vs. recorded) and the types of response required (pointing to pictures, same-different, right-wrong). But the essential approach to auditory discrimination testing has not changed; and all the published tests and informal tests, designed and used by professionals in communication disorders and learning disabilities, reflect this similarity. The *Test of Auditory Discrimination* brings nothing new to the process.

EUGENE C. SHEELEY, *Professor of Communicative Disorders and Director, Audiological Services, The University of Alabama, University, Alabama.*

The purpose of the test is to identify certain discrimination problems in order to provide auditory training and remediation with a view to improving reading ability. The test includes 125 items plus 55 optional items and is for use by the classroom or reading teacher. In the first five subtests the tasks are (a) to tell whether the beginning, middle, or final sound of a pair of words is the same, (b) to pick the two out

Test of Auditory Discrimination

of three words which have the same sound in the key position, and (c) for the optional items to say the sound (not the letter) which appears in a word in the key position. In constructing the first five subtests, the author has adopted some of the same criteria as those used for Wepman's *Auditory Discrimination Test:* monosyllabic words are used, contrasting words are matched for length, and contrasting consonants use the same manner of production, that is, nasal, stop-plosive and so on. In contrast to the use of minimal pairs in the ADT, these pairs almost always differ by more than one phoneme. For example, some pairs of words in the initial consonant subtest are *sad-zip, gab-ked,* and *lap-lug.* The last subtest is an auditory blending task similar to the sound blending subtest of the ITPA. One- to five-syllable words are divided in two to five parts, for example, *b-ase-b-all, as-so-ci-a-tion.*

Clear instructions to the child are provided. Directions for the administrator are generally satisfactory, except that there is no indication of how the sound blending items are to be spoken. The optional items are not discussed in terms of why they are included and when they are to be used. No performance criteria are given for the optional items or for the vowel subtest. For all other groups of test items, a score below 80 percent is said to indicate the need for remediation, specifically work on the sounds missed using the activities included in the manual. The use of a single criterion for failure regardless of grade level or age is inadequate since the norms for the ADT and the ITPA suggest that these skills continue to develop until eight years of age or later. The test manual should alert the user to the necessity of ruling out peripheral loss of hearing sensitivity as a possible reason for failure. The user should also be cautioned not to allow the child to watch the speaker's lips.

Eighty-one students in the first three grades (but not otherwise identified) were given the *Test of Auditory Discrimination* and the reading subtest of the *Metropolitan Achievement Test.* Although the auditory skills measured by the test correlate with and predict some reading skills for a certain population, the author goes beyond the data in saying the statistics show the skills are critical to reading achievement.

Some minor criticisms of the test might be

Test of Auditory Discrimination

made. In one subtest *ck* is considered a single consonant; in another subtest it is treated as a digraph. Although *ked* and *posh* are words, their relative unfamiliarity would make them equivalent to nonsense syllables for most children. The word *bade* is included with those containing long medial vowels although the preferred pronounciation is with a short *a.* The *ew* and *ow* in *brew* and *crow* are called "middle sounds." The individual item analysis sheets, which are not well designed, do not contain the same items as the test; specifically, *ew, ar, oa* and others are missing from the sheets, while *ai, ei, ie* and others are on the sheets but not found in the test.

The author has two excellent ideas: extending the test beyond the use of minimal pairs and same-different choices, and supplying a remediation program based on the errors in each subtest. In the absence of norms, validity data, and reliability data, however, the test is not recommended. Wepman's ADT is superior for same-different judgments because of its norms and data on validity and reliability. The sound blending subtest of the ITPA is superior because of its precise instructions for administration (including a phonograph recording); its suitability for children from 2 to 10 years because of its use of picture choices at the lower end and nonsense words at the upper end; and its norms, and validity and reliability data.

[949]

*Test of Listening Accuracy in Children.** Grades kgn–2, 2–6; 1962–74; TLAC; formerly called *Picture Speech Discrimination Test;* no data on validity; 1 form; 2 editions; postage extra; Merlin J. Mecham, J. Lorin Jex, and J. Dean Jones; Communication Research Associates, Inc. *

a) INDIVIDUAL TEST VERSION. Grades kgn–2; test administered by tape cassette; 1 form ('69, 92 picture cards, identical with pictures copyrighted 1962; 1973 printing includes slight format changes); manual ('73, 9 pages); record sheet ('73, 3 pages); $20 per set of testing materials including 25 record sheets; $1.50 per 25 record sheets; (20) minutes.

b) GROUP TEST VERSION. Grades 2–6; test administered by 3¾ ips tape recording and filmstrip; 1 form ('74); manual ('74, 9 pages); response sheet ('74, 1 page); $20 per set of testing materials including 35 response sheets ($15 if ordered in combination with a); $1.50 per 35 response sheets; (40–50) minutes.

See T2:2056 (2 references); for reviews by Ann Brickner and Richard E. Shine, see 7:946.

[950]

*Test of Nonverbal Auditory Discrimination.** Grades kgn–3; 1968–75; TENVAD; 6 scores: pitch, loudness, rhythm, duration, timbre, total; no data on reliability of part scores; no data presented in support of "expected ranges" for adequate and delayed auditory discrimination; no "expected ranges" presented for kindergarten; no data on reliability or validity of "expected range" categorizations; 1 form ('75) in 2 formats: 33⅓ rpm 12 inch record, tape cassette (not recommended for classroom use); manual ('75, 23 pages); response booklet ('75, 4 pages); $8.25 per set of testing materials including record, set of scoring stencils, and manual; $3.90 per 30 response booklets; $2.40 per set of manual, response booklet, and record excerpts; postage extra; (20) minutes; Norman A. Buktenica; Follett Publishing Co. *

See T2:2057 (9 references).

REFERENCES

1–9. See T2:2057.
10. LARKIN, MAUREEN A. *A Comparison of the Differences on Conventional Audiological Measures and Selected Auditory Instruments Between Reading Achievers and Underachievers.* Doctor's thesis, University of Kansas (Lawrence, Kan.), 1974. (*DAI* 35:5970A)
11. DiBACCO, JOHN PHILIP. *The Efficacy of Group and Individually Administered Perceptual Tests in Predicting Multi-Criteria First Grade Achievement.* Doctor's thesis, George Peabody College for Teachers (Nashville, Tenn.), 1975. (*DAI* 36:1901B)

NICHOLAS W. BANKSON, *Associate Professor of Speech Pathology and Audiology, Boston University, Boston, Massachusetts.*

The TENVAD was designed as a measure of nonverbal auditory discrimination for children from first through third grade. Test stimuli consist of high quality recordings of 50 pairs of pure tone stimuli which are presented via a phonograph to group or individual subjects. Testees are required to mark on a score sheet whether the pairs of pure tones that are presented are the same or different or, in some instances, the same or not the same. The 50 pairs are organized into five 10-pair units for each of the following subtests: pitch, loudness, rhythm, duration, and timbre.

In order for children to complete this test, they must have the concept of same-different and be able to associate "same" with putting a mark on a circle and "different" with putting a mark on a square. Two vertical columns, each comprised of rows containing a circle followed by a square, constitute the format of the scoring sheet. It is essential that the testee be able to follow moderately complex directions in order to take the test. It is also necessary that the child be able to provide sustained attention to an auditory stimulus.

Only the crudest type of norms are presented —mean scores of 33, 36, and 39 for the age levels 6, 7, and 8, respectively. The standardization sample consisted of 1,258 children made up of lower- and middle-class white children and lower-class black children in three Chicago schools. Since no measures of variability are provided, it is impossible to estimate the overlap in scores between age groups. The three-point increment from year to year seems small for a test with a possible score of 50. Children who score at or less than 28, 30, and 33 for age levels 6, 7, and 8, respectively, are described as having a "delayed range [of development in auditory discrimination] and probably need remediation." No data are presented in support of these arbitrary cutoff scores—it is impossible to interpret them intelligently. Even the teacher is warned to "seek corroborative evidence to support" test scores in the adequate or delayed range. The author should have presented more adequate norms and validity data.

The discrimination skills measured in TENVAD are reported to be precursors of the kinds of discrimination required for language functioning; however, there are few data presented to support this critical assumption. The subtests include rather difficult listening tasks, especially for children, as evidenced by an average score of 33 (out of 50) for the first-grade normative group. It is difficult to comprehend how such listening skills can be regarded as preceding linguistic development. The author reports that the test was "to some extent patterned after the *Seashore Test of Musical Talent,* in that pure tones are used throughout." Since the Seashore test was designed as a measure of musical aptitude, the possibility exists that this instrument may relate more closely to behaviors other than those considered linguistic in nature.

K-R 20 reliabilities of .75, .78, and .77 are reported for age groups 6, 7, and 8, respectively. The author implies that these reliabilities are adequate since "all these values are highly significant statistically." This is, of course, nonsense. "Significant statistically" has a very limited meaning—that the hypothesis that the true reliability in the population sampled is zero has been rejected at a specified level of significance. Even a reliability of .10 will be statistically significant if a large enough group is tested. The reliability of the total scores on TENVAD may be adequate for the measurement of groups but not for the measurement of individuals. No information is reported on the reliability of the five subtest scores.

The similarity between TENVAD and the Seashore test is cited as a source of face validity. Concurrent validity is claimed because of the test's correlation with Wepman's *Auditory Discrimination Test* (.40) and total scores on the *Primary Mental Abilities Test* (.45). The use of the ADT as a criterion of validity is questionable because of the uncertain validity of the Wepman test itself. In addition, the possibility exists that the correlation with the PMAT is reflective of underlying cognitive abilities required for each test. Other than the correlations, no information is presented regarding the group or groups tested—e.g., number of subjects, range of ages, means, and standard deviations.

The consumer should be careful in interpreting results he obtains with this test. The manual makes no claim to specific clinical applications that can be derived from the test results and, indeed, the clinical utility of the test data is a critical question for the user.

In summary, this test cannot be recommended because of its inadequate norms, low reliability, and lack of data in support of its claim to "identify" the child whose "auditory perceptual abilities are not sufficiently developed to allow him to communicate and learn adequately" so that he/she may be helped.

[951]

Verbal Auditory Screening for Children. Ages 3–6; 1964–71; VASC; for the detection of preschool children requiring "more specialized diagnostic testing"; no data on reliability and validity; no norms; tape cartridges with stepped attenuation of spondee words used with the *Zenith Speech Screening Audiometer*, Model ZA-111; 4 children may be tested simultaneously; manual ['71, 16 pages]; record form (no date, 1 page); $535 per audiometer, picture board, 25 record forms, and tape cartridge; postage extra; (3) minutes; Zenetron, Inc. *

See T2:2059 (1 reference) and 7:947 (6 references).

REFERENCES

1–6. See 7:947.
7. See T2:2059.
8. RITCHIE, BETTY CARAWAY, AND MERKLEIN, RICHARD A. "An Evaluation of the Efficiency of the Verbal Auditory Screening for Children (VASC)." *J Speech & Hearing Res* 15(2): 280–6 Je '72. *
9. NEAL, W. R., JR. "Verbal Auditory Screening With the Educable Mentally Retarded." *Training Sch B* 71(1):62–6 My '74. * (PA 53:1490)
10. BERNERO, RAYMOND J. "Review of Verbal Auditory Screening for Children," pp. 366–9. In *Pediatric Screening Tests.* Edited by William K. Frankenburg and Bonnie W. Camp. Springfield, Ill.: Charles C Thomas, Publisher, 1975. Pp. xii, 549. *
11. MENCHER, GEORGE T. "Review of Verbal Auditory Screening for Children," pp. 369–70. In *Pediatric Screening Tests.* Edited by William K. Frankenburg and Bonnie W. Camp. Springfield, Ill.: Charles C Thomas, Publisher, 1975. Pp. xii, 549. *

CHARLES V. ANDERSON, *Associate Professor of Speech Pathology and Audiology, The University of Iowa, Iowa City, Iowa.*

This hearing screening test, developed to identify hearing loss among young children, is designed to be administered by trained volunteers who then report screening results to professional staff for referral and identification purposes.

It was the intention of the developers of VASC to provide a reliable method for screening the hearing of preschool children. Among the several studies which have measured reliability, there appears to be agreement that the VASC is indeed reliable on a test-retest basis and equal in reliability to other hearing screening procedures such as individual pure-tone screening tests.

The question of validity remains controversial. Although otologic examination has been used as a criterion measure, the value has been limited since no study has been able to apply this criterion measure to all subjects. Often the otologic examination has been completed only on those subjects who failed the screening test; this prevents an evaluation of those falsely identified as having normal hearing. The more common criterion measure has been pure-tone screening. Agreement between these criterion measure results and those of VASC have varied greatly from study to study. The lack of uniform purposes, instrumentation, procedures, and criteria for identification of children with hearing losses have contributed to the variability reported in the literature. Certainly if one were to use only the words in the VASC signals, the ability to identify mild hearing losses and those hearing losses at frequencies of 1000 HZ and above are highly questionable.

The advantages of the VASC hearing screening procedure for preschool children are that standard equipment is available at a reasonable cost, volunteers can be trained in a short period of time to administer the test, most preschool children can learn the task, and test-retest reliability appears to be at least as positive as for any other procedure currently available. The major disadvantage of the VASC is the question of validity. A review of the literature leads one to the conclusion that for either health or educational purposes the VASC is no better at identifying the children with hearing loss than any other procedure and in many instances may be poorer than other procedures.

In summary, it appears that the VASC is a convenient test, easily administered by trained

Test of Nonverbal Auditory Discrimination

volunteers which relieves the time of professionals, portable, uses a task easily mastered by preschool children, and of good reliability as a hearing screening test. It is of no better validity than other procedures and for the same purposes may be poorer. The VASC is probably neither better nor worse than most hearing screening procedures available for use with preschool children for many purposes. It is best used in combination with other procedures such as pure-tone tests and acoustic impedance measures. The selection of procedures and criteria for identification remain dependent upon the purposes of the hearing screening. As with any hearing screening procedure, the VASC should be used as a part of an overall identification program and administered only under the direction of professional staff who understand the implications of the advantages and shortcomings of the procedure. Obviously, the equipment needs to be monitored regularly for calibration and taken out of use when not functioning properly.

[952]

Washington Speech Sound Discrimination Test.
Ages 3-5; 1971, c1969-71; WSSDT; no data on reliability of scores; norms consist of means and standard deviations; individual; 1 form (no date, 1 page and 5 cards); manual ('71, 16 pages); 2 demonstration cards (no date); $10.50 per set of testing materials including 64 forms; $2 per 64 forms; cash orders postpaid; (15) minutes; Elizabeth Prather, Adah Miner, Margaret Anne Addicott, and Linda Sunderland; Interstate Printers & Publishers, Inc. *

REFERENCES

1. ADDICOTT, JOHN PHILLIPS. *The Relationship Between Speech Sound Discrimination Skills and Language Abilities of Young Preschool Children.* Doctor's thesis, University of Washington (Seattle, Wash.), 1973. (*DAI* 34:1789B)

RAPHAEL M. HALLER, *Associate Professor of Speech Pathology and Audiology, Illinois State University, Normal, Illinois.*

Reading specialists, psychologists, and speech-language pathologists have long speculated that children's delays in articulatory and reading acquisition could be due to faulty speech sound discrimination, or the inability to differentiate auditorally between phonemes. The substantial experimental literature has yielded equivocal results. Many normal readers and normal speakers perform poorly on phoneme discrimination tasks, and the converse. Some children with articulatory defects are unable to discriminate only their own error sounds, lending support to the theory that one's production

of a phoneme enhances its perception even when it is uttered by someone else. This observation is familiar to adult speakers of English as a second language.

Despite these considerations, there exists a population of young children whose auditory perceptual deficits include those of phoneme discrimination. While what the most effective remediation or training strategies are is open to question, the need for basal data certainly exists. In this reviewer's opinion, the WSSDT is the best instrument thus far developed commercially for measuring this type of performance in preschool children. Unlike previous tests, the WSSDT focuses on only one word at a time and one that is familiar to the child. A picture illustrating that word is placed before the child, and he is instructed to point to it only when the examiner utters the word "correctly." Most of the foils are nonsense words although some are real words. Previous tests have employed two or more words or pictures, confounding this task with such presumed skills as auditory and visual memory and sequencing. A pretest training session is used, followed by 53 utterances relating to five pictures, presented one at a time.

The manual is seriously inadequate in reporting information on the statistical aspects which must be considered in constructing and evaluating a standardized test. No information is presented on its intertest reliability. The age norms are of little value because of the small numbers tested at each half-year level—20 children for age 3.5; 23 for age 4.0; and 21 for age 4.5. Kindergarten norms are based on 75 children. In addition, there is considerable overlap of scores amongst the youngest three age groups, further limiting the usefulness of the norms. No information is given about these norm groups or the time and place of testing. According to the manual, "the authors recognize that the standardization samples are small and that further testing is needed for stable normative scoring."

Most of the foils represent typical misarticulations of the target words, e.g., *thun* for *sun*. Thus, this test could compare the child's perception and production of the same phonemes. However, some of the foils represent dialectal pronunciations and, on that basis, could be logically identified as correct. For example, the

Eastern or Southern dialectal pronunciation of *cracker* is a foil in item 46, while frequent black dialectal pronunciations of *toothbrush* are foils in items 51 and 53.

As a result of these serious limitations, I recommend the use of this test only as a means of obtaining basal data, e.g., at the outset of remediation programs for children with presumed or documented auditory perceptual deficits. The examiner should have had coursework in phonetics and in geographic and social dialects, so that he can judge whether or not to include non-dialectal-free items for specific pupils.

LEIJA V. MCREYNOLDS, *Professor of Hearing and Speech, The University of Kansas Medical Center, Kansas City, Kansas.*

A constant and long-standing concern among clinicians has been the role that discrimination ability plays in the etiology and treatment of production problems in children. As noted by the authors of the WSSDT, speech sound discrimination tests developed to date frequently have weaknesses which prevent confident statements about discrimination performance. The present test is an effort to overcome some of these problems. In some respects the developers have accomplished this purpose; but unfortunately, their test also has weaknesses which appear to outweigh the assets.

Some of the problems are similar to problems in other speech sound discrimination tests; for example, the test is presented live voice so that production of any specific sound may vary considerably. The problem may be compounded in the WSSDT by the fact that the examiner produces errors which the child is expected to evaluate.

The test uses five pictures, that is, five words to test discrimination. The child's task is to point to a picture only when the examiner produces the word correctly as the picture is named repeatedly. For example, the word "fish" is produced 21 times, seven times accurately and 14 times inaccurately. The child is instructed to point to the picture of the fish only when he judges the examiner's production of the word to be correct. Inaccurate productions of "fish" range from omission of /f/ and /ʃ/ to various substitutions for these sounds according to place and manner features. The

exact model used for the test is not clear and a rationale for errors is not specified. Sometimes several features are changed in production; in other instances only one feature is changed. Clearly, a pointing response will not provide clues on the parameters which a child uses in judging the examiner's utterances.

Yet, one of the advantages of the test for nonverbal children, or children with limited language ability, is that a pointing response is required. Additionally, the authors have developed a rather elaborate preliminary teaching-testing procedure and a demonstration procedure to help the child understand the task prior to administration of the formal test. These procedures, however, differ from the actual testing procedure in that the child has an opportunity to use both visual and auditory information in pretraining, but not in testing. Furthermore, the correct and incorrect items alternate in pretraining, so a child could be learning an alternating response rather than responding to the acoustic aspects of the stimuli presented by the examiner.

In administering the test items, the examiner covers his mouth and attempts to control for visual cues, and intensity and inflection changes, which might constitute confounding variables. Live voice presentations are vulnerable to these variables; they can interfere with discrimination of the phonetic information which the test is supposed to be evaluating.

In the WSSDT, as in many similar tests, nonresponse by a child is difficult to interpret. If a child does not respond, the examiner has no way of determining whether the child can actually perform the discrimination.

Perhaps the most serious flaw is a lack of validity and reliability information. Validity is based on children's performance on an original set of 66 items from which 13 were eliminated because three or fewer children missed them. The WSSDT was not examined in relation to other speech sound discrimination tests or any other discrimination measure for validity purposes.

No data on test reliability are reported. Since the test is presented live voice, test-retest reliabilities using different examiners should have been possible. It can be speculated that scores from one administration to another would vary as considerable overlapping of scores was ob-

Washington Speech Sound Discrimination Test

tained, particularly for the 3.5 and 4.0 year old children.

A description of the population on which standardization was established is not included. Presumably the children were normal and represent a random sample, but this is not specified. Nor was the test administered to children with articulation and language problems to explore their performance in comparison to children developing normally. The authors report norms (means and standard deviations) based on extremely small groups: 20 children, age 3.5; 23, age 4.0; 21, age 4.5; and 75 kindergartners for whom ages are not reported. They caution that there is considerable variability among the groups, particularly for the two younger age groups. They suggest that the scores for the older groups can be interpreted more exactly, but lack of important information on test adequacy makes this suggestion a tentative one.

Although the authors' intentions were excellent, the test is not recommended for use at the present time. A great deal of developmental work is required before results from this test can be viewed with confidence.

[953]

Word Intelligibility by Picture Identification.
Hearing impaired children ages 5–13; 1971; WIPI; speech discrimination; norms consist of means and standard deviations; individual; forms 1, 2, 3, 4, (26 pages in manual); manual (19 pages plus test); score sheet (1 page); test may be administered with earphones or through pantomime; $13.25 per manual; 75¢ per 50 score sheets; postage extra; (2–10) minutes; Mark Ross and Jay Lerman; Stanwix House, Inc. *
    See T2:2061 (3 references).

REFERENCES

1–3. See T2:2061.
4. Ross, Mark; Kessler, Maureen E.; Phillips, Marion E.; and Lerman, Jay W. "Visual, Auditory, and Combined Mode Presentations of the WIPI Test to Hearing Impaired Children." *Volta R* 74(2):90–6 F '72. * (*PA* 48:5407)
5. Sanderson, Mary Elizabeth. *The Articulation Functions and Test-Retest Performance of Normal Hearing Children on Three Speech Discrimination Tests.* Doctor's thesis, Michigan State University (East Lansing, Mich.), 1972. (*DAI* 33:2394B)
6. Beasley, Daniel S.; Maki, Jean E.; and Orchik, Daniel J. "Children's Perception of Time-Compressed Speech on Two Measures of Speech Discrimination: PB-K 50 and Word Intelligibility by Picture Identification Tests." *J Speech & Hearing Disorders* 41(2):216–25 My '76. * (*PA* 56:1739)
7. Freeman, Barry Alan. *Performance of Reading Impaired and Normal Reading Children on Temporally Altered Monosyllables and Sentential Stimuli.* Doctor's thesis, Michigan State University (East Lansing, Mich.), 1976. (*DAI* 37:685B)
8. Sanderson-Leepa, Mary E., and Rintelmann, William F. "Articulation Functions and Test-Retest Performance of Normal-Hearing Children on Three Speech Discrimination Tests: WIPI, PBK-50, and N.U. Auditory Test No. 6." *J Speech & Hearing Disorders* 41(4):503–19 N '76. *

Leija V. McReynolds, *Professor of Hearing and Speech, The University of Kansas Medical Center, Kansas City, Kansas.*

This test was developed to fill a need for testing speech sound discrimination ability of difficult-to-test hearing impaired children whose verbal and language problems prohibit verbal and written responses. To overcome the problems, the test requires a pointing response rather than a verbal or written one. As noted by the developers, these children, even if they are able to produce verbal responses, are frequently unintelligible.

Thus, the test consists of 25 plates with six pictures on each plate. The pictures were selected on the basis of familiarity as established in a preliminary study involving 15 hearing impaired children. The examiner names a picture and the child is required to point to the picture named. Four lists of 25 words each form the test content, and the child is instructed in some manner that a pointing response is required. The test administration may be auditory, visual, or auditory and visual, depending on the kind of information sought by the examiner.

In several ways the test is an improvement over other speech discrimination tests for children whose verbal and language repertoires are limited or defective. On the other hand, a pointing response, of course, is limiting in the information it conveys concerning parameters on which judgments are made when several are changed simultaneously, as in some of the items in this test.

The problem of picture unfamiliarity is not entirely solved in this test, even though the preliminary identification test allowed elimination of unknown pictures. This procedure, although helpful, is not assurance that all hearing impaired children will recognize the pictures and names.

The four lists of words were equalized for inclusion of the same number of difficult and easy discriminations. The rationale for selection of the items was based partly on experience, partly on "acoustic phonetic considerations and partly on an a priori basis." These bases were listed, but not described or explained, in the manual. The equality of the lists was verified by presenting the four lists in different orders to hearing impaired children and running correlations. However, the rationale for selecting items for each discrimination task is not clear and is not readily identified by examining the phonetic content of the 25 words in each list.

A final evaluation of the test was conducted by presenting the test to 61 hearing impaired children with sensori-neural losses who ranged in age from 4.7 to 13.9 years. However, lack of detailed information on the children prevents determining the representative nature of the sample population.

Test-retest reliability was measured and results indicate that the four lists are highly reliable. Inter-examiner reliability is not presented. Evidence for validity is presented by providing information on the relationship between the discrimination scores on the WIPI and speech reception thresholds. A more direct measure of validity would have been an examination of the discrimination scores on the WIPI in relation to discrimination scores obtained on other commonly administered speech discrimination tests.

Interpreting the discrimination scores may present a problem, since limited norms and standardization data are available. It is difficult to know if a score of 60 percent, for example, represents a discrimination problem and, if so, how severe a problem. The developers suggest that the WIPI scores are not directly comparable to scores on other discrimination tests and tend to run about 25 percent higher. However, this appears to be a subjective conclusion, since no objective data are offered to support the accuracy of the statement.

The authors suggests that the WIPI would probably be too easy for children with conductive or minimal sensori-neural losses. It is, according to them, "suitable for children with moderate hearing losses from ages five or six and for children with severe hearing losses from ages seven or eight." Unfortunately, no data are presented to support this conclusion beyond the data for the 61 sensori-neural hearing impaired children.

Although the test needs additional development before it can be considered adequate, it offers another clinical tool for obtaining some information on a specific problem population. However, at this point the audiologist can make only subjective evaluations and statements of impressions concerning a child's performance.

ROBERT L. ROSENBAUM, *Assistant Professor of Communication Arts and Sciences and Associate Director, Speech and Hearing Clinic,* *Queens College of The City University of New York, Flushing, New York.*

The WIPI presents the audiologist with a useful format for determining speech discrimination ability of hearing impaired children. The test focuses on children from 5 to 6 years of age with moderate losses and children from 7 to 8 years of age with severe losses. It offers the opportunity for speech recognition without speech or writing as a response requirement; the test response requires the child to point to the appropriate picture.

The test words appear to be relatively simple, monosyllabic words that are represented pictorially. The authors discarded the concept of phonetic balance in the list preparation. While the departure from usual presentation is understandable, it would be desirable to obtain a larger number of children for the normative data to further validate the test. Further, an explanation of the acoustic phonetic consideration of the stimuli would be a useful aid to the audiologist.

The level of presentation depends upon the child and the test. Results are recorded under three conditions: auditory, visual, and combined. The opportunity to judge performance through another sensory channel provides an interesting view towards the child's functioning in the environment.

The stimuli are presented on plates of six pictures each. These pictures are clear and apparent representations of the items. Before the administration of the test the examiner must determine the child's ability to visually differentiate within the format. Children with associated learning disabilities may find the selection task visually difficult.

In summary, the WIPI is a successful and useful adjunct to the audiologist's battery of tests. While not appropriate to all hearing impaired clients, it should serve to aid the audiologist with specific categories of children.

SPEECH

[954]

The Arizona Articulation Proficiency Scale: Revised. Mental ages 2–14 and over; 1963–70; AAPS; norms for ages 3–11 only; individual; 1 form ('70, 50 cards, identical with cards copyrighted in 1963 except for format and 3 new items); sentence test ('70, 3 cards) may be administered to older children and adults; manual ('70, 9 pages plus sample copies of test materials); record booklet ('70, 4 pages); survey test form ('70, 1 page); $22.50 per kit of cards, 25 record booklets, 10 survey test forms, and manual; $12.50 per set of cards; $6.50 per 25 record booklets; $6.50 per 50 survey test forms; $3 per manual; 8% extra for postage and handling; (10–15) minutes; Janet Barker Fudala; Western Psychological Services. *

See T2:2065 (2 references), 7:948 (2 references), and 6:307a (2 references).

REFERENCES

1–2. See 6:307a.
3–4. See 7:948.
5–6. See T2:2065.
7. FUDALA, JANET BARKER; ENGLAND, GENE; AND GANOUNG, LAURA. "Utilization of Parents in a Speech Correction Program." *Excep Children* 38(5):407–12 Ja '72. * (*PA* 50:1475)
8. PROGER, BARTON B. "Review of the Arizona Articulation Proficiency Scale." *J Spec Ed* 6(3):285–9 f '72. *
9. KATAGI, ROLAND KENICHI. *A Follow-Up Study of Children With Previously Demonstrated Deviant Articulation Behavior.* Doctor's thesis, University of Oregon (Eugene, Ore.), 1973. (*DAI* 34:4736B)
10. DRUMWRIGHT, AMELIA F. "Review of Arizona Articulation Proficiency Scale, Revised," pp. 447+. In *Pediatric Screening Tests.* Edited by William K. Frankenburg and Bonnie W. Camp. Springfield, Ill.: Charles C Thomas, Publisher, 1975. Pp. xii, 549. *
11. WHITEHEAD, ROBERT L., AND MULLEN, PATRICIA A. "A Comparison of the Administration Times of Two Tests of Articulation." *Lang Speech & Hearing Services Sch* 6(3):150–3 Jl '75. *
12. BERRY, MAURIE MICHELE, AND MUNCY, MARGARET JEAN. *An Investigation of the Interrelationship Between Articulation, Receptive and Expressive Language Performance of Primary School Aged Children.* Doctor's thesis, University of Northern Colorado (Greeley, Colo.), 1976. (*DAI* 37:2107A)

RAPHAEL M. HALLER, *Associate Professor of Speech Pathology and Audiology, Illinois State University, Normal, Illinois.*

According to its manual, the AAPS aims at providing "a rapid and precise determination of misarticulations and of total articulatory proficiency" and a method for the "efficient and standardized interpretation of articulatory skill." Presumably developed for administration by a school speech-language pathologist, the test samples each American English consonant, most vowels and diphthongs, and several consonant clusters in single words, through picture naming, and in sentences, through oral reading. The unique feature of this test is that a weighted score is assigned to each target phoneme reflecting its relative frequency of occurrence in conversation. Thus, by subtracting the numerical values associated with all the misarticulations from 100 percent, the examiner arrives at a percentage representing the client's intelligibility. The manual recommends that these total scores be used for such purposes as establishing priorities for enrollment in speech therapy, evaluating progress in therapy, and in comparing the success of therapy approaches. The record booklet also contains norms for ages 3–11, ranges of test scores associated with various degrees of intelligibility, and recommended age cutoffs for the normal acquisition of the target phonemes.

While the use of a numerical score in any test may be advantageous, the author fails to justify her method of data quantification. First, the percentages associated with the target phonemes were obtained from a study in 1930 of the phonemes used by adults in telephone conversations. Whether the same frequencies of occurrence presently hold for children of various ages has not been determined. Secondly, the manual justifies the validity of these data by reference to a study in which judges rated the speech intelligibility of 10-second samples of connected speech on an equal-appearing interval scale. When the ratings were compared with the AAPS test scores obtained by the same children, a correlation coefficient of .92 was obtained. This result is suspect since all the judges were students at the same university (and thus received the same training), and neither the test manual nor the supporting references list the instructions given to the judges. On the other hand, there is considerable evidence in the literature that children's speech intelligibility is related to many articulatory variables, such as the number of defective phonemes.

The major improvement in the revised edition of the AAPS is the elimination of items eliciting intervocalic (medial) consonants, probably decreasing administration time by 10 to 20 percent. Several studies have indicated that children's production of intervocalic consonants is similar to their pre- and postvocalic production, so that no clinically significant information has been lost. The clarity of the pictures compares favorably with other tests, further decreasing test time. However, the author has opted for brevity at the cost of completeness. Except for a few clusters, each consonant is sampled in only one or two phonetic contexts, even though the articulation of most children through age 8 is inconsistent. Thus, this test is actually a screening instrument, identifying only phonemes which are usually—if not consistently—misarticulated, while ignoring contextual effects which might be of help in diagnosis and therapy planning. While the examiner is encouraged to enter on the test form whether each error is of the omission, substitution, or distortion type, the manual provides no information as to how these data may be utilized clinically. Perhaps the major limitation in the test design is its failure to incorporate the *type* of misarticulation with a phoneme's relative frequency of occurrence in scoring an individual response. For example, irrespective of a phoneme's relative frequency of occurrence, an omission would disrupt intelligibility more than would a distortion. Thus, it is conceivable that two children with identical AAPS scores might vary considerably in intelligibility.

The effect of error type on articulation performance is also ignored in the author's recommended procedures for interpreting test scores. For example, both the manual and the test form contain a table relating ranges of AAPS scores to degrees of speech intelligibility. However, the manual states only that these data were derived on the basis of "clinical and experimental experiences." It is hard to understand the author's statement that an AAPS total score ranging from 95 to *100* percent represents the category "Sound errors occasionally are noticed in continuous speech." The effect of error type is also ignored in the phoneme acquisition data on the test form. The acquisition age listed for each phoneme represents the lowest age at which at least 90 percent of the subjects articulated that phoneme in a standard manner, as reported in a 1957 study cited in the manual. Thus, even though the acquisition age for post-vocalic /s/ is listed as 11 years, the *omission* of this phoneme by even a 5-year-old would be sufficient to warrant a full speech and language evaluation. This reviewer agrees with the author that phoneme acquisition data might help "reduce parental anxiety and possible pressure to produce perfect articulation before the children are developmentally ready." However, parent counseling must take into account such factors as error type and consistency, to provide for early diagnosis and intervention.

As a further means of interpreting the test scores, the manual includes norms on mainstream children, based on a minimum of 25 boys and 25 girls at half-year intervals from 3.0 to 5.5 years of age and one-year intervals from 6 to 11 years. These norms are inadequate on several grounds. First, although 50 children per age level seems adequate, the SES and ethnicity of the standardization population is not specified. Thus, these norms could not be used on

nonmainstream, dialect-speaking children. Had larger Ns been used, scores representing percentile ranks within each category might have been presented. Second, the manual fails to explain how the cutoff scores were obtained. An inspection of the subjects' performance shows that the differences between "average" score at each age level were two percentage points or less in nine of the 12 comparisons. These differences would have been greater if error type had been incorporated into the score for each item.

Insufficient information is provided about the sentence form of the test to enable this reviewer to evaluate its usefulness. For example, the manual fails to mention whether, and to what degree, the sentences were used in the test's standardization, and whether children's performance on the picture and sentence stimuli were ever compared. However, inspection of the sentences suggests that, in many instances, production of the target phonemes could be facilitated or hampered by coarticulation effects. The manual states, without documentation, that the sentences are on the third grade level. While the sentences were developed for older children and adults, criteria for opting to administer the sentence form are not provided. In this reviewer's opinion, the semantic content of the sentences is at too low a level for teenagers or adults.

In conclusion, the revised version of the AAPS may be used by speech-language pathologists as a screening instrument to list the phonemes which are produced in a nonstandard manner by children of preschool and elementary school age. In terms of ease and required time of administration, the AAPS compares favorably with most of the other published screening tests. This reviewer does not recommend that the total score be utilized for parent counseling, establishing priorities for therapy, or evaluating the results of therapy. For these purposes, the clinician must have such information as error type, error consistency, stimulability, and anatomical and physiological support for speech. Finally, it is recommended that the sentence form be limited to elementary school-age children. While the author's attempts to develop a numerical measure of articulation performance are admirable, the AAPS as presently designed is based on too little information

Arizona Articulation Proficiency Scale

to support the interpretations suggested in the manual.

RONALD K. SOMMERS, *Professor of Speech and Coordinator, Division of Speech Pathology and Audiology, Kent State University, Kent, Ohio.*

This articulation test is basically a traditional instrument that uses pictures of common objects or sentences to be read to elicit a subject's production of consonants, some consonant blends, and vowels. It is unique in two ways. First of all, phonemes are never tested as they appear to exist in the middle of words because the author denies that medial position of consonants exists in connected speech (and most speech scientists respect this view). Secondly, the degree of speech intelligibility can be derived for an articulatory defective person by subtracting a weighted value for each consonant and vowel error from 100 percent intelligibility. The author claims that knowledge concerning the extent to which a person has reduced speech intelligibility due to misarticulations of sounds is valuable, since both professionals and lay consumers of this information will find it easily understandable and meaningful. However, experienced speech pathologists do not appear to have been attracted to the test because of the capability it has to generate a speech intelligibility index.

There appear to be two basic problems related to speech intelligibility determination. The first deals with the norms used to validate the assessment, and the second concerns the nature of the speech intelligibility construct.

Unfortunately, although this instrument is used most often with children, the normative data used to derive weighted values of speech intelligibility for each sound were gathered not on children but on adults. Furthermore, a substantial portion of the normative telephone conversation data was gathered over forty years ago.

The second problem relates to the nature of measurements of speech intelligibility. There are complex and largely unstudied important interactions between linguistic factors and the articulation (phonological) ones that also bear upon a determination of speech intelligibility. It is not just a sound in error or a combination of them that relate to losses in speech intelligibility, and the Arizona scale does not consider these very important additional variables. Articulation tests that measure a single unit, viz., one sound at a time in a word, are thought to be valuable only if the results obtained relate very well to how the speaker articulates in connected speech. Assumptions about losses of speech intelligibility in connected speech due to errors in the production of sounds are limited in that they fail to take into consideration the many other linguistic factors that interface with the articulatory one. The use of normative data based upon old telephone conversations makes the validity of this determination even more questionable.

Two types of measurements can be made of articulation using the AAPS. Picture word stimuli are used to elicit articulatory responses. The test also includes sentences in which the phonemes to be measured are embedded in words. The intent is that the sentence test be used with individuals mature enough to have some basic reading ability. Although the sentence form does allow an examiner to measure more than one phoneme per sentence, the word picture form of the test only allows for assessment of some vowels and vowel forms of /r/ in the same word. It would appear that many other consonant sounds could have been measured using the same picture word stimuli. This probably would have shortened the time required for the administration of the picture portion of the test. It should also be observed that the picture sentence portions of the test use different words to assess the articulation of the same sounds. This condition may restrict the test's usefulness as a research tool, particularly if a wide range of subjects are tested, since some variation in subjects' responses may occur if some receive the picture portion of the test and some the sentence portion. Another limitation of the scale is its lack of inclusion of consonant clusters of greater complexity.

The reviewer maintains that the *Deep Test of Articulation* or the *Templin-Darley Tests of Articulation* are superior instruments for assessment of consistency of misarticulation across numerous phonetic contexts and provide a more comprehensive profile of the articulatory status of speakers than does the Arizona scale.

J Spec Ed 6(3):285–9 f '72. *Barton B. Proger.* * Some validity studies on AAPS are available, but they are far fewer than one is led to believe from Fudala's preface to the revised edition's manual. * The AAPS manual does not clarify what the status of the test is (diagnostic versus screening), although it is quite clear the test should serve only as a screening device. * Depending upon the clinician's orientation, he might dislike the emphasis of AAPS on testing sounds in isolation, i.e., in initial or final positions within single words. Some specialists might also wish to sample a child's behavior in connected speech contexts * While the primary emphasis of AAPS is on consonants, vowel sounds are assessed by the *same* word that has yielded a sample of a consonant sound in question. Although this procedure might be economical in a screening test, it would seem less confusing to focus attention on only one sound in any given test word. In the sentence-test part of the stimulus book, eight to nine sentences are on a single plate. This may be a misplaced economy, resulting in distinct limitations. *Summary.* When one surveys all of the currently available diagnostic and screening devices in articulation testing, it is evident that the state of the art in test construction is primitive. * As a screening device, the unique error weighing value system of AAPS offers a noteworthy ease of interpretation. The standardization of the test is no worse than any of its counterparts. (This does not mean it is satisfactory!) Reliability and validity of AAPS are substantial.

[955]

Boston Diagnostic Aphasia Examination. Aphasic patients; 1972; BDAE; 44 scores: severity rating, fluency (articulation rating, phrase length, verbal agility), auditory comprehension (word discrimination, body part identification, commands, complex material), naming (responsive, confrontation, animal, body part), oral reading (word reading, oral sentence), repetition (words, high-probability sentences, low-probability sentences), paraphasia (neologistic distortion, literal, verbal, extended), automatized speech (sequences, reciting), reading comprehension (symbol discrimination, word recognition, oral spelling, word picture matching, sentences and paragraphs), writing (mechanics, serial writing, primer-level dictation, written confrontation naming, spelling to dictation, sentences to dictation, narrative writing), music (singing, rhythm), parietal (drawing to command, stick memory, total fingers, right-left, arithmetic, clock setting, 3-dimensional blocks) plus 7 ratings: melodic line, phrase length, articulatory agility, grammatical form, paraphasia in running speech, word finding, auditory comprehension; no data on validity; no norms; individual; 1 form consists of booklet (27 pages) and set of 16 stimulus cards; manual (17 pages plus booklet) avail-

able only in *1* below; $11.50 per book and set of stimulus cards; $12.50 per 25 booklets; postage extra; [75–150] minutes; Harold Goodglass with the collaboration of Edith Kaplan; Lea & Febiger. *

REFERENCES
1. GOODGLASS, HAROLD; WITH THE COLLABORATION OF EDITH KAPLAN. *The Assessment of Aphasia and Related Disorders.* Philadelphia, Pa.: Lea & Febiger, 1972. Pp. vii, 80, 28. *

DANIEL R. BOONE, *Professor of Speech and Hearing Sciences, The University of Arizona, Tucson, Arizona.*

This comprehensive test for the adult aphasic patient places greater emphasis on measuring conversational speech and overall oral expression than any other existing adult aphasia test. The authors designed and developed this test over a period of many years to meet particular goals: (*a*) diagnose the type of aphasia, providing "inferences concerning cerebral localization"; (*b*) determine a wide range of language performance from baseline testing to performance over time; and (*c*) serve as a language guide to therapy.

The major problem with the BDAE is that the complete test, including five sections, requires about three hours to administer. Although the authors provide no guidelines relative to administration times, this clinician working with 15 adult aphasic patients has averaged about 15 minutes for the first section, "Conversational and Expository Speech"; 45 for the second section, "Auditory Comprehension"; 60 for the third section, "Oral Expression" (much longer for patients with oral verbal apraxia); 35 for the fourth section, "Understanding Written Language"; and 75 for the fifth section, "Writing" (particularly difficult for patients writing with their left hands because of right hemiplegia). It requires perhaps three separate administrations of about one hour each to complete the whole test with the patient who has the stamina to stick to the task that long.

The advantage of administering the complete examination is that each of the 43 subtests yields a z score for that ability, comparing the individual patient to the total distribution of 207 patients in the standardization group. K-R reliability coefficients indicate good internal consistency within subtests. Each test patient is first rated on an Aphasia Severity Rating Scale, which is based on his comprehension and expression observed in the conversational tasks involved in the first section of the test. This six-point scale ranges from "no communication possible" to "no perceptible handicap." Characteristic z scores are presented for each of the six severity groups in the standardization population for each of the 43 subtests; that is, a particular patient's performance on each subtest may be compared with other patients in his particular severity grouping.

The outstanding feature of the *Boston Diagnostic Aphasia Examination* is its first section, which asks the examiner to tape record the patient's conversational responses. After testing, the examiner then rates on a seven-point scale these six features of the patient's conversation: melodic line (prosody), phrase length, articulatory agility, grammatical form (variety of grammatical constructions), paraphasia in running speech, and word-finding abilities. A judgment is also made on auditory verbal comprehension abilities, related to the appropriateness of the patient's conversational responses.

In general, the test items are easy to present. Test stimuli cards are large, $7'' \times 10''$, and present adult stimuli in various degrees of linguistic complexity. The complete test yields an enormous amount of information, perhaps more than is needed for either classifying the patient or planning his language rehabilitation program. This examiner has found the first two sections of the total test, "Conversational and Expository Speech" and "Auditory Comprehension," to provide in about one hour a thorough and valid look at the patient's decoding and encoding abilities for the spoken word. If patient and clinic time permits, the complete test should be administered, even if three or four separate testing periods are required. From the points of view of completeness, relevance of items, and standardization, the *Boston Diagnostic Aphasia Examination* is perhaps the best such instrument presently available for testing the adult aphasic patient.

MANFRED J. MEIER, *Professor of Psychology and Director, Neuropsychology Laboratory, University of Minnesota Medical School, Minneapolis, Minnesota.*

The development of a comprehensive set of procedures for the assessment of language and related disturbances of higher cortical function has been a primary goal of the Aphasia Research Center at the Boston Veterans Administration Hospital and the Department of Neurology, Boston University. The attainment of this goal was undertaken by Goodglass and Kaplan, clinical neuropsychologists experienced in the construction of psychological tests. The *Boston Diagnostic Aphasia Examination* is a distillation of the clinical procedures developed at the Center and constitutes a signal attempt to relate measures of the component language disturbances of the aphasic syndromes to regional cerebral localization doctrine. The instrument is designed to yield quantitative descriptions of the aphasic syndromes and provide specific guidelines for generating inferences about the neuroanatomical substrate for central language disorders. In addition to operational and interpretive criteria for identifying the aphasias, the test protocol can be used to evaluate longitudinal changes during spontaneous recovery or after appropriate therapeutic intervention.

Unlike many aphasia examinations, these procedures were developed to conform to the APA guidelines for the construction of tests. The major assessment goal to be fulfilled required a sampling of the many components of language which are known to be useful in identifying the aphasic syndromes. Careful attention is paid to difficulty, subtest length, procedural standardization, and normative information to assist the examiner in drawing comparisons of relative impairment across functions in aphasics. Where language functions are not readily reduced to pass-fail or level scores, rating scales and error classifications are provided. A refreshing inclusion is a responsible delineation of the limitations of the scores and the interpretive approach being espoused, yet the manual provides virtually all the supporting data available at inception, including a detailed description of the aphasic syndromes and an account of their neuroanatomical correlates as derived from the current literature.

The subtests are conceived as alternative avenues or "windows," selected for their relevance to a particular language capacity, from which inferences about the underlying capacity and the affected neuroanatomical structures are derived. The functional composition of the battery is based on a general consensus, exceptions noted, of the patterns of deficits observed in the major syndromes. A global aphasia severity control measure is based on a speech characteristics profile which incorporates ratings of melodic line, phrase length, articulatory agility, grammatical form, paraphasia in running speech, and word finding. Scored subtests are grouped to facilitate description of patterns of impairments in articulation, verbal fluency, word finding, repetition, seriatim speech, grammar and syntax, paraphasia, auditory comprehension, reading, and writing. Distinctions among literal, neologistic, verbal, and extended paraphasic speech are defined. Procedural variations for more definitive assessment of sometimes elusive or masked functions, such as auditory comprehension in severe apraxia, are described in detail. The importance of repetition in examining for aphasia is appropriately emphasized and explained. A special group of visuospatial, visuoconstructional, and somatognosic tasks provides complementary assessment of parietal lobe dysfunction. Test criteria for the identification of the aphasic syndromes and for inferring focal neuroanatomical involvement, functional relations among the components of the speech areas, and interactions between the speech areas and surrounding cortical structures are described.

A detailed statistical presentation provides unidentified K-R reliability coefficients for scored subtests (.80s and .90s with one exception). Linearly transformed standard scores are presented based on 207 aphasics of differing levels of severity. Intercorrelational matrices for 38 language and 11 nonlanguage subtests are provided. Results of factor analyses are discussed in detail in support of the conceptual model for the clinical approach. Limitations of large sample techniques for establishing the factorial independence of the aphasic syndromes are realistically acknowledged and selection of patients for these analyses justified. The second factor analysis, of 189 aphasic protocols, yielded somewhat different findings from the first one, but generally supported the conclusion that the factors separate the major syndromes when plotted as individual factor scores.

The rationale underlying the construction of the test protocol and the empirical bases for interpretation are clearly presented in the manual and provide the essential information for application of the test. Interpretive pitfalls and shortcomings of the approach are identified, thereby alerting the test consumer to the need for adequate conceptual and experiential preparation. Thus, the authors have minimized the likelihood of test misuse by experienced professionals and provided sufficient information for at least a marginally effective level of application by novices. Inexperienced examiners are advised to study carefully this comprehensive test protocol and to apply the procedures to a series of representative individual patients under the supervision of a qualified clinical neuropsychologist, speech pathologist, or behavioral neurologist. Establishment of a definitive clinical competency in language assessment requires a clinical background in aphasia commensurate with the conceptual, technological, and empirical content of the manual.

Adequate preparation in the use of this comprehensive language test protocol should improve remarkably the clinical contributions of psychologists working in neurological and rehabilitation settings. Inclusion of this battery and the necessary supervised clinical activity in the curriculum of relevant professional psychology training programs is clearly justified by the current level of refinement for both supporting knowledge and technique.

[956]

The Bzoch-League Receptive-Expressive Emergent Language Scale: For the Measurement of Language Skills in Infancy. Birth to age 3; 1970–71; also called *REEL Scale;* 3 scores: receptive, expressive, combined; no data on reliability of part scores; 1 form ('70, 8 pages); manual ('71, 46 pages plus scale) entitled *Assessing Language Skills in Infancy;* $15.50 per 25 scales and manual; $6.75 per 25 scales; $9.75 per manual; postage extra; (10) minutes; Kenneth R. Bzoch and Richard League; Anhinga Press. *

See T2:2067 (2 references).

REFERENCES

1–2. See T2:2067.
3. BANNATYNE, ALEX. "Review of the Bzoch-League Receptive-Expressive Emergent Language Scale." *J Learn Dis* 5(8): 512 O '72. *
4. BENDER, RUTH E. "Review of the Bzoch-League Receptive-Expressive Emergent Language Scale." *Volta R* 74(8):465 N '72. *
5. JOHNSON, DALE L. "Review of the Bzoch-League Receptive-Expressive Emergent Language Scale." *J Pers Assess* 37(6): 581–2 D '73. *
6. PLOTKIN, WILLIAM H. "Review of the Bzoch-League Receptive-Expressive Emergent Language Scale." *Am J Mental Def* 78(2):226–7 S '73. *
7. CRIPE, ANTJE E. "Review of Bzoch-League Receptive-Expressive Emergent Language Scale," pp. 463–5. In *Pediatric Screening Tests.* Edited by William K. Frankenburg and Bonnie W. Camp. Springfield, Ill.: Charles C Thomas, Publisher, 1975. Pp. xii, 549. *

J Learn Dis 5(8).512 O '72. Alex Bannatyne. REEL is an acronym of Receptive-Expressive Emergent Language Scale. The scale itself is a comprehensive disection of language development from birth to 36 months. It analyzes development in terms of both receptive (decoding) skills and expressive (encoding) skills. Also included is a Combined Language Age which combines the two dimensions of CNS maturation in terms of language functions and socio-cultural factors. * The authors' points of view largely mirror my own. I would suggest that in various ways the two types of language background largely result (in school) in the categories of neurological dysfunction dyslexia, genetic dyslexia and primary communicative dyslexia. However, returning to the *REEL* scale I can only fault it on two points. It relies on adult structured-choice interviews for information about the child's language development and the standardization was on a small sample of 50 linguistically competent infants. Perhaps this will be extended in the future in terms of both the total "n" and for other groups such as the socially disadvantaged. The reliability coefficient on test-retest (administrator to adult interviewed) is reasonable ($r_s = .71$). The glossary of terms and the rich detail of the *REEL* scale are nothing short of excellent. Everyone with even a remote interest in language development in infancy has to have the handbook. The *REEL* scale is easy to administer and score. It only takes 10 to 15 minutes and any professional can give it. Note that the best way to check out a child in the *REEL* scale (I think) is to observe the infant yourself for a considerable period of time.

J Pers Assess 37(6):581–2 D '73. Dale L. Johnson. [Review of the manual.] Very few measures of language ability of children in the birth to three years of age range exist. Most of those available are embedded in general tests of early development such as the Bayley Scales of Infant Development or the Gesell examination. Although there is now a fair amount of research on language development in this age range and the age of appearance of many key linguistic functions is rather well-defined, there have been few attempts to make use of this information in developing assessment procedures. Bzoch and League have taken advantage of this body of research in preparing their Receptive-Expressive Emergent Language Scale. The Scale is not administered to the child who is the subject of the study; instead, the

mother is interviewed about her child's language behavior. * The authors claim a high degree of validity for the Scale when the Stanford-Binet and Vineland Test of Social Maturity are used as criteria, but no data are reported. Why these measures were used rather than more linguistically relevant measures is not clear. * Test-retest reliability with three weeks intervening is .71. Although the Scale is offered as a means of obtaining early diagnoses for deafness, infantile autism, and mental retardation, no data at all are reported for results with these clinical groups. Again, a claim is made for the value of the Scale in assessing "functional learning disability" in children participating in early intervention programs, but no evidence is given that the Scale has ever actually been used for this purpose. Another serious lack is any report of the predictive powers of the measure. As a longitudinal study was done data on this must be available, but no results are reported. If the test is to be of diagnostic utility it should offer a high degree of predictability. While the scale is well-organized and clearly presented, many items are worded in ways that would almost certainly pose problems when interviewing a parent who has had little education. For example, how would the item, "Utterances now contain more consonants than at the 6-month stage," come across? There are several items of this type. The authors claim that the interview may be conducted successfully by relatively untrained examiners, but they include no documentation of their effectiveness with any but middle-class parents. The Scale would have been of much greater value if the authors had provided information on its use with a variety of subjects and had taken pains to see that the items would be communicated meaningfully to parents of varying degrees of sophistication. As it is, the Scale appears to have merit, but it was published prematurely.

J Spec Ed 5(4):383–8 w '71. Barton B. Proger. * REEL is an easily administered scale of graded language-behavior levels from birth through 36 months, consisting of two subtests— receptive language and expressive language. Each yields a developmental age score and together a combined language age. Each of these three developmental ages can be transformed into "quotients." The mother or father of the child is usually the interviewee who provides most of the data for the REEL items. * The REEL manual suggests general questioning to be used before asking specific items apparently to avoid contaminating the replies of the informant: "The important consideration is to form a general impression of linguistic performance before suggesting specific details to the informant for elaboration [p. 27]." This introductory questioning is apparently meant to answer some of the REEL items through general inquiry. However, it is difficult to see how one can accurately and easily translate these global replies into the structure of REEL's very specific item categories (e.g., "used vowel-like sounds similar to *O* and *U*.") The potential user of REEL is not told how to proceed with this translation activity. It would be desirable to have a supplementary set of directions on how to get around suggestiveness, documenting how this is done with actual examples of the translation process. Another problem is what the parent or educator should do with the REEL screening results, assuming they indicate difficulties: Should he go into more intensive diagnosis or formulate a practical remediational program? If the latter, just how would he go about it? Also missing is discussion on how large numbers of infants could be screened by means of individual test administrations. With respect to reliability, there should be separate test-retest coefficients for various chronological age levels for each of the three scores—receptive, expressive, and combined. The 3-week interval between testing and retesting that is used to determine test-retest reliability should be questioned because of the dramatic changes that occur in young children from week to week; test-retest reliability implies a fairly steady state of the trait being measured. Also, a sample of 28 used to assess test-retest reliability is not sufficient to avoid small-sample fluctuations in correlations. Validity studies should be conducted to determine whether the concepts of receptive- and expressive-language behavior can be differentiated meaningfully at these early ages. That is, if it is possible to identify children impaired (according to REEL's results) in receptive language, others impaired in expressive language, and still others developmentally "normal" in both expressive and receptive language, will expected differences result in performance on related but non-REEL tasks? It is also important to know how well REEL can predict future impairments in both receptive and expressive language at older levels, when the initial screening occurs very early (such as the first year). *Conclusions.* Clearly, there are few published instruments available for measuring the language of infants. REEL would appear to fulfill a definite need here. But is the interview method more effective than direct observation of child behavior? In the first stages of life, the obvious instability of children's behavior, especially behavior exhibited over relatively short, controlled periods of time, makes direct observational sampling appear questionable, especially if the evaluation tries to assess highly specific language or pre-language behavior in a fairly short time. REEL's informant-interview technique may therefore be the most appropriate approach at early ages. The REEL scale makes a definite contribution to early-childhood measurement by concentrating on language-linked behavior exclusively and by not allowing the usual motor behavior (e.g., lifting the head, turning on the side) to cloud the issues.

[957]

★Carrow Elicited Language Inventory. Ages 3–7; 1974; CELI; 18 scores: grammar (articles, adjectives, nouns, noun plurals, pronouns, verbs, negatives, contractions, adverbs, prepositions, demonstratives, conjunctions), type (substitutions, omissions, additions, transpositions, reversals), total; individual; no reading by examinees; 1 form; scoring/analysis form (4 pages); manual (49 pages); verb protocol (6 pages); training guide (51 pages); training tape, 5 inch reel or cassette; audio-tape equipment necessary for administration; $44.95 per set of testing materials including 25 scoring/analysis forms and 10 protocols; $4.50 per 25 tests; $4.50 per 25 protocols; cash orders postpaid; specimen set not available; [10–15] minutes; Elizabeth Carrow; Learning Concepts. *

REFERENCES

1. CARROW, ELIZABETH. "A Test Using Elicited Imitations in Assessing Grammatical Structure in Children." *J Speech & Hearing Disorders* 39(4):437–44 N '74. * (*PA* 53:9257)
2. CORNELIUS, SUZANNE. *A Comparison of the Elicited Language Inventory With the Developmental Syntax Scoring Procedure in Assessing Language Disorders in Children.* Master's thesis, University of Texas (Austin, Tex.), 1974.
3. DAMMANN, ELLY. *A Correlational Study of Three Tests of Language Comprehension/Expression and Auditory Processing.* Doctor's thesis, University of Oregon (Eugene, Ore.), 1976. (*DAI* 37:4412B)

COURTNEY B. CAZDEN, *Professor of Education, Harvard University, Cambridge, Massachusetts.*

As explained in the manual for the CELI, "one of the major problems in language testing has been the difficulty in obtaining specific and valid information about a child's [productive] language....in an efficient and reliable manner." Attempts can be divided into two categories: procedures for obtaining and scoring samples of a child's spontaneous speech, and a set of more structured elicitation frames we call a "test." When clinician's time is limited, as it so frequently is in this time of budget cuts and overburdened staff, tests are sought as a desirable alternative. The CELI is a test of children's productive use of selected aspects of language structure.

CELI is a set of 52 sentences which children are asked to imitate. The sentences vary in length from 2 to 10 words, and include a wide range of constructions. Scoring the imitations for number and types of errors (deviations from the model) can yield information about specific language structures that a child has not yet fully acquired and, if desired, also a single numerical score.

Sentence imitation tests are not new. The Stanford-Binet, for example, has included sentences for children to imitate ever since Binet's original research in 1905. Language acquisition research of the past 15 years has provided additional arguments for the validity of elicited imitations as a measure of children's knowledge of particular grammatical structures. As Carrow summarizes in correct and simple terms in the manual, many researchers have found that if children are asked to imitate sentences longer than their short-term memory capacity but within their span of comprehension, the sentences will be filtered through the same grammatical system that controls the child's spontaneous speech. In other words, the child will decode the underlying meaning of the model sentences and then recode that meaning into his own forms. For example, if a child's developing language system does not yet include the third person singular verb ending, the child will repeat "The train bumps the car" (item 8) as "The train bump the car." And if the child's system also does not yet include articles, the imitation will be simply "Train bump car." In contrast to analyses of spontaneous speech, sentence imitation tests can tap children's knowledge of structures that are not likely to appear spontaneously—e.g., rare verb forms such as "She would have liked to go" (item 27). While language researchers have used sentence imitation tasks for many years for these reasons,

CELI is the first set of sentences widely available for clinical use.

The test is administered by asking the child to "say the same thing I said," presenting each model sentence, and recording the child's imitation on a tape recorder. The child's responses are transcribed onto a scoring analysis form provided with the test. Here, for each sentence, each error is tallied according to type—substitution, omission, addition, transposition, or reversal—and according to grammatical category. The errors in the examples given above would be scored as omissions of verb ending and omissions of articles. The child's raw score is the total number of errors in all 52 sentences (to a maximum of one error per each word in the test). According to the manual, "the average time for administration, transcription, and scoring is 45 minutes" per child. In addition, a more detailed but optional analysis of verb errors can be done on a separate verb protocol sheet.

Because sentence imitation tests as used in language acquisition research and in CELI are designed to test children's knowledge of particular grammatical structures, they are in essence content-referenced tests. We care about the particular knowledge they tap. Such use is in contrast to the purpose of including them on the Stanford-Binet, for example, where the sentences are meant to be simply representative of a universe of sentences of similar length or complexity. For content-referenced purposes, the choice of the particular language structures included is very important, and one can always raise questions about the choices made.

On a criterion of completeness, one wonders why more complex embedded or coordinated sentences were deliberately excluded. Such an exclusion limits the test's usefulness with older or more advanced speakers. Within this limitation, CELI is reasonably complete.

Some structures that are included for their grammatical importance may cause problems specific to the sentence imitation context. For example, a question places a powerful constraint on the hearer, even the young child, to give an answer instead of a repetition. Clinicians may have to remind children not to answer "Where are the dolls?" (item 38) but to repeat it. For other sociolinguistic reasons, tag questions are not normally repeated in response to requests for clarification in ordinary conversation. And

Carrow Elicited Language Inventory

so children may omit the tag at the end of "That's not a baby, is it?" (item 15) for reasons of conversational abnormality rather than grammatical deficiency.

While one might expect that imitation tests would over-estimate a child's grammatical knowledge because of the availability of the presented model, that help seems to be countered by a corresponding and perhaps even more powerful hindrance: the unavailability in the imitation test context of any intentional and contextual support for the meaning expressed in the sentences. For example, Lois Bloom reports that whereas a 32-month-old boy spontaneously uttered "I'm trying to get this cow in here" when he was trying to get a colt's feet to fit into a barrel, he only repeated "Cow in here" when asked to repeat his own sentence out of context the following day. Thus, articles that appear sometimes but not consistently in a child's spontaneous speech may be totally absent from the imitations because more of the child's attention must be taken up with retaining the idea that the sentence given to him is supposed to express.

So far, these are minor problems. A more serious problem is the limitation on the children for whom the test as presented in the manual is valid. The manual wisely states that "CELI may not be useful with children who have certain problems": severe misarticulations, severe jargon speech, and echolalia. But, while the manual states clearly that "the standardization sample was composed of white middle class children from an urban community," it does not discuss the problems encountered if the test is used with children outside that category— children whose grammatical system may differ from the Standard English of the test sentences for reasons of social or ethnic dialect rather than individual immaturity or pathology of any kind. It is critically important that clinicians recognize those omissions or substitutions that are simply part of the prevailing way of speaking in the child's home community and take these into consideration in scoring the child's responses. It is unfortunate that the CELI manual does not include a discussion of this question.

For children from a standard English speaking community, the CELI is an extremely useful test, probably the most useful of the few productive language tests that now exist.

Carrow Elicited Language Inventory

[958]

★**The Denver Articulation Screening Exam.** Economically disadvantaged ages 2.5 to 6.0; 1971–73; DASE; individual; usually orally administered; 1 form; picture cards ('72, 22 cards) for use with "hard-to-test" children; manual ('71, 9 pages); record blank/profile ('71, 2 pages); training instructor's manual ('73, 14 pages for this and 3 other tests); training manual/workbook ('73, 44 pages); training and proficiency films or video cassettes; proficiency evaluation ('73, 5 pages); 60¢ per set of picture cards; 50¢ per 25 record blank/profiles; $3.25 per manual/ workbook; $250 per training and proficiency films including training instructor's manual and proficiency test (purchase), $25 (rental); $100 per video cassettes (purchase), $25 per week (rental); $2.50 per manual; 10% extra for postage and handling; (10–15) minutes; Amelia F. Drumwright; Ladoca Project and Publishing Foundation, Inc. *

REFERENCES

1. DRUMWRIGHT, AMELIA; VAN NATTA, PEARL; CAMP, BONNIE; FRANKENBURG, WILLIAM; AND DREXLER, HAZEL. "The Denver Articulation Screening Exam." *J Speech & Hearing Disorders* 38(1):3–14 F '73. *
2. SPRIESTERSBACH, BETTE R. "Review of the Denver Articulation Screening Exam." Letter. *J Speech & Hearing Disorders* 39(1):104–5 F '74. *
3. ARKEBAUER, HERBERT. "Review of Denver Articulation Screening Exam," pp. 452–3. In *Pediatric Screening Tests.* Edited by William K. Frankenburg and Bonnie W. Camp. Springfield, Ill.: Charles C Thomas, Publisher, 1975. Pp. xii, 549. *
4. CRIPE, ANTJE E. "Review of Denver Articulation Screening Exam," pp. 450–2. In *Pediatric Screening Tests.* Edited by William K. Frankenburg and Bonnie W. Camp. Springfield, Ill.: Charles C Thomas, Publisher, 1975. Pp. xii, 549. *

HAROLD A. PETERSON, *Professor of Audiology and Speech Pathology and Director, Hearing and Speech Center, The University of Tennessee, Knoxville, Tennessee.*

This test was designed to screen the articulation of culturally disadvantaged children, on the assumption that children learn articulation patterns of and from their environment (dialect). Implicit in this assumption is that "culturally different" children should not have the same standard of performance as their more "advantaged" counterparts. On this assumption, the authors screened 1,455 children described as culturally (economically) disadvantaged (defined primarily by income and residence in public housing). The children were approximately equally divided according to "cultural group" (white, black, and Mexican-American), with approximately equal numbers of boys and girls, at each half-year level from 2½ to 6 years of age. All were from the Denver, Colorado, area.

The sounds tested were taken from Templin's *Certain Language Skills in Children* as correctly produced by 85 percent of her six-year-old population. The final version of the DASE includes the 30 of 34 sounds which were correctly produced by at least 70 percent of the standardizing population and which showed a progressive growth in correct percentage of production with age. The 30 sounds represent 22 single phoneme consonants (primarily initial or final word-positions), one vowel (/er/), one glide plus vowel (/ju/), and six two-element combinations. The test is designed to be administered by the examiner saying the word containing the test sound and asking the child to repeat it. Pictures are included for the "hard-to-test child," it being assumed that the stimuli would then be auditory plus visual.

The DASE is a simple test to administer and score; so designed that it can be given by nonprofessionals. The examiner scores the test by counting the number of correct productions and interprets the results by consulting the back of the test form, which lists percentile rankings for number of correct productions by age. The authors have assigned the 15th percentile as the cutoff score for referral purposes.

Test-retest reliability of .95 was obtained when the same examiner tested 110 preschoolers four to eight days apart. The reliability would have been more meaningful if different examiners had been used with a longer interval between testings.

Validity is not as well demonstrated. The manual describes two studies in which the results on the DASE for 89 and 60 children (about half of whom scored as normal and half as abnormal) were compared to results on the Hejna articulation test to determine "copositivity" and "conegativity." Thus, results on two single-phoneme articulation tests were compared for agreement of "normal" vs. "abnormal" scores. Using another similar articulation test as the criterion does not provide adequate evidence of validity.

The manual describes the test as being designed "to detect common abnormal conditions such as hyponasality, hypernasality, lateral lisp and tongue thrust." There is no further comment in the test procedures or suggestions for scoring the interpretation as to how this should be accomplished. We would have to assume that the judgments of hypo- and hypernasality and observation of tongue thrust are not detectable from the *number* of correct or incorrect sounds. The /s/ sound was supposedly included primarily because of the increased probability of detecting lateral lisp and tongue thrust—but instructions are only for correct or incorrect scoring.

In summary, the test is easy to administer, and may be as reliable as other single-phoneme articulation tests. But until more adequate validation studies have been completed, I am not convinced that it does what it purports to do—separate adequate from inadequate articulation ability in culturally (economically) disadvantaged children.

[959]

The Edinburgh Articulation Test. Ages 3-0 to 6-0; 1971; EAT; individual; 1 form; picture book (42 pages); assessment sheets: quantitative (1 page), qualitative (5 pages); manual (93 pages); £13($37.50) per set of picture book, manual, and 50 sets of assessment sheets; £7.50($17.50) per 50 sets of assessment sheets; postage extra; specimen set not available; (10–20) minutes; T. T. S. Ingram, A. Anthony, D. Bogle, and M. W. McIsaac; Churchill Livingstone [Scotland]. * (United States distributor: Longman, Inc.)

See T2:2070 (1 reference).

REFERENCES

1. See T2:2070.
2. FAWCUS, ROBERT. "Review of the Edinburgh Articulation Test." *Develop Med & Child Neurol* (England) 14(1):122–3 F '72. *
3. FRANCIS, HAZEL. "Review of the Edinburgh Articulation Test." *Brit J Ed Psychol* 42(2):204 Je '72. *
4. HARRISON, P. MARGOT. "Review of the Edinburgh Articulation Test." *Brit J Dis Commun* 7(1):90–3 Ap '72. *
5. JONES, GARY W. *A Descriptive Analysis of the Articulation of a Stratified Random Sample of Children Aged 3.00 to 5.50 From School District #1 of Lewis County, New York as Evaluated by the Edinburgh Articulation Test.* Master's thesis, Bloomsburg State College (Bloomsburg, Pa.), 1972.
6. MORGAN, LINDA M. *A Descriptive Analysis of the Articulation of Children Between the Ages of Three and Six of the Hazelton Area School District as Evaluated by the Edinburgh Articulation Test—Shortened Form.* Master's thesis, Bloomsburg State College (Bloomsburg, Pa.), 1972.

HAROLD A. PETERSON, *Professor of Audiology and Speech Pathology and Director, Hearing and Speech Center, The University of Tennessee, Knoxville, Tennessee.*

This test was designed in Scotland as part of a study of speech maturation concerned with both phonological and linguistic development for later comparison with academics. This study is still in progress. The EAT is a 68-item revision of a preliminary test which contained 77 items.

The preliminary test utilized item analyses from 371 "normal" and 153 "speech retarded" children ranging in age from 2.5 to 6.0 years. The current EAT population consisted of 510 children ranging in age from 3.0 to 5.5 years. The conversion table for interpretation of test results is interpolated with three-month divisions, that is, age groups of 3.75 but less than

4.0 years, 4.0 but less than 4.25 years, etc. The data indicate that 5.5 to 6.0 years of age is the terminal level of the test, or approximately adult level performance. In its reported similarity to a "balanced and comprehensive picture of the consonants and consonantal clusters occurring in English at various positions in the word structure in monosyllabic, disyllabic and a few polysyllabic words," the test would appear to have face validity.

The standardization population was proportionately representative of the sex, social class, and familial status of the population in the Edinburgh area. Tabled values in the manual indicate slight differences for sex, social class, and family standing, but the differences are not statistically significant and the norms (conversion table for interpretation) do not now distinguish among the variables.

The EAT is overall a thoroughly well standardized test, which includes 41 words to spontaneously elicit 30 blends and 38 single phoneme consonants. Spontaneity is considered important. The authors selected the test words, at least partly, on the basis of lexical use and vocabulary recognition of the preliminary test population children. The original test protocol utilized some pictures and small toys as stimulus materials. The revised EAT uses only pictures. The authors note that the test is to be given as a spontaneous test, and if a word must be supplied by the examiner to be repeated by the child, that word is marked with "R" (for repeated). If a child self-corrects an error response, or if he changes his production of a sound in repeating a response, both productions are to be noted on the response sheet and the item is scored wrong.

The EAT was constructed to allow interpretation of normal performance which would include local dialectal variants. Since the local dialects used were Scottish, the variants accepted are not necessarily acceptable in English. For example, nine of the 68 test items are voiceless medial and final position plosives for which a glottal stop is considered a local (acceptable) variant. The idea of local variant is valid, e.g., a /d/ for /t/ sound as the medial position stop in the word "bottle," or "butter." However, an /o/ for /l/ substitution in the word "bottle" or as substitution for the final cluster in "milk" (as the author also suggests)

is not considered an acceptable variant in American English. The only validation data reported in the manual are in term of preliminary test (with toys) vs. the final test (with picture stimuli), which agree very well. A K-R 20 of .94 is reported for 510 children in the age range 3 to 6.0.

The manual describes a qualitative analysis to be performed with the quantitative right/wrong results. The degree of deviation illustrated by response examples has been assembled from the Scottish dialects used by the test population. The "values" implied on the continuum of right to wrong appear to be based on frequency of occurrence. For my biases, I would prefer this continuum to be expressed in frequency of manner and place feature substitutions. In any case, because the qualitative descriptions have been assembled from Scottish dialect variations, they do not appear particularly useful to the interpretation of an American child's English articulation.

The quantitative version of the test, however, is probably a valid base for interpretation of English speaking American children's articulation skills. I hope it will soon be standardized on an American population with both the quantitative and qualitative analyses, but in the meantime I recommend its use and, at least tentatively, consider the quantitative score to be valid.

JOEL STARK, *Director, Queens College Speech and Hearing Center, Queens College of The City University of New York, Flushing, New York.*

This test was the outgrowth of some research which was designed to study sequentially, at six monthly intervals, the speech maturation of groups of normal and slow children in Edinburgh. The researchers found that the few available tests of phonological development presented items which were too comprehensive. That is, all voiced and voiceless plosives were examined initially, medially, and finally—resulting in an unwieldy articulation test. After considerable preliminary sampling, a shortened more streamlined version, which requires 10 to 20 minutes to administer according to the age of a child, was developed.

The materials used in constructing the final version of the test came from two clearly sepa-

Edinburgh Articulation Test

rated groups of children as regards articulatory ability. The first was considered to have normal development, the second was retarded in speech development. A detailed item analysis was carried out on the 34,680 responses of 510 children to the 68 items in the test. A validation study was conducted with 74 children. The test provides both a qualitative and quantitative analysis of articulation ability.

The test procedure involves the examiner showing a child pictures in a book and inviting him to play a "naming game" explaining to him that each time she turns over a new picture he should tell her what it is. The aim is to elicit spontaneous utterances which are recorded immediately by the examiner in phonetic notation on the quantitative score sheet. The phonetic data are not scored until the test is fully completed.

While tests of articulation ability often rely on the pronunciation of words out of a communication context and are therefore limited, one is impressed with the painstaking and detailed analysis of the sample in the development of the EAT.

Brit J Dis Commun 7(1):90–3 Ap '72. P. Margot Harrison. This new and interesting quantitative and qualitative test of articulation for children aged 3 years to 6 years, has been produced as a result of some nine years work by the Edinburgh team. They are to be congratulated for the thoroughness of their investigations * It is important to remember that this test has been standardised on children in Edinburgh and that the adult norm for that area is the one referred to by the team and that the developmental patterns found in the qualitative assessment are those of the "normal" children in that area. * The team say that the pictures they have chosen are of words that a child could be expected to be familiar with. * The test is concerned solely with consonant articulation and the points in word structure that the team studied were :- word initial consonants; monosyllabic word final consonants; word initial consonant clusters; monosyllabic word final clusters; medial consonants between accented vowel and unaccented vowel in disyllabic words; medial consonant clusters between accented vowel and unaccented vowel in disyllabic words; final consonants following unaccented

vowel in disyllabic words; medial consonants and possible syllabic consonants in disyllabic words and consonants in trisyllabic words. The pictures are presented in book form, one side only, sturdily bound with a spiral wire. They are certainly robust enough for general clinical use, being printed on thin cards and coated with a plastic-type substance. Unfortunately, they tend to adhere to each other, making it difficult to turn a single page each time without error. The illustrations are of a good size, 6½ × 6½ inches, clearly and realistically drawn, with no unnecessary supplementary background features. The colouring is bright and cheerful without being harsh and they are very attractive to a child. Test procedure is clearly laid down on the first page and the therapist presents the pictures one by one in the form of a guessing game, thus trying to ensure that the child's attention be concentrated on naming the pictures, rather than pronouncing the words. The aim of the game is to elicit one word spontaneous utterances from the child. If the child does not produce the required response spontaneously, nor with the aid of clues, the therapist is instructed to give the relevant word and then ask the child to tell again what it is. In practice this works very nicely for a large proportion of the pictures, but there are nine pictures about which I should like to make comments. The picture of a train invokes the response of diesel and coming as the 4th picture can take a little of the shine off a child's eagerness. The picture for the word "stamps" is composed of five stamps in a block; a lot of children seem to be more familiar with a stamp on a letter. The picture for the word "clouds" is often not easily recognised and may require cluing from examination of the sky, which is a distracting process. The picture for sleeping is of a girl asleep in bed and this is a commonly produced answer. There is a picture of a ball of string, which many children identify as wool and when asked what they use to tie up a parcel, reply "sellotape." Surprisingly, the picture of the bowl of sugar with accompanying spoon causes difficulty, despite clues of, "what do you put in your tea, coffee, on your cereal" etc. There is a rather nice picture of an Indian smoking a peace-pipe, but unfortunately he does not wear a typical fully feathered head-dress, which, judging from the number of indignant

Edinburgh Articulation Test

remarks received would appear to be a fairly universal indian-type symbol. There is one really difficult picture in this test. It is of a desk, clearly presented as a large teacher's desk, with knee-hole and drawers. This seems to be an unknown quantity to many of the children in the age-range for which the test is designed. To illustrate this I quote just a selection of the responses most commonly received by therapists in our department :- dressing-table, sideboard, drawers, table with drawers, table, chest of drawers, cupboard, coffee table, shelves, telephone table, bookshelves and wardrobe. The tester's ingenuity and the child's imagination are certainly taxed on this one. The remaining pictures presented little difficulty to 300 local children aged 3 years, 4 years and 5 years, though queen, bridge, chimney, wings, garage, milk, feather, finger and thumb, in the main, frequently require a clue. None of our children refused, did not finish or became bored with the game, for it is appealing and not too terribly long. Under the heading of administration it is stated that the time taken to conduct the test varies from ten to twenty minutes and with a socalled normal child this is the case. However, for practical purposes it should be borne in mind that the children who visit a speech therapy clinic do not necessarily come into this category, frequently being a little more hyperactive and distractible or a little withdrawn and self-conscious. Taking this into consideration perhaps a slightly longer time would be a more realistic estimate. To use this test a therapist needs to be very familiar with both the material content and her International Phonetic Alphabet. She must play the game with her patient, watching carefully his face and mouth and phonetically transcribe the relevant parts of the responses received. As the handbook suggests it is very helpful to use a tape recorder, if this can be done without undue distraction, but certainly in the early stages the most effective help is another pair of trained ears and where two therapists can work together it is helpful for one to present the pictures and record and for the other to concentrate on watching, listening and transcribing the phonetic responses. Each test is scored in two ways, once quantitatively and once qualitatively. The quantitative score is very speedy. It is made solely on a right/wrong basis, the criteria for this decision

being the adult norm for the area. It is, therefore, essential for the therapist to be conversant with the adult norm for her community. * In the handbook some very interesting information concerning the findings of the team is given. * This pleasingly presented test, which gives a quantitative and qualitative analysis of consonant articulation is a valuable and useful piece of equipment for the therapist working with young children.

Brit J Ed Psychol 42(2):204 Je '72. *Hazel Francis.* * The test requires spontaneous naming of attractively drawn pictures, the responses being familiar words for young children. It is shown that an acceptable alternative in cases of incorrect or absent response is repetition of the tester's naming of the picture. In most responses two or three articulatory units are tested in different word positions, those which were found to discriminate well between different age levels and between normal and deviant speech being well represented. Only some consonantal phonemes and groups are included, the phonological system being sampled so that 41 words give 68 units for testing. * Only trained phoneticians can record the responses, their transcripts then being checked against a tape-recording before scoring is attempted. Each unit is scored right or wrong against the local adult norm as criterion. Examples of admissible forms in Edinburgh are given and the scoring has been standardised for each three month age group on a total sample of 510 children. One wonders, however, whether the inter-tester reliability reported for the two phoneticians who undertook most of the work would be maintained by others. To supplement the quantitative scoring a quantitative analysis of errors enables the tester to determine whether low scores are due to retarded or deviant development. Although the authors have produced a considerably improved form of articulation test the question of its usefulness for speech therapists generally and for students of speech and language development raises considerable problems. Unfortunately for the latter a screening test comprised of selected items cannot suffice for the study of the development of the phonological system. Furthermore, since doubt exists as to how far the phoneme is an appropriate unit for analysis of developing articulation, the test may be even more limited in its usefulness.

Edinburgh Articulation Test

Perhaps the most telling doubt, affecting both research and screening, is that until the test has been tried out in other localities it is impossible to say what changes of item and specification of acceptable forms might be required. The authors are, nevertheless, undoubtedly right to base their work on local speech norms, their tests offers the possibility of modification to suit other localities, and the quantitative analysis of error is a most valuable model for an approach to diagnosis and therapy.

Develop Med & Child Neurol (England) 14 (1):122–3 F '72. Robert Fawcus. The publication of the Edinburgh Articulation Test marks a major advance in the quantitative study of phonological development for both clinical and general linguistic purposes. The result of a collaboration between a paediatrician, two phoneticians, a statistician and two speech therapists, the test exhibits many signs of imagination, successful cooperation and planning. * an informative and well-presented manual * A number of obvious differences between the pronunciation of the Scottish sample and most other English dialect groups fortunately does not interfere with the scoring. In the qualitative section, a valuable means of assessing the relative importance of articulatory deviations is provided. The time-consuming nature of the latter exercise compared with the quantitative section makes one impatiently consider the possibility of a short-cut to the same information, but this may not be possible. In clinical use, a few of the pictures come in for criticism but these are definitely exceptions. The choice of vocabulary is admirable and covers the experience of children from a wide range of social strata. Some of the comments on relative maturity of certain allophones of specific consonants are heavily biased towards the Edinburgh sample. Observation would suggest, for example, that the development of the "r" sound in London takes a different path from that in Edinburgh. The difference between the mature forms would probably explain the divergence, and the structure of the test allows for a wide range of British dialects.

[960]

Fairview Language Evaluation Scale. Mentally retarded; 1971; FLES; rating scale of language age 0–72 months; 1 form (4 pages); manual (4 pages); $10 per 100 tests; 50¢ per manual; $1 per specimen set; postpaid; [10–60] minutes; Alan Boroskin; Research Department, Fairview State Hospital. *

REFERENCES
1. LAUDER, RONALD J. *Comparison of the Fairview Language Evaluation Scale With the ITPA Using a Sample of Institutionalized Mentally Retarded Patients.* Master's thesis, California State University (Fullerton, Calif.), 1972.
2. RAPP, DONALD WAYNE. *The Effects of Motor Training on a Sample Population of Blind, Severely and Profoundly Mentally Retarded Males.* Doctor's thesis, Boston College (Chestnut Hill, Mass.), 1975. (*DAI* 36:2138A)

RONALD K. SOMMERS, *Professor of Speech and Coordinator, Division of Speech Pathology and Audiology, Kent State University, Kent, Ohio.*

The *Fairview Language Evaluation Scale* is a primitive screening instrument intended for use by parents, caretakers, and other nonprofessionals to assess the language development of profoundly and severely retarded persons. Its ten levels of language performance have either six or eight items each. The examiner's task is to score each item pass or fail either through observation or through the administration of a simple test, e.g., digits forward, naming colors, and showing pictures.

The FLES is essentially unstandardized. The author has used items from a number of different tests and claims that normal subjects' performances on them have previously been determined. However, norms for the various levels of performance and total test score have not been reported.

Although a small amount of information has indicated that the test-retest reliability of the FLES is high, no validity information has been reported. Comparisons of subjects' performances on similar tests such as the *Preschool Language Scale* or the *Utah Test of Language Development* apparently have not been accomplished. The latter test is similar to the FLES, and comparison between language performances could have been made on both mentally retarded and normal subjects without difficulty.

The content validity of the language items within each of the ten language levels in the FLES is questionable. Many items at the lowest levels of language performance measure cognitive development. Although the relationships between cognition and what is usually meant by "language" appear to be high when the severely retarded or very young normal subjects are studied, claims that it is language per se that is being assessed in the FLES are probably debatable.

There are other problems with the items

within the ten language levels. Some items are so unstructured that choices made by examiners may yield different results. For example, item 5 in Level 3 is "Repeats 5 or 6 syllable sentence (e.g., The pony ran away)." Both the sentence length and the linguistic complexity of the content are known to affect subjects' performances on such a task. Thus allowing an examiner to use his own sentence probably introduces error into the measurement. A comparable problem can be see in item 1 in Level 2. The examiner asks the subject to follow "a 2-stage command (e.g., Pick up the ball and bring it to me)." If the examiner uses a different two-stage command, the task may be more difficult or easy for the subject to complete because of changes in the complexity of the linguistic material and changes in the length of the utterance.

The FLES allows nonprofessional personnel to make other choices and determinations that superficially appear simple but actually are difficult to accomplish if accuracy is important. For example, item 2 in Level 3 is "Fifty percent of speech is understandable to a stranger." Can ward technicians make such a judgment?

In summary, the FLES is a screening test which probably measures some aspects of cognitive development as well as language. It is quick to administer and score. It is basically untested and unstudied.

LAWRENCE J. TURTON, *Assistant Professor of Speech Pathology and Research Program Associate, Institute for the Study of Mental Retardation and Related Disabilities, The University of Michigan, Ann Arbor, Michigan.*

One of the principal goals of services to the severely retarded is the facilitation of a communication system commensurate with their cognitive development and their functional needs within their living environment. *The Fairview Language Evaluation Scale* represents an attempt to develop a rating scale system to provide assessment data on the target population using caretakers, principally ward technicians, as the raters. Despite the title, the FLES is not a true rating scale. It is basically a yes-no checklist. The items are not sequenced in any logical developmental order nor is the respondent asked to judge the behaviors on any scale of performance.

The most significant problem with the FLES can be found in the selection of items to be observed and scored. The author used two intelligence scales, a communication development chart, and the work of Gesell as the bases to generate the list of items. Research on natural language acquisition of normal children and the language skills of the mentally retarded was apparently ignored by the test author. In its present form, the scale does not reflect natural language acquisition from birth to six years of age.

More importantly, the scale is of questionable value for use with the target population. The items selected by the author, particularly at the five highest levels of the scale, violate the research findings on the language of the mentally retarded in terms of language form and function. For example, the severely retarded student is expected to repeat eight-to-ten word sentences at Level 2 (five-year-level). However, research with the mentally retarded would suggest that this task is outside the realm of possibility for the target population because it exceeds the average memory span for sentences of the mentally retarded and involves syntactic forms that are low probability for this population.

Furthermore, there is no logical sequence inherent between and within the ten levels used in the scale. Apparently, the items were randomly selected for each age level without a cohesive theory of language acquisition to guide the process. The scale forces the observer to score behaviors that involve attending to persons or objects, cognitive functions (numbers and colors), physiological functions (drooling and chewing), listening skills, as well as other forms of communication. The sequencing of the items, if used as a teaching format, would foster the development of splinter skills among the severely and profoundly mentally retarded.

The sampling procedures used to develop this scale were inadequate to justify its use. The manual includes reliability tables indicating relatively high intraobserver cofficient of correlations. Interobserver agreements are not reported.

The procedures to compute a language age described in the manual are relatively unclear. For each level of the test, the total number of items checked is multiplied by a constant value

Fairview Language Evaluation Scale

of one (Levels 7–10), two (Levels 5–6), or three (Levels 1–4). No explanation is provided for the weighting system or why the value changes across the levels of scale. After a total of the weighted points is obtained, a language age, language quotient, and language level can be derived for the subject.

In order to obtain a language age, the grand total is divided by two, the number which happens to be the mean of the weighted values originally assigned to the scores. Using a value of two would suggest that the score assigned to a subject is inflated by twice the items checked. A limit of 180 months (15 years) is placed upon the chronological age for computation of the language quotient. This is especially confusing because the items stop at a ceiling of six years and the mean age of the population used for a validity study was close to 16 years of age. The lack of a plausible statistical rationale for the weighted computations renders them non-functional for the purpose of establishing communication programs for severely retarded students.

In its present form, the FLES is unacceptable as a language evaluation scale for the severely and profoundly retarded. Until the problems in test development and standardization are resolved, the instrument is of questionable value for designing communication programs for the retarded. The instrument should be completely revised and standardized according to the accepted procedures for test development.

[961]

The Fisher-Logemann Test of Articulation Competence. Preschool to adult, grade 3 to adult; 1971; FLTAC; no data on reliability and validity; no norms; individual; 2 tests in a single portfolio (73 pages); manual (42 pages); record form (2 pages) for each test; $12.60 per test portfolio; $3.90 per 50 record forms; $2.40 per manual; postage extra; (40–45) minutes; Hilda B. Fisher and Jerilyn A. Logemann; Houghton Mifflin Co. *
a) PICTURE TEST. Preschool to adult; no scores, 3 areas: singleton consonants, consonant blends, vowel phonemes and diphthongs; a shortened screening form consisting of 11 of the singleton consonants may be administered.
b) SENTENCE ARTICULATION TEST. Grade 3 to adult; no scores, 5 areas: consonant pairs, singleton consonants, nasals, vowel phonemes, diphthongs.

MARIE C. FONTANA, *Assistant Professor of Communication Arts and Sciences, Queens College of The City University of New York, Flushing, New York.*

A more recent approach to the study of articulation has focused on the application of psycholinguistic theory and research. Through the application of distinctive feature theory, analysis of the evaluation of misarticulations has indicated that children do, in fact, have logical principles underlying their use of speech sounds which cause their production to be at variance with the adult system. Linguistic analysis, therefore, provides a model for understanding articulation disorders and a basis for more efficient remedial intervention. This test is an innovative articulatory inventory because it attempts an application of linguistic methodology of phonemic analysis. The authors state that the test grew out of a need for more specific and relevant information on the nature of articulation deficiencies.

The picture test consists of 109 attractive picture stimuli on 35 bound cards used to elicit spontaneous single word productions testing consonant singles, consonant blends, vowels, and diphthongs. Eleven selected cards, representing consonant phonemes which are most frequently misarticulated, comprise the screening portion. Marginal tabs are attached to the cards of the screening items for easy location. The sentence version of the test consists of 15 sentences to test all consonant singles, vowels, and diphthongs. Consonant blends are not evaluated in the sentence form.

The FLTAC has incorporated a recent approach to the study of consonant sounds as releasing or arresting phonemes of a syllable by examination in three syllabic positions: prevocalic (releasing), intervocalic, and postvocalic (arresting). Whether, in fact, intervocalic consonants serve, as the authors suggest, the "dual function of ending the preceding syllable and initiating the following syllable" is open to question. Selected consonant blends (/s/, /r/, and /l/), described as being "most critical," are tested in the initial position. There is no mention made of how or upon what basis the consonant blends selected for evaluation were originally determined as being "most critical." Twelve vowels and four phonemic diphthongs are also included in the test sample.

A unique feature of the FLTAC is the three-parameter system of distinctive feature analysis for consonant singles, including: place of articulation, manner of formation, and voicing. Place of articulation is further subdivided into areas from the most anterior to the most posterior parts of the oral cavity (from bilabial to glottal). Six categories of manner of formation are designated, such as stop, fricative, and nasal. The vowel portion, arranged for analysis according to the traditional vowel diagram, utilizes place of articulation (front, central, and back) and height of tongue blade (high, mid, and low), lip rounding, and degree of tension. The record form is well organized to allow for quick identification and analysis of the relationship between feature production and error sound. Analysis of the record form involves scanning the rows and columns for similarities in the type of misarticulations. This information is then interpreted in the summary section at the bottom of the record form.

Another unique feature of the FLTAC is its consideration of geographic and sociologic dialectal patterns of articulation. Dialectal notes in the manual enable the examiner to evaluate articulation performance within the framework of the individual's dialectal pattern. Speech pathologists have long awaited a test inventory which does not penalize speakers of other standard or prestige dialects.

The test procedure used in the FLTAC is similar to that used in other articulation inventories, such as the *Templin-Darley Tests of Articulation*. The recording of data, however, is more precise. The authors instruct the examiner to use allophonic or modifier symbols to describe distortions. Although these modifier symbols are outlined in the manual, it cannot be assumed that most speech pathologists are competent in understanding and using narrow transcription. Inclusion of the modifier symbols on the record form would be helpful for quick reference. Since the rationale for the test assumes a proficiency in narrow phonetic transcription, it would seem that reliability rests more with the examiner and his interpretation of results than with the test materials. No information on reliability is reported.

The question of validity for this test concerns itself with whether the test is actually measuring defective articulation. In terms of validity, no statistical evidence appears in the manual. How does the FLTAC correlate with other tests of articulation or outside criteria? There is, however, no reason to believe that discrepancies would occur, or that the FLTAC is

any less valid than other available tests of similar content.

Unlike earlier articulation inventories which were geared to the simple identification of defective phonemes, the FLTAC attempts to ferret out the "commonalities" of the errors. The FLTAC is innovative in its organization and procedure for recording, categorizing, and analyzing misarticulations. The major emphasis lies in discovering not only whether the phonemes are produced acceptably, but in what is done when sounds are misarticulated. It is the identification of feature violations which makes the FLTAC a unique diagnostic tool. The test provides information as to the nature of the misarticulation, the features requiring modification, and the direction for subsequent therapy.

LAWRENCE J. TURTON, *Assistant Professor of Speech Pathology and Research Program Associate, Institute for the Study of Mental Retardation and Related Disabilities, The University of Michigan, Ann Arbor, Michigan.*[1]

This test is best reviewed in the context of the purposes specified by the authors in the manual: "The test was planned with two uses in mind: (1) to achieve a more complete and systematized diagnosis of the speech deficiencies of a child with defective articulation, and (2) to furnish more reliable data for the researcher investigating the phonological development of normal children."

The question which must be answered by the potential user is simply "To what degree have the authors met their goals?" A second perspective in evaluating an articulation test is that speech and language pathology borrows heavily from other disciplines and the relationship between the date of publication of a test and the current theory of linguistics (or psychology or neurology) in vogue at that point in time is a critical variable.

The authors attempt to improve the diagnostic process for speech pathologists by incorporating the following features into their instrument: careful selection of words to be depicted in the stimulus items; careful attention to dialectical variations found in the speech of potential test subjects; specific instructions for the use of narrow phonetic transcription to

[1] The reviewer wishes to acknowledge with thanks the assistance of Carolyn M. Eckstein in the preparation of this review.

Fisher-Logemann Test of Articulation Competence

detect problems in allophonic variants of phonemes; and a data analysis procedure which incorporates a "distinctive feature analysis" and age level norms. Despite the apparent concern for detail in test construction, the test developers failed to use the same degree of rigorous standards in conceptualizing the use and interpretation of the test results. As with most commercially available articulation tests, a distinction must be made between the FLTAC as an organized collection of stimuli to obtain phonetic/phonemic data on children as opposed to a diagnostic (i.e., decision making) system.

In the first case, the FLTAC provides a clinician with a well-organized collection of stimuli and recording system for obtaining maximum information in a minimum amount of time. In terms of the latter function, interpretation and decision making, the test construction and procedures specified in the manual are not necessarily dependent upon the test stimuli. The recommended procedures can be used with any set of test results. The test is not diagnostic; it does not provide any more or less information than any other instrument.

The "diagnostic" function of articulation tests is a grossly misunderstood issue in speech pathology. The "systematized diagnosis" desired by the authors is a function of the tester (clinician) and not of an articulation test. No articulation test on the market today is diagnostic. The critical variable is the skill and knowledge which the *clinician* brings to the task. That is why the manual of the FLTAC is more important than the test booklet and the record forms.

Fisher and Logemann recommend that the clinician should attend to the age level norms provided on the record sheets, but they do not specify the source for the norms. We can assume with confidence that the norms were not derived from administration of this test to normal children. Narrow phonetic transcription is recommended as the scoring procedure. No data are provided by the authors to demonstrate that clinicians must use narrow transcriptions to make clinical judgments or, more importantly, that clinicians can reliably do narrow transcription under normal testing conditions. The complete absence of reliability and validity data in the manual reduces this "test" to a booklet of testing stimuli and a set of procedures for analyzing articulation patterns of children.

Assuming that any collection of articulation test results can be subjected to the analysis suggested in the FLTAC manual, the question regarding the value and rigor of these procedures must be answered. The manual suggests that a distinctive feature analysis should be performed with the data but then points out that the system used is not a distinctive feature but a "linguistic phonetics" analysis. The use of the term "distinctive feature analysis" is obviously questionable. The description of the procedures to do the analysis is somewhat weak. The clinician is not told how to reduce the results to a comprehensive statement of the child's articulation pattern to determine (a) the phonological rules controlling the pattern, (b) the level of severity to indicate the cutoff point to establish that a child needs treatment, and (c) the type of articulation treatment needed by the child. Even though blends are included in the single-word test stimuli (but, curiously, not in the sentence stimuli), concepts of imitation, stimulability, and the effects of phonetic context are basically ignored in the decision making process.

The FLTAC reflects one of the critical problems in human services. Collections of testing stimuli are packaged and sold under the rubric of a "test" without careful determination of the type of test intended, without rigorous standardization, particularly in terms of reliability measures for the scoring procedures, and without evidence that the instrument can reliably and consistently separate children who need services from those who do not. Before we can call a collection of stimuli a "test," the profession must insist that it conform to the standards of the American Psychological Association for test development. If the professionals do not insist upon such standards, they are open to valid criticism from their consumers.

Given the state of the art of articulation test development, the reviewer cannot recommend the FLTAC over any other instrument on the market or vice versa. Clinicians should be cognizant of the fact that their skills and abilities in interpreting testing results are more critical than the instrument. If clinicians know how to analyze phonology, to select children

Fisher-Logemann Test of Articulation Competence

who need services, and to program treatment, they will select the testing stimuli needed to answer their diagnostic questions. If they do not know how to function professionally, neither this instrument nor any other one on the market will serve as a substitute for professional knowledge or skill.

[962]

★Functional Communication Profile. Aphasic adults; 1956–69; FCP; ratings by experienced clinician following nonstructured interview; 6 scores: movement, speaking, understanding, reading, other, total; norms based on right hemiplegic patients who had suffered cerebrovascular accident; 1 form ('63, 2 pages); manual ('69, 35 pages); conversion chart ['63, 1 page]; $1 per 25 profiles and 2 conversion charts; $4 per manual; postpaid; (15–30) minutes for interview; Martha Taylor Sarno; Institute of Rehabilitation Medicine. *

REFERENCES

1. TAYLOR, MARTHA L. "A Measurement of Functional Communication in Aphasia." Arch Phys Med & Rehab 46:101–7 Ja '65. * (PA 39:16012)
2. SARNO, MARTHA TAYLOR. "Method for Multivariant Analysis of Aphasia Based on Studies of 235 Patients in a Rehabilitation Setting." Arch Phys Med & Rehab 49:210–6 Ap '68. *
3. GOODKIN, ROBERT. "Changes in Word Production, Sentence Production, and Relevance in an Aphasic Through Verbal Conditioning." Behav Res & Ther (England) 7(1):93–9 F '69. * (PA 43:9930)
4. SANDS, ELAINE S.; SARNO, MARTHA TAYLOR; AND SHANKWEILER, DONALD. "Long-Term Assessment of Language Function in Aphasia Due to Stroke." Arch Phys Med & Rehab 50(4):202–6+ Ap '69. *
5. SARNO, MARTHA TAYLOR. "A Survey of 100 Aphasic Medicare Patients in a Speech Pathology Program." J Am Geriatrics Soc 18(6):471–80 Je '70. *
6. SARNO, MARTHA TAYLOR; SILVERMAN, MARLA; AND SANDS, ELAINE. "Speech Therapy and Language Recovery in Severe Aphasia." J Speech & Hearing Res 13(3):607–23 S '70. *
7. LUDLOW, C. L., AND SWISHER, L. P. "The Audiometric Evaluation of Adult Aphasics." J Speech & Hearing Res 14(3): 535–43 S '71. * (PA 48:3504)
8. SARNO, JOHN E.; SARNO, MARTHA T.; AND LEVITA, ERIC. "Evaluating Language Improvement After Completed Stroke." Arch Phys Med & Rehab 52(2):73–8 F '71. *
9. SARNO, MARTHA TAYLOR, AND LEVITA, ERIC. "Natural Course of Recovery in Severe Aphasia." Arch Phys Med & Rehab 52(4):175–9 Ap '71. *
10. NEEDHAM, LESLIE SMITH, AND SWISHER, LINDA PECK. "A Comparison of Three Tests of Auditory Comprehension for Adult Aphasics." J Speech & Hearing Disorders 37(1):123–31 F '72. *
11. SARNO, MARTHA TAYLOR; SARNO, JOHN E.; AND DILLER, LEONARD. "The Effect of Hyperbaric Oxygen on Communication Function in Adults With Aphasia Secondary to Stroke." J Speech & Hearing Res 15(1):42–8 Mr '72. * (PA 49:11752)

RAPHAEL M. HALLER, Associate Professor of Speech Pathology and Audiology, Illinois State University, Normal, Illinois.

The Functional Communication Profile purports to be an informal inventory of daily communicative functioning of adult aphasics. According to the author, the FCP reflects the patient's "natural language use, in contrast to the 'clinical performance' elicited in formal language tests which often sample artificial behaviors." The current revision of the manual aims at updating the literature on the test while slightly altering its content and method of ad-

ministration and scoring. These alterations are not specified in the manual.

FCP data are obtained by casual interview with the patient, similar in format to the administration of the Vineland Social Maturity Scale. The examiner is cautioned to avoid taking notes or referring to the items. Videotaping is encouraged for subsequent analysis and data sheet completion. The author recognizes that the examiner must be thoroughly familiar with the behaviors to be rated, and therefore cautions that the examiner administer the inventory either frequently or not at all.

Forty-five communication behaviors are sampled, 5 under the heading of movement, 10 in speaking, 15 in understanding, 5 in reading, and 7 in other areas which include writing and numerical relationships. Each behavior is rated on a nine-point scale ranging from no response to the patient's presumed premorbid functioning level. The author's definitions of the intermediate ratings of poor, fair, and good are, unfortunately, limited to stating the percentage of the instances during the interview when the behavior under test occurred. While the author directs the examiner to attend to the consistency, speed, fluency, intelligibility, and frequency of each behavior, the relationship of these variables to the ratings is not discussed. The interrater agreement reported in the manual ranged from .87 to .97 on the various categories of the test when initially administered. Little information is available on interexaminer reliability on retest, so that the effect of increasing patient familiarity on the examiner's subsequent ratings is an open question.

FCP data entries may be analyzed in several ways. The data sheet is so organized that a patient's initial performance on each item appears in blue in bar-graph form. Retest entries are made in red, enabling the clinician to inspect readily changes in the patient's status at various stages of his medical course or therapy. Three scores are also obtained in each communication category: a raw score, a percentage of total score, and a weighted score. The maximum weighted scores in the categories are: 26 in movement, 18 in speaking, 24 in understanding, 18 in reading, and 14 in other. To explain these weightings, the manual states only that they "were derived from studies of post CVA, aphasic, right hemiplegic patients." Perhaps a detailed justification of these weightings, as well as their relevance to other populations of adult aphasics, will appear in a future revision of the manual.

In this reviewer's judgment, the FCP contains three major features which enhance its value for adult aphasics. First, it enables the speech pathologist to assess the patient's communication performance outside the clinical setting in a relatively nonthreatening manner. Second, it provides for mathematical comparison of a patient's communication abilities within and between testing sessions. Finally, it describes areas of functioning which are intelligible to other professionals, to the patient's family, and to fiscal intermediaries, which could result in better teamwork and patient care.

HARVEY HALPERN, *Professor of Communication Arts and Sciences, Queens College of The City University of New York, Flushing, New York.*

The purpose of the *Functional Communication Profile* is to objectively evaluate language in the adult aphasic. This is done by examining the "communication modalities" of movement, speaking, understanding, reading, and miscellaneous activities (writing, orientation, and calculation).

The FCP is administered through a series of five subtests representing the above modalities by employing a nonstructured interview method. As an example, speaking is tested by having the patient say greetings, own name, nouns, etc. Conversational interaction is achieved by having the examiner pose questions about the hospital stay, family, home, or vocation to the patient to elicit responses.

Scoring is done on a nine-point scale ranging from zero (no language) to normal and is based on an estimate of the patient's premorbid language level. Thus, a subscore for speaking of 62 percent means that the patient's speaking abilities are 62 percent of his premorbid level. A subscore for each of the "communication modalities" or a single overall score which indicates the patient's total functional communication can be achieved.

The test manual reports on research dealing with predictability of language recovery, reliability, and validity of the FCP. Predictability studies showed that scores on the FCP could effectively serve as a prognostic indicator for language rehabilitation. The higher the score on the FCP, the better the prognosis while a low score would make the prognosis more guarded. This is valuable since the severity of the aphasia at the onset of therapy is a known prognostic factor. Several reliability studies indicated that the FCP had a high degree of interrater and intrarater agreement.

From a number of validity studies reported, one study showed that the FCP had an "ordered relationship" (no statistics reported) with the *Minnesota Test for Differential Diagnosis of Aphasia.* Other studies showed "statistically significant relationships" (no statistics reported) between the FCP and "measures reflecting auditory attention span."

The unusual feature of the FCP is that it was designed to test the language performance of an aphasic patient in an informal and natural setting. Also, nonlinguistic variables and compensatory behavior are considered in the evaluation. This nontask-orientated approach can prove quite valuable with patients who are stymied by the typical confrontation task-orientated tests that are generally used in aphasia evaluations.

One limitation of the FCP is the subjective nature in arriving at the estimation of the patient's premorbid abilities. Age, educational level, and employment are considered in the assessment and while it may not be so difficult for the "average" patient, an evaluation of "superior" or "inferior" premorbid communication might make a rating especially difficult.

Another limitation is the claim that the profile can grossly differentiate among other types of verbal impairment. From the examples given in the test manuals, the profile scores of the patient with organic brain syndrome and not aphasia showed that the profile was able to grossly differentiate between those two syndromes. This was based on a good to normal rating in movement, speaking, understanding, and reading and a poor to fair rating in the "other" modality which included time orientation, writing, and calculating ability.

However, the second example in the manual was that of a patient with aphasia and verbal apraxia (apraxia of speech), and this profile showed the worst depression (poor to fair) in the speaking modality. There was no way of telling if the patient had verbal apraxia since the profile did not show whether the following symptoms were produced: inconsistency of articulatory error; trouble in starting; primarily substitution misarticulations; and in some, the ability to give a correct production after a number of faulty attempts. The profile did contain references to speaking attempts made during automatic and nonautomatic speech (correct production during automatic compared to non-automatic speech can be another sign of verbal apraxia) but no allusion was made to this in the interpretation of the profile.

In summation, the FCP was specifically designed to test the language performance of an aphasic patient in an informal and natural setting where scoring is based upon the patient's premorbid abilities. This nontask-orientated approach will prove to be quite valuable with patients who have excessive difficulty with the more formalized task-orientated tests. Some limitations of the FCP are the subjective nature in arriving at an estimation of the patient's premorbid abilities and the test's unclear ability to differentiate other types of verbal impairment. Because of these limitations, I would hesitate in using this test solely in making a comprehensive evaluation of the aphasic patient. I would rather use this as an adjunct to the other good tests used in aphasia with which the FCP compares rather favorably.

[963]

Halstead Aphasia Test. Adults; 1949–55; HAT; pocket-size version of the out-of-print *Halstead-Wepman Screening Test for Aphasia;* item responses grouped under 5 overlapping categories: agnosias (12 subcategories), apraxias (7), anomia, dysarthria, paraphasia (2); no data on reliability and validity; no norms; individual; Form M ['55, 15 cards]; record form ['55, 2 pages]; diagnostic code and profile must be reproduced locally; $12 per kit of test, 25 record sheets, and manual; postpaid; (30–60) minutes; Ward C. Halstead in cooperation with Joseph M. Wepman (test), Ralph M. Reitan (test), and Robert F. Heimburger (test); Industrial Relations Center, University of Chicago. *

See T2:2076 (2 references) and 7:953 (10 references).

REFERENCES

1–10. See 7:953.
11–12. See T2:2076; also includes a cumulative name index to the first 12 references for this test.
13. LEVINE, MAUREEN, AND FULLER, GERALD. "Psychological, Neuropsychological, and Educational Correlates of Reading Deficit." *J Learn Dis* 5(9):563–71 N '72. * (PA 49:9983)
14. TAYLOR, MICHAEL A.; ABRAMS, RICHARD; AND GAZTANAGA, PEDRO. "Manic-Depressive Illness and Schizophrenia: A Partial Validation of Research Diagnostic Criteria Utilizing Neuropsychological Testing." *Comprehen Psychiatry* 16(1):91–6 Ja–F '75. * (PA 54:1322)
15. GOLDSTEIN, DAVID. "Comprehension of Linguistic Ambiguity and Development of Classification." *Percept & Motor Skills* 43(3, pt 2):1050–8 D '76. * (PA 58:3097)

DANIEL R. BOONE, *Professor of Speech and Hearing Sciences, The University of Arizona, Tucson, Arizona.*

Some version of a Halstead aphasia test has been available for neurologists, psychologists, and speech pathologists since 1935. The most recent version, the *Halstead Aphasia Test,* Form M, was published in 1955 and contains basically the same stimuli and test item sequence as in the 1949 *Halstead-Wepman Aphasia Screening Test.* Form M is designed to fit in the pocket so that the neurologist can carry it with him and use it as needed "while making hospital rounds." The test booklet, only $2\frac{3}{8}$ inches by $3\frac{3}{4}$ inches, includes 51 test items. Most of the 51 test items require the patient to view the test stimuli through a small cutout window, 2 inches by $1\frac{1}{2}$ inches.

The majority of the items focus on testing agnosias and apraxias. In fact, the basic orientation of the test appears to be built around a sensory-motor dichotomy. The suggested diagnostic code and profile at the end of the test manual represent the type of diagnostic classification typically used in the 1940s, with patients classified into four types: global, expressive-receptive, expressive, and receptive. There is little descriptive terminology given to describe the kinds of aphasia the patient may demonstrate. In the category "paraphasia" there are seven items dealing with labels called "paragrammatism" and "agrammatism"; the actual task required on two of these items is to repeat after the examiner the phonemically difficult words "Massachusetts" and "Methodist Episcopal." In fact, there are only four items in the entire test that actually require the patient to attempt to formulate a spoken response beyond a naming task. A serious limitation of this test is that it does not ask the patient to say much as part of the 51 test items. The test predates present usage of linguistic concepts or terminology. There is no way to assess the patient's morphological or syntactical abilities except on four items. The clinician could probably obtain a more valid understanding of how the patient speaks by initiating a conversation with the patient rather than by administering this test.

Auditory verbal comprehension is not tested well, either. Apart from the fact that the test is orally administered, only eight items require the patient to respond to spoken item content. In administering the HAT to a small sample of aphasics, I found that it did not discriminate well between those patients who understand spoken language easily and those who understand it poorly. The majority of the test items focus on visual recognition of forms, letters, and words which require copying or writing responses. The primary deficits observed in most adult aphasic patients, auditory verbal comprehension difficulties and problems in formulating language, are only superficially tested.

While the test is easy to administer, taking only about 30 minutes for the typical patient, it does not identify well for the examiner what the particular patient's aphasic deficits may be. It also appeared to this examiner that occasional patients with hemianopsia experienced real difficulties seeing the visual stimuli appearing in the small test booklet window. Ease of administration and size convenience appear to be the test's two strongest points. Although there has been occasional literature citation of this test over the years, there has been no published attempt by the author to refine the test through item analysis, to report its reliability, or to update or change its items in the past 27 years.

In summary, the Halstead Aphasia Test does not assess aphasia in adults with the thoroughness provided by most other adult aphasia tests. The test might still be used by a neurologist who must make a quick judgment of possible visual agnosias or hand apraxias. To assess aphasia, however, the psychologist or the speech pathologist would be best advised to look beyond this test.

MANFRED J. MEIER, *Professor of Psychology and Director, Neuropsychology Laboratory, University of Minnesota, Minneapolis, Minnesota.*

Form M of the *Halstead Aphasia Test* was derived from an earlier version (1935) which introduced an innovation in format for the presentation of standard stimuli in a sequence. Stimuli were conveniently located on a cardboard dial; as a result, they could be readily used for screening purposes by military physicians during World War II. The current revision of this test introduces an innovation in test format which involves plastic stimulus cards bound flexibly in a black leather case. The manual and scoring sheets are similarly packaged in a compact form to allow ready application at bedside.

Quantitative scoring procedures and an extensive standardization were not intended to be incorporated into the development of this test. The materials were designed to elicit relatively specific signs of either localized or diffuse cerebral dysfunction utilizing assessment strategies demonstrated in the literature to be sensitive to impaired language behavior. The 1955 manual provides qualitative criteria for evaluating test responses judgmentally, utilizing verbatim response records, observation of nuances of gestures, voice, attitude, and general nonlanguage behavior of the patient, and inter-item response patterns.

As with most aphasia screening tests, formulation of inferences regarding etiology and location of the lesion must be based on the examiner's knowledge of the aphasic syndromes and their neuropathological determinants. The necessary background information is not provided in the manual. However, the criteria for interpreting the item responses and qualitative aspects of behavior observed during the data collection process are given more than cursory attention and should be quite helpful for applying the materials clinically. For example, suggestions are provided for comparing responses to interrelated items, for identifying perseverated responses, for estimating levels of severity of language disability, and for assessing verbal comprehension, paraphasic distortions, and disturbances in auditory, tactile, and visual recognition, and constructional behavior. While these suggestions for interpretation of responses may be helpful to the experienced assessor of aphasic disturbances, they would probably be insufficient for guiding the novice through effective application of the materials. This is not cited as an exclusive deficiency of this instrument, since most aphasia test manuals do not provide sufficient information to prepare the uninitiated for valid clinical application. It is provided to point up the necessity for consumers of such tests to develop the necessary clinical competencies, even for screening purposes.

It is the reviewer's impression that Form M is not in general use at this time. A later derivative of this instrument, developed by Ralph M.

Halstead Aphasia Test

Reitan and known as the Reitan-Indiana Aphasia Screening Test, has come into wider use as a result of its identification with the Halstead-Reitan neuropsychological test battery. This modification of the *Halstead-Wepman Aphasia Screening Test* (itself derived from the original Halstead aphasia test) improves upon the stimulus format found in earlier versions. The Reitan-Indiana version provides a similar format but differs in the number of stimuli included and in the size, distinctiveness, and separation of the stimuli from the instructional cues printed on the card for the benefit of the examiner. A manual of instructions can be obtained by ordering the revised materials directly from Reitan.

The necessary background information and professional competency preparation for utilizing these other materials are judged to be equivalent to those required for application of the *Halstead Aphasia Test*. Reitan (personal communication) has emphasized that the procedures are designed merely to elicit qualitative signs of disturbances in higher cortical function with implications for diffuse or focal cerebral disease. Generation of tentative hypotheses and inferences with respect to the presence and location of cerebral lesions, utilizing this approach, is part of a larger process involving an interpretation of an array of quantitative measures from the neuropsychological test battery. Much of the literature related to the Reitan-Indiana version of the test and earlier work with the *Halstead Aphasia Test* contains relevant documentation of findings in support of the conventional application of these procedures to the assessment of language disorders.

It is well known that these and related procedures are used routinely in neuropsychological test battery applications. Their use in generating hypotheses and inferences which can then be evaluated further by means of more extensive quantitative test procedures probably can be defended, provided the user has established definitive competencies in the area of language and nonlanguage disorders of focal cerebral origin. The convenience of the booklet forms has been acknowledged by the various disciplines that have utilized the test over the past few decades. For assessment requirements that transcend the screening level, more completely developed instruments, especially those with

Halstead Aphasia Test

standardization of subtests and extensive validity documentation, are recommended.

[964]

★**Language Sampling, Analysis, and Training.** Children with language delay; 1974; no data on reliability; no norms; individual; no reading by examinees; 1 form, 6 parts; manual (56 pages including sample worksheets); visual and verbal stimuli for eliciting language sample determined by examiner; tape recorder recommended to record responses; $16.50 per 25 sets of worksheets; $5 per 3 sets of worksheets and handbook; $3.25 per handbook; postage extra; Dorothy Tyack and Robert Gottsleben; Consulting Psychologists Press, Inc. *
a) TRANSCRIPTION SHEETS. 1 form (4 pages); $8 per 50 worksheets; (30–90) minutes.
b) WORD/MORPHEME TALLY AND SUMMARY. 6 scores: 3 totals (sentences, words, morphemes) and 3 means (words/sentence, morphemes/sentence, word-morpheme index); 1 form (1 page); $3.50 per 50 worksheets; (10) minutes.
c) SEQUENCE OF LANGUAGE ACQUISITION. Assessment of 6 areas: noun phrase constituents, verb phrase constituents, constructions, complex sentences, negation, questions; 1 form (4 pages); $8 per 50 worksheets; (30) minutes.
d) BASELINE AND GOAL DATA. 1 form (2 pages); $3.50 per 50 worksheets; (20) minutes.
e) TRAINING WORKSHEET. 1 form (2 pages); prices same as for *d*; (10) minutes.
f) SCORE SHEET. 1 form (1 page); prices same as for *d*; used during training lesson.

[965]

*National Teacher Examinations: Speech-Communication and Theatre.** College seniors and teachers; 1970–77; test administered 3 times annually (February, July, November) at centers established by the publisher; Forms ZNT1 ('77, 18 pages), ZNT2 ('77, 17 pages); descriptive booklet ('76, 7 pages); for program accessories, see 381; examination fee, $11 per candidate; 120(165) minutes; Educational Testing Service. *
For reviews of the testing program, see 381 (2 reviews) and 7:582 (2 reviews).

[966]

*National Teacher Examinations: Speech Pathology.** College seniors and teachers; 1970–77; test administered 3 times annually (February, July, November) at centers established by the publisher; Forms K-WNT ('74, 21 pages), ZNT1 ('77, 19 pages), ZNT2 ('77, 18 pages); descriptive booklet ('76, 8 pages); for program accessories, see 381; examination fee, $13 per candidate; 120(165) minutes; Educational Testing Service. *
For reviews of the testing program, see 381 (2 reviews) and 7:582 (2 reviews).

MARGARET C. BYRNE, *Professor of Speech Pathology and Audiology, University of Kansas, Lawrence, Kansas.* [Review of Form WNT.]

This is the examination taken by majors in speech pathology at the completion of their work for the M.A. degree or its equivalent. A passing score is one of the requirements for those who wish to obtain the Certificate of Clinical Competency (CCC) in speech pathology, issued by the Committee on Clinical Certification of the American Speech and Hearing Association. The Certificate is one indicator that its holder has sufficient basic knowledge in this field to be recommended to carry out clinical programs for those with communicative disorders.

The 150 questions for this test have been prepared by several experts in one facet of the field. The content areas include acoustics; anatomy and physiology of the speech and hearing mechanism; descriptive phonetics; instrumentation; normal and deficient articulation, language, voice, and fluency; linguistics; specific disorders associated with aphasia, cleft palate, laryngectomy, cerebral palsy, autism, mental retardation, dysarthrias; application of clinical principles and information to specific clinical cases; basic audiology; learning theory; intelligence and personality testing; research design and interpretation; and professional and ethical principles.

The questions are multiple choice, with the testee marking the best of five choices. Guessing is penalized. The test takes two hours. Eighty percent of the original sample completed all items within the time limit.

This 1974 edition was administered to 369 candidates, presumably representative of the training programs in speech pathology, although no information is provided about the sample in the in-house test analysis report, which does present several statistical analyses. The mean of correct answers was 60, and the standard deviation 23. All raw scores were converted to standard scores, using data on the 38 items common to this and to the earlier version. Thus, a raw score of 60 has a standard score of 610. Percentile ranks have also been provided. A score of 610 places the testee at the 46th percentile. The range of raw scores was 0 to 107, with a median of 63. Almost one-half of the scores fell between 55 and 80. Some testees got less than one-third of the items correct, and only a few (six) got more than two-thirds correct.

The 1974 edition has been updated to reflect new information in speech pathology. Approximately two-thirds of the total 150 questions are different from those in the 1972 edition.

This is the most carefully prepared and evaluated test in the field of speech pathology. It is factual and covers a wide range of topics from the total field of normal and pathologic communicative disorders. The testee must know structure, function, and breakdown. It should continue to be a primary measure of what the students know about speech pathology. Hopefully, training institutions will require more academic sophistication from their future students in training, so that the scores will rise as the students demonstrate their increased knowledge.

[967]

*Northwestern Syntax Screening Test.** Ages 3–7; 1969–71; NSST; 2 scores: receptive, expressive; no data on reliability; individual; 1 form ['69, 42 cards in manual]; manual ('71, 13 pages plus cards and record form); record form ('69, 1 page); $10.30 per kit including 50 record forms; $2.71 per 50 record forms; cash orders only; (15) minutes; Laura Lee; Northwestern University Press. *
See T2:2084 (3 references).

REFERENCES

1–3. See T2:2084.
4. FIESTER, ALAN R., AND GIAMBRA, LEONARD M. "Language Indices of Vocational Success in Mentally Retarded Adults." Am J Mental Def 77(3):332–7 N '72. * (PA 50:3442)
5. HANSON, IRENE. "The Use of Two Language Screening Tests With Kindergarten Children." El Engl 49(7):1102–5 N '72. *
6. LAW, SUSAN NOBLE. The Use of the Northwestern Syntax Screening Test as an Aid to Programing and Measurement of Language Change. Master's thesis, Utah State University (Logan, Utah), 1972.
7. TROTTER, GWENDOLYN TOWNSEND. An Exploration of the Syntactic Performance of Second and Third Grade Black Children. Doctor's thesis, Southern Illinois University (Carbondale, Ill.), 1972. (DAI 33:4991A)
8. BERRY, MARY D., AND ERICKSON, ROBERT L. "Speaking Rate: Effects on Children's Comprehension of Normal Speech." J Speech & Hearing Res 16(3):367–74 S '73. * (PA 51:8884)
9. FARRELL, MONA. The Predictive Relationship of Selected Oral Language Variables to Reading Achievement in First-Grade Inner-City Children. Doctor's thesis, McGill University (Montreal, Que., Canada), 1973. (DAI 34:3986A)
10. LIVELY-WEISS, MARY ANN, AND KOLLER, DONALD E. "Selected Language Characteristics of Middle-Class and Inner-City Children." J Commun Disorders (Netherlands) 6(4):293–302 D '73. * (PA 52:5300)
11. PRESSNELL, LUCILLE McKINNEY. "Hearing-Impaired Children's Comprehension and Production of Syntax in Oral Language." J Speech & Hearing Res 16(1):12–21 Mr '73. *
12. CARTWRIGHT, LYNN R., AND LASS, NORMAN J. "A Comparative Study of Children's Performance on the Token Test, Northwestern Syntax Screening Test, and Peabody Picture Vocabulary Test." Acta Symbolica 5(1):19–29 '74. * (PA 54:11386)
13. MATHENY, ADAM P., JR., AND DOLAN, ANNE BROWN. "A Twin Study of Genetic Influences in Reading Achievement." J Learn Dis 7(2):99–102 F '74. * (PA 52:6326)
14. PATELLA, CARMEN C. Performance of Aurally-Handicapped Children on the Receptive Portion of the Northwestern Syntax Screening Test Administered With and Without Cued Speech. Master's thesis, California State University (Sacramento, Calif.), 1974.
15. RAMSTAD, VIVIAN V., AND POTTER, ROBERT E. "Differences in Vocabulary and Syntax Usage Between Nez Perce Indian and White Kindergarten Children." J Learn Dis 7(8):491–7 O '74. * (PA 53:5278)
16. BALABAN, MAE JANET. Performance of Black and White Children on a Black Dialect and a Standard English Receptive Syntax Screening Test. Doctor's thesis, Columbia University (New York, N.Y.), 1975. (DAI 36:6595A)
17. BANNATYNE, MARYL. "Review of the Northwestern Syntax Screening Test." J Learn Dis 8(4):196–7 Ap '75. *
18. CRIPE, ANTJE E. "Review of Northwestern Syntax Screening Test," pp. 455–7. In Pediatric Screening Tests. Edited by William K. Frankenburg and Bonnie W. Camp.

Northwestern Syntax Screening Test

Springfield, Ill.: Charles C Thomas, Publisher, 1975. Pp. xii, 549. *

19. PANNBACKER, MARY. "Comment on the 'Expressive Portion of the NSST Compared to a Spontaneous Language Sample,' " Letter. Reply by Carol A. Prutting, Tanya M. Gallagher, and Anthony Mulac. *J Speech & Hearing Disorders* 40(4): 544–5 N '75. *

20. PRUTTING, CAROL A.; GALLAGHER, TANYA M.; AND MULAC, ANTHONY. "The Expressive Portion of the NSST Compared to a Spontaneous Language Sample." *J Speech & Hearing Disorders* 40(1):40–8 F '75. * (PA 54:1423)

21. RATUSNIK, DAVID L., AND KOENIGSKNECHT, ROY A. "Internal Consistency of the Northwestern Syntax Screening Test." *J Speech & Hearing Disorders* 40(1):59–68 F '75. * (PA 54:1424)

22. RIZZO, JEAN MICHALIK. *Performance of Children With Normal and Delayed Oral Language Production on a Set of Comprehension Tests.* Doctor's thesis, Purdue University (Lafayette, Ind.), 1975. (DAI 37:1192B)

23. SEMEL, ELEANOR M., AND WIIG, ELISABETH H. "Comprehension of Syntactic Structures and Critical Verbal Elements by Children With Learning Disabilities." *J Learn Dis* 8(1): 46–51 Ja '75. * (PA 53:11963)

24. WALKER, HOWARD J.; ROODIN, PAUL A.; AND LAMB, MARY JEANNE. "Relationship Between Linguistic Performance and Memory Deficits in Retarded Children." *Am J Mental Def* 79(5):545–52 Mr '75. * (PA 54:3447)

25. BERRY, MAURIE MICHELE, AND MUNCY, MARGARET JEAN. *An Investigation of the Interrelationship Between Articulation, Receptive and Expressive Language Performance of Primary School Aged Children.* Doctor's thesis, University of Northern Colorado (Greeley, Colo.), 1976. (DAI 37:2107A)

26. HERRON, BETTY JUNE. *Relationship Between Communication Channel Clearance and Linguistic Rules: Learning Disabled and Normal Learning Language Usage.* Doctor's thesis, University of Cincinnati (Cincinnati, Ohio), 1976. (DAI 37:1489A)

27. HOLDSTEIN, ILANA, AND BORUS, JUDITH F. "Kibbutz and City Children: A Comparative Study of Syntactic and Articulatory Abilities." *J Speech & Hear Dis* 41(1):10–5 F '76. * (PA 57:875)

28. LARSON, GEORGE W., AND SUMMERS, PATRICIA A. "Response Patterns of Pre-School-Age Children to the Northwestern Syntax Screening Test." *J Speech & Hear Dis* 41(4):486–97 N '76. *

29. LUTERMAN, DAVID M. "A Comparison of Language Skills of Hearing Impaired Children Trained in a Visual/Oral Method and an Auditory/Oral Method." *Am Ann Deaf* 121(4):389–93 Ag '76. * (PA 57:2009)

MARIE C. FONTANA, *Assistant Professor of Communication Arts and Sciences, Queens College of The City University of New York, Flushing, New York.*

This test was designed to identify children ages 3–7 who are "sufficiently deviant in syntactic development to warrant further study." As such, this test does not propose to measure a child's general language ability. Additionally, the author urges that the NSST not be considered as an in-depth measurement of syntactic ability but intends that it be used as a screening instrument to identify those in need of further study and analysis.

The test measures the reception and expression of sentence structure, transformations, and morphological forms in each of 20 sentence pairs. Both parts require the same linguistic tasks using different vocabulary and picture stimuli. The author suggests that the sentence pairs increase in difficulty of grammatic contrasts, but neither the nature of the grammatic contrasts nor the basis for the supposed differences in difficulty among sentence pairs is specified anywhere in the manual.

Northwestern Syntax Screening Test

Administration of the entire test can be accomplished in about 15 minutes. Receptive and expressive syntactic scores can be compared with normative data collected on 344 middle-class children. In order to use the normative data, one must give the entire test. The author advises, however, that the examiner may assume that a child will fail the segment tested if he demonstrates failure on the first 10 sentence pairs of that same segment.

The receptive portion of the test consists of 20 plates containing four line-drawn pictures per plate, two of which are decoy pictures. The remaining two pictures are to be identified by the child in the order prescribed on the record form. That is, the examiner is instructed to read the sentences in order as they appear on the record form but is to elicit the identification of the asterisked sentence of each pair first.

The expressive portion is similar to the receptive portion except that there are two pictures per plate, the decoy pictures having been eliminated. The child is instructed to listen to both sentences and to "copy" the examiner. Similarly, after *both* sentences are presented in order, the examiner elicits a verbal response to the asterisked one first by asking, "What's this picture?" After the child has responded, the examiner seeks a response to the picture corresponding to the unasterisked sentence. Whether this procedure examines a child's imitative ability more than his expressive syntactic ability is a question that deserves serious thought and has implictions for the validity of the test.

Scoring of the receptive portion involves recording one point for each correct identification made on each sentence. A perfect score on each part, receptive and expressive, is 40. Scoring the expressive syntactic items, however, is more problematic. The author indicates that failure on this part may be one of two kinds. If the child fails to use the grammatic structure of the test item as spoken by the examiner, or if the response contains a grammatic error, even though it is not the test item, it is scored as incorrect. Although some examples of correct and incorrect responses are included in the manual, the examiner could be hard put to make some decisions because the manual does not specify the grammatical distinctions sampled by each test item. The manual should include these distinctions to provide the scope of the test, as well as to assist the examiner in scoring responses.

There is no doubt that a test of this kind is sorely needed, especially to screen large populations of young children. To be useful, however, a test instrument must be valid and reliable. Screening tests can be useful if they provide a comparison of a child's performance with his peers. Although the author has included norms from scores collected on 344 children, validity of the test cannot be assumed. No statistical analysis indicating the criteria for item selection is included in the manual. This raises a serious question about the correlation of the NSST with outside criteria. For example, the nature of the expressive portion would have us conclude that a grammatical distinction has not been acquired on the basis of a child's failure to model a verbal expression which includes that grammatical construct. Prutting, Gallagher, and Mulac (20) compared the expressive portion with a spontaneous language sample and found that 30 percent of those syntactic structures incorrectly produced on the NSST were correctly produced in a spontaneous language sample. The discrepancy was attributed to the operational and psychological constraints of the NSST, which require the child to store and repeat a sentence which could be at variance with the response form he would use.

Despite these criticisms, the test has enjoyed widespread use as a screening tool. Its major strength is its application of current knowledge of language development to the assessment of syntactic ability. Earlier tests used for the rapid assessment of language ability focused on measures of receptive and expressive vocabulary. It must be emphasized, however, that the test should not be used beyond its stated purpose as a screening instrument. Screening tests, although useful, are of limited value. The examiner is cautioned to guard against overinterpretation of results. The expressive portion of this test may underestimate the child's spontaneous language performance. It is suggested, further, that information obtained should be supplemented by data from spontaneous speech.

R. Duane Logue, *Professor of Speech and Language and Auditory Pathology, East Carolina University, Greenville, North Carolina.*

This test is probably one of the most fre-
quently used instruments for the identification of children's deficits in the reception and expression of morphologic and syntactic forms. The author has been appropriately cautious in specifying the purposes of the NSST, indicating that it "is intended to be used as a screening instrument only; it is, in no sense, to be considered a measurement of a child's general language skill nor even as an 'in-depth' study of syntax." Paradoxically, it would seem that the misuse and misinterpretation of the NSST has reflected its greatest deficit and in turn has generated the most criticism. It has been frequently noted by this reviewer that the NSST is often employed by clinicians to provide information well beyond its specified scope as a screening device and sometimes even to develop treatment plans. This "overextending" should be avoided.

This test has receptive and expressive portions, each consisting of 20 items arranged in increasing order of difficulty. In the receptive section, the child is required to match a sentence spoken by the examiner with the proper pictorial reference from a set of four line drawings. The expressive section contains 20 sentence pairs sampling progressively more difficult syntactic forms. Each of the 20 items of the expressive subtest is referenced to two pictures on the same page and the examiner identifies both pictures using spoken sentences provided in the manual. In a grammatically and semantically correct sentence which does not change the test item, the child must repeat what the examiner has said. The grammatical items tested via the receptive and expressive sections include: prepositions, personal pronouns, plurals, negatives, verb tenses, reflexive pronouns, possessives, wh-questions, yes-no questions, passives, and indirect objects.

Each response is scored correct or incorrect. It is important to note that in the expressive portion, any response containing a grammatical error is considered a failure. This scoring decision has met with substantial criticism (20) because the specific grammatical distinction being tested may, in fact, be correct. This demand for precise speech imitation, sometimes in the absence of generative language potential, is the test's major deficiency.

Scores derived from the test are discussed in the test manual relative to statistical pertinence:

medians, standard deviations, and selected percentiles are given for chronological ages. Other general procedures for score interpretation and significance are provided. The so-called normative sample of 344 children was drawn from middle and upper middle income groups representing nursery and public schools. No reliability and validity assessment is given in the manual.

Linguistically deficient children were excluded from the sample. The sampling procedure and population studied precludes the use of the test, in any standardized fashion, with dialect groups other than standard American dialect.

The NSST is most definitely weakest in the expressive section, relying much too heavily on the imitative response mode, and in so doing, often penalizing the child who may in fact be a *language generator*. The reviewer's clinical experience with this test indicates that quite frequently the child, who upon more detailed spoken language sampling reflects syntactic competency, may well respond inaccurately and inconsistently to the NSST. The expressive portion would seem to provide minimal information relative to the morphology and syntax of a child's spoken language—even for screening purposes. Finally, the test is not semantically based and it is suggested that by analyzing syntax the screening procedure may in fact fail, even in a cursory form, to identify the pragmatic fundamentals of language development and usage in children.

J Learn Dis 8(4):196–7 Ap '75. Maryl Bannatyne. * Since the NSST is based on standard American dialect, it is an inappropriate language development test for other dialect groups. For example, one would not use this test with a disadvantaged or bilingual child to determine whether either was "language delayed" or "language deficient." It *could* be used with these children, however, to ascertain how well they, or children of another dialect group, *used* standard American dialect. The NSST involves only syntactic structure and is consequently intended to be a screening instrument. I highly recommend that preschool, kindergarten and first grade teachers use this test to identify children who deviate in syntactic development from their peers, especially in the area of expressive syntactic forms. NSST will assess specific areas of grammatical confusion and could provide teaching goals in an enrichment language program. Language research investigators will find it useful as a pre- and posttest measuring the acquisition of syntax.

[968]

★The Ohio State University Test for Identifying Misarticulations. Speech clinicians and senior speech majors; 1965; various titles used by publisher; "reliability of speech clinicians and researchers in the recognition of misarticulations"; 4 scores: isolated words, phrases, 3-word groups, total; for reliability data, see *1* below; 2 forms: Films A, B, (16 mm. sound); directions (2 pages, mimeographed); films may be rented ($10 per 3-day period, postage extra) or purchased ($175, postpaid); answer booklets must be reproduced locally; 22(30) minutes; Ruth Beckey Irwin; Department of Photography and Cinema, Ohio State University. *

REFERENCES

1. IRWIN, RUTH BECKEY, AND KRAFCHICK, IVAN PAUL. "An Audio-Visual Test for Evaluating the Ability to Recognize Phonetic Errors." *J Speech & Hearing Res* 8(3):281–90 S '65. *

[969]

Photo Articulation Test. Ages 3–12; 1969; PAT; 4 scores: tongue sounds, lip sounds, vowel sounds, total; individual; 1 form; 1 manual (19 pages plus 8 sheets of test pictures and record sheet); 72 individual picture cards for further diagnosis and therapy; record sheet (2 pages); $14.75 per manual and set of individual cards; $2 per 96 record sheets; cash orders postpaid; [2–20] minutes; Kathleen Pendergast, Stanley E. Dickey, John W. Selmar, and Anton L. Soder; Interstate Printers & Publishers, Inc. *
See 7:962 (2 references).

REFERENCES

1–2. See 7:962.
3. DREXLER, HAZEL G. "Review of Photo Articulation Test." pp. 459–60. In *Pediatric Screening Tests*. Edited by William K. Frankenburg and Bonnie W. Camp. Springfield, Ill.: Charles C Thomas, Publisher, 1975. Pp. xii, 549. *

LAWRENCE D. SHRIBERG, *Associate Professor of Speech Pathology, University of Wisconsin, Madison, Wisconsin.*

Speech clinicians will recognize the *Photo Articulation Test* as a conventional picture-naming procedure for obtaining a phonetic inventory from young children. As with some two dozen commercially available tests of this type, a child's articulation of English consonants and selected clusters, vowels, and diphthongs are evoked in word-initial, -medial, and -final position by means of pictured nouns. According to the authors, desirable features of this test are: (a) 72 color photographs of objects (arranged in arrays of nine per page in the test manual and included also on individual cards) have high recognizability with young children; (b) the stimuli and the test form are arranged to provide separate scores for tongue, lip, and vowel sounds; (c) the deck of individual photographs and a supplemental word list may be used to obtain information on consistency of error, effects of phonetic context, and stimulability; and (d) administration time is generally five minutes or less. Normative data for 684 white, middle class children are provided for the tongue, lip, and vowel subscales. Means and standard deviations are presented for boys and girls in six-month age groups from 3 to 12 years; at least 25 children of each sex were tested at each age group.

A fair critique of this articulation test must exclude from consideration reference to most of the recent theoretical and methodological issues in child phonology. Three-position articulation tests address only the "articulatory" level of speech behavior. More recent views of normal and deviant child phonology are concerned also with questions about children's comprehension of adult phonology, e.g., their knowledge of distributional rules and phonotactic, morphophonemic, and phonetic change rules. Three-position articulation testing is likely to be used for some time, however, for screening if not for diagnostic decisions. For such purposes, several aspects of the PAT warrant critical inspection: the stimuli, the format, validity and reliability data, and general information presented in the test manual.

Clinical experience with this test indicates that children do readily name the photographs used as stimuli. In the service of high recognition value, however, many linguistic attributes of these stimuli are uncontrolled. For example, the effects on production of syllabic structure, grammatical function, and phonetic context are all unknown sources of variance. To their credit, the authors suggest that all errors on test items be confirmed by having the child respond to words from the supplementary word list. In practice, however, three-position testing procedures are so well ingrained that clinicians are likely to ignore this suggestion.

The PAT's unique sequence of test items and format for recording responses is inefficient, if not counterproductive. Other three-position tests sequence items to either parallel the developmental ages associated with each sound or to facilitate a phonetic feature analysis (place nested within manner). The PAT, however, groups sounds by a hybrid logic, i.e., tongue sounds, lip sounds, and vowels. Testing begins by having the child produce five of the six sibilants (each in initial, medial, and final position), followed by four lingua-alveolars, a lingua-dental, a retroflex, and the two velar cognates—all of which are scored as a subscale for tongue sounds. The authors claim that this sequence promotes "diagnostic" observations about tongue tip behaviors, but they do not present information to amplify or substantiate this rationale. The organization is counterproductive in two ways. First, the initial 18 test items require production of the most difficult class of sounds to articulate—sibilants. Hence, most children with articulation errors experience failure during the entire first third of the test session. Second, for the clinician, the test data must be reshuffled in order to form a developmental (sound or feature class) perspective.

Validity and reliability data, as presented in a total of 13 lines in the manual, suggest barely a nod in the direction of psychometric rigor. Concurrent validity coefficients were obtained by comparing the responses on the PAT of 100 (unspecified) children to their responses on the *Templin-Darley Tests of Articulation* and one other test. Validity coefficients in the high .90s are based on "comparable items." Given the rationale and subscale norms for this test, validity coefficients at the subscale level would be more appropriate. Test-retest stability for 100 children is reported to be .99. Such spuriously high validity and reliability coefficients are essentially meaningless, in the absence of data at the level of error sounds, error type, and position of error for each age group.

In comparison to information presented in the manuals of the Templin-Darley, Goldman-Fristoe, and Fisher-Logemann articulation tests, the PAT manual is at best uninformative. Missing completely is test-related information on phonological development, sociolinguistic differences, diagnosis, and predictive indices. The stimulability directions are particularly sketchy. The suggestion to use the deck of individual photographs for therapy programs is ill-advised; such use precludes further use of these photographs as test stimuli to monitor a child's progress.

Overall, the one feature of the PAT that compares favorably with other commercially available three-position tests is that children do

Photo Articulation Test

respond readily to the photographs. This is of no small import to clinicians who value spontaneous testing and who need a rapid procedure for testing young children. On all other criteria, however, the Templin-Darley, Goldman-Fristoe, and Fisher-Logemann tests are more fully developed instruments. Clinicians should be aware that a new generation of phonological assessment procedures is currently in development. Administration and subsequent analyses using these procedures will require familiarity with recent developments in the study of normal and deviant child phonology.

[970]

★Picture Articulation & Language Screening Test. Grade 1; 1976; PALST; 3 parts: language abilities, initial and final sounds (administered only if part 1 score is below cutoff point), sounds in isolation (optional); no data on reliability; no norms; individual; 1 form; pictures and directions booklet (32 pages); no manual; record sheet (1 page); $18 per picture booklet and 24 record sheets; $1.50 per 24 record sheets; cash orders postpaid; (1–3) minutes; William C. Rodgers; Word Making Productions. *

[971]

Porch Index of Communicative Ability. Aphasic adults; 1967–71; PICA; for a downward extension, see 972; 22 scores: gestural (8 unnamed subtest scores and total), verbal (4 unnamed subtest scores and total), graphic (6 unnamed subtest scores and total), total; individual; 1 form ['67]: test objects, stimulus cards, and 6 graphic test sheets; revised administration manual ('71, 123 pages); technical manual ('67, 62 pages); format booklet ['67, 25 pages]; score sheet ('67, 1 page); 2 summary profiles ['67, 1 page]; $70 per set of materials for testing 25 subjects; $20 per 50 sets of graphic test sheets; $2.50 per 50 summary profiles; postage extra; (30–60) minutes; Bruce E. Porch; Consulting Psychologists Press, Inc. *

See T2:2087 (2 references); for a review by Daniel R. Boone, see 7:963 (1 reference).

REFERENCES

1. See 7:963.
2–3. See T2:2087.
4. HORSFALL, GEOFFREY HAMILTON. An Investigation of Selected Language Performance in Adult Schizophrenic Subjects. Doctor's thesis, University of Florida (Gainesville, Fla.), 1972. (DAI 34:452B)
5. MARSHALL, ROBERT C., AND KING, PHILIP S. "Effects of Fatigue Produced by Isokinetic Exercise on the Communication Ability of Aphasic Adults." J Speech & Hearing Res 16(2):222–30 Je '73. *
6. BROOKSHIRE, R. H. "Differences in Responding to Auditory Verbal Materials Among Aphasic Patients." Acta Symbolica 5(1):1–18 '74. * (PA 54:12078)
7. DEAL, JON L. "Consistency and Adaptation in Apraxia of Speech." J Commun Disorders 7(2):135–40 Je '74. *
8. McGEE, ANNELL. An Experimental Approach to the Assessment of Dyscalculia in Aphasia. Doctor's thesis, University of Denver (Denver, Colo.), 1974. (DAI 36:179B)
9. PORCH, BRUCE E. "Comments on Silverman's 'Psychometric Problem.'" Letter. J Speech & Hearing Disorders 39(2):226–7 My '74. *
10. SILVERMAN, FRANKLIN H. "The Porch Index of Communicative Ability (PICA): A Psychometric Problem and Its Solution." Letter. J Speech & Hearing Disorders 39(2):225–6 My '74. *
11. SKURDA, RAYMOND CARL. A Multivariate Battery and Regression Equation as a Predictor of Rehabilitation Outcome of Stroke Patients. Doctor's thesis, University of Detroit (Detroit, Mich.), 1974. (DAI 37:1930B)
12. VANDEMARK, ANN A. "Comment on PICA Interpretation." Letter. J Speech & Hearing Disorders 39(4):510–1 N '74. *
13. BARNES, JANICE ELLEN. Correlation of Test Performance on the Porch Index of Communicative Ability With the Localization of Cerebral Function in Patients With Tumors of the Brain. Doctor's thesis, Ohio State University (Columbus, Ohio), 1975. (DAI 36:1163B)
14. CHAPEY, ROBERTA. Divergent Semantic Behavior in Aphasia. Doctor's thesis, Columbia University (New York, N.Y.), 1975. (DAI 36:6091B)
15. CORLEW, MARILYN M., AND NATION, JAMES E. "Characteristics of Visual Stimuli and Naming Performance in Aphasic Adults." Cortex (Italy) 11(2):186–91 Je '75. * (PA 55:10099)
16. DiSIMONI, FRANK G.; KEITH, ROBERT L.; HOLT, DENNIS L.; AND DARLEY, FREDERIC L. "Practicality of Shortening the Porch Index of Communicative Ability." J Speech & Hearing Res 18(3):491–9 S '75. *
17. HELMICK, JOSEPH W.; WATAMORI, TOSHIKO S.; AND PALMER, JOHN M. "Spouses' Understanding of the Communication Disabilities of Aphasic Patients." J Speech & Hear Dis 41(2):238–43 My '76. * (PA 57:6154)

MARGARET C. BYRNE, Professor of Speech Pathology and Audiology, University of Kansas, Lawrence, Kansas.

This test was developed as a clinical tool for aphasic patients who had communication difficulties related to a medically diagnosed brain injury. It is based on a theoretical model of communication that has three parts: (a) input of information through visual, tactile, and auditory channels; (b) integration; and (c) output through gestural, verbal, and graphic modalities. It measures the three modalities of the output system in a series of 18 subtests. Each subtest uses the same 10 common objects, such as matches, fork, cigarette, and pen. Directions for all facets of the administration of the test and the analyses of the scores are easy to follow and complete. Interpretation of the test scores of an individual is based on the performance of other aphasic patients on whom the test was standardized. It is possible to classify the patient broadly in one of five clinical categories: uncomplicated aphasia; aphasia with verbal formulation problems; aphasia with accompanying illiteracy; bilateral brain damage; and nonaphasia.

The scoring system uses a multidimensional scale. It has 16 categories that take into account the problems that aphasic patients demonstrate in carrying out tasks. These problems are accuracy; responsiveness, the amount of information the patient needs to complete the task; completeness of the response; promptness in making a response; and efficiency, or facility in carrying out the motor aspects. To obtain 16 points the patient must provide an "accurate, responsive, complex, immediate, elaborative" answer. For 9 points he must give an accurate response, but either it is delayed or he requires a repetition of the instructions. For 2 points he attends but does not respond, and for 1, he shows "no awareness of the test item."

Any system as complex as this one requires stable clinical judgments. Both high intra-tester and inter-tester reliability must be developed initially and then maintained through some system of follow-up. A minimum of 40 hours of training supervised by a qualified examiner is crucial if the new tester is to obtain the level of competency needed to score responses. Maintenance of consistency in scoring is also essential so that interpretation of follow-up tests will be accurate.

In order to evaluate the stability of the multi-dimensional scoring, the test battery itself, and the scores as predictors of classes of communication deficits, 150 patients with varying degrees of communicative difficulty were tested over a two-year period. In the 1967 manual, the author reported that the statistical data support his contention that the test is sensitive in sorting out patients according to their abilities; that the subtests have internal consistency; that the scores when grouped by modalities show clusters of success or failure; and that the scoring system is highly reliable when used by those with special training on the PICA. Statistical analyses of test-retest scores of 40 patients for overall, and for each of the three modalities scores, yielded stability coefficients of at least .96.

Whether or not this is a valid instrument for the aphasic patient is open to question. It is difficult to determine validity for a test that has several unique features. Those clinicians who administer PICA routinely find it measures the three modalities and enables them to plan more adequate intervention. Since many clinicians prefer the *Minnesota Test for Differential Diagnosis of Aphasia,* or some other, we can only hypothesize that they do not consider it valid or that they have not been trained in its administration. The PICA is one defensible approach to the study of aphasia, but it is not the only one.

[972]

★**Porch Index of Communicative Ability in Children.** Prekgn–kgn, grades 1–6; 1973–74; PICAC; for the adult test, see 971; experimental; no data on reliability and validity; no norms; individual; 1 form ['73]: test objects, stimulus cards, and 2 graphic test sheets; 2 levels; manual, volume 2 ('74, 133 pages); format booklet ['74, 41 pages]; score sheet ['73, 1 page]; set of 3 profiles ['73, 1 page]; $52.50 per set of materials for testing 25 subjects; $20 per 50 sets of

profiles and graphic test sheets; postage extra; (30–120) minutes; Bruce E. Porch; Consulting Psychologists Press, Inc. *

a) BASIC BATTERY. Prekgn–kgn; 15 subtest scores: verbal (function, naming, completion, imitation), gestural function, auditory (function, commands, names), reading names, visual (pictures, matching), graphic (dictated, spelled, copying, geometric forms) plus 7 derived scores: overall, gestural, verbal, graphic, general comprehension, visual, auditory.

b) ADVANCED BATTERY. Grades 1–6; 20 subtest scores (same as for *a* except for deletion of visual matching and graphic geometric forms and the addition of reading [function, backwards], verbal description, graphic [function, names, drawing], drawing copying) plus 7 derived scores (same as for *a*).

LON L. EMERICK, *Professor of Speech Pathology, Northern Michigan University, Marquette, Michigan.*

This clinical test is designed to evaluate and quantify selected verbal, gestural, and graphic abilities in children. The format and scoring system for the PICAC are essentially similar to that of the *Porch Index of Communicative Ability* published more than a decade ago.

A distinctive feature of the Porch instruments is the scoring system. Employing the dimensions of "accuracy," "responsiveness," "completeness," "promptness," and "efficiency," each response is scored on a 16-category rating scale. The clearly written and well-organized PICAC manual specifies that the reliability of the diagnostician is critical; it is estimated that at least 40 hours of study and practice, preferably with assistance from a clinician trained in using the test, is necessary in order to use the instrument adequately. The author urges standard procedure when using the test so that comparisons between a given patient's scores and the norms for a standardizing population will have greater validity.

Although the PICAC is useful for establishing baseline data with respect to certain aspects of language functioning, its usefulness is limited for the following reasons: (*a*) There is a lack of subtests which tap verbal abilities. The Basic Battery features only four tests of verbal output and the Advanced Battery has only five tasks which assess oral/language production. (*b*) The scoring system does not allow for qualitative assessment of a child's linguistic performance; that is, it does not specifically evaluate the syntactical features a child is or is not using. (Parenthetically, the reviewer questions the use of means and standard deviations on data which are clearly ordinal in nature; the 16-category

Porch Index of Communicative Ability in Children

scoring system does not appear to be equal-interval in nature.) (*e*) Both batteries commence with a most complex language task—explaining the function of 10 standard objects. The evidence seems clear that if the patient fails on the initial task in a series of subtests, the impact of failure will seriously depress subsequent performance. (*d*) Most pre-educational children have little or no experience with reading and writing, and this reviewer can see little reason for the inclustion of three subtests assessing these areas on the Basic Battery. (*e*) The PICAC does not elicit "real" communication situations as Lee, Muma, Holland, and others advocate. It is obvious that a program of treatment is guided more appropriately by careful study of samples of a child's ongoing communicative behavior. (*f*) At the present time it is difficult to assess the PICAC since no data as to reliability and validity are available.

On balance, there are more accurate and efficient methods of obtaining a comprehensive sample of a child's language performance. Although the manual is complete, as far as it goes, a potential user of the PICAC should receive training in its use from someone skilled with the instrument. At the present time, we use portions of the test in a battery of tasks when assessing children with language impairments. Our opinion is that this is probably the only way or, at least, one of the few ways in which the instrument can be used with any kind of confidence at this time.

[973]

*Predictive Screening Test of Articulation. Grade 1; 1968–73; PSTA; identification of children unlikely to master normal articulation by end of grade 2 without speech therapy; individual; no reading by examinees; 1 form ('68, 9 pages presented in manual); manual, fourth edition ('75, 24 pages, identical with 1973 third edition manual); $1 per manual, postpaid; record sheets must be reproduced locally; (8) minutes; Charles Van Riper and Robert L. Erickson; Continuing Education Office, Western Michigan University. *
See T2:2088 (2 references) and 7:964 (1 reference).

REFERENCES

1. See 7:964.
2–3. See T2:2088.
4. CHASE, BRADLEY R. *A Method of Improving the Predictive Validity of the Predictive Screening Test of Articulation.* Master's thesis, Eastern Illinois University (Charleston, Ill.), 1973.
5. GIOVANNUCCI, JANICE E. *The Developmental Relationship of Language Skills and Articulation Skills.* Master's thesis, University of Maine (Orono, Me.), 1973.
6. MARKS, ALICE R. *The Validity of the Van Riper Predictive Test of Articulation.* Master's thesis, Illinois State University (Bloomington, Ill.), 1973.
7. BARRETT, MARK D., AND WELSH, JOHN W. "Predictive Articulation Screening." *Lang Speech & Hearing Services Sch* 6(2):91–5 Ap '75. *
8. DREXLER, HAZEL G. "Review of Predictive Screening Test of Articulation," pp. 462–3. In *Pediatric Screening Tests.* Edited by William K. Frankenburg and Bonnie W. Camp. Springfield, Ill.: Charles C Thomas, Publisher, 1975. Pp. xii, 549. *
9. DRUMWRIGHT, AMELIA F. "Review of Predictive Screening Test of Articulation," pp. 460–2. In *Pediatric Screening Tests.* Edited by William K. Frankenburg and Bonnie W. Camp. Springfield, Ill.: Charles C Thomas, Publisher, 1975. Pp. xii, 549. *
10. DALEY, WILLIAM THOMAS. *Predictive Articulation Testing for the Second Grade.* Doctor's thesis, Catholic University of America (Washington, D.C.), 1976. (*DAI* 37:1190B)

RALPH L. SHELTON, *Professor of Speech and Hearing Science, The University of Arizona, Tucson, Arizona.*

This test was developed to predict which first grade children who present functional articulation problems will acquire normal articulation by third grade without remedial work. From a literature survey and interviews of clinicians, the authors assembled a pool of 500 possible test items. The pool was cut to 111 items by eliminating those items that consumed too much time or were otherwise unsuited for use with first grade children. The 111 items were administered to 167 beginning first graders judged to have functional articulation errors. The speech of 134 of these children who were still available at the beginning of the third grade was sampled by use of a phonetic inventory and by elicitation of spontaneous connected speech, and 57 of the items differentiated at the .05 level of significance between the children who had acquired normal articulation and those who had not. Ten items were dropped because they required special materials; this left a test of 47 items that involved imitation of test sounds in words, syllables, and in isolation from context; imitation of a sentence; observation of tongue movement; discrimination of an articulation error; and ability to clap hands rhythmically.

The 47-item PSTA was then administered to two new groups of first grade misarticulating children, the members of which were classified at the beginning of third grade into those who had and those who had not developed normal articulation. Data from those subjects may be used for predictive purposes, and the manual contains tables which allow the test user to estimate the probability of false positive and false negative predictions in using the test. The authors note that when a recommended cutoff score is used to select children for therapy, 33 percent of the children tested will be misclassified; that is, either they will be scheduled for therapy even though they would clear their articulation errors without it or they will not get

Porch Index of Communicative Ability in Children

therapy they subseqeuntly appear to need. This error rate does not indicate precise prediction, but the authors cite several theses or unpublished reports of longitudinal observations which indicate higher levels of predictive success than were obtained in the standardization studies.

The authors caution the test user that the test was developed only with children who speak middle-American standard English, and they suggest that predictions based on the PSTA be confirmed by later observations of the children involved. All of the work done in standardizing the PSTA involved children who had previously been identified as presenting delayed articulation development. If the test is to be used only with children previously diagnosed as presenting articulation delay, then it constitutes a second step in a screening process. Probably the test could be used as a tool for initial identification of articulation defectiveness, but that issue is not addressed in the test manual.

Because of its high rate of prediction error, the PSTA would be of little value to a clinician wishing to predict future behavior of an individual child; however, when only a segment of a group of children with delayed articulation development can be scheduled for therapy, PSTA results might help select the children who are least likely to develop satisfactory articulation spontaneously. The predictive value of a test is dependent not only on its validity but also upon a selection ratio which is the percentage of all eligible persons that can be included in a program. If a clinician plans to schedule for remediation only a small percentage of the children identified as having articulation errors, then use of the PSTA may increase the probability of selecting for training those children who would otherwise continue to misarticulate. However, if most eligible children are to be scheduled for therapy, then selection of children on the basis of PSTA scores would be little or no better than chance selection.

The authors cite evidence that first grade children with lateral lisps or distorted vocalic /r/ sounds do not improve their articulation errors by third grade. Pattern information of this kind may eventually have more predictive value than screening test scores.

In summary, the authors of the PSTA identified possible items on the basis of clinicians' experience and then selected items for use in their test by determining which items identified children whose articulation errors disappeared with maturation. The authors then conducted crossvalidation studies that provided data used to score the test. While these steps involved extensive research of good quality, the test yields a 33 percent error rate for dichotomous predictions of whether or not an individual's articulation problem will clear spontaneously. Because of this error rate, use of the test in the diagnosis of individual clients is not recommended. However, the test will be useful to the clinician who can schedule for therapy only a relatively small segment of a group of misarticulating children. That is, when limited resources force the clinician to schedule only a subset of misarticulating first grade children for articulation therapy, PSTA scores can be helpful in making the administrative decision of who does and who does not receive therapy.

[974]

Reynell Developmental Language Scales, Experimental Edition. Ages 1–5 with delayed or deviant language development; 1969; RDLS; individual; 3 scales; manual (59 pages); graph for boys, girls, (1 page) for each scale; £48.50 per set of testing materials, 25 sets of record booklets and graphs, and manual; 55p per 25 graphs; £4.25 per manual; £4.60 per set of manual, record booklets, and graphs; postpaid within U.K.; (20) minutes; Joan Reynell; NFER Publishing Co. Ltd. [England]. *
a) VERBAL COMPREHENSION SCALE A. Requires no speech, but some hand function; 1 form; record booklet (4 pages); £1.55 per 25 record booklets.
b) VERBAL COMPREHENSION SCALE B. Adaptation of Scale A for use with children with neither speech nor hand function; 1 form; record booklet (4 pages); £1.55 per 25 record booklets.
c) EXPRESSIVE LANGUAGE SCALE. 4 scores: language structure, vocabulary, content, total; 1 form; record booklet (5 pages); £3.10 per 25 record booklets.
See T2:2025 (3 references).

REFERENCES

1–3. See T2:2025.
4. TIZARD, BARBARA; COOPERMAN, OLIVER; JOSEPH, ANNE; AND TIZARD, JACK. "Environmental Effects on Language Development: A Study of Young Children in Long-Stay Residential Nurseries." *Child Develop* 43(2):337–58 Je '72. * (*PA* 48:11260)
5. RICHMOND, DAWN M. "A Review and Evaluation of the Reynell Developmental Language Scales." *Slow Learning Child* (Australia) 20(2):102–16 Jl '73. *
6. PETRIE, IAN. "Characteristics and Progress of a Group of Language Disordered Children With Severe Receptive Difficulties." *Brit J Dis Commun* 10(2):123–33 O '75. * (*PA* 55:7421)

KATHARINE G. BUTLER, *Acting Dean of Graduate Studies and Research and Director, Speech and Hearing Center, San Jose State University, San Jose, California:*

The author notes that these scales are intended to be used as part of a comprehensive assessment and that the scores have limited value when used alone. Thus, the scales, while relatively brief, are not suitable for language screening purposes. The author also notes that the scales are intended for use only by examiners with training and experience in testing young children. The reviewer would suggest that, in addition, the examiner must have a solid foundation in linguistics, language sample, and qualitative analysis of basic cognitive skills in order to derive sufficient information from these scales.

The scales were developed as clinical tools to be used with handicapped children rather than being "based on a predetermined theoretical pattern." Later, two examiners normed the three scales on over 600 children, ranging in age from 6 months to 6 years, with the normative population selected, on the basis of age alone, from infant welfare centers and nursery schools in London and southeast England. While the cultural bias of the sample is not identified, the balance of socioeconomic groups, as assessed by the father's occupation, matches to some degree the socioeconomic census data for 1961.

Split-half reliabilities for the subtests vary from .77 to .92, with median .84. The scales are least reliable for the higher ages.

The Expressive Language Scale—consisting of 18 items related to language structure, 21 items related to vocabulary, and 5 items related to "content" (i.e., qualitative assessment of "creative" use of language)—should be administered to each child and *one* of the two Verbal Comprehension Scales. Scale A is the preferred scale for normal and mildly handicapped children, while Scale B is reserved for use with the severely handicapped who may need to use an "eye-pointing" response. While directions for administration are provided, they allow considerable latitude; scoring details are more specific.

A few of the items reflect lingustic differences between England and the United States, and items as "Show me which button is not *done up*" would need to be altered for use in the United States.

SUMMARY. The RDLS represents an effort to modify clinical assessment tools for use as a general language test for expression and comprehension for children ages 1 to 5. Developed almost a decade ago, the scales do not reflect

current linguistic concepts which are particularly helpful in assessing the language competency of children, such as language sampling. However, Verbal Comprehension Scale B, which does not require a verbal response and can be given to subjects with limited motor control, may be useful in clinical settings. If utilized, caution in the interpretation of the Expressive Language Scale is necessary, since current research would not support the author's statement that language structure reaches "a natural ceiling by 3½ to 4 years." It should be noted that the author has provided a considerable amount of normative data, to a degree not often found in experimental editions, and that the manual is extensive, providing the knowledgeable examiner with considerable information.

JOEL STARK, *Director, Queens College Speech and Hearing Center, Queens College of The City University of New York, Flushing, New York.*

These scales are intended to be used as part of a comprehensive assessment of a child's abilities, together with intelligence scales and tests of performance abilities. They are designed for the separate assessment of expressive language and verbal comprehension over the age range of 1 to 5 years. The author intended this experimental edition as a clinical tool for use particularly with handicapped children.

The scales have so far been standardized only on children from London and the southeast of England. Scores are given in terms of equivalent age levels and standard scores. The author points out that "the norms may not be quite the same for children coming from areas other than those in which the tests have so far been standardised."

There are three scales. Verbal Comprehension Scale A "follows the development of verbal comprehension from the earliest stage of selective recognition of certain word patterns on an affective level, through gradually increasing complexity of interpretation of different parts of speech, to the stage at which verbal interpretation extends to situations beyond the here and now." Scale B, a parallel scale, is intended for use with children who have no speech and no control over their hands or arms and often need to use their eyes as pointers (e.g., cerebral palsy children). Section 1 of the verbal comprehension scales is concerned with the stage of verbal preconcepts. Items include such tasks as looking at a familiar object or persons in response to naming. In the following sections of the scale, the stimuli become increasingly complex. The child is expected to understand more than noun-verb constructions, and content goes well beyond the stimulus items at hand. While toys are still used so that the child may respond by demonstration, the situation to which he is to respond is not enacted for him. For example, he must hear and understand: "This little boy has spilt his dinner. What must he do?" The child has to assimilate the instructions and use language to recreate the situation and carry out the sequence in terms of appropriate action with the toys.

The Expressive Language Scale is "divided into three sections, each being concerned with a different aspect of language." In Section 1, the structure and early stages of prelanguage are tapped. In Section 2, "the vocabulary increases in difficulty and yet the words are chosen so that they are within the experience of even the most housebound handicapped child." Section 3 involves more creative uses of language; the aim is to find out how far a child can use language creatively in describing a picture.

The major problem with the RDLS and other scales of its time, is that they fail to account for more recent developments in language acquisition. Specifically, language structure is analyzed in terms of parts of speech; there is little attention given to semantic intention or the functions of language.

[975]

The Riley Articulation and Language Test, Revised. Grades kgn-2; 1966-71; RALT; for screening of children most in need of speech therapy; 4 scores: language proficiency, intelligibility, articulation function, language function; reliability data for 1966 edition; no norms for language proficiency and intelligibility; norms for intelligibility and articulation consist of medians and 10th percentiles for the 1966 edition; norms for articulation and language for kgn and grade 2 are for 1966 edition; individual; 1 form; record booklet ('71, 4 pages); manual ('71, 7 pages plus record booklet); $8.50 per kit of 25 booklets and manual; $6.50 per 25 record booklets; $3 per manual; 8% extra for postage and handling; (3-5) minutes; Glyndon D. Riley; Western Psychological Services. *

For a review by Raphael M. Haller of the original edition, see 7:967 (1 reference).

REFERENCES

1. See 7:967.
2. DREXLER, HAZEL G. "Review of Riley Articulation and Language Test," pp. 466–8. In *Pediatric Screening Tests*.

Edited by William K. Frankenburg and Bonnie W. Camp. Springfield, Ill.: Charles C Thomas, Publisher, 1975. Pp. xii, 549. *

RALPH L. SHELTON, *Professor of Speech and Hearing Science, The University of Arizona, Tucson, Arizona.*

School speech pathologists face the abiding problem of screening large numbers of children to identify those who need diagnostic and perhaps remedial work for disorders of speech and language. The Riley test is intended to provide estimates of language proficiency, speech intelligibility, articulation loss, and language function. The test may be administered in 5 minutes or less.

The first of three parts of the test requires the examinee to tell a story, and the examiner is to rate language and intelligibility. The manual states that scores on this portion of the test are not sufficiently reliable "for meaningful norms to apply"; no data are presented for it.

The articulation subtest requires the child to repeat eight words after the examiner; when a child misarticulates a test sound, he or she is instructed to listen carefully and is then given two more opportunities to imitate the unit correctly. Errors are weighted for type of error (substitution, omission, and distortion) and for stimulability (whether or not correct responses were produced on the extra tries). The articulation items and scoring system were selected on the basis of six variables: (*a*) the degree to which an articulation error resembles a target sound, (*b*) correct production of a previously misarticulated sound in response to strong stimulation, (*c*) number of defective sounds, (*d*) error consistency—a given sound is always misarticulated or is sometimes produced correctly, (*e*) frequency of occurrence of the sound in the language, and (*f*) developmental order. These variables have credibility among persons who treat articulation clinically; however, their predictive value has not been well tested or developed. The authors rely on a study by Carter and Buck[1] to demonstrate the predictive value of stimulability. That study shows that stimulable first grade misarticulating children are more likely to make spontaneous articulation improvement than are less or nonstimulable children, but unfortunately (for the

[1] CARTER, EUNICE T., AND BUCK, MCKENZIE. "Prognostic Testing for Functional Articulation Disorders Among Children in the First Grade." *J Speech & Hearing Disorders* 23(2): 124–33 My '58. *

Riley Articulation and Language Test

point the author wishes to make) most of the subjects, whether stimulable or not, corrected their misarticulations without speech therapy or other services. The validity data reported for the articulation subtest are limited to a contingency correlation between scores on the Riley test and a 50-item Templin-Darley articulation test for 29 retarded or handicapped children.

The third part, language function, gives the child two chances to imitate each of six sentences which range in length from 4 to 14 syllables. This is based on a model with receptive, central processing, and expressive components, and on citation of a factor analytic study of adult aphasic patients. Validity data are again limited—this time to a contingency correlation between Riley scores and teacher ratings regarding the 29 children mentioned above.

This test is easily administered and scored. The only norms are medians and 10th percentiles for the articulation and language scores. Unfortunately, the validity data are so limited that the test user gains little information about persons to whom the test is administered. At best, the articulation data serve as an index to performance on another screening test. No studies have examined relationships between Riley scores and diagnostic assessments. No longitudinal data are presented regarding persons to whom the test has been administered. Administration of the test and comparison of the obtained scores with test norms allow no prediction of either spontaneous improvement or response to treatment. The information obtained provides no precise basis for decision making.

No articulation or language screening test known to the reviewer presents validity data needed to support inferences about individual clients. Clinicians faced with a screening task may be interested in the *Predictive Screening Test of Articulation* and in Irwin's Triota: A Computerized Screening Battery.[2] McDonald and McDonald have accumulated unpublished longitudinal and cross-sectional data that increase the predictive value of the *Screening Deep Test of Articulation*. The *Templin-Darley Tests of Articulation* include a screening test

as does the *Fisher-Logemann Test of Articulation Competence.*

In summary, the Riley test was constructed to serve the important screening function of identifying children in need of diagnostic and rehabilitative services. Unfortunately, it lacks the validity needed for accomplishment of the task.

LAWRENCE D. SHRIBERG, *Associate Professor of Speech Pathology, University of Wisconsin, Madison, Wisconsin.*

Two serious problems with this test are apparent. Each was briefly discussed by Haller in his critical review of the original RALT (7: 967), but with the exception of the addition of two normative tables that read simply "revised 1970," the manual for the revised RALT does not indicate that anything else has been revised.

The basic problem with this test is that the quantitative procedures for screening articulation and language (subtests B and C) lack face validity. As sampling procedures, testing articulation by word naming and language by sentence imitation are each fraught with problems. Neither the reliability data nor the criterion validity data, as presented in the manual, dispel concern with the inadequacy of these test procedures. No information is provided on the training given to the examiners for the reliability and validity studies. Because the manual does not specify characteristics for scoring responses to the sentence imitation tasks, and the language proficiency and intelligibility scales require wholly subjective judgments, the reported reliability data seem spuriously high (100 percent agreement on pass-fail). The test-retest and interjudge agreement data indicate that the samples contained mostly normal children; hence, high stability and examiner agreement are insured. The criterion validity study presented, involving only 29 "retarded" or "handicapped" children tested on both the RALT and the Templin-Darley, yielded an unimpressive 56 percent common variance.

The second problem concerns the failure of this screening instrument to account for speech and language differences associated with diverse cultural and ethnic backgrounds. The RALT purports to be a screening instrument for use with children of middle and low socioeconomic

---

[2] IRWIN, JOHN V. "The Triota Screening Battery: A Computerized Screening Battery." *Acta Symbolica* 3(1):26–38 sp 72. *

Riley Articulation and Language Test

background ("socially disadvantaged" children), yet the manual is entirely devoid of reference to the important sociolinguistic literature of the 60s. For example, no discussion or provision in the test accounts for speech and language differences associated with black vernacular or Spanish-influenced English, nor are the well-documented examiner-child effects acknowledged. In fact, several aspects of the RALT procedures are particularly ripe for cultural bias. Two examples: an omission of word-final *th* is considered an articulation error; a child is considered "somewhat" or "severely" subnormal depending on her/his "willingness to talk" to the examiner. Especially in light of the sketchy discussion of possible disorder "syndromes" that RALT scores might suggest, use of this test with children from varied linguistic backgrounds would be irresponsible.

Numerous other shortcomings in the manual for this instrument could be cited, ranging from typographical errors to misinterpretations of research literature. Given the proliferation of language measures in the last few years, clinicians should be able to assemble an effective and efficient screening battery. Importantly, any useful instrument must account for the linguistic backgrounds in the community served. This one does not.

[976]

Sklar Aphasia Scale, Revised 1973. Brain damaged adults; 1966–73; SAS; 5 scores: auditory decoding, visual decoding, oral encoding, graphic encoding, total; no data on reliability; no norms for part scores; scores consist of percentages of possible scores; no information on derivation of impairment categories equivalent to percentage scores; individual; 1 form; manual ('73, 18 pages plus record booklet and stimulus cards); record booklet ('73, 4 pages); $18.50 per kit of testing materials, 10 record booklets, and manual; $12.50 per set of testing materials; $6.50 per 25 record booklets; $3.50 per manual; 8% extra for postage and handling; [30–60] minutes; Maurice Sklar; Western Psychological Services. *

For reviews by Arthur L. Benton and Daniel R. Boone of the original edition, see 7:970; see also P:247 (2 references).

REFERENCES

1–2. See P:247.
3. SHEEHAN, JOSEPH G.; ASELTINE, SUZANNE; AND EDWARDS, ALAN E. "Aphasic Comprehension of Time Spacing." *J Speech & Hearing Res* 16(4):650–7 D '73. * (PA 52:8131)

MANFRED J. MEIER, *Professor of Psychology and Director, Neuropsychology Laboratory, University of Minnesota Medical School, Minneapolis, Minnesota.*

The 1973 revision of the *Sklar Aphasia Scale* introduces some minor but significant changes in format, scoring, and content which are designed to improve the clinical utility of the assessment materials for describing language impairments related to cerebral involvement. No new data or literature citations are provided in support of the instrument's validity for the differential diagnosis of the aphasias or for the prediction of recovery changes. Therefore, major limitations identified in previous reviews (7:970) have not been given any substantive consideration in this revision.

Changes of note include a more detailed 5-level scoring scale for each item, in contrast to the previous trilevel response categorizations. Some replacements of specific subtests have been made, presumably to strengthen the battery in selected areas of need. The revised manual contains guidelines for the conduct of a preliminary interview for assessing functional communication.

Also included is a classification of the aphasic syndromes as an aid to interpretation of language impairments elicited with the test materials. These aphasia classifications are in general use and have been derived from renewed attention to the neuroanatomical bases of the aphasic syndromes. It is somewhat surprising that the 1973 revision provides no documentation of the extensive recent literature involving the localization and etiology of cerebral lesions known to produce language impairments.

There is no dearth of aphasia examination procedures in the test literature. Most experienced evaluations of language impairment are likely to utilize the more extensively standardized and validated instruments. Less experienced consumers tend to use shorter, more readily administered instruments, primarily for screening purposes or for infrequent application. The Sklar appears to be directed at the occasional or perfunctory user and, therefore, should be sufficiently well documented to facilitate effective professional use by less experienced clinicians. Shortcomings cited by Benton in the Seventh MMY still apply and should be carefully reviewed. Application of an aphasia examination procedure requires some supervised clinical experience and greater documentation of supporting information than is provided in the Sklar manual.

[977]

★Stycar Language Test. Mental ages 11–20 months, 21 months–5.5 years, 3–6 years, with marked speech and language difficulties; 1976; SLT; no scores; no data on reliability; no norms; individual; 1 form; 3 levels; manual (57 pages); £50 per set of testing materials and manual; £1.65 per manual; postpaid within U.K.; (20–30) minutes; M. D. Sheridan; NFER Publishing Co. Ltd. [England]. *
a) COMMON OBJECTS TEST. Mental ages 11–20 months; 1 form; £24 per set of objects.
b) MINIATURE TOYS TEST. Mental ages 21 months–5.5 years; 1 form; £18.50 per set of toys.
c) PICTURE BOOK TEST. Mental ages 3–6; 1 form (26 pages); £5.85 per picture book.

REFERENCES

1. SHERIDAN, M. D. "The Stycar Language Test." *Develop Med & Child Neurol* (England) 17(2):164–74 Ap '75. * (PA 54:12093)

RONALD GOLDMAN, *Professor of Biocommunication, Center for Developmental and Learning Disorders, The University of Alabama in Birmingham, Birmingham, Alabama.*

The *Stycar Language Test* was designed to provide clinical information regarding a young child's ability to receive, comprehend, and express himself in oral language and his use of nonverbal communication. According to the author, the test, developed primarily for children under seven years of age, specifically assesses phonation, prosody, auditory competence, articulatory proficiency, vocabulary, semantics, grammar, and syntax.

Children taking the test are required to identify objects and pictures, define objects and pictures by function, repeat words and sentences, and, in some instances, draw and arrange pictures, blocks, and designs. Presumably, the results determine a child's auditory and visual intake abilities and his processing strategies relative to sounds, words, and sentences. Additionally, verbal expression can be assessed in greater detail for vocal quality and phonology as well as language.

Test materials include common objects (cup, spoon, bowl, etc.), miniature toys, pictures, blocks, and word and sentence lists. The use of these materials, according to the author, provides valuable information concerning a youngster's ability to effectively utilize "codemic" systems.

The test was designed to be administered individually. The author does not provide any indication of time required for test administration; however, the time commitment seems to be relatively short. Basically, the child will name objects, point to objects and pictures, and pantomime functions of these objects. In addi-

tion, the child will repeat words, sentences, and selected single speech sounds in order for the examiner to measure phonology as well as language. Finally, the youngster will be asked to arrange pictures and designs. The purpose of the varying activities is to provide an assessment of the child's skills in a single modality as well as across modalities.

According to the author, the SLT has the capacity for assessing numerous skills. She states, "After some experience in its clinical application with normal children, this test material provides, in very short time, an enormous amount of information concerning a child's hand-eye co-ordination, hearing, auditory discrimination, speech and language development, his general understanding interpersonal relationships and social competence, his alertness, drive and ability to maintain and shift attention, in space and time." In general, this reviewer feels that the test provides a number of potential opportunities for observing a variety of skills. The manual provides the reader with some interesting general information about normal speech and language development and it also describes some general procedures for use of the materials provided in the test protocol. It does not, however, provide a standardized test procedure or a structured set of instructions, and there is no response form from which meaningful interpretation can be derived. Furthermore, the manual fails to include a section to assist the examiner in making interpretations on the basis of test results. Although many practicing clinicians utilize observations to make judgments on language performance, the lack of structure and limited information on interpretation might render this test useless to a less experienced examiner. The only advantage provided by such a test is the accumulation of materials, hopefully, capable of eliciting various behaviors.

It also should be pointed out that the North American examiner would have to modify the procedures described by the author since some of the terms incorporated in the test protocol might be inappropriate for the children they are assessing. Because the test was designed in England, the use of such terms as "mummy," "pram," and "post a letter" might be unfamiliar to children being assessed.

A major criticism of this test is that it has

not been analyzed in any statistical manner to determine its reliability and validity. The author indicates, "It is not possible to be scientifically precise in defining 'norms' for so highly an individual process as that of language development." The reviewer is in disagreement with this philosophy since the measurement of reliability and validity is a critical factor in determining whether this procedure has clinical merit.

SUMMARY. The *Stycar Language Test* may provide a general inventory of certain aspects of language performance. This procedure may have some potential in assisting a clinician in making some decisions on a child's general adequacy in her/his receptive and expressive language skills. The test would have more credibility if standardized instructions for administration were presented, if test forms for summarizing performance were provided, and if information on reliability and validity was available. The value of such a screening device would be enormous if some of the criticisms indicated above were addressed.

[978]

★**The Test of Language Development.** Ages 4-0 to 8-11; 1977; TOLD; 6 principal scores (picture vocabulary, oral vocabulary, grammatic understanding, sentence imitation, grammatic completion, total) and 2 supplemental scores (word discrimination, word articulation); individual; 1 form; manual (41 pages); technical report (46 pages); scoring sheet (4 pages); picture book (77 pages); $39.95 per examiner's kit including 25 scoring sheets; $6.50 per 25 scoring sheets; cash orders postpaid; (35–45) minutes; Phyllis L. Newcomer and Donald D. Hammill; Empiric Press. *

[979]

*****UP Field Test in Drama and Theatre.** College; 1971–77; Form K-TUR ('71, 18 pages); descriptive booklet ('71, 15 pages); for UAP accessories, see 480; rental fee, $4 per test; rental and scoring fee, $5.50 per test; postage extra; 120(140) minutes; Educational Testing Service. *

[980]

★**The Vane Evaluation of Language Scale.** Ages 2.5 to 6.5; 1975; VELS, also called VANE-L; language acquisition; 3 scores: receptive language, expressive language, memory; no data on reliability and validity; individual; 1 form; record booklet (2 pages); manual (32 pages); class record sheet (2 pages); $15 per set of test objects, 50 record booklets, and manual; $3.50 per 50 record booklets; $8 per set of test objects; $5 per manual; cash orders postpaid; (10) minutes; Julia R. Vane; Clinical Psychology Publishing Co. *

REFERENCES

1. VANE, JULIA R. *Vane Evaluation of Language Scale* (The *Vane-L*). Archives of the Behavioral Sciences Monograph No. 49. Brandon, Vt.: Clinical Psychology Publishing Co., Inc., 1975. Pp. 32. *

ROBERT L. ROSENBAUM, *Assistant Professor of Communication Arts and Science and Associate Director, Speech and Hearing Clinic, Queens College of The City University of New York, Flushing, New York.*

This scale is designed to identify children ages 2.5 to 6.5 years with respect to receptive language, expressive language, memory, and handedness. The test is relatively simple to administer and can be completed within a short period of time.

The problem with screening tests is that the observation of the child in the environment takes precedent over specific test results. Test performance becomes a simplified and at times unrevealing statement of child behavior. The need for additional diagnostic information would be essential even though the test scores suggest appropriate functioning at age level. In effect, this screening test does not meaningfully differentiate between groups of children with respect to appropriate rate, form, and content of language behavior. A thorough study of test validity on representative samples of children would serve to give further credibility to this test.

In general, the scale is more successful in presenting material within the areas of receptive language than within the areas of expressive language.

Items requiring motor responses and block arrangements take relevant samples of behavior. Items requiring designation of relative quantity are presented in a format of beans in transparent containers. Items requiring tapping behavior serve to designate a form of auditory memory.

Within the area of expressive language, the information section is quick and sufficient for the screening. Estimates of speech intelligibility are difficult to make with respect to the author's severity levels of fair or poor. The judgment may reflect the adequacy of the language corpus and is likely to be subjective. Scoring for vocabulary is arbitrarily defined by the author. Estimates of zero scores are confusing insofar as some of the responses identify attributes of function and can be considered as credible responses.

In summary, this test is a superficial estimate of language acquisition and should not be substituted for existing tests that focus specifically on facets of language behavior.

Vane Evaluation of Language Scale

VOCATIONS

REVIEWS BY *Lewis E. Albright, Thomas S. Baldwin, Alan R. Bass, William C. Bingham, Jack L. Bodden, Fred H. Borgen, Walter C. Borman, Stephen L. Cohen, Nancy S. Cole, Charles J. Cranny, John O. Crites, Carolyn Dawson, Robert G. Demaree, Esther E. Diamond, Robert L. Dipboye, Robert H. Dolliver, George Domino, Jerome E. Doppelt, Lawrence W. Erickson, Richard C. Erickson, Lorraine D. Eyde, Robert Fitzpatrick, Austin C. Frank, Thomas T. Frantz, Leonard V. Gordon, Robert M. Guion, Jo-Ida C. Hansen, Lenore W. Harmon, David G. Hawkridge, David O. Herman, Emil H. Hoch, Daniel L. Householder, Richard T. Johnson, Richard W. Johnson, Ehud Jungwirth, Martin R. Katz, Raymond A. Katzell, Michael J. Kavanagh, Penelope Kegel-Flom, Paul Kline, Abraham K. Korman, Charles J. Krauskopf, Albert K. Kurtz, Elaine L. La Monica, Frank J. Landy, Wilbur L. Layton, Robert L. Linn, Gary E. Lintereur, Paul R. Lohnes, Patricia W. Lunneborg, Christine H. McGuire, Arthur C. MacKinney, Dean R. Malsbary, Richard S. Melton, C. Edward Meyers, William G. Mollenkopf, Stephan J. Motowidlo, Dean H. Nafziger, Charles W. Pendleton, Kenneth E. Poucher, James H. Ricks, Jr., Alice R. Rines, Frank L. Schmidt, Lyle F. Schoenfeldt, Stephen Sharp, Mary Lee Smith, Nick L. Smith, Stanley R. Strong, Alan R. Suess, Donald E. Super, Richard A. Swanson, Robert S. Swanson, Ronald N. Taylor, Paul W. Thayer, David V. Tiedeman, Thomas A. Tyler, William C. Ward, Tim L. Wentling, Bert W. Westbrook, Carl G. Willis, Sheldon Zedeck, and Donald G. Zytowski.*

[981]

*Flanagan Industrial Tests. Business and industry; 1960–75; FIT; short speeded forms of the *Flanagan Aptitude Classification Tests* designed for use with adults; 18 tests; the 7 Form AA tests are revisions of the corresponding Form A tests to make them more suitable for entry-level job applicants; reliability data for Form AA tests based on earlier forms; examiner's manual ('75, 36 pages); tape cassettes available for administration; $5.50 per 25 tests; $2.05 per scoring stencil for any one test (except Inspection, $4); $15 per tape cassette for any one test; $1.43 per manual; $7.10 per specimen set of any one test; postage extra; John C. Flanagan; Science Research Associates, Inc. *
a) ARITHMETIC. Form A ('60, 4 pages); 5(7) minutes.
b) ASSEMBLY. Form AA ('60, 4 pages); 10(13) minutes.
c) COMPONENTS. Form AA ('60, 4 pages); 10(12) minutes.
d) COORDINATION. Form A ('60, 4 pages); 5(7) minutes.
e) ELECTRONICS. Form AA ('60, 4 pages); 15(17) minutes.
f) EXPRESSION. Form A ('60, 4 pages); 5(8) minutes.
g) INGENUITY. Form AA ('60, 4 pages); 15(18) minutes.
h) INSPECTION. Form AA ('60, 4 pages); 5(9) minutes.
i) JUDGMENT AND COMPREHENSION. Form A ('62, 4 pages); 15(17) minutes.
j) MATHEMATICS AND REASONING. Form A ('60, 4 pages); 15(18) minutes.
k) MECHANICS. Form A ('60, 4 pages); 15(18) minutes.
l) MEMORY. Form AA ('63, 4 pages); 10(19) minutes.
m) PATTERNS. Form A ('60, 4 pages); 5(7) minutes.
n) PLANNING. Form A ('62, 4 pages); 15(18) minutes.
o) PRECISION. Form A ('60, 4 pages); 5(8) minutes.
p) SCALES. Form AA ('60, 4 pages); 5(7) minutes.
q) TABLES. Form A ('60, 4 pages); 5(8) minutes.
r) VOCABULARY. Form A ('60, 4 pages); 15(17) minutes.

For reviews by C. J. Adcock and Robert C. Droege

and an excerpted review by John L. Horn, see 7:977 (1 reference).

REFERENCES

1. See 7:977.
2. SCIENCE RESEARCH ASSOCIATES. *Validation: Procedures and Results: Part 2, Results From SRA Test Validation Studies.* Chicago, Ill.: Science Research Associates, Inc., 1972. Pp. ii, 62. *
3. TOOLE, DAVID L.; GAVIN, JAMES F.; MURDY, LEE B.; AND SELLS, SAUL B. "The Differential Validity of Personality, Personal History, and Aptitude Data for Minority and Nonminority Employees." *Personnel Psychol* 25(4):661–72 w '72. *
4. SCIENCE RESEARCH ASSOCIATES. *Validation: Procedures and Results: Part 3, Supplementary Results, Third Edition.* Chicago, Ill. Science Research Associates, 1974. Pp. ii, 90. *

DAVID O. HERMAN, *Assistant Director, Psychological Measurement Division, The Psychological Corporation, New York, New York.*

The *Flanagan Industrial Tests* represent an interesting application of the author's critical incident technique to the measurement of abilities and skills necessary in a variety of civilian occupations. At first glance, this multitest battery has three qualities that will be attractive to those responsible for personnel selection: the tests are short, easy to administer, and apparently comprehensive. The extensive domain that they cover is an unusual mixture of traditional measures of abilities that most people have learned through exposure to our culture, and measures of specific knowledge considered important for certain types of jobs.

The battery is not intended to be administered in full. Rather, a personnel administrator chooses a combination of tests to be used in selecting applicants for a particular job, on the basis of requirements identified through job analysis. The use of single tests is not recommended; for most jobs combinations of four to eight tests can be selected to reflect the important abilities. The published validity information should help identify tests that have relevance to specific occupations. Because each test is published as a separate consumable booklet, it will be easy to vary the choice of tests according to shifting needs.

ADMINISTRATION. Each test requires between 5 and 15 minutes of working time, and with one exception the time needed to present the directions is quite brief. Although the tests are easy to administer using the directions provided, the optional tape cassettes for presenting the directions and timing the administration should further simplify the work of a personnel clerk, and assure uniform testing times and conditions for examinees. The recorded voice is neutral in accent, and is clearly reproduced.

For certain tests, the directions to the examinee appear to be too brief to assure full clarity to those who are unfamiliar with objective tests. In addition, the directions for the Coordination and Precision tests do not give sufficient emphasis to the necessity for proceeding immediately to the next item as soon as an error has been made; examinees who do not heed this once-stated warning may be heavily penalized by the waste of time on these highly speeded tests.

SCORING. All of the tests except Coordination and Precision are scored with transparent plastic overlays, each of which bears its own scoring instructions. For three of the tests—Arithmetic, Inspection, and Tables—the official score is the number of correct answers less some function of errors. The printed portion of the scoring overlay for Patterns, which is slightly reduced in size, necessitates shifting the overlay a bit as each new item is scored—an inconvenience and, for this particular test, a potential source of error.

NORMS. Percentile and stanine norms are offered for three samples: business and industrial personnel, 12th grade students in a nationwide high school sample, and freshmen entering a selective men's university. The nature of the business-industrial norms is worth special comment, for they are based on samples that vary from test to test. According to the publisher, the data were gathered in connection with a validation project, so the norms for each test are based on a sample that is probably representative of groups that might be given the test in "real life." The only unfortunate consequence of this data-gathering procedure is that there are no industrial norms for four of the tests. This raises questions of the industrial relevance of Mathematics and Reasoning, Planning, and Vocabulary. According to the publisher, the lack of norms for Inspection is attributable to a record-keeping error.

A supporting table permits the user to determine the approximate composition of the industrial norms for each test according to the job titles included, type of industry, number of contributing companies, sex ratio, and proportion of nonwhites. (The samples may be described only approximately because the Ns in the table do not agree with those in the actual norms.) In addition, the industrial norms themselves are presented separately for majority- and minority-group individuals, as well as for the total group.

It is regrettable that these favorable comments must be qualified because of the omission of other information about the FIT normative data. As noted above, formula scoring is recommended for three of the tests. Nevertheless, according to the publisher, although formula scoring for these three tests was used in preparing the educational norms and the table of equivalent scores for FIT and FACT, the industrial norms for these are based on rights-only scoring. Many companies may, in fact, prefer this scoring method for all tests, as the manual suggests, but it would be less confusing to use a single scoring method for these three tests throughout. In any event, formula-scoring norms for the affected tests should be available to permit the use of the recommended scores.

A second issue concerns the replacement of seven of the original Form A tests with their Form AA revisions. It is essential to know which forms were used in preparing the various norms because the original and revised tests are not comparable in difficulty. This information is not given in the manual but, according to the publisher, the industrial norms and validity materials reflect the use of Form AA for the seven revised tests, while the norms for the two education groups reflect the use of Form A for all tests.

An earlier review of the FIT (7:977) ob-

Flanagan Industrial Tests

served that it took "a careful reading of the manual to realize that the table of FIT percentile norms for high school seniors is based on students tested on the FACT battery." The FIT norms were then prepared from the results through a table of FIT-FACT equivalents. This procedure is proper only when the corresponding tests are considered parallel —and some of the test-pairs do not seem to have this property, judging from their published intercorrelations. Further, the current manual nowhere discusses how the high school norms were developed. In all, the published normative data might be described as showing good intentions coupled with a bit of carelessness in presentation.

RELIABILITY. Earlier reviews of the FIT (7:977) criticized the absence of direct evidence of the battery's reliability. Little additional reliability information is available now, so this issue will only be summarized here. Briefly, the primary evidence consists of the correlations of corresponding pairs of tests on Form A of FIT and the FACT battery. Because, however, the corresponding tests of the two batteries differ in difficulty, length, and, at times, the item type used, the evidence presented is at best suggestive. At any rate, the interbattery coefficients for 17 test-pairs (none are available for Electronics, which does not have a counterpart on FACT) range from .28 to .79, with a median of .55. The manual speculates that alternate-form reliability coefficients, if they existed, would probably range between .50 and .90.

In view of the low reliability of many of the tests, the manual properly cautions the user not to allow a score on a single test to determine personnel decisions. That is, several tests should always be used, and their scores should be combined through a procedure such as a weighted sum, not a multiple-cutoff procedure. This point is well taken, and the manual's validity section follows it up by stressing the use of weighted test combinations as predictors.

VALIDITY. This review will consider two aspects of the FIT's validity—the tests' manifest content and their correlation with external criteria. Inspection of test content does raise questions about what is being measured beyond what the manual implies. The total process of

responding to the arithmetic items requires not only numerical, but also clerical-perceptual skills. This will tend to slow examinees down on this speeded test, as well as complicate and cloud the nature of what is measured. (The same criticism applies also to the scales test.) Furthermore, the five types of arithmetic problems are presented in separate groups, which means that the coverage of arithmetic skills is different for fast and slow examinees.

Perhaps one-sixth of the electronics items concern such nonelectronic material as household electricity, which confuses the interpretation of scores. While Ingenuity is described as tapping "the ability to devise ingenious procedures, equipment, or presentations," this test appears to measure a verbal skill close to that required for solving crossword puzzles. Whether this is significantly related to the kind of ingenuity needed to devise equipment may generously be called unproved.

Some potential users will question the proportion of items on Mathematics and Reasoning that cover definitions of terms and other strictly verbal aspects of mathematics. Inspection of the mechanics items also reveals many questions with a heavy verbal load which probably favors examinees whose knowledge comes more from reading than from shop experience. Furthermore, over half of Mechanics is specific to automotive mechanics, which may be undesirable in many personnel applications.

Vocabulary is a rather difficult test—the median score for high school seniors is 20 out of a possible 72—and it is doubtful that there are many industrial positions for which the test might be an efficient predictor of success. The quality of this test's items reflects lax editorial standards; flaws include having the correct answer a close etymological relative of the base word, mixing single words and entire phrases among the alternatives, using alternatives that are comparable in difficulty to the base words, and a pervasive legal flavor to the word list.

The reproduction of items within the test booklets is generally clear, but here too there are slips. As noted earlier, the format of Arithmetic and Scales introduces extraneous complexity to the examinee's task. The format of the inspection items is crowded on the page, and the relative positions of the stimulus figures and their answer spaces vary noticeably within each item so that it is not instantly clear which answer space corresponds to each figure. Thus, examinees may lose time needlessly when responding to these items. On the mechanics test the diagram of a two-cycle engine is so poorly printed that the letters identifying the different engine parts are hard to decipher.

Earlier reviews of the FIT were critical of the lack of industrial validation, and, to correct this, the publishers have undertaken a truly impressive program of gathering test and job-performance data for employees in a wide variety of occupations. The manual summarizes the results of 25 industrial validation studies, and additional validity material is presented in separate publications (*2, 4*). For each study, the manual reports the correlation of selected FIT tests with the criterion, together with the FIT means and standard deviations. For the larger validation groups, means and standard deviations are also reported for the majority- and minority-group portions of the sample.

Unhappily, the usefulness of this massive data-collection effort is weakened by the procedures used to analyze the data. In most of the studies the validity sample was divided into fourths on the criterion measure. Then the middle half of the sample was dropped, and the point-biserial correlation was computed between each test score and membership in the top or bottom 25 percent on the criterion. The resulting coefficients are, of course, systematic overestimates of validity. This problem is compounded by testing the coefficients for statistical significance using for N the total number of cases, including the excluded middle of the group. The results are improper and misleading. Still, the studies do serve to some degree their stated purposes—to suggest which FIT measures might be tried out in local validation studies, and to suggest which tests might be put to provisional use where local validation is not feasible.

EDITORIAL STANDARDS. Earlier portions of this review have commented on omitted or inconsistent information in the FIT manual, spottiness in item quality, and some cases of poor reproduction of items. To these should be added a few further examples of editorial carelessness. Means, standard deviations, and coefficients of correlation are reported to varying numbers of decimal places. The layout of the validity section of the manual is messy and a bit bothersome to follow. Between the manual and the separate validation report, the Ns are inconsistently reported for the validation samples of assemblers and electronic technicians. The method of responding to multiple choice items shifts inexplicably from test to test—on most tests a circle is filled in, while on others an "X" is made in the circle; and on one test a square is filled in. While each of these matters, taken singly, is trivial, together they make one wonder what other less easily detectable oversights might plague the battery.

SUMMARY. The *Flanagan Industrial Tests* have some clear strengths—ease and convenience of administration and scoring, ease of assembling special-purpose mini-batteries, and useful (though partly misleading) validity information. The availability of minority-group normative data is also praiseworthy. There are many weaknesses of the FIT; and, while some of these are merely inelegant and annoying, others compromise the utility of the battery. The gravest of these include the omission of essential information, which can lead the unwary to errors of scoring and interpretation; the absence of proper reliability information; and quirks in the constructs underlying some of the tests, as judged from their content and format. The prospective user will be wise to evaluate with more than usual care the relationships between test content and local job requirements, to heed the publisher's advice to use several tests in combination rather than one or two tests alone, and to pursue local validation as soon as conditions permit.

ARTHUR C. MACKINNEY, *Professor of Psychology and Vice Chancellor for Academic Affairs, University of Missouri, St. Louis, Missouri.*

The FIT battery is an excellent series of aptitude tests worthy of consideration for many personnel selection systems. Given the requirement for validation in each local situation, this statement is an expression of confidence that these tests have a good chance of being valid predictors of job performance in many settings. With local demonstration of validity, this reviewer judges that the personnel decisions resulting from the use of the tests should be defensible on both legal and ethical grounds.

Flanagan Industrial Tests

The FIT battery has the same roots as the older, longer, and somewhat lower-level FACT battery. FIT is an adaptation of FACT for industrial and business purposes. Both, therefore, originated with Flanagan's study of jobs which identified job components judged to be critically important for successful performance. Thus, neither a factor base nor criterion base provided the starting point for these tests. Rather, critical requirements were identified from descriptions of many jobs, grouped and clustered into higher-order categories, and aptitude measures for the most important ones were then hypothesized and developed. It is noteworthy that these tests originated in the content validity idea, based on judged relevance of the test dimensions. Recent development has carried the work well beyond this beginning, but the origin was content-oriented rather than construct- or criterion-oriented.

The bibliography accompanying these reviews is testimony to the fact that a great deal has been written about the FACT and FIT batteries. These references include, of course, reviews in earlier MMYs. There is no point in repeating here what has been said well elsewhere. The list includes excellent evaluations which are finely detailed, full of both praise and criticism, with some very prophetic views of these tests. This reviewer intends only to refer the serious investigator to these other important sources and concentrate here on what is new and different.

The latest FIT, reviewed here, incorporates a few relatively minor changes, plus one major one mentioned below. The best example of these minor points is the availability of a series of cassette tapes which record administration instructions. This would appear to provide a good service, particularly for relatively small organizations which lack a substantial professional staff. And, of course, recorded administration has the advantage of making conditions much more standard from time to time.

But the big change in FIT takes the form of substantial amounts of empirical validation information. Starting in the 1960s, a fairly large scale program of concurrent validation was initiated, and FIT was incorporated in many of these studies. As a result, a substantial amount of validity information has been accruing for many jobs and many work settings.

Perhaps more important yet is the fact that significant validity is being identified for these tests in many situations. This does *not* say universal validity, of course; no such thing exists so far as anyone has been able to tell. But many of these FIT subtests are producing significant validity in employment situations and significant contributions to selection decision-making.

The final chapter on validity of these tests has not yet been written. Thus far, empirical validity data are reported for 14 of the 18 subtests, and *all* of the studies that this reviewer has seen were concurrent rather than predictive in nature. Furthermore, the commonly used performance measure is a global rating. These are serious shortcomings, and users have a right to expect more studies of a broader range and of greater sophistication in the future.

On the other hand, many professional workers are coming to place at least some greater emphasis on content validation, to be followed by concurrent or predictive validation. The FIT battery seems very well adapted to this strategy. Since this battery, unlike many competitors, is available as 18 separate subtests, it is relatively easy to move from a job-description component to one of the aptitude subtests. This writer has used this battery for years in precisely this way. The job description provides the basis for hypothesizing what test dimensions seem likely to work, and subsequently concurrent or predictive validation is used to confirm or deny these content judgments.

It is probably unwise to use too few of these subtests alone, without combination with other subtests or with other predictors. These are short tests—sometimes very short indeed. The reliabilities reflect this fact, and, hence, it seems risky to base predictions about individual applicants on too few components. Multiple regression combination of predictors, including FIT components, provides a ready solution to the problem.

Given this precaution and, of course, local validation, the generalization with which this review opened, seems clearly to hold. Overall, this is a good series of aptitude tests, potentially useful in personnel selection.

[982]

★JEVS Work Sample Evaluation System. High school and adults; 1969–76; also called *Philadelphia J.E.V.S. Work Sample Battery;* simulated work ac-

Flanagan Industrial Tests

tivities for evaluation of performance, interest, and work behavior of rehabilitation, minority group, and school populations; 28 tests; 2 scores: time and quality ratings of 1 (lowest 40%), 2 (middle 20%), 3 (highest 40%) for each test, plus 27 ratings by evaluator: behavior in interpersonal situations (5 ratings), worker characteristics (9 ratings), learning and comprehension (6 ratings), discriminations, manipulative skills (5 ratings), significant worker characteristics (2 ratings); no data on reliability and validity; individual; 1 form; looseleaf handbook ('73, 213 pages); supplementary norms ('76, 26 pages); physical layout ('72, 1 page); hardware parts list ('73, 10 pages); guide to client orientation ('73, 3 pages); rules ('73, 1 page); motivational interview ('71, 1 page); general procedures ('73, 2 pages); worksample record ('74, c1975, 10 pages); worksample workslip ('69, c1975, 1 page); worksample evaluation report ('72, c1975, 10 pages); instructions for completing report ('72, 20 pages); supplement to report ('73, 3 pages); relationships of data-people-things hierarchies ('69, 3 pages); feedback interview form ('69, c1975, 1 page); referral form ('72, c1975, 1 page); definitions of factors ('72, 2 pages); distribution restricted to organizations which send at least 1 staff member to publisher's training course and agree to accept 1 consultation visit from a J.E.V.S. staff member; $6,345 per set of testing materials, postpaid; $700 per person for publisher's 2 week training course; $630 plus transportation for 1 consultation visit; 60% of examinees complete tests in administration times listed below; 5–7 days for 15 clients to complete battery; Jewish Employment and Vocational Service, Inc. *

a) WORK SAMPLE 1, NUT-BOLT-WASHER ASSEMBLY. (61) minutes.

b) 2, RUBBER STAMPING. (33) minutes.

c) 3, WASHER THREADING. (47) minutes.

d) 4, BUDGETTE ASSEMBLY. (54) minutes.

e) 5, SIGN MAKING. (46) minutes.

f) 10, TILE SORTING. (38) minutes.

g) 11, NUT PACKING. (34) minutes.

h) 12, COLLATING LEATHER SAMPLES. (7) minutes.

i) 20, GROMMET ASSEMBLY. (19) minutes.

j) 30, UNION ASSEMBLY. (20) minutes.

k) 31, BELT ASSEMBLY. (23) minutes.

l) 32, LADDER ASSEMBLY. (125) minutes.

m) 33, METAL SQUARE FABRICATION. (72) minutes.

n) 34, HARDWARE ASSEMBLY. (56) minutes.

o) 35, TELEPHONE ASSEMBLY. (73) minutes.

p) 36, LOCK ASSEMBLY. (59) minutes.

q) 40, FILING BY NUMBERS. (86) minutes.

r) 41, PROOFREADING. (54) minutes.

s) 50, FILING BY LETTERS. (101) minutes.

t) 51, NAIL AND SCREW SORTING. (22) minutes.

u) 52, ADDING MACHINE. (70) minutes.

v) 53, PAYROLL COMPUTATION. (62) minutes.

w) 54, COMPUTING POSTAGE. (62) minutes.

x) 60, RESISTOR READING. (67) minutes.

y) 70, PIPE ASSEMBLY. (57) minutes.

z) 80, BLOUSE MAKING. (194) minutes.

aa) 80a, VEST MAKING. (160) minutes.

bb) 90, CONDENSING PRINCIPLE. (153) minutes.

REFERENCES

1. KULMAN, HAROLD V., AND DRACHMAN, FRANKLIN. "New Developments in the Philadelphia JEVS Work Sample System." *Voc Eval & Work Adj B* 6(1):21–4 Mr '73. *
2. FLENNIKEN, DON. "Time-Quality Performance of Goodwill Clients Evaluated by the JEVS Work Sample Battery." *Work Eval & Work Adj B* 7(3):3–16 S '74. *
3. FLENNIKEN, DON. "Performance on the 1973 Revised Philadelphia JEVS Work Sample Battery." *Voc Eval & Work Adj B* 8(4):35–47 D '75. *

★**Position Analysis Questionnaire.** Business and industry; 1969–73; PAQ; "analysis of jobs in terms of 187 job elements that reflect....the basic human behaviors in jobs, regardless of the specific 'technological' area or level of the job"; each position should be rated by 3 or more analysts; 32 job dimension scores (watching devices/materials for information, interpreting what is heard or seen, using data originating with people, watching things from a distance, evaluating information from things, being aware of environmental conditions, being aware of body movement and balance, making decisions, processing information, controlling machines/processes, using hands and arms to control/modify, using feet/hands to operate equipment/vehicles, performing activities requiring general body movement, using hands and arms to move/position things, using fingers vs. general body movement, performing skilled/technical activities, communicating judgments-decisions-information, exchanging job-related information, performing staff/related activities, contacting supervisor or subordinates, dealing with the public, being in a hazardous/unpleasant environment, engaging in personally demanding situations, engaging in businesslike work situations, being alert to detail/changing conditions, performing unstructured vs. structured work, working on a variable vs. regular schedule, having decision making-communication-social responsibility, performing skilled activities, being physically active/related environmental conditions, operating equipment/vehicles, processing information) plus estimated means, standard deviations, and validity coefficients of 9 GATB scores (intelligence, verbal, numerical, spatial, form perception, clerical perception, motor coordination, finger dexterity, manual dexterity) for job incumbents; Form B ('69, 28 pages); technical manual ('72, 20 pages), user's manual ('73, 84 pages); separate answer sheets (Digitek) may be used; $1 per test; 15¢ per answer sheet; $2 per technical manual; $5 per user's manual; postage extra; $3 per specimen set (without user's manual), cash orders postpaid; information on scoring and statistical services available; (90–120) minutes; Ernest J. McCormick, P. R. Jeanneret, and Robert C. Mecham; published by PAQ Services, Inc.; distributed by University Book Store. *

REFERENCES

1. CUNNINGHAM, JOSEPH WILLIAM. *Worker-Oriented Job Variables: Their Factor Structure and Use in Determining Job Requirements.* Doctor's thesis, Purdue University (Lafayette, Ind.), 1964. (*DA* 26:2885)
2. PETERS, DAVID L., AND McCORMICK, ERNEST J. "Comparative Reliability of Numerically Anchored Versus Job-Task Anchored Rating Scales." *J Appl Psychol* 50:92–6 F '66. * (*PA* 40:4642)
3. McCORMICK, ERNEST J.; CUNNINGHAM, JOSEPH W.; AND GORDON, GEORGE G. "Job Dimensions Based on Factorial Analyses of Worker-Oriented Job Variables." *Personnel Psychol* 20:417–30 w '67. * (*PA* 42:7933)
4. McCORMICK, ERNEST J.; CUNNINGHAM, JOSEPH W.; AND THORNTON, GEORGE C. "The Prediction of Job Requirements by a Structured Job Analysis Procedure." *Personnel Psychol* 20: 431–40 w '67. *
5. McCORMICK, ERNEST J., AND MECHAM, ROBERT C. "Job Analysis Data as the Basis for Synthetic Test Validity." *Psychol Annual* 4:30–5 Mr '70. * (*PA* 46:3929)
6. McCORMICK, ERNEST J.; JEANNERET, P. R.; AND MECHAM, ROBERT C. "Application of a Structured Job Analysis Procedure." Abstract. *Proc 79th Ann Conv Am Psychol Assn* 6(2): 501–2 '71. * (*PA* 46:5868)
7. PRIEN, ERICH P., AND RONAN, WILLIAM W. "Job Analysis: A Review of Research Findings." *Personnel Psychol* 24(3): 371–96 au '71. * (*PA* 51:10007)
8. McCORMICK, ERNEST J.; JEANNERET, PAUL R.; AND MECHAM, ROBERT C. "A Study of Job Characteristics and Job Dimensions as Based on the Position Analysis Questionnaire (PAQ)." *J Appl Psychol* 56(4):347–68 Ag '72. * (*PA* 49: 1437)
9. BAUKUS, ERWIN JOHN. *The Relationship Between Synthetically Derived Job Profiles and a Personality Inventory*

Profile of First Line Supervisors. Doctor's thesis, Illinois Institute of Technology (Chicago, Ill.), 1973. (*DAI* 34:2350B)
   10. FRIELING, E.; KANNHEISER, W.; AND LINDBERG, R. "Some Results With the German Form of the Position Analysis Questionnaire (PAQ)." *J Appl Psychol* 59(6):741–7 D '74. * (*PA* 53:8452)
   11. MARQUARDT, LLOYD DAVID. *The Utility of Job Dimensions Based on the Position Analysis Questionnaire (PAQ) in a Job Component Validation Model.* Doctor's thesis, Purdue University (Lafayette, Ind.), 1974. (*DAI* 35:3079B)
   12. ROBINSON, DAVID D.; WAHLSTROM, OWEN W.; AND MECHAM, ROBERT C. "Comparison of Job Evaluation Methods: A 'Policy-Capturing' Approach Using the Position Analysis Questionnaire." *J Appl Psychol* 59(5):633–7 O '74. * (*PA* 53:6325)
   13. TOWNSEND, J. WILLIAM; PRIEN, ERICH P.; AND JOHNSON, JOHN T., JR. "The Use of the Position Analysis Questionnaire in Selecting Correlates of Job Performance Among Mentally Retarded Workers." *J Voc Behav* 4(2):181–92 Ap '74. * (*PA* 52:10445)
   14. ARVEY, RICHARD D., AND BEGALLA, MARTHA E. "Analyzing the Homemaker Job Using the Position Analysis Questionnaire (PAQ)." *J Appl Psychol* 60(4):513–7 Ag '75. * (*PA* 54:8582)
   15. ASH, RONALD A., AND EDGELL, STEVEN L. "A Note on the Readability of the Position Analysis Questionnaire (PAQ)." *J Appl Psychol* 60(6):765–6 '75. * (*PA* 55:3474)
   16. SMITH, JACK ELY. *Evaluation of the Position Analysis Questionnaire and Its Ramifications for Other Structured Job Analysis Questionnaires.* Doctor's thesis, Ohio State University (Columbus, Ohio), 1975. (*DAI* 36:5849B)
   17. ARVEY, RICHARD D.; PASSINO, EMILY M.; AND LOUNSBURY, JOHN W. "Job Analysis Results as Influenced by Sex of Incumbent and Sex of Analyst." *J Appl Psychol* 62(4):411–6 Ag '77. *

ALAN R. BASS, *Professor of Psychology, Wayne State University, Detroit, Michigan.*

A variety of techniques are available for conducting job and task analyses, such as the critical incidents technique, diary method, checklist methods, interviewing, and job observation. However, most of these procedures provide primarily qualitative, verbally descriptive rather than quantitative data; are rather subjective; and are dependent upon such factors as the verbal, interviewing, and observational skills of the job analyst. *The Position Analysis Questionnaire* is a structured job analysis questionnaire which provides quantitative data for each job analyzed on a number of job elements and dimensions.

The current version (Form B) of the PAQ consists of 194 items ("job elements") which the authors refer to as "worker-oriented" rather than "job-oriented" in nature. "Worker-oriented" job elements are relatively general in nature and are concerned with human behaviors which might be involved in a variety of jobs (e.g., coding, compiling, and transcribing information), whereas "job-oriented" elements are more job-specific and tend to deal with specialized technological processes of jobs (e.g., posting invoice receipts to general ledger).

The 194 job elements in the PAQ are grouped into six content divisions: information input (35 items); mental process (14 items);

work output (49 items); relationships with other persons (36 items); job context (19 items); and other job characteristics (41 items).

For most of the items in the PAQ a five-point response scale is provided, using response categories appropriate to that particular item (e.g., extent of use, importance to the job, amount of time, possibility of occurrence). In each case, a sixth response, "does not apply," is provided. For a few items, a two-point response scale (does or does not apply) is used.

The technical manual provides a summary of some of the extensive research which has been conducted with this instrument, and the user's manual provides detailed information on the appropriate use of the PAQ and on the kinds of data which can be provided for the user. Thus far, the authors have conducted quite extensive research on the dimensionality of the PAQ, reliabilities of PAQ responses, and on the use of the PAQ for job evaluation, job classification, and estimation of aptitude requirements for a wide variety of jobs.

On the basis of research which had been conducted at the time the manuals were prepared, the user is provided with information concerning factor scores which can be derived for a total of 27 divisional and five overall job dimensions, based on job data which had been identified at that time. However, subsequent research on a larger and broader sample of jobs has identified somewhat more and different job dimensions. McCormick (8) reports a total of 30 divisional and 14 general job dimensions based on job data.

Reliability studies have been primarily concerned with interanalyst agreement on the various job dimension scores. Interanalyst reliabilities have generally been in the .50s and higher, although some dimensions seem to be rated with considerably less agreement. Rate-rerate reliabilities are generally higher than the interanalyst reliabilities, as might be expected, and are reported in the .80s and .90s. The average interanalyst reliability coefficient across all items in the PAQ (based on a sample of 62 jobs) is reported as .79. Since these reliability coefficients are based on analyses of pairs of raters, it would be expected that reliabilities of dimension scores and of overall PAQ profiles would be higher if more than two analysts are used, which is often possible in job analysis studies.

One application of the PAQ has been in job evaluation, for the purpose of establishing compensation rates for jobs. A number of studies are reported in which job dimension scores obtained from the PAQ are used to predict actual job compensation rates, and the predicted rates are then compared with actual rates for these jobs. Overall, the PAQ appears to be a potentially useful instrument for obtaining data for use in job evaluation studies, and the user's manual provides "predicted job evaluation points" for each job analyzed, based on appropriate weighting of job dimension scores for that job as determined by previous research studies. Other applications are (a) in job classification, where it is desired to group a set of jobs into relatively homogeneous or comparable "job families" based on similarity of their job dimension profiles; and (b) the estimation of job-related aptitudes and abilities which might be appropriate for personnel selection purposes, based solely on job data obtained from the PAQ without the need for the usual empirical validation procedures. The authors refer to this technique as "job component validity" which is a variation of what has elsewhere been referred to as synthetic validity.

The authors have now conducted a number of research studies concerned with estimation of ability and aptitude requirements from data obtained with the PAQ. Thus far the aptitude and ability measures studied have been those obtained from the GATB, although the authors are currently in the process of extending this research to other commercially available tests. The job component validity studies have generally involved prediction of mean GATB test scores or of GATB validity coefficients, for a variety of jobs from job dimension scores obtained from the PAQ. A total of more than 3,800 jobs has been included in these studies, and the results have generally indicated reasonably good predictions of mean test scores from PAQ job dimensions. GATB test validity coefficients have generally not been as predictable as have the mean test scores.

The user's manual provides information on estimation of GATB test score means and validity coefficients for a particular job from the user's PAQ job dimension scores. The com-

puterized scoring service will also provide the user a "predicted use in selection" score for each GATB test for each job analyzed. Further, the three "best" tests for the job are identified, and predicted cutting scores are recommended for each of these three tests.

While the notion of job component validity is an intriguing one and may present a possible solution to the problems inherent in traditional criterion-related empirical validation studies, this technique has not yet been widely accepted as a legitimate alternative to traditional validation strategies. There are a number of problems which need to be dealt with, including decisions as to minimum standards for acceptance of a particular test as a selection procedure from job component validity data. It is not clear just when estimates of mean test scores and validity coefficients from job analysis data justify use of these tests for selection purposes. No minimal criteria such as level of statistical significance are available at this point.

Overall, the PAQ is a carefully developed, extensively and systematically researched instrument, which will be of value for many job analysis purposes. At the same time, some cautions are in order.

Even though the authors say they have attempted to make the present form reasonably simple to read and understand, it does appear that the instrument requires reasonably well-educated and/or trained analysts to achieve reliable and accurate job evaluations.

The value of this questionnaire to an organization will be limited by the extent to which the particular "worker-oriented" items and dimensions of the PAQ are applicable and useful for the jobs being analyzed and the purposes of the job analysis. It is entirely possible that an alternative job analysis approach or a tailormade questionnaire for the particular jobs being studied may be more valuable and appropriate in a given situation. Or a procedure which is more specifically oriented to a particular job or class of jobs might yield more appropriate job analysis information for some purposes than a more general instrument such as the PAQ. Nevertheless, if one wishes to obtain quantitative job analysis data on worker-oriented items and job dimensions for which considerable research has now been conducted and which has been shown to have utility for a number of applications

Position Analysis Questionnaire

(e.g., estimating aptitude requirements for jobs, job evaluation for compensation purposes, job classification), the PAQ is an excellent instrument for consideration.

[984]

★Social and Prevocational Information Battery. Educable mentally retarded (IQ 55–75) grades 7–12; 1975; SPIB; 10 scores: purchasing habits, budgeting, banking, job related behavior, job search skills, home management, health care, hygiene and grooming, functional signs, total; orally administered; 1 form; 2 editions: hand scored, machine scored (CompuScan), (16 pages); examiner's manual (62 pages); user's guide (27 pages); technical report (15 pages); $15 per 20 hand scored tests, $19 per 20 machine scored tests; $2.50 per technical report; $5 per specimen set; postage extra; CompuScan scoring service, 55¢ and over per test; (180–270) minutes in 3 or more sessions; Andrew Halpern, Paul Raffeld, Larry K. Irvin, and Robert Link; CTB/McGraw-Hill. *

REFERENCES

1. HALPERN, ANDREW S.; RAFFELD, PAUL; IRVIN, LARRY; AND LINK, ROBERT. "Measuring Social and Prevocational Awareness in Mildly Retarded Adolescents." *Am J Mental Def* 80(1):81–9 Jl '75. *
2. IRVIN, LARRY K., AND HALPERN, ANDREW S. "Reliability and Validity of the Social and Prevocational Information Battery for Mildly Retarded Individuals." *Am J Mental Def* 81(6):603–5 My '77. *

C. EDWARD MEYERS, *Research Psychologist, Neuropsychiatric Institute, University of California, Los Angeles, California.*

Preparing mildly mentally handicapped youth for employment and community living requires identifying and correcting their principal deficits in adaptation. One difficulty has been a lack of valid scores for selecting trainees, comparing and evaluating educational and treatment programs, and accountability reporting in terms of client status or change. Broad-ranged "adaptive behavior" scales may include items or subscales suited to such program planning but these are lean compared with a scale fully devoted to this group. The authors of this battery appear to have produced an instrument of high quality, filling some of the void.

The orally presented tests measure knowledge of salient aspects of employability and independent living. SPIB items and instructions are phrased simply to communicate the idea of the item to the educable mentally retarded (EMR); yet, appropriate language is used when it must be the substance of the tested competence, either in the examiner's spoken words or in the reading of advertisements or traffic or safety signs. No other reading is required. The authors hope to minimize subject fatigue by spreading testing over three sessions of about an hour each.

The manual stresses the importance that examinees respond appropriately. Reactions to trial questions are to be carefully observed and more help is to be given if required. Instructions for administration are precise and sequential, not wordy or preachy while making essential emphases. Though SPIB is a group test, the group should be limited, with adequate proctors present.

Each of the nine tests has from 26 to 30 items. The 277 items consist of 240 true-false items and 37 two-choice graphics. For example, an item concerned with "important things to budget for," requires a choice of pictured life necessities vs. luxuries.

Raw scores may be converted to percentage correct and percentile ranks, separately for the junior and the senior high groups. The SPIB was developed with 700 junior and 1,100 senior high EMR participants in Oregon, with reference group data on 453 of each level, ages 14–20 years. Most students were Caucasian; the sexes were about equally divided.

K-R 20 reliabilities for subtests range from .65 to .82, with median .75; for battery totals, .94 and .93. Test-retest correlations for two-week intervals had the same general magnitude.

EVALUATION. The SPIB is designed for use in programs which assist mildly retarded youth enter into hopefully normal adult life. Such youth, because they are slow to learn and often have been protected, are prone to experience difficulty in such prosaic matters as purchasing, applying for a job, and worker-boss relations. The SPIB seeks to measure the extent of such knowledge and thus to provide counselors and teachers with information about where needs are greatest so as to develop training priorities, as well as to have scores for use in selection and placement into sheltered workshops, community living facilities, etc. Given the paucity of psychometric tools in this area of use, the SPIB will be well received, though some reservations must be expressed. SPIB has sufficient total battery reliability for use in selection and placement of individuals. Some of the scale scores have insufficient reliability for individual use but are adequate for group use in evaluation of programs, description of a dependent population, accountability reporting, and the like. While one wishes the individual scales could demonstrate higher reliability than those reported, the reliabilities should be superior to the only other source of such information on subjects, i.e., ratings by teachers, parents, or counselors. If they follow a common practice in this work, many users will disregard reliability specifications in taking the scale scores or even the individual item failures as bases for instruction in specific skills.

Measuring information only and not actual competence, the tests can not reveal the extent to which the subject's implementation of his knowledge is impaired by any biomedical or emotional impediment, as often happens in a retarded population. Securing some such information by observation, rating, or checklist would seem a mandatory complement to SPIB in making key decisions. This reviewer tentatively accepts the claims for validity provided in the technical report and other publications. We are not provided with scores associated with comparative success-failure in specific settings such as rehabilitation training, sheltered workshop, or actual employment and hope such experience tables can soon be developed.

We regret the necessity for an Oregon-only, mostly Caucasian construction and norming. To add a few minority cases in Louisville and Anchorage fails to inform how the mid-city youth raised in the great apartment houses of our metropoles might perform; it is hoped such experience will soon accrue and be reported.

[985]

★Survey of Organizations: "A Machine-Scored Standardized Questionnaire Instrument." Employees; 1967-74; SOO; for measurement of groups, not individuals; 16 scores for each of 3 hierarchical groups (middle management, second line supervision, first line supervision): organizational climate (decision-making practices, communication flow, motivational conditions, human resources primacy, lower level influence, technological readiness), supervisory leadership (support, work facilitation, goal emphasis, team building), peer leadership (support, work facilitation, goal emphasis, team building), group process, satisfaction, plus 204 item scores; norms based on earlier editions; 1974 edition ('74, 8 pages, NCS scorable); no manual for 1974 edition; manual ('72, 167 pages) for superseded forms; norms ['72, 36 pages]; test materials and scoring service, $3.50 and over per test, postage extra; (30-45) minutes for salaried employees, (60-90) minutes for hourly employees; developed by the Organizational Development Research Program of the Center for Research on Utilization of Scientific Knowledge, Institute for Social Research, University of Michigan (manual by James C. Taylor and David G. Bowers); Institute for Social Research. *

REFERENCES

1. TAYLOR, J. C. "An Empirical Examination of a Four-Factor Theory of Leadership Using Smallest Space Analysis." Organiz Behav & Hum Perfor 6(3):249-66 My '71. * (PA 46:9883)
2. BOWERS, DAVID G. "OD Techniques and Their Results in 23 Organizations: The Michigan ICL Study." J Appl Behav Sci 9(1):21-43 Ja-F '73. * (PA 50:10086)
3. MICHAELSEN, LARRY K. "Leader Orientation, Leader Behavior, Group Effectiveness and Situational Favorability: An Empirical Extension of the Contingency Model." Organiz Behav & Hum Perfor 9(2):226-45 Ap '73. * (PA 50:12188)
4. TOPLIS, JOHN. "Review of the Survey of Organizations." Occup Psychol (England) 47(3-4):260-1 '73. *
5. COAD, ROSEMARY ANN. A Study of the Effects of Survey Feedback Data-Based Strategy Intervention Mode of Organization Development on the Educational Staffs of Four Wichita, Kansas, Public Schools. Doctor's thesis, Kansas State University (Manhattan, Kan.), 1975. (DAI 36:2524A)
6. EDEN, DOV, AND LEVIATAN, URI. "Implicit Leadership Theory as a Determinant of the Factor Structure Underlying Supervisory Behavior Scales." J Appl Psychol 60(6):736-41 D '75. *
7. FRANKLIN, JEROME L. "Relations Among Four Social-Psychological Aspects of Organizations." Adm Sci Q 20(3): 422-33 S '75. * (PA 56:6926)
8. HAUSSER, D. L.; PECORELLA, P. A.; AND WISSLER, A. L. Survey-Guided Development: A Manual for Consultants. Ann Arbor, Mich.: Organizational Development Research Program, Institute for Social Research, University of Michigan, 1975. Pp. ix, 183. *
9. WEINTRAUB, MARVIN. The Effect of an Educational Experience on Individual Perception Upon Reentry in the Work Organization. Doctor's thesis, Florida State University (Tallahassee, Fla.), 1975. (DAI 37:4070A)
10. FORREST, FRANK GOODWIN. Human Values Accounting as an Organization Development Diagnostic Technique. Doctor's thesis, United States International University (San Diego, Calif.), 1976. (DAI 37:1404B)
11. PARKER, WARRINGTON S., JR. "Black-White Differences in Leader Behavior Related to Subordinates' Reactions." J Appl Psychol 61(2):140-7 Ap '76. *
12. DREXLER, JOHN A., JR. "Organizational Climate: Its Homogeneity Within Organizations." J Appl Psychol 62(1): 38-42 F '77. * (PA 58:2375)

ROBERT FITZPATRICK, Director of Research, Psychological Service of Pittsburgh, Pittsburgh, Pennsylvania.

According to the manual, the Survey of Organizations "is best viewed, not as a 'morale' survey in the conventional sense of the word, but as a 'descriptive' survey of organizational conditions and practices." The items of this survey seem more complex and less down-to-earth than those in other surveys. For example, here is item 106, to be answered on a 5-point Likert-type scale of agreement: "To what extent are there times on your job when one person wants you to do one thing and someone else wants you to do something different."

Compare this with a roughly similar item on the SRA Employee Inventory, to be answered Agree, ?, or Disagree:

"Everybody in this organization tries to boss us around." The SOO emphasizes relations with the respondent's immediate work group and the supervisor of the group. There are no items concerning fringe benefits or the physical work environment.

The survey is designed to cover 19 "primary variables" considered to be the basic elements in organizational behavior, as conceived by Likert and his co-workers at the University of Michigan. Thus, it is both an embodiment of the

Likert theory of organizations and a tool in the further development and application of that theory.

The content and wording of the items in a survey imply something about the values of the organization involved. The SOO implies that workers at all levels should be given opportunities to discuss decisions before they are made, that cooperation and teamwork are quite important, that rewards should be based on performance, that disagreements are necessary and desirable if they are worked through, etc. Most of us would agree that these are good values, but they are not necessarily desirable for all organizations.

The ideas contained in the Likert theory, and hence in the SOO, are sophisticated. Do workers at all levels have a common understanding of what it means to "suppress" or "work through" a disagreement? Can everyone understand item 104: "To what extent does doing your job well lead to things like disapproval and rejection from those you work with?" The manual reports a study in which hourly workers from four plants in one company were interviewed about their responses to the survey. The study is said to show that misunderstandings of the survey were minor. However, the report of the study is sketchy and not convincing.

Much of the manual is poorly organized and hard to read. In large part, it is a rehash of previously published studies which are only partly congruent with the purposes of the manual. The manual contains many statements of doubtful merit and a few outright errors. For example: (a) the application of chi-square to the data in Tables 10 through 13 is inappropriate, since the cell entries are not derived from independent samplings; (b) no reference is made to any test of significance for the data of Table 15, but conclusions are drawn as if such tests had been made.

Nevertheless, the manual is to be applauded as a conscientious effort to compile for a survey the kind of information expected in a test manual. In particular, the authors deal constructively with the question of the survey's validity. They present convincing evidence that the content does in fact represent the Likert theory and conclude that it is therefore reasonably content valid. They also report several lines of evidence bearing on the construct and criterion-related

validity of the survey. On the whole, these efforts at validation are well conceived and suggest that the SOO is reasonably valid for its intended applications.

The manual presents detailed instructions for administration, even though it recommends that this administration be carried out by the Institute for Social Research of the University of Michigan. Also included in the manual are copies of three previous versions of the survey, along with discussion of reasons for some of the changes. A sketchy set of norms is provided separately, for several categories of employees but with no indication of the numbers of cases or organizations on which they are based.

No provision is made for comments by respondents. This seems unfortunate, since it is often possible for employees to clarify their responses by commenting on specific circumstances or events.

In general, the *Survey of Organizations* appears to have been competently developed and to be supported by a sound research program. If an organization finds the Likert concepts to be compatible or even acceptable, this instrument should definitely be considered. However, if what is wanted is simply a means by which to measure employee attitudes on the usual topics, the *Survey of Organizations* would not normally be suitable.

STEPHAN J. MOTOWIDLO, *Research Psychologist, Personnel Decisions Research Institute, Minneapolis, Minnesota.*

The *Survey of Organizations* is an instrument that purports to measure characteristics of organizations and organizational units according to variables reflecting features of organizational climate, managerial leadership, peer behavior, satisfaction, and group process. The SOO does not purport to measure characteristics of individual respondents but instead is analyzed and interpreted according to mean responses aggregated within organizational units such as primary work groups or within an entire organization. Although the SOO does include some frankly evaluative items—roughly a third of the 99 items in the 1969 version— that call for attitudinal or affective responses, the main thrust of the instrument seems to be toward providing descriptive measures of conditions prevailing in organizations as perceived by organizational members. In large part, then, the

Survey of Organizations

validity and usefulness of the SOO must rest on evidence that it accurately taps important, objective features of group and organizational environments of work settings.

The manual provides a great deal of information. It painstakingly spells out the development of the SOO, from the initial 1966 version to subsequent generations of machine scored versions up to the 1970 version. The various revisions testify to the care that has gone into the SOO's development and to the developers' dedication to its continual refinement and improvement. (Since the most recent version, 1974, is newer than the manual, it is, of course, not discussed in the manual.) The manual also includes detailed standardized instructions for administering the SOO, preparing cover letters in advance of administration, and gathering completed forms. All this should prove extremely helpful to persons wishing to administer and use the instrument. With respect to more substantive matters, however, such as the validity of scales included in the instrument, the manual could have been more thorough in reporting evidence, if such evidence exists, that mean perceptual scores derived from the SOO in fact reflect objective conditions in work groups or organizations.

The SOO includes four scales for managerial leadership: support, goal emphasis, work facilitation, and interaction facilitation. Despite arguments in the manual that these dimensions should not be collapsed into one overall leadership variable, the fact that their intercorrelations range from .72 to .81 certainly does not compel the conclusion that the four leadership scales possess a high degree of discriminant validity. To the contrary, the intercorrelations support the more skeptical view that the scales either reflect one, more parsimonious dimension of leadership behavior, whatever that dimension might be, or—and perhaps more probably—reflect a global, evaluative halo which may serve to distort presumed measures of how leaders actually behave.

The six scales said to measure dimensions of organizational climate (human resources primacy, communication flow, motivational conditions, decision-making practices, technological readiness, and lower level influence) are also highly intercorrelated (.41 to .78, with median .64). Once again, these high intercorrelations

point to the possibility that organizational climate as measured by these scales might more efficiently be conceptualized according to a single dimension of objective differences in climate or that they are severely handicapped by halo and contamination from affective or evaluative factors that introduce error into these perceptual measures.

The SOO includes one measure of overall satisfaction comprised of seven items. This scale was explicitly developed to tap differences in satisfaction among work groups, not among individuals, and is one of the few (if not the only) multi-item, self-report measures of satisfaction developed for that purpose. One would have more faith, however, that it does indeed measure group differences in satisfaction instead of (or in addition to) individual differences in satisfaction if there were evidence of significant between-group variance on this measure relative to within-group variance.

Seven items comprise a composite index of what is called "Group Process." They include items that tap perceptions about the extent to which the work group plans together and coordinates its efforts, really wants to meet its objectives successfully, is able to respond to unusual work demands, and consists of persons who are trusted by the questionnaire respondent. The precise conceptual nature of the *variable* which presumably underlies variance on this measure is a mystery, at least to me. There is no clear indication in the manual of what meaningful dimension of group process is tapped by this scale.

Some construct validity for some of the scales emerges from cross-lag correlational analyses that are reasonably consistent with theoretical assumptions about which SOO variables are causes of which other SOO variables. It would be far better, however, and, in fact, obligatory, to show that SOO perceptual measures of objective conditions in organizations are significantly related to other measures, including some more objective measures, of these same organizational conditions. Such multi-method evidence is conspicuously absent from the manual.

There is some other evidence that some of the SOO scales may, on some occasions, be significantly related to organizationally important outcomes such as efficiency and attendance. Although there may be more statistically signifi-

Survey of Organizations

cant correlations than would be expected by chance, they are generally rather low, certainly too low to warrant a great deal of enthusiasm for the predictive power of SOO scores for economic criteria of organizational effectiveness.

In sum, the SOO is one of the few available standardized instruments developed to measure characteristics of organizations and work units. I have little doubt that researchers will continue to revise, refine, and validate the scales. For now, however, the lack of validity evidence incorporating other measures of the objective organizational features which the SOO purports to measure and the high intercorrelations among scales which are said to measure meaningfully different dimensions give rise to skepticism about its usefulness as a diagnostic device. Possibly, some of the existing scales may be useful as flags or signals that something is right or wrong in an organization, but it is not likely that all the SOO scales provide nonredundant information of this sort. In my opinion, there is little evidence that SOO scales included in the core questionnaire yield much information about specifically *what* may be wrong, and therefore it is probably less useful for guiding efforts toward particular features of organizations that may need to be changed.

Occup Psychol (England) 47(3–4):260–1 '73. John Toplis. Criteria for judging the worth of psychological tests and other techniques for assessing individuals have been the subject of recommendations by both the British Psychological Society and the American Psychological Association. Taylor and Bowers believe that similar standards should be used to judge the worth of organisational survey methods and, in this monograph, describe the development of a standard questionnaire and the establishment of its technical properties. When the research began in 1966, Taylor, Bowers, and their associates had access to a sizeable pool of questionnaire items built up from earlier work at the Institute of Social Research, and the guidance of Dr. Rensis Likert together with his view of the basic elements in organisational development. The aims of the research were ambitious —to produce a questionnaire which would demand descriptive responses, which could be used in virtually all organisations without revisions, which could be quickly administered and tabulated and which would be soundly based on

organisation theories. There was the further aim of producing the survey results in a form which could be understood and used by work-group leaders in an organisation. The initial state of play is described in the first chapter, while subsequent chapters deal with the design of the questionnaire for machine scoring, technical problems of question design (such as stem reversal and position response bias) and the methods employed to measure "leadership," "organisational climate," "satisfaction" and "group processes." The final chapter contains information about reliability and validity (criteria used include "efficiency" and "manpower turnover" and "absence") and the remaining pages (over a third of the total) comprise appendices containing full copies of the questionnaires developed and details of the survey administration procedures. The copy of the monograph sent for review had an extra and unusual feature—a "Note of Caution" printed on green paper which had been slipped between the pages. This Note suggested that potential users should carefully examine their reasons for wanting to use the questionnaire and that the advice of people with relevant expertise should be sought. Taylor and Bowers certainly have made a good start towards their aim of "providing to potential users the technical information rightfully expected about any assessment device," and it is perhaps unfair to carp about omissions. But it is not clear whether the latest questionnaire can be used in a variety of situations without revisions or whether results can be understood and used by work-group leaders. Nor is there information as to whether responses vary with age, sex, length of service, type of work done, size of organisation and so on. Information about the administration of the questionnaire might have been more carefully selected too—for example, while four pages of the appendix comprise a guide to the construction of "drop boxes" in which to collect completed questionnaires, there is no mention of the way that the questionnaires might be introduced to suspicious trade union representatives or how to deal with absentees or individuals who do not wish to take part. In spite of these omissions, the monograph could well be used as a standard against which to evaluate the thoroughness of development of other organisational survey techniques. But it is a somewhat

Survey of Organizations

technical document and its appeal is likely to be limited by its turgid language and by some uncommon and ill-explained statistics. Perhaps this is not a bad thing because the greater the circulation the more people may be tempted to ignore the "Note of Caution" and plagiarise the questionnaire. All in all the quality of writing and editing does not match that of the research reported. But it is to be hoped that this is merely a first stage in reporting the series of development studies in which the questionnaire was used. An account of these studies detailing the questionnaire and other information collected, and the benefits to the organisations concerned, is likely to be well worth reading.

[986]

TAV Selection System. Adults; 1963–68; TAV; vocational selection and counseling; 7 tests; manual ('68, 65 pages); norms consist of means and standard deviations for 8 occupational groups (state traffic officers, municipal patrolmen, female high school teachers, male high school teachers, life insurance claims adjusters, life insurance salesmen, deputy sheriff cadets, female probation counselors); 1–50 sets of test-answer sheets (IBM 805 scorable) for the battery, $1 per set; $3 per set of scoring stencils for the battery; $2 per manual; $5 per specimen set; postage extra; (210) minutes for the battery, (15–20) minutes for any one test; R. R. Morman; TAV Selection System. *

a) TAV ADJECTIVE CHECKLIST. 1963–68; 3 scores: toward people (T), away from people (A), versus people (V); 1 form ('63, 2 pages); 1–50 test-answer sheets, 14¢ each.

b) TAV JUDGMENTS. 1964–68; 3 scores: same as in *a*; 1 form ('64, 4 pages on 2 sheets); 1–50 sets of the 2 test-answer sheets, 17¢ per set.

c) TAV PERSONAL DATA. 1964–68; 3 scores: same as in *a*; 1 form ('64, 4 pages on 2 sheets); 1–50 sets of the 2 test-answer sheets, 17¢ per set.

d) TAV PREFERENCES. 1963–68; 3 scores: same as in *a*; 1 form ('63, 2 pages); 1–50 tests, 14¢ each.

e) TAV PROVERBS AND SAYINGS. 1966–68; 3 scores: same as in *a*; 1 form ('66, 3 pages on 2 sheets); 1–50 sets of the 2 test-answer sheets, 17¢ per set.

f) TAV SALESMAN REACTIONS. 1967–68; 3 scores: same as in *a*; 1 form ('67, 4 pages on 2 sheets); 1–50 sets of the 2 test-answer sheets, 17¢ per set.

g) TAV MENTAL AGILITY. 1965–68; 3 scores: follow directions and carefulness, weights and balances, verbal comprehension; 1 form ('65, 3 pages on 2 sheets); 1–50 sets of the 2 test-answer sheets, 17¢ per set.

See T2:2113 (3 references); for an excerpted review by John O. Crites, see 7:983 (1 reference); see also P:263A (11 references).

REFERENCES

1–11. See P:263A.
12. See 7:983.
13–15. See T2:2113; also includes a cumulative name index to the first 15 references and 1 excerpt for this test.
16. MORMAN, R. R.; HANKEY, R. O.; LIDDLE, L. R.; AND CLEMENCE, R. "Multiple Relationship Between Age, Education, Police Experience and TAV Variables Correlated to Job Rating on 101 Female Deputy Sheriffs." *Police* 16(6):29–33 F '72. *

ROBERT G. DEMAREE, *Professor of Psychology and Professor in the Institute of Behavioral Research, Texas Christian University, Fort Worth, Texas.*[1]

The author's stated intention in constructing the TAV system is admirable: to devise a selection instrument based on measures of theoretically meaningful personality constructs. The theory from which the battery takes its name belongs to Karen Horney. "T" stands for interpersonal orientation *toward* people, "A" for interpersonal orientation *away* from people, and "V" for interpersonal orientation *versus* (against) people. Descriptive statements of global orientations do little to encompass an as yet uncharted content universe. Undaunted, the author concocted six personality "tests" which he claims measure "T," "A," and "V" adequately. In only two of the six, however, is there even a suggestion of adequate content validation, and in no instance have any item analyses been accomplished. The manual says that "undoubtedly Horney's impact on the author and her publications were foremost and provided practically all of the Adjective Check List [ACL] items."

The remaining tests are Personal Data (PD), Proverbs and Sayings (PS), Preferences (PREFS), Sales Reactions (SALES), Judgments (JUDG), and Mental Agility (MA). The latter comprises three 25-item subtests as follows: Following Directions and Carefulness (FDC), calling for the counting of the letters of the alphabet which have certain geometric characteristics; Weights and Balances (WB), involving statements about the balancing of a disc on which weights are placed; and Verbal Comprehension (VC), requiring judgments of same meaning, opposite meaning, or neither for pairs of proverbs. The manual describes item construction for all seven tests in unfortunate terms: "random thoughts of the author," "the author's memory," "an idea that just entered my mind while sunbathing," and the like.

The TAV is self-administering, the directions are simple, and responses for all six personality tests generally consist of marking words or phrases that "describe you," "appeal to you," and the like. (MA items are in multiple choice format.) There are 1,575 items in the full set of tests, which takes about 3½ hours to

[1] Technical assistance by Mr. Michael J. Gent in the preparation of this review is gratefully acknowledged.

complete. The manual states that the average reading difficulty is at the ninth grade level, based on 1949 norms for Flesch reading levels.

As was suggested previously, the ACL and PREFS items do appear to reflect, semantically at least, orientation toward, away from, and versus people. Whether the adjectives and preference statements chosen for each category are representative of Horney's constructs is another question. While the items appear to have face validity, they are also very vulnerable to social desirability responding. The makeup of the other four instruments appears to be a heterogeneous concoction of items which may share more method variance than any structural connectedness to underlying constructs.

The battery is being merchandised as a selection tool. Despite the author's protestations of theoretical saliency, validation data presented in the manual are actuarial in nature. References to TAV concepts explaining scale relationships to criteria measures are at this point a "phlogiston" explanation of fire. For each of the six personality "tests" the author derived three scale scores: the sums of responses to items coded "T," "A," and "V" within each instrument. In all but ACL and PREFS, classification of items into orientation scales was a priori and apparently mysterious. Notwithstanding, reported K-R 21 reliabilities for the six personality instruments are generally in the .70–.90 range, except for PD-T, PD-A, PD-V (all lower). In the four samples with MA scores, the median of the reliabilities is .84 for WB, .44 for FDC, and .21 for VC; in two samples the reliability for the last is reported to be .00. The only test-retest coefficients are for a sample of 48 deputy sheriff cadets; with a 16-week interval the correlations range from .36 for VC to .88 for PREFS-V, and have a median value of .72.

While full correlation results are not presented in the manual, a partial multi-trait/multi-method matrix can be pieced together. There is some evidence for convergent validity: different tests appear to measure the same T, A, or V orientation (this is particularly true for "toward" orientation). Discriminant validity, however, is notably lacking; with few exceptions the intercorrelations of the T, A, and V scores within tests are greater in magnitude than the correlations with TAV counterparts

from other tests. In fact, some of the intratest correlations of the TAV scores appear to have approached the upper limit indicated by the reliabilities. The TAV system measures something, or perhaps many things—but *what* is not apparent.

In a series of validation studies reported in the manual, weights are given to selected scales on the basis of step-wise regression results. Depending on the criterion and sample chosen, zero-order validity coefficients show reversals of signs with regression weights, and inconsistent patterns of predictive scales emerge. Thus, the author's insistence on maintaining a poorly enunciated theory that is even less adequately translated into test items and scales has the effect of producing unstable and virtually uninterpretable results.

Statements concerning the TAV system's utility as a selection device are at best equivocal. Of the 16 validation studies reported, 13 use concurrent criteria of dubious job relevance (mostly ratings and rankings). All are on small samples (24–78) drawn from groups of law enforcement personnel, salesmen, and teachers, with many multiple correlations in the .60–.80 range. The manual does not report any cross-validation results. Not atypical of the findings are those reported for predicting a criterion based on annual ratings for 45 male life insurance adjusters. A multiple correlation of .83, based on 12 of 24 predictors, is reported; the four largest beta-weights, by far, are for age, previous experience, ACL-V, and MA-FDC, but all these predictors were acting as suppressors. While the likelihood that these results would hold up in a crossvalidation is very slim, it is just as disturbing that the sum of the cross-products of the validity coefficients and beta weights reported should equal $.83^2$ but instead is negative in value. Obviously, something is wrong, and thus the reviewer is led to question the accuracy of results reported in the manual.

In addition to the fact that no confidence can be placed in reported validities for the TAV system, the selection utility data presented in the manual tend to be misleading. Close scrutiny of the selection results shows a number of high-scoring (and borderline) misses cropping up alongside some false positives with low scores on criterion measures. From the standpoint of job relevance in selection testing, even

TAV Selection System

though "success ratios" with testing are higher than chance, a pattern of close misses and extreme false positives is disturbing.

In summary, the TAV system appears to be a loosely constructed battery of six personality inventories and three ability measures of unknown construct validity. It is self-administering but lengthy. The author's contention that theoretically meaningful person-orientation scales are built into the personality tests is largely unsubstantiated. The results reported from criterion-validity studies are helter-skelter and flimsy in nature, and devoid of cross-validation. To say the very least, it would be most unwise to rely on the prediction equations or results offered in the manual.

[987]

Wide Range Employment Sample Test. Ages 16–54 (normal and handicapped); 1972–73; WREST; manual refers to the test as *The Jastak-King Work Samples;* originally developed for use with "mentally and physically handicapped" persons enrolled in a rehabilitation workshop for welfare clients; 12 scores: folding, stapling, bottle packaging, rice measuring, screw assembly, tag stringing, swatch pasting, collating, color and shade matching, pattern matching, total performance, total errors; no data on reliability of total scores; no data on validity; individual; manual ('72, 46 pages); manual supplement ('73, 42 pages); guide (no date, 3 pages); record form (no date, 1 page); $745 per set of testing materials (except manual and supplement) and 25 record forms; $5.70 per 50 record forms; $75 per resupply kit of consumable items; $14.60 per manual and supplement; postpaid; (90) minutes; J. F. Jastak and Dorothy E. King; Guidance Associates of Delaware, Inc. *

FRANK L. SCHMIDT, *Personnel Research Psychologist, United States Civil Service Commission, Washington, D.C.*

This test is essentially a low-level manual performance test—an aptitude test rather than a content-oriented test, designed for use with the mentally and/or physically handicapped. Representative of the 10 tasks that comprise the instrument is the stapling task, which requires the examinee to use an ordinary office stapler to place staples inside small rectangular boxes on a sheet of paper. There are 32 sheets of paper to be stapled; both time and number of errors are recorded.

CONSTRUCTION. Since the WREST is a work-oriented performance test, it is especially appropriate to ask how its content was determined. In their work in a workshop for the mentally and physically handicapped, Jastak and King found that many of the contracts the workshop had with local firms included "various types of assembly and packaging activities." King collected a number of work samples of various jobs for use as an informal tool in assigning trainees to work projects, i.e., as a classification test. Jastak "then selected the ten most representative sample items and developed standard time limits." No description is given as to how representativeness was determined or how the sample of tasks was selected for the WREST. Apparently, the process was based solely on Jastak's judgment, with neither input from expert judges nor empirical item analysis.

RELIABILITY. The story with respect to the reliability of the WREST is a strange one. First, the authors reject the very concept of reliability, as this quote illustrates:

Some people call inconsistent scores unreliable. Such people are either inexperienced in behavior observations in vivo or they depend on statistical methods that are erroneous. All so-called reliability coefficients presently used in test studies are unreliable and misleading in estimating the consistency of tests and work samples. From an observational point of view, reliability is an artificial concept created by statisticians who have had little or no experience in how people behave during work and test performances.

On the same page, the authors, in effect, argue that the WREST is unreliable. They state, "Time and error measures of work samples are subject to temporary moods" and "A person may organize the work better on some days than on others." If in fact the WREST is unreliable, it certainly should not be used as King and Jastak recommend. Uses they recommend for the WREST include: (*a*) determination of employability, (*b*) studying the industrial efficiency of an individual, (*c*) counseling the disadvantaged, and (*d*) determining trainability for employment.

Ironically, however, the WREST apparently does have good reliability. My calculations based on the subtask intercorrelation matrix in Table 12 of the manual supplement produced alpha coefficients of .82 and .83 for the male and female norm groups, respectively. This is a respectable internal consistency reliability. In addition, the authors present the correlations produced by immediate retest with the WREST. Although the authors reject the idea, these coefficients are obviously reliabilities. These values ranged from .84 to .92, again indicating good reliability. (Stability over time is, of course, another question.) The positive correlations among the WREST subscales indicate that the WREST is picking up a general factor of some kind. Whatever this factor is, it correlates about .45 with general mental ability.

Pages 24–27 of the manual supplement are apparently intended as part of what the authors substitute for a discussion of traditional reliability, but the content looks as if it came from the *Witchdoctor's Handbook of Fantasy-Based Personality Theories*. It consists of pompous and verbose expostulations on, for example, "lobal integration" of behavior, "global integration" of behavior, and "behavior organization." What this kind of thing is doing in a test manual is a question that would stump a Solomon.

VALIDITY. As in the case of reliability, the authors reject the concept of validity. The following quote is illustrative: "Again, there are no acceptable statistical methods to measure the validity of behavioral observations, because behavioral scientists need a behavioral (clinical) frame of reference to explain the statistical analyses." In reality, the WREST is an aptitude test (although of a performance nature) and both criterion validity and construct validity studies are appropriate and necessary. Neither are offered, nor is any other form of validity evidence presented.

INTERPRETATION. As an excellent example of misplaced priorities, the authors have devoted extensive efforts to the construction of norms as an aid in score interpretation, when the absence of any evidence for validity makes interpretation impossible—with or without norms. The norms, and the explanation of them, presented in the manual supplement can be understood only with some effort. One first obtains the raw time scores on each of the 10 tasks. These are then converted to "scaled scores" (ranging from 1 to 19) using one norm table. Scaled scores are then summed across the 10 tasks, and this sum is converted to "standard scores" (mean=100, SD=15), using a second norm table. For some unexplained reason, error scores are not handled this way: the raw error total is computed for the whole test, and these totals are then translated into five categories ranging from "very good" to "very poor."

The most important problem with the norms in the manual supplement, however, is the fact that they were apparently derived on a general sample of nonhandicapped individuals. If the meaning of WREST scores is murky for the handicapped, it is doubly so for the nonhandicapped. In contrast, the manual contains separate norms for "workshop" and "industrial" samples, although no description is given of either sample. The norms in the manual are presented in terms of stanines instead of scaled scores, and no table is given for converting the latter to standard scores.

INSTRUCTIONS AND SCORING. The instructions and scoring procedures given in the manual appear quite clear and are nicely supplemented with illustrating photos. The descriptions of the scoring procedures for the 10 tasks, though abbreviated, also appear to be clear and understandable. This is in contrast to the general vagueness and difficulty of the manual supplement.

In view of the casual manner in which this test was constructed, we have more than a little reason for doubting the optimality (for any purpose) of its content. Despite the apparently unsystematic methods used to select the 10 tasks comprising the test, the WREST may prove useful in assigning the mentally and physically handicapped to different work projects. Such usefulness remains to be demonstrated, however. But the WREST does yield a reliable total (time) score, indicating that low reliability, at least, is no barrier to validity. The WREST should probably be viewed as an experimental test, of the performance-aptitude variety, with apparently good reliability but completely unknown validity. For one considering use of a test of this kind, are there any alternatives to the WREST? To my knowledge, there is only one: The *JEVS Work Sample Evaluation System* developed by the Jewish Employment and Vocational Service for use in appraising and counseling the disadvantaged. Psychometrically, the JEVS, like the WREST, leaves a lot to be desired. But information is more complete on the JEVS, and this should certainly be carefully considered before the WREST is adopted for any purpose.

WILLIAM C. WARD, *Senior Research Psychologist, Educational Testing Service, Princeton, New Jersey.*

The WREST, consisting of 10 simple clerical and mechanical tasks, is intended for physically and mentally handicapped individuals who might be employed within a sheltered workshop environment. Suggested uses include determining employability, training, and providing suggestions as to the general kinds of jobs which would be appropriate for an individual.

Norms are based on 1,050 workers, who were selected by stratified sampling on level of general ability. Norms are presented separately for six age groups (Ns 45 to 150, median 82) within each sex. These include scaled time scores for each of the subtests, a standardized total time score, and an accuracy score based on total errors over all subtests.

Psychometric support for the instrument is entirely lacking. The manual supplement promises a clinical "factor analysis and a clinical interpretation of the total battery," but the publisher was unresponsive to a request for this analysis; it appears from the intercorrelations of the subtests that a substantial general factor would be found. "Reliability" coefficients are presented, but these are derived by way of an arcane manipulation on what is purportedly each subtest's unique variance. As for validity, it is argued that we lack both "adequate statistical logic and conceptual hypotheses," and so must be satisfied with "as objective clinical insights as can be obtained in the course of practical experience."

Unfortunately, such insights as are offered generally lack the precision which would be needed to make them useful, even if the user is prepared to overlook the lack of evidence. For example, it is suggested that "persons whose work sample efficiency reaches the low average level, either at the first trial or as a result of special training, may be potentially employable if they can find the right type of work and job." What special training and how much change it should produce are left to the imagination of the user, as is selecting the "right type of work and job" except for a recommendation to use an interest inventory from the same publisher. Similarly, "the differences between sub-samples [subtests] may, of course, be used as rough clues for estimating the general areas in which a person will work efficiently and happily. However, such differences may not and should not be used for the selection of specific jobs, identical to those of the work samples."

An instrument of the present kind could be extremely useful in assessing the trainability and work potential of severely handicapped individuals, if supported by appropriate studies of predictive relations to job performance of various sorts, of the effectiveness of various training regimens, and the like. So long as the user must develop all these on his own, the price (over $500) seems just a bit too high.

CAREERS AND INTERESTS

[988]

★AAMD-Becker Reading-Free Vocational Interest Inventory. Educable mentally retarded at the high school level; 1975; RFVII; 2 forms; manual (56 pages); profile (2 pages) for males; profile (2 pages) for females; $1 per test; $6 per manual; $10 per specimen set of 5 male booklets, 5 female booklets, and manual; 10% extra for postage and handling; (45) minutes; Ralph L. Becker; American Association on Mental Deficiency. *

a) MALE FORM. 11 scores: automotive, building trades, clerical, animal care, food service, patient care, horticulture, janitorial, personal service, laundry service, materials handling; 1 form (29 pages).

b) FEMALE FORM. 8 scores: laundry service, light industrial, clerical, personal service, food service, patient care, horticulture, housekeeping; 1 form (21 pages).

REFERENCES

1. BECKER, RALPH L., AND FERGUSON, ROY E. "Assessing Educable Retardates' Vocational Interest Through a Non-Reading Technique." Mental Retard 7(6):20–5 D '69. * (PA 45:2882)
2. BECKER, RALPH L., AND FERGUSON, ROY E. "A Vocational Picture Interest Inventory for Educable Retarded Youth." Excep Children 35(7):562–3 Mr '69. * (PA 44:17158)
3. BECKER, RALPH L. "The Reading-Free Vocational Interest Inventory: Measurement of Job Preference in the EMR." Mental Retard 11(4):11–5 Ag '73. * (PA 51:5933)
4. BECKER, RALPH L. "Vocational Choice: An Inventory Approach." Ed & Train Mental Retard 8(3):128–36 O '73. * (PA 52:1249)
5. GORNEY, ALLANA G. Use of Reading-Free Vocational Interest Inventory With Secondary Level Mentally Retarded Students. Master's thesis, Texas Woman's University (Denton, Tex.), 1975.
6. McCAWLEY, JAMES WILLIAM. The Development of Vocational Interests of Educable Mentally Retarded Students. Doctor's thesis, University of Oregon (Eugene, Ore.), 1975. (DAI 36:4402A)

ESTHER E. DIAMOND, Senior Project Director, Development, Science Research Associates, Chicago, Illinois.

This pictorial vocational interest inventory, for use with the educable mentally retarded at high school level, contains no verbal symbols or written statements; items are simple line drawings of vocationally-related tasks. Across all norm group samples, mean IQ range was 62 to 69. The trainable mentally retarded, generally defined as the group scoring just below the educable mentally retarded, and capable of learning very routine, repetitive tasks, were not involved in the development of the inventory. Research is needed to study the usefulness of redesigning and norming the inventory for this group.

The inventory provides scores in 11 interest areas for males and 8 for females; 6 areas are the same for both sexes.

Scales were developed by categorizing 134 specific jobs reported by the American Institutes of Research as being applicable to the employable retarded. Other than this information, however, there is no explanation of why scores on all scales are not provided for both sexes—a requirement now for Title IX compliance, and a way of broadening the options somewhat for a group whose range of options at best is quite narrow. No research evidence is presented to show that any of the occupations within the capabilities of the employable retardate are beyond those of one sex or the other.

The inventory is administered orally, and separate directions are provided for group and individual administration. The client compares the three pictorial items in each triad and circles the picture representing the task most appealing. The tasks are very clearly represented, with a minimum of detail and the same male or female worker appearing in each. A question does arise as to whether minority group retardates might have a problem identifying with the ubiquitous blond Caucasian worker. A second question concerns the marking of only the most-liked activities: Is valuable information lost by not also noting the least-liked activities? The manual does state that the preferences are presented in forced choice format and in effect ranked, but the only forced choice is the marking of the most-liked activity.

Norms tables give conversions from raw scores to T scores to percentile equivalents. Individual profile sheets are provided for profiling the percentile ranks for each examinee so that high, average, and low scores can easily be noted. Profiles are not provided to the examinees, and this reviewer wonders whether it might not be useful to provide each with a very simplified version of the profile, perhaps with each interest area represented by a drawing of a typical task from that area, taken from the test booklet itself. A modest research study to determine how well the examinee understands such a profile and what the affective gains of such feedback might be, should be interesting and possibly quite worthwhile.

Test-retest reliability coefficients reported in the manual, based on a two-week interval between testing, are mainly in the .70s and .80s. Greater reliability is indicated for the institutional subsamples, which represented an older and more experienced group of examinees. K-R 20 reliabilities range from .68 to .92, with a median of .82, for public school and institutional male group subsamples. These coefficients suggest an acceptable degree of internal consistency for the inventory.

Some evidence is presented for content, concurrent, and construct validity for some of the subsamples and some of the scales. Validity coefficients range from nearly zero to .82. Predictive validity has not been established.

In the absence of a choice of appropriate vocational interest inventories for this target group (there appears to be only one other such standardized inventory), the AAMD Becker fills a need which regular interest inventories cannot fill. Hopefully, too, its use will provide important evidence regarding its strengths and limitations about which there are insufficient data now. The validity data, for example, are adequate only for certain groups and certain scales. In addition, there is considerable overlapping of some of the scales. Usefulness of the full set of scales with both males and females also needs to be investigated. The inventory should therefore be used with caution, and as more of an exploratory than a decision-making device—particularly for those groups and those scales for which validity evidence is lacking.

GEORGE DOMINO, *Professor of Psychology, The University of Arizona, Tucson, Arizona.*

The RFVII is a vocational preference test for use with mentally retarded persons, particularly educable mentally retarded (EMR). As such it fills a much needed function, though how well is debatable.

The booklets contain instructions to be read aloud by the examiner. The instructions require the client to circle the one picture from a set of three that he or she "likes best." Unfortunately, the emphasis is on selecting the picture liked best rather than the work activity represented. The line drawings are generally clear and free of unnecessary details; they have a "dated" quality reminiscent of test items from the 1930s. Many of the triads contain items that, at least on the surface, appear unequal: for example, two items will each involve two interacting individuals while the third depicts only one person. No clear information is given as to how the specific triads were developed, nor is there any mention of social desirability or other possibly confounding variables.

Since the client indicates his responses directly on the booklet, the booklets are not reusable and the examiner needs to transcribe the responses on a grid. Both features are undesirable though possibly necessary.

The manual is very well written, attractively laid out, with large printing and sufficient but not overwhelming detail. Each of the interest areas is defined and occupational examples are given. The interest areas appear appropriate, though one may wonder if there are occupational areas not included and why the area of animal care is a male-only area.

The norms are based on nationwide samples of 3,407 male and 3,006 female educable mentally retarded persons in both public secondary day schools and residential institutions. There are separate norm tables for sex and for setting; the tables are clear and permit rapid translation of raw scores into T scores and percentiles (though the percentiles might have been better placed in a column adjacent to the T score column rather than in a separate area). The list of references is interesting but inappropriate since very few are cited in the manual.

The reliability of the RFVII is adequate and well documented. Test-retest reliability coefficients over a two-week period are primarily in the .70s and .80s, although a longer time period would seem more appropriate. The standard error of measurement is explained, albeit briefly, and standard errors are given. Finally, K-R 20 coefficients range from .68 to .92, with median .82.

Three types of validity are discussed: content, concurrent, and occupational. The discussion of content validity is brief and unclear; the reader is left with the impression that the items must be valid since they were looked at by various study teams and furthermore were subjected to a statistical analysis to determine their discriminating power! The discussion of concurrent validity is more reasonable and presents more clear cut evidence in the form of correlations between RFVII interest areas and similarly named areas on the *Geist Picture Interest Inventory* and the *Picture Interest Inventory*. The correlational patterns are adequate and meaningful and generally support the validity of the RFVII. The hard-nosed critic may wonder what the correlation coefficients between the RFVII and the other scales on the two picture interest inventories were like, since they are not given. Perhaps the most crucial type of validity discussed is occupational (or status) validity. The only study mentioned involved 891 males and 584 females in occupational groups (N for each group was between 35 and 55) covering the various interest areas. The manual states that each occupational group scored higher on the appropriate scale than on the other scales. Much more information is needed, particularly as to how membership in an occupational group was defined.

Thus the available validity information is positive but inadequate; hopefully, the future professional literature will correct this. For the present, one is left with the vague feeling that the individual client has been lost in the shuffle. For example, there is no evidence given linking expressed vocational interest and test-measured interest. Perhaps, just perhaps, vocational counseling clients, even if EMR, should be *asked* what their vocational preferences are. There is also no mention made as to whether the line drawings were ever presented to EMR for their evaluation, to see whether the artist's conception of, say, "collating papers" is in fact understandable to the client. Even the three-page section boldly titled "Interpreting the Individual Profile" seems to emphasize more psychometric than human aspects.

Finally, the manual gives the intercorrelations between interest areas and indicates that most are negative and low positive. No mention is made of the fact that this result may simply reflect the forced choice format; selection of an item in a forced choice situation not only enhances the score for that one interest area but also automatically depresses the scores for the other areas, resulting in spuriously low or negative intercorrelations.

The RFVII appears to be a useful test in

its early stages of development; while its use as a sole source of vocational decisions with an individual client may be premature, further research is to be encouraged.

[989]

*ACT Career Planning Program. Entrants to post-secondary educational institutions; 1970–76; CPP; 21 scores: 8 interest scores (business contact, business detail, trades, technology, science, health, creative arts, social service), 7 experience scores (same as interest, excluding health), and 6 ability scores (mechanical reasoning, numerical skills, space relations, reading skills, language usage, clerical skills) plus background and plans questions and 12 optional local items; national norms based on the previous edition; Form H ('76, 35 pages); handbook ('77, 98 pages); counselor's manual ('76, 32 pages); administration manual ('76, 20 pages); student's booklet ('76, 20 pages); separate answer folders (MRC) must be used; self-scoring answer folders for ability scales are available; $3.75 per test including scoring service; $3 per handbook; $1 per counselor's manual; $4 per specimen set; postage extra; optional institutional summary, $30 per report; (150–160) minutes; American College Testing Program. *

See T2:2101 (4 references).

REFERENCES

1–4. See T2:2101.
5. COLE, NANCY S. "On Measuring the Vocational Interests of Women." *ACT Res Rep* 49:1–11 Mr '72. * (*PA* 48:9970)
6. HANSON, GARY R., AND COLE, NANCY S. "Symposium: Tests and Counseling/Role Models? 5, The Career Planning Program—More Than a Test Battery." *Meas & Eval Guid* 5(3):415–9 O '72. * (*PA* 49:10145)
7. TEAL, JACK DEAN. *A Comparative Study of Four Placement Test Batteries at an Urban-Rural Community College.* Doctor's thesis, Illinois State University (Normal, Ill.), 1972. (*DAI* 33:2184A)
8. BARNETTE, W. LESLIE, JR. "Review of the ACT Career Planning Program." *J Counsel Psychol* 20(4):389–94 Jl '73. *
9. HANSON, GARY R., AND PREDIGER, DALE J. Chap. 6, "The Vocational Interests of Students in Career-Oriented Educational Programs," pp. 89–107. In *The Vocational Interests of Young Adults.* Edited by Gary R. Hanson and Nancy S. Cole. Iowa City, Iowa: American College Testing Program, 1973. Pp. vii, 132. *
10. HEALY, CHARLES C. "Review of the ACT Career Planning Program." *Meas & Eval Guid* 5(4):509–12 Ja '73. *
11. NICKENS, JOHN M., AND WATTENBARGER, JAMES L. "Characteristics of Students Enrolled in Florida Post High School Occupational Education Programs." *Fla J Ed Res* 15:57–68 '73. *
12. NOVICK, MELVIN R.; JONES, PAUL K.; AND COLE, NANCY S. "Predictions of Performance in Career Education." *ACT Res Rep* 55:1–17 F '73. * (*PA* 50:12194)
13. BAYLESS, DAVID L.; BERGSTEN, JANE W.; LEWIS, LOUISE H.; AND NOETH, RICHARD J. "Considerations and Procedures in National Norming: An Illustration Using the ACT Assessment of Career Development and ACT Career Planning Program, Grades 8–11." *ACT Res Rep* 65:1–32 Jl '74. * (*PA* 54:1965)
14. HANSON, GARY R.; LAMB, RICHARD R.; AND ENGLISH, EDWARD. "An Analysis of Holland's Interest Types for Women: A Comparison of the Strong-Holland and the ACT Vocational Interest Profile Scales for Women." *J Voc Behav* 4(2):259–69 Ap '74. * (*PA* 52:11116)
15. ROBERTS, CAROLE A., AND JOHANSSON, CHARLES B. "The Inheritance of Cognitive Interest Styles Among Twins." *J Voc Behav* 4(2):237–43 Ap '74. * (*PA* 52:9376)
16. SCHUSSEL, ROBERT. "Circularity of Vocational Interests: Spherical Analysis of VIP Items." *Meas & Eval Guid* 7(2):86–91 Jl '74. * (*PA* 53:2030)
17. SCOTT, CRAIG S.; FENSKE, ROBERT H.; AND MAXEY, E. JAMES. "Change in Vocational Choice as a Function of Initial Career Choice, Interests, Abilities, and Sex." *J Voc Behav* 5(2):285–92 O '74. * (*PA* 53:6256)
18. SCOTT, CRAIG S.; FENSKE, ROBERT H.; AND MAXEY, E. JAMES. "Vocational Choice Change Patterns of a National Sample of Community-Junior College Students." *ACT Res Rep* 64:1–10 My '74. * (*PA* 53:4117)
19. SCHUSSEL, ROBERT H. *The Use of Factor Analysis and Other Multivariate Techniques to Improve the Measurement of Vocational Interests Among Community College Students and to Develop an Empirically Derived Personality Inventory Constructed From Vocational Interest Items.* Doctor's thesis, Temple University (Philadelphia, Pa.), 1975. (*DAI* 36:3013B)
20. NOETH, RICHARD J. "Converting Student Data to Counseling Information." *Meas & Eval Guid* 9(2):60–9 Jl '76. *

Meas & Eval Guid 5(4):509–12 Ja '73. *Charles C. Healy.* * a set of tests and inventories designed to help students who are making career plans to use information about their measured aptitudes, inventoried interests, self-reported competencies, values, and grades * The *Student Report* is a well-organized, readily understandable, nonstatistical, one-page summary of the student's appraisal. * The scope of information furnished by the one-page report is impressive. Equally impressive is the manner in which the data is economically organized and clearly communicated. The report should be an effective communication device. It is hoped that ACT will test whether, in contrast to conventional dissemination methods, the *Student Report* increases student awareness and understanding of the data. * The *Counselor's Manual* devotes a chapter to the general use of the *Student Report* in counseling. However, specific procedures for helping students assimilate and interpret results are not provided. * The Vocational Interest Profile (VIP) assesses interests for the eight clusters. * Little data is presented to support the reliability and independence of the VIP scales. The number of items per scale is not given. Alpha coefficients indicate that the scales are internally consistent, but test-retest correlations based on 119 males and females indicate only moderate reliability. * The Technical and Science scales....are highly correlated, especially when their correlations are compared with their retest reliabilities. * VIP scales generally distribute the normative group in the manner suggested by the Roe and Holland clusters. This is impressive because it has been difficult to differentiate non-professional groups on the basis of interest. Data concerning the relation of the scales to other standardized interest measures such as the Kuder Preference Record or the Strong Vocational Interest Blank is not yet provided. Such information is needed to evaluate the meaning of the scales. Information about the relation of interest scores to grades or other achievement indices is not yet given either. * The eight abilities measured are important to a wide range of occupations. The tests were constructed to be short, relevant to performance in career education programs, and minimally verbal. * Limited data about the reliability of these measures is provided. It suggests moderate reliability. * correlations between corresponding GATB and CPP scores range from .35 to .72, and they generally support the validity of the CPP scales. In addition, correlations of the CPP scales with the GATB Verbal and General scores indicate that ACT achieved its goal of creating scales that are minimally influenced by verbal ability. * The individual Self-Report scales generally differentiate the training groups. Differentiation of groups by discriminant analysis of the VIP scales and the Self-Report scales is sufficient to permit statements about a student's similarity to students in different programs. * In deciding to use or not to use the CPP, one necessarily considers its relation to GATB and the Interest and Temperament measures of the Human Resources Development Agency. The CPP and GATB assess similar abilities, interests, and preferences. The GATB measures are longer and more reliable. Their validity is better demonstrated. The GATB and CPP use different norms, and their results are reported differently. The GATB's normative group is working adults; the CPP's is students entering training. The GATB results are given as a score for each test; a client and his counselor must relate those scores to different occupational profiles in order to use them in occupational exploration. In addition to individual test scores, the CPP reports the relevance of its results to eight occupational clusters and to the training programs within those clusters. The CPP and GATB offer different advantages. Choosing between them will not be easy. Each counselor will have to weigh their relative merits in terms of the needs of his students.

[990]

The Applied Biological and Agribusiness Interest Inventory. Grade 8; 1965–71; revision of *Vocational Agriculture Interest Inventory;* 5 scores: animals, plants, mechanics, business, total; no data on reliability; no norms; 1 form ('71, 8 pages); directions for administering ['71, 4 pages]; summary profile ('71, 1 page); separate answer sheets must be used; $3 per 20 tests; $1 per 20 answer sheets; 10¢ per set of scoring stencils; $1 per 20 summary profiles; $1.75 per specimen set; cash orders postpaid; [20–30] minutes; Robert W. Walker and Glenn Z. Stevens; Interstate Printers & Publishers, Inc. *

For a review by David P. Campbell of the original edition, see 7:1038 (4 references).

EHUD JUNGWIRTH, *Professor of Agricultural Education and Head of the Department, The Hebrew University of Jerusalem, Rehovot, Israel.*

This inventory is stated to be a valid and reliable help in assisting vocational agriculture teachers in identifying potential "high-interest" students at the 8th grade level for purposes of guidance. It also claims to provide interest-ratings in special areas of agriculture: animals, plants, mechanics, and business.

The test is characterized by an almost complete absence of the psychometric information needed to evaluate, and to use, a standardized test. Instead of a manual, there is a four-page leaflet giving the procedures for administering and scoring only. No information whatsoever is given on the reliability and validity of the inventory.

Without any explanation or supporting data, the authors claim that "scores ranging from 66 through 100 indicate high interest. A range of scores from 44 through 65 shows middle or 'lukewarm' interest, and scores below 44 are low." Apparently this revised edition has not been administered to any normative group, at least no such norms are reported by the authors and publisher.

Although the inventory has 100 items, only 59 items are scored—41 items are redundant. The authors do not explain the rationale of this puzzling scoring system. Positive credits are obtainable from 51 items by choosing either "like" (36 items) or "strongly like" (46 items); it is difficult to understand why for 5 items a positive credit is given for "like" but not for "strongly like." Several similar further questions can be raised about the scoring procedure.

The authors recommend a rather aggressive campaign to enroll high-interest students as identified by this test in agricultural education, including (*a*) the sending of letters to parents over the principal's signature, (*b*) the involvement of the guidance counselor, (*c*) student-interviews, and (*d*) home-visits. They claim that through the use of this inventory "guidance now becomes the art of helping students base their selection of courses on fact, not fancy." The "factual" character of the results of this particular inventory is very much to be doubted, turning this claim into something resembling a "flight of fancy."

In conclusion, this test has so many obvious faults that its use cannot be recommended.

[991]

*Assessment of Career Development. Grades 8–12; 1972–74; ACD; formerly called *ACT Assessment of Career Development;* 11 scores: occupational knowledge (occupational characteristics, occupational preparation requirements), exploratory occupational experiences (social-health-personal services, business sales and management, business operations, technologies and trades, natural-social-medical sciences, creative and applied arts, total), career planning (knowledge, involvement), plus statistical summaries of responses to 42 specific items and up to 19 locally developed items; norms for grades 10 and 12 are interpolated and extrapolated from norms for grades 8, 9, and 11; Form C ('73, 23 pages); administrator's manual ('73, 10 pages); handbook ('74, 92 pages); handbook supplement 1 ('74, 21 pages); norms for grades 10 and 12 (no date, 17 pages, available on request); student introduction ('73, 4 pages); separate answer sheets (MRC) must be used; $13.95 per 35 tests; $4.35 per 35 answer sheets; $4.95 per 35 student introductions; $1.95 per handbook; 84¢ per handbook supplement; 66¢ per administrator's manual; $3.60 per specimen set; postage extra; scoring service, 78¢ and over per test (minimum 50; scoring must be done by publisher); (125–135) minutes in 1 or 3 sessions; American College Testing Program; Houghton Mifflin Co. *

REFERENCES

1. PREDIGER, DALE; ROTH, JOHN; AND NOETH, RICHARD. "Nationwide Study of Student Career Development: Summary of Results." *ACT Res Rep* 61:1–54 N '73. *
2. BAYLESS, DAVID L.; BERGSTEN, JANE W.; LEWIS, LOUISE H.; AND NOETH, RICHARD J. "Considerations and Procedures in National Norming: An Illustration Using the ACT Assessment of Career Development and ACT Career Planning Program, Grades 8–11." *ACT Res Rep* 65:1–32 Jl '74. * (*PA* 54:1965)
3. DAVIDSON, TERENCE MAXWELL. *A Study of the Career Development of Visually Impaired Adolescents.* Doctor's thesis, University of Pittsburgh (Pittsburgh, Pa.), 1974. (*DAI* 35:7754A)
4. HANNA, GERALD S. "Review of the ACT Assessment of Career Development." *Meas & Eval Guid* 7(1):51–4 Ap '74. *
5. PREDIGER, DALE J.; ROTH, JOHN D.; AND NOETH, RICHARD J. "Career Development of Youth: A Nationwide Study." *Personnel & Guid J* 53(2):97–104 O '74. * (*PA* 54:4266)
6. WESTBROOK, BERT W. "Content Analysis of Six Career Development Tests." *Meas & Eval Guid* 7(3):172–80 O '74. * (*PA* 53:6473)
7. HITCH, CHARLES ROBERT. *The Effects of an Experimental Career Oriented Group Guidance Program on Selected Ninth Grade Students.* Doctor's thesis, Michigan State University (East Lansing, Mich.), 1975. (*DAI* 36:2127A)

MARTIN R. KATZ, *Senior Research Psychologist, Educational Testing Service, Princeton, New Jersey.*

The ACD is offered to develop guidance programs that fit students' needs and to evaluate effects of career guidance programs. Of the 11 ACD scales, three are said to measure knowledge: Occupational Characteristics (54 items); Occupational Preparation Requirements (18 items); and Career Planning Knowledge (40 items). Six scales are intended to indicate experiences in activities presumably related to each of six occupational clusters. Another scale is the sum of these six (90 items in all). Fin-

ally, a scale is labeled Career Planning Involvement (based on 32 items).

Along with the tests, the ACD booklet includes various questionnaire materials, including items about preferences, plans, needs for help, and reactions to school guidance programs. There is also a provision for schools to insert their own questions.

Reports to schools include score distributions, means and standard deviations of each group (presumably a class) on the 11 scales, response distributions on certain questions, and alphabetical listings of students' scores. It is expected that group performance will be compared with norms for individuals or with "expected performance levels" designated by a school. Interpretation of results to individuals is *"not recommended,"* according to the handbook.

The ACD is avowedly atheoretical. The handbook states, "instead of attempting to measure a psychological construct called vocational maturity, emphasis was placed on collecting those items of information most likely to help counselors identify the career development status and career guidance needs of students." Thus, the ACD associates itself with educational achievement tests generally in its reliance on "content validity" as evidence of its worth.

This reviewer finds the notion that content validity is "atheoretical" somewhat difficult to swallow, since some theory, at least about the components and structure of what is being measured, would seem to be prerequisite for specifying the content of an achievement test. There is less than universal agreement on what constitutes career development and career guidance. Furthermore, interpreting performances on well-defined achievement tests to individuals is generally much easier and much more useful than interpreting measures of psychological constructs. The explanation for the omission of an explicit theoretical foundation for the ACD seems, therefore, somewhat disingenuous.

It is noteworthy that, although the handbook does not recommend interpretation of results *to* individual students, it does suggest interpretation for decisions *about* individual students—such as placement in a special program. This reviewer, however, sees no more justification for the latter application than for the former.

Although the first sentence of the handbook states that the ACD is "a new kind of guidance assessment instrument," this reviewer could find nothing new in this potpourri of items, which closely resemble those that have appeared in measures developed over many years. Indeed, some of the items are taken or adapted (without acknowledgement) from a 20-year-old test. These shopworn items do not seem to be combined in any symbiotic way. Quantity alone is neither an innovation nor a virtue. The mere assembling of this mass of questions only serves to suggest that "more is less." Furthermore, notwithstanding the distinctions made between the ACD and the *Career Maturity Inventory* (which is the exemplar of the explicitly "theory-based" instrument), much of the content is not perceptibly different. Thus, items in the occupational characteristics scale of the former, very much like those in the occupational information scale of the latter, require selection of an occupational title to match a brief description. For example: "Having a friendly personality is especially important for success in which one of the following jobs? (A) ticket agent (B) sculptor (C) personnel assistant (D) auto salesperson." D is keyed correct. Aside from the clumsiness of this particular item (why use a vague construct, "friendly personality," when a specific behavioral description would do better?), the entire set of items is subject to the same criticisms made of the CMI scale (see 997). This kind of exercise is of dubious utility.

Similarly, the following item from the occupational preparation requirements scale illustrates deficiencies in item-writing as well as in content: "Which of the following jobs requires the *longest* period of specialized training? (A) meter reader (B) author (C) child care aide (D) bank teller." B is keyed correct. Since "author" is a notably uncredentialled occupation, one may readily argue with the key, especially because of the word, "requires." But again putting aside quarrels with the wording and key, one must question the use of exercises like these that appear to tap such miscellaneous scraps of information. It is difficult to believe that they represent the content of an effective guidance program, or provide a basis either for placement of any given individual in career development programs or for evaluating the merits of a guidance program. How many students would be expected to find

any item like the examples given above relevant for their career decision making and planning? Miscellaneous knowledge of the sort tapped by the ACD is probably correlated with reading comprehension and general information, but there are more effective ways of assessing those cognitive skills.

Since theory is not used to justify content, one must pay special attention to empirical justification. The 90-item exploratory occupational experiences scales comprise about 34 percent of the test. But from the data in the handbook, one must infer they are of very dubious utility and validity since mean scores on these six scales are shown to be the same for students in grades 8, 9, and 11. Surely, as the handbook states, one would expect 11th graders to have accumulated more experiences than students two or three years younger. What, then, can one make of such scores?

Looking for other empirical evidence of validity, one seizes on the statement in the handbook that data had been gathered in a series of studies using the ACD as a criterion measure to evaluate effects of guidance programs. It was hypothesized that ACD scores would differentiate between groups that did participate in extensive guidance activities and groups that did not. The handbook states that the data "are currently being analyzed" and that "results will be available early in 1974." In August 1977, the reviewer telephoned the ACD Director of Development to obtain a copy of the results and was told that the data had not yet been analyzed. This is surprising. Collection of data is often difficult and costly. But when that investment has been made, data processing and analyses—given the widespread availability of computers and technical competence—are relatively easy and inexpensive.

In short, to follow up the comparison of this inventory with the CMI, the latter is based on explicit theoretical formulations and shows signs of intellectual vigor in development and analysis. It can be criticized for errors in thinking, but thoughtfulness is pervasively evident. The ACD eschews theory and shows no such intellectual vigor; it is less interesting than the CMI, and no more deserving of use.

Assessment of Career Development

DAVID V. TIEDEMAN, *Professor of Education and Director, ERIC Clearinghouse in Career Education, Northern Illinois University, De-Kalb, Illinois.*

Career education is a means employed for the facilitation of career development. Career guidance, a function of career education, serves a similar end. *Assessment of Career Development* is offered as a planning instrumentality to the end of facilitating career development through the function of career guidance in career education. The ACD system consists of a student booklet with administrator's manual, a user's handbook for interpretation of group results, and a Guide for Increasing Student Career Development. The ACD system also acknowledges need for local initiative in planning for attainment of career development ends by allowing incorporation of the reporting of up to 19 locally developed items in the overall procedure.

Despite labeling the student booklet as the Student Test Booklet, the ACD is not a test and is not sold as a test. Instead, the ACD system is an assessment procedure in search of clever individuals able to make instructional and guidance sense out of its 11 scores, 42 item summaries, and 19 invitations to local initiative in needs-based assessment and career education planning.

No potential user can successfully adopt the ACD without thoughtful prior study of its intentions, contents, and potential reports, all of which are rather thoroughly revealed in the available examination kit. In the first place, considerable care will have to be given to weighing the correspondence of one's own meaning of career development with that revealed by the ACD. The ACD system offers no explicit structure for career development, just its own implicit one.

The needed care will have to start by comparing the user's and ACD's meanings of its key conceptions: "career," "occupation," and "job." For instance, in introducing the ACD to students, the authors indicate that "A CAREER is like a journey—a lifelong journey with a series of experiences and decisions related to EDUCATION AND WORK." Except for the limitation of "career" to education and work, this is a fine beginning. A career *is* a lifelong journey; in fact, career is a life-long journey in which individuals succeed in lending purpose to their existences. However, the ACD meaning of "career" is really limited to action in only education and work areas and little stress is placed upon the necessary repeated differentiation and reintegration of life purposes. Next, "work" is reduced to "occupations." Then "occupations" are aggregated to "occupational clusters." Finally, "occupations" and "occupational clusters" are renamed "jobs" and "job clusters" for students. For some reason or other, students are not considered bright enough to comprehend the more general conception of "occupation" as opposed to the more specific conception of "job," while ACD users are. Also, students are not expected to lend sense to the multifaceted skills and habits which the ACD reveals. And still the ACD is supposed to provide a "career development assessment," an even more general conception than that of "occupation"! Thus, in the ACD, authors' intentions and means really are not in very good correspondence with each other.

In weighing the authors' meaning of "career development" in relation to one's own meaning of it, care must also be given as to whether the user really wants an assessment of student development or not. If the user does, the ACD does not assess individual development well at all. Instead, the ACD largely compares individuals in terms of their occupational awareness, self-awareness, and knowledge and involvement in career planning and decision making. Individuals' integrations of these conceptions are not revealed in the assessment at all. In their attempt to play the lack of a scientific consensus about career development safely, the authors ignore any potential existence of it whatsoever.

The ACD seems to do its best job in the area of occupational awareness. Two subscores of occupational awareness indicate knowledge and overall exploratory experiences in occupations. The latter experiences are also further subdivided by occupational cluster so that counselors can get some idea of the clusters in which students' exploratory experiences exist. Such knowledge is obviously useful in relation to some preconceived model of expected exploratory experiences. However, the knowledge could also be useful to students except for the fact that the ACD's authors do not recommend that such information be shared with students.

In the occupational awareness area, the subscale for knowledge of occupational characteristics and the subscale for knowledge of occupational preparation requirements within their subsection are also both nicely balanced according to three subdivisions of the amount of formal education typically required in an occupation. In addition, the subscale dealing with knowledge of occupational characteristics in this same subsection is also balanced by duties, psychosocial aspects, and worker attributes. Finally, in this occupational awareness section, coverage by occupational cluster in both this subsection and the additional subsection on exploratory experiences lends particular value to these scores as three small elements in the larger career development picture.

Unfortunately, the direct career *development* sense associated with the ACD seems largely limited to the occupational awareness section. As indicated, that section yields well conceived and tested information about occupational knowledge and exploratory occupational experiences. Although information conveyed in the remaining two sections can all be useful to an informed career developmentalist, the user will have to supply utility to this information; the utility of the information for career development is not immediately evident in the booklet or the handbook. In the self-awareness section, three items indicate student value preferences and four, student preferences for working conditions. All seven of these items are in the preferred job characteristics subsection of self-awareness. One item in the career plans subsection indicates the student's educational plans; two items, the student's first and second preferences for an occupation noted within a cluster; and one, the student's certainty as to occupational preferences. Finally, the last subsection on perceived needs provides nine areas in which the student reports a need for help. All of this is fine for particular planning in career guidance and education, but such diverse data really cannot be put together to ascertain how far students have developed. In this regard, the ACD is weak, except for persons who have a clear prior conception of career development and its facilitation and elect to

know for school groups the particular fragments of self-awareness offered by the ACD.

Finally, the career planning and decision making section also provides fragmented but potentially useful indications of the knowledge which students have about both topics. However, the knowledge which is sought is largely that which career psychologists hold to be true about the timing of choice, the impact of work on life, reality in choosing, and the like. The individually elected decision frame of reference is not revealed; assimilation of society's frame of reference is all that is revealed. The section samples the individual's internalization of societal views but reveals little about the individual's developmental application of self-initiated, self-directed, self-corrected attitudes to the decisions associated with the "lifelong journey" that becomes career. Despite this fault, career guidance coordinators who are themselves familiar with career development might well want to use the knowledge of students' internalization of society's views about careers in planning next steps for facilitating the career developments of students within their responsibility.

Returning to more positive veins, the authors carefully attend to the psychometric properties of the ACD in keeping with just its intended needs assessment uses. The reliability and short-term stability of the 11 scales are reported. The content validity of the instrument is carefully discussed and presented. Several relevant statistical studies are reported. A well-defined set of norms is available for the scales and other items of the ACD. Those who care to infer development by comparisons among individuals are well served by the ACD for grades 8 through 12. Those who seek criterion-referenced measurement are also given help in establishing criteria for selected scales. Users of this procedure will, however, be hard pressed to lend career development meaning to criterion points on any of these scales.

In short, the ACD is a career development assessment device in search of those who understand career development well enough to make sense out of its many scale and item reports. Since the ACD reveals numerous pieces of career behavior, a user knowledgeable in career development can lend meaning to its behavioral reports. However, the ultimate choice becomes

Assessment of Career Development

whether such meaning can be more clearly revealed by assessment procedures constructed for one's own purposes or by use of the ACD, depending upon the relative costs of adaptation and of construction.

All that changes in individuals is not education. Neither is all that changes in individuals career development. Instead, both education and career development consist of growth in which the advantage of sense is realized in those educated and developing. Those who understand career development can lend career development sense to the ACD procedure. However, do not expect sense to be in the ACD procedure; the user has to put sense into it.

Meas & Eval Guid 7(1):51–4 Ap '74. Gerald S. Hanna. * The ACD is an integrated and useful blend of maximum-performance achievement tests, self-report inventories, and questionnaire data. * A productive combination of norm- and criterion-referenced interpretation is encouraged and facilitated by the use of the *Handbook* * Sound suggestions are offered for criterion-referenced interpretation of item and scale distributions. Since interpretation is primarily for groups, it would have been useful if school norms had been supplied in addition to those for individuals. * A few minor criticisms are noted. Career Planning Knowledge question 30 asks the student to select the best answer. The final choice is "any of the above." The answer "all of the above" and its variants are inappropriate for best-answer type multiple-choice questions. The directions for Job Knowledge questions 59 to 63 ask "Choose the minimum type of training the following jobs usually require." Each question stem consists of a job title. The directions strike the reviewer as being quite demanding for eighth-grade students to comprehend. Moreover, some choices seem to differ more in kind of preparation than in quantity of preparation, which the word "minimum" might imply. * The lack of distinction between general *education* that is reflected in some choices and job-specific *training* that is reflected in others is worrisome. * A central feature of the ACD is its wide band width and low fidelity compared with most instruments used by counselors. A lot of information (11 scores and assorted questionnaire items) is gathered in relatively little time. Since this is

accomplished at the expense of highly accurate measurement, scores tend to be less reliable than is normally demanded for individual interpretation. The publisher is to be commended for emphasizing this point, for explicitly recommending that individual interpretations not ordinarily be made, and for not supplying individual score labels. In view of the instrument's purposes, this wide band, low fidelity approach is sound. The reviewer's greatest misgiving about the ACD concerns its costs in student time and in money. Since its major and most defensible uses relate to group information, one wonders if the data could more economically be gathered for students in medium-sized and large schools either by administering the instrument to only a sample of students or by administering to each student only a sample of the total number of items. Either approach might be expected to yield data quite reliably descriptive of total groups while substantially reducing the amount of student time invested. Stated differently, the concern is that the reliability (fidelity), although lower than that of most instruments used for individual interpretations, may be uneconomically and unnecessarily high for an instrument designed for group interpretation. * The....*Manual*....provides the option of giving the ACD in three 45-minute periods or in one 125-minute session. A session in excess of two hours seems excessive for eighth graders. Implicit in this choice of scheduling is the claim that performance is thereby not affected, but no such evidence is provided. * Results of two cross sectional growth studies support the construct validity of the Career Planning Involvement scale and the three knowledge scales. However, in the study reporting scores on the Exploratory Occupational Experiences scales (which seem intended to reveal *cumulative* experiences) no gain between grades 8 and 11 was found. This finding casts a long shadow of doubt upon the construct validity of the seven scales in question. * The ACD is a well-articulated mix of tests, survey scales, and questionnaire items designed for use in "customizing" and evaluating local career guidance programs. It secures a large number of measures in relatively little testing time; therefore, its individual measures generally lack the level of reliability needed for individual interpretation, but are more than

Assessment of Career Development

sufficient for the norm- and criterion-referenced group interpretations for which the instrument is primarily intended. The *Handbook* reflects high professional standards of reporting. Although several criticisms were offered, the reviewer's general reaction to the ACD is favorable. It should prove to be a useful guidance aid and its value will likely be enhanced as new research reveals more of its characteristics.

[992]

*California Occupational Preference System. High school and college; 1966–76; COPS; also called *COPSystem* and *COPSystem Inventory;* revision of *California Occupational Preference Survey;* 14 scores: consumer economics, outdoor, clerical, communication, and 2 scores (skilled, professional) for each of the following: science, technology, business, arts, service; no data on validity; 1 form; 2 editions; manual ('75, 13 pages); technical manual ('76, 19 pages); profile and guide for high school, college, ('75, 6 pages); occupational cluster charts ('75, 16 pages); $4.75 per 25 profiles; $5 per 25 cluster charts; $1.25 per technical manual; $2.25 per specimen set (must be purchased to obtain manual); postage extra; (30–40) minutes; Robert R. Knapp and Lila Knapp; EdITS/Educational and Industrial Testing Service. *

a) CONSUMABLE EDITION. 1 form ('74, 5 pages); $8.25 per 25 tests.

b) REUSABLE EDITION. 1 form ('74, 4 pages); separate answer sheets (Digitek, IBM 1230) must be used; $9.75 per 25 tests; $4.75 per 50 answer sheets; $10 per set of IBM hand scoring stencils; scoring service, 85¢ or less per test.

See T2:2170 (2 references); for reviews by Jack L. Bodden and John W. French and an excerpted review by Robert H. Bauernfeind of the original edition, see 7:1012 (1 reference).

REFERENCES

1. See 7:1012.
2–3. See T2:2170.
4. LUX, PATRICIA L. *Evaluation of Self Administration, Self Scoring, and Self Interpretation of the California Occupational Preference Survey.* Master's thesis, California State University (Sacramento, Calif.), 1974.

JO-IDA C. HANSEN, *Assistant Professor of Psychology and Director, Center for Interest Measurement Research, University of Minnesota, Minneapolis, Minnesota.*

Like the earlier edition, this revision is designed to assist in career exploration by identifying activity interest scores that are keyed to the *Occupational Outlook Handbook* and the *Dictionary of Occupational Titles.*

One reason for the revision was to add new items that cover a wider range of occupational opportunities; another was to change the wording of some items to a lower reading level. Whether or not items were simplified enough to reduce the reading level is questionable.

The method of scale construction was refined in the revision to a factor analysis of single items and factor analysis of subclusters that had been constructed through content analysis. The revision slightly realigned the 14 original dimensions, collapsing the linguistic-professional and linguistic-skilled dimensions into a single scale called communication, and splitting technology into consumer economics, which contains food and textile occupations, and skilled and professional technology.

Issues of sex bias in interest measurement may also have stimulated the authors to revise their inventory at this time. Occupational titles in the interpretive materials have been changed to eliminate sex-bias titles.

The authors provide separate sex norms based on either a high school sample or a college sample. The high school sample was collected from five equally weighted geographic regions of the United States. Unfortunately, the technical manual reports data from only the Northeast Region, and does not provide means or standard deviations for the entire sample. Students in grades 7–12 were merged into one high school sample because the authors viewed grade-level differences as unmeaningful. Guidelines for meaningful differences are not presented in the manual, either in terms of raw scores or percentiles. This is one example of missing information that is important for interpretation. Although one scoring option is the college norms profile, no data for the college sample are reported in the technical manual, and no information is provided for choosing the norm group appropriate to the client.

The authors adhere to the philosophy that sex differences in vocational interests are occupationally relevant and, therefore, they present male and female norms rather than combined sex norms. Their method is intended to encourage females and males to explore occupations that in the past may have been closed to one sex or the other.

Census statistics of the distribution of female and male employment in the COPS clusters also are presented. These data should be eliminated for two reasons. First, the data were collected in 1970 and, therefore, are out of date, and second, that type of information is easily misinterpreted as approval of past sex restrictiveness in some occupations.

COPS is available in two scoring formats: machine-scorable, which also may be hand-scored with stencils, and self-scoring. A self-interpretive profile and guide is recommended for student use with the self-scoring test booklet. One of the few advantages of this instrument, compared to more extensively researched instruments, is the immediate feedback from the self-scoring format. Accuracy of the self-scoring has not been reported, even though a study on self-administration and scoring of the *Self-Directed Search* indicated that this is a legitimate concern.

Items are arranged systematically to accommodate the self-scoring format of the inventory, and the order readily reveals the 14 factors. To fake an interest in a particular area requires a minimum of skill. No data are presented in the manuals to evaluate this potential problem.

The factor analysis method of scale construction, that develops homogeneous scales, creates the problem of distinguishing vocational interests from work environments or avocational preferences. Even if a student's score does represent vocational interests, no occupational scores are presented as evidence to verify the relationship between high scores and the occupations listed for each cluster. One simply has to trust the intuitive skill of the authors for matching scale scores with occupations and courses of study. This is one example of the nonexistent validity data; not only are there no concurrent validity data, but there are no predictive validity data. COPS scores were correlated with other interest inventories, but these data are presented for only a few select scales leaving much to the imagination to determine construct validity.

Split-half reliability coefficients range from .86 to .95, and one week test-retest correlations for the 14 scales had a median of .87. The samples used for these studies are not described. The one year test-retest sample was composed of high school students at the middle and high school levels. The median correlation for the 14 scales was .70. The stability of COPS is impossible to judge without an adult sample study.

Technical data provided for COPS are not extensive or impressive, and one rarely would have reason to choose this instrument over better researched inventories such as the Strong and Kuder inventories.

The authors of COPS have provided easy-access interpretive aids that could be attractive for the first stages of vocational exploration. These aids include, for example, a set of over-head transparency masters to facilitate group testing. However, no guidelines, such as length of time required or reading level, are offered for using the transparencies, nor is their use explained.

COPS has the fundamentals for interest measurement in its 14 scales, but adequate technical data necessary for counseling or research have not been reported. Elementary questions regarding stability, validity, susceptibility to faking, and scoring accuracy are unanswered. Interpretive aids are a move in a creative direction but, as with the technical data, insufficient guidelines are provided for making sound counseling decisions.

WILBUR L. LAYTON, *Professor of Psychology, Iowa State University, Ames, Iowa.*

The *California Occupational Preference System* "is designed to assist students in career exploration" through providing "job activity interest scores based on occupational interest clusters."

The inventory consists of job activity items reflecting work performed in a wide variety of occupations. Response alternatives of "like very much," "like moderately," "dislike moderately," or "dislike very much" allow students to state their degree of like or dislike for each item.

There are 12 items for each of 14 scales for a total of 168 items. Every 14th item is scored on the same scale; that is, there are 12 clusters of 14 items each with items arranged in the same order by scale within each cluster. According to the authors, "Every item introduces a different occupation representing the broad spectrum of occupational opportunities in each cluster." The items are very obvious by content so the inventory must be easy to distort (fake). The authors present no evidence on this point. The reading difficulty level of the items appears to be quite high and, thus, the inventory may be too difficult for junior high school pupils. No data on reading difficulty level are available.

The item responses are differentially weighted. "Like" receives a weight of three; "like moderately," a weight of two; and "dislike moderately," a weight of one. "Dislike very much" is not scored, so it obviously receives a weight of zero. The rationale for and the efficacy of the standard item weights in defining the interest clusters and their relationship to occupational category are not given. They should be. The effect of differential weighting on cluster definition and separation should be determined and reported.

Three sets of scores composed of four items each were constructed through content analysis for each of the 14 COPS scales for a total of 42 variables. Subscores for these variables based on a sample of 590 junior and senior high school students in grades 7–12 were submitted to factor analysis. Intercorrelations among these group factors are presented in the technical manual. For some unknown reason, the correlations reported are based on only 241 high school students; however, from the data presented, it is clear that the group factor scales are significantly correlated and, hence, should not be considered as independent of each other.

Split-half reliability coefficients for the 14 scales, based on an unreported N and grade level, range from .86 to .95. Test-retest coefficients (N = 82) range from .77 to .91; again no grade level is indicated. One sample of seventh graders was tested again as eighth graders. For the 241 females tested, correlations ranged from .53 to .69; for the 256 males tested, the correlations ranged from .48 to .61. Also presented for the seventh- and eighth-grade groups are percentages of students whose first or second area of greatest interest remained in first or second place. For females, this percentage was 84 and for males 74. Considering the age of the students the stability demonstrated is reasonably good. No data on reliability are presented for college students although college norms are given.

The most serious shortcoming of COPS is the lack of evidence of predictive and concurrent validity. It would be highly desirable for the test authors to present evidence that persons currently employed in particular occupations do, indeed, score highest on the scale which one would expect them to. Even more desirable would be followup data of, say, seventh graders to determine the extent to which they distribute themselves eventually in occupations which would be predicted for them on the basis of

their seventh grade scores. Because COPS emphasizes career exploration and provides materials auxiliary to the test to aid in career exploration, it would be excellent if the authors could provide follow-up data supporting the efficacy of this approach.

The authors do present some theoretical concepts which are based on Roe's 1956 classification of occupations into major groups. This approach might be conceived as leading to construct validity.

If COPS lacks predictive validity, youngsters could be misled in their career exploration by being encouraged to explore some occupations which are not appropriate for them and to ignore occupations which might have proven to have been just right for them.

Male and female high school norms are based on a nationwide sample of over 7,000 boys and girls from public elementary and secondary schools in the United States. The 50 states and D.C. were grouped into five regions from which samples were taken. No information is given about exact sampling techniques used, so one cannot make inferences about the adequacy of sampling. "Inspection of grade level trends within the seventh to twelfth grade samples did not appear to be meaningful for interpretive purposes and consequently data from these grades were combined for computation of percentiles used in developing the High School Norms Profile." A college norms profile is available, but the only information available about these norms is an indication that they are based on a community college sample and on a four-year college sample.

CONCLUSION. The authors have devised a system with what might be considerable potential for encouraging career exploration especially at the high school level. However, because they have presented no evidence of concurrent or predictive validity, COPS should be used with considerable caution because there is a danger of leading pupils in the wrong direction in their career exploration.

[993]

★Career Assessment Inventory. "Individuals [grades 8 and over] seeking a career that does not generally require a four-year or advanced college degree"; 1975–76, c1973–76; CAI; vocational interests; 60 scores: 6 theme (realistic, investigative, artistic, social, enterprising, conventional), 22 basic interests (mechanical/fixing, electronics, carpentry, manual/skill trades, agriculture, nature/outdoors, animal service, science, numbers, writing, performing/entertaining, arts/crafts, social service, teaching, child care, medical service, religious activities, business, sales, office practices, clerical/clerking, food service), 32 occupational (auto mechanic, custodian-janitor, draftsperson, farmer/rancher, farrier-horseshoer, firefighter, operating room technician, pipefitter, police officer, truck driver, computer programmer, dental hygienist, advertising artist/writer, advertising executive, flight attendant, interior designer, dental assistant, funeral director, nurse L.P.N., nurse R.N., barber, buyer/merchandiser, food service manager, insurance agent, real estate agent, travel agent, accountant, cafeteria worker, executive housekeeper, innkeeper, secretary, waitress) ; norms for 22 occupational scales based on males only (14 scales) or females only (8 scales) ; Form 376 ('76, c1973–76, 4 pages, NCS scorable) ; manual ('76, 89 pages plus test) ; profile ('75, 2 pages) ; $8 per 50 test-answer sheets ; $5 per manual ; postage extra ; scoring service (scoring must be done by the publisher) : $1.90 or less per test, $5.50 or less per 15 page interpretive report (daily service), $1.20 or less per test ($30 minimum ; weekly service) ; (30) minutes ; Charles B. Johansson ; NCS Interpretive Scoring Systems. *

JACK L. BODDEN, *Area Director, Central Counties Center for MH-MR Services, Temple, Texas.*

At first glance, the *Career Assessment Inventory* looks very much like the *Strong-Campbell Interest Inventory,* and, in fact, a more thorough inspection reveals a degree of similarity which is more than cosmetic. The CAI is actually intended to be a "blue collar" version of the SCII.

In attempting to develop a vocational interest inventory primarily for persons seeking careers not requiring a college education, the CAI's author acknowledges his indebtedness to several existing instruments: the SCII, *Minnesota Vocational Interest Inventory, Vocational Preference Inventory, Self-Directed Search,* and the Kuder and Strong inventories.

The organizational format of the CAI is essentially the same as the SCII. It includes three main subsections: general themes (Holland's six types), basic interest areas (organized along the lines of Holland's typologies), and occupational scales. The test profile sheet is well laid-out and utilizes color to highlight important distinctions in groupings. A detailed explanation and interpretation of the scales and scores can be found on the reverse side of the profile sheet.

The manual carefully details the steps in construction of the test, which parallels closely the construction of the SCII. The manual also points out the care given to eliminating sex

biasing in item wording. Attention was also given to the reading level of the CAI. Apparently no reading level formula was applied to the test ; however, the author feels that the reading level required by the CAI is "at least eighth grade."

The CAI must be machine scored, which is a mixed blessing ; however, the disadvantages (expense and time lag in getting scores) are offset by the precision of machine scoring and the other desirable qualities of the test. It is interesting to note that the CAI answer sheets utilize a five choice response format, ranging from "like the activity very much" through "indifferent" to "dislike it very much." The test booklet also provides brief definitions for a few of the more esoteric occupations and school subjects. While this is probably a good idea, one might quibble with the definitional adequacy in a few instances.

Extensive reliability and validity data are presented in the manual for all three subsections of the CAI, and, in general, they seem quite acceptable. The construct validity data reveal the expected correlations with relevant instruments such as the VPI and SCII. Concurrent validity data utilized student and adult populations and are generally comparable to the evidence obtained with the SCII. Reliability data are primarily in the form of test-retest correlations, with median correlations usually at or above the .90 level.

The manual is quite impressive, especially for a newly developed test. The author of the CAI should be commended for his thorough and lucid treatment of practically all subjects relevant to the CAI's construction, usage, and interpretation. This reviewer has only one minor criticism of the manual, and that is that it lacks specific information of a descriptive sort on the nature of the normative sample used with the general themes and the basic interest sections.

In conclusion, the CAI is an excellent instrument and one which will probably receive wide acceptance and usage. It has an appropriate reason for being and should prove especially valuable to high school counselors in areas where a minority of students typically attend college. In addition to being a carefully constructed test designed to meet a genuine need, the CAI is built upon and ties into the

Career Assessment Inventory

theory and research of Holland, Strong, and Campbell. The only apparent limitation on the use of the CAI at present would appear to be the relatively small number of occupational scales (32). It is hoped that this number will be expanded with future revisions of the CAI. To counteract this minor limitation, one might consider using the CAI in conjunction with the SCII or MVII.

PAUL R. LOHNES, *Professor of Education, State University of New York at Buffalo, Buffalo, New York.*

The CAI is intended for an audience which is specialized in two respects: its members are *not* baccalaureate seekers, and they are indecisive about their vocational aspirations. The idea of specializing an interests inventory in these two ways is excellent. First, it can be demoralizing for a person with appropriately low educational aspirations to be endlessly reminded of the many exalted professional placements for which he cannot possibly hope to qualify. Second, research continues to show that an expressed vocational goal, when a goal is firmly expressed, remains the best predictor of the field in which vocational placement is eventually achieved. It is good to have an interests inventory which should not be administered to youths who know what they want in the world of work nor to youths who intend to pursue baccalaureate or graduate degrees. One of the silliest things that can happen in a school guidance program is the mass administration of an interest inventory. CAI's publishers have provided a painless, attractive, rather expensive package which should be administered selectively and which may be very useful to some of the youths for whom it is appropriate.

CAI is cheap to administer but expensive to score and interpret. The major question is whether the detail of the scoring scheme, which is what leads to a $5.50, 15-page interpretive report and probably to a lengthy client-counselor discussion, is really justified. Three separate sets of scales are reported: Holland's six vocational types, 22 basic interests, and 32 occupations. Assuming there is a demand in the marketplace for each of these approaches to scaling interests, so that the CAI has to use all three, it still may be that the number of scales of each type could be reduced, with im-

portant savings in detail and expense. I am not convinced that Holland's six categories are useful to this clientele. It seems noteworthy that the names for the six categories are not reproduced on the elaborate, multicolor profile sheet, where the categories are listed by the letters R, I, A, S, E, and C. How many professional readers of this review remember what these letters stand for in Holland's scheme? In the psychology of career development, Holland's hexagon is a fairly interesting idea, although the considerable correlations among the six vertices make it an avoidable idea. These clients are not career psychologists. I suspect that three categories, such as technical-manual, social-cultural, and business, would group interests suitably for these clients. Factor analysis of the Project TALENT data on the structure of interests in adolescents supported four uncorrelated factors, the three categories I have suggested plus science, which is not an available group of interests for these clients.[1] The list of 22 interests could perhaps be trimmed of science, writing, and teaching with some savings. The author has done a commendable job of restricting the list of 32 vocational titles to ones which do not require a baccalaureate degree, but it might be possible to define some titles broadly enough to subsume two or several of the presently listed titles, and so shorten the list.

CAI has a 100-page manual which is well organized, well written, and useful to the counselor. It gives a clear picture of what the history, purposes, and nature of CAI are, and good advice on how to employ it in counseling. The treatment of sex and race differences in the distribution of interests is sensible and adequate. Reliability, content, construct, and concurrent validities are adequately presented. The total absence of information about predictive validities must give us pause. How can the assessment of a pattern of interests help a youth to visualize and weigh his possible futures in the world of work when no statistical relationships between interests of youths and the later achievements of those same persons are demonstrated?

What America lacks is psychometric guidance systems firmly based upon regularly updated

[1] COOLEY, WILLIAM W., AND LOHNES, PAUL R. *Evaluation Research in Education.* New York: John Wiley & Sons, Inc., 1976. Pp. xi, 368. *

survey sample data bases and employing sophisticated multivariate statistical projection equations via a computerized delivery of information to clients and counselors. In such a scheme, interests and aptitudes would work together to transform a complete assessment of the client as he is presently measured into a reliable and informative sketch of his possible futures. Project TALENT has shown that such a guidance system could be created on the real predictive validities that such complete assessments possess. CAI could be incorporated as the interests part of such a complete assessment when the longitudinal data base and other features of such a guidance system are built. Meanwhile, it is reasonable to postulate an unresearched but nevertheless thinkable predictive validity for CAI within the penumbra of predictive validity for interests established by the Project TALENT research. I think the CAI manual would be improved if a review of the literature on prediction from interests were added to it. However, it would be unfair to ask that the documentation of a guidance tool provide a complete instruction on how to plan and operate a guidance program.

Obviously, I think that CAI can be improved, particularly by simplifications in its tripartite scoring scheme. As it stands, I judge it a good addition to the collection of interests inventories in print. It should be highly competitive. I give it especially high marks for the way it is tailored to a special clientele and would choose it myself if I had to counsel an indecisive youth who had properly ruled out seeking a baccalaureate education.

[994]

★**Career Awareness Inventory.** Grades 4–8; 1974–75; CAI; no norms for grades 4, 5, 7, and 8; 1 form ('74, 23 pages); teacher's manual ('74, 16 pages); scoring booklet ('75, 6 pages); separate answer sheets (NCS) may be used; $12 per 20 tests; $8.50 per 50 answer sheets; 50¢ per hand scoring stencil; postage extra; $1 per specimen set, cash orders only; scoring service, 72¢ per test; (60–90) minutes; LaVerna M. Fadale; Scholastic Testing Service, Inc. *

REFERENCES

1. SISCA, MARSHALL F. *Career Awareness: The Effect of a Career Education Program on Black and Non-Black Upper Elementary Grade Students.* Doctor's thesis, Brigham Young University (Provo, Utah), 1976. (*DAI* 36:7220A)

NANCY S. COLE, *Associate Professor of Education, University of Pittsburgh, Pittsburgh, Pennsylvania.*

The *Career Awareness Inventory* is in the genre of instruments developed in connection with the renewed interest in career education in the early 1970s. It is designed for use in grades 4–8, a level at which a prominent focus of most career education programs is career awareness—familiarity with and knowledge of a variety of careers. In particular, this inventory was constructed to conform with the awareness aspects of J. E. Taylor's model of career education involving 12 occupational clusters and information about the functions, contents, status, requirements, life-style, and experiences typical of occupations.

THE INSTRUMENT. The instrument is a 125-item inventory with seven parts: Part 1 (61 items)—identify pictured workers and related occupations; Part 2 (6 items)—identify which occupations require a college education; Part 3 (32 items)—specify whether or not you personally know a worker in the named occupations; Part 4 (4 items)—select the product (as opposed to service) occupation from a pictured pair; Part 5 (5 items)—select the higher status occupation from the pictured pair; Part 6 (10 items)—identify the occupation *not* belonging to the named occupational cluster; Part 7 (7 items)—recognize the type of activities usually liked by particular workers. The author claims that the subparts "may be useful in identifying specific strengths or weaknesses of individuals or groups" and in "planning career education programs that focus on specific aspects of career awareness." However, if part scores are to be used, most of the subparts are too short for adequate measurement.

There are several areas of concern regarding the instrument, the greatest being the reading level. Occupational titles are often long words; e.g., physical therapist, public service workers, choreographer, and pathologist. In addition, the concepts used are not simple; e.g., "most related to," "acquaintances," "performing a service," "higher prestige or status," "clusters," "natural resources," "manufacturing occupations," and "commerce." No reading-level data are presented, although it is noted that the scores correlated rather highly with intelligence scores when the inventory was group administered (38 percent common variance reported, thus apparently a correlation of 62) The correlations were considerably lower when administered as an interview (correlation about .3

on an unspecified sample). The high relationship to intelligence of the group administered instrument is almost insured by the frequently changing formats of each of the seven parts, requiring fairly long instructions in areas in which long, infrequently encountered words are the rule rather than the exception. The result is that one cannot very clearly separate career awareness as measured by this inventory from reading achievement and intelligence.

A second area of concern is the use of males and females in the pictures accompanying many of the items. Of the 36 unique pictures of people in occupations, 25 (or 69 percent) are males and only 11 are females. Of further concern is that 20 of the 25 males pictured are in stereotypical male roles such as doctor, lawyer, and construction worker; the other five males are pictured in sex-neutral roles. Only six of the 11 females are in female stereotypical roles such as nurse, secretary, and teacher; however, these stereotypically female pictures are repeated more often than others in the total test. No males are pictured in female stereotypical roles, whereas three females are pictured in male stereotypical roles (a research assistant, a telephone or electric line worker, and a draftsperson). Thus, only a minimal effort has been made to picture men and women in broad and balanced occupational roles. In addition, common sex-related occupational names (policeman, draftsman, salesman, postman, cameraman, fireman) are used throughout the inventory. Both the pictorial and language aspects violate the principles recommended for interest inventories by the "Guidelines for Assessment of Sex Bias and Sex Fairness in Career Interest Inventories" published by the National Institute of Education in 1974. The guidelines suggest sex balancing of occupational roles and use of sex-neutral language—both suggestions seem appropriate ones for the CAI.

Finally, as an easily corrected aspect of the inventory itself, I do not understand the confusing use of the same letters (A,B,C) to identify persons in the pictures as well as in the response options. One could end up selecting answer option C for person A and answer option A for person C. This potentially confusing situation could be helped by using X, Y, and Z for persons in the pictures.

TECHNICAL INFORMATION. There is a minimal amount of technical data in the manual, and the samples upon which particular results are reported are not described. We are told that "approximately 250 elementary children from urban and rural areas participated in the field testing of this inventory" and, further, that the stanine conversion table was "formulated from administration of the test to 120 sixth-grade pupils enrolled in a central school district in upstate New York." The smaller group is apparently the source of the reliability and other correlational data.

With the exception of the stanine scale for the 120 New York State sixth graders, no normative information is given. The split-half reliability is .80 for the 125-item test, which the author notes seems rather low (and I agree). Although the author attributes the lowness to the "inclusion of many very easy items and several very difficult items," the lack of intercorrelation among the seven subparts (discussed below) seems to me a more likely explanation.

The validity section of the manual appeals to content validity—reliance on the *Dictionary of Occupational Titles* and judgment by a panel of three specialists—and to construct validity—the relationship of scores to reading achievement and intelligence and the intercorrelations of the subparts. The level of relationship to reading achievement and intelligence ($r = .47$ and .62, respectively) which the author presents as evidence that the inventory "does measure a discrete factor," I interpret as suggesting too great a reading contamination. Similarly, the author views as desirable the quite low intercorrelations of the seven subparts ($-.14$ to .42, median .01) which I view as undesirable. One could question the appropriateness of combining scores from the seven quite unique subparts into one score called "career awareness" when there seem to be so many different, independent aspects of career awareness tapped by the inventory. No data comparing the CAI with any external measure of career awareness are reported.

SUMMARY. In some ways the CAI has been carefully done—it is neat, the layouts are attractive, the items have face validity, and the writing in the teacher's manual is clear and readable. The problem of measuring career awareness separate from reading skills and intelligence is not unique to this inventory but common to the entire career education area. The reported lower correlations of the inventory results with intelligence and reading achievement when the CAI is administered as an interview suggest the need to consider dictated or taped administration. It would seem very important to attempt to separate career awareness from academic skills much better than the inventory now achieves.

The use of sex stereotypical occupational roles should have been much better controlled in the inventory. The inventory reinforces the usual sex stereotypes which many career education programs may have been explicitly trying to overcome.

The technical data are inadequate. One would desire greater reliability for such a long measure and a more complete and documented validation. Consideration should be given to eliminating some of the subparts less related to the central intent of the instrument if only a total score is to be used. If subscores are to be used, as suggested by the author, the subparts need to be lengthened, and reliability, validity, and norms data need to be provided for them.

The *Career Awareness Inventory* is directed toward an area in which good instrumentation for program evaluation is definitely needed. Several fairly new options now exist and in its present form there seems little to recommend the CAI over other options, except possibly if Taylor's model is being implemented in the career education program and the subparts can be directly linked to the instructional goals. If so, the shortness of several subparts and lack of data on them remain a severe drawback. The inventory as it now stands needs some revision and much more research. At this stage it should definitely be marked "EXPERIMENTAL."

MARY LEE SMITH, *Director, Evaluation Research Services, Boulder, Colorado.*

The *Career Awareness Inventory* was designed to measure knowledge about the characteristics of vocations. Its principal use is in the evaluation of elementary school career education programs.

The inventory contains 131 items in seven sections. Part 1 contains line drawings of work scenes, such as a courtroom; the examinee is asked to name each worker in the picture (given five options for each worker). For each scene the examinee is also asked to identify which occupation is related to those in the scene. Part 2 contains six items for each of which the student is asked to identify the one of five occupations requiring a college education. Part 3 gives 32 types of worker (e.g., motel clerk, carpenter); the student is asked whether or not he is acquainted with anyone in these occupations. Part 4 asks whether or not eight work roles involve production rather than service as a product. Part 5 tests knowledge of the relative prestige associated with five pairs of occupations. Part 6 tests knowledge of which occupations cluster together. Part 7 tests knowledge of job duties.

All sections except Part 3 have a keyed correct response. The score on Part 3 is the number of the occupations with which the student reported familiarity. The total score is the sum of 211 parts, including Part 3.

The standardization data are based on 120 sixth-grade students. The only information given about these students is that they were "enrolled in a central school district in upstate New York." These data form the basis for a table of stanine scores with which the user can convert raw scores. The reliability (split-halves method) was .80, and the standard error of measurement was approximately one stanine score. The author confesses that this reliability is rather low but justifies it on the basis of a wide range of difficulty among items. This was viewed as a trade-off between reduced reliability and "a more pleasant and helpful testing situation."

In fact, that level of reliability is sufficient for the evaluation of group performance. It is questionable for making decisions about individuals. Unfortunately, the latter objective is suggested as one use of the test. To use the test to make decisions such as how to "form ability groups," a larger or more representative norm sample is required, and certainly more validity information is needed.

The evidence for validity is the congruence of items with information in the *Dictionary of Occupational Titles and Manpower Requirements* and with the judgment of a panel of three specialists. The author describes a correlational analysis of the test administered as it is, the same items administered in an interview format, and "intelligence/reading achievement scores." Unfortunately, she discusses the results of this analysis in narrative form ("The variance between reading achievement scores and career awareness scores increased to approximately 22 percent.") so that one cannot judge these data for oneself.

An obvious problem is the addition of Part 3 to the other sections to obtain total test scores. This procedure contaminates the assessment of knowledge of occupational characteristics with a self-report component. The problem should have been evident to the test developers by inspection of the table of intercorrelations of the test sections. Part 3 correlates −.08, −.07, −.11, −.14, −.02, and −.14 with Parts 1, 2, 4, 5, 6, and 7, respectively. Besides the deception (to self or others) possible in self-report items, the negative correlations of this part with others may be explained by the heavy loading of low-status occupations in this section. Children from lower social strata are both more likely to have had contact with these occupations and less likely to score high on knowledge-related tests. The inclusion of this subtest with the total score probably depresses total test reliability and validity.

Although the above problems can be corrected by further research by the author and publishers, other weaknesses may be more fundamental. Would the test stand up to review by equal opportunities commissions? None of the line drawings appears to contain dark faces. Although the research chemist is female, one wonders about the male doctor, lawyer, and judge and the female secretary, nurse, and teacher. Does career awareness relate to any variable of importance, such as job success or satisfaction? Although this test is tied to the theory of career development and programs of career education, no evidence is presented to establish the relationships hypothesized.

[995]

★Career Development Inventory. Grades 9–10 and out-of-school youth and adults; 1974–75; CDI; 17 scores: an occupational-consideration rating (low, moderate, or high) for 3 educational levels of entry (early, delayed, late) in each of 6 occupational groupings (technical/mechanical/skilled, scientific/theoretical [no early entry level], artistic/literary/musical, social/personal service, persuasive/managerial, clerical/computational); part 2, entitled *Kuder Career Interest*

Survey, is identical with *Kuder Occupational Interest Survey,* Form DD, copyrighted 1964; 1 form ('74, 4 pages); administrator's manual ('75, 8 pages); technical supplement ('75, 28 pages, minor revisions 1977); profile ('75, 1 page); student interpretive leaflet ('75, 4 pages); student directions leaflet ('75, 4 pages); may be used with the Career Development Program Planning Notebook; $33.55 per 25 sets of testing materials including scoring service (technical supplement included on request); $5.35 per specimen set; postage extra (except for return of profiles); (60–75) minutes; Esther E. Diamond and G. Frederic Kuder (test, part 2); Science Research Associates, Inc. *

REFERENCES

1. ZELKOWITZ, ROBIN SUSAN. *The Construction and Validation of a Measure of Vocational Maturity for Adult Males.* Doctor's thesis, Columbia University (New York, N.Y.), 1975. (DAI 36:1492B)

WILLIAM C. BINGHAM, *Professor of Education, Rutgers, The State University of New Jersey, New Brunswick, New Jersey.*

The CDI consists of two parts: a Personal Data Form of 46 biographical items and the *Kuder Occupational Interest Survey.* A student directions leaflet and an interpretive leaflet, both well planned and lucidly presented, make self-administration and self-interpretation possible, but the authors recommend that a resource person be available to assist when necessary.

Scores are reported on a computer-generated career development profile, an 18-cell matrix in which columns represent six clusters of occupational interests and rows represent entry level as early (high school or less), delayed (postsecondary education, training, or experience), and late (four years of college or more). With one exception, each cell is scored high, moderate, or low to suggest the degree of consideration a student ought to give to occupations falling in that cell. The complex procedures for arriving at high, moderate, and low scores is explained in detail in the technical supplement.

Sex bias in scoring was addressed systematically through score conversions which markedly reduced, but did not eliminate, gaps between male- and female-normed scales for the same occupation. Some curious sex differences remain, however. For example, correlations between academic level of interest scores (important in determining entry level) and occupational interest clusters tend to be slightly higher for males than females in most late-entry occupations, but substantially higher for females in the case of the late-entry artistic/literary/musical cluster. Proportions of females scoring high in late-entry technical/mechanical/

skilled and late-entry scientific/theoretical are low, while the same is true for males in late-entry artistic/literary/musical and late-entry social service/personal service. As the authors suggest, psychometric techniques may not be sufficient to counterbalance early socialization. Perhaps they are also insufficient to counterbalance response tendencies occasioned by the content or grouping of items.

No reliability or validity data are reported directly on the career development profile scores, but three kinds of data, obtained on a field-test random sample of 131 males and 199 females, and converted to T scores and ranks, are offered to assist with interpretation. Means and standard deviations are reported for 16 of the 18 cells of the profile, showing the same sex differences described in the preceding paragraph.

Intercorrelations among cells of the profile appear to be reasonable. For example, rank correlations between early- and late-entry occupations tend to be negative or close to zero, with one notable exception, .24 between early- and late-entry technical/mechanical/skilled occupations; among late-entry occupations, cells including social service/personal service occupations and those including persuasive/managerial are moderately related (.39), while those including technical/mechanical/skilled and social service/personal service are inversely related ($-.54$); the highest correlations are between early- and delayed-entry occupations in the same clusters (technical/mechanical/skilled, .86; clerical/computational, .81). These data indicate appropriate differentiations in classification.

Reliability of individual Kuder scores, checked by means of a test-retest comparison of sex-corrected scores for 50 male and 50 female college students over a two-week interval, ranged from "five cases....below .72" to .99, with median .93.

No reliability data are reported for the biographical items. While it can be expected that factual items on this part of the test will generate stable responses, some of the items are designed to tap values, attitudes, and other personal preferences. It would be helpful to users to know the stability of responses to such items. Appropriate data are not reported, and their absence is not noted, let alone explained.

Concurrent validity of occupational scales was checked by means of an errors-of-classification study of 202 males and 111 females. For males, 79 percent were classified correctly; for females, the correct classification rate was 76 percent.

No validity data are reported for biographical items, although item selection was consistent with procedures for establishing content validity. The absence of these data is only indirectly noted.

Although the technical supplement contains a variety of data and is reasonably thorough in describing the construction and development of the CDI, it falls short of meeting the APA test standards in three important respects: (a) failure to note the absence of some critical data; (b) inclusion of a great deal of data probably beyond the comprehension of likely users without sufficient explanation to bridge the gap; and (c) lack of reliability and validity data explicitly for grades 9 and 10, despite the authors' claim that the CDI is intended for use primarily in these grades.

As a reporting device, the career development profile is soundly conceived, although perhaps misnamed (career planning profile seems more accurate), and presents data to subjects in a way that facilitates exploration of suitable occupational alternatives and provides a convenient and usable link with sources of detailed occupational information, such as the *Dictionary of Occupational Titles*. For attaining these ends, the authors are to be commended. Actual efficacy of the profile, however, depends in large measure on the adequacy of the scores reported in each cell of the matrix. Until the technical data on that issue are more convincing, it seems reasonable to continue to use other instruments, such as Holland's *Self Directed Search*, which accomplish the same purposes of exploration and linkage with detailed data, but do so at less expense and inconvenience. In addition, while the authors' claims that the inventory has applicability with age groups and in settings other than ninth and tenth grade seem reasonable, no data are offered to support those claims.

JAMES H. RICKS, JR., *Senior Vice President, The Psychological Corporation, New York, New York.*

The *Career Development Inventory* is a variant of the *Kuder Career Interest Survey* or Form DD of the *Kuder Occupational Interest Survey* (reviewed previously, 7:1025), modified, expanded, and packaged.

Friends of testing for guidance purposes will see the packaging—the Planning Notebook—as an ingenious attempt to make it easier to convey to students and their parents what tests can help them discover about themselves, and to open up new horizons. Enemies of testing, or of private enterprise, will see it as an effort to extract approximately $3 from users for something which about $1.25 could have bought if the student or the counselor were willing to work a little harder. Or, worse, they will see it as one more effort to sort infinitely variable individuals into a few somewhat arbitrary categories.

Most readers of this review probably have already chosen their sides for or against this kind of offering. Too bad. Of more serious concern ought to be the modification and expansion of the parent instrument, and *then* one could make the cooler judgment as to how useful the CDI can be in a particular setting.

The KOIS reports 162 scores: 114 occupational (77 male, 37 female) and 48 college-major (29 male, 19 female) in the form of correlations (lambda coefficients) between the individual's responses and those of a criterion group. The CDI reports 17 in three-step ratings of low, moderate, or high, plus an academic level of interest score, a verification score, and some items of information gleaned from the Personal Data Form which precedes the Kuder items in the CDI. In place of numerical scores, that is, the CDI reports the three levels of probability mentioned above for entry into each of six fields at three levels of educational preparation (early, delayed, and late). (There are 17, not 18, because two cells are mutually exclusive.) The six broad categories replacing the occupations and the college majors of the earlier instrument closely resemble the six used by Holland.

The KOIS items form a little more than two-thirds of the CDI. To these 100 have been added 46 items in a Personal Data Form, including some questions of verifiable fact, some self-estimate reports, and some expressions of feelings or preferences. The present technical supplement to the manual provides no details as to how these items are scored or used, except

to note that some of them work as moderators of the academic level of interest score. (The items involved are primarily self-reports of marks in school and the education of parents and siblings; the publisher advises that future editions of the manual will contain more information regarding the scoring of these items.)

An aid to the questionnaire includes a list of 195 occupations, some overlapping and some much broader or narrower than others, from which the student selects an "ideal" and an "expected" future work. Necessarily the occupations differ considerably in degree of familiarity to different students; a descriptive index or glossary would be helpful. The list is laudably non-sexist in language—"repairer" rather than "repairman," for example.

The four-page form comprising the CDI probably presents no difficulty to a reasonably good reader with reasonably good eyesight. However, the typeface used is in the 7- to 9-point range and the ink is gray, sometimes backed by a lighter gray tint.

The Planning Notebook can be purchased without the CDI. In this case, it is suggested that the student plot a self-estimated profile anyway—but there are no data, of course, on the reliability or validity of this procedure.

Prospective users of the *Career Development Inventory* have two judgments to make. First, in the context of the Career Development Program, does an interest inventory provide the most important information needed? The program's notebook advises the student to consider "your abilities" as well as interests and other values and alternatives, but no provision is offered in the program for the measurement of the student's aptitudes or developed abilities. In counseling students and helping them plan, the latter are fundamental and should be measured first; interests do motivate and may be worth surveying, but also can be modified or molded by guidance toward particular exposures and experiences.

Second, if the decision is to use an interest inventory, is the CDI preferable to its parent instrument, the KOIS, and to other inventories available? To this question there is no one clearcut answer. For lack of evidence on the effect of the biodata obtained by the Personal Data Form, the desirability of its inclusion becomes a matter of the prospective purchaser's

Career Development Inventory

preference. Furthermore, while the combination of the KOIS's many scores into fewer categories and levels will make the results more easily digestible by more students, it will also constitute a step away from the empirical scoring base that is a major virtue of the parent. The KOIS or another good interest inventory would be the instrument of choice except for those to whom the appeal of the "packaged" counseling offered by the Career Planning Notebook outweighs its extra cost.

Meas & Eval Guid 10(4):244–6 Ja '78. Fred H. Borgen. More than a test, the Career Development Program is a set of materials intended to facilitate career development among diverse people ranging from ninth-grade students to adults. As the principal medium for career exploration, the planning notebook is the "integrative tool" designed to stimulate exploration and consideration of careers in a self-directed way or with greater counselor/teacher intervention, if desired. The planning notebook may be used with an optional, formal, self-report device, the Career Development Inventory (CDI). * As a novel, creative, and major extension of the conventional KOIS scoring, Occupational Cluster Scores are derived to show the person's interest similarity to people employed in the broad occupational classes represented by each of the 18 cells of the Profile. These new scores retain the lambda scoring system of KOIS, but apply it to occupational fields rather than single occupations. * This review focuses on this extension of the scoring and interpretation of the conventional KOIS because it: (a) reflects, in my view, the pivotal concept in the total program, (b) marks a significant departure in scoring and potential interpretation of the traditional KOIS, (c) involves primary efforts in reducing sex differences in the scores, (d) is the single part of the program that is formally a test, and (e) is the part of the program for which the technical manual presents descriptive and evaluative research. Concluding comments will also indicate my impression of the total package of materials as a career exploration tool. Two recent trends in interest measurement, led particularly by the work of John Holland, have been: (a) the development of simplified taxonomies of people and careers and (b) the increasing acceptance of self-directed tools for career exploration. The revised scoring system in the Kuder Career Interest Survey incorporates these features, and thus gains the advantages of these trends. In my view, it is particularly appropriate for people to begin career exploration in broadly defined domains and I applaud empirically based taxonomies that encourage this. The self-directed feature of the system makes it applicable on a wide scale to large numbers of people needing career facilitation. This is an advantage only if the system has effective characteristics. Present evidence suggests the promise of the total program but further research is clearly called for to substantiate the use of the system on a large scale. The technical manual effectively presents data supporting the reliability, factor structure, and concurrent validity of the Occupational Cluster Scores. Lacking are data on predictive validity. This research gap with the conventional KOIS has recently been addressed with Zytowski's KOIS follow-up study (1976). It would be valuable to rescore Zytowski's sample to evaluate the predictive validity of the Occupational Cluster Scores. The substantial sex differences in interest inventory scores have been probably the most controversial issue in the history of interest measurement. Vigorous efforts were made here to reduce sex differences by using a new correction formula. Evidence presented....for individual profiles scored with and without the correction formula shows that the ranks of scores shift to decrease sex differences when the correction formula is used. Other evidence for group comparisons....however, shows that the persisting sex differences for the CDI are as great, and in some cases considerably greater, than comparable comparisons (RIASEC) on the Holland Vocational Preference Inventory (VPI) and the Strong-Campbell Interest Inventory (SCII). (This observation is based on my calculation of sex differences in standard deviation units for data in each of the respective manuals.) Unfortunately, the magnitude of these persisting differences appears to be overlooked in the wake of enthusiasm over a new approach to a nettlesome psychometric problem. The VPI and SCII have often been viewed with concern because of the sex differences they yield; the data in Table 5 suggest equal problems for the CDI. Yet, it is too easy to read the promotional and technical

Career Development Inventory

materials for the CDI and conclude that some breakthrough in dealing with sex differences has been achieved. A particularly unfortunate overstatement appears in the brief fact sheet presenting the highlights of the Career Development Program: "The career interest scores reported on the Career Development Profile involve use of an equation that sharply reduces the influences of systematic sex differences in responses and consequently minimizes sex bias in individual scores." Although this statement is consistent with a portion of the data, it does not accurately depict the remaining substantial sex differences. Another index of sex differences is to look within each cell of the occupational grid at the relative frequencies of high, moderate, and low scores for males and females ....Although the patterns are not consistent throughout, there are cases where the sex differences are large. For example, the ratio of low scores on the late entry technical scale is 60 females to 8 males, and the ratio of high scores on the delayed entry persuasive scale is 32 males to 3 females. Inspection of the prime medium for the user, the planning notebook, shows many attractive features. The content throughout seems accurately to reflect current knowledge about career behavior and to treat important issues effectively. Ensuring individual stimulation, the workbook is attractively packaged, both graphically and stylistically. The materials are developmentally oriented for individual growth and vocational exploration. There are laudable emphases throughout on career exploration as a continuous process, on valuing self-perception, responsibility and autonomy, on stimulation of further exploration, information, and experience, and on sensitivity to issues such as sexual stereotyping in career behavior. The Career Development Program is an attractive tool with potential for use with large numbers of people. It is, therefore, especially incumbent on the publisher to undertake substantial research to generally evaluate the effectiveness of the package. Holland and his associates have begun research of this kind by evaluating the Self-Directed Search (SDS) in not only the usual psychometric way, but also in terms of impact on the self-assessment experiences on the user. I am favorably impressed by the central facilitation of career exploration, organized simply and understandably, around a reasonable

taxonomic system. In my experience, a counseling difficulty at times with the conventional KOIS is the lack of systematic scale organization; thus, this represents a clever and welcome extension of the KOIS to an organized taxonomic system. In fact, my pleasure with it leads me to strongly recommend that SRA provide users with such scores on the conventional KOIS profiles. The Career Development Program shows promise as an attractive tool for aiding....in career exploration. It appears to be a wise and creative merging of the established features of the KOIS and current knowledge about psychometrics, career behavior, and vocational counseling. Research presented on the interest scores is supportive although sex differences persist in the results, as they do for nearly all interest inventories. Major competing approaches for self-directed career assessment and exploration are Holland's SDS and the ACT 1977 Vocational Interest, Experience, and Skill Assessment (VIESA), both of which are self-scoring. The SDS has the current advantage of a larger body of evaluative research. All three approaches seem to have attractive features for individual users. All have much in common in that they are based on a common body of knowledge in vocational behavior and all use a taxonomic kind of occupational clustering to facilitate career exploration.

[996]

Career Guidance Inventory. Grades 7–13 students interested in trades, services, and technologies; 1972; CGI; 25 scores: 14 engineering related trades (carpentry and woodworking, masonry, mechanical repair, painting and decorating, plumbing and pipefitting, printing, tool and die making, sheet metal and welding, drafting and design, mechanical engineering, industrial production, civil and architectural engineering, electrical engineering, chemical and laboratory) and 11 nonengineering related services (environmental health, agriculture and forestry, business management, communications, data processing, sales, transportation services, protective services, medical laboratory, nursing, food service); 1 form (15 pages); manual (7 pages); separate answer sheets must be used; $1 per test; $7.50 per 25 self-marking answer sheets; cash orders postpaid; administration time not reported; James E. Oliver; Educational Guidance, Inc. *

BERT W. WESTBROOK, *Professor of Psychology, North Carolina State University, Raleigh, North Carolina.*

This inventory, designed "to aid counselors in the guidance of students with interest in the trades, services and technologies," consists of 250 pairs of statements which presumably describe the activities of persons employed in those areas. The manual does not indicate the total time needed to complete the test, but it is unlikely that many 7th graders can get through the 500 statements (250 paired items) in less than one hour. Some students will probably take much longer, perhaps two hours, to complete the inventory.

The directions for administration are very confusing, partly because of the wording and partly because the answer sheet does not have numbered answer positions beyond 25. The manual indicates that examinees may perform the mechanics of scoring their own answer sheet, but, unfortunately, it implies that the test is self-interpreting. More stress should be placed on the need for the help of a trained counselor in making interpretations.

The manual does not indicate what was done in planning and constructing the test to make it valid and useful, and there is no indication that an item analysis was made to determine item discrimination and difficulty.

The inventory provides a profile of 25 raw scores. Because all scales involve the same number of items, norms are viewed as unnecessary: "It is easy to attach meaning to your scores since they show your *relative* interest in major occupations." However, the statements which comprise a given scale may be preferred more or less than the statements which comprise a different scale. Hence, to know whether a high score reflects an individual's interests or only the popularity of statements, the user would need to consult a set of norms. Judgments cannot be made from raw scores because the manual does not present evidence that the statements (items) in each scale are a representative sample of that field.

Scores for each of the 25 scales are expressed in terms of seven descriptive phrases ranging from "very low" (3 or fewer items) to "very high" (18–20 items). A person with 10 or 11 preferences on a given scale is described as "average." The manual does not present evidence to support the interpretative statement presented to students: "the higher the score in a given area the greater the probability an individual will find that area attractive as a vocation or profession."

The author reports no data to demonstrate the validity of the test. Although he claims that "the *Career Guidance Inventory* has content validity," there is no indication that experts have been asked to judge whether the 25 scales are "of greatest value to the counselor and the student." The manual presents no evidence that a student's score predicts his satisfaction in a given type of job.

Reliability was determined by administering the inventory "to one hundred students pursuing terminal degrees in four different junior colleges" and computing split-half reliabilities (range .76 to .93, median .87) for each of the 25 scales.

The answer sheet is a combined self-scoring answer sheet and profile; therefore, the scoring and profiling are automatically achieved as the inventory is completed. The inventory includes a large enough sample of statements dealing with engineering-related trades and nonengineering-related services to give the student a variety of choices and therefore a more precise reading on areas of interest.

Unfortunately, the undesirable features of the inventory far outnumber the desirable ones. This reviewer is not convinced that a reasonable effort has been made to follow the recommendations in the *Standards for Educational and Psychological Tests*. The manual does not report the validity of the inventory for the type of inference for which it is recommended. The test manual does not indicate to what extent the inventory scores are stable; that is, how nearly constant the scores are likely to be if the inventory is repeated after time has lapsed. The confusing directions for administration should be rewritten and presented with a maximum of detail and clarity so as to reduce the likelihood of error.

The author of the *Career Guidance Inventory* has not furnished sufficient information to evaluate the inventory. Therefore, it should be distributed "for research use only" until the user is offered more extensive information on its development, its validity and reliability, its normative samples, the kinds of interpretations that are appropriate, and the uses for which the inventory can best be employed.

[997]

Career Maturity Inventory. Grades 6–12; 1973; CMI; formerly called *Vocational Development Inventory*; 2 tests; manual (53 pages); handbook (39 pages); profile (2 pages); separate answer sheets (CompuScan, Digitek, IBM 1230) must be used; $23.45

Career Guidance Inventory

per 35 sets of both tests; answer sheets: $4 per 50 CompuScan, $5 per 50 Digitek or IBM 1230; $2.50 per IBM 1230 scoring stencil; $5 per 100 profiles; $2.50 per handbook; $5 per specimen set; postage extra; scoring service ($50 minimum): 60¢ and over per student for both tests, 50¢ and over per student for either test; John O. Crites; CTB/McGraw-Hill. *

a) ATTITUDE SCALE. Form A-1 (7 pages); $6.65 per 35 tests; (25-35) minutes.

b) COMPETENCE TEST, RESEARCH EDITION. 5 scores: self-appraisal, occupational information, goal selection, planning, problem solving; Form A-1 (38 pages); $18.20 per 35 tests; (110-130) minutes.

See T2:2103 (35 references).

REFERENCES

1-35. See T2:2103; also includes a cumulative name index to the first 35 references for this test.

36. BYLER, BENNIE LEE. A Study of Factors Associated With the Vocational Development of High School Agricultural Occupations Students. Doctor's thesis, University of Illinois (Urbana, Ill.), 1972. (DAI 33:6245A)

37. COFFEY, MARTIN JAMES. Personality Orientation and Vocational Maturity: A Study of Profile Similarity. Doctor's thesis, University of Alabama (University, Ala.), 1972. (DAI 33:5488A)

38. ELMORE, THOMAS M.; GLADDING, SAMUEL T.; AND SOMMERS, JANE BELL. "Comparative Study of Psychological Anomie, Personality, and Vocational Aspiration and Maturity of the Disabled." Abstract. Proc 80th Ann Conv Am Psychol Assn 7(2):711-2 '72. * (PA 48:5385)

39. JORDAAN, JEAN PIERRE. "Vocational Maturity: The Construct, Its Measurement, and Its Validity." Proc Int Congr Appl Psychol 17(1):417-58 '72. *

40. KAPES, JEROME T. "Discriminating Among Successful and Unsuccessful Vocational and Academic 10th Grade Boys." J Indus Teach Ed 9(3):21-9 sp '72. *

41. PUCEL, DAVID J.; NELSON, HOWARD F.; HEITZMAN, DARRELL; AND WHEELER, DAVID N. "Vocational Maturity and Vocational Training." J Indus Teach Ed 9(3):30-8 sp '72. *

42. PUTNAM, BARBARA A., AND HANSEN, JAMES C. "Relationship of Self-Concept and Feminine Role Concept to Vocational Maturity in Young Women." J Counsel Psychol 19(5):436-40 S '72. * (PA 49:2499)

43. SAWYER, DAVID ERNEST. Differences in Vocational Maturity and Selected Behavioral Tendencies Between Part-Time Cooperative Education Participants and Nonparticipants in Selected Texas Secondary Schools. Doctor's thesis, Texas A & M University (College Station, Tex.), 1972. (DAI 33:4147A)

44. SMITH, EDWARD D., AND HERR, EDWIN L. "Sex Differences in the Maturation of Vocational Attitudes Among Adolescents." Voc Guid Q 20(3):177-82 Mr '72. *

45. WESTBROOK, BERT W., AND MASTIE, MARJORIE M. "On Pathfinding: Some Suggestions for Increasing Our Understanding of the Construct of Vocational Maturity." J. Indus Teach Ed 9(3):39-46 sp '72. *

46. WHITMAN, ROBERT LOWELL. The Vocational Attitude Maturity of Disadvantaged Eighth and Twelfth Grade Students in Rural Eastern Kentucky. Doctor's thesis, Pennsylvania State University (University Park, Pa.), 1972. (DAI 33:6812A)

47. AIKEN, JAMES, AND JOHNSTON, JOSEPH A. "Promoting Career Information Seeking Behaviors in College Students." J Voc Behav 3(1):81-7 Ja '73. * (PA 50:3658)

48. BLEDSOE, JOSEPH C., AND WIGGINS, R. GENE. "Academic Aspirations and Vocational Maturity of Ninth Grade Boys and Girls." Psychol Rep 32(2):674 Ap '73. * (PA 51:3888, title only)

49. BRANTNER, SEYMOUR T., AND ENDERLEIN, THOMAS E. "Identification of Potential Vocational High School Dropouts." J Indus Teach Ed 11(1):44-52 f '73. *

50. BURKHART, MARY QUINN. Vocational Decision-Making: A Comparison of the Rates of Development for Men and Women. Doctor's thesis, Florida State University (Tallahassee, Fla.), 1973. (DAI 34:1605A)

51. CAPEHART, JUNIUS LONG, JR. The Relationship of Vocational Maturity to Holland's Theory of Vocational Choice. Doctor's thesis, University of North Carolina (Chapel Hill, N.C.), 1973. (DAI 34:5618A)

52. CLAPSADDLE, DAVID K. "Career Development and Teacher Inservice Preparation." El Sch Guid & Counsel 8(2):92-7 D '73. *

53. CLAPSADDLE, DAVID KARL. The Relationship of Career Education Teacher Inservice Preparation to the Vocational Development of Sixth Grade School Children. Doctor's thesis, Kansas State University (Manhattan, Kan.), 1973. (DAI 34:4675A)

54. COSTARIS, MICHAEL J. Nonintellective Characteristics of Open Door Admittees to a Community College. Doctor's thesis, Rutgers—The State University (New Brunswick, N.J.), 1973. (DAI 34:6378A)

55. CRITES, JOHN O. "Career Maturity." Meas Ed 4(2):1-8 w '72-73 ['73]. *

56. CURRIE, LAWRENCE EVERETT. Vocational Awareness, Vocational Development, and Vocational Responses in Adolescents of Divergent Ethnic, Educational, and Socio-Economic Backgrounds. Doctor's thesis, Syracuse University (Syracuse, N.Y.), 1973. (DAI 34:7119A)

57. FAUROT, LYLE MARTIN. An Investigation of the Validity of Vocational Student Grades as a Criterion of Vocational Student Success and the Predictability of Vocational Student Grades Using Standardized Test Instruments. Doctor's thesis, University of Minnesota (Minneapolis, Minn.), 1973. (DAI 34:676A)

58. GREENE, STANLEY DEE. The Relationship Between a Developing Career Education Program and the Career Maturity of Secondary School Students. Doctor's thesis, Kansas State University (Manhattan, Kan.), 1973. (DAI 34:5817A)

59. HANSEN, JAMES C., AND ANSELL, EDGAR M. "Assessment of Vocational Maturity." J Voc Behav 3(1): 89-94 Ja '73. * (PA 50:3780)

60. McGEE, DONALD HUDSON. Psychological Needs and Vocational Maturity of Students in an Ohio Joint Vocational School. Doctor's thesis, Ohio State University (Columbus, Ohio), 1973. (DAI 34:861B)

61. MILLER, MICHAEL FOSTER. Effects of Information Complexity and Vocational Maturity on Pre-Decision Information Seeking. Doctor's thesis, New York University (New York, N.Y.), 1973. (DAI 34:3882A)

62. MUNLEY, PATRICK H. An Exploratory Investigation of the Relationship Between Erik Erikson's Theory of Psycho-Social Development and Vocational Behavior. Doctor's thesis, University of Maryland (College Park, Md.), 1973. (DAI 35:484B)

63. SAWYER, DAVID E. "The Worth of Part-Time Cooperative Education at the Secondary Level." J Indus Teach Ed 10(4): 22-35 su '73. *

64. SNYDER, FRANK W. "Vocational Development Inventory." Letter. Meas & Eval Guid 6(3):182-3 O '73. *

65. SWAILS, RICHARD BRAY. The Effects of Three Group Approaches on the Aptitude and Attitude Dimensions of Vocational Development of Ninth Grade High School Students. Doctor's thesis, Pennsylvania State University (University Park, Pa.), 1973. (DAI 34:4763A)

66. TINNEY, GLADYS ROSE FORIS. Occupational Maturity of Educable Mentally Retarded Students. Doctor's thesis, Kansas State University (Manhattan, Kan.), 1973. (DAI 35:333A)

67. TSENG, M. S., AND RHODES, C. I. "Correlates of the Perception of Occupational Prestige." J Counsel Psychol 20(6): 522-7 N '73. * (PA 51:8018)

68. WALSH, W. B.; HOWARD, P. R.; O'BRIEN, W. F.; SANTA-MARIA, M. L.; AND EDMONDSON, C. J. "Consistent Occupational Preferences and Satisfaction, Self Concept, Self Acceptance and Vocational Maturity." J Voc Behav 3(4):453-63 O '73. * (PA 52:1991)

69. WESTBROOK, BERT W., AND MASTIE, MARJORIE M. "Three Measures of Vocational Maturity: A Beginning to Know About." Meas & Eval Guid 6(1):8-16 Ap '73. * (PA 50:10259)

70. ADAMS, WILLIE GRAY. Influence of Career Education on Motivation and Aspiration of Middle School Age Educationally Disadvantaged Youth. Doctor's thesis, Pennsylvania State University (University Park, Pa.), 1974. (DAI 35:7641A)

71. BARNES, WILLIAM JAMES, JR. The Effect of Occupational Investigation Programs on Ninth Grade Students as Measured by the Career Maturity Inventory. Doctor's thesis, Texas A & M University (College Station, Tex.), 1974. (DAI 35:2129A)

72. BARTMAN, LEROY ROBERT. An Empirical Analysis of a Standardized Inventory of Vocational Maturity in Terms of Educational Cognitive Style. Doctor's thesis, Wayne State University (Detroit, Mich.), 1974. (DAI 35:7603A)

73. BINGHAM, GRACE D'AGOSTINO. Career Attitudes and Self-Esteem Among Boys With and Without Specific Learning Disabilities. Doctor's thesis, Rutgers—The State University (New Brunswick, N.J.), 1974. (DAI 36:815A)

74. BLEDSOE, JOSEPH C., AND WIGGINS, R. GENE. "Self-Concepts and Academic Aspirations of 'Understood' and 'Misunderstood' Boys and Girls in Ninth Grade." Psychol Rep 35(1, pt 1):57-8 Ag '74. * (PA 56:8737)

75. BROWN, RONALD ADRION. Influences of an Agricultural Career Orientation Unit on the Career Development of Selected Junior High School Students. Doctor's thesis, University of Illinois (Urbana, Ill.), 1974. (DAI 35:7794A)

76. CHAPIN, JAMES ARTHUR. Personality Correlates of Vocational Maturity. Doctor's thesis, Southern Illinois University (Carbondale, Ill.), 1974. (DAI 35:6066B)

77. CICCHETTI, ELRIC ANTHONY. The Effects of a Vocational Education Training Program on the Career Maturity Level of Disadvantaged Ninth Grade Junior High School Youth. Doctor's thesis, Rutgers—The State University (New Brunswick, N.J.), 1974. (DAI 36:856A)

78. CRITES, JOHN O. Chap. 2, "The Career Maturity Inventory," pp. 25-39. In Measuring Vocational Maturity for Counseling and Evaluation. Edited by Donald E. Super. Washington, D.C.: National Vocational Guidance Association, 1974. Pp. 169. *

Career Maturity Inventory

79. CRITES, JOHN O. Chap. 12, "Career Development Processes: A Model of Vocational Maturity," pp. 296–320. In *Vocational Guidance and Human Development*. Edited by Edwin L. Herr. Boston, Mass.: Houghton Mifflin Co., 1974. Pp. xi, 596. *

80. CRITES, JOHN O. "Methodological Issues in the Measurement of Career Maturity." *Meas & Eval Guid* 6(4):200–9 Ja '74. * (*PA* 52:1896)

81. ECONOMOU, NICK. *Relationships Between Identity Confusion, Identity Crisis Resolution, Self-Esteem and Career Choice Attitudes in Freshmen College Women.* Doctor's thesis, Rutgers—The State University (New Brunswick, N.J.), 1974. (*DAI* 36:703A)

82. ENDERLEIN, THOMAS ELLIS. *Causal Relationships of Student Characteristics Related to Satisfaction in Post High School Employment.* Doctor's thesis, Pennsylvania State University (University Park, Pa.), 1974. (*DAI* 35:7795A)

83. GILRAIN, JAMES BERNARD. *A Study of the Facilitation of Seventh Grade Students' Vocational Maturity Through the Integration of Vocational Development Material Into Existing Curricula, Utilizing Regular Teachers and Required Subjects in Lieu of Special Courses, Special Programs, and Special Personnel.* Doctor's thesis, St. John's University (Jamaica, N.Y.), 1974. (*DAI* 35:5812A)

84. GRAFF, ROBERT W., AND BEGGS, DONALD L. "Personal and Vocational Development in High School Students." *J Sch Psychol* 12(1):17–23 sp '74. * (*PA* 52:10949)

85. GRAVES, THOMAS D. *A Study of Vocational Maturity and College Students' Certainty and Commitment to Career Choice.* Doctor's thesis, University of Northern Colorado (Greeley, Colo.), 1974. (*DAI* 35:7056A)

86. HAMDANI, ASMA JAMILA. *Exploratory Behavior and Vocational Development Among Disadvantaged Inner-City Adolescents.* Doctor's thesis, Columbia University (New York, N.Y.), 1974. (*DAI* 35:3424A)

87. HANSEN, JO-IDA C. "Review of the Career Maturity Inventory." *J Counsel Psychol* 21(2):168–72 Mr '74. *

88. HARBAUGH, JAMES FORREST. *A Comparison of Career Maturity Attitudes of Industrial Arts Curriculum Project Students, Conventionally-Taught Industrial Arts Students and Non-Industrial Arts Students.* Doctor's thesis, Texas A & M University (College Station, Tex.), 1974. (*DAI* 36:164A)

89. HARMON, LENORE W. Chap. 6, "Problems in Measuring Vocational Maturity: A Counseling Perspective," pp. 81–6. In *Measuring Vocational Maturity for Counseling and Evaluation.* Edited by Donald E. Super. Washington, D.C.: National Vocational Guidance Association, 1974. Pp. 169. *

90. HILTON, THOMAS L. Chap. 12, "Using Measures of Vocational Maturity in Evaluation," pp. 145–59. In *Measuring Vocational Maturity for Counseling and Evaluation.* Edited by Donald E. Super. Washington, D.C.: National Vocational Guidance Association, 1974. Pp. 169. *

91. JOHNSON, DONALD GENE. *The Effects of a Career Guidance Component of a Career Education Program on Some Aspects of Career Maturity of Ninth Grade Students.* Doctor's thesis, Texas A & M University (College Station, Tex.), 1974. (*DAI* 35:5025A)

92. KERR, SAMMY WARREN. *The Effects of Career Education Inservice Classes on the Career Maturity of Sixth, Seventh, and Eighth Grade Students.* Doctor's thesis, Kansas State University (Manhattan, Kan.), 1974. (*DAI* 35:960A)

93. LAWRENCE, WILLIAM WESLEY. *The Relationship of Intelligence, Self Concept, Socio-Economic Status, Race and Sex to Level of Career Maturity of Twelfth-Grade Students.* Doctor's thesis, University of North Carolina (Chapel Hill, N.C.), 1974. (*DAI* 35:3426A)

94. LoCASCIO, RALPH. Chap. 10, "The Vocational Maturity of Diverse Groups: Theory and Measurement," pp. 123–33. In *Measuring Vocational Maturity for Counseling and Evaluation.* Edited by Donald E. Super. Washington, D.C.: National Vocational Guidance Association, 1974. Pp. 169. *

95. Mc GOWAN, ANDREW SCOTT. *Vocational Maturity and Anxiety Among Vocationally Undecided and Indecisive Students: The Effectiveness of the Self-Directed Search.* Doctor's thesis, Fordham University (New York, N.Y.), 1974. (*DAI* 35:2691A)

96. Mc NAMARA, LAURENCE CRAIG, JR. *Twelfth Graders' Vocational Maturity and Their Subsequent Vocational Adjustment.* Doctor's thesis, Rutgers—The State University (New Brunswick, N.J.), 1974. (*DAI* 36:710A)

97. MILLER, ESTHER JANE CRAFT. *A Comparative Study of the Impact of Curriculum Interventions on the Career Development of High School Students.* Doctor's thesis, University of Minnesota (Minneapolis, Minn.), 1974. (*DAI* 35:7655A)

98. MILLER, MICHAEL F. "Relationship of Vocational Maturity to Work Values." *J Voc Behav* 5(3):367–71 D '74. * (*PA* 53:12658)

99. NEW, ROSETTA HOLBROCK. *Relationship of Enrollment and Non-Enrollment in Home Economics Courses to Self-Concept and Career Maturity of Senior High School Students.* Doctor's thesis, Ohio State University (Columbus, Ohio), 1974. (*DAI* 35:7190A)

100. ORSINI, RONALD ARTHUR. *Career Attitude Development and the Educable Mentally Retarded Student.* Doctor's thesis, Ohio State University (Columbus, Ohio), 1974. (*DAI* 35:5177A)

101. PAGE, ELLIS B. Chap. 5, "Problems and Perspectives in Measuring Maturity," pp. 69–79. In *Measuring Vocational Maturity for Counseling and Evaluation.* Edited by Donald E. Super. Washington, D.C.: National Vocational Guidance Association, 1974. Pp. 169. *

102. PHETHEAN, DAVID GLENN. *Vocational Maturity of Tenth-Grade Students: Three Group Approaches.* Doctor's thesis, Pennsylvania State University (University Park, Pa.), 1974. (*DAI* 35:7068A)

103. POWERS, ROBERT J. "The Vocational Maturity of Inner-City Narcotic Addicts." *Rehab Counsel B* 17(4):210–4 Je '74. * (*PA* 52:12696)

104. SCHWAB, A. JOSEPH. *The Effects of Self Esteem and Vocational Maturity on the Level of Occupational Choice.* Doctor's thesis, University of Notre Dame (Notre Dame, Ind.), 1974. (*DAI* 35:3566B)

105. SMITH, ROY CARL. *A Study of the Vocational Maturity of Rural and Urban Students.* Doctor's thesis, University of Alabama (University, Ala.), 1974. (*DAI* 35:7070A)

106. SORENSON, GARTH. "Review of the Career Maturity Inventory." *Meas & Eval Guid* 7(1):54–7 Ap '74. *

107. SUPER, DONALD E. Chap. 13, "Retrospect, Circumspect, and Prospect," pp. 161–9. In his *Measuring Vocational Maturity for Counseling and Evaluation.* Washington, D.C.: National Vocational Guidance Association, 1974. Pp. 169. *

108. THOMAS, MARK J. *An Examination of the Relationship Between Locus of Control and Vocational Maturity, Choice Realism, and Job Knowledge Among Low Socio-Economic Status Black and White Male Youth.* Doctor's thesis, New York University (New York, N.Y.), 1974. (*DAI* 35:4264A)

109. WESTBROOK, BERT W. "Content Analysis of Six Career Development Tests." *Meas & Eval Guid* 7(3):172–80 O '74. * (*PA* 53:6473)

110. WINGETT, TERRY JEAN HAMILTON. *Career Attitude Maturity and Self Concept of Eighth Grade Girls After a Career Education Experience.* Doctor's thesis, University of Wyoming (Laramie, Wyo.), 1974. (*DAI* 35:4175A)

111. ACHEBE, CHRISTIE CHINWE. *Assessing the Vocational Maturity of Students in the East Central State of Nigeria.* Doctor's thesis, University of Massachusetts (Amherst, Mass.), 1975. (*DAI* 36:3396A)

112. BEARDEN, VANCE KEITH. *The Effects of an Occupational Exploration Course on Facilitating the Career Maturity of Ninth-Grade Male Students.* Doctor's thesis, East Texas State University (Commerce, Tex.), 1975. (*DAI* 36:1264A)

113. BERGWALL, EVAN HAROLD, JR. *The Effects of Personality Adjustment on Vocational Maturity in Eleventh Grade Adolescents.* Doctor's thesis, University of Notre Dame (Notre Dame, Ind.), 1975. (*DAI* 36:3020B)

114. BISCOGLIO, JOSEPH JOHN. *The Effect of a Decision-Making Program on Vocational Maturity.* Doctor's thesis, Fordham University (New York, N.Y.), 1975. (*DAI* 36:5033A)

115. BOYD, CINDERELLA. *Vocational Maturity and Occupational Realism Among Inner-City Disadvantaged College Bound High School Students.* Doctor's thesis, Fordham University (New York, N.Y.), 1975. (*DAI* 36:1298A)

116. BOYER, HARRY JOSEPH. *The Effect of a Cluster Oriented Career Guidance Program on the Occupational Maturity and Knowledge of Junior High Students in the LaFourche Parish School System.* Doctor's thesis, East Texas State University (Commerce, Tex.), 1975. (*DAI* 36:5235A)

117. COOGAN, JOHN PATRICK. *Work Experience Career Exploration Program Effect on 14- and 15-Year-Old Disadvantaged New Jersey Students as Measured by the Career Maturity Inventory.* Doctor's thesis, Rutgers—The State University (New Brunswick, N.J.), 1975. (*DAI* 36:6638A)

118. CROSS, ELLEN GAIL. *The Effects of a Vocational Exploration Group Program With Middle and High School Students.* Doctor's thesis, University of Florida (Gainesville, Fla.), 1975. (*DAI* 36:7863A)

119. DEVINE, HOWARD FRANCIS. *The Effects of a Computer-Based Career Counseling Program on the Vocational Maturity of Community College Students.* Doctor's thesis, University of Florida (Gainesville, Fla.), 1975. (*DAI* 36:7865A)

120. DILLARD, JOHN MILTON. *A Correlational Study of Middle Class Black Males' Vocational Maturity and Self-Concept.* Doctor's thesis, State University of New York (Buffalo, N.Y.), 1975. (*DAI* 36:6469A)

121. ENDERLEIN, THOMAS E. "Causal Patterns Related to Post High School Employment Satisfaction." *J Voc Behav* 7(1):67–80 Ag '75. * (*PA* 55:5810)

122. FELDMAN, HOWARD S., AND MARINELLI, ROBERT P. "Career Planning for Prison Inmates." *Voc Guid Q* 23(4):358–62 Je '75. * (*PA* 54:10698)

123. FLAKE, MURIEL HOWELL. *The Effects of Counseling by Same and Opposite Sex Counselors on Career Maturity of Tenth Grade Students.* Doctor's thesis, Texas A & M University (College Station, Tex.), 1975. (*DAI* 36:5041A)

124. FLAKE, MURIEL H.; ROACH, ARTHUR J., JR.; AND STENNING, WALTER F. "Effects of Short-Term Counseling on Career Maturity of Tenth-Grade Students." *J Voc Behav* 6(1):73–80 F '75. * (*PA* 53:12545)

125. FRANKLIN, HAROLD. *A Study of Career Maturity of Junior High School Students in Grades Seven Through Nine.*

Career Maturity Inventory

Doctor's thesis, Rutgers—The State University (New Brunswick, N.J.), 1975. (*DAI* 36:4439A)

126. GASPER, THEODORE HOWARD, JR. *The Relationship Between the Career Maturity and the Occupational Plans of Selected High School Juniors, and the Relationship or Difference of Each to Selected Student Variables.* Doctor's thesis, University of Kentucky (Lexington, Ky.), 1975. (*DAI* 37:255A)

127. GRAVES, LYDIA JEANETTE STAMEY. *The Effectiveness of a Junior High Career Information System for Increasing Career Knowledge and Maturity.* Doctor's thesis, University of Tennessee (Knoxville, Tenn.), 1975. (*DAI* 36:5242A)

128. HOLLAND, JOHN L., AND GOTTFREDSON, GARY D. "Predictive Value and Psychological Meaning of Vocational Aspirations." *J Voc Behav* 6(3):349–63 Je '75. * (*PA* 55:13649)

129. HOLLAND, JOHN L.; GOTTFREDSON, GARY D.; AND NAFZIGER, DEAN H. "Testing the Validity of Some Theoretical Signs of Vocational Decision-Making Ability." *J Counsel Psychol* 22(5):411–22 S '75. * (*PA* 54:12700)

130. KELSO, GEOFFREY I. "The Influences of Stage of Leaving School on Vocational Maturity and Realism of Vocational Choice." *J Voc Behav* 7(1):29–39 Ag '75. * (*PA* 55:5759)

131. KENNEDY, JOYCE SANDRA. *Comparative Effects of Three Career Guidance Strategies on Career Maturity of College Freshman and Sophomore Students With No Declared Educational Preference.* Doctor's thesis, Michigan State University (East Lansing, Mich.), 1975. (*DAI* 36:7868A)

132. LEE, CLIMON, III. *The Relationship of Vocational Maturity and Anxiety to Vocational Choice and Certainty of Vocational Choice of Tenth Grade Pre-Vocational Students.* Doctor's thesis, University of Akron (Akron, Ohio), 1975. (*DAI* 36:2634A)

133. LESTER, DAVID; NARKUNSKI, ABRAHAM; BURKMAN, J. HERBERT; AND GANDICA, ALFONSO. "An Exploratory Study of Correlates of Success in a Vocational Training Program for Ex-Addicts." *Psychol Rep* 37(3, pt 2):1212–4 D '75. * (*PA* 56:4588)

134. LILLOV, HIRAM WELLER. *Trait Anxiety and Career Maturity.* Doctor's thesis, University of Northern Colorado (Greeley, Colo.), 1975. (*DAI* 36:2449B)

135. MCCOY, VIVIAN ROGERS. *Impact of a Career Exploration Workshop for Student Wives on Selected Personality Factors, Career Maturity, Career Decision-Making and Career-Implementing Behaviors.* Doctor's thesis, Kansas State University (Manhattan, Kan.), 1975. (*DAI* 36:5052A)

136. MCFARLAND, PATRICIA BERO. *Analysis of Parent, Student and Counselor Competence in Accurately Interpreting Career Information.* Doctor's thesis, University of Maine (Orono, Me.), 1975. (*DAI* 36:6479A)

137. MUNLEY, PATRICK H. "Erik Erikson's Theory of Psychosocial Development and Vocational Behavior." *J Counsel Psychol* 22(4):314–9 Jl '75. * (*PA* 54:6412)

138. NORTHROP, LOIS CAROL. *Relationships Among Career Maturity, Achievement Motivation, Anxiety, Independence and Decisiveness in College Students.* Doctor's thesis, University of Maryland (College Park, Md.), 1975. (*DAI* 37:958B)

139. OLSEN, ROBERT EARL. *The Effect of a Career Decision-Making Skills Course of Study on Junior High School Students.* Doctor's thesis, University of Minnesota (Minneapolis, Minn.), 1975. (*DAI* 36:5054A)

140. OMVIG, CLAYTON P.; TULLOCH, RODNEY W.; AND THOMAS, EDWARD G. "The Effect of Career Education on Career Maturity." *J Voc Behav* 7(2):265–73 O '75. * (*PA* 55:11079)

141. SAVICKAS, MARK LEE. *Consistency of Expressed Interests as an Indicator of Vocational Maturity in College Freshmen.* Doctor's thesis, Kent State University (Kent, Ohio), 1975. (*DAI* 36:5838A)

142. SCHMOLL, ROBERT ROY. *A Study of Occupational Goals, Levels of Aspiration, and Career Maturity of Eighth Grade Gifted Boys.* Doctor's thesis, Brigham Young University (Provo, Utah), 1975. (*DAI* 36:1317A)

143. THOMAS, MARK J. "Assessing the Career Education Needs of High School Students." *Voc Guid Q* 24(1):76–9 S '75. * (*PA* 55:5737)

144. WALSH, W. BRUCE, AND HANLE, NANCY A. "Consistent Occupational Preferences, Vocational Maturity, and Academic Achievement." *J Voc Behav* 7(1):89–97 Ag '75. * (*PA* 55:5768)

145. WEBB, CHARLES ROYCE. *The Relationship of Certain Vocational Factors to Student Teaching Performance.* Doctor's thesis, Auburn University (Auburn, Ala.), 1975. (*DAI* 36:7362A)

146. WILLIAMS, VELMA HAYES. *A Survey of the Career Maturity of a Select Group of Black High School Students.* Doctor's thesis, Florida State University (Tallahassee, Fla.), 1975. (*DAI* 36:5066A)

147. WILSON, DIANE MICHELE SULLIVAN. *Locus of Control and Career Maturity: A Comparative Study of Secondary Students.* Doctor's thesis, St. Louis University (St. Louis, Mo.), 1975. (*DAI* 36:3422A)

148. ALEXANDER, GLIDA MYRA. *A Comparative Analysis Among Three Secondary Groups of Alabama's Urban Disadvantaged With Respect to Career Maturity.* Doctor's thesis, University of Tennessee (Knoxville, Tenn.), 1976. (*DAI* 37:5074A)

149. ANDERSON, AMEL. *The Validity of the Career Maturity Inventory as a Measure of Career Maturity Among First-Year Community College Students in Southwestern Virginia.* Doctor's thesis, Virginia Polytechnic Institute (Blacksburg, Va.), 1976. (*DAI* 37:5595A)

150. ARREDONDO, RODOLFO. *The Effect of Vocational Counseling on Career Maturity of Female Cooperative Health Education Students.* Doctor's thesis, Texas Tech University (Lubbock, Texas), 1976. (*DAI* 37:6263A)

151. BODER, CLARETTA KELSO. *The Relationship of Work Values, Career Decision-making and Career Maturity of Eleventh Grade Students in a Joint Vocational School.* Doctor's thesis, Ohio State University (Columbus, Ohio), 1976. (*DAI* 37:4853A)

152. BOURKE, GERARD JOSEPH. *The Expressed Career Choice Attitudes of Students in Jesuit High Schools in Japan and the United States.* Doctor's thesis, Fordham University (New York, N.Y.), 1976. (*DAI* 37:2628A)

153. BRESNAN, MARGARET THERESA. *The Effects of Ethnicity, Sex, and Locus of Control on Vocational Maturity of Disadvantaged High School Students.* Doctor's thesis, Fordham University (New York, N.Y.), 1976. (*DAI* 37:800A)

154. BURSON, LINDA SHARON. *Career Maturity: A Comparison of Affective and Cognitive Programs With College Freshmen Women.* Doctor's thesis, Mississippi State University (State College, Miss.), 1976. (*DAI* 37:1397A)

155. DILLARD, JOHN M. "Relationship Between Career Maturity and Self-Concepts of Suburban and Urban Middle- and Urban Lower-Class Preadolescent Black Males." *J Voc Behav* 9(3):311–20 D '76. * (*PA* 58:2131)

156. FROKE, BARBARA KAYE. *A Study of the Relationships Among Locus of Control, Maturity of Career Attitudes, and Consistency and Congruence of Career Choice.* Doctor's thesis, University of South Dakota (Vermillion, S.D.), 1976. (*DAI* 37:3417A)

157. GABLE, ROBERT K.; THOMPSON, DONALD L.; AND GLANSTEIN, PHYLLIS J. "Perceptions of Personal Control and Conformity of Vocational Choice as Correlates of Vocational Development." *J Voc Behav* 8(3):259–67 Je '76. *

158. GASPER, THEODORE H., JR., AND OMVIG, CLAYTON P. "The Relationship Between Career Maturity and Occupational Plans of High School Juniors." *J Voc Behav* 9(3):367–75 D '76. * (*PA* 58:2233)

159-60. HARRIS, DONALD EDWARD. *Affective Characteristics: Their Role in Candidate Selection for Baccalaureate Degree Programs in Vocational Industrial Education.* Doctor's thesis, Pennsylvania State University (University Park, Pa.), 1976. (*DAI* 37:7104A)

161. HERR, EDWIN L., AND ENDERLEIN, THOMAS E. "Vocational Maturity: The Effects of School, Grade, Curriculum and Sex." *J Voc Behav* 8(2):227–38 Ap '76. *

162. JONES, OCTAVIA M.; HANSEN, JAMES C.; AND PUTNAM, BARBARA A. "Relationship of Self-Concept and Vocational Maturity to Vocational Preferences of Adolescents." *J Voc Behav* 8(1):31–40 F '76. *

163. KARAYANNI, MOUSA. *Career Maturity of Emotionally Maladjusted High School Students.* Doctor's thesis, University of Florida (Gainesville, Fla.), 1976. (*DAI* 37:6276A)

164. KEITH, EDWIN MONROE, JR. *The Work Values and Career Maturity of Community College Transfer and Native Students.* Doctor's thesis, University of Florida (Gainesville, Fla.), 1976. (*DAI* 37:4135A)

165. LAWRENCE, WILLIAM, AND BROWN, DUANE. "An Investigation of Intelligence, Self-Concept, Socioeconomic Status, Race, and Sex as Predictors of Career Maturity." *J Voc Behav* 9(1):43–52 Ag '76. *

166. MARTENIS, FRANK BRUCE. *The Career Maturity of Eleventh and Twelfth Grade Adolescents Who Are Under the Supervision of the Court.* Doctor's thesis, Boston College (Chestnut Hill, Mass.), 1976. (*DAI* 37:811A)

167. MINTZER, RHODA GREENBERG. *Vocational Maturity and Its Relationship to Intelligence, Self-Concept, Sex Role Identification, and Grade Level.* Doctor's thesis, Fordham University (New York, N.Y.), 1976. (*DAI* 37:2643A)

168. MOORE, THOMAS LOWELL. *Measuring Vocational Maturity in a College Population: A Construct Validation Study of the Career Maturity Inventory Attitude Scale.* Doctor's thesis, University of Alabama (University, Ala.), 1976. (*DAI* 37:7546A)

169. MORACCO, JOHN C. "Vocational Maturity of Arab and American High School Students." *J Voc Behav* 8(3):367–73 Je '76. *

170. PENDLETON, BARBARA ANN. *A Comparison of High School Dropouts and Retainers on Career Choice Competencies.* Doctor's thesis, Virginia Polytechnic Institute (Charlottesville, Va.), 1976. (*DAI* 37:2820A)

171. ROSS, LANNY F. *Predicting Success in Vocational Programs From Permanent Record Data Versus Selected Non-Cognitive Variables.* Doctor's thesis, Pennsylvania State University (University Park, Pa.), 1976. (*DAI* 37:7108A)

172. SEAWARD, MARTY ROBERTSON. *A Comparison of the Career Maturity, Self Concept and Academic Achievement of Female Cooperative Vocational Office Training Students, Intensive Business Training Students, and Regular Business Education Students in Selected High Schools in Mississippi.* Doctor's

Career Maturity Inventory

thesis, Mississippi State University (State College, Miss.), 1976. (*DAI* 37:4321A)

173. SMITH, ELSIE J. "Reference Group Perspectives and the Vocational Maturity of Lower Socioeconomic Black Youth." *J Voc Behav* 8(3):321–36 Je '76. *

174. SMITH, KENNETH WAYNE. *Differences in Work Attitudes and Work Values of Disadvantaged and Non-Disadvantaged Eleventh Grade and Twelfth Grade Disadvantaged and Non-Disadvantaged Work Experience Students.* Doctor's thesis, Southern Illinois University (Carbondale, Ill.), 1976. (*DAI* 37:5784A)

175. STANSBURY, JAMES CLIFFORD. *Maturity of Vocational Attitudes and Locus of Control as Dimensions of Vocational Personality Types.* Doctor's thesis, Kansas State University (Manhattan, Kan.), 1976. (*DAI* 37:4147A)

176. SUTTON, RICHARD ALLAN. *Vocational Maturity as a Predictor of Delinquency Proneness in Male Juveniles: A Discriminant Analysis.* Doctor's thesis, University of Akron (Akron, Ohio), 1976. (*DAI* 37:1999A)

177. TILDEN, ARNOLD JOHN, JR. *A Cross Validation of the Career Development Inventory and a Study of Vocational Maturity in College Students.* Doctor's thesis, Temple University (Philadelphia, Pa.), 1976. (*DAI* 37:2088A)

178. TRAINOR, JOHN D. *Career Maturity and Information Exploration.* Doctor's thesis, Boston College (Chestnut Hill, Mass.), 1976. (*DAI* 37:4149A)

179. TUCKER, RUTH ELAINE. *The Relationship Between Perceptual-Motor Development and Academic Achievement.* Doctor's thesis, University of Alabama (University, Ala.), 1976. (*DAI* 37:7536A)

180. WESTBROOK, BERT W. "Criterion-Related and Construct Validity of the Career Maturity Inventory Competence Test With Ninth-Grade Pupils." *J Voc Behav* 9(3):377–83 D '76. * (*PA* 58:192)

181. WESTBROOK, BERT W. "Interrelationship of Career Choice Competencies and Career Choice Attitudes of Ninth-Grade Pupils: Testing Hypotheses Derived From Crites' Model of Career Maturity." *J Voc Behav* 8(1):1–12 F '76. *

182. WESTBROOK, BERT W. "The Relationship Between Career Choice Attitudes and Career Choice Competencies of Ninth-Grade Pupils." *J Voc Behav* 9(1):119–25 Ag '76. * (*PA* 58:192)

183. WESTBROOK, BERT W. "The Relationship Between Vocational Maturity and Appropriateness of Vocational Choices of Ninth-Grade Pupils." *Meas & Eval Guid* 9(2):75–80 Jl '76. *

184. WU, CHIEN DAVID. *Work Values in Relation to Cultures and Student Characteristics.* Doctor's thesis, Pennsylvania State University (University Park, Pa.), 1976. (*DAI* 37:7109A)

185. HAMBY, JEANNETTE K. JOHNSON. *An Analysis of the Effectiveness of a Career Education Cluster Curriculum as Reflected by Student Growth in Career Maturity.* Doctor's thesis, Oregon State University (Corvallis, Ore.), 1977. (*DAI* 37:4316A)

186. KELSO, GEOFFREY I. "The Relation of School Grade to Ages and Stages in Vocational Development." *Voc Behav* 10(3):287–301 Je '77. *

187. MOORE, THOMAS L., AND McLEAN, JAMES E. "Research in Brief: Short Reports of Research of Interest." *Meas & Eval Guid* 10(2):113–6 Jl '77. *

MARTIN R. KATZ, *Senior Research Psychologist, Educational Testing Service, Princeton, New Jersey.*

The CMI consists of a 50-item Attitude Scale and a Competence Test containing five subtests of 20 items each. The attitudes and competencies represented by the inventory are conceptualized, along with consistency and realism of career choices, as constituting a comprehensive model of the construct, career maturity in adolescence. Much thought and planning have gone into the development of CMI, and care has been taken to make the rationale explicit. Thus, whatever criticisms may be made, the critic must be grateful to the author for a well-organized theory and research handbook, replete with data.

It is not necessary to summarize here what is concisely stated in the handbook, except to note that a measure of "career maturity," as explicated by the author, requires a monotonic relationship between scores on the instrument and age (or grade). Thus, items for the Attitude Scale were selected, on the basis of differentiation between students in lower and higher grades, from a pool of items constructed to represent five logically deduced dimensions of attitudes presumably involved in "career maturity." By similar reasoning, the scoring key was derived from those item responses (true or false) that were endorsed by 51 percent or more of the 12th graders in the standardization sample.

It is interesting that all but 7 of the 50 items are keyed false. Falsity abounds, while truth is a rare event; thus, it is always easier to write items with false rather than true keys. This prevalence of items keyed false might lead one to infer that "maturity" means learning to be skeptical of items in inventories, or that naysayers are more mature than yea-sayers. It might also lead to the suspicion that scores are susceptible to response bias. The author cites a few studies on this point that, with one exception, fail to substantiate the suspicion. Still, one wonders why such a high proportion (86 percent) of the items were written for false keying; there is no mention of any attempt to strike a balance between true and false items. Must attitude items define "career maturity" almost entirely in terms of what it is not? If that is the case—if only 7 true statements out of 50 can be written to represent a "mature" attitude—one must question the operational definition (and validity) of the construct represented by the Attitude Scale.

Unfortunately, it is on the matter of keying and validity that the handbook veers most sharply from exposition to advocacy. It offers as empirical evidence of "content validity" the responses of 10 "expert judges" (counseling psychologists) to the items: there was agreement between 8 of the 10 judges and a majority of the 12th graders on 37 of the 50 items. Agreement between judges and keys hardly seems to represent content validity in the generally accepted sense. Rather it tends to substantiate (more or less, depending on how one rates 74 percent agreement) only the logic for keying the items. Indeed, would not counseling

Career Maturity Inventory

psychologists find it discomfiting to use a scale for assessment of guidance needs or for other purposes suggested in the handbook when they disagree with the keys for 26 percent of the items? Can they accept a majority response of 12th graders as a better definition of "career maturity" than their own responses? Perhaps the construct of "career maturity," made dependent by definition on the responses of 12th graders, has got in the way of constructing a useful measure of attitudes that are associated with effective career decision-making.

The handbook cites studies comparing scores on the Attitude Scale and other purported criteria of "career maturity" as evidence of "criterion-related validity," reporting correlations mostly in the .20s and .30s with several other measures. Correlations between the Attitude Scale and Super's Indices of Vocational Maturity (IVM), however, were nonsignificant. This is rather surprising, and speaks poorly for content validity since the IVM was derived from virtually the same definition of "career maturity" as the CMI. Relationships of the CMI with scholastic aptitude tests were found to be moderate (with correlations about .4 for secondary school students); these and correlations with personality scales, educational achievement, and other variables are cited as linking "career maturity" and educational achievement as components of overall adjustment. Alternative interpretations of these data are equally plausible, however. A "nomological net" there may be, but what does it hold?

In general, even though recognizing that many studies have been made of the Attitude Scale and many data are reported, one must, nevertheless, express reservations about the strong claims in the handbook and manual of categorical validity for various uses of the scale in guidance.

Since the Competence Test has been offered for use much more recently than the Attitude Scale, few data are available for report in the handbook. Therefore, it is appropriate to focus on the content and construction of the items in each of the five scales in turn.

Knowing Yourself (Self-Appraisal) has nothing to do with the "self" who is taking the test. Like the other parts, it is all about hypothetical others. The task is to read a vignette (4 to 7 lines) and select the appropriate appraisal, opinion, or action from a set of five options. The options from a typical item illustrate the distinct pattern:

A She has the makings of an astonomer [sic]; she should definitely go ahead with her plans.
B Before she decides about college, she should ask an astronomer's advice.
C Her interest in astronomy is strong enough, and she knows enough about it, to plan further study.
D She can't possibly decide if she has either aptitude or interest in astronomy from a backyard telescope.
E don't know

One option is always "don't know," as in E, and another involves dependence upon other people, such as an appeal for help or advice, as in B. The remaining three options are like Goldilocks' experience in the three bears' house: One is "too much"—an overinterpretation of the given information, or error toward a positive extreme, as in A; another is "too little" —an underinterpretation of the information, or error toward a negative extreme, as in D; and the third is "just right"—a balanced and moderate interpretation. as in C, which is keyed correct. It is apparent that recognition of this facet approach to the construction of items allows the test-taker to choose the keyed response without even reading the stems. Thus, these exercises called Knowing Yourself, or Self-Appraisal, not only fail to require knowledge of the self who is taking the test; they require no knowledge or appraisal of any person, real or hypothetical. Once the pattern has been perceived, they generally require only the ability to read the options well enough to differentiate the moderate statement from the two extreme statements, the dependent statement, and the "don't know." Perhaps it is just as well that the stems can be ignored, since they often provide very flimsy data for the kinds of decisions involved. It is also just as well that finer discriminations between options are not required. Consider, for example, this option, the "underinterpretation" for one item: "On the one hand, he might make a good doctor, but on the other, maybe he should be a guitarist. It's hard to say which he would be better at." This reviewer finds it difficult to distinguish the sense of this long-winded option from the more succinct "don't know."

Knowing about Jobs (Occupational Information) asks the student to match an occupational title to a description (5 to 8 lines) of work activities. The options are four occupational titles, plus "don't know." Roe's two-dimensional classification of occupations by level and field is used to determine the facets: one option is the right level, wrong field; another is the right field, wrong level; and a third is in a different level and field from the keyed occupation. Selecting the appropriate occupational title to match a description may measure reading comprehension and knowledge of occupational titles. But this kind of exercise is a very limited sample of the domain of occupational information and one of dubious utility. Perhaps the ability measured here is thought to be correlated with more useful knowledge. But cognitive abilities generally tend to be intercorrelated. Since the Competence Test is offered for diagnostic use, one would like to see the items in each subtest define as directly as possible the competency it purports to measure.

Choosing a Job (Goal Selection) provides statements (5 to 7 lines) about hypothetical persons and asks the student to select the "best occupation" for each. Again, as in subtest 2, the options reflect "field" and "level" facets, presumably corresponding to inferences drawn from the stem about abilities and interests. This exercise exemplifies the "trait-matching" approach to guidance at its worst. It makes bland and unvalidated assumptions about relationships between the inferred traits (sometimes the inferences must be quite weak) and success and satisfaction in a set of occupations. This reviewer would say that for the information given in the stem the best response would almost invariably be the "don't know" option. For example, consider this item:

Marty has many interests. He has been in the Debating Club for three years; he has written stories for the school newspaper; he has worked on the school yearbook; and, at the same time, he is one of the best students in the school. He is very good with words and can say exactly what he means. He is also quite persuasive and can often win people to his point of view.
Which one of the following occupations would be the best for him?

    F psychologist
    G literary agent
    H insurance agent
    J lawyer
    K don't know

The key is lawyer. Perhaps psychologist was ruled out by the trait "can say exactly what he means"! (But doesn't that exclude lawyer too?)

Looking Ahead (Planning) presents three steps a hypothetical person must take to enter a given occupation, and then asks the student to select the correct order of these three steps. The order is generally, first, take the appropriate training; second, get a job; third, pass an examination for certification or advancement. Again, one does not have to read the full stem or know the occupation involved, but can simply select the option that orders the three elements in this sequence. And again one feels that the items may be good measures of test-taking savvy, but miss the major components of the competency they purport to measure. The sequence of steps is not a decision students have to make—it takes care of itself. Planning requires, more centrally, knowing what the steps are—for example, knowing *what kind* of education or training is appropriate for each occupation, how long it will take, how much it will cost, and where it can be obtained, not whether it comes before or after getting a job in the occupation!

What Should They Do? (Problem Solving) is very much like the first subtest (Knowing Yourself). The stems are shorter, however—two sentences, presenting a thesis and an antithesis. Consider this item:

John wants to be an engineer and has the ability to be one. *But,* his grades are poor, and he thinks he may not get into college.
What should he do?
    A Work harder and get better grades.
    B Talk with his teachers or a counselor.
    C Expect to get into college despite his grades, because he has the ability.
    D Change his occupational choice to something else that doesn't require college.
    E don't know

The facets represented by the options are described as A, compensation; B, consultation; C, denial; D, compliance; and E, the ubiquitous "don't know," said to express confusion or indecisiveness. The key here is B. We encounter an interesting phenomenon when we compare the keys for these items with those for the so-called "Self-Appraisal" items in the first subtest. There consultation was said to represent "dependence upon others" and was taken as a sign of "career immaturity" or incompetence. Here it is taken as a sign of "career maturity" or competence! Even on the occasions when the consultation option is not the key, one must often quarrel with the option keyed correct on grounds of internal incon-

Career Maturity Inventory

sistency. For example, in one instance the author violates the very facets of level and field he has used as a criterion in subtests 2 and 3:

Betty wants to be a lawyer. *But,* her guidance tests indicate that she does not have enough ability.
What should she do?
    F Get married.
    G Go into law anyway; tests can be wrong.
    H Increase her ability to be a lawyer.
    J Enter a related field at a lower level, like legal
        secretary.
    K don't know

The key is J. Obviously, there is no reason to accept this response as a good one: legal secretary is not likely to provide experiences, rewards, and satisfactions similar to those of lawyer. But even (and especially) by the standards invoked in subtests 2 and 3 this keyed response is way off. According to the two-dimensional classification (after Roe) in the handbook, lawyer is level 1, field 7 in the matrix; secretary is level 4, field 3.

Finally, it should be mentioned that notwithstanding emphasis on the "maturity" construct, with selection of items on the basis of a monotonic curve increasing with grade, the 8th-grade means for four of the five competence tests are higher than the 9th-grade means in the standardization sample. Indeed, the 8th-grade mean is also higher than the 10th-grade mean on subtest 5 (Problem Solving).

In summary, although a great deal of thought and care have gone into the development of the Competence Test, this test cannot be recommended for use as a criterion of competencies involved in career decision-making or career development, for diagnostic measurement, or for any other purpose.

DONALD G. ZYTOWSKI, *Professor of Psychology and Counseling Psychologist, Iowa State University, Ames, Iowa.*

The author declares in the Administration and Use Manual that "the CMI can be profitably employed in....schools and colleges, business and industry, community agencies, hospitals, and other institutions and organizations.... to measure the maturity of attitudes and competencies that are critical in realistic career decision making." The CMI, previously known as the Vocational Development Inventory, has two parts: the Attitude Scale and the Competence Test.

ATTITUDE SCALE. This scale is described as having "its principal usefulness....in screening individuals for counseling and in evaluating the outcomes of career education and other didactic programs and interventive experiences." As well, it is recommended in the study of career development and to assess guidance needs.

The theoretical rationale for the construction of the scale is impressively detailed in the Theory and Research Handbook. Items relating to attitudes and beliefs about getting established in a career were generated both from Super's theory and from counseling practice, and were included in the scale if they showed an incremental relationship with grade level. This is a unique application of Binet's technique to attitude items, and required for a scale which must tap a developmental phenomenon such as career maturity. K-R 20 coefficients are reported for each grade level from 6 to 12. Curiously, the highest, .84, is for the sixth grade, while the lowest, .65, is for the ninth grade. The author says the coefficients are as expected, since the scale was formed from five conceptual clusters. Homogeneities for the clusters, or a factor analysis of the attitude scale, might have been undertaken in support of this assertion, but apparently none was. One stability coefficient of .71 is reported for a large sample of sixth through twelfth graders over a one-year interval. This figure is relatively low for an attitude measure, but Crites defends it, saying that it allows for "maturational variance." Presumably this term relates to Crites' description of career development as not developing uniformly, but sometimes in spurts and starts. While this *is* one explanation, the author owes us data to show that it is *the* explanation, and that the relatively low figure is not due to simple error or random variance in the scores. This level of reliability will be a problem if the Attitude Scale is to be used as a measure of individual or group change, since the standard error of measurement will be rather large in comparison to the amount of change which may occur naturally over an interval.

Much construct validity data are reported for the Attitude Scale. In general, it appears to be free from response biases, and to be related to things one would expect, such as other measures of maturity, ability, and certain personality variables. The author concludes that the

Career Maturity Inventory

scale is very closely tied to acceptance of white, middle-class, work-oriented values.

Evidence of the validity of the scale for the claimed uses is noticeably less extensive. Only five studies are cited in the handbook supporting the use of the scale in evaluating career education or counseling. Although the handbook is dated 1973, the latest year of any of these five studies is 1967. An afternoon of reading in *Dissertation Abstracts* and a couple of journals gave considerably more examples of successes—and failures—for the CMI. I fault Crites for not including more of these and for not attempting to clarify where the CMI is more successfully or validly applied and where it is not.

The norm tables in the manual are informative. Data are given to convert raw scores to percentiles for each of grades 6 through 12, although their use is not advocated, since "ultimately, the most appropriate reference group for an individual is the one he most resembles." This statement may have been prompted by the fact that differences between the means of groups from the various states which make up the norm group are often greater than the differences between the means of adjacent grade levels within any one of the states. Given his allowance for maturational variance, Crites might have said that the most appropriate point of reference for an individual should be his or her score the year before, or before becoming involved in career counseling or education.

Crites offers some interpretations of score levels in support of the utility of the scale as a screening device for career immaturity. "In general, those in the lowest quarter....can be considered as possibly delayed or impaired in their career development....and can be invited to participate in some facilitating experience." Shouldn't some test of the validity of such a cutting score be advanced? And what of the person whose score is higher than the lowest quartile, but is the same as it was a year ago?

Another problem is that the conversion tables show the average increment from grade to grade to be about 1.5 raw score points; an increase of only 11 correct answers, in a 50-item scale, from grade 6 to college freshman. In discussing sex differences in scores, the author states that reported mean differences of .99 (grade 8) and 1.09 (grade 10) on this variable

are negligible, and separate sex norms are not needed. However, three of the seven differences from grade to grade are no larger, and must therefore be negligible as well. What I take this to mean on the practical level is that gains springing from maturation or intervention are apt to be unimpressive in terms of the total possible score or standard error of measurement.

COMPETENCE TEST. This part of the CMI consists of five subtests of skills and knowledge derived from the elaboration of Super's career theory. Discussion of the conceptual definitions and item selection techniques forms the bulk of the section of the handbook devoted to the test, and Crites advances it as evidence of the test's "substantive validity as a measure of the relevant variables in contemporary career development theory." Apparently the item selection data obtained from 2,000 students in one California school district are also the source of the reliability and the sparse validity data. A cross-validation would be imperative to head off the possibility of inflation of the obtained figures. K-R 20 coefficients for the subtests ranging from .58 to .90, with a median of .83, are interpreted by the author as indicating that "within a subtest the items measure essentially the same variable." However, Nunnally does not accept K-R 20 as a measure of homogeneity. The "don't know" option among the alternatives, which the author says is to reduce response biases, must also inflate the reliability by siphoning off what would otherwise be random responding. For what is essentially an achievement test, these coefficients are low indeed, and argue against interpreting a score on one subtest to be higher or lower than a score on another, unless they are extremely divergent. Crites gratuitously points out that such interpretations must be based on reliable differences and demonstrated construct validity. No stability indexes whatever are reported. Intercorrelations of the subtests range from .25 to .73, with a mean of .54. The author states that "although the data must be interpreted cautiously, they appear to be consistent with the construct of career choice competencies." Crites does caution that the test "should be considered as being in an early state of development." I agree.

Percentile norms tables reveal that on the average, for each of the 20-item subtests, the twelfth graders answer correctly only 4.4 more items than do sixth graders.

CONCLUSIONS. The Attitude Scale does seem to be a fair representation of career development theory and thereby could be useful in other theoretical tests. Many studies, too few of which are reported in the manual, show that the Attitude Scale is sensitive to various kinds of attempts to enhance career development, although the exceptions illustrate the need to discover the limits or conditions of this application. Gains realized from such interventions are typically small and difficult to interpret, even though they may be statistically significant in large groups. Although Crites describes the scale's rather low reliabilities as permitting differential rates of development, he advances normative applications which would require much higher reliabilities.

The Competence Test is in the author's words, "at an early stage of development." Any application of it at the present time would be necessarily more fruitful for the author than the user, since it would reveal the qualities of the test which are not reported in the manual.

Throughout the materials, in-progress studies are mentioned and periodic supplements to the handbook are promised. None has appeared. The claims that introduced this review, I must conclude, are substantially overdrawn. The CMI may be a very popular criterion measure in doctoral dissertation program evaluations, but it appears to need a great deal more study, resulting perhaps in some revision, before it can receive better than this qualified endorsement for its extensive claimed uses.

Meas & Eval Guid 7(1):54–7 Ap '74. Garth Sorenson. The Career Maturity Inventory (CMI) is described by its publishers as a valid and reliable guide for assessing attitudes and competencies important to realistic career decisions in grades 6 to 12, as a useful tool both for elementary students below grade 6 as well as for adults, and an instrument that can be profitably employed by business and industry. The CMI is said to be good for purposes of counseling, evaluation, instruction, research, and as a means of identifying areas in career education where needs are currently not being met. * While the CMI may have a good deal of face validity, the data presented....do not persuade me that this test is valid for all the uses claimed by the publishers. * it seems to me that we need a criterion-referenced test battery that samples the entire domain of knowledge and skills that a student must master in the process of preparing for a career * the battery I am imagining would provide detailed information about what a student has learned at a particular point in his career and what he needed to learn next. It would reflect counterproductive as well as productive learning. Such a test would be truly diagnostic in that it would not only report a student's standing in relation to an absolute norm, but would also indicate his specific weaknesses and the kind of training he needed to correct those weaknesses. It would be valid for curriculum evaluation. Such a test would be complex and might be time-consuming; it would probably need to be constructed as a part of an instructional system. Of course Crites did not set out to build the kind of test I am imagining. * If it were not for the claims made for all the possible uses of the CMI, it would not be fair to criticize him for failing to do something he did not intend to do. But it is important that people concerned with career education not oversimplify the problem, and it is in this regard that my chief concern lies. The Competence Test, for example, is based on a number of untested assumptions, a basic assumption being that "individuals who can accurately appraise the career relevant capabilities of others are good self-appraisers." And in the case of the Competence Test item cited above, I do not know of any evidence that ability to respond correctly to a paper-pencil test is related to ability to cope with a girl who wants to get married. I don't even know that there is a "correct" response to the problem. The marriage item is only an illustration of the larger problem of oversimplification and perhaps an over-reliance on face validity. In sum, my view is that there is much that is commendable in the work Crites has already done, and it is to be hoped that he will continue to refine his model. The publisher's claims for the potential uses of the CMI do not appear to be supported. Some of the questions I have raised are empirical, and we can be confident that the answers will be forthcoming in due time.

Career Maturity Inventory

[998]

★Career Planning Program for Grades 8–12.
Grades 8–12; 1974; CPP; a downward extension of
ACT Career Planning Program; 18 scores: 6 interest
scores (social service, business contact, business detail,
technical, science, creative arts), 6 experience scores
(same as interest) and 6 ability scores (mechanical
reasoning, numerical skills, space relations, reading
skills, language usage, clerical skills); 1 form (82
pages in 2 booklets); manual (162 pages); supervisor's
manual (16 pages); norms supplement (12 pages);
separate answer folders (MRC) must be used; $41.20
per 35 tests; $7.35 per 35 MRC answer folders; 90¢
per norms supplement; 60¢ per supervisor's manual;
$3 per manual; $4.50 per specimen set; postage extra;
scoring service, 90¢ per test ($45 minimum); (150–
160) minutes; American College Testing Program;
Houghton Mifflin Co. *

RICHARD W. JOHNSON, *Associate Director,
Counseling Services, University of Wisconsin,
Madison, Wisconsin.*

The *Career Planning Program* for grades
8–12 combines individual assessment measures
of interests, experiences, and abilities with guidance materials which may be used in a "mini-
course" in career planning. The ability and
interest scores are used to identify a number of
career options ("exploration priorities") for
the student to consider. Each student is encouraged to explore a number of broad career possibilities by a series of exercises drawn from the
guidance materials.

ABILITY MEASURES. The six ability tests were
selected to assess both academic and nonacademic skills considered to be important in a
variety of careers. Each test is fairly short (25
to 48 items), with time limits ranging from 6 to
20 minutes. Clerical Skills is a speed test completed by only 25 percent of the 8th grade students. Each of the other tests is somewhat
speeded, with approximately 75 percent of the
8th graders and 80 percent of the 11th graders
(median values) completing all of the items.

The tests were normed on a national sample
of 8th, 9th, and 11th grade students enrolled
in 197 schools selected to represent different
regions of the country, different size communities, and different levels of socioeconomic
status. The results were weighted to take into
account disproportionate sampling, incomplete
sampling in some schools, and the refusal of
some schools to participate. The norms for 10th
grade students were interpolated from these
data. Recently, norms for 12th grade students
were extrapolated from these same data and
related data.

Test-retest reliabilities (9-week-interval) for
the ability tests, reported for grades 9 and 11
only, range from .59 to .87, with median .76.
Alpha coefficients reported for grades 8 and 11
for all tests excluding Clerical Skills tests are
higher, ranging from .77 to .91, with median
.86; these values, however, are still somewhat
low for the interpretation of test scores for
individuals. The authors have taken the relatively low reliabilities into account by the use
of stanine scores and bands which are three
stanines wide. The stanine bands are plotted
graphically beside the stanine scores on the
student report. As a result, students are encouraged to think in terms of broad categories
(lower quarter, middle half, and upper quarter)
rather than specific scores.

In spite of the modest reliabilities, the test
scores were relatively effective in predicting
grades in appropriate courses. Grades in social
studies and language arts were best predicted
by scores on reading skills (medians, .55 and
.47, respectively) while grades in science and
math, home economics, and industrial arts were
most highly correlated with scores on Numerical Skills (medians, .49, .62, and .37, respectively). Language Usage produced the highest
correlations with performance in business and
commercial courses (median, .42).

The correlations between the tests varied
from .20 to .70 for different samples of students
with median values of approximately .47. Although there is a fair amount of overlap among
the six measures, they are sufficiently independent to consider using them in combination to
predict academic or occupational success. In
many cases, the strength of the relationship
between the test scores and individual course
performance was increased substantially by the
use of multiple regression analysis.

The ability scores are used to suggest career
possibilities depending upon the magnitude of
the scores on relevant tests. Every student is
judged to have sufficient ability to succeed in
7 of the 25 job families (e.g., retail sales and
services and transportation equipment operation). For the remaining fields, only those students who obtain composite scores above a
certain percentile point on selected tests receive
"ability stars" on the Student Report.

The composite scores and the cutoff points
were determined by means of data collected

with the GATB and other instruments which have similar scales. Obviously, these judgments must be somewhat subjective and arbitrary; however, it is probably better to provide this information systematically than to expect counselors to be able quickly and easily to analyze the test scores for each student. The validities of the programmed interpretations need to be investigated.

INTEREST AND EXPERIENCE INVENTORIES. Interest scores in social service, business contact, business detail, technical, science, and creative arts are reported along with related experience scores. In contrast with the ability scales, separate norms are used for boys and girls. This appears to be both justifiable and necessary to counteract the effects of sex-role expectations which may artificially suppress the scores of females on the technical and science scales and of males on the social service, creative arts, and business detail scales.

The test-retest reliabilities reported for grades 9 and 11 only are relatively low. The test-retest reliabilities (9-week-interval) for the interest scales range from .70 to .85, with median .78; for the experience scales, the reliabilities range from .70 to .87, with median, .76.

The constructs underlying the interest and experience scales have been well established by the research of Holland, ACT research psychologists, and others. The six Holland categories have been refined further by a principal component analysis of the six interest scales. Approximately 53 percent of the variance in the six scales was accounted for by two principal components which reflected a data/ideas interest dimension and a people/things dimension. These two dimensions have been used to draw a world of work map for locating the 25 job families used in identifying a student's exploration priorities. Although the constructs measured by the principal components are relatively clear, it should be kept in mind that these two components, which are heavily emphasized in the interpretive materials, account for only one-half of the variance measured by the original six interest scales.

The experience scales are used primarily to help students evaluate interest in light of experiences. Presumably, interest scores should be more reliable and valid if they are backed by many experiences; however, no data are reported to support this proposition. Surprisingly, the norms for the experience scales show almost no differences between the mean scores of 8th grade and 12th grade students. These data call into question the validity of the experience scales. It seems reasonable to assume that seniors would report more career-related experiences than would 8th grade students.

GUIDANCE MATERIALS. CPP 8–12 includes a student workbook which may be used as part of a 9-unit mini-course in career planning. The handbook includes a detailed curriculum guide, a lengthy list of annotated resources, and instructions for developing a career information file based on the CPP job families. The use of such materials helps to place test scores in proper perspective and to insure that the students productively use the test information in career exploration. With a few additional instructions, it would be feasible for students to score their own answer sheets. By checking the individual items, the students could have a better understanding of the nature of their test scores. Such information would be valuable in a course on self-assessment and career planning. Unfortunately, the publishers have made no provisions for handscoring any of the formal assessment components.

SUMMARY. The goal of CPP is "to stimulate and facilitate self and career exploration, including the exploration of self in relation to careers." The CPP appears to be well designed for this purpose; however, the effectiveness of the program in achieving these goals has not been established. The tests and inventories cover a wide range of abilities, interests, and experiences which should foster broad exploration. Creative abilities, social skills, achievement needs, and work values are not formally measured; however, the student is encouraged to take these factors into consideration by a series of self-rating exercises in the student workbook. Holland's theory of careers, as modified by the authors, provides a comprehensive and fruitful organizational scheme for the test results and career information materials. The 25 job families, subdivisions of the 6 Holland categories, provide a suitable range of career fields for the type of "focused exploration" recommended by the authors.

In summary, CPP 8–12 offers a relatively complete program for career exploration and

Career Planning Program for Grades 8–12

planning for secondary school students. The program provides considerable information about one's self in relation to careers which may be best used to suggest, not verify, career possibilities. These possibilities may then be evaluated by means of the procedures outlined in the guidance materials.

[999]

★Comprehensive Career Assessment Scale. Grades 3–7, 8–12, teachers; 1974; CCAS; no norms; 1 form; 3 levels; technical report mentioned in the manual has not been published; profile-answer sheet (4 pages) for each level; separate answer sheets must be used; $1.95 per test; $3.75 per 25 profile-answer sheets; $2.95 per set of scoring stencils; $4.95 per manual; $10 per specimen set; cash orders postpaid; Stephan L. Jackson and Peggy M. Goulding; Learning Concepts. *
a) GRADES 3–7. 2 scores (familiarity, interest) in each of 15 areas: agribusiness and natural resources, business and office, communications and media, construction, consumer and homemaking education, environment, fine arts and humanities, health, hospitality and recreation, manufacturing, marine science, marketing and distribution, personal service, public service, transportation; 1 form (15 pages); manual (34 pages); [20–30] minutes.
b) GRADES 8–12. 30 scores: same as for grades 3–7; 1 form (7 pages); manual (33 pages); (20–30) minutes.
c) TEACHERS. 30 scores listed above plus supplementary scores for Part 2 (familiarity, attitude in each of 2 areas: career education concepts, implementing new educational programs) and Part 2 (essay); 1 form (7 pages); manual (29 pages); no data on reliability and validity for Parts 2 and 3; [20–30] minutes.

NANCY S. COLE, *Associate Professor of Education, University of Pittsburgh, Pittsburgh, Pennsylvania.*

The *Comprehensive Career Assessment Scale* is one of a variety of instruments developed in response to the growing concern in the early 1970s with career education. The scale was developed, in particular, to help with the assessment of needs in career education and to assist in program evaluation. In addition to the scale surveying students, there is also one for teachers, presumably designed to assess teacher training needs and teacher attitudes.

Each of the three levels consists of a list of 75 occupational titles, five in each of 15 occupational clusters. The testee responds to each title in terms of familiarity and interest. The occupations were chosen by career education specialists to be representative of the 15 clusters. However, one wonders about the advisability of using "egg candler" as an example item or of a few unusual occupations such as "kelp cutter" in the instrument itself. Most of

the occupations are stated in sex-neutral terms, a practice which seems appropriate and desirable.

The lower grade level instrument elicits answers on two three-point scales (know a lot about, know a little about, know nothing about; interesting, in between, not interesting). The other two age levels of the scale use seven-point responses labeled only at the ends as familiar–not familiar and interesting–not interesting.

As an attempt to measure the self-report of familiarity, the instrument is fairly straight-forward. The manual notes that the familiarity measure is simply a self-report; the user should carefully examine the type of measure needed in a particular situation. The self-report style would seem to limit the use of the instrument for program evaluation, since it is so clearly fakable. This instrument contrasts vividly with several instruments designed to test particular types of student knowledge and information about occupations. The latter give far more convincing evidence of familiarity, so a user should carefully consider if the type of familiarity given by this self-report scale is the desired information.

The second aspect measured is interest. The use of responses to occupational titles has been widely used in traditional interest measurement as part or all of an instrument when the target groups are high schoolers or older. Attempts have usually been made, even with high school youngsters, to seek other forms of presentation besides occupational titles (such as activities performed) in order to avoid the problem of familiarity with particular occupational titles. If a child is unfamiliar with or cannot read an occupational title, how can interest in the occupation be rated? I do not know of any other interest measure used with children as young as those in grades 3–7 which uses simply the occupational title format. I would guess that it is undesirable to do so.

The common response formats in interest measures of many types are three-point or five-point responses. It has generally been thought that more response options ask for finer judgments than most testees can make. The seven-point scales used in the high school and teacher version of this scale seem inappropriate. Since only the ends of the scale are anchored and there is no definition of the meaning of responses in between, the seven options can easily lead to different interpretations of the meaning of the scale by different testees.

Measuring the vocational interest of young adults is a relatively old and advanced field with mounds of available research evidence. By contrast, this foray into the field seems weak indeed in its technical documentation. In a field in which most available instrumentation is well-supported with technical documentation, norms, and validity studies, this scale presents essentially none.

All the versions of the scale underwent a field test from which the number of occupations in each cluster was narrowed from 10 to 5 on the basis of item statistics. No further results of the field test are given. The only reliability information presented in the manual is coefficient alpha, which is reported for overall familiarity and overall interest—scores which are not even calculated on the profile forms. Those figures, which are quite high, are irrelevant to the recommended use of the instrument in terms of scores by cluster.

Item-cluster correlations reported for both familiarity and interest appear relatively high. However, one must assume that the item itself is included in the total, in which case considerable spuriousness occurs. In fact, when some simplifying assumptions are made about item variances and intercorrelations (in the absence of the data), it appears that the item-cluster correlations reported in the manuals are inflated by .15 (for those above .80) to .30 (for those near .40). If one then estimates alpha coefficients for the five-point cluster scales from the corrected correlations, they range from zero to about .75. These values should be reduced even further, since the items were specifically selected because of their high correlations, apparently for the same sample of people for which the item-cluster correlations are reported. The cluster-score reliabilities are lowest for the grade 3–7 version, with at least half the scales having quite low reliabilities as estimated by this reviewer. Of course, it should be noted that low reliabilities for five-item scales are not unusual; but, unusual or not, the scales do not appear to be adequately reliable in this case to be useful for individual interpretation.

Data are not reported for test-retest reliability, an especially important consideration for the interest measures for the younger group, since vocational interest is likely to be less stable the younger the group tested. Since the form of the interest measure seems questionable for this age group because of variations in familiarity with and readability of the occupational titles, alternate form estimates of reliability are also needed.

No normative data of any kind are reported, and the authors recommend that only within-profile comparisons of scores be made. Such comparisons, however, require reliable difference scores between the already unreliable five-item scales. Thus, the within-profile comparisons recommended do not seem supported.

SUMMARY. In a new and developing area such as career education, one expects instrumentation to appear on the market without the wealth of background data common to instruments in more established fields with a much longer history. And users with pressing needs may often reasonably choose to use an apparently promising instrument with little technical back-up. For such a case, however, I have serious reservations about the usefulness of the *Comprehensive Career Assessment Scale*.

The instrument has several problems in its construction, and the reported technical data are not only incomplete but misleading. The internal reliabilities of the cluster scores are generally quite low, as would be expected from five-item scales, but, in contrast, the manual reports quite high alpha coefficients for the total (across cluster) scores—scores which are not even calculated in use of the instrument. The cluster scores seem to have insufficient reliability for individual use, especially at the lower age levels.

This instrument is not comprehensive as named, but, in fact, quite limited in what it attempts to measure. Although it might have some potential in needs assessment for groups, this use has not been developed nor the needed technical information considered by the authors.

A user buys a published test with one or both of two expectations: (*a*) that the test has been developed by professionals who can do a better job of instrument construction than could be done locally, and (*b*) that the test will have technical evidence insuring its quality—evidence which would be difficult and/or expensive to obtain on a locally developed instrument. The *Comprehensive Career Assessment Scale* seems to fulfill neither expectation.

THOMAS T. FRANTZ, *Associate Professor of Counseling Psychology, State University of New York at Buffalo, Buffalo, New York.*

Compared to other vocational interest inventories, the *Comprehensive Career Assessment Scale* (CCAS) purports to have two unique features. First, it provides an index of the *familiarity* with, or knowledge about, various occupations. Second, it is "designed to yield an index of the student's familiarity with and interest in each of the fifteen U.S.O.E. occupational clusters."

Recent federal interest in career education led the authors to construct the CCAS to meet two objectives: to assess the career education "needs of students across the country" and "to provide a means of evaluating the results of career education programs."

Each of the three levels contains 75 items (approximately two-thirds of which at any one level are identical items on each of the inventories at the other two levels), or occupational titles, to which the respondent is to indicate two things: his knowledge about the occupation and his interest in the occupation. Knowledge and interest are both indicated on a three-point scale at the elementary level and a seven-point scale at the secondary and faculty level.

Sturdy hand scoring stencil booklets are provided; but unfortunately the scoring procedure requires the scorer to twice (once for familiarity and once for interest) identify the proper numerical score for each item and then to twice add five such scores together for each scale and write the result in an unclearly designated space on the profile sheet. Such a scoring process, while clear if one goes slowly and carefully, is very likely to lead to scoring and recording errors. In addition, on the secondary and faculty inventories, since the scoring stencil does not permit the scorer to view the item number of the item he is scoring, the wrong item may be scored on occasion.

The three manuals contain much the same material and are terribly sparse. The USOE cluster concept on which the inventory is based is summarized, and a few references are given; but no discussion of, rationale for, or advantages of the concept are presented. Each scale score is derived from responses to only five items, which are likely to be too few to generate a stable score. Furthermore, occupational categories that include occupations like "kelp cutter" on the elementary form; that place "child care instructor," "fashion writer," and "food chemist" in the same category; and that group "policeman," "counselor," and "utility worker" together in another need justification. The concept of occupational level is ignored in this inventory.

By far the biggest problem with the CCAS is that the authors or publishers have not supplied the required data to warrant publishing what purports to be a standardized test. No norms of any kind are provided for any scale at any level! The manual states that the inventory is designed for "all children, regardless of social class, sex, or ethnic group." No data for social class, race, sex, or indeed of any kind at all, are provided. This is inexcusable.

Internal consistency alpha coefficients in the .90s are reported, but with no description whatsoever of the groups upon which they are based. Item/cluster correlations of unspecified nature and origin appear in the manual and average above .60 for all three levels. If one can take the item/cluster correlations at face value (which, without knowing how they were computed, is hard to do), the convergent validity of the items seems fine. The discriminant validity under these conditions is likely to be exceedingly poor; but no data are reported to assess it.

The manual refers to some "test-retesting" over a 10-day interval, data allegedly collected at an Alabama test site to assess stability of the inventory. Such data are neither presented nor mentioned in any way again. Explanations of what groups were tested or what students were included in various results are either lacking or confusing.

A strange aspect of the CCAS is the inclusion of a teacher's-level introduced in the manual by saying, "A demand has arisen for an instrument to be administered to teachers....to aid administrators to assess needs, plan curriculum, and evaluate the effects of career education programs as implemented." No support or justification is given for the above statement. A teacher's version may indeed be a worthwhile venture; but lacking a rationale or justification, one has difficulty seeing its value.

Furthermore, the teacher's version itself contains two sections not contained on the elementary and secondary levels. One section consists of ten items divided into two parts, one dealing with the teacher's familiarity with and attitude toward career education concepts. The second section contains three essay questions about career education. These last two sections appear to be haphazardly thrown into the inventory at the last minute with no rationale.

In summary, the CCAS is designed to assess both one's interest in and one's familiarity with (something seldom measured) the 15 occupational clusters developed through the USOE. The inventory is short, easy to take and administer, but possibly prone to hand-scoring errors. The manual is overly brief and misleading in places. The CCAS has apparently been published prematurely. No norms, reliability, discriminant validity, predictive or concurrent validity, scale mean or standard deviation data are reported. No adequate rationale for the nature of the inventory, for the inclusion of a teacher's version, or for the underlying cluster concept is offered.

[1000]

*Crowley Occupational Interests Blank. Secondary school pupils of average ability or less; 1970–76; COIB; 10 scores: 5 interest areas (active-outdoor, office, social, practical, artistic) and 5 sources of job satisfaction (financial gain, stability, companionship, working conditions, interest); 1 form ('76, 4 pages, spirit masters for local duplicating, unisex edition of formerly separate forms for boys and girls); manual ('76, 20 pages); £5.50 per set of spirit masters and scoring stencil; £3 per manual; postage extra; (20–30) minutes; A. D. Crowley; Hobsons Press (Cambridge) Ltd. for Careers Research Advisory Centre [England]. *

PAUL KLINE, *Reader in Psychometrics, University of Exeter, Exeter, Devon, England.*

The *Crowley Occupational Interests Blank* has a number of novel features which make it an interesting test. First, it is designed explicitly for children of average and below average ability. This is undoubtedly useful, since many children in Great Britain find tests such as the Kuder or Strong too difficult. Secondly, the test examines, in addition to interests, sources of job satisfaction. This too is useful, since the blank is envisaged not simply as a test for individual guidance but as a basis for

group discussion and as part of an integrated curriculum programme. This leads us to a third point: the manual contains a two-page section, "Basic principles of vocational guidance." All these features render the Crowley blank worthy of consideration.

However, this reviewer finds that the test has various flaws which in his view contraindicate its use, certainly for individual guidance.

There is a general air of what might be called British Amateurism which pervades the whole test and is used to avoid answering difficult questions. This is typified by the fact that users have to reproduce the test themselves from spirit-masters. More importantly, this air pervades the description of the aims of the test. For example, "the Blank, in common with other interest guides, is not an interest *test*—it does not measure strength of interest, participation, or motivation. It measures in the same way a compass measures—it indicates the direction of a person's occupational curiosity." Now, this analogy is perfectly useless: first, there actually is a magnetic North to which the compass is directed. Is there necessarily such a variable as occupational curiosity? If there is, how does this differ from interest? In what way are different curiosities directional? In any case, a compass always points the same way! Furthermore, as one gets nearer to the magnetic North, a compass becomes less and less accurate. There is no need to continue. However, this analogy indicates a lack of rigour in thinking about measurement, a failing which can be seen in other aspects of the test.

This test uses ipsative scores. Enough has been said now, in various reviews in the MMYs, about the problems of such scoring procedures. Crowley is well aware of these and agrees that the analysis of such scales by standard statistical procedures is dubious. However, since no more suitable techniques have been discovered, he offers the standard statistics. This is an unsatisfactory solution; it is better to abandon ipsative scales.

Despite the fact that the scales are ipsative and show only the *relative* strength of a pupil's interest (as Crowley points out with great care in his section on interpretation) norms are based on 600 boys and 606 girls. What meaning these might have is not explicated. This matter is particularly serious because the manual is clearly directed towards teachers rather than specialist psychologists who would be (hopefully) more cautious.

Despite these difficulties, if the scales were shown to be reliable and valid, all could be forgiven. The test-retest reliability coefficients for the interest scores are satisfactory. Except for one, they are all beyond .73 even after six months, although the sample size (40 girls) is somewhat small. The validity, however, is not so well attested although correlations with the *Rothwell-Miller Interest Blank* suggest that both are measuring much the same variables. How valid the Rothwell-Miller is, of course, is another question.

Crowley tries to show the independence of the scales from each other by presenting tables of correlations. In view of the ipsative scoring, however, the meaning of these correlations is unclear. Slightly more convincing are the percentile scores (based on the norms) of young workers in various jobs. These certainly make good sense.

So much for the test aspect of the Crowley blank. However, as the manual indicates, the blank can be used as a vehicle for discussion of jobs and for general vocational education. For such purposes it may well prove useful, although this is beyond the sphere of experience of this reviewer, and certainly any psychometric defects it may possess would then not be important. Whether it would prove more useful in stimulating discussion than any other similar blank would have to be put to the empirical test. However, even if it is thus valuable, is a "test" needed for such a purpose?

A final comment on the section of the manual on the principles of vocational guidance must be made. It is extraordinarily dogmatic: "Two personality traits are particularly important: outgoing versus self-contained, conforming versus self-reliant." Vocational advisers are told how to rate their pupils for these two traits. It states that "the terms introvert and extrovert tend to confuse these two quite independent traits." Forty years of research by the leading psychometrists in the world, Guilford, Eysenck, and Cattell, are dismissed out of hand without reference to evidence. Two rating scales are proposed in place of one of the few clearly established factors in the personality domain.

To this reviewer this is nonsense and indicates that Crowley's familiarity with anything beyond the narrowest strand of occupational psychology is slight.

The idea of compressing the principles of vocational guidance into two pages does disservice to the knowledge of vocational guidance that has gradually accumulated over the years. The fact that it contains such statements as found above illustrates that such compression is inevitably misleading. However, it is harmful also if it misleads teachers untrained in vocational guidance to use this test (or any other) for such a purpose and to make decisions about individuals on the strength of these psychometrically dubious scores.

Generally, therefore, one can conclude that the Crowley scales are reliable and give results in accord with common sense. However, there is no powerful evidence for validity, and the ipsative scoring makes the test difficult to use for quantitative research and for normative purposes. It could not, therefore, be recommended for serious psychological research into vocational psychology. Nor for the same reasons could it be recommended for individual guidance. The section on the principles of vocational guidance is positively misleading and potentially harmful. It the COIB has a use, it is in providing general vocational discussion among children and teachers. Here it may well be a valuable instrument, but in this usage it is hardly a psychological test.

STEPHEN SHARP, *Research Assistant, Newnham College, University of Cambridge, Cambridge, England.*

The COIB's main claim to fame is that it is one of the few tests designed for teenagers whose abilities are average or below average. Thus the occupations listed in the blank (and envisaged among the possibilities for the boys and girls when they leave school) do not generally demand academic qualifications; the instructions are easy to follow; and the terminology throughout is simple. The manual tells us that "the reading age required to cope with the blank is estimated to be at the 8¾–9 years level."

The blank comprises two parts, both being multiple choice and ipsatively scored. Part 1 requires the subjects to rank various occupa-

Crowley Occupational Interests Blank

tions in order of attractiveness, the aim being to infer the relative preference expressed by the subject for each of five types of jobs: active, office, social, practical, and artistic.

Part 2 consists of comparing statements about jobs so as to investigate the level of the subject's regard for five areas of job satisfaction: financial gain, security, companionship, working conditions, and job interest. These categories stemmed from the results of a "fourth-year leavers' careers project" (no further details given) which show "close agreement" (again no details) with a job dissatisfaction survey run by the National Youth Employment Council.

The results provided by the blank are then used to help structure the subject's thinking about his/her preferences for different types of employment. The blank is a guide, not a test, reflecting the relative rather than absolute level of interest shown by the subject in various job types and exploring only interests and not abilities. It is not intended to be used in isolation but as part of a vocational guidance programme, and a discussion of the role that the blank can play in such a programme is contained in the manual.

The raw profile from the COIB thus consists of ten scores on the ten scales mentioned above. Norms for these ten scales were obtained from a group of over 1,200 schoolchildren, the idea being to assign to each raw score one of five grades indicating its percentile position in the standardisation group. But in the case of the five Part 2 scales, the raw scores range only from 0 to 8, with the inevitable result that small changes in the raw score cause such large changes in the percentile grade as to deprive them of much of their value.

The five Part 1 scales show excellent split-half reliability (greater than .9) with samples of 100 and acceptable test-retest reliability (.64 to .92 over several months) with samples of 40. The five Part 2 scales show considerably poorer split-half reliability (.62 to .73) with a sample of 200 and also show lower test-retest reliability (.5 to .7 over 14 months) but with a sample of only 20. The reliability of the Part 2 scales, then, has yet to be established, although that of the Part 1 scales appears satisfactory.

The blank's construct validity is discussed in terms of item-total score correlations for each of the ten scales, and inter-scale correlation matrices. These calculations provide evidence of internal consistency and inter-scale independence, respectively, but are not strictly relevant to validity, as they reflect internal properties of the blank, rather than its success in vocational guidance. Results from the COIB are related to results from the *Rothwell-Miller Interest Blank,* but this relation is not discussed and its interpretation is unclear.

Concurrent validity is quite well demonstrated by a table showing that samples of 30 to 110 people in different occupations score highly on those scales which relate most closely to their jobs, e.g., "social" for nurses and "practical" for engineers. Similarly, predictive validity is demonstrated by comparing the number of job changes of each of a group of 201 subjects with the compatibility, as assessed by the blank, of the subject with his initial job; those subjects with high compatibility change less often (11 against 52 percent) than those with low compatibility

The other study cited in support of the blank is very threadbare; out of the occupations of 30 boys, 20 were predicted by the blank against 14 by "expressed interests" of the boys while still at school. This difference is not significant and would not mean much even if it were.

SUMMARY. The results of the blank constitute a basis for discussing vocational guidance which, in the hands of a skilled teacher, will provide a useful framework within which to start pupils thinking about jobs. But it is designed to do no more, and its usefulness is limited to this initial, though important, contribution.

[1001]

★**DAT Career Planning Program.** Grades 8–12; 1972–75; CPP; a counseling program based on the *Differential Aptitude Tests* (DAT) and the *DAT Career Planning Questionnaire* (CPQ); yields a computer printout for student, the *DAT Career Planning Report,* consisting of a profile of DAT scores and a page of narrative statements discussing compatibility of student's occupational preferences, school interests, educational aspirations, and tested abilities; no data on reliability and validity of narrative part of printout; 2 parts; counselor's manual ('73, 49 pages); glossary ('73, 2 pages); explanation of school summary report ('75, 4 pages); $15.50 per 50 combined questionnaire/DAT answer sheets; $1.25 per counselor's manual; $1.50 per specimen set (free if requested on letterhead by director of guidance or testing); postage extra; scoring service, 90¢ and over per student (scoring must be done by publisher); counselor's manual by Donald E. Super; Psychological Corporation. *
a) DIFFERENTIAL APTITUDE TESTS. Forms L, S, and T;

special MRC answer sheets must be used; see battery entry (485) for further details.

b) DAT CAREER PLANNING QUESTIONNAIRE. 1 form ('73, 2 pages plus 2-page MRC answer sheet for DAT); 2 editions: CPQ/Form L answer sheet, CPQ/Forms S and T answer sheet; (30) minutes.

For excerpted reviews of this and the DAT, see 485 (2 excerpts).

RICHARD W. JOHNSON, *Associate Director, Counseling Services, University of Wisconsin, Madison, Wisconsin.*

The DAT has enjoyed a well-deserved and long-established reputation as the best multiple-aptitude test battery for educational purposes since its publication in 1947. The original forms and subsequent revisions have been widely used in junior and senior high schools across the country.

The *DAT Career Planning Program* is a modification of the methods of collecting, interpreting, and reporting test data from the DAT in conjunction with additional information gathered about students at the time of testing. It consists, in addition to the DAT, of the *DAT Career Planning Questionnaire* and of the *DAT Career Planning Report.*

DAT CAREER PLANNING QUESTIONNAIRE. This form contains a 92-item interest inventory based on school subjects and activities and a 100-item interest inventory based on occupational titles. Additional items deal with educational plans and high school achievement.

The two interest inventories essentially serve as checklists that are used to help students identify their top three interest fields in both domains. The school subjects and activities are divided into 18 categories grouped on the basis of "prior work and manifest content." The occupational items have been placed in 20 categories derived from the 22 areas of work used in classifying the worker-trait groups for the *Dictionary of Occupational Titles.*

The various interest categories differ in both field and level. Within any one category, the items are sometimes relatively heterogeneous. For example, the occupational items librarian, editor, and lawyer are classified together under the broad title, Literary and Legal Occupations. Since some of the items may prove to be difficult for junior high school students (e.g., systems analyst, horticulture), a short glossary is provided for student use. The glossary probably should be expanded to include any item that

is not well known by most students (e.g., meteorologist, applied statistician).

Neither inventory has been standardized nor studied for reliability and validity. A student's responses may be used as interview aids; however, any assessments or predictions based on the responses must be extremely limited. Counselors should arrange to have the questionnaires returned to them after they are processed so that they may refer to the student's answers in their counseling sessions. The responses of a school or class may be analyzed as a group for help in curriculum planning.

DAT CAREER PLANNING REPORT. The test scores, school interests, and educational plans are related to the student's top three occupational interests by means of a computer program which provides a two-page, personalized, narrative report for each respondent.

Estimates of the amount of ability required for each of the 20 occupational categories are based on relevant research with the DAT, *General Aptitude Test Battery,* and other tests and rating scales. For this purpose, the DAT percentile scores have been grouped into five broad categories with the use of cutting scores at the 35th, 55th, 80th, and 95th percentiles. The rationale for these particular splits is not provided. The cutting score needed for "reasonable prospects of success" in an occupational group has been lowered by one category for each test to avoid "undesirable errors or exclusion." In most cases, the four abilities deemed to be most relevant for success in the occupation are used in determining occupational suitability.

Separate norms are used for men and women in relating the test scores to occupational fields. Because of the wide differences in the norms for men and women, women will qualify for technical occupations with lower raw scores than men on Mechanical Reasoning and Spatial Relations, while men will qualify for clerical occupations with lower raw scores than women on Clerical Speed and Accuracy, Spelling, and Language Usage. The use of the separate sex norms in establishing the cutoffs may help to combat the effects of social conditioning by encouraging men and women to consider nontraditional occupations; however, the validity of this technique in predicting job effectiveness needs to be examined and reported.

DAT Career Planning Program

The occupational choices are also compared with the student's school interests and educational plans. If either the school interests or the educational plans are incongruent with the student's occupational choices, the student is informed of this mismatch. For example, a student who has chosen Math and Physical Science Research as one of his occupational interest fields must also indicate an interest in either physical sciences or mathematics as school subjects and an intention to graduate from at least a four year college program. If neither one of the student's first two choices is fully supported by his or her abilities, school interests, and educational plans, a search is undertaken by the computer to identify occupational fields that would match each of these variables.

SUMMARY AND CONCLUSIONS. The authors of the DAT should be commended both for keeping the DAT updated and for expanding it into a career planning package. Although the *DAT Career Planning Program* is still in its initial stages of development, it promises to be a helpful tool for the secondary school counselor.

At the present time, the *DAT Career Planning Questionnaire* is most valuable in providing a structure for relating the student's occupational interests to his/her school interests, educational plans, and tested abilities. The questionnaire is not an adequate substitute for a standardized interest inventory. The reliability and validity of the questionnaire need to be investigated.

The interpretations in the *DAT Career Planning Report,* based on DAT scores and questionnaire responses, are probably more valid than those now drawn by most counselors. Because relatively low cutoff scores are used in determining occupational qualifications, the results should not be unnecessarily discouraging to most students.

The *DAT Career Planning Program* suffers from a lack of empirical evidence to support the judgments used in writing the planning reports. The DAT has been validated primarily against educational, not occupational, criteria. The validities of the interpretations generated by the computer program need to be ascertained.

The DAT program could profit from a student workbook and related curricular materials such as those provided in the *ACT Career Planning Program.* Ideally, a career planning program should help to stimulate and to guide information-seeking and exploratory behavior on the part of students. The DAT program materials should be beneficial in self-assessment; however, they fall short of a "program" for career planning and development.

STANLEY R. STRONG, *Professor of Psychology, University of Minnesota, Minneapolis, Minnesota.*

The *DAT Career Planning Program* uses a computer program to integrate information needed to help young people make educational and career plans, evaluate the appropriateness of the students' vocational aspirations, and report the findings in several short, sharply focused paragraphs in a computer printout. The manual urges that the reports be used as a basis or beginning point for the counselor's preparation for individual counseling. By examining the report, the counselor can check his own interpretations and judgments against those of the vocational psychologists who developed the program. The counselor is urged to use the instrument in counseling students and their parents as "the report serves as a bit of reality to be encountered by the student or parent," and the counselor is also urged to use the report in group counseling with students, training counselors, evaluation research, and curriculum development.

In using the report, the counselor relies solely on the expertise and judgment of the author of the manual; the counselor is given no reliability or validity data to buttress his confidence in the author's judgment. By providing the user with some independent basis of evaluating the usefulness of the program, the author could have acknowledged, met, and dispelled many serious questions about the way information is combined in the *DAT Career Planning Program* and in so doing greatly added to the user's confidence in the program.

It seems likely that the proposed relationships of DAT scores to occupations are influenced by the validation studies and cutoff criteria for the *General Aptitude Test Battery.* Elsewhere, Super and Crites [1] have cautioned against fully accepting the reported level of

[1] SUPER, DONALD E., AND CRITES, JOHN O. *Appraising Vocational Fitness by Means of Psychological Tests, Revised Edition.* New York: Harper & Row, Publishers, Inc., 1962. Pp. xv, 688. *

DAT Career Planning Program

validity of the GATB and have alerted readers that the scales in the DAT and the GATB are dissimilar. Yet the Career Planning Program manual does not present data showing the relationship between the DAT scales and the GATB scales. What about the effects of the ages of students taking the DAT versus the ages of those in the validational groups for the GATB? While such judgments can certainly be made, there is no attempt to inform the reader of relationships. This is especially serious in the use of the program when students' scores fall below the program cutoff levels for the students' occupational aspirations. Without evidence of the strength of relationship, a counselor does not know whether he should emphasize or de-emphasize these shortfalls. From a social psychological point of view, students will give high weight to the reports in decision-making because the reports are generated by "impartial scientific computers" on computer paper. It is unfortunate that data supporting the proposed DAT scale cutoff scores for occupational groups are not given. A brief description of this information would equip the counselor to make rational and humane use of the program reports.

Research on the SVIB, the Holland scales, and other research has shown relationships between school activities, job preferences, and occupational choice. Why hasn't Super presented the key findings he used so that the counselor may obtain a better idea of the meaning of the report? The report will at times discourage a student from entering occupations that do "not relate to his school activities or interests." Are the levels of relationships valid and strong enough to support such conclusions? More critically, what relationship does the *DAT Career Planning Questionnaire* have with occupations? No reliability or validity information on this new questionnaire is given. We are left in a situation of either accepting the word of the author or rejecting the entire program.

It is not enough to integrate the information needed for career planning in a splendid computer program such that the information is specific and pointed. It is not enough that a renowned vocational psychologist should prepare the integration of information. To document the relationships used in the program totally would doubtless require a lengthy book.

DAT Career Planning Program

Yet a manual that presents the key relationships and refers to supplementary or additional relationships would go a long way toward removing the total dependence on Super's judgment that the instrument now requires. To use this program a counselor must have a total command of vocational psychology to determine whether or not the reports are valid for use with each student. While no doubt this is an ideal for most counselors, it is seldom achieved. As a result, the program should not be used until the author and the publisher present more adquate information on the program's validity.

[1002]
*Educational Interest Inventory, Revised Edition.** High school and college; 1962-74; EII; 22 scores: literature, music, art, communications, education, business administration, engineering, industrial arts, agriculture, nursing, library arts, home economics, botany, zoology, physics, chemistry, earth science, history and political science, sociology, psychology, economics, mathematics; no high school norms; 1 form ('74, 12 pages, combined revision of formerly separate forms for males and females); manual ('74, 7 pages); separate answer sheet/profiles for men, women, ('74, 2 pages, self-marking); separate answer sheets must be used; $1 per test; $7.50 per 25 answer sheet/profiles for men or women; 50¢ per manual; $2 per specimen set; postage extra; [40-60] minutes; James E. Oliver; Educational Guidance, Inc. *
See T2:2178 (1 reference) and 7:1017 (6 references).

REFERENCES
1-6. See 7:1017.
7. See T2:2178.
8. WACHOWIAK, DALE G. "Personality Correlates of Vocational Counseling Outcome." *J Counsel Psychol* 20(6):567-8 N '73. * (PA 51:8022)

FRED H. BORGEN, *Associate Professor of Psychology and Director, Counseling Psychology Program, Iowa State University, Ames, Iowa.*

This inventory is designed, in the author's words, to measure "comparative strengths of interests in 22 major areas" of college study. It is intended for use with high school and college students who are making career and, particularly, curriculum decisions. Each of the 22 scales taps preference for the work activities typically encountered by graduates from a specific college curriculum. Thus, for example, a person who indicates preference for the activity "moderate discussion groups on a television show" receives a raw score increment on the communications scale.

The inventory uses a forced-choice format to minimize social desirability. Item stems were selected, apparently primarily by the author's judgment, to represent work activities typical of graduates from 22 college-level majors. Using a modified version of a full paired comparison design, stems for a given area are systematically paired with stems from 18 of the other areas. The result is an inventory composed of 198 pairs of items from each of which the respondent chooses the one which is "more interesting." Each choice adds one point to total score for the respective area of interest.

The 1974 revision introduced a single test booklet for use by both sexes, but separate answer sheets and norms continue to be used with each sex. Norms are based on a general group of 1,123 women and 1,643 men, also grouped separately to provide norms for "successful student majors" in most of the 22 curriculum areas. So far, norms are not available for each sex in three college-major areas: men in nursing, library arts, and home economics, and women in engineering, industrial arts, and agriculture.

The inventory is directly and simply self-scoring. With separate answer sheets for men and women, a cleverly designed carboned answer sheet produces a concealed impression which directly produces percentiled scores from the person's responses. However, a potential liability of the rather transparent answer format is that it may encourage a motivated respondent to distort answers. After answering a few pairs of items, one probably becomes aware that choices are beginning to gather in certain areas; it thus becomes fairly obvious how, if one chooses, to increase or decrease scores in a certain area.

When using the percentile norms for the college majors, users should be aware that a very small raw score shift can lead to a major shift in percentile rank. Thus, e.g., the economics score (for males) jumps from the 18th to the 59th percentile for majors with a raw score shift of three points. The reliability data, which are based on a different data base, are therefore probably misleading for use of percentile norms for specific major fields.

This instrument, like the *Edwards Personal Preference Schedule,* has combined elements of ipsative and normative measurement. The forced-choice format means the respondent, in effect, ranks his or her interests, but then the ranks are compared through norms with refer-

ence groups. The implications of this yoked intra- and inter-individual measurement are never discussed in the manual. Admittedly, this makes for a tricky interpretation, but the solution is certainly not benign neglect.

Inspection of the inventory reveals good *judgment* by the author in format, item writing, and ease of administration and interpretation. Unfortunately, the manual is altogether too brief, with too much credibility resting on trust in the author as expert. Description of the development of the inventory is so terse that insufficient information is given for an adequate independent appraisal. The manual contains less than four pages of text; few suggestions are made for interpreting the scores; no references to any published literature are given, either for supporting data or theory or for suggestions about where the user might go for further information.

The empirical data to evaluate the inventory are uncomfortably sparse. The manual contains six lines of terse discussion of reliability and a five-line comment on validity. The three pages of tabled data which accompany the discussion of reliability and validity *do* present, as far as they go, supportive evidence for the quality of the instrument. Both split-half and test-retest reliabilities are adequate. Concurrent validity can be inferred from the tabled means for each subgroup and from study of the percentiled norms on the answer sheets.

Validity is considered and dismissed as follows: "Content or intrinsic validity of the inventory is supported by both the objective measures of correlation and the subjective analysis of items. Moreover, the highly significant differences in the mean scores of 'College Students in General' and 'Successful Majors' provide meaningful statistical evidence of validity." I agree this is a first step for validity of the concurrent variety, but there is no evidence for predictive validity and no acknowledgement of its desirability.

In conclusion, this inventory has reasonable face validity and, in its physical simplicity and direct scoring features, has some appeal for measuring interest similarity in college major areas. Beginning data are presented to suggest promise for the instrument, but the manual is cavalier in its failure to provide more complete information and to acknowledge need for further study of the instrument. An alternative interest inventory to measure similarity to college students in major fields is the *Kuder Occupational Interest Survey*. Also, the basic interest scales of the *Strong-Campbell Interest Inventory* tap many of the same dimensions. Both of these inventories would seem preferable to the *Educational Interest Inventory* because of the comprehensiveness of their research base, accumulated lore for counseling use, and the availability of additional kinds of supplementary scales.

Thomas T. Frantz, *Associate Professor of Counseling Psychology, State University of New York at Buffalo, Buffalo, New York.*

Too many higher quality interest inventories are available to warrant much use of the *Educational Interest Inventory*. The EII contains 198 forced-choice items designed "to provide measures of interest in the specific areas of knowledge which can be studied in institutions of higher learning." Males and females respond to the same items but on separate self-scoring answer sheets containing norms for their respective sex only. It might be more useful to have one answer sheet with norms for both sexes. The answer sheet is somewhat unusual, consisting of 22 rows (one for each scale) of 18 boxes each (one for each item). Whenever the subject chooses a response on a given scale, he puts an X in the next open box in that row. Such procedure enables the subject to monitor his scores as he proceeds and introduces a likelihood of a response set producing a leveling of scale scores—e.g., the subject may think, I already have 10 Xs in this row, maybe I better put it in the row in which I have only one X to even things out a bit.

The overly brief (three pages of written material and three tables) manual indicates that the 22 scales correspond to the 22 most popular college majors as determined by an analysis of "the major fields of study in a large number of colleges and universities." The data from this study are not reported nor is any reference given for the study. The justification for including industrial arts, communications, library arts, and agriculture and omitting physical education, foreign language, anthropology, and geography is neither given nor apparent.

Item selection is perhaps the poorest part of the inventory. First, there are too many two-

part items; that is, items where the subject may agree with half of the item but not with the other half—e.g., "Write children's stories based on the classics." Second, items of virtually the same content appear in different scales—e.g., "Evaluate monthly selections for a book club" appears in the literature scale and "Make monthly selections for a book club" appears on the library arts scale. Third, items are remarkably unimaginative. The literature scale, for example, contains the following items: "Rewrite popular manuscripts for a condensed book club," "Evaluate monthly selections for a book club," "Rewrite classical manuscripts for a book club" (the latter two items are each repeated in another item on the same scale later in the inventory), "Prepare book reviews for a literary group," "Evaluate novels submitted to a publishing firm." Hence the same content is contained in seven of the 18 items on the literature scale. Fourth, a strange distribution of roles emerges from examining the items. Thirty-five choices involve the role of writer, 40 involve the role of teacher, and 149 (!!!) involve a role in research and development.

The inventory is designed for high school and college students; however, no norms are presented for high school students. The inventory was first published in 1962 and yet five scales of the women's norm tables and three scales of the men's are incomplete and hence of only limited use. No information describing the normative sample, other than that it consists of college students, is offered.

Test-retest and split-half reliability data of unknown origin on unknown subjects are presented for 19 of the men's scales and 17 of the women's scales. No data are offered on the remaining eight scales. The manual contains two sentences about validity, saying in part that "content or intrinsic validity of the inventory is supported by both the objective measures of correlation and the subjective analysis of the items." The sloppiness of the inventory's preparation is nowhere more evident. First, content validity is determined by expert evaluation of an inventory (none is reported), not by correlation coefficients. Second, no correlation data of any kind are reported. Third, no "subjective analysis of items" is reported or referred to.

In summary, because of questionable scale and item selection, a woefully inadequate man-

Educational Interest Inventory

ual, missing reliability and normative data, and a lack of validity to support its use, I do not recommend use of the *Educational Interest Inventory*. Existing interest inventories of comparable length and cost—such as the *Ohio Vocational Interest Survey*, the Kuder inventories, and the *Strong-Campbell Interest Inventory*—are more likely to be of help in situations where one might be tempted to use the *Educational Interest Inventory*.

[1003]

*Hall Occupational Orientation Inventory. Grades 3-7, 8-16 and adults, low-literate adults; 1968-76, c1965-76; HOOI; 22 scores: creativity-independence, risk, information-knowledge, belongingness, security, aspiration, esteem, self-actualization, personal satisfaction, routine-dependence, data orientation, things orientation, people orientation, location concern, aptitude concern, monetary concern, physical abilities concern, environment concern, co-worker concern, qualifications concern, time concern, defensiveness; 1 form; 3 levels; counselor's manual, third edition ('76, 54 pages); career education reader ('76, 35 pages); separate answer sheets (hand scored, NCS) must be used; $13 per 20 tests; $5 per 20 hand scored answer sheets; $5 per 20 interpretive folders; $1.50 per career education reader; $3.50 per manual; postage extra; $5.75 per specimen set ($2.50 without manual), cash orders only; scoring service (includes NCS answer sheets), 80¢ per test ($35 minimum); (30-40) minutes; L. G. Hall and R. B. Tarrier (manual); Scholastic Testing Service, Inc. *

a) INTERMEDIATE FORM. Grades 3-7; 1976; 1 form (7 pages); interpretive folder (7 pages).

b) [YOUNG ADULT FORM.] Grades 8-16 and adults; 1968-76, c1965-76; 1 form ('71, 12 pages); interpretive folders: young adult, college, ('76, 8 pages).

c) ADULT BASIC FORM. Low-literate adults; 1976; 1 form (7 pages); interpretive folder (8 pages).

See T2:2187 (3 references); for a review by Donald G. Zytowski of the original edition, see 7:1021 (4 references).

REFERENCES

1-4. See 7:1021.
5-7. See T2:2187.
8. BERTINETTI, JOSEPH FRANCIS. *A Comparison of Self Concepts, Values and Occupational Orientations Among Three Groups of Adolescents.* Doctor's thesis, University of New Mexico (Albuquerque, N.M.), 1972. (*DAI* 33:3278A)
9. BURGESS, GLORIA RUTH. *Self Esteem, Career Aspiration, and Selected Biographical Variables in Nurse Participants of Continuing Education.* Doctor's thesis, St. Louis University (St. Louis, Mo.), 1975. (*DAI* 36:2724B)
10. MADAK, PAUL JOSEPH. *The Expressed Moral and Occupational Values of Tenth and Twelfth Grade Students: A Comparison Between One Roman Catholic and One Public School.* Doctor's thesis, Kent State University (Kent, Ohio), 1975. (*DAI* 36:3297A)
11. PENTECOSTE, JOSEPH C. "Occupational Levels and Perceptions of the World of Work in the Inner City." *J Counsel Psychol* 22(5):437-9 S '75. * (*PA* 54:12657)
12. SMALL, JO ANN MORROW. *Sex Differences in Personality Characteristics of Workers in Selected Occupations.* Doctor's thesis, University of Houston (Houston, Tex.), 1975. (*DAI* 36:7877A)

ROBERT H. DOLLIVER, *Professor of Psychology and Counseling Psychologist, University of Missouri, Columbia, Missouri.*

Most of the comments in a previous MMY review by Zytowski are still applicable. The HOOI and the 1971 (second edition) manual have changed very little. The 1971 manual indicates these differences between the 1968 and 1971 Hall materials: 345 items reduced to 220, an expanded interpretative folder, a shortened and simplified answer sheet, and a "revised" and "expanded" manual. Dropping the "Extremeism" scale was an unacknowledged change, now leaving 22 scales of 10 items each. The 1971 manual provides only very general information about the methods used to select the present 220 items from among the previous 345 items: "Item analysis was conducted to insure significant item-scale correlation." The expansion of the 1971 manual is in the description of the Hall rationale and use; less psychometric information is presented. The 1971 manual presents some of the same information on the 220-item HOOI which had been presented in 1968 for the 345-item HOOI, usually for smaller numbers of subjects.

The 1976 (third edition) manual represents an extrapolation of trends evident in the 1971 manual. There is a 15-page section on the use of the inventory in group counseling and a five-page description of the "Tarrier-Hall model of occupational choice." Validity and reliability are reported in two and a half pages. Statistical data are presented in two tables and some of the data had already been presented in 1971; the only new data reported are the reliability coefficients for the newly developed intermediate and adult basic levels.

The inventory contains three major kinds of scales: (a) 10 values and needs, (b) 3 job characteristics, and (c) 8 worker traits, plus a validity scale ("defensiveness"). Abraham Maslow and Anne Roe provide the theoretical underpinnings for the values and needs scales. The US Department of Labor (USDL) is identified as the source for both the job characteristics and the worker traits scales. The connection is easily made between the HOOI job characteristics scales (data, things, and people orientations) with the USDL classification (ideas, things, and people). The connection is not easily made between the Hall worker traits scales (e.g., environmental concern, time concern) and the USDL classifications of job characteristics (e.g., able to see physical results of work, opportunity for self-expression). The worker traits scales appear to be a very loose constellation of ideas; for example, the environmental concern scale includes items having to do with whether (*a*) one works alone, (*b*) surroundings are free from pollution, (*c*) one travels by airplane, and (*d*) one must wear fashionable clothing. The 1976 manual states: "The new *Career Education Reader* presents information about various occupations which the U.S. Department of Labor has rated high for characteristics incorporated in the HALL scales." I do not find evidence in the cited USDL literature that the HOOI worker traits scale dimensions are comparable to USDL dimensions, nor do I find evidence that the USDL has rated those occupations in the manner presented in the Career Education Reader.

Empirical data are reported in the manuals without enough information to allow evaluation. Even the number of subjects is not reported for several studies. Very little information is presented about who the subjects are, and description of the methods of data collection is nonexistent. When reporting differences between groups, the authors do not indicate whether they had any reason to anticipate the obtained differences nor do they attempt to explain those results after-the-fact. No attempt is made to integrate the empirical findings into the theoretical views about the scales. Score differences are reported without indication of the absolute level of the scores or the actual amount of difference. The data on occupational group comparisons do not state whether the "scales that differentiate" are uniformly higher for the occupational groups than for the nongrouped workers. The sexual makeup of the groups is not specified. Reliability coefficients are reported for each scale on each edition; the authors provide no information about what kind of reliability is being reported for what time span for what subject groups. Only "(N = 425)" is reported.

The authors take a confusing stance on the "matching people with jobs" orientation: (*a*) The Career Education Reader lists occupations rated high on each of the scales. (*b*) The 1971 and 1976 manuals list occupations which showed empirical differences to nongrouped workers on various scales. The occupations listed in the manuals show little overlap with those listed in the Career Education Reader. (*c*) In the "Tarrier-Hall model of occupational choice," the authors stress that they have gone beyond the "matching" orientation to one which stresses "exploration."

I like the HOOI premise that promoting awareness of self and occupational characteristics is a useful activity. The inventory looks to me as though it could be a useful counseling or classroom method for promoting such awareness. However, I believe that most college and many high school students would already have the levels of self and occupational awareness represented in HOOI. The 1976 manual notes, "The primary aim of the HALL is instruction not measurement. The HALL is basically an instructional package cast in a measurement format." I do not see sufficient evidence in the 1976 manual to feel assured that the inventory does promote instruction. I find enough (*a*) diversity of items on the same scale, (*b*) doubts about the stated relationship to USDL ratings, (*c*) lack of specificity about data presented, and (*d*) confusing conceptual stance regarding the "matching" orientation to recommend caution to the HOOI user.

AUSTIN C. FRANK, *Director, Office of Student Affairs Research, University of California, Berkeley, California.*

The third edition of the HOOI, copyrighted in 1976, provides a marked set of changes from the original version published in 1968 and the modified second edition of 1971. The focus of the inventory as "basically....an instructional package cast in a measurement format" has been sharpened. New materials about the humanistic, theoretical commitments of the authors are presented, new teaching and guidance sections have been prepared, a career education reader has been created for supplemental reading, and two new forms of the inventory have been generated to provide materials for use with students in grades 3–7 and with adults in basic education programs. Simultaneously, there has been a *reduction* in the initially sketchy information available about reliability and validity.

The opening chapters of the 1976 manual set forth the theoretical foundations for the inventory and the "Tarrier-Hall model of occupational choice." In this self-proclaimed humanistic

Hall Occupational Orientation Inventory

framework, needs are considered the primary organizing principle for the individual's motivational life. Maslow's personality theory, Roe's theory of occupational choice, and worker traits and job characteristics assembled by the United States Department of Labor are the central elements of the authors' framework. In their occupational choice model "the counselor or teacher helps the individual move toward making decisions in terms of inner values, needs, beliefs, abilities, and interests that he or she feels are really important."

The inventory is merely the main vehicle or point of departure for group counseling "toward self-empowerment." Session-by-session uses of the inventory's items and scales are detailed, a variety of activities and simulations are suggested, and recommendations are provided for using the HOOI in groups in school, organizational, professional, and other settings. These include groups of women, senior citizens, veterans, prisoners, and clergy. Use of the inventory for individual counseling is given only minor attention.

The career education reader booklet is intended to accompany the group or course work central to the program. The booklet consists of brief statements about each of the inventory's scales: how the scale is occupationally relevant, why the individual who has taken the inventory should consider it, and lists of occupations at various levels of educational attainment which have been rated high on that characteristic.

The main version of the inventory itself is intended for young adults and college-age students. At the time of the second edition, it was shortened from the original 345 items and 23 scales to 220 items and 22 scales, and the third edition remains the same. Each scale has 10 items. The first 10 scales are considered values and needs, the next three are job characteristics, the next eight are called worker traits, and the final one, Defensiveness, is a verification scale. The items are statements, e.g., "You give people advice in your job" for which one is instructed to "rate each statement according to how you would feel about taking a job to which each statement applied." The five response options range from most desirable to very undesirable.

The scores for each scale are entered on a profile in the interpretive folder where they are designated low, average, or high. Brief one-paragraph descriptions of each scale are given, and the item numbers for the scale are listed so that the person taking the inventory can refer back to the items. The inventory taker is told to give particular attention to the items in the scales on which he/she has scored high or low and to all items in the inventory marked most desirable or very undesirable.

The Adult Basic Form has 110 items, 5 per scale, and is similar to the Young Adult Form except that both the items and the accompanying interpretive folder are written at a lower reading level. The Intermediate Form, with interpretive folder, intended for grades 3 to 7, also has 110 items, 5 per scale, but here the content is restructured to refer to a school setting.

If the inventory and its accompanying materials are used as recommended, with extensive group sessions, counselor-led discussion, and supplemental reading, it will probably be useful to people in most of its target populations in helping to clarify many of their occupationally relevant values and needs. This presumably will assist them in making better occupational choices. However, it is not clear that the HOOI, in its various forms, is the best instrument available for use in a variety of vocational guidance settings. Its psychometric characteristics, to the extent they are known, frequently leave a great deal to be desired, and *any* systematic exploration of personal characteristics in relation to occupational characteristics will likely be helpful to people with occupational-vocational uncertainties.

The authors make a point of the fact that the inventory is not normative or predictive but "designed to sample changing, dynamic personality variables." But the scale scores *are* said to be low, average, or high, and directions are given for interpreting them. How the classification (norming) is made is not described, nor is there any suggestion of differing mean scores for the various scales, for men or women, for individuals of different age or education levels, etc. Almost no attention is given to the fact that the last 8 scales are scored very differently from the first 13 and must be treated and interpreted differently.

Concerns such as these are dismissed with the following statement from the short manual section on validity and reliability : "Because of the dynamic nature of personality variables addressed by the Hall, the humanistic philosophy and model of occupational choice advanced, and the questionable role of predictive testing in counseling, the statistical concepts utilized in traditional measurement are not reported here." One table lists the scales on which members of 13 different occupational groups differed from a sample of 200 ungrouped adult workers, but such critical information as the direction of these differences—whether the occupational group is higher or lower on the scale —is not provided.

Another table lists reliability coefficients for each scale for each of the three forms, but the user is not told what kind of coefficients these are, test-retest, split-half, or what. The sample size is listed as 425, but is this three different samples of 425, or one sample for all forms? The data for the Young Adult Form are exactly the same as those reported in the second edition.

The catalogue of practical measurement problems inherent in the inventory is too long to enumerate. Suffice it to say that the problems in this area are many and important and should not be disregarded or dismissed, as they have been by the authors.

In sum, this is an inventory with the virtues of a point of view, some on-going development, and a package of materials which will probably be helpful to counselors who share its pervasive underlying humanistic perspective. However, the HOOI is dangerously and unnecessarily deficient in providing certain forms of essential interpretive material and cannot be well used by individuals working alone, outside of groups, and without a counselor. If the counselor carefully specifies his/her purposes in considering this inventory, other inventories and materials may well be found to serve the objectives better.

[1004]

★The Harrington/O'Shea System for Career Decision-Making. Grades 8–14 and adults ; 1974–76 ; CDM ; "self-administered and self-interpreted" inventory ; 6 scores (arts, business, clerical, crafts, scientific, social) used to identify 3 or more occupational areas, for intensive career exploration, from among 18 career clusters (art work, clerical work, customer services, data analysis, education work, entertainment, legal, literary work, management, manual work, math-science, medical-dental, music work, personal service, sales work, skilled crafts, social services, technical) and

questions in 5 areas (abilities, future plans, job values, occupational preferences, school subject preferences) ; 3 formats ; 3 reporting systems ; manual ('76, 57 pages) ; $2 per manual ; postage extra ; (40) minutes ; Thomas F. Harrington and Arthur J. O'Shea ; Career Planning Associates, Inc. ; distributed (except for NCS test-answer booklet) by Chronicle Guidance Publications, Inc. and (except for reusable booklet and separate answer sheets) by NCS Interpretive Scoring Systems. *

a) SYSTEM S–SELF SCORING REPORT. 1 form ('76, 12 pages) ; instructions for administration ['76, 2 pages] ; interpretive folder ('76, 4 pages) ; $21.25 per 25 tests ; $3 per CGP specimen set.

b) SYSTEMS I AND P [COMPUTERIZED REPORTS]. 1 form ; 2 formats : reusable booklet ('76, 8 pages), consumable NCS test-answer booklet ('75, 4 pages) ; interpretive folder ('76, 4 pages) for System P ; separate answer sheets (NCS) must be used with reusable edition ; 25¢ per reusable booklet ; $12.50 per 50 NCS test-answer booklets ; 2 reports available (scoring must be done by distributor) : System I (20–26 pages, interpretive report), System P (1 page, profile report) ; $5 ($8) per CGP specimen set of reusable test including prepaid profile (interpretive) report ; $10 per NCS specimen set of self scoring test and consumable test including prepaid interpretive report ; CGP scoring service (includes answer sheets) ; $9 or less per interpretive report, $1.85 or less per profile report ; NCS scoring service : $9 or less per interpretive report (daily service), $1.90 or less per profile report (daily service), $1.20 or less ($30 minimum, weekly service).

CARL G. WILLIS, *Counseling Psychologist, University of Missouri, Columbia, Missouri.*

In developing the CDM, the authors were convinced that many clients received interpretations of their interest test scores which were inadequately presented. "Even in those cases where clients have received competent assistance, counselors have been operating on the doubtful assumption that clients remembered in detail their very involved, sophisticated interpretations." I take exception to this statement. I have never believed that my clients have remembered or should remember everything in detail.

The rationale for the development of the CDM is the need for a vocational interest inventory with a sound theoretical base which is self-administered and self-interpreted. The report form was devised to "simulate the best career counseling techniques," whatever these are.

There are many career inventories on the market. Research sources are quoted to demonstrate that the lack of assistance to students in the career decision-making process is a major complaint about school counseling services. Although the CDM is offered as the answer to this problem, I doubt that it will resolve the problem by itself. Many uses are suggested for the CDM, but these uses are not supported by data in the manual.

The CDM manual provides an excellent discussion of the underlying rationale and development of the instrument, including specific efforts to eliminate sex bias. All occupational titles are presented in gender neutral terms, and the report system is based entirely on client responses independent of sex. Even the manual is presented in sex-free terms. The CDM has been cited by NIE-HEW as thoroughly incorporating criteria for eliminating sex bias. Yet, sex, grade, and age are still requested information on the answer sheet.

The authors view the *Vocational Preference Inventory* as a parallel instrument to the CDM. The hexagonal model of career development accounts for a majority of the variance of interest measurement of the CDM and other career inventories. The six scores reported for the VPI have been renamed for use in the CDM.

There are three systems for the CDM. System I—Interpretative Report and System P—Profile Report are scored and reported by a scoring service requiring a time lag for reporting scores. Group reports can be generated for Systems I and P to help in "planning curriculums, evaluating student readiness for career planning, and assessing student needs." No data are presented to support these contentions. System S—Self-Scoring can provide immediate feedback to the student. The test materials across the three systems can be confusing for a counselor, but a single system or format for a student is clearly presented. One item, "Work with slide rules" may be almost obsolete due to mass marketing of electronic calculators. Data are presented in the manual to support the use of the CDM as a self-scoring instrument. Correlations between student calculated scores and author calculated scores for the six scales range from .96 to .99. The authors still caution us to check client scoring, especially with younger students, the unmotivated, and those with limited reading skills.

All three systems provide a configuration of information for clients based on 18 career clusters, 14 job values, and 14 abilities. Students must self-rate themselves for the career clusters, job values, and abilities. Although the authors report prior research to justify the use

of self-ratings, they provide no information on the manner in which the 14 job values and 14 abilities incorporated in the CDM were selected. No information is presented showing the relationship of the self-ratings of abilities and job values directly to the six interest scores.

The CDM is not a criterion-based instrument. It relies on raw scores in suggesting career clusters for exploration. The career clusters were derived by applying Holland's occupational classification system to the worker trait groups in the *Dictionary of Occupational Titles*. Although there is no predictive validity, the manual presents an argument to support construct validity. Concurrent validity is based on the relationship to the VPI. Scale homogeneity is good. No item was selected by fewer than five percent of either sex. The lowest correlation of an item with an interest scale is .50, while the average item correlation within scale for all six scales ranges from .61 to .74. Alpha coefficients reported vary from .84 to .90 for the six interest scales. Test-retest correlations over a 30-day period range from .75 to .94. The normative sample seems well balanced compared to the 1970 census figures. Many sub norm groups are presented for comparison.

In summary, the CDM, as a test, is a shorter version of the *Vocational Preference Inventory*. As a self-scoring instrument, it is like the *Self-Directed Search*. The CDM adds nothing new to the testing market. However, the interpretative printout is a very thorough presentation, one of the best I have seen. The 20-plus page interpretation is that which good counselors should provide their clients. The interpretation provides more data than a counselor is likely to present, but the interpretation format has less flexibility than the typical counselor. Although the authors claim that the CDM is unique in surveying six critical elements in the career decision-making process, the *World of Work Inventory* is very similar.

[1005]

★**High School Interest Questionnaire.** "Coloured pupils" in standards 7–10; 1973–74; 8 scores: language, performing arts, fine arts, social, science, technical, business, office work; 1 form ('73, 17 pages, English and Afrikaans); manual ('74, 77 pages, English and Afrikaans); separate answer sheets (IBM 1230, hand scored) must be used; R2.50 per 10 tests; 25c per single copy; R5 per 100 IBM answer sheets; R2.50 per 100 hand scored answer sheets; R3 per manual; post-

High School Interest Questionnaire

paid within South Africa; (45–60) minutes; J. B. Wolfaardt; Human Sciences Research Council [South Africa]. *

[1006]

★Individual Career Exploration. Grades 8–12; 1976; ICE; self-administered and self-scored inventory of interests, experience, occupational choices, and abilities in 8 occupational groups: service, business contact, organization, technology, outdoor, science, general culture, arts and entertainment; 5 scores: first-choice occupational group, second-choice group, decision level (motivation), job values (most important, second most important); no data on reliability and validity; no norms; 1 form (23 pages); instructor's manual (7 pages); classification of occupations by group and level (21 pages); job information checklist (4 pages, for independent student research into a specific occupation); $20 per set of 20 tests, 25 classification booklets, 60 job information checklists, and manual; $5 per 20 tests or classification booklets; $8 per 60 checklists; postage extra; $1 per specimen set, cash orders only; (120) minutes; Anna Miller-Tiedeman in consultation with Anne Roe (classification of occupations booklet); Scholastic Testing Service, Inc. *

RICHARD S. MELTON, *Professor of Psychology, University of Cincinnati, Cincinnati, Ohio.*

The manual indicates that this inventory is "designed to help students focus on future occupations in relation to their current interests, experiences, abilities, and ambitions." Presumably after they have completed this inventory "students will have narrowed their occupational choices down to two occupational groups and two decision levels." The manual does not present any evidence, however, that these purposes are accomplished. In fact, there is no evidence presented that any of the assertions made to the students throughout the inventory are correct. Some examples: "When you finish this booklet, you will know which two groups are best for you." "After you answer these questions, you will be able to decide whether an occupation is really what you want: you will find out what the requirements are for the job, how much training you will need, about how much your salary will be, and how well the job fits in with your personal interests." These and similar assertions may or may not be correct. The problem is that in the process of responding to all the inventory items, totaling points for interests, experiences, occupations, decision levels, etc., a student (and even a nonpsychometrically trained adult) could be led to believe that there is validity for the whole system. Accordingly, a student might make some decisions about occupations based on the completion of the inventory. There simply are

no data to justify such decisions—no reliability data, no validity data, no norms, no validation of the scoring that is used, and no information on the sampling of items or the equivalence of items for the interest, experience, or occupations section of the inventory. Thus, for example, a student could get a higher total score on interest in service occupations than on interest in business contact occupations simply as a function of which activities in these domains were selected for inclusion in the inventory; no evidence is given for the equivalence of the items, i.e., item difficulty or item popularity or social desirability.

Thus, there is a complete lack of the kind of empirical evidence that would warrant a recommendation that the inventory be used with students. On the other hand, the inventory may be quite useful as a research tool provided that it is carefully explained to the participating students that their responses are for research uses only and that they should not attempt any interpretations of the results.

[1007]

★Introducing Career Concepts Inventory. Grades 5–7, 7–9; 1975; to be used as part of an instructional program; no data on reliability; no norms; 1 form (13 pages, self-marking, plus profile and worker interview); 2 levels; $16.33 per 25 tests; $3.27 per teacher's instructional guide; $4 per specimen set of either level; postage extra; [15] minutes; A. Joanne Holloway and Joan T. Naper; Science Research Associates, Inc. *
a) SERIES 1. Grades 5–7; 7 scores: interests, focus, school subjects, abilities, work features, work settings, total; teacher's guide (41 pages).
b) SERIES 2. Grades 7–9; 7 scores: work styles, work roles, skill development, training needs, income patterns, employment opportunities, total; teacher's guide (47 pages).

[1008]

★Knowledge of Occupations Test. High school; 1974; KOT; 9 scores: earnings, licensing and certification, job descriptions, employment trends, training, terminology, graphs, tools, total; no reliability data or norms for subtest scores; 1 form (8 pages); manual (8 pages); separate answer sheets must be used; $8.75 per 25 sets of test, answer sheet, and profile; $4.25 per 25 answer sheets; 75¢ per scoring stencil; $4.25 per 25 profiles; $3 per manual; $4.50 per specimen set; postage extra; 40(45) minutes; Leroy G. Baruth; Psychologists and Educators, Inc. *

REFERENCES
1. BARUTH, LEROY G. "KOT: Measuring Occupational Awareness." *Sch Shop* 34(2):47–8 O '74. *

DAVID O. HERMAN, *Assistant Director, Psychological Measurement Division, The Psychological Corporation, New York, New York.*

The *Knowledge of Occupations Test* attempts

to measure an important component of career development by means of 96 multiple choice questions, evenly divided among eight aspects of occupational information. According to the manual, the test may be used either with individuals for counseling purposes or with groups of students in connection with a career education program. For example, KOT results might be used to help plan course content, to evaluate an ongoing program, or to stimulate classroom discussion in this area of career exploration.

A brief section of the manual indicates that test content was determined and items selected for the final form according to technically adequate procedures. Nevertheless, certain characteristics of the published instrument must be questioned. Part 1 (Earnings) taps the examinee's knowledge of the average annual starting salary for workers in various occupations. While no one would deny that this information is important for making good vocational decisions, the keyed answers are likely to become dated rapidly. Furthermore, although the keyed answers may be accurate for the country as a whole, they may not reflect regional or urban-rural differences in typical salaries. The keying of at least one item does not agree with information in the 1976–77 *Occupational Outlook Handbook*: new veterinarians do not start work at an average salary of less than $8,000. Similarly Part 4, which covers expected employment trends, is tied to the 1970s and will require revision thereafter. While Part 7 (Graph Interpretation) covers a skill important for interpreting certain types of occupational information, some will feel that what amounts to a study skill has no place on an instrument of this kind. Clearly, potential users should carefully compare the test's coverage with local needs. The manual properly makes this point, but it merits emphasis.

The directions to the examinee are commendably clear, and the test should be virtually self-administering. However, a number of other details of the test materials are troublesome. The test booklet has been printed with typographical errors, some of which are likely to confuse some students. The scoring stencil is simply an answer sheet overprinted with the correct answers, and must be punched out by the user; this is difficult to do if one lacks a paper punch made for this purpose. Worst of all is the profile sheet

used for graphically illustrating the number of items correctly answered on each part of the test. No norms or reliability data are available for the eight part scores, but data presented in the manual show that the parts vary greatly in average item difficulty, so the absolute number of items answered correctly may not be compared from part to part. For these reasons, the profiled information is uninterpretable. The profile sheet is not recommended for use.

Percentile norms for the total score are presented for a group of 318 high school students in the Southwest. Although an ethnic breakdown of the sample is given, no information is presented about the number of schools or states represented in the standardization sample, nor is there a breakdown by grade. Since 41 percent of the sample was of Mexican-American background, the norms may not be generalizable for use outside the Southwest. Still, until users have developed their own local norms, the published percentiles should give a rough basis for interpreting the total score. A reliability estimate of .90 (K-R 20) indicates that the test has satisfactory reliability for most purposes.

The Competence Test of Crites's *Career Maturity Inventory* does overlap the KOT in measuring students' awareness of the duties of various jobs—and it does this in greater depth and with greater sophistication than does the corresponding 12-item section of the KOT. Schools that are content with shallower but broader coverage of occupational information may find the KOT useful in connection with their career education efforts. As indicated above, however, those considering its use should carefully review its content for suitability. The keying of the answers should also be checked locally for acceptability. And finally, users should avoid using the profile sheet, for it will tend to promote invalid and misleading interpretation.

DEAN H. NAFZIGER, *Director, Assessment Program, Northwest Regional Educational Laboratory, Portland, Oregon.*

The purpose of this test is to measure high school students' knowledge of occupations. According to the test manual, "Results of the test can be used in curriculum planning, instruction, and counseling."

The test consists of 96 items, 12 items in each of eight areas. Items are all multiple choice or matching. Test administration is limited to 40 minutes. Tests are hand scored with an accompanying scoring key. No information is given about scoring time, but this reviewer estimates that scoring will take less than five minutes per student. Although the test appears to address eight cogent areas about occupations, examination of the test raises serious questions about the thoroughness of the test development, appropriateness of the test content, and adequacy of the technical characteristics. Content of the test reflects the author's judgments about the importance of various types of information based upon his examination of vocational and career materials. The development of the test did not follow from any clearly discernible theoretical or empirical approach. There is no evidence that the author developed a blueprint describing any of the areas tested. Rather, the content results from the author's review of a limited amount of material, and decisions about test content seem arbitrary. As a result, even though the eight areas covered by the test seem cogent, the questions covering those areas do not seem representative or important.

The problem of the arbitrary selection of items is compounded by other difficulties with items in several of the sections. For example, the items dealing with average income in various jobs require students to classify average *starting* salaries of jobs into three ranges—below $8,000, between $8,000 and $12,000, and above $12,000. Since this range of salaries is very narrow, the probability of error is high even for students who are familiar with the occupations. Also, the salary figures do not reflect inflation since the test was written. Moreover, these items do not address issues about income that are most important: the range of income for people who are established in various jobs, the rate and likelihood of salary increases that might be expected in various jobs, and the comparative salaries in various types of jobs.

Items dealing with job descriptions suffer from severe problems. A marked lack of parallelism among the item stems causes confusion. A lack of agreement occurs between the item stems and the alternatives; most item stems use plural verbs, while all alternatives consist of singular nouns. The occupations included in this set of items are clerical, medical, or research related. In aggregate, these occupations account

for a small proportion of the work force, and most of those occupations (10 of 15) are those which demand extensive training beyond college. In short, these items poorly represent job descriptions students should know.

Problems similar to those noted above occur elsewhere throughout the test. In addition, there are other problems that bespeak a general lack of care in the development of the test. These problems include items that are keyed incorrectly, item alternatives that are neither parallel nor mutually exclusive, and matching items for which several correct matches are feasible.

According to the manual, the test is content valid because it is based upon the author's review of vocational and career guidance material. The author's selection of content was corroborated by experienced counselors and counselor educators. To the extent that the review was carefully conducted, content validity of the test has been enhanced. However, there is no evidence that the review process was extensive, and the lack of care that was given to the development of items serves as an unsettling indicator that the reviews were likewise limited. There is little evidence supporting the content validity of the test.

Reliability coefficients were not calculated for the eight separate sections of the test. Only a single K-R 20 (.90) across all 96 items of the test was calculated. Because each section of the test is complete within itself and differs from other sections in content and form, separate coefficients should have been provided.

The test was normed on a group of 318 high school students from the Southwestern United States. Teachers who believed they could use information from the test for their career education classes allowed their students to participate in the norming trial. No information is provided on the number of classrooms, schools, or cities included in the norming group or the distribution of students among age groups. The norm group clearly is restricted to students of only one region of the country, and there is no evidence that the group is representative of appropriate students in that region. Thus, the norm group seems totally inadequate as a basis for making test interpretations.

Use of the test has not been adequately planned. It is intended that scores be transformed to percentile scores for use. However,

Knowledge of Occupations Test

no clear commitment is made to the use of either the raw scores or norm-referenced scores, and no meaningful guidance about using test results is provided in the test manual. This particularly can be seen from the student profile sheet, which calls for students' raw scores to be plotted for each of the eight areas tested. The resulting profile of raw scores is displayed prominently.

However, the unavailability of percentiles for the eight areas contradicts the statement in the test manual that "raw scores on most tests are in themselves of but limited significance. In the case of this test meaningful interpretation of scores is made possible by percentile norms." The only percentile score provided for a student is for the entire test, and it receives little prominence on the profile sheet. The interpretations that can be made on the basis of this single percentile score are not meaningful. The format of the answer sheet, however, will clearly encourage teachers and students to use raw scores for making interpretations about strengths and weaknesses in each of the eight areas covered by the test.

SUMMARY. The *Knowledge of Occupations Test* is an effort to provide career education teachers with an instrument that can be used as a part of their classroom instruction. The test has little to offer these teachers, however. The content has not been adequately planned, and it does not measure important knowledge about jobs. The development of items is marked by a considerable lack of thoroughness and care. There is little evidence to support the validity of the test. Finally, insufficient attention has been given to the reporting of test results or to the use of the test.

A major redevelopment of the test is required before it can be regarded as making a contribution to the measurement of occupational knowledge. This reviewer sees no circumstances under which the use of the test would be advised.

[1009]

*Kuder General Interest Survey. Grades 6–12; 1934–76; KGIS; 11 scores: outdoor, mechanical, computational, scientific, persuasive, artistic, literary, musical, social service, clerical, verification; 1 form; 2 editions; $2.90 per specimen set of either edition; postage extra; (45–60) minutes; G. Frederic Kuder; Science Research Associates, Inc. *

a) SELF-SCORING CONSUMABLE EDITION. 1934–76; Form E ('76, 25 pages, identical to 1963 edition except for some minor word changes and the addition of a paragraph on separate sex norms); manual ('75, 53 pages,

essentially the same as the 1964 edition with the addition of a paragraph on separate sex norms); instructions ('70, 4 pages); $12 per 25 tests.
b) MACHINE SCORING EDITION. 1934–63; Form E ('63, 19 pages); DocuTran manual ('63, 15 pages); profile ('63, 1 page); separate answer sheets (NCS) must be used; test materials and scoring service, $27.50 per 25 tests.

For reviews by Barbara A. Kirk, Paul R. Lohnes, and John N. McCall, and excerpted reviews by T. R. Husek and Robert F. Stahmann, see 7:1024 (8 references).

REFERENCES

1–8. See 7:1024.
9. KARAGAN, NICHOLAS JAMES. *The Relationship Between Similarity of Teacher-Pupil Interests and School Grades.* Doctor's thesis, University of Iowa (Iowa City, Iowa), 1972. (*DAI* 33:4175A)
10. SHANN, MARY H. "The Interest Dimension as a Determinant of Career Choice of Vocational High School Boys." *Meas & Eval Guid* 4(4):197–205 Ja '72. * (*PA* 48:5723)
11. BECKER, SONIA. *The Relationship of Discrepancy Between Expressed and Inventoried Interest Scores to Selected Personality Variables: A Study of Adolescents.* Doctor's thesis, Loyola University (Chicago, Ill.), 1973. (*DAI* 34:129A)
12. CHANCE, DOUGLAS LEROY. *A Factorial Study of Certain Standardized Measurements for Inclusion in a Model Predicting Enrollment in a Non-College Preparatory Curriculum.* Doctor's thesis, McNeese State University (Lake Charles, La.), 1973. (*DAI* 34:2909A)
13. HARMON, LENORE W. "Sexual Bias in Interest Measurement." *Meas & Eval Guid* 5(4):496–501 Ja '73. * (*PA* 50:3999)
14. LOMBARD, JACK. *Career Guidance and the Kuder Interest Inventories.* Chicago, Ill.: Science Research Associates, 1973. Pp. iii, 41. *
15. ORTA, SIMON L. *Occupational Aspirations of Mexican-American and Anglo-American Senior High School Students.* Doctor's thesis, University of Nebraska (Lincoln, Neb.), 1973. (*DAI* 34:2342A)
16. PILATO, GUY T., AND MYERS, ROGER A. "Effects of Computer-Mediated Vocational Guidance Procedures: Accuracy of Self-Knowledge." *J Voc Behav* 3(2):167–74 Ap '73. * (*PA* 50:9978)
17. ROBINSON, HAROLD RAYMOND. *A Comparison of American Indian and White Student Occupational Interests With Respect to Family Background Factors.* Doctor's thesis, University of Nebraska (Lincoln, Neb.), 1973. (*DAI* 34:2312A)
18. McCARTHY, MAUREEN. "A Study of the Kuder General Interest Survey in a Nigerian Technical College." *West African J Ed & Voc Meas* (Nigeria) 2(1):1–6 D '74. * (*PA* 54:10654)
19. FALDET, BURTON W. *Relationships Between the Measured Interests of Seventh Grade Students and Their Parents.* Doctor's thesis, Northern Illinois University (DeKalb, Ill.), 1975. (*DAI* 36:6547A)
20. FREEMAN, ARTHUR. *Vocational Interest Patterns of Learning Disabled Adolescent Males.* Doctor's thesis, Columbia University (New York, N.Y.), 1975. (*DAI* 36:1388A)
21. KLINE, PAUL. *Psychology of Vocational Guidance,* pp. 136–9. New York: John Wiley & Sons, Inc., [1975]. Pp. xiii, 253. *
22. PILATO, GUY T., AND MYERS, ROGER A. "The Effects of Computer-Mediated Vocational Guidance Procedures on the Appropriateness of Vocational Preference." *J Voc Behav* 6(1):61–72 F '75. * (*PA* 53:12668)
23. COHEN, MARTIN PAUL. *Interest and Its Relationship to Problem-solving Ability Among Secondary School Mathematics Students.* Doctor's thesis, University of Texas (Austin, Texas), 1976. (*DAI* 37:4929A)
24. ZYTOWSKI, DONALD G. "Long-Term Profile Stability of the Kuder Occupational Interest Survey." *Ed & Psychol Meas* 36(3):689–92 au '76. * (*PA* 57:4780)

[1010]

*Kuder Occupational Interest Survey. Grades 11–16 and adults; 1956–76; KOIS; items same as those in *Kuder Preference Record—Occupational* but scored differently; 114 occupational scores and 48 college-major scores; Form DD ('64, NCS test-answer sheet); manual ('76, 69 pages); instructions ('74, 4 pages); interpretive leaflet ('74, 4 pages); $40 per 20 tests; purchase price includes scoring of tests which may be submitted in any quantity; $3.90 per specimen set (includes scoring); postage extra; (30–40) minutes; G. Frederic Kuder; Science Research Associates, Inc. *

See T2:2194 (13 references); for reviews by Robert H. Dolliver and W. Bruce Walsh, and excerpted reviews by Frederick G. Brown and Robert F. Stahmann, see 7:1025 (19 references).

REFERENCES

1–19. See 7:1025.
20–32. See T2:2194; also includes a cumulative name index to the first 32 references, 2 reviews, and 2 excerpts for this test.
33. HOHENSHIL, THOMAS H. *A Comparison of the Inventoried Interests of Selected Types of Guidance Specialists in Ohio.* Doctor's thesis, Kent State University (Kent, Ohio), 1971. (*DAI* 34:3872A)
34. CAREK, ROMAN. "Another Look at the Relationships Between Similar Scales on the Strong Vocational Interest Blank and Kuder Occupational Interest Survey." *J Counsel Psychol* 19(3):218–23 My '72. * (*PA* 48:9739)
35. COLE, NANCY S. "On Measuring the Vocational Interests of Women." *ACT Res Rep* 49:1–11 Mr '72. * (*PA* 48:9970)
36. O'SHEA, ARTHUR J., AND HARRINGTON, THOMAS F., JR. "Strong Vocational Interest Blank and Kuder Occupational Interest Survey Differences Reexamined in Terms of Holland's Vocational Theory." Comments by Wilbur L. Layton and Fred H. Borgen and reply by authors. *J Counsel Psychol* 19(5):455–63 S '72. * (*PA* 49:1536)
37. O'SHEA, ARTHUR J.; LYNCH, MERVIN D.; AND HARRINGTON, THOMAS F. "A Reply to Kuder's Criticism of SVIB-KOIS Comparative Studies." *Meas & Eval Guid* 5(1):306–9 Ap '72. * (*PA* 49:3524)
38. RICHMOND, LEE JOYCE. *A Comparison of Returning Women and Regular College Age Women at a Community College.* Doctor's thesis, University of Maryland (College Park, Md.), 1972. (*DAI* 33:1028A)
39. WYSOCK, RAYMOND ANTHONY. *An Analysis of the Relationships of Selected Occupational Interests, Aptitudes, and Grade Point Averages of Industrial Arts Education Students in the State of California.* Doctor's thesis, Utah State University (Logan, Utah), 1972. (*DAI* 33:5026A)
40. STERNE, DAVID M. "The Kuder Occupational Interest Survey With Hospitalized VA Counselees." *Newsl Res Psychol* 14(1):5–7 F '72. * (*PA* 50:9690)
41. ZYTOWSKI, DONALD G. "A Concurrent Test of Accuracy-of-Classification for the Strong Vocational Interest and Kuder Occupational Interest Survey." *J Voc Behav* 2(3):245–50 Jl '72. * (*PA* 49:5809)
42. ZYTOWSKI, DONALD G. "Equivalence of the Kuder Occupational Interest Survey and the Strong Vocational Interest Blank Revisited." *J Appl Psychol* 56(2):184–5 Ap '72. * (*PA* 48:7950)
43. BARNETTE, W. LESLIE, JR.; D'COSTA, AYRES; HARMON, LENORE W.; SUPER, DONALD E.; WEISS, DAVID J.; AND ZYTOWSKI, DONALD G. Chap. 9, "Illustrative Interpretations of Inventories," pp. 206–44. In *Contemporary Approaches to Interest Measurement.* Edited by Donald G. Zytowski. Minneapolis, Minn.: University of Minnesota Press, 1973. Pp. xi, 251. *
44. COLE, NANCY S. "On Measuring the Vocational Interests of Women." *J Counsel Psychol* 20(2):105–12 Mr '73. * (*PA* 50:3974)
45. GARDNER, RILEY W. "Relationships Between Similar Scales of Two Major Interest Inventories." *Percept & Motor Skills* 36(2):635–8 Ap '73. * (*PA* 51:3962)
46. HARMON, LENORE W. "Sexual Bias in Interest Measurement." *Meas & Eval Guid* 5(4):496–501 Ja '73. * (*PA* 50:3999)
47. STAHMANN, ROBERT F., AND MATHESON, GEORGE F. "The Kuder OIS as a Measure of Vocational Maturity." *Ed & Psychol Meas* 33(2):477–9 su '73. * (*PA* 51:6007)
48. ZYTOWSKI, DONALD G. Chap. 1, "Considerations in the Selection and Use of Interest Inventories," pp. 3–19. In his *Contemporary Approaches to Interest Measurement.* Minneapolis, Minn.: University of Minnesota Press, 1973. Pp. xi, 251. *
49. ZYTOWSKI, DONALD G. Chap. 5, "The Kuder Occupational Interest Survey," pp. 116–35. In his *Contemporary Approaches to Interest Measurement.* Minneapolis, Minn.: University of Minnesota Press, 1973. Pp. xi, 251. *
50. ANDERSON, J.; GALE, JANET; MARSDEN, P.; PETTINGALE, P. W.; SHAFFER, P.; AND TOMLINSON, R. W. S. "Vocational Preferences in Medicine and Dentistry at King's College Hospital Medical School." *Brit J Med Ed* 8(4):246–50 D '74. *
51. BROWN, RONALD HAYWOOD. *Class, Race and Athletics: A Study of Adolescent Aspiration, Intention and Interests.* Doctor's thesis, Boston University (Boston, Mass.), 1974. (*DAI* 35:6241A)
52. EPANCHIN, ALEXIS. *The Effect of Alternate Scoring Methods on Predictive Efficiencies for the Kuder Occupational Interest Inventories Used With Engineers.* Doctor's thesis, Duke University (Durham, N.C.), 1974. (*DAI* 35:5810A)
53. HERGER, CHARLES GEORGE. *Assessment of the Relationship of Selective Student Variables to Career Development in an Employer-Based Career Education Program.* Doctor's thesis, University of Washington (Seattle, Wash.), 1974. (*DAI* 35:3457A)
54. HOHENSHIL, THOMAS H. "Inventoried Vocational Interests of Vocational Counselors." *Voc Guid Q* 23(1):24–7 S '74. * (*PA* 53:12648)
55. HOHENSHIL, THOMAS H., AND HINKLE, DENNIS E. "A Comparison of the Inventoried Vocational Interests of Selected Types of School Counselors." *Meas & Eval Guid* 6(4):239–46 Ja '74. * (*PA* 52:1741)
56. NAFZIGER, DEAN H., AND HELMS, SAMUEL T. "Cluster Analyses of Interest Inventory Scales as Tests of Holland's Occupational Classification." *J Appl Psychol* 59(3):344–53 Je '74. * (*PA* 52:13320)
57. STERNE, DAVID M. "The Kuder OIS and Rankings of Vocational Preference." *Ed & Psychol Meas* 34(1):63–8 sp '74. * (*PA* 53:2048)
58. BIRK, JANICE M. Chap. 6, "Reducing Sex Bias: Factors Affecting the Client's View of the Use of Career Interest Inventories," pp. 101–21. In *Issues of Sex Bias and Sex Fairness in Career Interest Measurement.* Edited by Esther E. Diamond. Washington, D.C.: National Institute of Education, 1975. Pp. xxix, 219. *
59. GUNTER, KAY CHILCUTT. *Differential Effects of Three Types of Career Guidance Upon Community Junior College Students' Self Concepts and Vocational Crystallization.* Doctor's thesis, University of Southern Mississippi (Hattiesburg, Miss.), 1975. (*DAI* 36:2023A)
60. HOCKERT, SHELBY ANN. *The Relationship Between Personality Type and Choice of College Major.* Doctor's thesis, University of Minnesota (Minneapolis, Minn.), 1975. (*DAI* 36:3004B)
61. JOHANSSON, CHARLES B. Chap. 4, "Technical Aspects: Problems of Scale Development, Norms, Item Differences by Sex, and the Rate of Change in Occupational Group Characteristics," pp. 65–88. In *Issues of Sex Bias and Sex Fairness in Career Interest Measurement.* Edited by Esther E. Diamond. Washington, D.C.: National Institute of Education, 1975. Pp. xxix, 219. *
62. McCARTHY, THOMAS B. *An Investigation of the Occupational Goals, Abilities, Academic Achievement, and Occupational Interest of Brothers in Clerical Communities as Factors in Core Curriculum Development.* Doctor's thesis, Catholic University of America (Washington, D.C.), 1975. (*DAI* 36:1310A)
63. OLEJNIK, STEPHEN, AND PORTER, ANDREW C. "An Empirical Investigation Comparing the Effectiveness of Four Scoring Strategies on the Kuder Occupational Interest Survey Form DD." *Ed & Psychol Meas* 35(1):37–46 sp '75. *
64. TANNEY, MARY FAITH. Chap. 5, "Face Validity of Interest Measures: Sex-Role Stereotyping," pp. 89–99. In *Issues of Sex Bias and Sex Fairness in Career Interest Measurement.* Edited by Esther E. Diamond. Washington, D.C.: National Institute of Education, 1975. Pp. xxix, 219. *
65. WESTBROOK, FRANKLIN D. "High Scales on the Strong Vocational Interest Blank and the Kuder Occupational Interest Survey Using Holland's Occupational Codes." *J Counsel Psychol* 22(1):24–7 Ja '75. * (*PA* 53:8417)
66. AKPAN, MONDAY PAUL. *The Impact of Career Education Program Upon Measured Occupational Interests.* Doctor's thesis, Rutgers—The State University (New Brunswick, N.J.), 1976. (*DAI* 37:7714A)
67. DENKER, ELENOR RUBIN, AND TITTLE, CAROL KEHR. "'Reasonableness' of KOIS Results for Re-entry Women: Implications for Test Validity." *Ed & Psychol Meas* 36(2):495–500 su '76. *
68. TITTLE, CAROL KEHR, AND DENKER, ELENOR RUBIN. "Home-Career Conflict Reduction Revisited: The Effect of Experimental Directions on KOIS Scores for Women." *Ed & Psychol Meas* 36(4):1079–87 w '76. * (*PA* 58:187)
69. ZYTOWSKI, DONALD G. "Factor Analysis of the Kuder Occupational Interest Survey." *Meas & Eval Guid* 9(3):120–3 O '76. *
70. ZYTOWSKI, DONALD G. "Predictive Validity of the Kuder Occupational Interest Survey: A 12- to 19-Year Follow-up." *J Counsel Psychol* 23(3):221–33 My '76. * (*PA* 56:1671)
71. BECKER, SONIA. "Personality Correlates of the Discrepancy Between Expressed and Inventoried Interest Scores." *Meas & Eval Guid* 10(1):24–30 Ap '77. *
72. DIAMOND, STEPHEN R.; KELLER, HAROLD R.; AND MOBLEY, LINDA A. "Adults' Performance on Formal Operations: General Ability or Scientific Interest." *Percept & Motor Skills* 44(1):249–50 F '77. *
73. TITTLE, CAROL KEHR, AND DENKER, ELENOR RUBIN. "Kuder Occupational Interest Survey Profiles of Reentry Women." *J Counsel Psychol* 24(4):293–300 Jl '77. *

[1011]

Kuder Preference Record—Vocational. Grades 9–16 and adults; 1934–76; KPR–V; also called *Kuder C;* for revision and downward extension, see *Kuder General Interest Survey* (Kuder E); 11 scores: outdoor, mechanical, computational, scientific, persuasive, artistic, literary, musical, social service, clerical, verification; no data on reliability in manual; Form CP ('76, 16 pages plus answer pads, essentially the same as test copyrighted 1948); revised manual ('72, c1960, 27 pages); memorandum of instructions ('70, 4 pages); $15.75 per 25 tests; $5.50 per 25 pins and 25 backboards; $2.80 per specimen set; postage extra; manual free on request; (30–40) minutes; Frederic Kuder; Science Research Associates, Inc. *

See T2:2195 (302 references); for a review by Martin Katz, see 6:1063 (148 references); for reviews by Clifford P. Froehlich and John Pierce-Jones, see 5:863 (211 references); for reviews by Edward S. Bordin, Harold D. Carter, and H. M. Fowler, see 4:742 (144 references); for reviews by Ralph F. Berdie, E. G. Chambers, and Donald E. Super and an excerpted review by Arthur H. Brayfield of an earlier edition, see 3:640 (60 references); for reviews by A. B. Crawford and Arthur E. Traxler, see 2:1671 (2 references).

REFERENCES

1–2. See 2:1671.
3–62. See 3:640.
63–208. See 4:742.
209–419. See 5:863.
420–567. See 6:1063.
568–869. See T2:2195; also includes a cumulative name index to the first 869 references, 11 reviews, and 1 excerpt for this test.

870. THOMAS, CHARLES A. "Special Report on a Test Analysis of a Group of Time Study Men." *Adv Mgmt* 18:13 3–13 '53. * (*PA* 28:5097)
871. SINGH, HIRA; SRIVASTAVA, M. L.; AND GUPTA, G. L. "Interest Patterns of 300 Male Prisoners of Model Jail, Lucknow." *J Correct Work* (India) 10:80–7 O '63. *
872. MANN, HORACE, JR. *A Study of Selected Academic and Interest Variables in Relation to Achievement in a College of Engineering.* Doctor's thesis, Oklahoma State University (Stillwater, Okla.), 1971. (*DAI* 33:591A)
873. BEAUMONT, JOACHIM BALLIRIAIN. *Level of Item Specificity and the Measurement of Inventoried Interests.* Doctor's thesis, Columbia University (New York, N.Y.), 1972. (*DAI* 33:2365B)
874. BURGESS, MICHAEL M.; DUFFEY, MARGERY; AND TEMPLE, FRANCES G. "Two Studies of Prediction of Success in a Collegiate Program of Nursing." *Nursing Res* 21(4):357–66 Jl–Ag '72. *
875. BUTLER, F. J. J.; CRINNION, J.; AND MARTIN, JEAN. "The Kuder Preference Record in Adult Vocational Guidance." *Occup Psychol* (England) 46(2):99–104 '72. * (*PA* 51:12093)
876. DAY, H. I. "Intrinsic Motivation and Vocational Choice." *J Psychol* 81(1):3–6 My '72. * (*PA* 48:9971)
877. FRANK, DAVID S. *The Relationship of Psychometric Variables to the Prediction of Success of Vocational Rehabilitation.* Doctor's thesis, West Virginia University (Morgantown, W.Va.), 1972. (*DAI* 33:1602A)
878. GODFREY, ELLEN A., AND SCHULMAN, R. E. "Age and a Group Test Battery as Predictors of Types of Crime." *J Clin Psychol* 28(3):339–52 Jl '72. * (*PA* 51:3409)
879. HAKKIO, JOAN S. *A Comparison of 1958 and 1970 Women Student Leaders at Northwestern University: Their Characteristics, Self-Concepts, and Attitudes Toward the University.* Doctor's thesis, Northwestern University (Evanston, Ill.), 1972. (*DAI* 33:2710A)
880. SCHAFFER, KAY FRANKFORTHER. *Vocational Interests and Emotional Maladjustment.* Doctor's thesis, Ohio State University (Columbus, Ohio), 1972. (*DAI* 33:921B)
881. WILLIS, ROBERT JOHN. *A Search for Predictors of Growth Through Interpersonal Interaction.* Doctor's thesis, United States International University (San Diego, Calif.), 1972. (*DAI* 33:1300B)
882. ARBUTHNOT, JACK. "Relationships Between Maturity of Moral Judgment and Measures of Cognitive Abilities." *Psychol Rep* 33(3):945–6 D '73. * (*PA* 52:4395)
883. AZEN, STANLEY P.; SNIBBE, HOMA M.; AND MONTGOMERY, HUGH R. "A Longitudinal Predictive Study of Success and Performance of Law Enforcement Officers." *J Appl Psychol* 57(2):190–2 Ap '73. * (*PA* 53:4206)
884. GAFFNEY, JAMES PATRICK. *The Interrelationship of Scholastic Aptitude and Selected Personality Variables to Academic Achievement at the College Level.* Doctor's thesis, University of Cincinnati (Cincinnati, Ohio), 1973. (*DAI* 34:4617A)
885. GRIMSLEY, GLEN, AND JARRETT, HILTON F. "The Relation of Past Managerial Achievement to Test Measures Obtained in the Employment Situation: Methodology and Results." *Personnel Psychol* 26(1):31–48 sp '73. * (*PA* 51:2011)
886. HARMON, LENORE W. "Sexual Bias in Interest Measurement." *Meas & Eval Guid* 5(4):496–501 Ja '73. * (*PA* 50:3999)
887. LOEB, JANE, AND BOWERS, JOHN. "Programs of Study as a Basis for Selection, Placement and Guidance of College Students." *J Ed Meas* 10(2):131–9 su '73. * (*PA* 51:3970)
888. LOMBARD, JACK. *Career Guidance and the Kuder Interest Inventories.* Chicago, Ill.: Science Research Associates, 1973. Pp. iii, 41. *
889. RADTKE, ROLAND R. *A Comparison of the GATB, Kuder Preference, Henmon-Nelson, and Shopwork Scores of Ninth Grade Students at Brillion, Wisconsin, High School to Ascertain a Correlation for Vocational Guidance.* Master's thesis, University of Wisconsin (Platteville, Wis.), 1973.
890. STEPHENS, PHIL A. *The Effect of a Simulation Gaming Technique and Supplementary Activities on Modification of Occupational Interests Toward Congruence With Aptitudes of Ninth Grade Students.* Doctor's thesis, University of Southern California (Los Angeles, Calif.), 1973. (*DAI* 34:3891A)
891. TIEDEMAN, DAVID V. "Comment on Self-Estimate Ability in Adolescence." *J Counsel Psychol* 20(4):303–5 Jl '73. * (*PA* 51:3976)
892. TIERNEY, ROGER J., AND HERMAN, AL. "Self-Estimate Ability in Adolescence." *J Counsel Psychol* 20(4):298–302 Jl '73. * (*PA* 51:3977)
893. TORREY, DAVID ADRIAN. *The Validity of the Kuder Preference Record Vocational Form C as a Predictor of Future Occupational Behavior When Administered at the Ninth Grade Level in a Rural/Depressed Area.* Master's thesis, St. Bonaventure University (St. Bonaventure, N.Y.), 1973.
894. ZIMMERMAN, LAWRENCE EUGENE. *A Study of the Success of New Registrants When Programmed With and Without Counselor Use of the Science Research Associates—Test of Education Ability, the Kuder Preference Record-Vocational, and Test Result Feedback.* Doctor's thesis, University of Wyoming (Laramie, Wyo.), 1973. (*DAI* 34:2320A)
895. AYERS, JERRY B., AND ROHR, MICHAEL E. "Relationship of Selected Variables to Success in a Teacher Preparation Program." *Ed & Psychol Meas* 34(4):955–7 w '74. * (*PA* 54:6355)
896. HUNKE, EDMUND WILLIAM, JR. *A Multivariate Analysis of Selected Variables of Clergymen Serving High Achievement and Low Achievement Churches.* Doctor's thesis, Arizona State University (Tempe, Ariz.), 1974. (*DAI* 35:1744A)
897. SACCUZZO, DENNIS P.; HIGGINS, GWENDOLYN; AND LEWANDOWSKI, DENIS. "Program for Psychological Assessment of Law Enforcement Officers: Initial Evaluation." *Psychol Rep* 35(1, pt 2):651–4 Ag '74. * (*PA* 53:8440)
898. ZYTOWSKI, DONALD G. "Predictive Validity of the Kuder Preference Record, Form B, Over a 25-Year Span." *Meas & Eval Guid* 7(2):122–9 Jl '74. * (*PA* 53:4169)
899. GRIMSLEY, GLEN, AND JARRETT, HILTON F. "The Relation of Past Managerial Achievement to Test Measures Obtained in the Employment Situation: Methodology and Results-II." *Personnel Psychol* 28(2):215–31 su '75. * (*PA* 55:11144)
900. HOLLAND, JOHN L., AND NAFZIGER, DEAN H. "A Note on the Validity of the Self-Directed Search." *Meas & Eval Guid* 7(4):259–62 Ja '75. * (*PA* 53:12554)
901. LANGSTON, IRA WRIGHT, IV. *Curricular Program Effects on Vocational Interests and Academic Ability Over a Four Year Period.* Doctor's thesis, University of Illinois (Urbana, Ill.), 1975. (*DAI* 36:2633A)
902. HURT, DAVID J., AND HOLEN, MICHAEL C. "Work Values in Vocational Interest Exploration." *J Voc Behav* 8(1):89–93 F '76. *
903. KAUFMAN, JACK JUNIOR. *Development of an Instrument to be Used in Selecting Psychiatric Aides.* Doctor's thesis, Auburn University (Auburn, Ala.), 1976. (*DAI* 37:3347B)
904. PEIRCE, STEPHEN WALTER. *An Interbattery Factor Analysis of the Domains of Personality and Interest as Assessed by the GZTS and the KPR-V.* Doctor's thesis, University of Kansas (Lawrence, Kan.), 1976. (*DAI* 37:4869A)
905. DESCOMBES, JEAN-PIERRE. "Validation and Follow-Up Study of a French Adaptation of the Kuder Preference Record-Vocational on About 1800 Swiss French-Speaking Adolescents." *J Voc Behav* 11(1):31–50 Ag '77. *

LENORE W. HARMON, *Professor of Educational Psychology and Assistant Vice Chancellor, The University of Wisconsin-Milwaukee, Milwaukee, Wisconsin.*

The Kuder C seems to have been abandoned by its publishers, although it still could be a useful inventory for public use.

Interest inventories are constructed in one of two ways: empirically by selecting items which differentiate occupational groups or by selecting items which are related to form homogeneous scales. Empirical construction results in scales for specific occupations. Homogeneous construction results in broad general scales for types of occupations. The Kuder C was the early popular inventory of the homogeneous type. The first two published forms, A and B, are out of print and one gets the feeling that Form C will join them soon. If it does, its survivors will be the *Kuder General Interest Survey* (Form E), an inventory with homogeneous scales developed for children as young as sixth grade, and the *Kuder Occupational Interest Survey* (Form DD), an inventory with empirical scales, for grades 11–16 and adults. Since both differ in important ways from Form C its demise would leave a gap.

The manual for the Kuder C contains no information on the development of the inventory, the reliability or validity of the scales, or the composition of the norm groups for boys, girls, men, and women. Some of this information was previously available. Its disappearance leads me to conclude that the publishers have abandoned Form C and that the public should probably do so too, not because of poor quality but because of inadequate information.

Earlier reviews compared the Kuder inventories (A, B, and C) with the earlier forms of the *Strong Vocational Interest Blank*. This comparison was not necessarily a legitimate one since the Kuder inventories had homogeneous scales and the Strong scales were empirically derived. The two types of scales have utility with people in different stages of career development and need not be compared. At any rate, the Kuder inventories usually lost in this comparison because there was little evidence of predictive validity. However, Zytowski (*898*) has since presented evidence of predictive validity. In fact, there is more evidence of predictive validity for the Kuder inventories than for any of the other more recent entries into the field of interest measurement which utilize homogeneous scales. It is unfortunate that the only remaining form of the Kuder to which those findings can be generalized is accompanied by such an inadequate manual that it cannot be recommended. Test users should not use any inventory which is not accompanied by complete technical information no matter how good its reputation or sales record.

Kuder Preference Record—Vocational

[1012]

*Milwaukee Academic Interest Inventory. Grades 12–14; 1973-74; MAII; 8 scores: 6 field variables (physical science, healing occupations, behavioral science, economics, humanities-social studies, elementary education) plus 2 discriminant variables (commercial vs. nurturant interests, natural science vs. social studies interests); no data on reliability for discriminant variables; norms for discriminant variables consist of means only; 1 form ('73, 4 pages); manual ('73, 6 pages plus test); scoring directions ('74, 1 page); separate answer sheets must be used; $14 per kit of 10 tests, 25 answer sheets, manual, and scoring keys; $9.50 per 25 tests; $6.50 per set of scoring keys; $8.50 per 100 answer sheets; $2.50 per manual; 8% extra for postage and handling; (20–30) minutes; Andrew R. Baggaley; Western Psychological Services. *

See T2:2196 (4 references).

REFERENCES

1–4. See T2:2196.
5. BAGGALEY, ANDREW R. "The Stability of Interest Variables and Items During Adolescence." *J Multiv Exp Pers & Clin Psychol* 1(2):38–45 f '74. * (PA 56:6834)

AUSTIN C. FRANK, *Director, Office of Student Affairs Research, University of California, Berkeley, California.*

It is surprising that more than 50 years after the first sustained, successful attempts to measure interest, after all the intervening research, and after all the work that has been done establishing standards for test development and reportage, inventories continue to be presented which are relatively untouched by many of the major relevant events of the past. The MAII would have been an intriguing test in the early 1930s, but despite some competent developmental work and some reasonable supporting data, it lacks much that consumers today have a right to expect.

The inventory's purpose is "to aid in the counseling of college freshmen and sophomores and college-bound high school students." A student answers 150 items as "true," "false," or "?" and these are then hand-scored with overlay keys on eight scales. Six scales are called field variables (physical science, healing occupations, behavioral science, economics, humanities-social studies, and elementary education) and are based on aggregations of academic majors in those general areas. Scores on these scales are normed and profiled. Two other scales are called discriminant variables (commercial vs. nurturant interests, natural science vs. social studies interests) and were derived by factor and discriminant analyses. These raw scores are entered as a point on a bivariate graph which is printed with the locations of

19 academic fields of concentration for comparison purposes.

The development, validation, and interpretation materials in the slender six-page manual raise many significant questions, and mere reference to three journal articles by the author is not adequate. The items appear reasonable and straightforward, but the size of the subdivided developmental sample is very small by interest measurement standards.

The six field variable scales were developed by following a group of 313 tested freshmen, identifying those who were in particular academic fields 2½ years later, and contrasting their item responses with the pooled responses of all students used to create the scales. Facts related to important interest measurement issues such as the composition and representativeness of the reference group and size and nature of the criterion groups are not provided. The standard deviation of the scores obtained by the criterion groups is not given and it is impossible to know how much overlap there is of scores between students in one field and students in another, or students in general. What, then, constitutes a significant score? Are the scores of students who are juniors in college and majoring in a particular field really what we want to use as a standard for counseling college freshmen? Wouldn't the freshmen scores of graduating seniors or people who actually go into particular career areas be a better standard? Will women in various fields score differently than men on this inventory and possibly be counseled in different directions? How will minorities fare?

Quite a few well-developed interest inventories (e.g., the Strong-Campbell and Kuder instruments) are now available to college and high school counselors and provide for sex differences where they exist, and a direct assessment of interests both in the form of homogeneous scales such as mathematics and empirical scales keyed to occupational membership such as engineering. Many of these instruments are backed by research relating their scores directly to college majors so that they provide a potential wealth of material for educational as well as vocational counseling. Some are also linked to psychological theories helpful in counseling, such as those put forward by Holland. Under these circumstances it is difficult to imagine

situations in which the *Milwaukee Academic Interest Inventory* with its limited range of scales and problematic test-development underpinnings would be a first choice counseling and advising instrument.

[1013]

New Mexico Career Education Test Series. Grades 9–12; 1973; "designed to assess specific learner objectives in the area of career education"; criterion referenced; no reliability data or norms for grades 10 and 11; no suggested standards of mastery; 6 tests; manual (12 pages); separate answer sheets must be used; $8.50 per 35 tests; $2 per 35 answer sheets; $2.50 per manual; $17.50 per specimen set; postpaid; Charles C. Healy and Stephen P. Klein; Monitor. *

a) NM ATTITUDE TOWARD WORK TEST. NMATWT; 1 form (3 pages); $1 per scoring stencil; $3.75 per specimen set; 15(20) minutes.

b) NM CAREER PLANNING TEST. NMCPT; Forms A, B, (3 pages); prices same as for *a*; 20(25) minutes.

c) NM CAREER ORIENTED ACTIVITIES CHECKLIST. NM-COAC; 1 form (3 pages); $1.50 per set of scoring stencils; $3.75 per specimen set; 20(25) minutes.

d) NM KNOWLEDGE OF OCCUPATIONS TEST. NMKOT; 1 form (3 pages); $1 per scoring stencil; $3.75 per specimen set; 20(25) minutes.

e) NM JOB APPLICATION PROCEDURES TEST. NMJAPT; 1 form (3 pages); prices and time same as for *d*.

f) NM CAREER DEVELOPMENT TEST. NMCDT; 1 form (3 pages); prices and time same as for *d*.

REFERENCES
1. PREDIGER, DALE. "Review of the New Mexico Career Education Test Series." *Meas & Eval Guid* 8(4):260–2 Ja '76. *
2. WESTBROOK, BERT W. "Review of the New Mexico Career Education Test Series." *Meas & Eval Guid* 8(4):263–6 Ja '76. *

JACK L. BODDEN, *Area Director, Central Counties Center for MH-MR Services, Temple, Texas.*

Its authors claim that the NMCETS is a battery of criterion-referenced tests designed to assess specific learner objectives in the career education area. The subtests can presumably be used individually or collectively to evaluate the impact of high school career education programs. While this seems to be a reasonable and worthy objective to pursue, there is no evidence that the NMCETS even comes close to this goal.

The manual describes the tests as "criterion referenced," but it is unclear what this actually means. In psychometric terminology, a criterion-oriented approach to test construction means that items are selected for a test because they correlate with some specific "criteria" (usually some type of performance in daily life such as grades in school). If a criterion-oriented procedure was followed in developing the NMCETS, it is not made explicit by the manual.

The tests appear to be easy to administer and score. Directions in the manual for these purposes appear adequate. Each subtest has a time limit of either 15 or, in most cases, 20 minutes. Test-taking instructions appear clear and easy for students to understand; however, there are no data regarding the reading level required by the tests.

Frankly, it is difficult for this reviewer to find anything positive to say about the psychometric properties of the NMCETS. The internal-consistency reliability estimates range from .51 to .87, with the average near .66. Since these alpha coefficients represent upper limit estimates of the reliability of the tests, these reliabilities are not at all impressive. It should be noted that the relatively low reliabilities may be due, at least in part, to the small number of items making up the subtests.

The only evidence of validity offered by the authors is a table in the manual which shows that 12th graders score higher than 9th graders on the tests. The authors imply that this finding indicates that the tests are sensitive to gains in the students' vocational readiness. This reviewer feels that there is no basis for this implication. In essence, there is absolutely no evidence of the validity of the NMCETS. Since there are no validity data available, one has no way of knowing what, if anything, these tests are measuring. Even if it were possible to infer that the tests measured what their titles imply, there is still no empirical evidence that the measured variables have anything to do with vocational choice.

The manual is entirely inadequate for anything other than informing the potential user how to administer and score the tests. What data the manual does present are in the form of a series of tables; however, these data are either unnecessary or essentially meaningless. For example, the table of norms (which, strangely enough, omits norms for 10th and 11th graders) gives percentiles and stanine equivalents for raw scores, but nowhere is the reader given a clue as to the psychological meaning or interpretation of these scores. Also, the manual fails to inform the reader as to the manner in which the tests were constructed.

In conclusion, this reviewer feels that the stated purpose of the NMCETS is probably valid, but little or nothing else about the tests is. If the reader is concerned about evaluating the impact of a high school career education program, he would be well-advised to avoid the NMCETS. Instead, this reviewer suggests that program evaluators gather outcome data on the vocational behavior of students after the completion of a career education program. Such outcome behavior might include vocational satisfaction/satisfactoriness subsequent to initial employment or the number of job changes among essentially unrelated types of work during the first few years of employment. If program evaluators do not have the resources to follow up on program graduates to gain the type of data suggested above, they might wish to consider using test instruments which are more carefully developed and researched such as the *Career Maturity Inventory*.

Meas & Eval Guid 8(4):260–2 Ja '76. Dale Prediger. * very little information is available on the rationale, construction, norming, reliability, validity, or interpretation of the tests * it is not clear how....the NMCETS is "criterion-referenced" in the usual measurement sense of that term. Specifically, what criterion domain is referenced by each test? How was it determined? What are its boundaries? How was the domain sampled? Indeed, what was the source of the items? How were they written, tried out, revised, and selected? In short, what is the direct link between the test scores and the criterion that justifies the use of the term "criterion-referenced tests"? Healy and Klein do not provide the information needed to answer this crucial question. * The interpretation section of the manual consists of a single paragraph. One sentence is devoted to the mechanics of criterion-referenced program evaluation: "Goals such as '80 percent of the students will score higher than 20 points' can be easily evaluated by comparing the goal to the performance of the students" (p. 12). No information is given on how such goals are set or why they are meaningful. * the discussion of the use of NMCETS scores is woefully inadequate * At best, representative norms for New Mexico are provided. There is no discussion of the appropriateness of these norms for general use. * The reliabilities of most tests appear to be too low to justify the interpretation of scores to individuals as advocated in the manual. * Means for 9th and 12th graders in the norm group are

New Mexico Career Education Test Series

compared "to determine whether scores improve with exposure to the educational programs designed to make them improve" (p. 12). All t-tests between 9th and 12th grade means are statistically significant at the .001 level which "adds to the confidence that the tests are assessing incremental program effects" (p. 12). There is no description of the career education program, if any, experienced by the 12th graders but not by the 9th graders. No mention is made of control groups or expected growth increments. The fallacies in this use of normative data to assess "incremental program effects" should be obvious. No doubt, the difference in the heights of 9th and 12th graders would be statistically significant also. No information on the reading level of the NMCETS is given. However, all but the attitude test require a substantial amount of reading. * No information is provided on the sensitivity of the attitude scale to "faking good" or "putting one's best foot forward." * [In summary, the test series] has few redeeming qualities. The test series should be clearly marked experimental and its use restricted to studies needed to determine and improve its characteristics. Until these studies are completed, NMCETS results should not be used in ongoing educational programs. [See reply by author Charles C. Healy, in the same journal issue, pp. 266–8.]

Meas & Eval Guid 8(4):263–6 Ja '76. Bert W. Westbrook. * The manual does not document its claim that the subobjectives are those which are "frequently incorporated into career education programs." Coverage of career development behaviors is comprehensive. * The Attitude toward Work Test is a 25-item Likert-type scale about "attitudes toward work and careers." * Over half of the 25 items have unacceptable point biserials and should not have been included on the test. The result is a very ineffective and inefficient test which should be eliminated from the series immediately. * the coefficients of internal consistency are low, ranging from a few coefficients in the .50s to many in the middle .60s, with two in the .80s. These values raise questions about the value of some of the tests, particularly the Attitude toward Work Test which has a reliability of .52 in grade 9 and .51 in grade 12. * When the authors found that there was a statistically significant difference between the 9th-grade and

12th-grade raw score means, they concluded that "the significance of the t-values adds to the confidence that the tests are assessing incremental program effects." This reviewer is not convinced that these conclusions are valid. Since 9th-graders and 12th-graders differ in many respects, confounding represents a serious threat to the validity of these results. * The limited description of the norm groups raises several questions. * Some desirable features of the tests should be noted. First, although such classification is necessarily judgmental, the manual presents a table showing the classification of items according to subobjectives. Second, a distinguishing characteristic of this series is the inclusion of two areas identified by National Assessment of Educational Progress but omitted from other standardized measures: employment-seeking skills (Job Application Procedures Test) and generally useful on-the-job skills (Career Development Test). Third, the authors are to be commended for presenting item statistics for all the tests, thus allowing the reader to evaluate each item. Fourth, the Career-Oriented Activities Checklist possesses some characteristics that portend well for its future * Perhaps the most serious criticism of this series of tests concerns those things that were not done in planning and constructing the test to make it valid and useful: asking a team of experts to judge the appropriateness of the objectives; pretesting the items; analyzing the item statistics and eliminating or revising items which are weak, defective, or have unacceptable point biserials; and compiling preliminary test forms to provide a trial run on reliability before the final test form is compiled and administered for standardization purposes. This reviewer would not recommend the Attitude toward Work Test under any circumstances—it should be eliminated or substantially revised. The most promising of the six tests is the Career-Oriented Activities Checklist because it has very few statistically unsatisfactory items and its reliability is not seriously low. Future research studies should seek to establish its validity. Since the Job Application Procedures Test and the Career Development Test cover such important areas, an effort should be made to revise them so that they are reliable and valid. Many of the items on both tests should be replaced; alternate forms should be developed for both tests;

both tests should be subjected to a rigorous review by experts; and the authors should consider increasing the number of items on the Job Applications Procedures Test. The immediate goal of future revisions of the Career Education Test Series should be threefold: to survey the opinions of career education experts to determine which objectives should be assessed, to improve the quality of the items, and to establish the reliability of the tests. Until this research is completed, the Career Education Test Series should be considered as being in an early stage of development and should be used accordingly. [See reply by test author, Charles C. Healy, in the same journal issue, pp. 266–8.]

[1014]
★Occupational Check List. Ages 15 and over ("above average ability"); 1972–76; OCL; 6 scores: practical, enterprising, scientific, clerical, artistic, social; norms, for 5th-year students only, consist of means and standard deviations; 1 form ('72, 2 pages, spirit masters for local duplicating, printed forms no longer available); manual ('76, 16 pages); £4.50 per spirit master set and manual; postpaid within U.K.; (20) minutes; A. D. Crowley; Hobsons Press (Cambridge) Ltd. for Careers Research and Advisory Centre [England]. *

DAVID G. HAWKRIDGE, *Director, Institute of Educational Technology, The Open University, Milton Keynes, England.*

The *Occupational Check List* is a tool for pragmatic counsellors looking for a quick and rough indication of students' vocational interests as a basis for discussion.

This check list contains 108 activities drawn from a wide variety of jobs. It is not clear why activities are listed rather than jobs—the author reports that "neither method holds any substantial advantage in statistical validity." The manual provides a list of the titles represented by the statements of activities. There is considerable overlap; for example, community welfare, social work, probation work, citizens advisory work, and child-care work all appear as separate job titles. The author tries to avoid imbalance between broad occupational areas by arranging the statements in six panels which correspond to practical, enterprising, scientific, clerical, artistic, and social clusters of activities. The manual presents statistical data regarding the independence of the six panels, based on a small N of 124 boys and girls. Comparison of statements from different panels shows that there may be less difference between them than the

author may have wished; e.g., "Supervise young offenders on probation" is in the enterprising panel, while "Advise on the education of backward children" appears in the social panel. Much turns on the choice of verb, and such subtleties may be lost on respondents.

In constructing the check list, job titles were translated into activities. Something has been lost in the translation of a small number of the titles. For example, is "Develop coded languages for computer" a principal activity of computer programming? If "Sell insurance on life or property" is an activity in insurance, is it also correct to list "Value life and property for insurance policy risks" as an activity in insurance?

Completing the check list elicited puzzled remarks from one respondent about whether she should underline statements of what she would *like* to do (being very interested in that field), but knew was impossible. "I would very much like to be able to compose music for a living, but I know I will never be able to do it." One or two other statements have a similar unrealistic ring about them: "Investigate the structure of rock from the planets," and "Inspect sunken wrecks and salvage cargoes." No doubt these statements generate discussion, if only on account of their lack of realism for the majority of people. The instructions do say that respondents should underline those statements which they "would like to do if the opportunity arose."

However, these are minor criticisms of the 108 statements, which provide in total a stimulating range of possibilities to think and talk about. But if the check list is used principally for that purpose, then the statistical appendix in the manual is of little interest. Split-half reliabilities ranging from .82 to .90 seem satisfactory. Test-retest correlations are not satisfactory, ranging from .37 to .71; but that is to be expected as students' interests shift.

On the back of the check list the author provides a list of statements concerning occupational satisfaction. These statements receive little attention in the manual, even to the point of being omitted from all but one of the illustrated examples. The list is the least satisfactory part of the instrument. There are only 15 statements, but the overlap between a number of them makes responding difficult.

The manual is well laid out and provides a

modicum of interesting background information. The examples show that completion of the form is only the starting point for respondents: more fully-informed discussion with an adviser or counsellor must follow. There are some good ideas for group work; indeed, group work might well yield more valuable insights than individual counselling.

In summary, the *Occupational Check List* can be recommended. It is an inexpensive way of opening up students' visions of careers. It lacks the research backing of the *A.P.U. Occupational Interests Guide,* but is better than the *Connolly Occupational Interests Questionnaire* in this respect. Those intending to undertake advanced statistical analyses would be better off with another instrument.

[1015]

★Occupations and Careers Information BOX-SCORE. Grades 7–12; 1973; BOXSCORE; criterion referenced; no data on reliability; no norms; no suggested standards of mastery; 2 forms labeled Series A, B, (4 pages); teacher's guidebook (12 pages) for each form; $2.50 per 25 tests; 11¢ per single copy; postage extra; [45–55] minutes; S. Norman Feingold, Sol Swerdloff, and Joseph E. Barber; Chronicle Guidance Publications, Inc. *

WILLIAM C. BINGHAM, *Professor of Education, Rutgers, The State University of New Jersey, New Brunswick, New Jersey.*

This criterion-referenced test was designed (*a*) to provide an approximation of the individual pupil's knowledge of occupational information, (*b*) to evaluate instructional effectiveness in career education, and (*c*) to judge pupil fitness to make sound educational and vocational decisions.

The first objective is difficult to accomplish because it is virtually impossible to select and organize items to represent accurately a body of knowledge so complex and enormous as occupational information. The authors report that the accuracy of facts included in test items was verified by consulting suitable publications reporting labor force data. The authors address the complexity of the subject matter by organizing the test content in accordance with National Vocational Guidance Association (1971) guidelines. Thus, 40 items are grouped as general labor force data; 10, salaries; 20, educational requirements; 20, licensing requirements; and 10, type of work performed. In addition to consulting professional guidelines, it would have

been desirable to examine the compatibility of purposes between this test and the NVGA guidelines. The guidelines are intended to persuade producers of occupational information to provide the kinds of information needed by individuals to make informed decisions in selecting occupations. Are the same categories of information appropriate to the task of estimating mastery of occupational information in general? Obviously, an individual needs to know the specific educational and licensing requirements for those occupations he/she has under active consideration. But, is such an individual benefited, in terms of readiness to choose among occupations under consideration, by knowing the specific educational and licensing requirements for many occupations which are not under consideration?

The 40 items relating to the general labor force data are reasonably representative of the facts that people in general ought to have about the labor force, and the number is sufficient to permit an "approximation" of that body of knowledge. With each of the other groups of items, however, there is reason to question the representativeness of the selections. Since essentially the same conclusions can be drawn about each of the groups, only one will be analyzed.

Each of the 10 items about salaries gives the respondent two occupational titles with instructions to identify the one which generally offers the higher annual salary. The 20 occupational titles used in each form of the test are likely to be familiar to most pupils and are balanced in terms of field and level. Is it reasonable, however, to infer general knowledge about salaries from 10 judgments about these 20 occupations? If so, are these 20 occupational titles representative of the 23,000 or so titles listed in the *Dictionary of Occupational Titles?* The numbers are very small, making inference, at best, very hazardous. Further development of the test might well focus on determining successful applications and reporting relevant data to prospective users.

At times data on salaries are presented in different modes without a common base to facilitate comparison. For example, for item 44, Series B, hourly income of bricklayers is compared with weekly income of bank tellers.

How well the test meets its second purpose,

to evaluate instructional effectiveness in career education, is impossible to judge without data—none are given.

The authors report that the difficulty of the two forms is comparable, and they report one group of items as more difficult than the others. At the very least, it would be useful to know the difficulty levels of the items based on the responses of the 1,000 pupils on whom the items were pretested. It would also be useful to know whether the items were selected from a larger pool on the basis of their suitability for measuring growth. It is regrettable that these data were not made available.

Some test constructors might argue that, with criterion-referenced tests, the technical data need to be generated in the setting where the test is used. Whether that was the intention of these authors is not clear. If so, then some instructions about how to collect useful data and some cautions about possible misuse of the test would be in order. Since neither was offered, there is a serious prospect that unsophisticated test users will be left with the impression that the technical considerations are unimportant.

The third purpose, to judge pupil fitness to make sound educational and vocational decisions, is at least overstated. General knowledge about occupational information is indeed useful to individuals in making vocationally relevant decisions. In order that those decisions be personally rewarding, however, it is necessary that the individual have detailed and accurate information about specific occupations of particular interest. BOXSCORE offers a basis for judging fitness only in terms of the more general dimension of occupational information, not at all in terms of the more specific dimensions. In addition, other kinds of knowledge, such as self-understanding, are important in making educational and vocational decisions. The complexity of this decision-making process is alluded to in the introductory statements in the guidebooks, but is lost in the simplistic purpose statement about fitness to make decisions.

If this last purpose had been stated differently, perhaps as "to help to facilitate pupil career exploration," then it would have been consistent with the authors' introductory statements. The test can probably be used effectively to stimulate pupil discussion of work-related matters, to help pupils understand how much they know and do not know about work, to plan strategies to obtain additional needed information, etc. It may also be used to foster a search for self-understanding. Of course, each of these outcomes is more likely to be accomplished at the hands of a competent counselor who has a reasonably thorough understanding of vocational development than at the hands of a typical classroom teacher. It is this reviewer's opinion that, by and large, classroom teachers would need rather elaborate directions in order to generate, pursue, and capitalize on the exploratory behaviors that could arise from using this instrument. At present, directions of that kind are not available.

JAMES H. RICKS, JR., *Senior Vice President, The Psychological Corporation, New York, New York.*

Each of the two series asks 100 questions on occupations and careers. The questions call for information on work performed in the occupation, on entry requirements (schooling), on licensing requirements, on earnings, and on the "occupational outlook." A number of the questions require specific, perhaps trivial, information, e.g., the number of full-time officers employed by local police departments in 1972, or the number of flight attendants working for scheduled airlines in 1970.

As noted in the entry heading this review, the authors and publisher refer to BOXSCORE as "criterion-referenced." It seems that in their minds this justifies the absence not only of norms but of useful data of any sort. For example, the manual (Teacher's Guidebook) states that the two forms "are essentially comparable in difficulty"—but although each form is said to have been pretested on some hundreds of students, not even a pair of mean scores is offered in evidence. The manual *does* tell the user, however, that "an individual student's BOXSCORE is the percent of 100 questions on occupational information he was able to answer correctly. A student with a BOX-SCORE of 70 answered 70 percent of the questions correctly." The criterion to which the test is said to be referenced is nowhere specified.

Physically, the questionnaires and guidebooks are an odd and somewhat inconvenient size, $10\frac{3}{8}" \times 11"$; there is no apparent reason for their not having been made to fit in folders or other places along with conventional 8½″ × 11″ materials. For 20 items on each form, the options

1. Less than a high school diploma
2. A high school diploma
3. Some college
4. College degree (four years or more)

are printed twenty times instead of being stated once or perhaps placed in a four-column format which would permit presenting that section of the test in about one-fourth the space it now takes up. The manual states an intention to revise the two forms annually, but the questionnaires submitted for review in 1976 were the original forms copyrighted in 1973.

It is likely that students scoring higher on BOXSCORE are somewhat better informed about careers and occupations than those who score low. It is possible, also, that taking and scoring the test can stimulate some interest and discussion in a lesson or course on occupations. There is little else to support its use.

[1016]

Ohio Vocational Interest Survey. Grades 8–12; 1969–72; OVIS; 24 scores: manual work, machine work, personal services, caring for people or animals, clerical work, inspecting and testing, crafts and precise operations, customer services, nursing and related technical services, skilled personal services, training, literary, numerical, appraisal, agriculture, applied technology, promotion and communication, management and supervision, artistic, sales representative, music, entertainment and performing arts, teaching-counseling-social work, medical; norms consist of means and standard deviations; 1 form ('70, 16 pages); directions for administering ('70, 14 pages); manual for interpreting ('70, 74 pages); guide to career exploration ('72, 72 pages); separate answer sheets (MRC) or folders (NCS) must be used; supplementary directions for MRC ('70, 14 pages), for NCS (no date, 2 pages); $12.75 per 35 tests; $4.35 per 35 MRC answer sheets; $6.25 per 35 NCS answer folders; $7.25 per guide to career exploration; $5.25 per manual; $2.75 per specimen set; postage extra; tests cannot be scored locally; MRC scoring service, 80¢ and over per test; NCS scoring service: $1.75 per test (daily service), 95¢ and over per test (weekly service); (60–90) minutes; Ayres G. D'Costa, David W. Winefordner, John G. Odgers, and Paul B. Koons, Jr.; NCS scoring service available from NCS Interpretive Scoring Systems; Psychological Corporation. *

See T2:2201 (3 references); for reviews by Thomas T. Frantz and John W. M. Rothney, see 7:1029 (4 references).

REFERENCES

1–4. See 7:1029.
5–7. See T2:2201.
8. CLARK, CHARLES G. *An Assessment of Selected Variables in the Selection of Students for Secondary Area Vocational Programs.* Doctor's thesis, Michigan State University (East Lansing, Mich.), 1972. (*DAI* 33:4825A)
9. D'COSTA, AYRES G. "Symposium: Tests and Counseling/Role Models? 4, OVIS—A Nonpredicting Device." *Meas & Eval Guid* 5(3):411–4 O '72. *
10. FLUEGGE, LYNN ROY. *Pupillographic Study: Relationship Between Vocationally Oriented Stimuli and Selected OVIS Scale Scores.* Doctor's thesis, Purdue University (Lafayette, Ind.), 1972. (*DAI* 33:5053A)
11. MURPHY, WILLIAM HENRY. *The Concurrent and Predictive Validity of an Experimental Projective Vocational Interest Survey Using the OVIS as a Criterion.* Doctor's thesis, University of Cincinnati (Cincinnati, Ohio), 1972. (*DAI* 33:5559A)
12. OMVIG, CLAYTON P., AND DARLEY, LORRAINE K. "Expressed and Tested Vocational Interests of Black Inner-City Youth." *Voc Guid Q* 21(2):109–14 D '72. *
13. POULIN, DONALD ALPHONSE. *The Effects of Career Orientation on Vocational Interests and Occupational Plans.* Doctor's thesis, University of Connecticut (Storrs, Conn.), 1972. (*DAI* 33:2822A)
14. BARNETTE, W. LESLIE, JR.; D'COSTA, AYRES; HARMON, LENORE W.; SUPER, DONALD E.; WEISS, DAVID J.; AND ZYTOWSKI, DONALD G. Chap. 9, "Illustrative Interpretations of Inventories," pp. 206–44. In *Contemporary Approaches to Interest Measurement.* Edited by Donald G. Zytowski. Minneapolis, Minn. University of Minnesota Press, 1973. Pp. xi, 251. *
15. D'COSTA, AYRES. Chap. 7, "The Ohio Vocational Interest Survey," pp. 171–88. In *Contemporary Approaches to Interest Measurement.* Edited by Donald G. Zytowski. Minneapolis, Minn.: University of Minnesota Press, 1973. Pp. xi, 251. *
16. HARMON, LENORE W. "Sexual Bias in Interest Measurement." *Meas & Eval Guid* 5(4):496–501 Ja '73. * (*PA* 50:3999)
17. MARTIN, BETTY RADER. *Some Effects of Counseling on the Stability of OVIS Scores.* Doctor's thesis, North Carolina State University (Raleigh, N.C.), 1973. (*DAI* 34:3065A)
18. RHODES, CHARLES I. *An Evaluation of the Self Directed Search and the Effect of Group or Independent Use in Facilitating Career Development of Secondary School Students.* Doctor's thesis, West Virginia University (Morgantown, W.Va.), 1973. (*DAI* 34:1628A)
19. ROBERTSON, J. MARVIN. "Does Instruction Increase Occupational Interests?" *Ag Ed Mag* 45(8):188+ F '73. *
20. ZYTOWSKI, DONALD G. Chap. 1, "Considerations in the Selection and Use of Interest Inventories," pp. 3–19. In his *Contemporary Approaches to Interest Measurement.* Minneapolis, Minn.: University of Minnesota Press, 1973. Pp. xi, 251. *
21. BROWN, RONALD PAUL. *A Comparison of the Expressed and Inventoried Vocational Interests of 8th and 9th Grade Black and White Students at a Title I Inner City Junior High School.* Doctor's thesis, University of Akron (Akron, Ohio), 1974. (*DAI* 35:7052A)
22. CEGELKA, PATRICIA THOMAS; OMVIG, CLAYTON; AND LARIMORE, DAVID L. "Effects of Aptitude and Sex on Vocational Interests." *Meas & Eval Guid* 7(2):106–11 Jl '74. * (*PA* 53:4076)
23. OMVIG, CLAYTON P., AND THOMAS, EDWARD G. "A Socioeconomic Comparison of Vocational Interests: Implications for Counseling." *J Voc Behav* 5(1):147–55 Ag '74. * (*PA* 53:4108)
24. OMVIG, CLAYTON P., AND THOMAS, EDWARD G. "Vocational Interests of Affluent Suburban Students." *Voc Guid Q* 23(1):10–6 S '74. * (*PA* 53:12563)
25. STRICKLAND, CECIL LAFAYETTE, SR. *A Study of Occupational Interests and Educational Plans of High School Students in Greene County North Carolina: A Model for Program Planning.* Doctor's thesis, North Carolina State University (Raleigh, N.C.), 1974. (*DAI* 35:6590A)
26. WARNER, ANN BOWEN. *Home Economics Career Exploration Instruction and Vocational Interests of Eighth Grade Students in Selected Georgia Schools: An Exploratory Study.* Doctor's thesis, University of Georgia (Athens, Ga.), 1975. (*DAI* 36:8021A)
27. WATTERSON, DAVID GILCHRIST, JR. *Some Structural Dimensions of Career-Related Environmental Concerns and Their Relationship to Vocational Interests.* Doctor's thesis, University of Illinois (Urbana, Ill.), 1975. (*DAI* 36:2654A)
28. WOODBURY, ROGER. "Dimensions of the OVIS With Adjudicated Delinquents." *Meas & Eval Guid* 8(2):86–91 Jl '75. * (*PA* 54:12075)
29. KEITH, EDWIN MONROE, JR. *The Work Values and Career Maturity of Community College Transfer and Native Students.* Doctor's thesis, University of Florida (Gainesville, Fla.), 1976. (*DAI* 37:4135A)
30. STANSBURY, JAMES CLIFFORD. *Maturity of Vocational Attitudes and Locus of Control as Dimensions of Vocational Personality Types.* Doctor's thesis, Kansas State University (Manhattan, Kan.), 1976. (*DAI* 37:4147A)
31. WOODBURY, ROGER, AND PATE, DOVE HENRY. "Vocational Personality Dimensions of Adjudicated Delinquents." *Meas & Eval Guid* 10(2):106–112 Jl '77. *

[1017]

★**Ohio Work Values Inventory.** Grade 3–adults; 1971–74; OWVI; 11 scores: altruism, object orientation, security, control, self realization, independence, money, task satisfaction, solitude, ideas/data orientation, prestige; reliability data and norms for grades

4–8 and 11 only; 1 form ('73, 5 foldout panels plus detachable profile, identical with test copyrighted 1971 except for format); manual ('74, 40 pages); group profile ('71, 1 page); 25¢ per test; 5¢ per group profile; $1 per manual; $1.25 per specimen set; postage extra; (40–60) minutes including self-scoring; Bradford J. Fenner and Loyde W. Hales; Bradford J. Fenner. *

REFERENCES

1. FENNER, BRADFORD JOHN. *The Development of the Ohio Work Values Inventory: An Investigation of Internal Characteristics.* Doctor's thesis, Ohio University (Athens, Ohio), 1972. (*DAI* 33:1433A)
2. HALES, LOYDE W., AND FENNER, BRADFORD. "Work Values of 5th, 8th, and 11th Grade Students." *Voc Guid Q* 20(3):199–203 Mr '72. *
3. SEMBRIC, LORETTA JANE. *The Use of the Ohio Work Values Inventory to Determine the Work Values Held by Children According to Grade, Social Class, Race, and Sex.* Doctor's thesis, Ohio University (Athens, Ohio), 1972. (*DAI* 33:4101A)
4. HALES, LOYDE W., AND FENNER, BRADFORD J. "Sex and Social Class Differences in Work Values." *El Sch Guid & Counsel* 8(1):26–32 O '73. * (*PA* 51:5976)
5. HALES, LOYDE W., AND FENNER, BRADFORD J. "Measuring the Work Values of Children: The Ohio Work Values Inventory." *Meas & Eval Guid* 8(1):20–5 Ap '75. * (*PA* 54:4241)
6. KING, REED LEWIS. *A Comparison of Work Values of Emotionally Disturbed Adolescents and Normal Adolescents.* Doctor's thesis, Oregon State University (Corvallis, Ore.), 1975. (*DAI* 35:4324A)

[1018]

★Picture Interest Exploration Survey. Grades 7–12; 1974; PIES; career interest inventory based upon 156 slides, each showing "a worker's hands performing a task" representative of an occupation; 13 scores: industrial production, office, service, education, sales, construction, transportation activities, scientific and technical, mechanics and repairmen, health, social scientists and social service, art-design and communications, agriculture; no data on reliability and validity; no norms; 1 form; manual (54 pages); 156 color slides; 2 sets of career reference cards; tape cassette available for administration; separate response sheets must be used; $350 per set of testing materials including 50 response sheets; $5.50 per 50 response sheets; postage extra; (30–35) minutes; Elizabeth F. Mahoney; Education Achievement Corporation. *

[1019]

★Planning Career Goals. Grades 8–12; 1975–76; PCG; revision of tests in the 1960–61 *Project Talent Test Battery* (see T2:1058); values, abilities, information, and interests considered relevant to each of 12 occupational groups (engineering, physical sciences, mathematics, and architecture; medical and biological sciences; business administration; general teaching and social service; humanities, law, and social and behavioral sciences; fine arts and performing arts; technical jobs; proprietors and sales workers; mechanics and industrial trades; construction trades; secretarial-clerical and office workers; general labor and public and community service); no data on reliability for grade 12; normative data derived retrospectively from 1960 Project Talent data by means of a "1975 PCG/Project Talent equating study"; examiner's manual ('76, 45 pages); counselor's handbook ('76, 29 pages); career handbook ('76, 202 pages); student guide ('76, 55 pages); computer printout report ('76, 4 pages); technical bulletin ('77, 47 pages); separate answer booklets (CompuScan) must be used; $48.75 per 25 sets of tests, including examiner's manual; $25 per 50 CompuScan answer booklets and 50 consumable computation booklets; $25 per set of 10 scoring stencils; $1.50 per counselor's handbook; $7.95 per career hand-

book; $1.50 per student guide; $2.50 per technical bulletin; $5 per specimen set; postage extra; scoring service, $1 and over per student; (308–348) minutes in 2–6 sessions; American Institutes for Research; CTB/McGraw-Hill. *

a) LIFE AND CAREER PLANS. A 1–page questionnaire (printed as a part of the answer booklet) on occupational preferences and quality-of-life values; (10–15) minutes.

b) PCG ABILITY MEASURES. 10 scores: vocabulary, English, reading comprehension, creativity, mechanical reasoning, visualization, abstract reasoning, quantitative reasoning, mathematics, computation, plus a weighted average of stanine scores on the 3–5 tests which best predict membership in each of the 12 occupational groups; 1 form ('75, 80 pages in 2 booklets); 158(188–198) minutes.

c) PCG INFORMATION MEASURES. 12 occupational group scores as listed above; 1 form ('75, 28 pages); (80–90) minutes.

d) PCG INTEREST INVENTORY. 12 occupational group scores as listed above; no norms; raw score profiles may be compared with profiles of estimated median scores of students later entering one of 151 occupations; 1 form ('75, 11 pages); (30–45) minutes.

DEAN H. NAFZIGER, *Director, Assessment Program, Northwest Regional Educational Laboratory, Portland, Oregon.*

Planning Career Goals consists of career guidance materials centered about a set of tests and interest inventories developed as a part of the Project TALENT research conducted by the American Institutes for Research. The purpose of the PCG is to "assist guidance and counseling personnel in helping students in Grades 8–12 make realistic and long-lasting educational and career plans."

To their credit, the authors of PCG have attempted to produce a guidance device which includes assessment instruments, reporting mechanisms for students and counselors, and guidance materials. The intended use of the tests and materials is for students to take a battery of instruments comprising measures of values, interests in various careers, information about career-related areas, and abilities which can be compared with the high school profiles of persons in various occupations or occupational groups. The 12 occupational groups used as a basis for the comparison of profiles are listed in the descriptive entry above.

It is important for the user to understand that the research information underlying the PCG pertains to the characteristics of the assessment instruments and to the interpretative information that can be made on the basis of these instruments. However, no evaluative data are provided on the effectiveness of the battery and its related materials in meeting its purpose of promoting long-lasting plans.

TEST CONTENT. Four types of data are gathered from students by the test battery—values, interests, information, and abilities. Data regarding a student's values are gathered through 15 questions printed directly on the battery answer booklet. The student is asked to indicate the degree of importance of various needs and activities related to quality of life, e.g., material well-being, having and raising children, or expressing self. The responses are on a three-point scale ranging from "Of the greatest importance to me" to "Not very important to me."

Interest data are gathered through a separate Interest Inventory booklet comprising three parts. In the first part, students indicate the extent to which they think they would like each of 104 listed occupations. In the second part, students indicate how much they think they would enjoy each of 99 occupational activities. In the third part, students are asked to indicate how much they would enjoy each of 97 different activities which they are likely to find somewhat familiar. All responses are on a five-point scale (ranging from "dislike very much" to "like very much"). Responses are aggregated over the three parts of the Interest Inventory to yield one score for each of the 12 occupational categories.

Data about student information are gathered using a separate Information Measures booklet consisting of 240 items. The Information Measures items "sample knowledge that individuals would have acquired if they had studied about an occupation or participated in activities related to an occupation." Items were chosen to provide an indication of knowledge that individuals have gained in each of the 12 occupational categories.

Data about student abilities are gathered for 10 areas: reading comprehension (40 items), mathematics (24 items), abstract reasoning (22 items), creativity (24 items), mechanical reasoning (25 items), English (48 items), quantitative reasoning (22 items), vocabulary (60 items), visualization (25 items), and computation (76 items). Items for all areas except computation are included in the Ability Measures booklet. The computation scale, a speeded test, is in a separate booklet designed to facilitate finding and marking answers.

Taken together, the test battery provides a comprehensive assessment as a basis for career planning, and this is one of the prominent features of this test. At the same time, the comprehensiveness leads to a weakness in the test. Namely, it is difficult to learn and understand the different parts of the test and its related materials. This difficulty is compounded by the failure of any one of the accompanying descriptive documents to fully illuminate the test user and by some modest inconsistencies in the documents. Three descriptive documents accompany the test battery—an Examiner's Manual, a Counselor's Handbook, and Technical Bulletin No. 1.

SCORING AND REPORTING. Procedures for using and scoring the tests are well delineated, although this information is scattered among the three descriptive documents. Scoring may be done by hand scoring stencils or through a scoring service. Hand scoring the entire battery takes about one and a half hours per student and, for some sections of the battery, would be quite complex; it seems that there are few circumstances in which hand scoring would be advantageous.

The primary reporting mechanism for students is the career planning report, available only when scoring service is purchased. Three types of information are included in the report. First, students' responses on the interests, information, and abilities tests are summarized for each of the 12 occupational groups. Percentile ranks are given (for both male and female norm groups) for each of the 10 scores within the abilities test. Second, comparisons are shown between students' scores on values, interests, information, and abilities and the scores of individuals employed within each of the 12 occupational categories. Third, a computerized narrative report about certain of the responses is given.

The report provides considerable information to the students. However, except through portions of the narrative report, no synthesis of the information across the various types of data obtained on each student is provided. No overall career profile is developed, and it is not clear how a student should interpret results if different profiles result from different portions of the test. This plethora of information without a synthesis seems, to this reviewer, to put too much of an interpreting burden on the student. Users of this test should be prepared to provide considerable assistance to students in interpreting information.

A second reporting mechanism is the career planning profile, which can be purchased as an option from the scoring service or produced through handscoring. This report allows students to compare their interest and ability profiles with those of individuals in specific occupations as well as in occupational groups.

In addition to these individual student reports, group reports are also available.

TECHNICAL DATA. Means, standard deviations, and intercorrelation coefficients for the values items, Interest Inventory, Information Measures, and Ability Measures, and split-half reliability coefficients and standard errors of measurement on the latter three measures are reported for each of grades 8 through 11. There are no data for grade 12. Reported reliability coefficients for the Interest Inventory range from .84 to 1.00(?), from .63 to .89 for Information Measures, and from .68 to .94 for Ability Measures (with corrections made to prevent exaggerations that could occur because of the speededness of the computation section).

Because the PCG is based upon longitudinal data from a large national sample of students, validity data should be extensive. The test authors assert that predictive validity exists because the predictive weights for the occupational profiles are based upon data from people in various career groups obtained when they were in high school. However, important questions about the validity data remain. First, no evidence is presented to show that people within each career group are more similar on the measures used than they are to people in other career groups. Predictive validity is not meaningful if there is no differentiation among people in the various career groups. This problem is particularly important because the predictive data were gathered when students were in high school, a time when career interests and plans may be poorly defined. Second, the predictive weights were not derived by limiting the criterion group only to people who expressed satisfaction with their current occupation. Instead, all people for whom data were available were used in developing the predictive weights, and only 73 percent of the people upon whom

predictions are based indicated that they were satisfied or very satisfied with their occupations. Making predictions using all people in various career groups is a questionable procedure because it means that people who have made unsatisfactory career decisions are a part of the criterion group. Third, the authors placed no restriction on the minimum amount of time the members of the predictive groups had spent in the occupations, so there is no assurance of occupational stability for the criterion groups. Fourth, the test authors fail to note the number of people within each specific occupation or general occupational group upon whom the predictive weights are based. Because some occupations attract extremely small percentages of people, there is no assurance that predictions are made upon groups of sufficient size. These problems mean that, despite the extensive research behind the PCG, its validity has not been thoroughly demonstrated.

SUMMARY. *Planning Career Goals* is a comprehensive career guidance system, developed through a large-scale research effort, that gathers several types of data on students and provides guidance materials related to the assessment instruments. Despite its research base, users should be cautioned about some apparent shortcomings in the test battery. In particular, information from the test battery seems difficult to use because no synthesis of the results is provided, and the methods used for developing the predictive weights for the career profiles leave the validity of the profiles in question. The test developers should improve the descriptive documents so that each has a clear purpose and communicates to its intended audience. Users of the materials should be given guidelines on how to combine the information from all the parts of the test battery, especially when discrepancies occur. Data demonstrating the appropriateness of the criterion group for the development of the predictive weights should be provided. Finally, an evaluation of the PCG is needed to determine its effectiveness in meeting the goal of its authors to promote long-lasting and realistic career plans.

DONALD E. SUPER, *Honorary Director and Senior Fellow, National Institute for Careers Education and Counselling, Cambridge, England.*

The PCG was designed to collect, analyze,

and report career planning, values, interests, information, and abilities data to "assist guidance and counseling personnel in helping students in grades 8–12 make realistic and long-lasting educational and career plans."

Questionnaires and tests derived from those designed for use in Project Talent include a life and career plans survey and values inventory; an interest inventory of 300 occupational titles, occupational activity and related educational and avocational activities items scored for 12 occupational career groups; and an information measure of 240 items of occupational information.

Advertising describes the PCG as a "new battery" the interpretation of which is "based on a single, massive, data source—the 400,000-student Project Talent sample. No other instrument has such an extensive longitudinal data base to support it." *True:* the tests are new, but so developed as to facilitate calibration with the Talent tests and to make it legitimate to use the Talent norms. *False:* the sample does not consist of 400,000 students followed up in a longitudinal study, but only of the much smaller group of 11th and 12th graders who responded in the eleven-year follow-up, with an attrition rate which is not mentioned but which in other AIR publications varies from roughly 35 percent to roughly 65 percent. The reader is nowhere cautioned about the possible effects of the large numbers of nonrespondents on the representativeness of the various occupational samples. Despite this sampling problem, the data base is impressive.

The PCG is described as "a complete system of guidance and career information that allows the examinees to participate in the interpretation of information about themselves in forming career goals." *False:* it is a comprehensive system but not a complete one (examinees do not supply and do not use status data—academic, financial, racial, social—that have been shown to have a bearing on the attainability of educational and occupational objectives), and the student's participation is merely that of supplying and receiving information. This is an essential, laudable, but certainly low-level type of participation, in which the student does not contribute to decisions as to what data are important nor as to how to weight the data.

The Interest Inventory has 25 items relating to each of 12 "career" (actually occupational) groups, with split-half reliabilities which range from .84 to 1.00 [*sic*], with median .93. The reading level is at the 11th grade, but generally simple and relevant. The directions for the occupations section are perhaps misleading; for although they instruct the student to use what he knows about occupations and himself to decide how he would like to work in the job named, they then state: "Consider how well you could do the job, the working hours and environment, the pay and living conditions, and the training and effort required for success," thus naming extrinsic aspects of the job and implying that intrinsic interest in the work itself, liking what one does in it, is irrelevant to interest in an occupation!

The Information Measures contain 20 items for each occupational group, with reliabilities ranging from .63 to .89, with median .79. Because of the nature of occupational information, readability is again at the 11th grade level.

The Ability Measures contain typical items along with some new items which are quite ingenious. The reliabilities for the 10 tests range from .68 to .94, with median .86. The tests are arranged in a way which provides changes in the nature of the content and helps maintain interest.

Values are assessed by 15 items in Life and Career Plans. Each item, representing one aspect of the quality of life, is rated on a three-point scale of importance. The scoring involves a comparison of the ratings of each of the values with those given by each occupational group in the 11-year follow-up, the report reminding the student of his clustering of his most, moderately, and least important values. Occupational differences being slight, the worthwhileness of the values data is put into question.

The validity of the measures of interest, information, and abilities has "been shown to have predictive validity by analyzing data from the five- and 11-year Project Talent follow-up studies," from which are derived the weights used in combined scores for the 12 occupational groups. No data are reported, however, on the adequacy of the differentiation among occupational groups, and the reader is left to do his own research with the means and deviations of the occupational profiles. The validity data are thus, at this stage, to be taken on faith.

Planning Career Goals

The basic data, despite the loss of subjects over the years, are no doubt the best longitudinal occupational data now available on tests and inventories. But this is no reason for not presenting the evidence as to the ability of the PCG to predict membership in each of the occupational groups.

Interpreting results is provided for by the graphic profile and narrative printout made possible by computer scoring. Important too are the counselor's handbook as well as the career handbook, which is a combination of DOT and occupational outlook handbook job descriptions with test and inventory profiles for each of the 12 occupational groups and each of the 151 occupations.

Computer-printed, the career planning report resembles other profiles combined with narratives. Student scores are compared with those of people employed, 11 years after graduation from high school, in the two occupational groups which the student has indicated as first and second choices, and with those of people in the occupational group in which he has made, respectively, his three highest abilities scores and his two highest interest scores. This confrontation with his standing both on his "chosen" occupations and on others for which he has some of the important differentiating characteristics should help, as the manual claims on a priori grounds, to lead the student to consider more than one option and to see not only his strengths and weaknesses but also his multipotentiality. No consideration appears to be given, however, to the flat-profile, monopotential and/or nonpotential (low on all abilities tests) students, nor to the frequency with which such profiles arise—questions often raised, for example, by counselors using the *DAT Career Planning Program* in its attempts to cope with them in its printout.

A reusable "planning your career" handbook for student use is well-printed and illustrated, with all but one section written at the 8th or 9th grade level; the occupational titles and activities material require, as they generally do, 12th grade reading skill. As this section is designed to serve the student as a form of the career handbook, it is surprising that the attempt to make it more readable was not successful, even with occupational terminology as a problem. Attention has been paid to sex and ethnicity in the illustrations. The language is almost always unisexual; and in the few instances in which it is not, both sexes are referred to. The discussion of the wise and fair use of sex norms is very well handled.

Each section is summarized in outline form at the end; sections cover such topics as why and how to plan, steps in finding out about oneself, steps in learning about occupations, thumbnail sketches of the 12 occupational groups and 151 occupations, using the career planning report, and a final summary. The text is sometimes worrisome, as, for instance, "However, he was not told about his interests and abilities," when PCG Talent *scores* are surely meant, and especially "All your abilities may improve with time. Some can be improved greatly in a few months with much practice. Other abilities cannot be improved without some years of effort." Statements such as this surely encourage wishful thinking. The at-least-equally-true statements that the abilities of most people who do not go to college stabilize in the late teens or early twenties, and that many soon start declining through lack of use, are not made. Nor is anything said about the relative predictive validity of test scores earned with and without coaching. The term "career" is used throughout, in the current fadist manner, as a synonym for "occupation." Keeping options open, therefore, appears as keeping "the doors open to as many careers as possible," and nothing is done to help the student see how a sequence of occupations, with or without further education, can be so handled as to result in a satisfying career in the scientific sense of life or work history.

It is stated that "it is impossible to tell whether a person can do college work on the basis of Ability Measures obtained in the 8th or 9th grade." But this statement is followed by: "In the 1960 study, persons who completed a four-year college program generally scored above average in vocabulary, English." And this is followed by: "The decision to go or not to go to college should be based on your values, interests, and job preferences—not just on your abilities," put even more strongly in the section summary.

The career handbook is an important and usable counseling tool for students and for counselors. Its origins, contents, and use are briefly described and 182 pages list the occupations in each of the 12 career groups. Each of the specific occupations is treated by describing occupational activities, education and training, salary, interest, abilities, job satisfaction, and future opportunities through the mid-1980s, and the specific occupational profiles given. However, certain weaknesses in the handbook, not pointed out in it, need noting here.

The norms consist of 38,000 males and females tested in 11th and 12th grades in a scientifically chosen sample of American high schools in 1960 and followed up eleven years later. These 38,000, an impressive number in a domain which needs and has lacked impressive numbers, are the respondents of a sample of 400,000 students in grades 9 through 12, and, therefore, of some 160,000 (reviewer's estimate) 11th and 12th graders. The occupational norms must, therefore, be based on something like 25 percent of the original sample. As respondents are typically more successful than nonrespondents in follow-up studies, the PCG norms are probably higher than they should be. The setting of cutting scores classifies those who are near the mean as "Somewhat Alike," those who are about one stanine below the mean as "Not Much Alike," etc., thus not allowing for the fact that if nonresponding had not eliminated significant numbers from the samples the norms would no doubt be lower. If the reviewer is mistaken in this judgment, it is an argument which should have been dealt with in the technical manual; in any case, the attrition from testing to follow-up should have been reported in both the counselor's and career handbooks.

The occupational grouping handles the task of reducing the areas to be scanned to manageable numbers rather well, in that the occupations in a given group are reasonably homogeneous, but contain the usual defects in classification. Some of these are noted; for example, the fact that architects belong in both the engineering, etc., and the technical groups. Others are not. Some occupations are treated monolithically, all psychologists being in the humanities, law, and social and behavioural sciences group, with no recognition of the biological and engineering science interests of, for example, neuropsychologists and human factors psychologists.

Job activities are briefly described in DOT style. The usual problem in describing occupations is unresolved, for the reader must already be informed about an occupation in order to read understandingly about its duties, tools, etc.

Education and training present fewer problems. Salaries are described in a five-point scale in order to avoid problems of inflation and for clear communication with students, but the result is that some occupations are described in terms that may discourage students who would find them sufficiently rewarding. Descriptions of interest run into sampling problems when occupations are treated globally, as with psychologists whose profile shows that they dislike the medical and biological sciences, but who are saved from having this in the verbal description by the fact that they dislike the construction trades even more. The abilities of the occupational groups are generally well enough described on the basis of the tests, but the possibility of distortion because of grouping and sampling is not mentioned.

The counselor's handbook errs in not dealing with the sampling problem. It describes the measures well and makes good use of the ideas that information can be a sign of manifest interest, and that expressed or inventoried interest without information is evidence that information is needed. The effects of experience and of training on vocabulary, mechanical reasoning, and quantitative reasoning are discussed without citing evidence; the first two described as learned, respectively, in school and in out-of-school activities, the last as somewhat less affected by the number of mathematics courses taken than is the mathematics score. The treatment of the effects of training in this manual seems generally fair, but it may encourage vocabulary drill more than is warranted. The matter of sex norms is well handled, with data to support the use of both male and female norms and with suggestions as to using both with girls and women. Race and social status seem, however, to be nonexistent, but then AIR is not alone in trying to avoid discrimination by bypassing social handicaps.

Steps in planning and implementing the PCG program are well outlined, including the use of the students' manual, but the use of results with students is dealt with much too briefly and simplistically. Some good sample cases are described to help show the value and use of

Planning Career Goals

PCG data, but the section on the PCG in the total career education context is advertising rather than professional assistance material.

The technical bulletin covers standard topics, but many with surprising brevity. It is to be hoped that this bulletin will before long be replaced by a more adequate technical manual making good use of the rich data available on the AIR computer discs.

SUMMARY. Weaknesses to the contrary notwithstanding, the PCG battery and supporting materials are among the best vocational guidance tests available. Defects include sampling and too-rigid empiricism, the reading level of some sections, and excessive optimism about increasing abilities through study, and, some might add, testing time. But no other battery has norms as good as these, the reading-level problem is seemingly inevitable, and the excessive optimism aids and abets the ambitious disadvantaged student. The instruments are well designed and well produced. The assessment of occupationally important student characteristics requires and warrants time and money. The PCG should, however, be compared with materials of other publishers, especially those of the Psychological Corporation and the American College Testing Program.

[1020]

★**Priority Counseling Survey.** Grades 7–9, 9–12, 13–14; 1971–73; PCS; to identify educational and vocational counseling needs and priorities; no scores; individual student response report ['73, 1 page] consists of the items (with student responses) rearranged into 4 or 5 areas, 4 to 10 questions per area as listed below, plus up to 10 optional locally selected items; no data on reliability; no norms; 3 levels; no manual; uses (no date, 4 pages); separate answer sheets (Digitek) must be used; 25¢ per test; 95¢ per answer sheet including processing, yielding student response report (3 copies) and group report (minimum 50 tests; consists of counselor report and school/building and district/batch summaries); cash orders postpaid; specimen set free on request; [45–55] minutes; Thomas W. Smith and Clarence D. Johnson; Mincomp Corporation. *

a) JUNIOR HIGH SCHOOL—FORM A. Grades 7–9; 1972–73; 4 groups of 5 to 10 items: educational self-appraisal, educational help needed, career self-appraisal, career help needed; 1 form ('72, 6 pages).
b) [HIGH SCHOOL] FORM B. Grades 9–12; 1971–73; 5 groups of 4 to 6 items: educational self-appraisal, course of study and help needed, educational plans and help needed, career interests and skills and occupational choices, career plans and help needed; 1 form ('71, 6 pages); Spanish edition available.
c) JUNIOR COLLEGE—FORM C. Grades 13–14; 1972–73; 5 groups of 4 to 6 items: same as for b; 1 form ('72, 4 pages).

Planning Career Goals

[1021]

*Safran Student's Interest Inventory, Revised Edition.** Grades 8–12; 1960–76; SSII; revision of *Safran Vocational Interest Test;* 11 scores: 7 interest scores (economic, technical, outdoor, service, humane, artistic, scientific) and 4 ability self-ratings (academic, mechanical, social, clerical); all reliability and validity data based on initial form of test ('60); no norms for ability self-ratings (norms for interest scores based on earlier edition); 1 form ('76, 12 pages, essentially the same as test copyrighted 1969 except for sequence and wording changes); counsellor's manual ('76, 33 pages); student's manual ('76, 8 pages); Can $11.35 per 35 tests; $4.25 per 35 student's manuals; $2.95 per counsellor's manual; $3 per specimen set; postage extra; (40) minutes; Carl Safran, Douglas W. Feltham, and Edgar N. Wright; Thomas Nelson & Sons (Canada) Ltd. [Canada]. *

For a review by Thomas T. Frantz of an earlier edition, see 7:1035; see also 6:1069 (1 reference).

[1022]

The Self Directed Search: A Guide to Educational and Vocational Planning. High school and college and adults; 1970–73; SDS; "a self-administered, self-scored, and self-interpreted vocational counseling tool"; 6 scores (realistic, investigative, artistic, social, enterprising, conventional) for each of 3 scales (activities, competencies, occupations) and for self-ratings of abilities, summary; 2 forms; manual ('72, 36 pages); counsellor's guide ('71, 32 pages); $3 per manual; $1 per counsellor's guide; postage extra; (40–60) minutes; John L. Holland; Consulting Psychologists Press, Inc. *

a) [STANDARD FORM.] 1970–72; norms consist of means and standard deviations; 1 form ('70, 15 pages); revised occupations finder ('72, 8 pages); $14 per 25 tests; $5.25 per 25 occupations finders; $2 per specimen set (without manual).
b) FORM E. 1972–73; "simplified for a 4th grade reading level"; no data on reliability and validity; no norms; 1 form ('73, 15 pages); jobs finder ('72, 8 pages); $15 per 25 tests; $5.50 per 25 job finders; 75¢ per specimen set (without manual and counsellor's guide).

See T2:2211 (1 reference).

REFERENCES

1. See T2:2211.
2. BANIKIOTES, PAUL G., AND McCABE, SHERIDAN P. "Interest and Personality Measurement: Relationship Between Self-Directed Search and Eysenck Personality Inventory Scores." *Psychol Rep* 30(1):158 F '72. * (*PA* 48:7260)
3. BROWN, FRED. "Review of the Self-Directed Search." *Meas & Eval Guid* 5(1):315–6+ Ap '72. *
4. BROWN, JANE ELLA. *An Investigation of Holland's Theory of Vocational Choice Applied to High School Girls.* Doctor's thesis, University of Virginia (Charlottesville, Va.), 1972. (*DAI* 33:5486A)
5. COLLINS, ANNE M., AND SEDLACEK, WILLIAM E. "Comparison of Satisfied and Dissatisfied Users of Holland's Self-Directed Search." *J Counsel Psychol* 19(5):393–8 S '72. * (*PA* 49:3132)
6. EDWARDS, KEITH J., AND WHITNEY, DOUGLAS R. "Structural Analysis of Holland's Personality Types Using Factor and Configural Analysis." *J Counsel Psychol* 19(2):136–45 Mr '72. * (*PA* 48:7798)
7. GAFFEY, ROBERT LOUIS. *An Investigation of the Concurrent Validity of Holland's Theory.* Doctor's thesis, Ohio State University (Columbus, Ohio), 1972. (*DAI* 33:5490B)
8. LEWIS, ANN H., AND SEDLACEK, WILLIAM E. "Socioeconomic Level Differences on Holland's Self-Directed Search." Abstract. *Proc 80th Ann Conv Am Psychol Assn* 7(2):587–8 '72. *
9. REDMOND, RONALD E. *Increasing Vocational Information Seeking Behaviors of High School Students.* Doctor's thesis, University of Maryland (College Park, Md.), 1972 (*DAI* 34: 2311A)
10. ATTARIAN, PETER JAMES. *Early Recollections: Predictors of Vocational Preference.* Doctor's thesis, University of Arizona (Tucson, Ariz.), 1973. (*DAI* 34:3049A)

11. CAPEHART, JUNIUS LONG, JR. *The Relationship of Vocational Maturity to Holland's Theory of Vocational Choice.* Doctor's thesis, University of North Carolina (Chapel Hill, N.C.), 1973. (*DAI* 34:5618A)

12. FISHBURNE, FRANCIS JOSEPH, JR. *The Concurrent Validity of Two Measures Operationalizing Holland's Theory Using a Sample of Non-Professional Workers.* Doctor's thesis, Ohio State University (Columbus, Ohio), 1973. (*DAI* 34: 4016B)

12a. GELSO, CHARLES J.; COLLINS, ANNE M.; WILLIAMS, REBECCA O.; AND SEDLACEK, WILLIAM E. "The Accuracy of Self-Administration and Scoring on Holland's Self-Directed Search." *J Voc Behav* 3(3):375–82 Jl '73. * (*PA* 51:10027)

13. GESINDE, SAMUEL ADEBAYO. *Congruence of Basic Personal Orientation With Vocational Training: Its Relationship to Conditions of Choice and to Performance and Satisfaction in Selected Vocational Training Programs in Nigeria.* Doctor's thesis, Columbia University (New York, N.Y.), 1973. (*DAI* 34:2293A)

14. HOLLAND, JOHN L. *Making Vocational Choices: A Theory of Careers.* Englewood Cliffs, N.J.: Prentice-Hall, Inc., 1973. Pp. ix, 150. *

15. KIMBALL, RONALD L.; SEDLACEK, WILLIAM E.; AND BROOKS, GLENWOOD C., JR. "Black and White Vocational Interest on Holland's Self-Directed Search (SDS)." *J Negro Ed* 42(1):1–4 W '73. * (*PA* 50:9910)

16. NOLAN, JAMES JEREMIAH. *The Effectiveness of the Self-Directed Search Compared With Group Counseling in Promoting Information-Seeking Behavior and Realism of Vocational Choice.* Doctor's thesis, University of Maryland (College Park, Md.), 1973. (*DAI* 35:195A)

17. RHODES, CHARLES I. *An Evaluation of the Self Directed Search and the Effect of Group or Independent Use in Facilitating Career Development of Secondary School Students.* Doctor's thesis, West Virginia University (Morgantown, W.Va.), 1973. (*DAI* 34:1628A)

18. WALSH, W. B.; HOWARD, P. R.; O'BRIEN, W. F.; SANTA-MARIA, M. L.; AND EDMONDSON, C. J. "Consistent Occupational Preferences and Satisfaction, Self Concept, Self Acceptance and Vocational Maturity." *J Voc Behav* 3(4):453–63 O '73. * (*PA* 52:1991)

19. AVALLONE, VINCENT LOUIS. *A Comparative Study of the Effects of Two Vocational Guidance Systems: The Self-Directed Search and a Traditional Vocational Guidance Model.* Doctor's thesis, University of Northern Colorado (Greeley, Colo.), 1974. (*DAI* 35:2670A)

20. CHRISTENSEN, KATHLEEN C., AND SEDLACEK, WILLIAM E. "Diagnostic Use of Holland's Self-Directed Search." *Voc Guid Q* 22(3):214–7 Mr '74. * (*PA* 53:4176)

21. FRASER, FREDERICK DONALD. *Effect of the Strong Vocational Interest Blank and the Self Directed Search on Career Planning of College Students.* Doctor's thesis, University of Missouri (Columbia, Mo.), 1974. (*DAI* 36:1302A)

22. GAFFEY, ROBERT L., AND WALSH, W. BRUCE. "Concurrent Validity and Holland's Theory." *J Voc Behav* 5(1):41–51 Ag '74. * (*PA* 53:4138)

23. HOLLIFIELD, JOHN H. "An Examination of the Validity of the Self-Directed Search for Writers." *Meas & Eval Guid* 6(4):247 Ja '74. * (*PA* 52:56)

24. JONES, HELEN BORING. *The Effects of School Setting, Race, and Sex on the Occupational Interests of Tenth Grade Students.* Doctor's thesis, Ohio State University (Columbus, Ohio), 1974. (*DAI* 35:7060A)

25. KRIVATSY, SUSANA EVA. *Differential Effects of Three Vocational Counseling Treatments.* Doctor's thesis, University of Maryland (College Park, Md.), 1974. (*DAI* 36:707A)

26. McGOWAN, ANDREW SCOTT. *Vocational Maturity and Anxiety Among Vocationally Undecided and Indecisive Students: The Effectiveness of the Self-Directed Search.* Doctor's thesis, Fordham University (New York, N.Y.), 1974. (*DAI* 35:2691A)

27. RICHARDS, JAMES M., JR.; CALKINS, E. VIRGINIA; McCANSE, ANDREW; AND BURGESS, MICHAEL M. "Predicting Performance in a Combined Undergraduate and Medical Education Program." *Ed & Psychol Meas* 34(4):923–31 W '74. * (*PA* 54:6417)

28. SELIGMAN, RICHARD. "Review of the Self-Directed Search." *Meas & Eval Guid* 7(2):138–40 Jl '74. *

29. TOU, LOUIS ALOYSIUS. *A Study of Work Value Orientations of Chinese-American and White-American Students of the 7th and 8th Grades in Catholic Elementary Schools.* Doctor's thesis, Catholic University of America (Washington, D.C.), 1974. (*DAI* 35:831A)

30. WALSH, W. BRUCE. "Consistent Occupational Preferences and Personality." *J Voc Behav* 4(2):145–53 Ap '74. * (*PA* 52:10183)

31. BIRK, JANICE M. Chap. 6, "Reducing Sex Bias: Factors Affecting the Client's View of the Use of Career Interest Inventories," pp. 101–21. In *Issues of Sex Bias and Sex Fairness in Career Interest Measurement.* Edited by Esther E. Diamond. Washington, D.C.: National Institute of Education, 1975. Pp. xxix, 219. *

32. BOYD, VIVIAN STALLWORTH. *The Linguistic Structure of the Self-Directed Search: A Study in Sex-Role Stereotyping.* Doctor's thesis, University of Maryland (College Park, Md.),

1975. (*DAI* 36:3398A)

33. BROWN, STEPHEN J. "Career Planning Inventories: 'Do-It-Yourself' Won't Do." Comment by John L. Holland. *Personnel & Guid J* 53(7):512–9 Mr '75. * (*PA* 54:4232 and 54: 4248)

34. CHRISTENSEN, KATHLEEN C.; GELSO, CHARLES J.; WILLIAMS, REBECCA O.; AND SEDLACEK, WILLIAM E. "Variations in the Administration of the Self-Directed Search, Scoring Accuracy, and Satisfaction With Results." *J Counsel Psychol* 22(1):12–6 Ja '75. * (*PA* 53:6452)

35. ESPOSITO, RONALD PATRICK. *The Relationship Between the Motive to Avoid Success and Vocational Choice by Race and Sex.* Doctor's thesis, Fordham University (New York, N.Y.), 1975. (*DAI* 36:1302A)

36. GOTTFREDSON, GARY D., AND HOLLAND, JOHN L. "Vocational Choices of Men and Women: A Comparison of Predictors From the Self-Directed Search." *J Counsel Psychol* 22(1):28–34 Ja '75. * (*PA* 53:8393)

37. HELMS, SAMUEL THOMAS, III. *Perceived Person-Environment Congruency: A Test of Holland's Interaction Hypotheses.* Doctor's thesis, University of Maryland (College Park, Md.), 1975. (*DAI* 36:6472A)

38. HOLLAND, JOHN L. Chap. 2, "The Use and Evaluation of Interest Inventories and Simulations," pp. 19–44. In *Issues of Sex Bias and Sex Fairness in Career Interest Measurement.* Edited by Esther E. Diamond. Washington, D.C.: National Institute of Education, 1975. Pp. xxix, 219. *

39. HOLLAND, JOHN L., AND NAFZIGER, DEAN H. "A Note on the Validity of the Self-Directed Search." *Meas & Eval Guid* 7(4):259–62 Ja '75. * (*PA* 53:12554)

40. HOLLAND, JOHN L.; GOTTFREDSON, GARY D.; AND GOTTFREDSON, LINDA S. "Read Our Reports and Examine the Data: A Response to Prediger and Cole." *J Voc Behav* 7(2):253–9 O '75. * (*PA* 55:11075)

41. HOLLAND, JOHN L.; GOTTFREDSON, GARY D.; AND NAFZIGER, DEAN H. "Testing the Validity of Some Theoretical Signs of Vocational Decision-Making Ability." *J Counsel Psychol* 22(5):411–22 S '75. * (*PA* 54:12700)

42. HORTON, JOSEPH ANTHONY. *The Personality Characteristics of Professional Career Women: A Study of the Concurrent Validity of John Holland's Theory of Vocational Choice.* Doctor's thesis, Ohio State University (Columbus, Ohio), 1975. (*DAI* 36:3045B)

43. HURT, DAVID JAMES. *A Group Vocational Exploration Program to Facilitate Narrowing of Vocational Choice.* Doctor's thesis, Kansas State University (Manhattan, Kan.), 1975. (*DAI* 36:5247A)

44. KNOX, BARBARA RUTH SNYDER. *Effects of Values-Oriented Counseling on Leisure Attitudes, Career Preferences, and Self Concept.* Doctor's thesis, Catholic University of America (Washington, D.C.), 1975. (*DAI* 35:7653A)

45. KOONTZ, RONALD GENE. *The Influence of Supervised Experiences in Career Exploration on Certainty of Career Choice, Expressed Career Choice, Measured Career Interest and Similarity Between Expressed Career Choice to Measured Career Interest.* Doctor's thesis, University of Maryland (College Park, Md.), 1975. (*DAI* 36:6587A)

46. NAFZIGER, DEAN H.; HOLLAND, JOHN L.; AND GOTTFREDSON, GARY D. "Student-College Congruency as a Predictor of Satisfaction." *J Counsel Psychol* 22(2):132–9 Mr '75. * (*PA* 53:12561)

47. NELSON, RICHARD E. *A Comparison of the Effects of Three Career Group Counseling Techniques on Measures of Self Information, Cognitive Self Information Seeking Behavior, and Group Process Factors.* Doctor's thesis, University of Missouri (Columbia, Mo.), 1975. (*DAI* 36:6560A)

48. O'BRIEN, WILLIAM FRANCIS. *The Concurrent Validity of Holland's Theory of Vocational Development Using a Sample of Non-Professional Black Workers.* Doctor's thesis, Ohio State University (Columbus, Ohio), 1975. (*DAI* 36:3010B)

49. O'NEIL, JAMES MARTIN. *Predictiveness of Holland's Investigative Personality Type and Levels of Consistency Using the Self Directed Search.* Doctor's thesis, University of Maryland (College Park, Md.), 1975. (*DAI* 36:6482A)

50. PREDIGER, DALE J., AND COLE, NANCY S. "It Is Time to Face Some Issues: A Response to Holland, Gottfredson, and Gottfredson." *J Voc Behav* 7(2):261–3 O '75. * (*PA* 55:11082)

51. PREDIGER, DALE J., AND COLE, NANCY S. "Sex-Role Socialization and Employment Realities: Implications for Vocational Interest Measures." *J Voc Behav* 7(2):239–51 O '75. * (*PA* 55:11081)

52. REILLY, JANET ZAKRYK. *Birth Order and Vocational Choice Among Eighth-Grade Pupils.* Doctor's thesis, Fordham University (New York, N.Y.), 1975. (*DAI* 36:5159A)

53. TANNEY, MARY FAITH. Chap. 5, "Face Validity of Interest Measures: Sex-Role Stereotyping," pp. 89–99. In *Issues of Sex Bias and Sex Fairness in Career Interest Measurement.* Edited by Esther E. Diamond. Washington, D.C.: National Institute of Education, 1975. Pp. xxix, 219. *

54. VILLWOCK, JACLYN DOHM. *Holland's Personality Concepts as Predictors of Stability of Choice.* Doctor's thesis, University of Houston (Houston, Tex.), 1975. (*DAI* 36:2653A)

55. WALSH, W. BRUCE, AND HANLE, NANCY A. "Consistent Occupational Preferences, Vocational Maturity, and Academic

Achievement." *J Voc Behav* 7(1):89–97 Ag '75. * (*PA* 55:5768)

56. ARMSTRONG, PHILLIP JAMES. *The Relationship of Counselor-Counselee Background Experiences to High School Students' Evaluations of Counseling.* Doctor's thesis, Catholic University of America (Washington, D.C.), 1976. (*DAI* 37:4850A)

57. ARREDONDO, RODOLFO. *The Effect of Vocational Counseling on Career Maturity of Female Cooperative Health Education Students.* Doctor's thesis, Texas Tech University (Lubbock, Texas), 1976. (*DAI* 37:6263A)

58. BOYD, VIVIAN S. "Neutralizing Sexist Titles in Holland's Self-Directed Search: What Difference Does it Make?" *J Voc Behav* 9(2):191–9 O '76. *

59. CHATMAN, VERA A. STEVENS. *Career Planning in Decision Making: A Group Counseling Approach.* Doctor's thesis, George Peabody College for Teachers (Nashville, Tenn.), 1976. (*DAI* 37:1982A)

60. FISHBURNE, FRANCIS J., JR., AND WALSH, W. BRUCE. "Concurrent Validity of Holland's Theory for Non-College-Degreed Workers." *J Voc Behav* 8(1):77–84 F '76. *

61. GOTTFREDSON, GARY D. "A Note on Sexist Wording in Interest Measurement." *Meas & Eval Guid* 8(4):221–3 Ja '76. * (*PA* 56:4963)

62. HENDERSON, JOHN L. *Persistence and Nonpersistence Factors of Disadvantaged Vietnam-era Veterans in College.* Doctor's thesis, University of Cincinnati (Cincinnati, Ohio), 1976. (*DAI* 37:4133A)

63. HOLLAND, JOHN L. "Consistency and Raw Scores Survive Another Test: A Last Response to Prediger and His Colleagues." *Meas & Eval Guid* 9(3):132–5 O '76. *

64. HOLLAND, JOHN L. "The Virtues of the SDS and its Associated Typology: A Second Response to Prediger and Hanson." *J Voc Behav* 8(3):349–58 Je '76. * (*PA* 56:6884)

65. HOLLAND, JOHN L., AND GOTTFREDSON, GARY D. "Sex Differences, Item Revisions, Validity, and the Self-Directed Search." *Meas & Eval Guid* 8(4):224–8 Ja '76. * (*PA* 56:3232)

66. HORTON, JOSEPH A., AND WALSH, W. BRUCE. "Concurrent Validity of Holland's Theory for College Degreed Working Women." *J Voc Behav* 9(2):201–8 O '76. *

67. MEIR, ELCHANAN I., AND BEN-YEHUDA, AMALIA. "Inventories Based on Roe and Holland Yield Similar Results." *J Voc Behav* 8(3):269–74 Je '76. * (*PA* 56:5166)

68. NORD, CHARLES. *Personality Types of Undecided Students.* Doctor's thesis, The Florida State University (Tallahassee, Fla.), 1976. (*DAI* 37:3425A)

69. O'BRIEN, WILLIAM F., AND WALSH, W. BRUCE. "Concurrent Validity of Holland's Theory for Non-College Degreed Black Working Men." *J Voc Behav* 8(2):239–46 Ap '76. *

70. PENIX, LEVENIS. *The Influence of Selected Variables on the Prediction of High School Students' Outcome on Holland's Self Directed Search.* Doctor's thesis, East Texas State University (Commerce, Texas), 1976. (*DAI* 37:4141A)

71. PREDIGER, DALE J. "Alternatives for Validating Interest Inventories Against Group Membership Criteria." *ACT Res Rep* 76:1–5 Jl '76. *

72. PREDIGER, DALE J. "Do Raw Scores Deserve a D Minus? A Reply to Holland." *Meas & Eval Guid* 9(3):136–8 O '76. *

73. PREDIGER, DALE J. "The Viability of Holland's Consistency Construct and Raw Score Assessments of Personality." *Meas & Eval Guid* 9(3):124–31 O '76. *

74. PREDIGER, DALE J., AND HANSON, GARY R. "Holland's Theory of Careers Applied to Women and Men: Analysis of Implicit Assumptions." *J Voc Behav* 8(2):167–84 Ap '76. *

75. PREDIGER, DALE J., AND HANSON, GARY R. "A Theory of Careers Encounters Sex: Reply to Holland (1976)." *J Voc Behav* 8(3):359–66 Je '76. * (*PA* 56:6890)

76. SCHAEFER, BARBARA E. "Holland's SDS: Is its Effectiveness Contingent Upon Selected Variables?" *J Voc Behav* 8(1):113–23 F '76. *

77. SPOKANE, ARNOLD ROY. *Occupational Level, Sex and the Concurrent Validity of Holland's Theory in a Sample of Employed Adults.* Doctor's thesis, Ohio State University (Columbus, Ohio), 1976. (*DAI* 37:4122B)

78. VILLWOCK, JACLYN D.; SCHNITZEN, JOSEPH P.; AND CARBONARI, JOSEPH P. "Holland's Personality Constructs as Predictors of Stability of Choice." *J Voc Behav* 9(1):77–85 Ag '76. *

79. ZENER, THELMA BALDWIN, AND SCHNUELLE, LESLIE. "Effects of the Self-Directed Search on High School Students." *J Counsel Psychol* 23(4):353–9 Jl '76. * (*PA* 56:6865)

80. CUTTS, CATHERINE C. "Review of the Self-Directed Search." *Meas & Eval Guid* 10(2):117–20 Jl '77. *

81. DOLLIVER, ROBERT H., AND HANSEN, ROBERT N. "Review of the Self-Directed Search." *Meas & Eval Guid* 10(2):120–3 Jl '77. *

82. ESPOSITO, RONALD P. "The Relationship Between the Motive to Avoid Success and Vocational Choice." *Voc Behav* 10(3):347–57 Je '77. *

83. HODGSON, MARY L., AND CRAMER, STANLEY H. "The Relationship Between Selected Self Estimated and Measured Abilities in Adolescents." *Meas & Eval Guid* 10(2):98–105 Jl '77. *

84. KELSO, GEOFFREY I.; HOLLAND, JOHN L.; AND GOTTFRED-SON, GARY D. "The Relation of Self-Reported Competencies to Aptitude Test Scores." *Voc Behav* 10(1):99–103 F '77. *

85. McGOWAN, ANDREW S. "Vocational Maturity and Anxiety Among Vocationally Undecided and Indecisive Students." *Voc Behav* 10(2):196–204 Ap '77. *

86. O'NEIL, JAMES M., AND MAGOON, THOMAS M. "The Predictive Power of Holland's Investigative Personality Type and Consistency Levels Using the Self Directed Search." *Voc Behav* 10(1):39–46 F '77. *

87. PREDIGER, DALE J. "Alternatives for Validating Interest Inventories Against Group Membership Criteria." *Appl Psychol Meas* 1(2):275–80 sp '77. *

88. TOUCHTON, JUDITH GRAY, AND MAGOON, THOMAS M. "Occupational Daydreams as Predictors of Vocational Plans of College Women." *Voc Behav* 10(2):156–66 Ap '77. *

89. WALSH, W. BRUCE; HORTON, JOSEPH A.; AND GAFFEY, ROBERT L. "Holland's Theory and College Degreed Working Men and Women." *Voc Behav* 10(2):180–6 Ap '77. *

JOHN O. CRITES, *Professor of Psychology, University of Maryland, College Park, Maryland.*

Psychometrically, the *Self Directed Search* is "neither fish nor fowl": it is both a stimulus variable and a response measure. It is designed "to provide a vocational counseling experience for people who do not have access to professional counselors" and to assess an individual's competencies and preferences. As an intervention, the manual states that: "The SDS may be used for individual or group vocational counseling. In individual counseling, the SDS can be given to take home after a brief interview. In group counseling, the SDS can be used as a programmed experience." More generally, the SDS is used as a self-administered instrument without participation in vocational counseling. As an inventory, the SDS grew out of Holland's *Vocational Preference Inventory* and research on his theory of vocational choice, which proposes that there are six types of cognate personality orientations and environmental models: realistic (R), investigative (I), artistic (A), social (S), enterprising (E), and conventional (C). The central proposition of this theory, which is the Minnesota "matching men and jobs" approach of the 1930–40s decked out in contemporary trappings, is that if people go into a work environment congruent with their personality orientation, e.g., realistic person in realistic environment, then they will enjoy greater satisfaction, success, and stability in their vocation. The SDS was constructed to summarize the person's characteristics and relate them to appropriate occupations.

This process is pursued by filling out the self-assessment booklet, which consists of five major sections: occupational daydreams, activities, competencies, occupations, and self-estimates. Occupational daydreams asks respondents to list the careers they have daydreamed about as well as those they have discussed with others. These are then coded by using an occupations finder which gives the three-point codes (possible combinations of R, I, A, S, E, C taken three at a time) as determined rationally and empirically by Holland and others for 456 occupations in which more than 95 percent of the labor force are employed. Activities consists of statements such as "fix electrical things" and "sketch, draw, or paint," which describe activities classified in the six RIASEC categories. The respondent is directed to indicate either like or dislike for each stated activity, the latter response option also subsuming "those things you are indifferent to" or "have never done." Competencies uses the same format, except that the items are descriptions of skills or proficiencies, much like the old oral trade questions. The directions are to mark those activities which "you can do well or competently" and those which "you have never performed or performed poorly." Occupations is a reproduction of the VPI, which is comprised of occupational titles grouped into the various types. The respondent expresses liking or disliking for occupations in each type by answering yes or no. Self-estimates elicits two sets of ratings on seven-point scales of 14 abilities, each of which is assigned a three-point code. Following the RIASEC schema, the first set includes these abilities: mechanical, scientific, artistic, teaching, sales, and clerical; the second set is comprised of these skills and traits: manual, math, musical, friendliness, managerial, and office.

Once the five sections of the SDS are completed, a graph or profile for each is drawn and then these are compiled into a summary code. Thus, there is a graph for each of the self-estimates (a total of two), one for activities, one for competencies, and one for occupations. A three-point code is derived for each graph, and these five codes are summarized by weighting the three highest letter ratings. All first-place letters are given a weight of 3, second-place a weight of 2, and third-place a weight of 1. The summary code is calculated by adding the weighted totals for each letter and determining the letters with the three highest scores. Finally, the summary code is referred to the occupations finder to locate the occupations which are identical with or similar to the individual's high-point code. These occupations

are presumably ones to consider as possible choices.

The user of the occupations finder is reminded that "all responses are interpreted ipsatively, i.e., a person's typological resemblances are always determined relative to his own scores rather than the scores of a special normative group. These ipsative procedures orient the person toward the occupation that he [sic] most closely resembles." Although not explicitly articulated in the manual, the methodology assumed in this interpretative approach to the SDS is that of assessing profile similarity, with all of its inherent complexities and contradictions. First, in the computation of the summary code, *profile elevation* is lost by simply counting the number of times one of the RIASEC letters ranks highest, without preserving the numerical value of how high it is. For example: A person may rank highest on both activities and occupations, but with respective scores of 9 and 5, and yet still be counted equally in the summary code. Second, *profile shape* is lost by converting scores to letter ratings. Even the manual points out that "a code of RIE with scores of 12, 6, and 2 is different than the same code with scores of 12, 11, and 10." Third, *profile scatter* is lost because letter ratings are ranked without regard to score differences between them. These sources of error in the summary code are compounded when it is compared with codes in the occupations finder. An individual's summary code may be entirely different than an occupational code in profile elevation, shape, and scatter and yet have identical letter ratings!

A related problem concerns the differential weightings of the several sections of the SDS in the summary code. As compared with activities and competencies, which have 11-item scales for the RIASEC types, occupations (the VPI) has 14 items per scale. When adding these sections together in arriving at the summary code, occupations is more heavily weighted than activities and competencies, because raw scores, not transformed scores, are used. As a consequence, interests, for example, may contribute more to a high-point code than abilities, and thus lead to a possibly unrealistic career choice—one based more on preference than performance. The summary code is also more heavily weighted by competencies and self-estimates than by activities and occupations,

Self Directed Search

since the former contribute three codes and the latter two. Moreover, the weighting is differentially in favor of self-rated skills and proficiencies as compared with preferences for activities and occupations. Because of sex-stereotyping in the acquisition of skills and proficiencies, this differential may introduce sex bias into the SDS, particularly for females. The manual observes that: "The SDS is equally biased for and against women and for and against men. Men tend to get R, I, and E codes most frequently; these trends can be observed in the classification and in the score distributions of the SDS." What the manual fails to note, except by omission, is that women tend to get A, S, and C codes most frequently—largely due to the socialization of their abilities in these areas. It is possible, if not highly probable, therefore, for a woman with potential competencies for R, I, and E occupations to rate herself higher on skills and proficiencies (e.g., typing, teaching, and tea pouring) in A, S, and C occupations because she has not had R, I, and E experiences and opportunities.

The manual replies that: "Although the SDS incorporates this cultural experience [i.e., for women], the construction of the SDS and test data strongly imply that the SDS fosters the interests of women and other targets of discrimination." If women rate themselves on the ability sections of the SDS according to their largely sex-stereotyped experiences, however, and if these sections disproportionately contribute 60 percent to the summary code, then the construction of the SDS clearly does *not* "foster the interests of women." That it is also, but hardly equally, biased toward men does not mitigate its discrimination against women. That "test data" on the SDS demonstrate it fosters the interest of women is an unresolved issue. A voluminous literature has accumulated on whether the SDS is sex biased or not, but agreement cannot even be reached on what constitutes "sex bias." The problem is so many faceted, ranging from definition of terms through construction of same- and opposite-sex scales to transformation of scores, that no definitive conclusion can be drawn about the SDS. Suffice it to say that, if other counseling simulations or interest inventories are developed which appear to test users to be less sexist than the SDS, then they will be used, and the issue

of sex bias in the SDS will be settled pragmatically. At the present time, it apparently cannot be resolved psychometrically.

Other aspects of the SDS, and claims made for it in the manual and elsewhere, are more amenable to objective evaluation. The manual states that: "The language of the SDS is at an easy reading level, and the scoring, graphing, and computational tasks are also readily comprehensible." Evidence on the reading level of the SDS, except the occupations section, supports the first part of this statement, the Dale-Chall index of readability being between the 7th and 8th grade levels (ages 13–14). This does not mean, however, that all individuals in these grades can understand the SDS, because all of them do not necessarily read at these levels. Concerning the self-administration of the SDS, the evidence is less supportive. The manual advises that: "Generally, the SDS is most effective when it is given [to] an individual to take home or to fill out without supervision." The underlying assumption is that the respondent can accurately score the SDS and derive a correct summary code. At least two studies have investigated this procedure. In a group testing situation, Gelso et al. (*12a*) checked the self-administered SDSs of 221 incoming freshmen at the University of Maryland for six types of scoring errors, including computational, rating, and coding inaccuracies. They found that nearly all subjects made some kind of error and that 55 percent obtained an incorrect summary code! These results were replicated on an independent sample of 489 freshmen at the same university by Christensen et al. (*34*), leading them to conclude that "This sort of finding raises serious questions about whether the Self-Directed Search, as it currently stands, can be truly 'self-directed,' or at least as self-directed as its constructor has purported it to be."

Another claim made in the manual for the SDS is: "In general, people of all ages enjoy the experience." However, results of a study by Collins and Sedlacek (*5*) raise questions not only about this statement but also about the "self-directedness" of the SDS. From a large group of 4,631 incoming freshmen at the University of Maryland, 485 who were satisfied and 343 who were dissatisfied with their SDS codes were identified. The codes were then compared with the 48 codes for which no oc-

Self Directed Search

cupations are listed in the occupations finder, and it was found that 20 percent of the dissatisfied group as compared with 10 percent of the satisfied group obtained summary codes for "no occupation." For the satisfied and dissatisfied students combined, 14 percent did not have summary codes which correspond to those listed in the occupations finder. Collins and Sedlacek (5) caution:

From a counseling point of view, this 14% figure seems seriously high, especially if the Self-Directed Search is used without any formal supervision. Students who spend time to take and score the Search, and then find they do not "fit" the instrument, may become upset by the experience. Unless they took the Self-Directed Search under the supervision of a counselor or psychometrist there is little guarantee that they will receive further vocational guidance or even reassurance that they are not "weird," although the instructions on the Search suggest seeing a counselor if the person still has questions. If the Self-Directed Search is designed for use without such supervision, then further attention to the no-occupation codes is imperative.

Much is also made in the manual of the construct validity of the SDS: "The SDS is an outgrowth of a theory of vocational choice * The assessment and classification booklets which form the SDS are direct products of a theory of personality types and environmental models * The theoretical-empirical construction of the SDS should insure the validity of the occupational information transmitted in the use of the SDS." The core concept in SDS theory is "Holland's hexagon," which organizes and relates personality types to work environments. The hexagon presumably orders and represents the correlations among the RIASEC types: "The relationships among the major categories can be ordered according to a hexagon in which distances between occupational classes are inversely proportional to the size of the correlations between them." The principal purpose of this graphic arrangement was "to organize the classification booklet [occupations finder] so that occupations which are psychologically similar are located close together in the classification." Yet the hexagon shown in the manual is equilateral! For example, the correlation between R and I is .40 and the correlation between R and C is .51, but the legs of the hexagon connecting these points are the same length. At least two independent studies corroborate this anomaly. Using data on Occupational Reinforcer Patterns from Work Adjust-

ment Project, Toenjes and Borgen [1] concurred with Holland's RIASEC ordering (expressed in a clockwise fashion around the hexagon) but the shape of the hexagon was considerably distorted. Similarly, Schussel [2] replicated the RIASEC ordering with data from the *ACT Vocational Interest Profile* but not the shape. Moreover, there were sex differences: the configuration was U-shaped for males and Y-shaped for females. Clearly, "Holland's hexagon" is *not* a hexagon; it is more likely a 3-dimensional figure of unknown parameters. How pervasive the effect of this conceptual distortion is upon the construct validity of the SDS is presently unknown, but there is no question that the *linear* translation of summary codes into occupational codes is incorrect.

If there is one word that characterizes and summarizes the construction and development of the SDS it is "simplistic." Theoretically, its construct validity rests upon a geometric model that patently does not fit the empirical evidence. Moreover, it largely ignores the contemporary focus in vocational psychology upon career development during the past 25 years. The only mention in the manual of this theoretical emphasis is: "Because of its desirable characteristics, the SDS lends itself to repeated use. Such a periodic stock-taking is consistent with a developmental conception of vocational counseling." Psychometrically, its construction is wrought through with compounded errors attributable to naiveté concerning problems of profile analysis. The "matching model" is predicated upon the assessment of profile similarity, yet no attempt is made in the SDS to deal with the methodological shortcomings of this procedure. Instead, a mishmash of profile elevation, shape, and scatter is expressed in a summary code which is then compared with occupational codes based upon what is assumed to be a "hexagon" but isn't. Practically, there is sufficient evidence to question seriously the ethics of indiscriminately making the SDS available to the public (it is on sale at the University of Maryland bookstore, for example, without restrictions). Holland has recommended the SDS for mass consumption and has

[1] TOENJES, CAROL M., AND BORGEN, FRED H. "Validity Generalization of Holland's Hexagonal Model." *Meas & Eval Guid* 7(2):79–85 Jl '74. * (PA 53:2031)
[2] SCHUSSEL, ROBERT. "Circularity of Vocational Interests: Spherical Analysis of VIP Items." *Meas & Eval Guid* 7(2): 86–91 Jl '74. * (PA 53:2030)

Self Directed Search

intimated that it should largely replace vis-à-vis career counseling,[3] yet not only are the psychometrics of its coding questionable but most of its users make critical mistakes in its scoring, ones which affect the summary code obtained. Until sophisticated attention is given to these overly simplified theoretical, psychometric, and practical issues, the caveat to users of the *Self-Directed Search* is that it might better be thought of as the Mis-Directed Search.

Meas & Eval Guid 5(1):315–6+ Ap '72. *Fred Brown.* * Holland has attempted to provide a vehicle through which a person can make a systematic search of his own abilities and interests, then relate his assessments to the world of occupations. Not surprisingly, the search is organized around Holland's theory of vocational development. The SDS consists of a 15-page, self-administered booklet. During the assessment, a person does several things: He records his occupational daydreams * he answers a number of preference items about his interests; he indicates his competencies * he indicates whether certain occupations appeal to him; and he makes estimates of his abilities in six areas. These assessments are all organized according to Holland's major classes of occupations—realistic, investigative, enterprising, artistic, social, and conventional. After making these assessments, he constructs profiles of his activities, competencies, and occupational preferences; then he constructs a summary code based on all the assessments. He then uses the summary code to locate appropriate occupations in the accompanying *Occupations Finder,* a listing of 414 occupations. * My only negative reaction was to the use of the title "Occupational Daydreams" for one section; this section might better be given another title to reflect its purpose: to identify tentative occupational choices. The usefulness of the SDS depends on the answer to several questions: (a) Is Holland's classification of occupations a valid and useful one? (b) Can occupational choice and/or success be predicted from expressed interests? (c) Is the SDS a valid measure of expressed interests and occupational preferences? (d) Will the individual fill out the SDS without distorting his responses to produce a desired picture? Previous research by Holland and

others would seem to indicate that the first two questions can be answered "yes." There is also empirical support for a positive answer to the last question, especially if the person is motivated to present an honest picture of himself. However, it would seem that the arrangement of the assessment scales, with all items in a single area clustered together and with the dimension clearly labeled, might increase the tendency to distort. * The major question, then, is how accurate is the SDS in assessing vocational preferences? * the psychometric characteristics of the SDS are probably no worse or better than those of other self-report personality instruments. Certain improvements are obviously needed. More data on the reliability, validity, and score distribution of the scales, particularly data on samples other than college students, should be provided. For example, as the SDS is said to be useful from age 15 on, there should be data from high school students, whose assessments are likely to be less stable than those of college students. It would also be valuable to know how adults respond to the SDS and if it is useful with minority groups (at least one study has been done using black college students). Further, it would be informative to know how the SDS functions within the counseling process; does it, as suggested in the manual, facilitate the counseling process? Finally, and most important, Holland needs to develop a handbook that briefly explains the vocational choice process to the test-taker. Included should be a discussion of how the world of work is structured, what factors are important determiners of vocational success and satisfaction, and how to make a decision. Without such information, the person taking the test may place too much faith in the test results. The *Counselors Manual* does this for the counselor, but a similar description is needed for the person taking the test, especially if he is taking it outside the counseling process. Many counselors will probably look askance at the entire idea of the SDS, feeling that any process that does not utilize their skills somehow invalidates the process of selecting a vocation. And, without doubt, counselors do possess knowledge and skills that assist individuals to make more appropriate vocational decisions. But this view, perhaps, is from the wrong perspective. Holland is directing the SDS, at least in part, to persons

---

3 HOLLAND, JOHN L. "Career Counseling: Then, Now, and What's Next?" *Counsel Psychologist* 4(3):24–6 '74. *

who do not seek counseling. By forcing these persons, who otherwise might make their choices on more fanciful bases, to systematically look at their abilities and interests and relate them to our knowledge of the vocational world, the SDS may lead to better decisions. Also, Holland constantly reminds the user that professional counseling help is available through many sources and that the SDS user would be well advised to seek such help. In summary, I view the SDS as a good start, but only a start. I applaud Holland's attempt to provide a method that will encourage more people to think seriously about their careers. He should also be commended for attempting to accomplish this in a simple manner, yet one which takes into account our best knowledge about vocations. At its present stage of development the SDS could probably be best used in conjunction with group or individual counseling, as a vehicle for the counselee to focus his ideas about himself, occupations, and the choice process. *

Meas & Eval Guid 7(2):138–40 Jl '74. Richard Seligman. * The SDS does not require expensive computer hardware, software, or other gadgetry; the SDS does not require a trained counselor for the purpose of administration and/or interpretation. It is the client who administers the SDS to himself and then tabulates the results. The client receives assistance in the interpretation of the results through the use of appropriate portions of a companion booklet, the Jobs Finder, a copy of which is furnished with the test booklet. * Form E of the SDS is a shortened form of the version published in 1970 and is virtually identical to it. * Each subsection of the test presents items related to the six vocational and personality types which form the basis of Holland's theory of vocational choice: Realistic, Investigative, Artistic, Social, Enterprising, and Conventional. * Throughout the test the directions are clear and straightforward. One format problem was noted, however. The instructions in the competencies subtest say at one point, "Mark 'yes' if you know how *or think you could learn* how to do the following," while a few lines down the page, the statement changes to "I know how or *want to learn* how to...." (italics added). Clearly, there is a distinction to be made between what one *could* learn to do

and what one *wants* to learn to do. Although this discrepancy may not be crucial to the results obtained on the SDS, it should be eliminated in future editions. * The professional manual contains extensive technical data on the SDS. * The overwhelming impression is that the SDS is well grounded in both theory and empirical data. * The professional manual could be improved by a more cogent discussion of the meaning of validity, reliability, and norming in the SDS as distinguished from a standardized achievement test. Validity and reliability are discussed in the manual, but not in the same complete, concise, and jargon-free language which characterizes the SDS itself as well as other sections of the manual. Finally, Holland has given some thought to the essential knowledge which a counselor ought to possess in order to use the SDS appropriately. Accordingly he has included in the manual a mastery test, the successful passing of which suggests that a counselor possesses sufficient knowledge about the SDS to minimize the abuse of the instrument and the results obtained therefrom. This reviewer can strongly recommend the use of the Self-Directed Search as a helpful, inexpensive way for counselors to provide vocational guidance to a wide variety of clients. Potential users can be assured that the product in question has been well thought out, extensively tried out, and that it is being subjected to regular and continuing quality control. [See the original review for the author's comments on the review.]

Meas & Eval Guid 10(2):117–20 Jl '77. Catherine C. Cutts. * The SDS scales have a moderate degree of internal consistency. Samples of 2,000 to 6,000 college freshmen show the KR-20s range from .67 to .94. * The item content and format reflect clear content validity. * More research is needed to study the validity of the summary codes. * The SDS was built from a well-established theory and it is a test of many uses. Not only can it serve as a beginning vocational counseling tool but it can be used periodically throughout a person's entire career. It is also a useful tool at the present when counselors are concerned with planning for a changing society. The SDS offers many alternative occupations—not just a narrow selection. A possible flaw may occur in the test summary of females who have worked their way through college with clerical jobs. Their clerical competencies are reflected by the SDS and they tend to have a higher Conventional score even though their interests and plans do not lie in this area. It appears, however, that the advantages of the instrument outweigh the disadvantages, and the importance of the SDS as a vocational counseling tool should not be underestimated.

Meas & Eval Guid 10(2):120–3 Jl '77. Robert H. Dolliver and Robert N. Hansen. * Our experience with the SDS in a university counseling service indicates that....many undergraduate and gradute students do not read the directions carefully enough to correctly complete the SDS. Mistakes often occur multiplying the scores. * Directions for the SDS activities section are confusing: Mark "like" if you would like to do the activity, mark "dislike" if you have never done the activity. Those categories are not mutually exclusive; both could be true. * We believe that a counselor is needed to talk with the test taker about aspects of Holland's theory. * Holland does not sufficiently clarify the possibility that part of the Summary Code may reflect avocational interests. * The problems we have encountered with students reading, following directions, and doing simple multiplication indicate a need for clerical monitoring of SDS administration. Encouraging exploration of career possibilities suggested by the SDS and the explanation of the more complicated aspects of Holland's theory appears to us to require the assistance of a trained person. SDS respondents also need assistance using the *Occupations Finder*. * Our chief criticism of the *Manual* is the absence of data on the Occupational Daydreams and on the normative relationship between Daydreams and the Summary Code. * It seems strange that the *Manual* does not include reliability coefficients for the Summary Codes, although the reliabilities for each section are reported. * We are in agreement with Holland on major points. Our major disagreement is procedural: Our experience with the SDS does not support Holland's claim of its value as an entirely "self-directed" search. In addition, we feel that the appropriate use of the SDS rests on the user's awareness that Holland has constructed a *model* of personality/occupational functioning. Part of this model closely corresponds to the real world; part of it does not (such as the large number of three-letter codes without occupations that fit the code description). * Holland has done a service to the profession by pointing out the value of using in a straightforward (noncomputer scored) manner, the information that respondents' have about themselves. Holland has also provided a very useful theory for matching people with jobs, which is manifested in his SDS and Vocational Preference Inventory. These methods are less complex than are competing methods (such as Strong or Kuder). But the question inevitably is asked whether methods that are even less complex than the SDS are also productive (such as the SDS Daydreams section alone). A number of vocational assessment methods are helpful to some people. We would all benefit by achieving greater clarity about which methods are helpful for which people, under what circumstances. [See the original review for critical comments not excerpted; also see the author's comments on the reviews.]

[1023]
Strong-Campbell Interest Inventory. Ages 16 and over; 1927–77; SCII; revised unisex edition of *Strong Vocational Interest Blank for Men* and *Strong Vocational Interest Blank for Women;* 155 scoring scales (6 general occupational themes, 23 basic interest scales, 124 occupational scales, 2 special scales) and 23 administrative indexes; GENERAL OCCUPATIONAL THEMES: investigative, artistic, realistic, conventional, social, enterprising; BASIC INTEREST SCALES: adventure, agriculture, art, athletics, business management, domestic arts, law/politics, mathematics, mechanical activities, medical science, medical service, merchandising, military activities, music/dramatics, nature, office practices, public speaking, religious activities, sales, science, social service, teaching, writing; OCCUPATIONAL SCALES: accountant (2 scales: female, male), advertising executive (f, m), agribusiness manager (m), air force officer (m), architect (m), army officer (f, m), art teacher (f), artist (f, m), banker (f, m), beautician (f), biologist (m), business education teacher (f, m), buyer (f, m), cartographer (m), chamber of commerce executive (m), chemist (f), chiropractor (m), college professor (f, m), computer programmer (f, m), computer sales (m), credit manager (f, m), dental assistant (f), dental hygienist (f), dentist (f, m), department store manager (m), department store sales (f), dietitian (f, m), director—Christian education (f), elementary teacher (f, m), engineer (f, m), English teacher (f, m), entertainer (f), executive housekeeper (f), farmer (m), flight attendant (f), forester (m), funeral director (m), guidance counselor (f, m), highway patrol officer (m), home economics teacher (f), instrument assembler (f), interior decorator (f, m), investment fund manager (m), language interpreter (f), language teacher (f), lawyer (f, m), librarian (f, m), life insurance agent (f, m), mathematician (f, m), math-science teacher (f, m), medical technologist (f, m), merchant marine officer (m), minister (m),

musician (f, m), navy officer (m), nurse—licensed practical (f, m), nurse—registered (f, m), occupational therapist (f), optometrist (f, m), personnel director (m), pharmacist (f, m), photographer (m), physical education teacher (f), physical scientist (m), physical therapist (f, m), physician (f, m), physicist (f), police officer (m), priest (m), psychologist (f, m), public administrator (m), purchasing agent (m), radiologic technician (m), realtor (m), recreation leader (f, m), reporter (f, m), sales manager (m), school superintendent (m), secretary (f), skilled crafts (m), social science teacher (f, m), social scientist (m), social worker (f, m), speech pathologist (f, m), veterinarian (f, m), vocational agriculture teacher (m), YWCA staff (f); SPECIAL SCALES: academic orientation, introversion-extroversion; ADMINISTRATIVE INDEXES: total responses, infrequent responses, response percentages (like, indifferent, dislike) for each of the 7 inventory sections; no data on validity of general occupational themes; Form T325 ('74, 4 pages); 2 editions: reusable, NCS scorable; manual, second edition ('77, 143 pages); specimen brochure ['76, 16 pages]; profiles: for student, for counselor, ('76, 2 pages); separate answer sheets (NCS, OpScan) must be used with reusable edition; tests cannot be scored locally; (20-60) minutes; original inventory by Edward K. Strong, Jr., revision by David P. Campbell; Stanford University Press. * (All test materials and scoring services must be purchased from distributors. Scoring agencies authorized to score the tests are listed below.)

a) CONSULTING PSYCHOLOGISTS PRESS, INC. $6.25 per 25 reusable tests; $6.75 per 50 CPP OpScan answer sheets; $6.50 per manual; postage extra; scoring and profile report: $1.75 or less per test; 1 day service. *

b) EVALUATION SERVICES, INC. $1.75 per 25 OpScan answer sheets, postpaid; test booklets must be purchased elsewhere; scoring and 7-page interpretive report: $1.99 or less per test ($3 minimum). *

c) MINCOMP CORPORATION. Interpretive report manual, second edition ('77, 28 pages); descriptive tape cassette available; 25¢ per reusable test; $8.95 per tape; $6.50 per manual; $5 per interpretive report manual; 50¢ per specimen brochure; cash orders postpaid; answer sheet, scoring, and profile report: $1.95 or less per test; answer sheet, scoring, and 6-page interpretive report: $5 or less per test; 1 day service; interpretive report manual by Terry M. Wilmot and Alice M. Osterlund. *

d) NCS INTERPRETIVE SCORING SYSTEMS. Interpretive report manual ('74, 60 pages); $8 per 50 NCS scorable tests; $13 per 50 reusable tests; $6 per 50 answer sheets; $6.50 per manual; $5 per interpretive report manual; postage extra; scoring and profile report: $1.90 or less per test for 1 day service, $1.20 or less per test for weekly service ($30 minimum); scoring and interpretive report: $5.50 or less per test for 1 day service; interpretive report manual by Charles B. Johansson. *

e) ROCHE TESTING SERVICE. $3 per 25 NCS scorable tests, postpaid; scoring and profile report: $2 per test; 1 day service. *

For references on the *Strong Vocational Interest Blank for Men*, see T2:2212 (133 references); for reviews by Martin R. Katz and Charles J. Krauskopf and excerpted reviews by David P. Campbell and John W. M. Rothney, see 7:1036 (485 references); for reviews by Alexander W. Astin and Edward J. Furst, see 6:1070 (189 references); see also 5:868 (153 references); for reviews by Edward S. Bordin and Elmer D. Hinckley, see 4:747 (98 references); see also 3:647 (102 references); for reviews by Harold D. Carter, John G. Darley, and N. W. Morton, see 2:1680 (71

references); for a review by John G. Darley, see 1:1178.

For references on the *Strong Vocational Interest Blank for Women*, see T2:2213 (30 references); for reviews by Dorothy M. Clendenen and Barbara A. Kirk, see 7:1037 (92 references); see also 6:1071 (12 references) and 5:869 (19 references); for a review by Gwendolen Schneidler Dickson, see 3:649 (38 references); for a review by Ruth Stang, see 2:1681 (10 references); for a review by John G. Darley, see 1:1179.

References in this volume are for SVIB-M, SVIB-W, and SCII, with the numbering sequence continuing from the SVIB-M.

REFERENCES

1-71. See 2:1680.
72-175. See 3:647.
176-273. See 4:747.
274-426. See 5:868.
427-614. See 6:1070.
615-1099. See 7:1036.
1100-1232. See T2:2212; also includes a cumulative name index to the first 1232 references, 10 reviews, and 2 excerpts for this test.
1233. McCabe, Sheridan P. *The Self-Concept and Vocational Interest.* Washington, D.C.: Catholic University of America Press, 1958. Pp. v, 34. * (PA 33:6472)
1234. Heath, Douglas H. *Growing Up in College: Liberal Education and Maturity.* San Francisco, Calif.: Jossey-Bass Inc., Publishers, 1968. Pp. xvii, 326. *
1235. Blum, Richard H. Chap. 14, "Psychological Tests," pp. 232-41. In *Students and Drugs: Drugs II: College and High School Observations.* By Richard H. Blum and Associates. San Francisco, Calif.: Jossey-Bass Inc., Publishers, 1969. Pp. xix, 399. *
1236. Bayless, Polly Ann. *Personality Consistency as a Predictor of Vocational Counseling Success.* Doctor's thesis, University of Houston (Houston, Tex.), 1971. (DAI 33:897B)
1237. Eggenberger, John C. *The Application of the Strong Vocational Interest Blank to Holland's Theory.* Master's thesis, University of Calgary (Calgary, Alta., Canada), 1971.
1238. Finnegan, Rex Thomas. *A Study of Personality Differences of the Vocationally Undecided Student and the Effect of Vocational Counseling.* Doctor's thesis, Oklahoma State University (Stillwater, Okla.), 1971. (DAI 33:566A)
1239. Harrell, Thomas W. "Differences Between Men in Big and Small Business." *Personnel Psychol* 24(4):649-52 w '71. * (PA 51:4020)
1240. Anderson, Robert P., and Lawlis, G. Frank. "Strong Vocational Interest Blank and Culturally Handicapped Women." *J Counsel Psychol* 19(1):83-4 Ja '72. * (PA 47:9870)
1241. Apostal, Robert A., and Harper, Patricia. "Basic Interests in Personality." *J Counsel Psychol* 19(2):167-8 Mr '72. * (PA 48:5686)
1242. Baldwin, Lannes W., Jr. *The Effect of Sex and Type of Mental Status on Stimulus Preference in the Drawing-Completion Test.* Doctor's thesis, University of Oklahoma (Norman, Okla.), 1972. (DAI 33:1013A)
1243. Barron, Frank. *Artists in the Making.* New York: Seminar Press, Inc., 1972. Pp. xxi, 237. *
1244. Bascus, Joseph, and Eisenman, Russell. "Study of 'Adventure Clusters' of the Strong Vocational Interest Blank and the Personal Opinion Survey." *Percept & Motor Skills* 34(1):277-8 F '72. * (PA 48:7220)
1245. Blakeney, Roger N.; Matteson, Michael T.; and Holland, Thomas A. "A Research Note on the New SVIB Holland Scales." *J Voc Behav* 2(3):239-43 Jl '72. * (PA 49:8045)
1246. Borgen, Fred H. "Predicting Career Choices of Able College Men From Occupational and Basic Interest Scales of the Strong Vocational Interest Blank." *J Counsel Psychol* 19(3):202-11 My '72. * (PA 48:9736)
1247. Bradshaw, Harley Edward. *Predicting Holland Vocational Preference Inventory Scales From Strong Basic Interest Scales for Community College Males.* Doctor's thesis, Southern Illinois University (Carbondale, Ill.), 1972. (DAI 33:2097A)
1248. Brown, Jane Ella. *An Investigation of Holland's Theory of Vocational Choice Applied to High School Girls.* Doctor's thesis, University of Virginia (Charlottesville, Va.), 1972. (DAI 33:5486A)
1249. Campbell, David P., and Holland, John L. "A Merger in Vocational Interest Research: Applying Holland's Theory to Strong's Data." *J Voc Behav* 2(4):353-76 O '72. * (PA 50:7936)
1250. Campbell, David P., and Rossmann, Jack E. "Liberalism-Conservatism, Men and Women, and Occupations." Abstract. *Proc 80th Ann Conv Am Psychol Assn* 7(2):591-2 '72. *
1251. Carek, Roman. "Another Look at the Relationships

Between Similar Scales on the Strong Vocational Interest Blank and Kuder Occupational Interest Survey." *J Counsel Psychol* 19(3):218–23 My '72. * (*PA* 48:9739)

1252. COCKRIEL, IRVIN W. "Some Data Concerning the Vocational Preference Inventory Scales and the Strong Vocational Interest Blank." *J Voc Behav* 2(3):251–4 Jl '72. * (*PA* 49:7757)

1253. COLE, NANCY S. "On Measuring the Vocational Interests of Women." *ACT Res Rep* 49:1–11 Mr '72. * (*PA* 48:9970)

1254. DOLL, RICHARD E.; AMBLER, ROSALIE K.; LANE, NORMAN E.; AND BALE, RONALD M. "Vocational Interest Differences Between Students Completing the Naval Aviation Training Program and Students Voluntarily Withdrawing." Abstract. *Proc 80th Ann Conv Am Psychol Assn* 7(2):621–2 '72. * (*PA* 48:5941)

1255. DOLLIVER, ROBERT H., AND CLARK, JAMES A. "Status Faking on the SVIB-M." *J Voc Behav* 2(1):47–56 Ja '72. * (*PA* 48:3739)

1256. DOLLIVER, ROBERT H.; IRVIN, JAMES A.; AND BIGLEY, STEPHEN S. "Twelve-Year Follow-Up of the Strong Vocational Interest Blank." *J Counsel Psychol* 19(3):212–7 My '72. * (*PA* 48:9747)

1257. EGGENBERGER, JOHN, AND HERMAN, AL. "The Strong Inventory and Holland's Theory." *J Voc Behav* 2(4):447–56 O '72. * (*PA* 50:7948)

1258. FEENEY, HELEN MARIE. *Interest Values and Social Class as Related to Adult Women Who Are Continuing Their Education.* Doctor's thesis, New York University (New York, N.Y.), 1972. (*DAI* 33:5835A)

1259. FRANK, AUSTIN C. "Toward a College Student Typology: Semiempirical Student Clusters Using Ability, Interest, and Personality Tests Simultaneously." Abstract. *Proc 80th Ann Conv Am Psychol Assn* 7(2):605–6 '72. *

1260. FRANTZ, THOMAS T. "Reinterpretation of Flat SVIB Profiles." *J Voc Behav* 2(2):201–7 Ap '72. * (*PA* 48:9972)

1261. GANDY, GERALD LARMON. *The Relationship Between Birth Order and Vocational Interest.* Doctor's thesis, University of South Carolina (Columbia, S.C.), 1972. (*DAI* 32:6807A)

1262. GLENDY, DAVID G., AND CAPLE, RICHARD B. "Characteristics of Community/Junior College and University Counselors as Measured by the SVIB." *J Col Stud Personnel* 13(2):136–9 Mr '72. * (*PA* 48:7802)

1263. GOLDBERG, LEWIS R. "Student Personality Characteristics and Optimal College Learning Conditions: An Extensive Search for Trait-By-Treatment Interaction Effects." *Instructional Sci* (Netherlands) 1(2):153–210 Jl '72. *

1264. HANNAM, JOSEPH C. *Congruence of the Psychometric Assessment and Counselor Perceptions of Outcomes of Group Counseling With College Men and Women.* Doctor's thesis, St. John's University (Jamaica, N.Y.), 1972. (*DAI* 33:2810B)

1265. HANSEN, JO-IDA, AND JOHANSSON, CHARLES B. "The Application of Holland's Vocational Model to the Strong Vocational Interest Blank for Women." *J Voc Behav* 2(4):479–93 O '72. * (*PA* 50:7971)

1266. HARMON, LENORE W. "Variables Related to Women's Persistence in Educational Plans." *J Voc Behav* 2(2):143–53 Ap '72. * (*PA* 48:9756)

1267. HARRELL, THOMAS W. "High Earning MBA's." *Personnel Psychol* 25(3):523–30 au '72. * (*PA* 51:2013)

1268. HOLLENDER, JOHN. "Differential Parental Influences on Vocational Interest Development in Adolescent Males." *J Voc Behav* 2(1):67–76 Ja '72. * (*PA* 48:3751)

1269. HUGHES, HENRY M., JR. "Vocational Choice, Level, and Consistency: An Investigation of Holland's Theory on an Employed Sample." *J Voc Behav* 2(4):377–88 O '72. * (*PA* 50:7978)

1270. JOHANSSON, CHARLES B., AND HARMON, LENORE W. "Strong Vocational Interest Blank: One Form or Two?" *J Counsel Psychol* 19(5):404–10 S '72. * (*PA* 49:1526)

1271. JOHNSON, RICHARD W. "Content Analysis of the Strong Vocational Interest Blank for Men." *J Counsel Psychol* 19(6):479–86 N '72. * (*PA* 49:8093)

1272. JOHNSON, RICHARD W. "Contradictory Scores on the Strong Vocational Interest Blank." *J Counsel Psychol* 19(6):487–90 N '72. * (*PA* 49:8092)

1273. JOHNSON, RICHARD W., AND JOHANSSON, CHARLES B. "Moderating Effect of Basic Interests on Predictive Validity of SVIB Occupational Scales." Abstract. *Proc 80th Ann Conv Am Psychol Assn* 7(2):589–90 '72. *

1274. KELZ, JAMES W., AND FULLERTON, JOHN. "Rehabilitation Role Perceptions and Vocational Interests of Undergraduate Rehabilitation Students." *Voc Guid Q* 21(2):126–32 D '72. *

1275. KUNCE, JOSEPH T.; DOLLIVER, ROBERT H.; AND IRVIN, JAMES A. "Perspectives on Interpreting the Validity of the SVIB-M." *Voc Guid Q* 21(1):36–42 S '72. *

1276. LONNER, WALTER J., AND ADAMS, HENRY L. "Interest Patterns of Psychologists in Nine Western Nations." *J Appl Psychol* 56(2):146–51 Ap '72. * (*PA* 48:7948)

1277. LONNER, WALTER J., AND ADAMS, HENRY L. "A Multi-Nation Comparison of Psychologists Measured Interests." *South African J Psychol* 2:1–14 '72. *

1278. LONNER, W. J., AND ADAMS, H. L. "A Note on the Measured Interests of Australian and New Zealand Psychologists." *Austral Psychologist* 7(1):47–9 Mr '72. *

1279. LONNER, W. J., AND ADAMS, H. L. "A Note on the Measured Interests of British Psychologists." *B Brit Psychol Soc* 25(86): 29–30 Ja '72. * (*PA* 49:898)

1280. MARTUCCI, MARY ELIZABETH. *Difference in Self and Role Perceptions in Career Oriented and Non-Career Oriented College Women.* Doctor's thesis, University of Notre Dame (Notre Dame, Ind.), 1972. (*DAI* 33:5625A)

1281. MATTHEWS, CHARLES ODELL, II. *The Effect of Identification With the Technology of Society on the Identity Crisis of College Males as Postulated by Erik Erikson.* Doctor's thesis, Duke University (Durham, N.C.), 1972. (*DAI* 33:6094A)

1282. MEACCI, FRANK, JR. *The Effects of Three Career Counseling Approaches Upon College Freshmen Who Are Experiencing Career Uncertainty.* Doctor's thesis, University of Pittsburgh (Pittsburgh, Pa.), 1972. (*DAI* 33:6673A)

1283. MENGES, ROBERT J.; MARX, ROBERT; AND TRUMPETER, P. WILLIAM. "Effectiveness of Tutorial Assistance for High-Risk Students in Advanced College Courses." *J Counsel Psychol* 19(3):229–33 My '72. * (*PA* 48:9829)

1284. MULES, WILLIAM CURRAN. *A Comparison of Conventional Modes of Interpreting Strong Vocational Interest Blank Results to Modes Which Employ a Computer Generated, Prose Interpretation.* Doctor's thesis, University of Virginia (Charlottesville, Va.), 1972. (*DAI* 33:1445A)

1285. NAFISSI, GHOLAMREZA. *A Persian Version of the Strong Vocational Interest Blank.* Doctor's thesis, Purdue University (Lafayette, Ind.), 1972. (*DAI* 33:901B)

1286. O'SHEA, ARTHUR J., AND HARRINGTON, THOMAS F., JR. "Strong Vocational Interest Blank and Kuder Occupational Interest Survey Differences Reexamined in Terms of Holland's Vocational Theory." Comments by Wilbur L. Layton and Fred H. Borgen and reply by authors. *J Counsel Psychol* 19(5):455–63 S '72. * (*PA* 49:1536)

1287. O'SHEA, ARTHUR J.; LYNCH, MERVIN D.; AND HARRINGTON, THOMAS F. "A Reply to Kuder's Criticism of SVIB-KOIS Comparative Studies." *Meas & Eval Guid* 5(1):306–9 Ap '72. * (*PA* 49:3524)

1288. PETERSON, ROBERT A. "Vocational Interest Patterns of Male and Female Medical Students Over a Four-Year Period." *J Counsel Psychol* 19(1):21–5 Ja '72. * (*PA* 47:9767)

1289. PLETCHER, BERNARD PHILIP. *The Validity of a Required College of Education Screening Program for Transfer Students.* Doctor's thesis, University of Toledo (Toledo, Ohio), 1972. (*DAI* 33:4097A)

1290. RAYBURN, WENDELL GILBERT. *An Analysis of the Aspiration, Motivation, and Academic Achievement Levels of Disadvantaged Students as Compared to Advantaged Students at the University of Detroit.* Doctor's thesis, Wayne State University (Detroit, Mich.), 1972. (*DAI* 33:2134A)

1291. RAZIN, ANDREW MICHAEL. *The Relationship of the A-B Variable to Therapist Persuasiveness.* Doctor's thesis, Columbia University (New York, N.Y.), 1972. (*DAI* 33:449B)

1292. REICH, STEPHEN. *The Relationship of Personality Characteristics and Vocational Interests to Academic Achievement in a School of Law.* Doctor's thesis, Fordham University (New York, N.Y.), 1972. (*DAI* 33:449B)

1293. RHODE, JOHN GRANT, AND PETERSON, ROBERT A. "The Vocational Interests of Marketing Professionals." *J Voc Behav* 2(1):13–24 Ja '72. * (*PA* 48:3975)

1294. SANDLER, IRWIN N. "Characteristics of Women Working as Child Aides in a School-Based Preventive Mental Health Program." *J Consult & Clin Psychol* 39(1):56–61 Ag '72. * (*PA* 49:2550)

1295. SCOTT, WILLIAM E., JR., AND DAY, GERALD J. "Personality Dimensions and Vocational Interests Among Graduate Business Students." *J Counsel Psychol* 19(1):30–6 Ja '72. * (*PA* 47:9771)

1296. SINNETT, E. ROBERT; STONE, LEROY A.; AND MATTER, DARRYL E. "Clinical Judgment and the Strong Vocational Interest Blank." *J Counsel Psychol* 19(6):498–504 N '72. * (*PA* 49:8140)

1297. SOMMER, GARY. *Need for Achievement Motivation and Its Relationship to the Strong Vocational Interest Blank.* Master's thesis, California State University (Hayward, Calif.), 1972.

1298. STONE, LEROY A.; BASSETT, GERALD R.; BROSSEAU, JAMES D.; DEMERS, JUDY; AND STIENING, JOHN A. "Psychological Test Scores for a Group of MEDEX Trainees." *Psychol Rep* 31(3):827–31 D '72. * (*PA* 50:1183)

1299. SUE, DERALD W., AND KIRK, BARBARA A. "Psychological Characteristics of Chinese-American Students." *J Counsel Psychol* 19(6):471–8 N '72. * (*PA* 49:7002)

1300. TAYLOR, RONALD G., AND HANSON, GARY R. "Interest Change as a Function of Persistence and Transfer From an Engineering Major." *J Counsel Psychol* 19(2):130–5 Mr '72. * (*PA* 48:5729)

1301. TAYLOR, RONALD G., AND ROTH, JOHN D. "Relationships Between Minnesota Counseling Inventory and Strong Vocational Interest Blank Scores for Engineering Freshmen." *J Counsel Psychol* 19(2):104–11 Mr '72. * (*PA* 48:5728)

1302. TESTER, LEONARD W. *The Effect of Test Anxiety Desensitization on Scores on the Strong Vocational Interest Blank.* Master's thesis, Teachers College, Columbia University (New York, N.Y.), 1972.

1303. THOMPSON, JOHN KELL. *Personality Traits and Interest*

Strong-Campbell Interest Inventory

Characteristics of Graduate Students in a Rehabilitation Counselor Training Program. Doctor's thesis, University of Arizona (Tucson, Ariz.), 1972. (*DAI* 33:4858A)

1304. VAN SICKLE, ANETA LOUISE SMID. *Analysis of Intellective and Non-Intellective Differences Among Freshman Student Groups in the School of Humanities, Social Science and Education at Purdue University.* Doctor's thesis, Purdue University (Lafayette, Ind.), 1972. (*DAI* 33:578A)

1305. VAN TASSEL, JAMES McVAY. *Interrelationships Among Special Education Teacher Trainee Responses to Interest, Attitude and Personality Measures.* Doctor's thesis, Michigan State University (East Lansing, Mich.), 1972. (*DAI* 33:6209A)

1306. WADE, ARNOLD. *A Comparative Study of Unsuccessful Students Applying for Readmission in the School of Humanities, Social Science and Education at Purdue University.* Doctor's thesis, Purdue University (Lafayette, Ind.), 1972. (*DAI* 33:4859A)

1307. WILLOUGHBY, THEODORE C. "Are Programmers Paranoid?" *Proc Ann Computer Personnel Res Conf* 10:47–54 '72. *

1308. ZYTOWSKI, DONALD G. "A Concurrent Test of Accuracy-of-Classification for the Strong Vocational Interest and Kuder Occupational Interest Survey." *J Voc Behav* 2(3):245–50 Jl '72. * (*PA* 49:5809)

1309. ZYTOWSKI, DONALD G. "Equivalence of the Kuder Occupational Interest Survey and the Strong Vocational Interest Blank Revisited." *J Appl Psychol* 56(2):184–5 Ap '72. * (*PA* 48:7950)

1310. AMEG COMMISSION ON SEX BIAS IN MEASUREMENT. "AMEG Commission Report on Sex Bias in Interest Measurement." *Meas & Eval Guid* 6(3):171–7 O '73. * (*PA* 51:8001)

1311. ABRAHAMS, NORMAN M., AND NEUMANN, IDELL. "Predicting the Unpredictable: A Validation of the Strong Vocational Interest Blank for Predicting Military Aptitude Ratings of Naval Academy Midshipmen." Abstract. *Proc 81st Ann Conv Am Psychol Assn* 8(2):747–8 '73. * (*PA* 50:7924)

1312. BARNETTE, W. LESLIE, JR.; D'COSTA, AYRES; HARMON, LENORE W.; SUPER, DONALD E.; WEISS, DAVID J.; AND ZYTOWSKI, DONALD G. Chap. 9, "Illustrative Interpretations of Inventories," pp. 206–44. In *Contemporary Approaches to Interest Measurement.* Edited by Donald G. Zytowski. Minneapolis, Minn. University of Minnesota Press, 1973. Pp. xi, 251. *

1313. BEIT-HALLAHMI, BENJAMIN. "Counseling With the SVIB: The 'Ideal Self.'" *Personnel & Guid J* 52(4):256–61 D '73. * (*PA* 52:1964)

1314. BERGERON, ANDREW L. *The Relationship Between Selected SVIB Scales and Military Science Grade Point Averages.* Master's thesis, Alfred University (Alfred, N.Y.), 1973.

1315. BOGDAN, ARTHUR RICHARD. *Relationships Among Vocational Interests, Personal Needs, and Personality Characteristics.* Doctor's thesis, Rutgers—The State University (New Brunswick, N.J.), 1973. (*DAI* 34:3860A)

1316. BOHN, MARTIN J., JR. "Personality Variables in Successful Work-Study Performance." *J Col Stud Personnel* 14(2):135–40 Mr '73. * (*PA* 50:5632)

1317. BORGEN, FRED H., AND HARPER, GREGORY T. "Predictive Validity of Measured Vocational Interests With Black and White College Men." *Meas & Eval Guid* 6(1):19–27 Ap '73. * (*PA* 50:10216)

1318. CAMPBELL, DAVID P. "Reaction to the AMEG Commission Report on Sex Bias in Interest Measurement." *Meas & Eval Guid* 6(3):178–80 O '73. *

1319. CAMPBELL, DAVID P. Chap. 2, "The Strong Vocational Interest Blank for Men," pp. 20–57. (*PA* 51:1954, title only) In *Contemporary Approaches to Interest Measurement.* Edited by Donald G. Zytowski. Minneapolis, Minn.: University of Minnesota Press, 1973. Pp. xi, 251. *

1320. COLE, NANCY S. "On Measuring the Vocational Interests of Women." *J Counsel Psychol* 20(2):105–12 Mr '73. * (*PA* 50:3974)

1321. COLLINS, JAMES A., AND TAYLOR, RONALD G. "A Configural Approach to the Use of the Strong Vocational Interest Blank With Student Engineers." *J Voc Behav* 3(3):291–302 Jl '73. * (*PA* 51:10020)

1322. CONSTANTINOPLE, ANNE. "Masculinity-Femininity: An Exception to a Famous Dictum?" *Psychol B* 80(5):389–407 N '73. * (*PA* 51:9094)

1323. DAVIS, SANDRA LEE OTTSEN. *Factors Related to the Persistence of Women in a Four-Year Institute of Technology.* Doctor's thesis, University of Minnesota (Minneapolis, Minn.), 1973. (*DAI* 34:3460B)

1324. DOLLIVER, ROBERT H., AND KUNCE, JOSEPH T. "Who Drops Out of an SVIB Follow-Up Study?" *J Counsel Psychol* 20(2):188–9 Mr '73. * (*PA* 50:3982)

1325. DORÉ, RUSSELL, AND MEACHAM, MERLE. "Self-Concept and Interests Related to Job Satisfaction of Managers." *Personnel Psychol* 26(1):49–59 sp '73. * (*PA* 51:1984)

1326. DORR, DARWIN; COWEN, EMORY L.; SANDLER, IRWIN; AND PRATT, D. MICHAEL. "Dimensionality of a Test Battery for Nonprofessional Mental Health Workers." *J Consult & Clin Psychol* 41(2):181–5 O '73. * (*PA* 51:7199)

1327. EICHLER, LOIS S. *"Feminine Narcissism": An Empirical Investigation.* Doctor's thesis, Boston University (Boston, Mass.), 1973. (*DAI* 33:6074B)

1328. FOSTER, JAMES, AND GADE, ELDON. "Locus of Control, Consistency of Vocational Interest Patterns, and Academic Achievement." *J Counsel Psychol* 20(3):290–2 My '73. * (*PA* 50:11983)

1329. GANDY, GERALD L. "Birth Order and Vocational Interest." *Develop Psychol* 9(3):406–10 N '73. * (*PA* 51:4888)

1330. GARDNER, RILEY W. "Relationships Between Similar Scales of Two Major Interest Inventories." *Percept & Motor Skills* 36(2):635–8 Ap '73. * (*PA* 51:3962)

1331. HAMMEL, WILLIAM DONALD. *Predicting Multiple Criteria of College Success With Intellective and Nonintellective Predictors for New College of Liberal Arts Freshmen at the University of Minnesota.* Doctor's thesis, University of Minnesota (Minneapolis, Minn.), 1973. (*DAI* 34:7043A)

1332. HARMON, LENORE W. Chap. 3, "The 1969 Revision of the Strong Vocational Interest Blank for Women," pp. 58–96. (*PA* 51:1960, title only) In *Contemporary Approaches to Interest Measurement.* Edited by Donald G. Zytowski. Minneapolis, Minn.: University of Minnesota Press, 1973. Pp. xi, 251. *

1333. HARMON, LENORE W. "Sexual Bias in Interest Measurement." *Meas & Eval Guid* 5(4):496–501 Ja '73. * (*PA* 50:3999)

1334. HARMAN, ROBERT L. "Students Who Lack Vocational Identity." *Voc Guid Q* 21(3):169–73 Mr '73. *

1335. HARRELL, THOMAS W., AND HARRELL, MARGARET S. "The Personality of MBA's Who Reach General Management Early." *Personnel Psychol* 26(1):127–34 sp '73. * (*PA* 51:2012)

1336. HARRILL, THOMAS STEARN. *A Comparative Study of the Efficiency of Intellective and Nonintellective Measures as Predictors of Job Success and Job Satisfaction.* Doctor's thesis, Auburn University (Auburn, Ala.), 1973. (*DAI* 33:6665A)

1337. HARVEY, DAVID W., AND WHINFIELD, RICHARD W. "Extending Holland's Theory to Adult Women." *J Voc Behav* 3(2):115–27 Ap '73. * (*PA* 50:10120)

1338. HELSON, RAVENNA. "Heroic and Tender Modes in Women Authors of Fantasy." *J Personality* 41(4):493–512 D '73. * (*PA* 52:917)

1339. HIGGINS, PAUL S., AND ROSSMANN, JACK E. "Student Characteristics Preferred by the Faculty at a Liberal Arts College." *J Col Stud Personnel* 14(3):225–30 My '73. * (*PA* 52:1739)

1340. HOUNTRAS, PETER T.; LEE, DAVID L.; AND HEDAHL, BEULAH M. "Relationships Between SVIB Nonoccupational Scales and Achievement for Six Holland Personality Types." *J Voc Behav* 3(2):195–208 Ap '73. * (*PA* 50:9893)

1341. HUTH, CAROL MONNIK. "Measuring Women's Interests: How Useful?" Comment ("Women Deserve Better") by David P. Campbell. *Personnel & Guid J* 51(8):539–49 Ap '73. * (*PA* 50:10126)

1342. HUTH, CAROL MONNIK. "Reply to Campbell." Letter. *Personnel & Guid J* 51(10):697 Je '73. *

1343. JOHANSSON, CHARLES B., AND FLINT, ROBERT T. "Vocational Interests of Policemen." *Voc Guid Q* 22(1):40–2 S '73. * (*PA* 53:2022)

1344. KIRK, BARBARA A. "Characteristics of Users of Counseling Centers and Psychiatric Services on a College Campus." *J Counsel Psychol* 20(5):463–70 S '73. * (*PA* 51:9973)

1345. LANDOM, DAVE L. *The Strong Vocational Interest Blank Accounting Score, the ACT Mathematics Usage Score, and the ACT Self-Reported High School Average Grade in Mathematics as Predictors of Accounting Achievement.* Master's thesis, Black Hills State College (Spearfish, S.D.), 1973.

1346. LEE, DAVID L., AND HEDAHL, BEULAH. "Holland's Personality Types Applied to the SVIB Basic Interest Scales." *J Voc Behav* 3(1):61–8 Ja '73. * (*PA* 50:4014)

1347. LINDGREN, HENRY CLAY. "Strong's Psychologist Scale and Course Grades in Psychology." *Percept & Motor Skills* 36(1):58 F '73. * (*PA* 50:12040)

1348. LITTELL, WILLIAM J. *An Investigation of Possible Moderating Effects of Self-Esteem on Vocational Choice and Classification.* Doctor's thesis, University of Kansas (Lawrence, Kan.), 1973. (*DAI* 34:6196B)

1349. LONNER, WALTER J., AND ADAMS, HENRY L. "A Note on the Measured Interests of Canadian Psychologists." *Can Psychologist* 14(1):60–2 Ja '73. * (*PA* 50:3127)

1350. LORR, MAURICE, AND SUZIEDELIS, ANTANAS. "A Dimensional Approach to the Interests Measured by the SVIB." *J Counsel Psychol* 20(2):113–9 Mr '73. * (*PA* 50:4019)

1351. McMULLIN, JAMES D. *Differences Analyzed on EPPS Variables for Samples Selected on SVIB Criteria: A Test of Holland's Theory.* Doctor's thesis, Boston College (Chestnut Hill, Mass.), 1973. (*DAI* 34:6388A)

1352. MATTESON, MICHAEL T.; HOLLAND, THOMAS A.; BLAKENEY, ROGER N.; AND SCHNITZEN, JOSEPH P. "Empirical Derivation of SVIB-Holland Scales: A Brief Report." *J Voc Behav* 3(2):163–6 Ap '73. * (*PA* 50:10143)

1353. MULROY, JOHN PATRICK. *A Comparison of Differential Modes of Interpretation of the Strong Vocational Interest Blank With High School Juniors.* Doctor's thesis, University of Wyoming (Laramie, Wyo.), 1973. (*DAI* 34:4756A)

1354. MUNLEY, PATRICK H. *An Exploratory Investigation of the Relationship Between Erik Erikson's Theory of Psycho-Social Development and Vocational Behavior.* Doctor's thesis,

Strong-Campbell Interest Inventory

University of Maryland (College Park, Md.), 1973. (*DAI* 35: 484B).

1355. MUNLEY, PATRICK H.; FRETZ, BRUCE R.; AND MILLS, DAVID H. "Female College Students' Scores on the Men's and Women's Strong Vocational Interest Blanks." *J Counsel Psychol* 20(3):285–9 My '73. * (*PA* 50:12064)

1356. NYGARD, MELISSA WILCOX FARLEY. *Effect of Consciousness-Raising Groups Versus Lectures About Women on the Personalities and Career Interests and Homemaking Interests of Female Students in Nursing.* Doctor's thesis, University of Iowa (Iowa City, Iowa), 1973. (*DAI* 34:3151A)

1357. ONG, JIN, AND MARCHBANKS, ROBERT L. "Validity of Selected Academic and Non-Academic Predictors of Optometry Grades." *Am J Optom* 50(7):583–8 Jl '73. * (*PA* 51:5270)

1358. PANOS, GEORGE. *Variables Differentiating High-Achievers and Low-Achievers in Associate Degree Programs.* Doctor's thesis, University of South Carolina (Columbia, S.C.), 1973. (*DAI* 34:1654A)

1359. PETTIT, IRENE BERNADICOU. *Social Class, Values and Duration in Psychotherapy.* Doctor's thesis, New York University (New York, N.Y.), 1973. (*DAI* 34:1282B)

1360. PUGH, RICHARD C.; TURNER, RICHARD L.; JOSBERGER, MARIE C.; AND VAN NELSON, C. "A Profile of Individuals Engaged in Educational Development." *Improving Hum Perfor* 2(2):121–8 su '73. *

1361. REINHEIMER, GEORGE EDWARD. *A Comparative Study of the Vocational Interests and Values of Roman Catholic Priests Active in the Ministry and Roman Catholic Priests Who Have Left the Active Ministry.* Doctor's thesis, St. John's University (Jamaica, N.Y.), 1973. (*DAI* 34:6460A)

1362. SHAFFER, PHYLLIS E. "Academic Progress of Disadvantaged Minority Students: A Two-Year Study." *J Col Stud Personnel* 14(1):41–6 Ja '73. * (*PA* 50:7859)

1363. SILLIMAN, BENJAMIN DUANE. *The Interbattery Relationships Between the Domains of Personality and Interest as Assessed by Selected Scales of the MMPI and SVIB.* Doctor's thesis, University of Kansas (Lawrence, Kan.), 1973. (*DAI* 34:3889A)

1364. SNYDER, PATRICIA ANN SCOTT. *Small Group Facilitators: Analyses of Attitudes, Interests, and Values Among Three Types of Successful Group Leaders.* Doctor's thesis, University of Southern California (Los Angeles, Calif.), 1973. (*DAI* 34: 4008A)

1365. STAATS, ARTHUR W.; GROSS, MICHAEL C.; GUAY, PETER F.; AND CARLSON, CARL C. "Personality and Social Systems and Attitude-Reinforcer-Discriminative Theory: Interest (Attitude) Formation, Function, and Measurement." *J Pers & Social Psychol* 26(2):251–61 My '73. * (*PA* 50:10494)

1366. STONE, LEROY A., AND BROSSEAU, JAMES D. "Cross-Validation of a System for Predicting Training Success of Medex Trainees." *Psychol Rep* 33(3):917–8 D '73. * (*PA* 52:5492)

1367. STONE, LEROY A.; BASSETT, GERALD R.; BROSSEAU, JAMES D.; DEMERS, JUDY; AND STIENING, JOHN A. "Psychological Test Characteristics Associated With Training-Success in a Medex (Physician's Extension) Training Program." *Psychol Rep* 32(1):231–4 F '73. * (*PA* 51:4013)

1368. SUE, DERALD W., AND FRANK, AUSTIN C. "A Typological Approach to the Psychological Study of Chinese and Japanese American College Males." *J Social Issues* 29(2):129–48 '73. * (*PA* 51:6952)

1369. SUE, DERALD W., AND KIRK, BARBARA A. "Differential Characteristics of Japanese-American and Chinese-American College Students." *J Counsel Psychol* 20(2):142–8 Mr '73. * (*PA* 50:3922)

1370. VINITSKY, MICHAEL. "A Forty-Year Follow-Up on the Vocational Interests of Psychologists and Their Relationship to Career Development." *Am Psychologist* 28(11):1000–9 N '73. * (*PA* 51:11213)

1371. WAGNER, LOUIS GERALD. *An Interest Inventory of Agribusiness Managers.* Doctor's thesis, University of Minnesota (Minneapolis, Minn.), 1973. (*DAI* 34:3075A)

1372. WINER, ELLEN NAIOMI. *Interests, Attitudes and Work Satisfaction of Cooperative Education Students.* Doctor's thesis, Boston University (Boston, Mass.), 1973. (*DAI* 34:1664A)

1373. ZYTOWSKI, DONALD G. Chap. 1, "Considerations in the Selection and Use of Interest Inventories," pp. 3–19. (*PA* 51:59, title only) In his *Contemporary Approaches to Interest Measurement.* Minneapolis, Minn.: University of Minnesota Press, 1973. Pp. xi, 251. *

1374. ARMSTRONG, ROBERTA ANTOINETTE. *Interest Patterns on the Strong Vocational Interest Blank Characteristic of University of Minnesota Male Freshmen and Their Relationship to Persistence in the University Curriculum.* Doctor's thesis, University of Minnesota (Minneapolis, Minn.), 1974. (*DAI* 35: 4137B)

1375. BARNES, PATSY HARRIS. *A Study of Personality Characteristics of Selected Computer Programmers and Computer Programmer Trainees.* Doctor's thesis, Auburn University (Auburn, Ala.), 1974. (*DAI* 35:1440A)

1376. BIRK, JANICE M. "Interest Inventories: A Mixed Blessing." *Voc Guid Q* 22(4):280–6 Je '74. * (*PA* 53:12623)

1377. BUCHANAN, BERNICE F. *The Relationship of Work Values and Vocational Interest of Afro-American and Caucasian Generic Baccalaureate Nursing Students in Selected Colleges in the Washington Metropolitan Area.* Doctor's thesis, Catholic University of America (Washington, D.C.), 1974. (*DAI* 35: 5806A)

1378. CAMPBELL, DAVID P.; CRICHTON, LESLIE; HANSEN, JO IDA; AND WEBBER, PATRICIA. "A New Edition of the SVIB: The Strong-Campbell Interest Inventory." *Meas & Eval Guid* 7(2):92–5 Jl '74. * (*PA* 53:41)

1379. CASEY, TIMOTHY JOHN. *The Development of a Leadership Orientation Scale on the Strong Vocational Interest Blank for Women.* Doctor's thesis, University of Notre Dame (Notre Dame, Ind.), 1974. (*DAI* 34:3457B)

1380. CHOPE, ROBERT CRAWFORD, JR. *The Vocational Interests of Lawyers.* Doctor's thesis, University of Minnesota (Minneapolis, Minn.), 1974. (*DAI* 35:6066B)

1381. ECKERSLEY, EVERETT. *The Differences and Relationships of the Strong Vocational Interest Blank and Five Demographic Variables to the Prediction of Success in Vocational Rehabilitation.* Master's thesis, California State University (Hayward, Calif.), 1974.

1382. FIELDING, MICHAEL F., AND PAPPAS, JAMES P. "Internal-External Control of Reinforcement and the Strong Vocational Interest Blank: A Comparison Study." *J Counsel Psychol* 21(6):482–4 N '74. * (*PA* 53:6234)

1383. FRANK, AUSTIN C., AND KIRK, BARBARA A. "Factors Within the 1969 SVIB for Women and Relationships to Holland's Theory." *J Voc Behav* 5(1):79–94 Ag '74. * (*PA* 53:4137)

1384. FRASER, FREDERICK DONALD. *Effect of the Strong Vocational Interest Blank and the Self Directed Search on Career Planning of College Students.* Doctor's thesis, University of Missouri (Columbia, Mo.), 1974. (*DAI* 36:1302A)

1385. GAFFEY, ROBERT L., AND WALSH, W. BRUCE. "Concurrent Validity and Holland's Theory." *J Voc Behav* 5(1): 41–51 Ag '74. * (*PA* 53:4138)

1386. GROVES, D. L.; CAULEY, V. B., JR.; AND ROBERTS, R. K. "Some Underlying Interest and Occupational Orientation Factors of High School Students Interested in Natural Resource Occupations." *J Instruct Psychol* 1(4):28–39 f '74. * (*PA* 53:12550)

1387. HAGER, PAUL CALVIN. *The Prediction of the Educational Choice of College Women.* Doctor's thesis, University of Kentucky (Lexington, Ky.), 1974. (*DAI* 36:1306A)

1388. HANSEN, JO-IDA CHARLOTTE. *Coding Strong Vocational Interest Blank Items According to Holland's Theory of Personality Types.* Doctor's thesis, University of Minnesota (Minneapolis, Minn.), 1974. (*DAI* 35:2990B)

1389. HANSEN, JO-IDA C., AND JOHANSSON, CHARLES B. "Strong Vocational Interest Blank and Dogmatism." *J Counsel Psychol* 21(3):196–201 My '74. * (*PA* 52:8943)

1390. HANSON, GARY R.; LAMB, RICHARD R.; AND ENGLISH, EDWARD. "An Analysis of Holland's Interest Types for Women: A Comparison of the Strong-Holland and the ACT Vocational Interest Profile Scales for Women." *J Voc Behav* 4(2):259–69 Ap '74. * (*PA* 52:11116)

1391. HOLLAND, THOMAS A.; BLAKENEY, ROGER N.; MATTESON, MICHAEL T.; AND SCHNITZEN, JOSEPH P. "Empirical Derivation of SVIB-Holland Scales and Conversion Tables." *J Voc Behav* 5(1):23–9 Ag '74. * (*PA* 53:4140)

1392. HUNT, ANDREA P. *Changes in Gender-Related Vocational Interests Over a Thirty Year Interval.* Doctor's thesis, University of Minnesota (Minneapolis, Minn.), 1974. (*DAI* 35:6072B)

1393. JOHNSON, RICHARD W. "Content Analysis of the Strong Vocational Interest Blank for Women." *J Voc Behav* 5(1): 125–31 Ag '74. * (*PA* 53:2145)

1394. JOHNSON, RICHARD W., AND CAMPBELL, DAVID P. "Basic Interests of Men in 62 Occupations." *J Voc Behav* 5(3):373–80 D '74. * (*PA* 53:12649)

1395. KIRK, KENNETH W.; JOHNSON, RICHARD W.; AND OHVALL, RICHARD A. "Interests of Women Pharmacists." *Voc Guid Q* 22(3):200–8 Mr '74. * (*PA* 53:4148)

1396. KIRLIN, ELIZABETH ANNE. *A Personality Test Battery for Prediction and Planning in Graduate Social Work Education.* Doctor's thesis, University of Kentucky (Lexington, Ky.), 1974. (*DAI* 36:1331A)

1397. KRATZ, ROBERT CHARLES. *A Psychological Comparison of Alcoholism Counselors, Abstinent Alcoholics, and Chemically Dependent Inpatients.* Doctor's thesis, University of Minnesota (Minneapolis, Minn.), 1974. (*DAI* 35:3585B)

1398. KROGER, ROLF O. "Faking in Interest Measurement: A Social-Psychological Perspective." *Meas & Eval Guid* 7(2): 130–4 Jl '74. * (*PA* 53:3142)

1399. KUNCE, JOSEPH T., AND REEDER, CHARLES W. "SVIB Scores and Accident Proneness." *Meas & Eval Guid* 7(2): 118–21 Jl '74. * (*PA* 53:3143)

1400. MARTEL, IRA. *The Effect of the Deca Merit Awards Program on High School Student Interest Levels Toward Careers in Marketing.* Doctor's thesis, Oregon State University (Corvallis, Ore.), 1974. (*DAI* 35:2135A)

1401. MATHESON, GEORGE F., AND STAHMANN, ROBERT F. "Encouraging Vocational- and Self-Exploration Through the Strong Vocational Interest Blank." *J Col Stud Personnel* 15(2):151 Mr '74. *

1402. MAYES, JOHNNIE, JR. *A Comparative Analysis of the Basic and Occupational Interests of Transfer and Occupational*

Strong-Campbell Interest Inventory

Community College Students. Doctor's thesis, East Texas State University (Commerce, Tex.), 1974. (*DAI* 35:4197A)

1403. MUCHINSKY, PAUL M., AND HOYT, DONALD P. "Predicting Vocational Performance of Engineers From Selected Vocational Interest, Personality, and Scholastic Aptitude Variables." *J Voc Behav* 5(1):115–23 Ag '74. * (*PA* 53:4218)

1404. MUNLEY, PATRICK H. "Interests of Career and Home-making Oriented Women." *J Voc Behav* 4(1):43–8 Ja '74. * (*PA* 52:8729)

1405. NAFZIGER, DEAN H., AND HELMS, SAMUEL T. "Cluster Analyses of Interest Inventory Scales as Tests of Holland's Occupational Classification." *J Appl Psychol* 59(3):344–53 Je '74. * (*PA* 52:13320)

1406. O'BRIEN, BRIAN JOHN. *Internal and External Constructs as Predictors of Stability of Interests.* Doctor's thesis, Rutgers—The State University (New Brunswick, N.J.), 1974. (*DAI* 35:3029B)

1407. ODOM, KATHRINE POOL. *Comparative Study of Older and Younger Women Enrolled in an Undergraduate Degree Program at the Ohio State University.* Doctor's thesis, Ohio State University (Columbus, Ohio), 1974. (*DAI* 35:5033A)

1408. O'SHEA, ARTHUR J., AND HARRINGTON, THOMAS F., JR. "Measuring the Interests of Male and Female Students With the SVIB for Men." *Meas & Eval Guid* 7(2):112–7 Jl '74. * (*PA* 53:4107)

1409. PETTIT, IRENE B.; PETTIT, TUPPER F.; AND WELKO-WITZ, JOAN. "Relationship Between Values, Social Class, and Duration of Psychotherapy." *J Consult & Clin Psychol* 42(4):482–90 Ag '74. * (*PA* 52:12862)

1410. QUELET, THOMAS EDWARD. *Vocational Interests and Curriculum Choices of Eleventh Grade Students Attending the Larimer County Vocational-Technical School.* Doctor's thesis, Colorado State University (Ft. Collins, Colo.), 1974. (*DAI* 36:261A)

1411. ROBERTS, CAROLE A., AND JOHANSSON, CHARLES B. "The Inheritance of Cognitive Interest Styles Among Twins." *J Voc Behav* 4(2):237–43 Ap '74. * (*PA* 52:9376)

1412. SCHINKA, JOHN A., AND SINES, JACOB O. "Correlates of Accuracy in Personality Assessment." *J Clin Psychol* 30(3):374–7 Jl '74. * (*PA* 56:4669)

1413. SCHMIDT, FRANK L. "Probability and Utility Assumptions Underlying Use of the Strong Vocational Interest Blank." *J Appl Psychol* 59(4):456–64 Ag '74. * (*PA* 53:6327)

1414. SEIDMAN, EDWARD; GOLDING, STEPHEN L.; HOGAN, TERRENCE P.; AND LEBOW, MICHAEL D. "A Multidimensional Interpretation and Comparison of Three A-B Scales." *J Consult & Clin Psychol* 42(1):10–20 F '74. * (*PA* 52:5485)

1415. SHARP, NORMAN ROBERT. *A Multiple Regression Approach to Affective Sensitivity in Counselor Trainees.* Doctor's thesis, Western Michigan University (Kalamazoo, Mich.), 1974. (*DAI* 35:6488A)

1416. SHARP, W. HARRY, AND KIRK, BARBARA A. "A Longitudinal Study of Who Seeks Counseling When." *J Counsel Psychol* 21(1):43–50 Ja '74. * (*PA* 52:6400)

1417. SOUTH, J. C. "Early Career Performance of Engineers—Its Composition and Measurement." *Personnel Psychol* 27(2):225–43 su '74. *

1418. TONESK, XENIA; SUZIEDELIS, ANTANAS; AND LORR, MAURICE. "Vocational Interest Types of Men-in-General." *Meas & Eval Guid* 7(2):74–8 Jl '74. * (*PA* 53:2032)

1419. VRAA, CALVIN W. "Vocational Interest Orientations: A Comparison of Rural University and Junior College Freshmen." *J Voc Behav* 4(1):49–54 Ja '74. * (*PA* 52:8556)

1420. WEIR, W. DOUGLAS, AND JANTZ, ELEANORE M. "Attitudinal Grouping: A Rationale for Instructional Grouping of Medical Students." *J Med Ed* 49(8):785–6 Ag '74. * (*PA* 53:1931)

1421. WESSELL, TYRUS RAYMOND, JR. *A Comparative Analysis of the Psychological and Sociological Factors Relating to the Career Specialization Choices of Agency and School Counselors-in-Training.* Doctor's thesis, Western Michigan University (Kalamazoo, Mich.), 1974. (*DAI* 35:3441A)

1422. YAWORSKI, STEPHANIE EMILY. *An Analysis of the Interests, Personal and Educational Background of Selected Business Educators.* Doctor's thesis, University of North Dakota (Grand Forks, N.D.), 1974. (*DAI* 36:674A)

1423. ZAUGRA, JOHN F. *A Study of Selected Relationships Among Interests, Personality Traits, and Values Between Student Teachers and Experienced Teachers.* Doctor's thesis, University of Montana (Missoula, Mont.), 1974. (*DAI* 35:3444A)

1424. ALTMAN, SYDNEY L. *Women's Career Plans and Maternal Employment.* Doctor's thesis, Boston University (Boston, Mass.), 1975. (*DAI* 35:3569B)

1425. BELCASTRO, FRANK P. "Use of Selected Factors as Predictors of Success in Completing a Secondary Teacher Preparation Program." *Ed & Psychol Meas* 35(4):957–62 w '75. * (*PA* 55:13527)

1426. BENTON, ARTHUR L. "Inventoried Vocational Interests of Cartographers." *J Appl Psychol* 60(1):150–3 F '75. * (*PA* 53:12584)

1427. BIRK, JANICE M. Chap. 6, "Reducing Sex Bias: Factors Affecting the Client's View of the Use of Career Interest Inventories," pp. 101–21. In *Issues of Sex Bias and Sex Fairness in Career Interest Measurement.* Edited by Esther E. Diamond.

Washington, D.C.: National Institute of Education, 1975. Pp. xxix, 219. *

1428. BORGEN, FRED H., AND HELMS, JANET E. "Validity Generalization of the Men's Form of the Strong Vocational Interest Blank With Academically Able Women." *J Counsel Psychol* 22(3):210–6 My '75. * (*PA* 54:4456)

1429. BRENNY, AUDREY A. *A Study of the Inventoried Interests of Recent Graduates From Two Baccalaureate Nursing Programs and of Three Groups of Practicing Nurses.* Doctor's thesis, Marquette University (Milwaukee, Wis.), 1975. (*DAI* 36:4941B)

1430. BULL, PATRICK E. "Structure of Occupational Interests in New Zealand and America on Holland's Typology." *J Counsel Psychol* 22(6):554–6 N '75. * (*PA* 55:3477)

1431. CARITHERS, PHILIP L. *The Relationship of Pupillometric Response to Career Interests of Female College Students.* Doctor's thesis, Indiana State University (Terre Haute, Ind.), 1975. (*DAI* 36:4250A)

1432. CASEY, TIMOTHY J. "The Development of a Leadership Orientation Scale on the SVIB for Women." *Meas & Eval Guid* 8(2):96–100 Jl '75. * (*PA* 54:10825)

1433. CHU, MARK PING-HSIN. *Cross-Cultural Study of Vocational Interests Measured by the SCII.* Doctor's thesis, University of Wisconsin (Madison, Wis.), 1975. (*DAI* 36:4438A)

1434. CHU, PING-HSING. "Cross-Cultural Study of Vocational Interests Measured by the Strong-Campbell Interest Inventory." *Acta Psychologica Taiwanica* (Taiwan) 17:69–84 D '75. * (*PA* 55:11070)

1435. COOKE, PHYLISS. *Analysis of Data on Participants in Training to Become Elementary, Middle or Secondary School Counselors.* Doctor's thesis, Kent State University (Kent, Ohio), 1975. (*DAI* 36:3401A)

1436. COOPER, JACQUELINE FRIBUSH. *Impact of the Strong-Campbell Interest Inventory and the Vocational Card Sort on Career Salience and Vocational Exploration Behavior of Women.* Doctor's thesis, University of Maryland (College Park, Md.), 1975. (*DAI* 36:3401A)

1437. DEABLER, HERDIS L.; HARTL, EMIL M.; AND WILLIS, CONSTANCE A. "Physique and Personality: Somatotype and Vocational Interest." *Percept & Motor Skills* 41(2):382 O '75. * (*PA* 55:8454)

1438. DOLLIVER, ROBERT H. "Concurrent Prediction From the Strong Vocational Interest Blank." *J Counsel Psychol* 22(3):199–203 My '75. * (*PA* 54:4459)

1439. DOLLIVER, ROBERT H.; KUNCE, JOSEPH T.; AND IRVIN, JAMES A. "SVIB Revisions and Factors Affecting Scale Reliability." *J Voc Behav* 6(3):391–7 Je '75. * (*PA* 54:6581)

1440. FERRARA, THOMAS F. *The Influence of Race and Sex on the Development of Biodata and Interest Tests for Predicting Supervisory Success.* Doctor's thesis, American University (Washington, D.C.), 1975. (*DAI* 36:1486B)

1441. GOUGH, HARRISON G. "Strong Vocational Interest Blank Profiles of Women in Law, Mathematics, Medicine, and Psychology." *Psychol Rep* 37(1):127–34 Ag '75. * (*PA* 55:1623)

1442. GREEN, ELEANOR ALLISON. *Differential Effects of Modeling and an Instructional Procedure on Client Verbal Behavior in Vocational Counseling.* Doctor's thesis, Purdue University (Lafayette, Ind.), 1975. (*DAI* 36:4259A)

1443. HANSEN, JO-IDA C. Chap. 9, "Costs of Developing Interest Inventories and Implications for Change," pp. 161–75. In *Issues of Sex Bias and Sex Fairness in Career Interest Measurement.* Edited by Esther E. Diamond. Washington, D.C.: National Institute of Education, 1975. Pp. xxix, 219. *

1444. HARMON, LENORE W. Chap. 3, "Technical Aspects: Problems of Scale Development, Norms, Item Differences by Sex, and the Rate of Change in Occupational Group Characteristics—I," pp. 45–64. In *Issues of Sex Bias and Sex Fairness in Career Interest Measurement.* Edited by Esther E. Diamond. Washington, D.C.: National Institute of Education, 1975. Pp. xxix, 219. *

1445. HOMALL, GERALDINE M.; JUHASZ, SUZANNE; AND JUHASZ, JOSEPH. "Differences in Self-Perception and Vocational Aspirations of College Women." *Calif J Ed Res* 26(1):6–10 Ja '75. * (*PA* 54:1978)

1446. ISHIDA, HELEN. "Vocational Interests of Dental Hygienists." *Voc Guid Q* 23(3):257–62 Mr '75. *

1447. JOHANSSON, CHARLES B. Chap. 4, "Technical Aspects: Problems of Scale Development, Norms, Item Differences by Sex, and the Rate of Change in Occupational Group Characteristics," pp. 65–88. In *Issues of Sex Bias and Sex Fairness in Career Interest Measurement.* Edited by Esther E. Diamond. Washington, D.C.: National Institute of Education, 1975. Pp. xxix, 219. *

1448. JOHANSSON, CHARLES B. "Strong Vocational Interest Blank In-General Samples." *J Counsel Psychol* 22(2):113–6 Mr '75. * (*PA* 53:10715)

1449. JACKSON, DOUGLAS N., AND WILLIAMS, DAVID R. "Occupational Classification in Terms of Interest Patterns." *J Voc Behav* 6(2):269–80 Ap '75. * (*PA* 54:1980)

1450. JOHNSON, RICHARD W.; FLAMMER, DONALD P.; AND NELSON, J. GORDON. "Multiple Correlations Between Personality Factors and SVIB Occupational Scales." *J Counsel Psychol* 22(3):217–23 My '75. * (*PA* 54:6590)

Strong-Campbell Interest Inventory

1451. JOHNSON, RICHARD W.; KIRK, KENNETH W.; AND OHVALL, RICHARD A. "Predictive Validity of SVIB Pharmacist Scales." *Ed & Psychol Meas* 35(4):951–5 w '75. * (*PA* 55:13571)

1452. JOHNSON, RICHARD W.; NELSON, J. GORDON; NOLTING, EARL; ROTH, JOHN D.; AND TAYLOR, RONALD G. "Stability of Canonical Relationships Between the Strong Vocational Interest Blank and the Minnesota Counseling Inventory." *J Counsel Psychol* 22(3):247–51 My '75. * (*PA* 54:6589)

1453. JOHNSON, WILFRED ANTHONY. *A Study of the Attitudinal and Personality Traits of Students Accepted Into the Elementary Education and Special Education-Emotional Impairment Training Program at Michigan State University During Spring Term, 1974.* Doctor's thesis, Michigan State University (East Lansing, Mich.), 1975. (*DAI* 37:924A)

1454. KERLIN, BARBARA DRUMMOND. *A Study of John L. Holland's Theory of Careers as It Applies to Employed Adults.* Doctor's thesis, University of Maryland (College Park, Md.), 1975. (*DAI* 36:6640A)

1455. KLINE, PAUL. *Psychology of Vocational Guidance,* pp. 133–6. New York: John Wiley & Sons, Inc., [1975]. Pp. xiii, 253. *

1456. KREBS, DENNIS, AND ADINOLFI, ALLEN A. "Physical Attractiveness, Social Relations, and Personality Style." *J Pers & Social Psychol* 31(2):245–53 F '75. * (*PA* 53:11611)

1457. KUNCE, JOSEPH T.; COOK, DANIEL W.; AND MILLER, DOUGLAS E. "Random Variables and Correlational Overkill." *Ed & Psychol Meas* 35(3):529–34 au '75. * (*PA* 55:3558)

1458. LUNNEBORG, PATRICIA W. "Interpreting Other-Sex Scores on the Strong-Campbell Interest Inventory." *J Counsel Psychol* 22(6):494–9 N '75. * (*PA* 55:5937)

1459. MALETT, SHELDON DAVID. *The Effects of Information on the Expressed and Measured Vocational Interests of Private and Public School Graduates.* Doctor's thesis, University of Rochester (Rochester, N.Y.), 1975. (*DAI* 36:2105A)

1460. MINER, STEPHEN EDWARD. *An Analysis of Three Methods of Interpreting the Strong Vocational Interest Blank for Men.* Doctor's thesis, Purdue University (Lafayette, Ind.), 1975. (*DAI* 36:6480A)

1461. MUNLEY, PATRICK H. "Erik Erikson's Theory of Psychosocial Development and Vocational Behavior." *J Counsel Psychol* 22(4):314–9 Jl '75. * (*PA* 54:6412)

1462. NORTON, STEVEN, AND DIMARCO, NICHOLAS. "Personal and Vocational Interest Orientations: Comparison of Undergraduates in Two Programs." *Psychol Rep* 36(3):739–43 Je '75. * (*PA* 54:10659)

1463. OGG, THOMAS G. *A Descriptive Study of Student Persisters and Non-Persisters at St. Thomas Seminary From 1969 to 1973.* Doctor's thesis, University of Wyoming (Laramie, Wyo.), 1975. (*DAI* 36:2031A)

1464. PILLE, KLEMENS W. *Effects of the Novitiate on Personality and Vocational Decision in the Franciscan Formation Program.* Doctor's thesis, Catholic University of America (Washington, D.C.), 1975. (*DAI* 36:1468A)

1465. PRATT, ANN B. "Exploring Stereotypes of Popular and Unpopular Occupations Among Women-in-General." *J Voc Behav* 6(2):145–64 Ap '75. * (*PA* 54:963)

1466. RASKOPF, ROGER WILLIAM. *A Comparison of Correlates of Vocational Maturity Found in Episcopal Seminary Students Preparing for the Ministry as a Second Career With Those Found in Students Preparing for the Ministry as Their First Career.* Doctor's thesis, St. John's University (Jamaica, N.Y.), 1975. (*DAI* 36:5159A)

1467. ROBERTSON, DAVID WILLIAM. *Prediction of Naval Aviator Career Motivation and Job Satisfaction From the Strong Vocational Interest Blank.* Doctor's thesis, United States International University (San Diego, Calif.), 1975. (*DAI* 35:4244B)

1468. SCHUBERT, DANIEL S. P., AND WAGNER, MAZIE EARLE. "'A' Therapists as Creative and Personally Involved With Other People." *J Consult & Clin Psychol* 43(2):266 Ap '75. * (*PA* 54:1167)

1469. SCIMONELLI, FRANK JOSEPH. *A Study of Selected Variables Related to the Achievement of Music Majors in Two-Year Community Colleges.* Doctor's thesis, Catholic University of America (Washington, D.C.), 1975. (*DAI* 36:1366A)

1470. SCORDATO, ANGELO JOHN. *A Comparison of Interest, Personality and Biographical Characteristics of Seminary Persisters and Non-Persisters From St. Pius X Preparatory Seminary.* Doctor's thesis, University of Wyoming (Laramie, Wyo.), 1975. (*DAI* 36:7876A)

1471. SHARF, RICHARD S. "The Relationship Between the SVIB and the OAIS: Implications for Counseling." *Meas & Eval Guid* 7(4):215–9 Ja '75. * (*PA* 53:12572)

1472. SPIVEY, WILLIAM LANE. *A Study of the Self-Concept and Achievement Motivation of Black Versus White High School Male Achievers.* Doctor's thesis, California School of Professional Psychology (San Francisco, Calif.), 1975. (*DAI* 36:4711B)

1473. TANNEY, MARY FAITH. Chap. 5, "Face Validity of Interest Measures. Sex-Role Stereotyping," pp. 89–99. In *Issues of Sex Bias and Sex Fairness in Career Interest Measurement.* Edited by Esther E. Diamond. Washington, D.C.: National Institute of Education, 1975. Pp. xxix, 219. *

1474. WEBB, CHARLES ROYCE. *The Relationship of Certain Vocational Factors to Student Teaching Performance.* Doctor's thesis, Auburn University (Auburn, Ala.), 1975. (*DAI* 36:7362A)

1475. WELSH, GEORGE S. *Creativity and Intelligence: A Personality Approach.* Chapel Hill, N.C.: University of North Carolina, 1975. Pp. xi, 276. *

1476. WESTBROOK, FRANKLIN D. "High Scales on the Strong Vocational Interest Blank and the Kuder Occupational Interest Survey Using Holland's Occupational Codes." *J Counsel Psychol* 22(1):24–7 Ja '75. * (*PA* 53:8417)

1477. WHETSTONE, ROBERT D., AND HAYLES, V. ROBERT. "The SVIB and Black College Men." *Meas & Eval Guid* 8(2):105–9 Jl '75. * (*PA* 54:12670)

1478. WHITTON, MARY C. "Same-Sex and Cross-Sex Reliability and Concurrent Validity of the Strong-Campbell Interest Inventory." *J Counsel Psychol* 22(3):204–9 My '75. * (*PA* 54:4477)

1479. ANASTASI, ANNE. *Psychological Testing,* Fourth Edition, pp. 529–36. New York: Macmillan Publishing Co., Inc., 1976. Pp. xiii, 750. *

1480. BANRETI-FUCHS, K. M., AND MEADOWS, W. M. "Interest, Mental Health, and Attitudinal Correlates of Academic Achievement Among University Students." *Brit J Ed Psychol* 46(2):212–9 Je '76. * (*PA* 57:4357)

1481. CAMPBELL, DAVID P. "Review of the Strong-Campbell Interest Inventory." *Meas & Eval Guid* 9(1):45–6. Ap '76. *

1482. CAMPBELL, JEAN. "Differential Response for Female and Male Law Students on the Strong-Campbell Interest Inventory: The Question of Separate Sex Norms." *J Counsel Psychol* 23(2):130–5 Mr '76. * (*PA* 56:1497)

1483. CHARTOFF, SUSAN I. *A Comparison of Interests, Values, Personality Characteristics, and Past Experience With Life Crises of Hotline Volunteers, Nonvolunteers, and Selected Professional Groups.* Doctor's thesis, Rutgers, The State University of New Jersey (New Brunswick, N.J.), 1976. (*DAI* 37:3412A)

1484. COOPER, JACQUELINE FRIBUSH. "Comparative Impact of the SCII and the Vocational Card Sort on Career Salience and Career Exploration of Women." *J Counsel Psychol* 23(4): 348–52 Jl '76. * (*PA* 56:6881)

1485. CREASER, JAMES W. "Occupational Groupings of the Strong Vocational Interest Blank and the Strong-Campbell Interest Inventory." *J Appl Psychol* 61(2):238–41 Ap '76. * (*PA* 57:2048)

1486. CREASER, JAMES, AND CARSELLO, CARMEN. "Comparability of Cross-Sex Scores on the Strong-Campbell Interest Inventory." *J Counsel Psychol* 23(4):360–4 Jl '76. * (*PA* 56:5160)

1487. GOLDBERG, ROBERT W., AND GECHMAN, ARTHUR S. "Psychodynamic Inferences From the Strong Vocational Interest Blank." *J Pers Assess* 40(3):285–301 Je '76. *

1488. HANSEN, JO-IDA C. "Exploring New Directions for Strong-Campbell Interest Inventory Occupational Scale Construction." *J Voc Behav* 9(2):147–60 O '76. *

1489. HARMON, LENORE W., AND CONROE, FRANCES L. "Sex Stereotyping in Interest Items: Occupational Titles Versus Activities." *Meas & Eval Guid* 8(4):215–20 Ja '76. * (*PA* 56:5008)

1490. JOHNSON, RICHARD W. "Review of the Strong-Campbell Interest Inventory." *Meas & Eval Guid* 9(1):40–5 Ap '76. *

1491. KUNCE, JOSEPH T.; DECKER, GARY L.; AND ECKELMAN, C. CLEARY. "Strong Vocational Interest Blank Basic Interest Clusters and Occupational Satisfaction." *J Voc Behav* 9(3): 355–62 D '76. * (*PA* 58:2328)

1492. LAND, ANTHONY FRANK. *The Contribution of Vocational Interest Measures to the Prediction of Student Performance in Electrical and Mechanical Engineering Technology.* Doctor's thesis, Lehigh University (Bethlehem, Pa.), 1976. (*DAI* 37:6854A)

1493. LOITERSTEIN, SANDRA R. *Interpersonal Style and Interests of Graduate Students in Clinical and Non-Clinical Programs in Psychology.* Doctor's thesis, George Washington University (Washington, D.C.), 1976. (*DAI* 37:497B)

1494. MOSES, MARY LOUISE. *Predictors of Success or Failure of a Selected Group of Freshman Associate Degree Nursing Students.* Doctor's thesis, Texas Woman's University (Denton, Texas), 1976. (*DAI* 37:3871B)

1495. NOLTING, EARL, AND TAYLOR, RONALD G. "Vocational Interests of Engineering Students." *Meas & Eval Guid* 8(4): 245–51 Ja '76. * (*PA* 56:5014)

1496. PETILLO, JOHN J. *Career Interest Patterns of Priests With Measured Levels of Job Satisfaction Within the Chaplaincy, Teaching and Parochial Ministries.* Doctor's thesis, Fordham University (New York, N.Y.), 1976. (*DAI* 37:2648A)

1497. PREDIGER, DALE J., AND HANSON, GARY R. "Holland's Theory of Careers Applied to Women and Men: Analysis of Implicit Assumptions." *J Voc Behav* 8(2):167–84 Ap '76. *

1498. REICH, STEPHEN. "Strong Vocational Interest Blank Patterns Associated With Law School Achievement." *Psychol Rep* 39(3, pt 2):1343–6 D '76. *

1499. ROONEY, EDWARD JOSEPH. *The Use of the Strong Vocational Interest Blanks' Nonoccupational Scales in Counseling Freshmen in a Public Community College.* Doctor's thesis, Boston College (Chestnut Hill, Mass.), 1976. (*DAI* 36:7874A)

1500. ROSEN, NED; BILLINGS, ROBERT; AND TURNEY, JOHN. "The Emergence and Allocation of Leadership Resources Over Time in a Technical Organization." *Acad Mgmt J* 19(2):165–83 Je '76. *

1501. SCHREIER, JAMES W. *Identification and Comparison of Interest and Personality Profiles for College Business Students Based on Background and Intention for Entrepreneurial Activity.* Doctor's thesis, Marquette University (Milwaukee, Wis.), 1976. (*DAI* 37:1998A)

1502. STEINHAUER, JEAN C. "Review of the Strong-Campbell Interest Inventory." *Meas & Eval Guid* 9(1):47–8 Ap '76. *

1503. TIPTON, ROBERT M. "Attitudes Towards Women's Roles in Society and Vocational Interests." *J Voc Behav* 8(2):155–65 Ap '76. *

1504. UTZ, PATRICK, AND KORBEN, DONALD. "The Construct Validity of the Occupational Themes on the Strong-Campbell Interest Inventory." *J Voc Behav* 9(1):31–42 Ag '76. * (*PA* 57:125)

1505. WEBBER, PATRICIA LEE. *The Research Utility of Broad and Component Measures of Introversion-Extraversion.* Doctor's thesis, University of Minnesota (Minneapolis, Minn.), 1976. (*DAI* 37:6383A)

1506. WORTHINGTON, EVERETT LEE, JR. *As You Like It—Validity Studies of the Strong Vocational Interest Inventories.* Master's thesis, University of Missouri (Columbia, Mo.), 1976.

1507. WRIGHT, JOHN C. "The SVIB Academic Achievement Score and College Attrition." *Meas & Eval Guid* 8(4):258–9 Ja '76. * (*PA* 56:4997)

1508. CATRON, DAVID W., AND ZULTOWSKI, WALTER H. "Strong-Campbell General Occupational Themes: Profiles of Four Academic Divisions." *Meas & Eval Guid* 10(1):38–43 Ap '77. *

1509. CLOYD, LOUISA. "Effect of Acquaintanceship on Accuracy of Person Perception." *Percept & Motor Skills* 44(3, pt 1):819–26 Je '77. *

1510. COSTA, PAUL T., JR.; FOZARD, JAMES L.; AND MCCRAE, ROBERT R. "Personological Interpretation of Factors From the Strong Vocational Interest Blank Scales." *J Voc Behav* 10(2):231–43 Ap '77. *

1511. DOLLIVER, ROBERT H., AND WILL, JULIE A. "Ten-Year Follow-up of the Tyler Vocational Card Sort and the Strong Vocational Interest Blank." *J Counsel Psychol* 24(1):48–54 Ja '77. *

1512-4. FABRY, JULIAN, AND POGGIO, JOHN P. "The Factor Compatibility and Communality of Coded-Expressed and Inventoried Interests." *Meas & Eval Guid* 10(2):90–7 Jl '77. *

1515. GOODYEAR, RODNEY K., AND FRANK, AUSTIN C. "Introversion-Extroversion: Some Comparisons of the SVIB and OPI Scales." *Meas & Eval Guid* 9(4):206–11 Ja '77. *

1516. HANSEN, JO-IDA C. "Coding SCII Items According to Holland's Vocational Theory." *Meas & Eval Guid* 10(2):75–83 Jl '77. *

1516a. JOHNSON, RICHARD W. "Relationships Between Female and Male Interest Scales for the Same Occupations." *J Voc Behav* 11(2):239–52 O '77. *

1517. LUNNEBORG, PATRICIA W. "Construct Validity of the Strong-Campbell Interest Inventory and the Vocational Interest Inventory Among College Counseling Clients." *Voc Behav* 10(2):187–95 Ap '77. *

1518. LUNNEBORG, PATRICIA W., AND GERRY, MARIAN H. "Sex Differences in Changing Sex-Stereotyped Vocational Interests." *J Counsel Psychol* 24(3):247–50 My '77. *

1519. RAMANAIAH, NERELLA V., AND GOLDBERG, LEWIS R. "Stylistic Components of Human Judgment: The Generality of Individual Differences." *Appl Psychol Meas* 1(1):23–39 w '77. *

1520. TINSLEY, HOWARD E. A., AND TINSLEY, DIANE J. "Different Needs, Interests, and Abilities of Effective and Ineffective Counselor Trainees: Implications for Counselor Selection." *J Counsel Psychol* 24(1):83–6 Ja '77. *

1521. WORTHINGTON, EVERETT L., JR., AND DOLLIVER, ROBERT H. "Validity Studies of the Strong Vocational Interest Inventories." *J Counsel Psychol* 24(3):208–16 My '77. *

JOHN O. CRITES, *Professor of Psychology, University of Maryland, College Park, Maryland.*

Recognized as the paragon of applied behavioral measures and widely acclaimed as the bellwether of career counseling and personnel selection, the several editions of the *Strong Vocational Interest Blank* have a venerable history and reputation, dating back to the late 1920s and spanning the subsequent decades to its most recent revision in 1974. Literally thousands of studies have been conducted on the SVIB, and millions of copies have been sold.

It has launched and sustained careers, as well as assessing them, and it has served as a source of master's theses and doctoral dissertations. It seems almost presumptuous, therefore, to review the Strong, but such is the conscience of the testing community. Even the Strong must bear the scrutiny of critical analysis, although it may be difficult to find other than picayune flaws in it. Particularly is this true of the current edition, the *Strong-Campbell Interest Inventory,* which represents the culmination of almost 50 years of unparalleled "dustbowl empiricism" on the measurement of vocational interests. The SCII has been developed in response to the burgeoning concern among many during the early 1970s that even the 1966 and 1969 revisions of the SVIB men's form (blue booklet) and women's form (pink booklet) were somehow "sexist" in their conceptualization and construction (*1333*). The new, unisex form of the SCII (white booklet) has been designed to rectify this shortcoming.

In contrast to the older forms of the SVIB, the SCII has fewer items. It consists of 325 items drawn from the existing male and female booklets: 180 common to both the 1966 men's form and 1969 women's form; 74 from the men's form only; and 69 from the women's form only. Totaling these yields 254 items on which the male scales are scored and 249 on which the female scales are scored. In other words, "none of the scales can be used to score the samples of the other sex tested earlier with the older booklets." Eventually, of course, "when new occupational samples are tested with the combined booklet, this gap can be filled, but amassing useful long-term results will take years." In the meantime, some item statistics pertain only to the sex on which they were originally derived; also, there are two items which are brand new. These 325 items, then, appropriately updated during the revisions in the 1960s to eliminate dated items, and to correct the generic masculine where possible (e.g., policeman was changed to police officer but actor and actress were retained), constitute the pool from which the SCII scales were constructed.

There are three principal types of scales in the SCII. The general theme scales yield scores on each of Holland's "personality-interest" types: realistic, investigative, artistic, social, enterprising, and conventional (*1249*). Items were rationally selected to represent each type, with 20 items per scale. They were normed on a combined sample of 300 males and 300 females. Standard scores (mean 50, SD 10) were based upon the distribution for this total group, but the printed interpretive statements on the profile sheet ("Very high—94th and above," etc.) are based upon the respondent's own sex, since the raw scores for males and females were appreciably different. The basic interest scales (e.g., adventure, medical service, and teaching) were constructed largely empirically, the items in a given scale intercorrelating .30 or greater, except in certain instances when .20 was used. In either case, the correlations were quite low, reflecting the restricted variance on LID-type items. Again, the scales were normed on 300 males and 300 females, but each sex was treated separately. On the profile sheet, standard scores are reported on one scale for females and another for males. Finally, the occupational scales were developed by the familiar "group difference" method used in previous editions of the Strong. For each of the 325 items in the unisex booklet, 124 occupational "criterion" groups were contrasted with the men-in-general (MIG) and women-in-general (WIG) reference samples, and items were selected and assigned unit weights (+1, 0, or −1) if the groups differed by a certain percentage, which ranged from 16 percent up, the goal being approximately 50 items per scale. In addition, there are three administrative indices (total responses, infrequent responses, LID percentages) and two special scales (academic orientation scale and introversion-extroversion scale).

Rationally, the interrelationships among the SCII scales and, hence, their interpretation would seem to be fairly straightforward: cognate scales should be positively correlated with each other. The classification of all the scales according to Holland's types encourages this expectation. But certain disquieting anomalies occur. Because like and dislike responses to the items in the general theme and basic interest scales are weighted +1 and −1, respectively, their intercorrelations may be spuriously high or low depending upon the percentages of L and D responses. It is critical, therefore, to start the profile interpretation by examining the

administrative index for "yeasaying" and "naysaying" response styles. Similarly, the indifferent response is generally weighted 0, except on some occupational scales when the percentage difference with MIG or WIG exceeds 10 points. In effect, indifferent responses "don't count" and consequently tend to depress high scores and produce "flat profiles." The implication is, of course, that the SCII is largely useless with the modal client seen in career counseling—the passive dependent, "I don't know what I want to do" individual who characteristically makes a high percentage of indifferent responses and has few if any high scores. The administrative index for indifferent responses is also critical, therefore, in profile interpretation: if it is high, the scale scores may be disproportionately low.

Another inconsistency among the SCII scales involves the basic interest and occupational scales. For the SVIB, from which the SCII was largely taken, Johnson (*1272*) found approximately 20 percent inconsistencies among these scales. "The inconsistencies appear as highly contrasted scores on pairs of scales that are obviously related, such as art and artist, mathematics and mathematician, military activities and army officer." When these contradictions occur, the score on the BIS will usually be higher than the score on the corresponding occupational scale. In part this anomaly is a function of scale construction: the BIS consists of homogeneous sets of items. More basically, however, the two types of scales may disagree due to the weighting of LID responses. As mentioned previously, the BIS weights L responses +1 and D responses −1; in contrast, those occupational scales which disagree with the BIS tend to weight L responses −1 and D responses +1. Thus, a high score on the latter would be associated with a low score on the former. Again, the administrative index for L and D response percentages should be checked *before* profile interpretation. Furthermore, if the SCII is being used in career counseling with clients who "Yes, but" and who often have a large D percentage, the counselor should be cautious in interpreting high scores: they may be the result of indiscriminate "naysaying," or they may represent intrinsic dislikes akin to those of an occupational group comprised largely of "dislikers." Which of these interpretations applies is indeterminate from the SCII.

A third (last?) problem with the internal scale structure of the SCII scales concerns the relationship betwen the male and female keys for common occupations. Of the 124 occupational scales, there are 37 pairs which are the same for both sexes, e.g., female army officer and male army officer. Separate scales were constructed presumably because there are sometimes sex differences within an occupation. Given that there are, it follows that one would score higher on the like-sex scale, i.e., women would score higher, on the average, on the female than the male army officer scale. Paradoxically, the opposite is more often true. Why? Campbell comments that: "the tendency is for men to score higher on those pairs of scales dominated by 'male' items and for women to score higher on those pairs dominated by 'female' items. 'Male' and 'female', here, refer to items showing large differences in popularity between men- and women-in-general." Johnson explicates this inconsistency further: "Because of the widespread differences in the interests of men- and women-in-general, occupational scales for men and women for the same occupation will contain different items even when the interests of men and women within the occupation are the same. An occupational scale will consist of items reflecting interests (likes and dislikes) which are atypical for members of that sex * Individuals will [therefore] obtain spuriously high scores on those cross-sex occupational scales which represent interests usually preferred by members of their own sex."

In a study designed to test this hypothesis, Johnson (1516a) predicted that women would score higher on male occupational scales closely associated with general theme and basic interest scales preferred by females and equal/lower on male occupational scales related to GT and BI scales typical of males. For example, women should score higher on male artist and lower on male army officer than men. His findings clearly supported expectation for both the general theme and basic interest scales: "Both sexes obtained higher mean scores on the cross-sex Occupational scale than the same-sex scale if the former scale was highly correlated with basic interests preferred by that sex, but lower mean scores on the cross-sex scale if that scale

was closely associated with basic interests preferred by the other sex." From these results, which are consistent with earlier studies (1270, 1458, 1486), Johnson concludes: "In essence, both sexes obtained relatively high scores on cross-sex scales which represented 'traditional' occupations for their sex and relatively low scores on scales which represented 'nontraditional' occupations. Contrary to the opinion of many previous investigators, the use of the cross-sex scales has the net effect of strengthening, not reducing, the results of social conditioning." In this sense, the SCII is what Prediger and Hanson [1] have termed a "sex restrictive" instrument, i.e., an interest inventory in which the number of "career options suggested to males and females is disproportionate."

Complicating these internal interpretative problems with the SCII scales are external predictive difficulties recently revealed in a study by Dolliver, Irwin, and Bigley (1256). These investigators questioned the finding by Strong that the odds are about 3.5 to 1 that, if a man (Form SVIB-M) enters an occupation for which he has an "A" rating, he will stay in it for a long period of time (18–22 years), and conversely that the odds are approximately 5 to 1 that, if he enters an occupation for which he has a "C" rating, he will not stay in it. Based upon data collected on 220 former University of Missouri counseling center clients in a 12-year follow-up, Dolliver et al. found that the predictive validity of the SVIB was considerably less than that reported by Strong, the chances being about 1-to-1 for "A" ratings and 8-to-1 for "C" ratings. Moreover, the concurrent validity of the SVIB, as judged by how helpful clients thought its interpretation was in their career decision making, was even less: 34 percent considered it "helpful," 32 percent "some use," and 34 percent "misleading." A related finding was that they reported the SVIB information did not influence their career choice! In commenting upon this study in the SCII manual, Campbell appears to accept the major conclusion of Dolliver et al.: "All things considered, the hit rate looks to be about 50 percent."

Given these observations on the internal con-

1 PREDIGER, DALE J., AND HANSON, GARY R. "The Distinction Between Sex Restrictiveness and Sex Bias in Interest Inventories." *Meas & Eval Guid* 7(2):96–104 Jl '74. *

Strong-Campbell Interest Inventory

struction and external validity of the SCII, what can be inferred concerning its applicability and usefulness in assisting individuals in their career decision making? First, there seems to be no question that response style (percentages of LIDs) can affect scores on all of the SCII scales. Second, the cross-sex occupational scales should *not* be interpreted because they may simply represent sex-role stereotypes rather than vocational interests. Third, it should be recognized that, for this reason as well as others, the SCII may be sex restrictive. Fourth, low scores are considerably more predictive of eventual occupational membership than high scores. Scores in the "dissimilar" and "very dissimilar" ranges can be used to eliminate career options but scores in the "similar" and "very similar" ranges cannot be used with much confidence to select career options. Asking persons which occupation they intend to enter [P:283(35)] or using the base rates (983) is equally accurate, if not more so, than the SCII. Finally, clients did not see the Strong as significantly influencing their career decision making at the time it was interpreted to them or as appreciably related to their later job appropriateness.

To summarize, *if* a counselor decides to use an interest inventory with a client, without expecting it to necessarily influence her/his career decision making or planning, and *if* the primary purpose of the counseling is to eliminate higher level sex restrictive occupational options appropriate to the client's sex, and *if* the client is relatively bright (in order to qualify for upper range occupations) and is neither a "yeasayer" nor a "naysayer," then the *Strong-Campbell Interest Inventory* may be the best available.

ROBERT H. DOLLIVER, *Professor of Psychology and Counseling Psychologist, University of Missouri, Columbia, Missouri.*

The publication of the SCII was undoubtedly speeded up by what Campbell called "the biggest public relations blunder in the history of psychometrics"—a pink test booklet for females and a blue test booklet for males on the preceding SVIBs. The development of the SCII as a neuter vocational test was influenced by (*a*) criticism regarding separate test booklets and different occupational scales for men and women and (*b*) the Kuder DD, published in 1964, which uses the same test booklet for

men and women, and reports many of the same occupational scales for both sexes.

The SCII contains 325 items. Of those, 180 are items common to the women's 1969 SVIB (TW398) and the men's 1966 SVIB (T399). An additional 74 items found only on T399 and 69 items found only on TW398 are on the SCII. A total of 548 different, potential items were available from the T399 and TW398. The SCII manual gives no indication why the SCII is limited to 325 items. Inspection of the test booklet suggests that the item total may have been limited to accommodate printing the SCII on four pages. Another advantage, of course, is to save time for the test taker. A count of the item use on the six Holland scales, the 23 basic interest scales, the 124 occupational scales, and two special scales, indicates that each of the 325 items is used on an average of 19 scales.

The manual indicates that only two items are new. However, a comparison of the test items reveals that some 40 additional items have been changed by eradicating gender references, updating, and clarifying. One of the gender changes was apparently made at the last minute, leaving "flight attendant" the only occupational item out of alphabetical order, where the item "stewardess" had been. Some of the changes appear to have quite different response implications (e.g., artistic men to artistic persons, prominent businessmen to prominent business leaders, magazine writer to free-lance writer). Strong (610) contended that such changes in item wording would bring no change in response. Most of the SCII scales are based on that contention, because scales were constructed on responses to the originally worded items on TW398 and T399.

The SCII contains 67 male and 57 female occupational scales. On the 57 female scales, the median number of items dropped from 77 on the 1974 TW398 scales to 44 on the SCII; for the male scales, the drop was from 76 on the 1969 T399 scales to a median of 47 on the SCII scales. A shift in attitude about scale length is evident; Campbell (*1099*) had said that 40 items per scale are imperative for reliability; but on the SCII, 33 percent of the female occupational scales and 19 percent of the male occupational scales have fewer than that number. There is a small increase in the minimum percent difference of an item between the occupational criterion groups and the general groups. The increase is from a median of 16 percent on the 1969 TW398 and 17 percent on the 1966 T399 to a median of 18 percent for both female and male occupational scales on the SCII. The median SCII occupational scale test-retest reliability is reported to be .90 for 14 days and .88 for 30 days; median T399 occupational scale reliabilities of .91 for 14 and 30 days are reported in the 1966 SVIB manual.

Ten of the male occupational scales reflect criterion groups which were carried over (not renormed) from T399, 32 were renormed for the SCII, and 25 are new occupational groups. Four of the female scales are carryovers from the SVIB (Form W), 43 are carryovers from TW398, two were renormed for the SCII, and eight are new occupational groups. The median date of data collection of occupational samples was 1967 for the combined list of men's and women's SCII criterion groups. The female dentist criterion group is seriously out-of-date (1934-42). Fifteen percent of the criterion groups used to develop SCII occupational scales are limited to Minnesota. A discrepancy of 192 subjects exists between the listings of the criterion group for the female dietitian scale in the handbook and the SCII manual.

Of the 57 female and 67 male occupational scales, 37 are twin scales, that is, scales which have two scales for the same occupation, one normed on females and the other normed on males. That leaves 30 male nontwin and 20 female nontwin occupational scales. The manual points to an interpretative problem of the twin scales: General groups of females and males had higher average scores on the other-sex twin scales than they did on the same-sex twin scales. Research completed recently at the University of Missouri with male college graduates in one of the "twin" occupations indicates that those other-sex twin occupational scales have concurrent validity which exceeds that for the same-sex twin occupational scales. At this point, it seems clear that high scores on other-sex scales should not be construed as indications of the test taker's "masculinity/femininity" as represented by a scale on the preceding SVIB editions.

Overall, the manual does a very credible job of reporting data on the instrument. However, there are some significant gaps in the data.

The manual does not report the number of items on the introversion-extroversion and academic orientation scales, and the number of items on the general occupational theme scales is not reported. Those particular information gaps may stem from the publisher's decision not to report the content of the SCII scales for economic reasons. (Apparently several renegade scoring services grew up to score the SVIB, without paying royalties.) The secrecy regarding scale content is a small inconvenience to the practitioner but the secrecy could be a very large inconvenience to the researcher in making some kinds of research impossible. My experimentation indicates to me that 90 percent of the SCII theme scales item content is the same as the theme scales content reported for SVIB T399 in the handbook (1099). My additional experimentation indicates that about 90 percent of the content of the basic interest scales can be derived from the content of the original scales listed in the 1969 SVIB manual supplement and the description of the relationship between new and old basic interest scales which appears in the SCII manual. I can see justification for maintaining the secrecy of the empirically-derived occupational scales. I cannot see that any substantial economic risk is engendered by publishing the content of the theme and basic interest scales. Those scales can now be closely approximated; the missing 10 percent of the item content does not seem worth engendering the potential antagonism over this issue.

Also missing from the data presented in the manual are means and standard deviations for each occupational criterion group on all occupational scales and intercorrelations among occupational scales, which would allow estimates of scale overlap and of the potential for merging selected female and male occupational scales. There is no indication of the relationship between scores received on T399 and SCII occupational scales. The test user is left uncertain about the similarity of men's scales for the same occupations but based on a different general group, different criterion groups, and different item pools. The manual does not report means and standard deviations for general groups of men and of women on all occupational scales, other than the men-in-general (MIG) and women-in-general (WIG) groups. Since

Strong-Campbell Interest Inventory

the MIG and WIG groups were used in the construction of occupational scales, their scores would probably be spuriously low on the same-sex occupational scales. The descriptions of the criterion groups do not include references where more information could be gained about the construction of each occupational scale.

Some test users evaluate the SCII largely on the basis of its satisfactoriness in dealing with questions of sex bias. The SCII meets most of the criteria of an unbiased test by, for instance, using gender-neuter terms, and reporting some nontraditional female and male occupational scales. The big remaining question is whether occupational scales can be combined so that males and females are scored on the same items (perhaps with separate, perhaps with combined norms). In the SCII manual, Campbell addresses this question on an item level, showing, for example, a large female-male percent difference in responding to the SCII item, "Decorating a room with flowers." Campbell's consideration of combined scales apparently ended at the item level and did not explore departures from Strong's method of using separate MIG and WIG groups to find item-response rates for each sex separately. If diverse occupational groups can be combined into single scales (e.g., college professor, physical scientist, and social scientist), there seems promise for combining the same occupation constituted of males and females. Some experimenters have begun this work, mostly with individual occupations, but more work is needed to make an empirical resolution of the issue of combined versus separate sex occupational scales.

I conceptualize four levels of integration of a test for females and males: (a) separate test booklets, separate scales, separate norms; (b) combined test booklets, separate scales, separate norms; (c) combined test booklets, combined scales, and separate norms; and (d) combined test booklets, combined scales, and combined norms. Other prominent psychological tests (e.g., MMPI, EPPS, and Kuder DD) are at level (c) above. All earlier editions of the SVIB represent level (a) above. The SCII occupational scales and the infrequent response index represent (b) above. The SCII general theme scales and basic interest scales fall between (c) and (d) since the same items are

used and the same raw score receives the same standard score regardless of the test taker's sex. However, the interpretations differ; the same standard score could be described as average for a female but low for a male. The SCII special scales and most of the SCII administrative indices reflect (d) above. A test report for females and one for males, based on the same item responses, will typically show these differences: (a) the infrequent response index scores are different numbers, (b) the theme scales and the basic interest scales have different interpretative labels and/or different interpretative bands (although the score numbers are identical), and (c) the occupational scales are plotted with one set of marks for the same-sex and another set for other-sex scale scores (although, again, the score numbers are identical).

SUMMARY. The tone of this review has been largely negative in the focus on features of test construction, such as: (a) the use of TW 398 and T399 to build scales for the SCII so that changes in item wording and item array were assumed to be negligible; (b) the processing of TW398 and T399 in such a way that criterion groups of each sex responded to only about 250 items, which restricted the number of items for possible inclusion in the occupational scales for each sex; (c) the basing of 155 scales on 325 SCII items; and (d) the reduction of some 30 in the median number of items per SCII occupational scale from the number of items on the scales of the preceding SVIB. I consider those aspects of the SCII to be sacrifices to the concept of an integrated female/male vocational inventory, something achieved in only a limited way. Research recently completed at the University of Missouri (1506), however, indicates that the validity of the SCII exceeds that of the preceding T399 in making concurrent predictions for the group of male college graduates being studied. These very limited data indicate to me that the SCII will perform its basic function as well as the earlier male SVIB (T399).

The SCII appears to the reviewer to be the best vocational interest inventory available. Potential users may still have questions about the value of the SCII. Simply asking college students their vocational interests is as accurate as earlier editions of the SVIB, accurate for about 50 percent of those studied. The SVIBs

Strong-Campbell Interest Inventory

and SCII produce many "extraneous solutions" (*374*) (false positives) and not only the number but the percent of these occupational scales with high scores seems to have increased on the SCII (*1521*). Some potential users may object to the secrecy about the item content of the SCII scales, which denies test takers the opportunity to look at the items on a particular scale to see how they received the score they received. Other potential users may object to the confusion engendered in reporting other-sex occupational scales without any indication from the publishers about the validity of those results. Other potential users may wish to press for a greater degree of male/female integration on later SCII editions. In some instances, the "best" inventory may not be good enough for a particular use.

PATRICIA W. LUNNEBORG, *Associate Professor of Psychology, University of Washington, Seattle, Washington.*

A clear, concise, informative, and useful overview (to quote Campbell) of the *Strong-Campbell Interest Inventory* already exists (*1490*, excerpted below), obviating the need for another guided by the standard criteria of reliability, validity, normative samples, etc. Because sex bias in earlier Strong blanks led to creating the AMEG Commission on Sex Bias in Measurement, it seems more appropriate to review the new SCII according to test guidelines for sex fairness such as those of the NIE Career Education Program.[1] Just how successful, then, is merged Form T325 in avoiding sex bias, defined by NIE as "any factor that might influence a person to limit....consideration of a career solely on the basis of gender"?

As for the inventory itself, while the SCII conforms to the guideline calling for the same form for the sexes, client gender remains a salient feature, the first instruction on the NCS answer sheet being "Important: Mark One: Male, Female." We may well ask whether the uses to which the gender information is put are important enough to call attention to sex so blatantly as a factor in the world of work. An examination of these uses reveals absolutely no need for knowing gender. The first is that feed-

back is organized to emphasize occupational scores normed on groups of the same sex as the client. It is, however, easy to devise feedback reports which present a client with both male-normed and female-normed lists of occupations, together with an interpretive statement about emphasizing one's own sex. Such feedback could simultaneously remedy a weakness to the single score report, likewise adopted in line with Campbell's announced policy of providing all information for everyone. Currently in this single interpretive report, other-sex scores are fed back at the end in a long stream—*with* the (unvalidated) statement that own-sex data are "better predictors" and *without* Holland's RIASEC codes needed to explore *all* occupations to one's highest theme. This blanket discrediting of other-sex scores violates the spirit of the equalizing policy, serves no good counseling purpose, and misses a golden opportunity for educating clients about occupational sex stereotyping.

The second use of client gender is to produce different verbal messages to accompany general theme scores. Again, this violates the principle of all information for everyone. Why can't clients compare themselves with both norm groups? Why can't counselors use this comparing process to discuss traditional sex differences in RIASEC types, e.g., why a 60 on Realistic is average among males but high among females? The SCII scoring routine has no right to preempt this exploration. A related "technical" guideline that is also violated calls for publicizing the sexes' distributions of highest interest scores. Simply providing separate sex norms and reporting mean differences on scales does not satisfy this requirement. The distribution of Holland types in male and female samples is something clients should be told as well as counselors.

The NIE inventory guideline from which the SCII departs the most, however, has to do with removing item sex bias. It states that ideally items should be endorsed equally by the sexes, but that where this fails, items should be sex-balanced within sections of the test and within scales. The SCII clearly fails the first test, with half of the items showing 15 percent or larger sex difference, but also fails the second for making no attempt to balance either theoretical or empirical scales. Most discourag-

1 "Guidelines for Assessment of Sex Bias and Sex Fairness in Career Interest Inventories," pp. xxiii-xxix. In *Issues of Sex Bias and Sex Fairness in Career Interest Measurement.* Edited by Esther E. Diamond. Washington, D.C.: National Institute of Education, 1975. Pp. xxix, 219. *

ing, users have no way of knowing what bias or fairness lies therein. *The publisher's decision to keep secret the item content to all scales precludes research on this single most important guideline.*

Seven NIE guidelines concern technical information. Here again the problem is the publisher's decision to persist in separate treatment for the sexes—separate sex groups for the occupational scales and separate sex norms for homogeneous scales. The cross-sex research evidence cited for this decision is so scant and outdated as to suggest a purely economic rationale. And, absent from the manual are the minimal technical data that *should* have provided the decision's rationale and *should* be public for the sake of science: (*a*) extent of item overlap between same-named occupations, e.g., psychologist-f and psychologist-m, and (*b*) sex differences in endorsement for all items. Not only is item content necessary to clarify the meaning of Form T325's present scales, it is necessary for any attempt to develop occupational scales using combined sex samples.

Another technical deficiency has to do with the guideline calling for validity evidence when scales normed on one sex are used with the other sex. Widespread use of the SCII for over two years has certainly provided an extensive enough data base for the publisher now to report the predictive validity of other-sex scales. There is also a guideline specifying that norms be current. A count of the number of SCII occupational criterion groups tested in 1968 or later reveals that 67 of the 124 may well be obsolete. But more important than the datedness of the occupational groups for sex fairness is the present choice of the groups themselves. The number of unique female scales (20) is outnumbered by those normed on males (30). If we are to believe the manual—that same-sex scales have the greater validity—the effect of this imbalance is to restrict the options available to women. The character, as well as the number, of these options is also restrictive. Compared to the unique male scales, those for women reveal an abundance of low-level clerical jobs and a lack of realistic and enterprising options. This selection of the uniquely normed occupational groups is a striking example of sex bias against women in the SCII.

It is to the third class of guidelines regarding interpretive information, however, that SCII developers should turn immediate attention. *There is simply no good user's manual.* The present manual supplements the 1971 handbook as a technical resource. Counselors have only the back side of their copy of the client's profile to instruct them. The guidelines which are paramount in writing such a user's manual have to do with interpreting other-sex scores and with countering sex-role stereotyping by discussing how men and women have been influenced by early socialization, home vs. career conflict, etc., to be concentrated in certain RIASEC work environments and at certain levels of responsibility and pay. Case studies which portray women in a variety of jobs that go beyond traditional expectations are recommended. Further, in order to meet the guideline which demands full exploration of alternatives via interpretive materials, *all* SCII computerized feedback should be fully organized within the RIASEC framework, and the user's manual should include a variety of career and educational alternatives currently not represented by present occupational scales.

In summary, the major sex-bias defect in the SCII is the continued dependence upon separate sex groups for the occupational scales and separate sex norms for the homogeneous scales. While improved interpretive material will make this SCII more useful in counseling, the goal should be its replacement by one consisting of items not correlated with gender and of scales based upon mixed-sex reference and occupational groups.

Meas & Eval Guid 9(1):40–5 Ap '76. Richard W. Johnson. * One of the three scoring agencies....must be contacted to have the scales scored. Contrary to previous policy, the publisher does not plan to sell handscoring stencils or to publish the item content for any of the scales. This new policy has been adopted to prevent "scoring piracy" by unauthorized scoring firms. Most counselors will oppose this change. Knowledge of the item content is necessary to demystify the instrument and to clarify the meaning of the scores. The item lists may also be used to check for scoring accuracy. The new General Occupational Theme Scales.... measure the six types of personality and occupational environments identified by Holland. The six types—realistic, investigative, artistic,

Strong-Campbell Interest Inventory

social, enterprising, and conventional—are each represented by 20 items selected to fit Holland's descriptions. Each of the six scales is highly correlated ($r > .80$) with at least one of the Basic Interest Scales. As a consequence, the new scales do not provide much new information; however, they offer a theoretical framework that is helpful in organizing and interpreting the rest of the profile. * The differences between the interests of men and women conform with sex-role stereotypes. To a certain extent, respondents may simply be endorsing socially approved behavior for their sex when they answer the SCII items. For instance, female students do not need to express as many mechanical interests as males to be enrolled successfully in a science major. Separate sex norms should be used in interpreting the scores in order to take into account the differential effects of social conditioning. * The arrangement of the profile for the occupational scores has been changed so that average scores between 25 and 45 (the old C+, B—, B, and B+ letter grades) are presented in a narrow strip in the middle of the profile. As a result, many of the SCII profiles for individual clients appear to be relatively flat. Most clients are interested in detecting high or moderately high scores, not low scores. It would be better to group the low scores together if this procedure is necessary to save space on the profile. The interpretation of scores on the Occupational Scales is facilitated by the use of Holland letter codes to classify the scales. * The letter codes, which are arranged in descending order of importance, are based on the mean scores of the occupational criterion groups on the Holland scales. Surprisingly, the sex of the occupational criterion group was not taken into account in assigning the Holland codes. Because separate sex norms are used in interpreting the Holland codes for individuals, separate norms also should be used in assigning the Holland codes to the Occupational Scales. * Occupational scores based on the other sex are most misleading if they tap an interest area that shows large sex differences. For example, females tested by Campbell averaged 17 on the women's interior decorator scale, but 39 on the men's scale (SCII Manual, p. 74). Men averaged 33 on the men's Army officer scale, but their average score on the women's scale was 45. These differences

suggest that separate norms should be used in reporting the occupational scores for men and women. * The AOR [Academic Orientation] was normed on a combined sample of male and female PhDs, with a mean of 60 and a standard deviation of 10. This scale should be used cautiously. High scores reflect interest in investigative and artistic activities. As such, the scale is helpful in predicting persistence in liberal arts curricula, but it is less helpful in predicting academic longevity in other fields (e.g., business, counseling). In addition, scores on this scale are subject to greater change than on most interest scales. The mean score for University of Minnesota students increased 10 points during four years in college. * The like, indifferent, and dislike responses for the first five sections of the SCII are helpful in interpreting the rest of the profile. * The notations on the profile for the last two sections of the inventory ("preference between two activities" and "your characteristics") should be corrected to take into account the differences in item format for these two sections. The response patterns for these two sections cannot be interpreted in the same manner as the response patterns for the first five sections. *Conclusion.* The New SCII is well constructed. The reliability and validity figures reported for the new SCII scales are comparable to those reported for the SVIB scales. These values should improve as new keys are developed based on the total item pool. The new normative samples appear to be adequate in that they were selected to match the SVIB men-and-women-in-general samples that had been carefully assembled by Campbell a few years earlier. The interpretation of the new scales may present some problems. The item content should be made available, at least for the relatively short General Occupational Theme and Basic Interest Scales, so that counselors may refer to this information in attempting to explain the meaning of a particular score. The mean scores on the Basic Interest Scales for each of the occupational criterion groups should be published to facilitate the interpretation of the Occupational Scales. If the occupational scores based on one sex are to be reported for both sexes, they should be normed separately for men and women to take into account the effects of sexual stereotypes. In the past, the occupational scores for the middle third of men or women in gen-

Strong-Campbell Interest Inventory

eral were plotted on the SVIB-M and SVIB-W profiles. This same type of information should be provided on the SCII profile for each sex for all the Occupational Scales. A number of research studies are now made possible because of the single form for men and women and should be undertaken. Specifically, the validity of the occupational scores based on the opposite sex needs to be examined. The feasibility of developing occupational scales based on combined samples of men and women should be studied. Preliminary evidence indicates that combined-sex samples may be desirable in some circumstances, but not others. The use of Holland's theory as a framework for the SCII profile aids in interpreting the scores and in extending the results to other occupations and activities. A few problems require further attention. The Holland codes for the Occupational Scales should be based on normative samples that match the sex of the occupational criterion groups. The letter codes assigned by Campbell differ from those assigned by Holland for some occupations; for example, occupational therapist, librarian, and chiropractor were assigned RIA, A, and ESR codes, respectively, by Campbell, but these same occupations have been coded SRE, SAI, and ISR by Holland. Some of the occupations proved difficult to classify (e.g., lawyer). Because of the SCII emphasis on the profile sheet, there may be a tendency to place greater reliance on the Holland scales than on the other SCII scales; however, the Holland scales have not been validated as thoroughly as the other scales. Although some problems still need to be resolved, the new interest inventory is a timely and valuable contribution to counseling practice and research. Campbell and his co-workers not only have merged effectively the male and female forms, but also have improved substantially the interest inventory by eliminating undesirable items from the item pool, by adding a large number of new Occupational Scales, and by providing a theoretical structure for the empirical scales.

Meas & Eval Guid 9(1):45–6 Ap '76. David P. Campbell. "Author's Reaction to Johnson's Review." This is an informative, useful overview of the new inventory. It is clear, concise, occasionally critical; I like it. * Johnson raises one specific point that deserves some discussion—that is, the question of the security of

scoring weights. Should the composition of the scoring scales be released? There are two competing viewpoints and, uncomfortably, I agree with both of them. The first is that of the pure scientist and client-oriented counselor: "Of course, the scoring weights should be released, both for research purposes and to help the counselor understand the meaning of the scales." How can anyone disagree? The second viewpoint is that of the entrepreneur and pragmatic research scientist: "If you release the item weights, you can't control the scoring, which means you can't make any money, which means you have no research funds." It surprises many to learn that the Strong has not been a particularly lucrative enterprise. It is published by a university press (Stanford) that maintains a low profile, doesn't do much advertising, and has no sales force. The price of the inventory and its scoring is ludicrously low—less than $2 (ask yourself what the simplest test in a doctor's office costs), and the inventory has been mainly self-supporting—that is, research funds have come from sales income. To maintain the past level of research activity and at the same time to expand in order to cover all the new issues raised about testing requires a dependable source of income for the inventory. Because it is a commercial instrument, direct support from the government or other nonprofit agencies is not possible; consequently, the SCII has to generate its own funds. For the foreseeable future that will be done by controlling the scoring; I see no alternatives. *

Meas & Eval Guid 9(1):47–8 Ap '76. Jean C. Steinhauer. "Reaction to Johnson's Review—II." Although Johnson's is a sensitive and thorough review of the new Strong, he accepts the continuation of separate sex scales more easily than I do. My remarks will be directed toward the continuation of separate treatment for the sexes on the occupational scales, because I regard this as an issue that needs further attention. I do not argue with this solution as a practical step for the present revision. What I question is a stance that comes just short of declaring that the interests of men and women with respect to work are so different that the sexes *require* separate treatment on interest inventories. If such differences exist, if occupational identification requires tapping different interests for men and women in the same occupation, then it is a short distance to the conclusion that men and women actually do—perhaps even should do—different work. Given the current interest in the psychological differences between men and women and the social importance of issues related to women and work, I expect strong research for such a conclusion. In fact, research does not support this. * In fact, a careful review of SVIB research shows almost no research comparing differences between men and women in the same occupational groups. Exceptions are some early research reported by Strong in 1943 and research for the refinement of the masculinity-femininity scales for the 1966 restandardization of the Strong. It is this research which Campbell had to fall back on when the SCII was being developed. * I agree with Harmon that energy and resources should be used for the development of combined scales and that if there are differences between the sexes, this does not necessarily mean the differences are important enough to warrant separate sex scales. The point is the issues have not been thoroughly aired and researched. More work needs to be done. Aside from this, data used by Campbell to demonstrate sex differences for occupational groups are those items isolated for showing the greatest differences between the sexes on the masculinity-femininity scales. Indeed, these items discriminate between the sexes across occupations, but this finding seems somewhat circular since the items were selected as sensitive to sex differences in the first place. If separate sex scales are not necessary due to psychological differences but instead are primarily a pragmatic solution—and this appears to me to be the case—then the important social questions are whether this separate treatment reinforces sex differences with respect to work and whether this, in turn, contributes unnecessarily to discrimination. I think the answer to both questions is yes. Sex role is still a basic dimension of interest measurement with the new Strong. I hope that the future will see the development of combined scales. Further research is called for. It disturbs me that the Strong publisher intends to maintain tight control over who is to do research on the instrument—at least, this is what has been indicated to the Texas Tech Counseling Center. In my view, there are obvious questions of self-interest if

all the research is carried out and approved by the publisher and test developer. If the Strong needs protection because it is a business, then I have to say that monopoly in testing does not appeal to me any more than monopoly in, say, the pharmaceutical business. The profession needs to know on what basis research is to be allowed and to be assured that issues are dealt with by an openness of questioning within a community of scholars.

[1024]

Vocational Interest and Sophistication Assessment. Retarded adolescents and young adults; 1967-68; VISA; no data on reliability and validity; individual; separate forms for males, females; administration manual ('68, 50 pages); inquiry sheet ('68, 2 pages); $2 per 50 inquiry sheets; $1 per 25 response sheets; $1.50 per 25 profiles; $2 per manual; $7 per specimen set; cash orders postpaid; (30) minutes; Joseph J. Parnicky, Harris Kahn and Arthur D. Burdett; Joseph J. Parnicky. *
a) FORM FOR MALES. Interest and knowledge scores in each of 7 areas: garage, laundry, food service, maintenance, farm and grounds, materials handling, industry; 1 form ('67, 85 pictures); response sheet ('68, 1 page); profile ('68, 2 pages); $3 per picture booklet.
b) FORM FOR FEMALES. Interest and knowledge scores in each of 4 areas: business and clerical, housekeeping, food service, laundry and sewing; 1 form ('67, 60 pictures); response sheet ('68, 1 page); profile ('68, 2 pages); $2 per picture booklet.
See T2:2217 (1 reference) and 7:1039 (2 references).

REFERENCES

1-2. See 7:1030.
3. See T2:2217.
4. PEACH, WALTER. "Evaluation and Planning for the Secondary Educable Mentally Retarded: One Method and Analysis." *Slow Learning Child* (Australia) 19(2):109-16 Jl '72. * (*PA* 49:10021)
5. REITER, SHUNIT, AND WHELAN, EDWARD. "Vocational Counselling Of Mentally Retarded Young Adults." *Brit J Guid & Counsel* 3(1):93-106 Ja '75. * (*PA* 54:8210)
6. MIDDLETON, WILLIAM EUGENE. *Comparison of Social Maturity, Vocational Interest, and Vocational Sophistication of Institutionalized and Noninstitutionalized Mentally Retarded Persons.* Doctor's thesis, University of South Carolina (Columbia, S.C.), 1976. (*DAI* 37:6280A)

ESTHER E. DIAMOND, *Senior Project Director, Development, Science Research Associates, Chicago, Illinois.*

This interest inventory, for use with "mildly retarded" adolescents and young adults, contains no verbal symbols or statements. The vocational areas represented by the pictorial items are typical of those entered by retardates upon completion of training programs in schools, workshops, or institutions. It was standardized on 3,007 such subjects in seven northeastern states and Washington, D.C. In addition to assessing vocational interests, VISA provides a preliminary measure of sophistication, or knowledge of job requirements and conditions.

The female form is considerably more restricted than the male form, both in the number of sophistication and interest items and in the range of explorable options. There are only four corresponding sophistication and interest scales for females; there are seven for males.

For a given occupation, the work situation depicted varies very little from picture to picture, which should insure homogeneity of the scales. The workers and their supervisors are all faceless white males and females, which could be justified as thematic drawings rather than as drawings representative of a particular racial group. But the pictures are also quite crudely and often unnecessarily ambiguously drawn, so that it is sometimes difficult to determine exactly what the worker is doing. In one drawing of men sawing a log, it is difficult to identify the saw. In another, laundry is being emptied into a large machine, but one has to look closely to determine—or, rather, to infer—that the basket being emptied does indeed contain laundry. A mangle vaguely resembles a flat-bed press.

The technology in a number of pictures also seems outmoded. In one, a woman is seen beating a rug strung on a clothesline. In another, an old-fashioned mimeograph machine is shown instead of a more modern copying device. In other pictures, a worker seems to have only one arm, or an essential ladder rung is missing. Since scores for both the sophistication and the interest portions of the assessment are derived from responses to questions about the pictures, it would seem essential that they be as accurate and unambiguous as possible.

Scores of zero, 1, or 2 are assigned to each response on the basis of level of knowledge and, in general, the assignment of score points is unequivocal. There are, however, a few questionable instances. For example, the response "laundromat" to the question "In what kinds of places do people work as a laundry worker?" earns a score of zero. Yet laundromats often have attendants who help customers load the machine, put in the soap powder and bleach, and empty the driers if the customer is not there and others are waiting. The response "cooker" instead of "cook" to the question "What do you call someone who fries french fries?" receives a score of 1. It seems possible to this reviewer that the response might represent a vocabulary deficiency or an attempt to translate from another language rather than lack of knowledge about the job.

The interest portion of VISA appears to be independent of level of intelligence, chronological age, and job knowledge; correlations are negative or low. The sophistication inquiry is an added plus, since it indicates a level of confidence for interpretation of the interest inquiry responses. If sophistication scores are within the midrange or higher, the interest pattern is considered to have a basis in fairly adequate knowledge about the job areas covered. On the negative side, however, is the severely limited range of options for females—in apparent violation of Title IX; the poor quality of the pictorial representations; the weakness of the maintenance and materials handling scales; the geographically limited nature of the standardization sample; the absence of information on interpreting scores to examinees; and the inadequate treatment of standardization. It would be helpful if profile information—perhaps in pictorial form, using pictures from VISA to represent the various scales—could be shared with the examinee.

It must be considered that little else in the way of standardized vocational assessment tools is available for this group. As a device mainly for exploration until such time as some of its shortcomings have been corrected, VISA could be a helpful tool for use with retardates.

GEORGE DOMINO, *Professor of Psychology, The University of Arizona, Tucson, Arizona.*

VISA is a picture-inquiry technique designed to determine the interest pattern and career knowledge of mildly retarded adolescents. There are three phases to this technique: (*a*) a sophistication inquiry; (*b*) an explanatory presentation; and (*c*) an interest inquiry.

In the first phase, the examiner presents to the client a series of drawings in sequence (seven for males, four for females) depicting work activities, e.g., a man changing a tire, a woman filing papers. For each drawing the client is asked a standard series of questions, such as what the drawn person is doing, what his occupational label is, what settings does he work in, and how much money does he get paid.

In the second phase, three drawings are shown and the client is instructed to identify the central character as John (Jane), and a male and female supervisor. John (Jane) always has black hair, the male supervisor is getting bald and the female supervisor has her hair in a bun.

In the final phase, a series of drawings (75 for males, 53 for females) is presented in which John (Jane) is shown doing many different jobs and the client is asked to indicate whether he (she) would like to do the same kind of work.

There is great need for instruments designed to assist the mentally retarded in making vocational choices, so VISA could be potentially useful. Among its favorable aspects is its emphasis on the knowledge (sophistication) that the client possesses, so that misconceptions can be corrected by the examiner. The instructions are clear and include an explicit statement that responses should reflect liking rather than skill or familiarity. The responses to the sophistication inquiry are scored on a 3-point scale (0 for don't know, 1 for limited responses, and 2 for acceptable), and a clear and explicit scoring guide is included in the manual; in fact, the guide covers 22 of the 37 pages. The drawings are large, clear, and generally relevant. The response sheets are clear and make recording and scoring of the interest areas an easy task.

So much for the format of VISA. As a counseling or assessment technique, it is intriguing, but as a psychometric instrument, it is almost worthless. To begin with, the manual gives absolutely no data on reliability and validity. These are, in fact, not even mentioned, except for a brief reference to an in-house report. Normative tables are given for both the sophistication scores and the interest scores. The tables give minimum, mean, and maximum scores (plus points one-half an SD below and above the mean), but we are not told the size, composition, or nature of the normative sample, nor are there percentiles, standard scores, or other relevant interpretive data.

The manual gives no indication of how VISA was developed, how the interest areas were obtained, how the drawings were selected, the number of drawings in each interest area, and other essential information one would expect.

There are many additional minor criticisms that could be made. For example, why are DISLIKE responses scored +1? Why does the manual indicate that the drawings are sequen-

tially numbered when they are not? Why is no definition given of the interest clusters, or of their vocational-counseling implications?

There is one report on VISA in the literature (3); it is not, however, the type of report likely to be read by the user of VISA and it lacks clarity. This report indicates that the reliability of VISA was established earlier, and that the job clusters resulted from a factor analysis. The report itself discusses a study involving approximately 3,000 moderately to mildly retarded subjects drawn from institutions, workshops, and training schools in the Northeast.

Test-retest reliability coefficients are presented for both sexes over a one-month and a 12- to 18-month period. These coefficients are substantial but they are based on factor loadings rather than raw scores. Somewhat puzzling and possibly embarrassing is the fact that these cluster scores correlate significantly and negatively with both sophistication scores and IQ.

In its present form, VISA is not recommended and the potential user is urged to look elsewhere (e.g., the *AAMD-Becker Reading-Free Vocational Interest Inventory*). Much work needs to be done before VISA can qualify as a psychometric instrument.

[1025]

★Vocational Interest, Experience, and Skill Assessment. Grades 8-12; 1976; VIESA; abbreviated adaptation of *Career Planning Program;* norms consist of means and standard deviations; 1 form consists of 3 parts in 16-page career guidebook: interest inventory (2 detachable pages, self-marking), work-related experiences checklist (2 pages), and skill ratings (1 page); handbook (50 pages); $13.80 per 35 guidebooks; $2.55 per handbook; $2.85 per specimen set; postage extra; (40-45) minutes; American College Testing Program; Houghton Mifflin Co. *

CHARLES J. KRAUSKOPF, *Professor of Psychology, University of Missouri, Columbia, Missouri.*

The primary purpose of VIESA is to stimulate exploration of possible career choices, not necessarily to make a choice. It can also serve as the core for a short or "mini" course in vocational exploration. It is basically a short form of the *Career Planning Program for Grades 8-12,* which is, in turn, a downward extension of the *ACT Career Planning Program.*

If a student approaches the career guidebook as a programmed text, it is fairly easy to understand; however, the continual shifting back and forth from place to place in the booklet seems unnecessarily complicated. If one looks ahead to the next page, perhaps to get an idea of what is coming next, he/she may become quite confused. In other words, the scanning or overview which may be a part of good text-reading skill or test-taking skill is a disadvantage here. The teacher or counselor, on the other hand, faces a fairly sizable task preparing for the questions which any group of junior high or high school students will inevitably bring up. The handbook recommends thorough familiarity with it and the experience of filling out the same materials the student does. I would add the handbook for the *Career Planning Program*. If the counselor is not already familiar with the ACT system of classifying jobs and job families, it must be learned along with its relation to more familiar systems, such as Holland's or Roe's. This information is provided, but it takes some study.

Without thorough familiarity, some of the students' results may be more disturbing than helpful. My own interests, experiences, and skills come out in three different regions of the ACT work region chart. A little thought provided a rationalization satisfactory to me. Part of my interests and experiences come from interests which I know to be purely avocational. Without a thorough familiarity with the theory behind the vocational classification scheme, I can see a counselor recommending to me that I learn to repair lawnmowers. I know this sounds silly, but it is a common occurrence in college counseling centers to hear students report very similar recommendations.

I belabor the point about counselor preparation and familiarity for two reasons: (*a*) I see too many college students who missed the point of early vocational exploration, and (*b*) the VIESA materials emphasize wideband prediction and exploration to the point that the effect seems to be a message that details do not matter; only exposure does.

There are three assessment sections: an interest inventory, an experience inventory, and a self-rating of skills. They are all related to the ACT occupational classification system resulting in a pie chart cut into 12 regions with the students' results plotted in the regions. Each region suggests several occupations for later exploration.

The interest inventory is a short form of the Uni-sex ACT Interest Inventory (UNIACT

IV). Items were chosen to minimize sex-related differences in responses. Combined sex norms are also used. The idea is to remove as much of the sex stereotyping as possible in the measuring of interests. The rationale and procedures for constructing the interest scales are quite adequately explained in the handbook, as is the norming procedure. Split-half reliabilities for the two bipolar interest scales are .75 for the data/ideas dimension and .82 for the people/things dimension. The standard errors of measurement are reported to be less than 2.6 raw score points, .50 and .42 standard deviations, respectively, for reliabilities of .75 and .82. All other reliability information is "borrowed" from UNIACT IV.

The word validity does not appear in the table of contents for the VIESA handbook. There is, however, some validity related information, all of it borrowed from UNIACT IV. Since this is a short form of the UNIACT IV, this information probably has some relevance. UNIACT IV relates quite well to the Holland categories. The same-named scales correlate from .72 to .81. The factor structure is reported and shows that the two bipolar scales can be used to generate Holland categories very satisfactorily. Hopefully, the short form sufficiently retains these characteristics.

In summary, the purchaser of VIESA will get an interest test, which is psychometrically good for such a short form. As far as tests are concerned, that is all he gets. The rest of the complex (perhaps unnecessarily so) package is more of a programmed learning text on how to use the ACT occupational classification system.

[1026]

★Vocational Interest Questionnaire for [Black] Pupils in Forms I–V. 1974–75; VIQ; 10 scores: technical, outdoor, social service, natural science, office work (non-numerical, numerical), music, art, commerce, language; 1 form ('74, 17 pages, English and Afrikaans); manual ('75, 73 pages, English and Afrikaans); separate answer sheets (IBM 1230, hand scored) must be used; R5 per 10 tests; 50c per single copy; R5 per 100 IBM answer sheets; R1.75 per 100 hand scored answer sheets; R5.25 per manual; postpaid within South Africa; (60) minutes; T. M. Coetzee; Human Sciences Research Council [South Africa]. *

[1027]

Vocational Planning Inventory. Vocational students in grades 8–10, 11–12 and grade 13 entrants; 1968–70, c1954–70; VPI; the battery consists of the *SRA Arithmetic Index, SRA Pictorial Reasoning Test, SRA Verbal Form, Survey of Interpersonal Values, Survey of Personal Values*, Mechanics subtest of the *Flanagan Aptitude Classification Test,* and the following subtests of the *Flanagan Industrial Tests:* Arithmetic, Assembly (*a*), Expression (*a*), Memory (*a*), Scales (*b*), and Tables (*b*); tests cannot be locally scored; the student's copy of his test report presents predicted grades in 9 or 10 areas: agriculture (*a* only), business, construction trades, drafting and design, electronics and electrical trades, home economics and health, mechanics and mechanical maintenance, metal trades, general academic, general vocational; the counselor's copy of an individual test report also presents national percentile rank norms for the component tests: single scores for the 7 (or 8) nonpersonality tests and 12 value scores (practical mindedness, achievement, variety, decisiveness, orderliness, goal orientation, support, conformity, recognition, independence, benevolence, leadership) on the 2 personality tests; no information is presented on intercorrelations, means, variances, and multiple regression equations; 1 form; 2 levels; manual ('68, 37 pages); report forms ('68, 1 page) for counselor, student, and files; student interpretive leaflet ('68, 12 pages); separate answer sheets (MRC) must be used; $3.05 per specimen set of either level, postage extra; Science Research Associates, Inc. *

a) HIGH SCHOOL PREDICTION PROGRAM. Vocational students in grades 8–10; 1968–70, c1954–70; for predicting success in grades 9–12 in areas listed above; regression equations based upon testing and course grades in grade 12 only; 1 form ('68, 33 pages); examiner's manual ('68, 11 pages); interpretive supplement ('70, 9 pages); 130(200) minutes in 3 sessions.

　1) *Complete Rental Plan.* Rental and scoring service, $1.43 per student.

　2) *Scoring Only Plan.* $13.90 per 25 tests; scoring service, $1.32 per student.

b) POST-HIGH SCHOOL PREDICTION PROGRAM. Vocational students in grades 11–12 and grade 13 entrants; 1968, c1954–68; for predicting success in grade 13 in areas listed above; regression equations based upon testing and course grades in grade 13 only; 1 form ('68, 27 pages); examiner's manual ('68, 10 pages); scoring service and prices same as for *a*; 120(166) minutes in 2 sessions.

REFERENCES

1. CLARK, CHARLES G. *An Assessment of Selected Variables in the Selection of Students for Secondary Area Vocational Programs.* Doctor's thesis, Michigan State University (East Lansing, Mich.), 1972. (*DAI* 33:4825A)
2. JONES, W. PAUL, AND SCOTT, ISAIAH L. "High School and College Share Test Results." *Personnel & Guid J* 51(8): 562–5 Ap '73. *

PAUL R. LOHNES, *Professor of Education, State University of New York at Buffalo, Buffalo, New York.*

The *Vocational Planning Inventory* provides an ambitious assessment of aptitudes and values for noncollege-bound adolescents who are oriented toward vocational education. One form of the program is intended to serve the needs of students in grades 8 through 10 who are in the process of selecting a vocational curriculum for their high school experience; the other form provides guidance to older youths, nominally at grade levels 11 through 13, whose concern is planning post-high-school vocational education

tion matriculation. The program is very attractive in format, reasonable in time requirements and cost, supported by good report forms and manuals, unique (to my knowledge) in the prediction scheme on which interpretations of score profiles are based, and sound in the concepts of vocational guidance which it advances.

Some of the strengths of the program have to be described briefly to set the stage for comments on some of the weaknesses. A major strength is the attempt to survey aptitudes and proclivities which are known to be relevant to vocational choice for these clients on a broad spectrum. Thus, there are 9 or 10 tests (depending on form) ranging over verbal ability, arithmetic, mechanics, pictorial reasoning, tables, scales, memory, assembly, and a survey of values. Each test is short, since the required reliability will be for multiple regression functions based on all the tests. A possible weakness is that no interests survey is included. The program manual recommends that a Kuder be administered, but then the interests would not contribute to the multiple regression predictions of course grades, which are the main interpretive devices. Project TALENT research has established that inventoried interests can contribute substantially to vocational predictions when they are teamed with aptitudes. Factor analyses of the TALENT tests also established that a convenient, memorable factor transformation of the variance collected by diverse aptitude tests, such as those used in the VPI, is available. We may conclude that the breadth of the VPI assessment is impressive, but it could be improved in coverage of traits and in organization of scales.

A second major strength of the program is the casting of the reports to clients in terms of predicted grades in various vocational curriculum areas rather than in some form of scores for individual tests. These predicted grades are generated from what is termed a central prediction system, but one which cleverly adapts the regression equations to the local school situation by fitting an intercept constant to local achievement levels. The reason that VPI can have such an imaginative, useful central prediction system when many other testing programs do not is that an unusually ambitious norming research has been accomplished. In 1967, approximately 7,500 high school students in a nationwide sample provided test scores and high school record information to what amounted, almost, to an entrepreneurial Project TALENT. The resemblance to Project TALENT is improved by the stated intention to follow-up these subjects in order to make predictions of on-the-job success available. We can only wish the VPI researchers well in this endeavor. (Who are these able and ambitious authors of the VPI program? It's regrettable that they should be anonymous. One sees many clues that suggest the leadership of John Flanagan, Project TALENT's inventor and leader.)

While approving of the predictions of grades in various curriculum areas we yet may ask if prediction of placement in curricula or vocational membership groups would not be useful, also. VPI appears to have a marvelous opportunity to deploy multiple-group discriminant functions as a complementary central prediction scheme. Alternatively, centour predictions for each vocational curriculum could be provided. Project TALENT research has shown how information about the extent to which an individual resembles the membership of each criterion group can complement information about how successful that individual may be in each group. I personally believe that a better understanding of vocational opportunities and probable adjustments to various settings for one's career would be stimulated by assessment interpretations from a central prediction system which addressed both resemblance and success questions. Such a comprehensive view of career multipotentialities is within reach of the VPI program.

The interpretive supplement admits that the values survey scores contribute little to the multiple regressions. It seems to me that they might play a larger role in the recommended discriminant or centour calculations.

Two other comments may be in order. First, the student interpretive leaflet is a fine teaching text, but I wonder if the language level is not too high for the intended clients. Second, certain scores are reserved to the counselor in the reporting scheme. I am not sure this needs to be. It seems to me that these scores could be made available to the student if the text previously mentioned in this paragraph were extended to cover the understanding of these additional scores.

The VPI has a great deal going for it as a guidance program for adolescents who are oriented toward vocational curriculum placement, and no serious drawbacks. Although I have indicated some ways in which I would like to see it expanded, it seems to be an excellent program just as it stands.

RICHARD S. MELTON, *Professor of Psychology, University of Cincinnati, Cincinnati, Ohio.*

The VPI contains a good sampling of SRA tests for accomplishing its stated purpose of meeting the need for "expanded and more effective guidance services for vocationally oriented high school and post-high-school students and for young adults seeking to continue their training in vocational areas." The scores obtained on the various tests are used to make individual predictions of success in the major vocational curriculum areas at the high school and post-high-school levels. The multiple correlations reported in the manual are respectably large, ranging from .49 to .69 for the high school prediction battery, and from .39 to .70 for the post-high-school prediction battery. Crossvalidation correlations are also reported, and in only one instance was the shrinkage so great (from .54 to .16 for mechanics and mechanical maintenance at the high school level) as to warrant serious questioning of the operational usage of the prediction equations.

The manual devotes seven pages to a description of the research and development. It includes four tables giving frequencies and percentages of the 7,408 students tested by geographical and curriculum areas, and by sex and race. It then cautions the user that he or she should understand the nature of this reference group, because the prediction equations and the percentile norms are based upon it. The manual is somewhat lengthy for a user to study, but it is necessary if the program is to be used judiciously.

While the selection of tests for the VPI was sound and, in general, the research was well done, there are nevertheless a number of shortcomings. The primary one is that the two sexes were combined for all of the analyses. It would seem likely that the sexes would differ on most of the tests and probably on grade point averages in many of the curricula; accordingly, the

Vocational Planning Inventory

prediction equations would probably be different for each sex.

Secondly, the means and/or standard deviations are not reported in many of the tables (Tables 10, 11, 12, and 14). The reliability estimates for each test are reported in Table 13, but information on sample sizes, means, and standard deviations is not given. A personal inquiry to SRA revealed that the reliability estimates given in Table 13 were not based on the VPI standardization groups but rather on samples used in the original development of the tests. Hence, these reliability estimates, as well as the reliability estimates for the test batteries as a whole (.93 for the high school prediction battery and .90 for the post high school prediction battery) cannot be interpreted with confidence.

While the grade point predictions are focused on an individual's relative potential for success among the various curriculum areas, the manual indicates that "there are purposes for which information about absolute standing is of value." Accordingly, national percentile distributions of predicted grade points for the high school and post high school groups are presented. Norms tables of "predicted values" are quite rare, and until users are familiar with them and with methods for setting confidence intervals on values such as are given in these tables, the inclusion of such tables is questionable—particularly when the relevant means and standard deviations have not been presented in the manual.

There are also many highly commendable features of the manual and of the interpretive supplement, most notably the many cautious statements regarding interpretation. Two examples are: (a) "Ideally, the administration and interpretation of the VPI should be part of a comprehensive vocational counseling and planning program within the school," and (b) "to the extent that counseling resources are available, the greatest value from administering the program can be obtained by providing students with the opportunity, either individually or in groups, to talk over, in a counseling atmosphere, the questions raised by their VPI scores."

Also to be commended is the presentation of predicted grade average results in terms of ranges, as well as points, with the added explanation that if any pair of ranges overlap, the student should probably view his likelihood of success in the two curricula as equal.

One might question a few of the interpretive statements made to the student in the VPI report booklet, but taken together with the careful and extensive statements made to the counselor in the manual, the overall evaluation of the interpretive information must be quite positive.

[1028]

*Vocational Preference Inventory, Sixth Revision. High school and college and adults; 1953–75; VPI; "a personality inventory composed entirely of occupational titles"; formerly called *Holland Vocational Preference Inventory;* 11 scores: realistic, intellectual, social, conventional, enterprising, artistic, self-control, masculinity, status, infrequency, acquiescence; no data on reliability for high school; 1 form ('65, 2 pages); manual ('75, 31 pages); profile ['65, 2 pages]; separate answer sheets must be used; $1.75 per 25 tests; $4 per 50 sets of answer sheets and profiles; $1.50 per scoring stencil; $3.50 per manual; $5 per specimen set; postage extra; (15–30) minutes; John L. Holland; Consulting Psychologists Press, Inc. *

See T2:1430 (48 references); for reviews by Joseph A. Johnston and Paul R. Lohnes, see 7:157 (39 references); see also P:283 (31 references); for reviews by Robert L. French and H. Bradley Sagen of an earlier edition, see 6:115 (13 references).

REFERENCES

1–13. See 6:115.
14–44. See P:283.
45–83. See 7:157.
84–131. See T2:1430; also includes a cumulative name index to the first 131 references and 4 reviews for this test.
132. BLAKENEY, ROGER N.; MATTESON, MICHAEL T.; AND HOLLAND, THOMAS A. "A Research Note on the New SVIB Holland Scales." *J Voc Behav* 2(3):239–43 Jl '72. * (PA 49:8045)
133. BODDEN, JACK L., AND KLEIN, ALAN J. "Cognitive Complexity and Appropriate Vocational Choice: Another Look." *J Counsel Psychol* 19(3):257–8 My '72. * (PA 48:9968)
134. BRADSHAW, HARLEY EDWARD. *Predicting Holland Vocational Preference Inventory Scales From Strong Basic Interest Scales for Community College Males.* Doctor's thesis, Southern Illinois University (Carbondale, Ill.), 1972. (DAI 33:2097A)
135. COCKRIEL, IRVIN W. "Some Data Concerning the Vocational Preference Inventory Scales and the Strong Vocational Interest Blank." *J Voc Behav* 2(3):251–4 Jl '72. * (PA 49:7757)
136. COFFEY, MARTIN JAMES. *Personality Orientation and Vocational Maturity: A Study of Profile Similarity.* Doctor's thesis, University of Alabama (University, Ala.), 1972. (DAI 33:5488A)
137. COLE, NANCY S. "On Measuring the Vocational Interests of Women." *ACT Res Rep* 49:1–11 Mr '72. * (PA 48:9970)
138. CRAIG, DONALD HECTOR. *Student Personality Type as Related to Course Selection in a Relatively Choice-Free Curriculum.* Doctor's thesis, Ohio University (Athens, Ohio), 1972. (DAI 33:3282A)
139. DEMPSEY, DON GRAHAM. *Academic Achievement and Course Satisfaction: A Test of Holland's Theory of Vocational Choice.* Doctor's thesis, University of North Carolina (Chapel Hill, N.C.), 1972. (DAI 34:133A)
140. ELKINS, RICHARD LONSDALE. *An Investigation of Selected Factors Associated With the Success of Freshmen Engineering Students at the University of Maryland.* Doctor's thesis, University of Maryland (College Park, Md.), 1972. (DAI 33:2099A)
141. ELMENDORF, MARY ELIZABETH. *Occupational Stereotypes and Holland's Theory.* Doctor's thesis, Ohio State University (Columbus, Ohio), 1972. (DAI 33:5489B)
142. FRANTZ, THOMAS T. "Reinterpretation of Flat SVIB Profiles." *J Voc Behav* 2(2):201–7 Ap '72. * (PA 48:9972)
143. FRANTZ, THOMAS T., AND WALSH, E. PIERCE. "Ex-

ploration of Holland's Theory of Vocational Choice in Graduate School Environments." *J Voc Behav* 2(3):223–32 Jl '72. * (*PA* 49:8063)

144. GAFFEY, ROBERT LOUIS. *An Investigation of the Concurrent Validity of Holland's Theory.* Doctor's thesis, Ohio State University (Columbus, Ohio), 1972. (*DAI* 33:5490B)

145. GILBRIDE, THOMAS V. *A Study of Persisting and Nonpersisting Catholic Clergymen.* Doctor's thesis, Louisiana State University (Baton Rouge, La.), 1972. (*DAI* 33:4505B)

146. HILLIARD, TED R. *Rehabilitation Counselor Personal Characteristic Type Relationship to Counselor Performance Ratings.* Doctor's thesis, University of Florida (Gainesville, Fla.), 1972. (*DAI* 34:2933B)

147. HOGAN, ROBERT; HALL, ROBERT; AND BLANK, ESTHER. "An Extension of the Similarity-Attraction Hypothesis to the Study of Vocational Behavior." *J Counsel Psychol* 19(3):238–40 My '72. * (*PA* 48:9077)

148. HOUNTRAS, PETER T.; WILLIAMS, CONSTANCE M.; AND WILLIAMS, JOHN D. "Manifest Anxiety and Vocational Preference Among Male Graduate Students." *Psychol Rep* 30(3):886 Je '72. * (*PA* 49:2471)

149. HUGHES, HENRY M., JR. "Vocational Choice, Level, and Consistency: An Investigation of Holland's Theory on an Employed Sample." *J Voc Behav* 2(4):377–88 O '72. * (*PA* 50:7978)

150. JACOBS, S. S. "A Validity Study of the Acquiescence Scale of the Holland Vocational Preference Inventory." *Ed & Psychol Meas* 32(2):477–80 su '72. *

151. JOHNSON, RONALD BRUCE. *The Vocational Development of Undergraduate Students Enrolled in a Vocational-Educational Information Course.* Doctor's thesis, University of Iowa (Iowa City, Iowa), 1972. (*DAI* 33:6668A)

152. MARTIN, RANDALL BRENT. *Relationships Between Holland's Vocational Preference Inventory and Vocational-Technical Student Achievement.* Master's thesis, Pennsylvania State University (University Park, Pa.), 1972.

153. PERRY, FLOYD, JR. *Selected Variables Related to Academic Success of Black Freshmen Students at the University of Missouri-Columbia.* Doctor's thesis, University of Missouri (Columbia, Mo.), 1972. (*DAI* 33:4845A)

154. SALOMONE, PAUL R., AND MUTHARD, JOHN E. "Canonical Correlation of Vocational Needs and Vocational Style." *J Voc Behav* 2(2):163–71 Ap '72. * (*PA* 48:12343)

155. SOLIAH, DAVID CONRAD. *A Longitudinal Study of Academic Achievement Using Holland's Theory of Vocational Choice.* Doctor's thesis, University of North Dakota (Grand Forks, N.D.), 1972. (*DAI* 33:4854A)

156. STAHMANN, ROBERT F. "Review of the Holland Vocational Preference Inventory, Sixth Edition." *J Counsel Psychol* 19(1):85–6 Ja '72. *

157. VIERNSTEIN, MARY COWAN. "The Extension of Holland's Occupational Classification to All Occupations in the Dictionary of Occupational Titles." *J Voc Behav* 2(2):107–21 Ap '72. * (*PA* 48:12320)

158. WALSH, W. BRUCE. "Review of the Vocational Preference Inventory, Sixth Revision." *J Ed Meas* 9(2):167–9 su '72. *

159. WALSH, W. BRUCE, AND LEWIS, ROGER O. "Consistent, Inconsistent and Undecided Career Preferences and Personality." *J Voc Behav* 2(3):309–16 Jl '72. * (*PA* 49:8013)

160. WHITNEY, DOUGLAS R., AND WHITTLESEY, RICHARD R. "Two Hypotheses About Holland's Personality Types and Counseling Outcomes." *J Counsel Psychol* 19(4):323–7 Jl '72. * (*PA* 49:1384)

161. WILLIAMS, CONSTANCE M. "Occupational Choice of Male Graduate Students as Related to Values and Personality: A Test of Holland's Theory." *J Voc Behav* 2(1):39–46 Ja '72. * (*PA* 48:3923)

162. AIKEN, JAMES, AND JOHNSTON, JOSEPH A. "Promoting Career Information Seeking Behaviors in College Students." *J Voc Behav* 3(1):81–7 Ja '73. * (*PA* 50:3658)

163. ANDREWS, HANS A. "Personality Patterns and Vocational Choice: A Test of Holland's Theory With Adult Part-Time Community College Students." *J Counsel Psychol* 20(5):482–3 S '73. * (*PA* 51:9958)

164. BROOKS, JOHN ELBERT. *An Investigation to Determine Whether Selected Predictor Variables Discriminate Between Two Groups of Entering Freshmen Students at Wharton County Junior College.* Doctor's thesis, University of Houston (Houston, Tex.), 1973. (*DAI* 34:4729A)

165. CAIN, JOE L. *Decision Making and Disadvantaged College Students: "A Test of Holland's Theory."* Doctor's thesis, University of Tulsa (Tulsa, Okla.), 1973. (*DAI* 34:3862A)

166. CAMPBELL, RUTH M. *A Study of the Relationship Between Personality, Work and Leisure as It Applies to Men Who Work.* Doctor's thesis, State University of New York (Buffalo, N.Y.), 1973. (*DAI* 34:5617A)

167. COLE, NANCY S. "On Measuring the Vocational Interests of Women." *J Counsel Psychol* 20(2):105–12 Mr '73. * (*PA* 50:3974)

168. CURRIE, LAWRENCE EVERETT. *Vocational Awareness, Vocational Development, and Vocational Responses in Adolescents of Divergent Ethnic, Educational, and Socio-Economic Back-*

grounds. Doctor's thesis, Syracuse University (Syracuse, N.Y.), 1973. (*DAI* 34:7119A)

169. DIMOND, DAVID LAURENCE. *Differences in Selected Psychological Traits Between Pre-Service Male Secondary and Elementary Teachers in the University of Missouri System.* Doctor's thesis, University of Missouri (Columbia, Mo.), 1973. (*DAI* 35:744A)

170. DOWE, MARY CATHERINE. *A Study of the Characteristics of Two Selected Groups of Student Nurses.* Doctor's thesis, University of Kentucky (Lexington, Ky.), 1973. (*DAI* 35:1310B)

171. FISHBURNE, FRANCIS JOSEPH, JR. *The Concurrent Validity of Two Measures Operationalizing Holland's Theory Using a Sample of Non-Professional Workers.* Doctor's thesis, Ohio State University (Columbus, Ohio), 1973. (*DAI* 34:4016B)

172. FITCH, LANDON A. *The Vocational Preference Inventory as a Measure of Probable Teaching Effectiveness.* Master's thesis, Central Washington State College (Ellensburg, Wash.), 1973.

173. FLORENCE, JOHN WILLIAM. *A Further Investigation of Holland's Theory of Vocational Psychology.* Doctor's thesis, University of Tulsa (Tulsa, Okla.), 1973. (*DAI* 34:1076A)

174. FOLSOM, CLYDE H., JR. "Effects of Mental Abilities on Obtained Intercorrelations Among VPI Scales." *Meas & Eval Guid* 6(2):74–81 Jl '73. * (*PA* 51:9967)

175. GILBRIDE, THOMAS V. "Holland's Theory and Resignations From the Catholic Clergy." *J Counsel Psychol* 20(2):190–1 Mr '73. * (*PA* 50:2817)

176. HALL, HAROLD B. *Assignment to Residence Halls by Major: A Test of Holland's Theory of Vocational Choice.* Doctor's thesis, University of Missouri (Columbia, Mo.), 1973. (*DAI* 34:6975A)

177. HARVEY, DAVID W., AND WHINFIELD, RICHARD W. "Extending Holland's Theory to Adult Women." *J Voc Behav* 3(2):115–27 Ap '73. * (*PA* 50:10120)

178. HOLLAND, JOHN L. *Making Vocational Choices: A Theory of Careers.* Englewood Cliffs, N.J.: Prentice-Hall, Inc., 1973. Pp. ix, 150. *

179. HORTON, NOEL KENT. *A Descriptive Evaluation of Persisters and Non-persisters in Texas Community Colleges.* Doctor's thesis, Texas A & M University (College Station, Tex.), 1973. (*DAI* 34:7487A)

180. HOUNTRAS, PETER T.; LEE, DAVID L.; AND HEDAHL, BEULAH M. "Relationships Between SVIB Nonoccupational Scales and Achievement for Six Holland Personality Types." *J Voc Behav* 3(2):195–208 Ap '73. * (*PA* 50:9893)

181. JOHNSON, D. M., AND MOORE, J. C. "An Investigation of Holland's Theory of Vocational Psychology." *Meas & Eval Guid* 5(4):488–95 Ja '73. * (*PA* 50:4009)

182. JOHNSON, DALE M. "Relationships Between Selected Cognitive and Noncognitive Variables and Practical Nursing Achievement." *Nursing Res* 22(2):148–53 Mr–Ap '73. * (*PA* 50:9068)

183. LEE, DAVID L., AND HEDAHL, BEULAH. "Holland's Personality Types Applied to the SVIB Basic Interest Scales." *J Voc Behav* 3(1):61–8 Ja '73. * (*PA* 50:4014)

184. LEONARD, RUSSELL L., JR.; WALSH, W. BRUCE; AND OSIPOW, SAMUEL H. "Self-Esteem, Self-Consistency, and Second Vocational Choice." *J Counsel Psychol* 20(1):91–3 Ja '73. * (*PA* 50:2006)

185. LOMBARDI, ROBER ALFRED. *Are Community College Students With Majors Congruent With the Holland Vocational Inventory Typologies More Persistent in Their Pursuit of Educational Goals?* Doctor's thesis, University of Southern California (Los Angeles, Calif.), 1973. (*DAI* 34:2305A)

186. LOVELL, JOHN EDWARD. *Perceptions of the Psychological Climate of Purdue University in Relationship to Mode of College Residence.* Doctor's thesis, Purdue University (Lafayette, Ind.), 1973. (*DAI* 35:1448A)

187. MATTESON, MICHAEL T.; HOLLAND, THOMAS A.; BLAKENEY, ROGER N.; AND SCHNITZEN, JOSEPH P. "Empirical Derivation of SVIB-Holland Scales: A Brief Report." *J Voc Behav* 3(2):163–6 Ap '73. * (*PA* 50:10143)

188. PAULSON, DONALD L., JR., AND STAHMANN, ROBERT F. "High Risk Students Who Graduated: A Follow-Up Study." *J Col Stud Personnel* 14(2):149–52 Mr '73. * (*PA* 50:5819)

189. PETERSON, CARL D. "The Development and Achievement of Equal Opportunity Program Students." *J Col Stud Personnel* 14(1):34–7 Ja '73. * (*PA* 50:7824)

190. TAYLOR, K. F., AND KELSO, G. I. "Course of Study and Personality: An Australian Test of Holland's Theory." *Austral J Psychol* 25(3):199–209 D '73. * (*PA* 52:11086)

191. WAKEFIELD, JAMES A., JR., AND DOUGHTIE, EUGENE B. "The Geometric Relationship Between Holland's Personality Typology and the Vocational Preference Inventory." *J Counsel Psychol* 20(6):513–8 N '73. * (*PA* 51:8049)

192. WALSH, W. BRUCE, AND OSIPOW, SAMUEL H. "Career Preferences, Self-Concept, and Vocational Maturity." *Res Higher Ed* 1(3):287–95 '73. * (*PA* 51:6011)

193. WARRINGTON, MARILYN M. *Reality of Vocational Choice and Vocational Aspirations of Emotionally Disturbed/Socially Maladjusted and Normal Adolescents: A Comparison.* Doctor's thesis, University of Florida (Gainesville, Fla.), 1973. (*DAI* 35:916A)

Vocational Preference Inventory

194. WIGINGTON, JOHN H., AND APOSTAL, ROBERT A. "Personality Differences Among Men in Selected Air Force Specialties." *J Counsel Psychol* 20(5):454–8 S '73. * (*PA* 51:10051)

195. WILLIAMS, JOHN D., AND WILLIAMS, CONSTANCE M. "Canonical Analysis of the Vocational Preference Inventory and the Sixteen Personality Factor Questionnaire." *Psychol Rep* 32(1):211–4 F '73. * (*PA* 51:3979)

196. ANDERSON, GERALD LEE. *Anxiety, Risk, and Socioeconomic Class in Relation to Occupational Preference*. Doctor's thesis, East Texas State University (Commerce, Tex.), 1974. (*DAI* 35:7642A)

197. AUDETTE, EUGENE JOSEPH. *Teachers as Models for Vocational Choice of High School Students: A Study of Holland's Theory of Vocational Attraction*. Doctor's thesis, University of Iowa (Iowa City, Iowa), 1974. (*DAI* 35:2756A)

198. BOGNER, ROSELIND GULLO. *A Study of the Relationships Among John Holland's Vocational Types, Patterns of Need Satisfaction and Vocational Satisfaction*. Doctor's thesis, State University of New York (Buffalo, N.Y.), 1974. (*DAI* 35:7051A)

199. BUNCH, STEVEN CARL. *The Relationship of Dogmatism to Holland's Vocational Choice Theory Among Teacher Education Students*. Doctor's thesis, Washington State University (Pullman, Wash.), 1974. (*DAI* 35:3584A)

200. COX, JENNINGS GODDIN. *The Efficacy of Holland's Theoretical Model for Client-Counselor Matching in a Vocational Counseling Analogue Study*. Doctor's thesis, University of Missouri (Columbia, Mo.), 1974. (*DAI* 36:127A)

201. CRABTREE, PAUL D., AND HALES, LOYDE W. "Holland's Hexagonal Model Applied to Rural Youth." *Voc Guid Q* 22(3):218–23 Mr '74. * (*PA* 53:4080)

202. DI SCIPIO, WILLIAM J. "A Factor Analytic Validation of Holland's Vocational Preference Inventory." *J Voc Behav* 4(3):389–402 Je '74. * (*PA* 53:13252)

203. DREESE, CURTIS WILLIAM. *A Validation Study of Holland's Vocational Preference Inventory for College Education Majors*. Master's thesis, Washington State University (Pullman, Wash.), 1974.

204. EDWARDS, KEITH J.; NAFZIGER, DEAN H.; AND HOLLAND, JOHN L. "Differentiation of Occupational Perceptions Among Different Age Groups." *J Voc Behav* 4(3):311–8 Je '74. * (*PA* 52:13288)

205. ELKINS, RICHARD L., AND LUETKEMEYER, JOSEPH F. "Characteristics of Successful Freshmen Engineering Students." *Eng Ed* 65(2):189–91 N '74. *

206. FOX, LYNN H., AND DENHAM, SUSANNE A. Chap. 8, "Values and Career Interests of Mathematically and Scientifically Precocious Youth," pp. 140–75. In *Mathematical Talent: Discovery, Description, and Development*. Edited by Julian C. Stanley and others. Baltimore, Md.: Johns Hopkins University Press, 1974. Pp. xix, 215. *

207. GAFFEY, ROBERT L., AND WALSH, W. BRUCE. "Concurrent Validity and Holland's Theory." *J Voc Behav* 5(1):41–51 Ag '74. * (*PA* 53:4138)

208. GRANDY, THOMAS G., AND STAHMANN, ROBERT F. "Family Influence on College Students' Vocational Choice: Predicting Holland's Personality Types." *J Col Stud Personnel* 15(5):404–9 S '74. * (*PA* 53:5224)

209. HOLLAND, THOMAS A.; BLAKENEY, ROGER N.; MATTESON, MICHAEL T.; AND SCHNITZEN, JOSEPH P. "Empirical Derivation of SVIB-Holland Scales and Conversion Tables." *J Voc Behav* 5(1):23–9 Ag '74. * (*PA* 53:2143)

210. HUTCHINS, ARTHUR MICHAEL. *Selected Aspects of Vocational Maturity and Satisfaction With the University of Idaho in Older and Younger Male Undergraduate Students Using Holland's Theory of Vocational Choice*. Doctor's thesis, University of Idaho (Moscow, Idaho), 1974. (*DAI* 35:5024A)

211. LEWIS, ROGER OWEN, JR. *Consistent Career Preferences, Personality and Women's Perceptions of Male Views of Femininity*. Doctor's thesis, Ohio State University (Columbus, Ohio), 1974. (*DAI* 35:7062A)

212. LITTLE, DOLORES M., AND ROACH, ARTHUR J. "Videotape Modeling of Interest in Nontraditional Occupations for Women." *J Voc Behav* 5(1):133–8 Ag '74. * (*PA* 53:4099)

213. MAHRER, DAVID LEE. *Psychometric and Behavioral Correlates of an Index of Past Career Choice Stability*. Doctor's thesis, University of Arizona (Tucson, Ariz.), 1974. (*DAI* 35:7063A)

214. OLIVER, LAUREL W. "The Effect of Verbal Reinforcement on Career Choice Realism." *J Voc Behav* 5(2):275–84 O '74. * (*PA* 53:6252)

215. OLSEN, MILTON CURTIS. *A Study of the Effects of Training in Decision-Making on Selected Factors of Self-Concept, Certainty of Vocational Choice and Appropriateness of Vocational Choice*. Doctor's thesis, University of North Dakota (Grand Forks, N.D.), 1974. (*DAI* 35:2693A)

216. OLSON, RICHARD R. "Vocational Stability and Job Satisfaction Characteristics of Postsecondary Technology Instructors." *J Indus Teach Ed* 11(3):5–14 sp '74. *

217. PARKER, MELVIN SELBY, SR. *The Usefulness of the Holland Vocational Preference Inventory in Assessing the Congruency of Proposed Vocational Objectives of Veterans*. Doctor's thesis, University of Southern Mississippi (Hattiesburg, Miss.), 1974. (*DAI* 35:6465A)

218. PFEIFER, C. MICHAEL, JR., AND SEDLACEK, WILLIAM E. "Predicting Black Student Grades With Nonintellectual Measures." *J Negro Ed* 43(1):67–76 w '74. * (*PA* 54:4265)

219. SCHMITZ, CHARLES D., AND COCKRIEL, IRVIN W. "The Relationship Between Holland's Personality Types and Educational Achievement of Freshman Women." *J Nat Assn Women Deans & Counselors* 37(3):119–22 sp '74. *

220. SIBBISON, VIRGINIA HAYES. *Occupational Preferences and Expectations of Rural High School Males and Females: Background, Grade, and Sex-Role Correlates*. Doctor's thesis, Pennsylvania State University (University Park, Pa.), 1974. (*DAI* 35:7069A)

221. TOENJES, CAROL M., AND BORGEN, FRED H. "Validity Generalization of Holland's Hexagonal Model." *Meas & Eval Guid* 7(2):79–85 Jl '74. * (*PA* 53:2031)

222. TOU, LOUIS ALOYSIUS. *A Study of Work Value Orientations of Chinese-American and White-American Students of the 7th and 8th Grades in Catholic Elementary Schools*. Doctor's thesis, Catholic University of America (Washington, D.C.), 1974. (*DAI* 35:831A)

223. WAKEFIELD, JAMES A., JR.; ALSTON, HERBERT L.; YOM, B. LEE; AND DOUGHTIE, EUGENE B. "Related Factors of the Survey of Study Habits and Attitudes and the Vocational Preference Inventory." *J Voc Behav* 5(2):215–9 O '74. * (*PA* 53:6261)

224. WEISSMAN, SHELDON. *The Relationship Between Certain Early Childhood Social Indicators and Future Vocational Choice*. Doctor's thesis, State University of New York (Albany, N.Y.), 1974. (*DAI* 35:5044A)

225. WERNER, WAYNE E. "Effect of Role Choice on Vocational High School Students." *J Voc Behav* 4(1):77–84 Ja '74. * (*PA* 52:8747)

226. WIGGINS, JIMMY DALE. *The Relationship Between Job Satisfaction and Vocational Preferences of Teachers of the Educable Mentally Retarded*. Doctor's thesis, Indiana University (Bloomington, Ind.), 1974. (*DAI* 35:6545A)

227. WYMAN, SUZANNE ALISON. *Relationships of Organizational Climate to the Job Satisfaction and Satisfactoriness of the School Counselor*. Doctor's thesis, University of North Carolina (Chapel Hill, N.C.), 1974. (*DAI* 35:5046A)

228. ADERINTO, KAREN MCINTOSH. *Predicting Initial Academic Achievement of College Freshmen Using Holland's Constructs in an Urban, Private, Four Year Liberal Arts College*. Doctor's thesis, Fordham University (New York, N.Y.), 1975. (*DAI* 36:1297A)

229. ANDREWS, HANS A. "Beyond the High Point Code in Testing Holland's Theory." *J Voc Behav* 6(1):101–8 F '75. * (*PA* 53:12618)

230. ASTIN, HELEN S. "Sex Differences in Mathematical and Scientific Precocity." *J Spec Ed* 9(1):79–91 sp '75. * (*PA* 56:4812)

231. BENCH, JOSEPH EDWIN. *A Study of the Relationship Between Herzberg's Motivation-Hygiene Factors and Holland's Personality Patterns for Law Enforcement Personnel*. Doctor's thesis, West Virginia University (Morgantown, W.Va.), 1975. (*DAI* 36:7200A)

232. BITNEY, RAYMOND HOWARD, JR. *An Analysis of Occupational Choice and Selected Personality Characteristics*. Doctor's thesis, Washington State University (Pullman, Wash.), 1975. (*DAI* 36:699A)

233. BREME, FREDERICK J., AND COCKRIEL, IRVIN W. "Work Values and Work Interests: Are They the Same?" *J Voc Behav* 6(3):331–6 Je '75. * (*PA* 54:6578)

234. BURGGRAF, MARGARET ZEIDLER. *Holland's Vocational Preference Inventory: Its Applicability to a Group of Technical College Women and the Relationship of Social Level, Self Concept and Sex Role Identity to the Social Personality Type*. Doctor's thesis, Ohio University (Athens, Ohio), 1975. (*DAI* 36:6467A)

235. DESMOND, SARAH ELLEN. *Personality Orientation, Work Values and Other Characteristics of Pioneer and Traditional Academic Women*. Doctor's thesis, University of Pittsburgh (Pittsburgh, Pa.), 1975. (*DAI* 36:789A)

236. ELTON, CHARLES F., AND ROSE, HARRIETT A. "A Vocational Interest Test Minus Sex Bias." *J Voc Behav* 7(2):207–14 O '75. * (*PA* 55:8638)

237. FABRY, JULIAN J. "An Extended Concurrent Validation of the Vocational Preferences of Clergymen." *Psychol Rep* 36(3):947–50 Je '75. * (*PA* 54:9435)

238. FABRY, JULIAN J. *An Investigation of Holland's Vocational Theory Across and Within Selected Occupational Groups*. Doctor's thesis, University of Kansas (Lawrence, Kan.), 1975. (*DAI* 36:4256A)

239. FOOKS, GORDON M. *Selected Personality and Environmental Effects on the Vocational Choices of Black College Students*. Doctor's thesis, Pennsylvania State University (University Park, Pa.), 1975. (*DAI* 36:2019A)

240. GADE, ELDON M., AND GOODMAN, RONALD E. "Vocational Preferences of Daughters of Alcoholics." *Voc Guid Q* 24(1):41–7 S '75. * (*PA* 55:5756)

241. GADE, ELDON M., AND SOLIAH, DAVID. "Vocational Preference Inventory High Point Codes Versus Expressed Choices as Predictors of College Major and Career Entry." *J Counsel Psychol* 22(2):117–21 Mr '75. * (*PA* 53:12546)

242. GAUTHIER, EVELYN JANICE. *Holland Personality Types'*

Vocational Preference Inventory

Differences in Preference for Stimulus Complexity. Doctor's thesis, Ohio State University (Columbus, Ohio), 1975. (*DAI* 36:4130B)

243. GODIN, THOMAS J. *An Application of Holland's Theory to the Career Orientations and Job Satisfaction of College Alumnae.* Doctor's thesis, Boston College (Chestnut Hill, Mass.), 1975. (*DAI* 36:2021A)

244. GRABINSKI, JOSEPH. *A Study of the Transmission of Environmental Forces as They Affect Student Achievement in a Technical College.* Doctor's thesis, University of Massachusetts (Amherst, Mass.), 1975. (*DAI* 36:3617A)

245. HOLLAND, JOHN L. Chap. 2, "The Use and Evaluation of Interest Inventories and Simulations," pp. 19–44. In *Issues of Sex Bias and Sex Fairness in Career Interest Measurement.* Edited by Esther E. Diamond. Washington, D.C.: National Institute of Education, 1975. Pp. xxix, 219. *

246. HOLLAND, JOHN L., AND GOTTFREDSON, GARY D. "Predictive Value and Psychological Meaning of Vocational Aspirations." *J Voc Behav* 6(3):349–63 Je '75. * (*PA* 55:13649)

247. HORTON, JOSEPH ANTHONY. *The Personality Characteristics of Professional Career Women: A Study of the Concurrent Validity of John Holland's Theory of Vocational Choice.* Doctor's thesis, Ohio State University (Columbus, Ohio), 1975. (*DAI* 36:3045B)

248. KASPER, ANTHONY R. *The Relationship Between the Vocational Preference Inventory and the Personality Research Form.* Master's thesis, University of Calgary (Calgary, Alta., Canada), 1975.

249. KEATING, DANIEL P. "The Study of Mathematically Precocious Youth." *J Spec Ed* 9(1):45–62 sp '75. * (*PA* 56:4969)

250. LAUDEMAN, KENT ALLEN. *Vocational Personality Type, Personality Characteristics, and Satisfaction With College Major: An Investigation of Holland's Theory.* Doctor's thesis, Western Michigan University (Kalamazoo, Mich.), 1975. (*DAI* 36:5827A)

251. LUNNEBORG, CLIFFORD E., AND LUNNEBORG, PATRICIA W. "Factor Structure of the Vocational Interest Models of Roe and Holland." *J Voc Behav* 7(3):313–26 D '75. * (*PA* 55:11281)

252. LUNNEBORG, PATRICIA W. "Interest Differentiation in High School and Vocational Indecision in College." *J Voc Behav* 7(3):297–303 D '75. * (*PA* 55:13579)

253. MEADOWS, FERGUSON BOOKER, JR. *A Test of Holland's Hexagonal Model of Occupational Classification Using an Inner-City High School Population.* Doctor's thesis, Virginia Polytechnic Institute and State University (Blacksburg, Va.), 1975. (*DAI* 36:2638A)

254. MONTGOMERY, ELAINE FIELDS. *A Study of the Effects of Career and Personal Group Counseling on Retention Rates and Self-Actualization.* Doctor's thesis, University of Southern Mississippi (Hattiesburg, Miss.), 1975. (*DAI* 36:2028A)

255. O'BRIEN, WILLIAM FRANCIS. *The Concurrent Validity of Holland's Theory of Vocational Development Using a Sample of Non-Professional Black Workers.* Doctor's thesis, Ohio State University (Columbus, Ohio), 1975. (*DAI* 36:3010B)

256. ROWLAS, ANDREW D. *An Investigation of John L. Holland's Theory of Vocational Choice With High School Seniors.* Doctor's thesis, Indiana University (Bloomington, Ind.), 1975. (*DAI* 36:7218A)

257. SAVICKAS, MARK LEE. *Consistency of Expressed Interests as an Indicator of Vocational Maturity in College Freshmen.* Doctor's thesis, Kent State University (Kent, Ohio), 1975. (*DAI* 36:5838A)

258. SCOTT, NORMAN A., AND SEDLACEK, WILLIAM E. "Personality Differentiation and Prediction of Persistence in Physical Science and Engineering." *J Voc Behav* 6(2):205–16 Ap '75. * (*PA* 54:1847)

259. WAKEFIELD, JAMES A., JR.; ALSTON, HERBERT L.; YOM, B. LEE; DOUGHTIE, EUGENE B.; AND CHANG, WEI-NING C. "Personality Types and Traits in the Vocational Preference Inventory." *J Voc Behav* 6(1):19–26 F '75. * (*PA* 53:11761)

260. WAKEFIELD, JAMES A., JR., AND CUNNINGHAM, CLAUDE H. "Relationships Between the Vocational Preference Inventory and the Edwards Personal Preference Schedule." *J Voc Behav* 6(3):373–7 Je '75. * (*PA* 54:6609)

261. WAKEFIELD, JAMES A., JR.; CUNNINGHAM, CLAUDE H.; AND EDWARDS, DONALD D. "Teacher Attitudes and Personality." *Psychol Sch* 12(3):345–7 Jl '75. * (*PA* 54:12515)

262. WAKEFIELD, JAMES A., JR.; YOM, B. LEE; DOUGHTIE, EUGENE B.; CHANG, WEI-NING C.; AND ALSTON, HERBERT L. "The Geometric Relationship Between Holland's Personality Typology and the Vocational Preference Inventory for Blacks." *J Counsel Psychol* 22(1):58–60 Ja '75. * (*PA* 53:8416)

263. YOM, B. LEE; DOUGHTIE, EUGENE B.; CHANG, WEI-NING C.; ALSTON, HERBERT L.; AND WAKEFIELD, JAMES A. JR. "The Factor Structure of the Vocational Preference Inventory for Black and White College Students." *J Voc Behav* 6(1):15–8 F '75. * (*PA* 53:12715)

264. ALSTON, HERBERT L.; WAKEFIELD, JAMES A., JR.; DOUGHTIE, EUGENE B.; AND BOBELE, R. MONTE. "Correspondence of Constructs in Holland's Theory for Male and Female College Students." *J Voc Behav* 8(1):85–8 F '76. *

265. BARNES, EDWIN LEWIS. *Effects of Personality and*

266. BOBELE, R. MONTE; ALSTON, HERBERT L.; WAKEFIELD, JAMES A., JR.; AND DOUGHTIE, EUGENE B. "A Comparison of Holland's Model Using Constructs Measured by Two Different Methods." *J Voc Behav* 9(2):245–50 O '76. *

267. COOPER, SPENCER LEE. *A Test of Holland's Theory: A Comparative Study of the Expressed Vocational Choice of Black and White Students as Related to Race and Socioeconomic Factors.* Doctor's thesis, Ohio State University (Columbus, Ohio), 1976. (*DAI* 37:4112B)

268. DOUGHTIE, EUGENE B.; CHANG, WEI-NING C.; ALSTON, HERBERT L.; WAKEFIELD, JAMES A., JR.; AND YOM, B. LEE. "Black-White Differences on the Vocational Preference Inventory." *J Voc Behav* 8(1):41–4 F '76. *

269. DUBOYS, TIBBI. *Consistency, Congruency, Differentiation, and Job Satisfaction Among Female Clerical Workers.* Doctor's thesis, Fordham University (New York, N.Y.), 1976. (*DAI* 37:802A)

270. FABRY, JULIAN J. "An Investigation of Holland's Vocational Theory Across and Within Selected Occupational Groups." *J Voc Behav* 9(1):73–6 Ag '76. *

271. FISHBURNE, FRANCIS J., JR., AND WALSH, W. BRUCE. "Concurrent Validity of Holland's Theory for Non-College-Degreed Workers." *J Voc Behav* 8(1):77–84 F '76. *

272. FOREMAN, PETER E., AND ALLEN, LEON R. "Holland Vocational Preference Inventory: Norms for a Sample of Female Students of Therapy." *Psychol Rep* 39(2):446 O '76. * (*PA* 57:7174)

273. FROKE, BARBARA KAYE. *A Study of the Relationships Among Locus of Control, Maturity of Career Attitudes, and Consistency and Congruence of Career Choice.* Doctor's thesis, University of South Dakota (Vermillion, S.D.), 1976. (*DAI* 37:3417A)

274. GOTTFREDSON, GARY D. "A Note on Sexist Wording in Interest Measurement." *Meas & Eval Guid* 8(4):221–3 Ja '76. * (*PA* 56:4963)

275. HARRIS, DONALD EDWARD. *Affective Characteristics: Their Role in Candidate Selection for Baccalaureate Degree Programs in Vocational Industrial Education.* Doctor's thesis, Pennsylvania State University (University Park, Pa.), 1976. (*DAI* 37:7104A)

276. HOLLAND, JOHN L. "Consistency and Raw Scores Survive Another Test: A Last Response to Prediger and His Colleagues." *Meas & Eval Guid* 9(3):132–5 O '76. *

277. HOLLAND, JOHN L. "The Virtues of the SDS and its Associated Typology: A Second Response to Prediger and Hanson." *J Voc Behav* 8(3):349–58 Je '76. * (*PA* 56:6884)

278. HORTON, JOSEPH A., AND WALSH, W. BRUCE. "Concurrent Validity of Holland's Theory for College Degreed Working Women." *J Voc Behav* 9(2):201–8 O '76. *

279. JONES, OCTAVIA M.; HANSEN, JAMES C.; AND PUTNAM, BARBARA A. "Relationship of Self-Concept and Vocational Maturity to Vocational Preferences of Adolescents." *J Voc Behav* 8(1):31–40 F '76. *

280. KUNCE, JOSEPH T., AND KAPPES, BRUNO MAURICE. "The Vocational Preference Inventory Scores and Environmental Preferences." *J Voc Behav* 9(3):363–6 D '76. * (*PA* 58:2248)

281. LORCH, THOMAS DANIEL. *A Study of Holland's Theory of Careers as it Applies to the Job Satisfaction of Employed Adults.* Doctor's thesis, Indiana University (Bloomington, Ind.), 1976. (*DAI* 37:4866A)

282. O'BRIEN, WILLIAM F., AND WALSH, W. BRUCE. "Concurrent Validity of Holland's Theory for Non-College Degreed Black Working Men." *J Voc Behav* 8(2):239–46 Ap '76. *

283. PREDIGER, DALE J. "Do Raw Scores Deserve a D Minus? A Reply to Holland." *Meas & Eval Guid* 9(3):136–8 O '76. *

284. PREDIGER, DALE J., AND HANSON, GARY R. "Holland's Theory of Careers Applied to Women and Men: Analysis of Implicit Assumptions." *J Voc Behav* 8(2):167–84 Ap '76. *

285. PREDIGER, DALE J., AND HANSON, GARY R. "A Theory of Careers Encounters Sex: Reply to Holland (1976)." *J Voc Behav* 8(3):359–66 Je '76. * (*PA* 56:6890)

286. PREDIGER, DALE J. "The Viability of Holland's Consistency Construct and Raw Score Assessments of Personality." *Meas & Eval Guid* 9(3):124–31 O '76. *

287. PUIG-CASAURANC, MARIA DEL CARMEN. *Personality and Interest Characteristics of Females in Traditional and Nontraditional Fields of Academic Study and Their Relationship to Psychological Androgyny.* Doctor's thesis, Washington State University (Pullman, Wash.), 1976. (*DAI* 37:5001A)

288. ROARK, ELIZABETH ANNE BORDERS. *Relationship Between Administrator and Counselor Personality Characteristics and Training in Conflict Reduction.* Doctor's thesis, University of Colorado (Boulder, Colo.), 1976. (*DAI* 37:4762A)

289. ROBINSON-LASOFF, MARVA VERONICA. *An Analysis of Psychological and Sociological Factors Related to Congruence Between Expressed Vocational Choices and Inventoried Vocational Interests of Jamaican High School Seniors.* Doctor's thesis, University of Miami (Coral Gable, Fla.), 1976. (*DAI* 37:2484B)

290. ROSS, LANNY F. *Predicting Success in Vocational Pro-*

265a. Person-Environment Congruence on Job Satisfaction of Community College Faculty and Professional Staff. Doctor's thesis, Virginia Polytechnic Institute (Blacksburg, Va.), 1976. (*DAI* 37:1946A)

Vocational Preference Inventory

grams From Permanent Record Data Versus Selected Non-Cognitive Variables. Doctor's thesis, Pennsylvania State University (University Park, Pa.), 1976. (*DAI* 37:7108A)

291. SCHENK, GEORGE EDWARD. *Influence of a Career Group Experience on the Vocational Maturity of College Freshmen and Sophomores.* Doctor's thesis, University of Missouri (Columbia, Mo.), 1976. (*DAI* 37:5783A)

292. SPOKANE, ARNOLD ROY. *Occupational Level, Sex and the Concurrent Validity of Holland's Theory in a Sample of Employed Adults.* Doctor's thesis, Ohio State University (Columbus, Ohio), 1976. (*DAI* 37:4122B)

293. SWENSON, DANIEL HART. *Personality Type as a Factor in Predicting Academic Achievement, Satisfaction, Success, and Group Membership of Business and Distributive Education Teacher Candidates.* Doctor's thesis, Utah State University (Logan, Utah), 1976. (*DAI* 37:6284A)

294. TAYLOR, HOWARD THORNTON. *Work Values and Their Relationship to Certain Personality Types of Community College Students.* Doctor's thesis, College of William and Mary (Williamsburg, Va.), 1976. (*DAI* 37:2653A)

295. WARD, G. ROBERT; CUNNINGHAM, CLAUDE H.; AND WAKEFIELD, JAMES A., JR. "Relationships Between Holland's VPI and Cattell's 16PF." *J Voc Behav* 8(3):307–12 Je '76. * (*PA* 56:5171)

296. WERNER, PAUL J. *Parental Environment and Its Influence on Personality Development and Vocational Preference.* Doctor's thesis, Catholic University of America (Washington, D.C.), 1976. (*DAI* 36:7267A)

297. WESTBROOK, FRANKLIN D., AND MOLLA, BEKELE. "Unique Stereotypes for Holland's Personality Types, Testing the Traits Attributed to Men and Women in Holland's Typology." *J Voc Behav* 9(1):21–30 Ag '76. *

298. WIGGINS, J. D. "The Relation of Job Satisfaction to Vocational Preferences Among Teachers of the Educable Mentally Retarded." *J Voc Behav* 8(1):13–8 F '76. *

299. ZENER, THELMA BALDWIN, AND SCHNUELLE, LESLIE. "Effects of the Self-Directed Search on High School Students." *J Counsel Psychol* 21(4):353–9 Jl '74. * (*PA* 53:10051)

300. BROWN, NINA W. "Personality Characteristics of Black Adolescents." *Adolescence* 12(45):81–7 sp '77. *

301. COX, JENNINGS G., AND THORESON, RICHARD W. "Client-Counselor Matching: A Test of the Holland Model." *J Counsel Psychol* 24(2):158–61 Mr '77. * (*PA* 58:6450)

302. CUNNINGHAM, CLAUDE H.; ALSTON, HERBERT L.; DOUGHTIE, EUGENE B.; AND WAKEFIELD, JAMES A., JR. "Use of Holland's Vocational Theory With Potential High School Dropouts." *Voc Behav* 10(1):35–8 F '77. *

303. O'BRIEN, MARY JANE HEALY. *A Study to Determine the Accuracy of the Holland Types for Women Employed in Realistic and Social Occupations.* Doctor's thesis, Catholic University of America (Washington, D.C.), 1977. (*DAI* 37:7546A)

304. SMITH, PHYLLIS J. "Comparison of Counselees and Noncounselees With Reference to Holland's Theory." *J Counsel Psychol* 24(3):244–6 My '77. *

305. TURNER, ROBERT G., AND HIBBS, CLARENCE. "Vocational Interest and Personality Correlates of Differential Abilities." *Psychol Rep* 40(3, pt 1):727–30 Je '77. *

306. WALSH, W. BRUCE; HORTON, JOSEPH A.; AND GAFFEY, ROBERT L. "Holland's Theory and College Degreed Working Men and Women." *Voc Behav* 10(2):180–6 Ap '77. *

J Ed Meas 9(2):167–9 su '72. W. Bruce Walsh. * The rationale for the development of the VPI was based on the idea that preferences for occupations are expressions of personality. These preferences, while stereotypic, tend to be reliable and consistent with reality. To the degree an individual prefers a large number of occupations associated with a personality orientation, his favored coping behavior for dealing with interpersonal and environmental problems may be inferred. Thus, according to Holland, interest inventories are personality inventories, and vocational preferences represent a major facet of an individual's personality. * Although the primary purpose of the VPI is to assess personality, the inventory may also be used as an interest inventory and to stimulate occupational exploration. * The test-retest reliability for each scale of the VPI indicates that the

VPI has moderate to high reliability. * The manual contains a useful section on interpretation. * The VPI does have some limitations. Validity studies need to be conducted in the large non-college population. * Another limitation involves the use of the VPI with women. In its present form many of the occupational titles are not appropriate for women. In addition, as an interest inventory the VPI does not suggest specific occupational alternatives. Therefore, existing evidence suggests that the SVIB or the OIS would give an individual more information on the relationship between his likes and dislikes and the likes and dislikes of people in various occupations. Finally, research indicates that the personality types are not mutually exclusive and independent classes. * In general, the results of the validity studies lend support to the meaning attributed to the scales and to the rationale underlying the development of the inventory. The coefficients of stability indicate that the inventory has acceptable reliability. In terms of application Holland's theory and the VPI are easily translated into research terms. VPI data may also be useful in a counseling situation. If a counselor is aware of a client's personal orientation, he has a way of thinking about the client and a stimulus for developing hypotheses about this person's background, thinking, and behavior.

[1029]

Wide Range Interest-Opinion Test. Grades kgn–12 and adults; 1970–72; WRIOT; 25 scores: 18 occupational interests (art, literature, music, drama, sales, management, office work, personal service, protective service, social service, social science, biological science, physical science, number, mechanics, machine operation, outdoor, athletics), 7 vocational attitudes (sedentariness, risk, ambition, chosen skill level, activity by sex, agreement, interest spread); grade or age levels on which reliability data are based are not reported; no norms for grades kgn–7, 9, or 12; 1 form ('70, 154-page picture booklet); manual ('72, 103 pages); report form ('72, 2 pages, for hand scoring); separate answer sheets (Digitek) must be used; $9.60 per test; $5.70 per 50 answer sheets; $30 per set of scoring stencils; $5.70 per 50 report forms; $5.40 per manual; $46.50 per specimen set; postage extra; scoring service, 90¢ per test; (40–60) minutes; Joseph F. Jastak and Sarah R. Jastak; Guidance Associates of Delaware, Inc. *

DONALD G. ZYTOWSKI, *Professor of Psychology and Counseling Psychologist, Iowa State University, Ames, Iowa.*

The *Wide Range Interest-Opinion Test* (WRIOT) must have the most appealing acronym in all of testdom. Unhappily, for me that is the only appeal the test (actually inventory) has.

The chief distinction of the WRIOT is that its items consist exclusively of line drawings of persons doing things—mostly occupations, but a few leisure activities, arranged in triads to be judged most and least liked. Thus, it can be taken by persons not fluent in English or unable to read. The authors state that they do not assume that everyone attaches the same meanings to each item, so that the person who is suited for the inventory on account of his or her retardation need not understand that a certain item depicts a person writing a computer program, or teaching English, for example. It is implied that drawings yield a more valid measure of interests than verbal report.

Most of the persons represented in the drawings are males; the few women are doing sex-stereotyped activities—filing, waiting on customers, etc. Such stereotypic representation places its use under the shadow of the recent Title IX regulations.

To me, a real difficulty resides in the nature of the scales. After the items were drawn by the artist, they were assembled into 30 clusters by a rational process of the authors. They then calculated discrimination indices between the subjectively formed clusters and the items, which was the basis for the 18 interest scales and 7 attitude scales for which the WRIOT is scored. Unfortunately, none of the details of the analysis is reported. We don't find out who provided the data, what the number of subjects was, or what the mean index number was that admitted an item to a scale. This analysis also identified a number of items the rejection of which is scored positively. This is perfectly acceptable psychometrics, and it tends to reduce the chance of faking, but it makes problems for interpretation which will be discussed below.

The 18 interest scales are similar to the basic interest scales of the Strong blank: art, mechanical, number, outdoor, etc. Some of the seven opinion scales seem to reflect the kind of work or work environment the individual prefers: sedentariness, risk, ambition; while others seem to reflect general qualities of the profile: chosen skill level; activity by sex; interest spread; and agreement, which is a kind of popular-responses scale. All have brief descriptions on the profile

sheet, some of which tend to perpetuate the confusion between abilities and interests. The scales are more completely described in the manual. Each has a page showing what items are scored how, what other items are probably related, and occupational titles which are related. This last feature is something of a mixed blessing: for instance, in the list one finds such possibilities as "freak" and "churchgoer."

Administration is straightforward. The person responds on a well-organized optical scan answer sheet. The instructions specifically encourage the inventory-taker to disregard sex stereotypes, income, prestige, and social pressures. The answer sheets may be returned to the publisher for electronic scoring, or they may be hand scored with stencils. My experiences in hand scoring revealed that when the stencils were aligned on the edges of the answer sheet, some holes fell on the item number rather than the response position.

Norm groups are purported to include 15 percent from minorities, and are available for adults, 10th and 11th graders, and 8th graders, separately by gender. Scores are reported in T score form, and on the profile are further identified with verbal labels of "average," and three levels each above and below average. The manual, copyrighted 1972, states that norm groups are to be supplemented "soon" by 2,000 more cases on special new pages which may be inserted in the present manual. My materials, received in 1976, did not contain any additions.

One test of split-half reliability on a group of 150 males and 150 females, further undescribed, shows the scales to be admirably homogeneous. No coefficient is lower than .82. Presumably, this is on adults. One would be interested in a similar calculation for retardates or children, for whom the WRIOT seems especially made.

The authors take considerable pains to reject reporting the validities of the WRIOT, saying that the inventory will have to stand on its own merits and not on a table of coefficients. Then they report correlations between WRIOT scores and another pictorial interest inventory. They are high but illuminate nothing.

The manual reports, indirectly, the results of a correlation matrix of the 24 scales. About half the correlations obtained were significantly different from zero (Ns not reported). The

Wide Range Interest-Opinion Test

scales which correlate more than .30, positively or negatively, with each other scale are reported in the material which elaborates their meanings. Some scales had as few as four other scales so correlated; some as many as 17. The average appeared to be about 11. I conclude that the scales are not very independent. This is a virtue in the basic scales of the *Strong-Campbell Interest Inventory* and a sin in the *Kuder Preference Records*.

Interpretation of the WRIOT profile is illustrated by 10 sample cases. Curiously, despite the rationale given for the picture format, only one of these illustrative cases involves a person of questionable reading fluency. In the introductory material, the authors stress that interpretation should derive from the total record. They say that their experience has shown them, for example, that nursing students who score high on clerical interests as well as on biological sciences and service tend to leave training early. No such astuteness as this, it seems to me, is reflected in any of the sample case write-ups.

Machine scored answer sheets are apparently profiled by a line of pluses graphing T scores over 50, and a line of minuses for the scores of less than 50. The profile explanation clearly states that scores under 50 imply dislikes or rejection, and the converse for scores over 50. My investigation reveals that an 8th grader can reject all of the 15 positively keyed items on the art scale, and without any positive endorsement of art activities get a T score of 65, which is labelled "high" interest. This lack of clarity in concept, combined with the confusion in the scale descriptions of whether interests or abilities are being reported, simply does not inspire my confidence.

All in all, the WRIOT offers 25 interest and attitude scales, some of which appear (although we cannot be sure) to offer little information independent of that offered in other scales. They are of high internal consistency, but difficult to hand score with confidence, recommended with validity to be found in the using, missing promised new data, and with paradoxical meanings incorporated in the interpretative process. All of this is in exchange for a relaxation of the necessity to read. Why not simply read to the inventory-taker the items of, say, Holland's *Self-Directed Search* to gain this same benefit, and have at hand all the advantages of its clarity,

well-developed theoretical framework, associated research establishing its appropriate applications, and concurrent, discriminant, and predictive validity?

[1030]

Work Values Inventory. Grades 7–16 and adults; 1968–70; WVI; 15 scales: altruism, esthetics, creativity, intellectual stimulation, independence, achievement, prestige, management, economic returns, security, surroundings, supervisory relations, associates, variety, way of life; reliability data for grade 10 only; norms for grades 7–12 only; 1 form ('68, 4 pages, MRC scorable); manual ('70, 50 pages); $21.72 per 100 tests; $1.35 per specimen set; postage extra; scoring service, 51¢ per test ($25.50 minimum); (10–20) minutes; Donald E. Super; Houghton Mifflin Co. *

See T2:2221 (12 references); for reviews by Ralph F. Berdie and David V. Tiedeman, and an excerpted review by John W. French, see 7:1042 (33 references).

REFERENCES

1–33. See 7:1042.
34–45. See T2:2221; also includes a cumulative name index to the first 45 references, 2 reviews, and 1 excerpt for this test.
46. BYLER, BENNIE LEE. *A Study of Factors Associated With the Vocational Development of High School Agricultural Occupations Students.* Doctor's thesis, University of Illinois (Urbana, Ill.), 1972. (*DAI* 33:6245A)
47. FEENEY, HELEN MARIE. *Interest Values and Social Class as Related to Adult Women Who Are Continuing Their Education.* Doctor's thesis, New York University (New York, N.Y.), 1972. (*DAI* 33:5835A)
48. GABLE, ROBERT K. "Review of the Work Values Inventory." *J Counsel Psychol* 19(6):565–8 N '72. *
49. GELINA, ROBERT JOSEPH. *An Analysis of the Inter-Relationships of Selected Psychological Characteristics Inherent to Vocational Industrial Teachers.* Doctor's thesis, University of Maryland (College Park, Md.), 1972. (*DAI* 33:178A)
50. HURLEY, ROBERT BERNARD. *Race, Fatherlessness, and Vocational Development: An Exploration of Relationships Between Membership in Nuclear or Fatherless Families and Level of Occupational Aspiration and Expectation, Self-Esteem, Extrinsic Work Values and Person-Orientation Among a Sample of Black and White Adolescent Boys.* Doctor's thesis, New York University (New York, N.Y.), 1972. (*DAI* 33:6090A)
51. KENNEDY, JOHN JOSEPH, JR. *Familial and Cultural Factors Influencing the Occupational Choice of Women Who Are High Academic Achievers.* Doctor's thesis, New York University (New York, N.Y.), 1972. (*DAI* 33:570A)
52. McARDLE, H. ROY. *Work Values of Hawaii Public High School Seniors.* Doctor's thesis, University of New Mexico (Albuquerque, N.M.), 1972. (*DAI* 33:3297A)
53. McCARTHY, MARY MARGARET. *An Exploration Into the Measured Work Values of Counselors, the Measured Work Values of Their Eleventh Grade Clients, and the Counselors' Perceptions of Their Clients' Measured Work Values in Suburban Public High Schools.* Doctor's thesis, Boston College (Chestnut Hill, Mass.), 1972. (*DAI* 33:6671A)
54. RICHARDSON, MARY SUE. *Self Concepts and Role Concepts in the Career Orientation of College Women.* Doctor's thesis, Columbia University (New York, N.Y.), 1972. (*DAI* 33:5001B)
55. ZACCARIA, LUCY; JACOBS, MITCHELL; CREASER, JAMES; AND KLEHR, HAROLD. "Work Values of College-Bound Students." *Psychol Rep* 31(2):567–9 O '72. * (*PA* 49:8032)
56. BARNETTE, W. LESLIE, JR.; D'COSTA, AYRES; HARMON, LENORE W.; SUPER, DONALD E.; WEISS, DAVID J.; AND ZYTOWSKI, DONALD G. Chap. 9, "Illustrative Interpretations of Inventories," pp. 206–44. In *Contemporary Approaches to Interest Measurement.* Edited by Donald G. Zytowski. Minneapolis, Minn.: University of Minnesota Press, 1973. Pp. xi, 251. *
57. BHATTACHARYA, S. K. "A Study on Value System of Different Occupational Groups." *Indian J Psychol* 48(3):59–64 S '73. * (*PA* 54:5101)
58. DAVIS, JAMES FLOYD. *A Comparative Analysis of Eleventh Grade High School Students' Work Values.* Doctor's thesis, University of Maryland (College Park, Md.), 1973. (*DAI* 34:3246A)
59. GABLE, ROBERT K. "The Effect of Scale Modifications on the Factorial Dimensions and Reliability of Super's Work Values Inventory." *J Voc Behav* 3(3):303–22 Jl '73. * (*PA* 51:10026)
60. HALL, JOHN A., AND WIANT, HARRY V., JR. "Does School Desegregation Change Occupational Goals of Negro Males?" *J Voc Behav* 3(2):175–9 Ap '73. * (*PA* 50:9874)

61. HARRIS, EVERETT WAYNE. *A Study of Selected Factors Associated With the Participation in Employment of Rural Low Income Adults.* Doctor's thesis, University of Illinois (Urbana, Ill.), 1973. (*DAI* 34:6532A)

62. SELF, PATRICIA ANN PADDEN. *Self-Concepts, Attitudes, and Values of Women Honor Students.* Doctor's thesis, Texas A & M University (College Station, Tex.), 1973. (*DAI* 34: 7595A)

63. SUPER, DONALD E. Chap. 8, "The Work Values Inventory," pp. 189–205. In *Contemporary Approaches to Interest Measurement.* Edited by Donald G. Zytowski. Minneapolis, Minn.: University of Minnesota Press, 1973. Pp. xi, 251. *

64. THOMAS, JACK D. *Effectiveness of a Group Counseling Procedure in Changing Work Values of College Students.* Doctor's thesis, Texas A & M University (College Station, Tex.), 1973. (*DAI* 34:3893A)

65. TIEDEMAN, DAVID V. "Comment on Self-Estimate Ability in Adolescence." *J Counsel Psychol* 20(4):303–5 Jl '73. * (*PA* 51:3976)

66. TIERNEY, ROGER J., AND HERMAN, AL. "Self-Estimate Ability in Adolescence." *J Counsel Psychol* 20(4):298–302 Jl '73. * (*PA* 51:3977)

67. WOOLARD, GILBERT GARLAND, JR. *An Associational Study of Student Perceptions of the Importance of Occupational Relevancy in Adult Education Programs in North Carolina and South Carolina.* Doctor's thesis, North Carolina State University (Raleigh, N.C.), 1973. (*DAI* 34:5568A)

68. ZYTOWSKI, DONALD G. Chap. 1, "Considerations in the Selection and Use of Interest Inventories," pp. 3–19. (*PA* 51:59, title only) In his *Contemporary Approaches to Interest Measurement.* Minneapolis, Minn.: University of Minnesota Press, 1973. Pp. xi, 251. *

69. BENNETT, ROY M. "Work-Values of Trade and Technical Teachers." *J Indus Teach Ed* 12(1):33–7 f '74. *

70. BUCHANAN, BERNICE F. *The Relationship of Work Values and Vocational Interest of Afro-American and Caucasian Generic Baccalaureate Nursing Students in Selected Colleges in the Washington Metropolitan Area.* Doctor's thesis, Catholic University of America (Washington, D.C.), 1974. (*DAI* 35: 5806A)

71. CALLAHAN, RACHEL ANNE. *A Study of the Life and Work Values in High and Low Self-Actualized Adolescents.* Doctor's thesis, Catholic University of America (Washington, D.C.), 1974. (*DAI* 35:1904B)

72. GRACE, JANE CONSTANCE. *Work Values of Community College Students: An Exploratory Investigation of Freshmen at Middlesex Community College, Bedford, Massachusetts.* Doctor's thesis, Boston College (Chestnut Hill, Mass.), 1974. (*DAI* 35: 1977A)

73. MANHART, BETTY ANGE. *Correlation of Personal Orientation and Work Values of Student Teachers and Cooperating Teachers to Predict Compatibility.* Doctor's thesis, University of New Mexico (Albuquerque, N.M.), 1974. (*DAI* 36:1453A)

74. MILLER, MICHAEL F. "Relationship of Vocational Maturity to Work Values." *J Voc Behav* 5(3):367–71 D '74. * (*PA* 53:12658)

75. RICHARDSON, MARY SUE. "The Dimensions of Career and Work Orientation in College Women." *J Voc Behav* 5(1): 161–72 Ag '74. * (*PA* 53:4155)

76. THOMAS, HOLLIE B. "The Effects of Social Position, Race, and Sex on Work Values of Ninth-Grade Students." *J Voc Behav* 4(3):357–64 Je '74. * (*PA* 52:13284)

77. WESSELL, TYRUS RAYMOND, JR. *A Comparative Analysis of the Psychological and Sociological Factors Relating to the Career Specialization Choices of Agency and School Counselors-in-Training.* Doctor's thesis, Western Michigan University (Kalamazoo, Mich.), 1974. (*DAI* 35:3441A)

78. ZAUGRA, JOHN F. *A Study of Selected Relationships Among Interests, Personality Traits, and Values Between Student Teachers and Experienced Teachers.* Doctor's thesis, University of Montana (Missoula, Mont.), 1974. (*DAI* 35:3444A)

79. ABU-SABA, MARY BENTLEY. *An Evaluation of Vocational Alternatives Program for Men on Probation and Parole.* Doctor's thesis, University of Illinois (Urbana, Ill.), 1975. (*DAI* 36:5931A)

80. BARR, LOWELL LAWRENCE. *Business Knowledges and Work Values Acquired in Office Simulation and Cooperative Office Education Programs.* Doctor's thesis, University of North Dakota (Grand Forks, N.D.), 1975. (*DAI* 37:936A)

81. BOWDEN, SHIRLEY SMITH. *The Influence of Work Values in the Life Planning of Tenth Grade Girls.* Doctor's thesis, Oregon State University (Corvallis, Ore.), 1975. (*DAI* 35: 3428B)

82. BREME, FREDERICK J., AND COCKRIEL, IRVIN W. "Work Values and Work Interests: Are They the Same?" *J Voc Behav* 6(3):331–6 Je '75. * (*PA* 54:6578)

83. DATTLE, HARVEY JAY. *Interrelationships Between the Expression of Work Values and Grade Placement in School, Economic Community, and Sex.* Doctor's thesis, Ohio State University (Columbus, Ohio), 1975. (*DAI* 36:5241A)

84. DAVIS, JAMES F., AND HARRISON, PAUL E., JR. "An Analysis of Eleventh Grade High School Students' Work Values." *J Indus Teach Ed* 12(3):21–7 sp '75. *

85. DESMOND, SARAH ELLEN. *Personality Orientation, Work Values and Other Characteristics of Pioneer and Traditional Academic Women.* Doctor's thesis, University of Pittsburgh

(Pittsburgh, Pa.), 1975. (*DAI* 36:7891A)

86. SEARFOSS, KENNETH RAY. *A Comparison of Work Values Expressed by Employed Clerical Workers and Pre-Vocational Business Education Students.* Doctor's thesis, Bowling Green State University (Bowling Green, Ohio), 1975. (*DAI* 36: 4975A)

87. TRAIL, BILLIE M. *Comparison of Attitudes Toward Women and Measures of Interests Between Feminist, Traditional Female and Male University Students.* Doctor's thesis, Texas A & M University (College Station, Tex.), 1975. (*DAI* 36:4236B)

88. BODER, CLARETTA KELSO. *The Relationship of Work Values, Career Decision-making and Career Maturity of Eleventh Grade Students in a Joint Vocational School.* Doctor's thesis, Ohio State University (Columbus, Ohio), 1976. (*DAI* 37:4853A)

89. DRUMMOND, ROBERT J.; SKAGGS, CHARLES T.; AND RYAN, CHARLES W. "Work Values of Youthful Maine Workers, Ages 18–25, by Occupational Level." *Psychol Rep* 39(3, pt 2):1248–58 D '76. *

90. KHOSH, MARY SIVERT. *A Study of the Relationship to Career Objectives of Interests, Values and Selected Personality Factors of Mature Women Enrolled in Higher Education.* Doctor's thesis, Kent State University (Kent, Ohio), 1976. (*DAI* 37:2670A)

91. KUIPER, SHIRLEY. *Work Values and Problem Perceptions of Young Married Women in Clerical Occupations.* Doctor's thesis, Indiana University (Bloomington, Ind.), 1976. (*DAI* 37:5226A)

92. SMITH, KENNETH WAYNE. *Differences in Work Attitudes and Work Values of Disadvantaged and Non-Disadvantaged Eleventh Grade and Twelfth Grade Disadvantaged and Non-Disadvantaged Work Experience Students.* Doctor's thesis, Southern Illinois University (Carbondale, Ill.), 1976. (*DAI* 37:5784A)

93. TAYLOR, HOWARD THORNTON. *Work Values and Their Relationship to Certain Personality Types of Community College Students.* Doctor's thesis, College of William and Mary (Williamsburg, Va.), 1976. (*DAI* 37:2653A)

94. WHITE, LEON SAMUEL. *Dogmatism and Non-Intellective Factors Among Counselor and Non Counselor Trainees.* Doctor's thesis, Ohio State University (Columbus, Ohio), 1976. (*DAI* 37:6963A)

95. YUPASERT, PHONGPAN. *Work Values: A Comparative Study of American and Thai College Freshmen Students.* Doctor's thesis, University of Arizona (Tucson, Ariz.), 1976. (*DAI* 37:3435A)

96. DIETRICH, MARIE C. "Work Values Evolution in a Baccalaureate Student Nurse Population." *Voc Behav* 10(1): 25–34 F '77. *

97. DRUMMOND, ROBERT J.; McINTIRE, WALTER G.; AND SKAGGS, C. THOMAS. "Work Values and Job Satisfaction of Young Adult Males." *J Employ Counsel* 14(1):23–6 Mr '77. *

98. WOODBURY, ROGER, AND PATE, DOVE HENRY. "Vocational Personality Dimensions of Adjudicated Delinquents." *Meas & Eval Guid* 10(2):106–112 Jl '77. *

Meas & Eval Guid 4(3):189–90 O '71. Frederick Brown. * designed to assess 15 "values of particular importance in determining an individual's satisfaction and success in his vocation," "goals which motivate men to work." * Although the manual does not detail the test construction process (and even disclaims responsibility for doing so), it is clear that various procedures and formats were tried during the 20 years the test was under development: interviews, essay responses, sorting, item analysis, forced-choice, rank-ordering, and the present Likert-type scale. The published form of the test consists of 45 items which focus on aspects of the work situation—e.g., "Work in which you....have to keep solving new problems," "....help others." These statements are rated on a 5-point scale, from "very important" to "unimportant." The directions are clear, the vocabulary level is simple, and the inventory should easily be completed in 10 to 15 minutes, as suggested. * Although the manual states that the WVI is useful in academic and vocational counseling, the publisher is inconsistent regarding its usefulness in screening applicants for business and professional schools and for jobs; although the advertising flyer lists these functions as appropriate uses, the manual suggests caution. *Score interpretation.* Each of the 15 scales is composed of three items, with the scale score being the sum of the ratings on these three items. A brief description of each scale is included in the manual. Typically this is a one-sentence definition of the construct (value) plus assorted comments on sex differences, age trends, and the correlations between the scale and other instruments. These latter data are often based on such small samples as to be worthless. The manual suggests three possible methods of interpretation. First, the student can rank his raw scores, paying particular attention to the several highest and lowest scores. Second, raw scores can be converted to grade or adult percentile ranks; unfortunately, however, no adult percentile ranks are included in the manual. Third, a student can compare his scores to those of occupational criterion groups; again, however, no data are available in the manual. Separate norms are presented for each sex and grade (7 to 12). The sampling followed procedures used in Project TALENT and the samples are relatively large (n's = 672 to 949). However, the small range of scores on each scale (limits 5 to 15), coupled with a typical standard deviation of about two points, results in changes of one raw score point, often making a rank difference of 15 to 20 percentiles. It also results in such anomalies as a maximum percentile rank of 81 on one scale. Clearly, the score range of the scales is insufficient. *Reliability.* Reliability data are meager; the only data presented are based on one sample of 99 subjects. Retest reliabilities over a two-week interval ranged from .74 to .88, with a median of .83; inter-item correlations, within scales, averaged .65. In spite of the suggestion that profiles of scores be interpreted, no data on profile stability are presented. The manual states, "It is clear....that the 15 scales....are internally consistent and stable over a time interval of two weeks" (p. 27); this is certainly a gratuitous conclusion. *Validity.* Validity data, like reliability data, are virtually

nonexistent. In addition to a dearth of data, much of the data that are presented are from earlier forms of the test and/or small undefined samples. Furthermore, conclusions are presented without supporting data. Only the data on sex differences and age trends for grades 7 to 12 are anywhere near sufficient. If we can disregard the fact that they are based on samples too small to permit meaningful analysis, some of the factor analytic data are interesting. * *Summary.* It is rather inconceivable to me that anyone would market a test, particularly one presumably based on 20 years of research, which has so little supporting reliability and validity data, no occupational normative data, and a clearly inadequate score range. It appears that someone has labored long to bring forth a gnat.

[1031]

★World of Work Inventory. Grades 8–14 and adults; 1973–76; WWI; 35 scores in 3 areas: career interest activities (public service, the sciences, engineering, business relations, managerial, the arts, clerical, sales, service, primary outdoor, processing, machine work, bench work, structural work, mechanical and electrical work, graphic arts, mining), job satisfaction indicators (versatile, adaptable to repetitive work, adaptable to performing under specific instructions, dominant, gregarious, isolative, influencing, self-controlled, valuative, objective, subjective, rigorous), vocational training potentials (verbal, numerical, abstractions, spatial-form, mechanical-electrical, clerical); norms consist of means and standard deviations; 1 form ('75, 46 pages); revised administration manual ('75, 34 pages); interpretation manual ('76, 197 pages); occupational exploration worksheets ('73, 34 pages); separate answer sheets (NCS) must be used; $23.75 per 25 tests; $6 per 50 answer sheets; $1.25 per set of worksheets; $2.50 per administration manual; $6 per interpretation manual; $6 per specimen set (excluding interpretation manual); postage extra; scoring service (scoring must be done by publisher): $1.15 to $1.90 per test (daily service), 85¢ to $1.20 per test ($30 minimum; weekly service); (45–230) minutes; Robert E. Ripley and Marie J. Ripley (interpretation manual); NCS Interpretive Scoring Systems. *

REFERENCES

1. LOCKE, DON C. "Review of the World of Work Inventory." *Meas & Eval Guid* 10(1):62–4 Ap '77. *

WILBUR L. LAYTON, *Professor of Psychology, Iowa State University, Ames, Iowa.*

According to the authors, the *World of Work Inventory* was designed to provide from a single instrument scores on the more important phases of career identity and choice, to legitimatize and systematize vocational counseling, and to promote effective personal educational planning and job satisfaction. The authors recommend that it be used with secondary school and college students and with adults for career education; vocational guidance and counseling; employment, placement, and training; career development and occupational information courses; and research. Unfortunately, no evidence is provided to show that it has utility for any of these enterprises.

The WWI is essentially self-administering and can be taken in one, two, or three sittings, with between two and three hours usually required. A separate answer sheet has been designed for computer scoring.

The inventory consists of four sections: Identifying Information, Career Interest Activities, Vocational Training Potentials, and Job Satisfaction Indicators. The identifying information section allows the subject to record vital statistics, stated occupational choices, and best-liked school subjects. The career interest activities section, containing job-related activity items, is described as "force [sic] choice"; but it is not forced choice since the subject responds like, neutral, or dislike to each item. The vocational training potential section purportedly measures six aptitude-achievement areas: verbal, numerical, abstractions, spatial-form, clerical, and mechanical-electrical. The abstractions and spatial-form items are considered to be aptitude oriented, and the clerical and mechanical-electrical items are meant to be achievement oriented. The verbal and numerical items measure "the more traditional ability to do public school work of aptitude-achievement." The job satisfaction indicators section covers 12 job temperament areas; the subject is asked to respond like, dislike, or neutral to a job temperament indicator such as "Going to movies alone."

The authors consider the 17 scales in the career interest activities section and the 12 job temperament areas to be homogeneous. The career interest activities scales are keyed to the job classifications scheme in the *Dictionary of Occupational Titles,* and the job satisfaction indicators are keyed to the job temperaments listed in Volume 2 of the DOT. This attempt to coordinate the inventory with the DOT is about the only laudatory aspect of the WWI.

Seventeen basic occupational area worksheets containing 117 career family areas are coordinated with the inventory profile results. These worksheets were designed to allow for personal involvement in occupational exploration by the test taker.

DEVELOPMENT. Each of the items was written about job activities and tasks to maintain job relevancies. These items were then made into "homogeneous" scales in which an item was used only once and in only one scale. The career interest activities scales were reviewed by four or five judges for each of the 117 career families. The judges were people actually working in the occupation, supervisors of the workers, and teacher/trainers of the occupations. All judges had to agree on the use of an item before final placement in a particular scale. After many revisions, a final form of the instrument was developed, and stratified samples by age, sex, educational level, minority group membership, and occupational groupings were used to determine inter-item, intra-scale correlations and inter-scale correlations. No information is given as to the exact composition of the stratified sample, but it is probably the sample on which reliability was estimated and norms were based. The authors state that .9136 percent of the inter-item, intra-scale correlations were significant at or beyond the .001 level; I assume that they mean 91.36 percent. Inter-scale correlations of the 35 different scales are published in the administration manual. While the authors interpret these correlations to indicate that the three major areas of the inventory are measuring different factors, it is obvious that a factor analysis would yield considerably fewer than 35 factors. For example, the vocational training potential tests are rather strongly correlated. The lowest correlation is .307 (clerical vs. mechanical-electrical) and the highest is .651 (verbal vs. numerical).

RELIABILITY. Coefficient alpha was computed for each scale. The authors state that Spearman-Brown corrections were applied to the coefficients alpha because "the instrument was developed as a power test and therefore allows for this most sophisticated method of determining split-half reliability." This is the first time this reviewer has been aware of such an ingenious combination of coefficient alpha and Spearman-Brown! A stratified sample (N = 738) of approximately 58 percent females and 42 percent males representative of age groups from 14 through 62 was used to determine reliability; formal educational levels ranged from grade 8

World of Work Inventory

through grade 17; blacks, Chicanos, native Americans, and Anglos were represented in each group. The sample was composed of persons raised in seven geographical regions of the United States. There is no indication of how the sample was actually selected. The "corrected" coefficients alpha range from .81 to .94 for the career interest activities scales, from .81 to .89 for the job satisfaction indicators, and from .89 to .94 for the vocational training potentials (aptitude-achievement). The authors carry the coefficients to the fourth decimal place! The alpha coefficients are not given by the authors, and there is no indication of what values were substituted in the Spearman-Brown formula to arrive at the published "reliability" coefficients. If one assumes that the authors wanted to estimate the reliability of a test doubled in length and if one works the Spearman-Brown formula backwards one can estimate the authors' coefficients alpha. The lowest reliability estimate given by the test authors is reported as .8073 for the valuative score of the job satisfaction indicators, and the highest as .9418 for the verbal score of the vocational training potentials. Solving the Spearman-Brown formula for these two coefficients yields alpha estimates of .68 and .89, respectively. If the foregoing approach is correct then the scales are not as homogeneous as the authors present them to be.

Various tables in the interpretation manual give means, standard deviations, and standard errors of measurement for the various scales. Given the standard deviations and even with the inflated reliability coefficients the standard errors are certainly in error and drastically underestimated. For example, the following statistics are reported by the authors for the VTP verbal score for the total sample of 738 subjects: mean, 43.621; standard deviation, 8.948; and standard error of measurement, .329. Similar statistics are reported in one table alone for 126 groups broken down by sex, age, and education. Obviously, something is wrong. The authors reported standard errors of the mean rather than standard errors of measurement!

VALIDITY. As evidence of validity, the authors present mean scores earned by 37 real estate salespeople, 19 bank tellers, and 19 classroom teachers. Mean scores are given on the public service, clerical, and sales career interest activ-

ities areas for the three groups. The bank tellers and classroom teachers (both all-female groups) are then contrasted on all 35 scales of the inventory. Six of the mean differences are statistically significant at the one percent level and an additional six are significant at the five percent level.

The interpretation manual gives means and standard deviations for "selected" groups. The selection appears not to have a rational basis and probably reflects availability sampling. Also in the interpretation manual are presented correlations with miscellaneous interest, mechanical ability, and personality tests. The number of cases is small and of unlisted origin. From an examination of the correlations, one can only conclude that evidence for validity is meager and weak.

NORMS. No norms are presented. The vocational training potential scores are plotted on a profile form as low-average-high with the score determined by the number of correct responses. Low starts at 0, average signifies half of the items were marked correctly, and high represents a perfect score. On the verbal test 44 out of a possible 56 is the mean for the "general population." It is obvious that the test is too easy to discriminate well over the range of persons the author suggests as being the target population. The mean score given for ninth graders is 36, and for graduate students 51. The authors make a number of statements such as, "If the Numerical is higher than the Verbal, then as in other test results, this appears to indicate a reading problem." No research is reported to support such statements.

The scores on the career interest activities and job satisfaction indicators scales purport to reflect degree of liking or disliking things. The manual states that "the degree of liking to disliking was developed around a theoretical normal curve with a mean of 0 and a standard deviation of 20" and that "a score of 30 should be considered highly significant." Other than the means and standard deviations mentioned above, no further normative data are given.

SUMMARY. The authors are to be commended for their attempt to relate the WWI on an individualized basis to the *Dictionary of Occupational Titles* and the world of work. Unfortunately, the psychometric properties of the inventory are not developed to the point that this reviewer can recommend the use of the inventory in work with individuals. Given the governmental guidelines on nondiscriminatory use of tests, there is a need for the authors to provide ample evidence that the inventory is free of sex and ethnic group bias. Considerably more research covering reliability, validity, and norms must be carried out before the worth of the inventory for individual counseling can be ascertained.

CARL G. WILLIS, *Counseling Psychologist, University of Missouri, Columbia, Missouri.*

The WWI is "a comprehensive instrument which takes a wholistic [*sic*] approach to the individual and their [*sic*] vocational environment." The instrument is designed to assist test users in looking at themselves in their total environment and to increase self-awareness. Some of the authors' rhetoric is more subjective ("expand the horizons" and "measure the whole person") than objective. Many statements even seem tangential and/or inappropriate. The range of recommended groups and settings for which the WWI should be used appears inordinate.

The entire test is designed and packaged to parallel the *Dictionary of Occupational Titles* career classifications. The DOT is not an "add-on" concept as in other interest inventories.

The WWI is obviously the result of much thought and effort, especially the extensive presentation of career families and related information. The authors claim to fill a void in the testing market by starting the WWI's development with items based on job analysis and around activities that persons actually do on the job; that, therefore, it is job-relevant. Neither the qualifications of those many individuals completing the job analyses nor the number of job analyses completed are stated in the manual. Yet, the definition of specific jobs, roles, functions, and desirable job temperaments, as related to specific occupations and not to the people presently employed in the occupation, is a pleasant contrast to many career instruments. The job satisfaction indicators are "uniquely different from past tests or inventories of personality or temperament in that the types of situations in jobs requiring common adjustments in workers are utilized rather than traits or characteristics in people."

World of Work Inventory

The occupational exploration worksheet for each of the 17 career groups incorporates the three types of test scores with data or information in six other categories including the individual's personal occupational choice, best liked school subjects, school achievement, leisure time activities, other test data, and DOT codes. At this point, a subjective evaluation or interpretation must be made by the individual. The authors do not provide a system of weighting these categories to obtain maximum information or benefits.

The authors provide no information or data to justify linking leisure interests with vocations. There is no generally accepted taxonomy of leisure interests. In addition, leisure activities do not, and perhaps should not, always parallel vocational interests. There tends to be an age factor for some of the leisure activities for which it is very unlikely that eighth or ninth grade students would be involved.

The greatest criticism of the WWI is of the interpretation manual. It contains a number of grammatical and typographical errors and some omissions. Data that relate to validity are presented in a meager manner. Only five occupations have data for the user to peruse, and no other specific occupational groups are referenced. Many of the standard deviations reported for the scales are large.

While it appears that the WWI could be relatively easy to score manually, the authors have not provided any means to do this or any rationale for not making this option available. A scoring service must be used. No raw score information is provided, and a normative table is unavailable.

In summary, the WWI is a refreshing attempt to deal with career identity and choice. Considerable effort has been expended to this point in its development from the job analysis base; however, this effort may best be described as a good beginning which needs much more effort. There are many inadequacies in the validity information. Hand scoring keys and norms should be made available. The holistic approach to assessing the individual would better be accomplished by a selected battery of tests.

Meas & Eval Guid 10(1):62–4 Ap '77. Don C. Locke. * The manual contains no information on test-retest reliability. Correlations should be obtained over time spans since the stability of individual responses can provide an additional indication of the confidence which one can place in the instrument. Validity data on the WOWI is scanty; this lack is perhaps the greatest shortcoming of the test. * The information provided by the WOWI, when considered with other relevant information, can be of considerable value to the counselor. Responses on the WOWI may be considered as an initial attempt to communicate to the counselor an interest in a particular area. With this information, the D.O.T. becomes useful in further exploration of the career families. * The WOWI was designed to simultaneously assess vocational interest and measure aptitude or achievement. The inclusion of an aptitude measure is unique among interest inventories and is perhaps the greatest merit of the WOWI. The WOWI is probably most useful for clients who have less than a high school education. This recommendation is made since the aptitude measure seems geared to that educational level. Although these are important advantages, they are not significant enough to warrant recommendation of the WOWI over either the Strong Vocational Interest Blank or the Kuder Occupational Interest Survey. Both these measures have more reported validity and reliability data, more research, and more occupational normative data than the World of Work Inventory.

CLERICAL

[1032]

Appraisal of Occupational Aptitudes. High school and adult; 1971; AOA; "for predicting success in.... office occupations"; 8 tests in a single booklet (24 pages), any or all of which may be administered: checking letters, checking numbers, filing names, filing numbers, posting names, posting numbers, arithmetical computation and reasoning, desk calculator; no male norms for desk calculator test; 1 form; manual (22 pages); calculators necessary for administration of desk calculator test; $11.85 per 35 tests; $1.95 per manual; $1.35 per specimen set; postage extra; 93(110) minutes for the battery, 4(10) minutes each for checking tests, 5(10) minutes each for filing and posting tests, 30(35) minutes for arithmetic test, 35(40) minutes for desk calculator test; Aurelius A. Abbatiello; Houghton Mifflin Co. *

ROBERT FITZPATRICK, *Director of Research, Psychological Service of Pittsburgh, Pittsburgh, Pennsylvania.*

The *Appraisal of Occupational Aptitudes* is said by the manual to be a series which "provides accurate measures of aptitudes and developmental skills important in the successful performance of office tasks in business and industry." It is not clear how the eight tests were chosen or designed; their development was presumably based on a "job element approach," but none of the elements or their derivation is explained in the manual. The tests appear to be adaptations of tests commonly used for selecting clerical workers.

All eight tests are printed in a single booklet which is not intended to be reused. Answers are written by the examinee in the booklet; for example, in the Filing Names test, the examinee is to interpolate in handwriting 20 names in their proper alphabetical order within a longer list of names already alphabetized. This format has the advantage that it constitutes a direct simulation of a clerical task (though probably not a typical one; surely most clerks would type the list these days) without the artificialities of a separate answer sheet or of multiple choice format. However, it is expensive to use a test booklet for each examinee (especially if only one or two of the tests is to be administered). Hand scoring is required, and the answer spaces on each page have not been arranged to promote efficient scoring.

The test booklet is attractively printed and free of obvious errors. The directions to the examinee, however, are deficient. For example, in the Checking Numbers test, the directions say to compare sets of paired numbers, and the sample items consist entirely of numbers; but, upon turning the page to the test items, one finds that there are letters and other symbols interspersed in some of the number series. Should the examinee take these other symbols into account in deciding whether the pair is "alike" or not? The matter is not covered in the directions. The scoring key indicates the answer is yes, since a pair which differs only in that one contains a decimal point is scored unlike. The issue here is more than the obvious one that some examinees who might be excellent clerks could allow their test performance to be adversely affected by such confusing directions. More important in the long run is that examinees could get the impression from tests like this that test constructors are out to trick them rather than to help them learn about their own capabilities and other characteristics.

In several other instances, the test directions are misleading, or potentially so, to some examinees. For the Filing Names test, the sample answers in the test directions show the names written complete with initials; but the scoring key for this timed test says that inclusion of the initials is not necessary. There are several discrepancies between the directions and the scoring key for the Posting Numbers test. The directions for the Arithmetical Computation and Reasoning test give no hint as to whether fractions should be simplified, or indeed that fractions will be encountered.

A few of the items are ambiguous. Item 25 in Arithmetical Computation and Reasoning asks how much a purchaser saves when given a specified discount, but fails to indicate clearly the base against which the saving is to be measured. Several items in the Desk Calculator test are of the form $A \times B + C = ?$ There is an error in the scoring key for item 9 of Arithmetical Computation and Reasoning; the key incorrectly shows a minus sign.

All the tests are timed, but some are much more highly speeded than others. If the norm group is an appropriate target group for the tests, some of the tests are far too easy for efficient measurement.

However, the description of the norm group in the manual leaves a good deal to be desired. It is said that about 1,000 normative subjects were obtained variously from government agencies, industries, and schools. Students, job applicants, and job incumbents are lumped together into only two norm tables, one for men and one for women. Although the matter is not broached in the manual, in all cases except the Desk Calculator test, the men score significantly better than the women. This is odd, since women typically do well in clerical tasks. One cannot help but be concerned about the adequacy of the norms.

Norms for the Desk Calculator test are given for women only, separately for 234 who used "key driven" calculators and 153 who used "rotary" calculators. This test is, one presumes, intended for people who have had training or experience in the use of the particular type of calculator. Since the manual gives no indication of the level of training and experience of either

norm group, and since modern calculators may differ substantially from those used, it seems that special caution in the use of these norms is advisable.

The Desk Calculator norms are reported separately for what are labeled in the norm table as Power and Speed. However, this appears to be an error; the correct headings should apparently be Part I and Part II. The two parts, consisting of 30 and 48 items, respectively, are not separately timed. Although they are quite similar, there is no reason to suppose that they are equivalent. It is hard to understand why the test is divided into two parts, and the manual provides no explanation.

Split-half reliabilities are reported to be in the high .90s for the first five tests and in the .80s for the others. Numbers of cases and methods of splitting the tests into "equivalent halves" are not described in the manual. Split-half reliabilities are likely to be somewhat distorted for timed tests. Nevertheless, the reported reliabilities are high enough to engender some degree of confidence. Test-retest reliabilities over about six months are reported to range from .65 to .82. The manual suggests that the motivation of some subjects on the retest was poor. The reliabilities might be considered adequate with a reasonable number of cases. But the manual does not reveal the number of cases.

Results of two criterion-related validity studies are reported. The results are reasonably good, but the studies are not described in enough detail to allow an evaluation of their general worth or specific applicability. Again, numbers of cases are not reported. (Significance levels are shown, however, so that by working backwards, one can estimate that there were in the vicinity of 100 cases for each study.) In any case, two studies of the type reported here are entirely inadequate to support any general conclusion about the validity of the tests.

There are several good test batteries available to predict clerical and related abilities. The *Appraisal of Occupational Aptitudes* is not one of them. The directions are poor, scoring is difficult, norms are of doubtful value, the rationale for the tests is weak, and their validity has not been sufficiently investigated.

LEONARD V. GORDON, *Professor of Educational Psychology and Statistics, State University of New York at Albany, Albany, New York.*

Appraisal of Occupational Aptitudes

The intended uses of this test include counseling, selection, and differential placement of office personnel. The author states that the tests were developed on the basis of a critical appraisal of behaviors required in the clerical job family and represent selected job elements. The user is to identify job elements in a particular position under consideration and select appropriate tests for administration. All the tests, however, are printed in one booklet, which does not facilitate the selective usage suggested. Also, it is not clear why a verbal test is not included.

With one exception, the instructions for administering the tests appear to be adequate. For the Desk Calculator test, there are a few simple practice problems and then provision for the examinee to ask questions. Those who are unfamiliar with the particular model of calculator employed may fail to inquire about the more complex operations, and accordingly will be handicapped on the more complex problems in the test itself. Also, the interpretation of the scores for the Desk Calculator test is open to question. The two consecutive parts of this test are separately scored with the intention of providing respective measures of power and speed, but the parts are not separately timed. The amount of time the examinee spends on the "power" section will determine the amount of time available for the "speed" section. Thus, the second score cannot be properly interpreted as a speed measure.

Separate percentile norms are presented for 682 men and for 153 to 334 women. These normative groups are made up from a hodgepodge of subjects from business, government, industry, and schools. The proportions of cases from the various sources are not indicated. More important, the very large mean and distributional differences between the two sets of norms for some of the tests are suggestive of substantial differences in norm group composition. In the absence of clarifying information, the published norms cannot be taken as representative of any identifiable reference population, and their use, particularly for counseling, would be highly questionable.

The reliability information is misleading. Undoubtedly, values in one set are seriously inflated, in that split-half reliabilties were computed for the highly speeded tests. The author's statement that "these coefficients represent an adequate degree of reliability," and that "attempts to increase the reliabilty of the instrument beyond this will prove difficult if not impossible" is nonsense. The values in the upper .90s more likely indicate that the examinees completed about as many odd as even items. Test-retest coefficients, mostly in the upper .60s, may represent underestimates in that the interval between administrations was about six months. Sample sizes or descriptions do not accompany either set of data.

The intercorrelations among tests were based on the scores of about 1,000 subjects from a number of sources, seemingly the normative samples. This combining of groups precludes any meaningful interpretation of the elements of the correlation matrix, other than the likelihood that the values are inflated. For example, the correlation between the Desk Calculator and Filing Numbers tests, when corrected for attenuation on the basis of the reported reliabilities, is unity, and might be higher (?) if plausible reliability estimates were employed. Accordingly, the correlations between pairs of tests which involve the similar operations of checking, filing, and posting, cannot be taken to be alternate form reliabilities, as the author implies.

Several sets of data are presented as being supportive of the validity of the AOA. Correlations with grades of students enrolled in a Manpower Development Training Center program, and with whether they were hired or not hired would ordinarily be considered to be of satisfactory magnitude. However, there is no mention of the number of cases, the proportion of students hired, the type of coefficient employed with the dichotomous criterion, or whether the validities were predictive or concurrent. The set of correlations with supervisory ratings, presumably for a different sample, has only one bit of accompanying information, that cases from several industrial firms were combined, a procedure which renders the outcome even less interpretable. Correlations with several standardized achievement and mental ability measures for unspecified samples of undisclosed size are also presented.

Publishers have an obligation to provide potential test users with meaningful information regarding the characteristics of a given instrument and a reasonable basis for the interpretation of individual scores. This is not to be found

Appraisal of Occupational Aptitudes

in the present manual. In the absence of adequate technical information, it would be futile to speculate as to whether the tests are worth validating for employment purposes. The use of the test in counseling would be precluded on the basis of inadequate reliability and normative data alone. Pending the presentation of satisfactory information in a revised manual, one would be better advised to consider any of a number of available verbal, quantitative, or perceptual speed measures whose technical adequacy have been documented.

[1033]

General Clerical Test. Grades 9–16 and clerical job applicants; 1944–72; formerly called *Psychological Corporation General Clerical Test;* 4 scores: clerical speed and accuracy, numerical ability, verbal facility, total; partial booklets A (clerical and numerical tests) and B (verbal test) are available; 1 form ('44, 12 pages, reprinted with 1969 copyright identical except for slight word changes in 10 items); revised manual ('72, 29 pages); $8.75 per 25 tests; $1 per specimen set; postage extra; 47(57) minutes; Psychological Corporation. *

   British Edition: 1971–74; 1 form ('71, 12 pages, minor anglicizations); British technical manual ('74, 30 pages); technical manual by Peter Saville, Janice Hare, Laura Finlayson, and Stephen Blinkhorn; NFER Publishing Co. Ltd. [England]. *

   See T2:2129 (11 references); for reviews by Edward E. Cureton and G. A. Satter, see 4:730 (4 references); for reviews by Edward N. Hay, Thelma Hunt, Raymond A. Katzell, and E. F. Wonderlic, see 3:630.

REFERENCES

1–4. See 4:730.
5–15. See T2:2129; also includes a cumulative name index to the first 15 references, and 6 reviews for this test.
16. WHELCHEL, BARRY D. "A 'Tested' Procedure for Improving Clerical Selection." *J Col & Univ Personnel Assn* 23(3):68–73 My '72. *

CHARLES J. CRANNY, *Associate Professor of Psychology, Bowling Green State University, Bowling Green, Ohio.*

The *General Clerical Test* consists of nine parts, each separately timed. These are combined to yield three subscores—clerical, numerical, and verbal—and a total score. Time limits for the nine parts range from 3 to 8½ minutes. It would thus require approximately an hour to administer the complete test, and close attention of the examiner would be required. All parts are scored number right, and subscores are obtained by simply summing the appropriate part scores. Directions for administration are clear and complete. Scoring is unambiguous, but the lack of instructions for the use of the fan-key scoring device may bother some users.

The last substantial revision of test content was done in 1944. The present manual, published in 1972, replaces the 1950 version. Other than the manual, the only changes made since the test was last reviewed in the 4th MMY are described as "superficial," and consist of updating the content of 10 items.

A description of the test in the publisher's catalogue makes the claim that it is "useful in selecting and upgrading all types of clerical personnel." As is pointed out in the manual, high correlations between both subscores and total score and a number of measures of intellectual ability indicate that the test would be more appropriate for use with relatively high-level clerical positions. Available validity data are not sufficiently extensive to confirm this notion, however.

The major flaw in the test manual was mentioned by Satter in his review (4:730): there is no description of the process by which items were chosen or combined. The authors present no job analysis or similar data to support the claim that it measures abilities important in office work.

Despite the age of the test, no alternate form has been developed. The manual presents some evidence, in the form of retest reliability data, that means for each of the four scores increased by about half a standard deviation on retest after a one-month interval. Further attention should be paid to this aspect of score stability, since federal regulations require that unsuccessful applicants be allowed retesting.

The normative data have been updated in the 1972 manual, and the updating is quite extensive. The format is improved, and conversion to centile ranks is simplified by elimination of the need for interpolation. The norm tables from the 1950 manual are presented as an appendix to the 1972 manual. The manual quite properly stresses the importance of local norms, where possible, but could indicate more strongly that the 1950 norms will usually be much less appropriate than more recent norms.

Norm groups are well labeled with respect to sex, applicant or employee status, and whether they are educational or occupational groups. The "male and female" norm groups should identify the relative proportions of each sex included, particularly since the scores seem to exhibit sex differences. Information on age and racial or ethnic background of norm groups would also be helpful. Indeed, the development of separate minority group norms seems essential, since the high correlations of both the subtest and total scores with group intelligence tests, such as the *Wonderlic Personnel Test,* suggest the likelihood that significant racial and ethnic group differences may be found. Such differences could result in differential predictability for such subgroups, and the risk of illegal discrimination. Any test user should be alert to this possibility.

The 1972 manual reports data from two reliability studies, one of which was reported in the 1950 manual. The later study has only 51 subjects, but test-retest coefficients of .92, .88, .93, and .96 for clerical, numerical, verbal, and total, respectively, are closely comparable to those reported from the earlier study.

Presentation of validity data is much more extensive in the 1972 manual than was the case in 1950. Validity coefficients are reported for 22 different samples, 6 of which are educational and 16 are industrial groups. A problem in interpretation of these data is, with one exception, the lack of any indication of whether a particular validation study followed a predictive or concurrent design. Unless there were significant restriction in variance due to preselection or selective attrition, concurrent validity estimates are likely to overestimate predictive validity coefficients with tests of this type.

The criteria for the educational groups are grade point averages and course grades. Validity coefficients for total score range between .40 and .77. Most subscore coefficients are in the .40s and .50s. These data, and the test content, seem to indicate that the best use of the test is probably as a predictor of grades in commercial or secretarial courses. Of the 16 studies with industrial groups, about half show statistically significant validity coefficients for at least one score. These range from .16 to .56. The usual criteria were supervisory ratings. These data indicate that job performance criteria, especially supervisory ratings, are not predicted with nearly the consistency or accuracy as are grades.

This test compares favorably with other tests available in this area, especially for prediction with academic groups. The latest revision of the manual is a considerable improvement over the 1950 edition. Norm tables are more extensive than most, but racial, ethnic, and age differences

need attention. Problems with the use of the test in industrial settings include the lower validities in such settings and the lack of data supporting the content validity of the test for use with clerical jobs. The length of the test, with its separately timed parts, might also be a disadvantage. For those willing to take the time and trouble, and able to compile local normative and validity data, this test should be considered; otherwise, probably not.

[1034]
★N.B. Commercial Tests. Standards 6–8; 1962; 6 scores: arithmetic (computations, problems), comparison, synonyms, alphabetizing, spelling and punctuation; no data on validity; Forms A, B, (17 pages, English and Afrikaans); manual (30 pages, English and Afrikaans); separate answer sheets must be used; R2.75 per 10 tests; R3.80 per 100 answer sheets; R10 per scoring stencil; R7.50 per manual; postpaid within South Africa; specimen set not available; 57(70) minutes; Human Sciences Research Council [South Africa]. *

[1035]
★SRA Typing 5. Prospective employees; 1975; 3 tests, 2 scores for each: speed, accuracy; no data on reliability for accuracy scores; 1 form (3 pages); examiner's manual (8 pages); practice sheet (1 page); tape cassette available for administration; $6.60 per 25 tests; $2.50 per 25 practice sheets; $15 per tape cassette; 60¢ per manual; $1.85 per specimen set; postage extra; 5(12) minutes per test; Steven J. Stanard and LaVonne A. Macaitis (manual); Science Research Associates, Inc. *
a) FORM A—TYPING SPEED.
b) FORM B—BUSINESS LETTER.
c) FORM C—NUMERICAL.

CHARLES J. CRANNY, *Associate Professor of Psychology, Bowling Green State University, Bowling Green, Ohio.*

This test consists of three separately timed tests which claim to measure three kinds of typing skills: Form A, Typing Speed, involves typing straight copy only; Form B, Business Letter, is primarily straight copy in the form of a business letter, with two copy corrections; and Form C, Numerical, involves straight copy with 5 columns of numbers in tabular form.

The manual describes Form B as a measure of "the ability to set up a common business letter," and states that Form C allows assessment of "how well an individual can set up and type columns of numbers with headings." The format for both is shown in the test copy, which the subject is instructed to reproduce exactly. Variations in format are not scored in either test. For Form B, the manual states that, "the test user should, however, be aware of how well the typist is able to set up this kind of letter," but no standards are offered.

The manual claims that the three tests measure different typing skills yet no evidence, such as intercorrelations among scores on the three tests, is provided. This omission is difficult to understand, since the publishers have available scores from over 600 subjects in the norm samples, each of whom has scores on all three tests.

Although suggesting that employers may wish to use more than one of the tests, no advice is offered in the manual on the best order of administration, if any. No alternate forms are available, which is a disadvantage in an area where frequent retesting of applicants may be required.

Directions for administration are fairly clear and include appropriate stress on accuracy and consistency of directions and timing. An excellent feature in this regard is the availability of tape cassettes for the administration of a single test. The use of the cassette would be awkward, however, if more than one form were administered sequentially to the same subjects.

Each of the three tests is scored for speed and accuracy. Scoring directions are brief, and the possibility of inter-scorer differences exists, especially if vertical spacing in the typed copy is not perfectly correct. No data are provided regarding inter-scorer agreement, although such data would seem to be easy for the publisher to obtain.

The instructions for Form B may present the subject, and perhaps the scorer, with some problems. The subject is instructed to "use double spacing throughout" and to "reproduce the letter exactly as it appears." Since the letter appears with greater vertical spacing between some lines than others (e.g., address and salutation) these instructions are inconsistent.

Scoring problems result from the manner in which scores are computed. The speed score is obtained by dividing total words by 5. The accuracy score is obtained by subtracting total errors from total words, then dividing the remainder by total words. A cumulative word count appears at the left of each (double spaced) line on the typing sheet. This count is accurate and facilitates quick scoring only if each line typed matches the test letter line-for-line, if the copy is double spaced throughout, and if the copy begins on the appropriate line (which the in-

structions do not require). If these conditions are not met, the count of total words could be very laborious and time-consuming, with greater opportunity for scoring errors.

The data on reliability are clearly inadequate. Test-retest correlation coefficients are presented for the speed scores based on sample sizes of 72, 72, and 67 for Forms A, B, and C, respectively. There is no description of the sample, and the intertest interval is not reported. Means and standard deviations from the reliability sample are also missing, so that the calculation of an accurate estimate of the standard errors of measurement is impossible. The test-retest reliabilities of the accuracy scores are not mentioned, although they must be available from the raw data from the same sample. It is safe to assume that they are somewhat lower than the speed score reliabilities, since they involve difference scores.

The only comment in the manual regarding validity is the statement that "content validity is assumed in these tests of typing skill." Content validity should refer here to the appropriateness of these tests as a work sample for typing applicants, and more than an act of faith is required to make a convincing case. No data pertaining to aspects of validity relevant to the use of these tests as selection instruments, either content or criterion-related, are presented.

Norm tables are presented based on samples "from approximately 25 organizations and branch offices throughout the country." No further description of type of organization or job involved, other than the term "office applicants" is presented. The manual properly advised development of company specific norms. Certainly those presented here will be of limited use.

A table for conversion of speed and accuracy scores to percentile ranks is provided based on a combined group of experienced and inexperienced applicants, with separate distributions for majority and minority applicants on each test. Neither sample is described in any more detail than simply majority or minority. Separate norms by sex are not available.

Six other tables, two for each form, show the same sample broken down into experienced and inexperienced applicants, with majority and minority applicants combined. The terms "experienced" and "inexperienced" are not defined. Each group is then further subdivided into regional norm groups (North, South, East, West). These regions are not defined or described. Where the size of the regional norm sample is 66 or less (South and West) the manual advises the user to interpret the norms cautiously.

These tests have a number of severe limitations to their usefulness, not the least of which is the lack of disclosure of relevant data. The scoring may be inconvenient and sometimes inconsistent. Reliability data are either inadequate or totally missing, despite their apparent availabilty to the publisher. No validity data are offered, and the description of the norm samples is inadequate for their use. The best present use of the test is for research regarding reliability and validity for use as a selection or screening device. The publisher could help in this regard by the analysis and publication of available data.

LAWRENCE W. ERICKSON, *Professor of Education and Assistant Dean, Graduate School of Education, University of California, Los Angeles, California.*

This test was designed to measure a person's ability to type a particular kind of assignment in a business office. Supposedly, the three different subtests (Typing Speed, Business Letter, and Numerical) reflect typing requirements of office jobs.

The tests are scored for speed and accuracy. A word count is given for each line (total words typed) and the forms to be used for the typing tests provide spaces for recording errors per line.

The manual is easy to follow. Clear directions are given for administering and scoring the tests. An administration cassette, furnished with the tests, can be used to "ensure accuracy in timing" of the tests and to help "standardize the testing situation."

In constructing the tests, recognition was given to copy difficulty factors such as percent of high frequency words, syllable intensity, and average word length. However, no attempt was made to make each paragraph of uniform copy difficulty, without which both speed and accuracy may be affected.

In counting words, the spacing stroke was excluded. This approach is contrary to the accepted method of counting words in typewritten copy for determining the words-a-minute

(wam) typing rate. For example, the material of Form A contains 272 five-stroke typing words instead of the reported 215 five-stroke words. Consequently, the word count on all the tests is understated and the rate a typist makes on the copy would be from 5 to 15 words a minute below the true rate, depending on the speed of the typist. The understatement of the wam rate would be greatest for the fastest typists. Similarly, the syllable intensity (total syllables divided by actual words) and the average word length (total strokes divided by actual number of words) are understated. For example, paragraph 1 of Form A has an actual syllable intensity of 1.47 instead of the reported 1.64, and an average word length of 5.41 instead of the reported 4.34. This reviewer could not check the percent of high frequency words in the copy since the manual does not mention the name of the word list that was used.

Reliability of Forms A, B, and C was determined by the test-retest method to be .73, .84, and .82, respectively. Detailed tables showing the percentile rank of specific speed and accuracy scores for experienced and inexperienced office applicants in all regions of the United States (North, South, East, and West) are given. No information is given as to the validity of the test, although the statement is made that the "test items were written after a review of typing test literature and consultation with a typing expert." This reviewer, however, questions whether the tests really measure the ability to perform satisfactorily in a variety of office typing tasks. Comments on each form of the test follow:

FORM A—TYPING SPEED. This form, consisting of a series of paragraphs headed by a salutation and ended with a complimentary close and typed name, is to serve as a measure of straight copy typing speed and accuracy. The test is not a true measure of straight copy speed, since it contains the opening (salutation) and closing lines (complimentary close and typed name) of a letter, inclusion of which contaminates the measure of straight copy skill.

The manual suggests that "Form A may be used as a selection or screening tool for entry-level clerical personnel as well as for evaluating clerical personnel for advancement into a position that requires....a high volume of straight copy." In the reviewer's opinion, a measure of typing speed and accuracy of this type gives only partial information as to a typist's ability. As a screening device it may serve a useful purpose, but more information would be needed about overall typing skill of an applicant for an office position, or in evaluating clerical personnel for advancement into a position requiring a high volume of straight copy. As an example, a study by this reviewer indicated that a large percentage of the copy used by office typists for producing final copy is in rough-draft form. Such copy contained numerous, and often extensive, handwritten corrections.

FORM B—BUSINESS LETTER. In this five-minute writing, the testee is to reproduce a letter "exactly" as it appears in the test copy. This direction is confusing, as the copy contains two rough-draft corrections. To follow the "exactly" direction, the typist would type the incorrect words and then make the corrections in handwriting. In copy of this kind the direction should read: "Type the letter as it appears, making the corrections indicated in the copy." The entire letter is to be double-spaced, with no attention to proper spacing between letter parts. This approach is not realistic. Additionally, the closing parts of the letter are incorrectly displayed in the copy; yet, the testee is directed to "reproduce the letter *exactly* as it appears." Confusion compounded!

As was true for Form A, Form B is not a true measure of letter typing skill. It would be better to have the testee arrange the letter in some acceptable format while typing it so that the ability of the typist to place copy correctly on a sheet of paper could be evaluated, in addition to the letter copy rate. Furthermore, typing errors should be corrected, as would be done in an office typing situation.

The manual suggests that "Form B would be best used to test applicants for positions that require more experienced typists." In the opinion of this reviewer, Form B would give only limited information about the overall typing skill needed for most office typing jobs.

FORM C—NUMERICAL. As described in the manual, "Form C allows an employer to assess how well an individual can set up and type columns of numbers with headings. It also presents a measure of basic key-stroking ability." The material to be typed is a letter containing a four-column table. Again, the testee is directed

to type the letter "*exactly* as it appears"; consequently, the test does not actually measure the ability of a typist to "set up and type" a table. The table itself is relatively simple to type and presents little challenge as to its proper placement within the letter. The strength of Form C is that it does provide a measure of the number-typing skill.

SUMMARY. The redeeming features of the *SRA Typing 5* tests are the detailed tables of norms based on some 25 organizations and branch offices throughout the United States. The percentiles given for the speed and accuracy scores permit comparisons with individuals in the normative groups.

In the opinion of this reviewer, the tests themselves could be improved. As given, they do little to test the placement, problem-solving, and decision-making skills of a typist; nor do they adequately measure handling of rough-draft and related typing materials which make up the main source of copy for the office typist.

[1036]

*SRA Typing Skills. Applicants for clerical positions; 1947-73; 2 scores: speed, accuracy; no data on reliability; Forms A, B, ('47, 4 pages); manual ('47, 5 pages); supplementary norms ('73, 4 pages); tape cassette available for administration; $6.60 per 25 tests; $15 per tape cassette; 62¢ per manual; $1.70 per specimen set; postage extra; 10(17) minutes; Marion W. Richardson and Ruth A. Pedersen; Science Research Associates, Inc. *

See T2:792 (1 reference); for reviews by Lawrence W. Erickson and Jacob S. Orleans, see 6:51 (2 references).

[1037]

The Short Employment Tests. Applicants for clerical positions; 1951-72; SET; 4 scores: verbal, numerical, clerical, total; distribution of Form 1 restricted to banks which are members of the American Bankers Association; no data on reliability of total scores; 4 forms; 3 tests; revised manual ('72, 31 pages); $3.85 per 25 tests; $1.25 per specimen set; postage extra; 5(10) minutes per test; George K. Bennett and Marjorie Gelink; Psychological Corporation. *
a) v [VERBAL]. Forms 1, 2, 3, 4, ('51, 3 pages).
b) N[NUMERICAL]. Forms 1, 2, 3, 4, ('51, 4 pages).
c) CA [CLERICAL]. Forms 1, 2, 3, 4, ('51, 3 pages).

See T2:2151 (6 references); for a review by Leonard W. Ferguson, see 6:1045 (9 references); for a review by P. L. Mellenbruch, see 5:854 (16 references).

REFERENCES

1–16. See 5:854.
17–25. See 6:1045.
26–31. See T:2151; also includes a cumulative name index to the first 31 references and 2 reviews for this test.
32. CAMPION, JAMES E. "Work Sampling for Personnel Selection." *J Appl Psychol* 56(1):40–4 F '72. * (PA 47:11864)
33. ARVEY, RICHARD D., AND MUSSIO, STEPHEN J. "Determining the Existence of Unfair Test Discrimination for Female

Clerical Workers." *Personnel Psychol* 26(4):559–68 w '73. *
(*PA* 53:12619)
    34. ARVEY, RICHARD D., AND MUSSIO, STEPHEN J. "Test
Discrimination, Job Performance and Age." *Indus Gerontol*
16:22–9 w '73. * (*PA* 51:1950)
    35. MISHKEN, MARK ALLAN. *Self-Esteem as a Moderator in
the Relationship Between Job Ability and Job Performance.*
Doctor's thesis, University of Tennessee (Knoxville, Tenn.),
1973. (*DAI* 34:5731B)

RONALD N. TAYLOR, *Associate Professor of
Commerce and Business Administration, The
University of British Columbia, Vancouver,
British Columbia.*

The *Short Employment Tests,* a widely used
battery of clerical aptitude tests, have been previously reviewed. Since the last review, the
1972 revision of the SET manual has replaced
the 1956 manual and much additional psychometric evidence regarding the SET has appeared. Many reviewers in these yearbooks and
elsewhere have stressed the value and contributions made by the SET. In light of the psychometric evidence pertaining to the SET, however, this reviewer disagrees with many of the
advantages claimed for the tests and has serious
reservations about the validity of the tests.

Acceptance of the SET appears due in large
part to the authors' focus upon assessing three
aptitudes (verbal, numerical, and clerical) for
what the authors have described as a clearly
defined population—applicants for clerical work.
Yet, the term clerical work covers a great variety of jobs. The SET authors don't identify
what kinds of clerical workers are represented
in the validity studies reported in the 1972 revision of the manual. The 1956 manual provided
more information in listing bookkeepers, machine operators, policy-writing clerks, secretaries, stenographers, and typists. Many more
clerical jobs can be added and it is clear that
clerical work is not a homogeneous population.
Rather, the jobs for which the SET is suggested
for selecting employees represent considerable
diversity in duties; this diversity may have
contributed to the low validities reported for
the SET.

Evidence regarding both criterion-related
and construct validity are reported in the SET
manual, with predictive and concurrent validities being presented as evidence of criterion-
related validity. While the studies reported in
the 1956 manual were identified as either predictive or current, the distinction is not made
for the additional studies reported in the 1972
manual. This omission should be corrected.

The 72 criterion-related validity coefficients
reported in the 1956 manual have been supplemented by an additional 296 validity coefficients
in the 1972 manual. This large number of validity coefficients resulted in part from reporting
differential validities for sex and racial subgroups, but they also reflect 22 additional validity studies. A variety of criteria are used, but
most involve supervisory ratings. In summarizing the new validity coefficients for the separate
tests, the authors consider only the correlations
which are significantly different from zero at
the 5 percent level. This gives a distorted picture of the validity data. The authors report
the medians and ranges of the significant correlations as follows: verbal, .26 (−.28 to .46);
numerical, .26 (−.41 to .47); and clerical, .28
(.12 to .56). When all 296 validity coefficients
are considered, a more realistic summary is obtained: verbal, .13 (−.28 to .46); numerical,
.15 (−.41 to .50); clerical, .28 (−.22 to .57);
and total, .17 (−.21 to .59). Seventeen percent
of the 296 validity coefficients are negative, and
only 14 percent are .30 or higher.

Better understanding of the construct validity of the SET is needed, since it would be useful to know the logical dimensions represented
by the three subtests. Intercorrelations among
the three subtests of the SET provide some
insights into the dimensions contained in the
battery and raise questions regarding the independence of the subtests. The median intercorrelation reported is .36, with a range of .08 to
.60. The most highly correlated subtests are
numerical and clerical aptitude (.34 to .60);
the next most highly correlated subtests are
verbal and clerical aptitude (.13 to .51); and
the least correlated subtests are numerical and
verbal (.08 to .53). The authors conclude that
"In most cases the coefficients (.08 to .60,
median .36) are sufficiently small to indicate
that each test measures a relatively independent
aspect of clerical ability." Yet, this statement
contradicts their argument for validity. The
median of the 228 validity coefficients for these
three subtests is only .14. If the tests are "relatively independent" with a median intercorrelation of .36, one must conclude that the tests are
almost completely independent of the criteria
against which validity is being determined.

Evidence is also presented in the manual to
show the correlations of the SET with other

Short Employment Tests

tests purported to measure similar skills. Correlations with corresponding subtests from the *General Clerical Test* are the highest reported, with the pattern of intercorrelation indicating some convergent validity. More complete data regarding correlations with tests designed to measure similar aptitudes are needed if convergent and discriminant validity of these tests are to be assessed. While this approach constitutes a rigorous test of validity, enhancing the understanding of aptitude tests by taking a more theoretical approach would be beneficial for test construction and use.

Another limitation in the validation evidence reported for the SET is that trainability appears to have been used as a criterion in none of the validity studies reported in the 1956 manual and in only four of the 22 studies added for the 1972 manual. This is surprising in view of the opinion stated by the senior author [1] of the SET that "When aptitude tests are to be validated the most meaningful criterion is often trainability."

The authors are to be commended for reporting separate validity coefficients for sex and racial groups. The authors acknowledge that both female-male and minority-white differences in mean scores and in validity coefficients exist and suggest that, in setting cutoff scores, employers "must be aware of the relationship between minimum score requirements and selection ratio by ethnic category or by sex." Still, if a test is biased in favor of subgroups in the population of job applicants, it is difficult to know what form the correction should take.

The SET subtests appear reasonably reliable. Alternate-form reliability coefficients range from .86 for clerical aptitude to .92 for both verbal and numerical subtests. Test-retest scores over a two-year interval yielded stability coefficients of .84 for verbal, .75 for numerical, and .71 for clerical subtests. Although the authors recommend that all three tests be administered in most selection situations to increase validity, reliability for the total battery is not reported.

In conclusion, the evidence reported in the 1972 revision of the manual casts serious doubt upon the validity of the SET. In fact, 17 percent of the correlations report a negative validity. Rather than continuing to use general cleri-

cal test batteries such as the SET for selecting clerical workers, a more promising approach would appear to involve the use of job-specific tests. In view of the questionable validity of the SET, the reviewer cannot recommend that it be used for selecting clerical workers.

PAUL W. THAYER, *Professor of Psychology and Head of the Department, North Carolina State University, Raleigh, North Carolina.*

These tests were originally developed in 1951. One always runs the risk that some verbal items will become outdated. An examination of the verbal tests is reassuring; the words employed are still in current use.

Previous reviews by Ferguson and Mellenbruch state that, within limits, these tests meet three stated objectives of brevity, adequate test-retest reliability, and simple instructions and scoring. This reviewer would agree, adding that the alternate form reliabilities for the three tests are also quite adequate.

Evidence is presented, however, that clerical ability scores are susceptible to experience on clerical jobs. In one study in a bank, verbal and numerical mean scores over a two-year period increased very slightly, but clerical ability scores increased almost 6 points. For many of the normative groups, this would represent a substantial shift in percentile rank.

The 1972 edition of the manual is the sole new feature and the basis for this additional review. It reflects the increasing concern for and awareness of sex and race differences in applicant and employee populations. Extensive tables are given for female applicants and employees in several settings, for male applicants and employees, and for minority applicants and employees, the last separated by sex where possible. Racial differences are, in several instances, substantial. Sex differences are not quite as dramatic or consistent. Twelve pages of norms are reported in all. Such diligence in collecting and reporting is commendable. Unfortunately, the typical personnel officer may be bewildered as to which of these tables to use. The manual gives little or no help in choosing among them. It does, however, urge development of local norms where possible.

Such racial and sex differences obviously call for an examination of validity data. Four pages of data from 22 new sites are added to those

---

[1] BENNETT, GEORGE K. "Factors Affecting the Value of Validation Studies." *Personnel Psychol* 22(3):265–68 au '69. *

reported previously. The authors fail to provide information on the nature of the validity models used, concurrent or predictive, as they did for studies reported in 1956.

The verbal test has only 16 of 68 coefficients significant at the .05 level. They range from −.28 to .46, with a median of .26. Numerical has 21 of 83 significant coefficients, these ranging from −.41 to .47, with a median of .26. Clerical aptitude shows the highest validity, as 20 of 77 coefficients are significant. Those range from .12 to .56, with a median of .28. Almost all these studies suffer from the fact that the criteria are supervisory ratings of some sort. Despite this, about the same proportion of studies report significant relationships for males and females, while those for whites show twice the proportion of significant relationships as those for minorities. The authors give sound advice in urging local validation studies.

Their advice is less sound when they contend that lack of differences in validity coefficients among sexes or races makes it difficult to support the contention of unfairness. Although differential validity is an unusual finding, a comparison of correlation coefficients is insufficient in determining fairness. The aforementioned normative differences are certainly relevant.

In this reviewer's opinion, there is little doubt that the tests themselves have appropriate psychometric properties. The manual is extremely weak, however, in giving appropriate guidance to the employment officer. Greater assistance on the use of the normative tables, more thorough description of the validity studies, and more extended discussion of their significance and meaning to the user are essential. In addition, more explicit information should be given as to the implications of equal employment legislation and regulation.

The testing climate today puts greater demands on employers. Publishers have an *obligation* to provide proper information and guidance.

[1038]

Short Occupational Knowledge Test for Secretaries. Job applicants; 1969–70; score is pass, fail, or unclassifiable; 1 form ('69, 2 pages, self-marking); series manual ('70, 15 pages); tape cassette available for administration; $10.70 per 25 tests; $15 per tape cassette; $1.40 per manual; $7.10 per specimen set of the 12 tests in the series; postage extra; (10–15) minutes; Bruce A. Campbell and Suellen O. Johnson; Science Research Associates, Inc. *

ALBERT K. KURTZ, *1810 Ivy Lane, Winter Park, Florida.*

This 20-item multiple choice test is designed to differentiate between adequately trained secretaries and people with a modicum of interest and training who might apply for a job in the area. The items are described as "job-related with a practical, rather than theoretical, orientation."

Because the same 15-page manual is used for 12 occupations for which the Short tests are available, this reviewer wrote to the publisher asking for specific information about the tested secretaries. It took two letters to get the publisher to describe the secretaries and their control group. The secretaries included experienced secretaries, top students in the final stages of the secretarial training, and instructors in secretarial schools. The control group with which the secretaries were contrasted included typing students, typists, and students beginning secretarial training.

Now, how modern is this test which was published in 1969 or 1970? There is a reference to a carbon typewriter ribbon, but there is no evidence that the authors were familiar with electric typewriters, Xerox-type photocopiers, or the more recent liquid and paper erasing procedures, self-correcting typewriters, or magnetic typewriters with or without a memory. There are references to plastic or metal shields for erasing, to a mimeograph (called liquid duplicator), and to a collator; and one question is scored as correct only if the secretary says she should type "Miss" before a woman's name if her marital status is unknown! While only two or three items are really obsolete, it is a shame that more of the newer concepts are not included.

The K-R 20 reliability for the pretest sample of 213 is .74, and for the validation sample of 83, it is .73. This is clearly too low for the intended use in individual counseling and selection. By the simple expedient of lengthening the test to 30 to 65 items, the reliability could be increased to .80 or .90.

The manual refers to pretest and validation samples; and the manual has a section on validity. Despite this, not a single validity coefficient is given. The reviewer considered computing the validity from frequency distributions of scores given in the manual, but then realized that there were complications in its interpretation since the test is not designed to predict secretarial proficiency but merely to determine whether the examinee is a secretary or a member of another group. The authors avoided validity problems by grouping the scores, making predictions, and reporting the percent of accurate predictions after discarding the hard-to-predict middle group. This questionable procedure is discussed later.

The manual indicates that the examiner should read the directions (about 125 words) and then administer the test on an untimed basis, although the examinee should be able to complete the test in 10 to 15 minutes. In 1974, a cassette became available. One side gives the directions; the other side gives the directions and reads every item in the test. Since there is a pause of only 4 to 6 seconds for answering each item, and since most secretaries can read extremely well, this reading of all the items probably hinders rather than helps those taking this test. (For other tests in this series, this procedure, with more time for answers, may make sense since some of the tests are designed to be used with illiterates, tactfully described as having "a reading problem.")

Scoring is extremely simple. The test is self-marking and the examiner simply counts the Xs that appear in boxes connected by one long line.

The number right is converted into one of three classes. Scores of 12–20 are passing; those of 0–9 are failing; and those of 10 and 11 are considered unclassifiable. In the validation group, 41 people passed, 25 failed, and 13 were unclassifiable. All 41 who passed actually were secretaries, while 22 of the 25 who failed were not secretaries. The authors summarize this by reporting the percent unclassified as 16.5 and the percent of accurate predictions made after removing those subjects who were unclassifiable is 95.5. The reviewer regards the second statement as highly misleading. Instead of dividing 63 by 66 and getting 95.5 percent, the reviewer would divide 63 by 79 and state that the test gave 79.7 percent correct predictions. It also gave 3.8 percent incorrect predictions and was noncommittal on 16.5 percent. Note that these three percentages add up to 100 percent of the group, as they should. Note also that the test is doing a good job, being right 80 percent

of the time and wrong only 4 percent of the time, with the other 16 being, as the authors say, unclassifiable by this test. Finally, note that the reviewer's interpretation is not at all likely to mislead anybody about how well the test does the job that it was intended to do.

SUMMARY. If one's purpose is to find out whether or not an applicant for a secretarial position has knowledge of the content and concepts comparable to that of specialists in the secretarial field as opposed to those having limited knowledge, this is a good test to use. If the purpose is to select the best from a group of secretaries, forget it. A passing score thus may be regarded as a necessary but not a sufficient condition for locating an excellent secretary. Despite the shortcomings cited, this is a good test for differentiating between knowledgeable secretaries and people who are not familiar with the content and concepts of the field.

[1039]

*Short Tests of Clerical Ability. Applicants for office positions; 1959–73; STCA; 7 tests; 1 form ('59) ; manual ('73, 30 pages) ; tape cassettes available for administration; $6.50 per 25 tests; $1 per scoring stencil for any one test; $15 per tape cassette for any one test; 67¢ per manual; $3.80 per specimen set; postage extra; Jean M. Palormo; Science Research Associates, Inc. *

a) ARITHMETIC. 3 scores: computation, business arithmetic, total, no data on reliability for total score; Form A (2 pages) ; 9(14) minutes.

b) BUSINESS VOCABULARY. Form A (2 pages) ; 5(10) minutes.

c) CHECKING. Form A (2 pages) ; 5(10) minutes.

d) CODING. Form A (2 pages) ; 5(10) minutes.

e) DIRECTIONS—ORAL AND WRITTEN. Form A (5 pages in 2 parts) ; 5(10) minutes.

f) FILING. Form A (2 pages) ; 5(10) minutes.

g) LANGUAGE. Form A (2 pages) ; 5(10) minutes.

For reviews by Philip H. Kriedt and Paul W. Thayer, see 6:1046.

REFERENCES

1. Science Research Associates. *Validation: Procedures and Results: Part 3, Supplementary Results, Third Edition.* Chicago, Ill.: Science Research Associates, 1974. Pp. ii, 90. *

LORRAINE D. EYDE, *Personnel Research Psychologist, Personnel Research and Development Center, U.S. Civil Service Commission, Washington, D.C.*

The manual shows that considerable effort has been made to document the validity of seven tests for use in selecting office personnel in private industry and business. Ten concurrent criterion-related validity studies are presented in detail, seven of which were carried out after the passage of the 1964 Civil Rights Act. The manual points out the limitations of the methodologies and statistics used, noting for example, that the reported validity coefficients may be underestimates since the employees in the studies had for the most part been selected by means of tests. The author makes an effort to describe psychological concepts, and points out the need for carrying out local validity studies while making use of published normative data. The summary table of the STCA validity studies for general office personnel, general clerks, accounting clerks, and secretaries should provide test users with guidance on selecting the most appropriate tests for particular jobs. The manual, however, does not adequately focus on the tasks and critical worker requirements of the jobs, and in seven of the studies reference is made only to job titles.

Of the 10 validity studies, the three dealing with food chain jobs are the best documented. Not only are job tasks relating to clerical abilities identified for each of three jobs, but important job factors such as "relationships with coworkers and supervisors" and "attendance and punctuality" are also listed. The weights for the final test batteries are based on multiple correlations which include measures of adaptability and numerical skills in addition to the STCA. Furthermore, the weights have been crossvalidated on another sample and expectancy tables are provided to show the relationship between the weighted test scores and work-task ratings.

Another validity study shows a positive relationship between STCA test scores and progression from routine clerical jobs to advanced jobs for a group of 100 clerical workers (including 74 blacks) in a publishing house which had not had a testing program for the purpose of selection and placement for several years.

Intercorrelation data for the seven tests are reported, showing a median intercorrelation of .38. Unfortunately, correlations with other published clerical tests are not presented. It would also be interesting to know how well the STCA in combination with a measure of general intelligence and weighted biographical data predicts overall clerical job performance.

Instructions for these tests are now provided on tape cassettes, thus standardizing the timing for tests and easing the burden of test administration. These recordings are not always designed, however, to the advantage of the test taker. The general instructions are repeated—monotonously—before each test and may promise more than the examiner can deliver. For example, they say "The scores on these tests will help us decide what kind of office job you are likely to do best and therefore *like the best*." These instructions assume that the tests will be used for placement purposes and do not address the possibility that the applicants' interests may not be in the clerical area at all. The cassettes allow little time for questions and, as a result, less assertive examinees may fail to ask necessary questions. The cassette for the checking test contains background noise picked up during the test-taking interval. The directions test (oral and written), as presented on the cassette, is an anxiety producing and unreasonably difficult work sample. It is highly unlikely that clerical workers would be expected to absorb so many details in so short a period of time. Materials of this sort are usually presented to new employees in written form.

The language test is not ready for operational use in selecting individual clerical workers because its odd-even reliability based on an undefined group of 53 clerical employees is only .48, after being corrected by the Spearman-Brown formula. The test is scored—perhaps for administrative convenience—on the basis of the number of errors in each sentence. Actual errors are not marked; thus much information about the examinees' knowledge is lost. Also, this format probably encourages guessing.

All tests need to be edited for obsolete content. For example, the directions test refers to the now defunct Railway Express Agency and to mimeographing, which is no longer as prevalent as it once was. Throughout the tests, sex stereotyping perpetuates the myth that women's role in business is confined to lower-level clerical jobs. A general manager is referred to as "he," but a clerk who uses file folders is "she." The person who answers the phone is a "she," but a clerk who sells $500 worth of merchandise is "he." In the filing test, there are approximately five times as many names of men listed as there are women. On the other hand, male applicants and male clerical workers are briefly mentioned in two studies, but no descriptive data are reported for them. The author does, however, give descriptive statistics for small samples (8 to 12) of minority group members.

Short Tests of Clerical Ability

Normative data are provided for applicants by employed majority and minority group members, as well as by occupational groups. No norms are provided for mature applicants—particularly women. This group has been seeking to reenter the labor market in unprecedented numbers and might be adversely affected by the speeded nature of the tests, but once employed, they have, in general, proved to be effective workers showing low turnover.

The author provides the examinee with helpful hints on how to respond to some of the test questions; for example, for memorizing codes in the coding test. The filing test could be revised to include a few basic filing rules which may be learned quickly on the job.

In summary, the 1973 manual reports considerable progress in documenting the validity of the clerical tests. Additional attention needs to be given to the content and scoring of the language and directions tests. Editing for obsolete terms and sex-typing in the test content would greatly enhance the quality of this battery of tests. Six of the seven tests are ready for operational use in selection. The language test, however, has a number of problems and, if it is to be used in selecting workers, should be supplemented with additional information about the language skills of applicants.

DEAN R. MALSBARY, *Professor of Business and Vocational Education, The University of Connecticut, Storrs, Connecticut.*

This battery of seven short tests is designed to measure aptitudes and abilities that are generally considered important to successful performance of tasks commonly performed in the business office.

The test manual is well organized and written. Included are an overview of the tests and their purposes, description of their development, basic statistics and norms for each test, and instructions for administration.

This reviewer was impressed with the care and manner in which the battery was tested for reliability and validity. Reliability was determined by test-retest and split-half techniques. Validity studies, based on employed office personnel, consist of correlations with supervisors' ratings and work performance scores, by types of workers.

The numbers and types of workers tested are somewhat limited. Furthermore, correlation coefficients are not reported for all tests for each worker group. Nonetheless, the tables presenting correlations with supervisors' and work-task ratings and the expectancy tables (guides for making personnel selection decisions based on a weighted combination of predictor tests) should certainly be helpful, particularly to companies attempting to select employees for specific office roles. Such information might also prove of interest to business teachers preparing students for business office employment. Note should also be taken that the correlation coefficients are not high.

In the main, the tests appear to measure what they claim to measure. The instructions to the student are clear and well illustrated through practice examples. Although the tests are short, they are made up of a sufficient number of items to give some indication of the ability of the tested person.

The first part of the arithmetic test (9 minutes) consists of simple basic arithmetic computations and business arithmetic word problems. The type and variety of items are good and the word problems are clearly written.

The business vocabulary test (5 minutes) requires rapid reading, but, unlike most of the other tests in the series, can be completed within the time limit. The items include a considerable number of polysyllabic and infrequently used words, but generally there is good and diversified coverage.

The checking test (5 minutes) is a proofreading test requiring names and numbers to be checked accurately and rapidly against a correct list. Though demanding, the test appears to measure rather well what it claims to measure.

The coding test (5 minutes), in which students are asked to remember or quickly refer to and use simple codes, does seem to measure to some extent ability to adapt to office coding systems.

The directions test (5 minutes) is the most demanding of the series—probably much more demanding than the typical office worker would encounter in any modern office. In this test, the examinee is presented 14 areas of company policy on which rapid notes must be taken for use in responding to items dealing with the company policy. To get a good score, one must

Short Tests of Clerical Ability

listen very carefully, take very rapid notes, or have a very good memory. The test certainly does test those abilities. However, in reality, the office policies of most companies could be read out of or studied from company manuals. Perhaps too much of the success on this test depends upon notetaking or just plain writing speed. Furthermore, five minutes is much too little time to permit the testee to undertake many of the test items.

The filing test (5 minutes), particularly understanding the directions as to how to record responses, might take some getting used to. Nevertheless, the rather ingenious method of response is somewhat realistic in that the testee is required to index new names into an already established list—as would be the case in an office. The test does measure rather well the testee's ability to handle alphabetic filing. However, it does only that; the test does not "test knowledge of standard filing practices" as it claims to do.

In the language test (5 minutes), the examinee must record the number of spelling, grammar, punctuation, or capitalization errors in each sentence. The test items are representative and well written, and they do provide a good measure of ability in these four aspects of English usage.

SUMMARY. In the main, this test series should be useful in determining whether persons tested do possess certain abilities expected of them in the modern office. These tests, however, need revision and updating. Little attention is paid to the area of data processing—an area with which most office workers today have some contact or duties. And changes that have occurred in the office since 1959, the copyright date of the tests, might well influence the usefulness and interpretation of some of the items.

If the tests are to be used, the greatest value might be gained if the nature of the office duties to which the prospective worker would be assigned were first determined; and then only the test or tests most appropriate for obtaining some indication of that worker's ability to perform those duties were administered.

MANUAL DEXTERITY

[1040]

Manipulative Aptitude Test. Grades 9–12 and adults; 1967; MAT; 3 scores: left hand, right hand, total; no adult norms; 1 form; preliminary manual (14 pages); profile-record form (2 pages); $69.50 per set of testing materials including 10 record forms and manual; $6.50 per 25 record forms; $4.50 per manual; 8% extra for postage and handling; 5(7) minutes; Wesley S. Roeder; distributed by Western Psychological Services.*

LYLE F. SCHOENFELDT, *Professor of Management and Psychology, Rensselaer Polytechnic Institute, Troy, New York.*

The author suggests that this test measures eye-hand coordination and manual dexterity in executing prescribed "movements with the hands, arms, and fingers, particularly thrust and twisting movements." The apparatus consists of a rectangular plexiglass board with sockets embedded in four rows, 10 sockets to a row, and a T-bar.

There are two basic tasks. Using only the preferred hand, the examinee is first asked to pick up a rod, screw it into a socket, and then screw a cap onto the rod. The second task involves both hands and requires picking up two washers (one with each hand), slipping them on the T-bar (one on each side) and then doing the same with two nuts—repeating this cycle for 40 seconds.

The sections of the manual involving instructions for administering and scoring the test are clear and succinct. Unfortunately, other information is incomplete, therefore rendering the manual of limited value or worthless. For example, a retest reliability of .92 is given, but such details as the number of examinees and the inter-test interval are not mentioned, thus the coefficient has little meaning.

Two validity coefficients (.48 and .49) are indicated, but again they are meaningless as a result of incomplete information about the studies, such as data on the numbers of people involved and the specific nature of the criterion. A single norms table is provided for the total score as well as the optional left and right hand scores. According to the information provided, the norms are based on "over 4,600 administrations" of the test to high school students "in addition to various industrial groups." The description of this sample is confusing and no industrial norms are provided.

Two additional points: First, manipulative scores are known to improve with practice, and tests frequently allow two or three trials, with only the last being scored. The amount of practice to be allowed is not adequately standardized in the MAT. Second, the rods are threaded at both ends, but the threads allow only a half turn of the rod into the socket or the cap onto the rod. Agressive examinees might start the rod and/or cap out of alignment and damage the threads thus making the task more difficult for subsequent examinees. The threads should be examined from time to time, and damaged rods should be replaced.

Discussion in the manual along with the high school norms suggests that the author views the primary use of the test as a supplement to paper-and-pencil batteries for vocational counseling when differentiation on dexterity is sought. However, the cost of multiple apparatuses for group administration, the impracticality of large scale individual administration, and the limited utility of the information (given the cost) seem to weigh against inclusion of the MAT as a supplement to multiple aptitude batteries. Further, even if motor differentiation were sought, it is not clear that this should be restricted to finger dexterity—it could be argued that multi-limb coordination, reaction time, as well as other motor abilities might be of equal importance.

With regard to pre-employment screening, motor functions tend to have a high degree of specificity. If the job requires the finger movements of picking up, placing, and twisting of small parts (without tools), then the MAT could be useful as a pre-employment screening test. The matching of muscle groups involved in the job and the test is most important, for with the MAT as well as other manipulative tests, one is purchasing an apparatus more than anything else. In this regard the inadequacies of the manual are somewhat characteristic of tests of this type—potential users should plan to standardize pre-measurement practice and to develop job specific norms, reliability, and validity information for the test as used in their situation.

THOMAS A. TYLER, *President, Merit Employment Assessment Services, Inc., Flossmoor, Illinois.*

The primary component of the *Manipulative Aptitude Test* is a plastic board measuring approximately 25 by 30 centimeters. The board contains four rows of 10 embedded metal re-

ceptacles for the small threaded rods which are included with the test. Four shallow cups are arranged across the front of the board. The extreme rear of the board contains a receptacle for a "T-bar." The T-bar has a vertical post approximately five centimeters high and one centimeter in diameter with a horizontal shaft approximately 16 centimeters long and four millimeters in diameter. Those who wish to use this test would be well advised to attach non-slip material to the back of the board, as is recommended in the manual.

Two tasks are associated with performance on this test. The first task requires the subject to use the preferred hand to pick a rod from one of the cups, thread the rod into the board, and complete the assembly with the same preferred hand by threading a cap (acorn nut) on the rod. Time limit for this exercise is three minutes and the score for this part of the test is the total number of rods and caps assembled. The second task requires the subject to use both hands and to slide a washer and a hexagon nut alternately on both horizontal arms of the T-bar. The score for this part of the test is the sum of the number of nuts and washers which are strung on the T-bar. The total manipulative aptitude score is the simple sum of these two performances. The test also provides for left hand only or right hand only assembly of the washers and nuts on the T-bar.

In criticizing the apparatus, the shape of the receptacles on the front of the board may be a critical element. When the number of small nuts is diminished during the T-bar operation to the point where the pieces are one element deep on the bottom of the cup, it becomes nearly impossible to break the pattern to obtain the next nut. Since the number of pieces that are supplied with the board is unspecified, this critical period during the test performance will be achieved at different levels as the small pieces are lost over a period of time. It is recommended that those who wish to use this test carefully control the number of small parts that are provided to the subject. A changing number of pieces of hardware could be expected to affect the norms for the test seriously.

The manual contains several unsupported claims. For example, it suggests that performance on this test also measures an ability to follow verbal instructions. The manual suggests

Manipulative Aptitude Test

that the test would be related to manipulative aptitude and dexterity in as many as 80 courses in technical schools. The manual also mentions that intelligence test data in some cases were obtained in addition to the scores on the test. No such data or correlations are reported.

The administration instructions are well written and easy to follow. Scoring instructions are simple. The score record form is easy to use and contains graphical percentile rank profile scales for the total manipulative score, left hand performance, and right hand performance. Reported reliability by test-retest is .92. Sample size and description for the reliability analysis are not given. Results of two concurrent validity studies, both involving electronics assembly employees, are reported with coefficients of .48 and .49. Both studies used supervisor's ratings as the criterion. Sample size is not given and there is insufficient information to evaluate quality of these two validity studies.

Norms for this test are apparently based on a large sample of high school students. The norms for the single-handed performance of sliding washers and nuts on the horizontal bars are flawed by a lack of consideration of preferred hand; that is to say that the left-hand norms include the scores of right-handed subjects and left-handed subjects. The opposite is true for right-hand norms. For the major score on the test, the justification of summing the three-minute performance on rods and caps with the 40-second performance on washers and nuts with both hands is somewhat puzzling. Test users would prefer separate norms on these two aspects of the test and would also prefer separate norms for the rods and caps portion for left-handed and right-handed subjects by preferred and nonpreferred hand.

The most appealing aspect of this test is the hardware itself. Those who wish to predict performance on the assembly of small parts could modify the instructions to resemble more closely the task under study, collect their own normative data, and produce their own validity studies. These would probably be better than those supplied by the publisher.

Final comment on this apparatus is that no storage equipment is provided for the apparatus. Considering the number of small pieces of hardware, the user must devise something to keep the parts in order. If all parts are not at hand

and in order, no rational interpretation can be made of the test results.

MECHANICAL ABILITY

[1041]

*College Placement Test in Spatial Relations. Entering college freshmen; 1962–75, c1954–75; inactive forms of *College Board Special Aptitude Test in Spatial Relations* available for local administration and scoring; no data on reliability; Forms KPL1 ['62, reprint of 1955 test], KPL2 ['62, reprint of 1954 test] in a single booklet (27 pages); separate answer sheets (Digitek, IBM 805, IBM 1230) must be used; for program accessories, see 474; rental fee, $2 per student; 60(70) minutes; program administered for the College Entrance Examination Board by Educational Testing Service. *

See 6:1084 (4 references); for a review by Robert L. Thorndike of earlier forms, see 4:808. For a review of the CPT program, see 7:665.

[1042]

*Differential Aptitude Tests; Mechanical Reasoning. Grades 8–12 and adults; 1947–75; no reliability data or norms for adults; Form T ('72, 16 pages); no specific manual; battery directions and norms ('73, 66 pages); for additional battery accessories, see 485; separate answer sheets (IBM 805/ Digitek) must be used; directions for use of answer sheets ('73, 4 pages); $5.50 per 25 tests; $3 per 50 answer sheets; 90¢ per scoring stencil; $1 per battery directions and norms (free if requested with tests); $1.50 per specimen set; postage extra; scoring service, 35¢ and over per test; 30(40) minutes; George K. Bennett, Harold G. Seashore, and Alexander G. Wesman; Psychological Corporation. *

See T2:2256 (11 references). For reviews of the complete battery, see 485 (2 reviews, 3 excerpts), 7:673 (1 review, 1 excerpt), 6:767 (2 reviews), 5:605 (2 reviews), 4:711 (3 reviews), and 3:620 (1 excerpt).

REFERENCES

1–11. See T2:2256.
12. SETH, NIRMAL K., AND PRATAP, SWARN. "A Study of the Academic Performance, Intelligence and Aptitude of Engineering Students." *Ed & Psychol R* (India) 11(4):3–10 O '71. * (*PA* 50:3905)
13. CORRELL, LOU PERKINS. *Correlation of Student Attitudes, Mechanical Reasoning, and/or Personality Factors With Performance Ability in Operating Specified Audiovisual Equipment Through Self-Instruction.* Doctor's thesis, East Texas State University (Commerce, Tex.), 1974. (*DAI* 35:4122A)

[1043]

*Differential Aptitude Tests: Space Relations. Grades 8–12 and adults; 1947–75; no reliability data or norms for adults; Form T ('72, 15 pages, identical with 1962 Form M except for item sequence); no specific manual; battery directions and norms ('73, 66 pages); for additional battery accessories, see 485; separate answer sheets (IBM 805/Digitek) must be used; directions for use of answer sheets ('73, 4 pages); $5 per 25 tests; $3 per 50 answer sheets; 90¢ per scoring stencil; $1 per battery directions and norms (free if requested with tests); $1.50 per specimen set; postage extra; scoring service, 35¢ and over per test; 25(35) minutes; George K. Bennett, Harold G. Seashore, and Alexander G. Wesman; Psychological Corporation. *

See T2:2268 (18 references). For reviews of the

Differential Aptitude Tests: Space Relations

complete battery, see 485 (2 reviews, 3 excerpts), 7:673 (1 review, 1 excerpt), 6:767 (2 reviews), 5:605 (2 reviews), 4:711 (3 reviews), and 3:620 (1 excerpt).

REFERENCES

1–18. See T2:2268.
19. SETH, NIRMAL K., AND PRATAP, SWARN. "A Study of the Academic Performance, Intelligence and Aptitude of Engineering Students." *Ed & Psychol R* (India) 11(4):3–10 O '71. * (PA 50:3905)
20. SHERMAN, JULIA A. "Field Articulation, Sex, Spatial Visualization, Dependency, Practice, Laterality of the Brain and Birth Order." *Percept & Motor Skills* 38(3, pt 2):1223–35 Je '74. * (PA 53:247)

[1044]

*Group Test 81. Ages 14 and over; 1949–69; spatial perception; no data on reliability and validity; 1 form ['49, 11 pages]; mimeographed instructions ['69, 3 pages]; £1 per 10 tests; 35p per set of keys, directions, and norms; postpaid within U.K.; specimen set not available; 15(25) minutes; National Institute of Industrial Psychology; NFER Publishing Co. Ltd. [England]. *

See T2:2249 (6 references); for a review by E. G. Chambers, see 4:758 (5 references).

[1045]

★SRA Test of Mechanical Concepts. High school and adults; 1976; 4 scores: mechanical interrelationships, mechanical tools and devices, spatial relations, total; Forms A, B, (21 pages, self-marking); manual (19 pages); tape cassette available for administration; $17.50 per 25 tests; $15 per tape; 80¢ per manual; $2.75 per specimen set; postage extra; (30–40) minutes; Steven J. Stanard and Kathleen Wahl Bode; Science Research Associates, Inc. *

LORRAINE D. EYDE, *Personnel Research Psychologist, Personnel Research and Development Center, U.S. Civil Service Commission, Washington, D. C.*

The manual of the *SRA Test of Mechanical Concepts* states that the untimed test "is appropriate for evaluating individuals for hire, promotion, or training for such jobs as assembler, maintenance mechanic, machinist, and factory production worker," and goes on to state that the test "may also be used [for counseling purposes] to test individuals at all educational levels from junior high school through college." The manual documents national educational norms for 785 high school juniors and seniors and describes, though only briefly, three concurrent criterion-related validity studies involving auto mechanic trainees, maintenance mechanics, and machine operators. The workers, for whom the kind and amount of relevant training and job experience were left unspecified, were tested less than a year before the test manual was published.

An analysis of three studies of race, ethnic, and sex differences showed significant differences for the mechanical interrelationships and

mechanical tools and devices subtests, with white males scoring higher than black and Spanish-American males and higher than a sample of 45 females. Group differences were found on the spatial relations subtest for only one group, and that was the female group who on Form B scored significantly higher than a group of 870 males. In only one study, that of a small sample of 61 black and 55 white maintenance mechanics, were test scores related to supervisory ratings, and significant differences in the validity coefficients for blacks and whites were *not* found.

The test, viewed from the standpoint of test construction, leaves something to be desired. The examples are not always presented in the same format as the questions and contain ambiguities in phrases such as "uneven surface." The examples include a riveting hammer, which may not be familiar to many test users. The instructions in the spatial relations subtest are unrealistic and state, "In your mind, you may have to turn around some of the pieces or turn them over to make a *key figure*." Examinees sometimes sketch in the figures and, since it is often difficult to keep them from doing so, it would be wise to mention sketching as a possible option to the examinee.

The test has a higher verbal loading than is appropriate for persons seeking blue-collar jobs or training. The test items include unnecessary descriptive information. Nearly half of the items in the mechanical tools and devices subtest ask for the name of a tool. Examinees might know how to use a tool but might not know its exact name. Persons about to take this test should review the names of basic tools.

The test manual lacks adequate documentation. For example, the criteria for preparing equivalent forms are not described, and parallel-form reliabilities ranging from .69 to .88 are reported, with the time interval unspecified, on "an industrial population." A job analysis is reported in only one of the three validity studies and even then the worker requirements are stated in general terms such as "knowledge of the basic mechanical components of the equipment or machinery the person works with." In reporting the components of the industrial norms, the test user is informed that 304 of the 510 workers were from manufacturing companies, with no mention made of the kind of company and the job titles of the workers. The validity study involving maintenance mechanics reports that the job ratings were "purified" to reduce halo effect, but the manual does not say how the purifying was done. The standard deviations are missing from the t test tables.

The manual also needs editing. Test users would find it helpful if the table headings would include more information about their contents. The reviewer had to do considerable cross-referencing to identify which one of the validity samples was included in the data presented in the manual's 30 tables.

The most serious problem of all—one no doubt prevalent in the test publishing industry on the whole—is that the authors fail to consider trainability issues. John T. Dailey and Clinton A. Neyman, Jr., in their 1967 final report to the Office of Education, demonstrated that technical vocational talents are trainable. They used curriculum materials and demonstrations presented at a low verbal level, yet appealing to young adults, to train a large sample of eighth and ninth graders (including 504 girls) who were likely to enter a vocational training program. They documented the gains made through their simple training program by analyzing pre- and post-testing results, and comparing these to gains made each year in a project talent longitudinal study. The greatest gains were on measures of mechanical reasoning, visualization in two dimensions, and mechanics information, with the girls in general showing greater gains than the boys. Further research is needed to assess the impact of such training on job performance. Dailey and Neyman conclude that if culturally disadvantaged groups—in this case, women are among the disadvantaged—were trained on vocational talents, many more of these persons could qualify for military, governmental, or industrial training programs where selection is based on aptitude tests. Their training materials are now in use in a nationwide apprenticeship program run by the United Auto Workers.

In short, the authors would have been well advised to list their manual as a preliminary one or, better yet, to have taken the necessary time to better document their norms and their reliability and validity studies. There is a big gap between proposed uses of the tests and the evidence of its validity. Test users should carefully consider well-documented tests such as the *Bennett Mechanical Comprehension Test* and the *Revised Minnesota Paper Form Board Test* before adopting a relatively untested product such as the *SRA Test of Mechanical Concepts*.

LYLE F. SCHOENFELDT, *Professor of Management and Psychology, Rensselaer Polytechnic Institute, Troy, New York.*

The new *SRA Test of Mechanical Concepts* is designed to "measure....an individual's knowledge of common mechanical tools and devices" as well as his/her "ability to visualize and understand basic mechanical and spatial interrelationships." The test is available in two equivalent forms, each divided into three sections: (a) Mechanical Interrelationships, more commonly known as mechanical reasoning; (b) Mechanical Tools and Devices, most similar to what is commonly called a tool recognition test; and (c) Spatial Relations, a test of visualization in two dimensions.

The most elemental examination of a test is in terms of the quality of the items. Items were written by three consultants, and were reviewed by SRA's development staff and a fourth consultant. To be included in the test, "each item had to discriminate between high and low scores on the test [i.e., have a positive item-total correlation] and had to be of the proper level of difficulty."

Although the manual includes 30 tables, no information has been provided concerning the degree to which these item-selection criteria were met. Yet, many of the items are difficult in that they call for specialized knowledge, formulas from high school physics, and the like. The item difficulty is most apparent on Spatial Relations—the first items are easy, but subsequent items rapidly increase in difficulty, the result being that it is not unusual to find 10 percent, 20 percent, or, in one instance, 30 percent of the norm group examinees at or below the chance level on this subtest. With so much chance operating, it is hard to see that those responding "correctly" to several of these items would score higher on the test than those responding incorrectly. Thus, although the procedures for the screening of items seem reasonable, observations regarding the final products, the items, are seemingly at odds with the procedures followed.

SRA Test of Mechanical Concepts

One problem with the desire to test examinees on specialized knowledge is that the SRA staff and the independent consultant responsible for checking items may not have had the expertise to recognize a technically *incorrect* item. As an example, item 11 in the mechanical interrelationships section of Form A asks which of four projectiles will be in the air the longest, given certain assumptions. The correct answer is not the answer keyed as correct by the author and publisher. Further, it is possible for such items to pass the item analytic screen if the incorrect alternative keyed as correct is a popular response or if the item is difficult. The point is, there could be other such items—SRA should immediately have all items from both forms checked for technical correctness.

All items involve drawings, and these are of generally good quality with the usual amount of first edition oversights. Most of the deficiencies in the drawings will have only minimal bearing on the substance of the items. Some of the items are tricky, i.e., they require the noticing of small details unlikely to be seen by most examinees, even those knowledgeable in the area involved. As an example, for examinees knowing the principle involved, finding the correct answer to one item hinges on a decision as to which of four different shapes has the largest volume. The volume of the correct answer is only .03 cubic inches greater than the most attractive incorrect answer, a distinction that is likely to be difficult for the average examinee.

The subtest and total score reliabilities are in the high .80s, indicating that the consistency of measurement is acceptable. The parallel-form reliabilities are a little lower (between .69 and .88), but again are acceptable. No evidence is presented to indicate that the constructs intended are those actually being measured, although a check with the publisher revealed that the subtests are remarkably independent, with the subtest intercorrelations ranging between .28 and .33. This would suggest that the information contributed by each subtest to the total score is largely unique, and that the subtest overlap is less than is typical for paper-and-pencil subscales from the same form.

Normative data based on over 400 industrial and over 700 educational examinees are presented in 13 tables. Data are broken down by region, race, and sex as appropriate.

Results from three criterion validation studies are also presented in the manual, two based on job performance and the third based on training success. In all, 44 validity coefficients are presented, with 32 being in the .20s or .30s and the remaining 12 equally divided between the .40s and teens. Taken together they indicate that criterion-related validity is at the usual low-to-moderate levels for tests of this type, with the higher values resulting from correlating the SRA test with other paper-and-pencil measures, such as tests of training achievement. The subtest least likely to be valid is spatial relations.

Despite the prominence of the *Bennett Mechanical Comprehension Test* as a test of mechanical aptitude, no comparison data are given in the SRA manual. On the basis of examination of item content, the Bennett most closely resembles the mechanical interrelationships section of the SRA test, and bears least resemblance to the spatial relations subtest. However, even in comparison to the mechanical interrelationships section, the dissimilarity of the Bennett is as notable as its similarity. The SRA approach to mechanical aptitude seems more eclectic in that it involves specific formulas, plane geometry, general science information, etc., in addition to mechanical interrelationships, which is the major underlying construct of the Bennett. Both tests would be rated as convenient to use, although the Bennett would have a decided edge in terms of support research.

Any use of the *SRA Test of Mechanical Concepts* should best wait until the technical correctness has been checked by outside experts and appropriate revisions are implemented. Assuming the revised forms are of equivalent psychometric soundness, the test probably makes most sense as a "mini" aptitude battery for research or vocational counseling when differentiation of specific components of mechanical aptitude is sought. Employee selection is a more complicated business today than in former days, and it is not clear how the test would fit into this market, although it is probably the major application envisioned by the publisher. Current government and professional guidelines include caveats against making employment decisions on the basis of measures which are

SRA Test of Mechanical Concepts

normally learned in a brief orientation period. The tool recognition subtest might be hard to defend in this regard. On the basis of both content considerations and published validation data, the spatial relations subtest is likely to produce the weakest validities and thereby be the least useful of the subtests. The mechanical interrelationships test is likely to be most valuable, but for jobs that require the ability to understand mechanical concepts, the Bennett is an alternative that is probably: (a) more economical in terms of applicant time and effort; (b) more directly centered on the construct involved, i.e., a purer measure of mechanical ability; and (c) more thoroughly researched.

[1046]

★Shapes Analysis Test. Ages 14 and over; 1972; SAT; spatial perception; 3 scores: 2-dimensional, 3-dimensional, total; 1 form (15 pages); manual (20 pages); separate self-marking answer sheets must be used; £6.50 per 25 tests; £5.50 per 50 answer sheets; £1.75 per manual; £2.25 per specimen set; postage extra; 25(35) minutes; A. W. Heim, K. P. Watts, and V. Simmonds; Test Agency [England]. *

REFERENCES

1. HEIM, A. W., AND WATTS, K. P. "Contributions to Intelligence Testing and the Theory of Intelligence: V, An Experiment on Practice, Coaching and Discussion of Errors in Mental Testing." *Brit J Ed Psychol* 27:199–210 N '57. *
2. HEIM, A. W., AND SIMMONDS, V. "The Shapes Analysis, A Test of Spatial Perception." *Percept & Motor Skills* 20:158 F '65. * (*PA* 39:10073)

CHARLES T. MYERS, *Administrative Associate, Educational Testing Service, Princeton, New Jersey.*

This test was designed to be difficult and, from an examination of the test as well as from the norms data, it appears that the designers have achieved that aim. It contains 36 items to be given in a time limit of 25 minutes, and the manual states that people very rarely finish in the time limit. Six different item forms are used, but the test does appear to be factorially homogeneous; that is, probably all of the items would correlate highly with the total test score. However, there still may be several different ability factors in the test—a spatial factor, of course, but also a speed factor and a factor related to the ability to judge accurately the lengths of lines. It has been shown that judgments regarding shape and judgments regarding size depend on different abilities. How many factors contribute to total score variance is hard to determine and whether all the factors are valid for the purposes for which this test may be used is also hard to determine; but any-

one who takes this test would not doubt that it measures some kind of spatial ability.

The directions in the manual for administering the test are excellent and the 12 sample items provide an excellent introduction to the test. The print is clear and the items are well drawn. The items present a good variety of problems and cover a wide range of difficulty.

This test provides two subscores, a score for two-dimensional items and a score for three-dimensional items. It is clear that this distinction between two- and three-dimensional items is important to the test maker, but the reason for this distinction is never given in the manual. No interpretation is offered for the separate use of the two subscores. No evidence is offered to show that the two scores have different meanings. In fact, the correlations for various samples between these two scores are close to their reliabilities; e.g., .57 compared to .61. Strangely, all the so-called three-dimensional items may be solved without any consideration of the third dimension represented in the drawings, which are all, of course, two-dimensional drawings of flat three-dimensional objects something like pieces of a thick jigsaw puzzle. This is a disconcerting affair. One must assume that the test authors had some reason for providing the two subscores, but the reason remains a complete mystery and leaves one wondering how much to trust the authors' judgment.

This problem is compounded by the brevity of the manual. It seems to be a British custom with respect to test manuals to provide a list of references instead of providing extensive interpretive materials. This manual provides a list of 14 references, all of which were written before this test was published. It is hard to tell how relevant these references are for this particular test. It seems to be easy to overgeneralize about tests that are as generally unfamiliar as spatial ability tests are.

A number of different psychologists have done studies and written articles to describe what it is that spatial tests measure. In this reviewer's judgment there is not yet a usable consensus. Spatial ability cannot yet be better defined than by saying it is what spatial tests measure. This is even less satisfactory than the similar definition of intelligence. For a number of spatial tests a good deal of the variance does not seem to be related to anything but the variance in other spatial tests; but on the other hand, some spatial tests have had high correlations with socially significant criteria such as graduation versus nongraduation from engineering school. In this situation one must depend considerably on the intuition of the test maker. In this reviewer's judgment, the maker of this test has done a fine job.

Norms data for this test are in terms of British grammar school and university students. Data are given separately for boys and for girls and the usual sex difference for spatial tests is shown, with boys scoring higher than girls. Mean scores for 17 different faculties of university students are given, ranging from 15.9 for 34 zoology students to 20.8 for 142 mechanical engineering students. Test-retest reliabilities for three groups, with intervals between testing of from one to six weeks, range from .61 to .77.

Very little information is given in terms of correlations for concurrent or predictive validity. This reviewer would like to write favorably about this test because it made a very favorable impression; but in spite of, or perhaps because of, his many years of working with spatial tests he is skeptical of impressions.

[1047]

★Weber Advanced Spatial Perception Test. Ages 13–17; 1976, c1968–76; WASP; 5 scores: form recognition, pattern perception, shape analysis, reflected figures, total; no data on validity; 1 form consists of 2 parts: form recognition test booklet ('76, 10 pages, reusable) and "answer booklet" ('76, 21 pages, consumable) containing other 3 subtests and answer sheet for form recognition; manual ('68, 60 pages); not available for use in New South Wales; Aus 50¢ per form recognition test; 50¢ per "answer booklet"; $3.30 per set of scoring stencils; $3.30 per manual; $7.60 per specimen set; postpaid within Australia; 24(45) minutes; P. G. Weber: Australian Council for Educational Research [Australia]. *

MISCELLANEOUS

[1048]

★Group Encounter Survey. Group members; 1963–73; GES; feelings and behavior of individuals as members of task groups; 5 scores (individual attitudes, leadership preferences, conflict resolution, intergroup relations, total) for each of 5 group membership styles; 1 form ('73, 13 pages); no manual; score interpretation ('73, 11 pages); $3 per test, postage extra; statistical data free on request; [15–30] minutes; Jay Hall and Martha S. Williams; Teleometrics Int'l. *

REFERENCES

1. HALL, JAY, AND WILLIAMS, MARTHA S. "Personality and Group Encounter Style: A Multivariate Analysis of Traits and Preferences." J Pers & Social Psychol 18(2):163–72 My '71. * (PA 46:4952)

Shapes Analysis Test

2. NUTT, ANDREW TODD. *Decision Behavior of Group Members as a Factor in Group Performance Accountability*. Doctor's thesis, University of Texas (Austin, Texas), 1974. (DAI 35: 2596A)

[1049]

★Job Attitude Scale. Adults; 1971; JAS; intrinsic and extrinsic factors in job satisfaction and motivation; 17 scores: praise and recognition, growth in skill, creative work, responsibility, advancement, achievement, salary, security, personnel policies, competent supervision, relations-peers, relations-subordinates, relations-supervisor, working conditions, status, family needs, general intrinsic; data on reliability for general intrinsic score only; 1 form (5 pages); an abbreviated edition for obtaining only the general intrinsic score is available; manual (59 pages); separate answer sheets must be used; $15 per 100 tests; $5 per 100 answer sheets; $5 per manual and set of keys; $5 per specimen set; postage extra; [20] minutes; Shoukry D. Saleh; the Author [Canada].*

REFERENCES

1. SALEH, SHOUKRY D., AND OTIS, JAY L. "Sources of Job Satisfaction and Their Effects on Attitudes Toward Retirement." J Indus Psychol 1:101–6 D '63. * (PA 39:16570)
2. SALEH, SHOUKRY D. "A Study of Attitude Change in the Preretirement Period." J Appl Psychol 48:310–2 O '64. * (PA 39:6102)
3. SALEH, S. D., AND GRYGIER, T. G. "Psychodynamics of Intrinsic and Extrinsic Job Orientation." J Appl Psychol 53(6): 446–50 D '69. * (PA 44:5764)
4. SALEH, SHOUKRY D., AND LALLJEE, MANSUR. "Sex and Job Orientations." Personnel Psychol 22(4):465–71 w '69. * (PA 44:13496)
5. SALEH, SHOUKRY D. "Anxiety as a Function of Intrinsic-Extrinsic Job Orientation, the Presence or Absence of Observers, and Task Difficulty." J Appl Psychol 55(6):543–8 D '72. * (PA 47:9911)
6. SALEH, SHOUKRY D., AND BROWN, MARVIN. "Effects of Intrinsic vs. Extrinsic Job Orientation and Reported Anxiety Under Different Task Conditions." Can J Behav Sci 4(1):43–9 Ja '72. * (PA 48:2161)
7. GILMOUR-BARRETT, KAREN C. Managerial Systems and Interpersonal Treatment Processes in Residential Centres for Disturbed Youth. Doctor's thesis, University of Waterloo (Waterloo, Ont., Canada), 1974. (DAI 35:2428B)
8. SALEH, S. D., AND PASRICHA, V. "Job Orientation and Work Behavior." Acad Mgmt J 18(3):638–45 S '75. *
9. SALEH, S. D.; TOYE, J. R.; AND SIEVERT, H. A. "Occupational Values, Environments, and Levels." J Voc Behav 6(2): 235–43 Ap '75. * (PA 54:2074)

[1050]

*Minnesota Importance Questionnaire, 1975 Revision. Vocational counselees; 1967–75; MIQ; intrapersonal vocational needs of an individual for specified job-related reinforcers; 21 or 22 scores (20 of which parallel scores of *Minnesota Job Description Questionnaire* and *Minnesota Satisfaction Questionnaire*): ability utilization, achievement, activity, advancement, authority, company policies and practices, compensation, co-workers, creativity, independence, moral values, recognition, responsibility, security, social service, social status, supervision—human relations, supervision—technical, variety, working conditions, autonomy (ranked form only), validity; reliability data consists of lowest, highest, and median coefficients across 20 scales; no data on reliability of autonomy and validity scales; 2 forms: ranked form ('75, 10 pages), paired form ('75, 19 pages, identical with test copyrighted 1967); manual ('71, 93 pages); separate answer sheets must be used; 35¢ per test ($3.50 minimum); 5¢ per answer sheet ($2.50 minimum); postage extra; manual free with order; specimen set of sample pages free; scoring service, $1.10 and over per test; Spanish edition available; (15–25) minutes for ranked form, (30–40) minutes for paired form; David J. Weiss, René V. Dawis, Lloyd H. Lofquist, Evan G.

Gay, and Darwin D. Hendel (manual); Vocational Psychology Research. *
  See T2:2283 (8 references) and 7:1063 (29 references).

REFERENCES

1–29. See 7:1063.
30–37. See T2:2283; also includes a cumulative name index to the first 37 references for this test.
38. BITTER, JAMES A.; RAY, CHARLES C.; KUNCE, JOSEPH T.; LAWVER, DALE L.; AND MILLER, DOUGLAS E. "Vocational Values and Employment Outcomes of the Disadvantaged." *J Employ Counsel* 9(1):34–40 Mr '72. *
39. BUCHANAN, JOHN CLAYTON. *The Relationship Between Vocational Need and Ability Types.* Doctor's thesis, University of Minnesota (Minneapolis, Minn.), 1972. (*DAI* 33:4990B)
40. FITZGERALD, SHEILA MARY. *A Career Development Study of Elementary School Teachers.* Doctor's thesis, University of Minnesota (Minneapolis, Minn.), 1972. (*DAI* 33:3452A)
41. LAWLIS, G. FRANK, AND ANDERSON, ROBERT P. "MMPI Personality Factors as Predictors of Vocational Needs Assessed by Minnesota Importance Questionnaire." *Psychol Rep* 31(3):859–65 D '72. * (*PA* 50:1531)
42. PUCEL, DAVID J.; NELSON, HOWARD F.; HEITZMAN, DARRELL; AND WHEELER, DAVID N. "Vocational Maturity and Vocational Training." *J Indus Teach Ed* 9(3):30–8 Sp '72. *
43. SALOMONE, PAUL R., AND MUTHARD, JOHN E. "Canonical Correlation of Vocational Needs and Vocational Style." *J Voc Behav* 2(2):163–71 Ap '72. * (*PA* 48:12343)
44. SETNE, VERLIS LOUISE. *Rehabilitation Counselor Variables in Initial Interview and Assessment of Client Vocational Needs.* Doctor's thesis, Texas Tech University (Lubbock, Tex.), 1972. (*DAI* 33:3922B)
45. STEGER, JOSEPH MICHAEL. *Prediction of the Stability of Vocational Needs in Adult Males: A Methodological Study.* Doctor's thesis, University of Minnesota (Minneapolis, Minn.), 1972. (*DAI* 33:5558B)
46. WHELAN, ROBERT M. *The Effects of Part-Time Employment Upon the Vocational Need Patterns of Students Enrolled in Occupational Business Education Programs.* Doctor's thesis, State University of New York (Buffalo, N.Y.), 1972. (*DAI* 33:1089A)
47. WILLOUGHBY, THEODORE C. "Are Programmers Paranoid?" *Proc Ann Computer Personnel Res Conf* 10:47–54 '72. *
48. BARNETTE, W. LESLIE, JR.; D'COSTA, AYRES; HARMON, LENORE W.; SUPER, DONALD E.; WEISS, DAVID J.; AND ZYTOWSKI, DONALD G. Chap. 9, "Illustrative Interpretations of Inventories," pp. 206–44. In *Contemporary Approaches to Interest Measurement.* Edited by Donald G. Zytowski. Minneapolis, Minn.: University of Minnesota Press, 1973. Pp. xi, 251. *
49. BOGDAN, ARTHUR RICHARD. *Relationships Among Vocational Interests, Personal Needs, and Personality Characteristics.* Doctor's thesis, Rutgers—The State University (New Brunswick, N.J.), 1973. (*DAI* 34:3860A)
50. BURNICKAS, ALFRED ALPHONSE. *A Study of the Relationship Between Selected Personal Variables and the Vocational Need Profiles of a Sample of School and College Counselors.* Doctor's thesis, American University (Washington, D.C.), 1973. (*DAI* 34:3053A)
51. DUNN, DENNIS J., AND ALLEN, THOMAS. "Vocational Needs and Occupational Reinforcers of Vocational Evaluators." *Voc Eval & Work Adj B* 6(4):22–8 D '73. * (*PA* 52:8775)
52. FAUROT, LYLE MARTIN. *An Investigation of the Validity of Vocational Student Grades as a Criterion of Vocational Student Success and the Predictability of Vocational Student Grades Using Standardized Test Instruments.* Doctor's thesis, University of Minnesota (Minneapolis, Minn.), 1973. (*DAI* 34:676A)
53. LANEY, JOHN CLEMENS. *Vocational Needs of the Mexican American in South Texas.* Doctor's thesis, Texas Tech University (Lubbock, Tex.), 1973. (*DAI* 34:4668B)
54. MUNCRIEF, MARTHA CRAWFORD. *Work Adjustment of Vocational Education Teachers.* Doctor's thesis, Ohio State University (Columbus, Ohio), 1973. (*DAI* 34:2475A)
55. RICHARDSON, BILL K., AND OBERMANN, C. ESCO. "Relationship of Rehabilitation Counselor Characteristics to Supervisors' Ratings." *Counselor Ed & Sup* 13(2):94–104 D '73. * (*PA* 52:3082)
56. RIFKIND, LESLIE J. "Minnesota Importance Questionnaire," pp. 165–9. In *Measuring Human Behavior.* Edited by Dale G. Lake and others. New York: Teachers College Press, 1973. Pp. xviii, 422. *
57. SEILER, DALE A., AND LACEY, DAVID W. "Adapting the Work Adjustment Theory for Assessing Technical-Professional Utilization." *J Voc Behav* 3(4):443–51 O '73. * (*PA* 52:2005)
58. WEISS, DAVID J. Chap. 6, "The Minnesota Importance Questionnaire," pp. 136–70. In *Contemporary Approaches to Interest Measurement.* Edited by Donald G. Zytowski. Minneapolis, Minn.: University of Minnesota Press, 1973. Pp. xi, 251. *
59. ZYTOWSKI, DONALD G. Chap. 1, "Considerations in the Selection and Use of Interest Inventories," pp. 3–19. In his *Contemporary Approaches to Interest Measurement.* Minneapolis, Minn.: University of Minnesota Press, 1973. Pp. xi, 251. *
60. CORY, EDWARD DANA. *Job Satisfaction and Vocational Needs of Pennsylvania Vocational Teachers.* Doctor's thesis, Pennsylvania State University (University Park, Pa.), 1974. (*DAI* 35:1562A)
61. GRAY, BONNIE LEE. *A Longitudinal Study of Extracurricular Activities, Vocational Needs, and Individual Vocational Need Stability During Adolescence.* Doctor's thesis, University of Minnesota (Minneapolis, Minn.), 1974. (*DAI* 35:5082B)
62. McGRAW, MICHAEL JOHN. *Counselor Perception of the Vocational Needs of Welfare Recipients.* Doctor's thesis, University of Northern Colorado (Greeley, Colo.), 1974. (*DAI* 35:2692A)
63. McGRAW, MICHAEL J., AND BITTER, JAMES A. "Counselor Perception of Client Vocational Needs." *Rehab Counsel B* 18(2):83–9 D '74. *
64. McMILLAN, FLOYD WAYNE. *Psychological Variables Related to Effective Supervision in Health Care Agencies.* Doctor's thesis, Texas Tech University (Lubbock, Tex.), 1974. (*DAI* 35:6078B)
65. MOLINE, JOHN GILBERT. *Examination of Multivariate Relationships of Work-Value-Needs With Reported Antecedent Determinants and Concomitant Correlates.* Doctor's thesis, University of Connecticut (Storrs, Conn.), 1974. (*DAI* 35:7064A)
66. NOVAK, KATHLEEN DOBOSENSKI. *Preferred Job Reinforcers and the Job Satisfaction of Faculty in Minnesota's Area Vocational Technical Institutes.* Doctor's thesis, University of Minnesota (Minneapolis, Minn.), 1974. (*DAI* 35:7799A)
67. OLSON, HELEN LUCILE THOMAS. *The Relationship Between Needs-Reinforcer Correspondence and Job Satisfaction of Minnesota Secondary School Office Education Teacher Coordinators.* Doctor's thesis, University of Minnesota (Minneapolis, Minn.), 1974. (*DAI* 35:7599A)
68. PORRITT, D. "Applying a Model of Work Adjustment." *Austral Psychologist* 9(2):165–73 Jl '74. *
69. STULMAN, DAVID ALAN. *Experimental Validation of the Independence and Creativity Scales of the Minnesota Importance Questionnaire.* Doctor's thesis, University of Minnesota (Minneapolis, Minn.), 1974. (*DAI* 35:3075B)
70. D'ELIA, GEORGE PATRICK MICHAEL. *The Adjustment of Library School Graduates to the Job Environments of Librarianship: A Test of the Need Gratification and Expectation Fulfillment Theories of Job Satisfaction.* Doctor's thesis, Rutgers—The State University (New Brunswick, N.J.), 1975. (*DAI* 36:585A)
71. JENSON, GUST, III. *An Application of a Theory of Work Adjustment to Selection for Graduate Training in School Psychology.* Doctor's thesis, University of Minnesota (Minneapolis, Minn.), 1975. (*DAI* 37:440B)
72. LOFQUIST, LLOYD H., AND DAWIS, RENÉ V.; WITH THE ASSISTANCE OF DAVID J. WEISS. *Manual for the Counseling Use of the Minnesota Importance Questionnaire.* Minneapolis, Minn.: Vocational Psychology Research, Department of Psychology, University of Minnesota, 1975. Pp. v, 28. *
73. MERESMAN, JOEL FRANK. *Biographical Correlates of Vocational Needs.* Doctor's thesis, University of Minnesota (Minneapolis, Minn.), 1975. (*DAI* 36:3579B)
74. STULMAN, DAVID A., AND DAWIS, RENÉ V. "Experimental Validation of Two MIQ Scales." *J Voc Behav* 9(2):161–7 O '76. *
75. ELIZUR, DOV, AND TZINER, AHARON. "Vocational Needs, Job Rewards, and Satisfaction: A Canonical Analysis." *Voc Behav* 10(2):205–11 Ap '77. *
76. HENDEL, DARWIN D. "Behavioral Validation of a Vocational Needs Scale." *Appl Psychol Meas* 1(2):307–8 sp '77. *
77. TINSLEY, HOWARD E. A., AND TINSLEY, DIANE J. "Different Needs, Interests, and Abilities of Effective and Ineffective Counselor Trainees: Implications for Counselor Selection." *J Counsel Psychol* 24(1):83–6 Ja '77. *

LEWIS E. ALBRIGHT, *Director, Training and Development, Kaiser Aluminum and Chemical Corporation, Oakland, California.*

The *Minnesota Importance Questionnaire* was developed to measure vocational needs. "Needs" are defined as preferences for various reinforcers (conditions in which activity results in satisfaction) available in the work environment. The need statements comprising the questionnaire are based on earlier studies of job satisfaction. The 20 needs included may not be all-encompassing, but they should suffice for most situations. Item wording in the 1975 revision has been brought up to date by eliminating earlier male-oriented terminology; e.g., "My boss would train his men well" has been replaced by "My boss would train the workers well."

Some other items could also benefit from further rewording. For example, the statement representing the authority need, "I could tell people what to do," reflects a limited, rather quaint view of the concept of authority as it functions in most organizations. Not surprisingly, this need has a very low average rate of endorsement. The authors might consider equating their items for social desirability to minimize this problem.

The MIQ is one of the tools developed as part of the Minnesota Work Adjustment Project. The conceptual framework underlying this project is termed the Theory of Work Adjustment. In brief, this theory states that work adjustment can be predicted from the correspondence between an individual's work personality and the work environment; vocational needs, along with vocational abilities, constitute the major aspects of work personality. Ability requirements and the reinforcers present in jobs are identified as the significant aspects of the work environment. Thus, how well an individual's abilities correspond to the ability requirements of the job will predict the "satisfactoriness" of the worker, and how well the individual's needs correspond to the available reinforcers will predict job satisfaction.

Two forms of the MIQ are available in the 1975 edition. One is a paired-comparison format in which the subject is asked to consider each pair of the 20 needs and mark which need statement in the pair is more important in his/her ideal job ("the kind of job you would most like to have"). There are 190 paired items in this version, the complete pairing of all 20 statements being used. Many users evidently objected to the repetitiveness of the item pairings in this format and to the effort and time required for completion. Therefore, the authors have developed a ranked form. In this version, the statements are presented in blocks of five. The subject's task is to rank each set of five statements in terms of their importance in an

ideal job. In this format, there are only 105 required responses.

Both forms include a section in which the subject is asked to consider each of the 20 need statements one at a time and to check whether or not the item is important to have in an ideal job. These absolute judgments are used to determine a zero point for each subject to anchor the comparative judgments from the 20 need scales. Scoring of both forms is normally done by computer at the University of Minnesota, hand scoring being extremely laborious and prone to clerical error.

A research report accompanying the MIQ indicates that the two forms are similar in terms of their psychometric properties and that they yield generally similar results. The findings also indicate that the ranked form is preferred by two-thirds of the subjects, primarily because it is less repetitive and boring than the paired-comparison version.

One difference in the two forms, however, is that the ranked version requires the addition of a 21st need dimension in order to convert the ranked responses from the blocks of five statements to a complete set of paired-comparison responses. This new dimension (autonomy) is not scored, however, in order to make the two forms comparable. This discrepancy in item content raises a question as to why the authors elected to utilize a ranking method to shorten their questionnaire when there are partial pairing techniques which would have accomplished the same result.

For both versions, the user receives a computer generated report of the results containing the individual's profile of needs along with various interpretive information. The first score presented is a validity check based on the number of illogical comparisons (called circular triads); validity scores above a certain level indicate that random responding, or carelessness, fatigue, etc., on the part of the subject have rendered the profile invalid and no further analysis is performed. For the valid profiles, a comparison is made with patterns of reinforcers which have been determined for some 148 different occupations and a listing is provided of the 50 most similar and the 50 most dissimilar occupations. Presumably, the individual will be most satisfied in those occupations with

Minnesota Importance Questionnaire

reinforcer patterns most similar to his/her need patterns.

The counselor may also interpret the MIQ results in terms of clusters of occupations which have similar reinforcer patterns. Twelve such clusters have been identified. Cluster 1, for example, is named Social Service-Security since these are the important reinforcers for occupations in this cluster, e.g., janitor, hotel clerk, typist. Cluster 12 is titled Achievement-Autonomy-Social Service-Recognition-Variety and consists primarily of higher level professional occupations.

Regarding the reliability and validity of the MIQ, the manual presents considerable data, all based on the 1967 or earlier versions. The median internal consistency coefficients reported for all 20 scales with nine different groups of subjects range from .77 to .81, with a range of .30 to .95 for the individual scale scores. Test-retest reliability for the scale scores ranged from .19 (for a nine-month interval) to .93 (for an immediate retest), with median coefficients ranging from .48 to .89. The median stability coefficients of the MIQ profiles, rather than the scale scores themselves, are higher, ranging from .70 for a four-month interval to .95 for the immediate retest. Scale intercorrelations range from .05 to .77, with a median of .33. On balance, these findings suggest that the instrument has satisfactory internal consistency and stability, particularly the stability of the profiles, and an acceptable degree of scale independence.

The validity evidence is less satisfying, although that which is presented is suggestive that the MIQ functions in the way it was intended. Among other findings, concurrent validity studies are reported which indicate that four different occupational groups have MIQ profiles which tend to correspond to their occupational reinforcer patterns, the rank-order correlation coefficients ranging from .48 to .60. Convergent and discriminant validity were investigated by correlating the MIQ with the SVIB and GATB, respectively. The results, as would be expected, confirm that the MIQ resembles the SVIB more in what it measures than it does the GATB. Although other indications of validity are presented, there are, unfortunately, as yet no predictive validity studies which would answer the question of whether people who have been predicted to find satisfaction in certain occupations by the MIQ actually achieve a higher degree of satisfaction than if they had entered some other occupation.

In conclusion, the MIQ appears to be a potentially useful measure of vocational needs which is a product of extensive and ongoing research at the University of Minnesota. Although the MIQ is simple to use in terms of its ease of administration and readability (5th-grade difficulty level), it requires considerable understanding on the part of the counselor to interpret the results in relation to the underlying theory and other relevant vocational and technical information. As a suggestion, the authors could assist future users in this regard by developing a counselor's handbook in order to update and bring together the relevant materials now scattered throughout the various manuals, monographs, and research reports which accompany the MIQ.

Probably the best use of the MIQ at present is in university counseling centers or other vocational guidance facilities which employ highly experienced and well qualified personnel. The MIQ does not appear to be appropriate for use within most employee career planning programs, as these are now constituted in many organizations, unless counselors receive special training in use of the instrument.

SHELDON ZEDECK, *Associate Professor of Psychology, University of California, Berkeley, California.*

The MIQ assesses the worker's preferences for 20 specific job-related reinforcers or vocational needs. There are 210 items, 190 of which are in a paired comparison format in which each need dimension, represented by one item, is compared with all other need dimensions. The remaining 20 items require absolute judgments of the importance of each need dimension. All items are responded to in terms of the "ideal" jobs. The reading difficulty level is equivalent to the fifth grade.

The MIQ yields 20 adjusted scale scores (meaningful zero point and a "+" or "−" sign indicative of "important" or "not important," respectively), a total circular triad (TCT) score (an index of the extent of random guessing and other forms of invalid responding to the MIQ), and error bands (the extent of the limits to which the adjusted scale values

Minnesota Importance Questionnaire

could change if responses were perfectly consistent).

The Work Adjustment Project provides a computer scoring service which produces a three-page printout containing an analysis of TCT, adjusted scale values for the dimensions, and a measure of the correspondence between MIQ scores and occupational reinforcer patterns.

Conceptually, the MIQ is "on target" in measuring needs or preferences. The MIQ provides a within-person type of analysis which permits interpretation of the worker's importance of each need relative to his/her *own* other needs. This is in contrast to the more frequent, but less appropriate, strategy of normative assessments in which one worker's needs are compared to *other* workers' needs.

Psychometrically, the MIQ is a relatively well-developed, sound measurement instrument. Reliability is assessed in several manners. First, the median Hoyt reliability coefficients for nine different subgroups range from .77 to .81, thus indicating internal consistency. Second, the median stability coefficients of MIQ dimension scores for nine different test-retest intervals range from .48 (six-month interval) to .89 (immediate retesting). Third, median stability coefficients for profiles of dimension scores range from .70 (four-month interval) to .95 (immediate retesting).

The approaches to the assessment of validity are not as impressive as the means by which reliability was assessed, though the obtained validity data are adequate. Three strategies are reported. First, evidence for discriminant validity is based on the *lack* of relationship between the MIQ and the multifactor abilities of the *General Aptitude Test Battery* whereas evidence for convergent validity is based on canonical correlations of .78 and .74, for two groups, between the MIQ and the *Strong Vocational Interest Blank*. The second and third strategies for determining validity are based on pre-1967 forms and the 1967 edition, respectively. Both strategies involve validation by confirmation of expected group differences and hypotheses generated from the theory. Since the pre-1967 forms either required a Likert-type response or were from a form with twice as many items, the value of the validity evidence is minimized, though the results per se

are adequate. For the 1967 edition, an example of expected differences in needs was that found between experienced and nonexperienced workers.

Future validity research should (*a*) focus on predictive validity, (*b*) emphasize multivariate strategies of data analysis, and (*c*) examine relationships betwen the MIQ and other measures of ability, interest, or constructs suggested by the theory. Of particular necessity is research on the relationship between the MIQ and measures of satisfaction. A paragraph in the manual is devoted to one study (*20*) which tested one basic proposition of the theory that satisfaction (which in this study was measured by another product of the project) is a function of the correspondence between the reinforcer system of the work environment and the worker's needs. For two of three groups, data supported the proposition. Future studies should use satisfaction measures developed independently of the project.

The soundness of the MIQ is also evidenced by the dimension intercorrelations (median, .33) and factor composition. Results for the latter indicate common factor structures for three groups of subjects—vocational rehabilitation clients, employed workers, and college students.

The manual is deficient with regard to the use of the MIQ. About one page is devoted to the "Vocational Counseling Use of the MIQ"; it is suggested that the vocational rehabilitation counselor can help the counselee look at jobs in terms of the correspondence of the job's reinforcer systems to the counselee's vocational needs. Scores can now predict how satisfied the counselee will be in 148 occupations (*72*). Two figures in the manual present fictitious printouts of the kind of information available to a counselor. One shows that a counselee will be "satisfied" and "likely satisfied" in 2 and 79 occupations, respectively; the other shows that a counselee will be "satisfied," "likely satisfied," and "not likely satisfied" in 9, 70, and 2 occupations, respectively.

The discrimination among occupations in terms of "likely satisfaction" is so minimal that the usefulness to the counselee is questioned. This reviewer was more impressed with the recent counseling manual (*72*) for the counseling use of the MIQ and suggests that it be incorporated into a revision of the manual.

Several other limitations and deficiencies of the manual also should be corrected. First, more information is needed with regard to how the items and scales were chosen for the MIQ. The only information provided is a reference to two studies. Second, there should be more in terms of purpose, definition, and examples with regard to the concepts of "occupational reinforcement patterns" and "clusters," measures developed in other aspects of the project. One limitation of the MIQ is its reliance and dependence on other tools and strategies generated by the project. Does the MIQ have value in and of itself as a way of studying motivation; as a device for suggesting job redesign; as a means of establishing incentive programs? Does the MIQ correlate with other measures of needs or work values? Third, most of the data analyzed were obtained from approximately 10 "groups." Descriptions of these groups in terms of demographic and background factors, sampling procedures, subsamples within the groups (such as the subsamples within the "employed" group) are needed.

A final concern is the definition of the frame of reference for the respondent—the "ideal" job—which is the "kind of job you would most like to have." To determine respondent understanding, the manual suggests that the psychometrist ask the respondent to explain what the phrase "ideal job" means. Does this imply that more than one "ideal job" frame of reference is acceptable? Does it require that the individual consider the job he/she is "likely to get" or those for which he/she has requisite skills?

In summary, the data analyses, results, and research underlying the Work Adjustment Project, and particularly the MIQ, are generally impressive and suggest the potential for valuable contribution to the study, understanding, and prediction of work adjustment. But the work has not been completed. Only the test of time and future research will judge its utility adequately.

[1051]

Minnesota Job Description Questionnaire. Employees and supervisors; 1967–68; MJDQ; for research use only; primarily for group measurement of occupational reinforcer patterns (ORP's) to match with intrapersonal vocational needs as measured by *Minnesota Importance Questionnaire*; 22 scores (20 of

which parallel scores of *Minnesota Importance Questionnaire* and *Minnesota Satisfaction Questionnaire*): ability utilization, achievement, activity, advancement, authority, company policies and practices, compensation, coworkers, creativity, independence, moral values, recognition, responsibility, security, social service, social status, supervision—human relations, supervision—technical, variety, working conditions, autonomy, neutral point; Forms E ('68, 12 pages, for employees), S ('67, 8 pages, for supervisors); manual ('68, 96 pages); 20¢ per test (minimum 20); postage extra; manual free on request; scoring service, 90¢ or less (scoring must be done by publisher); [20] minutes; Fred H. Borgen, David J. Weiss, Howard E. A. Tinsley, René V. Dawis, and Lloyd H. Lofquist; Vocational Psychology Research. *

See T2:2284 (8 references).

REFERENCES

1–8. See T2:2284.
9. BORGEN, FRED H.; WEISS, DAVID J.; TINSLEY, HOWARD E. A.; DAWIS, RENE V.; AND LOFQUIST, LLOYD H. *Occupational Reinforcer Patterns (First Volume), Revised Edition.* Minneapolis, Minn.: Vocational Psychology Research, University of Minnesota, 1972. Pp. ix, 179. *
10. BORGEN, FRED H.; WEISS, DAVID J.; TINSLEY, HOWARD E. A.; DAWIS, RENE V.; AND LOFQUIST, LLOYD H. *Occupational Reinforcer Patterns (Second Volume).* Minneapolis, Minn.: Vocational Psychology Research, University of Minnesota, 1972. Pp. x, 263. *
11. WILLOUGHBY, THEODORE C. "Are Programmers Paranoid?" *Proc Ann Computer Personnel Res Conf* 10:47–54 '72. *
12. CASADY, MONA JOY CARLBERG. *Job Satisfaction of Magnetic Typewriter Operators in Word Processing.* Doctor's thesis, University of Minnesota (Minneapolis, Minn.), 1973. (*DAI* 34:4099A)
13. SEILER, DALE A., AND LACEY, DAVID W. "Adapting the Work Adjustment Theory for Assessing Technical-Professional Utilization." *J Voc Behav* 3(4):443–51 O '73. * (*PA* 52:2005)
14. WEISS, DAVID J. Chap. 6, "The Minnesota Importance Questionnaire," pp. 136–70. In *Contemporary Approaches to Interest Measurement.* Edited by Donald G. Zytowski. Minneapolis, Minn.: University of Minnesota Press, 1973. Pp. xi, 251. *
15. CORY, EDWARD DANA. *Job Satisfaction and Vocational Needs of Pennsylvania Vocational Teachers.* Doctor's thesis, Pennsylvania State University (University Park, Pa.), 1974. (*DAI* 35:1562A)
16. OLSON, HELEN LUCILE THOMAS. *The Relationship Between Needs-Reinforcer Correspondence and Job Satisfaction of Minnesota Secondary School Office Education Teacher Coordinators.* Doctor's thesis, University of Minnesota (Minneapolis, Minn.), 1974. (*DAI* 35:7599A)
17. PORRITT, D. "Applying a Model of Work Adjustment." *Austral Psychologist* 9(2):165–73 Jl '74. *
18. TINSLEY, HOWARD E. A., AND WEISS, DAVID J. "A Multivariate Investigation of the Reinforcer Structure of Occupations." *J Voc Behav* 4(1):97–113 Ja '74. * (*PA* 52:8802)
19. WALLS, RICHARD T., AND GULKUS, STEVEN P. "Reinforcers and Vocational Maturity in Occupational Aspiration, Expectation, and Goal Deflection." *J Voc Behav* 5(3):381–90 D '74. * (*PA* 53:12711)
20. WALLS, RICHARD T., AND GULKUS, STEVEN P. "Reinforcers, Values, and Vocational Maturity in Adults." *J Voc Behav* 4(3):325–32 Je '74. * (*PA* 52:13330)
21. D'ELIA, GEORGE PATRICK MICHAEL. *The Adjustment of Library School Graduates to the Job Environments of Librarianship: A Test of the Need Gratification and Expectation Fulfillment Theories of Job Satisfaction.* Doctor's thesis, Rutgers—The State University (New Brunswick, N.J.), 1975. (*DAI* 36:585A)
22. JENSON, GUST, III. *An Application of a Theory of Work Adjustment to Selection for Graduate Training in School Psychology.* Doctor's thesis, University of Minnesota (Minneapolis, Minn.), 1975. (*DAI* 37:440B)
23. ELIZUR, DOV, AND TZINER, AHARON. "Vocational Needs, Job Rewards, and Satisfaction: A Canonical Analysis." *Voc Behav* 10(2):205–11 Ap '77. *

SHELDON ZEDECK, *Associate Professor of Psychology, University of California, Berkeley, California.*

The *Minnesota Job Description Questionnaire* (MJDQ) is a product, along with the

Minnesota Importance Questionnaire (MIQ) and the *Minnesota Satisfaction Questionnaire* (MSQ), of the Work Adjustment Project which is a series of studies concerned with the problem of adjustment to work. These tools have been developed to test the basic propositions of the *Theory of Work Adjustment*,[1] which essentially proposes that the correspondence of the worker's needs and the reinforcers provided by the work environment is the primary factor behind work outcomes such as satisfaction and satisfactoriness.

The MJDQ is an instrument for measuring the work environments of single occupations through the combined evaluations of a group of individuals. The MJDQ uses combinations of 21 statements (20 of which parallel the MIQ and MSQ) to describe the reinforcer characteristics of work environments. The instructions are to rank the statements, which are in blocks of five each, in terms of "how well they describe a particular job." Each of the 21 statements appears in five ranking blocks, but each time with a different set of four other items. In general, the statements refer to observable kinds of behavior, though some require insights by the respondent into the "psychological environment" which the job provides. The obtained ranks provide information about the relative *importance* of reinforcers in the job. In addition, the respondent is asked to provide absolute judgments for each of the 21 statements in terms of whether the statement describes or does not describe the working environment. Thus, 22 scores are determined for each occupation. This relative and absolute information is provided by either a supervisor (Form S) or an employee (Form E). Form E also includes the short form of the MSQ.

The scores from the MJDQ are used to describe occupational reinforcer patterns (ORPs) for a given occupational environment. An ORP describes the stimulus conditions available in the work environment for the satisfaction of workers' needs. Those individuals whose needs, as measured by the MIQ, correspond with the ORP for a given occupation are predicted to be satisfied. Counselors can use the correspondence, or lack of it, in their advising and concern

[1] DAWIS, RENE V.; ENGLAND, GEORGE W.; AND LOFQUIST, LLOYD H. *A Theory of Work Adjustment.* University of Minnesota, Industrial Relations Center, Bulletin 38; Minnesota Studies in Vocational Rehabilitation 15. Minneapolis, Minn.: the Center, 1964. Pp. v, 27. *

Minnesota Job Description Questionnaire

for identifying several occupations for consideration by the counselee.

Evaluation of the MJDQ is a function of the ORPs produced by the MJDQ. The manual presents the development of the MJDQ as well as the profiles for 81 ORPs. ORPs are now described for 148 occupations with an additional 22 in press. Since the data for the 81 ORPs are based on *only* supervisors' responses, the reliability and validity presented in the manual are appropriate for Form S only. A compelling argument is made for supervisors as evaluators since they are close enough to the job to have a thorough and broad enough knowledge of the job with regard to how the stimulus conditions affect workers; their ratings are least likely to be influenced by their *own* job satisfaction since the rating is of *another* job. Yet, some of the newer ORPs are based on employee ratings (Form E) for occupations for which there were insufficient or even zero supervisors. Technical data, in summary form, concerning the use of employees as raters are available from the project; data exist which show supervisor-rated ORPs to be highly similar to employee-rated ORPs.

The reliability of Form S for the 81 ORPs is based on split-half reliability coefficients which range from .78 to .98, with a median of .91. Sample sizes in the split-half groups range from only 11 to 48. These data indicate exceptionally good agreement in assessments of work environment reinforcers. However, there may be a serious limitation. Since the ORPs serve, in part, to aid a counselee in his/her decisions to pursue or enter an occupation, the key question is whether the supervisors, raters, within an occupation were representative of the occupation-in-general. For example, 32 supervisors of "claim-adjuster" provided MJDQs. How many different companies were represented by these 32 supervisors? This important information is not presented in the manual. If the respondents represented a *few* companies, then the influence of variation in organizational climate, policy, administration, etc., is not taken into account and the representativeness of the available ORPs is limited. The high correlations may be a function of homogeneity of the rater group; heterogeneity of organizations within occupations may not have been examined.

The validity of ORPs is established by showing that different ORPs were obtained for different occupations. Results indicated that for each scale the 81 occupations were seen as having different amounts of relative reinforcement. In addition, patterns of scale values were used to differentiate groups of occupations. In a cluster analysis of the 81 ORPs, 59 were assigned to nine clusters or families of ORPs whereas 22 ORPs did not fit clearly into any cluster. The researchers "believed that the clusters which emerged are generally meaningful." This reviewer would be more impressed if the obtained clusters would fit any established taxonomy of occupations or if there was some demonstration of convergent validity between the MJDQ and other measures of job reinforcers.

A major concern is with the utility of the MJDQ to the test user. The use of the MJDQ per se for the "average test user" is not clear; the use is of the ORPs and the adoption of the entire strategy and propositions of the Work Adjustment Project. This reviewer feels that the considerations for item presentation and scoring are more than adequate. However, more research is necessary on reliability and validity, more description of the respondents and their organizations should be provided, and the suggestions for "Future Research on ORPs" as presented in the manual must be conducted before adoption of the ORPs (and consequently MJDQ) for counseling purposes can be recommended.

[1052]

Minnesota Satisfaction Questionnaire. Business and industry; 1963-67; MSQ; job satisfaction; 2 forms; manual free on request; David J. Weiss, René V. Dawis, George W. England, and Lloyd H. Lofquist; Vocational Psychology Research.*

a) LONG FORM. 21 scores: ability utilization, achievement, activity, advancement, authority, company policies and practices, compensation, coworkers, creativity, independence, moral values, recognition, responsibility, security, social service, social status, supervision—human relations, supervision—technical, variety, working conditions, general satisfaction; no reliability and validity data or norms for the 1967 revision; 2 editions: original edition ('63, 7 pages), 1967 revision ('67, 7 pages, identical with original edition except for response options, for research use only); 20¢ per test (minimum 15); scoring service, 55¢ per test; (15-20) minutes.

b) SHORT FORM. 3 scores: intrinsic, extrinsic, general; 1 form ('63, 4 pages); 10¢ per test (minimum 30); scoring service, 35¢ per test; (5-10) minutes.

See T2:2285 (11 references); for reviews by Lewis

E. Albright and John P. Foley, Jr., see 7:1064 (18 references).

REFERENCES

1-18. See 7:1064.
19-29. See T2:2285; also includes a cumulative name index to the first 29 references and 2 reviews for this test.
30. BILLUPS, MAURITA MILES. *The Job Satisfactions of Black School Administrators.* Doctor's thesis, Syracuse University (Syracuse, N.Y.), 1972. (*DAI* 33:5425A)
31. BORGEN, FRED H.; WEISS, DAVID J.; TINSLEY, HOWARD E. A.; DAWIS, RENE V.; AND LOFQUIST, LLOYD H. *Occupational Reinforcer Patterns (First Volume), Revised Edition.* Minneapolis, Minn.: Vocational Psychology Research, University of Minnesota, 1972. Pp. ix, 179. *
32. BORGEN, FRED H.; WEISS, DAVID J.; TINSLEY, HOWARD E. A.; DAWIS, RENE V.; AND LOFQUIST, LLOYD H. *Occupational Reinforcer Patterns (Second Volume).* Minneapolis, Minn.: Vocational Psychology Research, University of Minnesota, 1972. Pp. x, 263. *
33. BYRNES, JOSEPH LANNIN. *A Study of Certain Relationships Among Perceived Supervisory Style, Participativeness, and Teacher Job Satisfaction.* Doctor's thesis, Syracuse University (Syracuse, N.Y.), 1972. (*DAI* 33:5427A)
34. DELOREY, RUTH MARIE WOOD. *Job Satisfaction-Satisfactoriness and Characteristics of Minneapolis Business Graduates.* Doctor's thesis, University of Minnesota (Minneapolis, Minn.), 1972. (*DAI* 33:229A)
35. FITZGERALD, SHEILA MARY. *A Career Development Study of Elementary School Teachers.* Doctor's thesis, University of Minnesota (Minneapolis, Minn.), 1972. (*DAI* 33:3452A)
36. GILSRUD, RONALD DEAN. *Job Satisfaction of Formerly Disadvantaged Students as a Measure of Accountability for Vocational Office Education Programs.* Doctor's thesis, University of North Dakota (Grand Forks, N.D.), 1972. (*DAI* 33:6803A)
37. GREENSTEIN, GERALD. *A Study of Relationships Between Teachers' Feelings of General Satisfaction and the Needs and Expectations Fulfillment Qualities of Their Organizational Press.* Doctor's thesis, Syracuse University (Syracuse, N.Y.), 1972. (*DAI* 34:90A)
38. HORIUCHI, HERBERT SHIRO. *A Comparative Study of the Relationship of Organizational Climate to Job Satisfaction of Teachers in Selected Rural and Suburban Schools in Hawaii.* Doctor's thesis, Utah State University (Logan, Utah), 1972. (*DAI* 33:3197A)
39. LAROUCHE, VIATEUR. *A Multivariate Investigation of Biographical Factors in Job Satisfaction.* Doctor's thesis, University of Minnesota (Minneapolis, Minn.), 1972. (*DAI* 33:478B)
40. LEE, RICHARD HEATH, JR. *The Relationship Between Selected Life History Antecedents and the Job Satisfaction of School Principals.* Doctor's thesis, University of Northern Colorado (Greeley, Colo.), 1972. (*DAI* 33:929A)
41. LITTLE, WAYNE GERALD. *Relationships Between Certain Personality Characteristics of Post-Secondary Distributive Education Personnel and Job Satisfaction.* Doctor's thesis, University of Minnesota (Minneapolis, Minn.), 1972. (*DAI* 33:2252A)
42. PASSMORE, DAVID L. "The Usefulness of Weighting Test Item Responses." *J Indus Teach Ed* 10(1):59-67 f '72. *
43. PRITCHARD, ROBERT D.; DUNNETTE, MARVIN D.; AND JORGENSON, DALE O. "Effects of Perceptions of Equity and Inequity on Worker Performance and Satisfaction." *J Appl Psychol* 56(1):75-94 F '72. * (*PA* 47:11895)
44. TAYLOR, KENNETH E., AND WEISS, DAVID J. "Prediction of Individual Job Termination From Measured Job Satisfaction and Biographical Data." *J Voc Behav* 2(2):123-32 Ap '72. * (*PA* 48:10016)
45. WILLIAMS, EUGENE, SR. *Job Satisfaction and Self-Concept as Perceived by Black Female Paraprofessional Trainees.* Doctor's thesis, University of Miami (Coral Gables, Fla.), 1972. (*DAI* 33:5458A)
46. BOWLING, SUSAN RICHARDSON. *Leadership Behavior of Chief Student Personnel Administrators and Its Relationship to Morale and Job Satisfaction.* Doctor's thesis, University of Tennessee (Knoxville, Tenn.), 1973. (*DAI* 34:4772A)
47. CASADY, MONA JOY CARLBERG. *Job Satisfaction of Magnetic Typewriter Operators in Word Processing.* Doctor's thesis, University of Minnesota (Minneapolis, Minn.), 1973. (*DAI* 34:4099A)
48. CLEVELAND, ROBERT LATHROP, JR. *A Study of the Relationships Among Teacher Job Satisfaction, Teacher Morale and Categories of Teacher-Faculty Group Membership.* Doctor's thesis, Syracuse University (Syracuse, N.Y.), 1973. (*DAI* 34:6512A)
49. FAUROT, LYLE MARTIN. *An Investigation of the Validity of Vocational Student Grades as a Criterion of Vocational Student Success and the Predictability of Vocational Student Grades Using Standardized Test Instruments.* Doctor's thesis, University of Minnesota (Minneapolis, Minn.), 1973. (*DAI* 34:676A)
50. HARRILL, THOMAS STEARN. *A Comparative Study of the Efficiency of Intellective and Nonintellective Measures as*

Predictors of Job Success and Job Satisfaction. Doctor's thesis, Auburn University (Auburn, Ala.), 1973. (*DAI* 33:6665A)

51. HEBERT, CHARLES HENRY, JR. *An Analysis of Selected Factors Related to Rehabilitation Outcomes and Job Satisfaction of Disabled Persons Served by the Oklahoma Division of Vocational Rehabilitation.* Doctor's thesis, Oklahoma State University (Stillwater, Okla.), 1973. (*DAI* 34:6533A)

52. KEAN, HELEN E. *Person-Environment Congruence and Job Satisfaction in Counseling-Related Settings in Michigan: A Descriptive Study.* Doctor's thesis, Wayne State University (Detroit, Mich.), 1973. (*DAI* 34:7536A)

53. MILLER, DON E. *A Study of Relationships Between Job Satisfaction of Teachers and Their Perceptions of Bases of Social Influence of Their Principals.* Doctor's thesis. Syracuse University (Syracuse, N.Y.), 1973. (*DAI* 35:764A)

54. MUNCRIEF, MARTHA CRAWFORD. *Work Adjustment of Vocational Education Teachers.* Doctor's thesis, Ohio State University (Columbus, Ohio), 1973. (*DAI* 34:2475A)

55. PICCIRILLO, MARTIN LOUIS. *Organizational and Personal Dimensions of the New Haven Department of Police Service.* Doctor's thesis, Fordham University (New York, N.Y.), 1973. (*DAI* 34:2235A)

56. PRITCHARD, ROBERT D. "Effects of Varying Performance-Pay Instrumentalities on the Relationship Between Performance and Satisfaction: A Test of the Lawler and Porter Model." *J Appl Psychol* 58(1):122–5 Ag '73. * (*PA* 51:10070)

57. TRAVERS, JEROME A. *Relationships Between Overall Job Satisfaction and Intrinsic and Extrinsic Satisfaction of a Sample of Blue Collar Workers.* Doctor's thesis, Fordham University (New York, N.Y.), 1973. (*DAI* 34:4894A)

58. VESSEY, THOMAS MOORMAN. *A Longitudinal Study of the Prediction of Job Satisfaction as a Function of the Correspondence Between Needs and the Perceptions of Job Reinforcers in an Occupation.* Doctor's thesis, University of Minnesota (Minneapolis, Minn.), 1973. (*DAI* 34:2352B)

59. WANOUS, JOHN P. "Effects of a Realistic Job Preview on Job Acceptance, Job Attitudes, and Job Survival." *J Appl Psychol* 58(3):327–32 D '73. * (*PA* 52:8832)

60. WINTERS, ROBERT ARTHUR. *Relationships Between Job Satisfaction and Leisure Satisfaction.* Doctor's thesis, State University of New York (Buffalo, N.Y.), 1973. (*DAI* 34:3077A)

61. BULLOCK, JACK ARLEN. *An Investigation of the Personality Traits, Job Satisfaction Attitudes, Training and Experience Histories of Superior Teachers of Junior High School Instrumental Music in New York State.* Doctor's thesis, University of Miami (Coral Gables, Fla.), 1974. (*DAI* 35:2029A)

62. CAHOON, ALLAN RAY. *Managerial Behavior Under Conditions of Mandated Change in a Canadian Bureaucracy: An Empirical Study of the Relationships Among Job Satisfaction, Organizational Climate and Leadership Change Styles.* Doctor's thesis, Syracuse University (Syracuse, N.Y.), 1974. (*DAI* 35:7382A)

63. CORY, EDWARD DANA. *Job Satisfaction and Vocational Needs of Pennsylvania Vocational Teachers.* Doctor's thesis, Pennsylvania State University (University Park, Pa.), 1974. (*DAI* 35:1562A)

64. ENDERLEIN, THOMAS ELLIS. *Causal Relationships of Student Characteristics Related to Satisfaction in Post High School Employment.* Doctor's thesis, Pennsylvania State University (University Park, Pa.), 1974. (*DAI* 35:7795A)

65. GILLELAND, ROBERTA LOUISE. *The Relationship Between the WAIS and MMPI Subscale Scores and Work Adjustment Outcomes in Adult Blind and Partially Sighted Persons.* Doctor's thesis, Ohio State University (Columbus, Ohio), 1974. (*DAI* 35:5684B)

66. HULL, WESLEY TERRENCE. *Identification of Variables Related to the Job Satisfaction of California Elementary School Principals.* Doctor's thesis, University of the Pacific (Stockton, Calif.), 1974. (*DAI* 35:2581A)

67. LOFFREDO, MICHAEL JOSEPH, II. *A Study of the Relationships Between Various Personal Characteristics and Perceptions of Iowa Public School Principals and Their Attitudes Toward Educational Innovation.* Doctor's thesis, University of Iowa (Iowa City, Iowa), 1974. (*DAI* 35:4083A)

68. NOVAK, KATHLEEN DOBOSENSKI. *Preferred Job Reinforcers and the Job Satisfaction of Faculty in Minnesota's Area Vocational Technical Institutes.* Doctor's thesis, University of Minnesota (Minneapolis, Minn.), 1974. (*DAI* 35:7799A)

69. OLSON, HELEN LUCILE THOMAS. *The Relationship Between Needs-Reinforcer Correspondence and Job Satisfaction of Minnesota Secondary School Office Education Teacher Coordinators.* Doctor's thesis, University of Minnesota (Minneapolis, Minn.), 1974. (*DAI* 35:7599A)

70. PARKER, THOMAS MEREDITH, JR. *The Relationship Between Organizational Climate and Job Satisfaction of Elementary Teachers.* Doctor's thesis, University of Virginia (Charlottesville, Va.), 1974. (*DAI* 35:1937A)

71. PORRITT, D. "Applying a Model of Work Adjustment." *Austral Psychologist* 9(2):165–73 Jl '74. *

72. RANDLE, ELEANOR MOTHERSHED. *Staff Relationships, Morale, and Communications as They Affect a School System's*

Internal Public Relations. Doctor's thesis, Memphis State University (Memphis, Tenn.), 1974. (*DAI* 36:652A)

73. ROSS, NINA PRESTON, *An Assessment of the Effects of a Reading Workshop on Job Satisfaction of Elementary School Teachers.* Doctor's thesis, Memphis State University (Memphis, Tenn.), 1974. (*DAI* 35:5134A)

74. RUSSELL, EDDIE BAKER. *An Investigation of Predictor Variables of Selected Dimensions of Interpersonal Communications Among Correctional Personnel.* Doctor's thesis, University of Georgia (Athens, Ga.), 1974. (*DAI* 35:6467A)

75. SCHWAB, DONALD P. "Conflicting Impacts of Pay on Employee Motivation and Satisfaction." *Personnel J* 53(3):196–200 Mr '74. * (*PA* 53:4221)

76. SCHWAB, DONALD P., AND WALLACE, MARC J., JR. "Correlates of Employee Satisfaction With Pay." *Indus Relations* 13(1):78–89 F '74. *

77. WANOUS, JOHN P. "A Causal-Correlational Analysis of the Job Satisfaction and Performance Relationship." *J Appl Psychol* 59(2):139–44 Ap '74. * (*PA* 52:11150)

78. BURNS, ELLEN LOUISE. *Adaptiveness and Satisfaction in Educational Administration.* Doctor's thesis, University of Iowa (Iowa City, Iowa), 1975. (*DAI* 36:4890A)

79. CHANDLER, SARAH McKINNIE. *Teacher Stress and Job Satisfaction as They Relate to the Implementation of a Court-Ordered Desegregation Plan.* Doctor's thesis, University of Tennessee (Knoxville, Tenn.), 1975. (*DAI* 36:4144A)

80. D'ELIA, GEORGE PATRICK MICHAEL. *The Adjustment of Library School Graduates to the Job Environments of Librarianship: A Test of the Need Gratification and Expectation Fulfillment Theories of Job Satisfaction.* Doctor's thesis, Rutgers—The State University (New Brunswick, N.J.), 1975. (*DAI* 36:585A)

81. ENDERLEIN, THOMAS E. "Causal Patterns Related to Post High School Employment Satisfaction." *J Voc Behav* 7(1):67–80 Ag '75. * (*PA* 55:5810)

82. FINDLEY, BENJAMIN FLAVIOUS, JR. *The Relationship Among Selected Personal Variables and Job Satisfaction of College Business Teachers in Colorado.* Doctor's thesis, University of Northern Colorado (Greeley, Colo.), 1975. (*DAI* 36:4205A)

83. GASS, MARCELLE BURDETTE. *A Job Satisfactoriness and Job Satisfaction Study of College of Business Graduates.* Doctor's thesis, Kansas State University (Manhattan, Kan.), 1975. (*DAI* 37:829A)

84. GILLET, BERNARD, AND SCHWAB, DONALD P. "Convergent and Discriminant Validities of Corresponding Job Descriptive Index and Minnesota Satisfaction Questionnaire Scales." *J Appl Psychol* 60(3):313–7 Je '75. * (*PA* 54:6475)

85. JOHNSON, JOHN ROBERT. *Elementary Teacher Perceptions of Certain Organizational Processes and Job Satisfaction in Schools With Self-Contained and Differentiated Staffing Classrooms.* Doctor's thesis, Syracuse University (Syracuse, N.Y.), 1975. (*DAI* 36:6400A)

86. KAZANAS, H. C., AND GREGOR, TOM G. "Relationships of the Meaning of Work, Value of Work, Job Satisfaction, and Selected Demographic Variables of Vocational and Non-Vocational Teachers." *J Indus Teach Ed* 12(3):12–20 sp '75. *

87. KERLIN, BARBARA DRUMMOND. *A Study of John L. Holland's Theory of Careers as It Applies to Employed Adults.* Doctor's thesis, University of Maryland (College Park, Md.), 1975. (*DAI* 36:6640A)

88. LOFQUIST, LLOYD H., AND DAWIS, RENÉ V. "Vocational Needs, Work Reinforcers, and Job Satisfaction." *Voc Guid Q* 24(2):132–9 D '75. * (*PA* 55:11168)

89. PLATT, RICHARD A. *A Multitrait-Multifactor Approach to the Study of Job Satisfaction Attitudes of Mentally Retarded Workers.* Doctor's thesis, State University of New York (Buffalo, N.Y.), 1975. (*DAI* 36:5276B)

90. POUND, WINSDON NORWOOD MONTRESSEUR. *The Relationship Between School Calendar and Teacher Job Satisfaction.* Doctor's thesis, Virginia Polytechnic Institute and State University (Blacksburg, Va.), 1975. (*DAI* 36:1964A)

91. QUIRK, KEITH H. *The Work Adjustment of a Group of Mentally Retarded Persons From Coles County, Illinois.* Doctor's thesis, George Peabody College for Teachers (Nashville, Tenn.), 1975. (*DAI* 36:5201A)

92. RICHARDSON, JOHN GLENN. *A Comparison of Professional Institutional Corrections Workers and Professional Community Corrections Workers on Job Satisfaction and Self Concept.* Doctor's thesis, University of Cincinnati (Cincinnati, Ohio), 1975. (*DAI* 36:4268A)

93. SHAW, CHARLES ERNEST. *A Comparative Analysis of Organizational Climate and Job Satisfaction at Selected Public and Catholic Secondary Schools in Connecticut.* Doctor's thesis, University of Connecticut (Storrs, Conn.), 1975. (*DAI* 36:7796A)

94. ARVEY, RICHARD D., AND DEWHIRST, H. DUDLEY. "Goal-Setting Attributes, Personality Variables, and Job Satisfaction." *J Voc Behav* 9(2):179–89 O '76. *

95. ATTEBERRY, MARIE GETTY. *The Relationship Between Emotional Stability and Job Satisfaction of Elementary School Principals.* Doctor's thesis, Arizona State University (Tempe, Ariz.), 1976. (*DAI* 37:6163A)

96. BENOIT, SALLYE STARKS. *Job Satisfaction Among Faculty Women in Higher Education in the State University of*

Minnesota Satisfaction Questionnaire

Louisiana. Doctor's thesis, Louisiana State University (Baton Rouge, La.), 1976. (*DAI* 37:6969A)

97. DINGWALL, ROBERT WATSON. *Job Satisfaction as an Outcome Measure for Orthopedically Handicapped Clients of a Vocational Rehabilitation Program.* Doctor's thesis, University of Northern Colorado (Greeley, Colo.), 1976. (*DAI* 37:4268A)

98. HAFFORD, HELEN MARY. *The Measurement of Factors of Satisfaction and Dissatisfaction Which Affect Tennessee Teachers in Their Work.* Doctor's thesis, University of Tennessee (Knoxville, Tenn.), 1976. (*DAI* 37:5062A)

99. HENDERSON, LESTER F. *Elementary Teacher Satisfaction and Morale and Perceived Participation in Decision-Making.* Doctor's thesis, University of Arkansas (Fayetteville, Ark.), 1976. (*DAI* 37:2535A)

100. HIGGINS, EARL BERNARD. *Follow-Up Survey of Graduates of the Department of Counselor Education, 1970–1975.* Doctor's thesis, Auburn University (Auburn, Ala.), 1976. (*DAI* 37:807A)

101. HILL, MICHAEL DAVID. *Job Satisfaction Among the Rural and Urban Orthopedically Disabled in Wyoming: A Follow-up Study.* Doctor's thesis, University of Northern Colorado (Greeley, Colo.), 1976. (*DAI* 37:7638A)

102. HSIEH, WEN-CHYUAN. *A Comparative Study of Relationships Between Principals' Leadership Style and Teachers' Job Satisfaction in the Republic of China and the State of Iowa in the United States.* Doctor's thesis, University of Iowa (Iowa City, Iowa), 1976. (*DAI* 37:2540A)

103. ILGEN, DANIEL R., AND FUJII, DONALD S. "An Investigation of the Validity of Leader Behavior Descriptions Obtained from Subordinates." *J Appl Psychol* 61(5):642–51 O '76. * (*PA* 57:4682)

104. LORCH, THOMAS DANIEL. *A Study of Holland's Theory of Careers as it Applies to the Job Satisfaction of Employed Adults.* Doctor's thesis, Indiana University (Bloomington, Ind.), 1976. (*DAI* 37:4866A)

105. NEWSOME, EMANUEL T. *A Study of Relationships Between Job Satisfaction and Personality Trends of College Student Volunteers at Indiana State University.* Doctor's thesis, Indiana State University (Bloomington, Ind.), 1976. (*DAI* 37:3453A)

106. SAETTA, VINCENT ALBERT. *Organizational and Personal Dimensions of MBO and Non-MBO Public Schools in New York State.* Doctor's thesis, Fordham University (New York, N.Y.), 1976. (*DAI* 37:2562A)

107. SCHULT, HENRY ERNEST. *Need Fulfillment and Job Satisfaction of Principals Classified by Legal Status in New York State.* Doctor's thesis, Fordham University (New York, N.Y.), 1976. (*DAI* 37:2565A)

108. SMITH, JOHN JOSEPH. *Job Satisfaction of Connecticut Public Senior High School Principals as Related to School Location and School Size.* Doctor's thesis, University of Connecticut (Storrs, Conn.), 1976. (*DAI* 37:5517A)

109. WANOUS, JOHN P. "Organizational Entry: From Naive Expectations to Realistic Beliefs." *J Appl Psychol* 61(1):22–9 F '76. * (*PA* 55:11178)

110. ARVEY, RICHARD D., AND GROSS, RONALD H. "Satisfaction Levels and Correlates of Satisfaction in the Homemaker Job." *Voc Behav* 10(1):13–24 F '77. *

111. SCHWAB, DONALD P., AND HENEMAN, HERBERT G., III. "Age and Satisfaction With Dimensions of Work." *Voc Behav* 10(2):212–20 Ap '77. *

ROBERT M. GUION, *Professor of Psychology, Bowling Green State University, Bowling Green, Ohio.*

The 20 principal scales of the MSQ are intended to measure attitudes toward environmental "reinforcers" in the work situation that may satisfy categories of needs. An overall measure of general job satisfaction is obtained by summing across all 20 categories. Neither the theoretical foundations nor the psychometric history of the instrument is given in its manual; otherwise, the manual is quite informative. It describes the 20 scales, each with five items and each employing a five-point scale for response. Some items are nearly identical—is "the chance to be of service to others" really a different statement from "the chance to be of service to people"?

Perhaps because the items within a scale are so very close in meaning, the internal consistencies of the scales are generally high. There is less evidence on stability; what is reported, however, suggests that responses may not change any faster than the satisfactions they reflect.

Intercorrelations between many of the scales are quite substantial, but low relative to the reliability estimates. In general, they are low enough to indicate some substantial unique variance in the scales, yet high enough to justify adding scales together to form a twenty-first scale of general job satisfaction. Clearly, item analyses have been done even though not reported in detail; the manual points out that the general satisfaction score is found by using the one item in each set with the highest part-whole correlation.

Evidence of validity is limited to a few studies from which construct validity is implied. Nevertheless, the section on validity might well be imitated in other test manuals as a model of scholarly restraint; there are no heavy claims, and pains are taken to point out the scales not "performing according to theoretical expectations."

Part of that evidence consists of factor analyses of scale scores; results consistently include factors identified as intrinsic satisfactions and as extrinsic rewards. The short form (which uses those "best" items from each scale) is scored on the basis of these factors. Particularly important is the fact that normative tables are provided for 7 occupational groups for the short form and for 27 groups for the long form. Moreover, the normative data include both sample characteristics and summary statistics as well as percentile equivalents. Although some of the groups are small, the amount of sample description is something else to be imitated in other manuals.

Clearly, the MSQ gives reasonably reliable, valid, well-normed indications of general satisfaction at work and of 20 aspects of that satisfaction, collapsible into intrinsic and extrinsic components.

It seems appropriate to compare the MSQ with another widely used measure of job satisfaction, the Job Descriptive Index (7:B586). Like the MSQ, the JDI is a result of research in the 1960s, has an underlying rationale, is

Minnesota Satisfaction Questionnaire

based on extensive empirical research, provides reliable scores, has evidence of construct validity, and is extensively normed. Despite the similarities, the two are distinctly different.

First of all, the MSQ has four times as many scales. If these are independent, the MSQ gives more information. The JDI scales, on the other hand, are more nearly independent. The substantial intercorrelations among MSQ scales justify the global satisfaction score; the persistent efforts to create independence of JDI scales make an additive score inappropriate. Scale reliabilities (internal consistencies) are higher for the MSQ, but spuriously so, considering the near identity of items. Evaluations of construct validity for the MSQ are based on confirmation of predictions from theory; for the JDI they are based on factor analyses, yielding factors confirming the five scales. For the MSQ, factor analyses are based on scales; for the JDI, they are based on individual items. The MSQ manual provides occupational norms; the JDI manual provides norms on demographic groups.

Using data provided by Gillet and Schwab (84) a factor analysis [1] of a matrix including the 20 MSQ scales and the five JDI scales resulted in five factors, but they were not precisely the factors of the JDI itself. They have been identified as intrinsic satisfactions, financial rewards, supervision, co-workers, and status (or promotion). While these labels fit the five JDI scales, the scales themselves do not consistently have their principal loadings in the "right" places! Moreover, when these five factors (in oblique rotation) are themselves factored, the results return to the intrinsic and extrinsic categories of the MSQ.

In summary, the MSQ is well developed, it holds up well in comparison with a major alternate instrument, and it can give detailed diagnostics or parsimonious summary statements according to an investigator's needs. The only request the reviewer can make is that the next manual be more complete in describing the reasoning and the history basic to it.

[1053]

★Process Diagnostic. Group members; 1974-75; PD; ratings of self and fellow group members on individual contributions to group performance; 9 scores in 3 group climates: problem solving (integrative,

[1] I am indebted to Michael White for the analysis of the matrix.

Minnesota Satisfaction Questionnaire

content-bound, process-bound), fight (frustration, status-striving, perceptual difference), flight (fear, indifference, impotence) for each group member and total group; no data on reliability and validity; no norms; 1 form ('74, 8 pages); no manual; score interpretation ('75, 16 pages); $3 per test, postage extra; [15-30] minutes; Jay Hall; Teleometrics Int'l. *

PAUL W. THAYER, *Professor of Psychology and Head of the Department, North Carolina State University, Raleigh, North Carolina.*

Process Diagnostic is not a test in the usual sense. Yet, with the increasing emphasis upon group processes and the development of "learning aids" such as this device, it seems important to review the PD for the Eighth MMY. Perhaps such a review will stimulate the publisher to provide better and more complete information.

The author states that PD is designed to help a group become more aware of the processes through which it is attacking its tasks or problems. He accepts MacGregor's view that the effective group is self-conscious, aware of its internal processes. The author clearly falls into that group of theorists and practitioners who assume that a group or organization whose processes are judged effective, is effective. The orientation is inward, rather than outward toward identifiable goal accomplishments. In a personal communication, Hall said the PD is based "primarily on the work of Lee Bradford and Bion," the NTL group.

The basic purpose is to provide a diagnostic instrument to assist a group in understanding the processes it employs. If the group is bogged down in one way or another, the PD is designed to assist it in identifying its dominant modes of behavior and thereby to serve as a basis for discussion, self-revelation, and remedial action.

Those are noble goals! An examination of the device suggests that the PD might even help. Given the basic premise, this device seems to be the solution to whatever ails your decision-making group.

The description of the underlying theory is quite complete. After that, it gets spotty. The steps taken to develop the instrument are not described. Members of a group are to use a 36-item device to evaluate the performance of every member of the group on nine clusters and three modes of operation. Obviously, these items are heterogeneous. With one exception, all are included in two or more "clusters." It appears that the clusters are theoretically based. Statistical analysis might simplify the structure considerably—or elaborate upon it.

If the reader detects petulance on the part of the reviewer, the reader is perceptive. The reviewer recognizes the need for good process-diagnostic tools. The reviewer, however, is a little short on psychometric faith. The author should provide data.

Most annoying is the paucity of assistance given to the customer. One really must struggle and read carefully to comprehend both the administration and scoring of the PD. The catalog states that "group members may describe, evaluate, and interpret in a diagnostic way the contributions of fellow group members in a matter of minutes." In response to my letter, the author admitted that "rating and scoring takes the better part of an hour." Having plowed through the printed material, I would estimate that that time estimate assumes prior reading of the "manual."

Although no statistical data are provided in the printed material, Hall states that observers and participants were able to agree at the .05 level of confidence as to the decision processes employed in a small scale setting. One wishes more detail was available. The author presents no evidence in the printed material that the PD helps in group process work. His letter to me presents anecdotal evidence, for what that is worth.

My hunch is that this instrument might help if adequately researched, modified, and amplified. Right now, one accepts it on faith, has to plow through very muddy instructions, is very uncertain of scoring procedures, and has little or no assistance in implementation.

My guess is that Hall has used the PD locally with some positive feedback. He does not realize how difficult it is for someone to use this device without personal guidance. In addition, he has failed to provide evidence to support his process claims. Too bad. It might help.

In sum, before the PD is taken seriously or used widely, the author should provide the following: (a) a description of the test construction; (b) a description and discussion of the test's psychometric properties; (c) evidence that the PD does contribute to effective group

functioning; and (d) simple, clear, step-by-step instructions for administration and scoring. After all, shouldn't a "learning aid" utilize some of the things we know about learning?

[1054]

*SRA Attitude Survey. Employees; 1951–74; formerly called SRA Employee Inventory; employee attitudes toward work environment; for group measurement only; core survey plus 3 optional supplements; no data on reliability; administration manual ('74, 35 pages); descriptive booklet ('74, 18 pages); postage extra; specimen set free; Science Research Associates, Inc. *

a) THE CORE SURVEY. 1951–74; 78 item scores (percentages of both favorable response and no response for total group, subgroup) in 15 areas: job demands, working conditions, pay, employee benefits, friendliness and cooperation of fellow employees, supervisor-employee interpersonal relations, confidence in management, technical competence of supervision, effectiveness of administration, communication, job security, status and recognition, identification with company, growth and advancement opportunity, reactions to the inventory; 1 form ('72, 4 pages, identical with 1951 SRA Employee Inventory, Form A, except for 1 minor word change); test materials and scoring service, $3.50 per person ($350 minimum); French, Spanish, and Portuguese editions and a special edition for hospital employees are available; original survey by Robert K. Burns, L. L. Thurstone, David G. Moore, and Melany E. Baehr; (20–40) minutes.

b) ANONYMOUS COMMENTS. Optional supplement to a; 1 form (1 page of survey forms); report fee, $1 per person ($100 minimum); [15] minutes.

c) CUSTOM-BUILT SURVEY. Optional supplement to a of up to 21 custom items; no norms; test materials and scoring service, $300 plus $1.30 per person; [15] minutes.

d) FUNCTION-SPECIFIC SURVEYS. Supervisors and sales representatives; 1972–74; optional supplement to a; attitudes regarding their particular job areas and problems; 31 item scores (percentages of favorable response and no response for total group, subgroup) in 5 areas listed below; no norms; 2 surveys; test materials and scoring service, $2 per person ($100 minimum); [10] minutes.

1) Survey for Supervisors. 1 form ('72, 3 pages); 5 areas: job fulfillment conditions, authority and responsibility, relations with peers and subordinates, relations with superiors, management responsiveness. 2) Survey for Sales Representatives. 1 form ('72, 3 pages); 5 areas: training, sales support, demands and rewards, sales supervision, management responsiveness.

For reviews by Erwin K. Taylor and Albert S. Thompson of original edition of a, see 5:905 (10 references).

REFERENCES

1–10. See 5:905.
11. BAEHR, MELANY E. "A Simplified Procedure for the Measurement of Employee Attitudes." J Appl Psychol 37:163–7 Je '53. * (PA 28:3371)
12. BRUCE, MARTIN M. "Foreman's Attitudes, Pre- and Post-Strike." J Personnel Adm & Ind Rel 2:98–102 f '55. *
13. CALERO, THOMAS M. An Exploratory Study of the SRA Employee Inventory. Master's thesis, University of Chicago (Chicago, Ill.), 1956.
14. GRIVEST, MARY T., AND LYNCH, JOHN C. "Educational Implications of Personnel Inventory of Supervisors, Head Nurses and Staff Nurses in Selected Hospitals." J Exp Ed 26:179–84 D '57. * (PA 33:4805)

15. CORTNER, ROBERT HAROLD. *The Relation Between Morale and Informal Group Structure in Hospitals.* Doctor's thesis, St. Louis University (St. Louis, Mo.), 1961. (*DA* 22:4072)
16. BLOCK, JULES RICHARD. *Motivation, Satisfaction and Performance of Handicapped Workers.* Doctor's thesis, New York University (New York, N.Y.), 1962. (*DA* 24:819)
17. TOMPKINS, ELBERT LANGSTROTH, III. *Absenteeism as a Correlate of Job Satisfaction.* Doctor's thesis, Columbia University (New York, N.Y.), 1966. (*DA* 27:958B)
18. JOHANNESSON, RUSSELL EDWIN. *Job Satisfaction and Perceptually Measured Organizational Climate: An Investigation of Redundancy.* Doctor's thesis, Bowling Green State University (Bowling Green, Ohio), 1971. (*DAI* 32:2429B)
19. SAPIENZA, DUNNOVAN LEE. *The Introduction of the Adoption Process as a Conceptual Framework for Studying the Job Mobility Decision Behavior of Employees and an Analysis of the Processural Association of Selected Personal, Situational and Communicational Factors.* Doctor's thesis, Florida State University (Tallahassee, Fla.), 1971. (*DAI* 32:6734A)

[1055]

★**Team Effectiveness Survey.** Team members; 1968–69; TES; ratings of self and fellow team members on individual contributions to team action; 4 scores for each team member: exposure (open and candid expression of one's feelings), feedback (active solicitation of information from others), defensive, supportive, plus total team effectiveness score; no data on reliability and validity; no norms; 1 form ('68, 9 pages); no manual; score interpretation ('69, 7 pages); $3 per test, postage extra; [15–30] minutes; Jay Hall; Teleometrics Int'l.*

WILLIAM G. MOLLENKOPF, *Associate Manager of Personnel Administration, The Procter & Gamble Company, Cincinnati, Ohio.*

This instrument was designed as a means for assessing certain aspects of team effectiveness, especially those having to do with interpersonal styles, e.g., openness and candor, respect for others, readiness to help them, and welcoming help. Its main outputs are descriptions of how each member is seen by other team members, and by himself/herself. General team climate scores can also be derived.

Twenty behaviors are presented, in the form of bipolar statements, and each team member chooses a value on a scale ranging from 10 (extremely characteristic) to 1 (extremely uncharacteristic) to describe each of the other team members and then himself/herself. Except for the tiny type used to present the statements, the physical format is clear and attractive. The arrangements for team members to exchange information are neat. There are clearcut procedures for completing a well-designed worksheet so the team member can analyze how others view him/her and compare these views with the team member's self-perceptions.

The Johari Window is used as the central information processing model in the interpretation of data arising from administration of the TES. Thus, emphasis is placed on the extent to which the team member openly and candidly expresses feelings and knowledge (exposure), and on the team member's readiness to solicit information from others about how they view his/her behavior (feedback).

The author has provided little justification for omitting technical skills and knowledge from the factors in the TES. The only explanation offered—that "this may vary from team to team"—strikes the reviewer as a nonexplanation. Surely weaknesses in the various skills required to play a full part in a work team can have great impact on the effectiveness of the team and the quality of relationships among members of the team. If a team member can not pull his/her oar, it hurts the group output.

The reviewer wholeheartedly agrees with the author's statement that "it is what team members do with the data they get from the TES that will really determine its utility for achieving team effectiveness." Unfortunately, neither the manual nor the interpretive leaflet provides any information about how useful it has been in practice. Nevertheless, the reviewer believes that under appropriate circumstances this survey could be a helpful tool for team building, especially if it is used in conjunction with appropriate ways for giving due attention to technical skills and knowledge.

[1056]

★**Vocational Opinion Index.** Disadvantaged trainees in vocational skills programs, 1973–76; VOI; a measure of "Job Readiness Posture (JRP)....a term used to define an individual's attitudes, perceptions and motivations as they impact on his [or her] ability to obtain and maintain a job"; 7 to 11 scores in 3 areas (for 2 areas, attractions and losses, there are no subscores if there is an overall score): attractions to work (overall, benefits to children, benefits to worker, better life style, independence), losses associated with work (overall, personal freedom, time for family), barriers to employment (medical, child care and family, new situations and people, ability to get and hold a job, transportation); Forms A, FA, ('73, 7 pages, FA is out-of-program form for follow-up use, usually for research purposes); administration manual ('76, 4 pages); scoring manual ('74, 11 pages); project reports TTW II ('74, 90 pages), TTW III ('74, 95 pages); score sheet must be prepared locally when hand scored; 35¢ per Form A; $5 per set of manuals; reports free on request ($3.50 per additional copy of TTW III); test materials and scoring service: $1.25 per in-program form (plus $10 initial computer set-up fee), $2.75 per follow-up form, postpaid; $50 minimum first order; specimen copies of forms free on request; Spanish edition available; (45) minutes; Associates for Research in Behavior, Inc. *

[1057]

Work Information Inventory. Employee groups in industry; 1958; WII; morale; norms consist of means and standard deviations; 1 form (4 pages); manual (4 pages); $2.50 per 25 tests; $1.50 per specimen set (must be purchased to obtain manual); postage extra; (15) minutes; Raymond E. Bernberg; Psychometric Affiliates. *

ALBERT K. KURTZ, *1810 Ivy Lane, Winter Park, Florida.*

This test is specifically designed to get "away from the simple direct techniques of measurement" by the use of a projective technique. The person taking the test answers 34 two-choice questions about how people "in groups such as yours" feel or act. The resulting score, when averaged with scores of the others in the group, gives a measure of the average morale of the group. It probably does, but whether it does so (a) by averaging the N morale scores of the N persons in the group or (b) by averaging N guesses about the morale of the entire group is not specifically stated in the manual. This will matter when we discuss the validity of this test.

READABILITY AND APPEARANCE. The test is reproduced from copy prepared on a typewriter with a few defective letters and so out of alignment that the lower half of many capital letters is darkened. The test has one typographical error and at least two ungrammatical items. The four-page manual, however, is not nearly that good. It contains three uncorrected spelling or typographical errors, at least three grammatical errors, and inaccurate titles for two of the six references, one by the author himself. But the real objection to the manual is the shrinkage of the typing from 10 letters to the horizontal inch with 6 lines to the vertical inch to 16 letters to the inch with 9½ lines to the inch. This saves paper by getting 2½ times as many words on a page, but (even for a person with 20/20 vision) it is very difficult to read, especially since there is no space between paragraphs. True, the test is about 20 years old, but even 40 years ago many test materials were far better prepared.

PRACTICALITY. If we ignore the just cited misuse of the English language, the test is well written. Earlier versions were submitted to various groups and their comments have resulted in a test that can be understood by the intended audience. The language may be awkward in some places, but it is not stilted.

FACE VALIDITY. Since it is called *Work Information Inventory,* which the manual describes as a disguised morale scale, the test should have no face validity for the workers who take it, but it should appear to be a morale measure to the officials who arrange for it to be given. It probably meets both these objectives.

RELIABILITY. Although many people would prefer one of the Kuder-Richardson reliabilities, the split-half method used by the author is acceptable. The reliability of .86 is satisfactory for the group comparisons with which he seems to be concerned. If individual comparisons are to be made, the test could be lengthened to 50 items in order to obtain a reliability of .90.

VALIDITY. An awkward situation arises here. Perhaps this test is highly valid; perhaps it is merely reliable with completely unknown validity. Let us first look at item 16 of the test: "It has been found that in groups such as yours most people: a) do what is required; b) do more than is required." For the job I had in 1967, I would have answered "do what is required" solely because there is no alternative which says "do less than is required." I liked my job; I enjoyed my work; I was proud of what I did. If you believe that these last three facts indicate high morale, then such a test as this is neither accurate nor valid. But if you feel that my morale was low because I felt that most of my fellow-employees (but not my boss) were either lazy or incompetent, then this test may be valid for *individuals.* In either case, however, this reviewer will concede that it may be valid for measuring *groups.*

Just how valid is this test for measuring group morale? All we need to do is correlate scores on this test with a measure of morale. The author did this. He correlated the test scores with six performance indicators: absences, tardiness, short-time absences, medical-aid unit visits, merit rating, and a total performance indicator score. The highest of these six correlations was .06, so they would certainly qualify as six of the lowest validities on record.

The author then says, "To give an indication of validity of the test as well as provide a comparison of the morale tests, the appraisal of morale by the employees was used as a criterion." This measured "the degree to which he agreed with the proposition that 'On the whole, I believe that my work group has a high degree of morale. By that I mean the men work willingly and cheerfully as a well organized team.' "

Now compare the preceding paragraph with the opening paragraph of this review and the sample item quoted above. Is it any wonder that what a worker says about "my work group" agrees with his answers to 34 questions about what happens "in groups such as yours"? You are right; his two guesses about other people correlate .67. The author regards this as a validity coefficient. The reviewer regards it as the correlation between two guesses the worker makes about the work of his fellow employees. As such, it is the relation between two similar variables, but it is probably much closer to the reliability of either than it is to the validity of one of them. Stated bluntly, no proof or even hint is given about the accuracy of the projective notion that the employee is talking about himself when he answers about others. Further, the validity of this test is unknown—the reviewer's admission that it probably does measure group morale is just an opinion with no data to support it, while the author's notion that the validity is .67 cannot be accepted because of unwarranted similarity between the two variables.

SUMMARY AND CONCLUSION. Because (a) no evidence is given that this actually is a projective test that measures the worker who fills it out rather than his fellow-workers and, further, because (b) there is no proof that his own morale is being measured, the reviewer feels that this test should not be used for the measurement of any individual worker's morale. If someone wishes to use it to measure a group rather than the individual members of the group, it may be used although there will still remain the question as to whether it is measuring the group's morale rather than its sociability, friendliness, tendency to gossip, or something else. It is unfortunate that the author has given us no clearly acceptable information on the test's validity.

[1058]

★**Workshop Evaluation Scale.** Workshop participants; 1974; WES; 7 scores: organization, objectives, work of presenter, ideas and activities, scope, benefit, overall effectiveness; no data on reliability; 1 form (8 pages); manual (26 pages); profile-report form (4 pages); $3.75 per 25 scales, 25¢ per profile-report form; $2.95 per manual; $3.35 per specimen set; cash orders postpaid; (5–10) minutes; Earl McCallon; Learning Concepts. *

Work Information Inventory

SELECTION & RATING FORMS

[1059]

★**Job Performance Scale.** Employees; 1971; ratings by supervisors which may be used for local validation of *Wonderlic Personnel Test;* ratings in 3 areas: ability to perform, attitude, total; no data on reliability and validity; no norms; no data on scoring; 3 parts which may be used separately or in combination; no manual; only accessories are for conducting validation research; 5¢ per part ($5 minimum), postpaid; administration time not reported; E. F. Wonderlic & Associates, Inc. *
a) PRIMARY RATING NO. 1. [5–10] minutes.
b) PRIMARY RATING NO. 2. [5–15] minutes.
c) RATER'S PERFORMANCE SUMMARY. For ranking of all employees rated; [5–15] minutes.

[1060]

The McCormick Job Performance Measurement "Rate-$-Scales." Employees; 1971; 5 ratings by supervisors: responsibility, attitude, time in grade, efficiency, total; no data on reliability and validity; no norms; 1 form (4 pages); instructions (6 pages); $7.50 per 25 tests, postage extra; $3 per specimen set, postpaid; [5–10] minutes; Ronald R. McCormick, Trademark Design Products, Inc.*

REFERENCES

1. McCORMICK, RONALD R. "Can We Use Compensation Data to Measure Job Performance Behavior?" *Personnel J* 51(2):918–22 D '72. *

ALAN R. BASS, *Professor of Psychology, Wayne State University, Detroit, Michigan.*

This rating technique provides a method for evaluation of an employee's job performance in dollars and cents terms. All employees are rated on four job performance dimensions (*R*esponsibility, *A*ttitude, *T*ime in Grade, and *E*fficiency), the first letters of which result in the acronym RATE. In addition, the employee receives an overall job performance score. All ratings are made in dollar values rather than on more conventional fixed-point graphic rating scales. The overall performance score is simply the sum of the dollar values assigned to the four RATE dimensions, which then becomes the recommended total wage or salary to be paid to the employee.

In order to assist the rater in using the rating scales, the organization's personnel department is asked to provide a dollar value for the "fully qualified worker" on each of the four rating dimensions, as well as the fully qualified worker's total wage rate, which is the sum of those four dollar values. The fully qualified worker's total wage is recommended by the author to be at the midpoint of the wage range for that job classification. The rater is to use the dollar values provided as standards against which to evaluate each employee being rated. The author provides a method for allocation of the fully qualified worker's total wage rate among the four rating dimensions based on the level of the job in the organization, with more weight (i.e., a larger proportion of the total wage rate) given to the dimensions responsibility and attitude for higher-level job classifications and more weight given to time in grade and efficiency for lower-level jobs.

The rater, having available to him the dollar values allocated to each of the four rating dimensions and the total wage rate for a fully qualified worker, then assigns a dollar value to each rating dimension for each employee he rates. The four dollar values are to sum to the total wage rate which the rater wishes to recommend for the employee, thus providing a direct tie between pay and performance evaluation.

This rating technique cannot be evaluated in terms of the usual psychometric considerations, since no technical manual accompanies the rating scales and no data are presently available concerning psychometric properties of the scales. If the rating scales are used to obtain measures of individual differences in job performance (as a criterion measure in a test validation study, for example), then information concerning such matters as rate-rerate reliability, interrater agreement, correlations of the rating dimensions with one another and with the overall evaluation, correlations of the ratings with other variables, etc., would have to be obtained locally. However, there is no reason to believe that these rating scales should be any more valid or accurate measures of job performance or any more resistant to typical rater "errors," such as leniency and halo, than more conventional fixed-point graphic rating scales. The four rating dimensions are rather global and ambiguous, may be interpreted quite differently by different raters, and in some cases appear to be multifaceted (attitude, for example, is defined as including "good relationships with others, adherence to working rules, initiative, and growth in job knowledge").

On the other hand, it may not be entirely appropriate to evaluate this rating technique in terms of the usual psychometric considerations. The instructions which accompany the rating procedure seem to imply that the scales may be

more useful and appropriate as an organizational tool for establishing pay rates than as a measure of an employee's job performance. Therefore, it may be more appropriate to evaluate the rating procedure in terms of its effectiveness as a method of salary determination. The instruction booklet is rather specific in detailing the presumed advantages of using these rating scales, suggesting that the "RATE-$-SCALES" will increase job performance, control manpower costs, improve personnel budgeting, achieve greater employee job satisfaction, and develop better employer-employee communication. Again, however, no evidence is presented and apparently none is available to substantiate any of these claimed values of this rating technique.

It is likely that the typical rater using these scales would decide on the pay rate he wishes to recommend for a particular employee and then proceed to assign dollar values to the four rating dimensions so as to sum to the desired pay rate. It is not at all apparent that use of this technique is likely to result in improved job performance through increased employee motivation, higher job satisfaction, or better employer-employee communication.

The major problem, again, is that, like the typical graphic rating scale, the rating dimensions here are rather global and vague, and, contrary to the author's assertions, are not behaviorally-oriented. While each rating dimension is followed by a brief definition, e.g., responsibility: "Demonstrated ability to assume and carry out the job related responsibilities detailed in the job content," these definitions are themselves sufficiently general and ambiguous that the supervisor would probably find it difficult to use them, per se, as a basis for communicating to the subordinate what needs to be done to qualify for a higher wage raise in the future. It is entirely possible that ratees who receive relatively low ratings, and thus relatively low wage rates, will have little appreciation for the reasons for their ratings or for what needs to be done to improve their performance in the future. Defensive reactions, poor attitudes, and stable or even deteriorating performance could well ensue rather than the improved job performance and increased satisfaction which the author anticipates.

In the absence of evidence of any kind, one

McCormick Job Performance Measurement "Rate-$-Scales"

can only speculate about the possible values and consequences of using these rating scales. However, it would seem likely that whether the user wishes a valid and accurate measure of individual differences in job performance or a method for improving employee performance by tying pay directly to performance, a more behaviorally-oriented approach would be desirable. Evaluation of employee performance in terms of degree of achievement of specific goals or in terms of specific job behaviors determined by job analyses to be important for effective job performance might yield more valid job performance measures and result in better job performance and employee satisfaction than the scales reviewed here. In any event, even if one agrees on the desirability of tying pay directly to performance evaluation, it is difficult to see why this rating technique will achieve the goals suggested by the author or will be superior to other rating methods in achieving such goals.

[1061]

★Minnesota Satisfactoriness Scales. Employees; 1965-70; MSS; ratings by supervisors; 5 scores: performance, conformance, dependability, personal adjustment, general satisfactoriness; 1 form ('65, 3 pages); manual ('70, 53 pages plus test); hand scoring requires local reproduction of a scoring sheet ("Hand-Scoring Form") to which weighted response scores must be transferred; $3 per 30 tests; $3.20 per xerox copy of manual which is out of print; postage extra; scoring service, 30¢ to 50¢ per test; (5) minutes; Dennis L. Gibson, David J. Weiss, René V. Dawis, and Lloyd H. Lofquist; Vocational Psychology Research. *

REFERENCES

1. DELOREY, RUTH MARIE WOOD. Job Satisfaction-Satisfactoriness and Characteristics of Minneapolis Business Graduates. Doctor's thesis, University of Minnesota (Minneapolis, Minn.), 1972. (DAI 33:229A)
2. GILSRUD, RONALD DEAN. Job Satisfaction of Formerly Disadvantaged Students as a Measure of Accountability for Vocational Office Education Program. Doctor's thesis, University of North Dakota (Grand Forks, N.D.), 1972. (DAI 33: 6803A)
3. SEILER, DALE A., and LACEY, DAVID W. "Adapting the Work Adjustment Theory for Assessing Technical-Professional Utilization." J Voc Behav 3(4):443-51 O '73. * (PA 52:2005)
4. GILLELAND, ROBERTA LOUISE. The Relationship Between the WAIS and MMPI Subscale Scores and Work Adjustment Outcomes in Adult Blind and Partially Sighted Persons. Doctor's thesis, Ohio State University (Columbus, Ohio), 1974. (DAI 35:5684B)
5. McCULLOCH, ETTA SMITH. Factors Influencing Job Satisfaction and Job Satisfactoriness of Newly Licensed Nurses. Doctor's thesis, Florida State University (Tallahassee, Fla.), 1974. (DAI 35:2280B)
6. McPHERSON, TIMOTHY. Job Satisfaction and Performance of Elementary and Secondary Classroom Teachers in Region IX Service Center Area of Texas. Doctor's thesis, North Texas State University (Denton, Tex.), 1974. (DAI 35:7569A)
7. GASS, MARCELLE BURDETTE. A Job Satisfactoriness and Job Satisfaction Study of College of Business Graduates. Doctor's thesis, Kansas State University (Manhattan, Kan.), 1975. (DAI 37:829A)
8. NEELY, JERRY RICHARD. The Impact of a Substantial Pay Raise on Teacher Performance and Job Satisfaction in Region IX Service Center Area of Texas. Doctor's thesis, North Texas State University (Denton, Tex.), 1975. (DAI 36:7749A)
9. QUIRK, KEITH H. The Work Adjustment of a Group of Mentally Retarded Persons From Coles County, Illinois. Doctor's thesis, George Peabody College for Teachers (Nashville, Tenn.), 1975. (DAI 36:5201A)

JEROME E. DOPPELT, Director, Psychological Measurement Division, The Psychological Corporation, New York, New York.

The Minnesota Satisfactoriness Scales is one of the measurement devices that evolved from studies of adjustment to work, begun in 1957 by the Work Adjustment Project of the University of Minnesota. It is a 28-item questionnaire designed to assess the satisfactoriness of an individual as an employee. Indications of poor adjustment, as reflected in low scores on the MSS, suggest that the worker may need counseling that will lead him to an occupation that is better suited to him. For 27 of the items, three alternatives are provided for rating the worker in comparison with others in his work group. The last item calls for an overall evaluation and the ranking of the worker in one of four quartiles in comparison with his fellow workers. The questionnaire may be completed by a worker's immediate supervisor, a fellow worker, or the employee himself. Among the suggested applications of the MSS are these: by a counselor in a follow-up of counselees with their employers; in studies of the labor market, such as a comparison of MSS scores for counselees placed in different jobs; in counseling with an individual, as, for example, in determining a counselee's misperceptions of himself by comparing his own rating of his satisfactoriness with that given by a supervisor or a former employer.

The MSS yields scores on a general satisfactoriness scale based on all 28 items and four additional scales: performance, concerned with the employee's promotability and the quantity and quality of his work (9 items); conformance, reflecting how well the worker gets along with supervisors and co-workers and observes regulations (7 items); dependability, referring to the frequency of disciplinary problems created by the employee (4 items); and personal adjustment, dealing with the worker's emotional health (7 items). The first 27 items are scored 1, 2, or 3, and weights for the last item range from 1 to 4. A person's score on a scale is the sum of the weighted responses to the items that constitute that scale.

A hand-scoring form to which the rater's weighted responses are transferred is intended to facilitate scoring but the scoring procedure appears to be cumbersome and relatively time-consuming. Percentile norm tables are provided for five occupational groups and for a workers-in-general group which was constructed by combining cases randomly selected from the five groups in proportion to their frequency in the total labor force in 1968. The workers-in-general group is offered as the table to use for workers whose occupations are not represented among the five groups. Standard errors of measurement are given with each of the norm tables to permit the determination of a confidence band around each score.

The 28-item MSS is a revision of two previous forms. The range of internal consistency reliabilities for the five scales, as measured by Hoyt reliability coefficients, is .69 to .95, with median .87. Two-year test-retest (stability) correlation coefficients for four occupational groups ranged from .40 to .68, with median .50 for the 20 coefficients that were involved. The stability data were based on the MSS scores of persons rated in 1965 and 1967. Evidence of construct validity is presented and it is concluded, quite modestly, that there is some evidence that the MSS is a valid measure of satisfactoriness. Among "satisfied" workers, as judged by the extrinsic scale of the short-form *Minnesota Satisfaction Questionnaire,* those rated above the median on MSS performance were more likely to continue on the job over a two-year interval than were those rated below the median; MSS scores were related to age of employees in meaningful ways; general satisfactoriness and performance scores were highest for those between the age extremes of very young (inexperienced) or old (past their prime).

The MSS is a tool developed to measure one aspect of a worker's adjustment to a particular job. It has the advantages of being short, simply written, and concerned with activities that seem relevant to work performance. The questionnaire form shows a copyright date of 1965, a time when there was little concern about the exclusive use of the masculine form when refer-

ring to the worker. The MSS is replete with "his" and "him," with nary a single "her." In 1976, and subsequently, this might cause concern in some places. Norms data were collected before 1966. The occupational groups for which these data are presented are not likely to be representative of similarly-named occupational groups a decade later. More current data would be desirable.

The reliabilities seem remarkably high for short scales. Some of this is undoubtedly due to the refinement of the scales in successive revisions. But some of it may be due to redundancy of content or what might appear to be redundancy to the rater. For example, in the performance scale, "Transfer him to a job at a higher level?" and "Promote him to a position of more responsibility?" might seem quite similar and be rated accordingly, as might "Accept the direction of his supervisor?" and "Respect the authority of his supervisor?" in the conformance scale.

The MSS is consistent with a sound theory and its development reflects competence and caution. It should prove helpful in the vocational rehabilitation settings for which it is suggested. However, the data need updating and the authors should consider rewording some of the items to reduce sex bias. Perhaps one of the most important problems in the use of the MSS lies outside the instrument. Has the rater been adequately instructed in the rating of his workers so that a meaningful and objective evaluation is obtained? When such instruction can be given and the ratings can be based on relevant behaviors, the MSS may prove valuable not only in vocational rehabilitation practice but in particular companies that want to evaluate the performance of workers.

[1062]

★**Rehabilitation Client Rating Scale.** Vocational rehabilitation counselees; 1974; RCRS; formerly called *Queens Counsellor Rating Scale;* 5 scores: work attributes, impulsivity, emotional maladjustment, social adjustment, devious behavior; 1 form (2 pages); manual (28 pages); $1 per 100 tests; $2 per manual; $2 per specimen set; postpaid; program for computer scoring presented in manual; (10–15) minutes; John S. Hicks; the Author. *

REFERENCES

1. HICKS, JOHN; RAMSEY, PHILIP; AND BROWER, JULIAN. "The Queens Counsellor Rating Scale (QCRS) for Evaluating Client Performance in a Vocational Training Center." *Training Sch B* 71(2):71–9 Ag '74. *

SPECIFIC VOCATIONS

ACCOUNTING

[1063]

★**ACT Proficiency Examinations in Accounting.**
College and adults; 1973–77; for college accreditation
of nontraditional study, advanced placement, or assessment of educational achievement; tests (except *c*)
administered 4 times annually (February, May, August, November) at centers established by the publisher; developed and administered in New York
State as a part of their Regents External Degree Program; no data on reliability; 5 tests; study guides
('76, 2–3 pages) for each test; for further information
and program accessories, see 470; examination fees include reporting of scores to the candidate and one college; developed by the University of the State of New
York; American College Testing Program. *
a) LEVEL 1. 1973–76; 6 semester credits recommended;
Form ZZ ('76, 12 pages); earlier forms were used in
the College Proficiency Examination Program (1968–
72); examination fee, $35 per candidate; 180(210)
minutes.
b) LEVEL 2. 1973–77; 9 semester credits recommended;
single pass-fail grade; 2 parts: Form ZZ-objective
part ('73, 10 pages, reprinted with 1976 copyright),
Form XZ-essay part ('77, 8 pages); examination fee,
$75 per candidate; 240(270) minutes.
c) LEVEL 3. 1974–77; tests administered 2 times annually (May, November) at centers established by the
publisher; 3 essay tests; 12 semester credits recommended if all tests are passed; single pass-fail grade
for each test; examination fee, $75 per area; 180(210)
minutes per area.
   1) *Area 1, Business Law and Federal Income Taxa-
tion.* Form YZ ('77, 12 pages).
   2) *Area 2, Auditing and Cost Analysis.* Form YZ
('77, 11 pages).
   3) *Area 3, Advanced Theory and Special Problems.*
Form YZ ('77, 10 pages).

[1064]

*CLEP Subject Examination in Introductory
Accounting. 1 year or equivalent; 1970–76; for college accreditation of nontraditional study, advanced
placement, or assessment of educational achievement;
tests administered monthly at centers throughout the
United States; Forms YCT1 ('76, 15 pages), YCT2
('76, 16 pages); optional essay supplement scored by
college: Forms YCT-A, YCT-B, ('76, 3–4 pages);
for program accessories, see 473; rental and scoring
fee, $20 per student (includes reporting of scores to
the candidate and one college); postpaid; 90(95) minutes, same for essay supplement; program administered for the College Entrance Examination Board by
Educational Testing Service. *
   For reviews of the CLEP program, see 473 (3 reviews) and 7:664 (3 reviews).

BUSINESS

[1065]

★**ACT Proficiency Examination in Business Environment and Strategy.** College and adults; 1973–
77; for college accreditation of nontraditional study,
advanced placement, or assessment of educational
achievement; test administered 4 times annually (February, May, August, November) at centers established
by the publisher; developed and administered in New

York State as a part of their Regents External Degree Program; 6 semester credits recommended; single
pass-fail grade; no data on reliability; 2 parts: Form
ZZ-objective part ('73, 8 pages, reprinted with 1976
copyright); Form XZ-essay part ('77, 6 pages); study
guide ('76, 3 pages); for further information and program accessories, see 470; examination fee, $75 per
candidate (includes reporting of score to the candidate
and one college); 240(270) minutes; developed by the
University of the State of New York; American College Testing Program. *

[1066]

★**ACT Proficiency Examinations in Finance.**
College and adults; 1973–77; for college accreditation
of nontraditional study, advanced placement, or assessment of educational achievement; tests (except *c*)
administered 4 times annually (February, May, August, November) at centers established by the publisher; developed and administered in New York
State as a part of their Regents External Degree Program; no data on reliability; 3 tests; study guides
('76, 2–5 pages) for each test; for further information
and program accessories, see 470; examination fees
include reporting of scores to the candidate and one
college; developed by the University of the State of
New York; American College Testing Program. *
a) LEVEL 1. 1973–76; 9 semester credits recommended;
Form ZZ ('73, 12 pages, reprinted with 1976 copyright); examination fee, $35 per candidate; 180(210)
minutes.
b) LEVEL 2. 1973–77; 9 semester credits recommended; single pass-fail grade; 2 parts: Form ZZ-
objective part ('73, 7 pages, reprinted with 1976 copyright), Form XZ-essay part ('77, 5 pages); examination fee, $75 per candidate; 240(270) minutes.
c) LEVEL 3. 1974–77; test administered 2 times annually (May, November) at centers established by the
publisher; 12 semester credits recommended; single
pass-fail grade; essay test: Form YZ ('77, 11 pages);
examination fee, $150 per candidate; 420(480) min-
utes.

[1067]

★**ACT Proficiency Examinations in Management
of Human Resources.** College and adults; 1973–77;
for college accreditation of nontraditional study, advanced placement, or assessment of educational achievement; tests (except *c*) administered 4 times annually
(February, May, August, November) at centers established by the publisher; developed and administered
in New York State as a part of their Regents External Degree Program; no data on reliability; 3
tests; study guides ('76, 3–4 pages) for each test; for
further information and program accessories, see 470;
examination fees include reporting of scores to the
candidate and one college; developed by the University
of the State of New York; American College Testing
Program. *
a) LEVEL 1. 1973–76; 6 semester credits recommended; Form ZZ ('76, 10 pages); examination fee,
$35 per candidate; 180(210) minutes.
b) LEVEL 2. 1973–77; 9 semester credits recommended;
single pass-fail grade; 2 parts: Form ZZ-objective part
('73, 6 pages, reprinted with 1976 copyright), Form
YZ-essay part ('77, 3 pages); examination fee, $75 per
candidate; 240(270) minutes.
c) LEVEL 3. 1974–77; test administered 2 times annually (May, November) at centers established by the
publisher; 12 semester credits recommended; single
pass-fail grade; essay test: Form YZ ('77, 13 pages);

examination fee, $150 per candidate; 420(480) minutes.

[1068]

★ACT Proficiency Examinations in Marketing.
College and adults; 1973–77; for college accreditation of nontraditional study, advanced placement, or assessment of educational achievement; tests (except *c*) administered 4 times annually (February, May, August, November) at centers established by the publisher; developed and administered in New York State as a part of their Regents External Degree Program; no data on reliability; 3 tests; study guides ('76, 3–4 pages) for each test; for further information and program accessories, see 470; examination fees include reporting of scores to the candidate and one college; developed by the University of the State of New York; American College Testing Program. *
a) LEVEL 1. 1973–76; 3 semester credits recommended; Form ZZ ('73, 9 pages, reprinted with 1976 copyright); examination fee, $35 per candidate; 180(210) minutes.
b) LEVEL 2. 1973–77; 9 semester credits recommended; single pass-fail grade; 2 parts: Form ZZ-objective part ('73, 7 pages, reprinted with 1976 copyright), Form XZ-essay part ('77, 4 pages); examination fee, $75 per candidate; 240(270) minutes.
c) LEVEL 3. 1974–77; test administered 2 times annually (May, November) at centers established by the publisher; 12 semester credits recommended; single pass-fail grade; essay test: Form YZ ('77, 19 pages); examination fee, $150 per candidate; 420(480) minutes.

[1069]

★ACT Proficiency Examinations in Operations Management. College and adults; 1973–77; for college accreditation of nontraditional study, advanced placement, or assessment of educational achievement; tests (except *c*) administered 4 times annually (February, May, August, November) at centers established by the publisher; developed and administered in New York State as a part of their Regents External Degree Program; no data on reliability; 3 tests; study guide ('76, 2–5 pages) for each test; for further information and program accessories, see 470; examination fees include reporting of scores to the candidate and one college; developed by the University of the State of New York; American College Testing Program. *
a) LEVEL 1. 1973–76; 9 semester credits recommended; Form ZZ ('73, 10 pages, reprinted with 1976 copyright); examination fee, $35 per candidate; 180(210) minutes.
b) LEVEL 2. 1973–77; 9 semester credits recommended; single pass-fail grade; 2 parts: Form ZZ-objective part ('73, 6 pages, reprinted with 1976 copyright), Form XZ-essay part ('77, 5 pages); examination fee, $75 per candidate; 240(270) minutes.
c) LEVEL 3. 1974–77; test administered 2 times annually (May, November) at centers established by the publisher; 12 semester credits recommended; single pass-fail grade; essay test: Form YZ ('77, 9 pages); examination fee, $150 per candidate; 420(480) minutes.

[1070]

*CLEP Subject Examination in Introduction to Business Management. 1 semester or equivalent; 1969–76; for college accreditation of nontraditional study, advanced placement, or assessment of educational achievement; tests administered monthly at centers

throughout the United States; Forms SCT1 ('69, 14 pages), UCT1 ('73, 14 pages); optional essay supplement scored by college: Forms RCT1A, RCT1B, RCT2A, RCT2B, ('69, 2 pages); for program accessories, see 473; rental and scoring fee, $20 per student (includes reporting of scores to the candidate and one college); postpaid; 90(95) minutes, same for essay supplement; program administered for the College Entrance Examination Board by Educational Testing Service. *
For reviews of the CLEP program, see 473 (3 reviews) and 7:664 (3 reviews).

[1071]

*CLEP Subject Examination in Introductory Business Law. 1 semester or equivalent; 1970–76; for college accreditation of nontraditional study, advanced placement, or assessment of educational achievement; tests administered monthly at centers throughout the United States; Form XCT ('75, 15 pages); optional essay supplement scored by college: Forms SCT1A, SCT1B, SCT2A, SCT2B, ('70, 2 pages); for program accessories, see 473; rental and scoring fee, $20 per student (includes reporting of scores to the candidate and one college); postpaid; 90(95) minutes, same for essay supplement; program administered for the College Entrance Examination Board by Educational Testing Service. *
For reviews of the CLEP program, see 473 (3 reviews) and 7:664 (3 reviews).

[1072]

*CLEP Subject Examination in Introductory Marketing. 1 semester or equivalent; 1968–76; for college accreditation of nontraditional study, advanced placement, or assessment of educational achievement; tests administered monthly at centers throughout the United States; Forms K-QCT1, K-QCT2, ('68, 12 pages); optional essay supplement scored by college: Forms QCT1-A, QCT1-B, QCT2-A, QCT2-B, ('68, 2 pages); for program accessories, see 473; rental and scoring fee, $20 per student (includes reporting of scores to the candidate and one college); postpaid; 90(95) minutes, same for essay supplement; program administered for the College Entrance Examination Board by Educational Testing Service. *
For reviews of the CLEP program, see 473 (3 reviews) and 7:664 (3 reviews).

[1073]

*CLEP Subject Examination in Money and Banking. 1 semester or equivalent; 1967–76; for college accreditation of nontraditional study, advanced placement, or assessment of educational achievement; tests administered monthly at centers throughout the United States; Forms PCT1, PCT2, ('67, 16 pages); optional essay supplement scored by college: Forms PCT1-A, PCT1-B, K-PCT2-A, PCT2-B, ('67, 1–3 pages); for program accessories, see 473; rental and scoring fee, $20 per student (includes reporting of scores to the candidate and one college); postpaid; 90(95) minutes, same for essay supplement; program administered for the College Entrance Examination Board by Educational Testing Service. *
For reviews of the CLEP program, see 473 (3 reviews) and 7:664 (3 reviews).

[1074]

*Graduate Management Admission Test. Business graduate students; 1954–77; GMAT; formerly called *Admission Test for Graduate Study in Business;* test

Graduate Management Admission Test

administered 4 times annually (January, March, July, November) at centers established by the publisher; 3 scores: verbal, quantitative, total; 12 current forms ('67–77, 37–53 pages); supervisor's manual ('77, 26 pages); student guide ('77, 505 pages); bulletin for candidates ('77, 31 pages); score guide ('76, 15 pages); counselor's handbook ('74, 102 pages); separate answer sheets (MRC) must be used; examination fee, $12.50 per student (fee includes reporting of scores to 3 schools); $3.95 per student guide; $5 per counselor's handbook; postpaid; 180–190(240) minutes; Educational Testing Service. *

See T2:2325 (5 references); for reviews by Jerome E. Doppelt and Gary R. Hanson of earlier forms, see 7:1080 (10 references).

REFERENCES

1–10. See 7:1080.
11–15. See T2:2325; also includes a cumulative name index to the first 15 references and 2 reviews for this test.
16. HARRELL, THOMAS W. "Differences Between Men in Big and Small Business." *Personnel Psychol* 24(4):649–52 w '71. * (PA 51:4020)
17. EVANS, FRANKLIN R., AND REILLY, RICHARD R. "Test Speededness as a Potential Source of Bias in Quantitative Admissions Tests." Abstract. *Proc 80th Ann Conv Am Psychol Assn* 7(1):23–4 '72. * (PA 48:5619)
18. HARRELL, THOMAS W., AND HARRELL, MARGARET S. "The Personality of MBA's Who Reach General Management Early." *Personnel Psychol* 26(1):127–34 sp '73. * (PA 51:2012)
19. SRINIVASAN, V., AND WEINSTEIN, ALAN G. "Effects of Curtailment on an Admissions Model for a Graduate Management Program." *J Appl Psychol* 58(3):339–46 D '73. * (PA 52:8742)
20. NORD, WALTER R.; CONNELLY, FRANCIS; AND DAIGNAULT, GEORGE. "Locus of Control and Aptitude Test Scores as Predictors of Academic Achievement." *J Ed Psychol* 66(6):956–61 D '74. *
21. WEINSTEIN, ALAN G., AND SRINIVASAN, V. "Predicting Managerial Success of Master of Business Administration (MBA) Graduates." *J Appl Psychol* 59(2):207–12 Ap '74. * (PA 51:11153)
22. BAIRD, LEONARD L. "Comparative Prediction of First Year Graduate and Professional School Grades in Six Fields." *Ed & Psychol Meas* 35(4):941–6 w '75. * (PA 55:13523)
23. GOODRICH, JONATHAN N. "American Standardized Tests: Pseudo-Indicators of Ability?" *Ed Technol* 15(12):23–5 D '75. *
24. FOJTIK, CHARLES WILLIAM. *Individual Traits Associated With Characteristics of Subjective Probability Distributions.* Doctor's thesis, University of Southern California (Los Angeles, Calif.), 1976. (DAI 37:2287A)
25. EDUCATIONAL TESTING SERVICE. *Statistical Summary by Undergraduate Colleges Attended, 1957–1976.* Princeton, N.J.: Educational Testing Service, 1977. Pp. iv, 100. *
26. KURST, CHARLOTTE. *77/78 Graduate Study in Management: A Guide for Prospective Students.* Princeton, N.J.: Educational Testing Service, 1977. Pp. 512. *

[1075]

Organizational Value Dimensions Questionnaire: Business Form. Adults; 1965–66; OVDQ; for research use only; attitudes toward business and industrial firms in general; manual title is *Value Scale—The Business Firm;* 9 scores: organizational magnitude and structure, internal consideration, competition and strategy, social responsibility, quality, change, member identification and control, external political participation, member equality and participation; no data on reliability; no norms; Form BBR-65 ('65, 4 pages); manual ('66, 7 pages); separate answer sheets must be used; $2 per 25 tests; 2¢ per answer sheet; cash orders postpaid; specimen set free; (25) minutes; Carroll L. Shartle and Ralph M. Stogdill; University Publications Sales, Ohio State University. *

WILLIAM G. MOLLENKOPF, *Associate Manager of Personnel Administration, The Procter & Gamble Company, Cincinnati, Ohio.*

This questionnaire was an important stage in a research program aimed at devising a means for people to express "attitudinal values relating to business and industrial firms in general." However, the authors have apparently abandoned their project.

In view of their stated purpose, it seems unfortunate that the authors sought content mainly from academic sources—students, faculty, and the literature—and carried out experimental administrations only with college students. It is clearly evident that many items could have been improved, and that valuable ones on various topics might well have been added, had there been participation by people closer to the business world.

The authors carried out extensive analyses, both of their beginning set of 335 items, and of 140 of these, together with 175 new ones, using item, factor, and cluster analysis to study responses. This effort culminated in the present 100-item scale, measuring nine orthogonal factors.

The number of items per scale varies widely. The largest contains 25 items, but five contain only 4 to 6, and the others have 10, 11, and 15. Thirteen are not scored at all. Clearly, the breadth of coverage and the reliability per scale must vary considerably. No data are provided.

It is unfortunate that further work has not been done on the development of this instrument. In its present form, the reviewer believes it has very doubtful value even for research purposes.

COMPUTER PROGRAMMING

[1076]

*CLEP Subject Examination in Computers and Data Processing. 1–2 semesters or equivalent; 1968–76; for college accreditation of nontraditional study, advanced placement, or assessment of educational achievement; tests administered monthly at centers throughout the United States; Forms RCT1, UCT1, ('68, 14 pages); optional essay supplement scored by college: Forms QCT1-A, QCT1-B, QCT2-A, QCT2-B, ('68, 2 pages); for program accessories, see 473; rental and scoring fee, $20 per student (includes reporting of scores to the candidate and one college); postpaid; 90(95) minutes, same for essay supplement; program administered for the College Entrance Examination Board by Educational Testing Service. *

For reviews of the CLEP program, see 473 (3 reviews) and 7:664 (3 reviews).

[1077]

*CLEP Subject Examination in Elementary Computer Programming—Fortran IV. 1 semester or equivalent; 1971–76; for college accreditation of nontraditional study, advanced placement, or assessment of educational achievement; tests administered monthly at centers throughout the United States; Form TCT1 ('71, 14 pages); optional essay supplement scored by the college: Forms TCTA, TCTB, ('71, 3 pages); for program accessories, see 473; rental and scoring fee, $20 per student (includes reporting of scores to the candidate and one college); postpaid; 90(95) minutes, same for essay supplement; program administered for the College Entrance Examination Board by Educational Testing Service. *

For reviews of the CLEP program, see 473 (3 reviews).

[1078]

★Computer Operator Aptitude Battery. Experienced operators and trainees; 1973–74; COAB; 4 scores: sequence recognition, format checking, logical thinking, total; 1 form ('73, 25 pages); preliminary manual ('74, 19 pages); tape cassette available for administration; separate answer sheets must be used; $4 per test; $9.50 per 25 self-scoring answer sheets; $15 per tape cassette; $1.30 per manual; $5.60 per specimen set; postage extra; 45(55) minutes; A. Joanne Holloway; Science Research Associates, Inc. *

RICHARD T. JOHNSON, *Associate Professor of Education, Virginia Polytechnic Institute and State University, Reston, Virginia.*

The COAB claims predictive validity for two criteria: performance as a computer operator and predicted potential for learning computer programming. The test development was based on an analysis of the job requirements of an operator, using data from direct observation, training materials, discussions with supervisory personnel, and a literature review.

Six subtests were developed, three of which survived a purification phase. Since most test development begins with a set of items of which only a fraction are commercially viable, the discussion of the unusable material in the test manual seems unnecessary. Two of the three subtests are speeded, one requiring applicants to place a scrambled set of time-related events in correct order, and the other forcing them to decide which arrangements of numbers and letters conform to certain formats. In the third, generously timed, subtest applicants must analyze flowcharts.

Various estimates of reliability range from .71 to .95, probably adequate for the uses suggested. The lower values were based on draft alternate forms of the sequence recognition subtest as well as a test-retest procedure on the format checking, while the highest is a K-R 21 on the total battery for the initial validation group of 148 individuals. These 148 individuals were employed computer operators at five institutions in five states. Their immediate super-

visors ranked them on "demonstrated ability to perform the computer operator job." The rankings and raw scores were converted to standard scores within each institution before being combined for analysis.

Correlations of the subtest scores with ability to perform the job range from .15 to .33, and with years of experience from −.06 to −.21. (The latter values are not given in the manual, but were calculated from the data there.) Total scores correlate .33 with the ability ranking, which probably represents the core of the evidence for validity. A subsequent similar study shows a correlation of .42 for a smaller sample of 21 operators within a West Coast office.

In addition to using the COAB for choosing prospective operators, the author also presents an argument for using it as a predictor of potential for learning computer programming. Supervisors in three companies also ranked 87 of the operators on their "potential" as programmers, and the total score on the COAB correlates .44 with this estimate. Since the criterion was simply a guess, was probably contaminated by the halo effect, years of operator experience, and other influences, this use of the instrument seems less defensible than the first.

Directions for administration are generally adequate, except that if the applicants should ask about guessing, no direct answer is to be given except that they should make the best choice and go on. Furthermore, nothing is said about their using the white space on the answer sheet for scratch paper, which would simplify the sequence recognition subtest. However, any such marks would read through on the carboned self-scoring separate answer sheet and increase the difficulty of scoring. Instructions call for providing each person with two soft-lead pencils; an anachronistic holdover from an older generation of scoring machines. No score correction is made for guessing, and the expected guessing scores on the trainee norms are at the 10th, 45th, 10th, and 15th percentiles on the subtests and total score scales. A user probably should not hire anyone achieving a score below the 50th percentile.

Norms are based on data from 282 personnel (216 experienced and 66 trainees) in organizations which volunteered information. Significant differences exist between the means of the white and nonwhite norm subgroups, a problem the test author discusses but refrains from making any firm recommendations about handling in selection situations. No information is given concerning any possible sex differences in the scores.

The two norm tables in the manual present data for experienced operators and for trainees, providing percentile equivalents for each of the three subtests and the total scores. Since some data processing supervisors designate as trainees those persons who may have had a great deal of experience on other than their type of equipment, and since experience correlates negatively with COAB scores, the author should have defined the classification "trainee" more specifically.

The author gives no suggestion for the use of the subscales in selection, and only a minimum of assistance in general interpretation. Most of the advice appears inappropriate for small installations. In addition, the test author's assumed audience is not clear; in one paragraph users are encouraged to conduct local research which requires a fair amount of sophistication, and in the next paragraph are told that percentiles are spread out more at the ends of the distribution than in the middle. No bibliographic references are given to aid the inexperienced user.

The examiner's manual is accurately labeled "preliminary edition": data are sparse; validity, reliability, and norms are based on haphazard collections of inadequately specified groups; suggestions for use are meager; and superfluous material is presented. Hopefully the test author will correct these problems in the next edition of the manual.

However, the reliability and validity estimates are high enough to expect the COAB to be of some use in selection of potential computer operators, especially if only a few are to be chosen from among many applicants. A user would probably wish to augment this test with indicators (through tests or interviews) of obsessive-compulsiveness and other personality characteristics that might be helpful in the demands of the computer operator job, e.g., removing the write-protect ring from a tape or scheduling jobs in a multitask environment. Use of the COAB for choosing programmers seems ill-advised. If a company plans to promote a prospective operator to programmer, other in-struments such as the CPAB or IBM programmer aptitude tests are much more appropriate, either singly or in combination with the COAB.

NICK L. SMITH, *Senior Research Associate, Northwest Regional Educational Laboratory, Portland, Oregon.*

This test consists of three separately timed subtests designed to predict the job performance of computer operators. The first subtest, Sequence Recognition, is a speeded exercise requiring the examinee to place a scrambled set of time related events in proper order. For example, six common activities in fishing, such as cleaning a fish and baiting a hook, must be properly sequenced.

The second subtest, Format Checking, is also a speeded but more complicated exercise where substitutions are made to a series of numbers, letters, and punctuation marks according to a set of given rules. The examinee must determine whether the presented alternatives conform to the specified rules.

The third subtest, Logical Thinking, is a nonspeeded test described in the manual as "a test of ability to analyze the logical relations within problems and to visualize their solution in stepwise form." In fact, however, the subtest consists of a set of problem descriptions accompanied by a flowchart diagram illustrating how the problem is solved. The examinee must simply answer multiple choice questions about actions required at certain points in the flowchart.

The manual provides little useful information about the development of the test. An analysis of job requirements is mentioned and item types were supposedly selected for their "likelihood of measuring aptitudes important for learning and performing the tasks of a computer operator." However, few details are given and the discussion of item development and tryout is vague and incomplete.

Evidence of the test's reliability is also inadequate. Alternate-forms reliability estimates of .75 and .77 are reported for the sequence recognition subtest, but these estimates were obtained on trial versions of the test. There are no estimates of the reliability of the final version.

Three-week test-retest reliabilities ranging from .71 to .89 for samples of 9 to 16 junior college data processing students (47 total) are reported for the format checking subtest. Apparently none of these students was either a computer operator or an operator applicant and, as the author notes, these are small samples for estimating reliability. There is no indication how memory or practice effects may have influenced the estimates for the subtests with novel item formats.

Internal consistency estimates of .91 and .94 are reported for the logical thinking subtest. The internal consistency estimate of .95 reported for the total test is, unfortunately, based on the unacceptable practice of using an internal consistency measure on a test that contains speeded subtests.

The most serious deficiency of this test is the lack of evidence concerning its validity and job relevance. Two validity studies are reported; both are criterion-related and employ correlations between test scores and concurrent judgments of performance by immediate supervisors. In both studies the supervisors ranked all operators on actual job performance. Some of the supervisors in the first study also ranked their operators on their potential for learning computer programming. The subtest validities range from .15 to .39 for the job performance criterion and from .26 to .42 for the programmer-potential criterion.

Unfortunately, there is no information given about the reliability, deficiency, or contamination of the criterion measures nor about rater bias or reliability. A correction is made for years of experience, but there is no warning about the probable differences in motivation level between the employed operators tested and probable job applicants.

The author claims that this test measures computer operator "aptitude," but this term is never defined and no evidence of construct validity is given. Furthermore, the examinee is told that the logical thinking subtest "is a test of how logically you can think." Actually, the examinee is only required to interpret a flowchart diagram, and since there is no evidence of construct validity, this claim is also unsupported and misleading.

The manual states that "the test is intended to identify those applicants with potential to succeed in the operator job." However, this test's utility as a selection device is not supported by studies of predictive validity. In fact, the only information available on how job applicants perform is contained in a norm table obtained by voluntary submissions from organizations administering the test under unknown conditions.

There is no evidence given of the job relatedness of this test. The reported criterion-related validity would be evidence of job relatedness if the criterion measure were (a) a valid measure of overall job performance, (b) a construct related to job performance, or (c) a job sample. However, there is no information presented on the quality of the criterion, no construct validity information, and no evidence that the test behaviors constitute a job sample. Operator duties are never mentioned. The test, therefore, does not appear to be sufficiently job related as to comply with current legal standards (e.g., Griggs, et al. vs. Duke Power Company, 1971). In fact, the highest validities indicated are for the programmer-potential criterion, suggesting that the test is a better measure of programmer potential than a measure of operator ability.

The directions for administering the test are concise and easy to follow—sample items are explained and worked through in full. The test uses self-scoring answer sheets, but no corrections for guessing are made on the two speeded tests where they should be.

Percentile norm tables are provided for both experienced operators and trainees. They should be used cautiously, however, because the norms for experienced operators are based almost exclusively on male responses (93 percent) and the norms for trainees are based on a small sample of only 66.

The performance of minority persons on this test suggests that the test possibly discriminates illegally against nonwhite applicants. As the author points out, however, the data on this question are too sparse to provide a conclusive answer. There is no information on the possible sex bias of the test.

The manual does contain several sections designed to aid the test user in combining subtest scores, in interpreting the percentile norms, and in using the standard error of measurement estimates.

In summary, the considerable lack of evidence concerning construct validity, job-relatedness, and the test's utility as a selection device, and the possibility of social discrimination suggests that this test should be used *only* with

Computer Operator Aptitude Battery

extreme caution as an experimental device by selection personnel who should carefully collect their own research evidence.

[1079]

*Computer Programmer Aptitude Battery. Applicants for training or employment in computer programmer and systems analysis fields; 1964–74; CPAB; 6 scores: verbal meaning, reasoning, letter series, number ability, diagramming, total; 1 form ('64, 26 pages); revised manual ('74, 29 pages); tape cassette available for administration; separate answer sheets must be used; $4 per test; $9.50 per 25 self-marking answer sheets; $15 per tape cassette; $2 per manual; $6.75 per specimen set; postage extra; 79(90) minutes; Jean Maier Palormo; Science Research Associates, Inc. *

   British edition: 1964–71; standardization supplement by Peter Saville; NFER Publishing Co. Ltd. [England]. *

   See T2:2334 (2 references); for reviews by Richard T. Johnson and Donald J. Veldman, see 7:1089 (2 references).

REFERENCES

1–2. See 7:1089.
3–4. See T2:2334.
5. WOODROW, COLIN FRANCIS. *Moderator Variable Methodology Applied to Secondary School Computer Science Courses.* Doctor's thesis, University of Toronto (Toronto, Ont., Canada), 1972. (*DAI* 34:6472A)
6. KRATKIEWICZ, ROBERT FELIX. *The Relationship Between Student Variables and Achievement in a High School Computer Science Course Where Problem-Solving Is Done on a Terminal Connected to a Remote Time-Shared Computer.* Doctor's thesis, Wayne State University (Detroit, Mich.), 1973. (*DAI* 34: 6946A)
7. SCIENCE RESEARCH ASSOCIATES. *Validation: Procedures and Results: Part 3, Supplementary Results, Third Edition.* Chicago, Ill.: Science Research Associates, 1974. Pp. ii, 90. *

NICK L. SMITH, *Senior Research Associate, Northwest Regional Educational Laboratory, Portland, Oregon.*

This test, designed to select persons with an aptitude for computer programmer and systems analyst positions, is composed of five separately timed subtests: Verbal Meaning, a vocabulary test; Reasoning, an exercise in translating word problems into mathematical notation; Letter Series, a subtest of finding patterns in series of given letters; Number Ability, a testing requiring quick estimation of reasonable answers to numerical computations; and Diagramming, an exercise in interpreting flow-chart diagrams.

The manual has been revised and expanded since the 1967 edition and several improvements have been made. The section on the development of the test is lengthy and includes validities, item statistics, and intercorrelations with other tests. Although the reported reliabilities are acceptably high, they are based on the experimental forms of the tests developed over a decade ago. There are still no reliabilities for the final version of the test.

Of the ten validity studies reported in the manual, four employed programmer training outcomes as criteria. The predictive validities between total test score and training outcomes for these studies range from .30 to .71. The six additional validity studies used measures of job performance as criteria, but the concurrent and predictive validities for these studies are much lower, from .02 to .60. Each validity study is succinctly presented and its limitations adequately discussed. Overall, the test appears most useful for the selection of programmer trainees and somewhat less useful for predicting on-the-job performance. As the author points out, this is probably because ability, which is what this test is designed to measure, plays a larger role in determining short-term training success than long-term job performance, where personality factors, tenure, and supervisor bias are frequently very important.

The test is sufficiently job-related to be used as a screening device for selecting computer programmers as long as one follows the author's cautions and utilizes other sources of information before making a final selection decision. The test is not sufficiently valid or comprehensive to stand alone.

Although the author claims that systems analysts can also be selected by use of this instrument, most of the research concerns only programmers, and no attempt is made to discriminate between the two types of positions. Using the test to select analysts should be done cautiously.

The directions for administering the test are clear and easy to follow. In addition, a good quality cassette tape recording of the directions is provided. The test uses a self-scoring answer sheet, which is easy to use but does not provide the necessary correction for guessing on the two speeded tests.

A new section of the manual includes a discussion of the relationships between the following demographic variables and scores on the test: applicant status, sex, age, education, and race. The treatment of each variable is brief but informative.

Best sections of the manual include a discussion of certain types of needed local research on the test and a discussion of how to interpret the test scores from the norm tables. Percentile norms, means, standard deviations, and standard errors of measurement are provided for each subtest and for the total test for samples of 641 trainees and 299 experienced programmers.

Data presented in the manual show that there is little age or sex bias in the test. The limited available data do suggest, however, that the test may discriminate illegally against non-white applicants. A separate norm table for non-white trainees, based on a sample of 66, has therefore been provided.

Although there is still no information on the reliability of the final version of this test, the recent validity studies suggest that overall the CPAB is of sufficient quality for use in screening computer programmers for training. If the cautions outlined in the manual about local research are followed closely, the test could also be a useful predictor of one area of job performance. Because of the possibility of illegal discrimination, however, test scores should be interpreted with extreme care for non-white applicants.

[1080]

★The Graduate Record Examinations Advanced Computer Science Test. Graduate school candidates; 1976; test administered 3 times annually (April, October, December) at centers established by the publisher; 2 current forms ('76, 26–27 pages); descriptive booklet ('76, 14 pages); for program accessories, see 476; examination fee, $10.50 per candidate; 170(190) minutes; Educational Testing Service. *

DENTISTRY

[1081]

★CLEP Subject Examination in Dental Materials: Dental Auxiliary Education. Dental hygienists and assistants; 1976–77; for college accreditation of nontraditional study, advanced placement, or assessment of educational achievement; tests administered monthly at centers throughout the United States; Form YCTQ1 ('76, 10 pages); descriptive booklet ('77, 19 pages) for this and 3 other dental auxiliary education tests; for program accessories, see 473; rental and scoring fee, $20 per student (includes reporting of scores to the candidate and one college); postpaid; 45(50) minutes; program administered for the College Entrance Examination Board by Educational Testing Service. *
For reviews of the CLEP program, see 473 (3 reviews).

[1082]

★CLEP Subject Examination in Head, Neck, and Oral Anatomy: Dental Auxiliary Education. Dental hygienists and assistants; 1976–77; for college accreditation of nontraditional study, advanced placement, or assessment of educational achievement; tests administered monthly at centers throughout the United States; Forms YCT1 ('76, 8 pages), YCT2 ('76, 10

pages); descriptive booklet ('77, 19 pages) for this and 3 other dental auxiliary education tests; for program accessories, see 473; rental and scoring fee, $20 per student (includes reporting of scores to the candidate and one college); postpaid; 45(50) minutes; program administered for the College Entrance Examination Board by Educational Testing Service. *
For reviews of the CLEP program, see 473 (3 reviews).

[1083]

★CLEP Subject Examination in Oral Radiography: Dental Auxiliary Education. Dental hygienists and assistants; 1976–77; for college accreditation of nontraditional study, advanced placement, or assessment of educational achievement; tests administered monthly at centers throughout the United States; Forms YCT1 ('76, 13 pages), YCT2 ('76, 12 pages); descriptive booklet ('77, 19 pages) for this and 3 other dental auxiliary education tests; for program accessories, see 473; rental and scoring fee, $20 per student (includes reporting of scores to the candidate and one college); postpaid; 45(50) minutes; program administered for the College Entrance Examination Board by Educational Testing Service. *
For reviews of the CLEP program, see 473 (3 reviews).

[1084]

★CLEP Subject Examination in Tooth Morphology and Function: Dental Auxiliary Education. Dental hygienists and assistants; 1976–77; for college accreditation of nontraditional study, advanced placement, or assessment of educational achievement; tests administered monthly at centers throughout the United States; Forms YCT1, YCT2, ('76, 9 pages); descriptive booklet ('77, 19 pages) for this and 3 other dental auxiliary education tests; for program accessories, see 473; rental and scoring fee, $20 per student (includes reporting of scores to the candidate and one college); postpaid; 45(50) minutes; program administered for the College Entrance Examination Board by Educational Testing Service. *
For reviews of the CLEP program, see 473 (3 reviews).

[1085]

*Dental Admission Testing Program. Dental school applicants; 1946–77; DATP; formerly called *Dental Aptitude Testing Program;* tests administered 2 times annually (April, October) at centers established by the publisher; 5 tests, 12 scores: 10 scores listed below plus academic average (average of *a–c*) and perceptual-motor average (average of *d* and *e*); manual for administration (no date, 11 pages); preparation material for examinees ('77, 83 pages); score report explanation (no date, 2 pages); bulletin for applicants ('77, 16 pages); examination fee, $20 per student; fee includes reporting of scores to any 5 schools designated at time of application; $1 per additional report ($2 per report requested after examination); postpaid; 270(330) minutes in 2 sessions; Division of Educational Measurements, Council on Dental Education, American Dental Association. *
a) DENTAL ADMISSION QUANTITATIVE-VERBAL TEST. 1976–77; 3 scores: quantitative reasoning, verbal reasoning, total; forms 76A ('76, 11 pages), 76B ('77, 11 pages), 77 ('77, 11 pages); 60(70) minutes.
b) READING COMPREHENSION TEST. 1953–77; forms 68 ('73, 14 pages), 76A ('76, 10 pages), 76B ('75, 13 pages); 50(60) minutes.

c) SURVEY OF THE NATURAL SCIENCES. 1951–77; 4 scores: biology, inorganic chemistry, organic chemistry, total; forms 76A ('76, 14 pages), 76B ('77, 14 pages), 77 ('77, 13 pages); 90(100) minutes.
d) PERCEPTUAL-MOTOR ABILITY TEST/2D. 1968–77; forms 75A ('75, 19 pages), 76B ('77, 19 pages), 77 ('77, 19 pages); 35(45) minutes.
e) PERCEPTUAL-MOTOR ABILITY TEST/3D. 1968–77; forms 76A ('76, 21 pages), 76B ('77, 21 pages), 77 ('77, 21 pages); 35(45) minutes.
   See T2:2337 (8 references), 7:1091 (28 refrences), 5:916 (6 references), and 4:788 (2 references).

REFERENCES

1–2. See 4:788.
3–8. See 5:916.
9–36. See 7:1091.
37–44. See T2:2337; also includes a cumulative name index to the first 44 references for this test.
45. GRAHAM, JAMES W. "Factor Analysis of the Perceptual-Motor Ability Test." *J Dental Ed* 38(1):16–9 Ja '74. *
46. GRAHAM, JAMES W. "Substitution of Perceptual-Motor Ability Test for Chalk Carving in Dental Admission Testing Program." *J Dental Ed* 36(11):9–14 N '72. *
47. MALVITZ, DOLORES MARIE. *Correlates of Interpersonal Aspects of "Social Sensitivity" Among Students Entering the School of Dentistry, the University of Michigan, Fall, 1973.* Doctor's thesis, University of Michigan (Ann Arbor, Mich.), 1974. (*DAI* 35:4954B)
48. ROEBKER, DAVID LEE. *Personality, Values, Academic and Biographical Correlates Associated With Prediction of Location of Dental Practice.* Doctor's thesis, University of Kentucky (Lexington, Ky.), 1974. (*DAI* 35:5937A)
49. HOUSTON, JOHN B., AND MENSH, IVAN N. "Multiple Regression of Predictors and Criteria of Dental School Performance." *J Dental Res* 54(3):515–21 My–Je '75. *
50. KAPLAN, ALAN LEWIS. *Predicting General or Specialty Dental Practice From Admissions Data.* Doctor's thesis, University of Kentucky (Lexington, Ky.), 1975. (*DAI* 36:6555A)
51. GRAHAM, JAMES W. "Comparison of Males and Females in the Dental Admission Testing Program." *J Dental Ed* 40(12):783–6 D '76. *

ROBERT L. LINN, *Professor of Educational Psychology, University of Illinois, Urbana, Illinois.*

As the name implies, the Dental Admission Testing Program provides test scores to dental schools for use, along with other information, in making admissions decisions. The DATP consists of five separately timed examinations, which result in a total of 12 subscores and composite scores reported to dental schools and applicants. Except for part-whole relationships—e.g., organic chemistry with total science—the intercorrelations among the part scores are modest (generally about .4 or less) in the applicant population.

RELIABILITY. K-R 21 internal-consistency reliability estimates of the separately reported scores, while generally above .80, are rather low for some of the subscores. For example, the lowest reliability estimate in the April 1976 administration was .64 for inorganic chemistry. No estimates of parallel-form reliability or of score stability are provided.

VALIDITY. There is a substantial amount of evidence concerning the predictive validity of the test scores for freshman and sophomore grades in dental school, as well as for National Board scores. Validities for grades are reported for individual dental schools and for a national composite. Separate validity information is provided for grades in various content areas, such as histology and oral pathology. While the correlations of the test scores with grades or National Board scores are relatively low (typically in the range of .10 to .50), the level of documentation is impressive. The relatively low correlations with grades are not much different from what may be found in other graduate and professional school admissions contexts. The predictive accuracy of the tests is also about on a par with that of predental grade point average against grades in dental school.

There are many reasons to expect relatively low correlations of the admissions test scores with grades in dental school, including limitations of grades as a criterion measure and the effects of using already selected groups to perform validity studies. These limitations are substantial and are of concern in most applied selection contexts, especially where the selection is relatively severe. Nonetheless, the level of the reported correlation coefficients does not leave one feeling very sanguine about placing heavy reliance on the admissions test scores.

CODED SCORES. The coded scores, used in reporting, are integers that range from -1 to 9. These scores are obtained by dividing the observed frequency distribution for a test into intervals of one-half a standard deviation in length, except at the extremes where a standard score less than -2.0 is converted to a coded score of -1 and a standard score greater than 2.0 is converted to a coded score of 9. The coded scores have the potential advantage of limiting the overinterpretation of small score differences. For admissions purposes, however, they may be unnecessarily gross. For example, on a composite score such as the survey of natural sciences, which had a standard deviation of over 13 points in the April 1976 administration, a finer-grain scale would be justified. For that test, the current scale would mask differences of 6 raw score points within a single coded-score region and would exaggerate, by comparison, raw score differences of only 1 point for scores that fell on either side of the dividing line.

EQUATING. There is currently no procedure for equating scores from different test admin-

Dental Admission Testing Program

istrations. New forms of the tests are administered at each testing date, and observed frequency distributions are used to obtain nominally comparable coded scores. The tests previously have been given three times a year but will be given only twice a year starting in 1978. Without formal equating procedures there is no guarantee that the standard scores from different administrations are equivalent. The applicant population, as well as the test, may change from year to year. In addition, the groups that take the test on different dates within a year may be systematically different. Just in terms of the number of repeaters (i.e., examinees who have previously taken the DATP), for example, there were substantial differences in the October 1975, January 1976, and April 1976 administrations. At those three administrations there were, respectively, 42 percent, 47 percent, and 23 percent repeaters. It is at least conceivable that such a difference in percentage of repeaters influences the observed score distribution, and it is quite possible that there are other even more potent differences in the characteristics of the examinee populations at various administration dates.

In addition to possible differences in the populations taking the examinations at various administration dates, there may also be differences in what is measured by the forms of an examination which are changed at each administration. The comparability of what is measured from one form to the next may be particularly problematic for the reading comprehension test, which normally consists of a single passage followed by 50 multiple choice questions. Dependence of scores on unique characteristics of passages may make the equivalence of reading comprehension scores from different administrations questionable. Certainly, formal equating procedures would be highly desirable.

MANUALS. No technical manual is provided with the DATP, but there is generally good documentation available in a series of technical reports prepared each year. These technical reports provide most of the information one would expect to find in a professionally developed manual. Missing from these reports but provided to this reviewer by computer printouts or personal communication from the Director of the Division of Educational Measurements of the American Dental Association was

information about the intercorrelations of the examinations, multiple correlations, item development, item pretesting, and equating. It would be desirable to have such information available in a single source. Of greater importance, however, would be a publication that provided guidance on use of the DATP for people responsible for admission to dental school. Currently, assistance to users is provided in visits to dental schools by members of the Division of Educational Measurements. Although highly desirable, personal visits are not a substitute for written assistance.

SUMMARY. The DATP is a professionally developed, special-purpose admissions test battery. The tests have generally good internal consistencies and have modest predictive validities not unlike those found in similar testing programs in other specialities. The most serious defect of the DATP is the absence of an acceptable procedure for equating scores from different administrations of the test. Also lacking is a comprehensive technical manual and detailed written guidance for test users.

CHRISTINE H. McGUIRE, *Professor of Health Professions Education and Associate Director for Research and Development, Center for Educational Development, University of Illinois at the Medical Center, Chicago, Illinois.*

The Dental Admission Testing Program, conducted by the Council on Dental Education of the American Dental Association, is required of all applicants for admission to dental schools. The examination is designed to measure general academic ability, comprehension and knowledge of scientific information, and perceptual skills. The present test battery is composed of five separate examinations (see entry above) requiring one full day for administration.

The reading comprehension test is composed of a conventional set of multiple choice questions based on a single lengthy passage typical of a dental school text. The quantitative-verbal test is also composed of fairly conventional multiple choice items dealing with simple mathematical and word problems, including usage of mathematical concepts and elementary vocabulary. The perceptual-motor ability tests are composed of multiple choice items which require visualization of two and three dimensional patterns. The knowledge survey test is composed of relatively straightforward multiple choice questions most of which require recall of specific information. Despite claims to the contrary, few require anything but the most elementary application or problem-solving. The battery does NOT make any use of complex item formats or anything other than simple test instructions that should be readily understood by examinees.

The booklet announcing the program, available to all candidates and user institutions, contains an excellent description of the nature and contents of the several parts of the examination. The manual for administering the test is clear, precise, and well written to ensure that the test is administered under standard conditions in all testing centers.

The examinee and the schools to which he or she is applying receive an individual score report which includes scores on reading comprehension, quantitative reasoning, verbal reasoning, total of quantitative and verbal reasoning (a sum of the previous two scores), biology, inorganic chemistry, organic chemistry, total science (a sum of the previous three scores), perceptual-motor ability on two-dimensional problems, and perceptual-motor ability on three-dimensional problems. These scores are based on calculation of number of correct responses and are reported in standard score units ranging from −1 to +9, with a mean of 4 and a standard deviation of 2. In addition, two composite scores are reported: academic average (an average of the reading comprehension, quantitative reasoning, verbal reasoning, biology, and chemistry scores), and a perceptual-motor average (the average of the two perceptual-motor ability test scores). Percentile band equivalents are provided to facilitate interpretation of the standard scores.

Each school is also provided a set of summary statistics for each year's testing program, which includes a report of the raw score mean, standard deviation, distribution, and reliability (K-R 20) for each subtest of the battery, and an item analysis summary indicating the number of items in each subtest with unsatisfactory difficulty and/or discrimination indices. These data are based on the total group of candidates (5,000–9,000 for 1975–76) who take the examination at any given administration. Though the reported reliability coefficients are all .80 or over, and many approach .90, one must ques-

tion the confidence that can be placed in part scores based on, in one case, as few as 50 items. This reservation would seem particularly applicable to the reading comprehension test, which, in the edition submitted for review, contained only one set of items referring to the interpretation of a single passage.

Finally, the Division of Educational Measurements of the American Dental Association has accumulated a vast body of data relevant to the predictive validity of the various editions of the test battery. This information has been made available to the schools in the form of correlation studies relating performance on the various parts of the dental admission test and/or predental grade point average to freshman grades, to sophomore grades, and to National Board scores. These data are reported for each school separately and for the total national sample. As might be expected, most of the correlations are positive, but only very few exceed .50. In general, the magnitude of the coefficients varies in the expected direction; that is, scores on reading comprehension, verbal reasoning, and survey of natural sciences are somewhat more highly correlated with freshman grades than are scores on perceptual-motor ability; conversely, scores on perceptual-motor ability tend to be somewhat more highly correlated with grades on courses in technique.

The present admissions battery is based on an extensive survey conducted in late 1974 of all then-existing dental schools, requesting information on the importance which each attaches to various sources of information about applicants: high school transcript, predental general grade point average, predental science grade point average, predental advisor's rating, other recommendations, personal interviews, and the dental admission test in general. Most schools indicated that they placed fairly substantial importance on the last named, though they varied considerably in the relative importance attached to the various components of the present admission test and in the way in which they used each of the scores. In that sense the present test battery reflects the views of the constituency as to the kinds of skills and knowledge which are important to success in dental education. Furthermore, inspection of the test reveals that most of the items have a direct and fairly immediate relevance to the kinds of verbal, quantitative, reading, and technical operations which the student of dentistry is expected to perform.

Despite the extensive reliability and validity studies reported, some question must be raised about what may well be an overemphasis on conventional academic skills and an underemphasis on psychomotor skills. Secondly, though the available data do not suggest that a significant number of examinees fail to complete the tests, inspection of the tests in relation to the required time constraints strongly suggests that speed of response is an important factor in successful performance, and that its relevance should perhaps be questioned. Finally, in view of the complex intellectual tasks inherent in the practice of dentistry, the council would be well advised to consider increasing the number and sophistication of items requiring high level problem-solving skills.

[1086]

*Ohio Dental Assisting Achievement Test. Grades 11–12; 1970–77; ODAAT; available only as a part of the *Ohio Trade and Industrial Education Achievement Test Program* (see 1166 for more complete information); 16 scores: orientation, ethics, dental anatomy, dental and laboratory materials, microbiology and sterilization, preventive dentistry, operative-chairside assisting, specialties-chairside assisting, radiology, pharmacology, oral pathology, diet and nutrition, first aid and dental emergencies, human relations, office practice, total; no data on reliability of part scores; 1 form; parts 1 ('71, 19 pages), 2 ('71, 18 pages); no specific manual; series manual ('77, 32 pages); annual Ohio norms for juniors, seniors, ('77, 1 page each); occupational analysis (no date, 130 pages); rental and scoring service, $1.50 per student, postage extra; $3 per occupational analysis, postpaid; (300) minutes in 2 sessions; Instructional Materials Laboratory, Ohio State University. * [Test not available for review.]

ENGINEERING

[1087]

★Engineer Performance Description Form. Nonsupervisory college graduate engineers; 1975 (no date on test materials); EPDF; ratings by immediate supervisors; 7 scores yielding ratings for overall performance level plus 6 areas of development: communication, relating to others, administrative ability, motivation, technical knowledge and ability, self-sufficiency; no data on reliability and validity in manual; for reliability and validity data, see *1* below; no norms; 1 form (6 pages plus 2-page detachable profile); manual (13 pages); 45¢ per test; 40¢ per manual; postage extra; scoring service, 20¢ per test; [15–30] minutes; John C. South; the Author. *

REFERENCES

1. SOUTH, J. C. "Early Career Performance of Engineers—Its Composition and Measurement." *Personnel Psychol* 27(2): 225–43 su '74. *

[1088]

*The Graduate Record Examinations Advanced Engineering Test. Graduate school candidates; 1939–76; test administered 5 times annually (January, April, June, October, December) at centers established by the publisher; 3 scores: engineering, mathematics usage, total; 5 current forms ('73–76, 23–27 pages); descriptive booklet ('75, 12 pages); for program accessories, see 476; examination fee, $10.50 per candidate: 170(190) minutes; an inactive form is available for local administration (rental fee, $5.50 per test); Educational Testing Service. *

For reviews of the GRE program, see 7:667 (1 review) and 5:601 (1 review).

REFERENCES

1. SOUTH, J. C. "Early Career Performance of Engineers—Its Composition and Measurement." *Personnel Psychol* 27(2): 225–43 su '74. *

[1089]

*UP Field Test in Engineering. College; 1969–77; formerly called *The Undergraduate Record Examinations: Engineering Test;* Form TUR ('71, 21 pages); descriptive booklet ('71, 16 pages); for UAP accessories, see 480; rental fee, $4 per test, postage extra; 120(140) minutes; Educational Testing Service. *

LAW

[1090]

★ACT Proficiency Examination in Criminal Investigation. College and adults; 1975–76; for college accreditation of nontraditional study, advanced placement, or assessment of educational achievement; test administered 4 times annually (February, May, August, November) at centers established by the publisher; developed and administered in New York State as a part of their College Proficiency Examinations Program; 3 semester credits recommended; no data on reliability; Form YZ ('75, 13 pages, reprinted with 1976 copyright); study guide ('76, 3 pages); for further information and program accessories, see 470; examination fee, $25 per candidate (includes reporting of score to the candidate and one college); 180(210) minutes; developed by the New York State Education Department; American College Testing Program. *

[1091]

★ACT Proficiency Examination in Introduction to Criminal Justice. College and adults; 1975–76; for college accreditation of nontraditional study, advanced placement, or assessment of educational achievement; test administered 4 times annually (February, May, August, November) at centers established by the publisher; developed and administered in New York State as a part of their College Proficiency Examinations Program; 3 semester credits recommended; no data on reliability; Form ZZ ('75, 12 pages, reprinted with 1976 copyright); study guide ('76, 3 pages); for further information and program accessories, see 470; examination fee, $25 per candidate (includes reporting of score to the candidate and one college); 180(210) minutes; developed by the New York State Education Department; American College Testing Program. *

[1092]

★Correctional Policy Inventory: A Survey of Correctional Philosophy and Characteristic Methods of Dealing With Offenders. Correctional managers; 1970; 4 scores: reintegration, rehabilitation, reform, restraint; no data on reliability and validity; 1

form (6 pages); manual (6 pages); $2.60 per test, postage extra; [20] minutes; Vincent O'Leary; National Council on Crime and Delinquency. *

REFERENCES

1. DUFFEE, DAVID. "The Correction Officer Subculture and Organizational Change." *J Res Crime & Delinq* 11(2):155–72 Jl '74. *
2. CLAPP, JOHN ALBERT. *An Exploratory Study of Attitudes Toward Human Nature and Correctional Policies Among Criminal Justice Students and Faculty.* Doctor's thesis, California School of Professional Psychology (San Diego, Calif.), 1975.

[1093]

*Law School Admission Test.** Law school entrants; 1948–77; LSAT; test administered 5 times annually (February, April, July, October, December) at centers established by the publisher; 2 scores: aptitude (commonly referred to as the LSAT score), writing ability; Forms XLS1 ('76, 55 pages), XLS2 ('76, 54 pages), YLS3 ('76, 51 pages), YLS1–3 ('76, 53 pages), YLS2–2 ('76, 51 pages), YLS3–4 ('76, 51 pages), ZLS1–4 ('77, 54 pages), ZLS2–5 ('77, 55 pages); supervisor's manual ('76, 26 pages); bulletin for candidates ('77, 85 pages); interpretive booklet ('76, 15 pages); separate answer sheets (MRC) must be used; examination fee, $14 per candidate (fee includes reporting of scores to one law school); 210(270) minutes; Educational Testing Service. *

See T2:2349 (7 references); for a review by Leo A. Munday of earlier forms, see 7:1098 (23 references); see also 5:928 (7 references); for a review by Alexander G. Wesman, see 4:815 (6 references).

REFERENCES

1–6. See 4:815.
7–13. See 5:928.
14–36. See 7:1098.
37–43. See T2:2349; also includes a cumulative name index to the first 43 references and 2 reviews for this test.
44. EVANS, FRANKLIN R., AND REILLY, RICHARD R. "A Study of Speededness as a Source of Test Bias." *J Ed Meas* 9(2): 123–31 su '72. * (*PA* 50:3743)
45. LINN, ROBERT L.; KLEIN, STEPHEN P.; AND HART, FREDERICK M. "The Nature and Correlates of Law School Essay Grades." *Ed & Psychol Meas* 32(2):267–79 su '72. * (*PA* 49:9984)
46. REILLY, RICHARD R. "Contributions of Selected Transcript Information to Prediction of Law School Performance." *Ed & Psychol Meas* 32(2):411–24 su '72. *
47. BAIRD, LEONARD L. "Comparative Prediction of First Year Graduate and Professional School Grades in Six Fields." *Ed & Psychol Meas* 35(4):941–6 w '75. * (*PA* 55:13523)
48. BAIRD, LEONARD L. "Biographical and Educational Correlates of Graduate and Professional School Admissions Test Scores." *Ed & Psychol Meas* 36(2):415–20 su '76. *
49. EDUCATIONAL TESTING SERVICE. *Prelaw Handbook: 76–77 Annual Official Guide to ABA-Approved Law Schools.* Princeton, N.J.: Law School Admission Service, 1976. Pp. 375. *
50. LIN, PANG-CHIEH, AND HUMPHREYS, LLOYD G. "Predictions of Academic Performance in Graduate and Professional School." *Appl Psychol Meas* 1(2):249–57 sp '77. *

[1094]

★Multijurisdictional Policy Officer Examination. Prospective police officers; 1976; MPOE; no data on reliability; norms consist of means and standard deviations; form 165.1 (60 pages); technical report (195 pages); pretest study guide (38 pages); distribution restricted to public personnel agencies; separate answer sheets (IBM 1230) must be used; 1–50 tests (without scoring service), $30 plus $4.75 per test; 1–50 tests (including scoring service), $50 plus $5 per test; 35¢ per study guide; $10 per technical report; postage extra; 150(160) minutes; developed by Educational Testing Service for the International Association of Chiefs of Police and the publisher; technical report by Michael Rosenfeld and Richard F. Thornton; International Personnel Management Association. *

[1095]

*Police Officer J:A-1(M).** Prospective police officers; 1973; abbreviated revision of *Test for Police Officer A-1;* for validity data, see *1* below; norms consist of frequency distribution and summary data of raw scores; 1 form (19 pages); no specific manual; general instructions (no date, 1 page) and administration guide (no date, 4 pages); norms (2 pages); description of test (no date, 1 page); distribution restricted to public personnel agencies; separate answer sheets (IBM 1230, hand scored) must be used; tests rented only; rental fee, $15 ($30) basic fee plus $2 ($3) per test for member (nonmember) agencies; postpaid; specimen copy free; scoring and statistical analysis service, $25 plus 25¢ per test; 90(100) minutes; International Personnel Management Association. *

REFERENCES

1. WOLLACK, STEPHEN; CLANCY, JOHN J.; AND BEALS, STEPHEN. *The Validation of Entry-Level Law Enforcement Examinations in the States of California and Nevada.* Sacramento, Calif.: Selection Consulting Center, 1973. Pp. ix, 86. *

[1096]

★Police Sergeant. Prospective sergeants; 1975–77; various titles used by publisher; 6 scores: police supervisory principles and practices, legal knowledges, technical police knowledges, police judgment, understanding and interpreting police table and text materials, total; Forms ESV 1 ('75, 25 pages), ESV 2 ('75, 23 pages); no specific manual; general instructions (no date, 4 pages); candidate study booklet ('77, 23 pages); validation report ('75, 58 pages); distribution restricted to civil service commissions and municipal officials; separate answer sheets (IBM 805) must be used; tests rented only; rental and scoring service, $300 for first 5 candidates (additional candidates, $15 to $6 each); specimen set loaned for a fee of $15; 210(235) minutes; McCann Associates. *

MEDICINE

[1097]

*CLEP Subject Examination in Clinical Chemistry.** Medical technologists; 1972–76; for college accreditation of nontraditional study, advanced placement, or assessment of educational achievement; tests administered monthly at centers throughout the United States; Forms UCT1 ('72, 16 pages), UCT2 ('72, 18 pages); optional essay supplement scored by college: Forms UCT-A, UCT-B, ('72, 2 pages); for program accessories, see 473; rental and scoring fee, $20 per student (includes reporting of scores to the candidate and one college); postpaid; 90(95) minutes, same for essay supplement; program administered for the College Entrance Examination Board by Educational Testing Service. *

For reviews of the CLEP program, see 473 (3 reviews).

[1098]

*CLEP Subject Examination in Hematology.** Medical technologists; 1972–76; for college accreditation of nontraditional study, advanced placement, or assessment of educational achievement; tests administered monthly at centers throughout the United States; Forms UCT1 ('72, 14 pages), UCT2 ('72, 11 pages); optional essay supplement scored by college; Forms UCT-A, UCT-B, ('72, 2 pages); for program accessories, see 473; rental and scoring fee, $20 per student (includes reporting of scores to the candidate and one college) ; postpaid ; 90(95) minutes, same for essay supplement ; program administered for the College Entrance Examination Board by Educational Testing Service. *

For reviews of the CLEP program, see 473 (3 reviews).

[1099]

*CLEP Subject Examination in Immunohematology and Blood Banking. Medical technologists ; 1972–76 ; for college accreditation of nontraditional study, advanced placement, or assessment of educational achievement ; tests administered monthly at centers throughout the United States ; Forms UCT1 ('72, 17 pages), UCT2 ('72, 16 pages) ; optional essay supplement scored by college : Forms UCT-A, UCT-B, ('72, 2 pages) ; for program accessories, see 473 ; rental and scoring fee, $20 per student (includes reporting of scores to the candidate and one college) ; postpaid ; 90(95) minutes, same for essay supplement ; program administered for the College Entrance Examination Board by Educational Testing Service. *

For reviews of the CLEP program, see 473 (3 reviews).

[1100]

*CLEP Subject Examination in Microbiology. Medical technologists ; 1972–76 ; for college accreditation of nontraditional study, advanced placement, or assessment of educational achievement ; tests administered monthly at centers throughout the United States ; Forms UCT1 ('72, 15 pages), UCT2 ('72, 14 pages) ; optional essay supplement scored by college : Forms UCT-A, UCT-B, ('72, 2 pages) ; for program accessories, see 473 ; rental and scoring fee, $20 per student (includes reporting of scores to the candidate and one college) ; postpaid ; 90(95) minutes, same for essay supplement ; program administered for the College Entrance Examination Board by Educational Testing Service. *

For reviews of the CLEP program, see 473 (3 reviews).

[1101]

*New Medical College Admission Test. Applicants for admission to member colleges of the Association of American Medical Colleges and to other participating institutions ; 1946–77 ; New MCAT ; revision, first administered in spring 1977, of Medical College Admission Test; administered 2 times annually (spring, fall) at centers established by the publisher ; 6 scores : biology, chemistry, physics, science problems, skills analysis (reading, quantitative) ; Form 1 ('77) ; 4 parts : science knowledge (23 pages), science problems (15 pages), reading skills analysis (13 pages), quantitative skills analysis (13 pages) ; supervisor's manual ('77, 24 pages) ; interpretive manual ('77, 113 pages) ; student manual ('77, 78 pages) ; announcement ('77, 24 pages) ; separate answer sheets (MRC) must be used ; examination fee, $35 ($40 for foreign and Sunday administrations) ; $3.25 (4th class mail, postpaid) or $4 (priority mail) per student manual (available from Association of American Medical Colleges) ; 390 (450) minutes in 2 sessions ; constructed under the direction of AAMC by the American Institutes for Research ; program administered at the direction of AAMC by American College Testing Program. *

See T2:2355 (30 references) ; for reviews by Nancy S. Cole and James M. Richards, Jr. of earlier forms, see 7:1100 (57 references) ; for reviews by Robert L.

Ebel and Philip H. DuBois, see 6:1137 (43 references) ; for a review by Alexander G. Wesman, see 5:932 (4 references) ; for a review by Morey J. Wantman, see 4:817 (11 references).

REFERENCES

1–11. See 4:817.
12–15. See 5:932.
16–58. See 6:1137.
59–115. See 7:1100.
116–145. See T2:2355 ; also includes a cumulative name index to the first 145 references and 6 reviews for this test.
146. CHECKER, ARMAND; ERDMANN, JAMES B.; AND D'COSTA, AYRES. "Can the Choice of Medical Specialty Be Predicted by the Medical College Admission Test?" Abstract. Proc 80th Ann Conv Am Psychol Assn 7(2):595–6 '72. *
147. COLLISHAW, NEIL E., AND GRAINGER, ROBERT M. "Canadian Medical Student Selection and Some Characteristics of Applicants, 1970–71." J Med Ed 47(4):254–62 Ap '72. *
148. ERDMANN, JAMES B. "Separating Wheat From Chaff: Revision of the MCAT." Editorial. J Med Ed 47(9):747–9 S '72. *
149. HALEY, JOHN V., AND LERNER, MELVIN J. "The Characteristics and Performance of Medical Students During Preclinical Training." J Med Ed 47(6):446–52 Je '72. *
150. MATARAZZO, JOSEPH D., AND GOLDSTEIN, STEVEN G. "The Intellectual Caliber of Medical Students." J Med Ed 47(2):102–11 F '72. *
151. NELSON, BONNIE. "Medical College Admission Test." J Med Ed 47(9):750–2 S '72. *
152. NELSON, DAVID EDWARD. The Prediction of Student Performance in a College of Medicine by Biographical Information, Personality Scores and Academic Measures. Doctor's thesis, University of Utah (Salt Lake City, Utah), 1972. (DAI 32:6709B)
153. WEISMAN, ROBERT A.; WEINBERG, PAUL C.; AND WINSTEL, JAMES W. "On Achieving Greater Uniformity in Admissions Committee Decisions." J Med Ed 47(8):593–602 Ag '72. *
154. AMBROSINO, ROBERT J., AND BRADING, PAUL L. "An Analytical Computer-Based Methodology for Screening Medical School Applicants." J Med Ed 48(4):332–5 Ap '73. *
155. BECKER, MARSHALL H.; KATATSKY, MARILYNN E.; AND SEIDEL, HENRY M. "A Follow-up Study of Unsuccessful Applicants to Medical Schools." J Med Ed 48(11):991–1001 N '73. *
156. DUBÉ, W. F. "Applicants for the 1971–72 Medical School Entering Class." J Med Ed 48(4):380–2 Ap '73. *
157. DUBÉ, W. F. "Applicants for the 1972–73 Medical School Entering Class." J Med Ed 48(12):1161–3 D '73. *
158. DUBÉ, W. F.; JOHNSON, DAVIS G.; AND NELSON, BONNIE C. "Study of U.S. Medical School Applicants, 1971–72." J Med Ed 48(5):395–420 My '73. *
159. HALEY, JOHN V. "The Medical College Admission Test as a Predictor of Grade Factors." J Med Ed 48(1):98–100 Ja '73. *
160. NELSON, BONNIE C., AND SCHAFER, ANNE M. "Medical College Admission Test." J Med Ed 48(7):696–8 Jl '73. *
161. WEINBERG, ETHEL, AND ROONEY, JAMES F. "The Academic Performance of Women Students in Medical School." J Med Ed 48(3):240–7 Mr '73. *
162. BISHOP, BILLY MARION. A Study of Medical College Admission Test Scores and Grade-Point Averages on Undergraduate and Premedical Science College Courses in Predicting Academic Performance of First-Year Medical Students as Measured by a Prediction Index. Doctor's thesis, University of Mississippi (University, Miss.), 1974. (DAI 35:4060A)
163. CULLEN, THOMAS JOHN. The Prediction of Washington State Applicants' Acceptance to Medical School Using the Discriminant Function. Doctor's thesis, University of Washington (Seattle, Wash.), 1974. (DAI 35:4244A)
164. DUBÉ, W. F. "Applicants for the 1973–74 Medical School Entering Class." J Med Ed 49(11):1070–2 N '74. *
165. DUBÉ, W. F., AND JOHNSON, DAVIS G. "Study of U.S. Medical School Applicants, 1972–73." J Med Ed 49(9):849–69 S '74. *
166. FRUEN, MARY A.; ROTHMAN, ARTHUR I.; AND STEINER, JAN W. "Comparison of Characteristics of Male and Female Medical School Applicants." J Med Ed 49(2):137–45 F '74. * (PA 52:3062)
167–8. NELSON, BONNIE C. "Medical College Admission Test." J Med Ed 49(7):712–4 Jl '74. *
169. RHOADS, JOHN M.; GALLEMORE, JOHNNIE L., JR.; GIANTURCO, DANIEL T.; AND OSTERHOUT, SUYDAM. "Motivation, Medical School Admissions, and Student Performance." J Med Ed 49(12):1119–27 D '74. * (PA 53:9706)
170. SCHAEFFER, F. SAMUEL. Predictive Criteria for the Performance of Medical Students. Doctor's thesis, University of Toledo (Toledo, Ohio), 1974. (DAI 35:4943A)
171. TURNER, EDWARD V.; HELPER, MALCOLM M.; AND KRISKA, S. DAVID. "Predictors of Clinical Performance." J Med Ed 49(4):332–42 Ap '74. * (PA 53:3235)
172. WEINSTEIN, PHILIP, AND GIPPLE, CINDY. "The Relationship of Study Skills to Achievement in the First Two Years

of Medical School." *J Med Ed* 49(9):902–4 S '74. * (*PA* 53: 3238)

173. BAIRD, LEONARD L. "Comparative Prediction of First Year Graduate and Professional School Grades in Six Fields." *Ed & Psychol Meas* 35(4):941–6 w '75. * (*PA* 55:13523)

174. CLAPP, TERRY TILLMAN. *Comparison of Three Models for Selection of Applicants and Prediction of Success in Medical School.* Doctor's thesis, University of Missouri (Columbia, Mo.), 1975. (*DAI* 36:4145A)

175. DUBÉ, W. F. "Applicants for the 1974–75 First-Year Medical School Class." *J Med Ed* 50(12, pt 1):1134–6 D '75. *

176. DUBÉ, W. F., AND JOHNSON, DAVIS G. "Study of U.S. Medical School Applicants, 1973–74." *J Med Ed* 50(11):1015–32 N '75. *

177. EVANS, DORIS A.; JONES, PAUL K.; WORTMAN, RICHARD A.; AND JACKSON, EDGAR B., JR. "Traditional Criteria as Predictors of Minority Student Success in Medical School." *J Med Ed* 50(10):934–9 O '75. * (*PA* 55:5350)

178. GOUGH, HARRISON G., AND HALL, WALLACE B. "An Attempt to Predict Graduation From Medical School." *J Med Ed* 50(10):940–50 O '75. * (*PA* 55:5357)

179. PERLSTADT, HARRY. "MCAT: A Gate in Admissions and Internship Placements." *J Med Ed* 50(1):78–81 Ja '75. * (*PA* 53:11807)

180. ROESSLER, ROBERT; COLLINS, FORREST; AND MEFFERD, ROY B., JR. "Sex Similarities in Successful Medical School Applicants." *J Am Med Wom Assn* 30(6):254–7+ Je '75. *

181. SCHOFIELD, WILLIAM, AND GARRARD, JUDITH. "Longitudinal Study of Medical Students Selected for Admission to Medical School by Actuarial and Committee Methods." *Brit J Med Ed* 9(2):86–90 Je '75. *

182. BAIRD, LEONARD L. "Biographical and Educational Correlates of Graduate and Professional School Admissions Test Scores." *Ed & Psychol Meas* 36(2):415–20 su '76. *

183. FELDMAN, DIANE WHITLEY. *Characteristics Associated With Persistence in Premedical Education at Duke University: A Discriminant Analysis.* Doctor's thesis, Duke University (Durham, N.C.), 1976. (*DAI* 37:3514A)

184. KEYSOR, ROBERT ELLIS. *The Effect of "Test Wiseness" on Professional School Screening Test Scores.* Doctor's thesis, Brigham Young University (Provo, Utah), 1976. (*DAI* 37: 4652B)

185. GOUGH, HARRISON G., AND DUCKER, DALIA G. "Social Class in Relation to Medical School Performance and Choice of Specialty." *J Psychol* 96(1):31–43 My '77. *

[1102]

★Ohio Diversified Health Occupations Achievement Test. Grades 11–12; 1975–77; ODHOAT; available only as a part of the *Ohio Trade and Industrial Education Achievement Test Program* (see 1166 for more complete information); 16 scores: orientation, emergency first aid, dental assisting skills, medical assisting skills, communications and office skills, laboratory skills, preparing for the world of work, asepsis, vital signs, positioning and draping, physical examinations, transfer and ambulation, care of the patient unit, personal care of the patient, pre-operative and post-operative care, total; no data on reliability of part scores; 1 form; parts 1 ('75, 14 pages), 2 ('75, 18 pages); no specific manual; series manual ('77, 32 pages); annual Ohio norms for juniors, seniors, ('77, 1 page each); course outline ('75, 106 pages); rental and scoring service, $1.50 per student, postage extra; $2.50 per course outline, postpaid; (270) minutes in 2 sessions; Instructional Materials Laboratory, Ohio State University. * [Test not available for review.]

[1103]

★Ohio Medical Assisting Achievement Test. Grades 11–12; 1974–77; OMAAT; available only as a part of the *Ohio Trade and Industrial Education Achievement Test Program* (see 1166 for more complete information); 10 scores: orientation, body systems, clinical assistant skills, medications, sterilization, medical office skills, laboratory skills, electrocardiography, X-ray, total; no data on reliability of part scores; 1 form; parts 1 ('75, 14 pages), 2 ('75, 15 pages); no specific manual; series manual ('77, 32 pages); annual Ohio norms for juniors, seniors, ('77, 1 page each); occupational analysis (no date, 415 pages); rental and scoring service, $1.50 per student, postage extra; $6 per occupational analysis, postpaid;

New Medical College Admission Test

(240) minutes in 2 sessions; Instructional Materials Laboratory, Ohio State University. * [Test not available for review.]

[1104]

*Optometry College Admission Test. Optometry college applicants; 1971–76; OCAT; tests administered 3 times annually (January, March, November) at centers established by the publisher; 6 scores: biology, chemistry, physics, verbal ability, quantitative ability, study-reading; reliability data for form P only; there are 2–4 forms (P ['71], Q ['73], R ['74], S ['75]) of each subtest, which are used in various combinations in tests designated 02 ('73, P and Q subtests), 03 ('73, Q and R subtests), 04 ('75, R and S subtests), (33–35 pages in 2 booklets); directions ['74, 13 pages]; handbook ('73, 36 pages); results supplement ('75, 13 pages); validation supplement ('76, 19 pages); norms ('75, 1 page) for test 04; announcement ['76, 16 pages]; separate answer sheets (OpScan) must be used; examination fee, $25 per applicant; fee includes reporting of scores to applicant and 1–3 schools; $3 per additional report; 215(245) minutes; sponsored by the Association of Schools and Colleges of Optometry; prepared and administered by Psychological Corporation. *

REFERENCES

1. KEGEL-FLOM, PENELOPE. "Predicting Optometry Grades From the OCAT and Preoptometry Grades." *Am J Optom & Physiol Optics* 51(6):419–24 Je '74. *
2. WALLACE, WIMBURN L., AND LEVINE, NIRA R. "Optometry College Admission Test." *Am J Optom & Physiol Optics* 51(11):872–86 N '74. *
3. KATZELL, MILDRED E. "Characteristics of OCAT Applicants." *J Optom Ed* 2(1):12–14 sp '76. *

PENELOPE KEGEL-FLOM, *Research Psychologist, University of California, Berkeley, California.* [Review of Test 04.]

The OCAT is a carefully constructed, psychometrically sound test whose function is to provide a standardized assessment of the ability of applicants to succeed in optometry school. The test, required for admission to all optometry schools in the U.S., was taken by over 4,000 applicants in the 1975–76 program.

The OCAT (Test 04) consists of six subtests, a 26-item section requesting background information, and an experimental subtest. The first subtest, verbal ability, is a 20-minute test of vocabulary strength which measures knowledge of synonyms and antonyms of nonscientific words. Three 25-minute science tests follow: biology, emphasizing human biology; chemistry, organic and inorganic; and physics, emphasizing knowledge of light. Science questions rely primarily on factual recall and definitions of scientific words and very little on conceptual understanding of scientific principles. Quantitative ability is assessed in a 45-minute, 50-item test. The ability to read, organize, analyze, and remember new scientific material is assessed in a novel study-reading subtest. Questions on the candidate's background are inserted after the study-reading test and before a second, experimental biology section. The candidate is assured that the background questions are for research purposes only, yet their placement between test sections may lead some applicants to respond as they think an applicant "should." Scores are reported in percentiles for the six subtests; no composite scores are reported.

Percentile norms are based upon the performance of first year optometry students. Norming on a population other than the one (in this case, applicants) taking the test is somewhat unusual, and I found that some admissions officers were unaware of the actual norming population. Perhaps a better procedure would be to report two sets of norms, one based upon all applicants and the other on first year optometry students.

Subtest reliabilities for Form P (no data for other forms) are quite acceptable: K-R 20 coefficients, based upon 2,714 applicants, range from .82 to .89, with a median of .85. Intercorrelations among subtests range from .22 to .66, with median .50.

For 212 applicants who took both the OCAT and MCAT in 1971–72, substantial correlations, .73 and .78, were found between the verbal and quantitative scores, respectively, on the two tests. The MCAT science section correlated .68 with OCAT chemistry, .55 with OCAT biology, and .53 with OCAT physics.

From its inception in 1971, the validity of the OCAT to predict grades in optometry school has been carefully and continuously monitored by the Psychological Corporation. Unfortunately, the data accumulated has not always been presented in the most clear and useful manner. In the most recent OCAT handbook supplement (1976), correlations between each subtest and grades in the first year, first two years, first three years, and over four years are presented for each school; the range and median correlation for each subtest over all schools are also given.

For the first two, largely academic years of the optometry curriculum, median correlations (12 schools) between OCAT sections and GPA were: verbal ability, .23; biology, .31; chemistry, .32; physics, .30; quantitative, .40; and study-reading, .37.

The reason for cumulating GPA year after year is not explained; in view of the change in optometry curriculum emphasis from academic course work in the first two years to clinical practice in the latter two years, it would be more appropriate to report separate predictive validities for each year. Also, conclusions based upon cumulating fourth year GPA are misleading for schools in which the fourth year curriculum is ungraded.

In admissions, the primary usefulness of the OCAT lies in its potential ability to predict academic performance better than preoptometry grades alone can predict. In 6 of 11 schools, preoptometry GPA correlated more highly with three years' optometry GPA than did any single OCAT subtest, yet for all but one school, addition of OCAT scores in multiple regression enhanced the correlation with grades. The median multiple correlation over nine schools was .52 (range, .30 to .68) and the median increase in correlation over preoptometry grades was .12. While the reporting of multiple correlations by school and class is laudable, the individual school must also know the relative weighting of the subtests entering its predictive equation as well as the extent to which the combinations "hold" (cross-validate) from class to class. These data are not reported.

The importance of evaluating the predictive validity of the OCAT in the individual school cannot be overemphasized. Subtest validities for individual schools range from −.17 to .72 and variation within a subtest is considerable from school to school. Admissions officers need to be given examples of how to use the data for their school. The single example for data interpretation in the 1976 manual supplement is inadequate and misleading in making comparisons in validity coefficients over years, using different classes.

SUMMARY. The OCAT is a competently developed test whose considerable success in predicting optometry school grades lies in careful attention to the assessment of abilities closely related to the optometry curriculum. What is needed now is a more concise and understandable manual with examples for the use of validity data in the individual school.

Finally, it must be recognized that there are no data showing the relationship of OCAT scores to clinical performance in optometry school or to excellence in optometry practice.

Optometry College Admission Test

MISCELLANEOUS

[1105]

★**Change Agent Questionnaire.** Adults, whose work primarily concerns changing behavior of others; 1969–73; CAQ; "underlying assumptions and practical strategies employed by agents of change as they seek to influence others"; 4 scores (philosophy, strategy, evaluation, total) for each of 5 styles of change: client-centered, charismatic, custodial, credibility, compliance; no data on reliability and validity; 1 form ('73, 9 pages); no manual; score interpretation ('73, 11 pages); $3 per test, postage extra; [15–30] minutes; Jay Hall and Martha S. Williams; Teleometrics Int'l. *

[1106]

★**Entrance Level Firefighter.** Prospective firefighters; 1974–77; various titles used by publisher; 9 scores: 8 scores listed below plus total; 2 booklets; instructions (no date, 6 pages); validation report ('75, 53 pages); study guide ('77, 20 pages); distribution restricted to civil service commissions and municipal officials; separate answer sheets (IBM 805) must be used; tests rented only; rental and scoring service, $200 for first 5 candidates (additional candidates, $8 to $4 each); specimen set loaned for a fee of $15; McCann Associates. *
a) BOOK 1. 5 scores: interest in firefighting, compatibility, map reading, spatial relations, visual pursuit; Form ESV-1 ('77, 15 pages, essentially the same as test copyrighted 1975 except for format and minor wording changes; 66(75) minutes.
b) BOOK 2. 3 scores: understanding and interpreting table and test material about firefighting, basic building construction knowledges, mechanical aptitude; Form ESV-1 ('77, 15 pages, identical with test copyrighted 1975); 70(80) minutes.

[1107]

★**Field Work Performance Report.** Occupational therapy students; 1973–74; FWPR; ratings by supervisors; 6 scores: data gathering, treatment planning, treatment implementation, communication skills, professional characteristics, total; norms consist of means and minimal passing scores; 1 form ('73, 4 pages); manual ('74, 49 pages); $1 per test, postpaid; [60] minutes; Jane Estner Slaymaker, Linda M. Crocker, and John E. Muthard; American Occupational Therapy Association, Inc. *

REFERENCES

1. CROCKER, LINDA M.; MUTHARD, JOHN E.; SLAYMAKER, JANE ESTNER; AND SAMSON, LOUISE. "A Performance Rating Scale for Evaluating Clinical Competence of Occupational Therapy Students." *Am J Occup Ther* 29(2):81–6 F '75. * (*PA* 54:1201)

NURSING

[1108]

★**ACT Proficiency Examination in Adult Nursing.** College and adults; 1976; for college accreditation of nontraditional study, advanced placement, or assessment of educational achievement; test administered 4 times annually (February, May, August, November) at centers established by the publisher; developed and administered in New York State as a part of their College Proficiency Examinations Program; 12 semester credits recommended; no data on reliability; Forms YX, YY, (26 pages); study guide ('76, 2 pages); for further information and program acces-

sories, see 470; examination fee, $35 per candidate (includes reporting of score to the candidate and one college); 180(210) minutes; developed by the New York State Education Department; American College Testing Program. *

[1109]

★**ACT Proficiency Examination in Fundamentals of Nursing.** College and adults; 1969–76; for college accreditation of nontraditional study, advanced placement, or assessment of educational achievement; test administered 4 times annually (February, May, August, November) at centers established by the publisher; developed and administered in New York State as a part of their College Proficiency Examinations Program; 10 semester credits recommended; no data on reliability; Form ZZ ('76, 19 pages); study guide ('76, 2 pages); for further information and program accessories, see 470; examination fee, $30 per candidate (includes reporting of score to the candidate and one college); 180(210) minutes; developed by the New York State Education Department; American College Testing Program. *

[1110]

★**ACT Proficiency Examination in Nursing Health Care.** College and adults; 1973–76; for college accreditation of nontraditional study, advanced placement, or assessment of educational achievement; test administered 4 times annually (February, May, August, November) at centers established by the publisher; developed and administered in New York State as a part of their Regents External Degree Program; 4 semester credits recommended; no data on reliability; Form XZ ('76, 20 pages); study guide ('76, 4 pages); for further information and program accessories, see 470; examination fee, $35 per candidate (includes reporting of score to the candidate and one college); 180(210) minutes; developed by the University of the State of New York; American College Testing Program. *

[1111]

★**ACT Proficiency Examination in Occupational Strategy, Nursing.** College and adults; 1973–76; for college accreditation of nontraditional study, advanced placement, or assessment of educational achievement; test administered 4 times annually (February, May, August, November) at centers established by the publisher; developed and administered in New York State as a part of their Regents External Degree Program; 4 semester credits recommended; no data on reliability; Form XZ ('76, 20 pages); study guide ('76, 4 pages); for further information and program accessories, see 470; examination fee, $35 per candidate (includes reporting of score to the candidate and one college); 180(210) minutes; developed by the University of the State of New York; American College Testing Program. *

[1112]

★**ACT Proficiency Examination in Psychiatric/ Mental Health Nursing.** College and adults; 1968–76; for college accreditation of nontraditional study, advanced placement, or assessment of educational achievement; test administered 4 times annually (February, May, August, November) at centers established by the publisher; developed and administered in New York State as a part of their College Proficiency Examinations Program; 6 semester credits recommended; no data on reliability; Form ZY ('76, 28 pages); study guide ('76, 3 pages); for further information and program accessories, see 470; examination fee, $30 per candidate (includes reporting of score to the candidate and one college); 180(210) minutes; developed by the New York State Education Department; American College Testing Program. *

[1113]

★ACT Proficiency Examinations in Commonalities in Nursing Care. College and adults; 1973–76; for college accreditation of nontraditional study, advanced placement, or assessment of educational achievement; tests administered 4 times annually (February, May, August, November) at centers established by the publisher; developed and administered in New York State as a part of their Regents External Degree Program; no data on reliability; 2 tests; 4 semester credits recommended per test; study guide ('76, 5–6 pages) for each test; for further information and program accessories, see 470; examination fee, $35 per test (includes reporting of score to the candidate and one college); 180(210) minutes per test; developed by the University of the State of New York; American College Testing Program. *
a) AREA 1. Form XZ ('76, 20 pages).
b) AREA 2. Form XZ ('76, 21 pages).

[1114]

★ACT Proficiency Examinations in Differences in Nursing Care. College and adults; 1974–76; for college accreditation of nontraditional study, advanced placement, or assessment of educational achievement; tests administered 4 times annually (February, May, August, November) at centers established by the publisher; developed and administered in New York State as a part of their Regents External Degree Program; no data on reliability; 3 tests; 4 semester credits recommended per test; study guide ('76, 5 pages) for each test; for further information and program accessories, see 470; examination fee, $35 per test (includes reporting of score to the candidate and one college); 180(210) minutes per test; developed by the University of the State of New York; American College Testing Program. *
a) AREA 1. Form XZ ('76, 23 pages).
b) AREA 2. Form XZ ('76, 23 pages).
c) AREA 3. Form XZ ('76, 22 pages).

[1115]

★ACT Proficiency Examinations in Maternal and Child Nursing. College and adults; 1968–76; for college accreditation of nontraditional study, advanced placement, or assessment of educational achievement; tests administered 4 times annually (February, May, August, November) at centers established by the publisher; developed and administered in New York State as a part of their College Proficiency Examinations Program; no data on reliability; Form ZX ('76, 25 pages); 2 tests; study guide ('76, 3 pages) for each test; for further information and program accessories, see 470; 180(210) minutes per test; fee includes reporting of score to the candidate and one college; developed by the New York State Education Department; American College Testing Program. *
a) ASSOCIATE DEGREE. 1970–76; 6 semester credits recommended; examination fee, $30 per candidate.
b) BACCALAUREATE DEGREE. 1968–76; 12 semester credits recommended; examination fee, $35 per candidate.

[1116]

★CLEP Subject Examination in Anatomy, Physiology, Microbiology: North Carolina Nursing Equivalency Examinations. 1 year or equivalent; 1974–76; for college accreditation of nontraditional study, advanced placement, or assessment of educational achievement; tests administered monthly at centers throughout the United States; Form WCN ('74, 12 pages); descriptive booklet ('75, 11 pages) for this and 3 other nursing tests; for program accessories, see 473; rental and scoring fee, $20 per student (includes reporting of scores to the candidate and one college); postpaid; 90(95) minutes; program administered for the College Entrance Examination Board by Educational Testing Service. *
For reviews of the CLEP program, see 473 (3 reviews).

[1117]

★CLEP Subject Examination in Behavioral Sciences for Nurses: North Carolina Nursing Equivalency Examinations. 1 year or equivalent; 1974–76; for college accreditation of nontraditional study, advanced placement, or assessment of educational achievement; tests administered monthly at centers throughout the United States; Form WCN ('74, 10 pages); descriptive booklet ('75, 11 pages) for this and 3 other nursing tests; for program accessories, see 473; rental and scoring fee, $20 per student (includes reporting of scores to the candidate and one college); postpaid; 90(95) minutes; program administered for the College Entrance Examination Board by Educational Testing Service. *
For reviews of the CLEP program, see 473 (3 reviews).

[1118]

★CLEP Subject Examination in Fundamentals of Nursing: North Carolina Nursing Equivalency Examinations. 1 year or equivalent; 1974–76; for college accreditation of nontraditional study, advanced placement, or assessment of educational achievement; tests administered monthly at centers throughout the United States; Form WCN ('74, 12 pages); descriptive booklet ('75, 11 pages) for this and 3 other nursing tests; for program accessories, see 473; rental and scoring fee, $20 per student (includes reporting of scores to the candidate and one college); postpaid; 90(95) minutes; program administered for the College Entrance Examination Board by Educational Testing Service. *
For reviews of the CLEP program, see 473 (3 reviews).

ALICE R. RINES, *Associate Professor of Nursing Education, Teachers College, Columbia University, New York, New York.* [Review of Form WCN.]

This examination includes several of the areas normally taught in an associate degree nursing course in that area, but leaves out several significant areas. For instance, very little is included in such topics as vital signs, supporting the patient when lifting and moving, oxygenation, or irrigations. Nothing has been included in the areas of physical safety, bathing, back care (other than movement), use of equipment, electrolyte regulation, or charting. What has been included is not the equivalent of what is usually taught in ADN programs, but rather is more closely related to what a practical nurse would have to know. It is not surprising that the norming group found this examination easy.

In general, the examination deals with fundamental knowledge. However, some items refer to patient situations which assume knowledge of specific illnesses (7, 8, 20, 38, 59, 60, 69–71). One group of items (63–65) requires specific knowledge of diabetes mellitus to arrive at the correct answer. In the beginning stages of the program, where this course is usually taught, such knowledge should not be required.

Some of the items require only recall, while others also require application of knowledge. Even so, some, particularly the recall questions, deal with trivia (3, 14, 21, 24, 37, 57–8, 67, 75). In several items (12, 14, 23, 36, 64) there is more than one "best" answer, while in others all of the answers could be "best" (20, 58, 65, 67, 71, 74). None of the answers are correct or best in items 1, 18, 30, 34, 66, and 73. Many of the items stated in the negative form could be stated positively. Also, the format of items 10, 22, 26, and 37 is not generally recommended in writing items for standardized tests in nursing or even in teacher-made tests; many of the situations are unnecessary to answer the questions that follow. Only 21 of the 75 items are acceptable as they stand. The authors obviously had difficulty in finding a suitable fifth option; many of these items would be improved by reducing the options from five to four.

I do not believe this is a good examination and would not recommend its use in any associate degree nursing program. The basic question I have concerns its validity—the knowledge which it tests is not the equivalent of that generally considered important in an associate degree nursing program. I suggest that this examination be completely redeveloped.

[1119]

★CLEP Subject Examination in Medical-Surgical Nursing: North Carolina Nursing Equivalency Examinations. 1 year or equivalent; 1974–76; for college accreditation of nontraditional study, advanced placement, or assessment of educational achievement; tests administered monthly at centers throughout the United States; Form WCN ('74, 10 pages); descriptive booklet ('75, 11 pages) for this and 3 other nursing tests; for program accessories, see 473; rental and scoring fee, $20 per student (includes reporting of scores to the candidate and one college); postpaid; 90(95) minutes; program administered for the College Entrance Examination Board by Educational Testing Service. *

For reviews of the CLEP program, see 473 (3 reviews).

ELAINE L. LA MONICA, *Associate Professor of Nursing Education, Teachers College, Columbia University, New York, New York.*

Developed during the period of 1972 to 1973, this test is one of a four-part battery which includes anatomy, physiology, microbiology; behavioral sciences for nurses; fundamentals of nursing; and medical-surgical nursing. Its intent is to cover the first year of academic study in Associate Degree Nursing programs, thereby offering credit by examination or advanced placement. No equivalent forms are available.

The test consists of 75 multiple choice items answerable in a 90-minute time limit. A correaction-for-guessing formula is applied. Clear directions are provided for the respondent with haphazard guessing succinctly discouraged. No special training is required for the test administrator.

Items focus on cardiovascular, respiratory, digestive, and renal nursing plus the concepts of immobility and aging. They require recall comprehension and theoretical application. Upon review, the areas tested are considered advanced medical-surgical nursing content, usually given in second year ADN nursing programs. The first year of programs classically focuses on nursing fundamentals, beginning medical-surgical concepts, and maternal and child health. Moreover, ignoring the fact that the test measures advanced medical-surgical content in ADN programs while purporting to cover first level study usable for advanced placement, it remains incomplete in terms of medical-surgical content; e.g., gynecology, neurology and endocrinology, to name a few. It also combines a medical model of nursing study with an integrated mode, evident with the inclusion of the concepts of immobility and aging. Those factors rather strongly suggest that the test is not appropriate for the domain intended. Further support of this conclusion is based on the conspicuous absence of reported criteria for the inclusion of selected content areas, and item selection, preparation, and analysis. Even though review of the items suggests face validity for those areas tested as well as rigorous attention to principles of item development, no conclusive evidence is provided for content validity.

Correlations of .29, .43, .45, and .60 are reported between test scores and final grades. These moderate figures would seem to lend support to content validity but must be evaluated in terms of the population used in data collection: three programs were responsible for close to three-quarters of the sample, all being drawn from the single geographic area in which test development and data collection occurred. Furthermore, use of these correlations as evidence of validity becomes unfounded unless reports provide support that these levels are idiosyncratic to this instrument and could not have been achieved by comparing scores on tests from different areas such as reading, mathematics, intelligence, and verbal ability, with final nursing grades.

The population used for the normative studies involved 453 second-semester students from 13 of North Carolina's 24 ADN programs. Mean and percentile ranks of scaled scores are clearly presented. Comparisons of individual and institutional performance with various reference groups are explained with recommendations for credit allocation based on existing data.

The reported K-R 20 reliability of .81, based on 450 students, seems adequate. The standard error of measurement is also noted for this group. Unfortunately, no other reliability data are noted; coefficients of stability and equivalence should have been furnished.

Since ADN programs vary, it is advised that individual institutions decide if tested content parallels their curricular offerings. At the present time, it is difficult to conceive that this instrument be used as the single factor for credit by examination or advanced placement. Unfortunately, no other similar tests have been reported. Validity needs to be affirmed by more rigorous research. It is recommended that the test be used for assessment of educational achievement where tested content is appropriate to program offerings.

[1120]

★Clinical Experience Record for Nursing Students. Nursing students and nurses; 1960–75; CERNS; for recording by instructor of "critical incidents" (rated effective or ineffective) in 12 or 15 areas listed below; no scores; no data on reliability; no norms; 2 record forms; student orientation leaflet ['60, 2 pages]; additional instructional materials available; $10 per 100 record forms; $3.50 per 250 incident slips; 5¢ per student leaflet; $2.50 per manual; postage extra; specimen set not available; "a few minutes each day"; John C. Flanagan, Angeline C. Marchese, Grace Fivars, and Shirley A. Tuska (manual); Psychometric Techniques Associates. *

a) CLINICAL PERFORMANCE RECORD. 1960–75; 12 areas: planning and organizing and adapting nursing care, checking, meeting patient's adjustment and emotional needs, meeting patient's physical and medical needs, applying scientific principles to nursing care, observing and reporting and charting, adaptability to new or stressful situations, relations with co-workers and physicians and visitors, judgment regarding professional values, use of learning opportunities, acceptance of professional responsibility, personal appearance/conduct; 1 form ('72, 4 pages, essentially the same as 1960 form except for cover page, 3 new items, and minor wording changes); manual ('60, 45 pages) for 1960 form; incident slip ('61, 2 pages); list of behavior areas ('75, 2 pages, essentially the same as list copyrighted 1961); 7¢ per list of behavior areas.

b) PERFORMANCE/PROGRESS RECORD—PSYCHIATRIC/MENTALLY RETARDED PATIENT CARE. 1970; 15 areas: providing for comfort and hygiene and other physical needs, checking and observing, training the patient, controlling reluctant or undesirable behavior, recognizing and responding to emotional needs, preventing injury to patient, preventing injury to self or other staff members, coping with emergencies, using ingenuity, taking personal responsibility, maintaining ethical and moral behavior, contributing to effective ward management, interacting with families and visitors and the public, keeping records and reporting, supervising and assisting working patients; 1 form ('70, 4 pages); manual (no date, 24 pages); incident slip (no date, 2 pages).

REFERENCES

1. FLANAGAN, JOHN C.; GOSNELL, DORIS; AND FIVARS, GRACE. "Evaluating Student Performance." Am J Nursing 63(11): 96–9 N '63. *

[1121]

*Entrance Examination for Schools of Nursing. Applicants to schools of registered nursing; 1938–77; EESN; tests administered at centers established by the publisher; tests also available to schools for local administration; 7 scores: verbal ability, numerical ability, life sciences, physical sciences, reading skill, total (scholastic aptitude), arithmetic (first half of numerical ability subtest); no data on reliability of total score for Form 3; Forms 3 ('74, 23 pages), 4 ('76, 23 pages); directions for administering (no date, 11 pages); separate answer sheets (Digitek) must be used; examination fee, $10 per student; fee includes reporting of scores to the school of nursing through which application for examination was made; $2 per additional report; scores not reported to examinees; 125(150) minutes; Psychological Corporation. *

See T2:2379 (1 reference), 7:1115 (3 references), and 6:1156 (2 references).

CAROLYN DAWSON, *Assistant Professor of Nursing, University of Wisconsin-Madison, Madison, Wisconsin.*

As a nationally-normed examination, the EESN makes possible the comparison of applicants' academic abilities in reference to a common yardstick. Given the variability in high school grading systems, this fact alone makes it a useful tool in evaluating the relative academic strength of applicants to a program. However, in interpreting any specific applicant's standing, it is important to know the characteristics of the sample from which the norms were established. On the whole, the major users of the EESN have been hospital schools of nursing and associate degree programs. Consequently, the norms have been derived from a sample predominantly comprised of these potential candidates for nursing education. Baccalaureate schools of nursing would probably prefer to know their applicant's performance on tests which would provide information about the individual's standing relative to other college applicants, and to his or her potential for succeeding in a baccalaureate program.

The EESN emphasizes basic biological and physical science knowledge and quantitative ability. Even the content of the reading skill section is best described as biological and physical science material. The EESN does not include any test of ability in the broad area of the behavioral sciences. Those schools of nursing whose programs include a heavy behavioral science component and/or focus on the psychosocial aspects of patient care, may find this characteristic of the EESN a deficiency.

Basic statistical information is available only for Form 3 of the EESN. Form 4 is currently being administered for the purposes of gathering normative data.

Based on a sample of 1924 applicants, the publishers report K-R 20 reliabilities for the individual tests (Form 3) in the range of .82–.93. The equivalence of the two alternative forms of the examination has yet to be determined.

In addressing the issue of the validity of the EESN, the publishers do not report validity coefficients for Form 3. Rather, they graphically portray the relationship between nursing theory grades for 177 students in a New York school and percentile ranks on the EESN. The range of EESN scores received by the middle 50 percent of the students who achieved each grade are plotted. Information presented in this manner gives a visual image of correspondence between EESN percentiles and nursing theory grades without being substantive evidence for test validity. The basic validity question yet

to be answered is to what extent will EESN scores predict successful completion of specific educational programs in nursing. To this end, individual schools using this screening test will wish to collect data relevant to their own program and student body.

In summary, the EESN as a nationally normed examination is a potentially useful screening tool for hospital and technical programs preparing students for RN practice. Schools can compare the academic ability scores of their applicants to those of a national sample of similar potential students. An alternative form of the examination is available for those individuals wishing to repeat the test. Since it is a recently revised examination, normative data has not yet been obtained for the alternate form, and some reliability and validity questions are lacking studies.

CHRISTINE H. McGUIRE, *Professor of Health Professions Education and Associate Director for Research and Development, Center for Educational Development, University of Illinois at the Medical Center, Chicago, Illinois.*

The EESN consists of five subtests: verbal ability, numerical ability, life sciences, physical sciences, and reading skill. The life sciences subtest covers elementary biology with special emphasis on human biology. The physical sciences subtest gives special emphasis to chemistry. The reading subtest is designed to assess "the ability to read, understand, and analyze written materials similar to those found in nursing textbooks."

The manual describing the test provides adequate information to the user regarding the nature and content of each part of the examination and includes at least one sample item from each part. The instructions to examiners are sufficiently detailed and explicit to assure that standard testing conditions will prevail in all centers where the test is administered.

Each of the five tests comprising the examination is composed of 30 to 75 multiple choice questions with clear, easy-to-follow instructions that should not themselves produce any difficulty to candidates. In general, the questions are straightforward factual questions involving, at most, very simple manipulations of words or numbers. Most items can be defended as sampling information or operations that the student nurse will need to be able to perform. Few items involve any degree of problem solving or conceptualization, even at an elementary level. Given the nature and length of the examination and the time constraints, speed would seem to be a more important factor than intellectual skill in successful performance.

An individual report on each candidate's performance is returned to the applicant's school of choice. This report includes the maximum possible raw score, the examinee's actual raw score and percentile score on the total examination and on each part. The percentile data are also depicted by a profile presented in graphic form. Finally, a single overall prediction is made as to whether the applicant will find academic work "very easy," "easy," "average," "difficult," or "very difficult." The user bulletin accompanying the score reports includes a set of brief suggestions regarding the interpretation of a variety of score patterns, including alternative explanations of possible discrepancies between scores and/or between them and other data about the candidate. Some of these suggestions are presented in the form of questions, answers to which may help the user to understand and deal with any discrepancies which are identified. Finally, each user receives a two-page summary of basic statistics for the relevant form of the examination. For example, the statistics supplied in March 1975 on Form 3 were based on approximately 2,000 candidates. These statistics report the mean, maximum possible score, standard deviation, range, percentile norms, and reliability for each part of the examination and, except for reliability, for the composite total score. Despite the relative brevity of each part (30–75 items), K-R 20 reliability coefficients range from .82 to .93. Validity data are limited to illustrative graphs showing the relation between total score on this examination and first year grades in *one* theory course in *one* school. Inasmuch as such relationships can be expected to vary from school to school and, indeed, from course to course, provision of one simple illustrative scatterplot seems unduly conservative.

Content analysis suggests that most of the present examination samples knowledge and aptitude that, on a priori grounds, appear to relate closely to the prerequisites for success in schools of nursing. However, the health pro-

fessions are increasingly cognizant of the fact that success as a practicing professional involves many skills not sampled in the conventional scholastic aptitude tests and that selection criteria should include consideration of this broader universe. Given the increasingly sophisticated tasks nurses are required to perform and the varied settings in which they may practice, it can be hypothesized that sampling of more complex intellectual skills, of critical perceptual skills, and of essential psychomotor skills should be considered for inclusion in the further development of this examination. Finally, until such time as more definitive validity data are available on this examination, each school which uses it would be well advised to conduct local studies of its predictive validity.

[1122–3]

*Entrance Examination for Schools of Practical/ Vocational Nursing. Applicants to schools of practical nursing; 1942–75; EESPN; tests administered at regional centers established by the publisher; tests also available to schools for local administration; 7 scores: verbal ability, numerical ability, science, reading comprehension, total (academic ability), arithmetic (first half of numerical ability subtest), reading speed; no data on reliability of reading speed and total scores for Form 5; Forms 5 ('74, 21 pages), 6 ('75, 19 pages); directions for administering (no date, 10 pages); separate answer sheets (Digitek) must be used; examination fee, $10 per student; fee includes scoring service and reporting of scores to one school designated at time of application; $2 per additional report; scores not reported to examinees; 115(150) minutes; Psychological Corporation. *

See 7:1116 (2 references).

SALES

[1124]

★[Sales Motivation.] Sales managers, salespeople; 1972; 2 tests, 5 scores for each: basic-creature comfort, safety and order, belonging and affiliation, ego-status, actualization and self-expression; no data on reliability and validity; no norms; no manual; $3 per test, postage extra; [15–30] minutes per test; Jay Hall and Norman J. Seim; Teleometrics Int'l. *
a) INCENTIVES MANAGEMENT INDEX. Sales managers; IMI; practices and attitudes regarding motivational needs of subordinates; 1 form (17 pages); score interpretation (7 pages).
b) SALES MOTIVATION SURVEY. Salespeople; SMS; motivational needs and values; 1 form (17 pages); score interpretation (4 pages).

[1125]

★[Sales Relations.] Salespeople, customers; 1972; views regarding behavior in 20 sales situations; 2 tests (same items except for first and third person expression), 2 scores (exposure, feedback) in each of 3 areas (salesperson's views of his own behavior, customer's views of salesperson's behavior, customer's preferences for salesperson's behavior) plus categorization into 1 of 4 sales types (no sell, soft sell, hard sell, awareness sell); no data on reliability and validity; no norms; no manual; score interpretation (4 pages); $3 per test, postage extra; [15–30] minutes per test; Jay Hall and C. Leo Griffith (b); Teleometrics Int'l. *

a) SALES RELATIONS SURVEY. Salespeople; SRS; salesperson's views as to how he would behave; 1 form (5 pages plus 4 foldout scoring pages).

b) CUSTOMER REACTION SURVEY. Customers; CRS; customer's views of how a salesperson would behave and how customer would prefer that he behave; 1 form (7 pages plus 8 foldout scoring pages).

RAYMOND A. KATZELL, *Professor of Psychology, New York University, New York, New York.*

This pair of "learning instruments" is part of a series issued by the publisher. The three principal assumptions underlying the series are that social learning occurs when (a) the learner is *involved* in finding out relevant facts about the self, (b) there is *feedback* of accurate and meaningful information, and (c) there is subsequent discussion and self-reappraisal (called "*dampening*").

The particular instruments reviewed here are intended for use in applying that model in training sales personnel to relate more effectively to their customers. The two instruments, one to be filled out by the salesperson and the other by a customer, are parallel. The former, called the *Sales Relations Survey,* presents the salesperson with 20 hypothetical situations and asks which of two responses he or she would be more likely to make in each situation. These responses are then self-scored in terms of two dimensions: feedback, or the degree to which the respondent seeks information; and exposure, or the degree to which information is shared with the others involved.

The parallel instrument, called the *Customer Reaction Survey,* solicits descriptions from customers of how they think the salesperson would behave in those same 20 situations, and also how they would prefer that he behave. These descriptions are likewise scored in terms of feedback and exposure.

The general learning or change model noted above is one that probably would be accepted by most professionals concerned with personal change and development. The question remains, however, as to the degree to which the present instruments fit its requirements. Although, on their face, these kinds of instru-

ments may not look like conventional mental measurements, that question can be approached in psychometric terms. Specifically, we may ask about the degree to which they are: (a) reliable; (b) job-related, i.e., predictive of success on the job; (c) construct-valid, i.e., congruent with other manifestations of the underlying traits or behavioral dimensions; and (d) equipped with norms or standards so as to facilitate interpretation.

Since the instruments regrettably lack a conventional manual, we must turn for answers to the accompanying interpretative pamphlet and to the publisher's promotional literature on their "learning instruments."

Regarding reliability, the latter document states that, in developing the instruments, item analyses were performed to insure that all items correlate significantly with "criterion" (scale?) scores, and that no instrument was accepted with less than .65 test-retest reliability. Since no further information is provided, we do not know whether these specific instruments have higher test-retest reliability than the rather low minimum standard cited, or what the internal consistency of the scales actually is, or what samples were employed. In the case of the *Customer Reaction Survey,* it would also be important to know what the inter-rater agreement is.

Although the interpretative pamphlet refers to the relevance of the behavioral constructs measured to sales effectiveness and productivity, no mention is made of any criterion-related validation studies. The promotional brochure does allude to construct validation in the course of developing all their instruments, but no information is provided concerning studies involving particular ones. The approach to construct validation is described as "usually employing related personality inventories." It is difficult to envision what those would be in the present case, as the constructs which these instruments are designed to measure were based on a special model called the "Johari Window." That model, which is credited to Luft and Ingham, is described as featuring exposure and feedback as key interpersonal processes. To justify the validity of these instruments in terms of the model would require showing that (a) the model does in fact pertain to sales effectiveness, and (b) the instruments accu-

Sales Relations

rately assess the degree to which an individual's interpersonal style involves exposure and feedback. Neither of those demonstrations has been made.

The two scores are plotted on a bivariate graph with exposure on the ordinate and feedback on the abscissa. The interpretative pamphlet discusses four patterns of the two raw scores: both low, both high, and either one high with the other low. In each case, the associated interpersonal style is described, together with implications for selling performance. Neither norms nor criterion-related standards are provided for assisting in the interpretation. One is left with the impression that the interpretations are based on intuition or assumption, rather than on data.

On the basis of the information available, these instruments fall decidedly short of psychometric requirements. Whether they facilitate improvement when employed as sales training aids is a matter which remains to be demonstrated.

[1126]

★Sales Style Diagnosis Test. Salespeople; 1975; SSDT; salesperson's perception of own sales style; 6 scores: orientation (task, relationships), effectiveness, style (dominant, supporting, synthesis); no data on reliability and validity; no supporting data for cutoff points; 1 form (8 pages plus 5 pages of scoring directions); no manual; user's guide (1 page); Can $40 per 10 tests; $10 per specimen set; cash orders postpaid; (20–40) minutes; W. J. Reddin and David Forman; Organizational Tests Ltd. [Canada]. *

[1127–8]

★Sales Transaction Audit. Salespeople; 1972; STA; salesperson's views as to how he would handle 18 specific complaints, challenges, and uncertainties on the part of customers; 3 transaction scores (parent subsystem, adult subsystem, child subsystem) and 2 tension indexes (disruptive, constructive); no data on reliability and validity; no norms; 1 form (5 pages plus 4 foldout scoring pages); no manual; score interpretation (8 pages); $3 per test, postage extra; [15–30] minutes; Jay Hall and C. Leo Griffith; Teleometrics Int'l. *

STEPHEN L. COHEN, *Associate Professor of Industrial/Organizational Psychology, University of South Florida, Tampa, Florida; and Vice-President, Assessment Designs, Inc., Winter Park, Florida.*

This 18-item "learning instrument" alleges to assess sales style and its impact on salesman-customer transactions. For each item the respondent marks the one statement of three that best characterizes "If a customer said this to you, what would you feel like saying?" Each customer statement is preceded by an adverb describing the tone in which the comment should be stated (e.g., plaintively, despairingly, flatly, exasperatedly, and impishly). The development of the instrument is based on the work of Berne and Harris on transactional analysis. According to its authors, the STA "is designed to provide you, the salesman, with some information about the *effects* [italics added] that your feelings and sales practices in responding to customer comments have on the quality and subsequent success of your sales transactions." The intent of this instrument is admirable. But, this reviewer has some serious reservations about its capability of meeting its objectives. Quite simply, responses to paper-and-pencil audits do not necessarily generalize to actual behavioral responses in the real-world setting. In fact, the literature on attitude-discrepant behavior, social desirability, and reactivity of such instruments, suggests frequent inconsistent matches between responses to questionnaires and actual behaviors. Given this very feasible limitation, it behooves the instrument developer to carefully validate the construct or content in question and determine its reliability before claims about impact should be made. The developers of the STA do not provide any data supportive of this claim, nor even a manual for an administrator's or potential user's consumption. The only evidence, and this word is used lightly, for validity comes from a general catalogue of "Learning Instruments" provided by the publisher. A small paragraph in this catalogue answers the reliability and validity question in the following manner:

All materials are subjected to an item analysis and revised until all items correlate significantly with their criterion scores. Test-retest stability features are researched, and no instrument with less than .65 test-retest correlation is accepted. Construct validity studies are then conducted, usually employing related personality inventories. As far as can be determined, this procedure is the most complete of any used in the design and construction of learning aid materials.

It can be noted from the above passage that the authors tend to equate item analysis with some form of criterion-referenced validity. Furthermore, and more importantly, the criterion used appears to be defined by the internal scores of the audit itself, and not some more desirable external criterion source. The test-retest stability and construct validity studies alluded to would much better serve their purpose if referenced or included in a manual for each specific learning aid published.

As a learning aid, the STA can be classified as a training instrument. Training implies some type of change or modification in knowledge, attitude, or behavior as its primary goal. The STA may take a respondent through only the initial step of such a change process (i.e., self-awareness), yet it is claimed to have effects on sales performance. The utility of such an instrument rests on its capability to improve one's sales performance through insight into his/her likely reactions to customers, and consequently improve an organization's performance in general. Critical to this reviewer's reservations that either of the above can be improved measurably is the fact that the theoretical grounds on which the entire instrument is based are tenuous at best. Unlike some of the other learning aids published by Teleometrics (namely, the *Styles of Management Inventory*), the underlying theory and supporting evidence for transactional analysis is purely conjectural. While intuitively appealing, it is based on little, if any, hard evidence; certainly not enough to warrant the claim of improving sales performance. More importantly, the STA makes a questionable inferential leap in applying what may be a useful theory for psychoanalysis to principles of salesmanship. At its very best, the STA has the power only to *suggest* how a person *might* react to a customer who makes a certain type of comment. It is unlikely that it can do much else.

Let us assume, however, that the theoretical underpinning and evidence for the instrument are solid. What, then, can the respondent do with the information he/she receives? First, the respondent must score the instrument. The procedure for such scoring is provided by the authors as is the mechanism for transferring the scores to a transactional analysis framework (the parent, adult, or child subsystems model). The self-scoring procedure is not too difficult. Surely it could be handled by any parent or adult. However, the interpretation may push the limits of even a highly competent psychologist. The authors provide the respondents with an elaborate and lengthy interpretation guide which actually is a condensed version of transactional analysis theory. The guide is

very well done although it is difficult reading, and makes only minimal reference to the application of the theory to salesmanship. The use of the instrument would appear to require a very experienced and trained facilitator who could help the respondent translate this new-found knowledge into behaviors that might have an effective impact on the customer world. This reviewer does not see how it would be possible for the respondent, alone, to heed capably the authors' final statement that "the end result is up to you, the salesman, and whether or not you use this information to improve interpersonal relationships with your customers."

In sum, in this reviewer's opinion, the *Sales Transaction Audit* makes a host of assumptions about learning instrument construction, salesmanship, and transactional analysis that severely weaken its ability to fulfill the purposes for which it was designed.

SKILLED TRADES

[1129]

★NOCTI Examination: Air Conditioning and Refrigeration. Teachers and prospective teachers; 1973–77; test administered each spring and fall at centers approved by the publisher; 5 scores for written part (total and 4 subscores), 3 scores for performance part (process, product, total); no reliability data for performance part nor for subscores on written part; Form B ('74) in 2 parts: written (23 pages), performance (8 pages); manual ('74, 23 pages plus test) for performance part; for more complete information, see 1153; examination fee to centers, $100 per candidate (fee to candidate determined locally); postpaid; 180(195) minutes for written part, 300(330) minutes for performance part; National Occupational Competency Testing Institute. *

For a review of the NOCTI program, see 1153.

RICHARD A. SWANSON, *Professor of Industrial Education and Technology, Bowling Green State University, Bowling Green, Ohio.*

The Air Conditioning and Refrigeration (ACR) examination, including a written and a performance test, is one of 24 occupational examinations produced by the National Occupational Competency Testing Institute. The ACR written test is made up of 165 multiple choice questions taken within a three-hour period. The ACR performance test is made up of two major work-sample tasks, with a five-hour time limit. The ACR performance test requires subjective assessment by the examiner on several process and product criteria.

The major purpose of the ACR examination

is "to enable tradesmen to demonstrate the knowledge and skills they have acquired on the job." This may be for the purpose of recognition and/or advancement within the occupation, for partial certification as an industrial teacher, or for academic credit equivalency. The ACR has been available since 1974.

The NOCTI produces many publications, most of which deal with one aspect of all their occupational tests. No separate comprehensive manual for the ACR examination is available. Such a manual is needed.

The content validity of the ACR examination has been rigorously developed. Trade committees developed occupational analyses as the basis for the examination. Their consensus was utilized by test-writing experts. Prior to pilot testing, additional reviews were made by specialists across the United States. The methods by which the persons serving in the various capacities were selected are not identified.

The eight major content categories, subdivisions, and content weightings of the written test constitute a comprehensive measure of ACR occupational knowledge. Since the complex nature of performance testing makes comprehensive measures impossible, two representative work samples were selected: troubleshooting a major piece of equipment and constructing an air-conditioning and refrigeration subassembly. The criteria and process by which these tasks were selected are not described.

A separate NOCTI study completed in October 1976 explored the question of content validity for the State of Georgia. The State Department of Education wished to determine the validity of the ACR examination as a basis for certifying tradesmen aspiring to be air-conditioning and refrigeration teachers in vocational schools (one of the stated purposes of the examination). A six-person trade committee reviewed the tests for content, relative weight of content areas, appropriateness of each written test item, and representativeness of performance tasks and subtasks. Systematic responses to these questions, and statistical analysis of the committee judgments supported the content validity of the ACR written and performance tests for selection and certification of Georgia vocational school instructors.

The K-R 20 reliability of the ACR written test is reported as .907 (N = 49), with a 5.34 standard error of measurement. No measure of reliability is reported for the ACR performance test. Omission of this basic and essential information is a serious shortcoming. The matter is confounded by the subjective nature of the examiner's rating of examinees and the importance of the ACR performance test in maintaining the summative occupational performance purpose of the NOCTI program. With a correlation of .238 between ACR written and ACR performance test scores, the contention that the tests measure compatible, but different, behaviors was supported. This information was provided by NOCTI apart from information found in their official publications.

No assessment of concurrent validity, in terms of other ACR measures or actual job performance, has been reported—again, a serious shortcoming. Of less significance, but also ignored, is the construct validity of the ACR examination.

Summary item analysis statistics reported for the ACR written test are a mean item difficulty of .418 and a mean item discrimination of .256. Cumulative national norms based on data collected from spring 1974 through spring 1976 are presented for the written and the performance tests. The national sample included 106 and 84, respectively, ACR trade personnel who were aspiring to become ACR instructors. Scores are expressed in the form of percent achieved and can be easily converted to national percentile rank or to a T score through the chart provided. There was a much wider range of scores (4 to 100 percent correct) for the performance test than for the written test (38 to 84 percent correct).

NOCTI examinations are administered only through NOCTI area test centers. Strict guidelines for test centers and center test coordinators have been developed. Centers are operating in more than 30 states.

SUMMARY. The ACR examination has several serious deficiencies in terms of validation voids. It especially needs research in the areas of performance test reliability and of concurrent validity of both tests before it can be fully useful for its intended purposes.

Occupational competency testing is a complex and time-consuming venture. The ACR examination is but one of 24 being produced by

NOCTI. These tests are needed and once validated will prove useful to many institutions and individuals. Given the performance test component, it should not surprise the reader that no other ACR occupational competency examination is available commercially. The performance test provides the ACR examination its uniqueness and face validity.

It appears that the ACR examination will primarily be used for research and development purposes until more information is available on its ability to provide reliable and valid summative measurement of an individual's ACR occupational competency.

[1130]

★NOCTI Examination: Airframe and Power Plant Mechanic. Teachers and prospective teachers; 1973–77; test administered each spring and fall at centers approved by the publisher; 4 scores for written part (total, and 3 subscores), 3 scores for performance part (process, product, total); no reliability data for performance part nor for subscores on written part; Form B ('74) in 2 parts: written (29 pages), performance (7 pages); manual ('74, 22 pages plus test) for performance part; for more complete information, see 1153; examination fee to centers, $100 per candidate (fee to candidate determined locally); postpaid; 180(195) minutes for written part, 270(300) minutes for performance part; National Occupational Competency Testing Institute. *

For a review of the NOCTI program, see 1153.

[1131]

★NOCTI Examination: Architectural Drafting. Teachers and prospective teachers; 1973–77; test administered each spring and fall at centers approved by the publisher; 5 scores for written part (total and 4 subscores), 3 scores for performance part (process, product, total); no reliability data for performance part nor for subscores on written part; Form B ('74) in 2 parts: written (19 pages), performance (8 pages); manual ('74, 26 pages plus test) for performance part; for more complete information, see 1153; examination fee to centers, $100 per candidate (fee to candidate determined locally); postpaid; 180(195) minutes for written part, 300(330) minutes for performance part; National Occupational Competency Testing Institute. *

For a review of the NOCTI program, see 1153.

GARY E. LINTEREUR, *Assistant Professor of Industry and Technoloyy, Northern Illinois University, DeKalb, Illinois.*

These tests are directed toward individuals working in the architectural drafting field who wish certification to teach architectural drafting at the secondary or postsecondary level. It is important to note that the tests were not designed to measure aptitude for teaching, but rather purport to measure the individual's related technical knowledge and skills. The

following areas are covered in the written test: basic architectural data, planning and design, materials and methods of construction, and structural systems. The 150-question multiple choice examination is clearly written and can be easily machine scored. The performance test covers window details of a commercial building and transversal sections of a single-story residence. An evaluation form is provided for the performance test.

Some types of questions which could improve the quality of the written test relate to practical problem solving, environmental concerns, and symbol identification. These types of questions should be part of architectural drawing content but are noticeably missing in the present examination.

This type of examination addresses a real need in industrial/technical education—specifically, identifying individual competency gained from work experience. Most of the information covered on the written and performance tests is covered in architectural drawing courses at the senior high school, technical school, and college/university levels. The point is that, although these tests were designed to measure "trade experience," the examiner should be cognizant that an individual with formal instruction in architectural drawing could probably do very well on these examinations. There are few, if any, questions on the examination that are peculiar only to "tradesmen."

A content validation study using six judges from Georgia showed that "the standard of adequacy for the *related information* criterion on the written test was not reached." Regarding the content validation study, a few points need to be made. Content for the examination was derived through occupational analysis by trade committees and "experts" who were assigned to develop appropriate questions. However, of the six judges, all were high school/technical school teachers or directors from Georgia. It seems that practicing architectural draftsmen ought to be represented in the content validation process. Another interesting point is that the content validation study is for Georgia only. Any generalization to be drawn regarding the usability of the test in other states is not presented. This leads to the question of why a "national" representation of judges was not used to validate the content for

NOCTI Examination: Air Conditioning and Refrigeration

a supposedly national examination. No information regarding this point is available.

The reviewer is somewhat perplexed by the statistical treatment when in one table, 22 candidates are reported to have taken the examination in spring 1974 through spring 1976 and in the reliability and standard-error table an N of 58 is used for the same time period. This could be explained by a sample of 58 for reliability data and a sample of 22 for cumulative national norms (which is a rather small sample at best), but it does not explain why the two samples were not pooled to provide a more adequate sample for the cumulative norms. On the 150-question written test, candidate achievement ranged from 61 correct to 121 correct, with a mean of 98 and a median of 91. Scores on the 220-point performance test ranged from 73 to 220, with a mean of 173 and a median of 145.

The paramount question that needs to be asked about this type of testing—when most instructors allow an individual to "proficiency test out" of a course to obtain credit—is, does a national competency test of this type serve a purpose or is it just another test on the market? This reviewer would submit that this type of testing does serve a purpose; large samples could be collected, and validity, reliability, and usability of the instrument can be increased. The content covered is comprehensive in scope and equivalent to tests given to beginning architectural drafting students. The potential examiner must also realize that the candidate will not be involved in the time-honored (and time-consuming) task of building a model home of balsa wood, which usually is included in a course which covers this type of material. On the other hand, the reviewer cannot be overly optimistic about the acceptability of this type of testing. Most instructors have their own biases and "pet projects" that they want the candidate to be exposed to. Proficiency testing (equivalent testing) is not readily accepted by most teachers.

The content validation methodology and statistical treatment of data seem less than optimal, but the tests per se are comprehensive in scope. Comprehensive examiner directions are available for both the written test and the performance test, and a bulletin of relevant information for the candidate is also available.

NOCTI states that two- and four-year colleges have used these examinations to determine if credit should be given to candidates. This reviewer concludes with two suggestions: (a) If successful completion of the examinations is achieved by the candidate, credit should only be given for a beginning-level architectural drafting course because of the basic competencies covered; and (b) if the examinations are recognized for "tradesmen," they should also be available to a high school individual with architectural drafting background because the content covered is not peculiar to tradesmen only.

[1132]

★NOCTI Examination: Auto Body Repair. Teachers and prospective teachers; 1973–77; test administered each spring and fall at centers approved by the publisher; 5 scores for written part (total and 4 subscores), 3 scores for performance part (process, product, total); no reliability data for performance part nor for subscores on written part; Form B ('74) in 2 parts: written (21 pages), performance (6 pages); manual ('74, ?? pages plus test) for performance part; for more complete information, see 1153; examination fee to centers, $100 per candidate (fee to candidate determined locally); postpaid; 180(195) minutes for written part, 360(390) minutes for performance part; National Occupational Competency Testing Institute. *

For a review of the NOCTI program, see 1153.

[1133]

★NOCTI Examination: Auto Mechanic. Teachers and prospective teachers; 1973–77; test administered each spring and fall at centers approved by the publisher; 5 scores for written part (total and 4 subscores), 3 scores for performance part (process, product, total); no reliability data for performance part nor for subscores on written part; Form B ('74) in 2 parts: written (25 pages), performance (11 pages); manual ('74, 28 pages plus test) for performance part; for more complete information, see 1153; examination fee to centers, $100 per candidate (fee to candidate determined locally); postpaid; 180(195) minutes for written part, 300(330) minutes for performance part; National Occupational Competency Testing Institute. *

For a review of the NOCTI program, see 1153.

REFERENCES

1. COGSWELL, J. E. A Descriptive Study of the Texas Competency Testing Project for Vocational Industrial Teachers and Achievement Profile of the Participants. Doctor's thesis, East Texas State University (Commerce, Texas), 1976. (DAI 37: 4312A)

CHARLES W. PENDLETON, *Associate Professor of Automotive and Power Technology, Illinois State University, Normal, Illinois.*

This test was designed to enable trade personnel to demonstrate the knowledge and skills acquired from on-the-job experiences. Results of the tests are beneficial to state departments of education, industrial teacher-training institutions, and other organizations to ascertain who may: (*a*) enroll in an industrial teacher education program; (*b*) be certified as an industrial teacher, and (*c*) receive academic credit toward a degree. The test has two parts: a written test that measures knowledge gained on the job and a performance test that measures the manipulative skills a competent craftsperson uses in daily work. The written test requires three hours and the performance test five hours to complete. Candidates must take both parts.

The test seems to be carefully constructed and was initially designed for appropriateness in the certification of future vocational teachers in trade, industrial, and technical fields. Pilot testing of the exam at area test centers throughout the nation has resulted in fair and comprehensive samplings of the knowledge and skills the occupation demands.

Handbooks for test administration are comprehensive and succinctly written and should leave little doubt in the mind of the area test coordinator and test examiners as to their responsibilities.

Reliability (internal consistency) based on K-R 20 and K-R 21 for written test scores was .91 and .88, respectively, for the spring 1974 to spring 1976 test series. Subscore results for the written test indicate that candidates scored high in areas of basic shop principles and practices and in auto engines, and lower in areas of shop management and control, and auto accessories. Content validity was evaluated by a select trade committee of automotive instructors in Georgia. The subtopics and their respective weightings were judged by the committee to be appropriate and adequate for Georgia at the .01 confidence level. As the test becomes more utilized, a better evaluation of its validity can be determined.

This test for auto mechanics appears adequate for the purpose intended. The 200 multiple choice questions in the written part should measure the candidate's general knowledge of automobile service and repair. The 12 performance tasks are representative of service operations conducted by automotive mechanics in routine maintenance and repair.

The most serious deficiency found was in the construction of the written component of the test. Numerous typographical errors in both questions and answers could be misleading to the candidate. Component terminology is sometimes inconsistent from question to question and not in agreement with current service manuals and textbooks. Some questions pertain to mechanical devices that have not been used on automobiles for 15 to 20 years. The written test lacks emphasis in areas of automotive electronics, basic meters and their hookups, and electric and pneumatic-powered hand tools. The tests and their accompanying instructional booklets should be reread and corrected for sexist words or terms—i.e., tradesman, he, his, salesmanship, etc.—to be consistent with present publishing standards.

In summary, one should have a reasonable degree of confidence in using this two-part test as a measure of a candidate's knowledge and skill as an automotive mechanic. Since the future of the automobile and its associated technology is so unpredictable and rapidly changing, the written and performance test items should be continually updated and reflective of these changes.

KENNETH E. POUCHER, *Professor, Department of Industrial Education and Technology, Ball State University, Muncie, Indiana.*

The NOCTI Auto Mechanics Test was designed to evaluate vocational teachers for certification or selection. The test is composed of a written examination and an extensive performance examination.

The items selected for the written test appear to be very appropriate, in sufficient breadth, and in good proportion to the complexity of the technology.

Evidence of sufficient content validity of the written test was established by a panel of six secondary and postsecondary educators in the State of Georgia. Reliability data on the 200 test items are based on 78 examinees. The K-R 20 reliability coefficient is reported as .913, with a standard error of 5.55; the K-R 21 coefficient of equivalence derived is .878, with a standard error of 6.57. Reliability is deemed to be satisfactory.

Cumulative national norms for the written test for spring 1974 through spring 1976 are based on an N of 390. The sample on which the norms are based is not defined. Also provided is a table for converting percent correct to a national percentile rank or a T score (mean of 50 and standard deviation of 10).

NOCTI Examination: Auto Mechanic

The performance examination is composed of parts identification and 11 typical jobs with a maximum time allocated to perform each task. The tasks include disk brake assembly; front wheel alignment, ignition system and charging system diagnosis and repair; carburetor adjustment, engine diagnosis and repair; and drive train and air conditioning maintenance.

The examiner's manual for the performance test is a well-prepared document listing the tools, equipment, and materials necessary to set up each job. During administration of the performance test the candidate is observed and evaluated on a numerical scale for the subjective measure of workmanship and the quality of tasks performed. A formula yields a single final score as a measure of the individual's performance.

Content validation information provided indicates that the performance tasks are appropriate and typical, and utilize skills and knowledge representative of those expected of a vocational teacher in the State of Georgia.

Cumulative national norms are provided for the performance test, based on an N of 370, including the spring 1974 through spring 1976 administrations. No information is provided about these candidates.

The copyright date of the NOCTI Auto Mechanics written test and performance test is 1974, which indicates that the tests may lack some currency in their emission systems aspects.

It is this reviewer's opinion that, in addition to the stated purpose, the results of the test could also be used to assist in the selection of auto mechanics by industry, provided norms are available and appropriate.

[1134]

★NOCTI Examination: Cabinet Making and Millwork. Teachers and prospective teachers; 1973–77; test administered each spring and fall at centers approved by the publisher; 5 scores for written part (total and 4 subscores), 3 scores for performance part (process, product, total); no reliability data for performance part nor for subscores on written part; Form B ('74) in 2 parts: written (28 pages), performance (7 pages); manual ('74, 24 pages plus test) for performance part; for more complete information, see 1153; examination fee to centers, $100 per candidate (fee to candidate determined locally); postpaid; 180(195) minutes for written part, 300(330) minutes for performance part; National Occupational Competency Testing Institute. *

For a review of the NOCTI program, see 1153.

GARY E. LINTEREUR, *Assistant Professor of Industry and Technology, Northern Illinois University, DeKalb, Illinois.*

The purpose of this examination is to identify the competencies individuals have obtained while working in the occupational area of cabinet making and millwork. The tests are designed for individuals interested in teaching positions in trade and technical areas at the secondary or postsecondary level. NOCTI reports that some two- and four-year colleges use this examination to determine advanced standing of individuals in their programs. NOCTI also clearly states that it *does not* measure aptitude for teaching—it does purport to measure an individual's related technical knowledge and skills.

The scope of the written part of the examination covers planning, wood/stock selection, safety, machines and tools, joinery, assembly, and finishing. These areas are covered in the three-hour, 160-question, multiple choice test. The questions are very well constructed, with picture identification questions reproduced clearly. A machine-scanning answer sheet is used to record answers. NOCTI reports a K-R 20 reliability of .931, with standard error of 5.36. It should be noted that these statistics are based on only 23 candidates—a very small sample for this type of data. For a sample of 67, candidate achievement on the written test ranged from 58 correct to 130 correct, with a mean of 95 and a median of 93. The performance test encompasses layout and assembly of a counter kitchen cabinet, including a drawer construction, and producing a laminated top. A list of machines, tools, accessories, and materials required, and an easy-to-read drawing accompany the five-hour examination. Performance achievement on 425 points ranged from 162 to 421, with a mean of 326 and a median of 289. Comprehensive directions for examiners and candidates are available.

The written test can be readily used by high school instructors, technical school instructors, and college/university instructors. Most, if not all, of the material is covered in any good cabinet-making class, and little, if any, material is restricted to "tradesmen." The reviewer believes the written test is comprehensive in scope and addresses the basic cognitive competencies that vocational instructors should know regarding cabinet making and millwork. To reiterate, this test could be used for other purposes than specifically identifying tradesmen competencies. It would be interesting for the publishers to see how high school students enrolled in a good cabinet-making course perform on the test. Data of this nature are not available. Neither are data on characteristics of the norming population sample included, which would have been helpful to the potential user. Also missing is a content validation study and, as mentioned earlier, a very small sample was used to establish cumulative national norms. The preceding remarks are tempered by this reviewer in that the test does appear to have face validity.

Performance testing in this area seems somewhat difficult, to say the least. Having a "tradesman" make mortise, butt, and dado joints hardly seems to demonstrate rigorous journeyman cabinet making/millwork competencies. An inlaid "dutchman" would probably better exemplify a complex competency rather than cutting a dado joint. As a test for a tradesman to receive advanced standing in a program, this reviewer would have serious reservations—unless credit were given only for a very basic course in cabinet making.

Although this examination does an excellent job of identifying basic cognitive and psychomotor competencies, this reviewer has serious concern about the purpose for which it is to be used. This reviewer suggests that a potential examiner consider allowing the candidate to proficiency test out of a basic course using the instructor's own examination to insure that the candidate is exposed to all basic prerequisites before going into the next course in the sequence. It would be unfair to the candidate, unless the instructor's course did not go beyond the basic competencies identified in the tests, to accept successful completion of the NOCTI Cabinet Making and Millwork examination for advanced standing only to have the candidate struggle at the second-level course. This concern is proffered by the reviewer in the knowledge that some cabinet making and millwork operations specialize only in certain areas whereas a potential instructor needs breadth of experience which is usually offered in a survey course.

[1135]

★NOCTI Examination: Carpentry. Teachers and prospective teachers; 1973-77; test administered each spring and fall at centers approved by the publisher; 5 scores for written part (total and 4 subscores), 3 scores for performance part (process, product, total); no reliability data for performance part nor for subscores on written part; Form B ('74) in 2 parts: written (21 pages), performance (10 pages); manual ('74, 22 pages plus test) for performance part; for more complete information, see 1153; examination fee to centers, $100 per candidate (fee to candidate determined locally); postpaid; 180(195) minutes for written part, 300(330) minutes for performance part; National Occupational Competency Testing Institute. *

For a review of the NOCTI program, see 1153.

REFERENCES

1. COGSWELL, J. E. *A Descriptive Study of the Texas Competency Testing Project for Vocational Industrial Teachers and Achievement Profile of the Participants.* Doctor's thesis, East Texas State University (Commerce, Texas), 1976. (*DAI* 37: 4312A)

DANIEL L. HOUSEHOLDER, *Professor of Industrial Education, Texas A&M University, College Station, Texas.*

The Carpentry examination in the National Occupational Competency Testing Institute series provides a comprehensive combination of written and performance evaluation. The written test samples a good variety of topics generally associated with competent performance in the craft, while the performance test offers the individual an opportunity to demonstrate his skills at several typical trade tasks.

The sampling of test items from the respective areas of trade information appears skewed to some extent; a person who can compute simple cubic measures can obtain several points on the basis of that knowledge alone, without any experience in the trade. Overall performance on the written test should correlate closely with mastery of factual trade knowledge. Higher cognitive processes do not appear to be required to answer the written questions correctly.

The test relies heavily upon the traditional materials and methods used in the trade. Relatively few newly introduced materials and procedures are mentioned in the written test; none are utilized in the performance test. It would appear that considerable updating should be undertaken to avoid penalizing individuals who have acquired their trade experience in recent years.

Because of the variations in building codes and construction practices from one area to another, many of the items and subtests could yield misleading scores. Wood-frame floor construction, for example, is not standard in several geographic regions; yet is it the only floor construction procedure considered in the test. Similar problems arise in conventions for trim, wall framing, and roof framing. Some questions are based upon old size standards for dimension lumber ($1\frac{5}{8}''$ x $3\frac{5}{8}''$ for $2''$ x $4''$), others on the more recent ($1\frac{1}{2}''$ x $3\frac{1}{2}''$ for $2''$ x $4''$).

Since commercial and light industrial construction tasks are under-represented in the content coverage, a carpenter who specialized in residential construction would appear to have an advantage on the written test. If his experience were in the central portion of the country, he would have a distinct advantage on the performance sample, which requires construction of a small portion of a frame residential unit, to a reduced size, from standard components. However, the performance test incorporates a number of subtasks which are rarely performed in many sections of the country, such as the installation of bevel siding and the application of diagonal subflooring.

Ratings on the performance test depend upon interrater reliabilities for comparability. The attainment of a high level of objectivity within the guidelines provided the test administrators appears unlikely, though norms are provided by NOCTI. The lack of criterion-referenced scales is a serious handicap to the attainment of objective evaluation of performance.

While the norming population for the test is small (N = 57), reliabilities for the small group are impressive (K-R 20 = .925; K-R 21 = .903). Norms for the written and performance tests should be useful in assessing the competence of a tradesman in a general way.

General utility of the Carpentry examination should be relatively high in evaluating the backgrounds of prospective carpentry teachers. While gaps in content coverage remain a problem, the combination of written and performance assessment should yield an accurate evaluation.

[1136]

★NOCTI Examination: Civil Technology. Teachers and prospective teachers; 1973–77; test administered each spring and fall at centers approved by the publisher; 5 scores for written part (total and 4 subscores), 3 scores for performance part (process, product, total); no reliability data for performance part nor for subscores on written part; Form B ('74) in 2 parts: written (27 pages), performance (13 pages); manual ('74, 27 pages plus test) for perform-

ance part; for more complete information, see 1153; examination fee to centers, $100 per candidate (fee to candidate determined locally); postpaid; 180(195) minutes for written part, 300(330) minutes for performance part; National Occupational Competency Testing Institute.*

For a review of the NOCTI program, see 1153.

[1137]

★NOCTI Examination: Cosmetology. Teachers and prospective teachers; 1973–77; test administered each spring and fall at centers approved by the publisher; 5 scores for written part (total and 4 subscores), 3 scores for performance part (process, product, total); no reliability data for performance part nor for subscores on written part; Form B ('74) in 2 parts: written (14 pages), performance (8 pages); manual ('74, 23 pages plus test) for performance part; for more complete information, see 1153; examination fee to centers, $100 per candidate (fee to candidate determined locally); postpaid; 180(195) minutes for written part, 360(390) minutes for performance part; National Occupational Competency Testing Institute. *

For a review of the NOCTI program, see 1153.

[1138]

★NOCTI Examination: Diesel Engine Repair. Teachers and prospective teachers; 1973–77; test administered each spring and fall at centers approved by the publisher; 5 scores for written part (total and 4 subscores), 3 scores for performance part (process, product, total); no reliability data for performance part nor for subscores on written part; Form B ('74) in 2 parts: written (30 pages), performance (7 pages); manual (22 pages plus test) for performance part; for more complete information, see 1153; examination fee to centers, $100 per candidate (fee to candidate determined locally); postpaid; 180(195) minutes for written part, 300(330) minutes for performance part; National Occupational Competency Testing Institute.*

For a review of the NOCTI program, see 1153.

CHARLES W. PENDLETON, *Associate Professor of Automotive and Power Technology, Illinois State University, Normal, Illinois.*

The NOCTI Diesel Engine Repair examination, one of the products of the National Occupational Competency Testing Institute, is intended for those individuals experienced in skilled trades or occupations who need to present objective evidence of their competency to become vocational teachers, to obtain academic credit from an institution that recognizes the test results, or to become certified. The examination has two parts: a written part that measures the candidate's knowledge gained on the job and a performance part that measures the manipulative skills a competent diesel engine mechanic uses in daily work. The written test requires approximately three hours to complete, whereas the performance test requires approximately five hours for completion.

Instructional booklets for test administration

are provided. They clearly illustrate the duties, materials needed, check lists, and other forms that are needed by the examiners for total administration of both the written and performance components of the examination. A Bulletin of Information for Candidates indicates the scope of the written and performance tests, and explains how to register and whom to contact to find out when and where the NOCTI examinations will be administered, as well as answering other pre- and post-test procedural questions.

The Diesel Engine Repair test (like other NOCTI tests) was developed and norms established by skilled trade people and test development specialists throughout the nation. This test was reviewed by experienced diesel mechanics, and revised and pilot tested in area test centers in various states. To determine the appropriateness of the tests for the State of Georgia in the certification of vocational teachers in trade, industrial, and technical fields at both secondary and postsecondary levels, a select trade committee of educators from Georgia was selected. A content validity study was performed by a trade committee of postsecondary educators to determine adequacy of test coverage, weighting of subheadings, and appropriateness of written test items. The exam subtopics and their respective weightings were judged to be appropriate and adequate for Georgia at the .01 confidence level on six of seven criteria.

Written test reliabilities for a small sample (N = 24), based on K-R 20 and 21, were .94 and .92, respectively, for the spring 1974 to spring 1976 test series. This relatively high internal consistency should provide for consistent results whenever the test is used. The accuracy of this diesel engine repair test in measuring what it is supposed to measure should be determined by further validity studies. Tables have been provided for determining percentile rank and standard scores from the percentage of correct responses on the candidate's written test.

This test has many good features. Major emphasis is in the following areas: fuel injection pumps and nozzle repair and adjustment, hydraulic system troubleshooting and repair, electrical systems diagnosis and repair, power train

operation and repair, and basic engine diagnosis and repair.

Most test questions (both written and performance) are clearly written and thorough for the subject content designed, though some questions concerning the electrical system are inaccurate and misleading. The test questions provide a good coverage of basic diesel engines and their power trains as found in many applications, such as trucks, tractors, boats, locomotives, and other industrial equipment. The questions will not soon become obsolete.

In summary, the written and performance tests are superior to any diesel engine repair exam available on the market. A large degree of confidence could be placed in the ability of this test to differentiate between those with and those without adequate occupational competency in diesel engine repair.

[1139]

★NOCTI Examination: Electrical Installation. Teachers and prospective teachers; 1973–77; test administered each spring and fall at centers approved by the publisher; 5 scores for written part (total and 4 subscores), 3 scores for performance part (process, product, total); no reliability data for performance part nor for subscores on written part; Form B ('74) in 2 parts: written (25 pages), performance (13 pages); manual ('74, 29 pages plus test) for performance part; for more complete information, see 1153; examination fee to centers, $100 per candidate (fee to candidate determined locally); postpaid; 180(195) minutes for written part, 300(330) minutes for performance part; National Occupational Competency Testing Institute. *

For a review of the NOCTI program, see 1153.

REFERENCES

1. COGSWELL, J. E. *A Descriptive Study of the Texas Competency Testing Project for Vocational Industrial Teachers and Achievement Profile of the Participants*. Doctor's thesis, East Texas State University (Commerce, Texas), 1976. (*DAI* 37: 4312A)

ALAN R. SUESS, *Professor of Industrial Education and Education, Purdue University, West Lafayette, Indiana.*

The National Occupational Competency Testing Institute Electrical Installation examination consists of two parts. One part is a five-hour performance test. The second part is a 177-item, four-alternative, multiple choice test with a three-hour time limit. Form B of both tests was provided for review. None of the materials included in the review package indicated the number of forms available for this or any other NOCTI examination, but Form B appears to be the only available form.

The performance test is a comprehensive

sample of eight tasks common to electrical installation personnel. In deference to test confidentiality it would be wholly inappropriate to discuss the specifics of the tasks. However, the prospective user of this test can feel confident that they are genuinely representative of the tasks of electrical installers. Tasks include drawing procedures; tube bending; box installation; wiring problems requiring planning, splicing, and connecting; and motor (AC and DC) installation. The test samples activities that progress from relatively simple to fairly complex.

This reviewer has two important concerns about the performance test, despite its overall quality. First, the performance testing area is set up with eight different task stations. All participants use the same stations. If one or more participants experience difficulties, others may be deprived of access to the work station. While this reviewer does not claim trade competence, experience with the tools would indicate wide variations in the time required to complete each assignment. Provisions for multiple stations for the time-consuming tasks appears warranted when several candidates are participating in the testing sessions. A second difficulty is the lack of direction given the occupationally qualified performance examiner. Subtask points are assigned for each element of each performance task. The available cumulative national norms as of 1976 indicate surprisingly high mean achievement, with a substantially higher mean than median, possibly indicating evaluation that was more nearly "pass-fail" than continuous ratings.

The written test presents a balanced sample of items faithful to the item budget included in the series Bulletin of Information for Candidates. For example, questions relating to electronic control elements provide an excellent balance between vacuum tube, transistor, and logic devices. The computation questions are the only portion of the content sample that is of dubious quality. Some of the items are both artificially difficult and clearly unrealistic of in-field calculations.

The multiple choice items are flawed by violating nearly every standard of test construction. Correct alternatives are distributed as follows: "A," 36; "B," 43; "C," 58; "D," 40. Only minimal recall is required to identify three sets of questions that answer each other.

Two questions have as the correct alternative the single radically different alternative. A variety of other less serious flaws diminish the overall quality of the written test.

The physical appearance of the test makes it appear "homemade." One-third of a page of the answer section of the Directions to the Performance Examiner: Electrical Installation was not printed on this reviewer's copy. Typographical errors and typing irregularities are common. Typographical errors in the stems of three questions create problems for the examinee: one stem includes a schematic that is drawn as a short circuit; a stem reads "shatter" with alternatives dealing with motor chatter; and the third can be answered correctly only if the stem is read as "120–240 volt motor," not the printed "120–140 volt motor." The question dealing with a binary value has the number written backwards and is answerable only because the place values are also given. The drawings in a meter installation question are so poorly reproduced that it is not possible to determine subtle differences in contact location. Finally, the answer key is incorrect for one question.

The content selection of both the performance and written portions of the NOCTI Electrical Installation examination is basically sound. It is indeed unfortunate that the quality of the instrument has not progressed beyond what appears to be a first draft. Nationally standardized occupational competency examinations are long overdue. NOCTI has assumed leadership toward this goal, but has a responsibility to produce quality examinations to this end. The base for such an instrument is present in the Electrical Installation examination. Careful editing and minor revision of this examination can provide an outstanding evaluation of occupational competency.

[1140]

★NOCTI Examination: Electronics Communications. Teachers and prospective teachers; 1973–77; test administered each spring and fall at centers approved by the publisher; 5 scores for written part (total and 4 subscores), 3 scores for performance part (process, product, total); no reliability data for performance part nor for subscores on written part; Form B ('74) in 2 parts: written (22 pages), performance (15 pages); manual ('74, 24 pages plus test) for performance part; for more complete information, see 1153; examination fee to centers, $100 per candidate (fee to candidate determined locally); postpaid; 180(195) minutes for written part, 300(330) minutes for performance part; National Occupational Competency Testing Institute. *

For a review of the NOCTI program, see 1153.

EMIL H. HOCH, *Professor of Industrial Arts, State University College at Buffalo, Buffalo, New York.*

This examination helps to fill the void that has existed in the area of occupational competency testing in the field of electronic communications. The Electronics Communications examination has two distinct tests: a written test, of 130 four-option multiple choice items, with a three-hour time limit; and a five-hour performance test including nine jobs of which the candidate selects six. Both the written test and the performance test do an adequate job of covering the broad range of information, from simple to complex, necessary for the determination of an individual's skills and talents. The examination is rather comprehensive and it is of sufficient length to provide significant data relative to the candidate's ability.

A series Bulletin of Information for Candidates gives a brief description of the coverage of both the written test and the performance test. The emphasis placed on various topics is given as a percentage of the total test. The topics given the most weight within the written test include: basic electricity as applied to the electronics industry, 8%; electronic concepts applied to vacuum tube and solid state devices, 19%; amplifiers in cascade for RF and AF, 9%; single phase circuits, 12%; electronics circuits, 15%; and basic methods and procedures applied to maintenance correction and adjustment of units and component parts, 16%. The areas of testing covered in the performance test are: radio equipment, 33%; recording equipment, 17%; and television service, 50%.

The National Occupational Competency Testing Institute provides test developers with a sound foundational set of guidelines in their Handbook for Developing and Administering Occupational Competency Testing. The Institute also provides a Handbook for Area Test Center Organization and Administration which gives guidelines for establishing area test centers, for selecting the area test coordinator, for test administration procedures, etc. Such guidelines assure a relatively consistent procedure for administration of tests and the handling of data.

Detailed manuals for the administration of both the written test and the performance test are provided for the examiner. All possible points are thoroughly dealt with in a most judicious manner.

Cumulative national norms have been established using data collected from spring 1974 through spring 1976. Norms are presented separately for the written test and the performance test, based on 74 and 70 candidates, respectively. Tables show national percentile rank and T score—with a mean of 50 and a standard deviation of 10—for "percent score achieved" by candidate. Also, national norms for subscores on the written test are available, based on a very small number of candidates (14). For each of four subscore areas, the number of items, the minimum and maximum percent correct, the mean, standard deviation, and median are presented.

A pilot project was conducted by NOCTI for the State of Georgia "to demonstrate the feasibility of developing and administering a vocational competency testing program for new vocational teachers (secondary & postsecondary)." Analysis of data, collected on the project by NOCTI led to their conclusion that the examination was appropriate and adequate in terms of the stated criteria.

This reviewer found several items on the written test which may cause confusion for the candidate, including an inappropriate verb tense, a change in type of question stem (changed from a positive-type statement to a negative-type statement by using the word "not") without additional instructions, misspelled words, and inconsistency of alignment in numbers containing decimals. The performance test also includes a few minor points of possible confusion to the candidate. Students are told that the examiner will provide a schematic drawing in the instructions; however, in one problem the examiner is told to provide the schematic only if requested by the student. Terminology is not universally acceptable in all problems; e.g., "a three speed phone-player."

This reviewer believes that the Electronics Communication examination needs to have alternate forms developed because of the possibility of the retesting of any given candidate.

Overall, the reviewer was disappointed in the quality of test reproduction. There were frequent smudge marks on the copy provided, and it was somewhat distracting to have the test printed on both sides of the paper because the print was visible through the paper.

In summary, this occupational competency examination in Electronics Communication does help to fill a tremendous void which has existed. It is a rather noteworthy contribution to the profession and, even though it has relatively minor problems, does a good job of covering the field in both theory and performance. The minor flaws listed by this reviewer should not deter or prevent the use of this examination.

[1141]

★NOCTI Examination: Industrial Electrician. Teachers and prospective teachers; 1973–77; test administered each spring and fall at centers approved by the publisher; 5 scores for written part (total and 4 subscores), 3 scores for performance part (process, product, total); no reliability data for performance part nor for subscores on written part; Form B ('74) in 2 parts: written (25 pages), performance (9 pages); manual ('74, 24 pages plus test) for performance part; for more complete information, see 1153; examination fee to centers, $100 per candidate (fee to candidate determined locally); postpaid; 180(195) minutes for written part, 300(330) minutes for performance part; National Occupational Competency Testing Institute. *

For a review of the NOCTI program, see 1153.

ALAN R. SUESS, *Professor of Industrial Education and Education, Purdue University, West Lafayette, Indiana.*

The National Occupational Competency Testing Institute Industrial Electrician examination consists of two parts: a five-hour performance test including four tasks; and a three-hour multiple choice test. Materials provided by NOCTI to aid in this review report that the content selection procedures used for this examination duplicated the analysis procedure commonly used for curriculum development in occupational education. The content selection, item budget, etc., were the result of a job (task) analysis ultimately approved by a representative and occupationally competent advisory committee. None of the variety of analysis strategies possible with modern computer technology were used. The resulting content analysis is as traditional as the technique used for the analysis. Form B of both the performance and written tests was provided; it appears to be the only available form.

The performance test is evaluated by a trade-competent examiner. There are two types of evaluation for each task: one for process per-

formance, and a second for the overall quality of the finished product. Examiners rate performance on a variety of subtasks in both the process and product categories. Although the examiner is urged to use a range of scores, including fractional scores, the Directions to the Performance Examiner: Industrial Electrician is extremely vague about precise scoring procedures. Cumulative national norms for spring 1974 through spring 1976 indicate that only 29 individuals had completed the performance test for Industrial Electrician, with the mean achievement of 83.1 percent. One plausible reason for the high test scores could be a function of a virtual "pass-fail" scoring by the examiners. High performance test scores may also be attributed to the fact that two of the tasks involve identical tube-bending tasks; only the material to be bent changes. Thus, half of the tasks require the same knowledge and similar skill. The effect of the task selection decision is to greatly restrict the scope of the performance test. While all tasks included are appropriate to the occupation being tested, they are hardly a comprehensive sampling of possible tasks performed by industrial electricians.

The written test consists of 200 four-alternative items. If an examinee had a comprehensive basic electricity background, between 85 and 90 of these items could be answered without any practical experience as an industrial electrician. Similarly, if the examinee is "test-wise," instead of trade competent, there will almost certainly be a gain in score, since "C" is the dominant alternative (in 57 items) and "A" is the correct response only 39 times. The test is additionally flawed by questionable items requesting brand name products alleged to be superior, a question that does *not* reflect the most recent revision of the National Electrical Code, and by six sets of adjacent questions one of which gives important cues to the answer of the other. Two questions have as the correct alternative the single radically different alternative. Five questions have stems so ambiguous that it is not possible to answer them. Two questions have two answers, one the obvious response and a second correct alternative that the more sophisticated would consider correct. The examinee is faced with a genuine dilemma in a resonant circuit question, since the stem does not indicate whether the circuit is series or parallel and therefore the only plausible answer is not that indicated on the answer key. Finally, the test appears to have been constructed in a vacuum. Not one of the 200 questions deals with electronic or logic controls or devices.

The overall impression of the written test is one of a decidedly amateur appearance. Virtually every format, construction, and sequencing error that is commonly discussed in basic test construction books is present in this examination. As mentioned previously, the test appears to be the result of committee effort. Materials provided by NOCTI do not make clear whether the same committee that determined the content also wrote the items, but the items vary so in form and sophistication that it is obvious that several individuals wrote the questions. There can be no quarrel with having broadly representative committees develop test questions. The problem is that NOCTI has made no apparent effort to edit the questions into a uniform format. This problem must be faced if this test is to become a viable and legitimate evaluation of the knowledge and performance of experienced industrial electricians. With the omissions and flaws reported in this review, it is doubtful that either the performance or written test of the Industrial Electrician examination now meets this need. Considering the overall quality of the NOCTI Electrical Installation examination, reviewed elsewhere in this section, it may be that a more careful and modern analysis could reduce the electrical trades testing to a single examination.

[1142]

★NOCTI Examination: Industrial Electronics. Teachers and prospective teachers; 1973–77; test administered each spring and fall at centers approved by the publisher; 5 scores for written part (total and 4 subscores), 3 scores for performance part (process, product, total); no reliability data for performance part nor for subscores on written part; Form B ('74) in 2 parts: written (25 pages), performance (15 pages); manual ('74, 40 pages plus test) for performance part; for more complete information, see 1153; examination fee to centers, $100 per candidate (fee to candidate determined locally); postpaid; 180(195) minutes for written part, 300(330) minutes for performance part; National Occupational Competency Testing Institute. *

For a review of the NOCTI program, see 1153.

EMIL H. HOCH, *Professor of Industrial Arts, State University College at Buffalo, Buffalo, New York.*

NOCTI Examination: Industrial Electrician

The Industrial Electronics examination helps to fill the gap that has existed in occupational competency testing in this field. The examination is divided into two tests: a three-hour written test of 150 four-alternative multiple choice items, and a five-hour performance test of eight specific jobs. Both tests do a fine job of covering the range of information necessary for adequate measurement of individuals; the examination is comprehensive enough and of sufficient length.

A Bulletin of Information for Candidates gives a brief description of the topics covered by the written test and the performance test, and the percentage of the tests devoted to each of the topics. The topics and their weights for the written test are basic electronic fundamentals, 16%; digital circuits, 10%; network (passive), 6%; electronic control devices, 8%; amplifiers, detectors, and active circuits, 16%; components, 10%; use of instruments, 10%; troubleshooting, 10%; electronic assembly precautions, 2%; computer technology, 4%; energy conversion (servoloops), 4%; and transducers, 4%. Areas covered in the performance test include use of measuring instruments, 30%; measure, observe, and record, 25%; use of test equipment, 25%; and program simple problems, 15%.

The National Occupational Competency Testing Institute provides test users with a handbook for organizing and administering area test centers, assuring a relatively consistent procedure for administration of tests and the handling of data. Detailed manuals for the administration of both the written test and the performance test are provided for the examiner, covering all points judiciously.

Cumulative national norms for spring 1974 through spring 1976 are presented for the written test and the performance test, based on 83 and 81 candidates, respectively. No information is provided on the candidates. National norms for subscores on the written test are also available, based on only 15 candidates.

A project was conducted by NOCTI for Georgia to determine the appropriateness of the NOCTI test series for selection and certification of vocational and technical teachers in that state. Results of the collection of data from a team of four experts in the field of industrial electronics supported the position that the overall scope of the examination was appropriate and adequate in terms of the stated criteria.

Several items on the written test may cause confusion for the candidate. Two items are missing either a word or a numerical value (the numerical value is necessary to achieve an answer). The format of multiple choice items is changed from a positive to a negative statement by using the word "not," without any additional instructions to the test taker. There is a duplication of the use of the words "a/an" in at least one item. Not all choices using decimals are presented in a consistent format with decimals aligned. A few questions or statements are wordy and, therefore, somewhat confusing.

The development of alternate forms would be helpful to allow for the possibility of retesting of any given candidate.

This reviewer was disappointed in the quality of test reproduction. The test is printed on both sides of the paper, and it is somewhat distracting because the print is visible through the paper.

To sum up, this occupational competency examination in Industrial Electronics helps to fill a large void. It is a noteworthy contribution to the profession and, although less than perfect, does a fine job of covering the field in both theory and performance. The minor flaws noted here should not discourage the use of this valuable examination.

[1143]

★NOCTI Examination: Machine Drafting. Teachers and prospective teachers; 1973–77; test administered each spring and fall at centers approved by the publisher; 5 scores for written part (total and 4 subscores), 3 scores for performance part (process, product, total); no reliability data for performance part nor for subscores on written part; Form B ('74) in 2 parts: written (21 pages), performance (11 pages); manual ('74, 33 pages plus test) for performance part; for more complete information, see 1153; examination fee to centers, $100 per candidate (fee to candidate determined locally); postpaid; 180(195) minutes for written part, 360(390) minutes for performance part; National Occupational Competency Testing Institute. *

For a review of the NOCTI program, see 1153.

Tim L. Wentling, *Associate Professor of Vocational and Technical Education, University of Illinois, Urbana, Illinois.*

This test is one of 24 developed through a grant from the U.S. Office of Education. The NOCTI tests were originally designed to assist vocational teacher educators in selecting the occupationally best qualified individuals for their training programs. However, it is apparent that in some situations the tests are being utilized for certifying teachers and for the granting of college credit for technical competence.

The NOCTI tests represent a very positive initial developmental effort in the area of competency testing. The tests suffer somewhat from having had a limited grant for their development, but the NOCTI is to be commended for its work.

This test, like other NOCTI tests, has two segments: a written test and a performance test. The test has many accompanying booklets, including an administration manual for both written and performance segments, a subscore data booklet, a bulletin of information for candidates, and a handbook for area test center organization and administration. However, there exists no test manual of the type that accompanies most standardized tests.

CONTENT. The content for the written and performance tests was determined through job analyses and the use of experts from the trade. The written test is a three-hour, 135-item, four-option multiple choice test with 25 illustrations. This test focuses on nine content areas: drafting instruments, equipment, and media; basic machine drawing conventions; orthographic projection and pictorial drawings; standard machined parts; gears, cams, and pulleys; interpretation of drawings; related mathematical computations; general drafting room procedures; and manufacturing processes and practices. These nine content areas are collapsed into four for the reporting of subscores.

The performance test is a six-hour test that involves the use of drawing equipment, references, and materials. This test is both a process test and a product test that centers on five tasks, or jobs: redrawing a working drawing, constructing geometric shapes, producing a pictorial presentation, producing a sectional view presentation, and developing a working drawing.

In terms of content, both tests appear to be appropriately conceived. It is possible, however, in machine drafting to have geographic or industrial area differences that could affect the validity of the tests. For example, a person experienced in the aerospace industry of the

Northwest may take this test in the East and be examined by a person from the plastics industry. The instrument may not be sensitive to all nuances of industry. Also, very recent developments in dimensioning practices and in the use of metrics are not reflected in these tests.

ADMINISTRATION. This test, like all other NOCTI tests, is administered at 32 NOCTI area test centers. Each center has a coordinator who is responsible for carrying out functions of NOCTI within a specific region, including selecting qualified, occupationally competent examiners.

The examiners are responsible for administering individual tests and for scoring each examinee on the performance test. The examination procedures are standardized, and adequate documentation is presented to guide test setup, presenting of directions, and handling of irregularities in testing. However, a potential weakness in the process is in scoring of the performance test. Both the process and product measurement scales utilize a 4-point rating scale (ratings are 0, 1, 3, or 5), with several pages of rating recommendations to the examiner. These recommendations represent a commendable attempt at increasing interrater reliability; however, there exists potential for additional specificity. A training manual and training program for examiners might be warranted.

VALIDITY. The developmental process for this test involved tradespersons and test specialists. They were charged with ensuring content validity. An additional study conducted in Georgia involved rating of items by three machine drafting instructors. Beyond these efforts, lack of validation study is a major shortcoming of this test. The norm table provided (spring 1974 through spring 1976) shows that the written test has been administered to 144 individuals and the performance test to 129. However, no background information nor comparative information is provided for these examinee groups.

It is rather difficult to judge this instrument's ability to discriminate between competent and less-than-competent tradespersons when no comparative studies using an external criterion have been conducted. It is recommended that NOCTI pursue further study of their tests.

RELIABILITY. Indices of reliability are presented for the written test only. These are limited to coefficients of internal consistency. Reported K-R 20 reliability is .89 and K-R 21 reliability is reported as .85.

There exists a real need to assess the consistency of the performance test. The concern for more specificity in scoring instructions referred to in the administration section of this review relates to the potentially low interrater reliability of the performance test. Specific observational studies of several examiners, in addition to the central review of examinee products, could be conducted to establish reliability estimates.

UTILIZATION. This test has potential for use in screening applicants to teacher education programs, for certifying personnel, and in awarding college credit. The NOCTI provides no guidelines or suggestions for using results. This is a potential area for developmental work and for possible inclusion in a test manual.

SUMMARY. The NOCTI series represents an admirable initial attempt at improving competency testing within occupational areas. The following points summarize this review: (a) there is need for a test manual; (b) the content of the test appears to be appropriate, with minor exceptions; (c) scoring of the performance test needs to be made more objective; (d) there may be a need to train examiners; (e) validity information is lacking and further study of this test is needed; and (f) internal-consistency reliability is respectable.

[1144]

★NOCTI Examination: Machine Trades. Teachers and prospective teachers; 1973–77; test administered each spring and fall at centers approved by the publisher; 5 scores for written part (total and 4 subscores), 3 scores for performance part (process, product, total); no reliability data for performance part nor for subscores on written part; Form B ('74) in 2 parts: written (23 pages), performance (8 pages); manual ('74, 24 pages plus test) for performance part; for more complete information, see 1153; examination fee to centers, $100 per candidate (fee to candidate determined locally); postpaid; 180(195) minutes for written part, 300(330) minutes for performance part; National Occupational Competency Testing Institute. *

For a review of the NOCTI program, see 1153.

REFERENCES

1. COGSWELL, J. E. *A Descriptive Study of the Texas Competency Testing Project for Vocational Industrial Teachers and Achievement Profile of the Participants.* Doctor's thesis, East Texas State University (Commerce, Texas), 1976. (*DAI* 37: 4312A)

[1145]

★NOCTI Examination: Masonry. Teachers and prospective teachers; 1973–77; test administered each spring and fall at centers approved by the publisher;

5 scores for written part (total and 4 subscores), 3 scores for performance part (process, product, total); no reliability data for performance part nor for subscores on written part; Form B ('74) in 2 parts: written (13 pages), performance (6 pages); manual ('74, 26 pages plus test) for performance part; for more complete information, see 1153; examination fee to centers, $100 per candidate (fee to candidate determined locally); postpaid; 180(195) minutes for written part, 180(210) minutes for performance part; National Occupational Competency Testing Institute. *

For a review of the NOCTI program, see 1153.

[1146]

★NOCTI Examination: Mechanical Technology. Teachers and prospective teachers; 1973–77; test administered each spring and fall at centers approved by the publisher; 5 scores for written part (total and 4 subscores), 3 scores for performance part (process, product, total); no reliability data for performance part nor for subscores on written part; Form B ('74) in 2 parts: written (11 pages), performance (7 pages); manual (74, 22 pages plus test) for performance part; for more complete information, see 1153; examination fee to centers, $100 per candidate (fee to candidate determined locally); postpaid; 180(195) minutes for written part, 360(390) minutes for performance part; National Occupational Competency Testing Institute. *

For a review of the NOCTI program, see 1153.

[1147]

★NOCTI Examination: Plumbing. Teachers and prospective teachers; 1973–77; test administered each spring and fall at centers approved by the publisher; 5 scores for written part (total and 4 subscores), 3 scores for performance part (process, product, total); no reliability data for performance part nor for subscores on written part; Form B ('74) in 2 parts: written (29 pages), performance (7 pages); manual ('74, 25 pages plus test) for performance part; for more complete information, see 1153; examination fee to centers, $100 per candidate (fee to candidate determined locally); postpaid; 180(195) minutes for written part, 300(330) minutes for performance part; National Occupational Competency Testing Institute. *

For a review of the NOCTI program, see 1153.

RICHARD C. ERICKSON, *Professor of Practical Arts and Vocational-Technical Education and Chairman of the Department, University of Missouri, Columbia, Missouri.*

The NOCTI Plumbing written and performance examination has been prepared to enable candidates from the plumbing industry who wish to become vocational teachers to demonstrate the technical knowledge and manipulative skills expected of a competent worker in that field. The written test contains 167 multiple choice items and is comprehensive in its scope. The items generally are very well written; this reviewer found very few that were unclear or did not follow accepted guidelines for preparing multiple choice items. Items sample the technical content of the occupation very adequately

and elicit trade-related understandings as well as knowledge of tools, materials, processes, regulations, and the like.

The scope of the competencies to be demonstrated in the performance test is nearly as broad as the scope of the content covered in the written test. An adequate sample of the knowledge, understanding, and skills needed by trade-competent plumbers is included in the performance test. The performance evaluation form to be used by the performance examiner in rating both process and product aspects of performance is accompanied by a recommended listing of criteria or expectations for each area of concern to be rated. While these recommendations do appear to achieve their purpose to some degree, this reviewer feels that variation in performance examiners' expectations could be controlled to an even greater degree if a linear graphic scale (complete with descriptive categories and numbers for scale units positioned along the line) were incorporated in each of the eight process and four product ratings included on the performance evaluation form.

As is the case with many newly developed standardized instruments, those reported statistics important for judging reliability, level of difficulty, and ability to discriminate between qualified and unqualified candidates are of minimal use. They are based upon too few cases (10 in this instance), and little or no descriptive information is presented regarding the individuals included in this sample. K-R 20 and 21 reliability estimates for the written test are .885 and .813, respectively. The mean indices of item difficulty and discrimination are .386 and .208, respectively. Similar data are not presented for the performance examination. Empirical evidence regarding rater reliability and the degree to which the performance rating form is effective in controlling for variation in assessment due to differences among raters needs to be developed.

The validity of these examinations has not been demonstrated. Granted, both tests *appear* to be measuring what they were designed to measure, but it is necessary for the validity of these instruments to be *demonstrated* if they are to be used in any type of selection process, be it for vocational certification purposes or for purposes of granting academic credit for work experience.

The normative information presented for these examinations is very minimal. Only 47 persons were included in the norm group. Their levels of performance are presented in percentiles and in standard scores that are based upon percent of correct responses rather than upon obtained raw scores. Also of concern to this reviewer is the lack of a description of the persons included in the norming sample. Thus, it is extremely difficult for users to know how to relate scores attained by local candidates to the national norms. The only viable option for users at this point is to develop local norms and perhaps expectancy tables based upon local experience with these examinations, an option that is not only expensive and impractical but also defeats the original purpose and intent of the NOCTI exams.

A test manual of the type that usually accompanies standardized achievement tests needs to be developed for these examinations. Much of the content of such a manual has been developed. However, validity data, more descriptive norms, and guidelines and aids for interpreting and using the results of these tests (i.e., expectancy tables and cutoff scores based upon a large national sample) need to be developed and included in the much needed manual.

In summary, it is this reviewer's opinion that the NOCTI Plumbing examinations represent a giant step forward in developing a standardized means of assessing the trade competency of plumbers who desire to become vocational plumbing instructors. Considerable well-directed efforts have gone into their development and they are the best instruments of their kind that are readily available on a national scale. However, until they are accompanied by a sound manual that includes adequate validity and reliability data and norms, as well as expectancy tables, suggested cutoff scores, and/or other aids for interpreting locally obtained scores, these instruments (at their current costs in time and effort and for administration and scoring) offer the potential user expensive information that is of very limited, if not questionable, usefulness.

[1148]

★NOCTI Examination: Printing. Teachers and prospective teachers; 1973–77; test administered each spring and fall at centers approved by the publisher; 5 scores for written part (total and 4 subscores), 3 scores for performance part (process, product, total);

NOCTI Examination: Plumbing

no reliability data for performance part nor for subscores on written part; Form B ('74) in 2 parts: written (18 pages), performance (19 pages containing 2 tests: letterpress, offset; candidate elects one); manual ('74, 28 pages plus tests) for performance part; for more complete information, see 1153; examination fee to centers, $100 per candidate (fee to candidate determined locally); postpaid; 180(195) minutes for written part, 300(330) minutes for performance part; National Occupational Competency Testing Institute. *

For a review of the NOCTI program, see 1153.

[1149]

★NOCTI Examination: Quantity Food Preparation. Teachers and prospective teachers; 1973–77; test administered each spring and fall at centers approved by the publisher; 5 scores for written part (total and 4 subscores), 3 scores for performance part (process, product, total); no reliability data for performance part nor for subscores on written part; Form B ('74) in 2 parts: written (26 pages), performance (10 pages); manual ('74, 27 pages plus test) for performance part; for more complete information, see 1153; examination fee to centers, $100 per candidate (fee to candidate determined locally); postpaid; 180(195) minutes for written part, 150(180) minutes for performance part; National Occupational Competency Testing Institute. *

For a review of the NOCTI program, see 1153.

[1150]

★NOCTI Examination: Sheet Metal. Teachers and prospective teachers; 1973–77; test administered each spring and fall at centers approved by the publisher; 5 scores for written part (total and 4 subscores), 3 scores for performance part (process, product, total); no reliability data for performance part nor for subscores on written part; Form B ('74) in 2 parts: written (14 pages), performance (7 pages); manual ('74, 21 pages plus test) for performance part; for more complete information, see 1153; examination fee to centers, $100 per candidate (fee to candidate determined locally); postpaid; 180(195) minutes for written part, 300(330) minutes for performance part; National Occupational Competency Testing Institute. *

For a review of the NOCTI program, see 1153.

DANIEL L. HOUSEHOLDER, *Professor of Industrial Education, Texas A&M University, College Station, Texas.*

Development of standardized examinations for the sheet metal trade is an especially challenging task. Members of the trade practice their occupations in a variety of establishments, frequently specializing in a limited portion of the range of operations which may be categorized as falling within the trade. Identifying and preparing an appropriate sample of test items to cover the necessary cognitive information and psychomotor skills is quite complicated. The Sheet Metal examination developed by the National Occupational Competency Testing Institute endeavors to overcome these limitations.

Given the difficulty of the task, one must conclude that the test is at least partially successful.

The questions on the written portion of the examination provide a good sample of the cognitive content in sheet metal work. However, they concentrate upon mastery of factual knowledge to the exclusion of higher cognitive processes. Of particular concern is the omission of application items, an area of major importance to the tradesman. Considerable item redundancy is also evident, perhaps resulting from the need to develop a substantial number of items covering a restricted range of content. The test received for review (Form B) included several spelling errors and grammatical inconsistencies. Additional development and editorial work are clearly needed before the written test meets generally accepted commercial standards.

Norms provided by the publisher indicate an extremely small norming population (N = 20), casting considerable doubt upon the generalizability of the norms. Within this small group, however, reliability estimates appear to be within the anticipated range. With a larger norming population, the K-R 20 of .739 and K-R 21 of .637 might well be raised to acceptable figures. However, the small standard deviation of 7.8 and the restricted range of test scores combine to make the test of questionable value in differentiating between individuals, especially within the middle range of scores.

Utility of the test for assignment of college credit for occupational experience, one of the purposes in the development of the test, appears questionable. The materials available from the publisher do not provide data on the standards expected for awarding college credit; presumably that is the prerogative of the individual institution. Similarly, the test user is not given guidelines for an appropriate formula to be used to obtain a combination of the written and performance scores.

The performance portion of the Sheet Metal examination consists of one major task. Only one product is required: a somewhat unusual, difficult-to-produce transition piece. Each of several subtasks must be performed in sequence with a high level of accuracy if the total product is to be assigned a high mark. Failure to do very well on the complicated layout would effectively prohibit the attainment of an acceptable score on the total examination.

A larger sample of work tasks on the performance test would have been preferable. A series of independent work samples could have covered a wider variety of competencies and would have more accurately reflected the content coverage implied by the Bulletin of Information for Candidates. For instance, 10 percent of the total points on the performance examination are allocated to grinding and drilling, yet the product does not require the use of either process; and the examiner is not instructed to include a grinder among the equipment for the examination.

When all considerations are taken into account, the NOCTI examination in sheet metal has no direct competition. The potential market for such an examination restricts the likely competition in the area; it is hardly reasonable to expect more publishers to move into the development of sheet metal examinations. The potential test user is well advised to utilize the NOCTI examination, but to exercise considerable caution in the interpretation of results, pending the issuance of supplementary norms based upon a broader sample. The most regrettable feature of the examination, the utilization of a single work sample in the performance portion, may be amenable to local modification if the testing agency is anticipating the scalar rating of individuals completing the test. Testing agencies utilizing the examination with any frequency would do well to develop local norms, since the effects of local codes upon the performance of individuals on the examination is not dealt with in the publisher's materials.

[1151]

★NOCTI Examination: Small Engine Repair. Teachers and prospective teachers; 1973–77; test administered each spring and fall at centers approved by the publisher; 5 scores for written part (total and 4 subscores), 3 scores for performance part (process, product, total); no reliability data for performance part nor for subscores on written part; Form B ('74) in 2 parts: written (20 pages), performance (11 pages); manual ('74, 23 pages plus test) for performance part; for more complete information, see 1153; examination fee to centers, $100 per candidate (fee to candidate determined locally); postpaid; 180(195) minutes for written part, 300(330) minutes for performance part; National Occupational Competency Testing Institute. *
For a review of the NOCTI program, see 1153.

KENNETH E. POUCHER, *Professor of Industrial Education and Technology, Ball State University, Muncie, Indiana.*

The *NOCTI Examination in Small Engine Repair,* designed to evaluate vocational teachers for certification and selection, consists of an extensive performance test and a written test. The time allocated for the tests is liberal.

The multiple choice items on the written portion were evidently carefully selected to survey the broad spectrum of engine and systems theory, as well as transmission, maintenance, troubleshooting, trade science, and mathematics. The items selected are proportional to the emphasis and complexity generally devoted to engine systems. Further refinement of some 10 percent of the items would immeasurably improve the value of the test.

The manual contains no reference to the content validity for the written test. However, in this reviewer's judgment, the test has good content validity; it appears to sample adequately the major concepts involved in the technology.

Interpretation of the statistics presented in the manual is difficult because raw scores are used at times, and at other times percentages which the raw scores are of the possible score. National norms are presented in terms of percentages of possible scores, whereas raw scores —number of correct answers—are used in the table presenting data relevant to reliability. The national norms are based on only 35 or 36 candidates. No information is given about these candidates.

The reliability coefficients reported for the written test are quite high, a K-R 20 of .97 and a K-R 21 of .96. These coefficients are, however, inflated because the variability among the scores of the 18 subjects used to determine reliability is much greater than that in the norm group. Had the scores of the 35 examinees in the norm group been used, the K-R 21 reliability would have been only .70. No information is presented on the reliability of the performance scores.

The booklet on directions for administering the performance test is well prepared and lists the names and catalog numbers of the machines, power equipment, tools, instruments, and accessories required for each candidate. The tasks to be performed on the test are typical and provide knowledge of the candidate's skill in diagnosis, reconditioning, and repair, and in making recommendations for further maintenance. During the administration of the performance test the

candidate is observed and evaluated using a numerical rating ranging from inept to extremely competent. In the performance test, the candidate is rated on process and product; process being workmanship in performing the tasks, and product being the efficiency, correctness of method, and the accuracy of the tasks performed according to specifications. A formula yields a single final performance score.

The NOCTI Small Engine Repair examination needs further refinement, validation studies, and wider sampling and accumulation of normative data.

Generally, the examination is an excellent instrument for its stated purpose of assessing trade competencies for the certification of vocational teachers. Also, the examination would appear to be of value to postsecondary institutions wishing to grant advanced credit for occupational experiences.

[1152]

★NOCTI Examination: Welding. Teachers and prospective teachers; 1973–77; test administered each spring and fall at centers approved by the publisher; 5 scores for written part (total and 4 subscores), 3 scores for performance part (process, product, total); no reliability data for performance part nor for subscores on written part; Form B ('74) in 2 parts: written (20 pages), performance (6 pages); manual ('74, 23 pages plus test) for performance part; for more complete information, see 1153; examination fee to centers, $100 per candidate (fee to candidate determined locally); postpaid; 180(195) minutes for written part, 300(330) minutes for performance part; National Occupational Competency Testing Institute. *

For a review of the NOCTI program, see 1153.

RICHARD C. ERICKSON, *Professor of Practical Arts and Vocational-Technical Education and Chairman of the Department, University of Missouri, Columbia, Missouri.*

The NOCTI Welding written and performance examination has been prepared to enable candidates who are welders and who desire to become vocational welding teachers to demonstrate the technical knowledge and manipulative skills expected of a trade-competent welder. The written test contains 155 multiple choice items and is comprehensive in scope. It includes items that measure understanding as well as those that measure knowledge of terminology, equipment, procedures, standards, and the like. All the items reflect sound item-writing techniques. Moreover, they are clear in intent, concise in presentation, and singular in purpose.

The directions for administering both the

written examination and the performance test are clear, complete, and functional. The administrative procedures for the performance test are excellent. However, its scope is not as comprehensive as the written test. The performance test focuses on arc welding and oxy-acetylene brazing, and the written test focuses on these welding processes as well as several others including ultrasonic, resistance, and a variety of gas-shielded arc welding processes.

The normative data presented for both tests are minimal and based on percent of correct responses rather than obtained raw scores. Working backward from the normative data presented, one finds that these tests vary considerably in their ability to discriminate among the 115 candidates tested through spring 1976. For the written test, raw scores range from approximately 52 to 130 out of a possible 155 and have a standard deviation of approximately 15, whereas raw scores for these same persons on the performance test range from approximately 33 to 307 out of a possible 307, with a standard deviation of approximately 56. The large difference in the standard deviations for these two tests when administered to the same persons suggests to this reviewer that a significant portion of the variation in the raw scores for the performance evaluation is perhaps error variance—score differences due to differences in the performance standards used by the various performance test examiners at the various test sites.

The guidelines and procedures for establishing and operating the area test centers needed to administer the NOCTI examinations are clear, well thought-out, and functional. Only one aspect of the operation of the centers might be improved so far as the welding tests are concerned. Little formal training is provided for performance test examiners, and it appears as though such training is needed to standardize examiners' levels of expectation, their procedures for observing and measuring process and product, and their use of the performance evaluation form. These ends also could be achieved by incorporating within each of the ratings included on the performance evaluation form a linear graphic scale which includes descriptive categories and numbered scale units.

The validity of the two welding tests has not been demonstrated adequately. A content vali-

dation study has been conducted in which four trade experts found these examinations appeared to be measuring that which they were designed to measure. However, no predictive or concurrent validation studies have been conducted to demonstrate that these two instruments indeed can be used to differentiate accurately between those who have high degrees of the occupational competencies needed by vocational welding teachers and those who do not.

The developmental statistics reported provide little assistance in evaluating the potential value of these examinations. K-R 20 and 21 reliability estimates for the written test are .878 and .836, respectively, and the mean discrimination and difficulty indices for the 155 items included in the examination are .227 and .363, respectively. All these statistics are based on relatively few cases ($N=69$). Similar statistics are not presented for the performance test. Empirical evidence regarding rater reliability and the degree to which the performance rating form is able to control variation in assessments of candidates' performance due to differences among raters is needed.

The most glaring fault with regard to these instruments is the lack of a test manual of the type that usually accompanies standardized achievement tests designed to be administered on a national scale. All of the very fine procedures, guidelines, directions, as well as the extensive descriptive information and data concerning how the examinations were developed, should be included in the manual. To this should be added additional validity data, more descriptive norms, as well as guidelines and aids for interpreting and using the results of these tests. The latter might include expectancy tables and cutoff scores based upon a large national sample.

In summary, it is this reviewer's opinion that the NOCTI Welding examination represents a giant step forward in developing a standardized means of assessing the trade competency of welders who desire to become vocational welding instructors. Considerable well-directed effort has gone into its development, and the two tests are the best instruments of their kind that are readily available on a national scale. However, until they are accompanied by a sound testing manual that includes adequate validity and reliability data and norms, as well as expectancy tables, suggested cutoff scores, and/or

NOCTI Examination: Welding

other aids for interpreting locally obtained scores, these instruments (at their current costs in time and effort and for administration and scoring) offer the potential user expensive information that is of very limited, if not questionable, usefulness.

[1153]

★National Occupational Competency Testing Program. Teachers and prospective teachers in skilled trades; 1973–77; NOCTI; tests administered each spring and fall at centers approved by the publisher; 24 tests, also listed separately; 2 parts: written, performance; no reliability data for performance part nor for subscores on written part; manual ('74, 23 pages) for all written parts, manual ('74, 21–40 pages plus test) for each performance part; item analysis sheets ('73, 24 pages); information booklet ('74, 28 pages); test center handbook ('74, 27 pages); norms: total score ('76, 10 pages), subscore ('77, 10 pages); separate answer sheets (IBM 1230) must be used for written part; certain tools and materials must be supplied by examinee; examination fee to centers, $100 per candidate (fee to candidate determined locally); postpaid; 180(195) minutes for written part, 270–360 (300–390) minutes for performance part except as listed below; norms by Leon S. Tunkel and Raymond S. Klein; National Occupational Competency Testing Institute. *

a) AIR CONDITIONING AND REFRIGERATION.
b) AIRFRAME AND POWER PLANT MECHANIC.
c) ARCHITECTURAL DRAFTING.
d) AUTO BODY REPAIR.
e) AUTO MECHANIC.
f) CABINET MAKING AND MILLWORK.
g) CARPENTRY.
h) CIVIL TECHNOLOGY.
i) COSMETOLOGY.
j) DIESEL ENGINE REPAIR.
k) ELECTRICAL INSTALLATION.
l) ELECTRONICS COMMUNICATIONS.
m) INDUSTRIAL ELECTRICIAN.
n) INDUSTRIAL ELECTRONICS.
o) MACHINE DRAFTING.
p) MACHINE TRADES.
q) MASONRY. 180(210) minutes for performance part.
r) MECHANICAL TECHNOLOGY.
s) PLUMBING.
t) PRINTING.
u) QUANTITY FOOD PREPARATION. 210(240) minutes for performance part.
v) SHEET METAL.
w) SMALL ENGINE REPAIR.
x) WELDING.

For reviews of separate tests, see 1129 (1 review), 1131 (1 review), 1133 (2 reviews), 1134 (1 review), 1135 (1 review), 1138 (1 review), 1139 (1 review), 1140 (1 review), 1141 (1 review), 1142 (1 review), 1143 (1 review), 1147 (1 review), 1150 (1 review), 1151 (1 review), and 1152 (1 review).

REFERENCES

1. PANITZ, ADOLF, AND OLIVO, C. THOMAS. National Occupational Competency Testing Project, Phase 1: Planning—Organizing—Pilot Testing and Establishing the Feasibility of a National Consortium: Vol. 3, Handbook for Developing and Administering Occupational Competency Testing. An unpublished report to the U.S. Office of Education, Research Project No. 8–0474, Rutgers—The State University, 1971. Pp. xviii, 152. *
2. CORMAN, MYRON N. "Testing the Occupational Competency of T & I Teachers." Am Voc J 48(1):104–7 Ja '73. *
3. NELSON, RICHARD, AND OTHERS. A Consortium for Occupational Competency Testing of Trade and Industrial/Technical Teachers. An unpublished report to the U.S. Office of Education, Research Project No. 8–0474, Rutgers—The State University, 1973. Pp. xi, 185. *
4. PANITZ, ADOLF. "Performance Testing for Vo-Ed Teachers." Sch Shop 34(3):56–7 N '74. *
5. AKPAN, MONDAY PAUL. The Impact of Career Education Program Upon Measured Occupational Interests. Doctor's thesis, Rutgers, The State University of New Jersey (New Brunswick, N.J.), 1976. (DAI 37:7714A)
6. TUNKEL, LEON S., AND KLEIN, RAYMOND S. Vocational Competency Testing Project: Final Report, Vols. 1–3. An unpublished report to the State Department of Education, Atlanta, Georgia, under the terms of Grant Award Contract No. 7338, National Occupational Competency Testing Institute (Albany, N.Y.), 1976. Pp. v, 65; iii, 8; iii, 64. *

THOMAS S. BALDWIN, Lecturer in Social Work, The University of North Carolina, Chapel Hill, North Carolina.

The National Occupational Competency Testing Program is a response to a psychological testing problem so complex it has been avoided by even the large national psychological testing organizations. The stated purposes of the program are (a) "admission to trade and industrial/technical teacher education programs," (b) to provide "competency tests for temporary or permanent state certification," and (c) to provide "occupational competency tests for advanced standing in collegiate programs of study leading to the baccalaureate degree."

While occupational competency testing has been attempted for decades, this is the first effort to provide a standardized national program for various trade and technical occupations. In addition, most previous attempts have confined themselves to paper-and-pencil tests which measure primarily the "cognitive" component of occupational competency. Many attempts have been made to measure the performance or "psychomotor" aspects of occupational competency but these have been generally limited to local teacher-made tests or tests constructed by the military or other governmental or private industrial organizations. In these previous attempts the resources necessary to insure adequate reliability and validity of the instruments, standardization of testing procedures, and availability on a national scale have not been available. In this respect, then, the National Occupational Competency Testing Program can be considered the first major national effort to develop both cognitive and motor achievement tests in major trade and technical occupations.

In order to accomplish the fundamental task represented by the program, it was necessary

NOCTI Examination: Welding

after an initial feasibility study to develop a national organization, known as the National Occupational Competency Testing Institute, to administer the program. Since this undertaking was beyond the scope of a single state or federal agency, a national consortium of states was established, all of which had a major interest in the existence of such a program. Through the NOCTI, therefore, a program with wide impact was made possible.

NOCTI administers the testing program through a series of testing centers located throughout the United States. Through NOCTI, the trade and industrial occupation areas for which tests needed to be developed were determined and test development undertaken. Research on the validity and reliability of the tests developed for each area is a major responsibility of the institute, as well as the training of performance examiners who administer tests at the various centers. The institute conducts continuing research on the tests that it administers and operates the program in such a way as to insure test security, a major problem in occupational competency testing.

The institute currently offers occupational competency examinations in the 24 areas listed above. In each of these areas, both written and performance tests are administered. Technical reports on the project indicate that the entire test development process was carefully thought through and the various stages in the development of the institute and the tests themselves were accomplished with the input of noted national figures in occupational education and tests and measurement. Careful analyses of the state of the art of occupational competency testing were accomplished, and an overall plan for the development of the tests and administrative procedures were among the major planning efforts.

The overall administration of the program is through the area test coordinators, who must meet the institute's high standards in order to qualify for this role. The area test coordinator is responsible for disseminating information regarding the testing program, identifying test facilities and insuring that they meet the standards established by the institute, and obtaining qualified test examiners for both the written and performance tests. Various other administrative duties are assigned to the area test coordinator to insure the adequacy of test security and standardized conditions in the testing situation. The institute has also established specific criteria for qualifying as an area test center, to insure that the conditions of testing are equitable for all candidates. Very detailed instructions are provided for area test center organization and administration which should deal effectively with the difficult problem of standardized testing in the performance area, a major problem encountered in all performance testing.

While the institute has taken every reasonable precaution to insure standardized testing conditions for all candidates, it should be noted that performance testing presents some unique problems in this respect which are difficult, if not impossible, to overcome in their entirety. For example, equipment such as lathes and milling machines may vary somewhat from center to center even though made by the same manufacturer and presumably equivalent in all respects. While not a direct criticism of this testing program, this is a problem inherent in all performance testing, and for that matter all machine operation, that makes it difficult to standardize testing conditions with a high degree of precision.

The institute published cumulative national norms on the NOCTI examinations for the period of spring 1974 through spring 1976. While the national norms present considerable detailed information which permits the test user to convert test scores to percentiles and T scores, little information is provided for guidance in using the various tables presented in the norm booklet. The introduction states that the tables were developed with an N of 2,140 subjects; but from an examination of the tables it appears that this figure includes all 24 test areas, for an average of less than 100 subjects per test. The booklet also presents K-R 20 and K-R 21 reliability estimates for the written tests, based on a smaller sample in each area. In fact, the reliabilities are presented on samples as small as six subjects, too small a sample in which to place any confidence in the reliability. The largest number of subjects on which reliability data are presented is 108, an adequate number. There is no caution regarding the inadequacy of the sample size on which these reliability data are presented and the test user not familiar with the psychometric problems in determining reliability could be easily misled. The same is true of a table of the cumulative national norms on which the means and standard deviations are presented. In this table the number of candidates on which the data are based ranges from 2 to 390. There is no caution that statistics computed on small samples are of little value in interpreting test scores. While reliabilities of most of the tests seem to be in an acceptable range for making individual decisions, in the high .80s or .90s, some range as low as .53. There is no precautionary note regarding the use of such tests in making individual decisions about candidates for the several purposes for which these tests were devolped. While the shortcomings regarding sample size are undoubtedly a result of the relatively recent development and therefore the few number of candidates taking a particular test, the authors have the responsibility of cautioning the potential user where sample size is inadequate or where reliabilities are not sufficiently high for making individual decisions regarding candidates. In general, the booklet could be greatly improved by more detailed explanation of the various tables and by cautions regarding the use of various statistics computed on very small samples.

No data are presented on the reliabilities of the performance tests. Since the performance test scores are subjective evaluations by the evaluator which are functions of both the "process" and "product" of the examinee, such reliability data would of necessity require an inter-rater reliability approach. Since this would at least double the number of examiners for the entire series, the logistics of undertaking such an effort are undoubtedly the reason for the omission of this important information. Nevertheless, this should be a goal for the future. It should be pointed out that the notion of "process" and "product" is a particularly important one in performance testing. For example, a candidate might produce an adequate product using unsafe procedures in the process. If he were evaluated only on the product, his qualifications as a tradesman would suffer from a deficiency in terms of safety procedures followed.

Overall, the NOCTI program must be viewed as a continuing research and develop- ment effort that is at present in its infancy. Various research programs are currently being conducted by the institute, including a major project with the Department of Defense. In view of this, many of the criticisms made in this review, such as statistics computed on very small samples, will probably be invalid in the near future. The potential user of any test in the series should be advised to look into the adequacy of that particular test for his specific purposes.

The National Occupational Competency Testing Institute and the program of tests that it is currently conducting can be considered a major step forward in the use of tests and measurements in an industrialized country. Undoubtedly, as time and resources permit, the program will become more sophisticated and of greater utility to the potential test user. However, in its present stage of development the NOCTI testing program cannot be considered to have achieved the three purposes quoted in the first paragraph of this review.

The first purpose, "admission to trade and industrial/technical teacher education programs," is dependent upon what the institute refers to as "well-designed tests, properly validated and with their reliability thoroughly established." While the examinations may be considered to have a degree of content validity since they were developed with the aid of experts in the various trades and technologies, construct validity—as might be demonstrated by successively higher mean scores for higher levels of proficiency in a particular subject area—has not been demonstrated. One is at a loss to interpret what a given percentile score for an individual candidate means as the test data are now reported. For example, is a score equivalent to the 50th percentile to be interpreted as an acceptable level of proficiency for admission to industrial/technical teacher education programs? Further research is needed to establish a frame of reference for interpreting test scores. Furthermore, many of the tests do not have adequate reliability. This could be a real disservice to individual candidates, and is inconsistent with the institute's claim that such tests "provide measures that are fair to individual applicants." While admission to trade and industrial/technical teacher education programs is a legitimate purpose of such tests, data presented to date do not suggest that they are adequate to serve that purpose at this point in their development.

Similar criticisms can be made of the adequacy of data presented to support the examinations' use as "competency tests for temporary or permanent state certification." One is at a loss to interpret what a given score on a test means in this regard. While the tests do have the potential of fulfilling this purpose, further research is needed to demonstrate what level of performance on a test relates to excellence as a teacher in that particular occupational area.

With regard to using results of these examinations for "granting advanced standing in collegiate programs," again additional evidence will have to be provided if this purpose is to be met adequately. At present, the institute provides no evidence of the relationship of test scores to performance of students taking similar courses material in an approved program in a collegiate institution. It is left to the educational institution to determine, either through research or on a subjective basis, the meaning of test scores on the NOCTI series.

[1154]

*Ohio Auto Body Achievement Test. Grades 11–12; 1969–77; OABAT; available only as a part of the *Ohio Trade and Industrial Education Achievement Test Program* (see 1166 for more complete information); 16 scores: welding, metal forming, body filler, refinishing, trim and hardware, parts replacement, alignment, glass replacement, fiber glass repair, frame and unit body, electrical system, cooling and conditioning, shop management, applied science, applied math, total; no data on reliability of part scores; 1 form; parts 1 ('70, 13 pages), 2 ('70, 12 pages); no specific manual; series manual ('77, 32 pages); annual Ohio norms for juniors, seniors, ('77, 1 page each); occupational analysis ['77, 211 pages]; rental and scoring service, $1.50 per student, postage extra; $5.50 per occupational analysis, postpaid; (240) minutes in 2 sessions; Instructional Materials Laboratory, Ohio State University. * [Test not available for review.]

[1155]

*Ohio Automotive Mechanics Achievement Test. Grades 11–12; 1959–77; OAMAT; available only as a part of the *Ohio Trade and Industrial Education Achievement Test Program* (see 1166 for more complete information); 17 scores: service management, lubrication and preventive maintenance, engine, cooling systems, fuel and exhaust systems, ignition systems, cranking systems, charging system, accessory systems, transmissions, drive line, emission systems, brakes, steering, suspension, heating/ventilation/air conditioning, total; no data on reliability of part scores; 1 form; parts 1, 2, ('77, 15 pages); no specific manual; series manual ('77, 32 pages); annual Ohio norms for juniors, seniors, ('77, 1 page each); occupational analysis (no date, 109 pages); rental and

scoring service, $1.50 per student, postage extra; $2.75 per occupational analysis, postpaid; (300) minutes in 2 sessions; Instructional Materials Laboratory, Ohio State University. * [Test not available for review.]

REFERENCES

1. CLINE, HAYDEN DWIGHT. *A Study of the Relationship of Selected Factors and Student Achievement in Auto Mechanics.* Doctor's thesis, University of Kentucky (Lexington, Ky.), 1974. (*DAI* 35:2130A)

[1156]

*Ohio Carpentry Achievement Test. Grades 11–12; 1970–77; OCAT; available only as a part of the *Ohio Trade and Industrial Education Achievement Test Program* (see 1166 for more complete information); 14 scores: orientation, blueprint reading, applied math, applied science, foundations, floor framing, wall framing, roof framing, roofing, insulation, exterior finish, interior finish, special operations, total; no data on reliability of part scores; 1 form; parts 1 ('71, 17 pages), 2 ('71, 15 pages); no specific manual; series manual ('77, 32 pages); annual Ohio norms for juniors, seniors, ('77, 1 page each); occupational analysis (no date, 122 pages); rental and scoring service, $1.50 per student, postage extra; $3.25 per occupational analysis, postpaid; (300) minutes in 2 sessions; Instructional Materials Laboratory, Ohio State University. * [Test not available for review.]

| 1157 |

*Ohio Communication Products Electronics Achievement Test. Grades 11–12; 1973–77; OCPEAT; available only as a part of the *Ohio Trade and Industrial Education Achievement Test Program* (see 1166 for more complete information); 12 scores: orientation, D/C electricity, A/C electricity, electron tubes, semi-conductors, vacuum tube and solid state circuitry, audio devices, receivers, transmitters, television, business practices, total; no data on reliability of part scores; 1 form; parts 1, 2, ('74, 20 pages); part 1 is the *Ohio Electronics Achievement Test, Part 1;* no specific manual; series manual ('77, 32 pages); annual Ohio norms for juniors, seniors, ('77, 1 page each); occupational analysis (no date, 112 pages); rental and scoring service, $1.50 per student, postage extra; $2.75 per occupational analysis, postpaid; (300) minutes in 2 sessions; Instructional Materials Laboratory, Ohio State University. * [Test not available for review.]

[1158]

*Ohio Construction Electricity Achievement Test. Grades 11–12; 1973–77; OCEAT; available only as part of the *Ohio Trade and Industrial Education Achievement Test Program* (see 1166 for more complete information); 19 scores: orientation, D/C electricity, magnetism, D/C power sources, D/C motors and controllers, instrumentation, A/C electricity, A/C circuits, three-phase A/C electricity, transformers, A/C motors and starters, electronics, planning and layout, branch circuits, wiring methods, lighting, heating and air conditioning, low-voltage systems, total; no data on reliability of part scores; 1 form; parts 1 ('74, 18 pages), 2 ('74, 13 pages); no specific manual; series manual ('77, 32 pages); annual Ohio norms for juniors, seniors, ('77, 1 page each); occupational analysis (no date, 79 pages); rental and scoring service, $1.50 per student, postage extra; $2 per occupational analysis, postpaid; (270) minutes in 2 sessions; Instructional Materials Laboratory, Ohio State University. * [Test not available for review.]

Ohio Construction Electricity Achievement Test

[1159]

*Ohio Cosmetology Achievement Test. Grades 11–12; 1967–77; OCAT; available only as a part of the *Ohio Trade and Industrial Education Achievement Test Program* (see 1166 for more complete information); 14 scores: scalp, hands and feet, hair, hair tints and bleach, face information, facial, make-up, sanitation and bacteriology, applied science, anatomy and physiology, shop management, trade math, legal guidance, total; no data on reliability of part scores; 1 form; parts 1 ('69, 15 pages), 2 ('69, 12 pages); no specific manual; series manual ('77, 32 pages); annual Ohio norms for juniors, seniors, ('77, 1 page each); occupational analysis (no date, 221 pages); rental and scoring service, $1.50 per student, postage extra; $6 per occupational analysis, postpaid; (240) minutes in 2 sessions; Instructional Materials Laboratory, Ohio State University. * [Test not available for review.]

[1160]

*Ohio Drafting Achievement Test. Grades 11–12; 1962–77; ODAT; revision of *Ohio Mechanical Drafting Achievement Test;* available only as a part of the *Ohio Trade and Industrial Education Achievement Test Program* (see 1166 for more complete information); 18 scores: geometric drawing, orthographic projection, pictorial drawings, sectional views, auxiliary views, drafting materials/equipment/reproduction, dimensioning, production or working drawings, fastening methods, industrial materials and processes, intersections and developments, mechanisms, architectural drawings, structural drawings, electrical drawings, civil engineering drawings, mathematics, total; no data on reliability of part scores; 1 form; parts 1 ('77, 24 pages), 2 ('77, 19 pages); no specific manual; series manual ('77, 32 pages); annual Ohio norms for juniors, seniors, ('77, 1 page each); occupational analysis (no date, 145 pages); rental and scoring service, $1.50 per student, postage extra; $3.50 per occupational analysis, postpaid; (300) minutes in 2 sessions; Instructional Materials Laboratory, Ohio State University. * [Publisher did not supply test materials for review.]

See T2:2428 (1 reference).

RICHARD A. SWANSON, *Professor of Industrial Education and Technology, Bowling Green State University, Bowling Green, Ohio.* [Review of the 1963 test.]

This test is designed to measure cognitive achievement in the mechanical drafting trade. There are 18 subtests and a total of 151 multiple choice items. No manual for the OMDAT itself is available, and very little information is contained in the series manual.

No information about the content validity of this drafting test is given in the manual but users are told that the detailed trade course outline that is also produced by the Instructional Materials Laboratory served as a basis for the test, and that a team of experts developed the test, with a revision made after the first year it was disseminated. The 18 subtests correspond to the course outline. No measures of concurrent validity are reported in the series manual; however, one study (1) reported in the literature produced low correlations of .23 and .38 between OMDAT scores and end-of-year mechanical drafting course grades for juniors, and higher correlations of .43 and .53 for seniors; the four correlations were based on small groups, 26, 21, 9, and 16, respectively.

No studies of construct validity are presented. Likewise, there exists a void in the area of information dealing with test item information; however, the statement is made that an item analysis was utilized when the tests were revised.

The reliability seems to be quite high; K-R 20 reliabilities of .91 and .93 for total score are reported in the series manual; but there are no subtest reliabilities. The lack of subtest reliabilities is a serious shortcoming since IML contends that the primary purpose of the test is to improve instruction.

IML makes their tests available nationally to schools having "approved vocational programs." Approved is interpreted as programs receiving state-federal vocational funding. IML provides scoring services that include total and subtest scores (19 scores) for each student. The *Short Form Test of Academic Aptitude* must be taken along with each trade test of the OTATP. Norms, revised annually, are provided for each school, along with state norms.

SUMMARY. Even though IML would not supply test information for this review, and even though there is no manual for this test, the reviewer will summarize on a partially positive note. Through informal communications, this reviewer is convinced that the quality of the revised form (not listed above) is better than the 1963 form. The work of the IML constitutes a significant contribution to testing in vocational education since it is one of the few groups developing and distributing trade achievement tests. While they should be supported by the profession, the IML in return should meet its professional responsibility of reporting the data available on the OMDAT and they should continue to study its validity and report the results. It is unacceptable educational practice to promote tests of unknown quality (for use on a local, statewide, or national basis).

[1161]

★**Ohio Heating, Air Conditioning, and Refrigeration Achievement Test.** Grades 11–12; 1976–77; OHARAT; available only as a part of the *Ohio Trade and Industrial Education Achievement Test Program* (see 1166 for more complete information); 7 scores: refrigeration and air conditioning (installing, troubleshooting, service and repair), warm air heating system (installing, troubleshooting, service and repair), total; no data on reliability of part scores; 1 form; parts 1 ('77, 18 pages), 2 ('77, 19 pages); no specific manual; series manual ('77, 32 pages); annual Ohio norms for juniors, seniors, ('77, 1 page each); occupational analysis ('76, 161 pages); rental and scoring service, $1.50 per student, postage extra; $4.50 per occupational analysis, postpaid; (300) minutes in 2 sessions; Instructional Materials Laboratory, Ohio State University. * [Test not available for review.]

[1162]

Ohio Industrial Electronics Achievement Test. Grades 11–12; 1973–77; OIEAT; available only as a part of the *Ohio Trade and Industrial Education Achievement Test Program* (see 1166 for more complete information); 19 scores: orientation, D/C electricity, A/C electricity, electron tubes, semi-conductors, schematic drawings, power supplies, D/C timers, A/C timers, heavy current conductors, sequence timers, welding, sensors, heaters, magnetics, rotating machinery, servos, logic systems, total; no data on reliability of part scores; 1 form; parts 1, 2, ('74, 20 pages); Part 1 is the *Ohio Electronics Achievement Test, Part 1;* no specific manual; series manual ('77, 32 pages); annual Ohio norms for juniors, seniors, ('77, 1 page each); course outline ('73, 48 pages); rental and scoring service, $1.50 per student, postage extra; $2 per course outline, postpaid; (300) minutes in 2 sessions; Instructional Materials Laboratory, Ohio State University. * [Test not available for review.]

[1163]

★**Ohio Lithographic Printing Achievement Test.** Grades 11–12; 1976–77; OLPAT; available only as a part of the *Ohio Trade and Industrial Education Achievement Test Program* (see 1166 for more complete information); 10 scores: layout and design, composing, paste-up, proofing, camera and film processing, stripping, platemaking and proofs, offset presses, finishing operations, total; no data on reliability of part scores; 1 form; parts 1 ('77, 19 pages), 2 ('77, 17 pages); no specific manual; series manual ('77, 32 pages); annual Ohio norms for juniors, seniors, ('77, 1 page each); occupational analyses: cold type compositor ('76, 79 pages), offset cameraperson ['76, 65 pages], offset press operator ('76, 45 pages); rental and scoring service, $1.50 per student, postage extra; $3 per occupational analysis for cold type compositor, $2.50 for offset cameraperson, $3.50 for offset press operator, postpaid; (300) minutes in 2 sessions; Instructional Materials Laboratory, Ohio State University. * [Test not available for review.]

[1164]

Ohio Machine Trades Achievement Test. Grades 11–12; 1958–77; OMTAT; available only as a part of the *Ohio Trade and Industrial Education Achievement Test Program* (see 1166 for more complete information); 14 scores: orientation and safety, bench work, power sawing, drilling machines, engine lathes, turret lathes, blueprint reading, milling machine, shaper-planer, abrasive machining, heat treating and applied metallurgy, applied math, applied science, total; no data on reliability of part scores; 1 form; parts 1 ('75, 15 pages), 2 ('75, 17 pages); no specific manual; series manual ('77, 32 pages); annual Ohio norms for juniors, seniors, ('77, 1 page each); occupational analysis (no date, 257 pages); rental and scoring service, $1.50 per student, postage extra; $6 per occupational analysis, postpaid; (300) minutes in 2 sessions; Instructional Materials Laboratory, Ohio State University. * [Test not available for review.]

See T2:2427 (2 references).

[1165]

Ohio Sheet Metal Achievement Test. Grades 11–12; 1964–77; OSMAT; available only as a part of the *Ohio Trade and Industrial Education Achievement Test Program* (see 1166 for more complete information); 15 scores: blueprint reading, applied science, applied math, hand tool operations, machine operations, soldering, special operations, mechanical drawing, freehand sketching, metals, non-metallic, layout, fabricating, welding, total; no data on reliability of part scores; 1 form; parts 1 ('66, 13 pages), 2 ('64, 8 pages); no specific manual; series manual ('77, 32 pages); annual Ohio norms for juniors, seniors, ('77, 1 page each); course outline ['64, 8 pages]; rental and scoring service, $1.50 per student, postage extra; $2 per course outline, postpaid; (360) minutes in 2 sessions; Instructional Materials Laboratory, Ohio State University. * [Test not available for review.]

See T2:2430 (1 reference).

[1166]

Ohio Trade and Industrial Education Achievement Test Program. Grades 11–12; 1958–77; tests administered annually in March at participating schools; each student must take 2 tests: the intelligence test and a trade test; 1 form; revised manual ('77, 32 pages); instructions for administration ('77, 35 pages); separate answer booklets must be used; rental and scoring service, $1.50 per student; postage extra; individual state norms will be provided for minimum of 100 students and 5 or more schools per grade and trade; specimen set not available; (270–390) minutes in 3 sessions; Instructional Materials Laboratory, Ohio State University. * [Tests not available for review.]

a) INTELLIGENCE TEST. *Short Form Test of Academic Aptitude,* Level 5 (grades 9–12); see 202.

b) TRADE TESTS. 1958–77; 16 tests based on occupational analyses or course outlines prepared for use in Ohio.

1) *Ohio Auto Body Achievement Test.* See 1154.

2) *Ohio Automotive Mechanics Achievement Test.* See 1155.

3) *Ohio Carpentry Achievement Test.* See 1156.

4) *Ohio Communication Products Electronics Achievement Test.* See 1157.

5) *Ohio Construction Electricity Achievement Test.* See 1158.

6) *Ohio Cosmetology Achievement Test.* See 1159.

7) *Ohio Dental Assisting Achievement Test.* See 1086.

8) *Ohio Diversified Health Occupations Achievement Test.* See 1102.

9) *Ohio Drafting Achievement Test.* See 1160.

10) *Ohio Heating, Air Conditioning, and Refrigeration Achievement Test.* See 1161.

11) *Ohio Industrial Electronics Achievement Test.* See 1162.

12) *Ohio Lithographic Printing Achievement Test.*
See 1163.
13) *Ohio Machine Trades Achievement Test.* See
1164.
14) *Ohio Medical Assisting Achievement Test.* See
1103.
15) *Ohio Sheet Metal Achievement Test.* See 1165.
16) *Ohio Welding Achievement Test.* See 1167.
See T2:2431 (1 reference).

[1167]
*Ohio Welding Achievement Test. Grades 11–12;
1969–77; OWAT; available only as a part of the
*Ohio Trade and Industrial Education Achievement
Test Program* (see 1166 for more complete information); 12 scores: blueprint reading, flame cutting,
oxy-acetylene, arc welding, resistance welding, gas
tungsten—arc welding, gas metal arc welding, equipment, labor and management, applied math, applied
science, total; no data on reliability of part scores; 1
form; parts 1 ('70, 16 pages), 2 ('70, 11 pages); no
specific manual; series manual ('77, 32 pages);
annual Ohio norms for juniors, seniors, (77, 1 page
each); occupational analysis (no date, 77 pages);
rental and scoring service, $1.50 per student, postage
extra; $2 per occupational analysis, postpaid; (330)
minutes in 2 sessions; Instructional Materials Laboratory, Ohio State University. * [Test not available for
review.]

[1168]
**Purdue Trade Information Test in Welding,
Revised Edition.** Vocational school and adults;
1952; 1 form (8 pages); preliminary manual (3
pages); $5 per 25 tests, postage extra; 50¢ per speci-
men set, postpaid; (65–80) minutes; Joseph Tiffin
and Warren B. Griffin; distributed by University
Book Store. *
See T2:2438 (1 reference).

RICHARD A. SWANSON, *Professor of Industrial
Education and Technology, Bowling Green
State University, Bowling Green, Ohio.*

The authors state that this test is "designed
to aid industry and vocational schools in determining the amount of information in this field
that is possessed by applicants or students."
This test, developed in 1952, was validated
with a sample of 57 subjects and has not been
revised during its quarter-century lifetime. It
contains 70 multiple choice items with only 5
items having reference to illustrations or symbols.

The test is divided into the three sections of
general, gas welding, and electrical arc welding
knowledge. These three broad areas and the
specific content within each are based on a
pre-1952 literature review. The test does not
include any post-1952 developments in welding
technology (such as tungsten-arc welding) and
the new alloys being welded. The preliminary
150 questions were administered to 135 advanced vocational school students and then re-

duced to the final 70 items through an item
analysis. The odd-even reliability, based on 59
cases, is reported as .91. No item analysis information is provided in the manual. The
authors report a small study in which 11 journeymen welders scored significantly higher than
46 vocational school students who had completed a course in welding.

The test is not timed, but it is suggested that
60 minutes is quite sufficient. Scoring is awkward. Responses are entered directly onto the
eight-page test booklet, and a non-overlay key
is lined up edge to edge to obtain page scores.
These page scores are then added for a total
score.

SUMMARY. This test is outdated in content,
format, and scoring. It lacks current and comprehensive validity and reliability information.
Depending on the user's purposes, several more
effective tests are available; e.g., the *Short Occupational Knowledge Test for Welders* and the
Ohio Welding Achievement Test.

[1169]
**Short Occupational Knowledge Test for Car-
penters.** Job applicants; 1969–70; score is pass, fail,
or unclassifiable; 1 form ('69, 2 pages, self-marking);
series manual ('70, 15 pages); tape cassette available
for administration; $10.70 per 25 tests; $15 per tape
cassette; $1.40 per manual; $7.10 per specimen set of
the 12 tests in the series; postage extra; (10–15)
minutes; Bruce A. Campbell and Suellen O. Johnson;
Science Research Associates, Inc. *

ROBERT S. SWANSON, *Chancellor, University of
Wisconsin-Stout, Menomonie, Wisconsin.*

The *Short Occupational Knowledge Test for
Carpenters* is designed to determine how familiar a job applicant is with the content and concepts of carpentry. It is designed as a device
for quickly separating people who have knowledge of the trade, gained through experience
and training, from those who may have interest
in such work and possibly some experience but
little knowledge of important technical and
theoretical content.

The test consists of 20 multiple choice items,
generally testing four types of knowledge: technical terms associated with a particular problem common in carpentry, reasons for doing
something in a particular way, the theory on
which a particular practice is based, and specific
items of technical information.

The test manual describes the process and
gives adequate support data on the construc-

tion and validation of the test. A pool of about six times as many items as were needed was developed by at least three experts in carpentry training. The items were reviewed by other carpentry experts. To select the items for inclusion in the test, they were administered to two groups: (a) experienced carpenters and apprentices in their final stages of training, and (b) people with an interest in carpentry but with little formal training such as first year apprentices.

The items selected for the test were those which discriminated highly between these two groups.

Reliability was calculated on two samples of people by both an internal consistency technique (K-R 20) and alternate forms. The coefficients reported varied from .63 to .90, as high as one might expect from such a short test.

The test should be easy to administer; the directions are concise and easy to understand. Scoring is simple and provides three meaningful scores: pass, fail, and unclassifiable. A simple table translates the numerical score to one of the three categories. Only a score of 10, out of a possible 20, is regarded as "unclassifiable"; thus, there should not be a large group on which no decision is possible.

SUMMARY. For its purpose, this test is brief and easy to administer, and should very quickly separate persons with knowledge of carpentry gained in training and working from those without it. The items are more associated with house carpentry than with commercial, industrial building. They deal with wood framing of a rather traditional type and do not deal with manufactured homes or buildings or many of the specialized activities in which carpenters engage.

A person prepared in a vocational school program or a standard apprenticeship should easily have most of the knowledge called for by this test. A person who simply worked at the trade without much reading and formal study would probably not do well. As an initial selection device, this test is good.

[1170]

Short Occupational Knowledge Test for Draftsmen. Job applicants; 1969–70; score is pass, fail, or unclassifiable; 1 form ('69, 2 pages, self-marking); series manual ('70, 15 pages); tape cassette available for administration; $10.70 per 25 tests; $15 per tape

cassette; $1.40 per manual; $7.10 per specimen set of the 12 tests in the series; postage extra; (10–15) minutes; Bruce A. Campbell and Suellen O. Johnson; Science Research Associates, Inc. *

TIM L. WENTLING, *Associate Professor of Vocational and Technical Education, University of Illinois, Urbana, Illinois.*

This short, 19-item multiple choice test is designed to determine how familiar an applicant or employee is with the current content and concepts of the occupational area of drafting. The use of the test is as an "aid in the screening of applicants for hire, training, promotion, or transfer"; the authors state that scores on this test should function as only one information element in decision making.

The test is of the carbon-insert, self-scoring format that comprises two pages. A cassette tape is available for oral administration. This approach is commendable in terms of ensuring consistency of administration and in facilitating the testing of individuals with low verbal facility. The tape substantiates the authors' statement that "these tests are intended to be measures of job knowledge, not reading ability."

A primary concern in evaluation of this test pertains to its intended use. The conceptualization of drafting as an occupation may be oversimplified by the test authors. The test contains items relevant to general, machine, topographical, architectural, and electrical drawing. Within the technically specialized functions of most of our industries, personnel managers and employers (potential test users) would most likely want a more specialized instrument.

The instrument has undergone considerable tryout and validation with an administration to specialists and a control group. Items have been selected based upon their apparent discrimination power. However, a detailed description of the validation sample, in terms of their specific occupations, is not provided in the test manual. Also, the publication date of this test is 1969. It is possible that change has occurred in some occupations served by this test. It is suggested that the test be reanalyzed with more recent data and that the second form of the test, that was utilized in determining reliability, be published.

Validity was estimated by how well scores for the test (pass, fail, or unclassifiable) predicted an examinee's current status, i.e., specialist or control group. Specialists were "journeymen, competent experienced workers, last-year apprentices, and top advanced vocational students and instructors," while the control group was made up of first year apprentices, first year vocational students, and employees in a comparable area.

K-R 20 estimates for the pretest and validation samples are .73 (N = 235) and .78 (N = 79), respectively. The length of the test (19 items) may be a factor in this marginal reliability index. The parallel-form reliabilities are more respectable, .88 and .84 for the same samples.

To summarize, the following points may be made: (*a*) the use of this test for employment screening of specialized draftsmen is cautioned; (*b*) the test was published in 1969 and may not reflect current occupational advances; (*c*) predictive validity studies should be conducted with various industries; and (*d*) the use of an audio tape for administration is commendable.

[1171]

Short Occupational Knowledge Test for Welders. Job applicants; 1969–70; score is pass, fail, or unclassifiable; 1 form ('69, 2 pages, self-marking); series manual ('70, 15 pages); tape cassette available for administration; $10.70 per 25 tests; $15 per tape cassette; $1.40 per manual; $7.10 per specimen set of the 12 tests in the series; postage extra; (10–15) minutes; Bruce A. Campbell and Suellen O. Johnson; Science Research Associates, Inc. *

RICHARD A. SWANSON, *Professor of Industrial Education and Technology, Bowling Green State University, Bowling Green, Ohio.*

The purpose of this 20-item multiple choice test in welding is "to provide a means for setting knowledgeable applicants apart from those having only limited knowledge in the specific occupational area." The SOKTW is meant to serve as one element in the employee selection process and is of particular benefit to the personnel officer who is not an expert in welding.

The test yields scores of pass, fail, and unclassifiable. Pass (11 or more items correct) means attainment of job knowledge equivalent to practicing welding specialists, fail (8 or fewer correct) means a lack of that amount of knowledge, and unclassifiable is assigned to the scores 9 and 10.

A common manual for 12 short occupational knowledge tests is available. In the discussion of test validity and reliability some information is handled corporately and, thus, at too general

a level. Readers are assured that content validity was established via the item writing of three or more unnamed welding experts and a review of their work by additional unnamed experts.

All 100 of the original items were pretested within 12 companies or organizations having a total of 97 welding specialists and 203 control group subjects of first-year apprentices and vocational students. The appropriateness of the control group subjects is considered a strength of the SOKTW. The 100 items were reduced to 20, based on "extensive item analyses" and "comments by the examinees," yet no item analysis data are presented.

The K-R 20 reliability of the SOKTW was found to be .73 for both the pretest sample and the validation sample. While the stability is reassuring, the .73 coefficient is not. The alternate forms correlations are better estimates of the true reliability of the SOKTW because of their small number of items. These coefficients are .85 for the pretest sample and .90 in the validation sample. Beyond the reliability coefficients, item analysis information and the standard error of measurement would have been helpful to the user in judging the test.

The concurrent validity of the SOKTW was determined by the instrument's ability to sort the welding specialists and control subjects into their respective groups. In obtaining their "hits," the percentage of examinees properly classified by the test, the authors ignored those considered unclassifiable by the test, thus exaggerating the percentage of hits. The correct percentages of hits for the two groups of 167 and 108 are 75 and 83 percent, respectively— not 86 and 94 percent, as reported by the authors. Caution should be noted in the fact that the original categorization of subjects into the two groups had potential error. Beginning vocational students and apprentices may, in fact, have had the knowledge of specialists while experienced welders possibly do not.

Inasmuch as the test was developed in 1969, it would seem that a revision is in order. A revision based partially upon careful increases in item discrimination and difficulty would force a bi-modal distribution. This distribution, if validated through concurrent validity studies, would allow a greater definitiveness to the pass and fail categories and the possibility of having no or few subjects falling in the unclassifiable area.

SUMMARY. The SOKTW is an appropriate and adequate test for its intended purpose of functioning as only *one* element in the screening of welding job applicants. Simplicity, the strength of the SOKTW, is also its weakness. Applicants obtaining an "unclassifiable" score would most likely not be considered for employment while those obtaining "pass" scores would be. This major decision on an individual could be based on a score difference of one point (10 versus 11 correct). The shortness of the test and the three-category scoring can cause abuses through overinterpretation. While this is clearly the best such test available for its intended purpose, users should carefully follow the cautions and recommendations cited in the manual.

[1172]

★Sweet Technical Information Test. Ages 14–17; 1973–75; STIT; suitability of students "for technical and practical occupations at trade and subprofessional level"; 1 form ('75, 12 pages); manual ('73, 63 pages); separate answer sheets must be used; Aus 60¢ per test; 60¢ per 10 answer sheets; 80¢ per scoring stencil; $3.50 per manual; postpaid within Australia; 20(25) minutes; R. Sweet; Australian Council for Educational Research [Australia]. *

SUPERVISION

[1173]

★Conflict Management Survey. Adults; 1969–73; CMS; "manner in which individuals react to and attempt to manage differences between themselves and others"; 5 scores (personal orientation, interpersonal relationships, small group relationships, intergroup relationships, total) for each of 5 conflict management styles (based on varying degrees of concern for the relationship and concern for personal goals); norms based on males primarily in management positions; 1 form ('73, 12 pages); no manual; score interpretation ('73, 11 pages); $3 per test, postage extra; statistical data free on request; [15–30] minutes; Jay Hall; Teleometrics Int'l. *

REFERENCES

1. GRIFFITH, CHARLES LEO. *The Effects of Personal Preferences for Conflict Management on Decision Quality Under Cooperative and Competitive Conditions.* Doctor's thesis, Texas A & M University (College Station, Tex.), 1975. (*DAI* 36: 2713A)
2. THOMAS, KENNETH W., AND KILMANN, RALPH H. "The Social Desirability Variable in Organizational Research: An Alternative Explanation of Reported Findings." *Acad Mgmt J* 18(4):741–52 D '75. *

FRANK J. LANDY, *Associate Professor of Psychology, The Pennsylvania State University, University Park, Pennsylvania.*

In the brochure describing the various instruments published by Teleometrics Int'l., the following is stated about the *Conflict Management Survey:* "the underlying theory described in the accompanying handout material affords a stimulating and clarifying basis for studying conflict and its effects." On the basis of a careful examination of the instrument and its documentation, as well as a review of supporting research, I cannot argue with that description. I think that the "accompanying handout material" is first-rate. As a matter of fact, it might not be a bad idea for the publisher to market the handout material separately. As far as the instrument itself is concerned, it is as good as any other instrument for leading to a discussion of conflict, although more elaborate than most.

The research supporting the instrument is both sketchy and confusing—two paragraphs summarizing the results of one (or two?) studies—and evidently not routinely distributed with test materials. The only sample specifically described comprised 50 individuals, yet a factor analysis was done on 60 items somewhere along the line. We are told that the sample size for the normative profile is 1,050. The author states that "while the greatest proportion of responses are from persons in management positions with large organizations, data from ministers, trainers, law enforcement personnel, and labor contract negotiators are also represented in the sample." Without specific information to the contrary, the user should assume that the normative population consisted of upper-level managers. In addition to this material, I was presented with a table summarizing a canonical analysis of the CMS with the CPI, and a table of the bivariate relationships between CMS scores and CPI scores. I assume that these two tables are intended to make some point about the construct validity of the CMS. If they make any point, it is that social desirability would seem to be one of the major factors tapped by the CMS.

Some later studies assess more directly the properties of the CMS. An unpublished 1973 study by Thomas and Kilmann clearly demonstrates the enormous variance in the CMS accounted for by social desirability influences. Over 80 percent of the variance in item responses and 90 percent of the variance in scale scores can be accounted for by social desirability influences in this study. In fairness to the CMS, other similar instruments have not been significantly better. The conclusion is rather straightforward: When responding to questions about dealing with conflict, most people will respond in a manner intended to make themselves look good to the person asking the question, regardless of how they would actually behave in conflict situations. The interpretation booklet implies that this bias has been taken into account as evidenced by the conversion table for changing raw scores into T scores. It does not reduce the influence of social desirability.

The Thomas and Kilmann study also reports reliability coefficients considerably lower than those reported in the technical sheet sent to me by the publisher. Instead of values ranging from .70 to .87, as reported by the publisher, the values reported by Thomas and Kilmann range from .39 to .73. Finally, the Thomas and Kilmann work questions the value of two of the five conflict dimensions of the CMS on the basis of low convergent validities with other similar instruments intended to measure the same five modes. A briefer version of the Thomas and Kilmann paper was published in 1975 (2).

One final comment about the conceptual and verbal level of the test materials is in order. Both conceptually and verbally, the materials are at quite a high level. They require a high degree of verbal comprehension and analytic skill. Look the materials over carefully with these considerations in mind before deciding whether to use them.

The technical documentation of the CMS provided by the author is insufficient for anyone concerned with the development and actual properties of the scales. Coupled with the discouraging results of the Thomas and Kilmann study, there is little to justify the use of the instrument. Nevertheless, as a vehicle for generating discussion about the nature of conflict and its resolution in managerial settings, it does have some appeal due to the material accompanying it. Those who do decide to use the instrument and interpretation booklet for a training or development session would be wise to downplay the importance of the numbers representing the various subscale scores—the meaning of those numbers remains a mystery.

[1174]
Leader Behavior Description Questionnaire. Supervisors; 1957; LBDQ; "2 scores (consideration, initiating structure) based upon responses by 4–10 raters"; no norms; 2 tests; $2 per 25 tests, cash

Conflict Management Survey

orders postpaid; specimen set free; (10) minutes; original edition by John K. Hemphill and Alvin E. Coons; current edition by Personnel Research Board, Ohio State University; University Publication Sales, Ohio State University. *

a) LEADER BEHAVIOR DESCRIPTION QUESTIONNAIRE. Employee ratings of a specific supervisor; 1 form (3 pages); manual (10 pages); manual by Andrew W. Halpin.

b) IDEAL LEADER BEHAVIOR DESCRIPTION QUESTIONNAIRE. Employee ratings of what a supervisor ought to be; test booklet title is *Ideal Leader Behavior (What You Expect of Your Leader)*; no data on reliability; 1 form (3 pages); no manual.

See T2:2451 (35 references) and 7:1146 (108 references).

REFERENCES

1–108. See 7:1146.
109–143. See T2:2451; also includes a cumulative name index to the first 143 references for this test.
144. BEER, MICHAEL. *Leadership Employee Needs, and Motivation.* Ohio State University, Bureau of Business Research Monograph No. 129. Columbus, Ohio: the Bureau, 1966. Pp. xii, 100. *
145. BRYANT, GEORGE WENDELL. *Ideal Leader Behavior Descriptions of Appointed and Sociometrically Chosen Student Leaders.* Doctor's thesis, North Texas State University (Denton, Tex.), 1967. (*DA* 28:3497A)
146. STOGDILL, RALPH M., AND COADY, NICHOLAS P. "Preferences of Vocational Students for Different Styles of Supervisory Behavior." *Personnel Psychol* 23(3):309–12 au '70. * (*PA* 45:9117)
147. CARROLL, THOMAS BURGESS. *Leader Behavior of Community College Directors of Student Personnel as Viewed by Superiors and Subordinates.* Doctor's thesis, North Carolina State University (Raleigh, N.C.), 1971. (*DAI* 36:126A)
148. HENSLEY, STEPHEN RAY. *Leader Behavior of Biology Teachers and Principals and Its Relationship With Present Biology Curriculum Practices.* Doctor's thesis, Oklahoma State University (Stillwater, Okla.), 1971. (*DAI* 33:631A)
149. JOHNSON, MARY MAGDALENE. *Role Expectations That Supervisors, Teachers and Elementary School Principals Have for the Supervisor of Special Classes for Mentally Retarded Children.* Doctor's thesis, University of Maryland (College Park, Md.), 1971. (*DAI* 32:3613A)
150. LEE, WILFORD FRANKLIN. *A Study of the Relationship Between the Leader Behavior of Secondary School Principals and Biology Teachers' Attitudes Toward BSCS Biology.* Doctor's thesis, Oklahoma State University (Stillwater, Okla.), 1971. (*DAI* 33:632A)
151. McLENNAN, THOMAS DAVID. *An Analysis of the Leader-Behavior Preferences of Selected Suburban Residents From Three Socio-Economic Levels.* Doctor's thesis, Wayne State University (Detroit. Mich.), 1971. (*DAI* 32:2358A)
152. AMBROSIE, FRANK, AND HELLER, ROBERT W. "The Secondary School Administrator and Perceived Teacher Participation in the Decision-Making Process." *J Exp Ed* 40(4):6–13 su '72. *
153. CLAYPOOL, ROY CLIFFORD. *A Study of Organizational Climate, Leader Behavior and Their Relationships to Collective Bargaining Impasses.* Doctor's thesis, Lehigh University (Bethlehem, Pa.), 1972. (*DAI* 33:3181A)
154. CORNELL, JOSEPH PAUL. *Relationship Between Negotiation Function and Leadership Behavior of Superintendents of School Districts in the State of New Jersey.* Doctor's thesis, Fordham University (New York, N.Y.), 1972. (*DAI* 33:3182A)
155. DUFFY, JOSEPH PATRICK. *Relationships Between Educational Innovation, Principal's Leader Behavior, Faculty Belief System, and Organizational Climate in Jesuit High Schools in the United States.* Doctor's thesis, Fordham University (New York, N.Y.), 1972. (*DAI* 33:3996A)
156. EVANS, MARTIN G. "Leadership Behavior: Demographic Factors and Agreement Between Subordinate and Self-Descriptions." *Personnel Psychol* 25(4):649–53 w '72. *
157. FERGUSON, JON STANLEY. *The Relationship Between Pupil Control Ideology and Observed Leader Behavior of Public Secondary School Teachers.* Doctor's thesis, University of Kansas (Lawrence, Kan.), 1972. (*DAI* 33:6587A)
158. FLETCHER, MATTHEW ROYAL. *A Study of the Feasibility of Using the "Action Maze" Game to Identify the Behavioral Style of High School Principals.* Doctor's thesis, Syracuse University (Syracuse, N.Y.), 1972. (*DAI* 34:1019A)
159. GOODSELL, DAVID RAY ROBBINS. *Relationships Between Academic Dean Leader Behavior and Institutional Functioning as Perceived by the Faculty and Academic Deans of Selected Junior Colleges.* Doctor's thesis, University of Georgia (Athens, Ga.), 1972. (*DAI* 33:5513A)
160. GRAEN, GEORGE; DANSEREAU, FRED; AND MINAMI,

TAKAO. "Dysfunctional Leadership Styles." *Organiz Behav & Hum Perfor* 7(2):216–36 Ap '72. * *(PA* 48:3993)

161. GRAEN, GEORGE; DANSEREAU, FRED, JR.; AND MINAMI, TAKAO. "An Empirical Test of the Man-in-the-Middle Hypothesis Among Executives in a Hierarchical Organization Employing a Unit-Set Analysis." *Organiz Behav & Hum Perfor* 8(2):262–85 O '72. * *(PA* 49:8069)

162. HARRIS, WILLIE CHARLES. *The Use of Selected Leadership, Personality, Motivational, and Demographic Variables in the Identification of Successful Ministers.* Doctor's thesis, University of Tulsa (Tulsa, Okla.), 1972. *(DAI* 33:4833A)

163. HENNING, DORIS MAE MAXFIELD. *The Relationship Between Elementary Administrator's Self Perception and Effective Administrative Performance.* Doctor's thesis, University of Akron (Akron, Ohio), 1972. *(DAI* 33:526A)

164. HERMAN, JEANNE BRETT, AND HULIN, CHARLES L. "Studying Organizational Attitudes From Individual and Organizational Frames of Reference." *Organiz Behav & Hum Perfor* 8(1):84–108 Ag '72. * *(PA* 49:1422)

165. LUCAS, LARRY LESLIE. *The Relationship of Selected Variables to the Effectiveness of Secondary School Principals as Assessed by District Superintendents.* Doctor's thesis, University of Southern California (Los Angeles, Calif.), 1972. *(DAI* 33:1369A)

166. MC GRUDER, ROBERT CARL. *A Study of the Relationship Between Creativity and Leader Behavior of High School Principals.* Doctor's thesis, Syracuse University (Syracuse, N.Y.), 1972. *(DAI* 34:97A)

167. MADSON, JOHAN ALFRED. *A Description of the Leader Behavior of Residence Hall Directors at Three Selected State Universities.* Doctor's thesis, Ohio University (Athens, Ohio), 1972. *(DAI* 33:571A)

168. MAHER, EDWARD JOSEPH. *An Analysis of the Leadership Behavior of Elementary School Principals as Perceived by School Personnel in Selected Collective Negotiations Situations.* Doctor's thesis, University of Connecticut (Storrs, Conn.), 1972. *(DAI* 33:2659A)

169. MITCHELL, TERENCE R. "Cognitive Complexity and Group Performance." *J Social Psychol* 86(1):35–43 F '72. * *(PA* 47:10782)

170. MORRIS, LLOYD ERWIN. *The High School Athletic Director: A Comparative Study of Behavior.* Doctor's thesis, University of Utah (Salt Lake City, Utah), 1972. *(DAI* 33:931A)

171. MOY, JAMES YEE KIN. *Leadership Behavior and Organizational Environment: A Study of the Residence Life Program of Ohio University.* Doctor's thesis, Ohio University (Athens, Ohio), 1972. *(DAI* 33:6674A)

172. PRESTON, RICHARD L. *A Comparative Analysis of Learning Climate and Leader Behavior of Open Space Elementary and Traditional Elementary Schools.* Doctor's thesis, Miami University (Oxford, Ohio), 1972. *(DAI* 33:6029A)

173. ROEGIERS, CHARLES L. *An Experimental Study in Interpersonal Trust and Leadership in Problem-Solving Small Groups.* Doctor's thesis, University of Kansas (Lawrence, Kan.), 1972. *(DAI* 33:3057A)

174. STINSON, JOHN E. "'Least Preferred Coworker' as a Measure of Leadership Style." *Psychol Rep* 30(3):930 Je '72. * *(PA* 49:3452)

175. STONE, JOHN EDWARD. *Fulfillment of Expectations for Classroom Leadership as a Predictor of Student Ratings of College Teaching.* Doctor's thesis, University of Florida (Gainesville, Fla.), 1972. *(DAI* 34:178A)

176. SWEET, CODY. *Nonverbally Reading Initiating Structure and Consideration Dimensions of Administrative Behavior.* Doctor's thesis, Northwestern University (Evanston, Ill.), 1972. *(DAI* 33:3229A)

177. WEISSENBERG, PETER, AND KAVANAGH, MICHAEL J. "The Independence of Initiating Structure and Consideration: A Review of the Evidence." *Personnel Psychol* 25(1):119–30 sp '72. * *(PA* 49:12191)

178. WHITIS, JESSIE DILLARD. *A Study of the Leadership Role of Financial Aid Officers of the Western Association of Financial Aid Officers.* Doctor's thesis, Arizona State University (Tempe, Ariz.), 1972. *(DAI* 33:2058A)

179. AUSTIN, DEAN ALAN. *Leader Behavior Perceptions and Interpersonal Needs of Athletic Directors.* Doctor's thesis, University of Utah (Salt Lake City, Utah), 1973. *(DAI* 34:4828A)

180. BIMES, JAMES DAVID. *A Study of Social Studies Department Chairmen and Selected Leader Behavior Dimensions.* Doctor's thesis, University of Missouri (Columbia, Mo.), 1973. *(DAI* 35:738A)

181. CALL, MELVYN DOUGLAS. *Role-Expectations, Leader Behavior and Leadership Ideology of Academic Deans.* Doctor's thesis, West Virginia University (Morgantown, W.Va.), 1973. *(DAI* 35:4602A)

182. CARLSON, GERALD PAUL. *Perceptions of Physical Education Chairmen as Leaders.* Doctor's thesis, University of Utah (Salt Lake City, Utah), 1973. *(DAI* 34:3953A)

183. CASELLO, JOSEPH HARRIS. *The Superintendent's Leadership Style as It Affects His Role in the Collective Negotiation Process.* Doctor's thesis, Rutgers—The State University (New Brunswick, N.J.), 1973. *(DAI* 34:3735A)

184. DELUCIA, JOSEPH JAMES. *A Comparison of the Perceived Leadership Behavior of Principals in Schools Utilizing Differentiated Staffing Patterns With Schools Utilizing Traditional Staffing Patterns.* Doctor's thesis, University of Connecticut (Storrs, Conn.), 1973. *(DAI* 35:743A)

185. DISTEFANO, M. K., JR., AND PRYER, MARGARET W. "Comparisons of Leader and Subordinate Descriptions of Leadership Behavior." *Percept & Motor Skills* 37(3):714 D '73. * *(PA* 52:4177)

186. FLEMING, ROSE ANN. *The Relationship Between Administrative Behavior of the Principal and the Quality of Multi-Dimensional Organizational Output of Schools as Assessed by Teachers and Administrators of Catholic Elementary and Secondary Schools.* Doctor's thesis, Miami University (Oxford, Ohio), 1973. *(DAI* 34:3748A)

187. GRAEN, GEORGE; DANSEREAU, FRED, JR.; MINAMI, TAKAO; AND CASHMAN, JAMES. "Leadership Behaviors as Cues to Performance Evaluation." *Acad Mgmt J* 16(4):611–23 D '73. * *(PA* 52:4179)

188. GRUENFELD, LEOPOLD, AND KASSUM, SALEEM. "Supervisory Style and Organizational Effectiveness in a Pediatric Hospital." *Personnel Psychol* 26(4):531–44 w '73. * *(PA* 53:12721)

189. HALE, ROBERT EARL. *The Relationships Between Selected Personal Variables and Faculty Perception of the Leader Behavior of the Academic Dean.* Doctor's thesis, Ball State University (Muncie, Ind.), 1973. *(DAI* 34:2208A)

190. HARRIS, JOHNIE EDWARD. *An Investigation of Teachers' Perceptions of the Principal's Leadership Role and Parental Attitudes in Respect to School-Community Conflict.* Doctor's thesis, George Washington University (Washington, D.C.), 1973. *(DAI* 34:2210A)

191. HUETT, DENNIS LEE. *Impact of Subordinates on Leader Style.* Doctor's thesis, Colorado State University (Ft. Collins, Colo.), 1973. *(DAI* 34:1306B)

192. HUNT, J. G., AND LIEBSCHER, V. K. C. "Leadership Preference, Leadership Behavior, and Employee Satisfaction." *Organiz Behav & Hum Perfor* 9(1):59–77 F '73. * *(PA* 50:4007)

193. JOHNSON, PAUL O., AND BLEDSOE, JOSEPH C. "Morale as Related to Perceptions of Leader Behavior." *Personnel Psychol* 26(4):581–92 w '73. * *(PA* 53:12695)

194. KUNZ, DANIEL WALTER. *Leader Behavior of Principals and the Professional Zone of Acceptance of Teachers.* Doctor's thesis, Rutgers—The State University (New Brunswick, N.J.), 1973. *(DAI* 34:3770A)

195. LEWIS, JOSEPH WELBORN. *A Study to Determine the Relationship of Administrative Practices and Teacher Morale in the Post Secondary Vocational-Technical Programs of Mississippi.* Doctor's thesis, University of Southern Mississippi (Hattiesburg, Miss.), 1973. *(DAI* 34:4105A)

196. MILES, MATTHEW B. "Leader Behavior Description Questionnaire," pp. 129–32. In *Measuring Human Behavior.* Edited by Dale G. Lake and others. New York: Teachers College Press, 1973. Pp. xviii, 422. *

197. MITCHELL, BOBBY MACK, SR. *Analysis of the Perceptions of the Role of the Subordinate and Super-Ordinate With Respect to Authority, Responsibility, and Delegation in the Community Schools of Flint at the Attendance Center Level.* Doctor's thesis, Michigan State University (East Lansing, Mich.), 1973. *(DAI* 34:2979A)

198. MOLO, RAY DENNIS. *Teacher Perception of the Role of the Elementary Supervisor.* Doctor's thesis, McNeese State University (Lake Charles, La.), 1973. *(DAI* 34:1544A)

199. MOY, JAMES Y. K., AND HALES, LOYDE W. "Management Styles and Leadership Behavior Within a Residence Life Program." *J Exp Ed* 42(1):33–6 f '73. * *(PA* 52:2013)

200. POWERS, DAVID DURFEE. *The Relationships Between Faculty Morale and Perceived Leader Behavior of Department Chairmen at a Florida Metropolitan Community College.* Doctor's thesis, University of Miami (Coral Gables, Fla.), 1973. *(DAI* 34:2236A)

201. SHARMA, MOTI LAL. "Initiating Structure Behaviour of the Headmaster and School Climate." *Indian J Psychol* 48(4):30–6 D '73. * *(PA* 55:2970)

202. SPRANDEL, DENNIS STEUART. *Leader Behavior: An Analysis of the Athletic Director in Colleges of a Selected Midwestern Athletic Conference.* Doctor's thesis, Michigan State University (East Lansing, Mich.), 1973. *(DAI* 34:7574A)

203. STANLEY, WILLIAM LINCOLN, JR. *Perceived Principals' Leadership Behavior: The Relationship of Race in Selected Elementary Schools.* Doctor's thesis, Columbia University (New York, N.Y.), 1973. *(DAI* 34:107A)

204. STEVENS, CLARK ABEL. *Perceptions and Expectations of the Leadership Behavior of Selected Superintendents and Their Administrative Teams in Five Midwestern States.* Doctor's thesis, Iowa State University (Ames, Iowa), 1973. *(DAI* 34:2244A)

205. STINSON, JOHN E., AND ROBERTSON, JOHN H. "Follower-Maturity and Preference for Leader-Behavior Style." *Psychol Rep* 32(1):247–50 F '73. * *(PA* 51:3000)

206. STRAUB, RAYMOND RUSSELL, JR. *The Perceptions of the Leadership Behavior of the Director of Area Vocational-Technical Schools in Pennsylvania.* Doctor's thesis, Temple University (Philadelphia, Pa.), 1973. *(DAI* 34:4658A)

207. TEMPLER, ANDREW J. "A Study of the Relationship Between Psychological Differentiation and Management Style." *Personnel Psychol* 26(2):227–37 su '73. *

Leader Behavior Description Questionnaire

208. WAGNER, WILLIAM CHARLES. *A Study of Leader Behavior of College Administrators.* Doctor's thesis, Michigan State University (East Lansing, Mich.), 1973. (*DAI* 34: 5559A)

209. WHITE, DONALD AUSTIN. *Perceptual Style and Leader Behavior of Elementary Principals in Open Space Schools.* Doctor's thesis, Hofstra University (Hempstead, N.Y.), 1973. (*DAI* 34:546A)

210. ADAMS, EDDIE RAY. *Effects of a Performance Oriented Institute on Vocational Education Directors in Missouri.* Doctor's thesis, University of Missouri (Columbia, Mo.), 1974. (*DAI* 36:2165A)

211. COX, EDWARD WILTON. *Superiors' and Subordinates' Perceptions and Expectations of the Leader Behavior of the Dean of Instruction: A Survey of the North Carolina Community College System.* Doctor's thesis, University of North Carolina (Greensboro, N.C.), 1974. (*DAI* 35:2568A)

212. ELWELL, GORDON RICHEY. *Leadership and Situational Factors Related to Productivity and Turnover in Medical Laboratories.* Doctor's thesis, Georgia State University (Atlanta, Ga.), 1974. (*DAI* 35:6876A)

213. FOY, FRANCIS PATRICK. *An Analysis of the Leader Behavior of Texas Community Junior College Deans of Instruction.* Doctor's thesis, University of Texas (Austin, Tex.), 1974. (*DAI* 35:2575A)

214. FRANKLIN, EUGENE HOWSON. *The Relationship Between Principals' Leader Behavior and Their Perception of Changes Under Contractual Agreements.* Doctor's thesis, Oklahoma State University (Stillwater, Okla.), 1974. (*DAI* 36:6393A)

215. HENDERSHOTT, DANIEL JOSEPH. *Teacher Perceptions of Instructionally Related Leader Behaviors of Principals and Unit Leaders in Individually Guided Education/Multiunit Schools.* Doctor's thesis, Ball State University (Muncie, Ind.), 1974. (*DAI* 35:6391A)

216. JOSSELYN, LOUIS S., JR. *The Effectiveness of Secondary School Administrators-Leadership Behavior and Outside Activities.* Doctor's thesis, Boston University (Boston, Mass.), 1974. (*DAI* 35:1383A)

217. KERR, S.; SCHRIESHEIM, C. A.; MURPHY, C. J.; AND STOGDILL, R. "Toward a Contingency Theory of Leadership Based Upon the Consideration and Initiating Structure Literature." *Organiz Behav & Hum Perfor* 12(1):62–82 F '74. *

218. KERR, STEVEN, AND SCHRIESHEIM, CHESTER. "Consideration, Initiating Structure, and Organizational Criteria—An Update of Korman's 1966 Review." *Personnel Psychol* 27(4): 555–68 w '74. * (*PA* 55:1673)

219. LEFKOWITZ, JOEL. "Job Attitudes of Police: Overall Description and Demographic Correlates." *J Voc Behav* 5(2): 221–30 O '74. * (*PA* 53:6346)

220. LOCKRIDGE, BURMA LASSETER. *Determining the Validity of a Rating Scale to Measure Competencies for Supervision of Instruction.* Doctor's thesis, Georgia State University (Atlanta, Ga.), 1974. (*DAI* 35:6399A)

221. RICKARD, JACK WENTON. *Relationships Between Leadership Behavior and the Personal, Educational, and Occupational Characteristics of Adult Education Leaders.* Doctor's thesis, Arizona State University (Tempe, Ariz.), 1974. (*DAI* 35: 789A)

222. RIDER, LARRY HUGH. *Leader Behavior, Locus of Control and Consultation Effectiveness of School Psychologists.* Doctor's thesis, Ohio State University (Columbus, Ohio), 1974. (*DAI* 35:5134A)

223. SATENTES, MARCELO PUSA. *Study of the Factors Related to Teacher Morale in Five School Districts in the Province of Cotabato, Philippines.* Doctor's thesis, University of North Carolina (Chapel Hill, N.C.), 1974. (*DAI* 35:3361A)

224. SCHRIESHEIM, CHESTER, AND KERR, STEVEN. "Psychometric Properties of the Ohio State Leadership Scales." *Psychol B* 81(11):756–65 N '74. * (*PA* 53:5359)

225. SHIRLEY, THOMAS WILLIAM. *An Analysis of the Leader Behavior, Values and Pupil Control Ideologies of School Principals.* Doctor's thesis, Northwestern University (Evanston, Ill.), 1974. (*DAI* 35:6410A)

226. STOGDILL, RALPH M. *Handbook of Leadership: A Survey of Theory and Research,* pp. 128–41, passim. New York: Free Press, 1974. Pp. viii, 613. *

227. TRUITT, THOMAS E. *A Study of the Relationship Between the Leader Behavior of Principals and Organizational Outputs of High Schools in North Carolina.* Doctor's thesis, University of North Carolina (Chapel Hill, N.C.), 1974. (*DAI* 36:85A)

228. WOLF, LELAND RICHARD. *An Analysis of the Leader Behaviors of Career-Bound and Place-Bound Public School Superintendents in Iowa.* Doctor's thesis, Drake University (Des Moines, Iowa), 1974. (*DAI* 35:7009A)

229. AINSWORTH, RALPH SEGREST. *A Study of the Relationship of Teachers' Personal and Interpersonal Orientation Variables and the Teachers' Perceptions of Elementary and Secondary School Principals' Leadership Behavior.* Doctor's thesis, University of Southern Mississippi (Hattiesburg, Miss.), 1975. (*DAI* 36:4880A)

230. BLACHLY, MICHAEL DENNIS. *Personality and Leadership Behavior of Selected Student Leaders.* Doctor's thesis, University of Tennessee (Knoxville, Tenn.), 1975 (*DAI* 36:7284A)

231. BOZZOMO, LAWRENCE EGNAZIO. *An Analysis of Leader-*

ship and Its Relationship to Teacher Behavior in Open and Conventional Plan Schools. Doctor's thesis, Lehigh University (Bethlehem, Pa.), 1975. (*DAI* 36:2520A)

232. BRESHEARS, RONALD GENE. *Selected Characteristics and Qualifications Relating to Leader Behavior of University Administrators.* Doctor's thesis, University of Missouri (Columbia, Mo.), 1975. (*DAI* 36:4141A)

233. BROWN, KENNETH RAY. *The Leadership Role of the Elementary School Supervisor as Perceived by Elementary Teachers and Supervisors in Selected School Systems of Northeast Louisiana.* Doctor's thesis, Northeast Louisiana University (Monroe, La.), 1975. (*DAI* 36:1933A)

234. BUEHLMANN, DAVID MARVIN. *The Impact of Leadership Style on the Job Satisfaction, Turnover Perceptions, and Performance of Staff Accountants in Large Public Accounting Firms.* Doctor's thesis, University of Illinois (Urbana, Ill.), 1975. (*DAI* 36:6165A)

235. BURNS, ELLEN LOUISE. *Adaptiveness and Satisfaction in Educational Administration.* Doctor's thesis, University of Iowa (Iowa City, Iowa), 1975. (*DAI* 36:4890A)

236. CINCO, MA. ELENA SENO. *Leadership Behavior, Organizational Climate and Productivity of Catholic Secondary Schools in Mindanao, Philippines.* Doctor's thesis, Fordham University (New York, N.Y.), 1975. (*DAI* 36:4892A)

237. CONEY, CHARLES EDWARD. *Perceptions of the Role of the Middle School Principal in Selected School Systems of Southwest Louisiana.* Doctor's thesis, McNeese State University (Lake Charles, La.), 1975. (*DAI* 36:7765A)

238. CONNOLLY, JOHN P. *The Relationship of Selected Personal and Situational Characteristics to the Perceived Leader Behavior of Chief School Administrators.* Doctor's thesis, Columbia University (New York, N.Y.), 1975. (*DAI* 36:58A)

239. DOWNEY, H. KIRK; SHERIDAN, JOHN E.; AND SLOCUM, JOHN W., JR. "Analysis of Relationships Among Leader Behavior, Subordinate Job Performance and Satisfaction: A Path-Goal Approach." *Acad Mgmt J* 18(2):253–62 Je '75. * (*PA* 55:3367, title only)

240. DURRENCE, JESSE J. *Determining the Validity of an Instrument Designed to Measure Administrative Competencies.* Doctor's thesis, Georgia State University (Atlanta, Ga.), 1975. (*DAI* 36:4151A)

241. ELLIS, FRANK WILLIAM. *Leader Behavior of Secondary School Principals in Terms of Authoritarian Attitudes and Size of Organization.* Doctor's thesis, Temple University (Philadelphia, Pa.), 1975. (*DAI* 36:5679A)

242. GALINSKY, HARRY A. *The Relationship Between Leadership Motivation and Leadership Behavior as Moderated by the Favorableness of the Situation.* Doctor's thesis, Rutgers—The State University (New Brunswick, N.J.), 1975. (*DAI* 36:632A)

243. GORMAN, EDGAR JOHN. *A Study of the Relationships Between Leader Behavior and the Anxiety Levels of Selected Public School Principals.* Doctor's thesis, University of Connecticut (Storrs, Conn.), 1975. (*DAI* 36:4154A)

244. GREGG, GLORIA A. *An Examination of the Leader Behavior of Community Education Directors in the Advisory Council Setting.* Doctor's thesis, Western Michigan University (Kalamazoo, Mich.), 1975. (*DAI* 36:3280A)

245. JACOBS, HOWARD LEE. *A Critical Evaluation of Fiedler's Contingency Model of Leadership Effectiveness in Its Application to Inter-Disciplinary Task-Groups in Public School Settings.* Doctor's thesis, Columbia University (New York, N.Y.), 1975. (*DAI* 36:4912A)

246. LEWIS, CLARICE AILEEN. *An Empirical Investigation of the Relationship Between Size, Span of Control, Leadership Behavior and Organizational Climate in the Educational Organization.* Doctor's thesis, State University of New York (Buffalo, N.Y.), 1975. (*DAI* 36:3295A)

247. NOTHEIS, JOHN ARTHUR. *The Relationship Between Ideal and Real Leader Behavior as Perceived by Secondary School Teachers and Principals in the State of South Dakota.* Doctor's thesis, University of South Dakota (Vermillion, S.D.), 1975. (*DAI* 36:3302A)

248. PALMER, WILLIAM BERRY, I. *Leadership Behavior of Community College Deans of Instruction.* Doctor's thesis, Arizona State University (Tempe, Ariz.), 1975. (*DAI* 36:3305A)

249. PARKER, BARNEY CARL. *The Relationship of Organizational Position to the Expectations and Perceptions of the Leader Behavior of Selected Superintendents.* Doctor's thesis, University of Missouri (Columbia, Mo.), 1975. (*DAI* 36:4176A)

250. REALE, LOUIS D., JR. *Relationship Between Role-Personality Conflict in Teacher-Board Negotiations and the Leadership Behavior of Elementary School Principals in the School Districts of the State of New Jersey.* Doctor's thesis, Fordham University (New York, N.Y.), 1975. (*DAI* 36:4935A)

251. SCHRIESHEIM, CHESTER A., AND STOGDILL, RALPH M. "Differences in Factor Structure Across Three Versions of the Ohio State Leadership Scales." *Personnel Psychol* 28(2):189–206 su '75. * (*PA* 55:11126)

252. SHIN, JOONG SHIK. *A Study of the Relationships Among the Principal's Leadership Style, Teachers' Need-Orientation, and the Degree of Teachers' Satisfaction With Their Principal's Job Performance.* Doctor's thesis, University of Kentucky (Lexington, Ky), 1975. (*DAI* 37:84A)

253. SIKES, JUDSON VANN. *The Relationships Between the Morale of Georgia Directors of Curriculum and Instruction and*

Leader Behavior Description Questionnaire

the Perceived Leader Behavior of Georgia School Super-intendents. Doctor's thesis, University of Georgia (Athens, Ga.), 1975. (*DAI* 36:4943A)

254. SINGE, ANTHONY LOUIS. *A Study of the Relationship Between Work Group Performance and Leader Motivation, Leader Behavior, and Situational Favorableness: An Application of the Contingency Theory of Leadership Effectiveness to Group Supervision in Multi Unit Elementary Schools.* Doctor's thesis, University of Connecticut (Storrs, Conn.), 1975. (*DAI* 35:6999A)

255. STINSON, JOHN E. AND JOHNSON, THOMAS W. "The Path-Goal Theory of Leadership: A Partial Test and Suggested Refinement." *Acad Mgmt J* 18(2):242–52 Je '75. (*PA* 55:3382)

256. WALKER, JAMES GORDON. *A Study to Determine the Relationship Between Leader Behavior and Teacher Morale in Selected Elementary Schools.* Doctor's thesis, University of Southern Mississippi (Hattiesburg, Miss.), 1975. (*DAI* 36:4951A)

257. WASHINGTON, EARL MELVIN. *The Relationship Between College Department Chairperson's Leadership Style as Perceived by Teaching Faculty and That Faculty's Feelings of Job Satisfaction.* Doctor's thesis, Western Michigan University (Kalamazoo, Mich.), 1975. (*DAI* 36:3464A)

258. WHITTEN, JOAN ELIZABETH. *Women Teachers' Perceptions Concerning Career Aspirations of the Elementary Principalship in Selected Schools in Texas.* Doctor's thesis, University of Houston (Houston, Tex.), 1975. (*DAI* 36:2566A)

259. WORTHINGTON, JO ANN. *The Leadership Behavior of Secondary School Principals as Perceived by the Principal and Other Significant Educational Leaders.* Doctor's thesis, United States International University (San Diego, Calif.), 1975. (*DAI* 36:1237A)

260. AIKEN, WILLIAM CURTIS. *The Leadership Behavior of Selected Local Directors of Vocational Education in Tennessee.* Doctor's thesis, University of Tennessee (Knoxville, Tenn.), 1976. (*DAI* 37:5074A)

261. ANGELSON, ROBERT DRYDEN. *A Study of the Psycho-Social Characteristics of Teachers and the Interpersonal Climate of a County School System.* Doctor's thesis, University of Southern Mississippi (Hattiesburg, Miss.), 1976. (*DAI* 37:1964B)

262. BAYAT, ABBASGHOLI. *The Relationship of Leadership Behavior to the Academic Achievement of Students in Public Boys High Schools in Iran.* Doctor's thesis, Columbia University (New York, N.Y.), 1976. (*DAI* 36:7758A)

263. BERNARDIN, HAROLD JOHN, JR. *The Influence of Reinforcement Orientation on the Relationship Between Supervisory Style and Effectiveness Criteria.* Doctor's thesis, Bowling Green State University (Bowling Green, Ohio), 1976. (*DAI* 37:1018B)

264. DUNAGAN, FRANCES ACKER. *A Study of the Relationship Between Nursing Education Administrative Climate and Nursing Teacher Morale as Perceived by Teachers of Nursing.* Doctor's thesis, University of Southern Mississippi (Hattiesburg, Miss.), 1976. (*DAI* 37:5479A)

265. ERICKSON, JOHN MILTON. *Selected Characteristics and Qualifications Relating to Leader Behavior of Kansas and Missouri Community College Chief Administrators as Perceived by the Chief Administrators and Their Board of Trustees.* Doctor's thesis, Kansas State University (Manhattan, Kan.), 1976. (*DAI* 37:5549A)

266. FORSTALL, LIONEL JOSEPH. *Correlates of Administrative Leader Behavior in the Open Admissions Program of the City University of New York.* Doctor's thesis, Fordham University (New York, N.Y.), 1976. (*DAI* 37:728A)

267. HODGE, JOHN WESLY. *The Relationship Between Styles of Supervision and Need Satisfaction of Two Levels of Management Employees.* Doctor's thesis, Western Michigan University (Kalamazoo, Mich.), 1976. (*DAI* 37:1987A)

268. ILGEN, DANIEL R., AND FUJII, DONALD S. An Investigation of the Validity of Leader Behavior Descriptions Obtained from Subordinates." *J Appl Psychol* 61(5):642–51 O '76. * (*PA* 57:4682)

269. KIRCHHOFF, WILLIAM JAMES. *A Comparison of Teacher Perceptions of the Leader Behavior of Principals in Operating Lutheran Elementary Schools With Principals in Recently Closed Lutheran Elementary Schools.* Doctor's thesis, Northern Illinois University (DeKalb, Ill.), 1976. (*DAI* 37:7441A)

270. MILBURN, CORINNE M. *The Relationship Between Men and Women Secondary Teachers' Perceptions of Ideal and Real Leader Behavior of the Woman Secondary Principal in Public Schools.* Doctor's thesis, University of South Dakota (Vermillion, S.D.), 1976. (*DAI* 37:6392A)

271. MILNER, EDWARD KEITH. *A Comparative Study of Leadership Behavior of Male and Female Heads of Departments of Physical Education in Major Universities and Colleges.* Doctor's thesis, University of Iowa (Iowa City, Iowa), 1976. (*DAI* 37:2722A)

272. NICOL, SANFORD FRENCH. *The Academic Dean's Leadership Behavior in Selected Two Year Colleges as Viewed by Chief Executive Officers, Faculty, and Academic Deans.* Doctor's thesis, Temple University (Philadelphia, Pa.), 1976. (*DAI* 37:78A)

273. QUINN, KATHRYN IRENE. *Self-Perceptions of Leadership*

Behaviors and Decisionmaking Orientations of Men and Women Elementary School Principals in Chicago Public Schools. Doctor's thesis, University of Illinois (Urbana, Ill.), 1976. (*DAI* 37:6199A)

274. RIKE, GALEN EDWIN. *Staff Leadership Behavior of Directors of State Library Agencies: A Study of Role Expectations and Perceived Fulfillment.* Doctor's thesis, Florida State University (Tallahassee, Fla.), 1976. (*DAI* 37:7382A)

275. SANFORD, JAY W. *Perceptions of Autonomy, Security and Prestige of Locally and Centrally Selected Inner City Principals in New York City.* Doctor's thesis, Fordham University (New York, N.Y.), 1976. (*DAI* 37:2563A)

276. SCHRIESHEIM, CHESTER A.; HOUSE, ROBERT J.; AND KERR, STEVEN. "Leader Initiating Structure: A Reconciliation of Discrepant Research Results and Some Empirical Tests." *Organiz Behav & Hum Perfor* 15(2):297–331 Ap '76. * (*PA* 56:6933)

277. SHIELDS, RICHARD LAWRENCE. *A Study of the Validity of the Educational Administrative Style Diagnosis Test.* Doctor's thesis, American University (Washington, D.C.), 1976. (*DAI* 37:1344A)

278. ADAMS, EDWARD F.; LAKER, DENNIS R.; HULIN, CHARLES L. "An Investigation of the Influence of Job Level and Functional Specialty on Job Attitudes and Perceptions." *J Appl Psychol* 62(3):335–43 Jl '77. *

279. CHARLIER, PETER JOSEPH. *A Study of the Relationship Between Selected Personal and Interpersonal Dimensions of Elementary Principals and Their Leadership Behavior.* Doctor's thesis, Temple University (Philadelphia, Pa.), 1977. (*DAI* 37:7425A)

280. GILLIGAN, ARLENE KELLETT. *Elementary School Principals' Perceived Role Performance as it Relates to Analytic Style: A Study of Administrative Effectiveness.* Doctor's thesis, Hofstra University (Hempstead, N.Y.), 1977. (*DAI* 37:6870A)

281. LEE, DENNIS M., AND ALVARES, KENNETH M. "Effects of Sex on Descriptions and Evaluations of Supervisory Behavior in a Simulated Industrial Setting." *J Appl Psychol* 62(4):405–10 Ag '77. *

ROBERT L. DIPBOYE, *Assistant Professor of Industrial and Personnel Management, The University of Tennessee, Knoxville, Tennessee.*

A large amount of literature has been generated on the topic of leadership but the most influential research conducted in this century has been the Ohio State Leadership Studies. This research had as one objective the development of an objective measure of leader behaviors and as a second objective the determination of relationships existent between leader behavior and criteria such as job satisfaction and performance. Five widely used measures of leader behavior and attitudes toward leadership have resulted from the Ohio State studies: (*a*) *Leader Behavior Description Questionnaire,* (*b*) *Leader Behavior Description Questionnaire, Form 12,* (*c*) *Supervisory Behavior Description Questionnaire,* (*d*) *Ideal Leader Behavior Description Questionnaire,* and (*e*) the *Leadership Opinion Questionnaire.* The scales under consideration in this review are the LBDQ and the LBDQ-Ideal.

The meticulous fashion in which the LBDQ was developed in the late 1940s and early 1950s provides a stellar example of how a leadership scale or any psychological instrument should be developed. As an interdisciplinary venture led by Stogdill and Coons, nine a priori dimensions of leader behavior were developed and items for each dimension were generated by staff and students at the Ohio State University (*14*). From 1,790 items, 130 were selected for a preliminary questionnaire used in a study of bomber crews in the U.S. Air Force. Factor analysis revealed four factors, with initiating structure and consideration accounting for 83 percent of the variance. The final version of the LBDQ was constructed by selecting 15 items loading on the initiating structure factor (IS) and 15 items loading on the consideration factor (CS). Ten additional items were used as buffer items. The total scale consists of 40 items and is used by members of a work group to describe their leader's behavior. A consideration score is obtained by adding the 15 items loading on this factor and is defined as "behavior indicative of friendship, mutual trust, respect, and warmth in relationship between the leader and members of the group." The initiating structure score, obtained by adding another 15 items, is said to reflect the extent to which the leader organizes and defines the "relationship between himself and the members of his group," defines the role expected of each group member, endeavors "to establish well-defined patterns of organization," and communicates "ways of getting the job done."

The manual contains information on how the scale was developed, its reliability, procedures for administration and scoring, suggestions for interpretation of scores, and some normative data. The information on procedures for scoring and administration are clear, but the manual is old (1957) and is in dire need of updating. In particular, there has been a considerable amount of information gained from research since 1957 on the reliability and validity of the instrument and this information will not be found in the manual. Also, enough research has been conducted in the intervening 20 years to provide more adequate norm groups than the 395 aircraft commanders and 64 educational administrators whose LBDQ scores are summarized in the manual.

How shall we evaluate the reliability of the LBDQ in light of the 1957 manual and subsequent research? Both the IS and CS factors have been found to have high coefficients of internal consistency (*156, 188, 224*). Also, interrater agreement appears to be sufficiently high to justify procedures stated in the manual, i.e., averaging the ratings of a workgroup to obtain a score for that workgroup's leader. Although different subordinates appear to agree in their perceptions of a leader's behavior, correlations between the workgroup's ratings of the leader and the leader's self-rating on the LBDQ have been found to be low, indicating that while subordinates can agree among themselves on what behaviors the supervisor exhibits, subordinates and the supervisor do not often agree (*156*). No information exists on the test-retest reliability of the LBDQ scales at the time this review was written that would allow conclusions regarding the stability of the initiating structure and consideration scales over time.

In at least two respects, the LBDQ appears to possess validity as a measure of leadership behavior. In terms of face validity, the items are straightforward and seem to match commonsense descriptions of leader behavior in a variety of settings. While the instrument can be used across a variety of settings, users should examine the items carefully to ensure that they "make sense" for specific work groups under consideration. There are limits to the generality of the LBDQ's use. For instance, items such as "He assigns group members to particular tasks," "schedules the work to be done," "maintains definite standards of performance," or "sees to it that group members are working up to capacity" seem appropriate for describing a supervisor in a business organization but seem inappropriate for describing the leadership of a union official, or informal group leadership. The validity of the LBDQ as correlates of job satisfaction and work group performance seem fairly good in that most studies indicate significant correlations between the LBDQ scales and both satisfaction and performance, with the correlations being of low to moderate size. Several recent reviewers suggest that the direction of the correlations varies with several situational characteristics, including the routineness of the task, subordinate expectations, and subordinate need for information (*217*). However, almost all the research has been of a concurrent variety with performance or satisfaction at a particular time correlated with leadership measured at that same time (*53*). No evidence of the ability of the LBDQ to predict satisfaction and performance measured at later periods of time has been found by this reviewer.

Leader Behavior Description Questionnaire

Although the LBDQ scales appear to be related to such criteria as satisfaction with the job and performance, there is very little evidence as to whether or not the LBDQ correlates with other leadership scales purported to measure similar dimensions of leader behavior. Also, the initiating structure and consideration scales are not independent, contrary to the intent of the creators of these scales. They are positively correlated in most situations, indicating that a leader will be evaluated similarly on both (*226*). This lack of independence raises the question of whether or not a response bias such as halo is accounting for this convergence or whether these two dimensions naturally correlate. Given the data that exist on this instrument, definite conclusions cannot be reached, but halo and other response biases do seem to threaten the valid use of the LBDQ (*224*).

The LBDQ is sometimes called the LBDQ-Real scale to distinguish it from the LBDQ-Ideal, which is identical to the real version except that respondents are instructed to "describe the behavior of your supervisor, as you think he *should* act" and to "describe what an ideal leader *ought to do* in supervising his group." The ideal form is scored in the same manner as the real form but there is no manual associated with the LBDQ-Ideal. There is little information on the reliability of the ideal scale. A leader's own attitudes toward ideal leadership have not been found to reliably predict satisfaction or performance of his or her followers. However, discrepancies between subordinate attitudes toward ideal leadership and their descriptions on the LBDQ-Real form have been found to be highly and negatively related to subordinate satisfaction (*177*).

The LBDQ (ideal and real) seem to be most useful for research purposes. These scales also would be of value as measures of training outcomes or as a means of providing feedback to supervisors participating in training programs. Their use for purposes of job selection or placement should be discouraged given the lack of data on predictive validity or test-retest stability. In comparison to the other Ohio State Leadership scales, the LBDQ-Real seems superior to the SBDQ in having fewer items in the initiating structure scale that tap authoritarian or punitive supervision, dimensions that are extraneous to initiation of structure as conceived by Stogdill and his associates. However, the LBDQ-12 seems superior to either the LBDQ or the SBDQ in that it does not confound the initiating structure scale at all with punitive or authoritarian items and it measures more dimensions of leadership than either the LBDQ or SBDQ.

In summary, the LBDQ seems to possess internally consistent scales; raters appear to agree to a sufficient degree when using the scale to describe a leader's behavior; and the IS and CS scales appear to be related to such important criteria as satisfaction, performance, and grievances. However, a lack of data prevents any conclusion with regard to the test-retest reliability of the LBDQ (real or ideal), its ability to predict satisfaction or performance over time, or its convergence with similar measures of leadership. Serious defects of the scales include a confounding of authoritarian and punitive leadership with the initiating structure scale and the limitation of the instrument to only two dimensions of leader style. For most purposes, the LBDQ-12 would seem to be preferred to the original LBDQ.

[1175]

Leader Behavior Description Questionnaire, Form 12. Supervisors; 1957–63; LBDQ-12; revision of still-in-print *Leader Behavior Description Questionnaire* with 10 additional scores; for research use only; employee ratings of a supervisor; 12 scores: representation, demand reconciliation, tolerance of uncertainty, persuasiveness, initiation of structure, tolerance of freedom, role assumption, consideration, production emphasis, predictive accuracy, integration, superior orientation; scores based upon responses of 4 to 10 raters; no norms; 1 form ('62, 6 pages); manual ('63, 15 pages); record sheet ('63, 1 page); $4 per 25 tests, cash orders postpaid; specimen set free; (20) minutes; original edition by John K. Hemphill and Alvin E. Coons; manual by Ralph M. Stogdill; current edition by Bureau of Business Research, Ohio State University; University Publication Sales, Ohio State University. *

See T2:2452 (19 references) and 7:1147 (48 references).

REFERENCES

1–48. See 7:1147.
49–67. See T2:2452; also includes a cumulative name index to the first 67 references for this test.
68. STOGDILL, RALPH M. "Validity of Leader Behavior Descriptions." *Personnel Psychol* 22(2):153–8 su '69. * (PA 44:7419)
69. AIKEN, WILBUR J.; SMITS, STANLEY J.; AND LOLLAR, DONALD J. "Leadership Behavior and Job Satisfaction in State Rehabilitation Agencies." *Personnel Psychol* 25(1):65–73 sp '72. * (PA 49:11271)
70. CHRISTENSEN, FREDERICK GEORGE. *An Analysis of the Perceived Leader Behavior of the Dean in Selected Illinois High Schools.* Doctor's thesis, Northern Illinois University (DeKalb, Ill), 1972. (DAI 33:2008A)
71. DAY, DAVID R., AND STOGDILL, RALPH M. "Leader Behavior of Male and Female Supervisors: A Comparative Study." *Personnel Psychol* 25(2):353–60 su '72. * (PA 51:4038)
72. HOUSE, ROBERT J., AND RIZZO, JOHN R. "Role Conflict

and Ambiguity as Critical Variables in a Model of Organizational Behavior." *Organiz Behav & Hum Perfor* 7(3):467–505 Je '72. * (*PA* 49:1426)

73. LUTES, RONALD D. *Personal Variables of University Faculty Members as Related to Their Perception of the Leader Behavior of an Administrator.* Doctor's thesis, Purdue University (Lafayette, Ind.), 1972. (*DAI* 33:590A)

74. MOCK, RICHARD M., JR. *A Comparison of Selected Characteristics of Effective Resident Assistants at Three Liberal Arts Colleges.* Doctor's thesis, University of Oklahoma (Norman, Okla.), 1972. (*DAI* 33:592A)

75. NICHOLSON, EVERETT W., AND NULL, ELDON J. "Personal Variables of Teachers and Their Perception of Leader Behavior of Principals." *Am Sec Ed* 2(2):31–4 Mr '72. *

76. PAPPALARDO, JOSEPH LOUIS. *Organizational Climate of Secondary Schools as a Function of Faculty Size, Existence of a Negotiation Agreement and Principal's Leader Behavior.* Doctor's thesis, Boston University (Boston, Mass.), 1972. (*DAI* 33:1377A)

77. REASER, JOEL MONROE. *The Relationship Between Official and Leader Behaviors and the Performance and Job Satisfaction of Mental Health Employees.* Doctor's thesis, Southern Illinois University (Carbondale, Ill.), 1972. (*DAI* 34:1784B)

78. SIMPSON, DOUGLAS B., AND PETERSON, RICHARD B. "Leadership Behavior, Need Satisfactions, and Role Perceptions of Labor Leaders: A Behavioral Analysis." *Personnel Psychol* 25(4):673–86 w '72. *

79. TEGARDEN, ROBERT STEPHEN. *Teacher Perception of Leadership Behavior of School Principals as Related to Their Scores on the National Teacher Examinations.* Doctor's thesis, Purdue University (Lafayette, Ind.), 1972. (*DAI* 33:541A)

80. AYDIN, MUSTAFA. *Role Expectations and Performance of Turkish Teacher Training School Principals.* Doctor's thesis, Michigan State University (East Lansing, Mich.), 1973. (*DAI* 34:5505A)

81. COLEMAN, DONALD GENE. *A Two Dimensional Theoretical Model Measuring Organizational Achievement and Congruency.* Doctor's thesis, Ball State University (Muncie, Ind.), 1973. (*DAI* 34:6290A)

82. COOPER, JUDITH LOUISE. *The Relationship Between Principal Leadership Behavior and Organizational Characteristics of Nine Selected Indiana Elementary Schools: A Case Study.* Doctor's thesis, Indiana University (Bloomington, Ind.), 1973. (*DAI* 34:7462A)

83. DUFFY, PAUL J. *Lateral Interaction Orientation: An Expanded View of Leadership.* Doctor's thesis, Southern Illinois University (Carbondale, Ill.), 1973. (*DAI* 34:4727B)

84. FIORONI, RAYMOND J. *The Relationship Between the Agreement of Perceptions of the Senior High School Educational Environment and Leadership Behavior.* Doctor's thesis, University of Pittsburgh (Pittsburgh, Pa.), 1973. (*DAI* 34:2957A)

85. HILL, JAMES W., AND HUNT, JAMES G. Chap. 4, "Managerial Level, Leadership, and Employee Need-Satisfaction," pp. 86–104. In *Current Developments in the Study of Leadership.* Edited by Edwin A. Fleishman and James G. Hunt. Carbondale, Ill.: Southern Illinois University Press, 1973. Pp. xxi, 217. *

86. HUNT, J. G.; HILL, J. W.; AND REASER, J. M. "Correlates of Leadership Behavior at Two Managerial Levels in a Mental Institution." *J Appl Social Psychol* 3(2):174–85 Ap–Je '73. * (*PA* 51:12116)

87. HUNT, J. G., AND LIEBSCHER, V. K. C. "Leadership Preference, Leadership Behavior, and Employee Satisfaction." *Organiz Behav & Hum Perfor* 9(1):59–77 F '73. * (*PA* 50:4007)

88. KATT, DONALD CURTIS. *A Study of the Leader Behavior of the College and University Presidents at Fourteen of the Four Year Units of the State University of New York as Perceived by Members of the Local College Council, Administrative Staff, Faculty and Student Body.* Doctor's thesis, State University of New York (Albany, N.Y.), 1973. (*DAI* 34:6305A)

89. KUTKAT, JAMES HENRY. *The Awareness of Reciprocity of Administrative Assessment as a Factor in the Evaluation of Superintendents' Leadership Behavior by Principals.* Doctor's thesis, University of Iowa (Iowa City, Iowa), 1973. (*DAI* 35:131A)

90. LONGSTRETH, CATHERINE ARCHIBALD. *An Analysis of the Perceptions of the Leadership Behavior of Male and Female Secondary School Principals in Florida.* Doctor's thesis, University of Miami (Coral Gables, Fla.), 1973. (*DAI* 34:2224A)

91. PODEMSKI, RICHARD STEPHEN. *Leadership Behavior, Role Conflict, and Role Ambiguity: The University Department Chairman.* Doctor's thesis, State University of New York (Buffalo, N.Y.), 1973. (*DAI* 34:2986A)

92. PRYOR, NORMAN MARSHALL. *An Investigation of the Applicability of Multidimensional Scaling to the Domain of Performance Evaluation.* Doctor's thesis, University of Tennessee (Knoxville, Tenn.), 1973. (*DAI* 34:4109B)

93. RONNING, ROLF ONDECK. *A Study of the Leadership Role Behaviors of the College Presidents at Selected Institutions of Higher Education in New York State.* Doctor's thesis, State University of New York (Albany, N.Y.), 1973. (*DAI* 34:5548A)

94. SILVER, PAULA F. *The Relationships of Integrative Complexity and Interpersonal Environment Complexity to Perceived Leadership Styles in Selected Elementary Schools.* Doctor's thesis, New York University (New York, N.Y.), 1973. (*DAI* 35:145A)

95. TEMPLER, ANDREW J. "Self-Perceived and Others-Perceived Leadership Style Using the Leader Behavior Description Questionnaire." *Personnel Psychol* 26(3):359–67 au '73. * (*PA* 53:6376)

96. WRIGHT, KIRK LUDLOW. *Leader Behavior of Utah School Administrators.* Doctor's thesis, Brigham Young University (Provo, Utah), 1973. (*DAI* 34:5561A)

97. BEADON, MARY LUMLEY. "Achievement Motivation and Leader Behavior of Physical Education Administrators." *J Can Assn Health Phys Ed & Rec* 40(4):37–41 Mr-Ap '74. *

98. BUCKIEWICZ, DIANE RIMBY. *An Analysis of Leader Behavior in the Physical Education Departments of the Community Colleges of California, Oregon and Washington.* Doctor's thesis, University of Oregon (Eugene, Ore.), 1974. (*DAI* 35:5087A)

99. BUCKIEWICZ, FRANK ANTHONY. *An Investigation of Leadership Behavior in Athletic Departments of Selected Universities and Colleges.* Doctor's thesis, University of Oregon (Eugene, Ore.), 1974. (*DAI* 35:5087A)

100. CAWLEY, RICHARD THOMAS. *Leadership Behavior of Elementary School Principals as Perceived by Their Teachers and Superordinates United States Dependents Schools, European Area.* Doctor's thesis, University of Southern California (Los Angeles, Calif.), 1974. (*DAI* 35:4063A)

101. EVANS, MARTIN G. "Extensions of a Path-Goal Theory of Motivation." *J Appl Psychol* 59(2):172–8 Ap '74. * (*PA* 52:11094)

102. GERSTENBERGER, BESSIE KEENEY. *Relation of Task and Environment in Higher Education to Administrative Leader Behavior as Reflected by Recreation Department Chairmen.* Doctor's thesis, University of Illinois (Urbana, Ill.), 1974. (*DAI* 35:7077A)

103. GRESS, DONALD HERMAN. *Participatory Leadership: Leadership Characteristics of Secondary School Principals and Their Relationship to Perceived Subordinate Participation in the Decision-Making Process.* Doctor's thesis, Iowa State University (Ames, Iowa), 1974. (*DAI* 35:6975A)

104. HEROLD, DAVID M. "Interaction of Subordinate and Leader Characteristics in Moderating the Consideration-Satisfaction Relationship." *J Appl Psychol* 59(5):649–51 O '74. * (*PA* 53:6340)

105. KELLEY, WILLIE B. *A Study of Perceived and Expected Leadership Behavior of Inner-City Elementary School Principals as Viewed by Elementary Teachers and Upper Echelon Administrators.* Doctor's thesis, Memphis State University (Memphis, Tenn.), 1974. (*DAI* 35:4918A)

106. LAIRD, ROBERT EDWIN. *The Relationship of the Leader Behavior of Principals and Teacher Morale in the Vocational Centers of Maryland.* Doctor's thesis, University of Maryland (College Park, Md.), 1974. (*DAI* 35:3589A)

107. MEBERG, KENNETH PAUL. *Leadership Behavior and Organizational Profile of Principals Perceived as Successful.* Doctor's thesis, University of Southern California (Los Angeles, Calif.), 1974. (*DAI* 35:5737A)

108. MEISTER, ELLEN HEFTY. *Relationships Between Leader Behavior and Change, as Operationalized in Career Education Institutionalization.* Doctor's thesis, University of Wisconsin (Madison, Wis.), 1974. (*DAI* 35:1391A)

109. NAGLE, GEORGE CARVILLE. *Leader Behavior of Superintendents and Morale of Principals in Small Illinois Public School Systems.* Doctor's thesis, Purdue University (Lafayette, Ind.), 1974. (*DAI* 36:648A)

110. PETTY, M. M., AND PRYOR, NORMAN M. "A Note on the Predictive Validity of Initiating Structure and Consideration in ROTC Training." *J Appl Psychol* 59(3):383–5 Je '74. * (*PA* 52:13323)

111. REMSEN, ANN T. *The Relationship Between Teachers' Perceptions of Principals' Leadership Behavior and Individualization of the Teaching-Learning Process as Implemented in the Elementary Schools.* Doctor's thesis, New York University (New York, N.Y.), 1974. (*DAI* 35:6993A)

112. SCHERLING, STEVEN ARVID. *Cognitive Personality and Leadership Behavior of Vocational Rehabilitation Agency Supervisors.* Doctor's thesis, University of Oklahoma (Norman, Okla.), 1974. (*DAI* 35:4701B)

113. SCHRIESHEIM, CHESTER, AND KERR, STEVEN. "Psychometric Properties of the Ohio State Leadership Scales." *Psychol B* 81(11):756–65 N '74. * (*PA* 53:5359)

114. SCHUG, VICTOR LEWIS. *A Study of Perceptions of the Leader Behavior of the School Superintendent in Selected Michigan School Districts With Use of the LBDG.* Doctor's thesis, Michigan State University (East Lansing, Mich.), 1974. (*DAI* 35:3363A)

115. SMITH, WILSON SEXTEX, JR. *Organizational Role, Leader Behavior and Aspects of Problem Perception in Educational Administration.* Doctor's thesis, Ohio State University (Columbus, Ohio), 1974. (*DAI* 35:2612A)

116. STOGDILL, RALPH M. *Handbook of Leadership: A Survey of Theory and Research,* pp. 142–55, passim. New York: Free Press, 1974. Pp. viii, 613. *

117. BARTOL, KATHRYN M., AND WORTMAN, MAX S., JR. "Male Versus Female Leaders: Effects on Perceived Leader Behavior and Satisfaction in a Hospital." *Personnel Psychol* 28(4):533–47 w '75. *

Leader Behavior Description Questionnaire, Form 12

118. BILLINGS, ROLLAND GERALD. *A Comparative Case Study of the Relationship Between Administrative Organizational Leadership Patterns in Two Middle Schools and the Use of Educational Learning Resources.* Doctor's thesis, Wayne State University (Detroit, Mich.), 1975. (*DAI* 36:2520A)

119. BOULWARE, WINTHROP JONES. *A Descriptive Study of the Relationships Between Teachers' Perceptions of Leadership Behavior and Principals' Self-Concept and Interpersonal Values in the Virgin Islands.* Doctor's thesis, New York University (New York, N.Y.), 1975. (*DAI* 36:4139A)

120. BRISCOE, LLOYD WILLIAM. *The Rationale and Assessment of Faculties' Perceptions of the Leadership Behavior of Black and White Urban Elementary School Administrators.* Doctor's thesis, University of Pittsburgh (Pittsburgh, Pa.), 1975. (*DAI* 36:7742A)

121. DEROSIA, VICTOR LEE. *The Relationship Between Organizational Climate and Assumed Climate Determinants at the Senior High School Level in Jefferson County, Colorado.* Doctor's thesis, University of Colorado (Boulder, Colo.), 1975. (*DAI* 36:4898A)

122. GAUTHIER, WILLIAM JOSEPH, JR. *The Relationship of Organizational Structure, Leader Behavior of the Principal and Personality Orientation of the Principal to School Management Climate.* Doctor's thesis, University of Connecticut (Storrs, Conn.), 1975. (*DAI* 35:6973A)

123. GREENE, CHARLES N. "The Reciprocal Nature of Influence Between Leader and Subordinate." *J Appl Psychol* 60(2):187–93 Ap '75. * (*PA* 54:2083)

124. HUGHES, RALPH EUGENE. *Leader Behavior, Organizational Climate, Subclimate, and Job Satisfaction: An Exploration of Their Interrelations and the Effect of Organizational Level on These Interrelations.* Doctor's thesis, University of Kentucky (Lexington, Ky.), 1975. (*DAI* 36:6190A)

125. HUNT, J. G.; OSBORN, R. N.; AND LARSON, L. L. "Upper Level Technical Orientation and First Level Leadership Within a Noncontingency and Contingency Framework." *Acad Mgmt J* 18(3):476–88 S '75. *

126. INKPEN, THOMAS D. *A Study of the Relationships Between Perceived Teacher Participation in Decision Making and Administrator Leader Behavior Machiavellianism and Risk Taking.* Doctor's thesis, State University of New York (Albany, N.Y.), 1975. (*DAI* 35:7560A)

127. KAVANAGH, MICHAEL J. "Expected Supervisory Behavior, Interpersonal Trust and Environmental Preferences: Some Relationships Based on a Dyadic Model of Leadership." *Organiz Behav & Hum Perfor* 13(1):17–30 F '75. *

128. MONIOT, SARA HAMILL. *The Relationship Between Leader Behavior, Type of Organization, and Role Conflict.* Doctor's thesis, University of North Carolina (Greensboro, N.C.), 1975. (*DAI* 36:2311A)

129. MOONEYHAN, DAVID LEON. *Interrelationships of Characteristics Which Elementary School Teachers Ascribe to Elementary School Principals.* Doctor's thesis, George Peabody College for Teachers (Nashville, Tenn.), 1975. (*DAI* 36:1959A)

130. OSBORN, R. N., AND HUNT, J. G. "Relations Between Leadership, Size, and Subordinate Satisfaction in a Voluntary Organization." *J Appl Psychol* 60(6):730–5 D '75. * (*PA* 55:5800)

131. PINKNEY, HERCULES, JR. *A Study of the Leader Behavior of the Adult Education Administration in the District of Columbia Public Schools as Perceived by Two Reference Groups.* Doctor's thesis, Virginia Polytechnic Institute and State University (Blacksburg, Va.), 1975. (*DAI* 36:2555A)

132. RADIN, JOEL JOSEPH. *The Relationships Among the Personality Needs of Male Principals, Their Perceived Leadership Styles, and the Environmental Press of Selected Elementary Schools.* Doctor's thesis, New York University (New York, N.Y.), 1975. (*DAI* 36:4180A)

133. SCHRIESHEIM, CHESTER A., AND STOGDILL, RALPH M. "Differences in Factor Structure Across Three Versions of the Ohio State Leadership Scales." *Personnel Psychol* 28(2):189–206 su '75. * (*PA* 55:11126)

134. WALDENBERGER, ROBERT WESLEY. *An Analysis of Leader Behavior, Group Interaction and Organizational Climate in Physical Education Departments of Selected Canadian Universities.* Doctor's thesis, University of Oregon (Eugene, Ore.), 1975. (*DAI* 36:5927A)

135. ANGELLOZ, ROBERT EMILE. *A Study of the Psycho-Social Characteristics of Teachers and the Interpersonal Climate of a County School System.* Doctor's thesis, University of Southern Mississippi (Hattiesburg, Miss.), 1976. (*DAI* 37:1964B)

136. APKARIAN, K. GREGORY. *Leadership Behavior of High School Principals as Perceived by Teachers and Their Principals in North Sea District, United States Dependents Schools, European Area.* Doctor's thesis, University of Southern California (Los Angeles, Calif.), 1976. (*DAI* 36:7071A)

137. BARTOL, KATHRYN M.; AND WORTMAN, MAX S., JR. "Sex Effects in Leader Behavior Self-Descriptions and Job Satisfaction." *J Psychol* 94(2):177–83 N '76. *

138. BOETTCHER, BRIAN EDWARD. *An Analysis of Superordinate and Subordinate Perceptions of Secondary Principals' Leader Behavior and Its Relationship to Principals Collective Bargaining Units.* Doctor's thesis, University of Minnesota (Minneapolis, Minn.), 1976. (*DAI* 37:7422A)

139. COX, EDWARD PHILLIP. *The Degree of Congruence of Elementary Principals' Self-Perceptions and Teachers' Perceptions of Principals' Leadership Behavior.* Doctor's thesis, Northern Illinois University (DeKalb, Ill.), 1976. (*DAI* 37:1900A)

140. DAVENPORT, IRVIN WARREN. *Analysis of the Perceived Leader Behavior of Male and Female Elementary School Principals.* Doctor's thesis, University of Missouri (Columbia, Mo.), 1976. (*DAI* 37:5476A)

141. DEINES, JOSEPH M. *The Teacher's Perceived Value to the System as a Factor in the Evaluation of Principals' Leadership Behavior.* Doctor's thesis, University of Iowa (Iowa City, Iowa), 1976. (*DAI* 37:2530A)

142. DRAGON, ANDREA CLAIRE. *Self-Descriptions and Subordinate Descriptions of the Leader Behavior of Library Administrators.* Doctor's thesis, University of Minnesota (Minneapolis, Minn.), 1976. (*DAI* 37:7380A)

143. DURAND, DOUGLAS E., AND NORD, WALTER R. "Perceived Leader Behavior as a Function of Personality Characteristics of Supervisors and Subordinates." *Acad Mgmt J* 19(3):427–38 S '76. *

144. EPSTEIN, MAURRY HART. *Relationships Between Interpersonal Relations Orientations and Leader Behavior of Canadian Community College Administrative Leaders.* Doctor's thesis, George Peabody College for Teachers (Nashville, Tenn.), 1976. (*DAI* 37:1905A)

145. GIBBON, JOHN. *The Relationship Between the Leadership Style of Principals and the Organizational Climate in Secondary Schools in the Republic of South Africa.* Doctor's thesis, University of Virginia (Charlottesville, Va.), 1976. (*DAI* 37:1907A)

146. HALL, KIRBY DALE. *Leadership Style, Perceived Leader Behavior and Job Function Emphases of Secondary School Principals.* Doctor's thesis, Ohio State University (Athens, Ohio), 1976. (*DAI* 37:4742A)

147. HEDRICK, STANLEY HARRIS. *Leadership Behavior and Organizational Climate as Related to Department Chairpersons.* Doctor's thesis, University of Maryland (College Park, Md.), 1976. (*DAI* 37:3500A)

148. HSIEH, WEN-CHYUAN. *A Comparative Study of Relationships Between Principals' Leadership Style and Teachers' Job Satisfaction in the Republic of China and the State of Iowa in the United States.* Doctor's thesis, University of Iowa (Iowa City, Iowa), 1976. (*DAI* 37:2540A)

149. JACKSON, THOMAS EARL. *The Leadership Behavior and Role Expectations of Elementary School Principals as Perceived by Elementary School Secretaries, Building Representatives, and Principals.* Doctor's thesis, University of Michigan (Ann Arbor, Mich.), 1976. (*DAI* 37:3303A)

150. KEANE, FRANCIS JOSEPH. *The Relationship of Sex, Teacher Leadership Style, Teacher Leader Behavior in Teacher Student Interaction.* Doctor's thesis, Boston University (Boston, Mass.), 1976. (*DAI* 37:1497A)

151. KEENER, BARBARA JEAN. *An Analysis of the Perceptions of the Leadership Behavior of Male and Female University of Florida Administrators.* Doctor's thesis, University of Florida (Gainesville, Fla.), 1976. (*DAI* 37:4023A)

152. KORFHAGE, MARY MARGARETHA. *An Examination of the Leader Behavior of Chairpersons of Academic Departments in High and Low Paradigm Disciplines.* Doctor's thesis, Ohio State University (Columbus, Ohio), 1976. (*DAI* 37:4897A)

153. LAIRD, ROBERT, AND LUETKEMEYER, JOSEPH F. "The Relationship Between the Leader Behavior of Principals and Teacher Morale in the Vocational Centers of Maryland." *J Indus Teach Ed* 13(3):74–81 sp '76. *

154. LARSON, L. L.; HUNT, J. G.; AND OSBORN, R. N. "The Great Hi-Hi Leader Behavior Myth: A Lesson From Occam's Razor." *Acad Mgmt J* 19(4):628–41 D '76. *

155. MCCAMEY, WADE BYRON. *The Relationship Between Selected Factors of Leadership Behavior and Selected Factors of Teacher and Principal Self Concepts.* Doctor's thesis, East Tennessee State University (Commerce, Tenn.), 1976. (*DAI* 37:4031A)

156. MCCARTY, JIMMY LOUIS. *A Descriptive Study of Selected Faculty Members' Perceptions of Leader Behavior in Two Types of Virginia Institutions of Higher Education.* Doctor's thesis, Virginia Polytechnic Institute and State University (Charlottesville, Va.), 1976. (*DAI* 37:2551A)

157. MEAD, NEHEMIAH. *The Leadership Behavior of Jamaican High School Principals: Perceptions and Expectations of Teachers and Principals.* Doctor's thesis, Andrews University (Berrien Springs, Mich.), 1976. (*DAI* 37:7448A)

158. MOHAN, HOWARD DAVID. *Descriptive Analysis of the Leadership Behavior of Department Chairmen and Departmental Effectiveness in Industrial Teacher Education.* Doctor's thesis, Ohio State University (Columbus, Ohio), 1976. (*DAI* 37:2691A)

159. PRUITT, PEGGY JANE. *Perceived Leader Behavior of Male and Female Intercollegiate Athletic Directors in the United States.* Doctor's thesis, University of Illinois (Urbana, Ill.), 1976. (*DAI* 37:6199A)

160. SCHRIESHEIM, CHESTER A.; HOUSE, ROBERT J.; AND KERR, STEVEN. "Leader Initiating Structure: A Reconciliation of Discrepant Research Results and Some Empirical Tests." *Organiz Behav & Hum Perfor* 15(2):297–331 Ap '76. * (*PA* 56:6933)

161. SCHRIESHEIM, CHESTER A., AND MURPHY, CHARLES J. "Relationships Between Leader Behavior and Subordinate Satisfaction and Performance: A Test of Some Situational Moderators." *J Appl Psychol* 61(5):634–41 O '76. *

162. STAMM, RICHARD LeROY. *An Evaluation of the Leadership Role of Commanders of Battalion Sized Units as Perceived by Superiors, a Commander Self-Evaluation, and Subordinate Officers.* Doctor's thesis, Kansas State University (Manhattan, Kan.), 1976. (*DAI* 37:5457A)

163. STEVENS, DIXON GRANT. *The Leader Behavior of Selected New York State Community College Presidents as Perceived by Trustees, Administrators, and Faculty Leaders.* Doctor's thesis, State University of New York (Albany, N.Y.), 1976. (*DAI* 37:6230A)

164. SZILAGYI, ANDREW D., AND KELLER, ROBERT T. "A Comparative Investigation of the Supervisory Behavior Description Questionnaire (SBDQ) and the Revised Leader Behavior Description Questionnaire (LBDQ-Form XII)." *Acad Mgmt J* 19(4):642–9 D '76. *

165. TEPPER, LEON. *The Relationship Between District Negotiations on the Perceived Leader Behavior of the Principal and Teacher Representative in Selected New York State High Schools.* Doctor's thesis, Hofstra University (Hempstead, N.Y.), 1976. (*DAI* 37:2572A)

166. WEED, STAN E.; MITCHELL, TERENCE R.; AND MOFFITT, WELDON. "Leadership Style, Subordinate Personality, and Task Type as Predictors of Performance and Satisfaction With Supervision." *J Appl Psychol* 61(1):58–66 F '76. * (*PA* 55:11180)

167. WORTMAN, RANDY J. *Leadership Behavior of Secondary School Assistant Principals.* Doctor's thesis, Indiana University (Bloomington, Ind.), 1976. (*DAI* 37:4774A)

168. YUNKER, GARY W. AND HUNT, J. G. "An Empirical Comparison of the Michigan Four-Factor and Ohio State LBDQ Leadership Scales." *Organiz Behav & Hum Perfor* 17(1):45–65 O '76. * (*PA* 57:4778)

ROBERT L. DIPBOYE, *Assistant Professor of Industrial and Personnel Management, The University of Tennessee, Knoxville, Tennessee.*

Form 12 of the *Leadership Behavior Description Questionnaire* grew out of the original Ohio State research on the *Leadership Behavior Description Questionnaire* and the *Supervisory Behavior Description Questionnaire*. One major difference between the LBDQ-12 and the latter two instruments is that the LBDQ-12 measures twelve dimensions of leadership, while the LBDQ and SBDQ measure only two dimensions, initiation of structure and consideration. The twelve dimensions are listed in the entry above.

The manual contains information on the development of the instrument, definitions of the 12 factors, and keys for manual scoring. Also, the means, standard deviations, and internal consistency of each of the 12 scales are presented for nine different samples of leaders occupying high levels of authority (e.g., corporate presidents, labor union presidents, college presidents, senators). There are no other norms. Helpful instructions on administering the LBDQ-12 are provided in the manual, but there is very little information that would be of assistance to the user in interpreting the scores and providing feedback to participants.

Evidence exists to support the internal consistency, inter-rater reliability, and the test-retest reliability of several of the LBDQ-12

scales. The manual presents internal consistency coefficients that range from .38 to .91. Most of these coefficients are in the .70s and .80s, demonstrating reasonably good internal consistency. Stogdill reports a study of inter-rater reliability in which the scales with the highest degrees of inter-rater agreement were demand reconciliation, tolerance of uncertainty, persuasiveness, role retention, predictive accuracy, and influence with superiors. Those with the lowest inter-rater agreement were representation, tolerance of freedom, and integration (*116*). Greene reports test-retest reliability coefficients of between .57 and .72 for the initiation of structure scale and between .71 and .79 for the consideration scale (*123*).

Is the LBDQ-12 a valid measure of the leadership behaviors the authors of the scales claim to measure? One can approach this question by examining several facets of validity, including the item content, the correlation of the scales with external criteria, the ability to predict these criteria over time, and the correlation of the scales with other scales purported to measure similar dimensions of leader behavior. The content of the items contained in the initiation of structure scale is similar to the items contained in the structure scale of the LBDQ and SBDQ. However, an important difference, that renders the LBDQ-12 structure scale more content valid, is the elimination of items found in the LBDQ and SBDQ pertaining to authoritarian and punitive leadership (e.g., "He rules with an iron hand"). Other scales which seem to contain adequate samples of leader *behaviors* are the representation, tolerance for uncertainty, tolerance of freedom, role assumption, consideration, and production emphasis scales. However, the remaining scales sample what would be more appropriately called outcomes of leadership rather than descriptions of leader behaviors. For instance, the persuasion factor contains mostly items pertaining to whether or not the leader is persuasive (e.g., "His arguments are convincing," "He is a very persuasive talker," "He argues persuasively for his point of view," "He is very skillful in an argument") rather than how the leader goes about attempting to persuade others (sells, tells, listens, uses or does not use group discussion). The integration factor contains items pertaining to whether or not the leader achieves harmony

("He keeps the group working together as a team," "He settles conflicts when they occur in the group," "He sees to it that the work of the group is coordinated") rather than how the leader maintains harmony and resolves conflicts (smoothing over, confronting differences, forcing solutions to conflicts). Such scales are likely to be perceived as evaluations rather than descriptions and do not provide very rich detail on how the leader achieves important objectives or influences subordinates. Although leader behavior has been found to change with the situation, with individual subordinates, and with time, these leadership scales purport to measure a stable, recurring trait of leadership by averaging across subordinates and time, and ignoring individual subordinates or tasks. In this sense, all the Ohio State Leadership scales (SBDQ, LBDQ, and LBDQ-12) are inconsistent with the current trend of examining leader behavior and effectiveness as dependent on the situation.

There is very little evidence to support or deny the validity of the LBDQ-12 scales as psychological constructs. It has been found that raters can distinguish between actor performances on the consideration, structure, representation, tolerance of freedom, production emphasis, and superior orientation factors (68). Also, factor analyses of the LBDQ-12 scales have revealed factors that correspond closely to most of the twelve scales (116). Finally, one study found that the LBDQ-12 consideration, production emphasis, and structure scales were highly and positively correlated with the support, goal emphasis, and work facilitation scales of the Michigan Four-Factor Theory Questionnaire (168). However, all the scales were highly correlated, rather than just those scales measuring similar dimensions, suggesting that there was considerable halo error in both instruments. In this same study, the LBDQ-12 scales were found to predict satisfaction better and to have cleaner factor structures than the Michigan scales.

The LBDQ-12 initiation of structure and consideration are the most commonly used scales and have been found to correlate significantly with satisfaction and performance, although the direction of these correlations varies with situational differences. Stogdill (116) has reported evidence that the other ten dimensions also are related to member satisfaction and group performance. However, most of the research is of a concurrent nature, measuring criteria and leadership at the same point in time. Greene (123) has reported the only longitudinal study published as of this review, a study in which the LBDQ-12 was used to predict job satisfaction and performance. A causal analysis of his data suggests that consideration predicts and causes subordinate satisfaction but not performance. On the other hand, subordinate performance seemed to influence changes in initiation of structure and consideration but not vice versa. Also, an emphasis on structure by a leader seemed to cause higher performance only when the leader was high in consideration.

In summary, the LBDQ-12 would seem to possess reasonably good internal consistency, across all the twelve scales, high inter-rater agreement for some of the scales, and moderately high stability on the consideration and structure scales. The LBDQ-12 appears to possess concurrent validity in that its scales have been found to correlate with the external criteria of job satisfaction and performance and are capable of distinguishing between persons displaying behaviors corresponding to the dimensions. The instrument appears to be the best of the Ohio State Leadership Scales in that it provides a multifaceted measure of leader behaviors and traits and provides measures of initiation of structure and consideration that are unconfounded with punitive leadership items. Its best use would be as a research instrument, *not* as an instrument for personnel evaluation, selection, or placement. The LBDQ-12 also would appear to be an excellent basis for a multivariate evaluation of leadership training programs. However, the lack of norms lessens its value as an instrument that could be used in a training program to provide feedback to participants on their leadership styles.

[1176]

Leadership Evaluation and Development Scale. Prospective supervisors; 1964–65; LEADS; 1 form; 2 parts: casebook ('64, 11 pages), question booklet ('64, 8 pages); preliminary manual ('65, 4 pages); $17.50 per kit of 2 casebooks, 25 question booklets, scoring stencil, and manual; $7.50 per 10 casebooks; $22.50 per 50 question booklets; $3.50 per specimen set; postage extra; [40–50] minutes; Harley W. Mowry (question booklet and casebook, from materials prepared by the Armstrong Cork Company); Psychological Services, Inc. *

For a review by Cecil A. Gibb, see 7:1148 (1 reference).

WALTER C. BORMAN, *Executive Vice President and Director of Research, Personnel Decisions Research Institute, Minneapolis, Minnesota.*

LEADS is a test that purports to measure supervisory ability. It was designed to aid in promotion decisions related to supervisor positions. Very little data are available to suggest that it accomplishes this worthwhile goal.

LEADS consists of a casebook containing eight short vignettes about situations in which some kind of supervisory actions are or should be taken. Forty-four multiple choice questions require respondents to select what they consider the "best" action. The eight cases are easy to read and to understand—the required reading level is fifth or sixth grade. The cases seem realistic enough; they all involve unionized "shop" type settings, and the focus is on a first line, foreman kind of leadership rather than middle-level or higher management.

LEADS was developed primarily with the use of item analysis techniques on 150 multiple choice questions about 13 cases. The final form should be internally reliable because only items correlating significantly with the total test score were retained. Also, performance ratings of incumbent supervisors were used as criteria against which to correlate item responses. Items with low validities were eliminated.

The "Preliminary Manual" reports a split-half reliability of .81, using 113 manufacturing supervisors as a sample. With the same supervisors as a sample, LEADS correlated .36 with an objective performance criterion, while LOQ structure and consideration scores correlated only −.07 and .13, respectively, with the same criterion. LEADS did relate moderately to a verbal comprehension measure (.49). Still, this evidence is definitely favorable with respect to the practical validity of LEADS. Unfortunately, no other studies of the final form of LEADS were available to the reviewer. Thus, we are left not knowing how consistently successful LEADS might be in predicting supervisory success; and we are not even very informed about *what* LEADS is measuring, i.e., what kind of leadership ability or what type of supervisory knowledge or skills? For example, compare what we know about consideration and initiating structure as measured by the LOQ

with what is available to describe the kind of leadership ability measured by LEADS. At very least, more validity evidence is required before getting too excited over the use of LEADS as an indication of leadership potential.

It should also be pointed out that LEADS appears to be a "knowledge" rather than an "ability" test. Item content suggests that knowledge of generally approved supervisory practices would help considerably in scoring well on LEADS. Thus, the test may be less appropriate as a promotion tool than it is as an indicator of training needs or as a criterion of training success.

Also apparent is the possible discrepancy between what a respondent reports he/she *would* or *should* do and what the respondent might *actually do* in each of these situations. This potential difficulty is certainly not unique to LEADS, and it should not be interpreted as a severe criticism. Management assessment centers, for example, suffer the same potential conceptual problem. However, we should be aware of possible differences between what respondents say they will do and what they are likely to actually do in practice.

In summary, LEADS is easy to administer and score; the cases and questions seem realistic enough and, therefore, the test has some face validity. Available reliability and concurrent validity data are good, though more validity data are necessary before we know the stability of these results and the conditions under which we can and cannot expect to obtain useful validities. As a "knowledge test," LEADS might be most appropriately used to measure training needs and training progress.

FRANK J. LANDY, *Associate Professor of Psychology, The Pennsylvania State University, University Park, Pennsylvania.*

The *Leadership Evaluation and Development Scale* has been available commercially for 13 years. This is a sufficient period of time to determine its utility in either research or applied settings. Based on that criterion, the LEADS has failed completely to develop a reasonable reputation. The manual is entitled "Preliminary Manual." This implies that a "Final Manual" will eventually appear. The fact that no such final manual has appeared in 13 years, and that the one validity study on which that preliminary

Leadership Evaluation and Development Scale

manual was based remains the *only* validity study tells us either that further research on the scale was disappointing or that the scale failed to generate the enthusiasm or confidence necessary to assure its further use. In light of the absence of validity information and technical documentation beyond the most basic of pilot studies, the author's claim for its utility as a selection device is inappropriate.

In the manual, there is a section dealing with the rationale and development of the instrument. In that section, there is an implicit comparison made between LEADS and more traditional self-report inventories like the *Leadership Opinion Questionnaire*. The manual states that traditional supervisory "test items do not include enough background information to allow the examinee to come to a good conclusion." The manual suggests that a series of problems with multiple questions related to each problem is a better format for a supervisory test. There is simply no evidence to support such a claim. Nevertheless, for mangagement development sessions, as opposed to selection decisions, LEADS does provide a more useful vehicle for discussion than the LOQ or other similar devices which are not oriented around contextually based problems. This point was made by Gibb in an earlier MMY review (7:1148). But anyone working with management development groups, particularly in the area of leadership and supervision, should be capable of constructing problems just as real and more locally relevant than those in the casebook.

A more devastating criticism of the LEADS is the nature of the score obtained. There is no discussion of its meaning or interpretation. Its correlations with other measures provide little information. One might be tempted to guess that it is a measure of verbal comprehension rather than a more dynamic interpersonal construct.

In summary, the absence of technical and conceptual information about the nature of the LEADS suggests that it not be used either for selection decisions of any kind or as an exercise in assessment centers. Its use as a training tool or management development tool is also questionable on a cost/benefit basis.

[1177]

Leadership Opinion Questionnaire. Supervisors and prospective supervisors; 1960–69; LOQ; attitudes of supervisors toward ideal supervisory behavior; 2 scores: consideration, structure; 1 form ('60, 4 pages, self-marking); revised manual ('69, 15 pages); tape cassette available for administration; $11.70 per 25 tests; $15 per tape cassette; 82¢ per manual; $1.82 per specimen set; postage extra; (15–20) minutes; Edwin A. Fleishman; Science Research Associates, Inc. *

See T2:2454 (15 references); for a review by Cecil A. Gibb, see 7:1149 (41 references); for reviews by Jerome E. Doppelt and Wayne K. Kirchner, see 6:1190 (6 references).

REFERENCES

1–6. See 6:1190.
7–47. See 7:1149.
48–62. See T2:2454; also includes a cumulative name index to the first 62 references and 3 reviews for this test.
63. MILLER, DELBERT C. *Handbook of Research Design and Social Measurement, Second Edition*, pp. 303–7. New York: David McKay Co., Inc., 1970. Pp. xv, 432. *
64. HARRELL, THOMAS W. "Differences Between Men in Big and Small Business." *Personnel Psychol* 24(4):649–52 w '71. * (PA 51:4020)
65. ASHOUR, AHMED SAKR, AND ENGLAND, GEORGE. "Subordinate's Assigned Level of Discretion as a Function of Leader's Personality and Situational Variables." *J Appl Psychol* 56(2):120–3 Ap '72. * (PA 48:7991)
66. CUMMINS, ROBERT C. "Leader-Member Relations as a Moderator of the Effects of Leader Behavior and Attitude." *Personnel Psychol* 25(4):655–60 w '72. *
67. HAND, HERBERT H., AND SLOCUM, JOHN W., JR. "A Longitudinal Study of the Effects of a Human Relations Training Program on Managerial Effectiveness." *J Appl Psychol* 56(5):412–7 O '72. * (PA 50:8074)
68. HARRELL, THOMAS W. "High Earning MBA's." *Personnel Psychol* 25(3):523–30 au '72. * (PA 51:2013)
69. LEFKOWITZ, JOEL. "Evaluation of a Supervisory Training Program for Police Sergeants." *Personnel Psychol* 25(1):95–106 sp '72. * (PA 49:12160)
70. SIEGEL, JACOB P. "'Organizational' and 'Individual' Correlates of Leadership Attitudes." *Studies Personnel Psychol* 4(1):43–55 sp '72. * (PA 49:10179)
71. WEISSENBERG, PETER, AND KAVANAGH, MICHAEL J. "The Independence of Initiating Structure and Consideration: A Review of the Evidence." *Personnel Psychol* 25(1):119–30 sp '72. * (PA 49:12191)
72. FINNESSY, JOHN AUSTIN. *The Relationship Between Selected Personality Traits and Leadership Expectations of the Follower.* Doctor's thesis, Indiana University (Bloomington, Ind.), 1973. (DAI 33:6004A)
73. FLEISHMAN, EDWIN A. Chap. 1, "Twenty Years of Consideration and Structure," pp. 1–40. In *Current Developments in the Study of Leadership.* Edited by Edwin A. Fleishman and James G. Hunt. Carbondale, Ill.: Southern Illinois University Press, 1973. Pp. xxi, 217. *
74. HAND, HERBERT H.; RICHARDS, MAX D.; AND SLOCUM, JOHN W., JR. "Organizational Climate and the Effectiveness of a Human Relations Program." *Acad Mgmt J* 16(2):185–95 Je '73. * (PA 51:4052)
75. HARRELL, THOMAS W., AND HARRELL, MARGARET S. "The Personality of MBA's Who Reach General Management Early." *Personnel Psychol* 26(1):127–34 sp '73. * (PA 51:2012)
76. JOYNER, BETTY C. *The Influence of Instruction in Organizational Behavior on Some Aspects of Leadership Role Perception.* Doctor's thesis, Louisiana Tech University (Ruston, La.), 1973. (DAI 33:6519A)
77. NEWBY, JOHN HENRY, JR. *An Assessment of the Relationship Between Racial Perceptions and Patterns of Leadership Behavior Among Black and White Army Company Commanders.* Doctor's thesis, Catholic University of America (Washington, D.C.), 1973. (DAI 34:1366A)
78. ROSEN, RONALD. *Empathy and Opinions of Leadership Characteristics Between Selected Groups of Educators.* Doctor's thesis, State University of New York (Albany, N.Y.), 1973. (DAI 34:1553A)
79. TUCKER, BERNARD MARTIN. *Consideration, Initiating Structure and Leadership in Industry.* Doctor's thesis, Georgia State University (Atlanta, Ga.), 1973. (DAI 34:2839A)
80. WILLIAMS, AUDREY YVONNE. *An Analysis of the Relationship of Connecticut State Community College Central Administrators' Leadership Styles to Their Opinions of the Black Tradition in Higher Education.* Doctor's thesis, University of Connecticut (Storrs, Conn.), 1973. (DAI 34:6339A)
81. ADAMS, EDDIE RAY. *Effects of a Performance Oriented Institute on Vocational Education Directors in Missouri.* Doctor's thesis, University of Missouri (Columbia, Mo.), 1974. (DAI 36:2165A)
82. ANSTEY, JOHN ROBERT. *A Comparison of Chief Executive Leadership Styles and Personal Values With His Orientation Concerning the Firm's Social Responsibility in Air*

and Water Pollution. Doctor's thesis, University of Arkansas (Fayetteville, Ark.), 1974. (*DAI* 35:6298A)

83. ARVEY, RICHARD D., AND NEEL, C. WARREN. "Moderating Effects of Employee Expectancies on the Relationship Between Leadership Consideration and Job Performance of Engineers." *J Voc Behav* 4(2):213–22 Ap '74. * (*PA* 52: 11135)

84. BADIN, IRWIN J. "Some Moderator Influences on Relationships Between Consideration, Initiating Structure, and Organizational Criteria." *J Appl Psychol* 59(3):380–2 Je '74. * (*PA* 53:13335)

85. BEATTY, RICHARD W. "Supervisory Behavior Related to Job Success of Hard-Core Unemployed Over a Two-Year Period." *J Appl Psychol* 59(1):38–42 F '74. * (*PA* 52:4157)

86. DOWNS, CAL W. "The Impact of Laboratory Training on Leadership Orientation, Values, and Self-Image." *Speech Teach* 23(3):197–205 S '74. *

87. HARTLEY, GORDON EUGENE. *A Comparison of Baccalaureate and Associate Degree Nursing Students on Selected Personality Characteristics.* Doctor's thesis, Washington State University (Pullman, Wash.), 1974. (*DAI* 35:4963B)

88. HSU, CHRIS CHING-YANG, AND NEWTON, RICHARD R. "Relation Between Foremen's Leadership Attitudes and the Skill Level of Their Work Groups." *J Appl Psychol* 59(6): 771–2 D '74. * (*PA* 53:8496)

89. HUNT, PETER JAMES. *Women Supervisors: A Study of Their Performance and the Group Interaction in a Simulated Organization.* Doctor's thesis, University of Akron (Akron, Ohio), 1974. (*DAI* 35:1437B)

90. KERR, STEVEN, AND SCHRIESHEIM, CHESTER. "Consideration, Initiating Structure, and Organization Criteria— An Update of Korman's 1966 Review." *Personnel Psychol* 27(4):555–68 w '74. * (*PA* 55:1673)

91. LEFKOWITZ, JOEL. "Job Attitudes of Police: Overall Description and Demographic Correlates." *J Voc Behav* 5(2): 221–30 O '74. * (*PA* 53:6346)

92. MAUER, K. F. "The Utility of the Leadership Opinion Questionnaire in the South African Mining Industry." *J Behav Sci* (South Africa) 2(2):67–72 '74. * (*PA* 55:3375)

93. PALMER, WALTER J. "Management Effectiveness as a Function of Personality Traits of the Manager." *Personnel Psychol* 27(2):283–95 su '74. * (*PA* 54:4372)

94. PETTY, M. M., AND PRYOR, NORMAN M. "A Note on the Predictive Validity of Initiating Structure and Consideration in ROTC Training." *J Appl Psychol* 59(3):383–5 Je '74. * (*PA* 52:13323)

95. PURSLEY, ROBERT D. "Leadership and Community Identification Attitudes Among Two Categories of Police Chiefs: An Exploratory Inquiry." *J Police Sci & Adm* 2(4):414–22 D '74. * (*PA* 54:12736)

96. SCHERLING, STEVEN ARVID. *Cognitive Personality and Leadership Behavior of Vocational Rehabilitation Agency Supervisors.* Doctor's thesis, University of Oklahoma (Norman, Okla.), 1974. (*DAI* 35:4701B)

97. SCHLACK, MARILYN JOYCE. *A Comparison of Personal Characteristics and Leadership Styles of University Upper Management and Middle-Management Women Student Personnel Administrators.* Doctor's thesis, Western Michigan University (Kalamazoo, Mich.), 1974. (*DAI* 35:852A)

98. SCHMOOK, JAMES RAYMOND. *Effects of Race Relations Training on Leadership Attitudes of U.S. Navy Personnel.* Doctor's thesis, United States International University (San Diego, Calif.), 1974. (*DAI* 35:1443B)

99. SCHRIESHEIM, CHESTER, AND KERR, STEVEN. "Psychometric Properties of the Ohio State Leadership Scales." *Psychol B* 81(11):756–65 N '74. * (*PA* 53:5359)

100. SMITH, MARSHALL WAYNE. *The Use of an Autotelic Simulation Game to Teach Selected Concepts of Administrative Behavior.* Doctor's thesis, University of Alabama (University, Ala.), 1974. (*DAI* 35:7000A)

101. BOWMAN, BILLY RANDAL. *A Comparison of Self-Perceived Leadership Styles of Elementary Principals With Self-Perceived Leadership Styles in Problems Situations in Selected Texas Public Elementary Schools.* Doctor's thesis, Texas A & M University (College Station, Tex.), 1975. (*DAI* 36:4888A)

102. CAMP, JAMES HOWARD. *An Analysis of Leader Behavior Attitudes of Adult Basic Education Directors in the North Carolina Community College System.* Doctor's thesis, North Carolina State University (Raleigh, N.C.), 1975. (*DAI* 36: 4958A)

103. DIMARCO, NICHOLAS, AND WHITSITT, SUSAN E. "A Comparison of Female Supervisors in Business and Government Organizations." *J Voc Behav* 6(2):185–96 Ap '75. * (*PA* 54:2080)

104. DIMARCO, NICHOLAS; KUEHL, CHARLES; AND WIMS, EARL. "Leadership Style and Interpersonal Need Orientation as Moderators of Changes in Leadership Dimension Scores." *Personnel Psychol* 28(2):207–13 su '75. * (*PA* 55:11141)

105. HUDDLESTON, THOMAS JOE. *The Relationship Between Organizational Climate, Leadership Behavior, and Reciprocal Communication in Selected Missouri Elementary Schools.* Doctor's thesis, St. Louis University (St. Louis, Mo.), 1975. (*DAI* 36:3298A)

106. KRASNOW, BERNARD STEPHEN. *A Study of the Relationship Between Teacher Expected Ideal Leader Behavior of*

Elementary School Principals in New York State and Selected Situational Variables. Doctor's thesis, New York University (New York, N.Y.), 1975. (*DAI* 36:7783A)

107. KUEHL, CHARLES R.; DIMARCO, NICHOLAS; AND WIMS, EARL W. "Leadership Orientation as a Function of Interpersonal Need Structure." *J Appl Psychol* 60(1):143–5 F '75. * (*PA* 53:12727)

108. SPAUTZ, MICHAEL E. "A New Scale for Theories X and Y." *Austral J Psychol* 27(2):127–41 Ag '75. *

109. TEMPLETON, ROBERT MICHAEL. *The Leadership Vector Model: A Possible Method for Depicting Leadership Effectiveness in Organizations.* Doctor's thesis, United States International University (San Diego, Calif.), 1975. (*DAI* 36: 3110B)

110. CARPENO, LINDA. *Expectations of Male/Female Leadership Styles in an Educational Setting.* Doctor's thesis, Boston University (Boston, Mass.), 1976. (*DAI* 37:1482B)

111. HODGE, JOHN WESLY. *The Relationship Between Styles of Supervision and Need Satisfaction of Two Levels of Management Employees.* Doctor's thesis, Western Michigan University (Kalamazoo, Mich.), 1976. (*DAI* 37:1987A)

112. HOOK, JERRY MASON. *The Effects of Participation in a Collaborative Supervision Project on Student Teachers' and Cooperating Teachers' Attitudes Toward Leadership.* Doctor's thesis, University of Tennessee (Knoxville, Tenn.), 1976. (*DAI* 37:737A)

113. SCHRIESHEIM, CHESTER A.; HOUSE, ROBERT J.; AND KERR, STEVEN. "Leader Initiating Structure: A Reconciliation of Discrepant Research Results and Some Empirical Tests." *Organiz Behav & Hum Perfor* 15(2):297–331 Ap '76. * (*PA* 56:6933)

114. SUMRALL, CHARLOTTE CLAUDIA HERMANN. *A Study of the Relationship Between the Leadership Behavior of Instructional Supervisors and the Job Satisfaction of Teachers in Texas.* Doctor's thesis, University of Houston (Houston, Tex.), 1976. (*DAI* 37:2571)

[1178]

★**Management Relations Survey.** Managers; 1970; ratings by employees; 4 scores: exposure and feedback scores in each of 2 areas (your manager's practices, your practices with management); 1 form (7 pages, with 8 concealed pages for self-marking and scoring); manual (4 pages); $3 per test, postage extra; [15–30] minutes; Jay Hall; Teleometrics Int'l. *

REFERENCES

1. HALL, JAY. "Interpersonal Style and the Communication Dilemma: 2, Utility of the Johari Awareness Model for the Genotypic Diagnoses." *Hum Relations* (England) 28(8): 715–36 O '75. * (*PA* 55:7071)

WALTER C. BORMAN, *Executive Vice President and Director of Research, Personnel Decisions Research Institute, Minneapolis, Minnesota.*

The *Management Relations Survey* contains two 20-item inventories, the first of which asks the respondent to consider 20 different situations and for each situation to indicate the characteristic way that his/her boss would act. A probablistic framework is introduced by directing the respondent to divide five points between the two alternatives—e.g., 4–1, 2–3, etc. Here is an example item: "If in a discussion with me the conversation began to drift toward a subject about which my manager should be knowledgeable, but which in reality he was totally ignorant about, he would: (A) Try to steer the conversation in a different direction, lest his expertise be called into question, or (B) Confess his ignorance, whatever my reactions, and encourage continuation of the conversation."

The second part of the survey contains situations very similar to those appearing in the first part and requires the respondent to indicate how *he* or *she* would act in these interactions with the boss.

The responses are machine scored and returned in the form of a graphic "johari window" display. Essentially, this display indicates where a person stands on two dimensions of interpersonal style, "feedback" and "exposure." Scores on the two dimensions reveal the extent to which the person is Type A, B, C, or D, each type being defined in a four-page interpretation manual. As the interpretation manual states, the manager is to complete the MRS, focusing on how he/she see his/her own interpersonal style while the subordinate completes the MRS with the manager as the focal person and completes it again for him or herself. Then the two are to get together and have a discussion and critique, out of which supposedly can emerge a "stronger and more meaningful interpersonal relationship."

The goal of the MRS, then, is to foster improved and more effective interpersonal relationships between individuals who work together in organizations. The MRS is one of a number of instruments Hall and his colleagues suggest using in programs to diagnose communication and interpersonal relationship problems between bosses and subordinates and to deal with other problems related to organizational effectiveness. Hall writes that "one need not be a pro to use the materials but certainly the amount of mileage obtained may be enhanced by trainer skills."

How about research support for the effectiveness of the MRS? Hall claims in his sales catalog that the instruments he markets have at least a .65 test-retest reliability and the construct validity studies have been conducted usually by correlating scores on his inventory with scores on "related personality inventories." Hall also offers as research support data showing essentially that the higher the level of management, the higher the mean scores on each of the MRS dimensions. In addition, one of Hall's studies indicated that subordinates tend to adopt a "style" similar to their boss in terms of the MRS's interpersonal process model. And finally, Hall demonstrated that members of different organizational "types" score differently on the MRS.

I find this research on such a learning aid to be very commendable. Hall is obviously interested in selling a high quality product, one that possesses some of the positive psychometric properties usually required of psychological tests. The only problem I have with the kind of research support for the MRS offered by Hall and his colleagues is that it doesn't go far enough. To me, the critical dependent variable of interest here is organizational effectiveness. That is, the program associated with the MRS should have some positive impact on organizational or unit effectiveness—the organization's performance, the satisfaction of its members, etc. The utility of the "johari window" model in general, or the MRS program in particular, finally depends upon the degree to which organizational effectiveness is enhanced or improved by its application. This kind of research is seldom performed on instruments or programs designed to upgrade individuals' and organizations' effectiveness; so, given the "norms" in this area, Hall cannot be faulted for this lack. It would be helpful, however, to know more about the MRS's validity in terms of the criteria that really count.

Thus, if you are a manager, an in-house personnel type, or a consultant, if you deal with boss-subordinate interpersonal conflicts, and if you like the "johari window" concept for explaining individuals' interpersonal style, the MRS will probably be useful to you. The MRS seems easy to complete, the scores are fed back in an impressive package, and the interpretation manual explaining the scores is quite clear. The program seems down-to-earth enough for managers to accept and Hall has extensive norms to help give meaning to scores respondents receive. All of these points are positive ones. On the other hand, if you dislike the "johari window" concept or if you prefer some other model of interpersonal interaction, you might prefer some other "learning aid." The MRS has apparently been used by many organizations, some indication that it at least doesn't impact *negatively* on an organization or its members. And, as mentioned previously, the research on the instrument is commendable. Still, an important question that wasn't answered to my satisfaction is: To what extent is organizational effectiveness actually improved by the MRS and its accompanying program?

[1179]

★**Management Style Diagnosis Test, Second Edition.** Managers; 1965–75; MSDT; manager's perception of own managerial style; 8 managerial style scores (deserter, missionary, autocrat, compromiser, bureaucrat, developer, benevolent autocrat, executive) based upon combinations of dichotomized task orientation, relationships orientation, and effectiveness scores plus a style synthesis score (average of last 3 scores); no data on reliability and validity; 1 form ('72, 8 pages plus 6 pages of scoring directions); manual ('74, 6 pages); user's guide ('75, 1 page); style indicator ('70, 6 pages); Can $30 per 10 tests and user's guide; $10 per 10 style indicators; $10 per 10 manuals; $10 per specimen set; cash orders postpaid; (30–60) minutes; W. J. Reddin; Organizational Tests Ltd. [Canada]. *

REFERENCES

1. REDDIN, WILLIAM J. Chap. 19, "The Management-Style-Diagnosis Test," pp. 237–50. In his *Managerial Effectiveness.* New York: McGraw-Hill Book Co., Inc., 1970. Pp. xiv, 352. *
2. EDGINTON, CHRISTOPHER ROY. *A Study of the Relationships Between Management Style and Propensity for Risk-Taking Among Leisure Services Personnel.* Doctor's thesis, University of Iowa (Iowa City, Iowa), 1975. (*DAI* 36: 8292A)
3. DEPAUL, FRANK JOSEPH. *A Study of the Perceived Leadership Styles of Principals in ESEA Title I and Non Title I Elementary Schools in Chicago.* Doctor's thesis, University of Illinois (Urbana, Ill.), 1975. (*DAI* 36:5677A)
4. BECK, JACQUELINE BOLDEN. *Relationships Between Personality Type and Managerial Style of Leadership Personnel in Nursing.* Doctor's thesis, University of Florida (Gainesville, Fla.), 1976. (*DAI* 37:4988B)
5. SCHWARTZ, M. M.; ARANOFF, A.; AND REYNOLDS, W. F. "Responses of Middle Managers to Case Studies Under Conditions of Homogeneous and Heterogeneous Stylistic Grouping." *Psychol Rep* 38(3, pt 1):819–24 Je '76. *

ABRAHAM K. KORMAN, *Professor of Psychology, Baruch College, The City University of New York, New York, New York.*

It has now been about 16 years since this reviewer finished his doctoral training at that "dustbowl of empiricism," the University of Minnesota, and if somebody had told me then that I would be reviewing published tests toward the end of the 1970s that would fail on virtually every test guideline, I would have argued vehemently. After all, such guidelines have long been available; they have been accepted at least on a formal level by the psychological establishment, and they are not all that hard to meet.

Why, then, do we have tests like these in 1978? Descriptively, we have here a 64-item forced-choice measure based on the author's 3-D theory of management behavior, which generates scores along three dimensions: (*a*) task orientation—the extent to which the manager influences his subordinates toward task attainment; (*b*) relationships orientation—the extent to which the manager trusts his sub-

ordinates, respects their ideas, and has considerate and warm relationships with them; and (*c*) effectiveness—the extent to which the manager achieves the goals of his position. These dimensions are then combined to enable the respondent to be classified along each of a number of managerial styles: executive, developer, bureaucrat, benevolent autocrat, missionary, compromiser, deserter, and autocrat. The first four of these are defined as "more-effective" styles and the latter four as "less-effective." The respondents can be classified according to their most dominant styles, a synthesis of their styles, and their style profiles as well as their supporting styles.

For none of these scores or interpretations is there the slightest validity or justification. A number of descriptive studies with small samples are reported in the manual, but they provide no evidence, whatsoever, for construct validity for either the dimension scores or for the stylistic interpretation suggestions. Nor is there any recognition of the statistical and methodological problems in suggesting profile interpretations. To illustrate, there is no evidence presented as to the supposed greater effectiveness of the developer, executive, bureaucrat, and benevolent autocrat styles; there is no evidence presented as to the reliability of classification into any of the styles; there is no evidence presented as to the value of the different interpretations offered; and there is no recognition in the slightest of the questionable or, at best, contingent values of the initiating structure and consideration constructs as far as performance is concerned. Also, there is nothing that reflects the work of Mischel concerning the variability of personality and attitudinal constructs over time. Mischel's work is of significant importance to anyone who proposes to classify an individual along noncognitive dimensions.

Let me summarize my opinions about this measure in as succinct terms as possible. I would not use it; I do not recommend that anybody else use it; and I would hope that it would be withdrawn from the market as soon as possible, both for the benefit of the author and of the testing profession. *If* adequate validity data are ever developed, *if* convincing support is ever offered for the different types of interpretation, and *if* satisfactory reliability of the measure over time is ever established, it should come back on the market. But not until then !

[1180]

★**Management Transactions Audit.** Managers; 1973; MTA; manager's views as to how he would handle 18 specific complaints, challenges, and uncertainties on the part of subordinates, colleagues, and superiors; 3 transaction scores (parent subsystem, adult subsystem, child subsystem) and 2 tension indexes (disruptive, constructive) for each of 3 relationships (subordinates, colleagues, superiors); no data on reliability and validity; no norms; 1 form (9 pages plus 12 foldout scoring pages); no manual; score interpretation (11 pages); $3 per test, postage extra; [15–30] minutes; Jay Hall and C. Leo Griffith; Teleometrics Int'l. *

STEPHAN J. MOTOWIDLO, *Research Psychologist, Personnel Decisions Research Institute, Minneapolis, Minnesota.*

The *Management Transactions Audit* was designed for use as a learning aid in management training programs. The MTA's developers recommend that the instrument be completed by trainees before the training session, that one part of training include a presentation of theoretical material—in this case, presumably, principles of transactional analysis as spelled out by Berne, Harris, and others—and that trainees then score their own MTA's, interpret results, and discuss them with the trainer and others. Couched largely in the language of transactional analysis, the MTA yields scores which, one is told, reflect the following about an individual's interpersonal style: magnitude of "parent" component (judgmental, directive, and paternalistic tendencies), magnitude of "adult" component (rational, data-oriented tendencies), magnitude of "child" component (spontaneous, manipulative, self-pitying tendencies), potential for "disruptive tension" in interpersonal transactions (roughly, tendency toward inappropriate transactional patterns), and potential for "constructive tension" (tendency to change transactions to more appropriate patterns). These five scores are computed three times—in relation to transactions with subordinates, colleagues, and superiors. The three sets of parent, adult, and child scores are interpreted against norms from 848 management and supervisory personnel in a variety of organizations.

There seems to be no systematic evidence whatsoever about the reliability or validity of this instrument. There is no manual. Rather, the MTA is described sketchily in a promotional brochure with scoring and general interpretational guidance provided in the instrument itself and in a brief accompanying pamphlet. The promotional brochure is misleading where it implies that the MTA and other instruments marketed by the same firm possess adequate test-retest reliability. In fact, according to a letter from a representative of the firm, written in response to my request for information about the MTA, there is "no test-retest reliability data at this time." Also, there seems to be no systematic evidence that (*a*) that MTA scores reflect stable or reliable differences in individuals, (*b*) that MTA scores actually measure the constructs they purport to measure, (*c*) that MTA scores are associated with important behavioral patterns related to managerial or supervisory effectiveness, or (*d*) that managers or supervisors become more effective following training experiences because of knowledge or discussion about their MTA scores.

Because notions springing from transactional analysis likely have considerable intuitive appeal for laypersons, they may readily and uncritically accept MTA scores as accurate and valid assessments of their interpersonal styles. This sort of "face validity," however, without evidence of either empirical, content, or construct validity, gives rise to the dangerous possibility that laypersons who complete this instrument and interpret their scores may come to believe things about themselves that may not, in fact, be true. For these reasons, the MTA is not recommended as a feedback tool in training programs. Because there is no evidence that MTA scores are significantly related either to personal or work-related effectiveness, it is also not recommended for use as a tool for making decisions about individuals that may have important implications for human or economic consequences.

RONALD N. TAYLOR, *Associate Professor of Commerce and Business Administration, The University of British Columbia, Vancouver, British Columbia.*

Based on the popular transactional analysis (TA) theory of Eric Berne, the *Management Transactions Audit* purports to measure interpersonal transactions of managers in their relationships with subordinates, colleagues, and superiors. Fifty-four hypothetical statements attributed to either subordinates, colleagues, or superiors are presented to the subject who is asked to distribute five points among three responses to show how the subject would respond to these statements. Responses are scored as indicative of parent, adult, or child styles of interpersonal transactions. No time limit is prescribed for the instrument.

The instrument may be useful for illustrating the TA theory to participants in management development programs, but it appears that even in that limited context the instrument would be more misleading than helpful. Normative data are derived from 848 managers and supervisors in a variety of organizations, but this is the extent of psychometric data reported for the instrument. No information is provided to inform the user of item analyses used for selecting items, assigning items to scales, weighting of items or responses in deriving scale scores, reliability, or validity. Failure to report even the most rudimentary psychometric data makes the instrument unsuitable for assessment purposes.

Since the instrument is essentially an unknown quantity, the authors are urged to adhere to the principles of the APA-AERA-NCME *Standards for Educational and Psychological Tests* by informing potential users of the limitations of the instrument. Until much more is known about the psychometric properties of the MTA and appropriate reliability and validity information can be reported in a test manual, the use of the instrument for other than experimental purposes is definitely premature and in violation of the APA-AERA-NCME standards.

[1181]

★Managerial Philosophies Scale. Managers; 1975; MPS; "manager's assumptions and working theories about the nature of those whose activities he or she coordinates"; 2 scores: theory X (reductive management beliefs), theory Y (developmental management beliefs) ; no data on reliability and validity ; 1 form (5 pages plus 3 foldout scoring pages) ; no manual ; score interpretation (7 pages) ; $3 per test, postage extra; statistical data free on request; [15-30] minutes; Jacob Jacoby and James R. Terborg; Teleometrics Int'l. *

[1182]

★Managerial Style Questionnaire. Managers (of other managers or professional personnel) and subordinates; 1974; MSQ; "extent of goal use"; self-ratings or ratings by subordinates; 9 item scores (38

Management Transactions Audit

additional items are used in computing the 9 item scores) in 7 areas: controlling (2 scores), co-ordinating, motivating (2 scores), appraisal, compensation, personnel selection, training and developing, plus total; reliability and validity data available only in *1* below; no reliability and validity data or norms for ratings by subordinates; separate forms for managers, subordinates, ('74, 4 pages, both forms have identical items) ; no manual; mimeographed information and norms sheets ['74, 3 pages] ; hand scoring not recommended ("calculations are quite complex and should be computerized") ; $17.50 per 25 tests ; $50 per copy of Fortran computer program and scoring instructions; postage extra; specimen set not available; [10-20] minutes; Bruce A. Kirchhoff; the Author. *

REFERENCES

1. KIRCHHOFF, BRUCE A. "A Diagnostic Tool for Management by Objectives." *Personnel Psychol* 28(3):351–64 au '75. * (*PA* 56:6915)

FRANK L. SCHMIDT, *Personnel Research Psychologist, United States Civil Service Commission, Washington, D.C.*

The *Managerial Style Questionnaire* is one of the rash of new instruments emanating from the current ferment in the field of "organizational behavior." The focus of this instrument is on the management-by-objectives (MBO) technique. The stated purpose is to measure the extent to which MBO is actually being used in individual organizations. Indicators such as the presence of an MBO training program may be highly misleading. The author purports to derive the MSQ from his theory that MBO operates through three intervening variables: (*a*) Goal adequacy: the setting of appropriate goals; (*b*) Goal use: actual use of the goals; (*c*) Subordinate involvement in goal setting and use. Inexplicably, his purpose is to measure only goal use. No explanation is given for the neglect of the other two variables. A statement is made that goal use has never been measured, but there is no implication that the other two variables have been.

The intervening variables are apparently intended as individual differences dimensions (and this is how the MSQ is scored) but the avowed purpose of the instrument is the measurement of organizations, not individuals. Organizational differences are not the same as individual differences. This is the first of a number of conceptual confusions. All items require the respondent to rate the importance of the stated technique on a four-point scale. Item 16, for example, reads, "Meetings with subordinates to discuss and set objectives for their jobs." Why this keyed item (along with certain other similar items) measures "goal use" but not subordinate involvement "in processes of formulating and using goals" is not clear.

No information is given on how the items were evaluated or selected. The author reports that 18 managers, when presented with a list of the 11 keyed items and another list which was "a random selection of non-key items," were able in interviews to detect the goal-using theme in the former list. This fact is given as evidence that the instrument has "content validity."

SCORING. There are eight blocks of items with 4 to 7 items per block. The items in each block refer to a different managerial function, e.g., planning, appraisal, etc. Each block contains from 1 to 3 keyed items. The author provides, in addition to raw scores, a procedure for computing a standardized score for each keyed item based on the individual's mean and standard deviation for the items in that block. The standardized summary score is the sum of these scores across blocks. Kirchhoff feels that individual (and organizational) differences in level of response are due to undefined biases and that it is the *relative* importance of goal use and other procedures that matters. However, no rationale for this assumption is provided (although speculative *ex post facto* arguments based on scores of individual organizations are presented later).

RELIABILITY. Test-retest reliabilities for 40 middle managers from the same company over a 14-day period were .72 for total raw score and .62 for the standardized summary score. These reliabilities are relevant to the measurement of individuals. Reliabilities for organizations should be higher, since each organization's score would be the mean across its managers. However, the author once again fails to distinguish between the two measurement purposes. Internal consistency reliabilities are not reported, nor are correlations between Form M (self-description by managers) and Form S (subordinate description of managers).

VALIDITY. For various reasons, including structural restraints within organizations, the author postulates that goal use will be essentially uncorrelated across the eight management functions. Later, using reasoning that seems quite blurred, he hypothesizes that if individuals from different organizations are pooled, goal use will be positively correlated across management functions. He then shows that identically worded items (goal use and filler items) correlate well across blocks, while items different in meaning do not, and offers these findings as evidence of construct validity. He argues that identical items in different blocks are "different" measures of the same trait, and that the above findings therefore represent multi-trait, multi-method matrix validation for his instrument. Obviously, this claim is highly dubious.

The results of a factor analysis are also offered in support of the MSQ's construct validity. Although the factor analytic methods used were not ideal, the author did find that all but one of the 11 keyed items loaded highest on the second factor. (None of the other factors were interpreted.)

Two additional studies are cited as construct validity evidence. In the first, the author used four criteria (e.g., a policy requirement of goal setting) to classify 14 organizations as high or low on "goal adequacy." The mean MSQ score in the "high" group was higher on raw total scores and on standardized summary scores. In the second study, it was found that MSQ scores increased among managers in two organizations receiving MBO training. In the organization which modified management systems to be consistent with the MBO training, scores remained high two years after the original survey. In the other organization, scores declined to almost original levels after only 12 months. These two studies are supportive of the instrument, but they must be interpreted with caution: in studies of this sort, the organization, not the individual, is the unit of analysis. Thus the two studies are based on Ns of 11 and 2, respectively. Significance tests used by the author are mistakenly based on use of the individual respondent as the unit of analysis.

Obviously, the *Managerial Style Questionnaire* is less than ideal. How does it compare to other instruments designed to measure the variables with which research on management by objectives is concerned? This reviewer could locate only two competing instruments. The first is the Task-Goal Attribute Questionnaire [1] which purports to measure five dimensions of work goals: (a) employee participation in goal setting, (b) feedback on goal effort, (c) peer competition for goal attainment, (d) goal diffi-

---

[1] STEERS, ROBERT M. "Factors Affecting Job Attitudes in a Goal-Setting Environment." *Acad Mgmt J* 19(1):6–16 Mr '76. *

culty, (e) goal specificity. The second scale [2] has not been given a title. It is designed to assess only two dimensions: "Goal Clarity/Planning" and "Participation in Goal Setting." Although each of these scales appears to be based on a clearer, more plausible rationale than the MSQ, there is little evidence available on which to evaluate either. Thus, at the present time, there is little basis for an intelligent choice among competing scales of this type. But since goal setting and use in work environments is currently a popular research area, we can probably look forward to improvements in the future.

[1183]

★Personnel Relations Survey. Managers; 1967; 6 scores: exposure and feedback scores for each of 3 relationships (with colleagues, employees, and supervisors); no data on reliability and validity; 1 form (9 pages, with 12 concealed pages for self-marking and scoring); manual (6 pages); $3 per test, postage extra; [15–30] minutes; Jay Hall and Martha S. Williams; Teleometrics Int'l. *

REFERENCES
1. HALL, JAY. "Communication Revisited." Calif Mgmt R 15(3):56–67 sp '73. *
2. HALL, JAY. "Interpersonal Style and the Communication Dilemma: 2, Utility of the Johari Awareness Model for the Genotypic Diagnoses." Hum Relations (England) 28(8):715–36 O '75. * (PA 55:7071)
3. HALL, JAY. "To Achieve or Not: The Manager's Choice." Calif Mgmt R 18(4):5–18 su '76. *

ROBERT M. GUION, Professor of Psychology, Bowling Green State University, Bowling Green, Ohio.

The background of the test is the heuristic model of interpersonal relations called the "Johari window," a two-by-two, four-panel design representing information that is known (or unknown) to oneself and to others. Each panel has its own designation. Relevant information known both to self and the other is termed the "arena" of interpersonal communication. Information known by oneself but not by the other is one's "facade," while information known to the other but not to oneself is one's "blind spot." The fourth panel is "unknown." The larger the "arena" relative to the other three panels, the more desirable and effective is the interpersonal relationship. The size of the arena may be increased by two processes: "Exposure" of feelings, ideas, and other information and "Feedback," the "active solicitation by the self of information he feels others might have which

he does not"—the feelings, ideas, and other information to gain from the other or the other group.

The Personnel Relations Survey is based on these notions. It attempts to measure the exposure and feedback processes of a manager in three different kinds of interpersonal relationships, using the same questions (with only necessary changes in wording to designate the nature of the "other") for each group.

The concealed pages make possible immediate self-scoring. Normative data for both scales, exposure and feedback, are provided for in each of the three relationship categories. One may use raw scores or percentiles to draw his own "windows" for each of these three kinds of relationships. According to the insert, one ideally scores at the 80th percentile on both exposure and feedback. The basic concept is the size and shape of the arena: the larger and the more nearly square, the better.

The test is interesting in both format and in the self-scoring mechanisms. Each item is a brief statement of a problem with two alternatives for dealing with (or avoiding) that problem. Instead of choosing one over the other, the respondent allocates five points, in any desired combination, to the two options.

The senior author of the test has reported a number of research studies from which one may infer that the test has at least some construct validity; that is, it behaves in multivariate studies pretty much as he has predicted. Nevertheless, psychometric information of the sort one ordinarily expects to find in a test manual is both sparse and scattered. The "manual" offers only a description of the rationale and points one should consider in interpreting his scores. It gives no technical information at all on such matters as reliability, validity, sources of norms, sources of items, item analyses, developmental revisions, and the like.

So far as can be determined from research reports, reliabilities of the scales are modest. The only reliability report gives the average of the six reliability coefficients estimated from the scores of a group of 64 students (a small and inappropriate sample) retested after a six-week interval. That average is an unimpressive .71. No evidence of internal consistency, no item statistics, no intercorrelations among scales have been published. The theory seems based

[2] ARVEY, RICHARD D.; DEWHIRST, H. DUDLEY; AND DULING, JOHN C. "Relationships Between Goal Clarity, Participation in Goal Setting, and Personality Characteristics on Job Satisfaction in a Scientific Organization." J Appl Psychol 61(1):103–5 F '76. *

on orthogonal exposure and feedback dimensions, so at the very least there should be information showing whether the intercorrelations among these scales in the three sets of relationships are small relative to their own reliabilities. It seems unfortunate that such information is lacking when it could so easily be developed from normative data already available.

Normative data seem extensive enough, although the standardization sample is homogeneous only in that each person is male and in a management position. Management levels and functions, types of organizations, ages, and geographical locations vary widely. If any of these is associated with score variance (and management level certainly is), interpretations of one's score relative to others in like situations are not possible.

Although construct validity may be inferred indirectly from the existing research on hy potheses suggested by the theory, direct studies of validity would be preferable. Some old-fashioned criterion-related validity studies seem literally demanded by the basic concepts: Is it true that people high on an exposure scale do in fact communicate more effectively? Is it true that effectiveness of communication is a joint function of both exposure and feedback—a function that includes not only the two scores themselves but also a measure of their similarity? Research directly confronting these questions might permit validity inferences to be based as much on practical strength of relationships as on mere statistical significance.

Such information, even that which is already available, has not been assembled into a technical manual; the reason, it seems, is that the test is intended for use as a learning aid rather than as a tool for decisions. This is not a satisfactory reason. The user of a test for training purposes has a right to know what it is supposed to measure, what evidence exists that it does so, and how reliably it measures something. Otherwise, a trainer might as well write his own training aids, or borrow them from Sunday supplements.

The test clearly is better than this. It is a pity that evidence of its worth has not been more fully developed and assembled for psychometrically sophisticated users.

[1184]

The RAD Scales. Supervisors; 1957; RAD; experimental; self-ratings of perceived degrees of responsibility, authority, and delegation of authority; 3 scores: responsibility, authority, delegation; no norms; 1 form ('57, 4 pages); manual ['57, 7 pages]; $2 per 25 tests, cash orders postpaid; specimen set free; (5) minutes; Ralph M. Stogdill; University Publications Sales, Ohio State University. *

See T2:2457 (5 references) and 7:1150 (20 references).

REFERENCES

1–20. See 7:1150.
21–25. See T2:2457; also includes a cumulative name index to the first 25 references for this test.
26. HEMPHILL, JOHN K. "Leadership Behavior Associated With the Administrative Reputation of College Departments." *J Ed Psychol* 46:385–401 N '55. * (PA 31:3837)
27. MCCLAIN, BENJAMIN RICHARD. *Authority Relations in Bi-Racial High Schools: A Comparative Study.* Doctor's thesis, University of Michigan (Ann Arbor, Mich.), 1972. (DAI 33:4746A)
28. ARÉVALO, RODOLFO. *A Comparative Study of Mexican American and Anglo-American School Administrators' Perceptions of Responsibility, Authority and Delegation.* Doctor's thesis, University of Michigan (Ann Arbor, Mich.), 1973. (DAI 34:4595A)
29. MITCHELL, BOBBY MACK, SR. *Analysis of the Perceptions of the Role of the Subordinate and Super-Ordinate With Respect to Authority, Responsibility, and Delegation in the Community Schools of Flint at the Attendance Center Level.* Doctor's thesis, Michigan State University (East Lansing, Mich.), 1973. (DAI 34:2927A)
30. RIFKIND, LESLIE J. "Responsibility, Authority, and Delegation of Authority Scales," pp. 287–90. In *Measuring Human Behavior.* Edited by Dale G. Lake and others. New York: Teachers College Press, 1973. Pp. xviii, 422. *
31. STOGDILL, RALPH M. *Handbook of Leadership: A Survey of Theory and Research,* pp. 347–53. New York: Free Press, 1974. Pp. viii, 613. *

MICHAEL J. KAVANAGH, *Associate Professor of Organizational Behavior, State University of New York at Binghamton, Binghamton, New York.*

The RAD scales have been available for the past 20 years. However, little empirical work beyond the initial development has been done. This is quite unfortunate, since effective measurement of responsibility, authority, and delegation (as well as the related concept of power) would be most useful in the study of leadership and organizational functioning. These constructs are often invoked as explanatory concepts, both in research and practice, but they are rarely measured.

The RAD scales contain 48 items in six scales. There are two scales for each variable, and the scales are self-administered. The instructions require the respondent to "*double check* ($\vee\vee$) the single statement which most accurately describes your status and practices in carrying out your duties, and *check* ($\vee$) the next most descriptive statement" in each scale. Three scores are then computed from item scale values and a simple formula in the manual. These scores are assumed to measure perceived degrees of responsibility, authority, and delegation for the respondent. The format and instructions for the scales are well done and unambiguous. The scoring instructions are quite simple and could be easily adapted to computer scoring.

The manual was published in 1957 and has not been revised since then. The 7th MMY and TIP II list 25 references for the RAD scales. None of these are cited in the manual, including 12 studies published mostly by the Ohio State group from 1948–56. The manual clearly needs revision, but it does emphasize the strong and weak points of the scales. The strengths and weaknesses of the scales will be only briefly covered; interested readers are urged to obtain a copy of the manual bearing in mind its lack of revision.

The assigned scale values were carefully derived from several different studies. Items were selected with small dispersion values and in order to represent the full perceptual continuum for each scale. Split-half reliabilities in eight studies range from .60 to .88 (median .72) for responsibility, .28 to .82 (median .72) for authority, and .39 to .90 (median .78) for delegation. Test-retest reliabilities from one study are not quite as high—only .62, .55, and .73, respectively. As the author points out, the changing nature of organizational life may affect over-time consistency. These reliabilities are generally acceptable. However, due to the wide range of internal consistency reliabilities for authority and delegation, it would be wise for users to compute this index on their samples.

The author states that "No claims are made for the validity of the RAD scales." One study is cited that found for the responsibility scale fairly good agreement (.65 and .71) between self-descriptions by administrators and how they were perceived by their juniors and seniors. However, the correlations for authority and delegation in this study were low—correlations of .22 and .33 for authority and .28 and .39 for delegation.

Another weakness of the RAD scales is that there are no norms. A table of average scores for 29 different military officers for the three variables is included in the manual. Although this table cannot be used as norm data, it can be used for rough comparisons, depending on the needs of the user.

The manual states that "The RAD scales were developed for experimental purposes" and "should be used with caution by the practitioner." It seems obvious that the scales should not be used as diagnostic devices for applied purposes such as identification of organizational problems or training needs. However, based on good initial development work, the RAD scales could be used in some organizational development work. For example, if a change agent has established honest and open rapport with a vertical work team, the RAD scales could be used to investigate any problems concerned with authority, responsibility, or delegation relationships within the group. The RAD scales can be used by researchers concerned with investigating the three variables or related ones, such as power and power relationships in organizations, but users must be aware of the psychometric limitations of the scales. Researchers should be particularly aware of the weaknesses of the scales in terms of validity.

It appears the RAD scales cannot be used as advertised in the manual. Since no significant changes have been made in the manual since it was published in 1957, it is not a very good source for evaluating the scales. Although Stogdill (31) reports on additional research using the scales, there are not consistent results that would support the validity of the scales. Along with the widely ranging reliabilities, this questionable validity severely limits the use of the RAD scales at the individual level. As implied, however, it seems the scales would be appropriate for group measurement.

[1185]
★[Styles of Leadership and Management.] Views regarding leadership (a) or managerial (b) practices in 12 situations; 2 tests (same items except for first and third person expression); each test yields 5 scores (philosophy, planning and goal setting, implementation, evaluation, total) for each of 5 leadership (a) or managerial (b) styles (based on varying degrees of concern for people vs. concern for production); no data on reliability and validity; no manual; $3 per test, postage extra; [15–30] minutes per test; Jay Hall, Martha S. Williams (a1, b), and Jerry B. Harvey (b); Teleometrics Int'l. *
a) LEADERSHIP. Leaders, others; 1968–71; no norms.
  1) Styles of Leadership Survey. Leaders; 1968; SLS; leader's views of his own leadership practices and philosophy; 1 form (9 pages); score interpretation (4 pages).
  2) Leadership Appraisal Survey. Others; 1971; LAS; views of the practices and philosophy of one's leader; 1 form (8 pages); score interpretation (2 pages).
b) MANAGEMENT. Managers, employees; 1964–73.
  1) Styles of Management Inventory. Managers; 1964–73; SMI; manager's views of his own man-

agerial practices and attitudes; 1 form ('73, 9 pages); score interpretation ('73, 7 pages).

2) *Management Appraisal Survey.* Employees; 1967–73; MAS; employee's views on the managerial practices and attitudes of his superior; 1 form ('73, 8 pages); score interpretation ('73, 4 pages).

REFERENCES

1. GAROVE, WILLIAM EDWARD, JR., AND HANDLEY, EDWARD EUGENE. *The Effect of a Five-Day Simulation Training Experience in Reality-Based Simulation on Selected Management Behavior of Superintendents of Institutions for the Mentally Retarded.* Doctor's thesis, University of Pittsburgh (Pittsburgh, Pa.), 1972. (*DAI* 34:191A)
2. HALL, JAY. "Communication Revisited." *Calif Mgmt R* 15(3):56–67 sp '73. *
3. VIANO, EMILIO CESARE. *Styles of Management of Probation Administrators: A Methodological and Exploratory Study.* Doctor's thesis, New York University (New York, N.Y.), 1973. (*DAI* 34:3575A)
4. HALL, JAY. "Interpersonal Style and the Communication Dilemma: 1, Managerial Implications of the Johari Awareness Model." *Hum Relations* (England) 27(4):381–99 Ap '74. * (*PA* 54:4367)
5. HINOJOSA, THOMAS RODOLFO, JR. *The Influence of Idiographic Variables on Leadership Style: A Study of Special Education Administrators (Plan A) in Texas.* Doctor's thesis, University of Texas (Austin, Tex.), 1974. (*DAI* 35:2082A)
6. ALEXANDER, ROBERT. *A Study of Administrative Styles as Perceived by Principals of Selected Schools in Northeastern Ohio.* Doctor's thesis, University of Pittsburgh (Pittsburgh, Pa.), 1975. (*DAI* 36:7754A)
7. DUFFEE, DAVID. *Correctional Policy and Prison Organization,* pp. 136–54. New York: John Wiley & Sons, 1975. Pp. xiv, 232.
8. STINE, JOHN CARLTON. *A Study of Perceptions of the Relationship Between the Organizational Climate of Elementary Schools and Managerial Styles of Their Principals.* Doctor's thesis, University of Pittsburgh (Pittsburgh, Pa.), 1975. (*DAI* 36:4187A)

ABRAHAM K. KORMAN, *Professor of Psychology, Baruch College, The City University of New York, New York, New York.*

These are, supposedly, two pairs of instruments involving, in each case, a self-report instrument and an appraisal by others along similar dimensions. The underlying theory is the Blake-Mouton "grid" approach. It is proposed that scores should be used in providing diagnostic feedback to the leader (manager) for growth and development purposes.

I will be brief and to the point. So far as I could tell, there is absolutely no reason in the world why anyone would use any of these scales. To begin with the most minor point, the only substantive difference I could see between the scales was that one pair refers specifically to managers while the other refers to leaders in general. Everything else is similar, even the wording of what passes for the test manuals, except that in the leadership scales the word "purpose" is substituted for "production"! Considering the similarity of scales and items, were two pairs of instruments necessary?

Of more significant import is the poor psychometric justification for the instruments. Norms are provided for all instruments except the *Leadership Appraisal Survey,* but these are

poorly identified with no subgroup breakdowns according to age, occupation, etc. The information that the management instruments discriminate between low-, middle-, and high-achieving managers and between 13 organizational types, and that they have a test-retest correlation of .75, is provided not in the test manual but in a typed note, without sample sizes, occupational descriptions, criteria, etc., given. As unimpressive as this is, the data for the leadership instruments are even less impressive. No data are provided for the *Leadership Appraisal Survey* while a typed note reports that the *Styles of Leadership Survey* is affected by the number of people supervised, age and rank of the leader, and occupational and organizational type; however, no particulars are provided as to sample sizes, occupational groups, etc. That is it; there is nothing else.

Would I use the instruments? No! A statement in the catalogue that these are not "tests" but "learning aids" is not a legitimate explanation for the inadequacy of these instruments. Elsewhere in the catalogue they are called "tests"; they are sold as measuring instruments; the catalogue makes unsubstantiated claims for item-criteria correlational analysis and recommends them for use in self and other evaluation. The requirements for test rigor hold here, regardless of the author's claims! I do not know how many years it will take to get these types of measures off the market, but the process should begin.

[1186]

★**Supervisory Behavior Description.** Supervisors; 1970–72; SBD; ratings by subordinates; 2 scores: consideration, structure; 1 form ('70, 4 pages); manual ('72, 15 pages); scoring instructions/key ['72, 2 pages]; $9.50 per 25 tests; $3.50 per manual; $4 per specimen set; cash orders postpaid; (15–20) minutes; Edwin A. Fleishman; Management Research Institute. *

REFERENCES

1. FLEISHMAN, EDWIN A. "The Description of Supervisory Behavior." *J Appl Psychol* 37:1–6 F '53. * (*PA* 28:1635)
2. FLEISHMAN, EDWIN A. "Leadership Climate, Human Relations Training, and Supervisory Behavior." *Personnel Psychol* 6:205–22 su '53. * (*PA* 27:3376)
3. HARRIS, EDWIN F., AND FLEISHMAN, EDWIN A. "Human Relations Training and the Stability of Leadership Patterns." *J Appl Psychol* 39:20–5 F '55. * (*PA* 30:1741)
4. FLEISHMAN, EDWIN A. Chap. 9, "A Leader Behavior Description for Industry," pp. 103–19. In *Leader Behavior: Its Description and Measurement.* Edited by Ralph M. Stogdill and Alvin E. Coons. Ohio State University, Bureau of Business Research, Research Monograph No. 88. Columbus, Ohio: the Bureau, 1957. Pp. xv, 168. * (*PA* 32:1466)
5. FLEISHMAN, EDWIN A., AND HARRIS, EDWIN F. "Patterns of Leadership Behavior Related to Employee Grievances and Turnover." *Personnel Psychol* 15:43–56 sp '62. * (*PA* 37:3953)
6. OTIS, JAY L.; CAMPBELL, JOEL; AND PRIEN, ERIC. Sect.

7, "Leadership Characteristics of Chief Executives," pp. 149–77. In *Small Business Success: Operating and Executive Characteristics: A Study of 110 Successful Metalworking Plants in Ohio.* Edited by Kenneth Lawyer. Cleveland, Ohio: Bureau of Business Research, School of Business, Western Reserve University, 1963. Pp. xii, 183. *

7. HOLLOMAN, CHARLES R. "The Perceived Leadership Role of Military and Civilian Supervisors in a Military Setting." *Personnel Psychol* 20:199–210 su '67. * (PA 41:15905)

8. KROEN, CHARLES WILLIAM, JR. *Validation of Herzberg's Theory of Job Motivation and Its Relationship to Leadership Style.* Doctor's thesis, Colorado State University (Ft. Collins, Colo.), 1967. (DA 28:5225B)

9. SKINNER, ELIZABETH W. "Relationship Between Leadership Behavior Patterns and Organizational-Situational Variables." *Personnel Psychol* 22(4):489–94 w '69. *

10. FIMAN, BYRON GENE. *An Investigation of the Relationships Among Supervisory Attitudes, Behaviors, and Outputs: An Examination of McGregor's Theory Y.* Doctor's thesis, New York University (New York, N.Y.), 1970. (DAI 31:2338B)

11. FLEISHMAN, EDWIN A., AND SIMMONS, J. "Relationship Between Leadership Patterns and Effectiveness Ratings Among Israeli Foremen." *Personnel Psychol* 23(2):169–72 su '70. * (PA 45:7144)

12. MILLER, DELBERT C. *Handbook of Research Design and Social Measurement, Second Edition,* pp. 307–10. New York: David McKay Co., Inc., 1970. Pp. xv, 432. *

13. BLACK, CLIFFORD MERWYN. *Leader Behavior and Patterns of Religious Bureaucracy.* Doctor's thesis, Northwestern University (Evanston, Ill.), 1972. (DAI 33:5832A)

14. HAND, HERBERT H., AND SLOCUM, JOHN W., JR. "A Longitudinal Study of the Effects of a Human Relations Training Program on Managerial Effectiveness." *J Appl Psychol* 56(5):412–7 O '72. * (PA 49:8074)

15. WEISSENBERG, PETER, AND KAVANAGH, MICHAEL J. "The Independence of Initiating Structure and Consideration: A Review of the Evidence." *Personnel Psychol* 25(1):119–30 sp '72. *

16. FIMAN, BYRON G. "An Investigation of the Relationships Among Supervisory Attitudes, Behaviors, and Outputs: An Examination of McGregor's Theory Y." *Personnel Psychol* 26(1):95–105 sp '73. * (PA 51:1986)

17. FLEISHMAN, EDWIN A. Chap. 1, "Twenty Years of Consideration and Structure," pp. 1–40. In *Current Developments in the Study of Leadership.* Edited by Edwin A. Fleishman and James G. Hunt. Carbondale, Ill.: Southern Illinois University Press, 1973. Pp. xxi, 217. *

18. HAND, HERBERT H.; RICHARDS, MAX D.; AND SLOCUM, JOHN W., JR. "Organizational Climate and the Effectiveness of a Human Relations Program." *Acad Mgmt J* 16(2):185–95 Je '73. * (PA 51:4052)

19. HOWELL, JON PAUL. *A Study of the Relationship Between Individual Characteristics, Situational Variables, Leadership Behavior and Organizational Effectiveness in Community Mental Health Centers.* Doctor's thesis, University of California (Irvine, Calif.), 1973. (DAI 35:32A)

20. TSCHEULIN, D. "Leader Behavior Measurement in German Industry." *J Appl Psychol* 57(1):28–31 F '73. * (PA 50:4061)

21. KERR, STEVEN, AND SCHRIESHEIM, CHESTER. "Consideration, Initiating Structure, and Organizational Criteria—An Update of Korman's 1966 Review." *Personnel Psychol* 27(4):555–68 w '74. * (PA 55:1673)

22. SCHRIESHEIM, CHESTER, AND KERR, STEVEN. "Psychometric Properties of the Ohio State Leadership Scales." *Psychol B* 81(11):756–65 N '74. * (PA 53:5359)

23. SZILAGYI, ANDREW D., AND SIMS, HENRY P., JR. "Cross-Sample Stability of the Supervisory Behavior Description Questionnaire." *J Appl Psychol* 59(6):767–70 D '74. * (PA 53:8507)

24. SZILAGYI, ANDREW D., AND SIMS, HENRY P., JR. "An Exploration of the Path-Goal Theory of Leadership in a Health Care Environment." *Acad Mgmt J* 17(4):622–34 D '74. * (PA 53:10606)

25. PETTY, M. M., AND LEE, GORDON K., JR. "Moderating Effects of Sex of Supervisor and Subordinate on Relationships Between Supervisory Behavior and Subordinate Satisfaction." *J Appl Psychol* 60(5):624–8 O '75. * (PA 55:3377)

26. SCHRIESHEIM, CHESTER A., AND STOGDILL, RALPH M. "Differences in Factor Structure Across Three Versions of the Ohio State Leadership Scales." *Personnel Psychol* 28(2):189–206 su '75. * (PA 55:11126)

27. SIMS, HENRY P., JR., AND SZILAGYI, ANDREW D. "Leader Structure and Subordinate Satisfaction for Two Hospital Administrative Levels: A Path Analysis Approach." *J Appl Psychol* 60(2):194–7 Ap '75. * (PA 54:2090)

28. SWANSON, RONALD G., AND JOHNSON, DOUGLAS A. "Relation Between Peer Perception of Leader Behavior and Instructor-Pilot Performance." *J Appl Psychol* 60(2):198–200 Ap '75. * (PA 54:2075)

29. SCHRIESHEIM, CHESTER A.; HOUSE, ROBERT J.; AND KERR, STEVEN. "Leader Initiating Structure: A Reconciliation of Discrepant Research Results and Some Empirical Tests."

Organiz Behav & Hum Perfor 15(2):297–331 Ap '76. * (PA 56:6933)

30. SUMRALL, CHARLOTTE CLAUDIA HERMANN. *A Study of the Relationship Between the Leadership Behavior of Instructional Supervisors and the Job Satisfaction of Teachers in Texas.* Doctor's thesis, University of Houston (Houston, Tex.), 1976. (DAI 37:2571)

31. SZILAGYI, ANDREW D., AND KELLER, ROBERT T. "A Comparative Investigation of the Supervisory Behavior Description Questionnaire (SBDQ) and the Revised Leader Behavior Description Questionnaire (LBDQ-Form XII)." *Acad Mgmt J* 19(4):642–9 D '76. *

MICHAEL J. KAVANAGH, *Associate Professor of Organizational Behavior, State University of New York at Binghamton, Binghamton, New York.*

The measurement of leadership and leader behavior has been, and still is, of considerable interest for persons involved in either research or practice in the area of management/leadership. In terms of research, leadership behavior is assumed to be highly related, and in some cases, causally, to a variety of other important organizational variables, e.g., organizational effectiveness, subordinate productivity, and satisfaction. In addition, the effective measurement of leader behavior has many practical implications. Used as a diagnostic instrument, a scale to measure leader behavior can provide an assessment of current supervisory practices, and thus, in relation to other diagnostic information, could provide guidelines for organizational changes and training needs. These considerations argue for a leader behavior scale that meets the standards of measurement theory.

There are a number of methods of measuring *leadership,* including interviews, observation, self-reports, and other report questionnaires. It should be clearly understood that the SBD *does not measure leadership,* which is assumed to be a process between a leader and followers, but rather, it purports to measure leader behavior. When making this distinction, the number of available published instruments shrinks considerably; but still leaves the user with a choice as to which one to use in a given situation. The SBD is concerned with measuring the *frequency* of certain behaviors of supervisors as perceived by their subordinates. It is one of several questionnaires designed to measure leader behavior that evolved from the Ohio State University leadership studies. It is designed to measure two behavioral dimensions of supervisors, defined as follows: Consideration (C) "reflects the extent to which one's supervisor exhibits behavior indicative of friendship, mutual trust and respect, and good 'human relations' toward the members of his group." Structure (S) "reflects the extent to which one's supervisor exhibits the behavior of a leader in organizing and defining the relationships between himself and the group, defining interactions among group members, establishing ways of getting the job done, scheduling, criticizing, etc."

The questionnaire is self-administered and should require little supervision. The manual describes specific, important details with which the user must be concerned in administering the questionnaire, e.g., respondent anonymity. Scoring is quite straightforward, and a scoring key is provided. Thus, relative to practicality and simplicity, the SBD clearly passes.

The developmental evidence for the SBD is fairly adequate. Split-half reliabilities are generally strong—for C, .89 to .98, with median .92; and for S, .68 to .87, with median .78. Test-retest reliabilities are also quite acceptable—.56, .58, and .87 are reported for C; and .46, .53, and .75 for S. Interrater agreement is somewhat marginal—correlations for C range from .55 to .73, with median .64; and for S, .47 to .90, with median .57. These values meet acceptable standards for measurement. The norms presented in the manual are quite satisfactory; however, it would be useful to know the specific research studies on which the norms were based. This would allow the user to check as to which set of norms are most appropriate for use in a given situation.

However, there is one minor problem with this developmental evidence. Although the manual states that C and S are independent dimensions, this assertion has been questioned in the literature (15, 29). The author argues that an important feature of the SBD "is that the scores on each scale are independent of each other" and that the data "indicate that the dimensions of consideration and structure are most usefully considered as orthogonal coordinates against which the behavior of supervisors in different situations may be plotted." The data upon which this conclusion is based are six studies reporting correlations between C and S ranging from −.33 to .23, with median −.05. In an analysis of studies using the LBDQ and LOQ, Weissenberg and Kavanagh (15) found correlations between C and S ranging from −.57 to .70, with median .36. On the basis of these results, the independence of these scales must be ques-

tioned. However, in terms of use of the questionnaire in research or practice, this debate may not be terribly relevant. If the purpose of the measurement is to determine the level of supervisors' behavior on C and S in order to prescribe training and other corrective actions, the independence issue seems of limited importance. For research use, investigators should be aware of this potential problem, and adjust their results on the basis of their sample values.

The evidence for the validity of the scales is confusing. The author reports on several studies in which C and S were correlated with a variety of organization outcome variables, e.g., supervisory ratings, absenteeism, accidents, turnover, and grievances, all assumed to indicate supervisory effectiveness. The author states that "low consideration is more often indicative of an undesirable situation, and that some coupling of above-average consideration and structure optimizes more performance criteria." Although somewhat fuzzy, this statement implies that higher C and S behaviors are better for supervisory effectiveness. Frequently, the correlations which C and S have with specific criteria have different signs—one a positive correlation and the other a negative correlation; of the 22 pairs of correlations presented, 60 percent have different signs. The evidence for the validity of these scales is mixed, and the user should be aware of this fact, particularly if the scores are used to prescribe corrective action or a training program for supervisors. The validity evidence is not strong enough to justify use in these cases.

Finally, the construct validity of the SBD has been recently criticized (26, 29). These criticisms are primarily aimed at the S dimension, arguing that it contains excess meaning, not measuring S as advertised in the manual. The major concern has been that the SBD S scale also measures punitive and autocratic behaviors of supervisors. This is clearly a deficiency, and should be noted in future editions of the manual. There is an alternate scoring procedure suggested in Schriesheim, et al. (29) to attempt to deal with this problem. Although Schriesheim presents no norms, his other evidence indicates the original scoring of the S scale is incorrect. Users of the SBD may want to adjust their scoring dependent on their uses.

The development of the SBD was based on

solid empirical work, and it has been used in empirical studies too numerous to list. It is concerned with measuring an important variable in organizations—supervisory behavior patterns—and thus, has relevance to both the organizational researcher and practitioner. The evidence marshalled for its use more than meets acceptable standards, but the problems of predictive and constructive validity of the S dimension must be considered. The SBD seems highly appropriate as a descriptive measure of supervisory behavior in terms of C and S. The question of the "clearness" of the S dimension raised by Schriesheim, et al. (29) as well as the independence issue (15) indicate some care must be exercised in interpreting the scores.

In sum, the SBD is the best available measure of supervisory behavior in terms of C and S. It seems entirely appropriate for use as a diagnostic instrument to provide a description of current supervisory practices. It should not, however, be used carte blanche to prescribe training programs and changes in supervisory behavior. It could be useful to provide feedback to supervisors on the way their subordinates see their behavior, but no specific negative or positive advice for change should be given with the feedback. Unless C and S are strongly and significantly related to effectiveness in the user's organization, the use and interpretation of the SBD should be only descriptive.

[1187]

*Supervisory Practices Test, Revised. Supervisors; 1957–76; SPT; 1 form ('76, 4 pages, same as test copyrighted 1974 except for elimination of sex bias and identical with test copyrighted 1957 except for minor changes in 11 items); revised manual ('74, 15 pages); profile ('74, 2 pages); $8.80 per 20 tests; 45¢ per key; $3.85 per 20 profiles; $2.50 per manual; $3.15 per specimen set; cash orders postpaid; 10% extra on charge orders; French ('60) and German ('70) editions available; (20–30) minutes; Martin M. Bruce; Martin M. Bruce, Ph.D., Publishers. *

See T2:2466 (2 references) and 6:1194 (4 references); for reviews by Clifford E. Jurgensen and Mary Ellen Oliverio, see 5:955.

[1188]

The WPS Supervisor-Executive Tri-Dimensional Evaluation Scales. Supervisors; 1966; TES; the same questions about the individual being rated are answered by 3 persons—his supervisor, a colleague, and himself; 12 scores obtained from each of the 3 forms: knowledge, planning, results, delegating, leadership, morale, training, adaptability, communication, emotionality, growth, total; no data on reliability; no description of normative population; 3 forms: self-rating, colleague-rating, supervisor-rating, (6 pages); manual (9 pages plus forms); $10.50 per kit of manual and 10 sets of the 3 forms; $3.50 per manual; 8% extra for postage and handling; (30) minutes; Western Psychological Services. *

WILLIAM G. MOLLENKOPF, *Associate Manager of Personnel Administration, The Procter & Gamble Company, Cincinnati, Ohio.*

The title of these scales is both grandiose and misleading. There is little justification for inclusion of "executive," and "tri-dimensional" arises merely from the recommended arrangement of having three persons use variants of the same scale for carrying out the evaluation.

The 110 items are grouped into 11 areas. Apparently, these are believed to represent the areas that are important for effectiveness as a supervisor. However, no evidence is presented, and no references are cited, supporting these as providing an adequate coverage of the supervisory performance domain. An obvious omission is the lack of a scale dealing with coping with conflict.

Each item is presented in the form of a statement followed by two brief "answers." This forced-choice format would seem more appropriate in a personality test; indeed, a number of items unduly resemble those frequently found in such tests. Items are primarily oriented to the work of a first-line production supervisor. It is unfortunate that all pronouns used are masculine, and that the employees are always referred to as "men."

In the discussion of the analysis and interpretation of scores, the manual places greatest emphasis on the self-evaluation, less on the evaluation by the self-evaluator's supervisor, and still less on a colleague's evaluation. Much of the large literature on performance appraisal views a person's supervisor as being in the best position to evaluate that person. The assertion that the chief value of the supervisor's profile is to provide a control over the self-evaluation is quite out of line with this widely-held view.

It is never made clear whether, or in what way, the various evaluations are fed back to the person being evaluated. The manual states that the major purpose is "development by management of an *operational understanding* of a complex person: the *Self-Evaluator*," and later refers to use of the findings for "making decisions regarding work assignments, promotions, training, and discharge." In this reviewer's view, the use of findings from these scales in deciding about promotion or discharge would be both unwise and improper. Furthermore, a person called upon to make such a self-evaluation deserves to learn what emerges from the analyses of his own and others' responses.

The manual asserts that these scales "provide a new and penetrating approach for evaluating key personnel," and that they are "self-administered, easily scored and profiled, and readily interpreted." What one finds in the content, procedures, and recommendations for interpretation and application does not measure up to these bold promises. The reviewer is concerned that the possibilities for misuse, resulting in harm to those evaluated, may be serious. The use of the scales is not recommended.

THOMAS A. TYLER, *President, Merit Employment Assessment Services, Inc., Flossmoor, Illinois.*

The tri-dimensional aspect of this test is the completion of three parallel forms by the subject, a colleague, and the supervisor, respectively. All three forms include 110 short statements with two alternative responses, scored 1 or 2 on one of 11 different scales.

The manual provides instructions for administration and scoring, and offers a number of unsupported suggestions for interpretation. The profile chart included on each form implies that the test has been normed. No data are presented to suggest that this is true.

The test content appears to have face validity, although it should be noted that the content is phrased exclusively in the masculine person. In the absence of any empirical data, this test is recommended for research purposes only.

[1189 1]

★[Work Motivation.] Managers, employees; 1967–73; 2 tests, 5 scores for each: basic-creature comfort, safety and order, belonging and affiliation, ego-status, actualization and self-expression; no manual; $3 per test; postage extra; statistical data free on request; [15–30] minutes per test; Jay Hall and Martha Williams (*b*); Teleometrics Int'l. *
a) MANAGEMENT OF MOTIVES INDEX. Managers; 1968–73; MMI; assumptions and practices characterizing attempts to motivate employees; no norms; 1 form ('73, 13 pages); score interpretation ('73, 7 pages).
b) WORK MOTIVATION INVENTORY. Employees; 1967–73; WMI; motivational needs and values; norms consist of average scores; 1 form ('73, 13 pages); score interpretation ('73, 4 pages).

REFERENCES

1. CUNNINGHAM, CLAUDE H.; WAKEFIELD, JAMES A., JR.; AND WARD, G. ROBERT. "An Empirical Comparison of Maslow's and Murray's Needs Systems." *J Pers Assess* 39(6):594–6 D '75. * (PA 55:7195)
2. HALL, JAY. "To Achieve or Not: The Manager's Choice." *Calif Mgmt R* 18(4):5–18 su '76. *
3. JONES, HOWARD L.; SASEK, JAN.; AND WAKEFIELD, JAMES A., JR. "Maslow's Need Hierarchy and Cattell's 16PF." *J Clin Psychol* 32(1):74–6 Ja '76. * (PA 56:7045)

1 After all tests were numbered, 3 additional test entries were inserted and 8 were deleted, leaving a total of 1184 test entries in this volume. The inserted entries are 7A, 524A, and 726A. The deleted test entries are indicated by the compound numbers assigned to the immediately preceding entries: 275–6, 476–7, 537–8, 647–8, 808–9, 935–6, 1122–3, and 1127–8.

Books and Reviews

Books with no authors given are presented first, in alphabetical order by title, followed by books arranged alphabetically by author. A star preceding the entry denotes a book being listed in an MMY for the first time; an asterisk indicates a book which has been updated since it was last listed in an MMY.

[B1]

★**AAHPER Youth Fitness Test Manual, Revised 1976 Edition.** Washington, D.C.: American Alliance for Health, Physical Education, and Recreation, 1976. Pp. 91. Paper, $3.00. *

[B2]

★**CLEP Scores: Interpretation and Use.** Princeton, N.J.: Educational Testing Service, 1973. Pp. 43. Paper, $2.50. * For a later edition, see B3.

[B3]

*****CLEP Scores: Interpretation and Use.** Princeton, N.J.: Educational Testing Service, 1976. Pp. 47. Paper, $2.50. *

[B4]

★**Common Sense and Testing in English: Report of the Task Force on Measurement and Evaluation in the Study of English.** By Alan Purves, Beryl Bailey, Robert A. Bennett, Charles W. Daves, Helen Lodge, Olive S. Niles, Roy C. O'Donnell, Leo P. Ruth, Richard L. Venezky, and Robert E. Beck. Urbana, Ill.: National Council of Teachers of English, 1975. Pp. vi, 33. Paper, $1.50. *

[B5]

★**Interpretation System for the Guilford-Zimmerman Temperament Survey: A Program for Report Preparation.** Orange, Calif.: Sheridan Psychological Services, Inc., 1976. Pp. 30. $4.50. *

[B6]

★**Normative Data for the 1976–77 Freshman Class, University System of Georgia.** Atlanta, Ga.: Regents of the University System of Georgia, January 1977. Pp. vii, 114. Paper, lithotyped, gratis. *

[B7]

★**Releasing Test Scores: Educational Assessment Programs, How to Tell the Public.** Arlington, Va.: National School Public Relations Association, 1976. Pp. 64. Paper, $4.75. *

[B8]

★**Standardized Achievement Testing.** Washington, D.C.: National School Boards Association, 1977. Pp. 54. Paper, $3.70.

[B9]

*****Standards for Educational and Psychological Tests.** Prepared by a joint committee of the American Psychological Association, American Educational Research Association, and National Council on Measurement in Education. Frederick B. Davis, Chair. Washington, D.C.: American Psychological Association, Inc., 1974. Pp. iv, 76. Paper, $3.50. * For earlier editions, see the 1954 *Technical Recommendations for Psychological Tests and Techniques,* 5:B14 (reprinted in the 1961 *Tests in Print I*); the 1955 *Technical Recommendations for Achievement Tests,* 5:B13 (reprinted in the 1961 *Tests in Print I*); the 1966 *Standards for Educational and Psychological Tests and Manuals* (reprinted in the 1970 *Personality Tests and Reviews I*); the 1974 *Standards for Educational and Psychological Tests* (reprinted in the 1974 *Tests in Print II*). For reviews of the 1966 edition, see 7:B17 (8 excerpts). For a general historical analysis by the Editor, see pages 755–8 in the 1974 *Tests in Print II.*

[B10]

★**State Educational Assessment Programs, 1973 Revision.** Princeton, N.J.: Educational Testing Service, 1973. Pp. vii, 98. Paper, $4.00. *

J Ed Meas 12(1):55–6 sp '75. Joan Bollenbacher. This review....considers the publication primarily from the test user's point of view. * Most of the "something new" that has been added is an 18-page section on "Standards for the Use of Tests." The introduction states that the publication is "intended to guide both test developers and users." The user is defined as "one who chooses tests, interprets scores, or makes decisions based on test scores....Test users include clinical or industrial psychologists, research directors, school psychologists, counselors, employment supervisors, teachers, and various administrators who select or interpret tests for their organizations." This broad audience is in marked contrast to the narrower one described in the 1966 *Standards*. The earlier edition was directed to "readers who have training approximately equivalent to a level between the master's degree and the doctorate in education or psychology at a superior institution of higher learning." * the 1974 *Standards*....have much to say to everyone who uses tests in making decisions about people. The section on manuals and reports and the one on reliability and validity are of special concern to those responsible for choosing among available tests. But the section on "Standards for the Use of Tests" applies to all users and especially to those having responsibilities for large numbers of examinees—that is, school counselors, teachers, and school administrators. This section encompasses a broad diversity of test use ranging from individual diagnosis by clinicians to the classification of large groups of persons for purposes of instruction, guidance, and selection. * All except nine of the 58 test-use standards are accompanied by explanatory comments. Here, however, there is some inconsistency. Comments are appended to some standards which seem fairly obvious in themselves, while others, which might not be so obvious to some users, are left standing alone. * Several of the standards deserve special mention. Listed as "desirable" is Standard J2.1 which states that "an individual (or his agent or guardian) has the right to know his score." In view of the recent legislation covering release of personal information, this standard might now be more appropriately regarded as "essential." Two "essential" standards, J5.1 and J5.2, suggest that terms such as "IQ" and "grade equivalent" should be avoided. In the opinion of this reviewer, these are much-needed standards but probably the least likely to be observed. It is regrettable, however, that anyone who might wish to check quickly what the *Standards* say about "IQ" and "grade equivalent" would have something of a problem, since neither term is included in the index. The lack of a table of contents also contributes to the difficulty in using the *Standards* for ready reference. * it is the opinion of this reviewer that the *Standards* in their present form will probably have a minimal influence on many school people and others who use tests routinely in much of their work. Why? Because many teachers, administrators, and even counselors will continue to be unaware that any such body of standards exists. And many of those who are aware will hardly look forward to spending five dollars for a 76-page paperback. If the *Standards* are to serve the purpose intended, the sponsoring organizations—especially NCME—should make it their business to get the standards for test use disseminated in places where they will be read by users other than psychologists, researchers, and psychometrists. One way to do this would be to publish articles about the standards in the professional journals customarily read by teachers, counselors, and administrators—even if to do so might require rewriting the standards in a more popular (or palatable) style. * It is not known how much improvement has occurred since 1966, but by all accounts there is still room for much more. As the song says, "We've only just begun."

J Ed Meas 12(2):135-7 su '75. Roger T. Lennon. * Three elements account for the greater length of the 1974 version: (1) slightly expanded discussions of certain topics, particularly validity, (2) an increase in the number of standards related to tests and manuals, and (3) the addition of an entirely new section comprising 58 standards for test users. * the standards play an extremely useful, perhaps even necessary, role in test development, publication, and use. This reviewer does not hesitate to say that the earlier editions of the standards, beginning twenty years ago, have had a greatly beneficial impact on testing; the latest edition will prove at least as useful. The 1974 *Standards* adhere closely in scope and organization to the previous editions. * There is little substantive change in the standards relating to dissemination, aids to interpretation, administration and scoring, reliability, and scales and norms. The standards relating to validity show the greatest signs of rethinking; it is here, too, that the greatest number of new standards has been added. The discussion of validity that precedes the standards proper has been helpfully expanded, but no major conceptual differences from the 1966 treatment are introduced. The issue of test fairness and the problems of test use associated with equal employment have clearly been much on the Committee's mind. Several of the new standards address these problems. * Of the 245 standards, 142 are classified as ESSENTIAL, 74 as VERY DESIRABLE, and 27 as DESIRABLE. * Given the difficulty of making value judgments of this kind, and given the general tone and spirit of the *Standards* as a whole, the utility of this differentiation seems dubious, since a standard which may be ESSENTIAL for one type of test in one type of situation may be only DESIRABLE for another test in another situation. The Committee preparing the 1974 *Standards* has clearly succumbed to the belief that more is better, and that clarity and comprehensiveness are the fruits of expansion. Alas, it is not always necessarily so. A checklist of 187—not to say 245—items may be too much of a good thing. Perhaps because there are so many of them, the standards vary widely on a specificity-generality continuum. Some (e.g., A1.2.1, A1.2.2, B5.5, C2, E4.4, E7) are at such a level of generality, or obviousness, as to cause one to question their inclusion; the test maker needing to be told them is beyond redemption. Their inclusion has the regrettable consequence of trivializing the rest of the document. At the other extreme, highly specific standards (e.g., E8.1.1 and F5.3) may tend to relate to matters of preference or practice where the state of the art perhaps does not permit standardization. Some standards border on the doctrinaire; others are exceedingly difficult of realization in any practical framework. Having made these observations, this reviewer nevertheless is pleasantly aware of how infrequently he felt impelled to disagree violently with any of the standards. The major innovation in the 1974 revision is the inclusion of standards for test users. The 58 standards in this section cover user qualifications, choice of tests or methods, administration and scoring, and interpretation. Reviewers of the earlier editions have stressed the need for upgrading test use, if improved test making and reporting practices were to have full effect. The 1974 Committee has attempted to specify the knowledges, attitudes, and behaviors which the test user ought to bring to his role. (Concern for the role of the test user, incidentally, turns up not only in the test use section, but also in the section on reliability and validity where not a few of the standards appear to be guidelines for the test user rather than the test maker—e.g., E2, E2.1, E2.2, E2.3, E5.2.2, E7.3, E7.4.2, and E.11. Conversely, some of the standards in the test use section—e.g., I4.1, J5.5, and J.6—seem more properly to belong in other sections.) In general, this reviewer regretfully judges that the standards for test users are notably less helpful than the standards for test makers. Too many of them are obvious to the point of banality, too many at such a level of generality as to be meaningless in the concrete. One criterion which this reviewer applied to the *Standards* is whether they might serve as knowledge, understanding, or attitudinal objectives for a course in testing; for the most part, this reviewer found them lacking in the specificity appropriate for such a purpose. To sum up: The 1974 *Standards* are a useful updating of the earlier editions, and will serve equally well as a guide to test making and publishing, and to the training of persons for these endeavors. The work of the revision Committee, consisting of eleven persons widely respected by the testing profession, and chaired by Frederick B. Davis, merits the congratulations and gratitude of their colleagues. The Committee would be the last to suggest that all competent testing professionals would agree in every particular with this new set of standards; given the state of the art, such an expectation would be unrealistic. Still, no serious practitioner can fail to accord major deference to the *Standards,* and the level of excellence of test making and use will surely be related to the extent to which their spirit is observed.

[B11]

***State Testing Programs, 1973 Revision.** Princeton, N.J.: Educational Testing Service, 1973. Pp. vii, 59. Paper, $4.00. *

[B12]

★Testing for Impaired, Disabled and Handicapped Individuals. Washington, D.C.: American Alliance for Health, Physical Education and Recreation, [1975]. Pp. 110. Paper, $4.50. *

[B13]

★ABEL, THEODORA M. Psychological Testing in Cultural Contexts. New Haven, Conn.: College and University Press, 1973. Pp. 240. Paper, $3.45; cloth, $7.50. *

J Pers Assess 40(4):436–7 Ag '76. Earl X. Freed. This is an interesting book whose theme is an exposition of the influences of cultural and socioeconomic variables upon psychological testing, primarily projective testing. * There are many morals to this story. One is that psychologists need to be very attuned to cultural influences upon personality and behavior, not just test behavior. * Another message....is one of caution. Knowledge of one's test instrument is not enough. Confidence in one's ken can beguile. One needs to be aware of subtle, cultural impacts upon the nature of the test material and its stimulus value, the group on which it was standardized, the testing task per se and what it means to the subject to be "examined," the test setting, and the interpretation by an examiner with his own cultural biases—and all this is especially so when the assessment process represents a cross-cultural encounter. * I.... wonder about all of the psychological testing which takes place in institutions such as hospitals, nursing homes, prisons, therapeutic communities and the like. By virtue of the longer term care they afford, they exert cultural influences. They represent mini-societies in many cases and their influence upon personality needs to be factored into, not out of, interpretations of personality dynamics.

[B14]

★ABRAMS, STANLEY. **A Polygraph Handbook for Attorneys.** Lexington, Mass.: Lexington Books, D.C. Heath & Co., 1977. Pp. xii, 259. $16.95. *

[B15]

★ADAMS, ARTHUR A. **Test Your Personality.** New York: Hart Publishing Co., Inc., 1976. Pp. 192. Paper, $1.95. *

[B16]

★ADAMS, ARTHUR A. **Test Yourself.** New York: Hart Publishing Co., Inc., 1976. Pp. 158. Paper, $1.95. *

[B17]

*ADKINS, DOROTHY C. **Test Construction: Development and Interpretation of Achievement Tests, Second Edition.** Columbus, Ohio: Charles E. Merrill Publishing Co., 1974. Pp. xi, 160. Paper, $4.95. * For reviews of the first edition, see 6:B521 (3 excerpts).

Ed & Psychol Meas 34(3):713–5 au '74. Morris A. Okun and Joseph A. Sasfy. * The organization and content....[have] been substantially revised and amplified. * We have no reservations about the topics included in *Test Construction* but are disappointed that the issue of the relationship between marking and evaluation was not discussed. Based upon experience as instructors in educational psychology, we feel that there is a great deal of confusion concerning these two processes. The other substantive

aspect of the book which causes us some concern is the lack of attention paid to the use of the mastery approach in the chapter on assigning marks. Adkins has written this chapter from the perspective of a differential psychologist seeking to maximize differences between students. It is intimated that all teachers should create a distribution of final marks such that the entire range of letter marks are assigned to various members of the class. However, she fails to offer the reader the option of constructing mastery examinations whereby final marks are assigned according to the number of units completed. This is certainly a viable alternative to constructing weights for individual tests and imposing arbitrary cutoffs. Overall, the author has succeeded in her effort to present the basics of test construction on an elementary level. The concepts are discussed in a straightforward, easily comprehensible fashion. With respect to item construction, the concepts which are presented are complemented by numerous illustrative examples. In addition, the author has updated the book so that it touches on some of the "hot topics" in test construction. We feel that this book would be suitable for units on test construction in such courses as educational psychology. Though the author reports in the preface to the second edition of *Test Construction* that several university instructors have employed the first edition of this book as the basic text for a course in test construction, we feel that a more sophisticated textbook would be required for such a course.

J Ed Meas 12(2):137–8 su '75. William A. Mehrens. The first (1960) edition of this book proved very popular and the second edition will likely enjoy similar popularity. It is a good book. Adkins thinks clearly and writes well. * Approximately 3 pages are spent in differentiating between norm-referenced and content-referenced tests. Although I would have preferred a more expanded treatment of the topic, those three pages are written very well indeed. * While Adkins presents a very good discussion on planning objective tests in accord with test objectives, she does not make a similar case for essay tests. No mention is made of relating essay questions back to a table of specifications. * Chapter 10 is a completely new addition to this second edition and discusses some criticisms of tests. Some very good points are made in this chapter—particularly with respect to equity and validity in the use of selection tests. Although I have raised some points of criticism in the previous paragraphs, the book is in general, a very good one. It covers several important topics related to test construction clearly, concisely, and accurately. The few faults I find with the book relate almost entirely to errors of omission, not commission. But Adkins has been remarkably comprehensive considering that the textual portion of the book is only 135 pages long. I recommend it highly as a supplementary text or as a useful text for in-service workshops. I do not think it comprehensive or detailed enough to serve as a major text.

[B18]

★AHMANN, J. STANLEY. **How Much Are Our Young People Learning: The Story of the National Assessment.** Bloomington, Ind.: Phi Delta Kappa Educational Foundation, 1976. Pp. 37. Paper, $0.75. *

[B19]

*AHMANN, J. STANLEY, AND GLOCK, MARVIN D. **Evaluating Pupil Growth: Principles of Tests and Measurements, Fifth Edition.** Boston, Mass.: Allyn & Bacon, Inc., 1975. Pp. xi, 452. $14.95. * For reviews of earlier editions, see 7:B26 (1 excerpt) and 6:B33 (2 excerpts).

[B20]

*AHMANN, J. STANLEY, AND GLOCK, MARVIN D. **Measuring and Evaluating Educational Achievement, Second Edition.** Boston, Mass.: Allyn & Bacon, Inc., 1975. Pp. xi, 452. Paper, $7.95. * (The contents of this book first appeared as part of the authors' *Evaluating Pupil Growth: Principles of Tests and Measurements, Fifth Edition,* see B19.)

[B21]

AIKEN, LEWIS R., JR. **Psychological and Educational Testing.** Boston, Mass.: Allyn & Bacon, Inc., 1971. Pp. vi, 346. * *Out of print.* For the latest edition, see B22 (1 excerpt).

Ed & Psychol Meas 31(4):1031–3 w '71. Robert M. Colver. * the section on "Sources of information" is too brief * According to the preface "no previous exposure to statistics is assumed." Yet, it appears that this book in its section on statistical methods in testing tries to go too far too fast. * Chapter 2 concerns itself with the preparing, administering, scoring, and evaluating of tests and test items. This chapter is a very thoughtful and concise discussion of the problems and techniques in test preparation. It appears to be an excellent background for understanding the problems of test preparation, but does not appear to be adequate for instructing the classroom teacher in the preparation of classroom tests. Chapter 3 concerns itself primarily with the matter of the characteristics of

satisfactory measuring instruments such as the questions of reliability, validity, standardization and norming. This material appears to be very adequately covered and at a level of sophistication appropriate for the group for which this book is designed. * the author has made what appears to be an excellent and very up-to-date selection of the more widely used tests in these areas with a brief annotation and evaluation of these tests * Chapters 7, 8 and 9....cover the tests of special abilities, measures of interest, attitudes, and personality. * these three chapters serve as an excellent basic quick reference to up-to-date evaluation in these areas. Research and theories on general intelligence is the subject matter of Chapter 6. * this is a superior overview and review of this area and at a level of sophistication appropriate for the individuals for whom the book is designed. It does appear that sufficient distinction between the ratio IQ and the deviation IQ is missing throughout all discussion of intelligence and intelligence measurement in the book. The final chapter on current issues and developments is an excellent summary of the modern day problems in testing and a very realistic forward look to what could or might be happening in the area of testing. Overall the greatest strength in this book lies in well written up-to-date annotation and summary of the more common types of assessment devices currently in use in the schools. This does provide a valuable quick reference for the nonprofessional test user in assisting such persons in understanding the results obtained from testing programs as well as assisting in their communication with the professional test users. * The reviewer can recommend this book as a textbook or a source book for background information or training of the non-professional test user such as the classroom teacher and the school administrator who need to have understandings in this area.

J Ed Meas 9(3):245–6 f '72. Lee Sechrest. It is always easier and fundamentally more satisfying to be able to write a positive rather than a negative review of a book. Aside from one's natural disinclination to be harsh with a colleague, there is the nagging thought that after all someone originally found the book worth writing, and someone else found it worth publishing. Nonetheless, in the present case this reviewer can only insist that for whatever reasons, both the publisher and author were wrong. The book has literally nothing to recommend it.

That judgment is a harsh one but, unfortunately, merited. A fundamental difficulty with Aiken's book is that he seems never to have thought through the aims of the book in terms of the audience toward whom it is directed. It is very uneven in terms of its presentation, and it is difficult to imagine a class for which it would be appropriate. * The book ranges enormously from the almost absurdly simple to the highly complex. The difference, however, is that the absurdly simple things in Aiken's book are likely to be described at some length while the highly complex issues are presented with little if any explanation. "Likert-type" items are mentioned, but the definition of such items is not to be found anywhere. The Role Constructs Repertory Test is mentioned in a single sentence with almost no context to indicate to the student whether it is worth pursuing or not. There are very sketchy and virtually useless discussions of such topics as field independence and test fairness. The whole topic of response sets is dismissed with one footnote and a definition in the glossary, the "base rate problem" merits only a footnote, and there are many other similarly cavalier treatments of important topics in testing and assessment. Even in handling such traditional concepts as reliability Aiken's presentation is, in the reviewer's estimate, inadequate. Again, the inadequacy seems to stem from the inability of the author to decide whether he is writing a textbook for students who have had little more than an introduction to psychology, or whether he is writing for graduate students. * it seems to this reviewer that to discuss the matter of reliability at the present time in terms of Kuder-Richardson formulas without any mention of coefficient *alpha* is a poor way of proceeding. Probably it is understandable that in the first printing of a book there should be errors, but some in Aiken's book are fairly grievous. * a great deal of expense and effort was wasted in completely useless illustrations * The chapters devoted to individual tests are sketchy, and it is difficult to see how they might be particularly useful, either to students or to professionals who might want to use the book as a manual. Much of the material is too specific and too oriented toward particular applications to be very educational for students, and, on the other hand, it is far too superficial to be a good guide for people who must make a decision about which test to use. *

In conclusion, it appears to the reviewer that if the author had a goal when he began the preparation of his book, he rapidly lost sight of it and went completely astray. He states in the preface that the book was designed both as a text book for students and a source book of information and procedures for persons concerned with testing, but in the estimation of the reviewer the book would do a disservice to either group.

Meas & Eval Guid 7(3):195–6 O '74. Jeffrey L. Lorentz. * Aiken has produced a worthwhile addition to the literature * The brief test resumés are a salient characteristic of this particular book and would be quite helpful to both the novice and the experienced practitioner. Smaller school districts may find Aiken's book a worthwhile addition to their professional library as the one source book and resource on testing. The book is quite readable—with some exceptions—in a fairly nontechnical style. I found the presentation of various instruments to be essentially objective. Some users may wish, however, that Aiken had offered an opinion about the relative merits of the instruments when several alternatives are presented. * I found his treatment [of statistics] to be an unsatisfactory blend of simple explanation and complex computational formulas and procedures. I would have preferred fewer illustrations of computational procedures and more explanation of which statistics to use. The treatment is too brief to be useful to statisticians and so complex as to confuse the novice. On the other hand, I particularly appreciated his comprehensive treatment of test preparation, administration, and scoring. * The discussion of reliability and validity is handled well and Aiken's use of formulas here is appropriate without excessive computational detail. Aiken next discusses specific types of tests. It might have been helpful if he had used a taxonomic breakdown rather than the tropical approach which he chose. * Aiken devotes proportionately more attention to the problem of intelligence testing than to other areas. I felt that this was a good treatment with the major issues discussed at length. In his discussion of certain specialized instruments, Aiken neglects to mention the need for special training and/or restrictions on their administration. * Despite this flaw, the treatment of the various instruments is comprehensive and fairly exhaustive. I judged his treatment of personality measures to be weaker than his treatment of other measures * I felt that there was a need for closure at the end of chapters in the form of a summary. * Aiken did provide closure to the book with a good discussion of current problems and issues such as problems with objective tests, teachers and testing, and social issues such as race and tests. * In summary, *Psychological and Educational Testing* is an adequate, comprehensive treatment of the field. I would find it an adequate resource book, a good basic test, or a nice addition to a professional library.

[B22]

*AIKEN, LEWIS R., JR. **Psychological Testing and Assessment, Second Edition.** Boston, Mass.: Allyn & Bacon, Inc., 1976. Pp. viii, 360. $15.95. * For reviews of the first edition, see B21 (3 excerpts).

Ed & Psychol Meas 36(2):569–72 su '76. Brian Bolton. * The text is accompanied by a useful instructor's manual that contains, in addition to some 500 multiple-choice items, a bibliography of supplementary readings, a brief list of films and filmstrips, and answers to numerical problems presented in the text. All things considered, I believe that Dr. Aiken's revision meets his stated aim of being "comprehensive without being exhaustive." He has prepared a relatively brief (slightly over 300 pages of text and fewer than 200 references), extensively illustrated introduction to the principles and methods of psychological testing. In my opinion the level of presentation is most suitable for students majoring in various areas of applied psychology, e.g., special education, personnel management, social welfare, rehabilitation counseling, etc. This judgment is not meant to be a criticism; *Psychological testing and assessment* is well written and provides teachers of measurement courses with an additional choice among textbooks. Dr. Aiken's achievement is certainly a fitting tribute to Max Engelhart, to whom this book is dedicated. [See original review for additional critical comments not excerpted.]

[B23]

★AIKEN, LEWIS R., JR., EDITOR. **Readings in Psychological and Educational Testing.** Boston, Mass.: Allyn & Bacon, Inc., 1973. Pp. xi, 447. Paper, $6.95. *

Ed & Psychol Meas 33(4):999–1001 w '73. Max D. Engelhart. * excellent book of readings * a very useful anthology in the field of educational and psychological testing. In the opinion of this reviewer, it provides an effective means

of supplementing a current conventional text in measurement. Students using this anthology should acquire a much broader understanding of educational and psychological testing than from study of a textbook alone. This will be especially true if the instructor selects readings in terms of well-defined instructional objectives and prepares thought provoking questions relevant to those selected. *

Meas & Eval Guid 7(3):196–8 O '74. Jeffrey L. Lorentz. * Each of the nine sections includes four or five readings with a good introduction and summary by Aiken. * I found all of the readings to be of some relevance, and they would give depth and breadth to the novice in the field. The readings selected present a good blend of the theoretical and the practical. * Aiken's book is a good cross section of readings related to a broad spectrum of issues in testing. I found his mixture of theoretical articles with reports of research to be particularly appealing. The use of this book as a supplement to a course in psychological testing would certainly be worthwhile. Were I teaching such a course, I would certainly consider using it.

[B24]

★AKERET, ROBERT U. **Photoanalysis: How to Interpret the Hidden Psychological Meanings of Personal and Public Photographs.** New York: Pocket Books, 1975. Pp. xiii, 311. Paper, $1.75. *

[B25]

AMES, L. B.; MÉTRAUX, R. W.; AND WALKER, R. N. **Adolescent Rorschach Responses: Developmental Trends From 10 to 16 Years, Revised Edition.** New York: Brunner/Mazel, Inc., 1971. Pp. xvi, 319. $13.00. * For reviews of the earlier edition, see 6:B52 (2 excerpts).

Am J Psychiatry 129(2):246–7 Ag '72. H. Barry Molish. The reader who expects this edition of an earlier volume to be completely revised and expanded will be disappointed. * One gets the impression that this revision was a hurried effort to revive a text that has been out of print for some time. The format of the bibliography certainly adds to this impression. The new references are listed in poor style, with alphabetical subscripts inserted among the original bibliographical listings (pp. 305–307). The revised bibliography contains only 11 new references. The scope of the literature cited even in the first printing of this text was considered remiss by several reviewers for its omission of pertinent references. If there was one good reason for publishing this revised edition—beyond the recognized need of making available an out-of-print volume that was an excellent and classical source book for normative data— it is the revision of chapter 17. This chapter reports complete data on longitudinal Rorschach findings in 35 girls and 30 boys, each tested at yearly intervals from 10 to 16 years of age. * Many readers may be surprised to find that children are not remarkably different than they were a decade or more ago * The preeminent import of this revision is still essentially the same as that of the original text, as elaborated upon in detail by Piotrowski in the introduction to this revision, i.e., a presentation of "numerous needed guideposts for the one-timed and long-term study of individual children" (p. v). No one can deny the homage due this text from this point of view and, as with the original text, it will remain a classic.

Austral J Psychol 25(3):263–4 D '73. A. F. Condie. * contains only minor revisions * There are some significant shortcomings in the study which limit the usefulness of the norms; this is unfortunate in view of the tremendous amount of work that has obviously gone into the task of collecting, scoring and analysing the data. In the first place, the sample selected for study is anything but representative; the authors freely acknowledge that the children are well above average in intelligence (with a mean IQ. of 116), that they come from a very high socio-economic background, and that the sample is drawn from a limited geographical area. Secondly, the pool of protocols on which the norms were based was obtained from only 398 children, most of whom had contributed two or more test records; the readministration of the test to the same children at intervals of about 12 months appears to have led to a gradual reduction in their productivity and an increase in the number of card refusals, and must also have affected the norms in other significant but unspecifiable ways, leaving the clinical psychologist with doubts about the validity of comparing his "first-time" cases with these "repeat" norms. Finally, the authors use a scoring system which is somewhat idiosyncratic; it is derived mainly from Loosli-Usteri, whose scoring would be unfamiliar to most Australian psychologists, but includes also some elements of the Hertz and Klopfer systems as well as the authors' own method of scoring shading responses and W differentiation. Despite its shortcomings, this study, based as it is upon an impressive number of subjects, is an important milestone in the

continuing search for adequate norms for a test which, ironically, has now been in wide clinical use for over fifty years. One of the most interesting findings to emerge is that the "developmental trends" referred to in the title do not follow a smooth, consistent pattern; in fact there would appear to be very few scores in which the norms for 16 year olds would be significantly different from those for the 10 year olds. However, the authors have found an alternating personality pattern at successive age levels, with constriction, withdrawal and alienation at or around age 13 being followed by increased expansiveness at 14 years, further constriction around 15 years and further expansion at 16 years. This research also corrects a number of popular misconceptions, particularly the finding that some of the more malignant test "signs" derived from studies of adult psychiatric groups may occur quite frequently in a normal adolescent population. This second edition will continue to be of use to clinical psychologists who work with adolescents, and will also serve as a reference book in post-graduate courses on projective techniques.

J Sch Psychol 11(3):283–4 f '73. Richard R. Waite. This is a revised edition of a book written 12 years ago which reported the study of some 700 Rorschach protocols obtained from children ages ten through 16. For this revision the authors have re-evaluated the 700 records and have rewritten parts of the book, bringing to the study new knowledge and experience gained in the 12-year interim. In addition, they present and discuss test results obtained annually from each of 65 children seen from 10 to 16 years. * The subjects do not constitute a representative sample of American adolescents. Three-quarters of the subjects' fathers were classified as professional, semi-professional, or managerial. The estimated mean IQ of all subjects was 115.9. No indication is given of ethnic or cultural backgrounds of the subjects. Consequently, the degree to which the study's findings can be generalized is severely limited. Nevertheless, the results demonstrate the utility of a developmental approach to behavior (Rorschach responses), which is most often understood in terms of clinical considerations. Probably developmental factors are most important for testing in the preschool and adolescent years because of the rapid changes due to psychological growth during these periods. The analysis of the data is presented in detail, with the pertinent results sometimes difficult to differentiate from the mass of data. For the interested reader, these details can be helpful. For the reader attempting to understand the expected changes in Rorschach protocols as subjects grow from ten to 16, the section is not altogether helpful. It is in the second section that the book's major value can be found. Here the developmental trends are presented clearly. The authors present "composite Rorschachs" for each age level and indicate not only the central trends but also the features which are particularly prominent at each given age. The reader easily gains a feel for the kinds of test behavior to expect year by year. Many of the observations based upon the data clearly fit in with the prior developmental emphasis presented in their earlier writings * Thus, for the reader who is familiar with, and is accepting of, the developmental conceptualizations of the Gesell school, this study has a strong appeal. The more eclectic reader will be more likely to raise questions about the degree to which the study's conclusions were influenced by the authors' theoretical biases. The third section of the study, focusing on the longitudinal comparisons of protocols obtained on subjects who were tested yearly, is of value primarily as supporting evidence for the findings of the second section. Throughout the book the authors give special attention to sex differences in protocols. This emphasis is especially gratifying to the serious student of adolescent development. For the reader with strong interests in psychoanalytic theory, ego psychology, and perceptual and cognitive concepts, the authors' conclusions can be disappointing. Nevertheless, enough basic data are presented so that these kinds of readers will have an opportunity to explore the relevance of their own conceptualizations. On the whole, the book is a valuable contribution both to developmental and clinical psychology.

[B26]

*AMES, LOUISE BATES; MÉTRAUX, RUTH W.; RODELL, JANET LEARNED; AND WALKER, RICHARD N. **Child Rorschach Responses: Developmental Trends From Two to Ten Years, Second Edition.** New York: Brunner/Mazel, Inc., 1974. Pp. xiv, 321. $12.50. * For a review of the earlier edition see 5:B40.

J Pers Assess 39(3):312 Je '75. Denis J. Lynch. Since its publication in 1952, the first edition of this book has been a valuable addition to the library of the clinician working with children. There is an obvious yet critical need for

appropriate norms with which to evaluate children's Rorschach responses. The steady developmental changes occurring in childhood dictate the importance of separate norms at several age levels. However, one serious shortcoming of the previous edition was the nature of the normative sample. By the authors' own description, these children were, "mostly bright, healthy children of mostly highly educated parents." (p. xiii). While such a group might be generally comparable to the clientele of a private practitioner, the clinician in public supported agencies could only use the available norms as the best approximation of expectations for their client group and hope that he or she would not go too far wrong. In the second edition, however, findings from three other samples of different levels of socioeconomic status (including black inner city children) are presented. This supplement is probably the most significant and valuable change from the first edition. Other changes include the addition of longitudinal data accumulated by the authors during the interval between the publication of the first and second editions. * The material new to the second edition is found primarily in the final part, which includes the longitudinal data and socioeconomic comparisons mentioned previously, as well as a chapter on the Rorschach and evaluation. Studies relating "danger signals" on the Rorschach to childhood psychopathology and also on the prediction of reading problems from preschool Rorschach performances are reported. This final chapter left the reviewer somewhat unsatisfied since it did not deal in much depth with these important areas and seemed to be added almost as an afterthought. For any clinician who uses the Rorschach with children, this book is indispensable. Both the experienced clinician and the beginning student can find valuable content. The material dealing with administration, scoring and interpretation, while woven into the overall plan of the book, is presented clearly enough that the novice can appreciate it. The detailed normative information for children at various age levels and of different social classes is of inestimable value in the day-to-day work of even the most experienced clinician.

J Sch Psychol 12(4):341–2 w '74. John F. Tedesco. * The revised edition adds discussions on refined scoring techniques, longitudinal data, and data from the lower socioeconomic levels. Nearly 250 protocols have been added to the original sample. * In sum, this is a text for the school psychologist, clinical psychologist, or mental health worker who has had experience in administering and interpreting Rorschach data. Its major use is as a very excellent reference for age norms with samples comparable to the original sample. Secondly, the new longitudinal and socioeconomic data provide good basic data for further expansion and comparison. Finally, the new discussion of danger signals used to evaluate emotional disturbance was quite instructive. At first blush the huge amount of data makes it difficult for the reader to discern trends, and most of the developmental discussion appears to be based upon the Gesell school of thought. Upon second perusal, however, the text presents an excellent starting point for the serious student who is in the process of developing his own internal norms or for the professional interested in relating the results to his own view of human development.

[B27]

*AMES, LOUISE BATES; MÉTRAUX, RUTH W.; RODELL, JANET LEARNED; AND WALKER, RICHARD N. **Rorschach Responses in Old Age, [Revised Edition]**. New York: Brunner/Mazel, Inc., 1973. Pp. xvii, 219. $12.50. * For reviews of the earlier edition, see 5:B41 (2 excerpts).

Am J Psychiatry 132(2):213–4 F '75. Margaret Thaler Singer. This is a revised edition of the volume of the same name originally published in 1953. The changes between editions consist of the insertion of a page and a half of material on scoring whole responses, an increase from 8 to 61 in the number of persons retested, the deletion of several individual case examples to make room for a new short chapter on supplementary tests, and the addition of 10 new citations to the references. * The weaknesses of the book lie in its over-simplification of old age as a period of reverse growth and its efforts to locate individual aged persons at a single behavior level or level of intactness rather than using such concepts as dimensions or domains of behavior. * The authors' findings are far more complex and fascinating than their concepts of levels. The merits of the book lie in the qualitative sign checklists devised by the authors. One list of signs consists of those found in childrens' Rorschachs that do not appear in Rorschachs of normal adults. A second list of signs is composed of those which the writers feel do not characteristically appear in either normal adults' or normal childrens' records. These checklists become central in ordering the findings of this

research. In summary, one can recommend the sign checklists devised by the authors to quantify the qualitative features of Rorschach performance in aged persons without endorsing some of the theoretical underpinnings of the volume. This book had much to offer when it first appeared 20 years ago and still does.

J Pers Assess 38(4):389 Ag '74. Margaret Mercer. The Revised Edition....differs from the original version published in 1954 in reports of two longitudinal studies (Ames, 1960a, b) by the senior author, and reports (Pelz, Pike & Ames, 1961, 1962) of a selected group of preschool and school age tests (Ilg & Ames, 1972) given to discriminate between different levels of intactness of the elderly subjects. * The reader familiar with the original edition would do better to consult the complete reports mentioned above, than to purchase the new edition. For the beginner, the values of the original edition still hold. It provides good examples of records of subjects over 70 years of age who were reasonably healthy and alert. The careful analyses of their responses in relation to those of the children whom the authors have previously studied (Ames et al, 1973) are helpful in putting the changes of the aging process into a developmental perspective.

[B28]

*ANASTASI, ANNE. **Psychological Testing, Fourth Edition.** New York: Macmillan Publishing Co., Inc., 1976. Pp. xiii, 750. $15.95. * (Instructor's Manual by John T. Cowles. Pp. iii, 123. Paper, gratis. *) For reviews of earlier editions, see 7:B44 (4 excerpts), 6:B53 (3 excerpts), and 5:B42 (9 excerpts).

Brit J Psychiatry 129:393–7 O '76. Anne Broadhurst. Anastasi's *Psychological Testing* has rightly been revered since its original publication in 1954 as an authoritative and, above all, lucid account of practical psychometrics, of value to the expert as a ready reference book and to the beginner for its painstaking exposition of difficult material. Revised editions have appeared in 1961 and 1968 and now, before we have had opportunity to regard the 1968 edition as out of date, the tireless author has provided us with a fourth edition. * Anastasi's judgement and her skill in condensation are remarkable and combine to make a whole which lacks nothing vital from the past while incorporating much that is new. * This is one of those rare occasions when one can recommend a book entirely wholeheartedly. For those psychologists, psychiatrists and others interested in objective recording who do not already possess Anastasi, this edition is essential. Owners may still consider the new one worthwhile. The references bring one right up to 1975 and the price is right for today and the value of the contents.

J Ed Meas 13(2):167–9 su '76. W. B. Schrader. This new edition of a successful textbook by a distinguished psychologist incorporates timely changes in emphasis and a substantial amount of significant new material. * Nearly half of the references now cited did not appear in the preceding edition. Development of sensitivity to the social and ethical implications of testing has been elevated to the point where it is now one of the four major subgoals of the text, and the attention given to minority group testing has been markedly increased. Among the new topics covered are: criterion-referenced testing, adaptive testing, the impact of Piaget's conceptions on early childhood testing, the assessment of learning disabilities, the notion of heritability of intelligence, and the application of social learning theory to personality testing. A new "how-to" section on writing clinical reports and an outline for preparing a test evaluation have been added. Some changes in organization have been made, including the introduction of a full chapter—the third—on social and ethical implications. * Although the changes in the book are pervasive, there is nevertheless a strong continuity with previous editions. The essential conceptual structure of the book, the treatment of most methodological topics, and the discussion of many well-established tests are carried over from the third edition with little change. * the book has a remarkable intellectual coherence despite the complex, diverse, and often controversial field it seeks to encompass. This edition, like its predecessors, maintains a careful balance between stimulation for the top students and accessibility for marginal students. It also balances a strongly empirical approach with a recognition of values not adequately handled by available empirical methods. The overall impression one receives from the book is that the author has sought to be scrupulously fair to each idea, method, and test chosen for treatment. Not surprisingly, the style in which the book is written is also tightly disciplined. It is often highly condensed, but consistently clear and well-organized. Of particular interest is Anastasi's treatment of the testing of minority groups—a matter that she discusses under various appropriate headings

throughout the text. * The section on the *validity* of scores for minority group members warrants special comment. Much thought and research effort have been given to this topic during the past 10 years. In this section, a review of correlational studies clarifies technical issues and highlights the results. The essential analysis of covariance concepts are unusually well explained. The section as a whole is excellent, but the last few paragraphs are somewhat difficult to understand. * This book is admirably suited to serve as a textbook in a course for which a thorough grounding in the main ideas, methods, and instruments of present-day testing is a major objective. It should also be useful as a reference book and guide to the literature on psychological testing. I recommend it highly to test users who want to know more about current thinking in the testing field and who are willing to devote a reasonable amount of effort to working through the relevant chapters.

Personnel Psychol 30(3):464–7 au '77. Paul M. Muchinsky. * This version of the book does nothing to tarnish the impeccable quality of its predecessors, and further illustrates how Anastasi has made a truly masterful contribution to the profession of psychology. * the third chapter....is completely new. It reflects a major revision along the lines of "general orientation toward testing," involving such issues as protection of privacy, confidentiality, and testing and the civil rights of minorities. This chapter accurately portrays many of the problems and issues associated with the social implications of testing, but also omits several issues that I hope will be addressed in the next edition. In describing the fine line between freedom of information and the right to privacy, I feel some discussion of the "Buckley Amendment" is in order. This piece of legislation has a significant impact on the whole issue of confidentiality, especially in regard to information communicated via letters of reference which may contain information regarding test performance. This chapter would be the appropriate place in the book to include such a discourse. Secondly, I feel Anastasi should more fully embrace the theme of the *legal* (as well as the social and ethical) implications of testing. A recent symposium ("Federal Government Intervention in Psychological Testing: Is it Here?") published in *Personnel Psychology* (1976) speaks well to the salience of this topic for psychological testing. The referenced symposium is but one of a growing body of such programs attempting to resolve or at least understand the interface of psychological testing and federal legislation. In short I feel this topic is underrepresented in the book. Thirdly, while the 1970 EEOC guidelines and the 1974 OFCC guidelines are published in the appendices, only an ardent reader would detect that these two guidelines diverge in several places. Anastasi barely mentions the immense problem of employers having to deal with multiple guidelines that are by no means uniform. She does acknowledge via a footnote that the EEOCC was not successful in drafting a set of uniform guidelines, but she does not address the problem of compliance with divergent (and sometimes contradictory) guidelines. Lastly, in her discussion of testing and the civil rights of minorities, it would have been instructive had she cited some of the financial settlements that have resulted from litigation against employers for using invalid testing procedures. If nothing else this would serve to awaken readers to the fact that the impact of federal intervention in psychological testing is more than the propagation of bureaucratic red-tape. If there is a common theme running through my criticisms of this chapter, it would be the insufficient attention given to legalistic matters. While I fully realize that in their purest forms psychological testing and the law have little in common, in current practice they have become unnatural bedfellows which cannot be estranged. The second section of the book is entitled "Principles of Psychological Testing" and is a *tour de force*. The revisions in this section are primarily of the "substantive and methodological developments" type. In addition to her highly lucid presentations of the basic topics of norms, reliability, validity, etc., she discusses the increase in popularity of criterion-referenced and mastery testing, particularly in education. These testing procedures are explained in the context of entire educational programs involving computer-managed self-paced instructional systems. Anastasi does a nice job of explaining how various testing methods fit into large applied systems, such as educational or industrial settings. Her discussion of synthetic validity is itself a highly informative synthesis of previous writings on this sometimes elusive concept. Other recent additions include a discussion of decision theory applied to classification problems, and a straightforward presentation of test

bias and differential validity. The latter topics are not easily comprehended, but by separating regression analysis data into slope bias and intercept bias, these knotty issues are reduced in complexity. In addition to technical presentations, Anastasi offers her own opinions regarding the usefulness of statistical adjustments in test scores as a means of correcting social inequities. All in all, this section of the book gets very high marks. Sections three, four, and five are presentations of tests of intelligence, ability, and personality, respectively. The primary type of revision in these sections involves updating new tests that have been developed since the last edition, but also include some substantive and methodological developments. A major development....is a discussion of the Jensen controversy centering on the heritability and modifiability of intelligence. The content of the chapter devoted to occupational testing is similar to previous editions, and regrettably, the "tone" of the chapter is basically unchanged. Since publication of the previous edition, the overall use of occupational (ability and aptitude) tests is down, a product of the legal ramifications associated with psychological testing. It would have been instructive of Anastasi to comment on the lesser play given to such tests in recent times as a means of documenting the implications of federal intervention. However the content of the chapters is very thorough, as she describes recent research done with in-basket tests and work samples. The section on personality tests was written with increased emphasis on situational specificity and person-by-situation interactions in personality testing. The chapter dealing with vocational interest inventories is particularly strong, as Anastasi discusses how the Strong Vocational Interest Blank evolved into the Strong-Campbell Interest Inventory. Considerable attention is devoted to Holland's Hexagonal Model and the interrelationships among the various vocational interest measures. The final chapter is devoted to other assessment techniques and represents a grab-bag of situational stress tests, leaderless group discussions, peer evaluations, biographical inventory data, and perceived social climates. The content of this last chapter is extremely heterogeneous and doesn't flow as readily as previous chapters. However, the assessment techniques are well documented and clearly described despite their relative vagabond status within the book. In trying to describe the appropriate market for this book, it might be easier to list for whom the book would be *inappropriate*. It might be too general for laymen wanting a step-by-step cookbook description of how to validate a test. It would be too low-powered for methodologists concerned with statistical nuances of demonstrating test bias. Additionally, it probably would be too incomplete for the clinician who wanted a complete listing of all diagnostic tests. However, a book cannot be all things to all people. It provides enough information about test validation to inform the layman of relevant issues and problems. It does provide a clear account of test bias at a level that would satisfy most readers. Lastly, while the book is not a compendium of all psychological tests (Anastasi herself said her goal was not to write a miniature *Mental Measurements Yearbook*), this edition does contain over 100 tests that were initially published or revised since the last edition. In summary, this book should have a very broad market. Practitioners as well as academicians would benefit from having this book within arm's reach. While I certainly would not recommend changing the title of this well-known book, it should be apparent from this review that the book covers far more material than suggested by the title, or alternatively, *all* the ramifications of "psychological testing" are encompassed within this book. While I am critical of certain parts of the book (dealing almost exclusively with omissions), my criticisms are miniscule compared to the wealth of material presented by Anastasi. If my personal library could contain only five books to represent all of psychology, *Psychological Testing* would be one of them. This book is most deserving of its revered reputation. It continues to be the standard against which other texts are judged.

[B29]

★ANDERSON, BETTY R., AND ROGERS, MARTHA P., EDITORS. **Personnel Testing and Equal Employment Opportunity.** Washington, D.C.: U.S. Government Printing Office, 1970. Pp. viii, 48. Paper, $0.95. *

[B30]

★ANDERSON, JONATHAN. **Psycholinguistic Experiments in Foreign Language Testing.** St. Lucia, Australia: University of Queensland Press, 1976. Pp. x, 159. Aus $13.50. *

[B31]

ANDERSON, SCARVIA B.; BALL, SAMUEL; MURPHY, RICHARD T.; AND ASSOCIATES. **Encyclopedia of Educational Evaluation.** San Francisco, Calif.: Jossey-Bass Inc., Publishers, 1975. Pp. xxv, 515. $17.50. *

J Ed Meas 12(4):295–7 w '75. Donald M. Miller. * Presented as an encyclopedia....the volume is unsatisfactory in light of the many and varied purposes and functions that education and training evaluation is expected to serve. The book indeed is not an encyclopedia in the ordinarily accepted sense. It is neither sufficiently comprehensive, well-rounded, nor detailed to be so named. Rather it is a discursive technical glossary furnished with an apparatus of references and cross-references by which the reader interested in the topic briefly covered by a given entry may pursue the subject in somewhat greater depth. Without argument or justification the authors assert in the preface, "We recognize that *almost* everything there is to say about evaluation of education and training programs has already been said—or written— somewhere." By making this assertion and by calling their book an "encyclopedia" the authors seem to be giving the impression, especially to the lay public, that the field of evaluation is now mature and well-understood. But such is not the case. As this reviewer sees the situation, the field is still in the youth of its development with boundaries, subject matter, and methods imprecisely delineated. To suggest otherwise is to give the volume an illusory air of authority which the current capabilities of the field cannot sustain; for it is a field in which many questions of professional and public import are likely to remain unresolved for a long time to come. * major concepts and techniques are described in 144 "articles" presented in alphabetic sequence throughout the body of the book * A typical article—as this reviewer sees the modal pattern—begins with a discursive description of the topic and then expands to commentary on selected aspects and issues. This style provides the reader with a survey of the surface characteristics of the topic—a topographic view as it were—but gives little analytic depth or orientation in terms of implications for the practice of evaluating education and training programs. The several articles dealing specifically with statistics demonstrate the limitations of this style. * This lack of information and guidance is most apparent in the nearly complete absence of literature citations within the text of any article. * No explicit explanation or application of editorial guidelines is given for the inclusion or exclusion of concepts and techniques. So many areas and topics are absent from this volume that it can hardly be considered a definitive reference for the theory and practice of evaluation. RFPs are discussed, for instance, but no attention is given to the many other ways in which evaluation studies may be commissioned. Confidentiality of data is surveyed in one article, but only literature references give the reader clues as to the various other ethical and legal issues involved in evaluation. Dissemination of results is considered, but many of the facets of presenting and reporting evaluation outcomes are neglected. No recognition is given to ethnographic (and microethnographic) approaches to evaluation. Nor is mention made of jackknifing, the possible significance of outliers, budget and financial considerations, or the needs of clients and client-evaluator interrelationships. The authors partially state the guidelines which conditioned their choice or rejection of material, but they do not indicate how their editorial procedures determined the content domain for terminology discussed and for literature cited. A clue to the authors' guidelines is given cryptically in the preface where they put the reader on notice concerning some of their own values and viewpoints. There they say that they prefer "objective evidence over testimony....place high value on the construct validity of measures.... think that the common aspects of education and training should be emphasized rather than the distinctions." This last preference suggests that those concerned with the importance of diversity in bilingual-bicultural educational opportunities will find very limited use for this volume. The authors have recognized the need for a reference book in the field of evaluation and have concretely responded. But, in the opinion of this reviewer, the needed reference resource should be much broader in scope and more responsive to the diverse interests and needs of all types of participants in evaluative activities.

Meas & Eval Guid 8(3):208 O '75. Donald G. Zytowski. It really *is* an encyclopedia! The first entry is "accountability" and the last is "variance." (It could have been Z-scores!) There are no chapters; rather, each of approximately 130 entries are between 2 and as many as 20 pages. Each article is cross-referenced with other entries and is followed by a selected annotated bibliography. Some are on completely ordinary concepts—"grades"—while others concern the obscure—"Johnson-Neyman Technique" or "Lord's Paradox." * The problem with the book is how, or by whom, it is best used. A practicing evaluator probably already

knows a good deal about most of the concepts that are explained. The encyclopedia might be useful to the evaluator-in-training, who needs to get a broad but not deep knowledge of a number of evaluation concepts. It might be especially useful for the administrator who might run up against a concept treated in a proposal or a report and needs a quick and clean way to get a grasp of it. The bibliography given after each entry could be a quick refresher for the most pertinent sources, if you lost your grasp of, say, "Delphi technique" or "test anxiety."

[B32]

★ANDRULIS, RICHARD S. **Adult Assessment: A Source Book of Tests and Measures of Human Behavior.** Springfield, Ill.: Charles C Thomas, Publisher, 1977. Pp. xx, 325. Paper, spiral binding, $12.50. *

[B33]

★ANGOFF, WILLIAM H., AND MODU, CHRISTOPHER C. **Equating the Scales of the Prueba de Aptitud Acadímica and the Scholastic Aptitude Test.** College Entrance Examination Board, Research Report 3. New York: the Board, 1973. Pp. vi, 37. Paper, $1.50. *

[B34]

★ANNETT, JOHN. **Psychometrics.** Milton Keynes, England: Open University Press, 1974. Pp. 116. Paper, £1.95. * (New York: Open University Educational Media, Inc. $5.25.)

[B35]

★ANTHONY, H. SYLVIA. **An Experiment in Personality Assessment of Young Men Remanded in Custody.** Home Office Research Studies 13. London: Her Majesty's Stationery Office, 1972. Pp. viii, 79. 52.5p. *

[B36]

★APPLE, MICHAEL W.; SUBKOVIAK, MICHAEL J.; AND LUFLER, HENRY S., JR.; EDITORS. **Educational Evaluation: Analysis and Responsibility.** Berkeley, Calif.: McCutchan Publishing Corporation, 1974. Pp. xxi, 330. $13.50. *

J Ed Meas 13(3):239–41 f '76. Ingemar Wedman. * My general impression of this book is that its stated aims are worthwhile and that it accomplishes them to a very large extent. The reader is furnished with many convincing arguments: for example, that the evaluator must attend to the value systems in which schools operate, that the social phenomena affecting education are many and complex, and that, consequently, "solutions" to many of the problems we today face in our schools will not be reached easily. Apple's opening chapter nicely sets the stage for this approach. The chapters by Scriven and Jackson stand out in my mind as particularly valuable. And most of the remaining chapters contain much that the conscientious evaluator should ponder. Although the book is addressed primarily to professional evaluators, it should also be of interest to students preparing to enter the field and to the educational decision-makers who hire evaluators. [See original review for additional critical comments not excerpted.]

Meas & Eval Guid 8(3):207–8 O '75. Donald G. Zytowski. * a collection of papers from a conference on educational evaluation sponsored by the School of Education of the University of Wisconsin in 1973. * Most readers will probably find one or two topics of special interest. Mine were the two chapters, by Apple and by Karier, on the ideologies that condition our efforts and thinking about evaluations and on the need to be conscious of how they suggest what questions we ask, not to mention how we go about answering them. * Cook's extensive development of the idea of secondary evaluations was interesting too. * An interesting feature of the book is the critical response following each of the invited presentations, prepared by University of Wisconsin faculty members, and the reproduction of some of the questions and answers which ensued. They answer some of the questions that come to mind as you read; in any other book such questions wouldn't get answered. All in all, *Educational Evaluation* is an interesting book for the practicing or about-to-practice evaluator. It may make you conscious of some of your biases and may suggest some intriguing ways of evaluation that may rise above those biases.

[B37]

★ARNOLD, CHARLES B. **Could There Be a Medical Basis for the Declining SAT Scores? Appendixes to On Further Examination: Report of the Advisory Panel on the Scholastic Aptitude Test Score Decline.** New York: College Entrance Examination Board, 1977. Pp. 624. Paper, $2.00. * (For the summary report of the Advisory Panel, see B108.)

[B38]

★ARONOW, EDWARD, AND REZNIKOFF, MARVIN. **Rorschach Content Interpretation.** New York: Grune & Stratton, Inc., 1976. Pp. xv, 362. $19.50. *

J Pers Assess 41(5):549–50 O '77. Max R. Reed. * an outstanding work. It is not only that there are approximately 500 excellent references, ranging chronologically from 1897 to 1976, but that they are organized topically in such a way that the book is coherent, readable, and currently relevant. * The chapters provide excellent descriptions of the various approaches to content analysis combined with extensive

coverage of studies of reliability and validity for each major approach or system. The book abounds in helpful examples of scoring criteria for the various systems. The general findings reflect well reviewed research indicating that analysis with content categories, including verbalizations and behavioral styles, yields more valid, reliable results than previously used formal, perceptually focused analyses. Although the writers point up limitations necessarily imposed by validity and reliability findings for the various systems covered, they do express conviction that applying more flexible approaches to administration of the Rorschach is fruitful. * In summary, the authors state that the Rorschach test can simultaneously measure a host of personality characteristics in a relatively short period of time, but that the personality characteristics are likely to be measured with a relatively low degree of precision. They go on to contend that part of the problem arises from two divergent but often combined approaches to Rorschach interpretation, normative and idiographic. They decry the lack of normative data for content responses of various sorts which will of necessity, lead to errors in idiographic prediction. The authors present a rationale with principles and procedures which inform the unwary Rorschach user when not to interpret, and how to avoid wild analysis. Accompanying their comments that they see the idiographic approach as the most valuable source of information provided by the Rorschach test are warnings regarding limitations on the uses of such information. * In spite of this reviewer's mild objections to what, at times, seemed to him an inordinate number of warnings regarding dangers of Rorschach test use, he would wholeheartedly recommend this book for graduate students, researchers, and clinicians who have some knowledge of and interest in the Rorschach test and in personality assessment.

[B39]

★ASTIN, ALEXANDER W. **Predicting Academic Performance in College: Selectivity Data for 2300 American Colleges.** New York: Free Press, 1971. Pp. ix, 299. $12.95. *

[B40]

★AYLESWORTH, THOMAS G. **Graphology: A Guide to Handwriting Analysis.** New York: Franklin Watts, Inc., 1976. Pp. xii, 60. $4.90. *

[B41]

★BAIRD, LEONARD L. **Using Self-Reports to Predict Student Performance.** Research Monograph

No. 7. New York: College Entrance Examination Board, 1976. Pp. vi, 90. Paper, $5.00. *

J Pers Assess 41(2):186-7 Ap '77. Chadwick Karr. * Baird presents convincing evidence for the utility of brief self-reported information obtained from high school and college students. The evidence suggests that all one has to do is ask the person a simple question to get an accurate answer which has equal or greater predictive validity than the results obtained from published pencil-and-paper personality inventories. However, brief self-report questionnaires can be improved by the application of psychometric procedures such as item analysis and multiple regression. * The author makes a strong plea for the development of theoretical explanations for the empirical validity of brief self-reports. * Baird makes no mention of the technique of configural scoring which also can produce homogeneous subgroups. * Section I of the monograph provides evidence that students can report their grades accurately, but that this information has little predictive value with respect to successful performance beyond formal academic training (Section III). There is an erroneous implication when this lack of correlation is reported between grades or rank in class and subsequent level of income or other measure of success *within* a narrowly defined field of work such as a profession. This misleading implication which Baird does not dispel is that academic ability as measured by intelligence tests or by grades is unrelated to socio-economic status (SES). Taking the world of work at large, IQ and SES do have a positive relationship. * the monograph seems better suited to be a supplementary text for a graduate course in psychological assessment than as a guide to the development and use of questionnaires designed to provide brief self-report information. * One other type of information lacking in this monograph is an author and subject index. It would also help to have a listing of published brief self-report questionnaires, their publishers, and a brief description of each. The author's writing style is especially well suited to his topic. He is clear, succinct, and precise. The organization of the material is logical and internally consistent. Baird has achieved his purpose which was to provide a review of the value of brief self-report information obtained from high school and college students. He has done us all a service by showing us a promising direction to take in our efforts to make available better information to decision-makers, whether they be students, parents, counselors, advisors, teachers, administrators, or researchers. I especially recommend this monograph for classes in psychological assessment.

[B42]

*BARNETTE, W. LESLIE, JR., EDITOR. **Readings in Psychological Tests and Measurements, Third Edition.** New York: Oxford University Press, 1976. Pp. xiv, 415. Paper, $7.95. * For reviews of earlier editions, see 7:B59 (2 excerpts) and 7:B60 (1 excerpt).

J Pers Assess 40(6):643-6 D '76. Jon D. Swartz and Roland Dougherty. * Barnette has done a yeoman job of editing the selections: he has trimmed away superfluous parts from some of the readings, he has put considerable effort into his comments before (and sometimes, after) each reading, and on occasion he has even summarized other publications on the same and related topics. * there are minor errors * the Author Index seems to omit almost as many names mentioned in the text as it includes. * should prove to be an adequate textbook, or a valuable supplement to other teaching materials, in an undergraduate course in the psychology of testing. [See original review for additional critical comments not excerpted.]

J Sch Psychol 15(4):370-1 w '77. Everett E. Davis. * This book of readings....is "designed for advanced undergraduate majors in psychology." It probably, however, will be used at least equally often by psychologists in the field, for there is a vast literature in this area and the practitioner in no way can scan it all. As the editor suggests, there are seven other standard anthologies which with this volume "constitute a very complete and concise library of materials dealing with psychological tests and measurements." The format of this volume is convenient for the practitioner since many of these readings are merely excerpts; they are short and present a wide range of ideas. If the psychologist in the school can find a free 5 or 10 minutes during the busy day he can sample Barnette's selection and find grist which will enrich the produce of the mill of his mind. There is no questioning the eclecticism of the choices, and the ensuing sense of potpourri may be one of the reasons that reading this book is a mildly frustrating experience, especially for some of the earlier selections. Of the 52 presentations one-half are related in varying degrees to schools or education. These 26 articles and excerpts take up approximately 60% of pages of text and vary in length from about 2½ to 15 pages in length. It may be that undergraduates will benefit from the article on examinations for admission to the police academy in South Viet-Nam in 1955–1957, and the frankness of the author is highly commendable. As an example of psychometrics, though, the article seems amateurish, maybe because of its display of insensitivity to the customs and modes of conduct of cultures other than our own. Quite likely this selection was included because, as Barnette says, it was interest provoking, and one would hope that it was unusual. Although not as objectionable in tone, the report on testing in Nigeria seems elementary and longer than necessary. What might be considered a shortcoming is the inclusion of some studies which appear to be highly inadequate from a clean psychometric point of view. These comments are probably unfairly and unnecessarily adverse because as the editor states, he chose "readings of recent origin to supplement the basic text," including some that were "rather unusual and interest-provoking." This procedure was deliberately chosen to afford an opportunity for lively and wide-ranging discussion. Two of the more challenging selections are Jensen's "Understanding Readiness" and Cole and Bruner's "Cultural Differences and Inferences about Psychological Processes." One reason that Jensen's work is so widely discussed is that everyone can understand what he is saying. His article is easily readable, and one of the concepts with which it deals is the concept of "readiness." Jensen objects to teaching before the child is ready to learn. As he says, "The adverse effect of ignoring readiness by persisting in instruction beyond the child's present ability is to cause....'turning off.' This amounts to an increasing inhibition of the very behaviors that promote learning." In another vein Cole and Bruner stress the importance of the ecological environment in which the test item is administered. The gist of their article is that "cultural differences reside more in differences in the situations to which different cultural groups apply their skills than to differences in the skills possessed by the groups in question." This book contains an abundance of good pertinent material. One can mention in addition to the selections already noted the treatments of proficiency testing by Ebel and DuBois, the Pace articles on college and university atmosphere, Super's discussion of multifactor batteries, the Campbell

and Cooley selections. Some of the more topical, but less technically qualified, articles deal with people and situations not directly connected with the schools. This, however, is a rather superficial distinction, because testing which is begun in business or industry invariably later is used in schools, and testing which originates in the schools sooner or later is used in the world of work. The school psychologist will find it well worth his time to look at this collection of readings.

[B43]

★Beck, Samuel J. **The Rorschach Test Exemplified in Classics of Drama and Fiction.** New York: Stratton Intercontinental Medical Book Corp., 1976. Pp. ix, 134. Paper, $14.75. *

[B44]

★Beegle, Charles W., and Brandt, Richard M., Editors. **Observational Methods in the Classroom.** Washington, D.C.: Association for Supervision and Curriculum Development, 1973. Pp. ix, 85. Paper, $3.50. *

[B45]

★Beggs, Donald L., and Lewis, Ernest L. **Measurement and Evaluation in the Schools.** Boston, Mass.: Houghton Mifflin Co., 1975. Pp. xiii, 250. $11.50. *

[B46]

Bellak, Leopold; with the assistance of Ann Noll and Lynn Lustbader. **The Thematic Apperception Test and the Children's Apperception Test in Clinical Use, Second Edition.** New York: Grune & Stratton, Inc., 1971. Pp. xvi, 328. * *Out of print.* For reviews of the first edition, see 5:B63 (8 excerpts). For the latest edition, see B46A.

J Pers Assess 36(6):585 D '72. Sarah A. Alleman. This book is, for many psychologists, an old friend. * If a second edition tempts us to reread Bellak, it is more than worth the publishers' investment and ours. More than any other book on thematic analysis, Bellak's reawakens the sense of subtlety and excitement that is so easily lost in this age of ANOV. * The opening chapter provides an excellent grounding (or "apperceptive mass") for not only the TAT and CAT, but all projective tests. It is well worth periodic rereading. * A chapter on "The Study of Character and Defenses on the TAT" is particularly good, but all too brief. The author presents a series of protocols with analysis, referring to individual stories and including peripheral comments on how he came to his conclusions. As a teaching technique, this is unbeatable. He also analyzes briefly TAT stories by Julios Streicher and Alfred Rosenberg, Nazi war criminals, and short stories by Somerset Maugham. These are not only enlightening but fascinating, and provide an added extra-clinical dimension to thematic analysis. There are deficiencies. Some items and concepts are repeated verbatim at several points. While they may bear repeating, the impression is that whole paragraphs were lifted and duplicated. Other sections, particularly the discussion of Bellak TAT Blank scoring categories would profit from expansion and explication. On the whole, however, reading—or rereading—this book is a rewarding experience. The system of interpretation itself is an interesting one, and opens the door to insights into the subject's psychodynamics that may be easily overlooked. It is time-consuming, particularly at first, but well worth the effort even for the experienced clinician. This reviewer recommends that the reader choose a few protocols from his own files—particularly those who don't seem to "say much"—and go through a complete Bellak analysis. He may well be startled at how much he has missed in the past.

[B46A]

*BELLAK, LEOPOLD. **The Thematic Apperception Test, the Children's Apperception Test, and the Senior Apperception Technique in Clinical Use, Third Edition.** New York: Grune & Stratton, Inc., 1975. Pp. xvi, 320. $13.50. * For reviews of the earlier editions, see B46 (1 excerpt) and 5:B63 (8 excerpts).

[B47]

★BHATTACHARYA, SRINIBAS. **Psychometrics and Behavioural Research.** New Delhi, India: Sterling Publishers (P) Ltd., 1972. Pp. v, 254. (New York: International Publications Service, Collings Inc., $13.50.) *

[B48]

*BIELIAUSKAS, VYTAUTAS J. **The House-Tree-Person (H-T-P) Research Review: A Bibliography and Research Review, 1972 Edition.** Los Angeles, Calif.: Western Psychological Services, 1972. Pp. vi, 20. Paper, $5.50. *

[B49]

★BLALOCK, H. M., JR., EDITOR. **Measurement in the Social Sciences: Theories and Strategies.** Chicago, Ill.: Aldine Publishing Co., 1974. Pp. vii, 464. Paper, $8.95; cloth, $16.00. *

Meas & Eval Guid 9(2):85–6 Jl '76. Paul M. Muchinsky. * several chapters are exceptionally well written and offer insightful commentary about selected problems in measurement. For example, a chapter....entitled "Social Attitudes: Magnitude Measurement and Theory" describes the relationship between psychophysical scaling and attitude scaling in an uncharacteristically readable manner. Another chapter....on "Quantifying Unmeasured Variables" does a commendable job of explicating

the problems of quantifying relationships among observed variables and hypothetical constructs. Other chapters appear to be a potpourri of inscrutability, veritable epidemics of equations, arrows, and curves, with a heavy sprinkling of assorted etas, omicrons, and deltas. Such chapters made me feel that there must be an easier way to explain all of this. All of the chapters are highly technical—*caveat emptor!* I suspect that inwardly I would be proud to have this book assume a revered position at the end of my bookshelf along with other measurement books, primed and ready in the event I decide to plunge headlong into the intricacies of Zipf curves; however, at $16.00 it is a rather expensive bookend.

[B50]

★BLANTON, WILLIAM E.; FARR, ROGER; AND TUINMAN, J. JAAP, EDITORS. **Measuring Reading Performance.** Newark, Del.: International Reading Association, Inc., 1974. Pp. vi, 70. Paper, $3.50. *

[B51]

★BLANTON, WILLIAM; FARR, ROGER; AND TUINMAN, J. JAAP; EDITORS. **Reading Tests for the Secondary Grades.** Newark, Del.: International Reading Association, 1972. Pp. 55. Paper, $2.00.

J Read 16(5):405, 407 F '73. Edward Fry. On being asked to review *Reading Tests for the Secondary Grades* I am immediately faced with the same problem as the authors and the potential readers. This problem is expressed on page 53 of the booklet, "These excellent test reviews (in Buros' Mental Measurements Yearbooks) should be studied before a test consumer makes a final test selection." If the consumer should look in the MMY's anyway, why should he look in *Reading Tests for the Secondary Grades?* Now, given that little blast, *Reading Tests for the Secondary Grades* is not a bad little booklet. It certainly is not as complete as the MMY's in range of tests or in number of reviews per test. If one must pander to reading teachers by essentially telling them "you don't need to go to the best source which is all the way over in that nasty library," then this booklet is certainly better than nothing or than just reading the publisher's blurbs or even manuals. Professional reviewers often have insights as to what the manual did not say that might escape the average user. In scope the booklet is reasonably complete in covering the major reading tests for secondary schools. A couple of glaring exceptions are the Comprehensive Test of Basic Skills (California Test Bureau) and Raygor's

Basic Skills System (McGraw-Hill). The authors seem to have been a bit selective in omitting the Wide Range Achievement Test; it got bad reviews in the MMY, but it is often cited in the literature (a fact that you can learn from the MMY's because they include research citations as well as critical reviews) and because the Wide Range is often used by school psychologists and guidance workers in referring students to reading improvement classes. It is surprising that the Burnette Reading Series was omitted, as it was reviewed by Farr, one of the booklet editors, in the 7th MMY; hence, they can't claim they didn't know about it. The signed test reviews themselves are of generally good quality, but there is only one opinion per test. The authors state, "This book is intended primarily for classroom teachers" (page 1), yet we find such technical writing as: "Coefficients appear sufficiently high across all batteries with composite reliabilities on the multi-level edition equal to or greater than .97. Only the Kuder-Richardson Formula 20 was used to compute reliability. While this is one suitable attempt to estimate one source of variance....(p. 42)" I have a few questions about the introduction. Under Validity the editors state, "A reading achievement test should sample the decoding, vocabulary and comprehension skills taught." That is a pretty dogmatic statement for a book on secondary reading tests. It is obvious that most test authors disagree as few secondary tests include decoding. It is also strange in light of the fact that the editors themselves did not see fit to include the California Phonics Survey that is aimed at secondary students. In another section of the introduction the editors state, "The grade placement score has little instructional value" (p. 4). I would like to see this modified somewhat. In instances where there is some deviation from the norm it might have a lot of instructional value. A secondary student who gets a grade placement score of fourth grade on a reading test could probably have quite a bit of trouble reading most high school textbooks—an important instructional fact that is often overlooked in high schools. When the editors attempt to remedy the grade placement score problem they suggest that the teacher make an Informal Reading Inventory using a basal reader (in high school?). But I don't think many high school teachers will follow this direction because among other points, it suggests that "First it is necessary to obtain esti-

mates of reliability of the IRI," etc. * Though I agree that a grade placement score of 6.0 doesn't always mean a student can read sixth grade material, it is still more accurate than most IRI's or no test at all. Finally, most IRA members are surely aware of the current furor over standardized tests, particularly in the innercity. Some minority groups claim that they are unfairly penalized by standardized tests. It wasn't too long ago that the same minorities feared, probably correctly, that they were being excluded from civil service jobs because of favoritism and that objective testing was a fairer method of determining ability. As professionals in the field of reading, we should not bow to emotional criticism. Standardized reading tests do give us one source of valuable information. Yes, they can be misused to hurt children. But misuse does not apply only to tests; it also applies to just about everything: workbooks, films, textbooks, school budgets, sports. Standardized tests can be used to help children. They systematically help us to spot children who are in trouble. They give both the educators and the public some information on how well the schools are doing in teaching reading other than just subjective opinions. Hence, if *Reading Tests for the Secondary Grades* will help the profession to use standardized tests properly, I am all for it. Its chief problem is that it is not comprehensive enough for good teachers and is too hard to read for poor teachers. Its chief benefit is that it is small and limited to a specific area of interest. *

[B52]

★BLOCK, N. J., AND DWORKIN, GERALD, EDITORS. **The IQ Controversy: Critical Readings.** New York: Pantheon Books, 1976. Pp. xiii, 559. Paper, $6.95; cloth, $15.95. *

[B53]

★BLOOD, DON F., AND BUDD, WILLIAM C. **Educational Measurement and Evaluation.** New York: Harper & Row, Publishers, Inc., 1972. Pp. xi, 212. Paper, $7.50. *

J Ed Meas 10(1):75–6 sp '73. Richard C. Cox. * the book is written for present and soon-to-be classroom teachers, thus explaining the emphasis on classroom tests * There are instances throughout the book where the difficulty of text material varies considerably from sentence to sentence and where the intended audience is seemingly ignored. * In many places there are value judgments presented as if they are fact. This is a common phenomenon in introductory texts but not necessarily a good practice. As evidenced daily, a teacher with a little knowledge of measurement could be dangerous. A person with experience in measurement is able to identify and evaluate such judgments, but the layman may cling to such statements with fervor. * In most places the text is written in an understandable fashion and at the appropriate difficulty level. Also, the authors have succeeded in covering most topics relevant to the preparation of classroom tests. However, the absence of other substantive material on evaluation would make its inclusion in the title questionable. In comparison to other books, *Educational Measurement and Evaluation* is quite similar in length, topics covered, and intended audience to such works as Lindeman's *Educational Measurement* and Lindvall's *Measuring Pupil Achievement and Aptitude*. A personal opinion is that both these texts are written better and provide more depth on relevant topics than does the book under review.

Meas & Eval Guid 5(4):508 Ja '73. Ellen L. Betz. If you are looking for a how-to book on classroom tests and you don't mind encouraging a conviction that teacher knows best, you may like this book. It is generally easy to read and contains a lot of descriptive material about different kinds of classroom tests, items, and tally sheets. If, however, your purpose as an educator includes instilling a healthy respect for the potential error in all educational measurement (and its effects on individual students), especially the potential error in one's own tests, then you will have to look further. Not that this book does not contain chapters on topics like test reliability and validity and the related statistics. It does, but a cover-to-cover reading leaves the impression that these topics are really for the birds and that teachers can't seriously be expected to know much of anything about such technical matters. Perhaps this impression is due partly to a certain lack of logic in the order in which topics are presented, as well as to an inadequate integration of topics and principles. For example, the chapter on educational objectives is well written, presenting behavioral objectives as a useful and logical starting point in the development of a test. After a few pages on the topic, however, it is dropped cold: the chapters that follow overlook such objectives entirely; they are not even mentioned in the chapter on the selection and assessment of con-

tent coverage of a test. In turn, content coverage is discussed in relation to developing paper-and-pencil tests but is never mentioned in the preceding chapter on developing structured observational tests. To further confuse things, the text is based on the authors' own opinions as to what the terminology of measurement should be: what is commonly known in the field as validity is termed *relevance* in this book; the authors then redefine *validity* to mean an overall quality of a test, comprised of both reliability and relevance. Without evaluating here the specific redefinitions proposed by Blood and Budd, it seems to the present writer that such atypical definitions are out of place in an elementary textbook, leading to undue difficulty for students in later courses and in their use of other books or professional journals. In the introduction the authors contend that "....the production of good measuring instruments in education is more of an art than a science [p. x]." Unfortunately, there is not enough "art" in this book to compensate for its generally inconsistent presentation of the principles of measurement.

[B54]

BLOOM, BENJAMIN S.; HASTINGS, J. THOMAS; AND MADAUS, GEORGE F. **Handbook on Formative and Summative Evaluation of Student Learning.** New York: McGraw-Hill Book Co., Inc., 1971. Pp. xi, 923. $20.50. * For a review in addition to those below, see 7:B90.

Ed & Psychol Meas 31(4):1033–6 w '71. Warren G. Findley. * the reader may well ponder the opening chapter giving their "View of Education." They forthrightly declare a belief in the fundamental teachability of all children, arguing the considerable modifiability of social-class-linked learning factors of standard language development, motivation to secure maximum education, willingness to work for teacher approval and/or long-term goals, and acceptance of school learning tasks "with a minimum of rebellion." With evaluation turned from selection to development, a modern version of the "plan-test-teach-test-plan" model gives a place for not only fuller specification of instructional objectives in terms of behavioral outcomes, but insertion of formative evaluation and feedback as intervening steps in the "test-teach-test" sequence. Their argument for the primacy of structure of the learning process over structure of a subject seems moot in that there may be more need among their readers for those concerned with process to be attentive to subject structure than vice versa in the present cycle on that issue. Learning for mastery is given the full treatment it deserves. * One wonders whether the present shift from summative and predictive evaluation may not some day make it more natural to present these topics in their proper chronological sequence of placement, diagnosis, formative feedback, and summative evaluation. A third major section (105 pages) relates evaluation procedures to the several categories of the *Taxonomy of Educational Objectives* * The logic of the several levels of cognitive outcomes: knowledge, comprehension, application, analysis, synthesis and evaluation is clearly spelled out and well illustrated with items from college and academic high school levels. * One could wish for a broader set of references at many points. Creativity is discussed under "Synthesis" without mention or listing references to Guilford or Torrance. A warning against narrow interpretation of "Evaluation" as including mere preference is given without reference to the definitive research of Kropp and Stoker. And one misses any reference to the problem of presenting test exercises to young, slow, or foreign students less adept in the nuances of language taken for granted in the illustrations. Chapter 10 on "Evaluation Techniques for Affective Objectives" presents a strong case for including evaluation of the achievement of such objectives. * Short, efficient chapters are devoted to developing the technology of evaluation systems and emerging developments in evaluation. In the first of these, total evaluation systems are conceived as basic to helping the teacher help students learn by organizing a supporting technology and specialists to give leadership and guidance in its use. The second chapter seems unduly eclectic, quoting extensively from National Assessment, but omitting the systematic work of Guba and Stufflebeam and the whole concept of accountability. The subject chapters deserve separate review by separately competent specialists. Suffice it to say here, that this reviewer found the two chapters on preschool education especially rich with detailed illustration and definite comment. * Unfortunate omissions are chapters presumably originally planned in elementary social studies and mathematics. The chapter on secondary school social studies suffers most because of the still prevalent tendency to equate social studies at that level with history and government. Elementary social

studies is a ferment of disciplines, including rediscovery of geography. The chapter on secondary school mathematics will interest many because of the adaptation of the Bloom taxonomy to fit mathematics objectives. * here's to a truly elegant volume, in the best sense of that adjective. It is a reference that should stand long despite the shifting sands of curriculum and society.

J Ed Meas 9(1):86–7 sp '72. *Edward J. Furst.* The overriding purpose of this book is to help the teacher use evaluation to improve teaching and learning. Only incidentally is it intended to offer help on the evaluation of curricula. * They adapt Scriven's terms, which he had applied to curriculum evaluation. Formative evaluation here becomes the evaluation of the student's *learning* during its formation, and summative, at the end. This extension of Scriven's terms seems plausible, but elsewhere in the book overdone, as when one reads about "formative" and "summative" units of instruction and about "summative evaluation of short-term gains" (p. 329). In Part 1 the senior authors begin the attempt to convey the state of the art. Twelve chapters comprise a sound, competent, and up-to-date general survey of the fundamentals, with emphasis upon "mastery learning," formative and summative evaluation, and the two taxonomies produced by Bloom and associates. In Part 2 twelve relatively young but highly competent subject matter specialists present the state of the art in their respective areas (eleven in all). Each chapter follows much the same pattern, beginning with curriculum trends, followed by an overview of content and instructional objectives and culminating in a master table of specifications, an illustration of testing procedures, a short section on formative testing, and a discussion of standardized tests. It is commendable that the collaborating authors have had a rather free hand, particularly to adapt and supplement the two taxonomies as they saw fit. How they did this is, in the reviewer's judgment, one of the most valuable contributions of the entire book. The various chapters are well written, penetrating, and scholarly. * Is it sufficient for a teacher to have knowledge about accepted evaluation practices in order to provide effective instruction? This reviewer thinks not. The biggest problem for the teacher is going to be the decision about alternative instructional materials and procedures. It is here that he will need more comprehensive guides—instructional principles and strategies—that go well beyond the contribution that evaluation as such can make. The teacher needs to have sound hypotheses relating a particular student's characteristics to the kind of treatment best needed at that point (person-treatment interactions). Though the senior authors are aware of this need and discuss it, the chapters in Part 2 have little to offer on these instructional strategies, and perhaps this is all one should expect in a book on evaluation. Will the handbook serve teachers in various subjects and at various levels equally well? The answer has to be no, as the coverage in Part 2 is incomplete. The book does not cover all major subjects and fields. Major omissions are music, physical education, business education, and home economics. Also missing are elementary school mathematics and elementary school social studies, as well as economics, geography, political science, psychology, and a variety of other subjects or disciplines. Still, most teachers will find one of the chapters in Part 2, as well as chapters on the taxonomies in Part 1, of considerable value. Best served will be teachers of English, for the three chapters on language arts, literature, and writing will all be worth their study; these sections amount to about 166 of the 625 pages in Part 2. Teachers interested in only one of the chapters in Part 2—and this will include a great many—will understandably be reluctant to buy a book only half of which pertains to their interests. Specialists in curriculum and evaluation are likely to favor having the separate chapters in Part 2 in one book, but it is doubtful that teachers would. The book is rather too large for a handbook, but the economics of publishing have apparently worked against the publication of the chapters in Part 2 as separates. Even so, the bulk could have been kept down by limiting the treatment of the cognitive domain in Part 1 to one brief chapter and letting a revision of *Taxonomy I* do the main job. Overall, the reviewer would rate the handbook excellent as to quality and potential usefulness. It is, however, likely to be the last of its kind. The job is too big to be left to one omnibus book, and the main purpose would be better served by subject-matter handbooks focussed on instruction rather than evaluation. Nonetheless, future writers of such handbooks will find this one a valuable starting point.

[B55]

*BLUM, LUCILLE HOLLANDER; DAVIDSON, HELEN H.; AND FIELDSTEEL, NINA D. **A Rorschach Workbook, Revised Edition.** New York: International Universities Press, Inc., 1975. Pp. iv, 195. Spiral bound, $7.95; cloth, $10.00. * For reviews of the earlier edition, see 5:B73 (3 excerpts).

Brit J Social & Clin Psychol 15(2):222–3 Je '76. D. O. Fiddes. An updated version of the 1954 workbook adds a little data on expectations at different age levels and includes sample 5, 8 and 13 year old records as well as adult ones but the advice on adaptation of techniques with children and adolescents is very limited. Designed for the real beginner, a clear and concise account is given of the principles of scoring and the various scoring categories, together with sets of self-testing exercises. Whilst there is a wealth of simple examples the gradient of difficulty is very shallow indeed and it must be intensely frustrating for any worker to find no exposition at all of how the 'right' score is arrived at. The presentation of sets of keys alone does little to help the beginner who is inevitably faced with involved and problem responses, especially in the most troublesome areas of differentiation between texture, diffusion and vista and in the case of multiple determinants, where no guidance is given on precedence. The general impression is one of over-simplification. On the other hand the hideously patchy reproduction of the miniature blots throughout the review copy produces an unfavourable 'set' against something which looks so variable and complicated.

[B56]

★BOLANDER, KAREN. **Assessing Personality Through Tree Drawings.** New York: Basic Books, Inc., Publishers, 1977. Pp. xix, 421. $20.00. *

[B57]

★BOLTON, BRIAN, EDITOR. **Handbook of Measurement and Evaluation in Rehabilitation.** Baltimore, Md.: University Park Press, 1976. Pp. xxi, 362. $18.50. *

Ed & Psychol Meas 36(4):1115 w '76. Max D. Engelhart. * an excellent anthology of papers relevant to the measurement and evaluation of efforts to promote the rehabilitation of clients who are defective or disabled in various ways, including mental retardation and psychiatric disorders. Excellent discussions are given of the various ways that test and other measurement data should be used in counseling. The fundamentals of measurement are comprehensively explained. These include scores and norms, types of reliability and validity estimates, extensive reviews of numerous instruments: intelligence tests, interest inventories, and projective techniques. The book as a whole is a notable text in the general fields of measurement and evaluation.

[B58]

★Bolton, Dale L. **Selection and Evaluation of Teachers.** Berkeley, Calif.: McCutchan Publishing Corporation, 1973. Pp. xiv, 211. $12.00. *

[B59]

★Borich, Gary D., Editor. **Evaluating Educational Programs and Products.** Englewood Cliffs, N.J.: Educational Technology Publications, 1974. Pp. xxiii, 491. $14.95. *

Ed & Psychol Meas 35(4):1037–40 w '75. John L. Wasik. * The editor stated in the preface that the "book is not a textbook or collection of articles, but an especially prepared guide and handbook for planners, developers, and evaluations of educational programs and products (p. vii)." In light of this statement, the reviewer was struck by the lack of continuity. Since the editor stated a long (two years) and intensive R & D cycle of review and revision was performed in the production of the text, one would expect a smooth-flowing, balanced presentation of elements of formative evaluation. Unfortunately, this is not the case. The chapters appear to have been written without any consideration or, more likely, without any knowledge of what the other authors were doing. None of the contributed chapters contain a reference to any other chapter in the text. This was surprising in view of the unavoidable overlap in context treated by the several chapters. For example, the Prologue and Epilogue chapters present some suggestions as to information needs for prospective users of instructional products, the topic covered by Alkin and Fink and yet no reference is made to any of the other's ideas on the subject. Another example was the consideration of which unit of analysis is appropriate to use in evaluation studies. This topic is considered briefly by Edwards while Poynor devotes his whole chapter to this question and neither cites the other. This reviewer feels an individual who takes on the responsibility of coordinating the gathering of information from several authors should also use the review process to inform an individual author of what the other contributors have said that is relevant to their topic. This reviewer also feels a handbook should essentially cover the

field. Thus, a reasonable approach would be to identify a number of different aspects of the instructional product-program evaluation process and then to have specific chapters written to cover each of these areas. Thus, the overlap of topics treated and wide range of specificity of content covered in the chapters was surprising in view of the claims of careful planning and selection of topics. The extreme range of specificity is denoted at one end by one chapter in the methodology section which only covers the topics of appropriateness of units of analysis and at the other extreme by a chapter which exhaustively covers measuring instruments and associated operational procedures useful in formative evaluation. In conclusion, this reviewer feels the book will not serve as a basic reference for individuals performing formative evaluations of programs and products. However, by being selective, readers can benefit from the viewpoints and practical suggestions presented in the text. As one way of being selective and optimizing the investment of time, this reviewer suggests that the prospective reader cover the major part introductions and consult the readers' guide before turning to specific chapters.

[B60]

★Borich, Gary D., and Madden, Susan K. **Evaluating Classroom Instruction: A Sourcebook of Instruments.** Reading, Mass.: Addison-Wesley Publishing Co., Inc., 1977. Pp. v, 496. $15.75. *

[B61–2]

★Borich, Gary D.; with the assistance of Kathleen S. Fenton. **The Appraisal of Teaching: Concepts and Process.** Reading, Mass.: Addison-Wesley Publishing Co., Inc., 1977. Pp. xvi, 396. $12.50. *

[B63]

★Bracht, Glenn H.; Hopkins, Kenneth D.; and Stanley, Julian C.; Editors. **Perspectives in Educational and Psychological Measurement.** Englewood Cliffs, N.J.: Prentice-Hall, Inc., 1972. Pp. xvii, 357. Paper, $8.95; cloth, $11.95. * (A book of readings.)

Ed & Psychol Meas 33(2):512–3 su '73. Ronald K. Hambleton and Thomas F. Powers, Jr. * excellent collection of readings * The primary focus is on some of the recent developments and issues in the field. This we believe should enhance substantially the value of the book * since the focus of the book was to be on recent developments and issues in the field perhaps the book could have been improved by excluding some of the more factual papers and adding papers on some recent developments in areas such as tailored testing, scoring methods and assessment of the affective domain. Generally the selection of topical areas, the choice of articles and the amount of coverage given to each area is good * we would have expected to see more weight given to the norms section, and perhaps less to the section on testing intelligence and creativity. In summary, the editors should be commended for their excellent selection of important as well as interesting papers dealing with many of the more prominent issues and recent developments in the field. There is little doubt that the book will be well received by instructors of measurement classes and their students. The book is well organized and because technical articles were excluded, does not suffer from the usual problem of offering a multitude of notational systems to the student that tend to confuse him. In addition, the book seems to have less than the usual number of annoying typographical errors although one fairly serious error is that the general Spearman-Brown formula is reported incorrectly on page 160. Finally we should add that the book has been used for the last two semesters in our measurement courses at the University of Massachusetts with a great deal of success.

J Ed Meas 10(2):154-5 su '73. William Owen Scott. * A book of readings may usefully supplement a basic measurements text in a number of ways: providing more intensive treatment of a text topic (e.g., going into more detail, developing the theoretical frame of reference), providing more extensive treatment (e.g., broadening the context of application, presenting peripheral but relevant information), by treating other topics of interest to individual students, and by reporting supporting research. In assessing the readings in terms of these functions, reference will be made to the Stanley and Hopkins text as the basic text. The readings perform the first two functions reasonably well. For example, the selection by R. L. Thorndike on reliability is a more intensive treatment than that of the text; and the selection by Lennon on test norms and that by Anastasi on culture-fair tests provide more extensive treatments of these topics. In an instance or two, however, a selection is merely repetitive of the same topic in the text (e.g., the selection by R. L. Thorndike on school marks and marking systems). A number of selections serve the third function (e.g., the

selection by Frank Womer on the National Assessment of Educational Progress project and that by Gary Robertson on the development of the first group mental test). By choice of the editors, the fourth function is poorly served with only five research articles among the selections. Although many instructors will doubtless find these selections helpful, in the reviewer's judgment, they could be measurably improved by stressing research more and discussion less, and by focusing more directly on the measurements requirements of classroom teachers.

Meas & Eval Guid 7(3):199-201 O '74. David J. Weiss. * the selections are at a level which will retain the interest of many who are turned off by highly quantitative treatments of topics like reliability, validity, norms, measuring intelligence, creativity, interests, and personality * A unique idea is the reprinting of a test review from Buros' *Mental Measurements Yearbooks.* Yet with all the reviews available in Buros' volumes, the wisdom of devoting 20 pages of this book to a review of the Rorschach can be questioned. Few empirical papers are included in *Perspectives,* and those that are given are well chosen with respect to their level of difficulty. The editors are a bit too ambitious, however, when they state that "Part three provides a comprehensive discussion of test standards: reliability and validity." There is no way that part three's six chapters can be interpreted as "comprehensive" in the sense of being complete. "Representative" maybe, but "comprehensive," no. In these days of shrinking dollars the question of "Should I buy these books?" becomes very important to answer. You might want to take a look at *Perspectives,* although there is little in it of long-term reference value; perhaps you can borrow it from a nearby college or university library. If you've been exposed to a comprehensive measurement text such as Anastasi's or Cronbach's, *Educational and Psychological Measurement* has very little to offer, unless you're helping teachers build classroom tests. You might, however, want to recommend it to teachers with no previous background in measurement. Be sure to have them continue beyond this book to a more complete text to balance out some of the text's inadequacies.

[B64]

*BRASWELL, JAMES S., COMPILER; WITH THE ASSISTANCE OF DEBORAH WISSMAN. **Mathematics Tests Available in the United States, Fourth Edition.***

Reston, Va.: National Council of Teachers of Mathematics, Inc., 1976. Pp. 33. Paper, $1.80. *

Arith Teach 23(6):451 O '76. Edith Robinson. * tests are listed with only essential facts given (source, appropriate grade level, and so on). No evaluations are provided * However, when a review of a particular test is in print elsewhere, this information is included. * Since the list of mathematics tests covers mathematics from Kindergarten through grade fourteen, anyone with a need for standardized tests will find this pamphlet most useful.

[B65]

★BRAZELTON, T. BERRY. **Neonatal Behavioral Assessment Scale.** Clinics in Developmental Medicine No. 50. London: William Heinemann Medical Books Ltd., 1973. Pp. ix, 66. £2.50. (Philadelphia, Pa.: J. B. Lippincott Co. $10.50.) * For an excerpted review of the manual, see 208.

[B66]

★BRODY, ERNESS BRIGHT, AND BRODY, NATHAN. **Intelligence: Nature, Determinants, and Consequences.** New York: Academic Press, Inc., 1976. Pp. x, 241. $13.75. *

[B67]

★BROMAN, SARAH H.; NICHOLS, PAUL L.; AND KENNEDY, WALLACE A. **Preschool IQ: Prenatal and Early Developmental Correlates.** Hillsdale, N.J.: Lawrence Erlbaum Associates, Inc., Publishers, 1975. Pp. x, 326. $18.00. *

[B68]

BROWN, FREDERICK G. **Measurement and Evaluation.** Itasca, Ill.: F. E. Peacock Publishers, Inc., 1971. Pp. xiv, 199. * *Out of print.* For a review in addition to those below, see 7:B110.

Ed & Psychol Meas 31(2):569–70 su '71. Max D. Engelhart. * The discussion of the interpretations of test scores in terms of norm data and types of derived scores is well explained and illustrated. Commendably critical mention is made of criterion-referenced measurement. (This reviewer deplores the term criterion-referenced tests because of probable confusion with criterion-related validity. The idea of such interpretation of test data is almost as old as the measurement movement although tests have too seldom been designed to promote its accomplishment.) * The discussion of matching items is most inadequate. There could be much more explanation and illustration of matching exercises suitable for use with hand-scored or machine scored answer sheets. There should be some discussion of keylist exercises. These are especially useful with reference to quoted material in measurement of intellectual skills. * While the book has some minor limita-

tions, it should serve the purpose for which it was written. It is the opinion of this reviewer that it might also serve, when accompanied by one of the recent books of readings in the field, as a good choice for an undergraduate course in educational measurement.

J Ed Meas 8(4):345–6 w '71. James Diamond. * The strongest chapters, in this reviewer's opinion, are those dealing with classroom tests and evaluation of instruction * For the text as a whole, the writing and style are generally clear and precise. There were, however, some areas which seemed imprecise, and these serve to detract from the text's overall merits. The section dealing with reliability used terms such as "average intercorrelation between test items," "Kuder-Richardson formulae," "Spearman-Brown formula," and "Cronbach's coefficient alpha" with very little explanation. The important notion of the standard error of measurement is discussed in one-half of a page, indicating an appropriate confidence interval for a single true score. This limited discussion would appear to hamper the student who is interested in interpreting test scores with respect to differences either between individuals or within the same individual, i.e., measurement of change. * the type....[is] conducive to easy reading, with the tables and figures well-spaced and highly relevant * Brown has reached his....goal of showing....how tests "can be used in planning, conducting and evaluating instruction." However, the indicated problems in reliability discussion aside, this text has nothing to distinguish it from a dozen others on the market. In this reviewer's judgment, this text provides no new insights or explanations which one could not find in any basic measurement text such as those Professor Brown included in his end-of-chapter bibliographies. Those instructors seeking a text with an adequate explanation of classroom test procedures and curriculum evaluation, but with limited emphasis on the interpretation of scores, may find this text useful and informative.

Meas & Eval Guid 4(3):185–6 O '71. Fred Vallianos. * the author has accomplished the difficult task of presenting information in a nontechnical manner without distortion * Relatively difficult topics covered in Chapter 2, "Reliability and Validity," and Chapter 3, "Test Scores and Their Interpretation," are discussed with precision and simplicity. However, one may disagree with the implication found in Chapter 2 (p. 12) that only standardized instruments can be construed to be systematic and therefore meet the best definition of a test. * Chapter 8, "Grading," provides helpful hints for the teacher and should prove especially useful to the beginning teacher * Throughout the book helpful references are listed. The basic content and format of *Measurement and Evaluation* are traditional. Certain areas of primary interest to educators (e.g., the measurement and evaluation of creative behavior, assessment in individualized instruction, and interaction analysis) are given little or no attention. The major focus of this book is on classroom tests and other measures of achievement. Much less space is given to ability and personality tests. Despite an occasional and perhaps unavoidable shortcoming, there is little doubt that *Measurement and Evaluation* will make a valuable contribution as supplementary reading in areas related to educational psychology, learning, instructional methods, and measurement and evaluation.

[B69]

*BROWN, FREDERICK G. **Principles of Educational and Psychological Testing, Second Edition.** New York: Holt, Rinehart & Winston, Inc., 1976. Pp. viii, 504. $14.95. * For reviews of the first edition, see 7:B111 (4 excerpts).

[B70]

★BURNS, ROBERT C., AND KAUFMAN, S. HARVARD. **Actions, Styles and Symbols in Kinetic Family Drawings (K-F-D): An Interpretative Manual.** New York: Brunner/Mazel, Inc., 1972. Pp. xvi, 304. $15.00. *

[B71]

BURNS, ROBERT C., AND KAUFMAN, S. HARVARD. **Kinetic Family Drawings (K-F-D): An Introduction to Understanding Children Through Kinetic Drawings.** New York: Brunner/Mazel, Inc., 1970. Pp. 160. * *Out of print.* For a review in addition to the one below, see 7:B119.

Austral Psychologist 7(3):229–30 N '72. Leon Mann. * the child must draw everyone in the family *doing something.* The authors believe that these kinetic (or action) drawings are far more revealing of the feelings and attitudes of disturbed children than drawings obtained by more traditional instructions. A sample of over 60 of these kinetic family drawings selected from the author's files of over 10,000 are reproduced in this book. * Each drawing is accompanied by a brief description of the child who drew it and a discussion of how it illuminates his emotional problems. * We are shown only the drawings of so-called "disturbed" children,

and are given no "normal" children's drawings for comparison purposes. Second, the sample of drawings is very small, and it leads us to wonder whether they are truly representative or reflect the natural tendency of the clinician to demonstrate "interesting cases." * Burns and Kaufman are prepared to read a great deal of unconscious meanings into their material consistent with their clinical label for the child. Thus the kinetic drawings are often used and interpreted in the manner of a projective test. To assess their validity as clinical material it would be advisable to have the drawings submitted to the test of "blind" interpretation by a number of independent clinicians. My intention is not to question the potential value of kinetic drawings. They appear to be excellent material for analyzing the child's view of family relationships, and could be used as a gauge for assessing changes during the course of therapy. But one is left with the distinct impression that the interpretation of disturbed children's art is itself more of an art than a science.

[B72]

★BUROS, OSCAR KRISEN, EDITOR. **English Tests and Reviews: A Monograph Consisting of the English Sections of the Seven Mental Measurements Yearbooks (1938–72) and Tests in Print II (1974).** Highland Park, N.J.: Gryphon Press, 1975. Pp. xxv, 395. $25.00. *

[B73]

★BUROS, OSCAR KRISEN, EDITOR. **Foreign Language Tests and Reviews: A Monograph Consisting of the Foreign Language Sections of the Seven Mental Measurements Yearbooks (1938–72) and Tests in Print II (1974).** Highland Park, N.J.: Gryphon Press, 1975. Pp. xxiii, 312. $23.00. *

Meas & Eval Guid 9(3):156–7 O '76. Kemp Mabry. My reviewing a work of Oscar Buros is rather like an American tourist criticizing works of da Vinci or Michelangelo; the viewer or review is on trial. * Buros points out the discouraging fact that, for French, German, and Spanish, the most popular languages, there is only 1 published test each for use as low as grade 7 and no tests for lower grades. He deplores the lack of progress in quality and quantity of foreign language tests over the past 50 years. He would like to see nonprofit testing organizations expand their offerings to include more languages and tests for elementary grades, since there is little hope of much financial gain in publishing such tests. * Buros explains the organization of this monograph in much detail.

However, despite my four college degrees, I had difficulty using and differentiating the pagination and enumeration system of the *MMY*. As stated earlier, it is the reviewer who is on trial here.

Mod Lang J 60(3):138–9 Mr '76. Charles Stansfield. Few foreign language teachers are familiar with the long and glorious history of the *Mental Measurements Yearbook,* nor with the one-man crusade of its editor, Oscar Buros. * The fascinating history of this series led one *Journal of Educational Measurement* reviewer, Thomas F. Donlon of Educational Testing Service, to write, "It is as if one learned that the Washington Monument was the work of a single dedicated stonemason who built it from blocks donated by kindly quarry-owners." * a compendium of the foreign language sections of the seven *Mental Measurements Yearbooks* and *Tests in Print II* * contains 184 original test reviews by 66 specialists and 330 references to post-publication studies of their construction, use, and validity. The qualifications of the reviewers are generally excellent, although a number of test authorities are not included amongst them. Some of the more authoritative reviewers who have contributed include Frederick Agard, Nelson Brooks, John Carroll, John L. D. Clark, Paul Diederich, Harold Dunkel, Michio Hagiwara, Elton Hocking, Walter V. Kaulfers, Robert Lado, Hershel T. Manuel, Paul Pimsleur, and Mary Turnbull. The reviews vary considerably in length, from 600 to 3,500 words. Kaulfers' reviews tend to be the longest, with some of the most critical coming from Nelson Brooks. Following the reviews section is a 35 page index listing by subject areas all of the 2,467 tests included in *Tests in Print II.* I believe this could have been left out, and the twelve excerpted reviews of the seven books on foreign language testing which have appeared in the *MMY's,* substituted in its place. * As one can clearly ascertain, this book is a "must" reference for the serious student of foreign language testing due to the enormous quantity and quality of the information it contains. It is also invaluable to teachers, supervisors, curriculum specialists, administrators, and foreign language placement directors as a ready source of critical reviews on the appropriateness and merit of individual tests they may be considering or using. Hats off to Buros for producing this text! In view of its great utility, the price is meager.

[B74]

★Buros, Oscar Krisen, Editor. **Intelligence Tests and Reviews: A Monograph Consisting of the Intelligence Sections of the Seven Mental Measurements Yearbooks (1938–72) and Tests in Print II (1974).** Highland Park, N.J.: Gryphon Press, 1975. Pp. xxvii, 1129. $55.00. *

Austral J Psychol 28(3):183–4 '76. John Court. The *Mental Measurements Yearbooks* have established themselves since 1938 as authoritative sources of information on psychological tests of all kinds. The progressive updating of the yearbooks interspersed with a range of closely related sources such as *Tests in Print* has permitted new developments to be incorporated. The present compendium does not really offer anything new. It is essentially the repackaging of earlier material into a single volume devoted to intelligence. This streamlining down to a limited area should result in a volume of more manageable proportions than a yearbook covering the range of psychological tests. Regrettably, it does not because, as the editor states, it consists of "a monograph consisting of the intelligence sections of the seven *Mental Measurements Year Books* (1938–72) and *Tests in Print II* (1974)". The result is that the well-established tests such as the Stanford-Binet are reviewed up to six times in different parts of the volume. At the same time if one wishes to check out references in the literature it is necessary to move from review to review in order to be complete. It would have been a great deal more convenient for the reader if editorial revision had brought all the material together. These problems exemplify what comes through as an inherent tension for the editor. To be complete, exhaustive and authoritative, everything from the past 35 years has been retained virtually unchanged. In this sense it serves admirably as an archival source. On the other hand, the call for a single-volume compendium in a specific area is best served by presenting material in a heavily edited format allowing ease of cross-reference and the minimum of dead wood. If this is what was intended, and what the reader seeks, the outcome is a disappointment. No such work can be utterly complete and up to date. Its inherent limitations must be recognized. For example, while this edition was published in 1975, its reference sources stop well short of this at 1971 with the *Tests in Print II* source material. At the other end of the spectrum there are quite a number of out-of-date tests reviewed. It is difficult to see what point there is in such tests as the Wechsler-Bellevue being included in view of the subsequent revisions now universally used. Apart from tests which have been superseded there are others which have undergone modification over the years. It was appropriate for Keating in the *Second MMY* (1941) to comment on limitations to the Progressive Matrices Item E8 and on the absence of item analyses at that time. Subsequent revision, leading to the 1956 edition, together with extensive item analyses since that time make a reprint of the review somewhat anachronistic. Obviously the same point might be made regarding many reviews which by virtue of their constructive criticism at the time have now evoked a response in subsequent developments. Having said that, this compendium is admirable as an archival source and its value for certain types of research is clear. Many new university and research libraries will find this an economic volume to purchase failing the availability of the earlier yearbooks. For the individual reader, however, two further difficulties, apart from the price, may deter him from making this an investment. The practitioner wants to know what is currently available, not what was available several years before. Major advances in the development of intelligence tests occur but rarely. It would have been valuable to have waited long enough with this book to have been able to include an account of the WISC-R and the upcoming British Intelligence Scale. The researcher is more interested in gaining a complete appraisal of the literature on a given test but only the English literature is cited. In view of the international usage of some tests, and research reports available in many languages, a good case could be made for the inclusion of what can sometimes be keystone papers published in other languages.

Personnel Psychol 29(1):130–1 sp '76. Michael T. Wood. This reference volume is another of the Buros gems. It is unique in bringing together test information from earlier sources under the single substantive area of intelligence. The book is both intensive and extensive in its coverage, and, if one carefully reads the introduction, it is very easy to use. It should be a valuable source of information, and directions to further information, for test developers, users, and students of intelligence measurement. The book is essentially a monograph containing intelligence sections of the

(seven) *Mental Measurements Yearbooks* and *Tests in Print II* (1974). It is an outgrowth of the cumulative MMY and TIP efforts, and is one in a series of specialized volumes. (Others deal with reading, mathematics, science, etc. tests.) Its stated objective is to broaden readership by incorporating intelligence testing material in one complete and coherent source. The book consists of eight basic features: (1) an informative preface and introduction, which traces historical development of the monograph and its predecessors and tells the reader how to use the book; (2) a 146-page intelligence-section reprint from TIP II; (3) an 883-page section from the seven MMYs; (4) publisher's directory; (5) title index; (6) name index; (7) TIP scanning index, listing (2,467) tests in intelligence and other specialties; and (8) a concluding intelligence scanning index, identifying the intelligence tests in the TIP index. The magnitude of the editing task is conveyed by some summary figures. (1) TIP II lists 274 intelligence tests in print in 1974. This represents a 15% increase since 1960, which is largely due to a surge in creativity testing. Fourteen per cent of the tests are new since the seventh (1972) MMY. (2) Over 13,000 references on the construction, use, and validity of specific tests are reported. Fifty-nine tests, led by the Stanford-Binet with 1,408 references, account for 93% of the references. (3) the MMY section includes 574 test reviews, 145 excerpted reviews, and over 9,000 references. Even more impressive than the breadth of coverage is the depth and quality of the reviews. The test information available includes the following: title, test population, copyright date, acronym, special comments (e.g., "for research use only"), part scores, factual statements implying criticism (e.g., "no test manual"), author, publisher, foreign adaptations, sublistings of test parts or editions, test length, cost, scoring and reporting services, and administration time. It is to the editor's credit that only original publication sources are used, and most of the descriptions are based on first-hand examination of these sources. Moreover, the test reviews prepared by MMY reviewers are worthwhile, and in many cases necessary adjuncts to, or substitutes for, the original test manual descriptions. This reviewer did not read all of the reviews. However, a spot-check of some familiar, and some new tests showed first-class review preparation and editing. Where new research has been done on "old" tests, new reviews are included. In many cases, there are multiple reviews to provide evaluation from different perspectives. The only drawback is that this 1975 volume includes test references only through 1971 (based on the 1972 MMY). However, this should be brought up to date with Buros' intended publication of the eighth MMY and TIP III in the near future. The need for updating is reflected in Buros' estimate that knowledge is increasing at the rate of about 1,000 references (for intelligence tests) per year. One interested in the special field of intelligence testing could get the same information through earlier sources Buros has prepared, but with more effort. The present book serves a useful integrative function and should be a good addition to reference libraries.

Psychol Rep 38(1):339 F '76. R. B. Ammons and C. H. Ammons. [Also a review of *Personality Tests and Reviews II.*] Whether we know it or not, all psychologists are incredibly indebted to O. K. Buros for the enormous amount of work he has done over the years so we could be informed in an orderly way about tests available as means of assessing intelligence and personality. To achieve this he has provided descriptions and reviews by peers of materials and related research. Although there have been bones to pick and errors to correct, the over-all contribution has been effective and most helpful. Now, in these two volumes Dr. Buros provides a bit of historical perspective for us and has separated materials relevant to intelligence and personality into two books, put together in parallel format, one with which most of us are familiar—or ought to be. His titles tell all about these reprints, except there are indexes galore. There's one real trouble: these books are just about as big and heavy as any of the others!

[B75]

★Buros, Oscar Krisen, Editor. **Mathematics Tests and Reviews: A Monograph Consisting of the Mathematics Sections of the Seven Mental Measurements Yearbooks (1938–72) and Tests in Print II (1974).** Highland Park, N.J.: Gryphon Press, 1975. Pp. xxv, 435. $25.00. *

Arith Teach 23(8):632 D '76. Edith Robinson. This is a compilation of the mathematics sections of all of the seven Mental Measurements Yearbooks (1938–72) along with *Tests in Print* (1974). Most readers are probably familiar with the MMYs, and the policy that

solicited *critical* reviews in the true sense of that word. In this volume, a few reviews from other publications are included for completeness. The book is a most useful reference for anyone needing objective information on mathematics tests, either for research or for classroom testing.

Sch Sci & Math 75(7):663–4 N '75. George G. Mallinson. [Also a review of *Science Tests and Reviews.*] * Obviously, any professional interested in gathering information about tests in print in mathematics and science will find these monographs invaluable in that they publish in one place all the information that is available about these tests. Obviously this reduces greatly the time of literature search for information about tests. The caliber of the list of reviewers indicates that the descriptions and evaluations of the tests are probably as objective and valid as one could get. There is little doubt that these monographs should be available to mathematics and science educators, researchers in these areas, and anyone else interested in testing in these areas. In brief, they are invaluable.

[B76]

Buros, Oscar Krisen, Editor. **Personality Tests and Reviews I: Including an Index to The Mental Measurements Yearbooks.** Highland Park, N.J.: Gryphon Press, 1970. Pp. xxxi, 1659. $45.00. * For reviews in addition to those below, see 7:B120 (7 excerpts).

Brit J Social & Clin Psychol 10(3):295–6 S '71. H. J. Eysenck. * an invaluable addition to the many Mental Measurements Yearbooks and other texts which Buros has published since the early 1930s; it contains detailed information and reviews by experts of a vast number of personality tests, many of which even an expert might be forgiven for not knowing. Also given with each test is a bibliography of articles in which it has been used; where I have been able to check these bibliographies they have invariably been accurate and reasonably complete. * The reviews are usually very much to the point, contain valuable criticisms and enable the reader to form a reasonable judgment of the strength and weakness of a given test. * It is obvious that every psychological and psychiatric library must have a copy, and so, one would imagine, must everyone else actually working with personality tests. One of the values of the Buros series has always been that the critical comments of the reviewers would lead users into abandoning the less soundly based tests, and would encourage the producers of tests to mend their ways. Whether such a desirable outcome will in fact result is difficult to say; it is quite clear from the reviews that the majority of tests are still well below the level of competence in construction and validity which would mark them out as mediocre; far too many of even widely used tests are clearly bad and should be abandoned. This book is an important contribution to psychology; let us hope psychologists will make optimal use of it.

J Pers Assess 34(6):528–32 D '70. David C. Murray. This is a gigantic book, encyclopedic in design and execution, handsomely bound and attractively printed. It engenders a strong pride of ownership. The editor of this volume is probably known, at least by reputation, to almost every reader of this journal. For years psychologists and other test users have been overwhelmed by a seemingly bottomless cornucopia of tests possessing all possible degrees of validity and reliability. It has become impossible for the average psychologist even to be aware of all the tests available for various purposes, much less to personally survey the relevant manuals and research literature to determine the status of each test. Buros has performed this chore for test users with his six *Mental Measurements Yearbooks (MMYs)* published between 1938 and 1965. Were there no Buros, it would be essential to appoint someone to fill the role Buros has taken upon himself. * There is in existence today no other book which so uniquely and completely covers personality tests, the basic tools for personality assessment. * The Index of Names is a staggering listing of 27,549 items * The preface and the introduction in some ways are the most interesting sections of the book, for they detail something Buros' dogged struggle to publish his Yearbooks and the problems he faced, particularly the increasing risk of being overwhelmed by the proliferating volume of test references. * Best of all it gives the reader considerable information on the condition of personality testing today and Buros' own highly informative comments concerning this condition. This reviewer can but sympathize with his increasing discouragement "at the snail's pace at which we are advancing compared to the tremendous progress being made in the areas of medicine, science, and technology." Buros comments particularly on the "sterility of the research and experimental

writing on the Rorschach and the MMPI," a sterility "applicable to other personality tests," and wonders that 2,274 references have not thrown sufficient light on the MMPI to result in revision or replacement, that 3,747 Rorschach references have "not produced a body of knowledge generally accepted by competent psychologists." The introduction contains a documented account of the struggle for dominance among personality tests of the Rorschach and the MMPI, with the data suggesting that 1961 was the year in which the MMPI first forged ahead. It is clear that these two tests together still dominate the field of personality testing, accounting for about one-third of all references cited in this volume. As the MMPI has overtaken the Rorschach, so have objective tests overtaken the projectives. * It is perhaps a comment on the loyalty (or obtuseness) of projective test users that projective tests are longer lived than the objectives. * Reading the individual reviews of the tests as published in the various yearbooks is a fascinating exploration of changing trends. * The present author's impression after reading all....reviews of the Rorschach and the MMPI was that, except possibly as a screening device, the MMPI comes off no better than the Rorschach, which is to say that it come off very poorly. In some ways the MMPI seems to hold greater risk because of its appearance of objectivity and precision, which may lead unsophisticated users to have unwarranted confidence in making questionable inferences. Perhaps the Rorschach is less of a problem here because its mystic symbols may scare off the uninitiated. This leaves the question of why the MMPI seems so much more popular in university circles. The answer may lie in the greater ease of administering and scoring the MMPI. The process of research is greatly speeded up by the use of group administered paper and pencil tests which can be scored by graduate assistants. * Buros notes that "All published references have been examined to make sure that they meet our criteria for a test reference and to permit us to prepare accurate listings. Secondary sources are never used as the basis for listing published references." These are criteria that could profitably be followed by anyone preparing a list of references or a bibliography. * In a book already terribly long it seems unkind to suggest additions. This reviewer, even so, would have appreciated two additions. One would be a brief listing of tests never in print, such as Harrower's Most Unpleasant Concept Test, and David's Projective Questions. Test users need some convenient source of information about such tests. A short section on general reviews and books containing critiques of personality tests and personality testing would be useful. * The Scanning Index might better be just in front of the Personality Test Index, in the usual place for a table of contents. * anyone using this book for the first time will be more efficient if he turns first to the Introduction to get his bearings, and infrequent users may need to refresh their memories each time they use the book. Buros has a disconcerting, though understandable, ambivalence about some categories of tests. As an example, he includes aphasia tests in his Personality Test Index, but when the reader tries to find reviews of them in the reprinted *MMY* pages he cannot, as the sections on the aphasia tests were not reprinted, since aphasia tests apparently do not qualify for personality tests for this section of the Monograph. If the reader wants the specific reviews on these tests he must refer to the pertinent *MMY*. All of these criticisms are quite minor. In no case do they detract from the great usefulness of this book. *Personality Tests and Reviews* belongs on the reference shelves of every university library, and of most city libraries as well. Every professional employee of every organization which uses personality tests, whether a counseling clinic, public school, or personnel office, should have ready access to this volume, and indeed to all the Buros books. This book would be extremely useful to anyone doing research on personality, since it provides a ready reference list for so many tests and since it can help a researcher decide from among the available measures of a given aspect of personality. Certainly no student should complete a graduate program in psychology without being aware of the existence of this book and knowing something about is contents. [See original review for critical comments not excerpted.]

Manas (India) 17(2):135-7 N '70. J. M. Ojha. This big volume is one more useful addition to the series of unparalleled contributions Buros is making in form of MMYs and allied resource materials. It is back in 1940, that the entire objective of this type of presentation was specifically chalked out. It was also then, more specifically when 3rd MMY was being prepared, that Buros foresaw the immense growth

of testing and realised the need of compiling separate monographs for important categories of tests. An uphill task was persistently followed through several difficulties, most of them financial, which could have easily dampened even a most optimistic businessman. But Buros was also a psychologist of distinction with an unquenching interest in helping the profession and with an unusual tenacity he fought all difficulties. As a consequence, we are now in possession of the most distinguished series of these source books in testing, so painstakingly prepared. * The present volume is very comprehensive in presentation. * Buros has also included the APA, AERA & NCME Standards for Psychological Tests. This shows the extreme importance Buros as a conscientious professional psychologist places on correct use of these materials. This concern is also evident in the objectives for preparing the MMYs, (as quoted in the Introduction) and instructions to authors and reviews that he sends out. His thoroughness is evident from the fact that all materials included is seen by him. He cares for a correct entry, which is posted or reported several times to the publisher or author for correctness.

Psychologia Africana (South Africa) 13 (2-3):268-9 O '70. Y. H. Poortinga. * The high reputation and importance of the Mental Measurements series requires no restatement. A few specific comments may be made: (a) Those who are in possession of the Yearbooks will find the largest part of the present volume redundant. As it does contain new information which apparently will not be published separately, it will be necessary for many to obtain this issue. (b) No new reviews have been included. Reviews have always contributed significantly to the usefulness of the Yearbooks and this is felt to be a loss. (c) Some of the shorter chapters might well have been omitted. This criticism applies mainly to the classified test index and the book-review index which list no material appearing after the completion of the Sixth Yearbook, and to the alphabetic title index which has been brought up to date only for personality and reading tests. Indices could have been restricted to material directly relevant to the subject of this book, as in the "scanning index to tests." The more general indices might have been more appropriate in the new edition of Tests in Print which Buros intends publishing in 1972. The same applies to some parts of the introduction and to the "Standards for educational and psychological tests and manuals." (d) It might have been somewhat easier if the obsolete data from the Yearbooks had been excluded and all the information about a test put together. This lack of organization, which made reprinting possible, is more than compensated for by the reasonably low price. The reviewer has little doubt that many psychologists concerned with personality tests will welcome this comprehensive volume which has brought the information in the Mental Measurements Yearbooks on this subject up to date.

[B77–8]

★Buros, Oscar Krisen, Editor. **Personality Tests and Reviews II: A Monograph Consisting of the Personality Sections of the Seventh Mental Measurements Yearbook (1972) and Tests in Print II (1974).** Highland Park, N.J.: Gryphon Press, 1975. Pp. xxxi, 841. $45.00. * For reviews of *Personality Tests and Reviews I,* see B76 (4 excerpts) and 7:B120 (7 excerpts).

J Biol Psychol 17(1):57–9 Jl '75. Jon D. Swartz. * As stated in the Preface, for 50 years Buros has felt that "most standardized tests are poorly constructed, of questionable or unknown validity, pretentious in their claims, and likely to be misused more often than not" (p. xvii). After trying (and failing) to secure financial support for a test users' research organization—inspired by the founding of Consumers' Research, Inc. and *Your Money's Worth,* the book that led to it—Buros "settled" for the establishment of "a cooperative test reviewing service which would report on and evaluate standardized tests used in education, industry, and psychology" (p. xvii). The preliminary result (after three noncritical bibliographies in 1935, 1936, and 1937) was *The 1938 Mental Measurements Yearbook.* The ultimate result was the series of *Yearbooks,* and the other publications related to them, that have made Buros world famous and put all users of tests in his debt. (One cannot help but speculate about possible outcomes if Buros had been able to secure funding for his test users' research organization. Is it too farfetched to believe that such an organization might have prevented many of the testing abuses that have occurred during the past decade? I think not.) * almost 400 pages....of critical reviews by recognized authorities—and excerpted reviews by considerably less than recognized authorities. (One wonders at the wisdom of including even excerpted portions of reviews that appear liter-

ally *anywhere* in the "literature" by almost *anyone.* Every person who reviews in the literature is not the equal of every other, and certainly different journals have different standards. For example, at least one of the excerpted reviews that appears here is the direct result of a personal vendetta, one that Buros knew nothing about, of course.) * With 188 publishers, over 23,000 names, and approximately 52,000 documents (tests, reviews, excerpts, and references) contained between these covers, the result is little short of overwhelming! Yet the volume is easy to use, once one has mastered the book's organization. Buros, his wife Luella (the book's designer), and their associates are to be congratulated for their editorial work on this volume. Although his test users' research organization never came to pass, Buros's "scaled down objectives" have proved invaluable to all those involved in tests and testing during the past 40-plus years. *

J Pers Assess 40(5):554–5 O '76. Robert M. Allen. * Physically this book is well constructed and should endure years of usage * This reviewer has wondered about what could have motivated Dr. Buros to devote his time, energies, and finances to the tremendous task of editing and publishing the MMYs, TIPs, and PTRs as wholes and in monograph format. The sheer mountain of paper, the energy demanding correspondence, and the financial investment would repel rather than attract one to this task. Now, at last, Dr. Buros has committed his editorial autogenesis to print in PTR II: "It is my considered belief that most standardized tests are poorly constructed, of questionable or unknown validity, pretentious in their claims, and likely to be misused more often than not. This conviction began to form 48 to 50 years ago when I was taking courses in testing....I had the good fortune to read a book which was a landmark in the consumer movement—*Your Money's Worth* by Stuart Chase and F. J. Schlink....This book and the establishment of Consumers' Research stimulated me to begin thinking about a test users' research organization to evaluate tests (p. xvii)." Now this reviewer knows Dr. Buros' thinking *and* doing which have yielded a harvest for the applied psychologist in the form of another Book for the Tester's Bible, truly the conscience for the test user. * for each test in PTR II the reader is given a brief description, its publisher, reference(s) to "additional information" and reviews(s), and whether the test is still in print. These are followed by two innovations: *References Through 1971* and *Cumulative Name Index*. In these lists the inquirer has a definite resource for pursuing whatever interest there may be in each test. A third very helpful addition is the appearance of the names of the first and last tests on the bottoms of the right and left hand pages. * The cost of PTR II is high, but what isn't today? However, this and the 7th MMY should bring the test user up to date as of "early 1974." Obviously one cannot vote against information and PTR II is most certainly informative. It becomes a matter of how informed one wants to be. But this MMY Monograph (Buros' subtitle) should be in each University and/or psychology, counseling, and educational departmental libraries as a readily available reference source for students, faculty, and practitioners. *

Personnel Psychol 29(1):131–4 sp '76. Brian Bolton. It is [Buros']...."belief that most standardized tests are poorly constructed, of questionable or unknown validity, pretentious in their claims, and likely to be misused more often than not." Oscar Buros' opinion of psychological and educational tests was formed half a century ago when he was a graduate student at Minnesota and apparently remains unchanged today, having been restated in almost every one of his numerous publications. Doesn't Professor Buros believe that his monumental career effort has contributed to improvements in the construction and use of tests? In a presentation at the 1968 AMEG meeting he judged that the *Mental Measurements Yearbooks* (MMYs) have had some influence on some test publishers, but doubted whether the majority have been affected (Buros, 1968). However, he did feel that the major objective—to help test users select and use tests with discrimination—was being reasonably well achieved by the MMYs, although with less success than he had originally anticipated. An independent evaluation of the quality of tests reviewed between 1938 and 1958 by Engelhart and Beck (1963) was more optimistic: their analysis of the reviews in successive editions of the MMYs supported the conclusion that tests have improved over the years. They judged the improvement in personality inventories to have been small, however. *Personality Tests and Reviews II (PTR II)* is one of nine specialized reference volumes edited and published in 1975 by Professor Buros and his staff. * As the subtitle suggests, *PTR II* consists almost entirely of material reprinted from recent publications. Its primary purpose is simply to make the reviews and bibliographic information pertaining to personality tests available in one volume for the convenience of test users. One question immediately occurs to the reader: Is a separate publication of information which is already available in relatively convenient form warranted? The answer, of course, depends upon the needs (and financial resources) of the individual test user. In addition to the two major reprinted sections from the *Seventh MMY* and *Tests in Print II (TIP II)*, *PTR II* includes a scanning index of all tests listed in *TIP II*, a directory of 189 publishers of personality tests, cumulative author and title indexes covering both *PTR I* and *PTR II*, and an end-of-the-book scanning index for personality tests. In numerical terms, *PTR II* lists 445 personality tests and 12,376 references and contains 175 test reviews and 47 excerpted reviews. The specific test bibliographies may be the single most remarkable achievement in the entire MMY effort. *PTR I* and *PTR II* together list over 30,000 references for 445 copyrighted personality tests. In the Preface to *PTR II* Professor Buros states that, with the exception of unpublished theses, he personally examined every one of the 30,000 plus references to make sure that they met his criteria for relevancy. His personal investment in this enormous project is emphasized in the following paragraph where he reprimands authors who have obviously used the MMY test bibliographies without giving proper credit to the primary source. Professor Buros suggests that test authors and publishers refer readers to MMY test bibliographies and provide supplements where necessary. This is certainly a fair and reasonable recommendation. * Perhaps the most interesting and ironic piece of historical information surrounding the development of the MMYs is that Professor Buros' initial goal was to establish a test users' research organization. He attempted repeatedly over a period of 25 years to obtain funding for this project but was never successful (Buros, 1968). The test-reviewing service was only an after-thought. It is interesting to speculate as to whether there would be a reference series comparable to the MMYs today if Professor Buros' skills in grantsmanship had been more effective back in the 1930's. Oscar Buros probably would have made a notable contribution, though, regardless of any particular turn of events, because his view was future-oriented and he (obviously) possessed the capacity for hard work. He and his staff are already working on the *Eighth MMY* and *TIP III!* The well deserved praise should not obscure the fact that *PTR II* suffers from the same weakness that detracts from the utility of the seven MMYs—the test reviews are unstandardized, of uneven quality, and often reach contradictory conclusions. Who is the unsophisticated test user to believe when experts disagree? There is simply no substitute for an educated test user who can evaluate the test manual and available research studies in light of his/her own purposes and needs. I am confident that Professor Buros would concur with this statement. Even though there is very little that is new in *PTR II,* this volume and the other eight monographs will probably achieve Professor Buros' modest objective of broadening the readership of the reviews and make the bibliographic material available to a greater segment of the test using professions.

Psychol Rep 38(1):339 F '76. R. B. Ammons and C. H. Ammons. [Also a review for *Intelligence Tests and Reviews.*] Whether we know it or not, all psychologists are incredibly indebted to O. K. Buros for the enormous amount of work he has done over the years so we could be informed in an orderly way about tests available as means of assessing intelligence and personality. To achieve this he has provided descriptions and reviews by peers of materials and related research. Although there have been bones to pick and errors to correct, the over-all contribution has been effective and most helpful. Now, in these two volumes Dr. Buros provides a bit of historical perspective for us and has separated materials relevant to intelligence and personality into two books, put together in parallel format, one with which most of us are familiar—or ought to be. His titles tell all about these reprints, except there are indexes galore. There's one real trouble: these books are just about as big and heavy as any of the others!

[B79]

★Buros, Oscar Krisen, Editor. **Reading Tests and Reviews II: A Monograph Consisting of the Reading Sections of the Seventh Mental Measurements Yearbook (1972) and Tests in Print II (1974).** Highland Park, N.J.: Gryphon Press, 1975. Pp. xxvii, 257. $20.00. * For reviews of *Reading Tests and Reviews I,* see 7:B121 (7 excerpts).

Read World 15(4):245–6 My '76. Mary Jane Urbanowicz. * This monograph continues the long record of excellent publications by.... Buros. Teachers, administrators, curriculum supervisors, counselors, psychologists and researchers will find this publication to be the most desirable available source which deals with reading tests per se.

[B80]

★Buros, Oscar Krisen, Editor. **Science Tests and Reviews: A Monograph Consisting of the Science Sections of the Seven Mental Measurements Yearbooks (1938–72) and Tests in Print II (1974).** Highland Park, N.J.: Gryphon Press, 1975. Pp. xxiii, 296. $22.00. *

Sch Sci & Math 75(7):663–4 N '75. George G. Mallinson. [Also a review of *Mathematics Tests and Reviews.*] * Obviously, any professional interested in gathering information about tests in print in mathematics and science will find these monographs invaluable in that they publish in one place all the information that is available about these tests. Obviously this reduces greatly the time of literature search for information about tests. The caliber of the list of reviewers indicates that the descriptions and evaluations of the tests are probably as objective and valid as one could get. There is little doubt that these monographs should be available to mathematics and science educators, researchers in these areas, and anyone else interested in testing in these areas. In brief, they are invaluable.

Sci Teach 43(8):55 N '76. Janet Wall. Hardly a person in testing could doubt the value of *Tests in Print (TIP II)* and the seven *Mental Measurement Yearbooks (MMY)* as the most comprehensive reference guides available for selecting tests appropriate to a particular data-gathering operation. In *Science Tests and Reviews,* Oscar Buros reprints, in monograph form, entries dealing with science from both of the above publications, thus providing science educators with a handy reference on relevant tests. Entries (current through 1974) include both bibliographical listings (including test population, special comments and criticisms, foreign adaptations, and cross-references to *MMY*) as well as those more detailed reviews and test descriptions typical of *MMY.* An introduction gives the history and rationale of *TIP II* and *MMY.* Following the body of the book is the *TIP II* Scanning Index listing all tests by subject. (One drawback is that differing reviews of the same tests published in several of the yearbooks are not listed together.) A welcome addition to the personal library and an interesting historical view of test development in science. For science educators K–16.

[B81]

★Buros, Oscar Krisen, Editor. **The Seventh Mental Measurements Yearbook, Volumes 1 and 2.** Highland Park, N.J.: Gryphon Press, 1972, Pp. xl, vi, 1986. $85 per set. * For reviews of earlier yearbooks, see 7:B122 (9 excerpts), 6:B104 (14 excerpts), 5:B84 (19 excerpts), 4:B70 (4 excerpts), 4:B71 (18 excerpts), 3:788 (48 excerpts), and 2:B858 (57 excerpts).

Alberta J Ed Res (Canada) 18(3):234–5 S '72. John McLeish. What can one say about the Seventh Mental Measurements Yearbook adequately to convey the quality of the work? For a start, it appears to be twice as large as we are accustomed to see Buros. On inspection, it has all the qualities of the earlier yearbooks. Apparently it must be twice as good. Clearly, this is impossible! But it is still a quite remarkable achievement. Indeed it is extraordinary, in the class of a miracle that is always with us, that this two-"man" team, Oscar and Luella, with an associated small group of dedicated workers, have now spent over 34 years producing the "Yearbooks" as the most indispensable reference book in their field. The present volume is the crowning-piece of their achievement: it now seems very doubtful that another yearbook will appear under their imprint. These two volumes are a fitting continuation of the work begun three or more decades ago. More than 500 tests are reviewed by nearly 800 independent experts. These provide essential information about validity, reliability, norms and sources of tests as well as informed and frank comment about them. * The seven Yearbooks together, all of which are in print, provide the most comprehensive coverage of this area that one could possibly ask for. It is very helpful that the same format, the same layout, the same print, is used in this as in the earlier volumes. The valuable introduction provides a detailed breakdown of the volume itself which (fortunately) excuses the reviewer from making any attempt at a detailed analysis of the contents of this monumental work. It is indeed encyclopedic in its range. The maintenance of the critical and independent standpoint of the enterprise is shown by the editor's rather casual remark (which however is clearly a considered judgment with which many of us would agree) that

"at least half the tests currently on the market should never have been produced." That the proportion is not considerably higher than half is surely to be placed to the credit of the present series and their collaborating reviewers. * It is interesting in reading the reviews of the previous Yearbook, included (as usual) in the current volume, to discover that all the favourable things that one wishes to say about the present revision have already been said about its predecessor—"unique," "monumental," "indispensable," "unbelievable," "needing only a few Gustave Doré prints to heighten the illusion of a 'Bible'" etc. The niggling complaints which are generated in the casual user who fails to appreciate the nature of the work, have all been voiced before too—price, weight, an irritating and frustrating method of pagination and indexing, discursive and discordant opinions etc., etc. For those of us who use tests continually however, and who really want to know about them, it must be said that the new Seventh Yearbook has an exceptional value and will be blessed daily by students, librarians and research workers. It is beautifully bound in a sumptuous style, is printed in large, readable type, it contains exactly the kind of basic information about new and revised tests we need and it contains a fair sampling of the opinions of those leading experts who have actually used the tests they are reviewing. In a word, it is exactly the book we have been waiting for since 1965.

Austral J Psychol 25(1):115–6 Ap '73. * It is a pleasure to welcome the seventh edition of this reliable compendium which has done so much to raise the level of sophistication of test design and usage.

Brit J Ed Psychol 43(1):89–91 f '73. J. G. Morris. The preface to this seventh edition of a standard reference work on tests provides surprising information to the effect that the Gryphon Press consists of Buros and his wife. The work of producing both the *Mental Measurements Yearbooks* (MMY) and *Tests in Print* (TIP) is carried out by the editor and his wife, a practice which began with the 1940 edition, although Rutgers University, from which Buros has now retired, did produce two of the earlier works in the series. In 1973, there will be a second TIP and in 1975 it is hoped to produce an eighth MMY. After that someone else, whether individual or institution, will carry the burden. This is of interest because it is a mammoth task for two people, even allowing for editorial assistance and assistance from many outsiders. Finance has come from the sale of the product. It is an indication of the price of independence. The better mouse trap principle has, of course, operated and test constructors, editors of learned journals and reviewers have all been happy to be associated with the work. The objectives of all MMYs are very precise, to provide information on, and high quality evaluation of tests, by authoritative individuals and to provide extensive references and indicate sources of books on testing with the evaluative reviews of such books from the learned journals. Inevitably the authors have become crusaders for better tests with better background information to enable users to be better users who will also make a greater qualitative demand on test constructors. Like many other missionaries they have been frustrated, but in their case because of the gullibility of test users who will buy anything which is well-packaged and promoted, regardless of its inadequacies as a test and of claims for it which cannot be substantiated. Perhaps a measure of sympathy could be extended to teachers, educationists and psychologists desperately searching for instruments—however crude. An appropriate text for wall display is a quotation from Buros, "At least half of the tests currently on the market should never have been published." Few individuals will purchase this MMY, the first one to be produced in two volumes, partly because of the price and partly because of the system which inter-relates all editions of the MMY and related monographs with obsessive thoroughness. * each MMY is a supplement to its predecessors and should be used in conjunction with them. This determines that the series must be housed in an institution, but any institution serving individuals who are test users should hold the complete series. The young science of information retrieval would be critical of this system as it overwhelms even the most earnest seeker after truth by providing so much information. No concessions are made in presentation of information as in the commercial *Which* with its blobs for significance. Here you must read, and read—and read. Newcomers to this field would benefit greatly from a flowchart. * Although there is some duplication and overlap in the system yet there is little chance of an institution purchasing expensive books and then finding that it has a rapidly dating product on its hands. * Reviewers are

carefully chosen by the editor and precisely briefed as to what is required. There is an adequate mix of new and old reviewers and a good age spread. Most reviewers deal with one or two tests and overwhelmingly they are Americans, but 24 are from UK. Inevitably shrinkage of intent has occurred on the part of the editor by failure to achieve commitment on the part of some reviewers, a phenomenon known to most editors. The biggest growth area since the sixth MMY has been in references to literature published on tests in the English language and world wide with a 55 per cent increase here. * There is much new material on reviews of books on testing published in the last eight years in 86 journals and a striking feature is that 55 per cent of the books had no reviews worth excerpting from the journals. The problem then becomes one of determining whether the lack of a good review—or any review—is a criterion for the reader in choosing a book. The final section provides comprehensive indexes for periodicals, publishers of tests and test titles and names. With the mania for classification and analysis which characterises the book we are told *inter alia* that of the 99 journals agreeing to excerpting of reviews there are 16 British ones. This *Journal* is the most commonly used of these. Regarding publishers the situation is similar to that in Britain where there is a network inter-relationship of big companies. What is surprising is that there are so many small publishers producing just one test. * Only the most disciplined mind will ensure maintenance of original objective and eschew side-tracking as names and challenging statements catch the eye while going through the pages. The incidental learning is enormous. A useful bonus is the address lists provided by the contributing test reviewers and the index of periodicals. A brief overall evaluation would be sheer presumption but as R. H. Tawney said of the pillar-box, regarding communication in another era, so it can be said of this volume, "It is necessary." An interesting feature of this whole publishing venture in MMYs is that the 1938 and the 1940 MMYs have just been reissued. They indicate growth rates in this field by comparisons but also are useful source-books for contemporary reviews, i.e., what was thought about the 1937 Stanford-Binet revision at the time. Half of the book is given up to reviews of books on mental measurement, research and statistics, some of which have become classics. The 1940 MMY shows the precise direction of growth in giving more space to reviewers, encouraging more trenchant criticism and decisions on supplementary publication. The strong reactions of publishers and test authors to unfavourable reviews make fascinating reading as excerpted in the introduction. The other big change is in the ratio of test reviews to book reviews. Not all changes are in the form of increased growth. The periodical directory and index for the 1972 edition of MMY is smaller than that of the 1940 edition. One can see much more rigorous selection operating but in a period when the proliferation of scientific and learned journals has become a doomwatch phenomenon this is a move against the trend. A niggling doubt remains. What will happen to this massive collection of tests, books, journals and contacts when the Buros team cries, "Hold: enough"?

Brit J Ed Studies 21(2):233–4 Je '73. Gordon R. Cross. Widely acknowledged as an indispensable source of reference for students reading for higher degrees and diplomas in educational psychology the yearbook has expanded to such monumental proportions that in the seventh edition it is published in two volumes to facilitate ease of handling. Despite its increased size, all the qualities associated with previous volumes, excellence of scholarship, accuracy in recording information and speed of retrieving references have been retained. The yearbook does not simply list the full range of tests currently available in the English-speaking world, but frankly criticizes only those publications judged worthwhile by distinguished and experienced scholars with special practical knowledge of the tests they review. Bibliographies of references to tests are given in full, and are absolutely essential for [a] research worker. Finally the book includes original reviews and excerpted reviews from reputable international journals of books on mental testing and psychometric methods. For a number of decades Professor Buros has campaigned for higher standards in the construction, use and revision of published tests and has crusaded against tests of dubious value and the false and unsubstantiated claims which accompany them. In his own words, "at least half of the tests currently on the market should never have been published." That standards of practice have improved in recent years is in itself a magnificent personal tribute to the pro-

fessor; however, he would be the first to agree that a great deal more needs to be done before test users have complete confidence in all the instruments potentially available to them. Hence the need for a reliable mental measurements yearbook. Too many publishers "revise" a text without any substantial alteration in content or format in order to justify an increase in cost; this accusation can not be levied against the Gryphon Press. The seventh edition evaluates 1,157 tests and contains 798 test reviews, more than half these tests are new and all but a very small percentage have been revised since the sixth edition. It does not replace or make obsolete previous yearbooks, on the contrary it supplements them. The serious research worker needs to refer back constantly, and in doing so will gain useful insight into both the history of mental testing and the development of thinking in psychology generally. Trends in testing techniques are clearly shown in tables....of references; for example, the relatively greater expansion in personality and aptitude testing than in measuring general intelligence, or that the Rorschach test is losing ground to the M.M.P.I. and so forth. Newer areas such as psycholinguistics have not been overlooked, including a review of the filmed demonstration of the Illinois Test of Psycholinguistic Abilities. Knowing what tests to recommend to advanced students is a perennial problem, Buros does most of this ground work for us and we can all have confidence in his judgements.

Brit J Psychiatry 122(566):106–7 Ja '73. D. Bannister. There are three major perpetual works of reference in the field of psychology which a clinical psychology department might harbour. *Psychological Abstracts,* which are only for those so utterly devoted to "the literature" that they cannot bear to miss a drop of the waterfall as it descends upon our heads; *The Annual Review of Psychology,* which is eminently useful, particularly for those who have research inclinations; and *The Mental Measurements Yearbook* which is absolutely necessary for those who wish to use, and to avoid the pitfalls of, psychological tests. This seventh edition runs to a massive two volumes and maintains a high critical standard in reviewing tests and test-relevant books. Its coverage is exhaustive and exhausting. Each test has its rationale, procedures, standardization data and related literature carefully analysed, and the thousands of tests which psychologists have produced are reduced to a reasonable kind of evaluative and catalogue order. The indexing is of the kind which one operates by instinctive feel rather than by comprehending its logic, but so long as the great era of the psychological test remains with us, we need a Buros to guard and guide us.

Ed & Psychol Meas 32(3):843–6 au '72. Max D. Engelhart. * an analysis of the reviews in successive *Mental Measurements Yearbooks* reveals that tests have improved over the years by the fact that the proportions of adverse comments by increasingly sophisticated reviewers has progressively decreased. This is most true of achievement and aptitude tests and least true of personality instruments. An analysis of the yearbooks up to and including *The Fifth Yearbook* was reported in 1963 by this reviewer and John M. Beck. Such an analysis of the content of the *MMY* reviews should be repeated to obtain data concerning the characteristics and trends of criticism. * More than half of the tests, 55.6 per cent, are new tests listed for the first time in *The Seventh Yearbook*. In *The Sixth Yearbook* 51.5 per cent of the tests are listed for the first time. * In recent years a number of testing programs have developed for the purposes of accreditation of non-traditional study or for guidance and placement on the junior college level. These include the *College-Level Examination Program*, CLEP, administered for the College Entrance Examination Board by Educational Testing Service and the *Junior College Placement Program* of Science Research Associates. These programs are among those reviewed in *The Seventh Yearbook* pages 1009–1046. Another interesting development is the increasing use of high-speed electronic scoring machines....and of scoring services * There are numerous excellent reviews in *The Seventh Yearbook*. Among the most interesting are the reviews of *Analysis of Learning Potential* by Lee J. Cronbach and by Arthur R. Jensen. Other examples of reviews of more than usual interest are those of the *Rorschach* by Alvin G. Burstein and Charles C. McArthur. Also of unusual interest is the review of the *Illinois Test of Psycholinguistic Abilities* by John B. Carroll. Many more equally thought-provoking reviews could be listed. * since the publication of *The Sixth Yearbook*....the number of original test reviews has increased only from 795 to 798, but the number of references on the construction,

use, and validity of specific tests has increased from 7,967 to 12,372 * Given a use for such a list of references, it is extremely convenient to have such lists immediately available in this and earlier *MMY*'s. It has been suggested, for the sake of economy, that the lists of references and the more than 300 pages of excerpts from reviews of current books on measurements should be omitted from future mental measurements yearbooks. But such omissions, in the opinion of this reviewer, would be a false economy and would greatly lessen the impact of the yearbooks on the authors and publishers of tests. They would greatly decrease the usefulness of the yearbooks in the selection of tests, particularly for research purposes. The student and teacher of measurements would be seriously handicapped in acquiring more than textbook knowledge of the field. * It is difficult to find unused superlatives to characterize *The Seventh Yearbook* and its predecessors. They are indeed weighty—36 pounds on my bathroom scale. I can't believe I read the whole thing, but I have read enough to conclude by saying "Oscar, you are incredible!" To use an unused superlative, the *Mental Measurements Yearbooks* deserve to be *ubiquitous*.

Ed Leadership 33(1):69–70 O '75. James Raths. * the entire set of Mental Measurements Yearbooks (Vol. I–VII) would indubitably be invaluable for anyone with the responsibility for assessing student attributes (from interests and abilities through achievement) * The reviews....tend to be scholarly and technical. Neophytes to the testing field will rarely find useful and definitive judgments in reviews—such as "use this test by all means." As in most complex matters, the judgments are mixed with strong and weak points identified in technical language and in academic prose styles. To those who understand somewhat the lingo of the testing field, the reviews should prove helpful in making more intelligent uses of standardized tests. * [Both this volume and *Tests in Print II*] are valuable tools for anyone interested in research and/or evaluation. As alluded to earlier, they must be viewed as only a part of a much larger collection of needed resources. Although the comment may seem niggling, it would have been helpful if Buros had included in his citations ERIC access numbers. * (It would probably be fitting for an ERIC Clearinghouse to be assigned the responsibility of putting out similar Yearbooks once Oscar Buros decides to retire.) One final note. Although I have often used the Mental Measurements Yearbook as a resource and recommend it to my students, prior to undertaking this reviewing task, I don't think I really comprehended the enormity of the task that is represented in editing this material. Oscar Krisen Buros is to be congratulated for his outstanding contributions to the profession.

J Biol Psychol 14(2):50–1 D '72. Jon D. Swartz. * What else can one say in praise of the latest edition of such a valuable reference work that already has not been said time and time again by reviewers of previous editions, other than it is new and improved? Perhaps it will suffice to say that, in advising my students when they are writing a critical paper on *any* published test, I tell them first to check on the latest Buros in the library. * A highlight of every previous *Yearbook* and of the current edition is the editorial by the editor. In his present one Buros—in addition to briefly summarizing the purpose of the *Mental Measurements Yearbooks* and their companion volumes—compares the current with previous editions, reviews the publishing sources of tests and the reviews of them, and painstakingly leads the reader through a "How to Use This Yearbook" section (a highly necessary step for the novice, or even the old hand who hasn't picked up a *Yearbook* in a while). A great deal of credit belongs to Buros for this continuing monumental piece of work. As one who has had some personal correspondence with Buros, the reviewer knows just how exacting he is in securing accurate and complete references for the tests included. It truly is remarkable just how error-free the long lists of references are. Usually works of this nature abound with typographical mistakes, but not *The seventh MMY!* The reviewer's suggestion for improving an already indispensable work would involve the addition of a new bibliographical section on the most popular non-commercial tests used in research, such as Byrne's Repression-Sensitization Scale, Holtzman's Form Recognition Test, Van de Castle's Perceptual Maturity Scale, Moran's version of the Word Association Test, Kagan's experimental scales such as his Conceptual Styles Test and Visual Fractionation Test, etc. Some of these "unpublished" tests actually are in use more than some commerically published ones. To avoid making more work for the already overburdened

editor, the author of each test (who probably knows more about the research uses of his test than anyone else—and who may even keep up-to-date bibliographies on it) could supply this additional section himself. Those authors not taking the time to send in their sections would have only themselves to blame if their tests were not represented. Finally, a word of appreciation is due the designer of the set (Luella Buros) and the publisher, The Gryphon Press (O. K. *and* Luella Buros), for the attractive appearance of the *Yearbooks,* a beautifully printed and manufactured matched set of volumes. The reviewer looks forward to *The eighth MMY,* planned for 1975!

J Ed Meas 10(4):313–4 w '73. Elizabeth Hagen. * The 7th *MMY* is a difficult book to review simply because it is not like any other book. One might ask whether it really needs to be as voluminous as it is. Could the length be reduced? If the answer is yes, then what should be deleted? Perhaps two of the indices such as the Periodical Directory and Index and the Index of Names could be dropped. Such an action would not save much space, and there are probably many users who find these indices very useful. Perhaps the test references could be omitted. However, these bibliographies are extremely valuable, particularly to the novice in testing. Perhaps one could reduce the number of reviews of a particular test and have only one review of each test; but such a move would reduce the value of the reviews. If one scans a number of the tests that have two or more reviews, one finds that these tests have wide usage or are controversial. More than one review is needed to provide the desired objectivity and scholarly critique. Just a casual reading of the two or more reviews that accompany some tests shows that there is little repetition in the reviews and where there is repetition, it is needed particularly to warn the potential user about the limitations of the uses or interpretation of the test results. Perhaps one could limit all reviews to a specified length for a review, but this would be undesirable because different tests require different amounts of space for adequate review. There really is no way of reducing the length of the *MMY* without changing the fundamental nature of the book. The present reviewer has no desire to see this done. The reviews of tests in the 7th *MMY* are generally of high quality. The reviewers of most of the tests have attempted to look at what the authors of the tests have set out to do. Then the reviewers have tried to judge to what extent the authors have achieved their purposes. Many of the reviewers have pointed out specific misuses or misapplications of the reviewed tests and have suggested appropriate uses for the tests. Most of the reviews are written in such a way that a person with limited psychometric training can comprehend the issues that are discussed in the reviews. In other words, the 7th *MMY* is a book for the users of tests as well as for the specialist in testing. I just wish there were some law requiring anyone who proposes to use a test to read carefully the review of the test in the *MMY* before he is permitted to use it. The two volumes of the 7th *MMY* represent a monumental task accomplished primarily by the efforts of one man committed to the improvement of tests and to the wise use of tests and test results. All of us who construct tests are deeply indebted to Oscar Buros for his decision to continue the MMY after his retirement. Although all of us realize that we will not always have Oscar Buros to help us accomplish our objectives, let us hope that we will have a *Mental Measurement Yearbook*. In closing this review, I would like to say, "Thank you, Oscar. You have been more successful in achieving the objective listed on the first page of the introduction than you realize."

J Ed Meas 10(4):315–20 w '73. Henry S. Dyer. In the introduction to the *Seventh Mental Measurements Yearbook,* Buros restates the ten objectives that have guided his editorial efforts since the *MMY* series began in the 1930's. These ten objectives fall into two broad categories corresponding to the two major goals that have characterized the series from the outset. One of these is its encyclopedic goal: to make accessible all the available knowledge about tests and testing in the English-speaking world. Buros feels that he has done reasonably well on this one. The other main goal, which he calls his "crusade," has been to improve the science and practice of testing by trying to make test publishers, test users, and test experts more professionally conscientious in their work. Buros feels that his success along this line has been "disappointingly modest." One specific objective in the crusading category should be of special concern to measurement experts. It is objective (*h*): "to stimulate contributing reviewers to think through more carefully their

own beliefs and values relevant to testing [p.xxvii]." On this particular matter the evidence for success, or the lack of it, is not very clear-cut nor easy to come by. It is nevertheless a matter of large importance. In this essay, therefore, I shall see what can be done to find an answer to the single hard question: How carefully indeed have those who contributed reviews to *MMY–7* thought through their own beliefs and values relevant to testing? The reason this question is important rests on two fairly safe assumptions. The first is that the reviewers who get into the *MMY* constitute a reasonably representative sample of the population of experts in testing. The second assumption is that the level of thinking of these acknowledged experts defines a kind of upper bound for the quality of testing in the English-speaking world—regardless of the aberrations of test publishers and test users. My purpose then is to try to estimate where that upper bound may lie. In doing so I am relying solely on an assortment of hunches growing out of an analysis of the reviews produced by a ten percent random sample of the persons who contributed to *MMY–7*. The next section of this essay will describe the approach to the problem in the hope that somebody sometime might be moved to replicate it or indeed improve upon it. In the last section I shall display some of the data generated by the analysis, and make a few comments on them. * the prime question is whether Buros' efforts to make careful thinkers out of reviewers has in fact been "disappointingly modest." Or should it not perhaps be regarded as modestly disappointing? Considering the vast problems that testing is up against these days and the fact that testers are people, too, I prefer the latter interpretation. [See original review for details too extensive to excerpt.]

J Pers Assess 37(1):92–3 F '73. Robert M. Allen. More of the same, but even more of the new—this best characterizes the latest in the series of *Mental Measurements Yearbooks* (*MMY*s). * The 1972 *MMY* does not "supplant" any of the earlier editions, it "supplements" what has gone on before in the English-speaking testing movement. Herein lies a weakness for the psychological and educational test user who either does not have access to the *MMY*s or is insufficiently motivated to consult the earlier editions to obtain a more complete overview of the particular test(s) in which he is interested. Some of this has been minimized with the publication of *Personality Tests and Reviews* (Buros, 1970) which brought together in one large volume the cumulative information about personality tests and book reviews contained in the personality sections of the *MMY*s from 1938 to 1965, and supplementary data to 1970. * Buros and his staff have demonstrated an inordinate amount of dedication to the field of psychological and educational testing. This edition endeavors to update the data, reviews and information about tests and related books since the *MMY* of 1965 (the *Sixth*). Buros notes weaknesses still extant in the construction, publication, dissemination and use of tests. In the role of seemingly disheartened warrior, he writes (1972, p. xxvii):

Concomitantly, we attach considerable importance to other objectives of a crusading nature: (*f*) to impel test authors and publishers to publish better tests and to provide test users with detailed information on the validity and limitations of standardized tests; (*g*) to inculcate test users with a keener awareness of the values and limitations of standardized tests; (*h*) to stimulate contributing reviewers to think through more carefully their own beliefs and values relevant to testing; (*i*) to suggest to test users better methods of appraising tests in the light of their own particular needs; and (*j*) to impress test users with the need to suspect all tests unaccompanied by detailed data on their construction, validity, uses, and limitations—even when products of distinguished authors and reputable publishers.

Buros claims disappointingly modest success in attaining these five objectives, especially the last, (*j*), in which he cautions against validity by personal prestige. Your reviewer, who teaches graduate and undergraduate courses in test construction and test usage, sadly joins Buros in this bleak evaluation of too many colleagues. * There is no doubt that the *Seventh Mental Measurements Yearbook* offers the test user a resource for learning about the appropriateness and usefulness of a test or a battery in a particular applied situation. Even more apparent, a reading of the relevant test review(s) may persuade a potential test constructor to hesitate before cluttering up the literature with another test. Two suggestions need to be mentioned: First, there should be a brief content index at the end of Volume I in addition to the more detailed combined indexes in Volume II. Second, and this is more in the nature of a tongue-in-cheek offering, there should be an *On The Other Hand* section (cf. *Contemporary Psychology*) to enable those who feel maligned, misunderstood and/or slighted

to have their say. The psychologist who works with people, especially in the area of research and applied assessment and evaluation, should have all the *MMY*s on the bookshelf. If this seems to be too large an order, at least the *Seventh Mental Measurements Yearbook* should be there to supplement *Personality Tests and Reviews* (1970) and *Tests in Print* (1961). What a fine trio of source information!

Manas (India) 20(1):69–72 '73. J. M. Ojha. This is yet another-and latest-gift from Buros to the profession in his monumental series of Mental Measurements Yearbooks. It has been a distinguished service since the first *MMY* was launched in 1938. The objectives are clean and honest—they were intended not only to provide much needed information to the readers but to help improve the professional services rendered by the publishers and authors of tests. * The fact that these benefits—helping publication and development of better instruments—were actually thought of in the beginning and were made deliberately a part of the objectives of the MMYs, speaks highly of Buros and his dedication to the cause of better professional services. That volumes of ever increasing sizes are continued to be published with a regularity, precision and an impeccable editing, in spite of several financial crises, makes us admire Buros' faith in his mission. This spirit of crusading nature—a desire to put the material to fair examination—is evident in the way reviewers are selected. The same instruments are quite often reviewed by more than one reviewer and even where it is reviewed once, the underlying intention is to present various representative viewpoints. * For sheer coverage of material, 7th MMY is a highly prized volume. * An observation which is quite significant for this reviewer is that out of 242 publishers of tests, including this MMY, (of which an overwhelming majority is the US publishers) the field is dominated by some large US Corporations. 3% of the publishers account for 37.2% of the tests included in this MMY. 55% are one-test publishers accounting for only 11.5% of the tests. The top five test publishers of the USA who account for 30.2% of the tests, are actually two giant conglomerates who control these. It is obvious that test publishing in USA has become a monopoly business and is equal to any strong commercial venture where the standard of quality are not rigidly adhered to, as long as the tests have saleability and has the capability of bringing good returns. This is evident from Buros' own observation that at least half of the tests currently on market should never have been published—exaggerated, false or unsubstantiated claims are rule rather than the exception. A suggestion may be pertinent here. Buros may try to include foreign language published literature/bibliography for the tests reviewed in the MMYs. This of course may involve large work, a risk that they may not be actually verifiable by Buros and a necessity to increase pages, and expense. How far this can be possible is a matter for serious thought but the reviewer feels it will certainly add to the usefulness. Verifiability has been an important criterion with Buros; the bibliographies presented, foreign reviews and indexes are authoritative in the sense that they were checked and located in U.S. library or abroad.

Meas & Eval Guid 5(4):506–8 Ja '73. Fred H. Borgen. Even though the *Seventh Mental Measurements Yearbook* contains 798 test reviews contributed by 439 authors, there is no meaningful way it can be considered separately from the lives of Oscar and Luella Buros. Their personal story behind the MMYs has been poignantly recounted in this journal by Buros (*MEG,* 1968, vol. 1, no. 2). As psychometrics' resident crusader for forty years, Oscar Buros has pursued the protection of test consumers with a single-minded religious passion. Although Buros' crusades antedate Ralph Nader's by a generation, the two men have much in common. Both have shown a perseverance, independence of spirit, and self-sacrifice, and a work ethic which has an engaging blend of saintliness and compulsivity. Having come to expect these qualities from Buros, I was not surprised to discover that the latest MMY is even bigger and better than its predecessors. * it is clearly a new work, with over one-half of its tests new since 1964. In the primary period of coverage of this MMY, 1964–1970, the psychometric information explosion has hit with a vengeance. Buros and his tiny staff have personally examined 19,488 references for this period, two and one-half times more than for the sixth MMY. To cope with this growth, Buros has begun moving some recent material into monographs in specialized areas: the 1968 *Reading Tests and Reviews* and the 1970 *Personality Tests and Reviews* (reviewed in MEG by Eastman, 1970, vol. 3, no. 1). For many readers of this journal the latter volume will continue to be indispens-

able, since it contains 80 tests and over 7,000 recent references *not* in the current MMY. The heart of the MMY continues to be the reviews. Buros' professional and editorial skill is apparent in the way he has selected informed, careful, and appropriate reviewers who are capable of following his manifesto of "frankly critical reviews." * The reviewers are conscientious, though not equally courageous in delivering merited criticism. Few reviewers approached the candor of a British reviewer who reacted to one test by wondering whether "the MMY should have to concern itself with such disingenuous balderdash." Although the MMY approach of multiple test reviews is the best method around, there are frequent contradictions in the conclusions of reviewers who have examined the same evidence. For too many reviewers it is painfully obvious that their conclusions derive primarily from their psychometric preconceptions. This is true particularly in the evaluation of personality and interest measures, where the authors' views on such recurrent issues as response bias and empirical versus homogeneous scoring are often entangled in their evaluation of an instrument. These conflicting opinions by test experts should quickly disabuse the MMY reader of the notion that there is one accepted correct way to construct tests. * The strengths of the MMY, such as comprehensiveness and size, lead to some inevitable awkwardness, particularly for the casual user. The MMY is so complexly organized, with six indexes and parallel numbering systems, that one can easily get lost. Since there is no true subject index, I have occasionally found it difficult to locate test content which is unidentified in the test titles. For example, the key word "creativity" will locate only one test, listed under special intellectual measures. By tracing the names of researchers that I recall in the creativity area, I have also been able to find the Barron-Welsh Art Scale under personality measures and Taylor's Alpha Biographical Inventory among the vocational tests. Other creativity measures are hidden as subscales in various instruments. Despite its expense, most readers of this journal will profit by ready access to the latest yearbook in this classic series. The MMY is a continuing monument to the excellence of one dedicated individual and is without peer as a source (a) for facts and evaluations needed for selecting specific tests for counseling, evaluation, and research;

(b) for bibliographic information related to specific tests; and (c), to my mind, for just entertaining reading about diverse approaches in measurement.

Personnel Psychol 25(4):728–32 w '72. Philip Ash. Henry S. Dyer, in a review of the 6th MMY reprinted in the current opus (p. 1595) observed that "Oscar Buros has not only created, single-handed, an important institution in the field of educational and psychological measurement; he *is* the institution." It is frequently difficult enough to review a book; it is foolhardy to attempt to review an encyclopedia; it may be impossible to review an institution. In these parlous times, however, when tests have been taken out of the schools, the clinics, and the offices of industry and hailed before legislative bodies, commissions, and courts—in these times when the expertise of psychologists has given way to the strictures of sociologists, who have in turn been finessed by attorneys, and they in their turn trumped by the judiciary—in such times as these we cannot shirk the challenge. This reviewer will leave to others the encomiums deserved by Oscar Buros for this, the largest in the series of publications to which sophisticated test users and test developers resort to locate descriptions and evaluations of available tests. The statistics of the volumes themselves (a 23-page Introduction includes 10 tables of statistics on the content) boggle the mind; 2,032 double-columned pages, listing 1,157 tests (in 15 categories) with 12,372 references; 546 of the tests are evaluated in 798 original reviews by 439 reviewers; 181 review excerpts are given for 115 tests. * In short, the magnitude of the undertaking is enormous, and it is the widely-shared consensus of reviewers....that the set is "Indispensable....A special case of professional illiteracy is the fate of any teacher or student of educational and psychological tests and measurements who does not have access to Dr. Buros'....(7th MMY)...." (Psychological Corporation, 1972). The stamp of approval of one of the largest and most prestigious professional test publishers in the country attests to the excellence of the work, an almost omnibus compendium of testing practice and lore. It may be meretricious cavil, therefore, to take issue with the 7th MMY, not as it is, but as one reviewer, who must confess that he has not published a review of a single test, would have it be. * The institution has provided information, but the information has had only a slight impact on practice. The *possible* reasons for this state of affairs are suggested in the Russell Sage supported survey of testing (Holmen and Docter, 1972) and in a summary of criticisms of the Yearbooks by Melany Baehr (1967). The "frankly critical reviews" solicited by Dr. Buros were often criticized for apparent bias, lack of explicit standards against which tests were evaluated, a tone more negative than the test in question warranted, reviews more influenced by personal or professional biases than by the APA Standards manual (APA, 1966). Dr. Baehr cited a number of tests in the 6th MMY for which the reviews were contradictory (similar contradictions occur in the 7th MMY), and more likely to confuse than to enlighten the reader. Although it is perhaps impossible to compile a document like the MMY satisfactory in technical content and level of sophistication for all readers, another criticism is that the average review is written at a level beyond the comprehension of those test users who most need them. A reader's practices, to come back to the issue of disappointing impact, will not be modified by what he cannot understand. Previous reviewers have indeed suggested more structured and comparable reviews, or summaries after the style of *Consumer Reports* (e.g., T. L. Hilton's review of the 6th MMY, reprinted in the present volume, p. 1602). A data-based format that has appeared in the pages of this journal, and is best illustrated, perhaps, by Robert Guion's (1965) text, table 11.4, "Summary of validity studies for rative inventories" would be an excellent model to follow. It dispenses with both superlatives and pejoratives, and allows the reader to be the judge. Ghiselli's (1966) format, particularized as to tests rather than test categories, would also yield more precise and objective information. If the MMYs cannot go in this direction, there is still hope that the international associations (e.g., the International Association of Applied Psychology "Recommendations concerning....tests," July 28, 1971) or the national associations might fill these needs. The establishment of an Educational Resources Information Center (Holmen and Docter, p. 163) gives some promise, although it is difficult to discern on the near horizon any individual or organization that has the commitment to the problem clearly demonstrated by Dr. Buros and his wife. The preceding comments deal with the structure of the MMYs as an overall institution—leading either to the change of that institution or to the creation of another institution which will better serve more test users. Testing today, however, is facing, at every level of government, industry, and education, a particular challenge for which we look in vain for any but the most passing reference in a handful of reviews. This is, of course, the interaction of testing and equal employment opportunity. Given the truly staggering number of pages devoted to preface, introduction, text body, and indexes, it would not have been inappropriate, to the mind of this reviewer, to include the texts of the EEOC *Guidelines on Testing* (Equal Employment Opportunity Commission, 1970) and the OFCC *Order on Testing* (U.S. Department of Labor, 1968), both of which are setting the groundrules for the uses of tests in almost every context. * Dr. Buros, then, has done it again. Absent other alternatives, or bodies willing to undertake them, the MMYs will continue to serve those interests and needs which they chose to serve in the past. I hope it will not be considered captious cavil, however, to observe that other needs—indeed, those embodied in Dr. Buros' own "Crusading objectives"—have surfaced to demand urgent fulfillment. If the psychological profession does not rise to meet them it is perfectly obvious that other groups in our society will preempt the area and impose prescriptive solutions we may not at all relish. I venture with temerity the hope that Dr. Buros' 8th MMY, which he promises us by 1975, will at least take cognizance of the issues raised in this review.

Psychol Rep 30(3):1011 Je '72. Over the years there has been an increasing tendency to take for granted that one will find useful information about a test of interest in a book by Buros. We say, "Look in Buros." The work he has done to prepare descriptions, reviews, and comparisons of tests, bibliographic references to related research, lists of publishers, etc., has not gone unnoticed and certainly cannot fail to be appreciated by students and professional psychologists alike. However enthusiastic the reviews and casual our dependence on Buros, too little attention has been given to his excellent contribution to the sociology of assessment. In each of his introductory chapters, there are many wonderful bits of information about who reviews tests, where reviews of tests appear, how these are handled, what changes may be observed over the years in development of tests,

and in use. Buros never loses sight of his goals even though in this most comprehensive of his undertakings so far he is compelled to note with sadness the large increase in new tests which do not meet even minimum standards though they may find users because of their packaging. The present yearbook contains many new reviews and draws heavily on cooperative journals which publish reviews. It is noteworthy that many reviews from *Psychological Reports* and *Perceptual and Motor Skills* appear. Very often single reviews from one journal constitute the only comment on a test. The typesetting is very good. These reviewers feel that the present two volumes must be available to many professionals and that professionals must use them intelligently and validate their dependence on Buros by providing him and his staff with feedback. Consider these volumes a necessary and standard reference, a fine award for an outstanding student, and a source of pleasure for several hours' perusal.

[B82]

★Buros, Oscar Krisen, Editor. **Social Studies Tests and Reviews: A Monograph Consisting of the Social Studies Sections of the Seven Mental Measurements Yearbooks (1938–72) and Tests in Print II (1974).** Highland Park, N.J.: Gryphon Press, 1975. Pp. xxv, 227, $20.00. *

[B83]

★Buros, Oscar Krisen, Editor. **Tests in Print II: An Index to Tests, Test Reviews, and the Literature on Specific Tests.** Highland Park, N.J.: Gryphon Press, 1974. Pp. xxxix, 1107. $70.00. * For reviews of *Tests in Print I,* see 6:B105 (8 excerpts).

Austral J Psychol 28(3):197 '76. Don McNicol. Tests in Print is a comprehensive bibliography of almost 2,500 tests, most of which are of direct interest to psychologists—intelligence, personality, aptitude and reading tests—while others are of greater relevance to educators—foreign language, science, mathematics and social studies tests. Each test is listed together with information about its construction, use and validty, as well as an exhaustive reference list citing work in which it has been used. Buros does not attempt to evaluate the tests; this is done in his companion series, the *Mental Measurements Yearbooks.* T.I.P. is a valuable aid to all who use tests and are interested in their further development.

B Menninger Clinic 40(2):173-4 Mr '76. Sydney Smith. * But there are other factors to consider. The editorial costs in preparing this carefully documented reference work—the name of O. K. Buros guarantees its high standards—are estimated at a quarter of a million dollars. For forty years O. K. Buros has provided American psychology with the best researched, most accurate, painstaking inquiry into the quality and usefulness of tests. This volume contains 2,467 entries and provides a comprehensive bibliography for all tests published individually. * This book also....lists all of the published references to the test in the psychological literature. In fact, the bibliography contains 16,574 references which means the book will not soon be outdated, especially since these references will no longer be included in the *Mental Measurements Yearbook*. The great service Buros has provided the profession of psychology is his honest scientific appraisal of virtually every test in use. The book is, in this sense, the best consumer's manual published anywhere on a marketable product. Since many of us have learned the hard way that we cannot always trust what an overzealous author or a profit-making publisher has to say about their published tests, we turn to Buros to get a straight account of what we need to know before venturing the use of any test. The publication of this volume represents a major achievement in psychology, one dependent in large measure on the perseverance and dedication of its illustrious editor.

Behav Res & Ther (England) 13(4):344 O '75. D. R. Hemsley. * This massive work will be of interest to all concerned with assessment, including those involved in the assessment of the effects of therapeutic interventions. It includes a vital chapter on standards for educational and psychological tests, an extension of the document prepared in 1966 by the A.P.A. on this topic. The book is an essential work of reference for all psychologists.

Brit J Ed Studies 26(1):99–100 F '76. Jack Wrigley. This book should be on the shelves of all supervisors of students engaged in empirical educational research and should be consulted by anyone preparing to use an established test or about to construct his own. The book is invaluable as a source of information for all available tests, as a guide to informed comment on these tests, and even for information on tests which are now out of print. This volume is part of a famous series of publications by Oscar K. Buros which began in 1934 * *Tests in Print II* is itself much more than a mere catalogue of tests but it is most useful when used in conjunction with

the seven Mental Measurements Yearbooks. Using these books in combination, it is possible to find out about any test, gain some idea of its technical competence and, for the more important and popular tests, read the critical comments of informed reviewers. Not many readers will wish to buy the whole set of Yearbooks (though they are all still in print). There is a strong case for buying *Tests in Print II*, which virtually supplants *Tests in Print I*, and consulting the Yearbooks in the library. Such a comprehensive book could easily be unwieldy and indeed any reader would be well advised to study carefully the section in the introduction on "How to use this book." This done, the book is extremely clear and easy to follow. The reader is quickly guided to the appropriate tests in his chosen field, to reviews of the important tests, and to articles in learned journals which mention the tests. So real assistance in choice of tests is given. Those of us interested in mental measurement, especially those conscious of the need for critical appraisal of available tests, continue to be grateful for the amazing patience, ingenuity, integrity and accuracy of the editor of this series.

Brit J Social & Clin Psychol 14(4):439–40 N '75. Margaret Vaughn. * The vast amount of information contained in *Tests in Print II* is made easily accessible by a comprehensive indexing system. In addition to indices of names, titles and publishers, there is an invaluable scanning index in which tests are listed, according to function as they are in the body of the book. The main groups to which the tests are allocated may prove misleading, as there is no separate category for tests of brain damage. Most of these are subsumed under "Personality, Non-Projective," whilst a few are to be found under "Intelligence, Specific." In several cases no indication is given that the test is for brain damage. This imposes a minor limitation on the utility of the book. Nevertheless, *Tests in Print II* constitutes a useful preliminary reference volume for the potential test user who has some access to Buros' other works.

Develop Med & Child Neurol (England) 17(3):406 Je '75. R. C. MacKeith. This is a bibliographic dictionary of "all" in-print tests published for use with English-speaking subjects. It refers to reviews and relevant published articles on the various tests and lists descriptions of the populations for which each test is intended. There is a useful list of acronyms, which means the initials by which tests are known, and a list of authors of tests and of articles on tests. It is an American text and probably very comprehensive for American tests, but among English tests which I looked up I found Mary Sheridan's STYCAR tests but not Michael Reed's. Eleven tests of motor competence are cited, but the German Schilling KTK is not yet included. An enormous amount of hard work has gone into the making of this veritable tome and it will be extremely useful to workers in many fields.

Ed & Psychol Meas 35(2):515–7 su '75. Max D. Engelhart. * extremely useful volume * One cannot but be awed by the volume of business contemplated by Oscar Buros, his small staff, and his numerous contributors. In the INTRODUCTION are seven interesting and informative tables * As the president of Educational Testing Service, William Turnbull, said about him "If Oscar Buros didn't exist, we would have to create him."

Ed Leadership 33(1):69–70 O '75. James Raths. * *Tests in Print II* includes a bibliography of all known tests published for use with English-speaking subjects; a classified index to the contents of all of the previous Mental Measurements Yearbooks; extended bibliographies on the construction, use, and validity of specific tests; a list of tests that have gone out of print; a cumulative name index for each test; and a classified scanning index with a description of the population for which each test is intended. There are even more features—too numerous to mention, as they say. The expanded table of contents includes these headings of special interest to members of ASCD achievement batteries; multi-aptitude batteries; reading; science; social studies; and vocations. Each entry includes references to reviews in the *Mental Measurements Yearbooks* or to related articles in the professional literature. While it is possible to be confused at first by the variety of ways numerals are used in the text to cite references, to denote bibliographic listings, and to specify entries, the code can be cracked after only a brief exposure to the reference and a perusal of the notes on "how to use *Tests in Print II*" found in the front materials. It is important to bear in mind that the *Tests in Print II* reference contains almost no evaluative comments on the instruments it catalogues and only the barest of descriptions. To find out about a particular test, a reader must follow up on the cited references.

* [Both this volume and the *Seventh Mental Measurements Yearbook*] are valuable tools for anyone interested in research and/or evaluation. As alluded to earlier, they must be viewed as only a part of a much larger collection of needed resources. *

J Biol Psychol 17(1):57–9 Jl '75. Jon D. Swartz. * Also designed by Luella Buros—and published to serve as a master index to the nine previous Buros publications—*Tests in Print II*....is an impressive work too. Consisting of 1,156 two-column pages; 2,467 tests in print as of 1974; 16,574 references through 1971 on individual tests; a reprinting of the 1974 American Psychological Association-American Educational Research Association-National Council on Measurement in Education's "Standards for Educational and Psychological Tests" (why aren't all the outspoken critics of tests and testers required to read this document?); a directory of almost 500 publishers of tests with their published tests listed; an author index with references for each test; a title index including both in- and out-of-print tests; a cumulative author index to approximately 70,000 tests, reviews, excerpts, and references included in *Tests in Print II*, the seven *Mental Measurements Yearbooks, Personality Tests and Reviews,* and *Reading Tests and Reviews;* and a scanning index for locating tests for particular populations quickly. Indeed, *Tests in Print II* is the answer to a test user's prayer! * Concluding the Introduction is a bibliography of books listing information on unpublished tests—an item of information not covered in previous publications. While I doubt that my review of *The Seventh Mental Measurements Yearbook*....— in which I suggested that Buros add a new bibliographical section on the most popular non-commercial tests used in research—was responsible for this new section, I am immodest enough to hope that it may have contributed in some small fashion. (In this section, Buros points out that he has been compiling bibliographies on thousands of these unpublished tests for more than 30 years, something I was not aware of previously. Buros laments the fact that lack of resources probably will keep these bibliographies from ever being published. I wonder why a foundation could not be talked into financing such a worthwhile project?) *

J Ed Meas 12(3):216–8 f '75. Eleanor V. Horne. * a comprehensive, annotated bibliography of all in-print tests published as separates for use with English-speaking subjects. The tome serves as a master index to the test reviews and references in all the *Mental Measurement Yearbooks* (MMY), as well as in the monographs, *Personality Tests and Reviews* and *Reading Tests and Reviews*. The purpose of this volume is to encourage test consumers to choose tests more wisely by consulting the reviews in the MMY Series and the professional literature on the construction, use, and psychometric quality of the instruments. * Extensive, meticulously researched bibliographies are provided for many of the tests. Accompanying each such bibliography is a Cumulative Name Index which serves as a convenient point of entry. Items in these bibliographies have been screened for relevancy—and in effect represent a "research biography" of the instrument. The listing of these references is one of the major contributions of TIP II. Buros and his staff have thus greatly simplified the tedious and often frustrating task of retrieving references to tests, since most articles, books, or studies are not indexed by the measures used or discussed. These references form a substantial body of literature which supplements, expands, and often clarifies some of the comments in the MMY reviews themselves. In the opinion of this reviewer, however, the bibliographies could be further strengthened by including citations of documents available through the Educational Resources Information Center (ERIC) and other information systems that index the literature in the area covered by the test. * The test entries are listed alphabetically within approximately 100 broad categories such as; "Individual Intelligence Tests," "Diagnostic Reading Tests," "Mechanical Ability," etc. Generally, this classification is acceptable for this reference book with one major exception—personality tests. Although these measures comprise the largest grouping of tests (17.9%), they are divided into only two categories—projective and nonprojective. * It is extremely difficult to classify personality tests by the traits they purport to measure since many cover multiple factors. However, some effort along this line would be helpful for the user interested in identifying tests to measure some specific trait such as self concept, attitudes, values, or general adjustment. The Scanning Index, a feature new to TIP II, is a listing of all tests in the volume by category (the same categories mentioned above). For each test the intended population is listed. The function of

the Scanning Index is to identify tests that measure some knowledge, skill, or trait in a specific population. This feature works quite well with the exception of the personality category where the title and population may not provide sufficient information to enable the reader to decide whether or not a test warrants further investigation. Also provided in TIP II is an excellent Publishers' Directory and Index. Here tests are listed by publisher—an indispensible aid for the person who remembers the publisher but not the exact title of the instrument. The Title Index covers all tests listed in one of the fourteen volumes in the MMY Series. * Because of the presence of the Index of Names, I question the usefulness of the Cumulative Name Index that accompanies each of the bibliographies in the test entry section. * One of the outstanding features of TIP II is the fact that it is a cumulative index to all previous volumes in the MMY Series. * TIP II is far more than an index to earlier volumes. Approximately 395 of the tests have not been listed in any MMY and another 582 have been revised since the publication of the latest MMY. It would be desirable to have a more extensive entry—like those in the *Mental Measurements Yearbook*—for tests that are new and revised. * Ideally, the scope of coverage should be broadened by including entries for tests which are available as separates through information systems like the Educational Resources Information Center (ERIC) and the American Psychological Association's Journal Supplement Abstract Service (JSAS). * *Tests in Print II,* like its predecessors, is an indispensable volume for those involved in developing, using, criticizing, teaching, or disseminating information about tests. The "Buros Series" is certainly the most outstanding reference in educational and psychological testing and one of the best in the social sciences. For $70.00 TIP II is an excellent bargain.

J Learn Dis 9(1):55–6 Ja '76. Barry Bricklin. * *TIP II,* in contrast to the *Mental Measurements Yearbooks,* does not contain critical reviews of tests. But it does present a fantastic amount of material: a comprehensive bibliography of all known tests published as separates for use with English speaking subjects; a classified index to the contents of all *Mental Measurements Yearbooks* published to date; a reprinting of various APA and other group standards for educational and psychological tests; comprehensive bibliographies through 1971 on the construction, use and validity of specific tests (some of the bibliographies are complete in this volume while others supplement bibliographies in earlier publications); a classified list of tests which have gone out of print since the publication of *TIP I;* a cumulative name index for each test with references; title and name indexes covering all in print and out of print and all authors of tests, reviews, excerpts, and references in the seven *Mental Measurements Yearbooks* and *Personality Tests and Reviews;* a publisher's directory with a complete listing of each publisher's test titles; a classified scanning index with a description of the population for which each test is intended. This is indeed a monumental amount of information. Since Buros feels strongly committed to the fact that tests should be evaluated and chosen wisely, a person wishing to follow along with his advice would want to own the *Mental Measurements Yearbooks* to use along with *TIP II,* since the latter does not contain the critical reviews Buros feels are necessary to make proper test selections. To give some idea of the vastness of the information contained in *TIP II,* consider the fact that it contains 16,574 references. All seven *Mental Measurements Yearbooks* must be owned if one wants to be obsessively complete about information on available tests. The seventh yearbook was published in 1972. It is a tremendous two-volume work containing 2,032 pages. * With all of the work Buros has put into these books, one can readily understand and forgive his acting somewhat like an anxious, indeed vetching, mother. Comedians Mel Brooks and Carl Reiner do a skit in which Brooks plays a 2,000-year-old man. Reiner asks him if in the course of his 2,000 years he married and had children. Brooks indicates that indeed he has been married, and, in fact, has several thousand children. He plaintively adds: "....and not one of them comes to see me." In a similar vein, Buros says: "We are disturbed.... by the use of our material....without giving us credit....More than 60,000 references (have been) presented in (our volumes) at a tremendous cost in time and money. All references.... have been personally examined by me to make sure that they meet our criteria for relevancy with regard to specific tests....Yet, we regret to report that, to our knowledge, not one of these uniquely prepared bibliographies has ever been cited in a test manual, article, or book dealing

with a specific test (page xxiii)." If ever an author deserved to complain, Buros must be that person.

J Pers Assess 40(1):98–100 F '76. *Chadwick Karr.* Of all the books published in the field of psychology, none matches the scope, utility, and integrity of those published by Oscar Krisen Buros and his staff. Buros' awareness of psychology's lack of an established technology has not prevented him from publishing decade after decade a series of reference books on mental testing, most of which are indispensable to psychometrists and other applied practitioners. * Buros' *Tests in Print II* is....indispensable to anyone who is looking for a test. It is similar to a compendium of drugs for use by physicians, or a handbook for use by engineers. It differs from these two examples in that a great deal more is known about the composition and effects of drugs, and the physical facts tabled in an engineering handbook. Most of the tests listed in TIP II are of "....unknown or questionable validity" (p. xxii). Hence, this volume is designed primarily as an aid to the tester who is looking for a particular kind of test, and not for a recommendation of which test to use. * Fortunately for psychology, the work of Buros, his wife, and his unusually dedicated and competent staff has prevented the massive mental testing movement from generating its own self-serving myth of virtue and virtuosity. And yet among all those thousands of tests there are both discovered and undiscovered gems. Without ready access to Buros' publications, it would be almost impossible to find those tests which will meet our unique and special needs. To be fully functional, all testing centers require as a bare minimum *Tests in Print II* and the *Fifth, Sixth,* and *Seventh Mental Measurements Yearbooks.* Specialized testing centers would find valuable use for *Personality Tests and Reviews* (1970) and *Reading Tests and Reviews* (1968). All college and university libraries should have one or more complete sets of Buros' publications. Applied psychologists, psychometrists, teachers, and personnel directors need ready access to the more recent publications. Hopefully, enough organizations and institutions which need these publications will purchase them to guarantee the continuation of the series. Without the kind of effort represented by Buros and his staff, psychology could falter in its efforts to develop an effective and useful technology.

Meas & Eval Guid 9(1):37–8 Ap '76. *Donald*

G. Zytowski. * Besides the very complete descriptions for each entry and the bibliography accompanying them, it is a virtual cornucopia of indexes. There is a cumulative name index for each entry so that you can locate everything a single individual has written concerning any given test. You can discover what tests have gone out of print since the 1961 *Yearbook* and what tests have been revised or supplemented or are new since the last *Yearbook*. You may locate the material for any test in *TIP II* by means of an alphabetical index of titles, identify any test by means of its acronym, or you may find lists of all tests of a given type in a scanning index. A complete listing of the names and addresses of test publishers is included, and eleven test-scoring services or machines are identified and bibliographies given for those that have acquired references. An index of the names indexed in *TIP II* consumes 200 pages and permits one to find everything a given person has ever written relating to tests and testing, including any *Yearbook* review. What is more, the entire 1974 edition of the *Standards for Educational and Psychological Tests* is reprinted, properly credited to APA, AERA, and NCME. In the introduction, Buros gives us a glimpse of the history of his publications, especially of his hopes and the difficulties in attaining them. He also gives some analysis of the tests included in the volume, for example, the number of new or revised tests appearing each year since *TIP I,* which tests have the greatest number of references (Rorschach–4578; MMPI–3855), which tests have attracted the most references in the years 1969 to 1971 (the MMPI)—all in all, a very informative reflection of where testing appears to be going. The final section of the introduction reveals that Buros has been keeping bibliographies for thousands of tests that have not yet appeared as published separates, and he confesses that he will probably never find the resources to publish them. As if to make amends, he then lists 13 books which are mini-Buros of unpublished tests. Only one question remains: Where does Buros index the bibliography of reviews of the publications of the Institute of Mental Measurements? You'll find reviews (and presumably this one) under B (for Buros) in the books and reviews section of the *8th Yearbook* scheduled for 1975.

Personnel Psychol *28(3):403–4 au '75. Philip Ash.* * The uses of TIP II are manifold, and the interlocking indexes greatly simplify answering a variety of questions: identification of tests for particular populations or particular attributes (or both), location of test reviews through the bibliographies, location of publishers, etc. And, for those who have the time and interest, a place to browse through for a view of the testing establishment and testing as a preoccupation in American psychology. Given the behavioristic, objectivistic tradition of American psychology, for example, this reviewer at least cannot but view with continued astonishment that the three tests with the longest bibliographies (through 1971) are the Rorschach (4578), the MMPI (3855) and the TAT (1765)—psychology's black boxes of tricks. Indeed, personality tests predominate, accounting for 17.9% of all listings, followed by vocational tests (15.2%), intelligence tests (11.1%), and reading tests (10.1 percent). The plurality of personality tests may be a consequence of the old adage, "If you don't succeed at first, try, try, again." A comparison of TIP II with TIP I also provides some reflection on the pervasive inflation of the past thirteen years—an inflation to which Professor Buros alludes to some extent. The number of tests increased from 1961 to 1974 by 16.0%; the preface increased by 34.5%; the body of the text increased by 131.1%; and the price of the volume increased by 900.0%. But even at that, in these days of shrinking dollars and proliferating publications, TIP II is a very good buy for the serious user of tests.

Psychologia Africana (South Africa) 16(2): 147–8 Mr '76. D. W. Steyn. This massive new volume is a worthy and overdue successor to *Tests in Print* which was published in 1961. In spite of the anti-test sentiment that has become something of a fashion and a fad among certain parts of the populace, the sheer volume of tests published annually has shown no signs of abating. The industriousness and sometimes not too intelligent diligence of test producers in the English-speaking world have had the net result of not only bewildering the practical test user, but also of rendering the 1961 edition somewhat dated if not quaintly antique. One cannot but marvel at the impressive amount of work and meticulous attention to detail that must have gone into *Tests in Print II*. * There is little doubt that this ambitious volume is a veritable gold mine of information pertaining to the 2467 test entries. The classification of tests into different categories is done intelligently and the taxonomy adopted by the editor is easy to follow. The inclusion of the *Standards for Educational and Psychological Tests* is a valuable and welcome addition to a standard reference book of this nature and reflects the editor's concern with the maintenance of high standards for tests and the wise and prudent application of these instruments in practice. The usefulness of the volume in and of itself is perhaps more limited than the editor chooses to admit. It is invaluable, however, if used jointly with the *Mental Measurements Yearbooks* which include penetrating, thorough and thoughtful specialist reviews on a vast number of tests. The quality of printing and the general layout of the volume conform to the excellent standards that have become associated with Buros' work. In a volume of this sheer size, minor oversights can and do occur—reference to the Union of South Africa is a case in point. It is hoped that the magnitude of the task of keeping up to date will not discourage the editor from continuing with his commendable toils and that a time span of considerably less than thirteen years will elapse before *Tests in Print III* makes its appearance.

Read World 15(3):187–8 Mr '76. Wm. W. Anderson. Greatly expanded in both scope and size, TIP II presents a most impressively concise compilation of test data in a well-organized fashion. * This volume is designed to be used in conjunction with the various *Mental Measurements Yearbooks* and test monographs, but it is, nevertheless, a most valuable resource in its own right. A brief period spent in becoming acquainted with the unique structure of TIP II is a most rewarding venture. The reader who attempts to gain information from this time without a "get-acquainted" survey will find it a most frustrating experience. * Each successive volume of TIP is designed to supplement but not to supplant the others. Nevertheless, the publishers indicate that the comprehensive design of TIP II makes TIP I only of "marginal value." In summary, this work is an invaluable resource for researchers, guidance counselors, psychologists, curriculum planners, and anyone with an interest in tests and testing. The scholarship and clarity characteristic of Buros' earlier works coupled with the improved organizational features of TIP II will doubtlessly be received by professionals with well-deserved praise and appreciation.

Sch Sci & Math 75(6):572–3 O '75. George G. Mallinson. Those who have made use of the *Mental Measurements Yearbooks* and other compendia of analyses of tests during their educational careers can only stand in awe of the incredible, and no doubt grinding, effort expended by Oscar K. Buros and his staff in producing these publications. The amount of detail that must be checked for accuracy, the problems that no doubt arise with the vast numbers of those who review the tests; and the extensive reading of galleys and page proofs surely merit Dr. Buros, if nothing else, an additional rhinestone in his celestial crown. The most recent document reviewed here merits even another. * *Tests in Print II* differs from the *Mental Measurements Yearbooks* in that the narratives describe the general parameters of the tests and the purposes for which they are designed rather than reviewing them in detail with commentaries and judgments. However, the narratives are supplemented by lists of references, including those in the Buros publications and other studies and reviews, made of these tests and projects in which the tests were used. Obviously, the realm of tests covered is beyond science and mathematics. Yet for those who teach science and mathematics in colleges and universities, one of the greatest problems is the identification of reliable and valid tests for various student reports including theses and dissertations. Also, many elementary- and high-school teachers are searching for in-print tests for use with their students. *Tests in Print II* will provide the needed guidance. The publication deserves many kudos.

[B84]

★BUROS, OSCAR KRISEN, EDITOR. **Vocational Tests and Reviews: A Monograph Consisting of the Vocational Sections of the Seven Mental Measurements Yearbooks (1938–72) and Tests in Print II (1974).** Highland Park, N.J.: Gryphon Press, 1975. Pp. xxvii, 1087. $55.00. *

J Occup Psych 49(3):187 '76. J. C. Houston. * The MMY extracts are gathered together into seven sections one for each volume. The seven sections are further classified into the areas of interest for this volume, namely, business education, clerical, interests, manual dexterity, mechanical ability and so on. The reader will be familiar with the form these extracts take—full details about the tests and the famous reviews and bibliographies. The TIP II extracts are also classified under areas of interest. They contain information in short entries such as title, author, factual statement of criticism and cross references to MMYs. These entries are followed by bibliographic references, through 1971 and a cumulative index of authors' names with associated references. This enables the user to get quickly to any author he chooses. A list of out of print tests is given at the end of each section. * The index of titles distinguishes between in and out of print tests, and the authors index between books, reviews and excerpted reviews. * The introduction gives clear advice on how to use the book and there are also interesting statistics in the area of vocational tests about the tests and reviews associated with them. The preface explains more forcefully than ever Buros's views on the misuse of tests. This volume will continue the work of publicizing criticisms of tests so putting pressure on test constructors to do better, aiding users to choose the best tests for their purpose, and cathecting the thinking processes of reviewers. In conclusion, this rearrangement is a most useful and sophisticated development and further improvement is hard to envisage.

Meas & Eval Guid 9(4):214–5 Ja '77. Donald G. Zytowski. Why a monograph reprinting the vocational sections of the seven *Mental Measurements Yearbooks* and *Tests in Print II?* Mainly because, without the special monograph, it would cost $312 to buy all the *Yearbooks,* and users might be interested in only one type of test. What does this monograph include? There are sections for business education tests such as typing speed or bookkeeping knowledge, multi-aptitude test batteries such as the Differential Aptitude Test, multipurpose selection tests such as the Flanagan Aptitude Classification Test, selection tests for specific occupations, tests of dexterity or mechanical comprehension or supervisory skills, selection tests for professional schools such as nursing, selection and rating forms for employment, job satisfaction and employee morale surveys, and interest inventories. Everything the personnel director or career counselor might want to look up. * From my perspective, it is as much a museum of vocational testing and inventorying as it is a very useful reference work. * Anyone would probably want the *Monograph* to be arranged so that all the material from the seven *Yearbooks* would be assembled together under each test. Instead, the sections are arranged sequentially so that one has to look in each of seven sections plus the *Tests in Print* section for all the material on one test. Economics must

dictate this approach. And it should be understood that the coverage stops with 1971 even though the publication date is 1975. The next *Yearbook* is scheduled for 1977. I would urge Professor Buros to consider issuing his eighth both as a single volume and in sections so that prospective buyers might not be inhibited from extending their *Monograph* by the cost of acquiring everything!

Personnel Psychol 29(1):134–5 sp '76. Bernard P. Indik. This is a reference work in the Buros tradition of the Mental Measurements Yearbooks. In large part this is a reprint of material printed earlier in the seven Mental Measurements Yearbooks from 1938 through 1972....along with the above relevant sections of *Tests in Print II.* * Putting all of this very relevant material in this form makes the availability of tests and critical reviews of tests by topic areas of *most relevance* to personnel psychologists *centralized* in one volume and a *most useful* form. The areas include, of course, a much broader coverage in the seventh mental measurements yearbook than in the first mental measurements yearbook. The relevant segment of the first mental measurements yearbook covers only 11 pages while the seventh mental measurements yearbook covers 199 pages of test descriptions, references of studies and independent reviews of the various tests. Obviously, this is at least in part a reflection of the growth of the testing field particularly in the area of most concern to many personnel psychologists. This reorganized volume should be a useful shelf reference to most practicing personnel psychologists. There are two additional suggestions that I would make. First, that some considerable effort be made particularly in the selection testing field to assess the potential prejudicial effect of the utilization of tests for different subgroups within our society when most of the test development work that has been done on the mainstream of white people. Maybe there ought to be an added criteria in the BUROS type of review that questions the degree to which this has been considered and assessed for each test that is reviewed. Second, while there are a few reviews of measures of organizationally relevant individually measured concepts like the L.B.D.Q. and a few other measures of supervisory behavior and some job satisfaction measures, there are precious few reviews of other measures as a guide to the personnel psychologist. I would like to see more measures included for review by the psychometric criteria.

[B85]

★BURT, FORREST D., AND KING, SYLVIA, EDITORS. **Equivalency Testing: A Major Issue for College English.** Urbana, Ill.: National Council of Teachers of English, 1974. Pp. xii, 52. Paper, $2.25. *

[B86]

★BURTON, H. M. **Examinations in English: A Brief Guide for Candidates.** London: University of London Press Ltd., 1970. Pp. x, 60. Paper, 35p. *

[B87]

*BUTCHER, H. J. **Human Intelligence: Its Nature and Assessment.** New York: Harper & Row, Publishers, Inc., 1973, c1968. Pp. 343. Paper, $3.95. * For reviews, see 7:B124 (3 excerpts).

[B88]

★BUTCHER, H. J., AND LOMAX, D. E., EDITORS. **Readings in Human Intelligence.** London: Methuen & Co. Ltd., 1972. Pp. viii, 438. Paper, £3.50. *

Brit J Ed Psychol 44(1):98–9 F '74. Brian Dockrell. Readers who have found Butcher's lucid and wide ranging *Human Intelligence* to be an important item on their reading lists, will welcome this book of readings. The readings are specifically designed to provide familiarity with authors or schools of thought which are discussed in Butcher's original text. * The major strength is the breadth of approach to the workings of the human intelligence. These are certainly not readings in psychometrics. They range widely * Inevitably one has reservations. There is, of course, a logic in excluding Guilford's mental bloc from the book but it poses problems. Several of the articles included in the book refer to the "structure of intellect" model and it is hardly fair to Guilford to have his point of view presented solely through the eyes of his critics, especially since there is extensive discussion of this work in the text. Much more important is that the "building block" theory of intelligence as contrasted with the "g" plan is not represented at all. A lecturer can correct whatever he considers to be the deficiencies of Butcher's text in his lectures but the point of a book of readings is, as the editors point out, that it is difficult for students to have access to journal articles. How then can a lecturer who adopts this book of readings give his students the same direct experience of the point of view of the Thurstones, Guilford or their associates as they get of Burt and Spearman? A general deficiency of this kind is more important than cavilling at the inclusion of one representative of a point of view rather than another. Surely room could have been found by leaving out an article, like that of Warburton and his associates, which is of rather specialised interest. * We are long past the stage where it is necessary to produce a single book of readings—even one as good as this. Publishers here should now be willing to produce what we have seen for some years across the Atlantic—a set of readings tailored to meet the need of a particular course. If the publishers had been more flexible they could have printed separately two or three times as many articles as are included in this book, allowed each lecturer to make his own choice from this extended list and assembled the articles in loose leaf binders. In this way each lecturer could select readings to meet the needs of his own students and to compensate for the deficiencies of his own library. Equally important, it is possible in this way to avoid the inevitable deficiency of a book of readings—recent contributions are not included. This book will be used by students first in 1973 and then for many years after one expects, yet the most recent article included is one published in 1970 and that to my mind a technical article of peripheral interest to the general student. The loose leaf format makes it possible to include the more recent material that lecturers refer to in their lectures. * Until our publishers can be shaken out of their lethargy we must be grateful to Butcher and Lomax for a thoughtful, wide-ranging selection from the mass of literature on human intelligence produced in the last decade or so.

[B89]

★BUTCHER, JAMES N., EDITOR. **Objective Personality Assessment: Changing Perspectives.** New York: Academic Press, Inc., 1972. Pp. x, 212. $15.25. *

J Pers Assess 38(3):286–7 Je '74. James H. Johnson. This is a good book, but it is not *primarily* about the general issues surrounding objective personality assessment. It is about the MMPI, its limitations, future, and possible revision. General issues about objective testing are covered (and covered well), but in relation to the MMPI. What makes it an important book is the psychological impact of chapters by Hathaway, Meehl, and Dahlstrom on the present status of the MMPI, and the possible result on its future. The content of this edited volume may be summarized briefly. Butcher discusses various criticisms of objective personality testing. He suggests that while the MMPI was developed to correct shortcomings of earlier naive approaches, it is now known to have deficits of its own which are in need of correction. The remainder of the book is described as an attempt to deal with this issue. Hathaway questions why convincing progress in personality testing has not been made. He argues that it has lagged because psychologists have not identified the appropriate characteristics of personality to measure. * The attitude reflected in this book ought to be interesting to anyone with a psychometric bent. Hathaway, Meehl, and Dahlstrom write candidly about the status and the value of the MMPI. Hathaway projects pessimism over the fact that ordinary people are able to make personality judgments that psychologists with psychometric instrumentation are unable to improve on greatly. Meehl suggests that psychology is too hard for psychologists, and agrees that psychometrists have been overly optimistic in the face of weak personality theory. He argues for doing the best job possible with the present instrument. Dahlstrom does not believe the MMPI will be replaced readily, but feels that it should be improved through modification. Thus, these important figures convey disenchantment with progress to date on the MMPI—and without any clear agreement as to what viable alternatives should be pursued. In general, this is a comprehensive and well done collection of material pertaining to the MMPI. The text is not as inclusive as the title promises, and that is my only objection to it. The Minnesota view of testing and the MMPI are well discussed, but papers representing other psychometric approaches would have been helpful. I think this is an important book, however, for psychometrically inclined psychologists to read. When historically important "MMPIers" openly question the instrument, then it is my guess that the asymptote of interest has been reached. Therefore, this book probably marks the beginning of the end for large scale research on the present MMPI (despite Meehl's assertions). For this reason alone, it deserves reading.

[B90]

★BUTCHER, JAMES N., AND PANCHERI, PAOLO. **A Handbook of Cross-National MMPI Research.** Minneapolis, Minn.: University of Minnesota Press, 1976. Pp. viii, 470. $20.00. *

[B91]

★BYHAM, WILLIAM C., AND BOBIN, DONNA, EDITORS. **Alternatives to Paper and Pencil Testing: Pro-**ceedings of a Conference. Pittsburgh, Pa.: Graduate School of Business, University of Pittsburgh, 1973. Pp. iv, 142. *

Personnel Psychol 27(1):176–80 sp '74. *George W. Henderson, Jr.* * Carlson has produced what is essentially a "white paper" on the employment interview * His approach to this rather formidable task is a well organized one * this paper would profit from a distillation and re-write. In spite of these essentially stylistic deficiencies, it is a totally complete review, providing an insightful synthesis of judgmental techniques for industrial assessment. * His general conclusions hold no surprises, though his choice of examples to once again denigrate the interview seem out of date. * Carlson is convincing in claiming that at least three conditions are responsible for the failure of the interview to equal its competitors. These are: 1) lack of relevancy of the traditional interview's content; 2) the requirement for an interviewer to make an absolute judgment rather than relative judgments; and 3) the relative complexity of the individual interviewer's judgmental task. Attention to these three content and contextual variables should advance the interview's efficiency. * Carlson....wisely points out nevertheless that process and evaluative research strategies are complementary rather than competitive, and should be jointly pushed. * Thornton's address to the subject of performance testing begins with a dramatic example of the selection of bridge painters, and proceeds in a most interesting fashion into some practical and theoretical aspects of all achievement, i.e., performance testing. He challenges the adequacy of most efforts to construct representative work samples, and his claim that most such work samples are both unreliable and too low in difficulty level is believable and sobering. * An elegant address for its simplicity, and its synthesis of both old and new concepts, Dr. Thornton's remarks make good sense and represent a needed step away from the all too frequent armchairing of work samples. * the Cleff Computer Assisted Job Matching techniques sound very promising. The developers and their sponsors (the NAM) showed both courage and imagination in departing from the conventional. That they have succeeded seems apparent, but considerably more comparative research needs to be done before a full assessment of this technique can be given. * Byham presents his standard non-technical review of assessment centers, their administration, utility and operational validity. This represents a solid job of reporting for the lay audience, who will find this a clear exposition of what, where, how and why. For psychologists and personnel people familiar with this subject, this section could be lightly scanned. * Moses describes the application of the assessment center technology to lower levels—specifically to assessment of general supervisory skills, and for technical engineering potential * While thought-provoking and certainly a logical extension of the assessment center concept, the most significant value of these studies to this reviewer is Dr. Moses brief observation that such studies provoke managers into asking, "Do I really need to hire a college educated individual to do this job—or should I be looking for others without this education who could also be very successful?" This may be the major contribution of this very promising but very new extension of the assessment center to lower organizational levels.

[B92]

★Byham, William C., and Spitzer, Morton Edward. **The Law and Personnel Testing.** New York: American Management Association, 1971. Pp. xv, 238. * *Out of print.*

Personnel Psychol 25(4):715–9 w '72. James J. Kirkpatrick. * In general....the authors have reasonably met the objectives they set forth for their book. For a book aimed at the businessman, and within the limitation of about 190 pages of text, the coverage is a generally nontechnical survey of the problems and some approaches to possible answers. In addition, while both authors are psychologists with considerable industrial experience in personnel selection, and as expected somewhat protective of testing, they nevertheless are also strong advocates for equal opportunity. * the authors lay to rest one of the popular rationalizations still used by some employers that it is impossible to conduct validation studies or research on employment statistics on a racial group basis because it may be illegal * The authors also correctly state that government regulations permit an argument for content or rational validity for a test when a criterion-related validity study is not technically feasible. * Also commendably the authors take the position that differential validation studies, i.e., determining the fairness and validity of selection procedures for each racial group, are desirable from the standpoint of compliance

with the guidelines * Practical approaches for coping with the different forms of differential validity results are suggested. The important thing in this connection is that, rather than attempting to deny the existence of differential validity, the authors recognize the problem and deal with it constructively. Finally, the authors emphasize the necessity of comprehensive audits of the company's selection procedures. A practical guide for this purpose is included in the appendix, along with the testing guidelines issued by the EEOC and the OFCC, which employers are expected to follow. Thus, an employer who uses this book as an aid in compliance will find many valuable ideas and suggestions. * Of course, the perfect book has not yet been written, and this one has its share of relatively minor imperfections. For one thing, the book seems to be rather haphazardly organized, and as one result, there is some unnecessary repetition. ¹ Also, while the authors are sensitive to sex discrimination in employment, as well as race, and devote considerable discussion to it, their male chauvinism unfortunately occasionally slips through. * The authors seem to be incorrect in their statement regarding court cases involving the testing issue: "as far as can be determined, no test has been ruled irrelevant for lack of criterion-related validity statistics." Actually, the court cases in which the court found against testing have been decided because creditable criterion-related evidence was lacking, including the Supreme Court decision in Griggs, which is reproduced in the appendix. * for a book with under 190 pages of nontechnical text, without complicated graphs and formulas, the price of $14.00, even in today's book market, appears to be something of a "rip-off" on the part of the AMA, representing an exploitation of the desperate need employers have to find any sound guidance on these difficult personnel problems. A questionable statement is made comparing race and sex discrimination: "Sex discrimination in employment, in contrast with race discrimination, has often been quite openly practiced by companies." Certainly the way in which blacks and other racial minorities have been relegated to janitorial and laboring classifications in many companies would make it debatable as to which type of discrimination has been more obvious. In fact, considering union statistics, in which for example as late as 1969 a number of unions in the construction field had fewer than 2%

blacks in their national membership, it is difficult to find much more glaring examples of discrimination. Also, in the chapter dealing with government and union activities, the statement is made: "It appears that the unions may be going in the same direction as the government in demanding relevancy—both rational and criterion-related." This is doubtful as a generalization because in fact a number of unions have been sued in court cases, not only for discriminatory practices such as seniority and nepotism, but also for their unvalidated testing procedures, which had the effect of keeping the union membership virtually all white. Thus, it is difficult to understand the authors' inclination to place the union on the side of the government in questioning inappropriate testing practices. While unions have on occasion challenged management's use of testing, it has not been done in the spirit of equal opportunity. One more criticism. In two instances, the authors defend tests as not being essentially culturally biased * Theoretically speaking, this *may* be true. Yet, the way tests are typically used, the lower the score the more likely that individual will be rejected, regardless of whether the test is valid or not, or whether the low score was due to that individual's deficient education or disadvantaged background. * it accomplishes little to say to someone who is rejected for employment and is being denied an opportunity for a livelihood that the test wasn't culturally biased but that it was his background that was * In conclusion, and despite the foregoing criticisms, I can heartily recommend this book to the businessman who must be concerned with equal employment opportunities. Also, it is a valuable book for the personnel manager, psychologist, and those in the fair employment field because of its generally good overview of the problem. Perhaps its greatest virtue lies in the fact that there is no other book that brings so much material together in an attempt to meet the difficult challenge of providing equitable opportunity.

Personnel Psychol 25(4):719–22 w '72. *Floyd L. Ruch.* The very fact that this timely, broad-brush book is so sound in certain places serves to highlight other areas where the lopsided emphasis approaches downright error. An outstanding example of incomplete reporting which could lead to incorrect thinking on the part of the reader who is not familiar with the total literature in the relevant area is seen on page 63 where the authors state: "Various studies show that test scores of minority employees may be lower than those of whites, but job performance is the same." This statement may well have been based on the conclusions from some of the earlier and more poorly designed studies. It simply does not sum up the evidence. The hard fact is that the vast preponderance of evidence indicates, in black and white comparisons at least, that tests which are fair and valid for whites are equally fair and valid for blacks. Moreover, most studies show clearly that where small but statistically significant differences exist, aptitude tests tend to *overestimate* the performance of blacks. Since this book will probably have a wide circulation due to its timeliness, it is unfortunate that the authors do not put in proper perspective the classic work of Dr. Mary F. Gordon, published as Technical Report 53–34, Personnel Research Laboratory, Human Resources Research Center, Lackland Air Force Base, Texas, in November, 1953. The authors obviously were aware of this study since it is cited in the chapter reference on page 146. The important study was based on 8,888 male Air Force trainees of whom 1,384 were Negroes in seven different technical schools in which clerical and mechanical subjects were taught. A recent study by Guinn, Tupes and Alley entitled "Cultural Subgroup Differences in Relationships Between Air Force Aptitude Composites and Training Criteria" (AFHRL–TR–70–35, Lackland Air Force Base, Texas, Personnel Research Division, Air Force Human Resources Laboratory, 1970) is not cited nor discussed in the chapter on Differential Validity. Other studies published in 1971 are cited. This important work based on 19,734 subjects in 10 technical schools came to the same conclusion with regard to differential validity as a function of race that was arrived at in the study published some 18 years prior. Other competent studies were cited which came to the same conclusion as the Air Force studies but these were apparently given low weight by the authors as compared to the less well-designed studies of Lopez and Kirkpatrick et al. * These errors of omission are especially serious in view of the fact that the guidelines of the Equal Employment Opportunity Commission attempt to make the requirement that the employer conduct differential validity studies. The practical importance of this error, however, is greatly reduced by the fact that to the best of this reviewer's knowledge, no court has ever required an employer to conduct differential validity studies and in fact several Federal District Courts have ruled that the EEOC Guidelines are not legal standards and are, therefore, not binding. Byham and Spitzer have done a real service to employers, personnel people and to industrial psychologists in preparing this book. The service would have been greater had they evaluated the studies quoted in regard to differential validity on the soundness of their experimental design and the adequacy of the statistical analysis of their findings. Had they done so, this reviewer is certain the reader would come to accept the conclusion that the concept of differential validity has received far more attention and acceptance than the data justify. * Another serious deficiency in the book is that it deals almost entirely with tests as selection devices whereas the EEOC Guidelines and the OFCC Testing Order clearly state that other selection procedures such as the personal interview, the bio-data (application blank), work experience and education, arrest and conviction records are all "tests" and as such must be shown to be job-related if they have an adverse impact on minorities. Although some psychologists have endorsed the "total assessment" of the individual rather than reliance on a single test score or a composite score from a battery of tests and although some employers are giving up standardized tests in favor of assessment centers, both Title VII and the EEOC Guidelines as well as the OFCC Testing Order see no difference between the two approaches. When either has an adverse impact on minorities or women, the burden of proof is placed on the employer to show job-relatedness. This reviewer would have been happier had the authors seen fit to give the problems of sex discrimination the careful attention they deserve. Whereas objective tests of cognitive abilities have a well-recognized adverse impact on certain minorities (Blacks, Mexican American and American Indians), women (like Jews and Orientals) tend to excel male Anglos by a small margin and hence have different problems. The greatest deficiency in this book is the inadequate treatment of construct validity. On page 105 we are told: "EEOC and OFCC maintain that whenever technically feasible criterion-related validity *must* be established before a test or other objectively scored device can be used" (emphasis

added). They correctly point out, however, that courts have accepted both criterion-related and rational validity. This reviewer would have been happier to have seen the rational validity methods presented as superior to the criterion related validity methods for the reasons so well stated by Balma in the Autumn 1959 number of *Personnel Psychology*. They should have, I believe, emphasized the fact that rational validity methods are "color blind" and do not rely on subjective ratings by supervisors whose judgment may on occasion lack objectivity and who may be greatly influenced by race prejudice and ancient stereotypes. In this connection it is noted that the authors fail to cite the important work of Mullins and Usdin of the Air Force Human Resources Laboratory (AFHRL–TR–70–36) who showed that under conditions permissive of both rational and statistical validity determinations, the tests selected and weights given them are identical for all practical purposes. That is to say people who know the job can study the tests and people who know the tests can study the job and estimate regression weights which agree very closely with those revealed by the classical forward validation design. On page 174 the authors state: "In 'Project 100,000' for instance, the Defense Department inducted 100,000 men into the armed services who could not meet the usual selection-test standards. These men were given special training to compensate for their deficiencies. After two years the government reports about the same number of successes with these service men as it attains with regular inductees." Actually it was found that "the new standards" men who failed to measure up to the "old standards" passing scores were twice as likely to wash out of basic training as were those who did. The failure rate for entry job skill training was equal or higher. Thus the failure rate of the "new standards" exceeded that of the "old standards" group by a factor of four. The military services contrary to the implication of the above quoted statement have found this a "good business reason" for dropping the practice of accepting the "new standards" (lower passing score) individuals. Deserving of mention is one further point although it is not of a technical nature; on page 19 the authors appear to favor, at least they do not attack, the practice of EEOC trying cases in the news media rather than waiting for due process of law. On this page they state: "....the agency does have the means to cause a company adverse publicity." This reviewer, like most of his fellow Americans, has a profound respect for the judicial process which admittedly is slow but it is also fair. The judicial process embodies findings of fact and findings of law. The adversaries present their divergent views of the facts, the court weighs these facts, finds the governing law and makes a judgment. The release of statements by either adversary to the news media in advance of their presentation in open court is subversive to the concept of due process of law. The strengths of this book are obvious and it is hoped that the reader of this review, having been made aware of certain weaknesses, can think more realistically in this emotionally-loaded atmosphere.

[B93]

★Bzoch, Kenneth R., and League, Richard. **Assessing Language Skills in Infancy: A Handbook for the Multidimensional Analysis of Emergent Language.** Baltimore, Md.: University Park Press, 1971. Pp. 61. Paper, $9.75. *

[B94]

Campbell, David P. **Handbook for the Strong Vocational Interest Blank.** Stanford, Calif.: Stanford University Press, 1971. Pp. xxv, 516. $20.00. * For reviews of the test, see 1023 (3 reviews, 2 excerpts), 7:1036 (3 reviews, 2 excerpts), and 7:1037 (2 reviews).

Ed & Psychol Meas 32(2):503–5 su '72. Betty Corwin. * an important contribution to the literature on the SVIB * The *Handbook* should be a standard reference for anyone using the SVIB in either counseling or research until accumulated research or changes in the test make a revision necessary. The tables of intercorrelations and mean standard scores for occupational groups will be used by many readers, but the explanations are not dependent upon them. It would be unfortunate if some counselors using the test avoid the book because the mass of data makes it appear too statistical for their comprehension. * Campbell uses the organization of the SVIB, presenting rationale, development, reliability, and validity of each part of the profile as a unit. Some readers may wish he had presented all reliability data in one section and all validity information in another. However, the book is well indexed so that locating information on any topic will present no problem. * Those using the SVIB in counseling or research and those interested in general developments will appreciate both the book and the indication of an intent to continue work on the test.

Meas & Eval Guid 5(4):503–6 Ja '73. R. G. Taylor. * the validity and reliability of the SVIB well documented * Although Campbell claims that there is no psychological importance to the distribution of LP, IP, and DP, he presents four tables that indicate percentages of Like and Dislike responses for various occupations. Several noted researchers, including Glosser, Brown, Wegner, Stewart, Berdie, and Eisenberg, have studied the relevance of Like and Dislike percentage responses on the SVIB, arriving at fairly consistent results and conclusions that would indicate psychological relevance. The chapter on the interests of outstanding men is one of the most enjoyable and interesting. * The chapter on interpreting the profile is particularly valuable to the practicing counselor or psychologist who must respond to individual student or client questions regarding the SVIB. * In summary, this is an exceptionally well written handbook which attempts to weave dreary statistics and pages upon pages of tables with the brief, concise narrative style associated with much of Campbell's work. This is not meant to imply that Campbell was completely successful. Some of his comments are confusing. For example, in discussing the Total Response Index he states, "....it is prudent to explore what has happened whenever this number falls outside of the 390–410 range. (Note: some scoring services record the number of legitimate responses. Multiple responses, i.e., two responses to an item, are illegitimate and consequently are not counted, so the total number of responses can never be more than the total number of items.) [p. 249]." Since there are only 399 or 398 items, would a TR of 409 be a legitimate score? Some comments are even misleading—e.g., in discussing Like, Indifferent, and Dislike percentage scores Campbell states, "There will be those Psychologists who attribute psychological importance to the percentages of Likes versus Dislikes, or something such, but currently nothing is known about this." (Note the previous comment in this review regarding this question.) All in all, however, the *Handbook* represents an excellent effort to deal with the very complex problem of reporting in book form information typically seen in brief, annotated manuals.

[B95]

★Cancro, Robert, Editor. **Intelligence: Genetic and Environmental Influences.** New York: Grune & Stratton, Inc., 1971. Pp. xii, 312. $12.50. *

[B96]

★Cattell, Raymond B. **Abilities: Their Structure, Growth, and Action.** Boston, Mass.: Houghton Mifflin Co., 1971. Pp. xxiii, 581. *Out of print.*

[B97]

★Cattell, Raymond B. **Personality and Mood by Questionnaire.** San Francisco, Calif.: Jossey-Bass Inc., Publishers, 1973. Pp. xix, 532. $35.00. *

Brit J Social & Clin Psychol 14(2):213 Je '75. This book is modestly described by the publishers as a handbook of interpretive theory, psychometrics and practical procedures. It is much more than this. It represents the fruits of Professor Cattell's dedicated and creative effort in the development of this method of personality measurement. More than 700 studies, including many from cross-cultural research, are brought together. But the book is much more than that too. It reflects the considerable advances made by Professor Cattell in the development of theory and techniques, and their integration, since his first papers on "Temperament Tests" in the *British Journal of Psychology* in 1933. All libraries will need a copy of this book, and for psychologists concerned with these methods of personality study it will find a special place on the bookshelf.

*Ed & Psychol Meas 36(1):224–7 sp '76. Douglas Wardell. * a classic * promotes the importance of empirically-based structural personality theory as the frame for questionnaire development, interpretation, and evaluation * With missionary zeal and partisan zealotry, Cattell forcefully states arguments and defenses for psychometrics based on personality theory. * there is lots of material here that can be found elsewhere, particularly Cattell's own innumerable articles and other books, but it is gathered together and often updated here * the book presents a candid forum for Cattell to trace the historical development ("progressive rectification") of IPAT's adult and child questionnaires through over 25 years of voluminous research. New ideas and findings are reported * Besides being affronted by the exorbitant cost of this volume, some readers will likely be irritated by the typos (e.g., last lines on page 87, and formulae such as $V_{fe} = R_v^{-1} V_{fp} R_f^{-1}$ on page 341) and inadequate documentations and index. The style of the book compels one to treat many sections as one might treat a reference work, a catalogue, or even a telephone book. Some (particularly those struck by Cattell's venom) will be irritated by his indomitable way of confirming theory with factor analytic data: supporting studies are routinely applauded while non-supporting studies are soundly criticized on methodological grounds. Although these criticisms may well be trenchant, it is unfortunate that theoretical disputes so often dissolve into methodological prescriptions, particularly since those prescriptions have yet to be well vindicated. The development of theory from multivariate findings in personality remains pathetically stunted, despite the efforts of individuals such as Cattell. As many critics have reiterated, to end an investigation into personality with the results of a factor analysis truncates and trivializes personality theory in the same way that Watsonian behaviorism severely restricted the subject matter of psychology in an earlier laudable attempt to improve the relation of theory and data. *Personality and Mood* is most important when it shows that multivariate personality theory does not end with a list of factors and a set of specification equations relating factors to data variables. Professor Cattell continually points out that factors still need detailed theoretical development as source traits in a nomological net of further sensible and sensitive personality theory. Cattell, of course, besides being a primemover in multivariate psychology, is himself a very astute personality theorist. His chapter on the "natural history" of traits is probably the most exciting section of the present book, along with his discussions of "depth psychometry," for example, in the mutual interaction and spiral feedback theories of the development of higher-order factors (such as exvia and anxiety) from the primaries; and the development of surface traits (such as the neuroticism syndrome) from source traits. Factor analysts have been unfavourably compared, if we may borrow Abraham Kaplan's analogy, to ants, collecting data into a heap, and to spiders, spinning webs from their own substance. At its best, Cattell's book is better compared to the labour of a bee, transforming into honey the nectar it carefully gathers.

[B98]

★Chase, Clinton I. **Measurement for Educational Evaluation.** Reading, Mass.: Addison-Wesley Publishing Co., Inc., 1974. Pp. viii, 312. $11.25. *

Ed & Psychol Meas 35(1):204–5 sp '75. Max D. Engelhart. This excellent book should promote student acquisition of skills, knowledge, attitudes and interest in measurements. * The categories and related behaviors of the

Taxonomy of Educational Objectives produced by Benjamin Bloom and others, including this reviewer, are effectively summarized. * The writing and analysis of different types of objective items and essay questions are reasonably well explained * The measurement of general ability or intelligence and of special aptitudes is effectively explained * The appendices contain brief but lucid explanations of the computation of means, standard deviations, and coefficients of correlation. A useful list is given of names and addresses of ten important test publishers.

[B99]

★CHOPPIN, BRUCE, AND ORR, LEA. **Aptitude Testing at Eighteen-Plus.** Windsor. Berks., England: NFER Publishing Co. Ltd., 1976. Pp. vii, 151. Paper, £4.50. (Atlantic Highlands, N.J.: Humanities Press. $8.00.) *

[B100]

★CHUN, KI-TAEK; COBB, SIDNEY; AND FRENCH, JOHN R. P., JR. **Measures for Psychological Assessment: A Guide to 3,000 Original Sources and Their Applications.** Ann Arbor, Mich.: Institute for Social Research, University of Michigan, 1975. Pp. xxv, 664. $15.00. *

Personnel Psychol 28(4):581–5 w '75. Brian Bolton. * Despite the broad title, the range of instruments indexed in *Measures for Psychological Assessment* is fairly limited. In addition to those measures obviously related to mental health, the following are included: (a) measures of individual moods, traits, behaviors, and some attitudes, (b) measures of interpersonal relationships or behavior, and (c) measures of characteristics of organizations, cultures, or social groups. Measures of intelligence, aptitude, and most attitudinal measures were omitted, since they have been covered extensively in other reference volumes. The 3,000 scales and instruments which are indexed in *Measures* were located in a systematic search of 22 psychological and four sociological journals. * The authors state four objectives for *Measures:* (1) To provide a comprehensive bibliography of all measures of mental health and related concepts, (2) To aid the reader in selecting measures most appropriate to the intended use, (3) To provide readers with quick access to summaries of quantitative research in various content areas, and (4) To contribute toward improving the quality of measurement in mental health and related social science fields. I have no doubt that the volume will achieve immediate success in realizing the first and third objectives. But it does not address the real problem in "selecting measures most appropriate to the intended use."

The authors assume that, after reviewing the measures indexed in the primary references, the reader will be able to select the best one for any given purpose. In fact, few of the constructs or variables in psychology have been sufficiently explicated to make a reasonable choice possible. * The authors do allude to the problem of construct validity and suggest that *Measures* may stimulate needed methodological research: "Information on the multiplicity of measures for a given concept will hopefully encourage many research workers to examine the nature of the interrelationships among the measures." While additional research will provide the necessary data to eventually bring some order to the chaotic measurement field, it will not solve the immediate practical problem of test users who need to select the best available instrument for their purpose. It is my opinion that the near-term solution will require the efforts of a task force of measurement psychologists commissioned to evaluate those instruments and scales which meet minimal psychometric standards and recommend the better ones for application in specific situations. Furthermore, I believe that a moratorium on the development of new measures should be endorsed by the professional associations and remain in effect until the task force could prepare a comprehensive report on the state of the field. (A moratorium could virtually be assured if the professional journals adopted a policy of not accepting for publication any manuscript which included a new measurement scale.) While these suggestions may sound extreme, a brief perusal of *Measures* and other compendia should serve to convince the reader of the scope of the problems which currently exist. In fact, the single most important contribution that *Measures for Psychological Assessment* may make is to confront psychologists with the magnitude of the problem. The volume will certainly go a long way toward meeting the fourth objective which the authors have stated for it. E. Lowell Kelly's concluding remarks in the Foreword cannot be improved upon: "I am not so naive as to believe that the publication of this volume will suddenly halt the continued production of inadequate assessment devices, created on an ad hoc basis by relatively unsophisticated researchers and published in one of our journals. Hopefully, however, by making readily available the facts regarding the usually brief life history and the fate of similar devices previously developed by others, this unique volume will contribute to a somewhat more systematic approach to the development of better assessment instruments so essential for real progress in the social sciences." Unfortunately, the Repository is not being updated since neither of the authors' proposals—a long-range plan of incorporating the system into the *Psychological Abstracts* and an interim plan of continuously updating the system—was funded. Unless some constructive steps are taken in the near future psychological research and practice will be overwhelmed by the population explosion of measures.

[B101]

★CIMINERO, ANTHONY R.; CALHOUN, KAREN S.; AND ADAMS, HENRY E.; EDITORS. **Handbook of Behavioral Assessment.** New York: John Wiley & Sons, Inc., 1977. Pp. xiii, 751. $27.00. *

[B102]

★CLARK, JAMES P., AND THOMSON, SCOTT D. **Competency Tests and Graduation Requirements.** Reston, Va.: National Association of Secondary School Principals, 1976. Pp. v, 69. Paper, $3.00. *

[B103]

★CLARK, JOHN L. D. **Foreign Language Testing: Theory and Practice.** Philadelphia, Pa.: Chilton/Center for Curriculum Development, 1972. Pp. ix, 174. * (Distributed by Didier. Paper, $6.50.)

[B104]

*CLARKE, H. HARRISON. **Application of Measurement to Health and Physical Education, Fifth Edition.** Englewood Cliffs, N.J.: Prentice-Hall, Inc., 1976. Pp. xvii, 443. $14.95. * For reviews of earlier editions, see 7:B147 (1 excerpt), 4:B92 (1 excerpt), 3:805 (1 excerpt), and 3:806 (1 excerpt).

[B105]

★COFFMAN, WILLIAM E., EDITOR. **Frontiers of Educational Measurement and Information Systems—1973: Proceedings of an Invitational Conference on the Occasion of the Dedication of the Lindquist Center for Measurement, The University of Iowa, Iowa City, April 6–7, 1973.** Boston, Mass.: Houghton Mifflin Co., 1973. Pp. vi, 177. Paper, $6.00. *

J Ed Meas 12(1):60–2 sp '75. John E. Milholland. * proceedings of an invitational conference on the occasion of the dedication of the Lindquist Center for Measurement at the University of Iowa, April 6 and 7, 1973. The stature of the contributors and the quality of their offerings pay fitting tribute to the man being honored. It is good that he was there to enjoy it. * The paper by Robert L. Thorndike and the commentary by Benjamin Bloom provide valuable highlights of the work to date on the International Study of Educational Achievement. Bloom's list of seven effects of the studies is especially interesting. The paper by Stanley

Ahmann and his colleagues constitutes probably the best available succinct description of the sampling and data analysis methods used in the National Assessment of Educational Progress. Particularly illuminating are the discussion and the rationale for balancing comparisons among subgroups categorized on one dimension for disproportionalities on another (e.g. the effect of rural-urban imbalance on regional comparisons). * In the companion paper John Tukey.... comments further on the balancing process and makes the point, through a beautifully simple algebraic demonstration, that measured variables serve, to greater or less degrees, as "proxies" for those that have not been measured. * In conclusion, it is fair to say that the word "Frontiers" is quite appropriate in the title of this compendium. This of course makes it automatically susceptible to becoming outdated, but I suspect this will not happen too soon. For the present, it provides an excellent overview of where we now find ourselves in several of the fields in which Lindquist has left his indelible mark.

[B106]

★COHEN, RUDOLF. **Patterns of Personality Judgment.** Translated and edited by Dirk L. Schaeffer. New York: Academic Press, Inc., 1973. Pp. ix, 366. $27.00. * (Originally published in German as *Systematische Tendenzen Bei Personlichkeits-Beurteilungen.*)

[B107]

★COLEMAN, JAMES S., AND KARWEIT, NANCY L. **Information Systems and Performance Measures in Schools.** Englewood Cliffs, N.J.: Educational Technology Publications, 1972. Pp. xi, 130. $9.95. *

[B108]

★COLLEGE ENTRANCE EXAMINATION BOARD. **On Further Examination: Report of the Advisory Panel on the Scholastic Aptitude Test Score Decline.** Willard Wirtz, Chairman. New York: the Board, 1977. Pp. vii, 75. Paper, $4.00. * For an appendix, see B37. (The 26 additional appendixes were published too late for inclusion in this section.)

[B109]

*COLLINS, HAROLD W.; JOHANSEN, JOHN H.; AND JOHNSON, JAMES A. **Educational Measurement and Evaluation: A Worktext, Second Edition.** Glenview, Ill.: Scott, Foresman & Co., 1976. Pp. 285. Paper, $6.95. * For a review of the first edition, see 7:B152.

Ed & Psychol Meas 37(1):273–6 sp '77. Daniel Eignor and Ronald K. Hambleton. * In summary, it is our feeling that the book contains no substantial technical errors, and is written in a style that most teachers will understand. On the other hand, missing is a perspective on the field of educational testing and the role of testing within the field of education. We were distressed to discover the absence of some key topics, topics that should be thoroughly understood by classroom teachers. These topics include criterion-referenced testing, factors affecting the reliability and validity of test scores, and the social consequences of testing. Also, while the exercise section was perhaps the most unique section of the book, the anticipated gains will not be obtained because of the superficiality of many of the exercises and because of the failure of the authors to design exercises that make it possible to provide the readers with answers. Finally, we must say that we never felt any excitement in the book for the nature of the content, the direction the field of testing was taking, and so on. From our experience, this feature does exist in some other recent educational testing books and it is important for generating student interest and motivation to study the material. In our own rating of educational testing books intended for classroom teachers, we would position the book somewhere between the first and second quartile.

[B110]

★COMREY, ANDREW L.; BACKER, THOMAS E.; AND GLASER, EDWARD M. **A Sourcebook for Mental Health Measures.** Springfield, Va.: National Technical Information Service, 1973. Pp. vii, 462. Paper, $14.00. *

[B111]

★CONE, JOHN D., AND HAWKINS, ROBERT P., EDITORS. **Behavioral Assessment: New Directions in Clinical Psychology.** New York: Brunner/Mazel, Inc., 1977. Pp. xxiv, 440. $17.50. *

[B112]

★COOPER, CHARLES R. **Measuring Growth in Appreciation of Literature.** Newark, Del.: International Reading Association, 1972. Pp. 30. Paper, $2.00. *

J Read 16(8):648–9 My '73. Claire E. Morris. * written primarily for the researcher * First, it reviews a number of studies which measured appreciation of literature through the utilization of discrimination tests or through content analysis; second, it synthesizes these reviews by considering the questions of validity and feasibility; third, it recommends specific areas which need to be investigated in order to gain knowledge about the construct of appreciation of literature. In a succinct, easy-to-read form, the researcher has made available a summary and an analysis of past endeavors; consequently, the monograph would be an invaluable

aid. For those people conducting research in this area of appreciation, it is a "must."

[B113]

★COOPER, JOHN O. **Measurement and Analysis of Behavioral Techniques.** Columbus, Ohio: Charles E. Merrill Publishing Co., 1974. Pp. xii, 175. Paper, $6.95. *

[B114]

★COURT, J. H., COMPILER. **Researchers' Bibliography for Raven's Progressive Matrices and Mill Hill Vocabulary Scales, Fourth Edition.** Bedford Park, S.A., Australia: The Author, Flinders University, 1977. Pp. iv, 177. Paper, $8.00. *

[B115]

★CRADDICK, RAY A., AND L'ABATE, LUCIANO. **The Kahn Test of Symbol Arrangement: A Second Critical Review.** International Journal of Symbology Monograph No. 1. Atlanta, Ga.: International Society for the Study of Symbols, 1972. Pp. i, 33. Paper, gratis. *

[B116]

★CROMBAG, HANS F., AND DE GRUIJTER, DATO N., EDITORS. **Contemporary Issues in Educational Testing.** Proceedings of the International Symposium on Educational Testing. Elmsford, N.Y.: Mouton Publishers, 1974. Pp. iv, 344. $31.00. *

[B117]

★CRONBACH, L. J., AND DRENTH, P. J. D., EDITORS. **Mental Tests and Cultural Adaptation.** Elmsford, N.Y.: Mouton Publishers, 1972. Pp. xi, 495. Paper. (New York: Humanities Press, Inc.) $28.00. *

Austral J Psychol 27(1):89–90 Ap '75. George E. Kearney. This book contains 50 papers presented by just over one hundred participants at the NATO sponsored conference on the adaptation of mental tests to the cultural environment, which was held in Istanbul, Turkey, in July 1971. The papers discuss in detail both applied and theoretical problems associated with psychological assessments outside the mainstream technologically-based urbanized Western cultures. The volume seeks to answer difficult questions, which are applicable not only to the "developing" cultures but also to our own culture. * Unfortunately the book does not answer these questions and it is perhaps unfair to suggest it should do anything more than focus on the questions. This is especially true when it is realized that this was a paper-giving conference and not a working party. The editors have added a well balanced integration and summary at the end of the book which is of considerable use. * There is....an undue emphasis on factor analytic studies which may not in the long run be useful except for construct exploration. To evaluate the book as a whole is difficult, but it appears that apart from the fine theoretical points made by contributors such as Cronbach, Irvine, Berry and others much of the material will become a data base for future theoretical development and as such deserves a significant place in the annals of contemporary psychology. It also demonstrates forcibly that much of the important work is taking place in the non-Western non-English-speaking world. There are two disappointments: firstly, there is a relative absence of non-Western models and materials; secondly, multi-cultural Australia in multi-racial Asia had only one delegate at the conference. Even so, the book is essential for any serious reader in the area of testing or individual psychology.

Brit J Ed Psychol 44(3):322 N '74. J. B. Deregowski. This is a collection of 50 papers which were presented at a NATO sponsored conference in Istanbul in 1971. The papers are divided into eight sections dealing with the following problems: (1) Testing in its social framework; (2) Cross-cultural research strategy; (3) Testing procedure; (4) Testing devices; (5) Educational intervention and educational influence; (6) Correlates and determinants of test performance; (7) Factor analytic studies; (8) Technical issues and prospects. Thus the entire field of testing and selection is well covered, although certain subjects and geographical areas are better represented than others, and observations obtained from and related to "developing" countries dominate. * Over three-quarters of the papers deal specifically with cross-cultural issues. Of these about a third are concerned with application of tests and testing methods, now hallowed by usage in Western setting, to non-Western populations in general. * Such variety and the lack of cross-references (although Cronbach's and Drenth's "Summary and commentary" and editorial notes go some way to alleviate the latter defect) make this volume into a work of reference suitable for an educational or occupational psychologist involved in testing and selection rather than into a textbook. It provides a richness of ideas, none of which might be immediately applicable to a situation at hand, but many of which, *mutatis mutandis,* may prove very useful. The book can have yet another purpose: it can be used as a collection of readings in cross-cultural studies, dealing both with the above problems and the broader issues of cognition and perception.

Meas & Eval Guid 8(2):116-7 Jl '75. Gary M. Miller. * The readings are very comprehen-

sive and the research is reported in a clear, concise manner. I found these articles to be very enlightening * at times I struggled with the readings, for many had limited implications for testing in the United States, except to investigate the efforts and procedures of researchers in other lands. From a scholarly viewpoint this is an informative work, but I do not believe one would adopt this as a text or for supplemental reading unless it was for a special seminar dealing with research in testing. *

Occup Psychol (England) 47(3-4):254 '73. Denis McMahon. * the title of the book is deliberately ambiguous because the themes of the papers and discussion were diverse. Most papers are based on what are generally called cross-cultural studies and most corners of the earth seem to be represented. Most of the papers are concerned with intellectual functioning and its measurement, but the Editors say that participants in discussion found the old division between "cognitive" and "affective" activities an impediment to interpretation, seeing test performance as social, motivational and temperamental as well as "cognitive."

[B118]

★CRONBACH, LEE J., AND SNOW, RICHARD E. **Aptitudes and Instructional Methods: A Handbook for Research on Interactions.** New York: Irvington Publishers, Inc., 1977. Pp. xviii, 574. $34.50. *

[B119]

★CRONBACH, LEE J.; GLESER, GOLDINE C.; HARINDER, NANDA; AND RAJARATNAM, NAGESWARI. **The Dependability of Behavioral Measurements: Theory of Generalizability for Scores and Profiles.** New York: John Wiley & Sons, Inc., 1972. Pp. xix, 410. $18.25. *

Austral J Psychol 27(3):275-7 D '75. J. Lumsden. This book is an exposition of classical reliability theory, interpreted as generalizability, using analysis of variance estimation techniques. The observed score is treated as a sample from a universe of admissible observations. This universe should be defined by the test constructor or test user by the specification of a number of facets or dimensions and of permitted levels of them. Cronbach *et al.* consider facets such as forms, examiners and occasions. A particular observed score is obtained from one form of the test with a certain examiner and on a certain occasion. This score will typically differ from his *universe score* which is defined as the expected score over all admissible observations. After defining the universe of admissible observations the test constructor should carry out a G (generalizability) study which will permit variance components to be estimated for persons, forms, occasions and the interaction terms. Ideally the G study should be completely crossed but it is recognized that some nesting is inevitable. From the variance components an intra-class correlation is calculated which estimates the *coefficient of generalizability* defined as the ratio of universe score variance to expected observed score variance. It will be obvious that the universe score and the coefficient of generalizability are perfectly analogous to the true score and reliability coefficient of classical reliability theory. The test user should use the information derived from the G study in a D (decision) study which estimates the universe score which is described (p. 15) as the ideal datum on which to base decisions. Cronbach *et al.* open with an unevenly written introductory chapter which sets out the foregoing. They devote several chapters to discussions and illustrations of various designs for G and D studies. One chapter compares analysis of variance with the correlation approach and two are devoted to multivariate generalizability theory. The book ends with a somewhat biased summing up and consideration of criticisms. The book is in the great tradition of previous expositions of the true score model, Model T, by Thurstone, Gulliksen and Lord and Novick. It is a bad book as were the others because the true score model is inappropriate and unfruitful. Unfortunately, it is certain to be highly regarded, particularly by textbook writers and teachers. Because of this I ask the reader to forgive the tedious and elementary critique to follow. In all their designs for G studies Cronbach *et al.* advocate repeated measures without emphasizing the obvious dangers that main effects and interaction with persons are inextricably confounded with sequence effects and their interactions. Anything of value in the generalizability approach can be obtained without repeated measures; for example, by simple fully randomized designs main effects for form or for examiners can be estimated without confounding. The authors properly point out that the common practice of setting up confidence limits around the observed score is not correct. They recommend that universe scores should be estimated from the coefficient of generalizability via linear regression and confidence limits set around them using an equivalent of standard error of measurement. They realize that regres-

sion toward the general population mean is useless and suggest that regression should be toward sub-group means. This approach is subject to the criticism that the regression of true score on observed score is not linear and the standard error of measurement is not constant for all values of true score. If the reliability estimate is high then the departures from linearity cannot be great but in this case the regression estimates of the true or universe score will differ only trivially from the observed score. But even if these problems could be solved the approach remains useless. We do not need the true score. Cronbach *et al.* (p. 14) state very wisely that measuring procedures are to be used as the basis for decisions and that "the accuracy of measurement must in principle be examined separately for each application of the procedure." In the light of this why not simply examine the scatter diagram relating criterion performance to test performance and obtain from this the expected criterion score and the confidence limits *relevant to the decision?* For different subgroups we can if necessary set up different scatter diagrams. If we were foolish enough to calculate the regressed scores as recommended would we not, in principle, still need to consult the scatter diagrams to arrive at a sensible decision? And wouldn't these be exactly the same scatter diagrams with the numbers shifted a bit on one axis? Cronbach *et al.* go further and recommend....that profiles be plotted in universe scores with all the information from all the tests used to give a multiple regression estimate of the universe scores. The recommended practice is bad, indeed dangerous, because it erodes the extremes of the profile. It could lead, for example, to a gross misinterpretation when a poor reader was treated as within the normal range because his scores on an intelligence and an arithmetic test were high. The authors (Chapter 9) also strongly advocate the correction for attenuation without emphasizing that the correction typically produces an overestimate and that the attenuation paradox makes nonsense of the correction. It is clear....that Model T should be retired to a museum and replaced by an attribute based model, Model A. Model T in either its classical form or in generalizability trim cannot perform the task for which it was designed. The reliability coefficient and statistics calculated from it have no useful application. They should not be used to select tests, to estimate true scores, to estimate confidence limits for scores, in the correction for attenuation or for anything else. The problems for which these devices were alleged to be the solution can be handled more sensibly and fruitfully by simple regression methodology, i.e., by best validity practice. I have attempted to set the message of the Cronbach *et al.* book to music that attenuates its poison. Do not read it unless you know the tune.

Brit J Ed Psychol 43(3):310 N '73. J. W. Starr. * The term "universe score" is introduced as an alternative to the traditional "true score" on the grounds that the latter term is misleading; there is no unique "true score" corresponding to a particular "observed score" since one may choose to generalise in one of several different ways. The premise is, of course, true, but even the tyro is unlikely to confuse an "estimated true score" with what the authors call "in-the-eye-of God reality." Two chapters are devoted to the extension of multi facet analysis to multivariate data. The most interesting aspect of this is perhaps the use of all the data in a profile of scores to estimate, through multiple regression, the universe (i.e., true) score on any one of the variables. * The fundamental principles are clearly expounded, but the inter-collation of practical procedures with theoretical discussion tends to make the more esoteric parts of the argument rather obscure. Indeed, the authors concede that "the book is complexly organised and by no means simple to follow." The book does, nevertheless, make an important contribution to the field of measurement theory and is likely to be used as a reference work by researchers and graduate students. Its influence on day-to-day measurement procedures, in what the authors would describe as D situations, is unlikely to be very great for some time to come.

J Am Stat Assn 69(348):1050 D '74. Donald B. Rubin. * a monograph concentrating on mixed models analysis of variance designs, that is, designs in which factors are crossed or nested and fixed or random. Emphasis is given to the estimation of variance components and ratios of variance components, rather than the estimation and testing of effects for fixed factors as would be appropriate for designs based on randomized experiments. The basic concern seems to be with the populations to which the data analyst wishes to generalize results and how these affect statistical models, summaries, and conclusions. These issues are important and, in my experi-

ence, often misunderstood. However, I'm not sure this book will help to clarify the subject area for the typical data analyst. I found it not well outlined in the introductory sections, rather disorganized, and generally quite difficult to read. The authors seem to be aware that their presentation might not be reader-oriented: "...the book is complexly organized and by no means simple to follow (p. 3)." "The reader is certain to gain far more from his third reading of most sections than from his first or second (p. 4)." Perhaps part of the problem is the use of non-standard terminology and mathematical notation. This makes it quite difficult to skip or skim sections without feeling lost in later sections. For example, i and j are labels for "facets" (factors) whose conditions (levels) are indexed $i=A, B, C; j=a, b, c,$ where "distinct" conditions of facet i are labeled i or i', a "particular" condition of facet i is labeled i^* or i^{**}, and I is a set of conditions of facet i, I^* a particular set of conditions of facet i. Notational problems can be sticky, but relying on standard mathematical notation and standard terminology whenever possible would have helped, especially in a book that is disjointedly written. In conclusion, *The Dependability of Behavioral Measurements* covers important topics, but in such a way that it may be useful only to the highly motivated and sophisticated reader who is willing to struggle with the general style. Perhaps this review is unfair considering the authors' statement that "this volume is a theoretical monograph and not a textbook (p. 4)." Nevertheless, much of what is presented can be viewed as standard mixed model analysis of variance material, and even this often appears obscure and complex to me as well as to the authors:

Generalizability theory is both familiar and exotic. Its basic ideas have been well known to behavioral scientists at least since Fisherian analysis of variance came into prominence late in the 1940's. Even though the application of these ideas to measurement theory have with rare exceptions been limited to simplified cases, many of those applications are well known and embody most of the concepts with which this monograph deals. However, in the attempt to build a relatively comprehensive system, with assumptions somewhat more realistic than those of previous developments, we have constructed a maze of argument in which one can easily lose himself, and which is very difficult to see as a whole. Complicated as our argument is, it by no means goes into all the matters that will ultimately have a place in the theory.

A large part of our development is a restatement of classical theory in more general terms, displaying how the argument would look if derived from weaker assumptions. In the end, we are often forced back upon some of the classical simplifications in order to reach one or another conclusion (pp. 386–7).

The presentation of generally familiar material in complicated guise makes it difficult to push through and evaluate theoretical contributions.

[B120]

★CROOKS, LOIS A., EDITOR. An Investigation of Sources of Bias in the Prediction of Job Performance....A Six-Year Study: Proceedings of an Invitational Conference Held in New York City, June 22, 1972. Princeton, N.J.: Educational Testing Service, 1972. Pp. vii, 145. Paper, $3.00. *

Personnel Psychol 26(2):283–5 su '73. *William H. Mobley.* * The proceedings of this conference, along with the soon to be published complete technical report, should be required reading for all parties having an interest in issues related to testing in racially heterogeneous groups. This study may well become a "classic" in the area of testing. * The study is....a *model* for validation research; extensive job analysis; careful selection of tests; well developed multiple criteria including behaviorally anchored rating scales, job knowledge measures, and a work sample; large sample sizes; and appropriate statistical tests of the differential prediction hypothesis. The study also serves to document the feasibility of conducting large scale multi-location validation research as well as the expense, complexity, and time involved in such undertakings. Among the major findings summarized in the present report were: minority groups generally scored about one-half standard deviation below the Caucasian mean on aptitude tests; this difference was also reflected in the objective criterion measures (job knowledge and work samples) but not for the rating scales * a test which was valid for one ethnic group was, with few exceptions, valid for the other ethnic groups. Of particular interest and importance was the analysis of the differential prediction hypothesis. * The results....indicated that significant differences in ethnic subgroup regression parameters were the exception rather than the rule; when significant differences were found, it was most likely to be in the intercept; and that when such differences were found, the Caucasian regression line was generally *above* the minority regression lines. * When multiple regression equations from one ethnic group were applied to another ethnic group, it was found that minorities with low test scores had predicted criteria scores at least as high if not higher than when their own regression equation was used while

the reverse was true with high test scores. * There was a tendency for supervisors to give higher ratings, on the average, to members of one's own ethnic group. In addition, higher validities were found where Black supervisors have rated Black incumbents, while Mexican-American and Caucasian raters tend to produce higher validities when rating members of *other than* their own ethnic group. * Anastasi, Jacobson, and Wallace noted the relevance of careful job analysis for content validation efforts. The ability of this study to consistently demonstrate valid relationships was probably due in no small part to the careful job analysis. This should be a cardinal lesson for those conducting validation research. * To this observer, it is unfortunate that while much recent empirical research attention has been directed toward "proving" or "disproving" the differential validity hypothesis, relatively less attention has been directed to the question raised by these commentators and the question of what can be done to enhance the predicted job success of individuals for whom a reasonable level of job success cannot, at present, be predicted. With regard to the differential validity question, a number of the commentators including Brown, Albright, Jacobson, Guion, and Wallace suggested there is relatively little support for the differential validity hypothesis. In this regard, one would hope that this study, along with other recent studies which have reached the same conclusion, would be sufficient to warrant a decrease in the a priori rejection of the null hypothesis of no difference in subgroup prediction. A more tenable position would seem to be that the null hypothesis of no difference in subgroup prediction should be rejected only after the differential hypothesis has been tested with adequate sample sizes, adequate criteria, adequate score ranges, appropriate statistical analysis, and differential predictions are clearly warranted. Finally, Brown and Albright noted the importance of on-the-job training as a means of overcoming differences in performance. It is important to note that neither is suggesting an elimination of selection tests; rather, a combination of selection and training. To this observer, a portion of the current controversy regarding employment testing is attributable to a confounding of two distinguishable issues: (a) the valid prediction of job performance; and (b) what strategies, programs, or activities can and should be undertaken for those individuals for whom a reasonable level of performance cannot, at present, be predicted. Clearly the resolution of the second issue is not elimination of valid prediction. To focus on one issue to the exclusion of the other is not in the best interest of individuals, organizations, or the country. The suggestion by one of the commentators, R. C. Brown, Jr., that the basic approach be establishment of relatively low cutoff points for entry level jobs followed by on-the-job training would, in many situations, seem to be a reasonable response to both issues. In conclusion, the recommendation made in the second paragraph of this review is reiterated. This volume, together with the soon to be published complete technical report, should be required reading for all parties having an interest in issues related to testing in racially heterogenous groups!

[B121]
*DAHLSTROM, W. GRANT; WELSH, GEORGE SCHLAGER; AND DAHLSTROM, LEONA E. **An MMPI Handbook, Revised Edition: Volume 1, Clinical Interpretation.** Minneapolis, Minn.: University of Minnesota Press, 1972. Pp. xxvi, 507. $25.00. * For Volume 2, see B122 (2 excerpts). For a review of the earlier edition, see 6:B146.

Brit J Psychiatry 122(568):358–9 Mr '73. H. R. Beech. This first of a two-volume work represents a very considerable labour of compilation which aims to provide the clinician with material pertinent to the interpretation of individual MMPI records. No doubt we shall witness the usual bimodal reactions: many clinicians will find the information useful and will not question too closely the soundness of the data or opinions involved; others, on the other hand, will view with pessimism the publication of a work which affords little more than an independent authoritative source in support of fallible clinical judgement. As Hathaway points out in his foreword, work on the MMPI began at a time when there was general acceptance of the modernized Kraepelinian classificatory system. This purely diagnostic purpose is now regarded as of diminished importance, for "....only a small fraction of the published data relating clinical or experimental variables to its (the MMPI) scales or profiles can be understood in terms of the original approach. If the validity views of 1941 were the only support for the inventory, it could not survive." The surprising thing for the many critics of the MMPI is that the scale *has* survived in spite of failing in its original diagnostic purpose. How, they may ask, can what is in effect a

symptom check-list now be expected to perform the more elaborate and difficult task of describing facets of personality? The arguments that our tests often appear weak because we have failed to extract their real value merely gives emphasis to the shortcomings. Similarly, Hathaway's proffered justification that "....working psychologists cannot yet afford the luxury of throwing away a tool for its lack of constructural quality" does nothing to increase our confidence in the MMPI. The fact that one may have nothing better to offer is cold comfort indeed.

Ed & Psychol Meas 32(3):850–2 au '72. George M. Guthrie. * divided into three parts: administration, scoring, and categorizing profiles; interpreting the special scales which are designed to measure the patient's ability and intent to cooperate; and interpreting the profile of scores, particularly scores on the nine original scales. There are in addition, 15 appendices which list norms for various scales, an index of the items by key words, rules for profile discrimination and frequencies of patterns identified by the two highest scales. * In their scale-by-scale discussion the authors devote very little attention to the specific nature of the clinical group used in the development of each scale but a good deal of attention to personality differences which a number of investigators have found associated with high and low scores of normal subjects on various scales. There are many apparent contradictions in the adjectives which raters apply to those who are high on a given scale. One is led to ask whether an investigator interested in personality differences would not be well advised to use a personality test designed and validated for that purpose, such as the personality tests developed by Gough and by Jackson. * The final chapter, an example of profile interpretations by a clinician and by a number of computer programs, gives some sense of what can be said on the basis of an MMPI. It is by no means clear, however, how the statements were derived—certainly not from the material as reported in the preceding chapter. Because the patient in question terminated his contact before his evaluation was complete, we have no way of assessing the accuracy of the interpretations. Even if he had stayed and entered therapy it would still be difficult to evaluate how much additional and valid information was contained in the MMPI interpretations that was not available from his intake interview. A further question, which may be dealt with in Volume II, is the matter of how much information is available from the MMPI which makes any difference in how the patient is treated. It is difficult to review a book about a line of research without evaluating the research as well. The book itself is well written, with only as much specific vocabulary as is necessary. The most serious shortcoming, in the opinion of this reviewer, is the lack of evaluative and summarizing statements. One finding after another is presented without any attempt to give an overall picture. Nor are there evaluations of many of the studies cited. Surely, there were weaknesses in design or sampling; surely some findings have been confirmed by other investigators. In short, it reads too much like a well arranged annotated bibliography and not enough like a handbook. * The empiricist approach of MMPI advocates tends to minimize theories with the result that interpretations become speculative descriptions without implications for treatment. Without some sort of guiding theory one has no basis to choose which aspects of behavior to measure. Tradition alone seems to dictate the continued measurement of hypochondriacal concerns, depressive trends, etc. Possibly Volume II will indicate whether there is any reason to cling to the original nine scales other than the fact that users have developed an impressive body of statements associated with each scale, statements of unknown accuracy and utility.

J Pers Assess 38(1):76–7 F '74. Jerome D. Pauker. * A lot of work on and with the MMPI has been published in the 12 years between editions, and this is well-reflected in the book's contents. Among the approximately 600 literature citations in Volume I, a little more than half are to books and papers which have appeared since 1960. * Unfortunately, some will use this book not only "merely" as a how-to-do-it manual (it is actually a fine example of a manual), but unthinkingly as a how-to-do-it manual, without much heed to the discussions of base rates, population modifiers, possible scoring errors, and other cautions which have been emphasized throughout the book. It is this kind of injudicious and basically unethical use of tests and test results which has led some to throw out the bathtub along with the baby and the bathwater. I firmly believe that anybody who has not read and comprehended this book or its equivalent in the literature has absolutely

no business interpreting the MMPI in clinical practice, or, for that matter, in research. * There are some minor criticisms one might make. The writing is clear, but it gets a little pedantic in spots. There is at times more detail about the MMPI than most might wish to know—for example, some answer sheets no longer in print are described in detail, and the sizes of the scoring spaces are given down to the millimeter—but this also illustrates the encyclopedic nature of the Handbook. It is annoying that the asterisk and dagger markings which indicate items with special characteristics in the 14 tables of scale items are identified only at the bottom of the L scale table. It would have been more convenient to have the appendixes from Volumes I and II combined in one place (perhaps even as a separate, soft-cover addition to the two volumes). In using Table 4-6 on page 115 I found an error: the MMPI item listed in the table as booklet number 42 is really number 48. These little things pale before the significance of the whole work. The authors have done a magnificent service in writing this book, and I look forward to Volume II.

[B122]

*DAHLSTROM, W. GRANT; WELSH, GEORGE SCHLAGER; AND DAHLSTROM, LEONA E. **An MMPI Handbook, Revised Edition: Volume 2, Research Applications.** Minneapolis, Minn.: University of Minnesota Press, 1975. Pp. xiii, 586. $25.00. * For Volume 1, see B121 (3 excerpts). For a review of the earlier edition, see 6:B146.

Am J Psychiatry 133(4):460–1 Ap '76. David F. Berry. * This second volume, like the first, has the virtue of being useful to beginning MMPI students as well as to experts because it can save countless hours of searching the literature in an area one plans to investigate by providing complete bibliographies. It also introduces all of the important ideas about applying the test to a particular area of research. For sophisticated MMPI users this is a reference book. The book is well organized and clearly details the important research uses of the MMPI * The great usefulness of the MMPI lies not in predicting the old nosology (as it was originally constructed to do). The test is useful because of all that has been learned about it over the years. It is useful in the effort to recognize a variety of traits, qualities, and complex patterns of personality and behavior. The 10 clinical scales of the MMPI have become indices of numerous characteristics other than psychiatric diagnoses. Beyond the 10 clinical scales and 3 validity scales, which are described in the first volume, this second volume includes the items and directions for scoring the items for the 455 special scales that have been generated from the original item pool. These scales are indices of a variety of characteristics—from promiscuity to success in baseball and from headache proneness to pharisaic virtue. Both volumes of *An MMPI Handbook* provide access to the full usefulness of the MMPI. They bring all of the important ideas into one publication. The second volume includes a bibliography of over 6,000 significant references to the MMPI through the end of 1973.

J Pers Assess 40(6):646 D '76. Robert N. Sollod. * The Handbook's chief value is as a convenient, thorough, and helpful compendium of MMPI research. Were it not for the increased ease of doing computer searches of the literature, the Handbook would be an invaluable aid to the MMPI. Although the Handbook does have a valid role as a reference book, it is limited in other respects. The approach of the authors is prosaic, and their model of research is uninspiring. Their tone is often unnecessarily defensive. These faults will be harmful for the uncritical reader who may consequently feel that it is unnecessary to add any other instruments or possibly an interview to the MMPI while investigating a research problem. Empirical validity is the major strength of the MMPI, but often questions having to do with understanding psychological *processes* or with exploring areas only touched on superficially by the MMPI indices are much more relevant to good research than *a posteriori* hypothesis-free discriminant analyses. The MMPI as a research instrument would have been better served by a handbook which explored many of the issues involved with its effective and creative use and with its practical limitations. How can it be used as an early step in opening up a significant area of investigation? What studies are examples of both *un*imaginative as well as significant uses of the MMPI? What is the role of the MMPI as part of an overall test battery? * "How can the MMPI be used most appropriately and effectively in research?" The very validity, strength, popularity, and accessibility of the MMPI makes this issue a crucial one for an MMPI research handbook.

[B123]

★DAILEY, CHARLES A. **Assessment of Lives.** San Francisco, Calif.: Jossey-Bass Inc., Publishers, 1971. Pp. xix, 243. $12.95. *

Personnel Psychol 25(4):722–5 w '72. James L. Farr. Dailey's purpose....is to present a humanistic model of assessment as an alternative to the traditional behavioral and psychometric assessment models. Assessment is given a broad meaning in this book, referring to any situation in which a person is evaluated by others who make decisions affecting that person's life. This definition of assessment thus includes such diverse moments in an individual's life as when he applies for college, seeks a parole from prison, applies for a bank loan, applies for a job, or seeks membership in a professional organization. The traditional assessment model is viewed by Dailey as being credentials laden. By credentials Dailey refers to what might be called objective biographical data. Included here would be diplomas and degrees, previous jobs held, test scores on any sort of psychological instrument, prison records, awards, honors, grade point average, age, etc. Dailey assails credentials as being inherently prejudicial due to the fact that certain segments of society have been denied the opportunity to obtain acceptable credentials. Included among the members of society whom Dailey regards as victims of credentials discrimination are blacks, women, old people, and Mexican-Americans. Further compounding the inequities of an assessment system in which the success criteria are not uniformly available to all is the increasingly bureaucratic nature of all institutions. Bureaucracy stresses objectivity, impersonalness, and strict adherence to rules and procedures. Such an organizational design favors credentials as selection criteria because credentials give the appearance of being objective, impersonal, and amenable to rules and procedures. Dailey points out that, whereas credentials do look objective, their inclusion as standards in the assessment process is usually a subjective judgment. In other words, for example, the decision to hire only college graduates as management trainees in an organization is really a subjective one although it results in an objective requirement for job applicants. Basically, what really angers Dailey, and I think that "angers" is a good choice of words here, is that the traditional assessment model evaluates credentials and not the person. The alternative assessment model which Dailey proposes is humanistic. The basis of this approach to evaluation is an assessment philosophy based on the total life history of the assessee. Dailey relies upon the ideas of Henry Murray regarding life histories and their role in the assessment of individuals. A holistic view is espoused in which all significant data possible are integrated in an attempt to predict what an individual is trying to do in some situation. Significant data refer to all episodes in an individual's life which relate to need-fulfilling behaviors. That is, one gathers information about past ways in which the individual has attempted to fulfill various sorts of psychological needs. Dailey proposes to do this by means of an assessment interview in which the interviewer attempts to create or construct the life history of the assessee. The interviewer asks probing questions, generally concerned with reports of instances which the individual regards as especially meaningful to him. The interviewer attempts to sample events from the entirety of the person's life, both in terms of time and acquaintances. The episodes are placed in a temporal sequence. Dailey estimates that 50–100 episodes will usually be necessary in order to construct a complete life history. Finally, the interviewer asks the individual, on the basis of his now-constructed life history as well as his current thoughts, to relate his view of his future. Of special interest here are the person's goals in life, his subjective probabilities with regard to reaching these goals, and the presumed satisfactions he will feel upon attainment of his goals. The resulting life history is the basic data in Dailey's assessment model. The decision maker in a real world assessment situation would review the episodes in the life history and base his predictions of the individual's probability of success upon the information presented about the individual's behavior in past situations. * I now wish to review some of Dailey's statements and assumptions. First of all, Dailey has made many valid points concerning assessment as it is usually conducted. Among these is the point that assessment and evaluation follow a similar paradigm whether the institution involved be a college, industry, or hospital. It is also true that certain members of society have been denied an equal opportunity to participate in many of our culture's benefits. Many of Dailey's remarks concerning the place of credentials in our present assessment procedure are also correct. Credentials are very important and, as organiza-

tions become more bureaucratic, the assessment process becomes more impersonal and there is a greater reliance upon credentials. Some credentials often used as requirements for applying for a job may be of questionable validity. Berg's recent book has documented the often non-existent relationship between education and job performance, for example (Berg, 1970). In general, it is true that we do not currently know enough about the prediction of future success in educational or employment situations. These factual statements certainly provide a reason for assessment reform, but I have some reservations about the alternative model proposed in *Assessment of Lives*. There are some logical inconsistencies in Dailey's argument. On page 54 such credentials as age, sex, educational level, and IQ are stated to be important as modifiers, qualifiers, and verifiers of a life history. Yet in Chapter 1 and also on page 58 credentials are assailed as being invalid. If something is invalid, it does not appear to be a very good verifier of other data. In Chapter 1 Dailey discusses the well-known fact that objective tests and other credentials used for personnel selection are often not empirically validated. He further proclaims that, because of the large number of occupations, industries, and technologies, validation of psychological tests for all employment situations in which they are used is a hopeless task. That task is indeed formidable, but I ask Dailey why the task of validating his assessment model in all employment situations is no less difficult. At times Dailey seems to be saying that the life history is intrinsically valid. While it may be possible that that is true, I will have to be shown more data than are presented in *Assessment of Lives* before I am convinced. Certain omissions are also important. The most sticky problem of criteria is given slight mention. No mention is made of the assessment center (Bray and Grant, 1966) currently receiving much attention at AT and T, IBM, and other places. The use of multiple sources of data about individuals as is a part of the assessment center would seem in many ways to be congruent with Dailey's notions. Of particular relevance to *Assessment of Lives* would be the monograph by Rychlak and Bray (1967) concerned with the development of a life-theme method for the scoring of interviews with young managers. In summary, *Assessment of Lives* makes some good points regarding current assessment procedures, but the alternative presented has probably as many difficulties as the traditional model. I have not discussed the practical difficulties of implementing the life history approach because they seem quite evident. The book is interesting to read and does force one to examine the premises of assessment and evaluation.

[B124]

★DAVIS, JULIAN C., AND FOREYT, JOHN PAUL, EDITORS. **Mental Examiner's Source Book.** Springfield, Ill.: Charles C Thomas, Publisher, 1975. Pp. x, 238. $14.50. *

[B125]

★DAWES, ROBYN M. **Fundamentals of Attitude Measurement.** New York: John Wiley & Sons, Inc., 1972. Pp. xv, 165. Paper, $6.50. *

Austral J Psychol 25(1):107–8 Ap '73. E. R. Peay. * the author attempts to use the principles of measurement theory, a branch of mathematical psychology which has begun recently to make its impact felt, as a basis for analyzing the various types of techniques commonly used for attitude assessment * the book is intended to be (and certainly would be) suitable for "introductory courses in social psychology, attitudes, measurement, or even attitude measurement (p. vii)"; nevertheless, the subject matter, or at least the approach, might well be new to many who have been using (and devising) scales and other assessment techniques for years. Up to now, most measurement theorists have concentrated their substantive interests in such areas as decision-making and psychophysics. The application of measurement theory principles in the much more elusive area of attitudes must (at least for the present) be of less specificity, but possibly of even more value. That even those who are total novices in the field (second year students and even some of their elders) can use this approach as a basis for their understanding of attitude measurement is the special accomplishment of the book. While the size and aims of the book preclude an exhaustive presentation of existing techniques, a selection of the most widely-used ones, such as magnitude estimation, rating scales, unobtrusive measures, Thurstone and Guttman scaling, are demonstrated and analyzed. The book is quite lucid and readable, although its attempt to keep matters on a level which requires little background in the field, combined with its compactness, occasionally results in a bit of looseness (e.g., "....these distributions were of the type known as normal distributions (i.e., bell-shaped)...., p. 8"). Examples are frequent, apt, and con-

temporary, and the study questions at the ends of the sections are, for once, real study questions, having no pat answers and requiring an extension of the reader's thinking on the issues. The author also raises very cogently the ethical issues involved in some "indirect" attitude assessment techniques, although he then drops them in a somewhat unsatisfying way (with the old "we do it informally in everyday life anyway" argument). On the whole, the book is impressive in its clarity and could prove valuable both for introducing the student in a systematic way to the area of attitude measurement and for acquainting the more experienced person with a new approach which is becoming increasingly more important.

[B126]

★DeCATO, CLIFFORD M., AND WICKS, ROBERT J. **Case Studies of the Clinical Interpretation of the Bender Gestalt Test: Illustrations of the Interpretive Process for Graduate Training and Continuing Professional Education.** Springfield, Ill.: Charles C Thomas, Publisher, 1976. Pp. xi, 146. $9.75. *

[B127–8]

★DIAMOND, ESTHER E., EDITOR. **Issues of Sex Bias and Sex Fairness in Career Interest Measurement.** Washington, D.C.: National Institute of Education, 1975. Pp. xxix, 219. Paper, gratis. *

[B129]

★DIEDERICH, PAUL B. **Measuring Growth in English.** Urbana, Ill.: National Council of Teachers of English, 1974. Pp. iv, 103. Paper, $3.75. *

[B130]

★DI LEO, JOSEPH H. **Children's Drawings as Diagnostic Aids.** New York: Brunner/Mazel, Inc., 1973. Pp. ix, 227. $15.00. *

J Pers Assess 39(1):91–2 F '75. Donald P. Ogdon. * DiLeo's volume is profusely illustrated with nonverbal expressions of adjustment problems which range from mild emotional reactive conditions to psychotics and mental retardates with rare metabolic errors. * To some extent the major strength of this book implies its major weakness. It is a very graphic portrayal of children's drawings drawn from a very broad cross section of the author's varied clinical experience. It is short on objective analyses, virtually lacking in measures or statistics of any sort. Guidelines by which to separate normals from abnormals are not to be found, but one could use DiLeo's earlier volume for normal reference points. Primarily, he is simply sharing his vast clinical experience with children and their drawings with his readers. The pages are rich with interpretive hypotheses and hints for research. * One obvious lacuna.... is the absence of any reference to the work of

Buck, Hammer, or any of the House-Tree-Person Test literature. DiLeo develops the concept of a cognitive/affective ratio as an aid to the analysis of children's drawings. Some aspects of some children's drawings of a human figure are primarily the result of intellectual (cognitive) factors. This enables one to utilize the Harris-Goodenough technique to arrive at an index of intellectual ability. When the affective factors are strong, the importance of cognitive factors presumably diminishes. DiLeo sees this as a kind of see-saw effect. When cognitive factors are high, the affect factors must be low, and vice versa. His formulation should lead to some testable hypotheses. This reviewer remains of the opinion that the reciprocal effect of cognitive and affective processes may be an oversimplification which ignores other pertinent parameters. Various aspects of psychosocial and developmental, as well as physiological-maturational factors may be of equal importance. In any event this rather large volume, replete with illustrations, should be most helpful to graduate students in projective techniques classes, particularly to individuals who expect to work with children. The many and varied illustrations will serve to acquaint the student with a wide variety of drawing manifestations associated with diverse emotional and physical problems. It is a short cut to a great deal of experience. The student should be cautioned, however, that no matter how helpful this book may be, it is in fact no genuine substitute for clinical experience.

J Sch Psychol 13(2):163–4 su '75. Ronald J. Friedman. * If the reader of this book pays careful attention to the author's warning that the validity of interpretations of drawings is closely tied to the skill and experience of the examiner and that there can be no cookbook rules for interpreting human figure drawings of either normal or atypical subjects, this book should be of considerable value to those interested in developmental aspects of children's drawings. As a clinical tool, however, this work has serious drawbacks. DiLeo, after discussing drawings and developmental sequences in children, presents what is in essence a casebook based on his own experience. As rich and extensive as DiLeo's clinical experience may be, he offers no systematic normative data and no information with respect to the reliability or validity of the numerous signs that are presented as indicative of various psychological problems. In this regard the absence from the

bibliography of Swenson's (1968) excellent review of empirical evaluation of human figure drawings and Roback's (1968) discussion of drawings as a personality assessment device are striking. Although the book deals with the developmental aspects of children's drawings with sufficient clarity, discussion of drawings with respect to personality diagnosis suffers from a lack of systematically stated purpose. Furthermore, the book is largely atheoretical in this regard. Nor does the author offer even an implicit theory of personality to provide a framework to allow interpretation of unique aspects of children's drawings. This makes it of only very limited utility for school psychologists. This seems to be primarily an encyclopedia of deviant drawings. DiLeo includes discrete chapters or sections of chapters to detail the human figure drawings of hard of hearing children and children with phenylketonuria. Including these topics as separate chapters carries the implications that there are characteristic patterns of cognitive development and personality for these handicapped groups, a notion absolutely without basis in fact. It is well known that children with PKU, if untreated, typically score quite low on intelligence tests. Nonetheless, DiLeo presents several drawings of children with PKU and discusses the significance of the drawings with no reference to measured intelligence. There is no doubt that this systematically collected and well-constructed collection of children's drawings will be of interest to many psychologists and educators. However, as a clinical tool human figure drawings have generally failed to live up to the high expectations many people held out for them, and there is little in this book that will contribute to the school psychologist's diagnostic skills. Nonetheless, human figure drawings remain one of the most popular devices in the school psychologist's clinical repertoire. This continues despite the relative lack of success in substantiating the validity of these tools. It might be expected that this encyclopedia of children's drawings will have a high appeal to clinicians already using human figure drawings for personality assessment who feel comfortable ignoring the absence of any empirical research base upon which to rest their confidence in the test.

[B131]

★DOYLE, KENNETH O., JR. **Student Evaluation of Instruction.** Lexington, Mass.: Lexington Books, D.C. Heath & Co., 1975. Pp. xvii, 144. $15.00. *

[B132]

★DRAGUNS, JURIS G. **Assessment of Personality.** Homewood, Ill.: Learning Systems Co., 1975. Pp. v, 26. Paper, $1.50. *

[B133]

★DRESSEL, PAUL L. **Handbook of Academic Evaluation.** San Francisco, Calif.: Jossey-Bass Inc., Publishers, 1976. Pp. xix, 518. $17.50. *

[B134]

★DRUMMOND, MANSFORD E., JR. **Evaluation and Measurement Techniques for Digital Computer Systems.** Englewood Cliffs, N.J.: Prentice-Hall, Inc., 1973. Pp. xiv, 338. $19.95. *

[B135]

★DUBOIS, PHILIP H. **A History of Psychological Testing.** Boston, Mass.: Allyn & Bacon, Inc., 1970. Pp. xii, 173. * *Out of print.*

Personnel Psychol 24(3):539–43 au '71. Philip Ash. * a thoroughly delightful review of the origins and development of contemporary psychometric theory and technique, appropriate to the interests of all of us—in education, in psychodiagnostics, in business and industry—who use and work with tests. At the minimum, this brief treatise should be strongly encouraged collateral reading for all courses in tests and measurements, and for courses in personnel measurement. Students are too often left ignorant of the trials, the successes, and the failures of the past, and imagine creativity and innovation where there is only repetition. * The text is adorned with excellent line-drawing portraits of forty-four founders of psychometrics (admission only to those who made an important contribution to the field prior to the end of World War II) * Professor DuBois....has written a positive-thinking narrative, emphasizing successes and achievements, visiting upon neither our predecessors nor our contemporaries any significant criticism. (For example, as our industrial colleagues will recognize immediately, Professor DuBois is far too generous when he writes in connection with business and industry's response to the OFCC order on testing, that "While many industrial organizations *had already been conducting validity studies more or less routinely* (emphasis added by reviewer), this official step put psychological testing procedures in the framework of a governmental regulation." Would that this had in fact been true!) Finally, although Professor DuBois suggests that we may expect innovations in the future, he does not attempt to peer into a crystal ball to say what they may be. This is *his* book and, as I have indicated above, only pleasure and profit will come from reading it. A first attempt

to treat the history of psychometrics comprehensively, it succeeds admirably in doing so. Let what follows, therefore, be only a few marginal jottings for some future author whose account Professor Dubois himself invites. First, what I, for one, will look for in a somewhat more extended treatment is an account of the seminal work of the Occupational Research Program of the United States Employment Service (Stead and Masincup, 1941; Stead and Shartle, 1940) in the whole field of skill and aptitudinal measurement including, for example, the development (although not origination) of the technique of Oral Trade Questions tests and in the creation of multi-aptitude selection batteries culminating in the General Aptitude Test Battery (which is mentioned in passing in the text), the recently-published Non-reading Aptitude Test Battery (U.S. Department of Labor, 1969), and the procedures for establishing Occupational Aptitude Patterns. I missed any reference to Edwin Ghiselli whose studies have influenced a generation of industrial psychologists, for example, his provocative work on the use of moderator variables to improve prediction within Subgroups (Ghiselli, 1956, Ghiselli, 1960) and his painstaking summary (Ghiselli, 1966) of the results of almost four decades of industrial testing. Also, although Professor DuBois touches on predictive, concurrent, content and construct validity, there is no mention of synthetic validity, which is, in my judgment, one of the most exciting developments of the last twenty years. An industrial psychologist would also necessarily include a treatment of the Life Insurance Agency Management Association, with particular reference to the Aptitude Index as a model bio-data measurement device (Peterson and Wallace, 1966). Second, I would like to see shared with students and readers of a history of testing, one of the most painful facts facing us in industrial testing: in 1971 there is little in the field that did not already exist, if only in embryo form, by the end of the World War I, and over this span of half a century, while our statistical techniques have improved and our capacity for data-handling via computer has increased enormously, our validities have remained essentially constant—and low (e.g., Ghiselli's summary yields an overall average validity coefficient against performance criteria of .19, and an average validity coefficient of .29 against training criteria). As those of us who do validity studies know, the ablty to generalize from one study to another, from one company to another, still eludes us. There is as yet no coherent theory to explain why a predictor works in one place with one sample, and not in another. Third, and finally, I, for one, see around the corner radical changes in test methodology, emerging largely as a result of the efforts of my good friend and former colleague, Ernest J. Primoff and his associates at the United States Civil Service Commission. The first of these is the J-coefficient (Primoff, 1955), a lineal descendent of the Viteles Job Psychograph and a systematic, worked-out, application of the synthetic validity approach, which affords us a way to get around the problem of selecting tests on the basis of fallible, unreliable, and partial job performance criteria, particularly where only small samples of subjects can be obtained. The second, which takes selection methodology one step further, is the job-element method of examination—a method that, for the first time, puts sit-down written tests into the context of the overall structure of a job, and permits integration of test results *and* a variety of other inputs into a whole-job framework. Publication of these techniques in the professional journals has been limited, but their use is spreading by word-of-mouth. They are now integral to Federal civil service selection procedures. It may come about that, just as the ancient Chinese civil service examination was the model for British civil service examining in the nineteenth century and the progenitor of contemporary testing methodology, the work of the United States Civil Service Commission will be the well-spring from which tomorrow's selection and placement techniques emerge. The third is a job-person matching technique which reduces to quantifiable form the systematic comparison of job task requirements with applicant characteristics directly, without the mediation of a "test" as we now know it. The currently-available prototype of this approach to selection (Cleff and Hecht, 1971) in my judgment, leaves something to be desired, but that is largely an item-writing problem. We possess both the required computer hardware and software to apply the technique (essentially a correlation between job-attribute scores and people-attribute scores), and I believe that many psychologists have the item-writing skill needed to produce a reliable and valid instrument. In 1964, Morris Viteles (Viteles, 1964) expressed concern that the then developing legal involvements

of testing, and the adversary process such involvements entail, might threaten a significant reduction in experimentation and psychometric innovation, and a conservative defensive posture in the face of attacks on testing. I was then strongly inclined to agree with him (Ash, 1966). In the seven years that have passed since the decision in Myart vs. Motorola, we have indeed witnessed distressing defensiveness, sometimes unseemly (in my judgment) adversary proceedings in the course of which equally-accredited professional psychologists rendered before courts entirely contradictory evidence concerning the principles, procedures, and results of selection testing, and professional pronoucements that were bad mixtures of polemics and psychology. Viewed only from this vantage-point, the future of testing—in business and industry, in education, and in government—has appeared dim indeed. In fact, more than one commentator has called for a moratorium on testing altogether. The technological developments alluded to above, however—the *J*-coefficient, job-element examining, job-person matching techniques—have all buoyed my spirits and given me a certain degree of optimism about our future. I think that any history of testing that follows Professor DuBois' will be able legitimately to continue his positive-thinking approach, and to document important developments only dimly discerned now that will revitalize and expand psychometric methodology. We all owe Professor DuBois a deep debt of gratitude for having so ably brought our past into focus and for providing a foundation upon which to build the future. Who knows? Philip DuBois may himself rise to the challenge, and in four or five years give us the sequel which I, for one, hope it will be possible to write.

[B136–7]

★DUCKWORTH, JANE C., AND DUCKWORTH, EDWIN. **MMPI Interpretation Manual for Counselors and Clinicians.** Muncie, Ind.: Accelerated Development Inc., 1975. Pp. vi, 215. $6.95. *

[B138]

★DYSON, A. P. **Oral Examining in French.** London: Modern Language Association, 1972. Pp. 50. 40p.

[B139]

*EBEL, ROBERT L. **Essentials of Educational Measurement.** Englewood Cliffs, N.J.: Prentice Hall, Inc., 1972. Pp. xv, 622. $14.50. * (Previous edition entitled *Measuring Educational Achievement.* For reviews, see 7:B182 [2 excerpts].)

*Ed & Psychol Meas 32(3):853-5 au '72. Max D. Engelhart. * Chapter 7 and 8 deal respectively with true-false and multiple-choice items. Ebel discusses at some length the criticisms of the former—triviality, ambiguity, guessing, and harmful effect on learning. He then proceeds to their defense and to explanation of how to write effective true-false items. He almost convinces that this reviewer's own prejudice against such items is not very rational. But while directing the construction and use of comprehensive examinations in the various branches of the Chicago City Junior College, we tallied the item-test correlations of hundreds of items classified according to numbers of alternatives. These coefficients averaged much lower for the true-false items than for items with three, four, or five alternatives. * Chapter 8 on the writing of multiple-choice items is unequaled by other discussions of multiple-choice items. Especially noteworthy are the sample items on pages 193–195 and the later numerous contrasts between desirable and undesirable items. From each example the reader learns just what characteristic renders the items effective or ineffective. * Ebel mentions the usefulness of evaluation of items by a colleague and explains how item analysis can promote the improvement of items. This reviewer wishes that the values of cooperative efforts in defining instructional objectives in writing test material, in scoring tests, and in assigning marks had been given greater and more explicit emphasis. Chapter 9 deals admirably with such important testing problems as test anxiety, cheating, rapid hand or machine scoring, and correction for guessing. Chapter 10 is an excellent discussion of oral examinations. Such discussions are too seldom found in measurement texts. * Chapter 12 is a thorough discussion of marks and marking systems. * This reviewer is generally enthusiastic about this book, but a number of critical comments can be offered. The chapter summaries are very commendable, but there should also be questions for class discussion and possibly chapter bibliographies. In the history of educational measurement some mention should be made of the very influential *Progressive Eight Year Study* and the *Cooperative Study of General Education*. Something should have been said about the contributions to educational measurement made by Walter S. Monroe and his initiating the *Encyclopedias of Educational Research*. This reviewer's attitudes toward true-false items and neglect of items requiring interpretation of quoted materials have already been mentioned.

In using this text as the basis for a course in educational measurement, the instructor will need to define his objectives, since no definition of instructional objectives is given. In spite of these comments, *Essentials of Educational Measurement* deserves to be judged one of the two or three best books on educational measurement and, in spite of its advocacy of true-false items, the best book on classroom testing.

J Ed Meas 10(2):157–8 su '73. *Gerald Halpin.* The educator looking for a measurement text which places predominant emphasis on classroom achievement measures of a norm-referenced type will find *Essentials of Educational Measurement* an excellent choice. * Throughout the book the use of analogies is very effective in simplifying and emphasizing certain points. * Rather than adhere to the frequently used pessimistic approach to measurement in which the student is so warned of the associated problems and controversial issues to the point that he is skeptical of all measurement devices, Ebel goes to great length to capitalize on the positive attributes of measurement and brings many measurement problems into a realistic perspective. * Part I covers the history and philosophy of measurement relevant to education. Here Ebel communicates much thought and wisdom about the process of education and the role of measurement in this process. * this revised edition [is] particularly useful to those concerned with the development, selection, and use of educational tests. Other aspects which help to make this a useful and interesting book include the introductory quote at the beginning of each chapter which serves to stimulate thought. In addition, all chapters except chapter 1 are concluded with a summary consisting of a list of measurement propositions or principles presented in more detail in the chapter. Projects and problems included at the end of the book provide very good opportunities for students to apply the specific knowledge and skills presented in the preceding chapters * the coverage of some topics could be improved. For example, the impact of criterion-referenced measurement in recent years is....of sufficient magnitude to warrant a more positive and in-depth coverage. * The statistical concepts are presented on a level which most mathematically unsophisticated readers can grasp without much difficulty. In some instances, however, more conventional guidelines for statistical computations might be given. Extensive coverage is given to the construction of essay and multiple-choice tests, and a most optimistic treatment is given to true-false tests. However, only limited assistance is given the student who would like to develop skills in preparing completion and matching examinations. Overall, the book represents an excellent presentation of the *essentials* of educational measurement. It is, as it was designed to be, a comprehensive textbook for a solid introductory course in the use of tests in schools and colleges, and its aim—the presentation of sound ideas and procedures—is achieved.

[B140]

★EBEL, ROBERT L. **The Uses of Standardized Testing.** Bloomington, Ind.: Phi Delta Kappa Educational Foundation, 1977. Pp. 49. Paper, $0.75. *

[B141]

★EDWARDS, ALLEN J. **Individual Mental Testing, Part 2, Measurement.** New York: Intext Educational Publishers, 1972. Pp. xi, 204. Paper. * *Out of print.*

[B142]

★EDWARDS, ALLEN J. **Individual Mental Testing: Part 3, Research and Interpretation.** New York: Intext Educational Publishers, 1975. Pp. ix, 214. Paper, $5.75. *

[B143]

★ELLEY, WARWICK B., AND LIVINGSTONE, IAN D. **External Examinations and Internal Assessments.** Wellington, N.Z.: New Zealand Council for Educational Research, 1972. Pp. 192. NZ $5.00. *

Alberta J Ed Res (Canada) 20(1):100–2 Mr '74. Thomas O. Maguire. * In the book, Elley and Livingstone outline several alternate ways of providing some uniform standards for certification and university selection, while at the same time allowing for some flexibility within the classroom. * The major solution that is suggested can be described as moderated internal assessment. Briefly, the system is this: teachers rank the students in order of achievement on the year's work, then the scores on a standard reference test are used to determine the relative standings of schools. * A good reference test is one that correlates fairly well (.5 or greater) with examination results in each school subject (and university entrance). It should also be an exam that does not control the curriculum in the way that current external examinations do. Among the candidates for reference tests that are suggested and critically examined are the School Certificate Examination (English plus the scores in the best three others), standardized achievement tests, scholastic aptitude tests, and specially constructed tests. * In general, the book is written for the professional rather than the academic, and so the psychometrician will be disappointed in the lack of an elegant rationale, and in the lack of any evidence that the proposed system is "fairer" on the average than other alternatives like complete accreditation. No mention is made of other more traditional ways of dealing with the selection part of the problem * A second, and more significant criticism lies in the restrictive assumption that.... teachers can rank the students. This level of measurement is all that the moderating system requires, and it is all of the teacher's information that is used. Surely teachers can go beyond this. While it is difficult to provide an assessment of a student's *exact level of achievement,* most teachers can tell you if the achievement of one pair of students is more alike than the achievement of another pair. The effect of using the method described by Elley and Livingstone is to assume that all the students in a class are strung out evenly along the achievement continuum. * It is not uncommon in average classrooms to have a small number of students who have high (or low) achievement, with almost *no* detectable differences among them. The moderation system may force a distinction where none exists. Perhaps later models will capitalize on the teachers' ability to go beyond ordinal estimates. The purpose of the monograph is to provide a summary of the arguments concerning the role of external examinations in New Zealand secondary schools, and to suggest various ways that might be used to phase out external examinations while at the same time satisfying the demands that are presently being served by the current system. As the authors state, "It is hoped that this discussion paper will inform the debate, point to the implications of alternative policies and indicate at which points we need decisions, and where we need further inquiry." It is difficult to see how the authors could have been more successful in meeting their goals.

[B144]

★EMERICK, LON L., AND HATTEN, JOHN T. **Diagnosis and Evaluation in Speech Pathology.** Englewood Cliffs, N.J.: Prentice-Hall, Inc., 1974. Pp. xiii, 333. $14.95. *

[B145]

★ERICKSON, RICHARD C., AND WENTLING, TIM L. **Measuring Student Growth: Technique and Procedures for Occupational Education.** Boston, Mass.: Allyn & Bacon, Inc., 1976. Pp. xii, 443. $14.95. *

[B146]

★EXNER, JOHN E., JR. **The Rorschach: A Comprehensive System.** New York: John Wiley & Sons, Inc., 1974. Pp. xxi, 488. $32.50. *

J Pers Assess 40(1):103–4 F '76. Robert M. Allen. Once this book is put aside after having read it, thoughts come flooding in from all sides—what was it all about? Exner, the author of *The Rorschach Systems,* has unsuccessfully attempted to leave history in order to become part of it as Exner, the System Maker. This ambivalence between encyclopedist and systematizer permeates the entire volume *as if* the author could not free himself sufficiently from being the former to contribute spontaneously on his own. The book is haunted by the ghost and living presence of Klopfer, Beck, Piotrowski, Rapaport-Schafer, Hertz, and ABPP diplomates. This in itself is surely not a fault, up to a point. But diplomates responses to a questionnaire on their usage of the inkblot test is not research *qua* research but only a search. And frequency of usage is not a substitute for the validity of a test. So much for fault-finding. Now for what is good and why Exner's latest should be studied by Rorschach Test students and users. Exner is thorough. Very little about administration, scoring, and interpretation is lacking. He has gone into such detail as to justify the use of the terms "systematic" and "comprehensive." The chapter on Frequently Used Tables is an extra that could have been omitted without much loss to the book and the reader. Hertz (1970), Beck (1944), and Small (1956), among others, present a variety of location, determinant, form value, and content tables in much greater detail. Part III, Interpretation, and Part IV, Clinical Applications, reflect Exner at his best. These present his own ideas at work without constant and at times confusing (albeit informative) references to the theoretical and interpretive similarities and contradictions of the five major systematizers so often quoted and paraphrased in the first two Parts of this book. The language is not easy, but then, the subject-matter—human behavior and the Rorschach Test—is not a simple phenomenon. Exner has undertaken a difficult task and has delivered an excellent how-to historically-anchored manual on the Rorschach Psychodiagnostic Inkblot Test.

[B147]

★EYSENCK, H. J. **The IQ Argument: Race, Intelligence and Education.** LaSalle, Ill.: Open Court Publishing Co., 1971. Pp. xii, 156. $8.95. * (Also published in England with the title *Race, Intelligence and Education.*)

Ed & Psychol Meas 32(2):510–21 su '72.

Lita Furby. * Eysenck stated goals and attitudes are commendable. His intentions are the very best as revealed in his closing chapter on the social responsibility of science. But he fails disastrously in his analysis and interpretation of the data. There are serious methodological and logical fallacies in his evaluation of the evidence. This weakness is both unexpected and very disappointing since the reader is easily convinced by the introduction that it is only with much personal pain and in the face of irrefutable evidence that Eysenck will accept racial differences in intelligence. He sincerely thinks he is being objective and only facing the facts; actually he is over-interpreting the data and drawing unjustified conclusions. This book is remarkably full of statements supporting important scientific principles of analysis which are then contradicted by Eysenck in his own interpretation of the data. There is not much new here that hasn't been discussed by Jensen. But Eysenck analyzes the evidence less rigorously and both his stated and implied conclusions are more categorical on the race issue than Jensen's. While I agree with Eysenck that researching possible genetic differences in intelligence does not necessarily mean one is a racist, I cannot agree with his implication that disagreeing with Eysenck's evaluation of the evidence is a sign of "readers with closed minds (p. ii)." [See original review for additional critical comments not excerpted.]

Personnel Psychol 25(4):726–8 w '72. Robert L. Thorndike. * an extremely frustrating book to read! It is largely undocumented, though acknowledging major indebtedness to Jensen's presentation in "Environment, Heredity and Intelligence" and Shuey's volume, "The Testing of Negro Intelligence." As a consequence, it is replete with glib assertions * The argument proceeds, in general, in three stages: (1) Various lines of evidence indicate a substantial role for genetic factors in accounting for *individual* differences in IQ *within* the white population of the USA and England. (2) A large accumulation of evidence on many samples of blacks in the USA shows lower performance on existing intelligence tests, typically amounting to approximately one standard deviation of the general USA white population. (3) In the light of (1) and (2), it seems likely that some fraction of the black-white difference is attributable to genetic factors. Most psychologists would agree with (1), though they might differ in the proportion of variation that they would allocate to genetic factors. On (2), the evidence is clear and not a matter of debate. It is on (3) that the real battle starts. Eysenck admits clearly that we do not have knowledge—as we do in a few types of specialized mental deficiency—of the specifics of the genes involved or the manner in which they interact with pre-natal and post-natal environment to produce the living, performing individual. Thus, lines of evidence are all indirect, and add or detract from the probability of genetic factors being implicated. That the gene pool for whites and blacks is not identical is of course shown in outward appearance, incidence of blood types, and frequency of susceptibility to certain ailments such as sickle cell anemia. It is, therefore, plausible that the differences in this gene pool interact with the conditions of development to produce differences in behavior. The question is whether the differences in the gene pool are relatively trivial factors, so far as observed differences in behavior are concerned, or whether they account in large part for such differences as are observed. Eysenck appears to start out to defend the position that *some* consideration needs to be given to genetic factors in interpreting intelligence test score differences and to end up by concluding that the bulk of the mean score difference is attributable to genetic differences. * In arriving at this conclusion, he presents a variety of supporting evidence, largely from comparing performances of orientals, Mexicans, Indians and blacks in the USA. He also reports studies in which matching for gross indices of socio-economic status fails to reduce greatly the black-white difference in IQ. However, he never *really* faces up to the question of whether it is possible to equate black and white environments in the USA. The most severe criticisms of the aspect of Jensen's earlier paper dealing with black-white differences were addressed to this problem. Any attempt, especially by a white person, to comprehend fully what we might speak of as the "black experience" is probably doomed to failure. And even a black person may have difficulty in formulating it clearly and reducing it to experimentally measurable variables. So the problem of even defining the psychologically crucial aspects of environment, to say nothing of equating them, may be an insuperable one. If this *is* the case, the research to date is largely uninterpretable, and only highly sophisticated, expensive, and logisti-cally difficult studies will have the possibility of getting close to definitive results. At a time when a sincere and serious scientist gets shouted down in a professional meeting because the position that he has reached from his intensive review of the research in a field is unpopular with certain groups in our society, it is vital that someone speak out forcefully for the right and duty of the scientist to seek out the truth, and to report it as he sees it, even if that truth be socially unpopular or politically embarrassing. This Eysenck has done quite eloquently in *The IQ Argument*. The other thing that he has undertaken to do is to review the evidence on individual differences in intelligence test performance within the group of British and American Caucasians, and the evidence on differences in intelligence test performance between blacks and whites in the United States, in order to estimate how large a role genetic differences play in the two cases. In this, for the reasons that we have outlined, his effort falls short of being fully satisfying.

Phi Delta Kappan 53(5):331–3 Ja '72. Robert W. Friedrichs. * little more than a summary of the Shuey-Shockley-Jensen posture minus their documentation. This is not to say that it fails to make a contribution of its own; it is simply that the nature of the insight provided takes quite a different form from the one intended by the author. What the sophisticated reader should gain is a heightened appreciation of the relatively subtle assumptions that have governed the quasi-professional norms of the community of behavioral scientists over the past generation and the manner in which the contradictions that lay hidden within those assumptions are today erupting to divide each of the disciplines involved into hostile camps. Only then will he be in a position to comprehend how such a distinguished behavioral scientist as H. J. Eysenck....can, in the name of "objectivity" and "a dispassionate examination of the facts," produce an essay so cluttered with emotion, snide asides, and straw men, on an issue which he himself describes as empirically unresolved. * Eysenck is perceptive enough to be well aware of the inconsistency and ruthless enough to openly ridicule those who, when forced to bite the bullet, would elect the humane over the natural scientific component. He may not be quite as explicit as B. F. Skinner in moving "beyond freedom and dignity" in his natural scientific single-mindedness, for he does add a slim chapter on "The Social Responsibility of Science" after drawing a tentative "guilty until proven otherwise" verdict of genetic inferiority in I.Q. on the part of the average American black from the empirical evidence on hand. But even that chapter is misnamed, for it is not as much a plea for increased responsibility on the part of scientists as it is for an increase in a particular kind of responsibility on the part of nonscientists. No, you guessed wrong: He makes *no* plea for massive funds to radically reshape the 20% contribution which even he suggests the environment is potentially capable of contributing to a black's I.Q. *The plea is for the scientist, not for the black.* Scientists such as Jensen need greatly increased budgets for research. Why? Well, it *is* a bit embarrassing. For the fact of the matter is—and he makes this crystal clear in the book—that *the research to date doesn't really clinch the case for the inferiority of the American Negro gene pool as it affects I.Q.* In effect, then, top priority should be assigned the task of increasing the *credibility* of Jensen and Eysenck's indictment of the black American. Further research would then be warranted to spell out more clearly the quantitative profile or quality of that differential. Until these steps have been taken, we are admonished over and over, money spent in attempts to redress that balance cannot help but be largely wasted. If Eysenck's strategy is largely dictated by an unbridled identification of the student of man with the norms and interests of natural science, the book itself is an abortive product of a naive humanitarianism that failed to recognize the points at which the natural scientific mind-set contradicted it. For Eysenck was self-consciously sought out and commissioned by the liberal-to-left group identified with the British weekly, *New Society,* with the full expectation that he would demolish, on the basis of his rigid dedication to "objectivity," the edifice built by Arthur Jensen in his widely noted piece in the winter, 1969, issue of the *Harvard Educational Review.* Although all of *New Society's* editorial staff, with the exception of the chief editor, quickly went on public record as objecting to the resultant volume's polemical tone and less than scholarly substance, there is little reason to believe that they are yet aware of the roots of the debacle. The moral to the tale is simple: Natural science cannot be the lone support to the study, even the science, of man in society. The considerable mischief that Eysenck's book

will cause is directly attributable to both *New Society's* and Eysenck's lack of appreciation of this fact. * even after emphasizing that the evidence to date on the genetic basis of much of the I.Q. differential between American blacks and whites is inconclusive, goes ahead—as the natural scientist has every reason to do—to structure the evidence in favor of the hypothesis he would risk his reputation and invest his time in certifying. And, again with natural scientists in general, he seeks to persuade the sources of funds in the larger society that his hypothesis is likely to prove fruitful because he must induce its agents to invest some of their scarce and hotly contested resources in supporting research in its terms. What he does not do is weigh the impact of his strategy and campaign on other human beings, especially American blacks. The *social* scientist could in good conscience take no such easy liberty. He is—or should be—aware that he as scientist is one with the subject of his study, and that the immediate impact of his strategy in support of the funding of such research would, through the well-known process of the self-fulfilling prophecy, serve to reinforce the very environmental conditions which even Eysenck acknowledges as having a considerable role in creating the observed differences in I.Q. Again, because he studies people as inviolable as himself—in contrast to the inanimate matter or nonhuman forms of life that frame the traditional levels of credence acceptable to the natural scientist—he is more cognizant of the *human* risk involved when he accepts a given level of sampling or statistical error or generalizes from studies in which potentially crucial variables stand uncontrolled. In *no* study uncovered by Eysenck (and thus Shuey and Jensen as well) has the image of the American black's I.Q. potential (his own image and that of those about him) been "controlled," i.e., equated with those internalized by and enveloping whites. * the single enrichment program that sought to provide black infants from severely underprivileged homes with what approximated the supportive self-image available in the typical white middle-class home for a period of four years resulted, Eysenck notes, in I.Q.'s *excelling* normal white groups. What is his conclusion? "Such environmental manipulation....cannot of course be the answer. The cost is staggering...." (p. 130). Indeed, the cost would be staggering, approximately what it costs a white middle-class husband to maintain such a family environment for his children each year. The dedicated natural scientist's fundamental faith is, rather, in the value of research per se. Thus it really should be no surprise that even when an Eysenck openly acknowledges that the correct side to the "I.Q. argument" can never be certified short of the development of physiological or electro-encephalographic ("brain wave") criteria in some uncertain future, he calls for the massive funding of additional psychological research on the issue, while writing off action programs based upon an exceptionally successful environmental enrichment program as simply too expensive. This is not a book to assign as independent reading for high school children, white or black. Eysenck, with all his natural scientific shortsightedness (one of his recent books argued impressively against the now substantiated case which identifies cigarette smoking with lung cancer), has an awesome talent for the thrusts and parries, straw men and modest concessions, of debate. It is unlikely to confound the professional, however. Indeed, if educators respond to Eysenck in the manner in which a representative mail sampling of members of the American Psychological Association responded to the same essential posture as developed by Arthur Jensen, they will reject it overwhelmingly.

[B148]

★Eysenck, H. J. **The Measurement of Intelligence.** Lancaster, England: MTP Press Ltd., 1973. Pp. xii, 488. £13.95. (Baltimore, Md.: Williams & Wilkins Co. $22.00. *) (A facsimile reprinting of 28 journal articles.)

Am J Mental Def 79(5):612 Mr '75. Ronald J. Friedman. * The articles, particularly the early ones, are rich in historical (if not always theoretical) value in that they mark milestones in the development of the concept of intelligence as a scientific variable. * Each is introduced by the editor with a thoughtful discussion that helps focus on significant aspects of the articles in the ensuing section, and which (perhaps more importantly) serves to integrate the subject matter of the articles in a way consistent with the major theme of the book. * the articles.... taken as a whole, show that the concept of intelligence, conceived as "innate, general cognitive ability," rests on a firm theoretical foundation and is quantitative in nature. Furthermore, they indicate there is a scientific basis for the quantitative measurement and that the model permits deduction and testing. Little attention is given to the social, ethical, and

political issues associated with the measurement of intelligence. * This is an outstanding collection of contributions to the development of theory and measurement of intelligence. Because of this essential concern with issues of theory, measurement, and research methodology, it may not be appropriate as a basic textbook for most introductory courses in the applied use of intelligence tests. However, it would be a rich resource for anyone teaching a course dealing with theoretical issues in intellectual measurement; and, certainly, the material contained within this book is fundamental for anyone doing research in the area of psychological assessment or who is responsible for the application of the technology of intelligence testing.

Austral J Psychol 27(1):106 Ap '75. A collection of 29 reprinted articles, many of them quite old, on the concept and measurement of intelligence. As usual, Eysenck does not deal kindly with his critics, omitting them from the selection of papers, but weighing in against them in the brief introductory statements preceding each section. Incredibly, the race-intelligence controversy is not represented by any papers and is dealt with only superficially in several scattered pages. Eysenck also appears to have dispensed with a proof-reader: I found Galcurter (for Galanter) and conversation (for conservation) without looking very hard. At the price of $24.20, it is hard to see this book selling many copies.

Brit J Psychiatry 125:511 N '74. M. Berger. * A noteworthy section is devoted to the approach to intelligence measurement evolved by Eysenck and his colleagues. This includes the only previously unpublished paper in the volume. It is by Owen White of the Institute of Psychiatry, and describes a mathematical model for the analysis of problem solving which he is currently developing. This book is mainly for specialists, and its publication may serve to counter, if not silence, the recent upsurge of criticism of intelligence tests.

Meas & Eval Guid 8(2):120–1 Jl '75. Norman A. Scott. * The author's lucid style and frequent allusions to historical and methodological developments in the physical sciences paralleling those in the evolution of intellectual measurement make the entire work a delight to read for those enthralled by the history and philosophy of science. However, these introductions combined with the quantitative nature of the selections probably would not be comprehensible by the statistically naive nor appropriate for the beginning graduate student who has not had prior exposure to theories of measurement and intelligence. Eysenck's selection of material and arrangement of topics is superb and would handsomely augment the syllabus of most graduate courses in intellectual assessment. * This is an excellent collection, including not merely classic articles about intelligence but relatively recent (1972) presentations on the early intellectual development of twins and original theorizing and studies by Eysenck and his colleagues on their attempts to analyze intelligence test scores into components of speed, accuracy, and persistence. This valuable resource work is a scholarly and unified approach to the definition, measurement, and understanding of intelligence.

[B149]

★EYSENCK, H. J. **The Measurement of Personality.** Lancaster, England: MTP Press Ltd., 1976. Pp. xviii, 511. £13.95. (Baltimore, Md.: University Park Press. $29.50. *) (A facsimile reprinting of 67 journal articles.)

[B150]

EYSENCK, HANS J., AND EYSENCK, SYBIL B. G.; WITH THE HELP OF A. HENDRICKSON, S. RACHMAN, P. O. WHITE, AND M. I. SOUEIF. **Personality Structure and Measurement.** San Diego, Calif.: Robert R. Knapp, Publisher, 1969. Pp. xiii, 365. $8.95. * For reviews in addition to the one below, see 7:B200 (3 excerpts).

J Pers Assess 38(1):78–9 F '74. Russell Eisenman. * this book reviews in depth Eysenck's work on Intraversion-Extraversion and Neuroticism-Stability as two independent factors which account for much of personality. In fact, the evidence seems almost too good, with study after study being allegedly about other factors but actually, according to Eysenck and Eysenck, really being reducible to the two factors. The reason such a conception seems "too good" is that most people committed to understanding others via personality or clinical insights will find it hard to believe that just two factors are sufficient to get at the richness of the human personality. On the other hand, the Eysencks have made a good case, showing how factor analysis does lead one to these two factors, even when other researchers have found many factors. After this book, the burden would seem to be on those who wish to argue for more factors to refute the evidence the Eysencks have offered, or to come up with additional evidence. The Eysencks' claim for only two factors accounting for so much sounds intuitively unlikely, but science is supposed to proceed by data not just common sense alone. The Eysencks have also done a good job of discussing measurement in a broader context. Thus, measurement as a principle is discussed, with examples given from other sciences. This intelligent discussion of what measurement is all about would help make this an excellent text, were it not for the rather narrow focus of the rest of the book, which is mainly on the two factors. Students will still need their general text on measurement, but this book would make a good supplement, especially for considering (a) what is measurement? and (b) what is known about the two factors? *

[B151]

★EYSENCK, HANS, AND WILSON, GLENN. **Know Your Own Personality.** New York: Barnes & Noble Books, 1976. Pp. 206. $10.00.

J Pers Assess 41(1):101–3 F '77. * The professional usefulness of *Know Your Own Personality* for psychologists and students of personality assessment is limited. The book provides examples of a wide variety of personality questionnaires, which could be used for class projects and demonstrations. However, these people should approach the literature in the field critically. Technical questions concerning the reliability and validity of the questionnaires are not addressed in the book. When psychologists and students use the book, they will have to look elsewhere for references to the vast research literature that supports the inventories. Finally, the ethical question concerning whether a book containing self-administered personality questionnaires should be sold to the public must be raised. The authors' rationale for writing the book was that it would reduce the mystique surrounding personality measures. One of their defenses against the question of possible misuse of the questionnaires was that, to their knowledge, *Know Your Own I.Q.*, a similar book, had led to positive rather than negative results. Another was that most people like their personalities and are unlikely to be harmed by knowing their scores on personality questionnaires. Among professional psychologists, agreement with this position, as with much of Eysenck's work, is unlikely to be either unanimous or vigorous.

[B152]

★FAGAN, WILLIAM T.; COOPER, CHARLES R.; AND JENSEN, JULIE M. **Measures for Research and**

Evaluation in the English Language Arts. Urbana, Ill.: National Council of Teachers of English, 1975. Pp. xix, 235. Paper, $6.95. *

[B153]

★FALK, BARBARA, AND DOW, KWONG LEE. **The Assessment of University Teaching.** London: Society for Research Into Higher Education Ltd., 1971. Pp. iv, 47. Paper. *

[B154]

★FARR, ROGER. **Measurement of Reading Achievement: An Annotated Bibliography.** Newark, Del.: International Reading Association, 1971. Pp. 96. Paper, $1.50. *

Read Teach 25(6):553 Mr '72. Frank Greene. Eric/Crier's 1950 to 1969 entries related to reading achievement measurement are neatly organized in this compact book. * the book is clearly of immediate value to all who are concerned with reading achievement. *

[B155]

★FERGUSON, ROBERT J., JR., AND MILLER, ALLAN L. **The Polygraph in Court.** Springfield, Ill.: Charles C Thomas, Publisher, 1973. Pp. xxv, 346. $14.95. *

[B156]

★FINE, BENJAMIN. **The Stranglehold of the I.Q.** Garden City, N.Y.: Doubleday & Co., Inc., 1975. Pp. viii, 278. * *Out of print.*

Sci Teach 43(8):55 N '76. Paul Blackwood. As the title suggests, this book argues that the I.Q. testing movement has had and continues to have a largely negative impact on our educational system. The author looks at the movement's rationales and practices, case studies, and current research—ultimately concluding that a moratorium on I.Q. testing is long overdue. The book details how the I.Q. score is used to advance children, hold them back, deny them appropriate instruction, or otherwise handicap them. Further, that scores tend to shift according to test uses, tester, the changing experience and education of the child, and the child's motivation at test time. Can any score, then, be considered valid? Though we are not certain what I.Q. tests measure, we are sure they do not measure factors such as leadership, character, ambition, common sense, creativity, curiosity, integrity, native intelligence, or ability to adjust. The book includes a comprehensive bibliography on I.Q. and achievement testing. For teachers, counselors, and school administrators.

[B157]

FISKE, DONALD W. **Measuring the Concepts of Personality.** Chicago, Ill.: Aldine Publishing Co., 1971. Pp. xviii, 322. $9.95. *

Am J Mental Def 76(6):740–1 My '72. Jon D. Swartz. This book should be of interest to all who are concerned with personality measurement. * The author writes in a very readable style. Terms are defined both in the text and in the glossary, and the vocabulary used is appropriate for a wide range of readers. In addition, Fiske presents his material in such a clear and concise manner that the reader does not need extensive knowledge of statistics to understand it. In the reviewer's opinion the most interesting and provocative chapter is "A Human Being Takes a Test" (Chapter Ten) with its sections on what testing is like from the subject's point of view: the layman's view of testing, the psychology of the subject taking a test (kinds of stimuli, motives of subjects, examiner's relationship to the subject), the dimensions of test-taking behavior (response sets and other subject variables, such as test-wiseness and demographic characteristics), the ambiguity in questionnaire items, the process of responding to an item, the rights of the subject, and the need for a positive approach. While all the points made here certainly are not original with the author, he has fashioned them together in such a comprehensive manner that this chapter should be required reading for all persons involved in psychological testing. Another strength of the volume is its emphasis upon recent developments in personality measurement, such as Byrne's Repression-Sensitization Scale, the Holtzman Inkblot Technique, and the work of Gardner, Jourard, Witkin, Zuckerman, and their associates. * This text impresses the reviewer as being truly current, and the many recent publications in the reference list confirm this feeling. The major fault of the book—which is also the major fault of most volumes on personality written in the United States—is that it seems unduly culture-bound. This restriction has been recognized explicitly by Fiske, however, and he writes that the question of whether or not personality constructs and their interrelationships taken different forms in other cultures is a question for the future to answer since the amount of relevant research on this question still is quite small. * Using the stated intention of the author in writing this book, it must be concluded that his goal has been realized: "to further the progress of personology, the science of personality [p. xi]." This work can be recommended either as a text for advanced courses in personality theory and in the construction of tests or as a reference source for anyone conducting research in the broad area of personality assessment.

Brit J Psychol 63(3):484 Ag '72. L. B. Brown. Fiske presents a strictly conceptual, non-mathematical and even non-technical approach to the questions of personality measurement. * The emphasis throughout is on the ideas and the constructs of personality: it is described as "a textbook in the old tradition" (p. x). The argument rests heavily on an analysis of six modes of personality measurement or response. These are self-description, current experiencing, capabilities, prior behaviour, behavioural observation and psychophysiology. This is a useful scheme that facilitates a reiteration of the multi-trait, multi-method arguments. * There is a lot of good material in this text but one wonders where it will be used outside the American university system. There is continuous repetition of the main points and it ranges between the rather elementary and the highly sophisticated. Perhaps the comment on p. 197 that the discussion of change "is intended not to prepare the reader to conduct studies of change but rather to bring out some of the complexities" suggests its usefulness as a general introduction to an understanding of the concepts now being applied in personality measurement. But in doing this, one wonders why he kept returning to the Rorschach and to the related projective tests for his examples, and "personology" *is* an ugly word, even if it means "the science of personality." The book might also be useful for those "who are concerned with evaluating the measurement of personality in current research studies" (p. x) and for those generally interested in the logic of personality constructs.

Ed & Psychol Meas 32(2):523-6 su '72. Loretta A. Shepard. Fiske set out to present a view of measurement which is larger than a compendium of psychometric techniques. The result is a definitive work. Fiske, an expert and major contributor in the area of personality assessment, articulates the Gestalt as well as the details of his view of the field by dint of highly organized thought and a gift for uncluttered language. * a remarkably readable book considering the sophistication of the thinking. Fiske uses nontechnical language and avoids vocabulary with which only assessment methodologists are familiar. * can be highly recommended to research psychologists and graduate students in psychology, especially those among the latter

who have avoided taking assessment courses because of their highly mathematical or statistical content. The book is not, however, an ideal text for a basic course in personality measurement. One would lose the conceptual unity of the book if it were segmented for weekly discusions. The book would be put to its best use if graduate students in psychology read it during the first week of a semester course and subsequently applied its principles to specifying their own construct, devising test instruments, and carrying out some validation procedures. The book is also recommended reading for a researcher in education, business, and other applied behavioral sciences who is about to embark on a study requiring an assessment of personality variables. The most outstanding parts of the book are Chapter Six, "Specification of Constructs," and the treatment of construct validation. * One minor complaint must be recorded. The author used the Rorschach Inkblot Test and the Thematic Apperception Test as examples more frequently than any other instruments. It is acknowledged that the entire book is concerned with basic research and not with individual diagnosis and that, therefore, even relatively low positive correlations with a criterion may be of interest. However, these limitations on the use of the two tests are not specified; the sophisticated reader knows of the lack of empirical evidence that judges can agree in scoring the Rorschach and the TAT and that the obtained profiles do not correlate well with other measures of personality * The novice, who has so much to learn from this text, may be misled. The uninitiated reader is likely to generalize from Fiske's favoritism to uses outside of the research setting. Surprisingly Fiske used these examples even though they do not meet his criteria for good instrumentation; although the task specified for the subject is ambiguous and standardized for all subjects, neither the TAT nor the Rorschach can be considered homogeneous measures of a specified construct. Fiske's book will be read for two reasons: it is a comprehensive, well-integrated view of personality assessment, and it requires little prior experience in measurement theory to comprehend it. Although novice students will appreciate Fiske's ability to avoid sophisticated language, they are not the book's only audience. The author's work is so well done that his colleagues can learn from him.

[See the original review for additional critical comments not excerpted.]

[B158]

★FLANDERS, NED A. **Analyzing Teaching Behavior.** Reading, Mass.: Addison-Wesley Publishing Co., Inc., 1970. Pp. vii, 448. $16.50. *

[B159]

★FLAPAN, DOROTHY, AND NEUBAUER, PETER B. **The Assessment of Early Child Development.** New York: Jason Aronson, Inc., 1975. Pp. vii, 151. $10.00. *

[B160]

★FRANKENBURG, WILLIAM K., AND CAMP, BONNIE W., EDITORS. **Pediatric Screening Tests.** Springfield, Ill.: Charles C Thomas, Publisher, 1975. Pp. xii, 549. $24.75. *

J Learn Dis 9(10):680 D '76. Ruth Stekert. * an excellent reference text for those involved in the screening of children, i.e., physicians, nurses, educators, health administrators, etc. Part I lists 35 diseases for which widespread screening is recommended, discusses the principles in selecting diseases for screening, and explains the ten criteria in screening test selection. In the remainder of the text, Parts II through IV inclusive, the authors discuss specific conditions for which each screening test is administered, followed by a detailed description of the test. Test specifics include name, age range, availability, reliability, cost, time required in administration, and personnel required to administer the test. Over 100 tests are discussed in one of three categories: screening for physical problems, sensory processes, and psychotherapy. Discussions are relevant to the material presented in Part I. Following each test is a discussion and review by each of two experts in his/her field. Tables and graphs are clear, concise, and scientifically accurate. References are numerous, span 38 years, and are frequently of recent publications. The authors cite gaps in current screening program selection and development and stress the need for research in those areas. The pertinence of research need and its applicability to governmental mandates for screening programs are briefly discussed. This is a timely text. It was "designed to bring together, under one cover, as many as possible of what is known about screening procedures and the pediatric population." The authors meet their goal.

[B161]

★FRANKS, B. DON, AND DEUTSCH, HELGA. **Evaluating Performance in Physical Education.** New York: Academic Press, Inc., 1973. Pp. xviii, 226. $9.50. *

[B162]

★FREDERIKSEN, NORMAN; JENSEN, OLLIE; AND BEATON, ALBERT E. **Prediction of Organizational Behavior.** With a Contribution by Bruce Bloxom. New York: Pergamon Press Inc., 1972. Pp. x, 333. Paper, $9.00; cloth, $16.50. *

Occup Psychol (England) 47(3–4):253–4 '73. Brian Clarke. This....research traces its origins from a conference....which considered how to predict the behaviour of certain individuals whose acts could "affect the welfare and security of Americans." * experienced executives....each served as Chief of a "division of field services" during a two day research session. All had the same peers and subordinates and all dealt with identical problems. These problems took the form of letters and telephone calls which arrived in the "chief's" in-basket. The conditions under which the subjects worked were varied; for example, a "rules" climate would be different from an "innovation" climate. Conversations which are presented are considered against various climates and differ only slightly in presentation. A very impressive array of tables and examples accompanies the text and the enthusiasm with which the authors present their case is commendable. However.... one finds problems. In the chapter discussing the findings and their implications, we learn: "When correlations for the contrasting treatment groups are examined, a number of differences in correlation are found that are individually significant and interesting. But since the multivariate tests of slopes showed few significant differences, we must be careful in our interpretation." Then follows: "Any inclination to put into immediate practice personnel procedures that appear to be desirable on the basis of findings reported here will presumably be inhibited if one recalls that the study is based on performance in a simulated job." This really sums up the work. The theoretical approach is marred mainly by the fact that the subjects acted their role. Given a situation where their decisions would or might have had widespread effects or altered their position politically in the organisation, one cannot help but be suspicious about their honest dealing with problems. Whilst the authors are willing to discuss this caveat quie casually, the applied psychologist might take a rather different view. For students and others who plan a piece of research, this book is a useful guide. It demonstrates how easy it is to get carried away by research techniques and almost lose sight of what the research is trying to establish. It therefore becomes interesting, if somewhat complicated, reading, but should not be considered as an important contribution to research techniques.

[B163]

★FRIEDENHAIN, PAULA. **Write and Reveal: Interpretation of Handwriting.** London: Peter Owen Ltd., 1973. Pp. 183. $8.25.

J Pers Assess 38(5):493–4 O '74. Charles H. Steinmeyer. * This reviewer's orientation to handwriting analysis *per se* is skeptical but receptive to a good idea. * The Introduction presents the basic beliefs found throughout the book, for example, "Whatever Characteristics we have, they are likely to be shown in our writing [p. 7]," or "Slips of the pen sometimes occur and are as revealing as slips of the tongue [p. 7]." Chapter One attempts to summarize some of the basic principles of handwriting analysis [which] appear to be restatements of three other works, namely Saudek (1928), Saudek (1925), and Pulver (1931). The scope of scholarship throughout the book is limited to these three references, and there is no bibliography. Chapters Two through Ten are apparently attempts to demonstrate to the reader the utility of handwriting analysis in several domains, ranging from John Ruskin's personality to vocational guidance to mental disturbances. Rather intriguing psychodynamic vignettes are associated with several handwriting samples, and the implications for decision making in many situations are discussed. The impact of this discussion on this reviewer was limited by a number of concerns. The handwriting attributes which are supposedly rich in personality revelations are poorly defined and difficult to conceptualize without several specific examples and contrasting examples, especially with attributes such as "immaturity," "pasty," "aesthetic," or "unnaturalness." There is no discussion of, or even any concern shown for the problem of inter-rater reliability for determination of such attributes. The personality traits, dispositions, and dynamics that are revealed in the handwriting samples are generally common in both lay and psychodynamic literature, although an occasional quaint characteristic such as "degenerated refinement" or vaguely defined ones such as "intuition" do appear. No concern is shown for the reliability of the personality traits identified. In most examples of analysis beyond Chapter One, there is only infrequent articulation of the assumed relationships between the handwriting attributes and the personality characteristics revealed. It is in the Conclusion that the author at last states at least one of her goals, that is to "stimulate some of her colleagues to set out on extensive research." What, then, is the heuristic value of the book? The "Appendix of Complexes" which appears at the end of the book seems to be a summary of some of the personality-handwriting relationships used in the text. Ninety-six personality traits are arranged in alphabetical order, and under each are listed one to eleven handwriting attributes presumably associated with them. Perhaps these suggested relationships have heuristic value if they do stimulate research. However, the poorly defined terminology leaves much clarification yet to be done before any specific relationship can be studied empirically. At best, this book is an essay about ideas relating handwriting and personality which were already published more than 40 years ago. In no way is it a scholarly work, a clinical manual, or a research effort. While the contents might be interesting to a layman curious about how a person *might* reveal himself by his handwriting, it seems to offer relatively little to a clinical psychologist concerned with problems of assessment and with psychometrically hopeful variables.

[B164]

★FULTON, ROBERT T., AND LLOYD, LYLE L., EDITORS; HOYT, ROBERT, TECHNICAL EDITOR. **Auditory Assessment of the Difficult-to-Test.** Baltimore, Md.: Williams & Wilkins Co., 1975. Pp. xv, 297. $18.75. *

[B165]

★FULTS, ANNA CAROL; LUTZ, ROWENA; AND EDDLEMAN, JACQUIE; COMPILERS. **Readings in Evaluation: A Collection for Educators.** Danville, Ill.: Interstate Printers & Publishers, Inc., 1972. Pp. xvii, 399. Paper, $5.95. *

[B166]

★GARTNER, ALAN; GREER, COLIN; AND REISSMAN, FRANK; EDITORS. **The New Assault on Equality: IQ and Social Stratification.** New York: Harper & Row, Publishers, Inc., 1974. Pp. 225.

[B167]

★GAY, EVAN G.; WEISS, DAVID J.; HENDEL, DARWIN D.; DAWIS, RENÉ V.; AND LOFQUIST, LLOYD H. **Manual for the Minnesota Importance Questionnaire.** University of Minnesota, Minnesota Studies in Vocational Rehabilitation 28. Minneapolis, Minn.: Vocational Psychology Research, University of Minnesota, June 1971. Pp. x, 83. Paper, gratis. *

[B168]

★GEARHEART, BILL R., AND WILLENBERG, ERNEST P. **Application of Pupil Assessment Information: For the Special Education Teacher.** Denver, Colo.: Love Publishing Co., 1970. Pp. 93. Paper, $4.50. *

[B169]

*GEARHEART, BILL R., AND WILLENBERG, ERNEST P. **Application of Pupil Assessment Information: For the Special Education Teacher, Second Edition.** Denver, Colo.: Love Publishing Co., 1974. Pp. 148. Paper, $4.50. *

[B170]

★GENOVA, WILLIAM J.; MADOFF, MARJORIE K.; CHIN, ROBERT; AND THOMAS, GEORGE B. **Mutual Benefit Evaluation of Faculty and Administrators in Higher Education.** Cambridge, Mass.: Ballinger Publishing Co., 1976. Pp. xv, 222. $17.50. *

[B171]

★GLUECK, SHELDON, AND GLUECK, ELEANOR, EDITORS. **Identification of Predelinquents: Validation Studies and Some Suggested Uses of Glueck Table.** New York: Intercontinental Medical Book Corporation, 1972. Pp. viii, 150. $7.95. *

Am J Psychiatry 131(10):1165–6 O '74. Charles E. Smith. * a tribute to the lifelong efforts of Sheldon and Eleanor Glueck to explain the nature of delinquency. It has singular commemorative significance as the last joint publication of this most unusual husband and wife research team * The central objective.... was the development of prediction scales that would enable the identification of youngsters who are likely to become delinquent and would help in development of effective programs of prevention. Their efforts, which were made in the best traditions of science and humanitarianism, stress the importance of family life. * In the development of their predictive scale they gave heavy weight to factors relating to psychological and social development, with perhaps somewhat less refined measures of biological factors. * Whatever these papers may lack in methodological sophistication, they make up for in their authors' loyalty to the Gluecks, whose inspiration and influence provided the impetus for their work. In perusing these pages I am reminded once again of the fundamental desirability of employing research findings in social planning, particularly in the development of delinquency programs that are aimed at prevention rather than repression.

J Sch Psychol 13(2):164–5 su '75. Sandra R. Leichtman. * Some of the contributors have been remiss in considering methodology in their own reports. A paper by Elmering, for example, cited 25 retrospective studies purportedly validating the Table for the identification of predelinquents. Only one of these reported a matched group and several of the studies were not validated against a delinquent population. Two of the six other papers on validation studies used the same original sample but reported

different numbers of subjects. One of these studies excluded subjects with insufficient follow-up data, whereas the other classified the children lost to follow-up as nondelinquents. Despite these methodological weaknesses, the contributions to Part I suggest the Glueck Social Prediction Table can be a useful measure in identifying predelinquents, particularly in a socially and economically disadvantaged population. The importance of family cohesion and adequate parental supervision and discipline is again demonstrated and indicates that programs for the treatment and prevention of delinquency need to involve the family. * *Identification of Predelinquents* could have been more carefully edited by the Gluecks to avoid the weaknesses in a few contributed papers of poor methodology and inclusion of extraneous information. Reports of the same study by different authors should have been condensed into one paper. Despite these problems *Identification of Predelinquents* is a valuable contribution to research in delinquency in that it demonstrates the value of the Glueck Social Predictions Table in identifying predelinquents and offers suggestions for preventure intervention. Unfortunately, the factors which the Glueck Social Prediction Table uses to identify predelinquents are ones that may be particularly difficult to change. Multiproblem families, which are characterized by the Glueck factors of little family cohesiveness and inadequate parental discipline and supervision, are particularly difficult to involve in a cooperative prevention program. Thus, while Hodges and Tait (1963) found the Table to be successful in predicting future delinquents in a disadvantaged population, social casework treatment efforts were not successful in preventing delinquency. Future research might be directed toward finding means of motivating multiproblem families to attempt change in family structure and relationships.

[B172]

★GOLDBERG, DAVID P. **The Detection of Psychiatric Illness by Questionnaire: A Technique for the Identification and Assessment of Non-Psychotic Psychiatric Illness.** New York: Oxford University Press, 1972, Pp. 156. $11.25.

Austral & N Zeal J Psychiatry (Australia) 8(1):77–8 Mr '74. Russell Meares. * shows satisfactory reliability. The questionnaire is likely to have useful applications in the preventative aspects of developing community mental health programs. * Goldberg emphasizes that his questionnaire differs from Eysenck's well known neuroticism (N) scale, in that the latter supposedly scores an enduring "trait," while the new questionnaire measures "symptoms" and current emotional state. Goldberg's claim is based on face validity, and he does not pursue it in his investigation. It does, however, raise the interesting question of identification of "illness." Eysenck's scale and Goldberg's schedule each isolate approximately 15% of the population as abnormal (assuming that those beyond one standard deviation of the mean N are abnormal). If the groups are different as Goldberg believes, then it must be assumed that some people are "neurotic," in one sense, but not "cases," and vice versa. Thus, the possibility arises that "illness" is decided on other than symptomatic grounds. Goldberg's data provides some intriguing evidence in favour of this supposition. He compared 100 very ill and hospitalized psychiatric in-patients with 100 psychiatric out-patients, and 100 normals. The normals came from 162 people selected by National Opinion Polls as a random sample of the population. Thirty five of these were rejected on the grounds that they might be suffering from minor psychiatric disorder. Nevertheless, 16% of the remainder replied with "no more than usual" or "rather more than usual" to the question "Have you recently felt that life is entirely hopeless?" In addition, 14% admitted, by implication, to thoughts of doing away with themselves. Since these people were not patients, it might be presumed that "cases" are distinguished in terms of social function rather than symptomatically. Indeed Goldberg found this to be at least partly true, and a majority of the 12 items which best distinguished between normals and the ill, referred to coping. Having set out with the determination to distinguish "patients" on grounds which had face validity, he was forced to conclude that, "Although there may be strong theoretical reasons for measuring severity of illness in terms of the traditional phenomena of illness, many of the items that best define illness are inextricably connected with the patient's perceiving himself to be unable to cope with his problems and to deal with social difficulties." This side issue apart, Goldberg's work provides us with a useful epidemiological instrument of high sensitivity and specificity, for the detection of non-psychotic illness. His work is further evidence of the excellence of British research in social psychiatry.

Brit J Psychiatry 122(569):483 Ap '73. J. A. Baldwin. * From a very thorough examination of the theory and practice of questionnaires and other methods of estimation, the General Health Questionnaire (GHQ) has been derived and extensively tested, with results which appear to make it superior to other commonly used questionnaire types of rating. The recommended version consists of 60 symptom questions, each of which is answered on a four-point scale, and scored by an extremely simple technique. The resulting rating reflects current psychiatric status in relation to usual status, rather than to temporarily non-specific illness or personality traits. The GHQ does not purport to detect psychotic or severe organic psychiatric disorder and is intended only to detect potential minor disorder. * This work is remarkable for its thoroughness, originality (particularly the scoring technique), and practicality. As the author concludes, the GHQ will be useful to general practitioners and physicians in screening patients for minor psychiatric illness, and to epidemiologists and social psychiatrists for research. Comparisons of prevalence in populations, correlation of morbidity with social and other clinical variables, changes in morbidity levels in populations over time, and estimation of point prevalence (preferably with clinical assessment of potential cases detected) are the main classes of research use. The GHQ alone cannot provide a means of estimating incidence or of estimating period or life-time prevalence. Other possibilities are for assessment of the course of minor disorder and the outcome of care in general practice and, in conjunction with devices to detect psychotic illness and personality disorders, to provide a baseline against which to measure subsequent change in individuals. The book is clear, concise and readable. It will surely be a milestone in this baffling field.

Psychol Med (England) 3(2):257 My '73. D. D. Reid. * this volume reflects a commendable concern with the social or community aspects of psychiatry which is nevertheless tempered by a scientifically rigorous approach to the inherent problems * even psychiatrists find difficulty in agreeing on the definition and classification of the same case; and the disparity is even greater when clinicians have been trained in different countries. Moreover, extensive field surveys where large populations have to be screened cannot depend on the employment of a large staff of psychiatrists. Some way of sorting out for clinical study those most likely to be suffering from psychiatric disease is therefore required. This monograph describes the development of a self-completed questionnaire designed to do that (but not to provide any "diagnosis" in the usually accepted sense). There is an excellent review of earlier attempts to meet this need. * Instead of a Likert-type weighting along a scale from 0 to 3, the author proposes a scoring system which assigns zero weights to the first two classes and unit weights to the top two. This has the advantage that the score is less affected by tendencies to use either the extremes or the middle two scores to indicate the general severity of the symptom in question. On the other hand, this forced dichotomy allows no precise indication of the response and, to that extent at least, useful information might be lost. * [The book] will be useful to others working in this area for its critical review of past work, its honest appreciation of the pitfalls and limitations of the author's approach, and the systematic progress through to a most useful contribution to the methodology of psychiatric epidemiology.

[B173]

★GOLDBERG, LEWIS R. **Parameters of Personality Inventory Construction and Utilization: A Comparison of Prediction Strategies and Tactics.** MBR Monograph No. 72-2. Fort Worth, Tex.: Multivariate Behavioral Research, 1972. Pp. 59. Paper, $5.50. *

[B174]

★GOLDFRIED, MARVIN R.; STRICKER, GEORGE; AND WEINER, IRVING B. **Rorschach Handbook of Clinical Research Applications.** Englewood Cliffs, N.J.: Prentice-Hall, Inc., 1971. Pp. xii, 436. * *Out of print.*

Percept & Motor Skills 34(1):339 F '72. C. H. Ammons. * Only clinicians who are literate and also skilled with the Rorschach are likely to be happy with this book, but then they are the very persons for whom the book was prepared.

[B175]

★GOLDMAN, BERT A., AND SAUNDERS, JOHN L. **Directory of Unpublished Experimental Mental Measures, Vol. 1.** New York: Human Sciences Press, 1974. Pp. xiv, 223. $13.95. *

J Biol Psychol 17(1):57–9 Jl '75. Jon D. Swartz. * The....volume has many shortcomings. Tests listed are limited to those described in only the 1970 issues of a selected list of but 29 journals, those which "in the judgment of the authors (editors?), contained research involving instruments of value to researchers in edu-

cation, psychology and sociology" (p. xi). In addition, the editors selected for inclusion only those tests listed in the 1970 issues of these journals that they "deemed of possible value to researchers" (p. xii). So the work has definite limitations. One of the first limitations I noticed was the omission of an author index, something I should think would be of prime importance in such a directory. Perhaps this, and other, lamentable errors will be corrected in future volumes. There *is* a subject index provided, one that should prove very helpful for users of the volume. *

J Pers Assess 40(1):104–5 F '76. Philip Himelstein. This book is an attempt to do for non-commercially produced and experimental psychometric instruments what *Mental Measurements Yearbooks* have done for published standardized tests. * 29 journals published in 1970, were surveyed for experimental scales * such journals as the *Journal of Consulting and Clinical Psychology, Journal of Clinical Psychology, Journal of Abnormal Psychology* and many others likely to have studies employing unpublished instruments are omitted. * It is not clear what criteria were employed for inclusion in this volume. Almost certainly, the research potential of the instrument or the current interest in the trait or construct being measured are *not* factors in the selection of the mental measures. * Perhaps because of the educational slant of the editors many significant areas in measurement are omitted to make room for custom-built scales and instruments used apparently in one-shot studies of concern to a specific local setting. This volume is unlikely to be considered as a supplement to the Buros series of *Mental Measurements Yearbooks.* Only the sketchiest outlines of each test is provided, and without evaluation or critical examination. For example, the validity of the Social Desireability Questionnaire, in its entirety, is described as ".10 to −.55." The direction of the signs will have no meaning to the reader unfamiliar with the questionnaire. More important, however, is the omission of the nature of the sample and of the criterion. Reliability for the same instrument is ".80, .88." Test-retest or split half? What time interval for retest reliability and with what sample? In the absence of such information, one must assume that the editors assume that there is such an entity as *the* validity and *the* reliability of a test. Carelessness in editing and/or researching mars the book. D. L. Mosher's name is given as Masher three times. Included among the "unpublished" tests are the Lowenfeld Mosaic Test, that old saw, the Willoughby Personality Schedule, Human Figure Drawings, the Make a Picture-Story, and the Semantic Differential. There is much potential in a volume such as the editors have attempted to compile. For the researcher looking for an experimental scale with some research to substantiate its use, this series could be invaluable. To be of value, however, some selectivity would be necessary. Rather than including an instrument because it was mentioned in a journal article in a given year, it would be preferable to include only those scales that have sufficient research behind it to provide a basis for a critical review. Some improvement in organization so that personality assessment scales are not scattered under different but synonymous rubrics would also increase its value. In its present form, it would be best if the *Directory of Unpublished Experimental Mental Measurements* was itself unpublished.

[B176]

*Good, Patricia King-Ellison, and Brantner, John P. **A Practical Guide to the MMPI: An Introduction for Psychologists, Physicians, Social Workers, and Other Professionals.** Minneapolis, Minn.: University of Minnesota Press, 1974. Pp. vii, 102. $6.00. * (Revision of *The Physician's Guide to the MMPI.*) For a review of the earlier edition, see 6:B206.

Ed & Psychol Meas 36(2):582–3 su '76. William J. Richman. * a very modest revision * in the business of MMPI interpretation we now have a very complex domain with a large variety of resources. What....can a volume of less than a hundred pages accomplish? There are brief chapters on: (a) administration and scoring, (b) the validity scales, (c) the clinical scales, (d) the research scales (12 in all), (e) two digit codes, and (f) the MMPI in practice. Because of the many basic omissions, there is hardly enough here to begin the acquisition of interpretive skill. Consequently, it seems likely that the book is aimed at the consumer of test reports. There are many professionals and semi-professionals in education, medicine, corrections, etc. who have frequent contact with MMPI reports and, perhaps, MMPI profiles. Certainly there is an educational job to be done with the consumer. He should know the basic theory underlying the test and something about the accuracy of prediction/description. Otherwise, he is likely to over- or undervalue the

information he receives. Does the *Practical Guide* accomplish this purpose? I would have to give a resounding "No." Critical evaluation is almost entirely absent except for comments regarding the research scales. The virtues in the *Practical Guide* are those of simplicity and brevity. It is well written and there are no misstatements of fact that I could perceive. The sin is that of omission. Within the confines of its brief format there could have been more exploration of basic aspects of the MMPI, there could have been more critical evaluation, and there could have been more information on the best use of test reports. Certainly there is a need that is unmet by the current literature. My own graduate students in clinical psychology feel somewhat overwhelmed by the *MMPI Handbook* but there is no shorter, less complete, and less scientifically oriented book to serve as a true introduction. I attempt to bridge this gap with lecture material and advise use of the *Handbook* as just that. The broad audience of MMPI consumers, however, do not have that advantage; they must satisfy themselves with too much or too little, and perhaps, by virtue of that fact, deal with early disenchantment. One hopes that the ultimate consumer—the client or patient—is not damaged by the well meaning but less than skilled use of the MMPI data which often prevails.

J Pers Assess 39(6):647–8 D '75. Ray A. Craddick. This little book appears to do what it purports to do, namely to provide a practical guide for use of the MMPI. It updates its 1961 predecessor, *The Physician's Guide to the MMPI,* and will be valuable to workers, including physicians, who use the MMPI. * The description of the nine clinical scales (including the *Mf*) is well done * One chapter is devoted to the meaning and descriptions of the various research scales and is of particular value since it presents those scales which appear to have reasonable validity (e.g., *Si., A., R., Es., Re.*) and those which must be viewed as lacking proven validity (e.g., *Lb., Ca., Pr.*). A sixth chapter devoted to the description of two-digit code profiles is interesting and informative. * The overall impression of this book is that it is a valuable and useful guide for persons using the MMPI and knowing its limitations. Judicious use of this book as a guide will be valuable; haphazard use of it could be less than desirable. It will provide the beginning student some closure on what would otherwise be an overwhelming mass of MMPI research and data. It may permit such a student to understand possible hypotheses gleaned from high and low MMPI scales, but requires extensive knowledge of personality and psychopathology theory and also a good basic understanding of the underlying dynamics of both to fully integrate the various meanings attributed to the scale scores.

[B177]

★GOODGLASS, HAROLD; WITH THE COLLABORATION OF EDITH KAPLAN. **The Assessment of Aphasia and Related Disorders.** Philadelphia, Pa.: Lea & Febiger, 1972. Pp. vii, 80, 28. $11.50. *

[B178]

GOODSTEIN, LEONARD D., AND LANYON, RICHARD I., EDITORS. **Readings in Personality Assessment.** New York: John Wiley & Sons Inc., 1971. Pp. xv, 792. * Out of print.

Am J Psychiatry 129(1):106–7 Jl '72. Charles R. Shearn. * The collection of papers is quite current; about 75 percent of them have been published since 1960. The editors have provided a concise but very helpful introduction to each chapter, briefly commenting on the papers that are to follow in such a way as to highlight the major issues and explain the relationship of the papers to one another. The papers themselves seem to be well selected. They provide a cross section of writings by many different authors dealing with a broad range of issues in the field of personality assessment. About the only critical comment that might seem called for is that a number of these papers are quite technical, compared with the exposition presented in the textbook. Thus the student who finds the textbook to be at about the right technical level for his level of training might find some of the readings in this book too difficult; and the student who is able to understand and enjoy these readings might find the textbook presentation to be somewhat too simplified. *

Brit J Social & Clin Psychol 13(1):106–7 F '74. J. J. Kear-Colwell. * a very useful companion that can save a lot of time looking around libraries for references * On the whole the papers have been well selected and make interesting reading. *

Ed & Psychol Meas 32(2):530–3 su '72. David A. Hills. * The *Readings in Personality Assessment* volume edited by Goodstein and Lanyon is keyed to coordinate with *Personality Assessment.* The degree to which the articles

successfully amplify the main thrust of the parent book appears to be at least adequate. The most commendable features of the *Readings* book is the high density of contemporary material. Of the fifty-four selections, twenty are of 1966–1971 vintage. * *Readings in Personality Assessment* suffers from a subdued type face which flutters late at night and a design shortcoming in that the articles follow immediately upon the heels of the preceding selection along with an absence of identifying signposts at the top of the page to guide the reader who is hunting for an article. If one opens the book a page too soon or too late, there is no help but to return to the index. On the other hand, any publisher able to deliver a hardback book of nearly 800 pages in length for under $12.00 in these days is perhaps entitled to cut a few corners.

[B179]

★GORDEN, RAYMOND L. **Unidimensional Sealing of Social Variables: Concepts and Procedures.** New York: Free Press, 1977. Pp. xiii, 175. $10.95. *

[B180]

★GORDON, LEONARD V. **The Measurement of Interpersonal Values.** Chicago, Ill.: Science Research Associates, Inc., 1975. Pp. xii, 122. Paper, $6.50; cloth $9.50. *

[B181]

★GORTH, WILLIAM; O'REILLY, ROBERT P.; AND PINSKY, PAUL D. **Comprehensive Achievement Monitoring: A Criterion-Referenced Evaluation System.** Englewood Cliffs, N.J.: Educational Technology Publications, 1975. Pp. xii, 268. $13.95. *

[B182]

★GOTTMAN, JOHN MORDECHAI, AND CLASEN, ROBERT EARL. **Evaluation in Education: A Practitioner's Guide.** Itasca, Ill.: F. E. Peacock Publishers, Inc., 1972. Pp. xvii, 512. Paper. * Out of print.

J Ed Meas 10(1):76–8 sp '73. Thomas R. Owens. * a paperback textbook to teach the reader how to: 1) do a needs assessment, 2) write measurable objectives and design measurement procedures, 3) make flowcharts, and 4) design and use quality control procedures. Ralph Tyler's four familiar questions which need to be answered regarding any educational program—"why, what, how, and how will you know?"—form the structure of this book. * it appears that the book is designed for teachers and school administrators possessing little formal knowledge of statistics or measurement. No rationale appears in the book as to why certain content areas were presented and not others, except for the attempt to include some techniques under each of Tyler's questions regarding any educational program. The inclusion of needs assessment procedures, writing of measurable objectives and designing of measurement procedures appear essential for practitioners. The treatment of flowcharting and the use of time series analysis is more questionable, however. While flowcharting is one useful technique for organizing activities, it fails to account for an important component in the planning and execution of any project, namely the timelines involved. For this purpose, a discussion of PERT (Program Evaluation Review Technique) may have been more appropriate. The authors establish a good case for the importance of time series analysis as a way of providing quality control and continuous feedback about a program but fail to explain to teachers how to develop instructional measures appropriate for frequent use or how to account for the effects of repeated testing. * this book....omits many areas considered by other authors on evaluation and measurement as essential for classroom teachers or administrators....topics such as: purposes for evaluation, construction of teacher-made tests, writing test items, procedures for assessing standardized tests, use of criterion-referenced tests, grading practices, how to provide evaluation feedback to students and parents, and how to locate further information on existing tests and measurement procedures. Although an annotated booklist appears, it consists of only two pages and fails to mention works such as Buros' *Mental Measurements Yearbooks* or Bloom's *Taxonomy of Educational Objectives,* while including Lindsay's 1958 *New Techniques for Management Decision Making.* Evaluation is defined by Gottman and Clasen as "quality control of the processes and outcomes of an educational program." This definition is more restrictive than that used by most writers today, and no mention is made of alternate concepts of evaluation currently being used by Scriven, Stake, Stufflebeam and others. Organizationally, *Evaluation in Education* is confusing. The book has only three chapters and two appendices. Chapter 1 explains in seven pages why the book was written, chapter 2 contains 30 pages on the goals of the book and chapter 3, in 278 pages, concerns itself with "how this book will accomplish its objectives." The reader becomes dependent upon the flowcharts supplied by the authors to guide him through the maze. * In the section on needs assessment, a need is defined as a "....discrepancy which

should be zero. It may be a discrepancy between two populations on a variable or between an ideal and actual state." The authors provide illustrative data showing that discrepancies existed in a Wisconsin County between Indian and non-Indian third-grade students in reading on a standardized test while no discrepancies existed on the first-grade reading readiness test between the two groups. Such an example is confusing and can be easily misleading. The authors caution the reader about the problem in switching from the test of one publisher to that of another but fail to mention the fact that a reading readiness test measures skills quite different from those measured by the third-grade level of the *Cooperative Primary Test.* A more serious omission occurs in the authors' failure to distinguish between an existing need or discrepancy and the underlying problems which may cause the discrepancy. * No discussion occurs as to whether the educators, parents or students themselves should determine educational needs nor how to involve students and parents in helping to define needs. Although several interesting procedures such as the Delphi technique have been used successfully in the past few years to determine educational needs and priority among needs, these are not mentioned in this book. The section of the book dealing with writing measurable objectives has an ironic introduction. "If you feel very comfortable (this is the pretest) you will not need to read this section." In this reviewer's college teaching experience, it was not uncommon to find graduate students who thought they knew how to write behavioral objectives but really could not do this satisfactorily. Much of this section is well presented in a linear programmed instruction style with questions and answers. However, some of the blanks to be filled in by the reader are not related to the point being made. * in the section on writing process and product objectives, criteria are discussed for evaluating objectives. The consideration of criteria such as "realism, focus, worthiness, and likelihood for being accomplished" provides a useful addition to the existing literature on behavioral objectives. Over fifty pages of this book are devoted to the use of time-series analysis procedures. While the procedures for graphing unobtrusive time-series data are discussed in detail, no mention is made of the problems involved in developing classroom instruments appropriate for frequent administration nor of the threats to validity due to frequent testing. The last section....is entitled, "Troubleshooting guide for research and evaluation beyond this book." This label is a misnomer since the section provides neither framework or strategies for dealing with more complex problems in evaluation but instead merely serves as a glossary of selected research and statistical terms. * In summary, this book attempts to be an introductory statistics book and, at the same time, to cover some evaluation skills that the authors consider needed by practitioners. However, many of the basic skills needed in evaluation by a classroom teacher or administrator are omitted from this text, and the treatment of existing topics is often poor. With the number of recent alternate textbooks available as an introduction to educational evaluation, this reviewer would not recommend *Evaluation in Education, a Practitioner's Guide* for general use.

[B183]

★GRAHAM, JOHN R. **The MMPI: A Practical Guide.** New York: Oxford University Press, Inc., 1977. Pp. xv, 261. $8.50. *

[B184]

★GRANDY, JERILEE, AND SHEA, WALTER M. **The CLEP General Examinations in American Colleges and Universities.** Princeton, N.J.: Educational Testing Service, 1976. Pp. 23. Paper, $1.00. *

[B185-6]

★GREEN, DONALD ROSS. **The Aptitude-Achievement Distinction.** Monterey, Calif.: CTB/McGraw-Hill, 1973. Pp. vii, 384. $13.50. *

[B187]

★GREEN, JOAN L., AND STONE, JAMES C. **Curriculum Evaluation: Theory and Practice With a Case Study From Nursing Education.** New York: Springer Publishing Co., Inc., 1977. Pp. xv, 271. $14.95. *

[B188]

*GREEN, JOHN A. **Teacher-Made Tests, Second Edition.** New York: Harper & Row, Publishers, Inc., 1975. Pp. x, 211. Paper, $5.50. * For a review of the first edition, see 6:B211.

[B189]

★GREENBERGER, SUE M., AND THUM, SUSAN R. **S.T.E.P.: Sequential Testing and Educational Programming.** San Rafael, Calif.: Academic Therapy Publications, 1975. Pp. 235. Looseleaf, $27.50. *

[B190]

★GROMMON, ALFRED H., EDITOR. **Reviews of Selected Published Tests in English.** Urbana, Ill.: National Council of Teachers of English, 1976. Pp. v, 170. Paper, $5.50. *

[B191]

*GRONLUND, NORMAN E. **Constructing Achievement Tests, Second Edition.** Englewood Cliffs, N.J.: Prentice-Hall, Inc., 1977. Pp. x, 150. Paper, $4.95. * For reviews of the first edition, see 7:B260 (2 excerpts).

[B192]

★GRONLUND, NORMAN E. **Determining Accountability for Classroom Instruction.** New York: Macmillan Publishing Co., Inc., 1974. Pp. 57. Paper, $2.75. *

[B193]

★GRONLUND, NORMAN E. **Improving Marking and Reporting in Classroom Instruction.** New York: Macmillan Publishing Co., Inc., 1974. Pp. 58. Paper, $2.75. *

[B194]

★GRONLUND, NORMAN E. **Preparing Criterion-Referenced Tests for Classroom Instruction.** New York: Macmillan Publishing Co., Inc., 1973. Pp. 55. Paper, $2.75. *

Meas & Eval Guid 8(1):59 Ap '75. Glenn G. Dahlem. * Gronlund is rapidly establishing himself as a foremost authority on the pragmatic application of theoretical measurement principles to improving school instruction. This short work continues the Gronlund tradition of first setting forth a topic (in this case, criterion-referenced tests), then proceeding to delimit various aspects of the problem in terms which make sense to the average elementary or secondary teacher. Those who decry neo-behavioral learning theory and the current emphasis on behavioral objectives will not like this book. Anyone who considers these recent educational trends as dehumanizing and mechanistic will regard the Gronlund work as one more cookbook among a rash of how-to-do-it manuals for teachers. This reviewer will not be caught up in the controversy surrounding behavioral objectives and the companion concept, accountability. Perhaps they are a passing fad; perhaps they are the saving educational grace of the future—only time will tell. The Gronlund work must be judged on the success with which it achieves its stated goal, that of showing classroom teachers how to implement a systematic procedure for creating criterion-referenced tests. In short, this is a very worthwhile and readable book for the teacher who has a sketchy notion of what criterion-referenced tests are but lacks the expertise to develop a procedure for using them. It sets forth an orderly systematic methodology and is rich in tabular and graphical illustration. The text presupposes certain mathematical/statistical competencies on the part of the reader, but not to the point of going over the head of the average professional. The book will find its greatest readership among practicing elementary and secondary teachers and among master's level graduate students in education. It is not recommended for the undergraduate student who has not yet had actual classroom experience, nor will it be much help to the doctoral level and beyond educationist. And, indeed, this midlevel professional applicability is no doubt what Gronlund had in mind when he wrote it.

[B195]

GRONLUND, NORMAN E. **Stating Behavioral Objectives for Classroom Instruction.** New York: Macmillan Publishing Co., Inc., 1970. Pp. vi, 58. Paper. * *Out of print.* For a review in addition to the one below, see 7:B262. For the latest edition, see B196.

J Ed Meas 9(1):77–8 sp '72. C. Mauritz Lindvall. * a brief, but well organized, description of what is involved in identifying and stating instructional outcomes in a way which will be of greatest value in instruction and evaluation. In so doing, he introduces certain refinements in terms of specific suggestions for organizing and using objectives, refinements that are somewhat of a unique contribution of this book and that may be of considerable help to teachers attempting to employ objectives. * In its later chapters the book provides brief overviews of both the use of educational taxonomies as a source for objectives and of the use of objectives in instruction, in testing, and in marking. In treating these latter topics the author may be attempting to cover too much in such a brief book. The reviewer feels that this space might better have been devoted to more examples of the steps used in deriving and stating objectives in a variety of subject matter areas. Perhaps Gronlund should have dealt with the topics of testing and of marking by merely referring the reader to his rather complete coverage of these topics in his measurement texts. The book might be used with a unit on "instructional objectives" in a course on curriculum development or on evaluation. It might also be used as a type of basic outline for a course where pupils would be expected to do extensive additional reading. This latter use of the book would have been enhanced greatly by a listing of suggested additional readings at the end of each chapter (as Gronlund does in his *Measurement and Evaluation in Teaching*) and by the inclusion of specific student exercises which the reader could carry out in order to work with the described procedures.

[B196]

*GRONLUND, NORMAN E. **Stating Objectives for Classroom Instruction, Second Edition.** New York: Macmillan Publishing Co., Inc., 1978. Pp. vi,

74. Paper, $2.75. * For reviews of the first edition, see B195 (1 excerpt) and 7:B262 (1 excerpt).

[B197]

★GROTELUESCHEN, ARDEN D.; GOOLER, DENNIS D.; AND KNOX, ALAN B. **Evaluation in Adult Basic Education: How and Why.** Danville, Ill.: Interstate Printers & Publishers, Inc., 1976. Pp. xiii, 274. $12.50. *

[B198]

GUILFORD, J. P., AND HOEPFNER, RALPH. **The Analysis of Intelligence.** New York: McGraw-Hill Book Co., Inc., 1971. Pp. xiv, 514. $23.00. *

Ed & Psychol Meas 32(1):211–5 sp '72. A. Ralph Hakstian. This book will be of some interest to all those concerned with the study of human abilities, and of considerable interest to that somewhat smaller group who were swept up by the senior author's 1967 volume, *The Nature of Human Intelligence.* The present book, unlike the earlier one, in which a major theoretical position was enunciated and elaborated, reads like a long research paper, with the research reported firmly anchored in the senior author's "Structure of intellect" (SI) model. In addition to reporting the earlier studies which preceded the formulation of the SI model, the authors report results of research conducted since 1967, and, thus, the book can be considered, in part, an updating of SI thinking, with 98 of the 120 cells in the three-facet design now filled, as opposed to 77 in the 1967 treatment. Clearly, this book is a "must" for those serious students of human abilities who wish to keep abreast of Guilford's thinking in the area. * The book will prove to be of considerably less value, however, to those who either have not been persuaded by the SI organization of abilities or are just beginning the study of human intelligence. No theoretical refinements over the 1967 statement are apparent and results based on experimental procedures laden with subjectivity are frequent. * It is likely that the methodologically competent reader will find these two chapters on analysis procedures somewhat distasteful. A section entitled "Indices of Factorial Invariance," for example, contains a poor presentation of such indices, with several omissions and inaccuracies. A section on "Factor Extractions" reveals that, in general, more factors were retained in the subsequently reported analyses than would be by the vast majority of experienced factor analysts. Such criteria as the number of factors associated with latent roots of $R - U^2$ greater than .30, and the number of common factors accounting for 95% of the total communality were employed, helping to account for the unusual number of singlet "common" factors in the analyses reported later. Undoubtedly most distasteful of all, though, is the great dependence—in the more recent studies at least—on the Orthogonal Procrustes procedure (Schönemann, 1966) for rotation, a technique the authors refer to as "targeting." With this procedure, unrotated factor loading matrices are fitted, orthogonally and in a least-squares sense, to a target matrix which presumably embodies the hypothesis to be confirmed or disconfirmed. It has been pointed out by Horn (1967, 1971), however, that, given a large ratio of retained factors to variables, and a small number of marker variables per factor (both conditions are certainly met in the studies reported in this book), virtually any set of data can be fitted to any hypothesis. Knowing this fact, the reader may well consider tenuous, conclusions resulting from such subjective and potentially biased procedures. * Finally, Chapter 9 is devoted to an SI *content* category, *behavioral* abilities. It is in this area, largely identified with social intelligence....that has traditionally been excluded from the study of intelligence. The reader, thus, will likely find this chapter interesting; in addition, some clever tests to assess the constructs are described. * Although Guilford has stressed that the divergent production abilities in the SI model represent the important components of creativity and tend to be somewhat independent of IQ, the results presented, with seventh grade students, include higher correlations, on the average, between the divergent production abilities and IQ than between the former and teacher ratings of creativity. Also reported is a predictive validity study involving 15 selected SI abilities and grades in 10 subjects at the U.S. Coast Guard Academy. Of the resulting 150 correlations, only 31 were significantly different from 0 at the .05 level (one of the 31 was negative), and of these 31, the median *r* was only .23. Not one of the 15 SI abilities correlated significantly with grades in either algebra and plane geometry or communications. The reader must, therefore, be cautious in attributing much predictive efficacy to these logically derived SI constructs. * Regarded in its entirety, this book leaves several negative impressions. First, and least important, is the lifeless prose; most will likely find the book, in general, monotonous reading. More importantly, though, the content suffers too. It

is difficult to imagine those concerned with the nature of human intelligence being satisfied, upon reflection, with the notion that intelligence is most parsimoniously and efficaciously described in terms of 120 orthogonal dimensions. One suspects that the tendency, noted earlier, towards overfactoring may well have contributed to a substantial fragmentation of previously noted, broader, albeit unitary, constructs, and the alert reader will surely speculate about whether the 98 SI abilities currently "demonstrated" would prove empirically to be even nearly mutually uncorrelated. Most serious, though, are the previously noted hypothesis confirmation techniques employed. Although the authors appear to believe that the research reported in this book constitutes *empirical* support for the SI position, the apparent support is illusory. The student of human abilities may be expecting too much to demand—as many logical empiricists would—findings robust enough to emerge from analyses using a variety of techniques (see Harris, 1967, for a discussion of varying techniques in a factor analytic context), but he has the right to require that it be possible for hypotheses and theories tested to be disconfirmed. The procrustean techniques employed in the studies reported in this book all but preclude this possibility. The SI model, thus, has gained little if any empirical status on the strength of the reported research, and remains what it has always been—merely a *logical* organization of the field. In summary, *The analysis of intelligence* represents a comprehensive and up-to-date discussion of SI abilities and the relationship of other intellectual and non-intellectual traits to the SI model. The book is, thus, narrow, offering as it does, little view of alternative thinking about abilities; Cattell's (1963) well-received theory of fluid and crystallized intelligence, for example, is not mentioned once. The strength of the book would seem to revolve around its great detail and its comprehensive treatment of assessing—at times ingeniously—performance on a large number of extremely narrow and specific tasks. It is concluded, however, that the book can hardly be considered to make a substantial contribution to either the understanding of human intelligence or the techniques useful for its analysis.

[B199]

★GUILFORD, JOAN S.; ZIMMERMAN, WAYNE S.; AND GUILFORD, J. P. **Guilford-Zimmerman Temperament Survey Handbook: Twenty-five Years of**

Research and Application. San Diego, Calif.: EdITS Publishers, 1976. Pp. xv, 457. $14.95. *

Ed & Psychol Meas 37(1):276 sp '77. Max D. Engelhart. This valuable manual represents twenty-five years of research and discussion of application of results. * Especially valuable is the discussion of the uses of the scales in counseling and in clinics.

[B200]

★HAGGLUND, GEORGE, AND THOMPSON, DUANE, EDITORS. **Psychological Testing and Industrial Relations.** Monograph Series No. 14. Iowa City, Iowa: Center for Labor and Management, College of Business Administration, University of Iowa, November 1969. Pp. viii, 48. Paper, $1.50. *

[B201]

★HANSON, GARY R., AND COLE, NANCY S., EDITORS. **The Vocational Interests of Young Adults.** Iowa City, Iowa: American College Testing Program, 1973. Pp. vii, 132. Paper, $3.00. *

Ed & Psychol Meas 34(3):719–20 au '74. Max D. Engelhart. This challenging monograph should be of great interest to vocational guidance counselors and to everyone concerned with the classification of vocational interests. Especially worth noting is the "hexagonal model" for interpreting the intercorrelational matrix of vocational interest scales. * Particularly meaningful are the figures in the monograph resulting from spatial configuration analysis developed by Nancy and James W. L. Cole. * Particularly meaningful are the circular planar configurations of Holland's six Vocational Preference inventory scales, of 50 Strong Vocational Interest Blank occupational scales, and of the 23 Kuder Occupational Interest Survey scales. *

[B202]

★HARNISCHFEGER, ANNEGRET, AND WILEY, DAVID E. **Achievement Test Score Decline: Do We Need to Worry?** St. Louis, Mo.: CEMREL, Inc., 1976. Pp. xii, 160. Paper, $3.00. *

J Ed Meas 14(1):63–5 S '77. Roger D. Harrison. Over the last few years it has become evident that the average scores achieved by college-bound high school graduates on the Scholastic Aptitude Test (SAT) of the College Entrance Examination Board have been falling steadily and significantly. From an all time high in 1963 the drop has been about 40% of a standard deviation. The monograph under review presents these and other data very fully in both graphical and tabular form. * The authors, quite rightly, point out that there is insufficient evidence to establish which of these possible causes (or, more likely, which combination of

them) is responsible for the decline, and it is unlikely that such evidence can be obtained in retrospect. They recommend a number of additional studies of future cohorts of school pupils, which may eventually establish which causes are predominant, with particular emphasis on the effects of changes in school organization and curricula, since it is in these areas that effective remedial action can most easily be taken. In the opinion of this reviewer, the studies reported in this monograph appear to have been carried out competently and thoroughly, and the recommendations for further study seem both timely and pertinent. In one sense, however, the title is misleading. There is no discussion of the practical effects of the test score decline or of the steps which may be needed to live with it. These studies show that students entering colleges and universities have achieved less than their predecessors of ten years ago. This applies right across the ability range. One of the most disturbing features of the whole picture is that the proportion of college entrants achieving the highest grades has dropped significantly. What is not known is whether the decline is reversible or irreversible so far as the individual is concerned. Will the subsequent performance of these students be permanently impaired throughout their college careers and into adult life, or will they ultimately catch up if given better instruction and possibly a longer period of study? If the latter, the decline is probably not so serious, since it can be remedied by devoting more resources to higher education and vocational training. If the former, the situation could be much more serious and possibly presage the beginning of a decline of American Society. The changes would be irreversible if they could be traced to genetic causes or to factors in the physical environment such as radiation (from nuclear tests) or lead poisoning (from automobile exhausts). The latter possibility (not considered in the monograph) is one that is not very likely, but it cannot be ruled out. The decline of the Romans has been attributed, among other causes, to lead poisoning resulting from the storage of wine in lead containers! The evidence (particularly the greater loss of verbal aptitude among girls) suggests, however, that the decline is most probably due to changes in the behaviour and attitudes of young people, in which case there is no biological reason why it should be irreversible. Nevertheless, it is now rather well established that lack of stimulation during the early years of life results in an irreversible loss of mental potential later. Does this also apply to adolescents? Comparison of English and American university graduates suggests that it may not, and that it is possible for the individual to make up later for inadequate schooling, but this possibility is certainly not yet proven. Even if it is true, the economic costs could be astronomical. Clearly, as the monograph emphasizes, there is need for much further research in this field.

[B203]

★HARRIS, CHESTER W.; ALKIN, MARVIN C.; AND POPHAM, W. JAMES; EDITORS. **Problems in Criterion-Referenced Measurement.** CSE Monograph Series in Evaluation No. 3. Los Angeles, Calif.: Center for the Study of Evaluation, University of California, 1974. Pp. vii, 176. Paper, $3.50. *

[B204]

★HARRIS, CHESTER W.; PASTOROK, ANDREA; AND WILCOX, RAND R. **Achievement Test Items—Methods of Study.** CSE Monograph Series in Evaluation No. 6. Los Angeles, Calif.: Center for the Study of Evaluation, University of California, 1977. Pp. vii, 149. Paper, $4.50. *

[B205]

★HARTLAGE, LAWRENCE C., AND LUCAS, DAVID G. **Mental Development Evaluation of the Pediatric Patient.** Springfield, Ill.: Charles C Thomas, Publisher, 1973. Pp. x, 79. $6.50. *

J Learn Dis 7(7):402 Ag–S '74. *Alex Bannatyne.* * presents a series of mental development expectancies or norms for given ages against which the pediatrician can compare the children he sees, in much the same way that he compares a child's heart rate, height, or head circumference against a set of norms or expectancy tables. Although designed for use as a quick reference desk volume for pediatricians, this book will be consulted by child psychiatrists and psychologists, as well as educators and others interested in mental development evaluation of children.

[B206]

★HAYMAN, JOHN L., AND NAPIER, RODNEY N. **Evaluation in the Schools: A Human Process for Renewal.** Monterey, Calif.: Brooks/Cole Publishing Co., 1975. Pp. xi, 143. Paper, $3.95. *

Ed & Psychol Meas 35(4):1048–9 w '75. *Lewis R. Aiken, Jr.* This short, concise book may be read with profit by anyone concerned with evaluation in the schools. It is not a comprehensive treatise on evaluation, since many of the technical details about research design, statistical analysis, and instruments employed in evaluation studies are not presented. Matters

such as how to survey, interview, select tests, and the like are not discussed at all. Rather, what the authors stress are procedural matters and the human factors involved in evaluation, including process and subjective evaluation. Also emphasized are the facts that evaluation can be helpful or harmful, and it is the responsibility of the evaluator to determine which it shall be. The authors possess a penchant for outlining and schematizing, a talent that will facilitate the use of the book as a sourcebook and a text but which results in somewhat slow reading. * many undergraduates in educational fields could study the book with benefit, but most will probably find it fairly difficult reading. This reviewer considers the book's primary value to be in training educational evaluators—when supplemented extensively by books on educational measurement, administration, and psychology. * Every chapter is well written, if succinct, and contains a concluding summary. Throughout the chapters the point is repeated that feedback of the results of evaluation from evaluators to users is essential if evaluation is to be more than a futile exercise in wasting time. The first four chapters are highly structured, describing methods of planning, effecting, and utilizing evaluation, as well as input, process, and outcome variables. Beginning with Chapter 5 the orientation of the book becomes more psychological, or rather socio-psychological. The descriptions of group dynamics and process evaluation in Chapters 5 and 6 are especially good. Chapter 7 on accountability deals more with social psychology and management than with technical issues concerning the measurement of change. There is a good discussion of Dyer's multiple regression approach to accountability and a recognition of its shortcomings. The weaknesses of the multiple regression approach, and the necessity of complementing it with a "management-by-objectives" approach, are discussed. The latter approach, of course, also has weaknesses: getting participants to state objectives clearly; extensive administrative time required; the fact that the approach sometimes results in psycho therapeutic soul-searching more than realistic attempts to state and attain objectives. *

[B207]

★HAYNES, JUDITH M. **Educational Assessment of Immigrant Pupils.** Windsor, Berks., England: National Foundation for Educational Research in England and Wales, 1971. Pp. 121. £4.00. (Atlantic Highlands, N.J.: Humanities Press, Inc. $9.00.) *

[B208]

★HEATON, J. B. **Writing English Language Tests.** London and New York: Longman Group Ltd., 1975. Pp. xi, 236. Paper, £2.45; $5.95. *

[B209]

HEIM, ALICE. **Intelligence and Personality: Their Assessment and Relationship.** Harmondsworth, Middlesex, England and Baltimore, Md.: Penguin Books Ltd., 1970. Pp. 206. Paper, 30p; $1.25. *

Brit J Psychol 63(1):142–3 F '72. B. A. Akhurst. This is not a book that many psychologists will read with complacency for, in pursuance of her general theme of "the essential oneness of the human being" and the need for experience as well as overt behaviour to be accepted by psychologists as valid, indeed essential, evidence, Dr Heim delivers a series of vigorous attacks on some broad conceptual standpoints and specific tests and methodologies. Nor is the attack confined to academic issues. The morality as well as the applicability of much animal experimentation is criticized and there are scathing comments on the attitudes that some psychologists apparently take towards their human subjects. Dr Heim disapproves of schisms and dichotomies. Psychology, she maintains, is not the proper realm for their promotion. "Discrete variables are the exception rather than the rule." Some might question, however, whether discrete variables are commonly found in any field of science outside the artificial environment of the laboratory and her general stand on dichotomies is both open to and worthy of further debate. In pursuing her argument, however, Dr Heim has many thought provoking comments to make on such divisions as intelligence and personality, mental health and mental illness, intelligence and creativity, heredity and environment. The plea for a broader approach to the study of man also leads to interesting discussions of other important and diverse issues, including multiple-choice questions, validation, sex differences and the psychological aspects of ageing. The Brook Reaction Test and the Word-in-Context Test are described in some detail and presented as evidence for the practical as well as scientific usefulness of a broader approach to testing. A novel feature is the inclusion, at the end of the book, of notes on the technical terms used to which the reader may refer for further explanation. Whilst most of these are descriptive, others, such as those on "attenuation," involve further critical analysis and there is a danger that this could be missed by psychologists familiar with the terms. This is no cool, dispassionate account and, written as it is in a forthright and, at times, angry style, it is likely to elicit some equally forthright replies. If these lead to a re-examination of some basic concepts and precepts, I suspect that the book will have achieved one of its main functions.

[B210]

★HEIM, A. W. **Psychological Testing.** London: Oxford University Press, 1975. Pp. 16. Paper, 45p.

B Brit Psychol Soc 29:21 Ja '76. E. Anstey. * though....[this booklet is] intended primarily for non-psychologists, almost any psychologist would profit by reading it * presents a dialogue on the subject of sociological criticisms of psychological tests which sums up brilliantly in 30 lines or so the literally thousands of pages that have been written on this subject in countless books during the past 30 years * The booklet is written with an admirable economy of words, and yet contrives to be witty. * It has also some intriguing illustrations. *

[B211]

★HERRNSTEIN, RICHARD J. **I.Q. in the Meritocracy.** Boston, Mass.: Little, Brown & Co., 1973. Pp. xiii, 235. * *Out of print.*

Brit J Psychol 65(1):163–4 F '74. H. J. Eysenck. This is the book of the article—to wit, Herrnstein's famous (or notorious) article on IQ in the *Atlantic Monthly* in September 1971. That article brought down the wrath of the S.D.S. (Students for a Democratic Society) and other left-wing extremists on the author, who was accused of being a racist, fascist and a sexist (although he explicitly stated that he had nothing to say on the debate about racial differences in intelligence that was going on at the time, and nothing untoward is known about his sex life). He suffered persecution, had his classes broken up, was prevented from speaking in public, even about such innocuous topics as the mathematical analysis of learning in pigeons, and quite generally learned the hard way what is meant by "freedom of speech" by the S.D.S. and their camp-followers. Herrnstein provides a lengthy introductory chapter in which he recounts his experiences; regardless of what one may think about the main part of the book, this should be required reading for anyone concerned with academic work, and the freedom of the researcher to tell the truth as he sees it. There are close similarities between his experiences and those of Jensen, as recounted in the latter's book *Genetics and Education*. No one who is interested in preserving rational discourse as one of the important qualities of our universities can view these events without revulsion, particularly when contemplating the shameful conduct of many senior academic persons who should have known better. * Academically, this is a very straightforward account of the facts about the IQ; there is hardly anything here that was not contained, for instance, in my own first paperback, *Uses and Abuses of Psychology*, 25 years ago—without raising any kind of fuss at the time. * Herrnstein spells out a number of the social consequences of innate IQ differences in some welcome detail, and may thereby have started a long overdue discussion in the U.S.A., but essentially the book is not at all controversial, but almost overwhelmingly orthodox. There are one or two points on which one might fault the author, as is inevitable in a book covering such a wide territory. * In a semi-popular book like this, one demands accuracy and clarity; both are present. Herrnstein is to be congratulated on having presented, in a popular but accurate fashion, data which are of great social importance, and on having pointed out some of the social consequences of these data. * There is nothing "controversial" in Herrnstein's book; it simply reviews the evidence and comes to very commonplace conclusions which have been commonplace for many, many years. That the publication of such routine matters should produce such quite disproportionate excitement, and lead to the almost complete ostracism of the person responsible for the writing, is a fact of considerable interest; social psychologists ought to get busy and investigate the state of mind of those who refuse to look at the facts, or to allow those who have looked at the facts to write and speak about them. Here is a unique opportunity to observe and study the inquisition actually at work in their attempt to destroy the followers of Copernicus and Galileo; here we can actually experiment with the Aristotelians refusing to look through the telescope at the four moons of Jupiter! A solution to the question of why so many academic people refuse to acknowledge the simple facts about the IQ would be of considerable theoretical interest, and might even be of immense practical importance. The students of prejudice will never have a more clear-cut subject to investigate.

Phi Delta Kappan 55(4):277-8 D '73.

Nicholas J. Anastasiow. Herrnstein spends the first chapter documenting the abuse he experienced following the *Atlantic* article in which he first set forth his major thesis. His thesis is that if "mental capacity is to any degree inherited and if social standing reflects mental capacity, then social standing must be a mirror, albeit an imperfect one, of inherited ability" (p. 10), and "social position tends to run in families for genetic as well as for social reasons" (p. 13). Herrnstein reports that he was attacked, in written and verbal form, by radical student groups and members of his own faculty, as well as members of other universities. His account seems free of bitterness. He documents the harassment and misinterpretation of his position in a manner that only occasionally imputes motives to those who attacked him. Whether the "radicals" who attacked him are "like their precursors in Russia" remains to be seen, but hopefully men as capable as Jerome Kagan do not obscure "the subject of mental testing because its findings are troublesome" (p. 50). Few of us would have borne up as well as Herrnstein appears to have done under the onslaught of posters, letters, articles, and individuals who interrupted his classes and colloquia. Unfortunately, what immediately follows the opening chapter are two confusing chapters which attempt to present a picture of the history of intelligence testing and a definition of intelligence. Herrnstein's style does not lend itself to clarifying issues. He slips from abstract terminology to friendly, intimate appeals to common sense. In the process he makes some troublesome statements such as "Binet was too busy with his practical goals to dwell on hypotheses" (p. 78) and "we must sneak up on the answers" (p. 79), due to the costliness of doing tests. Equally questionable is the use of the terms "explain" or "blame" in connection with correlations. Correlations cannot be used to explain cause/effect relationship, and these terms imply that correlations may do so. To this reviewer, Herrnstein's examples do not add to his discussion, particularly in the case of using hair length and age to explain correlations. Herrnstein's major position can be summarized as follows: IQ influences schooling and success in school influences social class; therefore, IQ influences social class. Further, higher IQ (or more intelligent) persons are trained for more difficult professions (doctors, lawyers). These professions, in turn, are of higher prestige and social status. Therefore, argues Herrnstein, if IQ is inherited and social inequalities are removed, genetics will determine who achieves the more prestigious roles in our society. Herrnstein has been very selective in his choice of articles to support his thesis. He has not included substantive alternative arguments, nor has he dealt fairly with the critics of the genetic component of IQ. The larger questions are whether IQ is synonymous with intelligence and if IQ is the best predictor of intellectual functioning. Authors such as Herbert Ginsburg * seriously question whether the IQ score reflects fundamental differences in intelligence, whether IQ scores measure intellectual competence, and whether innate ability is unaffected by experience. Herrnstein's tendency is to dismiss opposing arguments as those held by extreme environmentalists or, as he states in his opening chapter, by "liberals," "leftists," or "radicals." A welcome inclusion would be the work of Emmy E. Werner and her colleagues, who reported recently in *Children of Kauki* * that mothers' child-rearing variables at age 2 are the best predictors of a child's academic achievement at age 12, or Sandra Scarr-Salapatekis's excellent work on genetic components of intelligence. Contrary to the position presented by Herrnstein in Chapter 4, most intervention projects are successful in raising children's IQs about six to 12 points. Donald Stedman et al., in their 1972 review of a major intervention project, found that the mother's child-rearing practices were the crucial variable determining whether a child maintained an IQ gain after he left the experimental program. Other recent data and articles could well have been integrated if the book's intent had been to present a balanced view. I find it hard to imagine why William Rohwer's work is not included, or Anne Anastasi's monumental and classical 1958 article on the whole subject, "Heredity and Environment and the Question How." It is clear that intelligence is in part inherited and, equally, that IQ is in part intelligence. These are such well-established findings that Herrnstein weakens his major thesis by fighting them. There are so many other issues involved in the question that a tract presenting a biased position does little for the profession. The important question for educators has always been, How can we maximize the probability of enabling a child to reach his inherited potential through environmental arrangement

and stimulation? Although Herrnstein argues for the genetic point of view, readers should be clear that his stand is neutral on racial differences in inherited intelligence. He points out that, in his opinion, there is insufficient data to support an environmental or genetic hypothesis for racial differences. Herrnstein states that "the overwhelming case is for believing that American blacks have been at an environmental disadvantage" (p. 186). But, curiously, he concludes, "At present, the most existing knowledge can tell us is that people had best be treated individually, without regard to race, ethnic or geographical origin, sex (except where sex is itself at issue), or whatever" (p. 188). Some of us hold the opinion that these are every citizen's moral and legal rights and should not need to be justified or stated. Is the inference that if differences can be determined to show one group's superiority to another, we should treat them differently? Herrnstein's main thesis appears to say yes. What alternatives there are to the rise in meritocracy are not clear from Herrnstein's book. In fact, I find it hard to understand why the author built his argument on the data he has; he could have built a much more powerful statement and suggested or pointed to rational solutions. Perhaps we should be alarmed by Herrnstein's warning. But given the large number of Americans who live in poverty and disease and the prevalence of bigotry and racism in the schools, the labor force, and society in general, it seems like a minor problem. Herrnstein states that educators assume they "must strive to blot out individual differences" (p. 200). This, to me, is a misreading of the goal of "individualizing" instruction. Herrnstein digs up more snakes than he can kill in this book. The first 11 pages and the last chapter set forth his thesis. What lies between is in the main accurate, at times overly optimistic in what IQ scores predict, but uniformly simplistic in its treatment of serious and complex social issues.

[B212]
★HERSEN, MICHEL, AND BELLACK, ALAN, S., EDITORS. **Behavioral Assessment: A Practical Handbook.** Elmsford, N.Y.: Pergamon Press, Inc., 1976. Pp. xi, 556. Paper, $19.50; cloth, $25.50. *

[B213]
★HETZEL, WILLIAM C., EDITOR. **Program Test Methods.** Englewood Cliffs, N.J.: Prentice-Hall, Inc., 1973. Pp. xi, 311. $15.00. *

[B214]

★HEYWOOD, JOHN. **Assessment in Higher Education.** London and New York: John Wiley & Sons Ltd., 1977. Pp. xiii, 289. £10.00; $24.50. *

[B215]

★HILL, EVELYN F. **The Holtzman Inkblot Technique.** San Francisco, Calif.: Jossey-Bass Inc., Publishers, 1972. Pp. xix, 313. $25.00. *

Percept & Motor Skills 35(2):679 O '72. *C. H. Ammons and R. B. Ammons.* * interesting and stimulating effort * This intensive treatment of the Holtzman Inkblot Technique is for the mature clinician but will provide much help for researchers in personality development and adult functioning. It is deserving of careful and continued study and will no doubt stimulate restudy of the Rorschach.

[B216]

★HILL, EVELYN F., AND PEIXOTTO, HELEN E. **Workbook for the Holtzman Inkblot Technique.** New York: Psychological Corporation, 1973. Pp. vi, 129. Paper, $3.50. *

[B217]

★HILLS, JOHN R. **Measurement and Evaluation in the Classroom.** Columbus, Ohio: Charles E. Merrill Publishing Co., 1976. Pp. vii, 359. Paper, $9.95. Exercises in Classroom Measurement. Pp. xvi, 174. Paper, $5.95. Audio Cassettes for Exercises in Classroom Measurement. 11 cassettes, $125.00. *

Ed & Psychol Meas 36(4):1117–20 w '76. *Warren G. Findley.* First off, this is a book on educational measurement and evaluation for preservice or beginning classroom teachers, but it is more than that. It is the central element of a system that includes a coordinated workbook, a series of cassette audiotapes coordinated with the workbook, an instructor's guide which suggests alternative schemes of conducting the course work and includes greater technical detail than is appropriate for general student reading, and finally very explicit working use of the *Mental Measurements Yearbooks.* The design makes great sense and has been extensively pretested. * The second section, on standardized tests, is quite complete and essentially as appropriate to school counselors and administrators as to teachers. * Individual testing of intelligence is unfortunately dismissed as requiring more specialized training than a classroom teacher would have, hence beyond the scope of this book. * The extensive third section on grading and marking goes into more detail than most treatments and ends with an important substantial discussion of legal implications of grading. * In the fourth section, much thought-provoking discussion is given to such uses of

tests as in bringing parents into curriculum planning; placing students in groups for best learning, including such subtopics as diagnostic testing and "ability" grouping; providing feedback during instruction; enhancing student memory for and application of learnings; evaluating the teacher's own effectiveness and/or the effectiveness of particular methods of teaching various topics. * The brief final section on measuring attitudes contains the appropriate caveats regarding the technical expertise required to produce usable instruments to measure attitudes together with a thoughtful discussion of the place of such measurement in the classroom situation. The author might have distinguished self-concept measures as especially appropriate for development or selection with moderate consultation. * this offering [is] highly promising. It puts a wholesome emphasis on the classroom, where the learning takes place, and which administrators, counselors and parents should view as their function to support as the fundamental source of learning outcomes. In its organization, the offering lends itself to flexible use. All the topics are there and the instructor may go as deeply or fully as he/she wishes within each major area. * The presentation....is generally thought-provoking. The instructor may take off in any direction from the material presented, by way of qualified disagreement or extension, comfortable in the feeling that his/her beginning teachers have been stimulated by the text to useful preliminary thinking about each topic. And the introduction of case law into the material is a distinct plus. * Perhaps this textbook gives what seems too extensive treatment to grading and marking * Perhaps in a second edition the author will be able to deemphasize traditional grading and marking and make less of the limitations on criterion-referenced testing as those expectations change. * the present offering provides a means of stimulating thought while providing the techniques for building and using tests in classrooms. * The present offering merits wide use.

[B218]

★HINES, GEORGE H., AND HINES, ANNE B. **Cultural Influences on the Validity of Psychological Testing of Leadership in Fiji.** Department of Business Studies, Occasional Paper No. 19. Palmerston North, N.Z.: Massey University. June 1977. Pp. v, 21. Paper, gratis. *

[B219]

★HIVELY, WELLS, EDITOR. **Domain-Referenced Testing.** Englewood Cliffs, N.J.: Educational Technology Publications, 1974. Pp. viii, 150. Paper, $6.95. * (Reprinted from *Educational Technology*, June 1974.)

[B220]

★HIVELY, WELLS, AND REYNOLDS, MAYNARD C., EDITORS. **Domain-Referenced Testing in Special Education.** Reston, Va.: Council for Exceptional Children, 1975. Pp. ix, 146. Paper, $4.00. *

[B221]

HOEPFNER, RALPH; STRICKLAND, GUY; STANGEL, GRETCHEN; JANSEN, PATRICE; AND PATALINO, MARIANNE. **CSE Elementary School Test Evaluations.** Los Angeles, Calif.: Center for the Study of Evaluation, University of California, 1970. Pp. xix, 146. $5.00. * For the latest edition, see B222.

Meas & Eval Guid 4(3):187 O '71. W. M. Eastman. This taxonomy of educational tests available for use in the elementary grades rates these characteristics: measurement validity, examine appropriateness, administrative usability, normed technical excellence, and total grades (an overall rating). This book should be an excellent reference document for the elementary school counselor or school psychologist.

[B222]

*HOEPFNER, RALPH, AND OTHERS. **CSE Elementary School Test Evaluations, 1976 Revision.** Los Angeles, Calif.: Center for the Study of Evaluation, University of California, 1976. Pp. xxxiii, 620. Paper, $12.50. * For a review of an earlier edition, see B221.

[B223]

★HOEPFNER, RALPH, AND OTHERS. **CSE Secondary School Test Evaluations: Grades 7 and 8.** Los Angeles, Calif.: Center for the Study of Evaluation, University of California, 1974. Pp. xxxvii, 225. Paper, $8.00. *

[B224]

★HOEPFNER, RALPH, AND OTHERS. **CSE Secondary School Test Evaluations: Grades 9 and 10.** Los Angeles, Calif.: Center for the Study of Evaluation, University of California, 1974. Pp. xxxvii, 299. Paper, $8.00. *

[B225]

★HOEPFNER, RALPH, AND OTHERS. **CSE Secondary School Test Evaluations: Grades 11 and 12.** Los Angeles, Calif.: Center for the Study of Evaluation, University of California, 1974. Pp. xxvii, 339. Paper, $8.00. *

[B226]

★HOEPFNER, RALPH; STERN, CAROLYN; AND NUMMEDAL, SUSAN G. **CSE-ECRC Preschool/Kindergarten Test Evaluations.** Los Angeles, Calif.: Center for the Study of Evaluation, University of California, 1971. Pp. xxiii, 54. Paper, $5.00. *

[B227]

★HOEPFNER, RALPH, AND OTHERS. **CSE-RBS Test Evaluations: Tests of Higher-Order Cognitive, Affective, and Interpersonal Skills.** Los Angeles, Calif.: Center for the Study of Evaluation, University of California, 1972. Pp. xxvii, 322. Paper, $8.50. *

[B228]

★HOFFER, ABRAM; KELM, HAROLD; OSMOND, HUMPHRY; EDITORS. **Clinical and Other Uses of** the Hoffer-Osmond Diagnostic Test. Huntington, N.Y.: Robert E. Krieger Publishing Co., Inc., 1975. Pp. xvi, 236. $12.50. *

[B229]

★HOLMEN, MILTON G., AND DOCTER, RICHARD. **Educational and Psychological Testing: A Study of the Industry and Its Practices.** New York: Russell Sage Foundation, 1972. Pp. ix, 218. $7.95. *

J Ed Meas 10(2):153–4 su '73. Lynnette B. Plumlee. * The discussion of test practices and issues is not comprehensive, nor does it appear to be intended as such. It calls attention to the various factors in test planning, development, and use which influence the effectiveness of testing and includes such matters as specialist and user qualifications, standards of testing, scoring facilities and interpretation devices, availability of information about testing, discrimination in employment testing, and invasion of privacy. Included is an informative discussion of the Federal Trade Commission's decision which has discouraged publishers in their efforts to control test use by selling only to qualified persons. The reviewer found the reporting reasonably objective and generally in accord with other available information. * persons who have administrative or legislative responsibility for testing but whose familiarity with the fundamentals is limited....might benefit from a better rationale for the continued existence of the testing industry than is found in the brief description of the major uses of testing and incidentally elsewhere. A summary of the sound and beneficial uses would have required little additional space and could have been done without giving the test specialist or user a sense of complacency. Some reference to the literature which covers the theory and proper use of tests would also appear helpful to such an audience. * no mention is made of the Educational Testing Service Test Collection which consists of an extensive library of tests and other measurement devices, publishers' catalogs and descriptive materials, information on scoring services and systems, test reviews, and reference materials on measurement and evaluation. The *Test Collection Bulletin,* started in 1967 and published bi-monthly, describes briefly the materials in the Test Collection (including new acquisitions) and provides references to reviews and other publications on testing. * The recommendations made for improving the use of tests seem sound for the most part. However, the recommendation that test records should be destroyed "when the purpose of the testing is served" neglects the need to retain data for purposes of validity studies. The book will give the reader an overview of the organizations and issues involved in testing, some of the steps which have been taken to insure proper use, and the continuing inadequacies.

J Pers Assess 37(6):585 D '73. *Dale Simmons*. Following the 1965 picketing of the American Psychological Association's national headquarters, the APA Board of Professional Affairs requested that a group of psychologists meet to plan a review of the psychological testing industry. One long-range consequence of that planning session is the Holmen and Docter book. * Psychologists appear to have been preoccupied with the test development subsystem to the detriment of their awareness of the takeover of the testing field by business and educational organizations. Of the six largest commercial test publishing companies five are profit-making corporations or divisions of profit-making corporations, ie, Harcourt Brace Jovanovich, Houghton Mifflin, Science Research Associates (a division of IBM), California Test Bureau (a division of McGraw Hill), Psychological Corporation (a division of Harcourt Brace Jovanovich). Educational Testing Service is nonprofit but clearly controlled by educational organizations. The testing industry would now seem to be functionally autonomous of the psychological wisdom which fostered it. * The book is well organized and easily read. The prospective audience would seem to be the generally well-educated person who is unfamiliar with the testing industry, however it is recommended that all psychologists who use tests read it so that they will be as informed as the "general well-educated" person. Possibly due to the prospective audience the authors have taken an objective rather than a critical point of review. For instance, they did not deal with the reality that a psychologist who sells his test to a publisher is absolved of any further ethical responsibility for the use of that test. Hence, it is possible for the individual psychologist to maintain a "pure" self-concept while receiving profits form the ungoverned use of his test by persons who are not beholders to any set of ethics, professional or otherwise. All in all the book is an excellent response to the BPA request, especially if the reader carries the facts to some of their natural conclusions.

Meas & Eval Guid 6(1):60–1 Ap '73. *Donald G. Zytowski*. * The authors were commissioned by the Russell Sage Foundation to survey the testing industry * Holmen and Docter are both psychologists; neither is closely identified with test development, although Docter is one of the authors of the EEOC guidelines. Their main source of data was structured interviews with persons associated with large and small test publishers, supplemented by questionnaires to users and visits to various meetings concerned with testing. To me, their best contribution is the formulation of what they call "criteria for a competent assessment system." These are described in terms of the following six subsystems, where one may look to evaluate the whole system: (a) definition of assessment-system requirements, (b) test development and standardization, (c) definition of subjects and test administration, (d) scoring and preparation of feedback documents, (e) feedback of test results, and (f) evaluation of the assessment system. These systems involve both test publisher and user and identify places where each is responsible for behavior that meets requirements of competence and ethics. * The book ends with an appendix, no doubt generated by their interviews, listing a number of test publishers and some of the tests they publish. It's uneven and probably not as useful as the too-large list in the back of Buros. It [the 7th MMY] includes all the publishers who send you a catalogue because you belong to APGA, many of the smaller, more specialized establishments, and an odd lot such as Barbara Boyle (Shipley Institute of Living Scale), Dow Chemical Company (Chemical Operators Selection Test), the Great Eastern Lumber Company (The Potter-Nash Test for Lumber Inspectors and Others Who Handle Lumber), and many more.

Occup Psychol (England) 47(1–2):88–9 '73. *Peter Saville*. To the British psychologist, this study by Holmen and Docter of the educational and psychological testing industry in the United States may at first sight appear rather curiously titled. However, the first chapter will leave the reader in little doubt that an industry it certainly is, albeit an unusual one. Indeed, testing is arguably the one activity which psychology has most widely lent to society, though many feel that, as from Pandora's box, more troubles than benefits have thereby been released to the world. From the authors' estimates of some 400 million answer sheets consumed yearly, it would seem that testing is almost as much part of the American way of life as brunch-burgers and blueberry pie. Sales certainly indicate a far greater use of psychological and educational tests than in Britain. Moreover, the discrepancies between British and American test practices are evident not only in terms of how much they are used, but also of where, by whom and for what purposes. It is estimated by the authors that approximately 65 per cent of all the educational and psychological measurement undertaken in the United States involves achievement testing. This figure reflects large testing programmes at both state and school district levels, where test results do much in shaping school curricula and the distribution of resources for remedial education. Apparently only about 5 per cent of North American test usage is in the counselling, guidance and clinical areas. This is a surprisingly small proportion, especially as these categories include the clinical psychologist and the school psychologist, the American counterpart of the British educational psychologist. It is probable that in Britain these practitioners account for a considerably greater percentage. Offset against this is the smaller British industrial usage of test materials in selection and placement, which account for some 30 per cent of the total American market. Holmen and Docter here provide us with an important insight into the American testing industry. Current problems concerning the use of psychological tests in occupational psychology, which have arisen since the establishment of the Equal Employment Opportunity Commission and the Office of Federal Contract Compliance, are especially well covered. Most disturbing is the reported marked discrepancy between professional standards and the actual testing practices of personnel departments. Chapters are also included on the various commercial test publishers. The authors comment favourably on large organizations, such as the Psychological Corporation and Harcourt Brace Jovanovich, which are able to devote considerable resources to test development and the advantages to be gained by broadening their responsibilities to include the evaluation of assessment systems, are stressed. The sections on test scoring and interpretation, the control of standards, and testing in relation to employment discrimination and invasion of privacy, supply useful comments on problems which are not confined to North America. The point is strongly made that good test practice can only result from good tests, good administration and

adequate feedback of results. Much misuse arises from improperly guided interpretation. Very often problems derive less from the tests themselves than from the way in which they are handled. Holmen and Docter end by stressing that tests must increasingly provide valid information for decisions, but they must not invade personal privacy nor inappropriately limit opportunities. With this message in mind, as with Pandora's box, hope remains.

[B230]

★Horn, Dorothy M. **The Writing of Multiple Choice Mathematics Test Items.** Toronto, Canada: Ontario Institute for Studies in Education, 1970. Pp. ii, 22. Paper. *Out of print.*

[B231]

★House, Ernest R., Editor. **School Evaluation: The Politics and Process.** Berkeley, Calif.: McCutchan Publishing Corporation, 1973. Pp. xii, 331. $13.50. *

J Ed Meas 11(3):222–4 f '74. Carol K. Tittle. * Several points can be made about the view of evaluation presented in this book of readings on school evaluation. In the first place, evaluation is presented as an omnibus term, suitable for application in almost all aspects of education from the classroom teacher to large-scale national programs such as Title I. * It may be possible for the administrator or educational consumer to skip among these various levels and activities labelled as evaluation and arrive at an understanding of the issues posed. However, this is an unlikely outcome, in this reviewer's opinion. The administrator is likely to be sensitive to one of the book's major themes—the political nature of evaluation—but also to have less understanding of the "world of evaluation," in terms of the issues, underlying assumptions and outcomes of various approaches to evaluation. The book is weakest in this last area, in dealing systematically with types of evaluations and results of these evaluations. This criticism leads to a second point and is not a criticism of the book as much as it is a criticism of the research on evaluation itself, however. The book has articles (justifiably) critical of the use of large scale testing programs and the ideas which accompany discussions of accountability. There is a rejection of much of the testing which the "state of the art" in testing leads to and on which much of the past work in evaluation has relied. However, there has not been to date an evaluation of the alternatives being proposed, and their "effects" on the school and decision making. The qualified view of the level and tools of present evaluation is well-founded, but alternatives are not yet clearly defined or tested. To this reviewer it would make sense to separate some of the functions described in the book under the label of school evaluation and to make more distinct the concepts of accountability, i.e., responsibility for the conduct of schools, and evaluation. The monitoring of the school is legally the responsibility of the state, and, by delegation, local school boards. The technical support and further strengthening of this responsibility surely needs development. In this respect, schools are in a position similar to that of many major societal institutions at the present time. We are struggling continually with the problem of effective monitoring and how to hold accountable business and government agencies as well. This problem, by its nature, is highly political and the outcomes are dependent on many vested interests. It is possible to see the concept of evaluation as comprising functions and problems distinct from this monitoring or accountability function for educational institutions, yet as eventually contributing to that same function. With current limitations to testing, however, alternative methods of monitoring need to be seriously pursued. To what extent could local school boards use self-study by schools and "site visits" by outside consultants to assist in monitoring and to provide the qualitative information referred to by Cohen as accompanying census-type data on schools and schooling? This review has taken the position that school evaluation is a concept distinct from that of school accountability. Evaluative research in education can be seen as one area of inquiry, part of the larger set of disciplined inquiries directed toward developing knowledge and understanding of social institutions, of the expectations or goals held and of attainments. Evaluative research in education has drawn extensively on the design of experiments and educational measurement for its basic tools. Adaptations and testing of methods from a variety of social and behavioral sciences will be required for the further development of evaluative research in education: the understanding and the assessment of the value of products, curricula, programs, and other facets of the complex social institution we label the school. At the very least, this book of readings will fulfill some of its purpose by informing the administrator that there is at present no consensus in the pluralistic world of educational evaluators.

Meas & Eval Guid 8(3)206–7 O '75. Douglas S. Baugh. The purpose of this book, according to the editor, is to give the administrator, the decision maker, the board member, and the educational consumer some feel for the political nature of evaluation in terms of what it may do to or for people involved. Evaluation is presented as a political animal, a process used to allocate resources, cover up mistakes, build reputations, make money, correct errors, improve programs, reward merit, and report to patrons what is happening to their children. The book is a collection of readings by various authors. The editor does a commendable job of describing the format of the text and summarizing the ideas expressed. The underlying rationale is that it is not necessary to understand the technologies of evaluation (there are enough people around who do) if a person understands the political nature of the process. But the proper role of evaluative data is to be useful, not to be the sole determiner or decision maker of policy. "Ultimately, human judgment must resolve the issues." For those who feel frustrated about the whole concept of evaluation, the book is must reading. It gives one a sense of reality about evaluation and the perspective needed to deal with it. It could also provide worthwhile material for a staff to chew over as a preliminary staff development project, prior to implementing evaluative programs. Spend the money for the book. Read it! Share it with your colleagues. At least launch your accountable evaluation program from a realistic knowledge base of the political process involved.

[B232]

★HOUTS, PAUL L., EDITOR. **The Myth of Measurability.** New York: Hart Publishing Co., Inc., 1977. Pp. 398. Paper, $5.95. *

J Ed Meas 14(4):403–6 w '77. Eric F. Gardner. One may take the title of this book in either of two ways: (1) as suggesting an exposure of the fictions perpetrated by the mental measurement community to support its biases regarding education and human development or (2) as suggesting a collection of fictions perpetrated by the editor and his authors in support of *their* biases regarding the mental measurement community. Although the editor and a good many of his authors seem to have had the first interpretation in mind, this reviewer feels that on balance the second might be more appropriate. For it is difficult to accept seriously the multiple attempts in the book to discredit the whole field of psychology that is associated with the discipline of educational and psychological measurement. With few exceptions the authors seem quite unaware of the large body of theoretical and empirical research in psychometrics that has been going on since the turn of the century and particularly in the last 50 years. The book consists of two series of articles that first appeared in the *National Elementary Principal* in 1975. The first series is made up of ten papers critical of the measurement of aptitudes. The second series consists of 18 papers assailing standardized tests of academic achievement from various viewpoints. Although the collection as a whole takes a negative approach, the presentations are, to a surprising degree, heterogeneous in quality. They range from one or two that reflect serious scholarship and a care for accuracy of reporting to several that are so loaded with misstatements as to be little more than exercises in journalistic fantasy. In between these extremes are some papers that rehearse a number of the criticisms of testing that can be found in any up-to-date textbook on educational and psychological measurement. Perhaps the most scholarly and well-written of the papers is one by Sheldon H. White tracing some of the important negative social and political implications of the IQ. * In the middle range are a number of papers devoted principally to criticisms of specific subject matter items found in widely used achievement tests. Many of the criticisms are appropriate and indeed resemble comparable passages on the criticism and construction of items which one can find in any good textbook of educational measurement. There are, however, a large number of comments in this vein which this reviewer finds either wrong or at best picayune. Among the better papers in this category is one by Janet H. and Dean K. Whitla discussing standardized tests in the social studies. They make the excellent point that achievement tests in the social studies cannot assess some of the most critical dimensions of behavior growth in that field, and Edwin F. Taylor, in a later article on science tests, makes a similar point. The Whitlas, for example, stress that "knowledge and skills in the social studies cannot be fully defined by specified content outcomes;

they involve sharing of learning, pleasure, and skill in expansion and exchange of ideas, along with personal immersion in knowledge and the process of knowing. Cognitive and psychosocial development go hand in hand. They must be seen as a unity, not divided into separate, sometimes competing arenas of learning." In accordance with this position, the Whitlas present samples of several interesting instruments that could be used in the classroom to obtain information about cooperative behavior in working toward an educational objective. In the book as a whole, however, this kind of positive contribution is rare. Although this reviewer agrees with the Whitlas that the kinds of variables they (and a few other contributors) describe are important, he takes exception to the low esteem in which they hold information-specific test items. Having in mind the 50 years of debate concerning the importance, or lack of importance, of such items, this reviewer remains deeply convinced that the measurement of factual information must play a necessary if not a sufficient role in the teaching-learning process. Pupils are unlikely to get very far in the pleasurable "exchange of ideas" etc. unless one can have some assurance that they share a common body of facts clothed in a common vocabulary by which to discuss their ideas. Among the articles in the book that this reviewer found most troubling are two—one by Paul A. Olson and the other by Sherwood D. Kohn—which are so careless about some ascertainable facts as to undermine any usefulness they might have had in furthering a productive dialogue about standardized testing in America. Olson's article, "Power and the National Assessment of Educational Progress," is little more than a flight of fancy about the nature, the urgencies, and the control of schooling in America. By larding his prose with a series of mostly irrelevant quotations, he purports to show that the NAEP was and is a nefarious plot hatched by wealthy foundations, the big testing companies, and the federal government to homogenize American education with a view to destroying the numerous subcultures that enrich American society. Unlike other similar articles, however Olson's is followed by a rejoinder from Ralph Tyler who was in at the creation of NAEP and who quietly disposes of much of the misinformation about its nature and its purposes upon which Olson relies in an attempt to make his case. This reviewer wonders why, in the interest of helping the reader to a more balanced view of things, the editor of the collection found it inconvenient to include similar rejoinders by similarly knowledgeable people to some of the other articles. Kohn's article, which carries the title, "The Numbers Game: How the Testing Industry Operates," is an example of investigative reporting that gives the illusion of objectivity by piling up facts, figures, and comments from sources inside and outside the testing profession. It is an unusually good example of how an accomplished and disingenuous writer can subtly impugn the motives of scholars in the measurement field by means of innuendo and colorful language that leans toward the position of those who would abolish standardized testing altogether as a "mindless, paranoid, stagnant, technology obsessed business that is hopelessly prone to all manner of abuses against the human spirit." For the knowledgeable reader, however, the credibility of the whole piece is impaired by a number of gaffes that make one wonder how carefully Kohn checked any of his facts. For instance, at one point he refers to the College Board's SAT (Scholastic Aptitude Test) as ETS's *Standard Achievement Test*. Again, he refers to "Otis and the other authors of the Stanford Achievement Test," when, as he should have known, Arthur Otis was the author of a widely used aptitude test, *not* a coauthor with Truman L. Kelley and Lewis M. Terman of the Stanford Achievement Test. Yet again, he refers to E. F. Lindquist as "the man who invented the test scoring computer," when, with a bit of research, he might have learned that the original adaptation of the analog computer to test scoring was the brain child of Ben D. Wood. Unfortunately the credibility of a number of useful criticisms of testing and the use of test results as stressed by the various authors is undermined by the tendency throughout the volume to be scornful of the entire testing enterprise as the work of "mere technicians" who are insensitive to the great issues that face American education. In the opinion of this reviewer, the majority of the issues raised are worthy of the most serious consideration by test makers and test users alike. If the book had presented those issues with more judicious attention to the pros and cons and less to the denigration of the testing community which has long been conversant with the problems cited,

it could have served a more useful purpose in raising the level of understanding in the education profession generally and in the public at large. Thus, to conclude, the book misses an excellent opportunity to achieve its objective as described by Paul Houts in his introduction: "Do we need testing? Of course we do. But we need many more kinds of tests that meet our current educational and social needs. Can we develop them? Of course. The education profession has met equally difficult challenges, and many effective forms of evaluation are already known to teachers and principals. Can the testing companies help in such future test development? Perhaps. Most any endeavor can benefit from broad participation and a wide range of viewpoints and knowledge. But we believe it is now imperative for the education profession to take the initiative in developing alternatives to current standardized tests." The book fails of this purpose just as a book stressing the use of tests in decision making would fail if it focused *only* on the successes and ignored both the false positives and the false negatives. The failure is due primarily to the fact that the many useful ideas and criticisms are drowned out by emotional language that is more than likely to divert the reader from an objective consideration of the issues. A problem as complex as measuring human abilities, knowledges, and skills needs all the brain power that can be marshalled. The solution is not to promote the idea that educational measurement is a discredited myth and that its instruments should be abolished because they are less than perfect. A more constructive approach would be to improve and add to the available tools, rather than, through the abolition of knowledge and products acquired during the past 100 years, to start from scratch at square one.

[B233]

★HUBBARD, JOHN P., AND SCHUMACHER, CHARLES F. **Measuring Medical Education: The Tests and Test Procedures of the National Board of Medical Examiners.** Philadelphia, Pa: Lea & Febiger, 1971. Pp. xiii, 180. $8.50. *

Ed & Psychol Meas 32(4):1141–4 w '72. *Lloyd A. Lewis.* The charge to the National Board of Medical Examiners is to produce a reliable and valid examination procedure for use in licensing physicians. The Board has accepted the challenging problem and has made a strong effort to overcome many testing evils. They have changed from an unreliable essay format to one of multiple-choice for Parts I and II of the examination. * Part III has been changed from unreliable oral examinations of clinical patient problems to multiple-choice and patient management simulations. * For the reader who does not wish to deal with the technicalities of test analysis, Hubbard's book is an informational account of construction of multiple-choice examinations. Part III, which deals with the assessment of clinical competence, is especially helpful. * two different kinds of testing were adopted. The first is a paper and pencil simulation of patient management problems. In this type of testing, a simulation of a visit with a patient is presented. As more information is required, the examinee chooses from a list of options; these may include relevant and irrelevant information about a physical examination, diagnostic tests of laboratory tests. When a student believes he has enough information, he chooses a diagnostic option followed by a treatment option from comprehensive lists. At each step only the information or result of a selected option is revealed. In essence, the student is scored on the basis of his wrong and right decisions as compared to the decisions of a group of experts. Initially he is given a "handicap score." For every error made, a point is subtracted; for every right decision, a point is added. The reliability of the programmed patient management problem is generally .80 to .85. * The way reliability of this unusual test was established was not explained. It seems the reliability issue ought to be further clarified. * The National Board is to be commended for the job done to date; however due to technical errors, their charge is far from being finished. Apparently the Board has produced a content valid examination and one which has high scoring reliability. However, it has not produced a test which maximizes validity for selection purposes. * The Board feels that it is reasonable to allow students to compensate for weakness in one section by doing better in another. * A counter argument could be advanced that students should meet a MPL on each section if a specific discipline represented by a section contributes unique and necessary information to a physician's competency. * the cutoff score ought to be based on the examiners' judgements of competency and not on how high or low the failure rate should be. Incompetents should be failed; competents should be passed. * the National Board is to be commended for the job it has done to date. It is hoped that the other health professions view their certification programs as diligently as the National Board of Medical Examiners have.

[B234]

★HUDSON, B., EDITOR. **Assessment Techniques: An Introduction.** London: Methuen & Co. Ltd., 1973. Pp. xii, 223. Paper, £1.35.

Brit J Ed Studies 21(3):350–1 O '73. E. A. Hewitt.
The editor rightly describes the book as a co-operative effort, for the individual members of the team have worked to a common plan and made appropriate reference to earlier or later chapters, though they have not entirely avoided the difficulties attendant upon collaboration. "Facility value," a simple enough concept, perhaps receives more than ample treatment in the four places to which one is referred by a useful index. The statement in the first chapter, that "those who were better at arts than at science can take consolation from the fact that...variability in standards and discrimination was a major reason why they never came top of the form," is unlikely to be intelligible to the readers for whom the book is intended until they have read chapter 2 on "Statistical Considerations" (and the more sophisticated reader may wonder how "standards" can be defined so as to make the statement a valid one). The seven chapters deal with planning an examination, relevant statistical concepts; assessment by essays, structured questions and objective tests; internal assessment, and moderation. There is a substantial list of references and suggestions for further reading, but at least two of the contributors refer the reader to the whole bibliography for further information on restricted topics, though the book titles alone are unlikely to provide adequate clues for selection. Perhaps the clearest exposition appears—where it is most needed— in the chapter on statistics in which such basic concepts as dispersion, standardisation, correlation, reliability and conversion of raw marks into grades are economically handled. In the last chapter too the account of moderating procedures is a commendably simplified one. The chapter on internal assessment will provide the reader who is not deterred by a somewhat pontifical tone with much information on oral examinations, practical tests, projects and the assessment of course work and of attitudes. The two chapters on structured questions and

objective tests respectively give detailed advice on how to construct test items, and the book as a whole should do much to dispel ignorance and misunderstanding of examination techniques that have been developed fairly recently in this country. It represents good value for money.

[B235]

★Hunt, J. McVicker, Editor. **Human Intelligence.** New Brunswick, N.J.: Transaction, Inc., 1972. Pp. vii, 283. Paper, $4.95. *

[B236]

*Hutt, Max L. **The Hutt Adaptation of the Bender-Gestalt Test, Third Edition.** New York: Grune & Stratton, Inc., 1977. Pp. viii, 279. $16.00. * For reviews of earlier editions, see 7:B320 (3 excerpts) and 6:B268 (2 excerpts).

[B237]

★Invitational Conference on Testing Problems. **Assessment in a Pluralistic Society.** Proceedings of the 1972 Invitational Conference on Testing Problems, October 28, 1972. Anne Anastasi, Chairman. Princeton, N.J.: Educational Testing Service, 1973. Pp. xvii, 126. Paper, $5.00. *

[B238]

★Invitational Conference on Testing Problems. **Educational Change: Implications for Measurement.** Proceedings of the 1971 Invitational Conference on Testing Problems, October 30, 1971. William E. Coffman, Chairman. Princeton, N.J.: Educational Testing Service, 1972. Pp. xvi, 139. Paper, $5.00. *

[B239]

★Invitational Conference on Testing Problems. **Measurement for Self-Understanding and Personal Development.** Proceedings of the 1973 Invitational Conference on Testing Problems, November 3, 1973. Henry Chauncey, Chairman. Princeton, N.J.: Educational Testing Service, 1974. Pp. xiii, 78. Paper, $5.00. *

[B240]

★Izard, J. F. **Construction and Analysis of Classroom Tests.** Hawthorn, Vic., Australia: Australian Council for Educational Research Ltd., 1977. Pp. viii, 74. Paper, Aus. $4.00. *

[B241]

★Jacobs, Paul I. **Up the IQ!** New York: Wyden Books, 1977. Pp. viii, 191. $10.95. *

[B242]

★Jacobson, Sherman, and Kovalinsky, Thomas. **Educational Interpretation of the Wechsler Intelligence Scale for Children—Revised (WISC-R).** Linden, N.J.: Remediation Associates, Inc., 1976. Pp. iv, 65. Paper, $3.00. *

[B243]

★Jansen, Abraham. **Validation of Graphological Judgments: An Experimental Study.** Elmsford, N.Y.: Mouton Publishers, 1973. Pp. xv, 189. Paper, $15.50. *

Behav Res & Ther (England) *13(1):70 F '75. H. J. Eysenck.* Graphology as a means of

assessing human personality is much more firmly entrenched on the Continent (particularly in Germany and Holland) than in this country, where scepticism (justified by a long string of negative experimental reports) has been more apparent. In 1955, on the initiative of the Nederlandse Vereniging voor Bedrijfspsychologie, a study group for graphology was set up; this report is one of the results of the efforts made by this group to come to grips with the problem of validity. Several experiments are described, all dealing with the personality dimension "energetic-weak." The main outcomes of these studies are not dissimilar from those reported by other investigators. There is a certain, very small, amount of evidence for validity, too small to be of any practical use; graphologists do not do better than do untrained persons; the content of the communication analysed may be more important in arriving at valid conclusions than the actual mode of handwriting. On the whole, the experiments here described are well executed, and their conclusions are quite acceptable. The practical use of graphology is certainly contra-indicated, but this will of course not prevent businessmen in Holland and Germany (who must be extremely credulous) from continuing to use "expert" graphologists in the selection of staff. Even more unfortunate in some ways, it will not prevent clinical psychologists from using this invalid method of assessment in their work with psychiatric patients. Let him who has used neither Rorschach nor T.A.T. throw the first stone.

[B244]

★Jarvik, Lissy F.; Eisdorfer, Carl; and Blum, June E.; Editors. **Intellectual Functioning in Adults: Psychological and Biological Influences.** New York: Springer Publishing Co., Inc., 1973. Pp. xiii, 177. $7.50. *

[B245]

★Jedrysek, Eleonora; Klapper, Zelda; Pope, Lillie; and Wortis, Joseph. **Psychoeducational Evaluation of the Preschool Child: A Manual Utilizing the Haeussermann Approach.** New York: Grune & Stratton, Inc., 1972. Pp. xii, 124. Spiral binding, $13.50. *

Am J Mental Def 78(2):231 S '73. A. Barclay. * In essence, this monograph is a test manual for the educational evaluation of preschoolers. Five areas of function are assessed: (*a*) physical and sensory status, (*b*) perceptual function, (*c*) learning competence, (*d*) language competence, and (*e*) cognitive functioning. Within each of these functional areas, items are arranged hierarchically in order of difficulty; and the purpose of the examination is to establish an individualized profile for each child. This profile can then (it is stated) be used for developing an individually prescribed teaching program that will hopefully both remediate specific weaknesses in the child's educational functioning and maximize his strength. Unfortunately, while the method of approach is laudable in that it treats each child as an individual and recognizes that each child has his own strengths and weaknesses, there are no empirical data that would allow for an evaluation of the adequacy of this test as a psychometric instrument. The authors have avowedly eschewed age and grade norms, using the rationale that classification of the child as being at a given level of development may lead to deleterious consequences. Given this position, the present material cannot be considered so much an instrument of measurement as a set of instructions for conducting a more or less "standardized" clinical observation procedure. Considered as such, the Haeussermann approach has merits of its own. Nonetheless, the generalizability of the technique and recommendations therefrom become essentially dependent upon the individual sensitivity of the clinician involved; so that its utility as a measurement procedure is limited. In the absence of any data regarding the reliability and validity of the technique, it must be concluded that while the approach is potentially a useful one, more empirical data are needed upon which to base a judgment as to whether the present instrument meets appropriate criteria for inclusion in the armamentarium of the clinician.

[B246]

★JENSEN, ARTHUR R. **Educability and Group Differences.** London: Methuen & Co. Ltd., 1973. Pp. xiii, 401. Paper, £3.90.

Brit J Ed Studies 22(1):102–3 F '74. N. Bolton. * The present book....is a testament to Jensen's determination to advance on all fronts in the battle against an extreme environmentalist view of intelligence and attainment. Thus, certain chapters consider the statistical problems involved in determining the relative influence of heredity and environment, there being an especially cogent account of the problem of the interaction between the two in which Jensen maintains that an additive, rather than a

multiplicative, model is to be favoured, whilst others look at social and racial differences in such aspects of behaviour as intelligence, scholastic attainment, language, and sensori-motor skills. In addition, Jensen examines the relationship between the physical environment and intelligence, the nature of social class, and the various programmes designed to accelerate attainment among deprived children. All this adds up to a powerful argument for the study of the genetic basis of behaviour. Jensen's great strength is his capacity to organise and interpret the available evidence in respect to all these aspects of the problem and to present his case with exemplary clarity. No doubt, he will fail again to appease a variety of academics. Sociologists and social psychologists will continue to affirm that Jensen grossly underestimates the influence of cultural norms and expectations; cognitive psychologists may argue that the course of intellectual development, as outlined by Piaget and others, is at variance with Jensen's psychometrics, for, although Piaget's theory might be described as biological in emphasis, it is questionable whether it is so in the straightforwardly deterministic manner implied by Jensen; and educationalists may object that in a book with the title of *Educability and Group Differences* the author has neglected to provide a very thorough and specific account of the educational implications of his work, since he limits himself to suggesting briefly and without elaboration that educational objectives should be threefold: we should seek interactions between aptitude and type of training, pay more attention to learning readiness, and introduce greater diversity of curricula and goals. Perhaps, eventually, he will follow in Bruner's footsteps and develop a theory of instruction to complement his psychology of intelligence. Despite these doubts, this book is necessary reading for all those interested in human behaviour in its biological and social contexts. "Jensenism" may, hopefully, become no more than a curious footnote in the history of psychology, but Jensen's work itself stands forth as a worthy achievement and a stimulus to thought.

[B247]

★JENSEN, ARTHUR R. **Educational Differences.** London: Methuen & Co. Ltd., 1973. Pp. 462. £5.75.

Brit J Psychol 65(4):553–4 N '74. D. A. Crawford. This is Professor Jensen's third book since the publication of his paper, "How much can we boost IQ and Scholastic Achievement?" in 1969, in the *Harvard Educational Review. * a collection of previously published papers, with a preface by the author. * apparently between 1967 and 1971, though the dates have to be teased out from cross-references in the papers themselves. * The most useful paper is perhaps the first one: "Hierarchical Theories of Mental Ability" which outlines some of the main theories of "intelligence," and Jensen's own theory of Level I and Level II ability. He also discusses the problem of cultural loading in tests such as the Terman-Merrill or Raven's Progressive Matrices, a topic which he takes up again at length in the fifth paper, "Another Look at Culture-fair Testing." There are many useful teaching points in both of these papers. * It may well be, as he and others whom he cites have found, that "culturally disadvantaged" and "minority children" are not at a disadvantage in terms of school provision, i.e. staffing and equipment, but these may not be the important variables. Can we afford to ignore reports like that of Jonathan Kozol in *Death at an Early Age* or, from another country, "A Letter to a Teacher" (from Barbiani) or more respectable (scientifically speaking) sources such as Joyce Morris's *Reading in Primary Schools* or Warburton's chapter in Wiseman's *Education and Environment,* which showed how important the variable of teachers' attitudes and interests in teaching were in relation to children's attainments in school. * he says some very useful things about tests and testing; the paper on "The Culturally Disadvantaged" shows more awareness than one might expect, even if he does not use any of the measurable items in his own investigations. The experiments on learning and the acquisition of learning sets in children are useful, and could be extended. The reviewer has a strong hereditarian bias herself (as befits one of Burt's students), bar not strong enough to accept Jensen's figures, nor indeed Burt's, nor to accept that the negro-white differences or social class differences are due mainly to genetic differences. This may be no more than an obstinate conviction; on the other hand, there is sufficient evidence about social classes, to make it worth considering the possibility that these adverse conditions may prevent the development of children's abilities to a greater extent than we have hitherto allowed for, and that the genetic contribution to individual and social class differences is much less than 80 per cent, though still a substantial one.

[B248–9]

★JENSEN, A. R. **Genetics and Education.** London: Methuen & Co. Ltd., 1972. Pp. vii, 379. £3.50.

Brit J Ed Studies 21(2):222–3 Je '73. W. D. Wall. * For the general reader and for those interested in the history of science and of ideas, Jensen's 67-page preface is perhaps the most interesting and chastening part of the book. It describes in detail the extraordinary public reaction provoked in part by the paper itself and in part by the various press accounts of it and demonstrates that even those claiming to be scientists may be far from a cool appraisal of evidence if their emotionally held convictions are called into question. The cleavage between the 'let's look' and 'let's hide' schools of thought was absolute; and the extraordinary feature of the whole affair was that this time it was those professing liberal ideas who tended towards McCarthyism—on both sides of the Atlantic. "La République n'a pas besoin de savants" was—and perhaps still is—more the mood than Montaigne's doctrine of tolerance. Jensen has been represented as holding extreme geneticist views—much as in this country Burt is. It is of the utmost importance therefore that those seriously concerned with the ideals of equality of opportunity in our society, with positive discrimination in favour of the socially disadvantaged, and with so-called compensatory education should read this book with great attention. What Jensen has done is to marshall an immense amount of evidence from studies of the cognitive performance of children from different social groups and different cultural and ethnological backgrounds. Most of the *facts* which he adduces are not in dispute. What are disputable are certain methods of analysis which he applies and the consequential inferences. For those equipped to evaluate the former, Jensen provides in the present volume theoretical discussions—for example, "A Note on Why Genetic Correlations are not Squared." So far as the inferences are concerned, whether one disagrees or not on ideological grounds, no one can legitimately challenge the scientific rigour with which they are drawn and presented—in marked contrast be it said to the work of many of his critics. Hence it becomes important that those who feel in their bones that he is wrong should study with great attention the paper on

"Primary and Secondary Familial Mental Retardation" which sets out his theory of Level I and Level II (respectively "associative" and "cognitive") abilities. * we may ask what....the famous Harvard Review article said more than other sober scientists of the stature of Vernon and Burt had said before? Jensen drew attention to obstinately persistent differences in mental functioning, to an array of facts which suggested that the origins of some considerable part of these might be present at birth, that explanations were to be sought in such matters as assortative mating and possible differences in gene-pools. He did not deny the influence of environment, even antenatal environment, nor the possibility of maximizing whatever potential there is by environmental means. Nor did he omit to point out that the relative weights of environment and heredity in the case of individuals and groups might considerably vary. One is forced to conclude that the heat engendered was motivated as much by the implied criticisms of programmes of compensatory education and the wish fulfilling ideologies on which many of them were based as it was by what in fact was said. Odium theologicum is a poor friend to scientific discussion; everyone concerned with education, and particularly the most generously motivated environmentalists, should study this book.

[B250]

★JESSUP, GILBERT, AND JESSUP, HELEN. **Selection and Assessment at Work.** London: Methuen and Co. Ltd, 1975. Pp. 143. Cloth, 75p; paper, £1.00. *

[B251]

★JOBE, FRED W. **Screening Vision in Schools.** Newark, Del.: International Reading Association, 1976. Pp. 64. Paper, $3.75.

Read Teach 31(2):231 N '77. S. Alan Cohen. * At last a vision expert who appears free of allegiance to either side of the O.D.-M.D. vendetta agreed to explain vision to the International Reading Association. That lack of allegiance, however, does not grant validity to Jobe's attempt to set aside "visual perception" from "seeing." At least he defines his parameters by limiting his content to those aspects "of clear, comfortable vision and the factors that interfere with it." Despite good intentions, visual perception keeps creeping into his descriptions of how we see. Forgive him, for he redeems himself with a key description of our visual apparatus. It is, he says, a mechanism we use to change the world so that we can function adequately. How delightful that IRA dares to publish someone who clearly announces that "visual problems are not necessarily visual defects," but interpretations of functions that are inefficient responses to real world demands. Not only reading experts, but many O.D.'s and M.D.'s would do well to diagnose visual functioning rather than visual defects. A critical reader will detect some fascinating discrepancies between Jobe's descriptions of vision and of visual diagnosis. On the one hand, he explains the key visual functions of accommodation (adjusting the crystalline lens to get a sharp image) and convergence (moving the two eyes in some sort of efficient consonance, or perhaps more accurately, getting two inputs into a "single," efficient perception) as functions that "must act together with some elasticity between them." If either functions "at the edge of this elasticity limit," then either function or both can break down. A few pages later, on the other hand, Jobe describes one technique doctors use to treat accommodation by patching an eye, thereby removing the convergence demand. And then a chapter later he describes separate tests of convergence and acuity. If one is a function of the other, how do we end up measuring or treating one function without the other? Is Jobe a faulty thinker? In fact, Jobe is accurate in both accounts. Yes, convergence and accommodation are interactive. Yes, doctors often act as if these functions operate in mutual isolation. And therein lies one reason for such problems as "overreferral" by sensitive reading clinicians and, perhaps, "underdiagnosis" by doctors who look at acuity eyeball by eyeball or at convergence without significant acuity demands. But that is just one of many problems that smart readers can consider in Fred W. Jobe's fine little book about vision. Read it.

[B252]

★JOHNS, JERRY L.; GARTON, SHARON; SCHOENFELDER, PAULA; AND SKIRBA, PATRICIA; COMPILERS. **Assessing Reading Behavior: Informal Reading Inventories—An Annotated Bibliography.** Newark, Del.: International Reading Association, 1977. Pp. 36. Paper, $2.00. *

[B253]

*JOHNSON, ORVAL G. **Tests and Measurements in Child Development: Handbook II, Vols. 1 and 2.** San Francisco, Calif.: Jossey-Bass Inc., Publishers, 1976. Pp. xiii, 674; xiii, 653. $50.00 per set. * For a review of the first handbook, see B254.

J Ed Res 70(6):344 Jl/Ag '77. Allan S. Cohen. * *Handbook II* represents a valuable update of unpublished measures of child development for social scientists in applied and research settings. It is perhaps most useful to professionals seeking brief introductions to the range of measures available on a particular topic. Appropriate choices between the measures described, however, will almost always require additional information from the references provided in the handbook. This should not be interpreted as a critical limitation of the handbook. To the contrary, researchers and clinicians seeking basic information on the alternatives available to measure a particular variable will find their task far easier through the use of the carefully constructed *Handbook II.* In combination with compilations of published measures, e.g., the *Mental Measurements Yearbook, Handbook II* provides an accessible resource for screening "what's available" and identifying "leads" for follow up, not necessarily for making final choices.

[B254]

JOHNSON, ORVAL G., AND BOMMARITO, JAMES W. **Tests and Measurements in Child Development: A Handbook.** San Francisco, Calif.: Jossey-Bass Inc., Publishers, 1971. Pp. xv, 518. $25.00. * For a review of the second handbook, see B253.

J Ed Meas 9(2):163–4 su '72. William J. Meyer. Johnson and Bommarito have performed an invaluable service to research workers concerned with children by producing this handbook. The job must certainly have been a tedious and a frequently frustrating one. They were able, however, to make available in one resource book tests and measurements that appear in a diversity of journals which could not possibly be covered by even the most diligent scholar. Their efforts uncovered over a thousand measures that have appeared in various periodicals during the ten-year period from 1956 through 1965 of which about one-third are included in this volume. * In addition to performing an excellent service to the profession, the book serves to provide the reader with a sense of where child workers have been placing their efforts during the past ten years. If one combines the cognitive and motor skills, brain injury, and sensory perception categories (a case could be made that the only basis for distinguishing these categories is on the basis of intended use rather than on some conceptual basis), it is clear that a high level of interest has been maintained in the general area of assessing intellectual competency. In addition,

it is encouraging to note that some seventy indices of personality and emotional characteristics appeared in the journals, suggesting, at least, the possibility that our theoretical conceptualizations in this area are beginning to bear operational fruit. On the other hand, it is also clear that interest in assessing physical attributes and attitudes and interests has been of relatively little concern to child workers. In summary, this handbook is extremely well done and should prove to be very useful to people engaged in research with children as well as to child workers in general.

[B255]

*JOLLES, ISAAC. **A Catalog for the Qualitative Interpretation of the House-Tree-Person (H-T-P), Revised 1971.** Los Angeles, Calif.: Western Psychological Services, 1971. Pp. ii, 192. Paper, $7.50. * For reviews of the earlier edition, see 5:B234 (2 excerpts).

[B256]

★JONES, ALAN, AND WHITTAKER, PETER. **Testing Industrial Skills.** New York: Halsted Press, 1975. Pp. xiii, 195. $14.50. *

B Brit Psychol Soc 29:310 S '76. Ray Adams. * a thorough workmanlike approach to the procedures and problems of developing performance tests. * A reader will find the advice is sensible and thorough, though not revolutionary. * a useful book for the beginning test designer or user to have at hand, in order to consult when needed. * an excellent supply of "selected further reading" for each chapter. * The reader who is concerned for the application of theory may not be completely satisfied. This book concentrates on the process of test development and is only concerned with the meta-theory of the subject. There is little attempt to show the application of theory in test development. This is a dangerous flaw. The appreciation and application of psychological theory is an essential ingredient in the development of performance tests for industrial skills. Clearly it is not possible to discuss all the relevant theories in a book of this size. It should be possible, at least, to illustrate the fact that the test developer can be guided by a good theory or model. Take the example of questionnaire design. There should be some indication of the existence of research in psycholinguistics and applied psychology on the comprehensibility of instructions. Testing development is not an independent subsection of applied psychology. If psychology is to progress it will be in the development of theory and its successful application to practical problems. The almost anti-theoretical start of this book could be moderated by the suggested further reading provided. Despite this one flaw, this text is a useful, practical source book. For the test developer or user, this book will be a useful reference.

Ed & Psychol Meas 36(1):228–9 sp '76. Brian Bolton. * a how-to-do-it manual for vocational instructors and industrial evaluation personnel. Yet, the examples and discussions of issues are fairly sophisticated, drawing extensively upon the authors' experience in performance testing and personnel assessment. The book is well organized, following an outline format generally, with lists of specific recommendations, questions, suggestions, and pros and cons of alternative procedures provided whenever feasible. * The eighth chapter begins with a good discussion of the relative merits and difficulties associated with criterion-referenced and norm-referenced interpretations of test performance * The strength of the book is clearly in its step-by-step organization and extensive use of illustrative material. Furthermore, the illustrations and examples were selected to avoid monotony * *Testing Industrial Skills* could be appropriately recommended to persons with little or no background in testing who are charged with responsibilities for assessing skill acquisition in vocational education and industrial training.

[B257]
★JONGSMA, EUGENE. **The Cloze Procedure as a Teaching Technique.** Newark, Del.: International Reading Association, 1971. Pp. 42. Paper, $2.25. *

[B258]
★KAHN, THEODORE C.; CAMERON, JAMES T.; AND GIFFEN, MARTIN B. **Methods and Evaluation in Clinical and Counseling Psychology.** Elmsford, N.Y.: Pergamon Press, Inc., 1975. Pp. xii, 329. Paper, $9.50; cloth, $15.00 *

Austral J Psychol 29(3):244–5 D '77. Kenneth R. Mitchell. * The contents of the thirteen chapters are by and large fairly sketchy, as I suppose they inevitably must be when you attempt to cover: the construction and use of psychological tests (12 pages); intelligence tests; evaluation and testing of children (11 pages); normals, behavioural disorders and differential diagnosis; neuroses; psychoses; organic brain impairment; approaches in counselling and psychotherapy (21 pages); new approaches in counselling and psychotherapy; psychological tests in vocational and educational guidance; clinical psychology, medicine, educa-

tion and law; and finally, five case illustrations (20 pages). The authors assert that they tried to answer as fully and clearly as possible the question: "What do modern practicing psychologists do, and how do they do it?" I think they failed, but to explain why would consume space better used in other ways. Suffice to say, that the authors totally ignored many functions and activities now accepted as part of the daily work role of the clinical and counselling psychologist, e.g., developmental and psycho-educational teaching, programme development, supervision and evaluation, social engineering, consultation, training non-professionals, etc. In my opinion this book does not achieve its major purpose nor does it succeed any better with its secondary aim, the exploration of new trends in clinical psychology and counselling—I do not regard sensitivity training, transactional analysis or biofeedback as new trends! Not recommended reading.

J Pers Assess 41(6):657–8 D '77. Eric C. Theiner. * The authors' purpose was to provide an overview of the current field of practicing psychology. And their approach has more than usual breadth since each of the authors adds a perspective that is rather different from that of the ordinary clinical practitioner. * The breadth of the book is wide, and so falls heir to what that necessarily implies. The text is a true overview in some areas, in others, quite specific. * the text ranges from providing contributions as purely philosophical as Kahn's discussion on Hominology, to as specific as giving "Psychoneurotic Indications on the Rorschach." The book will....be one of the most controversial designed for its intended audience. * On the one hand, the authors pay minimal attention to the hallowed traditions of such books—Freud has only five page mentions. On the other, there are some discussions that can be described only as radical departures from a scientific text. Professor Kahn has long enjoyed the reputation of being an iconoclast, and for good reason. Salted away throughout the text are statements guaranteed to set the teeth of many of the field's practitioners on edge. * The greatest contribution provided by this text is perhaps....the potential for expansion—mind expansion—in the most literal sense. The text is easier to read as one proceeds about it naively; to approach it with foregone conclusions makes the job that much harder. Many of the suggestions made in this text may well be seminal. And it is in this way that perhaps the book's value becomes more apparent. It is too glib to suggest that many of these concepts may be tradition breaking, but at the least, there is here much food for thought. The book makes a signal contribution. It proceeds at a pace which will be seen by its main audience as gently instructive. Many psychologists may occasionally find parts prosaic. Then at some point it changes. The nonpsychologist will blithely continue to feel gently instructed— and the traditionalists will go right up the wall. For the audience it is intended, the book is a good one. But perhaps its greatest value is for us—readers of journals like this. Not because of the ninety percent of the book which will be fairly apparent, but for the ten percent where their conceptual frameworks will feel assaulted. In closing, the book would be a solid addition to the library of most of today's psychologists. Moreover, perhaps it can be of more use to professionals who have been in the field long enough to have their engrams sated with traditional material, than for the audience for whom it is written—it is certainly capable of having a much greater impact on them, than the more naive. One thing for sure, it will stimulate an interest in areas not typically touched in ordinary training.

[B259]

★KAMIN, LEON J. **The Science and Politics of I.Q.** Hillsdale, N.J.: Lawrence Erlbaum Associates, Inc., Publishers, 1974. Pp. viii, 183. $10.95. *

B Brit Psychol Soc 28:352 Ag '75. H. J. Eysenck. Kamin is the only psychologist of note who can be said to be a 100% environmentalist, denying completely the determination of individual differences in IQ by hereditary causes. He sets out his reasons for doubting the evidence adduced for the orthodox beliefs in this book. Ideally, what should have been done would have been to state the many divergent types of proof which have been used, take each in turn, and submit it to a critical review, bearing in mind that alternative theories must also be stated clearly and coherently, so that a choice between competing systems of explanation becomes possible. This Kamin has not done. Instead, he has concentrated on a few arbitrarily chosen areas and persons, going in great detail into the chosen studies and criticizing them for various errors of omission and commission. * It is a pity that Kamin has shirked the larger labour; critics of orthodox positions are much

needed in science, and some at least of Kamin's attacks do find their target. Inevitably perhaps, studies planned and carried out 50 years ago do not stand up to comparisons with sophisticated modern methods; equally inevitably, many studies do not give all the information one might, with the benefit of hindsight, have liked them to contain. At times, errors have been committed, and these have occasionally found their way into textbooks and other secondary sources. A scavenging operation of the kind conducted by Kamin must therefore be welcome, and workers in the field will be grateful to him for pointing out weaknesses and errors which may have escaped their attention. Additionally, Kamin at times directs attention to data and to relations which have not previously been regarded as important; thus he shows that correlations between a twin and non-twin sibs are particularly low, suggesting some twin-interaction may have been responsible. Points such as these are valuable, and experts will need to consider them. However, Kamin does not see his book in this context; he sees it as *disproving* the claims of orthodoxy that heredity has been shown to play an important part in producing individual differences in IQ. This it does not do, although many readers predisposed to welcome such a demonstration may think that this is what it has done. The arbitrary choice of some topics, and the omission of others, make it impossible to take such claims seriously. There is no mention, for instance, of the remarkable regression effects which provide such a striking proof of inheritance, as well as making possible estimates of heritability. * there are many errors of commission, as well as of omission, details of which cannot be given in such a short review. The most desirable effect of his book would be if it sent readers back to the original literature, their minds made more critical by his strictures. I doubt very much if they will emerge agreeing with his conclusion. [See original review for additional critical comments not excerpted.]

[B260]

*KARMEL, LOUIS J., AND KARMEL, MARYLIN O. **Measurement and Evaluation in the Schools, Second Edition.** New York: Macmillan Publishing Co., Inc., 1978. Pp. xvii, 525. $13.95. * For reviews of the first edition, see 7:B353 (2 excerpts).

[B261]

★KARSON, SAMUEL, AND O'DELL, JERRY W. **A Guide to the Clinical Use of the 16 PF.** Champaign, Ill.: Institute for Personality and Ability Testing, 1976. Pp. xiii, 160. Paper, $5.95. *

J Pers Assess 41(5):552–3 O '77. J. M. Schuerger, M. Powers, and E. Franklin. * For a clinical or industrial psychologist already using the 16PF, the two or so hours required to read the guide should be more than justified by the sense of "hands-on" experience provided by the authors' perspective, background and style. A person unfamiliar with the 16PF may well find it the best general introduction to the test. It does not provide the wealth of research data available on occupational, clinical, and educational uses available in the *Handbook,* but does illustrate the breadth of coverage of the human personality by this inventory. From the perspective of a second-year clinical student, the book was "clear in style and structure, a guide rather than a tedious reference," which "made the 16PF immediately available clinically, yet served as an entree to more technical details available from other sources." In tone the book is familiar and concrete, as the authors merge psychodynamic concepts, research findings, and literary or historical personages with factor descriptions and clinical implications. * the authors were unable (despite some careful sidestepping), to avoid the sexism inherent in a consistent psychoanalytic point of view, primarily in discussions of dominance (factor E) and rebelliousness (factor Q_1). If there were any typos or demonstrable inaccuracies, they escaped notice. The authors do a friendly, well-organized, interesting tour of the 16PF against a clinical backdrop.

[B262]

★KEEPES, JILLIAN MALING, AND RECHTER, BERNARD. **English and Its Assessment.** Hawthorn, Vic., Australia: Australian Council for Educational Research Ltd., 1972. Paper, Aus. $3.60. *

[B263]

★KELLOGG, MARION S. **What to Do About Performance Appraisal, Revised Edition.** New York: AMACOM, 1975. Pp. x, 209. $10.95. *

Personnel Psychol 29(2):290–2 su '76. Oliver H. London. * First, Kellogg asks if appraisals are ethical and answers affirmatively. Not only are they ethical, but I feel it would be unethical not to do appraisals. * The second question then becomes, "Are the appraisals valid?" Kellogg suggests some general approaches to develop appraisals, but nothing specific. This is one of the big drawbacks of the entire book. She continually gives general ways to attack a problem, which sound good. However, by the time you try to make them specific, you don't know how. * It would have been helpful to suggest some of the typical job analysis techniques because they form the basis of performance appraisal. * Third, Kellogg sees the various uses of performance appraisal as part of one smooth system. It can be used for both coaching and salary purposes. However, Cummings et al. (1973) and Porter et al. (1975) agree with one another that major conflicts arise from these two purposes. * Fourth, I might suggest the method of more involvement on the part of the employee. Kellogg and I agree there should be feedback. The extent of that feedback is where we disagree. * I feel that input on the part of the subordinate is very important. He has different information than his superior because he is working on his job all the time. His superior is not. And certainly he has a different perspective of the job. Another very important reason for feedback is that if it is done properly it really does lead to improved performance. In a larger sense one important reason for feedback from the subordinate is participation * Fifth, Kellogg gives exhibits at the end of her book on sample forms that can be used in various parts of the appraisal system. Nowhere in the book does she discuss the various kinds of appraisal systems and the advantages and disadvantages of them. * Sixth, a crucial aspect of any appraisal system is the interview that should go along with it. Kellogg states at one point that in some situations it might be better not to tell the subordinate the conclusions the superior has come to. I feel the superior should be as open and honest as possible. The entire appraisal system can fail if the appraisal interview is not handled properly. * My review has sounded negative for two reasons: (1) it is easier to write about the negative and (2) I feel there are more negative parts to the book than positive. However, there are several really good aspects to the book. The emphasis on feedback is very important. The system of appraisal Kellogg discusses is valuable. Motivation is certainly the key to performance and therefore appraisal. In order to appraise anything you need to have criteria. My criteria have been the goal Kellogg stated in the flyleaf and my knowledge and experience with performance appraisal. The first is easy to objectify; the second is not. Perhaps your criteria would be different from mine. *

[B264]

★KIBLER, ROBERT J.; CEGALA, DONALD J.; BARKER, LARRY L.; AND MILES, DAVID T. **Objectives for Instruction and Evaluation, Revised Edition.** Boston, Mass.: Allyn & Bacon, Inc., 1974. Pp. x, 203. Paper, $5.95.

Ed & Psychol Meas 34(3):728–31 au '74. Joseph H. Sasfy and Morris Okun. * Given the persuasiveness with which the book proselytizes for the use of objectives and the thoroughness of its description of the implementation of objectives, I would expect this book to serve as sort of a "mini-bible" for those attempting to change the attitudes and instructional techniques of practitioners. The strength of the book's presentation lies in its wholistic approach to the use of objectives in instruction. The book makes it clear that the benefits that can be realized through the use of objectives depends on the rigorous and systematic implementation of objectives within an integrated instructional system. The detailed descriptions of techniques of writing objectives, adapting them to behavioral taxonomies, and devising appropriate criterion-referenced evaluation procedures should help teachers reach this goal. This book, in addition to being a practical manual for teachers, could serve as a useful supplementary text in a variety of education courses. The clarity of the text and its organization make it accessible to all levels of college students. Its systematic and logical presentation of the design and implementation of an instructional model renders the book a useful model, in itself, of the type of systematic and wholistic thinking teachers and educators should engage in when dealing with the instruction and learning process. One reservation I have about the book concerns itself with the book's tendency to gloss over some of the more serious educational and societal issues tied to the concepts of accountability and instructional objectives. This reviewer has the suspicion that much of the freedom teachers and educators have enjoyed has been related to the broad and generally innocuous and acceptable nature of educational objectives. If it becomes clear that behavioral goals can be successfully stated and attained for all types of outcomes, perhaps society will start to look at teachers and their role in a much different way.

[B265]

★KIRBY, JONELL H.; CULP, WILLIAM H.; AND KIRBY, JOE. **Manual for Users of Standardized Tests.** Bensenville, Ill.: Scholastic Testing Service, Inc., 1973. Pp. x, 179. Paper, $6.50. *

Meas & Eval Guid 9(1):35 Ap '76. Sandra T. Franklin. If you need both a programmed review of statistics in order to interpret standardized test data as well as a study of testing ethics through guidelines applied to a variety of cases then this manual may be a *Must* for you. * There are evaluations of two tests in the appendix that are applications of the authors' "self-estimate procedure for test interpretation." The procedure can be adapted for use with parents and teachers as well as students. Although the *MUST* publishers' own Educational Development Test is used as an example, its use is not offensive. In another example the procedure is applied to the General Aptitude Test Battery. * could be a welcome addition to many bookshelves.

[B266]

KIRK, SAMUEL A., AND KIRK, WINIFRED D. **Psycholinguistic Learning Disabilities: Diagnosis and Remediation.** Urbana, Ill.: University of Illinois Press, 1971. Pp. x, 198. Paper, $2.95. *

J Learn Dis 5(4):222–3 Ap '72. Margaret Scheffelin. * The Kirks have written a single-purpose book, useful for a wide variety of readers. The single purpose is to help people help children overcome their learning problems. The people range from teachers to school psychologists to college professors to parents to legislators to attorneys. Many myths have grown up about the words "learning disabilities" and "psycholinguistic." This brief, easy-to-read and remember book provides the reader with a clear, non-technical, and quotable series of descriptions and explanations. Two kinds of materials are presented on the Illinois Test of Psycholinguistic Abilities (ITPA). One kind is developmental and technical, meant primarily for test protocol interpreters and for researchers. The other kind is descriptive and interpretive, meant for teachers, consultants, and parents, as well as test interpreters, psychologists, educational specialists and researchers. * The book provides a systematic procedure for the study of an individual child, tracking clues for possible hidden trouble areas and collecting data to assist in organizing systematic remedial instruction. Properly applied, and widely used at an early age these procedures could benefit thousands of youngsters who now enter the schools poorly prepared for academic and social learning. * It gives me great professional pleasure to state that *Psycholinguistic Learning Disabilities* is the book of the year on learning disabilities of children.

Psychol Sch 9(4):460–1 O '72. Gilbert R. Gredler. * There is a helpful discussion of three types of learning disorders: academic, nonsymbolic, and symbolic. The chapter on selected research findings will acquaint the reader with some of the important investigations conducted with the ITPA. The section on the diagnostic process, while short, gives some helpful hints as to how to determine that a problem exists and describes correlates of disabilities. In addition to the ITPA test manual, the chapter on patterns of disabilities will aid the school psychologist to arrive at a diagnostic formulation. The section on specific guidance for remediation gives a helpful introductory paragraph on the major areas of the ITPA and their meaning for the educational process of the child. * Overall, this is a book that should be utilized by any school psychologist who wants to obtain a better understanding of the importance of the language process in the child. * Insufficient attention is paid to the fact that recommendations must be part of a specific program of remediation with constant feedback so that progress in strengthening a deficit area can be noted. In addition, there must be provision for on-going evaluation of the child's performance in academic areas. While the authors correctly state that the child's response to a series of learning situations should be noted in order to pinpoint areas in which he succeeds and fails, much more emphasis needs to be placed on this concept. Plans for individualized instruction (the diagnostic-remedial teacher plan, the resource room plan, the individualized class and the two-teacher class) are covered in one page. What is needed is more discussion of how the above plans have been combined with the specifics of ITPA remediation. * some psychologists have questioned the emphasis on the various deficit areas that Kirk and Kirk champion and emphasize rather an attentional deficit syndrome that could account for such deficits * Despite this glossing over of causative or "correlative" factors, Kirk and Kirk have put together a helpful book for those who want a better understanding of the use of the ITPA with children.

[B267]

★Kirk, Winifred D. **Aids and Precautions in Administering the Illinois Test of Psycholinguistic Abilities.** Urbana, Ill.: University of Illinois Press, 1974. Pp. v, 119. Paper, $2.95. *

[B268]

★Kline, P., Editor. **New Approaches in Psychological Measurement.** London and New York: John Wiley & Sons Ltd., 1973. Pp. ix, 269. * *Out of print.*

Brit J Ed Psychol 45(1):100 F '75. P. E. Vernon. * This collection of chapters, all but one by British authors, does focus on a theme which is likely to be useful to students and their lecturers, since new developments in testing occur so frequently that it is difficult to keep up with them. However, it does not quite come off because of inevitable unevenness in the way different authors approach their sub-topics. Five out of eight chapters admirably fulfil their purpose, but two are much more in the nature of research articles which, though interesting, take up far too much space and might have better appeared as journal articles. J. Holley's validation of the Rorschach by using Q technique factorisation is important, but unnecessarily detailed. And A. Gale, after making a good case for psychophysiological approaches to personality, requires 46 pages to analyse why a dozen experiments on the EEG and extraversion give contradictory results. The eighth chapter (actually the first in the book), by P. Levy gives a brilliant survey of developments in test theory. But parts of it are too technical for any who have not taken advanced courses in psychometrics and, therefore, likely to turn off aspiring readers. The five better balanced chapters are well worth the attention of educational psychologists. J. Butcher gives an able summary of "models" of intelligence (including Cattell's), of the heredity-environment controversy, and of creativity research. It is a pity that he was allowed only 23 pages. J. Hundleby, who has worked for some years with Cattell, provides a useful introduction to the latter's objective personality test batteries, including their difficulties as well as their merits. B. Semeonoff, well-known as an advocate of projective techniques, gives a scholarly and temperate review of the whole field (excluding only the standard Rorschach and TAT). D. Bannister and M. Bott have less novel material to present; but it is good for mental testers to be reminded of George Kelly's attacks on their trade, and there is a useful outline of the applications of the repertory grid method. Finally, the editor, P. Kline, takes up his favourite theme—the quantitative testing of psychodynamic hypotheses. The evidence, mainly from factorial studies, in favour of Freud's psychosexual stages,

Jungian typology, and other dynamic constructs, appears rather unconvincing, but at least shows that clinical and psychometric approaches can be combined.

Brit J Psychiatry 125:511 N '74. Lawrence Bartak. Most busy clinicians will have little time or appetite for huge compendia listing and evaluating psychological tests, such as the awe-inspiring volumes by Buros. Dr. Kline has produced a stimulating and useful book which is of manageable size and mostly written in clear and entertaining style. Specialist writers have each written on new developments in the field. * The coverage of the book is fairly selective (this reviewer's bias would have included chapters on assessment of children). However, within each chapter, reviews are cool, critical and reasonably comprehensive. There is constant examination of hard data and yet the book is happily free from those simplistic attempts to wish psychodynamic theory and practice away which often accompany moves to make us more scientific. This book is welcome and can be thoroughly recommended to both psychiatrists and clinical psychologists as an up-to-date collection of useful reference papers.

Brit J Psychol 66(4):538–9 N '75. Alan Dabbs. * The opening chapter by Professor Philip Levy is perhaps the most stimulating. He clearly sets out those questions every applied psychologist ought to be asking himself every time he employs a psychometric test. Levy argues that psychometric devices should be used to test hypotheses derived from observation rather than the normative test results serving as a generator for the production of a plethora of hypotheses. It is a chapter that merits inclusion as prescribed reading for all clinical and educational psychologists in training. The remaining contributions are of the literature survey type. J. D. Hundleby states: "in the area of objective tests of personality....the single test will disappear...." This is hardly surprising. The concept of personality has itself all but evaporated from my personal conceptual system. No doubt the tests in my cupboard will take rather long to turn to dust. Semenoff's chapter, "New Developments in Projective Testing," is discursive but oddly out of date when he speaks of the contribution of psychometrics to diagnosis and therapy. He suggests that projective techniques might be employed on the grounds of clinical expedience rather than claiming scientific validity, but he is never specific about the

kinds of questions these tests might answer. In contrast Jasper Holley presents a sophisticated statistical technique in his chapter, "Rorschach Analysis," which demonstrates that Rorschach responses can validly predict psychiatrists' discriminations between normals, neurotics and schizophrenics. One wonders why he bothered, though the statistical method bears further examination. Bannister tells us little new in his chapter, "Evaluating the Person." What is not said is that the interpretation of the grid matrix produced by any particular patient is as much a projective test for the psychologist as any TAT ever was. Bannister's validity safeguard would seem to be that he conveys the tentative grid analysis to the patient to see if he can make sense of it. The remaining contributions represent a degree of academic effort in that a great number of relevant publications are surveyed. Paul Kline in his chapter, "Assessment in Psychodynamic Psychology," concludes that "psychometrists with imagination and insight provide sound quantification into psychodynamic psychology...." This reviewer clearly is unimaginative and without insight. The Levy contribution apart, this book seems hardly worth £ 5.50.

J Pers Assess 39(2):184–5 Ap '75. Robert M. Allen. The reviewer of an edited book should tease out the common theme justifying the inclusion of the contributed chapters in a single volume. It would appear that the tie that binds is a critical and somewhat cynical view of current tests and testing procedures. Kline's rationale for this book is the effort to "scrutinize new developments in key areas of psychological measurement" (p. vii). In this limited sense Kline has achieved his objective. Most readers will be surprised and thoughtful about the "new" ideas and modifications of some of the traditionally accepted notions about psychological tests and measurements. The reader is cautioned to expect the pages to turn slowly. The style of writing, the rapid procession of ideas, the language itself, and the assumption of a prior body of knowledge converge to require reading and rereading to savor the depths of the concepts presented. Levy's chapter....makes a good case for the inadequacy of current tests and/or their usage. His overall message is clear: the present mode of test construction is test-centered and not people-centered. This reviewer felt the anti current-test bias of the author too keenly. However, Levy is not just critical. He is constructive in the wide variety of changes suggested for test-building rationales. Further, he calls for a break with the traditional concepts of validity and reliability and for an increased focus on the meaning of test items as they relate to validity criteria of a behavioral nature. In short, test people, not tests. The theme of "new" approaches to testing is extended in Holley's paper on Rorschach analysis. To describe this chapter as esoteric in content and difficult to understand is putting it mildly. Yet the basic concept is sound—to devise test procedures that are client-centered rather than test-centered is the name of this "new" game plan. Holley's defense of Rorschach's test in terms of people (and the varied quantitative manipulation of people's responses) has added, as a byproduct, a sense of validity to this test and, by extension, to other projective procedures used in the manner suggested in this chapter. Certainly this presentation is not addressed to the neophyte Rorschach Test user. "New" developments in projective testing reveal Semeonoff at his liberal understanding best. There is no condemnation of particular projective techniques, only evaluation. This, in itself, is sufficient to boost some and boot other tests (using the term "test" in the Mursellian, 1947, sense). His review of the development of projective procedures is intimately coupled with the characterization of each test as a useful tool in personality assessment. Aside from this brief presentation of tests, Semeonoff discusses in all too terse manner (due, no doubt, to editorially imposed space limitation) the issues of validity and reliability as these are used and abused in connection with projective test findings. * Semeonoff brilliantly makes the point that reliability is not equivalent to rigidity of responsiveness. * Kline's contribution focuses on the issues involved in assessment within the framework of psychodynamic psychology (read Freudian, neo-Freudian, and offbeat Freudian views). It is an interesting chapter somewhat not congruent with the thinking of Semeonoff and Holley * This volume is not for beginners in applied psychology. Its best audience would be those hardened testers who still have some flexibility for modifying their thinking about the objectives of personality assessment. Another group are those test authors and users who desire to buttress their arguments for a humanistic clinical view of human behavior that may not lend itself to easy computerization but

do adduce to better understanding. A final word—this is a good book. The ideas contained therein are not the unique property of British psychologists but these do deserve dissemination so as to bring about a naissance or renaissance of client-centered welfare to replace self-aggrandizing notoriety at the expense of good applied psychology.

[B269]

★KLINE, PAUL. **Psychological Testing: The Measurement of Intelligence, Ability, and Personality.** London: J. M. Dent & Sons Ltd., 1976. Pp. 168. £5.20. * (New York: Crane, Russak & Co., Inc. $10.50.)

Brit J Psychol 68(1):147–8 F '77. Chris Cullen. * for....the educated layman. * will not replace any of the more unusual sources to which practising clinicians will go for information. * I found three major criticisms. * I was not happy with the distinction he makes between fluid and crystallized ability, even though Cattell might believe it to be a real one. * My second major criticism is that he claims to be describing the Skinnerian approach to personality. In short, he is mistaken. * Finally, many will not be altogether happy with Kline's discussion of the social implications of psychological testing. * Notwithstanding these criticisms, I believe that Kline has written a useful and eminently readable book. His style, reflecting at times his background as a classicist, is witty and amusing. * The book points to some of the current controversies in psychology, and discusses clearly some of the uses and abuses of the more commonly used tests. It should help to dispel many of the false impressions the educated layman might have about psychology and psychologists, and is recommended for this. The price—which is steep for such a small book—might, however, prevent it from reaching the appropriate audience.

[B270]

KLOPFER, BRUNO; MEYER, MORTIMER M.; BRAWER, FLORENCE B.; AND KLOPFER, WALTER G. **Developments in the Rorschach Technique: Vol. 3, Aspects of Personality Structure.** New York: Harcourt Brace Jovanovich, Inc., 1970. Pp. xviii, 446. $12.50. *

J Pers Assess 37(5):494–5 O '73. A. I. Rabin. * Although Mayman's form-level scoring system has been used for quite some time by a number of workers, his "full dress" detailed presentation....is a highly desirable step. The description of the scores, the illustrative material and the supporting quantitative data, make it a useful contribution to those concerned with the systematic investigation of ego functioning by means of the Rorschach. The somewhat different approach to ego processes presented in the second chapter, by Meyer and Caruth, may be viewed as complimentary to that of Mayman. Their systematic integrative approach to the content, and the interrelating temporal aspects with cognitive and perceptual functions which result in seven ways of "evaluating ego processes," represent a very worthwhile contribution. By employing this approach, the clinician may certainly increase his diagnostic sensitivity; the researcher may find in it some useful hints for a more controlled examination of group data. With his usual stylistic felicity, Robert Holt discusses "artistic creativity and Rorschach measures of adaptive regression" in chapter 7. In addition to presenting a succinct up-to-date version of his scoring system which is introduced by a fine essay on the primary-secondary process dichotomy, he offers a review of nearly all studies that have employed it since he first introduced it. Although this chapter goes beyond the Holt and Havel (in Rickers-Ovsiankina) contribution some ten years earlier, it cannot serve as a substitute for the full version of the (mimeographed) manual. Mindness' chapter on the symbolic dimension in the Rorschach is much too brief to do justice to the subject. More integration with the existing literature would have aided the enterprise. The attempt to relate Piaget's developmental theory to the Rorschach method, by Wursten, is a good start. However, the articulation between the two is far from clear and in need of further effort and development. Two very "clinical" chapters present rather innovative developments. The potential of the "consensus Rorschach" is well illustrated in the chapter by Cutter and Farberow. One may not accept the nascent theoretical framework, but the demonstration of the method in the study of group and family dynamics is interesting, useful, and timely. Baker's illustration of the "post-diagnostic use of the Rorschach" points up a practical development in the field and the possible therapeutic potential of introducing the patient to his own responses. Actually, earlier work by Harrower, Holzberg, and others has introduced this approach. It is a pity that some of their findings are not integrated in the present chapter. Interesting clinical material is also introduced by Zellen who discusses Rorschach patterns in three generations of a family. The intergenerational transmission of pathology is illustrated by the author. Some methodological problems in the treatment of the data obtained will hopefully be worked out in the future. Finally, Brawer's last chapter which is a review of studies "in academic and vocational research" is hard to classify; it is neither clinical nor theoretical in the strict sense of the word, but it is useful. Although the subtitle of this volume (Aspects of Personality Structure) is a misnomer, and although many recent developments with the Rorschach have not been included (See Annual Review of Psychology and 6th & 7th Mental Measurements Yearbooks), there is much that is useful clinically and stimulating theoretically in this book. Rorschach workers can ill afford to ignore it.

[B271]

★KNAPP, ROBERT R. Handbook for the Personal Orientation Inventory. San Diego, Calif.: EdITS Publishers, 1976. Pp. xiv, 128. $12.95. *

[B272]

*KNOBLOCK, HILDA, AND PASAMANICK, BENJAMIN, EDITORS. Gesell and Amatruda's Developmental Diagnosis: The Evaluation and Management of Normal and Abnormal Neuropsychologic Development in Infancy and Early Childhood, Third Edition. New York: Harper & Row, Publishers, Inc., 1974. Pp. xxv, 538. $19.50. * For reviews of the first edition, see 3:277 (7 excerpts).

[B273]

*KOPPITZ, ELIZABETH MUNSTERBERG. The Bender Gestalt Test for Young Children, Vol. II: Research and Application, 1963–1973. New York: Grune & Stratton, Inc., 1975. Pp. xv, 205. $12.50. * For reviews of the first volume, see 7:B363 (2 excerpts).

J Pers Assess 41(2):188–9 Ap '77. Robert M. Allen. * complete coverage of the research, application, and theoretical views this test has evoked during the period of 1963 to 1973. * The 216 references provide a wealth of potential information about the Bender Test that a researcher and/or a practitioner might require. * For those new to the Bender Test, if there are any such, this volume may prove to be a boon, especially for the "how to" aspects of administering, scoring, and inference-making. Moreover, the less experienced may become so enamored of the quantitative approach to scoring the Bender Test protocol as to lead to cautious dependence on possible "global"-based flights of diagnostic formulation in interpretive fancies. Koppitz' second volume will go a long way to making the Bender Test less subjective. Both the test and the book are recommended reading and for a place in the clinician's roll call of test procedures.

[B274]
★KRUG, SAMUEL E., EDITOR. **Psychological Assessment in Medicine.** Champaign, Ill.: Institute for Personality and Ability Testing, 1977. Pp. xvi, 206. $17.25. *

[B275]
★KRYSPIN, WILLIAM J., AND FELDHUSEN, JOHN F. **Developing Classroom Tests: A Guide for Writing and Evaluating Test Items.** Minneapolis, Minn.: Burgess Publishing Co., 1974. Pp. xi, 168. Paper, $4.95. *

Ed & Psychol Meas 34(3):731–2 au '74. Nicholas M. Sanders. * With a few exceptions the reader will find this work a very clear and practical introduction to working on the kinds of tests most often used in the classroom. Discussions of terms, procedures and rationales are easy to follow, and the segmentation of text by tables, charts, other illustrations, and exercises is never distractingly abrupt, but instead provided for this reader a refreshing involvement throughout the book. The related exercises are well-chosen and feedback seems quite adequate. However, the concern expressed in earlier parts of the book that "higher order cognitive behaviors" are important objectives is not pursued in later item writing discussions. The reader is not guided in constructing multiple-choice tests for such objectives nor are there any examples of procedures for scoring essay tests for organization of ideas. These omissions are substantial ones, since the measurement of higher level objectives is presented as a major advantage of these types of items. This author also saw some shortcomings in the section on analyzing items. First, all examples and discussion is related to multiple-choice questions. Though Kryspin and Feldhusen do note that the techniques are applicable to other item types, examples would have allowed the reader to determine how. The second shortcoming to the item analysis section is its primary coverage of differentiation procedures, which represents a major departure from the general objectives-referenced testing orientation found elsewhere in the book. After presenting decision rules related to the difficulty level and discrimination index, the authors do engage in a discussion of the differentiation versus mastery issue, but are not very helpful in making practical suggestions for analyzing items for mastery tests. Thus, this section represents a discontinuity with the prior chapters that may leave the alert reader somewhat confused. Certainly if used in a course the above deficiencies may be easily overcome by supplemental information from the instructor. And, in balancing out the pros and cons of use of the book, I would say that the positive aspects far outweigh the negative.

[B276]
★KUDER, FREDERIC. **Activity Interests and Occupational Choice.** Chicago, Ill.: Science Research Associates, Inc., 1977. Pp. xvii, 326. $10.36. *

[B277]
★LACHAR, DAVID. **The MMPI: Clinical Assessment and Automated Interpretation.** Accompanied by 150 interpretive statement cards. Los Angeles, Calif.: Western Psychological Services, 1974. Pp. vii, 159. $21.50. *

[B278]
★LAKE, DALE G.; MILES, MATTHEW B.; AND EARLE, RALPH B., JR.; EDITORS. **Measuring Human Behavior: Tools for the Assessment of Social Functioning.** New York: Teachers College Press, 1973. Pp. xviii, 422. Paper, $9.75. *

J Ed Res 67(7):316 Mr '74. James Raths. * a valuable tool for researchers, especially those involved in advising graduate students in thesis research. The book is a catalog of measures and a compendia of research instruments. In a very brief introduction, the authors describe in convincing fashion the problems facing social science *vis-a-vis* measurement. * The volume is well indexed—by authors, by instruments, and by a "key word" procedure which allows users to look up by name terms they are interested in measuring. What is especially salutory about the authors' efforts is their recognition that still other compendia are needed. (A first reaction to the title of this reference might suggest that it deals with *all* human behavior.) Evidently, the authors see the need for additional works such as theirs. They, in a sense, challenge the rest of us to put together similar references for use by the research community. We will all benefit as the challenge is well met.

J Pers Assess 38(4):395–6 Ag '74. Robert M. Allen. * The authors set the stage for this tome by critiqueing the faults of testing as a tool of the psychologist. However, a close reading of their comments shows quite definitely that they are "test centered" rather than "client centered." Moreover, this reviewer is tempted to question their collective understanding of the real purpose of testing. * The authors, in their Introduction, shift between tests and test users so that it is difficult to follow their ideas. They cut too wide a swath with their generalizations about why support is not available for the testing movement. * Since the authors indicated that this tome contained tests which "By and large, have not been reviewed or discussed elsewhere in the recent literature," this reviewer checked the titles of the 84 tests with the *Seventh Mental Measurements Yearbook* (Buros, 1972). Of the 84 tests: 63 are listed in this book while 21 are listed in the *MMYB* for 1972. Moreover, since the reviewer confined the search to the 1972 edition, it is possible that more of the 63 are listed in previous editions of the *MMYB*. As a matter of fact, this reviewer recognized the names of several such tests as having been reviewed in the *Sixth MMYB* (Buros, 1965). The test compendia section contains a melange of tests, books, manuals and references for those social scientists and students of all facets of human behavior seeking a starting point from which to launch an investigation of background materials for a study or to select a battery of tests. Overall, there is a limited audience to which this book would appeal or even prove to be useful. But to those who need it, it can be valuable.

[B279]

★Lambert, Nadine M.; Wilcox, Margaret R.; and Gleason, W. Preston. **The Educationally Retarded Child: Comprehensive Assessment and Planning for Slow Learners and the Educable Mentally Retarded.** New York: Grune & Stratton, Inc., 1974. Pp. xiii, 197. Paper, $13.75. *

[B280]

Lanyon, Richard I., and Goodstein, Leonard D. **Personality Assessment.** New York: John Wiley & Sons, Inc., 1971. Pp. xiii, 267. $14.25. *

Am J Psychiatry 129(1):106–7 Jl '72. *Charles R. Shearn.* * The book is....well written and interesting. The excellent chapter summaries constitute an additional attractive feature. Perhaps most impressive of all is the continual reference to the journal literature pertaining to each of the many topics dealt with and the impartiality with which research findings are reported. * Lanyon and Goodstein have done a most impressive job in providing a comprehensive and up-to-the-minute survey of the field of personality assessment.

Brit J Psychol 63(4):650 N '72. Denis McMahon. * I would have preferred the behaviour samples and biographical data to have come earlier in the book. The only other small complaint—and this is essentially a reviewer's—is that one has to read every word because the authors don't waste any. Perhaps this is because one of the authors was an engineer before he came into clinical psychology. The parts I particularly liked were those on reliability and validity and the first-rate discussion on clinical versus actuarial prediction. The whole book could be read by those people whom British Association paper-givers are asked to bear in mind, "the intelligent educated laymen and scientists from other disciplines." The penultimate chapter of the book, devoted to the improper usage of personality assessment devices and the moral issues involved, should be obligatory reading for journalists and the over-enthusiastic pedlars of personality tests. The book has almost certainly taken a long time to compile, but it will stand for a very long time, even though research findings overtake the authors; the basis, the approach and temper of the whole book are *so* rational. *

Brit J Social & Clin Psychol 13(1):106–7 F '74. J. J. Kear-Colwell. * All the traditional approaches to personality assessment are well covered and discussed in a well-argued and rational fashion. However, the authors do not discuss in any detail more recent developments in personality assessment, e.g. the Repertory Grid and the Semantic Differential. The examples of tests used in the book tend to have a very strongly American bias but this does not detract from the usefulness of the text. Reliability, validity and response distortions are dealt with in some detail, but the arguments relating to reliability and validity are strictly related to traditional psychometrics and do not fully enter into many of the theoretical problems in the area of personality measurement. Towards the end of the book some of the problems of the clinical application of personality tests are again sensibly discussed by the authors, and the book finishes with a discussion of the types of criticism which have been levied, particularly in the United States, against the use of personality tests for the individual assessment. Finally there is a somewhat pedestrian discussion of new directions in personality assessment. *

Ed & Psychol Meas 32(2):530–3 su '72. David A. Hills. * In choosing to write an issues-oriented book, the authors will disappoint readers who are looking for a comprehensive review and evaluation of assessment instruments and technology. Also, those who are familiar with the authors' clinical experience and acumen may be unhappy with the absence of instruction in the applied arts of how to sensitively accumulate and meaningfully synthesize personality assessment data. However, for those who want a crisp, timely orientation to the theory and research in personality assessment, Lanyon and Goodstein should meet their expectations. * Lanyon and Goodstein commence with a review of the historical precursors of systematic personality assessment—astrology, palmistry, and phrenology. * the initial chapter is a pleasant and useful way to slip gently into the troubled waters * Next, the authors examine the fundamental logic of personality appraisal, establishing the assumptions underlying the various approaches to assessment. * Of particular value is a thoughtful discussion of the problems in establishing firm, standard definitions and concepts in personality assessment when personality theorists cannot agree among themselves upon a definition of personality. In succeeding chapters the authors expand upon current appraisal techniques and instruments as these derive from the rational-theoretical and empirical-statistical approaches. * Lanyon and Goodstein devote an entire chapter, and some unmistakable enthusiasm, to behavior sampling in natural settings, the unobtrusive observational methods, and biographic data collection. For the student or researcher who wants a compact review of both the research and arguments surrounding the nonstandard and improvizational personality assessment techniques, this chapter could be especially meaningful. The now traditional topics of reliability, validity, base rates, and clinical *vs* actuarial problems along with the political, ethical, and moral issues in personality assessment are soberly and conscientiously treated in several chapters. * *Personality Assessment* succeeds in the stated aim of the authors to provide a general introduction to personality assessment, and to lay the groundwork for clinical and research applications. Also, persons in fields allied to psychology and education seeking a relatively succinct summary and review of the current state of affairs in personality assessment should find their needs well met. *

[B281]

★LAUSTER, PETER. **The Personality Test.** London: Pan Books Ltd., 1976. Pp. 126. £0.70. (Radnor, Pa.: Chilton Book Co. Paper, $3.95; cloth, $6.95.) * (Originally published in German as *Der Personlichkeitstest.*)

[B282]

★LAZER, ROBERT I., AND WIKSTROM, WALTER S. **Appraising Managerial Performance: Current Practices and Future Directions.** New York: The Conference Board, Inc., 1977. Pp. ix, 122. Paper, $15.00. *

[B283]

★LEMKE, ELMER, AND WIERSMA, WILLIAM. **Principles of Psychological Measurement.** Chicago, Ill.: Rand McNally College Publishing Co., 1976. Pp. ix, 300. $15.95. * (Instructor's Manual. Pp. xi, 62. Gratis. *)

[B284]

★LEMON, NIGEL. **Attitudes and Their Measurement.** London: B. T. Batsford Ltd., 1973. Pp. viii, 294. £7.50. (New York: John Wiley & Sons, Inc. $11.50.) *

Brit J Social & Clin Psychol 14(4):437–8 N '75. Rex Rogers. * a predominantly empirically orientated text. As such, it can reasonably be expected to cater to the needs of those seeking an up-to-date treatment of the methodology of indexing attitudes. To a considerable extent it meets this expectation, covering a wide spectrum of approaches from interviewing through self-completion questionnaire techniques to indirect and unobtrusive methods—as well as issues of instrument validity and reliability. Further, many recent or sophisticated outcroppings of the attitude area find a place: salience, cognitive complexity, Guttman scales, factor analysis, latent structure analysis and multidimensional scaling. There are, however, equally areas where the text does not achieve a sense of roundness. Sparse consideration given, for example, to concepts such as values and beliefs that, while not in name "attitudes" are in fact essential adjuncts to the armourium of the investigator in this field. Again, the reader is largely left in the dark over areas like sampling, deception, subject attrition, missing data and other problems that beset the attitudinal researcher in the field. In the theoretical area Lemon's book proves consistently thinnest on the ground, both in terms of actual space and material. *Attitudes and Their Measurement* is certainly not the text for those who might wish to sample or to re-sample such positions as cognitive consistency approaches or dissonance theory, for example. The problem is implicit in the nature of the concept itself—attitude just does not lend itself to elucidation in 27 introductory pages. Unfortunately, this militates against any real bridging of one of Lemon's major concerns, "the widening gulf between the increasing sophistication of measurement and the relatively crude conceptualizations on which it is based...." Very much the same criticism can be raised against the other mainly theoretical chapter—that on attitudes and behaviour that ends the book. Without a detailed and very tight coverage of underlying theoretical and philosophical perspectives, this issue tends to degenerate into a mixture of depressing empirical studies on the one hand and ad hoc "explanations" of inconsistency on the other—a pitfall that the present treatment does not totally escape. Much that has been raised so far could perhaps be regarded as carping in the context of a text that does have many undoubted merits. Over one issue, however, the present reviewer feels that Lemon must be taken seriously to task. This is the almost total absence of any treatment of the crucially important issue of attitude change. Both at the conceptual level, where theories of attitude and theories of attitude change are almost synonymous, and at the methodological level where the meaning of change and its correct statistical treatment remain in dispute, change stands as the key issue. Without its consideration much that is important in the use of attitude measures as dependent variable in small-scale laboratory research and in longitudinal research must remain undiscussed. In conclusion, then, *Attitudes and Their Measurement* is a book whose title must be taken in a narrow sense rather than as implying a comprehensive overview. It nevertheless merits consideration as a text to consult alongside a number of recent publications that cater to specialized subsections of the attitude field (e.g. Triandis' *Attitude and Attitude Measurement,* Dawes' *Fundamentals of Attitude Measurement,* and Kiesler, Collins & Miller's *Attitude Change*).

[B285]

★LERNER, EDNA ALBERS. **The Projective Use of the Bender Gestalt.** Springfield, Ill.: Charles C Thomas, Publisher, 1972. Pp. viii, 86. Paper, $5.95; cloth, $10.75. *

[B286]

★LERNER, PAUL M., EDITOR. **Handbook of Rorschach Scales.** New York: International Universities Press, Inc., 1975. Pp. xii, 523. $25.00. *

[B287]

★LEVI, LENNART, EDITOR. **Emotions: Their Parameters and Measurement.** New York: Raven Press Publishers, 1975. Pp. xiii, 800. $33.00. *

[B288]

LEVINE, SAMUEL, AND ELZEY, FREEMAN F. **A Programmed Introduction to Educational and Psy-** **chological Measurement.** Belmont, Calif.: Brooks/ Cole Publishing Co., 1970. Pp. ix, 224. Paper. * *Out of print.*

J Ed Meas 9(2):159–60 su '72. Bert W. Westbrook. * The book contains extremes of quality in programming. A few frames are classic good examples of how to write a program. Unfortunately, in far greater abundance are frames which violate everything we know about S-R theories of learning. These frames require the student, at his first exposure to new material, to come up with the correct answer out of whole cloth, i.e., to guess blindly. The student faced with such tasks is very likely to guess incorrectly. After that, he has to undo the S-R connection he has established for himself and replace it with the one the authors had wanted but had not bothered to establish for him. This represents a serious weakness in the programming of the text. A large number of other types of poor examples exist. One type are those frames with meaningless foils in which the student can eliminate one choice as impossible without really knowing the material. Another irritating type of bad example occurs in the large number of careless typographical or grammatical errors. While such errors probably do not lessen the effectiveness of the program, they certainly do discredit it. Some bothersome format problems were found. Any attempt to identify a particular frame becomes clumsy because both page numbers and frame numbers have to be given. Also, the correct response to each frame is given immediately below the frame and must be kept covered until the response has been written. Such a format may not encourage some students to respond to the item before seeing the correct response. * In summary, it can be said that this book does have one very valid use (though certainly not that intended by its authors), namely, to serve as a concrete classroom example of what programming can do, at its best, and can't do, at its worst. The book should not be used in concentrated testing and measurement courses where it would likely create a false sense of security should the student consider himself "informed" after having digested the content of this text. In their introduction, the authors admit that an earlier version was found to have a fairly high error rate, due mainly to "typographical errors, poor wording, and poorly cued frames" (p. v). They go on to admit that no further testing was tried after their revisions, assuming that "undoubtedly the error rate for the present version of the text would be comparatively low." It is probably a more serious criticism to note that assumption (and hence the faulty research behind the text) than to point out all the features above, which are faulty precisely *because* the further examination which might have caught them was omitted.

[B289]

★LEVITT, EUGENE E., AND TRUUMAA, AARE. **The Rorschach Technique With Children and Adolescents: Applications and Norms.** New York: Grune & Stratton, Inc., 1972. Pp. 146. $12.50.

J Pers Assess 38(1):82–3 F '74. Robert Allen. This volume reflects, in a way, what is happening to the field of diagnostic evaluation (and is supported by the changes in names of this journal—from *Journal of Projective Techniques* to *Journal of Projective Techniques and Personality Assessment* to the current *Journal of Personality Assessment*) from knowing about the client or patient to knowing about the test period. The title of this book is a misnomer. The book does not focus on the use of the test with children and adolescents (the major portion of the title) but centers on the subtitle *Applications and Norms.* Even here the *Application* is thin. The emphasis is on *Norms.* There are 19 Tables and 15 Figures in the first 89 pages. Appendixes B, C, and E, 34 pages, contain 30 Tables and 17 Figures. The total numbers of statistical and graphic presentations are impressive: 49 Tables and 32 Figures. Unfortunately, these add little to understanding and interpreting the Rorschach Test protocol of a child or adolescent. Appendix D, Interpretation of Rorschach Factors by the "Systematizers" (actually an adaptation from a previous publication by the senior author, Levitt, 1972), is a definite contribution to the interpretation of the inkblot test factors *with no special reference to children, adolescents or adults.* Dr. Walter Klopfer's Foreword has high praise for this book. This reviewer disagrees that there is a value in it other than archival. It has missed its mark by a wide margin despite occasional references to children and adolescents beyond the chapter on administration. It would have been more appropriate as a *Psychological Bulletin* article. Furthermore, this reviewer cannot agree that the Rorschach technique has fallen from grace because of poor research. Rather, the finger should be pointed scornfully to the physical model into which the experi-

mental purists have pushed the Rorschach Test researcher. In place of the traditional "validity, reliability, objectivity and standardization" cliches perhaps it is time to recognize that research in human behavior still remains at the level of connotation and never has been, nor can it be, at the level of denotation. The latter fits well with the physical model. The former requires a new approach—the behavioral model. The suggestions by Cattell (1964) regarding the restructuring of the concept of reliability to apply "across occasions," "across tests," and "across people" would be more suitable to deriving conclusions regarding the usefulness of the Rorschach technique than the statistically manipulated raw score procedures prevalent in the Rorschach Test literature and in "how-to" books. This book has been written in terms of the physical model. Therefore the child and the adolescent as phenomenological focii have been neglected. Few clinicians will find this volume helpful for interpreting a child's or adolescent's inkblot protocol. It may be a boon to the statistically oriented researcher.

[B290]

★LEWIS, D. G. **Assessment in Education.** London: University of London Press Ltd., 1974. Pp. ix, 198. Paper, £1.60; cloth, £3.75. * (New York: Halsted Press. $12.50.)

Ed & Psychol Meas 37(2):559–60 su '77. Ronald K. Hambleton and Linda L. Cook. * provides an excellent review of the diverse types of educational tests available. The emphasis is on the principles of constructing different types of instruments. The reader is introduced to the intricacies of test development and testing problems in a non-technical and highly informative manner. Major strengths of the book include the author's insights and knowledge of the field which are reflected in the depth of coverage of the material. Basically, we liked the book very much. It is well-written, technically accurate, and interesting. In fact, the author has an engaging style of writing that makes it hard to put the book down. Certainly this was an unexpected pleasure for us to have such an experience reading a tests and measurements text! * The major limitation of the book for North American readers is that the author provides a British view of testing and testing problems. * Another shortcoming of the book is that it seems strangely out of date. Intelligence testing is discussed with no references, for example, to Jensen's work on the heredity/environment issue. Assessment in the affective domain, which has become so popular in the U.S., is only briefly discussed. The topics of test bias and content bias, and the broader topic of social and ethical consequences of testing, which has been so hotly debated in the press and the professional journals, are hardly discussed. The area of criterion-referenced testing receives only a brief mention in the book although there have been a large number of papers written on the topic, many criterion-referenced tests developed, and considerable discussion on the relative merits of norm-referenced tests and criterion-referenced tests. In fairness, the book is short and obviously was not written to provide a comprehensive coverage of the testing field. On the other hand, we feel the book as it is written may provide a narrow view of testing, at least as the testing field is being developed in Canada and the United States at the present time.

[B291]

★Lezak, Muriel Deutsch. **Neuropsychological Assessment.** New York: Oxford University Press, 1976. Pp. xvii, 549. $16.95. *

[B292]

*Lien, Arnold J. **Measurement and Evaluation of Learning, Third Edition.** Dubuque, Iowa: Wm. C. Brown Co. Publishers, 1976. Pp. xvi, 423. $9.95. * For reviews of the first edition, see 7:B387 (2 excerpts).

[B293]

*Lindvall, C. M., and Nitko, Anthony J. **Measuring Pupil Achievement and Aptitude, Second Edition.** New York: Harcourt Brace Jovanovich, Inc., 1975. Pp. xi, 237. Paper, $6.95. * For reviews of the first edition, see 7:B393 (2 excerpts).

Ed & Psychol Meas 35(3):739-40 au '75. Max D. Engelhart. * There is brief, but adequate, discussion of such characteristics of tests as validity, reliability, objectivity, and comprehensiveness, but no mention of machine scoring or analysis. * Chapter 4 explains the construction of teacher-made tests. It is most adequate with reference to rules for writing different types of objective items, but least adequate with reference to the production of thought-provoking exercises. Chapter 5 is devoted to the interpretation of test scores. It includes brief discussion of the difference between criterion-referenced and norm-referenced testing and brief, but adequate, explanations of percentile rank, mean, standard deviation, standard scores, normal distributions, and stanine scores. Table 5.4 presents excellent comparison of various kinds of norm-referenced scores. In Chapter 6 there is excellent elementary explanation of coefficients of correlation and of the kinds of test validity and of the means of assessing test reliability. * With some supplementation, this text would be an excellent basis of instruction for an introductory course in educational and psychological measurement.

[B294]

★Lippey, Gerald, Editor. **Computer-Assisted Test Construction.** Englewood Cliffs, N.J.: Educational Technology Publications, 1974. Pp. xii, 244. $13.95. *

J Ed Meas 12(4):294-5 w '75. Tse-Chi Hsu and Robert Glaser. This book deals with techniques for classifying, storing, assembling and printing items through computer assistance. It is concerned with test production and not with strategies of item construction or computer-assisted tailored testing, topics that might be implied by its title. The introductory chapter by Lippey contains an overview of test preparation functions which can be performed by a computer: (a) item banking, (b) item generation, (c) item attribute banking, (d) item selection, and (e) item printing. Most of these functions are discussed more fully in subsequent chapters of the book. Although the chapters were prepared by different authors, they are well integrated and form a concise and easy to read book. * the authors survey the test construction systems already in operation and compare alternative approaches and their possible pitfalls. The book offers an excellent survey of computer-assisted test construction systems currently in operation. A virtue of the book is its use of examples and reported experiences in many of the chapters rather than reliance on abstract conceptualizations. * Unfortunately, individualized tests cannot be produced from an item bank alone. To realize the potential of computer-assisted test construction, one must go beyond the concept of an item bank to concepts of online testing and data structures for instructional management. * The authors succeed well in describing computer uses for item classification, storage, and retrieval and for test production. The major shortcoming of the book is the authors' failure to consider whether their stated objectives for computer use might not be adequately justified both in terms of realizing the potential of computer support and in terms of cost effectiveness.

[B295]

★Liungman, Carl G. **What Is IQ? Intelligence, Heredity and Environment.** London: Gordon Cremonesi Ltd., 1975. Pp. vi, 234. Paper, £2.50. (New

York: Atheneum Publishers. Paper, $5.95.) * (First published as *Myten Om Intelligensen*, 1972.)

[B296]

★Loehlin, John C.; Lindzey, Gardner; and Spuhler, J. N. **Race Differences in Intelligence.** San Francisco, Calif.: W. H. Freeman & Co., 1975. Pp. xii, 380. Paper, $8.50; cloth, $16.00. *

Brit J Psychol 66(4):521–2 N '75. C. O. Carter. Loehlin, Lindzey and Spuhler, two psychologists and a human geneticist, are greatly to be commended for discussing the controversial topic of racial differences in intelligence with dispassionate competence. * On the issue of whether intelligence is best viewed as single general capacity, or a series of special abilities that tend to be positively intercorrelated, the authors comment that most of the time it does not matter. On heritability and the analysis of variance of intelligence test score the authors explain clearly the main concept and discuss the possible contributions of covariance, interaction, epistasis and assortative marriage. The authors make the important point that an estimate of heritability of a character refers to a particular trait in a particular population at a particular time. They discuss the limitations of measurements of heritability and note that such measurements are available at present mainly for Caucasian populations in the United States and Europe. They point out that estimates of broad heritability mostly lie between 0·60 and 0·85, and in an appendix dispose effectively of a recent claim that the data are consistent with zero heritability. The authors stress that high heritability of a trait within a population does not necessarily imply that no environmental training can modify that trait, but does imply that minor changes in environmental factors that already vary widely in a population are not likely to produce large changes in the levels of the trait. They also rightly stress that estimates of heritability within a population provide little, if any, information about the heritability of differences between the means of sub-populations. They note, however, that high within-group heritability does suggest that, if the between-group differences are largely environmental, the critical environmental factor concerned is likely to be one which sharply contrasts the groups. Such a factor would be racial prejudice. The algebra of heritability calculations is given in an appendix. In part II the authors summarize the observed differences in mean test score between races in America—essentially a significantly higher mean in Whites and Orientals than in Blacks and Amerindians. They then discuss the small amount and equivocal nature of the evidence that is yet available on the aetiology of these group differences. There is no consistent evidence of differences in heritability within the white and black populations of the U.S. There is no evidence that high scoring Blacks tend to be those with a substantial amount of white ancestry; but the last research study of this type was carried out nearly 30 years ago. The illegitimate offspring in Germany of white and black American soldiers do not show any significant differences in mean intelligence test score, suggesting no genetic difference between these particular samples of the white and black U.S. populations. On the whole Black-White differences have shown little change over several decades either in school children or military recruits; but some sub-populations have shown marked changes over this period, demonstrating that environmental changes can substantially alter the mean level of a group. With respect to the age at which racial differences appear, most studies show that differences on test score are well marked by 3 to 4 years of age, but not present at 1 or 2 years of age. This may well be because tests before the age of 3 or 4 do not measure "intelligence." During the school years the Black-White differences remain in general unchanged, though the scores of both white and black rural children fall over this period in comparison with urban white and black children. Socio-economic status (SES) is correlated with race in the United States. Those who regard SES differences in intelligence test score as largely due to environmental factors would see some of the Black-White differences as reflecting differences in SES grouping. It is, however, plausible to attribute SES differences at least in part to genetic differences, since social mobility up or down in each generation will be in part dependent on intelligence. In contrast there is no *a priori* reason to suppose that racial differences in one particular direction should be in part genetic. Further, mean test scores of Blacks are lower than those of Whites within each SES group. Black children of parents of high SES status tend to regress towards the black mean and white children towards the white mean; but the authors correctly point out that this would be expected whether the variation is due to genetic or environmental factors. Studies of racial profiles of intelligence are of interest, though again do not contribute to the main problem of the aetiology of the differences. Black children tend to score relatively well in verbal tests, less well in reasoning, and poorly in number and space tests. This is seen in both middle and lower SES groups, and is the opposite to the pattern seen in Amerindian and Oriental children. The latter often surpass Whites in numerical and spatial tests. In the last section of part II and an appendix the authors give a full account of the possible relationship of nutrition and intelligence. Here the authors appear to give too much weight to the possible effects of malnutrition on intelligence, perhaps as a result of experience limited to the United States, though they rightly note that some populations keep healthy and active (and intelligent) on food intakes which are grossly inadequate by current U.S. standards. In part III the authors summarize the empirical findings and state their main conclusions. These are that observed racial differences are in part environmental, in part genetic and in part due to inadequacies of the tests themselves. They stress, however, that racial differences must be seen in the perspective that the major part of variation is within and not between racial groups. They also emphasize that any differences observed should not be felt as a humiliation and should not be the occasion of a denial of opportunity in education, employment or social participation. They point out, however, that if the aim is to reduce race differences in intelligence test scores it is important to know the cause. The effect of some genetic differences might perhaps be more easily modified than environmental differences; but first the specific genetic and environmental factors must be elucidated. For the design of educational policies the authors stress that research into individual differences is more important than research into near-race differences. This book is much to be commended for technical competence and objectivity. Unfortunately, there are too few data to resolve the main issue, and indeed it is difficult to see how experiments that are presently practicable could be devised to resolve the issue in a way that would satisfy the scientists.

[B297]

★Loret, Peter G.; Seder, Alan; Bianchini, John C.; and Vale, Carol A. Anchor Test Study: Equivalence and Norms Tables for Selected Reading Achievement Tests (Grades 4, 5, 6). DHEW Publication S/N 1780-01312. Washington,

D.C.: U.S. Government Printing Office, 1974. Pp. ix, 92. Paper, $1.90. * For a later edition, see B298.

J Ed Meas 12(3):214-6 f '75. Margaret Fleming. * The study not only equated the tests, but also restandardized them to produce both individual norms and school mean norms. The following seven operations are some of those which the study has made possible for the three areas included in the eight reading tests—vocabulary, comprehension, and total reading: (1) An individual's raw score on one test can be converted to an equivalent raw score on any of the seven other tests. (2) An individual's raw score may be related to the national percentile rank and/or stanine based on Anchor Test Study individual score norms. (3) Publisher percentile ranks can be translated to Anchor Test national percentile ranks. (4) Anchor Test Study percentile ranks for individual pupils can be compared for the eight reading tests. (5) School mean raw scores for different tests can be compared via Anchor Test Study percentile ranks. (6) Mean raw scores of two or more schools using different tests can be compared via Anchor Test Study percentile ranks. (7) Summary data on one test—e.g., the median raw score, the 25th percentile, the 75th percentile—may be converted to the raw score of another test. As can be seen, a critical condition for use of the tables is the availability of raw scores for individual pupils or average raw scores of the schools to be compared. Comparisons are made through three types of tables: equivalency tables, tables of individual score norms, and tables of school mean norms. Directions for use of these tables are clear. Concise examples are included to demonstrate the steps to be taken in the various score conversion problems. * The manual of tables provides the information it purports to provide. Practitioners should be able to manage the translations with the information at hand. To the degree that they wish to translate the scores of the particular tests, editions, and grade levels involved in the study, then the study has accomplished its purposes. For those other practitioners, who have had more recent experience with federal, state, and local reading programs and have already made other provisions to avoid the dilemma of differences in reading tests—or who have moved to more recent editions—the resource offered by the study may not be all that indispensable to their efforts. Even for such practitioners, however, the data provided may contribute to their "trade talk" in selecting reading tests for evaluation. The six more recent instruments generated nearly comparable standings in both the Anchor Test Study norms and the publishers' norms—an outcome that should cause delight in some test publishing circles. The publishers' norms for one test of older vintage and the comprehension subtest in the case of another such test, for whatever reasons (number of items, content, format, difficulty level, varying socioeconomic status of norms groups, and the like) yielded pupil rankings less comparable to the Anchor Test Study norms. For these tests, the Anchor norms tend to show percentile ranks that are higher than the publisher norms. For those who yearned to compare reading performance across school districts and expected the Anchor Test Study to facilitate this process, there is scant advice. The term "district means" is mentioned casually just once in the discussion about the effect of equating errors on group data (page 8). Lest one be tempted to enter the school mean charts for the purpose of making interdistrict comparisons (when one has at hand the necessary individual pupil raw score data for generating district means), it is well to keep in mind that the tables give the distributions of school means, not district means. To be sure the manual of tables does not purport to provide district mean norms. But it would have been helpful to practitioners, if the authors of the Anchor Test Study had called attention more specifically to this limitation in the data. Consistent with its focus, the manual of tables does not address the technical issues of the study. These are treated in a series of reports of voluminous dimensions. Certain practical issues, however, do appear to deserve more emphasis, if not prominence, in the manual intended for users. For example, most practitioners would be concerned with the usefulness of the equivalence data with groups of socioeconomic status and racial characteristics different from those of the total equating sample. The manual calls on the users to exercise their "best professional judgment" in all matters of this type by selecting tests to begin with that are appropriate to their situation and by being prudent about any comparisons that can or should be made. It would have reinforced users' prudence more effectively if more emphasis had been given to these qualifying conditions and limitations.

[B298]
*LORET, PETER, G.; SEDER, ALAN; BIANCHINI, JOHN C.; AND VALE, CAROL A. Anchor Test Study: Equivalence and Norms Tables for Selected Reading Achievement Tests (Grades 4, 5, 6), Revised. DHEW Publication S/N 017-080-01409-2. Washington, D.C.: U.S. Government Printing Office, 1975. Pp. ix, 92. Paper, $2.25. * For a review of the first edition, see B297.

[B299]
McASHAN, H. H. Writing Behavioral Objectives: A New Approach. New York: Harper & Row, Publishers, Inc., 1970. Pp. xi, 116. Paper, $7.50. *

J Ed Meas 9(1):79-80 sp '72. C. Mauritz Lindvall. * This book proposes that a behavioral objective, written at the "desired level," should include five essential components. There should be an indication of (1) the learner, (2) the program variable (content), (3) the implied behavioral domain, (4) the activity to be assessed in evaluating achievement of the objective, and (5) the standard which tells how well the learner should be expected to perform the evaluative activity. Such a detailed outlining of the components of an objective should contribute to the development of goal statements that involve the specific detail needed for clear communication, and McAshan goes to considerable lengths in explaining his system and in providing examples of it. However, to the reviewer, this rather complex system does not seem to provide the clear cut guidance for stating objectives that is found in simpler approaches. Of course, this assessment may well be associated with the reviewer's long term involvement with older and more standard approaches such as those of Tyler and Mager. Evidently, the McAshan analysis has been found effective in a number of workshops in Florida.

[B300]
★McCLAFFERTY, JOHN. A Guide to Examinations in English for Foreign Students. London: Hamish Hamilton Ltd., 1972. Pp. 101. Paper, $2.00. For the latest edition, see B300A.

Mod Lang J 60(5-6):303-4 S-O '76. Charles W. Stansfield. Four modest sections and a conclusion (brief review) make up this useful little book for foreign students. The author's intent is to describe the three best known British examinations and to advise candidates on how to prepare for them. * most of Part I is a description of how to prepare for and answer such questions. It is suggested that preparation is best accomplished by enrolling in an examination course; then keeping extensive written notes, saving all compositions and homework papers that deal with the books on which one is to be examined, and writing summaries of the books themselves. The candidate should consult past examinations and prepare to answer the kinds of questions found therein. * A somewhat doubtful statement on page 31 is the following: "Never waste time by writing something you have not been asked for; never throw away marks by not writing something you have been asked for, or by writing something else instead." * One of several interesting observations about tests on literature is that if the candidate does not like a particular work, he should choose another one as it is difficult to construct an answer from purely negative responses (p. 45). No British examination would be complete without précis (summary) writing and quite logically the book includes a section on it. Generally one is asked to reduce a passage to about one third its length. One's knowledge of vocabulary and structure is put to test in devising alternate, more economical ways of saying things. However, aside from its value as a proficiency measure, the author leaves the impression that the British consider the ability to write a précis to be a useful accomplishment in itself. * The book is most informative, and one wonders why American publishers have not devised a similar guide of their own. The student information pamphlets commonly distributed are simply too brief to form an accurate impression of what to expect.

[B300A]

*McCLAFFERTY, JOHN. **A Guide to Examinations in English for Foreign Students, New Edition.** London: Hamish Hamilton Ltd., 1975. Pp. vii, 103. Paper, £1.50. *

[B301]

★McCLELLAND, DAVID C. **Assessing Human Motivation.** Morristown, N.J.: General Learning Press, 1971. Pp. 20. Paper, $1.80. *

[B302]

★McCULLY, ROBERT S. **Rorschach Theory and Symbolism: A Jungian Approach to Clinical Material.** Baltimore, Md.: Williams & Wilkins Co., 1971. Pp. xxi, 271. $15.75. *

Am J Psychiatry 130(11):1304–5 N '73. H. Barry Molish. This year will mark the 51st anniversary of Rorschach's death. The publication of this text is propitious if for no other reason than its historical significance as a continuing tribute to the genius of Rorschach and

his test. This text is bold, innovative, and certainly unconventional, to say the least, in its efforts to apply Jungian concepts of archetypes to content analysis of each of the ten Rorschach plates. * The illustrative case materials presented in chapter 7 are exotic and highly selected to illustrate the use of the Rorschach on the basis of their archetypal structures. Even though the interpretation is foreign to the classical Rorschach analysis and rejects the concepts of pathology and nosology, it would be helpful to at least present a "normal" subject for comparison. Some provocative questions could be presented. What is the relationship between the traditional Rorschach popular response in each card and its archetypes? How are the laws of symbol formation related to highly personal F minus responses? What are the developmental aspects of the Rorschach test on a longitudinal basis as related to the archetypal process (reference is made to Piaget's theories and to Ames's studies on p. 244). I have reviewed this text solely in terms of what it purports to do, i.e., to present a hypothetical method in the use of symbolism in the Rorschach test. To make it live up to Piotrowski's expectations that "eventually it will be improved in practice, systematized, and validated with gratifying results" (p. ix) will certainly require a Herculean and Sisyphean effort, to say the least. Yet this may be one of my own archetypal influences evoked by my own despair in viewing past efforts to objectify all that is subjective in projective test data.

Austral Psychologist 9(1):91–2 Mr '74. Alan Condie. This book breaks away from traditional approaches to Rorschach interpretation. McCully endeavours to apply Jungian theory, particularly his concept of the archetype, to the content analysis of selected Rorschach responses. * He concludes the book with....five spectacular and fascinating case studies which illustrate his approach to interpretation * This is a very interesting book. It presents a fresh approach, it provokes thinking about some fundamental issues in the field of personality and its assessment, and it should stimulate research directed towards validating some of the ideas presented by McCully. It has the potential to become one of the most significant of the many Rorschach books that have appeared during the past two or three decades. However, this potential will probably remain unrealized, mainly because the book's primary appeal will be to a rather restricted group of readers—hard-core Rorschachers with a strong Jungian bias. This will be unfortunate, as McCully presents material that would be relevant and helpful to many outside this limited field; the book could be read with profit by all who work with projective techniques, by those who are interested in extending their knowledge of psychic structure, and even by some who work in other disciplines such as anthropology, archaeology and philosophy.

Brit J Psychiatry 122(566):107 Ja '73. *Phillida Salmon.* This new contribution to an already crowded literature on the Rorschach is justified by its author on the perhaps questionable argument that the validity of the technique is implied by its continued use. The approach outlined in the book is based on the claim that the inkblots represent a direct link with the subject's unconscious via archetypal symbols. The author suggests some parallels between Jung and Rorschach, outlines the specific archetypal significance of each card, drawing upon a wide range of mythological, literary, religious and artistic analogies, and finally presents five illustrative case studies (selected, presumably, for their sensational nature rather than their typicality, as they include a man aged 167, a teenage homicide-suicide, and an auto-vampire). The book seems to offer little to the average Rorschach user. Location and determinant factors are not considered, and interpretation is based entirely on content; the approach therefore rests entirely on the dubious assumption of the universality of symbols. Secondly, despite McCully's own claim to an empirical approach, a great many theoretical assumptions are made, some of which are dogmatically presented as "laws" (for example "the law of mutual projection," "the law of psychic correspondence"). Finally, the analysis of Rorschach records presented in the text, though often interesting and imaginative, remains unconvincing; given the same theoretical approach, a different, but equally plausible, interpretation could usually have been made.

J Pers Assess 37(1):93–5 F '73. *Louise Bates Ames.* The Rorschach Inkblot Test has provided one of the most effective ways we have of measuring individuality. The fact that much Rorschach work has been carried out within a Freudian framework has proved to be both a strength and a weakness. This particular background has provided insights, but it has limited

imagination. As Robert McCully points out correctly, the Rorschach method has suffered because it has been generally regarded against Freud's libido theory. Through this a tremendous amount of research did grow, but it has about come to an end. McCully now offers a new approach to the interpretation of the familiar blots. Believing that the Rorschach has been too long in the service of a single theory, too embedded in a medical model, he substitutes Jung for Freud as a presiding genius and suggests that we consider the Rorschach as a means by which we can study and learn something about the archetypal forces that influence group behavior. * Though McCully keeps to the approach of symbolism which Jung followed, a knowledge of Jung is not presupposed for the reader. * For the individual not entirely familiar with Jung's writings on the archetypes, McCully's book offers an exciting and stimulating journey through a rather strange land. To this reviewer it is somewhat of an enchanted land. * The author's discussion of the basic and deepseated aspects of masculinity and femininity expressed in archetypes, though not aimed in their direction, would make rather interesting and somewhat devastating reading for enthusiasts of the Women's Liberation movement. For the developmental psychologist, his notion that if we could study the embryology of the psyche we might find that archetypes were the building blocks that led to the development of consciousness itself, is of interest. The author goes far beyond suggesting a new interpretation of the Rorschach for Rorschach clinicians. He goes so far as to suggest that the Rorschach method of investigation has usefulness for other disciplines such as archaeology, philosophy, and history. * This is a serious, scholarly, eye opening, creative and highly stimulating book. Whether or not one wishes to go all the way with McCully in his interest in archetypes as they relate to the individual's response to the Rorschach blots, I strongly recommend this book to any serious student or user of the Rorschach who wishes to broaden his horizons. As the author himself promises, it will liberate perspective and provide wider meanings. "That way the excitement of challenge sustains the task." This is a difficult book to read, but I do agree that the excitement of challenge does sustain the task. Revealing as the Rorschach has always been, one does sometimes have the feeling that there is more in it than some of us are getting out. McCully aims to offer that more.

[B303]

★McFie, John. **Assessment of Organic Intellectual Impairment.** London and New York: Academic Press, Inc., 1975. Pp. xii, 164. £5.20; $12.00 *

Am J Psychiatry 133(12):1481–2 D '76. David D. Daly. * The author....bases his exposition on the use of the Wechsler Adult Intelligence Scale alone. This has the advantage of using a test familiar to psychologists but the disadvantages that the subtests that make up the scale were not designed to tap specific neural functions and the concept of intelligence itself is too much dominated by holistic concepts. * Old concepts die hard, particularly if they have attained the dignity of such a name as "intellect." Thus McFie rightly rejects the concept of a single test for "brain damage" in his concluding chapter (p. 145). However, earlier, in discussing testing, he indicates that the examiner "will have been able to estimate to what extent the patient's disabilities are at the intellectual level or are at the *lower level* of disorders of language" (p. 16; my italics). What function of functions does McFie subsume under the term "intellectual," and how is this level "higher" than language? Inconsistencies such as this, overly simplified views of cognitive and linguistic functions, and narrowly restrictive concentration on a single psychometric test constitute, in my view, the major weaknesses of this book. For neurologists and psychiatrists who wish to learn more about neuropsychological testing it is too parochial and suffers in comparison with existing monographs on this subject.

Austral Psychologist 12(2):211–2 Jl '77. F. N. Cox. This is a small, practical book which describes and illustrates a technique of neuropsychological assessment and contains an extensive bibliography of over 200 references in this expanding field. McFie's basic premise is that "psychological testing is primarily an assessment of the function of the brain," so nonorganic influences receive scant attention. The orientation is genuinely clinical—the intensive study of the single case—and the measures are a mixture of unstandardised and standardised intelligence and memory tests. The measures have been administered to patients who have suffered relatively specific damage to parts of their brains, and the analysis attempts to associate damage to part of the brain with impairments of psychological functions, which include not only general intelligence but also particular abilities. McFie, offers, then a detailed account of his methodology, procedures and results. In addition, he provides a useful corrective to two prevailing trends in clinical practice: excessive emphasis on intervention (behaviour therapy, counselling and community psychology being three contemporary aspects of this bias) and belittling of assessment. At a more fundamental level, he reminds us of the vital importance of the dependence of all psychological functioning upon the pattern of neuronal discharges and chemical reactions which mediate between presentation of any stimulus and production of any response. His methodology is interesting. He is concerned with measuring the extent to which a given patient's symptomatology and pattern of test signs approximates to those characteristic of the disease or syndrome. With this objective in mind, McFie advocates contrasting relatively high with relatively low scores in any way which facilitates discrimination between criteria groups. Consequently, he cuts across functional groups of subtext scores on the Wechsler Scale and may, instead, simply rank scores in numerical order. The flexibility of this approach clearly has much to commend it, as does the author's use of well-established tests which happen to work for his particular purposes. In summary, this is a useful, practical book in the best tradition of British clinical psychology. It is unpretentious, economical and clearly written and should be required reading for graduate students who plan to work in any field of clinical practice.

J Psychosom Res (England) 21(1):94 '77. Anthony Mann. * the bulk of the book describes the administration of the WAIS and Memory tests, giving case histories to illustrate the variation in results obtained from subjects with different pathologies. The case histories are accompanied by the reasons why the author drew the conclusions he did. It is not necessary to agree with the conclusions to gain from reading these case histories. The book ends with useful chapters on psychogenic and cultural factors that affect test results.

[B304]

★McGee, Rosemary, and Drews, Fred. **Proficiency Testing for Physical Education.** Washington, D.C.: American Alliance for Health, Physical Education, and Recreation, 1974. Pp. v, 73. Paper, $3.75. *

[B305]

★MacGinitie, Walter H., Editor. **Assessment Problems in Reading.** Newark, Del.: International Reading Association, 1973. Pp. vi, 101. Paper, $4.50. *

Read Teach 27(7):732–3 Ap '74. *Donald Quick.* * a scholarly and thorough discussion of assessment and its varied ramifications that relate to improvement of reading. The book could most readily be used by classroom teachers, reading specialists, or professors of reading. It seemingly would serve best as a resource book for teachers seeking knowledge of assessment or for college professors who wish to supplement topics in their undergraduate or graduate courses. * provides some excellent information and should serve as useful resource material for nearly all personnel associated with the teaching of reading. It is certainly a worthwhile contribution to the education profession.

[B306]

★McGuire, Christine H.; Solomon, Lawrence M.; and Bashook, Philip G. **Construction and Use of Written Simulations.** New York: Psychological Corporation, 1976. Pp. xvii, 307. Paper, $17.95. *

[B307]

★Macintosh, Henry G. **Assessing Attainment in the Classroom.** London: Hodder & Stoughton Educational, 1977. Pp. 47. Paper, 80p. *

[B308]

*McReynolds, Paul, Editor. **Advances in Psychological Assessment, Vol. 2.** Palo Alto, Calif.: Science & Behavior Books, Inc., 1971. Pp. xii, 395. $11.50. * For reviews of the first volume, see 7:B414 (2 excerpts).

J Pers Assess 37(4):391–2 Ag '73. *Eric C. Theiner.* * McReynolds' stated target audience includes both the practical user of assessments and, at least for some of the chapters, the research worker. The former is reached rather more successfully than the latter. It could hardly have been otherwise. For it would be quite exceptional that for topical areas as broad as those noted above, a discussion of twenty to thirty pages could provide precision sufficient to offer the researcher more than an occasional hypothesis. Regardless of the intended audience, the large part of this book is oriented toward the user. * McReynolds has done his homework. Consequently, the second volume speaks to many of the more general criticisms of the first. The current chapters appear to be more balanced, more ready to consider negative findings as well as positive. Moreover, the overall tenor is more of comparison across, rather than within, topical areas. An example in Dunnette's

discussion of the incremental validity of multiple assessment procedures. On the other hand, the level of statistical sophistication remains unimpressive. Still, this criticism is mitigated by two factors. First, the primary audience for whom the book is intended is the generally non-statistically oriented user. Second, several of the articles concern areas that do not readily lend themselves to such treatment. Atypical for volumes comprised of contributions by multiple authors, the level of communication is relatively even—and relatively high. While style varies, the editing is done competently, and the discussions are generally clear. * the references on which the chapters are based are of considerable value. The last sixth of the book is comprised of a timely review of the literature * The large majority of the references are from 1960 on. Since a significant number are from sources not typically available (unpublished manuscripts, addresses, even B.A. theses), their value for researcher as well as user is clear. Finally, in these times of continuing inflation, the book represents a real value. While the price of Volume II over Volume I has increased 21%, size has increased almost correspondingly, 17%. So small an increase in the size/price ratio of almost anything deserves recognition. In sum, this book is recommended for any earnest user of assessments. It is a serious book competently done, and well worth the price.

[B309]

*McReynolds, Paul, Editor. **Advances in Psychological Assessment, Vol. 3.** San Francisco, Calif.: Jossey-Bass Inc., Publishers, 1975. Pp. xvi, 555. $17.50. * For a review of the second volume, see B308; for reviews of the first volume, see 7:B414 (2 excerpts).

[B310]

★Mager, Robert F. **Measuring Instructional Intent or Got a Match?** Belmont, Calif.: Fearon Publishers, 1973. Pp. vii, 159. Paper, $4.25. *

[B311]

★Maloney, Michael P., and Ward, Michael P. **Psychological Assessment: A Conceptual Approach.** New York: Oxford University Press, Inc., 1976. Pp. xv, 422. $14.00. *

Brit J Ed Psychol 47(2):219 Je '77. *Paul Kline.* * The first point to notice about this book is that psychometrically it is not advanced or up-to-date. Thus the descriptions of reliability make no mention of any unusual varieties, such as analysis of variance methods. Similarly, their discussion of validity is elementary although they utilise a concept of conceptual validity in terms of assessing an individual. Rather more importantly there is no discussion of item-scaling procedures such as Rasch scaling. However, even if elementary the material is clear and well-written. * Do the authors make their case that psychological testing alone is insufficient to assess an individual? As the arguments are presented in this book, they do. However, the multivariate approach, as advocated by Cattell and Eysenck, is never adequately discussed and although, at present, this is not perfected, ultimately, perhaps, as the specification equation and the dynamic calculus demonstrate, it might be. Thus, their Personal Construct model is not wholly convincing. * Although mention is made of Cattell's fluid and crystallised abilities, there is no discussion of Cattell's ADAC model which again makes this reviewer suspect that these clinical psychologists are not, as they say, into modern psychometrics. This deficiency permeates their later discussions of personality tests. Although factor-analytic tests are mentioned the fundamental distinction between factor analytic variables and criterion keyed variables in terms of psychological meaning is never dealt with. This then is the weakest side of the book. On the other side, however, the full discussion of cases, the sensitive use of test data together with case records and other information, the chapters on psychiatric diagnosis and brain damage make this book highly useful for the practical psychologist. In summary we would conclude that this book is welcome in that it stresses the importance of being able to assess the individual, rather than discriminate groups and it will be helpful in professional psychology. As an academic psychometric text, it cannot be recommended.

[B312]

★MARANELL, GARY M. **Scaling: A Sourcebook for Behavioral Scientists.** Chicago, Ill.: Aldine Publishing Co., 1974. Pp. xix, 436. Paper, $8.95; cloth, $19.50. *

Meas & Eval Guid 8(1):60–1 Ap '75. Nancy E. Betz. * a collection of articles written by some of the major contributors to scaling theory and methodology. Although one important purpose of the compilation is to familiarize the reader with the major methods of scaling, its more general purpose is to stress the importance of measurement in science and to suggest that the specific scaling methodologies given represent only some of the possible approaches to "the assignment of numbers to objects accord-

ing to rules." * Maranell has assembled a valuable collection of readings; I consider most of them must reading for any psychologist interested in measurement. The articles are interesting, informative, and provide a nice blend of philosophical and theoretical foundations with specific procedures and applications. They do not require great mathematical expertise and are at a level suitable for advanced undergraduate and graduate students. Maranell has provided good supporting features in his introductions to each section, an excellent selected bibliography, and a comprehensive index. *Scaling* would be worth using in a first course on scaling, perhaps in combination with a text such as Torgerson's *Theory and Methods of Scaling*. My only criticism of the book is the lack of any material on multidimensional scaling techniques, which are gaining increased use and which exceed unidimensional models in their potential for discovering and exploring the dimensionality of a domain. But in spite of its limitation to unidimensional models, this is a book well worth having.

[B313]

★MARKS, PHILIP A.; SEEMAN, WILLIAM; AND HALLER, DEBORAH L. **The Actuarial Use of the MMPI With Adolescents and Adults.** New York: Oxford University Press, 1974. Pp. xix, 324. $16.00. *

Am J Psychiatry 132(9):987 S '75. Bernard S. Glueck. I cannot improve upon the opening sentences of Drs. Starke Hathaway and Grant Dahlstrom's foreword to this book: "Readers familiar with....*Actuarial Description of Abnormal Personality* [(1)] will be pleased to learn of the publication of the present volume. In it they will find an expanded and updated version of the discussion of actuarial versus clinical procedures which delighted Prof. Meehl in that first edition, together with a reprinting of the data comprising the adult code types originally developed by the first two authors on their psychiatric cases....They will be pleasantly surprised that these data are now in a narrative format with somewhat less stringent typal defining criteria. The real bonus for them in this edition, however, will be the totally new set of code types and descriptors for adolescent subjects." The balance of the foreword puts the entire issue of the use of the MMPI as a statistical descriptor and predictor into historical perspective. It also brings the reader up-to-date about the development of the interpretive statements and the new descriptors of adolescent code types contained in the new volume. The opening chapters present a detailed description of the MMPI and a careful discussion of the actuarial description process, which is defined as a set of descriptive attributes assigned to individuals on the basis of a set of rules derived from experimentally and statistically demonstrated associations between the input data (e.g., MMPI profiles, Rorschach psychograms, word associations, etc.) and the descriptive statements that constitute the output. The authors then describe the 16 adult code types that were in the original volume. However, as indicated in the foreword, the personality description in this volume is in narrative form and therefore much more palatable to the average clinician than the earlier list. The next section of this volume is a new section on adolescent code types; 30 characteristic code types are discussed. A great deal of statistical information given for the adult types is not given in this section. Rather, the authors present extensive personality descriptions, emphasizing both the positive and negative aspects of the profiles. One possible criticism of the wealth of detailed description provided by the authors might be their failure to separate out some of the code types, e.g., the 4–9/9–4. Other authors have made a distinction between these code types and have described each separately. For most of the other codes, the combinations appear to be quite appropriate and serve as a useful condensation of what would otherwise be a very unwieldy set of profile types and codes. The final section of this book includes four appendices that provide the detailed information upon which the narrative descriptors of the code types is based. This information is invaluable to those who are interested in pursuing the development of MMPI types and those who are doing research using the MMPI. Although I hesitate to criticize the very carefully and beautifully detailed presentations in this volume, I would like to point out that a good deal of the work done by the authors in providing clinical interpretations for the profile types is becoming less and less essential for the clinical use of the MMPI because of the development of increasingly sophisticated computer programs for scoring and interpreting MMPI data. For the many mental health workers who may not have such computerized interpretations available to them but who can administer and hand-score the MMPI, however, the detailed clinical and demographic descriptors will continue to prove invaluable.

Brit J Ed Psychol 45(3):350–1 N '75. *Ronald R. Macdonald.* The problem of classification of mental illness has a long and not too successful history. Marks, Seeman and Haller in this work extend the approach they started in 1963. Their aim is to identify and describe typologies on the basis of the 10 clinical and four validity scales of the MMPI. The method they use is to apply the Hathaway coding system to 1411 MMPI profiles from patients admitted to the University of Kansas Medical Centre. This categorises profiles by the order of scales two standard deviations or more above the mean for normals. This first approximation to types is adjusted both to ensure that the numbers of any type are above a specified minimum and for within-type homogeneity. Although it is clear on what evidence the correction for homogeneity is based, its exact specification is not explicitly stated. The methodology is thus intuitively sensible but arbitrary and lacks theoretical justification. It should be noted however, that such techniques as discriminant function and cluster analyses may make unwarranted assumptions or involve a number of arbitrary decisions. The authors make much of the fact that their typologies are based on empirical data rather than the clinical experience of a number of therapists which has been used in some other studies. * The main extension to the 1963 work is in the application of similar techniques to a sample of 834 teenagers involved in psychotherapy. The coding system initially involved only the two highest MMPI scores and the subsequent adjustments to obtain the final typologies are explicit. In the case of the five adult types involving three scales at least two adolescent types out of a possible three are identified. Only one adult type involving two variables does not appear as an adolescent type, while 16 new types are identified. The considerable agreement between the two samples must strengthen the validity of the overall typologies, although it weakens the case for providing separate adolescent norms. The book gives an easily usable summary of a vast amount of material and should be of interest to any user of the MMPI. However, although it may be possible to use it to provide automated personality descriptions, such descriptions should not be overemphasised at the expense of other available information.

[B314]

MARSHALL, JON CLARK, AND HALES, LOYDE WESLEY. **Classroom Test Construction.** Reading, Mass.: Addison-Wesley Publishing Co., Inc., 1971. Pp. xiv, 335. $11.75. *

J Ed Meas 9(3):247–9 f '72. Joseph R. Jenkins. * All in all, the authors present a clearly written, well organized book. *Classroom Test Construction's* claim to uniqueness among the rising number of measurement texts lies in its exhaustive description of test forms. These forms include essay, completion, oral, multiple-choice, true-false, matching, and performance indices. The uses, advantages, weakness, construction, administration, scoring procedures, and "do's" and "don'ts" are described in detail for the various test forms. A second notable feature of this book is a brief review of the literature on examinations. This review includes such topics as grader reliability, question weighting, and response sets. In comparison to most other measurement texts currently available, the weaknesses of *Classroom Test Construction* are not unique. These weaknesses are all matters of exclusion resulting from what the authors have left unsaid. This book suffers in its failure to consider fully the issues of mastery, derivation of test items, sources of test items, and direct and continuous measurement. The issue of mastery receives little mention. Related to this issue, the authors' statement, "the primary purpose of testing is to determine the extent to which the objectives of the unit of study have been realized," needs further clarification. * In summary, prospective teachers who seek assistance in writing test items which employ the various and commonly used item-forms will find *Classroom Test Construction* a helpful book. However, should one adopt this text in a course, he would need to locate supplementary materials which focus on the many critical issues and problems which confront the classroom test writer. In its treatment of conventional test forms and analyses, this book succeeds in purpose. There still exists, however, a need for a more thorough and searching work on the full definition and delineation of testing.

[B315]

★MARSHALL, JON CLARK, AND HALES, LOYDE WESLEY. **Essentials of Testing.** Reading, Mass.: Addison-Wesley Publishing Co., Inc., 1972. Pp. xi, 162. Paper, $5.00. *

Ed & Psychol Meas 33(2):518–9 su '73. Richard Rovinelli and Daniel S. Sheehan. * The

most informative and also the best written section of the book consisted of the chapters which dealt with test construction and use. The authors carefully delineate test types and present the strengths and weaknesses of each form. They also list the "Do's and Don't's" with regards to the use of each test form. Teachers should find this section both practical and worthwhile. However, given the stated purposes of the book, two omissions are all too apparent. First, many of the new instructional models being implemented in the schools are dependent upon objective based curricula. The information required to evaluate student progress in these programs is clearly criterion-referenced. The authors' failure to provide more than one and a half pages for criterion-referenced testing is a serious deficiency for this book. * one would expect that any recent book on educational measurement would include information on instruments measuring performance or development from both domains. This book fails to provide any viable information for the assessment of objectives from the affective domain. While the format and style of the book make it easy to read, it is poorly organized and gives one the impression that it was hastily put together. * there are a number of terms such as power and speed tests, normal curve, and content validity which are utilized before they are defined. Also, the chapters on item analysis, reliability and validity and descriptive statistics do not augment each other but instead are disjoint, incomplete and isolated segments. In general we feel that teachers or anyone teaching an introductory course in educational measurement would receive as much or more practical information from sources such as the *Tests and Measurement Kit* prepared by the Educational Testing Service as from this book.

[B316]

★MARTUZA, VICTOR R. **Applying Norm-Referenced and Criterion-Referenced Measurement in Education.** Boston, Mass.: Allyn & Bacon, Inc., 1977. Pp. viii, 352. $13.50. *

[B317]

★MASH, ERIC J., AND TERDAL, LEIF G., EDITORS. **Behavior-Therapy Assessment: Diagnosis, Design, and Evaluation.** New York: Springer Publishing Co., Inc., 1976. Pp. xviii, 382. $14.95. *

[B318]

*MATARAZZO, JOSEPH D. **Wechsler's Measurement and Appraisal of Adult Intelligence, Fifth and Enlarged Edition.** New York: Oxford University Press, 1972. Pp. x, 572, $17.50. * For reviews of earlier editions, see 6:B503 (3 excerpts), 3:299 (7 excerpts),

3:300 (7 excerpts), 3:301 (5 excerpts), and 2:B1121 (10 excerpts).

Am J Mental Def 78(4):511–2 Ja '74. A. B. Silverstein. * a substantial departure from previous editions, with 8 of the 15 chapters entirely new, and only 4 essentially unchanged. * Historical attempts to define the nature of intelligence are treated in a way that proves history need not be dull. * There is no denying the key role that Wechsler has played in the measurement and appraisal of intelligence, and it is doubtful that a better choice than Matarazzo could have been made to "carry on the torch." Yet their collaboration—for the book is, in a sense, still collaborative effort—is not altogether successful. Previous editions centered around the theory, findings, and applications of the Wechsler-Bellevue and the WAIS. The present edition extends the scope and content considerably further, yet at some points it seems uncomfortably bound to these same scales. It is very nearly two books in one, and perhaps they should have remained separate. However, one book or two, Matarazzo's *Wechsler* is recommended reading not only for clinicians, but also for research workers and for students in psychology and related fields.

Brit J Psychol 65(3):461–3 Ag '74. A. Dabbs. * The revision is extremely lengthy and verbose. The first three parts of the book, comprising 260 pages, can best be characterized by the term "over-kill." There is little evidence of critical selectivity in his review of the field of intelligence. The final section, part 4, contains the more directly relevant material for practising clinical psychologists. Unfortunately it tends to be buried amid a welter of verbiage comprising 231 pages. There are three brief but pertinent appendices which refer as often to the W-BI as they do to the currently used WAIS. * The opening section of the book provides us with yet another attempt to define intelligence. Matarazzo traces the history of the concept in some detail from the earliest textbooks of modern psychology. He points out that in 1890 Baldwin succeeded in dealing with the topic in his textbook in two pages under the title of "Intellect." William James made only two references to the subject in his double-volume classic, *The Principles of Psychology.* Evidently this knowledge did little to help Matarazzo. After 133 pages reading, I did not feel any improvement had been made on David Wechsler's original definition. What seemed more disappointing was that Matarazzo does not seem to have considered how useful a concept like level of intelligence might be for the applied psychologist. Parts 2 and 3 of the book seek to demonstrate that classification of individuals on the basis of psychometric test results more or less coincides with those classifications made by most of us without the aid of IQ scores. University undergraduates reveal a higher mean test score than the average of young adults in the general population. What the tests do not tell us is why there are so many young adults in the general population of equivalent or better test scores than undergraduates but who do not enter university. Almost all the reported validational studies are retrospective * The final section of the book concentrates upon more practical issues. Certain statements stand out and merit further consideration, e.g. "The results of these three studies (Stice & Ekstron, 1964; Beinstock, 1967; Dillon, 1970) and the thousands of others which show an average correlation of about 0.50 between grades in school and IQ...." Another way of looking at it is to say that measured IQ only accounts for approximately 25 per cent of the variance in educational achievements. Educational psychologists might bear this in mind. The review of the nature-nurture issue in relation to intelligence under the title "Validity Indices, Exemplars and Correlates" is perhaps the most valuable section of the book. The argument is wide and impartial and succeeds in collating many different aspects of the problem. The subsequent chapters tread a well-beaten path over ground all too familiar to a previous generation of clinical psychologists. The section devoted to the application of Wechsler tests in the assessment of brain damage somehow never succeeds in grasping the nettle. Apparently Wechsler's psychometric devices can pick out many of the same patients whose brain lesions can be reliably indicated by EEG machines, neurological examinations and the like. We never learn about the apparently false positive results or the applications of these findings to rehabilitation programmes in an effort to improve the impaired psychomotor functioning of the brain-damaged patient. A study of Mathews, Shaw and Klove (*Cortex,* vol. 2, 1965) is quoted at some length, which reveals that the WAIS can predict which patients neurologists call neurological and psychiatrists call psychiatric. I imagine asking the particular physicians direct questions might have saved time. We also learn that there are more spastics in the lower half of the distribution of intelligence test scores than might be expected, compared with the general population, and that patients having undergone hemispherectomy produce similar WAIS scores as they did just prior to surgery when they still retained their severely diseased hemisphere of the brain. At least we are spared the serious consideration of subtest scatter and "psychographs" so beloved of Rapaport and earlier generations of clinical psychologists. Chapter 14 is related to psychiatric classification and Wechsler test scores, and merits a glance. My one reservation is a wonderment as to why these intelligence tests were administered to such a motley array of patients. A table is provided indicating IQ scores derived from 22 studies of "sociopaths" carried out by many different psychologists. Hundreds of patients must have been involved and the ultimate meaning is that the "sociopath" tends to have slightly lower verbal than performance IQ—or it could be that the so-called norms are incorrect and the difference would evaporate if we excluded all other identifiable groups, e.g. the higher range of educational attainers from the "normal" population. Matarazzo, or rather Wechsler, cannot have it both ways. If his tests claim to maximize objectivity on the part of the examiner, to minimize motivational differences in the subjects and to provide a fair estimate of global intelligence then they cannot at the same time be seriously considered as meaningful measures of personality variables. The book closes with a few case studies which serve to demonstrate that in the United States too much attention is paid to psychometric test results. It is not easy to summarize a book of this length and range of content. It reveals much painstaking effort but little original thought. The literature search is evidently comprehensive though rather unselective. Certain deficiencies stand out. The problem of Wechsler test scores, intelligence, and the effects of ageing are not adequately dealt with. On the other hand, there is much "hard data" which the applied psychologist would find useful. The references are copious and well set out. At the stated cost of the review edition it may be regarded as being a sensible requisite for all applied psychologists who might have cause to use the Wechsler tests.

Ed & Psychol Meas 33(4):1013–6 w '73. *James K. Dent.* * Matarazzo is concerned with issues in the philosophy of science as they relate to the origins and the development of the WAIS. By going back to original sources and through his own skillful writing, he has captured both the milieu and the excitement which surrounded the work of Binet, and later, of Wechsler. * Matarazzo is careful to tell us what kind of empirical evidence supports the findings he reports and the extent to which this evidence has been confirmed by other studies. He also reports promising new evidence not yet corroborated. The organization of the book is somewhat complex (like the subject), but the index is excellent and permits the reader to find what he wants. * The current "testing controversy" is so pressing, it overshadows the constructive contributions that have been made. I should like to devote the rest of this review to that issue. * Apparently, he sees the solution to the controversy in the distinction between group and individual testing. He contrasts the ivory-tower concern with *measurement* of intelligence through group testing, with the clinician's *assessment* of the individual through individual testing. While everyone will agree that individual testing permits assessment of a variety of relevant dimensions that group measurement does not, everyone will not agree that individual testing is going to make the problem go away. * There are two aspects to the problem. The first is a scientific question: What label shall be applied to the test scores? The second is a professional problem: To what use shall we put these scores? With respect to the first question the tests are labelled "intelligence" tests. Again and again, Matarazzo, as in the popular mind, defines "intelligence" as having to do with "success" (p. 65), "adapting to circumstances" (p. 66), "intellectual-behavioral-educational-occupational potential" (p. 68), and "ability to cope with the environment" (p. 77). Yet, over these same pages there are repeated assertions that intelligence, so defined, is also greatly influenced by nonintellective factors which are not measured directly by the tests. The time may soon come when we cannot have it both ways. * The second question is more complicated for it concerns our role and what we are trying to do with these tests. * Should our primary objective with these tests be to judge, or can we also use them as helpers? Are these tests to be viewed primarily as measures of adaptability or might they be useful also as aids to adaptation? Because of our judge-like responsibilities for admissions, transfers, and referrals, are we losing sight of our helper role? * It is true that we will never be able to shed the judge's role. Whatever these tests measure does indeed *correlate with* a wide variety of socially desirable behaviors and conditions. But in my view Matarazzo slights the helper's role. * It's fun to be a judge. But if our role is primarily that of identifying leaders and followers, we need to report more carefully, and pursue more avidly, the evidence surrounding the self-fulfilling prophecy. We need to understand and to measure how individuals "snow-ball" up or down in a society that is too busy to care much about such phenomena. But particularly we need to consider more fully what we can do to help people adapt, and how we can do it better. These issues are not raised as criticism, but in the spirit of debate. In his views Matarazzo has excellent company, and his book is a landmark in presenting these and other issues which are central to psychology and education.

Meas & Eval Guid 6(3):185–7 O '73. Everett E. Davis. * This really is two books; one is a polemic, and one is a handbook. The polemic results from the author's pre-occupation with the abuses associated with the impersonal, assembly-line nature of group testing. Although he concedes that testing has a scientific aspect, he looks upon psychological assessment as an art. * Probably no one is better qualified to write this book than Matarazzo, a noted clinical psychologist, who long has taught and practiced in the field. * There is a tremendous amount of information crammed into the text. In another way also this is two books; it is Wechsler's book, and it is Matarazzo's book * Occasionally this combination of viewpoints requires a certain cognitive agility on the part of the reader. * Yet it is usually quite obvious who has written each of the passages. Wechsler's writing is sprightly and unpretentious; Matarazzo's is detailed and occasionally labored. * This edition, in addition to the appendices and indices, has 507 pages of text in comparison with 237 in the fourth edition, and about two-fifths of the present edition is taken from the previous book. * In summary, this is an excellent textbook for advanced graduate courses. Also, any individual who is involved in the testing of adults should have this volume, or have access to it in the college or university library.

Psychol Sch 11(3):376–9 Jl '74. Robert J. Lovinger. The pattern of Matarazzo's book largely follows that of Wechsler's 1958 edition, but a little less than two-thirds is essentially new material within that structure. * The historical review in chapters one and two is interesting and valuable. His approach to assessment as a professional, clinical enterprise that relies upon scientific work but is not a scientific investigation as such, is an important point that requires courage to make so forthrightly. His sharp criticism of psychology's failure to control the misuse and misinterpretation of intelligence test results by nonpsychologists is much to the point. Matarazzo then goes on to discuss the problems in defining intelligence. His discussion of the various levels of definition and the processes whereby definitions are made can be read with profit by experienced workers in the field, particularly when at a loss to answer critical comments from hard-nosed colleagues. * On the negative side, Matarazzo occasionally assumes a knowledge that many beginning students may lack. For them a definition of functionalism or tetrad differences would not be out of place. They also might be confused by the statement on page 83 that every test on the Stanford-Binet between the ages of three and ten adds two months to the mental age score. This was true only of the 1916 revision, which is rarely seen now, and is not true of the 1937 or 1960 revisions. * The discussion of the development of concepts of mental retardation, the current state of thinking, and the nature of classification according to the AAMD Manual is illuminating and clearly set forth. * Part Three, basically chapters five, six and seven from Wechsler's 1958 edition, describes how and why the subtests were constructed and some correlates and interpretations associated with them. In general, these chapters are a straightforward setting-forth of data. The discussion of the standardization sample, particularly on the WAIS, tends to slide around some difficult questions that still are being argued with regard to the question of separate or combined norms for different ethnic, social and economic groups. * it would help the reader to give the page number in addition to the table or figure number, when a table is cross-referenced. Similarly, a list of tables and figures would be a real convenience. * Matarazzo states the IQ limit on the 1960 revision of the Stanford-Binet is 170–172. While this is true of the conversion tables, it is possible to compute deviation IQs beyond the tabular limits as described in Appendices A and C of the manual (Terman and Merrill, 1960). For this reviewer, Part Four was probably the most exciting and interesting section. Composed of five chapters that deal with validation, it contains mostly new material although their titles are similar to those in the 1958 edition. Matarazzo begins with a discussion of the factorial structure of the W-B I and the WAIS and concludes the chapter with an incisive discussion of validity. * Chapter twelve contains a wealth of material that is well organized and should prove useful even to experienced workers. * In this chapter, however, his treatment of ethnic factors in intelligence (Jensen, *et al*) is, to my mind, less than entirely straightforward. In one or two places he seems to misinterpret Jensen, although a supplementary comment or quotation then will correct the picture. In sum, on this topic he is too good a scientist to bend the data really out of shape but he is too much a humanist to like the data's apparent implications, so his exposition is sometimes erratic. Such a quality is the more noticeable when contrasted with his otherwise exceptionally clear and interesting writing style. The chapter on brain-behavior relationships provides a useful survey of much research not often available outside of specialized courses. * Matarazzo begins the chapter on personality correlates with a useful review of Wechsler's attempts at pattern analysis and some of the reasons that pattern analysis hasn't held up in studies. * The review of the Bayley and Honzik longitudinal growth studies is a good introduction for many students. I found the material on the Gittinger personality assessment system completely new and fascinating. Unfortunately, the presentation was not always easy to follow, and a diagram or specific examples would help. There weren't enough data to judge whether the Gittinger approach is a silly scheme or a fruitful one. Finally, in his last chapter he discusses qualitative aspects of interpretation and presents four interesting and illustrative cases. The book is dense but quite readable. Matarazzo has packed a wealth of data (505 references) as well as clinical wisdom into it, and he is not afraid to take stands and make judgments. As a result of reading it for this review, this writer selected it for a text in a graduate course in Intelligence Testing. Some of the students are intimidated by the amount of material, but others genuinely

like it. None are in great pain. In other ways though, this is a most remarkable book, for while collaborations between authors are common, I cannot recall another instance of a living author of Wechsler's stature to permit another to revise his work and take sole credit for the revision. It is a tribute to Wechsler's stature as a scientist and a person that he permitted this, and to Matarazzo's ability that he fully met this challenge. In all, the book is highly recommended.

[B319]
*MATHEWS, DONALD K. **Measurement in Physical Education, Fourth Edition.** Philadelphia, Pa.: W. B. Saunders Co., 1973. Pp. x, 467. $9.00. *

[B320]
★MAUSER, AUGUST J. **Assessing the Learning Disabled: Selected Instruments.** San Rafael, Calif.: Academic Therapy Publications, 1976. Pp. 95. Paper, $4.25. * For the latest edition, see B321.

Am J Mental Def 81(6):612 My '77. Richard A. Schere. * The book should serve well as a handy resource for those who seek to locate measures that may be appropriate for use with learning disabled persons. However, the scientific quality of the effort would have been improved with the inclusion of some data as to the reliability and validity of the assessments derived from the instruments. It is also interesting to note that of 16 learning disability tests listed in Buros' *Mental Measurements Yearbook,* only 6 were included in the present volume. However, this fact should not be construed as a criticism of Mauser's listings, which can be very helpful as a source of available instruments.

[B321]
*MAUSER, AUGUST J. **Assessing the Learning Disabled: Selected Instruments, Second Edition.** San Rafael, Calif.: Academic Therapy Publications, 1977. Pp. 109. Paper, $5.00. * For a review of the earlier edition, see B320.

[B322]
★MAYER, VICTOR J. **Unpublished Evaluation Instruments in Science Education: A Handbook.** Arlington, Va.: ERIC Document Reproduction Service, 1974. Pp. vi, 315. Paper, $4.05. *

[B323]
★MEEHL, PAUL E. **Psychodiagnosis: Selected Papers.** Minneapolis, Minn.: University of Minnesota Press, 1973. Pp. xxiii, 359. $14.50. *

J Pers Assess 38(5):486-7 O '74. Robert M. Allen. This is a compassionately provocative book containing papers written by one who is semantically down to earth, facile, esoteric, bitter, and determined. While the words must have flowed easily from his well-guided pen, Meehl's ideas are not assimilated as easily or as readily. But, then, this is a reflection of the editor-author of this book. At times he sails smoothly through a set of concepts. And then, without forewarning, he leads the reader into the rough waters of countervailing arguments and rationales of the duties, obligations and responsibilities of the psychologist as behavioral scientist and people-helper. There are several major thema enunciated and iterated in the 13 chapters which yield an impression of unevenness, perhaps ambivalence, in Meehl's effort to come to grips with Psychology as a scientific discipline and as an applied art. Certainly Meehl does not attempt to polarize these two conceptualizations despite his dogmatic language. Rather he seems to reflect an internal conflict as to how these two approaches to the problems of daily living may be reconciled in the service of the client and Psychology. * The....new materials are the "Preface" and Chapter 13. Meehl appears to have hurt feelings because of the alleged negative reaction by clinical psychologists to his *Clinical Versus Statistical Prediction opus.* This theme of hurt recurs several times in the selected papers of this volume. Because of this repetition, the reader may come away with the impression that the author actually resents these nonunderstanding clinicians. This personal concern and *non-apologia* are manifest in the "Preface" so that the reader may be given an early set toward what is to follow in the ensuing chapters. Fortunately, Meehl directs some of his rather strong (at times caustic) remarks at the psychiatrist, nurse, and social worker as a sort of digression for his bitterness. Then again, the very brilliance of his ideas and productive formulations do offer the reader some surcease. Meehl amply supports his claim that he is not opposed to diagnosis. It is poor diagnosis that offends him. He suggests a solution to the diagnosis-dilemma in his "Some Ruminations On The Validation Of Clinical Procedures," to wit (p. 102): "In order to employ dynamic constructs to arrive at predictions, it would be necessary to meet two conditions. In the first place we must have a sound theory about the determinative variables. Secondly, we must be in possession of an adequate technology for making measurements of those variables." Actually, isn't this what Psychology and people-helping is all about? Unfortunately, and this

reviewer agrees with Meehl, too many clinicians have been biased away from Meehl's essential appeal because they have either misread, half-read, or not read his 1954 *opus magnum.* The chapter on "Why I Do Not Attend Case Conferences" is a remarkable distillation of years of experience as a student, teacher, clinician, writer and thinker. His views are catholic so that efforts to pin him down as a "this-er" or "that-er" would be an exercise in futility. Essentially he believes in people and not in polemics. But this concern for people is spiced with doses of dogmatic verbalizations. Perhaps the language is stronger than the behavior, but all the reader has to go by is the printed word. Despite the authoritarian tone, this chapter should be required reading for all those who aspire to become, or who are already characterized as, people-helping psychologists (and related professions). Contradictory, easy and difficult to read, humanistic and Scientific—Meehl is all of these. But the appeals, the stories, the points made, and the admitted cathartic contents will offer the reader challenges far beyond the most avid expectations. There is one trivial question this reviewer would like to ask—Why is a premed student, albeit a bright under-graduate senior psychology major, "doing" psychotherapy with a potential-turned-actual suicidal patient? Finally, this volume of selected, edited, and authored papers may be considered to be a *festschrift* in honor of a psychology great— Paul E. Meehl.

[B324]

★MEGARGEE, EDWIN INGLEE. **The California Psychological Inventory Handbook.** San Francisco, Calif.: Jossey-Bass Inc., Publishers, 1972. Pp. xxvii, 298. $25.00. *

Ed & Psychol Meas 32(4):1144-7 w '72. Robert Hogan. Although the California Psychological Inventory (CPI) represents perhaps the most important advance in personality measurement since the MMPI, it is also the most poorly understood of the major inventories. This relative obscurity is due in part to the reluctance of the test's author, H. G. Gough, to discuss publically certain theoretical issues surrounding the development of the CPI, and in part to some misguided reviews which appeared early in the test's career. Most of these problems are resolved, however, with the appearance of Megargee's handbook for the CPI. * Counselors and clinicians will probably be most interested....in the third section wherein Megargee discusses test interpretation. * Several features of this handbook are noteworthy. First, it is not an "in-house" publication of the Institute of Personality Assessment and Research at Berkeley where the CPI was developed; it is definitely Megargee's book, a fact which is seen, for example, in the way he consistently distinguishes between his and Gough's attitudes toward the test. Second, the book is clearly written and easy to read. The clarity is perhaps most obvious in the discussion of such potentially obscure psychometric issues as strategies for item selection and criticisms of step-wise regression techniques. These and several other technical topics are handled with admirable lucidity and dispatch. Another valuable feature of the book is that it contains a good deal of imoprtant information that is literally unavailable elsewhere. Most people who know Gough well feel that his best ideas appear primarily in letters and private conversations. As Megargee notes, "Gough is one of the few test authors who has formally articulated his values and his philosophy of testing; unfortunately, the most cogent expression of his principles are contained in unpublished papers and personal correspondence" (p. 10). Megargee presents these principles in detail and, as a result, demystifies such otherwise puzzling features of the CPI as, for example, the arrangement of the scales on the profile sheet and the "value-loaded" names of many of the scales. A fourth commendable feature of the book is its superb review of the CPI literature. A wealth of data is summarzied, integrated, and evaluated in a judicious and balanced fashion. * Still another attractive feature is the detailed presentation of individual profile interpretations. * this section of the book should be quite useful to practitioners in a variety of settings (e.g., counseling centers, probation departments, and guidance clinics). The reviewer was particularly impressed with the manner in which Megargee discusses the "response-set problem." Although he presents correlations between CPI scales and measures of social desirability, he recognizes (a) that the CPI Good Impression scale was one of the earliest measures of social desirability to appear; and (b) that such variance is more often valid than artifactual. In addition, Megargee treats the topic of acquiescence response set with the benign neglect that it appears to deserve. From a history of science perspective, perhaps the most important con-

tribution of this book is to dispell some of the persistent myths that have haunted the CPI since its inception. For example, because the usual goal of personality inventories is trait specification (with the result that correlations with non-test criteria are considered "Peripheral"), the CPI has been roundly criticized for factorial impurity and heterogeneity of its scales. As Megargee points out, however, the CPI should be evaluated in terms of how well it achieves the goals that were originally set for it, rather than in terms of a reviewer's aesthetic predilections. The purpose of the CPI is to predict what an individual will do in a specified context and/or to forecast how he will be described by those who know him well. Consequently, scale homogeneity and factorial independence are relevant evaluative criteria for the CPI only if they can be shown to improve its predictive utility. Megargee also puts to rest the criticism that the CPI lacks any theoretical underpinnings. * A third persistent myth is that Gough doesn't understand the factor structure of his inventory, a fact reflected by the manner in which the scales are grouped on the CPI profile sheet. As Megargee observes, however, Gough arranged his scales to facilitate clinical interpretations of profiles rather than to reproduce psychometric factors or clusters. There are some points in the book that I would argue with, only one of which need be mentioned; i.e., Megargee asserts without documentation that "In recent years, research has been performed using Negro, Mexican-American, and American Indian subjects. The results of these studies are disquieting because they show that lower class minority-group members often obtain lower scores on most CPI scales" (p. 249). The reviewer's own data on this subject do not support Megargee's statement. In summary, this is a scholarly, well-written, and exceedingly helpful introduction to the CPI, a valuable and authoritative reference source for both practitioners and students, and an important contribution to the literature of personality assessment. It is also the most definitive study of the CPI available and as such should become required reading for students in a variety of applied areas of psychology.

[B325]

★MEHRENS, WILLIAM A., EDITOR. **Readings in Measurement and Evaluation in Education and Psy-**

chology. New York: Holt, Rinehart and Winston, Inc., 1976. Pp. x, 374. Paper, $7.95. *

[B326]

★MEHRENS, WILLIAM A., AND LEHMANN, IRVIN J. **Measurement and Evaluation in Education and Psychology.** New York: Holt, Rinehart and Winston, Inc., 1973. Pp. xv, 672. $13.50. * For the latest edition, see B327.

Ed & Psychol Meas 33(4):1011–3 w '73. Richard Hansen. * Much of the material in the book is concerned with the more practical aspects of classroom evaluation. A total of 6 of the 19 chapters deal directly with the preparation of teacher made tests. As would be expected, the discussion of item writing techniques is quite extensive. Check lists are provided for the evaluation of each of the major item types. These should be quite helpful to the teacher constructing his own tests. The extensive discussion of item writing techniques is perhaps the strongest aspect of the text. * The title of the textbook would tend to indicate that it is suitable as a beginning text for the student of psychology. However, in view of the rather abbreviated discussion of areas of concern to the psychologist it would seem to be somewhat more suited for the educator. Since the focus in the book is in classroom evaluation procedures it should be ideal as a first text in educational measurement at either the graduate or undergraduate level. In addition, it should make an outstanding basic reference work for the teacher or administrator with a concern for testing in a school. The student who masters the content is in an ideal position to avoid most of the pitfalls in the development and use of tests in schools.

J Ed Meas 11(1):68–70 sp '74. Jacinta Mann. * this reviewer finds the new Mehrens and Lehmann book to be as nearly ideal for her approach to teaching as any on the market and will adopt it forthwith. The authors claim that it "can serve as the main text in the first course in measurement and evaluation at either the undergraduate or graduate level" and that "no formal course work in either testing or statistics is necessary to understand" it. Both claims appear to be justified. A scan of measurement texts of the last decade reveals none which includes so many of the topics likely to be treated in a first course. Probably the entire text could not be covered in one semester, but the clarity and conciseness of the organization would make it simple for the teacher who

wishes to pick and choose. Most topics are covered thoroughly and in a manner that reflects the latest writing and thinking in the field. It is evident that the authors have truly read the works in the extensive and up-to-date list of references at the end of each chapter. Especially gratifying is the coverage given to the criterion- *vs* norm-referenced controversy. * the stance taken by the authors is a balanced one; they attempt to present both sides of the issue and in the process to alert the student of measurement to the practical aspects of each viewpoint. * The open-mindedness should appeal to and edify teachers. Students will appreciate the charmingly simple style in which many of the chapters are written as well as the constant use of practical examples to illustrate theoretical points. They will be attracted also to the many Peanuts cartoons which are used throughout, each of which is a humorous but telling measurement lesson. * Both teacher and student will welcome the lists of objectives that begin and the summary statements that end each chapter. * A few disappointments might be mentioned. * The scattergram seems too important a concept to have received such short treatment. * Chapter 7 which treats the planning stage of classroom testing has excellent content but is not organized as well as it might be for the most effective teaching. * in comparison with other works intended for the same audience, this reviewer would rank it higher than any she has seen. Its overriding advantage is that it avoids pompous erudition and yet manages to consistently reflect recent educational theory and research. This text should make quite a contribution to decreasing the lag between research and practice.

Meas & Eval Guid 6(4):248–9 Ja '74. Dean E. Rochester. * The material has been well organized, is presented clearly and simply, and follows a reasonable design usually associated with this type of text. * In general....material is presented logically and directly, with a minimum of technical verbiage. As they work to become proficient in test evaluation, students will find the analysis of specific tests in the various areas helpful. Our students found the discussions in the section entitled "Educational Testing: A Broader View" most helpful * Attention to the mechanics as well as the theoretical considerations of developing and administering a school testing program is most practical for embryo school counselors. The authors are particularly effective in opening current issues in test use in counseling for discussion. They are frank in their presentation of the real issues in the fairness of practices, cultural bias in tests, invasion of privacy, and the proper use of tests. Discussions are not overextended or defensive, yet pertinent points are tackled forthrightly in low-keyed, unequivocal language to which students react positively.

[B327]

*MEHRENS, WILLIAM A., AND LEHMANN, IRVIN J. **Measurement and Evaluation in Education and Psychology, Second Edition.** New York: Holt, Rinehart and Winston, Inc., 1978. Pp. viii, 759. $13.50. * For reviews of the first edition, see B326 (3 excerpts).

[B328]

*MEHRENS, WILLIAM A., AND LEHMANN, IRVIN J. **Standardized Tests in Education, Second Edition.** New York: Holt, Rinehart and Winston, Inc., 1975. Pp. xiii, 369. Paper, $8.50. * For reviews of the first edition, see 7:B427 (2 excerpts).

Meas & Eval Guid 9(2):84-5 Jl '76. Kemp Mabry. * When Norman Gronlund reviewed the first edition in the winter 1969 issue of the *Journal of Educational Measurement,* he said that it was, "well-written, concise, and understandable to the beginning student of measurement. Since it is limited to standardized testing in education, it would be most useful in courses that have that particular focus." The second edition deserves the same accolade. * the authors have done an admirable job.

[B329]

★MELLON, JOHN C. **National Assessment and the Teaching of English: Results of the First National Assessment of Educational Progress in Writing, Reading, and Literature—Implications for Teaching and Measurement in the English Language Arts.** Urbana, Ill.: National Council of Teachers of English, 1975. Pp. vi, 127. Paper, $4.95. *

[B330]

★MILLER, C. M. L., AND PARLETT, M. **Up to the Mark: A Study of the Examination Game.** London: Society for Research Into Higher Education, 1974. Pp. ix, 128. Paper, £2.20. *

Brit J Ed Psychol 45(2):243-4 Je '75. Desmond L. Nuttall. * Miller and Parlett studied the examinations of three faculties at Edinburgh University. * A substantial part of the text consists of quotations from interviews with staff and students; questionnaires and non-participant observation were also used, but in all cases, the authors were careful to incorporate cross-checking and independent judgments of their classifications. The short sections and an appendix on the methodology provide a convincing defence of techniques that might appear, on

the surface, to lack rigour, and amply demonstrate that the report is much more than a string of case studies, interspersed with the subjective interpretations of the authors. The strength of their techniques is made especially clear in their original work on "cue-consciousness." They identified three types of student: two, the "cue-conscious" and the "cue-seekers," were both very conscious of examination technique, but while the "cue-conscious" were content to pick up hints from staff and to notice the particular academic interests of staff, the "cue-seekers" actively tried to create a favourable impression on staff and button-holed them about examination questions * The coverage of the book is best illustrated by the five dimensions of assessment identified by the authors. These are task complexity (including reliability), the weight attached to the results (in their importance for the future) and consequent stress, task time, the predictability of the requirements of the task, and task distribution over time. Altogether this book provides a fascinating insight into the problems of university examinations, and the attitudes of staff and students. The postscript points to the importance of considering assessment methods in the context of the total circumstances—the ecological metaphor—and suggests a number of questions that flow from the metaphor. It is to be hoped that researchers will attempt to answer them. *

[B331]

★MILLER, DAVID MONROE. **Interpreting Test Scores.** New York: John Wiley & Sons, Inc., 1972. Pp. xi, 162. Paper, $3.95. *

[B332]

★MILLER, KENNETH M., EDITOR. **Psychological Testing in Personnel Assessment.** London: Gower Press Ltd., 1975. Pp. xv, 192. £7.50. (New York: John Wiley & Sons, Inc. $20.00. *)

Personnel Psychol 29(3):491-3 au '76. Paul M. Muchinsky. * this book was written by practitioners for practitioners. It is a very down-to-earth presentation of problems and issues associated with implementing personnel testing programs. * I was impressed with its clarity and the authors' willingness to discuss fundamental testing problems. * Given that the jacket describes the book to "be of special value to personnel managers with no specialist knowledge of psychological testing," the book does far more than an adequate job in fulfilling its purpose. * I feel somewhat guilty about giving this book less than a totally positive evaluation. It truly is a technically solid piece of work, well written and one that lives up to its billing. As such I feel this book has a lot to offer the practitioner about the mechanics of psychological testing. But somehow in my mind I can hear someone saying, "But what does this book have to say about psychological testing in light of the EEOC guidelines?" Regrettably the book does not address itself to the issue, nor was it expressly designed to. While no one can deny the value of technical competence in psychological testing, the whole area of psychological testing in personnel selection is currently ensnarled in a legal morass. The lesson learned from running afoul of the law can be financially devastating. No discussion of personnel selection in America today is complete without great attention being paid to the financial qua legal ramifications of psychological testing. Consequently the legal and social forces brought to bear upon contemporary testing procedures and issues make this book painfully anachronistic. Given the technical merit of the book, it deserves (but probably will not receive) a better fate.

[B333]

★MILLER, LaMar P., Editor. **The Testing of Black Students: A Symposium.** Englewood Cliffs, N.J.: Prentice-Hall, Inc., 1974. Pp. xi, 113. $9.50. *

J Ed Meas 12(2):138–40 su '75. Elizabeth A. Abramowitz. * ever since the civil rights movement got underway, it has generated increasingly heated debates over the position of Black people in our schools and other social institutions * Involved is the use of group and individual tests for selection and placement in ways that ultimately reward large numbers of white students while at the same time excluding large numbers of Black students. The resolution of the current debate over testing is of general interest, not because of the technical aspects of psychological assessment, but rather because of the social and public policy consequences for Black and white students themselves, for the civil rights movement, and for institutionalized white racism. The book under review is a readable, nontechnical work which does not resolve the debate but does much to advance its quality. * *The Testing of Black Students* is not an attempt to intellectualize the elimination of psychological and educational testing of minority students, nor is it a blind

defense or *apologia* for tests and measurements. What makes this book both unique and worth reading is that, in brief space, it succeeds in bringing the ideals of meritocracy that underlie the testing movement into harmony and peaceful coexistence with the ideals of pluralism that underlie the civil rights movement. This alone is a significant achievement.

J Higher Ed 46(6):739–41 D '75. Willie S. Williams. * an interesting and dynamic symposium that provides a positive view of the controversial issues regarding the testing of black students. The ten articles....vary in the depth of information related to testing. Some authors present their views with support from either various types of research or with very logical analyses. Several of the articles are direct, forthright, and informative, while others appear defensive and lacking in scholarly acumen. The salient issues of reliability, validity, and norming have extensive coverage, while noticeably missing from this volume are discussions of the use of various test batteries and profiles of students in the prediction of vocational and educational success. The contributors provide a practical approach to many situations which one faces in the educational as well as vocational testing of black students. The article by Robert L. Williams gives insight into some aspects of testing which portray the educational institutions and testing industries as a symbiotic biasing system. The bias that exists within the educational milieu also exists within the tests which were developed for evaluating the effectiveness of this milieu. The culturally biased educational system supports and feeds on the culturally biased testing system and vice versa. In order to reduce the effects of bias in the testing system, a number of researchers began to toy with notions of cultural free and cultural fair tests. As Williams states, the culture free or culture fair type tests are certainly inappropriate in culturally biased training situations. So, rather than work toward the development of a culture free or a culture fair test, researchers should direct efforts toward development of culture specific tests. While Mercer presents a similar analysis, she goes further to express such issues as legal considerations and alternative plans based on a multicultural approach to education. Her innovative discussion of manifest and latent use of tests is excellent. The articles by Williams and Mercer make this book a must for those who are interested in dealing with the problems of cultural bias in testing and in the educational and vocational opportunities of blacks. Traditional issues of the race and sex of the tester, as they relate to minority group children, are discussed. Some of the data suggest the need for separate facilities within institutions to assist black students. Epps demonstrates that various characteristics of testers tend to make a difference as far as scores are concerned. His data support the notion that racial differences of testers create variance in test scores of black children. Warren G. Findley lays out a very well-documented analysis of the controversy that relates to tracking students. He presents it from both the perspective of the British educational system and the American system, along with some alternatives to tracking. He also reports on a follow-up to the Coleman studies, and the traditional controversy over the halo effect and self-fulfilling prophesy of teacher expectation are covered extensively. Lawrence Plotkin writes a well documented, interesting, informative, and objective view of the issues of heredity versus environment in Negro intelligence. The analysis of various pieces of controversial research (e.g., that of Jensen and Yerkes) and the political use of such research which has not met the scientific rigor expected from a scholarly report is thorough. Information regarding I.Q. testing in school desegregation, employment testing, bussing, and other issues may be found in his article. Plotkin mentions the Anglo-Saxon bias against many groups even white groups who did not have the Anglo inheritance. All non-Anglo-Saxon immigrants were considered inherently inferior. This has created the foundation on which vitriolic inflammative attacks have been leveled on the abilities and potentials of certain groups by Garrett, Yerkes, Jensen, and others. The paper provides an excellent historical perspective regarding the problems of test bias in our schools and society. Roger T. Lennon appears very defensive in his article as he attempts to protect the established testing system. He seems to lack an understanding of the significance of the criticism to which he refers; or worse, he may be ignoring the criticism. The essential issue is test bias; he tends to infer there is none and that purely mechanical operations on the part of test publishers, such as inclusion of inner city or black subjects in new norm groups, would eliminate all semblances of test bias. Ronald Flaugher attempts

to clear some points of confusion regarding test bias in relation to the testing of black students. However, the polemics in which he deals tend to further obfuscate the issues. His article is lacking in sufficient references; and the development of his four points is, at most, mediocre. Although this volume covers a variety of topics and issues, it suffers, as most symposia, from limited information based upon controlled studies. A related problem found in this, and in other volumes of this type, is that most studies reported in social science literature lack valid replications. If the political, social, economical, and educational consequences of test bias were not so critical, then time could permit controlled studies for the exploration of some suggestions made in this book. Due to the insidious nature of racism in the educational and testing system, though, one cannot develop the kind of programs needed in the long run because short-run deficits and impairments of the opportunities for blacks and other minorities are too prevalent. As the author points out, "The primary reason for the development of this volume was to review some of the specific issues that underlie the testing controversy." The volume does this well and provides documented sources of support for those who intend to improve the educational and vocational plight of minorities.

[B334]
★MILLER, RICHARD I. **Evaluating Faculty Performance.** San Francisco, Calif.: Jossey-Bass Inc., Publishers, 1972. Pp. xvii, 145. $9.95. *

J Higher Ed 44(2):163–4 F '73. Donald P. Hoyt. In fifty-five pages of text and thirty-two pages of charts and illustrative forms, Miller tells more than is known about the complex activity of evaluating faculty performance. * By calling attention to the diversity of activities which describe the work of the faculty member, the book serves a useful purpose. Its emphasis on flexibility in establishing individualized "contracts" and on a variety of inputs in judging performances respond to common shortcomings in current practices. Its plea for quantification and objectivity is laudable. The naive reader may be misled by the numerous rating forms reproduced in the book. The only form with any supporting research is the teaching form; and it hardly qualifies as an instrument with established validity. Obvious weaknesses in the other forms include questionable relevance of items (e.g., "maintains accurate files" on the advising scale) and the impracticality of obtaining valid ratings (e.g., how colleagues at other institutions respond to a given publication). Miller makes a good case for improving faculty evaluation. Combined with his clear demonstration of how weak current appraisal devices and procedures are, his book may stimulate the research which the problem so badly needs. At least one hopes that this will be its impact, rather than a foolish, uncritical adoption of Miller's crude instruments.

[B335]

★MILTON, OHMER, AND EDGERLY, JOHN W. **The Testing and Grading of Students.** New Rochelle, N.Y.: Change Magazine, 1976. Pp. 62. Paper, $2.95. *

[B336]

★MITTLER, PETER, EDITOR. **Assessment for Learning in the Mentally Handicapped.** Edinburgh, Scotland: Churchill Livingstone, 1973. Pp. x, 313. * *Out of print.*

B Brit Psychol Soc 27:320 Jl '74. Simon Haskell. * Of the 28 Participants (26 psychologists and two physicians) not a single teacher or person substantially concerned with the day-to-day management of mentally retarded children was present at this symposium. It seems that the term "practitioner" was rather narrowly defined. Another notable group excluded was that of college of education lecturers running training courses for teachers of the mentally retarded. One wonders, therefore, for whom this book is intended. If it is for a small group of research workers, then the topics discussed have appeared in a variety of journals and books elsewhere. Most psychologists have been reminded *ad nauseam* that psychometric testing in itself is out, profile and functional analysis is in. Few research articles end without the ritualistic incantation that intervention and training programmes without evaluation are *passé*. If this book is intended for practitioners (and I include serving teachers) then none of my sophisticated and experienced teachers taking the advanced diploma course derived much inspiration or enlightenment from this volume. It is a pity that 26 sincere and gifted psychologists should choose to spend three days mutually reinforcing one another's beliefs, talking in that mystical in-language some psychologists use. I can think of no more effective way of alienating the earnest reader than the use of pretentious and tortuous descriptions of simple behaviour. Children no longer have arithmetical

difficulties, they "encounter problems in quantifying their environment." Military metaphors abound—strategy is used when what we mean is mode of behaviour. * The compelling concern and hope of parents of handicapped children in the 1970s will be that the plethora of such "methodologically impeccable research programmes" as automated assessment techniques, and experimental developments of functional analysis, will lead to prompt ameliorative action. This book does precious little to promote this aim.

Brit J Ed Psychol 44(3):330–1 N '74. O. C. Sampson. This book records the papers and discussions of a study group held at the Ciba Foundation under the auspices of the institute for Research into Mental Retardation. * Compilations such as this which include papers, bibliographies, semi-formal critiques, and contributions in open discussion, often provide rather unsatisfactory and uneasy reading material, but in this case, partly because of the quality of the discussants, this is by no means so. The main papers have been written or rewritten in such a way as to make them in style and approach suitable for the printed page and the individuality of the different points of view in the open discussions is so well preserved that they have an almost dramatic quality. * To select for special mention any of the 12 papers is invidious and must depend on personal interests to some extent. All are excellent in their particular way and are the fruit of exceptional individual expertise in different fields. * A final general discussion returns to some of the questions which have been exercising the study group during their deliberations such as what are the essential skills for which the subnormal should be trained, what is the appropriate role of parents in their training, and how are knowledge and suggestions to be disseminated? A book like this, excellent as it is, is only a part answer to the last question. It should certainly be read by all students, workers and research people. *

J Mental Def Res (England) 18(2):196–7 Je '74. B. H. Kirman. * The book reflects some of the current disillusions with simple "testing" and recognises the fact that expression of a social quotient or other reflection of social competence may be equally valuable. The discussion provided, however, a warning that there is a danger of moving from areas which lend themselves to fairly accurate measurement into nebulous and subjective reporting. John Corbett in discussion says something in defence of the intelligence quotient and the reviewer is alarmed by the suggestion that it is impossible to attempt a conventional assessment of all the children in E.S.N. (SSN) schools (ex-junior training centres). Admittedly this would be a formidable task: Peter Mittler estimates that some 35,000 children are involved. On the other hand work with autistic children has shown that a global estimate of intelligence is a useful guide to prognosis and certainly a measure of mental age is a helpful index for parent and teacher of appropriate starting points. Furthermore, discrepancies in more sophisticated assessment batteries are very useful cues as to aspects needing special attention in any remedial programme. It had seemed to the reviewer that a progressive trend has been the increasing involvement of psychologists in reliable assessment and it would seem to him retrograde to suggest that this work should be "off-loaded" on to teachers or medical practitioners who usually have less expertise in this area. The answer is surely a close-knit team approach. This book is well edited and produced. It is clearly and simply written. It should provide interested psychologists, teachers, psychiatrists and others concerned with child development an invaluable account of the exciting new happenings in this fascinating field.

[B337]

★MOKKEN, R. J. **A Theory and Procedure of Scale Analysis With Applications in Political Research.** Elmsford, N.Y.: Mouton Publishers, 1971. Pp. xiii, 353. $15.50. *

[B338]

★MOOS, RUDOLF H. **Evaluating Correctional and Community Settings.** New York: John Wiley & Sons, Inc., 1975. Pp. xxii, 377. $16.75. *

[B338A]

★NFER SCHOOL TO UNIVERSITY RESEARCH UNIT. **After A-Level? A Study of the Transition from School to Higher Education.** By B. H. L. Choppin and others. Slough, Bucks, England: NFER Publishing Co. Ltd., 1972. Pp. 30. Paper, £1.10.

Brit J Ed Psychol 44(1):92–6 F '74. N. J. *Entwistle.* [Not excerpted, see original review.]

[B339]

★NAFZIGER, DEAN H.; THOMPSON, R. BRENT; HISCOX, MICHAEL D.; AND OWEN, THOMAS R. **Tests of Functional Adult Literacy: An Evaluation of Currently Available Instruments.** Portland, Ore.: Northwest Regional Educational Laboratory, 1975. Pp. 110. Paper, $5.95. *

J Ed Res 70(4):230 Mr–Ap '77. *Eunice Askov.* * a paperback that gives us more than its title promises—that is, both a description and evaluation of current tests intended for ABE and GED classes. * the authors....have included a well-written introductory chapter on the problems of defining and measuring functional literacy. * The authors state that they intentionally do not include many tests presently used in adult programs that were originally developed for use in elementary or secondary schools. This decision limits the scope, and to some extent the usefulness, of the book, because one does not know which elementary or secondary reading tests might indeed be useful in adult programs. The descriptions of the tests may prove more useful than the test evaluations. The reader should be cautioned that some of the numerical weightings assigned to evaluation criteria seem debatable. Likewise, the selection of criteria seems biased toward a particular type of testing. The overall ratings of quality are questionable since zero points are awarded either for noncompliance with the criterion or for lack of information. Although the authors do point out some of these limitations, the reader should not accept the quality ratings at face value without considering whether or not their derivation is appropriate for the particular kind of test being considered. The book should prove to be a useful tool to teachers and administrators of ABE and GED programs in identifying appropriate tests for placement, diagnosis, or program evaluation. Although at least one other book of similar intent is presently available, this one is valuable for its authors' commentary and test descriptions.

[B340]

★NATIONAL ASSESSMENT OF EDUCATIONAL PROGRESS. **Adult Work Skills and Knowledge: Selected Results From the First National Assessment of Career and Occupational Development.** Career and Occupational Report No. 05–COD–01. Washington, D.C.: U.S. Government Printing Office, September 1976. Pp. xiii, 70. Paper, $3.65. *

[B341]

★NATIONAL ASSESSMENT OF EDUCATIONAL PROGRESS. **An Assessment of Attitudes Toward Music.** Music Report No. 03–MU–03. Washington, D.C.: U.S. Government Printing Office, September 1974. Pp. vii, 31. Paper, $1.10. *

[B342]

★NATIONAL ASSESSMENT OF EDUCATIONAL PROGRESS. **An Assessment of Career Development: Basic Work Skills: Selected Results From the First National Assessment of Career and Occupational Development.** Career and Occupational Development

Report No. 05–COD–02. Washington, D.C.: U.S. Government Printing Office, January 1977. Pp. xi, 32. Paper, $1.15. *

[B343]
★NATIONAL ASSESSMENT OF EDUCATIONAL PROGRESS. **Changes in Science Performance, 1969–1973: Exercise Volume.** Science Report No. 04–S–20. Washington, D.C.: U.S. Government Printing Office, December 1975. Pp. xiv, 317. Paper, $25.00. *

[B344]
★NATIONAL ASSESSMENT OF EDUCATIONAL PROGRESS. **Changes in Science Performance, 1969–73: Exercise Volume. Appendix (2 vols.).** Science Report No. 04–S–20. Washington, D.C.: U.S. Government Printing Office, April 1977. Pp. vii, 670, 847. Paper, $25.00. *

[B345]
★NATIONAL ASSESSMENT OF EDUCATIONAL PROGRESS. **Citizenship: National Results.** Report 2. Washington, D.C.: U.S. Government Printing Office, November 1970. Pp. ix, 125. Paper, $1.50. *

[B346]
★NATIONAL ASSESSMENT OF EDUCATIONAL PROGRESS. **Citizenship: 1969–1970 Assessment: Group Results for Parental Education, Color, Size and Type of Community.** National Assessment Report 9. Washington, D.C.: U.S. Government Printing Office, May 1972. Pp. iii, 115, G–1. Paper, $2.80. *

[B347]
★NATIONAL ASSESSMENT OF EDUCATIONAL PROGRESS. **Consumer Math: Selected Results from the First National Assessment of Mathematics.** Mathematics Report No. 04–MA–02. Washington, D.C.: U.S. Government Printing Office, June 1975. Pp. xii, 36. Paper, $2.00. *

[B348]
★NATIONAL ASSESSMENT OF EDUCATIONAL PROGRESS. **Critical Reading: Theme 8, Reading.** Report 02–R–08. Washington, D.C.: U.S. Government Printing Office, May 1973. Pp. xviii, 169. Paper, $3.70. *

[B349]
★NATIONAL ASSESSMENT OF EDUCATIONAL PROGRESS. **Drawing Inferences: Theme 7, Reading.** Report 02–R–07. Washington, D.C.: U.S. Government Printing Office, August 1973. Pp. xviii, 258. Paper, $5.00. *

[B350]
NATIONAL ASSESSMENT OF EDUCATIONAL PROGRESS. **Education for Citizenship: A Bicentennial Survey.** Citizenship/Social Studies Report No. 07–CS–01. Washington, D.C.: U.S. Government Printing Office, November 1976. Pp. ix, 35. Paper, $2.35. *

[B351]
★NATIONAL ASSESSMENT OF EDUCATIONAL PROGRESS. **Explanatory and Persuasive Letter Writing: Selected Results From the Second National Assessment of Writing.** Writing Report No. 05–W–03. Washington, D.C.: U.S. Government Printing Office, February 1977. Pp. xv, 21. Paper, $1.85. *

[B352]
★NATIONAL ASSESSMENT OF EDUCATIONAL PROGRESS. **Expressive Writing: Selected Results from the Second National Assessment of Writing.** Writing Report No. 05–W–02. Washington, D.C.: U.S. Government Printing Office, November 1976. Pp. xv, 49. Paper, $1.65. *

[B353]
★NATIONAL ASSESSMENT OF EDUCATIONAL PROGRESS. **The First Music Assessment: An Overview.** Report 03–MU–00. Washington, D.C.: U.S. Government Printing Office, August 1974. Pp. vi, 41. Paper, $1.00. *

[B354]
★NATIONAL ASSESSMENT OF EDUCATIONAL PROGRESS. **The First National Assessment of Career and Occupational Development: An Overview.** Career and Occupational Development Report No. 05–COD–00. Washington, D.C.: U.S. Government Printing Office, November 1976. Pp. xvi, 43. Paper, $1.60. *

[B355]
★NATIONAL ASSESSMENT OF EDUCATIONAL PROGRESS. **The First National Assessment of Mathematics: An Overview.** Mathematics Report No. 04–MA–00. Washington, D.C.: U.S. Government Printing Office, October 1975. Pp. xiv, 52. Paper, $1.80. *

[B356]
★NATIONAL ASSESSMENT OF EDUCATIONAL PROGRESS. **The First National Assessment of Musical Performance.** Report 03–MU–01. Washington, D.C.: U.S. Government Printing Office, February 1974. Pp. v, 29. Paper, $1.00. *

[B357]
★NATIONAL ASSESSMENT OF EDUCATIONAL PROGRESS. **The First Social Studies Assessment: An Overview.** Report 03–SS–00. Washington, D.C.: U.S. Government Printing Office, June 1974. Pp. vii, 71. Paper, $1.00. *

[B358]
★NATIONAL ASSESSMENT OF EDUCATIONAL PROGRESS. **Functional Literacy: Basic Reading Performance, A Brief Summary and Highlights of an Assessment of 17-Year-Old Students in 1974 and 1975.** Washington, D.C.: U.S. Government Printing Office, 1976. Pp. xii, 53. Paper, $2.10. *

[B359]
★NATIONAL ASSESSMENT OF EDUCATIONAL PROGRESS. **General Information Yearbook.** Report No. 03/04–GIY. Washington, D.C.: U.S. Government Printing Office, December 1974. Pp. viii, 55. Paper, $2.50. *

[B360]
★NATIONAL ASSESSMENT OF EDUCATIONAL PROGRESS. **Gleaning Significant Facts from Passages: Theme 5, Reading.** Report 02–R–05. Washington, D.C.: U.S. Government Printing Office, May 1973. Pp. xviii, 207. Paper, $4.50. *

[B361]
★NATIONAL ASSESSMENT OF EDUCATIONAL PROGRESS. **Graphic Materials: Theme 2, Reading.** Report 02–R–02. Washington, D.C.: U.S. Government Printing Office, June 1973. Pp. xv, 199. Paper, $4.20. *

[B362]
★NATIONAL ASSESSMENT OF EDUCATIONAL PROGRESS. **Hispanic Student Achievement in Five Learning Areas: 1971–75.** Report No. BR–2. Washington, D.C.: U.S. Government Printing Office, May 1977. Pp. ix, 78. Paper, $4.45. *

[B363]
★NATIONAL ASSESSMENT OF EDUCATIONAL PROGRESS. **Literature: Released Exercises.** Report 02–L–20. Washington, D.C.: U.S. Government Printing Office, April 1973. Pp. ii, 330. Paper, $6.00. *

[B364]

★NATIONAL ASSESSMENT OF EDUCATIONAL PROGRESS. **Literature: Summary Data.** Report 02-L-00. Washington, D.C.: U.S. Government Printing Office, June 1973. Pp. x, 105. Paper, $1.60. *

[B365]

★NATIONAL ASSESSMENT OF EDUCATIONAL PROGRESS. **Main Ideas and Organization: Theme 6, Reading.** Report 02-R-06. Washington, D.C.: U.S. Government Printing Office, July 1973. Pp. xviii, 139. Paper, $3.20. *

[B366]

★NATIONAL ASSESSMENT OF EDUCATIONAL PROGRESS. **Math Fundamentals: Selected Results From the First National Assessment of Mathematics.** Mathematics Report No. 04-MA-01. Washington, D.C.: U.S. Government Printing Office, January 1975. Pp. xiv, 41. Paper, $2.45. *

[B367]

★NATIONAL ASSESSMENT OF EDUCATIONAL PROGRESS. **Mathematics Technical Report: Exercise Volume.** Mathematics Report No. 04-MA-20. Washington, D.C.: U.S. Government Printing Office, February 1977. Pp. vii, 795. Paper, $25.00. *

[B368]

★NATIONAL ASSESSMENT OF EDUCATIONAL PROGRESS. **Mathematics Technical Report: Summary Volume.** Mathematics Report No. 04-MA-21. Washington, D.C.: U.S. Government Printing Office, September 1976. Pp. xi, 172. Paper, $19.50. *

[B369]

★NATIONAL ASSESSMENT OF EDUCATIONAL PROGRESS. **Music Technical Report: Exercise Volume.** Music Report No. 03-MU-20. Washington, D.C.: U.S. Government Printing Office, December 1975. Pp. viii, 1006. Paper, $25.00. *

[B370]

★NATIONAL ASSESSMENT OF EDUCATIONAL PROGRESS. **Music Technical Report: Summary Volume.** Music Report No. 03-MU-21. Washington, D.C.: U.S. Government Printing Office, November 1975. Pp. viii, 137. Paper, $4.40. *

[B371]

★NATIONAL ASSESSMENT OF EDUCATIONAL PROGRESS. **National Assessment and Social Studies Education: A Review of Assessments in Citizenship and Social Studies by the National Council for the Social Studies.** Edited by Jean Fair. Washington, D.C.: U.S. Government Printing Office, 1975. Pp. xii, 115. Paper, $1.95. *

[B372]

★NATIONAL ASSESSMENT OF EDUCATIONAL PROGRESS. **National Assessments of Science, 1969 and 1973: A Capsule Description of Changes in Science Achievement.** Science Report No. 04-S-00. Washington, D.C.: U.S. Government Printing Office, February 1975. Pp. xiii, 13. Paper, $1.00. *

[B373]

★NATIONAL ASSESSMENT OF EDUCATIONAL PROGRESS. **1969-1970 Citizenship: Group Results for Sex, Region, and Size of Community.** National Assessment Report 6. Washington, D.C.: U.S. Government Printing Office, July 1971. Pp. v, 49, E-4. Paper, $1.35. *

[B374]

★NATIONAL ASSESSMENT OF EDUCATIONAL PROGRESS. **1969-1970 Science: Group Results for Sex, Region, and Size of Community.** National Assessment Report 4. Washington, D.C.: U.S. Government Printing Office, April 1971. Pp. v, 65, 34. Paper, $1.00. *

[B375]

★NATIONAL ASSESSMENT OF EDUCATIONAL PROGRESS. **1969-1970 Science: National Results and Illustrations of Group Comparisons.** Report 1. Washington, D.C.: U.S. Government Printing Office, July 1970. Pp. xii, 160, F-1. Paper, $2.15. *

[B376]

★NATIONAL ASSESSMENT OF EDUCATIONAL PROGRESS. **1969-1970 Writing: Group Results for Sex, Region, and Size of Community.** National Assessment Report 5. Washington, D.C.: U.S. Government Printing Office, April 1971. Pp. vii, 59, C-13. Paper, $1.70. *

[B377]

★NATIONAL ASSESSMENT OF EDUCATIONAL PROGRESS. **1969-1970 Writing: National Results.** Report 3. Washington, D.C.: U.S. Government Printing Office, November 1970. Pp. ix, 115, E-1. Paper, $1.85. *

[B378]

★NATIONAL ASSESSMENT OF EDUCATIONAL PROGRESS. **A Perspective on the First Music Assessment.** Report 03-MU-02. Washington, D.C.: U.S. Government Printing Office, April 1974. Pp. v, 25. Paper, $1.00. *

[B379]

★NATIONAL ASSESSMENT OF EDUCATIONAL PROGRESS. **Political Knowledge and Attitudes: A Special Social Studies Report From the National Assessment of Educational Progress.** Report 03-SS-01. Washington, D.C.: U.S. Government Printing Office, December 1973. Pp. iii, 57. Paper, $1.00. *

[B380]

★NATIONAL ASSESSMENT OF EDUCATIONAL PROGRESS. **Reading and Literature: General Information Yearbook.** Report 02-GIY. Washington, D.C.: U.S. Government Printing Office, May 1972. Pp. vii, 102. Paper, $2.75. *

[B381]

★NATIONAL ASSESSMENT OF EDUCATIONAL PROGRESS. **Reading in America: A Perspective on Two Assessments.** Reading Report No. 06-R-01. Washington, D.C.: U.S. Government Printing Office, October 1976. Pp. xi, 30. Paper, $1.25. *

[B382]

★NATIONAL ASSESSMENT OF EDUCATIONAL PROGRESS. **Reading Rate and Comprehension.** Report 02-R-09. Washington, D.C.: U.S. Government Printing Office, December 1972. Pp. x, 225. Paper, $3.75. *

[B383]

★NATIONAL ASSESSMENT OF EDUCATIONAL PROGRESS. **Reading: Released Exercises.** Report 02-R-20. Washington, D.C.: U.S. Government Printing Office, July 1973. Pp. vii, 424. Paper, $11.15. *

[B384]

★NATIONAL ASSESSMENT OF EDUCATIONAL PROGRESS. **Reading: Summary Data.** Report 02-R-00. Washington, D.C.: U.S. Government Printing Office, July 1974. Pp. vi, 57. Paper, $1.00. *

[B385]

★NATIONAL ASSESSMENT OF EDUCATIONAL PROGRESS.
Recipes, Wrappers, Reasoning and Rate: A
Digest of the First Reading Assessment. Report
02–R–30. Washington, D.C.: U.S. Government Printing Office, April 1974. Pp. xiv, 65. Paper, $1.10. *

[B386]

★NATIONAL ASSESSMENT OF EDUCATIONAL PROGRESS.
Recognizing Literary Works and Characters:
Theme 3, Literature. Report 02–L–03. Washington,
D.C.: U.S. Government Printing Office, April 1973.
Pp. xiv, 198. Paper, $4.25. *

[B387]

★NATIONAL ASSESSMENT OF EDUCATIONAL PROGRESS.
Reference Materials: Theme 4, Reading. Report
02–R–04. Washington, D.C.: U.S. Government Printing Office, July 1973. Pp. xviii, 149. Paper, $3.55. *

[B388]

★NATIONAL ASSESSMENT OF EDUCATIONAL PROGRESS.
Responding to Literature: Theme 2, Literature.
Report 02–L–02. Washington, D.C.: U.S. Government
Printing Office, April 1973. Pp. xvii, 231. Paper,
$4.40. *

[B389]

★NATIONAL ASSESSMENT OF EDUCATIONAL PROGRESS.
Science Achievement: Racial and Regional
Trends, 1969–73. Background Report No. BRS–1.
Washington, D.C.: U.S. Government Printing Office,
March 1976. Pp. xiii, 46. Paper, $3.95. *

[B390]

★NATIONAL ASSESSMENT OF EDUCATIONAL PROGRESS.
Science: Group and Balanced Group Results for
Color, Parental Education, Size and Type of
Community and Balanced Group Results for
Region of the Country, Sex. Report 7. Washington,
D.C.: U.S. Government Printing Office, May 1973.
Pp. xxi, 195. Paper, $2.60. *

[B391]

★NATIONAL ASSESSMENT OF EDUCATIONAL PROGRESS.
Science: National Results. Summary of Report 1.
Washington, D.C.: U.S. Government Printing Office,
July 1970. Pp. iii, 15. Paper, $0.35. *

[B392]

★NATIONAL ASSESSMENT OF EDUCATIONAL PROGRESS.
Science Technical Report: Summary Volume.
Science Report No. 04–S–21. Washington, D.C.: U.S.
Government Printing Office, May 1977. Pp. xviii, 134.
Paper, $16.80. *

[B393]

★NATIONAL ASSESSMENT OF EDUCATIONAL PROGRESS.
Selected Essays and Letters: A Selection of
Papers Collected During the 1969–70 Assessment
of Writing. Report 10. Washington, D.C.: U.S. Gov-
ernment Printing Office, November 1972. Pp. iii, 1026.
Paper, $12.50. *

[B394]

★NATIONAL ASSESSMENT OF EDUCATIONAL PROGRESS.
Selected Results From the National Assessments
of Science: Attitude Questions. Science Report No.
04–S–03. Washington, D.C.: U.S. Government Printing Office, October 1975. Pp. ix, 75. Paper, $3.45. *

[B395]

★NATIONAL ASSESSMENT OF EDUCATIONAL PROGRESS.
Selected Results From the National Assessments

of Science: Energy Questions. Science Report No.
04–S–01. Washington, D.C.: U.S. Government Printing Office, May 1975. Pp. vii, 19. Paper, $1.45. *

[B396]

★NATIONAL ASSESSMENT OF EDUCATIONAL PROGRESS.
Selected Results From the National Assessments
of Science: Scientific Principles and Procedures.
Science Report No. 04–S–02. Washington, D.C.: U.S.
Government Printing Office, August 1975. Pp. xiii, 53.
Paper, $3.00. *

[B397]

★NATIONAL ASSESSMENT OF EDUCATIONAL PROGRESS.
Social Studies: Contemporary Social Issues. Re-
port 03–SS–02. Washington, D.C.: U.S. Government
Printing Office, July 1974. Pp. vii, 47. Paper, $1.20. *

[B398]

★NATIONAL ASSESSMENT OF EDUCATIONAL PROGRESS.
Social Studies Technical Report: Exercise Volume. Social Studies Report No. 03–SS–20. Washington, D.C.: U.S. Government Printing Office, December
1975. Pp. vii, 878. Paper, $25.00. *

[B399]

★NATIONAL ASSESSMENT OF EDUCATIONAL PROGRESS.
Social Studies Technical Report: Summary Volume. Social Studies Report No. 03–SS–21. Washington, D.C.: U.S. Government Printing Office, November 1975. Pp. viii, 113. Paper, $4.00. *

[B400]

★NATIONAL ASSESSMENT OF EDUCATIONAL PROGRESS.
A Survey of Reading Habits: Theme 4, Literature. Report 02–L–04. Washington, D.C.: U.S. Government Printing Office, May 1973. Pp. xiv, 261. Paper,
$4.80. *

[B401]

★NATIONAL ASSESSMENT OF EDUCATIONAL PROGRESS.
Understanding Imaginative Language: Theme 1
of the National Assessment of Literature. Report
02–L–01. Washington, D.C.: U.S. Government Printing Office, March 1973. Pp. xvi, 197. Paper, $4.15. *

[B402]

★NATIONAL ASSESSMENT OF EDUCATIONAL PROGRESS.
Understanding Words and Word Relationships:
Theme 1 of the National Assessment of Reading.
Report 02–R–01. Washington, D.C.: U.S. Government
Printing Office, April 1973. Pp. xx, 91. Paper, $2.35. *

[B403]

★NATIONAL ASSESSMENT OF EDUCATIONAL PROGRESS.
Writing: Group Results A and B for Objectively-
Scored Exercises—1969–70 Assessment: National
Results by Region, Sex, Color, Size and Type of
Community, and Parental Education. Report 11.
Washington, D.C.: U.S. Government Printing Office,
May 1973. Pp. xi, 80. Paper, $1.25. *

[B404]

★NATIONAL ASSESSMENT OF EDUCATIONAL PROGRESS.
Writing Mechanics, 1969–1974: A Capsule De-
scription of Changes in Writing Mechanics. Writ-
ing Report No. 05–W–01. Washington, D.C.: U.S.
Government Printing Office, October 1975. Pp. xi, 59.
Paper, $1.60. *

[B405]

★NATIONAL ASSESSMENT OF EDUCATIONAL PROGRESS.
Writing: National Results—Writing Mechanics.
Report 8. Washington, D.C.: U.S. Government Print-
ing Office, February 1972. Pp. viii, 202. Paper, $2.50. *

[B406]

★NATIONAL ASSESSMENT OF EDUCATIONAL PROGRESS. **Written Directions: Theme 3, Reading.** Report 02–R–03. Washington, D.C.: U.S. Government Printing Office, May 1973. Pp. xviii, 142. Paper, $3.35. *

[B407]

★NATIONAL EDUCATION ASSOCIATION. **Report of the NEA Task Force on Testing.** Reprinted from Reports of Committees, Councils and Task Forces, 1974–75. Washington, D.C.: National Education Association, July 1975. Pp. 10. Paper. * *Out of print.*

[B408]

★NATIONAL EDUCATION ASSOCIATION. **Standardized Testing Issues: Teachers' Perspectives.** Washington, D.C.: National Education Association, 1977. Pp. 96. Paper, $5.75. *

[B409]

★NEURINGER, CHARLES, EDITOR. **Psychological Assessment of Suicidal Risk.** Springfield, Ill.: Charles C Thomas, Publisher, 1974. Pp. xvi, 240. $11.75. *

Am J Psychiatry 131(12):1427 D '74. Norman Tabachnick. * this book will be of interest to all who wish to understand the nature of suicide and some of the available approaches and tools for predicting it.

[B410]

*NOLL, VICTOR H., AND SCANNELL, DALE P. **Introduction to Educational Measurement, Third Edition.** Boston, Mass.: Houghton Mifflin Co., 1972. Pp. xiv, 582. $15.50. * For reviews of the earlier editions, see 7:B451 (3 excerpts), 6:B396 (2 excerpts), and 5:B321 (1 excerpt).

Ed & Psychol Meas 33(1):197–200 sp '73. Max D. Engelhart. * presents....a clearly-written elementary discussion of statistical methods applicable to test data * Especially noteworthy is Chapter 6 emphasizing the importance of objectives to measurement. * The mechanical aspects of constructing completion, true-false, matching, and multiple-choice items are well treated, but some more thought-provoking items would have better served as models for teachers. It is gratifying to note the mention of key-list items although better illustrative examples could have been provided. The discussion of situational or interpretive exercises is among the best in the text. A number of helpful general suggestions for the writing of objective items are given toward the end of the chapter. Chapter 8 is similarly helpful in suggesting ways of organizing and trying out of the test material. * Included is a thoughtful discussion of the problem involved in testing the culturally disadvantaged. *

[B411]

★NOLL, VICTOR H.; SCANNELL, DALE P.; AND NOLL, RACHEL P.; EDITORS. **Introductory Readings in Educational Measurement.** Boston, Mass.: Houghton Mifflin Co., 1972. Pp. xiii, 447. Paper, $8.95. *

[B412]

★NORTH, MARION. **Personality Assessment Through Movement.** Boston, Mass.: Plays, Inc., 1975. Pp. xiii, 300. $12.95. *

[B413]

*NUNNALLY, JUM C.; WITH THE COLLABORATION OF NANCY ALMAND ATOR. **Educational Measurement and Evaluation, Second Edition.** New York: McGraw-Hill Book Co., Inc., 1972. Pp. x, 598. $17.50. * For reviews of the first edition, see 7:B454 (2 excerpts).

Ed & Psychol Meas 33(1):200–2 sp '73. Carl N. Shaw. * From a technical point of view, the book leaves little room for criticism. The coverage of basic principles of measurement and evaluation and teacher made tests is thorough and very complete for this level text. In fact students who do not have a fairly strong undergraduate background including some attention to measurement and related problems probably would find the text difficult. These sections are refreshing as they make minimal reference to published tests, forcing the reader to consider the concepts being discussed rather than attending to specific instruments. A major stylistic criticism is the disparaging comments concerning the training and ability of teachers. * When a teacher must construct a test every advantage should be afforded. * Nunnally has done a very good job of explaining the concepts and procedures a teacher would need. The sections on published tests are excellent. * However, the section on diagnostic tests (Chapter 10) is extremely depressing to read. This is not a fault of Nunnally but, rather reflects the state of affairs. * It appears that with all current emphasis on individualization of instruction with its accompanying need for diagnostic testing much is to be desired in this area. Nunnally might have expanded this area to point the way for further development. In summary it should be stated that this is a good book reflecting the state of the art. As has already been mentioned this reviewer was disappointed in that very little attempt was made to point out weaknesses in current thinking, nor was serious mention made of the special measurement problems accompanying educational innovation. Entirely missing is any mention of development of teacher made instruments to assess the affective outcomes of instruction, an area which is deserving of much attention.

[B414]

NUNNALLY, JUM C., JR. **Introduction to Psychological Measurement.** New York: McGraw-Hill Book Co., Inc., 1970. Pp. xv, 572. $17.50. *

J Ed Meas 9(1):82-3 sp '71. Charles Hanley. * Adopting construct validity as the goal of measurement and advocating factor analysis and homogeneous tests as the methods to achieve it, Nunnally does not—perhaps could not, given these preferences—deal with the effects of psychological measurement on life. * Chief among Nunnally's dislikes is criterion-oriented test construction, but he confines criticism of it to theory, not raising the issue in connection with the Strong VIB or the MMPI. Also rejected is the possibility that general traits do not exist in personality, an idea he restricts to idiographists and rules an "antiscientific point of view." That Lewin, Tryon, and Guthrie, among others, held this idea is not apparent in the text. * The book begins with the standard, unfortunate chapters psychologists write on the foundations and history of testing, followed by chapters on norms and correlations that are somewhat padded by statistical material not used later. The text gets down to business with chapters on reliability, buttressed by an excellent appendix section organized around the domain-sampling model, and validity, featured by a sympathetic presentation of construct validity. A clear chapter on scaling models uses trace lines effectively, but its title, "Psychophysical Methods and Theories," misleads: the book covers neither classical nor modern psychophysics. Completing the first half of the text, a chapter on test construction stresses theoretical relevance rather than utility. Because Nunnally does not give test utilization systematic attention, concepts like base rate and selection ratio are absent, as is any discussion of decision theory. * In all, the book is a legitimate descendant of its predecessor, achieving its author's aim to move away from tests toward measurement. Like the earlier book, it is suitable for upper-division undergraduates. The writing is clear, occasionally discursive, and friendly—but friendly like a professor, not a pal. Among its competitors, it most resembles Anastasi's *Psychological Testing* (1968) but is less formidable. Teachers who liked the original version will be happy with this revision.

[B415]

★NYFIELD, GILLIAN; SAVILLE, PETER; FIELD, JANICE; AND HODGKISS, JOHN. **British Supplement to the Watson-Glaser Thinking Appraisal (Form YM).** Windsor, Berks., England: NFER Publishing Co. Ltd., 1976. Pp. ii, 24. Paper, £4.00. *

[B416]

★OAKLAND, THOMAS, EDITOR. **Psychological and Educational Assessment of Minority Children.** New York: Brunner/Mazel, Inc., 1977. Pp. xiv, 241. $13.50. *

[B417]

★OMER, JANE L. **Evaluating the Audiogram.** Danville, Ill.: Interstate Printers & Publishers, 1976. Pp. 32. Paper, $1.00.

Read Teach 31(2):230 N '77. S. Alan Cohen. How to Draw an Audiogram: Plot tone on the X axis, intensity on the Y axis, use one symbol for air conduction, use another for bone conduction. With Jane Omer's pamphlet, a degree in special education and a few years of practice, you can spot acuity deficits and other juicy clues to peripheral or central defects. Verbiage, the professional educator's disease, is not in evidence here. Less than 100 words explain *pitch*. *Level* takes 103 words and *audiometer* requires about a dozen more than the other two. That is verbal precision. As for reading audiograms, one graph and two to four sentences per page do the trick. The rest is white space. Now answer these three questions: Do you know the psychoneurology of hearing? Do you understand the difference between perception and acuity? Do you know nothing about audiograms? If you answer all three questions with "yes," cable Danville, Illinois (east of Urbana and Champaign) and get this nifty pamphlet before they're sold out. If you answer any one as "no," forget Omer's book and find out about hearing.

[B418]

★OPPENHEIM, A. N., AND TORNEY, JUDITH. **The Measurement of Children's Civic Attitudes in Different Nations.** Stockholm, Sweden: Almqvist & Wiksell International, 1974. Pp. 84. Paper, Sw. kr. 26.00. (New York: John Wiley & Sons, Inc. $5.95.) *

B Brit Psychol Soc 28:352-3 Ag '75. G. Jahoda. * an ambitious study of various aspects of Civic Education. The project covered ten countries whose identity can mostly be ferreted out if one takes a little trouble (England, Federal Germany, Finland, Iran, Italy, Netherlands, New Zealand, Sweden, United States), though one escaped the present reviewer. A series of instruments was developed over the next few years and in 1971 administered to a massive sample of 35,000 children at three age levels * this monograph is confined to a description of the preliminary pilot work leading up to and including the final measures, which are given in an appendix * A number of ingenious projective techniques were devised which led at the next stage to the construction of scales of various kinds; factor analysis was employed to check comparability across countries in terms of similarity of structures, and the degree of consistency achieved was surprising. * The general impression one gains is that of a display of technical mastery in a difficult field. On the other hand, psychologists may have some reservations about the conceptual approach, which is in the tradition of "political socialization" as studied by political scientists and takes scant notice of the work of developmental psychologists. Some interesting problems of this kind are touched upon, as when children's responses were categorized into "egocentric" versus "sociocentric," but cognitive development seems to be insufficiently distinguished from information acquisition. It is not altogether clear for what type of readership the monograph is intended. Entirely self-contained (there being not a single reference to other work) it is obviously unsuitable for the beginner. Researchers in the area will be able to glean many useful ideas from it, and it may also prove valuable for research training purposes. In any case it whets one's appetite for the full report.

[B419]

★PARFIT, JESSIE. **Spotlight on Physical and Mental Assessment.** London: National Children's Bureau, 1971. Pp. xiv, 130. Paper, 50 p. *

[B420]

★PAYNE, DAVID A. **The Assessment of Learning: Cognitive and Affective.** Lexington, Mass.: D. C. Heath and Co., 1974. Pp. xvii, 524. $12.95. *

Ed & Psychol Meas 35(2):522–4 su '75. *Lewis R. Aiken, Jr.* * The book, a revision and expansion of his earlier paperback volume (Payne, 1968), is chock-full of facts and methods pertaining to educational assessment. Within its 524 pages are 18 chapters, several appendices including some useful statistical tables, a glossary of terms, and the usual prefatory and index material. * Cognitive objectives of learning are emphasized in the book, but somewhat unusual and timely is the comprehensive treatment of affective and psychomotor objectives. * The book possesses several other unusual features, but whether or not they are meritorious depends on one's point of view. It could be argued that the design and style of the chapters—summaries at the beginning rather

than the end; many lists, tables, flowcharts, etc.; technically competent but cumbersome and unflowing prose—is too reminiscent of journal articles in APA format. Personally, I found the emphasis on structure and handbook-like detail somewhat unstimulating and distracting at times. Whether fledgling students who frequently go through statistically-oriented courses in a hazy-dazy condition will appreciate this style is guesswork. Students do not invariably prefer the same textbooks as their professors, but it is usually wise to err on the simple side! Even with its shortcomings, there are numerous positive features to this book. Chapters 2 and 3 present a thorough coverage of educational objectives, Chapter 5 contains many helpful illustrations of good and poor item writing, and Chapter 8 gives excellent descriptions of self-report affective items and inventories. Chapter 10 on test interpretation, Chapter 13 on criterion-referenced measures, and Chapter 16 on the assessment of affective, performance, and product outcomes by direct observation are also noteworthy. I was also delighted to see a glossary in the appendix. On the other hand, rather than taking up so much space in Chapter 14 with critical reviews of standardized achievement tests, it would probably have been more helpful to harassed teachers if the author had simply given his recommendations as to which tests are most appropriate for particular situations and some comments on the uses of standardized achievement tests in the schools. Furthermore, I cannot imagine that prospective teachers would be interested in all of the details of specific instruments presented in Chapter 15. Among the topics receiving little or no attention, but deserving more, are the use of tests in accountability and performance contracting, gain scores, ethical and ethnical issues, the use of tests in prescriptive teaching as well as diagnosis of learning difficulties, and formative vs. summative evaluation. Chapter 9 is a good overview of statistics for testing, and unlike some authors this one did not confuse the definitions of percentile and percentile rank. Unfortunately, he was inconsistent in his definitions of variance and standard deviation: in the summary it's N, and in the chapter it's $N-1$ in the denominator. A set of problems and exercises, especially in the more statistical chapters, would also have been nice. Basically, David Payne has written a combination "how to do it" and reference book on assessment and evaluation for educators. He has done a good job of representing the current state of the art in educational testing. The book will serve well as a handbook or resource book for teachers and professional evaluators, and should also have its share of adoptions for courses on "educational," if not "psychological," measurement and testing. In designing a textbook for a first course in educational testing, however, the author and editor would have fared better if they had given more thought to motivational features. As the author would undoubtedly agree, affect, as well as cognition, must be taken into account by educators of every stripe—including textbook writers.

J Ed Meas 13(2):165–7 su '76. Robert L. Ebel. * a sound comprehensive, up-to-date textbook * Or measurement? The title of the book mentions assessment, but its content does not differ substantially from that found in current textbooks on educational measurement and evaluation. * The assessment of affective learnings is regarded as sufficiently important to be mentioned in the title of the book, and to occupy all or most of five chapters. This emphasis is perhaps the most distinctive feature of Prof. Payne's book. A teacher or a tester who is concerned with fostering affective learnings, or with assessing them, would surely want to read what this book has to say on the subject. * Payne argues that affective outcomes are important, and if sometimes controversial, they present issues that people need to face. He concludes, "By now the reader must agree that affective and cognitive outcomes are equally important, and deserve equal treatment and time" (p. 157). Here is one reader who does not agree. It may be true, in some sense, that cognitive abilities and affective dispositions are equally important to the individual who possesses them, though the process of demonstrating that equality might prove to be quite difficult, if not impossible. My main disagreement is with the latter part of the sentence quoted above. If I were a teacher or an administrator who had agreed to spend equal time on affective and cognitive outcomes, I would be hard put to know how to spend the affective half of the time, at least if I had to do it non-cognitively. * Allocation of equal school time to the development of affective outcomes clearly implies that these can be taught systematically. I question the correctness of that implication. Years ago I read the statement, "Attitudes can not be taught; they must be caught." * Interests, motives and

values, it seems to me, also are more "caught" than "taught." The belief that a school can profitably spend half its time in trying to teach affective learnings seems open to serious question. In discussing the nature of affective objectives the book relies heavily on the Krathwohl taxonomy, with its categories of receiving, responding, valuing, organization, and characterization. Later, in describing standardized measures of affective variables, the more familiar terms interest, motivations, attitudes, and values emerge as the major categories. The taxonomy categories grew out of the search for some "affective continuum" that could serve to order and relate the different affective outcomes. The continuum finally settled on was "internalization." Whether a continuum is necessary and whether internalization is the best continuum may be questioned. To use two sets of categories, the taxonomic and the popular, may complicate the task of the learner unduly. The relation between the two sets of categories is considered in the book (p. 153) without making completely clear and convincing the basis for the indicated relationship. None of these somewhat skeptical comments concerning the proportion of time schools should spend in direct pursuit of affective (noncognitive) outcomes is intended to suggest that educators should or can ignore pupil motivations, interests, attitudes and values. Measurements of these affective variables may sometimes be necessary or useful. Chapter 8 provides excellent suggestions for the development of affective items and inventories. * the author indicates his interest in showing how "—higher order mental abilities, skills and knowledges—" can be measured. This is commendable. He errs, however, in suggesting that this interest in general principles, understandings, and applications is a recent development. It is not true that "Only within the last several decades have professional educators moved away from the stultifying emphasis on recall of specific facts and information." Indeed it is difficult to think of any well known professional educator in any period of history who ever advocated emphasis on recall of specific facts as the principal goal of learning. Socrates did not. Neither did Quintillian, Comenius, Herbart, James, or Dewey, to name only a few. Viewed against a background of the many substantial and excellent qualities of this book, the faults I have noted in it are relatively minor. It is well written and attractively arranged and printed. I like the preview statements and the concrete illustrative materials. I do not deplore the absence of chapters on intelligence and aptitude tests. All in all it provides a generally sound and useful textbook for students of assessment-evaluation-measurement.

[B421]

★PAYNE, DAVID A. **Curriculum Evaluation: Commentaries on Purpose, Process, Product.** Lexington, Mass.: D. C. Heath & Co., 1974. Pp. x, 357. Paper. * *Out of print.*

J Ed Meas 12(1):62–3 sp '75. Paul B. Campbell. * a worthwhile collection because it brings together in one volume a number of thoughtful contributions to our understanding of the evaluation of curriculum * For those readers who are accustomed to dealing with information which appears to be in conflict or which is of doubtful relevance—i.e., seasoned evaluators—the material is rich in suggestions and illustrations. The curriculum worker who is looking for a source of guidance in solving real world evaluation problems is less likely to satisfy his needs. There is a good chance that he will turn away in confusion on the one hand, or, on the other, select the point of view presented in a single article, and thereby lose the significance of the alternative views that have been presented. * The curriculum worker who can see a possible fit of his evaluation problem to some workable model is in a position to communicate with the evaluator who will help him implement the evaluation. It is unfortunate that the editor did not present more of his own integrative material, supported by less numerous articles by others, in a series of alternative evaluation approaches. As *Curriculum Evaluation* now stands, it is a very useful collection of informative articles but, for the practicing curriculum worker, it may fall somewhat short of its primary objective because it does not provide the necessary linkage between the extensive ideas presented and a variety of implementable designs.

[B422]

*PAYNE, DAVID A., AND MCMORRIS, ROBERT F., EDITORS. **Educational and Psychological Measurement: Contributions to Theory and Practice,** Second Edition. Morristown, N.J.: General Learning Press, 1975. Pp. xxi, 397. Paper, $6.95. * (A book of readings.) (Booklet of test items. Pp. ix, 57. $1.00. *) For reviews of the first edition, see 7:B477 (2 excerpts).

[B423]

★PAYNE, JAMES L. **Principles of Social Science Measurement.** College Station, Tex.: Lytton Publishing Co., 1975. Pp. 157. Paper, $3.85. *

[B424]

★PEARCE, JOHN. **School Examinations.** London: Collier-Macmillan Publishers, 1972. Pp. 199. *Out of print.*

Brit J Ed Studies 21(1):114–5 F '73. John Roach. Mr. Pearce's book has been written with a polemical intention. His own experience of teaching and examining has left him dissatisfied with the way in which the system of G.C.E. examinations works. He criticizes the practical operation of the G.C.E. structure, though he pays a marked tribute to the efficiency of the Examining Boards. It should be noted that the author has not himself approached them for information. He has, he says, "tried to be fair to them on their public showing." He criticizes the social orientation of the present system which operates, in a meritocratic society, to select those who are to be schooled into positions of authority. Instead, he is anxious to achieve a pluralism in education which "is symbolic of and necessarily likely to foster a democratic style of community." In his final chapter Mr. Pearce sums up his aims. Those who assess school attainment should always themselves be school teachers, since they alone are directly in touch with the pupils. Pass-fail notions should be abandoned. The whole machinery should discriminate less, and more emphasis should be given to the imprecise nature of all assessments. Ways must be found of being more informative about attainments other than those assessed by final procedures. More weight should be given to concurrent and less to terminal assessment. In practice Mr. Pearce advocates the model presented by C.S.E. Mode III. Some of his criticism, for instance that G.C.E. "A" level syllabuses are both inexplicit in themselves and too diverse from one another to allow of reasonable comparability, may well be justified. The doubt remains whether exactly the same differences would not arise between the various C.S.E. Boards, unless some very rigid standardization were imposed which would be the antithesis of Mr. Pearce's arguments for a pluralized and decentralized system. Class teacher control might remove some problems but there are others which it would not touch. If examinations were put solely in the hands of class teachers, the system might be even more impervious to change than it is at the moment. One does not need to argue that the present G.C.E. Boards have achieved the best combination between academics, administrators and teachers to believe that some such partnership offers the best likelihood for improving school examinations in the future.

[B425]
★PERRONE, VITO. **The Abuses of Standardized Testing.** Bloomington, Ind.: Phi Delta Kappa Educational Foundation, 1977. Pp. 42. Paper, $0.75. *

[B426]
★PERRONE, VITO; COHEN, MONROE D.; AND MARTIN, LUCY PRETE. **Testing and Evaluation: New Views.** Washington, D.C.: Association for Childhood Education International, 1975. Pp. 64. Paper, $2.50. *

[B427]
★PFEIFFER, J. WILLIAM, AND HESLIN, RICHARD. **Instrumentation in Human Relations Training: A Guide to 75 Instruments With Wide Application to the Behavioral Sciences.** Iowa City, Iowa: University Associates, 1973. Pp. xiii, 306. Paper. * *Out of print.*

Personnel Psychol 27(1):173–6 sp '74. Ramon Henson. * the typical format for the description of the instruments includes the following information: length, time of administration and scoring, scales included, uses, positive features, concerns and information of where to order as well as cost. Aside from the short paragraph on "Positive Features," and possibly "Uses," and "Concerns," there is little evaluation of the tests. * Personnel psychologists who would be most interested in the section on instruments with an organizational focus will be disappointed. * the appendices include useful lists of authors, instruments, scales, and publishers. It also contains a small bibliography on the psychometrics and testing literature. The author with the most instruments represented in the book is Jay Hall (7), followed by William Schutz (6), and William Reddin (4). It is interesting to note that both Hall and Reddin are presidents of organizations that market these instruments. Yet, *not one* of Hall and Reddin's instruments reported contains any reliability or validity information, while some of their instruments (e.g., Hall's Management of Motives index) have parallels in the research literature (e.g., Porter's need deficiency instrument). Again, two issues particularly bother me about this book: the criteria for selecting the instruments, and the impact of books such as this on the development of human relations training. Certainly, the criterion of usefulness

was not discussed adequately. Again, to what extent was this based on the authors' own experiences, or on others' reports, or on just a priori judgments? Also, the proliferation of such instruments, unvalidated, and of questionable reliability, would only increase the gap between research and practice that neither the researchers nor practitioners would want. Although the authors take careful steps to provide the reader with some familiarity with test theory, I feel that their compromise is not really a good one unless coupled with advocacy of some of these implications. One can only hope that group facilitators will be concerned with the psychometric properties of their most used instruments. How does this book compare with other similar volumes in the market? In my judgment, it is one of the least research-oriented, and, because of its particular choice of instruments, has little overlap with the more established volumes (e.g., the ISR series, Shaw and Wright). In the latter sense, therefore, it represents a useful, though not too valuable, addition. To the group facilitator then, whoever or wherever you may be, a caveat that the instruments in this book may provide less than what they seem to offer. It would be wise to take the authors' advice to try the instruments out yourself first, and treat them as tools to be used and adapted for various purposes, and not as valid or reliable indicators of psychological reality. To the research-oriented personnel psychologist, you will learn little that you did not already know. This book may be handy as a reference and as a guide to developing instruments, but one would want to find out much more about some of the instruments than what is described before adopting them.

[B428]
★PHILLIPS, BEEMAN N., AND OAKLAND, THOMAS, EDITORS. **Assessing Minority Group Children: A Special Issue of Journal of School Psychology.** New York: Human Sciences Press, 1973. Pp. iv, 123. $9.95. *

J Pers Assess 40(3):332–4 Je '76. Rene A. Ruiz and Amado M. Padilla. This slim volume includes a group of articles originally published as a special issue of the *Journal of School Psychology.* * Although the intended audience may have been school psychologists—who presumably would be interested primarily, but not exclusively, in the assessment of achievement and aptitude—the recommendations, insights, and factual information included are highly appropriate for all professionals who use tests to evaluate the ethnic minority group child. * While most of the information in this book is not new, it seems sadly true that many professionals seem to operate without it. If the recommendations of the authors were put into practice, then the frequency of invalid examinations of minority children would decline. Only when test users become more knowledgeable about the limitations of their assessment devices and ethnic minority group cultures will these children be assessed fairly.

[B429]

★PICHOT, P., AND OLIVER-MARTIN, R., EDITORS. **Psychological Measurements in Psychopharmacology.** Modern Problems of Pharmacopsychiatry, Vol. 7. Basel, Switzerland: S. Karger, 1974. Pp. vi, 267. $49.00. *

Am J Psychiatry 132(8):887 Ag '75. Ralph A. O'Connell. * devoted to the most commonly used rating instruments in psychopharmacology research * valuable background reading for anyone conducting or evaluating research in psychopharmacology. The chapters are well written and not overly technical. The book may add an interesting dimension for those involved in the everyday use of rating scales.

J Psychosom Res (England) 19(2):162 Ap '75. Robin M. Murray. * [includes] a very interesting chapter on the quantification of manic behaviour from the National Institute of Mental Health. Anyone planning research involving assessment of patients with schizophrenia or affective illness would be foolish not to first study this book. Those more interested in neurotic illness will have to look elsewhere since instruments designed to measure phobic and obsessional symptoms are not well covered.

[B430]

★PIDGEON, DOUGLAS A., AND ALLEN, DAVID, EDITORS. **Measurement in Education.** London: BBC Publications, 1974. Pp. 96. Paper, £0.85. *

[B431]

★POPHAM, W. JAMES. **Classroom Implications of Criterion-Referenced Tests: Curriculum–Instruction–Evaluation.** Los Angeles, Calif.: Instructional Objectives Exchange, 1976. Pp. i, 19. Paper, $2.95. *

[B432]

★POPHAM, W. JAMES. **The Development of Criterion-Referenced Tests: Technical Considerations.** Los Angeles, Calif.: Instructional Objectives Exchange, 1976. Pp. i, 21. Paper, $2.95. *

[B433]

★POPHAM, W. JAMES. **Educational Evaluation.** Englewood Cliffs, N.J.: Prentice-Hall, Inc., 1975. Pp. vii, 328. $12.95. *

Ed & Psychol Meas 36(1):236-7 sp '76. Lewis R. Aiken, Jr. This book, reportedly written because the demand for educational evaluation and books on the subject is increasing, is designed for beginning students of the subject. It should serve this purpose well, but it is definitely an introductory textbook and will in no way substitute for courses in statistics, research design, educational measurement, or similar courses concerned with methodology. The coverage of the book is extensive, dealing with most topics in a rather general way and directing the reader to reference sources for in-depth treatments of particular matters. * Every chapter includes a set of useful discussion questions, practice exercises, answers to practice exercises, selected references and instructional aids. * In general, the book is well-written, avoiding the allegation of sexism by not employing he or his for an evaluator of indeterminate sex. There is some repetitious and awkward wording, and the author occasionally lapses into a folksy style. Furthermore, a number of cartoons and quips serve to brighten what might otherwise be dull reading, especially in the first three chapters. * quips and parenthetical puns may be a welcome relief to fledgling evaluators, but they are occasionally distracting to an old hand * It is.... heartwarming to observe that educational researchers are beginning to take a serious interest in cost analysis and other economic matters. After examining the details and labor involved in a cost analysis, however, one wonders why the cost of the cost analysis isn't taken into consideration. * this book....will serve well as the primary text in a beginning educational evaluation course, supplemented perhaps by Hayman and Napier's *Evaluation in the School: A Human Process for Renewal* (1975). Actually, the Hayman and Napier book contains more detailed examples and a more thorough discussion of the group dynamics of evaluation than Popham's book. But Popham's book is a longer and more comprehensive treatise, dealing with a wider variety of issues. Unfortunately, both of these books are testimonials to the short distance that we have traveled and how far we have to go in this field. As yet there is no exact science of educational evaluation.

J Ed Meas 13(4):319-21 w '76. Frank P. Stetz. The book jacket describes *Educational Evaluation* as "A practical single-source guide book of important issues facing the modern educational evaluator." Let us examine the book in this context to ascertain if the claim is justified. The book is indeed *practical*. It is written in an unintimidating, first-person style, seasoned with humor, cartoons, and wry accounts of *faux pas*. At the same time it conveys an important message to evaluators. * The analogies used to explain measurement and evaluation concepts are apt. One of Popham's major strengths is his ability to communicate information about quantitative matters to those users of evaluation who may be unfamiliar with quantitative concepts. *Educational Evaluation* is practical also in that it covers broadly most issues associated with the subject, and presents them in an historical perspective. * Does the book provide a *single-source* on educational evaluation? This reviewer sees the claim as a bit misleading. When conducting analyses of quantitative data, the reader will need to consult additional sources. * while educational administrators and other practitioners should find the book helpful in identifying the important issues in evaluation, anyone planning to engage in an in-depth study of the evaluation process must (as Popham himself recommends) rely heavily upon the supplementary references cited at the end of each chapter. Thus, the text by itself does not provide enough detail to support the claim * should be most useful as a guide for those who are newcomers to the field. * However, as a guide book for those already involved in educational evaluation, probably most of the topics covered and references cited will be quite familiar. But even the old hands should find much to ponder in the final chapter. Entitled "A Potpourri of Evaluation Issues," it discusses a range of topics too seldom given the attention they deserve * Impact of Educational Evaluation. This chapter should serve to raise the consciousness of everyone in the field. Of the many *important issues* discussed in the book, the topic of practical significance *versus* statistical significance should rank high. * Popham's step-by-step procedures for conducting a cost analysis should be helpful to all educational evaluators. * Some important issues not discussed in the book are the negotiation of the contract between the evaluator and the agency to be served, the financial costs of educational evaluations, and the evaluation of the evaluation itself. * Finally, can it be said that the book keeps in mind the reader as *the modern educational evaluator?* Indeed it does. * Popham's volume represents the first explicit attempt (1) to instruct the modern educational

evaluator in the variety of behaviors necessary for conducting an evaluation and (2) to grapple with some of the hard professional problems that evaluators come up against in their contacts with clients. Given the difficult task of surveying a relatively new professional field within some 300 pages, the author has done quite well. The problem of producing a text that is not only interesting and complete, but also concise and economical is, in these inflationary times, not an easy one. The innovativeness of some of the topics introduced and the scope of the book as a whole outweigh the unfortunate brevity with which some subjects have been treated.

[B434]

★POPHAM, W. JAMES. **Evaluating Instruction.** Englewood Cliffs, N.J.: Prentice-Hall, Inc., 1973. Pp. ix, 157. Paper. * *Out of print.*

J Ed Meas *11(1):70–1 sp '74. Tim L. Wentling* * consists of six programs, each preceded by a set of objectives. Opportunity for reader response is provided via detachable answer sheets. A mastery test (with answers) for each set of objectives is provided in the last pages of the book. * programs [1, 2, and 6] provide a clear, direct, concise, and useful orientation to evaluation terminology. Although Popham provides a good overview of current evaluation terminology in these programs, he mentions only one theoretical evaluation model. * Programs three, four, and five reflect Popham's traditional bias toward evaluation via student performance measurement. * Throughout the book, Popham has left unmentioned the value-laden constraints of his approach to instructional evaluation. These ideological assumptions are critical in examining his approach. For example, throughout programs three, four and five, Popham's emphasis is on product evaluation. He presents the evaluation of process as auxiliary to product evaluation— to be employed only when deficiencies in the product have been identified. This is a somewhat limited conception of evaluation. Although one is easily convinced by Popham that student performance is the ultimate goal and consequence of education, such product orientation has several shortcomings. Popham admits the possibility that interim measures might reasonably be construed to be product measures. For example, he contends that the frequency of smiles exhibited by students during instruction is most probably a process measure because it may be an indicator of post-instruction performance (product). However, he does not allow for the possibility that end-of-course performance may be a process criterion related to desired career performance, college success, or other real life situational behavior. In other words, an end-of-course performance measure may be interim and only penultimate. Moreover, evaluation that considers only prespecified student behavior may overlook many unintended outcomes. Popham discusses the importance of looking at unintended outcomes, but retains his emphasis on prespecified student performance throughout, never giving the reader any substantial assistance in measuring unintended outcomes. By de-emphasizing process measures, many trade-offs of paramount importance within the instructional milieu may be overlooked. Two teachers with similar objectives may utilize totally different approaches to instruction, yet both may achieve satisfactory results. Popham implies that in this case, process evaluation is inappropriate. However, if one of these teachers employs costly equipment while the other does not, a question of efficiency arises. Some methods may be uniquely suited to a particular teacher while others may not. Process information is valuable in assessing alternatives and improving the efficiency of the educational enterprise. If the reviewer had utilized Popham's approach in the evaluation of *Evaluating Instruction,* it would not have been necessary that he even see the text. It would only have been necessary that he obtain the performance measures of students who had read the book. Certainly, JEM's readers would be interested in this data. However, it would represent a rather limited evaluation of the text. A description of content, intended audience, cost and format of the text, as well as judgments regarding the author's viewpoint and philosophy would also be of interest to the readership. A thorough evaluation of this text would include all of these items, process and product. Overall, Popham does exceptionally well at bringing the reader to a general understanding of evaluation terminology, and effectively presents his strategies of supervision and teacher performance testing. This text would serve as an excellent introduction to an evaluation course or as a supplemental text for courses in teaching methods and instructional design.

[B435]

★POPHAM, W. JAMES. **An Evaluation Guidebook: A Set of Practical Guidelines for the Educational Evaluator.** Los Angeles, Calif.: Instructional Objectives Exchange, 1972. Pp. 89. Paper, $5.70. *

[B436]

★POPHAM, W. JAMES, EDITOR. **Criterion-Referenced Measurement: An Introduction.** Englewood Cliffs, N.J.: Educational Technology Publications, Inc., 1971. Pp. xviii, 108. $9.95. *

[B437]

★POPHAM, W. JAMES, EDITOR. **Evaluation in Education: Current Applications.** Berkeley, Calif.: McCutchan Publishing Corporation, 1974. Pp. xv, 585. $12.00. *

[B438]

★POPHAM, W. JAMES, AND BAKER, EVA L. **Establishing Instructional Goals.** Englewood Cliffs, N.J.: Prentice-Hall, Inc., 1970. Pp. vii, 130. Paper. $5.50.

J Ed Meas 9(1):80–1 sp '72. C. Mauritz Lindvall. * the authors have delimited the content to the problem of selecting, stating, and examining the worth of instructional goals. This approach has permitted them to deal quite intensively with these tasks without attempting also to deal with such related topics as test development and the design of instruction. In the reviewer's opinion, this book shares a minor weakness with most textbooks which use the programmed format. That is, although the reader is continually examining, criticizing, and revising instructional objectives, those objectives are always someone else's; i.e., examples shown in the text. The chances that the reader would make use of the steps advocated might be enhanced greatly if at certain points in his study, he became involved in such traditional textbook exercises as, "Define the objectives for one unit of work in a course you are now teaching and have these objectives criticized by one of your fellow students." Obviously this is a type of exercise that would be added by any good instructor using this text for a college course, but the inclusion of such suggested activities which would cause the student to work on his own problems might help to insure more worthwhile activity. The format and style of the Popham-Baker book makes it easy and interesting to read. The illustrations, the examples, and the frequent questions for the reader should tend to keep him involved with the content. Furthermore, all the procedures outlined are specific enough so that the reader should have little difficulty in applying them to his specific situation. Because of these qualities, this book should be effective, not only as required reading in a formal course, but also as a tool for independent study for any teacher who wishes to learn more about how to write and to use objectives.

[B439]

★Popovich, Dorothy. **A Prescriptive Behavioral Checklist for the Severely and Profoundly Retarded.** Baltimore, Md.: University Park Press, 1977. Pp. xi, 429. Paper, $14.95. *

[B440]

★Porter, Nancy, and Taylor, Nancy. **How to Assess the Moral Reasoning of Students: A Teacher's Guide to the Use of Lawrence Kohlberg's Stage Developmental Method.** Toronto, Canada: Ontario Institute for Studies in Education, 1972. Pp. v, 57. Paper, Can $3.25. *

[B441]

Potkay, Charles R. **The Rorschach Clinician: A New Research Approach and Its Application.** New York: Grune & Stratton, Inc., 1971. Pp. xiv, 223. $17.50. *

J Pers Assess 37(1):95 F '73. George Stricker. This book is primarily a study of how the Rorschach is used in a clinical situation, and only secondarily is concerned with the validity of the technique. It represents an attempt to identify what Rorschach information is being used, and in what sequence. * This problem was approached by a fascinating application of a technique developed by Rimoldi. Each bit of data is placed on a separate card and requested by the clinician if and when he feels he needs it. This allows the investigator to know which information is used, and in what order. The judgments were made by 36 clinicians, all of whom were experienced with and favorably disposed towards the Rorschach. They were asked to rate three separate cases, each one taken from the literature, and to respond to three different clinical problems. One was diagnostic, one was concerned with severity of anxiety, and one was an intellectual estimate. Unfortunately each case was always rated for the same problem, reducing the generalizability of the findings somewhat. The clear and overwhelming finding was that experienced clinicians rely most heavily on qualitative data. * The book represents an expansion of Potkay's doctoral dissertation and is an interesting and well conceived piece of work. It would have made an important and timely journal article, but there is some question about the ability of this one study to sustain a book length report. In fact, two-thirds of the book consists of each individual clinician's response, and is more of an appendix than a text. In light of this, without denigrating the contribution of the project, it is difficult to recommend the book to other than a serious researcher who might wish to replicate the method or the study. Hopefully, this form of presentation will not keep the findings from being widely circulated.

[B442]

★Povey, Robert M. **Intellectual Abilities: A Consideration of Their Development and Methods of Assessment.** London: University of London Press Ltd., 1972. Pp. 34. Paper, 35p. *

[B443]

★Powell, John L. **Selection for University in Scotland: A First Report on the Assessment for Higher Education Project.** Publications of the Scottish Council for Research in Education 64. London: University of London Press Ltd., 1973. Pp. 104. Paper, £0.80. *

B Brit Psychol Soc 26(92):255–6 Jl '73. Gordon Miller. * The testing of a measure of ability—a scholastic aptitude test—was one of the major tasks of the inquiry. Other data used included performance in the Scottish Certificate of Education, teachers' estimates and head teachers' forecasts of success in higher studies. The analysis of the comprehensive data was meticulously done using a carefully selected range of statistical procedures. The results show a familiar pattern. One important finding is that a Scholastic Aptitude Test does not have much value as a supplementary predictor to school performance. Headmasters' assessments were of lesser value than performance in the Scottish Certificate of Education. It was concluded that heads' assessments or predictions were of doubtful value whether on their own or supplementary to others. The best predictor of results in degree examinations was level of performance at the end of the first year's study in higher education. Compared with 9% of variance accounted for by heads' assessments—not to be sneezed at—first year performance accounted for 50% of the variance in performance in finals in arts and 72% of the variance in medicine. Although by their very nature the predictor variables and the pass/fail criterion of success are both imperfect, these results are quite impressive. However, other factors must come into the reckoning. Some failures might be due not so much to the inability of the student to obtain a degree but to his having attempted the wrong course, or that non-academic factors were at work, such as emotional upsets, bereavements, loss of financial support and a host of others. The relatively high predictive power of first year results suggests that a larger proportion of candidates should be admitted to first year, but the author argues that costs would rise and students might feel humiliated when failing first year. This reviewer does not find that argument very convincing. In spite of extra costs, it seems worth lowering the cut-off point in school results, or at least not raising it as has been done in the arts and social sciences in recent years. We must end on a pessimistic note. Although the search for improvement in prediction will no doubt continue, the outcome will be that predictors supplementary to school results will actually add very little if anything to accuracy in prediction. This must bring into question the usefulness of interviews. As the author quite sensibly points out, the weight of existing evidence is that when the target population is one at the upper end of the ability spectrum, scholastic aptitude tests are unlikely to discriminate successfully.

Brit J Ed Psychol 44(1):92–6 F '74. N. J. Entwistle. * In the Scottish study 9,801 pupils from 218 schools "met the criterion for inclusion....(and) can be regarded as constituting a virtually complete annual cohort." The sample entering the five well-established Scottish universities consisted of 2,781 students, all but 59 of whom were included in the final analyses. There can thus be no doubt at all about the representative nature of this sample of Scottish students—a tribute to the thoroughness with which the study was conducted. The main criterion used to assess validity was a simple dichotomy (pass/fail) based on degree result. Predictor variables included a variety of measures derived from performance in Scottish "Highers," teachers' scaled estimates of "Higher" grades, head teachers' estimates of degree potential, and verbal and mathematics scores from the American Scholastic Aptitude Test. * "The investigation has provided no grounds for supposing that the introduction of a Scholastic Aptitude Test such as the one employed would be of any value in selection for university entry in Scotland either as a sole predictor or as a predictor supplementary to SCE performance" (page 41). From this evidence there seems to be little future for these tests of academic aptitude as selection instruments in British higher education. *

Occup Psychol (England) 47(3–4):245–5 '73. D. McMahon. This is a typical report from The Scottish Council for Research in Education: not a word wasted, terse but highly readable (technical discussion of the analytical techniques employed is put in an appendix) and a bargain at 80p. What is also characteristic of the work of the SCRE is that the project which is reported was biased "towards providing guidance on practical problems arising from selection for University as practised in Scotland today: it has investigated only predictors currently accepted by, or likely to be acceptable to, the public." * Many readers will be disappointed to learn that the American Scholastic Aptitude Test turned out to be a very poor predictor of academic success. * "no evidence was found to suggest that headteachers' estimates of success at University are as good a predictor as performance in the SCE at Higher Grade or that they constitute a worthwhile supplementary measure." * I look forward to the reports on the follow-up of those pupils who did not enter Universities but went to Colleges of Education and other institutions of Higher Education.

[B444]
★PROVUS, MALCOLM. **Discrepancy Evaluation for Educational Program Improvement and Assessment.** Berkeley, Calif.: McCutchan Publishing Corporation, 1971. Pp. ix, 380. $14.00. *

[B445]
★PUMFREY, PETER D. **Measuring Reading Abilities: Concepts, Sources and Applications.** London: Hodder and Stoughton Educational, 1977. Pp. vii, 216. Paper, £2.85; cloth, £6.35. *

[B446]
★PUMFREY, PETER D. **Reading: Tests and Assessment Techniques.** London: Hodder and Stoughton Educational, 1976. Pp. 160. Paper, £2.60; cloth, £4.95. *

[B447]
★PURUSHOTHAMAN, M., COMPILER. **Secondary Mathematics Item Bank.** Windsor, Berks., England: NFER Publishing Co. Ltd., 1975. Pp. iii, 48. Paper, spiral binding, £2.69. *

[B448]
★PURVES, ALAN C., AND LEVINE, DANIEL H., EDITORS. **Educational Policy and International Assessment: Implications of the IEA Surveys of Achievement.** Berkeley, Calif.: McCutchan Publishing Corporation, 1975. Pp. xiv, 184. $11.00. *

[B449]
★RAVEN, J. C.; COURT, J. H.; AND RAVEN, J. **Manual for Raven's Progressive Matrices and Vocabulary Scales.** London: H. K. Lewis & Co. Ltd., 1977. Pp. vii, 217. Looseleaf, £11.00. *

[B450]
*REID, JOHN E., AND INBAU, FRED E. **Truth and Deception: The Polygraph ("Lie-Detector") Technique, Second Edition.** Baltimore, Md.: Williams & Wilkins Co., 1977. Pp. xvii, 430. $32.00. * For reviews of the first edition, see 7:B498 (2 excerpts).

[B451]

★RESNICK, LAUREN B., EDITOR. **The Nature of Intelligence.** Hillsdale, N.J.: Lawrence Erlbaum Associates, Inc., Publishers, 1976. Pp. xi, 364. $17.95. *

J Ed Res 70(4):228–9 Mr–Ap '77. Elmer A. Lemke. * This book is based on papers presented at a 1974 University of Pittsburgh conference where participants from many fields discussed a variety of intelligence-related topics. One conference product is this heady volume—appropriate reading for any professional who has systematically attempted to follow the developments in research on intelligence. * This volume is an excellent contribution to the evolving research on intelligence. It has a specific purpose and a specific audience; if you are a member of that audience, the stimulating chapters of this book will have great appeal.

[B452]

★RICHARDSON, KEN, AND SPEARS, DAVID, EDITORS. **Race and Intelligence: The Fallacies Behind the Race-IQ Controversy.** Baltimore, Md.: Penguin Books Inc., 1972. Pp. 205. Paper, $1.45. *

Brit J Social & Clin Psychol 11(4):418 D '72. Chris Brand and Halla Beloff. Here is a politically conscious, left-wing contribution to the arguments about intelligence, considering the problem of class differences as crucially similar to those of race. The contributors to this collection of papers "go well beyond the traditional confines of the race-IQ debate" in aspiring to find "a starting point from which we may proceed less divisively" in this troubled area. All of which involves the reader learning that IQ tests "largely test rote memory"; that correlation coefficients involve "anti-scientific absurdities"; and that the facts they yield may somehow be "more about tests than about people." Fortunately, perhaps, retreats from such starting points are numerous. Despite the rigged "immutability" of IQ scores, the dynamics of test situations receive attention for their possible effects; the potentially serious implications of the experiments of Katz and Rosenthal are rehearsed, albeit without consideration of the extensive work and criticism here by Shuey and Jensen. Improved nutrition would increase the abhorred IQ; but at least its use to enhance "cognitive development" is unexceptionable. While the "dogmatic scientism" of psychometrists is to be outlawed, the authors are confident that currently non-measurable social-caste effects—which do not seem to retard Mexicans and American Indians—could explain the black-white IQ differences. One further retreat is necessary. As the authors stress—with occasional brief references to Piaget's concept of intelligence—any characteristic develops as a complex interaction between genes and environment. Many of the ancient nature-nurture debates were thus futile. But there is still the question—separate from that of an individual's determinants—of how the differences *between* individuals are differentially determined by either set of factors. The complacency of some psychometrists should be shaken. New work on intellectual development and into the social psychology of tests and testing should be done. One awaits it eagerly from this group. For the present, thoughtless polemic is offered: Headstart may have *had* to be unsuccessful "because success would have led to fundamental social and political changes that the non-poor were not prepared to accept." These writers' ill-conceived protests against psychology's methods and results look like solipsism, while their doubts about psychology's applications look like nihilism. Such endeavours do not advance the cause of the serious environmentalist.

Meas & Eval Guid 6(2):124–5 Jl '73. Gary M. Miller. The controversy of heredity and environment is one with which behavioral scientists have been struggling for many years. As presented in the foreword of this book of essays, the controversy was regenerated by the publications of Arthur Jensen and H. J. Eysenck. Numerous articles and rejoinders have since appeared and questions posed to behavioral scientists. This compilation focuses on the concepts underlying the issues rather than the specific issues themselves; and as the editors indicate, they do not attempt to answer questions but to provide a view of the total problem. An opening presentation provides a perspective of the revival of the debate within a historical-political frame of reference. Three major sections of essays follow, with emphases on psychology, biology, and sociology. * My reactions to this book are positive. Being able to learn about this serious question through the perspective of writers from Great Britain was quite informative. Generally, the essays were well-prepared with sufficient but not elaborate documentation. The points of view of the writers were objectively presented and appropriately categorized in the three principal subsections. One assumption—that the reader has had some familiarity with the original writings of Galton,

Jensen, Eysenck, and Shuey—seems to exist throughout the essays. Because of this I would highly recommend reviewing the original works prior to reading the essays; this is too serious an issue to begin weighing and debating without adequate information. Hopefully, we will all be open to the varied points of view presented, for it appears that the debate will continue for some time to come.

[B453]

*RICKERS-OVSIANKINA, MARIA A., EDITOR. **Rorschach Psychology, Second Edition.** Huntington, N.Y.: Robert E. Krieger Publishing Co., Inc., 1977. Pp. xviii, 653. $24.50. * For reviews of the first edition, see 6:B409 (3 excerpts).

[B454–5]

★RILEY, PAMELA M. **The Cloze Procedure—A Selected Annotated Bibliography.** Lae, Papua New Guinea: Papua New Guinea University of Technology, 1973. Pp. vi, 33. Paper, Aus. $1.00. *

J Read 17(8):655 My '74. Nicholas J. Silvaroli. * This annotated bibliography provides ninety-two references to publications which have become available since 1972. In addition to classifying these publications into seven main categories, the author provides objective and insightful comments about each publication. Classroom teachers should find the categories related to readability and comprehension development especially useful. The overall publication is extremely well-done and will save time for anyone interested in a comprehensive review of current cloze literature.

[B456]

★ROBB, GEORGE P.; BERNARDONI, LOUIS C.; AND JOHNSON, RAY W. **Assessment of Individual Mental Ability.** New York: Harper & Row, Publishers, Inc., 1972. Pp. xiv, 354. $11.95. *

Psychol Sch 14(1):127 Ja '77. Gilbert R. Gredler. * integrates the theory and practice of mental ability testing. The authors attempt to provide background data on the beginning of mental testing, theoretical substructure of mental testing, and information as to the correct administration and scoring of mental tests. The reviewer feels that the authors have accomplished their purpose. * The book came out before the WISC-R appeared and thus is dated in that respect, but there is still meaningful material given on the WISC subtests which can be easily transferred to the present scale. Jensen's two-level theory of intelligence needs a more extended treatment, but the discussion of the WISC subtests is quite complete. The reader should definitely read the two-page sec-

tion on the digit span subtest of the WISC. This particular subtest is considered by many in the learning disability field to give a valid measure of the sequential processing ability of the child. Those with low scores on this test or the ASM subtest of the ITPA are frequently placed in "LD" classes. In rereading the authors' comments one is struck how performance on this type of test can supposedly reflect attention difficulties, negativism, anxiety, lack of flexibility, mental disturbance, compulsive trends, or organic impairment! The section ends with the comment: "The interpretation of scores achieved on this subtest must be made with extreme caution." (p. 224) Amen! All this goes to show that while many LD children definitely do have a sequential processing problem, this subtest or the similar one from the ITPA are hardly sufficient by themselves to arrive at an accurate assessment of sequential difficulty. The chapter on the psychological report is well done and quotes important authorities such as Goldman, L'Abate, and Freeman. Almost anyone involved in frequent report writing could profit from a rereading of this section. All in all, a helpful book.

[B457]

★ROBERTSON, E. WAYNE, EDITOR. **Educational Accountability Through Evaluation.** Englewood Cliffs, N.J.: Educational Technology Publications, 1971. Pp. 107. Paper, $4.95. *

[B458]

*ROBINSON, JOHN P., AND SHAVER, PHILLIP R. **Measures of Social Psychological Attitudes, Revised Edition.** Ann Arbor, Mich.: Institute for Social Research, University of Michigan, 1973. Pp. viii, 750. Paper, $10.00; cloth, $15.00. *

[B459]

★ROSS, G. ROBERT. **The Reliability of Clinical Ratings.** Charleston, S.C.: Medical University Press, 1977. Pp. iv, 24. Paper, $3.00. *

[B460]

★ROWE, B., AND BANKS, R. A. **New Objective Tests in English Language.** London: University of London Press Ltd., 1974. Pp. vi, 146. Paper, £0.85. *

[B461]

*ROWE, B., AND BANKS, R. A. **Objective Tests in English Language [Second Edition].** London: University of London Press Ltd., 1971. Pp. 128. Paper, £2.00. *

[B462]

*ROWE, HELGA A. H. **The Comparability of WISC and WISC-R.** Occasional Paper No. 10. Hawthorn, Victoria, Australia: Australian Council for Educational Research Ltd., 1976. Pp. ix, 47. Paper, Aus. $3.50. *

[B463]

★RUSSELL, ELBERT W.; NEURINGER, CHARLES; AND GOLDSTEIN, GERALD; WITH THE ASSISTANCE OF CAROLYN H. SHELLY. **Assessment of Brain Damage: A Neuropsychological Key Approach.** New York: Wiley-Interscience, 1970. Pp. xi, 167. $18.50. *

Brit J Social & Clin Psychol 11(4):416–7 D '72. Antonia Whitehead. Reitan's feats of neuropsychological diagnosis rank within the folk mythology of clinical psychology. Apart from the sceptics who feel that it is all part of some conjuring trick, there is an admiring populace who seek instead to learn how to emulate him. Undoubtedly, one of his major advantages is his knowledge not only of cortical function but also of cortical pathology. In an area where psychometric results can give 12 different answers, it is an advantage to be able to reject 11 of these as being neurologically silly. To attempt to objectify these techniques is patently worth while; the attempts of Wheeler using discriminant function analysis caused some excitement but, in this country, little change in neuropsychological behaviour. This book is another step in the same direction. Its aim is to develop "Keys" extracted from objective signs in the test battery. Once again, the battery is a form of the Halstead-Reitan; this is given in the neuropsychological laboratory by technicians and involves the patients in about 12 hours of testing. The scoring and extraction of scores is done by clerks; or the book supplies a computer program to reduce human labour still further. With major Keys and minor Keys echoing through the pages, the reader begins to get alarmed, but all is suddenly clarified into the Localization Key and the Process Key. The former says whether there is brain damage and, if so, whether it is left-sided, right-sided or diffuse. The Process Key indicates whether the damage is congenital, static or acute. Validation was by agreement with neurological examination. The authors realize that this is the lowest order of the normally adopted procedures for clinical ascertainment of the nature of cortical damage, but it appears that only a limited number of their patients had any higher order investigations. A further problem that they did not consider is that of criterion contamination. Among the factors taken into account by the neurologist would be certain aspects of cognitive functioning. As this was a retrospective study, there was no possibilty of extracting this contamination

from the neurological evaluation; it also meant that a psychologist had to interpret the neurological findings to assign patients to the categories used by the Keys. The results had also been assessed by a neuropsychologist, at the time of testing, so his opinion could also be compared with the Keys. Overall, the Keys tended to agree with the neurologist's opinion, but to a lesser extent than did the neuropsychologist's assessment. The authors feel that the use of the Keys can still be justified on the grounds of shortage of skilled time, but if a patient has invested 12 hours of his life in the proceedings, one feels that he is at least worth the courtesy of the best assessment methods available, be they computer or human. Although these Keys do not yet appear ready for clinical use, they do represent an interesting advance. One of the reasons for their present failure may well be their built-in obsolescence. The Key material has not changed since 1965; in that time neuropsychological knowledge has made some advances. Workers such as these must be prepared to evolve, take note of happenings on the world front, and build adaptability into their system; fortunately or unfortunately, the human neuropsychologist is almost infinitely variable.

[B464]

★RYAN, LEO ROBERT. **Clinical Interpretation of the FIRO-B.** Palo Alto, Calif.: Consulting Psychologists Press, Inc., 1970. Pp. iii, 24. Paper, $2.00. * (Reissued 1971 with minor revisions.) For the latest edition, see B465.

[B465]

*RYAN, LEO ROBERT. **Clinical Interpretation of the FIRO-B, 1977 Edition.** Palo Alto, Calif.: Consulting Psychologists Press, Inc., 1977. Pp. 39. Paper, $2.00. *

[B466]

★RYLE, ANTHONY. **Frames and Cages: The Repertory Grid Approach to Human Understanding.** London: Sussex University Press, 1975. Pp. v, 148. £4.50. (New York: International Universities Press, Inc. $11.50. *)

Brit J Psychol 67(2):284 My '76. Fay Fransella. This book is to be welcomed as the first on the subject of repertory grid technique since Bannister and Mair's *Evaluation of Personal Constructs* was published in 1968. *Frames and Cages* differs from its forerunner in many respects, but perhaps particularly in offering a practitioner's rather than an academic's approach to the study of grid technique. Ryle starts by giving a superficial coverage of personal construct theory and then compares this with other theories, particularly object relations theory. This is a worth-while attempt which fails. It fails because of Ryle's incomplete grasp of the fundamental ideas of construct theory. In some cases this results in confusion (as in his attempt to explain the difference between "construct" and "element" in the organization corollary), in others, erroneous deductions are made which are then used to criticize the theory. Next described is basic grid technique (mainly the rated grid), Slater's principal-components analysis and the interpretation of results. The following chapters on the interpretation of results in the light of psychoanalytic theory, the use of grid technique in the clinical situation and the case histories are of interest, the latter being particularly valuable to anyone new to the technique. But this is not a book for anyone who wants to evaluate critically the method. Ryle makes no attempt to discuss the literature concerning types of construct, validity, reliability, different sorts of grid and analyses, or its many reported uses as a measure of change in psychotherapy. In many cases it is apparent that he is unaware that such literature exists. Also, in many of the examples, inadequate data (e.g. correlations, loadings) are presented to enable the critical reader to follow how he reaches the conclusions he does. This is therefore a useful book for the psychologically unsophisticated reader who is looking for a general account of what grid technique is all about, but is unlikely to meet the needs of most psychologists.

[B467]

★SAFRIT, MARGARET J. **Evaluation in Physical Education: Assessing Motor Behavior.** Englewood Cliffs, N.J.: Prentice-Hall, Inc., 1973. Pp. xxi, 308. $12.95. *

J Ed Meas 11(1):72 sp '74. Aileene S. Lockhart. * Designed apparently for too diverse an audience, the text vacillates between simplistic understandings and technical controversies. The chapters on validity and reliability determinations and arguments surrounding these concepts are a welcome and interesting addition for the more advanced student, but require background not expected of the beginner. * Being oriented early in the text to the importance of three domains of behavior for which physical educators state objectives—the cognitive, the psychomotor, and the affective— the reader is disappointed not to find help in

evaluating the affective domain, an area of considerable current interest. * the chapters on basic statistics, concepts of validity and reliability, and the development of scales and norms....are well and clearly presented. Information on the construction of motor performance and written tests is more understandably described in other sources. The chapter on grading also leaves much to be desired. The usual chapter on administration of a measurement program is missing. The reviewer is surprised to find a chapter devoted to a consideration of specific tests of physical fitness in a text which deliberately omits consideration of specific tests of other objectives of physical education. Nevertheless the material on formative and summative evaluation, statistics which are needed to understand how to organize a set of raw scores and to understand measures of central tendency and variability, and the technical chapters on validity and reliability will add considerably to the tools and understandings of students of physical education. The presentation of reliability is accomplished with particular clarity. The book does achieve its purpose of suggesting ways in which educational decisions may be made with more objectivity. This reviewer wishes that the author had devoted herself more completely in intent to the more advanced student of physical education evaluation, believing the theoretical and philosophical to be neglected aspects in the preparation of many advanced physical education students and being convinced that the author of *Evaluation in Physical Education* is quite capable of rectifying this need.

[B468]

★SALVENDY, GAVRIEL, AND SEYMOUR, W. DOUGLAS. **Prediction and Development of Industrial Work Performance.** New York: John Wiley & Sons, Inc., 1973. Pp. xv, 351. * *Out of print.*

Personnel Psychol 27(4):663–5 w '74. Lowell M. Schipper and Robert M. Guion. * It seems a reasonable notion that both performance and satisfaction of individual workers will be improved if there can be once again a gathering of the clan so that those who work in the field of engineering psychology and those who work in the field of personnel selection psychology again begin to communicate with each other. With this as a frame of reference we looked forward with eagerness to the present book, the sixth in the Wiley Series in Human Factors. It begins with the material of traditional concern to the industrial engineer and moves to the material of traditional concern to the industrial psychologist. Surely, we thought, the result would be ideas about the design of work to match the characteristics of the worker and the selection of workers to provide economical homogeneity of such characteristics. We were disappointed. We found the book inadequate from both perspectives. Psychometric terms were used in peculiar ways. For example, cross validation was used only to refer to the notion of "double checking" when applied to job analysis, and, apparently, to the initial analysis in validating a battery of tests after the component tests of the battery had been declared reasonably valid. The use of the term has no implication in the evaluation of weights in a prediction equation. A definition of a criterion for selection purposes was given which in a few pages had become the concept of validity. Reliability is somehow, and not clearly, treated as distinct from a concept like homogeneity but is related to the newly introduced concept of "dependability." It is very difficult to understand what the authors mean by dependability as something different from reliability when they cite authorities whose work has dealt with reliability as supporting information for their material on dependability. The concept of linearity comes in for strange treatment when the authors ask whether criteria increase linearly, but do not indicate with regard to what it is that the criteria might increase linearly. It is difficult to distinguish between their use of the term "simulate" and the more conventional use of the term "predict." Notions of content validity become especially peculiar when the authors tell us that content validity can be assessed with multiple regression or factor analysis. We are told that if the content validity of criterion is low, "the standard error of the predictive validity coefficient will be high." But we are not told whether the "standard error" is the standard error of a correlation of zero used in significance testing or the standard error of estimate, or what. We know of no authority to tie the content validity of one measure to the predictive validity of another. The overall interpretation and explanation of statistical procedures, especially in Chap. 6, is atrocious. Symbols for "greater than" and "less than" are either improperly used many times or the book was poorly proofread. There seems to be apparent misuse of the simple Chi-square statistic (in Chap. 1) in tables where

entries appear not to be independent of one another. Although references to such highly respected statisticians as M. G. Kendall and J. E. Walsh are cited, some of the statements and interpretations are not those of the references. One example: "The greater the power of the statistical tests utilized, the more confidence can be had in the meaning of the significance." A rather broad positive statement that is simply not true. The authors have provided an adequate set of content references but here again they may be misleading. The work of Ghiselli is cited to support the notion that predictability of performance is not as good as the predictability of training because "....criteria measures at the early stages of acquisition of a skill exhibit higher validity coefficients than those we find when the measures are correlated with terminal performance." This is a far cry from Ghiselli's finding that trainability measures are more easily predicted than proficiency measures and we can't resist pointing out that Guion's *Personnel Testing* is cited as showing several methods for assessing "dependability" which was not done since that author's interpretation of this term is different. Sometimes, unfortunately, necessary references are not cited but that is not always a criticism. For example, the Thorndikian notions of immediate, intermediate, and ultimate criteria are used without citation to Thorndike himself. Just as well, since Thorndike's notion of the ultimate criteria never intended to say something about performance "after the completion of training." Overall, we come up disappointed. Some of the material is good, as case study data in special circumstances where the authors have done much work. The best circulation for this work appears to us to be in journals, monographs and technical reports. As a text offering a contribution to engineering and industrial psychology, it falls short of the mark.

[B469]

★SAMUDA, RONALD J. **Psychological Testing of American Minorities: Issues and Consequences.** New York: Harper & Row, Publishers, Inc., 1975. Pp. xv, 215. Paper, $9.50. *

Meas & Eval Guid 9(1):38–9 Ap '76. Kemp Mabry. Probably for the first time in one volume we have the theories, issues, and research findings on the intellectual assessment of American Minorities. * Samuda discusses quite well the technical problems found in the appraisal of behavior, including test validity and reliability and the concept and various theories of intelligence. After a lucid discussion of the age-old (and unresolved) nature-nurture issue, 37 pages are devoted to a well-documented presentation of environmental factors that influence test performance such as nutrition, self-concept, motivation, anxiety, test environment, and language. * A discussion of alternatives to traditional standardized tests is especially illuminating. Samuda reminds us that efforts of the culture-fair movement to bring about elimination of most biases in minority testing are laudable, but, to date, unfortunately, have not produced especially bias-free instruments. * In addition to 15 pages of excellent references, a significant aid to practitioners is a 27-page "compendium of tests" currently available for use with minority adolescents and adults. * *Psychological Testing of American Minorities* has the promise of becoming a minor classic. *

[B470]

★SANDVEN, JOHS. **Projectometry: A New Approach in the Psychological Study of Human Reaction Tendencies Exemplified by Research Pertaining to Education.** Oslo, Norway: Universitetsforlaget, 1975. Pp. 372. 90 N. kr. *

J Pers Assess 41(3):330–1 Je '77. Clifford H. Swensen. * an attempt to combine the advantages of objective methods of personality assessment with the advantages of the "projective" methods. Actually, Sandven calls objectively scored self-report instruments "subjective" since they are based upon self-report. He uses the term "objective" to refer to methods of behavior observation. His goal is to combine the advantages of the projective method, in which the subject is free to respond as he or she wills, with the advantages of the precise scoring of the "subjective" (self-report) methods. * Sandven has developed scales to measure four different variables, coreaction (the ability to put yourself into another person's shoes), the feeling of security, attitude toward education, and motivation for school achievement. * the author fails to make a case for the advantage of his method over other methods of personality assessment. In fact, he makes no case at all. He presents no studies which compare his method with other methods, in spite of the fact that the variables he chose to study have been studied extensively by others. * A second shortcoming in the book is the lack of reference to other research that is pertinent to the topics Sandven is studying. He is concerned with empathy, security, achieve-

ment, and school attitudes. All of these variables have been studied extensively. But Sandven develops hypotheses relative to these variables and school behavior with scarcely a reference to the work of others. Reading Sandven's book would give the uninformed reader no idea of the extent of the published literature on these subjects. Sandven set for himself the problem of developing a better method of personality assessment, and the application of this method to the measurement of certain specific personality variables. He developed a method for assessing personality variables, but he neglected to present the background of the efforts of others to measure these variables, and he failed to show how his method is superior to the methods developed by others.

[B471]

★SATTLER, JEROME M. **Assessment of Children's Intelligence, Revised Reprint.** Philadelphia, Pa.: W. B. Saunders Co., 1974. Pp. xxii, 591. $17.00. [Same as original edition except for additional appendices of 64 pages.] (Instructor's Manual. Pp. 85. Gratis.) *

Ed & Psychol Meas 34(4):1027–9 w '74. Nicholas J. Anastasiow. Sattler states....three main goals: (1) to assist the student in psychological evaluation, (2) to aid in selection of material, and (3) to summarize and integrate research findings concerned with individual intelligence tests. In his reviewer's opinion he has accomplished these goals. Sattler has written a lucid, comprehensive and exhaustive treatment of all the major issues dealing with individually administered intelligence tests. * The reference section alone covers thirty pages and includes more than 1200 entries, and reflects the care with which the text was prepared. Seminal research conducted at the turn of the century as well as current research is integrated into the discussion at appropriate points throughout the text. Sattler has not only enriched the text by his inclusion of references that extend the discussion but, in speaking of his own research, he has also included references and discussion of those who have disagreed with him. * Sattler deals exhaustively with the strengths and weaknesses of the Stanford-Binet and the various forms of the WISC. * Sattler presents advice concerning the need for special consideration in administering intelligence tests to handicapped children—the deaf, blind, and cerebral palsied, among others. * His cautions are well stated and he argues for a more complete rather than a simplistic diagnosis of a child. His discussion on the learning disabled is appropriately cautious and his chapter on Mental Retardation is excellent. His notion of "testing the limits" to find out how well a child can perform (as well as what he cannot do) is a useful notion. Throughout the text this reviewer received the impression that the author hoped his readers would administer intelligence tests for the purpose of assessing a child's strengths in order to provide suggestions on how to assist the child— rather than use the test score to categorize the child. * In summary, the text is comprehensive in its treatment of the full range of issues involved in choosing, administering and interpreting individually administered intelligence tests. It is a scholarly yet readable book. It contains not only suggestions derived from substantive findings but advice that appears to be founded on practical experience in schools and a heavy dose of common sense.

Ed & Psychol Meas 35(3):740–1 au '75. Lewis R. Aiken, Jr. * This large book possesses features of both a textbook and a source book, and this reviewer readily recommends it for graduate courses on intelligence testing. The book is well-written and clear, but the reader will need some knowledge of tests and measurements, developmental psychology, and abnormal psychology in order to derive the greatest benefit. An attractive feature for instruction is a manual of multiple choice questions. These questions, however, should be viewed as only a supplement to a more thorough evaluation of the students from observations of their performance in test situations and the quality of case reports. * The core of the book consists of detailed descriptions of the development, administration, and interpretation of the Stanford-Binet, WISC, and WPPSI. These chapters (8–17) by themselves constitute almost an entire course on intelligence testing of children. The reviewer found, however, that some of the most informative and useful material appears in Sections 2, 5, and 6. Admittedly, Section 5 (Diagnostic Implications) is a bit disappointing if one expects it to present clear-cut methods of diagnosing and prescribing for various disorders and exceptionalities. Such straightforward methods, of course, do not exist, and Jerome Sattler is no Pollyanna. Rather he is an empiricist and compiler who recognizes the limitations of intelligence tests for diagnostic and prescriptive purposes. Consequently, hundreds of empirical investigations are cited in this book, but

students and practicing psychologists who entertain unrealistic expectations about the diagnostic abilities of individual intelligence tests may "come out by that same door wherein (they) went." In short, the twenty-seven chapters make up a comprehensive handbook on intelligence testing of children. * Anyone planning to use the WISC-R would be well advised to examine Appendixes E and F of this book before proceeding. Unfortunately, not all individual intelligence testers possess the interpersonal sensitivity and statistical-technical expertise needed to draw sound diagnostic conclusions from test responses. To be sure, Jensen and Shockley have had some negative effects on the public image of intelligence testing. But this reviewer is convinced that vociferous critics of intelligence testing find ample ammunition in the errors of poorly-trained, and perhaps poorly-endowed, psychodiagnosticians. Many of these itinerant Binet-testers and WISC-testers might benefit from a serious study of Sattler's book. He has performed a useful scholarly service in collecting under one cover a great deal of material concerned with intelligence testing of children.

J Pers Assess 39(1):96–7 F '75. Robert J. Craig. * a penultimate contribution that should satisfy the clinician's thirst for increased understanding of the assessment process that goes beyond individual scores, as well as the scientist's rigor that demands the integration of research with clinical application. The author has organized his book into modular sections that provide excellent teaching presentations for the academician and student and which further provides excellent factual and interpretive understanding for the clinician-practitioner. The bulk of this book is devoted to the development, description, administering interpretation and evaluation of Stanford Binet, WISC and WPPSI, as well as other major individually administered intelligence tests. Sandwiched between these sections are some general issues related to intelligence testing....and the diagnostic application of intelligence tests with reference to special populations * The author ends with sections on synthesis of test findings, report writing and consultation. There are also a series of tables in the Appendices that are equally as valuable as the content in the body of the book. Sattler's style of meticulous detail, anchored in research, is consistent throughout. Not only are the chapter outlines logical, their analysis and content description are also thoroughly presented. Where conclusions can be based on empirical knowledge, the author provides convincing evidence; where areas are matters of speculation and unresolved conclusions, the author presents both sides of the issue for the reader's evaluation. Each chapter is followed by a summary that represents the best of its kind in a textbook. There are two potential shortcomings. The first is its emphasis on detail and facts which the student may find overwhelming, the clinician somewhat boring and the scientist somewhat delightful. The second is really no fault of the author. Since this book has been published, the WISC has been restandardized and revised. This obviates and accommodates many of Sattler's criticisms of the WISC. This may not prove to be too serious since many of the other statements of this test remain cogent. In no way does it drastically alter the diagnostic aspects indicated in this book. This book will be particularly helpful as a beginning textbook at the graduate level for courses related to the intellectual assessment of children. It should also be beneficial to school psychologists and to those psychologists engaged in private practice. Its helpfulness will be its up-to-date integration of empirical findings with its rich array of clinical methods to aid in the diagnostic and assessment process.

J Sch Psychol 14(4):368–70 w '76. Everett E. Davis. This is a long and rambling book which is packed with information, and it is the kind of book that should be in every educational diagnostician's office. * Although Sattler in his Preface states that this book is intended to be a text for a class in individual mental testing, it seems that it would serve better as a resource publication to supplement some briefer presentation. This work is useful and needed, but it is needed more by the individual who is occupied with professional testing than it is by the student who is trying to orient himself in the field of psychological testing. Although the student may be impressed by such scholarly prodigies as 1392 references, experience suggests that he more likely will be dumbfounded. There is no doubt concerning the effort and dedication that have gone into the preparation of this book. It is an impressive accomplishment, but some of the results noted in the review of research appear to be disappointingly trivial. Surely first-year graduate students must form academically unfavorable attitudes when they read a passage

such as the following, which pertains to how the examiner's prior opinion of the examinee's abilities affects test scores. "The primary difference among studies with these two outcomes is that in two of the three studies with significant expectancy effects, each examiner tested only two children, one under a positive expectancy and the other under a negative expectancy. In the studies reporting nonsignificant effects, the examiners tested four, five, six, or eight subjects." Not only is it shocking that such studies should be published in the first place, but it also is a disservice to graduate students if they gather the impression that administering as few as eight tests constitutes acceptable research. Sattler makes many points and for most of them he cites research—much of which is good. Often he points out the lack of support for many widely accepted assumptions and interpretations of intelligence test results. * Part of the disjointed impression left by the book is the result of the appearance of the WISC-R and the Revised Norms for the Stanford-Binet after Sattler's manuscript had gone to the printers. This Revised Reprint of the volume incorporates three new appendices dealing with these changed tests and occupying approximately 80 pages. As Sattler says, these are "excellent developments," but since he does not even mention the new and worthwhile McCarthy Scales of Children's Abilities, which also was published in 1972, one feels slightly chagrined. Overall this is an excellent book and has much valuable information which is not available anywhere else in a single consolidated form. * All the reservations noted so far have been rather picayune in comparison with the value of this commendable work. There is, however, one more minor detail that is annoying. In applying the technical definition of test validity, one normally is not able to say in a psychological report that the results of one administration of a test is valid. Results can be found to be valid only if they corroborate a current observation or predict some subsequent outcome. In six of the seven psychological reports in Chapter 25 there is a statement to the effect that the results "appear to be valid," and the seventh report says "There is some doubt about the validity of the test results because emotional factors....appear to be affecting his intellectual efficiency." It is suggested, since estimates of reliability can be stated with greater certainty, that they be included, but that estimates of validity be left for the future. The fact is that this book is a valuable contribution to the field of intelligence testing, and the very minor nature of the above criticism increases one's admiration for the vision and effort that went into its production. It should be available to every school psychologist.

Meas & Eval Guid 7(4):264–5 Ja '75. Joseph C. Finney. * Essentially, this is a textbook on the Stanford-Binet, the Wechsler Intelligence Scale for Children (WISC), and the Wechsler Preschool and Primary Scale of Intelligence (WPPSI). Only 1 of the 27 chapters deals with tests other than those three. * This book would be more generally useful....if a section on the Wechsler Adult Intelligence Scale were added. Within the chosen limits, the book gives thorough coverage of its subject—quite adequate for graduate courses. The appendices comprise 40 pages of useful tables. The 43 pages of references, the 13-page name index, and the 10-page subject index are well done. * an interesting chapter on testing minority group children, with a few pages each on Negroes, Mexican-Americans, Puerto Ricans, and North American Indians. The second section discusses some general problems of administering individual intelligence tests. The heart of the book is the third section on the Stanford-Binet and the fourth section on the WISC, the WPPSI, and other tests. Within each of these sections is one chapter on the history of the tests, one on administration, and one on test interpretation. The fifth section, covering diagnostic applications, includes a chapter on childhood schizophrenia, one on organic brain damage, and one on mental retardation. These are all well done. Sattler's treatment of Jensen's work is a study in tact and delicacy. In the early chapter on history and theory appear Jensen's concepts of associative and cognitive functions, of primary and secondary retardation, and of differences between socioeconomic classes (but not races). The tone of the discussion is neutral and not polemic. In the chapter on testing minority group children, Jensen's criteria for judging the status fairness of a test are well presented. Jensen's views on racial differences are not mentioned. The unwary reader is unaware of the storms that have swirled about this man. One of the worthiest features of the book is the discussion of report writing, which takes two chapters in the last section. Some good sample reports are shown. Wise and thoughtful advice

is given, some of it the author's, some quoted from others. This is one of the most valuable sections for graduate students; it enables them to avoid the common pitfalls. * Despite the unfortunate lack of a section on the WAIS, this book comes closer than any other to meeting the need for a textbook on individual intelligence testing. It will be widely used, and it deserves to be.

[B472]

★Savage, R. D.; Britton, P. G.; Bolton, N.; and Hall, E. H. **Intellectual Functioning in the Aged.** London: Methuen & Co. Ltd., 1973. Pp. 190. £4.85. *

[B473]

★Saville, Peter, and Blinkhorn, Steve. **Undergraduate Personality by Factored Scales: A Large Scale Study on Cattell's 16PF and the Eysenck Personality Inventory.** Windsor, Berks., England: NFER Publishing Co. Ltd., 1976. Pp. 176. Paper, £7.00. * (Atlantic Highlands, N.J.: Humanities Press, Inc. $15.75.)

[B474]

★Sax, Gilbert. **Principles of Educational Measurement and Evaluation.** Belmont, Calif.: Wadsworth Publishing Co., Inc., 1974. Pp. 642. $13.95. * (Accompanying Study Guide and Instructor's Manual. Pp. viii, 244; 122. Paper, $4.95; gratis.)

[B475]

★Scannell, Dale P. **Testing and Measurement in the Classroom.** Boston, Mass.: Houghton Mifflin Co., 1975. Pp. xi, 288. Paper, $7.25. *

[B476]

★Schildkrout, Mollie S.; Shenker, I. Ronald; and Sonnenblick, Marsha. **Human Figure Drawings in Adolescence.** New York: Brunner/Mazel, Inc., 1972. Pp. ix, 152. $8.95. *

Percept & Motor Skills 35(1):339 Ag '72. C. H. Ammons and R. B. Ammons. * This is an interesting volume and a useful one for those interested in the projective use of human figure drawings.

[B477]

★Schofield, Harry. **Assessment and Testing: An Introduction.** London: George Allen & Unwin Ltd., 1972. Pp. xiii, 209. Paper, £3.95; cloth, £7.00. * (New York: Crane, Russak & Co., Inc. $15.00.)

[B478–9]

★Scholl, Geraldine, and Schnur, Ronald. **Measures of Psychological, Vocational, and Educational Functioning in the Blind and Visually Handicapped.** New York: American Foundation for the Blind, Inc., 1976. Pp. v, 95. Paper, $5.00. *

[B480]

★Schools Council. **Assessment and Testing in the Secondary School.** By R. N. Deale. Examinations Bulletin 32. London: Evans/Methuen Educational, 1976. Pp. 191. Paper, £3.75. *

[B481]

★Schools Council. **Assessment of Attainment in Sixth-Form Science.** Examinations Bulletin 27. London: Evans/Methuen Educational, 1973. Pp. 77. Paper, £1.10. *

[B482–3]

★SCHOOLS COUNCIL. **British Examinations: Techniques of Analysis.** By Desmond L. Nuttall and Alan S. Willmott. Windsor, Berks., England: NFER Publishing Co. Ltd., 1972. Pp. 164. Paper, £4.20. * (Atlantic Highlands, N.J.: Humanities Press, Inc. $9.50.)

[B484]

★SCHOOLS COUNCIL. **CSE: Mode I Examination in Mathematics: A Study of Current Practice.** Examinations Bulletin 25. London: Evans/Methuen Educational, 1972. Pp. 40. Paper, 60p. *

[B485]

★SCHOOLS COUNCIL. **CSE: Two Research Studies.** By Diana E. Fowles. Examinations Bulletin 28. London: Evans/Methuen Educational, 1974. Pp. 143. Paper, £1.30. *

[B486]

★SCHOOLS COUNCIL. **A Common System of Examining at 16+.** Examinations Bulletin 23. London: Evans/Methuen Educational, 1971. Pp. 61. Paper, 80p. *

[B487]

★SCHOOLS COUNCIL. **Comparability of Standards Between Subjects.** By D. L. Nuttall, J. K. Backhouse, and A. S. Willmott. Examinations Bulletin 29. London: Evans/Methuen Educational, 1974. Pp. 112. Paper, £1.30. *

[B488]

★SCHOOLS COUNCIL. **Continuous Assessment in the CSE: Opinion and Practice.** By Roland Hoste and Barbara Bloomfield. Examinations Bulletin 31. London: Evans/Methuen Educational, 1975. Pp. 156. Paper, £3.10. *

[B489]

★SCHOOLS COUNCIL. **Examinations: Their Use in Curriculum Evaluation and Development.** By J. C. Mathews and J. R. Leece. Examinations Bulletin 33. London: Evans/Methuen Educational, 1976. Pp. 47. Paper, £1.10. *

[B490]

★SCHOOLS COUNCIL. **GCE and CSE: A Guide to Secondary-School Examinations for Teachers, Pupils, Parents and Employers.** London: Evans/Methuen Educational, 1973. Pp. 40. Paper, 55p. *

[B491]

★SCHOOLS COUNCIL. **Mode III Examinations in the CSE and GCE: A Survey of Current Practice.** By C. H. Smith. Examinations Bulletin 34. London: Evans/Methuen Educational, 1976. Pp. 112. Paper, £2.80. *

[B492]

★SCHOOLS COUNCIL. **Monitoring Grade Standards in English: The Value of Different Tests in Monitoring Grade Standards in English Language Examinations.** By Larry S. Skurnik. Working Paper 49. London: Evans/Methuen Educational, 1974. Pp. 63. Paper, 85p. *

[B493]

★SCHOOLS COUNCIL. **The 1967 CSE Monitoring Experiment.** By Larry S. Skurnik and Ian Connaughton. Working Paper 30. London: Evans/Methuen Educational, 1970. Pp. 30. Paper, 40p. *

[B494]

★SCHOOLS COUNCIL. **The 1968 CSE Monitoring Experiment.** By Desmond L. Nuttall. Working Paper 34. London: Evans/Methuen Educational, 1971. Pp. 71. Paper, 75p. *

[B495]

★SCHOOLS COUNCIL. **The Prediction of Academic Success.** By B. H. L. Choppin; L. Orr; S. D. M. Kurle; P. Fara; and G. James. Windsor, Berks., England: NFER Publishing Co. Ltd., 1973. Pp. 70. Paper, £2.00. (Atlantic Highlands, N.J.: Humanities Press, Inc. $4.50.) *

Brit J Ed Psychol 44(1):92–6 N '74. N. J. Entwistle. [Not excerpted, see original review.]

[B496]

★SCHOOLS COUNCIL. **The Predictive Value of CSE Grades for Further Education.** By I. C. Williams and N. C. Boreham. Examinations Bulletin 24. London: Evans/Methuen Educational, 1972. Pp. 88. Paper, £1.25. *

[B497]

★SCHOOLS COUNCIL. **Question Banking: An Approach Through Biology.** By Derek Duckworth and Roland Hoste. Examinations Bulletin 35. London: Evans/Methuen Educational, 1976. Pp. 116. Paper, £2.30. *

[B498]

★SCHOOLS COUNCIL. **Question Banks: Their Use in School Examinations.** Examinations Bulletin 22. London: Evans/Methuen Educational, 1971. Pp. 24. Paper, 40p. *

[B499]

★SCHOOLS COUNCIL. **The Reliability of Examinations at 16+.** By Alan S. Willmott and Desmond L. Nuttall. London: Macmillan Education Ltd., 1975. Pp. xii, 106. £4.65. *

[B500]

★SCHOOLS COUNCIL. **16–19: Growth and Response: 2, Examination Structure: Proposals From the Schools Council's Second Sixth Form Working Party.** Working Paper 46. London: Evans/Methuen Educational, 1973. Pp. 48. Paper, 50p. *

[B501]

*SCHUELL, HILDRED; REVISION BY JOYCE W. SEFER. **Differential Diagnosis of Aphasia With the Minnesota Test, Second Edition.** Minneapolis, Minn.: University of Minnesota Press, 1973. Pp. x, 108. $6.00. *

[B502]

★SCHUERGER, JAMES M., AND WATTERSON, DAVID G. **Using Tests and Other Information in Counseling: A Decision Model for Practitioners.** Champaign, Ill.: Institute for Personality and Ability Testing, 1977. Pp. v, 170. Paper, $7.95. *

[B503]

★SCHWARZ, PAUL A., AND KRUG, ROBERT E. **Ability Testing in Developing Countries: A Handbook of Principles and Techniques.** New York: Praeger Publishers, 1972. Pp. xviii, 244. $15.00. *

[B504]

★SEARLE, EVELYN F. **How to Use WISC Scores in Reading Diagnosis.** Newark, Del.: International Reading Association, Inc., 1975. Pp. v, 44. Paper, $3.00. *

[B505]

★SEMEONOFF, BORIS. **Projective Techniques.** New York: John Wiley & Sons, Inc., 1976. Pp. x, 336. Paper, $10.95; cloth, $21.95. *

[B506]

★SENNA, CARL, EDITOR. **The Fallacy of I.Q.** New York: Third Press, 1973. Pp. xv, 184. $7.95. *

Phi Delta Kappan 55(4):277 D '73. *Robert W. Friedrichs.* The present volume appears....to be as polemical an attempt to reach the layman, teacher, and high school student as H. J. Eysenck's *The I.Q. Argument,* but this time from the environmentalist's rather than the hereditarian's point of view. Fortunately, it *is* something more. Though a number of the essays included are unnecessarily pejorative—including the editor's own contributions—others do, to varying degrees, contribute more light than heat to the highly flammable issue kindled in 1969 with Arthur R. Jensen's now famous conclusion that the empirical evidence available suggested that American black/white IQ differentials were partially genetic in origin. For instance, Jane Mercer and Wayne Curtis Brown's intricately constructed and carefully reported study of the manner in which the statistical control of nine environmental factors led to the evaporation of the IQ differentials discovered between Anglo, Mexican-American, and black children in Riverside, California, is itself worth the book's price. It is important, also, to have generally accessible for the first time, in Strickland's "Can Slum Children Learn?" an account—though in far less detail than we need—of Rick Heber's ongoing "Milwaukee Study." In it a small sample of children of retarded mothers, provided the most enriched environments from infancy through (at the time of the preliminary report) their forty-second month that those in charge could devise, exhibited IQ scores an average of 33 points higher than their "controls." The scholar, however, will wish to balance that claim against Ellis Page's "Miracle in Milwaukee: Raising the IQ," in the *Educational Researcher,* January 10, 1972, which raises appropriate questions concerning the randomness of the assignment of the experimental and control groups, the degree to which subjects were specifically tutored for IQ tests, and the fact that the treatment methods appeared so "loose" as to be difficult to replicate with precision. * Layzer, Harvard astronomer, weakens his contribution by failing to identify the specific sources of most

of his quotations, but does an admirable job of warning the layman of the manner in which apparently sophisticated operational and statistical analyses crumble into insignificance when the assumptions upon which their use is based are examined. It is a pity that the volume was patched together before it could have considered the inclusion of an extremely important report by Stanford sociologists Elizabeth Cohen and Susan Roper (hidden though it is from the layman under an atrocious jargon-laden title) in the December, 1972, issue of the *American Sociological Review.* Here is behavioral science at its best: experimental (rather than correlational) design, with extreme care in extrapolation to remedial programs. But its conclusion is crystal clear: Equality of achievement cannot be reached among blacks and whites simply by raising the proficiency and morale of the blacks alone. Only when *whites* are led to conclude that blacks are as able as they do those whites *permit* a social climate to exist in which equality of achievement is possible. This is one horn of the responsible hereditarian's dilemma, for his hypothesis reinforces the white's resistance to such a possibility. The other horn is well known: It will be impossible to "control" fully for environmental differentials between blacks and whites until white society *assumes* the black is as potentially able as whites deem themselves to be.

[B507]

★SHERIDAN, MARY D. **Children's Developmental Progress From Birth to Five Years: The Stycar Sequences.** Windsor, Berks., England: NFER Publishing Co. Ltd., 1973. Pp. vi, 74. Paper, £2.10. *

[B508]

★SHOUKSMITH, GEORGE. **Intelligence, Creativity, and Cognitive Style.** New York: Wiley-Interscience, 1970. Pp. 240. $6.50.

J Pers Assess 37(3):289–90 Je '73. *Russell Eisenman.* This is a fascinating book, containing both historical perspective and data relevant to the three subject areas of intelligence, creativity, and cognitive styles. * The historical part is both impressive and disappointing. It is impressive because it puts some of the current research and theories in historical perspective, something which is often overlooked by the contemporary researcher. It is disappointing because the historical summaries are rather conventional histories. Someone else trying to do an historical summary would probably come up with much the same thing. This is all right, but lacks the depth of historical treatments by Jung (1964), Lewin (1964), or Mancuso and Dreisinger (1969) * Perhaps the best part of the book is the author's treatment of his data on intelligence, creativity, and cognitive style. He provides a factor analysis in Chapter 12, which indicates that creativity and intelligence measures do not necessarily correlate with each other, nor with themselves all the time. Thus, creativity and intelligence seem factorally complex, and there are interesting sex differences to further confuse the issue. Shouksmith's data do not allow for any easy answers, but at least they show the complexity of the problem, which is not always appreciated by those who talk glibly of "creativity" or "intelligence." This book contains some annoying shortcomings. Sometimes the author writes in such a way that the information is superficial if one already understands it, but probably is incomprehensible if one does not. * his semantic differential measure of cognitive style (p. 151) seems somewhat arbitrary and no validity data are presented. On page 168 the author presents a definition of "flexibility" which seems to fit what most researchers in the field would call "originality." On page 180 the author argues that a particular factor represents acquiescence, but no convincing evidence is presented, even though this interpretation is crucial to later explanations. In summary, this book covers important ground, and provides both an historical summary and original data. However, both are flawed, the former by superficiality and, at times, obtuse writing, the latter, at times, by poor reporting. In spite of these criticisms, there are valuable aspects to this book, *viz.*, the historical perspective and the thoughtful discussion of the author's original factor analytic data.

[B509]

★SILVERMAN, ROBERT J.; NOA, JOSLYN K.; AND RUSSELL, RANDALL H. **Oral Language Tests for Bilingual Students: An Evaluation of Language Dominance and Proficiency Instruments.** Portland, Ore.: Northwest Regional Educational Laboratory, 1976. Pp. 142. Paper, $6.25. *

J Ed Res 70(5):289-90 My/Je '77. Robert St. Clair. * this book is unique in that it provides a comprehensive survey of existing and emerging tests for language dominance and proficiency. Hence, it is highly recommended for those educators who must judge the bilingual ability of their students.

[B510]

★SIMON, FRANCES H. **Prediction Methods in Criminology: Including a Prediction Study of Young Men on Probation.** Home Office Research Studies 7. London: Her Majesty's Stationery Office, 1971. Pp. xi, 233. Paper, £1.25. *

Brit J Ed Psychol 42(2):218-9 Je '72. H. B. Gibson. This covers both a general review of prediction studies in criminology and an account of a particular study which was carried out with youths on probation. The author remarks, quite rightly, that prediction tables have been little used in administrative practice because their power is rather low. Their relative ineffectiveness is not surprising since what has to be predicted is not criminal activity but criminal conviction, and the latter involves a great ramification of chance variables involving the changing policies of local law-enforcement agencies, the accidents of the particular courts involved and many other variables irrelevant to the nature of the convicted person himself. * This is not an easy book to follow. It represents the fruit of an enormous amount of work by a large number of people over quite a period of time. Its style of presentation leaves something of a confusion in the reader's mind. Results, discussion of these data and of other people's data are often mixed together. One gets the feeling that the writer has lived with her material for so long that she has forgotten that other people are not as familiar with it as she is. As far as one can gather, the exercise was a resounding failure as far as prediction went, but the reader would need to do a very detailed post-mortem study to make up his mind *why* it was such a failure. A statistician might question the use made of regression analysis with dichotomous variables; a psychologist might wonder about the sort of use that was made of P.O.s as raters, and a social theorist might question the usefulness of the whole operation. In the author's final conclusions she argues that as we have failed to find any effective means of predicting success on probation, we should abandon such predictive research and turn to studying better means of treatment. This brings us back to the dilemma which faces all research workers in penology— the impossibility of doing controlled experimental work owing to the opposition of the administration. As long as the Home Office will sponsor research only with such limitations in this field, it is unlikely that we will get other than negative studies.

[B511]

★SINGER, E. **A Manual of Graphology.** London: Gerald Duckworth & Co. Ltd., 1973. Pp. 244. Paper, $1.50; cloth, $7.95.

Austral J Psychol 27(1):109 Ap '75. In the nineteenth century, Michon, a Frenchman, coined the term "graphology" and formulated most of the rules on which the system of deducing character from handwriting is based. In the early 1950s Eric Singer wrote three popular books on the subject: *Graphology for Everyman, The Graphologist's Alphabet* and *A Handwriting Quiz Book.* This is a reissue of those three books under a single title. Graphology may strike some as a fruitful projective technique, others as an enjoyable parlour game, and still others as pure bunkum. Either way, Singer's book makes for entertaining reading.

[B512]

★SLATER, PATRICK, EDITOR. **The Measurement of Intrapersonal Space by Grid Technique: Explorations of Intrapersonal Space, Vol. 1.** London and New York: John Wiley & Sons Ltd., 1976. Pp. viii, 258. £8.75; $23.50. *

*Brit J Ed Psychol 47(2):220 Je '77. Steve Duck. * Whilst the technique (which turns out to be several different ones, despite the Introduction) is originally derived from Kelly's personal construct theory, this reviewer at least was left wondering what the theoretical motor (and indeed theoretical outcome) is of some of the work reported. The chapters diverge and are diverse in their adherence to Kelly's theoretical beliefs and phrases like "castration anxiety" creep into the narrative at times. Some of the better chapters (Salmon's on children's thinking and Landfield's on suicide, for example) derive new and interesting conceptualisations of their respective concerns from Kelly's theory. The authors then turn, quite naturally, to the associated techniques to explore these insights. Other chapters employ Kelly-like views of thought processes but use them in informal and unstructured ways using grid technique, if for any reason at all, "because it's there." A third category of chapters appears based on the premise that if grid techniques exist they must be used and all that remains is the discovery of a problem to apply them to (i.e., Kelly's theory is incidental), whilst there are other examples where authors appear to wish simply to show that grids can be given to anyone, with a little ingenuity. One would not, in short, be surprised to find a chapter called "Grid Techniques applied to blind deaf mutes in the iron lung," and this raises precisely the issue of what advance of knowledge is represented by chapters in this latter category. In short, the theoretical impact of the book is hard to assess since so many of the issues it tackles appear to be *simply* examples of where the technique can be used, rather than comparisons of this *versus* that technique. Presumably any technique can be applied almost anywhere once the relationship of technique to theory is weakened. The theoretical assessment of the book is further complicated by the fact that it bears all the signs of having been long in the pipeline (written about 1972/1973 by the look of it) with later references being very few and largely confined to authors' own work. This is particularly important since those chapters that do make theoretically interesting statements have occasionally been overtaken by events when they have identified areas that need to be developed. One would certainly like to see a good book answering the challenge of Bannister and Fransella (1971) in showing the many new insights given to old problems by use of Kelly's theory and associated methods. Whilst this present book undoubtedly will be a useful "workshop manual" to those who use grid technique, it is not clear that it represents more than this.

[B513]

*SMITH, FRED M., AND ADAMS, SAM. **Educational Measurement for the Classroom Teacher, Second Edition.** New York: Harper & Row, Publishers, Inc., 1972. Pp. xiv, 370. $13.95. * For a review of the first edition, see 7:B584.

*Ed & Psychol Meas 33(3):756–8 au '73. Lloyd A. Lewis. * the authors apparently have managed to achieve their goal of attempting to concentrate "on those phases of measurement that are of specific interest to in-service or prospective classroom teachers." The authors make a reasonable attempt to discuss the fundamental nature of measurement and to place educational measurement in proper perspective. * Smith and Adams explore the concept of how measurement promotes learning, but no examples are used to show how poor measurement promotes worry, fear and anxiety in students who do not know how well they are doing. * The authors state that a novice to measurement "need not become overly concerned with whether or not a given test is criterion-referenced or norm-referenced." They go on to say that this decision should be left to specialists, yet they advocate that criterion-referenced tests be used whenever appropriate. Therein lies a problem; namely, they fail to give the teacher enough information so as to know which kind of test is used under what circumstances. The chapters on basic statistical operations, reliability, validity, and usability are well written and at the appropriate level of difficulty. * the authors do a good job of developing the sections on: (a) procedures in achievement testing, (b) selecting and writing objectives, (c) item writing techniques, (d) measuring achievement by direct observation, and (e) appraising achievement in the affective domain. In the evaluation of teacher made tests, some problems are encountered, the major one being that all discussion centers around norm-referenced tests. None of the material deals with the short criterion-referenced tests that teachers typically call a "quiz." * I would recommend this book for classroom use with some words of caution. I recommend it because it is clearly written and at the appropriate level of difficulty. Its chief fault lies in the fact that I seriously doubt if it persuades the classroom teacher that she is cheating her students when she does not use good classroom measurement techniques.

Meas & Eval Guid 6(1):61–2 Ap '73. Glenn G. Dahlem. This book is obviously intended to serve as an undergraduate text for the tests and measurements course of the teacher education curriculum. It has a possible secondary value as a professional development book for practicing classroom teachers who wish to update their measurement knowledges and concepts. On both these counts, the book appears adequate, and measures up well when compared with its several current competitors. Because of the broad scope demanded of a work of this type, many of the subtopical treatments, while excellent, are of necessity cursory. This fact somewhat limits its usefulness for those involved in graduate research and teaching and in standardized test creation and norming. This text covers a broad spectrum. * Just about every ramification and type of measurement is treated; hence, the great value of this book as a nuts-and-bolts kind of reference for practicing and neophyte teachers. The book reads like a lecture, in that all three persons of English grammar (we, you, it) are used by the authors. This somewhat colloquial rather than scholarly style probably will enhance its readability at the undergraduate level. Major weaknesses of the work lie in two areas. Although this is never stated, one guesses that the

authors have greater interest in secondary rather than elementary education and have organized their material accordingly. While conscious efforts are made to include elementary level material, the narrative rings truest where high school level evaluation is discussed. In addition, while many standardized tests are named in the text and are discussed, nowhere does one find a chart or listing of all instruments in a given category. Even the chapter on a schoolwide testing program, where one certainly would expect a chart of this type, contains none. Apparently the authors expect the reader to turn to one of the numerous chapter-end references (Bauernfeind, Buros, Cronbach, etc.) for information of this nature. Overall, despite the limitations cited, this book is a worthwhile acquisition for those interested in educational measurement at the neophyte level.

[B514]

★Smith, Judith M.; Smith, Donald E. P.; and Brink, James R. **A Technology of Reading and Writing: Vol. 2, Criterion-Referenced Tests for Reading and Writing.** New York: Academic Press, Inc., 1977. Pp. xii, 279. $13.75. *

Read Teach 31(4):461–3 Ja '78. Frank Greene. John Wilson (University of Maryland) has recently proposed that we talk of behavioral indicators, not of behavioral objectives. As often currently used, behavioral objectives are simply sets of test items which become the goal of instruction. But note what Wilson's renaming has done: the test items (behavioral objectives) are no longer the goal, they are simply indicators of competency from which someone has to make judgments (inferences) about whether the desired skills and attitudes have been acquired. Note that to talk of indicators also resolves the current confusion between measurement and evaluation that so fills our journals. Of course, evaluation is not measurement, but evaluation (making judgments) is never improved by having faulty data. Smith, Smith and Brink's book with all its talk of behavioral engineering, objectives and criterion referenced test items, etc. will upset people who have previously been shocked by the fragmented, minute, and often trivial behavioral objectives which have been applied to reading. To these upset people goes the caution to read carefully this book (and its rationale found in Volume 1)—for these authors are talking about "behavioral indicators," and about making inferences and, therefore, about teaching commitments. This is a book about teaching based on evaluation based on having precise and valid indicators of a pupil's skills. These authors clearly distinguish between learning to read and write and proficient reading and writing. This set of books concentrates on learning how to. The authors present some 350 specific tests, along with considerable data on the common ordering of the tasks based on the competency of pupils in grades one through six. The domain of concern is divided not by grade level or by inferred intellectual processes (word recognition, comprehension, etc.), but by the stimuli of language instruction (books, paragraphs, sentences, words, letters). The authors also present information on how to: reorganize test sequences to reflect local programs; write new tests which meet needed rigor for assessment; and use data generated for decision making about individual pupils, classes, grade levels, and schools. It is suggested that the data can be used for making within-classroom teaching decisions; within-building educational decisions; and within-district fiscal decisions. It is probable that Volume 1 needs to be read along with Volume 2, and that both will frequently be referred to after that. Possible solutions to many of today's pedagogic and/or measurement fights are already in this material. Even terms like engineered classroom become understandable: "....the important thing is whether the analysis leading to these and other instructional particulars is or is not the best available specification of components *with reference to* the capacity of an instructional system using the analysis to produce literacy in its clients. The constraints and rewards, in other words, are those associated with engineering, not science: the thing must be profound and elegant, but it must work" (p. 43). This is a most important book for anyone interested in teaching children to read and to write.

[B515]

★SPACHE, GEORGE D. **Diagnosing and Correcting Reading Disabilities.** Boston, Mass.: Allyn & Bacon, Inc., 1976. Pp. xiii, 397. $14.95. *

[B516]

★SPOONCER, FRANK A. **The Evaluation of Reading.** London: Hodder & Stoughton Educational, 1977. Pp. 31. Paper, 60p. *

[B517]

★STANLEY, JULIAN C., AND HOPKINS, KENNETH D. **Educational and Psychological Measurement and Evaluation.** Englewood Cliffs, N.J.: Prentice-Hall, Inc., 1972. Pp. xxiii, 520. $14.50. *

Ed & Psychol Meas 33(1):212–5 sp '73. *John H. Neel.* * While EPME was originally intended to be the 5th edition of *Measurement in Today's Schools* (MTS-Stanley, 1964); the authors believed the revisions were extensive enough to warrant a new title. * Reorganization is probably the most noticeable change in the book. This includes an expansion of material from 11 to 17 chapters with considerable regrouping of content. * Of all these additions, changes, and deletions the omission of grouped data calculation will probably have the greatest effect on the nature of a class using the text. With some portable electronic calculators now selling for as low as $50.00, calculation from grouped data does seem to be anachronistic. Class time formerly spent on those calculations can now be used for more necessary concepts. In its presentation, EPME seems to recognize this. The inclusion of some programmed material on statistics will probably be welcomed by students as will a 25 item test over statistical concepts at the end of Chapter 2. The general nature of the discussion of statistics seems greatly improved. * The separation and expansion of reliability and validity into two chapters is an improvement. * EPME Chapters 8 through 12 on test construction are well written but with one exception of a negative point on "semantic space" have little in them that differs from the usual listing of rules, examples and recommended procedures found in most introductory measurement texts. The "semantic space" concept is introduced on page 233 without adequate explanation. Students are presented with a figure and no explanation other than that it illustrates the concept of semantic space. * Instructors teaching a course primarily on test construction with some discussion of standardized tests will find EPME to be a good text. It certainly differs from MTS and should be given serious consideration even by those who may have rejected MTS.

J Ed Meas 10(2):155–7 su '73. *William Owen Scott.* * The format is attractive; the print, clear and easy to read, the writing style, terse and clear, and the tables and figures do clarify the narrative. Defects and errors in typography are commendably few * The comments which follow are predicated on the avowed purpose of the text—to meet the measurements needs of classroom teachers—and on the reviewer's judgment of these needs. * Among measurement topics of interest and importance to classroom teachers which the text does not consider are the following: 1. Specific application of item and test analyses to planning remedial instruction; 2. Making specific suggestions concerning the classroom use (or non-use) of intelligence test data; 3. Making specific suggestions for relating measurement to grading pupil achievement (in chapter 13 there are some general comments, but the teacher is left largely to her own devices); 4. Making specific suggestions with respect to measuring change in pupil achievement (admittedly this topic is complex, but in view of teacher interest and current stress on "educational accountability," it should be considered); and 5. Making specific suggestions concerning "pop" tests and "open-book" tests. With respect to the content which might be reasonably omitted, the general caveat of the reviewer is to appraise each topic in terms of its direct contribution to achievement of the text's major purpose. Some topics which do not measure up when so appraised, at least in this reviewer's judgment, include the following: most of chapters 6 and 7 (but leaving in the material on the unreliability of school marks and tests), most of chapter 14 (teachers have had other courses which consider the content of this chapter), and most of chapters 16 and 17. If the reviewer has seemed unduly harsh, this has not been his intention. This text is as good as, or better than, other basic measurements texts and can be used for its intended purpose, especially if the instructor exercises judgment in the selection and sequencing of the content.

Meas & Eval Guid 7(3):199–201 O '74. David J. Weiss. * The word "evaluation" in the title refers to the process of extracting meaning from test scores by attaching judgments to the results of testing. * This book is therefore not concerned with evaluation in the context of today's current use of the term, i.e., evaluation of educational programs or educational progress. Stanley and Hopkins' book is also not a comprehensive treatment of psychological testing; it will not replace Anastasi's *Psychological Testing* or Cronbach's *Essentials of Psychological Testing* on the counselor's bookshelf. Rather, as its title states, it is primarily concerned with *educational* measurement, although one chapter toward the end makes quick work of interest measurement, personality measurement, and "social measurement" (e.g., sociograms). In that chapter, the educator is briefly introduced to the Kuder and SVIB Inventories, as well as

a variety of personality instruments. The presentation is, of necessity, quite superficial. The main purpose in discussing personality instruments seems to be so that the authors can conclude: "Current personality inventory scores have generally been of little or no value for predicting future success in school, on the job, or in one's personal living. We believe no useful purpose is served by giving a personality or adjustment inventory, except perhaps in certain research projects (p. 396)." Such a biased statement, in a book likely to find use among school personnel, hardly makes counselors' jobs easier when they must administer personality inventories for clinical purposes such as understanding and helping a student. Similar instances of the book's lack of usefulness for the counselor can be found in Chapter 14, "Measuring Intelligence." As might be expected, much is made of the concept of IQ (which should follow the dodo to extinction), while only one and one-half pages are devoted to the considerably more useful multifactor ability tests. Hopkins and Stanley appear to consider tests of scholastic aptitude and "intelligence" to be interchangeable; with all the surplus meaning attached to the word "intelligence" (despite the authors' efforts to clarify its meaning within the context of the book), that term and the associated IQ could have been left out of the book with no loss at all. * The book is....intended for teachers. * A unique feature is the interweaving of conventional text format with programmed instruction. Although the conventional presentation and the programmed instruction are supposed to cover the same material, they really do not. Thus, while the idea is good, it is not very well implemented. The teacher would need to work through the entire chapter in order to learn all the material. * The chapter on test validity is disturbingly short (11 pages) with only one page devoted to the concept of construct validity. One of the purposes of the book is to assist educators in "interpreting" test scores, even though it is the concept of construct validity which helps in understanding what an instrument is measuring. Thus, construct validity needs to be developed in considerably more detail before educators should be turned loose on "interpreting" test scores. Only then can educators begin to realize that intelligence and scholastic aptitude cannot be measured by the same test. The chapter on reliability is fairly well done, although it is the only chapter in the book which seems to be a bit too technical for the beginning teacher. This chapter does include, however, one of the clearest available discussions of regression to the mean (p. 121–122). Since this concept is one of the least understood among persons using measurement techniques, everyone would benefit by reading these two pages. Part two of the book is really its major contribution. This part, entitled "The Development of Educational Measures," includes seven chapters and almost 200 pages. It is designed for the classroom teacher who needs to build his own multiple-choice or essay tests, wishes to assess certain noncognitive variables (remember that the authors say personality measurement is useless), or needs to assign grades based on test scores. These chapters include the expected information on all the various kinds of objective test items and methods of item analysis. However, there is very little continuity between this part of the book and the earlier discussions of reliability and validity. The book would be more valuable if the chapter on item analysis, for example, was more directly tied to the notions of reliability briefly discussed in earlier chapters. Item analysis is presented as simply something one does to obtain data on an item's "difficulty" and "discrimination," with reliability brought in as only a minor consideration. *

[B518]

★Stott, D. H.; Marston, N. C.; and Neill, Sara J. **Taxonomy of Behaviour Disturbance.** London: University of London Press Ltd., 1975. Pp. viii, 184. £4.75. *

[B519]

★Struening, Elmer L., and Guttentag, Marcia, Editors. **Handbook of Evaluation Research, Volumes 1 and 2.** Beverly Hills, Calif.: Sage Publications, Inc., 1975. Pp. viii, vii, 696, 736. $50.00 per set. *

Am J Psychiatry 133(10):1218 O '76. Lee B. Sechrest. Here is everything you wanted to know (well, almost) about evaluation research and a good bit besides. * Some of the material has appeared elsewhere in some form or another, but the collection of material is quite useful and of generally high quality and high reader interest. Volume 1 consists of basic material on evaluation research. * For the most part the material is well chosen and well presented, the ideas are up-to-date, and in general it is comprehensive and helpful. On the other hand, it must be noted that the presentation is scarcely geared to the novice; it will be most useful to

readers who already have a fair amount of experience or training in evaluation research. Volume 2 is oriented largely to program evaluation in the field of mental health and should be of distinct interest to professionals with responsibility for mental health programs, whether they have a direct responsibility for evaluation or not. There is an initial section on politics and values in evaluation research that is quite stimulating and should be of very general interest, as should the two subsequent chapters on cost-benefit and cost-effectiveness analysis. The latter two chapters will be especially helpful to social scientists with considerable interest and little training in economic analysis. A subsequent section on evaluation of mental health programs includes a mixed lot of chapters reporting specific evaluation efforts or reviewing literature in some area of program performance. These chapters will be of principal interest to professionals in the field of mental health. Volume 2 concludes with three chapters reporting evaluation efforts in the fields of early childhood educational interventions, public health programs, and new careers programs. All three make good reading for those with an interest in the content area. These two volumes were prepared and edited by thoughtful and experienced workers with a good bit of personal experience in evaluation. They chose materials very wisely from among those available, and they solicited and obtained pieces from some (one is tempted to say most) of the best known figures in evaluation research so that the work is both stimulating and authoritative. The cost of the two volumes together is high; not many individual readers may feel that the investment is worthwhile. However, I predict that persons with a continuing commitment to program evaluation at a professional level will, if they acquire these volumes, refer to them frequently and with profit.

Brit J Psychiatry 130:98 Ja '77. Alan Norton. This monster is no handbook ("a small book or treatise such as may be held in the hand": *Shorter Oxford Dictionary*), but is more of a "Handbuch" in the German sense. It weighs 2.7 kg, is in two volumes and has 1,400 pages and 45 authors. It is also unimaginably dull. Evaluation research, spawned by the social sciences, has crept up on us unawares in the last fifteen years or so. As the editors make clear, anyone carrying out research programmes in social science is all too prone to stumble: there may be faults in conceptualizing the problem; faults in research strategy, in design and in the choice of suitable means of measurements; and so forth. These volumes, comprehensive to a fault, give, one supposes, the definitive account of this new subject. Much of the second volume concerns the evaluation of mental health programmes. The chapters range widely. At one extreme is a new clear account (the only contribution from Europe) of Peter Sainsbury's well-known comparison of community-based and hospital-based psychiatric service in Chichester and Salisbury. At the other, one is deep into sociology and its soporific lingo. "Contracts constitute the *integrative function* for all human systems relationships at all social levels of systems organization." Some of the other chapters, notably Rabkin on attitudes towards mental illness, and Kreisman and Joy on family reactions to mental illness in a relative, are rewarding. But such nuggets are rare. Too many of the chapters are review articles; too many others are too political or too much concerned with economics or just too unreadable to make this work, at such a price, a worthwhile purchase for any but the largest psychiatric libraries.

Ed & Psychol Meas 37(2):562–6 su '77. John L. Wasik. * the *Handbook* was developed to achieve two purposes, one instructive and one demonstrative. With the mass of material presented within the two volume set, it may seem somewhat picayune to ask why the editors did not include some materials on this or that subject. However, this reviewer did feel that the *Handbook* could benefit by a discussion of evaluation models such as the CIPP model of Stufflebeam or the Goal-Free Evaluation approach of Scriven and expansion of the data analysis section to include discussion of the analysis of nontraditional measures of effectiveness. In contrast, it was pleasing to see the presentation of nonstatistically based methods for deriving indices of program effectiveness as presented by Levin and Rothenberg using cost benefit analysis and the Bayesian analysis approach presented by Edwards, et al. In general, this reviewer would conclude that the editors have achieved their goal of developing a set of "How to do it" instructional modules and providing examples of how evaluation methodology has been applied in real life setting. However, the question as to whether a cost benefit index can be determined for the use of

this text, which sells for $50 for both volumes, is beyond this reviewer's ability to estimate.

[B520]

★STUFFLEBEAM, DANIEL L., AND OTHERS. **Educational Evaluation and Decision Making.** Phi Delta Kappa National Study Committee on Evaluation. Itasca, Ill.: F. E. Peacock Publishers, Inc., 1971. Pp. xxviii, 368. $13.50.

Ed & Psychol Meas 32(1):219–23 sp '72. Carl A. Clark. * what the authors are really concerned with, is not evaluation as the term is ordinarily understood. What they are really concerned with is a theory of educational programming—how to set up a system of steps or a project to produce educational change. This can be seen in their re-definition of evaluation. "Educational evaluation is the process of delineating, obtaining, and providing useful information for judging decision alternatives." Evaluation in the sense of measurement and of judging the value of what has been done is thus relegated to a secondary function: secondary, though contributory, to the shaping of a given educational process. They present a "theory" of educational planning and implementation as involved in educational decision making, and in this respect the book has a great deal to offer, as one would expect from a group of experienced educators who have engaged in important educational projects. * Careful reading of the book should give to anyone interested in educational projects much insight into the complexities involved, the things to be thought of, the need for careful planning, including the need for communication at different levels with groups of persons concerned: parents, community, pupils, administrators, decision maker. Whether or not an "evaluator" reading the book may attempt to incorporate in his own system much of its methodology, there are likely to be some things of value that he could use. It is to be hoped, however, that a person preparing to undertake an evaluation will overlook some of the research viewpoints presented in the book. * Though the book is weak on the measurement and research design function of evaluation, it has much to offer concerning the organization and functioning of an educational project. Some of its value in this respect, however, is obscured through the organization of the book itself. There is a good deal of overlapping and repetition * Anyone who reads this book carefully, however, will certainly be stimulated to think, to analyze, and to reorganize his thoughts about educational evaluation and decision-making, even though he may disagree with much that is said. [See original review for additional critical comments not excerpted.]

J Ed Meas 9(3):251–2 f '72. Hulda Grobman. * represents a landmark in the development and codification of educational evaluation. It is both well written and up to date, and presents evaluation as a functional and respectable activity rather than as an illegitimate offspring of research. Though many of the comments and ideas are not new, the book is the most complete volume to date in terms of providing an overview of what evaluation should and can be, what it is and what it is not, and how it can better become what it should be. * One of the....potentially useful contributions is the end-of-book glossary of evaluation terms. Evaluation, as a relatively new area, has suffered from a dearth of standardized terminology. Although the terms used in this volume are neither all encompassing nor unique, the convenient listing could provide the nucleus for standardizing the vocabulary of evaluation. This would greatly simplify communications among evaluators and between evaluators and their audiences. This volume, while excellent, is certainly not the last word on evaluation, but it provides a good summary of where we are now and proposes some next steps. In so doing it should provide a useful point of departure for further theory and development in evaluation.

[B521]
★SUND, ROBERT B., AND PICARD, ANTHONY J. **Behavioral Objectives and Evaluational Measures: Science and Mathematics.** Columbus, Ohio: Charles E. Merrill Publishing Co., 1972. Pp. viii, 214. Paper, $3.95. *

[B522]
★SUNDBERG, NORMAN D. **Assessment of Persons.** Englewood Cliffs, N.J.: Prentice-Hall, Inc., 1977. Pp. xiii, 353. $12.95. *

[B523]
★SUYDAM, MARILYN N. **Evaluation in the Mathematics Classroom: From What and Why to How and Where.** Arlington, Va.: ERIC Document Reproduction Service, 1974. Pp. vii, 62. Paper, $2.10. *

[B524]
★SUYDAM, MARILYN N. **Unpublished Instruments for Evaluation in Mathematics Education: An Annotated Listing.** Arlington, Va.: ERIC Document Reproduction Service, 1974. Pp. iv, 259. Paper, $3.20. *

[B525]
★SWENSON, WENDELL M.; PEARSON, JOHN S.; AND OSBORNE, DAVID. **An MMPI Source Book: Basic Item, Scale, and Pattern Data on 50,000 Medical Patients.** Minneapolis, Minn.: University of Minnesota Press, 1973. Pp. ix, 150. $9.50. *

Am J Psychiatry 131(8):947 Ag '74. Bernard C. Glueck. This book is primarily a statistical report of the data obtained from the Minnesota Multiphasic Personality Inventory gathered on 50,000 patients, half of whom were men and half of whom were women, who were given the MMPI at the Mayo Clinic in Rochester, Minn., as part of their routine workup. * This book should be of particular interest and usefulness to research workers, students of personality theory, and all those concerned with the construction of personality inventories. In addition, it provides norms for medical patients that may be of value to clinicians as a comparison with their own patient population. We can only hope that this is but the first of a number of such reports to come from the Mayo Clinic group as they pursue further studies of the large populations of patients surveyed by use of the MMPI.

[B526]
★TANNER, J. M.; WHITEHOUSE, R. H.; MARSHALL, W. A.; HEALY, M. J. R.; AND GOLDSTEIN, H. **Assessment of Skeletal Maturity and Prediction of Adult Height (TW2 Method).** London and New York: Academic Press, Inc., 1975. Pp. vii, 99. £10.50; $22.25. *

[B527]
★TARCZAN, CONSTANCE. **An Educator's Guide to Psychological Tests: Descriptions and Classroom Implications.** Springfield, Ill.: Charles C Thomas, Publisher, 1972. Pp. xiv, 133. Paper, $6.50; cloth, $8.50. *

J Learn Dis 6(4):261–3 Ap '73. Margaret Scheffelin. * The praiseworthy aim of this book —informing teachers—does not appear to have been met. * I counted ten misstatements of facts and misleading statements in the chapter on tests, without attempting to locate *all* such statements. In my opinion, partially true information is less helpful than no information. Descriptions of projective tests may lead teachers to attempt clinical psychological interpretations of children's drawings and their responses to pictures. The chapter does not consistently designate the differential training necessary to choose, administer, score, and interpret the tests. * The teaching suggestions are general and minimal, but they are helpful, not harmful. * books such as this....provide partial and misleading information on tests and testing, mixed with potentially useful ideas on teaching * A reference guide must be scrupulously accurate.

This book is an example of inadequate editing and editorial research. In addition to the textual examples I have already cited, the bibliography is particularly in need of editing. *

Meas & Eval Guid 8(2)112–3 Jl '75. Richard J. Noeth. * Although the book is....more general in scope than its title implies, it might have made a valuable contribution if it helped teachers understand and use specific kinds of test data. But even this objective is only partially fulfilled. * The first chapter presents a narrow picture of psychological testing. * The second chapter inadequately covers the concept of intelligence and presents a traditional description of IQ. * The discussion of psychometrical terminology in the next chapter, although not a crash course in statistics, appears far too sketchy to be of any educational value. * The fourth chapter covers, at various lengths and in different degrees of detail, 64 specific tests. * Most noteworthy is the coverage of classroom implications (with remediation techniques) of test data—brief discussions which range from very good to slightly ambiguous. * Although the three achievement tests cited are sketchily covered, treatment of each of the perception tests is fairly complete and includes some excellent discussion of classroom implications. The introduction to the reading tests may cause teachers some concern. After stating that these tests "present little or no reliability, validity, or standardized-population description," the author recommends that the educator must "take it upon himself to check into the test and find out what it measures and how effectively." A tall order! * In general, the discussion of many of the specific tests is inadequate, uninformative, and sometimes misleading. * There are also some minor, but annoying, flaws in this book. Some studies which are referenced or discussed in the text are not included in the bibliography. The name index does not include all individuals mentioned in the text, and a number of page references in the index are incorrect. Books that help bridge the gap between psychological tests and classroom situations are important for the development of the individual as well as the total educational system. Unfortunately, although this book attempts to build such a bridge, it falls woefully short.

[B528]

★TAUBMAN, PAUL, AND WALES, TERENCE. **Mental Ability and Higher Educational Attainment in the 20th Century.** A Technical Report Prepared for the Carnegie Commission on Higher Education. New York: National Bureau of Economic Research, 1972. Pp. xvi, 47. Paper, $1.50. *

[B529]

★TAULBEE, EARL S.; WRIGHT, H. WILKES; AND STENMARK, DAVID E. **The Minnesota Multiphasic Personality Inventory (MMPI): A Comprehensive, Annotated Bibliography (1940–1965).** Troy, N.Y.: Whitston Publishing Co., Inc., 1977. Pp. xiii, 603. $35.00. *

Psychol Rep 41(3, pt 2):1347 D '77. R. B. Ammons and C. H. Ammons. Knowing how extensively the MMPI has been used in research and clinical assessment, if the title of this book does not catch your eye, the table of contents will, for it clearly indicates the thoroughness of the search. The chapters include the abstracts of MMPI articles (1–1310), non-abstracted MMPI articles (1311–1411), references to manifest anxiety (1412–1658), foreign references (1659–1769), doctoral dissertations (1770–2013), Master's theses and other unpublished items (2014–2108). Last appear books, reviews, and tests (2109–2144). This was quite an undertaking! But there are other tidbits: the expected author and subject indexes of course, then a list of scales with references to specific citations, special scoring procedures (13 are identified), a listing of special scales and subscales (their abbreviations, authors and citations), and last but not least two appendices of abbreviations of names and journals without which this book could not be read. In fact, any serious reader should begin here with what amounts to a glossary requisite for one to become an initiate. This nutshell library should become a frequently used reference, though the abstracts give but a hint as to the content and worth of items cited.

[B530]

★TAYLOR, JAMES C., AND BOWERS, DAVID G. **Survey of Organizations: A Machine-Scored Standardized Questionnaire Instrument.** Ann Arbor, Mich.: Center for Research on Utilization of Scientific Knowledge, Institute for Social Research, University of Michigan, 1972. Pp. vii, 165. $12.00.

[B531]

★TENBRINK, TERRY D. **Evaluation: A Practical Guide for Teachers.** New York: McGraw-Hill Book Co., Inc., 1974. Pp. xi, 493. $14.95. *

Ed & Psychol Meas 34(3):733–6 au '74. Dennis M. Roberts. * My general observations concerning TenBrink's book revolve around intrabook overlap of material, organization and usefulness of guidelines. First, there is substantial overlap from chapter to chapter. Norm-versus criterion referenced tests are discussed several places and the same kinds of information on data gathering devices are described in more or less detail in several chapters. I would estimate that judicious condensation and removal of redundancy would have shortened the book by 100 pages. Second, the basic organization of the book stems from the step-by-step model of evaluation given at the beginning. Within chapters, encircled boxes present series of steps and procedures on a given point, ask questions on the material and/or present examples of the object being discussed. This encircling technique is meant to be a highlighting device. However, too much of a good idea tends to blur its basic purpose. Almost every page has some boxed in material—many pages having only a few lines of "text" with several encircled sets of guidelines or examples. It makes for very fragmented reading. Third, the guidelines offered are, for the most part, practical and helpful. * In summary, I found *Evaluation: A practical guide for teachers* to be overly wordy and organizationally confusing. The model presented is useful though and should assist teachers in their work. I do feel, however, that drastic condensation of the material would have made for a more readable and useful guide.

Meas & Eval Guid 8(2):117–8 Jl '75. Kemp Mabry. * The book is written in a first person, easy-to-read style. It is the approach of a master teacher skillfully developing each concept, speaking directly to the student. There is enough content here for a graduate course, yet it is an admirable text for the math-shy undergraduate. The instructors' section is outstanding. It contains chapter summaries, learning activities, and discussion suggestions as well as a set of 20 masters for overhead transparencies. From 15 to 50 selection-type questions on each chapter are given in the manual. The most effective use of the book would be to require students to do what TenBrink describes and illustrates so well: (a) construct and use nontest instruments such as rating scales, (b) construct and use a classroom or teacher-made test, and (c) examine and follow his model for the use of standardized tests, using specimen sets. All of this and more is suggested. I like the model and I like the writing style. *

[B532]

★TERMAN, LEWIS M., AND MERRILL, MAUDE A. **Stanford-Binet Intelligence Scale: Manual for the Third Revision, Form L–M.** With revised IQ tables (pp. 257–349) by Samuel R. Pinneau and 1972 tables of norms (pp. 353–441) by Robert L. Thorndike.

Boston, Mass.: Houghton Mifflin Co., 1973. Pp. x, 455. $11.80. * (Same as 1960 edition except for addition of an appendix presenting 1972 norms.)

[B533]

★TERWILLIGER, JAMES S. **Assigning Grades to Students.** Glenview, Ill.: Scott, Foresman & Co., 1971. Pp. ix, 177. * *Out of print.*

J Ed Meas 10(3):235 f '73. William Clark Trow. * The target audience is presumably made up of classroom teachers. According to the preface, "the assignment of grades to students is a crucial part of the job of most teachers," but many, if not most, teachers would have considerable difficulty in following the rather technical explanations. Even having mastered them, they might well be disappointed to learn that the methods of deriving marks from data so meticulously described are so defective that (like grading on the curve), "it is impossible to justify the practice." Perhaps even more difficult to follow are some of the author's assumptions, both implicit and explicit. One, represented in common practice, is that the only legitimate procedure is to allow all pupils the same amount of time in which to master an uncertain number of facts and skills, i.e., to hold time instead of performance constant. A second is the assumption that the teacher should predict the proportion of students who will not thus master the "required" material and penalize them accordingly even though the stipulated numbers (per cents) of students to receive the different marks are given the currently popular name, "guide lines." A third dubious assumption is that the method used to determine the amount of the student-reward (or penalty) is a highly reliable process. In addition, it is assumed that the resulting mark is as valuable for the large number of purposes for which it is used as is claimed—an assumption rather effectively disproved by the author. Another dubious assumption is that all students should be expected to be highly motivated to learn all the details of a course they are taking whether or not it is required, even though there is no discernable interest or profit for them in such labor. And a final assumption seems to be that what pupils don't learn is not important for them to learn. If it *is* important, presumably it should be *taught;* if not, there is no need to trouble them about it. If this be treason,.....!

[B534]

*THORNDIKE, ROBERT L., EDITOR. **Educational Measurement, Second Edition.** Washington, D.C.: American Council on Education, 1971. Pp. xx, 768.

$18.00. * For reviews of the first edition, see 5:B269 (4 excerpts) and 4:B247 (5 excerpts).

Ed & Psychol Meas 31(4):1040–4 w '71. *Nicholas J. Anastasiow.* * This volume falls somewhere between an encyclopedia and a mechanics manual, it contains compendiums of current facts, step by step how-to-do-its, and theoretical discussions of varying levels of sophistication which range from very exciting to disappointing. The problem of single edited multi-authored, omnitopic volume is its unevenness. As encyclopedias vary in their descriptive excellence so do reference books of this nature. * The appropriate audience for this book is a diverse one and unhappily, to this reviewer one which does not include teachers and administrators. There are excellent chapters for the theoretician and the advanced student and some excellent sections for the test item writer, the printer, and the clerk in a testing department. However, a teacher turning to this reference work would find that the chapters which might be useful are overly drawn out, full of platitudes and display a suprising lack of sophistication about children and schooling. For the most part the articles contain psychometric theory by educational psychologists who are apparently much less versed in knowledge of schools, schooling and children. The first chapter of the book begins with an excellent overview by Robert Thorndike of the changes that have taken place during the past twenty years in the field of test and measurement. * Thorndike's discussion of the political and social problems of testing are only superficially summarized. The first section of this book covers *Test Design, Construction, Administration and Processing.* Chapter Two, *Defining and Assessing Educational Objectives,* is a disappointing chapter. The authors focus clearly on the need of test constructors to define pupil behavior and necessity of attempting to maximize the probability that the test be a measure of student learning. However, limited space was given to discussion of the critical issue of values and how the test developer selects objectives, i.e., how does the developer attempt to meet societal or humanistic needs. Lindquist's brilliant chapter in the 1951 *Educational Measurement (Preliminary Discussion in Objective Test Construction)* is quoted but his ideas are not developed nor applied as fully as one would hope, given the concerns of the 1970's. Chapter Three, *Planning the Objective Test,* is a compendium of folk lore and unvalidated common

sense assumptions. This is a very long chapter which could be greatly shortened by more concise writing. High points of the chapter are the editor's excellent note on the problem of guessing and the author's discussion on practical issues of reliability. Chapter Four, *Writing the Test Item,* should be useful to the clerk in a test production department. It contains many examples of items and the general suggestions for writing items are excellent. However, helpful though the chapter might be, it is unfortunately a composite of a multitude of unnecessary platitudes, i.e., "a good test is composed of well written items (81)." A more important criticism of this chapter is the author's suggestion to include test items to force teachers to attend to areas of the curriculum that they are ignoring even though the psychometric properties of the items may not be fully acceptable. This suggestion seems to this reviewer a very questionable procedure, both psychometrically and ethically. * Part two of the book covers *Special Types of Tests.* Chapters include *Performance and Product Evaluation, Essay Examinations, Prediction, Educational Outcomes.* All of the authors appear to be conversant with measurement techniques but weak on psychology. Some of the chapters in this section get carried away with rigidly applied procedures and rules as if our measuring instruments were perfect. Perhaps if all the authors in this section had read Cronbach, Jones and Davis, included elsewhere in the volume more levity could be applied to the current state of the art involving design and construction. The strongest section is section three, *Measurement Theory,* particularly Lyle Jones's *The Nature of Measurement,* Stanley's *Reliability,* and Cronbach's *Test Validation.* However in the same section, Angoff's otherwise excellent chapter on *Scales, Norms, and Equivalent Scores* is exhaustive beyond the point of relevancy and Cooley's *Techniques for Considering Multiple Measurements* is hardly above an annotated bibliography. Stanley's chapter is well written, makes complex ideas seem simple, deals exhaustively with reliability theory, and avoids cookbook procedures. However, readers of this chapter will have to have a background in statistical theory in order to apply its procedures. This reviewer would have profited from Stanley's including more discussion on "weak" and "strong" true score theory, however this is a minor point. Cronbach likewise writes clearly about complex issues. His presentation of construct validity is outstanding. He discusses his departure and agreement with Loevinger's earlier stand. He speaks to the ultraoperationalist and non-behavioralist as well. He and Stanley have the ability to write simple statements that assist the reader center on the basic issues of test theory, i.e., "one does not validate a test but the interpretation of data arising from a specified procedure (447)." Cronbach is immensely quotable. Angoff's chapter is very comprehensive in scope * Angoff's examples are frequently made to physical measurements and the analogies are somewhat debatable. * Jones's chapter on *The Nature of Measurement* covers a breadth of topics usually covered in test theory courses. He is readable. Jones stresses appropriately that the necessary prerequisite before measurement can be made is to define the attribute in quantifiable terms that contain meaning. This is an excellent point and he holds to it throughout his chapter. However, when he gives a case study to clarify the conception and perception of attributes he uses the example of the case history of length rather than an example from an educational setting. Likewise his example in his excellent section on classification and rankings are drawn from other than education and psychology. That is this reviewer's major critique of this chapter is of the tendency to use non-educational examples to make a point or to compare physical measurement scales for the purpose of developing a frame of references for the state of the art of educational measurement. Jones uses non-educational examples frequently in his otherwise excellent chapter. * Section Four, *Application of Tests to Educational Problems,* is a strong section of what has yet to be a well developed field, i.e., evaluation. Glaser's and Nitko's....discussion of instructional models are current and their discussion of norm versus criterion reference tests should be useful to program evaluators. Davis's use of *Measurement in Student Planning and Guidance* is useful but should be read in conjunction with Hill's chapter, *Use of Measurement in Selection and Prediction* which is largely aimed at college selecting. The Astin and Panos chapter, *The Evaluation of Educational Programs,* clearly defines evaluation as the collecting of information upon which to base a decision. However, in this reviewer's opinion they superficially overview the field. In addition, when they do draw upon the developmental needs of children they draw upon Bruner's 1961

work, Piaget's 1950 work and Erickson's 1950, even though Bruner's circa 1961 position was inconsistent with Piaget's circa 1950. This book has several chapters that will serve as a useful reference both for advanced students in educational psychology, particularly those in advanced measurement courses. Rarely does the volume contain new information for the professional. For the beginning test developer it will provide some useful hints and suggestions. Its strength is its weakness; it covers so much that users will have to be very selective in what they recommend to their students. The strong points have been mentioned above; its weakness is that there are all too few educational psychologists who specialize in measurement that can bring to bear a knowledge of children and curriculum. Isn't it about time we in education demanded that the level of scholarship about measurement be matched with an equally high level of scholarship about children and schools?

J Ed Meas 9(1):84–5 *sp '71. Paul L. Dressel.* The term "monumental" has been over used, yet it is the word that immediately comes to mind as one examines this volume. * a well-planned and edited volume, and the list of 24 authors (including Thorndike) is a veritable "Who's Who" of the measurement field * Chapter references are limited in number, but as far as I could judge, carefully chosen and adequate in coverage. At least three chapters have no parallel in the first edition. Thorndike's initial chapter, "Education in the Seventies," will be of interest to everyone concerned with measurement. His remarks on placement and classification as opposed to selection and his brief but pointed discussion of social and political issues are especially timely. * Chapter 11, "Prediction Instruments for Educational Outcomes" by Paul A. Schwarz, is also an innovation. It is a worthy one and constitutes a very useful review of this aspect of the field. Chapter 20, "The Evaluation of Educational Programs" by Alexander W. Astin and Robert J. Panos, is an especially meritorious addition to this edition. There has been all too little evaluation of educational programs, and much of what has appeared has been very sloppily done. This chapter should provide, for those who consult this volume for other purposes, a significant challenge to think through carefully any evaluation project they may be planning. * Thorndike and his associates are to be congratulated on their efforts, as is the American Council on Education and the Grant

Foundation for their vision in supporting its publication. It is truly a monumental volume.

J Ed Meas 9(4):325-7 w '72. John Doucette and Jason Millman. If you feel it worth your while to read this journal, then we commend you to become familiar with *Educational Measurement.* We know of no single volume which pulls together so much information related to the practice of educational measurement. In terms of sheer number of words, the present volume is roughly twice the size of the 1951 edition, a landmark effort in its own right. The chapters, written by different authors, vary greatly among themselves along the dimensions of superficial treatment/indepth reporting; easy to comprehend/technical dissertation; reviewing previous work/reconceptualizing the area. *Educational Measurement* contains something of interest and importance for all readers. Chapter 1 ("Educational Measurement for the Seventies" by Robert L. Thorndike) is an excellent, although brief, overview of many developments in measurement since the first edition of *Educational Measurement* twenty years ago. Unfortunately, there are few specific references given to guide further inquiry into the issues discussed, although further information on some of the topics can be obtained from other chapters in the volume. The seven chapters in Part I ("Test Design, Construction, Administration, and Processing") provide a comprehensive, step-by-step process for developing a test from its conceptual beginnings to its eventual administration and scoring. * All the chapters are full of examples of both good and bad procedures which can serve as models. One criticism of this section (and, to some extent, the entire volume) is that it deals almost exclusively with developing objective tests of academic achievement. The measurement of affective characteristics and the construction of any kind of instrument except an objective test are *not* specifically covered. * The chapter on reliability is very much what might be expected from its author, Julian C. Stanley. The development is extremely complete with great care given to the details of history, conceptualization and notation. Although the organization and detail make it less suitable as a first exposure to the topic for those less experienced in mathematics, the chapter will remain for some time as a first class documentation of much of the state-of-the-art in reliability theory. By far the most original chapter is Lee J. Cronbach's statement on validity.

More than giving us just a synthesis of previous thought, Cronbach presents a clear and compelling formulation of the concepts and processes of validity. Although it is an excellent introductory reference for the beginning student, it should be read and studied by measurement experts as well. Chapter 15 ("Scales, Norms and Equivalent Scores" by William H. Angoff) contains an excellent, nontechnical discussion of the nature and development of norms and scales for standardized tests. * The reader may wish to supplement this section of the book with parts of Flanagan's chapter in the 1951 volume. Chapter 16, written by William W. Cooley, is a very short presentation of common multivariate statistical procedures used in conjunction with test data. This introductory presentation is quite clear, especially if one understands matrix algebra. * The final chapter, written by Alexander W. Astin and Robert J. Panos, is admittedly a brief treatment of the application of measurement to program evaluation. A point of view is expressed. One would wish that other approaches and important facets had not been omitted, given the increasing general interest of educators in evaluation. This ambitious enterprise to produce a book rightfully titled *Educational Measurement* has once again attracted the very best men in our field. We owe much to these authors for the sometimes herculean task undertaken for the benefit of the profession. Special thanks are due Robert Thorndike whose editorial skill is much in evidence throughout the volume.

[B535]

*THORNDIKE, ROBERT L., AND HAGEN, ELIZABETH P. **Measurement and Evaluation in Psychology and Education, Fourth Edition.** New York: John Wiley & Sons, Inc., 1977. Pp. ix, 693. $16.95. * For reviews of earlier editions, see 7:B614 (3 excerpts), 6:B483 (3 excerpts), and 5:B424 (6 excerpts).

[B536]

★THYNE, JAMES M. **Principles of Examining.** London: University of London Press Ltd., 1974. Pp. ix, 278. Paper, £2.50. * (New York: Halsted Press. $10.50.)

Brit J Ed Psychol 45(2):243-4 Je '75. Desmond L. Nuttall. * a textbook which appears curiously out of touch with modern examining methods and with current research. A large part of the book is concerned with theory, with the topics of validity and the weighting of component parts of an examination treated at considerable length. The author often seems more concerned with logical and semantic precision, enlivened occasionally by his own cartoons, than with practical advice to the intending examiner. * Nevertheless, Thyne treats technical matters with competence and provides a useful discussion of norm-referenced and criterion-referenced testing. His advice on the preparation and marking of written questions (from true-false to open-ended) is sound, but the major weakness of the book is the omission of any discussion of other examining techniques such as oral and aural assessment, projects or dissertations, and continuous assessment. Ten years ago this book might have been useful to teachers; now there are many very much better and more comprehensive ones available.

[B537]

★TIEDEMAN, HERMAN R. **Fundamentals of Psychological and Educational Measurement.** Springfield, Ill.: Charles C Thomas, Publisher, 1972. Pp. ix, 134. $11.75. *

Ed & Psychol Meas 33(3):759–60 au '73. Thomas W. Durham. * The strong points include highly detailed examples for constructing percentile tables, computing measures of central tendency, and computing the standard deviation. Perhaps the best feature of the book is the chapter on correlation. * The above positive features of the book are, however, outweighed by several major weaknesses. First, the text is more adequate for use in an introductory statistics course than in a course of tests and measurements (for which the book is designed). The included material does not provide an adequate foundation in test theory; neither does it cover the basic fundamentals of measurement instruments. The validity and reliability sections are weak because they do not provide the reader with adequate definitions or examples. Second, the lack of stress on norms and normative data is seen as a weakness in a book designed to promote the understanding of tests, their use, and their interpretation. An overemphasis is placed on grade norms and the discussion of grade placement on pages 102 and 103 is likely to confuse the reader and cause misinterpretation of this concept. Thirdly, the discussion of a school testing program in Chapter 11 provides administrative information for maintaining standardized conditions, but the discussion totally avoids any information concerning the selection by the reader of proper tests for various situations and provides no criteria against which to select tests for use in these school testing programs. Finally, while the text does make an effort to warn the reader about the consequences of test mis-

use, these remarks are subtle and are not reinforced in the basic text background, thus leaving the reader falsely convinced that he is prepared for test evaluation. For these reasons, plus the relative high cost ($11.75) for a small book in size and in content, the book seems to be inadequate for the instructional unit for which it is designed. With the expansion of the statistical methods and calculation procedures, the book would be more suitable for a general statistics course. For use in a tests and measurements course, however, Tiedeman's text must be expanded in the areas of test evaluation, reliability, validity, and norms. Without modification in one direction or the other, the book seems to be unsuitable for general classroom use. Its generality precludes its use in a measurement course, and its lack of depth in statistical procedures precludes its use in a statistical course. These judgments lead to the recommendation that *Fundamental of Psychological and Educational Measurement* be given a long "shelf" life.

[B538]

★TITTLE, CAROL K.; McCARTHY, KAREN; AND STECKLER, JANE FAGGEN. **Women and Educational Testing: A Selective Review of the Research Literature and Testing Practices.** Princeton, N.J.: Educational Testing Service, 1974. Pp. x, 138. Paper, $4.00. *

Meas & Eval Guid 8(1):59–60 Ap '75. Patricia T. Cegelka. * The authors' analyses demonstrate that educational tests reflect the same general sex bias as other school instructional materials, drawing much more heavily on male examples, depicting active males and passive females, and using a much higher number of masculine than feminine noun referents. The inclusion in the appendix of the procedures used for determining sex-role stereotyping and for computing the language usage factors provides both for replication and extension of these analyses. The lengthy annotated bibliography is also helpful to anyone interested in pursuing research in this area. While the reviewer found the book poorly organized and would have preferred the authors to have developed more thoroughly the implications of and alternatives to current testing practices, the book does present a tantalizing overview of an important but much neglected area of discriminatory educational practices.

[B539]

★TOLLEFSON, NONA F. **Testing and Assessment in Elementary School Guidance Programs.** Hanover, N.H.: Time Share Corporation, 1975. Pp. ix, 94. Paper, $2.80. *

[B540]

★TRACTENBERG, PAUL L. **Testing the Teacher: How Urban School Districts Select Their Teachers and Supervisors.** New York: Agathon Press, Inc , 1973. Pp. xiv, 333. $10.00. *

[B541]

★TUCKMAN, BRUCE W. **Measuring Educational Outcomes: Fundamentals of Testing.** New York: Harcourt Brace Jovanovich, Inc., 1975. Pp. xix, 527. $13.95. *

Ed & Psychol Meas 36(2):590–3 su '76. John L. Wasik. * Tuckman appears to subscribe to the idea that a system's approach can be used to depict the educational process in operation. Specifically, he notes that the present trend in education is to regard the teacher as a manager of the learning process and that to make decisions, one has to have information on which to base decisions. Tests, if used appropriately, can be useful in making these decisions for planning individualized as well as group educational experiences. * He states, "Because people tend to equate measurement with statistics and to be wary of the difficult and relatively *useless* (italics mine) concepts they expect to encounter in a course in tests and measurements, this book uses some important techniques to make instruction about testing both comprehensible and useful (p. vii)." It seems that he is referring to the phenomenom of "symbol shock" so often demonstrated by students in education which leads to student attitudes of "I have always been poor in mathematics and I am afraid that I will do poorly in this course." Moreover, one must conclude that this statement is likely a result of his experiences in teaching these courses; I do not, however, accept the statement as an accurate representation of true state of affairs in the teaching of educational measurement and statistics courses. It must also be noted that Professor Tuckman provides no support for the statement. * The author has used a disciplined approach in writing this textbook which is demonstrated by attempts to relate content in each chapter to the textbook theme stated in the beginning of the text. Graphics in the form of cartoons, flow charts, and reproduction of text manual information are effectively used to instruct and motivate. However, the editorial work was not of the same high quality as indicated by textual errors such as failure to define terms (e g., probability, p. 256, median is referred to on p. 233, but not defined until p. 287), omitted footnotes (e.g., Figure 15.10) and an incomplete reference citation (e.g., p. 510). The

reviewer would hazard the guess that the systematic treatment of the content on the sections devoted to objectives and test development and evaluation would likely be quite well received by prospective as well as practicing teachers. Moreover, experienced teachers could also profit from the excellent discussion on criterion referenced tests. * Tuckman does present some sophisticated concepts, complete with equations for estimating psychometric characteristics of tests. However, there is no apparent heuristic breakthrough in presentation of these concepts to support the claims made by the author in the preface. Therefore, this reviewer feels the author has set up a "straw-man" which he has failed to exercise and this seems to be the only major criticism of an otherwise well thought-out and presented discussion of the development of procedures for measurement in education.

[B542]

TYLER, LEONA E. **Tests and Measurements, Second Edition.** Englewood Cliffs, N.J.: Prentice-Hall, Inc., 1971. Pp. xii, 99. Paper, $3.95. * For reviews of the first edition, see 6:B491 (2 excerpts).

Ed & Psychol Meas 32(1):231–2 sp '72. Glenn W. Durflinger. * Nothing is said about tests in the classroom. Obviously, then, the book is not written to supply the need for teachers to understand test construction, selection, administration, and interpretation. The book is written most lucidly and interestingly, as though the author were standing before a class in lecture sessions. Questions from the listeners are anticipated and answered. Relationships of the subject material to applications and uses are properly made. The historical backgrounds of the major topics are described and serve to enhance the reader's interest. * Some of this historical material is new, i.e., not found in other readily available books on the subject. The chapter on statistics....is clearly and well written. * The author brings the student-reader up-to-date in her discussion of testing or assessment in these three chapters. Particularly current and scarcely controversial is the material on (1) the IQ, (2) a test's fairness, (3) assessment of the total individual, and (4) proper interpretation and use of the results of testing. The reader becomes aware of the author's awareness of the criticisms of tests and measurements through her diplomatic suggestions designed to avoid a confrontation on the issues. One leaves the reading of this book with the impression that test users have been misusing and misinterpreting tests, particularly in employing measurement instruments to accomplish goals for which these instruments are not valid.

[B543]

★TYLER, RALPH W., AND WOLF, RICHARD M., EDITORS. **Crucial Issues in Testing.** National Society for the Study of Education Series on Contemporary Educational Issues. Berkeley, Calif.: McCutchan Publishing Corporation, 1974. Pp. x, 1970. $11.35. *

Ed & Psychol Meas 35(4):1061–4 w '75. Warren G. Findley. Any book that presumes to summarize issues in a diverse professional field presents its authors with a choice between giving balanced treatment (equal time?) to competing viewpoints or offering a considered judgment based on a review of the arguments or evidence, putting them in a coherent framework leading to whatever evaluative conclusion has been reached. Tyler and Wolf have chosen the latter alternative. Even where articles by others have been used to reflect different views, a conclusion emerges. Two questions need answering in the review of such a publication as this. First, did the authors choose the truly crucial issues? Second, how well did they summarize and generalize the state of the art? The seven-part table of contents answers the first question affirmatively, covering (1) the testing of minority groups, (2) selective testing for higher education, (3) testing for grouping students for instruction, (4) criterion-referenced testing, (5) assessing the educational achievement of schools or school systems, "accountability," (6) testing to evaluate effectiveness of programs, methods, and materials of instruction, and (7) testing and the invasion of privacy. Inevitably some of these topics overlap or involve interaction, e.g., ability grouping and the testing of minority groups, but the seven parts focus on definable areas of test use requiring attention by builders and users of tests in education without serious omission except possibly the use of tests in evaluating non-traditional acquisition of certifiable mastery of academic learning for high school or college credit. * *Crucial Issues in Testing* raises most of the critical issues to the point of visibility, is sometimes one-sidedly polemical, but elsewhere points the way to future realization of important new benefits and/or reconciliation of conflicting considerations. You'd better read it. [See original review for additional critical comments not excerpted.]

Meas & Eval Guid 9(2):82–3 Jl '76. Gary M. Miller. * This book addresses itself to cur-

rent concerns about testing in a manner that illuminates issues rather than clouding them in extensive statistical verbiage. The articles provide a perspective that I appreciated and found rewarding. The issues, as crucial as they are, will be around for some time, and I think forthright examination of them needs to continue. Efforts such as those presented in this volume obviously aid in that examination process. Consequently, anyone interested and concerned about testing would do well to spend some time reading and reflecting on this book.

Phi Delta Kappan 56(7):500 Mr '75. Gerald Halpin. * Part I of the book discusses some complex and often emotionally charged issues in testing individuals from minority groups. Parts II and III focus on the use of tests in selection for college entrance and grouping for instruction. Part IV treats norm-referenced versus criterion-referenced testing. Part V examines efforts at the national, state, and local levels to measure what students learn, and Part VI deals with the use of tests to measure the effectiveness of educational programs. Part VII goes into the controversial question of testing and the invasion of privacy. Called a "representative collection of discussions now under way," this book alone would be worthwhile reading for educators. They are encouraged to analyze and critically evaluate what they read, however, and to examine other books as well. This one small volume cannot deal with all the crucial issues in so broad a field as testing. Furthermore, it reflects the opinions and biases of the editors and contributing writers; it is certainly not the last word on the issues involved. To illustrate, criterion-referenced tests and the behavioristic psychology of learning are "heroes" in this book. Behavioristic learning theorists contend that almost anyone can learn almost anything, as John Watson boasted years ago, if educational procedures are appropriate. Criterion-referenced tests tell us when the learners have achieved the defined objectives. On the other hand, norm-referenced tests, which tell us how good an individual's performance is in relation to others, and differential psychology, which accentuates individual differences, are the villains. But norm-referenced testing and differential psychology have been acclaimed by other writers while criterion-referenced testing and behavioristic psychology have been denigrated. It is time to stop playing academic games with theoretical issues. If testing is to make the contributions it is capable of making to the educational process, we need to move toward a comprehensive theory of testing based not only on behavioristic psychology but also on differential psychology, humanistic psychology, and any other theoretical approach which might have something to say about testing. Such a comprehensive approach might be the necessary step to effect Tyler's concluding plea that testing must be and can be improved.

[B544]

★UzGIRIS, INA C., AND HUNT, J. McV. **Assessment in Infancy: Ordinal Scales of Psychological Development.** Urbana, Ill.: University of Illinois Press, 1975. Pp. xi, 263. $10.00. *

[B545]

★VALETT, ROBERT E. **Learning Disabilities: Diagnostic-Prescriptive Instruments.** Belmont, Calif.: Fearon-Pitman Publishers, 1973. Pp. xii, 176. Paper, $6.60; cloth, $8.80. *

J Learn Dis 7(7):401–2 Ag–S '74. Alex Bannatyne. * The book, taken as a whole, is a mine of practical information about learning disabilities, and students wishing to get a detailed overview of inventories, some tests, checklists, etc., will find what they are seeking. However, as I read through the lists and the prescriptions and remediations, I had the impression of a superficial almost "automatic" diagnostic-remedial system which was not based on any solid knowledge of the psychology of cognition, language structure and development, psycholinguistics (other than the entire ITPA) and motor-kinesthetic functioning. Almost every *term* used in connection with learning disabilities is mentioned somewhere in the book, but one of the most important ones, "motivation," is not even in the index. There was one line on "rewards" in one prescription. The case studies seemed to me to be over-tested and under-diagnosed while the recommendations were too broad and often naive. * In spite of these comments, there is much value to be found in this book especially if it is read as an example of how one group has worked effectively with learning disabled children.

[B546]

*VALETTE, REBECCA M. **Modern Language Testing, Second Edition.** New York: Harcourt Brace Jovanovich, Inc., 1977. Pp. xiv, 349. Paper, $6.95. * For reviews of the first edition, see 7:B621 (2 excerpts).

Mod Lang J 62(1–2):64 Ja–F '78. Ernest A. Franchette. Teachers will welcome this revised and expanded edition which has the twofold goal of acquainting them with terminology normally met in research on testing and of assisting them in the construction of better tests through a wealth of timely hints, suggestions, explanations, specific examples, and sample item types. * It is surprising that bilingual teachers were excluded since chapter twelve discusses testing in both ESL and bilingual programs. The preface of this second edition is longer, more descriptive, and more informative than that of the first edition. The book has a general orientation and is not specific to any course. It can be used in a methods course. The introduction gives some guidelines for using the book. Each chapter is preceded by a fairly thorough outline of its content, which should simplify one's search for any point(s) discussed therein. There are three entirely new chapters: the culture test, new in its content, directions in modern language testing, and testing in bilingual and ESL programs. An improvement over the previous edition is the inclusion of the English meaning for the varied sample test items in French, German, Italian, and Spanish. * Part one has been improved but is essentially much like that of the first edition. Part two, Methods of Evaluation, contains four chapters on language skills and two on culture and literature. There are new sample test items for each skill. * For culture, now in a separate chapter, the author deserves praise for a fine contribution in an area often neglected. Here one finds items on cultural awareness, cultural differences and values, and target culture analysis. The last chapter on the literature test is similar to that of the first edition. Part three, with two chapters on current developments, touches on language testing developments for measuring aptitude, affective goals, and command of the subject matter, and includes a discussion of testing in bilingual and ESL programs. Few item types are given and the treatment is rather limited. Because the book attempts to cover all conceivable types of test items there are obvious weaknesses such as some omissions and some inadequate coverage of important points, but its weaknesses are overshadowed by the tremendous amount of help it gives classroom teachers; they should not be without it

[B547]

★VENEZKY, RICHARD L. **Testing in Reading: Assessment and Instructional Decision Making.** Urbana, Ill.: National Council of Teachers of English, 1974. Pp. viii, 32. Paper, $1.50. *

[B548]

★Vincent, Denis, and Cresswell, Michael. **Reading Tests in the Classroom.** Windsor, Berks., England: NFER Publishing Co. Ltd., 1976. Pp. 185. Paper, £4.75; cloth, £12.05. * (Atlantic Highlands, N.J.: Humanities Press Inc. Paper, $10.75.)

Brit J Ed Psychol 47(2):223–4 Je '77. T. R. Miles. This book contains a large amount of good sense about the value and limitations of reading tests in a classroom situation. The authors are careful to avoid any suggestion of a "mystique," and are at pains to point out that a test is not invalidated because unskilled people misuse it. There is also some helpful guidance on statistical matters, and some very useful discussion of different types of test. I particularly enjoyed the excellent section on "criterion referenced testing." Briefly, such testing checks whether certain skills have been achieved rather than attempting to compare a child with some "norm." If this concept is taken seriously teachers will be encouraged to consider what are realistic "targets" for particular children and there will be fewer invidious comparisons between one child and another; more sensibly, each child will be compared with *himself.* The difficulties inherent in the notion of a "true" reading age are perhaps passed over somewhat lightly. (If the concept is a confused one, then placing inverted commas round "true" will not remedy the situation!) It was also a little disappointing that no mention was made of the Gillingham-Childs Phonics Proficiency Scales, and that Vernon (1957) is referred to in preference to Vernon (1971). The emphasis on reading skills as opposed to other kinds of language skill is, of course, deliberate, but I hope that this will not encourage teachers to concentrate too much on reading at the expense of spelling; in the experience of myself and colleagues this has particularly unfortunate effects in the case of children who display problems in certain specific areas of learning. All in all, however, this is a very sensible book.

[B549]

★Volle, Frank O. **Mental Evaluation of the Disability Claimant.** Springfield, Ill.: Charles C Thomas, Publisher, 1975. Pp. x, 121. $10.50. *

[B550]

★Walberg, Herbert J., Editor. **Evaluating Educational Performance: A Sourcebook of Methods, Instruments, and Examples.** Berkeley, Calif.: McCutchan Publishing Corporation, 1974. Pp. xxii, 395. $14.50. *

Ed & Psychol Meas 35(2):525–7 su '75. Brian Bolton. This collection of 19 papers addresses a variety of topics within the program evaluation/accountability realm of educational research. The editor's stated goal is to provide a practical orientation to evaluation of educational system effectiveness as a basis for policy formulation and decision making. The perspective is the macro-level of analysis with the school as subject. * the volume contains a variety of review articles and research studies which summarize instruments and findings and illustrate various research strategies and methodologies in educational program evaluation. The collection is uneven in style and quality, but this is unavoidable with contributed books. The value of the volume as a sourcebook is reduced due to the absence of a subject index.

Meas & Eval Guid 8(3):205–6 O '75. William B. Ware. * For those grappling with the difficult question of accountability, this book should come as a welcome relief, for it at least provides a point of departure from which one may venture into the evaluation of specific educational personnel and programs. Lest one conclude that "the answer" has arrived, let me hasten to add that such is not the case. Walberg presents research which is only a beginning. * Those professionals involved in competency/performance-based instruction and assessment will find the chapters "Teacher Effectiveness" and "Achievement Correlates" of particular interest. * This book does not address itself to many of the concerns of guidance per se. As in most educational research the guidance profession must make inferences and adapt and conduct research aimed specifically at the unique concerns of guidance. The book does, however, include three chapters directed to affective concerns that are often neglected or only vaguely referred to in educational evaluation research. The chapters "Classroom Climates," "Learning Environments," and "Affective Outcomes" present methodologies and instrumentation which are often avoided because of difficulty with specification. Guidance personnel will find these chapters significant. This book would seem to be most useful as a reference or sourcebook. For educators to base professional practice on sound evaluation and research, this book is an excellent resource.

[B551]

★Walker, Deborah Klein. **Socioemotional Measures for Preschool and Kindergarten Children: A Handbook.** San Francisco, Calif.: Jossey-Bass Inc., Publishers, 1973. Pp. xv, 362. $15.00. *

Brit J Social & Clin Psychol 15(2):219–20 Je '76. M. Vaughan. * The accumulation of so much important information in one place makes this book a worthwhile purchase for anyone interested in the socio-emotional assessment of young children.

J Pers Assess 40(2):196 Ap '76. Dale L. Johnson. * The....socioemotional measures.... include nearly every kind of measure except those clearly defined as measures of aptitude or achievement. The range is great, both across time and type of behavior concerned. * Limiting the collection to preschool and kindergarten age children is worthwhile. The linguistic and self-reflective limitations of young children present real research problems and the selection of research measures is often difficult. * The collection is divided into six parts with each part including a number of measures: attitudes (11 measures), general personality and emotional adjustment (38), interests or preferences (6), personality or behavior traits (41), self concept (18), and social skills or competency (28). * This catalog gives information on the authors, age range, measurement technique, sources in which the measure is described, address from which the measure can be obtained, a brief description of the measure, norms, validity and reliability. These items of information are given if available. It is some commentary on the state of psychology's technology that such basics as norms, validity and reliability are often not available. Walker has succeeded in compiling a useful catalog and she should be encouraged to keep it up-to-date. New measures are continually being developed and new information becomes available on old measures. We can hope that the catalog will appear again, if not each fall and winter, at least often enough to keep up with advances in the field.

Meas & Eval Guid 9(1):35–7 Ap '76. Alex Epanchin. * Part one....includes six very brief chapters presenting the rationale, sources for the book, and problems with and recommendations for the measurement of a young child's affective or socioemotional status. The author maintains that this is an important endeavor even though she is well aware of the present state of the art. Part two consists of data about 143 measures classified into six categories, for example, attitude, general personality and emotional adjustment, interest or preference. * The measures were gathered from Buros' yearbooks, Johnson and Bommarito's handbook, educa-

tional and psychological journals, standard textbooks, and government reports. The main criticism of this work is not the fault of the author. As Walker herself states, "The technical information available for these measures reveals that standardization procedures are practically non-existent, reliabilities generally moderate, and validity generally poor" (p. 39). In fact, she feels that the lack of a solid socioemotional developmental theory is responsible for the problems and shortcomings of socioemotional measurement technology. However, when one's appetite is whetted by the promise of the inclusion of norms even though one has been warned that technical information is scant, it is still disappointing to discover that two-thirds of all the measures have none to report. Most notably 88 percent of the measures of self-concept, and 78 percent of the measures of personality or behavior traits, have no available norms. The book's main contribution is that basic information about 143 affective measures for young children can now be found in one source. This contribution is not to be underestimated. The book refers readers to other sources for more specific details about the measures of interest to them, but it is certainly a convenient place to start and "let your fingers do the walking." This work is a timely publication because of the present emphasis (at least in North Carolina) for state-wide preschool screening, with an emphasis on the role that early socioemotional factors play in later school performance. It is certain to be of use to those interested in psychological measurement with young children, test specialists, child and school psychologists, researchers, and educators.

[B552]

★WALL, JANET, AND SUMMERLIN, LEE. **Standardized Science Achievement Tests: A Descriptive Listing.** Washington, D.C.: National Science Teachers Association, 1973. Pp. iv, 57. Paper, $1.50. *

[B553]

★WANAT, STANLEY F., EDITOR. **Issues in Evaluating Reading.** Papers in Applied Linguistics: Linguistics and Reading Series, 1. Arlington, Va.: Center for Applied Linguistics, 1977. Pp. xiii, 63. Paper, $4.95. *

[B554]

★WARD, ANNIE W.; BACKMAN, MARGARET E.; HALL, BRUCE W.; AND MAZUR, JOSEPH L.; EDITORS. **Guide for School Testing Programs.** East Lansing, Mich.: National Council on Measurement in Education, fall 1976. Pp. iv, 88. Paper, $3.50. *

[B555]

★WARDROP, JAMES L. **Standardized Testing in the Schools: Uses and Roles.** Monterey, Calif.: Brooks/Cole Publishing Co., 1976. Pp. xii, 130. Paper, $3.95. *

Ed & Psychol Meas 36(2):593 su '76. Max Engelhart. This little paperback contains an extraordinary amount of important information about the characteristics and uses of standardized tests. * The advantages and limitations of intelligence testing are well explained. Similar analysis is made of the various types of achievement testing and their uses in Chapter Six. Chapter Seven's discussion of the school testing program is excellent. Chapter Eight considers testing in relation to certain important issues: criterion referenced versus norm referenced measurement; standardized tests and educational accountability. The book concludes with an excellent list of selected references.

Ed & Psychol Meas 37(2):566–8 su '77. Richard L. Zweigenhaft. * In sum, Wardrop has written a useful little book, one that is simple enough for undergraduate students. The book raises important issues in an honest and forthright manner, and though the author does not sidestep the issues, he is not dogmatic in the position he takes. Anyone planning to teach or administrate at the primary or secondary level would benefit from reading this book. [See original review for critical comments not excerpted.]

[B556]

★WASKOW, IRENE E., AND PARLOFF, MORRIS B., EDITORS. **Psychotherapy Change Measures.** DHEW Publication No. (ADM) 74–120. Washington, D.C.: U.S. Government Printing Office, 1975. Pp. xi, 327. Paper, $3.05. *

[B557]

★WECHSLER, DAVID. **Manual for the Wechsler Intelligence Scale for Children, Revised Edition.** New York: Psychological Corporation, 1974. Pp. vii, 191. $6.85. *

Am J Mental Def 80(1):128–9 Jl '75. Ronald J. Friedman and Marlene Bird. * a lucid and thorough guide for the use of the test. A number of weaknesses in earlier WISC manuals have been eliminated. In the current manual, Wechsler includes a discussion of the WISC-R as a measure of general intelligence, offers an explicit statement that there is no claim that the test measures potential intelligence, and presents a clarification of his views of general intelligence, non-intellective factors involved in test performance, intelligence testing, and IQ interpretation. The 1949 WISC manual and subsequent modifications had been criticized for failing to include enough statistical data. The WISC-R is an improvement in this regard. There is a great deal of additional information.

* Validity data are still meager. Several concurrent validity studies are reported. On the whole, however, the manual provides clear and reasonably comprehensive statistical information. The manual is easy to use. It contains less paragraph and more point form. Spaces separate individual points. Directions to be read to the child stand out in brown ink, and information regarding starting points for testing discontinuation and directions for scoring are clearly separated and labeled. The starting points for different ages are well-marked, and page references for scoring criteria are given. Indeed, information in all sections of the manual is better organized than in earlier editions. Other revisions have also facilitated test administration. Instructions for the examiner are clearer. For instance, general testing principles are introduced early, and rules concerning timing, repetition, and probing are now separately grouped and clearly labeled. More general administrative concerns are also well-presented. Information concerning test environment and maintenance of rapport has been more appropriately grouped, separated, and labeled, and discussion of the latter has been given additional attention. Useful suggestions for the handling of special testing problems are also provided. * Scoring guidelines have been improved. A wider range of responses is now allowed for many questions. It is strongly emphasized to the examiner that scoring guides are illustrative and not exhaustive, and more sample 2-, 1-, and 0-point responses are given. Furthermore, there are more explicit statements of the general rules for scoring responses to each question, along with helpful explanations of the rationale behind them. These changes facilitate the classification of responses and will, hopefully, lead to greater interscorer reliability. A final note is that the WISC-R manual, while certainly a complete guide for those unfamiliar with the WISC, anticipates the special transition problems of experienced WISC users. So as to avoid confusion, Wechsler notes specific changes in content and procedure throughout the entire manual.

[B558]

★WEIDER, ARTHUR, EDITOR. **Psychodiagnostic Methods for the Behavioral Sciences, Expanded Edition.** Oceanside, N.Y.: Dabor Science Publications, 1977. Pp. xv, 390. $15.00. *

[B559]

★WEIMER, WAYNE, AND WEIMER, ANNE. **Reading Readiness Inventory.** Columbus, Ohio: Charles E. Merrill Publishing Co., 1977. Pp. 110. Paper, $3.95.

Read Teach 31(4):463–4 Ja '78. Nancy A. Mavrogenes. The RRI is proposed as a diagnostic tool for kindergarten and primary teachers wanting to individualize reading readiness and as an instrument for training teachers about readiness behavior. It consists of two forms of ten subtests: 1) Using the Pencil, 2) Visual Motor Activity, 3) Auditory Discrimination, 4) Verbalization, 5) Categories, 6) Reversals, 7) Matching Words, 8) Recognizing Words, 9) Recognizing Words, 10) Reproducing Words. Part Two is "Ongoing Evaluation" and Part Three, "Suggested Readiness Activities." A "Summary Record" enables the teacher to compare each student's score on a subtest with a "critical score." When the score is above any critical score, that area is "a probable high risk" for that child. Then the teacher checks possible deficiency areas ("Perceptual Motor," "Sensory Motor," "Comprehension"), based on subtest scores, and summarizes the student's needs. Individual administration time is claimed to be one hour per student and group administration time to be of "no significance" since the subtests are to be administered as part of a planned program during the school year. The book's introduction includes a general discussion of skills necessary for school and reading readiness. Since the inventory's subtests do not cover all the skills mentioned, the authors wisely recommend supplementing it with informal observations, parent interviews, and teacher-constructed tests. However, this inventory seems marked by questionable test-making procedures, incompleteness, and carelessness. For instance, the authors mention studies which show "a very high correlation between the individually administered test and the group administered test." But absolutely no statistical data are provided; nor can five of the ten subtests be group administered (numbers 1, 3, 4, 5, 8). Also, one wonders how the "critical scores" were determined, exactly how this instrument "has a potential for training prospective teachers unequaled by other types of learning activities," why there are no subtests on listening or letter recognition (skills considered pertinent for beginning reading instruction), why one reversal item is in cursive, and why all words in subtest 9 are in capitals. Furthermore, one might question the diagnostic

use of subtests which consist of a minimum of three up to a maximum of 11 items. And there are other questions. How are the forms really different, since three of 10 subtests are exactly the same (1, 4, 5), one consists of the same items in a different order (3), and one consists of half the same items (7)? Why does the list of references not include all the works referred to; why is the book on reading difficulties dated 1957 and the one on reading readiness 1950? How meaningful are the subtest titles for 8 and 9, both called "Recognizing Words," or for 2, "Visual Motor Activity," actually copying geometric figures—and why geometric figures when using letters or words is considered a more valid procedure? Why are some instructions incomplete? (In 9, should the words taught be left on the chalkboard?) Why are some letters printed so close together (pages 25 and 29) as to seem unclear to small children? In short, one wonders why buy this special inventory when most basic texts on reading include not only a rating scale for teacher judgments about reading readiness but also pages of specific readiness activities.

[B560]

★WELLS, L. EDWARD, AND MARWELL, GERALD. **Self-Esteem: Its Conceptualization and Measurement.** Beverly Hills, Calif.: Sage Publications, 1976. Pp. 260. Paper, $6.95; cloth, $14.00.

J Pers Assess 41(2):195–6 Ap '77. Lita Linzer Schwartz. One's initial reaction to the statement that this book grew out of a master's thesis (Wells') is that the thesis must have been an unusual piece of work. It has come at a time when a critical review of the concept of "self-esteem" and the varied approaches to its measurement is very much in order. * it is somewhat surprising that the work of Erik Erikson is omitted. * An extensive, and interesting, presentation of definitions of self-esteem leads to the conclusion that, although the definitions "sound fairly similar," their dependence on varying theoretical contexts do not "always lead to the same behavioral predictions (p. 69)." * The major part of the book deals with the measurement of self-esteem. Many techniques are examined, along with their manifold difficulties—verbal vs. nonverbal, nature of the stimuli, age limitations, validity. The proliferation of instruments, sometimes criticized on the basis of a homogeneous orientation (e.g., "white experience"), has compounded rather than eased the problem of meaningful measurement. Further, it is no secret that response bias has a major effect on the results obtained. Attempts to minimize this influence through the use of projective techniques are realistically evaluated. * There is one minor complaint in terms of editing. The use of numerals in brackets rather than superscript numerals to indicate chapter notes is distracting and confusing. * In summary, the Wells and Marwell book is impressive in its coverage, if necessarily inconclusive in resolving the questions of definitions and measurement. The authors can feel more secure in their self-esteem by reason of the competence they have brought to their work and the significance and utility that their work will bring to other social scientists.

[B561]
★WHALEY, DONALD L. **Psychological Testing and the Philosophy of Measurement.** Kalamazoo, Mich.: Behaviordelia, Inc., 1973. Pp. 58. Paper, $3.95. *

Personnel Psychol 26(2):293–5 su '73. *Michael T. Wood.* Dear Dr. Whaley: Since you have written such an unusual book, I thought I should write an equally unusual book review. However, I find it difficult to match your technique. Thus, I shall keep this short and sweet. You have provided a landmark in the pedagogic literature on psychological measurement, and, I suspect, enjoyed doing it. The emphasis on underlying philosophy of test development and use, and of the measurement process in general, is commendable. * I was favorably impressed by two characteristics of your treatment of the basic issues in testing. (1) You have effectively used an informal, humorous style to communicate your points, and (2) In so doing, you have not sacrificed scientific rigor or comprehension. * I would suggest that the discussion of types of validity left something to be desired. That is, while I laud the concern with predictive validity, construct validity seems to have been attributed the status of second-class citizen, being essentially nice but not necessary. * The personnel manager or professional psychologist will not be likely to learn a great deal of substance from reading your book. But wait—(as you say)— he may learn an innovative approach to teaching that material. He may also read it for pleasure or "light reading." If he has a sense of humor he might prefer to read it surreptitiously. The strange looks from one's colleagues as one laughs aloud (with you, not at you) while reading about testing and validity require some face-saving explanation. Your book is ideally suited

for an introductory base for further study of tests and measurement among a group of naive but hip undergraduates. * Congratulations on a fine book which I enjoyed reading. It may replace that malt liquor as the completely unique experience. I am eager to try the book and see how students respond. *

[B562]
★WHIMBEY, ARTHUR, AND WHIMBEY, LINDA SHAW. **Intelligence Can Be Taught.** New York: E. P. Dutton & Co., Inc., 1975. Pp. xi, 215. $7.95. *

[B563]
★WHYBREW, WILLIAM E. **Measurement and Evaluation in Music, Second Edition.** Dubuque, Iowa: Wm. C. Brown Co. Publishers, 1971. Pp. ix, 210. * *Out of print.*

J Res Music Ed 20(4):519 w '72. Paul R. Lehman. First published in 1962, this helpful work is intended to enable music teachers and prospective teachers to understand and utilize properly existing measures in music and to construct evaluative instruments of their own. The second edition includes summaries of several additional measures not described in the first * Other changes are minimal. Six of the twelve chapters contain no changes whatever. Whybrew's book is the only one in its field that provides specific instructions for computing many of the basic statistical measures * useful either as a text or as a reference book.

[B564]
*WICK, JOHN W. **Educational Measurement: Where Are We Going and How Will We Know When We Get There.** Columbus, Ohio: Charles E. Merrill Publishing Co., 1973. Pp. xi, 320. $11.95. *

J Ed Meas 11(3):219–20 f '74. Norma Reali. * Has the author succeeded in meeting his objectives? Has he written a book which should appeal to more than the major in measurement? Yes, I think he has. The coverage which he gives to topics, with the exception of the chapter on reliability, avoids tedious and confusing computations, using computation mostly to clarify. The book seems committed to furthering the understanding of the process of measurement. Yet, it never becomes simplistic and condescending to the reader. He has not included a chapter on specific tests and their uses (wisely he leaves this to Buros) which can only be of minor concern to most people taking the course. Further, he has a broad enough coverage of topics so that if a person never takes another measurement course, he at least has a speaking acquaintance with the important issues. Lastly, he did make it more palatable by his injection of humor (though this reviewer wonders if the people who identify with the educators he parodies, will agree). Is this book sufficiently different or better to consider it as an alternative to Cronbach, Thorndike and Hagen, and other similar texts? Again, the answer is yes, if two rather major flaws can be overlooked. One deals with the treatment of construct validity, the other with the omission of a comprehensive study of item analysis (the term "item analysis" does not even appear in the index). The author defines construct validity by saying "the results of a measure are independently tested against what reasonable people would expect to occur," and then gives extensive numbers of examples, testing the construct validity against this definition. When one thinks of the vast number of instruments claiming to measure a construct, it must be concluded that some people are more reasonable than others when it comes to accepting a measure. The treatment is totally unacceptable. The reviewer finds equally regrettable the lack of information on item analysis. However, there are virtually no measurement books which give this subject its due. Considering how important item selection is and how the results of a test can be biased by the method used, it is difficult to understand why this topic is given such incomplete coverage in almost all beginning measurement texts.

Meas & Eval Guid 6(3):184–5 O '73. Kemp Mabry. * This is a different kind of book. It is written in a relaxed, easy style that belies the author's considerable insight into the complexities of measurement. Here is the answer to the question posed several years ago by one of my graduate students, "Why must scholarly writing be so dull?" Wick is not dull. * I wish that Wick had not emphasized tired old grade equivalent scores quite so much * This book is an innovative approach to measurement. For maximum benefit I think students should examine numerous standardized tests as well as construct and administer a test to a class. I plan to adopt the book.

[B565]

★WIERSMA, WILLIAM, AND JURS, STEPHEN G. **Evaluation of Instruction in Individually Guided Education.** Reading, Mass.: Addison-Wesley Publishing Co., Inc., 1976. Pp. xv, 237. Paper, $6.95. *

[D566]

★WIGGINS, JERRY S. **Personality and Prediction: Principles of Personality Assessment.** Reading, Mass.: Addison-Wesley Publishing Co., Inc., 1973. Pp. xii, 656. $20.95. *

Austral J Psychol 27(1):103–4 Ap '75. John O'Gorman. Wiggins' book fills a need at the advanced level for a comprehensive and authoritative review of principles and procedures in personality assessment. * The strengths of the book are a thorough treatment of the mechanics of prediction models, a non-polemical review of the question of clinical judgment, a perceptive analysis of the problem of method variance common to observational and testing techniques, and concrete illustrations of the way in which decision theory can be used in evaluating assessment programmes. If the book has a weakness it is treating the interview, probably the most widely used technique of assessment, in only one paragraph. Wiggins' book because it is at once hard-headed and sympathetic to the practitioner would be a useful text for fourth year and postgraduate courses in clinical or industrial psychology which include a component on assessment. Its coverage of recent studies scattered in the periodical literature makes it a valuable reference for introductory courses in assessment as well as for practitioners who feel the need for a refresher course.

Ed & Psychol Meas 34(1):202–5 sp '74. George M. Guthrie. * In the domain of counseling and personnel selection the assessment of personality variables has not generally proven very useful. * those who have worked in this field have developed an elaborate set of procedures which, in theory, should account for a significant segment of the variance in later behavior. However, that accurate prediction, in a practical sense, is possible, has not been demonstrated, in this reviewer's opinion. Having expressed these misgivings, this reviewer hastens to add that this is an exceedingly well written book. The quality of the prose, the clarity and sequence of exposition, and the careful documentation mark it as a model for others to consider. It will be of great value to anyone concerned with the measurement of either individual differences or of experimental effects. * The author opens with an exposition of correlation and regression models, and suppressor variables. He continues with moderator variables and higher order functions, and actuarial strategies which are applicable with categorical rather than continuous variables. These three chapters are unusual in that the presentation is verbal rather than in mathematical notation. * In the second part....the discussion of observational techniques can stand by itself as lucid exposition of the problems of reliability and generalizability of observations as sources of data. * The final part....opens with an innovative attempt to relate measurement strategies to personality theories. Following Stern's categorization of analytic, synthetic and empirical approaches, he demonstrates the tenuous relationship which has prevailed between theorists and assessors of personality. The book closes with summaries of the OSS, MacKinnon IPAR, VA, Menninger, and Peace Corps projects which Wiggins calls "milestone studies" but which this reviewer would call "millstone studies" because of their lack of persuasive positive results. If there is a weakness in this book it is that insufficient attention is given to the problems of criteria. But this is a shortcoming common to almost all research in personality and prediction; and predictors have let themselves undertake tasks in which the odds were stacked against them. In each of the milestone studies the applicants were a highly homogeneous, self-selected lot and the final criteria were undefined or unreliable or both. In each study the criteria were supervisors' ratings which are subject to so many distortions that, had they been selector variables, no assessor would have accepted them. Although it is not appropriate to dwell on omitted topics, Wiggins did not include any discussion of projective techniques as assessment devices in spite of their widespread use. Furthermore, while categorization and differential treatment strategies are alluded to, the topic is not as well developed in the discussion as might seem to be warranted. Similarly, Wiggins does not discuss the shortcomings of the selection process most likely to affect his readers—the selection of admission to graduate school. This activity has also proved to be of dubious accuracy because of the homogeneity of applicants and the unreliability of criteria. Finally, we looked in vain for some estimates of future directions in this phase of psychology and for some summary of what appear at this point to be sound practices or common pitfalls. There is a need to reverse the order of approach of an assessment-predictor psychologist. Much more time needs to be spent on the criterion and on observation of factors which may influence criterion behavior, events which may occur after the predictions have been made or factors which are not assessed because their significance was not known. What happens is that the one doing the predicting gets out the same kit of tests regardless of the task at hand. The research of Stern, Stein and Bloom (1956) is one of the few exceptions to the tendency to use one's favorite test for any new task. The milestone studies listed above are prime examples of ignorance of the criterion and reliance on the old faithful, familiar predictor-test. Wiggins' favorable evaluation of peer ratings needs to be questioned because frequently the criterion data are the ratings of superiors which, in the Armed Forces, the Peace Corps and universities, are likely to have much variance in common with the predictors because of shared stereotypes. His evaluation of Peace Corps prediction activities would have been tempered by Harris' data (1973) which showed a steady decline over the years in the percentage of selected volunteers who completed their tours, so much so that Peace Corps abandoned much of their selection activity. The reviewer's own experience with the prediction of performance of Peace Corps volunteers also leads to a negative conclusion (Guthrie and Zektick, 1967). The criterion, in this instance, was judgments by Filipinos of the volunteers, collected in a research project operated by Filipinos and independent of the predicting agency and of Peace Corps staff in the Philippines. The correlation between the pooled judgments of the selection board and the performance criterion was .004. Peer ratings did even worse with a correlation with Filipinos' judgments of −.049! This is an important book because it presents measurement considerations in an understandable form, relates measurement to personality theory, and provides a basis on which we may begin to take into account both personality and situational variables rather than, as presently is the case, attending to one category while ignoring the other. A mastery of the theory of personality measurement as outlined by Wiggins will be of great value to any psychologist who looks at behavior (some seem not to do so), regardless of whether he is engaged in clinical assessment. This reviewer is persuaded, however, that prediction of performance in alien settings should be left to fortunetellers and public relations officers.

Meas & Eval Guid 8(2):114–6 Jl '75. Howard E. A. Tinsley. * one of the most authoritative, comprehensive, and interesting treatments of personality assessment to appear to date. Practitioners will find little of interest, since Wiggins makes no attempt to deal with personality assessment techniques from a how-to-do-it standpoint. Researchers and scholars, however, will find a sophisticated and scholarly treatment of the principles of personality research. The coverage is generally comprehensive, balanced, and informed. Wiggins gives an evenhanded presentation of viewpoints, refraining from expressing his own viewpoints and conclusions even when they might be warranted. He has the knack of writing about complex issues in a manner which makes them so easily understandable they sometimes look deceptively simple-minded. At times the discussion is heavily mathematical, but, with one exception in the first chapter, the mathematical treatments are clear, logically developed, easy to follow, and actually enhance the reader's understanding of the non-algebraic portions of the text. The book is genuinely interesting to read. The first six chapters are devoted to the principles of the prediction of human behavior and constitute the best part of the book. Here the reader will find a discussion of correlational analysis, regression and prediction, suppressor and moderator variables, the prediction of predictability, contingency tables, clinical and actuarial prediction, and decision theory. Wiggins' coverage of many of these topics is the best that I have yet read. * Chapters 7, 8, and 9....include an interesting summary of generalizability theory, an authoritative overview of the peer rating technique, and an integrated discussion of the work of Loevinger and that of Campbell and Fiske within the theoretical framework of construct validity. The final two chapters of the book are devoted to a coverage of the nature of personality theory, the use of personality theories as assessment models, and "American milestone studies" in personality assessment. This section was interesting but anticlimactic and of little practical value to contemporary researchers. * Some sections appear to be written in an elementary, discursive style appropriate as an introductory treatment for sophomores. Moreover, at points it appears that Wiggins did not do his homework sufficiently. In chapter 3, for example, he devotes several pages to the description of a cluster analysis procedure for identifying the initial categories from which an actuarial table can be constructed. From his discussion of the problems associated with this procedure, it appears that he is unaware of alternative cluster analytic techniques which would have avoided some of these problems. In the final analysis, however, the strengths of this

book significantly outweigh its defects. The book is generally written in an interesting style and presents complex concepts in such a clear, understandable fashion that I believe it could be used with above average undergraduate students. I would recommend it for use in beginning graduate classes in personality assessment, and advanced graduate students and professionals in the field will find much of interest and value in the book. I am pleased to add this volume to my bookshelf.

[B567]

★WILLINGHAM, WARREN W. **College Placement and Exemption.** New York: College Entrance Examination Board, 1974. Pp. xv, 272. Paper, $4.95; cloth, $6.95. *

Ed & Psychol Meas 35(3):741–3 au '75. Henry Moughamian. * Overall, the author of this text has done an admirable job in attempting to take widely diverse educational practices and programs and structuring them into a rational framework that could aid practitioners. There is no doubt that this type of endeavor has been long needed, especially in view of the increased access to higher education over approximately the last decade. * Despite this important limitation, as well as lack of adequate consideration of relevant significant psychometric problems, the models presented in Chapters 3 through 6 represent an outstanding attempt to bring some rational structure out of extreme diversity. Chapter 7, the conclusions, is an excellent discussion of the implications of these models in view of our educational setting and some of the current problems such as articulation. This text should be of immense value, not only to developing institutions, but to well-established institutions with placement and exemption programs. Its primary value lies not in how to develop and implement such programs, which is very much needed but beyond the scope of this book, but in giving institutions a framework upon which to proceed in developing such programs or a framework upon which to evaluate their existing programs. The author has, indeed, accomplished another purpose by reviewing extensively the relevant research literature, and even though much of the research presented cannot be considered as significant research, it nevertheless can be of help to individuals in getting a feel for the "lay of the land." Fragmentation of placement and exemption programs within institutions is a common symptom; this text can be profitable in the improvement of such programs with the end result of better meeting the needs of students.

[B568]

★WILLMOTT, ALAN S., AND FOWLES, DIANA E. **The Objective Interpretation of Test Performance: The Rasch Model Applied.** Windsor, Berks., England: NFER Publishing Co. Ltd., 1974. Pp. 94. Paper, £3.60. *

[B569]

★WILSON, JOHN. **The Assessment of Morality.** Windsor, Berks., England: NFER Publishing Co. Ltd., 1973. Pp. x, 115. Paper, £3.25. * (Atlantic Highlands, N.J.: Humanities Press, Inc. $7.50.)

Brit J Ed Psychol 44(2):217–8 Je '74. D. Graham. * The book is intended for research workers in psychology and the social sciences (though not restricted to these), and is primarily meant to clarify the conceptual difficulties which, the author holds, are at least as important as the purely empirical problems besetting the development of adequate methods of assessing morality. * Wilson's point is that much research in psychology, particularly in the field of moral development, has been bedevilled by lack of conceptual clarity and that productive research on morality is virtually impossible until some degree of conceptual clarity has been reached. * The present book is not long, but is both illuminating and stimulating. Not all who read it will agree with the author in all he says, but it should certainly be regarded as required reading for anyone interested in the field, and more particularly for anyone contemplating research.

[B570]

★WING, J. K.; COOPER, J. E.; AND SARTORIUS, N. **Measurement and Classification of Psychiatric Symptoms: An Instruction Manual for the PSE and Catego Program.** New York: Cambridge University Press, 1974. Pp. x, 233. $15.95. *

[B571]

WITTROCK, M. C., AND WILEY, DAVID E., EDITORS. **The Evaluation of Instruction: Issues and Problems.** New York: Holt, Rinehart & Winston, Inc., 1970. Pp. xiii, 494. $7.95. *

Ed & Psychol Meas 31(4):1047–50 w '71. James R. Sanders. * Evaluation specialists do not have a set of guidelines parallel to those provided to the research specialist by works such as the Campbell-Stanley treatment of experimental design. It is unfortunate that these expectations are not completely met by the Wittrock and Wiley book, although some excellent logical frameworks are provided. * The comments by Stake, Glass, and Scriven and the papers by Lortie and Alkin should be on all reading lists for evaluation courses. The paper by Gagné and the comments by Anderson, Postman, and Bormuth should be required reading for students of measurement. The paper by Wiley and those papers attached in the appendix of the volume are important readings for students of research design and analysis, measurement and evaluation. The volume fails to meet its promise in that many issues and few answers are provided for the practicing evaluator and that the promises of the book title and section headings are never fulfilled. These shortcomings are undoubtedly a function of the time at which the symposium was held. In 1967 much less had been written about the evaluation process than today. * There is no doubt that the volume will serve well as a reference in evaluation, statistics and research design, measurement, and educational psychology as well as a valuable historical document to students of evaluation. [See the original review for additional critical comments not excerpted.]

Meas & Eval Guid 4(3):184–5 O '71. Jacob G. Beard. * a report of a symposium on the evaluation of instruction held on the UCLA campus in December 1967. Four papers have been added to the conference proceedings to complete the volume. The major papers have been published separately by the Center for the Study of Evaluation of Instructional Programs. * Most of the formal papers are of the "armchair" type in which problems are well delineated, but rarely solved. They reflect a creative approach to the problem and will affect the thinking in this area for some time to come. The diversity of opinions among the many experienced evaluators participating in this symposium reflect the absence of an agreed-upon theory and methodology for the evaluation of instruction. The volume is of substantial value in helping to conceptualize the evaluation process. However, the beginning evaluator, who is more interested in "how-to-do-it," is referred to other sources, such as Suchman's *Principles and Practices of Evaluative Research* and the American Educational Research Association monograph series on evaluation.

[B572]

★WOLF, RICHARD M. **Achievement in America: National Report of the United States for International Educational Achievement Project.** New York: Teachers College Press, 1977. Pp. ix, 192. Paper, $7.95. *

[B573]

★WOLF, THETA H. **Alfred Binet.** Chicago, Ill.: University of Chicago Press, 1973. Pp. vi, 376. $13.75. *

Am J Mental Def 79(4):467–8 Ja '75. Henry Leland. It seems almost axiomatic in science that the closer the individual's name comes to being a "household word," the less one actually knows about him. This is certainly true of Alfred Binet. This biography exposes a long-neglected area in the history of child psychology and particularly that aspect of child psychology related to the development of research in growth and development and in developmental disability. Wolf has given us a fascinating, highly readable, scholarly work on Binet, the scientist; and she has left me very hungry for information on Binet, the man. One gets the impression of a bourgeois, conservative, somewhat snobbish, egocentric, somewhat isolated individual who, for example, would not even send his daughters to public school, but insisted on training them himself. This is a usual description of the upper-class intellectual Frenchmen of the late 19th and early 20th centuries. Nevertheless, it belies the image of Binet as a man who could work with his own two daughters and get from them vast amounts of descriptive and projective materials, who could work with other children (particularly those with developmental disabilities and mental retardation) and get good empathetic reception. Perhaps it will be a French biographer who can clarify this image of Binet. Wolf says that not too much is known, but what there is tickles the imagination. One may further wonder how much the history of psychology was affected by such interpersonal dynamics—recognizing, as Binet himself had to, that the personality of the researcher makes a tremendous impact upon his research. The book has been organized for the reader. The first chapter gives an overview of Binet's life touching all bases and making it possible for the more casual reader to get a very clear image of Binet's work in its historical context. Each of the next six chapters goes into the various details of specific periods of Binet's development, and each becomes in itself a short review in the history of psychology, both as it was affected by Binet and as it effected him. Here, Wolf has taken great pains to locate and document the opposing currents of that era, and the reader comes away with a very clear picture of the key issues, the major theoretical considerations, and indications of who was doing the research—as well as the

kind of research they were doing. What emerges is the description of a scientist who had his head in many areas (e.g., memory, physiology, natural science, hypnotism) and his finger in many pies, (e.g., legislations, laboratories, editing). He was a prolific writer and seemed interested in all aspects of the young science of psychology, whether one was dealing with research, clinical, experimental, or social-legal areas. He appears as the progenitor of the opposing approaches of both Piaget (who also took his doctorate in natural science) and Wallon (whom, unfortunately, Wolf ignores—except through his associate, Zazzo). The modern reader will find many of Binet's ideas still highly debatable. Also, some issues which we thought were settled have reappeared. In this regard, some of Binet's early theoretical and experimental approaches seemed to have been on the right track, and it is too bad that he abandoned them in favor of psychometric emphasis. It is interesting to note that the trouble that Binet got himself into with the scientific community in the 1880s centered around his failure to understand the effect of experimenter biases on experimental psychology; he seemingly did not understand that the psychological examiner had the same kind of effect on test results. It is also of interest that in 1903 he reproached Fechner and Wundt for "becoming so preoccupied with technical precision that they committed some enormous errors in subjective controls." Yet Binet apparently committed exactly the same errors in the development of his tests. Wolf emphasizes that the numerical result—the IQ—was not due to either Binet or Simon, that both were consistently opposed to this type of reporting, and that the real "villain" was Goddard [sic!]. Nonetheless, the tests were designed to lead to a unified or single concept of intelligence which, of course, immediately opened the door to IQ reporting by less conscientious or more harried clinicians. It is interesting, finally, to note that Binet's own concept of intelligence includes (along with rate of learning—which his test measures) a wide variety of variables which could well come under our rubrics of sensory-motor development, cognition, social awareness, and adaptation. However, he apparently got caught up in the expediency of an easily administered, clear-cut, relatively short measure, and he thus lost track of his push for individual differences. Binet seemed to view intelligence as a clinical entity, and modern writers using a multivariant approach, are in many respects forced to return to some of the earlier research of Binet's period because the overemphasis on the search for an IQ has left a tremendous void in available material. It may be that some of this current research will eventually redeem Binet's good name, and that it will serve, once and for all, to get it unhooked from the IQ model. This is an excellent volume in the history of psychology. It is much more than the biography of a great and famous psychologist; it is also a discussion and description of the ideas of his era, many of which still require research and understanding. Also, the description of Binet's methods indicates that, in many cases, he had a unique and important way of dealing with and observing field situations. By her selection of what to include and what to omit, the author has shown herself to be highly aware of the main lines of thought during that period. Thus, besides giving us the life of a psychologist, Wolf has given us a textbook in the early origins of child psychology and of work with mentally retarded children. I enjoyed the book and highly recommend it for both pleasure reading and improved understanding of the field.

[B574]

★WOMER, FRANK B. **Developing a Large Scale Assessment Program.** Denver, Colo.: Cooperative Accountability Project, Colorado Department of Education, 1973. Pp. 133. Paper. *

[B575]

★WONDERLIC, E. F., AND WONDERLIC, CHARLES F. **Negro Norms: A Study of 38,452 Job Applicants for Affirmative Action Programs.** Northfield, Ill.: E. F. Wonderlic & Associates, Inc., 1972. Pp. 80. Paper, $15.00. *

Personnel Psychol 26(1):171–6 sp '73. *William H. Mobley.* * The normative data are presented in a meaningful manner. Included are summary statistics, mean, medium, mode, N, standard deviation and quartile locations, as well as frequency distribution and cumulative centile ranks for the total Negro sample and for a variety of sub-categorizations. These sub-categorizations include summary statistics and distributions identified according to sex, age, education, geographic region, position applied for, various combinations of these variables, and in comparison to Caucasian samples. The industrial user of the Wonderlic will find this volume of norms a welcome adjunct to his local norms. Other publishers of tests for industrial (and other) use, would do well to provide so comprehensive a breakdown of normative infor-

mation. There are several important findings summarized in this report. The major finding is that Caucasian test performance is consistently higher than Negro performance on the Wonderlic. Whether looking at the total sample or subanalyses controlling for education, sex, age, geographic region or position applied for, the Negro and Caucasian means are generally about one standard deviation apart. Another interesting finding is the overall similarity in male and female Wonderlic means for the total sample and most sub-samples. However, Wonderlic's statement that, "No statistically significant differences occur in the Wonderlic Personnel Test relative to male and female populations" is an overgeneralization. For example, when the reviewer tested the significance of the difference in the means presented by Wonderlic for male vs. female Negro college level populations, the males were significantly higher ($p < .001$). * Although the norms are based on a large number of subjects applying for a variety of jobs in a variety of settings, it is not clear that the sample is representative of the total population of Wonderlic users. * Although the normative data are presented in a number of sub-categories and combination of sub-categories, there is no complete cross categorization. It would be useful to see a complete cross categorization based on race, sex, age, education, geographic region, and position applied for. * The *Negro Norms* are based on *all* forms of the test. * No data were presented....which permit analysis of the possible interaction of test form and racial group. * Wonderlic asserted that in the area of on-the-job training, "The Wonderlic Personnel Test serves as a highly accurate (valid) predictor of successful performance." Subsequently, he suggested, "As positions require various levels of 'ability to learn and ability to solve problems,' the Wonderlic Personnel Test can be shown to be valid....The only evidence presented which is relevant to these claims is a bar chart demonstrating that mean test scores increase systematically with increases in years of education. Elsewhere, Wonderlic (1970) has presented 'validity coefficients' based on the correlation of *average* test score and 10 levels of educational attainment. Wonderlic concluded that, 'The extremely high relationship between test score and educational attainment can be interpreted as Validity where Trainability is a job requirement.'" This statement must be taken with caution. First, the correlation between average test score and years of education is not the same as correlations between individual test score and years of education. By ignoring the variability in test score within each educational level, the reported correlations may be misleading from an individual difference viewpoint. Further, it is possible that factors other than "trainability" are involved in the decision to stay in or leave school, e.g., financial problems, domestic problems, temporary adjustment problems, etc. There is little reason to question the existence of a correlation between Wonderlic test scores and education. However, such a relation is insufficient to warrant the claim that the Wonderlic is a valid predictor of "trainability" or "ability to learn." It would seem imperative that Wonderlic present additional examples of empirical research supporting his claim. * Wonderlic's suggestion of considering "best qualified in class" on the basis of equivalent percentile relative to the appropriate racial distribution is not without merit. * Wonderlic's suggested strategy is that prediction equations for Negroes and Caucasians are likely to be significantly different * How viable is this hypothesized need for differential prediction based on racial subgroups? While there is still too little data relevant to this point, there would appear to be a growing body of evidence suggesting that when the differential prediction hypothesis is tested with adequate sample sizes and adequate criteria: differential validity and differential slopes may be the exception rather than the rule; if differences in prediction parameters are observed at all, the intercepts are most likely to differ; and that use of the common or majority regression equation may well *overestimate* minority criterion scores when compared to the minority regression line * Whether one chooses to follow Wonderlic's suggested interpretation and use of his normative data or alternatives, Wonderlic has, subject to the previously mentioned limitations, performed a useful and needed service by providing the *Negro Norms.*

[B576]

★Woods, Mary Lynn, and Moe, Alden J. **Analytical Reading Inventory.** Columbus, Ohio: Charles E. Merrill Publishing Co., 1977. Pp. 120. Paper, $3.95.

Read Teach 31(4):461–3 Ja '78. Frank Greene. * "The *Analytical Reading Inventory* is an informal reading inventory, intended for use by classroom teachers, reading specialists,

and prospective teachers. Because of the care given to the graded passages, the questions checking comprehension, and the instructions for use, users of the ARI may place greater faith in their analysis of the reading task than with IRI's previously available" (p. 3). "The teacher may use any of the three forms (A, B or C) since they are equivalent forms...." (p. 4). It may well be that the key word for users of this test is "faith." The authors present no information on reliability, equivalence of forms, or any sort of validity estimate. Since this is a test being marketed for use by others, it does not seem sufficient to excuse the lack of basic test data as an exercise in faith. No information is provided about the word lists: neither development of nor use of—other than as a means of determining where to start oral reading. Six categories of questions are presented with no information that they really measure different aspects of comprehension. Much information is provided about the readability of the passages. However, graded passages do not a comprehensive test make. The instructions for use are mechanical. The real problem of making sense out of what one is doing is handled by the cautions: "successful use of the ARI requires familiarity with informal reading inventory procedures...." (p. 15) and "because all deviations from the text should not be considered errors.... [included] is an optional Error Analysis Sheet, which some users may find helpful" (pp. 15–16). (N.B.: for anyone who might like to find out what to do with this Sheet, they are referred to a different commercially available reading test!) If the purpose of an IRI is to have individual teachers use their own materials on their own pupils and make their own decisions about what to teach, then one may question buying anyone else's informality. If the purpose of an IRI is to protect pupils from frustration by making sure they can easily handle assigned reading matter, then such precision of readability "by formula" is both unnecessary and silly: unnecessary because IRI standards are so conservative and the estimated reading level scores so broad (whole grade levels) that the pupil is "guaranteed" success at the instructional level; silly because the real criterion is the material available in the classroom the pupil is expected to read, not some other brief passages of artificial constraints never to be seen again. A considerable number of reading errors are best attributed to stress and are heard as inconsistent reading of words or seen as loss of place in the text. The format of the test seen by the pupil and the examiner of this test are NOT the same. If thee and they are looking at different layouts, it is very difficult to identify irregular losses of place. If it is not clear, I do like IRIs as a useful teaching strategy. But using someone else's and getting out of it only "estimated reading level scores" is limiting. Since this test provides no information on how or what to analyze in the reading task, what one is left with is a set of graded passages. But the cost is low, the printing clean and the zippered pages easy to remove. In summary, this is a fine example of a traditional IRI: with most of their possibilities and all of their faults.

[B577]
★WOODY, ROBERT HENLEY, AND WOODY, JANE DIVITA, EDITORS. **Clinical Assessment in Counseling and Psychotherapy.** New York: Appleton-Century-Crofts, 1972. Pp. xi, 370. $14.95. *

J Pers Assess 38(3):279–80 Je '74. Dale D. Simmons. Taking a rather "tough-minded" approach, seven authors have pieced together eight chapters to present a rather systematic, objectively-oriented critical analysis of the role of assessment in professional practice. * Although the book is not absolutely comprehensive the authors provide a rather thorough review of their selected topical areas. The book does not contain a review of selected assessment devices (i.e., tests) so the reader should look elsewhere for these. What is provided is an excellent review of assessment processes to precede training in the use of specific assessment devices.

[B578]
★WORNER, ROGER B. **Student Diagnosis, Placement, and Prescription: A Criterion-Referenced Approach.** Bloomington, Ind.: Indiana University Press, 1977. Pp. xiii, 237. $10.95. *

[B579]
★WYLIE, RUTH C. **The Self-Concept, Revised Edition: Vol. 1, A Review of Methodological Considerations and Measuring Instruments.** Lincoln, Neb.: University of Nebraska Press, 1974. Pp. xx, 433. $13.50. *

J Pers Assess 39(6):649–50 D '75. Arnold W. Vinson. * a masterful and provocative review of the problem of research in the field of self-concept. Wylie is concerned with the need to improve the science of personality, especially self-concept theorizing and its associated methodological problems. To emphasize the urgency of the situation she reminds the reader periodically throughout the book that there have been no constructive attempts in the last decade to improve self-concept theories and methodology in ways which could significantly promote more appropriate operationalyzing of self-referent constructs. Wylie also sharply criticizes self-concept researchers for their lack of rigor in experimental studies, and authors of introductory psychology text books for omitting recent findings of self-concept literature. One can detect, from the book, a challenge for self-concept theorists to improve drastically in methodology or abandon research altogether in the area of self-concept. One gets the feeling that the study of self-concept is in its last stage of scientific life and that this book is a prescription written in order to give the self-concept field a philosophical and methodological shot in the arm. * The author presents a frank and objective discussion of research topics drawn from extensive references and also provides a comprehensive bibliography. She makes no attempt to review or evaluate self-concept studies in the context of minority groups or any other specific populations, but rather, focuses on theoretical and methodological problems which arise in any type of self-concept research. Finally, this volume is not written for non- and semi-professional groups, but for graduate students, authors of introductory psychology texts and, more specifically, future self-concept researchers. There is a great need for a book of this type and certainly Dr. Wylie amply fills this need.

[B580]
★ZEITLIN, SHIRLEY. **Kindergarten Screening: Early Identification of Potential High Risk Learners.** Springfield, Ill.: Charles C Thomas, Publisher, 1976. Pp. xi, 289. $14.95. *

[B581]
★ZIMMERMAN, IRLA LEE, AND WOO-SAM, JAMES M.; WITH ALAN J. GLASSER. **Clinical Interpretation of the Wechsler Adult Intelligence Scale.** New York: Grune & Stratton, Inc., 1973. Pp. ix, 221. $11.50. *

Am J Mental Def 78(4):512–3 Ja '74. A. B. Silverstein. The title of a book should tell what it is about, and a preface should explain why the book was written and for whom. On these two points, the authors of the present volume earn poor grades. To be sure, they treat the Wechsler Adult Intelligence Scale (WAIS), but their emphasis is not on "clinical interpretation," at least as the reviewer understands that term (cf. Rapaport's classic treatment of the Wechsler-Bellevue in *Diagnostic Psychological Testing*). Moreover, their failure to provide a preface leaves one uncertain as to their reasons for writing the book and unable to judge how well they have succeeded in whatever it is they set out to do. *If,* however, their purpose was to prepare a WAIS handbook for students of clinical psychology, they have done rather well, and their grades should be raised accordingly. * In sum, the authors have reviewed the extensive WAIS literature, sorted it out, and presented a substantial portion of it in a well organized, easily digestible form. They have put relatively little of themselves, and their own clinical experience with the test, into the book. Had they done so, it would of course have been a different book, perhaps a better one, but presumably *not* the one they set out to write.

J Pers Assess 38(3):290–1 Je '74. Ronald E. Smith. In a way it is unfortunate that the publication of this book followed so closely in time that of Matarazzo's (1972) monumental revision of Wechsler's Measurement and Appraisal of Adult Intelligence, for its slim profile alone marks it as less detailed and comprehensive, and therefore, in the eyes of many, less worthwhile. Looks however are deceiving, for it provides the user of the WAIS with much useful material, which the Matarazzo book does not have, such as a comparison of other measures with the WAIS, as well as considerable additional information on administration and scoring. The writing style is terse and precise with no side-trips into personal opinion or philosophy. * The major portion of the book is devoted to an analysis of the WAIS subtests. Each is dealt with in its own chapter which is sequenced in the order in which the test is usually administered. * The inclusion of factorial information seems to this reviewer to be of doubtful value in a volume such as this. Different types of factor analysis tend to produce different results and a variety of sample variables affect factorial composition. When presented in the concise style characteristic of this book the factor data become contradictory and confusing to the unsophisticated reader. It quite possibly could have best been omitted. Sections on administration, scoring and interpretation will prove to be particularly helpful to the neophyte test administrator. * It has been estimated that as many as 90 percent of all WAISs administered are given in some abbreviated form. The inclusion here of a chapter on Adaptations and Brief Forms of the WAIS is not likely to contribute to a reduction of this number despite the inclusion by the authors of objections to this practice. The WAIS was not

designed to be a screening test and its use for this purpose in abbreviated form is a travesty except in the hands of the highly experienced clinician. The student, who will be the primary reader of this book would undoubtedly be better advised to consider the entire scale as a minimum rather than a maximum instrument subject to abbreviation. * It is not likely that this short volume will prove particularly useful to the experienced WAIS administrator, but it is of unquestionable value as a reference for the neophyte tester and the student enrolled in a course in intelligence measurement. One hopes that the authors, now that they have completed volumes on both the WISC and the WAIS, consider the task only two-thirds complete and are hard at work on the "Clinical Interpretation of the WPPSI."

Meas & Eval Guid 7(4):263 Ja '75. Norman A. Scott. * Their chapter-by-chapter dissection of the WAIS by subtests makes for a most thorough, usable, and practical understanding of not only the instrument, but also its interpretation. In a systematic way the authors present for each subtest a general description of what it measures along with factor analytic descriptions, information on administration, scoring, item placement and difficulty, the significance of differences between a given subtest and other subtests, relevant research, and a statement of advantages and limitations for each subtest. * a readable integrated work whose introductory chapters describe the development of the WAIS and compare it with other instruments through use of summary charts containing a wealth of information. Especially commendable are tables indicating for different probability levels the reliability of differences between subtest scale scores. * the book concludes with an all-too-brief discussion of test reports and sample protocols. The volume is well organized and presented, but it does have flaws in that it relies heavily upon a few WAIS factor analytic studies and makes only brief reference to test performance changes with age. Recent life span developmental findings and issues regarding cohort or generational influences in intellectual test performance are not included. A more serious deficit is the omission of cultural or minority group influences on WAIS performance and in assessment situations. For treatment of this topic a student or clinician should be referred to Jerome Sattler's *Assessment of Children's Intelligence.* Zimmerman and Woo-Sam have done a commendable job and their work deserves both praise and adoption either as a graduate course text, especially for assessment practica, or as a reference work for clinicians. This book is invaluable with respect to answering student questions concerning what test results mean. Use of this volume as a practica or lab text would nicely complement Sattler's book in intellectual assessment courses. It is likely that many students, interns, and clinicians will be indebted to Zimmerman and Woo-Sam for ingeniously and thoroughly explaining some of the puzzles and challenges of intellectual assessment.

[B582]

★ZYTOWSKI, DONALD G., EDITOR. **Contemporary Approaches to Interest Measurement.** Minneapolis, Minn.: University of Minnesota Press, 1973. Pp. xi, 251. $10.00. *

Ed & Psychol Meas 34(1):205-7 sp '74. Max D. Engelhart. * excellent anthology * Chapter 1 by Zytowski presents basic information on the selection and use of interest inventories. * Table 1.5 is especially valuable in its presentation of the characteristics of seven current interest inventories. * Harmon presents a....very interesting discussion of the special problems encountered in counseling women * This reviewer is impressed by the effort to relate the development of the *Ohio Vocational Interest Survey* to theory and to obtain validity, reliability, and to obtain normative data. * The last....chapter....contains numerous illustrative interpretations of profiles obtained for each of the inventories. This chapter should be very helpful to students of measurement and to counselors. The book as a whole is the best single source of information concerning the contemporary widely used vocational interest inventories. It deserves to be read with great care. Donald Zytowski and the other authors have made a significant contribution to our understanding of interest measurement.

Meas & Eval Guid 7(2):136-7 Jl '74. Richard S. Sharf. During 1968 and 1969 three workshops were held in different sections of the country to acquaint participants with interest inventories. These presentations have been polished, edited, and published in book form. The contents are broader than what is implied by the term "interest measurement" in the title. The book includes a measure of vocational needs and a work values inventory, as well as descriptions of four interest inventories. *

Generally, the eight contributors present only the highlights and essentials of their instruments and tend to pass over the weak points. * The attractiveness of this book is that it provides a bridge between the inventory user and the manual. With few exceptions, the chapters are well written and will stimulate readers to examine selected inventory manuals. Many complexities such as the lambda coefficient of the Kuder Occupational Interest Survey (KOIS) and the circular triads of the Minnesota Importance Questionnaire (MIQ) tend to be lost in the manuals, but are explained clearly in this book. * the chapters differ greatly in the degree to which the validity and reliability of the instrument is discussed. For example, Barnette's chapter on the Minnesota Vocational Interest Inventory (MVII) is almost exclusively devoted to validation studies of the MVII, with relatively little description of the scales themselves. This chapter stands out as being clearly different from the rest because of its concentration on the research the MVII has gathered rather than its use as a counseling tool. In contrast, Zytowski virtually ignores validity and reliability, preferring to discuss the counseling interpretation of the KOIS. * For counselors, the case studies illustrating interpretations of the inventories to clients will probably be the most useful aspect of the book. Harmon's chapter on the SVIB for women provides not only a good understanding of how it was developed, but also some excellent guidelines for use. The chapters describing the SVIB-M, KOIS, and OVIS also explain important concepts through illustrative examples of student profiles. With regard to the MVII and the WVI, the reader will learn little from the authors' chapters about how to use their instrument in counseling. The final chapter is a unique one in that it features each author interpreting the results of inventories taken by three clients. An opportunity to explain the meaning of his inventory in relation to biographical information is given to each author. This section also features answers by the authors to questions from workshop participants. This may be particularly helpful to beginning counselors because they can see test developers using their own products. In summary, a reader with limited time wishing to either briefly review a sampling of measures of vocational motivation or to understand the basic uses of such instruments will find Zytowski's book helpful.

Editor's Comments on Testing

FIFTY YEARS IN TESTING

PART I
SOME REMINISCENCES, CRITICISMS, AND SUGGESTIONS [1,2]

Oscar Krisen Buros

THE BUROS INSTITUTE OF MENTAL MEASUREMENTS

ALTHOUGH I would enjoy speaking about my experiences as a consumer advocate for test users over the past 45 years, I wish to speak to you about other things, without the restrictions I have always placed upon myself as editor of the *Mental Measurements Yearbooks*. Our work in serving as a clearinghouse of critical information on the merits and limitations of tests has consumed and dominated the lives of my wife and me and will continue to do so for two or three years more. Although I like to promote our *MMY* work whenever I can, I wish to reminisce over a wide range of my activities and beliefs, apart from the yearbooks. I shall speak about some historical developments over the past fifty years, express some of my early and current concerns in testing, and make some specific recommendations for change.

Many of you know that I consider that "most standardized tests are poorly constructed, of questionable or unknown validity, pretentious in their claims, and likely to be misused more often than not." I doubt, however, whether any of you are aware of the extent to which I am also critical of some of the most cherished tenets of the testing profession. It probably is foolhardy of me to present some of my criticisms in this distinguished stronghold of achievement testing at its best. Although I doubt whether I

shall win adherents to my views, I keep hoping that I just might.

In many ways, the year 1927 was a banner year in testing. I like to think of it as the approximate year in which the testing movement reached maturity. The unreasonably high expectations of earlier years were being replaced by more modest expectations of the usefulness of tests. The limitations of tests were beginning to be widely recognized. I cannot recall a year which produced so many scholarly books in testing: Kelley's *Interpretation of Educational Measurements,* Ruch and Stoddard's *Tests and Measurements in High School Instruction,* Symond's *Measurement in Secondary Education,* Well's *Mental Tests in Clinical Practice,* Bronner's *Manual of Individual Mental Tests and Testing,* Spearman's *Abilities of Man,* and Smith and Wright's *Second Revision of the Bibliography of Educational Measurements.*

If you would examine these books and the best of the achievement and intelligence tests then available, you might be surprised that so little progress has been made in the past fifty years—in fact, in some areas we are not doing as well. Except for the tremendous advances in electronic scoring, analysis, and reporting of test results, we don't have a great deal to show for fifty years of work. Essentially, achievement tests are being constructed today in the same way they were fifty years ago—the major changes being the use of more sophisticated statistical procedures for doing what we did then—mistakes and all.

[1] Reprinted from *Educational Researcher* 6(7):9–15 Jl–Ag '77.

[2] The first part of a lecture presented at Iowa City, Iowa, March 28, 1977, to a special seminar in education sponsored by the College of Education, University of Iowa and the American College Testing Program.

The year 1927 also can be related to the roots of this Lindquist Center for Measurement. It was in 1927 that Lindquist received his doctorate and embarked upon a career of remarkable accomplishments in testing, statistics, and electronic processing of tests. His contributions to testing have been truly monumental.

In 1927, the Smith-Wright standardized test bibliography listed 520 educational achievement tests compared to about 1500 today. Today's tests are more attractively printed and are generally machine scorable, but otherwise they show relatively little improvement. In the first quarter of this century, the developments in testing were truly remarkable. On the contrary, in the last fifty years, the improvements—except for the revolutionary electronic scoring machines and computers—have not been of enough consequence to permit us to have pride in what we have accomplished in the past half century. In fact, some of today's tests may even be poorer, because of the restrictions imposed by machine scoring. For example, the 1922 *Stanford Achievement Test* compares fairly well with the current test and, in fact, is probably better per unit of testing time. As incredible as it may seem, the methods of determining the reliability of the 1922 Stanford were better than those used by all but a few tests today. An approximation to interval estimation was even provided by printing vertical bars on the profiles to indicate the probable error of measurement for each test. If you examine the earliest editions of the *Stanford,* I am sure that you will be impressed by the quality of both the test and the manual.

In some areas, test users of thirty to fifty years ago had more tests to choose from than they have today. The most important area which receives little attention today compared to what it received forty to fifty years ago is character assessment. Edwin Starbuck of Iowa was an early pioneer in character measurement. The studies of character and deceit published in 1928, 1929, and 1930 by Hartshorne, May, and Shuttleworth stimulated the production of numerous rating scales and tests of attitudes, character, citizenship, conduct, moral knowledge, religious knowledge, and the like. For many years, we commonly spoke of character and personality tests. It probably is a reflection of the times, but today there are practically no published rating scales or tests available to assess character and closely related traits.

The history of testing has been characterized by periods of unwarranted optimism about the values of standardized tests in general and in specific kinds of tests. I shall briefly enumerate a few of the developments which once raised high hopes and were later quietly abandoned or rejected.

Sixty years ago, there was great excitement about the potentialities of standard tests in the evaluation of students, teachers, and school systems. In his editor's introduction to Monroe, DeVoss, and Kelley's *Educational Tests and Measurements* published in 1917, Cubberly praised the testing movement highly in these words:

To the teacher it cannot help but eventually mean not only concise and definite statements as to what she is expected to do in the different subjects of the course of study, but the reduction of instruction to those items which can be proved to be of importance in preparation for intelligent living and future usefulness in life. It will mean, too, an ultimate differentiation in training for the different types of children with which teachers now have to deal, and the specialization of work so as to enable teachers to obtain more satisfactory individual results. To the citizen the movement means the erection of standards of accomplishment which are definite, and by means of which he can judge for himself as to the efficiency of the schools he helps to support. For the superintendent it means the changing of school supervision from guesswork to scientific accuracy, and the establishment of standards of work by which he may defend what he is doing.

Within the next ten years, disillusionment set in. Now, however, despite the increasing criticism of testing by some, others are moving in the direction of similar unwarrantedly high expectations of sixty years ago—I refer to such movements as accountability, contract testing, and program evaluation.

In the 1930's and the 1940's, the American Council on Education played a leading role in the development of evaluation instruments for use in high schools and colleges. For many years it published annually a new form of Thurstone's famous *Psychological Examinations for College Freshmen.* Its cumulative record forms, personality rating scales, and Thurstone's *Tests of Primary Mental Abilities* never lived up to their widely publicized expectations. It also sponsored the preparation of seven achievement tests published by the World Book Co. Its most important project was, however, the founding of the Cooperative Test Service in 1930.

A grant of $50,000 per year for ten years was obtained from the General Education Board "to construct ten or more comparable forms of examinations in the fundamental subject matters of junior college and senior high schools, and to make them available to the colleges and schools, one form each year, at the lowest possible cost." The director of the Service, Ben D. Wood, referred to the tests as a "particular kind of scientific measuring instrument" and that the Service "aspires to serve the science and art of teaching in the same way in which a firm of instrument-makers serves physical science or the science of medicine."

In its first five years of existence, the Cooperative Test Service produced over thirty tests, many of them in three or four forms. Some of its most innovative tests—e.g., science tests covering specific objectives such as application of principles and interpretation of experiments—lasted only a few years. The expected demand for ten comparable forms never did materialize. Very few tests ever reached five forms. The goal of a new form each year was abandoned for all of its tests within ten years. The expectations of the founders were not realized.

Another widely publicized development in testing in the past fifty years was the Evaluation in the Eight Year Study project. Under the direction of Ralph Tyler, numerous innovative tests were constructed to measure behavioral objectives not covered by the available tests. Although practically all of these tests were published, none survived more than a few years.

I consider the Iowa Academic Contest, later called the Iowa Every-Pupil Testing Program, the most worthwhile of the numerous testing developments which have been abandoned or replaced within the past fifty years. The early reports on the program emphasized the competitive aspects with comparisons made by schools and school systems, as well as by individuals. The program attempted to improve Iowa education by motivating pupils, teachers, and school administrators "to an increased interest and greater effort in the improvement of instruction and learning." In 1931, Lindquist wrote:

The fundamental purposes of the Iowa Academic Contest are to assist high schools of the state in their attempts to: (1) Measure the achievements of pupils and the effectiveness of instruction; (2) Encourage *better* scholarship and *more effective* instruction; and (3) Make more rapid progress in the improvement of the *content* of instruction.

In 1941, ten years later, the objectives were essentially the same:

to provide superior instruments for the measurement of educational achievement, to facilitate improvement in high school instruction and in educational guidance, and to encourage better scholarship.

In 1942, the twelve subject tests were replaced by the *Iowa Tests of Educational Development,* a battery of tests designed to measure "the development of those abilities needed by a student to continue his own education." With such a goal, it was not surprising that the new battery appeared to many of us to be essentially a reading and scholastic aptitude test. It was in keeping with the trend to construct college achievement tests (e.g., those of the College Board) which place minimal coverage on content matter by the substitution of reading comprehension items based upon selections in the subject area of the test. It is hard to imagine a more drastic change than this 1942 shift from the Iowa subject-centered tests to the ITED reading-aptitude battery. Regardless of the generally accepted merits of the ITED, I think that the cost may have been too dear. We need high-quality subject tests of the kind provided in Iowa 35 to 45 years ago. I think it unfortunate that so much attention is being paid to predicting success at the next higher educational level, while less and less attention is being given to determining what was learned at earlier levels.

I shall not go on and mention other developments which started out with high hopes and expectations followed by disillusionment or abandonment. There have been so many disappointments, however, that I wonder which of the current developments will survive.

When I was an elementary school principal forty-six years ago, I was also in charge of testing in a small school system. When I analyzed the contents of the *Stanford Achievement Test,* I noticed that the History and Civics subtest dealt almost entirely with American history with very few items relevant to European backgrounds. Since we taught American history in the fifth grade and European backgrounds in the sixth grade, it was reasonable to expect that our sixth graders would do less well one year after completing their study of American history because of forgetting. On the contrary, our sixth graders did better. Further study of the excellent manual explained what at first seemed to be a paradox. On the basis of a preliminary item tryout, those items, about one-third, which did not show "a marked increase over a range of grades were eliminated." This meant, of course, that the sixth graders would necessarily do better than the fifth graders if our situation were similar to those in which the tryouts were made. This grade-by-grade improvement criterion—probably suggested by the age-to-age improvement criterion used in constructing intelligence tests—has been continuously accepted over a half a century as a requisite in the final selection of test items. This validation procedure is based upon assumptions which seem reasonable if not examined too closely. It was accepted as axiomatic that knowledge and skills of children improve as they progress through the grades. Consequently, a valid test should show grade-to-grade improvement in scores. It then seems logical to conclude that a valid item should also show grade-to-grade improvement.

In the construction of trade tests in the armed services sixty years ago, "the method of widely spaced groups" was used to make the final selection of items. Items which didn't differentiate in the expected direction between services, apprentices, journeymen, and experts were rejected. In 1925, Donald Paterson described the use of course grades in selecting what he called diagnostic items, that is, items which showed a progressive increase in the percent passing proceeding from the F to the A students.

In 1927, Ruch and Stoddard recommended that the total score on a tryout form of a test be used as a criterion for item selection. This procedure for validating items has been continuously used and advocated by testing specialists ever since.

Statistical methods such as these greatly simplify the task of the testmaker. The selection of the most discriminating items on the basis of a tryout requires no knowledge of the content matter of the test. It is a task which any testing specialist can perform. There is still another advantage in using discriminating items only— they will result in higher reliabilities.

These and related item-validation techniques play an important role in determining the characteristics of most standardized achievement tests. Although these techniques are widely used by our very best testmakers, it is my thesis that these techniques have been harmful to the development of the best possible measuring instruments. These statistical methods of item validation confuse differentiation with measurement and exaggerate differences among individ-

uals and between grades. I would like to see their use discontinued.

My first public criticism of those statistical methods of validating achievement items was made 42 years ago in a review of *Tests and Measurements in the Social Studies* by statistician Truman Kelley and historian A.C. Krey. This 1934 volume describes a five-year program of constructing tests, the items of which were statistically validated by requiring grade-to-grade increase in performance, usually from grade 4 through grade 12. The project also used total scores on tryout tests. In my 1935 criticism of these item validation procedures, I said: "The reviewer most deplores the reliance placed upon certain common rigid statistical techniques of selecting the items to be retained in the final test." According to Krey, the subject matter specialists

saw some questions which to them seemed among the best testing items dropped, while others relatively poor were retained. Items were selected on the basis of progressive performance grade by grade, the item showing the steadiest improvement apparently being regarded as the best. This resulted in the elimination of some questions which most teachers would regard as unusually good ones and the inclusion of others which seemed relatively poor questions....With these misgivings, but with a determination to follow out the dictates of objective measurement, nevertheless, the final tests were drawn up on that basis.

Commenting on this in my review, I said:

It is regrettable that the subject-matter specialists acquiesced so readily to the so-called "dictates of objective measurements." It seems inescapable that such methods of statistically validating achievement tests insidiously tend to strengthen the status quo, to impede curricular progress, to perpetuate our present grade classification, to differentiate rather than to measure, to conceal unlearning, and to give an illusory sense of continuous learning from grade to grade.

In a 1948 paper presented at the Invitational Conference on Testing Problems, I urged the abandonment of these statistical methods of validating test items as well as the practice of discarding items simply because they were either passed by all or failed by all. I urged that our goal should be measurement, not differentiation. Measurement may or may not result in differentiation. In the discussion which followed my presentation, Dr. Durost, one of the authors of the *Metropolitan Achievement Tests,* said:

I wonder if Mr. Buros realized—I am sure he must— that if we were to follow his plan we also would have to throw out all of the methods of interpreting test scores which we now use. If we had no gains in score from grade to grade, obviously we could have no grade equivalents....If we were to abandon the procedures which we currently use....we would have tests....which would be very unreliable....If most of our items did not differentiate between grade groups, being in effect non-functioning items, the range of scores on our tests would be seriously restricted, reliabilities would be very seriously lowered, and I wonder what publisher would venture to issue a test for use in schools under such circumstances.

Although I think that my criticisms of item validation procedures will not be acceptable to my fellow workers, I hope that some will give consideration and study to my suggestions. If we make it our goal to measure rather than to differentiate, most of our methods of constructing tests, measuring repeatability, assessing validity, and interpreting test results will need to be drastically changed.

Testing specialists claim that raw scores on objective tests have no meaning—that they become meaningful only when compared with the scores of other examinees. Unfortunately, authors, publishers and test users—except in the case of criterion-referenced tests—have accepted this view as axiomatic.

Even if a test user wanted to study the raw scores on a test, he frequently would have difficulty digging out this information—in some cases, it would be impossible. In most instances, I am sure that test authors and publishers do not want test users to study and use raw scores. Raw score equivalents to normed scores are likely to be disquieting to test users. It is much more comforting to consider normed scores which effectively cover up when little learning has taken place. We have allowed normed scores to serve as an effective barrier between test users and the achievement measured. Norms enable us to make certain interpretations of test results. Unfortunately, they also make it difficult or impossible to interpret raw scores.

This problem has been aggravated by the rapidly spreading practice of having tests scored by publishers. It becomes especially acute for secure tests which usually are not available for examination by persons wanting to interpret the scores. This is not the sort of information which publishers of secure tests like to reveal. For most secure tests, information on raw scores is confidential, for in-house use only.

I would like to see test authors and publishers go all out in making information available about raw scores both for individuals and items. We did this in the Army Specialized Training achievement testing program in World War II. In that program our interest was in

mean scores of colleges and not in individual scores. We profiled the mean scores of five or six achievement tests on the basis of standard deviation units away from the mean. We then presented for each test a frequency distribution of the college means. Along with each frequency we reported the mean percentage of items estimated to be known by the trainees and the college's percentile rank. These raw scores were most helpful—giving us information about both the college unit and the test.

You may be interested in some other features of the AST examination program. The test items were written by the Personnel Research Section of the Adjutant General's Office assisted by subject specialists in numerous colleges. All items were then sent to about five subject specialists for their criticisms. Item tryouts were not used. Profiled reports were sent to the commanding officers of each college unit. Our greatest concern was that test results would be misinterpreted and misused as bases for evaluating the quality of instruction. We enumerated other factors which could influence results. For example, variations in the quality of trainees received by a unit—this factor was emphasized by profiling Army General Classification Test as well as achievement test scores. Another disturbing factor was caused by variations in the number of failing trainees separated just before the examinations were administered. From the beginning we drew on each profile lines representing the 95 percent sampling limits built around the national means. Profiled points outside of these lines differed significantly at the five percent level from the national mean. Instructions were given for identifying statistically significant differences between the unit's mean scores on various tests. We pointed out that differences between a unit's mean scores and the national means may be statistically significant and yet not be educationally significant. For every test the profile also reported statistics usually found only in a manual: national raw score mean, mean percentage of items known, number of items, working time, reliability coefficient, units tested, trainees tested, and percentage of units with means below the national mean. Since the number of trainees in the units varied a great deal, the magnitude of statistically significant deviations from the national mean varied considerably. Near the end of the program we were experimenting with ways of identifying statistically significant differences which could also be considered educationally or socially significant. Unfortunately, then as now, statistical significance is mistaken for educational significance. This confusion has resulted in a great deal of sloppy thinking not only in testing but in all areas of research in the behavioral sciences.

Now to get back to my discussion of raw scores. I would like to see recording of normed scores on achievement tests—as well as some other tests—replaced by compound scores consisting of either two or three parts written as one continuous number except for the use of parentheses. Two-part scores should consist of the normed score and, immediately following in parentheses, the percentage of items estimated to be known. Three-part scores, which I prefer, might add the obtained percentile rank immediately following the closing parenthesis.

I would further publicize raw scores, expressed as estimated percentage of items known, by presenting unaltered frequency distributions of raw scores for the various normative groups along with means and standard deviations. I would also indicate the minimum raw score an examinee would need in order to reject at the five percent level the hypothesis that the items were answered at random.

Item scores might consist of two parts only: estimated percentage of items known and, immediately following in parentheses, the percentile rank.

The introduction of compound scores should be relatively simple in this computerized age. The consequences might well prove revolutionary. Their use will assist in interpreting and evaluating more effectively the scores of both examinees and items. We shall be forced to study tests more thoroughly in order to better understand the results. A small raw score improvement from one grade to the next will cause us to reconsider the significance of developmental progress expressed as one grade unit. If information of this kind were available for ACT and ETS college-level proficiency examinations, it would probably have a profound effect upon the choice of cutoff scores for granting college credit. The wide use of estimated percentage-of-items-known scores for both individuals and items will help to shift our emphasis from differentiation to measurement.

Publishers of secure tests not commercially available have been very good about making their confidential tests available to persons invited to review the tests for *The Mental Measurements Yearbook*. I deeply appreciate the wholehearted cooperation which we have received from the American College Testing Program, College Entrance Examination Board, Educational Testing Service, and other organizations. Nevertheless, I would like to point out that the information available to permit an adequate assessment to be made of these secure tests is quite unsatisfactory. Although our reviewers generally receive some in-house material, which is not available to other educators and psychologists, even this material is inadequate.

I would like to recommend that every secure test be accompanied by a manual describing the planning, construction, standardization, reliability, and validity of the test. Since the tests themselves can be examined only under highly restricted conditions, if at all, it becomes of greatest importance that detailed information be provided for secure tests. The important role which these tests play in influencing the lives of the examinees is much greater than the role of the commercially available tests. Yet far less information is available on these secure tests and, to make matters worse, much of the information which the publisher does possess is considered to be confidential—for in-house use only. If detailed information were made available simultaneously with the publication of tests, not only would educators and testing specialists be in a better position to evaluate the tests and to interpret the results more intelligently, but the publishers would be impelled to construct better tests, pointing out both their strengths and weaknesses.

Let me mention two important programs as examples of tests which provide far too little information. These programs are probably no worse than many of the other programs of secure tests. I refer to the College-Level Examination Program and the ACT Proficiency Examination Program, both of which provide examinations to permit students to receive college credit without taking the relevant college courses. The CLEP program, initiated thirteen years ago, is one of the most significant developments in testing in recent years. It has received extraordinarily wide publicity—it is regularly advertised on television, yet there is relatively little research data on the validity of these tests. Roadblocks have been placed between the test user and what the scores mean.

Only confidential house papers present raw score distributions. Such information should be routinely presented for every achievement test. The corresponding ACT PEP program is especially poor in the information it provides. I find it discouraging that two outstanding not-for-profit testing organizations have not provided test users with the hard data to permit them to assess more adequately the usefulness of the tests for the assignment of college credit.

I would like to repeat a statement which I made forty-two years ago:

Today it is practically impossible for a competent test technician or test consumer to make a thorough appraisal of the construction, validation, and use of most standardized tests being published because of the limited amount of trustworthy information supplied by test publishers and authors....If testing is to be of maximum value to schools, test authors and publishers must give more adequate information....It would be advantageous ....if test publishers would construct only one-fourth to one-half as many tests....and use the time saved for presenting the detailed information needed by test consumers.

Unfortunately, although some progress has been made, my 1935 complaint is equally applicable today to the majority of existing tests— and especially so for secure tests.

In 1924, Giles M. Ruch, an associate professor at this university, wrote one of the earliest books on the construction of new-type tests. In the preface to that volume, Ernest Horn, also of this university, pointed out that although standard tests performed a very useful service they had serious limitations. Standard tests rarely correspond closely to local instructional programs, they are greatly influenced by instructional materials closely resembling the test items, and they can not be used to measure the attainment of specific growth over short periods of time, such as a day, week, or month.

Professor Horn's comments are as appropriate today as they were 53 years ago. Not only should we devote more time to the construction of local examinations, but we should provide schools with commercially published tests which can be more easily adapted to local educational programs.

I suggest that achievement test batteries be of two types: tests for assessing the performance of groups and tests for assessing the performance of individuals. I shall refer to these two categories as group tests and individual tests, where the words "group" and "individual" refer to the targets being evaluated.

The group tests should be designed to mea-sure the achievement of schools, school systems, or other groups having common objectives and learning environments. Since our interest is in groups rather than individuals, each test could be quite short, requiring very little time to administer. In situations where the groups are fairly large, the tests could be subdivided into much shorter subtests with no student taking more than one subtest. The time now required to administer an achievement battery, sometimes as much as seven hours, could be reduced to thirty minutes. With group tests such as these, schools would be able to compare their performance on item, part, and total scores as well as their frequency distributions with those of normative groups. In addition to covering objectives common to most school systems, these group tests could be supplemented by subtests covering objectives not now included in standardized tests. The use of short group tests, each taken by only a fraction (say, one-fifth) of the students will greatly reduce the costs in time and money of testing. It will stimulate test publishers to give greater attention to problems involving group measurement and the interpretation of group results. A much wider range of objectives and curricular analyses could be covered. Relatively simple norms, raw scores means, frequency distributions of raw score means, both for total scores and item scores, would replace the complicated systems of norms now provided for individuals. I would not, however, limit the normative data to the particular grade for which the test was designed. The same normative data should be presented for the grades immediately below and above the target grade. The presentation of this comparative information for adjacent grades is especially important in the interpretation of tests built for measurement rather than for differentiation.

As is true of all achievement tests, scores on the group tests would be not only a function of what a student has learned, but also a function of the closeness with which the test covers the instructional objectives and curricular offerings of a local school system. Although these learning and curricular effects are confounded, I would like to experiment with ways of considering each of the effects separately. Let me suggest one way in which this might be done.

Let all normative groups provide information on the extent to which the test specifications and the test items are appropriate locally. Checklists could be provided requiring school officials or committees of teachers to classify each objective and each item into four categories for each grade: (1) taught in an earlier grade, (2) taught in the target grade, (3) taught in later grades, and (4) not taught in any grade. Item score norms might be presented for each of these categories. Other questions might well be directed to the importance of an objective or item. The normative groups might also be asked to indicate local objectives not covered by the group tests. Statistics such as these would enable school systems to compare both the performance of their students and the extent to which the objectives and content of the tests coincided with their local objective and instructional programs.

The use of different tests for measuring groups and individuals would permit school systems to abandon national norms altogether for individuals and to adapt and supplement commercially purchased tests and processing services to better meet local needs. Local norms would be far more meaningful than national norms. I would use compound scores consisting of a percentile rank within grade and the raw score (corrected for guessing) as a percentage of the possible score. Purchased tests could be supplemented by locally prepared examinations and integrated into the testing program.

Since there would be no national norms and statistical procedures for selecting items would not be used, the costs of final tryouts and normative testing would be eliminated. Local school systems would be free to adapt the tests in various ways to better meet their needs. Items could be dropped by not scoring and new items added in locally constructed tests. Time limits and administration procedures could be changed if desired. School systems would become more actively involved in the choice, study, adaptation, and supplementation of commercially purchased tests and processing services. Test authors and publishers should give local school systems assistance in formulating testing programs which are adapted to the local situation.

By better meeting local needs, publishers are likely to sell more tests to serve as a flexible core of the local testing program. Since computers would be necessary to provide local norms and reports for both students and test items, the data processing services of publishers would be needed more than ever.

I shall not take the time to enumerate further the advantages of using national norms for group measurement and local norms for individual measurement. If a school system were forced to choose only one of these two kinds of tests, I would have no hesitation in recommending the locally adapted and supplemented test with local norms.

PART 2

SOME COMMENTS ON TEST RELIABILITY [3, 4]

DURING the 25-year period ending in 1965, I did considerable research on test reliability and related statistical problems in testing. Although the results of my research were not published, I did lecture on my findings and circulated freely a great deal of mimeographed material to many testing specialists. I know that my thinking has influenced some of the leading writers on the subject. Nevertheless, I think that the scope and value of my wide-ranging schematization should be more widely known.

I started out from scratch by setting up four parametric models, each representing a commonly used score: standardized deviation scores, deviation scores, ranks or percentile ranks, and absolute scores. From these four models, I have been able to derive a great

[3] Reprinted from *Psychological Reports* 42(3):1023–9 Je '78.
[4] The second part of a lecture presented at Iowa City, Iowa, March 28, 1977, to a special seminar in education sponsored by the College of Education, University of Iowa and the American College Testing Program.

variety of formulas for reliability coefficients and error variances and to present new insights into their meaning.

Fifty years ago, all competent testing specialists agreed that parallel-form reliability coefficients were best and that split-half and test-retest reliabilities should be used only when parallel forms were not available. Furthermore, they set up high standards for minimum within-grade reliabilities for various purposes—generally .90 and higher for the measurement of individuals.

As editor of the *Mental Measurements Yearbooks,* I have had the opportunity to study the data on reliability and its interpretation in thousands of test manuals. Despite the tremendous literature which has been generated over the past fifty years, it is my considered conviction that we have gone backwards both in the techniques we use and in the standards of reliability we set for various uses of tests. If currently published tests presented the kind of information on reliability recommended and used by Kelley in 1927, we would have more trustworthy information on reliability than we now possess as well as a greater concern about the pervasiveness of errors in all of our measures. I hope that my views will not be shrugged off as those of an old testing specialist longing for the good old days of his youth. Although I have a great respect for the contributions of Spearman, Kelley, Otis, and others responsible for most of what we knew about test reliability in 1927, much of that theory now needs to be discarded.

Our emphasis on differentiation,[5] rather than measurement, and our use of correlational techniques to measure reliability are twin evils which aggravate and reinforce each other. Insofar as reliability is concerned, we would be better off had correlational measures never been developed. Since correlations are measures of covariation, they are applicable only when some differentiation has taken place, although they do not tell us how much. Their use as measures of reliability has caused us to develop and use statistical methods of selecting the most dis-

criminating test items with the result that we exaggerate differences among examinees and between grades. Although there is no need to use correlational measures of reliability, their use is so deeply rooted in our thinking that I doubt whether they will ever be discarded. The best I can hope for is that we better understand what the various measures are, their uses, and their limitations.

In order to identify and clarify the relationships among the numerous correlational reliability measures now in use, I have introduced some new terms which, if generally adopted, would help us to think more clearly about reliability.

All reliability coefficients are estimates of the *differential coincidence* of one of the following four kinds of scores: (1) Deviations from the mean; I shall refer to these as devscores. (2) Deviations from the mean expressed in standard deviation units, commonly called *z* scores or standard scores; I shall refer to these as stanscores. (3) Ranks or percentile ranks; I shall refer to these as ranscores. (4) Absolute scores which I shall call abscores. Abscores include all scores, such as normed scores, where our interest is in their absolute value.

Depending on how they are computed, reliability coefficients may be divided into two categories, those which are actually observed and computed directly, and those which are estimated by extrapolation procedures such as the Spearman-Brown formula. I shall refer to this second category as extrapolated reliability coefficients. It is obvious that extrapolated correlations are less trustworthy than observed correlations—extrapolation requires assumptions which may or may not be true. I shall also use the adjective "extrapolated" in referring to error variances obtained either by extrapolation or from extrapolated reliability coefficients.

Frequently, reliability coefficients are based upon one kind of score and then applied to another kind of score or, in the case of an abscore, to a different kind of abscore. I shall refer to such reliability coefficients and the accompanying error variances as "conjectural" to indicate their shaky basis.

The choice of a correlational measure depends on what scores we want to be differentially repeatable. Is our interest in abscores, devscores, ranscores, or stanscores? Our failure to make these distinctions is responsible for most of our misinterpretations and mislabeling of reliability

[5] In the first part of my Iowa paper, I pointed out that our methods of validating achievement test items wrongly assume that differentiation—rather than measurement *per se*—constitutes measurement. I wrote 40 years ago "that such methods of statistically validating achievement tests insidiously tend to strengthen the status quo, to impede curricular progress, to perpetuate our present grade classification, to differentiate rather than to measure, to conceal unlearning, and to give an illusory sense of continuous learning from grade to grade." If we measure with a given degree of precision, differentiation may or may not take place. Our goal should be measurement, not differentiation.

coefficients. Let me briefly indicate the correlational techniques appropriate for each of the four kinds of scores.

The terms abcorrelation, devcorrelation, rancorrelation, and stancorrelation will be used to indicate that the correlational measures are, respectively, measures of the differential repeatability of abscores, devscores, ranscores, and stanscores.

Stancorrelation, a generalization of the product-moment correlation coefficient, although widely used, is only appropriate as a measure of differential repeatability of stanscores. Stancorrelation will equal unity when every examinee has the same stanscore on both tests. Extrapolated stancorrelations, e.g., extrapolated from split-half correlations, are appropriate only if we are interested in the total or mean of a set of stanscores. This is rarely ever the case.

Abcorrelation, the intraclass correlation between abscores, is the appropriate measure of differential repeatability when our interest is in abscores. This is the correlational measure which should be used whenever we are interested in normed scores and have parallel forms. The extrapolated abcorrelation based upon item scores should be used whenever our interest is in total raw scores and we have only one form of a test. When the item scores are either zero or one, the abcorrelation is a measure of the differential repeatability of the item scores and the extrapolated abcorrelation is the Kuder-Richardson Formula 21. Although the contrary is commonly believed to be true, K-R 21 is a better measure than K-R 20.

Devcorrelation, the intraclass correlation between deviations from the mean, is the appropriate measure to use when our interest is in devscores. The extrapolated devcorrelation is Cronbach's alpha; when X is zero or one, it is the K-R 20; and when the correlation is between split-halves, it is the Otis-Rulon Formula.

My schematization of correlational techniques used in the measurement of differential repeatability is far more comprehensive than can be described here. I might add that all the correlations across test units have corresponding correlations across examinees—correlations which are measures of the differential repeatability of the four kinds of scores for test units. These across-examinee correlations can be used in profile analysis and the study of item and test difficulties.

Leading writers on test reliability have played an important role in adding to our misinformation. Extrapolated correlations such as the K-R formulas are mistakenly described as measures of homogeneity and internal consistency. Except in very rare instances, extrapolated correlations such as the K-R formulas approach one as the number of items increases. Obviously, the addition of more items does not increase their homogeneity. The nonextrapolated correlation, however, may be used as a measure of the differential repeatability of item scores. It should never be interpreted to mean that the items are measuring essentially the same ability or trait. A high correlation among items—say, .10 to .40—can be obtained from an obviously heterogeneous group of items. The correlation among items refers only to the differential repeatability of the item scores and nothing else.

Almost without exception, reliability measures such as the coefficient of stability and the coefficient of equivalence have been incorrectly used. These names imply that they are measures of the coincidence or repeatability of normed scores, that is, absolute scores. Unfortunately, the wrong correlational procedure, the product-moment correlation or stancorrelation, is used to measure stability and equivalence. As every student of testing knows but generally forgets, product-moment correlations are based upon stanscores—they are unaffected by differences in means and standard deviations. They are appropriate only for determining the differential repeatability of stanscores. All three editions of the *Test Standards* have played an important role in the dissemination of these erroneous concepts. Incidentally, no correlational technique can provide information about the repeatability or precision of scores generally, that is, regardless of the degree or absence of differentiation among examinees.

I have already mentioned my deep concern about the reinforcing interaction which has existed for the past 50 years and more between statistical methods of validating test items and the use of reliability measures which place a premium on differentiation. To make matters worse, Kuder and Richardson's 1937 discoveries of simple methods of estimating test reliability from item interrelationships have largely driven out better methods such as parallel-form coefficients. Since extrapolated correlations based upon internal analysis of a single test are reliability estimates for total raw scores only, their applicability to normed scores must always be described as conjectural. The use of extrapolated-conjectural correlations in making estimates of error variances is even more questionable. Test authors and publishers seem reluctant to present parallel-form reliabilities even when they have parallel forms. When such reliabilities are presented, they frequently are based on raw scores using the wrong correlational measure.

I would like to urge publishers and authors to provide reliability data for all of their normed scores. If they also use raw scores, which I recommend, reliability data should be provided for them too. In determining the reliability of normed scores, the abcorrelation should generally be applied to the normed scores on parallel tests. If only one form of a test is to be published, I suggest that it consist of two separately timed parallel subtests. Norms should be determined independently for each subtest and for the total test. Extrapolated correlations could then be estimated for each normed score.

Although every student of testing knows that correlational measures of reliability are functions both of the test and the examinees, we often forget this in practice. Fifty years ago, testing specialists pointed out that reliability coefficients should be based upon groups similar in variability to those in local school systems. This usually meant correlations were reported for each grade along with means and standard deviations to permit test users to decide whether the reliability measures were appropriate for local use. Many years later, some of our best students recommended that all reliability coefficients for specific grades be within school systems since the variability within schools is generally less than the variability in the national norming group.

It is discouraging that most authors and publishers fail to provide adequate data on the reliability of their tests. I shall enumerate some of the obvious shortcomings with respect to reliability: no data whatsoever reported, correlations based on wide grade range, and means and standard deviations not reported. These failings are bad enough, but at least they are obvious to many test users. Other shortcomings are not so obvious. I have already mentioned the use of the wrong correlational measures and the absence of reliability data on normed scores.

Some of our best publishers base their within-grade reliability coefficients on samples from the more variable normative populations. Finally, even our best publishers generally gloss over low reliabilities either by silence, mild cautions, or rationalizations. There are no longer any suggested standards of what reliabilities should be for various test uses. Apparently, the standards are whatever one obtains.

As noted earlier, correlational procedures are not necessary in studying test reliability. Error variances represent a more general approach. I shall not say more than a few words about my thinking in this area.

For every correlational measure there is a corresponding error variance. I refer to these as generalized error variances. A specific error variance can be computed for every examinee. A generalized error variance is the mean of the specific error variances. *The assignment of a generalized error variance to an individual examinee would have a parallel if we assigned the mean score to each examinee but with less dire consequences.* Error variances corresponding to conjectural reliability coefficients are also conjectural and consequently difficult to interpret.

Some concept such as true score must necessarily be used in interpreting error variances, whereas this is not the case in interpreting correlational measures of reliabilities. Error variances are estimates of the differential precision of our measuring instruments insofar as variable errors of measurement are concerned. Error variances provide no information about constant and systematic errors of measurement. Observed scores are made up of three components: the examinee's true score, a systematic error, and a variable error. Systematic errors are especially serious whenever we use norms. Fifty years ago, there was considerable interest in systematic or constant errors; today, they are rarely mentioned. Unfortunately, error variances give us no information about systematic errors.

The term "true score" needs to be replaced by the use of more definitive terms which distinguish between the two kinds of errors. I suggest the use of target parameters and asymptotic scores. The target parameter is the score which would be obtained if neither systematic nor variable errors were present. We are unable to make point or interval estimates of target parameters. The asymptotic score is the limiting value obtained as the variable errors of measurement approach zero. The asymptotic score plus the indeterminate systematic error equal the target parameter. Both point and interval estimates refer only to asymptotic scores and variable errors, never to the target parameters which would also involve systematic errors.

The point and interval estimates currently being made are not estimates of target parameters or the so-called true scores. Instead, they are estimates of asymptotic scores which may differ a great deal from the target parameters. When I first advocated the use of interval estimates about thirty years ago, I recommended the use of 95 percent interval estimates. The current usage of 68 percent interval estimates seems much too low to me; their use means that on the average, 32 percent of the interval estimates made for a group of examinees are wrong. Incidentally, "interval estimates" is a more appropriate term than "confidence limits" or "confidence interval." I recommend that the term "point estimate" also be used.

After this lengthy discussion of error variances, I should warn you that our repeated use of the same error variance is not supported by statistical theory. Even so, I think that they are better than nothing until we can devise more adequate measures. I have been thinking of various alternatives. In the case of raw scores consisting of item counts, the binomial distribution and its normal curve approximations yield point and interval estimates. Tests might be constructed in ways which will permit better estimates of specific error variances. If we were to make much greater use of raw scores and their linear transforms, it would greatly simplify the estimation of test reliability.

In summary, my major comments on reliability are: (1) In studying the repeatability of test results, we should use the appropriate procedure for the particular kind of score we are interested in. (2) We should discontinue applying conjectural measures of reliability to normed scores. This means that we must make more use of parallel-form and test-retest measures of reliability. (3) We should adopt terminology which describes accurately the four types of scores, correlational measures, and error variances as well as the use of the adjectives "extrapolated" and "conjectural" for reliability coefficients and error variances. (4) We should think of correlational reliabilities as measures of the differential repeatability of a particular kind of score. (5) We should make greater use of specific error variances and other techniques in determining the precision of individual measurements.

Periodical Directory and Index

References are to test and book entry numbers under which review excerpts from the given journal will be found, not to page numbers. Book entry numbers begin with the letter B. The name and address of the editor and the review editor are given for each journal. Test references are not indexed.

ALBERTA J ED RES—The Alberta Journal of Educational Research. Published by The University of Alberta. 4 issues; vol. 23 started Mr '77; Can $8 per year; $2.50 per issue; Henry W. Hodysh, editor, Faculty of Education, The University of Alberta, Edmonton, Alta., Canada T6G 2G5: B81, B143

Am J Mental Def—American Journal of Mental Deficiency. Published by the American Association on Mental Deficiency. 6 issues; vol. 82 started Jl '77; $40 per year; $8 per issue; H. Carl Haywood, editor, Box 503, Peabody College, Nashville, Tenn. 37203; Irv Bialer, book review editor, New York Department of Mental Hygiene, Long Island Research Institute, Health Sciences Center, T-10, Stony Brook, N.Y. 11794: 500, B148, B157, B245, B318, B320, B557, B573, B581

Am J Psychiatry—The American Journal of Psychiatry. Official journal of the American Psychiatric Association. 12 issues; vol. 134 started Ja '77; $18 per year; $2.25 per issue; Francis J. Braceland, editor, 1700 Eighteenth St. N.W., Washington, D.C. 20009: 546, 649, B25, B27, B122, B171, B178, B280, B302-3, B313, B409, B429, B519, B525

Arith Teach—The Arithmetic Teacher. An official journal of the National Council of Teachers of Mathematics. 8 issues (omitting Je, Jl, Ag, S); vol. '77 started S '77; $17 per year; $2.50 per issue; Jane M. Hill, managing editor, 1906 Association Drive, Reston, Va. 22091: B64, B75

Austral & N Zeal J Psychiatry—Australian and New Zealand Journal of Psychiatry. Official journal of the Royal Australian and New Zealand College of Psychiatrists. 4 issues; vol. 11 started Mr '77; Aus $20 per year; Roger C. Buckle, editor-in-chief; Donald Buckle, review editor; 107 Rathdowne St., Carlton, Victoria, 3053, Australia: B172

Austral J Psychol—Australian Journal of Psychology. Published by the Australian Psychological Society. 3 issues; vol. 29 started Ap '77; Aus $7.50 ($8.50) per year; Aus $3.50 per issue; R. H. Day, editor, Department of Psychology, Monash University, Melbourne, 3168, Australia; D. McNicol, book review editor, Department of Psychology, University of New South Wales, Kensington, N.S.W. 2033, Australia: B25, B74, B81, B83, B117, B119, B125, B148, B258, B511, B566

Austral Psychologist—Australian Psychologist. Published for the Australian Psychological Society. 3 issues; vol. 12 started Mr '77; Aus $9 per year; Aus $3 per issue; George E. Kearney, editor, University of Queensland, St. Lucia, Qd. 4067, Aus.; Leon Mann, book review editor, Flinders University of South Australia, Bedford Park, S. A. 5042, Australia: B71, B302-3

B BRIT PSYCHOL SOC—Bulletin of the British Psychological Society. 12 issues; vol. 30 started Ja '77; £6 per year; 50p per issue; John Wilding (Bedford College, University of London, Regent's Park, London NW1 4NS, England) and Norman Worrall, (Institute of Education, University of London, Malet St., London WC1E 7HS, England), editors: 649, B210, B256, B259, B336, B418, B443

B Menninger Clinic—Bulletin of the Menninger Clinic. Published by The Menninger Foundation. 6 issues; vol. 41 started Ja '77; $20 per year; $4 per issue; Sydney Smith, editor-in-chief; Virginia T. Eicholtz, managing editor, Box 829, Topeka, Kan. 66601: B83

Behav Res & Ther—Behavior Research and Therapy: An International Multi-disciplinary Journal. 24 issues; vol. 15 started Ja '77; $56 per year; H. J. Eysenck, editor-in-chief; D. Hemsley, book review editor; Institute of Psychiatry, Department of Psychology, DeCrespigny Park Rd., Denmark Hill, London, SE5 8AZ, England: 685, B83, B243

Brit J Dis Commun—The British Journal of Disorders of Communication. The Journal of the College of Speech Therapists, London. 2 issues; vol. 12 started Ap '77; £6 per year; B. Byers Brown, editor, Department of Audiology and Education of the Deaf, University of Manchester, England: 959

Brit J Ed Psychol—The British Journal of Educational Psychology. Published for the British Psychological Society and the Association of Teachers in Colleges and Departments of Education. 3 issues; vol. 47 started F '77; £8 per year; £3 per issue; N. J. Entwistle, editor, Department of Educational Research, University of Lancaster, Lancaster, England: 959, B81, B88, B117, B119, B268, B311, B313, B330, B336, B443, B479, B495, B510, B512, B536, B548, B569

Brit J Ed Studies—British Journal of Educational Studies. 3 issues; vol. 25 started F '77; £11.50 ($23) per year; Margaret B. Sutherland, executive editor, Education Department, University of Leeds, Leeds 2, England; R. Wilson, book review editor, School of Education, University of Reading, Reading, Berkshire, England: B81, B83, B234, B246, B248, B424

Brit J Psychiatry—The British Journal of Psychiatry. Published by the authority of the Royal College of Psychiatrists. 12 issues in 2 volumes; vol. 130 started Ja '77, vol. 131 started Jl '77; £55 per year; £6 per issue; J. L. Crammer, editor, 17 Belgrave Square, London SW1X 8PG, England: 208, B28, B81, B121, B148, B172, B268, B302, B519

Brit J Psychol—The British Journal of Psychology. A publication of the British Psychological Society. 4 issues; vol. 68 started F '77; £20 ($49.50) per year; £6 ($14) per issue; A. D. B. Clarke, editor; D. C. Kendrick, book review editor; Department of Psychology, The University, Hull, HU6 7RX, England: 649, B157, B209, B211, B247, B268-9, B280, B296, B318, B466

Brit J Social & Clin Psychol—The British Journal of Social and Clinical Psychology. A publication of the British Psychological Society. 4 issues; vol. 16 started F '77; £19 ($47.50) per year; £6 ($14) per issue; Halla Beloff, social psychology editor, Department of Psychology, University of Edinburgh, 60 Pleasance, Edinburgh EH8 9TJ, Scotland; H. R. Beech, clinical psychology editor, Department of Psychiatry, Withington Hospital, West Didsbury, Manchester M20 8LR, England; Vernon Hamilton, social psychology book review editor, Whiteknights Park, The University, Reading, Berks, England; Brian Sheffield, clinical psychology book review editor, Department of Psychiatry, Withington Hospital, West Didsbury, Manchester M20 8LR, England: B55, B76, B83, B97, B178, B280, B284, B452, B463, B551

DEVELOP MED & CHILD NEUROL—Developmental Medicine and Child Neurology. The official journal of the American Academy for Cerebral Palsy. 6 issues; vol. 19 started F '77; £18 ($44.75) per year; Martin Bax, senior editor, 5A Netherhall Gardens, London NW3 5RN, England: 810, 873, 959, B83

ED & PSYCHOL MEAS—Educational and Psychological Measurement: A Quarterly Journal Devoted to the Development and Application of Measures of Individual Differences. 4 issues; vol. 37 started sp '77; $20 per year; 5 per issue; W. Scott Gehman, editor; Robert D. Sawyer, book review editor; Box 6907, College Station, Durham, N.C. 27708: B17, B21-3, B54, B57, B59, B63, B68, B81, B83, B94, B97-8, B109, B121, B139, B147, B157, B176, B178, B198-9, B201, B206, B217, B233, B256, B264, B275, B280, B290, B293, B315, B318, B324, B326, B410, B413, B420, B434, B471, B513, B517, B519-20, B531, B534, B537, B541-3, B550, B555, B566-7, B571, B582

Ed Leadership—Educational Leadership: Journal of the Association for Supervision and Curriculum De-velopment, NEA. 8 issues (omitting Je, Jl, Ag, S); vol. 35 started O '77; $10 per year; $2 per issue; Robert R. Leeper, editor, 1701 K St. N.W., Washington, D.C. 20006: B81, B83

J AM STAT ASSN—Journal of the American Statistical Association. 4 issues; vol. 72 started Mr '77 (no. 359); $30 per year; $7.50 per issue; Steven E. Fienberg, coordinating and applications editor, University of Minnesota, St. Paul, Minn. 55108; Morris H. DeGroot, theory and methods editor, Carnegie-Mellon University, Pittsburgh, Pa. 15213; S. James Press, book review editor, University of California, Riverside, Calif. 92521: B119

J Biol Psychol—Journal of Biological Psychology. 2 issues; vol. 19 started Jl '77; $2.50 per issue; James V. McConnell, editor, Mental Health Research Institute, University of Michigan, Ann Arbor, Mich. 48107; Jon D. Swartz, book review editor, LAB 411, University of Texas-Permian, Odessa, Tex. 79762: 598, B77, B81, B83, B175, B553

J Child Psychol & Psychiatry—The Journal of Child Psychology and Psychiatry and Allied Disciplines. Official organ of the Association for Child Psychology and Psychiatry. 4 issues; vol. 18 started F '77; $50 per year; $9 per issue; L. A. Hersov (Children's Department, The Maudsley Hospital, Denmark Hill, London S.E.5 8AZ, England), and M. Berger (Department of Child Development and Educational Psychology, University of London, Institute of Education, Bedford Way, London WC1H OAL, England), editors: 810

J Ed Meas—Journal of Educational Measurement. Official publication of the National Council on Measurement in Education, Inc. 4 issues (sp, su, f, w); vol. 14 started sp '77; $15 per year; $4 per issue; Lorrie Shepard, editor, College of Education, University of Colorado, Boulder, Colo. 80302; George F. Madaus, review editor, McGuinn Hall, Boston College, Chestnut Hill, Mass. 02167: 7A, 29, 47, 70, 232, 244, 485, 730, 1028, B8, B17, B21, B28, B31, B36, B53-4, B63, B68, B81, B83, B105, B139, B182, B195, B202, B229, B231-2, B254, B288, B294, B297, B299, B314, B326, B333, B414, B420-1, B434-5, B467, B517, B520, B533-4, B564

J Ed Res—The Journal of Educational Research. 6 issues; vol. 70 started S-O '77; $15 per year; $3 per issue; Lynn E. Davie, Douglas R. Gross, Harold E. Mitzel, Willard E. North, Wayne Otto, and James D. Raths, executive editors, 4000 Albemarle St. N.W., Suite 510, Washington, D.C. 20016: B253, B278, B339, B451, B509

J Employ Counsel—Journal of Employment Counseling. Published by National Employment Counselors Association. 4 issues; vol. 14 started Mr '77; $10 per year; $2.50 per issue; David Meyer, editor, Oakland University, Rochester, Mich. 48063: 491

J Higher Ed—The Journal of Higher Education. Published in affiliation with the American Association for Higher Education. 6 issues; vol. 48 started Ja '77; $14 per year; $3 per issue; Robert J. Silverman, editor, 2070 Neil Ave., Columbus, Ohio 43210: B333-4

J Learn Dis—Journal of Learning Disabilities. 10 issues (combined issues: Je-Jl, Au-S); vol. 10 started Ja '77; $16 per year; Gerald Senf, editor-in-chief; 101 East Ontario St., Chicago, Ill. 60611: 24, 171, 305, 434-5, 485, 546, 601, 757, 775, 779, 938; 956, 967, B83, B160, B205, B266, B527, B545

J Marriage & Family—Journal of Marriage and the Family. Published by the National Council on Family Relations. 4 issues; vol. 39 started F '77; $20 per year; $5 per issue; Felix M. Berardo, editor, 1219 University Ave. S.E., Minneapolis, Minn. 55414: 338

J Mental Def Res—Journal of Mental Deficiency Research. Published by the National Society for Mentally Handicapped Children. 4 issues; vol. 21 started Mr '77; £10 ($30) per year; £2.50 ($7.50) per issue; B. W. Richards, editor, St. Lawrence's Hospital, Caterham, Surrey CR3 5YA, England; Helen Lang-Brown, book review editor, 22 Methuen Park, London, N10 2JS, England: B336

J Occup Psychol—Journal of Occupational Psychology. Published for the British Psychological Society. Title was *Occupational Psychology (q.v.)* through vol. 47, '74. 4 issues; vol. 50 started Mr '77; £15 ($34.50) per year; £5 ($11) per issue; B. Shackel, editor, Department of Human Sciences, University of Technology, Loughborough, Leics., England: B84

J Pers Assess—Journal of Personality Assessment. Official organ of the Society for Personality Assessment, Inc. 6 issues; vol. 41 started F '77; $22.50 per year; $3.75 per issue; Walter G. Klopfer, editor, 7840 S.W. 51st Ave., Portland, Ore. 97219; Max R. Reed, book review editor, 6201 S.W. Capitol Highway, Portland, Ore. 97201: 566, 598, 641, 873, 956, B13, B26-7, B38, B41-2, B46, B76-7, B81, B83, B89, B121-2, B130, B146, B150-1, B163, B175-6, B229, B258, B261, B268, B270, B273, B278, B289, B302, B308, B323, B428, B441, B470-1, B508, B551, B560, B577, B579, B581

J Psychosom Res—Journal of Psychosomatic Research. 6 issues; vol. 21 started Ja '77; $76 per year; Denis Leigh, editor-in-chief, The Maudsley Hospital, Denmark Hill, London S.E.5 8AZ, England: 649, B303, B429

J Read—Journal of Reading. A publication of the International Reading Association, Inc. 8 issues (omitting Je, Jl, Ag, S); vol. 21 started O '77; $15 per year; $2 per issue; Janet Ramage Binkley, editor, 800 Barksdale Road, Newark, Del. 19711: 740, 761, 779-80, 787, 814, B51, B112, B454

J Res Music Ed—Journal of Research in Music Education. A publication of the Society for Research in Music Education of the Music Educators National Conference. 4 issues (sp, su, f, w); vol. 25 started sp '77; $10 per year; $3 per issue; Robert G. Petzold, editor, 5545 Humanities Bldg., University of Wisconsin, Madison, Wisc. 53706: B563

J Sch Psychol—Journal of School Psychology. 4 issues; vol. 15 started sp '77; $35 per year; Beeman N. Philips, editor, College of Education, Department of Educational Psychology, University of Texas, Austin, Tex. 78712: 34, 202. 223, 431, 438, 625, 691, 757, 779, B25-6, B42, B130, B171, B471

J Spec Ed—The Journal of Special Education. 4 issues; vol. 11 started sp '77; $18.50 per year; Lester Mann, editor-in-chief, 3515 Woodhaven Road, Philadelphia, Pa. 19154: 24, 34, 203, 293, 439, 445-6, 498, 500, 513, 779, 794, 929, 954, 956

MANAS—Manas: A Journal of Scientific Psychology. 2 issues; vol. 24 started My '77; Rs. 25 ($6) per year; J. M. Ojha, executive editor, 32, Netaji Subhash Marg, New Delhi-110002, India: 546, B76, B81

Meas & Eval Guid—Measurement and Evaluation in Guidance. Published by the Association for Measurement and Evaluation in Guidance, a division of the American Personnel and Guidance Association. 4 issues; vol. 10 started Ap '77; $12 per year; $3.50 per issue; Donald G. Zytowski, editor, Student Counseling Service, Iowa State University, Ames, Iowa 50011; Bert Westbrook, test review editor, North Carolina State University, Raleigh, N.C. 27607; Kemp Mabry, book review editor, Georgia Southern College, Statesboro, Ga., 30458: 22, 178, 210, 219, 232, 485, 712, 730, 989, 991, 995, 997, 1013,

1022-3, 1030-1, B21, B23, B31, B36, B49, B53, B63, B68, B73, B81, B83-4, B94, B117, B148, B194, B221, B229, B231, B265, B312, B318, B326, B328, B452, B469, B471, B513, B517, B527, B531, B538, B543, B550-1, B564, B566, B571, B581-2

Mod Lang J—The Modern Language Journal. Published by The National Federation of Modern Language Teachers Associations, Inc. 6 issues (Ja-F, Mr, Ap, S-O, N, D); vol. 61 started Ja '77; $9 per year; $3 per issue; Charles L. King, editor; Charles W. Stansfield, test review editor; University of Colorado, Boulder, Colo. 80309: 120, 154, 156, 162-3, 167, 170-1, 427

OCCUP PSYCHOL—Occupational Psychology. Title changed to *Journal of Occupational Psychology (q.v.)* beginning with vol. 48, Mr '75: 985, B117, B229, B443

PERCEPT & MOTOR SKILLS—Perceptual and Motor Skills. 6 issues in 2 volumes; vol. 44 started F '77; vol. 45 started Ag '77; $91.40 per year; $20 per issue; R. B. Ammons and C. H. Ammons, editors, Box 9229, Missoula, Mont. 59807: 526, B174, B215, B476

Personnel Psychol—Personnel Psychology: A Journal of Applied Research. 4 issues (sp, su, au, w); vol. 30 started sp '77; $18 per year; $4.50 per issue; Milton D. Hakel, editor, Department of Psychology, The Ohio State University, 404-C West 17th Ave., Columbus, Ohio 43210; Theodore Kunin, book review editor, Psychological Consultant to Industry, 744 Henry W. Oliver Building, Pittsburgh, Pa. 15222: B28, B74, B77, B81, B83-4, B91-2, B100, B120, B123, B135, B147, B263, B332, B427, B468, B561, B575

Phi Delta Kappan—Phi Delta Kappan. 10 issues (omitting Jl, Ag); vol. 59 started S '77: $10 per year; $1.25 per issue; Stanley Elam, editor, Phi Delta Kappa, Inc., Eighth St. and Union Ave., Bloomington, Ind. 47401: B147, B211, B506, B543

Psychol Med—Psychological Medicine: A Journal for Research in Psychiatry and the Allied Sciences. 4 issues; vol. 7 started F '77; £24 ($56) per year; £7 ($16.50) per issue; Michael Shepherd, editor, Institute of Psychiatry, DeCrespigny Park, Denmark Hill, London SE5 8AF, England: B172

Psychol Rep—Psychological Reports. 6 issues in 2 volumes; vol. 40 started F '77; vol. 41 started Ag '77; $91.40 per year; $22 per issue; R. B. Ammons and C. H. Ammons, editors, Box 9229, Missoula, Mont. 59807: 219, 493, 691, B74, B81, B529

Psychol Sch—Psychology in the Schools. 4 issues; vol. 14 started Ja '77; $25 per year; $7.50 per issue; Gerald B. Fuller, editor, Department of Psychology, Central Michigan University, Mt. Pleasant, Mich. 48858: 4, 219, 232, 434, 487, 541, 877, 883, 941, B266, B318, B456

Psychologia Africana—Psychologia Africana. Journal of the National Institute for Personnel Research, South African Council for Scientific and Industrial Research. 1 or 2 issues per year; vol. 17 started F '77; R5 per volume of 3 issues; G. K. Nelson, editor-in-chief; M. A. Stent. managing editor: National Institute for Personnel Research, P. O. Box 10319, Johannesburg, South Africa: B76, B83

READ TEACH—The Reading Teacher. Published by the International Reading Association, Inc. 8 issues (omitting Je, Jl, Ag, S): vol. 30 started O '76; $15 per year: $2 per issue; Janet Ramage Binkley, editor, 800 Barksdale Road, Newark, Del. 19711: 29, 162, 170, 723, 757, 766, 768, 775, 810, B154, B251, B305, B417, B514, B559, B576

Read World—Reading World: The Journal of The College Reading Association. 4 issues; vol. 16 started O '77; $15 per year; $4 per issue; Samuel S. Zeman, editor, Box 462, Shippensburg State College, Shippensburg, Pa. 17257; Daniel T. Fishco, book review editor, Director of Institutional Development, Yavapai College, Prescott, Ariz. 86301: 746, 753, 781, 785, 803, 815, B74, B83

SCH SCI & MATH—School Science and Mathematics. The official journal of the School Science and Mathematics Association, Inc. 8 issues (omitting Je, Jl, Ag, S); vol. 77 started Ja '77; $12 per year; $1.50 per issue; George G. Mallinson, editor, Western Michigan University, Kalamazoo, Mich. 49008: B75, B80, B83

Sci Teach—The Science Teacher: Journal of the National Science Teachers Association. 9 issues (omitting Je, Jl, Ag); vol. 44 started Ja '77; $20 per year; $3.25 per issue; Rosemary Amidei, editor, 1742 Connecticut Ave. N.W., Washington, D.C. 20009: B80, B156

Publishers Directory and Index

References are to test and book entry numbers, not to page numbers. Book entry numbers begin with the letter B. For publishers of both tests and books, test entry numbers are given first.

American Psychological Association, Inc., 1200 Seventeenth St. N.W., Washington, D.C. 20036 : B9

Anhinga Press, Route 2, Box 513, Tallahassee, Fla. 32301 : 956

Appleton-Century-Crofts, 292 Madison Ave., New York, N.Y. 10017 : B577

Arden Press, P.O. Box 844, Huntington Beach, Calif. 92648 : 447, 510, 667, 795

Aronson (Jason), Inc., 59 Fourth Ave., New York, N.Y. 10003 : B159

Associates for Research in Behavior, Inc., The Science Center, 34th & Market Sts., Philadelphia, Pa. 19104 : 1056

Association for Childhood Education International, 3615 Wisconsin Ave. N.W., Washington, D.C. 20016 : B426

Association for Supervision and Curriculum Development, 1701 K St. N.W., Washington, D.C. 20006 : B44

Atheneum Publishers, 122 East 42nd St., New York, N.Y. 10017 : B295

Attwood (Madge), School of Education, University of Michigan, Ann Arbor, Mich. 48104 : 411

Audiotone, 2422 West Holly, Phoenix, Ariz. 85009 : 939

Australian Council for Educational Research, P.O. Box 210, Hawthorn, Vic. 3122, Australia : 89, 91, 174, 221, 562, 632, 696, 714, 738, 861, 1047, 1172, B240, B262, B462

Automated Psychological Assessment, Inc., 1270 Doris Road, Pontiac, Mich. 48057 : 618

BBC PUBLICATIONS, 35 Marylebone High St., London WIM 4AA, England : B430

BFA Educational Media, 2211 Michigan Ave., Santa Monica, Calif. 90406 : 768

Ballinger Publishing Co., 17 Dunster St., Harvard Square, Cambridge, Mass. 02138 : B170

Bardis (Panos D.), Professor of Sociology, University of Toledo, Toledo, Ohio 43606 : 331–2, 334–5, 337–8, 340–1, 350, 353, 357, 413, 464–5, 704, 922

Barnes & Noble Books, Division of Harper & Row Publishers, Inc., 10 East 53rd St., New York, N.Y. 10022 : B151

Basic Books, Inc., 10 East 53rd St., New York, N.Y. 10022 : B56

Batsford (B. T.), Ltd., 4 Fitzhardinge St., Portman Square, London W1H 0AH, England : B284

Behavior Arts Center, 77 Lyons Place, Westwood, N.J. 07675 : 631

Behavior Science Systems, Inc., P.O. Box 1108, Minneapolis, Minn. 55440 : 220

Behavioral Publications, Inc. See Human Sciences Press.

Behaviordelia, Inc., P.O. Box 1044, Kalamazoo, Mich. 49005 : B561

Behaviordyne, Inc., P.O. Box 3689, Stanford, Calif. 94305 : 515, 619

Behaviormetrics Publishing Co., Box 1168, Venice, Calif. 90291 : 534

Belwin-Mills Publishing Corporation, 25 Deshon Drive, Melville, N.Y. 11746 : 92

Berg (Ian), High Lands Adolescent Unit, Scalebor Park, Burley-in-Wharfedale, Ilkley, Yorkshire LS29 7AJ, England : 669

Bienvenu (Millard J.), Sr., 710 Watson Drive, Natchitoches, La. 71457 : 351, 589, 591

Bingham Button Test, 46211 North 125th St., East Lancaster, Calif. 93534 : 207

Bobbs-Merrill Co., Inc. (The), 4300 West 62nd St., Indianapolis, Ind. 46268 : 4, 40, 155, 213, 302, 597, 717, 792–3

Bond Publishing Co., 787 Willett Ave., Riverside, N.J. 02915 : 93

Boston Center for Blind Children, 147 Huntington Ave., Boston, Mass. 02130 : 321

Boyle (Barbara S.), 944 Bryant Ave., Chico, Calif. 95926 : 677

Brador Publications, Inc., Livonia, N.Y. 14487 : 772

Brandon House, Inc., 555 Riverdale Station, New York, N.Y. 10471 : 546

Brigham Young University Press. See Economy Co.

Brook Educational Publishing Ltd., P.O. Box 1171, Guelph, Ont., Canada : 881

Brooks/Cole Publishing Co., Subsidiary of Wadsworth Publishing Co., 555 Abrego St., Monterey, Calif. 93940 : B206, B288, B555

Brown (Wm. C.) Co. Publishers, 2460 Kerper Blvd. Dubuque, Iowa 52001 : 749, B292, B563

Bruce (Martin M.), 340 Oxford Road, New Rochelle, N.Y. 10804 : 1187

Brunner/Mazel, Inc., 19 Union Square West, New York, N.Y. 10003 : 601, B25–7, B70–1, B111, B130, B416, B476

Bureau of Educational Measurements, Emporia Kansas State College, Emporia, Kan. 66801 : 60, 74, 80, 164, 299, 404, 419, 467, 851, 893, 914–5

Bureau of Educational Research and Service, University of Iowa, Iowa City, Iowa 52242 : 97

Burgess Publishing Co., 7108 Ohms Lane, Minneapolis, Minn. 55435 : B275

CAL PRESS, Inc., 76 Madison Ave., New York, N.Y. 10016 : 812

CEMREL, Inc., 3120 Fifty-Ninth St., St. Louis, Mo. 63139 : B202

C.P.S., Inc., Box 83, Larchmont, N.Y. 10538 : 463, 676

CTB/McGraw Hill, Del Monte Research Park, Monterey, Calif. 93940 : 10, 12, 17–8, 33–4, 45, 51, 59, 172, 179, 202, 257, 264, 268, 287, 294, 497, 516, 719, 721, 753, 767, 769, 825, 860, 984, 997, 1019, B185

Caldwell Report, 3122 Santa Monica Blvd., Santa Monica, Calif. 90404 : 620

California Test Bureau. See CTB/McGraw-Hill.

Cambridge University Press, 32 East 57th St., New York, N.Y. 10022 : 649, B570

Camelot Behavioral Systems, P.O. Box 3447, Lawrence, Kan. 66044 : 517

Campus Publishers, 711 North University Ave., Ann Arbor, Mich. 48104 : 85

Careers Research and Advisory Centre. See Hobsons Press (Cambridge) Ltd.

Carroll Publications, 463 East Deerfield Road, Mt. Pleasant, Mich. 48858 : 449

Cassell (Wilfred A.), Alaska Psychiatric Institute, 2900 Providence Ave., Anchorage, Alaska 99504 : 518, 652

Center for Advanced Study in Theoretical Psychology, The University of Alberta, Edmonton, Alta. T6G 2E9 Canada : 653

Center for Applied Linguistics, 1611 North Kent St., Arlington, Va. 22209 : B553

Center for Labor and Management, College of Business Administration, University of Iowa, Iowa City, Iowa 52240 : B200

Center for Research on Utilization of Scientific Knowledge, Institute for Social Research, The University of Michigan, P.O. Box 1248, Ann Arbor, Mich. 48106 : B530

Center for the Study of Evaluation, University of California, Los Angeles, Calif. 90024 : B203–4, B221–7

Center for the Study of Sex Education in Medicine, University of Pennsylvania, 4025 Chestnut St., Suite 210, Philadelphia, Pa. 19104 : 352

Central Iowa Associates, Inc., 1408 Meadowlane Ave., Ames, Iowa 50010 : 524A

Change Magazine, NBW Tower, New Rochelle, N.Y. 10801: B335

Chilton Book Co., Chilton Way, Radnor, Pa. 19089: B281

Chilton/Center for Curriculum Development. See Didier.

Chronicle Guidance Publications, Inc., Moravia, N.Y. 13118: 1004, 1015

Churchill Livingston, 23 Ravelston Terrace, Edinburgh EH4, 3TL, Scotland: 959, B336

Clinical Psychology Publishing Co., Inc., 4 Conant Square, Brandon, Vt. 05733: 604, 872, 980

Coffin Associates, 21 Darling St., Marblehead, Mass. 01945: 318, 909

College and University Press, 263 Chapel St., New Haven, Conn. 06513: B13

College Entrance Examination Board, 888 Seventh Ave., New York, N.Y. 10019: 7, 8–9, 39, 42–4, 46, 48, 61, 64–8, 83, 90, 110, 112–3, 115–9, 126–31, 138–50, 153, 157–61, 182, 199, 254–6, 258–61, 289, 297, 309, 313–4, 364–5, 410, 459–60, 471–5, 479, 739, 824, 831–4, 846–9, 862–4, 886–90, 894–6, 907–8, 910–2, 919, 925, 1041, 1064, 1070–4, 1076–7, 1081–4, 1097–100, 1116–9, B33, B37, B41, B108, B567

Collier-Macmillan Publishers, 35 Red Lion Square, London WC1R 4SG, England: B424

Colorado Department of Education. See Cooperative Accountability Project.

Committee on Diagnostic Reading Tests, Inc., Mountain Home, N.C. 28758: 754

Communication Research Associates, Inc., Box 11012, Salt Lake City, Utah 84111: 949

Conference Board, Inc., 845 Third Ave., New York, N.Y. 10022: B282

Consulting Psychologists Press, Inc., 577 College Ave., Palo Alto, Calif. 94306: 452, 495, 500, 504, 512–4, 519, 521, 525, 531, 548, 550, 555, 557, 572–3, 576, 585, 594–5, 602, 630, 636, 642, 681–4, 700, 706, 713, 807, 871, 882, 964, 971–2, 1022–3, 1028, B464–5

Continuing Education Office, Western Michigan University, Kalamazoo, Mich. 49008: 973

Cooperative Accountability Project, Colorado Department of Education, 3262 Lincoln St., Denver, Colo. 80203: B574

Cooperative Tests and Services. See Addison-Wesley Publishing Co., Inc.

Cornell University Medical College, 1300 York Ave., Box 88, New York, N.Y. 10021: 530

Council for Exceptional Children, 1920 Association Drive, Reston, Va. 22091: B220

Council on Dental Education. See Division of Educational Measurements.

Counselor Recordings and Tests, Box 6184, Acklen Station, Nashville, Tenn. 37242: 646, 693

Court (J. H.), Flinders University, Bedford Park, S. A., Australia: B114

Crane Publishing Co., 1301 Hamilton Ave., P.O. Box 3713, Trenton, N.J. 08629: 162

Crane, Russak & Co., Inc., 347 Madison Ave., New York, N.Y. 10017: B269, B477

Cremonesi (Gordon) Ltd., New River House, 34 Seymour Road, London N8 OBE, England: B295

Crippled Children and Adults of Rhode Island, Inc., Meeting Street School, 667 Waterman Ave., East Providence, R.I. 02914: 435

Croft Educational Services, Inc., P.O. Box 15, Old Greenwich, Conn. 06870: 750

Curriculum Associates, Inc., 94 Bridge St., Newton, Mass. 02158. 6

Curtis Blake Child Development Center. See American International College.

Cutronics Educational Institute, 128 West 56th St., Bayonne, N.J. 07002: 426, 784

DABOR Science Publications, 297 Concord Ave., Oceanside, N.Y. 11572: B558

Dennis (William H.), Trumbull County Reading Clinic, 255 Bonnie Brae Ave. N.E., Warren, Ohio 44483: 212

Dent (J. M.) & Sons (Canada) Ltd., 100 Scarsdale Road, Don Mills, Ont. M3B 2R8, Canada: 928; Dent (J. M.) & Sons Ltd., Aldine House, 26 Albemarle St., London, England: B269

Department of Photography and Cinema, Ohio State University, 156 West 19th Ave., Columbus, Ohio 43210: 968

Department of Psychology, Oklahoma State University, 115 South Murray Hall, Stillwater, Okla. 74074; 680

Developmental Reading Distributors (DRD Press), 1944 Sheridan Ave., Laramie, Wyo. 82070: 731

Dial, Inc., 1233 Lincoln Ave. South, Highland Park, Ill. 60035: 428

Didier, 29 Lexington Road, Concord, Mass. 01742: B103

Division of Educational Measurements, Council on Dental Education, American Dental Association, 211 East Chicago Ave., Chicago, Ill. 60611: 1085

Division of Research and Evaluation. See Hahnemann Medical College and Hospital.

Doubleday & Co., Inc., 501 Franklin Ave., Garden City, N.Y. 11530: B156

Dreier Educational Systems, Inc., 300 Raritan Ave., Highland Park, N.J. 08904: 78, 761–2, 780, 787

Duckworth (Gerald) & Co., Ltd., The Old Piano Factory, 43 Gloucester Crescent, London NW1, England: B511

Dutton (E. P.) & Co., Inc., 201 Park Ave. South, New York, N.Y. 10003: B562

EdITS/EDUCATIONAL and Industrial Testing Service, P.O. Box 7234, San Diego, Calif. 92107: 238, 293, 333, 349, 527, 536, 553–4, 559, 596, 611, 628, 641, 651, 818, 992, B199, B271

ERIC Document Reproduction Service, P.O. Box 190, Arlington, Va. 22210: B322, B523–4

Economy Co., P.O. Box 25308, 1901 North Walnut, Oklahoma City, Okla. 73125: 746

Edcodyne Corporation, 16052 Beach Boulevard, Huntington Beach, Calif. 92647: 794

Education Achievement Corp., P.O. Box 7310, Waco, Tex. 76710: 1018

Educational Activities, Inc., P.O. Box 392, Freeport, N.Y. 11520: 694

Educational and Industrial Testing Service. See EdITS/Educational and Industrial Testing Service.

Educational Development Corporation, P.O. Box 45663, Tulsa, Okla. 74145: 275, 764, 880

Educational Guidance, Inc., P.O. Box 511, Main Post Office, Dearborn, Mich. 48121: 996, 1002

Educational Records Bureau, Box 619, Princeton, N.J. 08540: 15

Educational Resources, 19 Peacedale Grove, Nunawading 3131, Australia: 789

Educational Skills Development, Inc., 179 East Maxwell St., Lexington, Ky. 40508: 423, 502–3

Educational Technology Publications, 140 Sylvan Ave., Englewood Cliffs, N.J. 07632: B59, B107, B181, B219, B294, B436, B457

Educational Testing Service, Princeton, N.J. 08540: 7, 8–9, 36, 39, 42–4, 46, 48, 54, 61, 64–9, 71, 83, 86, 88, 90, 95, 99–101, 110, 112–3, 115–9, 121–2, 124–33, 136–51, 153, 157–61, 165–6, 169, 173, 182, 188, 199, 204, 254–6, 258–61, 272, 286, 289, 295, 297, 309, 313–4, 326, 330, 364–5, 372, 375, 381–8, 396, 398, 401, 406, 410, 414–5, 417, 420, 455–7, 459–62, 471–6, 478–80, 523–4, 586, 733–4, 739, 824, 828–9, 831–6, 846–9, 852, 854–6, 862–4, 866–7, 886–91, 894–7, 903–5, 907–8, 910–3, 916,

919, 921, 923–7, 931, 943, 965–6, 979, 1041, 1064, 1070–4, 1076–7, 1080–4, 1088–9, 1093, 1097–100, 1116–9, B2, B3, B10–1, B120, B184, B237–9, B538. See also Addison-Wesley Publishing Co., Inc.; College Entrance Examination Board; and Educational Records Bureau.

Educator Feedback Center, Western Michigan University, 12 Bigelow Annex, Kalamazoo, Mich. 49008: 362, 405

Educators Assistance Institute. See Pennant Press.

Educators Publishing Service, Inc., 75 Moulton St., Cambridge, Mass. 02138: 446, 760, 775, 944–5

Effective Study Materials, P.O. Box 603, San Marcos, Tex. 78666: 816, 819

El Paso Rehabilitation Center, 2630 Richmond St., El Paso, Tex. 79930: 211

Empiric Press, 333 Perry Brooks Bldg., Austin, Tex. 78701: 978

Emporia Kansas State College. See Bureau of Educational Measurements.

Endeavor Information Systems, Inc., 2407 Prospect Ave., Evanston, Ill. 60201: 370

English Language Institute, 2001 NU, University of Michigan, Ann Arbor, Mich. 48109: 102–3, 105–6

English Universities Press Ltd. See Hodder & Stoughton Educational.

Erlbaum (Lawrence) Associates, Inc., Publishers, P.O. Box 112, Hillsdale, N.J. 07642: B67, B259, B451

Evaluation Services, Inc., 4734 McKinley Drive, Boulder, Colo. 80303: 1023

Evans/Methuen Educational, 11 New Fetter Lane, London E.C.4, England: B480–1, B484–94, B496–8, B500

Examinations Committee, American Chemical Society, University of South Florida, Tampa, Fla. 33620: 837–45, 853

Executive Analysis Corporation. See Psychologists and Educators, Inc.

FACILITATION House, Box 611, Ottawa, Ill. 61350: 72, 265, 444, 755

Fairview State Hospital, Research Department, 2501 Harbor Blvd., Costa Mesa, Calif. 92626: 556, 960

Falcon Research & Development, 2350 Alamo Ave. S.E., Albuquerque, N.M. 87106: 191

Family Life Publications, Inc., P.O. Box 427, Saluda, N.C. 28773: 342, 345–6

Fast (Charles G.), Northeast Missouri State University, Kirkville, Mo. 63501: 412

Fearon Publishers, 6 Davis Drive, Belmont, Calif. 94002: 429, 438, 629, B310, B545

Fenner (Bradford J.), 2S 075 Avondale Lane, Lombard, Ill. 60148: 1017

Florida Educational Research and Development Council, College of Education, University of Florida, Gainesville, Fla. 32601: 580

Follett Publishing Co., 1010 West Washington Blvd., Chicago, Ill. 60607: 424, 870, 940, 950

Follett's Michigan Book Store. See English Language Institute.

Foster (Arthur L.), 248 Blossom Hill Road, Los Gatos, Calif. 95030: 355

Free Press, 866 Third Ave., New York, N.Y. 10022: 660, B39, B179

Freeman (W. H.), & Co., 660 Market St., San Francisco, Calif. 94104: B296

Friedman (Myles I.), College of Education, University of South Carolina, Columbia, S.C. 29208: 242

GENERAL Educational Development Testing Service, American Council on Education, 1 Dupont Circle, Washington, D.C. 20036: 35

General Learning Press, 250 James St., Morristown, N.J. 07960: B301, B422

Georgia State University. See International Society for the Study of Symbols.

Ginn & Co. Ltd. See NFER Publishing Co., Ltd.

Gleser (Goldine C.), University of Cincinnati Medical Center, Department of Psychiatry, 7110 College of Medicine, Cincinnati, Ohio 45267: 535

Gordon (Ira J.), School of Education, University of North Carolina, Chapel Hill, N.C. 27514: 580

Gough (Harrison G.), 2240 Piedmont Ave., University of California, Berkeley, Calif. 94720: 468

Gower Press Ltd., P.O. Box 5, Epping, Essex, England: B332

Goyer (Robert S.), Department of Interpersonal Communication, Ohio University, Athens, Ohio 45701: 817

Graduate School of Business, University of Pittsburgh, Pittsburgh, Pa. 15260: B91

Grassi (Joseph R.), 3501 Jackson Street #110, Hollywood, Fla. 33021: 430

Grune & Stratton, Inc., 111 Fifth Ave., New York, N.Y. 10003: 439, 661, 873, B38, B46, B46A, B95, B236, B245, B273, B279, B289, B441, B581

Gryphon Press, Box 978, Edison, N.J. 08817: B72–7, B79–84

Guidance Associates of Delaware, Inc., 1526 Gilpin Ave., Wilmington, Del. 19806: 37, 492, 987, 1029

Guidance Centre, University of Toronto, 1000 Yonge St., Toronto, Ont. M4W 2K8, Canada: 196, 266, 282, 560, 736

H & H ENTERPRISES, Inc., P.O. Box 3342, Lawrence, Kan. 66044: 689

Hahnemann Medical College and Hospital, Division of Research and Evaluation, 314 North Broad St., Philadelphia, Pa. 19102: 612

Halgren Tests, 873 Persimmon Ave., Sunnyvale, Calif. 94087: 660

Halsted Press, Division of John Wiley & Sons, Inc., 605 Third Ave., New York, N.Y. 10016: B256, B290, B536

Hamish Hamilton Ltd., 90 Great Russell St., London WC1B 3PT, England: B300, B300A

Harcourt Brace Jovanovich, Inc., 757 Third Ave., New York, N.Y. 10017: B270, B293, B541, B546. See also Psychological Corporation (The).

Harding (C. Chris.), P.O. Box 271, North Rockhampton, 4701 Queensland, Australia: 189

Harper & Row, Publishers, Inc., 10 East 53rd St., New York, N.Y. 10022: B53, B87, B166, B188, B272, B299, B456, B469, B513. See also Barnes & Noble Books.

Harrap (George C.) & Co., Ltd., P.O. Box 70, 182/4 High Holborn, London WC1V 7AX, England: 224

Hart Publishing Co., Inc., 510 Ave. of the Americas, New York, N.Y. 10011: B15–6, B232

Harvard University Press, 79 Garden St., Cambridge, Mass. 02138: 697

Harvey (O. J.), Department of Psychology, University of Colorado, Boulder Colo. 80302: 698

Heath (D. C.) & Co., 125 Spring St., Lexington, Mass. 02173: B420–1. See also T.E.D. Associates; and Lexington Books.

Heinemann Educational Australia Pty. Ltd., 85 Abinger St., Box 133, Richmond 3121, Australia: 726; Heinemann Educational Books Ltd., 26 Kilham Ave., Auckland, 9, P.O. Box 36064, New Zealand: 774; Heinemann (William) Medical Books Ltd., 23 Bedford Square, London WC1B 3HT, England: 208, B65

Her Majesty's Stationery Office, Atlantic House, Holborn Viaduct, London, E.C.2, England: B35, B510

Hicks (John S.), School of Education at Lincoln Center, Fordham University, New York, N.Y. 10023: 1062

Hill (Wm. Fawcett), California State Polytechnic University, Pomona, 3801 West Temple Ave., Pomona, Calif. 91768: 577

Hiskey (Marshall S.), 5640 Baldwin, Lincoln, Neb. 68507: 217

Hobsons Press (Cambridge) Ltd., Bateman St., Cambridge CB2 1LZ, England: 1000, 1014

Hodder & Stoughton Educational, P.O. Box 702, Dunton Green, Sevenoaks, Kent TN13 2YD, England: 76–7, 114, 197, 271, 273, 277, 301, 306, 553, 579, 596, 611, 724, 728–9, 742, 783, 791, 810, B86, B290, B307, B442–3, B445–6, B460–1, B516, B518, B536.

Hoffman LaRoche, Inc. See Roche Testing Service.

Holt, Rinehart & Winston, Inc., 383 Madison Ave., New York, N.Y. 10017: B69, B325–8, B571. See also Praeger Publishers.

Houghton Mifflin Co., 1 Beacon St., Boston, Mass. 02107: B45, B96, B105, B410–1, B475, B532, B539; Test Department, P.O. Box 1970, Iowa City, Iowa 52240: 19, 32, 47, 98, 181, 190, 223, 229, 244, 274, 300, 311, 319, 327, 686, 726A, 727, 735, 763, 796, 899, 961, 991, 998, 1025, 1030, 1032

Huber (Hans), Langgassstrasse 76, 3000 Bern 9, Switzerland: 661

Hubert (Edwina E.), 313 Wellesley S.E., Albuquerque, N.M. 87106: 603

Human Resources Center, Albertson, N.Y. 11507: 666

Human Sciences Press, 72 Fifth Ave., New York, N.Y. 10011: 369, 566, 570, 645, B175, B428

Human Sciences Research Council, Private Bag 41, Pretoria, Republic of South Africa: 55, 104, 107–9, 194, 281, 296, 308, 310, 315, 481–2, 520, 582, 587, 590, 597, 1005, 1026, 1034

Humanities Press, Inc., Atlantic Highlands, N.J. 07716: B99, B207, B473, B482, B495, B548, B569

IMPERIAL International Learning Corporation, Box 548, Kankakee, Ill. 60901: 303

Indiana University Press, Tenth & Morton Sts., Bloomington, Ind. 47401: B578

Industrial Psychology, Inc., 515 Madison Ave., New York, N.Y. 10022: 679

Industrial Relations Center, University of Chicago, 1225 East 60th St., Chicago, Ill. 60637: 963

Institute for Personality and Ability Testing, 1602 Coronado Drive, Champaign, Ill. 61820: 184, 484, 520, 522, 540, 547, 582–3, 597, 627, 668, 679, B261, B274, B502

Institute for Program Evaluation, Inc., Box 4654, Roanoke, Va. 24015: 638

Institute for Social Research, University of Michigan, P.O. Box 1248, Ann Arbor, Mich. 48106: 985, B100, B458. See also Center for Research on Utilization of Scientific Knowledge.

Institute of Clinical Analysis, 1000 East Broadway, Glendale, Calif. 91205: 621

Institute of Psychiatry, De Crespigny Park, Denmark Hill, London S.E.5, England: 565. See also Oxford University Press.

Institute of Psychological Research, Inc., 34 Fleury St. West, Montreal, Que. H3L 1S9, Canada: 21, 539, 695

Institute of Rehabilitation Medicine, New York University Medical Center, 400 East 34th St., New York, N.Y. 10016: 962

Instructional Materials Laboratory, Ohio State University, 1885 Neil Ave., Columbus, Ohio 43210: 1086, 1102–3, 1154–67

Instructional Objectives Exchange, Box 24095, Los Angeles, Calif. 90024: 53, 279, 771, 917, B431–2, B435

Intercontinental Medical Book Corporation, 381 Park Ave. South, New York, N.Y. 10016: B171

International Personnel Management Association, 1313 East 60th St., Chicago, Ill. 60637: 1094–5

International Publications Service Collings Inc., AB/9 Safdarjang Enclave, New Delhi-16, India: B47

International Reading Association, Inc., Box 8139, Newark, Del. 19711: B50–1, B112, B154, B251–2, B257, B305, B504

International Society for the Study of Symbols, Department of Psychology, Georgia State University, Atlanta, Ga. 30303: B115

International Tests, Inc., Box 634, Stevens Point, Wis. 54481: 487

International Universities Press, Inc., 315 Fifth Ave., New York, N.Y. 10016: B55, B286, B466

Interstate Printers & Publishers, Inc. (The), 19–27 North Jackson St., Danville, Ill. 61832: 344, 952, 969, 990, B165, B197, B417

Intext Educational Publishers, 10 East 53rd St., New York, N.Y. 10022: B141–2

Intran Corporation, 4555 West 77th St., Minneapolis, Minn. 55435: 489–91

Irvington Publishers, Inc., 551 Fifth Ave., New York, N.Y. 10017: B118

J-K SCREENING Service, 124 Solano St., San Rafael, Calif. 94901: 433

Jewish Employment and Vocational Service, Inc., 1624 Locust St., Philadelphia, Pa. 19103: 982

Joint Council on Economic Education, 1212 Ave. of the Americas, New York, N.Y. 10036: 898, 900–2

Jossey-Bass Inc., Publishers, 615 Montgomery St., San Francisco, Calif. 94111: 708, B31, B97, B123, B133, B215, B253–4, B309, B324, B334, B551

KAHN (Marvin W.), Department of Psychology, University of Arizona, Tuscon, Ariz. 85721: 511

Kaneko Shobo Publishers, 3–7, 3-chome Otsuka, Bunkyo-ku, Tokyo 112, Japan: 598

Karger (S.) AG, Medical and Scientific Publishers, Arnold-Bocklin-Strasse 25, CH-4011 Basel, Switzerland: B429

Katz (Martin M.), Clinical Research Branch, National Institute of Mental Health, 5600 Fishers Lane, Rockville, Md. 20852: 599

Katz (Phyllis A.), and Zalk (Sue R.), Institute for Research on Social Problems, 528 Pearl St., Boulder, Colorado 80302: 600

Kirchhoff (Bruce A.), College of Business, University of Nebraska at Omaha, Omaha, Neb. 68101: 1182

Knapp (Robert R.), P.O. Box 7234, San Diego, Calif. 92107: B150

Krieger (Robert E.) Publishing Co., Inc., 645 New York Ave., Huntington, N.Y. 11743: B228, B453

LABORATORY for Research on Higher Education, University of California, Graduate School of Education, Los Angeles, Calif. 90024: 397

Ladoca Project and Publishing Foundation, Inc., East 51st Ave. and Lincoln St., Denver, Colo. 80216: 958

Language Research Associates, Inc., P.O. Box 2085, Palm Springs, Calif. 92262: 448, 450, 876, 932–4

Larlin Corporation, P.O. Box 1523, Marietta, Ga. 30061: 821

Lawrence (Trudys), 5532 Poplar Blvd., Los Angeles, Calif. 90032: 567

Layton (Wilbur L.), 3604 Ross Road, Ames, Iowa 50010: 193

Lea & Febiger, 600 Washington Square, Philadelphia, Pa. 19106: 955, B177, B233

Lear Seigler, Inc./Fearon Publishers. See Fearon Publishers.

Learning Concepts, 2501 North Lamar, Austin, Tex. 78705: 81, 154, 167, 389, 395, 451, 454, 532–3, 650, 957, 999, 1058

Learning Institute of North Carolina, 1006 Lamond Ave., Durham, N.C. 27701: 647

Learning Pathways, Inc., Evergreen, Colo. 80439: 432

Learning Systems Co., 1818 Ridge Road, Homewood, Ill. 60430: B132

Leonard (Hal) Publishing Corporation, 960 East Mark St., Winona, Minn. 55987: 94

Lewis (H. K.) & Co. Ltd., P.O. Box 66, 136 Gower St., London WC1E 6BS, England: 200, B449

Lexington Books, D. C. Heath & Co., 125 Spring St., Lexington, Mass. 02173: B14, B131

Lippincott (J. B.) Co., East Washington Square, Philadelphia, Pa. 19105: 208, B65

Little, Brown & Co., 34 Beacon St., Boston, Mass. 02114: B211

Longman Group Ltd., Longman House, Burnt Mill, Harlow, Essex, England: B208; Longman Inc., 19 West 44th St., Suite 1012, New York, N.Y. 10036: 959, B208

Love Publishing Co., 6635 East Villanova Place, Denver, Colo. 80222: B168–9

Lucas Brothers Publishers, 909 Lowry, Columbia, Mo. 65201: 781

Lyons & Carnahan. See Rand McNally College Publishing Co.

Lytton Publishing Co., Drawer G, College Station, Tex. 77840: B423

M.A.A. COMMITTEE on High School Contests, University of Nebraska, Lincoln, Neb. 68508: 252

MTP Press Ltd., St. Leonards House, St. Leonard Gate, Lancaster, Lancashire, England: B148–9

Maas (James B.), Department of Psychology, 214 Uris Hall, Cornell University, Ithaca, N.Y. 14853: 367

McCann Associates, 2755 Philmont Ave., Huntington Valley, Pa. 19006: 1096, 1106

McCutchan Publishing Corporation, 2526 Grove St., P.O. Box 774A, Berkeley, Calif. 94701: B36, B58, B231, B437, B444, B448, B543, B550

McGrath Publishing Co., P.O. Box 535, Whitmore Lake, Mich. 48189: 765, 786, 788

McGraw-Hill Book Co., Inc., 1221 Ave. of the Americas, New York, N.Y. 10020: B54, B413–4, B531

Macmillan Education Ltd., Little Essex St., London WC2R 3LF, England: B499; Macmillan Publishing Co., Inc., 866 Third Ave., New York, N.Y. 10022: 790, 801, B28, B192–6, B260

Maferr Foundation, 124 East 28th St., New York, N.Y. 10016: 607–8

Mafex Associates, Inc., 90 Cherry St., Johnstown, Pa. 15902: 798

Management Research Institute, 305 East Melbourne Ave., Silver Spring, Md. 20901: 1186

Massey University, Palmerston North, New Zealand: B218

Matt-Jansky, 120 East 89th St., New York, N.Y. 10028: 800

Measurement and Research Center, Purdue University, Lafayette, Ind. 47907: 391

Measurement and Research Division, University of Illinois, 307 Engineering Hall, Urbana, Ill. 61801: 373–4

Medical University Press, 80 Barre St., Charleston, S.C. 29401: B459

Meeting Street School. See Crippled Children and Adults of Rhode Island, Inc.

Mens Sana Publishing Inc., P.O. Box 2966, Grand Central Station, New York, N.Y. 10017: 552

Merrell-National Laboratories, Division of Richardson-Merrell, Inc., Cincinnati, Ohio 45215: 675

Merrill (Charles E.) Publishing Co., 1300 Alum Creek Drive, Columbus, Ohio 43216: 874, 929, B17, B113, B217, B521, B559, B564, B576

Methuen & Co. Ltd., 11 New Fetter Lane, London ED4P 4EE, England: B88, B234, B246–8, B250, B472

Michigan State University. See National Council on Measurement in Education.

Midwest Music Tests, 1304 East University St., Bloomington, Ind. 47401: 96

Mincomp Corporation, 1780 South Bellaire, Suite 510, Denver, Colo. 80222: 1020, 1023

Modern Language Association, c/o Honorary Secretary S. R. Ingram, 33/35 Lewisham Way, London SE14 6PP, England: B138

Monitor, P.O. Box 2337, Hollywood, Calif. 90028: 82, 84, 247, 312, 317, 363, 416, 496, 544, 588, 699, 859, 1013

Morrison (James H.), 9804 Hadley, Overland Park, Kansas City, Mo. 66212: 605

Morstain (Barry R.), College of Urban Affairs and Public Policy, Raub Hall, University of Delaware, Newark, Del. 19711: 400

Mouton Publishers, 3 Westchester Plaza, Elmsford, N.Y. 10523: B116–7, B243, B337

Multivariate Behavioral Research, Texas Christian University, P.O. Box 30789, Fort Worth, Tex. 76129: B173

NCS INTERPRETIVE Scoring Systems, 4401 West 76th St., Minneapolis, Minn. 55435: 380, 485, 491, 778, 823, 993, 1004, 1023, 1031

NFER Publishing Co. Ltd., 2 Jennings Bldgs., Thames Ave., Windsor, Berks. SL4 1QS, England: 111, 175, 195, 230, 232, 234, 269, 494, 509, 539, 558, 597, 665, 711, 884, 930, 947, 974, 977, 1033, 1044, B99, B207, B338A, B415, B447, B473, B482, B495, B507, B548, B568–9

National Association of Secondary School Principals, 1904 Association Drive, Reston, Va. 22091: B102

National Bureau of Economic Research, Inc., 261 Madison Ave., New York, N.Y. 10016: B528

National Business Education Association, 1906 Association Drive, Reston, Va. 22091: 322–3, 325, 329

National Children's Bureau, 8 Wakley St., Islington, London EC1V 7QE, England: B419

National Council of Teachers of English, 1111 Kenyon Road, Urbana, Ill. 61801: B4, B85, B129, B152, B190, B329, B547

National Council of Teachers of Mathematics, Inc., 1906 Association Drive, Reston, Va. 22091: B64

National Council on Crime and Delinquency, Continental Plaza, 411 Hackensack Ave., Hackensack, N.J. 07601: 316, 1092

National Council on Measurement in Education, 206 South Kedzie, Michigan State University, East Lansing, Mich. 48824: B554

National Education Association, 1201 Sixteenth St., N.W., Washington, D.C. 20036: B407–8

National Educational Laboratory Publishers, Inc., P.O. Box 1003, Austin, Tex. 78767: 427

National Foundation for Educational Research in England and Wales. See NFER Publishing Co. Ltd.

National Institute for Personnel Research, P.O. Box 10319, Johannesburg, Republic of South Africa: 230

National Institute of Education, 1200 Nineteenth St. N.W., Washington, D.C. 20208: B127

National Merit Scholarship Corporation, 990 Grove Street, Evanston, Ill. 60201: 199

National Occupational Competency Testing Institute, 45 Colvin Ave., Albany, N.Y. 12206: 1129–53

National School Boards Association, 1055 Thomas Jefferson St. N.W., Washington, D.C. 20007: B8

National School Public Relations Association, 1801 North Moore St., Arlington, Va. 22209: B7

National Science Teachers Association, Affiliate of American Association for the Advancement of Science, 1724 Connecticut Ave. N.W., Washington, D.C. 20009 : B552

National Study of School Evaluation, 2201 Wilson Blvd., Arlington, Va. 22201 : 390, 399

National Technical Information Service, U.S. Department of Commerce, 5285 Port Royal Road, Springfield, Va. 22151 : B110

Natresources, Inc., 520 North Michigan Ave., Chicago, Ill. 60611 : 678

Nelson (Thomas) & Sons (Canada) Ltd., 81 Curlew Drive, Don Mills, Ont. M3A 2R1, Canada : 11, 180, 274, 284, 1021; Nelson (Thomas) & Sons Ltd., Lincoln Way, Windmill Road, Sunbury-on-Thames, Middlesex TW16 7HP, England : 25, 181, 747

New Dimensions in Education, Inc., 160 Dupont St., Plainview, N.Y. 11803 : 773

New York University Medical Center. See Institute of Rehabilitation Medicine.

New Zealand Council for Educational Research, Education House, 178 Willis St., Wellington 1, New Zealand : 288, 453, 738, B143

Newbury House Publishers, Inc., 54 Warehouse Lane, Rowley, Mass. 01969 : 58

Newland (T. Ernest), 702 South Race St., Urbana, Ill. 61801 : 320

Northwest Regional Educational Laboratory, Lindsay Building, 710 Southwest Second Ave., Portland, Ore. 97204 : B339, B509

Northwestern University Press, 1735 Benson Ave., Evanston, Ill. 60201 : 171, 967

OFFER (Daniel), Michael Reese Medical Center, 2959 South Ellis Ave., Chicago, Ill. 60616 : 633

Ohio State University. See Department of Photography and Cinema; Instructional Materials Laboratory; and University Publications Sales.

Oklahoma State University. See Department of Psychology.

Oliver & Boyd, Croyton House, 23 Ravelston Terrace, Edinburgh EH4 3TJ, Scotland : 756

Ontario Institute for Studies in Education, 252 Bloor St. West, Toronto, Ont. M5S IV6, Canada : 120, 737, B230, B440

Open Court Publishing Co., P.O. Box 599, LaSalle, Ill. 61301 : B147

Open University Educational Media, Inc., 110 East 59th St., New York, N.Y. 10022 : B34; Open University Press, Walton Hall, Milton Keynes MK7 6AB, England : B34

Organizational Tests Ltd., P.O. Box 324, Fredericton, N.B. E3B 4Y9, Canada : 1126, 1179

Owen (Peter) Ltd., 73 Kenway Road, London SW5, England : B163

Oxford University Press, Institute of Psychiatry, De Crespigny Park, Denmark Hill, London S.E. 5, England : 565, B210; 200 Madison Ave., New York, N.Y. 10016 : B42, B172, B183, B210, B291, B311, B313, B318

PAN Books Ltd., 18 Cavaye Place, London SW10 9PG, England : B281

Pantheon Books, 201 East 50th St., New York, N.Y. 10022 : B52

Papua New Guinea University of Technology, P.O. Box 793, Lae, Papua New Guinea : B454

Parauniversity Resources, 640 Northwest 36th Drive, Gainesville, Fla. 32607 : 378–9

Parnicky (Joseph J.), Nisonger Center, Ohio State University, 1580 Cannon Drive, Columbus, Ohio 43210 : 1024

Peacock (F. E.) Publishers, Inc., 401 West Irving Road, Itasca, Ill. 60143 : B68, B182, B520

Penguin Books, Inc., 7110 Ambassador Road, Baltimore, Md. 21207; B209, B452; Penguin Books Ltd.,

Bath Road, West Drayton UB7 0DA, Middlesex, England : B209

Pennant Press, 8265 Commercial St., Suite 14, La Mesa, Calif. 92041 : 564, 640, 659

Perceptual Learning Systems, P.O. Box 864, Dearborn, Mich. 48121 : 935, 946

Pergamon Press, Inc., Maxwell House, Fairview Park, Elmsford, N.Y. 10523 : B162, B212, B258

Personal Growth Press, Inc., Box M., Berea, Ohio 44017 : 348

Personnel Press, Education Center, P.O. Box 2649, Columbus, Ohio 43216 : 79, 248–9, 918

Personnel Security Corporation, 1301 West 22nd St., Oak Brook, Ill. 60521 : 644

Person-O-Metrics, Inc., 20504 Williamsburg Road, Dearborn Heights, Mich. 48127 : 551, 657, 670

Phi Delta Kappa, Inc., Eighth St. and Union Ave., Bloomington, Ind. 47401 : 16, B18, B140, B425

Pimm Consultants Ltd., Suite 211, 85 Sparks St., Ottawa 4, Ont., Canada : 637

Plays, Inc., 8 Arlington St., Boston, Mass. 02116 : B412

Pocket Books, 1230 Ave. of the Americas, New York, N.Y. 10020 : B24

Praeger Publishers, Division of Holt, Rinehart & Winston, Inc., 200 Park Ave., New York, N.Y. 10017 : B503

Prentice-Hall, Inc., Englewood Cliffs, N.J. 07632 : B63, B104, B134, B139, B144, B174, B191, B213, B333, B433–4, B438, B467, B517, B522, B542

Priority Innovations, Inc., P.O. Box 792, Skokie, Ill. 60076 : 445

Psychological Assessment and Services, Inc., P.O. Box 1031, Iowa City, Iowa 52240 : 625

Psychological Assessment Services, P.O. Box 1400, Tuscaloosa, Ala. 35401 : 622

Psychological Corporation (The), 757 Third Ave., New York, N.Y. 10017 : 2, 22, 29–31, 50, 73, 156, 177–8, 185–7, 192, 198, 200, 206, 209–10, 219, 224, 230, 232, 234, 236, 250, 267, 283, 291–2, 324, 377, 402, 485, 542, 568–9, 578, 616, 623, 626, 634, 663, 712, 730, 732, 745, 776–7, 785, 802–3, 820, 822, 1001, 1016, 1033, 1037, 1042–3, 1104, 1121–2, B216, B306, B557

Psychological Development Publications, P.O. Box 3198, Aspen, Colo. 81611 : 215

Psychological Publications, Inc., 5300 Hollywood Blvd., Los Angeles, Calif. 90027 : 692

Psychological Resources, Inc., 1422 West Peachtree St. N.W., Atlanta, Ga. 30309 : 507

Psychological Services, Inc., Suite 600, 4311 Wilshire Blvd., Los Angeles, Calif. 90010 : 1176

Psychological Test Publications, 107 Pilton St., Barnstaple, Devon, England : 571, 615

Psychological Test Specialists, Box 9229, Missoula, Mont. 59801 : 216, 225, 592, 613, 701

Psychologists and Educators, Inc., Suite 212, 211 West State St., Jacksonville, Ill. 62650 : 203, 231–3, 240, 347, 499, 505, 543, 609, 635, 664, 674, 805, 815, 1008

Psychometric Affiliates, Box 3167, Munster, Ind. 46321 : 226, 280, 656, 741, 1057

Psychometric Techniques Associates, 4614 Fifth Ave., Pittsburgh, Pa. 15213 : 1120

Purdue University. See Measurement and Research Center.

RAP RESEARCHERS, Sandy Lane, Marlborough, Conn. 06424 : 243

RIPIS, Box 9311, Providence, R.I. 02904 : 441

Rand McNally College Publishing Co., P.O. Box 7600, Chicago, Ill. 60680 : B283

Random House, Inc., 201 East 50th St., New York, N.Y. 10022 : 723

Raven Press Publishers, 1140 Ave. of the Americas, New York, N.Y. 10036 : B287

Evaluation; and Laboratory for Research on Higher Education.

University of Chicago. See Industrial Relations Center.

University of Chicago Press, 5801 South Ellis Ave., Chicago, Ill. 60637 : B573

University of Florida. See Florida Educational Research and Development Council.

University of Illinois. See Measurement and Research Division.

University of Illinois Press (The), Urbana, Ill. 61801 : 431, B266–7, B544

University of Iowa. See Bureau of Educational Research and Service; and Center for Labor and Management.

University of London Press Ltd. See Hodder & Stoughton Educational.

University of Michigan. See Center for Research on Utilization of Scientific Knowledge; English Language Institute; and Institute for Social Research.

University of Minnesota Press, 2037 University Ave. S.E., Minneapolis, Minn. 55455 : B90, B121–2, B176, B323, B501, B525, B582

University of Nebraska. See M.A.A. Committee on High School Contests.

University of Nebraska Press, 901 North 17th St., Lincoln, Neb. 68588 : B579

University of Pennsylvania. See Center for the Study of Sex Education in Medicine.

University of Pittsburgh. See Graduate School of Business.

University of Queensland Press, P.O. Box 42, St. Lucia, Queensland 4067, Australia : B30

University of South Florida. See Examinations Committee.

University of Sussex. See Sussex University Press.

University of Toronto. See Guidance Centre.

University Park Press, Chamber of Commerce Bldg., 213 East Redmond St., Baltimore, Md. 21202 : B57, B93, B149, B439

University Publications Sales, Ohio State University, 20 Lord Hall, 124 West 17th Ave., Columbus, Ohio 43210 : 1075, 1174–5, 1184

VIRGINIA Research Associates, Ltd., P.O. Box 5501, Charlottesville, Va. 22902 : 371

Vocational Psychology Research, Elliot Hall, University of Minnesota, Minneapolis, Minn. 55455 : 1050–8, 1061, B167

WADSWORTH Publishing Co., Inc., 10 Davis Drive, Belmont, Calif. 94002 : B474. See also Brooks/Cole Publishing Co.

Waetjen (Walter B.), President, Cleveland State University, Cleveland, Ohio 44115 : 671

Warwick Products Co., 7909 Rockside Road, Cleveland, Ohio 44131 : 490–1

Watts (Franklin), Inc., 730 Fifth Ave., New York, N.Y. 10019 : B40

Western Michigan University. See Continuing Education Office; and Educator Feedback Center.

Western Psychological Services, 12031 Wilshire Blvd., Los Angeles, Calif. 90025 : 246, 336, 356, 437, 541, 549, 561, 575, 584, 639, 655, 705, 710, 806, 875, 878–9, 954, 975–6, 1012, 1040, 1188, B48 B255, B277

Whitston Publishing Co., Inc., P.O. Box 322, Troy, N.Y. : B529

Wiley-Interscience. See Wiley (John) & Sons, Inc.

Wiley (John) & Sons, Inc., 605 Third Ave., New York, N.Y. 10016 : B101, B119, B125, B146, B178, B214, B268, B280, B284, B331–2, B338, B418, B463, B468, B505, B508, B512, B535; John Wiley & Sons Ltd., Baffin Lane, Chicester, Sussex, England : B214, B512. See also Halsted Press.

William, Lynde & Williams, 153 East Erie St., Painesville, Ohio 44077 : 205

Williams (Robert L.) and Associates, 7201 Creveling Drive, St. Louis, Mo. 63130 : 176

Williams & Wilkins Co., 428 East Preston St., Baltimore, Md. 21202 : B148, B164, B302, B450

Winch (B. L.) & Associates, P.O. Box 1185, Torrance, Calif. 90505 : 5, 253, 690, 718

Wonderlic (E. F.) & Associates, Inc., Box 7, Northfield, Ill. 60093 : 1059, B575

Word Making Productions, Inc., 70 West Louise Ave., Salt Lake City, Utah 84115 : 970

Wyden Books, 747 Third Ave., New York, N.Y. 10017 : B241

ZENETRON, Inc., 6501 West Grand Ave., Chicago, Ill. 60635 : 951

Zenith Hearing Aid Sales Corporation. See Zenetron, Inc.

Zweig (Richard L.) Associates, Inc., 20800 Beach Blvd., Huntington Beach, Calif. 92648 : 270, 725, 758

Index of Book Titles

References are to entry numbers, not to page numbers. The entry numbers for facing pages are given in the running heads next to the outside margins; the numbers next to the inside margins are page numbers. All entry numbers for books begin with the letter B.

AAHPER YOUTH Fitness Test Manual, Revised 1976 Edition, B1
Abilities: Their Structure, Growth, and Action, B96
Ability Testing in Developing Countries: A Handbook of Principles and Techniques, B503
Abuses of Standardized Testing, B425
Achievement in America: National Report of the United States for International Educational Achievement Project, B572
Achievement Test Items—Methods of Study, B204
Achievement Test Score Decline: Do We Need to Worry?, B202
Actions, Styles and Symbols in Kinetic Family Drawings (K-F-D): An Interpretative Manual, B70
Activity Interests and Occupational Choice, B276
Actuarial Use of the MMPI With Adolescents and Adults, B313
Adolescent Rorschach Responses: Developmental Trends From 10 to 16 Years, Revised Edition, B25
Adult Assessment: A Source Book of Tests and Measures of Human Behavior, B32
Adult Work Skills and Knowledge: Selected Results From the First National Assessment of Career and Occupational Development, B340
Advances in Psychological Assessment, Vol. 2, B308; Vol. 3, B309
After A-Level? A Study of the Transition from School to Higher Education, B338A
Aids and Precautions in Administering the Illinois Test of Psycholinguistic Abilities, B267
Alfred Binet, B573
Alternatives to Paper and Pencil Testing: Proceedings of a Conference, B91
Analysis of Intelligence, B198
Analytical Reading Inventory, B576
Analyzing Teaching Behavior, B158
Anchor Test Study: Equivalence and Norms Tables for Selected Reading Achievement Tests (Grades 4, 5, 6), B297; Revised, B298
Application of Measurement to Health and Physical Education, Fifth Edition, B104

Application of Pupil Assessment Information: For the Special Education Teacher, B168; Second Edition, B169
Applying Norm-Referenced and Criterion-Referenced Measurement in Education, B316
Appraisal of Teaching: Concepts and Process, B61
Appraising Managerial Performance: Current Practices and Future Directions, B282
Aptitude-Achievement Distinction, B185
Aptitude Testing at Eighteen-Plus, B99
Aptitudes and Instructional Methods: A Handbook for Research on Interactions, B118
Assessing Attainment in the Classroom, B307
Assessing Human Motivation, B301
Assessing Language Skills in Infancy: A Handbook for the Multidimensional Analysis of Emergent Language, B93
Assessing Minority Group Children: A Special Issue of Journal of School Psychology, B428
Assessing Personality Through Tree Drawings, B56
Assessing Reading Behavior: Informal Reading Inventories—An Annotated Bibliography, B252
Assessing the Learning Disabled: Selected Instruments, B320; Second Edition, B321
Assessment and Testing: An Introduction, B477
Assessment and Testing in the Secondary School, B480
Assessment for Learning in the Mentally Handicapped, B336
Assessment in a Pluralistic Society, B237
Assessment in Education, B290
Assessment in Higher Education, B214
Assessment in Infancy: Ordinal Scales of Psychological Development, B544
Assessment of Aphasia and Related Disorders, B177
Assessment of Attainment in Sixth-Form Science, B481
Assessment of Attitudes Toward Music, B341
Assessment of Brain Damage: A Neuropsychological Key Approach, B463
Assessment of Career Development: Basic Work Skills: Selected Results From the First National

Index of Test Titles

This title index lists all tests in this volume and all additional tests in Tests in Print II (TIP II). Citations are to test entry numbers, not to pages—e.g., 429 refers to test 429 in this volume; T2:1731 refers to test 1731 in TIP II. (The running-head numbers next to the outside margins in the test section refer to tests, not to pages.) Those titles consisting of two parts separated by a colon—e.g., Cooperative Science Tests: Chemistry—are also listed in inverted order. Tests which are a part of a series are also listed under the series title. Superseded titles are listed with cross references to current titles. Acronyms are presented for tests having 25 or more references in this volume. The title index in TIP II must be consulted for information about tests out of print as of late 1974.

AAHPER COOPERATIVE Health Education Test, T2:910

AAHPER Cooperative Physical Education Tests, T2:911

AAHPER-Kennedy Foundation Special Fitness Test for the Mentally Retarded, T2:912

AAHPER Sport Skills Tests, T2:913

AAHPER Youth Fitness Test, 407

AAMD Adaptive Behavior Scale, 493

AAMD-Becker Reading-Free Vocational Interest Inventory, 988

AATG German Test, see National German Examination for High School Students, 135

AATG National Standardized Testing Program, see National German Examination for High School Students, 135

ABC Inventory to Determine Kindergarten and School Readiness, T2:1691

A-B-C Vision Test for Ocular Dominance, T2:1905

ABS, AAMD Adaptive Behavior Scale, 493

AC Test of Creative Ability, T2:2340

A.C.E.R. Advanced Test B40, T2:323

A.C.E.R. Advanced Tests AL and AQ, T2:324

ACER & University of Melbourne Music Evaluation Kit, 89

A.C.E.R. Arithmetic Tests: Standardized for Use in New Zealand, T2:690

A.C.E.R. Higher Tests, T2:325

A.C.E.R. Intermediate Test A, T2:326

A.C.E.R. Intermediate Tests C and D, T2:327

A.C.E.R. Junior Non-Verbal Test, T2:328

A.C.E.R. Junior Test A, T2:329

A.C.E.R. Lower Grades General Ability Scale, T2:330

A.C.E.R. Lower Grades Reading Test, T2:1529

ACER Mathematics Tests: AM Series Topic Tests, T2:595

A.C.E.R. Mechanical Comprehension Test, T2:2237

A.C.E.R. Mechanical Reasoning Test, T2:2238

A.C.E.R. Number Test, T2:691

ACER Primary Reading Survey Tests, 714

ACER Short Clerical Test, T2:2117

A.C.E.R. Silent Reading Tests: Standardized for Use in New Zealand, T2:1531

A.C.E.R. Speed and Accuracy Tests, T2:2118

ACER Test of Learning Ability, 174

A.C.E.R. Word Knowledge Test, T2:163

ACL, Adjective Check List, 495

ACS Cooperative Examination Brief Course in Organic Chemistry, T2:1814.

A.C.S. Cooperative Examination for Graduate Placement in Organic Chemistry, see ACS Cooperative Examination in Organic Chemistry, 841

A.C.S. Cooperative Examination for Graduate Placement in Physical Chemistry, see ACS Cooperative Examination in Physical Chemistry, Graduate Level, 843

ACS Cooperative Examination in Analytical Chemistry, Graduate Level, T2:1815; in Biochemistry, T2:1816; in Brief Physical Chemistry, T2:1817; in Brief Qualitative Analysis, T2:1818; in General Chemistry, 837; in Inorganic Chemistry, 838; in Inorganic Chemistry, Graduate Level, T2:1821; in Inorganic-Organic-Biological Chemistry (for Allied Health Science Programs), 839; in Instrumental Analysis, T2:1823; in Organic Chemistry, 480, in Organic Chemistry, Graduate Level, 841; in Physical Chemistry, 842; in Physical Chemistry, Graduate Level, 843; in Qualitative Analysis, T2:1828; in Quantitative Analysis, T2:1829

A.C.S. Cooperative Organic Chemistry Test, see ACS Cooperative Examination in Organic Chemistry, 840

ACS-NSTA Cooperative Examination in High School

Chemistry, (Advanced Level), 844; in High School Chemistry, (Lower Level), 845
ACT, ACT Assessment, 469
ACT Assessment, 469
ACT Assessment of Career Development, *see* Assessment of Career Development, 991
ACT Career Planning Program, 989
ACT Guidance Profile, Two-Year College Edition, T2:2167
ACT Interest Inventory, 469b
ACT Mathematics Placement Examination, T2:596
ACT Proficiency Examination in Accounting, 1063; in Adult Nursing, 1108; in African and Afro-American History, 906; in Anatomy and Physiology, 857; in Business Environment and Strategy, 1065; in Corrective and Remedial Instruction in Reading, 715; in Criminal Investigation, 1090; in Earth Science, 858; in Educational Psychology, 458; in Freshman English, 38; in Fundamentals of Nursing, 1109; in History of American Education, 360; in Introduction to Criminal Justice, 1091; in Nursing Health Care, 1110; in Occupational Strategy, Nursing, 1111; in Philosophy of Education, 361; in Psychiatric/ Mental Health Nursing, 1112; in Reading Instruction in the Elementary School, 716; in Shakespeare, 63
ACT Proficiency Examination Program, 470
ACT Proficiency Examinations in Accounting, 1063; in American Literature, 62; in Commonalities in Nursing Care, 1113; in Differences in Nursing Care, 1114; in Finance, 1066; in Health, 408; in Management of Human Resources, 1067; in Marketing, 1068; in Maternal and Child Nursing, 1115; in Operations Management, 1069
ACT Test Battery, *see* ACT Assessment, 469
ADT, Auditory Discrimination Test, 932
AH2/AH3, 175
AH4, AH5, and AH6 Tests, T2:331
Ai3Q: A Measure of the Obsessional Personality or Anal Character, 494
A/9 Cumulative Record Folder, T2:1007
ANPA Foundation Newspaper Test, T2:1735
AO Sight Screener, T2:1906
APB Achievement Test, *see* American Political Behavior Achievement Test, 918
APE, Advanced Placement Examinations, 471
APELL Test: Assessment Program of Early Learning Levels, 794
APT Controlled Interview, T2:2294
APT Dictation Test, T2:2119
APT Manual Dexterity Test, T2:2222
APT Performance Test, T2:332
A.P.U. Arithmetic Test, 301
A.P.U. Occupational Interests Guide, T2:2168
A.P.U. Vocabulary Test, 77
A-S Reaction Study, T2:1090
ASK-Language Arts, *see* Analysis of Skills: Language Arts, 41
ASK-Mathematics, *see* Analysis of Skills: Mathematics, 251
ASK-Reading, *see* Analysis of Skills: Reading, 748
ASQ, IPAT Anxiety Scale Questionnaire, 582
ASVAB, Armed Services Vocational Aptitude Battery, 483
ATDP, Scale to Measure Attitudes Toward Disabled Persons, 666
ATDP Scale, *see* Scale to Measure Attitudes Toward Disabled Persons, 666
ATP, College Board Admissions Testing Program, 472
AVL, *see* Study of Values, 686
Abortion Scale, 331
Abstract Reasoning: Differential Aptitude Tests, 185

Abstract Spatial Relations Test, T2:541
Academic Alertness "AA," T2:334
Academic Aptitude Test, 481
Academic Aptitude Test: Non-Verbal Intelligence, T2:335; Verbal Intelligence, T2:336
Academic Freedom Survery, T2:852
Academic Proficiency Battery, T2:1
Academic Promise Tests, T2:1063
Academic Readiness Scale, 795
Academic-Technical Aptitude Tests, T2:1064
Account Clerk Test, T2:2322
Achievement Examinations for Secondary Schools: Advanced Algebra, T2:664; Bookkeeping, T2:775; Business Relations and Occupations, T2:779; Chemistry, T2:1834; Economic Geography, T2:1974; Elementary Algebra, T2:677; French I and II, T2:251; General Science III, T2:1786; German I and II, T2:268; Latin I and II, T2:294; Modern World History, T2:1997; Physics, T2:1870; Plane Geometry, T2:756; Spanish I and II, T2:320
Achievement Series: SRA Assessment Survey, 1
Achievement Test—Hebrew Language, T2:278
Achievement Test in Jewish History, T2:1020
Achievement Test—Jewish Life and Observances, T2:1021
Achievement Test—The State of Israel, T2:1022
Achievement Tests in Nursing, T2:2376
Achievement Tests in Practical Nursing, T2:2377
Acorn Achievement Tests: American History—Government—Problems of Democracy, T2:1936; Junior High School Mathematics Test, T2:624; Primary Reading Test, T2:1578
Acorn National Achievement Tests: Health Education Test, T2:928; Social Studies Test, T2:1950; World History Test, T2:2003
Acorn National Aptitude Tests: Academic Aptitude Test: Non-Verbal Intelligence, T2:335; Academic Aptitude Test: Verbal Intelligence, T2:336; Clerical Aptitude Test, T2:780; Inventory of Vocational Interests, T2:2192; Mechanical Aptitude Test, T2:2252
Action-Choice Tests for Competitive Sports Situations, T2:915
Activities Inventory, 7A(a1, b1)
Activity Vector Analysis, T2:1091
Adaptability Test, T2:337
Adaptive Behavior Scales, *see* AAMD Adaptive Behavior Scale, 493
Addiction Research Center Inventory, T2:1093
Adding Decorations: Creativity Tests for Children, 241a
Aden-Crosthwait Adolescent Psychology Achievement Test, T2:1001
Adjective Check List, 495
Adjustment Inventory, T2:1095
Adkins-McBride General Science Test, T2:1777
Administrator Image Questionnaire, 362
Admission Test for Graduate Study in Business, *see* Graduate Management Admission Test, 1074
Adolescent Alienation Index, 496
Adston Diagnostic Instruments in Elementary School Mathematics: Whole Numbers, T2:692
Adult Basic Education Student Survey, T2:2
Adult Basic Learning Examination, 2
Adult Basic Reading Inventory, 811
Adult Performance Level Survey, 3
Advanced Algebra: Achievement Examinations for Secondary Schools, T2:664
Advanced General Science: Cooperative Science Tests, 826
Advanced Mathematics (Including Trigonometry): Minnesota High School Achievement Examinations, T2:597

Fire Promotion Tests, T2:2361
Firefighter Test, T2:2362
Fireman Examination, T2:2363
First Grade Readiness Scale, *see* Basic School Skills Inventory, 424
First Grade Screening Test, T2:979
First Year Algebra Test: National Achievement Tests, T2:679
First Year Arabic Final Examination, T2:224
First Year French Test, T2:249
First Year Spanish Test, 164
Fisher-Logemann Test of Articulation Competence, 961
Five Task Test, T2:1460
Flags: A Test of Space Thinking, T2:2245
Flanagan Aptitude Classification Tests, T2:1072
Flanagan Industrial Tests, 981
Flash-X Sight Vocabulary Test, T2:1678
Flint Infant Security Scale, 560
Florida Cumulative Guidance Record, T2:1011
Flowers Auditory Test of Selective Attention, 935
Flowers-Costello Tests of Central Auditory Abilities, T2:2035
Following Directions, 737f
Ford-Hicks French Grammar Completion Tests, T2:250
Foreign Language Aptitude: Iowa Placement Examinations, T2:220
Foreign Language Prognosis Test, T2:218
Forer Structured Sentence Completion Test, T2:1461
Forer Vocational Survey, T2:1462
Form Perception Test, T2:2246
Form Relations Group Test, T2:2247
Forms From Diagnostic Methods in Speech Pathology, T2:2074
Forty-Eight Item Counseling Evaluation Test, 561
Fountain Valley Teacher Support System in Mathematics, 270; Reading, 725; Secondary Reading, 758
Four Tone Screening for Older Children and Adults, T2:2036
Franck Drawing Completion Test, 562
Freeman Anxiety Neurosis and Psychosomatic Test, T2:1188
French Comprehension Tests, 120
French: Graduate School Foreign Language Test, 122
French: MLA-Cooperative Foreign Language Tests, 123
French: National Teacher Examinations, 124
French I and II: Achievement Examinations for Secondary Schools, T2:251
French: Teacher Education Examination Program, T2:260
French Training: Iowa Placement Examinations, T2:254
Frost Self Description Questionnaire, 563
Frostig Movement Skills Test Battery, 871
Full-Range Picture Vocabulary Test, 216
Functional Communication Profile, 962
Functional Grammar Test, T2:82
Fundamental Achievement Series, T2:376
Furness Test of Aural Comprehension in Spanish, T2:310

GAP READING Comprehension Test, T2:1550
GAPADOL, 726
GATB, USES General Aptitude Test Battery, 490
GATB-NATB Screening Device, 490a1, 491a
G.C. Anecdotal Record Form, T2:1012
GED, Tests of General Educational Development, 35
GEFT, Group Embedded Figures Test, 572
GFW Auditory Memory Tests, 937c
GFW Auditory Selective Attention Test, 937a
G-F-W Battery, *see* Goldman-Fristoe-Woodcock Auditory Skills Test Battery, 937

GFW Diagnostic Auditory Discrimination Test, 937b
GFW Sound-Symbol Tests, 937d
GMAT, Graduate Management Admission Test, 1074
GMRT, Gates-MacGinitie Reading Tests, 726A
GPI, Gordon Personal Inventory, 568
GPP, Gordon Personal Profile, 569
GRE, Graduate Record Examinations, 476
GREAT, Graduate Record Examinations Aptitude Test, 188
GTSTD, Grid Test of Schizophrenic Thought Disorder, 571
GZTS, Guilford-Zimmerman Temperament Survey, 574
Gardner Analysis of Personality Survey, 564
Garnett College Test in Engineering Science, T2:2342
Gates-MacGinitie Reading Tests, 726A
Gates-MacGinitie Reading Tests: Readiness Skills, T2:1702
Gates-MacGinitie Reading Tests: Survey F, 727
Gates-McKillop Reading Diagnostic Tests, 759
Gates Reading Diagnostic Tests, *see* Gates-McKillop Reading Diagnostic Tests, 759
Geist Picture Interest Inventory, T2:2180; Deaf Form: Male, T2:2181
General Aptitude Test Battery, *see* USES General Aptitude Test Battery, 490
General Background in the Natural Sciences, T2:1787
General Biology Test: National Achievement Tests, T2:1810
General Chemistry Test: National Achievement Tests, T2:1842
General Clerical Ability Test: ETSA Test, T2:2128
General Clerical Test, 1033
General Concepts Test, *see* Tests of Basic Experiences, 34a
General Health Questionnaire, 565
General Industrial Arts: Cooperative Industrial Arts Test, T2:970
General Knowledge: Educational Goal Attainment Tests, 16e
General Mathematics III: Achievement Examinations for Secondary Schools, T2:617
General Mental Ability Test, T2:378
General Municipal Employees Performance (Efficiency) Rating System, T2:2364
General Office Clerical Test: National Business Entrance Tests, 325
General Physics Test: National Achievement Tests, T2:1865
General Professional Examinations: Teacher Education Examination Program, T2:41
General Science: Cooperative Science Tests, 827
General Science Test: National Achievement Tests, T2:1785
General Science Test [National Institute for Personnel Research], T2:1784
General Science III: Achievement Examinations for Secondary Schools, T2:1786
General Test on Traffic and Driving Knowledge, T2:846
General Tests of Language and Arithmetic, T2:14
General Tests of Language and Arithmetic for Students, T2:862
General Verbal Practice Tests G1–G3, T2:379
General Vocabulary: Iowa Tests of Educational Development, T2:166
Geography Test: Municipal Tests: National Achievement Tests, T2:1975
Geography Test: National Achievement Tests, T2:1976
Geometry: Cooperative Mathematics Tests, T2:746
Geometry (Including Plane and Solid Geometry): Minnesota High School Achievement Examinations, T2:748

NDRT, Nelson-Denny Reading Test, 735
N.I.I.P. Engineering Apprentice Selection Test Battery, T2:2345
NIIP Group Test 36, 195
NLN Achievement Test for Schools Preparing Registered Nurses, T2:2383
NLN Aide Selection Test, T2:2384
NLN Practical Nursing Achievement Tests, T2:2385
NLN Pre-Admission and Classification Examination, T2:2386
NLN Pre-Nursing and Guidance Examination, T2:2387
NM Attitude Toward Work Test, 1013a
NM Career Development Test, 1013f
NM Career Oriented Activities Checklist, 1013c
NM Career Planning Test, 1013b
NM Concepts of Ecology Test, 859
NM Consumer Mathematics Test, 312
NM Consumer Rights and Responsibilities Test, 416
NM Job Application Procedures Test, 1013e
NM Knowledge of Occupations Test, 1013d
NOCTI, National Occupational Competency Testing Program, 1153
NOCTI Examination: Air Conditioning and Refrigeration, 1129; Airframe and Power Plant Mechanic, 1130; Architectural Drafting, 1131; Auto Body Repair, 1132; Auto Mechanic, 1133; Cabinet Making and Millwork, 1134; Carpentry, 1135; Civil Technology, 1136; Cosmetology, 1137; Diesel Engine Repair, 1138; Electrical Installation, 1139; Electronics Communications, 1140; Industrial Electrician, 1141; Industrial Electronics, 1142; Machine Drafting, 1143; Machine Trades, 1144; Masonry, 1145; Mechanical Technology, 1146; Plumbing, 1147; Printing, 1148; Quantity Food Preparation, 1149; Sheet Metal, 1150; Small Engine Repair, 1151; Welding, 1152
NOSIE, Nurses' Observation Scale for Inpatient Evaluation, 631
NOSIE-30: A Treatment-Sensitive Ward Behavior Scale, *see* Nurses' Observation Scale for Inpatient Evaluation, 631
NSST, Northwestern Syntax Screening Test, 967
NTE, National Teacher Examinations, 381
Nagel Personnel Interviewing and Screening Forms, T2:2309
Names for Stories: Creativity Tests for Children, 241g
National Achievement Tests, T2:23; American History Test, T2:1984; Arithmetic Test, T2:701; Arithmetic Test (Fundamentals and Reasoning): Municipal Tests, T2:700; College English Test, T2:66; Elementary Science Test, T2:1782; English Test, T2:78; English Test: Municipal Tests, T2:77; First Year Algebra Test, T2:679; General Biology Test, T2:1810; General Physics Test, T2:1865; General Science Test, T2:1785; Geography Test, T2:1976; Geography Test: Municipal Tests, T2:1975; Health and Safety Education Test, T2:926; Health Knowledge Test for College Freshmen, T2:929; Health Test, T2:930; History and Civics Test: Municipal Tests, T2:1943; Literature Test, T2:139; Plane Geometry, T2:757; Plane Trigonometry, T2:764; Reading Test (Comprehension and Speed): Municipal Tests, 741; Social Studies Test, T2:1951; Solid Geometry, T2:759; Spelling Test, T2:161; Vocabulary Test, T2:178
National Business Entrance Tests, T2:786; Bookkeeping Test, 322; Business Fundamentals and General Information Test, 323; General Office Clerical Test, 325; Machine Calculation Test, T2:785; Stenographic Test, T2:795; Typewriting Test, 329
National Educational Development Tests, 23
National Engineering Aptitude Search Test, T2:2346
National German Contest for High School Students,

see National German Examination for High School Students, 135
National German Examination for High School Students, 135
National Guidance Testing Program, T2:1055
National Institute for Personnel Research Intermediate Battery, T2:1084; Normal Battery, T2:1085
National Inventory of Aptitudes and Abilities: Project Talent Test Battery, T2:1058
National Merit Scholarship Qualifying Test, *see* Preliminary Scholastic Aptitude Test/National Merit Scholarship Qualifying Test, 199
National Occupational Competency Testing Program, 1153
National Science Foundation Graduate Fellowship Testing Program, T2:1056
National Spanish Examination, 168
National Teacher Examinations, 381; Art Education, 86; Audiology, 943; Biology and General Science, 828; Business Education, 326; Chemistry, Physics and General Science, 829; Common Examinations, 382; Early Childhood Education, 383; Education in an Urban Setting, T2:871; Education in the Elementary School, 385; Education of the Mentally Retarded, 386; Educational Administration and Supervision, 384; English Language and Literature, 54; French, 124; German, 136; Guidance Counselor, 387; Home Economics Education, 417; Industrial Arts Education, 420; Introduction to the Teaching of Reading, 733; Mathematics, 286; Media Specialist—Library and Audio-Visual Services, 388; Music Education, 99; Physical Education, 414; Reading Specialist, 734; Social Studies, 891; Spanish, 169; Speech-Communication and Theatre, 965; Speech Pathology, 966; Texas Government, 923
National Test of Basic Words, T2:1667
National Test of Library Skills, T2:1762
Nationwide English Composition Examination, T2:97
Nationwide English Grammar Examination, T2:98
Nationwide English Vocabulary Examination, T2:169
Nationwide Library Skills Examination, T2:1763
Nationwide Speech Examination, T2:2083
Nationwide Spelling Examination, T2:154
Natural Sciences: CLEP General Examinations, 824
Naylor-Harwood Adult Intelligence Scale, 221
Neale Analysis of Reading Ability, T2:1683
Nebraska Test of Learning Aptitude, *see* Hiskey-Nebraska Test of Learning Aptitude, 217
Nelson Biology Test, T2:1812
Nelson-Denny Reading Test, 735
Nelson Reading Test, T2:1573
Netherne Study Difficulties Battery for Student Nurses, T2:2388
Neuroticism Scale Questionnaire, T2:1295
New Developmental Reading Tests, T2:1574
New Group Pure Tone Hearing Test, T2:2048
New Guinea Performance Scales, T2:510
New Iowa Spelling Scale, T2:155
New Junior Maudsley Inventory, T2:1296
New Medical College Admission Test, 1101
New Mexico Career Education Test Series, 1013
New Purdue Placement Test in English, T2:99
New South African Group Test, T2:411
New South African Individual Scale, T2:511
New Uses, T2:568
Newsweek NewsQuiz, T2:1959
19 Field Interest Inventory, T2:2198
1973 Stanford Mathematics Tests, *see* Stanford Achievement Test: Mathematics Tests, 291
1973 Stanford Reading Tests, *see* Stanford Achievement Test: Reading Tests, 745
Noises, 7A(a13)
Non-Language Test of Verbal Intelligence, T2:412
Non-Readers Intelligence Test, T2:413

Index of Names

This analytical name index indicates whether a citation refers to authorship of a test review, a test, a measurement book, an excerpted review, or a reference dealing with a specific test. Names mentioned in cross references are also indexed. References are to test and book entry numbers, not to page numbers. The abbreviations and numbers following the names may be interpreted thus: "rev, 68" indicates authorship of an original review of test 68; "test, 73" indicates authorship of test 73 or of some accessory mentioned within the entry for test 73; "bk, B16" indicates authorship of book B16; "exc, 110" (or "exc, B214") indicates authorship of an excerpted review of test 110 (or book B214); "ref, 123(34)" indicates authorship of reference 34 for test 123; "cross ref, 347" indicates authorship of an earlier review of test 347, to which a cross reference appears under test 347.

AMEG Commission on Sex Bias in Measurement: ref, 1023(1310)
Aanes, D.: ref, 493(27)
Aaron, I. E.: rev, 726, 768, 772
Aaron, P. G.: ref, 506(993)
Aaron, R.: ref, 720(167)
Aaronson, B. S.: ref, 549(10)
Aaronson, S.: ref, 720(269)
Abadzi, H.: ref, 106(8)
Abbas, R. D.: ref, 688(139)
Abbate, M. S.: test, 928
Abbatiello, A. A.: test, 1032
Abbott, E. B.: ref, 249(378), 520(92)
Abbott, J. C.: ref, 882(216)
Abbott, K.: ref, 514(1155)
Abbott, R. D.: ref, 198(51), 514(970, 1077), 542(1331, 1421–2), 616(3864, 4134), 641(292), 643(73–4, 100, 150), 679(1099)
Abbott, S. K.: ref, 616(3864)
Abel, E. L.: ref, 643(65)
Abel, T. M.: bk, B13; ref, 661(4660), 697(1839)
Abeles, N.: ref, 616(4653)
Abelman, A. K.: ref, 633(8)
Abelson, C.: ref, 882(173)
Abelson, W. D.: ref, 22(104), 24(14), 222(399–400), 467), 249(432)
Ables, J.: ref, 393(46, 56)
Aborn, M.: ref, 720(39–40)
Abraham, A.: ref, 553(392)
Abraham, T.: ref, 710(2)
Abrahams, N. M.: ref, 1023(1311)

Abrahamson, R. E.: ref, 187(393), 802(200)
Abram, H. S.: ref, 616(4960), 693(573)
Abramowitz, C. V.: ref, 641(401)
Abramowitz, E. A.: exc, B333
Abramowitz, S. I.: ref, 569(133), 641(401)
Abrams, H. I.: ref, 555(245)
Abrams, L.: ref, 244(163)
Abrams, L. M.: ref, 555(245)
Abrams, M. H.: ref, 542(1321), 616(4459), 679(933)
Abrams, R.: ref, 963(14)
Abrams, S.: bk, B14
Abramson, E. E.: ref, 628(147)
Abramson, L. M.: ref, 542(1638)
Abramson, P. R.: ref, 542(1638), 553(402), 578(300), 686(923)
Abudabbeh, N. N.: ref, 616(4391)
Abul-Hubb, D.: ref, 200(514), 377(443)
Abu-Saba, M. B.: ref, 595(24), 1030(79)
Acero, H. D.: ref, 469(386)
Achebe, C. C.: ref, 997(111)
Achenbach, T. M.: ref, 182(751), 229(1542)
Achord, C.: ref, 693(361)
Achord, C. D.: ref, 683(67, 154), 693(202)
Ackerman, P. T.: ref, 232(1454)
Acklen, L. M.: ref, 641(402), 693(362)
Acland, J.: ref, 22(117)
Acosta, F. X.: ref, 616(4591)

Acree, N. J.: ref, 616(4996)
Acuff, J.: ref, 656(12)
Adair, F. L.: rev, 617–20, 622–3
Adam, A. M.: ref, 536(10)
Adamczyk, F. J.: ref, 555(212)
Adamowicz, J. K.: ref, 579(66), 679(1120)
Adams, A. A.: bk, B15–6
Adams, A. C.: ref, 542(1605)
Adams, A. E.: ref, 693(363)
Adams, C.: ref, 469(471)
Adams, C. L.: ref, 542(1408), 820(140)
Adams, E. F.: ref, 1174(278)
Adams, E. P.: ref, 568(71), 569(134)
Adams, E. R.: ref, 688(168), 1174(210), 1177(81)
Adams, G.: ref, 616(4483)
Adams, G. S.: rev, 5, 508
Adams, H. B.: ref, 230(945), 616(3865)
Adams, H. E.: bk, B101; ref, 616(4870)
Adams, H. L.: ref, 542(1467), 1023(1276–9, 1349)
Adams, J.: ref, 187(413), 229(1458–9), 506(832–3), 882(930), 559(32, 38), 616(4135), 628(194), 703(193–4)
Adams, J. N.: ref, 523(241)
Adams, K. M.: ref, 616(4816), 617(76), 618(3)
Adams, M. F.: rev, 893, 901
Adams, M. S.: ref, 581(334)

Altshuler, K. Z.: *ref,* 224(265), 661(4856)
Altus, W. M.: *cross ref,* 216
Alumbaugh, R. V.: *ref,* 230(1000)
Alvares, K. M.: *ref,* 1174(281)
Alverno, L.: *ref,* 675(99)
Alviani, M. L.: *ref,* 469(483)
Amante, D.: *ref,* 506(931)
Amble, B. R.: *ref,* 431(408), 542 (1310), 679(908), 726A(27)
Ambler, R. K.: *ref,* 1023(1254)
Ambron, S. R.: *rev,* 7A
Ambrosie, F.: *ref,* 634(218), 1174 (152)
Ambrosino, R. J.: *ref,* 735(94), 1101(154)
Amburn, E.: *test,* 419
American Association of Teachers of German: *test,* 135
American Association of Teachers of Spanish and Portuguese: *test,* 168
American Automobile Association: *test,* 358–9
American Chemical Society: *test,* 837–45, 853; *ref,* 837(21–3), 838 (6), 839(1–2), 840(8), 841(3–4), 843(4), 845(18, 22, 28), 853(6)
American College Testing Program: *test,* 3, 469–70, 989, 991, 998, 1025; *ref,* 469(380, 387, 436, 482, 517, 547)
American Dental Association: *test,* 1085
American Institutes of Research: *test,* 1019
Amerson, V. M.: *cross ref,* 323
Ames, L. B.: *bk,* B25–7; *exc,* 601, B302; *ref,* 506(883), 601(3), 661 (4661–2, 4732–3, 4806)
Ames, S. G.: *ref,* 30(7)
Amir, Y.: *ref,* 548(327)
Ammons, C. H.: *test,* 225; *exc,* 219, 493, 526, 691, B74, B77, B174, B215, B476, B529; *ref,* 219(10), 493(14), 526(1), 691(4)
Ammons, H. S.: *test,* 216
Ammons, R. B.: *test,* 216, 225; *exc,* 219, 493, 526, 691, B74, B77, B215, B476, B529; *ref,* 219(10), 493(14), 526(1), 691(4)
Amolsch, T. J.: *ref,* 230(1178)
Anant, S. S.: *ref,* 686(1008)
Anastasi, A.: *rev,* 487, 702; *bk,* B28; *ref,* 229(1570), 230(1242), 232(1455), 234(158), 616(4820), 1023(1479); *cross ref,* 187, 190, 213, 486, 488, 492, 520, 643
Anastasiow, N. J.: *rev,* 439, 790; *exc,* B211, B471, B534
Anch, A. M.: *ref,* 616(4626)
Anchor, K. N.: *ref,* 683(108)
Andalib, A. A.: *ref,* 110(27), 182 (711), 469(518)
Anderegg, T.: *ref,* 495(462)
Anderhalter, O. F.: *test,* 41, 251, 748, 808–9; *cross ref,* 283
Anders, T. F.: *ref,* 206(59), 208 (15)
Andersen, D. O.: *ref,* 661(4787)
Andersen, P. A.: *ref,* 679(1210)
Anderson, A.: *ref,* 616(4614), 997 (149)
Anderson, A. H.: *ref,* 431(444)

Anderson, A. S.: *ref,* 688(140)
Anderson, B. R.: *bk,* B29
Anderson, C. C.: *ref,* 239(85), 529 (24)
Anderson, C. V.: *rev,* 951
Anderson, C. W.: *ref,* 675(55)
Anderson, D.: *ref,* 485(371)
Anderson, D. J.: *ref,* 790(12)
Anderson, E. A.: *ref,* 661(4807)
Anderson, E. I.: *ref,* 224(243), 548 (234)
Anderson, E. M.: *ref,* 597(150)
Anderson, E. R.: *ref,* 393(47)
Anderson, G. J.: *ref,* 190(103)
Anderson, G. L.: *ref,* 683(155), 1028(196)
Anderson, H. E.: *test,* 422; *ref,* 490(476)
Anderson, H. R.: *cross ref,* 887, 889
Anderson, I. H.: *cross ref,* 802
Anderson, J.: *test,* 726; *bk,* B30; *ref,* 179(120), 225(62), 679 (1422), 720(77, 113, 143, 180, 191, 227, 387), 1010(50)
Anderson, J. C.: *ref,* 495(356)
Anderson, J. D.: *ref,* 182(712)
Anderson, J. F.: *ref,* 377(520)
Anderson, J. M.: *cross ref,* 232, 882
Anderson, K. E.: *cross ref,* 837, 853
Anderson, L. K.: *ref,* 628(234)
Anderson, N. E.: *ref,* 222(395), 229(1493)
Anderson, P. A. S.: *ref,* 224(244)
Anderson, P. G.: *ref,* 641(208)
Anderson, R. F.: *ref,* 232(1048), 597(154), 668(14)
Anderson, R. H.: *ref,* 10(116)
Anderson, R. P.: *rev,* 425, 451; *ref,* 616(4006), 1023(1240), 1050(41)
Anderson, R. W.: *ref,* 616(4190)
Anderson, S. B.: *bk,* B31
Anderson, T.: *ref,* 506(940)
Anderson, T. H.: *ref,* 720(312)
Anderson, T. L. S.: *ref,* 514(1317)
Anderson, V. A.: *ref,* 187(394)
Anderson, W. F.: *ref,* 726A(20), 785(24), 882(169)
Anderson, W. H.: *ref,* 524(87)
Anderson, W. P.: *ref,* 616(4897)
Anderson, W. R.: *ref,* 616(5002)
Anderson, W. W.: *exc,* B83
Andert, J. N.: *ref,* 230(1279), 506 (970, 983)
Andes, D. A.: *ref,* 342(6)
Andrew, B. J.: *ref,* 616(4739)
Andrew, J. M.: *ref,* 230(1104–5), 232(1256), 250(93)
Andrews, E. S.: *ref,* 683(253)
Andrews, H. A.: *ref,* 1028(163, 229)
Andrews, H. B.: *ref,* 641(257), 679 (1005)
Andrews, J.: *ref,* 578(263), 660 (68)
Andrews, R. J.: *test,* 285, 743
Andrews, W. T.: *ref,* 200(529)
Andrieu, B. J. S.: *ref,* 679(1338)
Andrulis, R. S.: *bk,* B32
Andruss, H. A.: *cross ref,* 322
Andy, O. J.: *ref,* 230(1046), 506 (854), 613(91), 616(4495), 661 (4687)

Angelloz, R. E.: *ref,* 514(1318), 1174(261), 1175(135)
Angelone, J. V.: *ref,* 616(4815)
Angers, W. P.: *ref,* 616(4393)
Angoff, W. H.: *bk,* B33; *ref,* 110 (21–2), 182(617, 713), 199(24)
Angulu, U. A.: *ref,* 523(267)
Angus, G. D.: *ref,* 469(388), 630 (191), 679(918)
Anh, T.: *ref,* 660(193)
Aniol, L. J.: *ref,* 616(3868)
Annable, L.: *ref,* 585(200)
Annett, J.: *bk,* B34
Annett, M.: *ref,* 187(428), 222 (401)
Annis, L.: *ref,* 686(969)
Annis, L. V.: *ref,* 686(1009)
Ansara, A. S.: *test,* 446
Ansell, E. M.: *ref,* 997(59)
Ansley, M. Y.: *ref,* 555(316), 651 (48)
Anstett, R. R.: *ref,* 523(243)
Anstey, E.: *exc,* B210
Anstey, J. R.: *ref,* 1177(82)
Anthony, A.: *test,* 959
Anthony, H. S.: *bk,* B35
Anthony, J.: *test,* 558
Anthony, J. J.: *ref,* 176(2), 229 (1460), 232(1297), 234(110)
Anthony, N.: *ref,* 616(4821), 654 (34)
Anthony, N. C.: *ref,* 616(4137), 654(11)
Anthony, S. E.: *ref,* 542(1594)
Anthony, V. L.: *ref,* 514(1045), 641(294)
Anthony, W. A.: *ref,* 188(101), 192(154), 373(13)
Anthony, W. S.: *ref,* 553(403), 611(581)
Antill, J. K.: *ref,* 553(404)
Antoine, L. W.: *ref,* 553(319)
Anton, W. D.: *ref,* 683(213, 273)
Antone, E. J.: *ref,* 506(771)
Anttonen, R. G.: *ref,* 29(261)
Apfeldorf, M.: *ref,* 581(386–7), 616(4394–5, 4618, 4822), 686 (935)
Apkarian, K. G.: *ref,* 1175(136)
Apostal, R. A.: *ref,* 679(1432), 1023(1241), 1028(194)
Appel, M.: *ref,* 616(4235)
Appel, P.: *ref,* 683(328)
Appel, P. W.: *ref,* 230(1243)
Appelbaum, A. S.: *ref,* 222(503), 232(1548)
Apperson, J.: *ref,* 495(364), 693 (282)
Appignanesi, A.: *ref,* 249(418), 504(94), 682(83)
Apple, M. W.: *bk,* B36
Applebee, A. N.: *ref,* 37(128), 232 (1148), 726A(34)
Apps, R.: *ref,* 783(15)
Apstein, B.: *ref,* 43(2), 473(19)
Apter, A.: *ref,* 582(210), 611(582)
Apter, M. J.: *ref,* 553(587)
Aquino, M.: *ref,* 720(144, 145)
Arajarvi, T.: *ref,* 661(4595)
Aranoff, A.: *ref,* 1179(5)
Araoz, D. L.: *ref,* 697(1774)
Arbes, B. H.: *ref,* 528(5), 555 (213)
Arbet, L.: *ref,* 249(380), 596(53)

Becker, S.: *ref,* 249(439), 514
(1050), 1009(11), 1010(71)
Becker, W. C.: *ref,* 37(163), 227
(73)
Becker, W. E.: *ref,* 193(39)
Becker, W. M.: *ref,* 542(1470,
1546)
Beckman, L.: *ref,* 232(1550)
Beckner, J. A.: *ref,* 542(1471), 574
(538)
Bedeian, A. G.: *ref,* 495(491, 515)
Bedell, J. R.: *ref,* 683(215), 684
(17)
Bedell, R. C.: *cross ref,* 626
Bednar, R. L.: *ref,* 616(4625)
Bednarsky, R. A.: *ref,* 525(6), 681
(33)
Beech, H. R.: *exc,* B121
Beech, R. P.: *ref,* 660(40, 105, 183)
Beecham, W. M.: *ref,* 668(17)
Beegle, C. W.: *bk,* B44
Beeker, B. A.: *ref,* 634(339)
Beeker, C.: *ref,* 710(2)
Beer, M.: *ref,* 1174(144)
Beers, C. S.: *ref,* 238(37)
Beers, J. S.: *ref,* 693(285)
Berry, K. E.: *test,* 870
Begalla, M. E.: *ref,* 983(14)
Begelman, D. A.: *ref,* 559(39)
Beggs, D. L.: *bk,* B45 ; *ref,* 641
(427), 997(84)
Begle, E. G.: *rev,* 257
Behar, L.: *test,* 647–8
Behnke, R. B.: *ref,* 683(157)
Behr, J. J.: *ref,* 660(166)
Behre, C.: *ref,* 616(4315)
Beier, E. G.: *ref,* 232(1241)
Beischel, M. L.: *ref,* 572(6)
Beit-Hallahmi, B.: *ref,* 626(232–3,
260), 661(4606), 1023(1313)
Bejar, I. I.: *rev,* 156
Bekker, D.: *ref,* 535(33)
Belanger, D.: *ref,* 683(278)
Belanger, R. R.: *ref,* 514(946)
Belcastro, F. P.: *ref,* 542(1547),
1023(1425)
Belcher, T. L.: *ref,* 249(483–4)
Belding, H. H.: *ref,* 693(445)
Belford, B.: *ref,* 431(557)
Belinky, C. R.: *ref,* 661(4590)
Bell, A. E.: *ref,* 187(396), 227
(1427), 431(385), 506(772), 520
(116), 661(4607), 703(188)
Bell, A. W.: *ref,* 777(12)
Bell, C. R.: *ref,* 679(930), 686
(844)
Bell, D. B.: *ref,* 232(1048), 597
(154), 668(14)
Bell, E. C.: *ref,* 542(1472)
Bell, J. A.: *ref,* 377(560)
Bell, J. E.: *cross ref,* 558
Bell, J. M.: *ref,* 548(259), 581
(357)
Bell, M. L.: *ref,* 391(4), 679
(931–2)
Bell, R. M. S.: *ref,* 200(562)
Bell, R. Q.: *ref,* 206(54), 208(14),
209(55)
Bellack, A. S.: *bk,* B212 *ref,* 631
(67)
Bellak, L.: *test,* 463, 676 ; *bk,* B46,
B46A ; *ref,* 463(1), 676(1), 697
(1947)
Bellak, S. S.: *test,* 676

Bellamy, E.: *ref,* 542(1310), 679
(908)
Bellaterra, M.: *ref,* 683(311)
Bellaver, P. J.: *ref,* 555(248)
Bellico, R.: *ref,* 182(574)
Belmont, L.: *ref,* 200(644)
Beloff, H.: *test,* 597 ; *exc,* B452
Beltran, A. G.: *ref,* 503(1), 641
(501)
Belvedere, E.: *ref,* 514(1320)
Belvel, J.: *ref,* 506(773)
Bem, S. L.: *ref,* 514(1156), 574
(539)
Bemis, S. E.: *ref,* 490(480, 500)
Bench, J. E.: *ref,* 1028(231)
Bendel, R.: *ref,* 10(111), 200(574),
216(77), 488(389)
Bendel, R. B.: *ref,* 616(4924)
Bender, H. E.: *ref,* 549(11)
Bender, I. E.: *ref,* 686(946)
Bender, L.: *cross ref,* 506
Bender, M. L.: *test,* 868
Bender, P.: *ref,* 572(22)
Bender, R. E.: *ref,* 956(4)
Bendfeldt, F.: *ref,* 495(343), 616
(4020)
Bendich, S.: *ref,* 548(251), 581
(343)
Bene, E.: *test,* 558 ; *ref,* 558(27,
34), 661(4808)
Benenson, T. F.: *ref,* 450(1), 802
(204)
Benjamin, S. L.: *ref,* 527(44)
Benn, G. C.: *ref,* 523(289)
Benn, G. J.: *ref,* 495(454)
Bennet, R. W.: *ref,* 484(3)
Bennett, D. E.: *ref,* 488(382), 802
(228), 803(28)
Bennett, F. A.: *ref,* 493(26)
Bennett, G. K.: *test,* 50, 73, 185–6,
267, 485, 1037, 1042–3 ; *cross ref,*
244, 324
Bennett, L. F.: *ref,* 540(23)
Bennett, L. L. B.: *ref,* 693(535)
Bennett, M. J.: *ref,* 542(1548), 686
(973)
Bennett, R. A.: *bk,* B4
Bennett, R. M.: *ref,* 1030(69)
Bennett, R. N.: *ref,* 616(4044)
Bennett, R. R.: *ref,* 660(115, 141)
Bennett, S. M.: *ref,* 249(383)
Bennett, S. N.: *ref,* 237(61), 596
(54–5)
Bennett, S. W.: *ref,* 720(185)
Benning, B. M.: *ref,* 720(271)
Benningfield, M. F.: *ref,* 626(261),
641(404)
Benoit, S. S.: *ref,* 1052(96)
Benowitz, M. L.: *ref,* 506(934)
Benson, A. N.: *ref,* 577(40)
Bental, L. M.: *test,* 269
Bentham, J. E.: *ref,* 522(3), 542
(1410)
Bentler, P. M.: *test,* 238 ; *exc,* 22 ;
ref, 22(110), 238(21) ; *cross ref,*
646, 693
Bentley, M.: *ref,* 656(35)
Bentley, R. J.: *ref,* 200(645)
Bentley, R. R.: *test,* 391–3
Benton, A. L.: *test,* 236 ; *ref,* 236
(103), 1023(1426) ; *cross ref,*
506, 616, 697, 976
Benton, S. E.: *ref,* 398(8)
Bentz, C. M.: *ref,* 693(367)

Ben-Yehuda, A.: *ref,* 1022(67)
Berdie, R. F.: *test,* 1030; *ref,* 193
(37) ; *cross ref,* 485, 488, 1011
Bereiter, C.: *ref,* 10(117), 202(2)
Berenbaum, H. L.: *ref,* 506(869),
677(173)
Barends, M. L.: *ref,* 37(101), 759
(20)
Berez, W.: *ref,* 578(336)
Berg, H. D.: *rev,* 911 ; *cross ref,*
891, 907
Berg, I.: *test,* 669; *ref,* 596(42),
669(1–6)
Berg, S.: *ref,* 682(101)
Berg-Cross, G.: *ref,* 553(719)
Berg-Cross, L.: *ref,* 553(719)
Berger, A.: *rev,* 815, 818
Berger, F.: *ref,* 679(1499)
Berger, K. W.: *test,* 939; *ref,* 939
(2–3)
Berger, M.: *rev,* 25 ; *exc,* B148 ;
ref, 232(1368, 1453)
Berger, R. A.: *ref,* 182(622), 407
(154)
Bergeron, A. L.: *ref,* 1023(1314)
Bergeron, J.: *ref,* 683(278)
Bergeth, R. L.: *ref,* 393(44)
Bergin, A. E.: *ref,* 616(4460)
Berglas, W. W.: *ref,* 393(57)
Berglund, G. W.: *ref,* 183(351),
290(21)
Bergman, H.: *ref,* 548(270, 331)
Bergman, J. S.: *ref,* 542(1473),
548(192), 686(936)
Bergmann, K.: *ref,* 230(1146)
Bergquist, W. H.: *ref,* 616(4143–
4), 661(4634)
Bergsten, J. W.: *ref,* 19(106), 989
(13), 991(2)
Bergwall, E. H.: *ref,* 693(446), 997
(113)
Berk, R. J.: *ref,* 616(3874)
Berkowitz, L.: *ref,* 182(607)
Berlyne, G. M.: *ref,* 200(632), 232
(1338)
Berman, A.: *ref,* 232(1151)
Berman, A. L.: *ref,* 661(4608)
Berman, B. H.: *ref,* 641(405)
Berman, P. J.: *ref,* 188(110), 192
(160)
Bernabei, A.: *ref,* 683(311)
Bernal, E. M.: *ref,* 232(1258), 249
(440)
Bernal, G.: *ref,* 229(1472, 1520)
Bernardin, H. J.: *ref,* 679(1501),
1174(263)
Bernardoni, L. C.: *bk,* B456; *ref,*
229(1451), 230(1003), 232(1117),
234(103)
Bernay, T. M.: *ref,* 616(4826), 683
(279)
Bernberg, R. E.: *test,* 1057
Bernero, R. J.: *ref,* 951(10)
Bernstein, J.: *ref,* 616(4090)
Berrent, H. I.: *ref,* 720(356)
Berry, D. F.: *exc,* B122; *ref,* 613
(104), 616(3875, 4185)
Berry, F. M.: *ref,* 222(404)
Berry, G. L.: *ref,* 495(424), 626
(234)
Berry, J. W.: *ref,* 519(79), 548
(344)
Berry, M. D.: *ref,* 967(8)

Blanton, W.: *bk*, B51
Blanton, W. E.: *test*, 768; *bk*, B50; *ref*, 249(379), 720(384), 726A (22), 727(1), 802(226)
Blanz, L. T.: *ref*, 641(296), 693 (287)
Blaser, P.: *ref*, 616(4323)
Blashki, T. G.: *ref*, 675(59)
Blasi, E. R.: *ref*, 548(237)
Blass, J. H.: *ref*, 643(152), 686 (974)
Blatchley, R. J.: *ref*, 679(1217)
Blatt, S. J.: *ref*, 230(984, 1001, 1113), 611(616), 616(4014), 661 (4737–8, 4743, 4810, 4860, 4911), 675(102), 697(1803)
Blau, B. I.: *ref*, 616(4161)
Blazer, J. A.: *test*, 231; *ref*, 656 (26)
Bleckner, J. E.: *ref*, 616(4403), 661 (4739)
Blednick, G. A.: *ref*, 514(1240), 686(975)
Bledsoe, J. C.: *ref*, 10(102), 393 (64), 580(10, 12), 633(5), 709 (13), 997(48, 74), 1174(193)
Bleker, E. G.: *ref*, 661(4609)
Blenkner, M.: *ref*, 519(42)
Blessed, G.: *ref*, 230(972)
Bleyerveld, J.: *ref*, 224(246), 230 (973), 611(563)
Bleyle, D. M.: *ref*, 686(889), 693 (288)
Blick, K. A.: *ref*, 574(549)
Blinkhorn, S.: *test*, 1033; *bk*, B473; *ref*, 553(689–90), 582(269), 679 (1484–5), 726A(43)
Bliss, E.: *ref*, 495(430), 514(1174)
Bliss, F. H.: *ref*, 525(16–7), 681 (75–6)
Blizard, J.: *ref*, 597(142–6)
Bloch, S.: *ref*, 553(325)
Block, J.: *rev*, 554; *ref*, 514(937, 1052)
Block, J. H.: *ref*, 514(1052)
Block, J. R.: *test*, 666; *ref*, 666 (70), 1054(16)
Block, N. J.: *bk*, B52
Blocker, K.: *ref*, 576(35)
Blommers, P.: *cross ref*, 286, 298
Blood, D. F.: *bk*, B53; *ref*, 542 (1467)
Bloom, A. S.: *ref*, 229(1571, 1583), 232(1458, 1579)
Bloom, B. S.: *bk*, B54; *cross ref*, 36, 473
Bloom, J. W.: *ref*, 646(31)
Bloom, M.: *ref*, 519(42)
Bloom, R. B.: *ref*, 230(1182), 555 (215, 303), 616(4633)
Bloomer, R. H.: *test*, 772; *ref*, 720 (50, 78, 104, 118, 132)
Bloomfield, B.: *bk*, B488
Bloomfield, D. R.: *ref*, 574(549)
Bloxom, A. L.: *ref*, 616(4788)
Bloxom, B.: *cross ref*, 555, 641
Bloxom, B. M.: *rev*, 679
Blue, C. M.: *ref*, 938(18)
Blum, J. E.: *bk*, B244; *ref*, 229 (1429, 1441), 613(84)
Blum, L. H.: *test*, 210; *bk*, B55; *ref*, 661(4811)
Blum, M. L.: *cross ref*, 490
Blum, P. E.: *ref*, 582(193)

Blum, R. H.: *ref*, 514(933), 630 (188), 686(842), 1023(1235)
Blumberg, H. H.: *ref*, 634(294), 711(37)
Blumberg, H. M.: *ref*, 431(557)
Blume, S.: *ref*, 616(3994)
Blumenfeld, J. P.: *ref*, 720(56, 105)
Blumenfeld, W. S.: *ref*, 542(1323)
Blumenthal, M. D.: *ref*, 675(87–8)
Blumer, I.: *ref*, 688(178)
Blumetti, A. E.: *ref*, 616(3880)
Blumhagen, G. K. O.: *ref*, 607(20)
Blumstein, A. B.: *ref*, 661(4740)
Blumstein, E. M.: *ref*, 616(3881), 661(4610)
Bluvol, H.: *ref*, 697(1778)
Bly, D. F. H.: *ref*, 24(16)
Boardman, B. B.: *ref*, 693(448)
Boardman, W. K.: *ref*, 661(4823)
Boas, B.: *ref*, 616(4534)
Bobele, R. M.: *ref*, 236(126, 132), 495(488), 1028(264, 266)
Bobin, D.: *bk*, B91
Boblitt, W. E.: *ref*, 554(70), 559 (35)
Bochenek, W.: *ref*, 611(656)
Bock, R. D.: *ref*, 486(56), 488 (384)
Bodden, J. L.: *rev*, 993, 1013; *ref*, 820(131), 1028(133); *cross ref*, 992
Boddicker, R. F.: *ref*, 553(323), 628(148)
Bode, K. W.: *test*, 1045
Boder, C. K.: *ref*, 997(151), 1030 (88)
Bodi, S. L.: *ref*, 224(245), 581 (338)
Bödy, B.: *ref*, 393(90)
Boeck, B. G.: *ref*, 506(992)
Boecklen, W. A.: *ref*, 19(146), 232 (1371)
Boehm, A. E.: *test*, 178, 797; *ref*, 229(1502), 232(1264)
Boerger, A. R.: *ref*, 616(4404, 4634)
Boettcher, B. E.: *ref*, 1175(138)
Bogan, J. B.: *ref*, 230(1198), 616 (4658, 4847), 661(4864)
Bogard, M. E.: *ref*, 693(449)
Bogdan, A. R.: *ref*, 542(1411), 1023(1315), 1050(49)
Bogen, D.: *ref*, 493(27)
Bogle, D.: *test*, 959
Bognar, B. J.: *ref*, 656(36)
Bogner, R. G.: *ref*, 1028(198)
Bogue, E. G.: *ref*, 469(377)
Bohannon, K. M.: *ref*, 431(578)
Bohm, M. K.: *ref*, 232(1459)
Bohn, M. J.: *ref*, 495(366), 514 (1053), 1023(1316)
Bohrnstedt, G. W.: *ref*, 485(343)
Boice, R.: *ref*, 249(481)
Boileau, R. A.: *ref*, 407(162)
Bol, D. J.: *ref*, 692(26)
Bolan, S. L.: *ref*, 641(297)
Boland, B. K.: *ref*, 514(1054), 574 (520)
Boland, G. C.: *ref*, 597(181), 661 (4711)
Bolander, K.: *bk*, B56
Bolding, J. T.: *ref*, 679(931)
Boleloucky, Z.: *ref*, 615(27), 679 (1077, 1218–9)

Boles, B. K.: *ref*, 377(535)
Bolig, J. R.: *ref*, 802(229)
Boling, J. C.: *ref*, 495(489)
Boll, T. J.: *test*, 215; *ref*, 616 (4405)
Bolland, H. R.: *ref*, 578(264), 643 (70), 679(934)
Bollenbacher, J.: *exc*, B10; *cross ref*, 803
Boller, J. D.: *ref*, 611(614)
Bolling, B.: *ref*, 616(4496)
Bolton, B.: *bk*, B57, B550; *exc*, B22, B77, B100, B256; *ref*, 200 (563), 506(775, 836), 581 (339, 368), 616(4406, 4829), 661(4913), 679(1315), 693(369, 537)
Bolton, B. F.: *rev*, 217, 679
Bolton, D. L.: *bk*, B58
Bolton, N.: *bk*, B472; *exc*, B246; *ref*, 230(972, 1025, 1107, 1154, 1246), 239(90), 244(137), 250 (94, 121), 490(478, 531), 514 (1048, 1322), 553(406, 656), 579 (62, 82), 679 (1073, 1212, 1431)
Boltuch, B.: *ref*, 631(36)
Bommarito, J. W.: *bk*, B254
Bonar, J. R.: *ref*, 555(179)
Bonaventura, E.: *test*, 441; *ref*, 29 (228, 239), 441(1, 3, 5)
Bond, M. R.: *ref*, 553(412)
Bondell, J. A.: *ref*, 679(1340)
Bone, R. N.: *ref*, 553(324, 401), 616(4133), 679(1068)
Bonfield, R.: *ref*, 223(21)
Bonifacio, P. P.: *ref*, 235(120), 683 (158)
Bonk, E. C.: *ref*, 49(306), 377 (466–7, 505), 574(507–8, 528, 540), 616(4240), 641(243, 333–4), 677(170)
Bonner, D. J.: *ref*, 548(238), 655 (6)
Bonner, D. W.: *ref*, 523(210)
Bonner, R. L.: *ref*, 490(480, 500)
Bonomo, J.: *ref*, 720(272)
Bonsall, M. R.: *test*, 709
Book, R. M.: *ref*, 227(74), 506 (886), 802(258)
Bookbinder, G. E.: *test*, 791
Booker, H. E.: *ref*, 230(995)
Booker, I. A.: *cross ref*, 719, 730, 732, 735
Booker, L.: *ref*, 222(439), 227(82), 802(283), 882(217)
Boon, D. A.: *ref*, 574(546), 628 (209)
Boone, D. R.: *rev*, 955, 963; *cross ref*, 971, 976
Boone, J. A.: *ref*, 675(103), 677 (175)
Boone, L. E.: *ref*, 514(1157)
Boor, M.: *ref*, 230(947, 1183), 654 (12, 18)
Booth, R. F.: *ref*, 527(45, 48–9), 713(1–3)
Booth, S. R.: *ref*, 553(677)
Borchard, D. C.: *ref*, 461(576)
Bordeaux, J.: *ref*, 581(434)
Bordin, E. S.: *cross ref*, 1011, 1023
Boreham, N. C.: *bk*, B496
Borengasser, M. A.: *ref*, 616(4407)
Borg, S.: *ref*, 548(331)
Borgatta, E. F.: *ref*, 485(343)
Borgen, F. H.: *rev*, 700, 1002; *test*,

Csikszenthmihalyi, M.: *ref,* 679 (1091), 686(895)
Cubitt, G. H.: *ref,* 616(3911), 679 (947)
Cuchens, B. D.: *ref,* 580(13)
Cuculic, Z.: *ref,* 675(111)
Culbertson, R. G.: *ref,* 693(381), 693(458)
Culhane, J. W.: *ref,* 720(157, 172, 230, 278)
Cullen, C.: *exc,* B269
Cullen, T. J.: *ref,* 1101(163)
Culloty, M. B.: *exc,* 815; *ref,* 815 (3)
Culp, W. H.: *exc,* B265
Culpepper, B. W.: *ref,* 514(962), 661(4614)
Culver, C. M.: *ref,* 230(1118)
Culver, F. R.: *ref,* 98(45)
Cummings, B. S.: *test,* 917
Cummings, L. L.: *ref,* 235(125), 237(67), 239(102)
Cummins, M.: *ref,* 182(753)
Cummins, R. C.: *ref,* 1177(66)
Cundick, B. P.: *ref,* 506(776), 527(26), 613(82), 679(996)
Cunningham, C. H.: *ref,* 377(551, 559), 542(1557, 1598–9), 679 (1496–7, 1028(260–1, 295, 302), 1189(1)
Cunningham, J. W.: *ref,* 983(1, 3–4)
Cunningham, R. W.: *ref,* 630(220)
Cunningham, W. R.: *ref,* 200(570, 650), 230(1037, 1193)
Cunnington, B. F.: *test,* 248
Cureton, E. E.: *cross ref,* 1033
Cureton, K. J.: *ref,* 407(162)
Curlee, J.: *ref,* 616(4164)
Curley, J. F.: *ref,* 184(100), 200 (571), 222(360)
Curran, J.: *ref,* 547(2–3)
Curran, J. D.: *ref,* 553(521–2, 709), 682(87, 90), 820(171)
Curran, J. P.: *test,* 547; *ref,* 553 (623), 627(41), 679(948, 1474)
Curran, M. C.: *ref,* 660(172), 679 (1438)
Curran, S. F.: *ref,* 616(4486)
Currie, L. E.: *ref,* 997(56), 1028 (168)
Currie, S. F.: *ref,* 187(430), 232 (1270), 578(305)
Currie, S. R.: *ref,* 820(159)
Currin, M. S.: *ref,* 529(12)
Curtin, M. E.: *ref,* 616(4660)
Curtis Blake Child Development Center: *test,* 869
Curtis, G. C.: *ref,* 514(963), 628 (152), 661(4615)
Curtis, J. O.: *ref,* 634(222)
Curtis, R. H.: *ref,* 554(56)
Cusack, A. T.: *ref,* 574(522)
Cushing, J. F.: *ref,* 660(143)
Custer, R.: *ref,* 616(4201)
Cutler, C. M.: *ref,* 234(115)
Cutler, R.: *ref,* 693(226)
Cutrona, M. P.: *test,* 426, 784
Cutter, H.: *ref,* 616(3981)
Cutter, H. S. G.: *ref,* 611(585), 651(34, 42)
Cutts, C. C.: *exc,* 1022; *ref,* 1022 (80)
Cymbalisty, B. Y.: *ref,* 553(377)

Cysewski, B.: *ref,* 616(5005)
Cysewski, B. P.: *ref,* 628(219)
Czubalski, K. B.: *ref,* 611(656)

DAANE, C. J.: *ref,* 377(540)
D'Abadie, N. B.: *ref,* 578(306)
Dabbs, A.: *exc,* B268, B318
D'Afflitti, J. P.: *ref,* 675(102)
Daffron, W. C.: *ref,* 257(41)
Daggett, L.: *ref,* 599(27)
D'Agostino, C. A.: *ref,* 616(4837)
Dague, J. L.: *ref,* 542(1329)
Dahl, P. A.: *rev,* 844, 851
Dahl, T. A.: *exc,* 178; *ref,* 178(7)
Dahle, A. J.: *ref,* 932(91, 129)
Dahlem, G. G.: *exc,* B1944, B513
Dahlem, N. W.: *ref,* 232(1553), 431(636)
Dahlstrom, L. E.: *bk,* B121–2; *ref,* 616(3913, 4650), 617(55), 619 (12), 620(2), 621(7), 623(13), 624(19)
Dahlstrom, N. R.: *ref,* 506(841)
Dahlstrom, W. G.: *rev,* 604, 635; *bk,* B121–2; *exc,* 3912–3; *ref,* 616 (3872, 3912–3, 4650), 617(55), 619(12), 620(2) 621(7), 623 (13), 624(19)
Dahms, A. M.: *ref,* 698(18)
Daignault, G.: *ref,* 1074(20)
Dailey, C. A.: *bk,* B123
Dailey, J. N.: *ref,* 182(583)
Dailey, J. T.: *cross ref,* 182, 188, 192
Daily, W. E.: *ref,* 641(507)
Daines, D.: *ref,* 746(2), 749(2), 753(14), 759(22), 785(26)
Daitzman, R. J.: *ref,* 553(511), 554(65), 616(4436), 628(198–9), 643(130), 675(75)
Dale, J. B.: *ref,* 686(896)
Dale, J. D.: *ref,* 679(1398)
Dale, L. G.: *test,* 861
Dale, L. H.: *ref,* 720(158)
Daley, W. T.: *ref,* 973(10)
Dallara, R. F.: *ref,* 616(4639)
Dallas, J.: *ref,* 232(1098)
Dalpes, D.: *ref,* 616(5026)
Dalrymple, D. G.: *ref,* 553(334), 554(35, 43–4)
Dalton, J. C.: *ref,* 232(1381)
Dalton, J. L.: *ref,* 249(390)
Dalton, S.: *ref,* 30(7), 113(7), 126 (10), 153(4), 182(678–9, 755)
Daly, D. A.: *ref,* 932(91, 129)
Daly, D. D.: *exc,* B303
Daly, J.: *ref,* 200(562)
Daly, J. D.: *ref,* 469(401), 679 (949)
Daly, M. B.: *ref,* 530(157)
Damarin, F.: *rev,* 206, 209
Damarin, F. L.: *ref,* 616(4527)
D'Amico, D.: *ref,* 693(524)
Damino, J.: *ref,* 660(132)
Damm, V. J.: *ref,* 641(222)
Dammann, E.: *ref,* 957(3)
Damsbo, A. M.: *ref,* 461(508)
Dana, J. M.: *ref,* 661(4616)
Dana, R. H.: *rev,* 661; *ref,* 232 (1549), 661(4616, 4913); *cross ref,* 661–2, 697
Danahy, S.: *ref,* 616(4694)
Dangel, H. L.: *ref,* 232(1055)

D'Angeljan, A.: *exc,* 120; *ref,* 120 (1)
Daniel, E. H.: *ref,* 679(1240)
Daniel, K.: *ref,* 431(449)
Daniel, L. S.: *ref,* 553(428)
Daniels, J.: *ref,* 523(290)
Daniels, J. H.: *ref,* 666(83)
Daniels, H.: *ref,* 182(680)
Daniels, L. K.: *ref,* 229(1467), 687 (22)
Dannaway, J. C.: *ref,* 452(1558), 693(459)
Dansereau, F.: *ref,* 1174(160–1, 187)
Danzger, B.: *ref,* 208(5)
Daoud, F. S.: *ref,* 581(423)
Darbes, A.: *ref,* 575(38), 578(293, 308, 320)
Darby, C. A.: *ref,* 735(90)
Darden, E.: *ref,* 679(950)
Darden, L. A.: *ref,* 679(1353)
Dargel, R.: *ref,* 582(216)
Darley, F. L.: *ref,* 971(16)
Darley, J. G.: *cross ref,* 1023
Darley, L. K.: *ref,* 1016(12)
Darling, W. G.: *ref,* 634(253)
Darnell, D. K.: *ref,* 110(15), 720 (173)
Darnell, R. E.: *rev,* 868, 880
Darpli, F.: *ref,* 641(414)
Darr, A. D.: *ref,* 377(454), 679 (951)
Darr, R. E.: *ref,* 516(440)
Darrow, J. F.: *ref,* 485(355)
Darsa, S. D.: *ref,* 641(580)
Darsey, N. S.: *ref,* 574(550)
Das, J. P.: *ref,* 200(524, 572, 651–2), 222(452), 611(584), 613(83, 87–8, 110)
Dasberg, H.: *ref,* 236(116), 506 (880)
Dasen, P. R.: *ref,* 222(361)
Dasinger, E. M.: *ref,* 585(187), 599(32)
Dass, J.: *rev,* 275
Dates, B. G.: *ref,* 506(1013)
Datta, L. E.: *ref,* 187(448), 222 (453), 227(86)
Dattle, H. J :. *ref,* 1030(83)
Daubney, J. H.: *ref,* 661(4907)
D'Augelli, A. R.: *ref,* 683(161)
Daugherty, J.: *ref,* 720(200)
Daugs, D. R.: *ref,* 720(319)
Daugs, F.: *ref,* 720(319)
Dauw, D. C.: *ref,* 249(548), 641 (609)
Davenport, B. M.: *ref,* 22(120), 24 (33), 198(45)
Davenport, I. W.: *ref,* 1175(140)
Davenport, S.: *ref,* 616(4751)
Davens, E.: *ref,* 884(12)
Daves, C. W.: *bk,* B4
Davey, H.: *ref,* 230(968)
David, F.: *ref,* 249(488)
David, G.: *ref,* 225(72), 229(1555)
David, K. H.: *ref,* 224(257)
David, M. E.: *ref,* 649(1)
Davids, A.: *ref,* 661(4674–5), 697 (1846–7)
Davidson, A. D.: *ref,* 352(3)
Davidson, C. W.: *ref,* 377(455)
Davidson, H. H.: *bk,* B55; *ref,* 661 (4811)

Dinmore, G. C.: *ref,* 506(777)
Dinnan, J. A.: *ref,* 720(225)
Dinning, W. D.: *ref,* 230(1279), 232(1475), 506(970, 983), 616 (4973)
Dinoff, M.: *ref,* 683(93)
Dinsmore, S. C.: *ref,* 616(4446)
Dionne, M. T.: *ref,* 686(851)
Dipboye, R. L.: *rev,* 1174-5
Dirkes, M. A.: *ref,* 249(446)
Dirschel, K. M.: *ref,* 548(335)
Dischel, P. I.: *ref,* 683(117)
DiScipio, W. J.: *ref,* 549(31), 553 (382), 1028(202)
DiSiomi, F. G.: *ref,* 971(16)
Dissmore, L. F.: *ref,* 506(939)
Distefano, M. K.: *ref,* 628(246), 1174(185)
Dittes, J. E.: *ref,* 542(1311), 616 (3855)
Di Vesta, F. J.: *ref,* 519(89)
Divine, J. H.: *ref,* 732(58)
Dixon, C. C.: *ref,* 693(218)
Dixon, F. A.: *ref,* 514(1233)
Dixon, J. C.: *ref,* 611(620)
Dixon, P. W.: *ref,* 542(1416)
Dizzone, M. F.: *ref,* 225(58), 230 (1042)
Dlugokinski, E.: *ref,* 234(160)
Dmitruk, V. M.: *ref,* 606(306, 313), 660(74)
Doby, W. C.: *ref,* 182(682)
Dockrell, B.: *exc,* B88
Docter, R.: *bk,* B229
Docter, R. F.: *cross ref,* 224
Dodd, B. J.: *ref,* 206(33)
Dodd, C. D.: *ref,* 535(10), 616 (3920)
Dodge, H. E.: *ref,* 229(1417)
Dodge, R. L.: *ref,* 555(281), 693 (460)
Dodrill, C. B.: *ref,* 230(1196)
Dodson, J. A.: *ref,* 469(433)
Doehrman, S.: *ref,* 616(4400)
Doerr, H. A.: *ref,* 530(176), 616 (4317)
Doerr, H. O.: *ref,* 616(4316)
Doherty, E. G.: *ref,* 616(4654)
Doherty, M. T.: *ref,* 409(16)
Dokes, M. A.: *ref,* 802(262)
Dolan, A. B.: *ref,* 206(39), 232 (1407), 431(531), 520(112), 719 (89), 967(13)
Doland, D. J.: *ref,* 585(192)
Dole, A. A.: *ref,* 523(231)
Doles, R. D.: *ref,* 183(350)
Dolins, J. L.: *ref,* 514(1074)
Dolke, A. M.: *ref,* 490(519)
Doll, E. A.: *test,* 703
Doll, L. D.: *ref,* 569(139)
Doll, P. A.: *ref,* 592(59)
Doll, R.: *ref,* 701(5)
Doll, R. E.: *ref,* 1023(1254)
Dollar, R. J.: *ref,* 523(219)
Dollery, C. T.: *ref,* 615(37)
Dollimore, J.: *ref,* 232(1303), 234 (138)
Dolliver, R. H.: *rev,* 1003, 1023; *exc,* 1022; *ref,* 1022(81), 1023 (1255-6, 1275, 1324, 1438-9, 1511, 1521); *cross ref,* 1010
Dolnick, B.: *ref,* 660(98)
Doman, E. F.: *ref,* 523(304)

Domaracki, J.: *ref,* 753(25), 785 (38)
Domash, L.: *ref,* 187(463), 519 (84), 592(71)
Dombrowski, P. S.: *ref,* 616(4741)
Domino, G.: *rev,* 988, 1024; *ref,* 182(744), 235(117, 119), 237(62, 64, 72), 239(96), 244(148, 156, 160, 173, 177-8), 245(2, 4), 495 (374, 429, 480), 504(92, 96, 101, 110), 514(1169, 1300, 1309, 1331), 542(1483) 562(58-9, 63, 68-70), 578(288), 616(4789), 820(164); *cross ref,* 110, 656
Donah, C. E. H.: *ref,* 446(10)
Donahue, D. H.: *ref,* 679(954)
Donegan, R.: *test,* 898
Donham, R.: *ref,* 249(510)
Donlon, G.: *ref,* 232(1139, 1194)
Donlon, T. F.: *rev,* 33, 811
Donnelly, E. F.: *ref,* 230(1043, 1283), 250(98), 506(800), 616 (4173-4, 4447, 4655, 4840-1), 661 (4815)
Donnelly, F. A.: *ref,* 692(41)
Donnelly, M. E.: *ref,* 182(623)
Donner, L.: *ref,* 616(4086)
Donoghue, J. T.: *ref,* 200(683), 222(487)
Donoghue, R.: *ref,* 506(836), 581 (368)
Donoghue, R. J.: *ref,* 506(889)
Donohew, L.: *ref,* 720(107)
Donovan, D.: *ref,* 535(31)
Donovan, D. M.: *ref,* 535(27, 29, 38), 572(12, 16, 21, 31-2), 616 (4546, 4842, 4850, 4918, 5005), 693(461)
Donovan, J. M.: *ref,* 661(4816)
Doody, K. F.: *ref,* 616(4331)
Doppelt, J. E.: *rev,* 199, 1061; *ref,* 232(1562); *cross ref,* 1074, 1177
Doran, P. R.: *ref,* 485(334)
Doran, W. J.: *ref,* 523(255)
Dore, M. D.: *ref,* 555(253), 641 (417), 679(1242)
Dore, R.: *ref,* 1023(1325)
Doren, M.: *test,* 757
Dorhout, B.: *ref,* 616(4908)
Dorin, P. A.: *ref,* 514(1170)
Dorman, L.: *ref,* 229(1468)
Dorr, D.: *ref,* 516(498), 643(98), 1023(1326)
Dor-Shav, N. K.: *ref,* 548(348), 581(425)
Dorval, B.: *ref,* 200(569)
Doster, M. E.: *ref,* 29(236)
Doucette, J.: *exc,* B534
Dougherty, F. E.: *ref,* 555(308), 616(4843), 634(341), 641(581)
Dougherty, R.: *exc,* B42
Doughtie, E. B.: *ref,* 238(36), 431 (508, 600), 495(488), 616(4408, 4608, 4800, 4812), 820(157), 1028 (191, 223, 259, 262-4, 266, 268, 302)
Douglas, A. S.: *ref,* 553(318)
Douglas, J. W. B.: *ref,* 229(1433)
Douglas, R. L.: *ref,* 553(596), 582 (249), 683(220)
Douglas, S. A.: *ref,* 616(4844)
Douglas, V. I.: *ref,* 232(1051), 548 (240)
Douglass, E. B.: *ref,* 230(1143)

Douglass, L.: *ref,* 553(610)
Dove, J. L.: *ref,* 643(69)
Dow, K. L.: *bk,* B153
Dowd, R. F. D.: *ref,* 431(561)
Dowds, B. N.: *ref,* 638(4-5)
Dowe, M. C.: *ref,* 469(443), 634 (254), 1028(170)
Dowling, J. F.: *ref,* 616(4845)
Downer, J. W.: *ref,* 679(897)
Downey, H. K.: *ref,* 1174(239)
Downing, J.: *rev,* 807
Downing, R.: *ref,* 565(14)
Downing, R. W.: *ref,* 675(50, 61, 67)
Downs, C. W.: *ref,* 1177(86)
Downs, R. R.: *ref,* 230(1044)
Downs, T.: *ref,* 519(42)
Doyle, C. M.: *ref,* 553(687), 651 (46)
Doyle, J. A.: *ref,* 553(429, 657-8), 641(312, 509-10, 582-4)
Doyle, J. T.: *ref,* 720(279)
Doyle, K. O.: *rev,* 370, 391; *bk,* B131
Doyne, S. E.: *ref,* 693(219)
Draayer, D. R.: *ref,* 820(132)
Drachman, F.: *ref,* 982(1)
Draffan, J. W.: *ref,* 571(33, 39)
Dragon, A. C.: *ref,* 1175(142)
Draguns, J. G.: *bk,* B132
Draheim, C. K.: *ref,* 641(313), 820 (142)
Draheim, D. D.: *ref,* 249(392)
Drake, R. M.: *cross ref,* 184
Drake, S. V.: *ref,* 222(454), 802 (294-5)
Dreese, C. W.: *ref,* 1028(203)
Dreger, R. M.: *rev,* 678, 683; *ref,* 555(258), 616(4448), 679(1243, 1393), 683(89), 697(1945)
Dreher, E. R.: *ref,* 679(1097), 693 (300)
Dremuk, R.: *ref,* 476(49)
Drenth, P. J. D.: *bk,* B117
Dreskin, T.: *ref,* 641(360)
Dressel, P. L.: *rev.,* 471, 473; *bk,* B133; *exc,* B534; *cross ref,* 36, 290, 309, 523-4, 586
Drewery, J.: *ref,* 542(1378), 616 (4067)
Drews, F.: *bk,* B304
Drexler, H.: *ref,* 958(1)
Drexler, H. G.: *ref,* 969(3), 973 (8), 975(2)
Drexler, J. A.: *ref,* 985(12)
Dreyer, A. S.: *ref,* 519(46), 572(8)
Dreyer, C. A.: *ref.* 519(46)
Dreyer, P. H.: *rev,* 339, 557
Drichta, C. E.: *ref,* 431(608)
Drinkard, K.: *test,* 709
Drinkwater, J. S.: *ref,* 396(1)
Driscoll, L. A.: *rev,* 81, 500
Driscoll, M. C.: *ref,* 882(173)
Driskill, R. E.: *ref,* 732(62)
Driver, M. J.: *ref,* 611(548)
Droege, R. C.: *ref,* 490(451, 532-3), 491(7); *cross ref,* 981
Droppleman, L. F.: *test,* 651
Drossman, A. K.: *ref,* 585(165), 707(27)
Drowns-Garmize, K. S.: *ref,* 514 (1075)
Drude, K. P.: *ref,* 514(965), 641 (224), 693(220)

Fleming, E. E.: *test, 662*
Fleming, E. S.: *ref,* 29(261)
Fleming, J. B.: *ref,* 720(322)
Fleming, J. T.: *ref,* 720(245–6, 282, 339)
Fleming, M.: *exc,* B297
Fleming, R. A.: *ref,* 1174(186)
Fleminger, J. J.: *ref,* 250(114)
Flenniken, D.: *ref,* 982(2–3)
Flescher, B. E.: *ref,* 693(493)
Fleshler, H.: *ref,* 693(318)
Fletcher, G.: *test,* 80
Fletcher, G. O.: *ref,* 802(229)
Fletcher, J.: *ref,* 483(3)
Fletcher, J. D.: *ref,* 110(23), 745 (68)
Fletcher, J. E.: *ref,* 720(41)
Fletcher, J. M.: *ref,* 184(116), 200 (654), 230(1201)
Fletcher, M. R.: *ref,* 1174(158)
Fletcher, R.: *ref,* 542(1312)
Fletcher, R. K.: *ref,* 298(8)
Flick, G. L.: *ref,* 693(343)
Fling, S.: *ref,* 592(52)
Flink, E. W.: *ref,* 238(20)
Flint, B. M.: *test,* 560
Flint, G.: *ref,* 616(4256)
Flint, R. T.: *ref,* 1023(1343)
Flom, J. H.: *ref,* 96(11, 13)
Flook, W. M.: *ref,* 441(4)
Flora, R. R.: *ref,* 693(467)
Florence, J. W.: *ref,* 1028(173)
Flores, M. B.: *ref,* 200(527), 488 (371)
Floriani, B. P.: *ref,* 720(368)
Flouranzano, R.: *ref,* 697(1881)
Flowers, A.: *test,* 935–6, 946
Flowers, A. D.: *ref,* 182(586)
Floyd, J.: *ref,* 606(323)
Floyd, L. M.: *ref,* 555(283), 697 (1955)
Fluegge, L. R.: *ref,* 1016(10)
Flugsrud, M. R.: *ref,* 520(79)
Flynn, K. C.: *ref,* 536(19)
Flynn, S. K.: *ref,* 514(975)
Fogel, B.: *ref,* 232(1172), 661 (4678)
Fogel, F. R.: *ref,* 431(563)
Fogel, M. L.: *ref,* 514(963), 628 (152, 188), 661(4615)
Fogelberg, A. Q.: *ref,* 377(459)
Fogelgren, L. A.: *ref,* 697(1913)
Fogg, M. E.: *ref,* 616(4862)
Foggitt, R. H.: *ref,* 431(400)
Fogliatto, H.: *ref,* 563(4)
Fojtik, C. W.: *ref,* 568(98), 569 (169), 1074(24)
Foley, J. J.: *rev,* 57, 61
Foley, J. P.: *cross ref,* 1052
Foley, S. P. C.: *ref,* 596(63)
Folkins, C.: *ref,* 628(202)
Folkins, C. H.: *ref,* 495(498), 628 (240)
Folkins, L. D.: *ref,* 393(97)
Follingstad, D. R.: *ref,* 461(587, 599)
Follman, D. E.: *ref,* 222(408), 883 (5)
Follman, J.: *ref,* 179(101), 732(34)
Folman, R. Z.: *ref,* 548(277)
Folsom, C. H.: *ref,* 1028(174)
Fonda, C. P.: *ref,* 661(4916)
Fontana, A. F.: *ref,* 638(4–5)
Fontana, B. S.: *ref,* 222(409)

Fontana, M. C.: *rev,* 961, 967
Fontenelle, D. H.: *ref,* 553(339)
Fooks, G. M.: *ref,* 1028(239)
Foote, M.: *ref,* 634(322)
Forastieri, B. V.: *ref,* 684(16)
Forbes, A. R.: *ref,* 527(29, 36), 554 (40), 579(65), 679(906, 960)
Ford, C. V.: *ref,* 616(3937, 4187, 4858)
Ford, J. A.: *ref,* 628(155)
Ford, J. C.: *ref,* 524(115)
Ford, K.: *ref,* 631(53)
Ford, M. A.: *ref,* 187(431)
Ford, M. S.: *ref,* 681(78), 700(10)
Ford, S. F.: *ref,* 199(24)
Forde, J.: *ref,* 222(506)
Forehand, R.: *ref,* 229(1437)
Forell, E. R.: *ref,* 20(128), 232 (1206)
Foreman, P. E.: *ref,* 542(1606), 1028(272)
Foreman, P. J.: *ref,* 225(62)
Forer, B. R.: *cross ref,* 578
Foreyt, J. P.: *bk,* B124; *ref,* 616 (4651)
Forgone, C.: *ref,* 431(610), 882 (230)
Forinash, R. J.: *ref,* 630(277)
Forman, D.: *test,* 1126
Forman, S. G.: *ref,* 19(162), 488 (433)
Fornoff, F. J.: *rev,* 837, 853; *cross ref,* 838, 844–5
Forrer, S. E.: *ref,* 523(271, 292)
Forrest, A. R.: *ref,* 554(7), 596 (41)
Forrest, F. G.: *ref,* 985(10)
Forsberg, L. A.: *ref,* 519(47)
Forstall, L. J.: *ref,* 1174(266)
Forster, D. M.: *ref,* 641(228)
Forster, J. R.: *ref,* 679(1448)
Forsyth, R. A.: *rev,* 298, 735; *test,* 20; *ref,* 20(126), 616(4392)
Fosdick, C. J. H.: *ref,* 641(229)
Fosdick, D. H.: *ref,* 409(7), 679 (961)
Fosmire, F. R.: *ref,* 720(114)
Foss, R. V.: *ref,* 97(11, 15)
Fossen, G. J.: *ref,* 520(103), 540 (26)
Fosshage, J. L.: *ref,* 229(1429)
Foster, A. L.: *test,* 355
Foster, B. R.: *ref,* 469(447), 514 (1081), 626(253)
Foster, B. W.: *ref,* 693(227)
Foster, E. G.: *ref,* 679(962)
Foster, E. M.: *ref,* 230(1146)
Foster, F. G.: *ref,* 530(169)
Foster, G. G.: *ref,* 22(115), 181 (10), 506(992)
Foster, J.: *ref,* 469(448), 1023 (1328)
Foster, L. L.: *ref,* 616(4665), 638 (2)
Foster, L. M.: *ref,* 572(46)
Foster, R.: *test,* 452, 493
Foster, R. W.: *test,* 517; *ref,* 679 (1104)
Foster, S.: *ref,* 675(51), 683(75)
Foster, S. A.: *ref,* 585(187), 599 (31–2)
Foster, S. B.: *ref,* 683(164)
Foster, S. F.: *ref,* 641(230, 357)

Foulds, G. A.: *test,* 579; *ref,* 571 (29), 579(66), 679(1120)
Foulds, M. L.: *ref,* 514(1176), 641 (390, 489, 588)
Fournet, G. P.: *ref,* 179(122)
Fouse, A. B. F.: *ref,* 213(25), 506 (978), 779(5), 932(153)
Fowler, E. D.: *ref,* 732(43)
Fowler, H. M.: *cross ref,* 183, 190, 1011
Fowler, M. G.: *ref,* 495(325, 380, 494), 616(4859), 661(4870)
Fowler, R. D.: *rev,* 642, 649; *test,* 622, 624; *ref,* 616(3938, 4479, 4666, 4880), 617(18, 21–2, 28–31, 34–7, 40, 47, 57), 624(20)
Fowler, R. L.: *ref,* 229(1546)
Fowler, W. R.: *ref,* 232(1267), 542 (1486), 679(1246)
Fowles, D. E.: *bk,* B485, B568
Fox, B. R.: *ref,* 514(976)
Fox, D.: *test,* 607
Fox, D. B.: *ref,* 577(33)
Fox, D. C.: *ref,* 548(305)
Fox, D. J.: *test,* 608; *ref,* 607(14–5, 27), 608(3)
Fox, D. L.: *ref,* 579(1247)
Fox, J. A.: *ref,* 514(1255)
Fox, L. H.: *rev,* 183, 202; *ref,* 686 (942), 1028(206)
Fox, L. J.: *ref,* 692(28)
Fox, L. M.: *ref,* 693(308)
Fox, M.: *ref,* 249(519), 693(534)
Fox, R.: *ref,* 630(194), 872(41)
Fox, R. A.: *ref,* 571(34)
Fox, R. E.: *ref,* 514(979)
Foxgrover, P.: *ref,* 488(427), 778 (6), 803(31)
Foxman, P.: *ref,* 661(4871), 693 (545)
Foxman, P. N.: *ref,* 548(306), 661 (4752), 693(386)
Foy, F. P.: *ref,* 1174(213)
Fozard, J. L.: *ref,* 490(456–7), 679 (963), 1023(1510)
Fraas, L. A.: *ref,* 595(19), 692 (27–8)
Fracchia, J.: *ref,* 200(612, 665), 542 (1487, 1530–1, 1589–90), 549(15–6, 22–3, 26, 29), 616(4095–6, 4188–9, 4346–7, 4454–5), 617(66)
Fraconia, J.: *ref,* 506(893)
Fram, R. D.: *ref,* 720(233)
France, G. A.: *ref,* 555(254)
France, K.: *ref,* 222(364)
France, N.: *test,* 25
Franchette, E. A.: *exc,* B546
Francis, A.: *ref,* 554(77)
Francis, H.: *exc,* 959; *ref,* 959(3)
Francis, R.: *ref,* 527(28)
Francis, R. D.: *ref,* 553(432), 679 (964)
Francis-Williams, J. M.: *exc,* 810; *ref,* 810(1)
Franck, K.: *test,* 562
Franco, E. A.: *ref,* 548(362), 553 (673)
Franco, J. N.: *ref,* 683(224)
Franco, V. J.: *ref,* 599(29)
Frandsen, K. D.: *ref,* 555(199, 218)
Frank, A. C.: *rev,* 1003, 1012; *ref,* 183(327, 347), 634(227, 279, 344), 1023(1259, 1368, 1383, 1515)

Fugate, C. W.: *ref,* 35(111)
Fugita, S. S.: *ref,* 490(522)
Fugua, R. W.: *ref,* 249(491)
Fuhrer, M. J.: *ref,* 553(434)
Fuhrer, S.: *ref,* 298(6)
Fuhs, K.: *ref,* 495(321), 641(212)
Fujii, D. S.: *ref,* 514(1338), 1052 (103), 1174(268)
Fulchiero, C. F.: *ref,* 616(4669)
Fuld, P. A.: *exc,* 761, 780, 787; *ref,* 761(1), 780(1), 787(1)
Fuldauer, L. B.: *ref,* 375(17)
Fulkerson, R. V.: *ref,* 692(35)
Fulkerson, S. C.: *ref,* 506(851)
Fuller, A. R.: *ref,* 553(661)
Fuller, G.: *ref,* 37(114), 232(1091), 236(108), 597(172), 872(43-4, 49, 53), 963(13)
Fuller, G. B.: *test,* 872; *ref,* 20 (122), 37(167), 232(1280), 431 (512), 485(336), 872(47-8, 52, 54)
Fuller, H. E.: *ref,* 475(20)
Fuller, M.: *ref,* 581(346), 592(53)
Fuller, R.: *ref,* 37(178), 230(1159), 236(123)
Fuller, R. N.: *ref,* 229(1513)
Fuller, S. S.: *ref,* 683(225-6)
Fullerton, D. T.: *ref,* 549(6)
Fullerton, J.: *ref,* 1023(1274)
Fulmer, R. H.: *ref,* 616(4670)
Fulton, E. E.: *ref,* 461(513)
Fulton, J. T.: *ref,* 391(7), 679 (1105)
Fulton, R. T.: *bk,* B164
Fults, A. C.: *bk,* B165
Funk, W. R.: *ref,* 679(1106)
Funnell, M. R.: *ref,* 249(492), 529 (25)
Furby, L.: *exc,* B147
Furfey, P. H.: *cross ref,* 703
Furnell, J.: *ref,* 506(953)
Furry, C. A.: *ref,* 488(391)
Furst, E. J.: *rev,* 4; *exc,* B54; *cross ref,* 1023
Furth, J. D.: *ref,* 225(51)
Fyro, B.: *ref,* 548(331)

GABE, R.: *ref,* 19(150)
Gable, M.: *ref,* 555(312)
Gable, P.: *ref,* 616(4324)
Gable, R. K.: *test,* 442; *ref,* 475 (14), 693(309), 997(157), 1030 (48, 59)
Gaborit, M.: *ref,* 627(50), 679 (1096)
Gackenbach, J. I.: *ref,* 514(1256), 628(220)
Gadd, R. A.: *ref,* 615(34)
Gade, E.: *ref,* 469(448, 521), 1023 (1328)
Gade, E. M.: *ref,* 1028(240-1)
Gadza, G. M.: *ref,* 577(51)
Gadzella, B. M.: *ref,* 179(122), 816 (2), 820(172)
Gaensslen, H.: *ref,* 679(1107)
Gaffey, R. L.: *ref,* 1022(7, 22, 89), 1023(1385), 1028(144, 207, 306)
Gaffney, J. P.: *ref,* 182(628), 542 (1425), 1011(884)
Gaffney, M. J.: *ref,* 697(1854)
Gaffney, P. D.: *ref,* 232(1110)
Gage, N. L.: *cross ref,* 29, 686
Gagne, E. D.: *ref,* 182(649)

Gaillard, T. L.: *ref,* 182(724)
Gaines, L. S.: *ref,* 616(4459), 641 (479)
Gakhar, S.: *ref,* 553(435)
Galassi, J.: *ref,* 495(321), 641(212)
Galassi, J. P.: *ref,* 687(15)
Galaz, A.: *ref,* 611(559)
Galbraith, G. G.: *ref,* 663(131)
Galbraith, K. W.: *ref,* 238(30)
Galbraith, S. A.: *ref,* 542(1328), 555(182), 616(3905)
Galbreath, J. A.: *ref,* 666(57)
Galdieri, A. A.: *ref,* 232(1065)
Gale, A.: *ref,* 200(528), 553(553), 596(48), 820(150)
Gale, J.: *ref,* 1010(50)
Galen, R.: *ref,* 616(4743)
Galewski, J.: *ref,* 230(1002)
Galfo, A. J.: *ref,* 8(17)
Galinsky, H. A.: *ref,* 1174(242)
Gall, S. S.: *ref,* 179(108), 719(80)
Gallagher, A. F.: *ref,* 660(149)
Gallagher, F. D.: *ref,* 96(14)
Gallagher, J. E.: *ref,* 514(1257)
Gallagher, J. J.: *ref,* 679(1108)
Gallagher, J. M.: *ref,* 244(183), 572(49)
Gallagher, T. M.: *ref,* 967(20)
Galland, V. R.: *ref,* 495(458)
Gallant, D.: *ref,* 519(63), 616 (4428)
Gallant, D. H.: *ref,* 616(4647)
Gallant, R.: *ref,* 720(86)
Gallant, R. M. F.: *ref,* 720(69)
Gallegos, S.: *ref,* 469(522)
Gallemore, J. L.: *ref,* 616(3943), 1101(169)
Gallessich, J.: *ref,* 816(1)
Gallimore, R.: *ref,* 548(341)
Gallistel, E.: *ref,* 37(136), 745(61)
Gallo, J. G.: *ref,* 485(357)
Gallop, R.: *ref,* 679(1109), 686 (898)
Galloway, C.: *ref,* 628(182)
Galloway, C. G.: *ref,* 178(10)
Galloway, P.: *ref,* 720(284)
Galluzzi, E. G.: *ref,* 516(502), 646 (107)
Galvin, K. S.: *ref,* 553(535)
Gamble, K. R.: *ref,* 571(41, 44), 578(269), 661(4620)
Games, R. G.: *ref,* 660(122)
Gandica, A.: *ref,* 10(128), 542 (1574), 616(4716), 634(325), 712 (17), 997(133)
Gandy, G. L.: *ref,* 1023(1261, 1329)
Ganesan, V.: *ref,* 636(52)
Ganoung, L.: *ref,* 954(7)
Gant, R. W.: *ref,* 616(4861)
Garb, E.: *ref,* 641(295)
Garcia, C. R.: *ref,* 616(4487), 675 (76)
Gardener, S. H.: *ref,* 536(26), 582 (253), 628(225)
Gardiner, G. S.: *ref,* 697(1790)
Gardiner, H. W.: *ref,* 542(1426, 1617), 581(342)
Gardiner, J. M.: *ref,* 542(1335)
Gardner, A. J.: *ref,* 615(35)
Gardner, A. R.: *ref,* 615(35)
Gardner, E. F.: *rev,* 190, 401; *test,* 2, 29-31, 291-2, 745, 777; *exc,* B232; *cross ref,* 20, 272, 744, 802
Gardner, H. W.: *ref,* 581(391)

Gardner, L. E.: *test,* 564
Gardner, R. C.: *ref,* 593(4)
Gardner, R. W.: *ref,* 1010(45), 1023(1330)
Gardner, S.: *test,* 241
Gardos, G.: *ref,* 651(25)
Garetz, F. K.: *ref,* 616(4190)
Garfield, C. A.: *ref,* 514(1082), 656(28)
Garfield, N. J.: *ref,* 641(514)
Garfield, S. L.: *ref,* 616(4064, 4460)
Garfinkel, A.: *rev,* 155, 165
Garfinkel, R. S.: *ref,* 229(1553)
Gargan, M. A.: *ref,* 530(189), 582 (254)
Gargiulo, R. M.: *ref,* 249(560)
Garhart, C. K.: *ref,* 19(109), 249 (339), 516(442)
Garigliano, L. J.: *ref,* 291(33)
Garman, E. T.: *test,* 418
Garman, L. G.: *ref,* 514(1258)
Garmon, B. W.: *ref,* 616(4191)
Garove, W. E.: *ref,* 1185(1)
Garrard, J.: *ref,* 352(1), 1101(181)
Garrett, H. E.: *cross ref,* 488
Garrie, E. V.: *ref,* 683(165)
Garrie, S. A.: *ref,* 683(165)
Garris, C. W.: *ref,* 822(175)
Garrison, M.: *ref,* 694(6)
Garrison, R. K.: *ref,* 495(326), 693 (228)
Garrison, W. D.: *ref,* 377(460)
Garrity, L. I.: *ref,* 200(683), 222 (487)
Garrity, T. F.: *ref,* 634(347)
Garside, R. F.: *ref,* 536(14), 553 (452), 616(3957, 4075)
Garske, J. P.: *ref,* 553(691), 679 (1450)
Gartner, A.: *bk,* B166
Gartner, D.: *ref,* 616(3944), 662 (419)
Garton, S.: *bk,* B252
Garvey, F. J.: *ref,* 616(4240-1), 641(243, 333-4, 437), 677(170)
Garvey, R. M.: *ref,* 542(1336)
Garvin, B. S.: *ref,* 679(966)
Garwood, J.: *ref,* 661(4917)
Gary, V.: *ref,* 495(327)
Garza, R. T.: *ref,* 523(250)
Garza-Perez, J.: *ref,* 559(37), 582 (208)
Gasper, T. H.: *ref,* 997(126, 158)
Gass, M. B.: *ref,* 1052(83), 1061(7)
Gasser, E. S.: *ref,* 553(518)
Gasser, G. W.: *ref,* 469(496)
Gaston, G. W.: *ref,* 485(337), 630 (196)
Gaston, M. M.: *ref,* 693(229)
Gates, A. I.: *test,* 726A, 727-8, 759
Gates, J. A.: *ref,* 693(468)
Gates, S. L.: *ref,* 555(284), 693 (469)
Gates, W. K.: *ref,* 679(967)
Gatschenberger, J. M.: *ref,* 616 (4192)
Gatz, M.: *ref,* 506(974)
Gaudry, E.: *ref,* 683(66, 140, 227-8), 684(4)
Gault, U.: *ref,* 514(1259)
Gauthier, E. J.: *ref,* 1028(242)
Gauthier, W. J.: *ref,* 1175(122)
Gautt, P.: *ref,* 542(1561)
Gavin, J. F.: *ref,* 307(2), 574(532),

Ginn, R. O.: *ref*, 641(425, 516)
Ginsburg, A. B.: *ref*, 616(4464)
Ginther, D. W.: *ref*, 720(235)
Giovannucci, J. E.: *ref*, 973(5)
Gipple, C.: *ref*, 1101(172)
Girard, R.: *ref*, 527(30)
Giray, E. F.: *ref*, 230(1278)
Gironda, R. J.: *ref*, 232(1564)
Gittelman-Klein, R.: *ref*, 37(208), 232(1481), 585(163)
Gittinger, J. W.: *ref*, 230(1102)
Giuliano, J. R.: *ref*, 182(779)
Giurintano, L. P.: *ref*, 616(4495)
Gladding, S. T.: *ref*, 514(972), 630(193), 997(38)
Gladieux, J. D.: *ref*, 495(459), 642(2)
Glanstein, P. J.: *ref*, 514(1261), 997(157)
Glascott, B. J.: *ref*, 182(321)
Glaser, E. M.: *test*, 822; *bk*, B110
Glaser, F. B.: *ref*, 660(131)
Glaser, N. A.: *ref*, 726A(37)
Glaser, R.: *exc*, B294
Glass, A.: *ref*, 553(397)
Glass, D. C.: *ref*, 542(1612), 732(41), 932(113)
Glass, D. H.: *ref*, 616(4200)
Glass, G. V.: *rev*, 745, *ref*, 37(122), 230(1010), 232(1130)
Glasser, A. J.: *bk*, B581; *ref*, 229(1500)
Glatt, C. T.: *ref*, 661(4755)
Glaudin, V.: *ref*, 628(169)
Glavan, J. W.: *ref*, 431(401)
Glazzard, M.: *ref*, 726A(52)
Gleason, H. C.: *ref*, 377(543), 641(517)
Gleason, W. P.: *bk*, B279
Glen, A.: *ref*, 616(4201)
Glendy, D. G.: *ref*, 1023(1262)
Glenn, A. D.: *test*, 918
Glenn, L.: *ref*, 616(4535)
Gleser, G. C.: *rev*, 552, 607; *test*, 535; *bk*, B119; *ref*, 535(16), *cross ref*, 239, 575, 655
Glick, I. D.: *ref*, 585(193), 599(34)
Glick, M.: *ref*, 661(4860)
Glicksman, S. J.: *ref*, 232(1174)
Gligor, A. M.: *ref*, 616(4202)
Glittenberg, D. H.: *ref*, 698(31)
Globerson, T.: *ref*, 519(60)
Glock, M. D.: *bk*, B19-20
Glover, C. B.: *ref*, 683(166)
Glover, J. A.: *ref*, 249(533-5)
Glovinsky, M. A.: *ref*, 641(233), 693(230)
Glowinski, H.: *ref*, 250(100)
Gluck, E. A. T.: *ref*, 519(48)
Glueck, B. C.: *exc*, B525; *ref*, 617(7, 38, 43)
Glueck, B. S.: *exc*, B313
Glueck, E.: *bk*, B171
Glueck, S.: *bk*, B171
Glysh, E. A.: *ref*, 490(458)
Gnagney, T. D.: *test*, 72, 265, 444, 755
Gnewuch, M. M.: *ref*, 735(91)
Gobdel, B. C.: *ref*, 235(125), 237(67), 239(102)
Gockley, G. C.: *ref*, 646(33)
Godfrey, E. A.: *ref*, 490(459), 616(3856, 3946), 1011(878)

Godfrey Thomson Unit. See University of Edinburgh.
Godin, T. J.: *ref*, 1028(243)
Godwin, A.: *ref*, 37(209), 200(685), 232(1488)
Goebel, R. A.: *ref*, 230(1204)
Goerss, K. V. W.: *ref*, 641(518)
Goethals, G. R.: *ref*, 686(932)
Goethals, M. S.: *ref*, 693(546)
Goff, D. P.: *ref*, 697(1856)
Goggins, R.: *ref*, 553(523)
Goh, D. S.: *ref*, 222(507), 234(170), 553(437, 710), 554(68, 80)
Gold, K.: *ref*, 616(4743)
Goldberg, A. D.: *ref*, 529(19)
Goldberg, B.: *ref*, 628(202)
Goldberg, D.: *exc*, 649; *ref*, 649(19)
Goldberg, D. P.: *test*, 565; *bk*, B172, *ref*, 530(159), 565(1-5, 7, 14)
Goldberg, H. K.: *ref*, 213(17), 222(319), 236(106-7), 431(402-3), 732(35), 932(95)
Goldberg, H. L.: *ref*, 651(36)
Goldberg, J.: *ref*, 559(57), 651(25)
Goldberg, K.: *ref*, 572(33), 685(1)
Goldberg, L.: *test*, 702; *ref*, 578(290, 339), 697(1857), 702(2)
Goldberg, L. R.: *rev*, 593; *bk*, B173; *ref*, 182(588), 188(126), 495(329), 514(977-8, 1046, 1370, 1380), 542(1338, 1640), 616(3947, 5012), 627(42), 643(94, 185), 679(969), 820(134), 1023(1263, 1519)
Goldberg, L. S.: *ref*, 249(450)
Goldberg, P. A.: *ref*, 616(4465), 663(136)
Goldberg, R. W.: *ref*, 1023(1487)
Goldberg, S. A.: *ref*, 631(51)
Goldberg, S. C.: *ref*, 585(165, 194, 207), 599(36), 707(27)
Goldberg, L.: *ref*, 548(251), 581(335, 343), 661(4601)
Goldberger, N. I.: *ref*, 576(46)
Golden, C. J.: *ref*, 611(640), 616(4672), 679(1364)
Golden, E. E.: *ref*, 611(640), 616(4672), 679(1364)
Golden, G. M.: *ref*, 523(218)
Golden, J.: *ref*, 352(2)
Golden, M.: *ref*, 209(51), 229(1428)
Golden, S. S.: *ref*, 929(4)
Goldenberg, D.: *ref*, 428(1)
Goldenberg, D. S.: *test*, 428
Goldenthal, S.: *ref*, 683(230)
Goldfarb, A. I.: *ref*, 249(90)
Goldfarb, J.: *ref*, 225(60)
Goldfield, M. D.: *ref*, 585(193), 599(34)
Goldfried, M. R.: *bk*, B174; *ref*, 182(629), 628(221), 820(143)
Goldhamer, D.: *ref*, 562(49)
Golding, S. L.: *rev*, 654; *ref*, 643(140, 146), 661(4621), 1023(1414)
Goldman, B. A.: *bk*, B175; *cross ref*, 393
Goldman, E. L.: *ref*, 232(1175)
Goldman, H.: *ref*, 236(105), 506(782)

Goldman, J. A.: *ref*, 524(125), 641(519, 551-2, 589-90)
Goldman, L. A.: *ref*, 19(110)
Goldman, M.: *ref*, 232(1283), 514(1367)
Goldman, R.: *rev*, 947, 977; *test*, 937-8
Goldman, R. D.: *ref*, 182(630, 685-6, 725-7, 757-60), 200(605), 232(1482)
Goldman, W. J.: *ref*, 516(443)
Goldrick, R. B.: *ref*, 616(4203)
Goldschmid, M. L.: *test*, 238; *ref*, 232(1352), 238(21), 504(89), 555(209); *cross ref*, 181
Goldschmidt, J.: *ref*, 542(1490)
Goldsmith, E. B.: *ref*, 192(150)
Goldsmith, J. G.: *ref*, 643(133-4)
Goldsmith, R. W.: *ref*, 236(102), 506(770)
Goldstein, A.: *ref*, 230(1258), 800(13)
Goldstein, A. M.: *ref*, 616(3948), 617(58), 623(14)
Goldstein, A. P.: *ref*, 555(220), 651(26)
Goldstein, B. J.: *ref*, 631(50)
Goldstein, D.: *ref*, 963(15)
Goldstein, G.: *bk*, B463; *ref*, 230(970, 1051, 1128, 1205, 1280), 514(1180), 616(4741)
Goldstein, H.: *bk*, B526
Goldstein, H. S.: *ref*, 232(1483), 581(344), 616(3944), 662(419)
Goldstein, K. M.: *ref*, 553(411)
Goldstein, L. D.: *bk*, B178; *cross ref*, 675
Goldstein, L. P.: *ref*, 506(941)
Goldstein, M. J.: *ref*, 585(164, 179), 631(37), 697(2005)
Goldstein, S.: *ref*, 230(1012), 250(92), 616(4101)
Goldstein, S. G.: *ref*, 616(4464), 1101(150)
Goldstine, T.: *ref*, 697(1792)
Goldston, J.: *ref*, 816(2), 820(172)
Goldupp, O.: *ref*, 219(22)
Goleman, D. J.: *ref*, 683(284)
Golomb, C.: *ref*, 187(417), 581(372, 437)
Golomb, E.: *ref*, 661(4622)
Golub, S. B.: *ref*, 536(20), 683(167)
Gomberg, A. W.: *ref*, 720(389)
Gombosi, P. G.: *ref*, 661(4623)
Gomer, F. E.: *ref*, 236(105), 506(782)
Gomez-Mont, F.: *ref*, 616(4549)
Gomolka, E. G.: *ref*, 679(1250)
Gonyo, M. E.: *ref*, 882(231), 883(3)
Gonzalez-Reigosa, F.: *ref*, 683(76, 288)
Good, P. K. E.: *bk*, B176; *ref*, 616(4466)
Goodell, H.: *ref*, 230(985-6, 1065), 571(26)
Goodenough, D. R.: *ref*, 188(129), 572(50)
Goodenough, F. L.: *test*, 187; *cross ref*, 488
Goodglass, H.: *test*, 955; *bk*, B177; *ref*, 955(1)
Goodkin, R.: *ref*, 962(3)

Gray, J. A.: *ref*, 506(820), 554(38), 596(50), 611(575, 577)
Gray, J. D.: *ref*, 490(503)
Gray, J. E.: *ref*, 553(340, 436, 439, 440), 631(38), 872(42)
Gray, J. L.: *ref*, 19(139), 291(34), 745(73)
Gray, K.: *ref*, 823(3)
Gray, M. M.: *ref*, 29(226–7), 802 (213), 803(26)
Gray, R. M.: *test*, 400
Gray, S. C.: *ref*, 661(4625)
Gray, S. S.: *ref*, 693(471)
Gray, W. S.: *test*, 792–3
Gray-Little, B.: *ref*, 616(4468)
Grayson, H. M.: *ref*, 616(3952), 617(59), 621(8), 623(15), 624 (21)
Grayson, T. D.: *ref*, 514(1265), 845 (26)
Greaney, B. J.: *ref*, 229(1475), 431 (465), 870(18)
Greathouse, L. J.: *ref*, 720(390)
Gredler, G. R.: *exc*, B266, B456
Greebaum, G. H. C.: *ref*, 571(45)
Green, C.: *ref*, 553(377)
Green, C. B.: *ref*, 516(444), 693 (231)
Green, D. R.: *bk*, B185–6
Green, D. S.: *ref*, 22(121)
Green, E. A.: *ref*, 1023(1442)
Green, E. M.: *ref*, 222(411)
Green, F. A.: *ref*, 490(486)
Green, J. A.: *bk*, B188
Green, J. B.: *ref*, 232(1071, 1181)
Green, J. L.: *bk*, B187; *ref*, 542 (1340). 634(229)
Green, L. L.: *ref*, 514(1086)
Green, L. R.: *ref*, 611(585)
Green, M.: *ref*, 616(4691)
Green, M. D.: *ref*, 679(1437)
Green, M. S.: *ref*, 576(57)
Green, P. A.: *ref*, 232(1218), 431 (479)
Green, P. H.: *ref*, 616(3953)
Green, R.: *ref*, 548(208), 581(346), 592(53), 597(185), 697(1903)
Green, R. F.: *ref*, 230(971), 516 (498); *cross ref*, 183
Green, R. L.: *ref*, 675(86)
Green, V. D.: *ref*, 641(591)
Greenberg, F. A.: *ref*, 626(241), 679(971)
Greenberg, G.: *ref*, 627(49), 679 (1082)
Greenberg, G. J.: *ref*, 627(43)
Greenberg, H. C.: *ref*, 693(232)
Greenberg, J. B.: *ref*, 873(4)
Greenberg, J. S.: *ref*, 634(323)
Greenberg, J. W.: *ref*, 234(93), 506 (896)
Greenberg, M. D.: *ref*, 236(128), 250(115), 616(4675)
Greenberg, R. P.: *ref*, 514(974, 1087), 578(291), 616(3935), 661 4626, 4682), 697(1788)
Greenberger, S. M.: *bk*, B189
Greenburg, J. B.: *ref*, 232(1067)
Greenburg, J. W.: *ref*, 232(1068)
Greene, C. N.: *ref*, 1175(123)
Greene, C. S.: *ref*, 616(4581)
Greene, E. B.: *cross ref*, 490
Greene, F.: *exc*, 766, B154, B514, B576; *ref*, 766(1)

Greene, F. B.: *ref*, 720(87)
Greene, F. P.: *ref*, 720(70, 132)
Greene, G.: *ref*, 377(462), 686(856)
Greene, H. A.: *cross ref*, 45
Greene, H. R.: *ref*, 37(113, 137), 200(575)
Greene, J. F.: *test*, 533
Greene, L. R.: *ref*, 661(4878)
Greene, M. A.: *ref*, 377(501)
Greene, R. J.: *ref*, 683(77)
Greene, R. S.: *ref*, 514(1372), 574 (51, 62)
Greene, S.: *ref*, 675(98), 681(73–4), 706(30–1)
Greene, S. D.: *ref*, 997(58)
Greene, S. E.: *ref*, 679(1252)
Greenewald, M. J.: *ref*, 720(323)
Greenfield, G. J.: *ref*, 249(341)
Greenfield, N. S.: *ref*, 578(345)
Greenlee, W. E.: *ref*, 213(20)
Greeno, D. W.: *ref*, 569(141)
Greeno, J. G.: *ref*, 182(624)
Greenough, J.: *ref*, 244(154)
Greenough, T. J.: *ref*, 628(193)
Greenspan, S. B.: *ref*, 446(8), 882 (200)
Greenstein, G.: *ref*, 1052(37)
Greenstein, J.: *ref*, 305(10)
Greenstein, J. G.: *ref*, 305(8)
Greenstein, M.: *ref*, 548(265)
Greenstein, T.: *ref*, 660(115, 141)
Greenup, J.: *ref*, 230(1059), 611 (597), 615(23)
Greenwood, G. E.: *ref*, 393(63)
Greenwood, M. R.: *ref*, 679(1253), 693(389)
Greer, C.: *bk*, B166
Greer, F. S.: *ref*, 232(1069)
Greer, G. R.: *ref*, 616(4207)
Greer, P. C.: *ref*, 572(5), 616 (3954), 641(235)
Greer, R. M.: *ref*, 495(385), 616 (4208, 4676)
Greer, S.: *ref*, 553(606), 579(78), 582(218, 224)
Greer, W.: *ref*, 616(4302)
Greeson, L. E.: *ref*, 229(1440, 1472, 1520)
Greever, K. B.: *ref*, 514(1088)
Gregg, G. A.: *ref*, 1174(244)
Gregg, R.: *ref*, 229(1464)
Gregor, T. G.: *ref*, 1052(86)
Gregory, D.: *ref*, 616(4553)
Gregory, J.: *ref*, 576(36, 47), 682 (75, 88)
Gregory, R. J.: *ref*, 616(3955, 4469)
Gregory-Panopoulos, J. F.: *ref*, 720 (108)
Gregson, R. A. M.: *ref*, 553(410), 656(25)
Greif, E. B.: *ref*, 514(1089)
Greiner, F. D.: *ref*, 693(472)
Gress, D. H.: *ref*, 1175(103)
Gretsinger, A. F.: *ref*, 183(340)
Gretsky, N. E.: *ref*, 232(1098)
Gretzler, A. F.: *ref*, 229(1469)
Grewster, G.: *ref*, 182(761)
Gridley, N.: *ref*, 711(73)
Grier, M. E. S.: *ref*, 495(461), 555 (286)
Gries, K.: *cross ref*, 138, 145–6
Griesel, R. D.: *ref*, 234(163)
Griesmer, R.: *ref*, 641(520)
Griffin, C.: *ref*, 616(4108)

Griffin, H. R.: *ref*, 230(965)
Griffin, J. L.: *ref*, 616(4452, 4662, 4794, 4868)
Griffin, P.: *ref*, 183(328)
Griffin, R. S.: *ref*, 679(1111)
Griffin, W. B.: *test*, 1168
Griffith, C. L.: *test*, 1125, 1127–8, 1180; *ref*, 1173(1)
Griffith, G. M.: *ref*, 683(232)
Griffith, M.: *ref*, 542(1618), 553 (607), 559(61)
Griffiths, A. K.: *ref*, 553(665)
Griffiths, A. N.: *ref*, 232(1565)
Griffiths, A. W.: *ref*, 554(14)
Grigsby, D. P.: *ref*, 616(4869), 628 (241)
Grill, J. J.: *rev*, 428, 430; *ref*, 431 (637)
Grimes, J. E.: *ref*, 616(4470)
Grimm, J. E.: *ref*, 249(342)
Grimmer, D. J.: *ref*, 229(1515)
Grimmett, S.: *ref*, 200(597)
Grimsgård, A.: *ref*, 631(52)
Grimsley, G.: *ref*, 568(76, 93), 569 (142, 162), 574(524, 551), 686 (900, 986), 1011(885, 899)
Grimwade, J.: *ref*, 553(679)
Grindley, J.: *ref*, 627(52)
Grippin, P. C.: *ref*, 548(252)
Grisé, J.: *ref*, 643(102), 697(1858)
Grisell, J. L.: *ref*, 616(4899), 617 (78), 618(4)
Grisham, J. H.: *ref*, 641(236)
Grisso, J. T.: *ref*, 697(1859)
Grissom, J. J.: *ref*, 693(473)
Grissom, W. A.: *ref*, 693(547)
Grivest, M. T.: *ref*, 1054(14)
Grizzard, R.: *ref*, 230(1232)
Grob, P.: *ref*, 29(223)
Grobe, C. H.: *ref*, 833(6)
Grobman, H.: *rev*, 394, 902; *exc*, B520
Groden, G.: *ref*, 222(489), 229 (1579)
Grodzitsky, P.: *ref*, 592(61)
Groenman, N. H.: *ref*, 616(4991)
Groesch, S. J.: *ref*, 616(4982)
Groff, P.: *rev*, 761; *ref*, 932(143)
Groman, W. D.: *ref*, 611(647, 654)
Grommon, A. H.: *bk*, B190
Gronlund, N. E.: *rev*, 22, 33; *bk*, B191–6
Gronsky, S.: *ref*, 555(287)
Grosenbach, M. J.: *ref*, 630(279)
Gross, A. L.: *ref*, 182(688)
Gross, H.: *test*, 747
Gross, L. J.: *ref*, 22(114)
Gross, M. C.: *ref*, 1023(1365)
Gross, R. B.: *ref*, 548(239)
Gross, R. E.: *rev*, 886, 918; *cross ref*, 892
Gross, R. H.: *ref*, 1052(110)
Gross, S. J.: *ref*, 548(279), 641 (325)
Gross, S. M.: *ref*, 679(1112)
Gross, W. F.: *ref*, 542(1432), 643 (103–4, 170), 679(972, 1113, 1159, 1471)
Grossman, B. B.: *ref*, 641(592)
Grossman, J. C.: *ref*, 504(85), 661 (4627), 697(1860)
Grossnickle, F. E.: *cross ref*, 283
Grosz, R. D.: *ref*, 686(951)
Grotelueschen, A. D.: *bk*, B197

Heise, M. R.: *ref,* 661(4798)
Heisler, G.: *ref,* 183(330)
Heisler, J. T.: *ref,* 643(120)
Heist, P.: *test,* 634
Heitzman, A. J.: *ref,* 720(78, 118)
Heitzman, D.: *ref,* 490(472), 679 (1031), 997(41), 1050(42)
Hekmat, H.: *ref,* 553(626), 554 (54, 60–1, 84), 559(41), 654(28, 31–2, 39)
Held, M. L.: *ref,* 616(3977, 4352), 626(242)
Heller, M. E.: *ref,* 616(3978)
Heller, P. L.: *ref,* 338(7)
Heller, R. W.: *ref,* 634(218), 1174 (152)
Heller, S. S.: *ref,* 679(1261, 1280)
Helm, E. B.: *ref,* 720(287)
Helmberger, J. D.: *ref,* 193(39)
Helmes, E.: *ref,* 643(186)
Helmick, J. W.: *ref,* 971(17)
Helms, J. E.: *ref,* 1023(1428)
Helms, S. T.: *ref,* 1010(56), 1022 (37), 1023(1405)
Helmstadter, G. C.: *cross ref,* 504
Helper, M. M.: *ref,* 630(246), 634 (309), 679(1327), 1101(171)
Helson, R.: *ref,* 495(392–3), 514 (1094–5), 1023(1338)
Helton, J. R.: *ref,* 469(563)
Helwig, A. A.: *ref,* 490(461)
Helwig, H. D.: *ref,* 697(1793)
Helwig, L. D.: *ref,* 249(493–4)
Hemenway, J.: *test,* 247
Hemenway, T. S.: *ref,* 553(620), 616(4708)
Hemmel, J. J.: *ref,* 514(951), 553 (331)
Hemmendinger, L.: *ref,* 661(4918)
Hemphill, J. K.: *test,* 1174–5; *ref,* 1184(26); *cross ref,* 688
Hemsley, D.: *ref,* 236(118), 681 (73), 706(30)
Hemsley, D. R.: *exc,* B83; *ref,* 554 (55), 571(50)
Henard, K. F.: *ref,* 735(105)
Henard, R. E.: *ref,* 586(12)
Hendel, D. D.: *test,* 1050; *bk,* B167; *ref,* 1050(76)
Hendershott, D. J.: *ref,* 1174(215)
Henderson, A. S.: *ref,* 553(583), 565(6, 11), 579(59, 77), 679 (1333)
Henderson, A. W.: *ref,* 646(48)
Henderson, B.: *ref,* 178(21)
Henderson, D. W.: *ref,* 660(81)
Henderson, E. H.: *ref,* 802(199)
Henderson, G. W.: *exc,* B91; *ref,* 485(352), 486(55)
Henderson, J. L.: *ref,* 490(535), 1022(62)
Henderson, J. M.: *ref,* 641(525)
Henderson, J. T.: *ref,* 656(16), 693(233)
Henderson, L. F.: *ref,* 393(98), 1052(99)
Henderson, N. B.: *ref,* 37(141, 169), 187(418), 232(1169, 1182, 1289), 431(460), 506(844, 850, 898), 581(373)
Henderson, N. D.: *ref,* 703(190)
Henderson, R. W.: *test,* 205, 348; *ref,* 234(117)
Henderson, S.: *ref,* 579(84)

Henderson, S. E.: *test,* 881
Henderson, T. L.: *ref,* 377(463), 641(240)
Hendler, J. M.: *ref,* 697(1915)
Hendlin, S. J.: *ref,* 661(4824, 4882)
Hendrick, C.: *ref,* 542(1459), 611 (542)
Hendricks, M.: *test,* 82, 84
Hendrickson, A.: *bk,* B150
Hendrie, H. C.: *ref,* 616(4685)
Hendry, L. B.: *ref,* 539(28, 32–3), 553(610), 679(907, 977)
Hendy, C. M.: *ref,* 679(1366)
Heneman, H. G.: *ref,* 1052(111)
Henley, R. J.: *ref,* 679(1367)
Henman, J.: *ref,* 187(398), 222 (318), 519(39)
Hennessy, J. J.: *ref,* 10(132), 49 (321), 475(21, 26–7)
Henning, D. M. M.: *ref,* 1174(163)
Henning, G. H.: *ref,* 720(370)
Henning, J. J.: *ref,* 616(3979)
Henning, M. M.: *test,* 191
Henrich, L.: *ref,* 581(400)
Henrichs, T. F.: *ref,* 230(1178), 616(3980)
Henriques, E.: *ref,* 616(3981)
Henry, C. A.: *ref,* 182(700)
Henry, P. E.: *ref,* 720(154)
Henry, T. J.: *ref,* 627(58), 679 (1282)
Henryk-Gutt, R.: *ref,* 553(443), 616(4225)
Hensel, N. H.: *ref,* 249(399)
Hensley, B.: *ref,* 181(4), 232(1183, 1290), 882(201, 214), 932(131)
Hensley, B. L.: *ref,* 932(117)
Hensley, S. R.: *ref,* 1174(148)
Henson, K.: *exc,* B427
Henzlik, W. L. B.: *ref,* 184(109), 520(104)
Herbener, G. F.: *ref,* 679(1262)
Herbert, K.: *ref,* 144(1)
Herder, J.: *ref,* 616(5009), 628 (245), 683(332)
Hered, W.: *cross ref,* 837, 844–5, 848–9
Herger, C. G.: *ref,* 1010(53)
Heriot, J. T.: *ref,* 222(366, 415)
Heritage, J.: *ref,* 616(4913)
Herl, D.: *ref,* 616(4877)
Herman, A.: *ref,* 485(357), 628 (208), 693(409, 411), 1011(892), 1023(1257), 1030(66)
Herman, B. F.: *ref,* 661(4883)
Herman, D. O.: *rev,* 981, 1008; *ref,* 485(340)
Herman, J. B.: *ref,* 1174(164)
Hernandez, O. F.: *test,* 164
Hernandez Ch., E.: *test,* 156
Herndon, M. A.: *ref,* 720(241)
Herold, D. M.: *ref,* 1175(104)
Herr, E. L.: *ref,* 514(986), 997(44, 161)
Herrick, M. D.: *ref,* 542(1566), 630(256)
Herrick, V. E.: *cross ref,* 4, 19, 29
Herrin, M.: *ref,* 232(1486)
Herrmann, D. J.: *ref,* 679(1505)
Herrnstein, R. J.: *bk,* B211
Herron, B. J.: *ref,* 431(611), 967 (26)
Herron, E. W.: *test,* 578
Herron, M. J.: *ref,* 720(324)

Hersen, M.: *bk,* B212; *ref,* 559(39, 42)
Hertel, P.: *ref,* 616(4564)
Hertz, L.: *ref,* 578(283)
Hertz, M. R.: *ref,* 661(4919)
Hertzig, M. E.: *ref,* 37(150), 232 (1049, 1074)
Herzberg, F.: *ref,* 616(4477)
Herzberger, S.: *ref,* 28(48), 183 (366)
Herzog, E.: *ref,* 229(1438)
Hesbacher, P.: *ref,* 565(14)
Heskin, K. J.: *ref,* 230(1025, 1107, 1246), 250(94, 121), 490(478, 531), 514(1048, 1322), 553(406, 656), 579(62, 82), 679(1073, 1212, 1431)
Heslin, R.: *bk,* B427
Hess, A. K.: *ref,* 643(187), 651(27, 37), 683(126)
Hess, D.: *ref,* 495(435)
Hess, K. A.: *ref,* 514(1096)
Hess, L. R.: *ref,* 616(3982)
Hess, R. J.: *test,* 798; *ref,* 798(3)
Hesse, K. A.: *test,* 277, 306
Hester, R. T.: *ref,* 377(554)
Hetler, J. H.: *ref,* 616(4878)
Hetzel, R.: *ref,* 553(444)
Hetzel, W.: *ref,* 616(4536), 661 (4700, 4774), 663(137), 683 (190), 697(1928)
Hetzel, W. C.: *bk,* B213
Heuringer, C.: *ref,* 616(4157)
Heussenstamm, F. K.: *test,* 496, 588; *ref,* 496(2)
Hevner, K.: *test,* 96, *ref,* 96(1–2, 4–5)
Hewett, T. T.: *ref,* 555(255)
Hewitt, B. A.: *ref,* 46(38), 182 (578), 188(87), 258(6), 259(2), 472(50)
Hewitt, B. N.: *ref,* 182(686, 725–7, 757)
Hewitt, C. W.: *ref,* 616(4113)
Hewitt, E. A.: *exc,* B234
Heywood, J.: *bk,* B214
Heywood, J. S.: *ref,* 679(1263)
Hiat, A. B.: *ref,* 679(1368)
Hibbs, C.: *ref,* 679(1514), 1028 (305)
Hickcox, E. S.: *ref,* 192(166)
Hickey, K. L.: *ref,* 210(79)
Hickey, T.: *ref,* 187(402), 222 (321)
Hickman, M. A.: *ref,* 182(589)
Hicks, D. W.: *ref,* 720(325)
Hicks, J.: *ref,* 1062(1)
Hicks, J. P.: *ref,* 542(1498)
Hicks, J. S.: *test,* 1062
Hicks, R. A.: *ref,* 222(338), 232 (1112), 523(277)
Hicks, R. D.: *ref,* 719(76)
Hicks, R. E.: *ref,* 686(945)
Hielbrun, A. B.: *cross ref,* 542
Hieronymus, A. N.: *test,* 11, 19, 25, 284; *cross ref,* 2, 33, 57
Higdon, G.: *ref,* 249(559)
Higdon, J. F.: *ref,* 575(41), 616 (4226)
Higdon, M. C.: *ref,* 643(105)
Higgins, E. B.: *ref,* 1052(100)
Higgins, G.: *ref,* 616(4568), 1011 (897)
Higgins, K. E.: *ref,* 571(42)

Lyle, W.: *ref,* 431(408), 726A(27)
Lyman, H. B.: *cross ref,* 24, 222, 230
Lyman, M. H.: *ref,* 634(326)
Lyman, R. A. F.: *ref,* 616(4538, 4775), 663(138), 683(191)
Lynch, D. H.: *ref,* 469(463)
Lynch, D. J.: *exc,* B26; *ref,* 662 (435)
Lynch, F. D.: *ref,* 720(334)
Lynch, G. P.: *ref,* 223(23), 506 (798)
Lynch, J. C.: *ref,* 1054(14)
Lynch, L. R.: *ref,* 626(244)
Lynch, M. C.: *ref,* 662(422)
Lynch, M. D.: *ref,* 244(162), 697 (1862), 1010(37), 1023(1287)
Lynch, S.: *ref,* 628(182)
Lynn, A. W.: *ref,* 577(35), 641 (255), 693(243)
Lynn, C. W.: *ref,* 585(197)
Lynn, D. B.: *ref,* 514(993), 562 (55)
Lynn, R.: *ref,* 200(528), 596(48), 679(914, 1143)
Lynn, R. L.: *ref,* 375(10)
Lyon, L. P.: *test,* 409; *ref,* 409(9)
Lyon, M.: *ref,* 469(577)
Lyon, R. S.: *ref,* 514(1114)
Lyons, L.: *ref,* 643(175)
Lyttle, D.: *ref,* 616(4951)
Lytton, H.: *rev,* 513

MAAS, J. B.: *test,* 367
Mabe, R. L.: *ref,* 634(233)
Mabry, E.: *ref,* 553(713)
Mabry, E. A.: *ref,* 616(5026–7)
Mabry, K.: *exc,* B73, B328, B469, B531, B564
Mabry, N. K.: *ref,* 542(1507)
Mac, R. F.: *ref,* 616(4274)
McAdoo, W. G.: *ref,* 616(4275, 4385, 4517, 4721), 679(1204)
Macaitis, L.: *test,* 307, 813
Macaitis, L. A.: *test,* 1035
McAllister, H.: *ref,* 553(555), 615 (32)
McAllister, R. J.: *ref,* 200(540), 637(4), 726A(30)
Macaluso, R.: *ref,* 542(1447)
McArdle, H. R.: *ref,* 1030(52)
McAreavey, J. P.: *ref,* 37(192), 232(1403)
McAree, C. P.: *ref,* 616(4023)
McArthur, C. C.: *cross ref,* 661
McArthur, D. L.: *ref,* 488(408)
McArthur, D. S.: *ref,* 697(1991)
MacArthur, R.: *ref,* 200(586), 224 (252), 232(1201), 548(285)
McAshan, H. H.: *bk,* B299
Macauley, F. E.: *ref,* 514(1115)
McAvin, M. W.: *ref,* 688(188)
McAvoy, L. H.: *ref,* 693(407)
McBee, G. W.: *ref,* 616(4987)
Macbeth, H. M.: *ref,* 230(1130), 553(525)
McBrearty, J. F.: *ref,* 514(1304), 542(1588)
McBride, J. F.: *test,* 724
McCabe, J. J.: *ref,* 232(1202), 249 (412)
McCabe, J. J. C.: *ref,* 679(1144)
McCabe, O. L.: *ref,* 553(354), 616 (4024), 641(256)

McCabe, P.: *ref,* 200(657)
McCabe, S. P.: *ref,* 553(320), 1022 (2), 1023(1233)
McCahan, G. R.: *ref,* 693(324)
McCall, J. N.: *cross ref,* 1009
McCall, L. E.: *ref,* 29(237), 626 (256)
McCall, R. B.: *ref,* 229(1443)
McCall, R. J.: *ref,* 616(4276, 4518, 4992); *cross ref,* 661
McCall, T. D.: *ref,* 182(694)
McCalla, J. R.: *ref,* 393(99)
McCallon, E.: *test,* 395, 1058
McCallum, S.: *ref,* 232(1486)
McCamey, W. B.: *ref,* 693(555), 1175(155)
McCandless, B. R.: *ref,* 22(87), 222(343), 495(413), 562(60), 592(56), 732(54), 802(278); *cross ref,* 178, 225, 229, 232, 592
McCandless, R. W.: *ref,* 542(1356)
McCann, M. J.: *ref,* 559(52), 582 (243)
McCann, M. M.: *ref,* 641(351)
McCann Associates: *test,* 1096, 1106
McCanse, A.: *ref,* 616(4561), 677 (182), 1022(27)
McCardel, J.: *ref,* 641(454)
McCarley, D. G.: *test,* 545; *ref,* 545(1)
McCarron, L. T.: *ref,* 222(327), 230(988), 506(799)
McCarter, R. E.: *ref,* 559(38), 616 (4135)
McCarthy, C. E.: *ref,* 617(3)
McCarthy, D.: *test,* 219
McCarthy, D. P.: *ref,* 506(800, 949)
McCarthy, H.: *ref,* 581(375)
McCarthy, J. F.: *ref,* 98(51)
McCarthy, J. J.: *rev,* 428, 442; *test,* 431; *ref,* 431(525, 618), 660(57), 679(1145)
McCarthy, K.: *bk,* B538; *ref,* 182 (688)
McCarthy, K. A.: *ref,* 222(379), 719(82)
McCarthy, M.: *ref,* 200(619), 1009 (18)
McCarthy, M. M.: *ref,* 1030(53)
McCarthy, R. G.: *ref,* 222(306), 431(381)
McCarthy, S. V.: *ref,* 182(695)
McCarthy, T. B.: *ref,* 1010(62)
McCarthy, W.: *ref,* 230(1261)
McCartin, R.: *ref,* 506(815), 870 (17), 872(45)
McCartin, R. A.: *ref,* 222(303), 225(49), 232(1039), 431(375), 488(367), 802(198)
McCarty, J. L.: *ref,* 1175(156)
McCarver, R. B.: *ref,* 222(328)
McCary, J. L.: *rev,* 336, 345
McCary, P.: *ref,* 586(17), 683 (154), 693(361)
McCaskill, E. O.: *ref,* 249(503)
McCauley, A. A.: *ref,* 200(660), 229(1559), 232(1404)
McCauley, M. E.: *ref,* 222(380)
McCaulley, M. H.: *ref,* 630(230)
McCausland, D. F.: *ref,* 469(504), 820(152)

McCawley, J. W.: *ref,* 988(6)
Macchitelli, F. J.: *ref,* 574(531, 554), 616(4166, 4296–7, 4738)
McClafferty, J.: *bk,* B300, B300A
McClain, B. R.: *ref,* 1184(27)
McClain, D.: *ref,* 679(1048)
McClain, E. W.: *ref,* 542(1439), 641(257), 679(1005)
McClain, P. D.: *ref,* 238(16)
McClanahan, L. D.: *ref,* 559(58)
McClane, T. K.: *ref,* 675(45)
McClary, J. E.: *ref,* 490(476)
McClelland, D. C.: *bk,* B301; *ref,* 542(1357), 697(1804, 1875)
McClellen, L. A.: *ref,* 679(1287)
McCleskey, J.: *ref,* 802(269)
McCleskey, J. A.: *ref,* 802(242)
McCloud, T. E.: *ref,* 19(135)
McCloudy, C. W.: *ref,* 822(177)
McClung, C. J.: *ref,* 572(38)
McClure, C. A.: *ref,* 49(307), 183 (332), 490(467)
McClure, G.: *test,* 637
McClure, R. F.: *ref,* 469(382), 634 (216, 297–8)
McColloch, M. A.: *ref,* 514(998), 611(569), 616(3996–7, 4255)
McConaghy, N.: *ref,* 632(13–4)
McConnell, R. A.: *ref,* 661(4583), 662(417)
McConnell, T. R.: *test,* 634
McConville, M.: *ref,* 593(2)
McCook, J. E.: *ref,* 469(464)
McCord, M. T.: *ref,* 735(106), 753 (21)
McCormack, A. J.: *ref,* 249(504)
McCormick, C. H.: *ref,* 198(40), 283(14), 732(60)
McCormick, E. J.: *test,* 983; *ref,* 983(2–6, 8)
McCormick, J.: *ref,* 634(252)
McCormick, K.: *ref,* 553(624)
McCormick, P. J.: *ref,* 49(311)
McCormick, R. R.: *test,* 1060; *ref,* 1060(1)
McCormick, W. O.: *ref,* 611(645)
McCourt, E. L.: *ref,* 490(539)
McCoy, C. E.: *ref,* 523(258)
McCoy, J. G.: *ref,* 232(1576)
McCoy, P. B.: *ref,* 393(66)
McCoy, R. E.: *ref,* 542(1600), 626 (273, 276)
McCoy, V. R.: *ref,* 514(1282), 997 (135)
McCracken, A.: *ref,* 875(21)
McCrady, B.: *ref,* 654(36)
McCrae, R. R.: *ref,* 1023(1510)
McCraw, R. K.: *ref,* 506(968), 616 (4519), 661(4766, 4852, 4925)
McCreary, C.: *ref,* 616(4993, 5013)
McCreary, C. P.: *ref,* 616(4722–3, 4904)
MacCrimmon, D. J.: *ref,* 548(314)
McCue, P. A.: *ref,* 553(677)
McCullagh, D. J.: *ref,* 679(1288)
McCulloch, E. S.: *ref,* 1061(5)
McCullough, C. M.: *cross ref,* 45
McCullough, R. D.: *ref,* 514(1277), 542(1573)
McCully, R. S.: *bk,* B302; *ref,* 661 (4636, 4926)
McCurdy, M. E.: *ref,* 641(541)
McCutcheon, L. E.: *ref,* 679(1289)
McDaniel, E. L.: *test,* 584

Mider, P. A.: *ref,* 577(48)
Mihal, W. L.: *ref,* 183(341)
Mikaelian, S.: *ref,* 377(475)
Mikesell, R. H.: *ref,* 562(52), 693 (205)
Mikrut, J. J.: *ref,* 393(100), 569 (171)
Mikulka, P. J.: *ref,* 683(296)
Milam, D. R.: *ref,* 10(108)
Milburn, C. M.: *ref,* 1174(270)
Milby, H. B.: *ref,* 547(5), 582(267)
Milby, J. B.: *ref,* 525(13), 681(63)
Milchus, N. J.: *test,* 551, 657, 670
Miles, D. T.: *bk,* B264
Miles, J.: *ref,* 225(62)
Miles, J. E.: *ref,* 679(1392)
Miles, L. F.: *ref,* 686(911)
Miles, M. B.: *bk,* B278; *ref,* 555 (230), 628(186), 634(255), 1174 (196)
Miles, P. J.: *test,* 778
Miles, T. R.: *rev,* 437; *exc,* B548
Milgram, N. A.: *ref,* 693(557–8)
Milgram, R. M.: *ref,* 693(557–8)
Milholland, J. E.: *rev,* 8, 20; *exc,* B105; *ref,* 229(1551); *cross ref,* 184, 198, 488
Milillo, M. D.: *ref,* 616(4734), 683 (251)
Milkman, H.: *ref,* 626(233), 661 (4606)
Miller, A.: *ref,* 553(355)
Miller, A. G.: *ref,* 683(138), 698 (32)
Miller, A. L.: *bk,* B155
Miller, B.: *ref,* 222(329)
Miller, B. J.: *ref,* 431(579)
Miller, C.: *ref,* 495(462)
Miller, C. K.: *ref,* 37(122), 230 (1010), 232(1099, 1130, 1204)
Miller, C. M.: *ref,* 539(37), 616 (4911)
Miller, C. M. L.: *bk,* B330
Miller, D. C.: *ref,* 1177(63), 1186 (12)
Miller, D. E.: *ref,* 190(104), 485 (342), 683(196, 262), 1023 (1457), 1050(38), 1052(53)
Miller, D. L.: *ref,* 720(156)
Miller, D. M.: *bk,* B331; *exc,* B31; *ref,* 834(1)
Miller, E.: *ref,* 616(3854)
Miller, E. J. C.: *ref,* 997(97)
Miller, G.: *exc,* B443
Miller, G. A.: *ref,* 720(35)
Miller, G. D.: *ref,* 37(146), 679 (1154)
Miller, G. M.: *exc,* B117, B452, B543; *ref,* 679(1016)
Miller, G. R.: *ref,* 720(105, 122, 130)
Miller, H. D.: *ref,* 375(19)
Miller, H. K.: *ref,* 188(101), 192 (154)
Miller, H. M.: *ref,* 902(2)
Miller, J.: *ref,* 222(463), 232(1414)
Miller, J. B.: *ref,* 524(102)
Miller, J. C.: *ref,* 679(1285)
Miller, J. E.: *ref,* 576(61)
Miller, J. H.: *ref,* 688(173)
Miller, J. S.: *ref,* 660(85, 125)
Miller, J. W.: *ref,* 790(7)
Miller, K.: *ref,* 12(3)

Miller, K. M.: *test,* 271; *bk,* B332; *ref,* 720(42)
Miller, L.: *ref,* 19(154), 37(138), 232(1177), 769(5)
Miller, L. B.: *ref,* 229(1510)
Miller, L. C.: *rev,* 541, 625; *cross ref,* 493, 540
Miller, L. D.: *ref,* 524(103)
Miller, L. E.: *ref,* 641(261)
Miller, L. J.: *ref,* 506(943, 952, 984)
Miller, L. L.: *test,* 731
Miller, L. M.: *ref,* 616(4459)
Miller, L. P.: *bk,* B333
Miller, L. R.: *ref,* 686(953), 720 (376–7)
Miller, M.: *ref,* 230(1254), 516 (475), 616(3866)
Miller, M. D.: *ref,* 232(1504)
Miller, M. F.: *ref,* 997(61, 98), 1030(74)
Miller, M. L.: *ref,* 617(37, 40, 47)
Miller, M. M.: *test,* 164
Miller, R. A.: *ref,* 222(381), 523 (226)
Miller, R. I.: *bk,* B334
Miller, R. J.: *ref,* 576(72)
Miller, R. L.: *ref,* 548(353)
Miller, R. S.: *ref,* 555(191)
Miller, S. A.: *ref,* 548(345)
Miller, S. J.: *ref,* 531(10), 660 (126), 681(38), 686(960)
Miller, T. T.: *ref,* 182(773)
Miller, V. H.: *ref,* 555(231)
Miller, W. C.: *ref,* 230(1209, 1285), 553(671), 559(62), 613(111), 616(4705), 683(298), 872(59)
Miller, W. D.: *ref,* 222(330, 382–3), 227(54, 68–9), 719(78), 720 (337)
Miller, W. G.: *ref,* 634(295)
Miller, W. H.: *ref,* 616(4528), 800 (10)
Miller, W. R.: *ref,* 352(7), 469 (506), 628(229)
Miller, W. S.: *test,* 192
Miller-Tiedeman, A.: *test,* 1006
Millet, R.: *ref,* 548(283)
Millett, R.: *ref,* 613(93)
Millham, J.: *ref,* 229(1472)
Milligan, J. N.: *ref,* 548(345)
Milligan, J. R.: *ref,* 495(470), 514 (1285)
Milligan, W. L.: *ref,* 616(4236)
Millimet, C. R.: *ref,* 616(4291, 4735), 663(128), 697(1809)
Milling, M. E.: *ref,* 634(330)
Millman, J.: *rev,* 303, 776; *exc,* B534; *cross ref,* 727
Millman, J. E.: *ref,* 596(71)
Millott, R. F.: *ref,* 630(242, 245)
Mills, D. H.: *ref,* 542(1376), 1023 (1355)
Mills, F. M.: *ref,* 377(476)
Mills, H. A.: *ref,* 693(496)
Mills, J.: *ref,* 679(1408)
Mills, J. C.: *ref,* 802(244)
Mills, J. M.: *ref,* 553(583), 565 (11), 579(77), 679(1333)
Mills, N.: *ref,* 396(3)
Milne, N. D. M.: *ref,* 210(88), 232 (1310)
Milner, E. K.: *ref,* 1174(271)

Milner, J. S.: *ref,* 661(4769), 697 (1956, 1964)
Milstein, V.: *ref,* 230(1009, 1012), 250(92), 616(4101)
Milton, O.: *bk,* B335
Mina, E.: *ref,* 431(454)
Minami, T.: *ref,* 1174(160–1, 187)
Minard, J.: *ref,* 572(7)
Minard, J. G.: *ref,* 641(543)
Minars, E.: *ref,* 693(303)
Minde, K.: *ref,* 187(467)
Mindingall, A.: *ref,* 683(252)
Miner, A.: *test,* 952
Miner, B. B.: *ref,* 542(1435)
Miner, S. E.: *ref,* 1023(1460)
Minichiello, W.: *ref,* 495(321), 641 (212)
Minifie, E. L.: *ref,* 694(3)
Minkevich, G.: *ref,* 542(1337, 1366, 1427–8), 693(249)
Minkoff, J.: *ref,* 183(343)
Minnaar, G. G.: *test,* 590
Minnie, R.: *test,* 481
Minogue, B. M.: *ref,* 229(1416)
Minor, K. L.: *ref,* 524A(6)
Minor, M. J.: *ref,* 643(176)
Minskoff, E. H.: *ref,* 431(580, 620)
Minten, F.: *ref,* 553(355)
Minton, J. H.: *ref,* 802(214, 297)
Mintz, J.: *ref,* 250(103)
Mintz, J. R.: *ref,* 661(4587)
Mintzer, R. G.: *ref,* 997(167)
Mintzes, J. J.: *ref,* 679(1299)
Mirci, S. E.: *ref,* 693(559)
Miriani, C.: *ref,* 634(236)
Mirsky, A. F.: *ref,* 232(1323)
Mischel, F.: *ref,* 542(1367), 697 (1810)
Mishken, M. A.: *ref,* 1037(35)
Mishra, C.: *ref,* 200(621)
Misiewicz, J. J.: *ref,* 553(558), 615 (33)
Mitchell, B. M.: *ref,* 1174(197), 1184(29)
Mitchell, C.: *ref,* 178(24)
Mitchell, C. E. W.: *ref,* 641(463)
Mitchell, D. K.: *ref,* 542(1577)
Mitchell, H.: *ref,* 176(3), 578(314)
Mitchell, I.: *ref,* 611(567)
Mitchell, J. V.: *rev,* 381, 700; *cross ref,* 523
Mitchell, K. M.: *ref,* 525(3), 681 (24), 697(1926)
Mitchell, K. R.: *exc,* B258; *ref,* 687(6), 820(136, 162)
Mitchell, M. C.: *ref,* 200(636), 559(50), 677(185)
Mitchell, N. B.: *ref,* 232(1311)
Mitchell, R. R.: *ref,* 661(4770)
Mitchell, T. R.: *ref,* 1174(169), 1175(166)
Mitchell-Heggs, N.: *ref,* 230 (1059), 611(597), 615(23)
Mitroff, N. S.: *ref,* 4698)
Mittanck, R. G.: *ref,* 514(1202), 820(154)
Mittler, P.: *bk,* B336; *ref,* 431(416)
Mittman, A.: *rev,* 287, 289; *ref,* 236 (111); *cross ref,* 290
Mix, B. J.: *test,* 689
Miyashiro, C. M.: *ref,* 553(549)
Mlodnosky, L. B.: *ref,* 506(804), 882(180)

Mlott, S. R.: *ref*, 230(1285), 559 (51), 616(4040, 4292–3, 4529, 4736), 651(45)
Moan, C. A.: *ref*, 616(4496)
Moan, C. E.: *ref*, 224(250), 230 (1163), 616(4106, 4365–6), 677 (161)
Mobley, B. D.: *ref*, 693(327)
Mobley, L. A.: *ref*, 182(783), 184 (125), 1010(72)
Mobley, W. H.: *exc*, B120, B575
Mock, L. A. T.: *ref*, 628(230)
Mock, R. M.: *ref*, 1175(74)
Modern Language Association of America: *test*, 123, 134, 152
Modgil, S.: *ref*, 238(21), 597(168)
Modu, C.: *ref*, 113(5)
Modu, C. C.: *bk*, B33; *ref*, 113(6), 182(617), 862(5)
Moe, A. J.: *bk*, B576
Moelis, I.: *ref*, 661(4929)
Moerk, E. L.: *ref*, 514(1011), 578 (277), 693(328)
Moers, F.: *ref*, 29(263–4), 178(23)
Moffett, L. A.: *ref*, 679(1393)
Moffett, T. J.: *test*, 378; *ref*, 378 (1)
Moffitt, P.: *ref*, 222(362, 384), 234 (116, 126), 431(450, 474)
Moffitt, W.: *ref*, 1175(166)
Mogull, R. G.: *ref*, 485(344, 369)
Mohan, H. D.: *ref*, 1175(158)
Mohan, J.: *ref*, 494(7), 553(356, 466–7), 554(26), 661(4699)
Mohan, M.: *ref*, 249(356)
Mohan, V.: *ref*, 200(541–2, 591, 622, 663, 688), 553(468–9, 550, 680), 679(1017)
Mohns, L.: *ref*, 230(1254), 616 (4866)
Mohundro, L. W.: *ref*, 660(180)
Moilanen, P.: *ref*, 616(4717), 661 (4827)
Mokken, R. J.: *bk*, B337
Molina, H.: *rev*, 454; *exc*, 171; *ref*, 171(3)
Moline, J. G.: *ref*, 1050(65)
Molish, H. B.: *exc*, B25, B302; *ref*, 578(278), 661(4638), 697(1811)
Molla, B.: *ref*, 1028(297)
Mollach, F. L.: *ref*, 720(242)
Mollenkopf, W. G.: *rev*, 1055, 1075, 1188
Möller, A. T.: *ref*, 679(1079)
Molloy, G. N.: *ref*, 200(651), 222 (452), 613(110)
Molnar, G. E.: *ref*, 182(584, 648)
Molo, R. D.: *ref*, 1174(198)
Money, J.: *test*, 877; *ref*, 187(440), 506(905), 581(340)
Moniot, S. H.: *ref*, 1175(128)
Monroe, J. J.: *ref*, 616(3924)
Monroe, L. J.: *ref*, 616(5001)
Monroe, M.: *test*, 799
Monsalud, A.: *ref*, 679(1503)
Monson, M. A.: *ref*, 514(966–8, 1254)
Montagna, N. K.: *ref*, 514(1203)
Montague, D. J.: *ref*, 606(327)
Montalvo, H. S.: *ref*, 8(19)
Montare, A. P. S.: *test*, 16
Montero, E. F.: *ref*, 631(47)
Montgomery, E. F.: *ref*, 641(545), 1028(254)

Montgomery, H. R.: *ref*, 542 (1468), 574(517), 616(4139, 4396), 1011(883)
Montgomery, I. M.: *ref*, 565(6), 579(59)
Montgomery, J. R.: *ref*, 643(164)
Montgomery, L. E.: *ref*, 230(1125), 683(188), 684(5, 11–2, 19)
Montoye, H. J.: *ref*, 407(156, 161)
Montuori, J.: *test*, 684
Moody, W. E.: *ref*, 377(509)
Mooney, D. K.: *ref*, 611(653), 616 (4799)
Mooney, J. F.: *ref*, 232(1100), 431 (417)
Mooney, R. L.: *test*, 626
Mooney, T. F.: *ref*, 628(210)
Mooneyhan, D. L.: *ref*, 1175(129)
Moore, A.: *ref*, 10(124)
Moore, A. B.: *ref*, 693(250)
Moore, A. L.: *ref*, 469(533)
Moore, C. A.: *ref*, 188(129), 572 (50)
Moore, C. L.: *ref*, 234(125, 139)
Moore, C. M.: *ref*, 553(627)
Moore, D. G.: *test*, 1054
Moore, D. M.: *ref*, 431(581)
Moore, E. H.: *ref*, 516(487)
Moore, J. A.: *ref*, 641(465)
Moore, J. C.: *ref*, 35(126), 1028 (181)
Moore, J. E.: *ref*, 230(1009), 616 (4901, 4997–8), 641(464)
Moore, J. V.: *ref*, 616(4737)
Moore, J. W.: *ref*, 182(649)
Moore, K. T.: *ref*, 754(65)
Moore, L. F.: *ref*, 686(875)
Moore, M.: *ref*, 660(157)
Moore, M. G.: *ref*, 548(354)
Moore, M. L.: *ref*, 641(608), 822 (191)
Moore, M. R.: *ref*, 822(166)
Moore, N. C.: *ref*, 530(181, 195), 553(681)
Moore, P. L.: *ref*, 660(181)
Moore, R. C.: *ref*, 802(245)
Moore, R. J.: *ref*, 553(551)
Moore, S. C., *ref*, 35(117)
Moore, S. F.: *ref*, 548(279)
Moore, T.: *ref*, 183(352), 198(33)
Moore, T. L.: *ref*, 643(165), 997 (168, 187)
Moore, W. J.: *cross ref*, 70
Moores, D. F.: *ref*, 720(123, 183)
Moores, E. H.: *ref*, 183(353)
Moos, B. S.: *ref*, 557(2–3), 681(67, 80)
Moos, R.: *ref*, 525(1–2, 12), 681 (13, 15–6, 27, 29, 52), 706(10, 16–7)
Moos, R. H.: *test*, 521, 525, 531, 557, 573, 681, 700, 706, 713; *bk*, B338; *ref*, 521(1–2), 525(4–5, 8–11, 14, 16–7), 531(1–5, 13–5), 557(1–3), 628(231), 681(1–3, 6–7, 12–4, 17–20, 25–6, 28–30, 39–51, 54, 56–7, 64–71, 75–6, 79–80), 700 (1, 5, 8, 11), 706(1–2, 5, 11–2, 14–5, 18–25, 29)
Moos (R. H.) & Associates: *test*, 681
Moracco, J. C.: *ref*, 997(169)
Morado, C.: *ref*, 494(6)

Morales, C. A.: *ref*, 393(88), 630 (260)
Moran, P. A.: *ref*, 514(1012)
Morán, R. E.: *ref*, 200(543)
Moran, R. T.: *ref*, 514(1204)
Moran, S.: *ref*, 651(42)
Moray House College of Education: *test*, 724
Mordkoff, A. M.: *ref*, 576(66), 616 (3978), 682(100)
Morency, A.: *test*, 448, 450, 933–4; *ref*, 22(102), 448(1), 450(2), 932 (122), 933(2)
Morency, A. S.: *ref*, 933(1)
Moreno, J. M.: *ref*, 249(464, 547)
Moreno, S. S.: *ref*, 631(50)
Moretz, S. A.: *ref*, 12(4)
Morey, D. R.: *ref*, 634(302)
Morey, R. A.: *ref*, 523(281)
Morf, M. E.: *ref*, 539(37), 593(2), 616(4041, 4111, 4911), 617(52), 643(83, 87)
Morgan, A. H.: *ref*, 548(260), 682, 71, 80–1, 84, 95–6)
Morgan, C. D.: *ref*, 576(60)
Morgan, D. W.: *ref*, 616(3975, 4042), 617(62), 623(16)
Morgan, E. W.: *ref*, 802(215)
Morgan, G. A.: *ref*, 634(237)
Morgan, G. A. V.: *cross ref*, 19
Morgan, L. M.: *ref*, 959(6)
Morgan, M. K.: *ref*, 469(507), 634 (303)
Morgan, M. R.: *ref*, 679(1155)
Morgan, P.: *ref*, 232(1505)
Morgan, R. R.: *ref*, 469(534, 568), 542(1578, 1625)
Morgan, R. S. W.: *ref*, 616(4912), 643(177)
Morgan, W. P.: *ref*, 536(12), 553 (357)
Morgana, A.: *ref*, 617(77)
Morgenstern, F. S.: *ref*, 553(552)
Morgenstern, M.: *ref*, 37(147), 232(1205), 506(865)
Morin, S. F.: *ref*, 244(155)
Moritz, C.: *test*, 74
Moriwaki, S. Y.: *ref*, 666(60)
Mork, T. A.: *ref*, 720(212)
Morley, I. E.: *ref*, 553(371)
Morman, R. R.: *test*, 986; *ref*, 986 (16)
Moro, A. F.: *ref*, 377(529)
Moroz, M.: *ref*, 720(114)
Morris, C. E.: *exc*, B112
Morris, E. F.: *ref*, 542(1510), 679 (1300)
Morris, G. P.: *ref*, 514(1120)
Morris, H. G.: *ref*, 686(912)
Morris, J. D.: *ref*, 679(1394)
Morris, J. G.: *exc*, B81
Morris, J. L.: *ref*, 514(1013)
Morris, J. N.: *ref*, 675(96)
Morris, K. T.: *ref*, 693(439)
Morris, L.: *ref*, 651(34)
Morris, L. A.: *ref*, 616(4530)
Morris, L. E.: *ref*, 1174(170)
Morris, L. W.: *ref*, 628(166), 683 (139, 253)
Morris, M.: *ref*, 224(246), 230 (973), 611(563)
Morris, M. D.: *ref*, 20(130)
Morris, N. C.: *ref*, 683(253)
Morris, O. F.: *ref*, 785(29)

Netter-Munkelt, P.: *ref*, 553(359)
Nettlebeck, T.: *ref*, 230(1264)
Netusil, A. J.: *ref*, 524A(12)
Neubauer, P. B.: *bk*, B159
Neufeld, G. A.: *ref*, 938(19)
Neufeld, R. J.: *ref*, 553(360)
Neufeld, R. W. J.: *ref*, 628(200)
Neumann, G.: *ref*, 719(88)
Neumann, I.: *ref*, 1023(1311)
Neuringer, C.: *rev*, 609, 664; *bk*, B409, B463; *ref*, 616(4741, 4887), 661(4771-2), 697(1802)
Nevill, D.: *ref*, 548(315)
Neville, C. W.: *ref*, 616(4245, 4785), 679(1121)
Neville, D.: *ref*, 222(302), 232(1040), 431(377), 445(3), 643(187)
Neville, M. H.: *ref*, 720(338, 393)
Nevo, B.: *ref*, 514(1378)
New, R. H.: *ref*, 997(99)
Newbrough, J. R.: *ref*, 200(516)
Newby, J. H.: *ref*, 1177(77)
Newcomb, C.: *ref*, 229(1438)
Newcombe, A. G.: *ref*, 553(335), 711(25)
Newcombe, F. G.: *ref*, 230(1222)
Newcomer, B. F. B.: *ref*, 222(332)
Newcomer, P.: *ref*, 431(535-6, 564, 580, 586), 506(866), 883(1)
Newcomer, P. L.: *rev*, 425, 440; *test*, 978; *ref*, 10(126), 431(473, 583-5, 596, 622)
Newhauser, D. I.: *ref*, 675(107)
Newhouse, R. C.: *ref*, 646(62)
Newkome, M. C. M.: *ref*, 178(15)
Newland, T. E.: *test*, 320; *ref*, 320(1-2); *cross ref*, 210, 217, 223
Newman, A.: *ref*, 232(1508)
Newman, A. F.: *ref*, 19(115), 29(229), 232(1104), 506(806), 745(57), 802(217), 803(27), 932(100)
Newman, J.: *cross ref*, 236, 250
Newman, L. E.: *ref*, 630(262)
Newman, P. A.: *ref*, 616(4430)
Newmark, C. S.: *ref*, 232(1409), 616(4047-8, 4301-3, 4534-8, 4663, 4742-5, 4914-6, 5003-4), 661(4700, 4773-5, 4841), 663(137-8), 683(91-3, 189-91, 254), 684(13), 697(1881, 1928)
Newmark, L.: *ref*, 232(1409), 616(4537, 4744-5), 661(4841), 684(13)
New Mexico State Department of Education: *test*, 312, 416, 859
Newsome, E. T.: *ref*, 542(1626), 1052(105)
Newton, A. V.: *ref*, 679(1156)
Newton, F. B.: *ref*, 641(263)
Newton, F. E.: *ref*, 697(1815)
Newton, J. R.: *ref*, 495(443, 478)
Newton, M.: *ref*, 616(4304)
Newton, R. R.: *ref*, 1177(88)
New York State Education Department: *test*, 38, 62-3, 360-1, 408, 458, 715-6, 857, 906, 1090-1, 1108-9, 1112, 1115
Neziroglu, F.: *ref*, 616(4681, 4746)
Ng, K. T.: *ref*, 200(623), 687(6), 820(136)
Ngissah, P.: *ref*, 232(1524)
Ngo, N. A.: *ref*, 469(422)

Nias, D. K. B.: *ref*, 553(470), 554(27), 596(49), 711(27-9, 36, 50, 68, 91)
Nibbelink, W. H.: *rev*, 253, 280
Nicholl, C.: *ref*, 249(514)
Nicholls, J. G.: *ref*, 238(21)
Nichols, A. K.: *ref*, 679(904)
Nichols, C. B.: *ref*, 679(1303)
Nichols, D. A.: *ref*, 932(135)
Nichols, D. S.: *ref*, 616(4539)
Nichols, K.: *ref*, 596(42), 669(1)
Nichols, K. E.: *ref*, 679(941)
Nichols, M. A.: *ref*, 611(549), 616(3890)
Nichols, M. P.: *ref*, 522(8), 542(1368), 616(4049, 4540-1, 4828), 679(1509)
Nichols, P. L.: *bk*, B67; *ref*, 206(40, 47), 229(1430, 1543)
Nichols, R.: *ref*, 514(1352)
Nichols, R. C.: *rev*, 181, 203
Nichols, R. L.: *ref*, 182(739)
Nichols, R. W.: *ref*, 616(4542)
Nichols, T.: *ref*, 182(655)
Nicholsen, J.: *ref*, 377(548), 641(548)
Nicholson, C. L.: *ref*, 225(81), 227(44, 78), 232(1575)
Nicholson, E.: *ref*, 182(650), 472(53)
Nicholson, E. W.: *ref*, 377(477), 679(1022), 1175(75)
Nicholson, J. E.: *ref*, 206(37), 229(1487)
Nicholson, J. N.: *ref*, 596(50, 72)
Nickens, H. C.: *ref*, 523(230)
Nickens, J. M.: *ref*, 989(11)
Nickerson, E.: *ref*, 542(1608)
Nickles, L. A.: *ref*, 616(4243), 677(169), 707(28)
Nicol, M. A.: *ref*, 720(42)
Nicol, S. F.: *ref*, 1174(272)
Nicolay, R. C.: *ref*, 693(434)
Nicoletti, J.: *ref*, 610(2)
Nicoletti, J. A.: *ref*, 582(203)
Nicoll, R. C.: *ref*, 493(34)
Nicolosi, L.: *ref*, 222(333, 371)
Nidich, S.: *ref*, 641(274, 360)
Nieberding, J. E.: *ref*, 616(4747), 693(498)
Niederwerfer, M. B.: *ref*, 693(499)
Nielsen, E. C.: *ref*, 514(1376), 555(321), 582(263)
Nielsen, E. T.: *ref*, 686(878)
Nielsen, J.: *ref*, 230(1033), 611(635)
Nielsen, J. D.: *ref*, 236(119)
Nielsen, M.: *ref*, 519(50)
Nieratka, S.: *ref*, 790(8)
Nigam, A.: *ref*, 679(1185)
Nightingale, J. A.: *ref*, 630(205)
Nihira, K.: *test*, 493; *ref*, 493(13, 21, 36)
Nijhawan, N. K.: *ref*, 611(561)
Niles, J. A.: *ref*, 720(282, 326)
Niles, O. S.: *bk*, B4
Nillius, S. J.: *ref*, 553(433)
Nimnicht, G.: *ref*, 303(60)
Nimrod, G.: *ref*, 187(469), 520(120)
Ninio, A.: *ref*, 234(152)
Ninios, P. N.: *ref*, 230(1109)
Niquette, S.: *ref*, 488(427), 778(6), 803(31)

Nirmal, B.: *ref*, 184(123), 249(525)
Nisbet, J. D.: *ref*, 553(361), 596(51)
Nisbet, S.: *cross ref*, 271
Nisenson, R. A.: *ref*, 662(423)
Nisha, B.: *ref*, 611(599)
Nishiyama, T.: *ref*, 514(1124, 1287)
Niswander, K. R.: *ref*, 616(4050)
Nitko, A. J.: *rev*, 12, 279, 725; *bk*, B293
Nixon, G. F.: *ref*, 683(308, 331)
Nixon, J.: *ref*, 649(23)
Nixon, J. T.: *ref*, 822(168)
Njaa, L. J.: *ref*, 687(10)
Noa, J. K.: *bk*, B509
Nober, L. W.: *ref*, 932(123-4)
Noble, H.: *ref*, 37(138), 232(1177)
Noel, B.: *ref*, 661(4776), 697(1929)
Noeth, R.: *ref*, 991(1)
Noeth, R. J.: *exc*, B527; *ref*, 182(700), 989(13, 20), 991(2, 5)
Nogrady, M. E.: *test*, 709
Nolan, J. J.: *ref*, 1022(16)
Nolan, J. S.: *ref*, 12(5), 179(105)
Nolan, M. E.: *ref*, 660(86)
Noland, R. G.: *ref*, 187(424), 232(1208)
Noll, A.: *bk*, B46
Noll, G.: *ref*, 529(23), 641(474), 656(45)
Noll, G. A.: *ref*, 641(468)
Noll, R. L.: *ref*, 641(610)
Noll, R. P.: *bk*, B411
Noll, V. H.: *bk*, B410-1
Noller, R. B.: *ref*, 495(399)
Nolting, E.: *ref*, 1023(1452, 1495)
Noppe, L.: *ref*, 693(534)
Noppe, L. D.: *ref*, 244(183), 249(519), 572(49)
Norbert, N.: *ref*, 495(332), 616(3976)
Norcross, C. E.: *cross ref*, 29
Nord, C.: *ref*, 630(287), 1022(68)
Nord, W. R.: *ref*, 1074(20), 1175(143)
Nordland, F. H.: *ref*, 28(47), 182(731), 183(359), 744(37), 830(23)
Norem-Hebeisen, A.: *ref*, 616(4985)
Norfleet, M. A.: *ref*, 506(867)
Norlin, B.: *ref*, 548(331)
Norman, C. M.: *ref*, 490(511)
Norman, D.: *ref*, 720(354)
Norman, R. M. G.: *ref*, 553(683)
Norman, W. T.: *ref*, 616(4051); *cross ref*, 616
Norris, D. L.: *ref*, 576(50), 683(309)
Norris, L.: *ref*, 199(21)
Norris, T. A.: *ref*, 232(1314)
North, M.: *bk*, B412
North, R. D.: *cross ref*, 10, 27, 257
Northrop, L. C.: *ref*, 997(138)
Norton, A.: *exc*, B519
Norton, D. E.: *ref*, 790(26)
Norton, J. C.: *ref*, 230(1223), 616(4748)
Norton, R. S.: *ref*, 527(45, 48-9), 713(1-2)
Norton, S.: *ref*, 641(549), 1023(1462)

Ollendick, T. H.: *ref,* 24(29), 37 (195), 222(426, 495), 230(1124), 232(1170–1, 1316, 1412, 1509)
Oller, J. W.: *exc,* 156; *ref,* 110 (24), 156(3), 720(213–4, 247–9, 295–6, 327, 340)
Olley, M.: *ref,* 553(555), 615(32)
Olsen, J. E.: *ref,* 553(628)
Olsen, K. R.: *ref,* 506(808)
Olsen, M. C.: *ref,* 693(416), 1028 (215)
Olsen, R. E.: *ref,* 997(139)
Olson, A.: *ref,* 938(16)
Olson, C. J.: *cross ref,* 826
Olson, H. A.: *ref,* 661(4642)
Olson, H. L. T.: *ref,* 1050(67), 1051(8, 16), 1052(69)
Olson, J. L.: *ref,* 616(4576)
Olson, M.: *ref,* 683(83)
Olson, P. H.: *ref,* 732(64)
Olson, R. E.: *ref,* 216(76), 661 (4668)
Olson, R. R.: *ref,* 1028(216)
Olson, T. D.: *ref,* 616(4306)
Olthof, E. V.: *ref,* 232(1211)
Oltman, P. K.: *test,* 519, 548, 572; *ref,* 188(129), 232(1365), 519 (66), 548(324), 572(50), 581 (402)
O'Mahony, M. T.: *ref,* 469(425), 641(271), 679(1161)
O'Malley, J. J.: *ref,* 519(76–7)
O'Malley, P. M.: *ref,* 182(775), 225(78), 490(540)
O'Marra, M. M.: *ref,* 693(524)
Omer, J. L.: *bk,* B417
Ommanney, P. C.: *ref,* 641(320)
Omvig, C. P.: *ref,* 997(140, 158), 1016(12, 22–4)
O'Neil, C.: *ref,* 549(16)
O'Neil, H. F.: *ref,* 227(62), 230 (1054), 616(3923, 4516, 4751), 617(56, 74), 683(94, 125, 133, 180, 207)
O'Neil, J. M.: *ref,* 1022(49, 86)
O'Neil, P. M.: *ref,* 655(15)
O'Neil, M. F.: *ref,* 686(914), 688 (165)
O'Neil, M. R.: *ref,* 822(169)
O'Neill, P.: *ref,* 222(474), 519(78), 661(4854, 4894)
O'Neill, P. C.: *ref,* 222(474), 519 (78), 661(4854, 4894)
Oner, N.: *ref,* 683(302)
Ong, J.: *ref,* 183(345), 516(473), 686(915), 1023(1357)
Onoda, L.: *ref,* 495(444, 503), 553 (556)
Ontario Institute for Studies in Education: *test,* 196, 266, 736
Oothuizen, S.: *test,* 587
Opitz, E.: *ref,* 616(4392)
Oppel, W.: *ref,* 616(4138)
Oppenheim, A. N.: *bk,* B418
Orchik, D. J.: *ref,* 953(6)
O'Rear, J. M.: *ref,* 469(537), 679 (1396)
O'Reilly, P. A.: *ref,* 490(490)
O'Reilly, R.: *ref,* 183(360), 291 (33)
O'Reilly, R. P.: *bk,* B181
Orford, J.: *ref,* 553(557, 684)
Organ, D. W.: *ref,* 553(629–30, 685)

Organ, L. M.: *test,* 709
Orleans, J. S.: *cross ref,* 1, 1036
Orlett, M. J.: *ref,* 524(111), 634 (305)
Orloff, H.: *ref,* 37(149), 232 (1212), 516(485), 581(378), 697 (1882)
Orloff, L. J.: *ref,* 548(363)
Orloffsky, J. L.: *ref,* 697(1992)
Orme, J. E.: *ref,* 585(166, 168, 182, 201)
Orme, T. J.: *ref,* 473(25)
Ormond, H. A.: *ref,* 641(361), 656 (31)
Ormsby, V. J.: *ref,* 469(416)
Orndoff, R. K.: *ref,* 542(1534)
Orne, E. C.: *test,* 576; *ref,* 576(43)
Orne, M. T.: *ref,* 576(37), 682(69, 106)
Ornstein, A.: *ref,* 176(7)
Ornstein, P.: *ref,* 677(193)
Oros, J. A.: *ref,* 232(1105)
O'Rourke, A. M.: *ref,* 616(4919)
O'Rourke, T. W.: *ref,* 368(1)
O'Rourke, W. D.: *ref,* 656(61)
Orpen, C.: *ref,* 200(592), 225(63, 68), 514(1016, 1209), 553(315, 363, 686), 654(10, 23), 711(30, 51), 820(129)
Orpet, R. E.: *test,* 871; *ref,* 200 (544, 689), 217(28, 38), 232 (1101, 1510), 431(418, 623), 488 (377), 666(59)
Orr, D. B.: *cross ref,* 735
Orr, L.: *bk,* B99, B495
Orr, R. E.: *ref,* 555(299)
Orr, R. R.: *ref,* 222(513), 232 (1577)
Orr, W.: *ref,* 616(4578)
Orritt, C. P.: *ref,* 230(991)
Orsillo, D. G.: *ref,* 697(1883)
Orsini, R. A.: *ref,* 997(100)
Orta, S. L.: *ref,* 1009(15)
Ortar, G.: *ref,* 232(1106)
Orth, C. D.: *ref,* 686(868), 697 (1800)
Orth, L. L. J.: *ref,* 377(478)
Orvis, C. C.: *ref,* 469(459–60)
Orwig, M. D.: *ref,* 469(423)
Orwin, A.: *ref,* 553(578), 679 (1328)
Osanyinbi, J. A.: *ref,* 110(25)
Osborn, K. N.: *ref,* 213(22), 431 (538)
Osborn, M. E.: *ref,* 654(17)
Osborn, R. N.: *ref,* 1175(125, 130, 154)
Osborn, R. T.: *ref,* 19(152), 32(1), 181(9)
Osborne, A.: *rev,* 287
Osborne, D.: *bk,* B525; *ref,* 495 (349–50), 616(4088, 4368, 4972, 5006–7), 617(71), 623(17)
Osborne, F.: *ref,* 230(1061), 530 (173), 628(180)
Osborne, J. L.: *ref,* 468(10)
Osborne, J. W.: *ref,* 553(472)
Osborne, R. T.: *ref,* 19(152), 32 (1), 181(9), 232(1107); *cross ref,* 232
Osborne, W. L.: *ref,* 232(1464)
Osburn, W. J.: *cross ref,* 759, 802
Osgood, J. A.: *ref,* 630(206)

O'Shea, A. J.: *test,* 1004; *ref,* 1010 (36–7), 1023(1286–7, 1408)
Oshman, H.: *ref,* 616(4547)
Osicka, C. J.: *ref,* 222(496)
Osipow, S. H.: *ref,* 188(98), 693 (349), 1028(184, 192)
Oskamp, S.: *rev,* 659
Osman, A. C.: *ref,* 514(1126), 553 (473), 679(1162)
Osmond, H.: *test,* 552; *bk,* B228
Osofsky, J. D.: *ref,* 208(5)
Osterhoff, W. E.: *ref,* 616(4307)
Osterhouse, R.: *ref,* 820(131)
Osterhout, S.: *ref,* 1101(169)
Osterlund, A. M.: *test,* 1023
Osterrieth, P. A.: *ref,* 606(320)
Ostertag, R. H.: *ref,* 527(50)
Ostfeld, A. M.: *ref,* 616(4007)
Ostrand, J. L.: *ref,* 514(1127, 1350)
Ostrov, E.: *ref,* 230(996), 633(3), 661(4643)
Ostrowski, F. J.: *ref,* 628(168)
Oswald, W. T.: *ref,* 230(1288)
Otis, A. S.: *test,* 198; *ref,* 720(13)
Otis, J. L.: *ref,* 1049(1), 1186(6)
Ott, M. D.: *ref,* 182(740)
Ott, S.: *ref,* 595(20)
Otten, M. W.: *ref,* 641(553, 632)
Otto, B. J.: *ref,* 506(906)
Otto, J.: *ref,* 525(2, 11–2), 531(15), 681(16, 50, 52, 69)
Otto, J. A.: *ref,* 525(5), 681(28)
Otto, W.: *test,* 778, 823; *exc,* 757; *ref,* 757(5), 778(3, 7), 823(2)
Ottomanelli, G.: *ref,* 527(27), 574 (511), 616(4548)
Ottosson, J. O.: *ref,* 675(72)
Ousley, N. K.: *ref,* 616(5018)
Ovenstone, I. M. K.: *ref,* 530(174–5), 579(68–9), 649(13–4), 679 (1163–4)
Overall, J. E.: *ref,* 230(997, 1101), 578(279), 616(4054, 4127, 4308–11, 4549, 4752, 4920), 654(15, 22, 24–5), 679(1064)
Overholser, B. M.: *ref,* 720(159)
Overton, G. W.: *ref,* 222(335)
Overton, W.: *ref,* 200(650), 230 (1193)
Owen, D. R.: *ref,* 188(129), 232 (1108), 572(50), 625(7)
Owen, G.: *ref,* 585(166)
Owen, M.: *ref,* 616(4745)
Owen, T. R.: *test,* 367; *bk,* B339
Owens, E. K.: *ref,* 213(27), 232 (1511), 431(624), 938(21)
Owens, G. B.: *ref,* 616(4074)
Owens, J. M.: *ref,* 641(264)
Owens, N. J.: *ref,* 182(701), 183 (354), 490(512)
Owens, R. G.: *ref,* 542(1453)
Owens, T. R.: *exc,* B182
Owens, W. A.: *rev,* 247
Oxman, J. M.: *ref,* 646(99)
Oxman, K.: *ref,* 726A(29)
Ozehosky, J. R.: *ref,* 611(626), 616 (4550)
Oziel, L. D.: *ref,* 504(88)
Oziel, L. J.: *ref,* 244(147), 504 (88), 516(488), 611(552)
Ozmon, K. L.: *ref,* 616(3945), 654 (14)

Patterson, R. L.: *ref,* 683(108)
Patterson, T. W.: *ref,* 542(1543), 616(4887)
Pattison, D.: *ref,* 810(2)
Pattison, E. M.: *ref,* 530(176), 616 4316–7), 631(60)
Pattison, J. H.: *ref,* 651(33)
Patton, G. W. R.: *ref,* 616(4085)
Patton, M. J.: *ref,* 630(301)
Patton, W.: *ref,* 469(468)
Patton, W. F.: *ref,* 601(6)
Patty, R. A.: *ref,* 495(506)
Pauk, W.: *test,* 815
Pauker, J. D.: *rev,* 695, 881; *test,* 625; *exc,* B121; *ref,* 230(1224), 506(997), 625(8), 677(187); *cross ref,* 585
Paul, G. L.: *ref,* 585(172, 196), 631 (41, 59)
Paul, O.: *ref,* 616(4007)
Paul, O. D.: *ref,* 555(232)
Paulin, K. C.: *ref,* 686(995)
Paulson, D. E.: *ref,* 818(10)
Paulson, D. L.: *ref,* 1028(188)
Paulson, L.: *test,* 53, 771
Paulson, M. J.: *ref,* 616(4555, 4924)
Paulus, N. J.: *ref,* 732(53)
Pavek, B. J.: *ref,* 686(996)
Pawlik, K.: *ref,* 520(95), 597(170)
Paxton, N.: *test,* 53, 771
Paykel, E. S.: *ref,* 599(25), 611 (576, 601–3, 627), 685(4–5)
Payne, D. A.: *bk,* B420–2; *ref,* 182(651), 232(1523), 679(1168, 1365, 1398)
Payne, D. L.: *ref,* 182(571), 542 (1314)
Payne, F. D.: *ref,* 497(3), 616 (4059)
Payne, G.: *ref,* 616(3869)
Payne, H.: *ref,* 611(562)
Payne, I. R.: *test,* 507; *ref,* 507 (1–2)
Payne, J. L.: *bk,* B423
Payne, J. S.: *ref,* 222(336–7, 356), 229(1444, 1470, 1561)
Payne, R.: *ref,* 636(42)
Payne, R. W.: *rev,* 571, 632, 710; *cross ref,* 613
Payson, J. B.: *ref,* 679(1473)
Payson, S. L.: *ref,* 514(1210), 641 (472)
Payton, D. A.: *ref,* 555(193)
Payton-Miyazaki, M.: *ref,* 679 (1510)
Pazandak, C. H.: *ref,* 193(40), 469 (558)
Peace, H. L.: *ref,* 693(418)
Peach, W.: *ref,* 1024(4)
Pearce, J.: *bk,* B424
Pearce, R. M.: *ref,* 820(137)
Pearce, W. C.: *ref,* 475(28), 693 (563)
Pearlman, M. N.: *ref,* 514(1288)
Pearman, F. C.: *ref,* 686(997)
Pearson, B. F.: *ref,* 661(4844)
Pearson, J. S.: *test,* 623; *bk,* B525; *ref,* 616(4368), 617(3, 10–14, 26, 71), 623(12, 17)
Pearson, L. B.: *ref,* 187(456), 719 (94)
Pearson, N. S.: *ref,* 616(4060)
Pearson, P. D.: *rev,* 748, 755

Pearson, P. R.: *ref,* 548(261), 553 (365, 559), 656(44, 46, 56), 711 (87–8)
Pearson, S. A.: *ref,* 679(1308), 693 (419)
Pearson, V. L.: *ref,* 224(248)
Pease, D.: *ref,* 209(52), 229(1485)
Peatling, J. H.: *test,* 501
Peay, E. R.: *exc,* B125; *ref,* 660 (147)
Peck, R. L.: *ref,* 232(1111)
Peckford, T.: *ref,* 230(1225)
Pecorella, P. A.: *ref,* 985(8)
Pedder, J. R.: *ref,* 565(5)
Pedersen, D. M.: *ref,* 495(400), 611(604), 693(408)
Pedersen, F. A.: *ref,* 206(55)
Pedersen, L. G.: *ref,* 182(741)
Pedersen, R. A.: *test,* 1036
Pedhazur, E. J.: *rev,* 391, 711
Pedigo, E. A.: *ref,* 643(164)
Pedrini, B. C.: *ref,* 735(108)
Pedrini, B. M. C.: *ref,* 469(509)
Pedrini, B. S.: *ref,* 735(107)
Pedrini, D. T.: *ref,* 37(166), 222 (407), 229(1505), 735(107–8)
Peebles, P. R.: *ref,* 661(4845)
Peeler, J. M.: *ref,* 542(1519)
Peer, G. G.: *ref,* 182(776), 595(28)
Peirce, S. W.: *ref,* 574(563), 1011 (904)
Peisach, E. C.: *ref,* 720(92)
Peiser, K. B.: *ref,* 575(35)
Peitchinis, J.: *ref,* 542(1373)
Peixotto, H. E.: *bk,* B216; *ref,* 578 (294), 581(386), 616(4395)
Peizer, S. B.: *ref,* 612(11)
Pellegrini, R. J.: *ref,* 222(338), 232 (1112), 514(1129, 1289)
Pelusi, V. A.: *ref,* 431(478)
Pemberton, C. L.: *ref,* 182(702), 400(2)
Pender, R. H.: *ref,* 882(233)
Pendergast, K.: *test,* 969
Pendergrass, P. E.: *ref,* 525(13), 681(63)
Pendleton, B.: *ref,* 516(474)
Pendleton, B. A.: *ref,* 997(170)
Pendleton, C. W.: *rev,* 1133, 1138
Pendleton, R. F.: *ref,* 697(1884)
Penick, J. E.: *ref,* 249(417)
Penix, L.: *ref,* 1022(70)
Penk, W.: *ref,* 616(4925)
Penkava, R. A.: *ref,* 679(1309)
Penn, L. S.: *ref,* 495(472)
Penn, N. E.: *ref,* 542(1627)
Penn, W. I.: *ref,* 571(43)
Penna, J. P.: *rev,* 844, 850
Penner, K.: *ref,* 431(560)
Penner, L. A.: *ref,* 660(44, 193)
Penner, W.: *ref,* 634(273)
Penniman, T. L.: *ref,* 679(1310)
Pennock, C. D.: *ref,* 720(298–9)
Penny, J. L.: *ref,* 616(4926), 675 (108)
Penrod, J. P.: *ref,* 625(13)
Penrose, L. S.: *cross ref,* 616
Pentecoste, J. C.: *ref,* 1003(11)
Peoples, E. E.: *ref,* 555(264)
Pepper, S.: *ref,* 643(193)
Percell, L. P.: *ref,* 514(1130), 616 (4318)

Perdue, W. C.: *ref,* 611(624–5), 661(4633, 4644, 4691, 4701, 4762–4, 4779, 4836), 675(78–9)
Pereboom, M. J. G.: *ref,* 200(546), 227(55), 882(182)
Peretti, P. O.: *ref,* 229(1445), 485 (345), 495(446)
Peretz, M.: *ref,* 660(131)
Pereyra-Suarez, D. M.: *ref,* 942(5)
Pérez, A.: *ref,* 1(22), 514(1211)
Perez, F. I.: *ref,* 230(1226–7), 616 (4061), 661(4645)
Perez, T. L.: *ref,* 628(166)
Perez-Reyes, M. G.: *ref,* 616(4319)
Perilstein, J. P.: *ref,* 542(1581), 641(554)
Perin, C. T.: *ref,* 576(35)
Perino, J.: *ref,* 219(8)
Perkes, V. A.: *ref,* 634(333)
Perkins, C. J.: *ref,* 519(52), 613 (97)
Perkins, C. W.: *ref,* 536(24), 616 (4556), 677(181), 683(192)
Perkins, D. G.: *ref,* 574(513)
Perkins, E. M.: *ref,* 641(358)
Perkins, M. L.: *ref,* 439(5), 679 (1399)
Perkins, R. D.: *ref,* 697(1772), 698 (19)
Perley, R. L.: *ref,* 616(4793)
Perley, R. N.: *ref,* 616(4792)
Perlin, S.: *ref,* 599(26, 28), 651 (24)
Perlman, D.: *ref,* 643(151)
Perlman, S. M.: *ref,* 232(1215)
Perlstadt, H.: *ref,* 1101(179)
Perna, J. J.: *ref,* 581(431)
Perney, V. H.: *ref,* 548(355)
Perrin, D. W.: *ref,* 469(480)
Perris, C.: *ref,* 675(72)
Perrone, V.: *bk,* B425–6
Perruso, J. K.: *ref,* 249(549)
Perry, C.: *ref,* 249(418), 504(94), 682(82–3)
Perry, C. J. G.: *ref,* 514(962), 661 (4614)
Perry, C. M.: *ref,* 393(101)
Perry, D. K.: *ref,* 485(387)
Perry, F.: *ref,* 183(336), 1028(153)
Perry, H. W.: *ref,* 630(264)
Perry, N. W.: *ref,* 232(1576)
Perry, R. P.: *ref,* 495(322)
Perry, W. O.: *ref,* 349(5), 555 (265)
Perry, W. W.: *ref,* 96(10)
Pershad, D.: *ref,* 250(108, 113), 530(183–4), 661(4804)
Personnel Research Board, Ohio State University; *test,* 1174
Persons, C. I.: *ref,* 627(61)
Persson, G.: *ref,* 675(72)
Perullo, L. P.: *ref,* 393(68)
Pesick, M. N.: *ref,* 626(229)
Pess, A.: *ref,* 377(480), 542(1374)
Peter, C. J.: *ref,* 188(99)
Peters, D. L.: *ref,* 983(2)
Peters, H. D.: *ref,* 232(1512)
Peters, J. E.: *ref,* 232(1454), 576 (62)
Peters, N.: *ref,* 720(250, 300)
Peters, R. M.: *ref,* 110(29), 188 (125)
Petersen, C. G.: *ref,* 490(541)
Petersen, D. J.: *ref,* 693(254)

Plomin, R.: *ref,* 232(1217), 514 (1336), 611(660)

Plotkin, W. H.: *ref,* 956(6)

Plumlee, L. B.: *exc,* B229

Plummer, M.: *ref,* 711(21)

Plutchik, R.: *test,* 549; ref, 549(4, 7–8, 13–14, 19–21, 25, 27, 31), 616(4156, 4422)

Plutchik, R. R.: *ref,* 549(2–3), 628 (145)

Podel, B. M.: *ref,* 523(259)

Podemski, R. S.: *ref,* 1175(91)

Podhoretz, H.: *ref,* 542(1521)

Podietz, L.: *ref,* 872(57)

Poe, C. A.: *ref,* 542(1376, 1390)

Poeldinger, W. J.: *ref,* 616(4323)

Poetter, R.: *ref,* 559(58)

Poetter, R. A.: *ref,* 559(45)

Poggio, J. P.: *ref,* 520(86), 679 (1028), 1023(1512–4)

Pogul, L. J.: *ref,* 229(1527)

Pohler, M. J.: *ref,* 616(4074)

Pohlmann, J. T.: *test,* 376; *ref,* 376(3–6)

Pokorny, A. D.: *ref,* 585(184), 631 (71)

Poland, W. D.: *ref,* 636(46)

Polanski, H.: *ref,* 19(137), 200 (626), 249(468, 470)

Polirstok, S. R.: *ref,* 732(61)

Pollack, D.: *ref,* 249(421)

Pollack, R. H.: *ref,* 232(1311)

Pollack, S. N.: *ref,* 249(421)

Pollitt, J.: *ref,* 611(649, 652)

Pollock, J. M.: *ref,* 514(1018)

Pollock, S. W.: *ref,* 697(1807)

Polmantier, P. C.: *ref,* 377(493)

Polonsky, M. J.: *ref,* 693(420), 697 (1930)

Pond, R. L.: *ref,* 929(3)

Poole, A. D.: *ref,* 571(53)

Poole, C.: *ref,* 200(547), 683(227), 684(4)

Poole, D. R.: *ref,* 230(999)

Poole, F. R.: *ref,* 679(1400)

Poole, M. E.: *ref,* 720(251)

Poole, M. J.: *ref,* 227(77)

Pooler, A. E.: *ref,* 902(3)

Pooley, R. C.: *ref,* 660(88) ; *cross ref,* 39, 45–6, 48–9, 69

Poortinga, Y. H.: *exc,* B76

Pope, H. H.: *ref,* 382(2)

Pope, L.: *bk,* B245

Pope, P.: *ref,* 506(823), 932(108)

Pope, T.: *ref,* 661(4846)

Popham, R. J.: *test,* 53

Popham, W. J.: *test,* 53, 279, 771, 917; *bk,* B203, B431–8

Popoff, L. M.: *ref,* 675(43)

Popovich, D.: *bk,* B439

Popper, B. G.: *ref,* 693(502)

Popper, D. K.: *ref,* 646(80)

Porch, B. E.: *test,* 971–2; *ref,* 971 (9)

Porritt, D.: *ref,* 1050(68), 1051(9, 17), 1052(71)

Porter, A.: *ref,* 10(118), 202(3)

Porter, A. C.: *ref,* 1010(63)

Porter, D.: *ref,* 720(396)

Porter, D. T.: *ref,* 683(193)

Porter, M. J.: *ref,* 693(503)

Porter, N.: *bk,* B440

Porter, R. B.: *test,* 520

Porterfield, W. A.: *ref,* 693(331)

Porteus, J. H.: *ref,* 693(255)

Porteus, S. D.: *test,* 224

Portnoy, S.: *ref,* 514(1019), 542 (1377), 720(54, 76, 136)

Posada, A.: *ref,* 616(3886)

Posavac, E. J.: *ref,* 514(1213)

Posey, T. B.: *ref,* 230(1000), 582 (239)

Post, A. L.: *ref,* 679(1505)

Post, F.: *ref,* 553(420)

Post, R. D.: *ref,* 616(4661)

Post, W. L.: *cross ref,* 45

Posthuma, A. B.: *ref,* 555(234)

Posthuma, B. W.: *ref,* 555(234)

Potkay, C. R.: *bk,* B441, ref, 641 (293), 643(93), 661(4646, 4702), 697(1966)

Potter, E. L.: *ref,* 373(12)

Potter, N. D.: *ref,* 679(1311)

Potter, R. E.: *ref,* 222(428), 967 (15)

Potter, T. C.: *ref,* 720(137)

Poucher, K. E.: *rev,* 1151

Poulin, D. A.: *ref,* 490(470), 1016 (13)

Poulter, E. M.: *ref,* 431(422)

Pound, R. E.: *ref,* 693(504, 579)

Pound, W. N. M.: *ref,* 1052(90)

Pourier, J. E. E.: *ref,* 686(1022)

Povey, R. M.: *bk,* B442

Powell, A.: *ref,* 187(446), 200(548, 691), 222(442–3), 616(4324), 802 (285)

Powell, B. J.: *ref,* 548(290), 553 (476), 616(4683)

Powell, D. H.: *ref,* 514(1131), 683 (141)

Powell, E. R.: *ref,* 520(87)

Powell, J.: *ref,* 222(418)

Powell, J. A.: *ref,* 616(4682)

Powell, J. L.: *bk,* B443; *ref,* 182 (652)

Powell, L.: *ref,* 616(4924)

Powell, L. S.: *ref,* 229(1431), 234 (88), 431(388)

Powell, M. C.: *ref,* 572(41), 646 (100)

Powell, R. R.: *ref,* 200(627), 250 (109), 613(103), 631(61)

Power, J. H.: *ref,* 37(196), 232 (1416), 493(32), 506(956)

Power, R. P.: *ref,* 553(625, 631), 554(59), 596(43, 60), 611(628)

Powers, D. D.: *ref,* 1174(200)

Powers, J.: *ref,* 230(1083), 548 (268), 616(4358)

Powers, M.: *exc,* B261

Powers, R. J.: *ref,* 997(103)

Powers, S. M.: *ref,* 802(277)

Powers, T. F.: *exc,* B63

Powitzky, R. J.: *ref,* 708(23)

Poynton, C.: *ref,* 675(92)

Poznanski, E.: *ref,* 581(360), 661 (4647)

Prabhu, G. G.: *ref,* 553(477–8), 679(943)

Prado, W. M.: *ref,* 495(385), 616 (4208)

Prager, R. A.: *ref,* 616(4060, 4460)

Prandoni, J. R.: *ref,* 506(803), 661 (4703)

Prange, A. J.: *ref,* 585(197), 675 (45)

Prange, J. L.: *ref,* 198(28), 720 (302), 745(64)

Prasad, M.: *ref,* 578(329)

Pratap, S.: *ref,* 485(333), 1042 (12), 1043(19)

Prather, E.: *test,* 952

Pratt, A. B.: *ref,* 1023(1465)

Pratt, D. M.: *ref,* 643(98), 1023 (1326)

Pratt, W. E.: *test,* 4, 40, 302, 717

Pray, R. C.: *ref,* 187(451)

Prediger, D.: *exc,* 1013; *ref,* 991 (1), 1013(1)

Prediger, D. J.: *ref,* 469(511), 991(5), 1022(50–1, 71–5, 87), 1023(1497), 1028(283–6)

Preen, B.: *exc,* 810; *ref,* 810(3)

Preiser, M.: *ref,* 225(72), 229 (1555)

Preiss, L. C.: *ref,* 726A(51)

Prendergast, M. A.: *ref,* 693(505)

Prendergast, P. J.: *ref,* 679(1312)

Prentky, R. A.: *ref,* 553(632)

Prescott, G. A.: *test,* 22, 283, 732

Presly, A. S.: *ref,* 554(56), 679 (1291)

Pressnell, L. M.: *ref,* 967(11)

Presson, S. P.: *ref,* 192(153), 476 (51)

Preston, G. W.: *ref,* 493(29)

Preston, J.: *ref,* 230(1276)

Preston, J. H.: *ref,* 693(332)

Preston, R. C.: *cross ref,* 4, 29

Preston, R. L.: *ref,* 1174(172)

Preston, T. A.: *ref,* 616(4889)

Prestwood, J. S.: *ref,* 193(37)

Preucel, R. W.: *ref,* 616(4487), 675(76)

Price, B. B.: *ref,* 651(42)

Price, B. R.: *ref,* 539(35)

Price, E.: *ref,* 29(230), 802(220)

Price, F. F.: *ref,* 679(1029)

Price, F. W.: *ref,* 469(572)

Price, G. E.: *ref,* 641(612)

Price, H.: *ref,* 514(1020)

Price, J. A.: *test,* 391

Price, K. F.: *ref,* 542(1603)

Price, L.: *ref,* 486(59)

Price, M. G.: *ref,* 641(599)

Price, R. G.: *cross ref,* 322, 326

Price, R. H.: *ref,* 681(71), 706(29)

Price, R. L.: *ref,* 595(19)

Price, T. L.: *ref,* 506(998)

Price-Williams, D.: *ref,* 232(1365), 519(66), 548(324), 581(402)

Prickett, J.: *ref,* 238(39)

Priel, I.: *ref,* 662(424), 686(880)

Prien, E.: *ref,* 1186(6)

Prien, E. P.: *ref,* 568(82), 569 (147), 983(7, 13)

Prien, R. F.: *ref,* 582(173–5), 641 (475), 655(7–8)

Priest, R. G.: *ref,* 615(26)

Priggie, N. K.: *ref,* 679(1030)

Primavera, L. H.: *ref,* 542(1391–2, 1534, 1582, 1633)

Pringle, W. J.: *ref,* 557(4), 616 (4930), 681(81)

Prins, D.: *ref,* 515(452, 475)

Prinsloo, W. B. J.: *test,* 194

Prior, M. R.: *ref,* 632(15)

Pritchard, C.: *ref,* 596(42), 669(1)

Pritchard, D. A.: *ref,* 531(15), 681 (69)

Pritchard, R. D.: *ref,* 1052(43, 56)
Pritchett, B. J.: *ref,* 660(89)
Pritchett, E. M.: *test,* 305
Probasco, J. O.: *ref,* 35(112), 490 (471)
Prociuk, T. J.: *ref,* 820(155)
Proctor, J. A.: *ref,* 183(355)
Proger, B. B.: *rev,* 432, 443, 678, 771 ; *exc,* 24, 34, 203, 293, 439, 445–6, 498, 500, 513, 779, 794, 929, 954, 956 ; *ref,* 24(3), 34(1), 229 (1577), 232(1218), 293(2), 431 (479), 439(2), 498(5), 500(7), 513(2), 779(2), 954(8)
Prola, M.: *ref,* 697(1816–7)
Prosser, M. K.: *ref,* 693(302)
Prost, M. A.: *ref,* 578(354)
Protter, B. S.: *ref,* 697(1885)
Prout, H. T.: *ref,* 601(7)
Provus, M.: *bk,* B444
Prudent, S.: *ref,* 592(65)
Pruim, R. J.: *ref,* 585(187), 599 (31–2)
Pruitt, P. J.: *ref,* 1175(159)
Prusoff, B. A.: *ref,* 611(601–3, 627)
Prutsman, T. D.: *ref,* 37(137), 200 (575)
Prutting, C. A.: *ref,* 967(20)
Pryer, M. W.: *ref,* 626(252), 628 (246), 1174(185)
Pryor, A. B.: *ref,* 507(3)
Pryor, L. S.: *ref,* 529(26)
Pryor, N. M.: *ref,* 1175(92, 110), 1177(94)
Prytula, R. E.: *ref,* 581(361, 379, 412), 606(319, 327)
Pryzwansky, W. B.: *ref,* 227(78), 726A(31)
Psychological Corporation: *test,* 776, 1033, 1104, 1121–3
Ptacek, M.: *ref,* 616(4108)
Pucel, D. J.: *ref,* 490(472), 679 (1031), 997(41), 1050(42)
Puetz, W. J.: *ref,* 874(52)
Pugh, A. K.: *ref,* 720(338, 393)
Pugh, R. C.: *ref,* 634(343), 1023 (1360)
Pugliese, A. C.: *ref,* 616(4756)
Puhan, B. N.: *ref,* 184(113), 200 (628), 230(1151), 485(370)
Puig-Casauranc, M. del C.: *ref,* 542(1628), 1028(287)
Pulaski, R. E.: *ref,* 490(528)
Pullen, P. W.: *ref,* 574(514), 679 (1032)
Pulliam, G. P.: *ref,* 654(33)
Pullias, E. V.: *cross ref,* 22
Pullman, H. W.: *ref,* 182(602), 183 (337), 199(23)
Pulos, S. M.: *ref,* 661(4781)
Pumfrey, P. D.: *bk,* B445–6; *ref,* 431(626)
Pumroy, D. K.: *ref,* 616(3859), 617 (49), 621(6)
Puranajoti, T.: *ref,* 249(359)
Purcell, D.: *test,* 279
Purdie, M.: *ref,* 679(1033)
Pursley, R. D.: *ref,* 1177(95)
Purushothaman, M.: *bk,* B447
Purves, A.: *bk,* B4
Purves, A. C.: *rev,* 40, 45 ; *bk,* B448
Pusateri, P. D.: *ref,* 641(613)

Pusey, P. F.: *ref,* 582(223), 697 (1886)
Pusser, H. E.: *ref,* 732(54), 802 (278)
Pustel, G.: *ref,* 662(425)
Puthoff, F. T.: *ref,* 222(340), 575 (36)
Putkonen, A. R.: *ref,* 230(1167)
Putnam, B. A.: *ref,* 693(256, 551, 579), 997(42, 162), 1028(279)
Putnam, C. M.: *ref,* 495(402), 634 (275)
Putnam, L. R.: *ref,* 227(102)
Putnam, R. L.: *ref,* 409(4)
Pyle, R. R.: *ref,* 555(195)
Pyrczak, F.: *rev,* 19, 732; *ref,* 735 (87)

QUANE, R.: *ref,* 514(1327)
Quarrick, E.: *ref,* 210(91), 232 (1347), 703(201)
Quarter, J.: *ref,* 634(243)
Quast, W.: *ref,* 506(994)
Quay, A. T.: *ref,* 523(231)
Quay, L. C.: *ref,* 229(1447, 1528, 1562)
Queisser, H. R.: *ref,* 572(31)
Quelet, T. E.: *ref,* 1023(1410)
Quereshi, M. Y.: *rev,* 375, 486; *ref,* 230(1074, 1152), 232(114, 1219) ; *cross ref,* 485, 488, 527
Query, J. M.: *ref,* 542(1455), 578 (280)
Query, W. T.: *ref,* 542(1455), 578 (280)
Quezada, R.: *ref,* 802(292)
Quick, A. D.: *test,* 438; *ref,* 438(1)
Quick, D.: *exc,* B305
Quick, V. D.: *ref,* 523(282)
Quigley, G. L. S.: *ref,* 582(204)
Quigley, K.: *ref,* 542(1490)
Quinlan, D.: *ref,* 230(1061), 530 (173), 581(370), 611(612), 628 (180, 191), 661(4648, 4656, 4669, 4723, 4756, 4880), 675(69)
Quinlan, D. M.: *ref,* 230(1001), 232 (1228), 506(873), 530(167), 628 (174), 661(4649, 4782, 4894), 675 (102), 697(1848, 1890), 708(27)
Quinlan, M. M.: *ref,* 232(1318)
Quinn, E.: *ref,* 577(63)
Quinn, K. I.: *ref,* 1174(273)
Quinones, W. A.: *ref,* 24(36), 222 (497)
Quintard, G.: *ref,* 514(1182)
Quirk, K. H.: *ref,* 1052(91), 1061 (9)
Quirk, M. P.: *ref,* 641(265)
Quirk, T. J.: *ref,* 381(92, 95, 98)
Quiroga, I. R.: *ref,* 616(4065)

RAAB, M. K.: *ref,* 375(20)
Raab, T. J.: *ref,* 548(291), 581 (380)
Raanan, S. L.: *ref,* 641(363)
Rabin, A. I.: *exc,* B270; *cross ref,* 232, 661
Rabin, B. J.: *ref,* 679(915)
Rabinowitz, A.: *ref,* 663(143)
Raboch, J.: *ref,* 200(629)
Rabon, A. M.: *ref,* 675(45)
Rachman, S.: *bk,* B150
Radcliffe, J. A.: *test,* 627 ; *cross ref,* 542, 568–9, 686

Rader, C. M.: *ref,* 616(5011)
Rader, G.: *ref,* 535(34)
Rader, G. E.: *ref,* 661(4704), 697 (1887)
Rader, J. R.: *ref,* 238(33)
Rader, R. C.: *ref,* 660(159)
Raderman, R.: *ref,* 182(703)
Radin, J. J.: *ref,* 1175(132)
Radin, N.: *ref,* 222(341, 390), 229 (1448, 1486), 592(55)
Radley, A. R.: *ref,* 571(43)
Radtke, R. R.: *ref,* 190(110), 490 (496), 1011(889)
Radzin, A. B.: *ref,* 656(22)
Rae, G.: *ref,* 431(423), 553(633)
Rae, J. B.: *ref,* 542(1378), 616 (4066–7)
Raffeld, P.: *test,* 984; *ref,* 20(132), 984(1)
Rafferty, J. E.: *test,* 663
Raffini, J. P.: *ref,* 469(470)
Raggio, D. J.: *ref,* 232(1319)
Ragosin, E. M.: *ref,* 932(102)
Rahaim, F. J.: *ref,* 693(564)
Rahe, R. H.: *ref,* 530(154, 160, 165)
Rahman, W. R. A.: *ref,* 222(510)
Raina, M. K.: *ref,* 249(544)
Raina, T. N.: *ref,* 377(481)
Raisch, V.: *ref,* 777(9)
Raj, J. B.: *ref,* 553(317)
Rajagopal, J.: *ref,* 548(317)
Rajaratnam, N.: *bk,* B119
Rajinder: *ref,* 553(466–7)
Rakowski, A. J.: *ref,* 542(1308)
Ralls, E. M.: *ref,* 802(308)
Ralph, D. L.: *ref,* 469(573)
Ralph, R. S.: *ref,* 520(88)
Ralstin, M.: *ref,* 630(194), 872(41)
Ramanaiah, N. V.: *ref,* 232(1516), 514(1380), 542(1640), 616(5012), 820(163), 1023(1519)
Ramanauskas, S.: *ref,* 232(1220), 720(252–3)
Ramberg, M. L.: *test,* 823
Rambo, W. W.: *test,* 680; *ref,* 680 (1–2)
Ramey, C. T.: *ref,* 206(37), 229 (1487), 249(469)
Ramirez, M.: *ref,* 232(1365), 519 (66), 548(324), 581(402)
Ramon, S.: *ref,* 697(1818)
Rampton, G. M.: *ref,* 643(182)
Ramsaur, J. C.: *ref,* 542(1379)
Ramsay, C.: *ref,* 616(4757)
Ramsay, I.: *ref,* 582(218, 224)
Ramsay, W.: *ref,* 616(3962)
Ramsett, D. E.: *ref,* 469(471)
Ramsey, C. A.: *ref,* 200(630), 216 (75), 222(427)
Ramsey, P.: *ref,* 1062(1)
Ramsey, R. T.: *ref,* 688(151)
Ramsey, T. W.: *ref,* 393(53)
Ramseyer, J. A.: *ref,* 605(2)
Ramstad, V. V.: *ref,* 222(428), 967(15)
Ranck, S. A.: *ref,* 506(999), 873 (6), 882(234)
Rancourt, K. L.: *ref,* 719(83)
Rand, T. M.: *ref,* 575(45)
Randak, S.: *ref,* 28(47), 183(359)
Randall, A. M.: *ref,* 675(67)
Randel, M. A.: *ref,* 802(308)

Rider, V. J. E.: *ref,* 679(1173)
Ridgway, J. M. B.: *ref,* 616(4070)
Ridgway, R. W.: *ref,* 431(376)
Ridley, S. L.: *ref,* 514(950), 693 (388)
Rieder, W. B.: *ref,* 693(422)
Riedesel, C. A.: *rev,* 283, 293; *cross ref,* 291
Riedl, P. S.: *ref,* 932(149)
Rietz, E. G.: *cross ref,* 845
Rifkin, A.: *ref,* 230(1002), 616 (3877)
Rifkind, L. J.: *ref,* 628(186), 630 (265), 641(369), 1050(56), 1184 (30)
Riggs, D. E.: *ref,* 542(1456)
Riggs, P. M.: *ref,* 469(472)
Rijken, H. M.: *ref,* 559(40)
Rike, G. E.: *ref,* 1174(274)
Riklan, M.: *ref,* 616(4031, 4286, 4329), 628(164, 183, 187)
Riksen, B. O. M.: *ref,* 238(22)
Riley, C. M. D.: *test,* 806
Riley, G. D.: *test,* 879, 975
Riley, L.: *ref,* 675(46)
Riley, P. M.: *bk,* B454; *ref,* 720 (303)
Riley, R. T.: *ref,* 519(64)
Rim, Y.: *ref,* 611(629)
Rimmer, A.: *ref,* 506(812)
Rimmer, J. D.: *ref,* 182(657)
Rimoldi, H. J. A.: *ref,* 514(1296), 578(330)
Rincon, E.: *ref,* 542(1523), 555 (266)
Rincon, E. L.: *ref,* 232(1518)
Rines, A. R.: *rev,* 1118
Ring, D. G.: *ref,* 182(572)
Ringuette, E. L.: *ref,* 616(4071)
Rini, R. J.: *ref,* 516(485)
Rink, M. S.: *ref,* 626(257)
Rintelmann, W. F.: *ref,* 953(8)
Rios-Garcia, L. R.: *ref,* 616(4760), 683(258–9), 693(508)
Ripka, G. E.: *test,* 327
Ripley, M. J.: *test,* 1031
Ripley, R. E.: *test,* 1031
Risko, V.: *test,* 948
Ritch, P. A.: *ref,* 182(656)
Ritchie, B. C.: *ref,* 951(8)
Rith, D. G.: *ref,* 555(235)
Ritigstein, J. M.: *ref,* 535(21), 683 (195)
Ritter, D.: *ref,* 210(90), 227(71), 229(1488, 1529), 870(30)
Ritter, D. P.: *ref,* 656(64), 686 (1027)
Ritter, D. R.: *ref,* 29(262), 187 (442, 464), 200(692), 222 (431), 229(1530), 232(1519), 616(4562), 870(30)
Ritter, K. Y.: *ref,* 232(1324), 542 (1524)
Ritterman, S. I.: *ref,* 222(344)
Ritzler, B. A.: *ref,* 230(1113), 661 (4737–8, 4897)
Rivard, E.: *ref,* 661(4932)
Rivera, F. U.: *ref,* 506(909)
Rivera, J.: *test,* 395
Rivera, V. M.: *ref,* 230(1227)
Rivero, W. T.: *ref,* 683(260)
Riviere, M. S.: *ref,* 210(84), 222 (394), 229(1489), 232(1224)
Rivinus, E. M.: *ref,* 182(742)

Rivlin, H. N.: *test,* 372; *cross ref,* 381
Rizzo, J. L.: *ref,* 679(1011)
Rizzo, J. M.: *ref,* 178(22), 213 (24), 222(464), 452(2), 454(1), 967(22)
Rizzo, J. R.: *ref,* 1175(72)
Rizzo, R.: *ref,* 641(558)
Ro, M. H.: *ref,* 560(1), 582(255), 683(261)
Roach, A. J.: *ref,* 997(124), 1028 (212)
Roach, D. J.: *ref,* 720(255)
Roach, E. G.: *test,* 874
Roach, J.: *exc,* B424
Roach, M. E.: *ref,* 516(472)
Roach, R. E.: *ref,* 232(1044, 1116)
Roach, T.: *ref,* 225(59)
Roark, E. A. B.: *ref,* 529(28), 1028(288)
Roback, H. B.: *ref,* 606(322), 616 (4563)
Robb, G. P.: *bk,* B456; *ref,* 49 (306), 229(1451), 230(1003), 232(1117), 234(103), 377(466–7, 505), 574(507–8, 528)
Robb, J. A.: *ref,* 469(512), 679 (1314)
Robbins, D. M.: *ref,* 616(4428)
Robbins, E. L.: *test,* 768
Robbins, P. R.: *ref,* 542(1381), 697(1821)
Roberson, E. W.: *bk,* B457
Roberson, W. E.: *ref,* 377(484)
Roberts, A.: *ref,* 22(87)
Roberts, A. C.: *ref,* 616(4256)
Roberts, A. F.: *ref,* 679(1048)
Roberts, A. H.: *ref,* 224(260), 576 (51)
Roberts, A. L.: *ref,* 646(25)
Roberts, C. A.: *ref,* 989(15), 1023 (1411)
Roberts, C. D.: *ref,* 679(1403), 686 (1002)
Roberts, D. M.: *exc,* B531; *ref,* 820(161)
Roberts, D. R.: *ref,* 693(258)
Roberts, G. D.: *ref,* 688(175)
Roberts, G. W.: *ref,* 679(1037)
Roberts, H.: *cross ref,* 46, 48, 54, 730
Roberts, J.: *ref,* 187(400, 443), 232 (1325)
Roberts, J. E.: *ref,* 641(268)
Roberts, J. L.: *ref,* 697(1799)
Roberts, L. L.: *ref,* 630(289)
Roberts, M.: *ref,* 230(1140), 232 (1298)
Roberts, R.: *ref,* 37(202)
Roberts, R. D.: *ref,* 37(117), 232 (1119), 506(813)
Roberts, R. K.: *ref,* 1023(1386)
Roberts, R. S.: *ref,* 637(5)
Roberts, S. C.: *ref,* 24(5), 232 (1118), 431(424)
Roberts, T. K.: *ref,* 232(1427), 643 (113)
Robertson, A.: *ref,* 597(147), 711 (34, 54)
Robertson, D. W.: *ref,* 1023(1467)
Robertson, E. W.: *bk,* B457
Robertson, J.: *ref,* 232(1203), 703 (195)
Robertson, J. H.: *ref,* 1174(205)

Robertson, J. M.: *ref,* 1016(19)
Robertson, J. T.: *ref,* 553(368), 679(1038)
Robertson, L. M.: *ref,* 693(423)
Robertson, M.: *ref,* 230(946), 232 (1045), 616(3968)
Robey, J. S.: *ref,* 208(1)
Robinowitz, R.: *ref,* 616(4925)
Robinson, A.: *test,* 74
Robinson, B. C.: *ref,* 230(943)
Robinson, C.: *ref,* 553(635)
Robinson, C. L.: *ref,* 636(48)
Robinson, D. D.: *ref,* 983(12)
Robinson, E.: *exc,* B64, B75
Robinson, E. A.: *ref,* 641(587, 599)
Robinson, H.: *ref,* 553(368), 679 (1038)
Robinson, H. A.: *rev,* 734; *cross ref,* 732
Robinson, H. M.: *ref,* 932(103); *cross ref,* 745
Robinson, H. R.: *ref,* 1009(17)
Robinson, J. A.: *ref,* 616(4042)
Robinson, J. E.: *ref,* 19(139–40)
Robinson, J. P.: *bk,* B458
Robinson, J. S.: *ref,* 555(268), 693 (431)
Robinson, M. E.: *ref,* 506(872)
Robinson, P. E.: *ref,* 515(453), 660 (194)
Robinson, R.: *ref,* 720(204)
Robinson, R. D.: *rev,* 812, 815; *ref,* 29(231), 720(217, 256, 285, 304)
Robinson, S.: *ref,* 236(116), 506 (880), 616(4348)
Robinson, S. A.: *ref,* 616(4761)
Robinson, W. B.: *ref,* 580(14), 719 (95)
Robinson-Lasoff, M. V.: *ref,* 514 (1353), 1028(289)
Robison, L. R.: *ref,* 506(776), 613 (82)
Robl, R. M.: *ref,* 656(21)
Roblee, K. M.: *ref,* 182(743)
Robyak, J. E.: *ref,* 630(290, 301), 820(169)
Rocchio, P. D.: *ref,* 530(191), 616 (4808)
Rocco, J. A. *ref,* 516(490)
Rochester, D. E.: *exc,* B326
Rock, A. F.: *ref,* 616(4839)
Rock, D. A.: *ref,* 8(9)
Rock, M. H.: *ref,* 697(1967)
Rode, A.: *ref,* 679(1039)
Rodeheaver, R. E.: *ref,* 469(424)
Rodell, J. L.: *bk,* B26–7; *ref,* 661 (4662, 4733)
Rodenborn, L. V.: *ref,* 785(23)
Rodenwoldt, E.: *ref,* 711(51)
Rodgers, C. W.: *ref,* 542(1525), 576(63), 697(1889)
Rodgers, D.: *ref,* 13(2)
Rodgers, D. A.: *ref,* 514(932, 1084), 616(3847, 4198); *cross ref,* 616
Rodgers, W. C.: *test,* 970
Rodnick, E. H.: *ref,* 585(164, 179), 631(37), 697(2005)
Rodrigues, A.: *ref,* 527(37)
Rodrigues, M. C.: *test,* 796
Rodriguez, A.: *ref,* 693(259)
Rodriguez, T. N.: *ref,* 720(380)
Rodriguez, V. S.: *ref,* 646(26)

Rossman, J. E.: *ref,* 182(633, 637), 634(265), 686(905), 1023(1250, 1339)
Roth, A.: *ref,* 536(26), 582(253), 628(225)
Roth, C.: *ref,* 535(28)
Roth, D. R.: *ref,* 222(432)
Roth, G.: *ref,* 230(1006), 232(1306), 613(102)
Roth, J.: *ref,* 991(1)
Roth, J. D.: *ref,* 1023(1301, 1452)
Roth, L. D.: *ref,* 555(267)
Roth, M.: *ref,* 616(3957, 4075)
Roth, M. C.: *ref,* 514(1128)
Roth, R. S.: *ref,* 616(4965)
Roth, W. T.: *ref,* 553(687), 651(46)
Roth, Z.: *ref,* 679(1219)
Rothenberg, S.: *ref,* 651(42)
Rothkopf, E. Z.: *ref,* 720(61, 140)
Rothman, A. I.: *ref,* 200(595, 625), 643(117-8, 144), 1101(166)
Rothman, C.: *ref,* 232(1326)
Rothman, C. R.: *ref,* 232(1225)
Rothman, E.: *ref,* 616(4279)
Rothman, K. M.: *ref,* 561(4)
Rothman, L.: *ref,* 708(25)
Rothney, J. W. M.: *cross ref,* 229, 703, 709, 1016
Rothstein, G. H.: *ref,* 182(658)
Rothstein, W.: *ref,* 559(35, 38, 59), 616(4135)
Rothwell, P. S.: *ref,* 553(369, 482)
Rotter, J. B.: *test,* 663; *cross ref,* 616, 697
Roudabush, G. E.: *ref,* 769(3)
Rouff, L. L.: *ref,* 244(171-2)
Rourke, B. P.: *ref,* 37(151), 222(465, 513), 232(1226-7, 1417, 1577)
Rourke, P. G.: *ref,* 232(1228), 506(873), 697(1890)
Rousch, P. D.: *ref,* 720(257)
Roush, S. L.: *ref,* 490(476)
Roussell, N.: *ref,* 523(283)
Roussos, P. X.: *ref,* 33(1)
Roussos, V.: *ref,* 616(4933)
Routh, D. K.: *ref,* 37(117), 232(1119), 506(813), 616(4333), 641(489)
Routledge, L. M.: *ref,* 182(704)
Rouzer, D. L.: *ref,* 604(13), 616(3883)
Rovelli, V. A.: *ref,* 775(1)
Rovinelli, R.: *exc,* B315
Rowe, B.: *exc,* B460-1
Rowe, E. J.: *ref,* 200(633)
Rowe, A. H.: *bk,* B462; *ref,* 232(1520)
Rowe, J.: *ref,* 249(560)
Rowe, L. M.: *ref,* 35(113), 182(606)
Rowe, W.: *ref,* 641(291, 371-2)
Rowell, A. L.: *ref,* 182(659)
Rowell, E. H.: *ref,* 753(23)
Rowell, J. A.: *ref,* 553(638)
Roweton, W. E.: *ref,* 249(510)
Rowland, K. F.: *ref,* 641(599)
Rowland, T.: *ref,* 219(12), 229(1508)
Rowlas, A. D.: *ref,* 495(476), 1028(256)
Rowley, W. J.: *ref,* 641(559)
Rowswell, A. K.: *ref,* 393(102)

Roy, A.: *ref,* 553(688)
Roy, A. D.: *ref,* 35(124)
Royce, J. R.: *test,* 653; *ref,* 653(1-2)
Royer, F. L.: *ref,* 616(4201), 872(58)
Rozynko, V.: *ref,* 514(1227), 616(4586)
Rozynko, V. V.: *ref,* 616(4256)
Ruane, F. V.: *ref,* 630(229)
Rubenstein, A.: *ref,* 641(270)
Rubenstein, H.: *ref,* 720(39-40)
Rubenstein, J. L.: *ref,* 206(55)
Rubin, D. B.: *exc,* B119
Rubin, E. Z.: *ref,* 882(184)
Rubin, H. S.: *ref,* 469(425), 641(271)
Rubin, R.: *ref,* 431(425), 802(221)
Rubin, R. A.: *ref,* 37(152-3), 206(38), 229(1490-1), 232(1229-30), 431(481), 745(75), 802(249, 279)
Rubin, S. R.: *ref,* 244(166), 504(104)
Rubino, N. J.: *ref,* 393(103)
Rubinstein, R. P.: *ref,* 582(256)
Rubio, A.: *ref,* 616(3886)
Ruch, F. L.: *exc,* B92
Ruch, J. C.: *ref,* 576(74), 682(84, 96, 104)
Rucker, C. N.: *test,* 442
Ruddell, R. B.: *ref,* 720(62, 75, 97-9)
Rudder, C. S.: *ref,* 235(115), 697(1824)
Rude, R. T.: *ref,* 488(427), 778(4, 6-7), 802(250), 803(30-1)
Rudel, R. G.: *ref,* 232(1327, 1521)
Ruderman, G. H.: *ref,* 616(4076), 631(44)
Rudisill, E. M.: *ref,* 630(207)
Rudisill, J. R.: *ref,* 553(560)
Rudman, H. C.: *test,* 29, 291, 745
Rudolph, B.: *ref,* 495(462)
Rudolph, C. E.: *ref,* 227(72), 802(251)
Rudolph, L.: *ref,* 227(53), 230(993), 469(414)
Rudolph, P. M. J.: *ref,* 574(547), 662(444)
Rudy, K. P.: *ref,* 202(9)
Rueff, C. M.: *ref,* 227(80), 249(472), 431(540)
Rueff, S. D.: *ref,* 249(511)
Rueter, W. G.: *ref,* 679(1478)
Rufener, J. B.: *ref,* 720(258)
Ruff, C. F.: *ref,* 230(1085, 1225, 1286), 236(113), 507(877), 514(1229), 616(4370, 4620, 4764), 675(83)
Ruffer, W. A.: *ref,* 679(1407, 1479-82)
Rugel, R.: *ref,* 232(1328)
Rugel, R. P.: *ref,* 232(1329)
Ruger, M.: *ref,* 469(541)
Ruger, M. C.: *ref,* 469(540)
Ruh, R. A.: *ref,* 660(102)
Ruiz, R. A.: *exc,* B428
Rulla, L. M.: *ref,* 663(129), 697(1805, 1825)
Rummer, C. B.: *ref,* 516(498)
Rummo, J. H.: *ref,* 219(16)
Rumore, M. C.: *ref,* 200(588), 230(1069)

Rumsey, J. M. G.: *ref,* 232(1418)
Runde, P. C.: *ref,* 523(260)
Rungsinan, W.: *ref,* 249(551)
Runion, L. R.: *ref,* 553(639)
Runyon, J. C.: *ref,* 582(239)
Rupley, W. H.: *ref,* 720(305)
Rupp, J. D.: *ref,* 227(56), 506(814), 802(222), 932(104)
Rusalem, H. J.: *ref,* 24(6), 431(426)
Ruschival, M. L.: *ref,* 229(1423)
Rushall, B. S.: *ref,* 679(1043, 1176)
Russakoff, S.: *ref,* 616(5025)
Russel, R. K.: *ref,* 683(262)
Russell, C. N.: *ref,* 523(284)
Russell, D.: *ref,* 37(154)
Russell, D. H.: *cross ref,* 792
Russell, D. L.: *ref,* 553(549)
Russell, E. B.: *ref,* 198(35), 679(1316), 1052(74)
Russell, E. W.: *bk,* B463; *ref,* 190(111), 230(1007, 1153), 250(119), 506(1000), 616(4765, 5015)
Russell, J.: *ref,* 244(181)
Russell, J. K.: *ref,* 641(476), 693(424)
Russell, J. M.: *ref,* 553(321)
Russell, M. W.: *ref,* 616(4044)
Russell, P. L.: *ref,* 553(560), 643(145)
Russell, R. H.: *bk,* B509
Russell, R. K.: *ref,* 683(196, 262)
Russell, T. L.: *ref,* 616(3940), 628(156)
Russell, W. J. C.: *ref,* 200(613), 222(413)
Russie, R. E.: *ref,* 641(560)
Russo, A. J.: *ref,* 692(32)
Rust, J.: *ref,* 554(57)
Rust, M. A.: *ref,* 570(2)
Rustad, L. C.: *ref,* 553(640)
Ruth, L. P.: *rev,* 46, 64; *bk,* B4
Ruth, R. A.: *rev,* 801
Rutherford, B. M.: *ref,* 19(113), 249(355)
Rutkin, R.: *ref,* 662(445)
Rutkowski, K.: *ref,* 182(744), 514(1300) 820(164)
Rutkowski, K. S.: *ref,* 514(1354)
Rutland, E.: *ref,* 182(573)
Rutledge, P. B.: *ref,* 502(7)
Rutley, B.: *ref,* 581(346), 592(53)
Rutschmann, J.: *ref,* 628(189)
Rutter, D. R.: *ref,* 553(370-1)
Rutter, M.: *ref,* 232(1368, 1453)
Ryan, C. W.: *ref,* 1030(89)
Ryan, D. V.: *ref,* 616(4334)
Ryan, J. J.: *ref,* 19(160), 229(1494), 230(1257), 232(1234)
Ryan, J. S.: *ref,* 187(459)
Ryan, K. J.: *ref,* 693(509)
Ryan, L. E.: *ref,* 37(155), 232(1231)
Ryan, L. M. J.: *ref,* 643(181), 686(1023)
Ryan, L. R.: *bk,* B464-5; *ref,* 555(177)
Ryan, M.: *ref,* 616(4413), 643(126)
Ryan, M. M.: *ref,* 641(477)
Ryan, R. A.: *ref,* 37(156), 431(482), 643(119), 745(65)
Ryan, T. A.: *ref,* 616(4165)

Shreve, E. E.: *ref,* 646(38), 693 (340)
Shriberg, L. D.: *rev,* 969, 975; *ref,* 553(380)
Shugar, R.: *ref,* 559(47), 582(227), 611(611)
Shukla, T. R.: *ref,* 578(284, 313, 317, 329)
Shull, W. B.: *ref,* 182(746), 469 (542)
Shulman, A. D.: *ref,* 641(278)
Shulman, E.: *ref,* 572(9)
Shulman, K.: *ref,* 232(1038)
Shulte, T.: *ref,* 555(201)
Shumaker, D. G.: *ref,* 661(4849)
Shuman, J. B.: *ref,* 229(1513)
Shuman, R.: *ref,* 616(4502)
Shure, M. B.: *ref,* 612(3)
Shurling, J.: *ref,* 595(27)
Shurtleff, H. D.: *ref,* 377(513)
Shutt, D. L.: *ref,* 217(33), 232 (1342)
Shutte, P.: *ref,* 711(66)
Shweder, R. A.: *ref,* 616(4779)
Siann, G.: *ref,* 548(262)
Sibbison, V. H.: *ref,* 1028(220)
Sica, M. G.: *test,* 899
Sidell, F. R.: *ref,* 616(3997)
Siderits, M. A.: *ref,* 616(4992)
Sidhu, K.: *ref,* 184(97), 582(200), 611(566)
Sidman, J.: *ref,* 681(29), 706(17)
Siegel, A. W.: *ref,* 230(1060)
Siegel, B.: *ref,* 661(4890)
Siegel, C. L. F.: *ref,* 661(4717)
Siegel, J.: *ref,* 616(4942)
Siegel, J. M.: *ref,* 612(8, 10–1), 616(4928)
Siegel, J. P.: *ref,* 1177(70)
Siegel, L.: *ref,* 662(425)
Siegelman, M.: *ref,* 679(1184)
Siegenthaler, B. M.: *ref,* 232(1126)
Siegman, A. B.: *ref,* 514(1136)
Siegmeister, J. S.: *ref,* 298(11)
Sierra, V. R.: *ref,* 198(49), 249 (553)
Siess, T. F.: *ref,* 582(266), 643 (121)
Sievert, H. A.: *ref,* 1049(9)
Sievert, N. W.: *ref,* 490(489)
Sigal, J.: *ref,* 516(501)
Sigal, J. J.: *ref,* 548(314)
Sigueland, M. L.: *test,* 435
Siipola, E.: *ref,* 697(1787)
Sikes, H. C.: *ref,* 720(219)
Sikes, J. V.: *ref,* 1174(253)
Sikula, A. F.: *ref,* 660(94–5, 163)
Sikula, J. P.: *ref,* 660(163, 184)
Silapalikitporn, T.: *ref,* 555(238)
Silberberg, M. C.: *ref,* 37(119, 216), 187(407), 785(39)
Silberberg, N. E.: *ref,* 37(119, 216), 187(407), 785(39)
Silbergeld, S.: *ref,* 577(64)
Silberzahn, M.: *ref,* 875(22)
Silliman, B. D.: *ref,* 616(4350), 1023(1363)
Silva, E. R.: *ref,* 393(70)
Silvaroli, N. J.: *test,* 749; *exc,* B454
Silver, M. J.: *ref,* 661(4789), 682 (98)
Silver, P. F.: *ref,* 1175(94)

Silverblank, F.: *ref,* 569(129, 149), 582(207, 226)
Silverman, A. I.: *ref,* 712(13)
Silverman, A. J.: *ref,* 548(308–9)
Silverman, B. I.: *ref,* 469(577), 553(567), 660(56, 136, 185)
Silverman, F. H.: *ref,* 971(10)
Silverman, G.: *ref,* 720(260)
Silverman, I.: *ref,* 232(1579), 634 (278)
Silverman, L. H.: *ref,* 697(1830)
Silverman, M.: *ref,* 962(6)
Silverman, M. R. J.: *ref,* 641(377)
Silverman, R.: *ref,* 222(372, 420), 249(406, 459), 613(94, 100)
Silverman, R. H.: *test,* 82, 84
Silverman, R. J.: *bk,* B509
Silverman, S. H.: *ref,* 688(155)
Silverman, W.: *ref,* 488(404), 679 (1214)
Silvers, R. J.: *ref,* 641(617)
Silverstein, A. B.: *rev,* 213, 219; *exc,* 500, B318, B581; *ref,* 229 (1534), 230(1078, 1268), 232 (1236–7, 1343, 1423–4, 1527–8, 1580), 234(166), 431(632), 500 (6), 641(279–80, 378, 563), 882 (186, 207, 236); *cross ref,* 234
Silverstein, L.: *ref,* 703(206)
Silverstone, J. T.: *ref,* 553(381)
Silzer, J. C. K.: *ref,* 585(176)
Simcoe, G.: *ref,* 683(202)
Simensen, R. J.: *ref,* 232(1344–5), 439(3), 506(821, 913–4), 613 (105)
Simmers, P. R.: *ref,* 514(1223)
Simmonds, V.: *test,* 175, 509, 1046; *ref,* 175(1), 1046(2)
Simmons, D.: *exc,* B229
Simmons, D. D.: *exc,* B577; *ref,* 611(661)
Simmons, J.: *ref,* 1186(11)
Simmons, J. B.: *ref,* 693(428)
Simmons, J. L.: *ref,* 688(184)
Simmons, J. P.: *ref,* 660(64)
Simmons, J. W.: *ref,* 514(1137), 611(606)
Simmons, M.: *ref,* 802(289)
Simmons, P. R.: *ref,* 660(137)
Simmons, T. W.: *ref,* 182(780)
Simmons, W. L.: *ref,* 661(4694)
Simnegar, R. R.: *ref,* 616(4700)
Simon, A.: *ref,* 230(943), 597 (182), 822(179)
Simon, A. J.: *ref,* 222(434, 499)
Simon, F. H.: *bk,* B510
Simon, M. G.: *ref,* 542(1534)
Simon, R.: *ref,* 649(10)
Simon, W. E.: *ref,* 542(1391–2, 1460, 1533–4, 1582, 1633)
Simonds, J. F.: *ref,* 37(177), 232 (1346)
Simono, R. B.: *ref,* 616(4780)
Simonton, D. K.: *ref,* 504(108)
Simopoulos, A. M.: *ref,* 631(62)
Simpson, B. K.: *test,* 640
Simpson, B. R.: *ref,* 720(4)
Simpson, C.: *ref,* 679(1319)
Simpson, C. K.: *ref,* 693(513)
Simpson, D. B.: *ref,* 1175(78)
Simpson, G. F.: *ref,* 19(128)
Simpson, G. M.: *ref,* 553(350), 675 (111)
Simpson, K.: *ref,* 675(83)

Simpson, R. D.: *ref,* 471(13)
Simpson, S. A.: *ref,* 236(122), 506 (915)
Simpson, S. B.: *ref,* 506(822)
Simpson, W. A.: *ref,* 693(514)
Sims, C. A.: *exc,* 649; *ref,* 601(9), 649(22)
Sims, H. P.: *ref,* 1186(23–4, 27)
Sims, V. M.: *cross ref,* 37, 516
Sinaiko, H. W.: *ref,* 720(240, 261)
Sinatra, W. J.: *ref,* 555(301)
Sinclair, E. D.: *ref,* 679(902)
Sinclair, I.: *ref,* 200(596), 611 (607)
Sinclair, I. A. C.: *ref,* 553(568)
Sinclair, W. A.: *ref,* 516(479), 871(4)
Sindberg, R. M.: *ref,* 542(1453), 679(1048)
Sines, J. O.: *rev,* 540, 577; *test,* 625; *ref,* 616(4571), 617(19), 1023(1412)
Sines, L. K.: *test,* 625; *ref,* 616 (4047)
Singa, S. P.: *ref,* 662(437)
Singe, A. L.: *ref,* 1174(254)
Singer, D. L.: *ref,* 182(607)
Singer, E.: *bk,* B511
Singer, H.: *rev,* 759, 790; *ref,* 431 (573), 759(26); *cross ref,* 802–3
Singer, H. A.: *ref,* 686(923)
Singer, J.: *ref,* 616(4050)
Singer, J. E.: *ref,* 732(41), 932 (113)
Singer, J. L.: *ref,* 643(135, 189)
Singer, K.: *ref,* 530(178), 611 (608)
Singer, M.: *ref,* 616(4050)
Singer, M. T.: *exc,* B27; *ref,* 661 (4935)
Singh, A.: *ref,* 200(553), 542(1393)
Singh, A. K.: *ref,* 596(74)
Singh, A. N.: *ref,* 599(33)
Singh, B.: *ref,* 230(1013–4)
Singh, B. K.: *ref,* 553(487), 611 (609)
Singh, G.: *ref,* 200(609)
Singh, H.: *ref,* 1011(871)
Singh, M.: *ref,* 683(145)
Singh, M. M.: *ref,* 553(382)
Singh, M. V.: *ref,* 506(958)
Singh, R.: *ref,* 200(545), 611(554)
Singh, R. I. P.: *ref,* 611(574)
Singh, S.: *ref,* 611(593), 679(1370)
Singh, S. B.: *ref,* 679(1185)
Singh, S. N.: *ref,* 597(203), 626 (248, 271)
Singh, U. P.: *ref,* 611(546, 578, 610, 632)
Singh, V. K.: *ref,* 661(4850)
Singhal, S.: *ref,* 506(847), 582 (217)
Singleton, M. H.: *ref,* 548(359), 661(4903), 697(1996)
Sinha, A. K.: *ref,* 506(922), 581 (399), 661(4794), 697(1937)
Sinha, J. K.: *ref,* 553(351), 569 (125)
Sinha, L. N. K.: *ref,* 611(544)
Sinha, M.: *ref,* 187(408–9), 200 (554)
Sinha, N. C.: *ref,* 553(383)
Sinha, N. C. P.: *ref,* 553(488)

Smith, T. A.: *exc,* 223; *ref,* 223 (26)
Smith, T. T.: *ref,* 393(72)
Smith, T. W.: *test,* 1020; *ref,* 611 (662)
Smith, W. A. S.: *ref,* 653(1–2)
Smith, W. B.: *ref,* 697(1933)
Smith, W. J.: *ref,* 549(387), 581 (386), 616(4395), 686(935)
Smith, W. L.: *rev,* 720; *ref,* 720 (163)
Smith, W. P.: *ref,* 555(240)
Smith, W. S.: *ref,* 1175(115)
Smithers, A. G.: *ref,* 553(571), 660(153), 679(1378)
Smits, S. J.: *ref,* 1175(69)
Smittle, P.: *ref,* 693(221, 372), 745 (55)
Smock, C. D.: *cross ref,* 178
Smukler, A. J.: *ref,* 527(43), 616 (4782)
Smyth, L.: *ref,* 535(29), 572(32), 616(4850), 693(461)
Snaith, R. P.: *ref,* 611(663)
Sneddon, P. M.: *ref,* 697(1773)
Sneed, G. A.: *ref,* 232(1426)
Snibbe, H. M.: *ref,* 542(1468), 574(517), 616(4139, 4396), 679 (1412), 1011(883)
Snibbe, J. R.: *ref,* 37(174), 184 (111), 683(182), 686(958)
Snider, B.: *ref,* 616(4392)
Snijders, J. T.: *test,* 228
Snijders-Oomen, N.: *test,* 228
Snodgrass, J. E.: *ref,* 646(87)
Snodgrass, R. W.: *ref,* 616(5017)
Snortum, J. R.: *ref,* 630(243)
Snow, D. L.: *ref,* 616(3977, 4352), 626(242)
Snow, G. D.: *ref,* 488(402), 506 (875), 581(382)
Snow, R. E.: *bk,* B118
Snow, S. T.: *ref,* 663(130)
Snowden, L.: *ref,* 616(4353)
Snyder, C. R.: *ref,* 683(99)
Snyder, F. W.: *ref,* 997(64)
Snyder, H. C.: *ref,* 490(473)
Snyder, P. A. S.: *ref,* 1023(1364)
Snyder, P. P.: *ref,* 506(916)
Snyder, Q. C.: *ref,* 514(1027)
Snyder, R.: *ref,* 506(823), 697 (1777), 932(108)
Snyder, R. T.: *ref,* 506(915), 646 (109)
Soar, R. S.: *ref,* 393(63)
Soares, A. T.: *test,* 673; *ref,* 673 (1)
Soares, L. M.: *test,* 673; *ref,* 673 (1)
Soat, D. M.: *ref,* 693(429)
Sobel, H.: *ref,* 601(17)
Sobel, W.: *ref,* 601(17)
Sobocinski, D.: *ref,* 628(221)
Society of Actuaries: *test,* 252
Sockloff, A. L.: *ref,* 524(119)
Socks, M. H.: *ref,* 649(26)
Soder, A. L.: *test,* 696
Soderstrom, D.: *ref,* 656(65)
Soethe, J. W.: *ref,* 24(7), 37(121), 232(1128)
Sofer, S.: *ref,* 581(429)
Soh, K. C.: *ref,* 597(183), 616 (4099), 668(19)
Sohn, M.: *ref,* 600(3)

Sola, S.: *ref,* 616(4815)
Solberg, K. B.: *ref,* 681(9–10), 706 (7–8)
Soliah, D.: *ref,* 469(521), 1028 (241)
Soliah, D. C.: *ref,* 1028(155)
Solkoff, N.: *ref,* 208(12), 232 (1129, 1348)
Solla, J.: *ref,* 519(70)
Sollod, R. N.: *exc,* B122
Solmon, L. C.: *ref,* 182(661)
Solomon, A. O.: *ref,* 249(474)
Solomon, L. M.: *bk,* B306
Solomon, R. J.: *cross ref,* 35
Solomons, G.: *ref,* 206(53)
Solomons, H. C.: *ref,* 206(53)
Soltz, Z.: *ref,* 697(1972)
Solway, K. S.: *ref,* 232(1268, 1427, 1529–30), 589(4), 616(4945)
Solyom, C.: *ref,* 559(37, 47), 582 (208, 227), 611(611)
Solyom, L.: *ref,* 559(37, 47), 582 (208, 227), 611(611)
Somes, G. W.: *ref,* 634(347)
Sommer, G.: *ref,* 1023(1297)
Sommerfield, R. E.: *ref,* 239(104)
Sommers, D. D.: *ref,* 182(662)
Sommers, J. B.: *ref,* 514(972), 630 (193), 997(38)
Sommers, M. S.: *ref,* 569(141)
Sommers, P.: *ref,* 531(14), 681 (68)
Sommers, R. K.: *rev,* 954, 960
Sommerschield, H.: *ref,* 697(1895)
Somogye, R. J.: *ref,* 495(407)
Son, N. H.: *ref,* 183(362)
Sones, R. A.: *test,* 541
Sonnenblick, M.: *bk,* B476
Soper, R. E.: *ref,* 554(69)
Sopher, J. T.: *ref,* 616(4783)
Sorensen, N. C.: *ref,* 232(1531)
Sorenson, G.: *exc,* 997; *ref,* 997 (106)
Sorge, D. H.: *ref,* 377(526)
Soskin, R. A.: *ref,* 616(4354), 679 (1189)
Sostek, A. M.: *rev,* 208; *ref,* 206 (59), 208(15)
Sotile, W. M.: *ref,* 628(242), 641 (598)
Soto, D.: *ref,* 232(1524)
Soueif, M. I.: *bk,* B150
Soule, A. B.: *ref,* 208(6)
Sousa-Poza, J. F.: *ref,* 572(9)
South, J. C.: *test,* 1087; *ref,* 1023 (1417), 1087(1), 1088(1)
South, J. J.: *ref,* 735(98)
Southern, M. L.: *ref,* 22(88), 222 (339), 223(24), 229(1446), 230 (954), 234(102, 107), 431(421, 433), 514(1028, 1226), 802(219)
Southwest Educational Development Laboratory: *test,* 172
Southworth, A.: *ref,* 495(321), 641 (212)
Southworth, B. T.: *ref,* 641(482), 681(55), 700(6)
Sowder, L.: *rev,* 263, 292
Sowell, L. H.: *ref,* 232(1239)
Sowell, V.: *ref,* 431(616), 506 (989), 932(154)
Spaan, M.: *test,* 102, 105–6
Spache, G. D.: *test,* 753; *bk,* B515; *cross ref,* 759

Spain, D. H.: *ref,* 661(4655), 697 (1832)
Spalding, D.: *ref,* 530(177), 542 (1454), 582(222)
Spangler, C. M.: *ref,* 523(234)
Spangler, P. F.: *ref,* 24(23)
Spanier, D.: *ref,* 641(386), 693 (346)
Spanos, N. P.: *ref,* 576(75), 585 (205)
Sparks, D. C.: *ref,* 693(568)
Sparks, E. L.: *ref,* 523(235)
Sparks, J. C.: *ref,* 654(20)
Spaulding, R. C.: *ref,* 616(4187)
Spaulding, W. D.: *ref,* 585(206)
Spautz, M. E.: *ref,* 686(1007), 1177 (108)
Spear, G. E.: *ref,* 660(65)
Speare, J.: *ref,* 616(4100)
Spearman, C.: *cross ref,* 488
Spears, D.: *bk,* B452
Spears, L.: *ref,* 469(543)
Speedie, S. M.: *ref,* 249(476)
Speer, R. K.: *test,* 741
Spellacy, F.: *ref,* 222(345)
Speller, K. G.: *ref,* 235(129)
Spellman, A.: *ref,* 530(156)
Spelman, M. S.: *ref,* 571(30)
Spence, A. C.: *ref,* 693(430)
Spencer, D.: *cross ref,* 516
Spencer, H. L.: *ref,* 249(510)
Spencer, L. A.: *ref,* 222(346), 431 (434)
Spencer, P. L.: *cross ref,* 283
Spencer, R. E.: *test,* 373–4; *ref,* 373(6)
Spencer, T. M.: *ref,* 183(363), 475 (24)
Sperry, R. W.: *ref,* 200(600), 236 (125), 250(111), 431(555), 613 (108)
Spielberg, L.: *ref,* 662(445)
Spielberger, C. D.: *rev,* 559, 639; *test,* 683–4; *ref,* 616(4355), 651 (19), 661(4597), 683(66, 69, 72, 100, 114–5, 129, 144–5, 207, 228, 265, 280, 299, 314–5), 684(14, 16)
Spiers, P.: *ref,* 643(194)
Spiker, J.: *ref,* 431(615)
Spilman, H.: *ref,* 283(11)
Spinelli, P. R.: *ref,* 610(2)
Spink, J. P.: *ref,* 641(282), 660 (66)
Spinks, W. B.: *ref,* 616(4585)
Spiro, J. H.: *ref,* 643(169)
Spitz, H. H.: *ref,* 230(1082)
Spitzer, M. E.: *bk,* B92
Spivack, G.: *test,* 612; *ref,* 612(1–3, 5–9)
Spivey, D. R.: *ref,* 679(1050)
Spivey, W. L.: *ref,* 693(519), 1023 (1472)
Spokane, A. R.: *ref,* 1022(77), 1028 (292)
Spooncer, F. A.: *test,* 728; *bk,* B516
Sprafkin, R. P.: *ref,* 514(1029)
Sprandel, D. S.: *ref,* 1174(202)
Sprankel, C. M.: *ref,* 469(578)
Spray, G. D.: *ref,* 720(307)
Spreen, O.: *cross ref,* 613
Spriestersbach, D. C.: *ref,* 958(2)
Spriggs, A. J.: *test,* 246
Spring, K. S.: *ref,* 720(382)

Stern, M. J.: *ref*, 679(1053)
Stern, S. L.: *ref*, 548(279)
Sternbach, R. A.: *ref*, 578(345), 616(4356, 4603)
Sternberg, D. P.: *ref*, 232(1131, 1241)
Sternberg, R. I.: *ref*, 229(1582)
Sternberg, S. E.: *ref*, 230(1269), 697(1999)
Sterne, A. L.: *ref*, 616(4730, 4906, 4997-8)
Sterne, D. M.: *ref*, 224(253), 236(112), 1010(40, 57)
Sterner, K. M.: *ref*, 536(15), 616(4357)
Sternlicht, M.: *ref*, 662(425)
Sterns, H. L.: *ref*, 575(59)
Stettler, H. F.: *ref*, 182(605)
Stetz, F. P.: *exc*, B434
Steuber, D. J.: *ref*, 37(123), 222(347), 229(1453), 232(1132)
Steuber, H. B.: *ref*, 514(1228, 1307), 616(4589, 4787)
Stevens, C. A.: *ref*, 1174(204)
Stevens, D. G.: *ref*, 1175(163)
Stevens, G. Z.: *test*, 990
Stevens, H. A.: *ref*, 500(3)
Stevens, H. I.: *ref*, 177(3)
Stevens, J. R.: *ref*, 230(1012), 250(92), 616(4101)
Stevens, J. T.: *ref*, 542(1396), 822(160)
Stevens, N. B.: *ref*, 22(92), 198(21), 516(454)
Stevens, T. B.: *ref*, 679(1190), 686(924)
Stevenson, D. K.: *ref*, 110(26)
Stevenson, F. B.: *ref*, 514(1141)
Stevenson, H. W.: *ref*, 37(213), 187(470), 222(500), 232(1533), 506(1002), 932(156)
Stevenson, M. R.: *ref*, 182(747), 472(55)
Stevenson, R. D.: *ref*, 679(939, 1196)
Stewart, A. J.: *ref*, 697(1934)
Stewart, C. G.: *ref*, 576(65)
Stewart, D. J.: *ref*, 230(1083), 616(4358), 697(1898)
Stewart, D. M.: *test*, 778, 823
Stewart, D. W.: *ref*, 232(1534, 1581), 431(544, 633, 642), 514(1382), 589(3), 626(275), 627(68), 679(1511-2), 693(582)
Stewart, D. Y.: *ref*, 553(508)
Stewart, E. W.: *ref*, 720(125)
Stewart, J. T.: *ref*, 542(1397)
Stewart, K. D.: *ref*, 227(81, 104), 229(1538)
Stewart, K. J.: *ref*, 230(1161), 628(213)
Stewart, L.: *ref*, 409(5)
Stewart, L. H.: *ref*, 634(246)
Stewart, M.: *ref*, 232(1109)
Stewart, N.: *cross ref*, 187, 606, 709
Stewart, N. E.: *ref*, 469(504), 820(152)
Stewart, R A C.: *ref*, 542(1464), 596(77), 616(4590), 641(383, 391), 679(1191), 686(925), 688(166), 711(57-8)
Stewart, R. R.: *ref*, 553(376)
Stewart, W. D.: *ref*, 679(1414)

Stewin, L.: *ref*, 529(24)
Steyn, D. W.: *exc*, B83
Stiening, J. A.: *ref*, 490(474), 542(1398), 616(4102, 4359), 1023(1298, 1367)
Stiffler, E. J.: *ref*, 641(484)
Stikeleather, R. A.: *ref*, 585(197)
Stiles, D. B.: *ref*, 641(384)
Stillion, J. M.: *ref*, 249(478), 708(18)
Stillman, B. W.: *test*, 760
Stills, A. B.: *ref*, 523(299)
Stilwell, W. E.: *ref*, 502(1, 3)
Stine, J. C.: *ref*, 1185(8)
Stingle, S. F.: *ref*, 581(383). 592(62)
Stinson, J. E.: *ref*, 1174(174, 205, 255)
Stith, R. C.: *ref*, 698(26)
Stitt, J. A.: *ref*, 726A(46)
Stob, W. K.: *ref*, 523(300)
Stockbridge, F. P.: *ref*, 720(16)
Stockdale, D. F.: *ref*, 209(52), 229(1485)
Stocker, J. M.: *ref*, 683(146)
Stocker, R. B.: *ref*, 660(85)
Stockton, J. J.: *ref*, 182(700)
Stofac, R.: *ref*, 616(4554)
Stoffelmayr, B. E.: *ref*, 711(31, 52)
Stofflet, F.: *ref*, 1(23)
Stogdill, R.: *ref*, 1174(217)
Stogdill, R. M.: *test*, 1075, 1175, 1184; *ref*, 1174(146, 226, 251), 1175(68, 71, 116, 133), 1184(31), 1186(26)
Stokes, J. D.: *ref*, 627(54)
Stokes, R.: *ref*, 182(748)
Stole, P. D.: *ref*, 488(379)
Stoll, P. D.: *ref*, 488(379), 777(11), 785(27)
Stolurow, L. M.: *ref*, 720(240)
Stone, A. G.: *ref*, 630(244)
Stone, A. R.: *test*, 685; *ref*, 685(2-3)
Stone, C. P.: *test*, 250
Stone, C. R.: *cross ref*, 792-3
Stone, D. A.: *ref*, 597(197)
Stone, J. C.: *bk*, B187; *ref*, 542(1340), 634(229)
Stone, J. D.: *ref*, 693(342)
Stone, J. E.: *ref*, 1174(175)
Stone, J. M.: *ref*, 607(34), 693(522)
Stone, L. A.: *ref*, 490(474), 542(1398), 616(4102, 4267, 4359-60), 661(4720), 1023(1296, 1298, 1366-7)
Stone, M.: *ref*, 227(94)
Stone, N. M.: *ref*, 661(4851, 4904)
Stone, W. J.: *ref*, 679(1343)
Stoneburner, R. L.: *ref*, 232(1350), 431(545)
Stonehill, E.: *ref*, 553(558), 615(19, 33)
Stoner, S.: *ref*, 542(1535), 553(575)
Stones, M. J.: *ref*, 553(698, 718)
Stones, R. W. H.: *ref*, 200(519), 553(330)
Stonner, D.: *ref*, 553(609)
Stoops, J. W.: *ref*, 625(14)
Stoppard, J. M.: *ref*, 596(43, 60)
Storandt, M.: *ref*, 230(1028, 1114,

1184, 1233), 250(120), 506(960), 686(934)
Storck, P. A.: *ref*, 200(556), 229(1454, 1496)
Storms, L.: *ref*, 578(355)
Storms, L. H.: *ref*, 613(85), 616(4013, 4591)
Story, G. E.: *ref*, 630(212)
Story, L. E.: *ref*, 822(180)
Stotsky, B. A.: *ref*, 631(46), 675(60)
Stott, D. H.: *test*, 665, 881; *bk*, B518; *ref*, 881(6)
Stoudenmire, J.: *ref*, 553(388), 628(171), 683(101, 147, 266)
Stouffer, G. A. W.: *test*, 4, 40, 302, 717
Stouffer, S. A.: *test*, 23
Stout, A. L.: *ref*, 559(59)
Stowe, W. A.: *ref*, 506(824)
Strade, B. W.: *test*, 699
Strader, S. G.: *ref*, 785(35)
Strag, G. A.: *ref*, 932(128)
Strahan, R.: *ref*, 553(495), 572(27)
Strain, P. S.: *ref*, 305(10)
Strait, J.: *test*, 467
Strand, A. L.: *test*, 644
Strand, E. M.: *ref*, 485(348)
Strand, K. H.: *ref*, 555(278)
Strang, H. R.: *ref*, 222(353), 232(1265, 1351)
Strange, A.: *ref*, 392(4)
Stranges, R. J.: *ref*, 2(4)
Strassberg, D.: *ref*, 616(4563)
Strassberg, D. S.: *ref*, 555(268), 582(228), 693(431)
Strassfield, R.: *ref*, 232(1499), 506(991)
Strattner, N. S.: *ref*, 555(175)
Stratton, L. O.: *ref*, 693(343)
Straub, J. C.: *ref*, 542(1591), 568(96), 569(164)
Straub, R. R.: *ref*, 1174(206)
Straub, W. F.: *ref*, 514(1043), 679(916)
Strauch, M.: *ref*, 535(39), 679(1513)
Strauch-Rahauser, G.: *ref*, 535(39), 679(1513)
Strauss, B. P. A.: *test*, 481
Strauss, F. F.: *ref*, 616(5018)
Strauss, J. J.: *ref*, 649(26)
Strauss, J. S.: *ref*, 585(177), 649(11, 25)
Strauss, M. E.: *ref*, 616(4592, 4892), 661(4839)
Street, C. P.: *ref*, 616(4946), 693(569)
Street, R. F.: *ref*, 720(101)
Streff, J.: *ref*, 506(879)
Streib, R.: *ref*, 720(397)
Strein, W.: *ref*, 222(436), 320(4)
Strein, W. O.: *ref*, 320(3)
Streiner, D. L.: *ref*, 548(314), 616(4361, 5019), 677(177)
Stricker, G.: *bk*, B174; *exc*, B441; *ref*, 559(34)
Stricker, L. J.: *rev*, 550, 554; *ref*, 616(4593), 643(122, 147), 679(1323); *cross ref*, 542
Strickland, B. R.: *ref*, 628(234)
Strickland, C. L.: *ref*, 1016(25)
Strickland, G.: *bk*, B221
Strickland, G. P.: *test*, 363

Taff, L. R.: *ref,* 688(149)
Taffin, J.: *test,* 1168
Taft, R.: *ref,* 235(107)
Taguiri, R.: *ref,* 686(837)
Taina, T. N.: *ref,* 377(481)
Talbott, B. L.: *ref,* 1(25)
Tallent, N.: *ref,* 616(3901)
Talley, E. E.: *ref,* 222(344)
Talley, L.: *ref,* 469(392)
Talley, T.: *ref,* 20(133), 616(4790)
Talone, J. M.: *ref,* 576(36, 76), 682 (88, 105)
Tamayo, A.: *ref,* 529(29)
Tammerk, H. A.: *ref,* 514(1220), 553(566)
Tan, G.: *ref,* 349(8)
Tanabe, E. M. N.: *ref,* 524(105), 693(345)
Tanaka, M.: *test,* 106
Tanck, M. L.: *test,* 898
Tanck, R. H.: *ref,* 542(1381), 697 (1821)
Tancredi, F. N.: *ref,* 616(4791)
Tandon, P. N.: *ref,* 230(1013–4)
Tangeman, A.: *ref,* 726A(29)
Tangudtaisuk, P. V.: *ref,* 29(260), 697(1974)
Tannenbaum, A. J.: *cross ref,* 184
Tannenbaum, P. H.: *ref,* 720(82, 164)
Tanner, B. A.: *ref,* 616(4598)
Tanner, J. M.: *bk,* B526
Tanners, H.: *ref,* 223(30), 229 (1516)
Tanney, M. F.: *ref,* 495(328), 1010 (64), 1022(53), 1023(1473)
Tanpraphat, A.: *ref,* 29(266), 249 (555)
Tansey, D. A.: *ref,* 230(1164), 597 (198)
Tapp, G. S.: *ref,* 502(2, 8)
Tapp, J. T.: *ref,* 641(386), 693 (346)
Tapscott, B. M.: *ref,* 732(55)
Tarczan, C.: *bk,* B527
Tardibuono, J. S.: *ref,* 232(1126)
Tardo, K.: *ref,* 519(72)
Tarr, L. H.: *ref,* 495(410), 616 (4369)
Tarrier, R. B.: *test,* 1003
Tartaglione, S.: *ref,* 683(311)
Tarter, R. E.: *ref,* 225(65), 230 (1084), 514(1310, 1362), 616 (4792–3, 4948)
Taschow, H. G.: *ref,* 735(93)
Tate, J. C.: *ref,* 475(16), 686(882)
Tatham, C. B.: *ref,* 182(706)
Tatham, E. L.: *ref,* 182(706)
Tatsuoka, M. M.: *test,* 679
Tatum, B. J.: *ref,* 790(9)
Taub, H. A.: *ref,* 230(1015)
Taub, M. J.: *ref,* 693(265–6)
Tauber, C. E.: *ref,* 506(900)
Taubman, P.: *bk,* B528
Tauger, H.: *ref,* 693(297)
Taulbee, E. S.: *rev,* 706–7; *bk,* B529; *ref,* 578(340), 581(428), 616(4355, 4599, 5020), 661(4886), 683(144), 697(1988)
Tava, E. G.: *ref,* 232(1133)
Tavormina, J.: *ref,* 187(432), 506 (895), 616(4862)
Tavormina, J. B.: *ref,* 222(316,

415), 596(76), 625(15), 646 (102), 654(37)
Taylor, A. J. W.: *ref,* 711(22)
Taylor, A. P.: *ref,* 87
Taylor, C. L.: *ref,* 20(135), 198 (50)
Taylor, D.: *ref,* 230(1000)
Taylor, D. J.: *ref,* 495(411), 542 (1462)
Taylor, D. R.: *ref,* 198(36)
Taylor, E. K.: *ref,* 485(352), 486 (55); *cross ref,* 1054
Taylor, F. R. D.: *ref,* 683(102)
Taylor, G. A.: *ref,* 616(4836)
Taylor, H. A.: *ref,* 651(17)
Taylor, H. C.: *ref,* 542(1467)
Taylor, H. D.: *ref,* 506(807, 825–6)
Taylor, H. R.: *cross ref,* 490
Taylor, H. T.: *ref,* 1028(294), 1030 (93)
Taylor, I. A.: *ref,* 249(366)
Taylor, J. B.: *ref,* 616(4108, 4949)
Taylor, J. C.: *test,* 985; *bk,* B530; *ref,* 985(1)
Taylor, J. F.: *ref,* 393(54), 616 (4600)
Taylor, J. R.: *ref,* 491(22, 37)
Taylor, K. E.: *ref,* 1052(44)
Taylor, K. F.: *ref,* 514(1142), 1028 (190)
Taylor, L.: *ref,* 222(384), 234 (126), 431(474), 548(282)
Taylor, L. B.: *test,* 640
Taylor, L. E.: *ref,* 679(1055, 1416), 822(161)
Taylor, L. J.: *ref,* 200(693), 222 (348, 362, 396, 437, 469), 234 (116), 431(450), 661(4792–3), 701(12)
Taylor, M. A.: *ref,* 963(14)
Taylor, M. J.: *ref,* 232(1537)
Taylor, M. L.: *ref,* 962(1)
Taylor, N.: *bk,* B440; *ref,* 882 (206)
Taylor, P. H.: *ref,* 381(89), 627 (38), 679(917)
Taylor, R. G.: *exc,* B94; *ref,* 469 (441), 1023(1300–1, 1321, 1452, 1495)
Taylor, R. L.: *ref,* 230(1226–7)
Taylor, R. M.: *test,* 692
Taylor, R. N.: *rev,* 1037, 1180
Taylor, S.: *ref,* 616(4426), 633(7)
Taylor, V.: *ref,* 630(240)
Taylor, W.: *ref,* 720(132)
Taylor, W. G.: *ref,* 514(1311), 679 (1417)
Taylor, W. L.: *ref,* 375(28), 720 (28, 30, 32, 36, 188, 263)
Teagarden, F. M.: *cross ref,* 209, 703
Teague, M.: *ref,* 616(4751)
Teahan, J. E.: *ref,* 660(164)
Teal, J. D.: *ref,* 469(429), 475(17), 485(349), 989(7)
Teasdale, G. R.: *ref,* 222(349, 438), 431(437, 546, 590, 599)
Teasdale, J.: *ref,* 681(73), 706(30)
Teasdale, J. D.: *ref,* 554(18), 675 (98), 681(74), 706(31)
Tedesco, J. F.: *exc,* B26
Tedford, W. H.: *ref,* 578(262)
Teevan, J. J.: *ref,* 660(98)

Teevan, R. C.: *ref,* 559(54), 697 (1949, 1975)
Tegarden, R. S.: *ref,* 381(93), 1175 (79)
Teich, H. E.: *ref,* 222(470)
Teichman, Y.: *ref,* 683(210)
Teichmann, H.: *ref,* 200(536), 230 (980)
Teigland, D. W.: *ref,* 555(243)
Tekippe, D. J.: *ref,* 693(343)
Telegdi, M. S.: *ref,* 578(275)
Telegdy, G. A.: *ref,* 37(200), 222 (501), 232(1242), 506(918–9, 961), 802(280–1, 298)
Tellegen, A.: *rev,* 553–4; *ref,* 576 (51, 64)
Teller, H. C.: *ref,* 232(1429), 703 (204)
Temkin, S. M.: *ref,* 568(97), 569 (165)
Temple, F. G.: *ref,* 183(325), 230 (950), 244(134), 616(3888), 1011 (874)
Templer, A. J.: *ref,* 553(389), 582 (209), 1174(207), 1175(95)
Templer, D. I.: *ref,* 225(65), 230 (1084–5, 1225, 1270, 1286), 232 (1543), 236(105, 113), 506(782, 877), 514(1229), 553(390), 616 (4370, 4601, 4620, 4764, 4793, 4950), 675(83)
Templeton, R. M.: *ref,* 1177(109)
Templin, M. C.: *cross ref,* 217
TenBrink, T. D.: *bk,* B531
Tennyson, R. D.: *ref,* 683(149)
Tepper, D.: *ref,* 495(321), 641 (212)
Tepper, L.: *ref,* 1175(165)
Terborg, J. R.: *test,* 1181
Terdal, L. G.: *bk,* B317
Terezakis, M. S.: *ref,* 555(317), 679(1490)
Terhune, K. W.: *ref,* 697(1936)
Terman, L. M.: *test,* 229; *bk,* B532; *ref,* 229(1497), 720(2, 5, 15)
Terry, R. L.: *ref,* 679(1194, 1324), 697(1869)
Terry, T. D.: *ref,* 393(55)
Terwilliger, J. S.: *bk,* B533
Teschner, R. V.: *exc,* 163; *ref,* 163(2)
Teskey, G. M.: *ref,* 11(1)
Tessin, M. J.: *ref,* 688(158)
Tester, L. W.: *ref,* 1023(1302)
Tetenbaum, T. J.: *ref,* 643(149, 170)
Teters, J. E. W.: *ref,* 686(966)
Teubner, J.: *ref,* 249(430)
Tew, B.: *ref,* 232(1353–4, 1583), 882(237)
Thacker, A. J.: *ref,* 188(105)
Thacker, B. T.: *ref,* 249(367)
Thackray, D.: *test,* 810
Thackray, L.: *test,* 810
Thackray, R. I.: *ref,* 553(576)
Thaipanich, N.: *ref,* 377(515)
Thakar, B.: *ref,* 679(1325)
Thakur, G. P.: *ref,* 553(497)
Thakur, M.: *ref,* 553(497)
Thaler, J. S.: *ref,* 631(51)
Thames, J. A.: *ref,* 23(4), 26(3), 182(664), 818(7)
Tharp, R. G.: *ref,* 616(4602)

Todd, G. A.: *ref*, 697(1898a)
Todd, J.: *ref*, 184(116), 200(654), 230(1201, 1289)
Todd, L. W.: *ref*, 543(1), 693(375)
Todorov, J. C.: *ref*, 182(599)
Toel, P.: *ref*, 616(4459)
Toenjes, C. M.: *ref*, 1028(221)
Tokar, E. B.: *ref*, 1(23)
Toler, C.: *ref*, 660(139, 165)
Tollefson, N. F.: *bk*, B539
Tolor, A.: *ref*, 542(1539), 553(647), 581(398), 606(329), 693(524, 571)
Tolor, B.: *ref*, 581(398)
Tomanelli, A. R.: *ref*, 235(130), 611(651)
Tomasini, J.: *ref*, 582(229)
Tomko, M. A.: *ref*, 616(4372)
Tomlinson, R. F.: *ref*, 504(99)
Tomlinson, R. W. S.: *ref*, 1010(50)
Tompkins, E. L.: *ref*, 1054(17)
Tondow, M.: *ref*, 616(4664)
Tonesk, X.: *ref*, 1023(1418)
Tong, J. E.: *ref*, 661(4582)
Toole, D. L.: *ref*, 307(2), 574(532), 679(1058, 1158), 686(913), 745(62), 813(2), 981(3)
Toomer, J. E.: *ref*, 555(270), 654(26)
Toomey, T.: *ref*, 616(4048)
Toomey, T. C.: *ref*, 230(1016), 548(288), 616(4604)
Toops, H. A.: *cross ref*, 193
Toplis, J.: *exc*, 985; *ref*, 985(4)
Topp, E. J.: *ref*, 35(115), 469(430)
Torbert, M. R.: *ref*, 646(27)
Torgerson, T. L.: *cross ref*, 759
Tori, C. A.: *ref*, 616(4178), 660(75)
Tori, C. D.: *ref*, 643(64)
Torney, J.: *bk*, B418
Toronto, A. S.: *test*, 171, 427
Torrance, E. P.: *test*, 248–9; *ref*, 249(352, 368–72, 396–8, 410, 452, 515)
Torres-Matrullo, C.: *ref*, 495(452)
Torrey, D. A.: *ref*, 1011(893)
Tortelli, J. P.: *ref*, 790(17)
Tortorella, W. M.: *ref*, 230(1089), 616(4373)
Tosi, D. J.: *exc*, 641; *ref*, 641(283, 567)
Tou, L. A.: *ref*, 1022(29), 1028(222)
Touchstone, R. M.: *ref*, 553(576)
Touchton, J. G.: *ref*, 1022(88)
Touliatos, J.: *test*, 317; *ref*, 10(134), 697(1976)
Tousignant, M.: *ref*, 693(525)
Tovey, D.: *ref*, 679(1419)
Towell, R. D.: *ref*, 249(373)
Tower, D. Q.: *ref*, 882(238)
Towle, N. J.: *ref*, 683(267)
Townes, W.: *ref*, 599(26)
Townley, J. L.: *ref*, 679(1199)
Towns, W.: *ref*, 599(39)
Townsend, A.: *cross ref*, 717, 735, 745
Townsend, J. W.: *ref*, 983(13)
Townsend, M. A. R.: *ref*, 200(695), 453(2)
Toye, J. R.: *ref*, 1049(9)
Trabue, M. R.: *ref*, 720(9, 11, 16)
Trachsel, M. D.: *ref*, 616(4374)

Trachtman, J. P.: *ref*, 257(44), 693(526)
Tractenberg, P. L.: *bk*, B540
Tracy, J. F. L.: *ref*, 693(527)
Tracy, P.: *test*, 736–7
Trail, B. M.: *ref*, 1030(87)
Trainor, J. D.: *ref*, 997(178)
Trainor, J. J.: *ref*, 514(1030), 548(264)
Tramel, S.: *ref*, 249(535)
Tramer, R. R.: *ref*, 200(634), 519(65)
Trammel, G. B.: *ref*, 712(15)
Trask, T. H.: *ref*, 523(286)
Travers, J. A.: *ref*, 1052(57)
Travers, K. J.: *cross ref*, 298
Travers, R. M. W.: *cross ref*, 830
Travis, C. B.: *ref*, 542(1594)
Travis, R. J.: *ref*, 616(4152)
Travis, T. A.: *ref*, 553(577)
Travis, V. K.: *ref*, 693(271)
Travis, W. P.: *ref*, 641(622)
Traw, L. S.: *ref*, 49(309), 188(94), 192(147), 372(20)
Traweek, A. R.: *ref*, 616(4700)
Traxler, A. E.: *cross ref*, 23, 745, 1011
Traxler, A. J.: *ref*, 10(114), 200(590), 227(63–4, 67), 232(1196), 431(467), 582(244)
Treadway, K. A.: *ref*, 222(473), 234(154), 431(591), 802(299)
Tredoux, M.: *test*, 482
Treffinger, D. J.: *ref*, 249(363, 476)
Treherne, A. D.: *ref*, 872(42)
Trenberth, G. I.: *ref*, 641(623)
Trent, E. R.: *ref*, 548(320)
Trent, R.: *test*, 782
Trentham, L. L.: *ref*, 249(374, 516)
Treppa, J. A.: *ref*, 616(4110), 641(284)
Treul, S.: *ref*, 675(99)
Trevelyan, M. H.: *ref*, 530(158)
Trickett, E. J.: *test*, 521; *ref*, 521(1, 2), 531(3), 681(17–8, 30, 56–7), 706(12)
Triebe, J. K.: *ref*, 606(307)
Triffinger, D. J.: *ref*, 239(103)
Trilling, B. A.: *ref*, 495(481)
Trimakas, K. A.: *ref*, 693(434)
Trimble, A. C.: *ref*, 800(4)
Trimble, D. M.: *ref*, 222(502), 232(1538)
Trimble, H. C.: *rev*, 266, 288; *cross ref*, 291
Trimboli, F.: *ref*, 679(1059)
Trimmer, H.: *ref*, 490(515)
Trimmer, J. R.: *ref*, 679(1326), 693(435)
Triplett, C. M.: *ref*, 514(1031), 574(516)
Triplett, N. M.: *ref*, 582(268)
Tripp, V. A.: *ref*, 520(100)
Trittschuh, D. A.: *ref*, 469(379)
Tronick, E.: *ref*, 208(13)
Troop, J.: *ref*, 553(568)
Troth, W. A.: *ref*, 683(178)
Trott, D. M.: *ref*, 616(4111), 643(87)
Trott, J. D.: *ref*, 523(236)
Trotter, G. T.: *ref*, 222(350), 431(438), 967(7)
Troupin, A. S.: *ref*, 230(1196)
Trow, W. C.: *exc*, B533

Truax, C. B.: *ref*, 616(4375)
True, J. F.: *ref*, 523(237)
Truesdell, A. B.: *ref*, 469(431)
Truex, S.: *ref*, 753(25), 785(38)
Truitt, T. E.: *ref*, 1174(227)
Trumpeter, P. W.: *ref*, 183(335), 1023(1283)
Truumaa, A.: *bk*, B289
Truxal, J. R.: *ref*, 37(124, 158), 230(1017, 1090), 514(1032), 597(164), 616(4112)
Trybus, R. J.: *ref*, 616(4113)
Tryon, G. S.: *ref*, 520(77), 616(3861, 4952)
Tryon, R. C.: *cross ref*, 488
Tryon, W.: *ref*, 616(4202)
Tryon, W. W.: *ref*, 616(4952), 656(22)
Tryphonopoulos, S.: *ref*, 628(182)
Tseng, M. S.: *ref*, 37(125), 230(1018), 370(1018), 506(827), 514(1088), 542(1400), 613(86), 666(61), 679(1060, 1200), 997(67)
Tsushima, W. T.: *ref*, 19(153), 230(1290), 616(4795)
Tubbs, R.: *ref*, 230(1048)
Tuck, B. F.: *ref*, 232(1430), 267(12), 485(350)
Tucker, B. M.: *ref*, 1177(79)
Tucker, D. L.: *ref*, 229(1539)
Tucker, D. M.: *ref*, 616(4965)
Tucker, G.: *ref*, 581(370), 661(4648–9, 4669)
Tucker, G. J.: *ref*, 611(612), 628(191), 661(4656, 4723), 675(69)
Tucker, G. R.: *ref*, 22(116), 200(669), 720(351)
Tucker, L.: *ref*, 398(10)
Tucker, M. A.: *ref*, 461(487)
Tucker, R. E.: *ref*, 469(579), 870(35), 874(55), 997(179)
Tucker, S. J.: *ref*, 542(1595)
Tuckman, B. W.: *rev*, 489, 491; *test*, 16; *bk*, B541; *exc*, 244; *ref*, 244(131)
Tudor, T. G.: *ref*, 616(4376), 683(151)
Tufano, L. G.: *ref*, 232(1432)
Tuffli, C. S.: *ref*, 249(421)
Tuinman, J.: *ref*, 720(223)
Tuinman, J. J.: *rev*, 779, 782; *bk*, B50–1; *ref*, 19(105, 142), 719(91), 720(194, 222, 264–5, 309, 384), 732(56)
Tulkin, S. R.: *ref*, 200(516)
Tulloch, R. W.: *ref*, 997(140)
Tully, G. E.: *ref*, 8(25), 471(17), 473(26)
Tuma, J. M.: *ref*, 222(503), 232(1548), 661(4852, 4925)
Tumilty, T. N.: *ref*, 553(511), 616(4436), 628(199), 643(130)
Tunkel, L. S.: *test*, 1153; *ref*, 1153(6)
Tunstall, O. A.: *ref*, 200(557), 553(396)
Tuoti, P. L.: *ref*, 506(920)
Tupin, J. P.: *ref*, 616(3940), 628(156)
Turaids, D.: *test*, 876
Turnbull, A. A.: *ref*, 553(699)
Turnbull, W.: *ref*, 616(3862, 4713)

(1255, 1437), 238(36), 377(551, 559), 431(498–9, 508, 592, 600), 495(488, 512–3), 506(1010), 514 (1364), 542(1557, 1598–9), 554 (70, 75), 616(4380, 4408, 4608, 4800, 4812, 4957), 630(296), 634 (345), 679(1449, 1459, 1496–7), 769(5), 820(157), 1028(191, 223, 259, 260–4, 266, 268, 295, 302), 1189(1, 3)
Wakefield, M. W.: *ref,* 232(1246), 431(489)
Wakefield, W. M.: *ref,* 542(1541)
Wakeman, R. J.: *ref,* 683(269)
Walberg, H. J.: *bk,* B550; *ref,* 488 (403, 423–4)
Waldenberger, J. J.: *ref,* 1175(134)
Walder, J. M.: *ref,* 641(569)
Walder, L. O.: *ref,* 616(3925, 4260)
Waldman, I. N.: *ref,* 616(4841), 720(188)
Waldman, K.: *ref,* 708(24)
Waldron, J. A.: *ref,* 616(4801)
Waldron, K. A.: *ref,* 646(90)
Waldton, S.: *ref,* 585(167)
Wales, B.: *ref,* 616(4118)
Wales, T.: *bk,* B528
Walizer, D. G.: *ref,* 524A(8), 686 (928)
Walizer, W. B.: *ref,* 524A(8)
Walker, B.: *test,* 49
Walker, C.: *ref,* 219(24, 28), 229 (1575), 232(1560), 431(607)
Walker, C. A.: *ref,* 230(1019), 232 (1135)
Walker, C. E.: *ref,* 232(1372), 553 (607), 616(4027), 654(35)
Walker, D. K.: *bk,* B551
Walker, G. R.: *ref,* 495(416), 542 (1463)
Walker, H. A.: *ref,* 232(1358)
Walker, H. J.: *ref,* 232(1438), 431 (593), 967(24)
Walker, J. C.: *ref,* 222(488), 232 (1480)
Walker, J. G.: *ref,* 393(92), 1174 (256)
Walker, K. P.: *ref,* 230(1019), 232 (1135)
Walker, L.: *ref,* 661(4700)
Walker, L. B.: *ref,* 495(359), 697 (28)
Walker, N.: *ref,* 485(372)
Walker, N. W.: *ref,* 232(1439)
Walker, R. E.: *ref,* 230(968), 628 (190), 641(376, 630)
Walker, R. N.: *bk,* B25–7; *ref,* 506 (879), 661(4662, 4733)
Walker, R. W.: *test,* 990
Walker, W. R.: *ref,* 585(190)
Walkey, F. H.: *ref,* 679(1209)
Wall, J.: *bk,* B552; *exc,* B80
Wall, T. W.: *ref,* 530(186)
Wall, W. D.: *exc,* B248; *cross ref,* 200
Wallace, B.: *ref,* 576(55)
Wallace, D. H.: *ref,* 660(100)
Wallace, L. M. V.: *ref,* 431(490)
Wallace, M. E.: *ref,* 574(536), 686 (929)
Wallace, M. J.: *ref,* 188(124), 1052 (76)
Wallace, S. H.: *ref,* 634(346)

Wallace, W. L.: *rev,* 473; *ref,* 1104(2); *cross ref,* 182, 469
Wallach, C.: *ref,* 697(1973)
Wallach, M. A.: *ref,* 182(569), 581 (366, 434)
Wallbrown, F. H.: *ref,* 227(84, 95–6), 230(1166), 232(1263, 1359–60, 1440–2), 234(128), 431 (550, 594), 506(926, 963–5, 977, 1004–5, 1018), 800(11, 14), 802 (286), 872(60), 932(138, 151)
Wallbrown, J. D.: *ref,* 227(84, 96), 232(1359, 1440–1, 1443, 1476), 431 (550, 594), 506(926, 964–5, 1004–5, 1018), 800(11, 14), 802(286), 872(60), 932(138, 151)
Wallen, N. E.: *cross ref,* 190, 634
Waller, S.: *ref,* 553(557)
Waller, S. L.: *ref,* 553(558), 615 (33)
Wallhermfechtel, J.: *ref,* 616(4592)
Wallhermfechtel, J. H.: *ref,* 641 (624)
Wallington, S.: *ref,* 661(4880)
Wallmark, M.: *ref,* 461(13)
Wallner, N. K.: *ref,* 29(248), 802 (225, 287)
Walls, R.: *ref,* 616(5022)
Walls, R. T.: *ref,* 1051(19–20)
Wallston, B. S.: *ref,* 666(76)
Wallston, K. A.: *ref,* 666(76)
Walpole, J. W.: *ref,* 693(347)
Walsh, E. P.: *ref,* 1028(143)
Walsh, J.: *ref,* 237(72), 244(177), 245(4), 504(110), 562(69)
Walsh, J. A.: *rev,* 610, 679; *cross ref,* 514, 535
Walsh, R. P.: *ref,* 514(1349)
Walsh, W. B.: *exc,* 1028; *ref,* 188 (98), 469(432, 544), 514(1231), 523(222), 524A(9), 634(245, 311), 693(348–9), 997(68, 144), 1022(18, 22, 30, 55, 60, 66, 69, 89), 1023(1385), 1028(158–9, 184, 192, 207, 271, 278, 282, 306); *cross ref,* 1010
Walster, G. W.: *ref,* 183(326)
Walter, C. L.: *ref,* 581(387)
Walter, J. E.: *ref,* 686(879)
Walter, R. B.: *ref,* 720(310)
Walthall, J. E.: *ref,* 580(15)
Waltimo, O.: *ref,* 230(1167)
Waltmann, R. H.: *ref,* 617(15)
Walton, C. E.: *test,* 60
Walton, J. M.: *ref,* 542(1542)
Wamhoff, M. J.: *ref,* 580(9)
Wanat, S. F.: *bk,* B553
Wanberg, K. W.: *ref,* 616(4235, 4483)
Wandt, E.: *cross ref,* 381
Wang, H. S.: *ref,* 230(1094, 1168–9)
Wang, R. I.: *ref,* 675(99)
Wanko, G. J.: *ref,* 523(301), 641 (570)
Wanous, J. P.: *ref,* 1052(59, 77, 109)
Wantman, M. J.: *cross ref,* 1101
Warberg, W. B.: *ref,* 485(373)
Warbin, R.: *ref,* 616(4212)
Warbin, R. W.: *ref,* 616(3867, 3960–1, 4119, 4136, 4213–7), 617 (53, 60–1, 64, 67–70)
Ward, A. W.: *bk,* B554

Ward, C.: *ref,* 582(246)
Ward, C. F.: *ref,* 490(449)
Ward, C. S.: *ref,* 641(625)
Ward, D. L.: *ref,* 686(930)
Ward, E. F.: *ref,* 661(4646)
Ward, G. R.: *ref,* 542(1475, 1557), 679(1497), 1028(295), 1189(1)
Ward, J. S.: *ref,* 577(39)
Ward, L. O.: *ref,* 597(182), 822 (179)
Ward, M. P.: *bk,* B311; *ref,* 225 (61), 230(1070, 1262), 616 (4905), 661(4891)
Ward, S. H.: *ref,* 646(29)
Ward, S. S.: *ref,* 643(164)
Ward, W. C.: *rev,* 246, 987; *ref,* 244(174)
Ward, W. D.: *ref,* 230(1052), 585 (181), 592(58, 63)
Wardell, D.: *exc,* B97; *ref,* 553 (581), 679(1331)
Wardrop, J. L.: *rev,* 744, 746; *bk,* B555; *ref,* 720(311)
Ware, W. B.: *exc,* B550
Warehime, R. G.: *ref,* 641(390, 489)
Waring, E. M.: *ref,* 565(10)
Wark, D. M.: *ref,* 193(38)
Warnath, C. F.: *rev,* 335, 348, 546
Warncke, E.: *ref,* 232(1247), 257 (40)
Warner, A. B.: *ref,* 1016(26)
Warner, M. O.: *ref,* 628(205)
Warner, R. S.: *ref,* 37(126–7), 227(57), 232(1136), 506(828)
Warner, R. W.: *ref,* 514(986)
Warner, W. R.: *ref,* 882(175)
Warren, G. H.: *ref,* 651(22)
Warren, J. R.: *test,* 401; *ref,* 401 (1)
Warren, N.: *ref,* 238(21)
Warren, S. A.: *ref,* 229(1498), 232 (1248)
Warren, V. M.: *ref,* 661(4727)
Warren, W. G.: *ref,* 523(302)
Warrick, P.: *ref,* 842(7)
Warrington, E. K.: *ref,* 232(1313)
Warrington, M. M.: *ref,* 1023(193)
Warrington, W. G.: *cross ref,* 845
Waser, C. J.: *ref,* 641(571)
Washinger, K. C.: *ref,* 182(666)
Washington, D. J.: *ref,* 227(85)
Washington, E. M.: *ref,* 1174(257)
Washington, R.: *ref,* 626(258)
Wasik, B. H.: *ref,* 230(1020), 234 (108), 238(41)
Wasik, J. L.: *exc,* B59, B519, B541; *ref,* 230(1020), 234(108), 238(41), 298(9)
Waskow, I. E.: *bk,* B556
Wass, J.: *ref,* 225(71), 230(1203), 485(376)
Wasung, R. S. K.: *ref,* 37(201), 232(1444)
Wasyluk, G.: *ref,* 660(79–80)
Watamori, T. S.: *ref,* 971(17)
Waterman, A. S.: *ref,* 524(98, 125)
Waterman, L.: *ref,* 238(42)
Waterman, L. J.: *ref,* 230(1288)
Waters, C. C.: *ref,* 607(39)
Waters, C. W.: *ref,* 182(707)
Waters, D. E.: *ref,* 634(281)
Waters, E. C.: *ref,* 349(6), 679 (1332)

Waters, W. B.: *ref,* 182(613)
Waters, W. F.: *ref,* 616(3980)
Watkins, B.: *ref,* 616(5009), 628
 (245), 683(332)
Watkins, B. A.: *ref,* 616(4649)
Watkins, D.: *ref,* 553(386, 702),
 554(30)
Watkins, D. A.: *ref,* 506(966)
Watkins, J. M.: *ref,* 506(966)
Watkins, J. T.: *ref,* 529(23), 641
 (468, 474, 512), 656(45, 58)
Watkins, J. V.: *ref,* 555(272)
Watkins, R. W.: *rev,* 392
Watman, M.: *ref,* 542(1535), 553
 (575)
Watrous, B.: *ref,* 697(1834)
Watrous, B. G.: *ref,* 697(1767)
Watson, B. L.: *ref,* 431(446)
Watson, C. D.: *ref,* 785(35)
Watson, C. G.: *ref,* 179(111, 119),
 184(114, 121), 187(465), 190
 (115–6), 200(638, 672), 224(261,
 264), 225(76–7), 227(97–8), 230
 (1021, 1095–6, 1170, 1237–8,
 1274), 236(114), 616(4117, 4120–
 2, 4381, 4958, 5009, 5023–4), 628
 (245), 655(10–2), 677(162, 188),
 683(332)
Watson, D.: *ref,* 616(4602)
Watson, D. J.: *ref,* 790(10–1)
Watson, G.: *test,* 822
Watson, G. T.: *ref,* 542(1636), 679
 (1498)
Watson, H. W.: *ref,* 641(285)
Watson, J. G.: *ref,* 697(1938, 2003)
Watson, J. R.: *ref,* 515(456)
Watson, L. D.: *ref,* 553(683)
Watson, M. A.: *ref,* 222(397), 431
 (491), 938(13)
Watson, P.: *ref,* 232(1249)
Watson, P. C.: *ref,* 24(8)
Watson, R. G.: *ref,* 646(30), 693
 (273)
Watson, R. I.: *ref,* 662(429), 697
 (1875)
Watt, S. L.: *ref,* 596(76), 625(15),
 646(102), 654(37)
Wattenbarger, J. L.: *ref,* 989(11)
Watterson, D. G.: *bk,* B502; *ref,*
 1016(27)
Watts, G. P.: *ref,* 585(191), 663
 (133)
Watts, K. P.: *test,* 175, 509, 1046;
 ref, 175(1), 1046(1)
Watts, T.: *ref,* 28(47), 183(359)
Watts, W. A.: *ref,* 469(478), 628
 (182)
Waugh, D. B.: *ref,* 662(446)
Waugh, N. C.: *ref,* 490(457)
Waugh, R.: *ref,* 431(493)
Waugh, R. P.: *exc,* 431; *ref,* 431
 (492, 595)
Waxer, P.: *ref,* 616(4959)
Way, J. G.: *ref,* 229(1423)
Waynant, L. F.: *ref,* 785(28)
Wayne, D.: *ref,* 701(2)
Wayne, H.: *ref,* 230(1077) 506
 (874), 616(4093), 661(4715)
Wayne, K. S.: *ref,* 677(163)
Weade, B. L.: *ref,* 229(1459), 703
 (194)
Wearing, A. J.: *ref,* 686(884)
Weart, D. N.: *ref,* 555(207)
Weaver, A.: *ref,* 558(26)

Weaver, J. F.: *cross ref,* 302
Weaver, J. W.: *ref,* 679(1421)
Weaver, K. E.: *ref,* 660(101)
Weaver, S. J.: *ref,* 558(26)
Weaver, W. W.: *ref,* 720(49, 63,
 103, 120, 126, 132, 141, 165, 178,
 184, 190, 224–5)
Webb, A. P.: *ref,* 230(1097)
Webb, C. R.: *ref,* 997(145), 1023
 (1474)
Webb, J. B.: *ref,* 232(1137)
Webb, J. T.: *ref,* 616(4441, 4605),
 617(40, 45–7)
Webb, R. P.: *ref,* 469(581)
Webb, S. L.: *ref,* 802(288)
Webb, W. W.: *ref,* 616(4450, 4563,
 4960), 693(573)
Webber, G. D.: *ref,* 200(673), 227
 (99), 232(1445)
Webber, M. S.: *ref,* 932(110)
Webber, P.: *ref,* 1023(1378)
Webber, P. L.: *ref,* 553(703), 1023
 (1505)
Weber, C. A.: *ref,* 393(73)
Weber, D. S.: *ref,* 511(5)
Weber, E. S. P.: *ref,* 616(4389)
Weber, L.: *ref,* 490(499)
Weber, P. G.: *test,* 1047
Weber, R. G.: *ref,* 616(4461)
Webster, A. C.: *ref,* 542(1464),
 641(391), 711(58)
Webster, E. G.: *ref,* 527(49), 713
 (1–2)
Webster, H.: *test,* 634
Webster, R. E.: *ref,* 230(1171)
Wechsler, D.: *test,* 230, 232, 234,
 250; *bk,* B557; *cross ref,* 200
Weckowicz, T. E.: *rev,* 651, 655;
 ref, 230(1022)
Wedel, G. J.: *ref,* 35(122)
Wedell, K.: *ref,* 431(394), 882
 (171)
Wedman, I.: *exc,* B36
Weed, S. E.: *ref,* 1175(166)
Weeks, R. T.: *ref,* 485(362)
Weeks, S. R.: *ref,* 616(4682)
Weeks, T. H.: *ref,* 377(517), 391
 (9), 392(5)
Weener, P.: *ref,* 431(483), 720
 (291–2)
Wefring, L. R.: *ref,* 616(3986)
Wegner, K. W.: *ref,* 601(15), 616
 (4224)
Wehner, W. L.: *rev,* 93–4
Wehr, M.: *ref,* 679(1066, 1201)
Weidenaar, D. J.: *ref,* 469(433)
Weider, A.: *bk,* B558
Weidmann, R. E.: *ref,* 182(708)
Weidner, W. E.: *ref,* 932(102)
Weigel, R. G.: *ref,* 617(27)
Weijola, M. J.: *test,* 614
Weikel, W. J.: *ref,* 643(174)
Weil, A. T.: *ref,* 720(166)
Weil, G. R.: *test,* 691
Weil, M. B.: *ref,* 669(1925)
Weimer, A.: *bk,* B559
Weimer, W.: *bk,* B559
Weimer, W. R.: *ref,* 800(7)
Weinberg, E.: *ref,* 1101(161)
Weinberg, J.: *ref,* 230(959)
Weinberg, P. C.: *ref,* 1101(153)
Weinberg, R. A.: *ref,* 232(1155)
Weinberg, S. F.: *ref,* 381(95)

Weinberg, W. A.: *ref,* 37(180),
 222(444), 232(1361)
Weinberger, A.: *ref,* 683(317)
Weiner, B. J.: *ref,* 553(648), 628
 (197), 693(473)
Weiner, E. A.: *ref,* 555(269), 628
 (192, 197, 219, 235), 656(48),
 693(473)
Weiner, F. J.: *ref,* 661(4912)
Weiner, I. B.: *bk,* B174; *ref,* 661
 (4939)
Weiner, M.: *ref,* 8(10, 21), 182
 (614), 199(29), 283(11)
Weiner, M. M.: *ref,* 391(11), 392
 (6)
Weiner, P. S.: *ref,* 222(398), 431
 (494), 932(111), 938(14)
Weinman, B.: *ref,* 631(48), 693
 (329)
Weinrach, S. G.: *ref,* 641(286, 626)
Weinstein, A. G.: *ref,* 1074(19, 21)
Weinstein, B.: *ref,* 549(19)
Weinstein, C. G.: *ref,* 641(572)
Weinstein, E. A.: *ref,* 250(90)
Weinstein, J. M.: *ref,* 641(392)
Weinstein, M. S.: *ref,* 495(483)
Weinstein, N.: *ref,* 616(4036), 628
 (165), 675(54)
Weinstein, P.: *ref,* 1101(172)
Weinstein, S. P.: *ref,* 693(350)
Weintraub, M.: *ref,* 536(25), 985
 (9)
Weintraub, S.: *ref,* 720(142)
Weintraub, S. A.: *rev,* 497, 501;
 cross ref, 519, 595
Weir, D. M.: *ref,* 630(267)
Weir, T.: *ref,* 555(277, 305)
Weir, W. D.: *ref,* 1023(1420)
Weisenberg, M.: *ref,* 683(212, 270)
Weiser, H. E.: *ref,* 393(83)
Weisman, A. D.: *ref,* 616(4811),
 651(43)
Weisman, R. A.: *ref,* 1101(153)
Weiss, A. A.: *ref,* 236(115–6, 124),
 506(812, 880, 884, 967), 661
 (4888)
Weiss, A. P.: *ref,* 720(6)
Weiss, D.: *ref,* 514(1232, 1280)
Weiss, D. J.: *rev,* 483, 492; *test,*
 1050–2, 1061, *bk,* B167; *exc,* B63,
 B517; *ref,* 490(483), 1010(43),
 1016(14), 1023(1312), 1030(56),
 1050(48, 58, 72), 1051(9–10, 14,
 18), 1052(31–2, 44); *cross ref,*
 490
Weiss, D. S.: *ref,* 514(1188)
Weiss, G. H.: *ref,* 555(208)
Weiss, J. L.: *ref,* 519(63), 616
 (3903, 4428–9, 4647)
Weiss, J. M. A.: *ref,* 616(4382)
Weiss, M. F.: *ref,* 616(4383)
Weiss, N. L.: *ref,* 506(927)
Weiss, R. H.: *ref,* 661(4593)
Weiss, R. W.: *ref,* 616(5025)
Weiss, S.: *ref,* 234(160), 599(27)
Weiss, V. A.: *ref,* 230(958)
Weiss, W. U.: *ref,* 230(1121), 661
 (4747, 4799)
Weissbach, T. A.: *ref,* 679(1202)
Weissenberg, P.: *ref,* 548(280,
 307), 1174(177), 1177(71), 1186
 (15)
Weisskopf-Joelson, E.: *ref,* 697
 (1835)

White, M. L. V.: *ref,* 693(354)
White, O.: *ref,* 554(67)
White, P. O.: *bk,* B150
White, R. B.: *ref,* 506(968, 1006), 616(4515), 661(4766)
White, R. K.: *ref,* 641(395)
White, R. T.: *test,* 696
White, W. A.: *ref,* 661(4923)
White, W. C.: *ref,* 616(3853, 4385, 4804), 662(449), 679(1204, 1499)
White, W. E.: *ref,* 616(4611)
White, W. F.: *ref,* 179(120), 520 (87), 679(1422), 720(141, 165, 167, 400), 802(289)
White, W. G.: *ref,* 616(4612)
Whitehead, A.: *exc,* B463; *ref,* 230 (1099, 1172), 553(420), 651(39)
Whitehead, G.: *ref,* 679(1220), 683 (293, 326)
Whitehead, G. I.: *ref,* 679(1458)
Whitehead, P. C.: *ref,* 616(4410)
Whitehead, R. G.: *ref,* 183(357)
Whitehead, R. L.: *ref,* 954(11)
Whitehouse, R. H.: *bk,* B526
Whitehurst, M. R.: *ref,* 515(447), 688(167)
Whiteside, M. J.: *ref,* 693(355)
Whiting, H. T. A.: *ref,* 539(28), 553(394), 679(977)
Whiting, R. E.: *ref,* 582(247)
Whitis, J. D.: *ref,* 1174(178)
Whitla, D. K.: *cross ref,* 472
Whitlock, F. A.: *ref,* 553(539), 616(4494), 679(1273)
Whitlock, J.: *ref,* 182(654), 514 (1132)
Whitman, R. L.: *ref,* 198(22), 997 (46)
Whitmer, M.: *ref,* 553(567)
Whitmer, R. L.: *ref,* 720(385-6)
Whitmyre, J. W.: *ref,* 616(4386)
Whitney, D. R.: *ref,* 469(480, 495, 515), 473(17), 900(2), 1022(6), 1028(160)
Whitsitt, S. E.: *ref,* 555(280), 1177 (103)
Whittaker, P.: *bk,* B256
Whittaker, W. S.: *ref,* 697(1836)
Whitten, J. E.: *ref,* 1174(258)
Whitten, J. R.: *ref,* 225(55), 232 (1121)
Whitten, M. R.: *ref,* 679(1374)
Whittlesey, J. R. B.: *test,* 882; *ref,* 1028(160)
Whitton, M. C.: *ref,* 1023(1478)
Whitworth, R. H.: *rev,* 232
Whybrew, W. E.: *bk,* B563
Whyte, H. M.: *ref,* 616(4203)
Wiant, H. V.: *ref,* 1030(60)
Wiater, R. T.: *ref,* 222(475)
Wick, J. W.: *bk,* B564
Wickert, J.: *ref,* 405(1)
Wickramasekera, I.: *ref,* 682(86)
Wicks, R. J.: *bk,* B126; *ref,* 506 (976)
Widawski, M. H.: *ref,* 182(759-60)
Widdop, J. H.: *ref,* 514(1316), 542 (1601), 582(261), 679(1423)
Widdop, V. A.: *ref,* 514(1316), 542 (1601), 582(261), 679(1423)
Widlak, F. W.: *ref,* 230(1152), 249 (520)
Widlake, P.: *ref,* 703(196)
Widom, C. S.: *ref,* 616(4975)

Wiebe, B.: *ref,* 686(1024)
Wiebe, M. J.: *ref,* 219(29), 229 (1586), 232(1567)
Wiechelman, D. S.: *ref,* 720(226)
Wiederholt, J. L.: *rev,* 426, 431; *ref,* 22(97), 227(61), 802(236), 882(189, 199)
Wiedl, K. H.: *ref,* 200(679, 696)
Wiehe, V. R.: *ref,* 495(514)
Wiekhorst, C. L.: *ref,* 683(152)
Wiener, Y.: *ref,* 514(1185), 616 (4477)
Wiens, A. N.: *ref,* 176(8), 230 (1072, 1219, 1284)
Wiersma, W.: *bk,* B283, B565
Wiesen, L. E.: *ref,* 616(4477)
Wig, N. N.: *ref,* 530(183-5), 554 (31), 606(312)
Wigdor, B. T.: *ref,* 616(4253)
Wigent, P. A.: *ref,* 542(1404, 1544)
Wiggins, J. D.: *ref,* 1028(226, 298)
Wiggins, J. G.: *test,* 348
Wiggins, J. S.: *bk,* B566; *ref,* 616 (4059); *cross ref,* 643
Wiggins, N.: *ref,* 616(4524), 661 (4677)
Wiggins, R. G.: *ref,* 580(10-2), 633 (5-6), 997(48, 74)
Wiggins, T. W.: *ref,* 555(210), 636 (43), 688(159)
Wigington, J. H.: *ref,* 1028(194)
Wigley, M.: *ref,* 230(1130), 553 (525)
Wiig, E. H.: *ref,* 230(1173), 232 (1363), 431(551), 452(3), 967 (23)
Wijesinghe, B.: *ref,* 711(43)
Wikstrom, W. S.: *bk,* B282
Wilborn, B. L.: *ref,* 232(1544), 431 (635)
Wilbur, C. B.: *ref,* 495(343), 616 (4020)
Wilbur, R. H.: *ref,* 485(363)
Wilburn, D. J.: *ref,* 802(253)
Wilcock, J. A.: *ref,* 679(1062)
Wilcox, B. L.: *ref,* 681(83), 700 (12)
Wilcox, L.: *ref,* 110(18), 182(619)
Wilcox, M. R.: *bk,* B279; *ref,* 491 (29)
Wilcox, R.: *ref,* 520(101)
Wilcox, R. R.: *bk,* B204
Wild, C. M.: *ref,* 661(4902)
Wildblood, R. W.: *ref,* 693(276)
Wilde, V.: *ref,* 542(1460)
Wilder, S.: *ref,* 249(418), 504(94), 682(83)
Wilding, J. M.: *ref,* 553(395)
Wildman, L.: *ref,* 523(237)
Wildman, R. W.: *ref,* 506(969), 616(4805), 661(4855), 697(1977)
Wilee, C. T.: *ref,* 581(435)
Wilensky, H.: *ref,* 578(339)
Wiley, D. E.: *bk,* B202, B571; *ref,* 12(12), 19(157), 20(134), 182 (763-4), 193(41), 199(30), 469 (562)
Wiley, R. C.: *ref,* 641(494)
Wilgosh, L.: *ref,* 37(183), 200 (640)
Wilhelm, K.: *ref,* 630(247)
Wilhelm, P.: *ref,* 641(311)
Wilhelm, P. G.: *ref,* 641(475)
Wilke, F. L.: *ref,* 230(1100)

Wilkie, F.: *ref,* 230(1046, 1174)
Wilkins, G.: *ref,* 529(17)
Wilkins, J. L.: *ref,* 616(4613)
Wilkins, K. A.: *ref,* 232(1275)
Wilkinson, A.: *ref,* 37(213), 187 (470), 222(500), 232(1533), 506 (1002), 932(156)
Wilkinson, J. M.: *ref,* 182(669), 641(396)
Wilkinson, L.: *ref,* 531(6-7), 681 (31-2)
Will, J. A.: *ref,* 1023(1511)
Willard, D.: *ref,* 20(124), 643(88)
Willenberg, E. P.: *bk,* B168-9
Willerman, L.: *ref,* 206(44-5), 229 (1540), 230(1272-3), 232(1092), 431(504), 616(4955), 679(1491-2)
Williams, A. F.: *ref,* 643(123)
Williams, A. M.: *ref,* 222(352), 431(441)
Williams, A. Y.: *ref,* 1177(80)
Williams, C.: *ref,* 469(545), 490 (530)
Williams, C. C.: *ref,* 719(96), 830 (24), 892(15)
Williams, C. L.: *ref,* 553(583), 565(11), 579(77), 679(1333)
Williams, C. M.: *ref,* 679(1063, 1205), 686(885), 1028(148, 161, 195)
Williams, D. D.: *ref,* 630(269), 693 (277)
Williams, D. G.: *ref,* 553(503)
Williams, D. L.: *ref,* 529(10), 630 (214)
Williams, D. M.: *ref,* 660(67)
Williams, D. R.: *ref,* 1023(1449)
Williams, E.: *ref,* 693(278), 1052 (45)
Williams, E. C.: *ref,* 542(1465)
Williams, F.: *ref,* 720(67, 82, 164)
Williams, F. C.: *ref,* 1(19), 732 (45), 736(45), 932(125)
Williams, F. E.: *ref,* 377(489)
Williams, G.: *ref,* 661(4863), 697 (1981)
Williams, G. D.: *ref,* 524(99), 643 (89)
Williams, H. L.: *test,* 665
Williams, I. C.: *bk,* B496
Williams, J. D.: *ref,* 187(429), 230 (1101), 249(430), 488(385-6, 418), 529(16), 616(4010, 4127, 4310), 679(1064, 1205), 726A (35-6), 749(5), 1028(148, 195)
Williams, J. E.: *ref,* 495(520)
Williams, J. H.: *ref,* 396(4), 514 (1150), 606(317)
Williams, J. K.: *ref,* 514(1038), 641 (288), 693(279)
Williams, J. R.: *ref,* 693(532)
Williams, J. W.: *ref,* 469(481)
Williams, K. G.: *ref,* 222(410)
Williams, K. L.: *ref,* 692(29)
Williams, L.: *ref,* 661(4853)
Williams, L. C.: *ref,* 19(161), 181 (12)
Williams, M.: *test,* 1189; *ref,* 495 (435), 553(719)
Williams, M. G.: *ref,* 495(360), 641 (289)
Williams, M. J. S.: *ref,* 431(552)

Scanning Index

This scanning index is a classified index to all tests in this volume and all additional tests in Tests in Print II (*TIP II*). Foreign tests are identified by listing the country of origin in brackets immediately after the title. Within each classification, the tests are listed in two alphabetical sequences: first the tests included in this yearbook; and second, set in smaller type size, tests listed in *TIP II* but not in this yearbook. The numbers preceding the larger-type titles and those following the smaller-type titles refer to test entry numbers, not to pages—e.g., 467 refers to test 467 in this volume; T2:1832 refers to test 1832 in TIP II. (In the running heads of the *Tests and Reviews* section, entry numbers are next to the outside margins; page numbers are next to the inside margins.) Among the titles set in larger type, stars (★) indicate tests not previously listed in publications of The Buros Institute of Mental Measurements; asterisks (*) indicate tests revised or supplemented since last listed. Among the titles set in smaller type (tests listed in TIP II but not in this yearbook), double daggers (‡) indicate tests new since the 7th MMY and daggers (†) indicate tests revised or supplemented since the 7th MMY. The following additional information is given for each test: the population for which the test is intended; range of copyright dates; number of reviews, excerpts, and references in either this volume (larger-type titles) or TIP II (smaller-type titles); and, following the word "cited," the number of reviews, excerpts, and references in earlier publications.

VOLUME I

ACHIEVEMENT BATTERIES

1. *Achievement Series: SRA Assessment Survey. Grades 1–9; 1954–75; 2 reviews, 11 references; cited; 5 reviews, 15 references.

2. *Adult Basic Learning Examination. Adults with achievement levels grades 1–12; 1967–74; 4 references; cited; 1 review, 2 excerpts, 3 references.

3. ★Adult Performance Level Survey. High school and adults; 1976.

4. *American School Achievement Tests. Grades 1–9; 1941–75; 2 reviews, 1 excerpt, 1 reference; cited: 7 reviews, 2 references.

5. ★Basic Educational Skills Inventory. Grades kgn–6; 1972–73; 2 reviews.

6. ★Brigance Diagnostic Inventory of Basic Skills. Grades kgn–6; 1976.

7. ★CGP Self-Scoring Placement Tests in English and Mathematics. Students entering postsecondary institutions with open-door policies; 1976; 2 reviews.

7A. ★CIRCUS. Nursery school, kgn, and first grade entrants; 1974–76; 2 reviews, 2 excerpts, 3 references.

8. *CLEP General Examinations. 1–2 years of college or equivalent; 1964–76; 2 reviews, 20 references; cited: 7 references.

9. *CLEP General Examinations: Humanities. 1–2 years of college or equivalent; 1964–76; 1 review, 1 reference.

10. *California Achievement Tests. Grades 1.5–12; 1934–74; 2 reviews, 33 references; cited: 10 reviews, 1 excerpt, 101 references.

11. *Canadian Tests of Basic Skills [Canada]. Grades 1.7–8; 1955–74; 1 reference; cited: 1 review.

12. *Comprehensive Tests of Basic Skills. Grades kgn–12.9; 1968–76; 2 reviews, 13 references; cited: 2 reviews, 2 excerpts, 1 reference.

13. Cooperative Primary Tests. Grades 1.5–3; 1965–67; 1 review, 1 reference; cited: 2 excerpts, 1 reference.

14. ★Criterion Test of Basic Skills. Grades kgn–8; 1976.

15. ★ERB Comprehensive Testing Program. Grades 1–12; 1974–77.

16. ★Educational Goal Attainment Tests. Grades 7–12; 1975.

17. Educational Skills Tests: College Edition. Open-door college entrants; 1971; 1 review.

18. ★Everyday Skills Tests. Grades 6–12; 1975; 2 reviews.

19. *Iowa Tests of Basic Skills, Forms 5 and 6. Grades 1.7–9; 1955–75; 2 reviews, 58 references; cited: 3 reviews, 1 excerpt, 104 references.

20. *Iowa Tests of Educational Development: SRA

Assessment Survey. Grades 9–12; 1942–74; 2 reviews, 15 references; cited: 8 reviews, 120 references.

21. Ligondé Equivalence Test [Canada]. Adults who left elementary or secondary school 15 to 20 years ago; 1967; 1 review.

22. *Metropolitan Achievement Tests. Grades kgn.7–9.5; 1931–73; 2 reviews, 1 excerpt, 41 references; cited: 8 reviews, 81 references.

23. *National Educational Development Tests. Grades 7–10; 1959–74; 1 review, 2 references; cited: 3 reviews, 3 references.

24. Peabody Individual Achievement Test. Grades kgn–12; 1970; 2 excerpts, 36 references; cited: 1 review, 2 references.

25. ★Richmond Tests of Basic Skills [England]. Junior school and secondary school (ages 8–1 to 14–0); 1975; 2 reviews.

26. *STS Closed High School Placement Test. Grade 9 entrants; 1955–77; 2 reviews, 1 reference; cited: 4 reviews, 2 references.

27. *STS Educational Development Series: Scholastic Tests. Grades 2–12; 1963–76; 2 reviews; cited: 1 review, 1 reference.

28. Sequential Tests of Educational Progress, Series II. Grades 4–14; 1956–72; 2 reviews, 5 references; cited: 4 reviews, 1 excerpt, 43 references.

29. *Stanford Achievement Test. Grades 1.5–9.5; 1923–75; 2 reviews, 2 excerpts, 49 references; cited: 6 reviews, 2 excerpts, 216 references.

30. Stanford Early School Achievement Test. Grades kgn.1–1.8; 1969–71; 1 review, 6 references; cited: 2 reviews, 1 reference.

31. Stanford Test of Academic Skills. Grades 8–13; 1972–75; 2 reviews.

32. Tests of Academic Progress. Grades 9–12; 1964–72; 2 reviews, 1 reference; cited: 1 review.

33. *Tests of Adult Basic Education. Adults at reading levels grades 2–9; 1967–76; 2 reviews, 1 reference; cited: 1 review, 1 excerpt.

34. *Tests of Basic Experiences. Prekgn–grade 1 (Level L); 1970–75; 1 review, 2 excerpts, 8 references; cited: 1 review.

35. *Tests of General Educational Development. Candidates for high school equivalency certificates; 1944–76; 20 references; cited: 7 reviews, 98 references.

36. *UP Area Tests. College; 1954–77; 2 references; cited: 4 reviews, 17 references.

37. *Wide Range Achievement Test. Ages 5 and over; 1940–76; 117 references; cited: 5 reviews, 99 references.

For other tests, see in *Tests in Print II:*

Academic Proficiency Battery [South Africa], T2:1. College entrants; 1969.
Adult Basic Education Student Survey, T2:2. Poorly educated adults in basic education classes; 1966–67; cited: 2 reviews.
Bristol Achievement Tests [England], T2:5. Ages 8–13; 1969; cited: 2 reviews.
Classification and Placement Examination, T2:9. Grade 8 and high school entrants; 1967–68; cited: 1 review.
General Tests of Language and Arithmetic [South Africa], T2:14. Standards 5–7; 1964–67.
Gray-Votaw-Rogers General Achievement Tests, T2:15. Grades 1–9; 1934–63; cited: 9 reviews, 5 references.
‡Guidance Test for Junior Secondary Bantu Pupils in Form 3 [South Africa], T2:16. 1969–71.
High School Fundamentals Evaluation Test, T2:17. Grades 9–12; 1955–59; cited: 4 reviews, 1 reference.
Iowa High School Content Examination, T2:18. Grades 11–13; 1924–43; 21 references; cited: 2 reviews, 11 references.
National Achievement Tests, T2:23. Grades 4–9; 1954–62; cited: 1 review.
‡Primary Survey Tests, T2:27. Grades 2–3; 1973.
Public School Achievement Tests, T2:28. Grades 3–8; 1928–61; 2 references; cited: 2 reviews, 2 references.
†SRA High School Placement Test, T2:31. Grade 9 entrants; 1957–73; 2 references; cited: 4 reviews, 11 references.
†Scholastic Proficiency Battery [South Africa], T2:34. Standards 8–10; 1969–71.
Stanford Achievement Test: High School Basic Battery, T2:37. Grades 9–12; 1965–66; cited: 2 reviews.

Survey of College Achievement, T2:40. Grades 13–14; 1966–69; cited: 2 reviews.
†Teacher Education Examination Program: General Professional Examinations, T2:41. College seniors preparing to teach; 1957–72.
†Test for High School Entrants, T2:42. High school entrants; 1945–69; cited: 2 reviews.
Test of Reading and Number: Inter-American Series, T2:43. Grade 4 entrants; 1969.
‡Tests of Arithmetic and Language for Indian South Africans [South Africa], T2:46. Standards 6–8; 1968.

ENGLISH

38. ★ACT Proficiency Examination in Freshman English. College and adults; 1964–77.

39. *Advanced Placement Examination in English. High school students desiring credit for college level courses and admission to advanced courses; 1954–77; 1 review; cited: 2 reviews, 3 references.

40. *American School Achievement Tests: Part 3, Language and Spelling. Grades 2–9; 1941–75; 1 review; cited: 2 reviews, 1 reference.

41. ★Analysis of Skills: Language Arts. Grades 2–8; 1975–76.

42. *CLEP General Examinations: English Composition. 1–2 years of college or equivalent; 1964–76; 4 references; cited: 1 reference.

43. *CLEP Subject Examination in College Composition. 1 year of college or equivalent; 1965–76; 1 review, 2 references; cited: 1 review.

44. *CLEP Subject Examination in Freshman English. 1 year of college or equivalent; 1973–76; 1 review, 1 reference.

45. *California Achievement Tests: Language. Grades 1.5–12; 1933–74; 2 reviews, 1 reference; cited: 7 reviews, 10 references.

46. *College Board Achievement Test in English Composition. Candidates for college entrance; 1943–76; 2 reviews, 2 references; cited: 4 reviews, 37 references.

47. College English Placement Test. College entrants; 1969; 1 excerpt, 2 references; cited: 2 reviews, 2 references.

48. *College Placement Tests in English Composition. Entering college freshmen; 1962–75; cited: 5 reviews, 3 references.

49. Cooperative English Tests. Grades 9–14; 1940–65; 20 references; cited: 5 reviews, 1 excerpt, 300 references.

50. *Differential Aptitude Tests: Language Usage. Grades 8–12 and adults; 1947–75; cited: 2 references.

51. ★Educational Skills Tests: English, College Edition. Open-door college entrants; 1971.

52. ★Illinois Tests in the Teaching of English. High school English teachers; 1969–72; 1 reference.

53. ★Language Arts: IOX Objectives-Based Tests. Grades kgn–6; 1973–74; 2 reviews.

54. *National Teacher Examinations: English Language and Literature. College seniors and teachers; 1940–76; 1 review; cited: 1 review, 1 reference.

55. ★Scholastic Achievement Tests for English First Language [South Africa]. Grade 2/sub B, standards 1–4, 6, 9–10; 1973–75.

56. Sequential Tests of Educational Progress: English Expression, Series II. Grades 4–14; 1969–72; 2 reviews.

57. Sequential Tests of Educational Progress: Mechanics of Writing, Series II. Grades 4–12; 1956–72; 1 review, 3 references; cited: 5 reviews, 1 excerpt, 16 references.

58. ★Structure Tests—English Language. High school and over; 1976.

59. Tests of Basic Experiences: Language. Prekgn–grade 1; 1970–72; 1 review.

60. Walton-Sanders English Test. 1–2 semesters in grades 9–13; 1962–64; 1 review.

61. ★Written English Expression Placement Test.

Students entering postsecondary institutions with open-door policies; 1976; 2 reviews.

FOR OTHER TESTS, see in *Tests in Print II:*

Analytical Survey Test in English Fundamentals, T2:53. Grades 9–13; 1932–57; 3 references; cited: 2 reviews, 2 references.

Barrett-Ryan English Test, T2:54. Grades 7–13; 1926–61; 1 reference; cited: 2 reviews, 2 references.

‡Berry-Talbott Language Test: Comprehension of Grammar, T2:55. Ages 5–8; 1966.

Bristol Achievement Tests: English Language [England], T2:56. Ages 8–13; 1969; cited: 1 review.

Business English Test: Dailey Vocational Tests, T2:57. Grades 8–12 and adults; 1964–65.

†Canadian Achievement Test in English [Canada], T2:62. Grade 10; 1961–68; cited: 1 review, 2 references.

†Canadian English Achievement Test [Canada], T2:63. Grades 8.5–9; 1959–68; cited: 2 reviews, 2 references.

‡Canadian English Language Achievement Test [Canada], T2:63A. Candidates for college entrance; 1968–73; 4 references.

College English Test: National Achievement Tests, T2:66. Grades 12–13; 1937–43; cited: 3 reviews.

†Comprehensive Tests of Basic Skills: Language, T2:68. Grades 2.5–12; 1968–71.

Cooperative Primary Tests: Writing Skills, T2:70. Grades 2.5–3; 1965–67.

†Cotswold Junior English Ability Test [Scotland], T2:71. Ages 8.5–10.5; 1949–70; cited: 2 reviews.

†Cotswold Measurement of Ability: English [Scotland], T2:72. Ages 10–12; 1947–69; cited: 2 reviews.

English Expression: Cooperative English Tests, T2:73. Grades 9–14; 1940–60; cited: 3 reviews.

English IX–XII: Achievement Examinations for Secondary Schools, T2:74. Grades 9–12; 1951–54; 1 reference.

†English Progress Tests [England], T2:75. Ages 7–3 to 15–6; 1952–72; cited: 2 reviews.

English Test FG [England], T2:76. Ages 12–13; 1952; cited: 3 reviews.

English Test: Municipal Tests, T2:77. Grades 3–8; 1 reference.

English Test: National Achievement Tests, T2:78. Grades 3–12; 1936–57; 1 reference; cited: 2 reviews.

English Tests (Adv.) [England], T2:79. Ages 12–13; 1954–67; cited: 2 reviews.

†English Tests 14–20 and 22 [England], T2:80. Ages 10–11; 1951–71; cited: 3 reviews, 1 reference.

Essentials of English Tests, T2:81. Grades 7–13; 1939–61; 1 reference; cited: 3 reviews, 1 excerpt.

‡Functional Grammar Test, T2:82. High school and college; 1970.

†Grammar and Usage Test Series, T2:83. Grades 7–12; 1950–70.

Grammar, Usage, and Structure Test and Vocabulary Test, T2:84. College entrants; 1963–68.

Hoyum-Sanders English Tests, T2:85. 1–2 semesters in grades 2–8; 1962–64; cited: 1 review.

Iowa Placement Examinations: English Aptitude, T2:86. Grades 12–13; 1925–26; 1 reference; cited: 3 reviews, 14 references.

Iowa Placement Examinations: English Training, T2:87. Grades 12–13; 1925–44; 6 references; cited: 3 reviews, 20 references.

†Iowa Tests of Educational Development: Correctness and Appropriateness of Expression, T2:88. Grades 9–12; 1942–67; cited: 1 reference.

‡Language Arts Diagnostic Probes, T2:89. Grades 3–9; 1970.

Language Arts: Minnesota High School Achievement Examinations, T2:90. Grades 7–12; 1951–70; cited: 2 reviews.

Language Arts Tests: Content Evaluation Series, T2:91. Grades 7–9; 1969; cited: 2 reviews.

Language Perception Test, T2:92. Business and industry; 1959–63.

Moray House English Tests [England], T2:95. Ages 8.5–14; 1935–70; 6 references; cited: 1 review, 8 references.

Nationwide English Composition Examination, T2:97. Grades 4–12; 1959–63.

Nationwide English Grammar Examination, T2:98. Grades 4–12; 1957–63.

New Purdue Placement Test in English, T2:99. Grades 11–16; 1931–55; 7 references; cited: 2 reviews, 14 references.

†Objective Tests in Constructive English, T2:100. Grades 7–12; 1955–64.

†Objective Tests in Punctuation, T2:101. Grades 7–12; 1955–64.

Pacific Tests of English Attainment and Skills: Pacific Test Series [Australia], T2:102. Job applicants in Papua and New Guinea; 1933–68.

Picture Story Language Test, T2:103. Ages 7–17; 1965; 1 reference; cited: 2 reviews, 2 excerpts, 5 references.

Pressey Diagnostic Tests in English Composition, T2:104. Grades 7–12; 1923–24; 7 references; cited: 2 reviews.

Purdue High School English Test, T2:105. Grades 9–12; 1931–62; 12 references; cited: 2 reviews.

RBH Spelling Test and Word Meaning Test, T2:106. Business and industry; 1949–63.

RBH Test of Language Skills, T2:107. Business and industry; 1949–63.

SRA Achievement Series: Language Arts, T2:108. Grades 2–9; 1954–69; 1 reference; cited: 3 reviews, 1 reference.

Schonell Diagnostic English Tests [Scotland], T2:110. Ages 9.5–16; 1940; 1 reference; cited: 2 reviews.

†Senior English Test [England], T2:111. Technical college entrants; 1963–71; cited: 2 reviews.

Stanford Achievement Test: High School English and Spelling Tests, T2:114. Grades 9–12; 1965–66; cited: 2 reviews.

Stanford Achievement Test: Spelling and Language Tests, T2:115. Grades 4–9; 1940–68; 1 reference; cited: 2 reviews.

Survey Tests of English Usage, T2:116. Grades 9–13; 1947–49; cited: 1 review, 1 reference.

†Teacher Education Examination Program: English Language and Literature, T2:117. College seniors preparing to teach secondary school; 1957–72.

Test of English Usage [India], T2:118. English-speaking high school and college students and adults; 1963–64.

Tests of Academic Progress: Composition, T2:119. Grades 9–12; 1964–66; cited: 2 reviews, 1 reference.

Tressler English Minimum Essentials Test, T2:121. Grades 8–12; 1932–56; cited: 2 reviews, 1 reference.

Watson English Usage and Appreciation Test [Canada], T2:123. Grades 4–8; 1966; cited: 1 review.

Writing Skills Test, T2:124. Grades 9–12; 1961; cited: 2 reviews.

Writing Test: McGraw-Hill Basic Skills System, T2:125. Grades 11–14; 1970; cited: 1 review.

LITERATURE

62. ★ACT Proficiency Examinations in American Literature. College and adults; 1975–76.

63. ★ACT Proficiency Examination in Shakespeare. College and adults; 1964–76.

64. *CLEP Subject Examination in American Literature. 1 year of college or equivalent; 1971–76; 1 review.

65. *CLEP Subject Examination in Analysis and Interpretation of Literature. 1 year of college or equivalent; 1964–76; 1 review, 1 reference.

66. *CLEP Subject Examination in English Literature. 1 year of college or equivalent; 1970–76; 1 review.

67. *College Board Achievement Test in Literature. Candidates for college entrance; 1968–76; cited: 2 references.

68. *College Placement Test in Literature. Entering college freshmen; 1968–75.

69. *Graduate Record Examinations Advanced Literature in English Test. Graduate school candidates; 1939–76; 1 review; cited: 1 review, 1 reference.

70. Look at Literature: NCTE Cooperative Test of Critical Reading and Appreciation. Grades 4–6; 1968–69; 1 excerpt, 3 references; cited: 2 reviews.

71. *UP Field Test in Literature. College; 1969–77; cited: 1 reference.

FOR OTHER TESTS, see in *Tests in Print II:*

†American Literature Anthology Tests, T2:126. High school; 1959–70.

‡Cooperative Literature Tests, T2:132. Grades 9–12; 1972–73.

†English Literature Anthology Tests, T2:133. High school; 1959–70.

English Tests for Outside Reading, T2:134. Grades 9–12; 1939.

Hollingsworth-Sanders Junior High School Literature Test, T2:136. Grades 7–8; 1962–64; cited: 1 review.

Hoskins-Sanders Literature Test, T2:137. 1, 2 semesters in grades 9–13; 1962–64; cited: 1 review.

†Iowa Tests of Educational Development: Ability to Interpret Literary Materials, T2:138. Grades 9–12; 1942–67; 2 references; cited: 1 reference.

Literature Test: National Achievement Tests, T2:139. Grades 7–12; 1937–57; cited: 2 reviews.

†Literature Tests/Objective, T2:140. High school; 1929–71.

‡Poetry Test/Objective, T2:142. Grades 7–12; 1968.

Tests of Academic Progress: Literature, T2:143. Grades 9–12; 1964–66; cited: 3 reviews, 1 reference.

‡World Literature Anthology Tests, T2:145. High school; 1964–70.

SPELLING

72. ★Diagnostic Screening Test: Spelling. Grades 1–12; 1976.

73. *Differential Aptitude Tests: Spelling. Grades 8–12 and adults; 1947–75; cited: 2 references.

74. Kansas Spelling Tests. Grades 3–8; 1962–64; 1 review.

75. ★Larsen-Hammill Test of Written Spelling. Grades 1–8; 1976.
76. ★SPAR Spelling Test [England]. Ages 7–0 to 15–11; 1976; 1 review.

FOR OTHER TESTS, see in *Tests in Print II:*

Buckingham Extension of the Ayres Spelling Scale, T2:146. Grades 2–9; [1918?]; 9 references.
‡Correct Spelling, T2:147. Grades 10–13; 1967.
Group Diagnostic Spelling Test, T2:148. Grades 9–13; 1958.
Iowa Spelling Scales, T2:149. Grades 2–8; 1921–45; 2 references.
Kelvin Measurement of Spelling Ability [Scotland], T2:151. Ages 7–12; 1933.
Lincoln Diagnostic Spelling Tests, T2:152. Grades 2–12; 1941–62; 3 references; cited: 3 reviews, 6 references.
N.B. Spelling Tests [South Africa], T2:153. Standards 1–10 for English pupils and 3–10 for Afrikaans pupils; [1962–64].
Nationwide Spelling Examination, T2:154. Grades 4–12; 1959–63.
New Iowa Spelling Scale, T2:155. Grades 2–8; 1954; cited: 1 reference.
Sanders-Fletcher Spelling Test, T2:156. Grades 9–13; 1962–63; cited: 1 review.
Spelling Errors Test, T2:158. Grades 2–8; 1948–55; cited: 1 reference.
Spelling Test for Clerical Workers, T2:159. Stenographic applicants and high school; 1947; 1 reference; cited: 1 review.
Spelling Test: McGraw-Hill Basic Skills System, T2:160. Grades 11–14; 1970; cited: 2 reviews.
Spelling Test: National Achievement Tests, T2:161. Grades 3–12; 1936–57; cited: 2 reviews.
Traxler High School Spelling Test, T2:162. Grades 9–12; 1937–55; cited: 2 reviews.

VOCABULARY

77. ★A.P.U. Vocabulary Test [England]. Ages 11–17; 1976.
78. ★Basic Word Vocabulary Test. Grades 4 and over; 1975; 2 reviews, 1 reference.
79. ★Johnson Basic Sight Vocabulary Test. Grades 1–2; 1976; 1 review.
80. Sanders-Fletcher Vocabulary Test. 1–2 semesters in grades 9–13; 1938–64; 2 reviews.
81. ★Vocabulary Comprehension Scale. Ages 2–6; 1975; 1 review.
82. Word Understanding. Grades 6–12; 1969; 1 review.

FOR OTHER TESTS, see in *Tests in Print II:*

A.C.E.R. Word Knowledge Test [Australia], T2:163. Ages 18 and over; 1933–60; cited: 1 reference.
American Literacy Test, T2:164. Adults; 1962; cited: 1 review.
Bruce Vocabulary Inventory, T2:165. Business and industry; 1959–67; cited: 2 reviews.
†Iowa Tests of Educational Development: General Vocabulary, T2:166. Grades 9–12; 1942–67.
Johnson O'Connor English Vocabulary Worksamples, T2:167. Ages 9 and over; 1934–62; 2 references; cited: 5 references.
Johnson O'Connor Vocabulary Tests, T2:168. Professionals; 1937–58.
Nationwide English Vocabulary Examination, T2:169. Grades 4–12; 1959–63.
Purdue Industrial Supervisors Word-Meaning Test, T2:170. Supervisors; 1952; 3 references; cited: 2 reviews, 2 references.
RBH Vocabulary Test, T2:171. Applicants for clerical and stenographic positions; 1948–63; cited: 1 review.
Survey Test of Vocabulary, T2:173. Grades 3–12; 1931–65; 2 references; cited: 2 reviews, 4 references.
Test of Active Vocabulary, T2:174. Grades 9–12; 1961.
‡Vocabulary Survey Test, T2:175. Grades kgn–1; 1971.
Vocabulary Test for High School Students and College Freshmen, T2:176. Grades 9–13; 1964; cited: 1 review, 1 excerpt, 1 reference.
Vocabulary Test: McGraw-Hill Basic Skills System, T2:177. Grades 11–14; 1970; cited: 1 review.
Vocabulary Test: National Achievement Tests, T2:178. Grades 3–12; 1939–57; cited: 1 review.
Wide Range Vocabulary Test, T2:179. Ages 8 and over; 1937–45; 4 references; cited: 1 review, 1 reference.
Word Clue Tests, T2:180. Grades 7–13 and adults; 1962–65.
Word Dexterity Test, T2:181. Grades 7–16; 1942–50; cited: 2 references.

FINE ARTS
ART

83. *Advanced Placement Examinations in Art. High school students desiring credit for college level courses and admission to advanced courses; 1972–77.
84. Art Vocabulary. Grades 6–12; 1969; 2 reviews.
85. ★Bryant-Schwan Design Test, Part 1. Grades kgn–12 and the mentally retarded; 1973; 1 reference.
86. *National Teacher Examinations: Art Education. College seniors and teachers; 1961–76; 1 review; cited: 1 review.
87. ★Taylor-Helmstadter Pair Comparison Scale of Aesthetic Judgement. Ages 4 and over; 1973.
88. *UP Field Test in Art History. College; 1970–77.

FOR OTHER TESTS, see in *Tests in Print II:*

Graves Design Judgment Test, T2:185. Grades 7–16 and adults; 1948; 22 references; cited: 2 reviews, 1 excerpt, 2 references.
Horn Art Aptitude Inventory, T2:186. Grades 12–16 and adults; 1939–53; cited: 2 reviews, 1 reference.
Knauber Art Ability Test, T2:187. Grades 7–16; 1932–35; 2 references; cited: 2 reviews, 4 references.
Knauber Art Vocabulary Test, T2:188. Grades 7–16; 1932–35; cited: 3 reviews, 6 references.
Meier Art Tests, T2:189. Grades 7–16 and adults; 1929–63; 5 references; cited: 5 reviews, 1 excerpt, 43 references.
‡Teacher Education Examination Program: Art Education, T2:191. College seniors preparing to teach secondary school; 1971–72.

MUSIC

89. ★ACER & University of Melbourne Music Evaluation Kit [Australia]. Beginning of secondary school; 1976.
90. *Advanced Placement Examination in Music. High school students desiring credit for college level courses and admission to advanced courses; 1971–77.
91. ★Australian Test for Advanced Music Studies [Australia]. Tertiary education entrance level; 1974; 1 review.
92. Belwin-Mills Singing Achievement Test. Grades 5–16; 1971; 1 review.
93. ★Farnum Music Test. Grades 4–9; 1969–70; 2 reviews.
94. ★Farnum String Scale: A Performance Scale for All String Instruments. Grades 7–12; 1969; 1 review.
95. *Graduate Record Examinations Advanced Music Test. Graduate school candidates; 1951–76; cited: 1 review.
96. ★Indiana-Oregon Music Discrimination Test. Grades 5 through graduate school; 1934–75; 2 reviews, 16 references.
97. Iowa Tests of Music Literacy. Grades 4–12; 1970–71; 1 review, 16 references; cited: 7 references.
98. Musical Aptitude Profile. Grades 4–12; 1965; 25 references; cited: 2 reviews, 44 references.
99. *National Teacher Examinations: Music Education. College seniors and teachers; 1957–76; cited: 3 reviews.
100. *UP Field Test in Music. College; 1969–77; cited: 1 review.

FOR OTHER TESTS, see in *Tests in Print II:*

Aliferis-Stecklein Music Achievement Tests, T2:194. Music students college level entrance and over; 1954–62; 5 references; cited: 3 reviews, 10 references.
‡Elementary Rhythm and Pitch Test, T2:196. Grades 4–8; 1937–70; 1 reference.
Gretsch-Tilson Musical Aptitude Test, T2:198. Grades 4–12; 1938; cited: 2 references.
Jones Music Recognition Test, T2:200. Grades 4–16; 1949; cited: 1 review.
Knuth Achievement Tests in Music, T2:201. Grades 3–12; 1936–68; 5 references; cited: 3 reviews, 2 references.
Kwalwasser-Dykema Music Tests, T2:202. Grades 4–16 and adults; 1930; 25 references; cited: 1 review, 29 references.

Kwalwasser Music Talent Test, T2:203. Grades 4–16 and adults; 1953; 4 references; cited: 2 reviews.
Kwalwasser-Ruch Test of Musical Accomplishment, T2:204. Grades 4–12; 1924–27; 6 references; cited: 2 reviews, 1 reference.
Kwalwasser Test of Music Information and Appreciation, T2:205. High school and college; 1927; 2 references; cited: 2 reviews, 1 reference.
Measures of Musical Abilities [England], T2:206. Ages 7–14; 1966; 3 references; cited: 2 reviews, 2 excerpts, 13 references.
Music Achievement Tests, T2:207. Grades 3–12; 1967–70; 5 references; cited: 1 review, 5 references.
‡Music Aptitude Test, T2:208. Grades 4–8; 1948–55; 2 references.
Seashore Measures of Musical Talents, T2:211. Grades 4–16 and adults; 1919–60; 97 references; cited: 7 reviews, 144 references.
Snyder Knuth Music Achievement Test, T2:212. Elementary education and music majors; 1968; cited: 2 reviews, 3 references.
†Teacher Education Examination Program: Music Education, T2:213. College seniors preparing to teach secondary school; 1958–72.
Test of Musicality, T2:214. Grades 4–12; 1942–58; 11 references; cited: 2 reviews, 1 reference.
Watkins-Farnum Performance Scale, T2:216. Music students; 1942–62; 4 references; cited: 1 review, 2 references.
Wing Standardised Tests of Musical Intelligence [England], T2:217. Ages 8 and over; 1939–61; 14 references; cited: 3 reviews, 16 references.

FOREIGN LANGUAGES

101. *Graduate School Foreign Language Testing Program. Graduate level degree candidates required to demonstrate foreign language reading proficiency; 1963–76; cited: 3 references.

FOR OTHER TESTS, see in *Tests in Print II:*
Foreign Language Prognosis Test, T2:218. Grades 8–9; 1930–59; cited: 3 reviews, 7 references.
Iowa Placement Examinations: Foreign Language Aptitude, T2:220. Grades 12–13; 1925–44; 9 references; cited: 1 review, 7 references.
Modern Language Aptitude Test, T2:221. Grades 9 and over; 1959; 34 references; cited: 2 reviews, 4 excerpts, 10 references.
Modern Language Aptitude Test—Elementary, T2:222. Grades 3–6; 1960–67; 1 reference; cited: 1 review.
Pimsleur Language Aptitude Battery, T2:223. Grades 6–12; 1966–67; 5 references; cited: 1 review, 1 excerpt, 5 references.

ARABIC

FOR A TEST, see in *Tests in Print II:*
†First Year Arabic Final Examination, T2:224. 1 year college; 1964–72.

CHINESE

FOR A TEST, see in *Tests in Print II:*
Harvard-MLA Tests of Chinese Language Proficiency, T2:225. College and adults; 1959–65.

ENGLISH

102. English Placement Test. Entrants to courses in English as a second language; 1972; 1 review.
103. Examination in Structure (English as a Foreign Language). Non-native speakers of English; 1947; 1 review; cited: 1 reference.
104. ★Language Proficiency Tests in English [South Africa]. Black pupils in forms IV, V; 1974–75.
105. Michigan Test of Aural Comprehension. College applicants from non-English language countries; 1969–72; 1 review.
106. *Michigan Test of English Language Proficiency. College applicants from non-English language countries; 1961–77; 1 review, 5 references; cited: 1 review, 3 references.
107. ★Scholastic Achievement Test for English Lower Standards 2 and 3. Standards 2–3; 1973–74.
108. ★Scholastic Achievement Test for English Lower Standards 9 and 10 [South Africa]. Standards 9–10; 1973.

109. ★Scholastic Achievement Test for English Second Language Standard 1 [South Africa]. Standard 1; 1974–75.
110. *Test of English as a Foreign Language. College applicants from non-English language countries; 1964–77; 15 references; cited: 2 reviews, 14 references.
111. ★Tests of Proficiency in English. Non-native speakers of English ages 7–11; 1973; 1 review.

FOR OTHER TESTS, see in *Tests in Print II:*
Comprehensive English Language Test for Speakers of English as a Second Language, T2:226. Non-native speakers of English; 1970; cited: 1 review.
Diagnostic Test for Students of English as a Second Language, T2:227. Applicants from non-English language countries for admission to American colleges; 1953; 1 reference; cited: 2 reviews.
English Knowledge and Comprehensive Test [India], T2:228. High school; 1965.
†English Usage Test for Non-Native Speakers of English, T2:230. Non-native speakers of English; 1955–72.
Oral Rating Form for Rating Language Proficiency in Speaking and Understanding English, T2:234. Non-native speakers of English; 1959–67.
‡Test A/65: English Language Achievement Test [South Africa], T2:235. Matriculants and higher; [1956?].
Test of Aural Perception in English for Japanese Students, T2:236. Japanese students in American colleges; 1950; 1 reference.
Test of Aural Perception in English for Latin-American Students, T2:237. Latin-American students of English; 1947–57; 2 references.
†Vocabulary and Reading Test for Students of English as a Second Language, T2:239. Non-native speakers of English; 1960–72.

FRENCH

112. ★Advanced Placement Examination in French Language, Level 3. High school students desiring credit for college level courses and admission to advanced courses; 1971–77; 1 review.
113. *Advanced Placement Examination in French Literature, Level 3. High school students desiring credit for college level courses and admission to advanced courses; 1954–77; 2 reviews, 3 references; cited: 4 references.
114. ★Basic Proficiency in French Tests. Ages 14–16; 1976; 1 review.
115. ★CLEP Subject Examination in College French, Levels 1 and 2. 1–2 years of college or equivalent; 1975–76; 1 review.
116. *College Board Achievement Test in French Reading. Candidates for college entrance with 2–4 years high school French; 1901–76; 1 review; cited: 1 review, 13 references.
117. *College Placement Test in French Listening Comprehension. Entering college freshmen; 1962–75; 1 reference; cited: 1 reference.
118. *College Placement Test in French Listening-Reading. Entering college freshmen; 1971–75.
119. *College Placement Test in French Reading. Entering college freshmen; 1962–75; 1 reference; cited: 1 review, 1 reference.
120. ★French Comprehension Tests. Grades kgn–5; 1975–76; 1 excerpt, 1 reference.
121. *Graduate Record Examinations Advanced French Test. Graduate school candidates; 1939–76; 2 reviews; cited: 2 reviews.
122. *Graduate School Foreign Language Test: French. Graduate level degree candidates required to demonstrate reading proficiency in French; 1963–76; 1 review; cited: 1 review, 3 references.
123. MLA-Cooperative Foreign Language Tests: French. 1–4 years high school or 2 and 4 semesters college; 1963–65; 1 review, 1 reference; cited: 1 review, 1 excerpt, 6 references.
124. *National Teacher Examinations: French. College seniors and teachers; 1970–76; 1 review.
125. *UP Field Test in French. College; 1969–77; cited: 1 review.

FOR OTHER TESTS, see in *Tests in Print II:*

Baltimore County French Test, T2:241. 1 year high school; 1962; cited: 2 reviews, 1 reference.

†Canadian Achievement Test in French [Canada], T2:242. Grade 10; 1961–68; cited: 1 review, 2 references.

‡College Board Achievement Test in French Listening-Reading, T2:243. Candidates for college entrance with 2–4 years high school French; 1971–73.

Cooperative French Listening Comprehension Test, T2:248. 2–5 semesters high school or college; 1955; 4 references; cited: 2 reviews, 1 reference.

First Year French Test, T2:249. High school and college; 1956–68; cited: 2 reviews.

Ford-Hicks French Grammar Completion Tests [Canada], T2:250. High school; 1944.

French I and II: Achievement Examinations for Secondary Schools, T2:251. 1–2 years high school; 1951–60; cited: 2 reviews.

Iowa Placement Examinations: French Training, T2:254. Grades 12–13; 1925–26; 3 references; cited: 1 review, 4 references.

MLA Cooperative Foreign Language Proficiency Tests: French, T2:255. French majors and advanced students in college; 1960–68; 2 references; cited: 4 reviews, 12 references.

Pimsleur French Proficiency Tests, T2:258. Grades 7–16; 1967; cited: 2 reviews, 1 excerpt.

Second Year French Test, T2:259. High school and college; 1956–68; cited: 3 reviews.

†Teacher Education Examination Program: French, T2:260. College seniors preparing to teach secondary school; 1957–72.

GERMAN

126. *Advanced Placement Examination in German Literature, Level 3. High school students desiring credit for college level courses and admission to advanced courses; 1954–77; 1 review, 1 reference; cited: 1 review, 9 references.

127. ★CLEP Subject Examination in College German, Levels 1 and 2. 1–2 years of college or equivalent; 1975–76; 2 reviews.

128. *College Board Achievement Test in German Reading. Candidates for college entrance with 2–4 years high school German; 1901–76; 1 review; cited: 3 reviews, 6 references.

129. *College Placement Test in German Listening Comprehension. Entering college freshmen; 1962–75; 1 reference; cited: 2 reviews, 2 references.

130. *College Placement Test in German Listening-Reading. Entering college freshmen; 1971–75; 1 reference.

131. *College Placement Test in German Reading. Entering college freshmen; 1962–75; cited: 3 reviews, 2 references.

132. *Graduate Record Examinations Advanced German Test. Graduate school candidates; 1939–76; 1 review; cited: 1 reference.

133. *Graduate School Foreign Language Test: German. Graduate level degree candidates required to demonstrate reading proficiency in German; 1963–76; 1 review; cited: 1 review, 3 references.

134. MLA-Cooperative Foreign Language Tests: German. 1–4 years high school or 2 and 4 semesters college; 1963–65; 1 review, 1 reference; cited: 1 review, 1 excerpt, 3 references.

135. *National German Examination for High School Students. 2–4 years high school; 1960–76; cited: 2 reviews.

136. *National Teacher Examinations: German. College seniors and teachers; 1970–76; 1 review.

137. *UP Field Test in German. College; 1969–77.

FOR OTHER TESTS, see in *Tests in Print II:*

‡College Board Achievement Test in German Listening-Reading, T2:263. Candidates for college entrance with 2–4 years high school German; 1971–73.

German I and II: Achievement Examinations for Secondary Schools, T2:268. 1–2 years high school; 1951–60; cited: 1 review.

MLA Cooperative Foreign Language Proficiency Tests: German, T2:271. German majors and advanced students in college; 1960–68; 1 reference; cited: 2 reviews, 11 references.

Pimsleur German Proficiency Tests, T2:275. Grades 7–16; 1967; cited: 2 reviews, 1 excerpt.

GREEK

138. *College Placement Test in Greek Reading. Entering college freshmen; 1962–75; cited: 1 review.

HEBREW

139. *College Board Achievement Test in Hebrew. Candidates for college entrance with 2–4 years high school Hebrew; 1961–76.

140. *College Placement Test in Hebrew Reading. Entering college freshmen; 1962–75.

FOR OTHER TESTS, see in *Tests in Print II:*

‡Achievement Test—Hebrew Language, T2:278. Grades 5–7; 1973.

NCRI Achievement Tests in Hebrew, T2:281. Grades 5–9; 1965–67; 1 reference.

Test on the Fundamentals of Hebrew, T2:282. Grades 2–7; 1955–59.

ITALIAN

141. *College Placement Test in Italian Listening Comprehension. Entering college freshmen; 1962–75; cited: 1 review.

142. *College Placement Test in Italian Listening-Reading. Entering college freshmen; 1971–75.

143. *College Placement Test in Italian Reading. Entering college freshmen; 1962–75; cited: 1 review.

FOR OTHER TESTS, see in *Tests in Print II:*

MLA Cooperative Foreign Language Proficiency Tests: Italian, T2:286. Italian majors and advanced students in college; 1961–68; cited: 1 review, 5 references.

MLA-Cooperative Foreign Language Tests: Italian, T2:287. 1–4 years high school or 1–2 years college; 1963–65; cited: 1 review.

LATIN

144. *Advanced Placement Examination in Classics. High school students desiring credit for college level courses and admission to advanced courses; 1954–77; 3 references.

145. *College Board Achievement Test in Latin. Candidates for college entrance with 2–4 years high school Latin; 1901–76; cited: 2 reviews, 3 references.

146. *College Placement Test in Latin Reading. Entering college freshmen; 1962–75; cited: 2 reviews.

FOR OTHER TESTS, see in *Tests in Print II:*

Cooperative Latin Test: Elementary and Advanced Levels, T2:291. Grades 9–16; 1932–41; 2 references; cited: 4 reviews, 1 reference.

Emporia First Year Latin Test, T2:292. 1 year high school; 1962–64.

Emporia Second Year Latin Test, T2:293. 2 years high school; 1962–64.

Latin I and II: Achievmeent Examinations for Secondary Schools, T2:294. 1–2 years high school; 1951–59.

RUSSIAN

147. *College Board Achievement Test in Russian Reading. Candidates for college entrance with 2–4 years high school Russian; 1961–76; 1 review.

148. *College Placement Test in Russian Listening Comprehension. Entering college freshmen; 1962–75; cited: 1 reference.

149. *College Placement Test in Russian Listening-Reading. Entering college freshmen; 1971–75.

150. *College Placement Test in Russian Reading. Entering college freshmen; 1962–75.

151. *Graduate School Foreign Language Test: Russian. Graduate level degree candidates required to demonstrate reading proficiency in Russian; 1963–76; 1 review; cited: 4 references.

152. MLA-Cooperative Foreign Language Tests: Russian. 1–4 years high school or 2 and 4 semesters college; 1963–65; 1 review; cited: 2 excerpts, 3 references.

For OTHER TESTS, see in *Tests in Print II*:

‡College Board Achievement Test in Russian Listening-Reading, T2:295. Candidates for college entrance with 2–4 years high school Russian; 1971–73.

MLA Cooperative Foreign Language Proficiency Tests: Russian, T2:300. Russian majors and advanced students in college; 1960–68; cited: 1 review, 6 references.

SPANISH

153. *Advanced Placement Examinations in Spanish. High school students desiring credit for college level courses and admission to advanced courses; 1954–77; 1 review, 1 reference; cited: 3 references.

154. ★Austin Spanish Articulation Test. Ages 3–12; 1974; 1 review, 1 excerpt, 1 reference.

155. Baltimore County Spanish Test. 1 year high school; 1962; 1 review; cited: 1 review.

156. ★Bilingual Syntax Measure. Bilingual children grades kgn–2; 1973–76; 2 reviews, 1 excerpt, 4 references.

157. ★CLEP Subject Examination in College Spanish, Levels 1 and 2. 1–2 years of college or equivalent; 1975–76.

158. *College Board Achievement Test in Spanish Reading. Candidates for college entrance with 2–4 years high school Spanish; 1902–76; cited: 5 references.

159. *College Placement Test in Spanish Listening Comprehension. Entering college freshmen; 1962–75; 1 reference; cited: 2 references.

160. *College Placement Test in Spanish Listening-Reading. Entering college freshmen; 1971–75.

161. *College Placement Test in Spanish Reading. Entering college freshmen; 1962–75; 1 reference; cited: 1 reference.

162. ★Crane Oral Dominance Test: Spanish/English. Ages 4–8; 1976; 2 excerpts, 1 reference.

163. ★Dos Amigos Verbal Language Scales. Ages 5-0 to 13-5; 1973–74; 1 excerpt, 2 references.

164. First Year Spanish Test. High school and college; 1947–68; 1 review.

165. *Graduate Record Examinations Advanced Spanish Test. Graduate school candidates; 1946–76; 1 review; cited: 1 review.

166. *Graduate School Foreign Language Test: Spanish. Graduate level degree candidates required to demonstrate reading proficiency in Spanish; 1963–76; cited: 1 review, 3 references.

167. ★James Language Dominance Test. Mexican-Americans ages 5–6; 1974; 1 review, 1 excerpt, 1 reference.

168. *National Spanish Examination. 1–5 years junior high school and high school; 1957–76; 2 references; cited: 1 review, 9 references.

169. *National Teacher Examinations: Spanish. College seniors and teachers; 1970–76; 1 review.

170. ★SOBER-Español. Grades kgn–3; 1975; 2 excerpts, 2 references.

171. ★Screening Test of Spanish Grammar. Spanish-speaking children ages 3–6; 1973; 1 review, 2 excerpts, 3 references.

172. ★Spanish/English Language Performance Screening. Ages 4–5; 1976; 1 review.

173. *UP Field Test in Spanish. College; 1969–77.

For OTHER TESTS, see in *Tests in Print II*:

‡College Board Achievement Test in Spanish Listening-Reading, T2:304. Candidates for college entrance with 2–4 years high school Spanish; 1971–73.

Furness Test of Aural Comprehension in Spanish, T2:310. 1–3 years high school or 1–2 years college; 1945–51; 1 reference; cited: 2 reviews.

Iowa Placement Examinations: Spanish Training, T2:313. Grades 12–13; 1925–26; 3 references; cited: 1 review, 2 references.

MLA Cooperative Foreign Language Proficiency Tests: Spanish, T2:314. Spanish majors and advanced students in college; 1960–68; 1 reference; cited: 2 reviews, 9 references.

MLA-Cooperative Foreign Language Tests: Spanish, T2:315.

1–4 years high school or 1–2 years college; 1963–65; cited: 1 review, 2 references.

Pimsleur Spanish Proficiency Tests, T2:318. Grades 7–16; 1967; cited: 1 review, 1 excerpt.

Second Year Spanish Test, T2:319. High school and college; 1953–68.

Spanish I and II: Achievement Examinations for Secondary Schools, T2:320. 1–2 years high school; 1951–55.

†Teacher Education Examination Program: Spanish, T2:321. College seniors preparing to teach secondary school; 1957–72.

INTELLIGENCE

GROUP

174. ★ACER Test of Learning Ability [Australia]. Grades 4 and 6; 1976.

175. ★AH2/AH3 [England]. Ages 9 and over; 1974–75; 1 reference.

176. BITCH Test (Black Intelligence Test of Cultural Homogeneity). Adolescents and adults; 1972; 2 reviews, 8 references.

177. ★Barranquilla Rapid Survey Intelligence Test. Spanish-speaking children (grades 3–6) and adults (educational levels grades 3–6); 1957–58; 1 review, 3 references.

178. Boehm Test of Basic Concepts. Grades kgn–2; 1967–71; 1 excerpt, 22 references; cited: 2 reviews, 4 excerpts, 2 references.

179. California Short-Form Test of Mental Maturity. Grades kgn–16 and adults; 1938–65; 28 references; cited: 2 reviews, 1 excerpt, 95 references.

180. *Canadian Cognitive Abilities Test [Canada]. Grades kgn–9; 1954–74; 2 references.

181. *Cognitive Abilities Test. Grades kgn–12; 1954–74; 2 reviews, 12 references; cited: 2 reviews, 1 excerpt.

182. *College Board Scholastic Aptitude Test and Test of Standard Written English. Candidates for college entrance; 1926–77; 215 references; cited: 6 reviews, 567 references.

183. Cooperative School and College Ability Tests, Series II. Grades 4–14; 1955–73; 2 reviews, 48 references; cited: 5 reviews, 3 excerpts, 319 references.

184. Culture Fair Intelligence Test. Ages 4 and over (mentally retarded, average, and superior intelligence); 1933–73; 38 references; cited: 5 reviews, 89 references.

185. *Differential Aptitude Tests: Abstract Reasoning. Grades 8–12 and adults; 1947–75; 3 references; cited: 7 references.

186. *Differential Aptitude Tests: Verbal Reasoning. Grades 8–12 and adults; 1947–75; cited: 12 references.

187. Goodenough-Harris Drawing Test. Ages 3–15; 1926–63; 87 references; cited: 3 reviews, 6 excerpts, 388 references.

188. *Graduate Record Examinations Aptitude Test. Graduate school candidates; 1949–76; 45 references; cited: 5 reviews, 84 references.

189. ★Harding Skyscraper [Australia]. Ages 17 and over with intelligence level in top 1% of population; 1973–75; 2 references.

190. *Henmon-Nelson Tests of Mental Ability. Grades kgn–12; 1931–74; 1 review, 14 references; cited: 8 reviews, 3 excerpts, 102 references.

191. ★Learning Ability Profile. Grades 5–16 and adults; 1975–76.

192. *Miller Analogies Test. Candidates for graduate school; 1926–75; 31 references; cited: 6 reviews, 142 references.

193. *Minnesota Scholastic Aptitude Test. High school and college; 1969–72; 1 review, 10 references; cited: 31 references.

194. ★NB Group Tests [South Africa]. "Coloured pupils" in standards 4–10; 1966–74.

195. *NIIP Group Test 36 [England]. Ages 10–13; 1937–74; cited: 4 references.

196. OISE Picture Reasoning Test: Primary

[Canada]. Grades 1–2; 1969–70; 1 review.

197. Oral Verbal Intelligence Test [England]. Ages 7.5–14; 1973; 1 review.

198. Otis-Lennon Mental Ability Test. Grades kgn–12; 1936–70; 35 references; cited: 1 review, 2 excerpts, 16 references.

199. *Preliminary Scholastic Aptitude Test/National Merit Scholarship Qualifying Test. Grades 10–12; 1959–76; 2 reviews, 15 references; cited: 1 review, 16 references.

200. Progressive Matrices [England]. Ages 5 and over; 1938–65; 190 references; cited: 7 reviews, 509 references.

201. ★Ross Test of High Cognitive Processes. Grades 4–6; 1976.

202. *Short Form Test of Academic Aptitude. Grades 1.5–12; 1936–74; 1 review, 1 excerpt, 9 references.

203. *Test of Perceptual Organization. "Normals and psychiatric patients ages 12 and over"; 1967–70; 2 reviews, 1 excerpt; cited: 1 reference.

204. *UP Aptitude Test. Grades 15–16; 1969–77; 1 reference.

205. WLW Employment Inventory III. Job applicants; 1954–72; 1 review.

FOR OTHER TESTS, see in *Tests in Print II:*

A.C.E.R. Advanced Test B40 [Australia], T2:323. Ages 13 and over; 1940–66; 6 references; cited: 1 review, 7 references.

†A.C.E.R. Advanced Tests AL and AQ [Australia], T2:324. College and superior adults; 1953–73; 3 references; cited: 1 review.

†A.C.E.R. Higher Tests [Australia], T2:325. Ages 13 and over; 1944–73; 1 reference; cited: 1 review, 1 reference.

A.C.E.R. Intermediate Test A [Australia], T2:326. Ages 10–13; 1938–61.

†A.C.E.R. Intermediate Tests C and D, T2:327. Ages 10–13; 1939–72; 1 reference; cited: 1 review, 2 references.

A.C.E.R. Junior Non-Verbal Test [Australia], T2:328. Ages 8.5–11; 1949–53; 3 references; cited: 1 review, 1 reference.

A.C.E.R. Junior Test A [Australia], T2:329. Ages 8.5–11; 1946–58; cited: 1 review.

A.C.E.R. Lower Grades General Ability Scale [Australia], T2:330. Ages 6.6 to 9.1; 1962–66; 1 reference.

†AH4, AH5, and AH6 Tests [England], T2:331. Ages 10 and over; 1955–73; 20 references; cited: 4 reviews, 23 references.

APT Performance Test, T2:332. Adults; 1954–57; 1 reference.

Academic Alterness "AA," T2:334. Adults; 1957–66; cited: 1 review.

Academic Aptitude Test: Non-Verbal Intelligence: Acorn National Aptitude Tests, T2:335. Grades 7–16 and adults; 1943–57; cited: 1 review.

Academic Aptitude Test: Verbal Intelligence: Acorn National Aptitude Tests, T2:336. Grades 7–16 and adults; 1943–52; cited: 2 reviews.

Adaptability Test, T2:337. Job applicants; 1942–67; 3 references; cited: 3 reviews, 22 references.

Advanced Test N [Australia], T2:338. Ages 15 and over; 1951–52; cited: 2 reviews.

American School Intelligence Test, T2:339. Grades kgn–12; 1961–63; cited: 2 reviews, 1 reference.

†Analysis of Learning Potential, T2:340. Grades 1–12; 1970–71; 2 references; cited: 2 reviews.

Analysis of Relationships, T2:341. Grades 12–16 and industry; 1960; 1 reference; cited: 2 reviews, 2 references.

Army Alpha Examination: First Nebraska Revision, T2:341A. Grades 6–16 and adults; 1937–40; cited: 2 reviews, 5 references.

Army General Classification Test, First Civilian Edition, T2:342. Grades 9–16 and adults; 1940–60; 27 references; cited: 3 reviews, 1 excerpt, 51 references.

†Business Test, T2:345. Clerical workers; 1952–71; cited: 2 reviews.

CGA Mental Ability Tests [Canada], T2:346. Grades 6–12; 1957–68.

‡C.P. 66 Test [England], T2:347. Ages 13 and over; 1966; 1 reference.

California Test of Mental Maturity, T2:349. Grades kgn–16 and adults; 1936–65; 72 references; cited: 10 reviews, 4 excerpts, 205 references.

Canadian Academic Aptitude Test [Canada], T2:350. Grades 8.5–9.0; 1959–68; cited: 2 reviews, 3 references.

Canadian Lorge-Thorndike Intelligence Tests [Canada], T2:352. Grades 3–9; 1954–67.

‡Canadian Scholastic Aptitude Test [Canada], T2:353. Candidates for college entrance; 1968–73; 6 references.

Cattell Intelligence Tests [England], T2:354. Mental ages 4 and over; 1930–52; 3 references; cited: 2 reviews, 12 references.

Chicago Non-Verbal Examination, T2:355. Ages 6 and over; 1936–54; 6 references; cited: 4 reviews, 10 references.

College Qualification Tests, T2:358. Candidates for college entrance; 1955–61; 15 references; cited: 5 reviews, 35 references.

Concept Mastery Test, T2:359. Grades 15–16 and graduate students and applicants for executive and research positions; 1956; 28 references; cited: 2 reviews, 12 references.

Cooperative Academic Ability Test, T2:360. Superior grade 12 students; 1963–64; cited: 2 reviews, 1 excerpt, 3 references.

†Cotswold Junior Ability Tests [Scotland], T2:362. Ages 8.5–10.5; 1949–69.

†Cotswold Measurement of Ability [Scotland], T2:363. Ages 10–12; 1947–70; 1 reference; cited: 1 review.

D48 Test, T2:365–6. Grades 5 and over; 1963; 13 references; cited: 2 reviews, 3 references.

Deeside Non-Verbal Reasoning Test [England], T2:367. Ages 10–12; 1961–63.

Deeside Picture Puzzles [England], T2:368. Ages 6.5–8.5; 1956–58; cited: 2 reviews.

Dennis Test of Scholastic Aptitude, T2:369. Grades 4–8; 1961–63.

Detroit General Intelligence Examination, T2:370. Grades 7–12; 1938–54.

Doppelt Mathematical Reasoning Test, T2:371. Grades 16–17 and employees; 1954–68; cited: 1 review, 4 references.

Draw-A-Man Test for Indian Children [India], T2:372. Ages 6–10; 1956–66; 1 reference; cited: 1 excerpt, 4 references.

Essential Intelligence Test [Scotland], T2:373. Ages 8–12; 1940–52; 7 references; cited: 2 reviews.

Executive Employment Review, T2:374. Applicants for executive level positions; 1964–70.

Figure Reasoning Test [England], T2:375. Ages 10 and over; 1949–62; 1 reference; cited: 3 reviews, 1 excerpt, 1 reference.

†Fundamental Achievement Series, T2:376–7. Semiliterate job applicants and employees; 1968–70; cited: 1 review, 1 excerpt.

†General Mental Ability Test, T2:378. Job applicants; 1960–72.

General Verbal Practice Test G1–G3 [England], T2:379. Ages 10–11; 1954–61.

†Gilliland Learning Potential Examination, T2:380. Ages 6 and over; 1966–71; cited: 2 reviews.

‡Group Test for Indian South Africans [South Africa], T2:383. Standards 4–10; 1967–71.

Group Test 75 [England], T2:385. Ages 12–13; 1957; 1 reference.

Group Test 91 [England], T2:386. Industrial applicants; 1949–68; 1 reference.

‡Group Test 95 [England], T2:386A. Ages 14 and over; [1972].

†Group Test of Learning Capacity: Dominion Tests [Canada], T2:387. Grades kgn–1, 4–12 and adults; 1934–70; 3 references; cited: 4 reviews, 3 references.

Group Tests 70 and 70B [England], T2:388. Ages 15 and over; 1939–70; 9 references; cited: 1 review, 10 references.

Group Tests 72 and 73 [England], T2:389. Industrial applicants; 1949–68; cited: 1 reference.

Group Tests 90A and 90B [England], T2:390. Ages 15 and over; 1950–70; 2 references; cited: 1 review, 1 reference.

Illinois Index of Scholastic Aptitude, T2:392. Grades 9–12; 1966; cited: 2 reviews.

Inventory No. 2, T2:393. Ages 16 and over; 1956.

Junior Scholastic Aptitude Test, T2:394. Grades 7–9; 1935–60; 4 references; cited: 1 review, 15 references.

Kelvin Measurement of Ability in Infant Classes [Scotland], T2:395. Ages 5–8; 1935; 1 reference.

Kelvin Measurement of Mental Ability [Scotland], T2:396. Ages 8–12; 1933.

Kingston Test of Intelligence [England], T2:397. Ages 10–12; 1953–63; cited: 2 reviews.

†Kuhlmann-Anderson Test, T2:398. Grades kgn–12; 1927–67; 53 references; cited: 10 reviews, 1 excerpt, 76 references.

Kuhlmann-Finch Tests, T2:399. Grades 1–12; 1951–60; 6 references; cited: 3 reviews, 3 references.

Lorge-Thorndike Intelligence Tests, T2:400. Grades kgn–13; 1954–66; 38 references; cited: 4 reviews, 112 references.

Lorge-Thorndike Intelligence Tests, College Edition, T2:401. Grades 12–13; 1954–66; cited: 3 reviews.

†Mental Alertness: Tests A/1 and A/2 [South Africa], T2:402. Job applicants with 9 or more years of education; 1945–68.

Mill Hill Vocabulary Scale [England], T2:403. Ages 4 and over; 1943–58; 32 references; cited: 2 reviews, 26 references.

Mitchell Vocabulary Test [England], T2:406. Adults; 1958; cited: 1 reference.

Modified Alpha Examination Form 9, T2:407. Grades 7–12 and adults; 1941–51; 2 references; cited: 1 review, 8 references.

Moray House Picture Tests [England], T2:408. Ages 6.5–8.5; 1944–61; 7 references; cited: 2 reviews, 5 references.

†Moray House Verbal Reasoning Tests [England], T2:409. Ages 8.5 and over; 1930–72; 18 references; cited: 2 reviews, 20 references.

N.B. Group Tests [South Africa], T2:410. Ages 5–8; 1958.
New South African Group Test [South Africa], T2:411. Ages 8–17; 1931–65; 1 reference; cited: 3 references.
‡Non-Language Test of Verbal Intelligence [India], T2:412. Class 8 (ages 11–13); 1968; 2 references.
Non-Readers Intelligence Test [England], T2:413. Ages 6–8; 1964.
Non-Verbal Reasoning Test, T2:414. Job applicants and industrial employees; 1961; 2 references; cited: 2 reviews.
Non-Verbal Tests [England], T2:415. Ages 8–15; 1947–65; 12 references; cited: 4 reviews, 6 references.
Northumberland Mental Tests [England], T2:416. Ages 10–12.5; 1922; 10 references.
Ohio Penal Classification Test, T2:418. Penal institutions; 1952–54; 2 references; cited: 1 review.
†Ohio State University Psychological Test, T2:419. Grades 9–16 and adults; 1919–68; 89 references; cited: 6 reviews, 80 references.
Oregon Academic Ranking Test, T2:420. Gifted children grades 3–7; 1965; cited: 1 review.
O'Rourke General Classification Test, T2:421. Grades 12–13 and adults; 1927–42; 2 references; cited: 1 review, 3 references.
"Orton" Intelligence Test, No. 4 [Scotland], T2:422. Ages 10–14; 1931.
Otis Employment Tests, T2:423. Applicants for employment; 1943; 11 references.
Otis Quick-Scoring Mental Ability Tests, T2:425. Grades 1–16; 1936–54; 136 references; cited: 7 reviews, 2 excerpts, 66 references.
Otis Self-Administering Tests of Mental Ability, T2:426. Grades 4–16; 1922–29; 139 references; cited: 1 review, 123 references.
Pacific Reasoning Series Tests [Australia], T2:427. Job applicants in Papua New Guinea; 1962–68; 1 reference.
Pattern Perception Test [England], T2:428. Ages 6 and over; 1943; 1 reference; cited: 1 review, 3 references.
Performance Alertness "PA" (With Pictures), T2:429. Adults; 1961–66; cited: 1 review.
Personal Classification Test, T2:430. Business and industry; 1953–59.
Personnel Research Institute Classification Test, T2:431. Adults; 1943–54; 1 reference; cited: 2 reviews, 2 references.
Personnel Research Institute Factory Series Test, T2:432. Applicants for routine industrial positions; 1950–56; cited: 1 review.
Personnel Tests for Industry, T2:433. Trade school and adults; 1945–69; 5 references; cited: 4 reviews, 4 references.
Picture Test A [England], T2:434. Ages 7·0 to 8·1; 1955–70; cited: 2 reviews.
†Pintner-Cunningham Primary Test [England], T2:435. Grades kgn–2; 1923–66; 41 references; cited: 1 excerpt.
‡Preschool and Early Primary Skill Survey, T2:437. Ages 3·3 to 7·2; 1971.
Pressey Classification and Verifying Tests, T2:438. Grades 1–12 and adults; 1922–58; 15 references; cited: 1 review, 11 references.
Proverbs Test, T2:440. Grades 5–16 and adults; 1954–56; 33 references; cited: 2 reviews, 4 references.
Public School Primary Intelligence Test, T2:441. Grades 2–4; 1924–56; 4 references; cited: 1 review.
Purdue Non-Language Personnel Test, T2:442. Business and industry; 1957–69; 1 reference; cited: 2 reviews.
Quantitative Evaluative Device, T2:443. Entering graduate students; 1959–62; 1 reference; cited: 1 reference.
RBH Test of Learning Ability, T2:444. Business and industry; 1947–63; 1 reference; cited: 1 review, 4 references.
RBH Test of Non-Verbal Reasoning, T2:445. Business and industry; 1948–63; cited: 1 review, 4 references.
Reasoning Tests for Higher Levels of Intelligence [Scotland], T2:446. College entrants; 1954; 7 references; cited: 1 review.
Revised Beta Examination, T2:447. Ages 16–59; 1931–57; 29 references; cited: 5 reviews, 36 references.
Ryburn Group Intelligence Tests [Scotland], T2:448. Ages 6.5–15.5; [1936–40].
†SRA Nonverbal Form, T2:449. Ages 12 and over; 1946–73; 12 references; cited: 1 review, 1 excerpt.
†SRA Pictorial Reasoning Test, T2:450. Ages 14 and over; 1966–73; cited: 2 reviews, 1 excerpt.
†SRA Short Test of Educational Ability, T2:451. Grades kgn–12; 1966–72; 1 reference; cited: 2 reviews, 1 excerpt, 2 references.
†SRA Verbal Form, T2:452. Grades 7–16 and adults; 1946–73; 1 reference; citde: 2 reviews, 2 references.
Safran Culture Reduced Intelligence Test [Canada], T2:453. Grades 1 and over; 1960–69; 1 reference; cited: 1 review, 7 references.
Scholastic Mental Ability Tests, T2:454. Grades kgn–8; 1953–67; cited: 2 reviews.
Schubert General Ability Battery, T2:455. Grades 12–16 and adults; 1946–65; cited: 1 review, 1 reference.
Scott Company Mental Alertness Test, T2:456. Applicants for office positions; 1923; 1 reference.
Ship Destination Test, T2:457. Grades 9 and over; 1955–56; 13 references; cited: 2 reviews, 8 references.
Simplex GNV Intelligence Tests [England], T2:459. Ages 11–12; 1952–57; cited: 1 review, 2 references.

Simplex Group Intelligence Scale [England], T2:460. Ages 10 and over; 1922–39; 3 references; cited: 1 review.
Simplex Junior Intelligence Tests [England], T2:461. Ages 7–14; 1932–51; 5 references; cited: 1 review, 3 references.
Sleight Non-Verbal Intelligence Test [England], T2:462. Ages 6–10; 1931–63; 3 references; cited: 2 reviews, 1 reference.
Southend Test of Intelligence [England], T2:463. Ages 10–12; 1939–53; cited: 2 reviews, 1 excerpt, 1 reference.
Spiral Nines [South Africa], T2:464. Job applicants with 7–8 years of education; 1960–65; cited: 2 references.
Test of Adult College Aptitude, T2:465. Evening college entrants; 1966; cited: 1 review.
Tests of General Ability, T2:467. Grades kgn–12; 1959–60; 8 references; cited: 2 reviews, 1 excerpt.
†Tests of General Ability: Inter-American Series, T2:468. Preschool and grades kgn–13.5; 1961–73; 1 reference; cited: 4 reviews, 10 references.
Thurstone Test of Mental Alertness, T2:469. Grades 9–12 and adults; 1943–68; 5 references; cited: 4 reviews, 7 references.
Verbal Power Test of Concept Equivalence, T2:471. Ages 14 and over; 1959–63; 3 references; cited: 1 review, 3 references.
Verbal Reasoning, T2:472. Job applicants and industrial employees; 1958–61; cited: 2 reviews.
Verbal Tests (Adv.) [England], T2:474. Ages 12–13; 1954–67; cited: 2 reviews.
Verbal Tests BC, CD, C, and D [England], T2:475. Ages 8–11; 1953–66; cited: 2 reviews.
Verbal Tests EF and GH [England], T2:476. Ages 11–14; 1960–66; cited: 1 review.
†Verbal Tests 15–23 and 69 [England], T2:477. Ages 10–12; 1951–72; cited: 2 reviews, 1 reference.
‡WLW Mental Alertness Inventory, T2:479. Job applicants; 1955.
Wesman Personnel Classification Test, T2:480. Grades 8–16 and adults; 1946–65; 2 references; cited: 3 reviews, 2 excerpts, 18 references.
Western Personnel Tests, T2:481. College and adults; 1962; 1 reference; cited: 2 reviews.
†Wonderlic Personnel Test, T2:482. Adults; 1938–72; 10 references; cited: 7 reviews, 113 references.

INDIVIDUAL

206. Bayley Scales of Infant Development. Ages 2–30 months; 1969; 1 review, 28 references; cited: 2 reviews, 31 references.
207. Bingham Button Test. Disadvantaged children ages 3–6; 1967; 1 review.
208. ★Brazelton Neonatal Assessment Scale [England]. Ages 3 days to 4 weeks; 1973; 1 review, 1 excerpt, 15 references.
209. Cattell Infant Intelligence Scale. Ages 3–30 months; 1940–60; 1 review, 7 references; cited: 2 reviews, 5 excerpts, 49 references.
210. Columbia Mental Maturity Scale. Ages 3–6 to 9–11; 1954–72; 2 reviews, 1 excerpt, 18 references; cited: 2 reviews, 78 references.
211. ★Comprehensive Developmental Evaluation Chart. Developmental ages birth to 3 years; 1975.
212. ★Dennis Test of Child Development. Grades kgn–1; 1966–74.
213. *Detroit Tests of Learning Aptitude. Ages 3 and over; 1935–75; 1 review, 14 references; cited: 3 reviews, 1 excerpt, 14 references.
214. ★Developmental Activities Screening Inventory. Ages 6–60 months; 1977.
215. ★Developmental Profile. Birth to age 12; 1972; 1 review, 1 reference.
216. Full-Range Picture Vocabulary Test. Ages 2 and over; 1948; 1 review, 6 references; cited: 2 reviews, 73 references.
217. Hiskey-Nebraska Test of Learning Aptitude. Ages 3–17 (deaf and hearing); 1941–66; 1 review, 11 references; cited: 3 reviews, 27 references.
218. ★Kaufman Development Scale. Birth to age 9 and mentally retarded all ages; 1972–74; 1 review.
219. McCarthy Scales of Children's Abilities. Ages 2.5–8.5; 1972; 3 reviews, 4 excerpts, 29 references.
220. Minnesota Child Development Inventory. Ages 6 months to 6.5 years; 1968–72; 1 review, 3 references.
221. ★Naylor-Harwood Adult Intelligence Scale [Australia]. Ages 18 and over; 1955–72.
222. Peabody Picture Vocabulary Test. Ages 2.5–18;

1959–65; 209 references; cited: 2 reviews, 299 references.

223. Pictorial Test of Intelligence. Ages 3–8; 1964; 1 excerpt, 11 references; cited: 2 reviews, 20 references.

224. Porteus Maze Test. Ages 3 and over; 1914–65; 25 references; cited: 4 reviews, 4 excerpts, 241 references.

225. Quick Test. Ages 2 and over; 1958–62; 33 references; cited: 2 reviews, 2 excerpts, 48 references.

226. *Ring and Peg Tests of Behavior Development. Birth to age 6; 1958–75; cited: 2 reviews.

227. Slosson Intelligence Test. Ages 2 weeks and over; 1961–63; 62 references; cited: 2 reviews, 43 references.

228. *Snijders-Oomen Non-Verbal Intelligence Scale for Young Children [The Netherlands]. Ages 2.5–7; 1939–76; cited: 1 review, 7 references.

229. Stanford-Binet Intelligence Scale. Ages 2 and over; 1916–73; 176 references; cited: 8 reviews, 8 excerpts, 1408 references.

230. Wechsler Adult Intelligence Scale. Ages 16 and over; 1939–55; 351 references; cited: 4 reviews, 938 references.

231. ★[Re Wechsler Adult Intelligence Scale] WAIS Mental Description Sheet. Ages 16 and over; 1974.

232. *Wechsler Intelligence Scale for Children. Ages 5–16; 1949–74; 2 reviews, 3 excerpts, 548 references; cited: 9 reviews, 1 excerpt, 1036 references.

233. ★[Re Wechsler Intelligence Scale for Children—Revised] WISC-R Profile Form. Ages 6–17; 1974.

234. Wechsler Preschool and Primary Scale of Intelligence. Ages 4–6.5; 1967; 84 references; cited: 2 reviews, 2 excerpts, 86 references.

FOR OTHER TESTS, see in *Tests in Print II:*

Arthur Point Scale of Performance Tests, T2:483. Ages 4.5 to superior adults; 1925–47; 21 references; cited: 3 reviews, 2 excerpts, 47 references.

Canadian Intelligence Test [Canada], T2:486. Ages 3–16; 1940–66; cited: 2 reviews, 2 excerpts, 1 reference.

‡Classification Tasks [Australia], T2:488. Ages 5–9; 1971; 1 reference.

Cooperative Preschool Inventory, T2:490. Ages 3–6; 1965–70; 4 references; cited: 1 review, 1 excerpt, 5 references.

Crichton Vocabulary Scale [England], T2:491. Ages 4–11; 1950; 3 references; cited: 3 reviews, 1 reference.

Denver Developmental Screening Test, T2:492. Ages 2 weeks to 6 years; 1968–70; 6 references; cited: 2 reviews, 6 references.

Developmental Screening Inventory, T2:494. Ages 1–18 months; 1966; 2 references; cited: 1 reference.

†English Picture Vocabulary Test [England], T2:495. Ages 5 and over; 1962–68; 4 references; cited: 3 reviews, 5 references.

Gesell Developmental Schedules, T2:497. Ages 4 weeks to 6 years; 1925–49; 48 references; cited: 3 reviews, 60 references.

Haptic Intelligence Scale for Adult Blind, T2:498. Blind and partially sighted adults; 1964; 1 reference; cited: 1 review, 9 references.

Immediate Test: A Quick Verbal Intelligence Test, T2:500. Adults; 1951; 2 references; cited: 2 reviews, 1 reference.

‡Individual Scale for Indian South Africans [South Africa], T2:501. Ages 8–17; 1971.

Kahn Intelligence Tests, T2:502. Ages 1 month and over (particularly the verbally or culturally handicapped); 1960; 1 reference; cited: 1 review, 8 references.

Kent Series of Emergency Scales, T2:503. Ages 5–14; 1932–46; 27 references; cited: 4 reviews, 34 references.

†Leiter Adult Intelligence Scale, T2:504. Adults; 1949–72; 12 references; cited: 4 reviews, 4 excerpts, 19 references.

Leiter International Performance Scale, T2:505. Ages 2–18; 1936–55; 18 references; cited: 2 reviews, 1 excerpt, 52 references.

Merrill-Palmer Scale of Mental Tests, T2:507. Ages 24–63 months; 1926–31; 17 references; cited: 5 reviews, 29 references.

Minnesota Preschool Scale, T2:509. Ages 1.5–6.0; 1932–40; 2 references; cited: 5 reviews, 10 references.

New Guinea Performance Scales [Papua New Guinea], T2:510. Pre-literates ages 17 and over; 1961–71; cited: 4 references.

New South African Individual Scale [South Africa], T2:511. Ages 6–17; 1964; cited: 1 reference.

Ohwaki-Kohs Tactile Block Design Intelligence Test for the Blind, T2:513. Blind ages 6 and over; 1965; 1 reference; cited: 1 excerpt, 4 references.

Pacific Design Construction Test [Australia], T2:514. Illiterates and semiliterates in Papua New Guinea; 1962–68; 1 reference; cited: 3 references.

Passalong Test: A Performance Test of Intelligence, T2:515. Ages 8 and over; 1932–37; 15 references; cited: 3 reviews, 5 references.

Preschool Attainment Record, T2:519. Ages 6 months to 7 years; 1966–67; 2 references; cited: 1 review, 1 excerpt, 5 references.

Queensland Test [Australia], T2:520. Ages 7 and over; 1968–70; 1 reference; cited: 7 references.

Quick Screening Scale of Mental Development, T2:521. Ages 6 months to 10 years; 1963; cited: 1 review.

[Re Stanford-Binet Intelligence Scale] A Clinical Profile for the Stanford Binet Intelligence Scale (L-M), T2:526. Ages 5 and over; 1965.

Stanford-Ohwaki-Kohs Block Design Intelligence Test for the Blind, T2:527. Blind and partially sighted ages 16 and over; 1965–66.

Vane Kindergarten Test, T2:528. Ages 4–6; 1968; 7 references; cited: 2 reviews, 3 references.

[Re Wechsler Adult Intelligence Scale] Rhodes WAIS Scatter Profile, T2:530. Ages 16 and over; 1971.

‡[Re Wechsler Adult Intelligence Scale] WAIS Test Profile, T2:531. Ages 16 and over; 1968–69.

Wechsler-Bellevue Intelligence Scale, T2:532. Ages 10 and over; 1939–47; 243 references; cited: 4 reviews, 2 excerpts, 747 references.

[Re Wechsler Intelligence Scale for Children] California Abbreviated WISC, T2:534. Educable mentally retarded ages 8–13.5, intellectually gifted elementary school children; 1966; cited: 1 review, 1 reference.

[Re Wechsler Intelligence Scale for Children] Rhodes WISC Scatter Profile, T2:535. Ages 5–15; 1969.

‡[Re Wechsler Intelligence Scale for Children] WISC Mental Description Sheet, T2:536. Ages 5–15; 1970–71.

‡[Re Wechsler Intelligence Scale for Children] WISC Test Profile, T2:537. Ages 5–15; 1968–69.

‡[Re Wechsler Preschool and Primary Scale for Children] WPPSI Test Profile, T2:539. Ages 4–6.5; 1968–69.

Williams Intelligence Test for Children With Defective Vision [England], T2:540. Blind and partially sighted ages 5–15; 1956; 1 reference; cited: 1 review, 2 references.

SPECIFIC

235. Alternate Uses. Grades 6–16 and adults; 1960; 32 references; cited: 101 references.

236. *Benton Visual Retention Test. Ages 8 and over; 1946–74; 32 references; cited: 4 reviews, 101 references.

237. Christensen-Guilford Fluency Tests. Grades 7–16 and adults; 1957–73; 20 references; cited: 2 reviews, 52 references.

238. Concept Assessment Kit—Conservation. Ages 4–7; 1968; 32 references; cited: 1 review, 3 excerpts, 10 references.

239. Consequences. Grades 9–16 and adults; 1958; 23 references; cited: 1 review, 84 references.

240. Creativity Attitude Survey. Grades 4–6; 1971; 2 reviews, 1 reference; cited: 1 reference.

241. *Creativity Tests for Children. Grades 4–6; 1971–76; 2 reviews, 1 reference.

242. ★Predictive Ability Test, Adult Edition. Ages 17 and over; 1974; 1 reference.

243. ★Relevant Aspects of Potential. Low socioeconomic and minority high school students and college candidates; 1974; 2 reviews.

244. Remote Associates Test. College and adults; 1967; 1 excerpt, 55 references; cited: 3 reviews, 129 references.

245. Similes. Grades 4–16; 1971; 2 reviews, 3 references; cited: 1 reference.

246. Test of Concept Utilization. Ages 4.5–18.5; 1972; 1 review; cited: 1 reference.

247. Test of Creative Potential. Grades 2–12 and adults; 1973; 2 reviews.

248. Thinking Creatively With Sounds and Words. Grades 3–12 and adults; 1973; 2 reviews, 16 references; cited: 17 references.

248. *Torrance Tests of Creative Thinking. Kgn through graduate school; 1966–74; 229 references; cited: 2 reviews, 3 excerpts, 331 references.

250. Wechsler Memory Scale. Adults; 1945–46; 36 references; cited: 3 reviews, 88 references.

FOR OTHER TESTS, see in *Tests in Print II:*

‡Abstract Spatial Relations Test [South Africa], T2:541. Bantu industrial workers with 0–12 years of education; ?–1969; 1 reference.
‡Biographical Inventory—Creativity, T2:544. "Adolescents and young adults"; 1970; 2 references.
Block-Design Test, T2:545. Mental ages 5–20; [1919]; 74 references.
Closure Flexibility (Concealed Figures), T2:547. Industrial employees; 1956–65; 9 references; cited: 1 review, 13 references.
Closure Speed (Gestalt Completion), T2:548. Industrial employees; 1956–66; 1 reference; cited: 1 review, 5 references.
‡Concept Attainment Test [South Africa], T2:550. College and adults; 1959.
‡Consequences [South Africa], T2:552. Ages 15 and over; 1972.
Decorations, T2:555. Grades 9–16 and adults; 1963; 5 references; cited: 1 reference.
Feature Profile Test: Pintner-Paterson Modification, T2:556. Ages 4 and over; [1917–23]; 1 reference.
‡Gottschaldt Figures [South Africa], T2:557. Job applicants with at least 10 years of education; 1943–56.
Healy Pictorial Completion Tests, T2:558. Ages 5 and over; [1914–21]; 37 references.
Hidden Figures Test, T2:559. Grades 6–16; 1962–63; 18 references; cited: 31 references.
Higgins-Wertman Test: Threshold of Visual Closure, T2:560. Ages 5–15; 1968; 1 reference; cited: 1 reference.
Jensen Alternation Board, T2:560A. Ages 5 and over; 1959–60; 3 references; cited: 2 references.
Kit of Reference Tests for Cognitive Factors, T2:561. Grades 6–16; 1954–63; 103 references.
Making Objects, T2:562. Grades 9–16 and adults; 1963; 8 references; cited: 1 reference.
Manikin Test, T2:563. Ages 2 and over; [1917]; 1 reference.
Match Problems, T2:564. Grades 9–16 and adults; 1963; 15 references; cited: 7 references.
†Match Problems 5, T2:565. Grades 9–16; 1962–69.
‡Memory for Events, T2:566. Grades 9–13; 1969.
†Memory for Meanings, T2:567. Grades 7–16; 1969.
†New Uses, T2:568. Grades 10–16; 1962–69.
‡Pattern Relations Test [South Africa], T2:569. College graduates; 1968–69.
Perceptual Speed (Identical Forms), T2:570. Grades 9–16 and industrial employees; 1956–66; 2 references; cited: 1 review, 2 references.
Pertinent Questions, T2:571. Grades 9–16 and adults; 1960; 1 reference; cited: 3 references.
†Plot Titles, T2:572. Grades 9–16; 1962–69; 23 references.
Possible Jobs, T2:573. Grades 6–16 and adults; 1963; 9 references; cited: 1 reference.
Rutgers Drawing Test, T2:575. Ages 4–9; 1952–69; cited: 1 review, 8 references.
‡Seeing Faults [South Africa], T2:576. Ages 15 and over; 1971.
†Seeing Problems, T2:577. Grades 9–16; 1962–69; 15 references.
Seguin-Goddard Formboard, T2:578. Ages 5–14; [1911]; 25 references.
†Simile Interpretations, T2:579. Grades 10–16; 1962–69; 1 reference.
‡Sketches, T2:581. Grades 9 and over; 1967; 1 reference.
Subsumed Abilities Test, T2:582. Ages 9 and over; 1957–63; 2 references; cited: 1 reference.
‡Symbol Identities, T2:583. Grades 10 and over; 1967.
Symbol Series Test [South Africa], T2:584. Illiterate and semiliterate adults; 1969.
Time Appreciation Test, T2:588. Ages 10 and over; 1943–46; 5 references; cited: 2 reviews, 2 references.
Two-Figure Formboard, T2:590. Ages 4 and over; [1917].
†Utility Test, T2:591. Grades 9–12; 1962–69; 14 references.
‡Willner Instance Similarities Test, T2:593. Adults; 1971.
Word Fluency, T2:594. Industrial employees; 1959–61; 2 references; cited: 1 review.

MATHEMATICS

251. ★Analysis of Skills: Mathematics. Grades 1–8; 1974–76; 1 review.
252. *Annual High School Mathematics Examination. High school students competing for individual and school awards; 1950–76; 1 review, 1 reference; cited: 3 references.
253. ★Basic Educational Skills Inventory: Math. Grades kgn–6; 1972–73; 1 review.
254. *CLEP General Examinations: Mathematics. 1–2 years of college or equivalent; 1964–76; 1 review, 1 reference.

255. ★CLEP Subject Examination in Calculus With Analytic Geometry. 1 year of college or equivalent; 1974–76; 1 review.
256. *CLEP Subject Examination in College Algebra and Trigonometry. 1 semester of college or equivalent; 1968–76; 1 review, 1 reference; cited: 1 review.
257. *California Achievement Tests: Mathematics. Grades 1.5–12; 1933–74; 1 review, 8 references; cited: 5 reviews, 37 references.
258. *College Board Achievement Test in Mathematics, Level 1. Candidates for college entrance; 1901–76; 2 reviews, 4 references; cited: 4 references.
259. *College Board Achievement Test in Mathematics, Level 2. Candidates for college entrance; 1901–76; 1 reference; cited: 1 reference.
260. *College Placement Test in Mathematics, Level 1. Entering college freshmen; 1964–75.
261. *College Placement Test in Mathematics, Level 2. Entering college freshmen; 1965–75.
262. Cooperative Primary Tests: Mathematics. Grades 1.5–3; 1965–67; 2 reviews.
263. ★Diagnosis: An Instructional Aid: Mathematics. Grades 1–6; 1972–74; 2 reviews.
264. *Diagnostic Mathematics Inventory. Grades 1.5–8.5; 1971–75; 2 reviews.
265. ★Diagnostic Screening Test: Math. Grades 1–12; 1976.
266. Diagnostic Test in Mathematics—Level 1 [Canada]. Grades 8–9; 1970; 2 reviews.
267. *Differential Aptitude Tests: Numerical Ability. Grades 8–12 and adults; 1947–75; 2 references; cited: 11 references.
268. ★Educational Skills Tests: Mathematics, College Edition. Open-door college entrants; 1971.
269. ★Essential Mathematics [England]. Ages 7–14; 1976.
270. ★Fountain Valley Teacher Support System in Mathematics. Grades kgn–8; 1972–74; 1 review.
271. *Graded Arithmetic-Mathematics Test [England]. Ages 6–21; 1949–76; cited: 1 review, 8 references.
272. *Graduate Record Examinations Advanced Mathematics Test. Graduate school candidates; 1939–76; 1 reference; cited: 2 reviews, 1 reference.
273. Group Mathematics Test [England]. Ages 6.5–8.5; 1970; 1 review.
274. ★Individual Pupil Monitoring System—Mathematics. Grades 1–8; 1973; 2 reviews.
275-6. ★Individualized Criterion Referenced Testing: Math. Grades 1–8; 1973–77; 1 review.
277. *Leicester Number Test: Basic Number Concepts [England]. Ages 7-1 to 9-0; 1970–73; 1 review.
278. ★Mastery: An Evaluation Tool: Mathematics. Grades kgn–9; 1974–76; 1 review.
279. ★Mathematics: IOX Objectives-Based Tests. Grades kgn–9; 1973–76; 2 reviews.
280. Mathematics Test for Grades Four, Five and Six. Grades 4–6; 1969; 1 review.
281. ★Mathematics Test for Seniors [South Africa]. Standards 9–10; 1973.
282. ★Mathematics Topic Tests: Elementary Level. Various grades 4–9; 1974; 1 review.
283. *Metropolitan Achievement Tests: Mathematics Tests. Grades 3.5–9.5; 1932–73; 1 review, 5 references; cited: 7 reviews, 9 references.
284. ★Modern Mathematics Supplement to the Canadian Tests of Basic Skills [Canada]. Grades 3–8; 1968–70.
285. *Moreton Mathematics Tests. Grades 3–7; 1970–74; cited: 1 reference.
286. *National Teacher Examinations: Mathematics. College seniors and teachers; 1940–76; cited: 1 review.
287. ★Objectives-Referenced Bank of Items and

Tests: Mathematics. Grades kgn–12 and adults; 1975; 2 reviews.

288. ★Progressive Achievement Tests of Mathematics [New Zealand]. Standards 2–4 and Forms I–IV (ages 8–14); 1974–75; 1 review.

289. ★Self-Scoring Mathematics Placement Tests. Students entering postsecondary institutions with open-door policies; 1976; 1 review.

290. Sequential Tests of Educational Progress: Mathematics, Series II. Grades 4–14; 1956–72; 1 review, 1 reference; cited: 5 reviews, 20 references.

291. *Stanford Achievement Test: Mathematics Tests. Grades 1.5–9.5; 1923–75; 2 reviews, 5 references; cited: 3 reviews, 30 references.

292. ★Stanford Diagnostic Mathematics Test. Grades 1.5–13; 1976; 2 reviews.

293. *Tests of Achievement in Basic Skills: Mathematics. Preschool–grade 12; 1970–76; 2 reviews, 1 excerpt, 2 references; cited: 1 reference.

294. Tests of Basic Experiences: Mathematics. Prekgn–grade 1; 1970–72; 1 review.

295. *UP Field Test in Mathematics. College; 1969–77.

FOR OTHER TESTS, see in *Tests in Print II*:

‡ACER Mathematics Tests [Australia], T2:595. Grades 4–6; 1971–72.
ACT Mathematics Placement Examination, T2:596. College entrants; 1968; 1 reference; cited: 1 review, 1 reference.
†Advanced Mathematics (Including Trigonometry): Minnesota High School Achievement Examinations, T2:597. High school; 1951–70; cited: 3 reviews.
†Basic Mathematics Tests [England] T2:599. Ages 7–14.5; 1969–72.
Bristol Achievement Tests: Mathematics [England] T2:600. Ages 8–13; 1969; cited: 1 review.
†Canadian Achievement Test in Mathematics [Canada], T2:604. Grade 10; 1961–68; 2 references; cited: 1 review.
†Canadian Achievement Test in Technical and Commercial Mathematics [Canada], T2:605. Grade 10; 1961–68; 2 references; cited: 1 review.
†Canadian Mathematics Achievement Test [Canada], T2:606. Grades 8.5–9.0; 1959–68; 2 references; cited: 2 reviews.
†College Placement Test in Advanced Mathematics, T2:609. Entering college freshmen; 1962–72.
†College Placement Test in Intermediate Mathematics, T2:610. Entering college freshmen; 1962–72.
Cooperative Mathematics Tests: Structure of the Number System, T2:613. Grades 7–8; 1963–65; 1 reference; cited: 2 reviews.
†ERB Modern Mathematics Test, T2:616. Grades 7–8; 1965–71; cited: 1 reference.
General Mathematics III: Achievement Examinations for Secondary Schools, T2:617. Grade 9; 1951–54.
Iowa Placement Examinations: Mathematics Aptiutde, T2:621. Grades 12–13; 1925–44; 17 references; cited: 2 reviews, 18 references.
Iowa Placement Examinations: Mathematics Training, T2:622. Grades 12–13; 1925–26; 6 references; cited: 2 reviews, 8 references.
†Iowa Tests of Educational Development: Ability to Do Quantitative Thinking, T2:623. Grades 9–12; 1942–67; 1 reference; cited: 1 review.
Junior High School Mathematics Test: Acorn Achievement Tests, T2:624. Grades 7–9; 1942–52; cited: 2 reviews.
‡Mathematics Attainment Test EF [England], T2:626. Ages 11–12; 1965–69.
Mathematics Attainment Tests C1 and C3 [England], T2:627. Ages 9–3 to 10–8; 1965–69; cited: 1 review.
Mathematics Attainment Tests DE1 and DE2 [England], T2:628. Ages 10–11; 1966–70.
†Mathematics Attainment Tests (Oral) [England], T2:629. Ages 7 to 9.8; 1965–72.
‡Mathematics Inventory Tests, T2:630. Grades 4–12; 1970.
†Mathematics: Minnesota High School Achievement Examinations, T2:631. Grades 7–9; 1951–70; cited: 1 review.
†Mathematics Test (Adv.) 6 [England], T2:632. Ages 12–13; 1954–72; cited: 1 review.
Mathematics Test: Content Evaluation Series, T2:633. Grades 7–9; 1969; cited: 1 review.
Mathematics Test: McGraw-Hill Basic Skills System, T2:635. Grades 11–14; 1970; cited: 2 reviews.
†Mathematics Tests 20–22 [England], T2:636. Ages 10–11; 1951–71; cited: 1 reference.
†Minimum Essentials for Modern Mathematics, T2:638. Grades 6–8; 1963–71; cited: 1 review.
Modern Mathematics Supplement to the Iowa Tests of Basic Skills, T2:639. Grades 3–9; 1968; cited: 2 reviews.
Moray House Mathematics Tests [England]. Ages 8.5–12; 1964–70.

N.B. Mathematics Tests [South Africa], T2:642. Standards 7–8 (ages 14–15); 1967.
‡Objective Tests in Mathematics: Arithmetic and Trigonometry [England], T2:645. Ages 15 and over; 1970.
†Portland Prognostic Test for Mathematics, T2:646. Grades 6.9–8; 1960–71; 1 reference; cited: 1 review, 1 reference.
‡Prescriptive Mathematics Inventory, T2:647. Grades 4–8; 1971–72.
‡Prescriptive Mathematics Inventory Interim Evaluation Tests, T2:648. Grades 4–7; 1973.
‡Primary Mathematics Survey Tests, T2:649. Grades 2–3; 1973.
Purdue Industrial Mathematics Test, T2:650. Adults; 1946; 6 references; cited: 2 reviews.
†Senior Mathematics Test [England], T2:651. Technical college entrants; 1963–71.
Stanford Achievement Test: High School Mathematics Test, T2:653. Grades 9–12; 1965–66; cited: 2 reviews.
Stanford Achievement Test: High School Numerical Competence Test, T2:654. Grades 9–12; 1965–66; cited: 2 reviews.
Stanford Modern Mathematics Concepts Test, T2:656. Grades 5.5–9.5; 1965; cited: 1 review, 1 excerpt, 3 references.
†Teacher Education Examination Program: Mathematics, T2:657. College seniors preparing to teach secondary school; 1957–72.
‡Test A/16: Mathematical Achievement Test [South Africa], T2:658. Job applicants with at least 10 years of education; 1957–63.
Test of Academic Progress: Mathematics, T2:659. Grades 9–12; 1964–66; 1 reference.
‡Watson Diagnosis Mathematics Test: Computation [Canada], T2:663. Grades 1–10; 1973.

ALGEBRA

296. ★Algebra Test for Stds 9 and 10 [South Africa]. Standards 9–10; 1973.

297. *CLEP Subject Examination in College Algebra. 1 semester of college or equivalent; 1968–76; 1 review.

298. Cooperative Mathematics Tests: Algebra I and II. Grades 8–12; 1962–65; 1 review, 7 references; cited: 2 reviews, 2 excerpts, 4 references.

299. ★Emporia State Algebra II Test. High school; 1974.

300. Modern Algebra Test: Content Evaluation Series. 1 year high school; 1972; 2 reviews.

FOR OTHER TESTS, see in *Tests in Print II*:

Advanced Algebra: Achievement Examinations for Secondary Schools, T2:664. High school; 1951–54.
Algebra Readiness Test, T2:665. Grades 8–9; 1947; cited: 1 review.
Algebra Test for Engineering and Science, T2:666–7. College entrants; 1958–61; cited: 1 review.
Blyth Second-Year Algebra Test, T2:668. Grades 9–12; 1953–66; cited: 4 reviews.
Breslich Algebra Survey Test, T2:669. 1–2 semesters high school; 1930–31; cited: 1 review.
California Algebra Aptitude Test, T2:671. High school; 1940–58; 3 references; cited: 2 reviews.
Cooperative Mathematics Tests: Algebra III, T2:673. High school and college; 1963–65; 1 reference; cited: 2 reviews, 2 excerpts.
Diagnostic Test in Basic Algebra [Australia], T2:674. 2–3 semesters high school; 1956.
†ERB Modern Elementary Algebra Test, T2:675. Grades 8–9; 1965–71; 1 reference.
ERB Modern Second Year Algebra Test, T2:676. High school; 1968–69.
Elementary Algebra: Achievement Examinations for Secondary Schools, T2:677. High school; 1951–54.
†Elementary Algebra: Minnesota High School Achievement Examinations, T2:678. High school; 1951–70; cited: 1 review.
First Year Algebra Test: National Achievement Tests, T2:679. 1 year high school; 1958–62; cited: 1 review.
Illinois Algebra Test, T2:680. 1–2 semesters high school; 1956–58; cited: 2 reviews.
Iowa Algebra Aptitude Test, T2:681. Grade 8; 1931–69; 11 references; cited: 7 reviews, 1 excerpt, 6 references.
Kepner Mid-Year Algebra Achievement Tests, T2:682. 1 semester high school; 1969; cited: 1 review, 1 excerpt.
Lankton First-Year Algebra Test, T2:683. Grades 8–12; 1950–65; 1 reference; cited: 4 reviews, 4 references.
Lee Test of Algebraic Ability, T2:684. Grades 7–8; 1930–64; 3 references; cited: 3 reviews, 1 excerpt, 3 references.
Mid-Year Algebra Test, T2:685. High school; 1968; cited: 1 review.
‡Objective Tests in Mathematics: Algebra [England], T2:687. Ages 15 and over; 1970.
Orleans-Hanna Algebra Prognosis Test, T2:688. Grades 7–11; 1928–69; 11 references; cited: 5 reviews, 8 references.

Survey Test of Algebraic Aptitude, T2:689. Grade 8; 1959; 2 references; cited: 2 reviews.

ARITHMETIC

301. ★A.P.U. Arithmetic Test [England]. Ages 11–18; 1976.

302. *American School Achievement Tests: Part 2, Arithmetic. Grades 2–9; 1941–75; 1 review; cited: 2 reviews, 1 reference.

303. ★Basic Arithmetic Skill Evaluation. Grades 1–9; 1973–74; 1 review.

304. ★Diagnostic Math Test. Grades 1–8; 1974.

305. *KeyMath Diagnostic Arithmetic Test. Preschool–grade 6; 1971–76; 1 excerpt, 10 references.

306. ★Nottingham Number Test [England]. Ages 9-1 to 11-0; 1973.

307. *SRA Arithmetic Index. Job applicants ages 14 and over with poor educational backgrounds; 1968–74; 3 references; cited: 1 review.

308. ★Scholastic Achievement Test in Arithmetic. Grades 1/substandard A, 2/substandard B, standards 1–4; 1973–74.

For other tests, see in *Tests in Print II:*

A.C.E.R. Arithmetic Tests: Standardized for Use in New Zealand [New Zealand], T2:690. Ages 9–12; 1957; 1 reference.

A.C.E.R. Number Test [Australia], T2:691. Ages 13.5 and over; 1942–55; 2 references; cited: 1 review.

‡Adston Diagnostic Instruments in Elementary School Mathematics: Whole Numbers, T2:692. Grades 4–8; 1971.

American Numerical Test, T2:693. Adults in "that great middle and upper middle block of vocations which emphasize shop and white collar skills involving number competence"; 1962; cited: 2 reviews.

American School Achievement Tests: Arithmetic Readiness, T2:694. Grades kgn–1; 1941–55; cited: 1 review.

Analytical Survey Test in Computational Arithmetic, T2:696. Grades 7–12; 1930–57; 3 references; cited: 1 review.

Arithmetic Computation: Public School Achievement Tests, T2:697. Grades 3–8; 1928–59.

Arithmetic Reasoning: Public School Achievement Tests, T2:698. Grades 3–8; 1928–59; 1 reference.

Arithmetic Reasoning Test, T2:699. Clerical applicants and high school; 1948.

Arithmetic Test (Fundamentals and Reasoning): Municipal Tests, T2:700. Grades 3–8; 1938–56; cited: 2 reviews.

Arithmetic Test: National Achievement Tests, T2:701. Grades 3–8; 1936–61; cited: 4 reviews.

†Arithmetic Tests EA2A and EA4 [England], T2:702. Ages 14.5 and over; 1947–72.

†Arithmetical Problems: Test A/68 [South Africa], T2:703. Job applicants with at least 10 years of education; 1955–62.

Basic Skills in Arithmetic Test, T2:704. Grades 6–12; 1945; 1 reference; cited: 2 reviews.

Bobbs-Merrill Arithmetic Achievement Tests, T2:705. Grades 1–9; 1963; cited: 1 review.

Brief Survey of Arithmetic Skills, T2:706. Grades 7–12; 1947–53; 1 reference; cited: 3 reviews, 1 reference.

†Comprehensive Tests of Basic Skills: Arithmetic, T2:707. Grades 2.5–12; 1968–71; 1 reference; cited: 2 reviews.

Computation Test A/67 [South Africa], T2:708. Job applicants with at least 6 years of education; 1956–63.

Cooperative Mathematics Tests: Arithmetic, T2:709. Grades 7–9; 1962–65; 2 references; cited: 2 reviews, 2 excerpts, 2 references.

†Cotswold Junior Arithmetic Ability Tests [Scotland], T2:710. Ages 8.5–10.5; 1949–70; cited: 2 reviews.

†Cotswold Measurement of Ability: Arithmetic [Scotland], T2:711. Ages 10–12; 1947–68; cited: 1 review.

†Diagnostic Arithmetic Tests [South Africa], T2:712. Standards 2–5 (ages 9–12); 1951–66.

Diagnostic Chart for Fundamental Processes in Arithmetic, T2:713. Grades 2–8; 1925; 2 references; cited: 3 reviews, 1 reference.

‡Diagnostic Decimal Tests 1–3 [Australia], T2:714. Ages 9–13; 1966.

Diagnostic Fractions Test 3 [Australia], T2:715. Ages 7–11; 1957–66.

Diagnostic Number Tests 1–2 [Australia], T2:716. Ages 8–12; 1951–66.

Diagnostic Tests and Self-Helps in Arithmetic, T2:717. Grades 3–12; 1955; cited: 1 review.

†ERB Modern Arithmetic Test, T2:718. Grades 5–6; 1969–71.

Emporia Arithmetic Tests, T2:719. Grades 1–8; 1962–64; cited: 2 reviews.

Kelvin Measurement of Ability in Arithmetic [Scotland], T2:720. Ages 7–12; 1933.

Moray House Arithmetic Test [England], T2:722. Ages 10–12; 1935–69; 5 references; cited: 1 review, 9 references.

‡Moreton Arithmetic Tests [Australia], T2:723. Grades 6–7; 1967; 1 reference.

N.B. Arithmetic Tests [South Africa], T2:724. Standards 2–8 (ages 9–15), 1961–63.

Number Test DE [England], T2:725. Ages 10.5–12.5; 1965.

†Office Arithmetic Test, T2:726. Job applicants; 1960–72.

RBH Arithmetic Fundamentals Test, T2:727. Business and industry 1951–63; cited: 1 review.

RBH Arithmetic Reasoning Test, T2:728. Business and industry; 1948–63; cited: 1 review.

RBH Shop Arithmetic Test, T2:729. Industry; 1948–63; 1 reference; cited: 1 review, 2 references.

Revised Southend Attainment Test in Mechanical Arithmetic [England], T2:730. Ages 7–15; 1939–50.

SRA Achievement Series: Arithmetic, T2:731. Grades 1–9; 1954–69; cited: 4 reviews.

Schonell Diagnostic Arithmetic Tests [Scotland], T2:734. Ages 7–13; 1936–57; cited: 2 reviews, 4 references.

†Seeing Through Arithmetic Tests, T2:735. Grades 1–6; 1960–69; cited: 1 review.

Southend Attainment Test in Mechanical Arithmetic [England], T2:736. Ages 6–14; 1939; 1 reference; cited: 1 review.

Staffordshire Arithmetic Test [England], T2:737. Ages 7–15; 1938–58.

Stanford Diagnostic Arithmetic Test, T2:738. Grades 2.5–8.5; 1966–68; cited: 1 review.

Survey Tests of Arithmetic Fundamentals [Canada], T2:739. Grades 3–8; 1957–58; cited: 1 review.

Test A/8: Arithmetic [South Africa], T2:740. Technical college students and applicants for clerical and trade positions with 8–12 years of education; 1943–57; 2 references.

Watson Number-Readiness Test [Canada], T2:741. Grades kgn–1; 1963.

CALCULUS

309. *Advanced Placement Examinations in Mathematics. High school students desiring credit for college level courses and admission to advanced courses; 1954–77; 1 reference; cited: 1 review, 7 references.

For other tests, see in *Tests in Print II:*

†CLEP Subject Examination in Introductory Calculus, T2:743. 1 year of college or equivalent; 1964–73.

Cooperative Mathematics Tests: Calculus, T2:744. High school and college; 1963–65; cited: 2 reviews, 2 excerpts.

GEOMETRY

310. ★Geometry Test for Stds 9 and 10 [South Africa]. Standards 9–10; 1973.

311. Modern Geometry Test: Content Evaluation Series. Grades 10–12; 1971; 2 reviews.

For other tests, see in *Tests in Print II:*

Cooperative Mathematics Tests: Analytic Geometry, T2:745. High school and college; 1963–65; cited: 1 review, 2 excerpts.

Cooperative Mathematics Tests: Geometry, T2:746. Grades 10–12; 1963–65; cited: 1 review, 2 excerpts, 3 references.

Diagnostic Test in Basic Geometry [Australia], T2:747. 1–2 years high school; 1962.

Geometry (Including Plane and Solid Geometry): Minnesota High School Achievement Examinations, T2:748–9. High school; 1969–71.

Howell Geometry Test, T2:750. Grades 9–12; 1969; cited: 2 reviews.

Iowa Geometry Aptitude Test, T2:751. High school; 1935–69; 2 references; cited: 4 reviews, 2 references.

Mid-Year Geometry Test, T2:752. High school; 1968; cited: 1 review.

‡Objective Tests in Mathematics: Geometry [England], T2:754. Ages 15 and over; 1970.

Orleans-Hanna Geometry Prognosis Test, T2:755. Grades 8–11; 1929–68; 5 references; cited: 3 reviews, 9 references.

Plane Geometry: Achievement Examinations for Secondary Schools, T2:756. High school; 1951–68; cited: 1 review.

Plane Geometry: National Achievement Tests, T2:757. High school; 1958–70; cited: 1 review.

†Solid Geometry: Achievement Examinations for Secondary Schools, T2:758. High school; 1951–68.

Solid Geometry: National Achievement Tests, T2:759. High school; 1958–60; cited: 1 review.

SPECIAL FIELDS

312. NM Consumer Mathematics Test. Grades 9–12; 1973; 2 reviews.

For another test, see in *Tests in Print II:*

‡Decimal Currency Test [England], T2:760. Primary and secondary school; 1969.

STATISTICS

313. *CLEP Subject Examination in Statistics. 1 semester of college or equivalent; 1967–76.

FOR ANOTHER TEST, see in *Tests in Print II*:
‡Objective Tests in Mathematics: Statistics [England], T2:1043. Ages 15 and over; 1970.

TRIGONOMETRY

314. *CLEP Subject Examination in Trigonometry. 1 semester of college or equivalent; 1968–76.
315. ★Trigonometry Test for Stds 9 and 10 [South Africa]. Standards 9–10; 1973.

FOR OTHER TESTS, see in *Tests in Print II*:
Cooperative Mathematics Tests: Trigonometry, T2:763. High school and college; 1962–65; cited: 1 review, 2 excerpts.
Plane Trigonometry: National Achievement Tests, T2:764. Grades 10–16; 1958–60.
†Trigonometry: Minnesota High School Achievement Examinations, T2:765. High school; 1961–70.

MISCELLANEOUS

316. ★Juvenile Justice Policy Inventory. Juvenile justice professionals; 1973.
317. ★Motivation and Potential for Adoptive Parenthood Scale. Adults seeking to adopt children; 1977.
318. ★Multi-Ethnic Awareness Survey. Grades 7–12 and teachers; 1977.

FOR ANOTHER TEST, see in *Tests in Print II*:
Modern Photography Comprehension Test, T2:766. Photography students; 1953–69; cited: 1 review.

AGRICULTURE

319. Agribusiness Achievement Test: Content Evaluation Series. Grades 9–12; 1973; 2 reviews.

BLIND

320. ★Blind Learning Aptitude Test. Blind ages 6–20; 1971; 2 reviews, 4 references.
321. ★Developmental Checklist. Visually impaired multihandicapped children ages 1–8; 1974.

FOR OTHER TESTS, see in *Tests in Print II*:
Colorado Braille Battery: Literary Code Tests, T2:769. Grades 1 and over; 1963–66; 1 reference.
Colorado Braille Battery: Nemeth Code Tests, T2:770. Grades 4 and over; 1963–66; 2 references.
Lorimer Braille Recognition Test [England], T2:771. Students (ages 7–13) in grade 2 Braille; 1962; 1 reference.
Roughness Discrimination Test, T2:772. Blind children in grades kgn–1; 1965; cited: 4 references.
‡Stanford Multi-Modality Imagery Test, T2:773. Blind and partially sighted ages 16 and over; 1972; 1 reference.
Tooze Braille Speed Test [England], T2:774. Students (ages 7–13) in grades 1 or 2 Braille; 1962.

BUSINESS EDUCATION

322. Bookkeeping Test: National Business Entrance Tests. Grades 11–16 and adults; 1938–72; 1 review, 1 reference; cited: 2 reviews.
323. Business Fundamentals and General Information Test: National Business Entrance Tests. Grades 11–16 and adults; 1938–72; 1 review, 1 reference; cited: 2 reviews.
324. *Differential Aptitude Tests: Clerical Speed and Accuracy. Grades 8–12 and adults; 1947–75; cited: 2 references.
325. General Office Clerical Test: National Business Entrance Tests. Grades 11–16 and adults; 1948–72; 1 review; cited: 1 reference.
326. *National Teacher Examinations: Business Education. College seniors and teachers; 1956–77; 1 review; cited: 1 review.
327. Office Information and Skills Test: Content Evaluation Series. Grade 12; 1971–72; 1 review.

328. *SRA Clerical Aptitudes. Grades 9–12 and adults; 1947–73; cited: 2 reviews, 2 references.
329. Typewriting Test: National Business Entrance Tests. Grades 11–16 and adults; 1941–72; 1 review; cited: 4 reviews, 2 references.
330. *UP Field Test in Business. College; 1969–77.

FOR OTHER TESTS, see in *Tests in Print II*:
Bookkeeping: Achievement Examinations for Secondary Schools, T2:775. High school; 1951–54.
†Bookkeeping: Minnesota High School Achievement Examinations, T2:776. High school; 1951–70; cited: 2 reviews.
†Business Relations and Occupations: Achievement Examinations for Secondary Schools, T2:779. High school; 1951–61.
Clerical Aptitude Test: Acorn National Aptitude Tests, T2:780. Grades 7–16 and adults; 1943–50; 1 reference; cited: 4 reviews.
Clerical Tests FG and 2 [England], T2:781A. Ages 12–13; 1952–54.
Detroit Clerical Aptitudes Examination, T2:782. Grades 9–12; 1937–44; 3 references; cited: 3 reviews.
Hiett Simplified Shorthand Test (Gregg), T2:784. 1–2 semesters high school; 1951–63; cited: 1 review.
†Machine Calculation Test: National Business Entrance Tests, T2:785. Grades 11–16 and adults; 1941–72; cited: 2 reviews.
†National Business Entrance Tests, T2:786. Grades 11–16 and adults; 1938–72; cited: 5 reviews, 16 references.
Reicherter-Sanders Typewriting I and II, T2:789. 1–2 semesters high school; 1962–64; cited: 1 review.
Russell-Sanders Bookkeeping Test, T2:790. 1–2 semesters high school; 1962–64; cited: 1 review.
Shorthand Aptitude Test [Australia], T2:793. High school; 1953–54; cited: 1 review.
Stenographic Aptitude Test, T2:794. Grades 9–16; 1939–46; 2 references; cited: 2 reviews, 2 references.
†Stenographic Test: National Business Entrance Tests, T2:795. Grades 11–16 and adults; 1938–72; 3 references; cited: 3 reviews, 1 reference.
†Tapping Test: A Predictor of Typing and Other Tapping Operations, T2:796. High school; 1959–70; 3 references; cited: 2 reviews, 2 references.
†Teacher Education Examination Program: Business Education, T2:797. College seniors preparing to teach secondary school; 1957–72.
Turse Shorthand Aptitude Test, T2:798. Grades 8 and over; 1937–40; 11 references; cited: 2 reviews, 5 references.
United States Typewriting Tests, T2:801. 1–4 semesters; 1932–58.

COMPUTATIONAL & TESTING DEVICES

FOR TESTS, see in *Tests in Print II*:
‡Bowman Chronological Age Calculator, T2:802. 1964.
Bowman M.A. and I.Q. Kalculator, T2:803. 1957.
†Chronological Age Computer, T2:804. Ages 3–7 to 19–5; 1961–73.
Dominion Table for Converting Mental Age to I.Q. [Canada], T2:805. 1948.
Grade Averaging Charts, T2:806. 1956–61.
I.Q. Calculator, T2:807. 1952.
‡Mental Age Calculator, T2:808. 1952.
†Multiple Purpose Self Trainer, T2:809. High school and adults; 1951–67.
Psychometric Research and Service Chart Showing the Davis Difficulty and Discrimination Indices for Item Analysis [India], T2:810. 1962; cited: 1 excerpt.
Rapid-Rater, T2:811. 1961–68.
‡Ratio I.Q. Computer, T2:812. 1966.

COURTSHIP & MARRIAGE

331. ★Abortion Scale. Older adolescents and adults; 1972.
332. ★Borromean Family Index. Adolescents and adults; 1975; 1 reference.
333. *Caring Relationship Inventory. Premarital and marital counselees; 1966–75; 2 reviews, 5 references; cited: 1 review.
334. ★Coitometer. Older adolescents and adults; 1974.
335. ★Dating Scale. Adolescents and adults; 1962; 1 review, 3 references.
336. *El Senoussi Multiphasic Marital Inventory. Premarital and marital counselees; 1963–73; 2 reviews, 1 reference; cited: 1 review.
337. ★Erotometer: A Technique for the Measurement of Heterosexual Love. Older adolescents and adults; 1971; 1 reference.

338. ★Familism Scale. Adolescents and adults : 1959; 1 excerpt, 8 references.

339. ★Family Pre-Counseling Inventory. Adolescents and their parents; 1975; 2 reviews.

340. ★Family Violence Scale. Adolescents and adults; 1973; 1 reference.

341. ★Gravidometer. Older adolescents and adults; 1974.

342. Marital Communication Inventory. Adults; 1968–69; 1 review, 6 references; cited: 2 references.

343. ★Marital Pre-Counseling Inventory. Married couples beginning counseling; 1972–73.

344. ★Marriage Counseling Kit. Premarital couples; 1972.

345. Marriage Expectation Inventories. Engaged and married couples; 1972; 1 review.

346. ★Marriage Inventory. Married couples in counseling; 1971; 1 review.

347. Marriage Scale (For Measuring Compatibility of Interests). Premarital and marital counselees; 1970–73.

348. Marriage Skills Analysis. Marital counselees; 1970; 1 review.

349. Pair Attraction Inventory. College and adults; 1970–71; 1 review, 10 references.

350. ★Pill Scale. Older adolescents and adults; 1969; 3 references.

351. ★Premarital Communication Inventory. Premarital counselees; 1968–74; 1 review.

352. ★Sex Knowledge and Attitude Test. College and adults; 1971–73; 1 review, 7 references.

353. ★Sexometer. Adolescents and adults; 1974; 1 reference.

354. ★Sexual Adjustment Inventory. 1975.

355. ★Sexual Compatibility Test. Couples; 1974–76.

356. *Thorman Family Relations Technique. Families receiving therapy; 1965–71; 2 reviews.

357. ★Vasectomy Scale: Attitudes. Older adolescents and adults; 1974.

FOR OTHER TESTS, see in *Tests in Print II:*

‡Albert Mate Selection Check List, T2:813. Premarital counselees; 1971.

California Marriage Readiness Evaluation, T2:814. Premarital counselees; 1965; cited: 1 review.

Courtship Analysis, T2:816. Adults; 1961–66; cited: 1 review.

Dating Problems Checklist, T2:817. High school and college; 1961; cited: 2 reviews.

‡I-Am Sentence Completion Test, T2:819. Marital counselees; 1971.

Individual and Family Developmental Review, T2:820. Counselees and therapy patients; 1969; cited: 1 excerpt.

‡Love Attitudes Inventory, T2:821. Grades 12–16; 1971; 1 reference.

Male Impotence Test, T2:822. Adult males; 1964; cited: 1 review.

‡Marital Diagnostic Inventory, T2:824. Marital counselees; 1973.

Marital Roles Inventory, T2:825. Marital counselees; 1961; 2 references; cited: 1 review, 3 references.

Marriage Adjustment Form, T2:826. Adults; 1938–61; 3 references; cited: 1 review, 1 reference.

Marriage Adjustment Inventory, T2:827. Marital counselees; 1962; cited: 2 reviews.

Marriage Adjustment Sentence Completion Survey, T2:828. Marital counselees; 1962–65; cited: 1 review.

Marriage Analysis, T2:829. Married couples in counseling; 1966; cited: 2 reviews.

Marriage-Personality Inventory, T2:831. Individuals and couples; 1963–69; cited: 2 reviews.

Marriage Prediction Schedule, T2:832. Adults; 1939–61; cited: 1 review, 8 references.

Marriage Role Expectation Inventory, T2:833. Adolescents and adults; 1960–63; cited: 1 review, 6 references.

Otto Pre-Marital Counseling Schedules, T2:836. Adult couples; 1961; cited: 2 reviews, 2 references.

Sex Knowledge Inventory, T2:838. Sex education classes in high school and college and adults; 1950–68; 2 references; cited: 2 reviews, 1 excerpt, 9 references.

Sexual Development Scale for Females, T2:839. Adult females; 1968–69; cited: 1 review.

DRIVING & SAFETY EDUCATION

358. ★How to Drive Tests. Beginning and experienced drivers; 1958–72.

359. ★Motorcycle Operator's Test. Motorcycle operators; 1968–70.

FOR OTHER TESTS, see in *Tests in Print II:*

†American Automobile Association Driver Testing Apparatus, T2:842. Drivers; 1939–72; 1 reference.

†Bicycle Safety—Performance and Skill Tests, T2:843. Ages 10–16; 1940–62.

Driver Attitude Survey, T2:844. Drivers; 1962–70; 4 references; cited: 3 references.

‡Driving Skill Exercises, T2:845. Automobile drivers; 1961.

General Test on Traffic and Driving Knowledge, T2:846. Drivers; 1949–50.

Hannaford Industrial Safety Attitude Scales, T2:847. Industry; 1959; cited: 1 review.

McGlade Road Test for Use in Driver Licensing, Education and Employment, T2:848. Prospective drivers; 1961–62; cited: 1 reference.

Road Test Check List for Passenger Car Drivers, T2:849. Passenger car drivers; 1947–55.

Siebrecht Attitude Scale, T2:850. Grades 9–16 and adults; 1941–58; 2 references; cited: 3 references.

‡Simplified Road Test, T2:851. Drivers; 1969.

EDUCATION

360. ★ACT Proficiency Examination in History of American Education. College and adults; 1965–77.

361. ★ACT Proficiency Examination in Philosophy of Education. College and adults; 1966–77.

362. ★Administrator Image Questionnaire. School administrators; 1968; 2 reviews, 1 reference.

363. ★Attitude to School Questionnaire. Grades kgn–2; 1976.

364. *CLEP Subject Examination in History of American Education. 1 semester of college or equivalent; 1967–76.

365. *CLEP Subject Examination in Tests and Measurements. 1 semester of college or equivalent; 1964–76; 1 review.

366. Classroom Atmosphere Questionnaire. Grades 4–9; 1971; 1 review.

367. ★Cornell Inventory for Student Appraisal of Teaching and Courses. College teachers; 1972–73; 1 review.

368. Course Evaluation Questionnaire. High school and college; 1971–72; 2 reviews, 1 reference.

369. Educational Values Assessment Questionnaire. Adults; 1973; 1 review.

370. ★Endeavor Instructional Rating System. College; 1973–74; 1 review, 5 references.

371. ★Estes Attitude Scales. End of grade 2 to grade 12; 1975–76; 5 references.

372. *Graduate Record Examinations Advanced Education Test. Graduate school candidates; 1946–76; 3 references; cited: 2 reviews, 16 references.

373. *Illinois Course Evaluation Questionnaire. College; 1965–74; 1 review, 10 references; cited: 3 references.

374. Illinois Teacher Evaluation Questionnaire. Grades 7–12; 1968–70; 1 review, 1 reference.

375. *Institutional Goals Inventory. College faculty and students and other subgroups; 1972–77; 2 reviews, 31 references; cited: 2 references.

376. ★Instructional Improvement Questionnaire. College teachers; 1972–75; 1 review, 6 references.

377. Minnesota Teacher Attitude Inventory. Teachers and (prospective) education majors in grades 12–17; 1951; 119 references; cited: 2 reviews, 442 references.

378. ★Multidimensional Assessment of Gains in School. Grades 4–6; 1970–73; 2 references.

379. ★Multidimensional Assessment of Philosophy of Education. Teachers and prospective teachers; 1973–76; 1 reference.

380. ★NCS Student Survey. High school and college; 1973-75; 2 reviews.

381. *National Teacher Examinations. College seniors and teachers; 1940-77; 2 reviews, 15 references; cited: 7 reviews, 87 references.

382. *National Teacher Examinations: Common Examinations. College seniors and teachers; 1940-76; 2 references.

383. *National Teacher Examinations: Early Childhood Education. College seniors and teachers; 1953-77.

384. *National Teacher Examinations: Educational Administration and Supervision. Prospective school administrators; 1971-77.

385. *National Teacher Examinations: Education in the Elementary School. College seniors and teachers; 1940-76.

386. *National Teacher Examinations: Education of the Mentally Retarded. College seniors and teachers; 1970-77.

387. *National Teacher Examinations: Guidance Counselor. Prospective guidance counselors; 1972-76.

388. *National Teacher Examinations: Media Specialist—Library and Audio-Visual Services. College seniors and teachers; 1970-76.

389. ★Open School Evaluation System. School evaluators, school personnel, and parents; 1975.

390. ★Parent Opinion Inventory. Parents of school children; 1976.

391. *Purdue Student-Teacher Opinionaire. Student teachers; 1969-76; 2 reviews, 8 references; cited: 3 references.

392. *Purdue Teacher Evaluation Scale. Teachers grades 7-12; 1969-75; 2 reviews, 5 references; cited: 1 reference.

393. *Purdue Teacher Opinionaire. Teachers; 1961-75; 63 references; cited: 2 reviews, 42 references.

394. School Atmosphere Questionnaire. Grades 7-12; 1971; 1 review.

395. School Attitude Test. Grades kgn-6; 1973; 2 reviews.

396. *Secondary School Research Program. High school students, teachers and administrators; 1971-75; 1 review, 4 references.

397. ★Student Information Form. Entering college freshmen; 1966-76; 1 review, 15 references.

398. *Student Instructional Report. College teachers; 1971-77; 2 reviews, 16 references; cited: 1 reference.

399. ★Student Opinion Inventory. High school; 1974.

400. ★Student Orientations Survey. College students; 1971-76; 2 reviews, 4 references.

401. *Student Reactions to College. 1 or more semesters of a two-year college; 1971-74; 2 reviews, 1 reference.

402. ★Survey of School Attitudes. Grades 1-8; 1975-77; 2 reviews.

403. ★Teacher Attitude Inventory [India]. Teachers and prospective teachers; 1974.

404. ★Teacher Evaluation by Objectives. Teachers; 1974.

405. ★Teacher-Image Questionnaire. Grades 7-12; 1968; 1 review, 2 references.

406. *UP Field Test in Education. College; 1969-77; 1 reference.

For OTHER TESTS, see in *Tests in Print II:*
Academic Freedom Survey, T2:852. College students and faculty; 1954.
‡Comprehensive Teaching and Training Evaluation, T2:856. College and training programs; 1969.
‡Counseling Services Assessment Blank, T2:857. College and adult counseling clients; 1968; 3 references.
Diagnostic Teacher-Rating Scale, T2:859. Grades 4-12; 1938-52; cited: 1 review, 7 references.
Faculty Morale Scale for Institutional Improvement, T2:861. College faculty; 1954-63.

‡General Tests of Language and Arithmetic for Students [South Africa], T2:862. First and second year Bantu candidates for primary teacher's certificate; 1972-73.
Illinois Ratings of Teacher Effectiveness, T2:865. Grades 9-12; 1967; cited: 1 review.
†Junior Index of Motivation, T2:867. Grades 7-12; 1965-70; 7 references.
†National Teacher Examinations: Education in an Urban Setting, T2:871. College seniors and teachers; 1970-73.
Ohio Teaching Record: Anecdotal Observation Form, T2:877. Teachers; 1940-45; cited: 1 excerpt, 1 reference.
Pictographic Self Rating Scale, T2:879. High school and college; 1955-57; cited: 2 reviews, 2 references.
Purdue Instructor Performance Indicator, T2:880. College teachers; 1960; 1 reference; cited: 1 review, 3 references.
Purdue Rating Scale for Instruction, T2:881. College teachers; 1927-65; cited: 2 reviews.
Remmlein's School Law Test, T2:885. Teacher education classes in school law; 1957.
‡School Administration and Supervision, T2:886. Prospective elementary school administrators and supervisors; 1968-71.
‡School Personnel Research and Evaluation Services, T2:889. Teachers and prospective administrators and supervisors; 1971.
‡School Survey of Interpersonal Relationships, T2:890. Teachers; 1971; 2 references.
‡Secondary School Administration, T2:891. Prospective secondary school administrators; 1968-71.
‡Secondary School Supervision, T2:892. Prospective secondary school supervisors; 1968-71.
Self Appraisal Scale for Teachers, T2:893. Teachers; 1957.
†Student's Rating Scale of an Instructor, T2:896. High school and college; 1952-60; 1 reference; cited: 1 review.
‡Survey of Educational Leadership Practices, T2:897. Teachers and school administrators; 1955-67; 1 reference.
†Teacher Education Examination Program, T2:898. College seniors preparing to teach; 1957-72; 2 references; cited: 1 review.
†Teacher Education Examination Program: Early Childhood Education, T2:899. College seniors preparing to teach kgn-grade 3; 1957-72.
†Teacher Education Examination Program: Elementary School Education, T2:900. College seniors preparing to teach grades 1-8; 1957-72.
Teacher Opinionaire on Democracy, T2:901. Teachers; 1949; 2 references; cited: 2 reviews.
Teacher Preference Schedule, T2:902. Elementary school teachers and prospective teachers; [1960]; 4 references.
‡Teacher Self-Rating Inventory, T2:903. Teachers; 1971.
Teaching Aptitude Test, T2:904. Grades 12-16; 1927; 2 references; cited: 2 reviews, 8 references.
Teaching Evaluation Record, T2:905. Teachers; 1953-56; 5 references.
Wilson Teacher-Appraisal Scale, T2:907. Ratings by students in grades 7-16; 1948-57; cited: 1 review.

HANDWRITING

For OTHER TESTS, see in *Tests in Print II:*
Ayres Measuring Scale for Handwriting: Gettysburg Edition, T2:908. Grades 5-8; 1912-17; 20 references; cited: 1 review, 9 references.
†Expressional Growth Through Handwriting Evaluation Scale, T2:909. Grades 1-12; 1958-68; cited: 1 review, 2 references.

HEALTH & PHYSICAL EDUCATION

407. *AAHPER Youth Fitness Test. Grades 5-12; 1958-76; 15 references; cited: 1 review, 147 references.

408. ★ACT Proficiency Examinations in Health. College and adults; 1971-76.

409. ★Athletic Motivation Inventory. Athletes ages 13 and over; 1969-77; 1 review, 19 references.

410. *CLEP Subject Examination in Human Growth and Development. 1 semester of college or equivalent; 1969-76.

411. Drug Abuse Knowledge Test. Grades 10-12; 1972-73; 1 review.

412. ★Fast-Tyson Health Knowledge Test. High school and college; 1970-75; 1 review.

413. ★Menometer. Adolescents and adults; 1974.

414. *National Teacher Examinations: Physical Education. College seniors and teachers; 1954-77.

415. *UP Field Test in Physical Education. College; 1969-77.

For OTHER TESTS, see in *Tests in Print II:*
‡AAHPER Cooperative Health Education Test, T2:910. Grades 5-9; 1971-72.

AAHPER Cooperative Physical Education Tests, T2:911. Grades 4–12; 1970; 1 reference.
AAHPER-Kennedy Foundation Special Fitness Test for the Mentally Retarded, T2:912. Ages 8–18; 1968; cited: 2 references.
AAHPER Sport Skills Tests, T2:913. Ages 10–18; 1965–69; cited: 3 references.
Action-Choice Tests for Competitive Sports Situations, T2:915. High school and college; 1960; cited: 2 references.
Attitude Inventory, T2:916. College women; [1959].
Basic Fitness Tests, T2:917. Ages 12–18; 1964; 6 references; cited: 1 review, 1 excerpt, 8 references.
Belmont Measures of Athletic Performance, T2:918. Females grades 9–16; 1963–64; cited: 2 references.
†CAHPER Fitness-Performance Test [Canada], T2:919. Ages 7–44; 1966–71; 2 references; cited: 1 reference.
College Health Knowledge Test, T2:921. College; 1950–59; 4 references; cited: 3 reviews, 4 references.
Drug Knowledge Inventory, T2:923. Grades 7–16 and adults; 1969–70; cited: 1 review.
Emporia Elementary Health Test, T2:924. Grades 6–8; 1962–64; cited: 1 review.
Emporia High School Health Test, T2:925. High school and college; 1962–64.
Health and Safety Education Test, T2:926. Grades 3–6; 1947–60; cited: 1 review.
Health Behavior Inventory, T2:927. Grades 3–16; 1962–66; 2 references; cited: 2 reviews, 4 references.
Health Education Test: Knowledge and Application, T2:928. Grades 7–13; 1946–56; 1 reference; cited: 2 reviews, 1 reference.
Health Knowledge Test for College Freshmen, T2:929. Grade 13; 1956; cited: 1 review, 3 references.
Health Test: National Achievement Tests, T2:930. Grades 3–8; 1937–57; cited: 2 reviews.
Illinois Ratings of Character in Physical Education, T2:931. High school, 1969.
Indiana Physical Fitness Test, T2:932. Grades 4–12; 1964.
†Information Test on Drugs and Drug Abuse, T2:933. Grades 9–16 and adults; 1957–68.
†Information Test on Human Reproduction, T2:934. Grades 9–16 and adults; 1950–67; 1 reference.
Kilander-Leach Health Knowledge Test, T2:935. Grades 12–16; 1936–72; 5 references; cited: 1 review, 1 excerpt, 5 references.
†Modified Sjöstrand Physical Work Capacity Test [Canada], T2:936. Ages 7–44; 1968–71; 1 reference; cited: 6 references.
Patient's Self-History Form, T2:939. Patients; 1948–58.
‡Self Administered Health Questionnaire for Secondary School Students, T2:940. High school; 1968; 2 references.
Swimming Ability Scales for Boys in Secondary Schools: National Swimming Norms [England], T2:941. Boys ages 11–18; 1964.
†Teacher Education Examination Program: Physical Education, T2:942. College seniors preparing to teach secondary school; 1957–72.
‡Tests for Venereal Disease Education, T2:943. Junior high school, high school and college; 1965–67; 2 references.
‡Thompson Smoking and Tobacco Knowledge Test, T2:944. Grades 7–16; 1964–67; 2 references.
‡VD Knowledge Test, T2:946. Grades 6 and over; 1973.
Wetzel Grid Charts, T2:947. Ages birth–18; 1940–48; 19 references; cited: 1 review, 35 references.

HOME ECONOMICS

416. NM Consumer Rights and Responsibilities Test. Grades 9–12; 2 reviews.
417. *National Teacher Examinations: Home Economics Education. College seniors and teachers; 1960–77.
418. ★Test of Consumer Competencies. Grades 8–12; 1975–76; 1 review, 1 reference.

FOR OTHER TESTS, see in *Tests in Print II:*

Compton Fabric Preference Test, T2:948. Females in grades 7 and over; 1965; 2 references; cited: 1 review, 9 references.
Emporia Clothing Test, T2:949. High school; 1962–64.
Emporia Foods Test, T2:950. High school; 1962–64.
Minnesota Check List for Food Preparation and Serving, T2:951. Grades 7–16 and adults; 1938–51; cited: 1 excerpt, 1 reference.
†Nutrition Information Test, T2:953. Grades 9–16 and adults; 1942–68; 2 references; cited: 1 reference.
Scales for Appraising High School Homemaking Programs, T2:954. Pupils, teachers, community members, and administrators; 1953.
‡Teacher Education Examination Program: Home Economics Education, T2:955. College seniors preparing to teach secondary school; 1971–72.
‡Test of Family Life Knowledge and Attitudes, T2:956. Grade 12 boys and girls seeking Betty Crocker college scholarships and awards; 1955–73.

INDUSTRIAL ARTS

419. ★Industrial Arts Aptitude Battery: Woodworking Test. Grades 7–14; 1974; 1 reference.
420. *National Teacher Examinations: Industrial Arts Education. College seniors and teachers; 1947–76.

FOR OTHER TESTS, see in *Tests in Print II:*

Drawing: Cooperative Industrial Arts Tests, T2:967. 1 semester grades 7–9; 1969–70; 1 reference; cited: 1 review.
Electricity/Electronics: Cooperative Industrial Arts Tests, T2:968. 1 semester grades 7–9; 1969–70; 1 reference; cited: 1 review.
Emporia Industrial Arts Test, T2:969. High school; 1962–63.
General Industrial Arts: Cooperative Industrial Arts Tests, T2:970. 1 year grades 7–9; 1969–70; 1 reference; cited: 1 review.
Metals: Cooperative Industrial Arts Tests, T2:971. 1 semester grades 7–9; 1969–70; 1 reference.
†Teacher Education Examination Program: Industrial Arts, T2:973. College seniors preparing to teach secondary school; 1957–72.
Technical and Scholastic Test: Dailey Vocational Tests, T2:974. Grades 8–12 and adults; 1964–65.
Woods: Cooperative Industrial Arts Tests, T2:975. 1 semester grades 7–9; 1969–70; 1 reference; cited: 1 review.

LEARNING DISABILITIES

421. ★Auditory Pointing Test. Ages 5–10; 1974; 2 reviews, 1 reference.
422. ★BACKS: Basic Achievement of Common Knowledge and Skills. Mentally and educationally retarded or culturally deprived adolescents and adults; 1969; 2 reviews, 1 reference.
423. ★Barclay Early Childhood Skill Assessment Guide. Preschool–grade 1; 1973–76; 2 reviews.
424. ★Basic School Skills Inventory. Ages 4–6; 1975; 2 reviews, 2 references.
425. ★Comprehensive Identification Process. Ages 2.5–5.5; 1975; 2 reviews, 1 reference.
426. *Cutrona Child Study Profile of Psycho-Educational Abilities. Grades kgn–3 and special education classes; 1970–75; 1 review.
427. ★Del Rio Language Screening Test. Ages 3 to 6–11; 1975; 1 excerpt, 1 reference.
428. ★Developmental Indicators for the Assessment of Learning. Ages 2.5–5.5; 1975; 2 reviews, 3 references.
429. ★Developmental Task Analysis. Grades kgn–6; 1969.
430. Grassi Basic Cognitive Evaluation. Ages 3–9; 1973; 2 reviews.
431. Illinois Test of Psycholinguistic Abilities. Ages 2–10; 1961–68; 2 reviews, 1 excerpt, 270 references; cited: 2 reviews, 374 references.
432. *Individual Learning Disabilities Classroom Screening Instrument. Preschool–grade 12; 1970–73; 2 reviews; cited: 1 reference.
433. ★Johnson-Kenney Screening Test. Ages 5.5–6.5; 1970–73; 1 review, 2 references.
434. ★Jordan Left-Right Reversal Test. Ages 5–12; 1973–74; 2 reviews, 2 excerpts, 5 references.
435. Meeting Street School Screening Test. Grades kgn–1; 1969; 1 review, 1 excerpt, 8 references; cited: 1 excerpt, 5 references.
436. ★Melvin-Smith Receptive-Expressive Observation. Grades 1–12; 1973–76; 1 reference.
437. ★Mertens Visual Perception Test. Grades kgn–1; 1969–74; 2 reviews.
438. ★Project MEMPHIS Instruments for Individual Program Planning and Evaluation. Preschool handicapped children; 1974; 1 excerpt, 2 references.
439. Pupil Rating Scale: Screening for Learning Disabilities. Grades 3–4; 1971; 1 review, 1 excerpt, 5 references.
440. ★Pupil Record of Educational Behavior. Preschool through "lower intermediate levels"; 1971; 1 review.

441. ★Rhode Island Pupil Identification Scale. Grades kgn–2; 1972; 1 review, 5 references.

442. ★Rucker-Gable Educational Programming Scale. Teachers and administrators; 1973–74; 1 review, 9 references.

443. ★SCREEN. Grades kgn–3; 1975; 1 review, 2 references.

444. ★School Problem Screening Inventory. Grades kgn–12; 1974.

445. Screening Test for the Assignment of Remedial Treatments. Ages 4-6 to 6-5; 1968; 1 excerpt, 2 references; cited: 1 review, 1 reference.

446. *Screening Tests for Identifying Children With Specific Language Disability. Grades 1–6; 1962–74; 1 excerpt, 3 references; cited: 2 reviews, 7 references.

447. ★Student Disability Survey. Grades 1–9; 1975; 1 review.

448. ★Visual Discrimination Test. Ages 5–8; 1975; 2 reviews, 1 reference.

449. ★Visual Memory Scale. Ages 5–6; 1971–75; 2 references.

450. ★Visual Memory Test. Ages 5–8; 1975; 1 review, 2 references.

451. ★Yellow Brick Road. Ages 3–6; 1975; 2 reviews.

FOR OTHER TESTS, see in *Tests in Print II*:

‡Automated Graphogestalt Technique, T2:976. Grades 1–4; 1970–72.
‡Basic Screening and Referral Form for Children With Suspected Learning and Behavioral Disabilities, T2:977. Grades 1–12; 1972.
First Grade Screening Test, T2:979. First grade entrants; 1966–69; 3 references; cited: 1 excerpt.
[Re Illinois Test of Psycholinguistic Abilities] Filmed Demonstration of the ITPA, T2:982. 1969; cited: 1 excerpt.
‡Psychoeducational Inventory of Basic Learning Abilities, T2:985. Ages 5–12 with suspected learning disabilities; 1968.
Psychoeducational Profile of Basic Learning Abilities, T2:986. Ages 2–14 with learning disabilities; 1966.
Specific Language Disability Test, T:990. "Average to high IQ" children in grades 6–8; 1967–68; cited: 2 reviews.
Valett Developmental Survey of Basic Learning Abilities, T2:991. Ages 2–7; 1966; 1 reference; cited: 2 reviews, 2 references.

LISTENING COMPREHENSION

452. *Assessment of Children's Language Comprehension. Ages 3–7; 1969–74; 1 review, 3 references.

453. Progressive Achievement Tests of Listening Comprehension [New Zealand]. Standards 1–4 and Forms I–IV (ages 7–14); 1971–72; 1 review, 2 references.

454. Tests for Auditory Comprehension of Language. Ages 3–6; 1973; 2 reviews, 6 references; cited: 2 references.

FOR OTHER TESTS, see in *Tests in Print II*:

Brown-Carlsen Listening Comprehension Test, T2:993. Grades 9–16 and adults; 1953–55; 21 references; cited: 2 reviews, 22 references.
Cooperative Primary Tests: Listening, T:994. Grades 1.5–3; 1965–67.
Orr-Graham Listening Test, T2:995. Junior high school boys; 1968; cited: 2 reviews, 5 references.
Sequential Tests of Educational Progress: Listening, T2:997. Grades 4–14; 1956–63; 24 references; cited: 2 reviews, 11 references.

PHILOSOPHY

455. *Graduate Record Examinations Advanced Philosophy Test. Graduate school candidates; 1939–76; cited: 1 reference.

456. *UP Field Test in Philosophy. College; 1969–77.

457. *UP Field Test in Scholastic Philosophy. College; 1969–77.

PSYCHOLOGY

458. ★ACT Proficiency Examination in Educational Psychology. College and adults; 1964–76.

459. *CLEP Subject Examination in Educational Psychology. 1 semester of college or equivalent; 1967–76.

460. *CLEP Subject Examination in General Psychology. 1 semester of college or equivalent; 1967–76; 1 review.

461. *Graduate Record Examinations Advanced Psychology Test. Graduate school candidates; 1939–76; 3 references; cited: 1 review, 11 references.

462. *UP Field Test in Psychology. College; 1969–77.

FOR OTHER TESTS, see in *Tests in Print II*:

Aden-Crosthwait Adolescent Psychology Achievement Test, T2:1001. College; 1963–70; cited: 1 reference.
Cass-Sanders Psychology Test, T2:1004. High school and college; 1964.

RECORD & REPORT FORMS

463. *Psychodiagnostic Test Report Blank. Psychologists; 1965–74; 1 reference.

FOR OTHER TESTS, see in *Tests in Print II*:

†A/9 Cumulative Record Folder, T2:1007. Grades kgn–12; 1951–72.
American Council on Education Cumulative Record Folders, T2:1008. Grades 1–16; 1928–47; cited: 3 reviews.
California Cumulative Record and Health Insert, T2:1009. Grades 1–12; 1944–58; cited: 1 review.
†Cassel Developmental Record, T2:1010. Birth to death; 1955–71; cited: 1 review.
Florida Cumulative Guidance Record, T2:1011. Grades 1–12; 1950–59.
G.C. Anecdotal Record Form [Canada], T2:1012. Teachers' recordings of student actions; 1943.
†Guidance Cumulative Folder and Record Forms, T2:1013. Grades kgn–12; 1941–70.
†Height Weight Interpretation Folders, T2:1014. Ages 4–17; 1947–64; 1 reference; cited: 1 reference.
Junior High School Record, T2:1015. Grades 7–10; 1955.
†Ontario School Record System [Canada], T2:1016. Grades kgn–13; 1950–72.
‡Permanent Record Folder, T2:1017. Exceptional children; 1966.
†Secondary-School Record, T2:1019. Grades 9–12; 1941–64; cited: 1 reference.

RELIGIOUS EDUCATION

464. ★Partial Index of Modernization: Measurement of Attitudes Toward Morality. Children and adults; 1972; 1 reference.

465. ★Religion Scale. Adolescents and adults; 1961; 2 references.

466. *Standardized Bible Content Tests. Bible college; 1956–76; cited: 1 reference.

467. ★Strait Biblical Knowledge Test. Grades 9–16 and adults; 1975.

FOR OTHER TESTS, see in *Tests in Print II*:

Achievement Test in Jewish History, T2:1020. Junior high school; 1962.
‡Achievement Test—Jewish Life and Observances, T2:1021. Grades 5–7; 1973.
‡Achievement Test—The State of Israel, T2:1022. "Pupils who have completed an organized course of study on the State of Israel"; 1973.
‡Bible and You, T2:1023. Ages 13 and over; 1961–64.
‡Biblical Survey Test, T2:1024. College; 1961.
†Concordia Bible Information Inventory, T2:1025. Grades 4–8; 1954–71; 1 reference.
†Inventory of Religious Activities and Interests, T2:1025A. High school and college students considering church-related occupations and theological school students; 1967–70; 2 references; cited: 1 review.
Religious Attitudes Inventory, T2:1026. Religious counselees; 1964.
†Theological School Inventory, T2:1028. Incoming seminary students; 1962–72; 7 references; cited: 5 references.
†Youth Research Survey, T2:1029. Ages 13–19; 1958–71; 1 reference; cited: 2 references.

SCORING MACHINES & SERVICES

FOR TESTS, see in *Tests in Print II*:

†Automata EDT 1200 Educational Data Terminal, T2:1030. 1967–72.
Hankes Scoring Service, T2:1031. 1946–62; 8 references; cited: 6 references.

IBM 1230 Optical Mark Scoring Reader, T2:1032. 1962–63; 19 references.
‡IBM 3881 Optical Mark Reader, T2:1033. 1972.
†MRC Scoring and Reporting Services, T2:1034. 1956–71; cited: 2 references.
NCS Scoring and Reporting Services, T2:1035. 1962–68; cited: 6 references.
NCS Sentry 70, T2:1036. 1962–70; cited: 2 reviews.
†OpScan Test Scoring and Document Scanning System, T2:1037. 1963–70; cited: 2 reviews, 3 references.
Psychological Resources, T2:1038. 1970.

SOCIOECONOMIC STATUS

468. *Home Index. Grades 4–16; 1949–74; 3 references; cited: 8 references.

FOR OTHER TESTS, see in *Tests in Print II:*
American Home Scale, T2:1039. Grades 8–16; 1942; 5 references; cited: 2 reviews, 9 references.
Environmental Participation Index, T2:1040. Culturally disadvantaged ages 12 and over; 1966–67; cited: 1 review, 2 references.
Socio-Economic Status Scales [India], T2:1041. Urban students, adults, and rural families; 1962–64; 1 reference; cited: 4 excerpts, 2 references.

TEST PROGRAMS

469. *ACT Assessment. Candidates for college entrance; 1959–77; 1 review, 208 references; cited: 3 reviews, 1 excerpt, 376 references.
470. ★ACT Proficiency Examination Program. College and adults; 1964–77.
471. *Advanced Placement Examinations. High school students desiring credit for college level courses or admission to advanced courses; 1954–76; 2 reviews, 5 references; cited: 2 reviews, 12 references.
472. *College Board Admissions Testing Program. Candidates for college entrance; 1901–77; 6 references; cited: 2 reviews, 49 references.
473. *College-Level Examination Program. 1–2 years of college or equivalent; 1964–77; 3 reviews, 15 references; cited: 3 reviews, 11 references.
474. *College Placement Tests. Entering college freshmen; 1962–75; cited: 1 review.
475. *Comparative Guidance and Placement Program. Entrants to postsecondary institutions; 1969–75; 1 review, 18 references; cited: 2 reviews, 8 references.
476-7. *Graduate Record Examinations: National Program for Graduate School Selection. Graduate school candidates; 1939–76; 6 references; cited: 2 reviews, 47 references.
478. *Secondary School Admission Test: General School Ability and Reading. Grades 5–10; 1957–77; cited: 2 reviews, 2 references.
479. *Testing Academic Achievement. High school graduates and college students; 1973–76.
480. ★Undergraduate Assessment Program. College; 1976–77.

FOR OTHER TESTS, see in *Tests in Print II:*
†Canadian Test Battery, Grade 10 [Canada], T2:1046. 1961–68.
†Canadian Test Battery, Grades 8–9 [Canada], T2:1047. Grades 8.5–9.0; 1959–68.
‡College Guidance Program. T2:1049. Grade 11; 1972–73.
Junior College Placement Program, T2:1054. Junior college entrants; 1967–69; cited: 3 reviews, 1 reference.
†National Guidance Testing Program, T2:1055. Grades 1.5–14; 1958–71.
†National Science Foundation Graduate Fellowship Testing Program, T2:1056. Applicants for N.S.F. fellowships for graduate study in the sciences; 1951–72.
‡Ohio Survey Tests, T2:1057. Grades 4, 6, 8, and 10; 1965–73.
Project Talent Test Battery, T2:1058. Grades 9–12; 1960–61; 11 references; cited: 5 references.
‡Service for Admission to College and University Testing Program [Canada], T2:1060. Candidates for college entrance; 1968–73; 3 references.

MULTI-APTITUDE BATTERIES

481. ★Academic Aptitude Test [South Africa]. Bantu pupils in Form V, first-year university; 1974–76.

482. ★Aptitude Tests for School Beginners [South Africa]. Grade 1 entrants; 1974–76.
483. *Armed Services Vocational Aptitude Battery. High school (some seniors must be included); 1967–76; 1 review, 4 references; cited: 1 reference.
484. ★Comprehensive Ability Battery. Ages 15 and over; 1975–77; 2 reviews, 3 references.
485. *Differential Aptitude Tests. Grades 8–12 and adults; 1947–75; 2 reviews, 3 excerpts, 56 references; cited: 8 reviews, 1 excerpt, 331 references.
486. Guilford-Zimmerman Aptitude Survey. Grades 9–16 and adults; 1947–56; 1 review, 9 references; cited: 4 reviews, 51 references.
487. International Primary Factors Test Battery. Grades 5–16 and adults; 1973; 2 reviews, 1 excerpt, 1 reference.
488. SRA Primary Mental Abilities. Grades kgn–12; 1946–65; 67 references; cited: 19 reviews, 2 excerpts, 368 references.
489. ★USES Basic Occupational Literacy Test. Educationally disadvantaged adults; 1971–74; 2 reviews.
490. *USES General Aptitude Test Battery. Grades 9–12 and adults; 1946–77; 96 references; cited: 9 reviews, 447 references.
491. USES Nonreading Aptitude Test Battery. Disadvantaged grades 9–12 and adults; 1965–73; 1 review, 1 excerpt, 5 references; cited: 3 references.
492. *Wide Range Intelligence and Personality Test. Ages 9.5–54; 1958–74; 1 review, 1 reference; cited: 2 reviews, 2 excerpts, 3 references.

FOR OTHER TESTS, see in *Tests in Print II:*
Academic Promise Tests, T2:1063. Grades 6–9; 1959–69; 1 reference; cited: 2 reviews, 6 references.
‡Academic-Technical Aptitude Tests [South Africa], T2:1064. "Coloured pupils" in standards 6–8; 1970.
‡Aptitude Test for Junior Secondary Pupils [South Africa], T2:1065. Bantus in Form I; 1970–72.
Aptitude Tests for Occupations, T2:1066. Grades 9–13 and adults; 1951; 3 references; cited: 2 reviews; 1 excerpt.
Detroit General Aptitudes Examination, T2:1068. Grades 6–12; 1938–54; 3 references; cited: 3 reviews.
Differential Test Battery [England], T2:1070. Ages 7 to "top university level"; 1955–59; 6 references; cited: 3 reviews.
Employee Aptitude Survey, T2:1071. Ages 16 and over; 1952–63; 14 references; cited: 4 reviews, 1 excerpt, 4 references.
Flanagan Aptitude Classification Tests, T2:1072. Grades 9–12 and adults; 1951–60; 1 reference; cited: 5 reviews, 1 excerpt, 17 references.
†High Level Battery: Test A/75 [South Africa], T2:1075. Adults with at least 12 years of education; 1960–72; cited: 1 reference.
Job-Tests Program, T2:1078. Adults; 1947–60; 12 references; cited: 4 reviews, 1 excerpt, 1 reference.
‡Junior Aptitude Tests for Indian South Africans [South Africa], T2:1079. Standards 6–8; 1971.
Measurement of Skill, T2:1080. Adults; 1956–67; cited: 3 reviews, 6 references.
Multi-Aptitude Test, T2:1081. College courses in testing; 1955; cited: 1 review, 1 reference.
Multiple Aptitude Tests, T2:1082. Grades 7–13; 1955–60; 6 references; cited: 4 reviews, 1 excerpt, 8 references.
N.B. Aptitude Tests (Junior) [South Africa], T2:1083. Standards 4–8; 1961–62.
National Institute for Personnel Research Intermediate Battery [South Africa], T2:1084. Standards 7–10 and job applicants with 9–12 years of education; 1964–69; 1 reference.
†National Institute for Personnel Research Normal Battery [South Africa], T2:1085. Standards 6–10 and job applicants with 8–11 years of education; 1960–73; 2 references.
†Senior Aptitude Tests [South Africa], T2:1088. Standards 8–10 and college and adults; 1969–71.

PERSONALITY

493. *AAMD Adaptive Behavior Scale. Mentally retarded and emotionally maladjusted ages 3–adult, grades 2–6; 1969–75; 1 review, 1 excerpt, 25 references; cited: 2 reviews, 12 references.
494. Ai3Q: A Measure of the Obsessional Personality or Anal Character [England]. Sixth form and intelligent adults; 1971; 2 reviews, 3 references; cited: 5 references.

495. Adjective Check List. Grades 9–16 and adults; 1952–65; 202 references; cited: 2 reviews, 318 references.

496. Adolescent Alienation Index. Ages 12–19; 1971; 2 reviews, 1 reference; cited: 1 reference.

497. *Animal Crackers: A Test of Motivation to Achieve. Preschool–grade 1; 1973–75; 1 review, 5 references.

498. Anxiety Scale for the Blind. Blind and partially sighted ages 13 and over; 1966–68; 1 excerpt, 1 reference; cited: 4 references.

499. ★Arlin-Hills Attitude Surveys. Grades kgn–12; 1976; 1 reference.

500. *Balthazar Scales of Adaptive Behavior. "Profoundly and severely mentally retarded adults and the younger less retarded"; 1971–76; 2 reviews, 2 excerpts, 7 references; cited: 2 references.

501. ★Barber Scales of Self-Regard for Preschool Children. Ages 2–5; 1975–76; 2 reviews, 1 reference.

502. Barclay Classroom Climate Inventory. Grades 3–6; 1971–74; 1 review, 10 references.

503. ★Barclay Learning Needs Assessment Inventory. Grades 6–16; 1975; 1 review, 1 reference.

504. Barron-Welsh Art Scale: A Portion of the Welsh Figure Preference Test. Ages 6 and over; 1959–63; 30 references; cited: 2 reviews, 83 references.

505. Behavior Status Inventory. Psychiatric inpatients; 1969; 1 review.

506. [Bender-Gestalt Test.] Ages 4 and over; 1938–46; 252 references; cited: 4 reviews, 1 excerpt, 765 references.

507. ★Bipolar Psychological Inventory. College and adults; 1971–72; 11 references.

508. ★Bradfield Classroom Interaction Analysis. Grades kgn–12; 1973; 1 review.

509. Brook Reaction Test [England]. Ages 13 and over; 1969; 2 reviews, 2 references; cited: 11 references.

510. Burks' Behavior Rating Scale for Organic Brain Dysfunction. Grades kgn–6; 1968; 2 reviews, 1 reference.

511. ★CPH Patient Attitude Scale. Mental patients; 1972–74; 6 references.

512. Caine-Levine Social Competency Scale. Mentally retarded children ages 5–13; 1963; 1 review, 2 references; cited: 1 review, 8 references.

513. California Preschool Social Competency Scale. Ages 2.5–5.5; 1969; 2 reviews, 1 excerpt, 2 references.

514. *California Psychological Inventory. Ages 13 and over; 1956–75; 1 review, 452 references; cited: 5 reviews, 2 excerpts, 934 references.

515. *[Re California Psychological Inventory.] Behaviordyne Psychodiagnostic Laboratory Service. 1969–76; 1 reference.

516. California Test of Personality. Grades kgn–14 and adults; 1939–53; 67 references; cited: 6 reviews, 2 excerpts, 438 references.

517. ★Camelot Behavioral Checklist. Mentally retarded; 1974.

518. ★Cassell's Somatic Inkblots. Mental patients and normals; 1969–77; 2 references.

519. Children's Embedded Figures Test. Ages 5–12; 1963–71; 53 references; cited; 1 review, 38 references.

520. *Children's Personality Questionnaire [South Africa]. Ages 8–12; 1959–75; 1 review, 46 references; cited: 3 reviews, 76 references.

521. ★Classroom Environment Scale. Students and teachers in grades 7–12; 1974; 2 reviews, 3 references.

522. *Clinical Analysis Questionnaire. Ages 18 and over; 1970–75; 1 review, 7 references; cited: 2 references.

523. College and University Environment Scales. College; 1962–69; 100 references; cited: 2 reviews, 208 references.

524. College Student Questionnaires. College entrants, students; 1965–69; 39 references; cited: 2 reviews, 86 references.

524A. College Student Satisfaction Questionnaire. College; 1971; 1 review, 9 references; cited: 3 references.

525. ★Community Oriented Programs Environment Scale. Patients and staff of community oriented psychiatric facilities; 1974; 1 review, 17 references.

526. ★Complex Figure Test [The Netherlands]. Ages 16 and over; 1970–73; 1 excerpt, 1 reference.

527. Comrey Personality Scales. Ages 16 and over; 1970; 1 review, 28 references; cited: 2 reviews, 24 references.

528. Concept-Specific Anxiety Scale. College and adults; 1972; 1 review, 4 references; cited: 3 references.

529. Conceptual Systems Test. Grades 7 and over; 1971; 1 review, 24 references; cited: 5 references.

530. Cornell Medical Index—Health Questionnaire. Ages 14 and over; 1949–56; 46 references; cited: 2 reviews, 151 references.

531. ★Correctional Institutions Environment Scale. Residents and staff of juvenile and adult correctional facilities; 1974; 1 review, 16 references.

532. ★Cultural Attitude Inventories. Grades 4–16 and adults; 1974.

533. *Cultural Attitude Scales. Grades kgn–6; 1971–74; 1 review.

534. ★[Daily Behavior System.] Children and adults with problem behaviors; 1971–74.

535. Defense Mechanism Inventory. Ages 16 and over; 1968–69; 30 references; cited: 1 review, 9 references.

536. Depression Adjective Check Lists. Grades 9–16 and adults; 1967; 20 references; cited: 2 reviews, 9 references.

537–8. ★Dimock L Inventory. High school and adults; 1969–74.

539. *Dynamic Personality Inventory [Canada]. Ages 15 or 17 and over with IQs of 80 and over; 1956–76; 1 review, 12 references; cited: 1 review, 26 references.

540. *Early School Personality Questionnaire. Ages 6–8; 1966–76; 2 reviews, 8 references; cited: 1 review, 18 references.

541. Education Apperception Test. Preschool and elementary school; 1973; 1 review, 1 excerpt, 1 reference; cited: 1 reference.

542. Edwards Personal Preference Schedule. College and adults; 1953–59; 334 references; cited: 7 reviews, 3 excerpts, 1314 references.

543. ★Ego Development Scale. Grades 4–16 and adults; 1974; 2 reviews, 2 references.

544. Ego-Ideal and Conscience Development Test. Ages 12–18; 1969; 1 review; cited: 5 references.

545. ★Ego State Inventory. Adolescents and adults; 1974; 2 reviews, 1 reference.

546. ★Eidetic Parents Test. Clinical patients and marriage and family counselees; 1972; 1 review, 3 excerpts, 8 references.

547. ★Eight State Questionnaire. Ages 16 and over; 1976; 1 review, 5 references.

548. Embedded Figures Test. Ages 10 and over; 1950–71; 134 references; cited: 2 reviews, 229 references.

549. ★Emotions Profile Index. College and adults; 1974; 1 review, 33 references.

550. ★Environmental Response Inventory. College and adults; 1971–74; 2 reviews, 1 reference.

551. ★Evaluation Disposition Toward the Environment. High school and college; 1976.

552. Experiential World Inventory. Disturbed

adolescents and adults; 1970; 2 reviews, 2 references; cited: 1 reference.

553. *Eysenck Personality Inventory [England]. Grades 9–16 and adults; 1963–69; 1 review, 404 references; cited: 3 reviews, 2 excerpts, 314 references.

554. ★Eysenck Personality Questionnaire [England]. Ages 7 and over; 1975–76; 4 reviews, 84 references.

555. *FIRO Scales. Grades 4–16 and adults; 1957–77; 147 references; cited: 1 review, 173 references.

556. *Fairview Development Scale: For the Infirm Mentally Retarded. Severely and profoundly mentally retarded; 1971–74.

557. ★Family Environment Scale. Family members; 1974; 2 reviews, 4 references.

558. *Family Relations Test. Ages 3 and over; 1957–76; 18 references; cited: 3 reviews, 1 excerpt, 24 references.

559. *Fear Survey Schedule. College and adults; 1964–77; 1 review, 32 references; cited: 1 review, 31 references.

560. ★Flint Infant Security Scale [Canada]. Ages 3–24 months; 1974; 1 review, 1 reference.

561. Forty-Eight Item Counseling Evaluation Test. Adolescents and adults; 1963–71; 1 review, 2 references; cited: 1 review, 2 references.

562. *Franck Drawing Completion Test [Australia]. Ages 6 and over; 1951–76; 23 references; cited: 1 review, 48 references.

563. Frost Self Description Questionnaire [Canada]. Ages 8–14; 1972–73; 1 review, 1 reference; cited: 3 references.

564. ★Gardner Analysis of Personality Survey. Grades 7–12 and adults; 1972; 1 review, 1 reference.

565. ★General Health Questionnaire [England]. Adults; 1969–72; 15 references.

566. Gerontological Apperception Test. Ages 66 and over; 1971; 1 review, 1 excerpt, 5 references; cited: 2 references.

567. *Getting Along. Grades 7–9; 1964–65; cited: 2 references.

568. Gordon Personal Inventory. Grades 9–16 and adults; 1956–63; 34 references; cited: 4 reviews, 2 excerpts, 64 references.

569. Gordon Personal Profile. Grades 9–16 and adults; 1953–63; 52 references; cited: 4 reviews, 1 excerpt, 120 references.

570. ★Gottesfield Community Mental Health Critical Issues Test. Mental health professionals; 1974; 1 review, 2 references.

571. Grid Test of Schizophrenic Thought Disorder [England]. Adults; 1967; 1 review, 30 references; cited: 1 review, 23 references.

572. Group Embedded Figures Test. Ages 10 and over; 1971; 2 reviews, 47 references; cited: 3 references.

573. ★Group Environment Scale. Group members and leaders; 1974; 2 reviews.

574. Guilford-Zimmerman Temperament Survey. Grades 12–16 and adults; 1949–55; 72 references; cited: 3 reviews, 1 excerpt, 493 references.

575. Hand Test. Ages 6 and over; 1959–71; 29 references; cited: 1 review, 1 excerpt, 33 references.

576. Harvard Group Scale of Hypnotic Susceptibility. College and adults; 1959–62; 46 references; cited: 1 review, 35 references.

577. Hill Interaction Matrix. Psychotherapy groups; 1954–68; 35 references; cited: 29 references.

578. Holtzman Inkblot Technique. Ages 5 and over; 1958–66; 1 review, 96 references; cited: 4 reviews, 2 excerpts, 260 references.

579. Hostility and Direction of Hostility Questionnaire: Personality and Personal Illness Questionnaires. Mental patients and normals; 1967; 28 references; cited: 2 reviews, 56 references.

580. How I see Myself Scale. Grades 3–12; 1966–68; 2 reviews, 11 references; cited: 6 references.

581. Human Figure Drawing Techniques. 108 references; cited: 331 references.

582. *IPAT Anxiety Scale Questionnaire. Ages 14 and over; 1957–76; 2 reviews, 85 references; cited: 3 reviews, 1 excerpt, 188 references.

583. ★IPAT Depression Scale. Adults; 1976; 2 reviews.

584. Inferred Self-Concept Scale. Grades 1–6; 1969–73; 1 review; cited: 1 reference.

585. Inpatient Multidimensional Psychiatric Scale. Hospitalized mental patients; 1953–67; 46 references; cited: 1 review, 161 references.

586. Institutional Functioning Inventory. College faculty and administrators; 1968–70; 24 references; cited: 2 reviews, 5 references.

587. ★Intermediate Personality Questionnaire for Indian Pupils [South Africa]. Standards 6–8; 1974.

588. Inter-Person Perception Test. Ages 6 and over; 1969; 2 reviews.

589. *Interpersonal Communication Inventory. Grades 9–16 and adults; 1969–76; 3 references; cited: 1 reference.

590. ★Intra- and Interpersonal Relations Scale [South Africa]. Bantu pupils in Forms IV and V; 1973–75.

591. ★Inventory of Anger Communication. High school and adults; 1974–76; 1 reference.

592. It Scale for Children. Ages 5–6; 1956; 23 references; cited: 2 reviews, 50 references.

593. ★Jackson Personality Inventory. Grades 10–16 and adults; 1976; 2 reviews, 6 references.

594. Jesness Behavior Checklist. Ages 10 and over; 1970–71; 2 reviews, 3 references.

595. Jesness Inventory. Disturbed children and adolescents ages 8–18 and adults; 1962–72; 1 review, 14 references; cited: 1 review, 18 references.

596. Junior Eysenck Personality Inventory. Ages 7–15; 1963–70; 37 references; cited: 2 reviews, 2 excerpts, 40 references.

597. *Jr.-Sr. High School Personality Questionnaire. Ages 12–18; 1953–75; 68 references; cited: 4 reviews, 140 references.

598. Ka-Ro Inkblot Test [Japan]. Ages 3 and over; 1970; 2 excerpts, 4 references; cited: 1 reference.

599. *Katz Adjustment Scales. Normal and mentally disordered adults; 1961–76; 26 references; cited: 22 references.

600. ★Katz-Zalk Opinion Questionnaire. Grades 1–6; 1973–75; 3 references.

601. ★Kinetic Family Drawings. Ages 5–20; 1970–72; 2 reviews, 1 excerpt, 17 references.

602. ★Leisure Activities Blank. Ages 15 and over; 1974–75; 2 reviews, 3 references.

603. ★Leisure Interest Inventory. High school, college, and adults; 1969.

604. M-B History Record: Self-Administered Form. Psychiatric patients and penal groups; 1957–72; 2 reviews, 3 references; cited: 12 references.

605. M-Scale: An Inventory of Attitudes Toward Black/White Relations in the United States. College and adults; 1968–69; 1 review, 1 reference; cited: 1 reference.

606. Machover Draw-A-Person Test. Ages 2 and over; 1949; 26 references; cited: 3 reviews, 304 references.

607. *Maferr Inventory of Feminine Values. Junior and senior high school, older adolescents and adults; 1955–76; 2 reviews, 28 references; cited: 11 references.

608. *Maferr Inventory of Masculine Values. Junior and senior high school, older adolescents and adults; 1966–76; 1 review, 4 references; cited: 1 reference.

609. Martin S-D Inventory. Clients and patients; 1970; 1 review, 1 reference.

610. Mathematics Anxiety Rating Scale. College and adults; 1972; 2 reviews, 3 references.

611. Maudsley Personality Inventory [England]. College and adults; 1959–62; 129 references; cited: 4 reviews, 3 excerpts, 542 references.

612. ★Means-Ends Problem-Solving Procedure. Adults; 1975; 11 references.

613. Memory-For-Designs Test. Ages 8.5 and over; 1946–60; 34 references; cited: 2 reviews, 80 references.

614. ★Merrill-Demos DD Scale: An Attitude Scale for the Identification of Potential or Actual Primary and Secondary Drug Abuse and Delinquent Behavior. Grades 3–9; 1971.

615. Middlesex Hospital Questionnaire [England]. Psychiatric and nonpsychiatric patients ages 18 and over; 1970; 2 reviews, 26 references; cited: 1 review, 13 references.

616. Minnesota Multiphasic Personality Inventory. Ages 16 and over; 1943–67; 2 reviews, 1188 references; cited: 11 reviews, 3855 references.

617. *[Re Minnesota Multiphasic Personality Inventory.] Computerized scoring and Interpreting Services. 2 reviews, 79 references.

618. ★[Re Minnesota Multiphasic Personality Inventory.] Automated Psychological Assessment. 1976; 2 reviews, 4 references.

619. *[Re Minnesota Multiphasic Personality Inventory.] Behaviordyne Psychodiagnostic Laboratory Service. 1969–76; 2 reviews, 5 references; cited: 1 review, 11 references.

620. ★[Re Minnesota Multiphasic Personality Inventory.] Caldwell Report: An MMPI Interpretation. 1969; 2 reviews, 4 references.

621. [Re Minnesota Multiphasic Personality Inventory.] MMPI-ICA Computer Report. 1963–67; 1 review, 5 references; cited: 1 review, 5 references.

622. ★[Re Minnesota Multiphasic Personality Inventory.] Psychological Assessment Services. 1973–75; 2 reviews.

623. [Re Minnesota Multiphasic Personality Inventory.] The Psychological Corporation MMPI Reporting Service. 1967; 2 reviews, 7 references; cited: 1 review, 11 references.

624. *[Re Minnesota Multiphasic Personality Inventory.] Roche MMPI Computerized Interpretation Service. 1966–76; 1 review, 7 references; cited: 2 reviews, 17 references.

625. Missouri Children's Picture Series. Ages 5–16; 1971; 2 reviews, 1 excerpt, 11 references; cited: 4 references.

626. Mooney Problem Check List. Grades 7–16 and adults; 1941–50; 48 references; cited: 5 reviews, 228 references.

627. *Motivation Analysis Test. Ages 17 and over; 1959–75; 31 references; cited: 2 reviews, 1 excerpt, 37 references.

628. Multiple Affect Adjective Check List. Grades 8–16 and adults; 1960–67; 102 references; cited: 2 reviews, 144 references.

629. ★My Self Checklist. Grades 1–9; 1973.

630. *Myers-Briggs Type Indicator. Grades 9–16 and adults; 1943–76; 1 review, 115 references; cited: 2 reviews, 1 excerpt, 186 references.

631. Nurses' Observation Scale for Inpatient Evaluation. Mental patients; 1965–66; 1 review, 37 references; cited: 35 references.

632. Object Sorting Scales [Australia]. Ages 16 and over; 1966; 1 review, 5 references; cited: 11 references.

633. ★Offer Self-Image Questionnaire for Adolescents. Ages 14–18; 1971–74; 10 references.

634. Omnibus Personality Inventory. College; 1968; 1 review, 135 references; cited: 4 reviews, 1 excerpt, 215 references.

635. Opinions Toward Adolescents. College and adults; 1971–72; 1 review.

636. *Orientation Inventory. College and industry; 1962–77; 1 review, 15 references; cited: 2 reviews, 41 references.

637. Ottawa School Behavior Check List. Ages 6–12; 1967–69; 1 review, 2 references; cited: 3 references.

638. ★PARS Scale. Mental patients and clinical clients; 1974–75; 1 review, 6 references.

639. *Pain Apperception Test. Adults; 1956–75; 1 review, 3 references; cited: 10 references.

640. ★Perception of Values Inventory. Grades kgn-12 and adults; 1973–74; 1 review, 1 reference.

641. Personal Orientation Inventory. Grades 9–16 and adults; 1962–68; 1 excerpt, 431 references; cited: 2 reviews, 203 references.

642. Personal Values Abstract. Ages 13 and over; 1972; 2 reviews, 3 references.

643. *Personality Research Form. Grades 7–16, college, and adults; 1965–74; 1 review, 132 references; cited: 3 reviews, 3 excerpts, 63 references.

644. ★Personnel Security Preview. Job applicants; 1967–75.

645. ★Physiognomic Cue Test. College and adults; 1974–75.

646. Piers-Harris Children's Self Concept Scale (The Way I Feel About Myself). Grades 3–12; 1969; 95 references; cited: 1 review, 18 references.

647-8. ★Preschool Behavior Questionnaire. Ages 3–6; 1974.

649. ★Present State Examination. Adult psychiatric patients; 1967–74; 1 review, 4 excerpts, 26 references.

650. *Primary Self-Concept Inventory. Grades kgn-6; 1973–74; 1 review, 6 references.

651. Profile of Mood States. College and psychiatric out-patients; 1971; 2 reviews, 33 references; cited: 16 references.

652. ★Projective Index of Body Awareness. Mental patients; 1969.

653. ★Psycho-Epistemological Profile [Canada]. College juniors and seniors and adults; 1968–76; 2 references.

654. Psychological Screening Inventory. Ages 16 and over; 1968–73; 1 review, 32 references; cited: 7 references.

655. Psychotic Inpatient Profile. Mental patients; 1961–68; 1 review, 10 references; cited: 1 review, 5 references.

656. Purpose in Life Test. Adults; 1962–69; 54 references; cited: 2 reviews, 11 references.

657. ★QUESTS: A Life-Choice Inventory. Grades 9–12; 1974–76.

658. *Reid Report. Job applicants; 1969–76; 1 review, 3 references; cited: 2 references.

659. *Risk-Taking-Attitude-Values Inventory. Ages 3 and over; 1972–76; 1 review, 1 reference; cited: 1 review, 1 reference.

660. Rokeach Value Survey. Ages 11 and over; 1967–73; 2 reviews, 154 references; cited: 39 references.

661. Rorschach [Switzerland]. Ages 3 and over; 1921–51; 2 reviews, 360 references; cited: 15 reviews, 4,582 references.

662. Rosenzweig Picture-Frustration Study. Ages 4 and over; 1944–64; 39 references; cited: 5 reviews, 416 references.

663. Rotter Incomplete Sentences Blank. Grades 9–16 and adults; 1950; 21 references; cited: 2 reviews, 1 excerpt, 124 references.

664. S-D Proneness Checklist. Clients and patients; 1970; 1 review.

665. ★Scale of Effectiveness Motivation [England]. Ages 3–5; 1976.

666. Scale to Measure Attitudes Toward Disabled Persons. Disabled and nondisabled adults; 1957–66; 31 references; cited: 54 references.

667. School Attitude Survey: Feelings I Have About School. Grades 3–6; 1970; 1 review; cited: 1 reference.

668. School Motivation Analysis Test. Ages 12–17; 1961–76; 2 reviews, 11 references; cited: 12 references.

669. ★Self-Administered Dependency Questionnaire [England]. Ages 8–15; 1973–74; 6 references.

670. Self-Concept and Motivation Inventory: What Face Would You Wear? Age 4 and grades kgn–12; 1967–77; 1 review, 3 references.

671. ★Self-Concept as a Learner Scale. Grades 4–12; 1967–72; 1 reference.

672. Self-Esteem Questionnaire. Ages 9 and over; 1971–76; 1 review.

673. ★Self Perception Inventory [ALSO Corporation, Inc.]. Grades 9–12 and adults; 1965–75; 1 review, 2 references.

674. Self Perception Inventory [Psychologists and Educators, Inc.]. Ages 12 and over; 1967–69; 1 review, 1 reference; cited: 3 references.

675. *Self-Rating Depression Scale. Adults; 1965–74; 72 references; cited: 42 references.

676. ★Senior Apperception Technique. Ages 65 and over; 1973; 1 review, 1 reference.

677. Shipley-Institute of Living Scale for Measuring Intellectual Impairment. Adults; 1939–46; 39 references; cited: 4 reviews, 154 references.

678. Situational Attitude Scale. College and adults; 1972; 2 reviews, 1 reference; cited: 3 references.

679. *Sixteen Personality Factor Questionnaire. Ages 16 and over; 1949–76; 3 reviews, 619 references; cited: 7 reviews, 898 references.

680. ★Social Attitude Scale. High school graduates and above; 1971–72; 2 references.

681. ★Social Climate Scales. Members of various groups; 1974; 1 review, 84 references.

682. Stanford Hypnotic Susceptibility Scale. College and adults; 1959–62; 40 references; cited: 2 reviews, 66 references.

683. State-Trait Anxiety Inventory. Grades 9–16 and adults; 1968–70; 2 reviews, 267 references; cited: 65 references.

684. State-Trait Anxiety Inventory for Children. Grades 4–6; 1970–73; 1 review, 19 references; cited: 2 references.

685. Structured and Scaled Interview to Assess Maladjustment. Mental patients; 1974; 1 review, 1 excerpt, 7 references.

686. Study of Values: A Scale for Measuring the Dominant Interests in Personality. Grades 10–16 and adults; 1931–70; 191 references; cited: 7 reviews, 1 excerpt, 836 references.

687. Suinn Test Anxiety Behavior Scale. College and adults; 1971; 1 review, 20 references; cited: 3 references.

688. *Survey of Interpersonal Values. Grades 9–16 and adults; 1960–76; 2 reviews, 51 references; cited: 3 reviews, 1 excerpt, 138 references.

689. ★TARC Assessment Inventory for Severely Handicapped Children. Severely handicapped ages 3–16; 1975.

690. ★Target Behavior. Grades kgn–8; 1973.

691. Tasks of Emotional Development Test. Ages 6–18; 1960–71; 2 excerpts, 7 references; cited: 3 references.

692. *Taylor - Johnson Temperament Analysis. Grades 7–16 and adults; 1941–77; 1 review, 18 references; cited: 3 reviews, 23 references.

693. Tennessee Self Concept Scale. Ages 12 and over; 1964–65; 382 references; cited: 2 reviews, 1 excerpt, 198 references.

649. ★Test of Social Inferences. Normals (ages 7–13), mildly retarded (ages 9 and over), and moderately retarded (ages 12 and over); 1974; 10 references.

695. Test of Work Competency and Stability [Canada]. Ages 21 and over; 1960–61; 1 review; cited: 3 references.

696. ★Tests of Perception of Scientists and Self. Grades 9–12; 1976.

697. Thematic Apperception Test. Ages 4 and over; 1935–43; 1 review, 242 references; cited: 9 reviews, 1,765 references.

698. This I Believe Test. Grades 10 and over; 1971–74; 1 review, 27 references; cited: 11 references.

699. ★Transactional Analysis Life Position Survey. Ages 18 and over; 1976.

700. ★University Residence Environment Scale. Students in university living groups; 1974; 2 reviews, 12 references.

701. ★Uses Test. Ages 11–13; 1974; 15 references.

702. ★Values Inventory for Children. Grades 1–7; 1976; 1 review, 3 references.

703. Vineland Social Maturity Scale. Birth to maturity; 1935–65; 23 references; cited: 7 reviews, 185 references.

704. ★Violence Scale. Adolescents and adults; 1973; 1 reference.

705. Wahler Self-Description Inventory. Grades 7 and over and psychiatric patients; 1971; 1 review; cited: 3 references.

706. ★Ward Atmosphere Scale. Patients and staff of hospital-based psychiatric treatment programs; 1974; 1 review, 31 references.

707. Ward Behavior Inventory. Mental patients; 1959–68; 1 review, 4 references; cited: 26 references.

708. Washington University Sentence Completion Test. Ages 12 and over; 1962–70; 26 references; cited: 6 references.

709. *What I Like to Do: An Inventory of Students' Interests. Grades 4–7; 1954–75; 1 review, 1 reference; cited: 2 reviews, 1 excerpt, 12 references.

710. Whitaker Index of Schizophrenic Thinking. Mental patients; 1973; 2 reviews, 4 references.

711. *Wilson-Patterson Attitude Inventory [England]. Ages 14 and over; 1970–75; 2 reviews, 78 references; cited: 18 references.

712. Work Environment Preference Schedule. Grades 11–16 and adults; 1973; 1 review, 1 excerpt, 13 references; cited: 8 references.

713. ★Work Environment Scale. Employees and supervisors; 1974; 3 references.

FOR OTHER TESTS, see in *Tests in Print II:*

A-S Reaction Study, T2:1090. College and adults; 1928–39; 36 references; cited: 3 reviews, 65 references.

†Activity Vector Analysis, T2:1091. Ages 16 and over; 1945–72; 10 references; cited: 5 reviews, 48 references.

Addiction Research Center Inventory, T2:1093. Drug addicts; 1961–67; 8 references; cited: 15 references.

Adjustment Inventory, T2:1095. Grades 9–16 and adults; 1934–63; 77 references; cited: 11 reviews, 2 excerpts, 172 references.

‡Affect Scale, T2:1097. College; 1960–71.

Alcadd Test, T2:1098. Adults; 1949; 1 reference; cited: 3 reviews, 9 references.

Attitudes-Interest Analysis Test, T2:1101. Early adolescents and adults; 1936–38; 18 references; cited: 1 review, 41 references.

Attitudes Toward Industrialization, T2:1102. Adults; 1959; cited: 1 review.

Attitudes Toward Parental Control of Children, T2:1103. Adults; 1936; cited: 2 references.

Ayres Space Test, T2:1104. Ages 3 and over; 1962; 4 references; cited: 2 reviews, 5 references.

Babcock Test of Mental Efficiency, T2:1105. Ages 7 and over; 1930–65; 8 references; cited: 3 reviews, 60 references.

Baker-Schulberg Community Mental Health Ideology Scale, T2:1106. Mental health professionals; 1967; 3 references; cited: 2 reviews, 3 references.

Behavior Cards, T2:1110. Delinquents having a reading grade score 4.5 or higher; 1941–50; cited: 2 reviews, 4 references.

Bristol Social Adjustment Guides [England], T2:1112. Ages 5–15; 1956–66; 17 references; cited: 2 reviews, 5 excerpts, 19 references.

Burks' Behavior Rating Scales, T2:1115. Preschool and grades kgn–8; 1968–69; 1 reference; cited: 2 references.

C-R Opinionaire, T2:1116. Grades 11–16 and adults; 1935–46; 7 references; cited: 3 reviews, 13 references.

California Life Goals Evaluation Schedules, T2:1118. Ages 15 and over; 1966–69; 2 references; cited: 1 review, 3 references.

California Medical Survey, T2:1119. Medical patients ages 10–18 and adults; 1962.

Cassel Group Level of Aspiration Test, T2:1124. Grades 5–16 and adults; 1952–57; 8 references; cited: 3 reviews, 2 excerpts, 6 references.

Chapin Social Insight Test, T2:1125. Ages 13 and over; 1967–68; cited: 2 reviews, 3 references.

Child Behavior Rating Scale, T2:1126. Grades kgn–3; 1960–62; cited: 1 review, 1 reference.

Children's Hypnotic Susceptibility Scale, T2:1128. Ages 5–16; 1963; 4 references; cited: 2 reviews, 1 excerpt, 6 references.

Client-Centered Counseling Progress Record, T2:1130. Adults and children undergoing psychotherapeutic counseling; 1950–60; cited: 1 review.

Clinical Behavior Check List and Rating Scale, T2:1132. Clinical clients; 1965.

College Inventory of Academic Adjustment, T2:1134. College; 1949; 5 references; cited: 3 reviews, 23 references.

Community Adaptation Schedule, T2:1137. Normals and psychiatric patients; 1965–68; 3 references; cited: 2 reviews, 6 references.

Community Improvement Scale, T2:1138. Adults; 1955; cited: 1 review.

Concept Formation Test, T2:1140. Normal and schizophrenic adults; 1940; 9 references; cited: 2 reviews, 47 references.

Conservatism Scale [England], T2:1143. Ages 12 and over; 1970; 9 references; cited: 9 references.

Cornell Index, T2:1144. Ages 18 and over; 1944–49; 28 references; cited: 3 reviews, 70 references.

Cornell Word Form 2, T2:1146. Adults; 1946–55; 1 reference; cited: 1 review, 14 references.

Cotswold Personality Assessment P.A.1 [Scotland], T2:1147. Ages 11–16; 1960; cited: 2 reviews, 1 reference.

‡Crawford Psychological Adjustment Scale, T2:1148. Psychiatric patients; 1968; 1 reference.

Cree Questionnaire, T2:1149. Industrial employees; 1957–59; 1 reference; cited: 2 reviews, 3 references.

Current and Past Psychopathology Scales, T2:1150. Psychiatric patients and nonpatients; 1966–68; cited: 2 reviews, 4 references.

DF Opinion Survey, T2:1151. Grades 12–16 and adults; 1954–56; 7 references; cited: 3 reviews, 12 references.

Demos D Scale: An Attitude Scale for the Identification of Dropouts, T2:1153. Grades 7–12; 1965–70; 1 reference; cited: 2 reviews.

Detroit Adjustment Inventory, T2:1155. Grades kgn–12; 1942–54; 2 references; cited: 2 reviews, 2 references.

Developmental Potential of Preschool Children, T2:1156. Handicapped children ages 2–6; 1958–62.

Devereux Adolescent Behavior Rating Scale, T2:1157. Normal and emotionally disturbed children ages 13–18; 1967; cited: 1 review, 1 reference.

Devereux Child Behavior Rating Scale, T2:1158. Emotionally disturbed and mentally retarded children ages 8–12; 1966; 1 reference; cited: 1 review, 3 references.

Devereux Elementary School Behavior Rating Scale, T2:1159. Grades kgn–6; 1966–67; 3 references; cited: 1 review, 3 references.

Diplomacy Test of Empathy, T2:1160. Business and industry; 1957–60; 1 reference; cited: 3 reviews, 3 references.

‡Discharge Readiness Inventory, T2:1161. Psychiatric patients; 1968–72; 5 references.

Edwards Personality Inventory, T2:1165. Grades 11–16 and adults; 1966–67; 4 references; cited: 2 reviews, 2 excerpts, 11 references.

Ego Strength Q-Sort Test, T2:1167. Grades 9–16 and adults; 1956–58; 1 reference; cited: 2 reviews, 3 references.

Elizur Test of Psycho-Organicity, T2:1168. Ages 6 and over; 1959–69; cited: 2 reviews, 1 excerpt, 5 references.

Emo Questionnaire, T2:1170. Adults; 1958–60; 1 reference; cited: 2 reviews, 1 reference.

Empathy Test, T2:1171. Ages 13 and over; 1947–61; 10 references; cited: 2 reviews, 30 references.

Evaluation Modality Test, T2:1172. Adults; 1956; cited: 1 review.

Eysenck-Withers Personality Inventory [England], T2:1175. Institutionalized subnormal adults; 1963–66; cited: 2 reviews, 3 references.

‡Fairview Problem Behavior Record, T2:1178. Mentally retarded; 1971.

‡Fairview Self-Help Scale, T2:1179. Mentally retarded; 1969–70; 3 references.

‡Fairview Social Skills Scale, T2:1180. Mentally retarded; 1971–74.

Family Adjustment Test, T2:1181. Ages 12 and over; 1952–54; 12 references; cited: 2 reviews, 7 references.

Famous Sayings, T2:1183. Grades 9–16 and business and industry; 1958; 8 references; cited: 2 reviews, 21 references.

Fatigue Scales Kit, T2:1184. Adults; 1944–54; cited: 1 review, 1 reference.

Fels Parent Behavior Rating Scales, T2:1186. Parents; 1937–49; 6 references; cited: 1 review, 23 references.

Freeman Anxiety Neurosis and Psychosomatic Test, T2:1188. Mental patients; 1952–55; cited: 2 reviews, 7 references.

Gibson Spiral Maze [England], T2:1191. Ages 8.5 and over; 1961–65; 3 references; cited: 1 review, 2 excerpts, 6 references.

Goldstein-Scheerer Tests of Abstract and Concrete Thinking, T2:1192. Brain damaged adults; 1941–51; 36 references; cited: 4 reviews, 91 references.

Gottschalk-Gleser Content Analysis Scales, T2:1195. Ages 14 and over; 1969; 26 references; cited: 1 review, 1 excerpt, 10 references.

Grassi Block Substitution Test, T2:1196. Mental patients; 1947–66; 7 references; cited: 2 excerpts, 18 references.

Grayson Perceptualization Test, T2:1197. Detection of cortical impairment; 1950–57; 1 reference; cited: 2 reviews, 1 reference.

Group Cohesiveness: A Study of Group Morale, T2:1199. Adults; 1958; 1 reference; cited: 2 reviews, 1 reference.

Group Dimensions Descriptions Questionnaire, T2:1200. College and adult groups; 1956; 14 references; cited: 7 references.

Group Psychotherapy Suitability Evaluation Scale, T2:1202. Patients in group therapy; 1965–68; cited: 1 reference.

†Guidance Inventory, T2:1203. High school; 1960–73; cited: 1 review.

Guilford-Holley L Inventory, T2:1204. College and adults; 1953–63; 1 reference; cited: 2 reviews, 1 reference.

Guilford-Martin Inventory of Factors GAMIN, T2:1205. Grades 12–16 and adults; 1943–48; 29 references; cited: 3 reviews, 83 references.

Guilford-Martin Personnel Inventory, T2:1206. Adults; 1943–46; 18 references; cited: 3 reviews, 69 references.

‡Hahan Self Psychoevaluation Materials, T2:1208. Ages 40 and over; 1967–73.

‡Hahnemann High School Behavior Rating Scale, T2:1209. Grades 7–12; 1971–72.

Handicap Problems Inventory, T2:1210. Ages 16 and over with physical disabilities; 1960; 7 references; cited: 1 review, 2 references.

†Hartman Value Profile, T2:1211. Ages 12 and over; 1965–72; 2 references; cited: 2 reviews.

Hellenic Affiliation Scale, T2:1213. College; 1967; 1 reference.

Hoffer-Osmond Diagnostic Test, T2:1215. Mental patients; 1961–67; 6 references; cited: 2 reviews, 28 references.

Hooper Visual Organization Test, T2:1216. Ages 14 and over; 1957–66; 5 references; cited: 2 reviews, 11 references.

Hospital Adjustment Scale, T2:1217. Mental patients; 1951–53; 19 references; cited: 2 reviews, 14 references.

How Well Do You Know Yourself?, T2:1220. High school, college, office and factory workers; 1959–61; 2 references; cited: 2 reviews, 2 excerpts, 2 references.

Human Relations Inventory, T2:1221. Grades 9–16 and adults; 1954–59; 4 references; cited: 2 reviews, 7 references.

Humm-Wadsworth Temperament Scale, T2:1222. Adults; 1934–60; 2 references; cited: 8 reviews, 70 references.

†Hunt-Minnesota Test for Organic Brain Damage, T2:1223. Chronological ages 16–70 and mental ages 8 and over; 1943–66; 3 references; cited: 3 reviews, 24 references.

Hysteroid-Obsessoid Questionnaire [England], T2:1224. Mental patients and normals; 1967; 8 references; cited: 2 reviews, 26 references.

IPAT Contact Personality Factor Test, T2:1226. High school and adults; 1954–56; 2 references; cited: 2 reviews, 7 references.

†IPAT 8-Parallel-Form Anxiety Battery, T2:1227. Ages 14 or 15 and over; 1960–73; 26 references; cited: 2 reviews, 12 references.

IPAT Humor Test of Personality, T2:1228. High school and adults; 1949–66; 2 references; cited: 3 reviews, 13 references.

IPAT Neurotic Personality Factor Test, T2:1229. Grades 9–16 and adults; 1955; cited: 2 reviews, 7 references.

Independent Activities Questionnaire, T2:1230. High school and college; 1965–67; 1 reference; cited: 2 references.

Institute of Child Study Security Test [Canada], T2:1233. Grades 1–8; 1957–68; 1 reference; cited: 1 review, 4 references.

Institutional Self-Study Service Survey, T2:1236. College students; 1969–71; 4 references; cited: 1 review.

Integration Level Test Series, T2:1237. Adults; 1965–66; 5 references; cited: 12 references.

Interest Inventory for Elementary Grades, T2:1238. Grades 4–6; 1941; 1 reference; cited: 2 reviews, 5 references.

†Interpersonal Check List, T2:1240. Adults; 1955–73; 115 references; cited: 1 review, 109 references.

‡Interpersonal Orientation Scale, T2:1242. College and adults; 1965–71; 9 references.

Interpersonal Perception Method [England], T2:1243. Married

Social Competence Inventories, T2:1385. Adults; 1951–68; cited: 2 reviews.

Social Intelligence Test, T2:1386. Grades 9–16 and adults; 1930–55; 15 references; cited: 3 reviews, 53 references.

Spiral Aftereffect Test, T2:1387. Ages 5 and over; 1958; 28 references; cited: 2 reviews, 60 references.

†Stamp Behaviour Study Technique [Australia], T2:1388. Preschool–kgn; 1968–72.

Stanford Profile Scales of Hypnotic Susceptibility, T2:1390. College and adults; 1963–67; 3 references; cited: 2 reviews, 4 references.

Stereopathy-Acquiescence Schedule, T2:1393. College; [1960]; 2 references.

†Stern Activities Index, T2:1394. Grades 7–16 and adults; 1950–72; 23 references; cited: 2 reviews, 129 references.

†Stern Environment Indexes, T2:1395. Grades 7 through graduate school; 1957–72; 38 references; cited: 2 reviews, 143 references.

Stockton Geriatric Rating Scale, T2:1396. Hospital or nursing home patients aged 65 and over; 1964–66; 1 reference; cited: 2 references.

Structured Clinical Interview, T2:1398. Mental patients; 1963–69; 6 references; cited: 2 reviews, 1 excerpt, 7 references.

Student Attitude Inventory [Australia], T2:1399. College; 1967; cited: 2 references.

Student Description Form, T2:1400. Grades 9–12; 1964.

‡Student Evaluation Scale, T2:1401. Grades 1–12; 1970.

Study of Choices, T2:1402. Ages 16 and over; 1948; 1 reference.

Study of Values: British Edition [England], T2:1404. College and adults; 1965; 4 references.

Style of Mind Inventory, T2:1405. College and adults; 1958–61.

Survey of Personal Attitude "SPA" (With Pictures), T2:1408. Adults; 1960–66; cited: 2 reviews.

Survey of Personal Values, T2:1409. Grades 11–16 and adults; 1964–67; 5 references; cited: 1 review, 9 references.

Symptom Sign Inventory [England], T2:1410. Mental patients; 1968; 12 references; cited: 2 reviews, 1 excerpt, 31 references.

Systematic Interview Guides [England], T2:1411. Mothers; 1967; cited: 1 excerpt.

‡T.M.R. Performance Profile for the Severely and Moderately Retarded, T2:1412. Ages 4 and over; 1963–67; 1 reference.

Temperament Comparator, T2:1413. Adults; 1958–61; 1 reference; cited: 2 reviews, 1 reference.

‡Temperament Questionnaire [South Africa], T2:1414. Standards 8 and over; 1964–68; 1 reference.

Test for Developmental Age in Girls, T2:1416. Girls ages 8–18; 1933–34; 2 references; cited: 1 reference.

Test of Basic Assumptions, T2:1417. Adults; 1959–68.

Test of Behavioral Rigidity, T2:1418. Ages 21 and over; 1960; 9 references; cited: 2 reviews, 13 references.

Test of Social Insight, T2:1419. Grades 6–16 and adults; 1959–63; 3 references; cited: 2 reviews, 1 excerpt, 4 references.

Tests of Social Intelligence, T2:1421. High school and adults; 1965–66; 4 references; cited: 1 review, 3 references.

Thorndike Dimensions of Temperament, T2:1422. Grades 11–16 and adults; 1963–66; 1 reference; cited: 2 reviews, 3 excerpts, 8 references.

Thurstone Temperament Schedule, T2:1423. Grades 9–16 and adults; 1949–53; 32 references; cited: 4 reviews, 1 excerpt, 49 references.

Trait Evaluation Index, T2:1424. College and adults; 1967–68; 1 reference; cited: 2 reviews, 1 reference.

Triadal Equated Personality Inventory, T2:1425. Adult males; 1960–63; cited: 1 review.

Tulane Factors of Liberalism-Conservatism, T2:1427. Social science students; 1946–55; 1 reference; cited: 2 reviews, 2 references.

Visual-Verbal Test, T2:1429. Schizophrenic patients; 1959–60; cited: 2 reviews, 8 references.

WLW Personal Attitude Invnetory, T2:1431. Business and industry; 1954–69; cited: 1 review.

‡Wahler Physical Symptoms Inventory, T2:1432. Psychiatric patients and counselees; 1973; 1 reference.

Walker Problem Behavior Identification Checklist, T2:1434. Grades 4–6; 1970; cited: 1 reference.

Weighted-Score Likability Rating Scale, T2:1436. Ages 6 and over; 1946.

Welsh Figure Preference Test, T2:1437. Ages 6 and over; 1959; 34 references; cited: 1 review, 1 excerpt, 44 references.

Western Personality Inventory, T2:1438. Adults; 1948–63.

†William, Lynde & Williams Analysis of Personal Values, T2:1441. Business and industry; 1958–71; cited: 1 review.

‡Y.E.M.R. Performance Profile for the Young Moderately and Mildly Retarded, T2:1443. Ages 3–9; 1967.

African T.A.T. [South Africa], T2:1444. Urban African adults; 1960–61; 2 references; cited: 2 references.

Association Adjustment Inventory, T2:1445. Normal and institutionalized adults; 1959; cited: 2 reviews, 1 excerpt.

Auditory Apperception Test, T2:1446. Grades 9 and over; 1953; cited: 2 reviews, 3 references.

Blacky Pictures, T2:1448. Ages 5 and over; 1950–67; 47 references; cited: 3 reviews, 4 excerpts, 118 references.

Braverman-Chevigny Auditory Projective Test, T2:1449. Ages 4 and over; 1955–64; 2 references; cited: 2 references.

Buttons, T2:1450. Grades 7–9; 1963; cited: 1 review.

Children's Apperception Test, T2:1451. Ages 3–10; 1949–74; 23 references; cited: 6 reviews, 5 excerpts, 54 references.

Color Pyramid Test [Switzerland], T2:1452. Ages 6 and over; 1951–65; 6 references; cited: 2 reviews, 3 excerpts, 10 references.

Columbus: Picture Analysis of Growth Towards Maturity [Switzerland], T2:1453. Ages 5–20; 1969; cited: 2 excerpts, 1 reference.

Curtis Completion Form, T2:1454. Grades 11–16 and adults; 1950–68; 1 reference; cited: 3 reviews, 5 references.

Draw-A-Person, T2:1455. Ages 5 and over; 1963; cited: 2 reviews.

Draw-A-Person Quality Scale, T2:1456. Ages 16–25; 1955–65; cited: 1 review, 6 references.

Driscoll Play Kit, T2:1457. Ages 2–10; 1952; 1 reference; cited: 2 references.

Family Relations Indicator, T2:1459. Emotionally disturbed children and their parents; 1962–67; cited: 3 reviews, 2 excerpts, 4 references.

Five Task Test, T2:1460. Ages 8 and over; 1955; cited: 2 reviews, 1 excerpt.

†Forer Structured Sentence Completion Test, T2:1461. Ages 10–18 and adults; 1957–67; 3 references; cited: 2 reviews, 1 excerpt, 9 references.

Forer Vocational Survey, T2:1462. Adolescents and adults; 1957; 2 reviews, 1 excerpt.

Graphoscopic Scale, T2:1465. Ages 5–16 and over; 1953–69; 1 reference; cited: 8 references.

Group Personality Projective Test, T2:1466. Ages 11 and over; 1956–61; 5 references; cited: 3 reviews, 14 references.

Group Projection Sketches for the Study of Small Groups, T2:1467. Ages 16 and over; 1949; 1 reference; cited: 3 reviews, 1 reference.

HFD Test, T2:1468. Ages 5–12; 1968; 5 references; cited: 1 review, 15 references.

H-T-P: House-Tree-Person Projective Technique, T2:1469. Ages 3 and over; 1946–66; 61 references; cited: 6 reviews, 1 excerpt, 136 references.

[Re Holtzman Inkblot Technique] Computer Scoring Service for the Holtzman Inkblot Technique, T2:1472. 1966–68; 4 references; cited: 5 references.

Howard Ink Blot Test, T2:1473. Adults; 1953–60; cited: 3 reviews, 3 excerpts, 5 references.

IES Test, T2:1475. Ages 10 and over and latency period girls; 1956–58; 16 references; cited: 2 reviews, 1 excerpt, 41 references.

Incomplete Sentence Test, T2:1476. Employees and college; 1949–53; cited: 1 review.

Industrial Sentence Completion Form, T2:1477. Employee applicants; 1963.

Kahn Test of Symbol Arrangement, T2:1478. Ages 6 and over; 1949–60; 27 references; cited: 3 reviews, 1 excerpt, 64 references.

Kent-Rosanoff Free Association Test, T2:1480. Ages 4 and over; 1910; 44 references; cited: 1 review, 116 references.

Make a Picture Story, T2:1482. Ages 6 and over; 1947–52; 10 references; cited: 3 reviews, 51 references.

Measurement of Self Concept in Kindergarten Children, T2:1483. Kgn; 1967.

Miner Sentence Completion Scale, T2:1484. Managers and management trainees; 1961–64; 4 references; cited: 1 review, 7 references.

†Object Relations Technique [England], T2:1486. Ages 11 and over; 1955–73; 5 references; cited: 2 reviews, 1 excerpt, 18 references.

PRADI Draw-A-Person Test, T2:1487. Clinical clients; 1966.

Pickford Projective Pictures [England], T2:1489. Ages 5–15; 1963; cited: 1 review, 5 excerpts, 5 references.

†Picture Identification Test, T2:1490. High school and college; 1959–71; 2 references; cited: 17 references.

Picture Impressions Test, T2:1491. Adolescents and adults; 1956–69; cited: 1 review, 1 excerpt, 4 references.

‡Picture Situation Test [South Africa], T2:1492. Adult males; 1971.

Picture Story Test Blank, T2:1493. Clinical clients; 1965–66.

Picture World Test, T2:1494. Ages 6 and over; 1955–65; cited: 1 review, 1 excerpt, 1 reference.

‡Politte Sentence Completion Test, T2:1495. Grades 1–12; 1970–71.

Psychiatric Attitudes Battery, T2:1496. Adults; 1955–61; cited: 12 references.

Rock-A-Bye, Baby, T2:1497. Ages 5–10; 1959; 1 reference; cited: 4 references.

Rohde Sentence Completions Test, T2:1498. Ages 12 and over; 1940–57; 2 references; cited: 2 reviews, 1 excerpt, 9 references.

Ruth Fry Symbolic Profile, T2:1502. Ages 14 and over; 1959–61.

School Apperception Method, T2:1503. Grades kgn–9; 1968; cited: 2 reviews, 3 references.

VOLUME II

READING

714. *ACER Primary Reading Survey Tests [Australia]. Grades 1–6; 1971–73.

715. ★ACT Proficiency Examination in Corrective Remedial Instruction in Reading. College and adults; 1975–76.

716. ★ACT Proficiency Examination in Reading Instruction in the Elementary School. College and adults; 1973–76.

717. *American School Achievement Tests: Part 1, Reading. Grades 2–9; 1941–75; 1 review, 1 reference; cited: 2 reviews.

718. ★Basic Educational Skills Inventory: Reading. Grades kgn–6; 1972–73; 1 review.

719. *California Achievement Tests: Reading. Grades 1.5–12; 1933–74; 2 reviews, 26 references; cited: 5 reviews, 1 excerpt, 74 references.

720. ★Cloze Procedure [Ebbinghaus Completion Method] as Applied to Reading. 3 reviews, 399 references.

721. *Comprehensive Tests of Basic Skills: Reading. Grades kgn. 6–12.9; 1968–76;; 1 review, 9 references.

722. Cooperative Primary Tests: Reading. Grades 1.5–3; 1965–67; 2 reviews, 1 reference.

723. ★Criterion Reading: Individualized Learning Management System. Grades kgn–adult basic education; 1970–71; 1 excerpt, 2 references.

724. Edinburgh Reading Tests [England]. Ages 8.5–12.5; 1972–73; 2 reviews.

725. ★Fountain Valley Teacher Support System in Reading. Grades 1–6; 1971–75; 2 reviews, 1 reference.

726. GAPADOL [Australia]. Ages 10–16; 1972; 1 review.

726A. Gates-MacGinitie Reading Tests. Grades 1–9; 1926–72; 34 references.

727. Gates-MacGinitie Reading Tests: Survey F. Grades 10–12; 1969–72; 1 review, 2 references; cited: 1 review.

728. Group Reading Assessment [England]. End of first year junior school; 1962–64; 2 reviews.

729. Group Reading Test [England]. Ages 6–10; 1968–69; 1 review.

730. Iowa Silent Reading Tests. Grades 6–16; 1927–73; 2 reviews, 2 excerpts, 9 references; cited: 5 reviews, 2 excerpts, 109 references.

731. *Maintaining Reading Efficiency Tests. Grades 7–16 and adults; 1966–74; 1 review.

732. Metropolitan Achievement Tests: Reading Tests. Grades 2.5–9.5; 1931–73; 2 reviews, 32 references; cited: 6 reviews, 32 references.

733. ★National Teacher Examinations: Introduction to the Teaching of Reading. College seniors and teachers; 1972–76.

734. *National Teacher Examinations: Reading Specialist. College seniors and teachers; 1969–76; 1 review.

735. *Nelson-Denny Reading Test, Forms C and D. Grades 9–16 and adults; 1929–76; 2 reviews, 31 references; cited: 4 reviews, 1 excerpt, 82 references.

736. OISE Achievement Tests in Silent Reading: Advanced Primary Battery [Canada]. Grade 2; 1969–71; 1 review.

737. ★Primary Reading Assessment Units [Canada]. Grades 1–3; 1973.

738. Progressive Achievement Tests of Reading [New Zealand]. Standards 2–4 and Forms I–IV; 1969–70; 1 review, 1 reference; cited: 2 excerpts, 1 reference.

739. ★Reading Placement Test. Students entering post-secondary institutions with open-door policies; 1976.

740. *Reading Progress Scale. Grades 3–14; 1970–75; 1 review, 1 excerpt, 2 references.

741. Reading (Comprehension and Speed): Municipal Tests: National Achievement Tests. Grades 3–8; 1938–57; 1 review.

742. ★SPAR Reading Test [England]. Ages 7-0 to 15-11; 1976; 1 review.

743. ★St. Lucia Reading Comprehension Test [Australia]. Grades 2–4; 1974.

744. Sequential Tests of Educational Progress: Reading, Series II. Grades 4–14; 1956–72; 2 reviews, 7 references; cited: 5 reviews, 31 references.

745. *Stanford Achievement Test: Reading Tests. Grades 1.5–9.5; 1923–75; 2 reviews, 22 references; cited: 5 reviews, 53 references.

746. *Sucher-Allred Reading Placement Inventory. Reading level grades 1–9; 1968–73; 2 reviews, 2 excerpts, 3 references; cited: 1 reference.

747. Wide-span Reading Test [England]. Ages 7–15; 1972; 2 reviews.

Commerce Reading Comprehension Test, T2:1538. Grades 12–16 and adults; 1956–58; 1 reference.

Comprehension Test for Training College Students [England], T2:1539. Training college students and applicants for admission; 1962.

Comprehensive Primary Reading Scales, T2:1540. Grade 1; 1956–60.

Comprehensive Reading Scales, T2:1541. Grades 4–12; 1948–53.

Cooperative Reading Comprehensive Test, Form Y [Australia], T2:1544. Secondary forms 5–6 and university; 1948–64; 6 references.

Cooperative Reading Comprehension Test, Forms L and M [Australia], T2:1545. Secondary forms 2–4; 1960–67.

Davis Reading Test, T2:1546. Grades 8–13; 1956–62; 18 references; cited: 3 reviews, 2 references.

Delaware County Silent Reading Test, T2:1547. Grades 1.5–8; 1965; cited: 1 review.

Emporia Reading Tests, T2:1549. Grades 1–8; 1962–64; cited: 1 review.

GAP Reading Comprehension Test [Australia], T2:1550. Grades 2–7; 1965–70; 3 references; cited: 2 reviews.

High School Reading Test: National Achievement Tests, T2:1556. Grades 7–12; 1939–52; cited: 3 reviews.

Individual Reading Test [Australia], T2:1557. Ages 6-0 to 9-9; 1935–36; cited: 1 review.

‡Informal Reading Assessment Tests [Canada], T2:1558. Grades 1–3; 1971.

‡Inventory-Survey Tests, T2:1559. Grades 4–8; 1968–69.

Kelvin Measurement of Reading Ability [Scotland], T2:1561. Ages 8–12; 1933.

Kingston Test of Silent Reading [England], T2:1562. Ages 7–11; 1953–54; cited: 2 reviews.

Lee-Clark Reading Test, T2:1563. Grades 1–2; 1931–65; 2 references; cited: 3 reviews.

McGrath Test of Reading Skills, T2:1564. Grades 1–13; 1965–67; cited: 1 review.

McMenemy Measure of Reading Ability, T2:1565. Grades 3 and 5–8; 1964–68; cited: 2 reviews.

Minnesota Reading Examination for College Students, T2:1568. Grades 9–16; 1930–35; 7 references; cited: 3 reviews, 6 references.

Monroe's Standardized Silent Reading Test, T2:1569. Grades 3–12; 1919–59; 27 references; cited: 2 reviews, 5 references.

N.B. Silent Reading Tests (Beginners): Reading Comprehension Test [South Africa], T2:1570. Substandard B; 1961.

Nelson Reading Test, T2:1573. Grades 3–9; 1931–62; 5 references; cited: 3 reviews, 1 excerpt, 1 reference.

New Developmental Reading Tests, T2:1574. Grades 1–6; 1955–68; 2 references; cited: 4 reviews, 4 references.

Pressey Diagnostic Reading Tests, T2:1576. Grades 3–9; 1929; 3 references.

‡Primary Reading Survey Tests, T2:1577. Grades 2–3; 1973.

Primary Reading Test: Acorn Achievement Tests, T2:1578. Grades 2–3; 1943–57; cited: 1 review.

RBH Basic Reading and Word Test, T2:1580. Disadvantaged adults; 1968–69; cited: 1 review.

RBH Test of Reading Comprehension, T2:1581. Business and industry; 1951–63; cited: 2 reviews.

†Reading Comprehension: Canadian English Achievement Test [Canada], T2:1582. Grades 8.5–9.0; 1959–68; cited: 2 reviews.

Reading Comprehension: Cooperative English Tests, T2:1583. Grades 9–14; 1940–60; 51 references; cited: 4 reviews, 70 references.

Reading Comprehension Test, T2:1584. College entrants; 1963–68.

†Reading Comprehension Test DE [England], T2:1585. Ages 10–12.5; 1963–71.

Reading Comprehension Test: National Achievement Tests [Crow, Kuhlmann, and Crow], T2:1586. Grades 4–9; 1953–57.

Reading Comprehension Test: National Achievement Tests [Speer and Smith], T2:1587. Grades 3–8; 1938–57; cited: 1 review.

†Reading for Understanding Placement Test, T2:1588. Grades 3–16; 1959–69; 2 references.

Reading: Public School Achievement Tests, T2:1590. Grades 3–8; 1928–59.

Reading Test AD [England], T2:1591. Ages 7-6 to 11-1; 1956–70; 3 references; cited: 2 reviews.

Reading Test: McGraw-Hill Basic Skills System, T2:1593. Grades 11–14; 1970; cited: 1 review.

†Reading Tests A and BD [England], T2:1594. 1–4 years primary school; 1967–73.

Reading Tests EH 1–3 [England], T2:1595. First 4 years of secondary school; 1961–66.

SRA Achievement Series: Reading, T2:1596. Grades 1–9; 1954–69; 9 references; cited: 4 reviews, 6 references.

SRA Reading Record, T2:1597. Grades 6–12; 1947–59; 1 reference; cited: 2 reviews, 1 excerpt, 2 references.

Schrammel-Gray High School and College Reading Test, T2:1598. Grades 7–16; 1940–42; 2 references; cited: 2 reviews, 1 excerpt.

Silent Reading Tests [South Africa], T2:1600. Standards 1–10 (ages 7–17); 1947–63.

Southgate Group Reading Tests [England], T2:1601. Ages 6–8; 1960–62; cited: 2 reviews, 1 excerpt.

Stanford Achievement Test: High School Reading Test, T2:1602. Grades 9–12; 1965–66; 1 reference; cited: 2 reviews.

Survey of Primary Reading Development, T2:1605. Grades 1–4; 1957–64; cited: 3 reviews.

Survey of Reading Achievement, T2:1606. Grades 7–12; 1959; cited: 2 reviews.

Survey Tests of Reading, T2:1607. Grades 3–13; 1931–32.

Tests of Academic Progress: Reading, T2:1608. Grades 9–12; 1964–66; cited: 1 review, 2 references.

Tests of Reading: Inter-American Series, T2:1609. Grades 1–13; 1950–73; cited: 3 reviews, 12 references.

Traxler High School Reading Test, T2:1610. Grades 10–12; 1938–67; 3 references; cited: 5 reviews, 2 excerpts, 4 references.

Traxler Silent Reading Test, T2:1611. Grades 7–10; 1934–69; 1 reference; cited: 6 reviews, 1 excerpt, 5 references.

Van Wagenen Analytical Reading Scales, T2:1612. Grades 4–12; 1953–54.

W.A.L. English Comprehension Test [Australia], T2:1613. High school; 1962–65.

Williams Primary Reading Test, T2:1615. Grades 1–3; 1926–55; 2 references; cited: 1 review.

Williams Reading Test for Grades 4–9, T2:1616. 1929; 1 reference.

DIAGNOSTIC

748. ★Analysis of Skills: Reading. Grades 1–8; 1974–76; 2 reviews.

749. *Classroom Reading Inventory. Grades 2–10; 1965–76; 1 review, 6 references; cited: 1 excerpt, 1 reference.

750. Cooper-McGuire Diagnostic Word-Analysis Test. Grades 1–5 and over; 1970–72; 1 review.

751. Cooperative Primary Tests: Word Analysis. Grades 1.5–3; 1965–67; 1 review.

752. ★Diagnosis: An Instructional Aid: Reading. Grades 1–6; 1973–74; 1 review.

753. *Diagnostic Reading Scales. Grades 1–6 and poor readers in grades 7–12; 1963–75; 2 reviews, 1 excerpt, 15 references; cited: 2 reviews, 11 references.

754. *Diagnostic Reading Tests. Various grades kgn–13; 1947–74; 4 references; cited: 5 reviews, 61 references.

755. ★Diagnostic Screening Test: Reading. Grades 1–12; 1976; 1 review.

756. ★Domain Phonic Tests [Scotland]. Ages 5–9; 1972.

757. Doren Diagnostic Reading Test of Word Recognition Skills. Grades 1–4; 1956–73; 1 review, 3 excerpts, 3 references; cited: 2 reviews, 2 references.

758. ★Fountain Valley Teacher Support System in Secondary Reading. Grades 7–12; 1976; 2 reviews.

759. Gates-McKillop Reading Diagnostic Tests. Grades 2-9 to 6-0; 1926–62; 1 review, 8 references; cited: 5 reviews, 18 references.

760. Gillingham-Childs Phonics Proficiency Scales. Grades 2–8; 1966–72; 2 reviews.

761. Group Phonics Analysis. Reading Level grades 1–3 1971; 1 review, 1 excerpt, 1 reference.

762. Individual Phonics Criterion Test. Grades 1–8; 1971; 1 review.

763. ★Individual Pupil Monitoring System—Reading. Grades 1–6; 1974; 2 reviews.

764. ★Individualized Criterion Referenced Testing: Reading. Grades kgn–8; 1973–76; 2 reviews.

765. ★McGrath Diagnostic Reading Test. Grades 1–13; 1974–76.

766. ★Mastery: An Evaluation Tool: Reading. Grades kgn–9; 1974–76; 1 review, 1 excerpt, 1 reference.

767. ★Objectives-Referenced Bank of Items and Tests: Reading and Communication Skills. Grades kgn–12 and adults; 1975.

768. ★Power Reading Survey Test. Grades 1–12; 1973–75; 2 reviews, 1 excerpt, 1 reference.

769. *Prescriptive Reading Inventory. Grades kgn.0–

6.5; 1972–77; 2 reviews, 5 references.
2 reviews, 5 references.

770. ★Ransom Program Reading Tests. Grades kgn–6; 1974–75; 1 review.

771. ★Reading: IOX Objectives-Based Tests. Grades kgn–6; 1973–76; 2 reviews.

772. *Reading Skills Diagnostic Test. Grades 2–8; 1967–71; 2 reviews; cited: 1 reference.

773. SPIRE Individual Reading Evaluation. Reading levels grades primer–10; 1970–73; 2 reviews, 1 reference.

774. ★Sand: Concepts About Print Test [New Zealand]. Ages 5–7; 1972.

775. Sipay Word Analysis Tests. Grades 1–adult; 1974; 2 reviews, 2 excerpts, 4 references.

776. ★Skills Monitoring System: Reading. Grades 3–5; 1974–75; 1 review.

777. *Stanford Diagnostic Reading Test. Grades 1.5–13; 1966–76; 1 review, 13 references; cited: 1 review, 5 references.

778. Wisconsin Tests of Reading Skill Development: Word Attack. Grades kgn–6; 1970–72; 2 reviews, 6 references; cited: 1 reference.

779. Woodcock Reading Mastery Tests. Grades kgn–12; 1972–73; 2 reviews, 4 excerpts, 7 references.

FOR OTHER TESTS, see in *Tests in Print II:*

California Phonics Survey, T2:1619. Grades 7–12 and college, 1956–63; 1 reference; cited: 2 reviews, 2 references.
Denver Public Schools Inventory, T2:1621. Grades 1–8; 1965–68.
Diagnostic Examination of Silent Reading Abilities, T2:1622. Grades 4–12; 1939–54; 7 references; cited: 3 reviews, 1 excerpt, 2 references.
Diagnostic Reading Examination for Diagnosis of Special Difficulty in Reading, T2:1623. Grades 1–4; [1928–29]; 4 references.
Diagnostic Reading Test: Pupil Progress Series, T2:1625. Grades 1.9–8; 1956–70; 1 reference; cited: 3 reviews.
Durrell Analysis of Reading Difficulty, T2:1628. Grades 1–6; 1937–55; 18 references; cited: 6 reviews, 2 references.
Group Diagnostic Reading Aptitude and Achievement Tests, T2:1631. Grades 3–9; 1939; 3 references.
‡LRA Standard Mastery Tasks in Language, T2:1633. Grades 1–2; 1970.
McCullough Word-Analysis Tests, T2:1634. Grades 4–6; 1962–63; 1 reference; cited: 3 reviews, 2 references.
‡McGuire-Bumpus Diagnostic Comprehensive Test, T2:1635. Reading levels grades 2.5–6; 1971–72.
Phonics Knowledge Survey, T2:1637. Grades 1–6; 1964; cited: 2 reviews.
Phonovisual Diagnostic Test, T2:1638. Grades 3–12; 1949–58; cited: 2 reviews.
‡Prescriptive Reading Inventory Interim Tests, T2:1640. Grades 1.5–6.5; 1973.
Primary Reading Profiles, T2:1641. Grades 1–3; 1953–68; 2 references; cited: 2 reviews.
‡Reading Diagnostic Probes, T2:1642. Grades 2–9; 1970.
Roswell-Chall Diagnostic Reading Test of Word Analysis Skills, T2:1643. Grades 2–6; 1956–59; 2 references; cited: 3 reviews, 1 reference.
Schonell Reading Tests [Scotland], T2:1646. Ages 5–15; 1942–55; 18 references; cited: 3 reviews, 7 references.
Silent Reading Diagnostic Tests, T2:1647. Grades 2–6; 1955–70; 3 references; cited: 4 reviews, 8 references.
Standard Reading Inventory, T2:1649. Grades 1–7; 1966; 2 references; cited: 1 review, 8 references.
Standard Reading Tests [England], T2:1650. Reading ages up to 9; 1958; 1 reference; cited: 2 reviews, 1 reference.
‡Swansea Test of Phonic Skills [England], T2:1652. Reading ages below 7.5; 1970–71.
†Test of Individual Needs in Reading, T2:1653. Grades 1–6; 1961–71; cited: 2 references.
‡Test of Phonic Skills, T2:1654. Reading level grades kgn–3; 1971; cited: 2 reviews.

MISCELLANEOUS

780. Instant Word Recognition Test. Reading level grades 1–4; 1971; 1 review, 1 excerpt, 1 reference.

781. *Inventory of Teacher Knowledge of Reading. Elementary school teachers and college students in methods courses; 1971–75; 1 excerpt, 6 references.

782. ★Speed Scale for Determining Independent Reading Level. Grades 1–12; 1975; 1 review.

FOR OTHER TESTS, see in *Tests in Print II:*

Basic Sight Word Test, T2:1657. Grades 1–2; 1942; 5 references.
Botel Reading Inventory, T2:1658. Grades 1–12; 1961–70; 2 references; cited: 2 reviews, 5 references.
Cumulative Reading Record, T2:1659. Grades 9–12; 1933–56.
Durrell Listening-Reading Series, T2:1660. Grades 1–9; 1969–70; 3 references; cited: 2 reviews, 3 references.
Durrell-Sullivan Reading Capacity and Achievement Tests, T2:1661. Grades 2.5–6; 1937–45; 12 references; cited: 4 reviews, 1 excerpt, 9 references.
Dyslexia Schedule, T2:1662. Children having reading difficulties and first grade entrants; 1968–69; cited: 1 review, 3 references.
Individual Reading Placement Inventory, T2:1663. Youth and adults with reading levels up to grade 7; 1969; 1 reference; 2 reviews.
Learning Methods Test, T2:1666. Grades kgn–3; 1954–55; 3 references; cited: 2 reviews, 1 reference.
‡National Test of Basic Words, T2:1667. Grades 1–5; 1970.
OC Diagnostic Syllabizing Test, T2:1668. Grades 4–6; 1960–62.
Phonics Test for Teachers, T2:1669. Reading methods courses; 1964; cited: 2 reviews, 2 references.
Reader Rater With Self-Scoring Profile, T2:1670. Ages 15 and over; 1959–65.
Reader's Inventory, T2:1671. Entrants to a reading improvement course for secondary and college students and adults; 1963; cited: 2 reviews.
Reading Eye II, T2:1672. Grades 1–16 and adults; 1959–69; 5 references; cited: 3 reviews, 12 references.
Reading Versatility Test, T2:1673. Grades 5–16; 1961–68; 1 reference; cited: 1 review.
Roswell-Chall Auditory Blending Test, T2:1674. Grades 1–4; 1963; 7 references; cited: 2 reviews, 2 references.
Word Discrimination Test, T2:1675. Grades 1–8; 1958; cited: 2 references.
‡Word Recognition Test [England], T2:1676. Preschool to age 8.5; 1970.

ORAL

783. *Burt Word Reading Test [England]. Ages 5 and over; 1921–76; 5 references; cited: 10 references.

784. ★Cutrona Reading Inventory. Grades kgn–12 and adult; 1975.

785. Gilmore Oral Reading Test. Grades 1–8; 1951–68; 1 excerpt, 17 references; cited: 4 reviews, 22 references.

786. ★McGrath's Preliminary Screening Test in Reading. Grades 1–13; 1973–76.

787. Oral Reading Criterion Test. Reading level grades 1–7; 1971; 1 excerpt, 1 reference.

788. ★Oral Word-Recognition Test. Grades 1–13; 1973.

789. ★Reading Classification Test [Australia]. Ages 7.5–11.5; 1972–76; 1 reference.

790. Reading Miscue Inventory. Grades 1–8; 1972; 2 reviews, 27 references; cited: 1 reference.

791. ★Salford Sentence Reading Test [England]. Ages 6-10 to 10-6; 1976; 1 review.

792. Standardized Oral Reading Check Tests. Grades 1–8; 1 review; cited: 2 reviews, 8 references.

793. Standardized Oral Reading Paragraphs. Grades 1–8; 1915; 1 review; cited: 2 reviews, 26 references.

FOR OTHER TESTS, see in *Tests in Print II:*

‡Concise Word Reading Tests [Australia], T2:1677. Ages 7–12; 1969.
Flash-X Sight Vocabulary Test, T2:1678. Grades 1–2; 1961.
Gray Oral Reading Test, T2:1681. Grades 1–16 and adults; 1963–67; 11 references; cited: 3 reviews.
Holborn Reading Scale [England], T2:1682. Ages 5.5–10; 1948; 2 references; cited: 2 reviews, 1 reference.
†Neale Analysis of Reading Ability [England], T2:1683. Ages 6–13; 1957–66; 7 references; cited: 2 reviews, 1 excerpt.
Oral Word Reading Test [New Zealand], T2:1685. Ages 7–11; 1952; 2 references; cited: 2 reviews.
‡St. Lucia Graded Word Reading Test [Australia], T2:1687. Grades 2–7; 1969.
Slosson Oral Reading Test, T2:1688. Grades 1–8 and high school; 1963; 5 references.

READINESS

794. APELL Test: Assessment Program of Early Learning Levels. Ages 4.5–7; 1969; 1 excerpt; cited: 1 reference.

795. Academic Readiness Scale. First grade entrants; 1968; 2 reviews, 1 reference; cited: 1 reference.

796. Analysis of Readiness Skills: Reading and Mathematics. Grades kgn–1; 1972; 2 reviews.

797. ★Cognitive Skills Assessment Battery. Prekgn–kgn; 1974; 2 reviews.

798. ★Hess School Readiness Scale. Ages 3.5–7.0; 1975; 1 review, 3 references.

799. Initial Survey Test. First grade entrants; 1970–72; 2 reviews, 1 reference.

800. ★Jansky Screening Index. Kgn; 1972; 14 references.

801. Macmillan Reading Readiness Test. First grade entrants; 1965–70; 2 reviews, 3 references.

802. *Metropolitan Readiness Tests. Kgn and first grade entrants; 1933–76; 111 references; cited: 5 reviews, 1 excerpt, 197 references.

803. Murphy-Durrell Reading Readiness Analysis. First grade entrants; 1949–65; 1 excerpt, 13 references; cited: 4 reviews, 21 references.

804. ★PMA Readiness Level. Grades kgn–1; 1946–74; 1 review.

805. PreReading Expectancy Screening Scales. First grade entrants; 1973; 2 reviews, 1 reference.

806. Riley Preschool Developmental Screening Inventory. Ages 3–5; 1969; 1 review.

807. *School Readiness Survey. Ages 4–6; 1967–75; 1 review, 3 references; cited 2 excerpts.

808–9. ★School Readiness Test. Grades kgn–1; 1974–77; 1 review.

810. ★Thackray Reading Readiness Profiles [England]. Ages 4–8 to 5–8; 1974; 3 excerpts, 4 references.

FOR OTHER TESTS, see in *Tests in Print II*:

ABC Inventory to Determine Kindergarten and School Readiness, T2:1691. Entrants to kgn and grade 1; 1965; 2 references; cited: 1 review, 2 references.
American School Reading Readiness Test, T2:1694. First grade entrants; 1941–64; cited: 4 reviews, 3 references.
Anton Brenner Developmental Gestalt Test of School Readiness, T2:1696. Ages 5–6; 1964; cited: 1 review, 16 references.
Basic Concept Inventory, T2:1697. Preschool and kgn; 1967; cited: 2 reviews, 2 references.
Binion-Beck Reading Readiness Test for Kindergarten and First Grade, T2:1698. Grades kgn–1; 1945; cited: 2 reviews, 1 reference.
Clymer-Barrett Prereading Battery, T2:1699. First grade entrants; 1966–69; 2 references; cited: 2 reviews, 2 references.
Contemporary School Readiness Test, T2:1700. First grade entrants; 1970; cited: 1 review.
‡Delco Readiness Test, T2:1701. First grade entrants; 1970.
Gates-MacGinitie Reading Tests: Readiness Skills, T2:1702. Grades kgn–1; 1939–69; 2 references; cited: 5 reviews, 2 excerpts, 27 references.
†Gesell Developmental Tests, T2:1703. Ages 5–10; 1964–71; 4 references; cited: 2 excerpts, 5 references.
Group Test of Reading Readiness. T2:1704. Grades kgn–1; 1949–59; 1 reference; cited: 1 review.
Harrison-Stroud Reading Readiness Profiles, T2:1705. Grades kgn–1; 1949–56; 17 references; cited: 2 reviews, 2 references.
‡Inventory of Primary Skills, T2:1707. Grades kgn–1; 1970.
‡Kindergarten Behavioural Index [Australia], T2:1708. Grades kgn–1; 1972.
Kindergarten Evaluation of Learning Potential, T2:1709. Kgn; 1963–69; cited: 1 excerpt, 5 references.
‡LRS Seriation Test, T2:1710. Ages 4–6; 1968; 3 references.
Lee-Clark Reading Readiness Test, T2:1711. Grades kgn–1; 1931–62; 13 references; cited: 4 reviews, 24 references.
†Lippincott Reading Readiness Test, T2:1712. Grades kgn–1; 1965–73; cited: 1 review, 1 reference.
McHugh-McParland Reading Readiness Test, T2:1713. Grades kgn–1; 1966–68; cited: 2 reviews.
Maturity Level for School Entrance and Reading Readiness, T2:1715. Grades kgn–1; 1950–59; 3 references; cited: 1 review.
Parent Readiness Evaluation of Preschoolers, T2:1718. Ages 3–9 to 5–8; 1968–69; cited: 3 reviews.
‡Pre-Reading Assessment Kit [Canada], T2:1719. Grades kgn–1; 1971–72.
Pre-Reading Screening Procedures, T2:1721. First grade entrants of average or superior intelligence; 1968–69; 1 reference; cited: 2 reviews, 1 reference.
‡Preschool and Kindergarten Performance Profile, T2:1722. Preschool and kgn; 1970.
Primary Academic Sentiment Scale, T2:1723. Ages 4–4 to 7–3;

1968; cited: 1 review.
Reading Aptitude Tests, T2:1724. Grades kgn–1; 1935; 16 references; cited: 1 review, 5 references.
‡Reading Inventory Probe 1, T2:1725. Grades 1–2; 1970–73.
Reversal Test [Sweden], T2:1726. Grade 1 entrants; 1954.
School Readiness Checklist, T2:1728. Ages 5–6; 1963–68; cited: 1 review.
Screening Test of Academic Readiness, T2:1730. Ages 4–0 to 6–5; 1966; cited: 1 review, 1 excerpt, 5 references.
Sprigle School Readiness Screening Test, T2:1731. Ages 4–6 to 6–9; 1965; 2 references; cited: 2 reviews, 4 references.
Steinbach Test of Reading Readiness, T2:1732. Grades kgn–1; 1965–66; 1 reference.
Van Wagenen Reading Readiness Scales, T2:1733. First grade entrants; 1933–58; 3 references; cited: 1 review, 4 references.
Watson Reading-Readiness Test [Canada], T2:1734. Grades kgn–1; 1960.

SPECIAL FIELDS

811. Adult Basic Reading Inventory. Functionally illiterate adolescents and adults; 1966; 1 review; cited: 1 review.

812. Reading/Everyday Activities in Life. Ages 10 and over; 1972; 2 reviews, 1 reference.

813. *SRA Reading Index. Job applicants ages 14 and over with poor educational backgrounds; 1968–74; 3 references; cited: 1 review.

FOR OTHER TESTS, see in *Tests in Print II*:

†ANPA Foundation Newspaper Test, T2:1735. Grades 7–12; 1969–72.
†Iowa Tests of Educational Development: Ability to Interpret Reading Materials in the Social Studies, T2:1737. Grades 9–12; 1942–67; 2 references.
†Iowa Tests of Educational Development: Ability to Interpret Reading Materials in the Natural Sciences, T2:1738. Grades 9–12; 1942–67; 2 references.
Purdue Reading Test for Industrial Supervisors, T2:1739. Supervisors; 1955; 3 references; cited: 2 reviews, 1 reference.
RBH Scientific Reading Test, T2:1740. Employees in technical companies; 1950–69; cited: 1 review.
Reading Adequacy "READ" Test: Individual Placement Series, T2:1741. Adults in industry; 1961–66; cited: 1 review.
Reading: Adult Basic Education Student Survey, T2:1742. Poorly educated adults; 1966–67.
Reading Comprehension Test for Personnel Selection [England], T2:1743. Applicants for technical training programs with high verbal content; 1965–66; cited: 2 reviews, 3 references.
Robinson-Hall Reading Tests, T2:1745. College; 1940–49; 2 references; cited: 1 review, 5 references.
Understanding Communication (Verbal Comprehension), T2:1747. Industrial employees at the skilled level or below; 1959; 1 reference; cited: 2 reviews.

SPEED

814. Basic Reading Rate Scale. Grades 3–16; 1970–71; 1 review, 1 excerpt, 1 reference; cited: 1 review.

FOR ANOTHER TEST, see in *Tests in Print II*:

Minnesota Speed of Reading Test for College Students, T2:1749. Grades 12–16; 1936; 13 references; cited: 3 reviews, 2 references.

STUDY SKILLS

815. Cornell Learning and Study Skills Inventory. Grades 7–16; 1970; 2 reviews, 1 excerpt, 1 reference; cited: 2 references.

816. ★Effective Study Test. Grades 8–13; 1964–72; 1 review, 2 references.

817. ★Goyer Organization of Ideas Test. College; 1966–68; 1 reference.

818. *Study Attitudes and Methods Survey. High school and college; 1972–76; 2 reviews, 6 references; cited: 4 references.

819. ★Study Skills Surveys. Grades 9–16; 1965–70.

820. Survey of Study Habits and Attitudes. Grades 7–14; 1953–67; 45 references; cited: 3 reviews, 2 excerpts, 128 references.

821. ★Test of Library/Study Skills. Grades 2–12; 1975.

822. Watson-Glaser Critical Thinking Appraisal. Grades 9–16 and adults; 1942–64; 49 references; cited: 3 reviews, 3 excerpts, 144 references.

823. Wisconsin Tests of Reading Skill Development: Study Skills. Grades kgn–7; 1970–73; 1 review, 3 references.

For other tests, see in *Tests in Print II*:

Bristol Achievement Tests: Study Skills [England], T2:1750. Ages 8–13; 1969; cited: 1 review.
College Adjustment and Study Skills Inventory, T2:1751. College; 1968; cited: 2 reviews.
†Comprehensive Tests of Basic Skills: Study Skills, T2:1752. Grades 2.5–12; 1968–71; cited: 1 review.
‡Cornell Class-Reasoning Test, T2:1753. Grades 4–12; 1964; 1 reference.
‡Cornell Conditional-Reasoning Test, T2:1754. Grades 4–12; 1964; 1 reference.
Cornell Critical Thinking Test, T2:1755. Grades 7–16; 1961–71; 2 references; cited: 10 references.
Evaluation Aptitude Test, T2:1757. Candidates for college and graduate school entrance; 1951–52; cited: 2 reviews.
†Iowa Tests of Educational Development: Use of Sources of Information, T2:1758. Grades 9–12; 1942–67; 1 reference.
Library Orientation Test for College Freshmen, T2:1759. Grade 13; 1950–61; 1 reference; cited: 3 reviews, 1 reference.
‡Library Tests, T2:1760. College; 1967–72.
Logical Reasoning, T2:1761. Grades 9–16 and adults; 1955; 10 references; cited: 2 reviews, 1 reference.
‡National Test of Library Skills, T2:1762. Grades 2–12; 1967–71.
Nationwide Library Skills Examination, T2:1763. Grades 4–12; 1962–63.
OC Diagnostic Dictionary Test, T2:1764. Grades 5–8; 1960.
SRA Achievement Series: Work-Study Skills, T2:1765. Grades 4–9; 1955–69; cited: 2 reviews.
Study Habits Checklist, T2:1767. Grades 9–14; 1957–67; 3 references.
Study Habits Inventory, T2:1768. Grades 12–16; 1934–41; 14 references; cited: 3 reviews, 8 references.
Study Performance Test, T2:1769. High school and college; 1934–43.
Study Skills Counseling Evaluation, T2:1770. High school and college; 1962; cited: 2 reviews.
Study Skills Test: McGraw-Hill Basic Skills System, T2:1771. Grades 11–14; 1970; cited: 1 review.
Test on Use of the Dictionary, T2:1773. High school and college; 1955–63.
‡Uncritical Inference Test, T2:1774. College; 1955–67; 5 references.

SCIENCE

824. *CLEP General Examinations: Natural Sciences. 1–2 years of college or equivalent; 1964–76; 1 review, 2 references.

825. ★Comprehensive Tests of Basic Skills: Science. Grades 4.5–8.9; 1973–76; 1 review.

826. Cooperative Science Tests: Advanced General Science. Grades 8–9; 1962–65; 1 review; cited: 1 review, 2 excerpts, 1 reference.

827. Cooperative Science Tests: General Science. Grades 7–9; 1962–65; cited: 1 review, 2 excerpts, 1 reference.

828. *National Teacher Examinations: Biology and General Science. College seniors and teachers; 1940–77.

829. *National Teacher Examinations: Chemistry, Physics, and General Science. College seniors and teachers; 1940–77; 1 review.

830. Sequential Tests of Educational Progress: Science, Series II. Grades 4–14; 1956–72; 2 reviews, 4 references; cited: 5 reviews, 20 references.

For other tests, see in *Tests in Print II*:

Adkins-McBride General Science Test, T2:1777. High school; 1969; cited: 1 review.
Borman-Sanders Elementary Science Test, T2:1778. Grades 5–8; 1964; cited: 1 review.
Elementary Science Test: National Achievement Tests, T2:1782. Grades 4–6; 1948–58; 1 reference; cited: 1 review.
Emporia General Science Test, T2:1783. 1–2 semesters high school; 1962–64; cited: 1 review.
‡General Science Test [South Africa], T2:1784. Matriculants and higher; 1955(?)–70; 1 reference.
General Science Test: National Achievement Tests, T2:1785.

Grades 7–9; 1936–50; cited: 3 reviews.
General Science III: Achievement Examinations for Secondary Schools, T2:1786. High school; 1951–54.
†Iowa Tests of Educational Development: General Background in the Natural Sciences, T2:1787. Grades 9–12; 1942–67; 2 references; cited: 2 reviews, 1 reference.
SRA Achievement Series: Science, T2:1790. Grades 4–9; 1963–69; cited: 1 review.
†Science: Minnesota High School Achievement Examinations, T2:1791. Grades 7–9; 1951–70; cited: 2 reviews.
Science Tests: Content Evaluation Series, T2:1792. Grades 8–9; 1969; cited: 1 review.
Scientific Knowledge and Aptitude Test [India], T2:1793. High school; 1964; 1 reference; cited: 1 reference.
Stanford Achievement Test: High School Science Test, T2:1795. Grades 9–12; 1965–66; cited: 2 reviews.
Stanford Achievement Test: Science, T2:1796. Grades 5.5–9.9; 1940–68; cited: 3 reviews, 1 reference.
†Teacher Education Examination Program: Biology and General Science, T2:1797. College seniors preparing to teach secondary school; 1957–72.
†Teacher Education Examination Program: Chemistry, Physics and General Science, T2:1798. College seniors preparing to teach secondary school; 1957–72.
Tests of Academic Progress: Science, T2:1799. Grades 9–12; 1964–66; cited: 1 review, 1 reference.

BIOLOGY

831. *Advanced Placement Examination in Biology. High school students desiring credit for college level courses and admission to advanced courses; 1956–77; 1 reference; cited: 2 reviews, 2 references.

832. *CLEP Subject Examination in Biology. 1 year of college or equivalent; 1970–76; 1 review.

833. *College Board Achievement Test in Biology. Candidates for college entrance; 1915–76; 1 reference; cited: 2 reviews, 5 references.

834. *College Placement Test in Biology. Entering college freshman; 1962–75; 1 reference; cited: 2 reviews.

835. *Graduate Record Examinations Advanced Biology Test. Graduate school candidates; 1939–76; cited: 1 review.

836. *UP Field Test in Biology. College; 1969–77; 1 review.

For other tests, see in *Tests in Print II*:

†BSCS Achievement Tests, T2:1801. Grade 10; 1962–70.
†Biological Science: Interaction of Experiments and Ideas, T2:1802. Grades 10–12; 1963–70.
†Biology: Minnesota High School Achievement Examinations, T2:1803. High school; 1951–70; cited: 1 review.
†Cooperative Biology Test: Educational Records Bureau Edition, T2:1807. High school; 1941–70; 1 reference; cited: 3 references.
Cooperative Science Tests: Biology, T2:1808. Grades 10–12; 1963–65; cited: 1 review.
Emporia Biology Test, T2:1809. 1–2 semesters high school; 1962–64.
General Biology Test: National Achievement Tests, T2:1810. High school; 1951; cited: 2 reviews.
Nelson Biology Test, T2:1812. Grades 9–13; 1950–65; 1 reference; cited: 4 reviews, 1 excerpt, 3 references.

CHEMISTRY

837. *ACS Cooperative Examination in General Chemistry. 1 year college; 1934–76; 1 review, 3 references; cited: 7 reviews, 1 excerpt, 20 references.

838. *ACS Cooperative Examination in Inorganic Chemistry. College juniors and seniors (Form 1976 for graduate level also); 1961–76; 2 references; cited: 1 review, 1 excerpt, 4 references.

839. *ACS Cooperative Examination in Inorganic-Organic-Biological Chemistry (for Allied Health Science Programs). 1–4 quarters of chemistry for para-medical students; 1970–74; 2 references.

840. *ACS Cooperative Examination in Organic Chemistry. 1 year college; 1942–74; 3 references; cited: 1 review, 7 references.

841. *ACS Cooperative Examination in Organic Chemistry, Graduate Level. Entering graduate students; 1961–74; 2 references; cited: 2 references.

842. *ACS Cooperative Examination in Physical Chemistry. 1 year college; 1946–76; 1 review, 2 references; cited: 1 review, 5 references.

843. ACS Cooperative Examination in Physical Chemistry, Graduate Level. Entering graduate students; 1961–72; 1 review, 1 reference; cited: 3 references.

844. *ACS-NSTA Cooperative Examination in High School Chemistry, [Advanced Level]. Advanced high school classes; 1963–74; 2 reviews, 1 reference; cited: 3 reviews, 3 references.

845. *ACS-NSTA Cooperative Examination in High School Chemistry, [Lower Level]. 1 year high school; 1957–75; 1 review, 11 references; cited: 6 reviews, 2 excerpts, 17 references.

846. *Advanced Placement Examination in Chemistry. High school students desiring credit for college level courses and admission to advanced courses; 1954–77; 1 review, cited: 1 review, 2 references.

847. *CLEP Subject Examination in General Chemistry. 1 year of college or equivalent; 1964–76; 1 review.

848. *College Board Achievement Test in Chemistry. Candidates for college entrance; 1901–76; cited: 3 reviews, 13 references.

849. *College Placement Test in Chemistry. Entering college freshmen; 1962–75; cited: 3 reviews.

850. Cooperative Science Tests: Chemistry. Grades 9–12; 1963–65; 2 reviews; cited: 2 excerpts.

851. Emporia Chemistry Test. 1–2 semesters high school; 1962–64; 1 review.

852. *Graduate Record Examinations Advanced Chemistry Test. Graduate school candidates; 1939–76; 1 reference; cited: 1 review, 1 reference.

853. *Toledo Chemistry Placement Examination. College entrants; 1959–74; 1 review, 3 references; cited: 2 reviews, 3 references.

854. *UP Field Test in Chemistry. College; 1969–77.

For other tests, see in *Tests in Print II:*
ACS Cooperative Examination Brief Course in Organic Chemistry, T2:1814. 1 semester college; 1956–70; cited: 1 excerpt, 1 reference.
†ACS Cooperative Examination in Analytical Chemistry, Graduate Level, T2:1815. Entering graduate students; 1961–73; 1 reference; cited: 2 references.
†ACS Cooperative Examination in Biochemistry, T2:1816. College; 1947–72; cited: 1 excerpt, 3 references.
ACS Cooperative Examination in Brief Physical Chemistry, T2:1817. 1 semester college; 1968; 1 reference.
†ACS Cooperative Examination in Brief Qualitative Analysis, T2:1818. College; 1961–73; 4 references; cited: 1 excerpt, 4 references.
ACS Cooperative Examination in Inorganic Chemistry, Graduate Level, T2:1821. Entering graduate students; 1965–70; 1 reference.
†ACS Cooperative Examination in Instrumental Analysis, T2:1823. Grades 15–16; 1966–72; cited: 1 reference.
ACS Cooperative Examination in Qualitative Analysis, T2:1828. College; 1939–69; cited: 3 reviews, 1 excerpt, 4 references.
†ACS Cooperative Examination in Quantitative Analysis, T2:1829. College; 1944–74; cited: 2 reviews, 1 excerpt, 2 references.
Chemistry: Achievement Examinations for Secondary Schools, T2:1834. High school; 1951–54; cited: 1 review.
Chemistry Achievement Test for CHEM Study or Equivalent, T2:1835. High school; 1968–69.
†Chemistry: Minnesota High School Achievement Examinations, T2:1836. High school; 1955–73; cited: 1 review.
†Cooperative Chemistry Test: Educational Records Bureau Edition, T2:1839. High school; 1941–70; 1 reference; cited: 1 review, 3 references.
General Chemistry Test: National Achievement Tests, T2:1842. Grades 10–16; 1958–59; cited: 1 review.
Iowa Placement Examinations: Chemistry Aptitude, T2:1044. Grades 12–13; 1925–44; 11 references; cited: 2 reviews, 20 references.
Iowa Placement Examinations: Chemistry Training, T2:1845. Grades 12–13; 1925–26; 2 references; cited: 2 reviews, 15 references.
RBH Test of Chemical Comprehension, T2:1846. Employee applicants and applicants for nurses' training; 1951–68.

GEOLOGY

855. *Graduate Record Examinations Advanced Geology Test. Graduate school candidates; 1939–76; cited: 1 reference.

856. *UP Field Test in Geology. College; 1969–77.

For another test, see in *Tests in Print II:*
†CLEP Subject Examination in Geology, T2:1849. 1 year of college or equivalent; 1965–73.

MISCELLANEOUS

857. ★ACT Proficiency Examination in Anatomy and Physiology. College and adults; 1975–76.

858. ★ACT Proficiency Examination in Earth Science. College and adults; 1966–76.

859. NM Concepts of Ecology Test. Grades 6–12; 1973; 1 review.

860. Tests of Basic Experiences: Science. Prekgngrade 1; 1970–72; 1 review.

861. ★Understanding in Science Test [Australia]. Grades 7–9; 1975.

For other tests, see in *Tests in Print II:*
Butler Life Science Concept Test, T2:1852. Grades 1–6; 1965–69; cited: 1 review.
Dubins Earth Science Test, T2:1853. Grades 8–12; 1969; cited: 1 review.
‡Science Attitude Questionnaire [England], T2:1855. Secondary school; 1970–71.
Test on Understanding Science, T2:1856. Grades 9–12; 1961; 11 references; cited: 2 reviews, 33 references.

PHYSICS

862. *Advanced Placement Examinations in Physics. High school students desiring credit for college level courses and admission to advanced courses; 1954–77; 1 review, 3 references; cited: 1 review, 2 references.

863. *College Board Achievement Test in Physics. Candidates for college entrance; 1901–76; 1 reference; cited: 2 reviews, 11 references.

864. *College Placement Test in Physics. Entering college freshman; 1962–75; cited: 2 reviews.

865. Cooperative Science Tests: Physics. Grades 10–12; 1963–65; 1 review; cited: 1 review, 2 excerpts.

866. *Graduate Record Examinations Advanced Physics Test. Graduate school candidates; 1939–76; 1 reference; cited: 2 reviews.

867. *UP Field Test in Physics. College; 1969–77.

For other tests, see in *Tests in Print II:*
†Cooperative Physics Test: Educational Records Bureau Edition, T2:1861. High school; 1941–70; 1 reference; cited: 3 references.
Dunning-Abeles Physics Test, T2:1863. Grades 10–13; 1950–67; cited: 3 reviews, 2 references.
Emporia Physics Test, T2:1864. 1–2 semesters high school; 1962–64; cited: 1 review.
General Physics Test: National Achievement Tests, T2:1865. Grades 10–16; 1958–62; cited: 1 review.
Iowa Placement Examinations: Physics Aptitude, T2:1867. Grades 12–13; 1925–44; 1 reference; cited: 2 reviews, 6 references.
Iowa Placement Examinations: Physics Training, T2:1868. Grades 12–13; 1925–26; 1 reference; cited: 1 review, 2 references.
‡Objective Tests in Physics, T2:1869. High school; 1971.
Physics: Achievement Examinations for Secondary Schools, T2:1870. High school; 1951–54; cited: 1 review.
†Physics: Minnesota High School Achievement Examinations, T2:1871. High school; 1951–70; cited: 1 review.
Tests of the Physical Science Study Committee, T2:1872. High school; 1959–67; 1 reference; cited: 2 reviews, 1 excerpt, 1 reference.

SENSORY MOTOR

868. ★Bender-Purdue Reflex Test: For Signs of Symmetric Tonic Neck Reflex Immaturity. Ages 6–12; 1976; 1 review.

869. ★Cleary-Now Test of Perceptual-Motor Readiness. Grades kgn–1; 1973–74.

870. Developmental Test of Visual-Motor Integration. Ages 2–15; 1967; 2 reviews, 24 references; cited: 1 review, 11 references.

871. Frostig Movement Skills Test Battery. Ages 6–12; 1972; 2 reviews, 4 references.

872. Minnesota Percepto-Diagnostic Test. Ages 5–16; 1962–69; 22 references; cited: 2 reviews, 38 references.

873. Primary Visual Motor Test. Ages 4–8; 1964–70; 2 excerpts, 5 references; cited: 1 review, 1 excerpt, 1 reference.

874. Purdue Perceptual-Motor Survey. Ages 6–10; 1966; 21 references; cited: 2 reviews, 34 references.

875. Southern California Sensory Integration Tests. Ages 4–10 with learning problems; 1962–72; 2 reviews, 5 references; cited: 18 references.

876. *Spatial Orientation Memory Test. Ages 5–9; 1971–75; 1 review.

877. Standardized Road-Map Test of Direction Sense. Ages 7–18; 1965; 1 excerpt, 2 references; cited: 1 review, 2 excerpts, 6 references.

878. Symbol Digit Modalities Test. Ages 8 and over; 1973; 2 reviews; cited: 4 references.

FOR OTHER TESTS, see in *Tests in Print II:*

D-K Scale of Lateral Dominance, T2:1874. Grades 2–6; 1969; cited: 1 review, 1 reference.

Harris Tests of Lateral Dominance, T2:1877. Ages 7 and over; 1947–58; 20 references; cited: 2 reviews, 1 excerpt, 1 reference.

†Leavell Hand-Eye Coordinator Tests, T2:1878. Ages 8–14; 1958–61.

MKM Picture Arrangement Test, T2:1879. Grades kgn–6; 1963–65.

†Moore Eye-Hand Coordination and Color-Matching Test, T2:1880. Ages 2 and over; 1949–68; 2 references; cited: 2 reviews, 7 references.

Perceptual Forms Test, T2:1881. Ages 5–8; 1955–69; 1 reference; cited: 3 reviews, 14 references.

‡Rosner Perceptual Survey, T2:1884. Ages 5–12; 1968.

Southern California Kinesthesia and Tactile Perception Tests, T2:1885. Ages 4–8; 1966; 2 references; cited: 1 review, 2 references.

Southern California Perceptual-Motor Tests, T2:1886. Ages 4–8; 1965–69; 2 references; cited: 1 review, 1 excerpt, 5 references.

Trankell's Laterality Tests [Sweden], T2:1890. Left-handed children in grades 1–2; [1951].

‡Wold Digit-Symbol Test, T2:1891. Ages 6–16; 1967–70.

‡Wold Sentence Copying Test, T2:1892. Grades 2–8; 1967–70.

‡Wold Visuo-Motor Test, T2:1893. Ages 6–16; 1967–70.

MOTOR

879. Motor Problems Inventory. Preschool through grade 5; 1972; 1 review.

880. ★Perceptual Motor Test. Grades 1–3; 1972–73; 2 reviews.

881. Test of Motor Impairment. Ages 5–14; 1972; 1 review, 2 references; cited: 4 references.

FOR OTHER TESTS, see in *Tests in Print II:*

‡Devereux Test of Extremity Coordination, T2:1894. Emotionally handicapped and neurologically impaired ages 4–10; 1971–73; 1 reference.

Lincoln-Oseretsky Motor Development Scale, T2:1895. Ages 6–14; 1948–56; 27 references; cited: 1 review, 10 references.

‡Manual Accuracy and Speed Test, T2:1896. Ages 4 and over; 1971; 1 reference.

Oseretsky Tests of Motor Proficiency: A Translation From the Portuguese Adaptation, T2:1898. Ages 4–16; 1946; 15 references; cited: 1 review, 1 excerpt, 16 references.

Perrin Motor Coordination Test, T2:1899. Adults; [1921].

Rail-Walking Test, T2:1900. Ages 5 and over; 1941–44; 8 references; cited: 1 review, 7 references.

Smedley Hand Dynamometer, T2:1901. Ages 6–18; [1920(?)–53]; 10 references.

Southern California Motor Accuracy Test, T2:1902. Ages 4–7 with nervous system dysfunction; 1964; 2 references; cited: 1 review, 1 excerpt, 9 references.

‡Teaching Research Motor-Development Scale, T2:1903. Moderately and severely retarded (preschool–grade 12); 1972.

VISION

882. Marianne Frostig Developmental Test of Visual Perception. Ages 3–8; 1961–66; 72 references; cited: 5 reviews, 167 references.

883. Motor-Free Visual Perception Test. Ages 4–8; 1972; 1 review, 1 excerpt, 9 references.

884. *Stycar Vision Tests [England]. Normal and handicapped children 6 months and over; 1958–76; 8 references; cited: 5 references.

885. 3-D Test of Visualization Skill. Ages 3–8; 1972; 1 review.

FOR OTHER TESTS, see in *Tests in Print II:*

A-B-C Vision Test for Ocular Dominance, T2:1905. Ages 5 and over; 1927–46; 5 references; cited: 1 review, 5 references.

AO Sight Screener, T2:1906. Adults; 1945–56; 8 references; cited: 2 reviews, 15 references.

Atlantic City Eye Test, T2:1907. Grades 1 and over; 1953–61; 1 reference; cited: 1 reference.

Basic Screen Test—Vision: Measurement of Skill Test 12, T2:1908. Job applicants; 1963–69.

Burnham-Clark-Munsell Color Memory Test, T2:1909. Adults; 1955–56; 2 references; cited: 1 reference.

Dennis Visual Perception Scale, T2:1910. Grades 1–6; 1969; cited: 1 review, 1 reference.

Dvorine Pseudo-Isochromatic Plates, T2:1911. Ages 3 and over; 1944–58; 13 references; cited: 7 excerpts, 30 references.

Farnsworth Dichotomous Test for Color Blindness: Panel D-15, T2:1912. Ages 12 and over; 1947; 16 references; cited: 1 review, 1 excerpt, 2 references.

Farnsworth-Munsell 100-Hue Test for the Examination of Color Discrimination, T2:1913. Mental ages 12 and over; 1942–57; 23 references; cited: 1 review, 3 references.

‡Guy's Colour Vision Test for Young Children [England], T2:1914. Ages 3–5 and handicapped; 1972.

†Inter-Society Color Council Color Aptitude Test, T2:1915. Adults; 1944–64; 11 references; cited: 5 references.

Keystone Ready-to-Read Tests, T2:1916. School entrants; 1954.

Keystone Tests of Binocular Skill, T2:1917. Grades 1 and over; 1938–49; cited: 1 reference.

†Keystone Visual Screening Tests, T2:1918. Preschool and over; 1933–71; 27 references; cited: 1 review, 1 excerpt, 61 references.

MKM Binocular Preschool Test, T2:1919. Preschool; 1963–65.

MKM Monocular and Binocular Reading Test, T2:1920. Grades 1 and over; 1963–64; 1 reference.

Ortho-Rater, T2:1923. Adults; 1942–58; 31 references; cited: 2 reviews, 100 references.

†Pseudo-Isochromatic Plates for Testing Color Perception, T2:1924. Ages 7 and over; 1940–65; 21 references; cited: 1 excerpt, 17 references.

School Vision Tester, T2:1925. Grades kgn and over; 1957–74; cited: 2 reviews, 3 references.

‡Sheridan Gardiner Test of Visual Acuity [England], T2:1926. Ages 5 and over; 1970; 1 reference.

‡Sloan Achromatopsia Test, T2:1927. Individuals suspected of total color blindness; 1955–61.

Southern California Figure-Ground Visual Perception Test, T2:1928. Ages 4–10; 1966; 4 references; cited: 1 review, 2 references.

Spache Binocular Reading Test, T2:1929. Nonreaders and grades 1 and over; 1943–55; 2 references; cited: 2 reviews, 8 references.

‡Speed of Color Discrimination Test, T2:1930. College; 1964; 1 reference.

Test for Colour-Blindness [Japan], T2:1932. Ages 4 and over; 1917–70; 29 references; cited: 71 references.

Titmus Vision Tester, T2:1934. Ages 3 and over; 1958–69; 6 references; cited: 1 reference.

‡Visualization Test of Three Dimensional Orthographic Shape, T2:1935. High school and college; 1971.

SOCIAL STUDIES

886. *CLEP General Examinations: Social Sciences and History. 1–2 years of college or equivalent; 1964–76; 1 review, 1 reference.

887. *College Board Achievement Test in American History and Social Studies. Candidates for college entrance; 1901–76; cited: 3 reviews, 10 references.

888. *College Board Achievement Test in European History and World Cultures. Candidates for college entrance; 1901–76; cited: 1 review.

889. *College Placement Test in American History and Social Studies. Entering college freshmen; 1962–75; cited: 3 reviews.

890. *College Placement Test in European History and World Cultures. Entering college freshmen; 1963–75; cited: 1 review.

891. *National Teacher Examinations: Social Studies. College seniors and teachers; 1940–76; 1 review, cited: 1 review.

892. Sequential Tests of Educational Progress: Social Studies, Series II. Grades 4–14; 1956–72; 2 reviews, 1 reference; cited: 5 reviews, 14 references.

893. Zimmerman-Sanders Social Studies Test. Grades 7–8; 1962–64; 1 review.

For OTHER TESTS, see in *Tests in Print II:*
American History—Government—Problems of Democracy: Acorn Achievement Tests, T2:1936. Grades 9–16; 1942–53; cited: 2 reviews.
American School Achievement Tests: Social Studies and Science, T2:1937. Grades 4–9; 1941–63.
History and Civics Test: Municipal Tests, T2:1943. Grades 3–8; 1938–55; cited: 2 reviews.
†Iowa Tests of Educational Development: Understanding of Basic Social Concepts, T2:1944. Grades 9–12; 1942–67; 1 reference; cited: 1 review.
Primary Social Studies Test, T2:1946. Grades 1–3; 1967; cited: 1 review.
SRA Achievement Series: Social Studies, T2:1947. Grades 4–9; 1963–69.
†Social Studies: Minnesota High School Achievement Examinations, T2:1949. Grades 7–9; 1961–70.
Social Studies Test: Acorn National Achievement Tests, T2:1950 Grades 7–9; 1946–50; cited: 1 review.
Social Studies Test: National Achievement Tests, T2:1951. Grades 4–9; 1937–57; cited: 1 review.
Stanford Achievement Test: High School Social Studies Test, T2:1952. Grades 9–12; 1965–66; 1 reference.
Stanford Achievement Test: Social Studies Tests, T2:1953. Grades 5.5–9; 1940–68; cited: 3 reviews.
†Teacher Education Examination Program: Social Studies, T2:1954. College seniors preparing to teach secondary school; 1957–72.
Tests of Academic Progress: Social Studies, T2:1955. Grades 9–12; 1964–66; cited: 1 review, 1 reference.
†Tests of Basic Experiences: Social Studies, T2:1956. Prekgn–grade 1; 1970–72.

CONTEMPORARY AFFAIRS

For TESTS, see in *Tests in Print II:*
†Current News Test, T2:1958. Grades 9–12; 1951–74.
†Newsweek NewsQuiz, T2:1959. Grades 9–12; 1951–74.
†School Weekly News Quiz, T2:1960. High school; 1947–74.
†Time Current Affairs Test, T2:1961. Grades 9–12 and adults; 1935–74.
‡Time Monthly News Quiz, T2:1962. Grades 9–12 and adults; 1969–74.

ECONOMICS

894. ★CLEP Subject Examination in Introductory Macroeconomics. 1 semester of college or equivalent; 1974–76.

895. ★CLEP Subject Examination in Introductory Micro- and Macroeconomics. 1–2 semesters of college or equivalent; 1974–76.

896. ★CLEP Subject Examination in Introductory Microeconomics. 1 semester of college or equivalent; 1974–76.

897. *Graduate Record Examinations Advanced Economics Test. Graduate school candidates; 1939–76; 1 review; cited: 1 reference.

898. ★Junior High School Test of Economics. Grades 7–9; 1973–74; 1 review.

899. Modern Economics Test: Content Evaluation Series. Grades 10–12; 1971; 2 reviews.

900. Primary Test of Economic Understanding. Grades 2–3; 1971; 2 reviews, 1 reference; cited: 1 reference.

901. Test of Elementary Economics. Grades 4–6; 1971; 2 reviews, 1 reference.

902. Test of Understanding in Personal Economics. High School; 1971; 1 review, 5 references.

903. *UP Field Test in Economics. College; 1969–73.

For OTHER TESTS, see in *Tests in Print II:*
†CLEP Subject Examination in Introductory Economics, T2:1963. 1 year of college or equivalent; 1964–73.
‡Economics/Objective Tests, T2:1964. 1 semester high school; 1970.
Test of Economic Understanding, T2:1968. High school and college; 1963–64; 19 references; cited: 2 reviews, 1 excerpt, 10 references.
Test of Understanding in College Economics, T2:1970. 1–2 semesters college; 1967–68; 10 references; cited: 1 review.

GEOGRAPHY

904. *Graduate Record Examinations Advanced Geography Test. Graduate school candidates; 1966–76.

905. *UP Field Test in Geography. College; 1969–77.

For OTHER TESTS, see in *Tests in Print II:*
Brandywine Achievement Test in Geography for Secondary Schools, T2:1973. Grades 7–12; 1962.
†Economic Geography: Achievement Examinations for Secondary Schools, T2:1974. High school; 1951–61.
Geography Test: Municipal Tests, T2:1975. Grades 3–8; 1938–52; cited: 1 review.
Geography Test: National Achievement Tests, T2:1976. Grades 6–8; 1938–49; cited: 1 review.
Hollingsworth-Sanders Geography Test, T2:1978. Grades 5–7; 1962–64; cited: 1 review.

HISTORY

906. ★ACT Proficiency Examination in African and Afro-American History. College and adults; 1972–76.

907. *Advanced Placement Examination in American History. High school students desiring credit for college level courses and admission to advanced courses; 1956–77; cited: 3 reviews, 2 references.

908. *Advanced Placement Examination in European History. High school students desiring credit for college level courses and admission to advanced courses; 1956–77; 1 reference; cited: 2 references.

909. ★Black History: A Test to Create Awareness and Arouse Interest. Teachers; 1974; 1 reference.

910. *CLEP Subject Examination in Afro-American History. 1 semester of college or equivalent; 1973–76.

911. *CLEP Subject Examination in American History. 1 year of college or equivalent; 1970–76; 1 review.

912. *CLEP Subject Examination in Western Civilization. 1 year of college or equivalent; 1964–76.

913. *Graduate Record Examinations Advanced History Test. Graduate school candidates; 1939–76; cited: 1 review, 1 reference.

914. Hollingsworth-Sanders Intermediate History Test. Grades 5–6; 1962–64; 1 review.

915. Meares-Sanders Junior High School History Test. Grades 7–8; 1962–64; 1 review.

916. *UP Field Test in History. College; 1969–77.

For OTHER TESTS, see in *Tests in Print II:*
‡American History: Junior High—Objective, T2:1982. Grades 7–9; 1963–70.
†American History: Senior High—Objective, T2:1983. 1–2 semesters high school; 1960–70.
American History Test: National Achievement Tests, T2:1984. Grades 7–8; 1937–56; cited: 2 reviews.
Cooperative Social Studies Tests: American History, T2:1988. Grades 7–8, 10–12; 1964–65; 1 reference; cited: 1 review.
Cooperative Social Studies Tests: Modern European History, T2:1989. Grades 10–12; 1964–65; cited: 1 review.
Cooperative Social Studies Tests: World History, T2:1990. Grades 10–12; 1964–65.
Cooperative Topical Tests in American History, T2:1991. High school; 1963–65; cited: 1 review.
Crary American History Test, T2:1992. Grades 10–13; 1950–65; 1 reference; cited: 3 reviews, 2 references.
Emporia American History Test, T2:1993. 1–2 semesters high school; 1962–64; cited: 1 review.
Modern World History: Achievement Examinations for Secondary Schools, T2:1997. High school; 1951–54.
Sanders-Buller World History Test, T2:1998. 1–2 semesters high school; 1962–64; cited: 1 review.
†Social Studies Grade 10 (American History): Minnesota High School Achievement Examinations, T2:1999. Grade 10; 1951–70; cited: 1 review.

†Social Studies Grade 11 (World History): Minnesota High School Achievement Examinations, T2:2000. Grade 11; 1951–70.
†World History/Objective Tests, T2:2002. 1–2 semesters high school; 1961–70.
World History Test: Acorn National Achievement Tests, T2:2003. High school and college; 1948–57; cited: 1 review.

POLITICAL SCIENCE

917. ★American Government: IOX Objectives-Based Tests. Grades 10–12; 1973–74; 2 reviews.
918. ★American Political Behavior Achievement Test. High school; 1974; 1 review.
919. *CLEP Subject Examination in American Government. 1 semester of college or equivalent; 1965–76; 1 review.
920. Cooperative Social Studies Tests: Civics. Grades 8–9; 1964–65; 1 review; cited: 1 review.
921. *Graduate Record Examinations Advanced Political Science Test. Graduate school candidates; 1939–76; cited: 1 review.
922. ★Informeter: An International Technique for the Measurement of Political Information. Older adolescents and adults; 1972.
923. *National Teacher Examinations: Texas Government. College seniors and teachers; 1972–76.
924. *UP Field Test in Political Science. College; 1969–77.

For other tests, see in *Tests in Print II:*

Cooperative Social Studies Tests: American Government, T2:2005. Grades 10–12; 1964–65; cited: 1 review.
Cooperative Social Studies Tests: Problems of Democracy, T2:2007. Grades 10–12; 1964–65; cited: 1 review, 1 reference.
‡Government/Objective Tests, T2:2008. 1 semester grades 11–12; 1970.
Patterson Test or Study Exercises on the Constitution of the United States, T2:2011. Grades 9–16 and adults; 1931–53.
Principles of Democracy Test, T2:2012. Grades 9–12; 1961; cited: 2 reviews.
Sare-Sanders American Government Test, T2:2013. High school and college; 1962–64; cited: 1 review.
Sare-Sanders Constitution Test, T2:2014. High school and college; 1962–64.
†Social Studies Grade 12 (American Problems): Minnesota High School Achievement Examinations, T2:2015. Grade 12; 1951–70.

SOCIOLOGY

925. *CLEP Subject Examination in Introductory Sociology. 1 year of college or equivalent; 1965–76.
926. *Graduate Record Examinations Advanced Sociology Test. Graduate school candidates; 1939–76; cited: 1 review.
927. *UP Field Test in Sociology. College; 1969–77.

For another test, see in *Tests in Print II:*

Sare-Sanders Sociology Test, T2:2019. High school and college; 1958; cited: 1 review.

SPEECH & HEARING

928. Ohio Tests of Articulation and Perception of Sounds. Ages 5–8; 1973; 1 review, 4 references; cited: 4 references.
929. Preschool Language Scale. Ages 2–6; 1969; 1 excerpt, 3 references; cited: 1 review, 1 excerpt, 1 reference.
930. ★Symbolic Play Test [England]. Ages 1–3; 1976.
931. *UP Field Test in Speech Pathology and Audiology. College; 1969–77; 1 review.

For other tests, see in *Tests in Print II:*

‡Diagnostic Test of Speechreading, T2:2021. Deaf children ages 4–9; 1970.
‡Multiple-Choice Intelligibility Test, T2:2022. College; 1963; 6 references.

HEARING

932. Auditory Discrimination Test. Ages 5–8; 1958–73; 74 references; cited: 1 review, 84 references.
933. Auditory Memory Span Test. Ages 5–8; 1973; 1 review, 2 references.
934. Auditory Sequential Memory Test. Ages 5–8; 1973; 1 review.
935–6. ★F.A.T.S.A. Test (Flowers Auditory Test of Selective Attention). Grades 1–6; 1972; 2 reviews.
937. ★Goldman-Fristoe-Woodcock Auditory Skills Test Battery. Ages 3 and over; 1974–76; 2 reviews.
938. Goldman-Fristoe-Woodcock Test of Auditory Discrimination. Ages 4 and over; 1970; 1 excerpt, 18 references; cited: 2 reviews, 1 excerpt, 4 references.
939. ★K.S.U. Speech Discrimination Test. Persons with hearing loss grades 3 and over; 1967–69; 1 review, 3 references.
940. Kindergarten Auditory Screening Test. Grades kgn–1; 1971; 1 review, 3 references.
941. ★Language-Structured Auditory Retention Span Test. Mental ages 3.6 to adult; 1973–75; 1 review, 1 excerpt, 1 reference.
942. Lindamood Auditory Conceptualization Test. Grades kgn–12; 1971; 2 reviews, 5 references.
943. *National Teacher Examinations: Audiology. College seniors and teachers; 1970–77.
944. Oliphant Auditory Discrimination Memory Test. Grades 1–8; 1971; 1 review; cited: 1 reference.
945. Oliphant Auditory Synthesizing Test. Grades 1–8; 1971; 1 review, cited: 1 reference.
946. ★STARS Test (Short Term Auditory Retrieval and Storage). Grades 1–6; 1972.
947. *Stycar Hearing Tests [England]. Ages 6 months to 7 years; 1958–76; 1 review.
948. ★Test of Auditory Discrimination. Grades kgn–6; 1975; 2 reviews.
949. *Test of Listening Accuracy in Children. Grades kgn–6; 1962–74; cited: 2 reviews, 2 references.
950. *Test of Nonverbal Auditory Discrimination. Grades kgn–3; 1968–75; 1 review, 2 references; cited: 9 references.
951. Verbal Auditory Screening for Children. Ages 3–6; 1964–71; 1 review, 4 references; cited: 7 references.
952. Washington Speech Sound Discrimination Test. Ages 3–5; 1971; 2 reviews, 1 reference.
953. Word Intelligibility by Picture Identification. Hearing impaired children ages 5–13; 1971; 2 reviews, 5 references; cited 3 references.

For other tests, see in *Tests in Print II:*

†Ambco Audiometers, T2:2027. Ages 10 and over; 1954–70.
Ambco Speech Test Record, T2:2027A. Ages 3 and over; [1958].
Auditory Tests, T2:2031. Grades 2 and over; 1951–56; 30 references; cited: 20 references.
†Beltone Audiometers, T2:2032. Grades kgn and over; 1954–73; 1 reference.
Comprehension of Oral Language: Inter-American Series, T2:2033. Grade 1; 1968.
†Eckstein Audiometers, T2:2034. Grades kgn and over; 1959–72.
‡Flowers-Costello Tests of Central Auditory Abilities, T2:2035. Grades kgn–6; 1970; 2 references.
‡Four Tone Screening for Older Children and Adults, T2:2036. Ages 8 and over; 1973.
†Grason-Stadler Audiometers, T2:2038. Ages 6 and over; 1950–73; 11 references; cited: 6 references.
Hearing of Speech Tests, T2:2039. Ages 3–12; 1966; 1 reference; cited: 1 review, 7 references.
Hollien-Thompson Group Hearing Test, T2:2040. Grades 1 and over; 1968; cited: 3 references.
†Maico Audiometers, T2:2043. Grades kgn and over; 1936–72; 1 reference; cited: 6 references.
†Maico Hearing Impairment Calculator, T2:2044. 1959–65.
Massachusetts Hearing Test, T2:2045. Grades 1–16 and adults; 1948; 1 reference; cited: 10 references.
Modified Rhyme Hearing Test, T2:2046. Grades 4 and over; 1963–68; 4 references; cited: 7 references.

New Group Pure Tone Hearing Test, T2:2048. Grades 1 and over; 1952–58; cited: 3 referneces.

Pritchard-Fox Phoneme Auditory Discrimination Tests: Test Four, T2:2051. Kgn and over; 1970.

Robbins Speech Sound Discrimination and Verbal Imagery Type Tests, T2:2052. Ages 4 and over; 1948–58; cited: 1 review.

Rush Hughes (PB 50): Phonetically Balanced Lists 5–12, T2:2053. Grades 2 and over; 1951; 6 references; cited: 6 references.

Screening Test for Auditory Perception, T2:2054. Grades 2–6; 1969; cited: 2 reviews, 1 reference.

‡Tracor Audiometers, T2:2058. Infants and older; 1955[?]–73.

‡ZECO Pure Tone Screening for Children, T2:2062. Ages 3–8; 1972.

†Zenith Audiometers, T2:2063–4. Preschool and over; 1959–73.

SPEECH

954. Arizona Articulation Proficiency Scale. Mental ages 2–14 and over; 1963–70; 2 reviews, 1 excerpt, 5 references; cited: 6 references.

955. Boston Diagnostic Aphasia Examination. Aphasic patients; 1972; 2 reviews, 1 reference.

956. Bzoch-League Receptive-Expressive Emergent Language Scale: For the Measurement of Language Skills in Infancy. Birth to age 3; 1970–71; 3 excerpts, 5 references; cited: 2 references.

957. ★Carrow Elicited Language Inventory. Ages 3–7; 1974; 1 review, 3 references.

958. ★Denver Articulation Screening Exam. Economically disadvantaged ages 2.5 to 6.0; 1971–73; 1 review, 4 references.

959. Edinburgh Articulation Test [Scotland]. Ages 3–0 to 6–0; 1971; 2 reviews, 3 excerpts, 5 references; cited: 1 reference.

960. Fairview Language Evaluation Scale. Mentally retarded; 1971; 2 reviews, 2 references.

961. Fisher-Logemann Test of Articulation Competence. Preschool to adult; 1971; 2 reviews.

962. ★Functional Communication Profile. Aphasic adults; 1956–69; 2 reviews, 11 references.

963. Halstead Aphasia Test. Adults; 1949–55; 2 reviews, 5 references; cited: 12 references.

964. ★Language Sampling, Analysis, and Training. Children with language delay; 1974.

965. *National Teacher Examinations: Speech-Communication and Theatre. College seniors and teachers; 1970–77.

966. *National Teacher Examinations: Speech Pathology. College seniors and teachers; 1970–77; 1 review.

967. *Northwestern Syntax Screening Test. Ages 3–7; 1969–71; 2 reviews, 1 excerpt, 26 references; cited: 3 references.

968. ★Ohio State University Test for Identifying Misarticulations. Speech clinicians and senior speech majors; 1965; 1 reference.

969. Photo Articulation Test. Ages 3–12; 1969; 1 review; cited: 2 references.

970. ★Picture Articulation & Language Screening Test. Grade 1; 1976.

971. Porch Index of Communicative Ability. Aphasic adults; 1967–71; 1 review, 14 references; cited: 1 review, 3 references.

972. ★Porch Index of Communicative Ability in Children. Prekgn–grade 6; 1973–74; 1 review.

973. *Predictive Screening Test of Articulation. Grade 1; 1968–73; 1 review, 9 references; cited: 3 references.

974. Reynell Developmental Language Scales [England]. Ages 1–5 with delayed or deviant language development; 1969; 2 reviews, 3 references; cited: 3 references.

975. Riley Articulation and Language Test. Grades kgn–2; 1966–71; 2 reviews, 1 reference; cited: 1 reference.

976. Sklar Aphasia Scale. Brain damaged adults;

1966–73; 1 review, 1 reference; cited: 2 reviews, 2 references.

977. ★Stycar Language Test [England]. Mental ages 11 months–6 years, with marked speech and language difficulties; 1976; 1 review, 1 reference.

978. ★Test of Language Development. Ages 4–0 to 8–11; 1977.

979. *UP Field Test in Drama and Theatre. College; 1971–77.

980. ★Vane Evaluation of Language Scale. Ages 2.5–6.5; 1975; 1 review, 1 reference.

For other tests, see in *Tests in Print II:*

Communicative Evaluation Chart From Infancy to Five Years, T2:2068. 1963–64.

Deep Test of Articulation, T2:2069. All reading levels; 1964; 2 references; cited: 2 reviews, 6 references.

Examining for Aphasia, T2:2071. Adolescents and adults; 1946–54; 3 references; cited: 3 reviews, 5 excerpts, 5 references.

Forms From Diagnostic Methods in Speech Pathology, T2:2074. Children and adults with speech problems; 1952–63; cited: 1 reference.

†Goldman-Fristoe Test of Articulation, T2:2075. Ages 2 and over; 1969–72; cited: 2 reviews, 1 excerpt, 4 references.

Houston Test for Language Development, T2:2077. Ages 6 months to 6 years; 1958–63; cited: 2 reviews, 1 excerpt, 1 reference.

Language Facility Test, T2:2078. Ages 3 and over; 1965–68; cited: 1 review, 1 reference.

Language Modalities Test for Aphasia, T2:2079. Adults; 1961; 2 references; cited: 2 reviews, 12 references.

†Minnesota Test for Differential Diagnosis of Aphasia, T2:2080. Adults; 1965–73; 4 references; cited: 2 reviews, 15 references.

Nationwide Speech Examination, T2:2083. Grades 4–12; 1959–63.

Orzeck Aphasia Evaluation, T2:2085. Mental and brain damaged patients; 1964–66; cited: 2 reviews.

Screening Deep Test of Articulation, T2:2090. Grades kgn and over; 1968; 1 reference; cited: 2 reviews, 2 references.

†Screening Speech Articulation Test, T2:2091. Ages 3.5–8.5; 1955–70.

Speech Defect Questionnaire, T2:2093. Ages 6 and over; 1933.

Speech Diagnostic Chart, T2:2094. Grades 1–8; 1937–51.

Templin-Darley Tests of Articulation, T2:2095. Ages 3 and over; 1960–69; 8 references; cited: 1 review, 2 excerpts, 25 references.

Utah Test of Language Development, T2:2097. Ages 1.5 to 14.5; 1958–67; 4 references; cited: 2 reviews.

†Verbal Language Development Scale, T2:2098. Birth to age 15; 1958–71; 4 references; cited: 2 reviews, 8 references.

Weidner-Fensch Speech Screening Test, T2:2099. Grades 1–3; 1955; cited: 1 review.

VOCATIONS

981. *Flanagan Industrial Tests. Business and industry; 1960–75; 2 reviews, 3 references; cited: 2 reviews, 1 excerpt, 1 reference.

982. ★JEVS Work Sample Evaluaton System. High school and adults; 1969–76; 3 references.

983. ★Position Analysis Questionnaire. Business and industry; 1969–73; 1 review, 17 references.

984. ★Social and Prevocational Information Battery. Educable mentally retarded (IQ 55–75) grades 7–12; 1975; 1 review, 2 references.

985. ★Survey of Organizations: "A Machine-Scored Standardized Questionnaire Instrument." Employees; 1967–74; 2 reviews, 1 excerpt, 12 references.

986. TAV Selection System. Adults; 1963–68; 1 review, 1 reference; cited: 1 excerpt, 15 references.

987. Wide Range Employment Sample Test. Ages 16–54 (normal and handicapped); 1972–73; 2 reviews.

For other tests, see in *Tests in Print II:*

†Aptitude Inventory, T2:2102. Employee applicants; 1957–71; 1 reference; cited: 2 reviews, 1 excerpt, 1 reference.

‡Classification Test Battery [South Africa], T2:2104. Illiterate and semiliterate applicants for unskilled and semiskilled mining jobs; 1970–71.

Dailey Vocational Tests, T2:2105. Grades 8–12 and adults; 1964–65; 1 reference; cited: 2 reviews, 2 excerpts, 5 references.

†ETSA Tests, T2:2106. Job applicants; 1960–73; cited: 2 reviews.

Individual Placement Series, T2:2108. High school and adults; 1957–66.
Personal History Index, T2:2110. Job applicants; 1963–67; cited: 1 review, 5 references.
Steward Basic Factors Inventory, T2:2111. Applicants for sales and office positions; 1957–63; cited: 2 reviews.
Steward Personnel Tests, T2:2112. Applicants for sales and office positions; 1957–58; cited: 2 reviews.
WLW Employment Inventory, T2:2115. Adults; 1957–64.

CAREERS & INTERESTS

988. ★AAMD-Becker Reading-Free Vocational Interest Inventory. Educable mentally retarded at the high school level; 1975; 2 reviews, 6 references.
989. *ACT Career Planning Program. Entrants to postsecondary educational institutions; 1970–76; 1 excerpt, 16 references; cited: 4 references.
990. Applied Biological and Agribusiness Interest Inventory. Grade 8; 1965–71; 1 review; cited: 1 review, 4 references.
991. *Assessment of Career Development. Grades 8–12; 1972–74; 2 reviews, 1 excerpt, 7 references.
992. *California Occupational Preference System. High school and college; 1966–76; 2 reviews, 1 reference; cited: 2 reviews, 1 excerpt, 3 references.
993. ★Career Assessment Inventory. "Individuals [grades 8 and over] seeking a career that does not generally require a four-year or advanced college degree"; 1975–76; 2 reviews.
994. ★Career Awareness Inventory. Grades 4–8; 1974–75; 2 reviews, 1 reference.
995. ★Career Development Inventory. Grades 9–10 and out-of-school youth and adults; 1974–75; 2 reviews, 1 excerpt, 1 reference.
996. Career Guidance Inventory. Grades 7–13 students interested in trades, services, and technologies; 1972; 1 review.
997. Career Maturity Inventory. Grades 6–12; 1973; 2 reviews, 1 excerpt, 151 references; cited: 35 references.
998. ★Career Planning Program for Grades 8–12. Grades 8–12; 1974; 1 review.
999. ★Comprehensive Career Assessment Scale. Grades 3–12 and teachers; 1974; 2 reviews.
1000. *Crowley Occupational Interests Blank [England]. Secondary school pupils of average ability or less; 1970–76; 2 reviews.
1001. ★DAT Career Planning Program. Grades 8–12; 1972–75; 2 reviews.
1002. *Educational Interest Inventory. High school and college; 1962–74; 2 reviews, 1 reference; cited: 7 references.
1003. *Hall Occupational Orientation Inventory. Grades 3–16 and adults and low-literate adults; 1968–76; 2 reviews, 5 references; cited: 1 review, 7 references.
1004. ★Harrington/O'Shea System for Career Decision-Making. Grades 8–14 and adults; 1974–76; 1 review.
1005. ★High School Interest Questionnaire [South Africa]. "Coloured pupils" in standards 7–10; 1973–74.
1006. ★Individual Career Exploration. Grades 8–12; 1976; 1 review.
1007. ★Introducing Career Concepts Inventory. Grades 5–9; 1975.
1008. ★Knowledge of Occupations Test. High school; 1974; 2 reviews, 1 reference.
1009. *Kuder General Interest Survey. Grades 6–12; 1934–76; 16 references; cited: 3 reviews, 2 excerpts, 8 references.
1010. *Kuder Occupational Interest Survey. Grades 11–16 and adults; 1956–76; 41 references; cited: 2 reviews, 2 excerpts, 32 references.
1011. Kuder Preference Record—Vocational. Grades 9–16 and adults; 1934–76; 1 review, 36 references; cited: 11 reviews, 1 excerpt, 867 references.
1012. *Milwaukee Academic Interest Inventory. Grades 12–14; 1973–74; 1 review, 1 reference; cited: 4 references.
1013. New Mexico Career Education Test Series. Grades 9–12; 1973; 1 review, 2 excerpts, 2 references.
1014. ★Occupational Check List [England]. Ages 15 and over ("above average ability"); 1972–76; 1 review.
1015. ★Occupations and Careers Information BOX-SCORE. Grades 7–12; 1973; 2 reviews.
1016. Ohio Vocational Interest Survey. Grades 8–12; 1969–72; 24 references; cited: 2 reviews, 7 references.
1017. ★Ohio Work Values Inventory. Grade 3–adults; 1971–74; 6 references.
1018. ★Picture Interest Exploration Survey. Grades 7–12; 1974.
1019. ★Planning Career Goals. Grades 8–12; 1975–76; 2 reviews.
1020. ★Priority Counseling Survey. Grades 7–14; 1971–73.
1021. *Safran Student's Interest Inventory [Canada]. Grades 8–12; 1960–76; cited: 1 review, 1 reference.
1022. Self Directed Search: A Guide to Educational and Vocational Planning. High school and college and adults; 1970–73; 1 review, 4 excerpts, 89 references; cited: 1 reference.
1023. *Strong-Campbell Interest Inventory. Ages 16 and over; 1927–77; 3 reviews, 3 excerpts, 288 references; cited: 15 reviews, 2 excerpts, 1,432 references.
1024. Vocational Interest and Sophistication Assessment. Retarded adolescents and young adults; 1967–68; 2 reviews, 3 references; cited: 3 references.
1025. ★Vocational Interest, Experience, and Skill Assessment. Grades 8–12; 1976; 1 review.
1026. ★Vocational Interest Questionnaire for [Black] Pupils in Forms I–V [South Africa]. 1974–75.
1027. Vocational Planning Inventory. Vocational students in grades 8–13; 1968–70; 2 reviews, 2 references.
1028. *Vocational Preference Inventory. High school and college and adults; 1953–75; 1 excerpt, 175 references; cited: 4 reviews, 131 references.
1029. Wide Range Interest-Opinion Test. Grades kgn–12 and adults; 1970–72; 1 review.
1030. Work Values Inventory. Grades 7–16 and adults; 1968–70; 1 excerpt, 53 references; cited: 2 reviews, 1 excerpt, 45 references.
1031. ★World of Work Inventory. Grades 8–14 and adults; 1973–76; 2 reviews, 1 excerpt, 1 reference.

For other tests, see in *Tests in Print II:*
ACT Guidance Profile, T2:2167. Junior college; 1965–69; 2 references; cited: 1 review, 2 references.
A.P.U. Occupational Interests Guide [England], T2:2168. Ages 14–18; 1966–69; 2 references; cited: 2 reviews, 1 reference.
California Pre-Counseling Self-Analysis Protocol Booklet, T2:2171. Student counselees; 1965.
Chatterji's Non-Language Preference Record [India], T2:2173. Ages 11–16; 1962; 6 references.
College Interest Inventory, T2:2174. Grades 11–16; 1967; cited: 2 reviews.
Connolly Occupational Interests Questionnaire [England], T2:2175. Ages 15 and over; 1967–70; cited: 1 review, 2 references.
Curtis Interest Scale, T2:2177. Grades 9–16 and adults; 1959; 1 reference; cited: 2 reviews.
Factorial Interest Blank [England], T2:2179. Ages 11–16; 1967; 1 reference; cited: 2 reviews, 1 reference.
†Geist Picture Interest Inventory, T2:2180. Grades 8–16 and adults; 1959–71; 18 references; cited: 2 reviews, 1 excerpt, 12 references.
Geist Picture Interest Inventory: Deaf Form: Male, T2:2181. Deaf and hard of hearing males (grades 7–16 and adults); 1962; 1 reference; cited: 1 reference.
Gordon Occupational Check List, T2:2182. High school students not planning to enter college; 1961–67; cited: 4 reviews.
Gregory Academic Interest Inventory, T2:2183. Grades 13–16; 1946; 2 references; cited: 3 reviews, 1 reference.

Guilford-Shneidman-Zimmerman Interest Survey, T2:2184. Grades 9–16 and adults; 1948; 2 references; cited: 2 reviews, 2 references.

Guilford-Zimmerman Interest Inventory, T2:2185. Grades 10–16 and adults; 1962–63; 7 references; cited: 1 review.

Hackman-Gaither Vocational Interest Inventory, T2:2186. Grades 9–12 and adults; 1962–68; cited: 1 review, 25 references.

Henderson Analysis of Interest, T2:2188. Grades 9–16 and adults; 1950; cited: 2 reviews.

How Well Do You Know Your Interests, T2:2189. High school, college, adults; 1957–70; cited: 3 reviews, 1 excerpt, 3 references.

†Interest Check List, T2:2190. Grades 9 and over; 1946–67; 2 references; cited: 2 reviews.

‡Interest Questionnaire for Indian South Africans [South Africa], T2:2191. Standards 6–10; 1969–71.

Inventory of Vocational Interests: Acorn National Aptitude Tests, T2:2192. Grades 7–16 and adults; 1943–60; cited: 5 reviews.

Minnesota Vocational Interest Inventory, T2:2197. Males ages 15 and over not planning to attend college; 1965–66; 11 references; cited: 2 reviews, 3 excerpts, 45 references.

19 Field Interest Inventory [South Africa], T2:2198. Standards 8–10 and college and adults; 1970–71.

Occupational Interest Inventory, T2:2199. Grades 7–16 and adults; 1943–58; 23 references; cited: 5 reviews, 45 references.

Occupational Interest Survey (With Pictures), T2:2200. Industrial applicants and employees; 1959–66; cited: 2 reviews.

Phillips Occupational Preference Scale [Australia], T2:2202. Ages 14 and over; 1959–65.

Pictorial Interest Inventory, T2:2203. Adult males, particularly poor readers and nonreaders; 1959; 4 references.

‡Pictorial Inventory of Careers, T2:2204. Grades 3–14 and disadvantaged adults; 1972.

Picture Interest Inventory, T2:2205. Grades 7 and over; 1958; 7 references; cited: 2 reviews, 1 excerpt, 4 references.

Preference Analysis [South Africa], T2:2206–7. Standards 8 and over; 1968–69.

Rothwell-Miller Interest Blank [Australia], T2:2208. Ages 13 and over; 1958.

Rothwell-Miller Interest Blank, British Edition [England], T2:2209. Ages 11 and over; 1958–68; cited: 2 reviews, 2 references.

Thurstone Interest Schedule, T2:2214. Grades 9–16 and adults; 1947; 20 references; cited: 2 reviews, 1 reference.

VALCAN Vocational Interest Profile [Canada], T2:2215. Ages 15 and over; 1960–61.

Vocational Apperception Test, T2:2216. College; 1949; cited: 2 reviews, 1 excerpt, 4 references.

Vocational Interest Profile [Canada], T2:2218. Ages 15 and over; 1960–66; cited: 1 reference.

†William, Lynde & Williams Analysis of Interest, T2:2220. Male adults; 1956–71; cited: 1 review.

CLERICAL

1032. Appraisal of Occupational Aptitudes. High school and adults; 1971; 2 reviews.

1033. General Clerical Test. Grades 9–16 and clerical job applicants; 1944–72; 1 review, 1 reference; cited: 6 reviews, 15 references.

1034. ★N.B. Commercial Tests [South Africa]. Standards 6–8; 1962.

1035. ★SRA Typing 5. Prospective employees; 1975; 2 reviews.

1036. *SRA Typing Skills. Applicants for clerical positions; 1947–73; cited: 2 reviews, 3 references.

1037. Short Employment Tests. Applicants for clerical positions; 1951–72; 2 reviews, 4 references; cited: 2 reviews, 31 references.

1038. Short Occupational Knowledge Test for Secretaries. Job applicants; 1969–70; 1 review.

1039. *Short Tests of Clerical Ability. Applicants for office positions; 1959–73; 2 reviews, 1 reference; cited: 2 reviews.

FOR OTHER TESTS, see in *Tests in Print II:*

ACER Short Clerical Test—Form C [Australia], T2:2117. Ages 13 and over; 1953–67.

A.C.E.R. Speed and Accuracy Tests [Australia], T2:2118. Ages 13.5 and over; 1942–62; 1 reference; cited: 1 review, 2 references.

APT Dictation Test, T2:2119. Stenographers; 1955.

Clerical Skills Series, T2:2121. Clerical workers and applicants; 1966–69; cited: 1 review.

Clerical Tests, T2:2122. Applicants for clerical positions; 1951–66.

Clerical Tests, Series N, T2:2123. Applicants for clerical positions not involving frequent use of typewriter or verbal skill; 1940–59.

Clerical Tests, Series V, T2:2124. Applicants for typing and stenographic positions; 1940–59.

Clerical Worker Examination, T2:2125. Clerical workers; 1962–63.

Cross Reference Test, T2:2126. Clerical job applicants; 1959; cited: 1 review.

Curtis Verbal-Clerical Skills Tests, T2:2127. Applicants for clerical positions; 1963–65.

†General Clerical Ability Test, T2:2128. Job applicants; 1960–72.

†Group Test 20 [England], T2:2130. Ages 15 and over; 1936–72; 1 reference; cited: 1 review, 2 references.

†Group Tests 61A, 64, and 66A [England], T2:2131. Clerical applicants; 1956–72.

†Hay Clerical Test Battery, T2:2132. Applicants for clerical positions; 1941–72; 2 references; cited: 2 reviews, 10 references.

L & L Clerical Tests, T2:2133. Applicants for office positions; 1964.

McCann Typing Tests, T2:2134. Applicants for typing positions; 1961–64.

Minnesota Clerical Test, T2:2135. Grades 8–12 and adults; 1933–59; 23 references; cited: 6 reviews, 96 references.

Office Skills Achievement Test, T2:2136. Employees; 1962–63; cited: 2 reviews.

†Office Worker Test, T2:2137. Office workers; 1956–72; cited: 2 reviews.

O'Rourke Clerical Aptitude Test, Junior Grade, T2:2138. Applicants for clerical positions; 1926–58; 1 reference; cited: 1 review, 4 references.

Personnel Institute Clerical Tests, T2:2139. Clerical personnel and typists-stenographers-secretaries; 1922–67.

Personnel Research Institute Clerical Battery, T2:2140. Applicants for clerical positions; 1945–48; 6 references; cited: 2 reviews.

Personnel Research Institute Test of Shorthand Skills, T2:2141. Stenographers; 1951–54; cited: 1 review.

Purdue Clerical Adaptability Test, T2:2142. Applicants for clerical positions; 1949–56; 2 references; cited: 5 reviews, 2 references.

RBH Checking Test, T2:2143. Applicants for clerical and stenographic positions; 1948–63; cited: 1 review.

RBH Classifying Test, T2:2144. Business and industry; 1950–63; cited: 1 review.

RBH Number Checking Test, T2:2145. Business and industry; 1957–63; cited: 1 review.

†RBH Test of Dictation Speed, T2:2146. Stenographers; 1958–63.

RBH Test of Typing Speed, T2:2147. Applicants for clerical positions; 1958–63.

Seashore-Bennett Stenographic Proficiency Test, T2:2148. Adults; 1946–56; cited: 2 reviews, 3 references.

Secretarial Performance Analysis, T2:2149. Employees; 1969.

Selection Tests for Office Personnel, T2:2150. Insurance office workers and applicants; 1962–64.

Short Occupational Knowledge Test for Bookkeepers, T2:2152. Job applicants; 1970.

Short Occupational Knowledge Test for Office Machine Operators, T2:2153. Job applicants; 1970.

Shorthand Test: Individual Placement Series, T2:2156. Adults; 1960–66.

Skill in Typing: Measurement of Skill Test 9, T2:2157. Job applicants; 1966–68.

Stenographic Dictation Test, T2:2158. Applicants for stenographic positions; 1962–64.

†Stenographic Skill-Dictation Test, T2:2159. Applicants for stenographic positions; 1950–73; cited: 2 reviews.

†Stenographic Skills Test, T2:2160. Job applicants; 1960–72.

Survey of Clerical Skills: Individual Placement Series, T2:2161. Adults; 1959–66.

Thurstone Employment Tests, T2:2162. Applicants for clerical and typing positions; 1922; 2 references; cited: 2 reviews, 6 references.

†Typing Skill, T2:2163. Typists; 1952–71; cited: 1 review.

Typing Test for Business, T2:2164. Applicants for typing positions; 1967–68; cited: 2 reviews.

Typing Test: Individual Placement Series, T2:2165. Adults; 1959–66; cited: 1 review.

USES Clerical Skills Tests, T2:2166. Applicants for clerical positions; 1968; cited: 1 reference.

MANUAL DEXTERITY

1040. Manipulative Aptitude Test. Grades 9–12 and adults; 1967; 2 reviews.

FOR OTHER TESTS, see in *Tests in Print II:*

†APT Manual Dexterity Test, T2:2222. Automobile and truck mechanics and mechanics' helpers; 1960–63.

Crawford Small Parts Dexterity Test, T2:2223. High school and adults; 1946–56; 12 references; cited: 3 reviews, 8 references.

Crissey Dexterity Test, T2:2224. Job applicants; 1964; cited: 1 review, 1 reference.
Hand-Tool Dexterity Test, T2:2225. Adolescents and adults; 1946–65; cited: 2 reviews, 6 references.
Minnesota Rate of Manipulation Test, T2:2227. Grade 7 to adults; 1931–69; 10 references; cited: 5 reviews, 1 excerpt, 61 references.
O'Connor Finger Dexterity Test, T2:2228. Ages 14 and over; 1920–26(?); 14 references; cited: 1 review, 47 references.
O'Connor Tweezer Dexterity Test, T2:2229. Ages 14 and over; 1920–28(?); 9 references; cited: 1 review, 36 references.
‡One Hole Test, T2:2230. Job applicants; 1972; 1 reference.
Pennsylvania Bi-Manual Worksample, T2:2231. Ages 16 and over; 1943–45; 8 references; cited: 4 reviews, 3 references.
Practical Dexterity Board, T2:2232. Ages 8 and over; 1962.
†Purdue Hand Precision Test, T2:2233. Ages 17 and over; 1941; cited: 2 references.
†Purdue Pegboard, T2:2234. Grades 9–16 and adults; 1941–68; 51 references; cited: 4 reviews, 41 references.
Stromberg Dexterity Test, T2:2235. Trade school and adults; 1945–51; 8 references; cited: 1 review, 1 reference.
Yarn Dexterity Test, T2:2236. Textile workers and applicants; 1964–65.

MECHANICAL ABILITY

1041. *College Placement Test in Spatial Relations. Entering college freshmen; 1962–75; cited: 1 review, 4 references.
1042. *Differential Aptitude Tests: Mechanical Reasoning. Grades 8–12 and adults; 1947–75; 2 references; cited: 11 references.
1043. *Differential Aptitude Tests: Space Relations. Grades 8–12 and adults; 1947–75; 2 references; cited: 18 references.
1044. *Group Test 81 [England]. Ages 14 and over; 1949–69; cited: 1 review, 11 references.
1045. ★SRA Test of Mechanical Concepts. High school and adults; 1976; 2 reviews.
1046. ★Shapes Analysis Test [England]. Ages 14 and over; 1972; 1 review, 2 references.
1047. ★Weber Advanced Spatial Perception Test [Australia]. Ages 13–17; 1976.

FOR OTHER TESTS, see in *Tests in Print II*:
A.C.E.R. Mechanical Comprehension Test [Australia], T2:2237. Ages 13.5 and over; 1942–53; cited: 3 reviews, 2 references.
A.C.E.R. Mechanical Reasoning Test [Australia], T2:2238. Ages 13–9 and over; 1951–62; 3 references; cited: 2 reviews.
Bennett Mechanical Comprehension Test [England], T2:2239. Grades 9–12 and adults; 1940–70; 9 references; cited: 6 reviews, 1 excerpt, 130 references.
Chriswell Structural Dexterity Test, T2:2240. Grades 7–9; 1953–63; cited: 1 review, 1 reference.
Cox Mechanical and Manual Tests [England], T2:2242. Boys ages 10 and over; 1928–34; 8 references; cited: 2 reviews, 4 references.
Curtis Object Completion and Space Form Tests, T2:2243. Applicants for mechanical and technical jobs; 1960–61; cited: 2 reviews.
Detroit Mechanical Aptitudes Examination, T2:2244. Grades 7–16; 1928–39; 11 references; cited: 3 reviews, 1 excerpt, 4 references.
Flags: A Test of Space Thinking, T2:2245. Industrial employees; 1959; 1 reference; cited: 1 review.
Form Perception Test [South Africa], T2:2246. Illiterate and semiliterate adults; 1966–68.
Form Relations Group Test [England], T2:2247. Ages 14 and over; 1926–46; 9 references; cited: 1 review, 10 references.
Group Test 80A [England], T2:2248. Ages 15 and over; 1943–51; 2 references; cited: 2 reviews.
Group Test 82 [England], T2:2250. Ages 14.5 and over; 1959–70.
MacQuarrie Test for Mechanical Ability, T2:2251. Grades 7 and over; 1925–43; 38 references; cited: 3 reviews, 58 references.
Mechanical Aptitude Test: Acorn National Aptitude Tests, T2:2252. Grades 7–16 and adults; 1943–52; cited: 3 reviews.
Mechanical Comprehension Test [South Africa], T2:2253. Male technical apprentices and trainee engineer applicants; 1966–68.
Mechanical Information Test [England], T2:2254. Ages 15 and over; 1948–70; cited: 2 reviews.
Mechanical Movements: A Test of Mechanical Comprehension, T2:2255. Industrial employees; 1959–63; cited: 1 review.
Mellenbruch Mechanical Motivation Test, T2:2257. Grades 6–16 and adults; 1944–57; 2 references; cited: 4 reviews.
Minnesota Spatial Relations Test, T2:2258. Ages 11 and over; 1930; 23 references; cited: 2 reviews, 28 references.

O'Connor Wiggly Block, T2:2259. Ages 16 and over; 1928–51; 3 references; cited: 27 references.
O'Rourke Mechanical Aptitude Test, T2:2260. Grades 7–12 and adults; 1926–57; 1 reference; cited: 3 reviews, 8 references.
Perceptual Battery [South Africa], T2:2261. Job applicants with at least 10 years of education; 1961–63.
Primary Mechanical Ability Tests, T2:2262. Applicants for positions requiring mechanical ability; 1940–50.
Purdue Mechanical Adaptability Test, T2:2263. Males ages 15 and over; 1945–50; 5 references; cited: 2 reviews, 6 references.
RBH Three-Dimensional Space Test, T2:2264. Industrial workers in mechanical fields; 1950–63.
RBH Two-Dimensional Space Test, T2:2265. Business and industry; 1948–63.
Revised Minnesota Paper Form Board Test, T2:2266. Grades 9–16 and adults; 1930–70; 37 references; cited: 5 reviews, 159 references.
SRA Mechanical Aptitudes, T2:2267. Grades 9–12 and adults; 1947–50; 8 references; cited: 2 reviews.
Spatial Tests EG, 2, and 3 [England], T2:2269. Ages 10–13 and 15–17; 1950–63; 2 references; cited: 3 reviews, 5 references.
Spatial Visualization Test: Dailey Vocational Tests, T2:2270. Grades 8–12 and adults; 1964–65.
Vincent Mechanical Diagrams Test [England], T2:2271. Ages 15 and over; 1936–70.
Weights and Pulleys: A Test of Intuitive Mechanics, T2:2272. Engineering students and industrial employees; 1959; cited: 1 review.

MISCELLANEOUS

1048. ★Group Encounter Survey. Group members; 1963–73; 2 references.
1049. ★Job Attitude Scale [Canada]. Adults; 1971; 9 references.
1050. *Minnesota Importance Questionnaire. Vocational counselees; 1967–75; 2 reviews, 40 references; cited: 37 references.
1051. Minnesota Job Description Questionnaire. Employees and supervisors; 1967–68; 1 review, 15 references; cited: 8 references.
1052. Minnesota Satisfaction Questionnaire. Business and industry; 1963–67; 1 review, 82 references; cited: 2 reviews, 29 references.
1053. ★Process Diagnostic. Group members; 1974–75; 1 review.
1054. *SRA Attitude Survey. Employees; 1951–74; 9 references; cited: 2 reviews, 10 references.
1055. ★Team Effectiveness Survey. Team members; 1968–69; 1 review.
1056. ★Vocational Opinion Index. Disadvantaged trainees in vocational skills programs; 1973–76.
1057. Work Information Inventory. Employee groups in industry; 1958; 1 review.
1058. ★Workshop Evaluation Scale. Workshop participants; 1974.

FOR OTHER TESTS, see in *Tests in Print II*:
Alpha Biographical Inventory, T2:2273. Grades 9–12; 1968; 3 references; cited: 2 reviews, 16 references.
Biographical Index, T2:2274. College and industry; 1961–62; cited: 2 reviews.
Business Judgment Test, T2:2275. Adults; 1953–69; 1 reference; cited: 2 reviews, 1 excerpt, 5 references.
†Conference Evaluation, T2:2276. Conference participants; 1969–71.
Conference Meeting Rating Scale, T2:2277. Conference leaders and participants; 1959.
‡Continuous Letter Checking and Continuous Symbol Checking [South Africa], T2:2278-9. Ages 12 and over; 1967–72.
Gullo Workshop and Seminar Evaluation, T2:2280. Workshop and seminar participants; 1969.
Job Attitude Analysis, T2:2281. Production and clerical workers; 1961–70; cited: 1 reference.
Mathematical and Technical Test [England], T2:2282. Ages 11 and over; 1948; cited: 2 reviews.
Per-Flu-Dex Tests, T2:2286. College and industry; 1955; 2 references; cited: 2 reviews.
RBH Breadth of Information, T2:2287. Business and industry; 1957–63.
Self-Rating Scale for Leadership Qualifications, T2:2288. Adults; 1942–48.
Tear Ballot for Industry, T2:2289. Employees in industry; 1944–62; 1 reference; cited: 2 reviews, 1 excerpt, 9 references.

Test Orientation Procedure, T2:2290. Job applicants and trainees; 1967; cited: 1 review.
Tests A/9 and A/10 [South Africa], T2:2291. Applicants for technical and apprentice jobs; 1955–57.
Whisler Strategy Test, T2:2292. Business and industry; 1959–61; 1 reference; cited: 2 reviews, 1 reference.

SELECTION & RATING FORMS

1059. ★Job Performance Scale. Employees; 1971.
1060. McCormick Job Performance Measurement "Rate-$-Scales." Employees; 1971; 1 review, 1 reference.
1061. ★Minnesota Satisfactoriness Scales. Employees; 1965–70; 1 review, 9 references.
1062. ★Rehabilitation Client Rating Scale. Vocational rehabilitation counselees; 1974; 1 reference.

FOR OTHER TESTS, see in *Tests in Print II*:
APT Controlled Interview, T2:2294. Applicants for employment; 1945–56.
Application Interview Screening Form, T2:2295. Job applicants; 1965.
Career Counseling Personal Data Form, T2:2296. Vocational counselees; 1962.
Employee Competency Scale, T2:2297. Employees; 1969.
Employee Evaluation Form for Interviewrs, T2:2298. Adults; 1943; cited: 2 reviews, 2 excerpts.
Employee Performance Appraisal, T2:2299. Business and industry; 1962; cited: 1 review.
‡Employee Progress Appraisal Form, T2:2300. Rating of office employees; 1944.
†Employee Rating and Development Forms, T2:2301. Executive, industrial, office, and sales personnel; 1950–65; cited: 3 reviews.
†Executive, Industrial, and Sales Personnel Forms, T2:2302. Applicants for executive, industrial, office, or sales positions; 1949–68; cited: 2 reviews, 1 reference.
†Job Application Forms, T2:2303. Job applicants and employees; 1957–71.
Lawshe-Kephart Personnel Comparison System, T2:2304. For rating any aspect of employee performance by the paired comparison technique; 1946–48; cited: 1 review, 1 reference.
McQuaig Manpower Selection Series, T2:2306. Applicants for office and sales positions; 1957.
†Martin Performance Appraisal, T2:2307. Employees; 1966–69.
Merit Rating Series, T2:2308. Industry; 1948–59; cited: 2 reviews, 1 reference.
Nagel Personnel Interviewing and Screening Forms, T2:2309. Job applicants; 1963.
Performance Review Forms, T2:2310. Employees and managers; 1960–61.
Personal Data Blank, T2:2311. Counselees ages 15 and over; 1934–52; cited: 3 reviews.
Personnel Interviewing Forms, T2:2312. Business and industry; 1956.
Personnel Rating Scale, T2:2313. Employees; 1965–66.
RBH Individual Background Survey, T2:2314. Business and industry; 1949–69; cited: 2 references.
San Francisco Vocational Competency Scale, T2:2315. Mentally retarded adults; 1968; 1 reference.
Selection Interview Forms, T2:2316. Business and industry; 1962.
Speech-Appearance Record, T2:2317. Job applicants; 1967.
†Stevens-Thurow Personnel Forms, T2:2318. Business and industry; 1951–72.
‡Tickmaster, T2:2319. Job applicants; 1954–65.
Wonderlic Personnel Selection Procedure, T2:2320. Applicants for employment; 1967–69.
Work Reference Check, T2:2321. Job applicants; 1965.

SPECIFIC VOCATIONS

ACCOUNTING

1063. ★ACT Proficiency Examinations in Accounting. College and adults; 1973–77.
1064. *CLEP Subject Examination in Introductory Accounting. 1 year of college or equivalent; 1970–76.

FOR OTHER TESTS, see in *Tests in Print II*:
Account Clerk Test, T2:2322. Job applicants; 1957–66.
†American Institute of Certified Public Accountants Testing Programs, T2:2323. Grades 13–16 and accountants; 1946–72; 7 references; cited: 21 references.

BUSINESS

1065. ★ACT Proficiency Examination in Business Environment and Strategy. College and adults; 1973–77.

1066. ★ACT Proficiency Examinations in Finance. College and adults; 1973–77.
1067. ★ACT Proficiency Examinations in Management of Human Resources. College and adults; 1973–77.
1068. ★ACT Proficiency Examinations in Marketing. College and adults; 1973–77.
1069. ★ACT Proficiency Examinations in Operations Management. College and adults; 1973–77.
1070. *CLEP Subject Examination in Introduction to Business Management. 1 semester of college or equivalent; 1969–76.
1071. *CLEP Subject Examination in Introductory Business Law. 1 semester of college or equivalent; 1970–76.
1072. *CLEP Subject Examination in Introductory Marketing. 1 semester of college or equivalent; 1968–76.
1073. *CLEP Subject Examination in Money and Banking. 1 semester of college or equivalent; 1967–76.
1074. *Graduate Management Admission Test. Business graduate students; 1954–77; 11 references; cited: 2 reviews, 15 references.
1075. Organizational Value Dimensions Questionnaire: Business Form. Adults; 1965–66; 1 review.

COMPUTER PROGRAMMING

1076. *CLEP Subject Examination in Computers and Data Processing. 1–2 semesters of college or equivalent; 1968–76.
1077. *CLEP Subject Examination in Elementary Computer Programming—Fortran IV. 1 semester of college or equivalent; 1971–76.
1078. ★Computer Operator Aptitude Battery. Experienced operators and trainees; 1973–74; 2 reviews.
1079. *Computer Programmer Aptitude Battery. Applicants for training or employment in computer programmer and systems analysis fields; 1964–74; 1 review, 3 references; cited: 2 reviews, 4 references.
1080. ★Graduate Record Examinations Advanced Computer Science Test. Graduate school candidates; 1976.

FOR OTHER TESTS, see in *Tests in Print II*:
Aptitude Assessment Battery: Programming, T2:2331. Programmers and trainees; 1967–69; cited: 1 reference.
Diebold Personnel Tests, T2:2335. Programmers and systems analysts for automatic data processing and computing installations; 1959.
‡Programmer Aptitude/Competence Test System, T2:2336. Computer programmers and applicants for programmer training; 1970; 1 reference.

DENTISTRY

1081. ★CLEP Subject Examination in Dental Materials: Dental Auxiliary Education. Dental hygienists and assistants; 1976–77.
1082. ★CLEP Subject Examination in Head, Neck, and Oral Anatomy: Dental Auxiliary Education. Dental hygienists and assistants; 1976–77.
1083. ★CLEP Subject Examination in Oral Radiography: Dental Auxiliary Education. Dental hygienists and assistants; 1976–77.
1084. ★CLEP Subject Examination in Tooth Morphology and Function; Dental Auxiliary Education. Dental hygienists and assistants; 1976–77.
1085. *Dental Admission Testing Program. Dental school applicants; 1946–77; 2 reviews, 7 references; cited: 44 references.
1086. *Ohio Dental Assistanting Achievement Test. Grades 11–12; 1970–77.

FOR ANOTHER TEST, see in *Tests in Print II*:
Dental Hygiene Aptitude Testing Program, T2:2338. Dental hygiene school applicants; 1947–72.

ENGINEERING

1087. ★Engineer Performance Description Form. Nonsupervisory college graduate engineers; 1975; 1 reference.

1088. *Graduate Record Examinations Advanced Engineering Test. Graduate school candidates; 1939–76; 1 reference.

1089. *UP Field Test in Engineering. College; 1969–77.

For other tests, see in *Tests in Print II:*

AC Test of Creative Ability, T2:2340. Engineers and supervisors; 1953–60; 23 references; cited: 3 reviews, 1 reference.
Engineering Aide Test, T2:2341. Engineering aides; 1957–60.
†Garnett College Test in Engineering Science [England], T2:2342. 1–2 years technical college; 1966–71.
Minnesota Engineering Analogies Test, T2:2344. Candidates for graduate school and industry; 1954–70; cited: 2 reviews, 10 references.
†N.I.I.P. Engineering Apprentice Selection Test Battery [England], T2:2345. Engineering apprentices; 1936–72; cited: 1 reference.
†National Engineering Aptitude Search Test: The Junior Engineering Technical Society, T2:2346. Grades 9–12; 1963–71.
Purdue Creativity Test, T2:2347. Applicants for engineering positions; 1960; 1 reference; cited: 2 reviews, 2 references.

LAW

1090. ★ACT Proficiency Examination in Criminal Investigation. College and adults; 1975–76.

1091. ★ACT Proficiency Examination in Introduction to Criminal Justice. College and adults; 1975–76.

1092. ★Correctional Policy Inventory: A Survey of Correctional Philosophy and Characteristic Methods of Dealing With Offenders. Correctional managers; 1970; 2 references.

1093. *Law School Admission Test. Law school entrants; 1948–77; 7 references; cited: 2 reviews, 43 references.

1094. ★Multijurisdictional Police Officer Examination. Prospective police officers; 1976.

1095. *Police Officer J:A-1(M). Prospective police officers; 1973; 1 reference.

1096. ★Police Sergeant. Prospective sergeants; 1975–77.

MEDICINE

1097. *CLEP Subject Examination in Clinical Chemistry. Medical technologists; 1972–76.

1098. *CLEP Subject Examination in Hematology. Medical technologists; 1972–76.

1099. *CLEP Subject Examination in Immunohematology and Blood Banking. Medical technologists; 1972–76.

1100. *CLEP Subject Examination in Microbiology. Medical technologists; 1972–76.

1101. *New Medical College Admission Test. Applicants for admission to member colleges of the Association of American Medical Colleges and to other participating institutions; 1946–77; 39 references; cited: 6 reviews, 145 references.

1102. ★Ohio Diversified Health Occupations Achievement Test. Grades 11–12;; 1975–77.

1103. ★Ohio Medical Assisting Achievement Test. Grades 11–12; 1974–77.

1104. *Optometry College Admission Test. Optometry college applicants; 1971–76; 1 review, 3 references.

For other tests, see in *Tests in Print II:*

†Colleges of Podiatry Admission Test, T2:2354. Grades 14 and over; 1968–72.
Medical School Instructor Attitude Inventory, T2:2356. Medical school faculty members; 1961; cited: 1 reference.
†Veterinary Aptitude Test, T2:2358. Veterinary school applicants; 1951–73; 1 reference; cited: 6 references.

MISCELLANEOUS

1105. ★Change Agent Questionnaire. Adults whose work primarily concerns changing behavior of others; 1969–73.

1106. ★Entrance Level Firefighter. Prospective firefighters; 1974–77.

1107. ★Field Work Performance Report. Occupational therapy students; 1973–74; 1 reference.

For other tests, see in *Tests in Print II:*

†Architectural School Aptitude Test, T2:2359. Architectural school applicants; 1963–73; cited: 2 references.
Chemical Operators Selection Test, T2:2360. Chemical operators and applicants; 1958–71; cited: 1 reference.
Fire Promotion Tests, T2:2361 Prospective firemen promotees; 1960–69.
†Firefighter Test, T2:2362. Prospective firemen; 1954–72.
Fireman Examination, T2:2363. Prospective firemen; 1961–62.
General Municipal Employees Performance (Efficiency) Rating System, T2:2364. Municipal employees; 1967–69.
Journalism Test, T2:2365. High school; 1957.
‡Law Enforcement Perception Questionnaire, T2:2366. Law enforcement personnel; 1970.
Memory and Observation Tests for Policeman, T2:2367. Prospective policemen; 1962.
Police Performance Rating System, T2:2368. Policemen; 1964–69.
Police Promotion Tests, T2:2369. Prospective policemen promotees; 1960–69.
Policeman Examination, T2:2370. Prospective policemen; 1960–62.
Policeman Test, T2:2371. Policemen and prospective policemen; 1953–65.
Potter-Nash Aptitude Test for Lumber Inspectors and Other General Personnel Who Handle Lumber, T2:2372. Employees in woodworking industries; 1958.
‡Test for Firefighter B-1, T2:2373. Firemen and prospective firemen; 1973.
Visual Comprehension Test for Detective, T2:2375. Prospective police detectives; 1963.

NURSING

1108. ★ACT Proficiency Examination in Adult Nursing. College and adults; 1976.

1109. ★ACT Proficiency Examination in Fundamentals of Nursing. College and adults; 1969–76.

1110. ★ACT Proficiency Examination in Nursing Health Care. College and adults; 1973–76.

1111. ★ACT Proficiency Examination in Occupational Strategy, Nursing. College and adults; 1973–76.

1112. ★ACT Proficiency Examination in Psychiatric/Mental Health Nursing. College and adults; 1968–76.

1113. ★ACT Proficiency Examinations in Commonalities in Nursing Care. College and adults; 1973–76.

1114. ★ACT Proficiency Examinations in Differences in Nursing Care. College and adults; 1974–76.

1115. ★ACT Proficiency Examinations in Maternal and Child Nursing. College and adults; 1968–76.

1116. ★CLEP Subject Examination in Anatomy, Physiology, Microbiology: North Carolina Nursing Equivalency Examinations. 1 year of college or equivalent; 1974–76.

1117. ★CLEP Subject Examination in Behavioral Sciences for Nurses; North Carolina Nursing Equivalency Examinations. 1 year of college or equivalent; 1974–76.

1118. ★CLEP Subject Examination in Fundamentals of Nursing: North Carolina Nursing Equivalency Examinations. 1 year of college or equivalent; 1974–76; 1 review.

1119. ★CLEP Subject Examination in Medical-Surgical Nursing: North Carolina Nursing Equivalency Examinations. 1 year of college or equivalent; 1974–76; 1 review.

1120. ★Clinical Experience Record for Nursing Students. Nursing students and nurses; 1960–75; 1 reference.

1121. *Entrance Examination for Schools of Nursing. Applicants to schools of registered nursing; 1938–77; 2 reviews; cited: 6 references.

1122–3. *Entrance Examination for Schools of Practical/Vocational Nursing. Applicants to schools of practical nursing; 1942–75; cited: 2 references.

For other tests, see in *Tests in Print II:*

Achievement Tests in Nursing, T2:2376. Students in schools of registered nursing; 1952–71.

Achievement Tests in Practical Nursing, T2:2377. Practical nursing students; 1957–67; cited: 1 reference.

Empathy Inventory, T2:2378. Nursing instructors; 1966–70; cited: 2 references.

George Washington University Series Nursing Tests, T2:2381. Prospective nurses; 1931–50; 3 references; cited: 8 references.

Luther Hospital Sentence Completions, T2:2382. Prospective nursing students; 1959–70; 2 references; cited: 5 references.

†NLN Achievement Tests for Schools Preparing Registered Nurses, T2:2383. Students in state-approved schools preparing registered nurses; 1943–73; 4 references; cited: 11 references.

NLN Aide Selection Test, T2:2384. Applicants for aide positions in hospitals and home health agencies; 1970.

NLN Practical Nursing Achievement Tests, T2:2385. Students in state-approved schools of practical nursing; 1950–64; 2 references; cited: 1 reference.

NLN Pre-Admission and Classification Examination, T2:2386. Practical nursing school entrants; 1950–63; 5 references; cited: 1 reference.

†NLN Pre-Nursing and Guidance Examination, T2:2387. Applicants for admission to state-approved schools preparing registered nurses; 1941–72; 18 references; cited: 8 references.

Netherne Study Difficulties Battery for Student Nurses [England], T2:2388. Student nurses; 1964–69.

Nurse Attitudes Inventory, T2:2389. Prospective nursing students; 1965–70; cited: 5 references.

†PSB-Aptitude for Practical Nursing Examination, T2:2390. Applicants for admission to practical nursing schools; 1961–72.

RESEARCH

For tests, see in *Tests in Print II:*

Research Personnel Review Form, T2:2391. Research and engineering and scientific firms; 1959–60.

Supervisor's Evaluation of Research Personnel, T2:2392. Research personnel; 1960; 2 references; cited: 1 review, 1 excerpt, 3 references.

Surveys of Research Administration and Environment, T2:2393. Research and engineering and scientific firms; 1959–60.

Technical Personnel Recruiting Inventory, T2:2394. Research and engineering and scientific firms; 1959–60.

SALES

1124. ★[Sales Motivation.] Sales managers, salespeople; 1972.

1125. ★[Sales Relations.] Salespeople, customers; 1972; 1 review.

1126. ★Sales Style Diagnosis Test [Canada]. Salespeople; 1975.

1127–8. ★Sales Transaction Audit. Salespeople; 1972; 1 review.

For other tests, see in *Tests in Print II:*

Aptitudes Associates Test of Sales Aptitude, T2:2395. Applicants for sales positions; 1947–60; cited: 2 reviews, 6 references.

Combination Inventory, Form 2, T2:2396. Prospective debit life insurance salesmen; 1954–66; cited: 1 reference.

Detroit Retail Selling Inventory, T2:2397. Candidates for training in retail selling; 1940; 2 references: cited: 2 reviews, 2 excerpts.

Evaluation Record, T2:2398. Prospective life insurance agency managers; 1947–63.

Hall Salespower Inventory, T2:2399. Salesmen; 1946–57.

Hanes Sales Selection Inventory, T2:2400. Insurance and printing salesmen; 1954–55; cited: 2 reviews.

†Information Index, T2:2401. Life and health insurance agents; 1951–72; 1 reference; cited: 4 references.

LIAMA Inventory of Job Attitudes, T2:2402. Life insurance field personnel; 1956–70.

Personnel Institute Hiring Kit, T2:2403. Applicants for sales positions; 1954–62; 1 reference; cited: 3 references.

SRA Sales Attitudes Check List T2:2404. Applicants for sales positions; 1960; cited: 1 review.

†Sales Aptitude Test, T2:2405. Job applicants; 1960–72.

†Sales Comprehension Test, T2:2406. Applicants for sales positions; 1947–71; 3 references; cited: 1 review, 17 references.

†Sales Method Index, T2:2407. Life insurance agents; 1948–71.

†Sales Motivation Inventory, T2:2408. Applicants for sales positions; 1953–69; 5 references; cited: 1 review, 2 references.

Sales Sentence Completion Blank, T2:2409. Applicants for sales positions; 1961; cited: 1 review, 1 excerpt.

Steward Life Insurance Knowledge Test, T2:2410. Applicants for life insurance agent or supervisory positions; 1952–56.

Steward Occupational Objectives Inventory, T2:2411. Applicants for supervisory positions in life insurance companies or agencies; 1956–57.

Steward Personal Background Inventory, T2:2412. Applicants for sales positions; 1949–60; cited: 2 reviews.

Test for Ability to Sell: George Washington University Series, T2:2413. Grades 7–16 and adults; 1929–50; cited: 1 review.

‡Test of Retail Sales Insight, T2:2414. Retail clerks and students; 1960–71.

SKILLED TRADES

1129. ★NOCTI Examination: Air Conditioning and Refrigeration. Teachers and prospective teachers; 1973–77; 1 review.

1130. ★NOCTI Examination: Airframe and Power Plant Mechanic. Teachers and prospective teachers; 1973–77.

1131. ★NOCTI Examination: Architectural Drafting. Teachers and prospective teachers; 1973–77; 1 review.

1132. ★NOCTI Examination: Auto Body Repair. Teachers and prospective teachers; 1973–77.

1133. ★NOCTI Examination: Auto Mechanic. Teachers and prospective teachers; 1973–77; 2 reviews, 1 reference.

1134. ★NOCTI Examination: Cabinet Making and Millwork. Teachers and prospective teachers; 1973–77; 1 review.

1135. ★NOCTI Examination: Carpentry. Teachers and prospective teachers; 1973–77; 1 review, 1 reference.

1136. ★NOCTI Examination: Civil Technology. Teachers and prospective teachers; 1973–77.

1137. ★NOCTI Examination: Cosmetology. Teachers and prospective teachers; 1973–77.

1138. ★NOCTI Examination: Diesel Engine Repair. Teachers and prospective teachers; 1973–77; 1 review.

1139. ★NOCTI Examination: Electrical Installation. Teachers and prospective teachers; 1973–77; 1 review, 1 reference.

1140. ★NOCTI Examination: Electronics Communications. Teachers and prospective teachers; 1973–77; 1 review.

1141. ★NOCTI Examination: Industrial Electrician. Teachers and prospective teachers; 1973–77; 1 review.

1142. ★NOCTI Examination: Industrial Electronics. Teachers and prospective teachers; 1973–77; 1 review.

1143. ★NOCTI Examination: Machine Drafting. Teachers and prospective teachers; 1973–77; 1 review.

1144. ★NOCTI Examination: Machine Trades. Teachers and prospective teachers; 1973–77; 1 reference.

1145. ★NOCTI Examination: Masonry. Teachers and prospective teachers; 1973–77.

1146. ★NOCTI Examination: Mechanical Technology. Teachers and prospective teachers; 1973–77.

1147. ★NOCTI Examination: Plumbing. Teachers and prospective teachers; 1973–77; 1 review.

1148. ★NOCTI Examination: Printing. Teachers and prospective teachers; 1973–77.

1149. ★NOCTI Examination: Quantity Food Preparation. Teachers and prospective teachers; 1973–77.

1150. ★NOCTI Examination: Sheet Metal. Teachers and prospective teachers; 1973–77; 1 review.

1151. ★NOCTI Examination: Small Engine Repair. Teachers and prospective teachers; 1973–77; 1 review.

1152. ★NOCTI Examination: Welding. Teachers and prospective teachers; 1973–77; 1 review.

1153. ★National Occupational Competency Testing Program. Teachers and prospective teachers in skilled trades; 1973–77; 1 review, 6 references.

1154. *Ohio Auto Body Achievement Test. Grades 11–12; 1969–77.

1155. *Ohio Automotive Mechanics Achievement Test. Grades 11–12; 1959–77; 1 reference.

1156. *Ohio Carpentry Achievement Test. Grades 11–12; 1970–77.

1157. *Ohio Communication Products Electronics Achievement Test. Grades 11–12; 1973–77.

1158. *Ohio Construction Electricity Achievement Test. Grades 11–12; 1973–77.

1159. *Ohio Cosmetology Achievement Test. Grades 11–12; 1967–77.

1160. *Ohio Drafting Achievement Test. Grades 11–12; 1962–77; 1 review.

1161. ★Ohio Heating, Air Conditioning, and Refrigeration Achievement Test. Grades 11–12; 1976–77.

1162. *Ohio Industrial Electronics Achievement Test. Grades 11–12; 1973–77.

1163. ★Ohio Lithographic Printing Achievement Test. Grades 11–12; 1976–77.

1164. *Ohio Machine Trades Achievement Test. Grades 11–12; 1958–77; cited: 2 references.

1165. *Ohio Sheet Metal Achievement Test. Grades 11–12; 1964–77; cited: 1 reference.

1166. *Ohio Trade and Industrial Education Achievement Test Program. Grades 11–12; 1958–77; cited: 1 reference.

1167. *Ohio Welding Achievement Test. Grades 11–12; 1969–77.

1168. Purdue Trade Information Test in Welding. Vocational school and adults; 1952; 1 review; cited: 1 reference.

1169. Short Occupational Knowledge Test for Carpenters. Job applicants; 1969–70; 1 review.

1170. Short Occupational Knowledge Test for Draftsmen. Job applicants; 1969–70; 1 review.

1171. Short Occupational Knowledge Test for Welders. Job applicants; 1969–70; 1 review.

1172. ★Sweet Technical Information Test [Australia]. Ages 14–17; 1973–75.

FOR OTHER TESTS, see in *Tests in Print II*:

Electrical Sophistication Test, T2:2415. Job applicants; 1963–65; cited: 1 review.
Fiesenheiser Test of Ability to Read Drawings, T2:2416. Trade school and adults; 1955; cited: 1 review.
†Mechanical Familiarity Test, T2:2417. Job applicants; 1960–72.
Mechanical Handyman Test, T2:2418. Maintenance workers; 1957–65.
†Mechanical Knowledge Test, T2:2419. Job applicants; 1960–72.
†Ohio Printing Achievement Test, T2:2429. Grades 11–12; 1963–73; 1 reference.
Purdue Industrial Training Classification Test, T2:2433. Grades 9–12 and adults; 1942; 2 references; cited: 2 reviews, 2 references.
Purdue Interview Aids, T2:2434. Applicants for industrial employment; 1943; cited: 1 review.
Purdue Trade Information Test for Sheetmetal Workers, T2:2435. Sheetmetal workers; 1958.
Purdue Trade Information Test in Carpentry, T2:2436. Vocational school and adults; 1952; cited: 1 review, 1 reference.
Purdue Trade Information Test in Engine Lathe Operation, T2:2437. Vocational school and adults; 1955; cited: 1 review.
Short Occupational Knowledge Test for Auto Mechanics, T2:2439. Job applicants; 1969–70; cited: 1 review.
Short Occupational Knowledge Test for Electricians, T2:2442. Job applicants; 1969–70; cited: 1 review.
Short Occupational Knowledge Test for Machinists, T2:2443. Job applicants; 1969–70.
Short Occupational Knowledge Test for Plumbers, T2:2444. Job applicants; 1970.
Short Occupational Knowledge Test for Tool and Die Makers, T2:2445. Job applicants; 1970.

Technical Tests [South Africa], T2:2447. Standards 6–8 (ages 13–15); 1962.

SUPERVISION

1173. ★Conflict Management Survey. Adults; 1969–73; 1 review, 2 references.

1174. Leader Behavior Description Questionnaire. Supervisors; 1957; 1 review, 138 references; cited: 143 references.

1175. Leader Behavior Description Questionnaire, Form 12. Supervisors; 1957–63; 1 review, 101 references; cited: 67 references.

1176. Leadership Evaluation and Development Scale. Prospective supervisors: 1964–65; 2 reviews; cited: 1 review, 1 reference.

1177. Leadership Opinion Questionnaire. Supervisors and prospective supervisors; 1960–69; 52 references; cited: 3 reviews, 62 references.

1178. ★Management Relations Survey. Managers; 1970; 1 review, 1 reference.

1179. ★Management Style Diagnosis Test [Canada]. Managers; 1965–75; 1 review, 5 references.

1180. ★Management Transactions Audit. Managers; 1973; 2 reviews.

1181. ★Managerial Philosophies Scale. Managers; 1975.

1182. ★Managerial Style Questionnaire. Managers (of other managers or professional personnel) and subordinates; 1974; 1 review, 1 reference.

1183. ★Personnel Relations Survey. Managers; 1967; 1 review, 3 references.

1184. RAD Scales. Supervisors; 1957; 1 review, 6 references; cited: 25 references.

1185. ★[Styles of Leadership and Management.] Leaders, managers, employees, and others; 1964–73; 1 review, 8 references.

1186. ★Supervisory Behavior Description. Supervisors; 1970–72; 1 review, 31 references.

1187. *Supervisory Practices Test. Supervisors; 1957–76; cited: 2 reviews, 6 references.

1188. WPS Supervisor-Executive Tri-Dimensional Evaluation Scales. Supervisors; 1966; 2 reviews.

1189. ★[Work Motivation.] Managers, employees; 1967–73; 3 references.

FOR OTHER TESTS, see in *Tests in Print II*:

†How Supervise?, T2:2448. Supervisors; 1943–71; 11 references; cited: 5 reviews, 40 references.
‡In-Basket Test [South Africa], T2:2450. Applicants for high level executive positions; 1961–66.
‡Leadership Practices Inventory, T2:2455. Supervisors: 1955–67.
Managerial Scale for Enterprise Improvement, T2:2456. Supervisors; 1955; cited: 2 reviews.
RHB Test of Supervisory Judgment, T2:2458. Business and industry; 1949–63; 1 reference.
Supervisory Index, T2:2459. Supervisors; 1960–69; 1 reference; cited: 2 reviews, 2 references.
†Supervisory Inventory on Communication, T2:2460. Supervisors and prospective supervisors; 1965–72; cited: 1 reference.
‡Supervisory Inventory on Discipline, T2:2461. Supervisors; 1973.
‡Supervisory Inventory on Grievances, T2:2462. Supervisors; 1970.
†Supervisory Inventory on Human Relations, T2:2463. Supervisors and prospective supervisors; 1960–72; 1 reference; cited: 1 review, 1 reference.
‡Supervisory Inventory on Labor Relations, T2:2464. Supervisors in unionized firms; 1972.
Supervisory Inventory on Safety, T2:2465. Supervisors and prospective supervisors; 1967–69.
‡Survey of Management Perception, T2:2467. Supervisors; 1956–58.

TRANSPORTATION

FOR TESTS, see in *Tests in Print II*:

American Transit Association Tests, T2:2469. Transit operating personnel; 1941–51; 1 reference; cited: 3 reviews, 1 reference.

†Driver Selection Forms and Tests, T2:2470. Truck drivers; 1943–73; cited: 2 reviews.

McGuire Safe Driver Scale and Interview Guide, T2:2471. Prospective motor vehicle operators; 1961–62; 1 reference; cited: 2 reviews, 1 reference.

Road Test Check List for Testing, Selecting, Rating, and Training Coach Operators, T2:2472. Bus drivers; 1958.

Road Test in Traffic for Testing, Selecting, Rating, and Train-ing Truck Drivers ,T2:2473. Truck drivers; 1943–55.

Short Occupational Knowledge Test for Truck Drivers, T2:2474. Job applicants; 1970.

†Truck Driver Test, T2:2475. Drivers of light and medium trucks; 1957–72; cited: 2 reviews.

†Wilson Driver Selection Test, T2:2476. Prospective motor vehicle operators; 1961–72; cited: 2 reviews.